John Milton
N. Scott Momaday
Marianne Moore
Frederick Morgan
Arakida Moritake
Howard Moss
Marilyn Nelson
Howard Nemerov
Pablo Neruda
Lorine Niedecker
John Frederick Nims
Yone Noguchi
Sharon Olds
Olga Orozco
Wilfred Owen
Neiji Ozawa
José Emilio Pacheco
Dorothy Parker
Linda Pastan
Octavio Paz
Robert Phillips
Robert Pinsky
Sylvia Plath
Edgar Allan Poe
Alexander Pope
Ezra Pound

Craig Raine
Dudley Randall
John Crowe Ransom
Henry Reed
James Reeves
Alastair Reid
Adrienne Rich
John Ridland
Rainer Maria Rilke
Edwin Arlington Robinson
Theodore Roethke
Wendy Rose
Christina Rossetti
Clare Rossini
Run D. M. C.
Kay Ryan
Benjamin Alire Sáenz
Mary Jo Salter
Carl Sandburg
Carole Satyamurti
Gjertrud Schnackenberg
Anne Sexton
William Shakespeare
Percy Bysshe Shelley
Charles Simic
Paul Simon

Louis Simpson
David Slavitt
Christopher Smart
Bessie Smith
Stevie Smith
William Jay Smith
Gary Snyder
Cathy Song
Sor Juana
William Stafford
A. E. Stallings
Jon Stallworthy
Timothy Steele
James Stephens
Wallace Stevens
Anne Stevenson
Michael Stillman
Ruth Stone
Alfonsina Storni
Jonathan Swift
Stephen Tapscott
Henry Taylor
Sara Teasdale
Alfred, Lord Tennyson
Cornelius Ter Maat
Diane Thiel

Dylan Thomas
Chidiock Tichborne
Charles Tomlinson
Jean Toomer
Grace Treasone
Natasha Trethewey
John Updike
Amy Uyematsu
César Vallejo
Hakuro Wada
Derek Walcott
Arthur Waley
Edmund Waller
Walt Whitman
Richard Wilbur
C. K. Williams
Clarence Williams
William Carlos Williams
William Wordsworth
James Wright
Mary Sidney Wroth
Sir Thomas Wyatt
William Butler Yeats
Chryss Yost

PLAYWRIGHTS

Susan Glaspell
Beth Henley
David Henry Hwang
Henrik Ibsen

David Ives
Jane Martin
Terrence McNally
Arthur Miller

Milcha Sanchez-Scott
William Shakespeare
Sophocles
John Millington Synge

Tennessee Williams
August Wilson

WRITING RESOURCES

Chapter 40 Writing About Literature, p. 2119
  Using Critical Sources and Maintaining
     Academic Integrity
  Drafting and Revising
  The Form of Your Finished Paper
Chapter 41 Writing About a Story, p. 2130
  Explicating
  Analyzing
  Comparing and Contrasting
Chapter 42 Writing About a Poem, p. 2147
  Explicating
  Analyzing
  Comparing and Contrasting
  How to Quote a Poem
Chapter 43 Writing About a Play, p. 2167
  Methods
  How to Quote a Play
  Reviewing a Play
Chapter 44 Writing a Research Paper, p. 2179
  Doing Research for an Essay
  Evaluating and Using Internet Sources
  Guarding Academic Integrity
  Acknowledging and Documenting Sources
Reference Guide for Citations, p. 2194

13 Student Essays, 1 Review, 2 Card Reports
Analysis:
   Symbolism in Steinbeck's "The Chrysanthemums,"
     p. 280
   The Hearer of the Tell-Tale Heart, p. 2136
   Word Choice in Roethke's "My Papa's Waltz," p. 745
   Imagery in Elizabeth Bishop's "The Fish," p. 809
   The Design of Frost's "Design," p. 2154
   Othello: Tragedy or Soap Opera?, p. 1800

Argument: Helmer vs. Helmer, p. 1888

Comparison and Contrast:
   "Wing Spread" Does a Dip, p. 2158
   Outside *Trifles*, p. 1351

Explication:
   By Lantern Light ["The Tell-Tale Heart"], p. 2132
   The Bonds Between Love and Hatred in H. D.'s
     "Helen," p. 997
   An Unfolding of Frost's "Design," p. 2149

Research Paper: Kafka's Greatness, p. 374

Review: *Trifles* Scores Mixed Success, p. 2175

Card Report:
   "The Tell-Tale Heart," p. 2140
   Trifles, p. 2172

LITERATURE

LITERATURE

LITERATURE

An Introduction to
Fiction, Poetry, and Drama

Ninth Edition

X. J. KENNEDY
DANA GIOIA

PEARSON
Longman

New York Boston San Francisco
London Toronto Sydney Tokyo Singapore Madrid
Mexico City Munich Paris Cape Town Hong Kong Montreal

Vice President and Editor-in-Chief: Joseph Terry
Development Manager: Janet Lanphier
Development Editor: Katharine Glynn
Senior Marketing Manager: Melanie Craig
Senior Supplements Editor: Donna Campion
Media Supplements Editor: Nancy Garcia
Production Manager: Joseph Vella
Project Coordination, Text Design, and Electronic Page Makeup: Nesbitt Graphics, Inc.
Cover Design Manager: John Callahan
Cover Designer: Mary McDonnell
Cover Image: *Gloucester Harbor* by Winslow Homer, © Francis G. Mayer/Corbis
Photo Research: Photosearch, Inc.
Manufacturing Buyer: Roy L. Pickering, Jr.
Printer and Binder: Quebecor World, Taunton
Cover Printer: The Lehigh Press

For permission to use copyrighted material, grateful acknowledgment is made to the copyright holders on pp. A1–A18, which are hereby made part of this copyright page.

Library of Congress Cataloging-in-Publication Data
Literature: an introduction to fiction, poetry, and drama / [compiled by]
X. J. Kennedy, Dana Gioia.—9th ed.
    p. cm
  ISBN 0-321-24551-2 (Literature)—ISBN 0-321-18330-4 (Literature Interactive)
    1. Literature—Collections. I. Kennedy, X. J. II. Gioia, Dana.
PN6014.L58 2005
808—dc22

2003027420

Copyright © 2005 by X. J. Kennedy and Dana Gioia

Please visit us at http://www.ablongman.com/kennedy

ISBN 0-321-24551-2 (Literature)
ISBN 0-321-18330-4 (Literature Interactive)
ISBN 0-321-27260-9 (Schools)

1 2 3 4 5 6 7 8 9 10—QWT—07 06 05 04

Contents

Preface xlv
To the Instructor xlix
About the Authors lxi

FICTION 1

1 Reading a Story 3

FABLE, PARABLE, AND TALES 4

W. Somerset Maugham, THE APPOINTMENT IN SAMARRA 4
A servant tries to gallop away from Death in this brief sardonic fable retold in memorable form by a popular storyteller.

Aesop, THE FOX AND THE GRAPES 5
Ever wonder where the phrase "sour grapes" comes from? Find out in this classic fable.

Bidpai, THE CAMEL AND HIS FRIENDS 6
With friends like these, you can guess what the camel doesn't need.

Chuang Tzu, INDEPENDENCE 8
The Prince of Ch'u asks the philosopher Chuang Tzu to become his advisor and gets a surprising reply in this classic Chinese fable.

Jakob and Wilhelm Grimm, GODFATHER DEATH 9
Neither God nor the Devil came to the christening. In this stark folktale, a young man receives magical powers with a string attached.

PLOT 12

THE SHORT STORY 13

John Updike, A & P 15
In walk three girls in nothing but bathing suits, and Sammy finds himself no longer an aproned checkout clerk but an armored knight.

WRITER'S PERSPECTIVE
John Updike on Writing, WHY WRITE?   20

WRITING CRITICALLY
What's the Plot?   21

WRITING ASSIGNMENT   22
FURTHER SUGGESTIONS FOR WRITING   22

2   Point of View   23

William Faulkner, A ROSE FOR EMILY   29
  Proud, imperious Emily Grierson defied the town from the fortress of her mansion. Who could have guessed the secret that lay within?

Jhumpa Lahiri, INTERPRETER OF MALADIES   37
  Mr. Kapasi's life had settled into a quiet pattern—and then Mrs. Das and her family came into it.

James Baldwin, SONNY'S BLUES   53
  Two brothers in Harlem see life differently. The older brother is the sensible family man, but Sonny wants to be a jazz musician.

Eudora Welty, WHY I LIVE AT THE P.O.   77
  Since no one appreciated Sister, she decides to live at the Post Office. After meeting her family, you won't blame her.

WRITER'S PERSPECTIVE
James Baldwin on Writing, RACE AND THE AFRICAN AMERICAN
  WRITER   87

WRITING CRITICALLY
How Point of View Shapes a Story   89

WRITING ASSIGNMENT   89
FURTHER SUGGESTIONS FOR WRITING   90

3   Character   91

Katherine Anne Porter, THE JILTING OF GRANNY WEATHERALL   94
  For sixty years Ellen Weatherall has fought back the memory of that terrible day, but now once more the priest waits in the house.

Alice Walker, EVERYDAY USE   102
  When successful Dee visits from the city, she has changed her name. Her mother and sister notice other things have changed, too.

Raymond Carver, CATHEDRAL 109
> He had never expected to find himself trying to describe a cathedral to a blind man. He hadn't even wanted to meet this odd, old friend of his wife.

WRITER'S PERSPECTIVE

Raymond Carver on Writing, COMMONPLACE BUT PRECISE LANGUAGE 121

WRITING CRITICALLY

How Character Creates Action 122

WRITING ASSIGNMENT 123
FURTHER SUGGESTIONS FOR WRITING 123

4 Setting 124

Kate Chopin, THE STORM 127
> Even with her husband away, Calixta feels happily, securely married. Why then should she not shelter an old admirer from the rain?

Jack London, TO BUILD A FIRE 132
> Seventy-five degrees below zero. Alone except for one mistrustful wolf dog, a man finds himself battling a relentless force.

T. Coraghessan Boyle, GREASY LAKE 143
> Murky and strewn with beer cans, the lake appears a wasteland. On its shore three "dangerous characters" learn a lesson one grim night.

Amy Tan, A PAIR OF TICKETS 152
> A young woman flies with her father to China to meet two half sisters she never knew existed.

WRITER'S PERSPECTIVE

Amy Tan on Writing, SETTING THE VOICE 167

WRITING CRITICALLY

How Time and Place Set a Story 168

WRITING ASSIGNMENT 169
FURTHER SUGGESTIONS FOR WRITING 169

5 Tone and Style 170

Ernest Hemingway, A CLEAN, WELL-LIGHTED PLACE 174
> All by himself each night, the old man lingers in the bright café. What does he need more than brandy? One other knew.

William Faulkner, Barn Burning   178

This time when Ab Snopes wields his blazing torch, his son Sarty faces a dilemma: whether to obey or defy the vengeful old man.

Irony   192

Guy de Maupassant, The Necklace   193

Having no jewels to wear to the ball, a young woman borrows her rich friend's diamond necklace—with disastrous results.

Ha Jin, Saboteur   200

When the police unfairly arrest Mr. Chiu, he hopes for justice. After witnessing their brutality, he quietly plans revenge.

Writer's Perspective

Ernest Hemingway on Writing, The Direct Style   209

Writing Critically

Be Style-Conscious   210

Writing Assignment   211
Further Suggestions for Writing   211

6   Theme   212

Stephen Crane, The Open Boat   215

In a lifeboat circled by sharks, tantalized by glimpses of land, a reporter scrutinizes Fate and learns about comradeship.

Alice Munro, Day of the Butterfly   234

A sixth-grader is surprised by some of her own reactions when one of her classmates becomes seriously ill.

Luke 15: 11–32, The Parable of the Prodigal Son   241

A father has two sons. One demands his inheritance now and leaves to spend it with ruinous results.

Kurt Vonnegut, Jr., Harrison Bergeron   242

Are you handsome? Off with your eyebrows! Are you brainy? Let a transmitter sound thought-shattering beeps inside your ear.

Writer's Perspective

Kurt Vonnegut, Jr. on Writing, The Themes of Science Fiction   248

Writing Critically

Stating the Theme   249

Writing Assignment   250
Further Suggestions for Writing   250

7 Symbol 251

John Steinbeck, THE CHRYSANTHEMUMS 253
Fenced-in Elisa feels emotionally starved—then her life promises to blossom with the arrival of the scissors-grinding man.

Shirley Jackson, THE LOTTERY 262
Splintered and faded, the sinister black box had worked its annual terror for longer than anyone in town could remember.

Elizabeth Tallent, NO ONE'S A MYSTERY 269
A two-page story speaks volumes about an open-hearted girl and her married lover.

Ursula K. Le Guin, THE ONES WHO WALK AWAY FROM OMELAS 272
Omelas is the perfect city. All of its inhabitants are happy. But everyone's prosperity depends on a hidden evil.

WRITER'S PERSPECTIVE
Ursula K. Le Guin on Writing, NOTE ON "THE ONES WHO WALK AWAY FROM OMELAS" 278

WRITING CRITICALLY
Recognizing Symbols 279
WRITING ASSIGNMENT 279

STUDENT ESSAY
An Analysis of the Symbolism in Steinbeck's "The Chrysanthemums" 280

FURTHER SUGGESTIONS FOR WRITING 283

8 Evaluating a Story 284

WRITING CRITICALLY
Know What You're Judging 286
WRITING ASSIGNMENT 287
FURTHER SUGGESTIONS FOR WRITING 287

9 Reading Long Stories and Novels 288

Leo Tolstoy, THE DEATH OF IVAN ILYCH 294
The supreme Russian novelist tells how a petty, ambitious judge, near the end of his wasted life, discovers a harrowing truth.

Franz Kafka, THE METAMORPHOSIS   336

> *"When Gregor Samsa awoke one morning from troubled dreams, he found himself transformed in his bed into a monstrous insect." Kafka's famous opening sentence introduces one of the most chilling stories in world literature.*

WRITER'S PERSPECTIVE
Franz Kafka on Writing, DISCUSSING *The Metamorphosis*   371

WRITING CRITICALLY
Leaving Things Out   373

WRITING ASSIGNMENT—RESEARCH PAPER   373

STUDENT RESEARCH PAPER
Kafka's Greatness   374

FURTHER SUGGESTIONS FOR WRITING   380

10 *Two Critical Casebooks: Edgar Allan Poe and Flannery O'Connor*   381

EDGAR ALLAN POE   381

~ STORIES

THE TELL-TALE HEART   382

> *The smoldering eye at last extinguished, a murderer finds that, despite all his attempts at a cover-up, his victim will be heard.*

THE MASQUE OF THE RED DEATH   386

> *The uninvited guest at Prince Prospero's masquerade ball changes the life of everyone present in this masterpiece of mood and effect.*

THE FALL OF THE HOUSE OF USHER   391

> *A letter from a boyhood friend turns out to be an invitation to a world of horror and doom.*

~ EDGAR ALLAN POE ON EDGAR ALLAN POE

THE TALE AND ITS EFFECT   405
ON IMAGINATION   406
THE PHILOSOPHY OF COMPOSITION   407

~ CRITICS ON EDGAR ALLAN POE

Daniel Hoffman, THE FATHER-FIGURE IN "THE TELL-TALE HEART"   408
Marie Bonaparte, A PSYCHOANALYTIC READING OF "THE MASQUE OF THE RED DEATH"   410

Charles Baudelaire, On Poe's Genius   412
James Tuttleton, Poe's Quest for Supernal Beauty   413

FLANNERY O'CONNOR   415

⌁ STORIES

Good Country People   416
> *Joy's mother thought the Bible salesman was a nice young man, but Joy
> will soon discover otherwise.*

A Good Man Is Hard to Find   431
> *Wanted: The Misfit, a cold-blooded killer. An ordinary family vacation
> leads to horror—and one moment of redeeming grace.*

Revelation   443
> *Mrs. Turpin thinks herself Jesus' favorite child, until she meets a troubled
> college girl. Soon violence flares in a doctor's waiting room.*

⌁ FLANNERY O'CONNOR ON FLANNERY O'CONNOR

Excerpt from "On Her Own Work": The Element of Suspense
in "A Good Man Is Hard to Find"   459
On Her Catholic Faith   462
Excerpt from "The Grotesque in Southern Fiction":
The Serious Writer and the Tired Reader   462
Yearbook Cartoons   464

⌁ CRITICS ON FLANNERY O'CONNOR

Robert Brinkmeyer Jr., Flannery O'Connor and Her
Readers   465
J. O. Tate, A Good Source Is Not So Hard to Find:
The Real Life Misfit   468
Mary Jane Schenck, Deconstructing "A Good Man Is Hard
to Find"   470
Kathleen Feeley, Comic Perversion in "Good Country
People"   472

WRITING CRITICALLY

How One Story Illuminates Another   473

Writing Assignment   473
Further Suggestions for Writing on Edgar Allan Poe   473
Further Suggestions for Writing on Flannery O'Connor   474

11 *Stories for Further Reading*   475

Chinua Achebe, Dead Men's Path   475
> *The new headmaster of the village school was determined to fight
> superstition, but the villagers did not agree.*

Isabel Allende, THE JUDGE'S WIFE   478
   Revenge can take many different forms, but few are as strange as the revenge taken in this passionate tale.

Anjana Appachana, THE PROPHECY   485
   Seventeen years old and pregnant, Amrita doesn't know what to do, but before she visits the gynecologist, she consults a fortune teller.

Margaret Atwood, HAPPY ENDINGS   497
   John and Mary meet. What happens next? This witty experimental story offers five different outcomes.

Ambrose Bierce, AN OCCURRENCE AT OWL CREEK BRIDGE   501
   At last, Peyton Farquhar's neck is in the noose. Reality mingles with dream in this classic story of the American Civil War.

Jorge Luis Borges, THE GOSPEL ACCORDING TO MARK   508
   A young man from Buenos Aires is trapped by a flood on an isolated ranch. To pass the time he reads the Gospel to a family with unforeseen results.

Willa Cather, PAUL'S CASE   513
   Paul's teachers can't understand the boy. Then one day, with stolen cash, he boards a train for New York and the life of his dreams.

John Cheever, THE FIVE-FORTY-EIGHT   528
   After their brief affair, Blake fired his secretary. He never expected she would seek revenge.

Anton Chekhov, THE LADY WITH THE PET DOG   539
   Lonely and bored at a seaside resort, they had sought a merely casual affair. How could they know it might deepen and trouble their separate marriages?

Kate Chopin, THE STORY OF AN HOUR   552
   "There was something coming to her and she was waiting for it, fearfully. What was it? She did not know; it was too subtle and elusive to name."

Sandra Cisneros, THE HOUSE ON MANGO STREET   554
   Does where we live tell what we are? A little girl dreams of a new house, but things don't always turn out the way we want them to.

Ralph Ellison, BATTLE ROYAL   555
   A young black man is invited to deliver his high school graduation speech to a gathering of a Southern town's leading white citizens. What promises to be an honor turns into a nightmare of violence, humiliation, and painful self-discovery.

Gabriel García Márquez, THE HANDSOMEST DROWNED MAN IN THE WORLD   566
   Even in death, a mysterious stranger has a profound effect on all of the people in the village.

Charlotte Perkins Gilman, THE YELLOW WALLPAPER   571
   *Her husband the doctor prescribed complete rest in the isolated and
   mysterious country house they rented for the summer. The cure proves
   worse than the disease in this gothic classic.*

Nathaniel Hawthorne, YOUNG GOODMAN BROWN   584
   *Urged on through deepening woods, a young Puritan sees—or dreams he
   sees—good villagers hasten toward a diabolic rite.*

Zora Neale Hurston, SWEAT   594
   *Delia's hard work paid for her small house. Now her drunken husband
   Sykes has promised it to another woman.*

Kazuo Ishiguro, A FAMILY SUPPER   604
   *Something very odd lurks beneath the surface of this family supper, and it
   might prove fatal.*

James Joyce, ARABY   612
   *If only he can find her a token, she might love him in return. As night
   falls, a Dublin boy hurries to make his dream come true.*

Jamaica Kincaid, GIRL   617
   *"Try to walk like a lady, and not like the slut you are so bent on
   becoming." An old-fashioned mother tells her daughter how to live.*

D. H. Lawrence, THE ROCKING-HORSE WINNER   619
   *Wild-eyed "as if something were going to explode in him," the boy
   predicts each winning horse, and gamblers rush to bet a thousand pounds.*

Bernard Malamud, ANGEL LEVINE   631
   *Broke, ill, and desperate, the tailor Manischevitz begs God for help. But
   when he discovers a black man in his living room who claims to be a
   Jewish angel, the tailor refuses to believe. A comic classic of how grace
   and need overcome prejudice.*

Katherine Mansfield, MISS BRILL   639
   *Sundays had long brought joy to solitary Miss Brill, until one fateful day
   when she happened to share a bench with two lovers in the park.*

Bobbie Ann Mason, SHILOH   643
   *After the accident Leroy could no longer work as a truck driver. He
   hoped to make a new life with his wife, but she seemed strangely different.*

Joyce Carol Oates, WHERE ARE YOU GOING, WHERE HAVE
   YOU BEEN?   654
   *Alone in the house, Connie finds herself helpless before the advances of a
   spellbinding imitation teenager, Arnold Friend.*

Tim O'Brien, THE THINGS THEY CARRIED   667
   *What each soldier carried into the combat zone was largely determined by
   necessity, but each man's necessities differed.*

Frank O'Connor, First Confession   680
A sympathetic Irish priest cross-examines a boy who takes a bread knife
to his sister and wants to chop up his grandmother besides.

Tillie Olsen, I Stand Here Ironing   687
Deserted by her husband, forced to send away her child, a woman
remembers how both she and her daughter managed to survive.

Leslie Marmon Silko, The Man to Send Rain Clouds   693
When old Teofilo dies, his friends give him a tribal burial to ensure that
the rains will come for the pueblo. But can they also convince Father Paul
to take part in the pagan ceremony?

Poetry   697

12   Reading a Poem   701

William Butler Yeats, The Lake Isle of Innisfree   703

Lyric Poetry   706
D. H. Lawrence, Piano   706
Adrienne Rich, Aunt Jennifer's Tigers   707

Narrative Poetry   708
Anonymous, Sir Patrick Spence   708
Robert Frost, "Out, Out—"   710

Dramatic Poetry   711
Robert Browning, My Last Duchess   712

Writer's Perspective
Adrienne Rich on Writing, Recalling "Aunt Jennifer's
Tigers"   714

Writing Critically
Can a Poem be Paraphrased?   715
William Stafford, Ask Me   715
William Stafford, A Paraphrase of "Ask Me"   716

Writing Assignment   716

13   Listening to a Voice   717

Tone   717
Theodore Roethke, My Papa's Waltz   718
Countee Cullen, For a Lady I Know   719

Anne Bradstreet, THE AUTHOR TO HER BOOK   719
Walt Whitman, TO A LOCOMOTIVE IN WINTER   720
Emily Dickinson, I LIKE TO SEE IT LAP THE MILES   721
Benjamin Alire Sáenz, TO THE DESERT   722
Weldon Kees, FOR MY DAUGHTER   723

THE PERSON IN THE POEM   723

Natasha Trethewey, WHITE LIES   724
Edwin Arlington Robinson, LUKE HAVERGAL   725
Ted Hughes, HAWK ROOSTING   726
William Wordsworth, I WANDERED LONELY AS A CLOUD   727
Dorothy Wordsworth, JOURNAL ENTRY   728
James Stephens, A GLASS OF BEER   729
Anne Sexton, HER KIND   730
William Carlos Williams, THE RED WHEELBARROW   731

IRONY   731

Robert Creeley, OH NO   732
W. H. Auden, THE UNKNOWN CITIZEN   733
Sharon Olds, RITES OF PASSAGE   734
John Betjeman, IN WESTMINSTER ABBEY   735
Sarah N. Cleghorn, THE GOLF LINKS   736
Josephine Miles, CIVILIAN   737
Connie Bensley, THE COVETOUS CAT   737
Thomas Hardy, THE WORKBOX   738

FOR REVIEW AND FURTHER STUDY

William Blake, THE CHIMNEY SWEEPER   739
Robert McDowell, AT HOME WITH DOLLFACE   740
William Stafford, AT THE UN-NATIONAL MONUMENT ALONG THE
   CANADIAN BORDER   740
H. L. Hix, I LOVE THE WORLD, AS DOES ANY DANCER   741
Richard Lovelace, TO LUCASTA   741
Wilfred Owen, DULCE ET DECORUM EST   742

WRITER'S PERSPECTIVE

Wilfred Owen on Writing, WAR POETRY   743

WRITING CRITICALLY

Paying Attention to the Obvious   744

WRITING ASSIGNMENT   744

STUDENT ESSAY

**Word Choice, Tone, and Point of View in Roethke's
"My Papa's Waltz"**   745

FURTHER SUGGESTIONS FOR WRITING   748

14 Words 749

Literal Meaning: What a Poem Says First 749

William Carlos Williams, This Is Just to Say 750
Marianne Moore, Silence 751
Robert Graves, Down, Wanton, Down! 752
John Donne, Batter my heart, three-personed God,
for You 753

The Value of a Dictionary 754

Henry Wadsworth Longfellow, Aftermath 755
John Clare, Mouse's Nest 756
J. V. Cunningham, Friend, on this scaffold Thomas More
lies dead 757
Kelly Cherry, Advice to a Friend Who Paints 758
Carl Sandburg, Grass 758

Word Choice and Word Order 758

Robert Herrick, Upon Julia's Clothes 761
Kay Ryan, Blandeur 763
Thomas Hardy, The Ruined Maid 764
Richard Eberhart, The Fury of Aerial Bombardment 765
Wendy Cope, Lonely Hearts 766

For Review and Further Study

E. E. Cummings, anyone lived in a pretty how town 767
Billy Collins, The Names 768
Anonymous, Carnation Milk 770
William Wordsworth, My heart leaps up when I behold 770
William Wordsworth, Mutability 770
Anonymous, Scottsboro 771
Lewis Carroll, Jabberwocky 771

Writer's Perspective

Lewis Carroll on Writing, Humpty Dumpty Explicates
"Jabberwocky" 773

Writing Critically

How Much Difference Does a Word Make? 774

Writing Assignment 775
Further Suggestions for Writing 775

15 *Saying and Suggesting* 776

John Masefield, Cargoes 777
William Blake, London 778
Wallace Stevens, Disillusionment of Ten O'Clock 780
Gwendolyn Brooks, the independent man 781
Timothy Steele, Epitaph 781
Geoffrey Hill, Merlin 782
Walter de la Mare, The Listeners 782
Robert Frost, Fire and Ice 784
Clare Rossini, Final Love Note 784
Alfred, Lord Tennyson, Tears, Idle Tears 785
Richard Wilbur, Love Calls Us to the Things of
    This World 786

Writer's Perspective

Richard Wilbur on Writing, Concerning "Love Calls Us to the
    Things of This World" 787

Writing Critically

The Ways a Poem Suggests 788

Writing Assignment 789
Further Suggestions for Writing 789

16 *Imagery* 790

Ezra Pound, In a Station of the Metro 790
Taniguchi Buson, The piercing chill I feel 790
T. S. Eliot, The winter evening settles down 792
Theodore Roethke, Root Cellar 792
Elizabeth Bishop, The Fish 793
Anne Stevenson, The Victory 795
Charles Simic, Fork 796
Emily Dickinson, A Route of Evanescence 796
Jean Toomer, Reapers 797
Gerard Manley Hopkins, Pied Beauty 797

About Haiku 798

Arakida Moritake, The falling flower 798
Matsuo Basho, Heat-lightning streak 799
Matsuo Basho, In the old stone pool 799
Taniguchi Buson, On the one-ton temple bell 799
Taniguchi Buson, I go 799
Kobayashi Issa, only one guy 799
Kobayashi Issa, Cricket 799

Suiko Matsushita, Rain shower from mountain 800
Suiko Matsushita, Cosmos in bloom 800
Neiji Ozawa, War forced us from California 800
Neiji Ozawa, The war 800
Hakuro Wada, Even the croaking of frogs 800
Etheridge Knight, Lee Gurga, Penny Harter, Jennifer Brutschy,
   John Ridland, Connie Bensley, Adelle Foley, A Selection
   of Haiku 800–801

For Review and Further Study

John Keats, Bright star! would I were steadfast as
   thou art 801
Walt Whitman, The Runner 802
T. E. Hulme, Image 802
Chana Bloch, Tired Sex 802
Robert Bly, Driving to Town Late to Mail a Letter 803
Gary Snyder, Piute Creek 803
H. D., Heat 804
Louise Glück, Mock Orange 804
Billy Collins, Embrace 805
John Haines, Winter News 805
Stevie Smith, Not Waving but Drowning 806

Writer's Perspective

Ezra Pound on Writing, The Image 807

Writing Critically

Analyzing Images 808

Writing Assignment 809

Student Essay

Elizabeth Bishop's Use of Imagery in "The Fish" 809

Further Suggestions for Writing 813

17 Figures of Speech 814

Why Speak Figuratively? 814

Alfred, Lord Tennyson, The Eagle 815
William Shakespeare, Shall I compare thee to a
   summer's day? 815
Howard Moss, Shall I Compare Thee to a Summer's Day? 816

Metaphor and Simile 817

Emily Dickinson, My Life had stood – a Loaded Gun 818

Alfred, Lord Tennyson, FLOWER IN THE CRANNIED WALL   819
William Blake, TO SEE A WORLD IN A GRAIN OF SAND   820
Sylvia Plath, METAPHORS   820
N. Scott Momaday, SIMILE   820
Emily Dickinson, IT DROPPED SO LOW – IN MY REGARD   821
Craig Raine, A MARTIAN SENDS A POSTCARD HOME   821

OTHER FIGURES   824

James Stephens, THE WIND   825
Chidiock Tichborne, ELEGY, WRITTEN WITH HIS OWN HAND IN
   THE TOWER BEFORE HIS EXECUTION   827
Margaret Atwood, YOU FIT INTO ME   828
John Ashbery, THE CATHEDRAL IS   828
George Herbert, THE PULLEY   828
Louis MacNeice, PLAIN SPEAKING   829

FOR REVIEW AND FURTHER STUDY

Robert Frost, THE SILKEN TENT   830
Denise Levertov, LEAVING FOREVER   831
Jane Kenyon, THE SUITOR   831
Robert Frost, THE SECRET SITS   832
H. D., LOVE THAT I BEAR   832
A. R. Ammons, COWARD   832
Kay Ryan, TURTLE   832
Robinson Jeffers, HANDS   833
Robert Burns, OH, MY LOVE IS LIKE A RED, RED ROSE   833

WRITER'S PERSPECTIVE

Robert Frost on Writing, THE IMPORTANCE OF POETIC
   METAPHOR   834

WRITING CRITICALLY

How Metaphors Enlarge a Poem's Meaning   835

WRITING ASSIGNMENT   836
FURTHER SUGGESTIONS FOR WRITING   836

18 *Song*   837

SINGING AND SAYING   837

Ben Jonson, TO CELIA   838
Anonymous, THE CRUEL MOTHER   839
William Shakespeare, TAKE, O, TAKE THOSE LIPS AWAY   841
Edwin Arlington Robinson, RICHARD CORY   842
Paul Simon, RICHARD CORY   843

BALLADS 844

Anonymous, BONNY BARBARA ALLAN 844
Dudley Randall, BALLAD OF BIRMINGHAM 847

BLUES 848

Bessie Smith with Clarence Williams, JAILHOUSE BLUES 849
W. H. Auden, FUNERAL BLUES 850

RAP 850

Run D.M.C., from PETER PIPER 852

FOR REVIEW AND FURTHER STUDY

John Lennon and Paul McCartney, ELEANOR RIGBY 853
Bob Dylan, THE TIMES THEY ARE A-CHANGIN' 854
Gwendolyn Brooks, QUEEN OF THE BLUES 856

WRITER'S PERSPECTIVE

Paul McCartney on Writing, CREATING "ELEANOR RIGBY" 858

WRITING CRITICALLY

Is There a Difference Between Poetry and Song? 859

WRITING ASSIGNMENT 860
FURTHER SUGGESTIONS FOR WRITING 860

19 *Sound* 861

SOUND AS MEANING 861

Alexander Pope, TRUE EASE IN WRITING COMES FROM ART,
 NOT CHANCE 862
William Butler Yeats, WHO GOES WITH FERGUS? 864
John Updike, RECITAL 865
William Wordsworth, A SLUMBER DID MY SPIRIT SEAL 865
Emanuel di Pasquale, RAIN 866
Aphra Behn, WHEN MAIDENS ARE YOUNG 866

ALLITERATION AND ASSONANCE 866

A. E. Housman, EIGHT O'CLOCK 868
Robert Herrick, UPON JULIA'S VOICE 868
Alfred, Lord Tennyson, THE SPLENDOR FALLS ON
 CASTLE WALLS 869

RIME 869

William Cole, ON MY BOAT ON LAKE CAYUGA 870
James Reeves, ROUGH WEATHER 872

Hilaire Belloc, THE HIPPOPOTAMUS 873
William Butler Yeats, LEDA AND THE SWAN 874
Gerard Manley Hopkins, GOD'S GRANDEUR 875
Fred Chappell, NARCISSUS AND ECHO · 875
Robert Frost, DESERT PLACES 876

READING AND HEARING POEMS ALOUD 877

Michael Stillman, IN MEMORIAM JOHN COLTRANE 879
William Shakespeare, FULL FATHOM FIVE THY FATHER LIES 879
Chryss Yost, LAI WITH SOUNDS OF SKIN 880
T. S. Eliot, VIRGINIA 880

WRITER'S PERSPECTIVE

T. S. Eliot on Writing, THE MUSIC OF POETRY 881

WRITING CRITICALLY

Is it Possible to Write About Sound? 882

WRITING ASSIGNMENT 882
FURTHER SUGGESTIONS FOR WRITING 882

20 *Rhythm* 884

STRESSES AND PAUSES 884

Gwendolyn Brooks, WE REAL COOL 889
Alfred, Lord Tennyson, BREAK, BREAK, BREAK 889
Ben Jonson, SLOW, SLOW, FRESH FOUNT, KEEP TIME WITH
  MY SALT TEARS 890
Alexander Pope, ATTICUS 891
Sir Thomas Wyatt, WITH SERVING STILL 892
Dorothy Parker, RÉSUMÉ 892

METER 892

Max Beerbohm, ON THE IMPRINT OF THE FIRST ENGLISH EDITION OF
  THE WORKS OF MAX BEERBOHM 893
Thomas Campion, ROSE-CHEEKED LAURA, COME 899
Vachel Lindsay, FACTORY WINDOWS ARE ALWAYS BROKEN 900
Edna St. Vincent Millay, COUNTING-OUT RHYME 901
A. E. Housman, WHEN I WAS ONE-AND-TWENTY 902
William Carlos Williams, HEEL & TOE TO THE END 902
Walt Whitman, BEAT! BEAT! DRUMS! 903
David Mason, SONG OF THE POWERS 904
Langston Hughes, DREAM BOOGIE 904

WRITER'S PERSPECTIVE

Gwendolyn Brooks on Writing, HEARING "WE REAL COOL"   905

WRITING CRITICALLY

Freeze-Framing the Sound   906

WRITING ASSIGNMENT   907
FURTHER SUGGESTIONS FOR WRITING   907

21   *Closed Form*   908

FORMAL PATTERNS   909

John Keats, THIS LIVING HAND, NOW WARM AND CAPABLE   910
Robert Graves, COUNTING THE BEATS   912
John Donne, SONG ("GO AND CATCH A FALLING STAR")   913
Phillis Levin, BRIEF BIO   914
Ronald Gross, YIELD   915

THE SONNET   917

William Shakespeare, LET ME NOT TO THE MARRIAGE OF
   TRUE MINDS   917
Michael Drayton, SINCE THERE'S NO HELP, COME LET US KISS
   AND PART   918
Edna St. Vincent Millay, WHAT LIPS MY LIPS HAVE KISSED,
   AND WHERE, AND WHY   919
Robert Frost, ACQUAINTED WITH THE NIGHT   919
Kim Addonizio, FIRST POEM FOR YOU   920
Mark Jarman, UNHOLY SONNET: AFTER THE PRAYING   920
R. S. Gwynn, SCENES FROM THE PLAYROOM   921
Timothy Steele, SUMMER   922
A. E. Stallings, SINE QUA NON   922

THE EPIGRAM   923

*Alexander Pope, Sir John Harrington, Robert Herrick, William
   Blake, E. E. Cummings, Langston Hughes, J. V. Cunningham,
   John Frederick Nims, Stevie Smith, Brad Leithauser, Dick
   Davis, Anonymous, Hilaire Belloc, Wendy Cope,* A SELECTION
   OF EPIGRAMS   923–925
*W. H. Auden, Edmund Clerihew Bentley, Cornelius J.
   Ter Maat,* CLERIHEWS   925–926

OTHER FORMS   926

Robert Pinsky, ABC   926
Dylan Thomas, DO NOT GO GENTLE INTO THAT GOOD NIGHT   927

Robert Bridges, Triolet   927
Elizabeth Bishop, Sestina   928

Writer's Perspective
Robert Graves on Writing, Poetic Inspiration and
   Poetic Form   930

Writing Critically
Turning Points   931

Writing Assignment   932
Further Suggestions for Writing   932

22 Open Form   933

Denise Levertov, Ancient Stairway   933
E. E. Cummings, Buffalo Bill 's   938
W. S. Merwin, For the Anniversary of My Death   938
William Carlos Williams, The Dance   939
Stephen Crane, The Heart   940
Walt Whitman, Cavalry Crossing a Ford   940
Ezra Pound, The Garret   941
Wallace Stevens, Thirteen Ways of Looking
   at a Blackbird   941
Carolyn Forché, The Colonel   944

Visual Poetry   944

George Herbert, Easter Wings   945
John Hollander, Swan and Shadow   946
Terry Ehret, from Papyrus   947
Dorthi Charles, Concrete Cat   948

Seeing the Logic of Open Form Verse   949

E. E. Cummings, in Just-   949
Lucille Clifton, Homage to my hips   950
Carole Satyamurti, I Shall Paint My Nails Red   951
Alice Fulton, What I Like   951

Writer's Perspective
Walt Whitman on Writing, The Poetry of the Future   952

Writing Critically
Lining Up for Free Verse   953

Writing Assignment   953
Further Suggestions for Writing   954

23 Symbol 955

T. S. Eliot, THE BOSTON EVENING TRANSCRIPT 956
Emily Dickinson, THE LIGHTNING IS A YELLOW FORK 957
Thomas Hardy, NEUTRAL TONES 959
Matthew 13: 24-30, THE PARABLE OF THE GOOD SEED 960
George Herbert, THE WORLD 960
John Ciardi, MOST LIKE AN ARCH THIS MARRIAGE 961
Robert Frost, THE ROAD NOT TAKEN 962
Christina Rossetti, UPHILL 963
Gjertrud Schnackenberg, SUPERNATURAL LOVE 963

FOR REVIEW AND FURTHER STUDY

Robinson Jeffers, THE BEAKS OF EAGLES 965
Sara Teasdale, THE FLIGHT 966
William Carlos Williams, THE TERM 967
Ted Kooser, CARRIE 968
Rafael Campo, WHAT THE BODY TOLD 968
Jon Stallworthy, AN EVENING WALK 969
Lorine Niedecker, POPCORN-CAN COVER 970
Wallace Stevens, ANECDOTE OF THE JAR 970

WRITER'S PERSPECTIVE

William Butler Yeats On Writing, POETIC SYMBOLS 971

WRITING CRITICALLY

How to Read a Symbol 972

WRITING ASSIGNMENT 972
FURTHER SUGGESTIONS FOR WRITING 973

24 Myth and Narrative 974

Robert Frost, NOTHING GOLD CAN STAY 976
D. H. Lawrence, BAVARIAN GENTIANS 977
Thomas Hardy, THE OXEN 977
William Wordsworth, THE WORLD IS TOO MUCH WITH US 978
H. D., HELEN 979

ARCHETYPE 979

Louise Bogan, MEDUSA 980

PERSONAL MYTH 981

William Butler Yeats, THE SECOND COMING 982
Jonathan Holden, THE NAMES OF THE RAPIDS 983

James Dickey, THE HEAVEN OF ANIMALS 984
Diane Thiel, MEMENTO MORI IN MIDDLE SCHOOL 985

MYTH AND POPULAR CULTURE 987
Charles Martin, TAKEN UP 988
A. D. Hope, IMPERIAL ADAM 989
Anne Sexton, CINDERELLA 990

WRITER'S PERSPECTIVE
Anne Sexton on Writing, TRANSFORMING FAIRY TALES 994

WRITING CRITICALLY
Demystifying Myth 995
WRITING ASSIGNMENT 996

STUDENT ESSAY
The Bonds Between Love and Hatred In H. D.'s "Helen" 997
FURTHER SUGGESTIONS FOR WRITING 1001

25 Poetry and Personal Identity 1002

Sylvia Plath, LADY LAZARUS 1003
Julia Alvarez, THE WOMEN ON MY MOTHER'S SIDE
  WERE KNOWN 1006

CULTURE, RACE, AND ETHNICITY 1007
Claude McKay, AMERICA 1007
Rhina Espaillat, BILINGUAL/BILINGÜE 1008
Samuel Menashe, THE SHRINE WHOSE SHAPE I AM 1010
Francisco X. Alarcón, THE X IN MY NAME 1010
Wendy Rose, FOR THE WHITE POETS WHO WOULD
  BE INDIAN 1011
Sherman Alexie, INDIAN BOY LOVE SONG (#1) 1012
Yusef Komunyakaa, FACING IT 1012

GENDER 1013
Anne Stevenson, SOUS-ENTENDU 1014
Emily Grosholz, LISTENING 1014
Donald Justice, MEN AT FORTY 1015
Adrienne Rich, WOMEN 1016

FOR REVIEW AND FURTHER STUDY
Shirley Geok-Lin Lim, LEARNING TO LOVE AMERICA 1016
Andrew Hudgins, ELEGY FOR MY FATHER, WHO IS
  NOT DEAD 1017

Judith Ortiz Cofer, QUINCEAÑERA 1018
Alastair Reid, SPEAKING A FOREIGN LANGUAGE 1019
Philip Larkin, AUBADE 1019

WRITER'S PERSPECTIVE
Rhina Espaillat, BEING A BILINGUAL WRITER 1021

WRITING CRITICALLY
Poetic Voice and Personal Identity 1022

WRITING ASSIGNMENT 1023
FURTHER SUGGESTIONS FOR WRITING 1023

26 Translation 1024

IS POETIC TRANSLATION POSSIBLE? 1024
Rainer Maria Rilke, EINGANG 1025
Rainer Maria Rilke, translated by Dana Gioia,
    ENTRANCE 1025

WORLD POETRY 1025
Li Po, DRINKING ALONE BENEATH THE MOON (CHINESE
    TEXT) 1026
Li Po, YUEH HSIA TU CHO, MOON-BENEATH ALONE DRINK
    (LITERAL TRANSLATION) 1027
Li Po, translated by Arthur Waley, DRINKING ALONE BY
    MOONLIGHT 1027
Horace, ODES I (11) (Carpe Diem) 1028
Horace, translated by Edwin Arlington Robinson, James Michie,
    A. E. Stallings, ODES I 1027–1030
Omar Khayyam, RUBAI 1031
Omar Khayyam, translated by Edward FitzGerald,
    Robert Graves and Omar Ali-Shah, Dick Davis, RUBAI 1031

PARODY 1032
Anonymous, WE FOUR LADS FROM LIVERPOOL ARE 1033
Wendy Cope, A NURSERY RHYME (AS IT MIGHT HAVE BEEN WRITTEN
    BY WILLIAM WORDSWORTH) 1034
Hugh Kingsmill, WHAT, STILL ALIVE AT TWENTY-TWO? 1034
Bruce Bennett, THE LADY SPEAKS AGAIN 1035
Gene Fehler, IF RICHARD LOVELACE BECAME A FREE AGENT 1035
Aaron Abeyta, THIRTEEN WAYS OF LOOKING AT A TORTILLA 1036

WRITER'S PERSPECTIVE
Arthur Waley on Writing, THE METHOD OF TRANSLATION 1038

WRITING CRITICALLY

Parody Is the Sincerest Form of Flattery 1039

WRITING ASSIGNMENT 1039
FURTHER SUGGESTIONS FOR WRITING 1040

27 *Critical Casebook: Latin American Poetry* 1041

SOR JUANA 1043

ASEGURA LA CONFIANZA DE QUE OCULTURÁ DE TODO UN
SECRETO 1044
   Translated by Diane Thiel, SHE PROMISES TO HOLD A SECRET
   IN CONFIDENCE 1044
PRESENTE EN QUE EL CARIÑO HACE REGALO LA LLANEZA 1044
   Translated by Diane Thiel, A SIMPLE GIFT MADE RICH BY
   AFFECTION 1044

PABLO NERUDA 1045

MUCHOS SOMOS 1046
   Translated by Alastair Reid, WE ARE MANY 1046
CIEN SONETOS DE AMOR (V) 1047
   Translated by Stephen Tapscott, ONE HUNDRED LOVE
   SONNETS (V) 1048

JORGE LUIS BORGES 1049

AMOROSA ANTICIPACIÓN 1050
   Translated by Robert Fitzgerald, ANTICIPATION
   OF LOVE 1050
LOS ENIGMAS 1051
   Translated by John Updike, THE ENIGMAS 1051

OCTAVIO PAZ 1052

CON LOS OJOS CERRADOS 1053
   Translated by John Felstiner, WITH OUR EYES SHUT 1053
CERTEZA 1053
   Translated by Charles Tomlinson, CERTAINTY 1053

SURREALISM IN LATIN AMERICAN POETRY 1053

Frida Kahlo, THE TWO FRIDAS 1055
César Vallejo, LA CÓLERA QUE QUIEBRA AL HOMBRE
   EN NIÑOS 1055
César Vallejo, Translated by Thomas Merton, ANGER 1056
Olga Orozco, LA REALIDAD Y EL DESEO 1056
Olga Orozco, Translated by Stephen Tapscott, REALITY AND
   DESIRE 1057

POEMS FOR FURTHER READING

Alfonsina Storni, Peso Ancestral 1058

Alfonsina Stoni, Translated by Diane Thiel, Ancestral
   Burden 1058

José Emilio Pacheco, Alta Traición 1058

José Emilio Pacheco, Translated by Alastair Reid, High
   Treason 1059

~ Latin American Poets on Poetry

Sor Juana, Reply to Sor Philothea 1059

Pablo Neruda, Towards the Splendid City 1060

Jorge Luis Borges, The Riddle of Poetry 1061

Octavio Paz, In Search of the Present 1062

~ Critics on Latin American Poetry

Stephanie Merrim, Endgames: Sor Juana Inés de la
   Cruz 1062

Alastair Reid, Translating Neruda 1063

Emir Rodríguez Monegal, Borges and Paz 1064

Suggestions for Writing 1065

28 *Recognizing Excellence* 1066

Anonymous, O Moon, when I gaze on thy beautiful face 1068

Grace Treasone, Life 1068

Emily Dickinson, A Dying Tiger—moaned for Drink 1069

Rod McKuen, Thoughts on Capital Punishment 1072

William Stafford, Traveling Through the Dark 1072

Wallace McRae, Reincarnation 1073

Recognizing Excellence 1075

William Butler Yeats, Sailing to Byzantium 1075

Arthur Guiterman, On the Vanity of Earthly Greatness 1078

Percy Bysshe Shelley, Ozymandias 1078

Robert Hayden, The Whipping 1079

Elizabeth Bishop, One Art 1080

W. H. Auden, September 1, 1939 1081

Walt Whitman, O Captain! My Captain! 1084

Carl Sandburg, Fog 1086

Emma Lazarus, The New Colossus 1087

Edgar Allan Poe, Annabel Lee 1088

WRITER'S PERSPECTIVE

Edgar Allan Poe on Writing, A LONG POEM DOES
NOT EXIST 1089

WRITING CRITICALLY

How to Begin Evaluating a Poem 1089

WRITING ASSIGNMENT 1090
FURTHER SUGGESTIONS FOR WRITING 1091

29 *What Is Poetry?* 1092

Archibald MacLeish, ARS POETICA 1092
*Dante, Samuel Johnson, Samuel Taylor Coleridge,
William Wordsworth, Thomas Carlyle, Thomas Hardy,
Emily Dickinson, Gerard Manley Hopkins, Robert Frost,
Wallace Stevens, Mina Loy, T. S. Eliot, W. H. Auden,
J. V. Cunningham, Elizabeth Bishop, Jorge Luis Borges,
Octavio Paz, William Stafford, Gwendolyn Brooks, Robert Bly,*
SOME DEFINITIONS OF POETRY 1093–1094
Ha Jin, MISSED TIME 1096

30 *Two Critical Casebooks: Emily Dickinson
and Langston Hughes* 1097

EMILY DICKINSON 1097

〜 POEMS

SUCCESS IS COUNTED SWEETEST 1098
WILD NIGHTS – WILD NIGHTS! 1098
THERE'S A CERTAIN SLANT OF LIGHT 1099
I FELT A FUNERAL, IN MY BRAIN 1099
I'M NOBODY! WHO ARE YOU? 1100
THE SOUL SELECTS HER OWN SOCIETY 1100
SOME KEEP THE SABBATH GOING TO CHURCH 1101
AFTER GREAT PAIN, A FORMAL FEELING COMES 1101
MUCH MADNESS IS DIVINEST SENSE 1101
THIS IS MY LETTER TO THE WORLD 1102
I HEARD A FLY BUZZ – WHEN I DIED 1102
I STARTED EARLY – TOOK MY DOG 1102
BECAUSE I COULD NOT STOP FOR DEATH 1103
THE BUSTLE IN A HOUSE 1104
TELL ALL THE TRUTH BUT TELL IT SLANT 1104

~ EMILY DICKINSON ON EMILY DICKINSON

RECOGNIZING POETRY 1105
SELF-DESCRIPTION 1106

~ CRITICS ON EMILY DICKINSON

Thomas Wentworth Higginson, MEETING EMILY DICKINSON 1108
Thomas H. Johnson, THE DISCOVERY OF EMILY DICKINSON'S
  MANUSCRIPTS 1109
Richard Wilbur, THE THREE PRIVATIONS OF EMILY DICKINSON 1111
Cynthia Griffin Wolff, DICKINSON AND DEATH (A READING OF
  "BECAUSE I COULD NOT STOP FOR DEATH") 1112
Judith Farr, A READING OF "MY LIFE HAD STOOD – A LOADED
  GUN" 1114

LANGSTON HUGHES 1116

~ POEMS

THE NEGRO SPEAKS OF RIVERS 1117
MOTHER TO SON 1117
DREAM VARIATIONS 1118
I, TOO 1118
THE WEARY BLUES 1119
SONG FOR A DARK GIRL 1120
DESIRE 1120
PRAYER 1120
BATTLE OF THE LANDLORD 1121
END 1122
ISLAND 1122
THEME FOR ENGLISH B 1122
SUBWAY RUSH HOUR 1123
SLIVER 1124
HARLEM [DREAM DEFERRED] 1124

~ LANGSTON HUGHES ON LANGSTON HUGHES

THE NEGRO ARTIST AND THE RACIAL MOUNTAIN 1125
THE HARLEM RENAISSANCE 1126

~ CRITICS ON LANGSTON HUGHES

Arnold Rampersad, HUGHES AS AN EXPERIMENTALIST 1128
Rita Dove and Marilyn Nelson, LANGSTON HUGHES
  AND HARLEM 1129
Darryl Pinckney, BLACK IDENTITY IN LANGSTON HUGHES 1131
Peter Townsend, LANGSTON HUGHES AND JAZZ 1132
Onwuchekwa Jemie, A READING OF "DREAM DEFERRED" 1134

FOR FURTHER READING 1136
SUGGESTIONS FOR WRITING 1136

31 *Poems for Further Reading* 1137

Anonymous, LORD RANDALL 1138

Anonymous, THE THREE RAVENS 1139

Anonymous, THE TWA CORBIES 1140

Anonymous, WESTERN WIND 1141

Anonymous, LAST WORDS OF THE PROPHET 1141

Matthew Arnold, DOVER BEACH 1141

John Ashbery, AT NORTH FARM 1142

Margaret Atwood, ROMANTIC 1143

W. H. Auden, AS I WALKED OUT ONE EVENING 1144

W. H. Auden, MUSÉE DES BEAUX ARTS 1146

Elizabeth Bishop, FILLING STATION 1147

William Blake, THE TYGER 1149

William Blake, THE SICK ROSE 1150

Eavan Boland, ANOREXIC 1151

Gwendolyn Brooks, THE MOTHER 1152

Gwendolyn Brooks, THE PREACHER RUMINATES: BEHIND THE
SERMON 1153

Elizabeth Barrett Browning, How DO I LOVE THEE? LET ME
COUNT THE WAYS 1154

Robert Browning, SOLILOQUY OF THE SPANISH CLOISTER 1154

Geoffrey Chaucer, MERCILESS BEAUTY 1156

G. K. Chesterton, THE DONKEY 1157

Samuel Taylor Coleridge, KUBLA KHAN 1158

Billy Collins, CARE AND FEEDING 1159

Hart Crane, MY GRANDMOTHER'S LOVE LETTERS 1160

E. E. Cummings, SOMEWHERE I HAVE NEVER TRAVELLED,
GLADLY BEYOND 1161

John Donne, DEATH BE NOT PROUD 1162

John Donne, THE FLEA 1163

John Donne, A VALEDICTION: FORBIDDING MOURNING 1164

Rita Dove, SUMMIT BEACH, 1921 1165

John Dryden, TO THE MEMORY OF MR. OLDHAM 1166

T.S. Eliot, JOURNEY OF THE MAGI 1167

T.S. Eliot, THE LOVE SONG OF J. ALFRED PRUFROCK 1169

Louise Erdrich, INDIAN BOARDING SCHOOL:
THE RUNAWAYS 1173

B. H. Fairchild, A STARLIT NIGHT 1174

Robert Frost, BIRCHES 1175

Robert Frost, MENDING WALL 1176

Robert Frost, STOPPING BY WOODS ON A SNOWY EVENING 1177

Allen Ginsberg, A SUPERMARKET IN CALIFORNIA 1178

Dana Gioia, CALIFORNIA HILLS IN AUGUST 1179

Thom Gunn, THE MAN WITH NIGHT SWEATS 1180

Donald Hall, NAMES OF HORSES 1181

Thomas Hardy, THE CONVERGENCE OF THE TWAIN   1182
Thomas Hardy, THE DARKLING THRUSH   1183
Thomas Hardy, HAP   1184
Robert Hayden, THOSE WINTER SUNDAYS   1185
Seamus Heaney, DIGGING   1186
Seamus Heaney, MOTHER OF THE GROOM   1187
Anthony Hecht, ADAM   1188
George Herbert, LOVE   1190
Robert Herrick, TO THE VIRGINS, TO MAKE MUCH OF TIME   1191
Gerard Manley Hopkins, SPRING AND FALL   1191
Gerard Manley Hopkins, NO WORST, THERE IS NONE   1192
Gerard Manley Hopkins, THE WINDHOVER   1193
A. E. Housman, LOVELIEST OF TREES, THE CHERRY NOW   1193
A. E. Housman, TO AN ATHLETE DYING YOUNG   1194
Randall Jarrell, THE DEATH OF THE BALL TURRET GUNNER   1195
Robinson Jeffers, TO THE STONE-CUTTERS   1196
Ben Jonson, ON MY FIRST SON   1196
Donald Justice, COUNTING THE MAD   1197
John Keats, ODE ON A GRECIAN URN   1197
John Keats, ON FIRST LOOKING INTO CHAPMAN'S HOMER   1199
John Keats, WHEN I HAVE FEARS THAT I MAY CEASE TO BE   1200
John Keats, TO AUTUMN   1201
Philip Larkin, HOME IS SO SAD   1202
Philip Larkin, POETRY OF DEPARTURES   1203
Irving Layton, THE BULL CALF   1204
Philip Levine, THEY FEED THEY LION   1205
Adrian Louis, LOOKING FOR JUDAS   1206
Robert Lowell, SKUNK HOUR   1206
Andrew Marvell, TO HIS COY MISTRESS   1208
James Merrill, KITE POEM   1209
Charlotte Mew, THE FARMER'S BRIDE   1210
Edna St. Vincent Millay, RECUERDO   1211
John Milton, HOW SOON HATH TIME   1212
John Milton, WHEN I CONSIDER HOW MY LIGHT IS SPENT   1212
Marianne Moore, POETRY   1213
Frederick Morgan, THE MASTER   1214
Marilyn Nelson, A STRANGE BEAUTIFUL WOMAN   1215
Howard Nemerov, THE WAR IN THE AIR   1216
Lorine Niedecker, SORROW MOVES IN WIDE WAVES   1217
Yone Noguchi, A SELECTION OF HOKKU   1218
Sharon Olds, THE ONE GIRL AT THE BOYS' PARTY   1219
Wilfred Owen, ANTHEM FOR DOOMED YOUTH   1220
Linda Pastan, ETHICS   1220
Robert Phillips, RUNNING ON EMPTY   1221
Sylvia Plath, DADDY   1222

Edgar Allan Poe, A Dream within a Dream 1225

Alexander Pope, A little Learning is a dang'rous
  Thing 1226

Ezra Pound, The River-Merchant's Wife: a Letter 1226

Dudley Randall, A Different Image 1228

John Crowe Ransom, Piazza Piece 1229

Henry Reed, Naming of Parts 1229

Adrienne Rich, Living in Sin 1230

Adrienne Rich, Power 1231

Edwin Arlington Robinson, Miniver Cheevy 1232

Theodore Roethke, Elegy for Jane 1233

Mary Jo Salter, Welcome to Hiroshima 1234

William Shakespeare, When, in disgrace with Fortune
  and men's eyes 1236

William Shakespeare, Not marble nor the gilded
  monuments 1237

William Shakespeare, Weary with toil, I haste me
  to my bed 1237

William Shakespeare, That time of year thou mayst
  in me behold 1238

William Shakespeare, My mistress' eyes are nothing
  like the sun 1238

Louis Simpson, American Poetry 1239

David R. Slavitt, Titanic 1239

Christopher Smart, For I will consider my Cat Jeoffry 1240

William Jay Smith, American Primitive 1242

Cathy Song, Stamp Collecting 1243

William Stafford, The Farm on the Great Plains 1244

Wallace Stevens, Peter Quince at the Clavier 1245

Wallace Stevens, The Emperor of Ice-Cream 1247

Ruth Stone, Second Hand Coat 1248

Jonathan Swift, A Description of the Morning 1248

Alfred, Lord Tennyson, Dark house, by which once
  more I stand 1249

Alfred, Lord Tennyson, Ulysses 1250

Dylan Thomas, Fern Hill 1252

John Updike, Ex-Basketball Player 1253

Amy Uyematsu, The Ten Million Flames of
  Los Angeles 1255

Derek Walcott, The Virgins 1257

Edmund Waller, Go, Lovely Rose 1258

Walt Whitman, A Noiseless Patient Spider 1258

Walt Whitman, I Hear America Singing 1259

Richard Wilbur, The Writer 1260

C. K. Williams, Elms 1261

William Carlos Williams, SPRING AND ALL 1261
William Carlos Williams, TO WAKEN AN OLD LADY 1262
William Wordsworth, COMPOSED UPON
  WESTMINSTER BRIDGE 1263
James Wright, A BLESSING 1264
James Wright, AUTUMN BEGINS IN MARTINS FERRY, OHIO 1265
Mary Sidney Wroth, IN THIS STRANGE LABYRINTH 1265
Sir Thomas Wyatt, THEY FLEE FROM ME THAT SOMETIME
  DID ME SEKË 1266
William Butler Yeats, CRAZY JANE TALKS WITH THE BISHOP 1267
William Butler Yeats, THE MAGI 1268
William Butler Yeats, WHEN YOU ARE OLD 1268

32 *Lives of the Poets* 1269

DRAMA 1299

33 *Reading a Play* 1303

A PLAY IN ITS ELEMENTS 1305

Susan Glaspell, TRIFLES 1305
> Was Minnie Wright to blame for the death of her husband? While the
> menfolk try to unravel a mystery, two women in the kitchen turn up
> revealing clues.

TRAGEDY 1321

John Millington Synge, RIDERS TO THE SEA 1322
> From her island home off the west coast of Ireland, Maurya has already
> lost seven loved ones to the sea. How can she stop her youngest son from
> venturing forth?

COMEDY 1331

David Ives, SURE THING 1334
> Bill wants to pick up Betty in a cafe, but he makes every mistake in the
> book. Luckily, he not only gets a second chance, but a third and a fourth
> as well.

Jane Martin, BEAUTY 1343
> We've all wanted to be someone else at one time or another. But what
> would happen if we got our wish?

WRITER'S PERSPECTIVE
Susan Glaspell on Drama, CREATING TRIFLES 1349

WRITING CRITICALLY
Conflict Resolution 1350

WRITING ASSIGNMENT 1351

STUDENT ESSAY
Outside Trifles 1351

FURTHER SUGGESTIONS FOR WRITING 1356

34 *Critical Casebook: Sophocles* 1357

THE THEATER OF SOPHOCLES 1357

STAGING 1357

THE CIVIC ROLE OF GREEK DRAMA 1361

ARISTOTLE'S CONCEPT OF TRAGEDY 1362

SOPHOCLES 1364

〜 PLAYS

THE ORIGINS OF OEDIPUS THE KING 1364
Sophocles, OEDIPUS THE KING *(Translated by Robert Fagles)* 1365
  *"Who is the man the voice of god denounces / resounding out of the rocky
  gorge of Delphi? / the horror too dark to tell / whose ruthless bloody hands
  have done the work?"*

THE BACKGROUND OF ANTIGONE 1434
Sophocles, ANTIGONE *(Translated by Robert Fagles)* 1435
  *In one of the great plays of classical Greek drama, a daughter of Oedipus
  strives to give the body of her slain brother a proper burial. Soon she finds
  herself in conflict with a king.*

〜 ROBERT FITZGERALD ON SOPHOCLES
Robert Fitzgerald, TRANSLATING SOPHOCLES 1489

〜 CRITICS ON SOPHOCLES
Aristotle, DEFINING TRAGEDY 1490
Sigmund Freud, THE DESTINY OF OEDIPUS 1491

E. R. Dodds, ON MISUNDERSTANDING OEDIPUS   1492
A. E. Haigh, THE IRONY OF SOPHOCLES   1493
Patricia M. Lines, ANTIGONE'S FLAW   1495

WRITING CRITICALLY
Some Things Change, Some Things Don't   1497

WRITING ASSIGNMENT   1498
FURTHER SUGGESTIONS FOR WRITING   1498

35 *Critical Casebook: Shakespeare*   1499

THE THEATER OF SHAKESPEARE   1499

WILLIAM SHAKESPEARE   1501

⟞ PLAYS

A NOTE ON OTHELLO   1501
William Shakespeare, OTHELLO, THE MOOR OF VENICE   1502
  *Here is a story of jealousy, that "green-eyed monster which doth mock /
  The meat it feeds on"—of a passionate, suspicious man and his blameless
  wife, of a serpent masked as a friend.*

THE BACKGROUND OF HAMLET   1603
William Shakespeare, HAMLET, PRINCE OF DENMARK   1604
  *In perhaps the most celebrated play in English, a ghost demands that
  young Prince Hamlet avenge his father's "most foul and unnatural
  murder." But how can Hamlet be sure that the apparition is indeed his
  father's spirit?*

THE BACKGROUND OF A MIDSUMMER NIGHT'S DREAM   1722
William Shakespeare, A MIDSUMMER NIGHT'S DREAM   1723
  *"The course of true love never did run smooth" is the right motto for this
  romantic comedy in which love, magic, and mistaken identity combine for
  madcap results.*

⟞ BEN JONSON ON SHAKESPEARE

Ben Jonson, ON HIS FRIEND AND RIVAL
  WILLIAM SHAKESPEARE   1786

⟞ CRITICS ON SHAKESPEARE

A. C. Bradley, HAMLET'S MELANCHOLY   1787
Rebecca West, HAMLET AND OPHELIA   1788

Jan Kott, PRODUCING HAMLET   1789

Joel Wingard, READER-RESPONSE ISSUES IN HAMLET   1791

W. H. Auden, IAGO AS A TRIUMPHANT VILLAIN   1792

Maud Bodkin, LUCIFER IN SHAKESPEARE'S OTHELLO   1792

Virginia Mason Vaughan, BLACK AND WHITE IN OTHELLO   1793

Anthony Burgess, AN ASIAN CULTURE LOOKS
   AT SHAKESPEARE   1794

John Russell Brown, RECOGNIZING LOVE IN A MIDSUMMER
   NIGHT'S DREAM   1795

Germaine Greer, SHAKESPEARE'S "HONEST MIRTH"   1797

Linda Bamber, FEMALE POWER IN A MIDSUMMER
   NIGHT'S DREAM   1797

WRITING CRITICALLY

Breaking the Language Barrier   1799

WRITING ASSIGNMENT   1799

STUDENT ESSAY

Othello: *Tragedy or Soap Opera?*   1800

FURTHER SUGGESTIONS FOR WRITING   1805

36 *The Modern Theater*   1806

REALISM AND NATURALISM   1806

Henrik Ibsen, A DOLL'S HOUSE (*Translated by*
James McFarlane)   1809
   The founder of modern drama portrays a troubled marriage. Helmer, the
   bank manager, regards his wife Nora as a chuckleheaded pet—not
   knowing the truth may shatter his smug world.

WRITER'S PERSPECTIVE

George Bernard Shaw on Drama, IBSEN AND THE FAMILIAR
   SITUATION   1867

TRAGICOMEDY AND THE ABSURD   1868

Milcha Sanchez-Scott, THE CUBAN SWIMMER   1870
   Nineteen-year-old Margarita Suárez wants to win a Southern California
   distance swimming race. Is her family behind her? Quite literally!

WRITER'S PERSPECTIVE

Milcha Sanchez-Scott on Drama, WRITING THE CUBAN
   SWIMMER   1885

WRITING CRITICALLY

What's So Realistic About Realism? 1886

WRITING ASSIGNMENT 1887

STUDENT ESSAY

Helmer vs. Helmer 1888

FURTHER SUGGESTIONS FOR WRITING 1891

37 *Evaluating a Play* 1892

WRITING CRITICALLY

Critical Performance 1893

WRITING ASSIGNMENT 1894
FURTHER SUGGESTIONS FOR WRITING 1894

38 *Plays for Further Reading* 1896

Arthur Miller, DEATH OF A SALESMAN 1897
Willy Loman has bright dreams for himself and his two sons, but he is an aging salesman whose only assets are a shoeshine and a smile. A modern classic about the downfall of an ordinary American.

WRITER'S PERSPECTIVE

Arthur Miller on Drama, TRAGEDY AND THE
    COMMON MAN 1969

Tennessee Williams, THE GLASS MENAGERIE 1972
Painfully shy and retiring, shunning love, Laura dwells in a world as fragile as her collection of tiny figurines—until one memorable night a gentleman comes to call.

WRITER'S PERSPECTIVE

Tennessee Williams on Drama, HOW TO STAGE THE GLASS
    MENAGERIE 2023

39 *New Voices in American Drama* 2026

Beth Henley, AM I BLUE 2026
His friends want to give John Polk a good time for his eighteenth birthday, but he finds something much more valuable instead.

WRITER'S PERSPECTIVE

Beth Henley on Drama, A PLAYWRIGHT IS BORN 2043

David Henry Hwang, THE SOUND OF A VOICE   2044
> *A strange man arrives at a solitary woman's home in the remote countryside. As they fall in love, they discover disturbing secrets about one another's past.*

WRITER'S PERSPECTIVE
David Henry Hwang on Drama, MULTICULTURAL
 THEATER   2059

Terrence McNally, ANDRE'S MOTHER   2060
> *After Andre's funeral the four people who loved him most walk into Central Park together. Three of them talk about their grief, but Andre's mother remains silent about her son, dead of AIDS.*

WRITER'S PERSPECTIVE
Terrence McNally on Drama, HOW TO WRITE A PLAY   2063

August Wilson, JOE TURNER'S COME AND GONE   2064
> *When Herald Loomis turns up at Seth Holly's boardinghouse, he arouses suspicion. And why is the voodoo man out in the garden burying a pigeon and praying over its blood?*

WRITER'S PERSPECTIVE
August Wilson on Drama, BLACK EXPERIENCE IN AMERICA   2114

WRITING   2117

40 *Writing About Literature*   2119

BEGINNING   2119

KEEPING A JOURNAL   2120

USING CRITICAL SOURCES AND
 MAINTAINING ACADEMIC INTEGRITY   2121

DISCOVERING ESSAY IDEAS   2121

DRAFTING AND REVISING, OR
 CREATIVITY VS. ANALYSIS   2124

THE FORM OF YOUR FINISHED PAPER   2127

USING SPELL-CHECK AND GRAMMER-CHECK
PROGRAMS 2127
Anonymous (after a poem by Jerrold H. Zar), A LITTLE POEM
REGARDING COMPUTER SPELL CHECKERS 2128

41 *Writing About a Story* 2130

EXPLICATING 2130
Sample Student Essay (Explication) 2132

ANALYZING 2135
Sample Student Essay (Analysis) 2136
Sample Student Card Report 2140

COMPARING AND CONTRASTING 2142

SUGGESTIONS FOR WRITING 2143

42 *Writing About a Poem* 2147

EXPLICATING 2148
Robert Frost, DESIGN 2149
Sample Student Essay (Explication) 2149

ANALYZING 2153
Sample Student Essay (Analysis) 2154

COMPARING AND CONTRASTING 2156
Abbie Huston Evans, WING-SPREAD 2157
Sample Student Essay (Comparison) 2158

HOW TO QUOTE A POEM 2160

BEFORE YOU BEGIN 2162

SUGGESTIONS FOR WRITING 2163
Robert Frost, IN WHITE (*early draft of* "DESIGN") 2165

43 *Writing About a Play* 2167

METHODS 2167

HOW TO QUOTE A PLAY 2169

WRITING A CARD REPORT   2170
Sample Student Card Report   2172

REVIEWING A PLAY   2174
Sample Student Drama Review   2175

SUGGESTIONS FOR WRITING   2176

44 Writing a Research Paper   2179

DOING RESEARCH FOR AN ESSAY   2179

EVALUATING AND USING INTERNET SOURCES   2181

GUARDING ACADEMIC INTEGRITY   2184

ACKNOWLEDGING AND DOCUMENTING SOURCES   2184

SAMPLE STUDENT RESEARCH PAPER   2193

CONCLUDING THOUGHTS   2193

REFERENCE GUIDE FOR CITATIONS   2194

45 Critical Approaches to Literature   2201

FORMALIST CRITICISM   2202
Cleanth Brooks, THE FORMALIST CRITIC   2203
Michael Clark, LIGHT AND DARKNESS IN "SONNY'S BLUES"   2204
Robert Langbaum, ON ROBERT BROWNING'S
"MY LAST DUCHESS"   2205

BIOGRAPHICAL CRITICISM   2207
Virginia Llewellyn Smith, CHEKHOV'S ATTITUDE TO
ROMANTIC LOVE   2208
Brett C. Millier, ON ELIZABETH BISHOP'S "ONE ART"   2210
Emily Toth, THE SOURCE FOR ALCÉE LABALLIÈRE IN
"THE STORM"   2211

HISTORICAL CRITICISM   2212
Hugh Kenner, IMAGISM   2213
Joseph Moldenhauer, "TO HIS COY MISTRESS" AND THE
RENAISSANCE TRADITION   2215

Barbara T. Christian, "Everyday Use" and the Black Power
    Movement   2216

Psychological Criticism   2218

Sigmund Freud, The Nature of Dreams   2219
Gretchen Schulz and R. J. R. Rockwood, Fairy Tale Motifs in
    "Where Are You Going, Where Have You Been?"   2220
Harold Bloom, Poetic Influence   2222

Mythological Criticism   2223

C. G. Jung, The Collective Unconscious
    and Archetypes   2223
Northrop Frye, Mythic Archetypes   2224
Edmond Volpe, Myth in Faulkner's "Barn Burning"   2225

Sociological Criticism   2227

Georg Lukacs, Content Determines Form   2228
Daniel P. Watkins, Money and Labor in "The Rocking-Horse
    Winner"   2229
Alfred Kazin, Walt Whitman and Abraham Lincoln   2230

Gender Criticism   2231

Elaine Showalter, Toward a Feminist Poetics   2232
Juliann Fleenor, Gender and Pathology in "The Yellow
    Wallpaper"   2233
Sandra M. Gilbert and Susan Gubar, The Freedom
    of Emily Dickinson   2234

Reader-Response Criticism   2235

Stanley Fish, An Eskimo "A Rose for Emily"   2236
Robert Scholes, "How Do We Make a Poem?"   2237
Michael J. Colacurcio, The End of Young Goodman
    Brown   2239

Deconstructionist Criticism   2240

Roland Barthes, The Death of the Author   2241
Barbara Johnson, Rigorous Unreliability   2242
Geoffrey Hartman, On Wordsworth's "A Slumber Did My
    Spirit Seal"   2243

Cultural Studies   2245

Vincent B. Leitch, Poststructuralist Cultural
    Critique   2246
Mark Bauerlein, What Is Cultural Studies?   2247
Heather Glen, The Stance of Observation in William Blake's
    "London"   2249

Glossary of Literary Terms   G1

Acknowledgments   A1
Photo Acknowledgments   A17
Index of Authors and Titles   I1
List of Authors (front endpapers)
Index of Literary Terms (back endpapers)

Preface

Literature, Ninth Edition—the book in your hands—is really four interlocking volumes sharing one cover. Each of the first three sections is devoted to one of the major literary forms—fiction, poetry, and drama. The fourth section is a comprehensive introduction to critical writing. All together, the book is an attempt to provide the college student with a reasonably compact introduction to the study and appreciation of stories, poems, and plays—as well as practical advice on the sort of writing expected in a college English course.

We assume that appreciation begins in delighted attention to words on a page. Speed reading has its uses; but at times, as Robert Frost said, the person who reads for speed "misses the best part of what a good writer puts into it." Close reading, then, is essential. Still, we do not believe that close reading tells us everything, that it is wrong to read a literary work by any light except that of the work itself. At times we suggest different approaches such as referring to the facts of an author's life, looking for myth, or seeing the conventions that typify a kind of writing—noticing, for instance, that an old mansion, cobwebbed and creaking, is the setting for a Gothic horror story.

Although we cannot help having a few convictions about the meanings of stories, poems, and plays, we have tried to step back and give you room to make up your own mind. Here and there, in the wording of a question, our opinions may occasionally stick out. If you should notice any, please feel free to ignore them. Be assured that no one interpretation, laid down by authority, is the only right one for any work of literature. Trust your own interpretation—provided that in making it you have looked clearly and carefully at the evidence.

Reading literature often will provide you with reason to write. At the back of the book, there are several chapters that give the student writer some practical advice. It will guide you, step-by-step, in finding a topic, planning an essay, writing, revising, and putting your paper into finished form. Further, you will find there specific help in writing about fiction, poetry, and drama. There are also short features at the end of every chapter that provide help and perspective on writing about literature. In a few places we have even offered some suggestions about writing your own stories or poems—in case reading the selections in this book inspires you to try your hand at imaginative writing.

A WORD ABOUT CAREERS

Most students agree that to read celebrated writers such as William Faulkner, Emily Dickinson, and William Shakespeare is probably good for the spirit. Most students even take some pleasure in the experience. But many, not planning to teach English and impatient to begin some other career, wonder if the study of literature, however enjoyable, isn't a waste of time—or at least, an annoying obstacle.

This objection may seem reasonable at first glance, but it rests on a shaky assumption. Success in a career does not depend merely on learning the specialized information and skills required to join a profession. In most careers, according to one senior business executive, people often fail not because they don't understand their jobs, but because they don't understand their co-workers, their clients, or their customers. They don't ever see the world from another person's point of view. Their problem is a failure of imagination.

To leap over the wall of self and to look through another's eyes is valuable experience that literature offers. If you are lucky, you may never meet (or have to do business with) anyone *exactly* like Mrs. Turpin in the story "Revelation," and yet you will learn much about the kind of person she is from Flannery O'Connor's fictional portrait of her. What is it like to be black, a white may wonder? James Baldwin, Gwendolyn Brooks, Rita Dove, Langston Hughes, Zora Neale Hurston, Alice Walker, August Wilson, and others have knowledge to impart. What is it like to be a woman? If a man would learn, let him read (for a start) Sandra Cisneros, Kate Chopin, Susan Glaspell, Alice Munro, Sylvia Plath, Katherine Anne Porter, Flannery O'Connor, Tillie Olsen, Adrienne Rich, and Amy Tan, and perhaps, too, Henrik Ibsen's A *Doll's House* and John Steinbeck's "The Chrysanthemums."

Plodding single-mindedly toward careers, some people are like horses wearing blinders. For many, the goals looked fixed and predictable. Competent nurses, accountants, and dental technicians seem always in demand. Others may find that in our society some careers, like waves in the sea, will rise or fall unexpectedly. Think how many professions we now take for granted, which a few years ago didn't even exist: genetic engineering, energy conservation, digital editing, and Web site design. Others that once looked like lifetime meal tickets have been cut back and nearly ruined: shoe repairing, commercial fishing, railroading.

In a perpetually changing society, it may be risky to lock yourself on one track to a career, refusing to consider any other. "We are moving," writes John Naisbitt in *Megatrends*, a study of our changing society, "from the specialist, soon obsolete, to the generalist who can adapt." Perhaps the greatest opportunity in your whole life lies in a career that has yet to be invented. If you do change your career as you go along, you will be like most people. According to a U.S. Bureau of Labor Statistics survey conducted in April, 2000, the average person holds over nine jobs between the ages of 18 and 34—often completely changing his or her basic occupation. When for some unforeseen reason you have to make such a change, basic skills—and a knowledge of humanity—may be your most valuable credentials.

Literature has much practical knowledge to offer you. An art of words, it can help you become more sensitive to language—both your own and other people's. It can make you aware of the difference between the word that is exactly right and the word that is merely good enough—Mark Twain calls it "the difference between the lightning and the lightning-bug." Read a fine work of literature alertly, and some of its writer's sensitivity to words may grow on you. A Supreme Court Justice, John Paul Stevens, once remarked that the best preparation for law school is to study poetry. Why? George D. Gopen, an English professor with a law degree, says it may be because "no other discipline so closely replicates the central question asked in the study of legal thinking: Here is a text; in how many ways can it have meaning?"

Many careers today, besides law, call for close reading and clear writing—as well as careful listening and thoughtful speech. Lately, college placement directors have reported more demand for graduates who are good readers and writers. The reason is evident: employers need people who can handle words. In a survey conducted by Cornell University, business executives were asked to rank in importance the traits they look for when hiring. Leadership was first, but skill in writing and speaking came in fourth, ahead of both managerial and analytical skills. Times change, but to think cogently and to express yourself well will always be the abilities the world needs.

KEY LITERARY TERMS

Every discipline has its own terminology. This book introduces a large range of critical terms that may help you in both your reading and writing. When these important words and phrases are first defined, they are printed in **boldface.** If you find a critical term anywhere in this book you don't know or don't recall (for example, what is a *carpe diem* poem or a *dramatic question*?), just look it up in the "Glossary of Literary Terms" in the back of the book.

TEXTS AND DATES

Every effort has been made to supply each selection in its most accurate text and (where necessary) in a lively, faithful translation. For the reader who wishes to know when a work was written, at the right of each title appears the date of its first publication in book form. Parentheses around a date indicate the work's date of composition or first magazine publication, given when it was composed much earlier than when it was first published in book form.

A POSSIBLY PUZZLING ASTERISK

Throughout the poetry section of *Literature*, you will often notice an asterisk (*) after a poet's byline. This asterisk indicates that there is a short biography of the author in Chapter 32, "Lives of the Poets." This special chapter offers 79 biographies of the poets represented in the anthology by two or more poems. For easy reference we have tucked them into one place. The only exceptions are the more extensive biographical notes on Sor Juana, Pablo Neruda, Jorge Luis Borges, and Octavio Paz, the poets collected in Chapter 27, "Critical Casebook:

Latin American Poetry," and Emily Dickinson and Langston Hughes, which appear (with substantial selections of their work) in Chapter 30, "Two Critical Casebooks: Emily Dickinson and Langston Hughes." (All writers featured in the fiction and drama sections have individual biographies preceding their stories or plays.)

But enough housekeeping, let's enjoy ourselves and read some unforgettable stories, poems, and plays.

X. J. K. AND D. G.

To the Instructor

Literature, Ninth Edition, is a book divided into four more or less equal parts—fiction, poetry, drama, and writing. The aim of the book is first to introduce college students to the appreciation and experience of literature in its major forms. Second, the book tries to develop the student's ability to think critically and to communicate effectively through writing.

Both editors of this volume are writers. We believe that textbooks should not only be informative and accurate but also lively, accessible, and engaging. Our intent has always been to write a book that students will read eagerly and enjoy.

The new edition of *Literature* offers a number of compelling features:

- **Diverse and exciting stories**—65 stories from familiar classics to contemporary work from around the globe.
- **Great poems old and new**—Over 500 poems mixing classic favorites with exciting contemporary work.
- **A rich array of plays**—17 plays from the classical tragedies by Sophocles to contemporary works by Beth Henley, Jane Martin, and Milcha Sanchez-Scott, plus three plays by Shakespeare.
- **New and revised author casebooks**—a new casebook on Edgar Allan Poe joins the features on Flannery O'Connor, Emily Dickinson, Langston Hughes, Sophocles, and Shakespeare. Multiple selections by each author are given along with reflections by the author, critical articles, and other contextual material.
- **New Casebook on Latin American Poetry**—invites students to experience an important world poetry in a different language and translation. Poems from Sor Juana, Pablo Neruda, Jorge Luis Borges, Octavio Paz, and others illuminate different cultural experiences.
- **Abundant critical coverage**—117 critical excerpts including a comprehensive survey of ten major schools of literary criticism and theory.
- **Writing coverage**—integrated into every chapter with exercises, sample papers, and pragmatic advice. Five complete chapters are devoted to writing about literature and include student drafts and completed papers.
- **New chapter on writing a research paper**—offers helpful advice on such topics as getting started, evaluating and using Internet sources, guarding academic integrity, plagiarism, and acknowledging and documenting sources. A student research paper appears in Chapter 9.
- **Real student writing**—16 student essays and reports by real students provide credible examples on how to write about literature.

All in all, we have tried to create a book to help readers develop sensitivity to language, culture, and identity to lead them beyond the boundaries of their own selves and see the world through the eyes of others. This book is built on the assumption that great literature can enrich and enlarge the lives it touches.

FEATURES IN THIS EDITION

We have revised the ninth edition of *Literature* with the simple aim of introducing useful new features and selections without losing the best liked material. We have been guided in this effort by scores of instructors and students who use the book in their classrooms. Teaching is a kind of conversation between instructor and student and between reader and text. By revising *Literature*, we try to help keep this conversation fresh by mixing the classic with the new and the familiar with the surprising.

CASEBOOKS ON MAJOR AUTHORS

We continue to include six substantial casebooks on major authors. These special chapters present a variety of material—biographies, photographs, critical commentaries, statements by the authors, and a deep selection of the featured writer's work. Our aim has been to provide everything a student might need to begin an in-depth study of each author. Two major writers from each basic literary form have been featured.

For fiction, the casebooks showcase Edgar Allan Poe (new to this edition) and Flannery O'Connor with six selections from each author (three stories and three critical statements), as well as a selection of responses from eight critics. For poetry, we present in-depth selections from Emily Dickinson and Langston Hughes with fifteen poems each—supplemented by others elsewhere in the volume—as well as ten critical articles, photographs, facsimiles, letters, and statements. For drama we have created two extensive chapters on Sophocles and Shakespeare. The critical casebook on Sophocles offers commentary, photographs, and diagrams as well as a selection of critical articles. The casebook on Shakespeare includes three complete plays—not only *Hamlet* and *Othello*, but also *A Midsummer Night's Dream*, as well as a dozen critical excerpts on the author and his plays.

NEW LATIN AMERICAN POETRY CASEBOOK

Experiencing poetry in a different language and in translation gives students the opportunity to see how poetry represents and illuminates a different cultural experience. A new thematic casebook, "Latin American Poetry," gives students this enriching and challenging experience with voices including Sor Juana, Pablo Neruda, Jorge Luis Borges, and Octavio Paz. Students are also introduced to the role of surrealism in Latin American poetry with an image from Frida Kahlo and words from César Vallejo and Olga Orozco. We feel this important and unique new chapter will not only broaden most students' knowledge of world poetry, but will also recognize the richness of Spanish-language poetry in the literature of the Americas—a very relevant subject to today's multicultural classrooms.

GLOSSARY OF LITERARY TERMS

The comprehensive "Glossary of Literary Terms" at the back of the book has been retained by popular demand from the previous edition. It includes every term highlighted in boldface throughout the text as well as other important terms—over 350 entries in all—providing a clear and accurate definition usually with cross references to related terms. The purpose of the glossary is to provide a single accessible reference for students of all key literary terms.

WRITING MATERIAL

All the main chapters still include a Writer's Perspective, a Writing Critically feature, and Further Suggestions for Writing. The extremely popular Writer's Perspective provides an author's own comments on his or her work reprinted in the chapter. These 50 statements range across the literary spectrum from Franz Kafka discussing *The Metamorphosis* and Gwendolyn Brooks explaining "We Real Cool," to Tennessee Williams describing an ideal production of *A Glass Menagerie* and Amy Tan recalling how she developed a narrative voice. Meanwhile the Writing Critically feature provides students with practical advice on planning and composing critical essays as well as offering specific assignments for possible term papers.

We have also reprinted 13 complete student papers to provide models for critical writing, including a research paper. (There are also two card reports and a review.) Five of the papers are found in final chapters, "Writing About Fiction," "Writing About Poetry," and "Writing About Drama," where they illustrate three different approaches to critical writing—explication, analysis, and comparison—as well as a drama review. Eight papers will be found in earlier chapters. Each of these papers focus on a single work or author in the book (John Steinbeck's "The Chrysanthemums," Franz Kafka, Theodore Roethke's "My Papa's Waltz," Elizabeth Bishop's "The Fish," H. D.'s "Helen," Susan Glaspell's *Trifles*, Shakespeare's *Othello*, and Henrik Ibsen's *A Doll's House*). The papers also provide close readings of the literary works that emphasize specific elements of their structure and meaning. The final chapters on critical writing have also been revised and updated.

NEW CHAPTER, "WRITING A RESEARCH PAPER"

A new addition to the writing section is Chapter 44, "Writing a Research Paper." Guiding students through the research process, the chapter covers such topics as getting started, evaluating and using Internet sources, guarding academic integrity, plagiarism, and acknowledging and documenting sources. A student research paper appears in Chapter 9.

NEW STORIES, POEMS, AND PLAYS

There are many new selections in the book. A great deal of help came from both instructors and students who use the book. Their suggestions helped confirm the new stories, poems, and plays that work best in the classroom while identifying older selections that seemed less valuable and could be retired to make room for new work.

FICTION

The fiction section now includes many new stories, bringing the total selection to 65. (There are also 22 pieces of critical prose.) We have added several new stories to broaden and update our coverage. Many of the new stories deepen our international and multicultural coverage such as Isabel Allende's "The Judge's Wife"; Sandra Cisneros's "The House on Mango Street"; Gabriel García Márquez's "The Handsomest Drowned Man in the World"; and Jhumpa Lahiri's "Interpreter of Maladies." We've brought back Elizabeth Tallent's "No One's a Mystery" and added a new story, "Day of the Butterfly," by Alice Munro.

A few classic stories also have been added including two stories by Edgar Allan Poe—"The Masque of the Red Death" and "The Fall of the House of Usher." We've kept Leo Tolstoy's harrowing novella, *The Death of Ivan Ilyich*—due to the impassioned requests of several instructors. Also retained by popular demand is Kurt Vonnegut's mordant satire "Harrison Bergeron," a contemporary science-fiction classic that has become a classroom favorite. Vonnegut's story helps maintain our coverage of popular fictional genres—a long-standing interest of this anthology. The current edition contains classic examples of the Gothic tale (Gilman, Poe), the adventure story (London, Crane), science fiction (Vonnegut, Le Guin), as well as Magical Realism (García Márquez, Borges). These selections combine with traditional realist and modernist stories to demonstrate the full range of the short story's possibilities.

POETRY

Literature proudly provides the most extensive selection of poems found in any comparable book in the field—over 500 poems in the new edition. We have added more than 70 new poems to the book—to freshen the selections, update our coverage of contemporary work, and expand our presentation of Asian and Latin American poetry.

The new Latin American poetry casebook includes a pair of poems by Sor Juana, Pablo Neruda, Jorge Luis Borges, and Octavio Paz. Surrealism in Latin American poetry is explored through an image from Frida Kahlo and words from César Vallejo and Olga Orozco. Works from other fine contemporary Latin American poets are included.

Many other fine new poems have been added by writers including Sherman Alexie, W. H. Auden, Connie Bensley, Gwendolyn Brooks, Billy Collins, Wendy Cope, Rita Dove, B. H. Fairchild, Donald Justice, Louis MacNeice,

Suiko Matsushita, Robert McDowell, Josephine Miles, John Milton, Rainer Maria Rilke, Gary Snyder, Natasha Trethewey, Amy Uyematsu, and William Carlos Williams. Not only are Dickinson and Hughes presented in depth, but the reader will also find multiple selections by W. H. Auden, William Blake, Gwendolyn Brooks, E. E. Cummings, John Donne, T. S. Eliot, Robert Frost, Thomas Hardy, Gerard Manley Hopkins, John Keats, Edna St. Vincent Millay, Adrienne Rich, William Shakespeare, Wallace Stevens, Alfred, Lord Tennyson, Walt Whitman, William Carlos Williams, William Wordsworth, and William Butler Yeats.

DRAMA

We have added two contemporary new plays to the drama section: Jane Martin's *Beauty* and Beth Henley's *Am I Blue*. We have also kept our coverage of both comedy and Shakespeare by including *A Midsummer Night's Dream*. Both Sophocles and Shakespeare are the subjects of extensive casebooks, which include 18 critical commentaries on the dramatists. Illustrations have been extensively integrated into the text to provide students with visual reference points to the texts.

CRITICAL APPROACHES TO LITERATURE

Chapter 45, "Critical Approaches to Literature," has proven so popular in the last few editions that we have kept and slightly updated it in the new *Literature*. There are three selections for every major critical school—30 selections in all. The critical excerpts have been carefully chosen both to illustrate the major theoretical approaches and to be accessible to beginning students. All the critical selections focus on literary works found in the present edition. Among the new critical excerpts are examinations of works by Kate Chopin, Alice Walker, and Joyce Carol Oates. Taken together with the many commentaries in the casebooks and Writer's Perspectives, *Literature* now includes a total of 117 critical excerpts. This expanded coverage gives *Literature* both more depth and flexibility for instructors who prefer to incorporate literary theory and criticism into their introductory courses.

OTHER EDITIONS AVAILABLE

Instructors who wish to use only the fiction section or only the poetry section of this book are assured that *An Introduction to Fiction*, Ninth Edition, and *An Introduction to Poetry*, Eleventh Edition, contain the full and complete contents of these sections. Each book has writing chapters applicable to its subject, as well as the chapters "Writing About Literature," "Writing a Research Paper," and "Critical Approaches to Literature."

There is also a compact edition in paperback of *Literature: An Introduction to Fiction, Poetry, and Drama*, Fourth Edition, for instructors who find the full edition "too much book." Although this compact version offers a slightly abridged table of contents, it still covers the complete range of topics presented in the full edition.

For instructors who want to incorporate media into their class, interactive editions of *Literature* and of *Compact Literature* come packaged with *The Craft of Literature* CD-ROM (see below) and contain icons in the margins identifying authors and selections featured on the CD-ROM and the book's Companion Website.

RESOURCES FOR STUDENTS AND INSTRUCTORS

FOR STUDENTS

THE CRAFT OF LITERATURE CD-ROM

Organized around *Literature's* table of contents, *The Craft of Literature* is a multimedia CD-ROM offering film footage, audio, photographs, Web links, interactive readings, critical articles, and student papers. Every entry on the CD-ROM is accompanied by critical thinking questions or writing prompts. Instructors can assign the projects for students to submit via e-mail, or students can use the questions independently to deepen their appreciation and understanding of the featured selections. CD-ROM icons in the Interactive Edition of *Literature* identify authors and selections featured in *The Craft of Literature*. You can order *The Craft of Literature* free with this textbook or order the special Interactive Edition of *Literature*, Ninth Edition. Contact your Longman publisher's representative for more information.

COMPANION WEBSITE TO LITERATURE, NINTH EDITION

(http://www.ablongman.com/kennedy)
The text-specific site includes biographies, bibliographies, and links to sites about many of the authors found in *Literature*, Ninth Edition.

HANDBOOK OF LITERARY TERMS

Handbook of Literary Terms by X. J. Kennedy, Dana Gioia, and Mark Bauerlein is a user-friendly primer of over 350 critical terms brought to life with literary examples, pronunciation guides, and scholarly yet accessible explanations. Aimed at undergraduates getting their first taste of serious literary study, the volume will help students engage with the humanities canon and become critical readers and writers ready to experience the insights and joy of great fiction, poetry, and drama.

RESPONDING TO LITERATURE: A WRITER'S JOURNAL

This free journal provides students with their own personal space for writing. Helpful writing prompts for responding to fiction, poetry, and drama are also included.

EVALUATING PLAYS ON FILM AND VIDEO

This guide walks students through the process of analyzing and writing about plays on film, whether in a short review or a longer essay. It covers each stage of the process, from preparing and analyzing material through writing the piece. The four appendices include writing and editing tips and a glossary of film terms. The final portion of the guide offers worksheets to help students organize their notes and thoughts before they begin writing.

EVALUATING A PERFORMANCE

Perfect for the student assigned to review a local production, this free supplement offers students a convenient place to record their evaluation. Useful tips and suggestions of things to consider when evaluating a production are included.

LITERATURE TIMELINE

This accessible and visually appealing timeline provides students with a chronological overview of major literary works written throughout history. The timeline also lists the major sociocultural and political events that occurred contemporaneously with these major works of literature, providing students with historical and contextual insights into the impact historical events have had on writers and their works and vice versa.

RESEARCH NAVIGATOR GUIDE FOR ENGLISH

Designed to teach students how to conduct high-quality online research and to document it properly, *Research Navigator* guides provide discipline-specific academic resources in addition to helpful tips on the writing process, online research, and finding and citing valid sources. Free when packaged with any Longman text, *Research Navigator* guides include an access code to Research Navigator™, providing access to thousands of academic journals and periodicals, the New York Times Search by Subject Archive, Link Library, Library Guides, and more.

FOR INSTRUCTORS

INSTRUCTOR'S MANUAL

A separate *Instructor's Manual* is available to instructors. If you have never seen our *Instructor's Manual* before, don't prejudge it. We actually write the manual ourselves, and we work hard to make it as interesting, lively, and informed as the parent text. It offers commentary and teaching ideas for every selection in the book. It also contains additional commentary, debate, qualifications and information—including scores of classroom ideas—from over one hundred teachers and authors. As you will see, our *Instructor's Manual* is no ordinary book.

TEACHING COMPOSITION WITH LITERATURE

For instructors who either use *Literature* in expository writing courses or have a special emphasis on writing in their literature courses, there is an invaluable supplement, *Teaching Composition with Literature: 101 Writing Assignments from College Instructors*. Edited by Dana Gioia and Patricia Wagner, *Teaching Composition with Literature* collects proven writing assignments and classroom exercises from scores of instructors across North America. Each assignment or exercise uses one or more selections in *Literature* as its departure point. A great many instructors have enthusiastically shared their best writing assignments for *Teaching Composition with Literature*.

PENGUIN DISCOUNT NOVEL PROGRAM

In cooperation with Penguin Putnam, Inc., one of our sibling companies, Longman is proud to offer a variety of Penguin paperbacks at a significant discount when packaged with any Longman title. Excellent additions to any literature course, Penguin titles give students the opportunity to explore contemporary and classical fiction and drama. The available titles include works by authors as diverse as Toni Morrison, Julia Alvarez, Mary Shelley, and Shakespeare. To review the complete list of titles available, visit the Longman-Penguin-Putnam website: *http://www.ablongman.com/penguin*.

VIDEO PROGRAM

For qualified adopters, an impressive selection of videotapes is available to enrich students' experience of literature. The videos include selections from William Shakespeare, Sylvia Plath, Ezra Pound, and Alice Walker. Contact your Allyn & Bacon/Longman sales representative to see if you qualify.

TEACHING LITERATURE ON-LINE, SECOND EDITION

Concise and practical, *Teaching Literature On-line* provides instructors with strategies and advice for incorporating elements of computer technology into the literature classroom. Offering a range of information and examples, this manual provides ideas and activities for enhancing literature courses with the help of technology.

THE LONGMAN ELECTRONIC TESTBANK FOR LITERATURE

This electronic test bank features various objective questions on major works of fiction, short fiction, poetry, and drama. With this user-friendly CD-ROM, instructors simply choose questions from the electronic test bank, then print out the completed test for distribution.

CONTACT US

For examination copies of any of these books, CDs, videos, and programs, please contact your Allyn & Bacon/Longman sales representative, or write to Literature Marketing Manager, Longman Publishers, 1185 Avenue of the Americas, New York, NY 10036. For examination copies only, call (800) 922-0579. To order an examination copy via the Internet: *http://www.ablongman.com* or E-mail: *exam.copies@ablongman.com*.

THANKS

The collaboration necessary to create this new edition goes far beyond the partnership of its two editors. *Literature: An Introduction to Fiction, Poetry, and Drama* has once again been revised, corrected, and shaped by wisdom and advice from instructors who actually put it to the test—also from a number who, in teaching literature, preferred other textbooks to it, but who generously criticized this book anyway and made suggestions for it. (Some responded to the book in part, focusing their comments on the previous editions of *An Introduction to Poetry* and *An Introduction to Fiction*.)

Deep thanks to Alvaro Aleman, University of Florida; Jonathan Alexander, University of Southern Colorado; Ann P. Allen, Salisbury State University; Brian Anderson, Central Piedmont Community College; Kimberly Green Angel, Georgia State University; Carmela A. Arnoldt, Glendale Community College; Herman Asarnow, University of Portland; Beverly Bailey, Seminole Community College; Carolyn Baker, San Antonio College; Rosemary Baker, State University of New York at Morrisville; Lee Barnes, Community College of Southern Nevada, Las Vegas; Sandra Barnhill, South Plains College; Bob Baron, Mesa Community College; Ellen Dugan-Barrette, Brescia University; Melinda Barth, El Camino Community College; Robin Barrow, University of Iowa; Joseph Bathanti, Mitchell Community College; Judith Baumel, Adelphi University; Anis Bawarski, University of Kansas; Bruce Beckum, Colorado Mountain College; Elaine Bender, El Camino Community College; Pamela Benson, Tarrant County Junior College; Jennifer Black, McLennan Community College; Brian Blackley, North Carolina State University; Paul Buchanan, Biola University; Andrew Burke, University of Georgia; Jolayne Call, Utah Valley State College; Stasia Callan, Monroe Community College; Uzzie T. Cannon, University of North Carolina at Greensboro; Al Capovilla, Folsom Lake Community College; Eleanor Carducci, Sussex County Community College; Thomas Carper, University of Southern Maine; Jean W. Cash, James Madison University; Michael Cass, Mercer University; Dr. Patricia Cearley, South Plains College; Fred Chancey, Chemeketa Community College; Kitty Chen, Nassau Community College; Edward M. Cifelli, County College of Morris; Marc Cirigliano, Empire State College; Maria Clayton, Middle Tennessee State University; Cheryl Clements, Blinn College; Jerry Coats, Tarrant County Community College; Peggy Cole, Arapahoe Community College; Patricia Connors, University of Memphis; Steve Cooper, California State University, Long Beach; Cynthia Cornell, DePauw University; Ruth Corson, NCTC, Norwalk; James Finn Cotter, Mount St. Mary College; Dessa Crawford, Delaware Community College; Janis Adams Crowe, Furman University; Allison M. Cummings, University of Wisconsin, Madison; Elizabeth Curtin, Salisbury State University; Robert Darling, Keuka College; Denise David, Niagara County Community College; Alan Davis, Moorhead State University; Kathleen De Grave, Pittsburg State University; Apryl Denny, Viterbo University; Fred Dings, University of South Carolina; Dr. Leo Doobad, Stetson University; Dennis Driewald, Laredo Community College; David Driscoll, Benedictine College; John Drury, University of Cincinnati; Victoria Duckworth, Santa Rosa Junior College; Dixie Durman, Chapman University; Janet Eber, County College of Morris; Terry Ehret, Santa Rosa Junior College; George Ellenbogen, Bentley College; Peggy Ellsberg, Barnard College; Toni Empringham, El Camino Community College; Lin Enger, Moorhead State University; Alexina Fagan, Virginia Commonwealth University; Lynn Fauth, Oxnard College; Annie Finch, Miami University; Katie Fischer, Clarke College; Susan Fitzgerald, University of Memphis; Juliann Fleenor, Harper College; Richard Flynn, Georgia Southern University; Deborah Ford, University of Southern Mississippi; James E. Ford, University of Nebraska, Lincoln; Peter Fortunato, Ithaca College; Ray Foster, Scottsdale Community College; Maryanne Garbowsky, County College of Morris; John Gery, University of New Orleans; Mary Frances Gibbons, Richland College; Maggie Gordon, University of Mississippi; Joseph Green, Lower Columbia College; William E. Gruber, Emory University; Huey Guagliardo, Louisana State University; R. S. Gwynn, Lamar University; Steven K. Hale, DeKalb College; Renée Harlow, Southern Connecticut State University; John Harper, Seminole Community College; Iris Rose Hart, Santa Fe Community College; Karen Hatch, California State University, Chico; Jim Hauser, William Patterson College; Jennifer Heller, Johnson County Community College; Mary Piering Hiltbrand, University of Southern Colorado; Jan Hodge, Morningside College; Dr. David E. Hoffman, Averett University; Patricia Hymson, Delaware County Community College; Alan Jacobs, Wheaton College; Kimberlie Johnson, Seminole Community College; Peter Johnson, Providence College; Ted E. Johnston, El Paso Community College; Dr. Cris Karmas, Graceland University; D. S. Koelling, Northwest College; Dennis Kriewald, Laredo Community College; Paul Lake, Arkansas Technical University; Susan Lang, Southern Illinois University; Sherry Little, San Diego State University; Alfred Guy Litton, Texas Woman's University; Heather Lobban-Viravong, Grinnell College; Karen Locke, Lane Community College; Eric Loring, Scottsdale Community College; Gerald Luboff, County College of Morris; Susan Popkin Mach, UCLA; Samuel Maio, California State University, San Jose; Paul Marx, University of New Haven; David Mason, Colorado College; Mike Matthews, Tarrant County Junior College; Janet McCann, Texas A&M; Susan McClure, Indiana University of PA; Kim McCollum-Clark, Millersville University; David McCracken, Texas A&M; Nellie McCrory, Gaston College; Robert McPhillips, Iona College; Dr. Jim

McWilliams, Dickinson State University; Elizabeth Meador, Wayne Community College; Bruce Meyer, Toronto; Tom Miller, University of Arizona; Joseph Mills, University of California at Davis; Cindy Milwe, Santa Monica High School; Mary Alice Morgan, Mercer University; Samantha Morgan, University of Tennessee; Bernard Morris, Modesto Junior College; Brian T. Murphy, Burlington Community College; Madeleine Mysko, Johns Hopkins University; Kevin Nebergall, Kirkwood Community College; Eric Nelson, Georgia Southern University; Jeff Newberry, University of West Florida; Marsha Nourse, Dean College; Hillary Nunn, University of Akron; James Obertino, Central Missouri State University; Julia O'Brien, Meredith College; Sally O'Friel, John Carroll University; Elizabeth Oness, Viterbo College; Regina B. Oost, Wesleyan College; Mike Osborne, Central Piedmont Community College; Jim Owen, Columbus State University; Jeannette Palmer, Motlow State Community College; Mark Palmer, Tacoma Community College; Dianne Peich, Delaware County Community College; Betty Jo Peters, Morehead State University; Timothy Peters, Boston University; Norm Peterson, County College of Morris; Louis Phillips, School of Visual Arts; Robert Phillips, University of Houston; Rodney Phillips, New York Public Library; Teresa Point, Emory University; Deborah Prickett, Jacksonville State University; William Provost, University of Georgia; Wyatt Prunty, University of the South, Sewanee; Allen Ramsey, Central Missouri State University; Ron Rash, Tri-County Technical College; Michael W. Raymond, Stetson University; Mary Anne Reiss, Elizabethtown Community College; Barbara Rhodes, Central Missouri State University; Diane Richard-Alludya, Lynn University; Gary Richardson, Mercer University; Fred Robbins, Southern Illinois University; Daniel Robinson, Colorado State University; Dawn Rodrigues, University of Texas, Brownsville; Linda C. Rollins, Motlow State Community College; Laura Ross, Seminole Community College; Jude Roy, Madisonville Community College; M. Runyon, Saddleback College; Mark Sanders, College of the Mainland; Kay Satre, Carroll College; Ben Sattersfield, Mercer University; SueAnn Schatz, University of New Mexico; Roy Scheele, Doane College; Bill Schmidt, Seminole Community College; Beverly Schneller, Millersville University; Meg Schoerke, San Francisco State University; William Scurrah, Pima Community College; Susan Semrow, Northeastern State University; Tom Sexton, University of Alaska, Anchorage; Chenliang Sheng, Northern Kentucky University; Phillip Skaar, Texas A&M; Michael Slaughter, Illinois Central College; Richard Spiese, California State, Long Beach; Lisa S. Starks, Texas A&M; John R. Stephenson, Lake Superior State University; Jack Stewart, East Georgia College; Dabney Stuart, Washington and Lee University; David Sudol, Arizona State University; Stan Sulkes, Raymond Walters College; Gerald Sullivan, Savio Preparatory School; Henry Taylor, American University; Jean Tobin, University of Wisconsin Center, Sheboygan County; Linda Travers, University of Massachusetts, Amherst; Tom Treffinger, Greenville Technical College; Lee Upton, Lafayette College; Rex Veeder, St. Cloud University; Deborah Viles, University of Colorado, Boulder; Joyce Walker, Southern Illinois University-Carbondale; Sue Walker, University of Southern Alabama; Irene Ward,

Kansas State University; Penelope Warren, Laredo Community College; Barbara Wenner, University of Cincinnati; Mary Wilder, Mercer University; Terry Witek, Stetson University; Sallie Wolf, Arapahoe Community College; Beth Rapp Young, University of Alabama; William Zander, Fairleigh Dickinson University; and Tom Zaniello, Northern Kentucky University.

Three distinguished writers made invaluable contributions to the new edition. Michael Palma scrupulously examined and updated every chapter from the previous edition. His deep knowledge of literature and crisp sense of style kept the new edition fresh, informed, and accessible. Diane Thiel of the University of New Mexico, Albuquerque, masterminded the new Latin American poetry casebook. Working with the editors, she drafted the chapter and helped select the poems—providing three superb new translations especially for this edition. Susan Balée selected the critical materials for the Edgar Allan Poe casebook as well as co-authored the new chapter on writing a research paper. Ongoing thanks also goes to Mark Bernier of Blinn College in Brenham, Texas, who helped make the writing material exemplary in both quality and practicality, and to John Swensson of De Anza College who provided ongoing excellent practical suggestions from the classroom.

We would also like to again thank and congratulate the eight youngest authors in the book—the eight students who allowed us to use their exemplary essays. We consider it an honor to have hosted the literary debuts of Samantha Brown, El Camino College; Heather Burke, Wesleyan University; Stephanie Crowe, Mercer University; Janet Housden, El Camino College; Kim Larsen, Lake Community College; Carlota Llarena, Folsam Lake Center College; Tara Mazzuca, Millersville University; and Becki Woods, Blinn College.

On the publisher's staff, Joseph Terry, Katharine Glynn, Janet Lanphier, and Melanie Craig made many contributions to the development and revisions for the new edition. Joe Vella and Lois Lombardo directed the complex job of managing production of the book from manuscript to the final printed form. Virginia Creeden handled the difficult job of permissions. Shaie Dively supervised the expansion of photographs and artwork in the new edition; Nancy Garcia oversaw work on the Website for the book.

Mary Gioia was involved in every stage of planning, editing, and execution. Not only could the book have not been done without her capable hand and careful eye, but her expert guidance made every chapter better.

Past debts that will never be repaid are outstanding to hundreds of instructors named in prefaces past and to Dorothy M. Kennedy.

X. J. K. AND D. G.

About the Authors

X. J. KENNEDY, after graduation from Seton Hall and Columbia, became a journalist second class in the Navy ("Actually, I was pretty eighth class"). His poems, some published in the *New Yorker*, were first collected in *Nude Descending a Staircase* (1961). Since then he has written six more collections, several widely adopted literature and writing textbooks, and seventeen books for children, including two novels. He has taught at Michigan, North Carolina (Greensboro), California (Irvine), Wellesley, Tufts, and Leeds. Cited in *Bartlett's Familiar Quotations* and reprinted in some 200 anthologies, his verse has brought him a Guggenheim fellowship, a Lamont Award, a *Los Angeles Times* Book Prize, an award from the American Academy and Institute of Arts and Letters, an Aiken-Taylor prize, and the Award for Poetry for Children from the National Council of Teachers of English. He now lives in Lexington, Massachusetts, where he and his wife Dorothy have collaborated on four books and five children.

DANA GIOIA is a poet, critic, and teacher. Born in Los Angeles of Italian and Mexican ancestry, he attended Stanford and Harvard before taking a detour into business. ("Not many poets have a Stanford M.B.A., thank goodness!") After years of writing and reading late in the evenings after work, he quit a vice presidency to write and teach. He has published three collections of poetry, *Daily Horoscope* (1986), *The Gods of Winter* (1991), and *Interrogations at Noon* (2001), which won the American Book Award, an opera libretto, *Nosferatu* (2001), and three critical volumes, including *Can Poetry Matter?* (1992), an influential study of poetry's place in contemporary America. Gioia has taught at Johns Hopkins, Sarah Lawrence, Wesleyan (Connecticut), Mercer, and Colorado College. He is also the co-founder of the summer poetry conference at West Chester University in Pennsylvania and "Teaching Poetry" in Santa Rosa, California. In 2003 he became Chairman of the National Endowment for the Arts. He currently lives in Washington, D.C, with his wife Mary, two sons, and an uncontrollable cat.

(The surname Gioia is pronounced JOY-A. As some of you may have already guessed, *gioia* is the Italian word for *joy*.)

LITERATURE

FICTION

Ernest Hemingway at his desk in Sun Valley, Idaho, c. 1940.

Here is a story, one of the shortest ever written and one of the most difficult to forget:

> A woman is sitting in her old, shuttered house. She knows that she is alone in the whole world; every other thing is dead.
>
> The doorbell rings.

In a brief space this small tale of terror, credited to Thomas Bailey Aldrich, makes itself memorable. It sets a promising scene—is this a haunted house?—introduces a character, and places her in a strange and intriguing situation. Although in reading a story that is over so quickly we don't come to know the character well, for a moment we enter her thoughts and begin to share her feelings. Then something amazing happens. The story leaves us to wonder: who or what rang that bell?

Like many richer, longer, more complicated stories, this one, in its few words, engages the imagination. Evidently, how much a story contains and suggests doesn't depend on its size. In the opening chapter of this book, we will look first at other brief stories—examples of three ancient kinds of fiction, a fable, a parable and a tale— then at a contemporary short story. We will consider the elements of fiction one after another. By seeing a few short stories broken into their parts, you will come to a keener sense of how a story is put together. Not all stories are short, of course; later in the book, you will find a chapter on reading long stories and novels.

All in all, here are sixty-five stories. Among them, may you find at least a few you'll enjoy and care to remember.

1 Reading a Story

After the shipwreck that marooned him on his desert island, Robinson Crusoe, in the novel by Daniel Defoe, stood gazing over the water where pieces of cargo from his ship were floating by. Along came "two shoes, not mates." It is the qualification *not mates* that makes the detail memorable. We could well believe that a thing so striking and odd must have been seen, and not invented. But in truth Defoe, like other masters of the art of fiction, had the power to make us believe his imaginings. Borne along by the art of the storyteller, we trust what we are told, even though the story may be sheer fantasy.

Fiction (from the Latin *fictio*, "a shaping, a counterfeiting") is a name for stories not entirely factual, but at least partially shaped, made up, imagined. It is true that in some fiction, such as a historical novel, a writer draws on factual information in presenting scenes, events, and characters. But the factual information in a historical novel, unlike that in a history book, is of secondary importance. Many firsthand accounts of the American Civil War were written by men who had fought in it, but few eyewitnesses give us so keen a sense of actual life on the battlefront as the author of *The Red Badge of Courage*, Stephen Crane, born after the war was over. In fiction, the "facts" may or may not be true, and a story is none the worse for their being entirely imaginary. We expect from fiction a sense of how people act, not an authentic chronicle of how, at some past time, a few people acted.

As children, we used to read (if we were lucky and formed the habit) to steep ourselves in romance, mystery, and adventure. As adults, we still do: at an airport, while waiting for a flight, we pass the time with some newsstand paperback full of fast action and brisk dialogue. Certain fiction, of course, calls for closer attention. To read a novel by the Russian master Dostoevsky instead of a James Bond thriller is somewhat like playing chess instead of a game of tic-tac-toe. Not that a great novel does not provide entertainment. In fact, it may offer more deeply satisfying entertainment than a novel of violence and soft-core pornography, in which stick figures connive, go to bed, and kill one another in accord with some market-tested formula. Reading literary fiction (as distinguished from fiction as a commercial product—the formula kind of spy, detective, Western, romance, or science fiction story), we are not necessarily led on by the promise of thrills; we do not keep reading mainly to find out what happens next. Indeed, a literary story might even disclose in its opening lines everything that happened, then spend the rest of its length revealing what that happening meant. Reading literary fiction is no merely passive activity, but one that demands both attention and insight-lending participation. In return, it offers rewards. In some works of literary fiction, such as Stephen Crane's "The Open Boat" and Flannery O'Connor's "Revelation," we see more deeply into the minds and hearts of the characters than we ever see into those of our family, our close friends, our lovers—or even ourselves.

FABLE, PARABLE, AND TALES

Modern literary fiction in English has been dominated by two forms: the novel and the short story. The two have many elements in common (and in this book a further discussion of the novel as a special form will be given in Chapter Nine). Perhaps we will be able to define the short story more meaningfully—for it has traits more essential than just a particular length—if first, for comparison, we consider some related varieties of fiction: the fable and the tale. Ancient forms whose origins date back to the time of word-of-mouth storytelling, the fable and the tale are relatively simple in structure; in them we can plainly see elements also found in the short story (and in the novel). To begin, here is a **fable:** a brief story that sets forth some pointed statement of truth. The writer, W. Somerset Maugham (1874–1965), an English novelist and playwright, is retelling an Arabian folk story. (Samarra, by the way, is a city sixty miles from Bagdad.)

W. Somerset Maugham

THE APPOINTMENT IN SAMARRA   1933

Death speaks: There was a merchant in Bagdad who sent his servant to market to buy provisions and in a little while the servant came back, white and trembling, and said, Master, just now when I was in the marketplace I was jostled by a woman in the crowd and when I turned I saw it was Death that jostled me. She looked at me and made a threatening gesture; now, lend me your horse, and I will ride away from this city and avoid my fate. I will go to Samarra and there Death will not find me. The merchant lent him his horse, and the servant mounted it, and he dug his spurs in its flanks and as fast as the horse could gallop he went. Then the merchant went down to the marketplace and he saw me standing in the crowd and he came to me and said, Why did you make a threatening gesture to my servant when you saw him this morning? That was not a threatening gesture, I said, it was only a start of surprise. I was astonished to see him in Bagdad, for I had an appointment with him tonight in Samarra.

This brief story seems practically all skin and bones; that is, it contains little decoration. For in a fable everything leads directly to the **moral,** or message, sometimes stated at the end (moral: "Haste makes waste"). In "The Appointment in Samarra" the moral isn't stated outright, it is merely implied. How would you state it in your own words?

You are probably acquainted with some of the fables credited to the Greek slave Aesop (about 620–560 B.C.), whose stories seem designed to teach lessons about human life. Such is the fable of "The Goose That Laid the Golden Eggs," in which the owner of this marvelous creature slaughters her to get at the great treasure that he thinks is inside her, but finds nothing (implied moral: "Be content with what you have"). Another is the fable of "The Tortoise and the Hare" (implied moral: "Slow, steady plodding wins the race"). The characters in a fable may be talking animals (as in many of Aesop's fables), inanimate objects, or people and supernatural beings (as in "The Appointment in Samarra"). Whoever they may be, these characters are merely sketched, not greatly developed. Evidently, it would not have helped Maugham's fable to put across its point if he had portrayed the merchant, the servant, and Death in fuller detail. A more elaborate description of the marketplace would not have improved the story. Probably, such a description would strike us as unnecessary and distracting. By its very bareness and simplicity, a fable fixes itself— and its message—in memory.

Aesop

THE FOX AND THE GRAPES   6TH CENTURY B.C.

TRANSLATED BY V. S. VERNON JONES

Very little is known with certainty about the man called Aesop (sixth century B.C.), but several accounts and many traditions survive from antiquity. According to the Greek historian Herodotus, Aesop was a slave on the island of Samos. He gained great fame from his fables, but he somehow met his death at the hands of the people of Delphi. The later historian Plutarch claims the Delphians hurled the author to his death from a cliff as a punishment for sacrilege. According to a less reliable tradition, Aesop was an ugly and misshapen man who charmed and amused people with his stories. No one knows if Aesop himself wrote down any of his fables, but they circulated widely in ancient Greece and were praised by Plato, Aristotle, and numerous other authors. His short and witty tales with their incisive morals influenced innumerable later writers. For two and a half millennia Aesop's fables have maintained constant popularity.

A hungry fox saw some fine bunches of grapes hanging from a vine that was trained along a high trellis, and did his best to reach them by jumping as high as he could into the air. But it was all in vain, for they were just out of reach: so he gave up trying, and walked away with an air of dignity and unconcern, remarking, "I thought those grapes were ripe, but I see now they are quite sour."

Moral: It is easy to despise what you cannot get.

1. In fables, the fox is usually clever and frequently successful. Is that the case here?
2. The original Greek word for the fox's description of the grapes is *omphakes*, which more precisely means "unripe." Does the translator's use of the word "sour" add any further level of meaning to the fable?
3. How well does the closing moral fit the fable?

We are so accustomed to the phrase *Aesop's fables* that we might almost start to think the two words inseparable, but in fact there have been fabulists (creators or writers of fables) in virtually every culture throughout recorded history. Here is another fable from many centuries ago, this time from India.

Bidpai

THE CAMEL AND HIS FRIENDS   C. 4TH CENTURY

RETOLD IN ENGLISH BY ARUNDHATI KHANWALKAR

The Panchatantra (Pañca-tantra), a collection of beast fables from India, is attributed to its narrator, a sage named Bidpai, who is a legendary figure about whom almost nothing is known for certain. The Panchatantra, which means the Five Chapters *in Sanskrit, is based on earlier oral folklore. The collection was composed some time between 100 B.C. and 500 A.D. in a Sanskrit original now lost, and is primarily known through an Arabic version of the eighth century and a twelfth-century Hebrew translation, which is the source of most Western versions of the tales. Other translations spread the fables as far as central Europe, Asia, and Indonesia.*

Like many collections of fables, The Panchatantra is a frame-tale, with an introduction containing verse and aphorisms spoken by an eighty-year-old Brahmin teacher named Vishnusharman, who tells the stories over a period of six months for the edification of three foolish princes named Rich-Power, Fierce-Power, and Endless-Power. The stories are didactic, teaching niti, *the wise conduct of life, and* artha, *practical wisdom that stresses cleverness and self-reliance above more altruistic virtues.*

Once a merchant was leading a caravan of heavily-laden camels through a jungle when one of them, overcome by fatigue, collapsed. The merchant decided to leave the camel in the jungle and go on his way. Later, when the camel recovered his strength, he realized that he was alone in a strange jungle. Fortunately there was plenty of grass, and he survived.

One day the king of the jungle, a lion, arrived along with his three friends—a leopard, a fox, and a crow. The king lion wondered what the camel was doing in the jungle! He came near the camel and asked how he, a creature of the desert, had ended up in the hostile jungle. The camel tearfully explained what happened. The lion took pity on him and said, "You have nothing to fear now. Henceforth, you are under my protection and can stay with us." The camel began to live happily in the jungle.

Then one day the lion was wounded in a fight with an elephant. He retired to his cave and stayed there for several days. His friends came to offer their sympathy. They tried to catch prey for the hungry lion but failed. The camel had no problem as he lived on grass while the others were starving.

The fox came up with a plan. He secretly went to the lion and suggested that the camel be sacrificed for the good of the others. The lion got furious, "I can never kill an animal who is under my protection."

The fox humbly said, "But Lord, you have provided us food all the time. If 5 any one of us voluntarily offered himself to save your life, I hope you won't mind!" The hungry lion did not object to that and agreed to take the offer.

The fox went back to his companions and said, "Friends, our king is dying of starvation. Let us go and beg him to eat one of us. It is the least we can do for such a noble soul."

So they went to the king and the crow offered his life. The fox interrupted, and said, "You are a small creature, the master's hunger will hardly be appeased by eating you. May I humbly offer my life to satisfy my master's hunger."

The leopard stepped forward and said, "You are no bigger than the crow, it is me whom our master should eat."

The foolish camel thought, "Everyone has offered to lay down their lives for the king, but he has not hurt any one. It is now my turn to offer myself." So he stepped forward and said, "Stand aside friend leopard, the king and you have close family ties. It is me whom the master must eat."

An ominous silence greeted the camel's offer. Then the king gladly said, "I 10 accept your offer, O noble camel." And in no time he was killed by the three rogues, the false friends.

Moral: Be careful in choosing your friends.

Another traditional form of storytelling is the **parable.** Like the fable, a parable is a brief narrative that teaches a moral, but unlike the fable, its plot is plausibly realistic, and the main characters are human rather than anthropomorphized animals or natural forces. The other key difference is that parables usually possess a more mysterious and suggestive tone. A fable customarily ends by explicitly stating its moral, but parables often present their morals implicitly, and their meanings can be open to several interpretations.

In the Western tradition, the literary conventions of the parable are largely based on the brief stories told by Jesus in his preaching. The forty-three parables recounted in the four gospels reveal how frequently he used the form to teach. Jesus designed his parables to have two levels of meaning—a literal story that could immediately be understood by the crowds he addressed and a deeper meaning fully comprehended only by his disciples, an inner circle who understood the nature of his ministry. (You can see the richness of interpretations suggested by Jesus' parables by reading and analyzing "The Parable of the Prodigal Son" from St. Luke's gospel, which appears in Chapter Six.) The parable was also widely used by Eastern philosophers. The Taoist sage Chuang Tzu often portrayed the principles of Tao—which he called the "Way of Nature"—in witty parables like the following one traditionally titled, "Independence."

Chuang Tzu

INDEPENDENCE

CHOU DYNASTY (4TH CENTURY B.C.)

TRANSLATED BY HERBERT GILES

Chuang Chou, usually known as Chuang Tzu (approximately 390–365 B.C.), was one of the great philosophers of the Chou period in China. He was born in the Sung feudal state and received an excellent education. Unlike most educated men, however, Chuang Tzu did not seek public office or political power. Influenced by Taoist philosophy, he believed that individuals should transcend their desire for success and wealth, as well as their fear of failure and poverty. True freedom, he maintained, came from escaping the distractions of worldly affairs. Chuang Tzu's writings have been particularly praised for their combination of humor and wisdom. His parables and stories are classics of Chinese literature.

Chuang Tzu was one day fishing, when the Prince of Ch'u sent two high officials to interview him, saying that his Highness would be glad of Chuang Tzu's assistance in the administration of his government. The latter quietly fished on, and without looking round, replied, "I have heard that in the State of Ch'u there is a sacred tortoise, which has been dead three thousand years, and which the prince keeps packed up in a box on the altar in his ancestral shrine. Now do you think that tortoise would rather be dead and have its remains thus honoured, or be alive and wagging its tail in the mud?" The two officials answered that no doubt it would rather be alive and wagging its tail in the mud; whereupon Chuang Tzu cried out "Begone! I too elect to remain wagging my tail in the mud."

QUESTIONS

1. What part of this story is the exposition? How many sentences does Chuang Tzu use to set up the dramatic situation?
2. Why does the protagonist change the subject and mention the sacred tortoise? Why doesn't he answer the request directly and immediately? Does it serve any purpose that Chuang Tzu makes the officials answer a question to which he knows the answer?
3. What does this story tell us about the protagonist Chuang Tzu's personality?

The name *tale* (from the Old English *talu*, "speech") is sometimes applied to any story, whether short or long, true or fictitious. *Tale* being a more evocative name than *story*, writers sometimes call their stories "tales" as if to imply something handed down from the past. But defined in a more limited sense, a **tale** is a story, usually short, that sets forth strange and wonderful events in more or less bare summary, without detailed character-drawing. "Tale" is pretty much synonymous with "yarn," for it implies a story in which the goal is revelation of the marvelous rather than revelation of character. In the English folktale "Jack and the Beanstalk," we take away a more vivid impression of the miraculous beanstalk and the giant who dwells at its top than of Jack's mind or personality. Because such venerable stories were told aloud before someone set them down in writing, the storytellers had to limit themselves to brief descriptions. Probably spoken around a fire or hearth, such a tale tends to be less complicated and less closely detailed than a story written for the printed page, whose reader can linger over it. Still, such tales *can* be complicated. It is not merely greater length that makes a short story different from a tale or a fable: a mark of a short story is a fully delineated character.

Even modern tales favor supernatural or fantastic events: for instance, the **tall tale,** that variety of folk story which recounts the deeds of a superhero (Paul Bunyan, John Henry, Sally Ann Thunder) or of the storyteller. If the storyteller is telling about his or her own imaginary experience, the bragging yarn is usually told with a straight face to listeners who take pleasure in scoffing at it. Although the **fairy tale,** set in a world of magic and enchantment, is sometimes the work of a modern author (notably Hans Christian Andersen), well-known examples are those German folktales that probably originated in the Middle Ages, collected by the brothers Grimm. The label *fairy tale* is something of an English misnomer, for in the Grimm stories, though witches and goblins abound, fairies are a minority.

Jakob and Wilhelm Grimm

GODFATHER DEATH   1812 (FROM ORAL TRADITION)

TRANSLATED BY DANA GIOIA

Jakob Grimm (1785–1863) and Wilhelm Grimm (1786–1859), brothers and scholars, were born near Frankfurt-am-Main, Germany. For most of their lives they worked together— lived together, too, even when in 1825 Wilhelm married. In 1838, as librarians, they began toiling on their Deutsch Wörterbuch, *or German dictionary, a vast project that was to outlive them by a century. (It was completed only in 1960.) In 1840 King Friedrich Wilhelm IV appointed both brothers to the Royal Academy of Sciences, and both taught at the University of Berlin for the rest of their days. Although Jakob had a side career as a diplomat, wrote a great* Deutsche Grammatik, *or German grammar (1819–37),*

Jakob and Wilhelm Grimm

and propounded Grimm's Law (an explanation of shifts in consonant sounds, of interest to students of linguistics), the name Grimm is best known to us for that splendid collection of ancient German folk stories we call Grimm's Fairy Tales—in German, Kinder- und Hausmärchen ("Childhood and Household Tales," 1812–15). This classic work spread German children's stories around the world. Many tales we hear early in life were collected by the Grimms: "Hansel and Gretel," "Snow White and the Seven Dwarfs," "Rapunzel," "Tom Thumb," "Little Red Riding Hood," "Rumpelstiltskin." Versions of some of these

tales had been written down as early as the sixteenth century, but mainly the brothers relied
on the memories of Hessian peasants who recited the stories aloud for them.

A poor man had twelve children and had to work day and night just to give them bread. Now when the thirteenth came into the world, he did not know what to do, so he ran out onto the main highway intending to ask the first one he met to be the child's godfather.

The first person he met was the good Lord God, who knew very well what was weighing on the man's heart. And He said to him, "Poor man, I am sorry for you. I will hold your child at the baptismal font. I will take care of him and fill his days with happiness."

The man asked, "Who are you?"

"I am the good Lord."

"Then I don't want you as godfather. You give to the rich and let the poor   5
starve."

The man spoke thus because he did not know how wisely God portions out wealth and poverty. So he turned away from the Lord and went on.

Then the Devil came up to him and said, "What are you looking for? If you take me as your child's sponsor, I will give him gold heaped high and wide and all the joys of this world."

The man asked, "Who are you?"

"I am the Devil."

"Then I don't want you as godfather," said the man. "You trick men and   10
lead them astray."

He went on, and bone-thin Death strode up to him and said, "Choose me as godfather."

The man asked, "Who are you?"

"I am Death, who makes all men equal."

Then the man said, "You are the right one. You take the rich and the poor without distinction. You will be the godfather."

Death answered, "I will make your child rich and famous. Whoever has me   15
as a friend shall lack for nothing."

The man said, "The baptism is next Sunday. Be there on time."

Death appeared just as he had promised and stood there as a proper godfather.

When the boy had grown up, his godfather walked in one day and said to come along with him. Death led him out into the woods, showed him an herb, and said, "Now you are going to get your christening present. I am making you a famous doctor. When you are called to a patient, I will always appear to you. If I stand next to the sick person's head, you may speak boldly that you will make him healthy again. Give him some of this herb, and he will recover. But if you see me standing by the sick person's feet, then he is mine. You must say that nothing can be done and that no doctor in the world can save him. But beware of using the herb against my will, or it will turn out badly for you."

It was not long before the young man was the most famous doctor in the whole world. "He needs only to look at the sick person," everyone said, "and then he knows how things stand—whether the patient will get well again or whether he must die." People came from far and wide to bring their sick and gave him so much gold that he quickly became quite rich.

Now it soon happened that the king grew ill, and the doctor was summoned to say whether a recovery was possible. But when he came to the bed, Death was standing at the sick man's feet, and now no herb grown could save him.

"If I cheat Death this one time," thought the doctor, "he will be angry, but since I am his godson, he will turn a blind eye, so I will risk it." He took up the sick man and turned him around so that his head was now where Death stood. Then he gave the king some of the herb. The king recovered and grew healthy again.

But Death then came to the doctor with a dark and angry face and threatened him with his finger. "You have hoodwinked me this time," he said, "And I will forgive you once because you are my godson. But if you try such a thing again, it will be your neck, and I will take you away with me."

Not long after, the king's daughter fell into a serious illness. She was his only child, and he wept day and night until his eyes went blind. He let it be known that whoever saved her from death would become her husband and inherit the crown.

When the doctor came to the sick girl's bed, he saw Death standing at her feet. He should have remembered his godfather's warning, but the princess's great beauty and the happy prospect of becoming her husband so infatuated him that he flung all caution to the wind. He didn't notice that Death stared at him angrily or that he raised his hand and shook his bony fist. The doctor picked up the sick girl and turned her around to place her head where her feet had been. He gave her the herb, and right away her cheeks grew rosy and she stirred again with life.

When Death saw that he had been cheated out of his property a second time, he strode with long steps up to the doctor and said, "It is all over for you. Now it's your turn." Death seized him so firmly with his ice-cold hand that the doctor could not resist. He led him into an underground cavern. There the doctor saw thousands and thousands of candles burning in endless rows. Some were tall, others medium-sized, and others quite small. Every moment some went out and others lit up, so that the tiny flames seemed to jump to and fro in perpetual motion.

"Look," said Death, "these are the life lights of mankind. The tall ones belong to children, the middle-size ones to married people in the prime of life, and the short ones to the very old. But sometimes even children and young people have only a short candle."

"Show me my life light," said the doctor, assuming it would be very tall.

Death pointed to the small stub that seemed about to flicker out.

"Oh, dear godfather!" cried the terrified doctor. "Light a new candle for me. If you love me, do it, so that I may enjoy my life, become king, and marry the beautiful princess."

"That I cannot do," Death replied. "One candle must first go out before a 30
new one is lighted."

"Then put my old one on top of a new candle that will keep burning when
the old one goes out," begged the doctor.

Death acted as if he were going to grant the wish and picked up a tall new
candle. But because he wanted revenge, he deliberately fumbled in placing the
new candle, and the stub toppled over and went out. The doctor immediately
dropped to the ground and fell into the hands of Death.

PLOT

Like a fable, the Grimm brothers' tale seems stark in its lack of detail and in the
swiftness of its telling. Compared with the fully portrayed characters of many modern
stories, the characters of father, son, king, princess, and even Death himself seem
hardly more than stick figures. It may have been that to draw ample characters would
not have contributed to the storytellers' design; that, indeed, to have done so would
have been inartistic. Yet "Godfather Death" is a compelling story. By what methods
does it arouse and sustain our interest?

From the opening sentence of the tale, we watch the unfolding of a **dramatic situation:** a person is involved in some conflict. First, this character is a poor man with
children to feed, in conflict with the world; very soon, we find him in conflict with
God and with the Devil besides. Drama in fiction occurs in any clash of wills, desires,
or powers—whether it be a conflict of character against character, character against
society, character against some natural force, or, as in "Godfather Death," character
against some supernatural entity.

Like any shapely tale, "Godfather Death" has a beginning, a middle, and an end.
In fact, it is unusual to find a story so clearly displaying the elements of structure that
critics have found in many classic works of fiction and drama. The tale begins with
an **exposition:** the opening portion that sets the scene (if any), introduces the main
characters, tells us what happened before the story opened, and provides any other
background information that we need in order to understand and care about the
events to follow. In "Godfather Death," the exposition is brief—all in the opening
paragraph. The middle section of the story begins with Death's giving the herb to the
boy and his warning not to defy him. This moment introduces a new conflict (a
complication), and by this time it is clear that the son and not the father is to be the
central human character of the story. Death's godson is the principal person who
strives: the **protagonist** (a better term than **hero,** for it may apply equally well to a
central character who is not especially brave or virtuous).

The **suspense,** the pleasurable anxiety we feel that heightens our attention to
the story, inheres in our wondering how it will all turn out. Will the doctor triumph
over Death? Even though we suspect, early in the story, that the doctor stands no
chance against such a superhuman **antagonist,** we want to see for ourselves the outcome of his defiance. A storyteller can try to incite our anticipation by giving us
some **foreshadowing** or indication of events to come. In "Godfather Death" the foreshadowings are apparent in Death's warnings ("But if you try such a thing again, it

will be your neck"). When the doctor defies his godfather for the first time—when he saves the king—we have a **crisis,** a moment of high tension. The tension is momentarily resolved when Death lets him off. Then an even greater crisis—the turning point in the action—occurs with the doctor's second defiance in restoring the princess to life. In the last section of the story, with the doctor in the underworld, events come to a **climax,** the moment of greatest tension at which the outcome is to be decided, when the terrified doctor begs for a new candle. Will Death grant him one? Will he live, become king, and marry the princess? The outcome or **conclusion**—also called the **resolution** or **dénouement** ("the untying of the knot")— quickly follows as Death allows the little candle to go out.

Such a structure of events arising out of a conflict may be called the plot of the story. Like many terms used in literary discussion, *plot* is blessed with several meanings. Sometimes it refers simply to the events in a story. In this book, **plot** will mean the artistic arrangement of those events. Different arrangements of the same material are possible. A writer might decide to tell of the events in chronological order, beginning with the earliest; or he or she might open the story with the last event, then tell what led up to it. Sometimes a writer chooses to skip rapidly over the exposition and begin *in medias res* (Latin, "in the midst of things"), first presenting some exciting or significant moment, then filling in what happened earlier. This method is by no means a modern invention: Homer begins the *Odyssey* with his hero mysteriously late in returning from war and his son searching for him; John Milton's *Paradise Lost* opens with Satan already defeated in his revolt against the Lord. A device useful to writers for filling in what happened earlier is the **flashback** (or **retrospect**), a scene relived in a character's memory.

To have a plot, a story does not need an intense, sustained conflict such as we find in "Godfather Death," a tale especially economical in its structure of crisis, climax, and conclusion. Although a highly dramatic story may tend to assume such a clearly recognizable structure, many contemporary writers avoid it, considering it too contrived and arbitrary. In commercial fiction, in which exciting conflict is everything and in which the writer has to manufacture all possible suspense, such a structure is often obvious. In popular detective, Western, and adventure novels; in juvenile fiction (the perennial Hardy Boys and Nancy Drew books); and in popular series on television (soap operas, police and hospital dramas, mysteries, and the *Star Trek* series), it is often easy to recognize crisis, climax, and conclusion. The presence of these elements does not necessarily indicate inferior literature (as "Godfather Death" shows); yet when they are reduced to parts of a formula, the result may seem stale and contrived.[1]

THE SHORT STORY

The teller of a tale relies heavily on the method of **summary:** terse, general narration as in "Godfather Death" ("It was not long before the young man was the most famous doctor in the whole world"). But in a **short story,** a form more realistic than the tale

---

[1]In the heyday of the **pulp magazines** (so called for their cheap wood-pulp paper), some professional writers even relied on a mechanical device called Plotto: a tin arrow-spinner pointed to numbers and the writer looked them up in a book that listed necessary ingredients—type of hero, type of villain, type of conflict, crisis, climax, conclusion.

and of modern origin, the writer usually presents the main events in greater fullness. Fine writers of short stories, although they may use summary at times (often to give some portion of a story less emphasis), are skilled in rendering a **scene:** a vivid or dramatic moment described in enough detail to create the illusion that the reader is practically there. Avoiding long summary, they try to *show* rather than simply to *tell*, as if following Mark Twain's advice to authors: "Don't say, 'The old lady screamed.' Bring her on and let her scream."

A short story is more than just a sequence of happenings. A finely wrought short story has the richness and conciseness of an excellent lyric poem. Spontaneous and natural as the finished story may seem, the writer has crafted it so artfully that there is meaning in even seemingly casual speeches and apparently trivial details. If we skim it hastily, skipping the descriptive passages, we miss significant parts. Some literary short stories, unlike commercial fiction in which the main interest is in physical action or conflict, tell of an **epiphany:** some moment of insight, discovery, or revelation by which a character's life, or view of life, is greatly altered.[2] (For such moments in fiction, see the stories in this book by James Joyce, John Steinbeck, and Joyce Carol Oates.) Other short stories tell of a character initiated into experience or maturity: one such **story of initiation** is William Faulkner's "Barn Burning" (Chapter Five), in which a boy finds it necessary to defy his father and suddenly to grow into manhood. Less obviously dramatic, perhaps, than "Godfather Death," such a story may be no less powerful.

The fable and the tale are ancient forms; the short story is of more recent origin. In the nineteenth century, writers of fiction were encouraged by a large, literate audience of middle-class readers who wanted to see their lives reflected in faithful mirrors. Skillfully representing ordinary life, many writers perfected the art of the short story: in Russia, Anton Chekhov; in France, Honoré de Balzac, Gustave Flaubert, and Guy de Maupassant; and in America, Nathaniel Hawthorne and Edgar Allan Poe (although the Americans seem less fond of everyday life than of dream and fantasy). It would be false to claim that, in passing from the fable and the tale to the short story, fiction has made a triumphant progress; or to claim that, because short stories are modern, they are superior to fables and tales. Fable, tale, and short story are distinct forms, each achieving its own effects. (Incidentally, fable and tale are far from being extinct today: you can find many recent examples.) In the hands of Jorge Luis Borges, Joyce Carol Oates, Gabriel García Márquez, and other innovative writers, the conventions of the short story underwent great changes in the second half of the twentieth century; and, at present, stories of epiphany and initiation are not as prevalent as they once were.

But let us begin with a contemporary short story whose protagonist *does* undergo an initiation into maturity. To notice the difference between a short story and a tale, you may find it helpful to compare John Updike's "A & P" with "Godfather Death." Although Updike's short story is centuries distant from the Grimm tale in its method of telling and in its setting, you may be reminded of "Godfather Death" in the main

[2]From the Greek *epiphainein*, "to show forth." In Christian tradition, the Feast of the Epiphany commemorates the revelation to the Magi of the birth of Christ.

character's dramatic situation. To defend a young woman, a young man has to defy his mentor—here, the boss of a supermarket! In so doing, he places himself in jeopardy. Updike has the protagonist tell his own story, amply and with humor. How does it differ from a tale?

John Updike

A & P   1961

John Updike, born in Pennsylvania in 1932, received his B.A. from Harvard, then went to Oxford to study drawing and fine art. In the mid-1950s he worked on the staff of the New Yorker, at times doing errands for the aged James Thurber. Although he left the magazine to become a full-time writer, Updike has continued to supply it with memorable stories, witty light verse, and searching reviews. A famously prolific writer, he has published more than fifty books. Updike is best known as a hardworking, versatile, highly productive writer of fiction. For his novel The Centaur (1963) he received a National Book Award, and for Rabbit Is Rich (1982) a Pulitzer Prize and an American Book Award. The fourth and last Rabbit Angstrom novel, Rabbit at Rest (1990), won him a second Pulitzer. Licks of Love (2000), a collection of stories, contains a long footnote to the tetraology, a novella called "Rabbit Remembered," in which Rabbit Angstrom's friends reminisce about him after his death. Updike's many other novels include The Witches of Eastwick (1984), made into a successful film starring Jack Nicholson; S. (1988), partly inspired by Nathaniel Hawthorne's The Scarlet Letter; Gertrude and Claudius (2000), derived from Shakespeare's Hamlet; and Seek My Face (2002), Updike's twentieth novel. Compilations of his work include Collected Poems (1993), The Complete Henry Bech (2001), and The Early Stories, 1953–1975 (2003).

Almost unique among living American writers, Updike has moved back and forth successfully among a variety of literary genres: light verse, serious poetry, drama, criticism, children's books, novels, and short stories. But it is perhaps in short fiction that he has done his finest work. Updike has been quietly innovative in expanding the forms of short fiction, especially in his volumes of interlocked stories built around recurrent characters, as in the Maple family stories in Too Far to Go (1979) and his three collections that depict the ups and downs of fictional writer Henry Bech. Despite Updike's achievements as a novelist, some critics such as Washington Post writer Jonathan Yardley believe that "It is in his short stories that we find Updike's most assured work, and no doubt it is upon the best of them that his reputation ultimately will rest."

In walks three girls in nothing but bathing suits. I'm in the third check-out slot, with my back to the door, so I don't see them until they're over by the bread. The one that caught my eye first was the one in the plaid green two-piece. She was a chunky kid, with a good tan and a sweet broad soft-looking can with those two crescents of white just under it, where the sun never seems to hit, at the top of the backs of her legs. I stood there with my hand on a box of HiHo crackers trying to remember if I rang it up or not. I ring it up again and the customer starts giving me hell. She's one of these cash-register-watchers, a witch about fifty with rouge on her cheekbones and no eyebrows, and I know it made her day to trip me up. She'd been watching cash registers for fifty years and probably never seen a mistake before.

By the time I got her feathers smoothed and her goodies into a bag—she gives me a little snort in passing, if she'd been born at the right time they would have burned her over in Salem—by the time I get her on her way the girls had circled around the bread and were coming back, without a pushcart, back my way along the counters, in the aisle between the check-outs and the Special bins. They didn't even have shoes on. There was this chunky one, with the two-piece—it was bright green and the seams on the bra were still sharp and her belly was still pretty pale so I guessed she just got it (the suit)—there was this one, with one of those chubby berry-faces, the lips all bunched together under her nose, this one, and a tall one, with black hair that hadn't quite frizzed right, and one of these sunburns right across under the eyes, and a chin that was too long—you know, the kind of girl other girls think is very "striking" and "attractive" but never quite makes it, as they very well know, which is why they like her so much—and then the third one, that wasn't quite so tall. She was the queen. She kind of led them, the other two peeking around and making their shoulders round. She didn't look around, not this queen, she just walked straight on slowly, on these long white prima-donna legs. She came down a little hard on her heels, as if she didn't walk in her bare feet that much, putting down her heels and then letting the weight move along to her toes as if she was testing the floor with every step, putting a little deliberate extra action into it. You never know for sure how girls' minds work (do you really think it's a mind in there or just a little buzz like a bee in a glass jar?) but you got the idea she had talked the other two into coming in here with her, and now she was showing them how to do it, walk slow and hold yourself straight.

She had on a kind of dirty-pink—beige maybe, I don't know—bathing suit with a little nubble all over it and, what got me, the straps were down. They were off her shoulders looped loose around the cool tops of her arms, and I guess as a result the suit had slipped a little on her, so all around the top of the cloth there was this shining rim. If it hadn't been there you wouldn't have known there could have been anything whiter than those shoulders. With the straps pushed off, there was nothing between the top of the suit and the top of her head except just *her*, this clean bare plane of the top of her chest down from the shoulder bones like a dented sheet of metal tilted in the light. I mean, it was more than pretty.

She had sort of oaky hair that the sun and salt had bleached, done up in a bun that was unraveling, and a kind of prim face. Walking into the A & P with your straps down, I suppose it's the only kind of face you *can* have. She held her head so high her neck, coming up out of those white shoulders, looked kind of stretched, but I didn't mind. The longer her neck was, the more of her there was.

She must have felt in the corner of her eye me and over my shoulder   5
Stokesie in the second slot watching, but she didn't tip. Not this queen. She kept her eyes moving across the racks, and stopped, and turned so slow it made my stomach rub the inside of my apron, and buzzed to the other two, who kind of huddled against her for relief, and they all three of them went up the cat-and-dog-food-breakfast-cereal-macaroni-rice-raisins-seasonings-spreads-spaghetti-soft-drinks-crackers-and-cookies aisle. From the third slot I look straight up this

aisle to the meat counter, and I watched them all the way. The fat one with the tan sort of fumbled with the cookies, but on second thought she put the packages back. The sheep pushing their carts down the aisle—the girls were walking against the usual traffic (not that we have one-way signs or anything)—were pretty hilarious. You could see them, when Queenie's white shoulders dawned on them, kind of jerk, or hop, or hiccup, but their eyes snapped back to their own baskets and on they pushed. I bet you could set off dynamite in an A & P and the people would by and large keep reaching and checking oatmeal off their lists and muttering "Let me see, there was a third thing, began with A, asparagus, no, ah, yes, applesauce!" or whatever it is they do mutter. But there was no doubt, this jiggled them. A few houseslaves in pin curlers even looked around after pushing their carts past to make sure what they had seen was correct.

You know, it's one thing to have a girl in a bathing suit down on the beach, where what with the glare nobody can look at each other much anyway, and another thing in the cool of the A & P, under the fluorescent lights, against all those stacked packages, with her feet padding along naked over our checker-board green-and-cream rubber-tile floor.

"Oh Daddy," Stokesie said beside me. "I feel so faint."

"Darling," I said. "Hold me tight." Stokesie's married, with two babies chalked up on his fuselage already, but as far as I can tell that's the only difference. He's twenty-two, and I was nineteen this April.

"Is it done?" he asks, the responsible married man finding his voice. I forgot to say he thinks he's going to be manager some sunny day, maybe in 1990 when it's called the Great Alexandrov and Petrooshki Tea Company or something.

What he meant was, our town is five miles from a beach, with a big summer colony out on the Point, but we're right in the middle of town, and the women generally put on a shirt or shorts or something before they get out of the car into the street. And anyway these are usually women with six children and varicose veins mapping their legs and nobody, including them, could care less. As I say, we're right in the middle of town, and if you stand at our front doors you can see two banks and the Congregational church and the newspaper store and three real-estate offices and about twenty-seven old freeloaders tearing up Central Street because the sewer broke again. It's not as if we're on the Cape; we're north of Boston and there's people in this town haven't seen the ocean for twenty years. The girls had reached the meat counter and were asking McMahon something. He pointed, they pointed, and they shuffled out of sight behind a pyramid of Diet Delight peaches. All that was left for us to see was old McMahon patting his mouth and looking after them sizing up their joints. Poor kids, I began to feel sorry for them, they couldn't help it.

Now here comes the sad part of the story, at least my family says it's sad but I don't think it's sad myself. The store's pretty empty, it being Thursday afternoon, so there was nothing much to do except lean on the register and wait for the girls to show up again. The whole store was like a pinball machine and I didn't know which tunnel they'd come out of. After a while they come around out of the far aisle, around the light bulbs, records at discount of the Caribbean Six or Tony

10

Martin Sings or some such gunk you wonder they waste the wax on, six-packs of candy bars, and plastic toys done up in cellophane that fall apart when a kid looks at them anyway. Around they come, Queenie still leading the way, and holding a little gray jar in her hand. Slots Three through Seven are unmanned and I could see her wondering between Stokes and me, but Stokesie with his usual luck draws an old party in baggy gray pants who stumbles up with four giant cans of pineapple juice (what do these bums *do* with all that pineapple juice? I've often asked myself) so the girls come to me. Queenie puts down the jar and I take it into my fingers icy cold. Kingfish Fancy Herring Snacks in Pure Sour Cream: 49¢. Now her hands are empty, not a ring or a bracelet, bare as God made them, and I wonder where the money's coming from. Still with that prim look she lifts a folded dollar bill out of the hollow at the center of her nubbled pink top. The jar went heavy in my hand. Really, I thought that was so cute.

Then everybody's luck begins to run out. Lengel comes in from haggling with a truck full of cabbages on the lot and is about to scuttle into that door marked MANAGER behind which he hides all day when the girls touch his eye. Lengel's pretty dreary, teaches Sunday school and the rest, but he doesn't miss that much. He comes over and says, "Girls, this isn't the beach."

Queenie blushes, though maybe it's just a brush of sunburn I was noticing for the first time, now that she was so close. "My mother asked me to pick up a jar of herring snacks." Her voice kind of startled me, the way voices do when you see the people first, coming out so flat and dumb yet kind of tony, too, the way it ticked over "pick up" and "snacks." All of a sudden I slid right down her voice into her living room. Her father and the other men were standing around in ice-cream coats and bow ties and the women were in sandals picking up herring snacks on toothpicks off a big plate and they were all holding drinks the color of water with olives and sprigs of mint in them. When my parents have somebody over they get lemonade and if it's a real racy affair Schlitz in tall glasses with "They'll Do It Every Time" cartoons stencilled on.

"That's all right," Lengel said. "But this isn't the beach." His repeating this struck me as funny, as if it had just occurred to him, and he had been thinking all these years the A & P was a great big dune and he was the head lifeguard. He didn't like my smiling—as I say he doesn't miss much—but he concentrates on giving the girls that sad Sunday-school-superintendent stare.

Queenie's blush is no sunburn now, and the plump one in plaid, that I liked better from the back—a really sweet can—pipes up, "We weren't doing any shopping. We just came in for the one thing."

"That makes no difference," Lengel tells her, and I could see from the way his eyes went that he hadn't noticed she was wearing a two-piece before. "We want you decently dressed when you come in here."

"We *are* decent," Queenie says suddenly, her lower lip pushing, getting sore now that she remembers her place, a place from which the crowd that runs the A & P must look pretty crummy. Fancy Herring Snacks flashed in her very blue eyes.

"Girls, I don't want to argue with you. After this come in here with your shoulders covered. It's our policy." He turns his back. That's policy for you. Policy is what the kingpins want. What the others want is juvenile delinquency.

All this while, the customers had been showing up with their carts but, you know, sheep, seeing a scene, they had all bunched up on Stokesie, who shook open a paper bag as gently as peeling a peach, not wanting to miss a word. I could feel in the silence everybody getting nervous, most of all Lengel, who asks me, "Sammy, have you rung up this purchase?"

I thought and said "No" but it wasn't about that I was thinking. I go through 20
the punches, 4, 9, GROC, TOT—it's more complicated than you think, and after you do it often enough, it begins to make a little song, that you hear words to, in my case "Hello (*bing*) there, you (*gung*) hap-py *pee*-pul (*splat*)!"—the *splat* being the drawer flying out. I uncrease the bill, tenderly as you may imagine, it just having come from between the two smoothest scoops of vanilla I had ever known were there, and pass a half and a penny into her narrow pink palm, and nestle the herrings in a bag and twist its neck and hand it over, all the time thinking.

The girls, and who'd blame them, are in a hurry to get out, so I say "I quit" to Lengel quick enough for them to hear, hoping they'll stop and watch me, their unsuspected hero. They keep right on going, into the electric eye; the door flies open and they flicker across the lot to their car, Queenie and Plaid and Big Tall Goony-Goony (not that as raw material she was so bad), leaving me with Lengel and a kink in his eyebrow.

"Did you say something, Sammy?"

"I said I quit."

"I thought you did."

"You didn't have to embarrass them." 25

"It was they who were embarrassing us."

I started to say something that came out "Fiddle-de-doo." It's a saying of my grandmother's, and I know she would have been pleased.

"I don't think you know what you're saying," Lengel said.

"I know you don't," I said. "But I do." I pull the bow at the back of my apron and start shrugging it off my shoulders. A couple customers that had been heading for my slot begin to knock against each other, like scared pigs in a chute.

Lengel sighs and begins to look very patient and old and gray. He's been a 30
friend of my parents for years. "Sammy, you don't want to do this to your Mom and Dad," he tells me. It's true, I don't. But it seems to me that once you begin a gesture it's fatal not to go through with it. I fold the apron, "Sammy" stitched in red on the pocket, and put it on the counter, and drop the bow tie on top of it. The bow tie is theirs, if you've ever wondered. "You'll feel this for the rest of your life," Lengel says, and I know that's true, too, but remembering how he made that pretty girl blush makes me so scrunchy inside I punch the No Sale tab and the machine whirs "pee-pul" and the drawer splats out. One advantage to this scene taking place in summer, I can follow this up with a clean exit, there's no fumbling around getting your coat and galoshes, I just saunter into the electric eye in my white shirt that my mother ironed the night before, and the door heaves itself open, and outside the sunshine is skating around on the asphalt.

I look around for my girls, but they're gone, of course. There wasn't anybody but some young married screaming with her children about some candy they didn't get by the door of a powder-blue Falcon station wagon. Looking back in the big windows, over the bags of peat moss and aluminum lawn furniture stacked on the pavement, I could see Lengel in my place in the slot, checking the sheep through. His face was dark gray and his back stiff, as if he'd just had an injection of iron, and my stomach kind of fell as I felt how hard the world was going to be to me hereafter.

QUESTIONS

1. Notice how artfully Updike arranges details to set the story in a perfectly ordinary supermarket. What details stand out for you as particularly true to life? What does this close attention to detail contribute to the story?
2. How fully does Updike draw the character of Sammy? What traits (admirable or otherwise) does Sammy show? Is he any less a hero for wanting the girls to notice his heroism? To what extent is he more thoroughly and fully portrayed than the doctor in "Godfather Death"?
3. What part of the story seems to be the exposition? (See the definition of *exposition* in the discussion of plot earlier in the chapter and in the Glossary.) Of what value to the story is the carefully detailed portrait of Queenie, the leader of the three girls?
4. As the story develops, do you detect any change in Sammy's feelings toward the girls?
5. Where in "A & P" does the dramatic conflict become apparent? What moment in the story brings the crisis? What is the climax of the story?
6. Why, exactly, does Sammy quit his job?
7. Does anything lead you to *expect* Sammy to make some gesture of sympathy for the three girls? What incident earlier in the story (before Sammy quits) seems a foreshadowing?
8. What do you understand from the conclusion of the story? What does Sammy mean when he acknowledges "how hard the world was going to be . . . hereafter"?
9. What comment does Updike—through Sammy—make on supermarket society?

WRITER'S PERSPECTIVE

John Updike

John Updike on Writing

WHY WRITE? 1975

The ancients said the purpose of poetry, of writing, was to entertain and to instruct; Aristotle put forward the still fascinating notion that a dramatic action, however terrible and piteous, carries off at the end, in catharsis, the morbid, personal, subjective impurities of our emotions. The enlargement of sympathy, through identification with the lives of fictional others, is frequently presented as an aim of narrative; D. H. Lawrence, with characteristic fervor, wrote, "And here lies the vast importance of the novel, properly handled. It can inform and lead into new places the flows of our sympathetic consciousness, and can lead our sympathy away in recoil from things that are dead." Kafka wrote that a book is an ax to break the frozen sea within us.

Most people sensibly assume that writing is propaganda. Of course, they admit, there is bad propaganda, like the boy-meets-tractor novels of socialist realism, and old-fashioned propaganda, like Christian melodrama and the capitalist success stories of Horatio Alger or Samuel Smiles. But that some message is intended, wrapped in the story like a piece of crystal carefully mailed in cardboard and excelsior, is not doubted. Scarcely a day passes in my native land that I don't receive some letter from a student or teacher asking me *what I meant to say* in such a book, asking me to elaborate more fully on some sentence I deliberately whittled into minimal shape, or inviting me to speak on some topic, usually theological or sexual, on which it is pleasantly assumed I am an expert. The writer as hero, as Hemingway or Saint-Exupéry or D'Annunzio, a tradition of which Camus was perhaps the last example, has been replaced in America by the writer as educationist. Most writers teach, a great many teach writing; writing is furiously taught in the colleges even as the death knell of the book and the written word is monotonously tolled; any writer, it is assumed, can give a lecture, and the purer products of his academic mind, the "writings" themselves, are sifted and, if found of sufficient quality, installed in their places on the assembly belt of study, as objects of educational contemplation.

How dare one confess, to the politely but firmly inquiring letter-writer who takes for granted that as a remote but functioning element of his education you are duty-bound to provide the information and elucidating essay that will enable him to complete his term paper, or his Ph.D. thesis, or his critical *opus*—how dare one confess that the absence of a swiftly expressible message is, often, *the* message; that reticence is as important a tool to the writer as expression; that the hasty filling out of a questionnaire is not merely irrelevant but *inimical* to the writer's proper activity; that this activity is rather curiously private and finicking, a matter of exorcism and manufacture rather than of toplofty proclamation; that what he makes is ideally as ambiguous and opaque as life itself.

From "Why Write?"

⊷⊷⊏⊐ WRITING CRITICALLY ⊏⊐⊷⊷

What's the Plot?

If a friend asks you, "What was the story you just read about?" you will probably reply by summarizing the plot. The plot of a short story is the element most readers notice first and remember longest. Plotting is such an obvious aspect of fiction that in analyzing a short story, it is easy to overlook its importance. It seems much more profound to dig into imagery, style, or symbolism to discover hidden meanings. Although discussing those other elements can often be illuminating, don't forget the central importance of the plot in expressing the meaning of a story.

Remember that a plot is usually not just a linear sequence of events ("and then . . . and then . . . and then . . ."). Plotting is a *pattern* of actions, events, and situations. Some patterns are simple, but others are complex. The plot is also an expressive device. In a well-written work of fiction, this narrative pattern has been carefully organized by the author to create a certain effect or set of effects on the reader—suspense, humor, sadness, excitement, terror. The organization of a plot also suggests or emphasizes the relationship among characters, events, and situations. The true nature of characters is almost always revealed not by what they say in a story but by what they do.

In writing about a short story, never ignore the surface narrative. It is possible to uncover important and even profound things by focusing on the plot.

WRITING ASSIGNMENT

Summarize the plot of John Updike's "A & P" (or any other selection). In one paragraph of no more than 200 words, clearly and accurately present the key characters and events of the story.

Now write a second paragraph of similar length in which you discuss how much of the story comes through in your summary. How much of the story's effect carries over in your version? How much is lost? List several specific qualities that manage to survive your condensation. Also, list some qualities of the original story that disappear in your summary.

FURTHER SUGGESTIONS FOR WRITING

1. In a paragraph or two, referring to John Updike's "A & P," consider this remark: "Sammy is a male chauvinist who suddenly sees the light." What evidence supporting (or refuting) this comment do you find in the story?
2. Imagining you are Sammy, write a brief letter to a friend explaining why you quit your job.
3. Look up Anne Sexton's retelling of the Grimm tale "Godfather Death" in her book of poems *Transformations* (1971); it is also included in *The Complete Poems of Anne Sexton* (1981). In a short essay of three to five paragraphs, discuss the differences you find between the Grimm and Sexton versions. What is the effect of Sexton's retelling? What does she retain from the original? Which version of the story do you prefer? Why?
4. If you have had an experience in telling stories aloud (to children or to others), write a brief but detailed account of your experience, giving tips to adults who wish to become storytellers.
5. Write a brief fable of your own invention, perhaps illustrating some familiar proverb ("Too many cooks spoil the broth," "A rolling stone gathers no moss"). Your fable might be inspired by "The Appointment in Samarra" or "The Fox and the Grapes." You can state a moral at the end, or, if you prefer, let the moral be unstated but obvious.
6. After you have written such a fable, write a short account of your writing process. Tell of the problems you encountered in thinking up your fable and in writing it, and how you surmounted them.

2 Point of View

In the opening lines of *Adventures of Huckleberry Finn*, Mark Twain takes care to separate himself from the leading character, who is to tell his own story:

> You don't know about me, without you have read a book by the name of *The Adventures of Tom Sawyer*, but that ain't no matter. That book was made by Mr. Mark Twain, and he told the truth, mainly.

Twain wrote the novel, but the **narrator** or speaker is Huck Finn, the one from whose perspective the story is told. Obviously, in *Huckleberry Finn*, the narrator of the story is not the same person as the "real-life" author, the one given the byline. In employing Huck as his narrator, Twain selects a special angle of vision: not his own, exactly, but that of a resourceful boy moving through the thick of events, with a mind at times shrewd, at other times innocent. Through Huck's eyes, Twain takes in certain scenes, actions, and characters and—as only Huck's angle of vision could have enabled Twain to do so well—records them memorably.

Not every narrator in fiction is, like Huck Finn, a main character, one in the thick of events. Some narrators play only minor parts in the stories they tell; others take no active part at all. In the tale of "Godfather Death," we have a narrator who does not participate in the events he recounts. He is not a character in the story but is someone not even named, who stands at some distance from the action recording what the main characters say and do; recording also, at times, what they think, feel, or desire. He seems to have unlimited knowledge: he even knows the mind of Death, who "because he wanted revenge" let the doctor's candle go out. More humanly restricted in their knowledge, other narrators can see into the mind of only one character. They may be less willing to express opinions than the narrator of "Godfather Death" ("He ought to have remembered his godfather's warning"). A story may even be told by a narrator who seems so impartial and aloof that he limits himself to reporting only overheard conversation and to describing, without comment or opinion, the appearances of things. Evidently, narrators greatly differ in kind; however, because stories usually are told by someone, almost every story has some kind of narrator.[1] It is rare in modern fiction for the "real-life" author to try to step out from behind the typewriter and tell the story. Real persons can tell stories, but when such a story is *written*, the result is usually *nonfiction*: a memoir, an account of travels, an autobiography.[2]

To identify the narrator of a story, describing any part he or she plays in the events and any limits placed on his or her knowledge, is to identify the story's **point of view.** In a short story, it is usual for the writer to maintain one point of view from beginning to end, but there is nothing to stop him or her from introducing other points of view as well. In his long, panoramic novel *War and Peace*, encompassing the vast drama of Napoleon's invasion of Russia, Leo Tolstoy freely shifts the point of view in and out of the minds of many characters, among them Napoleon himself.

Theoretically, a great many points of view are possible. A narrator who says "I" might conceivably be involved in events to a much greater or a much lesser degree: as the protagonist, as some other major character, as some minor character, as a mere passive spectator, or even as a character who arrives late upon the scene and then tries to piece together what happened. Evidently, too, a narrator's knowledge might vary in gradations from total omniscience to almost total ignorance. But in reading fiction, again and again we encounter familiar and recognizable points of view. Here is a list of them—admittedly just a rough abstraction—that may provide a few terms with which to discuss the stories that you read and to describe their points of view:

Narrator a Participant (Writing in the First Person):
1. a major character
2. a minor character

Narrator a Nonparticipant (Writing in the Third Person):
3. all-knowing (seeing into any of the characters)
4. seeing into one major character
5. seeing into one minor character
6. objective (not seeing into any characters)

When the narrator is cast as a **participant** in the events of the story, he or she is a dramatized character who says "I." Such a narrator may be the protagonist (Huck Finn) or may be an **observer,** a minor character standing a little to one side, watching a story unfold that mainly involves someone else.

A narrator who remains a **nonparticipant** does not appear in the story as a character. Viewing the characters, perhaps seeing into the minds of one or more of them,

---

[1]Some theorists reserve the term *narrator* for a character who tells a story in the first person. We use it in a wider sense: to mean a recording consciousness that an author creates, who may or may not be a participant in the events of the story. In the view of Wayne C. Booth, the term *narrator* can be dispensed with in dealing with a rigorously impersonal "fly-on-the-wall" story, containing no editorializing and confined to the presentation of surfaces: "In Hemingway's 'The Killers,' for example, there is no narrator other than the implicit second self that Hemingway creates as he writes" (*The Rhetoric of Fiction* [Chicago: U of Chicago P, 1961] 151).

[2]Another relationship between the author and the story will be discussed in Chapter Five, "Tone and Style."

such a narrator refers to them as "he," "she," or "they." When **all-knowing** (or **omniscient**), the narrator sees into the minds of all (or some) characters, moving when necessary from one to another. This is the point of view in "Godfather Death," in which the narrator knows the feelings and motives of the father, of the doctor, and even of Death himself. In that he adds an occasional comment or opinion, this narrator may be said also to show **editorial omniscience** (as we can tell from his disapproving remark that the doctor "ought to have remembered" and his observation that the father did not understand "how wisely God shares out wealth and poverty"). A narrator who shows **impartial omniscience** presents the thoughts and actions of the characters, but does not judge them or comment on them.

When a nonparticipating narrator sees events through the eyes of a single character, whether a major character or a minor one, the resulting point of view is sometimes called **limited omniscience** or **selective omniscience.** The author, of course, selects which character to see through; the omniscience is his and not the narrator's. In William Faulkner's "Barn Burning" (Chapter Five), the narrator is almost entirely confined to knowing the thoughts and perceptions of a boy, the central character. Here is another example. Early in his novel *Madame Bovary*, Gustave Flaubert tells of the first time a young country doctor, Charles Bovary, meets Emma, the woman later to become his wife. The doctor has been summoned late at night to set the broken leg of a farmer, Emma's father.

A young woman wearing a blue merino dress with three flounces came to the door of the house to greet Monsieur Bovary, and she ushered him into the kitchen, where a big open fire was blazing. Around its edges the farm hands' breakfast was bubbling in small pots of assorted sizes. Damp clothes were drying inside the vast chimney-opening. The fire shovel, the tongs, and the nose of the bellows, all of colossal proportions, shone like polished steel; and along the walls hung a lavish array of kitchen utensils, glimmering in the bright light of the fire and in the first rays of the sun that were now beginning to come in through the window-panes.

Charles went upstairs to see the patient. He found him in bed, sweating under blankets, his nightcap lying where he had flung it. He was a stocky little man of fifty, fair-skinned, blue-eyed, bald in front and wearing earrings. On a chair beside him was a big decanter of brandy: he had been pouring himself drinks to keep up his courage. But as soon as he saw the doctor he dropped his bluster, and instead of cursing as he had been doing for the past twelve hours he began to groan weakly.

The fracture was a simple one, without complications of any kind. Charles couldn't have wished for anything easier. Then he recalled his teachers' bedside manner in accident cases, and proceeded to cheer up his patient with all kinds of facetious remarks—a truly surgical attention, like the oiling of a scalpel. For splints, they sent someone to bring a bundle of laths from the carriage shed. Charles selected one, cut it into lengths and smoothed it down with a piece of broken window glass, while the maidservant tore sheets for bandages and Mademoiselle Emma tried to sew some pads. She was a long time finding her workbox, and her father showed his impatience. She made no reply; but as she sewed she kept pricking her fingers and raising them to her mouth to suck.

Charles was surprised by the whiteness of her fingernails. They were almond-shaped, tapering, as polished and shining as Dieppe ivories. Her hands, however, were not pretty—not pale enough, perhaps, a little rough at the knuckles; and they were too long, without softness of line. The finest thing about her was her eyes. They were brown, but seemed black under the long eyelashes; and she had an open gaze that met yours with fearless candor.[3]

In this famous scene, Charles Bovary is beholding people and objects in a natural sequence. On first meeting Emma, he notices only her dress, as though less interested in the woman who opens the door than in passing through to the warm fire. Needing pads for his patient's splint, the doctor observes just the hands of the woman sewing them. Obliged to wait for the splints, he then has the leisure to notice her face, her remarkable eyes. (By the way, notice the effect of the word *yours* in the last sentence of the passage. It is as if the reader, seeing through the doctor's eyes, suddenly became one with him.) Who is the narrator? Not Charles Bovary, nor Gustave Flaubert, but someone able to enter the minds of others—here limited to knowing the thoughts and perceptions of one character.

In the **objective point of view,** the narrator does not enter the mind of any character but describes events from the outside. Telling us what people say and how their faces look, he or she leaves us to infer their thoughts and feelings. So inconspicuous is the narrator that this point of view has been called "the fly on the wall." This metaphor assumes the existence of a fly with a highly discriminating gaze, who knows which details to look for to communicate the deepest meaning. Some critics would say that in the objective point of view, the narrator disappears altogether. Consider this passage by a writer famous for remaining objective, Dashiell Hammett, in his mystery novel *The Maltese Falcon*, describing his private detective Sam Spade:

Spade's thick fingers made a cigarette with deliberate care, sifting a measured quantity of tan flakes down into curved paper, spreading the flakes so that they lay equal at the ends with a slight depression in the middle, thumbs rolling the paper's inner edge down and up under the outer edge as forefingers pressed it over, thumb and fingers sliding to the paper cylinder's ends to hold it even while tongue licked the flap, left forefinger and thumb pinching their ends while right forefinger and thumb smoothed the damp seam, right forefinger and thumb twisting their end and lifting the other to Spade's mouth.[4]

In Hammett's novel, this sentence comes at a moment of crisis: just after Spade has been roused from bed in the middle of the night by a phone call telling him that his partner has been murdered. Even in times of stress (we infer) Spade is deliberate, cool, efficient, and painstaking. Hammett refrains from applying all those adjectives

[3]*Madame Bovary*, translated by Francis Steegmuller (New York: Random, 1957) 16–17.
[4]Chapter Two, "Death in the Fog," *The Maltese Falcon* (New York: Knopf, 1929).

to Spade; to do so would be to exercise editorial omniscience and to destroy the objective point of view.

Besides the common points of view just listed, uncommon points of view are possible. In *Flush,* a fictional biography of Elizabeth Barrett Browning, Virginia Woolf employs an unusual observer as narrator: the poet's pet cocker spaniel. In "The Circular Valley," a short story by Paul Bowles, a man and a woman are watched by a sinister spirit trying to take possession of them, and we see the human characters through the spirit's vague consciousness.

Also possible, but unusual, is a story written in the second person, *you.* This point of view results in an attention-getting directness, as in Jay McInerney's novel *Bright Lights, Big City* (1985), which begins:

> You are not the kind of guy who would be at a place like this at this time of the morning. But here you are, and you cannot say that the terrain is entirely unfamiliar, although the details are *fuzzy.* You are at a nightclub talking to a girl with a shaved head.

This arresting way to tell a story is effective, too, in a novel by Carlos Fuentes, *Aura* (1962), and in some startling stories by Lorrie Moore in *Self-Help* (1985).

The attitudes and opinions of a narrator aren't necessarily those of the author; in fact, we may notice a lively conflict between what we are told and what, apparently, we are meant to believe. A story may be told by an **innocent narrator** or a **naive narrator,** a character who fails to understand all the implications of the story. One such innocent narrator (despite his sometimes shrewd perceptions) is Huckleberry Finn. Because Huck accepts without question the morality and lawfulness of slavery, he feels guilty about helping Jim, a runaway slave. But, far from condemning Huck for his defiance of the law—"All right, then, I'll *go* to hell," Huck tells himself, deciding against returning Jim to captivity—the author, and the reader along with him, silently applaud. Naive in the extreme is the narrator of one part of William Faulkner's novel *The Sound and the Fury,* the idiot Benjy, a grown man with the intellect of a child. In a story told by an **unreliable narrator,** the point of view is that of a person who, we perceive, is deceptive, self-deceptive, deluded, or deranged. As though seeking ways to be faithful to uncertainty, contemporary writers have been particularly fond of unreliable narrators.

Virginia Woolf compared life to "a luminous halo, a semi-transparent envelope surrounding us from the beginning of consciousness to the end."[5] To capture such a reality, modern writers of fiction have employed many strategies. One is the method of writing called **stream of consciousness,** from a phrase coined by psychologist William James to describe the procession of thoughts passing through the mind. In fiction, the stream of consciousness is a kind of selective omniscience: the presentation of thoughts and sense impressions in a lifelike fashion—not in a sequence arranged by logic, but mingled randomly. When in his novel *Ulysses* James Joyce takes us into the mind of Leopold Bloom, an ordinary Dublin mind well-stocked with trivia and fragments of odd learning, the reader may have an impression not of a

---

[5]"Modern Fiction," *Collected Essays* (New York: Harcourt, 1967).

smoothly flowing stream but of an ocean of miscellaneous things, all crowded and jostling.

> As he set foot on O'Connell bridge a puffball of smoke plumed up from the parapet. Brewery barge with export stout. England. Sea air sours it, I heard. Be interesting some day to get a pass through Hancock to see the brewery. Regular world in itself. Vats of porter, wonderful. Rats get in too. Drink themselves bloated as big as a collie floating.[6]

Perceptions—such as the smoke from the brewery barge—trigger Bloom's reflections. A moment later, as he casts a crumpled paper ball off the bridge, he recalls a bit of science he learned in school, the rate of speed of a falling body: "thirty-two feet per sec."

Stream-of-consciousness writing usually occurs in relatively short passages, but in *Ulysses* Joyce employs it extensively. Similar in method, an **interior monologue** is an extended presentation of a character's thoughts, not in the seemingly helter-skelter order of a stream of consciousness, but in an arrangement as if the character were speaking out loud to himself, for us to overhear. A famous interior monologue comes at the end of *Ulysses* when Joyce gives us the rambling memories and reflections of earth-mother Molly Bloom.

Every point of view has limitations. Even **total omniscience,** a knowledge of the minds of all the characters, has its disadvantages. Such a point of view requires high skill to manage, without the storyteller's losing his way in a multitude of perspectives. In fact, there are evident advantages in having a narrator not know everything. We are accustomed to seeing the world through one pair of eyes, to having truths gradually occur to us. Henry James, whose theory and practice of fiction have been influential, held that an excellent way to tell a story was through the fine but bewildered mind of an observer. "It seems probable," James wrote, "that if we were never bewildered there would never be a story to tell about us; we should partake of the superior nature of the all-knowing immortals whose annals are dreadfully dull so long as flurried humans are not, for the positive relief of bored Olympians, mixed up with them."[7]

By using a particular point of view, an author may artfully withhold information, if need be, rather than immediately present it to us. If, for instance, the suspense in a story depends on our not knowing until the end that the protagonist is a spy, the author would be ill advised to tell the story from the protagonist's point of view. If a character acts as the narrator, the author must make sure that the character possesses (or can obtain) enough information to tell the story adequately. Clearly, the author makes a fundamental decision in selecting, from many possibilities, a story's point of view. What we readers admire, if the story is effective, is not only skill in execution, but also judicious choice.

Here is a short story memorable for many reasons, among them its point of view.

---

[6]*Ulysses* (New York: Random, 1934) 150.
[7]Preface, *The Princess Casamassima*, reprinted in *The Art of the Novel*, ed. R. P. Blackmur (New York: Scribner's, 1934).

William Faulkner

A ROSE FOR EMILY

1931

William Faulkner (1897–1962) spent most of his days in Oxford, Mississippi, where he attended the University of Mississippi and where he served as postmaster until angry townspeople ejected him because they had failed to receive mail. During World War I he served with the Royal Canadian Air Force and afterward worked as a feature writer for the New Orleans Times-Picayune. Faulkner's private life was a long struggle to stay solvent: even after fame came to him, he had to write Hollywood scripts and teach at the University of Virginia to support himself. His violent comic novel Sanctuary (1931) caused a stir and turned a profit, but critics tend most to admire The Sound and the Fury (1929), a tale partially told through the eyes of an idiot; As I Lay Dying (1930); Light in August

William Faulkner

(1932); Absalom, Absalom (1936); and The Hamlet (1940). Beginning with Sartoris (1929), Faulkner in his fiction imagines a Mississippi county named Yoknapatawpha and traces the fortunes of several of its families, including the aristocratic Compsons and Sartorises and the white-trash, dollar-grabbing Snopeses, from the Civil War to modern times. His influence on his fellow Southern writers (and others) has been profound. In 1950 he received the Nobel Prize for literature. Although we think of Faulkner primarily as a novelist, he wrote nearly a hundred short stories. Forty-two of the best are available in his Collected Stories (1950; 1995).

I

When Miss Emily Grierson died, our whole town went to her funeral: the men through a sort of respectful affection for a fallen monument, the women mostly out of curiosity to see the inside of her house, which no one save an old manservant—a combined gardener and cook—had seen in at least ten years.

It was a big, squarish frame house that had once been white, decorated with cupolas and spires and scrolled balconies in the heavily lightsome style of the seventies, set on what had once been our most select street. But garages and cotton gins had encroached and obliterated even the august names of that neighborhood; only Miss Emily's house was left, lifting its stubborn and coquettish decay above the cotton wagons and the gasoline pumps—an eyesore among eyesores. And now Miss Emily had gone to join the representatives of those august names where they lay in the cedar-bemused cemetery among the ranked and anonymous graves of Union and Confederate soldiers who fell at the battle of Jefferson.

Alive, Miss Emily had been a tradition, a duty, and a care; a sort of hereditary obligation upon the town, dating from that day in 1894 when Colonel Sartoris, the mayor—he who fathered the edict that no Negro woman should appear on the streets without an apron—remitted her taxes, the dispensation dating from the death of her father on into perpetuity. Not that Miss Emily would have accepted charity. Colonel Sartoris invented an involved tale to the effect that Miss Emily's father had loaned money to the town, which the town, as a matter of business, preferred this way of repaying. Only a man of Colonel Sartoris' generation and thought could have invented it, and only a woman could have believed it.

When the next generation, with its more modern ideas, became mayors and aldermen, this arrangement created some little dissatisfaction. On the first of the year they mailed her a tax notice. February came, and there was no reply. They wrote her a formal letter, asking her to call at the sheriff's office at her convenience. A week later the mayor wrote her himself, offering to call or to send his car for her, and received in reply a note on paper of an archaic shape, in a thin, flowing calligraphy in faded ink, to the effect that she no longer went out at all. The tax notice was also enclosed, without comment.

They called a special meeting of the Board of Aldermen. A deputation 5 waited upon her, knocked at the door through which no visitor had passed since she ceased giving china-painting lessons eight or ten years earlier. They were admitted by the old Negro into a dim hall from which a stairway mounted into still more shadow. It smelled of dust and disuse—a close, dank smell. The Negro led them into the parlor. It was furnished in heavy, leather-covered furniture. When the Negro opened the blinds of one window, they could see that the leather was cracked; and when they sat down, a faint dust rose sluggishly about their thighs, spinning with slow motes in the single sun-ray. On a tarnished gilt easel before the fireplace stood a crayon portrait of Miss Emily's father.

They rose when she entered—a small, fat woman in black, with a thin gold chain descending to her waist and vanishing into her belt, leaning on an ebony cane with a tarnished gold head. Her skeleton was small and spare; perhaps that was why what would have been merely plumpness in another was obesity in her. She looked bloated, like a body long submerged in motionless water, and of that pallid hue. Her eyes, lost in the fatty ridges of her face, looked like two small pieces of coal pressed into a lump of dough as they moved from one face to another while the visitors stated their errand.

She did not ask them to sit. She just stood in the door and listened quietly until the spokesman came to a stumbling halt. Then they could hear the invisible watch ticking at the end of the gold chain.

Her voice was dry and cold. "I have no taxes in Jefferson. Colonel Sartoris explained it to me. Perhaps one of you can gain access to the city records and satisfy yourselves."

"But we have. We are the city authorities, Miss Emily. Didn't you get a notice from the sheriff, signed by him?"

"I received a paper, yes," Miss Emily said. "Perhaps he considers himself the sheriff . . . I have no taxes in Jefferson." 10

"But there is nothing on the books to show that, you see. We must go by the—"

"See Colonel Sartoris. I have no taxes in Jefferson."

"But, Miss Emily—"

"See Colonel Sartoris." (Colonel Sartoris had been dead almost ten years.) "I have no taxes in Jefferson. Tobe!" The Negro appeared. "Show these gentlemen out."

II

So she vanquished them, horse and foot, just as she had vanquished their fa- 15 thers thirty years before about the smell. That was two years after her father's death and a short time after her sweetheart—the one we believed would marry her—had deserted her. After her father's death she went out very little; after her sweetheart went away, people hardly saw her at all. A few of the ladies had the temerity to call, but were not received, and the only sign of life about the place was the Negro man—a young man then—going in and out with a market basket.

"Just as if a man—any man—could keep a kitchen properly," the ladies said; so they were not surprised when the smell developed. It was another link between the gross, teeming world and the high and mighty Griersons.

A neighbor, a woman, complained to the mayor, Judge Stevens, eighty years old.

"But what will you have me do about it, madam?" he said.

"Why, send her word to stop it," the woman said. "Isn't there a law?"

"I'm sure that won't be necessary," Judge Stevens said. "It's probably just a 20 snake or a rat that nigger of hers killed in the yard. I'll speak to him about it."

The next day he received two more complaints, one from a man who came in diffident deprecation. "We really must do something about it, Judge. I'd be the last one in the world to bother Miss Emily, but we've got to do something." That night the Board of Aldermen met—three graybeards and one younger man, a member of the rising generation.

"It's simple enough," he said. "Send her word to have her place cleaned up. Give her a certain time to do it in, and if she don't . . ."

"Dammit, sir," Judge Stevens said, "will you accuse a lady to her face of smelling bad?"

So the next night, after midnight, four men crossed Miss Emily's lawn and slunk about the house like burglars, sniffing along the base of the brickwork and at the cellar openings while one of them performed a regular sowing motion with his hand out of a sack slung from his shoulder. They broke open the cellar door and sprinkled lime there, and in all the outbuildings. As they recrossed the lawn, a window that had been dark was lighted and Miss Emily sat in it, the light behind her, and her upright torso motionless as that of an idol. They crept quietly across the lawn and into the shadow of the locusts that lined the street. After a week or two the smell went away.

That was when people had begun to feel really sorry for her. People in our town, remembering how old lady Wyatt, her great-aunt, had gone completely crazy at last, believed that the Griersons held themselves a little too high for what they really were. None of the young men were quite good enough for Miss Emily and such. We had long thought of them as a tableau, Miss Emily a slender figure in white in the background, her father a spraddled silhouette in the foreground, his back to her and clutching a horsewhip, the two of them framed by the back-flung front door. So when she got to be thirty and was still single, we were not pleased exactly, but vindicated; even with insanity in the family she wouldn't have turned down all of her chances if they had really materialized.

When her father died, it got about that the house was all that was left to her; and in a way, people were glad. At last they could pity Miss Emily. Being left alone, and a pauper, she had become humanized. Now she too would know the old thrill and the old despair of a penny more or less.

The day after his death all the ladies prepared to call at the house and offer condolence and aid, as is our custom. Miss Emily met them at the door, dressed as usual and with no trace of grief on her face. She told them that her father was not dead. She did that for three days, with the ministers calling on her, and the doctors, trying to persuade her to let them dispose of the body. Just as they were about to resort to law and force, she broke down, and they buried her father quickly.

We did not say she was crazy then. We believed she had to do that. We remembered all the young men her father had driven away, and we knew that with nothing left, she would have to cling to that which had robbed her, as people will.

III

She was sick for a long time. When we saw her again, her hair was cut short, making her look like a girl, with a vague resemblance to those angels in colored church windows—sort of tragic and serene.

The town had just let the contracts for paving the sidewalks, and in the 30 summer after her father's death they began the work. The construction company came with niggers and mules and machinery, and a foreman named Homer Barron, a Yankee—a big, dark, ready man, with a big voice and eyes lighter than his face. The little boys would follow in groups to hear him cuss the niggers, and the niggers singing in time to the rise and fall of picks. Pretty soon he knew everybody in town. Whenever you heard a lot of laughing anywhere about the square, Homer Barron would be in the center of the group. Presently we began to see him and Miss Emily on Sunday afternoons driving in the yellow-wheeled buggy and the matched team of bays from the livery stable.

32   POINT OF VIEW

At first we were glad that Miss Emily would have an interest, because the ladies all said, "Of course a Grierson would not think seriously of a Northerner, a day laborer." But there were still others, older people, who said that even grief could not cause a real lady to forget *noblesse oblige°*—without calling it *noblesse oblige*. They just said, "Poor Emily. Her kinsfolk should come to her." She had some kin in Alabama; but years ago her father had fallen out with them over the estate of old lady Wyatt, the crazy woman, and there was no communication between the two families. They had not even been represented at the funeral.

And as soon as the old people said, "Poor Emily," the whispering began. "Do you suppose it's really so?" they said to one another. "Of course it is. What else could . . ." This behind their hands; rustling of craned silk and satin behind jalousies closed upon the sun of Sunday afternoon as the thin, swift clop-clop-clop of the matched team passed: "Poor Emily."

She carried her head high enough—even when we believed that she was fallen. It was as if she demanded more than ever the recognition of her dignity as the last Grierson; as if it had wanted that touch of earthiness to reaffirm her imperviousness. Like when she bought the rat poison, the arsenic. That was over a year after they had begun to say "Poor Emily," and while the two female cousins were visiting her.

"I want some poison," she said to the druggist. She was over thirty then, still a slight woman, though thinner than usual, with cold, haughty black eyes in a face the flesh of which was strained across the temples and about the eye-sockets as you imagine a lighthouse-keeper's face ought to look. "I want some poison," she said.

"Yes, Miss Emily. What kind? For rats and such? I'd recom—"   35

"I want the best you have. I don't care what kind."

The druggist named several. "They'll kill anything up to an elephant. But what you want is—"

"Arsenic," Miss Emily said. "Is that a good one?"

"Is . . . arsenic? Yes, ma'am. But what you want—"

"I want arsenic."   40

The druggist looked down at her. She looked back at him, erect, her face like a strained flag. "Why, of course," the druggist said. "If that's what you want. But the law requires you to tell what you are going to use it for."

Miss Emily just stared at him, her head tilted back in order to look him eye for eye, until he looked away and went and got the arsenic and wrapped it up. The Negro delivery boy brought her the package; the druggist didn't come back. When she opened the package at home there was written on the box, under the skull and bones: "For rats."

---

noblesse oblige: the obligation of a member of the nobility to behave with honor and dignity.

IV

So the next day we all said, "She will kill herself"; and we said it would be the best thing. When she had first begun to be seen with Homer Barron, we had said, "She will marry him." Then we said, "She will persuade him yet," because Homer himself had remarked—he liked men, and it was known that he drank with the younger men in the Elks' Club—that he was not a marrying man. Later we said, "Poor Emily," behind the jalousies as they passed on Sunday afternoon in the glittering buggy, Miss Emily with her head high and Homer Barron with his hat cocked and a cigar in his teeth, reins and whip in a yellow glove.

Then some of the ladies began to say that it was a disgrace to the town and a bad example to the young people. The men did not want to interfere, but at last the ladies forced the Baptist minister—Miss Emily's people were Episcopal—to call upon her. He would never divulge what happened during that interview, but he refused to go back again. The next Sunday they again drove about the streets, and the following day the minister's wife wrote to Miss Emily's relations in Alabama.

So she had blood-kin under her roof again and we sat back to watch developments. At first nothing happened. Then we were sure that they were to be married. We learned that Miss Emily had been to the jeweler's and ordered a man's toilet set in silver, with the letters H.B. on each piece. Two days later we learned that she had bought a complete outfit of men's clothing, including a nightshirt, and we said, "They are married." We were really glad. We were glad because the two female cousins were even more Grierson than Miss Emily had ever been.

So we were not surprised when Homer Barron—the streets had been finished some time since—was gone. We were a little disappointed that there was not a public blowing-off, but we believed that he had gone on to prepare for Miss Emily's coming, or to give her a chance to get rid of the cousins. (By that time it was a cabal, and we were all Miss Emily's allies to help circumvent the cousins.) Sure enough, after another week they departed. And, as we had expected all along, within three days Homer Barron was back in town. A neighbor saw the Negro man admit him at the kitchen door at dusk one evening.

And that was the last we saw of Homer Barron. And of Miss Emily for some time. The Negro man went in and out with the market basket, but the front door remained closed. Now and then we would see her at a window for a moment, as the men did that night when they sprinkled the lime, but for almost six months she did not appear on the streets. Then we knew that this was to be expected too; as if that quality of her father which had thwarted her woman's life so many times had been too virulent and too furious to die.

When we next saw Miss Emily, she had grown fat and her hair was turning gray. During the next few years it grew grayer and grayer until it attained an even pepper-and-salt iron-gray, when it ceased turning. Up to the day of her death at seventy-four it was still that vigorous iron-gray, like the hair of an active man.

From that time on her front door remained closed, save for a period of six or seven years, when she was about forty, during which she gave lessons in china-painting. She fitted up a studio in one of the downstairs rooms, where the daughters and granddaughters of Colonel Sartoris' contemporaries were sent to her with the same regularity and in the same spirit that they were sent to church on Sundays with a twenty-five-cent piece for the collection plate. Meanwhile her taxes had been remitted.

Then the newer generation became the backbone and the spirit of the town, and the painting pupils grew up and fell away and did not send their children to her with boxes of color and tedious brushes and pictures cut from the ladies' magazines. The front door closed upon the last one and remained closed for good. When the town got free postal delivery, Miss Emily alone refused to let them fasten the metal numbers above her door and attach a mailbox to it. She would not listen to them.

Daily, monthly, yearly we watched the Negro grow grayer and more stooped, going in and out with the market basket. Each December we sent her a tax notice, which would be returned by the post office a week later, unclaimed. Now and then we would see her in one of the downstairs windows—she had evidently shut up the top floor of the house—like the carven torso of an idol in a niche, looking or not looking at us, we could never tell which. Thus she passed from generation to generation—dear, inescapable, impervious, tranquil, and perverse.

And so she died. Fell ill in the house filled with dust and shadows, with only a doddering Negro man to wait on her. We did not even know she was sick; we had long since given up trying to get any information from the Negro. He talked to no one, probably not even to her, for his voice had grown harsh and rusty, as if from disuse.

She died in one of the downstairs rooms, in a heavy walnut bed with a curtain, her gray head propped on a pillow yellow and moldy with age and lack of sunlight.

V

The Negro met the first of the ladies at the front door and let them in, with their hushed, sibilant voices and their quick, curious glances, and then he disappeared. He walked right through the house and out the back and was not seen again.

The two female cousins came at once. They held the funeral on the second day, with the town coming to look at Miss Emily beneath a mass of bought flowers, with the crayon face of her father musing profoundly above the bier and the ladies sibilant and macabre; and the very old men—some in their brushed Confederate uniforms—on the porch and the lawn, talking of Miss Emily as if she had been a contemporary of theirs, believing that they had danced with her and courted her perhaps, confusing time with its mathematical progression, as the old do, to whom all the past is not a diminishing road but, instead, a huge meadow which no winter ever quite touches, divided from them now by the narrow bottleneck of the most recent decade of years.

Already we knew that there was one room in that region above stairs which no one had seen in forty years, and which would have to be forced. They waited until Miss Emily was decently in the ground before they opened it.

The violence of breaking down the door seemed to fill this room with pervading dust. A thin, acrid pall as of the tomb seemed to lie everywhere upon this room decked and furnished as for a bridal: upon the valance curtains of faded rose color, upon the rose-shaded lights, upon the dressing table, upon the delicate array of crystal and the man's toilet things backed with tarnished silver, silver so tarnished that the monogram was obscured. Among them lay collar and tie, as if they had just been removed, which, lifted, left upon the surface a pale crescent in the dust. Upon a chair hung the suit, carefully folded; beneath it the two mute shoes and the discarded socks.

The man himself lay in the bed.

For a long while we just stood there, looking down at the profound and fleshless grin. The body had apparently once lain in the attitude of an embrace, but now the long sleep that outlasts love, that conquers even the grimace of love, had cuckolded him. What was left of him, rotted beneath what was left of the nightshirt, had become inextricable from the bed in which he lay; and upon him and upon the pillow beside him lay that even coating of the patient and biding dust.

Then we noticed that in the second pillow was the indentation of a head. 60 One of us lifted something from it, and leaning forward, that faint and invisible dust dry and acrid in the nostrils, we saw a long strand of iron-gray hair.

QUESTIONS

1. What is meaningful in the final detail that the strand of hair on the second pillow is *iron-gray*?
2. Who is the unnamed narrator? For whom does he profess to be speaking?
3. Why does "A Rose for Emily" seem better told from his point of view than if it were told (like John Updike's "A & P") from the point of view of the main character?
4. What foreshadowings of the discovery of the body of Homer Barron are we given earlier in the story? Share your experience in reading "A Rose for Emily": did the foreshadowings give away the ending for you? Did they heighten your interest?
5. What contrasts does the narrator draw between changing reality and Emily's refusal or inability to recognize change?
6. How do the character and background of Emily Grierson differ from those of Homer Barron? What general observations about the society that Faulkner depicts can be made from his portraits of these two characters and from his account of life in this one Mississippi town?
7. Does the story seem to you totally grim, or do you find any humor in it?
8. What do you infer to be the author's attitude toward Emily Grierson? Is she simply a murderous madwoman? Why do you suppose Faulkner calls his story "A Rose . . ."?

Jhumpa Lahiri

INTERPRETER OF MALADIES

Jhumpa Lahiri

Jhumpa Lahiri was born in London in 1967 and grew up in Rhode Island. Her father, a librarian, and her mother, a teacher, had emigrated from their native India, to which Lahiri has made a number of extended visits. After writing a great deal of fiction as a child and teenager, she wrote none at all during her college years. She graduated from Barnard College with a B.A. in English literature, and after all her graduate school applications had been rejected, she went to work as a research assistant for a nonprofit organization. She began staying late after work to use her office computer to write short stories, on the strength of which she was accepted into the creative writing program at Boston University. Earning an M.A. in creative writing, Lahiri stayed on to complete an M.A. in English, an M.A. in comparative literature and the arts, and a Ph.D. in Renaissance studies. "In the process," she has said, "it became clear to me that I was not meant to be a scholar. It was something I did out of a sense of duty and practicality, but it was never something I loved. . . . The year I finished my dissertation, I was also accepted to the Fine Arts Work Center in Provincetown, and that changed everything." During her seven-month residency at the center, she found an agent, had a story published in the New Yorker, and sold a collection of her stories to a publisher. That volume, Interpreter of Maladies, appeared in 1999 to excellent reviews and was awarded the Pulitzer Prize for fiction. Its title story was also selected for both an O. Henry Award and publication in The Best American Short Stories. Lahiri's second book and first novel, The Namesake, was published in 2003. She has taught creative writing at Boston University and the Rhode Island School of Design. She lives in New York.

At the tea stall Mr. and Mrs. Das bickered about who should take Tina to the toilet. Eventually Mrs. Das relented when Mr. Das pointed out that he had given the girl her bath the night before. In the rearview mirror Mr. Kapasi watched as Mrs. Das emerged slowly from his bulky white Ambassador, dragging her shaved, largely bare legs across the back seat. She did not hold the little girl's hand as they walked to the rest room.

They were on their way to see the Sun Temple at Konarak. It was a dry, bright Saturday, the mid-July heat tempered by a steady ocean breeze, ideal weather for sightseeing. Ordinarily Mr. Kapasi would not have stopped so soon along the way, but less than five minutes after he'd picked up the family that morning in front of Hotel Sandy Villa, the little girl had complained. The first thing Mr. Kapasi had noticed when he saw Mr. and Mrs. Das, standing with their children under the portico of the hotel, was that they were very young, perhaps not even thirty. In addition to Tina they had two boys, Ronny and Bobby, who appeared very close in age and had teeth covered in a network of flashing silver wires. The family looked Indian but dressed as foreigners did, the children in stiff, brightly colored clothing and caps with translucent visors. Mr. Kapasi was accustomed to foreign tourists; he was assigned to them regularly because he could speak English. Yesterday he had driven an elderly couple from Scotland, both with spotted faces and fluffy white hair so thin it exposed their sunburnt scalps. In comparison, the tanned, youthful faces of Mr. and Mrs. Das were all the more striking. When he'd introduced himself, Mr. Kapasi had pressed his palms together in greeting, but Mr. Das squeezed hands like an American so that Mr. Kapasi felt it in his elbow. Mrs. Das, for her part, had flexed one side of her mouth, smiling dutifully at Mr. Kapasi, without displaying any interest in him.

As they waited at the tea stall, Ronny, who looked like the older of the two boys, clambered suddenly out of the back seat, intrigued by a goat tied to a stake in the ground.

"Don't touch it," Mr. Das said. He glanced up from his paperback tour book, which said "INDIA" in yellow letters and looked as if it had been published abroad. His voice, somehow tentative and a little shrill, sounded as though it had not yet settled into maturity.

"I want to give it a piece of gum," the boy called back as he trotted ahead.   5

Mr. Das stepped out of the car and stretched his legs by squatting briefly to the ground. A clean-shaven man, he looked exactly like a magnified version of Ronny. He had a sapphire blue visor, and was dressed in shorts, sneakers, and a T-shirt. The camera slung around his neck, with an impressive telephoto lens and numerous buttons and markings, was the only complicated thing he wore. He frowned, watching as Ronny rushed toward the goat, but appeared to have no intention of intervening. "Bobby, make sure that your brother doesn't do anything stupid."

"I don't feel like it," Bobby said, not moving. He was sitting in the front seat beside Mr. Kapasi, studying a picture of the elephant god taped to the glove compartment.

"No need to worry," Mr. Kapasi said. "They are quite tame." Mr. Kapasi was forty-six years old, with receding hair that had gone completely silver, but his butterscotch complexion and his unlined brow, which he treated in spare moments to dabs of lotus-oil balm, made it easy to imagine what he must have looked like at an earlier age. He wore gray trousers and a matching jacket-style shirt, tapered at the waist, with short sleeves and a large pointed collar, made of a thin but durable synthetic material. He had specified both the cut and the fabric to his tailor—it was his preferred uniform for giving tours because it did not get crushed during his long hours behind the wheel. Through the windshield he watched as Ronny circled around the goat, touched it quickly on its side, then trotted back to the car.

"You left India as a child?" Mr. Kapasi asked when Mr. Das had settled once again into the passenger seat.

"Oh, Mina and I were both born in America," Mr. Das announced with an air of sudden confidence. "Born and raised. Our parents live here now, in Assansol.° They retired. We visit them every couple years." He turned to watch as the little girl ran toward the car, the wide purple bows of her sundress flopping on her narrow brown shoulders. She was holding to her chest a doll with yellow hair that looked as if it had been chopped, as a punitive measure, with a pair of dull scissors. "This is Tina's first trip to India, isn't it, Tina?"

"I don't have to go to the bathroom anymore," Tina announced.

"Where's Mina?" Mr. Das asked.

Mr. Kapasi found it strange that Mr. Das should refer to his wife by her first name when speaking to the little girl. Tina pointed to where Mrs. Das was purchasing something from one of the shirtless men who worked at the tea stall. Mr. Kapasi heard one of the shirtless men sing a phrase from a popular Hindi love song as Mrs. Das walked back to the car, but she did not appear to understand the words of the song, for she did not express irritation, or embarrassment, or react in any other way to the man's declarations.

He observed her. She wore a red-and-white-checkered skirt that stopped above her knees, slip-on shoes with a square wooden heel, and a close-fitting blouse styled like a man's undershirt. The blouse was decorated at chest-level with a calico appliqué in the shape of a strawberry. She was a short woman, with small hands like paws, her frosty pink fingernails painted to match her lips, and was slightly plump in her figure. Her hair, shorn only a little longer than her husband's, was parted far to one side. She was wearing large dark brown sunglasses with a pinkish tint to them, and carried a big straw bag, almost as big as her torso, shaped like a bowl, with a water bottle poking out of it. She walked slowly, carrying some puffed rice tossed with peanuts and chili peppers in a large packet made from newspapers. Mr. Kapasi turned to Mr. Das.

"Where in America do you live?"

"New Brunswick, New Jersey."

"Next to New York?"

"Exactly. I teach middle school there."

"What subject?"

"Science. In fact, every year I take my students on a trip to the Museum of Natural History in New York City. In a way we have a lot in common, you could say, you and I. How long have you been a tour guide, Mr. Kapasi?"

"Five years."

Mrs. Das reached the car. "How long's the trip?" she asked, shutting the door.

"About two and a half hours," Mr. Kapasi replied.

At this Mrs. Das gave an impatient sigh, as if she had been traveling her whole life without pause. She fanned herself with a folded Bombay film magazine written in English.

"I thought that the Sun Temple is only eighteen miles north of Puri," Mr. Das said, tapping on the tour book.

Assansol: a city in the state of West Bengal in northeastern India.

"The roads to Konarak are poor. Actually it is a distance of fifty-two miles," Mr. Kapasi explained.

Mr. Das nodded, readjusting the camera strap where it had begun to chafe the back of his neck.

Before starting the ignition, Mr. Kapasi reached back to make sure the cranklike locks on the inside of each of the back doors were secured. As soon as the car began to move the little girl began to play with the lock on her side, clicking it with some effort forward and backward, but Mrs. Das said nothing to stop her. She sat a bit slouched at one end of the back seat, not offering her puffed rice to anyone. Ronny and Tina sat on either side of her, both snapping bright green gum.

"Look," Bobby said as the car began to gather speed. He pointed with his finger to the tall trees that lined the road. "Look."

"Monkeys!" Ronny shrieked. "Wow!"   30

They were seated in groups along the branches, with shining black faces, silver bodies, horizontal eyebrows, and crested heads. Their long gray tails dangled like a series of ropes among the leaves. A few scratched themselves with black leathery hands, or swung their feet, staring as the car passed.

"We call them the hanuman," Mr. Kapasi said. "They are quite common in the area."

As soon as he spoke, one of the monkeys leaped into the middle of the road, causing Mr. Kapasi to brake suddenly. Another bounced onto the hood of the car, then sprang away. Mr. Kapasi beeped his horn. The children began to get excited, sucking in their breath and covering their faces partly with their hands. They had never seen monkeys outside of a zoo, Mr. Das explained. He asked Mr. Kapasi to stop the car so that he could take a picture.

While Mr. Das adjusted his telephoto lens, Mrs. Das reached into her straw bag and pulled out a bottle of colorless nail polish, which she proceeded to stroke on the tip of her index finger.

The little girl stuck out a hand. "Mine too. Mommy, do mine too."   35

"Leave me alone," Mrs. Das said, blowing on her nail and turning her body slightly. "You're making me mess up."

The little girl occupied herself by buttoning and unbuttoning a pinafore on the doll's plastic body.

"All set," Mr. Das said, replacing the lens cap.

The car rattled considerably as it raced along the dusty road, causing them all to pop up from their seats every now and then, but Mrs. Das continued to polish her nails. Mr. Kapasi eased up on the accelerator, hoping to produce a smoother ride. When he reached for the gearshift the boy in front accommodated him by swinging his hairless knees out of the way. Mr. Kapasi noted that this boy was slightly paler than the other children. "Daddy, why is the driver sitting on the wrong side in this car, too?" the boy asked.

"They all do that here, dummy," Ronny said.   40

"Don't call your brother a dummy," Mr. Das said. He turned to Mr. Kapasi. "In America, you know . . . it confuses them."

"Oh yes, I am well aware," Mr. Kapasi said. As delicately as he could, he shifted gears again, accelerating as they approached a hill in the road. "I see it on *Dallas*,° the steering wheels are on the left-hand side."

"What's *Dallas*?" Tina asked, banging her now naked doll on the seat behind Mr. Kapasi.

"It went off the air," Mr. Das explained. "It's a television show."

They were all like siblings, Mr. Kapasi thought as they passed a row of date   45
trees. Mr. and Mrs. Das behaved like an older brother and sister, not parents. It seemed that they were in charge of the children only for the day; it was hard to believe they were regularly responsible for anything other than themselves. Mr. Das tapped on his lens cap, and his tour book, dragging his thumbnail occasionally across the pages so that they made a scraping sound. Mrs. Das continued to polish her nails. She had still not removed her sunglasses. Every now and then Tina renewed her plea that she wanted her nails done, too, and so at one point Mrs. Das flicked a drop of polish on the little girl's finger before depositing the bottle back inside her straw bag.

"Isn't this an air-conditioned car?" she asked, still blowing on her hand. The window on Tina's side was broken and could not be rolled down.

"Quit complaining," Mr. Das said. "It isn't so hot."

"I told you to get a car with air-conditioning," Mrs. Das continued. "Why do you do this, Raj, just to save a few stupid rupees. What are you saving us, fifty cents?"

Their accents sounded just like the ones Mr. Kapasi heard on American television programs, though not like the ones on *Dallas*.

"Doesn't it get tiresome, Mr. Kapasi, showing people the same thing every   50
day?" Mr. Das asked, rolling down his own window all the way. "Hey, do you mind stopping the car? I just want to get a shot of this guy."

Mr. Kapasi pulled over to the side of the road as Mr. Das took a picture of a barefoot man, his head wrapped in a dirty turban, seated on top of a cart of grain sacks pulled by a pair of bullocks.° Both the man and the bullocks were emaciated. In the back seat Mrs. Das gazed out another window, at the sky, where nearly transparent clouds passed quickly in front of one another.

"I look forward to it, actually," Mr. Kapasi said as they continued on their way. "The Sun Temple is one of my favorite places. In that way it is a reward for me. I give tours on Fridays and Saturdays only. I have another job during the week."

"Oh? Where?" Mr. Das asked.

"I work in a doctor's office."

"You're a doctor?"   55

"I am not a doctor. I work with one. As an interpreter."

"What does a doctor need an interpreter for?"

Dallas: extremely popular 1980s television drama centered on the professional and romantic affairs of unscrupulous oil baron J. R. Ewing and his family.   *bullocks:* young or castrated bulls; steer.

"He has a number of Gujarati patients. My father was Gujarati, but many people do not speak Gujarati in this area, including the doctor. And so the doctor asked me to work in his office, interpreting what the patients say."

"Interesting. I've never heard of anything like that," Mr. Das said.

Mr. Kapasi shrugged. "It is a job like any other." 60

"But so romantic," Mrs. Das said dreamily, breaking her extended silence. She lifted her pinkish brown sunglasses and arranged them on top of her head like a tiara. For the first time, her eyes met Mr. Kapasi's in the rearview mirror: pale, a bit small, their gaze fixed but drowsy.

Mr. Das craned to look at her. "What's so romantic about it?"

"I don't know. Something." She shrugged, knitting her brows together for an instant. "Would you like a piece of gum, Mr. Kapasi?" she asked brightly. She reached into her straw bag and handed him a small square wrapped in green-and-white-striped paper. As soon as Mr. Kapasi put the gum in his mouth a thick sweet liquid burst onto his tongue.

"Tell us more about your job, Mr. Kapasi," Mrs. Das said.

"What would you like to know, madame?" 65

"I don't know," she shrugged, munching on some puffed rice and licking the mustard oil from the corners of her mouth. "Tell us a typical situation." She settled back in her seat, her head tilted in a patch of sun, and closed her eyes. "I want to picture what happens."

"Very well. The other day a man came in with a pain in his throat."

"Did he smoke cigarettes?"

"No. It was very curious. He complained that he felt as if there were long pieces of straw stuck in his throat. When I told the doctor he was able to prescribe the proper medication."

"That's so neat."

"Yes," Mr. Kapasi agreed after some hesitation. 70

"So these patients are totally dependent on you," Mrs. Das said. She spoke slowly, as if she were thinking aloud. "In a way, more dependent on you than the doctor."

"How do you mean? How could it be?"

"Well, for example, you could tell the doctor that the pain felt like a burning, not straw. The patient would never know what you had told the doctor, and the doctor wouldn't know that you had told the wrong thing. It's a big responsibility."

"Yes, a big responsibility you have there, Mr. Kapasi," Mr. Das agreed. 75

Mr. Kapasi had never thought of his job in such complimentary terms. To him it was a thankless occupation. He found nothing noble in interpreting people's maladies, assiduously translating the symptoms of so many swollen bones, countless cramps of bellies and bowels, spots on people's palms that changed color, shape, or size. The doctor, nearly half his age, had an affinity for bell-bottom trousers and made humorless jokes about the Congress party.°

the Congress party: India's governing party for five decades after independence in 1947, widely perceived as corrupt.

Together they worked in a stale little infirmary where Mr. Kapasi's smartly tailored clothes clung to him in the heat, in spite of the blackened blades of a ceiling fan churning over their heads.

The job was a sign of his failings. In his youth he'd been a devoted scholar of foreign languages, the owner of an impressive collection of dictionaries. He had dreamed of being an interpreter for diplomats and dignitaries, resolving conflicts between people and nations, settling disputes of which he alone could understand both sides. He was a self-educated man. In a series of notebooks, in the evenings before his parents settled his marriage, he had listed the common etymologies of words, and at one point in his life he was confident that he could converse, if given the opportunity, in English, French, Russian, Portuguese, and Italian, not to mention Hindi, Bengali, Orissi, and Gujarati. Now only a handful of European phrases remained in his memory, scattered words for things like saucers and chairs. English was the only non-Indian language he spoke fluently anymore. Mr. Kapasi knew it was not a remarkable talent. Sometimes he feared that his children knew better English than he did, just from watching television. Still, it came in handy for the tours.

He had taken the job as an interpreter after his first son, at the age of seven, contracted typhoid—that was how he had first made the acquaintance of the doctor. At the time Mr. Kapasi had been teaching English in a grammar school, and he bartered his skills as an interpreter to pay the increasingly exorbitant medical bills. In the end the boy had died one evening in his mother's arms, his limbs burning with fever, but then there was the funeral to pay for, and the other children who were born soon enough, and the newer, bigger house, and the good schools and tutors, and the fine shoes and the television, and the countless other ways he tried to console his wife and to keep her from crying in her sleep, and so when the doctor offered to pay him twice as much as he earned at the grammar school, he accepted. Mr. Kapasi knew that his wife had little regard for his career as an interpreter. He knew it reminded her of the son she'd lost, and that she resented the other lives he helped, in his own small way, to save. If ever she referred to his position, she used the phrase "doctor's assistant," as if the process of interpretation were equal to taking someone's temperature, or changing a bedpan. She never asked him about the patients who came to the doctor's office, or said that his job was a big responsibility.

For this reason it flattered Mr. Kapasi that Mrs. Das was so intrigued by his job. Unlike his wife, she had reminded him of its intellectual challenges. She had also used the word "romantic." She did not behave in a romantic way toward her husband, and yet she had used the word to describe him. He wondered if Mr. and Mrs. Das were a bad match, just as he and his wife were. Perhaps they, too, had little in common apart from three children and a decade of their lives. The signs he recognized from his own marriage were there—the bickering, the indifference, the protracted silences. Her sudden interest in him, an interest she did not express in either her husband or her children, was mildly intoxicating. When Mr. Kapasi thought once again about how she had said "romantic," the feeling of intoxication grew.

He began to check his reflection in the rearview mirror as he drove, feeling grateful that he had chosen the gray suit that morning and not the brown one, which tended to sag a little in the knees. From time to time he glanced through the mirror at Mrs. Das. In addition to glancing at her face he glanced at the strawberry between her breasts, and the golden brown hollow in her throat. He decided to tell Mrs. Das about another patient, and another: the young woman who had complained of a sensation of raindrops in her spine, the gentleman whose birthmark had begun to sprout hairs. Mrs. Das listened attentively, stroking her hair with a small plastic brush that resembled an oval bed of nails, asking more questions, for yet another example. The children were quiet, intent on spotting more monkeys in the trees, and Mr. Das was absorbed by his tour book, so it seemed like a private conversation between Mr. Kapasi and Mrs. Das. In this manner the next half hour passed, and when they stopped for lunch at a roadside restaurant that sold fritters and omelette sandwiches, usually something Mr. Kapasi looked forward to on his tours so that he could sit in peace and enjoy some hot tea, he was disappointed. As the Das family settled together under a magenta umbrella fringed with white and orange tassels, and placed their orders with one of the waiters who marched about in tricornered caps, Mr. Kapasi reluctantly headed toward a neighboring table.

"Mr. Kapasi, wait. There's room here," Mrs. Das called out. She gathered Tina onto her lap, insisting that he accompany them. And so, together, they had bottled mango juice and sandwiches and plates of onions and potatoes deep-fried in graham-flour batter. After finishing two omelette sandwiches Mr. Das took more pictures of the group as they ate.

"How much longer?" he asked Mr. Kapasi as he paused to load a new roll of film in the camera.

"About half an hour more."

By now the children had gotten up from the table to look at more monkeys perched in a nearby tree, so there was a considerable space between Mrs. Das and Mr. Kapasi. Mr. Das placed the camera to his face and squeezed one eye shut, his tongue exposed at one corner of his mouth. "This looks funny. Mina, you need to lean in closer to Mr. Kapasi."

She did. He could smell a scent on her skin, like a mixture of whiskey and rosewater. He worried suddenly that she could smell his perspiration, which he knew had collected beneath the synthetic material of his shirt. He polished off his mango juice in one gulp and smoothed his silver hair with his hands. A bit of the juice dripped onto his chin. He wondered if Mrs. Das had noticed.

She had not. "What's your address, Mr. Kapasi?" she inquired, fishing for something inside her straw bag.

"You would like my address?"

"So we can send you copies," she said. "Of the pictures." She handed him a scrap of paper which she had hastily ripped from a page of her film magazine. The blank portion was limited, for the narrow strip was crowded by lines of text and a tiny picture of a hero and heroine embracing under a eucalyptus tree.

The paper curled as Mr. Kapasi wrote his address in clear, careful letters. She would write to him, asking about his days interpreting at the doctor's office, and he would respond eloquently, choosing only the most entertaining anecdotes, ones that would make her laugh out loud as she read them in her house in New Jersey. In time she would reveal the disappointment of her marriage, and he his. In this way their friendship would grow, and flourish. He would possess a picture of the two of them, eating fried onions under a magenta umbrella, which he would keep, he decided, safely tucked between the pages of his Russian grammar. As his mind raced, Mr. Kapasi experienced a mild and pleasant shock. It was similar to a feeling he used to experience long ago when, after months of translating with the aid of a dictionary, he would finally read a passage from a French novel, or an Italian sonnet, and understand the words, one after another, unencumbered by his own efforts. In those moments Mr. Kapasi used to believe that all was right with the world, that all struggles were rewarded, that all of life's mistakes made sense in the end. The promise that he would hear from Mrs. Das now filled him with the same belief.

When he finished writing his address Mr. Kapasi handed her the paper, but 90 as soon as he did so he worried that he had either misspelled his name, or accidentally reversed the numbers of his postal code. He dreaded the possibility of a lost letter, the photograph never reaching him, hovering somewhere in Orissa,° close but ultimately unattainable. He thought of asking for the slip of paper again, just to make sure he had written his address accurately, but Mrs. Das had already dropped it into the jumble of her bag.

They reached Konarak at two-thirty. The temple, made of sandstone, was a massive pyramid-like structure in the shape of a chariot. It was dedicated to the great master of life, the sun, which struck three sides of the edifice as it made its journey each day across the sky. Twenty-four giant wheels were carved on the north and south sides of the plinth. The whole thing was drawn by a team of seven horses, speeding as if through the heavens. As they approached, Mr. Kapasi explained that the temple had been built between A.D. 1243 and 1255, with the efforts of twelve hundred artisans, by the great ruler of the Ganga dynasty, King Narasimhadeva the First, to commemorate his victory against the Muslim army.

"It says the temple occupies about a hundred and seventy acres of land," Mr. Das said, reading from his book.

"It's like a desert," Ronny said, his eyes wandering across the sand that stretched on all sides beyond the temple.

"The Chandrabhaga River once flowed one mile north of here. It is dry now," Mr. Kapasi said, turning off the engine.

They got out and walked toward the temple, posing first for pictures by the 95 pair of lions that flanked the steps. Mr. Kapasi led them next to one of the wheels of the chariot, higher than any human being, nine feet in diameter.

Orissa: a state on the southwest border of West Bengal.

"'The wheels are supposed to symbolize the wheel of life,'" Mr. Das read. "'They depict the cycle of creation, preservation, and achievement of realization.' Cool." He turned the page of his book. "'Each wheel is divided into eight thick and thin spokes, dividing the day into eight equal parts. The rims are carved with designs of birds and animals, whereas the medallions in the spokes are carved with women in luxurious poses, largely erotic in nature.'"

What he referred to were the countless friezes of entwined naked bodies, making love in various positions, women clinging to the necks of men, their knees wrapped eternally around their lovers' thighs. In addition to these were assorted scenes from daily life, of hunting and trading, of deer being killed with bows and arrows and marching warriors holding swords in their hands.

It was no longer possible to enter the temple, for it had filled with rubble years ago, but they admired the exterior, as did all the tourists Mr. Kapasi brought there, slowly strolling along each of its sides. Mr. Das trailed behind, taking pictures. The children ran ahead, pointing to figures of naked people, intrigued in particular by the Nagamithunas, the half-human, half-serpentine couples who were said, Mr. Kapasi told them, to live in the deepest waters of the sea. Mr. Kapasi was pleased that they liked the temple, pleased especially that it appealed to Mrs. Das. She stopped every three or four paces, staring silently at the carved lovers, and the processions of elephants, and the topless female musicians beating on two-sided drums.

Though Mr. Kapasi had been to the temple countless times, it occurred to him, as he, too, gazed at the topless women, that he had never seen his own wife fully naked. Even when they had made love she kept the panels of her blouse hooked together, the string of her petticoat knotted around her waist. He had never admired the backs of his wife's legs the way he now admired those of Mrs. Das, walking as if for his benefit alone. He had, of course, seen plenty of bare limbs before, belonging to the American and European ladies who took his tours. But Mrs. Das was different. Unlike the other women, who had an interest only in the temple, and kept their noses buried in a guidebook, or their eyes behind the lens of a camera, Mrs. Das had taken an interest in him.

Mr. Kapasi was anxious to be alone with her, to continue their private conversation, yet he felt nervous to walk at her side. She was lost behind her sunglasses, ignoring her husband's requests that she pose for another picture, walking past her children as if they were strangers. Worried that he might disturb her, Mr. Kapasi walked ahead, to admire, as he always did, the three life-sized bronze avatars of Surya, the sun god, each emerging from its own niche on the temple facade to greet the sun at dawn, noon, and evening. They wore elaborate headdresses, their languid, elongated eyes closed, their bare chests draped with carved chains and amulets. Hibiscus petals, offerings from previous visitors, were strewn at their gray-green feet. The last statue, on the northern wall of the temple, was Mr. Kapasi's favorite. This Surya had a tired expression, weary after a hard day of work, sitting astride a horse with folded legs. Even his horse's eyes were drowsy. Around his body were smaller sculptures of women in pairs, their hips thrust to one side.

"Who's that?" Mrs. Das asked. He was startled to see that she was standing beside him.

"He is the Astachala-Surya," Mr. Kapasi said. "The setting sun."

"So in a couple of hours the sun will set right here?" She slipped a foot out of one of her square-heeled shoes, rubbed her toes on the back of her other leg.

"That is correct."

She raised her sunglasses for a moment, then put them back on again. "Neat." 105

Mr. Kapasi was not certain exactly what the word suggested, but he had a feeling it was a favorable response. He hoped that Mrs. Das had understood Surya's beauty, his power. Perhaps they would discuss it further in their letters. He would explain things to her, things about India, and she would explain things to him about America. In its own way this correspondence would fulfill his dream, of serving as an interpreter between nations. He looked at her straw bag, delighted that his address lay nestled among its contents. When he pictured her so many thousands of miles away he plummeted, so much so that he had an overwhelming urge to wrap his arms around her, to freeze with her, even for an instant, in an embrace witnessed by his favorite Surya. But Mrs. Das had already started walking.

"When do you return to America?" he asked, trying to sound placid.

"In ten days."

He calculated: A week to settle in, a week to develop the pictures, a few days to compose her letter, two weeks to get to India by air. According to his schedule, allowing room for delays, he would hear from Mrs. Das in approximately six weeks' time.

110

The family was silent as Mr. Kapasi drove them back, a little past four-thirty, to Hotel Sandy Villa. The children had bought miniature granite versions of the chariot's wheels at a souvenir stand, and they turned them round in their hands. Mr. Das continued to read his book. Mrs. Das untangled Tina's hair with her brush and divided it into two little ponytails.

Mr. Kapasi was beginning to dread the thought of dropping them off. He was not prepared to begin his six-week wait to hear from Mrs. Das. As he stole glances at her in the rearview mirror, wrapping elastic bands around Tina's hair, he wondered how he might make the tour last a little longer. Ordinarily he sped back to Puri using a shortcut, eager to return home, scrub his feet and hands with sandalwood soap, and enjoy the evening newspaper and a cup of tea that his wife would serve him in silence. The thought of that silence, something to which he'd long been resigned, now oppressed him. It was then that he suggested visiting the hills at Udayagiri and Khandagiri, where a number of monastic dwellings were hewn out of the ground, facing one another across a defile. It was some miles away, but well worth seeing, Mr. Kapasi told them.

"Oh yeah, there's something mentioned about it in this book," Mr. Das said. "Built by a Jain° king or something."

Jain: an adherent of Jainism, a dualistic, ascetic religion founded in the sixth century B.C. in revolt against the Hindu caste system.

"Shall we go then?" Mr. Kapasi asked. He paused at a turn in the road. "It's to the left."

Mr. Das turned to look at Mrs. Das. Both of them shrugged.

"Left, left," the children chanted.

Mr. Kapasi turned the wheel, almost delirious with relief. He did not know what he would do or say to Mrs. Das once they arrived at the hills. Perhaps he would tell her what a pleasing smile she had. Perhaps he would compliment her strawberry shirt, which he found irresistibly becoming. Perhaps, when Mr. Das was busy taking a picture, he would take her hand.

He did not have to worry. When they got to the hills, divided by a steep path thick with trees, Mrs. Das refused to get out of the car. All along the path, dozens of monkeys were seated on stones, as well as on the branches of the trees. Their hind legs were stretched out in front and raised to shoulder level, their arms resting on their knees.

"My legs are tired," she said, sinking low in her seat. "I'll stay here."

"Why did you have to wear those stupid shoes?" Mr. Das said. "You won't be in the pictures."

"Pretend I'm there."

"But we could use one of these pictures for our Christmas card this year. We didn't get one of all five of us at the Sun Temple. Mr. Kapasi could take it."

"I'm not coming. Anyway, those monkeys give me the creeps."

"But they're harmless," Mr. Das said. He turned to Mr. Kapasi. "Aren't they?"

"They are more hungry than dangerous," Mr. Kapasi said. "Do not provoke them with food, and they will not bother you."

Mr. Das headed up the defile with the children, the boys at his side, the little girl on his shoulders. Mr. Kapasi watched as they crossed paths with a Japanese man and woman, the only other tourists there, who paused for a final photograph, then stepped into a nearby car and drove away. As the car disappeared out of view some of the monkeys called out, emitting soft whooping sounds, and then walked on their flat black hands and feet up the path. At one point a group of them formed a little ring around Mr. Das and the children. Tina screamed in delight. Ronny ran in circles around his father. Bobby bent down and picked up a fat stick on the ground. When he extended it, one of the monkeys approached him and snatched it, then briefly beat the ground.

"I'll join them," Mr. Kapasi said, unlocking the door on his side. "There is much to explain about the caves."

"No. Stay a minute," Mrs. Das said. She got out of the back seat and slipped in beside Mr. Kapasi. "Raj has his dumb book anyway." Together, through the windshield, Mrs. Das and Mr. Kapasi watched as Bobby and the monkey passed the stick back and forth between them.

"A brave little boy," Mr. Kapasi commented.

"It's not so surprising," Mrs. Das said.

"No?"

"He's not his."

"I beg your pardon?"

48   POINT OF VIEW

"Raj's. He's not Raj's son."

Mr. Kapasi felt a prickle on his skin. He reached into his shirt pocket for the small tin of lotus-oil balm he carried with him at all times, and applied it to three spots on his forehead. He knew that Mrs. Das was watching him, but he did not turn to face her. Instead he watched as the figures of Mr. Das and the children grew smaller, climbing up the steep path, pausing every now and then for a picture, surrounded by a growing number of monkeys.

"Are you surprised?" The way she put it made him choose his words with care. 135

"It's not the type of thing one assumes," Mr. Kapasi replied slowly. He put the tin of lotus-oil balm back in his pocket.

"No, of course not. And no one knows, of course. No one at all. I've kept it a secret for eight whole years." She looked at Mr. Kapasi, tilting her chin as if to gain a fresh perspective. "But now I've told you."

Mr. Kapasi nodded. He felt suddenly parched, and his forehead was warm and slightly numb from the balm. He considered asking Mrs. Das for a sip of water, then decided against it.

"We met when we were very young," she said. She reached into her straw bag in search of something, then pulled out a packet of puffed rice. "Want some?"

"No, thank you." 140

She put a fistful in her mouth, sank into the seat a little, and looked away from Mr. Kapasi, out the window on her side of the car. "We married when we were still in college. We were in high school when he proposed. We went to the same college, of course. Back then we couldn't stand the thought of being separated, not for a day, not for a minute. Our parents were best friends who lived in the same town. My entire life I saw him every weekend, either at our house or theirs. We were sent upstairs to play together while our parents joked about our marriage. Imagine! They never caught us at anything, though in a way I think it was all more or less a setup. The things we did those Friday and Saturday nights, while our parents sat downstairs drinking tea . . . I could tell you stories, Mr. Kapasi."

As a result of spending all her time in college with Raj, she continued, she did not make many close friends. There was no one to confide in about him at the end of a difficult day, or to share a passing thought or a worry. Her parents now lived on the other side of the world, but she had never been very close to them, anyway. After marrying so young she was overwhelmed by it all, having a child so quickly, and nursing, and warming up bottles of milk and testing their temperature against her wrist while Raj was at work, dressed in sweaters and corduroy pants, teaching his students about rocks and dinosaurs. Raj never looked cross or harried, or plump as she had become after the first baby.

Always tired, she declined invitations from her one or two college girlfriends, to have lunch or shop in Manhattan. Eventually the friends stopped calling her, so that she was left at home all day with the baby, surrounded by toys that made her trip when she walked or wince when she sat, always cross and tired. Only occasionally did they go out after Ronny was born, and even more rarely did they entertain. Raj didn't mind; he looked forward to coming home from teaching and watching television and bouncing Ronny on his knee. She had been outraged when Raj told her that a Punjabi° friend, someone whom she had once met but did not remember, would be staying with them for a week for some job interviews in the New Brunswick area.

Bobby was conceived in the afternoon, on a sofa littered with rubber teething toys, after the friend learned that a London pharmaceutical company had hired him, while Ronny cried to be freed from his playpen. She made no protest when the friend touched the small of her back as she was about to make a pot of coffee, then pulled her against his crisp navy suit. He made love to her swiftly, in silence, with an expertise she had never known, without the meaningful expressions and smiles Raj always insisted on afterward. The next day Raj drove the friend to JFK. He was married now, to a Punjabi girl, and they lived in London still, and every year they exchanged Christmas cards with Raj and Mina, each couple tucking photos of their families into the envelopes. He did not know that he was Bobby's father. He never would.

"I beg your pardon, Mrs. Das, but why have you told me this information?" 145
Mr. Kapasi asked when she had finally finished speaking, and had turned to face him once again.

"For God's sake, stop calling me Mrs. Das. I'm twenty-eight. You probably have children my age."

"Not quite." It disturbed Mr. Kapasi to learn that she thought of him as a parent. The feeling he had had toward her, that had made him check his reflection in the rearview mirror as they drove, evaporated a little.

"I told you because of your talents." She put the packet of puffed rice back into her bag without folding over the top.

"I don't understand," Mr. Kapasi said.

"Don't you see? For eight years I haven't been able to express this to any- 150
body, not to friends, certainly not to Raj. He doesn't even suspect it. He thinks I'm still in love with him. Well, don't you have anything to say?"

"About what?"

"About what I've just told you. About my secret, and about how terrible it makes me feel. I feel terrible looking at my children, and at Raj, always terrible. I have terrible urges, Mr. Kapasi, to throw things away. One day I had the urge to throw everything I own out the window, the television, the children, everything. Don't you think it's unhealthy?"

He was silent.

"Mr. Kapasi, don't you have anything to say? I thought that was your job."

"My job is to give tours, Mrs. Das." 155

"Not that. Your other job. As an interpreter."

"But we do not face a language barrier. What need is there for an interpreter?"

"That's not what I mean. I would never have told you otherwise. Don't you realize what it means for me to tell you?"

"What does it mean?"

Punjabi: a native of Punjab, a state in northwest India.

"It means that I'm tired of feeling so terrible all the time. Eight years, Mr. 160
Kapasi, I've been in pain eight years. I was hoping you could help me feel better,
say the right thing. Suggest some kind of remedy."

He looked at her, in her red plaid skirt and strawberry T-shirt, a woman not
yet thirty, who loved neither her husband nor her children, who had already
fallen out of love with life. Her confession depressed him, depressed him all the
more when he thought of Mr. Das at the top of the path, Tina clinging to his
shoulders, taking pictures of ancient monastic cells cut into the hills to show his
students in America, unsuspecting and unaware that one of his sons was not his
own. Mr. Kapasi felt insulted that Mrs. Das should ask him to interpret her
common, trivial little secret. She did not resemble the patients in the doctor's
office, those who came glassy-eyed and desperate, unable to sleep or breathe or
urinate with ease, unable, above all, to give words to their pains. Still, Mr. Kapasi believed it was his duty to assist Mrs. Das. Perhaps he ought to tell her to
confess the truth to Mr. Das. He would explain that honesty was the best policy.
Honesty, surely, would help her feel better, as she'd put it. Perhaps he would
offer to preside over the discussion, as a mediator. He decided to begin with the
most obvious question, to get to the heart of the matter, and so he asked, "Is it
really pain you feel, Mrs. Das, or is it guilt?"

She turned to him and glared, mustard oil thick on her frosty pink lips. She
opened her mouth to say something, but as she glared at Mr. Kapasi some certain
knowledge seemed to pass before her eyes, and she stopped. It crushed him; he
knew at that moment that he was not even important enough to be properly insulted. She opened the car door and began walking up the path, wobbling a little
on her square wooden heels, reaching into her straw bag to eat handfuls of puffed
rice. It fell through her fingers, leaving a zigzagging trail, causing a monkey to
leap down from a tree and devour the little white grains. In search of more, the
monkey began to follow Mrs. Das. Others joined him, so that she was soon being
followed by about half a dozen of them, their velvety tails dragging behind.

Mr. Kapasi stepped out of the car. He wanted to holler, to alert her in some
way, but he worried that if she knew they were behind her, she would grow nervous. Perhaps she would lose her balance. Perhaps they would pull at her bag or
her hair. He began to jog up the path, taking a fallen branch in his hand to scare
away the monkeys. Mrs. Das continued walking, oblivious, trailing grains of puffed
rice. Near the top of the incline, before a group of cells fronted by a row of squat
stone pillars, Mr. Das was kneeling on the ground focusing the lens of his camera.
The children stood under the arcade, now hiding, now emerging from view.

"Wait for me," Mrs. Das called out. "I'm coming."

Tina jumped up and down. "Here comes Mommy!" 165

"Great," Mr. Das said without looking up. "Just in time. We'll get Mr. Kapasi to take a picture of the five of us."

Mr. Kapasi quickened his pace, waving his branch so that the monkeys
scampered away, distracted, in another direction.

"Where's Bobby?" Mrs. Das asked when she stopped.

Mr. Das looked up from the camera. "I don't know. Ronny, where's Bobby?" Ronny shrugged, "I thought he was right here."

"Where is he?" Mrs. Das repeated sharply. "What's wrong with all of you?"

They began calling his name, wandering up and down the path a bit. Because they were calling, they did not initially hear the boy's screams. When they found him, a little farther down the path under a tree, he was surrounded by a group of monkeys, over a dozen of them, pulling at his T-shirt with their long black fingers. The puffed rice Mrs. Das had spilled was scattered at his feet, raked over by the monkeys' hands. The boy was silent, his body frozen, swift tears running down his startled face. His bare legs were dusty and red with welts from where one of the monkeys struck him repeatedly with the stick he had given to it earlier.

"Daddy, the monkey's hurting Bobby," Tina said.

Mr. Das wiped his palms on the front of his shorts. In his nervousness he accidentally pressed the shutter on his camera; the whirring noise of the advancing film excited the monkeys, and the one with the stick began to beat Bobby more intently. "What are we supposed to do? What if they start attacking?"

"Mr. Kapasi," Mrs. Das shrieked, noticing him standing to one side. "Do something, for God's sake, do something!"

Mr. Kapasi took his branch and shooed them away, hissing at the ones that remained, stomping his feet to scare them. The animals retreated slowly, with a measured gait, obedient but unintimidated. Mr. Kapasi gathered Bobby in his arms and brought him back to where his parents and siblings were standing. As he carried him he was tempted to whisper a secret into the boy's ear. But Bobby was stunned, and shivering with fright, his legs bleeding slightly where the stick had broken the skin. When Mr. Kapasi delivered him to his parents, Mr. Das brushed some dirt off the boy's T-shirt and put the visor on him the right way. Mrs. Das reached into her straw bag to find a bandage which she taped over the cut on his knee. Ronny offered his brother a fresh piece of gum. "He's fine. Just a little scared, right, Bobby?" Mr. Das said, patting the top of his head.

"God, let's get out of here," Mrs. Das said. She folded her arms across the strawberry on her chest. "This place gives me the creeps."

"Yeah. Back to the hotel, definitely," Mr. Das agreed.

"Poor Bobby," Mrs. Das said. "Come here a second. Let Mommy fix your hair." Again she reached into her straw bag, this time for her hairbrush, and began to run it around the edges of the translucent visor. When she whipped out the hairbrush, the slip of paper with Mr. Kapasi's address on it fluttered away in the wind. No one but Mr. Kapasi noticed. He watched as it rose, carried higher and higher by the breeze, into the trees where the monkeys now sat, solemnly observing the scene below. Mr. Kapasi observed it too, knowing that this was the picture of the Das family he would preserve forever in his mind.

QUESTIONS

1. From whose point of view is the story told? How would you characterize the method employed—omniscient, limited omniscient, or objective?

2. Mr. Das tells Mr. Kapasi (paragraph 20), " In a way we have a lot in common . . ." What does he mean by this? Do they in fact have much in common? Explain.
3. What can we determine about the relationship of Mr. and Mrs. Das from the details given in the first few pages of the story?
4. On one level, "Interpreter of Maladies" is about a clash of cultures. In what ways do the members of the Das family seem particularly American to Mr. Kapasi? How are these characteristics contrasted with Indian life and behavior?
5. When Mrs. Das comments on Mr. Kapasi's responsibilities as an interpreter of maladies (paragraph 74), her remarks underline the importance of subjective perceptions. People don't usually change in the space of an afternoon, but our perceptions of them can shift profoundly, especially if we don't know them very well. How would you characterize and describe the separate stages of Mr. Kapasi's evolving feelings about Mrs. Das?
6. Why does Mrs. Das tell Mr. Kapasi such intimate details about her life? How does she respond to his interpretation of her malady? How accurate, in your view, is his interpretation? Explain.

James Baldwin
SONNY'S BLUES   1957

James Baldwin (1924–1987) was born in Harlem, in New York City. His father was a Pentecostal minister, and the young Baldwin initially planned to become a clergyman. While still in high school, he preached sermons in a storefront church. At seventeen, however, Baldwin left home to live in Greenwich Village, where he worked at menial jobs and began publishing articles in Commentary *and the* Nation. *Later he embarked on a series of travels that eventually brought him to France. Baldwin soon regarded France as a second home, a country in which he could avoid the racial discrimination he felt in America. Baldwin's first novel,* Go Tell It on the Mountain *(1953), which described a single day in the lives of the members of a Harlem church, immediately earned him a position as a leading African American writer. His next two novels,* Giovanni's Room *(1956) and* Another Country *(1962), dealt with homosexual themes and drew criticism from some of his early champions. His collection of essays* Notes of a Native Son *(1955) remains one of the key books of the civil rights movement. His short stories were not collected until* Going to Meet the Man *was published in 1965. Although he spent nearly forty years in France, Baldwin still considered himself an American. He was not an expatriate, he claimed, but a "commuter." He died in St. Paul de Vence, France, but was buried in Ardsley, New York.*

I read about it in the paper, in the subway, on my way to work. I read it, and I couldn't believe it, and I read it again. Then perhaps I just stared at it, at the newsprint spelling out his name, spelling out the story. I stared at it in the swinging lights of the subway car, and in the faces and bodies of the people, and in my own face, trapped in the darkness which roared outside.

It was not to be believed and I kept telling myself that, as I walked from the subway station to the high school. And at the same time I couldn't doubt it. I was scared, scared for Sonny. He became real to me again. A great block of ice got settled in my belly and kept melting there slowly all day long, while I taught my classes algebra. It was a special kind of ice. It kept melting, sending trickles of ice water all up and down my veins, but it never got less. Sometimes it hardened and seemed to expand until I felt my guts were going to come spilling out or that I was going to choke or scream. This would always be at a moment when I was remembering some specific thing Sonny had once said or done.

When he was about as old as the boys in my classes his face had been bright and open, there was a lot of copper in it; and he'd had wonderfully direct brown eyes, and great gentleness and privacy. I wondered what he looked like now. He had been picked up, the evening before, in a raid on an apartment downtown, for peddling and using heroin.

I couldn't believe it: but what I mean by that is that I couldn't find any room for it anywhere inside me. I had kept it outside me for a long time. I hadn't wanted to know. I had had suspicions, but I didn't name them, I kept putting them away. I told myself that Sonny was wild, but he wasn't crazy. And he'd always been a good boy, he hadn't ever turned hard or evil or disrespectful, the way kids can, so quick, so quick, especially in Harlem. I didn't want to believe that I'd ever see my brother going down, coming to nothing, all that light in his face gone out, in the condition I'd already seen so many others. Yet it had happened and here I was, talking about algebra to a lot of boys who might, every one of them for all I knew, be popping off needles every time they went to the head. Maybe it did more for them than algebra could.

I was sure that the first time Sonny had ever had horse,° he couldn't have been much older than these boys were now. These boys, now, were living as we'd been living then, they were growing up with a rush and their heads bumped abruptly against the low ceiling of their actual possibilities. They were filled with rage. All they really knew were two darknesses, the darkness of their lives, which was now closing in on them, and the darkness of the movies, which had blinded them to that other darkness, and in which they now, vindictively, dreamed, at once more together than they were at any other time, and more alone. 5

When the last bell rang, the last class ended, I let out my breath. It seemed I'd been holding it for all that time. My clothes were wet—I may have looked as though I'd been sitting in a steam bath, all dressed up, all afternoon. I sat alone in the classroom a long time. I listened to the boys outside, downstairs, shouting and cursing and laughing. Their laughter struck me for perhaps the first time. It was not the joyous laughter which—God knows why—one associates with children. It was mocking and insular, its intent to denigrate. It was disenchanted, and in this, also, lay the authority of their curses. Perhaps I was listening to them because I was thinking about my brother and in them I heard my brother. And myself.

One boy was whistling a tune, at once very complicated and very simple, it seemed to be pouring out of him as though he were a bird, and it sounded very cool and moving through all that harsh, bright air, only just holding its own through all those other sounds.

horse: heroin.

I stood up and walked over to the window and looked down into the court-yard. It was the beginning of the spring and the sap was rising in the boys. A teacher passed through them every now and again, quickly, as though he or she couldn't wait to get out of that courtyard, to get those boys out of their sight and off their minds. I started collecting my stuff. I thought I'd better get home and talk to Isabel.

The courtyard was almost deserted by the time I got downstairs. I saw this boy standing in the shadow of a doorway, looking just like Sonny. I almost called his name. Then I saw that it wasn't Sonny, but somebody we used to know, a boy from around our block. He'd been Sonny's friend. He'd never been mine, having been too young for me, and, anyway, I'd never liked him. And now, even though he was a grown-up man, he still hung around that block, still spent hours on the street corners, was always high and raggy. I used to run into him from time to time and he'd often work around to asking me for a quarter or fifty cents. He always had some real good excuse, too, and I always gave it to him, I don't know why.

But now, abruptly, I hated him. I couldn't stand the way he looked at me,   10 partly like a dog, partly like a cunning child. I wanted to ask him what the hell he was doing in the school courtyard.

He sort of shuffled over to me, and he said, "I see you got the papers. So you already know about it."

"You mean about Sonny? Yes, I already know about it. How come they didn't get you?"

He grinned. It made him repulsive and it also brought to mind what he'd looked like as a kid. "I wasn't there. I stay away from them people."

"Good for you." I offered him a cigarette and I watched him through the smoke. "You come all the way down here just to tell me about Sonny?"

"That's right." He was sort of shaking his head and his eyes looked strange,   15 as though they were about to cross. The bright sun deadened his damp dark brown skin and it made his eyes look yellow and showed up the dirt in his kinked hair. He smelled funky. I moved a little away from him and I said, "Well, thanks. But I already know about it and I got to get home."

"I'll walk you a little ways," he said. We started walking. There were a couple of kids still loitering in the courtyard and one of them said goodnight to me and looked strangely at the boy beside me.

"What're you going to do?" he asked me. "I mean, about Sonny?"

"Look. I haven't seen Sonny for over a year. I'm not sure I'm going to do anything. Anyway, what the hell *can* I do?"

"That's right," he said quickly, "ain't nothing you can do. Can't much help old Sonny no more, I guess."

It was what I was thinking and so it seemed to me he had no right to say it.   20

"I'm surprised at Sonny, though," he went on—he had a funny way of talking, he looked straight ahead as though he were talking to himself—"I thought Sonny was a smart boy, I thought he was too smart to get hung."

"I guess he thought so too," I said sharply, "and that's how he got hung. And how about you? You're pretty goddamn smart, I bet."

Then he looked directly at me, just for a minute. "I ain't smart," he said. "If I was smart, I'd have reached for a pistol a long time ago."

"Look. Don't tell *me* your sad story, if it was up to me, I'd give you one." Then I felt guilty—guilty, probably, for never having supposed that the poor bastard *had* a story of his own, much less a sad one, and I asked, quickly, "What's going to happen to him now?"

He didn't answer this. He was off by himself some place. "Funny thing," he said, and from his tone we might have been discussing the quickest way to get to Brooklyn, "when I saw the papers this morning, the first thing I asked myself was if I had anything to do with it. I felt sort of responsible." 25

I began to listen more carefully. The subway station was on the corner, just before us, and I stopped. He stopped, too. We were in front of a bar and he ducked slightly, peering in, but whoever he was looking for didn't seem to be there. The juke box was blasting away with something black and bouncy and I half watched the barmaid as she danced her way from the juke box to her place behind the bar. And I watched her face as she laughingly responded to something someone said to her, still keeping time to the music. When she smiled one saw the little girl, one sensed the doomed, still-struggling woman beneath the battered face of the semiwhore.

"I never *give* Sonny nothing," the boy said finally, "but a long time ago I come to school high and Sonny asked me how it felt." He paused, I couldn't bear to watch him, I watched the barmaid, and I listened to the music which seemed to be causing the pavement to shake. "I told him it felt great." The music stopped, the barmaid paused and watched the juke box until the music began again. "It did."

All this was carrying me some place I didn't want to go. I certainly didn't want to know how it felt. It filled everything, the people, the houses, the music, the dark, quicksilver barmaid, with menace; and this menace was their reality.

"What's going to happen to him now?" I asked again.

"They'll send him away some place and they'll try to cure him." He shook his head. "Maybe he'll even think he's kicked the habit. Then they'll let him loose"—he gestured, throwing his cigarette into the gutter. "That's all." 30

"What do you mean, that's *all?*"

But I knew what he meant.

"I *mean*, that's *all*." He turned his head and looked at me, pulling down the corners of his mouth. "Don't you know what I mean?" he asked, softly.

"How the hell *would* I know what you mean?" I almost whispered it, I don't know why.

"That's right," he said to the air, "how would *he* know what I mean?" He turned toward me again, patient and calm, and yet I somehow felt him shaking, shaking as though he were going to fall apart. I felt that ice in my guts again, the dread I'd felt all afternoon; and again I watched the barmaid, moving about the bar, washing glasses, and singing. "Listen. They'll let him out and then it'll just start all over again. That's what I mean." 35

"You mean—they'll let him out. And then he'll just start working his way back in again. You mean he'll never kick the habit. Is that what you mean?"

"That's right," he said, cheerfully. "*You* see what I mean."

"Tell me," I said at last, "why does he want to die? He must want to die, he's killing himself, why does he want to die?"

He looked at me in surprise. He licked his lips. "He don't want to die. He wants to live. Don't nobody want to die, ever."

Then I wanted to ask him—too many things. He could not have answered, or if he had, I could not have borne the answers. I started walking. "Well, I guess it's none of my business." 40

"It's going to be rough on old Sonny," he said. We reached the subway station. "This is your station?" he asked. I nodded. I took one step down. "Damn!" he said, suddenly. I looked up at him. He grinned again. "Damn it if I didn't leave all my money home. You ain't got a dollar on you, have you? Just for a couple of days, is all."

All at once something inside gave and threatened to come pouring out of me. I didn't hate him any more. I felt that in another moment I'd start crying like a child.

"Sure," I said. "Don't sweat." I looked in my wallet and didn't have a dollar, I only had a five. "Here," I said. "That hold you?"

He didn't look at it—he didn't want to look at it. A terrible closed look came over his face, as though he were keeping the number on the bill a secret from him and me. "Thanks," he said, and now he was dying to see me go. "Don't worry about Sonny. Maybe I'll write him or something."

"Sure," I said. "You do that. So long." 45

"Be seeing you," he said. I went on down the steps.

And I didn't write Sonny or send him anything for a long time. When I finally did, it was just after my little girl died, he wrote me back a letter which made me feel like a bastard.

Here's what he said:

Dear brother,

You don't know how much I needed to hear from you. I wanted to write you many a time but I dug how much I must have hurt you and so I didn't write. But now I feel like a man who's been trying to climb up out of some deep, real deep and funky hole and just saw the sun up there, outside. I got to get outside.

I can't tell you much about how I got here. I mean I don't know how to tell you. I guess I was afraid of something or I was trying to escape from something and you know I have never been very strong in the head (smile). I'm glad Mama and Daddy are dead and can't see what's happened to their son and I swear if I'd known what I was doing I would never have hurt you so, you and a lot of other fine people who were nice to me and who believed in me.

I don't want you to think it had anything to do with me being a musician. It's more than that. Or maybe less than that. I can't get anything straight in my head down here and I try not to think about what's going to happen to me when I get outside again. Sometime I think I'm going to flip and *never* get outside and sometime I think I'll come straight back. I tell you one thing, though, I'd rather blow my brains out than go through this again. But that's what they all say, so they tell me. If I tell you when I'm coming to New York and if you could meet me, I sure would appreciate it. Give my love to Isabel and the kids and I was sure sorry to hear about little Gracie. I wish I could be like Mama and say the Lord's will be done, but I don't know it seems to me that trouble is the one thing that never does get stopped and I don't know what good it does to blame it on the Lord. But maybe it does some good if you believe it.

Your brother,
Sonny

Then I kept in constant touch with him and I sent him whatever I could and I went to meet him when he came back to New York. When I saw him many things I thought I had forgotten came flooding back to me. This was because I had begun, finally, to wonder about Sonny, about the life that Sonny lived inside. This life, whatever it was, had made him older and thinner and it had deepened the distant stillness in which he had always moved. He looked very unlike my baby brother. Yet, when he smiled, when we shook hands, the baby brother I'd never known looked out from the depths of his private life, like an animal waiting to be coaxed into the light.

"How you been keeping?" he asked me.   50

"All right. And you?"

"Just fine." He was smiling all over his face. "It's good to see you again."

"It's good to see you."

The seven years' difference in our ages lay between us like a chasm: I wondered if these years would ever operate between us as a bridge. I was remembering, and it made it hard to catch my breath, that I had been there when he was born; and I had heard the first words he had ever spoken. When he started to walk, he walked from our mother straight to me. I caught him just before he fell when he took the first steps he ever took in this world.

"How's Isabel?"   55

"Just fine. She's dying to see you."

"And the boys?"

"They're fine, too. They're anxious to see their uncle."

"Oh, come on. You know they don't remember me."

"Are you kidding? Of course they remember you."   60

He grinned again. We got into a taxi. We had a lot to say to each other, far too much to know how to begin.

As the taxi began to move, I asked, "You still want to go to India?"

He laughed. "You still remember that. Hell, no. This place is Indian enough for me."

"It used to belong to them," I said.

And he laughed again. "They damn sure knew what they were doing when 65
they got rid of it."

Years ago, when he was around fourteen, he'd been all hipped on the idea of
going to India. He read books about people sitting on rocks, naked, in all kinds
of weather, but mostly bad, naturally, and walking barefoot through hot coals
and arriving at wisdom. I used to say that it sounded to me as though they were
getting away from wisdom as fast as they could. I think he sort of looked down on
me for that.

"Do you mind," he asked, "if we have the driver drive alongside the park?
On the west side—I haven't seen the city in so long."

"Of course not," I said. I was afraid that I might sound as though I were hu-
moring him, but I hoped he wouldn't take it that way.

So we drove along, between the green of the park and the stony, lifeless elegance of hotels and apartment buildings, toward the vivid, killing streets of
our childhood. These streets hadn't changed, though housing projects jutted up
out of them now like rocks in the middle of a boiling sea. Most of the houses in
which we had grown up had vanished, as had the stores from which we had
stolen, the basements in which we had first tried sex, the rooftops from which
we had hurled tin cans and bricks. But houses exactly like the houses of our past
yet dominated the landscape, boys exactly like the boys we once had been
found themselves smothering in these houses, came down into the streets for
light and air and found themselves encircled by disaster. Some escaped the trap,
most didn't. Those who got out always left something of themselves behind, as
some animals amputate a leg and leave it in the trap. It might be said, perhaps,
that I had escaped, after all, I was a school teacher; or that Sonny had, he
hadn't lived in Harlem for years. Yet, as the cab moved uptown through streets
which seemed, with a rush, to darken with dark people, and as I covertly
studied Sonny's face, it came to me that what we both were seeking through
our separate cab windows was that part of ourselves which had been left behind.
It's always at the hour of trouble and confrontation that the missing member
aches.

We hit 110th Street and started rolling up Lenox Avenue. And I'd known 70
this avenue all my life, but it seemed to me again, as it had seemed on the day I'd
first heard about Sonny's trouble, filled with a hidden menace which was its very
breath of life.

"We almost there," said Sonny.

"Almost." We were both too nervous to say anything more.

We live in a housing project. It hasn't been up long. A few days after it was
up it seemed uninhabitably new, now, of course, it's already rundown. It looks
like a parody of the good, clean, faceless life—God knows the people who live in
it do their best to make it a parody. The beat-looking grass lying around isn't
enough to make their lives green, the hedges will never hold out the streets, and
they know it. The big windows fool no one, they aren't big enough to make
space out of no space. They don't bother with the windows, they watch the TV
screen instead. The playground is most popular with the children who don't play

at jacks, or skip rope, or roller skate, or swing, and they can be found in it after dark. We moved in partly because it's not too far from where I teach, and partly for the kids; but it's really just like the houses in which Sonny and I grew up. The same things happen, they'll have the same things to remember. The moment Sonny and I started into the house I had the feeling that I was simply bringing him back into the danger he had almost died trying to escape.

Sonny has never been talkative. So I don't know why I was sure he'd be dying to talk to me when supper was over the first night. Everything went fine, the oldest boy remembered him, and the youngest boy liked him, and Sonny had remembered to bring something for each of them; and Isabel, who is really much nicer than I am, more open and giving, had gone to a lot of trouble about dinner and was genuinely glad to see him. And she's always been able to tease Sonny in a way that I haven't. It was nice to see her face so vivid again and to hear her laugh and watch her make Sonny laugh. She wasn't, or, anyway, she didn't seem to be, at all uneasy or embarrassed. She chatted as though there were no subject which had to be avoided and she got Sonny past his first, faint stiffness. And thank God she was there, for I was filled with that icy dread again. Everything I did seemed awkward to me, and everything I said sounded freighted with hidden meaning. I was trying to remember everything I'd heard about dope addiction and I couldn't help watching Sonny for signs. I wasn't doing it out of malice. I was trying to find out something about my brother. I was dying to hear him tell me he was safe.

"Safe!" my father grunted, whenever Mama suggested trying to move to a neighborhood which might be safer for children. "Safe, hell! Ain't no place safe for kids, nor nobody." 75

He always went on like this, but he wasn't, ever, really as bad as he sounded, not even on weekends, when he got drunk. As a matter of fact, he was always on the lookout for "something a little better," but he died before he found it. He died suddenly, during a drunken weekend in the middle of the war, when Sonny was fifteen. He and Sonny hadn't ever got on too well. And this was partly because Sonny was the apple of his father's eye. It was because he loved Sonny so much and was frightened for him, that he was always fighting with him. It doesn't do any good to fight with Sonny. Sonny just moves back, inside himself, where he can't be reached. But the principal reason that they never hit it off is that they were so much alike. Daddy was big and rough and loud-talking, just the opposite of Sonny, but they both had—that same privacy.

Mama tried to tell me something about this, just after Daddy died. I was home on leave from the army.

This was the last time I ever saw my mother alive. Just the same, this picture gets all mixed up in my mind with pictures I had of her when she was younger. The way I always see her is the way she used to be on a Sunday afternoon, say, when the old folks were talking after the big Sunday dinner. I always see her wearing pale blue. She'd be sitting on the sofa. And my father would be sitting in the easy chair, not far from her. And the living room would be full of church folks and relatives. There they sit, in chairs all around the living room, and the night is creeping up outside, but nobody knows it yet. You can see the darkness growing against the windowpanes and you hear the street noises every now and again, or maybe the jangling beat of a tambourine from one of the churches close by, but it's real quiet in the room. For a moment nobody's talking, but every face looks darkening, like the sky outside. And my mother rocks a little from the waist, and my father's eyes are closed. Everyone is looking at something a child can't see. For a minute they've forgotten the children. Maybe a kid is lying on the rug, half asleep. Maybe somebody's got a kid in his lap and is absent-mindedly stroking the kid's head. Maybe there's a kid, quiet and big-eyed, curled up in a big chair in the corner. The silence, the darkness coming, and the darkness in the faces frightens the child obscurely. He hopes that the hand which strokes his forehead will never stop—will never die. He hopes that there will never come a time when the old folks won't be sitting around the living room, talking about where they've come from, and what they've seen, and what's happened to them and their kinfolk.

But something deep and watchful in the child knows that this is bound to end, is already ending. In a moment someone will get up and turn on the light. Then the old folks will remember the children and they won't talk any more that day. And when light fills the room, the child is filled with darkness. He knows that everytime this happens he's moved just a little closer to that darkness outside. The darkness outside is what the old folks have been talking about. It's what they've come from. It's what they endure. The child knows that they won't talk any more because if he knows too much about what's happened to *them*, he'll know too much too soon, about what's going to happen to *him*.

The last time I talked to my mother, I remember I was restless. I wanted to get out and see Isabel. We weren't married then and we had a lot to straighten out between us.

There Mama sat, in black, by the window. She was humming an old church song, *Lord, you brought me from a long ways off*. Sonny was out somewhere. Mama kept watching the streets.

"I don't know," she said, "if I'll ever see you again, after you go off from here. But I hope you'll remember the things I tried to teach you."

"Don't talk like that," I said, and smiled. "You'll be here a long time yet."

She smiled, too, but she said nothing. She was quiet for a long time. And I said, "Mama, don't you worry about nothing. I'll be writing all the time, and you be getting the checks . . ."

"I want to talk to you about your brother," she said, suddenly. "If anything happens to me he ain't going to have nobody to look out for him."

"Mama," I said, "ain't nothing going to happen to you *or* Sonny. Sonny's all right. He's a good boy and he's got good sense."

"It ain't a question of his being a good boy," Mama said, "nor of his having good sense. It ain't only the bad ones, nor yet the dumb ones that gets sucked under." She stopped, looking at me. "Your Daddy once had a brother," she said, and she smiled in a way that made me feel she was in pain. "You didn't never know that, did you?"

"No," I said, "I never knew that," and I watched her face.

"Oh, yes," she said, "your Daddy had a brother." She looked out of the window again. "I know you never saw your Daddy cry. But I did—many a time, through all these years."

I asked her, "What happened to his brother? How come nobody's ever talked about him?" 90

This was the first time I ever saw my mother look old.

"His brother got killed," she said, "when he was just a little younger than you are now. I knew him. He was a fine boy. He was maybe a little full of the devil, but he didn't mean nobody no harm."

Then she stopped and the room was silent, exactly as it had sometimes been on those Sunday afternoons. Mama kept looking out into the streets.

"He used to have a job in the mill," she said, "and, like all young folks, he just liked to perform on Saturday nights. Saturday nights, him and your father would drift around to different places, go to dances and things like that, or just sit around with people they knew, and your father's brother would sing, he had a fine voice, and play along with himself on his guitar. Well, this particular Saturday night, him and your father was coming home from some place, and they were both a little drunk and there was a moon that night, it was bright like day. Your father's brother was feeling kind of good, and he was whistling to himself, and he had his guitar slung over his shoulder. They was coming down a hill and beneath them was a road that turned off from the highway. Well, your father's brother, being always kind of frisky, decided to run down this hill, and he did, with that guitar banging and clanging behind him, and he ran across the road, and he was making water behind a tree. And your father was sort of amused at him and he was still coming down the hill, kind of slow. Then he heard a car motor and that same minute his brother stepped from behind the tree, into the road, in the moonlight. And he started to cross the road. And your father started to run down the hill, he says he don't know why. This car was full of white men. They was all drunk, and when they seen your father's brother they let out a great whoop and holler and they aimed the car straight at him. They was having fun, they just wanted to scare him, the way they do sometimes, you know. But they was drunk. And I guess the boy, being drunk, too, and scared, kind of lost his head. By the time he jumped it was too late. Your father says he heard his brother scream when the car rolled over him, and he heard the wood of that guitar when it give, and he heard them strings go flying, and he heard them white men shouting, and the car kept on a-going and it ain't stopped till this day. And, time your father got down the hill, his brother weren't nothing but blood and pulp."

Tears were gleaming on my mother's face. There wasn't anything I could say. 95

"He never mentioned it," she said, "because I never let him mention it before you children. Your Daddy was like a crazy man that night and for many a night thereafter. He says he never in his life seen anything as dark as that road after the lights of that car had gone away. Weren't nothing, weren't nobody on that road, just your Daddy and his brother and that busted guitar. Oh, yes. Your Daddy never did really get right again. Till the day he died he weren't sure but that every white man he saw was the man that killed his brother."

She stopped and took out her handkerchief and dried her eyes and looked at me.

"I ain't telling you all this," she said, "to make you scared or bitter or to make you hate nobody. I'm telling you this because you got a brother. And the world ain't changed."

I guess I didn't want to believe this. I guess she saw this in my face. She turned away from me, toward the window again, searching those streets.

"But I praise my Redeemer," she said at last, "that He called your Daddy home before me. I ain't saying it to throw no flowers at myself, but, I declare, it keeps me from feeling too cast down to know I helped your father get safely through this world. Your father always acted like he was the roughest, strongest man on earth. And everybody took him to be like that. But if he hadn't had *me* there—to see his tears!"

She was crying again. Still, I couldn't move. I said, "Lord, Lord, Mama, I didn't know it was like that."

"Oh, honey," she said, "there's a lot that you don't know. But you are going to find it out." She stood up from the window and came over to me. "You got to hold on to your brother," she said, "and don't let him fall, no matter what it looks like is happening to him and no matter how evil you gets with him. You going to be evil with him many a time. But don't you forget what I told you, you hear?"

"I won't forget," I said. "Don't you worry, I won't forget. I won't let nothing happen to Sonny."

My mother smiled as though she were amused at something she saw in my face. Then, "You may not be able to stop nothing from happening. But you got to let him know you's *there*."

Two days later I was married, and then I was gone. And I had a lot of things on my mind and I pretty well forgot my promise to Mama until I got shipped home on a special furlough for her funeral.

And, after the funeral, with just Sonny and me alone in the empty kitchen, I tried to find out something about him.

"What do you want to do?" I asked him.

"I'm going to be a musician," he said.

For he had graduated, in the time I had been away, from dancing to the juke box to finding out who was playing what, and what they were doing with it, and he had bought himself a set of drums.

"You mean, you want to be a drummer?" I somehow had the feeling that being a drummer might be all right for other people but not for my brother Sonny.

"I don't think," he said, looking at me very gravely, "that I'll ever be a good drummer. But I think I can play a piano."

I frowned. I'd never played the role of the older brother quite so seriously before, had scarcely ever, in fact, *asked* Sonny a damn thing. I sensed myself in the presence of something I didn't really know how to handle, didn't understand. So I made my frown a little deeper as I asked: "What kind of musician do you want to be?"

He grinned. "How many kinds do you think there are?"

"Be *serious*," I said.

He laughed, throwing his head back, and then looked at me. "I *am* serious." 115

"Well, then, for Christ's sake, stop kidding around and answer a serious question. I mean, do you want to be a concert pianist, you want to play classical music and all that, or—or what?" Long before I finished he was laughing again. "For Christ's *sake*, Sonny!"

He sobered, but with difficulty. "I'm sorry. But you sound so—*scared!*" and he was off again.

"Well, you may think it's funny now, baby, but it's not going to be so funny when you have to make your living at it, let me tell you *that.*" I was furious because I knew he was laughing at me and I didn't know why.

"No," he said, very sober now, and afraid, perhaps, that he'd hurt me, "I don't want to be a classical pianist. That isn't what interests me. I mean"—he paused, looking hard at me, as though his eyes would help me to understand, and then gestured helplessly, as though perhaps his hand would help—"I mean, I'll have a lot of studying to do, and I'll have to study *everything*, but, I mean, I want to play *with*—jazz musicians." He stopped. "I want to play jazz," he said.

Well, the word had never before sounded as heavy, as real, as it sounded 120 that afternoon in Sonny's mouth. I just looked at him and I was probably frowning a real frown by this time. I simply couldn't see why on earth he'd want to spend his time hanging around nightclubs, clowning around on bandstands, while people pushed each other around a dance floor. It seemed—beneath him, somehow. I had never thought about it before, had never been forced to, but I suppose I had always put jazz musicians in a class with what Daddy called "good-time people."

"Are you *serious?*"

"Hell, *yes*, I'm serious."

He looked more helpless than ever, and annoyed, and deeply hurt.

I suggested, helpfully: "You mean—like Louis Armstrong?"°

His face closed as though I'd struck him. "No. I'm not talking about none of 125 that old-time, down home crap."

"Well, look, Sonny, I'm sorry, don't get mad. I just don't altogether get it, that's all. Name somebody—you know, a jazz musician you admire."

"Bird."

"Who?"

"Bird! Charlie Parker!° Don't they teach you nothing in the goddamn army?"

I lit a cigarette. I was surprised and then a little amused to discover that I 130 was trembling. "I've been out of touch," I said. "You'll have to be patient with me. Now. Who's this Parker character?"

Louis Armstrong: jazz trumpeter and vocalist (1900–1971) born in New Orleans. In the 1950s his music would have been considered conservative by progressive jazz fans.   *Charlie Parker:* a jazz saxophonist (1920–1955) who helped create the progressive jazz style called bebop. Parker was a heroin addict who died at an early age.

"He's just one of the greatest jazz musicians alive," said Sonny, sullenly, his hands in his pockets, his back to me. "Maybe *the* greatest," he added, bitterly, "that's probably why *you* never heard of him."

"All right," I said, "I'm ignorant. I'm sorry. I'll go out and buy all the cat's records right away, all right?"

"It don't," said Sonny, with dignity, "make any difference to me. I don't care what you listen to. Don't do me no favors."

I was beginning to realize that I'd never seen him so upset before. With another part of my mind I was thinking that this would probably turn out to be one of those things kids go through and that I shouldn't make it seem important by pushing it too hard. Still, I didn't think it would do any harm to ask: "Doesn't all this take a lot of time? Can you make a living at it?"

He turned back to me and half leaned, half sat, on the kitchen table. 135 "Everything takes time," he said, "and—well, yes, sure, I can make a living at it. But what I don't seem to be able to make you understand is that it's the only thing I want to do."

"Well, Sonny," I said, gently, "you know people can't always do exactly what they *want* to do—"

"*No,* I don't know that," said Sonny, surprising me. "I think people *ought* to do what they want to do, what else are they alive for?"

"You getting to be a big boy," I said desperately, "it's time you started thinking about your future."

"I'm thinking about my future," said Sonny, grimly. "I think about it all the time."

I gave up. I decided, if he didn't change his mind, that we could always talk 140 about it later. "In the meantime," I said, "you got to finish school." We had already decided that he'd have to move in with Isabel and her folks. I knew this wasn't the ideal arrangement because Isabel's folks are inclined to be dicty and they hadn't especially wanted Isabel to marry me. But I didn't know what else to do. "And we have to get you fixed up at Isabel's."

There was a long silence. He moved from the kitchen table to the window. "That's a terrible idea. You know it yourself."

"Do you have a *better* idea?"

He just walked up and down the kitchen for a minute. He was as tall as I was. He had started to shave. I suddenly had the feeling that I didn't know him at all.

He stopped at the kitchen table and picked up my cigarettes. Looking at me with a kind of mocking, amused defiance, he put one between his lips. "You mind?"

"You smoking already?" 145

He lit the cigarette and nodded, watching me through the smoke. "I just wanted to see if I'd have the courage to smoke in front of you." He grinned and blew a great cloud of smoke to the ceiling. "It was easy." He looked at my face. "Come on, now. I bet you was smoking at my age, tell the truth."

I didn't say anything but the truth was on my face, and he laughed. But now there was something very strained in his laugh. "Sure. And I bet that ain't all you was doing."

He was frightening me a little. "Cut the crap," I said. "We already decided that you was going to go and live at Isabel's. Now what's got into you all of a sudden?"

"*You* decided it," he pointed out. "*I* didn't decide nothing." He stopped in front of me, leaning against the stove, arms loosely folded. "Look, brother. I don't want to stay in Harlem no more, I really don't." He was very earnest. He looked at me, then over toward the kitchen window. There was something in his eyes I'd never seen before, some thoughtfulness, some worry all his own. He rubbed the muscle of one arm. "It's time I was getting out of here."

"Where do you want to *go*, Sonny?"   150

"I want to join the army. Or the navy, I don't care. If I say I'm old enough, they'll believe me."

Then I got mad. It was because I was so scared. "You must be crazy. You goddamn fool, what the hell do you want to go and join the *army* for?"

"I just told you. To get out of Harlem."

"Sonny, you haven't even finished *school*. And if you really want to be a musician, how do you expect to study if you're in the *army*?"

He looked at me, trapped, and in anguish. "There's ways. I might be able to   155
work out some kind of deal. Anyway, I'll have the G.I. Bill when I come out."

"*If* you come out." We stared at each other. "Sonny, please. Be reasonable. I know the setup is far from perfect. But we got to do the best we can."

"I ain't learning nothing in school," he said. "Even when I go." He turned away from me and opened the window and threw his cigarette out into the narrow alley. I watched his back. "At least, I ain't learning nothing you'd want me to learn." He slammed the window so hard I thought the glass would fly out, and turned back to me. "And I'm sick of the stink of these garbage cans!"

"Sonny," I said, "I know how you feel. But if you don't finish school now, you're going to be sorry later that you didn't." I grabbed him by the shoulders. "And you only got another year. It ain't so bad. And I'll come back and I swear I'll help you do *whatever* you want to do. Just try to put up with it till I come back. Will you please do that? For me?"

He didn't answer and he wouldn't look at me.

"Sonny. You hear me?"   160

He pulled away. "I hear you. But you never hear anything *I* say."

I didn't know what to say to that. He looked out of the window and then back at me. "OK," he said, and sighed. "I'll try."

Then I said, trying to cheer him up a little, "They got a piano at Isabel's. You can practice on it."

And as a matter of fact, it did cheer him up for a minute. "That's right," he said to himself. "I forgot that." His face relaxed a little. But the worry, the thoughtfulness, played on it still, the way shadows play on a face which is staring into the fire.

But I thought I'd never hear the end of that piano. At first, Isabel would write   165
me, saying how nice it was that Sonny was so serious about his music and how, as soon as he came in from school, or wherever he had been when he was supposed

to be at school, he went straight to that piano and stayed there until suppertime. And, after supper, he went back to that piano and stayed there until everybody went to bed. He was at the piano all day Saturday and all day Sunday. Then he bought a record player and started playing records. He'd play one record over and over again, all day long sometimes, and he'd improvise along with it on the piano. Or he'd play one section of the record, one chord, one change, one progression, then he'd do it on the piano. Then back to the record. Then back to the piano.

Well, I really don't know how they stood it. Isabel finally confessed that it wasn't like living with a person at all, it was like living with sound. And the sound didn't make any sense to her, didn't make any sense to any of them—naturally. They began, in a way, to be afflicted by this presence that was living in their home. It was as though Sonny were some sort of god, or monster. He moved in an atmosphere which wasn't like theirs at all. They fed him and he ate, he washed himself, he walked in and out of their door; he certainly wasn't nasty or unpleasant or rude, Sonny isn't any of those things; but it was as though he were all wrapped up in some cloud, some fire, some vision all his own; and there wasn't any way to reach him.

At the same time, he wasn't really a man yet, he was still a child, and they had to watch out for him in all kinds of ways. They certainly couldn't throw him out. Neither did they dare to make a great scene about that piano because even they dimly sensed, as I sensed, from so many thousands of miles away, that Sonny was at that piano playing for his life.

But he hadn't been going to school. One day a letter came from the school board and Isabel's mother got it—there had, apparently, been other letters but Sonny had torn them up. This day, when Sonny came in, Isabel's mother showed him the letter and asked where he'd been spending his time. And she finally got it out of him that he'd been down in Greenwich Village, with musicians and other characters, in a white girl's apartment. And this scared her and she started to scream at him and what came up, once she began—though she denies it to this day—was what sacrifices they were making to give Sonny a decent home and how little he appreciated it.

Sonny didn't play the piano that day. By evening, Isabel's mother had calmed down but then there was the old man to deal with, and Isabel herself. Isabel says she did her best to be calm but she broke down and started crying. She says she just watched Sonny's face. She could tell, by watching him, what was happening with him. And what was happening was that they penetrated his cloud, they had reached him. Even if their fingers had been a thousand times more gentle than human fingers ever are, he could hardly help feeling that they had stripped him naked and were spitting on that nakedness. For he also had to see that his presence, that music, which was life or death to him, had been torture for them and that they had endured it, not at all for his sake, but only for mine. And Sonny couldn't take that. He can take it a little better today than he could then but he's still not very good at it and, frankly, I don't know anybody who is.

The silence of the next few days must have been louder than the sound of all ₁₇₀ the music ever played since time began. One morning, before she went to work,

Isabel was in his room for something and she suddenly realized that all of his records were gone. And she knew for certain that he was gone. And he was. He went as far as the navy would carry him. He finally sent me a postcard from some place in Greece and that was the first I knew that Sonny was still alive. I didn't see him any more until we were both back in New York and the war had long been over.

He was a man by then, of course, but I wasn't willing to see it. He came by the house from time to time, but we fought almost every time we met. I didn't like the way he carried himself, loose and dreamlike all the time, and I didn't like his friends, and his music seemed to be merely an excuse for the life he led. It sounded just that weird and disordered.

Then we had a fight, a pretty awful fight, and I didn't see him for months. By and by I looked him up, where he was living, in a furnished room in the Village, and I tried to make it up. But there were lots of people in the room and Sonny just lay on his bed, and he wouldn't come downstairs with me, and he treated these other people as though they were his family and I weren't. So I got mad and then he got mad, and then I told him that he might just as well be dead as live the way he was living. Then he stood up and he told me not to worry about him any more in life, that he *was* dead as far as I was concerned. Then he pushed me to the door and the other people looked on as though nothing were happening, and he slammed the door behind me. I stood in the hallway, staring at the door. I heard somebody laugh in the room and then the tears came to my eyes. I started down the steps, whistling to keep from crying, I kept whistling to myself, *You going to need me, baby, one of these cold, rainy days.*

I read about Sonny's trouble in the spring. Little Grace died in the fall. She was a beautiful little girl. But she only lived a little over two years. She died of polio and she suffered. She had a slight fever for a couple of days, but it didn't seem like anything and we just kept her in bed. And we would certainly have called the doctor, but the fever dropped, she seemed to be all right. So we thought it had just been a cold. Then, one day, she was up, playing, Isabel was in the kitchen fixing lunch for the two boys when they'd come in from school, and she heard Grace fall down in the living room. When you have a lot of children you don't always start running when one of them falls, unless they start screaming or something. And, this time, Grace was quiet. Yet, Isabel says that when she heard that *thump* and then that silence, something happened in her to make her afraid. And she ran to the living room and there was little Grace on the floor, all twisted up, and the reason she hadn't screamed was that she couldn't get her breath. And when she did scream, it was the worst sound, Isabel says, that she'd ever heard in all her life, and she still hears it sometimes in her dreams. Isabel will sometimes wake me up with a low, moaning, strangled sound and I have to be quick to awaken her and hold her to me and where Isabel is weeping against me seems a mortal wound.

I think I may have written Sonny the very day that little Grace was buried. I was sitting in the living room in the dark, by myself, and I suddenly thought of Sonny. My trouble made his real.

One Saturday afternoon, when Sonny had been living with us, or, anyway, been in our house, for nearly two weeks, I found myself wandering aimlessly about 175 the living room, drinking from a can of beer, and trying to work up the courage to search Sonny's room. He was out, he was usually out whenever I was home, and Isabel had taken the children to see their grandparents. Suddenly I was standing still in front of the living room window, watching Seventh Avenue. The idea of searching Sonny's room made me still. I scarcely dared to admit to myself what I'd be searching for. I didn't know what I'd do if I found it. Or if I didn't.

On the sidewalk across from me, near the entrance to a barbecue joint, some people were holding an old-fashioned revival meeting. The barbecue cook, wearing a dirty white apron, his conked hair reddish and metallic in the pale sun, and a cigarette between his lips, stood in the doorway, watching them. Kids and older people paused in their errands and stood there, along with some older men and a couple of very tough-looking women who watched everything that happened on the avenue, as though they owned it, or were maybe owned by it. Well, they were watching this, too. The revival was being carried on by three sisters in black, and a brother. All they had were their voices and their Bibles and a tambourine. The brother was testifying and while he testified two of the sisters stood together, seeming to say, amen, and the third sister walked around with the tambourine outstretched and a couple of people dropped coins into it. Then the brother's testimony ended and the sister who had been taking up the collection dumped the coins into her palm and transferred them to the pocket of her long black robe. Then she raised both hands, striking the tambourine against the air, and then against one hand, and she started to sing. And the two other sisters and the brother joined in.

It was strange, suddenly, to watch, though I had been seeing these street meetings all my life. So, of course, had everybody else down there. Yet, they paused and watched and listened and I stood still at the window. *"Tis the old ship of Zion,"* they sang, and the sister with the tambourine kept a steady, jangling beat, *"it has rescued many a thousand!"* Not a soul under the sound of their voices was hearing this song for the first time, not one of them had been rescued. Nor had they seen much in the way of rescue work being done around them. Neither did they especially believe in the holiness of the three sisters and the brother, they knew too much about them, knew where they lived, and how. The woman with the tambourine, whose voice dominated the air, whose face was bright with joy, was divided by very little from the woman who stood watching her, a cigarette between her heavy, chapped lips, her hair a cuckoo's nest, her face scarred and swollen from many beatings, and her black eyes glittering like coal. Perhaps they both knew this, which was why, when, as rarely, they addressed each other, they addressed each other as Sister. As the singing filled the air the watching, listening faces underwent a change, the eyes focusing on something within; the music seemed to soothe a poison out of them; and time seemed, nearly, to fall away from the sullen, belligerent, battered faces, as though they were fleeing back to their first condition, while dreaming of their last. The barbecue cook half shook his head and smiled, and dropped his cigarette and disappeared into his joint. A man fumbled in his pockets for change and stood holding it in his hand impatiently, as though he had just remembered a pressing appointment further up the avenue. He looked furious. Then I saw Sonny, standing on the edge of the crowd. He was carrying a wide, flat notebook with a green cover, and it made him look, from where I was standing, almost like a schoolboy. The coppery sun brought out the copper in his skin, he was very faintly smiling, standing very still. Then the singing stopped, the tambourine turned into a collection plate again. The furious man dropped in his coins and vanished, so did a couple of the women, and Sonny dropped some change in the plate, looking directly at the woman with a little smile. He started across the avenue, toward the house. He has a slow, loping walk, something like the way Harlem hipsters walk, only he's imposed on this his own half-beat. I had never really noticed it before.

I stayed at the window, both relieved and apprehensive. As Sonny disappeared from my sight, they began singing again. And they were still singing when his key turned in the lock.

"Hey," he said.

"Hey, yourself. You want some beer?"

"No. Well, maybe." But he came up to the window and stood beside me, looking out. "What a warm voice," he said.   180

They were singing *If I could only hear my mother pray again!*

"Yes," I said, "and she can sure beat that tambourine."

"But what a terrible song," he said, and laughed. He dropped his notebook on the sofa and disappeared into the kitchen. "Where's Isabel and the kids?"

"I think they went to see their grandparents. You hungry?"   185

"No." He came back into the living room with his can of beer. "You want to come some place with me tonight?"

I sensed, I don't know how, that I couldn't possibly say no. "Sure. Where?"

He sat down on the sofa and picked up his notebook and started leafing through it. "I'm going to sit in with some fellows in a joint in the Village."

"You mean, you're going to play, tonight?"

"That's right." He took a swallow of his beer and moved back to the   190
window. He gave me a sidelong look. "If you can stand it."

"I'll try," I said.

He smiled to himself and we both watched as the meeting across the way broke up. The three sisters and the brother, heads bowed, were singing *God be with you till we meet again*. The faces around them were very quiet. Then the song ended. The small crowd dispersed. We watched the three women and the lone man walk slowly up the avenue.

"When she was singing before," said Sonny, abruptly, "her voice reminded me for a minute of what heroin feels like sometimes—when it's in your veins. It makes you feel sort of warm and cool at the same time. And distant. And—and sure." He sipped his beer, very deliberately not looking at me. I watched his face. "It makes you feel—in control. Sometimes you've got to have that feeling."

"Do you?" I sat down slowly in the easy chair.

"Sometimes." He went to the sofa and picked up his notebook again. "Some   195
people do."

"In order," I asked, "to play?" And my voice was very ugly, full of contempt and anger.

"Well"—he looked at me with great, troubled eyes, as though, in fact, he hoped his eyes would tell me things he could never otherwise say—"they *think* so. And *if* they think so—!"

"And what do *you* think?" I asked.

He sat on the sofa and put his can of beer on the floor. "I don't know," he said, and I couldn't be sure if he were answering my question or pursuing his thoughts. His face didn't tell me. "It's not so much to *play*. It's to *stand* it, to be able to make it at all. On any level." He frowned and smiled: "In order to keep from shaking to pieces."

"But these friends of yours," I said, "they seem to shake themselves to pieces 200 pretty goddamn fast."

"Maybe." He played with the notebook. And something told me that I should curb my tongue, that Sonny was doing his best to talk, that I should listen. "But of course you only know the ones that've gone to pieces. Some don't—or at least they haven't *yet* and that's just about all *any* of us can say." He paused. "And then there are some who just live, really, in hell, and they know it and they see what's happening and they go right on. I don't know." He sighed, dropped the notebook, folded his arms. "Some guys, you can tell from the way they play, they on something *all* the time. And you can see that, well, it makes something real for them. But of course," he picked up his beer from the floor and sipped it and put the can down again, "they *want* to, too, you've got to see that. Even some of them that say they don't—*some*, not all."

"And what about you?" I asked—I couldn't help it. "What about you? Do *you* want to?"

He stood up and walked to the window and remained silent for a long time. Then he sighed. "Me," he said. Then: "While I was downstairs before, on my way here, listening to that woman sing, it struck me all of a sudden how much suffering she must have had to go through—to sing like that. It's *repulsive* to think you have to suffer that much."

I said: "But there's no way not to suffer—is there, Sonny?"

"I believe not," he said and smiled, "but that's never stopped anyone from 205 trying." He looked at me. "Has it?" I realized, with this mocking look, that there stood between us, forever, beyond the power of time or forgiveness, the fact that I had held silence—so long!—when he had needed human speech to help him. He turned back to the window. "No, there's no way not to suffer. But you try all kinds of ways to keep from drowning in it, to keep on top of it, and to make it seem—well, like *you*. Like you did something, all right, and now you're suffering for it. You know?" I said nothing. "Well you know," he said, impatiently, "why *do* people suffer? Maybe it's better to do something to give it a reason, *any* reason."

"But we just agreed," I said "that there's no way not to suffer. Isn't it better, then, just to—take it?"

"But nobody just takes it," Sonny cried, "that's what I'm telling you! *Everybody* tries not to. You're just hung up on the *way* some people try—it's not *your* way!"

The hair on my face began to itch, my face felt wet. "That's not true," I said, "that's not true. I don't give a damn what other people do, I don't even care how they suffer. I just care how *you* suffer." And he looked at me. "Please believe me," I said, "I don't want to see you—die—trying not to suffer."

"I won't," he said, flatly, "die trying not to suffer. At least, not any faster than anybody else."

"But there's no need," I said, trying to laugh, "is there? in killing yourself." 210

I wanted to say more, but I couldn't. I wanted to talk about will power and how life could be—well, beautiful. I wanted to say that it was all within; but was it? or, rather, wasn't that exactly the trouble? And I wanted to promise that I would never fail him again. But it would all have sounded—empty words and lies.

So I made the promise to myself and prayed that I would keep it.

"It's terrible sometimes, inside," he said, "that's what's the trouble. You walk these streets, black and funky and cold, and there's not really a living ass to talk to, and there's nothing shaking, and there's no way of getting it out—that storm inside. You can't talk it and you can't make love with it, and when you finally try to get with it and play it, you realize *nobody's* listening. So *you've* got to listen. You got to find a way to listen."

And then he walked away from the window and sat on the sofa again, as though all the wind had suddenly been knocked out of him. "Sometimes you'll do *anything* to play, even cut your mother's throat." He laughed and looked at me. "Or your brother's." Then he sobered. "Or your own." Then: "Don't worry. I'm all right now and I think I'll *be* all right. But I can't forget—where I've been. I don't mean just the physical place I've been, I mean where I've *been*. And *what* I've been."

"What have you been, Sonny?" I asked. 215

He smiled—but sat sideways on the sofa, his elbow resting on the back, his fingers playing with his mouth and chin, not looking at me. "I've been something I didn't recognize, didn't know I could be. Didn't know anybody could be." He stopped, looking inward, looking helplessly young, looking old. "I'm not talking about it now because I feel *guilty* or anything like that—maybe it would be better if I did, I don't know. Anyway, I can't really talk about it. Not to you, not to anybody," and now he turned and faced me. "Sometimes, you know, and it was actually when I was most *out* of the world, I felt that I was in it, that I was *with* it, really, and I could play or I didn't really have to *play*, it just came out of me, it was there. And I don't know how I played, thinking about it now, but I know I did awful things, those times, sometimes, to people. Or it wasn't that I *did* anything to them—it was that they weren't real." He picked up the beer can; it was empty; he rolled it between his palms: "And other times—well, I needed a fix, I needed to find a place to lean, I needed to clear a space to *listen*—and I couldn't find it, and I—went crazy, I did terrible things to *me*, I was terrible *for* me." He began pressing the beer can between his hands, I watched the metal begin to give. It glittered, as he played with it, like a knife, and I was afraid he would cut himself, but I said nothing. "Oh well. I can never tell you. I was all by myself at the bottom of something, stinking and sweating and crying and shaking, and I smelled it, you know? *my* stink, and I thought I'd die if I couldn't get away from it and yet, all the same, I knew that everything I was doing was just locking me in with it. And I didn't know," he paused, still flattening the beer can, "I didn't know, I still *don't* know, something kept telling me that maybe it was good to smell your own stink, but I didn't think that *that* was what I'd been trying to do—and—who can stand it?" and he abruptly dropped the ruined beer can, looking at me with a small, still smile, and then rose, walking to the window as though it were the lodestone rock. I watched his face, he watched the avenue. "I couldn't tell you when Mama died—but the reason I wanted to leave Harlem so bad was to get away from drugs. And then, when I ran away, that's what I was running from—really. When I came back, nothing had changed, *I* hadn't changed, I was just—older." And he stopped, drumming with his fingers on the windowpane. The sun had vanished, soon darkness would fall. I watched his face. "It can come again," he said, almost as though speaking to himself. Then he turned to me. "It can come again," he repeated. "I just want you to know that."

"All right," I said, at last. "So it can come again. All right."

He smiled, but the smile was sorrowful. "I had to try to tell you," he said.

"Yes," I said. "I understand that."

"You're my brother," he said, looking straight at me, and not smiling at all. 220

"Yes," I repeated, "yes. I understand that."

He turned back to the window, looking out. "All that hatred down there," he said, "all that hatred and misery and love. It's a wonder it doesn't blow the avenue apart."

We went to the only nightclub on a short, dark street, downtown. We squeezed through the narrow, chattering, jam-packed bar to the entrance of the big room, where the bandstand was. And we stood there for a moment, for the lights were very dim in this room and we couldn't see. Then, "Hello, boy," said a voice and an enormous black man, much older than Sonny or myself, erupted out of all that atmospheric lighting and put an arm around Sonny's shoulder. "I been sitting right here," he said, "waiting for you."

He had a big voice, too, and heads in the darkness turned toward us.

Sonny grinned and pulled a little away, and said, "Creole, this is my brother. 225 I told you about him."

Creole shook my hand. "I'm glad to meet you, son," he said, and it was clear that he was glad to meet me *there*, for Sonny's sake. And he smiled, "You got a real musician in *your* family," and he took his arm from Sonny's shoulder and slapped him, lightly, affectionately, with the back of his hand.

"Well. Now I've heard it all," said a voice behind us. This was another musician, and a friend of Sonny's, a coal-black, cheerful-looking man, built close to the ground. He immediately began confiding to me, at the top of his lungs, the most terrible things about Sonny, his teeth gleaming like a lighthouse and his laugh coming up out of him like the beginning of an earthquake. And it turned out that everyone at the bar knew Sonny, or almost everyone; some were musicians, working there, or nearby, or not working, some were simply hangers-on, and some were there to hear Sonny play. I was introduced to all of them and they were all very polite to me. Yet, it was clear that, for them, I was only Sonny's brother. Here, I was in Sonny's world. Or, rather: his kingdom. Here, it was not even a question that his veins bore royal blood.

They were going to play soon and Creole installed me, by myself, at a table in a dark corner. Then I watched them, Creole, and the little black man, and Sonny, and the others, while they horsed around, standing just below the bandstand. The light from the bandstand spilled just a little short of them and, watching them laughing and gesturing and moving about, I had the feeling that they, nevertheless, were being most careful not to step into that circle of light too suddenly: that if they moved into the light too suddenly, without thinking, they would perish in flame. Then, while I watched, one of them, the small, black man, moved into the light and crossed the bandstand and started fooling around with his drums. Then—being funny and being, also, extremely ceremonious—Creole took Sonny by the arm and led him to the piano. A woman's voice called Sonny's name and a few hands started clapping. And Sonny, also being funny and being ceremonious, and so touched, I think, that he could have cried, but neither hiding it nor showing it, riding it like a man, grinned, and put both hands to his heart and bowed from the waist.

Creole then went to the bass fiddle and a lean, very bright-skinned brown man jumped up on the bandstand and picked up his horn. So there they were, and the atmosphere on the bandstand and in the room began to change and tighten. Someone stepped up to the microphone and announced them. Then there were all kinds of murmurs. Some people at the bar shushed others. The waitress ran around, frantically getting in the last orders, guys and chicks got closer to each other, and the lights on the bandstand, on the quartet, turned to a kind of indigo. Then they all looked different there. Creole looked about him for the last time, as though he were making certain that all his chickens were in the coop, and then he—jumped and struck the fiddle. And there they were.

All I know about music is that not many people ever really hear it. And 230 even then, on the rare occasions when something opens within, and the music enters, what we mainly hear, or hear corroborated, are personal, private, vanishing evocations. But the man who creates the music is hearing something else, is dealing with the roar rising from the void and imposing order on it as it hits the air. What is evoked in him, then, is of another order, more terrible because it has no words, and triumphant, too, for that same reason. And his triumph, when he triumphs, is ours. I just watched Sonny's face. His face was troubled, he was working hard, but he wasn't with it. And I had the feeling that, in a way, everyone on the bandstand was waiting for him, both waiting for him and pushing him along. But as I began to watch Creole, I realized that it was Creole who held them all back. He had them on a short rein. Up there, keeping the beat with his whole body, wailing on the fiddle, with his eyes half closed, he was listening to everything, but he was listening to Sonny. He was having a dialogue with Sonny. He wanted Sonny to leave the shoreline and strike out for the deep water. He was Sonny's witness that deep water and drowning were not the same thing—he had been there, and he knew. And he wanted Sonny to know. He was waiting for Sonny to do the things on the keys which would let Creole know that Sonny was in the water.

And, while Creole listened, Sonny moved, deep within, exactly like someone in torment. I had never before thought of how awful the relationship must be between the musician and his instrument. He has to fill it, this instrument, with the breath of life, his own. He has to make it do what he wants it to do. And a piano is just a piano. It's made out of so much wood and wires and little hammers and big ones, and ivory. While there's only so much you can do with it, the only way to find this out is to try; to try and make it do everything.

And Sonny hadn't been near a piano for over a year. And he wasn't on much better terms with his life, not the life that stretched before him now. He and the piano stammered, started one way, got scared, stopped; started another way, panicked, marked time, started again; then seemed to have found a direction, panicked again, got stuck. And the face I saw on Sonny I'd never seen before. Everything had been burned out of it, and, at the same time, things usually hidden were being burned in, by the fire and fury of the battle which was occurring in him up there.

Yet, watching Creole's face as they neared the end of the first set, I had the feeling that something had happened, something I hadn't heard. Then they finished, there was scattered applause, and then, without an instant's warning, Creole started into something else, it was almost sardonic, it was *Am I Blue*. And, as though he commanded, Sonny began to play. Something began to happen. And Creole let out the reins. The dry, low, black man said something awful on the drums, Creole answered, and the drums talked back. Then the horn insisted, sweet and high, slightly detached perhaps, and Creole listened, commenting now and then, dry, and driving, beautiful and calm and old. Then they all came together again, and Sonny was part of the family again. I could tell this from his face. He seemed to have found, right there beneath his fingers, a damn brand-new piano. It seemed that he couldn't get over it. Then, for awhile, just being happy with Sonny, they seemed to be agreeing with him that brand-new pianos certainly were a gas.

Then Creole stepped forward to remind them that what they were playing was the blues. He hit something in all of them, he hit something in me, myself, and the music tightened and deepened, apprehension began to beat the air. Creole began to tell us what the blues were all about. They were not about anything very new. He and his boys up there were keeping it new, at the risk of ruin, destruction, madness, and death, in order to find new ways to make us listen. For, while the tale of how we suffer, and how we are delighted, and how we may triumph is never new, it always must be heard. There isn't any other tale to tell, it's the only light we've got in all this darkness.

And this tale, according to that face, that body, those strong hands on those 235 strings, has another aspect in every country, and a new depth in every generation. Listen, Creole seemed to be saying, listen. Now these are Sonny's blues. He made the little black man on the drums know it, and the bright, brown man on the horn. Creole wasn't trying any longer to get Sonny in the water. He was wishing him Godspeed.° Then he stepped back, very slowly, filling the air with the immense suggestion that Sonny speak for himself.

Then they all gathered around Sonny and Sonny played. Every now and again one of them seemed to say, amen. Sonny's fingers filled the air with life, his life. But that life contained so many others. And Sonny went all the way back, he really began with the spare, flat statement of the opening phrase of the song. Then he began to make it his. It was very beautiful because it wasn't hurried and it was no longer a lament. I seemed to hear with what burning he had made it his, with what burning we had yet to make it ours, how we could cease lamenting. Freedom lurked around us and I understood, at last, that he could help us to be free if we would listen, that he would never be free until we did. Yet, there was no battle in his face now. I heard what he had gone through, and would continue to go through until he came to rest in earth. He had made it his: that long line, of which we knew only Mama and Daddy. And he was giving it back, as everything must be given back, so that, passing through death, it can live forever. I saw my mother's face again, and felt, for the first time, how the stones of the road she had walked on must have bruised her feet. I saw the moon-lit road where my father's brother died. And it brought something else back to me, and carried me past it. I saw my little girl again and felt Isabel's tears again, and I felt my own tears begin to rise. And I was yet aware that this was only a moment, that the world waited outside, as hungry as a tiger, and that trouble stretched above us, longer than the sky.

Then it was over. Creole and Sonny let out their breath, both soaking wet, and grinning. There was a lot of applause and some of it was real. In the dark, the girl came by and I asked her to take drinks to the bandstand. There was a long pause, while they talked up there in the indigo light and after awhile I saw the girl put a Scotch and milk on top of the piano for Sonny. He didn't seem to notice it, but just before they started playing again, he sipped from it and looked toward me, and nodded. Then he put it back on top of the piano. For me, then, as they began to play again, it glowed and shook above my brother's head like the very cup of trembling.

QUESTIONS

1. From whose point of view is "Sonny's Blues" told? How do the narrator's values and experiences affect his view of the story?
2. What is the older brother's profession? Does it suggest anything about his personality?
3. How would this story change if it were told by Sonny?
4. What event prompts the narrator to write his brother?
5. What does the narrator's mother ask him to do for Sonny? Does the older brother keep his promise?
6. The major characters in this story are called Mama, Daddy, and Sonny (the older brother is never named or even nicknamed). How do these names affect our sense of the story?
7. Reread the last four paragraphs and explain the significance of the statement "Now these are Sonny's blues." How has Sonny made this music his own?

wishing him Godspeed: to wish success.

Eudora Welty

Why I Live at the P.O.

Eudora Welty

Eudora Welty (1909–2001) was born in Jackson, Mississippi, daughter of an insurance company president. Like William Faulkner, another Mississippi writer, she stayed close to her roots for practically all her life, except for short sojourns at the University of Wisconsin, where she took her B.A., and in New York City, where she studied advertising. She lived most of her life in her childhood home in Jackson, within a stone's throw of the state capitol. Although Welty was a novelist distinguished for The Robber Bridegroom *(1942),* Delta Wedding *(1946),* The Ponder Heart *(1954), and* Losing Battles *(1970), many critics think her finest work was in the short-story form.* The Collected Stories of Eudora Welty *(1980) gathers the work of more than forty years. Welty's other books include memoirs,* The Optimist's Daughter *(1972) and* One Writer's Beginnings *(1984), and* The Eye of the Story *(1977), a book of sympathetic criticism on the fiction of other writers, including Willa Cather, Virginia Woolf, Katherine Anne Porter, and Isak Dinesen.* One Time, One Place, *a book of photographs of everyday life that Welty took in Mississippi during the Depression, was republished in a revised edition in 1996.*

I was getting along fine with Mama, Papa-Daddy, and Uncle Rondo until my sister Stella-Rondo just separated from her husband and came back home again. Mr. Whitaker! Of course I went with Mr. Whitaker first, when he first appeared here in China Grove, taking "Pose Yourself" photos, and Stella-Rondo broke us up. Told him I was one-sided. Bigger on one side than the other, which is a deliberate, calculated falsehood: I'm the same. Stella-Rondo is exactly twelve months to the day younger than I am and for that reason she's spoiled.

She's always had anything in the world she wanted and then she'd throw it away. Papa-Daddy gave her this gorgeous Add-a-Pearl necklace when she was eight years old and she threw it away playing baseball when she was nine, with only two pearls.

So as soon as she got married and moved away from home the first thing she did was separate! From Mr. Whitaker! This photographer with the popeyes she said she trusted. Came home from one of those towns up in Illinois and to our complete surprise brought this child of two.

Mama said she like to make her drop dead for a second. "Here you had this marvelous blonde child and never so much as wrote your mother a word about it," says Mama. "I'm thoroughly ashamed of you." But of course she wasn't.

Stella-Rondo just calmly takes off this *hat.* I wish you could see it. She says,   5 "Why, Mama, Shirley-T.'s adopted, I can prove it."

"How?" says Mama, but all I says was, "H'm!" There I was over the hot stove, trying to stretch two chickens over five people and a completely unexpected child into the bargain, without one moment's notice.

"What do you mean—'H'm!'?" says Stella-Rondo, and Mama says, "I heard that, Sister."

I said that oh, I didn't mean a thing, only that whoever Shirley-T. was, she was the spit-image of Papa-Daddy if he'd cut off his beard, which of course he'd never do in the world. Papa-Daddy's Mama's papa and sulks.

Stella-Rondo got furious! She said, "Sister, I don't need to tell you you got a lot of nerve and always did have and I'll thank you to make no future reference to my adopted child whatsoever."

"Very well," I said. "Very well, very well. Of course I noticed at once she looks like Mr. Whitaker's side too. That frown. She looks like a cross between Mr. Whitaker and Papa-Daddy." 10

"Well, all I can say is she isn't."

"She looks exactly like Shirley Temple to me," says Mama, but Shirley-T. just ran away from her.

So the first thing Stella-Rondo did at the table was turn Papa-Daddy against me.

"Papa-Daddy," she says. He was trying to cut up his meat. "Papa-Daddy!" I was taken completely by surprise. Papa-Daddy is about a million years old and's got this long-long beard. "Papa-Daddy, Sister says she fails to understand why you don't cut off your beard."

So Papa Daddy l-a-y-s down his knife and fork! He's real rich. Mama says he is, he says he isn't. So he says, "Have I heard correctly? You don't understand why I don't cut off my beard?" 15

"Why," I says, "Papa-Daddy, of course I understand, I did not say any such of a thing, the idea!"

He says, "Hussy!"

I says, "Papa-Daddy, you know I wouldn't any more want you to cut off your beard than the man in the moon. It was the farthest thing from my mind! Stella-Rondo sat there and made that up while she was eating breast of chicken."

But he says, "So the postmistress fails to understand why I don't cut off my beard. Which job I got you through my influence with the government. 'Bird's nest'—is that what you call it?"

Not that it isn't the next to smallest P.O. in the entire state of Mississippi. 20

I says, "Oh, Papa-Daddy," I says, "I didn't say any such of a thing, I never dreamed it was a bird's nest, I have always been grateful though this is the next to smallest P.O. in the state of Mississippi, and I do not enjoy being referred to as a hussy by my own grandfather."

But Stella-Rondo says, "Yes, you did say it too. Anybody in the world could of heard you, that had ears."

"Stop right there," says Mama, looking at *me*.

So I pulled my napkin straight back through the napkin ring and left the table.

As soon as I was out of the room Mama says, "Call her back, or she'll starve   25
to death," but Papa-Daddy says, "This is the beard I started growing on the Coast
when I was fifteen years old." He would of gone on till nightfall if Shirley-T.
hadn't lost the Milky Way she ate in Cairo.

So Papa-Daddy says, "I am going out and lie in the hammock, and you can
all sit here and remember my words: I'll never cut off my beard as long as I live,
even one inch, and I don't appreciate it in you at all." Passed right by me in the
hall and went straight out and got in the hammock.

It would be a holiday. It wasn't five minutes before Uncle Rondo suddenly
appeared in the hall in one of Stella-Rondo's flesh-colored kimonos, all cut on
the bias, like something Mr. Whitaker probably thought was gorgeous.

"Uncle Rondo!" I says. "I didn't know who that was! Where are you going?"

"Sister," he says, "get out of my way, I'm poisoned."

"If you're poisoned stay away from Papa-Daddy," I says. "Keep out of the   30
hammock. Papa-Daddy will certainly beat you on the head if you come within
forty miles of him. He thinks I deliberately said he ought to cut off his beard after
he got me the P.O., and I've told him and told him and told him, and he acts
like he just don't hear me. Papa-Daddy must of gone stone deaf."

"He picked a fine day to do it then," says Uncle Rondo, and before you
could say "Jack Robinson" flew out in the yard.

What he'd really done, he'd drunk another bottle of that prescription. He
does it every single Fourth of July as sure as shooting, and it's horribly expensive.
Then he falls over in the hammock and snores. So he insisted on zigzagging right
on out to the hammock, looking like a half-wit.

Papa-Daddy woke up with this horrible yell and right there without moving
an inch he tried to turn Uncle Rondo against me. I heard every word he said.
Oh, he told Uncle Rondo I didn't learn to read till I was eight years old and he
didn't see how in the world I ever got the mail put up at the P.O., much less read
it all, and he said if Uncle Rondo could only fathom the lengths he had gone to
get me that job! And he said on the other hand he thought Stella-Rondo had a
brilliant mind and deserved credit for getting out of town. All the time he was
just lying there swinging as pretty as you please and looping out his beard, and
poor Uncle Rondo was *pleading* with him to slow down the hammock, it was
making him as dizzy as a witch to watch it. But that's what Papa-Daddy likes
about a hammock. So Uncle Rondo was too dizzy to get turned against me for
the time being. He's Mama's only brother and is a good case of a one-track mind.
Ask anybody. A certified pharmacist.

Just then I heard Stella-Rondo raising the upstairs window. While she was
married she got this peculiar idea that it's cooler with the windows shut and
locked. So she has to raise the window before she can make a soul hear her outdoors.

So she raises the window and says, "Oh!" You would have thought she was   35
mortally wounded.

Uncle Rondo and Papa-Daddy didn't even look up, but kept right on with
what they were doing. I had to laugh.

I flew up the stairs and threw the door open! I says, "What in the wide world's the matter, Stella-Rondo? You mortally wounded?"

"No," she says, "I am not mortally wounded but I wish you would do me the favor of looking out that window there and telling me what you see."

So I shade my eyes and look out the window.

"I see the front yard," I says.

"Don't you see any human beings?" she says.

"I see Uncle Rondo trying to run Papa-Daddy out of the hammock," I says. "Nothing more. Naturally, it's so suffocating-hot in the house, with all the windows shut and locked, everybody who cares to stay in their right mind will have to go out and get in the hammock before the Fourth of July is over."

"Don't you notice anything different about Uncle Rondo?" asks Stella-Rondo.

"Why, no, except he's got on some terrible-looking flesh-colored contraption I wouldn't be found dead in, is all I can see," I says.

"Never mind, you won't be found dead in it, because it happens to be part of my trousseau, and Mr. Whitaker took several dozen photographs of me in it," says Stella-Rondo. "What on earth could Uncle Rondo *mean* by wearing part of my trousseau out in the broad open daylight without saying so much as 'Kiss my foot,' *knowing* I only got home this morning after my separation and hung my negligee up on the bathroom door, just as nervous as I could be?"

"I'm sure I don't know, and what do you expect me to do about it?" I says. "Jump out the window?"

"No, I expect nothing of the kind. I simply declare that Uncle Rondo looks like a fool in it, that's all," she says. "It makes me sick to my stomach."

"Well, he looks as good as he can," I says. "As good as anybody in reason could." I stood up for Uncle Rondo, please remember. And I said to Stella-Rondo, "I think I would do well not to criticize so freely if I were you and came home with a two-year-old child I had never said a word about, and no explanation whatever about my separation."

"I asked you the instant I entered this house not to refer one more time to my adopted child, and you gave me your word of honor you would not," was all Stella-Rondo would say, and started pulling out every one of her eyebrows with some cheap Kress tweezers.

So I merely slammed the door behind me and went down and made some green-tomato pickle. Somebody had to do it. Of course Mama had turned both the niggers loose; she always said no earthly power could hold one anyway on the Fourth of July, so she wouldn't even try. It turned out that Jaypan fell in the lake and came within a very narrow limit of drowning.

So Mama trots in. Lifts up the lid and says, "H'm! Not very good for your Uncle Rondo in his precarious condition, I must say. Or poor little adopted Shirley-T. Shame on you!"

That made me tired. I says, "Well, Stella-Rondo had better thank her lucky stars it was her instead of me came trotting in with that very peculiar-looking child. Now if it had been me that trotted in from Illinois and brought a peculiar-

40

45

50

looking child of two, I shudder to think of the reception I'd of got, much less controlled the diet of an entire family."

"But you must remember, Sister, that you were never married to Mr. Whitaker in the first place and didn't go up to Illinois to live," says Mama, shaking a spoon in my face. If you had I would have been just as overjoyed to see you and your little adopted girl as I was to see Stella-Rondo, when you wound up with your separation and came on back home."

"You would not," I says.

"Don't contradict me, I would," says Mama.   55

But I said she couldn't convince me though she talked till she was blue in the face. Then I said, "Besides, you know as well as I do that that child is not adopted."

"She most certainly is adopted," says Mama, stiff as a poker.

I says, "Why, Mama, Stella-Rondo had her just as sure as anything in this world, and just too stuck up to admit it."

"Why Sister," said Mama. "Here I thought we were going to have a pleasant Fourth of July, and you start right out not believing a word your own baby sister tells you!"

"Just like Cousin Annie Flo. Went to her grave denying the facts of life," I   60
remind Mama.

"I told you if you ever mentioned Annie Flo's name I'd slap your face," says Mama, and slaps my face.

"All right, you wait and see," I says.

"I," says Mama, "I prefer to take my children's word for anything when it's humanly possible." You ought to see Mama, she weighs two hundred pounds and has real tiny feet.

Just then something perfectly horrible occurred to me.

"Mama," I says, "can that child talk?" I simply had to whisper! "Mama, I   65
wonder if that child can be—you know—in any way? Do you realize," I says, "that she hasn't spoken one single, solitary word to a human being up to this minute? This is the way she looks," I says, and I looked like this.

Well, Mama and I just stood there and stared at each other. It was horrible!

"I remember well that Joe Whitaker frequently drank like a fish," says Mama. "I believed to my soul he drank *chemicals*." And without another word she marches to the foot of the stairs and calls Stella-Rondo.

"Stella-Rondo? O-o-o-o-o! Stella-Rondo!"

"What?" says Stella-Rondo from upstairs. Not even the grace to get up off the bed.

"Can that child of yours talk?" asks Mama.   70

Stella-Rondo yells back, "Can she what?"

"Talk! Talk!" says Mama. "Burdyburdyburdyburdy!"

So Stella-Rondo yells back, "Who says she can't talk?"

"Sister says so," says Mama.

"You didn't have to tell me, I know whose word of honor don't mean a thing   75
in this house," says Stella-Rondo.

And in a minute the loudest Yankee voice I ever heard in my life yells out, "OE'm Pop-OE the Sailor-r-r Ma-a-an!" and then somebody jumps up and down in the upstairs hall. In another second the house would of fallen down.

"Not only talks, she can tap-dance!" calls Stella-Rondo. "Which is more than some people I won't name can do."

"Why, the little precious darling thing!" Mama says, so surprised. "Just as smart as she can be!" Starts talking baby talk right there. Then she turns on me. "Sister, you ought to be thoroughly ashamed! Run upstairs this instant and apologize to Stella-Rondo and Shirley-T."

"Apologize for what?" I says. "I merely wondered if the child was normal, that's all. Now that she's proved she is, why, I have nothing further to say."

But Mama just turned on her heel and flew out, furious. She ran right upstairs and hugged the baby. She believed it was adopted. Stella-Rondo hadn't done a thing but turn her against me from upstairs while I stood there helpless over the hot stove. So that made Mama, Papa-Daddy, and the baby all on Stella-Rondo's side.

Next, Uncle Rondo.

I must say that Uncle Rondo has been marvelous to me at various times in the past and I was completely unprepared to be made to jump out of my skin, the way it turned out. Once Stella-Rondo did something perfectly horrible to him— broke a chain letter from Flanders Field°—and he took the radio back he had given her and gave it to me. Stella-Rondo was furious! For six months we all had to call her Stella instead of Stella-Rondo, or she wouldn't answer. I always thought Uncle Rondo had all the brains of the entire family. Another time he sent me to Mammoth Cave,° with all expenses paid.

But this would be the day he was drinking that prescription, the Fourth of July.

So at supper Stella-Rondo speaks up and says she thinks Uncle Rondo ought to try to eat a little something. So finally Uncle Rondo said he would try a little cold biscuits and ketchup, but that was all. So *she* brought it to him.

"Do you think it is wise to disport with ketchup in Stella-Rondo's flesh-colored kimono?" I says. Trying to be considerate! If Stella-Rondo couldn't watch out for her trousseau, somebody had to.

"Any objections?" asks Uncle Rondo, just about to pour out all the ketchup.

"Don't mind what she says, Uncle Rondo," says Stella-Rondo. "Sister has been devoting this solid afternoon to sneering out my bedroom window at the way you look."

"What's that?" says Uncle Rondo. Uncle Rondo has got the most terrible temper in the world. Anything is liable to make him tear the house down if it comes at the wrong time.

Flanders Field: an Allied military cemetery in Belgium for the dead of World War I, it was made famous by a poem by John McCrae. The artificial red poppies still sold for charity on Veteran's Day commemorate the cemetery and poem.   *Mammoth Cave:* a network of natural underground caverns in Kentucky.

So Stella-Rondo says, "Sister says, 'Uncle Rondo certainly does look like a fool in that pink kimono!'"

Do you remember who it was really said that?

Uncle Rondo spills out all the ketchup and jumps out of his chair and tears off the kimono and throws it down on the dirty floor and puts his foot on it. It had to be sent all the way to Jackson to the cleaners and re-pleated.

"So that's your opinion of your Uncle Rondo, is it?" he says. "I look like a fool, do I? Well, that's the last straw. A whole day in this house with nothing to do, and then to hear you come out with a remark like that behind my back!"

"I didn't say any such of a thing, Uncle Rondo," I says, "and I'm not saying who did, either. Why, I think you look all right. Just try to take care of yourself and not talk and eat at the same time," I says. "I think you better go lie down."

"Lie down my foot," says Uncle Rondo. I ought to of known by that he was fixing to do something perfectly horrible.

So he didn't do anything that night in the precarious state he was in—just played Casino with Mama and Stella-Rondo and Shirley-T. and gave Shirley-T. a nickel with a head on both sides. It tickled her nearly to death, and she called him "Papa." But at 6:30 A.M. the next morning, he threw a whole five-cent package of some unsold one-inch firecrackers from the store as hard as he could into my bedroom and they every one went off. Not one bad one in the string. Anybody else, there'd be one that wouldn't go off.

Well, I'm just terribly susceptible to noise of any kind, the doctor has always told me I was the most sensitive person he had ever seen in his whole life, and I was simply prostrated. I couldn't eat! People tell me they heard it as far as the cemetery, and old Aunt Jep Patterson, that had been holding her own so good, thought it was Judgment Day and she was going to meet her whole family. It's usually so quiet here.

And I'll tell you it didn't take me any longer than a minute to make up my mind what to do. There I was with the whole entire house on Stella-Rondo's side and turned against me. If I have anything at all I have pride.

So I just decided I'd go straight down to the P.O. There's plenty of room there in the back, I says to myself.

Well! I made no bones about letting the family catch on to what I was up to. I didn't try to conceal it.

The first thing they knew, I marched in where they were all playing Old Maid and pulled the electric oscillating fan out by the plug, and everything got real hot. Next I snatched the pillow I'd done the needlepoint on right off the davenport from behind Papa-Daddy. He went "Ugh!" I beat Stella-Rondo up the stairs and finally found my charm bracelet in her bureau drawer under a picture of Nelson Eddy.°

Nelson Eddy: a popular singer (1901–1967) who appeared in romantic musical films during the Depression era.

"So that's the way the land lies," says Uncle Rondo. There he was, piecing on the ham. "Well, Sister, I'll be glad to donate my army cot if you got any place to set it up, providing you'll leave right this minute and let me get some peace." Uncle Rondo was in France.

"Thank you kindly for the cot and 'peace' is hardly the word I would select if I had to resort to firecrackers at 6:30 A.M. in a young girl's bedroom," I says back to him. "And as to where I intend to go, you seem to forget my position as post-mistress of China Grove, Mississippi," I says. "I've always got the P.O."

Well, that made them all sit up and take notice.

I went out front and started digging up some four-o'clocks to plant around the P.O.

"Ah-ah-ah!" says Mama, raising the window. "Those happen to be my four-o'clocks. Everything planted in that star is mine. I've never known you to make anything grow in your life." 105

"Very well," I says. "But I take the fern. Even you, Mama, can't stand there and deny that I'm the one watered that fern. And I happen to know where I can send in a box top and get a packet of one thousand mixed seeds, no two the same kind, free."

"Oh, where?" Mama wants to know.

But I says, "Too late. You 'tend to your house, and I'll 'tend to mine. You hear things like that all the time if you know how to listen to the radio. Perfectly marvelous offers. Get anything you want free."

So I hope to tell you I marched in and got that radio, and they could of all bit a nail in two, especially Stella-Rondo, that it used to belong to, and she well knew she couldn't get it back, I'd sue for it like a shot. And I very politely took the sewing-machine motor I helped pay the most on to give Mama for Christmas back in 1929, and a good big calendar, with the first-aid remedies on it. The thermometer and the Hawaiian ukulele certainly were rightfully mine, and I stood on the step-ladder and got all my watermelon-rind preserves and every fruit and vegetable I'd put up, every jar. Then I began to pull the tacks out of the bluebird wall vases on the archway to the dining room.

"Who told you you could have those, Miss Priss?" says Mama, fanning as hard as she could. 110

"I bought 'em and I'll keep track of 'em," I says. "I'll tack 'em up one on each side the post-office window, and you can see 'em when you come to ask me for your mail, if you're so dead to see 'em."

"Not I! I'll never darken the door to that post office again if I live to be a hundred," Mama says. "Ungrateful child! After all the money we spent on you at the Normal."°

"Me either," says Stella-Rondo. "You can just let my mail lie there and *rot*, for all I care. I'll never come and relieve you of a single, solitary piece."

"I should worry," I says. "And who you think's going to sit down and write you all those big fat letters and postcards, by the way? Mr. Whitaker? Just be-

---

Normal: normal school, a two-year college for the training of elementary school teachers.

cause he was the only man ever dropped down in China Grove and you got him—unfairly—is he going to sit down and write you a lengthy correspondence after you come home giving no rhyme nor reason whatsoever for your separation and no explanation for the presence of that child? I may not have your brilliant mind, but I fail to see it."

So Mama says, "Sister, I've told you a thousand times that Stella-Rondo   115
simply got homesick, and this child is far too big to be hers," and she says, "Now, why don't you just sit down and play Casino?"

Then Shirley-T. sticks out her tongue at me in this perfectly horrible way. She has no more manners than the man in the moon. I told her she was going to cross her eyes like that some day and they'd stick.

"It's too late to stop me now," I says. "You should have tried that yesterday. I'm going to the P.O. and the only way you can possibly see me is to visit me there."

So Papa-Daddy says, "You'll never catch me setting foot in that post office, even if I should take a notion into my head to write a letter some place." He says, "I won't have you reachin' out of that little old window with a pair of shears and cuttin' off any beard of mine. I'm too smart for you!"

"We all are," says Stella-Rondo.

But I said, "If you're so smart, where's Mr. Whitaker?"   120

So then Uncle Rondo says, "I'll thank you from now on to stop reading all the orders I get on postcards and telling everybody in China Grove what you think is the matter with them," but I says, "I draw my own conclusions and will continue in the future to draw them." I says, "If people want to write their inmost secrets on penny postcards, there's nothing in the wide world you can do about it, Uncle Rondo."

"And if you think we'll ever *write* another postcard you're sadly mistaken," says Mama.

"Cutting off your nose to spite your face then," I says. "But if you're all determined to have no more to do with the U.S. mail, think of this: What will Stella-Rondo do now, if she wants to tell Mr. Whitaker to come after her?"

"Wah!" says Stella-Rondo. I knew she'd cry. She had a conniption fit right there in the kitchen.

"It will be interesting to see how long she holds out," I says. "And now—I   125
am leaving."

"Good-bye," says Uncle Rondo.

"Oh, I declare," says Mama, "to think that a family of mine should quarrel on the Fourth of July, or the day after, over Stella-Rondo leaving old Mr. Whitaker and having the sweetest little adopted child! It looks like we'd all be glad!"

"Wah!" says Stella-Rondo, and has a fresh conniption fit.

"*He* left *her*—you mark my words," I says. "That's Mr. Whitaker. I know Mr. Whitaker. After all, I knew him first. I said from the beginning he'd up and leave her. I foretold every single thing that's happened."

"Where did he go?" asks Mama.   130

"Probably to the North Pole, if he knows what's good for him," I says.

But Stella-Rondo just bawled and wouldn't say another word. She flew to her room and slammed the door.

"Now look what you've gone and done, Sister," says Mama. "You go apologize."

"I haven't got time, I'm leaving," I says.

"Well, what are you waiting around for?" asks Uncle Rondo.   135

So I just picked up the kitchen clock and marched off, without saying "Kiss my foot," or anything, and never did tell Stella-Rondo good-bye.

There was a nigger girl going along on a little wagon right in front.

"Nigger girl," I says, "come help me haul these things down the hill, I'm going to live in the post office."

Took her nine trips in her express wagon. Uncle Rondo came out on the porch and threw her a nickel.

And that's the last I've laid eyes on any of my family or my family laid eyes   140
on me for five solid days and nights. Stella-Rondo may be telling the most horrible tales in the world about Mr. Whitaker, but I haven't heard them. As I tell everybody, I draw my own conclusions.

But oh, I like it here. It's ideal, as I've been saying. You see, I've got everything cater-cornered, the way I like it. Hear the radio? All the war news. Radio, sewing machine, book ends, ironing board and that great big piano lamp— peace, that's what I like. Butter-bean vines planted all along the front where the strings are.

Of course, there's not much mail. My family are naturally the main people in China Grove, and if they prefer to vanish from the face of the earth, for all the mail they get or the mail they write, why, I'm not going to open my mouth. Some of the folks here in town are taking up for me and some turned against me. I know which is which. There are always people who will quit buying stamps just to get on the right side of Papa-Daddy.

But here I am, and here I'll stay. I want the world to know I'm happy.

And if Stella-Rondo should come to me this minute, on bended knees, and *attempt* to explain the incidents of her life with Mr. Whitaker, I'd simply put my fingers in both my ears and refuse to listen.

QUESTIONS

1. Can we equate the narrator's voice with Welty's? What clues does the author give that Sister's opinions are not her own?
2. What statements does the narrator make that seem unreliable?
3. Describe Sister's personality. Is she slightly crazy or is her odd behavior a justified revolt against her family?
4. Sister uses the word "nigger" several times in the story, and she is clearly a racist. What does her attitude toward African Americans tell you about the time and place of the story?
5. Why does Sister fight so much with her family?

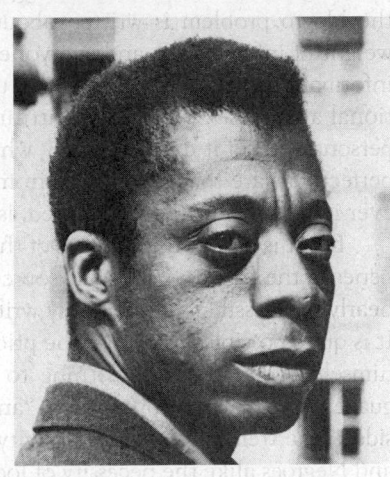

James Baldwin

James Baldwin on Writing

RACE AND THE AFRICAN AMERICAN WRITER   1955

I was born in Harlem thirty-one years ago. I began plotting novels at about the time I learned to read. The story of my childhood is the usual bleak fantasy, and we can dismiss it with the unrestrained observation that I certainly would not consider living it again. . . .

Any writer, I suppose, feels that the world into which he was born is nothing less than a conspiracy against the cultivation of his talent—which attitude certainly has a great deal to support it. On the other hand, it is only because the world looks on his talent with such a frightening indifference that the artist is compelled to make his talent important. So that any writer, looking back over even so short a span of time as I am here forced to assess, finds that the things which hurt him and the things which helped him cannot be divorced from each other; he could be helped in a certain way only because he was hurt in a certain way; and his help is simply to be enabled to move from one conundrum to the next—one is tempted to say that he moves from one disaster to the next. When one begins looking for influences one finds them by the score. I haven't thought much about my own, not enough anyway; I hazard that the King James Bible, the rhetoric of the store-front church, something ironic and violent and perpetually understated in Negro speech—and something of Dickens' love for bravura—have something to do with me today; but I wouldn't stake my life on it. Likewise, innumerable people have helped me in many ways; but finally, I suppose, the most difficult (and most rewarding) thing in my life has been the fact that I was born a Negro and was forced, therefore, to effect some kind of truce with this reality. (Truce, by the way, is the best one can hope for.)

One of the difficulties about being a Negro writer (and this is not special pleading, since I don't mean to suggest that he has it worse than anybody else) is that the Negro problem is written about so widely. The bookshelves groan under the weight of information, and everyone therefore considers himself informed. And this information, furthermore, operates usually (generally, popularly) to reinforce traditional attitudes. Of traditional attitudes there are only two—For or Against—and I, personally, find it difficult to say which attitude has caused me the most pain. I am perfectly aware that the change from ill-will to good-will, however motivated, however imperfect, however expressed, is better than no change at all.

But it is part of the business of the writer—as I see it—to examine attitudes, to go beneath the surface, to tap the source. From this point of view the Negro problem is nearly inaccessible. It is not only written about so widely; it is written about so badly. It is quite possible to say that the price a Negro pays for becoming articulate is to find himself, at length, with nothing to be articulate about. ("You taught me the language," says Caliban to Prospero, "and my profit on't is I know how to curse.") Consider: The tremendous social activity that this problem generates imposes on whites and Negroes alike the necessity of looking forward, of working to bring about a better day. This is fine, it keeps the waters troubled; it is all, indeed, that has made possible the Negro's progress. Nevertheless, social affairs are not generally speaking the writer's prime concern, whether they ought to be or not; it is absolutely necessary that he establish between himself and these affairs a distance that will allow, at least, for clarity, so that before he can look forward in any meaningful sense, he must first be allowed to take a long look back. In the context of the Negro problem neither whites nor blacks, for excellent reasons of their own, have the faintest desire to look back; but I think that the past is all that makes the present coherent, and further, that the past will remain horrible for exactly as long as we refuse to assess it honestly.

I know, in any case, that the most crucial time in my own development came when I was forced to recognize that I was a kind of bastard of the West; when I followed the line of my past I did not find myself in Europe but in Africa. And this meant that in some subtle way, in a really profound way, I brought to Shakespeare, Bach, Rembrandt, to the stones of Paris, to the cathedral at Chartres, and to the Empire State Building, a special attitude. These were not really my creations, they did not contain my history; I might search in them in vain forever for any reflection of myself. I was an interloper; this was not my heritage. At the same time I had no other heritage which I could possibly hope to use—I had certainly been unfitted for the jungle or the tribe. I would have to appropriate these white centuries, I would have to make them mine—I would have to accept my special attitude, my special place in this scheme—otherwise I would have no place in *any* scheme. What was the most difficult was the fact that I was forced to admit something I had always hidden from myself, which the American Negro has had to hide from himself as the price of his public progress; that I hated and feared the world. And this meant, not only that I thus gave the world an altogether murderous power over me, but also that in such a self-destroying limbo I could never hope to write.

One writes out of one thing only—one's own experience. Everything depends on how relentlessly one forces from this experience the last drop, sweet or bitter, it can possibly give. This is the only real concern of the artist, to recreate out of the disorder of life that order which is art. The difficulty then, for me, of being a Negro writer was the fact that I was, in effect, prohibited from examining my own experience too closely by the tremendous demands and the very real dangers of my social situation.

I don't think the dilemma outlined above is uncommon. I do think, since writers work in the disastrously explicit medium of language, that it goes a little way towards explaining why, out of the enormous resources of Negro speech and life, and despite the example of Negro music, prose written by Negroes has been generally speaking so pallid and so harsh. I have not written about being a Negro at such length because I expect that to be my only subject, but only because it was the gate I had to unlock before I could hope to write about anything else.

From "Autobiographical Notes"

◄■□►WRITING CRITICALLY◄■►

How Point of View Shapes a Story

The point of view from which a narrative work is told does not merely affect the story; it is an important part of the story. From the first sentence until the final word, the point of view shapes what the reader experiences in a work of fiction.

Often the point of view also demonstrates how well readers will understand a story's theme. A third-person omniscient point of view, for example, may give the reader a sense of authority and stability that makes the narrative seem reliable. A first-person narrator, however, often suggests a certain bias, especially when the narrator describes events in which he or she played a part. In such cases the narrator sometimes has an obvious interest in the audience's accepting his or her particular version of the story as truth.

In analyzing a story, always determine the point of view from which it is narrated. If the tale is told by a participant in the action, question the speaker's motivation. What is the speaker's main reason for telling the story? Does he or she have something to gain by the version of the facts presented? Sometimes the narrator's special point of view greatly enriches a story that might not seem as memorable from another narrative angle. Do we gain something from the speaker's perspective that we might not discover elsewhere? Understanding the limits and rewards of a narrator's point of view is a key to interpreting everything a story says.

WRITING ASSIGNMENT

Select a story from this chapter (or elsewhere in the book) and discuss how the author's choice of a particular point of view helps communicate a central theme of the tale. Develop a clear argument to show how the narrator's point of view is essential to the audience's recognizing and understanding the theme. Support your argument with specific observations and analysis.

Quote and document according to the guidelines in the chapter "Writing About Literature" at the back of the book.

Possible selections to choose from in Chapter Eleven, "Stories for Further Reading," are Ambrose Bierce's "An Occurrence at Owl Creek Bridge," Charlotte Perkins Gilman's "The Yellow Wallpaper," and Zora Neale Hurston's "Sweat," or in Chapter One, John Updike's "A & P."

FURTHER SUGGESTIONS FOR WRITING

1. Here is a writing exercise to help you sense what a difference a point of view makes. Write a short statement from the point of view of one of these characters: William Faulkner's Homer Barron (on "My Affair with Miss Emily"); John Updike's store manager Lengel (on "What's Wrong with That Kid Sammy Anyway?")

2. Write a brief narrative account of a decisive moment in your life—one that changed your outlook or your future—from two quite different, contrasting points of view. One instance: a memory of buying a first car, told in two ways: from (1) the first-person point of view of the buyer and (2) the third-person point of view of a worried parent or a gloating car dealer. Another example: An account of meeting a person who profoundly affected your life, from (1) your point of view and then (2) the point of view of that other person.

3. Topic for an essay of two or three paragraphs: How William Faulkner Sees North and South in "A Rose for Emily."

4. Taking examples from short stories in other chapters, point out some differences between male and female ways of looking at things. Some stories especially to consider: "A & P," "The Jilting of Granny Weatherall," "The Five-Forty-Eight," "First Confession," and "I Stand Here Ironing." (Note: The fact that a character holds a certain attitude in a specific situation doesn't oblige you to argue that such an attitude is universally held by women or men.)

5. Adopt the point of view of a naive, innocent commentator—either a younger, less-knowing version of yourself, or some imagined character. From this point of view, discuss a proposed ban on nuclear weapons, the case for legislation against the sale of pornography, or another issue in the news. Sound off like a true ignoramus. An effective paper will make clear to your reader that your speaker is full of malarkey. (This task means that you, the knowing writer, and not the uninformed speaker who is your mask, will need to know something about your subject.)

6. Choosing one of the "Stories for Further Reading" in Chapter Eleven, briefly describe whatever point of view you find in it. Then, in a paragraph or two, explain why this angle of vision seems right and fitting to the telling of this story. If you like, you may argue that the story might be told more effectively from some other point of view.

7. Write a one-paragraph story in the first person. Some recent small event in your life is a possible subject. Then rewrite your story from the *objective*, or "fly-on-the-wall," point of view. (See the passage by Dashiell Hammett at the beginning of Chapter Two for an illustration.) Following your two terse stories, write a comment summing up what this exercise told you about point of view.

3 Character

From popular fiction and drama, both classic and contemporary, we are acquainted with many stereotyped characters. Called **stock characters,** they are often known by some outstanding trait or traits: the *bragging* soldier of Greek and Roman comedy, the Prince *Charming* of fairy tales, the *mad* scientist of horror movies, the *fearlessly reckless* police detective of urban action films, the *greedy* explorer of Tarzan films, the *brilliant but alcoholic* brain surgeon of medical thrillers on television. Stock characters are especially convenient for writers of commercial fiction: they require little detailed portraiture, for we already know them well. Most writers of the literary story, however, attempt to create characters who strike us not as stereotypes but as unique individuals. Although stock characters tend to have single dominant virtues and vices, characters in the finest contemporary short stories tend to have many facets, like people we meet.

A **character,** then, is presumably an imagined person who inhabits a story—although that simple definition may admit to a few exceptions. In George Stewart's novel *Storm,* the protagonist is the wind; in Richard Adams's *Watership Down,* the main characters are rabbits. But usually we recognize, in the main characters of a story, human personalities that become familiar to us. If the story seems "true to life," we generally find that its characters act in a reasonably consistent manner and that the author has provided them with **motivation:** sufficient reason to behave as they do. Should a character behave in a sudden and unexpected way, seeming to deny what we have been told about his or her nature or personality, we trust that there was a reason for this behavior and that sooner or later we will discover it. This is not to claim that *all* authors insist that their characters behave with absolute consistency, for (as we shall see later in this chapter) some contemporary stories feature characters who sometimes act without apparent reason. Nor can we say that, in good fiction, characters never change or develop. In *A Christmas Carol,* Charles Dickens tells how Ebenezer Scrooge, a tightfisted miser, reforms overnight, suddenly gives to the poor, and endeavors to assist his clerk's struggling family. But Dickens amply demonstrates why Scrooge had such a change of heart: four ghostly visitors, stirring kind memories the old miser had forgotten and also warning him of the probable consequences of his habits, provide the character (and hence the story) with adequate motivation.

To borrow the useful terms of the English novelist E. M. Forster, characters may seem **flat** or **round,** depending on whether a writer sketches or sculpts them. A flat character has only one outstanding trait or feature, or at most a few distinguishing marks: for example, the familiar stock character of the mad scientist, with his lust for absolute power and his crazily gleaming eyes. Flat characters, however, need not be stock characters: in all of literature there is probably only one Tiny Tim, though his functions in *A Christmas Carol* are mainly to invoke blessings and to remind others of their Christian duties. Some writers, notably Balzac, who peopled his many novels with hosts of characters, try to distinguish the flat ones by giving each a single odd physical feature or mannerism—a nervous twitch, a piercing gaze, an obsessive fondness for oysters. Round characters, however, present us with more facets—that is, their authors portray them in greater depth and in more generous detail. Such a round character may appear to us only as he appears to the other characters in the story. If their views of him differ, we will see him from more than one side. In other stories, we enter a character's mind and come to know him through his own thoughts, feelings, and perceptions. By the time we finish reading James Baldwin's "Sonny's Blues" (in Chapter Two), we are well acquainted with the central characters and find them amply three-dimensional.

Flat characters tend to stay the same throughout a story, but round characters often change—learn or become enlightened, grow or deteriorate. In William Faulkner's "Barn Burning" (Chapter Five), the boy Sarty Snopes, driven to defy his proud and violent father, becomes at the story's end more knowing and more mature. (Some critics call a fixed character **static;** a changing one, **dynamic.**) This is not to damn a flat character as an inferior work of art. In most fiction—even the greatest—minor characters tend to be flat instead of round. Why? Rounding them would cost time and space; and so enlarged, they might only distract us from the main characters.

"A character, first of all, is the noise of his name," according to novelist William Gass.[1] Names, chosen artfully, can indicate natures. A simple illustration is the completely virtuous Squire Allworthy, the foster father in *Tom Jones* by Henry Fielding. Subtler, perhaps, is the custom of giving a character a name that makes an **allusion:** a reference to some famous person, place, or thing in history, in other fiction, or in actuality. For his central characters in *Moby-Dick*, Herman Melville chose names from the Old Testament, calling his tragic and domineering Ahab after a Biblical tyrant who came to a bad end, and his wandering narrator Ishmael after a Biblical outcast. Whether or not it includes an allusion, a good name often reveals the character of the character. Charles Dickens, a vigorous and richly suggestive christener, named a charming confidence man Mr. Jingle (suggesting something jingly, light, and superficially pleasant), named a couple of shyster lawyers Dodgson and Fogg (suggesting dodging evasiveness and foglike obfuscation), and named two heartless educators, who grimly drill their schoolchildren in "hard facts," Gradgind and M'Choakumchild. Henry James, who so loved names that he kept lists of them for characters he

[1]"The Concept of Character in Fiction," *Fiction and the Figures of Life* (New York: Knopf, 1970).

might someday conceive, chose for a sensitive, cultured gentleman the name of Lambert Strether; for a down-to-earth, benevolent individual, the name of Mrs. Bread. (But James may have wished to indicate that names cannot be identified with people absolutely, in giving the fragile, considerate heroine of *The Spoils of Poynton* the harsh-sounding name of Fleda Vetch.)

Instead of a hero, many a recent novel has featured an **antihero:** a protagonist conspicuously lacking in one or more of the usual attributes of a traditional hero (bravery, skill, idealism, sense of purpose). The antihero is an ordinary, unglorious citizen of the modern world, usually drawn (according to Sean O'Faolain) as someone "groping, puzzled, cross, mocking, frustrated, and isolated."[2] (Obviously, there are antiheroines, too: Ellen, for instance, is the aimlessly drifting central character of Edna O'Brien's novel *August Is a Wicked Month*.) If epic poets once drew their heroes as decisive leaders of their people, embodying their people's highest ideals, antiheroes tend to be loners, without perfections, just barely able to survive. Antiheroes lack "character," as defined by psychologist Anthony Quinton to mean a person's conduct or "persistence and consistency in seeking to realize his long-term aims."[3] A gulf separates Leopold Bloom, antihero of James Joyce's novel *Ulysses*, from the hero of the Greek *Odyssey*. In Homer's epic, Ulysses wanders the Mediterranean, battling monsters and overcoming enchantments. In Joyce's novel, Bloom wanders the littered streets of Dublin, peddling advertising space. Meursault, the title character of Albert Camus's novel *The Stranger*, is so alienated from his own life that he is unmoved at the news of his mother's death.

Evidently, not only fashions in heroes but also attitudes toward human nature have undergone change. In the eighteenth century, Scottish philosopher David Hume argued that the nature of an individual is relatively fixed and unalterable. Hume mentioned, however, a few exceptions: "A person of an obliging disposition gives a peevish answer; but he has the toothache or has not dined. A stupid fellow discovers an obvious alacrity in his carriage; but he has met with a sudden piece of good fortune." For a long time after Hume, novelists and short-story writers seem to have assumed that characters nearly always behave in a predictable fashion and that their actions ought to be consistent with their personalities. Now and again, a writer differed: Jane Austen in *Pride and Prejudice* has her protagonist Elizabeth Bennet remark to the citified Mr. Darcy, who fears that life in the country cannot be amusing, "But people themselves alter so much, that there is something to be observed in them forever."

Many contemporary writers of fiction would deny even that people have definite selves to alter. Following Sigmund Freud and other modern psychologists, they assume that a large part of human behavior is shaped in the unconscious—that, for instance, a person might fear horses, not because of a basically timid nature, but because of unconscious memories of having been nearly trampled by a horse when a child. To some writers it now appears that what Hume called a "disposition" (what we call a "personality") is more vulnerable to change from such causes as age, disease,

[2]*The Vanishing Hero* (Boston: Little, 1957).
[3]"The Continuity of Persons," *Times Literary Supplement*, 27 July 1973.

neurosis, psychic shock, or brainwashing than was once believed. Hence, some characters in modern fiction appear to be shifting bundles of impulses. "You mustn't look in my novel for the old stable ego of character," wrote D. H. Lawrence to a friend about *The Rainbow;* and in that novel and others Lawrence demonstrated his view of individuals as bits of one vast Life Force, spurred to act by incomprehensible passions and urges—the "dark gods" in them. The idea of the **gratuitous act,** a deed without cause or motive, is explored in André Gide's novel *Lafcadio's Adventures,* in which an ordinary young man without homicidal tendencies abruptly and for no reason pushes a stranger from a speeding train. The usual limits of character are playfully violated by Virginia Woolf in *Orlando,* a novel whose protagonist, defying time, lives right on from Elizabethan days into the present, changing in midstory from a man into a woman. Characterization, as practiced by nineteenth-century novelists, almost entirely disappears in Franz Kafka's *The Castle,* whose protagonist has no home, no family, no definite appearance—not even a name, just the initial K. Characters are things of the past, insists the contemporary French novelist Alain Robbe-Grillet. Still, many writers of fiction go on portraying them.

Katherine Anne Porter

THE JILTING OF GRANNY WEATHERALL
1930

Katherine Anne Porter (1890–1980) was born in Indian Creek, Texas. Her mother died when she was two, and Porter was raised by a grandmother who surrounded the growing girl with books. At sixteen she ran away from school and soon married a railway clerk in Louisiana. Three years later, she divorced her husband and began supporting herself as a reporter in Chicago, Denver, and Fort Worth, and sometimes as an actress and ballad singer while traveling through the South. Sojourns in Europe and in Mexico supplied her with material for some of her finest stories. Her brilliant, sensitive short fiction, first collected in Flowering Judas *(1930), won her a high reputation. Her one novel,* Ship of Fools *(1962), with which she had struggled for twenty years, received harsh critical notices, but proved a commercial success. Made into a movie, it ended Porter's lifelong struggle to earn a living. In 1965 her* Collected Stories *received a Pulitzer Prize and a National Book Award.*

Katherine Anne Porter (© Jill Krementz, Inc.)

She flicked her wrist neatly out of Doctor Harry's pudgy careful fingers and pulled the sheet up to her chin. The brat ought to be in knee breeches. Doctoring around the country with spectacles on his nose! "Get along now, take your schoolbooks and go. There's nothing wrong with me."

Doctor Harry spread a warm paw like a cushion on her forehead where the forked green vein danced and made her eyelids twitch. "Now, now, be a good girl, and we'll have you up in no time."

"That's no way to speak to a woman nearly eighty years old just because she's down. I'd have you respect your elders, young man."

"Well, Missy, excuse me." Doctor Harry patted her cheek. "But I've got to warn you, haven't I? You're a marvel, but you must be careful or you're going to be good and sorry."

"Don't tell me what I'm going to be. I'm on my feet now, morally speaking.   5 It's Cornelia. I had to go to bed to get rid of her."

Her bones felt loose, and floated around in her skin, and Doctor Harry floated like a balloon around the foot of the bed. He floated and pulled down his waistcoat and swung his glasses on a cord. "Well, stay where you are, it certainly can't hurt you."

"Get along and doctor your sick," said Granny Weatherall. "Leave a well woman alone. I'll call for you when I want you. . . . Where were you forty years ago when I pulled through milk-leg and double pneumonia? You weren't even born. Don't let Cornelia lead you on," she shouted, because Doctor Harry appeared to float up to the ceiling and out. "I pay my own bills, and I don't throw my money away on nonsense!"

She meant to wave good-by, but it was too much trouble. Her eyes closed of themselves, it was like a dark curtain drawn around the bed. The pillow rose and floated under her, pleasant as a hammock in a light wind. She listened to the leaves rustling outside the window. No, somebody was swishing newspapers: no, Cornelia and Doctor Harry were whispering together. She leaped broad awake, thinking they whispered in her ear.

"She was never like this, *never* like this!" "Well, what can we expect?" "Yes, eighty years old. . . ."

Well, and what if she was? She still had ears. It was like Cornelia to whisper   10 around doors. She always kept things secret in such a public way. She was always being tactful and kind. Cornelia was dutiful; that was the trouble with her. Dutiful and good: "So good and dutiful," said Granny, "that I'd like to spank her." She saw herself spanking Cornelia and making a fine job of it.

"What'd you say, Mother?"

Granny felt her face tying up in hard knots.

"Can't a body think, I'd like to know?"

"I thought you might want something."

"I do. I want a lot of things. First off, go away and don't whisper."   15

She lay and drowsed, hoping in her sleep that the children would keep out and let her rest a minute. It had been a long day. Not that she was tired. It was always pleasant to snatch a minute now and then. There was always so much to be done, let me see: tomorrow.

Tomorrow was far away and there was nothing to trouble about. Things were finished somehow when the time came; thank God there was always a little margin over for peace: then a person could spread out the plan of life and tuck in the edges orderly. It was good to have everything clean and folded away, with the hair brushes and tonic bottles sitting straight on the white embroidered linen: the day started without fuss and the pantry shelves laid out with rows of jelly glasses and brown jugs and white stone-china jars with blue whirligigs and words painted on them: coffee, tea, sugar, ginger, cinnamon, allspice: and the bronze clock with the lion on top nicely dusted off. The dust that lion could collect in twenty-four hours! The box in the attic with all those letters tied up, well, she'd have to go through that tomorrow. All those letters—George's letters and John's letters and her letters to them both—lying around for the children to find afterwards made her uneasy. Yes, that would be tomorrow's business. No use to let them know how silly she had been once.

While she was rummaging around she found death in her mind and it felt clammy and unfamiliar. She had spent so much time preparing for death there was no need for bringing it up again. Let it take care of itself now. When she was sixty she had felt very old, finished, and went around making farewell trips to see her children and grandchildren, with a secret in her mind: This is the very last of your mother, children! Then she made her will and came down with a long fever. That was all just a notion like a lot of other things, but it was lucky too, for she had once for all got over the idea of dying for a long time. Now she couldn't be worried. She hoped she had better sense now. Her father had lived to be one hundred and two years old and had drunk a noggin of strong hot toddy on his last birthday. He told the reporters it was his daily habit, and he owed his long life to it. He had made quite a scandal and was very pleased about it. She believed she'd just plague Cornelia a little.

"Cornelia! Cornelia!" No footsteps, but a sudden hand on her cheek. "Bless you, where have you been?"

"Here, Mother."

"Well, Cornelia, I want a noggin of hot toddy."

"Are you cold, darling?"

"I'm chilly, Cornelia. Lying in bed stops the circulation. I must have told you that a thousand times."

Well, she could just hear Cornelia telling her husband that Mother was getting a little childish and they'd have to humor her. The thing that most annoyed her was that Cornelia thought she was deaf, dumb, and blind. Little hasty glances and tiny gestures tossed around her and over her head saying, "Don't cross her, let her have her way, she's eighty years old," and she sitting there as if she lived in a thin glass cage. Sometimes Granny almost made up her mind to pack up and move back to her own house where nobody could remind her every minute that she was old. Wait, wait, Cornelia, till your own children whisper behind your back!

In her day she had kept a better house and had got more work done. She wasn't too old yet for Lydia to be driving eighty miles for advice when one of the children jumped the track, and Jimmy still dropped in and talked things over: "Now, Mammy, you've a good business head, I want to know what you think of this? . . ." Old. Cornelia couldn't change the furniture around without asking. Little things, little things! They had been so sweet when they were little.

Granny wished the old days were back again with the children young and everything to be done over. It had been a hard pull, but not too much for her. When she thought of all the food she had cooked, and all the clothes she had cut and sewed, and all the gardens she had made—well, the children showed it. There they were, made out of her, and they couldn't get away from that. Sometimes she wanted to see John again and point to them and say, Well, I didn't do so badly, did I? But that would have to wait. That was for tomorrow. She used to think of him as a man, but now all the children were older than their father, and he would be a child beside her if she saw him now. It seemed strange and there was something wrong in the idea. Why, he couldn't possibly recognize her. She had fenced in a hundred acres once, digging the post holes herself and clamping the wires with just a negro boy to help. That changed a woman. John would be looking for a young woman with the peaked Spanish comb in her hair and the painted fan. Digging post holes changed a woman. Riding country roads in the winter when women had their babies was another thing: sitting up nights with sick horses and sick negroes and sick children and hardly ever losing one. John, I hardly ever lost one of them! John would see that in a minute, that would be something he could understand, she wouldn't have to explain anything!

It made her feel like rolling up her sleeves and putting the whole place to rights again. No matter if Cornelia was determined to be everywhere at once, there were a great many things left undone on this place. She would start tomorrow and do them. It was good to be strong enough for everything, even if all you made melted and changed and slipped under your hands, so that by the time you finished you almost forgot what you were working for. What was it I set out to do? she asked herself intently, but she could not remember. A fog rose over the valley, she saw it marching across the creek swallowing the trees and moving up the hill like an army of ghosts. Soon it would be at the near edge of the orchard, and then it was time to go in and light the lamps. Come in, children, don't stay out in the night air.

Lighting the lamps had been beautiful. The children huddled up to her and breathed like little calves waiting at the bars in the twilight. Their eyes followed the match and watched the flame rise and settle in a blue curve, then they moved away from her. The lamp was lit, they didn't have to be scared and hang on to mother any more. Never, never, never more. God, for all my life I thank Thee. Without Thee, my God, I could never have done it. Hail, Mary, full of grace.

I want you to pick all the fruit this year and see that nothing is wasted. There's always someone who can use it. Don't let good things rot for want of using. You waste life when you waste good food. Don't let things get lost. It's bitter to lose things. Now, don't let me get to thinking, not when I am tired and taking a little nap before supper. . . .

The pillow rose about her shoulders and pressed against her heart and the memory was being squeezed out of it: oh, push down the pillow, somebody: it would smother her if she tried to hold it. Such a fresh breeze blowing and such a green day with no threats in it. But he had not come, just the same. What does a woman do when she has put on the white veil and set out the white cake for a man and he doesn't come? She tried to remember. No, I swear he never harmed me but in that. He never harmed me but in that . . . and what if he did? There was the day, the day, but a whirl of dark smoke rose and covered it, crept up and over into the bright field where everything was planted so carefully in orderly rows. That was hell, she knew hell when she saw it. For sixty years she had prayed against remembering him and against losing her soul in the deep pit of hell, and now the two things were mingled in one and the thought of him was a smoky cloud from hell that moved and crept in her head when she had just got rid of Doctor Harry and was trying to rest a minute. Wounded vanity, Ellen, said a sharp voice in the top of her mind. Don't let your wounded vanity get the upper hand of you. Plenty of girls get jilted. You were jilted, weren't you? Then stand up to it. Her eyelids wavered and let in streamers of blue-gray light like tissue paper over her eyes. She must get up and pull the shades down or she'd never sleep. She was in bed again and the shades were not down. How could that happen? Better turn over, hide from the light, sleeping in the light gave you nightmares. "Mother, how do you feel now?" and a stinging wetness on her fore-head. But I don't like having my face washed in cold water!

Hapsy? George? Lydia? Jimmy? No, Cornelia, and her features were swollen   30
and full of little puddles. "They're coming, darling, they'll all be here soon." Go wash your face, child, you look funny.

Instead of obeying, Cornelia knelt down and put her head on the pillow. She seemed to be talking but there was no sound. "Well, are you tongue-tied? Whose birthday is it? Are you going to give a party?"

Cornelia's mouth moved urgently in strange shapes. "Don't do that, you bother me, daughter."

"Oh, no, Mother. Oh, no. . . ."

Nonsense. It was strange about children. They disputed your every word. "No what, Cornelia?"

"Here's Doctor Harry."   35

"I won't see that boy again. He just left three minutes ago."

"That was this morning, Mother. It's night now. Here's the nurse."

"This is Doctor Harry, Mrs. Weatherall. I never saw you look so young and happy!"

"Ah, I'll never be young again—but I'd be happy if they'd let me lie in peace and get rested."

She thought she spoke up loudly, but no one answered. A warm weight on   40
her forehead, a warm bracelet on her wrist, and a breeze went on whispering, trying to tell her something. A shuffle of leaves in the everlasting hand of God. He blew on them and they danced and rattled. "Mother, don't mind, we're going to give you a little hypodermic." "Look here, daughter, how do ants get in this bed? I saw sugar ants yesterday." Did you send for Hapsy too?

It was Hapsy she really wanted. She had to go a long way back through a great many rooms to find Hapsy standing with a baby on her arm. She seemed to herself to be Hapsy also, and the baby on Hapsy's arm was Hapsy and himself and herself, all at once, and there was no surprise in the meeting. Then Hapsy melted from within and turned flimsy as gray gauze and the baby was a gauzy shadow, and Hapsy came up close and said, "I thought you'd never come," and looked at her very searchingly and said, "You haven't changed a bit!" They leaned forward to kiss, when Cornelia began whispering from a long way off, "Oh, is there anything you want to tell me? Is there anything I can do for you?"

Yes, she had changed her mind after sixty years and she would like to see George. I want you to find George. Find him and be sure to tell him I forgot him. I want him to know I had my husband just the same and my children and my house like any other woman. A good house too and a good husband that I loved and fine children out of him. Better than I hoped for even. Tell him I was given back everything he took away and more. Oh, no, oh, God, no, there was something else besides the house and the man and the children. Oh, surely they were not all? What was it? Something not given back. . . . Her breath crowded down under her ribs and grew into a monstrous frightening shape with cutting edges; it bored up into her head, and the agony was unbelievable: Yes, John, get the Doctor now, no more talk, my time has come.

When this one was born it should be the last. The last. It should have been born first, for it was the one she had truly wanted. Everything came in good time. Nothing left out, left over. She was strong, in three days she would be as well as ever. Better. A woman needed milk in her to have her full health.

"Mother, do you hear me?"

"I've been telling you—" 45

"Mother, Father Connolly's here."

"I went to Holy Communion only last week. Tell him I'm not so sinful as all that."

"Father just wants to speak to you."

He could speak as much as he pleased. It was like him to drop in and inquire about her soul as if it were a teething baby, and then stay on for a cup of tea and a round of cards and gossip. He always had a funny story of some sort, usually about an Irishman who made his little mistakes and confessed them, and the point lay in some absurd thing he would blurt out in the confessional showing his struggles between native piety and original sin. Granny felt easy about her soul. Cornelia, where are your manners? Give Father Connolly a chair. She had her secret comfortable understanding with a few favorite saints who cleared a straight road to God for her. All as surely signed and sealed as the papers for the new Forty Acres. Forever . . . heirs and assigns forever. Since the day the wedding cake was not cut, but thrown out and wasted. The whole bottom dropped out of the world, and there she was blind and sweating with nothing under her feet and the walls falling away. His hand had caught her under the breast, she had not fallen, there was the freshly polished floor with the green rug on it, just as before. He had cursed like a sailor's parrot and said, "I'll kill him for you." Don't lay a hand on him, for my sake leave something to God. "Now, Ellen, you must believe what I tell you. . . ."

So there was nothing, nothing to worry about any more, except sometimes 50
in the night one of the children screamed in a nightmare, and they both hustled

out shaking and hunting for the matches and calling, "There, wait a minute, here we are!" John, get the doctor now, Hapsy's time has come. But there was Hapsy standing by the bed in a white cap. "Cornelia, tell Hapsy to take off her cap. I can't see her plain."

Her eyes opened very wide and the room stood out like a picture she had seen somewhere. Dark colors with the shadows rising towards the ceiling in long angles. The tall black dresser gleamed with nothing on it but John's picture, enlarged from a little one, with John's eyes very black when they should have been blue. You never saw him, so how do you know how he looked? But the man insisted the copy was perfect, it was very rich and handsome. For a picture, yes, but it's not my husband. The table by the bed had a linen cover and a candle and a crucifix. The light was blue from Cornelia's silk lampshades. No sort of light at all, just frippery. You had to live forty years with kerosene lamps to appreciate honest electricity. She felt very strong and she saw Doctor Harry with a rosy nimbus around him.

"You look like a saint, Doctor Harry, and I vow that's as near as you'll ever come to it."

"She's saying something."

"I heard you, Cornelia. What's all this carrying-on?"

"Father Connolly's saying—"

Cornelia's voice staggered and bumped like a cart in a bad road. It rounded corners and turned back again and arrived nowhere. Granny stepped up in the cart very lightly and reached for the reins, but a man sat beside her and she knew him by his hands, driving the cart. She did not look in his face, for she knew without seeing, but looked instead down the road where the trees leaned over and bowed to each other and a thousand birds were singing a Mass. She felt like singing too, but she put her hand in the bosom of her dress and pulled out a rosary, and Father Connolly murmured Latin in a very solemn voice and tickled her feet. My God, will you stop that nonsense? I'm a married woman. What if he did run away and leave me to face the priest by myself? I found another a whole world better. I wouldn't have exchanged my husband for anybody except St. Michael himself, and you may tell him that for me with a thank you in the bargain.

Light flashed on her closed eyelids, and a deep roaring shook her. Cornelia, is that lightning? I hear thunder. There's going to be a storm. Close all the windows. Call the children in. . . ." Mother, here we are, all of us." "Is that you, Hapsy?" "Oh, no, I'm Lydia. We drove as fast as we could." Their faces drifted above her, drifted away. The rosary fell out of her hands and Lydia put it back. Jimmy tried to help, their hands fumbled together, and Granny closed two fingers around Jimmy's thumb. Beads wouldn't do, it must be something alive. She was so amazed her thoughts ran round and round. So, my dear Lord, this is my death and I wasn't even thinking about it. My children have come to see me die. But I can't, it's not time. Oh, I always hated surprises. I wanted to give Cornelia the amethyst set—Cornelia, you're to have the amethyst set, but Hapsy's to wear it when she wants, and, Doctor Harry, do shut up. Nobody sent for you. Oh, my dear Lord, do wait a minute. I meant to do something about the Forty Acres, Jimmy doesn't need it and Lydia will later on, with that worthless husband of hers. I meant to finish the altar cloth and send six bottles of wine to Sister Borgia for her dyspepsia. I want to send six bottles of wine to Sister Borgia, Father Connolly, now don't let me forget.

Cornelia's voice made short turns and tilted over and crashed, "Oh, Mother, oh, Mother, oh, Mother. . . ."

"I'm not going, Cornelia. I'm taken by surprise. I can't go."

You'll see Hapsy again. What about her? "I thought you'd never come." 60 Granny made a long journey outward, looking for Hapsy. What if I don't find her? What then? Her heart sank down and down, there was no bottom to death, she couldn't come to the end of it. The blue light from Cornelia's lampshade drew into a tiny point in the center of her brain, it flickered and winked like an eye, quietly it fluttered and dwindled. Granny lay curled down within herself, amazed and watchful, staring at the point of light that was herself; her body was now only a deeper mass of shadow in an endless darkness and this darkness would curl around the light and swallow it up. God, give a sign!

For the second time there was no sign. Again no bridegroom and the priest in the house. She could not remember any other sorrow because this grief wiped them all away. Oh, no, there's nothing more cruel than this—I'll never forgive it. She stretched herself with a deep breath and blew out the light.

QUESTIONS

1. In the very first paragraph, what does the writer tell us about Ellen (Granny) Weatherall?
2. What does the name of Weatherall have to do with Granny's nature (or her life story)? What other traits or qualities do you find in her?
3. "Her bones felt loose, and floated around in her skin, and Doctor Harry floated like a balloon" (paragraph 6). What do you understand from this statement? By what other remarks does the writer indicate Granny's condition? In paragraph 56, why does Father Connolly tickle Granny's feet? At what other moments in the story does she fail to understand what is happening, or confuse the present with the past?
4. Exactly what happened to Ellen Weatherall sixty years earlier? What effects did this event have on her?
5. In paragraph 49, who do you guess to be the man who "cursed like a sailor's parrot"? In paragraph 56, who do you assume to be the man driving the cart? Is the fact that these persons are not clearly labeled and identified a failure on the author's part?
6. What is stream of consciousness? Would you call "The Jilting of Granny Weatherall" a stream of consciousness story? Refer to the story in your reply.
7. Sum up the character of the daughter Cornelia.
8. Why doesn't Granny's last child Hapsy come to her mother's deathbed?
9. Would you call the character of Doctor Harry "flat" or "round"? Why is his flatness (or roundness) appropriate to the story?
10. How is this the story of another "jilting"? What is similar between that fateful day of sixty years ago (described in paragraphs 29, 49, and 61) and the moment when Granny is dying? This time, who is the "bridegroom" not in the house?
11. "This is the story of an eighty-year-old woman lying in bed, getting groggy, and dying. I can't see why it should interest anybody." How would you answer this critic?

Alice Walker

EVERYDAY USE

Alice Walker, a leading black writer and social activist, was born in 1944 in Eatonton, Georgia, the youngest of eight children. Her father, a sharecropper and dairy farmer, usually earned about $300 a year; her mother helped by working as a maid. Both entertained their children by telling stories. When Alice Walker was eight, she was accidentally struck by a pellet from a brother's BB gun. She lost the sight of one eye because the Walkers had no car to rush her to the hospital. Later she attended Spelman College in Atlanta and finished college at Sarah Lawrence College on a scholarship. While working for the civil rights movement in Mississippi, she met a young lawyer, Melvyn Leventhal. In 1967 they settled in Jackson, Mississippi, the first legally married interracial couple in town. They re-turned to New York in 1974 and were later divorced. First known as a poet, Walker has published four books of her verse. She also has edited a collection of the work of the neglected black writer Zora Neale Hurston, and has written a study of Langston Hughes. In a collection of essays, In Search of Our Mothers' Gardens: Womanist Prose (1983), she recalls her mother and addresses her own daughter. (By womanist she means "black feminist.") But the largest part of Walker's reading audience know her fiction: three story collections, In Love and Trouble (1973), from which "Everyday Use" is taken, You Can't Keep a Good Woman Down (1981), and The Way Forward Is with a Broken Heart (2000); and her novels, The Third Life of Grange Copeland (1970) and Meridian (1976). Her best known novel, The Color Purple (1982), won a Pulitzer Prize and was made into a film by Steven Spielberg in 1985. Her recent novels include The Temple of My Familiar (1989), Possessing the Secret of Joy (1992), and By the Light of My Father's Smile (1998). Walker now lives in northern California.

Alice Walker

FOR YOUR GRANDMAMA

I will wait for her in the yard that Maggie and I made so clean and wavy yesterday afternoon. A yard like this is more comfortable than most people know. It is not just a yard. It is like an extended living room. When the hard clay is swept clean as a floor and the fine sand around the edges lined with tiny, irregular grooves anyone can come and sit and look up into the elm tree and wait for the breezes that never come inside the house.

Maggie will be nervous until after her sister goes: she will stand hopelessly in corners, homely and ashamed of the burn scars down her arms and legs, eyeing her sister with a mixture of envy and awe. She thinks her sister has held life always in the palm of one hand, that "no" is a word the world never learned to say to her.

You've no doubt seen those TV shows where the child who has "made it" is confronted, as a surprise, by her own mother and father, tottering in weakly from backstage. (A pleasant surprise, of course: What would they do if parent and child came on the show only to curse out and insult each other?) On TV mother and child embrace and smile into each other's faces. Sometimes the mother and father weep, the child wraps them in her arms and leans across the table to tell how she would not have made it without their help. I have seen these programs.°

Sometimes I dream a dream in which Dee and I are suddenly brought together on a TV program of this sort. Out of a dark and soft-seated limousine I am ushered into a bright room filled with many people. There I meet a smiling, gray, sporty man like Johnny Carson who shakes my hand and tells me what a fine girl I have. Then we are on the stage and Dee is embracing me with tears in her eyes. She pins on my dress a large orchid, even though she has told me once that she thinks orchids are tacky flowers.

In real life I am a large, big-boned woman with rough, man-working hands.   5
In the winter I wear flannel nightgowns to bed and overalls during the day. I can kill and clean a hog as mercilessly as a man. My fat keeps me hot in zero weather. I can work outside all day, breaking ice to get water for washing. I can eat pork liver cooked over the open fire minutes after it comes steaming from the hog. One winter I knocked a bull calf straight in the brain between the eyes with a sledge hammer and had the meat hung up to chill before nightfall. But of course all this does not show on television. I am the way my daughter would want me to be: a hundred pounds lighter, my skin like an uncooked barley pancake. My hair glistens in the hot bright lights. Johnny Carson has much to do to keep up with my quick and witty tongue.

But that is a mistake. I know even before I wake up. Who ever knew a Johnson with a quick tongue? Who can even imagine me looking a strange white man in the eye? It seems to me I have talked to them always with one foot raised in flight, with my head turned in whichever way is farthest from them. Dee, though. She would always look anyone in the eye. Hesitation was no part of her nature.

"How do I look, Mama?" Maggie says, showing just enough of her thin body enveloped in pink skirt and red blouse for me to know she's there, almost hidden by the door.

"Come out into the yard," I say.

Have you ever seen a lame animal, perhaps a dog run over by some careless person rich enough to own a car, sidle up to someone who is ignorant enough to

---

these programs: On the NBC television show *This Is Your Life*, people were publicly and often tearfully reunited with friends, relatives, and teachers they had not seen in years.

be kind to him? That is the way my Maggie walks. She has been like this, chin on chest, eyes on ground, feet in shuffle, ever since the fire that burned the other house to the ground.

Dee is lighter than Maggie, with nicer hair and a fuller figure. She's a woman now, though sometimes I forget. How long ago was it that the other house burned? Ten, twelve years? Sometimes I can still hear the flames and feel Maggie's arms sticking to me, her hair smoking and her dress falling off her in little black papery flakes. Her eyes seemed stretched open, blazed open by the flames reflected in them. And Dee. I see her standing off under the sweet gum tree she used to dig gum out of; a look of concentration on her face as she watched the last dingy gray board of the house fall in toward the red-hot brick chimney. Why don't you do a dance around the ashes? I'd wanted to ask her. She had hated the house that much.

I used to think she hated Maggie, too. But that was before we raised the money, the church and me, to send her to Augusta to school. She used to read to us without pity; forcing words, lies, other folks' habits, whole lives upon us two, sitting trapped and ignorant underneath her voice. She washed us in a river of make-believe, burned us with a lot of knowledge we didn't necessarily need to know. Pressed us to her with the serious way she read, to shove us away at just the moment, like dimwits, we seemed about to understand.

Dee wanted nice things. A yellow organdy dress to wear to her graduation from high school; black pumps to match a green suit she'd made from an old suit somebody gave me. She was determined to stare down any disaster in her efforts. Her eyelids would not flicker for minutes at a time. Often I fought off the temptation to shake her. At sixteen she had a style of her own: and knew what style was.

I never had an education myself. After second grade the school was closed down. Don't ask me why: in 1927 colored asked fewer questions than they do now. Sometimes Maggie reads to me. She stumbles along good-naturedly but can't see well. She knows she is not bright. Like good looks and money, quickness passed her by. She will marry John Thomas (who has mossy teeth in an earnest face) and then I'll be free to sit here and I guess just sing church songs to myself. Although I never was a good singer. Never could carry a tune. I was always better at a man's job. I used to love to milk till I was hoofed in the side in '49. Cows are soothing and slow and don't bother you, unless you try to milk them the wrong way.

I have deliberately turned my back on the house. It is three rooms, just like the one that burned, except the roof is tin; they don't make shingle roofs any more. There are no real windows, just some holes cut in the sides, like the portholes in a ship, but not round and not square, with rawhide holding the shutters up on the outside. This house is in a pasture, too, like the other one. No doubt when Dee sees it she will want to tear it down. She wrote me once that no matter where we "choose" to live, she will manage to come see us. But she will never bring her friends. Maggie and I thought about this and Maggie asked me, "Mama, when did Dee ever *have* any friends?"

She had a few. Furtive boys in pink shirts hanging about on washday after ¹⁵ school. Nervous girls who never laughed. Impressed with her they worshiped the well-turned phrase, the cute shape, the scalding humor that erupted like bubbles in lye. She read to them.

When she was courting Jimmy T she didn't have much time to pay to us, but turned all her faultfinding power on him. He *flew* to marry a cheap city girl from a family of ignorant flashy people. She hardly had time to recompose herself.

When she comes I will meet—but there they are!

Maggie attempts to make a dash for the house, in her shuffling way, but I stay her with my hand. "Come back here," I say. And she stops and tries to dig a well in the sand with her toe.

It is hard to see them clearly through the strong sun. But even the first glimpse of leg out of the car tells me it is Dee. Her feet were always neat-looking, as if God himself had shaped them with a certain style. From the other side of the car comes a short, stocky man. Hair is all over his head a foot long and hanging from his chin like a kinky mule tail. I hear Maggie suck in her breath. "Uhnnnh," is what it sounds like. Like when you see the wriggling end of a snake just in front of your foot on the road. "Uhnnnh."

Dee next. A dress down to the ground, in this hot weather. A dress so loud ²⁰ it hurts my eyes. There are yellows and oranges enough to throw back the light of the sun. I feel my whole face warming from the heat waves it throws out. Earrings, too, gold and hanging down to her shoulders. Bracelets dangling and making noises when she moves her arm up to shake the folds of the dress out of her armpits. The dress is loose and flows, and as she walks closer, I like it. I hear Maggie go "Uhnnnh" again. It is her sister's hair. It stands straight up like the wool on a sheep. It is black as night and around the edges are two long pigtails that rope about like small lizards disappearing behind her ears.

"Wa-su-zo-Tean-o!"° she says, coming on in that gliding way the dress makes her move. The short stocky fellow with the hair to his navel is all grinning and he follows up with "Asalamalakim,° my mother and sister!" He moves to hug Maggie but she falls back, right up against the back of my chair. I feel her trembling there and when I look up I see the perspiration falling off her chin.

"Don't get up," says Dee. Since I am stout it takes something of a push. You can see me trying to move a second or two before I make it. She turns, showing white heels through her sandals, and goes back to the car. Out she peeks next with a Polaroid. She stoops down quickly and lines up picture after picture of me sitting there in front of the house with Maggie cowering behind me. She never takes a shot without making sure the house is included. When a cow comes nibbling around the edge of the yard she snaps it and me and Maggie *and* the house. Then she puts the Polaroid in the back seat of the car, and comes up and kisses me on the forehead.

Wa-su-zo-Tean-o!: salutation in Swahili, an African language. Notice that Dee has to sound it out, syllable by syllable. *Asalamalakim*: salutation in Arabic: "Peace be upon you."

Meanwhile Asalamalakim is going through the motions with Maggie's hand. Maggie's hand is as limp as a fish, and probably as cold, despite the sweat, and she keeps trying to pull it back. It looks like Asalamalakim wants to shake hands but wants to do it fancy. Or maybe he don't know how people shake hands. Anyhow, he soon gives up on Maggie.

"Well," I say. "Dee."

"No, Mama," she says. "Not 'Dee,' Wangero Leewanika Kemanjo!"   25

"What happened to 'Dee'?" I wanted to know.

"She's dead," Wangero said. "I couldn't bear it any longer, being named after the people who oppress me."

"You know as well as me you was named after your aunt Dicie," I said. Dicie is my sister. She named Dee. We called her "Big Dee" after Dee was born.

"But who was *she* named after?" asked Wangero.

"I guess after Grandma Dee," I said.   30

"And who was she named after?" asked Wangero.

"Her mother," I said, and saw Wangero was getting tired. "That's about as far back as I can trace it," I said. Though, in fact, I probably could have carried it back beyond the Civil War through the branches.

"Well," said Asalamalakim, "there you are."

"Uhnnnh," I heard Maggie say.

"There I was not," I said, "before 'Dicie' cropped up in our family, so why   35
should I try to trace it that far back?"

He just stood there grinning, looking down on me like somebody inspecting a Model A car.° Every once in a while he and Wangero sent eye signals over my head.

"How do you pronounce this name?" I asked.

"You don't have to call me by it if you don't want to," said Wangero.

"Why shouldn't I?" I asked. "If that's what you want us to call you, we'll call you."

"I know it might sound awkward at first," said Wangero.   40

"I'll get used to it," I said. "Ream it out again."

Well, soon we got the name out of the way. Asalamalakim had a name twice as long and three times as hard. After I tripped over it two or three times he told me to just call him Hakim-a-barber. I wanted to ask him was he a barber, but I didn't really think he was, so I didn't ask.

"You must belong to those beef-cattle peoples down the road," I said. They said "Asalamalakim" when they met you, too, but they didn't shake hands. Always too busy: feeding the cattle, fixing the fences, putting up salt-lick shelters, throwing down hay. When the white folks poisoned some of the herd the men stayed up all night with rifles in their hands. I walked a mile and a half just to see the sight.

Hakim-a-barber said, "I accept some of their doctrines, but farming and raising cattle is not my style." (They didn't tell me, and I didn't ask, whether Wangero (Dee) had really gone and married him.)

Model A *car:* popular low-priced automobile introduced by the Ford Motor Company in 1927.

We sat down to eat and right away he said he didn't eat collards and pork was unclean. Wangero, though, went on through the chitlins and corn bread, the greens and everything else. She talked a blue streak over the sweet potatoes. Everything delighted her. Even the fact that we still used the benches her daddy made for the table when we couldn't afford to buy chairs.

"Oh, Mama!" she cried. Then turned to Hakim-a-barber. "I never knew how lovely these benches are. You can feel the rump prints," she said, running her hands underneath her and along the bench. Then she gave a sigh and her hand closed over Grandma Dee's butter dish. "That's it!" she said. "I knew there was something I wanted to ask you if I could have." She jumped up from the table and went over in the corner where the churn stood, the milk in it clabber° by now. She looked at the churn and looked at it.

"This churn top is what I need," she said. "Didn't Uncle Buddy whittle it out of a tree you all used to have?"

"Yes," I said.

"Uh huh," she said happily. "And I want the dasher, too."

"Uncle Buddy whittle that, too?" asked the barber.

Dee (Wangero) looked up at me.

"Aunt Dee's first husband whittled the dash," said Maggie so low you almost couldn't hear her. "His name was Henry, but they called him Stash."

"Maggie's brain is like an elephant's," Wangero said, laughing. "I can use the churn top as a centerpiece for the alcove table," she said, sliding a plate over the churn, "and I'll think of something artistic to do with the dasher."

When she finished wrapping the dasher the handle stuck out. I took it for a moment in my hands. You didn't even have to look close to see where hands pushing the dasher up and down to make butter had left a kind of sink in the wood. In fact, there were a lot of small sinks; you could see where thumbs and fingers had sunk into the wood. It was beautiful light yellow wood, from a tree that grew in the yard where Big Dee and Stash had lived.

After dinner Dee (Wangero) went to the trunk at the foot of my bed and started rifling through it. Maggie hung back in the kitchen over the dishpan. Out came Wangero with two quilts. They had been pieced by Grandma Dee and then Big Dee and me had hung them on the quilt frames on the front porch and quilted them. One was in the Lone Star pattern. The other was Walk Around the Mountain. In both of them were scraps of dresses Grandma Dee had worn fifty and more years ago. Bits and pieces of Grandpa Jarrell's paisley shirts. And one teeny faded blue piece, about the piece of a penny matchbox, that was from Great Grandpa Ezra's uniform that he wore in the Civil War.

"Mama," Wangero said sweet as a bird. "Can I have these old quilts?"

I heard something fall in the kitchen, and a minute later the kitchen door slammed.

---

clabber: sour milk or buttermilk.

"Why don't you take one or two of the others?" I asked. "These old things was just done by me and Big Dee from some tops your grandma pieced before she died."

"No," said Wangero. "I don't want those. They are stitched around the borders by machine."

"That'll make them last better," I said.

60

"That's not the point," said Wangero. "These are all pieces of dresses Grandma used to wear. She did all this stitching by hand. Imagine!" She held the quilts securely in her arms, stroking them.

"Some of the pieces, like those lavender ones, come from old clothes her mother handed down to her," I said, moving up to touch the quilts. Dee (Wangero) moved back just enough so that I couldn't reach the quilts. They already belonged to her.

"Imagine!" she breathed again, clutching them closely to her bosom.

"The truth is," I said, "I promised to give them quilts to Maggie, for when she marries John Thomas."

She gasped like a bee had stung her.

65

"Maggie can't appreciate these quilts!" she said. "She'd probably be backward enough to put them to everyday use."

"I reckon she would," I said. "God knows I been saving 'em for long enough with nobody using 'em. I hope she will!" I didn't want to bring up how I had offered Dee (Wangero) a quilt when she went away to college. Then she had told me they were old-fashioned, out of style.

"But they're *priceless!*" she was saying now, furiously; for she has a temper. "Maggie would put them on the bed and in five years they'd be in rags. Less than that!"

"She can always make some more," I said. "Maggie knows how to quilt."

Dee (Wangero) looked at me with hatred. "You just will not understand. The point is these quilts, *these* quilts!"

70

"Well," I said, stumped. "What would *you* do with them?"

"Hang them," she said. As if that was the only thing you *could* do with quilts.

Maggie by now was standing in the door. I could almost hear the sound her feet made as they scraped over each other.

"She can have them, Mama," she said, like somebody used to never winning anything, or having anything reserved for her. "I can 'member Grandma Dee without the quilts."

I looked at her hard. She had filled her bottom lip with checkerberry snuff and it gave her face a kind of dopey, hangdog look. It was Grandma Dee and Big Dee who taught her how to quilt herself. She stood there with her scarred hands hidden in the folds of her skirt. She looked at her sister with something like fear but she wasn't mad at her. This was Maggie's portion. This was the way she knew God to work.

75

When I looked at her like that something hit me in the top of my head and ran down to the soles of my feet. Just like when I'm in church and the spirit of

God touches me and I get happy and shout. I did something I never had done before: hugged Maggie to me, then dragged her on into the room, snatched the quilts out of Miss Wangero's hands and dumped them into Maggie's lap. Maggie just sat there on my bed with her mouth open.

"Take one or two of the others," I said to Dee.

But she turned without a word and went out to Hakim-a-barber.

"You just don't understand," she said, as Maggie and I came out to the car.

"What don't I understand?" I wanted to know.   80

"Your heritage," she said. And then she turned to Maggie, kissed her, and said, "You ought to try to make something of yourself, too, Maggie. It's really a new day for us. But from the way you and Mama still live you'd never know it."

She put on some sunglasses that hid everything above the tip of her nose and her chin.

Maggie smiled; maybe at the sunglasses. But a real smile, not scared. After we watched the car dust settle I asked Maggie to bring me a dip of snuff. And then the two of us sat there just enjoying, until it was time to go in the house and go to bed.

QUESTIONS

1. What is the basic conflict in "Everyday Use"?
2. What is the tone of Walker's story? By what means does the author communicate it?
3. From whose point of view is "Everyday Use" told? What does the story gain from this point of view—instead of, say, from the point of view of Dee (Wangero)?
4. What does the narrator of the story feel toward Dee? What seems to be Dee's present attitude toward her mother and sister?
5. What do you take to be the author's attitude toward each of her characters? How does she convey it?
6. What levels of meaning do you find in the story's title?
7. Contrast Dee's attitude toward her heritage with the attitudes of her mother and sister. How much truth is there in Dee's accusation that her mother and sister don't understand their heritage?
8. Does the knowledge that "Everyday Use" was written by a black writer in any way influence your reactions to it? Explain.

Raymond Carver

CATHEDRAL   1983

Born in Clatskanie, Oregon, Raymond Carver (1938–1988) moved at three with his parents to Yakima, Washington, where his father found employment as a sawmill worker. In his early years Carver worked briefly at a lumber mill and at other unskilled jobs, including a stint as a tulip-picker. Married with two children before he was twenty, he experienced blue-collar desperation on terms more intimate than have most American writers, though he once quipped that, until he read critics' reactions to his works, he never realized that the characters in his stories "were so bad off." Carver attended several universities, including Chico State College, where he studied with novelist John Gardner, and Humboldt State College (now California State University, Humboldt), where he earned a degree in 1963. He briefly attended the Writers' Workshop of the University of Iowa, but pressured by the need to support his family, he returned to California, working for three years as a hospital custodian before finding a job editing textbooks. In 1967 he met Gordon Lish, the influential editor who would publish several of his stories in Esquire, and had one of his early stories selected for publication in The Best American Short Stories of 1967. Under Lish's demanding tutelage, Carver learned to strip his fiction of everything but the essentials. Through the early 1970s, though plagued with bankruptcies, increasing dependency on alcohol, and marital problems, Carver began teaching in various one-year appointments at several universities.

Carver's publishing career began with a collection of poems, Near Klamath (1968). His collections of short stories include Will You Please Be Quiet, Please? (1977), What We Talk About When We Talk About Love (1981), Cathedral (1983), and Where I'm Calling From (1988), which contained new and selected work. The compression of language he learned as a poet may in part account for the lean quality of his prose, what has been termed "minimalist," a term Carver himself did not like, complaining that the term "smacks of smallness of vision and execution." In his last decade Carver taught creative writing at Syracuse University, living with the poet Tess Gallagher, whom he married in 1988. His receipt of the Mildred and Harold Strauss Living Award in 1983 finally allowed him to devote his full time to writing. He divided his remaining years between Syracuse and Port Angeles, Washington. Carver's personal victory in 1977 over decades of alcoholism underscored the many professional triumphs of his final decade. He once said, "If you want the truth, I'm prouder of that, that I quit drinking, than I am of anything in my life." His reputation as a master craftsman of the contemporary short story was still growing at the end of his life, which ended prematurely after a struggle with lung cancer.

This blind man, an old friend of my wife's, he was on his way to spend the night. His wife had died. So he was visiting the dead wife's relatives in Connecticut. He called my wife from his in-laws'. Arrangements were made. He would come by train, a five-hour trip, and my wife would meet him at the station. She hadn't seen him since she worked for him one summer in Seattle ten years ago. But she and the blind man had kept in touch. They made tapes and mailed them back and forth. I wasn't enthusiastic about his visit. He was no one I knew. And his being blind bothered me. My idea of blindness came from the movies. In the movies, the blind moved slowly and never laughed. Sometimes they were led by seeing-eye dogs. A blind man in my house was not something I looked forward to.

That summer in Seattle she had needed a job. She didn't have any money. The man she was going to marry at the end of the summer was in officers' training school. He didn't have any money, either. But she was in love with the guy, and he was in love with her, etc. She'd seen something in the paper: HELP WANTED—Reading to Blind Man, and a telephone number. She phoned and went over, was hired on the spot. She'd worked with this blind man all summer. She read stuff to him, case studies, reports, that sort of thing. She helped him organize his little office in the county social-service department. They'd become good friends, my wife and the blind man. How do I know these things? She told me. And she told me something else. On her last day in the office, the blind man asked if he could touch her face. She agreed to this. She told me he touched his fingers to every part of her face, her nose—even her neck! She never forgot it. She even tried to write a poem about it. She was always trying to write a poem. She wrote a poem or two every year, usually after something really important had happened to her.

When we first started going out together, she showed me the poem. In the poem, she recalled his fingers and the way they had moved around over her face. In the poem, she talked about what she had felt at the time, about what went through her mind when the blind man touched her nose and lips. I can remember I didn't think much of the poem. Of course, I didn't tell her that. Maybe I just don't understand poetry. I admit it's not the first thing I reach for when I pick up something to read.

Anyway, this man who'd first enjoyed her favors, the officer-to-be, he'd been her childhood sweetheart. So okay. I'm saying that at the end of the summer she let the blind man run his hands over her face, said good-bye to him, married her childhood etc., who was now a commissioned officer, and she moved away from Seattle. But they'd kept in touch, she and the blind man. She made the first contact after a year or so. She called him up one night from an Air Force base in Alabama. She wanted to talk. They talked. He asked her to send a tape and tell him about her life. She did this. She sent the tape. On the tape, she told the blind man about her husband and about their life together in the military. She told the blind man she loved her husband but she didn't like it where they lived and she didn't like it that he was part of the military-industrial thing. She told the blind man she'd written a poem and he was in it. She told him that she was writing a poem about what it was like to be an Air Force officer's wife. The poem wasn't finished yet. She was still writing it. The blind man made a tape. He sent her the tape. She made a tape. This went on for years. My wife's officer was posted to one base and then another. She sent tapes from Moody AFB, McGuire, McConnell, and finally Travis, near Sacramento, where one night she got to feeling lonely and cut off from people she kept losing in that moving-around life. She got to feeling she couldn't go it another step. She went in and swallowed all the pills and capsules in the medicine chest and washed them down with a bottle of gin. Then she got into a hot bath and passed out.

But instead of dying, she got sick. She threw up. Her officer—why should   5
he have a name? he was the childhood sweetheart, and what more does he want?—came home from somewhere, found her, and called the ambulance. In time, she put it all on a tape and sent the tape to the blind man. Over the years, she put all kinds of stuff on tapes and sent the tapes off lickety-split. Next to writing a poem every year, I think it was her chief means of recreation. On one tape, she told the blind man she'd decided to live away from her officer for a time. On another tape, she told him about her divorce. She and I began going out, and of course she told her blind man about it. She told him everything, or so it seemed to me. Once she asked me if I'd like to hear the latest tape from the blind man. This was a year ago. I was on the tape, she said. So I said okay, I'd

listen to it. I got us drinks and we settled down in the living room. We made ready to listen. First she inserted the tape into the player and adjusted a couple of dials. Then she pushed a lever. The tape squeaked and someone began to talk in this loud voice. She lowered the volume. After a few minutes of harmless chitchat, I heard my own name in the mouth of this stranger, this blind man I didn't even know! And then this: "From all you've said about him, I can only conclude—" But we were interrupted, a knock at the door, something, and we didn't ever get back to the tape. Maybe it was just as well. I'd heard all I wanted to.

Now this same blind man was coming to sleep in my house.

"Maybe I could take him bowling," I said to my wife. She was at the draining board doing scalloped potatoes. She put down the knife she was using and turned around.

"If you love me," she said, "you can do this for me. If you don't love me, okay. But if you had a friend, any friend, and the friend came to visit, I'd make him feel comfortable." She wiped her hands with the dish towel.

"I don't have any blind friends," I said.

"You don't have *any* friends," she said. "Period. Besides," she said, "god- 10 damn it, his wife's just died! Don't you understand that? The man's lost his wife!"

I didn't answer. She'd told me a little about the blind man's wife. Her name was Beulah. Beulah! That's a name for a colored woman.

"Was his wife a Negro?" I asked.

"Are you crazy?" my wife said. "Have you just flipped or something?" She picked up a potato. I saw it hit the floor, then roll under the stove. "What's wrong with you?" she said. "Are you drunk?"

"I'm just asking," I said.

Right then my wife filled me in with more detail than I cared to know. I 15 made a drink and sat at the kitchen table to listen. Pieces of the story began to fall into place.

Beulah had gone to work for the blind man the summer after my wife had stopped working for him. Pretty soon Beulah and the blind man had themselves a church wedding. It was a little wedding—who'd want to go to such a wedding in the first place?—just the two of them, plus the minister and the minister's wife. But it was a church wedding just the same. It was what Beulah had wanted, he'd said. But even then Beulah must have been carrying the cancer in her glands. After they had been inseparable for eight years—my wife's word, *inseparable*—Beulah's health went into a rapid decline. She died in a Seattle hospital room, the blind man sitting beside the bed and holding on to her hand. They'd married, lived and worked together, slept together—had sex, sure—and then the blind man had to bury her. All this without his having ever seen what the goddamned woman looked like. It was beyond my understanding. Hearing this, I felt sorry for the blind man for a little bit. And then I found myself thinking what a pitiful life this woman must have led. Imagine a woman who could never see herself as she was seen in the eyes of her loved one. A woman who could go on day after day and never receive the smallest compliment from her beloved. A woman whose husband could never read the expression on her face, be it misery or something better. Someone who could wear makeup or not—what difference to him? She could, if she wanted, wear green eye-shadow around one eye, a straight pin in her nostril, yellow slacks, and purple shoes, no matter. And then to slip off into death, the blind man's hand on her hand, his blind eyes streaming tears—I'm imagining now—her last thought maybe this: that he never even knew what she looked like, and she on an express to the grave. Robert was left with a small insurance policy and a half of a twenty-peso Mexican coin. The other half of the coin went into the box with her. Pathetic.

So when the time rolled around, my wife went to the depot to pick him up. With nothing to do but wait—sure, I blamed him for that—I was having a drink and watching the TV when I heard the car pull into the drive. I got up from the sofa with my drink and went to the window to have a look.

I saw my wife laughing as she parked the car. I saw her get out of the car and shut the door. She was still wearing a smile. Just amazing. She went around to the other side of the car to where the blind man was already starting to get out. This blind man, feature this, he was wearing a full beard! A beard on a blind man! Too much, I say. The blind man reached into the backseat and dragged out a suitcase. My wife took his arm, shut the car door, and, talking all the way, moved him down the drive and then up the steps to the front porch. I turned off the TV. I finished my drink, rinsed the glass, dried my hands. Then I went to the door.

My wife said, "I want you to meet Robert. Robert, this is my husband. I've told you all about him." She was beaming. She had this blind man by his coat sleeve.

The blind man let go of his suitcase and up came his hand.   20

I took it. He squeezed hard, held my hand, and then he let it go.

"I feel like we've already met," he boomed.

"Likewise," I said. I didn't know what else to say. Then I said, "Welcome. I've heard a lot about you." We began to move then, a little group, from the porch into the living room, my wife guiding him by the arm. The blind man was carrying his suitcase in his other hand. My wife said things like, "To your left here, Robert. That's right. Now watch it, there's a chair. That's it. Sit down right here. This is the sofa. We just bought this sofa two weeks ago."

I started to say something about the old sofa. I'd liked that old sofa. But I didn't say anything. Then I wanted to say something else, small-talk, about the scenic ride along the Hudson. How going *to* New York, you should sit on the right-hand side of the train, and coming *from* New York, the left-hand side.

"Did you have a good train ride?" I said. "Which side of the train did you sit   25 on, by the way?"

"What a question, which side!" my wife said. "What's it matter which side?" she said.

"I just asked," I said.

"Right side," the blind man said. "I hadn't been on a train in nearly forty years. Not since I was a kid. With my folks. That's been a long time. I'd nearly forgotten the sensation. I have winter in my beard now," he said. "So I've been told, anyway. Do I look distinguished, my dear?" the blind man said to my wife.

"You look distinguished, Robert," she said. "Robert," she said. "Robert, it's just so good to see you."

My wife finally took her eyes off the blind man and looked at me. I had the feeling she didn't like what she saw. I shrugged.

I've never met, or personally known, anyone who was blind. This blind man was late forties, a heavy-set, balding man with stooped shoulders, as if he carried a great weight there. He wore brown slacks, brown shoes, a light-brown shirt, a tie, a sports coat. Spiffy. He also had this full beard. But he didn't use a cane and he didn't wear dark glasses. I'd always thought dark glasses were a must for the blind. Fact was, I wished he had a pair. At first glance, his eyes looked like anyone else's eyes. But if you looked close, there was something different about them. Too much white in the iris, for one thing, and the pupils seemed to move around in the sockets without his knowing it or being able to stop it. Creepy. As I stared at his face, I saw the left pupil turn in toward his nose while the other made an effort to keep in one place. But it was only an effort, for that eye was on the roam without his knowing it or wanting it to be.

I said, "Let me get you a drink. What's your pleasure? We have a little of everything. It's one of our pastimes."

"Bub, I'm a Scotch man myself," he said fast enough in this big voice.

"Right," I said. Bub! "Sure you are. I knew it."

He let his fingers touch his suitcase, which was sitting alongside the sofa. He was taking his bearings. I didn't blame him for that.

"I'll move that up to your room," my wife said.

"No, that's fine," the blind man said loudly. "It can go up when I go up."

"A little water with the Scotch?" I said.

"Very little," he said.

"I knew it," I said.

He said, "Just a tad. The Irish actor, Barry Fitzgerald? I'm like that fellow. When I drink water, Fitzgerald said, I drink water. When I drink whiskey, I drink whiskey." My wife laughed. The blind man brought his hand up under his beard. He lifted his beard slowly and let it drop.

I did the drinks, three big glasses of Scotch with a splash of water in each. Then we made ourselves comfortable and talked about Robert's travels. First the long flight from the West Coast to Connecticut, we covered that. Then from Connecticut up here by train. We had another drink concerning that leg of the trip.

I remembered having read somewhere that the blind didn't smoke because, as speculation had it, they couldn't see the smoke they exhaled. I thought I knew that much and that much only about blind people. But this blind man smoked his cigarette down to the nubbin and then lit another one. This blind man filled his ashtray and my wife emptied it.

When we sat down at the table for dinner, we had another drink. My wife heaped Robert's plate with cube steak, scalloped potatoes, green beans. I buttered him up two slices of bread. I said, "Here's bread and butter for you." I swallowed some of my drink. "Now let us pray," I said, and the blind man lowered his head. My wife looked at me, her mouth agape. "Pray the phone won't ring and the food doesn't get cold," I said.

We dug in. We ate everything there was to eat on the table. We ate like 45 there was no tomorrow. We didn't talk. We ate. We scarfed. We grazed that table. We were into serious eating. The blind man had right away located his foods, he knew just where everything was on his plate. I watched with admiration as he used his knife and fork on the meat. He'd cut two pieces of meat, fork the meat into his mouth, and then go all out for the scalloped potatoes, the beans next, and then he'd tear off a hunk of buttered bread and eat that. He'd follow this up with a big drink of milk. It didn't seem to bother him to use his fingers once in a while, either.

We finished everything, including half a strawberry pie. For a few moments, we sat as if stunned. Sweat beaded on our faces. Finally, we got up from the table and left the dirty plates. We didn't look back. We took ourselves into the living room and sank into our places again. Robert and my wife sat on the sofa. I took the big chair. We had us two or three more drinks while they talked about the major things that had come to pass for them in the past ten years. For the most part, I just listened. Now and then I joined in. I didn't want him to think I'd left the room, and I didn't want her to think I was feeling left out. They talked of things that had happened to them—to them!—these past ten years. I waited in vain to hear my name on my wife's sweet lips: "And then my dear husband came into my life"—something like that. But I heard nothing of the sort. More talk of Robert. Robert had done a little of everything, it seemed, a regular blind jack-of-all-trades. But most recently he and his wife had had an Amway distributorship, from which, I gathered, they'd earned their living, such as it was. The blind man was also a ham radio operator. He talked in his loud voice about conversations he'd had with fellow operators in Guam, in the Philippines, in Alaska, and even in Tahiti. He said he'd have a lot of friends there if he ever wanted to go visit those places. From time to time, he'd turn his blind face toward me, put his hand under his beard, ask me something. How long had I been in my present position? (Three years.) Did I like my work? (I didn't.) Was I going to stay with it? (What were the options?) Finally, when I thought he was beginning to run down, I got up and turned on the TV.

My wife looked at me with irritation. She was heading toward a boil. Then she looked at the blind man and said, "Robert, do you have a TV?"

The blind man said, "My dear, I have two TVs. I have a color set and a black-and-white thing, an old relic. It's funny, but if I turn the TV on, and I'm always turning it on, I turn on the color set. It's funny, don't you think?"

I didn't know what to say to that. I had absolutely nothing to say to that. No opinion. So I watched the news program and tried to listen to what the announcer was saying.

"This is a color TV," the blind man said. "Don't ask me how, but I can tell." 50

"We traded up a while ago," I said.

The blind man had another taste of this drink. He lifted his beard, sniffed it, and let it fall. He leaned forward on the sofa. He positioned his ashtray on the coffee table, then put the lighter to his cigarette. He leaned back on the sofa and crossed his legs at the ankles.

My wife covered her mouth, and then she yawned. She stretched. She said, "I think I'll go upstairs and put on my robe. I think I'll change into something else. Robert, you make yourself comfortable," she said.

"I'm comfortable," the blind man said.

"I want you to feel comfortable in this house," she said.

"I am comfortable," the blind man said.

After she'd left the room, he and I listened to the weather report and then to the sports roundup. By that time, she'd been gone so long I didn't know if she was going to come back. I thought she might have gone to bed. I wished she'd come back downstairs. I didn't want to be left alone with a blind man. I asked him if he wanted another drink, and he said sure. Then I asked if he wanted to smoke some dope with me. I said I'd just rolled a number. I hadn't, but I planned to do so in about two shakes.

"I'll try some with you," he said.

"Damm right," I said. "That's the stuff."

"I got our drinks and sat down on the sofa with him. Then I rolled us two fat numbers. I lit one and passed it. I brought it to his fingers. He took it and inhaled.

"Hold it as long as you can," I said. I could tell he didn't know the first thing.

My wife came back downstairs wearing her pink robe and her pink slippers.

"What do I smell?" she said.

"We thought we'd have us some cannabis," I said.

My wife gave me a savage look. Then she looked at the blind man and said, "Robert, I didn't know you smoked."

He said, "I do now, my dear. There's a first time for everything. But I don't feel anything yet."

"This stuff is pretty mellow," I said. "This stuff is mild. It's dope you can reason with," I said. "It doesn't mess you up."

"Not much it doesn't, bub," he said, and laughed.

My wife sat on the sofa between the blind man and me. I passed her the number. She took it and toked and then passed it back to me. "Which way is this going?" she said. Then she said, "I shouldn't be smoking this. I can hardly keep my eyes open as it is. That dinner did me in. I shouldn't have eaten so much."

"It was the strawberry pie," the blind man said. "That's what did it," he said, and he laughed his big laugh. Then he shook his head.

"There's more strawberry pie," I said.

"Do you want some more, Robert?" my wife said.

"Maybe in a little while," he said.

We gave our attention to the TV. My wife yawned again. She said, "Your bed is made up when you feel like going to bed, Robert. I know you must have had a long day. When you're ready to go to bed, say so." She pulled his arm. "Robert?"

He came to and said, "I've had a real nice time. This beats tapes, doesn't it?"

I said, "Coming at you," and I put the number between his fingers. He inhaled, held the smoke, and then let it go. It was like he'd been doing it since he was nine years old.

"Thanks, bub," he said. "But I think this is all for me. I think I'm beginning to feel it," he said. He held the burning roach out for my wife.

"Same here," she said. "Ditto. Me, too." She took the roach and passed it to me. "I may just sit here for a while between you two guys with my eyes closed. But don't let me bother you, okay? Either one of you. If it bothers you, say so. Otherwise, I may just sit here with my eyes closed until you're ready to go to bed," she said. "Your bed's made up, Robert, when you're ready. It's right next to our room at the top of the stairs. We'll show you up when you're ready. You wake me up now, you guys, if I fall asleep." She said that and then she closed her eyes and went to sleep.

The news program ended. I got up and changed the channel. I sat back down on the sofa. I wished my wife hadn't pooped out. Her head lay across the back of the sofa, her mouth open. She'd turned so that her robe slipped away from her legs, exposing a juicy thigh. I reached to draw her robe back over her, and it was then that I glanced at the blind man. What the hell! I flipped the robe open again.

"You say when you want some strawberry pie," I said.   80

"I will," he said.

I said, "Are you tired? Do you want me to take you up to your bed? Are you ready to hit the hay?"

"Not yet," he said. "No, I'll stay up with you, bub. If that's all right. I'll stay up until you're ready to turn in. We haven't had a chance to talk. Know what I mean? I feel like me and her monopolized the evening." He lifted his beard and he let it fall. He picked up his cigarettes and his lighter.

"That's all right," I said. Then I said, "I'm glad for the company."

And I guess I was. Every night I smoked dope and stayed up as long as I   85
could before I fell asleep. My wife and I hardly ever went to bed at the same time. When I did go to sleep, I had these dreams. Sometimes I'd wake up from one of them, my heart going crazy.

Something about the church and the Middle Ages was on the TV. Not your run-of-the-mill TV fare. I wanted to watch something else. I turned to the other channels. But there was nothing on them, either. So I turned back to the first channel and apologized.

"Bub, it's all right," the blind man said. "It's fine with me. Whatever you want to watch is okay. I'm always learning something. Learning never ends. It won't hurt me to learn something tonight. I got ears," he said.

We didn't say anything for a time. He was leaning forward with his head turned at me, his right ear aimed in the direction of the set. Very disconcerting. Now and then his eyelids drooped and then they snapped open again. Now and then he put his fingers into his beard and tugged, like he was thinking about something he was hearing on the television.

On the screen, a group of men wearing cowls was being set upon and tormented by men dressed in skeleton costumes and men dressed as devils. The men dressed as devils wore devil masks, horns, and long tails. This pageant was part of a procession. The Englishman who was narrating the thing said it took place in Spain once a year. I tried to explain to the blind man what was happening.

"Skeletons," he said. "I know about skeletons," he said, and he nodded.

The TV showed this one cathedral. Then there was a long, slow look at another one. Finally, the picture switched to the famous one in Paris, with its flying buttresses and its spires reaching up to the clouds. The camera pulled away to show the whole of the cathedral rising above the skyline.

There were times when the Englishman who was telling the thing would shut up, would simply let the camera move around the cathedrals. Or else the camera would tour the countryside, men in fields walking behind oxen. I waited as long as I could. Then I felt I had to say something. I said, "They're showing the outside of this cathedral now. Gargoyles. Little statues carved to look like monsters. Now I guess they're in Italy. Yeah, they're in Italy. There's paintings on the walls of this one church."

"Are those fresco paintings, bub?" he asked, and he sipped from his drink.

I reached for my glass. But it was empty. I tried to remember what I could remember. "You're asking me are those frescoes?" I said. "That's a good question. I don't know."

The camera moved to a cathedral outside Lisbon. The differences in the Portuguese cathedral compared with the French and Italian were not that great. But they were there. Mostly the interior stuff. Then something occurred to me, and I said, "Something has occurred to me. Do you have any idea what a cathedral is? What they look like, that is? Do you follow me? If somebody says cathedral to you, do you have any notion what they're talking about? Do you know the difference between that and a Baptist church, say?"

He let the smoke dribble from his mouth. "I know they took hundreds of workers fifty or a hundred years to build," he said. "I just heard the man say that, of course. I know generations of the same families worked on a cathedral. I heard him say that, too. The men who began their life's work on them, they never lived to see the completion of their work. In that wise, bub, they're no different from the rest of us, right?" He laughed. Then his eyelids drooped again. His head nodded. He seemed to be snoozing. Maybe he was imagining himself in Portugal. The TV was showing another cathedral now. This one was in Germany. The Englishman's voice droned on. "Cathedrals," the blind man said. He sat up and rolled his head back and forth. "If you want the truth, bub, that's about all I know. What I just said. What I heard him say. But maybe you could describe one to me? I wish you'd do it. I'd like that. If you want to know, I really don't have a good idea."

I stared hard at the shot of the cathedral on the TV. How could I even begin to describe it? But say my life depended on it. Say my life was being threatened by an insane guy who said I had to do it or else.

I stared some more at the cathedral before the picture flipped off into the countryside. There was no use. I turned to the blind man and said, "To begin with, they're very tall." I was looking around the room for clues. "They reach way up. Up and up. Toward the sky. They're so big, some of them, they have to have these supports. To help hold them up, so to speak. These supports are called buttresses. They remind me of viaducts, for some reason. But maybe you don't know viaducts, either? Sometimes the cathedrals have devils and such carved into the front. Sometimes lords and ladies. Don't ask me why this is," I said.

He was nodding. The whole upper part of his body seemed to be moving back and forth.

"I'm not doing so good, am I?" I said.

He stopped nodding and leaned forward on the edge of the sofa. As he listened to me, he was running his fingers through his beard. I wasn't getting through to him, I could see that. But he waited for me to go on just the same. He nodded, like he was trying to encourage me. I tried to think what else to say. "They're really big," I said. "They're massive. They're built of stone. Marble, too, sometimes. In those olden days, when they built cathedrals, men wanted to be close to God. In those olden days, God was an important part of everyone's life. You could tell this from their cathedral-building. I'm sorry," I said, "but it looks like that's the best I can do for you. I'm just no good at it."

"That's all right, bub," the blind man said. "Hey, listen. I hope you don't mind my asking you. Can I ask you something? Let me ask you a simple question, yes or no. I'm just curious and there's no offense. You're my host. But let me ask if you are in any way religious? You don't mind my asking?"

I shook my head. He couldn't see that, though. A wink is the same as a nod to a blind man. "I guess I don't believe in it. In anything. Sometimes it's hard. You know what I'm saying?"

"Sure, I do," he said.

"Right," I said.

The Englishman was still holding forth. My wife sighed in her sleep. She drew a long breath and went on with her sleeping.

"You'll have to forgive me," I said. "But I can't tell you what a cathedral looks like. It just isn't in me to do it. I can't do any more than I've done."

The blind man sat very still, his head down, as he listened to me.

I said, "The truth is, cathedrals don't mean anything special to me. Nothing. Cathedrals. They're something to look at on late-night TV. That's all they are."

It was then that the blind man cleared his throat. He brought something up. He took a handkerchief from his back pocket. Then he said, "I get it, bub. It's okay. It happens. Don't worry about it," he said. "Hey, listen to me. Will you do me a favor? I got an idea. Why don't you find us some heavy paper? And a pen. We'll do something. We'll draw one together. Get us a pen and some heavy paper. Go on, bud, get the stuff," he said.

So I went upstairs. My legs felt like they didn't have any strength in them. They felt like they did after I'd done some running. In my wife's room I looked around. I found some ballpoints in a little basket on her table. And then I tried to think where to look for the kind of paper he was talking about.

Downstairs, in the kitchen, I found a shopping bag with onion skins in the bottom of the bag. I emptied the bag and shook it. I brought it into the living room and sat down with it near his legs. I moved some things, smoothed the wrinkles from the bag, spread it out on the coffee table.

The blind man got down from the sofa and sat next to me on the carpet.

He ran his fingers over the paper. He went up and down the sides of the paper. The edges, even the edges. He fingered the corners.

"All right," he said. "All right, let's do her." 115

He found my hand, the hand with the pen. He closed his hand over my hand. "Go ahead, bub, draw," he said. "Draw. You'll see. I'll follow along with you. It'll be okay. Just begin now like I'm telling you. You'll see. Draw," the blind man said.

So I began. First I drew a box that looked like a house. It could have been the house I lived in. Then I put a roof on it. At either end of the roof, I drew spires. Crazy.

"Swell," he said. "Terrific. You're doing fine," he said. "Never thought anything like this could happen in your lifetime, did you, bub? Well, it's a strange life, we all know that. Go on now. Keep it up."

I put in windows with arches. I drew flying buttresses. I hung great doors. I couldn't stop. The TV station went off the air. I put down the pen and closed and opened my fingers. The blind man felt around over the paper. He moved the tips of his fingers over the paper, all over what I had drawn, and he nodded.

"Doing fine," the blind man said. 120

I took up the pen again, and he found my hand. I kept at it. I'm no artist. But I kept drawing just the same.

My wife opened up her eyes and gazed at us. She sat up on the sofa, her robe hanging open. She said, "What are you doing? Tell me, I want to know."

I didn't answer her.

The blind man said, "We're drawing a cathedral. Me and him are working on it. Press hard," he said to me. "That's right. That's good," he said. "Sure. You got it, bub, I can tell. You didn't think you could. But you can, can't you? You're cooking with gas now. You know what I'm saying? We're going to really have us something here in a minute. How's the old arm?" he said. "Put some people in there now. What's a cathedral without people?"

My wife said, "What's going on? Robert, what are you doing? What's going 125 on?"

"It's all right," he said to her. "Close your eyes now," the blind man said to me.

I did it. I closed them just like he said.

"Are they closed?" he said. "Don't fudge."

"They're closed," I said.

"Keep them that way," he said. He said, "Don't stop now. Draw." 130

So we kept on with it. His fingers rode my fingers as my hand went over the paper. It was like nothing else in my life up to now.

Then he said, "I think that's it. I think you got it," he said. "Take a look. What do you think?"

But I had my eyes closed. I thought I'd keep them that way for a little longer. I thought it was something I ought to do.

"Well?" he said. "Are you looking?"

My eyes were still closed. I was in my house. I knew that. But I didn't feel like I was inside anything.

"It's really something," I said.

1. What details in "Cathedral" make clear the narrator's initial attitude toward blind people? What hints does the author give about the reasons for this attitude? At what point in the story do the narrator's preconceptions about blind people start to change?
2. For what reason does the wife keep asking Robert if he'd like to go to bed (paragraphs 74–78)? What motivates the narrator to make the same suggestion in paragraph 82? What effect does Robert's reply have on the narrator?
3. What makes the narrator start explaining what he's seeing on television?
4. How does the point of view contribute to the effectiveness of the story?
5. At the end, the narrator has an epiphany. How would you describe it?
6. Would you describe the narrator as an antihero? Use specific details from the story to back up your response.
7. Is the wife a flat or a round character? What about Robert? Support your conclusion about each of them.
8. In a good story, a character doesn't suddenly become a completely different sort of person. Find details early in the story that show the narrator's more sensitive side and thus help to make his development credible and persuasive.

WRITER'S PERSPECTIVE

Raymond Carver

Raymond Carver on Writing

COMMONPLACE BUT PRECISE LANGUAGE   1983

It's possible, in a poem or short story, to write about commonplace things and objects using commonplace but precise language, and to endow those things—a chair, a window curtain, a fork, a stone, a woman's earring—with immense, even startling power. It is possible to write a line of seemingly innocuous dialogue and have it send a chill along the reader's spine—the source of artistic delight, as Nabokov would have it. That's the kind of writing that most interests me. I hate sloppy or haphazard writing whether it flies under the banner of experimentation or else is just clumsily rendered realism. In Isaac Babel's wonderful short story, "Guy de Maupassant," the narrator has this to say about the writing of fiction: "No iron can pierce the heart with such force as a period put just at the right place." This too ought to go on a three-by-five.

Evan Connell said once that he knew he was finished with a short story when he found himself going through it and taking out commas and then going through the story again and putting commas back in the same places. I like that way of working on something. I respect that kind of care for what is being done. That's all we have, finally, the words, and they had better be the right ones, with the punctuation in the right places so that they can best say what they are meant to say. If the words are heavy with the writer's own unbridled emotions, or if they are imprecise and inaccurate for some reason—if the words are in any way blurred—the reader's eyes will slide right over them and nothing will be achieved. The reader's own artistic sense will simply not be engaged. Henry James called this sort of hapless writing "weak specification."

I have friends who've told me they had to hurry a book because they needed the money, their editor or their wife was leaning on them or leaving them—something, some apology for the writing not being very good. "It would have been better if I'd taken the time." I was dumbfounded when I heard a novelist friend say this. I still am, if I think about it, which I don't. It's none of my business. But if the writing can't be made as good as it is within us to make it, then why do it? In the end, the satisfaction of having done our best, and the proof of that labor, is the one thing we can take into the grave.

From "On Writing"

<hr>

━━▭▷ WRITING CRITICALLY ◁▭━━

How Character Creates Action

Although the average reader may consider plot the basic element of fiction, writers often remark that stories begin with characters. They imagine a certain person and then wait to see what that character will do. "By the time I write a story," remarked Katherine Anne Porter, "my people are up and alive and walking around and taking things into their own hands." The action of a story usually grows out of the personality of its protagonist and the situation he or she faces. As critic Phyllis Bottome observed, "If a writer is true to his characters they will give him his plot."

In writing about the protagonist (or any other figure) in a short story, novel, or other literary work, begin by studying his or her personality. What makes this individual different from the other characters in the story? Jot down a quick list of individual physical, mental, moral, or behavioral traits the character displays. Does one trait seem especially significant? Do any of these qualities foreshadow the action of the story? Now jot down what the character's primary motivation appears to be. Does this motivation seem as reasonable to the reader as it does to the protagonist? If not, what does the gap between the protagonist's motivation and the reader's reaction suggest? (In John Updike's "A & P," for instance, Sammy's nasty observations about the other customers—especially their physical appearance—might suggest to us that his reasons for defending the girls are not quite as noble as he thinks.) Does the protagonist fully understand his or her own motivation?

Asking these simple questions and writing down a few specific observations will give you a solid foundation for critical analysis.

WRITING ASSIGNMENT

Using a story from the book, write a short essay that explains why a protagonist takes a crucial, life-changing action. What motivates this character to do something that seems bold or surprising? Some possible topics include:

- Why does Dee's mother refuse to give her the quilt she wants in "Everyday Use" by Alice Walker?
- What motivates the narrator to overcome his instinctive antipathy to the blind man in "Cathedral"?
- What motivates the older brother to write to Sonny during his incarceration in "Sonny's Blues" by James Baldwin?

FURTHER SUGGESTIONS FOR WRITING

1. Here is a topic for a lively essay if you are familiar with some variety of popular fiction—detective stories, science fiction, Gothic novels, romances, "adolescent agony" novels written for teenagers, or other kinds of paperback storytelling. Portray some of the stock characters you find prevalent in this type of fiction. Suggestion: It might be simplistic to condemn stock characters as bad. They have long been valuable ingredients in much excellent literature. (See the beginning of this chapter for a discussion of stock characters.)
2. Alternative topic: Portray a few stock characters we meet in current television programs. It might focus your essay to confine it to just one variety of stock character (for instance, the little man who peddles information to the police, the glamorous spy), or to just one kind of program (situation comedies or soap operas or police thrillers).
3. In a brief essay, study a dynamic character in a story, showing exactly how that character changed, or grew and developed. Possible subjects: Granny Weatherall, Sammy in John Updike's "A & P," the narrator in T. Coraghessan Boyle's "Greasy Lake," the boy Sarty Snopes in William Faulkner's "Barn Burning," and the narrator in Raymond Carver's "Cathedral." (See the beginning of this chapter for a discussion of dynamic characters.)
4. Alternative topic: Have you ever known anyone whose character, over months or years, has altered deeply? If so, try to explain what may have caused that person to be a "dynamic character."

4 Setting

By the **setting** of a story, we mean its time and place. The word might remind you of the metal that holds a diamond in a ring, or of a *set* used in a play—perhaps a bare chair in front of a slab of painted canvas. But often, in an effective short story, setting may figure as more than mere background or underpinning. It can make things happen. It can prompt characters to act, bring them to realizations, or cause them to reveal their inmost natures.

To be sure, the idea of setting includes the physical environment of a story: a house, a street, a city, a landscape, a region. (*Where* a story takes place is sometimes called its **locale.**) Physical places mattered so greatly to French novelist Honoré de Balzac that sometimes, before writing a story set in a particular town, he would visit that town, select a few houses, and describe them in detail, down to their very smells. "The place in which an event occurred," Henry James admiringly said of him, "was in his view of equal moment with the event itself . . . it had a part to play; it needed to be made as definite as anything else."

But besides place, setting may crucially involve the *time* of the story—hour, year, or century. It might matter greatly that a story takes place at dawn, or on the day of the first moon landing. When we begin to read a historical novel, we are soon made aware that we aren't reading about life in the twenty-first century. In *The Scarlet Letter*, nineteenth-century author Nathaniel Hawthorne, by a long introduction and a vivid opening scene at a prison door, prepares us to witness events in the Puritan community of Boston in the earlier seventeenth century. This setting, together with scenes of Puritan times we recall from high school history, helps us understand what happens in the novel. We can appreciate the shocked agitation in town when a woman is accused of adultery: she has given illegitimate birth. Such an event might seem common today, but in the stern, God-fearing New England Puritan community, it was a flagrant defiance of church and state, which were all-powerful (and were all one). That reader will make no sense of *The Scarlet Letter* who ignores its setting—if to ignore the setting is even possible, given how much attention Hawthorne pays to it.

That Hawthorne's novel takes place in a time remote from our own leads us to expect different customs and different attitudes. Some critics and teachers regard the setting of a story as its whole society, including the beliefs and assumptions of its characters. Still, we suggest that for now you keep your working definition of *setting* simple. Call it time and place. If later you should feel that your definition needs widening and deepening, you can always expand it.

Besides time and place, setting may also include the weather, which in some stories may be crucial. Climate seems as substantial as any character in William Faulkner's "Dry September." After sixty-two rainless days, a long unbroken spell of late-summer heat has frayed every nerve in a small town and caused the main character, a hotheaded white supremacist, to feel more and more irritation. The weather, someone remarks, is "enough to make a man do anything." When a false report circulates that a white woman has been raped by a black man, the rumor, like a match flung into a dry field, ignites rage and provokes a lynching. Evidently, to understand the story we have to recognize its locale, a small town in Mississippi in the 1930s during an infernal heat wave. Fully to take in the meaning of Faulkner's story, we have to take in the setting in its entirety.

Physical place, by the way, is especially vital to a regional writer, who usually sets stories (or other work) in one geographic area. Such a writer, often a native of the place, tries to bring it alive to readers who live elsewhere. William Faulkner, a distinguished regional writer, almost always sets his novels and stories in his native Mississippi. Though born in St. Louis, Kate Chopin became known as a regional writer for writing about Louisiana in many of her short stories and in her novel *The Awakening*. Willa Cather, for her novels of frontier Nebraska, often is regarded as another outstanding regionalist (though she also set fiction in Quebec, the Southwest, and, in "Paul's Case," in Pittsburgh and New York). There is often something arbitrary, however, about calling an author a regional writer. The label often has a political tinge; it means that the author describes an area outside the political and economic centers of a society. In a sense, we might think of James Joyce as a regional writer, in that all his fiction takes place in the city of Dublin, but instead we usually call him an Irish one.

As such writers show, a place can profoundly affect the character who grew up in it. Willa Cather is fond of portraying strong-minded, independent women, such as the heroine of her novel *My Antonía*, strengthened in part by years of coping with the hardships of life on the wind-lashed prairie. Not that every writer of stories in which a place matters greatly will draw the characters as helpless puppets of their environment. Few writers do so, although that may be what you find in novels of **naturalism**—fiction of grim realism, in which the writer observes human characters like a scientist observing ants, seeing them as the products and victims of environment and heredity.[1] Theodore Dreiser carries on the tradition of naturalism in such

---

[1] The founder of naturalism in fiction was French novelist Émile Zola (1840–1902), who in a vast series of twenty novels about the family Rougon-Macquart traced a case of syphilis through several generations. In America, Stephen Crane wrote an early naturalist novel, *Maggie: A Girl of the Streets* (1893), and showed the way for later novelists such as Theodore Dreiser, Upton Sinclair, and James T. Farrell.

novels as *The Financier* (1912). It begins in a city setting. A young lad (who will grow up to be a ruthless industrialist) is watching a battle to the death between a lobster and a squid in a fish-market tank. Dented for the rest of his life by this grim scene, he decides that's exactly the way to live in human society.

Setting may operate more subtly than that fish tank. Often, setting and character will reveal each other. Recall how Faulkner, at the start of "A Rose for Emily," depicts Emily Grierson's house, once handsome but now "an eyesore among eyesores" surrounded by gas stations. Still standing, refusing to yield its old-time horse-and-buggy splendor to the age of the automobile, the house in "its stubborn and coquettish decay" embodies the character of its owner. In some fiction, setting is closely bound with theme (what the story is saying)—as you will find in John Steinbeck's "The Chrysanthemums" (Chapter Seven), a story beginning with a fog that has sealed off a valley from the rest of the world—a fog like the lid on a pot. In *The Scarlet Letter*, even small details contain powerful hints. At the beginning of his novel, Hawthorne remarks of a colonial jailhouse:

> Before this ugly edifice, and between it and the wheel-track of the street, was a grass-plot, much overgrown with burdock, pigweed, apple-peru, and such unsightly vegetation, which evidently found something congenial in the soil that had so early borne the black flower of civilized society, a prison. But, on one side of the portal, and rooted almost at the threshold, was a wild rose-bush, covered, in this month of June, with its delicate gems, which might be imagined to offer their fragrance and fragile beauty to the prisoner as he went in, and to the condemned criminal as he came forth to his doom, in token that the deep heart of Nature could pity and be kind to him.

Apparently, Hawthorne wishes to show us that Puritan Boston, a town of rutted streets and an ugly jail with a tangled grass-plot, may be rough but has beauty in it. As the story unfolds, he will further suggest (among other things) that secret sin and a beautiful child may go together like pigweed and wild roses. In his artfully crafted novel, setting is one with—not separate from—characters, theme, and symbols.

In some stories, a writer will seem to draw a setting mainly to evoke atmosphere. In such a story, setting starts us feeling whatever the storyteller would have us feel. In "The Tell-Tale Heart," Poe's setting the action in an old, dark, lantern-lit house greatly contributes to our sense of unease—and so helps the story's effectiveness. (Old, dark mansions are favorite settings for the Gothic story, a long-popular kind of fiction mentioned again in Chapter Eight.)

But be warned: you'll meet stories in which setting appears hardly to matter. In W. Somerset Maugham's fable, "The Appointment in Samarra," all we need to be told about the setting is that it is a marketplace in Bagdad. In that brief fable, the inevitability of death is the point, not an exotic setting. In this chapter, though, you will meet four fine stories in which setting, for one reason or another, counts greatly. Without it, none of these stories could happen.

Kate Chopin

THE STORM

1898

Kate Chopin

Kate Chopin (1851–1904) was born Katherine O'Flaherty in St. Louis, daughter of an Irish immigrant grown wealthy in retailing. On his death, young Kate was raised by her mother's family: aristocratic Creoles, descendants of the French and Spaniards who had colonized Louisiana. Young Kate received a convent schooling, and at nineteen married Oscar Chopin, a Creole cotton broker from New Orleans. Later, the Chopins lived on a plantation near Cloutierville, Louisiana, a region whose varied people—Creoles, Cajuns, blacks—Kate Chopin was later to write about with loving care in Bayou Folk (1894) and A Night in Arcadia (1897). The shock of her husband's sudden death in 1883, which left her with the raising of six children, seems to have plunged Kate Chopin into writing. She read and admired fine woman writers of her day, such as the Maine realist Sarah Orne Jewett. She also read Maupassant, Zola, and other new (and scandalous) French naturalist writers. She began to bring into American fiction some of their hard-eyed observation and their passion for telling unpleasant truths. Determined, in defiance of her times, frankly to show the sexual feelings of her characters, Chopin suffered from neglect and censorship. When her major novel, The Awakening, appeared in 1899, critics were outraged by her candid portrait of a woman who seeks sexual and professional independence. After causing such a literary scandal, Chopin was unable to get her later work published, and wrote little more before she died. The Awakening and many of her stories had to wait seven decades for a sympathetic audience.

I

The leaves were so still that even Bibi thought it was going to rain. Bobinôt, who was accustomed to converse on terms of perfect equality with his little son, called the child's attention to certain somber clouds that were rolling with sinister intention from the west, accompanied by a sullen, threatening roar. They were at Friedheimer's store and decided to remain there till the storm had passed. They sat within the door on two empty kegs. Bibi was four years old and looked very wise.

"Mama'll be 'fraid, yes," he suggested with blinking eyes.

"She'll shut the house. Maybe she got Sylvie helpin' her this evenin'," Bobinôt responded reassuringly.

"No; she ent got Sylvie. Sylvie was helpin' her yistiday," piped Bibi.

Bobinôt arose and going across to the counter purchased a can of shrimps, of   5
which Calixta was very fond. Then he returned to his perch on the keg and sat
stolidly holding the can of shrimps while the storm burst. It shook the wooden
store and seemed to be ripping great furrows in the distant field. Bibi laid his
little hand on his father's knee and was not afraid.

II

Calixta, at home, felt no uneasiness for their safety. She sat at a side window
sewing furiously on a sewing machine. She was greatly occupied and did not notice the approaching storm. But she felt very warm and often stopped to mop her
face on which the perspiration gathered in beads. She unfastened her white
sacque at the throat. It began to grow dark, and suddenly realizing the situation
she got up hurriedly and went about closing windows and doors.

Out on the small front gallery she had hung Bobinôt's Sunday clothes to air
and she hastened out to gather them before the rain fell. As she stepped outside,
Alcée Laballière rode in at the gate. She had not seen him very often since her
marriage, and never alone. She stood there with Bobinôt's coat in her hands,
and the big rain drops began to fall. Alcée rode his horse under the shelter of a
side projection where the chickens had huddled and there were plows and a
harrow piled up in the corner.

"May I come and wait on your gallery till the storm is over, Calixta?" he
asked.

"Come 'long in, M'sieur Alcée."

His voice and her own startled her as if from a trance, and she seized   10
Bobinôt's vest. Alcée, mounting to the porch, grabbed the trousers and snatched
Bibi's braided jacket that was about to be carried away by a sudden gust of wind.
He expressed an intention to remain outside, but it was soon apparent that he
might as well have been out in the open: the water beat in upon the boards in
driving sheets, and he went inside, closing the door after him. It was even necessary to put something beneath the door to keep the water out.

"My! what a rain! It's good two years sence it rain like that," exclaimed Calixta as she rolled up a piece of bagging and Alcée helped her to thrust it beneath
the crack.

She was a little fuller of figure than five years before when she married; but
she had lost nothing of her vivacity. Her blue eyes still retained their melting
quality; and her yellow hair, dishevelled by the wind and rain, kinked more stubbornly than ever about her ears and temples.

The rain beat upon the low, shingled roof with a force and clatter that
threatened to break an entrance and deluge them there. They were in the dining
room—the sitting room—the general utility room. Adjoining was her bed room,
with Bibi's couch along side her own. The door stood open, and the room with
its white, monumental bed, its closed shutters, looked dim and mysterious.

Alcée flung himself into a rocker and Calixta nervously began to gather up
from the floor the lengths of a cotton sheet which she had been sewing.

"If this keeps up, *Dieu sait*° if the levees goin' to stan' it!" she exclaimed.

"What have you got to do with the levees?"

"I got enough to do! An' there's Bobinôt with Bibi out in that storm—if he only didn' left Friedheimer's!"

"Let us hope, Calixta, that Bobinôt's got sense enough to come in out of a cyclone."

She went and stood at the window with a greatly disturbed look on her face. She wiped the frame that was clouded with moisture. It was stiflingly hot. Alcée got up and joined her at the window, looking over her shoulder. The rain was coming down in sheets obscuring the view of far-off cabins and enveloping the distant wood in a gray mist. The playing of the lightning was incessant. A bolt struck a tall chinaberry tree at the edge of the field. It filled all visible space with a blinding glare and the crash seemed to invade the very boards they stood upon.

Calixta put her hands to her eyes, and with a cry, staggered backward. Alcée's arm encircled her, and for an instant he drew her close and spasmodically to him.

"*Bonté!*"° she cried, releasing herself from his encircling arm and retreating from the window, "the house'll go next! If I only knew w'ere Bibi was!" She would not compose herself; she would not be seated. Alcée clasped her shoulders and looked into her face. The contact of her warm, palpitating body when he had unthinkingly drawn her into his arms, had aroused all the old-time infatuation and desire for her flesh.

"Calixta," he said, "don't be frightened. Nothing can happen. The house is too low to be struck, with so many tall trees standing about. There! aren't you going to be quiet? say, aren't you?" He pushed her hair back from her face that was warm and steaming. Her lips were as red and moist as pomegranate seed. Her white neck and a glimpse of her full, firm bosom disturbed him powerfully. As she glanced up at him the fear in her liquid blue eyes had given place to a drowsy gleam that unconsciously betrayed a sensuous desire. He looked down into her eyes and there was nothing for him to do but gather her lips in a kiss. It reminded him of Assumption.°

"Do you remember—in Assumption, Calixta?" he asked in a low voice broken by passion. Oh! she remembered; for in Assumption he had kissed her and kissed and kissed her; until his senses would well nigh fail, and to save her he would resort to a desperate flight. If she was not an immaculate dove in those days, she was still inviolate; a passionate creature whose very defenselessness had made her defense, against which his honor forbade him to prevail. Now—well, now—her lips seemed in a manner free to be tasted, as well as her round, white throat and her whiter breasts.

They did not heed the crashing torrents, and the roar of the elements made her laugh as she lay in his arms. She was a revelation in that dim, mysterious

---

Dieu sait: God only knows.   *Bonté!:* Heavens!   *Assumption:* a parish west of New Orleans.

chamber; as white as the couch she lay upon. Her firm, elastic flesh that was knowing for the first time its birthright, was like a creamy lily that the sun invites to contribute its breath and perfume to the undying life of the world.

The generous abundance of her passion, without guile or trickery, was like a white flame which penetrated and found response in depths of his own sensuous nature that had never yet been reached. 25

When he touched her breasts they gave themselves up in quivering ecstasy, inviting his lips. Her mouth was a fountain of delight. And when he possessed her, they seemed to swoon together at the very borderland of life's mystery.

He stayed cushioned upon her, breathless, dazed, enervated, with his heart beating like a hammer upon her. With one hand she clasped his head, her lips lightly touching his forehead. The other hand stroked with a soothing rhythm his muscular shoulders.

The growl of the thunder was distant and passing away. The rain beat softly upon the shingles, inviting them to drowsiness and sleep. But they dared not yield.

The rain was over; and the sun was turning the glistening green world into a palace of gems. Calixta, on the gallery, watched Alcée ride away. He turned and smiled at her with a beaming face; and she lifted her pretty chin in the air and laughed aloud.

III

Bobinôt and Bibi, trudging home, stopped without at the cistern to make themselves presentable. 30

"My! Bibi, w'at will yo' mama say! You ought to be ashame'. You oughtn' put on those good pants. Look at 'em! An' that mud on yo' collar! How you got that mud on yo' collar, Bibi? I never saw such a boy!" Bibi was the picture of pathetic resignation. Bobinôt was the embodiment of serious solicitude as he strove to remove from his own person and his son's the signs of their tramp over heavy roads and through wet fields. He scraped the mud off Bibi's bare legs and feet with a stick and carefully removed all traces from his heavy brogans. Then, prepared for the worst—the meeting with an overscrupulous housewife, they entered cautiously at the back door.

Calixta was preparing supper. She had set the table and was dripping coffee at the hearth. She sprang up as they came in.

"Oh, Bobinôt! You back! My! but I was uneasy. W'ere you been during the rain? An' Bibi? he ain't wet? he ain't hurt?" She had clasped Bibi and was kissing him effusively. Bobinôt's explanations and apologies which he had been composing all along the way, died on his lips as Calixta felt him to see if he were dry, and seemed to express nothing but satisfaction at their safe return.

"I brought you some shrimps, Calixta," offered Bobinôt, hauling the can from his ample side pocket and laying it on the table.

"Shrimps! Oh, Bobinôt! you too good fo' anything!" and she gave him a   35
smacking kiss on the cheek that resounded. "*J'vous réponds,*° we'll have feas' to
night! umph-umph!"

Bobinôt and Bibi began to relax and enjoy themselves, and when the three
seated themselves at table they laughed much and so loud that anyone might
have heard them as far away as Laballière's.

IV

Alcée Laballière wrote to his wife, Clarisse, that night. It was a loving letter,
full of tender solicitude. He told her not to hurry back, but if she and the babies
liked it at Biloxi, to stay a month longer. He was getting on nicely; and though
he missed them, he was willing to bear the separation a while longer—realizing
that their health and pleasure were the first things to be considered.

V

As for Clarisse, she was charmed upon receiving her husband's letter. She
and the babies were doing well. The society was agreeable; many of her old
friends and acquaintances were at the bay. And the first free breath since her
marriage seemed to restore the pleasant liberty of her maiden days. Devoted as
she was to her husband, their intimate conjugal life was something which she
was more than willing to forego for a while.

So the storm passed and everyone was happy.

QUESTIONS

1. Exactly where does Chopin's story take place? How can you tell?
2. What circumstances introduced in Part I turn out to have a profound effect on events in the story?
3. What details in "The Storm" emphasize the fact that Bobinôt loves his wife? What details reveal how imperfectly he comprehends her nature?
4. What general attitudes toward sex, love, and marriage does Chopin imply? Cite evidence to support your answer.
5. What meanings do you find in the title "The Storm"?
6. In the story as a whole, how do setting and plot reinforce each other?

J'vous réponds: Let me tell you.

Jack London

To Build a Fire

Jack London (1876–1916), born in San Fran-cisco, won a large popular audience for his novels of the sea and the Yukon: The Call of the Wild (1903), The Sea-Wolf (1904), and White Fang (1906). Like Ernest Hemingway, he was a writer who lived a strenuous life. In 1893, he marched cross-country in Coxey's Army, an or-ganized protest of the unemployed; in 1897, he took part in the Klondike gold rush; and later as a reporter, he covered the Russo-Japanese war and the Mexican Revolution. Son of an unmarried mother and a father who denied his paternity, London grew up in poverty. At fourteen, he began holding hard jobs: working in a canning factory and a jute-mill, serving as a deck hand,

Jack London

pirating oysters in San Francisco Bay. These experiences persuaded him to join the Socialist Labor Party and crusade for workers' rights. In his political novel The Iron Heel (1908), London envisions a grim totalitarian America. Like himself, the hero of his novel Martin Eden (1909) is a man of brief schooling who gains fame as a writer, works for a cause, loses faith in it, and finds life without meaning. Though endowed with immense physical energy—he wrote fifty volumes—London drank hard, spent fast, and played out early. While his rep-utation as a novelist may have declined since his own day, some of his short stories have lasted triumphantly.

Day had broken cold and gray, exceedingly cold and gray, when the man turned aside from the main Yukon trail and climbed the high earth-bank, where a dim and little-travelled trail led eastward through the fat spruce timberland. It was a steep bank, and he paused for breath at the top, excusing the act to himself by looking at his watch. It was nine o'clock. There was no sun nor hint of sun, though there was not a cloud in the sky. It was a clear day, and yet there seemed an intangible pall over the face of things, a subtle gloom that made the day dark, and that was due to the absence of sun. This fact did not worry the man. He was used to the lack of sun. It had been days since he had seen the sun, and he knew that a few more days must pass before that cheerful orb, due south, would just peep above the sky line and dip immediately from view.

The man flung a look back along the way he had come. The Yukon lay a mile wide and hidden under three feet of ice. On top of this ice were as many feet of snow. It was all pure white, rolling in gentle undulations where the ice jams of the freeze-up had formed. North and south, as far as the eye could see, it was unbroken white, save for a dark hairline that curved and twisted from around the spruce-covered island to the south, and that curved and twisted away into the north, where it disappeared behind another spruce-covered island. This dark hairline was the trail—the main trail—that led south five hundred miles to the Chilcoot Pass, Dyea, and salt water; and that led north seventy miles to Dawson, and still on to the north a thousand miles to Nulato, and finally to St. Michael, on Bering Sea, a thousand miles and half a thousand more.

But all this—the mysterious, far-reaching hairline trail, the absence of sun from the sky, the tremendous cold, and the strangeness and weirdness of it all—made no impression on the man. It was not because he was long used to it. He was a newcomer in the land, a *chechaquo*, and this was his first winter. The trouble with him was that he was without imagination. He was quick and alert in the things of life, but only in the things, and not in the significances. Fifty degrees below zero meant eighty-odd degrees of frost. Such fact impressed him as being cold and uncomfortable, and that was all. It did not lead him to meditate upon his frailty as a creature of temperature, and upon man's frailty in general, able only to live within certain narrow limits of heat and cold; and from there on it did not lead him to the conjectural field of immortality and man's place in the universe. Fifty degrees below zero stood for a bite of frost that hurt and that must be guarded against by the use of mittens, ear flaps, warm moccasins, and thick socks. Fifty degrees below zero was to him just precisely fifty degrees below zero. That there should be anything more to it than that was a thought that never entered his head.

As he turned to go on, he spat speculatively. There was a sharp, explosive crackle that startled him. He spat again. And again, in the air, before it could fall to the snow, the spittle crackled. He knew that at fifty below spittle crackled on the snow, but this spittle had crackled in the air. Undoubtedly it was colder than fifty below—how much colder he did not know. But the temperature did not matter. He was bound for the old claim on the left fork of Henderson Creek, where the boys were already. They had come over across the divide from the Indian Creek country, while he had come the roundabout way to take a look at the possibilities of getting out logs in the spring from the islands in the Yukon. He would be in to camp by six o'clock; a bit after dark, it was true, but the boys would be there, a fire would be going, and a hot supper would be ready. As for lunch, he pressed his hand against the protruding bundle under his jacket. It was also under his shirt, wrapped up in a handkerchief and lying against the naked skin. It was the only way to keep the biscuits from freezing. He smiled agreeably to himself as he thought of those biscuits, each cut open and sopped in bacon grease, and each enclosing a generous slice of fried bacon.

He plunged in among the big spruce trees. The trail was faint. A foot of snow had fallen since the last sled had passed over, and he was glad he was without a sled, travelling light. In fact, he carried nothing but the lunch wrapped in the handkerchief. He was surprised, however, at the cold. It certainly was cold, he concluded, as he rubbed his numb nose and cheekbones with his mittened hand. He was a warm-whiskered man, but the hair on his face did not protect the high cheekbones and the eager nose that thrust itself aggressively into the frosty air.

At the man's heels trotted a dog, a big native husky, the proper wolf dog, gray-coated and without any visible or temperamental difference from its brother, the wild wolf. The animal was depressed by the tremendous cold. It knew that it was no time for travelling. Its instinct told it a truer tale than was told to the man by the man's judgment. In reality, it was not merely colder than fifty below zero; it was colder than sixty below, than seventy below. It was seventy-five below zero. Since the freezing point is thirty-two above zero, it meant that one hundred and seven degrees of frost obtained. The dog did not know anything about thermometers. Possibly in its brain there was no sharp consciousness of a condition of very cold such as was in the man's brain. But the brute had its instinct. It experienced a vague but menacing apprehension that subdued it and made it slink along at the man's heels, and that made it question eagerly every unwonted movement of the man as if expecting him to go into camp or to seek shelter somewhere and build a fire. The dog had learned fire, and it wanted fire, or else to burrow under the snow and cuddle its warmth away from the air.

The frozen moisture of its breathing had settled on its fur in a fine powder of frost, and especially were its jowls, muzzle, and eyelashes whitened by its crystalled breath. The man's red beard and mustache were likewise frosted, but more solidly, the deposit taking the form of ice and increasing with every warm, moist breath he exhaled. Also, the man was chewing tobacco, and the muzzle of ice held his lips so rigidly that he was unable to clear his chin when he expelled the juice. The result was that a crystal beard of the color and solidity of amber was increasing its length on his chin. If he fell down it would shatter itself, like glass, into brittle fragments. But he did not mind the appendage. It was the penalty all tobacco chewers paid in that country, and he had been out before in two cold snaps. They had not been so cold as this, he knew, but by the spirit thermometer at Sixty Mile he knew they had been registered at fifty below and at fifty-five.

He held on through the level stretch of woods for several miles, crossed a wide flat, and dropped down a bank to the frozen bed of a small stream. This was Henderson Creek, and he knew he was ten miles from the forks. He looked at his watch. It was ten o'clock. He was making four miles an hour, and he calculated that he would arrive at the forks at half-past twelve. He decided to celebrate that event by eating his lunch there.

The dog dropped in again at his heels, with a tail drooping discouragement, as the man swung along the creek bed. The furrow of the old sled trail was plainly visible, but a dozen inches of snow covered the marks of the last runners. In a month no man had come up or down that silent creek. The man held steadily on. He was not much given to thinking, and just then particularly he had nothing to think about save that he would eat lunch at the forks and that at six o'clock he would be in camp with the boys. There was nobody to talk to; and, had there been, speech would have been impossible because of the ice muzzle on his mouth. So he continued monotonously to chew tobacco and to increase the length of his amber beard.

Once in a while the thought reiterated itself that it was very cold and that he had never experienced such cold. As he walked along he rubbed his cheekbones and nose with the back of his mittened hand. He did this automatically, now and again changing hands. But, rub as he would, the instant he stopped his cheekbones were numb, and the following instant the end of his nose went numb. He was sure to frost his cheeks; he knew that, and experienced a pang of

10

regret that he had not devised a nose strap of the sort Bud wore in cold snaps. Such a strap passed across the cheeks, as well, and saved them. But it didn't matter much, after all. What were frosted cheeks? A bit painful, that was all; they were never serious.

Empty as the man's mind was of thoughts, he was keenly observant, and he noticed the changes in the creek, the curves and bends and timber jams, and always he sharply noted where he placed his feet. Once, coming around a bend, he shied abruptly, like a startled horse, curved away from the place where he had been walking, and retreated several paces back along the trail. The creek he knew was frozen clear to the bottom—no creek could contain water in that arctic winter—but he knew also that there were springs that bubbled out from the hillsides and ran along under the snow and on top the ice of the creek. He knew that the coldest snaps never froze these springs, and he knew likewise their danger. They were traps. They hid pools of water under the snow that might be three inches deep, or three feet. Sometimes a skin of ice half an inch thick covered them, and in turn was covered by the snow. Sometimes there were alternate layers of water and ice skin, so that when one broke through he kept on breaking through for a while, sometimes wetting himself to the waist.

That was why he had shied in such panic. He had felt the give under his feet and heard the crackle of a snow-hidden ice skin. And to get his feet wet in such a temperature meant trouble and danger. At the very least it meant delay, for he would be forced to stop and build a fire, and under its protection to bare his feet while he dried his socks and moccasins. He stood and studied the creek bed and its banks, and decided that the flow of water came from the right. He reflected awhile, rubbing his nose and cheeks, then skirted to the left, stepping gingerly and testing the footing for each step. Once clear of the danger, he took a fresh chew of tobacco and swung along at his four-mile gait.

In the course of the next two hours he came upon several similar traps. Usually the snow above the hidden pools had a sunken, candied appearance that advertised the danger. Once again, however, he had a close call; and once, suspecting danger, he compelled the dog to go on in front. The dog did not want to go. It hung back until the man shoved it forward, and then it went quickly across the white, unbroken surface. Suddenly it broke through, floundered to one side, and got away to firmer footing. It had wet its forefeet and legs, and almost immediately the water that clung to it turned to ice. It made quick efforts to lick the ice off its legs, then dropped down in the snow and began to bite out the ice that had formed between the toes. This was a matter of instinct. To permit the ice to remain would mean sore feet. It did not know this. It merely obeyed the mysterious prompting that arose from the deep crypts of its being. But the man knew, having achieved a judgment on the subject, and he removed the mitten from his right hand and helped tear out the ice particles. He did not expose his fingers more than a minute, and was astonished at the swift numbness that smote them. It certainly was cold. He pulled on the mitten hastily, and beat the hand savagely across his chest.

At twelve o'clock the day was at its brightest. Yet the sun was too far south on its winter journey to clear the horizon. The bulge of the earth intervened between it and Henderson Creek, where the men walked under a clear sky at noon and cast no shadow. At half-past twelve, to the minute, he arrived at the forks of the creek. He was pleased at the speed he had made. If he kept it up, he would certainly be with the boys by six. He unbuttoned his jacket and shirt and drew forth his lunch. The action consumed no more than a quarter of a minute, yet in that brief moment the numbness laid hold of the exposed fingers. He did not put the mitten on, but, instead, struck the fingers a dozen sharp smashes against his leg. Then he sat down on a snow-covered log to eat. The sting that followed upon the striking of his fingers against his leg ceased so quickly that he was startled. He had had no chance to take a bite of biscuit. He struck the fingers repeatedly and returned them to the mitten, baring the other hand for the purpose of eating. He tried to take a mouthful, but the ice muzzle prevented. He had forgotten to build a fire and thaw out. He chuckled at his foolishness, and as he chuckled he noted the numbness creeping into the exposed fingers. Also, he noted that the stinging which had first come to his toes when he sat down was already passing away. He wondered whether the toes were warm or numb. He moved them inside the moccasins and decided that they were numb.

He pulled the mitten on hurriedly and stood up. He was a bit frightened. He stamped up and down until the stinging returned into the feet. It certainly was cold, was his thought. That man from Sulphur Creek had spoken the truth when telling how cold it sometimes got in the country. And he had laughed at him at the time! That showed one must not be too sure of things. There was no mistake about it, it *was* cold. He strode up and down, stamping his feet and threshing his arms, until reassured by the returning warmth. Then he got out matches and proceeded to make a fire. From the undergrowth, where high water of the previous spring had lodged a supply of seasoned twigs, he got his firewood. Working carefully from a small beginning, he soon had a roaring fire, over which he thawed the ice from his face and in the protection of which he ate his biscuits. For the moment the cold of space was outwitted. The dog took satisfaction in the fire, stretching out close enough for warmth and far enough away to escape being singed.

When the man had finished, he filled his pipe and took his comfortable time over a smoke. Then he pulled on his mittens, settled the ear flaps of his cap firmly about his ears, and took the creek trail up the left fork. The dog was disappointed and yearned back toward the fire. This man did not know cold. Possibly all the generations of his ancestry had been ignorant of cold, of real cold, of cold one hundred and seven degrees below freezing point. But the dog knew; all its ancestry knew, and it had inherited the knowledge. And it knew that it was not good to walk abroad in such fearful cold. It was the time to lie snug in a hole in the snow and wait for a curtain of cloud to be drawn across the face of outer space whence this cold came. On the other hand, there was no keen intimacy between the dog and the man. The one was the toil slave of the other, and the only caresses it had ever received were the caresses of the whip lash and of harsh and menacing throat sounds that threatened the whip lash. So the dog made no effort to communicate its apprehension to the man. It was not concerned in the welfare of the man; it was for its own sake that it yearned back toward the fire. But the man whistled, and spoke to it with the sound of whip lashes, and the dog swung in at the man's heels and followed after.

The man took a chew of tobacco and proceeded to start a new amber beard. Also, his moist breath quickly powdered with white his mustache, eyebrows, and lashes. There did not seem to be so many springs on the left fork of the Henderson, and for half an hour the man saw no signs of any. And then it happened. At a place where there were no signs, where the soft, unbroken snow seemed to advertise solidity beneath, the man broke through. It was not deep. He wet himself halfway to the knees before he floundered out to the firm crust.

He was angry, and cursed his luck aloud. He had hoped to get into camp with the boys at six o'clock, and this would delay him an hour, for he would have to build a fire and dry out his footgear. This was imperative at that low temperature—he knew that much; and he turned aside to the bank, which he climbed. On top, tangled in the underbrush about the trunks of several small spruce trees, was a high-water deposit of dry firewood—sticks and twigs, principally, but also larger portions of seasoned branches and fine, dry, last year's grasses. He threw down several large pieces on top of the snow. This served for a foundation and prevented the young flame from drowning itself in the snow it otherwise would melt. The flame he got by touching a match to a small shred of birch bark that he took from his pocket. This burned even more readily than paper. Placing it on the foundation, he fed the young flame with wisps of dry grass and with the tiniest dry twigs.

He worked slowly and carefully, keenly aware of his danger. Gradually, as the flame grew stronger, he increased the size of the twigs with which he fed it. He squatted in the snow, pulling the twigs out from their entanglement in the brush and feeding directly to the flame. He knew there must be no failure. When it is seventy-five below zero, a man must not fail in his first attempt to build a fire—that is, if his feet are wet. If his feet are dry, and he fails, he can run along the trail for half a mile and restore his circulation. But the circulation of wet and freezing feet cannot be restored by running when it is seventy-five below. No matter how fast he runs, the wet feet will freeze the harder.

All this the man knew. The old-timer on Sulphur Creek had told him about 20 it the previous fall, and now he was appreciating the advice. Already all sensation had gone out of his feet. To build the fire he had been forced to remove his mittens, and the fingers had quickly gone numb. His pace of four miles an hour had kept his heart pumping blood to the surface of his body and to all the extremities. But the instant he stopped, the action of the pump eased down. The cold of space smote the unprotected tip of the planet, and he, being on that unprotected tip, received the full force of the blow. The blood of his body recoiled before it. The blood was alive, like the dog, and like the dog it wanted to hide away and cover itself up from the fearful cold. So long as he walked four miles an hour, he pumped that blood, willy-nilly, to the surface; but now it ebbed away and sank down into the recesses of his body. The extremities were the first to feel its absence. His wet feet froze the faster, and his exposed fingers numbed the faster, though they had not yet begun to freeze. Nose and cheeks were already freezing, while the skin of all his body chilled as it lost its blood.

But he was safe. Toes and nose and cheeks would be only touched by the frost, for the fire was beginning to burn with strength. He was feeding it with twigs the size of his finger. In another minute he would be able to feed it with branches the size of his wrist, and then he could remove his wet footgear, and, while it dried, he could keep his naked feet warm by the fire, rubbing them at first, of course, with snow. The fire was a success. He was safe. He remembered the advice of the old-timer on Sulphur Creek, and smiled. The old-timer had been very serious in laying down the law that no man must travel alone in the Klondike after fifty below. Well, here he was; he had had the accident; he was alone; and he had saved himself. Those old-timers were rather womanish, some of them, he thought. All a man had to do was to keep his head, and he was all right. Any man who was a man could travel alone. But it was surprising, the rapidity with which his cheeks and nose were freezing. And he had not thought his fingers could go lifeless in so short a time. Lifeless they were, for he could scarcely make them move together to grip a twig, and they seemed remote from his body and from him. When he touched a twig, he had to look and see whether or not he had hold of it. The wires were pretty well down between him and his finger ends.

All of which counted for little. There was the fire, snapping and crackling and promising life with every dancing flame. He started to untie his moccasins. They were coated with ice; the thick German socks were like sheaths of iron halfway to the knees; and the moccasin strings were like rods of steel all twisted and knotted as by some conflagration. For a moment he tugged with his numb fingers, then, realizing the folly of it, he drew his sheath knife.

But before he could cut the strings, it happened. It was his own fault or, rather, his mistake. He should not have built the fire under the spruce tree. He should have built it in the open. But it had been easier to pull the twigs from the brush and drop them directly on the fire. Now the tree under which he had done this carried a weight of snow on its boughs. No wind had blown for weeks, and each bough was fully freighted. Each time he had pulled a twig he had communicated a slight agitation to the tree—an imperceptible agitation, so far as he was concerned, but an agitation sufficient to bring about the disaster. High up in the tree one bough capsized its load of snow. This fell on the boughs beneath, capsizing them. This process continued, spreading out and involving the whole tree. It grew like an avalanche, and it descended without warning upon the man and the fire, and the fire was blotted out! Where it had burned was a mantle of fresh and disordered snow.

The man was shocked. It was as though he had just heard his own sentence of death. For a moment he sat and stared at the spot where the fire had been. Then he grew very calm. Perhaps the old-timer on Sulphur Creek was right. If he had only had a trail mate he would have been in no danger now. The trail mate could have built the fire. Well, it was up to him to build the fire over again, and this second time there must be no failure. Even if he succeeded, he would most likely lose some toes. His feet must be badly frozen by now, and there would be some time before the second fire was ready.

Such were his thoughts, but he did not sit and think them. He was busy all the time they were passing through his mind. He made a new foundation for a fire, this time in the open, where no treacherous tree could blot it out. Next he gathered dry grasses and tiny twigs from the high-water flotsam. He could not bring his fingers together to pull them out, but he was able to gather them by the handful. In this

25

way he got many rotten twigs and bits of green moss that were undesirable, but it was the best he could do. He worked methodically, even collecting an armful of the larger branches to be used later when the fire gathered strength. And all the while the dog sat and watched him, a certain yearning wistfulness in its eye, for it looked upon him as the fire provider, and the fire was slow in coming.

When all was ready, the man reached in his pocket for a second piece of birch bark. He knew the bark was there, and, though he could not feel it with his fingers, he could hear its crisp rustling as he fumbled for it. Try as he would, he could not clutch hold of it. And all the time, in his consciousness, was the knowledge that each instant his feet were freezing. This thought tended to put him in a panic, but he fought against it and kept calm. He pulled on his mittens with his teeth, and threshed his arms back and forth, beating his hands with all his might against his sides. He did this sitting down, and he stood up to do it; and all the while the dog sat in the snow, its wolf brush of a tail curled around warmly over its forefeet, its sharp wolf ears pricked forward intently as it watched the man. And the man, as he beat and threshed with his arms and hands, felt a great surge of envy as he regarded the creature that was warm and secure in its natural covering.

After a time he was aware of the first faraway signals of sensation in his beaten fingers. The faint tingling grew stronger till it evolved into a stinging ache that was excruciating, but which the man hailed with satisfaction. He stripped the mitten from his right hand and fetched forth the birch bark. The exposed fingers were quickly going numb again. Next he brought out his bunch of sulphur matches. But the tremendous cold had already driven the life out of his fingers. In his effort to separate one match from the others, the whole bunch fell in the snow. He tried to pick it out of the snow, but failed. The dead fingers could neither touch nor clutch. He was very careful. He drove the thought of his freezing feet, and nose, and cheeks, out of his mind, devoting his whole soul to the matches. He watched, using the sense of vision in place of that of touch, and when he saw his fingers on each side the bunch, he closed them—that is, he willed to close them, for the wires were down, and the fingers did not obey. He pulled the mitten on the right hand, and beat it fiercely against his knee. Then, with both mittened hands, he scooped the bunch of matches, along with much snow, into his lap. Yet he was no better off.

After some manipulation he managed to get the bunch between the heels of his mittened hands. In this fashion he carried it to his mouth. The ice crackled and snapped when by a violent effort he opened his mouth. He drew the lower jaw in, curled the upper lip out of the way, and scraped the bunch with his upper teeth in order to separate a match. He succeeded in getting one, which he dropped on his lap. He was no better off. He could not pick it up. Then he devised a way. He picked it up in his teeth and scratched it on his leg. Twenty times he scratched before he succeeded in lighting it. As it flamed he held it with his teeth to the birch bark. But the burning brimstone went up his nostrils and into his lungs, causing him to cough spasmodically. The match fell into the snow and went out.

The old-timer on Sulphur Creek was right, he thought in the moment of controlled despair that ensued: after fifty below, a man should travel with a partner. He beat his hands, but failed in exciting any sensation. Suddenly he bared both hands, removing the mittens with his teeth. He caught the whole bunch between the heels of his hands. His arm muscles not being frozen enabled him to press the hand heels tightly against the matches. Then he scratched the bunch along his leg. It flared into flame, seventy sulphur matches at once! There was no wind to blow them out. He kept his head to one side to escape the strangling fumes, and held the blazing bunch to the birch bark. As he so held it, he became aware of sensation in his hand. His flesh was burning. He could smell it. Deep down below the surface he could feel it. The sensation developed into pain that grew acute. And still he endured it, holding the flame of the matches clumsily to the bark that would not light readily because his own burning hands were in the way, absorbing most of the flame.

At last, when he could endure no more, he jerked his hands apart. The 30 blazing matches fell sizzling into the snow, but the birch bark was alight. He began laying dry grasses and the tiniest twigs on the flame. He could not pick and choose, for he had to lift the fuel between the heels of his hands. Small pieces of rotten wood and green moss clung to the twigs, and he bit them off as well as he could with his teeth. He cherished the flame carefully and awkwardly. It meant life, and it must not perish. The withdrawal of blood from the surface of his body now made him begin to shiver, and he grew more awkward. A large piece of green moss fell squarely on the little fire. He tried to poke it out with his fingers, but his shivering frame made him poke too far, and he disrupted the nucleus of the little fire, the burning grasses and tiny twigs separating and scattering. He tried to poke them together again, but in spite of the tenseness of the effort, his shivering got away from him, and the twigs were hopelessly scattered. Each twig gushed a puff of smoke and went out. The fire provider had failed. As he looked apathetically about him, his eyes chanced on the dog, sitting across the ruins of the fire from him, in the snow, making restless, hunching movements, slightly lifting one forefoot and then the other, shifting its weight back and forth on them with wistful eagerness.

The sight of the dog put a wild idea into his head. He remembered the tale of the man, caught in the blizzard, who killed a steer and crawled inside the carcass, and so was saved. He would kill the dog and bury his hands in the warm body until the numbness went out of them. Then he could build another fire. He spoke to the dog, calling it to him; but in his voice was a strange note of fear that frightened the animal, who had never known the man to speak in such a way before. Something was the matter, and its suspicious nature sensed danger—it knew not what danger, but somewhere, somehow, in its brain arose an apprehension of the man. It flattened its ears down at the sound of the man's voice, and its restless, hunching movements and the liftings and shiftings of its forefeet became more pronounced; but it would not come to the man. He got on his hands and knees and crawled toward the dog. This unusual posture again excited suspicion, and the animal sidled mincingly away.

The man sat up in the snow for a moment and struggled for calmness. Then he pulled on his mittens, by means of his teeth, and got upon his feet. He glanced down at first in order to assure himself that he was really standing up, for the absence of sensation in his feet left him unrelated to the earth. His erect position in itself started to drive the webs of suspicion from the dog's mind; and when he spoke peremptorily, with the sound of whip lashes in his voice, the dog rendered its customary allegiance and came to him. As it came within reaching distance, the man lost his control. His arms flashed out to the dog, and he experienced genuine surprise when he discovered that his hands could not clutch, that there was neither bend nor feeling in the fingers. He had forgotten for the moment that they were frozen and that they were freezing more and more. All this happened quickly, and before the animal could get away, he encircled its body with his arms. He sat down in the snow, and in this fashion held the dog, while it snarled and whined and struggled.

But it was all he could do, hold its body encircled in his arms and sit there. He realized that he could not kill the dog. There was no way to do it. With his helpless hands he could neither draw nor hold his sheath knife nor throttle the animal. He released it, and it plunged wildly away, with tail between its legs, and still snarling. It halted forty feet away and surveyed him curiously, with ears sharply pricked forward.

The man looked down at his hands in order to locate them, and found them hanging on the ends of his arms. It struck him as curious that one should have to use his eyes in order to find out where his hands were. He began threshing his arms back and forth, beating the mittened hands against his sides. He did this for five minutes, violently, and his heart pumped enough blood up to the surface to put a stop to his shivering. But no sensation was aroused in the hands. He had an impression that they hung like weights on the ends of his arms, but when he tried to run the impression down, he could not find it.

A certain fear of death, dull and oppressive, came to him. This fear quickly   35
became poignant as he realized that it was no longer a mere matter of freezing his fingers and toes, or of losing his hands and feet, but that it was a matter of life and death with the chances against him. This threw him into a panic, and he turned and ran up the creek bed along the old, dim trail. The dog joined in behind and kept up with him. He ran blindly, without intention, in fear such as he had never known in his life. Slowly, as he plowed and floundered through the snow, he began to see things again—the banks of the creek, the old timber jams, the leafless aspens, and the sky. The running made him feel better. He did not shiver. Maybe, if he ran on, his feet would thaw out; and anyway, if he ran far enough, he would reach camp and the boys. Without doubt he would lose some fingers and toes and some of his face; but the boys would take care of him, and save the rest of him when he got there. And at the same time there was another thought in his mind that said he would never get to the camp and the boys; that it was too many miles away, that the freezing had too great a start on him, and that he would soon be stiff and dead. This thought he kept in the background and refused to consider. Sometimes it pushed itself forward and demanded to be heard, but he thrust it back and strove to think of other things.

It struck him as curious that he could run at all on feet so frozen that he could not feel them when they struck the earth and took the weight of his body. He seemed to himself to skim along above the surface, and to have no connection with the earth. Somewhere he had once seen a winged Mercury, and he wondered if Mercury felt as he felt when skimming over the earth.

His theory of running until he reached the camp and the boys had one flaw in it: he lacked the endurance. Several times he stumbled, and finally he tottered, crumpled up, and fell. When he tried to rise, he failed. He must sit and rest, he decided, and next time he would merely walk and keep on going. As he sat and regained his breath, he noted that he was feeling quite warm and comfortable. He was not shivering, and it even seemed that a warm glow had come to his chest and trunk. And yet, when he touched his nose and cheeks, there was no sensation. Running would not thaw them out. Nor would it thaw out his hands and feet. Then the thought came to him that the frozen portions of his body must be extending. He tried to keep this thought down, to forget it, to think of something else; he was aware of the panicky feeling that it caused, and he was afraid of the panic. But the thought asserted itself, and persisted, until it produced a vision of his body totally frozen. This was too much, and he made another wild run along the trail. Once he slowed down to a walk, but the thought of the freezing extending itself made him run again.

And all the time the dog ran with him, at his heels. When he fell down a second time, it curled its tail over its forefeet and sat in front of him, facing him, curiously eager and intent. The warmth and security of the animal angered him, and he cursed it till it flattened down its ears appeasingly. This time the shivering came more quickly upon the man. He was losing in his battle with the frost. It was creeping into his body from all sides. The thought of it drove him on, but he ran no more than a hundred feet, when he staggered and pitched headlong. It was his last panic. When he had recovered his breath and control, he sat up and entertained in his mind the conception of meeting death with dignity. However, the conception did not come to him in such terms. His idea of it was that he had been making a fool of himself, running around like a chicken with its head cut off—such was the simile that occurred to him. Well, he was bound to freeze anyway, and he might as well take it decently. With this newfound peace of mind came the first glimmerings of drowsiness. A good idea, he thought, to sleep off to death. It was like taking an anesthetic. Freezing was not so bad as people thought. There were lots worse ways to die.

He pictured the boys finding his body next day. Suddenly he found himself with them, coming along the trail and looking for himself. And, still with them, he came around a turn in the trail and found himself lying in the snow. He did not belong with himself any more, for even then he was out of himself, standing with the boys and looking at himself in the snow. It certainly was cold, was his thought. When he got back to the States he could tell the folks what real cold was. He drifted on from this to a vision of the old-timer on Sulphur Creek. He could see him quite clearly, warm and comfortable, and smoking a pipe.

"You were right, old hoss; you were right," the man mumbled to the old-timer of Sulphur Creek.

Then the man drowsed off into what seemed to him the most comfortable and satisfying sleep he had ever known. The dog sat facing him and waiting. The brief day drew to a close in a long, slow twilight. There were no signs of a fire to be made, and, besides, never in the dog's experience had it known a man to sit like that in the snow and make no fire. As the twilight drew on, its eager yearning for the fire mastered it, and with a great lifting and shifting of forefeet, it whined softly, then flattened its ears down in anticipation of being chidden by the man. But the man remained silent. Later the dog whined loudly. And still later it crept close to the man and caught the scent of death. This made the animal bristle and back away. A little longer it delayed, howling under the stars that leaped and danced and shone brightly in the cold sky. Then it turned and trotted up the trail in the direction of the camp it knew, where were the other food providers and fire providers.

QUESTIONS

1. Roughly how much of London's story is devoted to describing the setting? What particular details make it memorable?
2. To what extent does setting determine what happens in this story?
3. From what point of view is London's story told?
4. In "To Build a Fire" the man is never given a name. What is the effect of his being called simply "the man" throughout the story?
5. From the evidence London gives us, what stages are involved in the process of freezing to death? What does the story gain from London's detailed account of the man's experience with each successive stage?
6. What are the most serious mistakes the man makes? To what factors do you attribute these errors?

T. Coraghessan Boyle

GREASY LAKE   1985

T. Coraghessan Boyle (the T. stands for Tom) was born in 1948 in Peekskill, New York, the son of Irish immigrants. He grew up, he recalls, "as a sort of pampered punk" who did not read a book until he was eighteen. After a brief period as a high school teacher, he studied in the University of Iowa Writers' Workshop, submitting a collection of stories for his Ph.D. He now teaches writing at the University of Southern California and sometimes plays saxophone in a rockabilly band. His stories in Esquire, Paris Review, *the* Atlantic, *and other magazines quickly won him notice for their outrageous macabre humor and bizarre inventiveness. Boyle has published six*

T. Coraghessan Boyle

volumes of short stories, including Greasy Lake *(1985),* T.C. Boyle Stories *(1998), and* After the Plague *(2001). He has also published nine novels that are quite unlike anything else in contemporary American fiction. The subjects of some Boyle novels reveal his wide-ranging and idiosyncratic interests.* Water Music *(1982) concerns an eighteenth-century expedition to Africa.* Budding Prospects *(1984) is a picaresque romp among adventurous marijuana growers.* East Is East *(1990) is a half-serious, half-comic story of a Japanese fugitive in an American writers' colony.* The Road to Wellville *(1993), which was made into a film with Anthony Hopkins and Matthew Broderick, takes place in 1907 in a sanitarium run by Dr. John Harvey Kellogg of corn flakes fame, with cameo appearances by Henry Ford, Thomas Edison, and Harvey Firestone. His most recent novels include* A Friend of the Earth *(2000) and* Drop City *(2003). Boyle lives in southern California.*

It's about a mile down on the dark side of Route 88.
                    —Bruce Springsteen

There was a time when courtesy and winning ways went out of style, when it was good to be bad, when you cultivated decadence like a taste. We were all dangerous characters then. We wore torn-up leather jackets, slouched around with toothpicks in our mouths, sniffed glue and ether and what somebody claimed was cocaine. When we wheeled our parents' whining station wagons out onto the street we left a patch of rubber half a block long. We drank gin and grape juice, Tango, Thunderbird, and Bali Hai. We were nineteen. We were bad. We read André Gide° and struck elaborate poses to show that we didn't give a shit about anything. At night, we went up to Greasy Lake.

Through the center of town, up the strip, past the housing developments and shopping malls, street lights giving way to the thin streaming illumination of the headlights, trees crowding the asphalt in a black unbroken wall: that was the way out to Greasy Lake. The Indians had called it Wakan, a reference to the clarity of its waters. Now it was fetid and murky, the mud banks glittering with broken glass and strewn with beer cans and the charred remains of bonfires. There was a single ravaged island a hundred yards from shore, so stripped of vegetation it looked as if the air force had strafed it. We went up to the lake because everyone went there, because we wanted to snuff the rich scent of possibility on the breeze, watch a girl take off her clothes and plunge into the festering murk, drink beer, smoke pot, howl at the stars, savor the incongruous full-throated roar of rock and roll against the primeval susurrus of frogs and crickets. This was nature.

I was there one night, late, in the company of two dangerous characters. Digby wore a gold star in his right ear and allowed his father to pay his tuition at Cornell; Jeff was thinking of quitting school to become a painter/musician/head-shop proprietor. They were both expert in the social graces, quick with a sneer, able to manage a Ford with lousy shocks over a rutted and gutted blacktop road at eighty-five while rolling a joint as compact as a Tootsie Roll Pop stick. They could lounge against a bank of booming speakers and trade "man"s with the best of them or roll out across the dance floor as if their joints worked on bearings.

André Gide: controversial French writer (1869–1951) whose novels, including *The Counterfeiters* and *Lafcadio's Adventures,* often show individuals in conflict with accepted morality.

They were slick and quick and they wore their mirror shades at breakfast and dinner, in the shower, in closets and caves. In short, they were bad.

I drove. Digby pounded the dashboard and shouted along with Toots & the Maytals while Jeff hung his head out the window and streaked the side of my mother's Bel Air with vomit. It was early June, the air soft as a hand on your cheek, the third night of summer vacation. The first two nights we'd been out till dawn, looking for something we never found. On this, the third night, we'd cruised the strip sixty-seven times, been in and out of every bar and club we could think of in a twenty-mile radius, stopped twice for bucket chicken and forty-cent hamburgers, debated going to a party at the house of a girl Jeff's sister knew, and chucked two dozen raw eggs at mailboxes and hitchhikers. It was 2:00 A.M.; the bars were closing. There was nothing to do but take a bottle of lemon-flavored gin up to Greasy Lake.

The taillights of a single car winked at us as we swung into the dirt lot with   5
its tufts of weed and washboard corrugations; '57 Chevy, mint, metallic blue. On the far side of the lot, like the exoskeleton of some gaunt chrome insect, a chopper leaned against its kickstand. And that was it for excitement: some junkie halfwit biker and a car freak pumping his girlfriend. Whatever it was we were looking for, we weren't about to find it at Greasy Lake. Not that night.

But then all of a sudden Digby was fighting for the wheel. "Hey, that's Tony Lovett's car! Hey!" he shouted, while I stabbed at the brake pedal and the Bel Air nosed up to the gleaming bumper of the parked Chevy. Digby leaned on the horn, laughing, and instructed me to put my brights on. I flicked on the brights. This was hilarious. A joke. Tony would experience premature withdrawal and expect to be confronted by grim-looking state troopers with flashlights. We hit the horn, strobed the lights, and then jumped out of the car to press our witty faces to Tony's windows; for all we knew we might even catch a glimpse of some little fox's tit, and then we could slap backs with red-faced Tony, roughhouse a little, and go on to new heights of adventure and daring.

The first mistake, the one that opened the whole floodgate, was losing my grip on the keys. In the excitement, leaping from the car with the gin in one hand and a roach clip in the other, I spilled them in the grass—in the dark, rank, mysterious nighttime grass of Greasy Lake. This was a tactical error, as damaging and irreversible in its way as Westmoreland's decision to dig in at Khe Sanh.° I felt it like a jab of intuition, and I stopped there by the open door, peering vaguely into the night that puddled up round my feet.

The second mistake—and this was inextricably bound up with the first—was identifying the car as Tony Lovett's. Even before the very bad character in greasy jeans and engineer boots ripped out of the driver's door, I began to realize

---

Westmoreland's decision . . . Khe Sanh: General William C. Westmoreland commanded U.S. troops in Vietnam (1964–68). In late 1967 the North Vietnamese and Viet Cong forces attacked Khe Sanh (or Khesanh) with a show of strength, causing Westmoreland to expend great effort to defend a plateau of relatively little tactical importance.

that this chrome blue was much lighter than the robin's-egg of Tony's car, and that Tony's car didn't have rear-mounted speakers. Judging from their expressions, Digby and Jeff were privately groping toward the same inevitable and unsettling conclusion as I was.

In any case, there was no reasoning with this bad greasy character—clearly he was a man of action. The first lusty Rockette° kick of his steel-toed boot caught me under the chin, chipped my favorite tooth, and left me sprawled in the dirt. Like a fool, I'd gone down on one knee to comb the stiff hacked grass for the keys, my mind making connections in the most dragged-out, testudineous way, knowing that things had gone wrong, that I was in a lot of trouble, and that the lost ignition key was my grail and my salvation. The three or four succeeding blows were mainly absorbed by my right buttock and the tough piece of bone at the base of my spine.

Meanwhile, Digby vaulted the kissing bumpers and delivered a savage kung-fu blow to the greasy character's collarbone. Digby had just finished a course in martial arts for phys-ed credit and had spent the better part of the past two nights telling us apocryphal tales of Bruce Lee types and of the raw power invested in lightning blows shot from coiled wrists, ankles, and elbows. The greasy character was unimpressed. He merely backed off a step, his face like a Toltec mask, and laid Digby out with a single whistling roundhouse blow . . . but by now Jeff had got into the act, and I was beginning to extricate myself from the dirt, a tinny compound of shock, rage, and impotence wadded in my throat.

Jeff was on the guy's back, biting at his ear. Digby was on the ground, cursing. I went for the tire iron I kept under the driver's seat. I kept it there because bad characters always keep tire irons under the driver's seat, for just such an occasion as this. Never mind that I hadn't been involved in a fight since sixth grade, when a kid with a sleepy eye and two streams of mucus depending from his nostrils hit me in the knee with a Louisville slugger,° never mind that I'd touched the tire iron exactly twice before, to change tires: it was there. And I went for it.

I was terrified. Blood was beating in my ears, my hands were shaking, my heart turning over like a dirtbike in the wrong gear. My antagonist was shirtless, and a single cord of muscle flashed across his chest as he bent forward to peel Jeff from his back like a wet overcoat. "Motherfucker," he spat, over and over, and I was aware in that instant that all four of us—Digby, Jeff, and myself included—were chanting "motherfucker, motherfucker," as if it were a battle cry. (What happened next? the detective asks the murderer from beneath the turned-down brim of his porkpie hat. I don't know, the murderer says, something came over me. Exactly.)

10

Rockette: member of a dancing troupe in the stage show at Radio City Music Hall, New York, famous for its ability to kick fast and high with wonderful coordination. *Louisville slugger:* a brand of baseball bat.

Digby poked the flat of his hand in the bad character's face and I came at him like a kamikaze, mindless, raging, stung with humiliation—the whole thing, from the initial boot in the chin to this murderous primal instant involving no more than sixty hyperventilating, gland-flooding seconds—I came at him and brought the tire iron down across his ear. The effect was instantaneous, astonishing. He was a stunt man and this was Hollywood, he was a big grimacing toothy balloon and I was a man with a straight pin. He collapsed. Wet his pants. Went loose in his boots.

A single second, big as a zeppelin, floated by. We were standing over him in a circle, gritting our teeth, jerking our necks, our limbs and hands and feet twitching with glandular discharges. No one said anything. We just stared down at the guy, the car freak, the lover, the bad greasy character laid low. Digby looked at me; so did Jeff. I was still holding the tire iron, a tuft of hair clinging to the crook like dandelion fluff, like down. Rattled, I dropped it in the dirt, already envisioning the headlines, the pitted faces of the police inquisitors, the gleam of handcuffs, clank of bars, the big black shadows rising from the back of the cell . . . when suddenly a raw torn shriek cut through me like all the juice in all the electric chairs in the country.

It was the fox. She was short, barefoot, dressed in panties and a man's shirt.   15 "Animals!" she screamed, running at us with her fists clenched and wisps of blow-dried hair in her face. There was a silver chain round her ankle, and her toenails flashed in the glare of the headlights. I think it was the toenails that did it. Sure, the gin and the cannabis and even the Kentucky Fried may have had a hand in it, but it was the sight of those flaming toes that set us off—the toad emerging from the loaf in *Virgin Spring,*° lipstick smeared on a child; she was already tainted. We were on her like Bergman's deranged brothers—see no evil, hear none, speak none—panting, wheezing, tearing at her clothes, grabbing for flesh. We were bad characters, and we were scared and hot and three steps over the line—anything could have happened.

It didn't.

Before we could pin her to the hood of the car, our eyes masked with lust and greed and the purest primal badness, a pair of headlights swung into the lot. There we were, dirty, bloody, guilty, dissociated from humanity and civilization, the first of the *Ur*-crimes behind us, the second in progress, shreds of nylon panty and spandex brassiere dangling from our fingers, our flies open, lips licked—there we were, caught in the spotlight. Nailed.

We bolted. First for the car, and then, realizing we had no way of starting it, for the woods. I thought nothing. I thought escape. The headlights came at me like accusing fingers. I was gone.

Ram-bam-bam, across the parking lot, past the chopper and into the feculent undergrowth at the lake's edge, insects flying up in my face, weeds whipping,

---

Virgin Spring: film by Swedish director Ingmar Bergman.

frogs and snakes and red-eyed turtles splashing off into the night: I was already ankle-deep in muck and tepid water and still going strong. Behind me, the girl's screams rose in intensity, disconsolate, incriminating, the screams of the Sabine women,° the Christian martyrs, Anne Frank° dragged from the garret. I kept going, pursued by those cries, imagining cops and bloodhounds. The water was up to my knees when I realized what I was doing: I was going to swim for it. Swim the breadth of Greasy Lake and hide myself in the thick clot of woods on the far side. They'd never find me there.

I was breathing in sobs, in gasps. The water lapped at my waist as I looked   20
out over the moon-burnished ripples, the mats of algae that clung to the surface like scabs. Digby and Jeff had vanished. I paused. Listened. The girl was quieter now, screams tapering to sobs, but there were male voices, angry, excited, and the high-pitched ticking of the second car's engine. I waded deeper, stealthy, hunted, the ooze sucking at my sneakers. As I was about to take the plunge—at the very instant I dropped my shoulder for the first slashing stroke—I blundered into something. Something unspeakable, obscene, something soft, wet, moss-grown. A patch of weed? A log? When I reached out to touch it, it gave like a rubber duck, it gave like flesh.

In one of those nasty little epiphanies for which we are prepared by films and TV and childhood visits to the funeral home to ponder the shrunken painted forms of dead grandparents, I understood what it was that bobbed there so inadmissibly in the dark. Understood, and stumbled back in horror and revulsion, my mind yanked in six different directions (I was nineteen, a mere child, an infant, and here in the space of five minutes I'd struck down one greasy character and blundered into the waterlogged carcass of a second), thinking, The keys, the keys, why did I have to go and lose the keys? I stumbled back, but the muck took hold of my feet—a sneaker snagged, balance lost—and suddenly I was pitching face forward into the buoyant black mass, throwing out my hands in desperation while simultaneously conjuring the image of reeking frogs and muskrats revolving in slicks of their own deliquescing juices. AAAAArrrgh! I shot from the water like a torpedo, the dead man rotating to expose a mossy beard and eyes cold as the moon. I must have shouted out, thrashing around in the weeds, because the voices behind me suddenly became animated.

"What was that?"

"It's them, it's them: they tried to, tried to . . . *rape* me!" Sobs.

A man's voice, flat Midwestern accent. "You sons a bitches, we'll kill you!"

Frogs, crickets.   25

Sabine women: members of an ancient tribe in Italy, according to legend, forcibly carried off by the early Romans under Romulus to be their wives. The incident is depicted in a famous painting, "The Rape of the Sabine Women," by seventeenth-century French artist Nicolas Poussin.   *Anne Frank:* German Jewish girl (1929–1945) whose diary written during the Nazi occupation of the Netherlands later became world famous. She hid with her family in a secret attic in Amsterdam, but was caught by the Gestapo and sent to the concentration camp at Belsen, where she died.

Then another voice, harsh, *r*-less, Lower East Side: "Motherfucker!" I recognized the verbal virtuosity of the bad greasy character in the engineer boots. Tooth chipped, sneakers gone, coated in mud and slime and worse, crouching breathless in the weeds waiting to have my ass thoroughly and definitively kicked and fresh from the hideous stinking embrace of a three-days-dead-corpse, I suddenly felt a rush of joy and vindication: the son of a bitch was alive! Just as quickly, my bowels turned to ice. "Come on out of there, you pansy mothers!" the bad greasy character was screaming. He shouted curses till he was out of breath.

The crickets started up again, then the frogs. I held my breath. All at once was a sound in the reeds, a swishing, a splash: thunk-a-thunk. They were throwing rocks. The frogs fell silent. I cradled my head. Swish, swish, thunk-a-thunk. A wedge of feldspar the size of a cue ball glanced off my knee. I bit my finger.

It was then that they turned to the car. I heard a door slam, a curse, and then the sound of the headlights shattering—almost a good-natured sound, celebratory, like corks popping from the necks of bottles. This was succeeded by the dull booming of the fenders, metal on metal, and then the icy crash of the windshield. I inched forward, elbows and knees, my belly pressed to the muck, thinking of guerrillas and commandos and *The Naked and the Dead*.° I parted the weeds and squinted the length of the parking lot.

The second car—it was a Trans-Am—was still running, its high beams washing the scene in a lurid stagy light. Tire iron flailing, the greasy bad character was laying into the side of my mother's Bel Air like an avenging demon, his shadow riding up the trunks of the trees. Whomp. Whomp. Whomp-whomp. The other two guys—blond types, in fraternity jackets—were helping out with tree branches and skull-sized boulders. One of them was gathering up bottles, rocks, muck, candy wrappers, used condoms, poptops, and other refuse and pitching it through the window on the driver's side. I could see the fox, a white bulb behind the windshield of the '57 Chevy. "Bobbie," she whined over the thumping, "come on." The greasy character paused a moment, took one good swipe at the left taillight, and then heaved the tire iron halfway across the lake. Then he fired up the '57 and was gone.

Blond head nodded at blond head. One said something to the other, too low   30
for me to catch. They were no doubt thinking that in helping to annihilate my mother's car they'd committed a fairly rash act, and thinking too that there were three bad characters connected with that very car watching them from the woods. Perhaps other possibilities occurred to them as well—police, jail cells, justices of the peace, reparations, lawyers, irate parents, fraternal censure. Whatever they were thinking, they suddenly dropped branches, bottles, and rocks and sprang for their car in unison, as if they'd choreographed it. Five seconds. That's all it took. The engine shrieked, the tires squealed, a cloud of dust rose from the rutted lot and then settled back on darkness.

The Naked and the Dead: novel (1948) by Norman Mailer, about U.S. Army life in World War II.

I don't know how long I lay there, the bad breath of decay all around me, my jacket heavy as a bear, the primordial ooze subtly reconstituting itself to accommodate my upper thighs and testicles. My jaws ached, my knee throbbed, my coccyx was on fire. I contemplated suicide, wondered if I'd need bridgework, scraped the recesses of my brain for some sort of excuse to give my parents—a tree had fallen on the car, I was blinded by a bread truck, hit and run, vandals had got to it while we were playing chess at Digby's. Then I thought of the dead man. He was probably the only person on the planet worse off than I was. I thought about him, fog on the lake, insects chirring eerily, and felt the tug of fear, felt the darkness opening up inside me like a set of jaws. Who was he, I wondered, this victim of time and circumstance bobbing sorrowfully in the lake at my back. The owner of the chopper, no doubt, a bad older character come to this. Shot during a murky drug deal, drowned while drunkenly frolicking in the lake. Another headline. My car was wrecked; he was dead.

When the eastern half of the sky went from black to cobalt and the trees began to separate themselves from the shadows, I pushed myself up from the mud and stepped out into the open. By now the birds had begun to take over for the crickets, and dew lay slick on the leaves. There was a smell in the air, raw and sweet at the same time, the smell of the sun firing buds and opening blossoms. I contemplated the car. It lay there like a wreck along the highway, like a steel sculpture left over from a vanished civilization. Everything was still. This was nature.

I was circling the car, as dazed and bedraggled as the sole survivor of an air blitz, when Digby and Jeff emerged from the trees behind me. Digby's face was crosshatched with smears of dirt; Jeff's jacket was gone and his shirt was torn across the shoulder. They slouched across the lot, looking sheepish, and silently came up beside me to gape at the ravaged automobile. No one said a word. After a while Jeff swung open the driver's door and began to scoop the broken glass and garbage off the seat. I looked at Digby. He shrugged. "At least they didn't slash the tires," he said.

It was true: the tires were intact. There was no windshield, the headlights were staved in, and the body looked as if it had been sledge-hammered for a quarter a shot at the county fair, but the tires were inflated to regulation pressure. The car was drivable. In silence, all three of us bent to scrape the mud and shattered glass from the interior. I said nothing about the biker. When we were finished, I reached in my pocket for the keys, experienced a nasty stab of recollection, cursed myself, and turned to search the grass. I spotted them almost immediately, no more than five feet from the open door, glinting like jewels in the first tapering shaft of sunlight. There was no reason to get philosophical about it: I eased into the seat and turned the engine over.

It was at that precise moment that the silver Mustang with the flame decals rumbled into the lot. All three of us froze; then Digby and Jeff slid into the car and slammed the door. We watched as the Mustang rocked and bobbed across the ruts and finally jerked to a halt beside the forlorn chopper at the far end of the lot. "Let's go," Digby said. I hesitated, the Bel Air wheezing beneath me.

Two girls emerged from the Mustang. Tight jeans, stiletto heels, hair like frozen fur. They bent over the motorcycle, paced back and forth aimlessly, glanced once or twice at us, and then ambled over to where the reeds sprang up in a green fence round the perimeter of the lake. One of them cupped her hands to her mouth. "Al," she called. "Hey, Al!"

"Come on," Digby hissed. "Let's get out of here."

But it was too late. The second girl was picking her way across the lot, unsteady on her heels, looking up at us and then away. She was older—twenty-five or -six—and as she came closer we could see there was something wrong with her: she was stoned or drunk, lurching now and waving her arms for balance. I gripped the steering wheel as if it were the ejection lever of a flaming jet, and Digby spat out my name, twice, terse and impatient.

"Hi," the girl said.

We looked at her like zombies, like war veterans, like deaf-and-dumb pencil   40 peddlers.

She smiled, her lips cracked and dry. "Listen," she said, bending from the waist to look in the window, "you guys seen Al?" Her pupils were pinpoints, her eyes glass. She jerked her neck. "That's his bike over there—Al's. You seen him?"

Al. I didn't know what to say. I wanted to get out of the car and retch, I wanted to go home to my parents' house and crawl into bed. Digby poked me in the ribs. "We haven't seen anybody," I said.

The girl seemed to consider this, reaching out a slim veiny arm to brace herself against the car. "No matter," she said, slurring the *t*'s, "he'll turn up." And then, as if she'd just taken stock of the whole scene—the ravaged car and our battered faces, the desolation of the place—she said: "Hey, you guys look like some pretty bad characters—been fightin', huh?" We stared straight ahead, rigid as catatonics. She was fumbling in her pocket and muttering something. Finally she held out a handful of tablets in glassine wrappers: "Hey, you want to party, you want to do some of these with me and Sarah?"

I just looked at her. I thought I was going to cry. Digby broke the silence. "No, thanks," he said, leaning over me. "Some other time."

I put the car in gear and it inched forward with a groan, shaking off pellets   45 of glass like an old dog shedding water after a bath, heaving over the ruts on its worn springs, creeping toward the highway. There was a sheen of sun on the lake. I looked back. The girl was still standing there, watching us, her shoulders slumped, hand outstretched.

QUESTIONS

1. Around what year, would you say, was it that "courtesy and winning ways went out of style, when it was good to be bad, when you cultivated decadence like a taste"?
2. What is it about Digby and Jeff that inspires the narrator to call them "bad"?
3. Twice in "Greasy Lake"—in paragraphs 2 and 32—appear the words, "This was nature." What contrasts do you find between the "nature" of the narrator's earlier and later views?
4. What makes the narrator and his friends run off into the woods?

5. How does the heroes' encounter with the two girls at the end of the story differ from their earlier encounter with the girl from the blue Chevy? How do you account for the difference? When at the end of the story the girl offers to party with the three friends, what makes the narrator say, "I thought I was going to cry"?
6. How important to what happens in this story is Greasy Lake itself? What details about the lake and its shores strike you as particularly memorable (whether funny, disgusting, or both)?

Amy Tan

A PAIR OF TICKETS   1989

Amy Tan was born in Oakland, California, in 1952. Both of her parents were recent Chinese immigrants. Her father was an electrical engineer (as well as a Baptist minister); her mother was a vocational nurse. When her father and older brother both died of brain tumors, the fifteen-year-old Tan moved with her mother and younger brother to Switzerland, where she attended high school. On their return to the United States Tan attended Linfield College, a Baptist school in Oregon, but she eventually transferred to California State University at San Jose. At this time Tan and her mother argued about her future. The mother insisted her daughter pursue premedical studies in preparation for becoming a neurosurgeon, but Tan wanted to do something else. For six months the two did not speak to one another. Tan worked for IBM writing computer manuals and also wrote freelance business articles under a pseudonym. In 1987 she and her mother visited China together. This experience, which is reflected in "A Pair of Tickets," deepened Tan's sense of her Chinese American identity. "As soon as my feet touched China," she wrote, "I became Chinese." Soon after, she began writing her first novel, The Joy Luck Club *(1989), which consists of sixteen interrelated stories about a group of Chinese American mothers and their daughters. (The club of the title is a woman's social group.)* The Joy Luck Club *became both a critical success and a best-seller, and was made into a movie in 1993. In 1991 Tan published her second novel,* The Kitchen God's Wife. *Her later novels include* The Hundred Secret Senses *(1995) and* The Bonesetter's Daughter *(2001). She has also published two books for children,* The Moon Lady *(1992) and* The Chinese Siamese Cat *(1994). In 2003, she published* The Opposite of Fate: A Book of Musings, *a collection of autobiographical writings. Tan performs with a "vintage garage" band called the Rock Bottom Remainders, which also includes, among others, Stephen King, Dave Barry, and Scott Turow. She lives in San Francisco with her husband.*

The minute our train leaves the Hong Kong border and enters Shenzhen, China, I feel different. I can feel the skin on my forehead tingling, my blood rushing through a new course, my bones aching with a familiar old pain. And I think, My mother was right. I am becoming Chinese.

"Cannot be helped," my mother said when I was fifteen and had vigorously denied that I had any Chinese whatsoever below my skin. I was a sophomore at Galileo High in San Francisco, and all my Caucasian friends agreed: I was about as Chinese as they were. But my mother had studied at a famous nursing school in Shanghai, and she said she knew all about genetics. So there was no doubt in her mind, whether I agreed or not: Once you are born Chinese, you cannot help but feel and think Chinese.

"Someday you will see," said my mother. "It is in your blood, waiting to be let go."

And when she said this, I saw myself transforming like a werewolf, a mutant tag of DNA suddenly triggered, replicating itself insidiously into a *syndrome*,° a cluster of telltale Chinese behaviors, all those things my mother did to embarrass me—haggling with store owners, pecking her mouth with a toothpick in public, being color-blind to the fact that lemon yellow and pale pink are not good combinations for winter clothes.

But today I realize I've never really known what it means to be Chinese. I am thirty-six years old. My mother is dead and I am on a train, carrying with me her dreams of coming home. I am going to China. 5

We are first going to Guangzhou, my seventy-two-year-old father, Canning Woo, and I, where we will visit his aunt, whom he has not seen since he was ten years old. And I don't know whether it's the prospect of seeing his aunt or if it's because he's back in China, but now he looks like he's a young boy, so innocent and happy I want to button his sweater and pat his head. We are sitting across from each other, separated by a little table with two cold cups of tea. For the first time I can ever remember, my father has tears in his eyes, and all he is seeing out the train window is a sectioned field of yellow, green, and brown, a narrow canal flanking the tracks, low rising hills, and three people in blue jackets riding an ox-driven cart on this early October morning. And I can't help myself. I also have misty eyes, as if I had seen this a long, long time ago, and had almost forgotten.

In less than three hours, we will be in Guangzhou, which my guidebook tells me is how one properly refers to Canton these days. It seems all the cities I have heard of, except Shanghai, have changed their spellings. I think they are saying China has changed in other ways as well. Chungking is Chongqing. And Kweilin is Guilin. I have looked these names up, because after we see my father's aunt in Guangzhou, we will catch a plane to Shanghai, where I will meet my two half-sisters for the first time.

They are my mother's twin daughters from her first marriage, little babies she was forced to abandon on a road as she was fleeing Kweilin for Chungking in 1944. That was all my mother had told me about these daughters, so they had remained babies in my mind, all these years, sitting on the side of a road, listening to bombs whistling in the distance while sucking their patient red thumbs.

And it was only this year that someone found them and wrote with this joyful news. A letter came from Shanghai, addressed to my mother. When I first heard about this, that they were alive, I imagined my identical sisters transforming from little babies into six-year-old girls. In my mind, they were seated next to each other at a table, taking turns with the fountain pen. One would

syndrome: a group of symptoms that occur together as the sign of a particular disease or abnormality.

write a neat row of characters: *Dearest Mama. We are alive.* She would brush back her wispy bangs and hand the other sister the pen, and she would write: *Come get us. Please hurry.*

Of course they could not know that my mother had died three months be- 10 fore, suddenly, when a blood vessel in her brain burst. One minute she was talking to my father, complaining about the tenants upstairs, scheming how to evict them under the pretense that relatives from China were moving in. The next minute she was holding her head, her eyes squeezed shut, groping for the sofa, and then crumpling softly to the floor with fluttering hands.

So my father had been the first one to open the letter, a long letter it turned out. And they did call her Mama. They said they always revered her as their true mother. They kept a framed picture of her. They told her about their life, from the time my mother last saw them on the road leaving Kweilin to when they were finally found.

And the letter had broken my father's heart so much—these daughters calling my mother from another life he never knew—that he gave the letter to my mother's old friend Auntie Lindo and asked her to write back and tell my sisters, in the gentlest way possible, that my mother was dead.

But instead Auntie Lindo took the letter to the Joy Luck Club and discussed with Auntie Ying and Auntie An-mei what should be done, because they had known for many years about my mother's search for her twin daughters, her endless hope. Auntie Lindo and the others cried over this double tragedy, of losing my mother three months before, and now again. And so they couldn't help but think of some miracle, some possible way of reviving her from the dead, so my mother could fulfill her dream.

So this is what they wrote to my sisters in Shanghai: "Dearest Daughters, I too have never forgotten you in my memory or in my heart. I never gave up hope that we would see each other again in a joyous reunion. I am only sorry it has been too long. I want to tell you everything about my life since I last saw you. I want to tell you this when our family comes to see you in China. . . ." They signed it with my mother's name.

It wasn't until all this had been done that they first told me about my sisters, 15 the letter they received, the one they wrote back.

"They'll think she's coming, then," I murmured. And I had imagined my sisters now being ten or eleven, jumping up and down, holding hands, their pigtails bouncing, excited that their mother—*their* mother—was coming, whereas my mother was dead.

"How can you say she is not coming in a letter?" said Auntie Lindo. "She is their mother. She is your mother. You must be the one to tell them. All these years, they have been dreaming of her." And I thought she was right.

But then I started dreaming, too, of my mother and my sisters and how it would be if I arrived in Shanghai. All these years, while they waited to be found, I had lived with my mother and then had lost her. I imagined seeing my sisters at the airport. They would be standing on their tip-toes, looking anxiously, scanning from one dark head to another as we got off the plane. And I would recognize them instantly, their faces with the identical worried look.

"*Jyejye, Jyejye*. Sister, Sister. We are here," I saw myself saying in my poor version of Chinese.

"Where is Mama?" they would say, and look around, still smiling, two flushed and eager faces. "Is she hiding?" And this would have been like my mother, to stand behind just a bit, to tease a little and make people's patience pull a little on their hearts. I would shake my head and tell my sisters she was not hiding.

"Oh, that must be Mama, no?" one of my sisters would whisper excitedly, pointing to another small woman completely engulfed in a tower of presents. And that, too, would have been like my mother, to bring mountains of gifts, food, and toys for children—all bought on sale—shunning thanks, saying the gifts were nothing, and later turning the labels over to show my sisters, "Calvin Klein, 100% wool."

I imagined myself starting to say, "Sisters, I am sorry, I have come alone . . ." and before I could tell them—they could see it in my face—they were wailing, pulling their hair, their lips twisted in pain, as they ran away from me. And then I saw myself getting back on the plane and coming home.

After I had dreamed this scene many times—watching their despair turn from horror into anger—I begged Auntie Lindo to write another letter. And at first she refused.

"How can I say she is dead? I cannot write this," said Auntie Lindo with a stubborn look.

"But it's cruel to have them believe she's coming on the plane," I said. "When they see it's just me, they'll hate me."

"Hate you? Cannot be." She was scowling. "You are their own sister, their only family."

"You don't understand," I protested.

"What I don't understand?" she said.

And I whispered, "They'll think I'm responsible, that she died because I didn't appreciate her."

And Auntie Lindo looked satisfied and sad at the same time, as if this were true and I had finally realized it. She sat down for an hour, and when she stood up she handed me a two-page letter. She had tears in her eyes. I realized that the very thing I had feared, she had done. So even if she had written the news of my mother's death in English, I wouldn't have had the heart to read it.

"Thank you," I whispered.

The landscape has become gray, filled with low flat cement buildings, old factories, and then tracks and more tracks filled with trains like ours passing by in the opposite direction. I see platforms crowded with people wearing drab Western clothes, with spots of bright colors: little children wearing pink and yellow, red and peach. And there are soldiers in olive green and red, and old ladies in gray tops and pants that stop mid-calf. We are in Guangzhou.

Before the train even comes to a stop, people are bringing down their belongings from above their seats. For a moment there is a dangerous shower of heavy suitcases laden with gifts to relatives, half-broken boxes wrapped in miles of string to keep the contents from spilling out, plastic bags filled with yarn and vegetables and packages of dried mushrooms, and camera cases. And then we are caught in a stream of people rushing, shoving, pushing us along, until we find ourselves in one of a dozen lines waiting to go through customs. I feel as if I were getting on the number 30 Stockton bus in San Francisco. I am in China, I remind myself. And somehow the crowds don't bother me. It feels right. I start pushing too.

I take out the declaration forms and my passport. "Woo," it says at the top, and below that, "June May," who was born in "California, U.S.A.," in 1951. I wonder if the customs people will question whether I'm the same person in the passport photo. In this picture, my chin-length hair is swept back and artfully styled. I am wearing false eyelashes, eye shadow, and lip liner. My cheeks are hollowed out by bronze blusher. But I had not expected the heat in October. And now my hair hangs limp with the humidity. I wear no makeup; in Hong Kong my mascara had melted into dark circles and everything else had felt like layers of grease. So today my face is plain, unadorned except for a thin mist of shiny sweat on my forehead and nose.

Even without makeup, I could never pass for true Chinese. I stand five-foot-six, and my head pokes above the crowd so that I am eye level only with other tourists. My mother once told me my height came from my grandfather, who was a northerner, and may have even had some Mongol blood. "This is what your grandmother once told me," explained my mother. "But now it is too late to ask her. They are all dead, your grandparents, your uncles, and their wives and children, all killed in the war, when a bomb fell on our house. So many generations in one instant."

She had said this so matter-of-factly that I thought she had long since gotten over any grief she had. And then I wondered how she knew they were all dead.

"Maybe they left the house before the bomb fell," I suggested.

"No," said my mother. "Our whole family is gone. It is just you and I."

"But how do you know? Some of them could have escaped."

"Cannot be," said my mother, this time almost angrily. And then her frown was washed over by a puzzled blank look, and she began to talk as if she were trying to remember where she had misplaced something. "I went back to that house. I kept looking up to where the house used to be. And it wasn't a house, just the sky. And below, underneath my feet, were four stories of burnt bricks and wood, all the life of our house. Then off to the side I saw things blown into the yard, nothing valuable. There was a bed someone used to sleep in, really just a metal frame twisted up at one corner. And a book, I don't know what kind, because every page had turned black. And I saw a teacup which was unbroken but filled with ashes. And then I found my doll, with her hands and legs broken, her hair burned off. . . . When I was a little girl, I had cried for that doll, seeing it all alone in the store window, and my mother had bought it for me. It was an American doll with yellow hair. It could turn its legs and arms. The eyes moved up and down. And when I married and left my family home, I gave the doll to my youngest niece, because she was like me. She cried if that doll was not with her always. Do you see? If she was in the house with that doll, her parents were there, and so everybody was there, waiting together, because that's how our family was."

The woman in the customs booth stares at my documents, then glances at me briefly, and with two quick movements stamps everything and sternly nods me along. And soon my father and I find ourselves in a large area filled with thousands of people and suitcases. I feel lost and my father looks helpless.

"Excuse me," I say to a man who looks like an American. "Can you tell me where I can get a taxi?" He mumbles something that sounds Swedish or Dutch.

"Syau Yen! Syau Yen!" I hear a piercing voice shout from behind me. An old woman in a yellow knit beret is holding up a pink plastic bag filled with wrapped trinkets. I guess she is trying to sell us something. But my father is staring down at this tiny sparrow of a woman, squinting into her eyes. And then his eyes widen, his face opens up and he smiles like a pleased little boy.

"Aiyi! Aiyi!" —Auntie Auntie!—he says softly.

"Syau Yen!" coos my great-aunt. I think it's funny she has just called my fa- 45 ther "Little Wild Goose." It must be his baby milk name, the name used to discourage ghosts from stealing children.

They clasp each other's hands—they do not hug—and hold on like this, taking turns saying, "Look at you! You are so old. Look how old you've become!" They are both crying openly, laughing at the same time, and I bite my lip, trying not to cry. I'm afraid to feel their joy. Because I am thinking how different our arrival in Shanghai will be tomorrow, how awkward it will feel.

Now Aiyi beams and points to a Polaroid picture of my father. My father had wisely sent pictures when he wrote and said we were coming. See how smart she was, she seems to intone as she compares the picture to my father. In the letter, my father had said we would call her from the hotel once we arrived, so this is a surprise, that they've come to meet us. I wonder if my sisters will be at the airport.

It is only then that I remember the camera. I had meant to take a picture of my father and his aunt the moment they met. It's not too late.

"Here, stand together over here," I say, holding up the Polaroid. The camera flashes and I hand them the snapshot. Aiyi and my father still stand close together, each of them holding a corner of the picture, watching as their images begin to form. They are almost reverentially quiet. Aiyi is only five years older than my father, which makes her around seventy-seven. But she looks ancient, shrunken, a mummified relic. Her thin hair is pure white, her teeth are brown with decay. So much for stories of Chinese women looking young forever, I think to myself.

Now Aiyi is crooning to me: "Jandale." So big already. She looks up at me, 50 at my full height, and then peers into her pink plastic bag—her gifts to us, I have figured out—as if she is wondering what she will give to me, now that I am so old and big. And then she grabs my elbow with her sharp pincerlike grasp and turns me around. A man and woman in their fifties are shaking hands with my father, everybody smiling and saying, "Ah! Ah!" They are Aiyi's oldest son and his wife, and standing next to them are four other people, around my age, and a little girl who's around ten. The introductions go by so fast, all I know is that one of them is Aiyi's grandson, with his wife, and the other is her granddaughter, with her husband. And the little girl is Lili, Aiyi's great-granddaughter.

Aiyi and my father speak the Mandarin dialect from their childhood, but the rest of the family speaks only the Cantonese of their village. I understand only Mandarin but can't speak it that well. So Aiyi and my father gossip unrestrained in Mandarin, exchanging news about people from their old village. And they stop only occasionally to talk to the rest of us, sometimes in Cantonese, sometimes in English.

"Oh, it is as I suspected," says my father, turning to me. "He died last summer." And I already understood this. I just don't know who this person, Li Gong, is. I feel as if I were in the United Nations and the translators had run amok.

"Hello," I say to the little girl. "My name is Jing-mei." But the little girl squirms to look away, causing her parents to laugh with embarrassment. I try to think of Cantonese words I can say to her, stuff I learned from friends in China-town, but all I can think of are swear words, terms for bodily functions, and short phrases like "tastes good," "tastes like garbage," and "she's really ugly." And then I have another plan: I hold up the Polaroid camera, beckoning Lili with my finger. She immediately jumps forward, places one hand on her hip in the manner of a fashion model, juts out her chest, and flashes me a toothy smile. As soon as I take the picture she is standing next to me, jumping and giggling every few seconds as she watches herself appear on the greenish film.

By the time we hail taxis for the ride to the hotel, Lili is holding tight onto my hand, pulling me along.

In the taxi, Aiyi talks nonstop, so I have no chance to ask her about the different sights we are passing by.

"You wrote and said you would come only for one day," says Aiyi to my father in an agitated tone. "One day! How can you see your family in one day! Toishan is many hours' drive from Guangzhou. And this idea to call us when you arrive. This is nonsense. We have no telephone."

My heart races a little. I wonder if Auntie Lindo told my sisters we would call from the hotel in Shanghai?

Aiyi continues to scold my father. "I was so beside myself, ask my son, almost turned heaven and earth upside down trying to think of a way! So we decided the best was for us to take the bus from Toishan and come into Guangzhou—meet you right from the start."

And now I am holding my breath as the taxi driver dodges between trucks and buses, honking his horn constantly. We seem to be on some sort of long freeway overpass, like a bridge above the city. I can see row after row of apartments, each floor cluttered with laundry hanging out to dry on the balcony. We pass a public bus, with people jammed in so tight their faces are nearly wedged

55

against the window. Then I see the skyline of what must be downtown Guangzhou. From a distance, it looks like a major American city, with high rises and construction going on everywhere. As we slow down in the more congested part of the city, I see scores of little shops, dark inside, lined with counters and shelves. And then there is a building, its front laced with scaffolding made of bamboo poles held together with plastic strips. Men and women are standing on narrow platforms, scraping the sides, working without safety straps or helmets. Oh, would OSHA° have a field day here, I think.

Aiyi's shrill voice rises up again: "So it is a shame you can't see our village,   60 our house. My sons have been quite successful, selling our vegetables in the free market. We had enough these last few years to build a big house, three stories, all of new brick, big enough for our whole family and then some. And every year, the money is even better. You Americans aren't the only ones who know how to get rich!"

The taxi stops and I assume we've arrived, but then I peer out at what looks like a grander version of the Hyatt Regency. "This is communist China?" I wonder out loud. And then I shake my head toward my father. "This must be the wrong hotel." I quickly pull out our itinerary, travel tickets, and reservations. I had explicitly instructed my travel agent to choose something inexpensive, in the thirty-to-forty-dollar range. I'm sure of this. And there it says on our itinerary: Garden Hotel, Huanshi Dong Lu. Well, our travel agent had better be prepared to eat the extra, that's all I have to say.

The hotel is magnificent. A bellboy complete with uniform and sharp-creased cap jumps forward and begins to carry our bags into the lobby. Inside, the hotel looks like an orgy of shopping arcades and restaurants all encased in granite and glass. And rather than be impressed, I am worried about the expense, as well as the appearance it must give Aiyi, that we rich Americans cannot be without our luxuries even for one night.

But when I step up to the reservation desk, ready to haggle over this booking mistake, it is confirmed. Our rooms are prepaid, thirty-four dollars each. I feel sheepish, and Aiyi and the others seem delighted by our temporary surroundings. Lili is looking wide-eyed at an arcade filled with video games.

Our whole family crowds into one elevator, and the bellboy waves, saying he will meet us on the eighteenth floor. As soon as the elevator door shuts, everybody becomes very quiet, and when the door finally opens again, everybody talks at once in what sounds like relieved voices. I have the feeling Aiyi and the others have never been on such a long elevator ride.

Our rooms are next to each other and are identical. The rugs, drapes, bed-   65 spreads are all in shades of taupe. There's a color television with remote-control panels built into the lamp table between the two twin beds. The bathroom has marble walls and floors. I find a built-in wet bar with a small refrigerator stocked with Heineken beer, Coke Classic, and Seven-Up, mini-bottles of Johnnie

OSHA: Occupation, Safety, and Health Administration, a federal agency that regulates and monitors workplace safety conditions.

Walker Red, Bacardi rum, and Smirnoff vodka, and packets of M & M's, honey-roasted cashews, and Cadbury chocolate bars. And again I say out loud, "This is communist China?"

My father comes into my room. "They decided we should just stay here and visit," he says, shrugging his shoulders. "They say, Less trouble that way. More time to talk."

"What about dinner?" I ask. I have been envisioning my first real Chinese feast for many days already, a big banquet with one of those soups steaming out of a carved winter melon, chicken wrapped in clay, Peking duck, the works.

My father walks over and picks up a room service book next to a *Travel & Leisure* magazine. He flips through the pages quickly and then points to the menu. "This is what they want," says my father.

So it's decided. We are going to dine tonight in our rooms, with our family, sharing hamburgers, french fries, and apple pie à la mode.

Aiyi and her family are browsing the shops while we clean up. After a hot ride on the train, I'm eager for a shower and cooler clothes. 70

The hotel has provided little packets of shampoo which, upon opening, I discover is the consistency and color of hoisin sauce. This is more like it, I think. This is China. And I rub some in my damp hair.

Standing in the shower, I realize this is the first time I've been by myself in what seems like days. But instead of feeling relieved, I feel forlorn. I think about what my mother said, about activating my genes and becoming Chinese. And I wonder what she meant.

Right after my mother died, I asked myself a lot of things, things that couldn't be answered, to force myself to grieve more. It seemed as if I wanted to sustain my grief, to assure myself that I had cared deeply enough.

But now I ask the questions mostly because I want to know the answers. What was that pork stuff she used to make that had the texture of sawdust? What were the names of the uncles who died in Shanghai? What had she dreamt all these years about her other daughters? All the times when she got mad at me, was she really thinking about them? Did she wish I were they? Did she regret that I wasn't?

At one o'clock in the morning, I awake to tapping sounds on the window. I must have dozed off and now I feel my body uncramping itself. I'm sitting on the floor, leaning against one of the twin beds. Lili is lying next to me. The others are asleep, too, sprawled out on the beds and floor. Aiyi is seated at a little table, looking very sleepy. And my father is staring out the window, tapping his fingers on the glass. The last time I listened my father was telling Aiyi about his life since he last saw her. How he had gone to Yenching University, later got a post with a newspaper in Chungking, met my mother there, a young widow. How they later fled together to Shanghai to try to find my mother's family house, but there was nothing there. And then they traveled eventually to Canton and then to Hong Kong, then Haiphong and finally to San Francisco. . . . 75

"Suyuan didn't tell me she was trying all these years to find her daughters," he is now saying in a quiet voice. "Naturally, I did not discuss her daughters with her. I thought she was ashamed she had left them behind."

"Where did she leave them?" asks Aiyi. "How were they found?"

I am wide awake now. Although I have heard parts of this story from my mother's friends.

"It happened when the Japanese took over Kweilin," says my father.

"Japanese in Kweilin?" says Aiyi. "That was never the case. Couldn't be. The Japanese never came to Kweilin." 80

"Yes, that is what the newspapers reported. I know this because I was working for the news bureau at the time. The Kuomintang often told us what we could say and could not say. But we knew the Japanese had come into Kwangsi Province. We had sources who told us how they had captured the Wuchang-Canton railway. How they were coming overland, making very fast progress, marching toward the provincial capital."

Aiyi looks astonished. "If people did not know this, how could Suyuan know the Japanese were coming?"

"An officer of the Kuomintang secretly warned her," explains my father. "Suyuan's husband also was an officer and everybody knew that officers and their families would be the first to be killed. So she gathered a few possessions and, in the middle of the night, she picked up her daughters and fled on foot. The babies were not even one year old."

"How could she give up those babies!" sighs Aiyi. "Twin girls. We have never had such luck in our family." And then she yawns again.

"What were they named?" she asks. I listen carefully. I had been planning 85 on using just the familiar "Sister" to address them both. But now I want to know how to pronounce their names.

"They have their father's surname, Wang," says my father. "And their given names are Chwun Yu and Chwun Hwa."

"What do the names mean?" I ask.

"Ah." My father draws imaginary characters on the window. "One means 'Spring Rain,' the other 'Spring Flower,'" he explains in English, "because they born in the spring, and of course rain come before flower, same order these girls are born. Your mother like a poet, don't you think?"

I nod my head. I see Aiyi nod her head forward, too. But it falls forward and stays there. She is breathing deeply, noisily. She is asleep.

"And what does Ma's name mean?" I whisper. 90

"'Suyuan,'" he says, writing more invisible characters on the glass. "The way she write it in Chinese, it mean 'Long-Cherished Wish.' Quite a fancy name, not so ordinary like flower name. See this first character, it mean something like 'Forever Never Forgotten.' But there is another way to write 'Suyuan.' Sound exactly the same, but the meaning is opposite." His finger creates the brushstrokes of another character. "The first part look the same: 'Never Forgotten.' But the last part add to first part make the whole word mean 'Long-Held Grudge.' Your mother get angry with me, I tell her her name should be Grudge."

My father is looking at me, moist-eyed. "See, I pretty clever, too, hah?"

I nod, wishing I could find some way to comfort him. "And what about my name," I ask, "what does 'Jing-mei' mean?"

"Your name also special," he says. I wonder if any name in Chinese is not something special. " 'Jing' like excellent *jing*. Not just good, it's something pure, essential, the best quality. *Jing* is good leftover stuff when you take impurities out of something like gold, or rice, or salt. So what is left—just pure essence. And 'Mei,' this is common *mei*, as in *meimei*, 'younger sister.' "

I think about this. My mother's long-cherished wish. Me, the younger   95
sister who was supposed to be the essence of the others. I feed myself with the old grief, wondering how disappointed my mother must have been. Tiny Aiyi stirs suddenly, her head rolls and then falls back, her mouth opens as if to answer my question. She grunts in her sleep, tucking her body more closely into the chair.

"So why did she abandon those babies on the road?" I need to know, because now I feel abandoned too.

"Long time I wondered this myself," says my father. "But then I read that letter from her daughters in Shanghai now, and I talk to Auntie Lindo, all the others. And then I knew. No shame in what she done. None."

"What happened?"

"Your mother running away—" begins my father.

"No, tell me in Chinese," I interrupt. "Really, I can understand."   100

He begins to talk, still standing at the window, looking into the night.

After fleeing Kweilin, your mother walked for several days trying to find a main road. Her thought was to catch a ride on a truck or wagon, to catch enough rides until she reached Chungking, where her husband was stationed.

She had sewn money and jewelry into the lining of her dress, enough, she thought, to barter rides all the way. If I am lucky, she thought, I will not have to trade the heavy gold bracelet and jade ring. These were things from her mother, your grandmother.

By the third day, she had traded nothing. The roads were filled with people, everybody running and begging for rides from passing trucks. The trucks rushed by, afraid to stop. So your mother found no rides, only the start of dysentery pains in her stomach.

Her shoulders ached from the two babies swinging from scarf slings. Blisters   105
grew on her palms from holding two leather suitcases. And then the blisters burst and began to bleed. After a while, she left the suitcases behind, keeping only the food and a few clothes. And later she also dropped the bags of wheat flour and rice and kept walking like this for many miles, singing songs to her little girls, until she was delirious with pain and fever.

Finally, there was not one more step left in her body. She didn't have the strength to carry those babies any farther. She slumped to the ground. She knew she would die of her sickness, or perhaps from thirst, from starvation, or from the Japanese, who she was sure were marching right behind her.

She took the babies out of the slings and sat them on the side of the road, then lay down next to them. You babies are so good, she said, so quiet. They smiled back, reaching their chubby hands for her, wanting to be picked up again. And then she knew she could not bear to watch her babies die with her.

She saw a family with three young children in a cart going by. "Take my babies, I beg you," she cried to them. But they stared back with empty eyes and never stopped.

She saw another person pass and called out again. This time a man turned around, and he had such a terrible expression—your mother said it looked like death itself—she shivered and looked away.

When the road grew quiet, she tore open the lining of her dress, and stuffed 110 jewelry under the shirt of one baby and money under the other. She reached into her pocket and drew out the photos of her family, the picture of her father and mother, the picture of herself and her husband on their wedding day. And she wrote on the back of each the names of the babies and this same message: "Please care for these babies with the money and valuables provided. When it is safe to come, if you bring them to Shanghai, 9 Weichang Lu, the Li family will be glad to give you a generous reward. Li Suyuan and Wang Fuchi."

And then she touched each baby's cheek and told her not to cry. She would go down the road to find them some food and would be back. And without looking back, she walked down the road, stumbling and crying, thinking only of this one last hope, that her daughters would be found by a kindhearted person who would care for them. She would not allow herself to imagine anything else.

She did not remember how far she walked, which direction she went, when she fainted, or how she was found. When she awoke, she was in the back of a bouncing truck with several other sick people, all moaning. And she began to scream, thinking she was now on a journey to Buddhist hell. But the face of an American missionary lady bent over her and smiled, talking to her in a soothing language she did not understand. And yet she could somehow understand. She had been saved for no good reason, and it was now too late to go back and save her babies.

When she arrived in Chungking, she learned her husband had died two weeks before. She told me later she laughed when the officers told her this news, she was so delirious with madness and disease. To come so far, to lose so much and to find nothing.

I met her in a hospital. She was lying on a cot, hardly able to move, her dysentery had drained her so thin. I had come in for my foot, my missing toe, which was cut off by a piece of falling rubble. She was talking to herself, mumbling.

"Look at these clothes," she said, and I saw she had on a rather unusual dress 115 for wartime. It was silk satin, quite dirty, but there was no doubt it was a beautiful dress.

"Look at this face," she said, and I saw her dusty face and hollow cheeks, her eyes shining back. "Do you see my foolish hope?"

"I thought I had lost everything, except these two things," she murmured. "And I wondered which I would lose next. Clothes or hope? Hope or clothes?"

"But now, see here, look what is happening," she said, laughing, as if all her prayers had been answered. And she was pulling hair out of her head as easily as one lifts new wheat from wet soil.

It was an old peasant woman who found them. "How could I resist?" the peasant woman later told your sisters when they were older. They were still sitting obediently near where your mother had left them, looking like little fairy queens waiting for their sedan to arrive.

The woman, Mei Ching, and her husband, Mei Han, lived in a stone cave. 120 There were thousands of hidden caves like that in and around Kweilin so secret that the people remained hidden even after the war ended. The Meis would come out of their cave every few days and forage for food supplies left on the road, and sometimes they would see something that they both agreed was a tragedy to leave behind. So one day they took back to their cave a delicately painted set of rice bowls, another day a little footstool with a velvet cushion and two new wedding blankets. And once, it was your sisters.

They were pious people, Muslims, who believed the twin babies were a sign of double luck, and they were sure of this when, later in the evening, they discovered how valuable the babies were. She and her husband had never seen rings and bracelets like those. And while they admired the pictures, knowing the babies came from a good family, neither of them could read or write. It was not until many months later that Mei Ching found someone who could read the writing on the back. By then, she loved these baby girls like her own.

In 1952 Mei Han, the husband, died. The twins were already eight years old, and Mei Ching now decided it was time to find your sisters' true family.

She showed the girls the picture of their mother and told them they had been born into a great family and she would take them back to see their true mother and grandparents. Mei Ching told them about the reward, but she swore she would refuse it. She loved these girls so much, she only wanted them to have what they were entitled to—a better life, a fine house, educated ways. Maybe the family would let her stay on as the girls' amah. Yes, she was certain they would insist.

Of course, when she found the place at 9 Weichang Lu, in the old French Concession, it was something completely different. It was the site of a factory building, recently constructed, and none of the workers knew what had become of the family whose house had burned down on that spot.

Mei Ching could not have known, of course, that your mother and I, her 125 new husband, had already returned to that same place in 1945 in hopes of finding both her family and her daughters.

Your mother and I stayed in China until 1947. We went to many different cities—back to Kweilin, to Changsha, as far south as Kunming. She was always looking out of one corner of her eye for twin babies, then little girls. Later we went to Hong Kong, and when we finally left in 1949 for the United States, I think she was even looking for them on the boat. But when we arrived, she no longer talked about them. I thought, At last, they have died in her heart.

When letters could be openly exchanged between China and the United States, she wrote immediately to old friends in Shanghai and Kweilin. I did not know she did this. Auntie Lindo told me. But of course, by then, all the street names had changed. Some people had died, others had moved away. So it took many years to find a contact. And when she did find an old schoolmate's address and wrote asking her to look for her daughters, her friend wrote back and said this was impossible, like looking for a needle on the bottom of the ocean. How did she know her daughters were in Shanghai and not somewhere else in China? The friend, of course, did not ask, How do you know your daughters are still alive?

So her schoolmate did not look. Finding babies lost during the war was a matter of foolish imagination, and she had no time for that.

But every year, your mother wrote to different people. And this last year, I think she got a big idea in her head, to go to China and find them herself. I remember she told me, "Canning, we should go, before it is too late, before we are too old." And I told her we were already too old, it was already too late.

I just thought she wanted to be a tourist! I didn't know she wanted to go and look for her daughters. So when I said it was too late, that must have put a terrible thought in her head that her daughters might be dead. And I think this possibility grew bigger and bigger in her head, until it killed her.

Maybe it was your mother's dead spirit who guided her Shanghai schoolmate to find her daughters. Because after your mother died, the schoolmate saw your sisters, by chance, while shopping for shoes at the Number One Department Store on Nanjing Dong Road. She said it was like a dream, seeing these two women who looked so much alike, moving down the stairs together. There was something about their facial expressions that reminded the schoolmate of your mother.

She quickly walked over to them and called their names, which of course, they did not recognize at first, because Mei Ching had changed their names. But your mother's friend was so sure, she persisted. "Are you not Wang Chwun Yu and Wang Chwun Hwa?" she asked them. And then these double-image women became very excited, because they remembered the names written on the back of an old photo, a photo of a young man and woman they still honored, as their much-loved first parents, who had died and become spirit ghosts still roaming the earth looking for them.

At the airport, I am exhausted. I could not sleep last night. Aiyi had followed me into my room at three in the morning, and she instantly fell asleep on one of the twin beds, snoring with the might of a lumberjack. I lay awake thinking about my mother's story, realizing how much I have never known about her, grieving that my sisters and I had both lost her.

And now at the airport, after shaking hands with everybody, waving good-bye, I think about all the different ways we leave people in this world. Cheerily waving good-bye to some at airports, knowing we'll never see each other again. Leaving others on the side of the road, hoping that we will. Finding my mother in my father's story and saying good-bye before I have a chance to know her better.

Aiyi smiles at me as we wait for our gate to be called. She is so old. I put one arm around her and one around Lili. They are the same size, it seems. And then it's time. As we wave good-bye one more time and enter the waiting area, I get the sense I am going from one funeral to another. In my hand I'm clutching a pair of tickets to Shanghai. In two hours we'll be there.

The plane takes off. I close my eyes. How can I describe to them in my broken Chinese about our mother's life? Where should I begin?

"Wake up, we're here," says my father. And I awake with my heart pounding in my throat. I look out the window and we're already on the runway. It's gray outside.

And now I'm walking down the steps of the plane, onto the tarmac and toward the building. If only, I think, if only my mother had lived long enough to be the one walking toward them. I am so nervous I cannot even feel my feet. I am just moving somehow.

Somebody shouts, "She's arrived!" And then I see her. Her short hair. Her small body. And that same look on her face. She has the back of her hand pressed hard against her mouth. She is crying as though she had gone through a terrible ordeal and were happy it is over.

And I know it's not my mother, yet it is the same look she had when I was five and had disappeared all afternoon, for such a long time, that she was convinced I was dead. And when I miraculously appeared, sleepy-eyed, crawling from underneath my bed, she wept and laughed, biting the back of her hand to make sure it was true.

And now I see her again, two of her, waving, and in one hand there is a photo, the Polaroid I sent them. As soon as I get beyond the gate, we run toward each other, all three of us embracing, all hesitations and expectations forgotten.

"Mama, Mama," we all murmur, as if she is among us.

My sisters look at me, proudly. "Meimei jandale," says one sister proudly to the other. "Little Sister has grown up." I look at their faces again and I see no trace of my mother in them. Yet they still look familiar. And now I also see what part of me is Chinese. It is so obvious. It is my family. It is in our blood. After all these years, it can finally be let go.

My sisters and I stand, arms around each other, laughing and wiping the tears from each other's eyes. The flash of the Polaroid goes off and my father hands me the snapshot. My sisters and I watch quietly together, eager to see what develops.

The gray-green surface changes to the bright colors of our three images, sharpening and deepening all at once. And although we don't speak, I know we all see it: Together we look like our mother. Her same eyes, her same mouth, open in surprise to see, at last, her long-cherished wish.

QUESTIONS

1. How is the external setting of "A Pair of Tickets" essential to what happens internally to the narrator in the course of this story?
2. How does the narrator's view of her father change by seeing him in a different setting?
3. In what ways does the narrator feel at home in China? In what ways does she feel foreign?
4. What do the narrator and her half-sisters have in common? How does this factor relate to the theme of the story?
5. In what ways does the story explore specifically Chinese American experiences? In what other ways is the story grounded in universal family issues?

WRITER'S PERSPECTIVE

Amy Tan

Amy Tan on Writing

SETTING THE VOICE   1989

Lately, I've been giving more thought to the kind of English my mother speaks. Like others, I have described it to people as "broken" or "fractured" English. But I wince when I say that. It has always bothered me that I can think of no way to describe it other than "broken," as if it were damaged and needed to be fixed, as if it lacked a certain wholeness and soundness. I've heard other terms used, "limited English," for example. But they seem just as bad, as if everything is limited, including people's perceptions of the limited English speaker.

I know this for a fact, because when I was growing up, my mother's "limited" English limited *my* perception of her. I was ashamed of her English. I believed that her English reflected the quality of what she had to say. That is, because she expressed them imperfectly, her thoughts were imperfect. And I had plenty of empirical evidence to support me: the fact that people in department stores, at banks, and at restaurants did not take her seriously, did not give her good service, pretended not to understand her, or even acted as if they did not hear her.

· · · ·

But it wasn't until 1985 that I finally began to write fiction. And at first I wrote using what I thought to be wittily crafted sentences, sentences that would finally prove I had mastery over the English language. Here's an example from the first draft of a story that later made its way into *The Joy Luck Club*, but without this line: "That was my mental quandary in its nascent state." A terrible line, which I can barely pronounce.

Fortunately, for reasons I won't get into today, I later decided I should envision a reader for the stories I would write. And the reader I decided upon was my mother, because these were stories about mothers. So with this reader in mind—and in fact she did read my early drafts—I began to write stories using all the Englishes I grew up with: the English I spoke to my mother, which for lack of a better term might be described as "simple"; the English she used with me, which for lack of a better term might be described as "broken"; my translation of her Chinese, which could certainly be described as "watered down"; and what I imagined to be her translation of her Chinese if she could speak in perfect English, her internal language, and for that I sought to preserve the essence, but neither an English nor a Chinese structure. I wanted to capture what language ability tests can never reveal: her intent, her passion, her imagery, the rhythms of her speech and the nature of her thoughts.

Apart from what any critic had to say about my writing, I knew I had succeeded where it counted when my mother finished reading my book and gave me her verdict: "So easy to read."

From "Mother Tongue"

WRITING CRITICALLY

How Time and Place Set a Story

When you write about a short story, do not consider only the plot and characters— the *what* and *who* of the tale. What happens and who is involved are essential, but those two elements are not the whole story. You should also examine *where* and *when* the story unfolds.

A story's setting constitutes the external reality that surrounds the internal reality of the character's personalities. The external pressure of the setting is often the key factor that compels or invites the protagonist into action. To write about a story's setting, therefore, invites you to study not only the setting itself but also its relation to the protagonist.

Before writing about the setting, it may help to ask yourself the following questions:

- When does the story take place? Is the time of year or time of day of any significance?
- Does the weather play a meaningful role in the story's action?
- Where does the story take place? Does its location suggest anything about the characters' lives?

- Do different characters become associated with different locations?
- Do any external elements of time or place suggest something about the protagonists?

WRITING ASSIGNMENT

Taking any story from this chapter, show how the setting relates to the inner life of the protagonist. Two possible topics would be:

- Discuss how the protagonist's arrival in China (in Amy Tan's "A Pair of Tickets") helps her arrive at a new understanding of her identity.
- Analyze how the dirty, remote lake (in T. Coraghessan Boyle's "Greasy Lake") brings out behavior that the characters would not demonstrate elsewhere.

FURTHER SUGGESTIONS FOR WRITING

1. In a few paragraphs, not necessarily a complete essay or story, recreate a time and place you know intimately. Write about it like a fiction writer, giving reality to a setting in which a story is about to unfold. Imagine this setting in detail—or, if you can, go take a fresh look at it. Ensure that your reader can virtually see, hear, smell, and taste your chosen time and place.

   You might find it revealing to choose for your subject some nearby, present-day place that your audience will recognize, then read your paper aloud in class. If, without your dropping place names or giving them other obvious clues, your listeners can identify your subject, then you will have written well.

2. From a different chapter of this book, or from "Stories for Further Reading" (Chapter Eleven), choose a story that particularly interests you. Start out by defining for your reader its exact time and place. Then, in two or three more paragraphs, go on to show how this setting functions in the story. Does the setting supply atmosphere? Make things happen? Reveal the natures of certain people? Prompt a character to a realization? Suggested stories to work on: "A Clean, Well-Lighted Place," "Barn Burning," "Araby," "Young Goodman Brown," "The Chrysanthemums," "The Five-Forty-Eight," and "The Gospel According to Mark."

3. Rewrite the first page or two of a story you have read, picking up the characters and putting them down in an entirely different setting. This new time and place might be the setting of another story, or it might be some actual place your readers will recognize. As you write, you might find yourself deciding to seek laughs, or you might decide to make the rewrite serious. You might try, for instance, a satire in the vein of *Monty Python*, shifting Hawthorne's "Young Goodman Brown" to the setting of Updike's "A & P." Or, without trying to be funny, you might rewrite the opening of Joyce's "Araby," setting the story in the neighborhood where you grew up.

   End with a short comment in answer to the question: "What did this exercise prove to you?" If your attempt should seem to you a failure, try to explain why the original story proved so reluctant to give up its time and place. (The purpose of this exercise is not to produce a new masterpiece, but to experience firsthand how the setting of a story works.)

5 *Tone and Style*

In many Victorian novels it was customary for some commentator, presumably the author, to interrupt the story from time to time, remarking on the action, offering philosophical asides, or explaining the procedures to be followed in telling the story.

> Two hours later, Dorothea was seated in an inner room or boudoir of a handsome apartment in the Via Sistina. I am sorry to add that she was sobbing bitterly. . . .
>
> —George Eliot in *Middlemarch* (1873)

> But let the gentle-hearted reader be under no apprehension whatsoever. It is not destined that Eleanor shall marry Mr. Slope or Bertie Stanhope.
>
> —Anthony Trollope in *Barchester Towers* (1857)

> And, as we bring our characters forward, I will ask leave, as a man and a brother, not only to introduce, but occasionally step down from the platform, and talk about them: if they are good and kindly, to love them and shake them by the hand; if they are silly, to laugh at them confidentially in the reader's sleeve; if they are wicked and heartless, to abuse them in the strongest terms which politeness admits of.
>
> —William Makepeace Thackeray in *Vanity Fair* (1847–1848)

Of course, the voice of this commentator was not identical with that of the "real-life" author—the one toiling over an inkpot, worrying about publication deadlines and whether the rent would be paid. At times the living author might have been far different in personality from that usually wise and cheerful intruder who kept addressing the reader of the book. Much of the time, to be sure, the author probably agreed with whatever attitudes this alter ego expressed. But, in effect, the author created the character of a commentator to speak for him or her and throughout the novel artfully sustained that character's voice.

Such intrusions, although sometimes useful to the "real" author and enjoyable to the reader, are today rare. Modern storytellers, carefully keeping out of sight, seldom comment on their plots and characters. Apparently they agree with Anton Chekhov that a writer should not judge the characters but should serve as their "impartial witness." And yet, no less definitely than Victorian novelists who introduced commentators, writers of effective stories no doubt have feelings toward their characters and events. The authors presumably care about these imaginary people and, in order for the story to grasp and sustain our interest, have to make us see these people in such a way that we, too, will care about them. When at the beginning of the short story "In Exile" Chekhov introduces us to a character, he does so with a description that arouses sympathy:

> The Tartar was worn out and ill, and wrapping himself in his rags, he talked about how good it was in the province of Simbirsk, and what a beautiful and clever wife he had left at home. He was not more than twenty-five, and in the firelight his pale, sickly face and woebegone expression made him seem like a boy.

Other than the comparison of the Tartar to a child, the details in this passage seem mostly factual: the young man's illness, ragged clothes, facial expression, and topics of conversation. But these details form a portrait that stirs pity. By his selection of these imaginary details out of countless others that he might have included, Chekhov firmly directs our feelings about the Tartar, so miserable and pathetic in his sickness and his homesickness. We cannot know, of course, exactly what the living Chekhov felt; but at least we can be sure that we are supposed to share the compassion and tenderness of the narrator—Chekhov's impartial (but human) witness.

Not only the author's choice of details may lead us to infer his or her attitude, but also choice of characters, events, and situations, and choice of words. When the narrator of Joseph Conrad's *Heart of Darkness* comes upon an African outpost littered with abandoned machines and notices "a boiler wallowing in the grass," the exact word *wallowing* conveys an attitude: that there is something swinish about this scene of careless waste. Whatever leads us to infer the author's attitude is commonly called **tone.** Like a tone of voice, the tone of a story may communicate amusement, anger, affection, sorrow, contempt. It implies the feelings of the author, so far as we can sense them. Those feelings may be similar to feelings expressed by the narrator of the story (or by any character), but sometimes they may be dissimilar, even sharply opposed. The characters in a story may regard an event as sad, but we sense that the author regards it as funny. To understand the tone of a story, then, is to understand some attitude more fundamental to the story than whatever attitude the characters explicitly declare.

The tone of a story, like a tone of voice, may convey not simply one attitude, but a medley. Reading "A & P" (Chapter One), we have mingled feelings about Sammy: delight in his wicked comments about other people and his skewering of hypocrisy; irritation at his smugness and condescension; admiration for his readiness to take a stand; sympathy for the pain of his disillusionment. Often the tone of a literary story will be too rich and complicated to sum up in one or two words. But to try to describe the tone of such a story may be a useful way to penetrate to its center and to grasp the whole of it.

One of the clearest indications of the tone of a story is the **style** in which it is written. In general, style refers to the individual traits or characteristics of a piece of writing: to a writer's particular ways of managing words that we come to recognize as habitual or customary. A distinctive style marks the work of a fine writer: we can tell his or her work from that of anyone else. From one story to another, however, the writer may fittingly change style; and in some stories, style may be altered meaningfully as the story goes along. In his novel *As I Lay Dying*, William Faulkner changes narrators with every chapter, and he distinguishes the narrators one from another by giving each an individual style or manner of speaking. Though each narrator has his or her own style, the book as a whole demonstrates Faulkner's style as well. For instance, one chapter is written from the point of view of a small boy, Vardaman Bundren, member of a family of poor Mississippi tenant farmers, whose view of a horse in a barn reads like this:

> It is as though the dark were resolving him out of his integrity, into an unrelated scattering of components—snuffings and stampings; smells of cooling flesh and ammoniac hair; an illusion of a coordinated whole of splotched hide and strong bones within which, detached and secret and familiar, an *is* different from my is.[1]

How can a small boy unaccustomed to libraries use words like *integrity, components, illusion,* and *coordinated?* Elsewhere in the story, Vardaman says aloud, with no trace of literacy, "Hit was a-laying right there on the ground." Apparently, in the passage it is not the voice of the boy that we are hearing, but something resembling the voice of William Faulkner, elevated and passionate, expressing the boy's thoughts in a style that admits Faulknerian words.

Usually, *style* indicates a mode of expression: the language a writer uses. In this sense, the notion of style includes such traits as the length and complexity of sentences, and **diction,** or choice of words: abstract or concrete, bookish ("unrelated scattering of components") or close to speech ("Hit was a-laying right there on the ground"). Involved in the idea of style, too, is any habitual use of imagery, patterns of sound, figures of speech, or other devices.

More recently, several writers of realistic fiction, called **minimalists**—Ann Beattie, Raymond Carver, Bobbie Ann Mason—have written with a flat, laid-back, unemotional tone, in an appropriately bare, unadorned style. Minimalists seem to give nothing but facts drawn from ordinary life, sometimes in picayune detail. Here is a sample passage, from Raymond Carver's story "A Small, Good Thing":

> She pulled into the driveway and cut the engine. She closed her eyes and leaned her head against the wheel for a minute. She listened to the ticking sounds the engine made as it began to cool. Then she got out of the car. She could hear the dog barking inside the house. She went to the front door,

[1]Modern Library edition (New York: Random, 1930) 379.

which was unlocked. She went inside and turned on lights and put on a kettle of water for tea. She opened some dog food and fed Slug on the back porch. The dog ate in hungry little smacks. It kept running into the kitchen to see that she was going to stay.

Explicit feeling and showy language are kept at a minimum here. Taken out of context, this description may strike you as banal, as if the writer himself were bored; but it works effectively as a part of Carver's entire story. As in all good writing, the style here seems a faithful mirror of what is said in it. At its best, such writing achieves "a hard-won reduction, a painful stripping away of richness, a baring of bone."[2]

To see what style means, compare the stories in this chapter by William Faulkner ("Barn Burning") and by Ernest Hemingway ("A Clean, Well-Lighted Place"). Faulkner frequently falls into a style in which a statement, as soon as uttered, is followed by another statement expressing the idea in a more emphatic way. Sentences are interrupted with parenthetical elements (asides, like this) thrust into them unexpectedly. At times, Faulkner writes of seemingly ordinary matters as if giving a speech in a towering passion. Here, from "Barn Burning," is a description of how a boy's father delivers a rug:

> "Don't you want me to help?" he whispered. His father did not answer and now he heard again that stiff foot striking the hollow portico with that wooden and clocklike deliberation, that outrageous overstatement of the weight it carried. The rug, hunched, not flung (the boy could tell that even in the darkness) from his father's shoulder struck the angle of wall and floor with a sound unbelievably loud, thunderous, then the foot again, unhurried and enormous; a light came on in the house and the boy sat, tense, breathing steadily and quietly and just a little fast, though the foot itself did not increase its beat at all, descending the steps now; now the boy could see him.

Faulkner is not merely indulging in language for its own sake. As you will find when you read the whole story, this rug delivery is vital to the story, and so too is the father's profound defiance—indicated by his walk. By devices of style—by *metaphor* and *simile* ("wooden and clocklike"), by exact qualification ("not flung"), by emphatic adjectives ("loud, thunderous")—Faulkner is carefully placing his emphases. By the words he selects to describe the father's stride, Faulkner directs how we feel toward the man and perhaps also indicates his own wondering but skeptical attitude toward a character whose very footfall is "outrageous" and "enormous." (Fond of long sentences like the last one in the quoted passage, Faulkner remarked that there are sentences that need to be written in the way a circus acrobat pedals a bicycle on a high wire: rapidly, so as not to fall off.)

Hemingway's famous style includes both short sentences and long, but when the sentences are long, they tend to be relatively simple in construction. Hemingway

[2]Letter in the *New York Times Book Review*, June 5, 1988.

likes long compound sentences (clause plus clause plus clause), sometimes joined with "ands." He interrupts such a sentence with a dependent clause or a parenthetical element much less frequently than Faulkner does. The effect is like listening to speech:

> In the day time the street was dusty, but at night the dew settled the dust and the old man liked to sit late because he was deaf and now at night it was quiet and he felt the difference.

Hemingway is a master of swift, terse dialogue, and often casts whole scenes in the form of conversation. As if he were a closemouthed speaker unwilling to let his feelings loose, the narrator of a Hemingway story often addresses us in understatement, implying greater depths of feeling than he puts into words. Read the following story and you will see that its style and tone cannot be separated.

Ernest Hemingway

A CLEAN, WELL-LIGHTED PLACE   1933

Ernest Hemingway (1899–1961), born in Oak Park, Illinois, bypassed college to be a cub reporter. In World War I, as an eighteen-year-old volunteer ambulance driver in Italy, he was wounded in action. In 1922 he settled in Paris, then aswarm with writers; he later recalled that time in A Moveable Feast *(1964). Hemingway won swift acclaim for his early stories,* In Our Time *(1925), and for his first, perhaps finest, novel,* The Sun Also Rises *(1926), portraying a "lost generation" of postwar American drifters in France and Spain. For Whom the Bell Tolls (1940) depicts life during the Spanish Civil War. Hemingway became a celebrity, often photographed as a marlin fisherman or a lion hunter. A fan of bullfighting, he wrote two nonfiction books on the subject:* Death in the Afternoon *(1932) and* The Dangerous Summer *(1985). After World War II, with his fourth wife, journalist Mary Welsh, he made his home in Cuba, where he wrote* The Old Man and the Sea *(1952). The Nobel Prize for literature came his way in 1954. In 1961, mentally distressed and physically ailing, he shot himself. Hemingway brought a hard-bitten realism to American fiction. His heroes live dangerously, by personal codes of honor, courage, and endurance. Hemingway's distinctively crisp, unadorned style left American literature permanently changed.*

It was late and every one had left the café except an old man who sat in the shadow the leaves of the tree made against the electric light. In the day time the street was dusty, but at night the dew settled the dust and the old man liked to sit late because he was deaf and now at night it was quiet and he felt the difference. The two waiters inside the café knew that the old man was a little drunk, and while he was a good client they knew that if he became too drunk he would leave without paying, so they kept watch on him.

"Last week he tried to commit suicide," one waiter said.

"Why?"

"He was in despair."

"What about?"

"Nothing."

"How do you know it was nothing?"

"He has plenty of money."

They sat together at a table that was close against the wall near the door of the café and looked at the terrace where the tables were all empty except where the old man sat in the shadow of the leaves of the tree that moved slightly in the wind. A girl and a soldier went by in the street. The street light shone on the brass number on his collar. The girl wore no head covering and hurried beside him.

"The guard will pick him up," one waiter said.

"What does it matter if he gets what he's after?"

"He had better get off the street now. The guard will get him. They went by five minutes ago."

The old man sitting in the shadow rapped on his saucer with his glass. The younger waiter went over to him.

"What do you want?"

The old man looked at him. "Another brandy," he said.

"You'll be drunk," the waiter said. The old man looked at him. The waiter went away.

"He'll stay all night," he said to his colleague. "I'm sleepy now. I never get into bed before three o'clock. He should have killed himself last week."

The waiter took the brandy bottle and another saucer from the counter inside the café and marched out to the old man's table. He put down the saucer and poured the glass full of brandy.

"You should have killed yourself last week," he said to the deaf man. The old man motioned with his finger. "A little more," he said. The waiter poured on into the glass so that the brandy slopped over and ran down the stem into the top saucer of the pile. "Thank you," the old man said. The waiter took the bottle back inside the café. He sat down at the table with his colleague again.

"He's drunk now," he said.

"He's drunk every night."°

"What did he want to kill himself for?"

"How should I know?"

"How did he do it?"

"He hung himself with a rope."

"Who cut him down?"

"His niece."

"Why did they do it?"

"Fear for his soul."

"How much money has he got?"

"He's got plenty."

"He's drunk now," he said. "He's drunk every night": The younger waiter perhaps says both these lines. A device of Hemingway's style is sometimes to have a character pause, then speak again—as often happens in actual speech

"He must be eighty years old."

"Anyway I should say he was eighty."°

"I wish he would go home. I never get to bed before three o'clock. What kind of hour is that to go to bed?"

"He stays up because he likes it."   35

"He's lonely. I'm not lonely. I have a wife waiting in bed for me."

"He had a wife once too."

"A wife would be no good to him now."

"You can't tell. He might be better with a wife."

"His niece looks after him."   40

"I know. You said she cut him down."

"I wouldn't want to be that old. An old man is a nasty thing."

"Not always. This old man is clean. He drinks without spilling. Even now, drunk. Look at him."

"I don't want to look at him. I wish he would go home. He has no regard for those who must work."

The old man looked from his glass across the square, then over at the waiters.   45

"Another brandy," he said, pointing to his glass. The waiter who was in a hurry came over.

"Finished," he said, speaking with that omission of syntax stupid people employ when talking to drunken people or foreigners. "No more tonight. Close now."

"Another," said the old man.

"No. Finished." The waiter wiped the edge of the table with a towel and shook his head.

The old man stood up, slowly counted the saucers, took a leather coin purse   50
from his pocket and paid for the drinks, leaving half a peseta tip.

The waiter watched him go down the street, a very old man walking unsteadily but with dignity.

"Why didn't you let him stay and drink?" the unhurried waiter asked. They were putting up the shutters. "It is not half-past two."

"I want to go home to bed."

"What is an hour?"

"More to me than to him."   55

"An hour is the same."

"You talk like an old man yourself. He can buy a bottle and drink at home."

"It's not the same."

"No, it is not," agreed the waiter with a wife. He did not wish to be unjust. He was only in a hurry.

"And you? You have no fear of going home before the usual hour?"   60

"*He must be eighty years old.*" "*Anyway I should say he was eighty*": Is this another instance of the same character's speaking twice? Clearly, it is the younger waiter who says the next line, "I wish he would go home."

"Are you trying to insult me?"

"No, hombre, only to make a joke."

"No," the waiter who was in a hurry said, rising from pulling down the metal shutters. "I have confidence. I am all confidence."

"You have youth, confidence, and a job," the older waiter said. "You have everything."

"And what do you lack?"

"Everything but work."

"You have everything I have."

"No. I have never had confidence and I am not young."

"Come on. Stop talking nonsense and lock up."

"I am of those who like to stay late at the café," the older waiter said. "With all those who do not want to go to bed. With all those who need a light for the night."

"I want to go home and into bed."

"We are of two different kinds," the older waiter said. He was not dressed to go home. "It is not only a question of youth and confidence although those things are very beautiful. Each night I am reluctant to close up because there may be some one who needs the café."

"Hombre, there are bodegas° open all night long."

"You do not understand. This is a clean and pleasant café. It is well lighted. The light is very good and also, now, there are shadows of the leaves."

"Good night," said the younger waiter.

"Good night," the other said. Turning off the electric light he continued the conversation with himself. It is the light of course but it is necessary that the place be clean and pleasant. You do not want music. Certainly you do not want music. Nor can you stand before a bar with dignity although that is all that is provided for these hours. What did he fear? It was not fear or dread. It was a nothing that he knew too well. It was all a nothing and a man was nothing too. It was only that and light was all it needed and a certain cleanness and order. Some lived in it and never felt it but he knew it all was nada y pues nada y nada y pues nada.° Our nada who art in nada, nada be thy name thy kingdom nada thy will be nada in nada as it is in nada. Give us this nada our daily nada and nada us our nada as we nada our nadas and nada us not into nada but deliver us from nada; pues nada. Hail nothing full of nothing, nothing is with thee. He smiled and stood before a bar with a shining steam pressure coffee machine.

"What's yours?" asked the barman.

"Nada."

"Otro loco más,"° said the barman and turned away.

"A little cup," said the waiter.

The barman poured it for him.

---

bodegas: wineshops.   nada y pues . . . nada: nothing and then nothing and nothing and then nothing.   Otro loco más: another lunatic.

"The light is very bright and pleasant but the bar is unpolished," the waiter said.

The barman looked at him but did not answer. It was too late at night for conversation.

"You want another copita?"° the barman asked.

"No, thank you," said the waiter and went out. He disliked bars and bodegas. A clean, well-lighted café was a very different thing. Now, without thinking further, he would go home to his room. He would lie in the bed and finally, with daylight, he would go to sleep. After all, he said to himself, it is probably only insomnia. Many must have it. 85

QUESTIONS

1. What besides insomnia makes the older waiter reluctant to go to bed? Comment especially on his meditation with its *nada* refrain. Why does he so well understand the old man's need for a café? What does the café represent for the two of them?
2. Compare the younger waiter and the older waiter in their attitudes toward the old man. Whose attitude do you take to be closer to that of the author? Even though Hemingway does not editorially state his own feelings, how does he make them clear to us?
3. Point to sentences that establish the style of the story. What is distinctive in them? What repetitions of words or phrases seem particularly effective? Does Hemingway seem to favor a simple or an erudite vocabulary?
4. What is the story's point of view? Discuss its appropriateness.

William Faulkner

BARN BURNING   1939

William Faulkner (1897–1962) receives a capsule biography in Chapter Two, page 29, along with his story "A Rose for Emily." His "Barn Burning" is among his many contributions to the history of Yoknapatawpha, an imaginary Mississippi county in which the Sartorises and the de Spains are landed aristocrats living by a code of honor and the Snopeses— most of them—are shiftless ne'er-do-wells.

The store in which the Justice of the Peace's court was sitting smelled of cheese. The boy, crouched on his nail keg at the back of the crowded room, knew he smelled cheese, and more: from where he sat he could see the ranked shelves close-packed with the solid, squat, dynamic shapes of tin cans whose labels his stomach read, not from the lettering which meant nothing to his mind but from the scarlet devils and the silver curve of fish—this, the cheese which he knew he smelled and the hermetic meat which his intestines believed he smelled coming in intermittent gusts momentary and brief between the other constant one, the smell and sense just a little of fear because mostly of despair and grief, the old fierce pull of blood. He could not see the table where the Justice sat and

---

copita: little cup.

before which his father and his father's enemy (*our enemy* he thought in that despair: *ourn! mine and hisn both! He's my father!*) stood, but he could hear them, the two of them that is, because his father had said no word yet:

"But what proof have you, Mr. Harris?"

"I told you. The hog got into my corn. I caught it up and sent it back to him. He had no fence that would hold it. I told him so, warned him. The next time I put the hog in my pen. When he came to get it I gave him enough wire to patch up his pen. The next time I put the hog up and kept it. I rode down to his house and saw the wire I gave him still rolled on to the spool in his yard. I told him he could have the hog when he paid me a dollar pound fee. That evening a nigger came with the dollar and got the hog. He was a strange nigger. He said, 'He say to tell you wood and hay kin burn.' I said, 'What?' 'That whut he say to tell you,' the nigger said. 'Wood and hay kin burn.' That night my barn burned. I got the stock out but I lost the barn."

"Where's the nigger? Have you got him?"

"He was a strange nigger, I tell you. I don't know what became of him." 5

"But that's not proof. Don't you see that's not proof?"

"Get that boy up here. He knows." For a moment the boy thought too that the man meant his older brother until Harris said, "Not him. The little one. The boy," and, crouching, small for his age, small and wiry like his father, in patched and faded jeans even too small for him, with straight, uncombed, brown hair and eyes gray and wild as storm scud, he saw the men between himself and the table part and become a lane of grim faces, at the end of which he saw the Justice, a shabby, collarless, graying man in spectacles, beckoning him. He felt no floor under his bare feet; he seemed to walk beneath the palpable weight of the grim turning faces. His father, still in his black Sunday coat donned not for the trial but for the moving, did not even look at him. *He aims for me to lie*, he thought, again with that frantic grief and despair. *And I will have to do hit.*

"What's your name, boy?" the Justice said.

"Colonel Sartoris Snopes," the boy whispered.

"Hey?" the Justice said. "Talk louder. Colonel Sartoris? I reckon anybody 10 named for Colonel Sartoris in this country can't help but tell the truth, can they?" The boy said nothing. *Enemy! Enemy!* he thought; for a moment he could not even see, could not see that the Justice's face was kindly nor discern that his voice was troubled when he spoke to the man named Harris: "Do you want me to question this boy?" But he could hear, and during those subsequent long seconds while there was absolutely no sound in the crowded little room save that of quiet and intent breathing it was as if he had swung outward at the end of a grape vine, over a ravine, and at the top of the swing had been caught in a prolonged instant of mesmerized gravity, weightless in time.

"No!" Harris said violently, explosively. "Damnation! Send him out of here!" Now time, the fluid world, rushed beneath him again, the voices coming to him again through the smell of cheese and sealed meat, the fear and despair and the old grief of blood:

"This case is closed. I can't find against you, Snopes, but I can give you advice. Leave this country and don't come back to it."

His father spoke for the first time, his voice cold and harsh, level, without emphasis: "I aim to. I don't figure to stay in a country among people who . . ." he said something unprintable and vile, addressed to no one.

"That'll do," the Justice said. "Take your wagon and get out of this country before dark. Case dismissed."

His father turned, and he followed the stiff black coat, the wiry figure walking a little stiffly from where a Confederate provost's man's musket ball had taken him in the heel on a stolen horse thirty years ago, followed the two backs now, since his older brother had appeared from somewhere in the crowd, no taller than the father but thicker, chewing tobacco steadily, between the two lines of grim-faced men and out of the store and across the worn gallery and down the sagging steps and among the dogs and half-grown boys in the mild May dust, where as he passed a voice hissed:

"Barn burner!"

Again he could not see, whirling; there was a face in a red haze, moonlike, bigger than the full moon, the owner of it half again his size, he leaping in the red haze toward the face, feeling no blow, feeling no shock when his head struck the earth, scrabbling up and leaping again, feeling no blow this time either and tasting no blood, scrabbling up to see the other boy in full flight and himself already leaping into pursuit as his father's hand jerked him back, the harsh, cold voice speaking above him: "Go get in the wagon."

It stood in a grove of locusts and mulberries across the road. His two hulking sisters in their Sunday dresses and his mother and her sister in calico and sunbonnets were already in it, sitting on and among the sorry residue of the dozen and more movings which even the boy could remember—the battered stove, the broken beds and chairs, the clock inlaid with mother-of-pearl, which would not run, stopped at some fourteen minutes past two o'clock of a dead and forgotten day and time, which had been his mother's dowry. She was crying, though when she saw him she drew her sleeve across her face and began to descend from the wagon. "Get back," the father said.

"He's hurt. I got to get some water and wash his . . ."

"Get back in the wagon," his father said. He got in too, over the tail-gate. His father mounted to the seat where the older brother already sat and struck the gaunt mules two savage blows with the peeled willow, but without heat. It was not even sadistic; it was exactly that same quality which in later years would cause his descendants to over-run the engine before putting a motor car into motion, striking and reining back in the same movement. The wagon went on, the store with its quiet crowd of grimly watching men dropped behind; a curve in the road hid it. *Forever* he thought. *Maybe he's done satisfied now, now that he has . . .* stopping himself, not to say it aloud even to himself. His mother's hand touched his shoulder.

"Does hit hurt?" she said.

"Naw," he said. "Hit don't hurt. Lemme be."

"Can't you wipe some of the blood off before hit dries?"

"I'll wash to-night," he said. "Lemme be, I tell you."

The wagon went on. He did not know where they were going. None of them ever did or ever asked, because it was always somewhere, always a house of sorts waiting for them a day or two days or even three days away. Likely his father had already arranged to make a crop on another farm before he . . . Again he had to stop himself. He (the father) always did. There was something about his wolflike independence and even courage when the advantage was at least neutral which impressed strangers, as if they got from his latent ravening ferocity not so much a sense of dependability as a feeling that his ferocious conviction in the rightness of his own actions would be of advantage to all whose interest lay with his.

That night they camped, in a grove of oaks and beeches where a spring ran. The nights were still cool and they had a fire against it, of a rail lifted from a nearby fence and cut into lengths—a small fire, neat, niggard almost, a shrewd fire; such fires were his father's habit and custom always, even in freezing weather. Older, the boy might have remarked this and wondered why not a big one; why should not a man who had not only seen the waste and extravagance of war, but who had in his blood an inherent voracious prodigality with material not his own, have burned everything in sight? Then he might have gone a step farther and thought that that was the reason: that niggard blaze was the living fruit of nights passed during those four years in the woods hiding from all men, blue and gray, with his strings of horses (captured horses, he called them). And older still, he might have divined the true reason: that the element of fire spoke to some deep mainspring of his father's being, as the element of steel or of powder spoke to other men, as the one weapon for the preservation of integrity, else breath were not worth the breathing, and hence to be regarded with respect and used with discretion.

But he did not think this now and he had seen those same niggard blazes all his life. He merely ate his supper beside it and was already half asleep over his iron plate when his father called him, and once more he followed the stiff back, the stiff and ruthless limp, up the slope and on to the starlit road where, turning, he could see his father against the stars but without face or depth—a shape black, flat, and bloodless as though cut from tin in the iron folds of the frockcoat which had not been made for him, the voice harsh like tin and without heat like tin:

"You were fixing to tell them. You would have told him."

He didn't answer. His father struck him with the flat of his hand on the side of the head, hard but without heat, exactly as he had struck the two mules at the store, exactly as he would strike either of them with any stick in order to kill a horse fly, his voice without heat or anger: "You're getting to be a man. You got to learn. You got to learn to stick to your own blood or you ain't going to have any blood to stick to you. Do you think either of them, any man there this morning, would? Don't you know all they wanted was a chance to get at me because they knew I had them beat? Eh?" Later, twenty years later, he was to tell himself, "If I had said they wanted only truth, justice, he would have hit me again." But now he said nothing. He was not crying. He just stood there. "Answer me," his father said.

"Yes," he whispered. His father turned.

"Get on to bed. We'll be there tomorrow."

Tomorrow they were there. In the early afternoon the wagon stopped before a paintless two-room house identical almost with the dozen others it had stopped before even in the boy's ten years, and again, as on the other dozen occasions, his mother and aunt got down and began to unload the wagon, although his two sisters and his father and brother had not moved.

"Likely hit ain't fitten for hawgs," one of the sisters said.

"Nevertheless, fit it will and you'll hog it and like it," his father said. "Get out of them chairs and help your Ma unload."

The two sisters got down, big, bovine, in a flutter of cheap ribbons; one of them drew from the jumbled wagon bed a battered lantern, the other a worn broom. His father handed the reins to the older son and began to climb stiffly over the wheel. "When they get unloaded, take the team to the barn and feed them." Then he said, and at first the boy thought he was still speaking to his brother: "Come with me."

"Me?" he said.

"Yes," his father said. "You."

"Abner," his mother said. His father paused and looked back—the harsh level stare beneath the shaggy, graying, irascible brows.

"I reckon I'll have a word with the man that aims to begin tomorrow owning me body and soul for the next eight months."

They went back up the road. A week ago—or before last night, that is—he would have asked where they were going, but not now. His father had struck him before last night but never before had he paused afterward to explain why; it was as if the blow and the following calm, outrageous voice still rang, repercussed, divulging nothing to him save the terrible handicap of being young, the light weight of his few years, just heavy enough to prevent his soaring free of the world as it seemed to be ordered but not heavy enough to keep him footed solid in it, to resist it and try to change the course of its events.

Presently he could see the grove of oaks and cedars and the other flowering trees and shrubs where the house would be, though not the house yet. They walked beside a fence massed with honeysuckle and Cherokee roses and came to a gate swinging open between two brick pillars, and now, beyond a sweep of drive, he saw the house for the first time and at that instant he forgot his father and the terror and despair both, and even when he remembered his father again (who had not stopped) the terror and despair did not return. Because, for all the twelve movings, they had sojourned until now in a poor country, a land of small farms and fields and houses, and he had never seen a house like this before. *Hit's big as a courthouse* he thought quietly, with a surge of peace and joy whose reason he could not have thought into words, being too young for that: *They are safe from him. People whose lives are a part of this peace and dignity are beyond his touch, he no more to them than a buzzing wasp: capable of stinging for a little moment but*

Margin line numbers: 30, 35, 40

that's all; the spell of this peace and dignity rendering even the barns and stable and cribs which belong to it impervious to the puny flames he might contrive . . . this, the peace and joy, ebbing for an instant as he looked again at the stiff black back, the stiff and implacable limp of the figure which was not dwarfed by the house, for the reason that it had never looked big anywhere and which now, against the serene columned backdrop, had more than ever that impervious quality of something cut ruthlessly from tin, depthless, as though, sidewise to the sun, it would cast no shadow. Watching him, the boy remarked the absolutely undeviating course which his father held and saw the stiff foot come squarely down in a pile of fresh droppings where a horse had stood in the drive and which his father could have avoided by a simple change of stride. But it ebbed only a moment, though he could not have thought this into words either, walking on in the spell of the house, which he could even want but without envy, without sorrow, certainly never with that ravening and jealous rage which unknown to him walked in the ironlike black coat before him: *Maybe he will feel it too. Maybe it will even change him now from what maybe he couldn't help but be.*

They crossed the portico. Now he could hear his father's stiff foot as it came down on the boards with clocklike finality, a sound out of all proportion to the displacement of the body it bore and which was not dwarfed either by the white door before it, as though it had attained to a sort of vicious and ravening minimum not to be dwarfed by anything—the flat, wide, black hat, the formal coat of broadcloth which had once been black but which had now that friction-glazed greenish cast of the bodies of old house flies, the lifted sleeve which was too large, the lifted hand like a curled claw. The door opened so promptly that the boy knew the Negro must have been watching them all the time, an old man with neat grizzled hair, in a linen jacket, who stood barring the door with his body, saying, "Wipe yo foots, white man, fo you come in here. Major ain't home nohow."

"Get out of my way, nigger," his father said, without heat too, flinging the door back and the Negro also and entering, his hat still on his head. And now the boy saw the prints of the stiff foot on the doorjamb and saw them appear on the pale rug behind the machinelike deliberation of the foot which seemed to bear (or transmit) twice the weight which the body compassed. The Negro was shouting "Miss Lula! Miss Lula!" somewhere behind them, then the boy, deluged as though by a warm wave by a suave turn of the carpeted stair and a pendant glitter of chandeliers and a mute gleam of gold frames, heard the swift feet and saw her too, a lady—perhaps he had never seen her like before either—in a gray, smooth gown with lace at the throat and an apron tied at the waist and the sleeves turned back, wiping cake or biscuit dough from her hands with a towel as she came up the hall, looking not at his father at all but at the tracks on the blond rug with an expression of incredulous amazement.

"I tried," the Negro cried. "I tole him to . . ."

"Will you please go away?" she said in a shaking voice. "Major de Spain is not at home. Will you please go away?"

His father had not spoken again. He did not speak again. He did not even look at her. He just stood stiff in the center of the rug, in his hat, the shaggy iron-gray brows twitching slightly above the pebble-colored eyes as he appeared to examine the house with brief deliberation. Then with the same deliberation he turned; the boy watched him pivot on the good leg and saw the stiff foot drag around the arc of the turning, leaving a final long and fading smear. His father never looked at it, he never once looked down at the rug. The Negro held the door. It closed behind them, upon the hysteric and indistinguishable woman-wail. His father stopped at the top of the steps and scraped his boot clean on the edge of it. At the gate he stopped again. He stood for a moment, planted stiffly on the stiff foot, looking back at the house. "Pretty and white, ain't it?" he said. "That's sweat. Nigger sweat. Maybe it ain't white enough yet to suit him. Maybe he wants to mix some white sweat with it."

Two hours later the boy was chopping wood behind the house within which his mother and aunt and the two sisters (the mother and aunt, not the two girls, he knew that; even at this distance and muffled by walls the flat loud voices of the two girls emanated an incorrigible idle inertia) were setting up the stove to prepare a meal, when he heard the hooves and saw the linen-clad man on a fine sorrel mare, whom he recognized even before he saw the rolled rug in front of the Negro youth following on a fat bay carriage horse—a suffused, angry face van-ishing, still at full gallop, beyond the corner of the house where his father and brother were sitting in the two tilted chairs; and a moment later, almost before he could have put the axe down, he heard the hooves again and watched the sorrel mare go back out of the yard, already galloping again. Then his father began to shout one of the sisters' names, who presently emerged backward from the kitchen door dragging the rolled rug along the ground by one end while the other sister walked behind it.

"If you ain't going to tote, go on and set up the wash pot," the first said.

"You, Sarty!" the second shouted. "Set up the wash pot!" His father ap-peared at the door, framed against that shabbiness, as he had been against that other bland perfection, impervious to either, the mother's anxious face at his shoulder.

"Go on," the father said. "Pick it up." The two sisters stooped, broad, 50 lethargic; stooping, they presented an incredible expanse of pale cloth and a flutter of tawdry ribbons.

"If I thought enough of a rug to have to git hit all the way from France I wouldn't keep hit where folks coming in would have to tromp on hit," the first said. They raised the rug.

"Abner," the mother said. "Let me do it."

"You go back and git dinner," his father said. "I'll tend to this."

From the woodpile through the rest of the afternoon the boy watched them, the rug spread flat in the dust beside the bubbling wash pot, the two sisters stooping over it with that profound and lethargic reluctance, while the father stood over them in turn, implacable and grim, driving them though never raising his voice again. He could smell the harsh homemade lye they were using; he saw his mother come to the door once and look toward them with an expression not anxious now but very like despair; he saw his father turn, and he fell to with the axe and saw from the corner of his eye his father raise from the ground a flattish fragment of field stone and examine it and return to the pot, and this time his mother actually spoke: "Abner. Abner. Please don't. Please, Abner."

Then he was done too. It was dusk; the whippoorwills had already begun. He could smell coffee from the room where they would presently eat the cold food remaining from the mid-afternoon meal, though when he entered the house he realized they were having coffee again probably because there was a fire on the hearth, before which the rug now lay spread over the backs of the two chairs. The tracks of his father's foot were gone. Where they had been were now long, water-cloudy scoriations resembling the sporadic course of a lilliputian mowing machine.

It still hung there while they ate the cold food and then went to bed, scattered without order or claim up and down the two rooms, his mother in one bed, where his father would later lie, the older brother in the other, himself, the aunt, and the two sisters on pallets on the floor. But his father was not in bed yet. The last thing the boy remembered was the depthless, harsh silhouette of the hat and coat bending over the rug and it seemed to him that he had not even closed his eyes when the silhouette was standing over him, the fire almost dead behind it, the stiff foot prodding him awake. "Catch up the mule," his father said.

When he returned with the mule his father was standing in the back door, the rolled rug over his shoulder. "Ain't you going to ride?" he said.

"No. Give me your foot."

He bent his knee into his father's hand, the wiry, surprising power flowed smoothly, rising, he rising with it, on to the mule's bare back (they had owned a saddle once; the boy could remember it though not when or where) and with the same effortlessness his father swung the rug up in front of him. Now in the starlight they retraced the afternoon's path, up the dusty road rife with honeysuckle, through the gate and up the black tunnel of the drive to the lightless house, where he sat on the mule and felt the rough warp of the rug drag across his thighs and vanish.

"Don't you want me to help?" he whispered. His father did not answer and now he heard again that stiff foot striking the hollow portico with that wooden and clocklike deliberation, that outrageous overstatement of the weight it carried. The rug, hunched, not flung (the boy could tell that even in the darkness) from his father's shoulder struck the angle of wall and floor with a sound unbelievably loud, thunderous, then the foot again, unhurried and enormous; a light came on in the house and the boy sat, tense, breathing steadily and quietly and just a little fast, though the foot itself did not increase its beat at all, descending the steps now; now the boy could see him.

"Don't you want to ride now?" he whispered. "We kin both ride now," the light within the house altering now, flaring up and sinking. *He's coming down the stairs now,* he thought. He had already ridden the mule up beside the horse block; presently his father was up behind him and he doubled the reins over and slashed the mule across the neck, but before the animal could begin to trot the hard, thin arm came around him, the hard, knotted hand jerking the mule back to a walk.

In the first red rays of the sun they were in the lot, putting plow gear on the mules. This time the sorrel mare was in the lot before he heard it at all, the rider collarless and even bareheaded, trembling, speaking in a shaking voice as the woman in the house had done, his father merely looking up once before stooping again to the hame he was buckling, so that the man on the mare spoke to his stooping back:

"You must realize you have ruined that rug. Wasn't there anybody here, any of your women . . ." he ceased, shaking, the boy watching him, the older brother leaning now in the stable door, chewing, blinking slowly and steadily at nothing apparently. "It cost a hundred dollars. But you never had a hundred dollars. You never will. So I'm going to charge you twenty bushels of corn against your crop. I'll add it in your contract and when you come to the commissary you can sign it. That won't keep Mrs. de Spain quiet but maybe it will teach you to wipe your feet off before you enter her house again."

Then he was gone. The boy looked at his father, who still had not spoken or even looked up again, who was now adjusting the logger-head in the hame.

"Pap," he said. His father looked at him—the inscrutable face, the shaggy 65 brows beneath where the gray eyes glinted coldly. Suddenly the boy went toward him, fast, stopping as suddenly. "You done the best you could!" he cried. "If he wanted hit done different why didn't he wait and tell you how? He won't git no twenty bushels! He won't git none! We'll gather hit and hide hit! I kin watch . . ."

"Did you put the cutter back in that straight stock like I told you?"

"No, sir," he said.

"Then go do it."

That was Wednesday. During the rest of that week he worked steadily, at what was within his scope and some which was beyond it, with an industry that did not need to be driven nor even commanded twice; he had this from his mother, with the difference that some at least of what he did he liked to do, such as splitting wood with the half-size axe which his mother and aunt had earned, or saved money somehow, to present him with at Christmas. In company with the two older women (and on one afternoon, even one of the sisters), he built pens for the shoat and the cow which were a part of his father's contract with the landlord, and one afternoon, his father being absent, gone somewhere on one of the mules, he went to the field.

They were running a middle buster now, his brother holding the plow 70 straight while he handled the reins, and walking beside the straining mule, the rich black soil shearing cool and damp against his bare ankles, he thought *Maybe this is the end of it. Maybe even that twenty bushels that seems hard to have to pay for just a rug will be a cheap price for him to stop forever and always from being what he used to be*; thinking, dreaming now, so that his brother had to speak sharply to him to mind the mule: *Maybe he even won't collect the twenty bushels. Maybe it will all add up and balance and vanish—corn, rug, fire; the terror and grief; the being pulled two ways like between two teams of horses—gone, done with for ever and ever.*

Then it was Saturday; he looked up from beneath the mule he was harnessing and saw his father in the black coat and hat. "Not that," his father said. "The wagon gear." And then, two hours later, sitting in the wagon bed behind his father and brother on the seat, the wagon accomplished a final curve, and he saw the weathered paintless store with its tattered tobacco- and patent-medicine posters and the tethered wagons and saddle animals below the gallery. He mounted the gnawed steps behind his father and brother, and there again was the lane of quiet, watching faces for the three of them to walk through. He saw the man in spectacles sitting at the plank table and he did not need to be told this was a Justice of the Peace; he sent one glare of fierce, exultant, partisan defiance at the man in collar and cravat now, whom he had seen but twice before in his life, and that on a galloping horse, who now wore on his face an expression not of rage but of amazed unbelief which the boy could not have known was at the incredible circumstance of being sued by one of his own tenants, and came and stood against his father and cried at the Justice: "He ain't done it! He ain't burnt . . ."

"Go back to the wagon," his father said.

"Burnt?" the Justice said. "Do I understand this rug was burned too?"

"Does anybody here claim it was?" his father said. "Go back to the wagon." But he did not, he merely retreated to the rear of the room, crowded as that other had been, but not to sit down this time, instead, to stand pressing among the motionless bodies, listening to the voices:

"And you claim twenty bushels of corn is too high for the damage you did to the rug?" 75

"He brought the rug to me and said he wanted the tracks washed out of it. I washed the tracks out and took the rug back to him."

"But you didn't carry the rug back to him in the same condition it was in before you made the tracks on it."

His father did not answer, and now for perhaps half a minute there was no sound at all save that of breathing, the faint, steady suspiration of complete and intent listening.

"You decline to answer that, Mr. Snopes?" Again his father did not answer. "I'm going to find against you, Mr. Snopes. I'm going to find that you were responsible for the injury to Major de Spain's rug and hold you liable for it. But twenty bushels of corn seems a little high for a man in your circumstances to have to pay. Major de Spain claims it cost a hundred dollars. October corn will be worth about fifty cents. I figure that if Major de Spain can stand a ninety-five dollar loss on something he paid cash for, you can stand a five-dollar loss you haven't earned yet. I hold you in damages to Major de Spain to the amount of ten bushels of corn over and above your contract with him, to be paid to him out of your crop at gathering time. Court adjourned."

It had taken no time hardly, the morning was but half begun. He thought 80 they would return home and perhaps back to the field, since they were late, far behind all other farmers. But instead his father passed on behind the wagon, merely indicating with his hand for the older brother to follow with it, and crossed the road toward the blacksmith shop opposite, pressing on after his father, overtaking him, speaking, whispering up at the harsh, calm face beneath the weathered hat: "He won't git no ten bushels either. He won't git one. We'll . . ." until his father glanced for an instant down at him, the face absolutely calm, the grizzled eyebrows tangled above the cold eyes, the voice almost pleasant, almost gentle:

"You think so? Well, we'll wait till October anyway."

The matter of the wagon—the setting of a spoke or two and the tightening of the tires—did not take long either, the business of the tires accomplished by driving the wagon into the spring branch behind the shop and letting it stand there, the mules nuzzling into the water from time to time, and the boy on the seat with the idle reins, looking up the slope and through the sooty tunnel of the shed where the slow hammer rang and where his father sat on an upended cypress bolt, easily, either talking or listening, still sitting there when the boy brought the dripping wagon up out of the branch and halted it before the door.

"Take them on to the shade and hitch," his father said. He did so and returned. His father and the smith and a third man squatting on his heels inside the door were talking, about crops and animals; the boy, squatting too in the ammoniac dust and hoof-parings and scales of rust, heard his father tell a long and unhurried story out of the time before the birth of the older brother even when he had been a professional horsetrader. And then his father came up beside him where he stood before a tattered last year's circus poster on the other side of the store, gazing rapt and quiet at the scarlet horses, the incredible poisings and convulsions of tulle and tights and the painted leers of comedians, and said, "It's time to eat."

But not at home. Squatting beside his brother against the front wall, he watched his father emerge from the store and produce from a paper sack a segment of cheese and divide it carefully and deliberately into three with his pocket knife and produce crackers from the same sack. They all three squatted on the gallery and ate, slowly, without talking; then in the store again, they drank from a tin dipper tepid water smelling of the cedar bucket and of living beech trees. And still they did not go home. It was a horse lot this time, a tall rail fence upon and along which men stood and sat and out of which one by one horses were led, to be walked and trotted and then cantered back and forth along the road while the slow swapping and buying went on and the sun began to slant westward, they—the three of them—watching and listening, the older brother with his muddy eyes and his steady, inevitable tobacco, the father commenting now and then on certain of the animals, to no one in particular.

It was after sundown when they reached home. They ate supper by lamplight, then, sitting on the doorstep, the boy watched the night fully accomplish, listening to the whippoorwills and the frogs, when he heard his mother's voice: "Abner! No! No! Oh, God. Oh, God. Abner!" and he rose, whirled, and saw the altered light through the door where a candle stub now burned in a bottle neck on the table and his father, still in the hat and coat, at once formal and burlesque as though dressed carefully for some shabby and ceremonial violence, emptying the reservoir of the lamp back into the five-gallon kerosene can from which it had been filled, while the mother tugged at his arm until he shifted the lamp to the other hand and flung her back, not savagely or viciously, just hard, into the wall, her hands flung out against the wall for balance, her mouth open and in her face the same quality of hopeless despair as had been in her voice. Then his father saw him standing in the door.

"Go to the barn and get that can of oil we were oiling the wagon with," he said. The boy did not move. Then he could speak.

"What . . ." he cried. "What are you . . ."

"Go get that oil," his father said. "Go."

Then he was moving, running, outside the house, toward the stable: this the old habit, the old blood which he had not been permitted to choose for himself, which had been bequeathed him willy nilly and which had run for so long (and who knew where, battening on what of outrage and savagery and lust) before it came to him. *I could keep on*, he thought. *I could run on and on and never look back, never need to see his face again. Only I can't. I can't*, the rusted can in his hand now, the liquid sploshing in it as he ran back to the house and into it, into the sound of his mother's weeping in the next room, and handed the can to his father.

"Ain't you going to even send a nigger?" he cried. "At least you sent a nigger before!"   90

This time his father didn't strike him. The hand came even faster than the blow had, the same hand which had set the can on the table with almost excruciating care flashing from the can toward him too quick for him to follow it, gripping him by the back of his shirt and on to tiptoe before he had seen it quit the can, the face stooping at him in breathless and frozen ferocity, the cold, dead voice speaking over him to the older brother who leaned against the table, chewing with that steady, curious, sidewise motion of cows:

"Empty the can into the big one and go on. I'll catch up with you."

"Better tie him up to the bedpost," the brother said.

"Do like I told you," the father said. Then the boy was moving, his bunched shirt and the hard, bony hand between his shoulder-blades, his toes just touching the floor, across the room and into the other one, past the sisters sitting with spread heavy thighs in the two chairs over the cold hearth, and to where his mother and aunt sat side by side on the bed, the aunt's arm about his mother's shoulders.

"Hold him," the father said. The aunt made a startled movement. "Not   95
you," the father said. "Lennie. Take hold of him. I want to see you do it." His mother took him by the wrist. "You'll hold him better than that. If he gets loose don't you know what he is going to do? He will go up yonder." He jerked his head toward the road. "Maybe I'd better tie him."

"I'll hold him," his mother whispered.

"See you do then." Then his father was gone, the stiff foot heavy and measured upon the boards, ceasing at last.

Then he began to struggle. His mother caught him in both arms, he jerking and wrenching at them. He would be stronger in the end, he knew that. But he had no time to wait for it. "Lemme go!" he cried. "I don't want to have to hit you!"

"Let him go!" the aunt said. "If he don't go, before God, I am going up there myself!"

"Don't you see I can't?" his mother cried. "Sarty! Sarty! No! No! Help me, Lizzie!" 100

Then he was free. His aunt grasped at him but it was too late. He whirled, running, his mother stumbled forward on to her knees behind him, crying to the nearer sister: "Catch him, Net! Catch him!" But that was too late too, the sister (the sisters were twins, born at the same time, yet either of them now gave the impression of being, encompassing as much living meat and volume and weight as any other two of the family) not yet having begun to rise from the chair, her head, face, alone merely turned, presenting to him in the flying instant an aston-ishing expanse of young female features untroubled by any surprise even, wearing only an expression of bovine interest. Then he was out of the room, out of the house, in the mild dust of the starlit road and the heavy rifeness of honeysuckle, the pale ribbon unspooling with terrific slowness under his running feet, reaching the gate at last and turning in, running, his heart and lungs drumming, on up the drive toward the lighted house, the lighted door. He did not knock, he burst in, sobbing for breath, incapable for the moment of speech; he saw the as-tonished face of the Negro in the linen jacket without knowing when the Negro had appeared.

"De Spain!" he cried, panted. "Where's . . ." then he saw the white man too emerging from a white door down the hall. "Barn!" he cried. "Barn!"

"What?" the white man said. "Barn?"

"Yes!" the boy cried. "Barn!"

"Catch him!" the white man shouted. 105

But it was too late this time too. The Negro grasped his shirt, but the entire sleeve, rotten with washing, carried away, and he was out that door too and in the drive again, and had actually never ceased to run even while he was screaming into the white man's face.

Behind him the white man was shouting. "My horse! Fetch my horse!" and he thought for an instant of cutting across the park and climbing the fence into the road, but he did not know the park nor how the vine-massed fence might be and he dared not risk it. So he ran on down the drive, blood and breath roaring; presently he was in the road again though he could not see it. He could not hear either: the galloping mare was almost upon him before he heard her, and even then he held his course, as if the very urgency of his wild grief and need must in a moment more find him wings, waiting until the ultimate instant to hurl him-self aside and into the weed-choked roadside ditch as the horse thundered past and on, for an instant in furious silhouette against the stars, the tranquil early summer night sky which, even before the shape of the horse and rider vanished, stained abruptly and violently upward: a long, swirling roar incredible and soundless, blotting the stars, and he springing up and into the road again, run-ning again, knowing it was too late yet still running even after he heard the shot and an instant later, two shots, pausing now without knowing he had ceased to run, crying, "Pap! Pap!", running again before he knew he had begun to run, stumbling, tripping over something and scrabbling up again without ceasing to run, looking backward over his shoulder at the glare as he got up, running on among the invisible trees, panting, sobbing, "Father! Father!"

At midnight he was sitting on the crest of a hill. He did not know it was midnight and he did not know how far he had come. But there was no glare behind him now and he sat now, his back toward what he had called home for four days anyhow, his face toward the dark woods which he would enter when breath was strong again, small, shaking steadily in the chill darkness, hugging himself into the remainder of his thin, rotten shirt, the grief and despair now no longer terror and fear but just grief and despair. *Father. My father,* he thought. "He was brave!" he cried suddenly, aloud but not loud, no more than a whisper. "He was! He was in the war! He was in Colonel Sartoris' cav'ry!" not knowing that his father had gone to that war a private in the fine old European sense, wearing no uniform, admitting the authority of and giving fidelity to no man or army or flag, going to war as Malbrouck° himself did: for booty—it meant nothing and less than nothing to him if it were enemy booty or his own.

The slow constellations wheeled on. It would be dawn and then sun-up after a while and he would be hungry. But that would be tomorrow and now he was only cold, and walking would cure that. His breathing was easier now and he decided to get up and go on, and then he found that he had been asleep because he knew it was almost dawn, the night almost over. He could tell that from the whippoorwills. They were everywhere now among the dark trees below him, constant and inflectioned and ceaseless, so that, as the instant for giving over to the day birds drew nearer and nearer, there was no interval at all between them. He got up. He was a little stiff, but walking would cure that too as it would the cold, and soon there would be the sun. He went on down the hill, toward the dark woods within which the liquid silver voices of the birds called unceasing—the rapid and urgent beating of the urgent and quiring heart of the late spring night. He did not look back.

Questions

1. After delivering his warning to Major de Spain, the boy Snopes does not actually witness what happens to his father and brother, nor what happens to the Major's barn. But what do you assume happens? What evidence is given in the story?
2. What do you understand to be Faulkner's opinion of Abner Snopes? Make a guess, indicating details in the story that convey attitudes.
3. Which adjectives best describe the general tone of the story: calm, amused, disinterested, scornful, marveling, excited, impassioned? Point out passages that may be so described. What do you notice about the style in which these passages are written?

Malbrouck: John Churchill, Duke of Marlborough (1650–1722), English general victorious in the Battle of Blenheim (1704), which triumph drove the French army out of Germany. The French called him Malbrouck, a name they found easier to pronounce.

4. In tone and style, how does "Barn Burning" compare with Faulkner's story "A Rose for Emily" (Chapter Two)? To what do you attribute any differences?
5. Suppose that, instead of "Barn Burning," Faulkner had written another story told by Abner Snopes in the first person. Why would such a story need a style different from that of "Barn Burning"? (Suggestion: Notice Faulkner's descriptions of Abner Snopes's voice.)
6. Although "Barn Burning" takes place some thirty years after the Civil War, how does the war figure in it?

IRONY

If a friend declares, "Oh, sure, I just *love* to have four papers due on the same day," you detect that the statement contains **irony.** This is **verbal irony,** the most familiar kind, in which we understand the speaker's meaning to be far from the usual meaning of the words—in this case, quite the opposite. (When the irony is found, as here, in a somewhat sour statement tinged with mockery, it is called **sarcasm.**)

Irony, of course, occurs in writing as well as in conversation. When in a comic moment in Isaac Bashevis Singer's "Gimpel the Fool" the sexton announces, "The wealthy Reb Gimpel invites the congregation to a feast in honor of the birth of a son," the people at the synagogue burst into laughter. They know that Gimpel, in contrast to the sexton's words, is not a wealthy man but a humble baker; that the son is not his own but his wife's lover's; and that the birth brings no honor to anybody. Verbal irony, then, implies a contrast or discrepancy between what is *said* and what is *meant.* But stories often contain other kinds of irony besides such verbal irony. A situation, for example, can be ironic if it contains some wry contrast or incongruity. In Jack London's "To Build a Fire" (Chapter Four), it is ironic that a freezing man, desperately trying to strike a match to light a fire and save himself, accidentally ignites all his remaining matches.

An entire story may be told from an **ironic point of view.** Whenever we sense a sharp distinction between the narrator of a story and the author, irony is likely to occur—especially when the narrator is telling us something that we are clearly expected to doubt or to interpret very differently. In "A & P," Sammy (who tells his own story) makes many smug and cruel observations about the people around him; but the author makes clear to us that much of his superiority is based on immaturity and lack of self-knowledge. (This irony, by the way, does not negate the fact that Sammy makes some very telling comments about society's superficial values and rigid and judgmental attitudes, comments that Updike seems to endorse and wants us to endorse as well.) And when we read Hemingway's "A Clean, Well-Lighted Place," surely we feel that most of the time the older waiter speaks for the author. Though the waiter gives us a respectful, compassionate view of a lonely old man, and we don't doubt that the view is Hemingway's, still, in the closing lines of the story we are reminded that author and waiter are not identical. Musing on the sleepless night ahead of him, the waiter tries to shrug off his problem—"After all, it is probably only insomnia"—but the reader, who recalls the waiter's bleak view of *nada*, nothingness, knows that it certainly isn't mere insomnia that keeps him awake but a dread of solitude and death. At that crucial moment, Hemingway and the older waiter part company, and we perceive an ironic point of view, and also a verbal irony, "After all, it is probably only insomnia."

Storytellers are sometimes fond of ironic twists of fate—developments that reveal a terrible distance between what people deserve and what they get, between what is and what ought to be. In the novels of Thomas Hardy, some hostile fate keeps playing tricks to thwart the main characters. In *Tess of the D'Urbervilles*, an all-important letter, thrust under a door, by chance slides beneath a carpet and is not received. An obvious prank of fate occurs in O. Henry's short story "The Gift of the Magi," in which a young wife sells her beautiful hair to buy her poor young husband a watch chain for Christmas, not knowing that, to buy combs for her hair, he has sold his watch. Such an irony is sometimes called an **irony of fate** or a **cosmic irony,** for it suggests that some malicious fate (or other spirit in the universe) is deliberately frustrating human efforts. (In O. Henry's story, however, the twist of fate leads to a happy ending; for the author suggests that, by their futile sacrifices, the lovers are drawn closer together.) Evidently, there is an irony of fate in the servant's futile attempt to escape Death in the fable "The Appointment in Samarra," and perhaps in the flaring up of the all-precious matches in "To Build a Fire" as well.

To notice an irony gives pleasure. It may move us to laughter, make us feel wonder, or arouse our sympathy. By so involving us, irony—whether in a statement, a situation, an unexpected event, or a point of view—can render a story more likely to strike us, to affect us, and to be remembered.

Guy de Maupassant

THE NECKLACE   1884

TRANSLATED BY MARJORIE LAURIE

Guy de Maupassant (1850–1893) was born in a rented castle in Normandy. The son of minor aristocrats (the de *in his surname denotes a noble family), Maupassant grew up overshadowed by his parents' unhappy marriage. His mother was a friend of the novelist Gustave Flaubert who took the teenage boy under his tutelage. Whenever the novelist stayed in Paris, he invited Maupassant to lunch. The meal was served with literary lectures and writing lessons. "He is my disciple," Flaubert declared, "and I love him like a son." For the young Maupassant, the child of a broken marriage, the older novelist served as the crucial figure in his life. Maupassant studied law, but the Franco-Prussian war of 1870 inspired him to enlist as a soldier. After the war he worked briefly*

Guy de Maupassant

as a minor bureaucrat while continuing to study privately with Flaubert. In 1880 he pub-lished his first short story, "Boule de Suif" ("Ball of Fat"), a story of a prostitute, which caused a literary sensation. He soon quit his government job, and dedicated himself to litera-ture, writing over 360 short stories, six novels, and three travel books in the decade before his untimely death. Maupassant became wealthy and internationally famous from his sto-ries; the hardworking author lived a luxurious and often dissipated life. Having contracted syphilis (then incurable) in his twenties, Maupassant watched his own health and sanity de-teriorate. He died one month before his forty-third birthday. Maupassant not only ranks as France's greatest writer of short fiction; he is also one of the key inventors of the modern short story. Concise, clear, and often ironic, his stories present well-plotted and engaging in-cidents without imposing moral judgments on the characters. His work influenced most of the major short story writers of the next two generations—including Anton Chekhov, Henry James, Isaac Babel, Somerset Maugham, Ernest Hemingway, and Kate Chopin.

She was one of those pretty and charming girls who are sometimes, as if by a mistake of destiny, born in a family of clerks. She had no dowry, no expecta-tions, no means of being known, understood, loved, wedded by any rich and dis-tinguished man; and she let herself be married to a little clerk at the Ministry of Public Instruction.

She dressed plainly because she could not dress well, but she was as unhappy as though she had really fallen from her proper station, since with women there is neither caste nor rank: and beauty, grace and charm act instead of family and birth. Natural fineness, instinct for what is elegant, suppleness of wit, are the sole hierarchy, and make from women of the people the equals of the very greatest ladies.

She suffered ceaselessly, feeling herself born for all the delicacies and all the luxuries. She suffered from the poverty of her dwelling, from the wretched look of the walls, from the worn-out chairs, from the ugliness of the curtains. All those things, of which another woman of her rank would never even have been con-scious, tortured her and made her angry. The sight of the little Breton peasant who did her humble housework aroused in her regrets which were despairing, and distracted dreams. She thought of the silent antechambers hung with Oriental ta-pestry, lit by tall bronze candelabra, and of the two great footmen in knee breeches who sleep in the big armchairs, made drowsy by the heavy warmth of the hot-air stove. She thought of the long *salons*° fitted up with ancient silk, of the delicate furniture carrying priceless curiosities, and of the coquettish perfumed boudoirs made for talks at five o'clock with intimate friends, with men famous and sought after, whom all women envy and whose attention they all desire.

When she sat down to dinner, before the round table covered with a table-cloth three days old, opposite her husband, who uncovered the soup tureen and declared with an enchanted air, "Ah, the good *pot-au-feu!*° I don't know anything better than that," she thought of dainty dinners, of shining silverware, of tapestry which peopled the walls with ancient personages and with strange birds flying in

salons: drawing-rooms.   *pot-au-feu:* stew.

the midst of a fairy forest; and she thought of delicious dishes served on marvelous plates, and of the whispered gallantries which you listen to with a sphinxlike smile, while you are eating the pink flesh of a trout or the wings of a quail.

She had no dresses, no jewels, nothing. And she loved nothing but that; she felt made for that. She would so have liked to please, to be envied, to be charming, to be sought after.

She had a friend, a former schoolmate at the convent, who was rich, and whom she did not like to go and see any more, because she suffered so much when she came back.

But one evening, her husband returned home with a triumphant air, and holding a large envelope in his hand.

"There," said he. "Here is something for you."

She tore the paper sharply, and drew out a printed card which bore these words:

"The Minister of Public Instruction and Mme. Georges Ramponneau request the honor of M. and Mme. Loisel's company at the palace of the Ministry on Monday evening, January eighteenth."

Instead of being delighted, as her husband hoped, she threw the invitation on the table with disdain, murmuring:

"What do you want me to do with that?"

"But, my dear, I thought you would be glad. You never go out, and this is such a fine opportunity. I had awful trouble to get it. Everyone wants to go; it is very select, and they are not giving many invitations to clerks. The whole official world will be there."

She looked at him with an irritated glance, and said, impatiently:

"And what do you want me to put on my back?"

He had not thought of that; he stammered:

"Why, the dress you go to the theater in. It looks very well, to me."

He stopped, distracted, seeing his wife was crying. Two great tears descended slowly from the corners of her eyes toward the corners of her mouth. He stuttered:

"What's the matter? What's the matter?"

But, by violent effort, she had conquered her grief, and she replied, with a calm voice, while she wiped her wet cheeks:

"Nothing. Only I have no dress and therefore I can't go to this ball. Give your card to some colleague whose wife is better equipped than I."

He was in despair. He resumed:

"Come, let us see, Mathilde. How much would it cost, a suitable dress, which you could use on other occasions, something very simple?"

She reflected several seconds, making her calculations and wondering also what sum she could ask without drawing on herself an immediate refusal and a frightened exclamation from the economical clerk.

Finally, she replied, hesitatingly:

"I don't know exactly, but I think I could manage it with four hundred francs."

He had grown a little pale, because he was laying aside just that amount to buy a gun and treat himself to a little shooting next summer on the plain of Nanterre, with several friends who went to shoot larks down there, of a Sunday.

But he said:

"All right. I will give you four hundred francs. And try to have a pretty dress."

The day of the ball drew near, and Mme. Loisel seemed sad, uneasy, anxious. Her dress was ready, however. Her husband said to her one evening: 30

"What is the matter? Come, you've been so queer these last three days."

And she answered:

"It annoys me not to have a single jewel, not a single stone, nothing to put on. I shall look like distress. I should almost rather not go at all."

He resumed:

"You might wear natural flowers. It's very stylish at this time of the year. For 35 ten francs you can get two or three magnificent roses."

She was not convinced.

"No; there's nothing more humiliating than to look poor among other women who are rich."

But her husband cried:

"How stupid you are! Go look up your friend Mme. Forestier, and ask her to lend you some jewels. You're quite thick enough with her to do that."

She uttered a cry of joy: 40

"It's true. I never thought of it."

The next day she went to her friend and told of her distress.

Mme. Forestier went to a wardrobe with a glass door, took out a large jewelbox, brought it back, opened it, and said to Mme. Loisel:

"Choose, my dear."

She saw first of all some bracelets, then a pearl necklace, then a Venetian 45 cross, gold and precious stones of admirable workmanship. She tried on the ornaments before the glass, hesitated, could not make up her mind to part with them, to give them back. She kept asking:

"Haven't you any more?"

"Why, yes. Look. I don't know what you like."

All of a sudden she discovered, in a black satin box, a superb necklace of diamonds, and her heart began to beat with an immoderate desire. Her hands trembled as she took it. She fastened it around her throat, outside her highnecked dress, and remained lost in ecstasy at the sight of herself.

Then she asked, hesitating, filled with anguish:

"Can you lend me that, only that?" 50

"Why, yes, certainly."

She sprang upon the neck of her friend, kissed her passionately, then fled with her treasure.

The day of the ball arrived. Mme. Loisel made a great success. She was prettier than them all, elegant, gracious, smiling, and crazy with joy. All the men looked at her, asked her name, endeavored to be introduced. All the attachés of the Cabinet wanted to waltz with her. She was remarked by the minister himself.

She danced with intoxication, with passion, made drunk by pleasure, forgetting all, in the triumph of her beauty, in the glory of her success, in a sort of cloud of happiness composed of all this homage, of all this admiration, of all these awakened desires, and of that sense of complete victory which is so sweet to a woman's heart.

She went away about four o'clock in the morning. Her husband had been sleeping since midnight, in a little deserted anteroom, with three other gentlemen whose wives were having a very good time. He threw over her shoulders the wraps which he had brought, modest wraps of common life, whose poverty contrasted with the elegance of the ball dress. She felt this, and wanted to escape so as not to be remarked by the other women, who were enveloping themselves in costly furs.

Loisel held her back.

"Wait a bit. You will catch cold outside. I will go and call a cab."

But she did not listen to him, and rapidly descended the stairs. When they were in the street they did not find a carriage; and they began to look for one, shouting after the cabmen whom they saw passing by at a distance.

They went down toward the Seine, in despair, shivering with cold. At last they found on the quay one of those ancient noctambulant coupés which, exactly as if they were ashamed to show their misery during the day, are never seen round Paris until after nightfall.

It took them to their door in the Rue des Martyrs, and once more, sadly, they climbed up homeward. All was ended, for her. And as to him, he reflected that he must be at the Ministry at ten o'clock.

She removed the wraps which covered her shoulders, before the glass, so as once more to see herself in all her glory. But suddenly she uttered a cry. She no longer had the necklace around her neck!

Her husband, already half undressed, demanded:

"What is the matter with you?"

She turned madly towards him:

"I have—I have—I've lost Mme. Forestier's necklace."

He stood up, distracted.

"What!—how?—impossible!"

And they looked in the folds of her dress, in the folds of her cloak, in her pockets, everywhere. They did not find it.

He asked:

"You're sure you had it on when you left the ball?"

"Yes, I felt it in the vestibule of the palace."

"But if you had lost it in the street we should have heard it fall. It must be in the cab."

"Yes. Probably. Did you take his number?"

"No. And you, didn't you notice it?"

"No."

They looked, thunderstruck, at one another. At last Loisel put on his clothes.

"I shall go back on foot," said he, "over the whole route which we have taken to see if I can find it."

And he went out. She sat waiting on a chair in her ball dress, without strength to go to bed, overwhelmed, without fire, without a thought.

Her husband came back about seven o'clock. He had found nothing.

He went to Police Headquarters, to the newspaper offices, to offer a reward; he went to the cab companies—everywhere, in fact, whither he was urged by the least suspicion of hope.

She waited all day, in the same condition of mad fear before this terrible calamity.

Loisel returned at night with a hollow, pale face; he had discovered nothing.

"You must write to your friend," said he, "that you have broken the clasp of her necklace and that you are having it mended. That will give us time to turn round."

She wrote at his dictation.

At the end of a week they had lost all hope.

And Loisel, who had aged five years, declared:

"We must consider how to replace that ornament."

The next day they took the box which had contained it, and they went to the jeweler whose name was found within. He consulted his books.

"It was not I, madame, who sold that necklace; I must simply have furnished the case."

Then they went from jeweler to jeweler, searching for a necklace like the other, consulting their memories, sick both of them with chagrin and anguish.

They found, in a shop at the Palais Royal, a string of diamonds which seemed to them exactly like the one they looked for. It was worth forty thousand francs. They could have it for thirty-six.

So they begged the jeweler not to sell it for three days yet. And they made a bargain that he should buy it back for thirty-four thousand francs, in case they found the other one before the end of February.

Loisel possessed eighteen thousand francs which his father had left him. He would borrow the rest.

He did borrow, asking a thousand francs of one, five hundred of another, five louis here, three louis there. He gave notes, took up ruinous obligations, dealt with usurers and all the race of lenders. He compromised all the rest of his life, risked his signature without even knowing if he could meet it; and, frightened by the pains yet to come, by the black misery which was about to fall upon him, by the prospect of all the physical privation and of all the moral tortures which he was to suffer, he went to get the new necklace, putting down upon the merchant's counter thirty-six thousand francs.

When Mme. Loisel took back the necklace, Mme. Forestier said to her, with a chilly manner:

"You should have returned it sooner; I might have needed it."

She did not open the case, as her friend had so much feared. If she had detected the substitution, what would she have thought, what would she have said? Would she not have taken Mme. Loisel for a thief?

Mme. Loisel now knew the horrible existence of the needy. She took her part, moreover, all of a sudden, with heroism. That dreadful debt must be paid. She would pay it. They dismissed their servant; they changed their lodgings; they rented a garret under the roof.

She came to know what heavy housework meant and the odious cares of the kitchen. She washed the dishes, using her rosy nails on the greasy pots and pans. She washed the dirty linen, the shirts, and the dishcloths, which she dried upon a line; she carried the slops down to the street every morning, and carried up the water, stopping for breath at every landing. And, dressed like a woman of the people, she went to the fruiterer, the grocer, the butcher, her basket on her arm, bargaining, insulted, defending her miserable money sou by sou.

Each month they had to meet some notes, renew others, obtain more time. 100

Her husband worked in the evening making a fair copy of some tradesman's accounts, and late at night he often copied manuscript for five sous a page.

And this life lasted for ten years.

At the end of ten years, they had paid everything, everything, with the rates of usury, and the accumulations of the compound interest.

Mme. Loisel looked old now. She had become the woman of impoverished households—strong and hard and rough. With frowsy hair, skirts askew, and red hands, she talked loud while washing the floor with great swishes of water. But sometimes, when her husband was at the office, she sat down near the window, and she thought of that gay evening of long ago, of the ball where she had been so beautiful and so fêted.

What would have happened if she had not lost that necklace? Who knows? 105 Who knows? How life is strange and changeful! How little a thing is needed for us to be lost or to be saved!

But, one Sunday, having gone to take a walk in the Champs Elysées to refresh herself from the labor of the week, she suddenly perceived a woman who was leading a child. It was Mme. Forestier, still young, still beautiful, still charming.

Mme. Loisel felt moved. Was she going to speak to her? Yes, certainly. And now that she had paid, she was going to tell her all about it. Why not?

She went up.

"Good day, Jeanne."

The other, astonished to be familiarly addressed by this plain goodwife, did 110 not recognize her at all, and stammered:

"But—madam!—I do not know—You must be mistaken."

"No. I am Mathilde Loisel."

Her friend uttered a cry.

"Oh, my poor Mathilde! How you are changed!"

"Yes, I have had days hard enough, since I have seen you, days wretched 115 enough—and that because of you!"

"Of me! How so?"

"Do you remember that diamond necklace which you lent me to wear at the ministerial ball?"

"Yes. Well?"

"Well, I lost it."

"What do you mean? You brought it back."   120

"I brought you back another just like it. And for this we have been ten years paying. You can understand that it was not easy for us, us who had nothing. At last it is ended, and I am very glad."

Mme. Forestier had stopped.

"You say that you bought a necklace of diamonds to replace mine?"

"Yes. You never noticed it, then! They were very like."

And she smiled with a joy which was proud and naïve at once.   125

Mme. Forestier, strongly moved, took her two hands.

"Oh, my poor Mathilde! Why, my necklace was paste. It was worth at most five hundred francs!"

QUESTIONS

1. Why does Mathilde Loisel borrow her friend's diamond necklace for the ball? What do her motivations reveal about her character?
2. Why does the protagonist not admit to her friend that she has lost the necklace?
3. How do the Loisels afford the new necklace? What obligations does its purchase involve?
4. What is ironic about the story's conclusion?
5. What other ironic elements are present in this story?

Ha Jin

SABOTEUR   2000

Ha Jin is the pen name for Xuefei Jin who was born in Liaoning, China, in 1956. The son of a military officer and a worker, Jin grew up during the turbulent Cultural Revolution, a ten-year upheaval initiated by the Communist Party in 1966 to transform China into a Marxist worker's society by destroying all remnants of the nation's ancient past. During this period many schools and universities were closed and intellectuals were required to work in proletariat jobs. At fourteen, Jin joined the People's Liberation Army, where he remained for nearly six years, and later worked as a telegraph operator for a railroad company. Jin then attended Heilongjiang University, where in 1981 he received a B.A. in English. After earning an M.A. in American literature from Shangdong University in 1984, Jin traveled to the United States to work on a Ph.D. at Brandeis University. He

Ha Jin

intended to return to China, but the Communist Party's violent suppression of the student movement in 1989 made him decide to stay in the United States and only write in English. "It's such a brutal government," he commented, "I was very angry, and I decided not to return to China." "Writing in English became my means of survival," he remarked, "of spending or wasting my life, of retrieving losses, mine, and those of others." He completed his Ph.D. in 1993.

Jin has published three books of poetry, Between Silences (1990), Facing Shadows (1996), and Wreckage (2001); and three novels, In the Pond (1998), Waiting (1999), which won the National Book Award, and The Crazed (2002). His first volume of short fiction, Ocean of Words (1996), drawn from his experience in the People's Liberation Army, won the PEN/Hemingway Award. His subsequent collections of stories are Under the Red Flag (1997, Flannery O'Connor Award) and The Bridegroom (2000, Asian American Literary Award). He is a professor of English at Boston University.

Mr. Chiu and his bride were having lunch in the square before Muji Train Station. On the table between them were two bottles of soda spewing out brown foam and two paper boxes of rice and sautéed cucumber and pork. "Let's eat," he said to her, and broke the connected ends of the chopsticks. He picked up a slice of streaky pork and put it into his mouth. As he was chewing, a few crinkles appeared on his thin jaw.

To his right, at another table, two railroad policemen were drinking tea and laughing; it seemed that the stout, middle-aged man was telling a joke to his young comrade, who was tall and of athletic build. Now and again they would steal a glance at Mr. Chiu's table.

The air smelled of rotten melon. A few flies kept buzzing above the couple's lunch. Hundreds of people were rushing around to get on the platform or to catch buses to downtown. Food and fruit vendors were crying for customers in lazy voices. About a dozen young women, representing the local hotels, held up placards which displayed the daily prices and words as large as a palm, like FREE MEALS, AIR-CONDITIONING, and ON THE RIVER. In the center of the square stood a concrete statue of Chairman Mao, at whose feet peasants were napping, their backs on the warm granite and their faces toward the sunny sky. A flock of pigeons perched on the Chairman's raised hand and forearm.

The rice and cucumber tasted good, and Mr. Chiu was eating unhurriedly. His sallow face showed exhaustion. He was glad that the honeymoon was finally over and that he and his bride were heading back for Harbin. During the two weeks' vacation, he had been worried about his liver, because three months ago he had suffered from acute hepatitis; he was afraid he might have a relapse. But he had had no severe symptoms, despite his liver being still big and tender. On the whole he was pleased with his health, which could endure even the strain of a honeymoon; indeed, he was on the course of recovery. He looked at his bride, who took off her wire glasses, kneading the root of her nose with her fingertips. Beads of sweat coated her pale cheeks.

"Are you all right, sweetheart?" he asked.

"I have a headache. I didn't sleep well last night."

"Take an aspirin, will you?"

"It's not that serious. Tomorrow is Sunday and I can sleep in. Don't worry."

As they were talking, the stout policeman at the next table stood up and threw a bowl of tea in their direction. Both Mr. Chiu's and his bride's sandals were wet instantly.

"Hooligan!" she said in a low voice.

Mr. Chiu got to his feet and said out loud, "Comrade Policeman, why did you do this?" He stretched out his right foot to show the wet sandal.

"Do what?" the stout man asked huskily, glaring at Mr. Chiu while the young fellow was whistling.

"See, you dumped tea on our feet."

"You're lying. You wet your shoes yourself."

"Comrade Policemen, your duty is to keep order, but you purposely tortured us common citizens. Why violate the law you are supposed to enforce?" As Mr. Chiu was speaking, dozens of people began gathering around.

With a wave of his hand, the man said to the young fellow, "Let's get hold of him!"

They grabbed Mr. Chiu and clamped handcuffs around his wrists. He cried, "You can't do this to me. This is utterly unreasonable."

"Shut up!" The man pulled out his pistol. "You can use your tongue at our headquarters."

The young fellow added, "You're a saboteur, you know that? You're disrupting public order."

The bride was too petrified to say anything coherent. She was a recent college graduate, had majored in fine arts, and had never seen the police make an arrest. All she could say was, "Oh, please, please!"

The policemen were pulling Mr. Chiu, but he refused to go with them, holding the corner of the table and shouting, "We have a train to catch. We already bought the tickets."

The stout man punched him in the chest. "Shut up. Let your ticket expire." With the pistol butt he chopped Mr. Chiu's hands, which at once released the table. Together the two men were dragging him away to the police station.

Realizing he had to go with them, Mr. Chiu turned his head and shouted to his bride, "Don't wait for me here. Take the train. If I'm not back by tomorrow morning, send someone over to get me out."

She nodded, covering her sobbing mouth with her palm.

After removing his belt, they locked Mr. Chiu into a cell in the back of the Railroad Police Station. The single window in the room was blocked by six steel bars; it faced a spacious yard, in which stood a few pines. Beyond the trees, two swings hung from an iron frame, swaying gently in the breeze. Somewhere in the building a cleaver was chopping rhythmically. There must be a kitchen upstairs, Mr. Chiu thought.

He was too exhausted to worry about what they would do to him, so he lay down on the narrow bed and shut his eyes. He wasn't afraid. The Cultural Revolution was over already, and recently the Party had been propagating the idea that all citizens were equal before the law. The police ought to be a law-abiding model for common people. As long as he remained coolheaded and reasoned with them, they probably wouldn't harm him.

Late in the afternoon he was taken to the Interrogation Bureau on the second floor. On his way there, in the stairwell, he ran into the middle-aged policeman who had manhandled him. The man grinned, rolling his bulgy eyes and pointing his fingers at him as if firing a pistol. Egg of a tortoise! Mr. Chiu cursed mentally.

The moment he sat down in the office, he burped, his palm shielding his mouth. In front of him, across a long desk, sat the chief of the bureau and a donkey-faced man. On the glass desktop was a folder containing information on his case. He felt it bizarre that in just a matter of hours they had accumulated a small pile of writing about him. On second thought he began to wonder whether they had kept a file on him all the time. How could this have happened? He lived and worked in Harbin, more than three hundred miles away, and this was his first time in Muji City.

The chief of the bureau was a thin, bald man who looked serene and intelligent. His slim hands handled the written pages in the folder in the manner of a lecturing scholar. To Mr. Chiu's left sat a young scribe, with a clipboard on his knee and a black fountain pen in his hand.

"Your name?" the chief asked, apparently reading out the question from a form. 30

"Chiu Maguang."

"Age?"

"Thirty-four."

"Profession?"

"Lecturer." 35

"Work unit?"

"Harbin University."

"Political status?"

"Communist Party member."

The chief put down the paper and began to speak. "Your crime is sabotage, 40 although it hasn't induced serious consequences yet. Because you are a Party member, you should be punished more. You have failed to be a model for the masses and you—"

"Excuse me, sir," Mr. Chiu cut him off.

"What?"

"I didn't do anything. Your men are the saboteurs of our social order. They threw hot tea on my feet and on my wife's feet. Logically speaking, you should criticize them, if not punish them."

"That statement is groundless. You have no witness. Why should I believe you?" the chief said matter-of-factly.

"This is my evidence." He raised his right hand. "Your man hit my fingers with a pistol."

"That doesn't prove how your feet got wet. Besides, you could have hurt your fingers yourself."

"But I am telling the truth!" Anger flared up in Mr. Chiu. "Your police station owes me an apology. My train ticket has expired, my new leather sandals are ruined, and I am late for a conference in the provincial capital. You must compensate me for the damage and losses. Don't mistake me for a common citizen who would tremble when you sneeze. I'm a scholar, a philosopher, and an expert in dialectical materialism. If necessary, we will argue about this in *The Northeastern Daily,* or we will go to the highest People's Court in Beijing. Tell me, what's your name?" He got carried away with his harangue, which was by no means trivial and had worked to his advantage on numerous occasions.

"Stop bluffing us," the donkey-faced man broke in. "We have seen a lot of your kind. We can easily prove you are guilty. Here are some of the statements given by eyewitnesses." He pushed a few sheets of paper toward Mr. Chiu.

Mr. Chiu was dazed to see the different handwritings, which all stated that he had shouted in the square to attract attention and refused to obey the police. One of the witnesses had identified herself as a purchasing agent from a shipyard in Shanghai. Something stirred in Mr. Chiu's stomach, a pain rising to his rib. He gave out a faint moan.

"Now you have to admit you are guilty," the chief said. "Although it's a serious crime, we won't punish you severely, provided you write out a self-criticism and promise that you won't disrupt the public order again. In other words, your release will depend on your attitude toward this crime."

"You're daydreaming," Mr. Chiu cried. "I won't write a word, because I'm innocent. I demand that you provide me with a letter of apology so I can explain to my university why I'm late."

Both the interrogators smiled contemptuously. "Well, we've never done that," said the chief, taking a puff of his cigarette.

"Then make this a precedent."

"That's unnecessary. We are pretty certain that you will comply with our wishes." The chief blew a column of smoke toward Mr. Chiu's face.

At the tilt of the chief's head, two guards stepped forward and grabbed the criminal by the arms. Mr. Chiu meanwhile went on saying, "I shall report you to the Provincial Administration. You'll have to pay for this! You are worse than the Japanese military police."

They dragged him out of the room.

After dinner, which consisted of a bowl of millet porridge, a corn bun, and a piece of pickled turnip, Mr. Chiu began to have a fever, shaking with a chill and sweating profusely. He knew that the fire of anger had gotten into his liver and that he was probably having a relapse. No medicine was available, because his briefcase had been left with his bride. At home it would have been time for him to sit in front of their color TV, drinking jasmine tea and watching the evening news. It was so lonesome in here. The orange bulb above the single bed was the only source of light, which enabled the guards to keep him under surveillance at night. A moment ago he had asked them for a newspaper or a magazine to read, but they turned him down.

Through the small opening on the door noises came in. It seemed that the police on duty were playing cards or chess in a nearby office; shouts and laughter could be heard now and then. Meanwhile, an accordion kept coughing from a remote corner in the building. Looking at the ballpoint and the letter paper left for him by the guards when they took him back from the Interrogation Bureau, Mr. Chiu remembered the old saying, "When a scholar runs into soldiers, the more he argues, the muddier his point becomes." How ridiculous this whole thing was. He ruffled his thick hair with his fingers.

He felt miserable, massaging his stomach continually. To tell the truth, he was more upset than frightened, because he would have to catch up with his work once he was back home—a paper that was due at the printers next week, and two dozen books he ought to read for the courses he was going to teach in the fall.

A human shadow flitted across the opening. Mr. Chiu rushed to the door   60
and shouted through the hole, "Comrade Guard, Comrade Guard!"

"What do you want?" a voice rasped.

"I want you to inform your leaders that I'm very sick. I have heart disease and hepatitis. I may die here if you keep me like this without medication."

"No leader is on duty on the weekend. You have to wait till Monday."

"What? You mean I'll stay in here tomorrow?"

"Yes."   65

"Your station will be held responsible if anything happens to me."

"We know that. Take it easy, you won't die."

It seemed illogical that Mr. Chiu slept quite well that night, though the light above his head had been on all the time and the straw mattress was hard and infested with fleas. He was afraid of ticks, mosquitoes, cockroaches—any kind of insect but fleas and bedbugs. Once, in the countryside, where his school's faculty and staff had helped the peasants harvest crops for a week, his colleagues had joked about his flesh, which they said must have tasted nonhuman to fleas. Except for him, they were all afflicted with hundreds of bites.

More amazing now, he didn't miss his bride a lot. He even enjoyed sleeping alone, perhaps because the honeymoon had tired him out and he needed more rest.

The backyard was quiet on Sunday morning. Pale sunlight streamed through   70
the pine branches. A few sparrows were jumping on the ground, catching caterpillars and ladybugs. Holding the steel bars, Mr. Chiu inhaled the morning air, which smelled meaty. There must have been an eatery or a cooked-meat stand nearby. He reminded himself that he should take this detention with ease. A sentence that Chairman Mao had written to a hospitalized friend rose in his mind: "Since you are already in here, you may as well stay and make the best of it."

His desire for peace of mind originated in his fear that his hepatitis might get worse. He tried to remain unperturbed. However, he was sure that his liver was swelling up, since the fever still persisted. For a whole day he lay in bed, thinking about his paper on the nature of contradictions. Time and again he was overwhelmed by anger, cursing aloud, "A bunch of thugs!" He swore that once he was out, he would write an article about this experience. He had better find out some of the policemen's names.

It turned out to be a restful day for the most part; he was certain that his university would send somebody to his rescue. All he should do now was remain calm and wait patiently. Sooner or later the police would have to release him, although they had no idea that he might refuse to leave unless they wrote him an apology. Damn those hoodlums, they had ordered more than they could eat!

When he woke up on Monday morning, it was already light. Somewhere a man was moaning; the sound came from the backyard. After a long yawn, and kicking off the tattered blanket, Mr. Chiu climbed out of bed and went to the window. In the middle of the yard, a young man was fastened to a pine, his wrists handcuffed around the trunk from behind. He was wriggling and swearing loudly, but there was no sight of anyone else in the yard. He looked familiar to Mr. Chiu.

Mr. Chiu squinted his eyes to see who it was. To his astonishment, he recognized the man, who was Fenjin, a recent graduate from the Law Department at Harbin University. Two years ago Mr. Chiu had taught a course in Marxist materialism, in which Fenjin had enrolled. Now, how on earth had this young devil landed here?

Then it dawned on him that Fenjin must have been sent over by his bride. 75
What a stupid woman! A bookworm, who only knew how to read foreign novels! He had expected that she would contact the school's Security Section, which would for sure send a cadre here. Fenjin held no official position; he merely worked in a private law firm that had just two lawyers; in fact, they had little business except for some detective work for men and women who suspected their spouses of having extramarital affairs. Mr. Chiu was overcome with a wave of nausea.

Should he call out to let his student know he was nearby? He decided not to, because he didn't know what had happened. Fenjin must have quarreled with the police to incur such a punishment. Yet this could never have occurred if Fenjin hadn't come to his rescue. So no matter what, Mr. Chiu had to do something. But what could he do?

It was going to be a scorcher. He could see purple steam shimmering and rising from the ground among the pines. Poor devil, he thought, as he raised a bowl of corn glue to his mouth, sipped, and took a bite of a piece of salted celery.

When a guard came to collect the bowl and the chopsticks, Mr. Chiu asked him what had happened to the man in the backyard. "He called our boss 'bandit.' " the guard said. "He claimed he was a lawyer or something. An arrogant son of a rabbit."

Now it was obvious to Mr. Chiu that he had to do something to help his rescuer. Before he could figure out a way, a scream broke out in the backyard. He rushed to the window and saw a tall policeman standing before Fenjin, an iron bucket on the ground. It was the same young fellow who had arrested Mr. Chiu in the square two days before. The man pinched Fenjin's nose, then raised his hand, which stayed in the air for a few seconds, then slapped the lawyer across the face. As Fenjin was groaning, the man lifted up the bucket and poured water on his head.

"This will keep you from getting sunstroke, boy. I'll give you some more every hour," the man said loudly.   80

Fenjin kept his eyes shut, yet his wry face showed that he was struggling to hold back from cursing the policeman, or, more likely, that he was sobbing in silence. He sneezed, then raised his face and shouted, "Let me go take a piss."

"Oh, yeah?" the man bawled. "Pee in your pants."

Still Mr. Chiu didn't make any noise, gripping the steel bars with both hands, his fingers white. The policeman turned and glanced at the cell's window; his pistol, partly holstered, glittered in the sun. With a snort he spat his cigarette butt to the ground and stamped it into the dust.

Then the door opened and the guards motioned Mr. Chiu to come out. Again they took him upstairs to the Interrogation Bureau.

The same men were in the office, though this time the scribe was sitting   85
there empty-handed. At the sight of Mr. Chiu the chief said, "Ah, here you are. Please be seated."

After Mr. Chiu sat down, the chief waved a white silk fan and said to him, "You may have seen your lawyer. He's a young man without manners, so our director had him taught a crash course in the backyard."

"It's illegal to do that. Aren't you afraid to appear in a newspaper?"

"No, we are not, not even on TV. What else can you do? We are not afraid of any story you make up. We call it fiction. What we do care about is that you cooperate with us. That is to say, you must admit your crime."

"What if I refuse to cooperate?"

"Then your lawyer will continue his education in the sunshine."   90

A swoon swayed Mr. Chiu, and he held the arms of the chair to steady himself. A numb pain stung him in the upper stomach and nauseated him, and his head was throbbing. He was sure that the hepatitis was finally attacking him. Anger was flaming up in his chest; his throat was tight and clogged.

The chief resumed, "As a matter of fact, you don't even have to write out your self-criticism. We have your crime described clearly here. All we need is your signature."

Holding back his rage, Mr. Chiu said, "Let me look at that."

With a smirk the donkey-faced man handed him a sheet which carried these words:

I hereby admit that on July 13 I disrupted public order at Muji Train Station, and that I refused to listen to reason when the railroad police issued their warning. Thus I myself am responsible for my arrest. After two days' detention, I have realized the reactionary nature of my crime. From now on, I shall continue to educate myself with all my effort and shall never commit this kind of crime again.

A voice started screaming in Mr. Chiu's ears, "Lie, lie!" But he shook his head and forced the voice away. He asked the chief, "If I sign this, will you release both my lawyer and me?"   95

"Of course, we'll do that." The chief was drumming his fingers on the blue folder—their file on him.

Mr. Chiu signed his name and put his thumbprint under his signature.

"Now you are free to go," the chief said with a smile, and handed him a piece of paper to wipe his thumb with.

Mr. Chiu was so sick that he couldn't stand up from the chair at first try. Then he doubled his effort and rose to his feet. He staggered out of the building to meet his lawyer in the backyard, having forgotten to ask for his belt back. In his chest he felt as though there were a bomb. If he were able to, he would have razed the entire police station and eliminated all their families. Though he knew he could do nothing like that, he made up his mind to do something.

"I'm sorry about this torture, Fenjin," Mr. Chiu said when they met.   100

"It doesn't matter. They are savages." The lawyer brushed a patch of dirt off his jacket with trembling fingers. Water was still dribbling from the bottoms of his trouser legs.

"Let's go now," the teacher said.

The moment they came out of the police station, Mr. Chiu caught sight of a tea stand. He grabbed Fenjin's arm and walked over to the old woman at the table. "Two bowls of black tea," he said and handed her a one-yuan note.

After the first bowl, they each had another one. Then they set out for the train station. But before they walked fifty yards, Mr. Chiu insisted on eating a bowl of tree-ear soup at a food stand. Fenjin agreed. He told his teacher, "You mustn't treat me like a guest."

"No, I want to eat something myself."   105

As if dying of hunger, Mr. Chiu dragged his lawyer from restaurant to restaurant near the police station, but at each place he ordered no more than two bowls of food. Fenjin wondered why his teacher wouldn't stay at one place and eat his fill.

Mr. Chiu bought noodles, wonton, eight-grain porridge, and chicken soup, respectively, at four restaurants. While eating, he kept saying through his teeth, "If only I could kill all the bastards!" At the last place he merely took a few sips of the soup without tasting the chicken cubes and mushrooms.

Fenjin was baffled by his teacher, who looked ferocious and muttered to himself mysteriously, and whose jaundiced face was covered with dark puckers. For the first time Fenjin thought of Mr. Chiu as an ugly man.

Within a month over eight hundred people contracted acute hepatitis in Muji. Six died of the disease, including two children. Nobody knew how the epidemic had started.

QUESTIONS

1. Why is Mr. Chiu in Muji?
2. In the story's second paragraph, two railroad policemen are sitting next to Mr. Chiu and his wife. Why do you think they are laughing and looking at the newly wed couple?
3. With what specific crime is Mr. Chiu charged? Is he guilty?
4. What is Mr. Chiu's initial reaction to his arrest?
5. Why does Mr. Chiu initially refuse to sign a confession? Why does he eventually decide to sign it?
6. What is ironic about Mr. Chiu's arrest? What is ironic about his ultimate confession?
7. When does Mr. Chiu decide to revenge himself on the police?
8. Is Mr. Chiu's revenge justified? Are the effects of his revenge proportionate to his own suffering?
9. What is ironic about the story's title? Who is the saboteur?

WRITER'S PERSPECTIVE

Ernest Hemingway

Ernest Hemingway on Writing

THE DIRECT STYLE   1964

"When you write," he [Hemingway] said, "Your object is to convey every sensation, sight, feeling, emotion, to the reader. So you have to work over what you write. If you use a pencil, you get three different views of it to see if you are getting it across the way you want to. First, when you read it over, then when it is typed, and again in proof. And it keeps it fluid longer so that you can improve it easier."

"How do you ever learn to convey every sensation, sight and feeling to the reader? Just keep working at it for forty-odd years the way you have? Are there any tricks?"

"No. The hardest trade in the world to do is the writing of straight, honest prose about human beings. But there are ways you can train yourself."

"How?"

"When you walk into a room and you get a certain feeling or emotion, remember back until you see exactly what it was that gave you the emotion. Remember what the noises and smells were and what was said. Then write it down, making it clear so the reader will see it too and have the same feeling you had. And watch people, observe, try to put yourself in somebody else's head. If two men argue, don't just think who is right and who is wrong. Think what both their sides are. As a man, you know who is right and who is wrong; you have to judge. As a writer, you should not judge, you should understand."

From "An Afternoon with Hemingway" by Edward Stafford

═══▶ WRITING CRITICALLY ◀═══

Be Style-Conscious

If you look around a crowded classroom, you will notice—consciously or not—the styles of your fellow students. The way they dress, talk, and even sit conveys information on their attitudes. A haircut, a tattoo, a piece of jewelry all silently say something. Style is not merely a literary concept, it is a phenomenon we encounter every day in society.

Use the same powers of observation when discussing a writer's style. It may help to begin with a checklist of four elements—diction, sentence structure, tone, and organization:

1. *Diction:* Does the writer use word choice in a distinctive way? In "A Clean, Well-Lighted Place," for example, Hemingway favors simple, unemotional, and descriptive language, whereas in "The Storm" Chopin uses extravagant and emotionally charged diction. Each choice reveals something important about the story.

2. *Sentence Structure:* Does the author characteristically use long or short sentences? Are there perhaps even sentence fragments? Hemingway is famous for his short, clipped sentences, which often repeat certain key words. Faulkner, however, favors long, elaborate syntax that immerses the reader in the emotional situation of the narrative.

3. *Tone:* What is the writer's evident attitude toward the material? In "The Gospel According to Mark," Borges unfolds the story over a central irony, a tragic misunderstanding that will doom his protagonist. Tan's "A Pair of Tickets," by contrast, creates a tone of hushed excitement and direct emotional involvement. The tone of each story is an important element in its total design.

4. *Organization:* How does a writer go about arranging the material of the story? Borges presents his story in a straightforward, chronological manner, which eventually makes it possible for us to appreciate the tale's complex undercurrents.

Focus on the specifics of the story you are discussing. Examine the obvious elements of style and note what seems characteristic. Remember that style is personality.

WRITING ASSIGNMENT

Consider a short story in which the narrator is the central character: perhaps "A & P," "Greasy Lake," "Araby," "I Stand Here Ironing," or "Cathedral." In a brief essay, show how the character of the narrator determines the style of the story. Examine language in particular—words or phrases, slang expressions, figures of speech, local or regional speech.

FURTHER SUGGESTIONS FOR WRITING

1. Choose a subject you admire greatly: some person, place, film, sports team, work of fiction, or whatever. In a paragraph, describe it so that you make clear your admiration. Then rewrite the paragraph from the point of view of someone who detests the same subject. Try not to declare "I love this" or "I hate this," but select details and characteristics of your subject that will make the tone of each paragraph unmistakable.
2. Take a short story or novel not included in this book—one by a writer of high reputation and distinctive style, such as William Faulkner, Ernest Hemingway, Eudora Welty, Raymond Carver, Flannery O'Connor, or another writer suggested by your instructor. Then write a passage of your own, in which you imitate the writer's style as closely as possible. Pay attention to tone, vocabulary, length and variety of sentences, amount of description. Find some place in the story to insert your original passage. Then type out two or three pages of the story, including your forgery, and make copies for the other members of the class. See if anyone can tell where the writer's prose stops and yours begins.
3. Freewrite for fifteen or twenty minutes, rapidly jotting down any thoughts you may have in answer to this question: From your daily contacts with people, what ironies do you at times become aware of? Consider ironies of language (in deliberately misleading or sarcastic remarks), ironies of situation (here you are, a trained computer programmer unable to convince a counterperson in a fast-food joint that you can correctly add up a check). Then, using any good perceptions you have generated, write and polish a short answer to the question, illustrating your remarks by reference to your own recalled experience and recent observations. Of course you might also find it useful to cite some ironies in any stories about everyday life.
4. Here are some other topics: "Irony in 'A Rose for Emily.'" "Irony in 'Greasy Lake.'" "Cosmic irony in Borges's 'The Gospel According to Mark.'" "Irony in 'The Jilting of Granny Weatherall.'" (Or, use another story that you have read that more keenly interests you.) What sorts of irony make the story more effective? In dealing with any of them, you may find the method of analysis a help to you. Before you write, read about this useful method in the chapter "Writing About a Story" later in the book.

6 Theme

The **theme** of a story is whatever general idea or insight the entire story reveals. In some stories the theme is unmistakable. At the end of Aesop's fable about the council of the mice that can't decide who will bell the cat, the theme is stated in the moral: *It is easier to propose a thing than to carry it out.* In a work of commercial fiction, too, the theme (if any) is usually obvious. Consider a typical detective thriller in which, say, a rookie police officer trained in scientific methods of crime detection sets out to solve a mystery sooner than his or her rival, a veteran sleuth whose only laboratory is carried under his hat. Perhaps the veteran solves the case, leading to the conclusion (and the theme), "The old ways are the best ways after all." Another story by the same writer might dramatize the same rivalry but reverse the outcome, having the rookie win, thereby reversing the theme: "The times are changing! Let's shake loose from old-fashioned ways." In such commercial entertainments, a theme is like a length of rope with which the writer, patently and mechanically, trusses the story neatly (usually too neatly) into meaningful shape.

In literary fiction, a theme is seldom so obvious. That is, a theme need not be a moral or a message; it may be what the happenings add up to, what the story is about. When we come to the end of a finely wrought short story such as Ernest Hemingway's "A Clean, Well-Lighted Place" (Chapter Five), it may be easy to sum up the plot—to say what happens—but it is more difficult to sum up the story's main idea. Evidently, Hemingway relates events—how a younger waiter gets rid of an old man and how an older waiter then goes to a coffee bar—but in themselves these events seem relatively slight, though the story as a whole seems large (for its size) and full of meaning. For the meaning, we must look to other elements in the story besides what happens in it. And it is clear that Hemingway is most deeply interested in the thoughts and feelings of the older waiter, the character who has more and more to say as the story progresses, until at the end the story is entirely confined to his thoughts and perceptions. What is meaningful in these thoughts and perceptions? The older waiter understands the old man and sympathizes with his need for a clean, well-lighted place. If we say that, we are still talking about what happens in the story, though we have gone beyond merely recording its external events. But a theme is usually stated in *general* words. Another try: "Solitary people who cannot sleep need a cheerful, orderly place where they can drink with dignity." That's a little better. We have indicated, at least, that Hemingway's story is about more than just an old man and a couple of waiters. But what about the older waiter's meditation on *nada*, nothingness? Coming near the end of the story, it takes great emphasis, and probably no good statement of Hemingway's theme can leave it out. Still another try at a statement: "Solitary people need a place of refuge from their terrible awareness that their lives (or, perhaps, human lives) are essentially meaningless." Neither this nor any other statement of the story's theme is unarguably right, but at least the sentence helps the reader to bring into focus one primary idea that Hemingway seems to be driving at. When we finish reading "A Clean, Well-Lighted Place," we feel that there is such a theme, a unifying vision, even though we cannot reduce it absolutely to a tag. Like some freshwater lake alive with creatures, Hemingway's story is a broad expanse, reflecting in many directions. No wonder that many readers will view it differently.

Moral inferences may be drawn from the story, no doubt, for Hemingway is indirectly giving us advice for properly regarding and sympathizing with the lonely, the uncertain, and the old. But the story doesn't set forth a lesson that we are supposed to put into practice. One could argue that "A Clean, Well-Lighted Place" contains *several* themes, and other statements could be made to take in Hemingway's views of love, of communication between people, of dignity. Great short stories, like great symphonies, frequently have more than one theme.

In many a fine short story, theme is the center, the moving force, the principle of unity. Clearly, such a theme is something other than the characters and events of its story. To say of James Joyce's "Araby" (Chapter Eleven) that it is about a boy who goes to a bazaar to buy a gift for a young woman, only to arrive too late, is to summarize plot, not theme. (The theme *might* be put, "The illusions of a romantic child are vulnerable," or it might be put in any of a few hundred other ways.) Although the title of Shirley Jackson's "The Lottery" (Chapter Seven), with its hint of the lure of easy riches, may arouse pleasant expectations, which the neutral tone of the narrative does nothing to dispel, the theme—the larger realization that the story leaves us with—has to do with the ways in which cruel and insensitive attitudes can come to seem like normal and natural ones.

Sometimes you will hear it said that the theme of a story (say, Faulkner's "Barn Burning") is "loss of innocence" or "initiation into maturity"; or that the theme of some other story (Hurston's "Sweat," for instance) is "the revolt of the downtrodden." This is to use *theme* in a larger and more abstract sense than we use it here. Although such general descriptions of theme can be useful—as in sorting a large number of stories into rough categories—we suggest that, in the beginning, you look for whatever truth or insight you think the writer of a story reveals. Try to sum it up *in a sentence*. By doing so, you will find yourself looking closely at the story, trying to define its principal meaning. You may find it helpful, in making your sentence-statement of theme, to consider these points:

1. Look back once more at the title of the story. From what you have read, what does it indicate?
2. Does the main character in any way change in the story? Does this character arrive at any eventual realization or understanding? Are you left with any realization or understanding you did not have before?
3. Does the author make any general observations about life or human nature? Do the characters make any? (Caution: Characters now and again will utter opinions with which the reader is not necessarily supposed to agree.)
4. Does the story contain any especially curious objects, mysterious flat characters, significant animals, repeated names, song titles, or whatever, that hint at meanings larger than such things ordinarily have? In literary stories, such symbols may point to central themes. (For a short discussion of symbolism and a few illustrations, see Chapter Seven.)
5. When you have worded your statement of theme, have you cast your statement into general language, not just given a plot summary?
6. Does your statement hold true for the story as a whole, not for just part of it?

In distilling a statement of theme from a rich and complicated story, we have, of course, no more encompassed the whole story than a paleontologist taking a plaster mold of a petrified footprint has captured a living brontosaurus. A writer (other than a fabulist) does not usually set out with theme in hand, determined to make every detail in the story work to demonstrate it. Well then, the skeptical reader may ask, if only *some* stories have themes, if those themes may be hard to sum up, and if readers will probably disagree in their summations, why bother to state themes? Isn't it too much trouble? Surely it is, unless the effort to state a theme ends in pleasure and profit. Trying to sum up the point of a story in our own words is merely one way to make ourselves better aware of whatever we may have understood vaguely and tentatively. Attempted with loving care, such statements may bring into focus our scattered impressions of a rewarding story, may help to clarify and hold fast whatever wisdom the storyteller has offered us.

Stephen Crane

THE OPEN BOAT

Stephen Crane (1871–1900) was born in Newark, New Jersey, a Methodist minister's last and fourteenth child. After flunking out of both Lafayette College and Syracuse University, he became a journalist in New York, specializing in grim life among the down-and-out who people his early self-published novel Maggie: A Girl of the Streets *(1893). Restlessly generating material for stories, Crane trekked to the Southwest, New Orleans, and Mexico. "The Open Boat" is based on experience. En route to Havana to report the Cuban revolution for the New York Press, Crane was shipwrecked when the SS Commodore sank in heavy seas east of New Smyrna, Florida, on January 2, 1897. He escaped in a ten-foot lifeboat with the captain and two members of the crew. Later that year, Crane moved*

Stephen Crane (courtesy of The Newark Public Library)

into a stately home in England with Cora Taylor, former madam of a Florida brothel, hobnobbed with literary greats, and lived beyond his means. Hounded by creditors, afflicted by tuberculosis, he died in Germany at twenty-eight. Crane has been called the first writer of American realism. His famed novel The Red Badge of Courage *(1895) gives an imagined but convincing account of a young Union soldier's initiation into battle. A handful of his short stories appear immortal. He was an original poet, too, writing terse, sardonic poems in open forms, at the time considered radical. In his short life, Crane greatly helped American literature to come of age.*

A TALE INTENDED TO BE AFTER THE FACT:
BEING THE EXPERIENCE OF FOUR MEN FROM THE SUNK STEAMER COMMODORE

I

None of them knew the color of the sky. Their eyes glanced level, and were fastened upon the waves that swept toward them. These waves were of the hue of slate, save for the tops, which were of foaming white, and all of the men knew the colors of the sea. The horizon narrowed and widened, and dipped and rose, and at all times its edge was jagged with waves that seemed thrust up in points like rocks.

Many a man ought to have a bathtub larger than the boat which here rode upon the sea. These waves were most wrongfully and barbarously abrupt and tall, and each frothtop was a problem in small-boat navigation.

The cook squatted in the bottom, and looked with both eyes at the six inches of gunwale which separated him from the ocean. His sleeves were rolled over his fat forearms, and the two flaps of his unbuttoned vest dangled as he bent to bail out the boat. Often he said, "Gawd! that was a narrow clip." As he remarked it he invariably gazed eastward over the broken sea.

The oiler, steering with one of the two oars in the boat, sometimes raised himself suddenly to keep clear of water that swirled in over the stern. It was a thin little oar, and it seemed often ready to snap.

The correspondent,° pulling at the other oar, watched the waves and wondered why he was there. 5

The injured captain, lying in the bow, was at this time buried in that profound dejection and indifference which comes, temporarily at least, to even the bravest and most enduring when, willy-nilly, the firm fails, the army loses, the ship goes down. The mind of the master of a vessel is rooted deep in the timbers of her, though he command for a day or a decade; and this captain had on him the stern impression of a scene in the grays of dawn of seven turned faces, and later a stump of a topmast with a white ball on it, that slashed to and fro at the waves, went low and lower, and down. Thereafter there was something strange in his voice. Although steady, it was deep with mourning, and of a quality beyond oration or tears.

"Keep 'er a little more south, Billie," said he.

"A little more south, sir," said the oiler in the stern.

A seat in this boat was not unlike a seat upon a bucking broncho, and by the same token a broncho is not much smaller. The craft pranced and reared and plunged like an animal. As each wave came, and she rose for it, she seemed like a horse making at a fence outrageously high. The manner of her scramble over these walls of water is a mystic thing, and, moreover, at the top of them were ordinarily these problems in white water, the foam racing down from the summit of each wave requiring a new leap, and a leap from the air. Then, after scornfully bumping a crest, she would slide and race and splash down a long incline, and arrive bobbing and nodding in front of the next menace.

A singular disadvantage of the sea lies in the fact that after successfully surmounting one wave you discover that there is another behind it just as important and just as nervously anxious to do something effective in the way of swamping boats. In a ten-foot dinghy one can get an idea of the resources of the sea in the line of waves that is not probable to the average experience which is never at sea in a dinghy. As each slaty wall of water approached, it shut all else from the view of the men in the boat, and it was not difficult to imagine that this particular wave was the final outburst of the ocean, the last effort of the grim water. There was a terrible grace in the move of the waves, and they came in silence, save for the snarling of the crests. 10

In the wan light the faces of the men must have been gray. Their eyes must have glinted in strange ways as they gazed steadily astern. Viewed from a bal-

---

correspondent: foreign correspondent, newspaper reporter.

cony, the whole thing would doubtless have been weirdly picturesque. But the men in the boat had no time to see it, and if they had had leisure, there were other things to occupy their minds. The sun swung steadily up the sky, and they knew it was broad day because the color of the sea changed from slate to emerald green streaked with amber lights, and the foam was like tumbling snow. The process of the breaking day was unknown to them. They were aware only of this effect upon the color of the waves that rolled toward them.

In disjointed sentences the cook and the correspondent argued as to the difference between a life-saving station and a house of refuge. The cook had said: "There's a house of refuge just north of the Mosquito Inlet Light, and as soon as they see us they'll come off in their boat and pick us up."

"As soon as who see us?" said the correspondent.

"The crew," said the cook.

"Houses of refuge don't have crews," said the correspondent. "As I under-   15
stand them, they are only places where clothes and grub are stored for the benefit of shipwrecked people. They don't carry crews."

"Oh, yes, they do," said the cook.

"No, they don't," said the correspondent.

"Well, we're not there yet, anyhow," said the oiler, in the stern.

"Well," said the cook, "perhaps it's not a house of refuge that I'm thinking of as being near Mosquito Inlet Light; perhaps it's a life-saving station."

"We're not there yet," said the oiler in the stern.   20

II

As the boat bounced from the top of each wave the wind tore through the hair of the hatless men, and as the craft plopped her stern down again the spray slashed past them. The crest of each of these waves was a hill, from the top of which the men surveyed for a moment a broad tumultuous expanse, shining and wind-riven. It was probably splendid, it was probably glorious, this play of the free sea, wild with lights of emerald and white and amber.

"Bully good thing it's an on-shore wind," said the cook. "If not, where would we be? Wouldn't have a show."

"That's right," said the correspondent.

The busy oiler nodded his assent.

Then the captain, in the bow, chuckled in a way that expressed humor, con-   25
tempt, tragedy, all in one. "Do you think we've got much of a show now, boys?" said he.

Whereupon the three were silent, save for a trifle of hemming and hawing. To express any particular optimism at this time they felt to be childish and stupid, but they all doubtless possessed this sense of the situation in their minds. A young man thinks doggedly at such times. On the other hand, the ethics of their condition was decidedly against any open suggestion of hopelessness. So they were silent.

"Oh, well," said the captain, soothing his children, "we'll get ashore all right."

But there was that in his tone which made them think; so the oiler quoth, "Yes! if this wind holds."

The cook was bailing. "Yes! if we don't catch hell in the surf."

Canton-flannel gulls flew near and far. Sometimes they sat down on the sea, near patches of brown seaweed that rolled over the waves with a movement like carpets on a line in a gale. The birds sat comfortably in groups, and they were envied by some in the dinghy, for the wrath of the sea was no more to them than it was to a covey of prairie chickens a thousand miles inland. Often they came very close and stared at the men with black bead-like eyes. At these times they were uncanny and sinister in their unblinking scrutiny, and the men hooted angrily at them, telling them to be gone. One came, and evidently decided to alight on the top of the captain's head. The bird flew parallel to the boat and did not circle, but made short sidelong jumps in the air in chicken-fashion. His black eyes were wistfully fixed upon the captain's head. "Ugly brute," said the oiler to the bird. "You look as if you were made with a jacknife." The cook and the correspondent swore darkly at the creature. The captain naturally wished to knock it away with the end of the heavy painter, but he did not dare do it, because anything resembling an emphatic gesture would have capsized this freighted boat; and so, with his open hand, the captain gently and carefully waved the gull away. After it had been discouraged from the pursuit the captain breathed easier on account of his hair, and others breathed easier because the bird struck their minds at this time as being somehow gruesome and ominous.

In the meantime the oiler and the correspondent rowed. And also they rowed. They sat together in the same seat, and each rowed an oar. Then the oiler took both oars; then the correspondent took both oars; then the oiler; then the correspondent. They rowed and they rowed. The very ticklish part of the business was when the time came for the reclining one in the stern to take his turn at the oars. By the very last star of truth, it is easier to steal eggs from under a hen than it was to change seats in the dinghy. First the man in the stern slid his hand along the thwart and moved with care, as if he were of Sèvres.° Then the man in the rowing-seat slid his hand along the other thwart. It was all done with the most extraordinary care. As the two sidled past each other, the whole party kept watchful eyes on the coming wave, and the captain cried: "Look out, now! Steady, there!"

The brown mats of seaweed that appeared from time to time were like islands, bits of earth. They were travelling, apparently, neither one way nor the other. They were, to all intents, stationary. They informed the men in the boat that it was making progress slowly toward the land.

The captain, rearing cautiously in the bow after the dinghy soared on a great swell, said that he had seen the lighthouse at Mosquito Inlet. Presently the cook remarked that he had seen it. The correspondent was at the oars then, and for

Sèvres: chinaware made in this French town.

some reason he too wished to look at the lighthouse; but his back was toward the far shore, and the waves were important, and for some time he could not seize an opportunity to turn his head. But at last there came a wave more gentle than the others, and when at the crest of it he swiftly scoured the western horizon.

"See it?" said the captain.

"No," said the correspondent, slowly; "I didn't see anything."   35

"Look again," said the captain. He pointed. "It's exactly in that direction."

At the top of another wave the correspondent did as he was bid, and this time his eyes chanced on a small, still thing on the edge of the swaying horizon. It was precisely like the point of a pin. It took an anxious eye to find a lighthouse so tiny.

"Think we'll make it, Captain?"

"If this wind holds and the boat don't swamp, we can't do much else," said the captain.

The little boat, lifted by each towering sea and splashed viciously by the   40 crests, made progress that in the absence of seaweed was not apparent to those in her. She seemed just a wee thing wallowing, miraculously top up, at the mercy of five oceans. Occasionally a great spread of water, like white flames, swarmed into her.

"Bail her, cook," said the captain, serenely.

"All right, Captain," said the cheerful cook.

III

It would be difficult to describe the subtle brotherhood of men that was here established on the seas. No one said that it was so. No one mentioned it. But it dwelt in the boat, and each man felt it warm him. They were a captain, an oiler, a cook, and a correspondent, and they were friends—friends in a more curiously iron-bound degree than may be common. The hurt captain, lying against the water-jar in the bow, spoke always in a low voice and calmly; but he could never command a more ready and swiftly obedient crew than the motley three of the dinghy. It was more than a mere recognition of what was best for the common safety. There was surely in it a quality that was personal and heart-felt. And after this devotion to the commander of the boat, there was this comradeship, that the correspondent, for instance, who had been taught to be cynical of men, knew even at the time was the best experience of his life. But no one said that it was so. No one mentioned it.

"I wish we had a sail," remarked the captain. "We might try my overcoat on the end of an oar, and give you two boys a chance to rest." So the cook and the correspondent held the mast and spread wide the overcoat; the oiler steered; and the little boat made good way with her new rig. Sometimes the oiler had to scull sharply to keep a sea from breaking into the boat, but other-wise sailing was a success.

Meanwhile the lighthouse had been growing slowly larger. It had now al-   45 most assumed color, and appeared like a little gray shadow on the sky. The man at the oars could not be prevented from turning his head rather often to try for a glimpse of this little gray shadow.

At last, from the top of each wave, the men in the tossing boat could see land. Even as the lighthouse was an upright shadow on the sky, this land seemed but a long black shadow on the sea. It certainly was thinner than paper. "We must be about opposite New Smyrna," said the cook, who had coasted this shore often in schooners. "Captain, by the way, I believe they abandoned that life-saving station there about a year ago."

"Did they?" said the captain.

The wind slowly died away. The cook and the correspondent were not now obliged to slave in order to hold high the oar. But the waves continued their old impetuous swooping at the dinghy, and the little craft, no longer under way, struggled woundily over them. The oiler or the correspondent took the oars again.

Shipwrecks are apropos of nothing. If men could only train for them and have them occur when the men had reached pink condition, there would be less drowning at sea. Of the four in the dinghy none had slept any time worth mentioning for two days and two nights previous to embarking in the dinghy, and in the excitement of clambering about the deck of a foundering ship they had also forgotten to eat heartily.

For these reasons, and for others, neither the oiler nor the correspondent was fond of rowing at this time. The correspondent wondered ingenuously how in the name of all that was sane could there be people who thought it amusing to row a boat. It was not an amusement; it was a diabolical punishment, and even a genius of mental aberrations could never conclude that it was anything but a horror to the muscles and crime against the back. He mentioned to the boat in general how the amusement of rowing struck him, and the weary-faced oiler smiled in full sympathy. Previously to the foundering, by the way, the oiler had worked double watch in the engine-room of the ship. [50]

"Take her easy now, boys," said the captain. "Don't spend yourselves. If we have to run a surf you'll need all your strength, because we'll sure have to swim for it. Take your time."

Slowly the land arose from the sea. From a black line it became a line of black and a line of white—trees and sand. Finally the captain said that he could make out a house on the shore. "That's the house of refuge, sure," said the cook. "They'll see us before long, and come out after us."

The distant lighthouse reared high. "The keeper ought to be able to make us out now, if he's looking through a glass," said the captain. "He'll notify the life-saving people."

"None of those other boats could have got ashore to give word of the wreck," said the oiler, in a low voice, "else the life-boat would be out hunting us."

Slowly and beautifully the land loomed out of the sea. The wind came again. It had veered from the north-east to the south-east. Finally a new sound struck the ears of the men in the boat. It was the low thunder of the surf on the shore. "We'll never be able to make the lighthouse now," said the captain. "Swing her head a little more north, Billie." [55]

"A little more north, sir," said the oiler.

Whereupon the little boat turned her nose once more down the wind, and all but the oarsman watched the shore grow. Under the influence of this expansion doubt and direful apprehension were leaving the minds of the men. The management of the boat was still most absorbing, but it could not prevent a quiet cheerfulness. In an hour, perhaps, they would be ashore.

Their backbones had become thoroughly used to balancing in the boat, and they now rode this wild colt of a dinghy like circus men. The correspondent thought that he had been drenched to the skin, but happening to feel in the top pocket of his coat, he found therein eight cigars. Four of them were soaked with seawater; four were perfectly scatheless. After a search, somebody produced three dry matches; and thereupon the four waifs rode impudently in their little boat and, with an assurance of an impending rescue shining in their eyes, puffed at the big cigars, and judged well and ill of all men. Everybody took a drink of water.

IV

"Cook," remarked the captain, "there don't seem to be any signs of life about your house of refuge."

"No," replied the cook. "Funny they don't see us!"   60

A broad stretch of lowly coast lay before the eyes of the men. It was of low dunes topped with dark vegetation. The roar of the surf was plain, and sometimes they could see the white lip of a wave as it spun up the beach. A tiny house was blocked out black upon the sky. Southward, the slim lighthouse lifted its little gray length.

Tide, wind, and waves were swinging the dinghy northward. "Funny they don't see us," said the men.

The surf's roar was here dulled, but its tone was nevertheless thunderous and mighty. As the boat swam over the great rollers the men sat listening to this roar. "We'll swamp sure," said everybody.

It is fair to say here that there was not a life-saving station within twenty miles in either direction; but the men did not know this fact, and in consequence they made dark and opprobrious remarks concerning the eyesight of the nation's life-savers. Four scowling men sat in the dinghy and surpassed records in the invention of epithets.

"Funny they don't see us."   65

The light-heartedness of a former time had completely faded. To their sharpened minds it was easy to conjure pictures of all kinds of incompetency and blindness and, indeed, cowardice. There was the shore of the populous land, and it was bitter and bitter to them that from it came no sign.

"Well," said the captain, ultimately, "I suppose we'll have to make a try for ourselves. If we stay out here too long, we'll none of us have strength left to swim after the boat swamps."

And so the oiler, who was at the oars, turned the boat straight for the shore. There was a sudden tightening of muscles. There was some thinking.

"If we don't all get ashore," said the captain—"if we don't all get ashore, I suppose you fellows know where to send news of my finish?"

They then briefly exchanged some addresses and admonitions. As for the re-flections of the men, there was a great deal of rage in them. Perchance they might be formulated thus: "If I am going to be drowned—if I am going to be drowned—if I am going to be drowned, why, in the name of the seven mad gods who rule the sea, was I allowed to come thus far and contemplate sand and trees? Was I brought here merely to have my nose dragged away as I was about to nibble the sacred cheese of life? It is preposterous. If this old ninny-woman, Fate, cannot do better than this, she should be deprived of the management of men's fortunes. She is an old hen who knows not her intention. If she has decided to drown me, why did she not do it in the beginning and save me all this trouble? The whole affair is absurd.—But no; she cannot mean to drown me. She dare not drown me. She cannot drown me. Not after all this work." Afterward the man might have had an impulse to shake his fist at the clouds. "Just you drown me, now, and then hear what I call you!"

The billows that came at this time were more formidable. They seemed al-ways just about to break and roll over the little boat in a turmoil of foam. There was a preparatory and long growl in the speech of them. No mind unused to the sea would have concluded that the dinghy could ascend these sheer heights in time. The shore was still afar. The oiler was a wily surfman. "Boys," he said swiftly, "she won't live three minutes more, and we're too far out to swim. Shall I take her to sea again, Captain?

"Yes; go ahead!" said the captain.

This oiler, by a series of quick miracles and fast and steady oarsmanship, turned the boat in the middle of the surf and took her safely to sea again.

There was a considerable silence as the boat bumped over the furrowed sea to deeper water. Then somebody in gloom spoke: "Well, anyhow, they must have seen us from the shore by now."

The gulls went in slanting flight up the wind toward the gray, desolate east. A squall, marked by dinghy clouds and clouds brick-red like smoke from a burning building, appeared from the south-east.

"What do you think of those life-saving people? Ain't they peaches?"

"Funny they haven't seen us."

"Maybe they think we're out here for sport! Maybe they think we're fishin'. Maybe they think we're damned fools."

It was a long afternoon. A changed tide tried to force them southward, but wind and wave said northward. Far ahead, where coast-line, sea, and sky formed their mighty angle, there were little dots which seemed to indicate a city on the shore.

"St. Augustine?"

The captain shook his head. "Too near Mosquito Inlet."

And the oiler rowed, and then the correspondent rowed; then the oiler rowed. It was a weary business. The human back can become the seat of more aches and pains than are registered in books for the composite anatomy of a regiment. It is a limited area, but it can become the theatre of innumerable muscular conflicts, tangles, wrenches, knots, and other comforts.

"Did you ever like to row, Billie?" asked the correspondent.

"No," said the oiler; "hang it!"

When one exchanged the rowing-seat for a place in the bottom of the boat, he suffered a bodily depression that caused him to be careless of everything save an obligation to wiggle one finger. There was cold sea-water swashing to and fro in the boat, and he lay in it. His head, pillowed on a thwart, was within an inch of the swirl of a wave-crest, and sometimes a particularly obstreperous sea came inboard and drenched him once more. But these matters did not annoy him. It is almost certain that if the boat had capsized he would have tumbled comfortably upon the ocean as if he felt sure that it was a great soft mattress.

"Look! There's a man on the shore!"

"Where?"

"There! See 'im?"

"Yes, sure! He's walking along."

"Now he's stopped. Look! He's facing us!"

"He's waving at us!"

"So he is! By thunder!"

"Ah, now we're all right! Now we're all right! There'll be a boat out here for us in half an hour."

"He's going on. He's running. He's going up to that house there."

The remote beach seemed lower than the sea, and it required a searching glance to discern the little black figure. The captain saw a floating stick, and they rowed to it. A bath towel was by some weird chance in the boat, and, tying this on the stick, the captain waved it. The oarsman did not dare turn his head, so he was obliged to ask questions.

"What's he doing now?"

"He's standing still again. He's looking, I think.—There he goes again—toward the house.—Now he's stopped again."

"Is he waving at us?"

"No, not now; he was, though."

"Look! There comes another man!"

"He's running."

"Look at him go, would you!"

"Why, he's on a bicycle. Now he's met the other man. They're both waving at us. Look!"

"There comes something up the beach."

"What the devil is that thing?"

"Why, it looks like a boat."

"Why, certainly, it's a boat."

"No; it's on wheels."

"Yes, so it is. Well, that must be the life-boat. They drag them along shore on a wagon."

"That's the life-boat, sure."

85

90

95

100

105

110

"No, by God, it's—it's an omnibus."

"I tell you it's a life-boat."

"It is not! It's an omnibus. I can see it plain. See? One of the these big hotel omnibuses."

"By thunder, you're right. It's an omnibus, sure as fate. What do you suppose they are doing with an omnibus? Maybe they are going around collecting the life-crew, hey?"

"That's it, likely. Look! There's a fellow waving a little black flag. He's standing on the steps of the omnibus. There come those other two fellows. Now they're all talking together. Look at the fellow with the flag. Maybe he ain't waving it!" 115

"That ain't a flag, is it? That's his coat. Why, certainly, that's his coat."

"So it is; it's his coat. He's taken it off and is waving it around his head. But would you look at him swing it!"

"Oh, say, there isn't any life-saving station there. That's just a winter-resort hotel omnibus that has brought over some of the boarders to see us drown."

"What's that idiot with the coat mean? What's he signalling, anyhow?"

"It looks as if he were trying to tell us to go north. There must be a life-saving station up there." 120

"No; he thinks we're fishing. Just giving us a merry hand. See? Ah, there, Willie!"

"Well, I wish I could make something out of those signals. What do you suppose he means?"

"He don't mean anything; he's just playing."

"Well, if he'd just signal us to try the surf again, or to go to sea and wait, or go north, or go south, or go to hell, there would be some reason in it. But look at him! He just stands there and keeps his coat revolving like a wheel. The ass!"

"There come more people." 125

"Now there's quite a mob. Look! Isn't that a boat?"

"Where? Oh, I see where you mean. No, that's no boat."

"That fellow is still waving his coat."

"He must think we like to see him do that. Why don't he quit it? It don't mean anything."

"I don't know. I think he is trying to make us go north. It must be that there's a life-saving station there somewhere." 130

"Say, he ain't tired yet. Look at 'im wave!"

"Wonder how long he can keep that up. He's been revolving his coat ever since he caught sight of us. He's an idiot. Why aren't they getting men to bring a boat out? A fishing boat—one of those big yawls—could come out here all right. Why don't he do something?"

"Oh, it's all right now."

"They'll have a boat out here for us in less than no time, now that they've seen us."

A faint yellow tone came into the sky over the low land. The shadows on the sea slowly deepened. The wind bore coldness with it, and the men began to shiver. 135

"Holy smoke!" said one, allowing his voice to express his impious mood, "If we keep on monkeying out here! If we've got to flounder out here all night!"

"Oh, we'll never have to stay here all night! Don't you worry. They've seen us now, and it won't be long before they'll come chasing out after us."

The shore grew dusky. The man waving a coat blended gradually into this gloom, and it swallowed in the same manner the omnibus and the group of people. The spray, when it dashed uproariously over the side, made the voyagers shrink and swear like men who were being branded.

"I'd like to catch the chump who waved the coat. I feel like socking him one, just for luck."

"Why? What did he do?"   140

"Oh, nothing, but then he seemed so damned cheerful."

In the meantime the oiler rowed, and then the correspondent rowed, and then the oiler rowed. Gray-faced and bowed forward, they mechanically, turn by turn, plied the leaden oars. The form of the lighthouse had vanished from the southern horizon, but finally a pale star appeared, just lifting from the sea. The streaked saffron in the west passed before the all-merging darkness, and the sea to the east was black. The land had vanished, and was expressed only by the low and drear thunder of the surf.

"If I am going to be drowned—if I am going to be drowned—if I am going to be drowned, why, in the name of the seven mad gods who rule the sea, was I allowed to come thus far and contemplate sand and trees? Was I brought here merely to have my nose dragged away as I was about to nibble the sacred cheese of life?"

The patient captain, drooped over the water-jar, was sometimes obliged to speak to the oarsman.

"Keep her head up! Keep her head up!"   145

"Keep her head, up, sir." The voices were weary and low.

This was surely a quiet evening. All save the oarsman lay heavily and listlessly in the boat's bottom. As for him, his eyes were just capable of noting the tall black waves that swept forward in a most sinister silence, save for an occasional subdued growl of a crest.

The cook's head was on a thwart, and he looked without interest at the water under this nose. He was deep in other scenes. Finally he spoke. "Billie," he murmured, dreamfully, "what kind of pie do you like best?"

V

"Pie!" said the oiler and the correspondent, agitatedly. "Don't talk about those things, blast you!"

"Well," said the cook, "I was just thinking about ham sandwiches, and—"   150

A night on the sea in an open boat is a long night. As darkness settled finally, the shine of the light, lifting from the sea in the south, changed to full gold. On the northern horizon a new light appeared, a small bluish gleam on the edge of the waters. These two lights were the furniture of the world. Otherwise there was nothing but waves.

Two men huddled in the stern, and distances were so magnificent in the dinghy that the rower was enabled to keep his feet partly warm by thrusting them under his companions. Their legs indeed extended far under the rowingseat until they touched the feet of the captain forward. Sometimes, despite the efforts of the tired oarsman, a wave came piling into the boat, an icy wave of the night, and the chilling water soaked them anew. They would twist their bodies for a moment and groan, and sleep the dead sleep once more, while the water in the boat gurgled about them as the craft rocked.

The plan of the oiler and the correspondent was for one to row until he lost the ability, and then arouse the other from his sea-water couch in the bottom of the boat.

The oiler plied the oars until his head drooped forward and the overpowering sleep blinded him; and he rowed yet afterward. Then he touched a man in the bottom of the boat, and called his name. "Will you spell me for a little while?" he said meekly.

"Sure, Billie," said the correspondent, awaking and dragging himself to a sit- 155 ting position. They exchanged places carefully, and the oiler, cuddling down in the sea-water at the cook's side, seemed to go to sleep instantly.

The particular violence of the sea had ceased. The waves came without snarling. The obligation of the man at the oars was to keep the boat headed so that the tilt of the roller would not capsize her, and to preserve her from filling when the crests rushed past. The black waves were silent and hard to be seen in the darkness. Often one was almost upon the boat before the oarsman was aware.

In a low voice the correspondent addressed the captain. He was not sure that the captain was awake, although this iron man seemed to be always awake. "Captain, shall I keep her making for that light north, sir?"

The same steady voice answered him. "Yes. Keep it about two points off the port bow."

The cook had tied a life-belt around himself in order to get even the warmth which this clumsy cork contrivance could donate, and he seemed almost stovelike when a rower, whose teeth invariably chattered wildly as soon as he ceased his labor, dropped down to sleep.

The correspondent, as he rowed, looked down at the two men sleeping un- 160 derfoot. The cook's arm was around the oiler's shoulders, and, with their fragmentary clothing and haggard faces, they were the babes of the sea—a grotesque rendering of the old babes in the wood.

Later he must have grown stupid at his work, for suddenly there was a growling of water, and a crest came with a roar and a swash into the boat, and it was a wonder that it did not set the cook afloat in his life-belt. The cook continued to sleep, but the oiler sat up, blinking his eyes and shaking with the new cold.

"Oh, I'm awful sorry, Billie," said the correspondent, contritely.

"That's all right, old boy," said the oiler, and lay down again and was asleep.

Presently it seemed that even the captain dozed, and the correspondent thought that he was the one man afloat on all the oceans. The wind had a voice as it came over the waves, and it was sadder than the end.

There was a long, loud swishing astern of the boat, and a gleaming trail of phosphorescence, like blue flame, was furrowed on the black waters. It might have been made by a monstrous knife.

Then there came a stillness, while the correspondent breathed with open mouth and looked at the sea.

Suddenly there was another swish and another long flash of bluish light, and this time it was alongside the boat, and might almost have been reached with an oar. The correspondent saw an enormous fin speed like a shadow through the water, hurling the crystalline spray and leaving the long glowing trail.

The correspondent looked over his shoulder at the captain. His face was hidden, and he seemed to be asleep. He looked at the babes of the sea. They certainly were asleep. So, being bereft of sympathy, he leaned a little way to one side and swore softly into the sea.

But the thing did not then leave the vicinity of the boat. Ahead or astern, on one side or the other, at intervals long or short, fled the long sparkling streak, and there was to be heard the *whirroo* of the dark fin. The speed and power of the thing was greatly to be admired. It cut the water like a gigantic and keen projectile.

The presence of this biding thing did not affect the man with the same horror that it would if he had been a picnicker. He simply looked at the sea dully and swore in an undertone.

Nevertheless, it is true that he did not wish to be alone with the thing. He wished one of his companions to awake by chance and keep him company with it. But the captain hung motionless over the water-jar, and the oiler and the cook in the bottom of the boat were plunged in slumber.

VI

"If I am going to be drowned—if I am going to be drowned—if I am going to be drowned, why, in the name of the seven mad gods who rule the sea, was I allowed to come thus far and contemplate sand and trees?"

During this dismal night, it may be remarked that a man would conclude that it was really the intention of the seven mad gods to drown him, despite the abominable injustice of it. For it was certainly an abominable injustice to drown a man who had worked so hard, so hard. The man felt it would be a crime most unnatural. Other people had drowned at sea since galleys swarmed with painted sails, but still—

When it occurs to a man that nature does not regard him as important, and that she feels she would not maim the universe by disposing of him, he at first wishes to throw bricks at the temple, and he hates deeply the fact that there are no bricks and no temples. Any visible expression of nature would surely be pelleted with his jeers.

Then, if there be no tangible thing to hoot, he feels, perhaps, the desire to confront a personification and indulge in pleas, bowed to one knee, and with hands supplicant, saying, "Yes, but I love myself."

A high cold star on a winter's night is the word he feels that she says to him. Thereafter he knows the pathos of his situation.

The men in the dinghy had not discussed these matters, but each had, no doubt, reflected upon them in silence and according to his mind. There was seldom any expression upon their faces save the general one of complete weariness. Speech was devoted to the business of the boat.

To chime the notes of his emotion, a verse mysteriously entered the correspondent's head. He had even forgotten that he had forgotten this verse, but it suddenly was in his mind.

> A soldier of the Legion lay dying in Algiers;
> There was lack of woman's nursing, there was dearth of woman's tears;
> But a comrade stood beside him, and he took that comrade's hand,
> And he said, "I never more shall see my own, my native land."°

In his childhood the correspondent had been made acquainted with the fact that a soldier of the Legion lay dying in Algiers, but he had never regarded the fact as important. Myriads of his school-fellows had informed him of the soldier's plight, but the dinning had naturally ended by making him perfectly indifferent. He had never considered it his affair that a soldier of the Legion lay dying in Algiers, nor had it appeared to him as a matter for sorrow. It was less to him than the breaking of a pencil's point.

Now, however, it quaintly came to him as a human, living thing. It was no 180 longer merely a picture of a few throes in the breast of a poet, meanwhile drinking tea and warming his feet at the grate; it was an actuality—stern, mournful, and fine.

The correspondent plainly saw the soldier. He lay on the sand with his feet out straight and still. While his pale left hand was upon his chest in an attempt to thwart the going of his life, the blood came between his fingers. In the far Algerian distance, a city of low square forms was set against a sky that was faint with the last sunset hues. The correspondent, plying the oars and dreaming of the slow and slower movements of the lips of the soldier, was moved by a profound and perfectly impersonal comprehension. He was sorry for the soldier of the Legion who lay dying in Algiers.

The thing which had followed the boat and waited had evidently grown bored at the delay. There was no longer to be heard the slash of the cutwater, and there was no longer the flame of the long trail. The light in the north still glimmered, but it was apparently no nearer to the boat. Sometimes the boom of the surf rang in the correspondent's ears, and he turned the craft seaward then and rowed harder. Southward, some one had evidently built a watch-fire on the beach. It was too low and too far to be seen, but it made a shimmering, roseate reflection upon the bluff in back of it, and this could be discerned from the boat. The wind came stronger, and sometimes a wave suddenly raged out like a mountain cat, and there was to be seen the sheen and sparkle of a broken crest.

A soldier of the Legion . . . native land: The correspondent remembers a Victorian ballad about a German dying in the French Foreign Legion, "Bingen on the Rhine" by Caroline Norton.

The captain, in the bow, moved on his water-jar and sat erect. "Pretty long night," he observed to the correspondent. He looked at the shore. "Those life-saving people take their time."

"Did you see that shark playing around?"

"Yes, I saw him. He was a big fellow, all right."   185

"Wish I had known you were awake."

Later the correspondent spoke into the bottom of the boat.

"Billie!" There was a slow and gradual disentanglement.

"Billie, will you spell me?"

"Sure," said the oiler.   190

As soon as the correspondent touched the cold, comfortable sea-water in the bottom of the boat and had huddled close to the cook's life-belt he was deep in sleep, despite the fact that his teeth played all the popular airs. This sleep was so good to him that it was but a moment before he heard a voice call his name in a tone that demonstrated the last stages of exhaustion. "Will you spell me?"

"Sure, Billie."

The light in the north had mysteriously vanished, but the correspondent took his course from the wide-awake captain.

Later in the night they took the boat farther out to sea, and the captain directed the cook to take one oar at the stern and keep the boat facing the seas. He was to call out if he should hear the thunder of the surf. This plan enabled the oiler and the correspondent to get respite together. "We'll give those boys a chance to get into shape again," said the captain. They curled down and, after a few preliminary chatterings and trembles, slept once more the dead sleep. Neither knew they had bequeathed to the cook the company of another shark, or perhaps the same shark.

As the boat caroused on the waves, spray occasionally bumped over the side   195
and gave them a fresh soaking, but this had no power to break their repose. The ominous slash of the wind and the water affected them as it would have affected mummies.

"Boys," said the cook, with the notes of every reluctance in his voice, "she's drifted in pretty close. I guess one of you had better take her to sea again." The correspondent, aroused, heard the crash of the toppled crests.

As he was rowing, the captain gave him some whisky-and-water, and this steadied the chills out of him. "If I ever get ashore and anybody shows me even a photograph of an oar—"

At last there was a short conversation.

"Billie!—Billie, will you spell me?"

"Sure," said the oiler.   200

VII

When the correspondent again opened his eyes, the sea and sky were each of the gray hue of the dawning. Later, carmine and gold was painted upon the waters. The morning appeared finally, in its splendor, with a sky of pure blue, and the sunlight flamed on the tips of the waves.

On the distant dunes were set many little black cottages, and a tall white windmill reared above them. No man, nor dog, nor bicycle appeared on the beach. The cottages might have formed a deserted village.

The voyagers scanned the shore. A conference was held in the boat. "Well," said the captain, "if no help is coming, we might better try a run through the surf right away. If we stay out here much longer we will be too weak to do anything for ourselves at all." The others silently acquiesced in this reasoning. The boat was headed for the beach. The correspondent wondered if none ever ascended the tall wind-tower, and if they never looked seaward. This tower was a giant, standing with its back to the plight of the ants. It represented in a degree, to the correspondent, the serenity of nature amid the struggles of the individual—nature in the wind, and nature in the vision of men. She did not seem cruel to him then, nor beneficent, nor treacherous, nor wise. But she was indifferent, flatly indifferent. It is, perhaps, plausible that a man in this situation, impressed with the unconcern of the universe, should see the innumerable flaws of life, and have them taste wickedly in his mind, and wish for another chance. A distinction between right and wrong seems absurdly clear to him, then, in this new ignorance of the grave-edge, and he understands that if he were given another opportunity he would mend his conduct and his words, and be better and brighter during an introduction or at a tea.

"Now, boys," said the captain, "she is going to swamp sure. All we can do is to work her in as far as possible, and then when she swamps, pile out and scramble for the beach. Keep cool now, and don't jump until she swamps sure."

The oiler took the oars. Over his shoulders he scanned the surf. "Captain," he said, "I think I'd better bring her about and keep her head-on to the seas and back her in."

"All right, Billie," said the captain. "Back her in." The oiler swung the boat then, and, seated in the stern, the cook and the correspondent were obliged to look over their shoulders to contemplate the lonely and indifferent shore.

The monstrous inshore rollers heaved the boat high until the men were again enabled to see the white sheets of water scudding up the slanted beach. "We won't get in very close," said the captain. Each time a man could wrest his attention from the rollers, he turned his glance toward the shore, and in the expression of the eyes during this contemplation there was a singular quality. The correspondent, observing the others, knew that they were not afraid, but the full meaning of their glances was shrouded.

As for himself, he was too tired to grapple fundamentally with the fact. He tried to coerce his mind into thinking of it, but the mind was dominated at this time by the muscles, and the muscles said they did not care. It merely occurred to him that if he should drown it would be a shame.

There were no hurried words, no pallor, no plain agitation. The men simply looked at the shore. "Now, remember to get well clear of the boat when you jump," said the captain.

Seaward the crest of a roller suddenly fell with a thunderous crash, and the 210
long white comber came roaring down upon the boat.

"Steady now," said the captain. The men were silent. They turned their eyes
from the shore to the comber and waited. The boat slid up the incline, leaped at
the furious top, bounced over it, and swung down the long back of the wave.
Some water had been shipped, and the cook bailed it out.

But the next crest crashed also. The tumbling, boiling flood of white water
caught the boat and whirled it almost perpendicular. Water swarmed in from all
sides. The correspondent had his hands on the gunwale at this time, and when
the water entered at that place he swiftly withdrew his fingers, as if he objected
to wetting them.

The little boat, drunken with this weight of water, reeled and snuggled
deeper into the sea.

"Bail her out, cook! Bail her out!" said the captain.

"All right, Captain," said the cook. 215

"Now, boys, the next one will do for us sure," said the oiler. "Mind to jump
clear of the boat."

The third wave moved forward, huge, furious, implacable. It fairly swallowed the dinghy, and almost simultaneously the men tumbled into the sea. A
piece of life-belt had lain in the bottom of the boat, and as the correspondent
went overboard he held this to his chest with his left hand.

The January water was icy, and he reflected immediately that it was colder
than he had expected to find it off the coast of Florida. This appeared to his
dazed mind as a fact important enough to be noted at the time. The coldness of
the water was sad; it was tragic. This fact was somehow mixed and confused with
his opinion of his own situation, so that it seemed almost a proper reason for
tears. The water was cold.

When he came to the surface he was conscious of little but the noisy water.
Afterward he saw his companions in the sea. The oiler was ahead in the race. He
was swimming strongly and rapidly. Off to the correspondent's left, the cook's
great white and corked back bulged out of the water; and in the rear the captain
was hanging with his one good hand to the keel of the overturned dinghy.

There is a certain immovable quality to a shore, and the correspondent 220
wondered at it amid the confusion of the sea.

It seemed also very attractive; but the correspondent knew that it was a long
journey, and he paddled leisurely. The piece of life-preserver lay under him, and
sometimes he whirled down the incline of a wave as if he were on a handsled.

But finally he arrived at a place in the sea where travel was beset with difficulty.
He did not pause swimming to inquire what manner of current had caught him, but
there his progress ceased. The shore was set before him like a bit of scenery on a
stage, and he looked at it and understood with his eyes each detail of it.

As the cook passed, much farther to the left, the captain was calling to him,
"Turn over on your back, cook! Turn over on your back and use the oar."

"All right, sir." The cook turned on his back, and, paddling with an oar,
went ahead as if he were a canoe.

Presently the boat also passed to the left of the correspondent, with the captain clinging with one hand to the keel. He would have appeared like a man
raising himself to look over a board fence if it were not for the extraordinary
gymnastics of the boat. The correspondent marvelled that the captain could still
hold to it.

They passed on nearer to shore—the oiler, the cook, the captain—and following them went the water-jar, bouncing gaily over the seas.

The correspondent remained in the grip of this strange new enemy—a current. The shore, with its white slope of sand and its green bluff topped with little
silent cottages, was spread like a picture before him. It was very near to him
then, but he was impressed as one who, in a gallery, looks at a scene from Brit-
tany or Algiers.

He thought: "I am going to drown? Can it be possible? Can it be possible?
Can it be possible?" Perhaps an individual must consider his own death to be the
final phenomenon of nature.

But later a wave perhaps whirled him out of this small deadly current, for he
found suddenly that he could again make progress toward the shore. Later still he
was aware that the captain, clinging with one hand to the keel of the dinghy,
had his face turned away from the shore and toward him, and was calling his
name. "Come to the boat! Come to the boat!"

In his struggle to reach the captain and the boat, he reflected that when one
gets properly wearied drowning must really be a comfortable arrangement—a
cessation of hostilities accompanied by a large degree of relief; and he was glad of
it, for the main thing in his mind for some moments had been horror of the temporary agony. He did not wish to be hurt.

Presently he saw a man running along the shore. He was undressing with
most remarkable speed. Coat, trousers, shirt, everything flew magically off him.

"Come to the boat!" called the captain.

"All right, Captain." As the correspondent paddled, he saw the captain let
himself down to bottom and leave the boat. Then the correspondent performed
his one little marvel of the voyage. A large wave caught him and flung him with
ease and supreme speed completely over the boat and far beyond it. It struck him
even then as an event in gymnastics and a true miracle of the sea. An overturned
boat in the surf is not a plaything to a swimming man.

The correspondent arrived in water that reached only to his waist, but his
condition did not enable him to stand for more than a moment. Each wave
knocked him into a heap, and the undertow pulled at him.

Then he saw the man who had been running and undressing, and undressing and running, come bounding into the water. He dragged ashore the
cook, and then waded toward the captain; but the captain waved him away and
sent him to the correspondent. He was naked—naked as a tree in winter; but a
halo was about his head, and he shone like a saint. He gave a strong pull, and a
long drag, and a bully heave at the correspondent's hand. The correspondent,
schooled in the minor formulae, said, "Thanks, old man." But suddenly the man
cried, "What's that?" He pointed a swift finger. The correspondent said, "Go."

In the shallows, face downward, lay the oiler. His forehead touched sand that was periodically, between each wave, clear of the sea.

The correspondent did not know all that transpired afterward. When he achieved safe ground he fell, striking the sand with each particular part of his body. It was as if he had dropped from a roof, but the thud was grateful to him.

It seems that instantly the beach was populated with men with blankets, clothes, and flasks, and women with coffee-pots and all the remedies sacred to their minds. The welcome of the land to the men from the sea was warm and generous; but a still and dripping shape was carried slowly up the beach, and the land's welcome for it could only be the different and sinister hospitality of the grave.

When it came night, the white waves paced to and fro in the moonlight, and the wind brought the sound of the great sea's voice to the men on the shore, and they felt that they could then be interpreters.

QUESTIONS

1. In actuality, Crane, the captain of the *Commodore*, and the two crew members spent nearly thirty hours in the open boat. William Higgins, the oiler, was drowned as Crane describes. Does a knowledge of these facts in any way affect your response to the story? Would you admire the story less if you believed it to be pure fiction?

2. Sum up the personalities of each of the four men in the boat: captain, cook, oiler, and correspondent.

3. What is the point of view of the story?

4. In paragraph 9, we are told that as each wave came, the boat "seemed like a horse making at a fence outrageously high." Point to the other vivid similes or figures of speech. What do they contribute to the story's effectiveness?

5. Notice some of the ways in which Crane, as a storyteller conscious of plot, builds suspense. What enemies or obstacles do the men in the boat confront? What is the effect of the scene of the men who wave from the beach (paragraphs 86–141)? What is the climax of the story? (If you need to be refreshed on the meaning of *climax*, see the discussion of plot in Chapter One and in the Glossary.)

6. In paragraph 70 (and again in paragraph 143), the men wonder, "Was I brought here merely to have my nose dragged away as I was about to nibble the sacred cheese of life?" What variety of irony do you find in this quotation?

7. Why does the scrap of verse about the soldier dying in Algiers (paragraph 178) suddenly come to mean so much to the correspondent?

8. What theme in "The Open Boat" seems most important to you? Where is it stated?

9. What secondary themes also enrich the story? See for instance paragraph 43 (the thoughts on comradeship).

10. How do you define *heroism*? Who is a hero in "The Open Boat"?

Alice Munro

DAY OF THE BUTTERFLY

Alice Munro, one of the most widely admired contemporary writers in Canada, was born of farm parents in 1931 in Wingham, in south-western Ontario, an area in which she has spent most of her life. Its small town people figure in many of her stories. For two years, she attended the University of Western Ontario, but dropped out at twenty, after her first marriage. The mother of three daughters, Munro is a particularly sensitive explorer of the relations between parents and children, yet she ranges widely in choosing her themes. She has published ten remarkable collections of short fiction, including Dance of the Happy Shades (1968), Something I've Been Meaning to Tell You (1974), The Beggar Maid (1982), Open Secrets (1994), The Love of a Good Woman (1998),

Alice Munro

and Hateship, Friendship, Courtship, Loveship, Marriage (2001). Munro's Selected Stories appeared in 1996, comfirming her position as one of the greatest living masters of short fiction. Three of her books have won Canada's prestigious Governor General's Literary Award; in the United States she has won the National Book Critics Circle Award. The short story is her true medium, and she has declared her preference for "the story that will zero in and give you intense, but not connected, moments of experience."

I do not remember when Myra Sayla came to town, though she must have been in our class at school for two or three years. I start remembering her in the last year, when her little brother Jimmy Sayla was in Grade One. Jimmy Sayla was not used to going to the bathroom by himself and he would have to come to the Grade Six door and ask for Myra and she would take him downstairs. Quite often he would not get to Myra in time and there would be a big dark stain on his little button-on cotton pants. Then Myra had to come and ask the teacher: "Please may I take my brother home, he has wet himself?"

That was what she said the first time and everybody in the front seats heard her—though Myra's voice was the lightest singsong—and there was a muted giggling which alerted the rest of the class. Our teacher, a cold gentle girl who wore glasses with thin gold rims and in the stiff solicitude of certain poses resembled a giraffe, wrote something on a piece of paper and showed it to Myra. And Myra recited uncertainly: "My brother has had an accident, please, teacher."

Everybody knew of Jimmy Sayla's shame and at recess (if he was not being kept in, as he often was, for doing something he shouldn't in school) he did not dare go out on the school grounds, where the other little boys, and some bigger ones, were waiting to chase him and corner him against the back fence and thrash him with tree branches. He had to stay with Myra. But at our school there were the two sides, the Boys' Side and the Girls' Side, and it was believed that if you so much as stepped on the side that was not your own you might easily get the strap. Jimmy could not go out on the Girls' Side and Myra could not go out on the Boys' Side, and no one was allowed to stay in the school unless it was raining or snowing. So Myra and Jimmy spent every recess standing in the little back porch between the two sides. Perhaps they watched the baseball games, the tag and skipping and building of leaf houses in the fall and snow forts in the winter; perhaps they did not watch at all. Whenever you happened to look at them their heads were slightly bent, their narrow bodies hunched in, quite still. They had long smooth oval faces, melancholy and discreet—dark, oily, shining hair. The little boy's was long, clipped at home, and Myra's was worn in heavy braids coiled on top of her head so that she looked, from a distance, as if she was wearing a turban too big for her. Over their dark eyes the lids were never fully raised; they had a weary look. But it was more than that. They were like children in a medieval painting, they were like small figures carved of wood, for worship or magic, with faces smooth and aged, and meekly, cryptically uncommunicative.

Most of the teachers at our school had been teaching for a long time and at recess they would disappear into the teachers' room and not bother us. But our own teacher, the young woman of the fragile gold-rimmed glasses, was apt to watch us from a window and sometimes come out, looking brisk and uncomfortable, to stop a fight among the little girls or start a running game among the big ones, who had been huddled together playing Truth or Secrets. One day she came out and called, "Girls in Grade Six, I want to talk to you!" She smiled persuasively, earnestly, and with dreadful unease, showing fine gold rims around her teeth. She said, "There is a girl in Grade Six called Myra Sayla. She *is* in your grade, isn't she?"

We mumbled. But there was a coo from Gladys Healey. "Yes, Miss Darling!" 5

"Well, why is she never playing with the rest of you? Every day I see her standing in the back porch, never playing. Do you think she looks very happy standing back there? Do you think you would be very happy, if *you* were left back there?"

Nobody answered; we faced Miss Darling, all respectful, self-possessed, and bored with the unreality of her question. Then Gladys said, "Myra can't come out with us, Miss Darling. Myra has to look after her little brother!"

"Oh," said Miss Darling dubiously. "Well you ought to try to be nicer to her anyway. Don't you think so? Don't you? You will try to be nicer, won't you? I *know* you will." Poor Miss Darling! Her campaigns were soon confused, her persuasions turned to bleating and uncertain pleas.

When she had gone Gladys Healey said softly, "You will try to be nicer, won't you? I *know* you will!" and then drawing her lip back over her big teeth she yelled exuberantly, "I don't care if it rains or freezes."° She went through the

"*I don't care if it rains or freezes*": opening line of the song "Plastic Jesus," variously attributed to Ernie Marrs (1932–1998) and others; the song became well known through its use in the film *Cool Hand Luke* (1967).

whole verse and ended it with a spectacular twirl of her Royal Stuart tartan skirt. Mr. Healey ran a Dry Goods and Ladies' Wear, and his daughter's leadership in our class was partly due to her flashing plaid skirts and organdie blouses and velvet jackets with brass buttons, but also to her early-maturing bust and the fine brutal force of her personality. Now we all began to imitate Miss Darling.

We had not paid much attention to Myra before this. But now a game was 10 developed; it started with saying, "Let's be nice to Myra!" Then we would walk up to her in formal groups of three or four and at a signal, say together, "Hel-lo Myra, Hello My-ra!" and follow up with something like, "What do you wash your hair in, Myra, it's so nice and shiny, My-ra." "Oh she washes it in cod-liver oil, don't you, Myra, she washes it in cod-liver oil, can't you smell it?"

And to tell the truth there was a smell about Myra, but it was a rotten-sweetish smell as of bad fruit. That was what the Saylas did, kept a little fruit store. Her father sat all day on a stool by the window, with his shirt open over his swelling stomach and tufts of black hair showing around his belly button; he chewed garlic. But if you went into the store it was Mrs. Sayla who came to wait on you, appearing silently between the limp print curtains hung across the back of the store. Her hair was crimped in black waves and she smiled with her full lips held together, stretched as far as they would go; she told you the price in a little rapping voice, daring you to challenge her and, when you did not, handed you the bag of fruit with open mockery in her eyes.

One morning in the winter I was walking up the school hill very early; a neighbour had given me a ride into town. I lived about half a mile out of town, on a farm, and I should not have been going to the town school at all, but to a country school nearby where there were half a dozen pupils and a teacher a little demented since her change of life. But my mother, who was an ambitious woman, had prevailed on the town trustees to accept me and my father to pay the extra tuition, and I went to school in town. I was the only one in the class who carried a lunch pail and ate peanut-butter sandwiches in the high, bare, mustard-colored cloakroom, the only one who had to wear rubber boots in the spring, when the roads were heavy with mud. I felt a little danger, on account of this; but I could not tell exactly what it was.

I saw Myra and Jimmy ahead of me on the hill; they always went to school very early—sometimes so early that they had to stand outside waiting for the janitor to open the door. They were walking slowly, and now and then Myra half turned around. I had often loitered in that way, wanting to walk with some important girl who was behind me, and not quite daring to stop and wait. Now it occurred to me that Myra might be doing this with me. I did not know what to do. I could not afford to be seen walking with her, and I did not even want to— but, on the other hand, the flattery of those humble, hopeful turnings was not lost on me. A role was shaping for me that I could not resist playing. I felt a great pleasurable rush of self-conscious benevolence; before I thought what I was doing I called, "Myra! Hey, Myra, wait up, I got some Cracker Jack!" and I quickened my pace as she stopped.

Myra waited, but she did not look at me; she waited in the withdrawn and rigid attitude with which she always met us. Perhaps she thought I was playing a trick on her, perhaps she expected me to run past and throw an empty Cracker Jack box in her face. And I opened the box and held it out to her. She took a little. Jimmy ducked behind her coat and would not take any when I offered the box to him.

"He's shy," I said reassuringly. "A lot of little kids are shy like that. He'll probably grow out of it."

"Yes," said Myra.

"I have a brother four," I said. "He's awfully shy." He wasn't. "Have some more Cracker Jack," I said. "I used to eat Cracker Jack all the time but I don't any more. I think it's bad for your complexion."

There was a silence.

"Do you like Art?" said Myra faintly.

"No. I like Social Studies and Spelling and Health."

"I like Art and Arithmetic." Myra could add and multiply in her head faster than anyone else in the class.

"I wish I was as good as you. In Arithmetic," I said, and felt magnanimous.

"But I am no good at Spelling," said Myra. "I make the most mistakes, I'll fail maybe." She did not sound unhappy about this, but pleased to have such a thing to say. She kept her head turned away from me staring at the dirty snowbanks along Victoria Street, and as she talked she made a sound as if she was wetting her lips with her tongue.

"You won't fail," I said. "You are too good in Arithmetic. What are you going to be when you grow up?"

She looked bewildered. "I will help my mother," she said. "And work in the store."

"Well I am going to be an airplane hostess," I said. "But don't mention it to anybody. I haven't told many people."

"No, I won't," said Myra. "Do you read Steve Canyon in the paper?"

"Yes." It was queer to think that Myra, too, read the comics, or that she did anything at all, apart from her role at the school. "Do you read Rip Kirby?"

"Do you read Orphan Annie?"

"Do you read Betsy and the Boys?"

"You haven't had hardly any Cracker Jack," I said. "Have some. Take a whole handful."

Myra looked into the box. "There's a prize in there," she said. She pulled it out. It was a brooch, a little tin butterfly, painted gold with bits of colored glass stuck onto it to look like jewels. She held it in her brown hand, smiling slightly.

I said, "Do you like that?"

Myra said, "I like them blue stones. Blue stones are sapphires."

"I know. My birthstone is sapphire. What is your birthstone?"

"I don't know."

"When is your birthday?"

"July."

"Then yours is ruby."

"I like sapphire better," said Myra. "I like yours." She handed me the 40
brooch.

"You keep it," I said. "Finders keepers."

Myra kept holding it out, as if she did not know what I meant. "Finders keepers," I said.

"It was your Cracker Jack," said Myra, scared and solemn. "You bought it."

"Well you found it."

"No—" said Myra. 45

"Go on!" I said. "Here, I'll *give* it to you." I took the brooch from her and pushed it back into her hand.

We were both surprised. We looked at each other; I flushed but Myra did not. I realized the pledge as our fingers touched; I was panicky, but *all right*. I thought, I can come early and walk with her other mornings. I can go and talk to her at recess. Why not? *Why not?*

Myra put the brooch in her pocket. She said, "I can wear it on my good dress. My good dress is blue."

I knew it would be. Myra wore out her good dresses at school. Even in mid-winter among the plaid wool skirts and serge tunics, she glimmered sadly in sky-blue taffeta, in dusty turquoise crepe, a grown woman's dress made over, weighted by a big bow at the v of the neck and folding empty over Myra's narrow chest.

And I was glad she had not put it on. If someone asked her where she got it, 50 and she told them, what would I say?

It was the day after this, or the week after, that Myra did not come to school. Often she was kept at home to help. But this time she did not come back. For a week, then two weeks, her desk was empty. Then we had a moving day at school and Myra's books were taken out of her desk and put on a shelf in the closet. Miss Darling said, "We'll find a seat when she comes back." And she stopped calling Myra's name when she took attendance.

Jimmy Sayla did not come to school either, having no one to take him to the bathroom.

In the fourth week or the fifth, that Myra had been away, Gladys Healey came to school and said, "Do you know what—Myra Sayla is sick in the hospital."

It was true. Gladys Healey had an aunt who was a nurse. Gladys put up her hand in the middle of Spelling and told Miss Darling. "I thought you might like to know," she said. "Oh yes," said Miss Darling. "I do know."

"What has she got?" we said to Gladys. 55

And Gladys said, "Akemia, or something. And she has blood transfusions." She said to Miss Darling, "My aunt is a nurse."

So Miss Darling had the whole class write Myra a letter, in which everybody said, "Dear Myra, We are all writing you a letter. We hope you will soon be better and be back to school, Yours truly. . . ." And Miss Darling said, "I've thought of something. Who would like to go up to the hospital and visit Myra on the twentieth of March, for a birthday party?"

I said, "Her birthday's in July."

"I know," said Miss Darling. "It's the twentieth of July. So this year she could have it on the twentieth of March, because she's sick."

"But her *birthday* is in July."

"Because she's sick," said Miss Darling, with a warning shrillness. "The cook at the hospital would make a cake and you could all give a little present, twenty-five cents or so. It would have to be between two and four, because that's visiting hours. And we couldn't all go, it'd be too many. So who wants to go and who wants to stay here and do supplementary reading?"

We all put up our hands. Miss Darling got out the spelling records and picked out the first fifteen, twelve girls and three boys. Then the three boys did not want to go so she picked out the next three girls. And I do not know when it was, but I think it was probably at this moment that the birthday party of Myra Sayla became fashionable.

Perhaps it was because Gladys Healey had an aunt who was a nurse, perhaps it was the excitement of sickness and hospitals, or simply the fact that Myra was so entirely, impressively set free of all the rules and conditions of our lives. We began to talk of her as if she were something we owned, and her party became a cause; with womanly heaviness we discussed it at recess, and decided that twenty-five cents was too low.

We all went up to the hospital on a sunny afternoon when the snow was melting, carrying our presents, and a nurse led us upstairs, single file, and down a hall past half-closed doors and dim conversations. She and Miss Darling kept saying, "Sh-sh," but we were going on tiptoe anyway; our hospital demeanor was perfect.

At this small country hospital there was no children's ward, and Myra was not really a child; they had put her in with two grey old women. A nurse was putting screens around them as we came in.

Myra was sitting up in bed, in a bulky stiff hospital gown. Her hair was down, the long braids falling over her shoulders and down the coverlet. But her face was the same, always the same.

She had been told something about the party, Miss Darling said, so the surprise would not upset her; but it seemed she had not believed, or had not understood what it was. She watched us as she used to watch in the school grounds when we played.

"Well, here we are!" said Miss Darling. "Here we are!"

And we said, "Happy birthday, Myra! Hello, Myra, happy birthday!" Myra said, "My birthday is in July." Her voice was lighter than ever, drifting, expressionless.

"Never mind when it is, really," said Miss Darling. "Pretend it's now! How old are you, Myra?"

"Eleven," Myra said. "In July."

Then we all took off our coats and emerged in our party dresses, and laid our presents, in their pale flowery wrappings on Myra's bed. Some of our mothers had made immense, complicated bows of fine satin ribbon, some of them had even taped on little bouquets of imitation roses and lilies of the valley. "Here Myra," we said, "here Myra, happy birthday." Myra did not look at us, but at the ribbons, pink and blue and speckled with silver, and the miniature bouquets; they pleased her, as the butterfly had done. An innocent look came into her face, a partial, private smile.

"Open them, Myra," said Miss Darling. "They're for you!"

Myra gathered the presents around her, fingering them, with this smile, and a cautious realization, an unexpected pride. She said, "Saturday I'm going to London° to St. Joseph's Hospital."

"That's where my mother was at," somebody said. "We went and saw her. They've got all nuns there." 75

"My father's sister is a nun," said Myra calmly.

She began to unwrap the presents, with an air that not even Gladys could have bettered, folding the tissue paper and the ribbons, and drawing out books and puzzles and cutouts as if they were all prizes she had won. Miss Darling said that maybe she should say thank you, and the person's name with every gift she opened, to make sure she knew whom it was from, and so Myra said, "Thank you, Mary Louise, thank you, Carol," and when she came to mine she said, "Thank you, Helen." Everyone explained their presents to her and there was talking and excitement and a little gaiety, which Myra presided over, though she was not gay. A cake was brought in with *Happy Birthday Myra* written on it, pink on white, and eleven candles. Miss Darling lit the candles and we all sang Happy Birthday to You, and cried, "Make a wish, Myra, make a wish—" and Myra blew them out. Then we all had cake and strawberry ice cream.

At four o'clock a buzzer sounded and the nurse took out what was left of the cake, and the dirty dishes, and we put on our coats to go home. Everybody said, "Goodbye, Myra," and Myra sat in the bed watching us go, her back straight, not supported by any pillow, her hands resting on the gifts. But at the door I heard her call; she called, "Helen!" Only a couple of the others heard; Miss Darling did not hear, she had gone out ahead. I went back to the bed.

Myra said, "I got too many things. You take something."

"What?" I said. "It's for your birthday. You always get a lot at a birthday." 80

"Well you take something," Myra said. She picked up a leatherette case with a mirror in it, a comb and a nail file and a natural lipstick and a small handkerchief edged with gold thread. I had noticed it before. "You take that," she said.

"Don't you want it?"

"You take it." She put it into my hand. Our fingers touched again.

"When I come back from London," Myra said, "you can come and play at my place after school."

"Okay," I said. Outside the hospital window there was a clear carrying sound 85 of somebody playing in the street, maybe chasing with the last snowballs of the year. This sound made Myra, her triumph and her bounty, and most of all her

London: a city in southern Ontario, Canada.

future in which she had found this place for me, turn shadowy, turn dark. All the presents on the bed, the folded paper and ribbons, those guilt-tinged offerings, had passed into this shadow, they were no longer innocent objects to be touched, exchanged, accepted without danger. I didn't want to take the case now but I could not think how to get out of it, what lie to tell. I'll give it away, I thought, I won't ever play with it. I would let my little brother pull it apart.

The nurse came back, carrying a glass of chocolate milk.

"What's the matter, didn't you hear the buzzer?"

So I was released, set free by the barriers which now closed about Myra, her unknown, exalted, ether-smelling hospital world, and by the treachery of my own heart. "Well thank you," I said. "Thank you for the thing. Goodbye."

Did Myra ever say goodbye? Not likely. She sat in her high bed, her delicate brown neck, rising out of a hospital gown too big for her, her brown carved face immune to treachery, her offering perhaps already forgotten, prepared to be set apart for legendary uses, as she was even in the back porch at school.

QUESTIONS

1. A work's title will often guide us in discovering the theme of the work. What is the "day of the butterfly" in this story, and why is it significant?
2. Almost everything about the Saylas emphasizes their status as outsiders in the community. Find—and comment on—as many details as you can to support this viewpoint.
3. Discuss Gladys Healey (paragraph 9) as a *foil* to Myra (foils are characters whose personal attributes or situations are emphasized by the contrast between them).
4. What explanation does Helen give us for her friendliness toward Myra? Does the text suggest any other (perhaps unconscious) motivations?
5. Why does Helen tell Myra (paragraph 17) that her little brother is shy too?
6. Why does Miss Darling want to celebrate Myra's birthday in March? Why do you think this makes Helen angry?
7. How—and why—does Helen feel she has betrayed Myra at the end of the story?

Luke 15:11–32

THE PARABLE OF THE PRODIGAL SON   (Authorized or King James Version, 1611)

And he said, A certain man had two sons: And the younger of them said to his father, Father, give me the portion of goods that falleth to me. And he divided unto them his living. And not many days after the younger son gathered all together, and took his journey into a far country, and there wasted his substance with riotous living. And when he had spent all, there arose a mighty famine in that land; and he began to be in want. And he went and joined himself to a citizen of that country; and he sent him into his fields to feed swine. And he would fain have filled his belly with the husks that the swine did eat: and no man gave unto him. And when he came to himself, he said, How many hired servants of my father's have bread enough and to spare, and I perish with hunger! I will arise and go to my father, and will say unto him, Father I have sinned against heaven, and before thee, and am no more worthy to be called thy son;

make me as one of thy hired servants. And he arose, and came to his father. But when he was yet a great way off, his father saw him, and had compassion, and ran, and fell on his neck, and kissed him. And the son said unto him, Father I have sinned against heaven, and in thy sight, and am no more worthy to be called thy son. But the father said to his servants, Bring forth the best robe, and put it on him; and put a ring on his hand, and shoes on his feet: And bring hither the fatted calf, and kill it; and let us eat, and be merry: For this my son was dead, and is alive again; he was lost, and is found. And they began to be merry. Now his elder son was in the field: and he came and drew nigh to the house, he heard music and dancing. And he called one of the servants, and asked what these things meant. And he said unto him, Thy brother is come; and thy father hath killed the fatted calf, because he hath received him safe and sound. And he was angry, and would not go in: therefore came his father out, and entreated him. And he answering said to his father, Lo, these many years do I serve thee, neither transgressed I at any time thy commandment; and yet thou never gavest me a kid, that I might make merry with my friends: But as soon as this thy son was come, which hath devoured thy living with harlots, thou hast killed for him the fatted calf. And he said unto him, Son thou art ever with me, and all that I have is thine. It was meet that we should make merry, and be glad: for this thy brother was dead, and is alive again; and was lost, and is found.

QUESTIONS

1. This story has traditionally been called "The Parable of the Prodigal Son." What does *prodigal* mean? Which of the two brothers is prodigal?
2. What position does the younger son expect when he returns to his father's house? What does the father give him?
3. When the older brother sees the celebration for his younger brother's return, he gets angry. He makes a very reasonable set of complaints to his father. He has indeed been a loyal and moral son, but what virtue does the older brother lack?
4. Is the father fair to the elder son? Explain your answer.
5. Theologians have discussed this parable's religious significance for two thousand years. What, in your own words, is the human theme of the story?

Kurt Vonnegut, Jr.

HARRISON BERGERON   1961

Kurt Vonnegut, Jr. was born in Indianapolis in 1922. During the Depression his father, a well-to-do architect, had virtually no work, and the family lived in reduced circumstances. He attended Cornell University, where he studied sciences but also became managing editor for the daily student newspaper. In 1943 Vonnegut enlisted in the U.S. Army. During the Battle of the Bulge he was captured by German troops and interned as a prisoner of war in Dresden, where he survived the massive Allied firebombing, which killed over 130,000 people, mostly civilians. (The firebombing of Dresden became the central incident in Vonnegut's best-selling 1969 novel, Slaughterhouse Five.) After the war Vonnegut worked as a reporter and later as a public relations man for General Electric in Schenectady. After publishing several science fiction stories in national magazines, he quit his job in 1951 to write full-time. His first novel, Player Piano, *appeared in 1952, followed by* Sirens of Titan (1959), Mother Night (1962), *and his first best-seller,* Cat's Cradle (1963)—all *now considered classics of literary science fiction. Among his many later books are* Jailbird (1979), Bluebird (1987), Hocus Pocus (1990), Timequake (1997), *and* God Bless You, Dr. Kevorkian (2000). *His short fiction is collected in* Welcome to the Monkey House (1968) *and* Bagombo Snuff Box (1999). *He was named New York State Author for the period 2001–2003. Vonnegut is a singular figure in modern American fiction. An ingenious comic writer, he has combined the popular genre of science fiction with the literary tradition of dark satire—a combination splendidly realized in "Harrison Bergeron."*

The year was 2081, and everybody was finally equal. They weren't only equal before God and the law. They were equal every which way. Nobody was smarter than anybody else. Nobody was better looking than anybody else. Nobody was stronger or quicker than anybody else. All this equality was due to the 211th, 212th, and 213th Amendments to the Constitution, and to the unceasing vigilance of agents of the United States Handicapper General.

Some things about living still weren't quite right, though. April, for instance, still drove people crazy by not being springtime. And it was in that clammy month that the H-G men took George and Hazel Bergeron's fourteen-year-old son, Harrison, away.

It was tragic, all right, but George and Hazel couldn't think about it very hard. Hazel had a perfectly average intelligence, which meant she couldn't think about anything except in short bursts. And George, while his intelligence was way above normal, had a little mental handicap radio in his ear. He was required by law to wear it at all times. It was tuned to a government transmitter. Every twenty seconds or so, the transmitter would send out some sharp noise to keep people like George from taking unfair advantage of their brains.

George and Hazel were watching television. There were tears on Hazel's cheeks, but she'd forgotten for the moment what they were about.

On the television screen were ballerinas.   5

A buzzer sounded in George's head. His thoughts fled in panic, like bandits from a burglar alarm.

"That was a real pretty dance, that dance they just did," said Hazel.

"Huh?" said George.

"That dance—it was nice," said Hazel.

"Yup," said George. He tried to think a little about the ballerinas. They   10
weren't really very good—no better than anybody else would have been, anyway. They were burdened with sashweights and bags of birdshot, and their faces were masked, so that no one, seeing a free and graceful gesture or a pretty face, would feel like something the cat drug in. George was toying with the vague notion that maybe dancers shouldn't be handicapped. But he didn't get very far with it before another noise in his ear radio scattered his thoughts.

George winced. So did two out of the eight ballerinas.

Hazel saw him wince. Having no mental handicap herself, she had to ask George what the latest sound had been.

"Sounded like somebody hitting a milk bottle with a ball peen hammer," said George.

"I'd think it would be real interesting, hearing all the different sounds," said Hazel, a little envious. "All the things they think up."

"Um," said George.

"Only, if I was Handicapper General, you know what I would do?" said Hazel. Hazel, as a matter of fact, bore a strong resemblance to the Handicapper General, a woman named Diana Moon Glampers. "If I was Diana Moon Glampers," said Hazel, "I'd have chimes on Sunday—just chimes. Kind of in honor of religion."

"I could think, if it was just chimes," said George.

"Well—maybe make 'em real loud," said Hazel. "I think I'd make a good Handicapper General."

"Good as anybody else," said George.

"Who knows better'n I do what normal is?" said Hazel.

"Right," said George. He began to think glimmeringly about his abnormal son who was now in jail, about Harrison, but a twenty-one-gun salute in his head stopped that.

"Boy!" said Hazel, "that was a doozy, wasn't it?"

It was such a doozy that George was white and trembling, and tears stood on the rims of his red eyes. Two of the eight ballerinas had collapsed to the studio floor, were holding their temples.

"All of a sudden you look so tired," said Hazel. "Why don't you stretch out on the sofa, so's you can rest your handicap bag on the pillows, honeybunch." She was referring to the forty-seven pounds of birdshot in a canvas bag, which was padlocked around George's neck. "Go on and rest the bag for a little while," she said. "I don't care if you're not equal to me for a while."

George weighed the bag with his hands. "I don't mind it," he said. "I don't notice it any more. It's just a part of me."

"You been so tired lately—kind of wore out," said Hazel. "If there was just some way we could make a little hole in the bottom of the bag, and just take out a few of them lead balls. Just a few."

"Two years in prison and two thousand dollars fine for every ball I took out," said George. "I don't call that a bargain."

"If you could just take a few out when you came home from work," said Hazel. "I mean—you don't compete with anybody around here. You just set around."

"If I tried to get away with it," said George, "then other people'd get away with it—and pretty soon we'd be right back to the dark ages again, with everybody competing against everybody else. You wouldn't like that, would you?"

"I'd hate it," said Hazel.

"There you are," said George. "The minute people start cheating on laws, what do you think happens to society?"

If Hazel hadn't been able to come up with an answer to this question, George couldn't have supplied one. A siren was going off in his head.

"Reckon it'd fall all apart," said Hazel.

"What would?" said George blankly.

"Society," said Hazel uncertainly. "Wasn't that what you just said?"   35

"Who knows?" said George.

The television program was suddenly interrupted for a news bulletin. It wasn't clear at first as to what the bulletin was about, since the announcer, like all announcers, had a serious speech impediment. For about half a minute, and in a state of high excitement, the announcer tried to say, "Ladies and gentlemen—"

He finally gave up, handed the bulletin to a ballerina to read.

"That's all right—" Hazel said of the announcer, "he tried. That's the big thing. He tried to do the best he could with what God gave him. He should get a nice raise for trying so hard."

"Ladies and gentlemen—" said the ballerina, reading the bulletin. She must   40 have been extraordinarily beautiful, because the mask she wore was hideous. And it was easy to see that she was the strongest and most graceful of all the dancers, for her handicap bags were as big as those worn by two-hundred-pound men.

And she had to apologize at once for her voice, which was a very unfair voice for a woman to use. Her voice was a warm, luminous, timeless melody. "Excuse me—" she said, and she began again, making her voice absolutely uncompetitive.

"Harrison Bergeron, age fourteen," she said in a grackle squawk, "has just escaped from jail, where he was held on suspicion of plotting to overthrow the government. He is a genius and an athlete, is under-handicapped, and should be regarded as extremely dangerous."

A police photograph of Harrison Bergeron was flashed on the screen upside down, then sideways, upside down again, then right side up. The picture showed the full length of Harrison against a background calibrated in feet and inches. He was exactly seven feet tall.

The rest of Harrison's appearance was Halloween and hardware. Nobody had ever borne heavier handicaps. He had outgrown hindrances faster than the H-G men could think them up. Instead of a little ear radio for a mental handicap, he wore a tremendous pair of earphones, and spectacles with thick wavy lenses. The spectacles were intended to make him not only half blind, but to give him whanging headaches besides.

Scrap metal was hung all over him. Ordinarily, there was a certain symmetry,   45 a military neatness to the handicaps issued to strong people, but Harrison looked like a walking junkyard. In the race of life, Harrison carried three hundred pounds.

And to offset his good looks, the H-G men required that he wear at all times a red rubber ball for a nose, keep his eyebrows shaved off, and cover his even white teeth with black caps at snaggle-tooth random.

"If you see this boy," said the ballerina, "do not—I repeat, do not—try to reason with him."

There was the shriek of a door being torn from its hinges.

Screams and barking cries of consternation came from the television set. The photograph of Harrison Bergeron on the screen jumped again and again, as though dancing to the tune of an earthquake.

George Bergeron correctly identified the earthquake, and well he might   50
have—for many was the time his own home had danced to the same crashing
tune. "My God—" said George, "that must be Harrison!"

The realization was blasted from his mind instantly by the sound of an automobile collision in his head.

When George could open his eyes again, the photograph of Harrison was
gone. A living, breathing Harrison filled the screen.

Clanking, clownish, and huge, Harrison stood in the center of the studio. The
knob of the uprooted studio door was still in his hand. Ballerinas, technicians, musicians, and announcers cowered on their knees before him, expecting to die.

"I am the Emperor!" cried Harrison. "Do you hear? I am the Emperor! Everybody must do what I say at once!" He stamped his foot and the studio shook.

"Even as I stand here—" he bellowed, "crippled, hobbled, sickened—I am a   55
greater ruler than any man who ever lived! Now watch me become what I *can*
become!"

Harrison tore the straps of his handicap harness like wet tissue paper, tore
straps guaranteed to support five thousand pounds.

Harrison's scrap-iron handicaps crashed to the floor.

Harrison thrust his thumbs under the bar of the padlock that secured his
head harness. The bar snapped like celery. Harrison smashed his headphones
and spectacles against the wall.

He flung away his rubber-ball nose, revealed a man that would have awed
Thor, the god of thunder.

"I shall now select my Empress!" he said, looking down on the cowering   60
people. "Let the first woman who dares rise to her feet claim her mate and her
throne!"

A moment passed, and then a ballerina arose, swaying like a willow.

Harrison plucked the mental handicap from her ear, snapped off her physical handicaps with marvelous delicacy. Last of all, he removed her mask.

She was blindingly beautiful.

"Now—" said Harrison, taking her hand, "shall we show the people the
meaning of the word dance? Music!" he commanded.

The musicians scrambled back into their chairs, and Harrison stripped them   65
of their handicaps, too. "Play your best," he told them, "and I'll make you barons
and dukes and earls."

The music began. It was normal at first—cheap, silly, false. But Harrison
snatched two musicians from their chairs, waved them like batons as he sang the
music as he wanted it played. He slammed them back into their chairs.

The music began again and was much improved.

Harrison and his Empress merely listened to the music for a while—listened
gravely, as though synchronizing their heartbeats with it.

They shifted their weights to their toes.

Harrison placed his big hands on the girl's tiny waist, letting her sense the   70
weightlessness that would soon be hers.

And then, in an explosion of joy and grace, into the air they sprang!

Not only were the laws of the land abandoned, but the law of gravity and the laws of motion as well.

They reeled, whirled, swiveled, flounced, capered, gamboled, and spun.

They leaped like deer on the moon.

The studio ceiling was thirty feet high, but each leap brought the dancers   75
nearer to it.

It became their obvious intention to kiss the ceiling.

They kissed it.

And then, neutralizing gravity with love and pure will, they remained suspended in air inches below the ceiling, and they kissed each other for a long, long time.

It was then that Diana Moon Glampers, the Handicapper General, came into the studio with a double-barreled ten-gauge shotgun. She fired twice, and the Emperor and the Empress were dead before they hit the floor.

Diana Moon Glampers loaded the gun again. She aimed it at the musicians   80
and told them they had ten seconds to get their handicaps back on.

It was then that the Bergerons' television tube burned out.

Hazel turned to comment about the blackout to George. But George had gone out into the kitchen for a can of beer.

George came back in with the beer, paused while a handicap signal shook him up. And then he sat down again. "You been crying?" he said to Hazel.

"Yup," she said.

"What about?" he said.   85

"I forget," she said. "Something real sad on television."

"What was it?" he said.

"It's all kind of mixed up in my mind," said Hazel.

"Forget sad things," said George.

"I always do," said Hazel.   90

"That's my girl," said George. He winced. There was the sound of a rivetting gun in his head.

"Gee—I could tell that one was a doozy," said Hazel.

"You can say that again," said George.

"Gee—" said Hazel, "I could tell that one was a doozy."

QUESTIONS

1. What tendencies in present-day American society is Vonnegut satirizing? Does the story argue *for* anything? How would you sum up its theme?
2. Is Diana Moon Glampers a "flat" or a "round" character? (If you need to review these terms, see the discussion of character in Chapter Three and in the Glossary.) Would you call Vonnegut's characterization of her "realistic"? If not, why doesn't it need to be?
3. From what point of view is the story told? Why is it more effective than if Harrison Bergeron had told his own story in the first person?
4. Two sympathetic critics of Vonnegut's work, Karen and Charles Wood, have said of his stories: "Vonnegut proves repeatedly . . . that men and women remain fundamentally the same, no matter what technology surrounds them." Try applying this comment to "Harrison Bergeron." Do you agree?

5. Stanislaw Lem, Polish author of *Solaris* and other novels, once made this thoughtful criticism of many of his contemporaries among science fiction writers:

> The revolt against the machine and against civilization, the praise of the "aesthetic" nature of catastrophe, the dead-end course of human civilization—these are their foremost problems, the intellectual content of their works. Such SF is as it were *a priori* vitiated by pessimism, in the sense that anything that may happen will be for the worse. ("The Time-Travel Story and Related Matters of SF Structuring," *Science Fiction Studies* 1 [1974], 143–54.)

How might Lem's objection be raised against "Harrison Bergeron"? In your opinion, does it negate the value of Vonnegut's story?

WRITER'S PERSPECTIVE

Kurt Vonnegut, Jr.

Kurt Vonnegut, Jr., on Writing

THE THEMES OF SCIENCE FICTION   1971, 1973

INTERVIEWER: You talked a lot about the difficulties you had when you first began. For instance, I think you gave one of the reasons for using the science fiction form as the fact that you were a professional writer and had to do something which was popular.

VONNEGUT: In the beginning I was writing about what concerned me, and what was all around me was machinery. I myself had had some training in engineering and chemistry rather than in the arts and I was working for General Electric in a big factory city, Schenectady. So the first book I wrote was about Schenectady, which is full of machinery and engineers. And I was classified as a science fiction writer. Well, in the past, science fiction writers have been beneath the attention of any serious critic. That is, far above you are the people dealing with the really important, beautiful issues and using great skills and so forth. It used to be that if you were a science fiction writer you really didn't belong in the arts at all, and other artists wouldn't talk to you. You just had this scruffy little gang of your own.

. . . .

INTERVIEWER: What attracted you to using the form [of science fiction] yourself?

VONNEGUT: . . . I saw a milling machine for cutting the rotors on jet engines, gas turbines. This was a very expensive thing for a machinist to do, to cut what is essentially one of those Brancusi forms. So they had a computer-operated milling machine built to cut the blades, and I was fascinated by that. This was in 1949 and the guys who were working on it were foreseeing all sorts of machines being run by little boxes and punched cards. *Player Piano* was my response to the implications of having everything run by little boxes. The idea of doing that, you know, made sense, perfect sense. To have a little clicking box make all the decisions wasn't a vicious thing to do. But it was too bad for the human beings who got their dignity from their jobs.

INTERVIEWER: So science fiction seemed like the best way to write about your thoughts on the subject.

VONNEGUT: There was no avoiding it, since General Electric Company *was* science fiction.

From interviews with Laurie Clancy and David Standish

WRITING CRITICALLY

Stating the Theme

Finding the central theme of a story is only part of the challenge in writing about a work of fiction. It is also necessary to state the theme concisely and accurately in words. In a story we have read with understanding and enjoyment, we often recognize the major theme intuitively. But how do we express that often slightly vague recognition in clear language?

One method is to do a bit of freewriting. Rapidly jot down a list of everything you associate with the central point of the story. If you are discussing Stephen Crane's "The Open Boat," for example, you might write down a list like: "man against nature, life-and-death struggle, camaraderie of people in crisis, blindness of fate, courage in face of danger, bravery not enough." After completing your list, circle the two or three most important points and then try to combine them into a short sentence. For Crane, you might summarize the key point as: "The central theme of 'The Open Boat' is nature's indifference to the fate of even the most courageous individuals."

Once you have clearly and concisely stated the central theme, it will be easy to relate particular details of the story to it. If other elements do not demonstrate some connection to your theme, you might want to reevaluate your summation. Is there some important aspect you have missed? Or have you put some secondary idea into the theme? There is no shame in starting over. Recognizing our own mistakes is an important step in critical thinking.

Writing Assignment

Pick any story not found in this chapter and state, in your own words, its main theme. Then indicate what you find in the story that makes this theme clear. Some likely stories to discuss are "Barn Burning," "The Chrysanthemums," "I Stand Here Ironing," "Cathedral," and "Everyday Use."

Further Suggestions for Writing

1. Have you, like the narrator of "The Open Boat," ever been in physical danger? Not that your life needs to be a television thriller, but think and see what you can recall. What have you learned from your experience? Tell of it, comparing your memory with what Crane observes of people in danger, with what Crane's correspondent reporter notices within himself.

    Note: In a sense, you are sometimes in real danger from forces sometimes beyond your control (storms, criminals, terrorists, disease carriers). In a way, passively to face such ordinary perils may seem less heroic than rowing an open boat in a heaving sea. In another way—well, if you're looking for a danger to recall, you might think about this comparison. Reading Crane's story, do you feel that, in any sense, you and the news correspondent are in the same boat?

2. In "The Open Boat," recall the poem that comes to matter greatly to the correspondent (paragraphs 178–181). Have you ever been in a situation in which a story, an Aesop fable, a saying, a line of poetry, or a song lyric took on fresh and immediate meaning for you? If so, relate your experience. (If no such experience has befallen you, don't make one up.)

3. Does the relationship of Myra and Helen in "Day of the Butterfly" remind you of any relationship of your own in grade school? Which of the two characters more closely reflects your role in that relationship? Which of the two do you more closely identify with now?

4. Compare two stories similar in theme. Both Joyce in "Araby" and Sister in "Why I Live at the P.O." set forth a conflict between illusion and reality. Flannery O'Connor's "A Good Man Is Hard to Find" and "Revelation" show how, by the grace of God, an ordinary individual can receive enlightenment. Browse through other chapters and "Stories for Further Reading" (Chapter Eleven) and see what other pairs of stories go together in theme. Then set them side by side and point out their similarities and differences. This topic will lead you to compare and contrast, as discussed in the chapter "Writing About a Story" at the back of the book.

5. Here is a topic for science fiction fans: Trace a general theme in two or more science fiction novels or stories you know. Choose works that express similar views. Suggestion: If you know two science fiction writers who distrust the benefits of technology, or who take a keen interest in the future of women, look closely at their work and you will probably find an intriguing theme.

7 Symbol

In F. Scott Fitzgerald's novel *The Great Gatsby*, a huge pair of bespectacled eyes stares across a wilderness of ash heaps, from a billboard advertising the services of an oculist. Repeatedly entering into the story, the advertisement comes to mean more than simply the availability of eye examinations. Fitzgerald has a character liken it to the eyes of God; he hints that some sad, compassionate spirit is brooding as it watches the passing procession of humanity. Such an object is a **symbol:** in literature, a thing that suggests more than its literal meaning. Symbols generally do not "stand for" any one meaning, nor for anything absolutely definite; they point, they hint, or, as Henry James put it, they cast long shadows. To take a large example: in Herman Melville's *Moby-Dick*, the great white whale of the book's title apparently means more than the literal dictionary-definition meaning of an aquatic mammal. He also suggests more than the devil, to whom some of the characters liken him. The great whale, as the story unfolds, comes to imply an amplitude of meanings, among them the forces of nature and the whole created universe.

This indefinite multiplicity of meanings is characteristic of a symbolic story and distinguishes it from an **allegory,** a story in which persons, places, and things form a system of clearly labeled equivalents. In a simple allegory, characters and other elements often stand for other definite meanings, which are often abstractions. You will meet such a character in another story in this book, Nathaniel Hawthorne's "Young Goodman Brown." This tale's main female character, Faith, represents the religious virtue suggested by her name. Supreme allegories are found in some biblical parables ("The Kingdom of Heaven is like a man who sowed good seed in his field . . . ," Matthew 13:24–30). A classic allegory is the medieval play *Everyman*, whose hero represents us all, and who, deserted by false friends called Kindred and Goods, faces the judgment of God accompanied only by a faithful friend called Good Deeds. In John Bunyan's seventeenth-century allegory *Pilgrim's Progress*, the protagonist, Christian, struggles along the difficult road toward salvation, meeting along the way persons such as Mr. Worldly Wiseman, who directs him into a more comfortable path (a wrong turn), and the residents of a town called Fair Speech, among them a hypocrite named Mr. Facing-both-ways. Not all allegories are simple: Dante's *Divine Comedy*, written in the Middle Ages, continues to reveal new meanings to careful readers. Allegory was much beloved in the Middle Ages, but in contemporary fiction it is rare. One modern instance is George Orwell's long fable *Animal Farm*, in which (among its double meanings) barnyard animals stand for human victims and totalitarian oppressors.

Symbols in fiction are not generally abstract terms such as *love* or *truth*, but are likely to be perceptible objects (or worded descriptions that cause us to imagine them). In William Faulkner's "A Rose for Emily" (Chapter Two), Miss Emily's invisible watch ticking at the end of a golden chain not only indicates the passage of time, but also suggests that time passes without even being noticed by the watch's owner, and the golden chain carries suggestions of wealth and authority. Objects (and creatures) that seem insignificant in themselves can take on a symbolic importance in the larger context: in "Interpreter of Maladies" (Chapter Two) the piece of gum that Mrs. Das gives Mr. Kapasi—"As soon as Mr. Kapasi put the gum in his mouth a thick sweet liquid burst onto his tongue"—underscores her effect on his slumbering senses, as does his later comment on the wild monkeys: "They are more hungry than dangerous. . . . Do not provoke them with food, and they will not bother you." Often the symbols we meet in fiction are inanimate objects, but other things also may function symbolically. In James Joyce's "Araby" (Chapter Eleven), the very name of the bazaar, Araby—the poetic name for Arabia—suggests magic, romance, and *The Arabian Nights;* its syllables (the narrator tells us) "cast an Eastern enchantment over me." Even a locale, or a feature of physical topography, can provide rich suggestions. Recall Ernest Hemingway's "A Clean, Well-Lighted Place" (Chapter Five), in which the café is not merely a café, but an island of refuge from night, chaos, loneliness, old age, and impending death.

In some novels and stories, symbolic characters make brief cameo appearances. Such characters often are not well-rounded and fully known, but are seen fleetingly and remain slightly mysterious. In *Heart of Darkness,* a short novel by Joseph Conrad, a steamship company that hires men to work in the Congo maintains in its waiting room two women who knit black wool—like the classical Fates. Usually such a symbolic character is more a portrait than a person—or somewhat portraitlike, as Faulkner's Miss Emily, who twice appears at a window of her house "like the carven torso of an idol in a niche." Though Faulkner invests Miss Emily with life and vigor, he also clothes her in symbolic hints: she seems almost to personify the vanishing aristocracy of the antebellum South, still maintaining a black servant and being ruthlessly betrayed by a moneymaking Yankee. Sometimes a part of a character's body or an attribute may convey symbolic meaning: a baleful eye, as in Edgar Allan Poe's "The Tell-Tale Heart" (Chapter Ten).

Much as a symbolic whale holds more meaning than an ordinary whale, a **symbolic act** is a gesture with larger significance than usual. For the boy's father in Faulkner's "Barn Burning" (Chapter Five), the act of destroying a barn is no mere act of spite, but an expression of his profound hatred for anything not belonging to him. Faulkner adds that burning a barn reflects the father's memories of the "waste and extravagance of war," and further adds that "the element of fire spoke to some deep mainspring" in his being. A symbolic act, however, doesn't have to be a gesture as large as starting a conflagration. Before setting out in pursuit of the great white whale, Melville's Captain Ahab in *Moby-Dick* deliberately snaps his tobacco pipe and throws it away, as if to suggest (among other things) that he will let no pleasure or pastime distract him from his vengeance.

Why do writers have to symbolize—why don't they tell us outright? One advantage of a symbol is that it is so compact, and yet so fully laden. Both starkly concrete and slightly mysterious, like Miss Emily's invisible ticking watch, it may impress us with all the force of something beheld in a dream or in a nightmare. The watch suggests, among other things, the slow and invisible passage of time. What this symbol says, it says more fully and more memorably than could be said, perhaps, in a long essay on the subject.

To some extent (it may be claimed), all stories are symbolic. Merely by holding up for our inspection these characters and their actions, the writer lends them *some* special significance. But this is to think of *symbol* in an extremely broad and inclusive way. For the usual purposes of reading a story and understanding it, there is probably little point in looking for symbolism in every word, in every stick or stone, in every striking of a match, in every minor character. Still, to be on the alert for symbols when reading fiction is perhaps wiser than to ignore them. Not to admit that symbolic meanings may be present, or to refuse to think about them, would be another way to misread a story—or to read no further than its outer edges.

How, then, do you recognize a symbol in fiction when you meet it? Fortunately, the storyteller often gives the symbol particular emphasis. It may be mentioned repeatedly throughout the story; it may even supply the story with a title ("Barn Burning," "A Clean, Well-Lighted Place," "Araby"). At times, a crucial symbol will open a story or end it. Unless an object, act, or character is given some such special emphasis and importance, we may generally feel safe in taking it at face value. Probably it isn't a symbol if it points clearly and unmistakably toward some one meaning, like a whistle in a factory, whose blast at noon means lunch. But an object, an act, or a character is surely symbolic (and almost as surely displays high literary art) if, when we finish the story, we realize that it was that item—those gigantic eyes; that clean, well-lighted café; that burning of a barn—which led us to the author's theme, the essential meaning.

John Steinbeck

THE CHRYSANTHEMUMS   1938

John Steinbeck (1902–1968) was born in Salinas, California, in the fertile valley he remembers in "The Chrysanthemums." Off and on, he attended Stanford University, then sojourned in New York as a reporter and a bricklayer. After years of struggle to earn his living by fiction, Steinbeck reached a large audience with Tortilla Flat *(1935), a loosely woven novel portraying Mexican Americans in Monterey with fondness and sympathy. Great acclaim greeted* The Grapes of Wrath *(1939), the story of a family of Oklahoma farmers who, ruined by dust storms in the 1930s, join a mass migration to California. Like Ernest Hemingway and Stephen Crane, Steinbeck prided himself on his journalism: in World War II, he filed dispatches from* John Steinbeck *battlefronts in Italy and Africa, and in 1966 he wrote a column from South Vietnam.*

Known widely behind the Iron Curtain, Steinbeck accepted an invitation to visit the Soviet Union, and reported on his trip in A Russian Journal *(1948). In 1962 he became the seventh American to win the Nobel Prize for literature, but critics have never placed Steinbeck on the same high shelf with Faulkner and Hemingway. He wrote much, not all good, and yet his best work adds to an impressive total. Besides* The Grapes of Wrath, *it includes* In Dubious Battle *(1936), a novel of an apple-pickers' strike;* Of Mice and Men *(1937), a powerful short novel (also a play) of comradeship between a hobo and a retarded man;* The Log from the Sea of Cortez *(1951), a nonfiction account of a marine biological expedition; and the short stories in* The Long Valley *(1938). Throughout the fiction he wrote in his prime, Steinbeck maintains an appealing sympathy for the poor and downtrodden, the lonely and dispossessed.*

The high grey-flannel fog of winter closed off the Salinas Valley° from the sky and from all the rest of the world. On every side it sat like a lid on the mountains and made of the great valley a closed pot. On the broad, level land floor the gang plows bit deep and left the black earth shining like metal where the shares had cut. On the foothill ranches across the Salinas River, the yellow stubble fields seemed to be bathed in pale cold sunshine, but there was no sunshine in the valley now in December. The thick willow scrub along the river flamed with sharp and positive yellow leaves.

It was a time of quiet and of waiting. The air was cold and tender. A light wind blew up from the southwest so that the farmers were mildly hopeful of a good rain before long; but fog and rain do not go together.

Across the river, on Henry Allen's foothill ranch there was little work to be done, for the hay was cut and stored and the orchards were plowed up to receive the rain deeply when it should come. The cattle on the higher slopes were becoming shaggy and rough-coated.

Elisa Allen, working in her flower garden, looked down across the yard and saw Henry, her husband, talking to two men in business suits. The three of them stood by the tractor shed, each man with one foot on the side of the little Fordson. They smoked cigarettes and studied the machine as they talked.

Elisa watched them for a moment and then went back to her work. She was 5 thirty-five. Her face was lean and strong and her eyes were as clear as water. Her figure looked blocked and heavy in her gardening costume, a man's black hat pulled low down over her eyes, clod-hopper shoes, a figured print dress almost completely covered by a big corduroy apron with four big pockets to hold the snips, the trowel and scratcher, the seeds and the knife she worked with. She wore heavy leather gloves to protect her hands while she worked.

She was cutting down the old year's chrysanthemum stalks with a pair of short and powerful scissors. She looked down toward the men by the tractor shed now and then. Her face was eager and mature and handsome; even her work with the scissors was over-eager, over-powerful. The chrysanthemum stems seemed too small and easy for her energy.

She brushed a cloud of hair out of her eyes with the back of her glove, and left a smudge of earth on her cheek in doing it. Behind her stood the neat white

Salinas Valley: south of San Francisco in the Coast Ranges region of California.

farm house with red geraniums close-banked around it as high as the windows. It was a hard-swept looking little house with hard-polished windows, and a clean mud-mat on the front steps.

Elisa cast another glance toward the tractor shed. The strangers were getting into their Ford coupe. She took off a glove and put her strong fingers down into the forest of new green chrysanthemum sprouts that were growing around the old roots. She spread the leaves and looked down among the close-growing stems. No aphids were there, no sowbugs or snails or cutworms. Her terrier fingers destroyed such pests before they could get started.

Elisa started at the sound of her husband's voice. He had come near quietly, and he leaned over the wire fence that protected her flower garden from cattle and dogs and chickens.

"At it again," he said. "You've got a strong new crop coming."   10

Elisa straightened her back and pulled on the gardening glove again. "Yes. They'll be strong this coming year." In her tone and on her face there was a little smugness.

"You've got a gift with things," Henry observed. "Some of those yellow chrysanthemums you had this year were ten inches across. I wish you'd work out in the orchard and raise some apples that big."

Her eyes sharpened. "Maybe I could do it, too. I've a gift with things, all right. My mother had it. She could stick anything in the ground and make it grow. She said it was having planters' hands that knew how to do it."

"Well, it sure works with flowers," he said.

"Henry, who were those men you were talking to?"   15

"Why, sure, that's what I came to tell you. They were from the Western Meat Company. I sold those thirty head of three-year-old steers. Got nearly my own price, too."

"Good," she said. "Good for you."

"And I thought," he continued, "I thought how it's Saturday afternoon, and we might go into Salinas for dinner at a restaurant, and then to a picture show— to celebrate, you see."

"Good," she repeated. "Oh, yes. That will be good."

Henry put on his joking tone. "There's fights tonight. How'd you like to go   20 to the fights?"

"Oh, no," she said breathlessly. "No, I wouldn't like fights."

"Just fooling, Elisa. We'll go to a movie. Let's see. It's two now. I'm going to take Scotty and bring down those steers from the hill. It'll take us maybe two hours. We'll go in town about five and have dinner at the Cominos Hotel. Like that?"

"Of course I'll like it. It's good to eat away from home."

"All right, then. I'll go get up a couple of horses."

She said, "I'll have plenty of time to transplant some of these sets, I guess."   25

She heard her husband calling Scotty down by the barn. And a little later she saw the two men ride up the pale yellow hillside in search of the steers.

There was a little square sandy bed kept for rooting the chrysanthemums. With her trowel she turned the soil over and over, and smoothed it and patted it firm. Then she dug ten parallel trenches to receive the sets. Back at the chrysan-themum bed she pulled out the little crisp shoots, trimmed off the leaves of each one with her scissors and laid it on a small orderly pile.

A squeak of wheels and plod of hoofs came from the road. Elisa looked up. The country road ran along the dense bank of willows and cottonwoods that bordered the river, and up this road came a curious vehicle, curiously drawn. It was an old spring-wagon, with a round canvas top on it like the cover of a prairie schooner. It was drawn by an old bay horse and a little grey-and-white burro. A big stubble-bearded man sat between the cover flaps and drove the crawling team. Underneath the wagon, between the hind wheels, a lean and rangy mon-grel dog walked sedately. Words were painted on the canvas, in clumsy, crooked letters. "Pots, pans, knives, sisors, lawn mores, Fixed." Two rows of articles, and the triumphantly definitive "Fixed" below. The black paint had run down in little sharp points beneath each letter.

Elisa, squatting on the ground, watched to see the crazy, loose-jointed wagon pass by. But it didn't pass. It turned into the farm road in front of her house, crooked old wheels skirling and squeaking. The rangy dog darted from be-tween the wheels and ran ahead. Instantly the two ranch shepherds flew out at him. Then all three stopped, and with stiff and quivering tails, with taut straight legs, with ambassadorial dignity, they slowly circled, sniffing daintily. The car-avan pulled up to Elisa's wire fence and stopped. Now the newcomer dog, feeling out-numbered, lowered his tail and retired under the wagon with raised hackles and bared teeth.

The man on the wagon seat called out, "That's a bad dog in a fight when he gets started."   30

Elisa laughed. "I see he is. How soon does he generally get started?"

The man caught up her laughter and echoed it heartily. "Sometimes not for weeks and weeks," he said. He climbed stiffly down, over the wheel. The horse and the donkey drooped like unwatered flowers.

Elisa saw that he was a very big man. Although his hair and beard were greying, he did not look old. His worn black suit was wrinkled and spotted with grease. The laughter had disappeared from his face and eyes the moment his laughing voice ceased. His eyes were dark, and they were full of the brooding that gets in the eyes of teamsters and of sailors. The calloused hands he rested on the wire fence were cracked, and every crack was a black line. He took off his battered hat.

"I'm off my general road, ma'am," he said. "Does this dirt road cut over across the river to the Los Angeles highway?"

Elisa stood up and shoved the thick scissors in her apron pocket. "Well, yes,   35
it does, but it winds around and then fords the river. I don't think your team could pull through the sand."

He replied with some asperity. "It might surprise you what them beasts can pull through."

"When they get started?" she asked.

He smiled for a second. "Yes. When they get started."

"Well," said Elisa, "I think you'll save time if you go back to the Salinas road and pick up the highway there."

He drew a big finger down the chicken wire and made it sing. "I ain't in any hurry, ma'am. I go from Seattle to San Diego and back every year. Takes all my time. About six months each way. I aim to follow nice weather."

Elisa took off her gloves and stuffed them in the apron pocket with the scissors. She touched the under edge of her man's hat, searching for fugitive hairs. "That sounds like a nice kind of a way to live," she said.

He leaned confidentially over the fence. "Maybe you noticed the writing on my wagon. I mend pots and sharpen knives and scissors. You got any of them things to do?"

"Oh, no," she said quickly. "Nothing like that." Her eyes hardened with resistance.

"Scissors is the worst thing," he explained. "Most people just ruin scissors trying to sharpen 'em, but I know how. I got a special tool. It's a little bobbit kind of thing, and patented. But it sure does the trick."

"No. My scissors are all sharp."

"All right, then. Take a pot," he continued earnestly, "a bent pot, or a pot with a hole. I can make it like new so you don't have to buy no new ones. That's a saving for you."

"No," she said shortly. "I tell you I have nothing like that for you to do."

His face fell to an exaggerated sadness. His voice took on a whining undertone. "I ain't had a thing to do today. Maybe I won't have no supper tonight. You see I'm off my regular road. I know folks on the highway clear from Seattle to San Diego. They save their things for me to sharpen up because they know I do it so good and save them money."

"I'm sorry," Elisa said irritably. "I haven't anything for you to do."

His eyes left her face and fell to searching the ground. They roamed about until they came to the chrysanthemum bed where she had been working. "What's them plants, ma'am?"

The irritation and resistance melted from Elisa's face. "Oh, those are chrysanthemums, giant whites and yellows. I raise them every year, bigger than anybody around here."

"Kind of a long-stemmed flower? Looks like a quick puff of colored smoke?" he asked.

"That's it. What a nice way to describe them."

"They smell kind of nasty till you get used to them," he said.

"It's a good bitter smell," she retorted, "not nasty at all."

He changed his tone quickly. "I like the smell myself."

"I had ten-inch blooms this year," she said.

The man leaned farther over the fence. "Look. I know a lady down the road a piece, has got the nicest garden you ever seen. Got nearly every kind of flower but no chrysanthemums. Last time I was mending a copper-bottom washtub for her (that's a hard job but I do it good), she said to me, 'If you ever run acrost some nice chrysanthemums I wish you'd try to get me a few seeds.' That's what she told me."

Elisa's eyes grew alert and eager. "She couldn't have known much about chrysanthemums. You *can* raise them from seed, but it's much easier to root the little sprouts you see there."

"Oh," he said. "I s'pose I can't take none to her, then." 60

"Why yes you can," Elisa cried. "I can put some in damp sand, and you can carry them right along with you. They'll take root in the pot if you keep them damp. And then she can transplant them."

"She'd sure like to have some, ma'am. You say they're nice ones?"

"Beautiful," she said. "Oh, beautiful." Her eyes shone. She tore off the battered hat and shook out her dark pretty hair. "I'll put them in a flower pot, and you can take them right with you. Come into the yard."

While the man came through the picket gate Elisa ran excitedly along the geranium-bordered path to the back of the house. And she returned carrying a big red flower pot. The gloves were forgotten now. She kneeled on the ground by the starting bed and dug up the sandy soil with her fingers and scooped it into the bright new flower pot. Then she picked up the little pile of shoots she had prepared. With her strong fingers she pressed them in the sand and tamped around them with her knuckles. The man stood over her. "I'll tell you what to do," she said. "You remember so you can tell the lady."

"Yes, I'll try to remember." 65

"Well, look. These will take root in about a month. Then she must set them out, about a foot apart in good rich earth like this, see?" She lifted a handful of dark soil for him to look at. "They'll grow fast and tall. Now remember this: In July tell her to cut them down, about eight inches from the ground."

"Before they bloom?" he asked.

"Yes, before they bloom." Her face was tight with eagerness. "They'll grow right up again. About the last of September the buds will start."

She stopped and seemed perplexed. "It's the budding that takes the most care," she said hesitantly. "I don't know how to tell you." She looked deep into his eyes, searchingly. Her mouth opened a little, and she seemed to be listening. "I'll try to tell you," she said. "Did you ever hear of planting hands?"

"Can't say I have, ma'am." 70

"Well, I can only tell you what it feels like. It's when you're picking off the buds you don't want. Everything goes right down into your fingertips. You watch your fingers work. They do it themselves. You can feel how it is. They pick and pick the buds. They never make a mistake. They're with the plant. Do you see? Your fingers and the plant. You can feel that, right up your arm. They know. They never make a mistake. You can feel it. When you're like that you can't do anything wrong. Do you see that? Can you understand that?"

She was kneeling on the ground looking up at him. Her breast swelled passionately.

The man's eyes narrowed. He looked away self-consciously. "Maybe I know," he said. "Sometimes in the night in the wagon there—"

Elisa's voice grew husky. She broke in on him, "I've never lived as you do, but I know what you mean. When the night is dark—why, the stars are sharp-pointed, and there's quiet. Why, you rise up and up! Every pointed star gets driven into your body. It's like that. Hot and sharp and—lovely."

Kneeling there, her hand went out toward his legs in the greasy black 75 trousers. Her hesitant fingers almost touched the cloth. Then her hand dropped to the ground. She crouched low like a fawning dog.

He said, "It's nice, just like you say. Only when you don't have no dinner, it ain't."

She stood up then, very straight, and her face was ashamed. She held the flower pot out to him and placed it gently in his arms. "Here. Put it in your wagon, on the seat, where you can watch it. Maybe I can find something for you to do."

At the back of the house she dug in the can pile and found two old and battered aluminum saucepans. She carried them back and gave them to him. "Here, maybe you can fix these."

His manner changed. He became professional. "Good as new I can fix them." At the back of his wagon he set a little anvil, and out of an oily tool box dug a small machine hammer. Elisa came through the gate to watch him while he pounded out the dents in the kettles. His mouth grew sure and knowing. At a difficult part of the work he sucked his under-lip.

"You sleep right in the wagon?" Elisa asked. 80

"Right in the wagon, ma'am. Rain or shine I'm dry as a cow in there."

"It must be nice," she said. "It must be very nice. I wish women could do such things."

"It ain't the right kind of a life for a woman."

Her upper lip raised a little, showing her teeth. "How do you know? How can you tell?" she said.

"I don't know, ma'am," he protested. "Of course I don't know. Now here's 85 your kettles, done. You don't have to buy no new ones."

"How much?"

"Oh, fifty cents'll do. I keep my prices down and my work good. That's why I have all them satisfied customers up and down the highway."

Elisa brought him a fifty-cent piece from the house and dropped it in his hand. "You might be surprised to have a rival some time. I can sharpen scissors, too. And I can beat the dents out of little pots. I could show you what a woman might do."

He put his hammer back in the oily box and shoved the little anvil out of sight. "It would be a lonely life for a woman, ma'am, and a scarey life, too, with animals creeping under the wagon all night." He climbed over the singletree, steadying himself with a hand on the burro's white rump. He settled himself in the seat, picked up the lines. "Thank you kindly, ma'am," he said. "I'll do like you told me; I'll go back and catch the Salinas road."

"Mind," she called, "if you're long in getting there, keep the sand damp." 90

"Sand, ma'am? . . . Sand? Oh, sure. You mean around the chrysanthemums. Sure I will." He clucked his tongue. The beasts leaned luxuriously into their collars. The mongrel dog took his place between the back wheels. The wagon turned and crawled out the entrance road and back the way it had come, along the river.

Elisa stood in front of her wire fence watching the slow progress of the caravan. Her shoulders were straight, her head thrown back, her eyes half-closed, so that the scene came vaguely into them. Her lips moved silently, forming the words "Good-bye—good-bye." Then she whispered, "That's a bright direction. There's a glowing there." The sound of her whisper startled her. She shook herself free and looked about to see whether anyone had been listening. Only the dogs had heard. They lifted their heads toward her from their sleeping in the dust, and then stretched out their chins and settled asleep again. Elisa turned and ran hurriedly into the house.

In the kitchen she reached behind the stove and felt the water tank. It was full of hot water from the noonday cooking. In the bathroom she tore off her soiled clothes and flung them into the corner. And then she scrubbed herself with a little block of pumice, legs and thighs, loins and chest and arms, until her skin was scratched and red. When she had dried herself she stood in front of a mirror in her bedroom and looked at her body. She tightened her stomach and threw out her chest. She turned and looked over her shoulder at her back.

After a while she began to dress, slowly. She put on her newest underclothing and her nicest stockings and the dress which was the symbol of her prettiness. She worked carefully on her hair, penciled her eyebrows and rouged her lips.

Before she was finished she heard the little thunder of hoofs and the shouts 95
of Henry and his helper as they drove the red steers into the corral. She heard the gate bang shut and set herself for Henry's arrival.

His step sounded on the porch. He entered the house calling, "Elisa, where are you?"

"In my room, dressing. I'm not ready. There's hot water for your bath. Hurry up. It's getting late."

When she heard him splashing in the tub, Elisa laid his dark suit on the bed, and shirt and socks and tie beside it. She stood his polished shoes on the floor beside the bed. Then she went to the porch and sat primly and stiffly down. She looked toward the river road where the willow-line was still yellow with frosted leaves so that under the high grey fog they seemed a thin band of sunshine. This was the only color in the grey afternoon. She sat unmoving for a long time. Her eyes blinked rarely.

Henry came banging out of the door, shoving his tie inside his vest as he came. Elisa stiffened and her face grew tight. Henry stopped short and looked at her. "Why—why, Elisa. You look so nice!"

"Nice? You think I look nice? What do you mean by 'nice'?" 100

Henry blundered on. "I don't know. I mean you look different, strong and happy."

"I am strong? Yes, strong. What do you mean 'strong'?"

He looked bewildered. "You're playing some kind of a game," he said help-lessly. "It's a kind of a play. You look strong enough to break a calf over your knee, happy enough to eat it like a watermelon."

For a second she lost her rigidity. "Henry! Don't talk like that. You didn't know what you said." She grew complete again. "I'm strong," she boasted. "I never knew before how strong."

Henry looked down toward the tractor shed, and when he brought his eyes back to her, they were his own again. "I'll get out the car. You can put on your coat while I'm starting." 105

Elisa went into the house. She heard him drive to the gate and idle down his motor, and then she took a long time to put on her hat. She pulled it here and pressed it there. When Henry turned the motor off she slipped into her coat and went out.

The little roadster bounced along on the dirt road by the river, raising the birds and driving the rabbits into the brush. Two cranes flapped heavily over the willow-line and dropped into the river-bed.

Far ahead on the road Elisa saw a dark speck. She knew.

She tried not to look as they passed it, but her eyes would not obey. She whispered to herself sadly, "He might have thrown them off the road. That wouldn't have been much trouble, not very much. But he kept the pot," she ex-plained. "He had to keep the pot. That's why he couldn't get them off the road."

The roadster turned a bend and she saw the caravan ahead. She swung full around toward her husband so she could not see the little covered wagon and the mismatched team as the car passed them. 110

In a moment it was over. The thing was done. She did not look back.

She said loudly, to be heard above the motor, "It will be good, tonight, a good dinner."

"Now you're changed again," Henry complained. He took one hand from the wheel and patted her knee. "I ought to take you in to dinner oftener. It would be good for both of us. We get so heavy out on the ranch."

"Henry," she asked, "could we have wine at dinner?"

"Sure we could. Say! That will be fine." 115

She was silent for a while; then she said, "Henry, at those prize fights, do the men hurt each other very much?"

"Sometimes a little, not often. Why?"

"Well, I've read how they break noses, and blood runs down their chests. I've read how the fighting gloves get heavy and soggy with blood."

He looked around at her. "What's the matter, Elisa? I didn't know you read things like that." He brought the car to a stop, then turned to the right over the Salinas River bridge.

"Do any women ever go to the fights?" she asked. 120

"Oh, sure, some. What's the matter, Elisa? Do you want to go? I don't think you'd like it, but I'll take you if you really want to go."

She relaxed limply in the seat. "Oh, no. No. I don't want to go. I'm sure I don't." Her face was turned away from him. "It will be enough if we can have wine. It will be plenty." She turned up her coat collar so he could not see that she was crying weakly—like an old woman.

QUESTIONS

1. When we first meet Elisa in her garden, with what details does Steinbeck delineate her character for us?
2. Elisa works inside a "wire fence that protected her flower garden from cattle and dogs and chickens" (paragraph 9). What does this wire fence suggest?
3. How would you describe Henry and Elisa's marriage? Cite details from the story.
4. For what motive does the traveling salesman take an interest in Elisa's chrysanthemums? What immediate effect does his interest have on Elisa?
5. For what possible purpose does Steinbeck give us such a detailed account of Elisa's preparations for her evening out? Notice her tearing off her soiled clothes, her scrubbing her body with pumice (paragraphs 93–94).
6. Of what significance to Elisa is the sight of the contents of the flower pot discarded in the road? Notice that, as her husband's car overtakes the covered wagon, Elisa averts her eyes; and then Steinbeck adds, "In a moment it was over. The thing was done. She did not look back" (paragraph 111). Explain this passage.
7. How do you interpret Elisa's asking for wine with dinner? How do you account for her new interest in prizefights?
8. In a sentence, try to state this short story's theme.
9. Why are Elisa Allen's chrysanthemums so important to this story? Sum up what you understand them to mean.

Shirley Jackson

THE LOTTERY   1948

*Shirley Jackson (1919–1965), a native of San Francisco, moved in her teens to Rochester, New York. She started college at the University of Rochester, but had to drop out, stricken by severe depression, a problem that was to recur at intervals throughout her life. Later she graduated from Syracuse University. With her husband Stanley Edgar Hyman, a literary critic, she settled in Bennington, Vermont, in a sprawling house built in the nineteenth century. There Jackson conscientiously set herself to produce a fixed number of words each day. She wrote novels—*The Road Through the Wall *(1948)—and three psychological thrillers—*

Shirley Jackson

Hangsaman *(1951),* The Haunting of Hill House *(1959), and* We Have Always Lived in the Castle *(1962). She wrote light, witty articles for* Good Housekeeping *and other popular magazines about the horrors of housekeeping and rearing four children, collected in* Life Among the Savages *(1953) and* Raising Demons *(1957); but she claimed to have written these only for money. When "The Lottery" appeared in the New Yorker in 1948, that issue of the magazine quickly sold out. Her purpose in writing the story, Jackson declared, had been "to shock the story's readers with a graphic demonstration of the pointless violence and general inhumanity in their own lives."*

The morning of June 27th was clear and sunny, with the fresh warmth of a full-summer day; the flowers were blossoming profusely and the grass was richly green. The people of the village began to gather in the square, between the post office and the bank, around ten o'clock; in some towns there were so many people that the lottery took two days and had to be started on June 26th, but in this village, where there were only about three hundred people, the whole lottery took less than two hours, so it could begin at ten o'clock in the morning and still be through in time to allow the villagers to get home for noon dinner.

The children assembled first, of course. School was recently over for the summer, and the feeling of liberty sat uneasily on most of them; they tended to gather together quietly for a while before they broke into boisterous play, and their talk was still of the classroom and the teacher, of books and reprimands. Bobby Martin had already stuffed his pockets full of stones, and the other boys soon followed his example, selecting the smoothest and roundest stones; Bobby and Harry Jones and Dickie Delacroix—the villagers pronounced this name "Dellacroy"—eventually made a great pile of stones in one corner of the square and guarded it against the raids of the other boys. The girls stood aside, talking among themselves, looking over their shoulders at the boys, and the very small children rolled in the dust or clung to the hands of their older brothers or sisters.

Soon the men began to gather, surveying their own children, speaking of planting and rain, tractors and taxes. They stood together, away from the pile of stones in the corner, and their jokes were quiet and they smiled rather than laughed. The women, wearing faded house dresses and sweaters, came shortly after their menfolk. They greeted one another and exchanged bits of gossip as they went to join their husbands. Soon the women, standing by their husbands, began to call to their children, and the children came reluctantly, having to be called four or five times. Bobby Martin ducked under his mother's grasping hand and ran, laughing, back to the pile of stones. His father spoke up sharply, and Bobby came quickly and took his place between his father and his oldest brother.

The lottery was conducted—as were the square dances, the teenage club, the Halloween program—by Mr. Summers, who had time and energy to devote to civic activities. He was a roundfaced, jovial man and he ran the coal business, and people were sorry for him, because he had no children and his wife was a scold. When he arrived in the square, carrying the black wooden box, there was a murmur of conversation among the villagers and he waved and called, "Little late today, folks." The postmaster, Mr. Graves, followed him, carrying a three-legged stool, and the stool was put in the center of the square and Mr. Summers set the black box down on it. The villagers kept their distance, leaving a space between themselves and the stool, and when Mr. Summers said, "Some of you fellows want to give me a hand?" there was a hesitation before two men, Mr.

Martin and his oldest son, Baxter, came forward to hold the box steady on the stool while Mr. Summers stirred up the papers inside it.

The original paraphernalia for the lottery had been lost long ago, and the 5 black box now resting on the stool had been put into use even before Old Man Warner, the oldest man in town, was born. Mr. Summers spoke frequently to the villagers about making a new box, but no one liked to upset even as much tradition as was represented by the black box. There was a story that the present box had been made with some pieces of the box that had preceded it, the one that had been constructed when the first people settled down to make a village here. Every year, after the lottery, Mr. Summers began talking again about a new box, but every year the subject was allowed to fade off without anything's being done. The black box grew shabbier each year; by now it was no longer completely black but splintered badly along one side to show the original wood color, and in some places faded or stained.

Mr. Martin and his oldest son, Baxter, held the black box securely on the stool until Mr. Summers had stirred the papers thoroughly with his hand. Because so much of the ritual had been forgotten or discarded, Mr. Summers had been successful in having slips of paper substituted for the chips of wood that had been used for generations. Chips of wood, Mr. Summers had argued, had been all very well when the village was tiny, but now that the population was more than three hundred and likely to keep on growing, it was necessary to use something that would fit more easily into the black box. The night before the lottery, Mr. Summers and Mr. Graves made up the slips of paper and put them in the box, and it was then taken to the safe of Mr. Summers's coal company and locked up until Mr. Summers was ready to take it to the square next morning. The rest of the year, the box was put away, sometimes one place, sometimes another; it had spent one year in Mr. Graves's barn and another year underfoot in the post office, and sometimes it was set on a shelf in the Martin grocery and left there.

There was a great deal of fussing to be done before Mr. Summers declared the lottery open. There were lists to make up—of heads of families, heads of households in each family, members of each household in each family. There was the proper swearing-in of Mr. Summers by the postmaster, as the official of the lottery; at one time, some people remembered, there had been a recital of some sort, performed by the official of the lottery, a perfunctory, tuneless chant that had been rattled off duly each year; some people believed that the official of the lottery used to stand just so when he said or sang it, others believed that he was supposed to walk among the people, but years and years ago this part of the ritual had been allowed to lapse. There had been, also, a ritual salute, which the official of the lottery had had to use in addressing each person who came up to draw from the box, but this also had changed with time, until now it was felt necessary only for the official to speak to each person approaching. Mr. Summers was very good at all this; in his clean white shirt and blue jeans, with one hand resting carelessly on the black box, he seemed very proper and important as he talked interminably to Mr. Graves and the Martins.

Just as Mr. Summers finally left off talking and turned to the assembled villagers, Mrs. Hutchinson came hurriedly along the path to the square, her sweater thrown over her shoulders, and slid into place in the back of the crowd. "Clean forgot what day it was," she said to Mrs. Delacroix, who stood next to her, and they both laughed softly. "Thought my old man was out back stacking wood," Mrs. Hutchinson went on, "and then I looked out the window and the kids were gone, and then I remembered it was the twenty-seventh and came a-running." She dried her hands on her apron, and Mrs. Delacroix said, "You're in time, though. They're still talking away up there."

Mrs. Hutchinson craned her neck to see through the crowd and found her husband and children standing near the front. She tapped Mrs. Delacroix on the arm as a farewell and began to make her way through the crowd. The people separated good-humoredly to let her through; two or three people said, in voices just loud enough to be heard across the crowd, "Here comes your Missus, Hutchinson," and "Bill, she made it after all." Mrs. Hutchinson reached her husband, and Mr. Summers, who had been waiting, said cheerfully, "Thought we were going to have to get on without you, Tessie." Mrs. Hutchinson said, grinning, "Wouldn't have me leave m'dishes in the sink, now would you, Joe?" and soft laughter ran through the crowd as the people stirred back into position after Mrs. Hutchinson's arrival.

"Well, now," Mr. Summers said soberly, "guess we better get started, get this 10
over with, so's we can go back to work. Anybody ain't here?"

"Dunbar," several people said. "Dunbar, Dunbar."

Mr. Summers consulted his list. "Clyde Dunbar," he said. "That's right. He's broke his leg, hasn't he? Who's drawing for him?"

"Me, I guess," a woman said, and Mr. Summers turned to look at her. "Wife draws for her husband," Mr. Summers said. "Don't you have a grown boy to do it for you, Janey?" Although Mr. Summers and everyone else in the village knew the answer perfectly well, it was the business of the official of the lottery to ask such questions formally. Mr. Summers waited with an expression of polite interest while Mrs. Dunbar answered.

"Horace's not but sixteen yet," Mrs. Dunbar said regretfully. "Guess I gotta fill in for the old man this year."

"Right," Mr. Summers said. He made a note on the list he was holding. 15
Then he asked, "Watson boy drawing this year?"

A tall boy in the crowd raised his hand. "Here," he said. "I'm drawing for m'mother and me." He blinked his eyes nervously and ducked his head as several voices in the crowd said things like "Good fellow, Jack," and "Glad to see your mother's got a man to do it."

"Well," Mr. Summers said, "guess that's everyone. Old Man Warner make it?"

"Here," a voice said, and Mr. Summers nodded.

A sudden hush fell on the crowd as Mr. Summers cleared his throat and looked at the list. "All ready?" he called. "Now, I'll read the names—heads of families first—and the men come up and take a paper out of the box. Keep the paper folded in your hand without looking at it until everyone has had a turn. Everything clear?"

The people had done it so many times that they only half listened to the di- 20
rections; most of them were quiet, wetting their lips, not looking around. Then Mr. Summers raised one hand high and said, "Adams." A man disengaged himself

from the crowd and came forward. "Hi, Steve," Mr. Summers said, and Mr. Adams said, "Hi, Joe." They grinned at one another humorlessly and nervously. Then Mr. Adams reached into the black box and took out a folded paper. He held it firmly by one corner as he turned and went hastily back to his place in the crowd, where he stood a little apart from his family, not looking down at his hand.

"Allen," Mr. Summers said. "Anderson. . . . Bentham."

"Seems like there's no time at all between lotteries any more," Mrs. Delacroix said to Mrs. Graves in the back row. "Seems like we got through with the last one only last week."

"Time sure goes fast," Mrs. Graves said.

"Clark. . . . Delacroix."

"There goes my old man," Mrs. Delacroix said. She held her breath while 25 her husband went forward.

"Dunbar," Mr. Summers said, and Mrs. Dunbar went steadily to the box while one of the women said, "Go on, Janey," and another said, "There she goes."

"We're next," Mrs. Graves said. She watched while Mr. Graves came around from the side of the box, greeted Mr. Summers gravely, and selected a slip of paper from the box. By now, all through the crowd there were men holding the small folded papers in their large hands, turning them over and over nervously. Mrs. Dunbar and her two sons stood together, Mrs. Dunbar holding the slip of paper.

"Harburt. . . . Hutchinson."

"Get up there, Bill," Mrs. Hutchinson said, and the people near her laughed.

"Jones." 30

"They do say," Mr. Adams said to Old Man Warner, who stood next to him, "that over in the north village they're talking of giving up the lottery."

Old Man Warner snorted. "Pack of crazy fools," he said. "Listening to the young folks, nothing's good enough for *them*. Next thing you know, they'll be wanting to go back to living in caves, nobody work any more, live *that* way for a while. Used to be a saying about 'Lottery in June, corn be heavy soon.' First thing you know, we'd all be eating stewed chickweed and acorns. There's *always* been a lottery," he added petulantly. "Bad enough to see young Joe Summers up there joking with everybody."

"Some places have already quit lotteries," Mrs. Adams said.

"Nothing but trouble in *that*, " Old Man Warner said stoutly. "Pack of young fools."

"Martin." And Bobby Martin watched his father go forward. "Overdyke. . . . 35 Percy."

"I wish they'd hurry," Mrs. Dunbar said to her older son. "I wish they'd hurry."

"They're almost through," her son said.

"You get ready to run tell Dad," Mrs. Dunbar said.

Mr. Summers called his own name and then stepped forward precisely and selected a slip from the box. Then he called, "Warner."

"Seventy-seventh year I been in the lottery," Old Man Warner said as he 40 went through the crowd. "Seventy-seventh time."

"Watson." The tall boy came awkwardly through the crowd. Someone said, "Don't be nervous, Jack," and Mr. Summers said, "Take your time, son."

"Zanini."

After that, there was a long pause, a breathless pause, until Mr. Summers, holding his slip of paper in the air, said, "All right, fellows." For a minute, no one moved, and then all the slips of paper were opened. Suddenly, all women began to speak at once, saying, "Who is it?" "Who's got it?" "Is it the Dunbars?" "Is it the Watsons?" Then the voices began to say, "It's Hutchinson. It's Bill." "Bill Hutchinson's got it."

"Go tell your father," Mrs. Dunbar said to her older son.

People began to look around to see the Hutchinsons. Bill Hutchinson was   45
standing quiet, staring down at the paper in his hand. Suddenly, Tessie Hutchinson shouted to Mr. Summers, "You didn't give him time enough to take any paper he wanted. I saw you. It wasn't fair!"

"Be a good sport, Tessie," Mrs. Delacroix called, and Mrs. Graves said, "All of us took the same chance."

"Shut up, Tessie," Bill Hutchinson said.

"Well, everyone," Mr. Summers said, "that was done pretty fast, and now we've got to be hurrying a little more to get done in time." He consulted his next list. "Bill," he said, "you draw for the Hutchinson family. You got any other households in the Hutchinsons?"

"There's Don and Eva," Mrs. Hutchinson yelled. "Make them take their chance!"

"Daughters draw with their husbands' families, Tessie," Mr. Summers said   50
gently. "You know that as well as anyone else."

"It wasn't fair," Tessie said.

"I guess not, Joe," Bill Hutchinson said regretfully. "My daughter draws with her husband's family, that's only fair. And I've got no other family except the kids."

"Then, as far as drawing for families is concerned, it's you," Mr. Summers said in explanation, "and as far as drawing for households is concerned, that's you, too. Right?"

"Right," Bill Hutchinson said.

"How many kids, Bill?" Mr. Summers asked formally.   55

"Three," Bill Hutchinson said. "There's Bill, Jr., and Nancy, and little Dave. And Tessie and me."

"All right, then," Mr. Summers said. "Harry, you got their tickets back?"

Mr. Graves nodded and held up the slips of paper. "Put them in the box, then," Mr. Summers directed. "Take Bill's and put it in."

"I think we ought to start over," Mrs. Hutchinson said, as quietly as she could. "I tell you it wasn't *fair*. You didn't give him time enough to choose. *Everybody* saw that."

Mr. Graves had selected the five slips and put them in the box, and he   60
dropped all the papers but those onto the ground, where the breeze caught them and lifted them off.

"Listen, everybody," Mrs. Hutchinson was saying to the people around her.

"Ready, Bill?" Mr. Summers asked, and Bill Hutchinson, with one quick glance around at his wife and children, nodded.

"Remember," Mr. Summers said, "take the slips and keep them folded until each person has taken one. Harry, you help little Dave." Mr. Graves took the hand of the little boy, who came willingly with him up to the box. "Take a paper out of the box, Davy," Mr. Summers said. Davy put his hand into the box and laughed. "Take just *one* paper," Mr. Summers said. "Harry, you hold it for him." Mr. Graves took the child's hand and removed the folded paper from the tight fist and held it while little Dave stood next to him and looked up at him wonderingly.

"Nancy next," Mr. Summers said. Nancy was twelve, and her school friends breathed heavily as she went forward, switching her skirt, and took a slip daintily from the box. "Bill, Jr.," Mr. Summers said, and Billy, his face red and his feet over-large, nearly knocked the box over as he got a paper out. "Tessie," Mr. Summers said. She hesitated for a minute, looking around defiantly, and then set her lips and went up to the box. She snatched a paper out and held it behind her.

"Bill," Mr. Summers said, and Bill Hutchinson reached into the box and felt   65
around, bringing his hand out at last with the slip of paper in it.

The crowd was quiet. A girl whispered, "I hope it's not Nancy," and the sound of the whisper reached the edges of the crowd.

"It's not the way it used to be," Old Man Warner said clearly. "People ain't the way they used to be."

"All right," Mr. Summers said. "Open the papers. Harry, you open little Dave's."

Mr. Graves opened the slip of paper and there was a general sigh through the crowd as he held it up and everyone could see that it was blank. Nancy and Bill, Jr., opened theirs at the same time, and both beamed and laughed, turning around to the crowd and holding their slips of paper above their heads.

"Tessie," Mr. Summers said. There was a pause, and then Mr. Summers   70
looked at Bill Hutchinson, and Bill unfolded his paper and showed it. It was blank.

"It's Tessie," Mr. Summers said, and his voice was hushed. "Show us her paper, Bill."

Bill Hutchinson went over to his wife and forced the slip of paper out of her hand. It had a black spot on it, the black spot Mr. Summers had made the night before with the heavy pencil in the coal-company office. Bill Hutchinson held it up, and there was a stir in the crowd.

"All right, folks," Mr. Summers said, "let's finish quickly."

Although the villagers had forgotten the ritual and lost the original black box, they still remembered to use stones. The pile of stones the boys had made earlier was ready; there were stones on the ground with the blowing scraps of paper that had come out of the box. Mrs. Delacroix selected a stone so large she had to pick it up with both hands and turned to Mrs. Dunbar. "Come on," she said. "Hurry up."

Mrs. Dunbar had small stones in both hands, and she said, gasping for   75
breath, "I can't run at all. You'll have to go ahead and I'll catch up with you."

The children had stones already, and someone gave little Davy Hutchinson a few pebbles.

Tessie Hutchinson was in the center of a cleared space by now, and she held her hands out desperately as the villagers moved in on her. "It isn't fair," she said. A stone hit her on the side of the head.

Old Man Warner was saying, "Come on, come on, everyone." Steve Adams was in the front of the crowd of villagers, with Mrs. Graves beside him.

"It isn't fair, it isn't right," Mrs. Hutchinson screamed, and then they were upon her.

QUESTIONS

1. Where do you think "The Lottery" takes place? What purpose do you suppose the writer has in making this setting appear so familiar and ordinary?
2. In paragraphs 2 and 3, what details foreshadow the ending of the story?
3. Take a close look at Jackson's description of the black wooden box (paragraph 5) and of the black spot on the fatal slip of paper (paragraph 72). What do these objects suggest to you? Are there any other symbols in the story?
4. What do you understand to be the writer's own attitude toward the lottery and the stoning? Exactly what in the story makes her attitude clear to us?
5. What do you make of Old Man Warner's saying, "Lottery in June, corn be heavy soon"?
6. What do you think Shirley Jackson is driving at? Consider each of the following interpretations and, looking at the story, see if you can find any evidence for it:

> Jackson takes a primitive fertility rite and playfully transfers it to a small town in North America.
>
> Jackson, writing her story soon after World War II, indirectly expresses her horror at the Holocaust. She assumes that the massacre of the Jews was carried out by unwitting, obedient people, like these villagers.
>
> Jackson is satirizing our own society, in which men are selected for the army by lottery.
>
> Jackson is just writing a memorable story that signifies nothing at all.

Elizabeth Tallent

NO ONE'S A MYSTERY   1987

Elizabeth Tallent was born in Washington, D.C., in 1954. Her father was a research chemist, her mother a speech therapist who gave up her job to raise Tallent and her two younger siblings. She attended Illinois State University, where she majored in anthropology. Tallent initially planned to do graduate work in anthropology, but instead she pursued a literary career, living for many years in Santa Fe, New Mexico. Her first published short story, "Ice," appeared in the New Yorker *in 1980. Her first collection of stories,* In Constant Flight, *was published in 1983, followed by a novel,* Museum Pieces, *in 1985. Two subsequent collections of short stories have appeared,* Time With Children *(1987) and* Honey *(1993). Winner of an O. Henry*

Elizabeth Tallent

Award and a National Endowment for the Arts fellowship, Tallent has also published a critical study of John Updike's fiction. She currently teaches in the creative writing program at Stanford University. "No One's a Mystery" originally appeared in Harper's *in 1985 and is in the collection* Time With Children.

For my eighteenth birthday Jack gave me a five-year diary with a latch and a little key, light as a dime. I was sitting beside him scratching at the lock, which didn't want to work, when he thought he saw his wife's Cadillac in the distance, coming toward us. He pushed me down onto the dirty floor of the pickup and kept one hand on my head while I inhaled the musk of his cigarettes in the dashboard ashtray and sang along with Rosanne Cash on the tape deck. We'd been drinking tequila and the bottle was between his legs, resting up against his crotch, where the seam of his Levi's was bleached linen-white, though the Levi's were nearly new. I don't know why his Levi's always bleached like that, along the seams and at the knees. In a curve of cloth his zipper glinted, gold.

"It's her," he said. "She keeps the lights on in the daytime. I can't think of a single habit in a woman that irritates me more than that." When he saw that I was going to stay still he took his hand from my head and ran it through his own dark hair.

"Why does she?" I said.

"She thinks it's safer. Why does she need to be safer? She's driving exactly fifty-five miles an hour. She believes in those signs: 'Speed Monitored by Aircraft.' It doesn't matter that you can look up and see that the sky is empty."

"She'll see your lips move, Jack. She'll know you're talking to someone." 5

"She'll think I'm singing along with the radio."

He didn't lift his hand, just raised the fingers in salute while the pressure of his palm steadied the wheel, and I heard the Cadillac honk twice, musically; he was driving easily eighty miles an hour. I studied his boots. The elk heads stitched into the leather were bearded with frayed thread, the toes were scuffed, and there was a compact wedge of muddy manure between the heel and the sole—the same boots he'd been wearing for the two years I'd known him. On the tape deck Rosanne Cash sang, "Nobody's into me, no one's a mystery."°

"Do you think she's getting famous because of who her daddy is or for herself?" Jack said.

"There are about a hundred pop tops on the floor, did you know that? Some little kid could cut a bare foot on one of these, Jack."

"No little kids get into this truck except for you." 10

"How come you let it get so dirty?"

"'How come,'" he mocked. "You even sound like a kid. You can get back into the seat now, if you want. She's not going to look over her shoulder and see you."

"*Nobody's into me, no one's a mystery*": from the song "It Hasn't Happened Yet" by John Hiatt, recorded in 1982 by Rosanne Cash, daughter of Johnny Cash. The song's speaker claims to feel none of the heartache predicted for her after a broken romance.

"How do you know?"

"I just know," he said. "Like I know I'm going to get meat loaf for supper. It's in the air. Like I know what you'll be writing in that diary."

"What will I be writing?" I knelt on my side of the seat and craned around to look at the butterfly of dust printed on my jeans. Outside the window Wyoming was dazzling in the heat. The wheat was fawn and yellow and parted smoothly by the thin dirt road. I could smell the water in the irrigation ditches hidden in the wheat.

"Tonight you'll write, 'I love Jack. This is my birthday present from him. I can't imagine anybody loving anybody more than I love Jack.'"

"I can't."

"In a year you'll write, 'I wonder what I ever really saw in Jack. I wonder why I spent so many days just riding around in his pickup. It's true he taught me something about sex. It's true there wasn't ever much else to do in Cheyenne.'"

"I won't write that."

"In two years you'll write, 'I wonder what that old guy's name was, the one with the curly hair and the filthy dirty pickup truck and time on his hands.'"

"I won't write that."

"No?"

"Tonight I'll write, 'I love Jack. This is my birthday present from him. I can't imagine anybody loving anybody more than I love Jack.'"

"No, you can't," he says. "You can't imagine it."

"In a year I'll write, 'Jack should be home any minute now. The table's set— my grandmother's linen and her old silver and the yellow candles left over from the wedding—but I don't know if I can wait until after the trout *à la Navarra* to make love to him.'"

"It must have been a fast divorce."

"In two years I'll write, 'Jack should be home by now. Little Jack is hungry for his supper. He said his first word today besides "Mama" and "Papa." He said, "Caca."'"

Jack laughed. "He was probably trying to fingerpaint with caca on the bathroom wall when you heard him say it."

"In three years I'll write, 'My nipples are a little sore from nursing Eliza Rosamund.'"

"Rosamund. Every little girl should have a middle name she hates."

"'Her breath smells like vanilla and her eyes are just Jack's color of blue.'"

"That's nice," Jack said.

"So? Which one do you like?"

"I like yours," he said. "But I believe mine."

"It doesn't matter. I believe mine."

"Not in your heart of hearts, you don't."

"You're wrong."

"I'm not wrong," he said. "And her breath would smell like your milk, and it's kind of a bittersweet smell, if you want to know the truth."

Questions

1. How does Jack's present to the narrator, the "five-year diary with a latch and a little key," function symbolically in the story?
2. What do we learn about Jack's marriage? Through what details are these insights communicated?
3. What does each character's version of their future tell us about him or her?
4. The story ends with Jack's words, "if you want to know the truth." Do you think that the narrator does want to know the truth? Explain.
5. A quoted phrase can often take on new meanings in a new context. Consider the story's title: Is its application to the story literal or ironic?

Ursula K. Le Guin

THE ONES WHO WALK AWAY FROM OMELAS   1975

Ursala Kroeber Le Guin was born in 1929 on St. Ursula's Day (October 21) in Berkeley, California, the only daughter and youngest child of Theodora Kroeber, a folklorist, and Alfred Kroeber, a renowned anthropologist. Both parents had been widowed in previous marriages, and they created an intellectually lively and happy home for their four children. Le Guin attended Radcliffe College, where she graduated Phi Beta Kappa, and then entered Columbia University to do graduate work in French and Italian literature. While completing her M.A., she wrote her first stories. On a Fulbright fellowship to France, she met Charles Le Guin, a professor of French history, whom she married in Paris in 1953. Over the next decade Le Guin reared three children and worked on her writing in private.

In the early sixties Le Guin began publishing in both science fiction pulp magazines such as Amazing Stories *and academic journals such as* Western Humanities Review. *In 1966 her first novel,* Rocannon's World, *was published as an Ace science fiction paperback original—hardly a respectable format for the debut of one of America's premier writers.* Rocannon's World *began Le Guin's cycle of "Hainish" novels, a loosely structured but subtly interlocked series about intergalactic civilizations.* Planet of Exiles (1966) *and* City of Illusions (1967), *also paperback originals, quickly followed in the cycle. In 1968 Le Guin published* A Wizard of Earthsea, *the first novel in her Earthsea Trilogy—now considered a classic of children's literature. The next two volumes,* The Tombs of Atuan (1971), *which won a Newbery citation, and* The Farthest Shore (1972), *which won a National Book Award, brought Le Guin mainstream acclaim. (In recent years Le Guin has augmented both cycles, publishing a new Hainish novel,* The Telling, *in 2000 and two new Earthsea volumes,* The Other Wind *and* Tales from Earthsea, *in 2001.)*

Meanwhile, Le Guin's next adult book, The Left Hand of Darkness (1969), *won both the Hugo and the Nebula awards—science fiction's two most prized honors—for the year's best science fiction novel. Her novel* The Dispossessed (1974) *also won both awards—an unprecedented feat in the history of the genre. She has also twice won Hugos for best short story, including the 1974 award for "The Ones Who Walk Away from Omelas." Le Guin has published more than thirty novels and volumes of short stories. Other recent books of hers include a volume of poems,* Sixty Odd (1999), *and two short-story collections,* The Birthday of the World (2002) *and* Changing Planes (2003). *In 2002 Le Guin received the PEN/Malamud Award for excellence in the art of short fiction. She lives in Portland Oregon.*

One of the few science fiction writers whose work has earned general critical acclaim, Le Guin belongs most naturally in the company of major novelists of ideas such as Aldous Huxley, George Orwell, or Anthony Burgess who have used the genre of science fiction to explore the possible consequences of ideological rather than technological change. Bringing a social scientist's eye and a feminist's sensibility to the task, Le Guin has employed this notably speculative genre to critique contemporary civilization. She has been especially concerned with issues of social justice and equality, whether between classes, genders, or races. In short stories—such as "The Ones Who Walk Away from Omelas"—she creates complex imaginary civilizations, envisioned with anthropological authority, and her aim is less to imagine alien cultures than to explore humanity.

With a clamor of bells that set the swallows soaring, the Festival of Summer came to the city. Omelas, bright-towered by the sea. The rigging of the boats in harbor sparkled with flags. In the streets between houses with red roofs and painted walls, between old moss-grown gardens and under avenues of trees, past great parks and public buildings, processions moved. Some were decorous: old people in long stiff robes of mauve and grey, grave master workmen, quiet, merry women carrying their babies and chatting as they walked. In other streets the music beat faster, a shimmering of gong and tambourine, and the people went dancing, the procession was a dance. Children dodged in and out, their high calls rising like the swallows' crossing flights over the music and the singing. All the processions wound towards the north side of the city, where on the great water-meadow called the Green Fields boys and girls, naked in the bright air, with mud-stained feet and ankles and long, lithe arms, exercised their restive horses before the race. The horses wore no gear at all but a halter without bit. Their manes were braided with streamers of silver, gold, and green. They flared their nostrils and pranced and boasted to one another; they were vastly excited, the horse being the only animal who has adopted our ceremonies as his own. Far off to the north and west the mountains stood up half encircling Omelas on her bay. The air of morning was so clear that the snow still crowning the Eighteen Peaks burned with white-gold fire across the miles of sunlit air, under the dark blue of the sky. There was just enough wind to make the banners that marked the racecourse snap and flutter now and then. In the silence of the broad green meadows one could hear the music winding through the city streets, farther and nearer and ever approaching, a cheerful faint sweetness of the air that from time to time trembled and gathered together and broke out into the great joyous clanging of the bells.

Joyous! How is one to tell about joy? How describe the citizens of Omelas?

They were not simple folk, you see, though they were happy. But we do not say the words of cheer much any more. All smiles have become archaic. Given a description such as this one tends to make certain assumptions. Given a description such as this one tends to look next for the King, mounted on a splendid stallion and surrounded by his noble knights, or perhaps in a golden litter borne by great-muscled slaves. But there was no king. They did not use swords, or keep slaves. They were not barbarians. I do not know the rules and laws of their society, but I suspect that they were singularly few. As they did without monarchy and slavery, so they also got on without the stock exchange, the advertisement, the secret police, and the bomb. Yet I repeat that these were not simple folk, not dulcet shepherds, noble savages, bland utopians. They were not less complex than us. The trouble is that we have a bad habit, encouraged by pedants and sophisticates, of considering happiness as something rather stupid. Only pain is intellectual, only evil interesting. This is the treason of the artist: a refusal to admit the banality of evil and the terrible boredom of pain. If you can't lick 'em, join 'em. If it hurts, repeat it. But to praise despair is to condemn delight, to embrace violence is to lose hold of everything else. We have almost lost hold; we can no longer describe a happy man, nor make any celebration of joy. How can I tell you about the people of Omelas? They were not naïve and happy children—though their children were, in fact, happy. They were mature, intelligent, passionate adults whose lives were not wretched. O miracle! but I wish I could describe it better. I wish I could convince you. Omelas sounds in my words like a city in a fairy tale, long ago and far away, once upon a time. Perhaps it would be best if you imagined it as your own fancy bids, assuming it will rise to the occasion, for certainly I cannot suit you all. For instance, how about technology? I think that there would be no cars or helicopters in and above the streets; this follows from the fact that the people of Omelas are happy people. Happiness is based on a just discrimination of what is necessary, what is neither necessary nor destructive, and what is destructive. In the middle category, however—that of the unnecessary but undestructive, that of comfort, luxury, exuberance, etc.— they could perfectly well have central heating, subway trains, washing machines, and all kinds of marvelous devices not yet invented here, floating light-sources, fuelless power, a cure for the common cold. Or they could have none of that: it doesn't matter. As you like it. I incline to think that people from towns up and down the coast have been coming in to Omelas during the last days before the Festival on very fast little trains and double-decked trams and that the train station of Omelas is actually the handsomest building in town, though plainer than the magnificent Farmers' Market. But even granted trains, I fear that Omelas so far strikes some of you as goody-goody. Smiles, bells, parades, horses, bleh. If so, please add an orgy. If an orgy would help, don't hesitate. Let us not, however, have temples from which issue beautiful nude priests and priestesses already half in ecstasy and ready to copulate with any man or woman, lover or stranger, who desires union with the deep godhead of the blood, although that was my first idea. But really it would be better not to have any temples in Omelas—at least, not manned temples. Religion yes, clergy no. Surely the beautiful nudes can just wander about, offering themselves like divine soufflés to the hunger of the needy and the rapture of the flesh. Let them join the processions. Let tambourines be struck above the copulations, and the glory of desire be proclaimed upon the gongs, and (a not unimportant point) let the offspring of these delightful rituals be beloved and looked after by all. One thing I know there is none of in Omelas is guilt. But what else should there be? I thought at first there were no drugs, but that is puritanical. For those who like it, the faint insistent sweetness of *drooz* may perfume the ways of the city, drooz which first brings a great lightness and brilliance to the mind and limbs, and then after some hours a dreamy languor, and wonderful visions at last of the very arcana and inmost secrets of the Universe, as well as exciting the pleasure of sex beyond all belief; and it is not habit-forming. For more modest tastes I think there ought to be beer. What else, what else belongs in the joyous city? The sense of victory, surely, the celebration of courage. But as we did without clergy, let us do without soldiers. The joy built upon successful slaughter is not the right kind of joy; it will not do; it is fearful and it is trivial. A boundless and generous contentment, a magnanimous triumph felt not against some outer enemy but in communion with the finest and fairest in the souls of all men everywhere and the splendor of the world's summer: this is what swells the hearts of the people of Omelas, and the victory they celebrate is that of life. I really don't think many of them need to take *drooz*.

Most of the processions have reached the Green Fields by now. A marvelous smell of cooking goes forth from the red and blue tents of the provisioners. The faces of small children are amiably sticky; in the benign grey beard of a man a couple of crumbs of rich pastry are entangled. The youths and girls have mounted their horses and are beginning to group around the starting line of the course. An old woman, small, fat, and laughing, is passing out flowers from a basket, and tall young men wear her flowers in their shining hair. A child of nine or ten sits at the edge of the crowd, alone, playing on a wooden flute. People pause to listen, and they smile, but they do not speak to him, for he never ceases playing and never sees them, his dark eyes wholly rapt in the sweet, thin magic of the tune.

He finishes, and slowly lowers his hands holding the wooden flute.   5

As if that little private silence were the signal, all at once a trumpet sounds from the pavillion near the starting line: imperious, melancholy, piercing. The horses rear on their slender legs, and some of them neigh in answer. Sober-faced, the young riders stroke the horses' necks and soothe them, whispering, "Quiet, quiet, there my beauty, my hope. . . ." They begin to form in rank along the starting line. The crowds along the racecourse are like a field of grass and flowers in the wind. The Festival of Summer has begun.

Do you believe? Do you accept the festival, the city, the joy? No? Then let me describe one more thing.

In a basement under one of the beautiful public buildings of Omelas, or perhaps in the cellar of one of its spacious private homes, there is a room. It has one locked door, and no window. A little light seeps in dustily between cracks in the boards, secondhand from a cobwebbed window somewhere across the cellar. In one corner of the little room a couple of mops, with stiff, clotted, foul-smelling heads, stand near a rusty bucket. The floor is dirt, a little damp to the touch, as cellar dirt usually is. The room is about three paces long and two wide: a mere broom closet or disused tool room. In the room a child is sitting. It could be a boy or a girl. It looks about six, but actually is nearly ten. It is feeble-minded. Perhaps it was born defective, or perhaps it has become imbecile through fear, malnutrition, and neglect. It picks its nose and occasionally fumbles vaguely with its toes or genitals, as it sits hunched in the corner farthest from the bucket and the two mops. It is afraid of the mops. It finds them horrible. It shuts its eyes, but it knows the mops are still standing there; and the door is locked; and nobody will come. The door is always locked; and nobody ever comes, except that sometimes—the child has no understanding of time or interval—sometimes the door rattles terribly and opens, and a person, or several people, are there. One of them may come in and kick the child to make it stand up. The others never come close, but peer in at it with frightened, disgusted eyes. The food bowl and the water jug are hastily filled, the door is locked, the eyes disappear. The people at the door never say anything, but the child, who has not always lived in the tool room, and can remember sunlight and its mother's voice, sometimes speaks. "I will be good," it says. "Please let me out. I will be good!" They never answer. The child used to scream for help at night, and cry a good deal, but now it only makes a kind of whining, "eh-haa, eh-haa," and it speaks less and less often. It is so thin there are no calves to its legs; its belly protrudes; it lives on a half-bowl of corn meal and grease a day. It is naked. Its buttocks and thighs are a mass of festered sores, as it sits in its own excrement continually.

They all know it is there, all the people of Omelas. Some of them have come to see it, others are content merely to know it is there. They all know that it has to be there. Some of them understand why, and some do not, but they all understand that their happiness, the beauty of their city, the tenderness of their friendships, the health of their children, the wisdom of their scholars, the skill of their makers, even the abundance of their harvest and the kindly weathers of their skies, depend wholly on this child's abominable misery.

This is usually explained to children when they are between eight and 10
twelve, whenever they seem capable of understanding; and most of those who come to see the child are young people, though often enough an adult comes, or comes back, to see the child. No matter how well the matter has been explained to them, these young spectators are always shocked and sickened at the sight. They feel disgust, which they had thought themselves superior to. They feel anger, outrage, impotence, despite all the explanations. They would like to do something for the child. But there is nothing they can do. If the child were brought up into the sunlight out of that vile place, if it were cleaned and fed and comforted, that would be a good thing, indeed; but if it were done, in that day and hour all the prosperity and beauty and delight of Omelas would wither and be destroyed. Those are the terms. To exchange all the goodness and grace of every life in Omelas for that single, small improvement: to throw away the happiness of thousands for the chance of the happiness of one: that would be to let guilt within the walls indeed.

The terms are strict and absolute; there may not even be a kind word spoken to the child.

Often the young people go home in tears, or in a tearless rage, when they have seen the child and faced this terrible paradox. They may brood over it for weeks or years. But as time goes on they begin to realize that even if the child

could be released, it would not get much good of its freedom: a little vague pleasure of warmth and food, no doubt, but little more. It is too degraded and imbecile to know any real joy. It has been afraid too long ever to be free of fear. Its
habits are too uncouth for it to respond to humane treatment. Indeed, after so
long it would probably be wretched without walls about it to protect it, and darkness for its eyes, and its own excrement to sit in. Their tears at the bitter injustice dry when they begin to perceive the terrible justice of reality and to accept
it. Yet it is their tears and anger, the trying of their generosity and the acceptance of their helplessness, which are perhaps the true source of the splendor of
their lives. Theirs is no vapid, irresponsible happiness. They know that they, like
the child, are not free. They know compassion. It is the existence of the child,
and their knowledge of its existence, that makes possible the nobility of their architecture, the poignancy of their music, the profundity of their science. It is because of the child that they are so gentle with children. They know that if the
wretched one were not there snivelling in the dark, the other one, the flute-
player, could make no joyful music as the young riders line up in their beauty for
the race in the sunlight of the first morning of summer.

Now do you believe in them? Are they not more credible? But there is one
more thing to tell, and this is quite incredible.

At times one of the adolescent girls or boys who go to see the child does not
go home to weep or rage, does not, in fact, go home at all. Sometimes also a man
or woman much older falls silent for a day or two, and then leaves home. These
people go out into the street, and walk down the street alone. They keep walking,
and walk straight out of the city of Omelas, through the beautiful gates. They
keep walking across the farmlands of Omelas. Each one goes alone, youth or girl,
man or woman. Night falls; the traveler must pass down village streets, between
the houses with yellow-lit windows, and on out into the darkness of the fields.
Each alone, they go west or north, towards the mountains. They go on. They
leave Omelas, they walk ahead into the darkness, and they do not come back.
The place they go towards is a place even less imaginable to most of us than the
city of happiness. I cannot describe it at all. It is possible that it does not exist.
But they seem to know where they are going, the ones who walk away from
Omelas.

QUESTIONS

1. Does the narrator live in Omelas? What do we know about the narrator's society?
2. What is the narrator's opinion of Omelas? Does the author seem to share that opinion?
3. What is the narrator's attitude toward "the ones who walk away from Omelas"? Would
   the narrator have been one of those who walked away?
4. How do you account for the narrator's willingness to let us readers add to the story anything we like?—"If an orgy would help, don't hesitate" (paragraph 3). Doesn't Ursula Le
   Guin care what her story includes?
5. What does the locked, dark cellar in which the child sits suggest? What other details in
   the story are suggestive enough to be called symbolic?
6. Do you find in the story any implied criticism of our own society?

Ursula K. Le Guin

Ursula K. Le Guin on Writing

NOTE ON "THE ONES WHO WALK AWAY FROM OMELAS" 1975

The central idea of this psychomyth, the scapegoat, turns up in Dostoyevsky's *Brothers Karamazov*, and several people have asked me, rather suspiciously, why I gave the credit to William James. The fact is, I haven't been able to re-read Dostoyevsky, much as I loved him, since I was twenty-five, and I'd simply forgotten he used the idea. But when I met it in James's "The Moral Philosopher and the Moral Life," it was with a shock of recognition. Here is how James puts it:

> Or if the hypothesis were offered us of a world in which Messrs. Fourier's and Bellamy's and Morris's utopias should all be outdone, and millions kept permanently happy on the one simple condition that a certain lost soul on the far-off edge of things should lead a life of lonely torment, what except a specific and independent sort of emotion can it be which would make us immediately feel, even though an impulse arose within us to clutch at the happiness so offered, how hideous a thing would be its enjoyment when deliberately accepted as the fruit of such a bargain?

The dilemma of the American conscience can hardly be better stated. Dostoyevsky was a great artist, and a radical one, but his early social radicalism reversed itself, leaving him a violent reactionary. Whereas the American James, who seems so mild, so naïvely gentlemanly—look how he says "us," assuming all his readers are as decent as himself—was, and remained, and remains, a genuinely radical thinker. Directly after the "lost soul" passage he goes on,

> All the higher, more penetrating ideals are revolutionary. They present themselves far less in the guise of effects of past experience than in that of

probable causes of future experience, factors to which the environment and the lessons it has so far taught us must learn to bend.

The application of those two sentences to this story, and to science fiction, and to all thinking about the future, is quite direct. Ideals as "the probable causes of future experience"—that is a subtle and an exhilarating remark!

Of course I didn't read James and sit down and say, Now I'll write a story about that "lost soul." It seldom works that simply. I sat down and started a story, just because I felt like it, with nothing but the word "Omelas" in mind. It came from a road sign: Salem (Oregon) backwards. Don't you read road signs backwards? POTS, WOLS nerdlihc. Ocsicnarf Nas . . . Salem equals schelomo equals salaam equals Peace. Melas. O melas. Omelas. Homme hélas. "Where *do* you get your ideas from, Ms. Le Guin?" From forgetting Dostoyevsky and reading road signs backwards, naturally. Where else?

From *The Wind's Twelve Quarters*

╾╼▶ WRITING CRITICALLY ◀╾╼

Recognizing Symbols

The most important thing to remember when writing about symbolism is to avoid far-fetched interpretations. Not every image or event in a short story is symbolic. In literature, few symbols are hidden; most are right out in the open. Don't hunt for symbols. As you read or reread a story, any real symbol will usually find you.

An image that has acquired symbolic resonance in the course of a story will feel different to the reader. It has acquired enough associations to suggest something else. A genuine symbol has an emotional or intellectual power beyond its literal importance. You will recognize its power intuitively, even if you don't initially understand why.

If recognizing a symbol can be done by most experienced readers, understanding its meaning requires critical analysis. The temptation is usually to make the symbol mean too much or too little—to limit it to one narrow association or else to claim it summons up many different things.

In writing about a symbol, avoid vagueness. Begin by listing the specific object, people, and ideas with which a particular symbol is associated. Don't be subjective. Identify an exact place in the story where the symbol links itself to the other thing. A list of associations does not need to be long, it only needs to be accurate and reasonable.

WRITING ASSIGNMENT

Find a story in this book in which there is a strong central symbol. Citing specific moments in the text, demonstrate how the symbol helps communicate the meaning of the story. Here is an example of a paper written on that topic by Samantha L. Brown, a student of Melinda Barth at El Camino College.

Samantha L. Brown
Professor Barth
English 210
26 May 20xx

An Analysis of the Symbolism in Steinbeck's
"The Chrysanthemums"

Symbols are used in literature to convey a special meaning to the reader. In his short story "The Chrysanthemums," John Steinbeck uses chrysanthemums for both realistic and symbolic purposes. The chrysanthemums advance the plot by creating the story's central conflict. They also help define the character of Elisa, provide a greater understanding of the setting, and play a vital part in revealing the story's theme.

In the plot, the chrysanthemums cause the conflict that animates the story. The only reason Elisa talked to the tinker was because of his admiration of her chrysanthemums. Their conversation initiates the story's central conflict. The reader sees that Elisa is unhappy and emotionally isolated from her husband. When she is talking with the tinker, she feels that she has finally met someone she can be intimate with emotionally. This illusion is shattered, however, when she discovers her plant starts on the side of the road. The discarded, dying plants symbolize her shortened life. Therefore, without the chrysanthemums, there wouldn't have been a conflict. Without a conflict, Elisa's story would not have happened.

The chrysanthemums also provide the reader with insight into Elisa. The reader better understands her character through her gardening, her discussion with the tinker, and her realization of what the tinker had done with her plant starts. Elisa is a passionate person. When she is gardening, one can see where her passion is funneled. She has a sexual attachment to her flowers. The tinker's admiration causes her to develop sexual feelings about him. Furthermore, when she sees her plant starts discarded on the side of the road, the reader can deduce two things about her character. First, one can see that Elisa does not have an emotional bond with her husband. Second, one comprehends how deeply she feels defeated. Once again, the chrysanthemums initiate both insights. Without the flowers, the reader would not understand Elisa. Her reaction concerning her flowers defines her character.

"The Chrysanthemums" is set in rural Monterey in the 1930s. The setting has great importance to the story. Elisa could have never grown her ten-inch blooms in contemporary New York City. The chrysanthemums and her garden also create further images of the rural area Elisa lives in. This is important because the reader must understand the isolation of Elisa from the world. Her isolation is also implied in Elisa's comment to the tinker that she didn't know the woman down the road. One would assume that Elisa would know the women on neighboring farms. They should be her friends. Hence, the chrysanthemums help define the setting and create a better understanding of the story itself. Elisa's physical and emotional isolation, which is exemplified in the setting, is one of the reasons for her reaction to the tinker and her actions with her husband.

The theme of a story is the main message the writer hopes to convey to the reader. The chrysanthemums are vital to Steinbeck's presentation of the theme. The function of this story is to better understand Elisa's real character. At the beginning of the story, Elisa is presented as a strong woman, one who is strong enough to break the back of a calf. She regards herself as strong, as does her husband. At the end of story, Elisa is seen huddled like an old woman, crying weakly. The newly revealed Elisa is not the strong woman that she or her husband thought she was. Like most people, she is deluded about her emotional strength. It wasn't until Elisa saw the plant starts on the side of the road that she felt the sting of her rejection and isolation. Until that moment, her gardening had protected--or at least distracted--her from her loneliness, isolation, and feelings of inadequacy.

Elisa's chrysanthemums play a critical role in illuminating the story's theme. Without seeing the sprouts on the side of the road, the reader could not have concluded two of the major points in the understanding of this story. First, Elisa is a sad, lonely woman. Second, she is emotionally detached from her husband. That is the picture Steinbeck intended his reader to understand. This lonely, emotionally detached woman puts all her passion and energy into her flowers.

Elisa's chrysanthemums are central to this story. Understanding how they function as a symbol is imperative to understanding the story. Elisa's character completely revolves around her flowers. The conflict in the story is created through the flowers. Finally, the theme emerges from understanding this woman and the importance of her chrysanthemums. To understand Steinbeck's symbolism, therefore, is essential to understanding how the story works.

FURTHER SUGGESTIONS FOR WRITING

1. Reexamine one of these stories you have already read: "A Rose for Emily," "Interpreter of Maladies," "Greasy Lake," "Barn Burning," "A Clean, Well-Lighted Place," "The Storm," "Everyday Use," "The Open Boat." In writing, indicate what actions and objects now seem to you symbolic in their suggestions. Do these actions or objects point toward any central theme in the story?

2. For an alternative topic, look for symbols in a story you have not read before. In "Stories for Further Reading" (Chapter Eleven), you might take a look at D. H. Lawrence's "The Rocking-Horse Winner," Charlotte Perkins Gilman's "The Yellow Wallpaper," or Joyce Carol Oates's "Where Are You Going, Where Have You Been?"

3. Write a short comment inspired by the title "Absolutely Nothing Is Symbolic" or "There Isn't a Thing You Can't Make a Symbol of." Draw on your experiences in reading the stories in this chapter, or any other literature. Give concrete examples.

4. Pick a tangible *thing* that intrigues you—an animal, a plant, or another part of nature; a house or another man-made object. Recall it, observe it, meditate on it. Then write an opening paragraph for a story that will make a symbol of that object, doing your best to fill the passage with hints.

5. Write an essay in which you compare the symbolic use of the scapegoat in "The Lottery" and "The Ones Who Walk Away from Omelas," focusing not only on the similarities between the two, but also on their differences—for example, the prevailing mood or spirit of each society, and the degree of dissent, if any, in each.

8 Evaluating a Story

When we **evaluate** a story, we consider it and place a value on it. Perhaps we decide that it is a masterpiece, or a bit of trash, or (like most fiction we read) a work of some value in between. No cut-and-dried method of judgment will work on every story, and so in this chapter we have none to propose. Still, there are things we can look for in a story—usually clear indications of its author's competence.

In judging the quality of a baseball glove, we first have to be aware that a catcher's mitt differs—for good reasons—from a first baseman's glove. It is no less true that, before evaluating a story, we need to recognize its nature. To see, for instance, that a story is a fable (or perhaps a tale) may save us from condemning it as a failed short story.

Good critics of literature have at least a working knowledge of some of its conventions. By **conventions** we mean usual devices and features of a literary work, by which we can recognize its kind. When in movies or on television we watch a yarn about a sinister old mansion full of horrors, we recognize the conventions of that long-lived species of fiction, the **Gothic story.** *The Castle of Otranto, A Gothic Story* (1764), by English author Horace Walpole, started the genre, supplied its name, and established its favorite trappings. In Walpole's short novel, Otranto is a cobwebbed ruin full of underground passages and massive doors that slam unexpectedly. There are awful objects: a statue that bleeds, a portrait that steps from its frame, a giant helmet that falls and leaves its victim "dashed to pieces." Atmosphere is essential to a Gothic story: dusty halls, shadowy landscapes, whispering servants "seen at a distance imperfectly through the dusk" (the quotation is from Ann Radcliffe's novel *The Mysteries of Udolpho*, 1794). In Charlotte Brontë's *Jane Eyre* (1847), we find the model for a legion of heroines in the Gothic fiction of our own day. In the best-selling Gothic romances of Victoria Holt, Phyllis A. Whitney, and others, young women similarly find love while working as governesses in ominous mansions. Lacking English castles, American authors of Gothic fiction have had to make do with dark old houses—like those in Nathaniel Hawthorne's novel *The House of the Seven Gables*, in

Charlotte Perkins Gilman's "The Yellow Wallpaper," and in the short stories of Edgar Allan Poe, such as "The Tell-Tale Heart." William Faulkner, who brought the tradition to Mississippi, gives "A Rose for Emily" some familiar conventions: a run-down mansion, a mysterious servant, a madwoman, a hideous secret. But Faulkner's story, in its portrait of an aristocrat who refuses to admit that her world has vanished, goes far beyond Gothic conventions. When you set up court as a judge of stories, to recognize such conventions will be an advantage. Knowing a Gothic story for what it is, you won't condemn it for lacking "realism." And being aware of the Gothic elements in "A Rose for Emily" may help you see how original Faulkner manages to be, in spite of employing some handed-down conventions.

Is the story a piece of commercial fiction tailored to a formula, or is it unique in its design? You can't demand the subtlety of a Katherine Anne Porter from a writer of hard-boiled detective stories. Neither can you put down "The Jilting of Granny Weatherall" for lacking slam-bang action. Some stories are no more than light, entertaining bits of fluff—no point in damning them, unless you dislike fluff or find them badly written. Of course, you are within your rights to prefer solidity to fluff, or to prefer a Porter story to a typical paperback romance by a hack writer. Kurt Vonnegut's "Harrison Bergeron," though a simpler and briefer story than Franz Kafka's *The Metamorphosis*, is no less finished, complete, and satisfactory as a work of art. Yet, considered in another light, Kafka's short novel may well seem a greater work than Vonnegut's. It reveals greater depths of meaning and enfolds more life.

Masterpieces often have flaws; and so, whenever we can, we need to consider a story in its entirety. Some novels by Thomas Hardy and by Theodore Dreiser impress (on the whole), despite passages of stilted dialogue and other clumsy writing. If a story totally fails to enlist our sympathies, probably it suffers from some basic ineptitude: choice of an inappropriate point of view, a style ill-suited to its theme, or possibly insufficient knowledge of human beings. In some ineffectual stories, things important to the writer (and to the story) remain private and unmentioned. In other stories, the writer's interests may be perfectly clear but they may not interest the reader, for they are not presented with sufficient art.

Some stories fail from **sentimentality,** a defect in a work whose writer seems to feel tremendous emotion and implies that we too should feel it, but does not provide us enough reason to share such feelings. Sentimentality is rampant in televised weekday afternoon soap operas, whose characters usually palpitate with passion for reasons not quite known, and who speak in melodramatic tones as if heralding the end of the world. In some fiction, conventional objects (locks of baby hair, posthumously awarded medals, pressed roses) frequently signal, "Let's have a good cry!" Visiting home after her marriage, the character Amelia in William Makepeace Thackeray's *Vanity Fair* effuses about the bed she slept in when a virgin: "Dear little bed! how many a long night had she wept on its pillow."[1] Teary sentimentality is

---

[1]Sentimentality in fiction is older than the Victorians. Popular in eighteenth-century England, the sentimental novel (or novel of sensibility) specialized in characters whose ability to shed quick and copious tears signified their virtuous hearts. Oliver Goldsmith's *The Vicar of Wakefield* (1766) and Henry Mackenzie's *The Man of Feeling* (1771) are classics of the genre. An abundance of tears does not prevent such novels from having merit.

more common in nineteenth-century fiction than in ours. We have gone to the other extreme, some critics think, into a sentimentality of the violent and the hard-boiled. But in a grossly sentimental work of any kind, failure inheres in our refusal to go along with the author's implied attitudes. We smirk when we are expected to cry, feel delight when we are supposed to be horrified. As Oscar Wilde said about a notoriously drawn-out and overwritten death scene in Charles Dickens's *The Old Curiosity Shop*: "One must have a heart of stone to read the death of Little Nell without laughing."

In evaluating a story, we may usefully ask a few questions:

1. What is the tone of the story? By what means and how effectively is it communicated?

2. What is the point of view? Does it seem appropriate and effective in this story? Imagine the story told from a different point of view; would such a change be for the worse or for the better?

3. Does the story show us unique and individual scenes, events, and characters—or weary stereotypes?

4. Are any symbols evident? If so, do they direct us to the story's central theme, or do they distract us from it?

5. How appropriate to the theme of the story, and to its subject matter, are its tone and style? Is it ever difficult or impossible to sympathize with the attitudes of the author (insofar as we can tell what they are)?

6. Does our interest in the story mainly depend on following its plot, on finding out what will happen next? Or does the author go beyond the events to show us what they mean? Are the events (however fantastic) credible, or are they incredibly melodramatic? Does the plot greatly depend on far-fetched coincidence?

7. Has the writer caused characters, events, and settings to come alive? Are they full of breath and motion, or simply told about in the abstract ("She was a lovable girl whose life had been highly exciting")? Unless the story is a fable or a tale, which needs no detailed description or deep portrayal of character, then we may well expect the story to contain enough vividly imagined detail to make us believe in it.

<hr />

◄━━━▪ WRITING CRITICALLY ▪━━━►

Know What You're Judging

The ancient Romans had a proverb that we still quote today, "*De gustibus non disputandum est*," which is to say, "there is no arguing about taste." In every field of human endeavor, individuals have their personal favorites—a baseball team, a movie star, a rock group—that no amount of persuasion, rational or otherwise, will convince them to abandon for another. Works of literature elicit the same deep sorts of responses for many people. How do we strive to evaluate a story by some perspective other than the narrowly personal?

Although it may never be possible—or perhaps even desirable—to exclude our own subjective responses in judging a short story, it is possible to begin any formal process of evaluation by asking how the work itself asks to be judged. What effect does the story intend—humor, horror, suspense, introspection? Do the other elements in the story meaningfully contribute to this goal? Does the story belong to any recognizable genre (or literary type) of fiction—an adventure tale, a coming-of-age story, a fable, a romantic comedy?

Identifying the type or genre of a story usually tells us how the author intends it to be read. We will not necessarily expect depth of psychological characterization in a science fiction story, but we would be hard-pressed to admire a realistic coming-of-age story that lacked it.

Begin evaluating a story by finding some point of reference in the work itself. If possible, determine in strictly literary terms how the story asks to be read. The best strategy is not to deny your personal response but to find some other perspective by which to analyze your response in relation to the text.

WRITING ASSIGNMENT

Write a short essay evaluating any story in Chapter Eleven, "Stories for Further Reading." Begin by discussing the type of story the author seems to have written. What effects does the story try to create? Then evaluate how well you think the author succeeds (or how badly he or she fails) in achieving this.

FURTHER SUGGESTIONS FOR WRITING

1. In a short essay, take two stories that you find differing markedly in quality and evaluate them, giving evidence to support your judgments. Stories similar enough to compare might include two character studies of women, as in "The Jilting of Granny Weatherall" and "The Chrysanthemums."
2. Write a blast against a story in this book that you dislike intensely. Stick to the text of the story in making your criticisms and support your charges with plenty of evidence.
3. Find two stories that strike you as similar in some important way (e.g., "Greasy Lake" and "Barn Burning" are both stories about hard-won maturity). Write a comparison of the two stories that serves to evaluate them.

9 Reading Long Stories and Novels

Among the forms of imaginative literature in our language, the novel has been the favorite of both writers and readers for more than two hundred years. Broadly defined, a **novel** is a book-length story in prose, whose author tries to create the sense that while we read, we experience actual life.

This sense of actuality, also found in artful short stories, may be the quality that sets the novel apart from other long prose narratives. Why do we not apply the name *novel* to, for instance, *Gulliver's Travels?* In his marvel-filled account of Lemuel Gulliver's voyages among pygmies, giants, civilized horses, and noxious humanoid swine, Jonathan Swift does not seem primarily to care if we find his story credible. Though he arrays the adventures of Gulliver in painstaking detail (and, ironically, has Gulliver swear to the truth of them), Swift neither attempts nor achieves a convincing illusion of life. For his book is a fantastic satire that finds resemblances between noble horses and man's reasoning faculties, between debased apes and man's kinship with the beasts.

Unlike other major literary forms—drama, lyric, ballad, and epic—the novel is a relative newcomer. Originally, the drama in ancient Greece came alive only when actors performed it; the epic or heroic poem (from the classic *Iliad* through the Old English *Beowulf*), only when a bard sang or chanted it. But the English novel came to maturity in literate times, in the eighteenth century, and by its nature was something different: a story to be communicated silently, at whatever moment and at whatever pace (whether quickly or slowly and meditatively) the reader desired.

Some definitions of the novel would more strictly limit its province. "The Novel is a picture of real life and manners, and of the time in which it was written," declared Clara Reeve in 1785, thus distinguishing the novel from the romance, which "describes what never happened nor is likely to happen." By so specifying that the novel depicts life in the present day, the critic was probably observing the derivation of the word *novel*. Akin to the French word for "news" (*nouvelles*), it comes from the

Italian *novella* ("something new and small"), a term applied to a newly made story taking place in recent times, and not a traditional story taking place long ago.

Also drawing a line between novel and romance, Nathaniel Hawthorne, in his preface to *The House of the Seven Gables* (1851), restricted the novel "not merely to the possible, but to the probable and ordinary course of man's experience." A **romance** had no such limitations. Such a definition would deny the name of *novel* to any fantastic or speculative story—to, say, the Gothic novel and the science fiction novel. Carefully bestowed, the labels *novel* and *romance* may be useful to distinguish between the true-to-life story of usual people in ordinary places (such as George Eliot's *Silas Marner* or Amy Tan's *The Joy Luck Club*) and the larger-than-life story of daring deeds and high adventure, set in the past or future or in some timeless land (such as Walter Scott's *Ivanhoe* or J. R. R. Tolkien's *Lord of the Rings*). But the labels are difficult to apply to much modern fiction, in which ordinary life is sometimes mingled with outlandishness. Who can say that James Joyce's *Ulysses* is not a novel, for though it contains moments of dream and drunken hallucination, the total effect, as in any successful novel, is a sense of the actual.

This sense of the actual is, perhaps, the hallmark of a novel, whether or not the events it relates are literally possible. To achieve this sense, novelists have employed many devices, and frequently have tried to pass off their storytelling as reporting. Nathaniel Hawthorne, in his introduction to *The Scarlet Letter*, gives a minute account of his finding documents tied with a faded red ribbon and gathering dust in a customshouse, on which he claims to base his novel. Vladimir Nabokov's *Pale Fire* (1962) tells its story in the form of a scholarly edition of a 999-line poem, complete with a biographical commentary by a friend of the late poet. The major characters of Max Apple's 1987 novel *The Propheteers* include Walt Disney, Howard Johnson, C. W. Post, and Clarence Birdseye (the inventor of frozen vegetables). Mixing historical fact with shameless invention, Apple creates a story of entrepreneurial vision and eccentricity weird enough to seem true.

Many early novels were told in the form of letters. Sometimes these **epistolary novels** contained letters by only one character; often they contained letters by several of the characters in the book. By casting his novel *Pamela* (1740) into the form of personal letters, Samuel Richardson helped give the story the appearance of being not invented but discovered from real documents. Alice Walker's *The Color Purple* (1982) is a more recent epistolary novel, though some of the letters that tell the story are addressed to God. Another method favored by novelists is to write as though setting down a memoir or an autobiography. Daniel Defoe, whose skill in feigning such memoirs was phenomenal, even succeeded in writing the supposedly true confessions of a woman retired from a life of crime, *Moll Flanders* (1722), and in maintaining a vivid truthfulness:

> Going through Aldersgate Street, there was a pretty little child who had been at a dancing-school, and was going home all alone: and my prompter, like a true devil, set me upon this innocent creature. I talked to it, and it prattled to me again, and I took it by the hand and led it along till I came to

a paved alley that goes into Bartholomew Close, and I led it in there. The child said that was not its way home. I said, "Yes, my dear, it is; I'll show you the way home." The child had a little necklace on of gold beads, and I had my eye upon that, and in the dark of the alley I stooped, pretending to mend the child's clog that was loose, and took off her necklace, and the child never felt it, and so led the child on again. Here, I say, the devil put me upon killing the child in the dark alley, that it might not cry, but the very thought frighted me so that I was ready to drop down; but I turned the child about and bade it go back again. . . . The last affair left no great concern upon me, for as I did the poor child no harm, I only said to myself, I had given the parents a just reproof for their negligence in leaving the poor little lamb to come home by itself, and it would teach them to take more care of it another time.

What could sound more like the voice of an experienced child-robber than this manner of excusing her crime, and even justifying it?

Informed that a student had given up the study of mathematics to become a novelist, the logician David Hilbert drily remarked, "It was just as well: he did not have enough imagination to become a first-rate mathematician."[1] It is true that some novelists place great emphasis on research and notetaking. James A. Michener, the internationally best-selling author of novels such as *Centennnial* (which tracks life in Colorado from prehistory through modern times) and *Chesapeake* (which describes 400 years of events on Maryland's Eastern Shore), started work on a book by studying everything available about his chosen subject. He also traveled to locations that might appear in the book, interviewed local people, and compiled immense amounts of scientific, historical, and cultural data. Research alone, however, is not enough to finish a novel. A novel grows to completion only through the slow mental process of creation, selection, and arrangement. But raw facts can sometimes provide a beginning. Many novels started when the author read some arresting episode in a newspaper or magazine. Theodore Dreiser's impressive study of a murder, *An American Tragedy* (1925), for example, was inspired by a journalist's account of a real-life case.

Since both the novel and journalism try to capture the fabric of everyday life, there has long been a close relationship between the two literary forms. Many novelists, among them Ernest Hemingway, Stephen Crane, and Jack London, began their writing careers as cub reporters. Ambrose Bierce was the most influential newspaper satirist of his day. The two modes of writing, however, remain different. "Literature is the art of writing something that will be read twice," commented critic and novelist Cyril Connolly, "journalism what will be grasped at once." Journalism greatly influences how novelists depict the world around them. Stephen Crane's "The Open Boat" (Chapter Six) began as a newspaper account of his actual experiences in a

[1]Quoted by William H. Gass, *Fiction and the Figures of Life* (New York: Knopf, 1970).

small rowboat after the sinking of the *Commodore* in 1897. A journalist might have been content with such a gripping first-person story of surviving a shipwreck, but a great fiction writer has the gift of turning personal bad luck into art, and Crane eventually created a masterpiece of fiction based on fact.

In the 1960s there was a great deal of talk about the **nonfiction novel,** in which the author presents actual people and events in story form. The vogue of the nonfiction novel was created by Truman Capote's *In Cold Blood* (1966), which depicts an actual multiple murder and the resulting trial in Kansas. Capote traveled to the scene of the crime and interviewed all of the principal parties, including the murderers. Norman Mailer wrote a similar novel, *The Executioner's Song* (1979), chronicling the life and death of Gary Gilmore, the Utah murderer who demanded his own execution. More recently, John Berendt's darkly comic 1994 account of the upperclass and underclass of Savannah, Georgia, *Midnight in the Garden of Good and Evil* (which also centers on a murder and the subsequent trial) revived interest in the form. Perhaps the name "nonfiction novel" (Capote's term for it) or "true life novel" (as Mailer calls his Gilmore story) is newer than the form. In the past, writers of autobiography have cast their memoirs into what looks like novel form: Richard Wright in *Black Boy* (1945), William Burroughs in *Junkie* (1953). Derived not from the author's memory but from his reporting, John Hersey's *Hiroshima* (1946) reconstructs the lives of six survivors of the atom bomb as if they were fictional. In reading such works we may nearly forget we are reading literal truth, so well do the techniques of the novel lend remembered facts an air of immediacy.

A familiar kind of fiction that claims a basis in fact is the **historical novel,** a detailed reconstruction of life in another time, perhaps in another place. In some historical novels the author attempts a faithful picture of daily life in another era, as does Robert Graves in *I, Claudius* (1934), a novel of patrician Rome. More often, history is a backdrop for an exciting story of love and heroic adventure. Nathaniel Hawthorne's *The Scarlet Letter* (set in Puritan Boston), Herman Melville's *Moby-Dick* (set in the heyday of Yankee whalers), and Stephen Crane's *The Red Badge of Courage* (set on the battlefields of the Civil War) are historical novels in that their authors lived considerably later than the scenes and events that they depicted—and strove for truthfulness, by imaginative means.

Other varieties of novel will be familiar to anyone who scans the racks of paperback books in any drugstore: the mystery or detective novel, the Western novel, the science fiction novel, and other enduring types. Classified according to less well-known species, novels are sometimes said to belong to a category if they contain some recognizable kind of structure or theme. Such a category is the *Bildungsroman* (German for a "novel of growth or development"), sometimes called the **apprenticeship novel** after its classic example, *Wilhelm Meister's Apprenticeship* (1796) by Johann Wolfgang von Goethe. This is the kind of novel in which a youth struggles toward maturity, seeking, perhaps, some consistent worldview or philosophy of life. Sometimes the apprenticeship novel is evidently the author's recollection of his own early life: James Joyce's *Portrait of the Artist as a Young Man* and Mark Twain's *Tom Sawyer*.

In a **picaresque novel** (another famous category), a likable scoundrel wanders through adventures, living by his wits, duping the straight citizenry. The name comes from Spanish: *pícaro*, "rascal" or "rogue." The classic picaresque novel is the anonymous Spanish *Life of Lazarillo de Tormes* (1554), imitated by many English writers, among them Henry Fielding in his story of a London thief and racketeer, *Jonathan Wild* (1743). Mark Twain's *Huckleberry Finn* owes something to the tradition; like early picaresque novels, it is told in episodes rather than in one all-unifying plot and is narrated in the first person by a hero at odds with respectable society ("dismal regular and decent," Huck Finn calls it). In Twain's novel, however, the traveling swindlers who claim to be a duke and a dauphin are much more typical rogues of picaresque fiction than Huck himself, an honest innocent. Modern novels worthy of the name include J. P. Donleavy's *The Ginger Man* (1965), Saul Bellow's *The Adventures of Augie March* (1953), Erica Jong's *Fanny* (1981), and Seth Morgan's *Homeboy* (1990).

The term **short novel** (or **novella**) mainly describes the size of a narrative; it refers to a narrative midway in length between a short story and a novel. (E. M. Forster once said that a novel should be at least 50,000 words in length, and most editors and publishers would agree with that definition.) Generally a short novel, like a short story, focuses on just one or two characters; but, unlike a short story, it has room to examine them in great depth and detail. A short novel also often explores its characters over a greater period of time. Many writers, such as Thomas Mann, Henry James, Joseph Conrad, and Willa Cather, favored the novella (called **nouvelle** in France) as a perfect medium between the necessary compression of the short story and the potential sprawl of the novel. Franz Kafka's famous novella *The Metamorphosis* is included in this book. When the term **novelette** is used, it usually refers (often disapprovingly) to a short novel written for a popular magazine, especially in such fields as science fiction, romance, Westerns, and horror.

Trying to perceive a novel as a whole, we may find it helpful to look for the same elements that we have noticed in reading short stories. By asking ourselves leading questions, we may be drawn more deeply into the novel's world, and may come to recognize and appreciate the techniques of the novelist. Does the novel have themes, or an overall theme? Who is its main character? What is the author's kind of narrative voice? What do we know about the tone, style, and use of irony? Why is this novel written from one point of view rather than from another? If the novel in question is large and thickly populated, it may help to read it with a pencil and take brief notes. Forced to put the novel aside and later return to it, the reader may find that the notes refresh the memory. Notetaking habits differ, but perhaps these might be no more than, say, "Theme introduced, p. 27," or, "Old clothes dealer, p. 109—walking symbol?" Some readers find it useful to list briefly whatever each chapter accomplishes. Others make lists of a novel's characters, especially when reading classic Russian novels in which the reader has to recall that Dostoyevsky's Alexey Karamazov is also identified by his pet name Alyosha, or that, in Leo Tolstoy's *Anna Karenina*, Princess Catherine Alexándrovna Shcherbátskaya and "Kitty" are one and the same.

Once our reading of a novel is finished and we prepare to discuss it or write about it, it may be a good idea to browse through it again, rereading brief portions. This method of overall browsing may also help when first approaching a bulky and difficult novel. Just as an explorer mapping unfamiliar territory may find it best to begin by taking an aerial view of it, so too the reader approaching an exceptionally thick and demanding novel may wish, at the start, to look for its general shape. This is the method of some professional book reviewers, who size up a novel (even an easy-to-read spy story, because they are not reading for pleasure) by skimming the first chapter, a middle chapter or two, and the last chapter; then going back and browsing at top speed through the rest. Reading a novel in this grim fashion, of course, the reviewer does not really know it thoroughly, any more than a tourist knows the mind and heart of a foreign people after just strolling in a capital city and riding a tour bus to a few monuments. The reviewer's method will, however, provide a general notion of what the author is doing, and at the very least will tell something of his or her tone, style, point of view, and competence. We suggest this method only as a way to *approach* a book that, otherwise, the reader might not want to approach at all. It may be a comfort in studying some obdurate-looking or highly experimental novel, such as James Joyce's *Ulysses* or Henry James's *The Sacred Fount*. But the reader will find it necessary to return to the book, in order to know it, and to read it honestly, in detail. There is, of course, no shortcut to novel reading, and probably the best method is to settle in comfort and read the book through: with your own eyes, not with the borrowed glasses of literary criticism.

The death of the novel has been frequently announced. Competition from television, DVDs, video games, and the Internet, critics claim, will overwhelm the habit of reading; the public is lazy and will follow the easiest route available for entertainment. But in England and America television and films have been sending people back in vast numbers to the books they dramatize. Jane Austen has never lacked readers, but films such as *Emma, Persuasion*, and *Sense and Sensibility* (not to mention *Clueless*, a teenage version of *Emma* set in Beverly Hills) made her one of the world's best-selling novelists. Stylish adaptations of Philip K. Dick's offbeat science fiction, including *Blade Runner, Total Recall*, and *Minority Report*, have created a cult for his once neglected work. Even experimental novels such as Virginia Woolf's *Orlando* and William Burroughs's *Naked Lunch* have become successful films that have in turn sent a new generation of readers back to the books. Sometimes Hollywood even helps bring a good book into print. No one would publish Thomas Disch's sophisticated children's novella, *The Brave Little Toaster* until Walt Disney turned it into a cartoon movie. A major publisher then not only rushed it into print, but commissioned a sequel as well.

Meanwhile, each year new novels by the hundreds continue to appear, their authors wistfully looking for a public. A chosen few reach tens of thousands of readers through book clubs, and, through paperback reprint editions, occasionally millions more. To forecast the end of the novel seems risky, for the novel exercises the imagination of the beholder. At any hour, at a touch of the hand, it opens and (with no warm-up) begins to speak. Once printed, it consumes no further energy. Often so small it may be carried in a pocket, it may yet survive by its ability to contain multitudes (a "capacious vessel," Henry James called it): a thing that is both a work of art and an amazingly compact system for the storage and retrieval of imagined life.

Leo Tolstoy

THE DEATH OF IVAN ILYCH

1886

TRANSLATED BY LOUISE AND AYLMER MAUDE

The complex and contradictory Leo Nikolaevich Tolstoy (1828–1910) is generally considered the greatest Russian novelist. Born on his aristocratic family's country estate, Yasnaya Polyana, in central Russia, he was orphaned at nine and raised by his aunts. At sixteen, Tolstoy entered Kazan University to study law, but soon returned to the family estate. The young count took off for St. Petersburg and Moscow, where he led a profligate life—carefully listing his moral transgressions in his diary. In 1851 Tolstoy joined the army and fought in the Caucasus. It was there that he completed his first book, Childhood (1852), a lyrical memoir. Having served in the Crimean War, he left the army in 1856 to become a writer.

Leo Tolstoy

For the next six decades the brilliant and perpetually dissatisfied Tolstoy tried to settle in Yasnaya Polyana, but frequently escaped to St. Petersburg and Western Europe. In 1862 he wed Sonya Bers, an intellectual middle-class woman. Initially happy, the marriage was eventually undermined by the sex-obsessed and guilt-ridden Tolstoy, who engaged in many infidelities (which were sometimes followed by the author's unsuccessful renunciations of sex). Despite its many problems, the marriage produced thirteen children. At Yasnaya Polyana, Tolstoy wrote his two greatest novels, the six-volume War and Peace (1863–1869), which depicts the lives of five aristocratic Russian families during the Napoleonic Wars, and Anna Karenina (1877), which tells the tragic story of a woman led by romantic illusions into a destructive adulterous liaison. As Tolstoy grew older, he became obsessed with early Christianity. He formulated his own version of Christ's teachings, stressing simplicity, love, nonviolence, and community property. Excommunicated by the Orthodox Church, the count, who now dressed in peasant clothing, preached his "Christian anarchism" to the Russian intelligentsia in streams of books and pamphlets. Upset by his ruined marriage and his inability to renounce his personal wealth, the eighty-two-year-old Tolstoy fled home one night to enter a monastery. He died of pneumonia a few days later in a provincial railway station.

Tolstoy is one of the great masters of European Realism. His fame came early and has never been seriously challenged. Much of his fiction examines a tragic predicament of human existence—the difficult search for truth and justice in a world of limited knowledge and ethical imperfection. Tolstoy resolutely believed in the moral development of humanity, but was also painfully aware of the obstacles to genuine progress. His gripping novella The Death of Ivan Ilyich dramatizes Tolstoy's central spiritual concerns. His antiheroic Everyman faces death with the horrifying realization that he has not lived a correct or meaningful life.

I

During an interval in the Melvinski trial in the large building of the Law Courts, the members and public prosecutor met in Ivan Egorovich Shebek's private room, where the conversation turned on the celebrated Krasovski case. Fëdor Vasilievich warmly maintained that it was not subject to their jurisdiction, Ivan Egorovich maintained the contrary, while Peter Ivanovich, not having entered into the discussion at the start, took no part in it but looked through the *Gazette* which had just been handed in.

"Gentlemen," he said, "Ivan Ilych has died!"

"You don't say so!"

"Here, read it yourself," replied Peter Ivanovich, handing Fëdor Vasilievich the paper still damp from the press. Surrounded by a black border were the words: "Praskovya Fëdorovna Golviná, with profound sorrow, informs relatives and friends of the demise of her beloved husband Ivan Ilych Golovin, Member of the Court of Justice, which occurred on February the 4th of this year 1882. The funeral will take place on Friday at one o'clock in the afternoon."

Ivan Ilych had been a colleague of the gentlemen present and was liked by them all. He had been ill for some weeks with an illness said to be incurable. His post had been kept open for him, but there had been conjectures that in case of his death Alexeev might receive his appointment, and that either Vinnikov or Shtabel would succeed Alexeev. So on receiving the news of Ivan Ilych's death the first thought of each of the gentlemen in that private room was of the changes and promotions it might occasion among themselves or their acquaintances.

"I shall be sure to get Shtabel's place or Vinnikov's," thought Fëdor Vasilievich. "I was promised that long ago, and the promotion means an extra eight hundred rubles a year for me besides the allowance."

"Now I must apply for my brother-in-law's transfer from Kaluga," thought Peter Ivanovich. "My wife will be very glad, and then she won't be able to say that I never do anything for her relations."

"I thought he would never leave his bed again," said Peter Ivanovich aloud. "It's very sad."

"But what really was the matter with him?"

"The doctors couldn't say—at least they could, but each of them said something different. When last I saw him I thought he was getting better."

"And I haven't been to see him since the holidays. I always meant to go."

"Had he any property?"

"I think his wife had a little—but something quite trifling."

"We shall have to go to see her, but they live so terribly far away."

"Far away from you, you mean. Everything's far away from your place."

"You see, he never can forgive my living on the other side of the river," said Peter Ivanovich, smiling at Shebek. Then, still talking of the distances between different parts of the city, they returned to the Court.

Besides considerations as to the possible transfers and promotions likely to result from Ivan Ilych's death, the mere fact of the death of a near acquaintance

5

10

15

aroused, as usual, in all who heard of it the complacent feeling that "it is he who is dead and not I."

Each one thought or felt, "Well, he's dead but I'm alive!" But the more intimate of Ivan Ilych's acquaintances, his so-called friends, could not help thinking also that they would now have to fulfil the very tiresome demands of propriety by attending the funeral service and paying a visit of condolence to the widow.

Fëdor Vasilievich and Peter Ivanovich had been his nearest acquaintances. Peter Ivanovich had studied law with Ivan Ilych and had considered himself to be under obligations to him.

Having told his wife at dinner-time of Ivan Ilych's death and of his conjecture that it might be possible to get her brother transferred to their circuit, Peter Ivanovich sacrificed his usual nap, put on his evening clothes, and drove to Ivan Ilych's house. 20

At the entrance stood a carriage and two cabs. Leaning against the wall in the hall downstairs near the cloak-stand was a coffin-lid covered with cloth of gold, ornamented with gold cord and tassels, that had been polished up with metal powder. Two ladies in black were taking off their fur cloaks. Peter Ivanovich recognized one of them as Ivan Ilych's sister, but the other was a stranger to him. His colleague Schwartz was just coming downstairs, but on seeing Peter Ivanovich enter he stopped and winked at him, as if to say: "Ivan Ilych has made a mess of things—not like you and me."

Schwartz's face with his Piccadilly whiskers and his slim figure in evening dress had as usual an air of elegant solemnity which contrasted with the playfulness of his character and had a special piquancy here, or so it seemed to Peter Ivanovich.

Peter Ivanovich allowed the ladies to precede him and slowly followed them upstairs. Schwartz did not come down but remained where he was, and Peter Ivanovich understood that he wanted to arrange where they should play bridge that evening. The ladies went upstairs to the widow's room, and Schwartz with seriously compressed lips but a playful look in his eyes, indicated by a twist of his eyebrows the room to the right where the body lay.

Peter Ivanovich, like everyone else on such occasions, entered feeling uncertain what he would have to do. All he knew was that at such times it is always safe to cross oneself. But he was not quite sure whether one should make obeisances while doing so. He therefore adopted a middle course. On entering the room he began crossing himself and made a slight movement resembling a bow. At the same time, as far as the motion of his head and arm allowed, he surveyed the room. Two young men—apparently nephews, one of whom was a high-school pupil—were leaving the room, crossing themselves as they did so. An old woman was standing motionless, and a lady with strangely arched eyebrows was saying something to her in a whisper. A vigorous, resolute Church Reader, in a frock-coat, was reading something in a loud voice with an expression that precluded any contradiction. The butler's assistant, Gerasim, stepping lightly in front of Peter Ivanovich, was strewing something on the floor. Noticing this, Peter Ivanovich was immediately aware of a faint odor of a decomposing body.

The last time he had called on Ivan Ilych, Peter Ivanovich had seen Gerasim in the study. Ivan Ilych had been particularly fond of him and he was performing the duty of a sick nurse.

Peter Ivanovich continued to make the sign of the cross, slightly inclining his head in an intermediate direction between the coffin, the Reader, and the icons on the table in a corner of the room. Afterwards, when it seemed to him that this movement of his arm in crossing himself had gone on too long, he stopped and began to look at the corpse.

The dead man lay, as dead men always lie, in a specially heavy way, his rigid limbs sunk in the soft cushions of the coffin, with the head forever bowed on the pillow. His yellow waxen brow with bald patches over his sunken temples was thrust up in the way peculiar to the dead, the protruding nose seeming to press on the upper lip. He was much changed and had grown even thinner since Peter Ivanovich had last seen him, but, as is always the case with the dead, his face was handsomer and above all more dignified than when he was alive. The expression on the face said that what was necessary had been accomplished, and accomplished rightly. Besides this there was in that expression a reproach and a warning to the living. This warning seemed to Peter Ivanovich out of place, or at least not applicable to him. He felt a certain discomfort and so he hurriedly crossed himself once more and turned and went out the door—too hurriedly and too regardless of propriety, as he himself was aware.

Schwartz was waiting for him in the adjoining room with legs spread wide apart and both hands toying with his top-hat behind his back. The mere sight of that playful, well-groomed, and elegant figure refreshed Peter Ivanovich. He felt that Schwartz was above all these happenings and would not surrender to any depressing influences. His very look said that this incident of a church service for Ivan Ilych could not be a sufficient reason for infringing the order of the session—in other words, that it would certainly not prevent his unwrapping a new pack of cards and shuffling them that evening while a footman placed four fresh candles on the table: in fact, that there was no reason for supposing that this incident would hinder their spending the evening agreeably. Indeed he said this in a whisper as Peter Ivanovich passed him, proposing that they should meet for a game at Fëdor Vasilievich's. But apparently Peter Ivanovich was not destined to play bridge that evening. Praskovya Fëdorovna (a short, fat woman who despite all efforts to the contrary had continued to broaden steadily from her shoulders downwards and who had the same extraordinarily arched eyebrows as the lady who had been standing by the coffin), dressed all in black, her head covered with lace, came out of her own room with some other ladies, conducted them to the room where the dead body lay, and said: "The service will begin immediately. Please go in."

Schwartz, making an indefinite bow, stood still, evidently neither accepting nor declining this invitation. Praskovya Fëdorovna, recognizing Peter Ivanovich, sighed, went close up to him, took his hand, and said: "I know you were a true friend to Ivan Ilych . . ." and looked at him awaiting some suitable response. And Peter Ivanovich knew that, just as it had been the right thing to cross himself in that room, so what he had to do here was to press her hand, sigh, and say, "Believe me. . . ." So he did all this and as he did it felt that the desired result had been achieved: that both he and she were touched.

"Come with me. I want to speak to you before it begins," said the widow. 30 "Give me your arm."

Peter Ivanovich gave her his arm and they went to the inner rooms, passing Schwartz, who winked at Peter Ivanovich compassionately.

"That does for our bridge! Don't object if we find another player. Perhaps you can cut in when you do escape," said his playful look.

Peter Ivanovich sighed still more deeply and despondently, and Praskovya Fëdorovna pressed his arm gratefully. When they reached the drawing-room, upholstered in pink cretonne and lighted by a dim lamp, they sat down at the table—she on a sofa and Peter Ivanovich on a low pouffe, the springs of which yielded spasmodically under his weight. Praskovya Fëdorovna had been on the point of warning him to take another seat, but felt that such a warning was out of keeping with her present condition and so changed her mind. As he sat down on the pouffe Peter Ivanovich recalled how Ivan Ilych had arranged this room and had consulted him regarding this pink cretonne with green leaves. The whole room was full of furniture and knick-knacks, and on her way to the sofa the lace of the widow's black shawl caught on the carved edge of the table. Peter Ivanovich rose to detach it, and the springs of the pouffe, relieved of his weight, rose also and gave him a push. The widow began detaching her shawl herself, and Peter Ivanovich again sat down, suppressing the rebellious springs of the pouffe under him. But the widow had not quite freed herself and Peter Ivanovich got up again, and again the pouffe rebelled and even creaked. When this was all over she took out a clean cambric handkerchief and began to weep. The episode with the shawl and the struggle with the pouffe had cooled Peter Ivanovich's emotions and he sat there with a sullen look on his face. This awkward situation was interrupted by Sokolov, Ivan Ilych's butler, who came to report that the plot in the cemetery that Praskovya Fëdorovna had chosen would cost two hundred rubles. She stopped weeping and, looking at Peter Ivanovich with the air of a victim, remarked in French that it was very hard for her. Peter Ivanovich made a silent gesture signifying his full conviction that it must indeed be so.

"Please smoke," she said in a magnanimous yet crushed voice, and turned to discuss with Sokolov the price of the plot for the grave.

Peter Ivanovich while lighting his cigarette heard her inquiring very cir- 35 cumstantially into the prices of different plots in the cemetery and finally decide which she would take. When that was done she gave instructions about engaging the choir. Sokolov then left the room.

"I look after everything myself," she told Peter Ivanovich, shifting the albums that lay on the table; and noticing that the table was endangered by his cigarette-ash, she immediately passed him an ashtray, saying as she did so: "I consider it an affectation to say that my grief prevents my attending to practical affairs. On the contrary, if anything can—I won't say console me, but—distract me, it is seeing to everything concerning him." She again took out her handkerchief as if preparing to cry, but suddenly, as if mastering her feeling, she shook herself and began to speak calmly. "But there is something I want to talk to you about."

Peter Ivanovich bowed, keeping control of the springs of the pouffe, which immediately began quivering under him.

"He suffered terribly the last few days."

"Did he?" said Peter Ivanovich.

"Oh, terribly! He screamed unceasingly, not for minutes but for hours. For the last three days he screamed incessantly. It was unendurable. I cannot understand how I bore it; you could hear him three rooms off. Oh, what I have suffered!" 40

"Is it possible that he was conscious all that time?" asked Peter Ivanovich.

"Yes," she whispered. "To the last moment. He took leave of us a quarter of an hour before he died, and asked us to take Vasya away."

The thought of the sufferings of this man he had known so intimately, first as a merry little boy, then as a school-mate, and later as a grown-up colleague, suddenly struck Peter Ivanovich with horror, despite an unpleasant consciousness of his own and this woman's dissimulation. He again saw that brow, and that nose pressing down on the lip, and felt afraid for himself.

"Three days of frightful suffering and then death! Why, that might suddenly, at any time, happen to me," he thought, and for a moment felt terrified. But—he did not himself know how—the customary reflection at once occurred to him that this had happened to Ivan Ilych and not to him, and that it should not and could not happen to him, and that to think that it could would be yielding to depression which he ought not to do, as Schwartz's expression plainly showed. After which reflection Peter Ivanovich felt reassured, and began to ask with interest about the details of Ivan Ilych's death, as though death was an accident natural to Ivan Ilych but certainly not to himself.

After many details of the really dreadful physical sufferings Ivan Ilych had endured (which details he learnt only from the effect those sufferings had produced on Praskovya Fëdorovna's nerves) the widow apparently found it necessary to get to business. 45

"Oh, Peter Ivanovich, how hard it is! How terribly, terribly hard!" and she again began to weep.

Peter Ivanovich sighed and waited for her to finish blowing her nose. When she had done so he said, "Believe me . . ." and she again began talking and brought out what was evidently her chief concern with him—namely, to question him as to how she could obtain a grant of money from the government on the occasion of her husband's death. She made it appear that she was asking Peter Ivanovich's advice about her pension, but he soon saw that she already knew about that to the minutest detail, more even than he did himself. She knew how much could be got out of the government in consequence of her husband's death, but wanted to find out whether she could not possibly extract something more. Peter Ivanovich tried to think of some means of doing so, but after reflecting for a while and, out of propriety, condemning the government for its niggardliness, he said he thought that nothing more could be got. Then she sighed and evidently began to devise means of getting rid of her visitor. Noticing this, he put out his cigarette, rose, pressed her hand, and went out into the anteroom.

In the dining-room where the clock stood that Ivan Ilych had liked so much and had bought at an antique shop, Peter Ivanovich met a priest and a few acquaintances who had come to attend the service, and he recognized Ivan Ilych's daughter, a handsome young woman. She was in black and her slim figure appeared slimmer than ever. She had a gloomy, determined, almost angry expression, and bowed to Peter Ivanovich as though he were in some way to blame. Behind her, with the same offended look, stood a wealthy young man, an examining magistrate, whom Peter Ivanovich also knew and who was her fiancé, as he had heard. He bowed mournfully to them and was about to pass into the death-chamber, when from under the stairs appeared the figure of Ivan Ilych's schoolboy son, who was extremely like his father. He seemed a little Ivan Ilych, such as Peter Ivanovich remembered when they studied law together. His tear-stained eyes had in them the look that is seen in the eyes of boys of thirteen or fourteen who are not pureminded. When he saw Peter Ivanovich he scowled morosely and shamefacedly. Peter Ivanovich nodded to him and entered the death-chamber. The service began: candles, groans, incense, tears, and sobs. Peter Ivanovich stood looking gloomily down at his feet. He did not look once at the dead man, did not yield to any depressing influence, and was one of the first to leave the room. There was no one in the anteroom, but Gerasim darted out of the dead man's room, rummaged with his strong hands among the fur coats to find Peter Ivanovich's, and helped him on with it.

"Well, friend Gerasim," said Peter Ivanovich, so as to say something. "It's a sad affair, isn't it?"

"It's God's will. We shall all come to it some day," said Gerasim, displaying his teeth—the even, white teeth of a healthy peasant—and, like a man in the thick of urgent work, he briskly opened the front door, called the coachman, helped Peter Ivanovich into the sledge, and sprang back to the porch as if in readiness for what he had to do next. 50

Peter Ivanovich found the fresh air particularly pleasant after the smell of incense, the dead body, and carbolic acid.

"Where to, sir?" asked the coachman.

"It's not too late even now . . . I'll call round on Fëdor Vasilievich."

He accordingly drove there and found them just finishing the first rubber, so that it was quite convenient for him to cut in.

II

Ivan Ilych's life had been most simple and most ordinary and therefore most terrible. 55

He had been a member of the Court of Justice, and died at the age of forty-five. His father had been an official who after serving in various ministries and departments in Petersburg had made the sort of career which brings men to positions from which by reason of their long service they cannot be dismissed, though they are obviously unfit to hold any responsible position, and for whom therefore posts are specially created, which, though fictitious, carry salaries of from six to ten thousand rubles that are not fictitious, and in receipt of which they live on to a great age.

Such was the Privy Councillor and superfluous member of various superfluous institutions, Ilya Epimovich Golovin.

He had three sons, of whom Ivan Ilych was the second. The eldest son was following in his father's footsteps only in another department, and was already approaching that stage in the service at which a similar sinecure would be reached. The third son was a failure. He had ruined his prospects in a number of positions and was now serving in the railway department. His father and brothers, and still more their wives, not merely disliked meeting him, but avoided remembering his existence unless compelled to do so. His sister had married Baron Greff, a Petersburg official of her father's type. Ivan Ilych was *le phénix de la famille*° as people said. He was neither as cold and formal as his elder brother nor as wild as the younger, but was a happy mean between them—an intelligent, polished, lively, and agreeable man. He had studied with his younger brother at the School of Law, but the latter had failed to complete the course and was expelled when he was in the fifth class. Ivan Ilych finished the course well. Even when he was at the School of Law he was just what he remained for the rest of his life: a capable, cheerful, good-natured, and sociable man, though strict in the fulfillment of what he considered to be his duty: and he considered his duty to be what was so considered by those in authority. Neither as a boy nor as a man was he a toady, but from early youth was by nature attracted to people of high station as a fly is drawn to the light, assimilating their ways and views of life and establishing friendly relations with them. All the enthusiasms of childhood and youth passed without leaving much trace on him; he succumbed to sensuality, to vanity, and latterly among the highest classes to liberalism, but always within limits which his instinct unfailingly indicated to him as correct.

At school he had done things which had formerly seemed to him very horrid and made him feel disgusted with himself when he did them; but when later on he saw that such actions were done by people of good position and that they did not regard them as wrong, he was able not exactly to regard them as right, but to forget about them entirely or not be at all troubled at remembering them.

Having graduated from the School of Law and qualified for the tenth rank of the civil service, and having received money from his father for his equipment, Ivan Ilych ordered himself clothes at Scharmer's, the fashionable tailor, hung a medallion inscribed *respice finem*° on his watch-chain, took leave of his professor and the prince who was patron of the school, had a farewell dinner with his comrades at Donon's first-class restaurant, and with his new and fashionable portmanteau, linen, clothes, shaving and other toilet appliances, and a traveling rug

60

---

le phénix de la famille: French for "the prize of the family."   *respice finem:* Latin for "Think of the end (of your life)."

all purchased at the best shops, he set off for one of the provinces where through his father's influence, he had been attached to the Governor as an official for special service.

In the province Ivan Ilych soon arranged as easy and agreeable a position for himself as he had had at the School of Law. He performed his official tasks, made his career, and at the same time amused himself pleasantly and decorously. Occasionally he paid official visits to country districts, where he behaved with dignity both to his superiors and inferiors, and performed the duties entrusted to him, which related chiefly to the sectarians,° with an exactness and incorruptible honesty of which he could not but feel proud.

In official matters, despite his youth and taste for frivolous gaiety, he was exceedingly reserved, punctilious, and even severe; but in society he was often amusing and witty, and always good-natured, correct in his manner, and *bon enfant,* ° as the Governor and his wife—with whom he was like one of the family—used to say of him.

In the province he had an affair with a lady who made advances to the elegant young lawyer, and there was also a milliner; and there were carousals with aides-de-camp who visited the district, and after-supper visits to a certain outlying street of doubtful reputation; and there was too some obsequiousness to his chief and even to his chief's wife, but all this was done with such a tone of good breeding that no hard names could be applied to it. It all came under the heading of the French saying: *"Il faut que jeunesse se passe."* ° It was all done with clean hands, in clean linen, with French phrases, and above all among people of the best society and consequently with the approval of people of rank.

So Ivan Ilych served for five years and then came a change in his official life. The new and reformed judicial institutions were introduced, and new men were needed. Ivan Ilych became such a new man. He was offered the post of examining magistrate, and he accepted it though the post was in another province and obliged him to give up the connections he had formed and to make new ones. His friends met to give him a send-off; they had a group-photograph taken and presented him with a silver cigarette-case, and he set off to his new post.

As examining magistrate Ivan Ilych was just as *comme il faut*° and decorous a man, inspiring general respect and capable of separating his official duties from his private life, as he had been when acting as an official on special service. His duties now as examining magistrate were far more interesting and attractive than before. In his former position it had been pleasant to wear an undress uniform made by Scharmer, and to pass through the crowd of petitioners and officials who were timorously awaiting an audience with the Governor, and who envied him as with free and easy gait he went straight into his chief's private room to have a cup of tea and a cigarette with him. But not many people had been directly dependent on him—only police officials and the sectarians when he went

---

sectarians: dissenters from the Orthodox Church. *bon enfant:* French for "a well-behaved child." *"Il faut que jeunesse se passe":* "Youth doesn't last." *comme il faut:* "as required," ruleabiding.

on special missions—and he liked to treat them politely, almost as comrades, as if he were letting them feel that he who had the power to crush them was treating them in this simple, friendly way. There were then but few such people. But now, as an examining magistrate, Ivan Ilych felt that everyone without exception, even the most important and self-satisfied, was in his power, and that he need only write a few words on a sheet of paper with a certain heading, and this or that important, self-satisfied person would be brought before him in the role of an accused person or a witness, and if he did not choose to allow him to sit down, would have to stand before him and answer his questions. Ivan Ilych never abused his power; he tried on the contrary to soften its expression, but the consciousness of it and of the possibility of softening its effect, supplied the chief interest and attraction of his office. In his work itself, especially in his examinations, he very soon acquired a method of eliminating all considerations irrelevant to the legal aspect of the case, and reducing even the most complicated case to a form in which it would be presented on paper only in its externals, completely excluding his personal opinion of the matter, while above all observing every prescribed formality. The work was new and Ivan Ilych was one of the first men to apply the new Code of 1864.°

On taking up the post of examining magistrate in a new town, he made new acquaintances and connections, placed himself on a new footing, and assumed a somewhat different tone. He took up an attitude of rather dignified aloofness towards the provincial authorities, but picked out the best circle of legal gentlemen and wealthy gentry living in the town and assumed a tone of slight dissatisfaction with the government, of moderate liberalism, and of enlightened citizenship. At the same time, without at all altering the elegance of his toilet, he ceased shaving his chin and allowed his beard to grow as it pleased.

Ivan Ilych settled down very pleasantly in this new town. The society there, which inclined towards opposition to the Governor, was friendly, his salary was larger, and he began to play vint, ° which he found added not a little to the pleasure of life, for he had a capacity for cards, played good-humoredly, and calculated rapidly and astutely, so that he usually won.

After living there for two years he met his future wife, Praskovya Fëdorovna Mikhel, who was the most attractive, clever, and brilliant girl of the set in which he moved, and among other amusements and relaxations from his labors as examining magistrate, Ivan Ilych established light and playful relations with her.

While he had been an official on special service he had been accustomed to dance, but now as an examining magistrate it was exceptional for him to do so. If he danced now, he did it as if to show that though he served under the reformed order of things, and had reached the fifth official rank, yet when it came to

Code of 1864: The emancipation of the serfs in 1861 was followed by a thorough all-round reform of judicial proceedings. [Translators' note.]   vint: a form of bridge. [Translators' note.]

dancing he could do it better than most people. So at the end of an evening he sometimes danced with Praskovya Fëdorovna, and it was chiefly during these dances that he captivated her. She fell in love with him. Ivan Ilych had at first no definite intention of marrying, but when the girl fell in love with him he said to himself: "Really, why shouldn't I marry?"

Praskovya Fëdorovna came of a good family, was not bad-looking, and had some little property. Ivan Ilych might have aspired to a more brilliant match, but even this was good. He had his salary, and she, he hoped, would have an equal income. She was well connected, and was a sweet, pretty, and thoroughly correct young woman. To say that Ivan Ilych married because he fell in love with Praskovya Fëdorovna and found that she sympathized with his views of life would be as incorrect as to say that he married because his social circle approved of the match. He was swayed by both these considerations: the marriage gave him personal satisfaction, and at the same time it was considered the right thing by the most highly placed of his associates.

So Ivan Ilych got married.

The preparations for marriage and the beginning of married life, with its conjugal caresses, the new furniture, new crockery, and new linen, were very pleasant until his wife became pregnant—so that Ivan Ilych had begun to think that marriage would not impair the easy, agreeable, gay, and always decorous character of his life, approved of by society and regarded by himself as natural, but would even improve it. But from the first months of his wife's pregnancy, something new, unpleasant, depressing, and unseemly, and from which there was no way of escape, unexpectedly showed itself.

His wife, without any reason—*de gaieté de coeur*° as Ivan Ilych expressed it to himself—began to disturb the pleasure and propriety of their life. She began to be jealous without any cause, expected him to devote his whole attention to her, found fault with everything, and made coarse and ill-mannered scenes.

At first Ivan Ilych hoped to escape from the unpleasantness of this state of affairs by the same easy and decorous relation to life that had served him heretofore: he tried to ignore his wife's disagreeable moods, continued to live in his usual easy and pleasant way, invited friends to his house for a game of cards, and also tried going out to his club or spending his evenings with friends. But one day his wife began upbraiding him so vigorously, using such coarse words, and continued to abuse him every time he did not fulfil her demands, so resolutely and with such evident determination not to give way till he submitted—that is, till he stayed at home and was bored just as she was—that he became alarmed. He now realized that matrimony—at any rate with Praskovya Fëdorovna—was not always conducive to the pleasures and amenities of life, but on the contrary often infringed both comfort and propriety, and that he must therefore entrench himself against such infringement. And Ivan Ilych began to seek for means of doing so. His official duties were the one thing that imposed upon Praskovya Fëdorovna,

de gaieté de coeur: "from pure whim."

and by means of his official work and the duties attached to it he began struggling with his wife to secure his own independence.

With the birth of their child, the attempts to feed it and the various failures in doing so, and with the real and imaginary illnesses of mother and child, in which Ivan Ilych's sympathy was demanded but about which he understood nothing, the need of securing for himself an existence outside his family life became still more imperative.

As his wife grew more irritable and exacting and Ivan Ilych transferred the center of gravity of his life more and more to his official work, so did he grow to like his work better and became more ambitious than before.

Very soon, within a year of his wedding, Ivan Ilych had realized that marriage, though it may add some comforts to life, is in fact a very intricate and difficult affair towards which in order to perform one's duty, that is, to lead a decorous life approved of by society, one must adopt a definite attitude just as towards one's official duties.

And Ivan Ilych evolved such an attitude towards married life. He only required of it those conveniences—dinner at home, housewife, and bed—which it could give him, and above all that propriety of external forms required by public opinion. For the rest he looked for light-hearted pleasure and propriety, and was very thankful when he found them, but if he met with antagonism and querulousness he at once retired into his separate fenced-off world of official duties, where he found satisfaction.

Ivan Ilych was esteemed a good official, and after three years was made Assistant Public Prosecutor. His new duties, their importance, the possibility of indicting and imprisoning anyone he chose, the publicity his speeches received, and the success he had in all these things, made his work still more attractive.

More children came. His wife became more and more querulous and ill-tempered, but the attitude Ivan Ilych had adopted towards his home life rendered him almost impervious to her grumbling.

After seven years' service in that town he was transferred to another province as Public Prosecutor. They moved, but were short of money and his wife did not like the place they moved to. Though the salary was higher the cost of living was greater, besides which two of their children died and family life became still more unpleasant for him.

Praskovya Fëdorovna blamed her husband for every inconvenience they encountered in their new home. Most of the conversations between husband and wife, especially as to the children's education, led to topics which recalled former disputes, and those disputes were apt to flare up again at any moment. There remained only those rare periods of amorousness which still came to them at times but did not last long. These were islets at which they anchored for a while and then again set out upon that ocean of veiled hostility which showed itself in their aloofness from one another. This aloofness might have grieved Ivan Ilych had he considered that it ought not to exist, but he now regarded the position as normal, and even made it the goal at which he aimed in family life. His aim was to free himself more and more from those unpleasantnesses and to give them a semblance of harmlessness and propriety. He attained this by spending less and less time with his family, and when obliged to be at home he tried to safeguard his position by the presence of outsiders. The chief thing, however, was that he had his official duties. The whole interest of his life now centered in the official world and that interest absorbed him. The consciousness of his power, being able to ruin anybody he wished to ruin, the importance, even the external dignity of his entry into court, or meetings with his subordinates, his success with superiors and inferiors, and above all his masterly handling of cases, of which he was conscious—all this gave him pleasure and filled his life, together with chats with his colleagues, dinners, and bridge. So that on the whole Ivan Ilych's life continued to flow as he considered it should do—pleasantly and properly.

So things continued for another seven years. His eldest daughter was already sixteen, another child had died, and only one son was left, a schoolboy and a subject of dissension. Ivan Ilych wanted to put him in the School of Law, but to spite him Praskovya Fëdorovna entered him at the High School. The daughter had been educated at home and had turned out well: the boy did not learn badly either.

III

So Ivan Ilych lived for seventeen years after his marriage. He was already a Public Prosecutor of long standing, and had declined several proposed transfers while awaiting a more desirable post, when an unanticipated and unpleasant occurrence quite upset the peaceful course of his life. He was expecting to be offered the post of presiding judge in a University town, but Happe somehow came to the front and obtained the appointment instead. Ivan Ilych became irritable, reproached Happe, and quarreled both with him and with his immediate superiors—who became colder to him and again passed him over when other appointments were made.

This was in 1880, the hardest year of Ivan Ilych's life. It was then that it became evident on the one hand that his salary was insufficient for them to live on, and on the other that he had been forgotten, and not only this, but that what was for him the greatest and most cruel injustice appeared to others a quite ordinary occurrence. Even his father did not consider it his duty to help him. Ivan Ilych felt himself abandoned by everyone, and that they regarded his position with a salary of 3,500 rubles as quite normal and even fortunate. He alone knew that with the consciousness of the injustices done him, with his wife's incessant nagging, and with the debts he had contracted by living beyond his means, his position was far from normal.

In order to save money that summer he obtained leave of absence and went with his wife to live in the country at her brother's place.

In the country, without his work, he experienced *ennui* for the first time in his life, and not only *ennui* but intolerable depression, and he decided that it was impossible to go on living like that, and that it was necessary to take energetic measures.

Having passed a sleepless night pacing up and down the veranda, he decided to go to Petersburg and bestir himself, in order to punish those who had failed to appreciate him and to get transferred to another ministry.

Next day, despite many protests from his wife and her brother, he started for Petersburg with the sole object of obtaining a post with a salary of five thousand rubles a year. He was no longer bent on any particular department, or tendency, or kind of activity. All he now wanted was an appointment to another post with a salary of five thousand rubles, either in the administration, in the banks, with the railways, in one of the Empress Marya's Institutions,° or even in the customs—but it had to carry with it a salary of five thousand rubles and be in a ministry other than that in which they had failed to appreciate him.

And this quest of Ivan Ilych's was crowned with remarkable and unexpected success. At Kursk an acquaintance of his, F. I. Ilyin, got into the first-class carriage, sat down beside Ivan Ilych, and told him of a telegram just received by the Governor of Kursk announcing that a change was about to take place in the ministry: Peter Ivanovich was to be superseded by Ivan Semënovich.

The proposed change, apart from its significance for Russia, had a special significance for Ivan Ilych, because by bringing forward a new man, Peter Petrovich, and consequently his friend Zachar Ivanovich, it was highly favorable for Ivan Ilych, since Zachar Ivanovich was a friend and colleague of his.

In Moscow this news was confirmed, and on reaching Petersburg Ivan Ilych found Zachar Ivanovich and received a definite promise of an appointment in his former department of Justice.

A week later he telegraphed to his wife: "Zachar in Miller's place. I shall receive appointment on presentation of report."

Thanks to this change of personnel, Ivan Ilych had unexpectedly obtained an appointment in his former ministry which placed him two stages above his former colleagues besides giving him five thousand rubles salary and three thousand five hundred rubles for expenses connected with his removal. All his ill humor towards his former enemies and the whole department vanished, and Ivan Ilych was completely happy.

He returned to the country more cheerful and contented than he had been for a long time. Praskovya Fëdorovna also cheered up and a truce was arranged between them. Ivan Ilych told of how he had been fêted by everybody in Petersburg, how all those who had been his enemies were put to shame and now fawned on him, how envious they were of his appointment, and how much everybody in Petersburg had liked him.

Praskovya Fëdorovna listened to all this and appeared to believe it. She did not contradict anything, but only made plans for their life in the town to which they were going. Ivan Ilych saw with delight that these plans were his plans, that

90

95

Empress Marya's Institutions: orphanages.

he and his wife agreed, and that, after a stumble, his life was regaining its due and natural character of pleasant lightheartedness and decorum.

Ivan Ilych had come back for a short time only, for he had to take up his new duties on the 10th of September. Moreover, he needed time to settle into the new place, to move all his belongings from the province, and to buy and order many additional things: in a word, to make such arrangements as he had resolved on, which were almost exactly what Praskovya Fëdorovna too had decided on.

Now that everything had happened so fortunately, and that he and his wife were at one in their aims and moreover saw so little of one another, they got on together better than they had done since the first years of marriage. Ivan Ilych had thought of taking his family away with him at once, but the insistence of his wife's brother and her sister-in-law, who had suddenly become particularly amiable and friendly to him and his family, induced him to depart alone.

So he departed, and the cheerful state of mind induced by his success and by the harmony between his wife and himself, the one intensifying the other, did not leave him. He found a delightful house, just the thing both he and his wife had dreamt of. Spacious, lofty reception rooms in the old style, a convenient and dignified study, rooms for his wife and daughter, a study for his son—it might have been specially built for them. Ivan Ilych himself superintended the arrangements, chose the wallpapers, supplemented the furniture (preferably with antiques which he considered particularly *comme il faut*), and supervised the upholstering. Everything progressed and progressed and approached the ideal he had set himself: even when things were only half completed they exceeded his expectations. He saw what a refined and elegant character, free from vulgarity, it would all have when it was ready. On falling asleep he pictured to himself how the reception-room would look. Looking at the yet unfinished drawing-room he could see the fireplace, the screen, the what-not, the little chairs dotted here and there, the dishes and plates on the walls, and the bronzes, as they would be when everything was in place. He was pleased by the thought of how his wife and daughter, who shared his taste in this matter, would be impressed by it. They were certainly not expecting as much. He had been particularly successful in finding, and buying cheaply, antiques which gave a particularly aristocratic character to the whole place. But in his letters he intentionally understated everything in order to be able to surprise them. All this so absorbed him that his new duties—though he liked his official work—interested him less than he had expected. Sometimes he even had moments of absentmindedness during the Court Sessions, and would consider whether he should have straight or curved cornices for his curtains. He was so interested in it all that he often did things himself, rearranging the furniture, or rehanging the curtains. Once when mounting a stepladder to show the upholsterer, who did not understand, how he wanted the hangings draped, he made a false step and slipped, but being a strong and agile man he clung on and only knocked his side against the knob of the window frame. The bruised place was painful but the pain soon passed, and he felt particularly bright and well just then. He wrote: "I feel fifteen years younger." He thought he would have everything ready by September, but it dragged on till mid-October. But the result was charming not only in his eyes but to everyone who saw it.

In reality it was just what is usually seen in the houses of people of mod- 100 erate means who want to appear rich, and therefore succeed only in resembling others like themselves: there were damasks, dark wood, plants, rugs, and dull and polished bronzes—all the things people of a certain class have in order to resemble other people of that class. His house was so like the others that it would never have been noticed, but to him it all seemed to be quite excep- tional. He was very happy when he met his family at the station and brought them to the newly furnished house all lit up, where a footman in a white tie opened the door into the hall decorated with plants, and when they went on into the drawing-room and the study uttering exclamations of delight. He con- ducted them everywhere, drank in their praises eagerly, and beamed with plea- sure. At tea that evening, when Praskovya Fëdorovna among other things asked him about his fall, he laughed and showed them how he had gone flying and had frightened the upholsterer.

"It's a good thing I'm a bit of an athlete. Another man might have been killed, but I merely knocked myself, just there; it hurts when it's touched, but it's passing off already—it's only a bruise."

So they began living in their new home—in which, as always happens, when they got thoroughly settled in they found they were just one room short— and with the increased income, which as always was just a little (some five hun- dred rubles) too little, but it was all very nice.

Things went particularly well at first, before everything was finally arranged and while something had still to be done: this thing bought, that thing ordered, another thing moved, and something else adjusted. Though there were some dis- putes between husband and wife, they were both so well satisfied and had so much to do that it all passed off without any serious quarrels. When nothing was left to arrange it became rather dull and something seemed to be lacking, but they were then making acquaintances, forming habits, and life was growing fuller.

Ivan Ilych spent his mornings at the law courts and came home to dinner, and at first he was generally in a good humor, though he occasionally became ir- ritable just on account of his house. (Every spot on the tablecloth or the uphol- stery, and every broken window-blind string, irritated him. He had devoted so much trouble to arranging it all that every disturbance of it distressed him.) But on the whole his life ran its course as he believed life should do: easily, pleas- antly, and decorously.

He got up at nine, drank his coffee, read the paper, and then put on his un- 105 dress uniform and went to the law courts. There the harness in which he worked had already been stretched to fit him and he donned it without a hitch: peti- tioners, inquiries at the chancery, the chancery itself, and the sittings public and administrative. In all this the thing was to exclude everything fresh and vital, which always disturbs the regular course of official business, and to admit only official relations with people, and then only on official grounds. A man would come, for instance, wanting some information. Ivan Ilych, as one in whose sphere the matter did not lie, would have nothing to do with him: but if the man had some business with him in his official capacity, something that could be expressed on officially stamped paper, he would do everything, positively everything he could within the limits of such relations, and in doing so would maintain the semblance of friendly human relations, that is, would observe the courtesies of life. As soon as the official relations ended, so did everything else. Ivan Ilych possessed this capacity to separate his real life from the official side of affairs and not mix the two, in the highest degree, and by long practice and natural aptitude had brought it to such a pitch that sometimes, in the manner of a virtuoso, he would even allow himself to let the human and official relations mingle. He let himself do this just because he felt that he could at any time he chose resume the strictly official attitude again and drop the human relation. And he did it all easily, pleasantly, correctly, and even artistically. In the intervals between the sessions he smoked, drank tea, chatted a little about politics, a little about general topics, a little about cards, but most of all about official appointments. Tired, but with the feelings of a virtuoso—one of the first violins who has played his part in an orchestra with precision—he would return home to find that his wife and daughter had been out paying calls, or had a visitor, and that his son had been to school, had done his homework with his tutor, and was duly learning what is taught at High Schools. Everything was as it should be. After dinner, if they had no visitors, Ivan Ilych sometimes read a book that was being much discussed at the time, and in the evening settled down to work, that is, read official papers, compared the depositions of witnesses, and noted paragraphs of the Code applying to them. This was neither dull nor amusing. It was dull when he might have been playing bridge, but if no bridge was available it was at any rate better than doing nothing or sitting with his wife. Ivan Ilych's chief pleasure was giving little dinners to which he invited men and women of good social position, and just as his drawing-room resembled all other drawing-rooms so did his enjoyable little parties resemble all other such parties.

Once they even gave a dance. Ivan Ilych enjoyed it and everything went off well, except that it led to a violent quarrel with his wife about the cakes and sweets. Praskovya Fëdorovna had made her own plans, but Ivan Ilych insisted on getting everything from an expensive confectioner and ordered too many cakes, and the quarrel occurred because some of those cakes were left over and the confectioner's bill came to forty-five rubles. It was a great and disagreeable quarrel. Praskovya Fëdorovna called him "a fool and an imbecile," and he clutched at his head and made angry allusions to divorce.

But the dance itself had been enjoyable. The best people were there, and Ivan Ilych had danced with Princess Trufonova, a sister of the distinguished founder of the Society "Bear My Burden."

The pleasures connected with his work were pleasures of ambition; his social pleasures were those of vanity; but Ivan Ilych's greatest pleasure was playing bridge. He acknowledged that whatever disagreeable incident happened in his life, the pleasure that beamed like a ray of light above everything else was to sit down to bridge with good players, not noisy partners, and of course to four-handed bridge (with five players it was annoying to have to stand out, though one pretended not to mind), to play a clever and serious game (when the cards allowed it), and then to have supper and drink a glass of wine. After a game of bridge, especially if he had won a little (to win a large sum was unpleasant), Ivan Ilych went to bed in specially good humor.

So they lived. They formed a circle of acquaintances among the best people and were visited by people of importance and by young folk. In their views as to their acquaintances, husband, wife, and daughter were entirely agreed, and tacitly and unanimously kept at arm's length and shook off the various shabby friends and relations who, with much show of affection, gushed into the drawing-room with its Japanese plates on the walls. Soon these shabby friends ceased to obtrude themselves and only the best people remained in the Golovins' set.

Young men made up to Lisa, and Petrishchev, an examining magistrate and Dmitri Ivanovich Petrishchev's son and sole heir, began to be so attentive to her that Ivan Ilych had already spoken to Praskovya Fëdorovna about it, and considered whether they should not arrange a party for them, or get up some private theatricals.

So they lived, and all went well, without change, and life flowed pleasantly.

IV

They were all in good health. It could not be called ill health if Ivan Ilych sometimes said that he had a queer taste in his mouth and felt some discomfort in his left side.

But this discomfort increased and, though not exactly painful, grew into a sense of pressure in his side accompanied by ill humor. And his irritability became worse and worse and began to mar the agreeable, easy, and correct life that had established itself in the Golovin family. Quarrels between husband and wife became more and more frequent, and soon the ease and amenity disappeared and even the decorum was barely maintained. Scenes again became frequent, and very few of those islets remained on which husband and wife could meet without an explosion. Praskovya Fëdorovna now had good reason to say that her husband's temper was trying. With characteristic exaggeration she said he had always had a dreadful temper, and that it had needed all her good nature to put up with it for twenty years. It was true that now the quarrels were started by him. His bursts of temper always came just before dinner, often just as he began to eat his soup. Sometimes he noticed that a plate or dish was chipped, or the food was not right, or his son put his elbow on the table, or his daughter's hair was not done as he liked it, and for all this he blamed Praskovya Fëdorovna. At first she retorted and said disagreeable things to him, but once or twice he fell into such a rage at the beginning of dinner that she realized it was due to some physical derangement brought on by taking food, and so she restrained herself and did not answer, but only hurried to get the dinner over. She regarded this self-restraint as highly praiseworthy. Having come to the conclusion that her husband had a dreadful temper and made her life miserable, she began to feel sorry for herself, and the more she pitied herself the more she hated her husband. She began to wish he would die; yet she did not want him to die because then his salary would cease. And this irritated her against him still more. She considered herself dreadfully unhappy just because not even his death could save her, and though she concealed her exasperation, that hidden exasperation of hers increased his irritation also.

After one scene in which Ivan Ilych had been particularly unfair and after which he had said in explanation that he certainly was irritable but that it was due to his not being well, she said that if he was ill it should be attended to, and insisted on his going to see a celebrated doctor.

He went. Everything took place as he had expected and as it always does. There was the usual waiting and the important air assumed by the doctor, with which he was so familiar (resembling that which he himself assumed in court), and the sounding and listening, and the questions which called for answers that were foregone conclusions and were evidently unnecessary, and the look of importance which implied that "if only you put yourself in our hands we will arrange everything—we know indubitably how it has to be done, always in the same way for everybody alike." It was all just as it was in the law courts. The doctor put on just the same air towards him as he himself put on towards an accused person. 115

The doctor said that so-and-so indicated that there was so-and-so inside the patient, but if the investigation of so-and-so did not confirm this, then he must assume that and that. If he assumed that and that, then . . . and so on. To Ivan Ilych only one question was important: was his case serious or not? But the doctor ignored that inappropriate question. From his point of view it was not the one under consideration, the real question was to decide between a floating kidney, chronic catarrh, or appendicitis. It was not a question of Ivan Ilych's life or death, but one between a floating kidney and appendicitis. And that question the doctor solved brilliantly, as it seemed to Ivan Ilych, in favor of the appendix, with the reservation that should an examination of the urine give fresh indications the matter would be reconsidered. All this was just what Ivan Ilych had himself brilliantly accomplished a thousand times in dealing with men on trial. The doctor summed up just as brilliantly, looking over his spectacles triumphantly and even gaily at the accused. From the doctor's summing up Ivan Ilych concluded that things were bad, but that for the doctor, and perhaps for everybody else, it was a matter of indifference, though for him it was bad. And this conclusion struck him painfully, arousing in him a great feeling of pity for himself and of bitterness towards the doctor's indifference to a matter of such importance.

He said nothing of this, but rose, placed the doctor's fee on the table, and remarked with a sigh: "We sick people probably often put inappropriate questions. But tell me, in general, is this complaint dangerous, or not? . . ."

The doctor looked at him sternly over his spectacles with one eye, as if to say: "Prisoner, if you will not keep to the questions put to you, I shall be obliged to have you removed from the court."

"I have already told you what I consider necessary and proper. The analysis may show something more." And the doctor bowed.

Ivan Ilych went out slowly, seated himself disconsolately in his sledge, and 120 drove home. All the way home he was going over what the doctor had said, trying to translate those complicated, obscure, scientific phrases into plain language and find in them an answer to the question: "Is my condition bad? Is it very bad? Or is there as yet nothing much wrong?" And it seemed to him that the meaning of what the doctor had said was that it was very bad. Everything in the streets seemed depressing. The cabmen, the houses, the passers-by, and the shops, were dismal. His ache, this dull gnawing ache that never ceased for a moment, seemed to have acquired a new and more serious significance from the doctor's dubious remarks. Ivan Ilych now watched it with a new and oppressive feeling.

He reached home and began to tell his wife about it. She listened, but in the middle of his account his daughter came in with her hat on, ready to go out with her mother. She sat down reluctantly to listen to this tedious story, but could not stand it long, and her mother too did not hear him to the end.

"Well, I am very glad," she said. "Mind now to take your medicine regularly. Give me the prescription and I'll send Gerasim to the chemist's." And she went to get ready to go out.

While she was in the room Ivan Ilych had hardly taken time to breathe, but he sighed deeply when she left it.

"Well," he thought, "perhaps it isn't so bad after all."

He began taking his medicine and following the doctor's directions, which 125 had been altered after the examination of the urine. But then it happened that there was a contradiction between the indications drawn from the examination of the urine and the symptoms that showed themselves. It turned out that what was happening differed from what the doctor had told him, and that he had either forgotten, or blundered, or hidden something from him. He could not, however, be blamed for that, and Ivan Ilych still obeyed his orders implicitly and at first derived some comfort from doing so.

From the time of his visit to the doctor, Ivan Ilych's chief occupation was the exact fulfillment of the doctor's instructions regarding hygiene and the taking of medicine, and the observation of his pain and his excretions. His chief interests came to be people's ailments and people's health. When sickness, deaths, or recoveries were mentioned in his presence, especially when the illness resembled his own, he listened with agitation which he tried to hide, asked questions, and applied what he heard to his own case.

The pain did not grow less, but Ivan Ilych made efforts to force himself to think that he was better. And he could do this so long as nothing agitated him. But as soon as he had any unpleasantness with his wife, any lack of success in his official work, or held bad cards at bridge, he was at once acutely sensible of his disease. He had formerly borne such mischances, hoping soon to adjust what was wrong, to master it and attain success, or make a grand slam. But now every mischance upset him and plunged him into despair. He would say to himself: "There now, just as I was beginning to get better and the medicine had begun to take effect, comes this accursed misfortune, or unpleasantness. . . ." And he was furious with the mishap, or with the people who were causing the unpleasantness and killing him, for he felt that this fury was killing him but could not restrain it. One would have thought that it should have been clear to him that this exasperation with circumstances and people aggravated his illness, and that he ought therefore to ignore unpleasant occurrences. But he drew the very opposite conclusion: he said that he needed peace, and he watched for everything that might disturb it and became irritable at the slightest infringement of it. His condition was rendered worse by the fact that he read medical books and consulted doctors. The progress of his disease was so gradual that he could deceive himself when comparing one day with another—the difference was so slight. But when he consulted the doctors it seemed to him that he was getting worse, and even very rapidly. Yet despite this he was continually consulting them.

That month he went to see another celebrity, who told him almost the same as the first had done but put his questions rather differently, and the interview with this celebrity only increased Ivan Ilych's doubts and fears. A friend of a friend of his, a very good doctor, diagnosed his illness again quite differently from the others, and though he predicted recovery, his questions and suppositions bewildered Ivan Ilych still more and increased his doubts. A homeopathist diagnosed the disease in yet another way, and prescribed medicine which Ivan Ilych took secretly for a week. But after a week, not feeling any improvement and having lost confidence both in the former doctor's treatment and in this one's, he became still more despondent. One day a lady acquaintance mentioned a cure effected by a wonder-working icon. Ivan Ilych caught himself listening attentively and beginning to believe that it had occurred. This incident alarmed him. "Has my mind really weakened to such an extent?" he asked himself. "Nonsense! It's all rubbish. I mustn't give way to nervous fears but having chosen a doctor must keep strictly to his treatment. That is what I will do. Now it's all settled. I won't think about it, but will follow the treatment seriously till summer, and then we shall see. From now there must be no more of this wavering!" This was easy to say but impossible to carry out. The pain in his side oppressed him and seemed to grow worse and more incessant, while the taste in his mouth grew stranger and stranger. It seemed to him that his breath had a disgusting smell, and he was conscious of a loss of appetite and strength. There was no deceiving himself: something terrible, new, and more important than anything before in his life, was taking place within him of which he alone was aware. Those about him did not understand or would not understand it, but thought everything in the world was going on as usual. That tormented Ivan Ilych more than anything. He saw that his household, especially his wife and daughter who were in a perfect whirl of visiting, did not understand anything of it and were annoyed that he was so depressed and so exacting, as if he were to blame for it. Though they tried to disguise it he saw that he was an obstacle in their path, and that his wife had adopted a definite line in regard to his illness and kept to it regardless of anything he said or did. Her attitude was this: "You know," she would say to her friends, "Ivan Ilych can't do as other people do, and keep to the treatment prescribed for him. One day he'll take his drops and keep strictly to his diet and go to bed in good time, but the next day unless I watch him he'll suddenly forget his medicine, eat sturgeon—which is forbidden—and sit up playing cards till one o'clock in the morning."

"Oh, come, when was that?" Ivan Ilych would ask in vexation. "Only once at Peter Ivanovich's."

"And yesterday with Shebek."   130

"Well, even if I hadn't stayed up, this pain would have kept me awake."

"Be that as it may you'll never get well like that, but will always make us wretched."

Praskovya Fëdorovna's attitude to Ivan Ilych's illness, as she expressed it both to others and to him, was that it was his own fault and was another of the annoyances he caused her. Ivan Ilych felt that this opinion escaped her involuntarily—but that did not make it easier for him.

At the law courts too, Ivan Ilych noticed, or thought he noticed, a strange attitude towards himself. It sometimes seemed to him that people were watching him inquisitively as a man whose place might soon be vacant. Then again, his friends would suddenly begin to chaff him in a friendly way about his low spirits, as if the awful, horrible, and unheard-of thing that was going on within him, incessantly gnawing at him and irresistibly drawing him away, was a very agreeable subject for jests. Schwartz in particular irritated him by his jocularity, vivacity, and *savoir-faire*, which reminded him of what he himself had been ten years ago.

Friends came to make up a set and they sat down to cards. They dealt, 135 bending the new cards to soften them, and he sorted the diamonds in his hand and found he had seven. His partner said "No trumps" and supported him with two diamonds. What more could be wished for? It ought to be jolly and lively. They would make a grand slam. But suddenly Ivan Ilych was conscious of that gnawing pain, that taste in his mouth, and it seemed ridiculous that in such circumstances he should be pleased to make a grand slam.

He looked at his partner Mikhail Mikhaylovich, who rapped the table with his strong hand and instead of snatching up the tricks pushed the cards courteously and indulgently towards Ivan Ilych that he might have the pleasure of gathering them up without the trouble of stretching out his hand for them. "Does he think I am too weak to stretch out my arm?" thought Ivan Ilych, and forgetting what he was doing he over-trumped his partner, missing the grand slam by three tricks. And what was most awful of all was that he saw how upset Mikhail Mikhaylovich was about it but did not himself care. And it was dreadful to realize why he did not care.

They all saw that he was suffering, and said: "We can stop if you are tired. Take a rest." Lie down? No, he was not at all tired, and he finished the rubber. All were gloomy and silent. Ivan Ilych felt that he had diffused this gloom over them and could not dispel it. They had supper and went away, and Ivan Ilych was left alone with the consciousness that his life was poisoned and was poisoning the lives of others, and that this poison did not weaken but penetrated more and more deeply into his whole being.

With this consciousness, and with physical pain besides the terror, he must go to bed, often to lie awake the greater part of the night. Next morning he had to get up again, dress, go to the law courts, speak, and write; or if he did not go out, spend at home those twenty-four hours a day each of which was a torture. And he had to live thus all alone on the brink of an abyss, with no one who understood or pitied him.

V

So one month passed and then another. Just before the New Year his brother-in-law came to town and stayed at their house. Ivan Ilych was at the law courts and Praskovya Fëdorovna had gone shopping. When Ivan Ilych came home and entered his study he found his brother-in-law there—a healthy, florid man—unpacking his portmanteau himself. He raised his head on hearing Ivan Ilych's footsteps and looked up at him for a moment without a word. That stare told Ivan Ilych everything. His brother-in-law opened his mouth to utter an exclamation of surprise but checked himself, and that action confirmed it all.

"I have changed, eh?" 140

"Yes, there is a change."

And after that, try as he would to get his brother-in-law to return to the subject of his looks, the latter would say nothing about it. Praskovya Fëdorovna came home and her brother went out to her. Ivan Ilych locked the door and began to examine himself in the glass, first full face, then in profile. He took up a portrait of himself taken with his wife, and compared it with what he saw in the glass. The change in him was immense. Then he bared his arms to the elbow, looked at them, drew the sleeves down again, sat down on an ottoman, and grew blacker than night.

"No, no, this won't do!" he said to himself, and jumped up, went to the table, took up some law papers, and began to read them, but could not continue. He unlocked the door and went into the reception-room. The door leading to the drawing-room was shut. He approached it on tiptoe and listened.

"No, you are exaggerating!" Praskovya Fëdorovna was saying.

"Exaggerating! Don't you see it? Why, he's a dead man! Look at his eyes— 145 there's no light in them. But what is it that is wrong with him?"

"No one knows. Nikolaevich said something, but I don't know what. And Leshchetitsky° said quite the contrary . . ."

Ivan Ilych walked away, went to his own room, lay down, and began musing: "The kidney, a floating kidney." He recalled all the doctors had told him of how it detached itself and swayed about. And by an effort of imagination he tried to catch that kidney and arrest it and support it. So little was needed for

Nikolaevich, Leshchetitsky: two doctors, the latter a celebrated specialist. [Translators' note.]

this, it seemed to him. "No, I'll go to see Peter Ivanovich° again." He rang, ordered the carriage, and got ready to go.

"Where are you going, Jean?" asked his wife, with a specially sad and exceptionally kind look.

This exceptionally kind look irritated him. He looked morosely at her.

"I must go to see Peter Ivanovich." 150

He went to see Peter Ivanovich, and together they went to see his friend, the doctor. He was in, and Ivan Ilych had a long talk with him.

Reviewing the anatomical and physiological details of what in the doctor's opinion was going on inside him, he understood it all.

There was something, a small thing, in the vermiform appendix. It might all come right. Only stimulate the energy of one organ and check the activity of another, then absorption would take place and everything would come right. He got home rather late for dinner, ate his dinner, and conversed cheerfully, but could not for a long time bring himself to go back to work in his room. At last, however, he went to his study and did what was necessary, but the consciousness that he had put something aside—an important, intimate matter which he would revert to when his work was done—never left him. When he had finished his work he remembered that this intimate matter was the thought of his vermiform appendix. But he did not give himself up to it, and went to the drawingroom for tea. There were callers there, including the examining magistrate who was a desirable match for his daughter, and they were conversing, playing the piano, and singing. Ivan Ilych, as Praskovya Fëdorovna remarked, spent that evening more cheerfully than usual, but he never for a moment forgot that he had postponed the important matter of the appendix. At eleven o'clock he said good-night and went to his bedroom. Since his illness he had slept alone in a small room next to his study. He undressed and took up a novel by Zola, but instead of reading it he fell into thought, and in his imagination that desired improvement in the vermiform appendix occurred. There was the absorption and evacuation and the re-establishment of normal activity. "Yes, that's it!" he said to himself. "One need only assist nature, that's all." He remembered his medicine, rose, took it, and lay down on his back watching for the beneficent action of the medicine and for it to lessen the pain. "I need only take it regularly and avoid all injurious influences. I am already feeling better, much better." He began touching his side: it was not painful to the touch. "There, I really don't feel it. It's much better already." He put out the light and turned on his side . . . "The appendix is getting better, absorption is occurring." Suddenly he felt the old, familiar, dull, gnawing pain, stubborn and serious. There was the same familiar loathsome taste in his mouth. His heart sank and he felt dazed. "My God! My God!" he muttered. "Again, again! and it will never cease." And suddenly the matter presented itself in a quite different aspect. "Vermiform appendix! Kidney!" he said to himself. "It's not a question of appendix or kidney, but of life and . . . death. Yes, life was there and now it is going, going and I cannot stop it.

Peter Ivanovich: That was the friend whose friend was a doctor. [Translators' note.]

Yes. Why deceive myself? Isn't it obvious to everyone but me that I'm dying, and that it's only a question of weeks, days . . . it may happen this moment. There was light and now there is darkness. I was here and now I'm going there! Where?" A chill came over him, his breathing ceased, and he felt only the throbbing of his heart.

"When I am not, what will there be? There will be nothing. Then where shall I be when I am no more? Can this be dying? No, I don't want to!" He jumped up and tried to light the candle, felt for it with trembling hands, dropped candle and candlestick on the floor, and fell back on his pillow.

"What's the use? It makes no difference," he said to himself, staring with   155
wide-open eyes into the darkness. "Death. Yes, death. And none of them know or wish to know it, and they have no pity for me. Now they are playing." (He heard through the door the distant sound of a song and its accompaniment.) "It's all the same to them, but they will die too! Fools! I first, and they later, but it will be the same for them. And now they are merry . . . . the beasts!"

Anger choked him and he was agonizingly, unbearably miserable. "It is impossible that all men have been doomed to suffer this awful horror!" He raised himself.

"Something must be wrong. I must calm myself—must think it all over from the beginning." And he again began thinking. "Yes, the beginning of my illness: I knocked my side, but I was still quite well that day and the next. It hurt a little, then rather more. I saw the doctors, then followed despondency and anguish, more doctors, and I drew nearer to the abyss. My strength grew less and I kept coming nearer and nearer, and now I have wasted away and there is no light in my eyes. I think of the appendix—but this is death! I think of mending the appendix, and all the while here is death! Can it really be death?" Again terror seized him and he gasped for breath. He leant down and began feeling for the matches, pressing with his elbow on the stand beside the bed. It was in his way and hurt him, he grew furious with it, pressed on it still harder, and upset it. Breathless and in despair he fell on his back, expecting death to come immediately.

Meanwhile the visitors were leaving. Praskovya Fëdorovna was seeing them off. She heard something fall and came in.

"What has happened?"

"Nothing. I knocked it over accidentally."   160

She went out and returned with a candle. He lay there panting heavily, like a man who has run a thousand yards, and stared upwards at her with a fixed look.

"What is it, Jean?"

"No . . . o . . . thing. I upset it." ("Why speak of it? She won't understand," he thought.)

And in truth she did not understand. She picked up the stand, lit his candle, and hurried away to see another visitor off. When she came back he still lay on his back, looking upwards.

"What is it? Do you feel worse?"   165

"Yes."

She shook her head and sat down.

"Do you know, Jean, I think we must ask Leshchetitsky to come and see you here."

This meant calling in the famous specialist, regardless of expense. He smiled malignantly and said "No." She remained a little longer and then went up to him and kissed his forehead.

While she was kissing him he hated her from the bottom of his soul and 170 with difficulty refrained from pushing her away.

"Good-night. Please God you'll sleep."

"Yes."

VI

Ivan Ilych saw that he was dying, and he was in continual despair.

In the depth of his heart he knew he was dying, but not only was he not accustomed to the thought, he simply did not and could not grasp it.

The syllogism he had learnt from Kiezewetter's Logic: "Caius is a man, men 175 are mortal, therefore Caius is mortal," had always seemed to him correct as applied to Caius, but certainly not as applied to himself. That Caius—man in the abstract—was mortal, was perfectly correct, but he was not Caius, not an abstract man, but a creature quite, quite separate from all others. He had been little Vanya, with a mamma and a papa, with Mitya and Volodya, with the toys, a coachman and a nurse, afterwards with Katenka and with all the joys, griefs, and delights of childhood, boyhood, and youth. What did Caius know of the smell of that striped leather ball Vanya had been so fond of? Had Caius kissed his mother's hand like that, and did the silk of her dress rustle so for Caius? Had he rioted like that at school when the pastry was bad? Had Caius been in love like that? Could Caius preside at a session as he did? "Caius really was mortal, and it was right for him to die; but for me, little Vanya, Ivan Ilych, with all my thoughts and emotions, it's altogether a different matter. It cannot be that I ought to die. That would be too terrible."

Such was his feeling.

"If I had to die like Caius I should have known it was so. An inner voice would have told me so, but there was nothing of the sort in me and I and all my friends felt that our case was quite different from that of Caius. And now here it is!" he said to himself. "It can't be. It's impossible! But here it is. How is this? How is one to understand it?"

He could not understand it, and tried to drive this false, incorrect, morbid thought away and to replace it by other proper and healthy thoughts. But that thought, and not the thought only but the reality itself, seemed to come and confront him.

And to replace that thought he called up a succession of others, hoping to find in them some support. He tried to get back into the former current of thoughts that had once screened the thought of death from him. But strange to say, all that had formerly shut off, hidden, and destroyed his consciousness of death, no longer had that effect. Ivan Ilych now spent most of his time in attempting to re-establish that old current. He would say to himself: "I will take up my duties again—after all I used to live by them." And banishing all doubts he would go to the law courts, enter into conversation with his colleagues, and sit carelessly as was his wont, scanning the crowd with a thoughtful look and leaning both his emaciated arms on the arms of his oak chair; bending over as usual to a colleague and drawing his papers nearer he would interchange whispers with him, and then suddenly raising his eyes and sitting erect would pronounce certain words and open the proceedings. But suddenly in the midst of those proceedings the pain in his side, regardless of the stage the proceedings had reached, would begin its own gnawing work. Ivan Ilych would turn his attention to it and try to drive the thought of it away, but without success. It would come and stand before him and look at him, and he would be petrified and the light would die out of his eyes, and he would again begin asking himself whether It alone was true. And his colleagues and subordinates would see with surprise and distress that he, the brilliant and subtle judge, was becoming confused and making mistakes. He would shake himself, try to pull himself together, manage somehow to bring the sitting to a close, and return home with the sorrowful consciousness that his judicial labors could not as formerly hide from him what he wanted them to hide, and could not deliver him from It. And what was worst of all was that It drew his attention to itself not in order to make him take some action but only that he should look at It, look it straight in the face: look at it and, without doing anything, suffer inexpressibly.

And to save himself from this condition Ivan Ilych looked for consolation— new screens—and new screens were found and for a while seemed to save him, but then they immediately fell to pieces or rather became transparent, as if It penetrated them and nothing could veil It.

In these latter days he would go into the drawing-room he had arranged— that drawing-room where he had fallen and for the sake of which (how bitterly ridiculous it seemed) he had sacrificed his life—for he knew that his illness originated with that knock. He would enter and see that something had scratched the polished table. He would look for the cause of this and find that it was the bronze ornamentation of an album, that had got bent. He would take up the expensive album which he had lovingly arranged, and feel vexed with his daughter and her friends for their untidiness—for the album was torn here and there and some of the photographs turned upside down. He would put it carefully in order and bend the ornamentation back into position. Then it would occur to him to place all those things in another corner of the room, near the plants. He could call the footman, but his daughter or wife would come to help him. They would not agree, and his wife would contradict him, and he would dispute and grow angry. But that was all right, for then he did not think about It. It was invisible.

But then, when he was moving something himself, his wife would say: "Let the servants do it. You will hurt yourself again." And suddenly It would flash through the screen and he would see it. It was just a flash, and he hoped it would

180

disappear, but he would involuntarily pay attention to his side. "It sits there as before, gnawing just the same!" And he could no longer forget It, but could distinctly see it looking at him from behind the flowers. "What is it all for?"

"It really is so! I lost my life over that curtain as I might have done when storming a fort. Is that possible? How terrible and how stupid. It can't be true! It can't, but it is."

He would go to his study, lie down, and again be alone with It: face to face with It. And nothing could be done with It except to look at it and shudder.

VII

How it happened it is impossible to say because it came about step by step, 185
unnoticed, but in the third month of Ivan Ilych's illness, his wife, his daughter, his son, his acquaintances, the doctors, the servants, and above all he himself, were aware that the whole interest he had for other people was whether he would soon vacate his place, and at last release the living from the discomfort caused by his presence and be himself released from his sufferings.

He slept less and less. He was given opium and hypodermic injections of morphine, but this did not relieve him. The dull depression he experienced in a somnolent condition at first gave him a little relief, but only as something new, afterwards it became as distressing as the pain itself or even more so.

Special foods were prepared for him by the doctors' orders, but all those foods became increasingly distasteful and disgusting to him.

For his excretions also special arrangements had to be made, and this was a torment to him every time—a torment from the uncleanliness, the unseemliness, and the smell, and from knowing that another person had to take part in it.

But just through this most unpleasant matter, Ivan Ilych obtained comfort. Gerasim, the butler's young assistant, always came in to carry the things out. Gerasim was a clean, fresh peasant lad, grown stout on town food and always cheerful and bright. At first the sight of him, in his clean Russian peasant costume, engaged on that disgusting task embarrassed Ivan Ilych.

Once when he got up from the commode too weak to draw up his trousers, 190
he dropped into a soft armchair and looked with horror at his bare, enfeebled thighs with the muscles so sharply marked on them.

Gerasim with a firm light tread, his heavy boots emitting a pleasant smell of tar and fresh winter air, came in wearing a clean Hessian apron, the sleeves of his print shirt tucked up over his strong, bare young arms; and refraining from looking at his sick master out of consideration for his feelings, and restraining the joy of life that beamed from his face, he went up to the commode.

"Gerasim!" said Ivan Ilych in a weak voice.

Gerasim started, evidently afraid he might have committed some blunder, and with a rapid movement turned his fresh, kind, simple young face which just showed the first downy signs of a beard.

"Yes, sir?"

"That must be very unpleasant for you. You must forgive me. I am helpless." 195

"Oh, why, sir," and Gerasim's eyes beamed and he showed his glistening white teeth, "what's a little trouble? It's a case of illness with you, sir."

And his deft strong hands did their accustomed task, and he went out of the room stepping lightly. Five minutes later he as lightly returned.

Ivan Ilych was still sitting in the same position in the armchair.

"Gerasim," he said when the latter had replaced the freshly washed utensil. "Please come here and help me." Gerasim went up to him. "Lift me up. It is hard for me to get up, and I have sent Dmitri away."

Gerasim went up to him, grasped his master with his strong arms deftly but 200 gently, in the same way that he stepped—lifted him, supported him with one hand, and with the other drew up his trousers and would have set him down again, but Ivan Ilych asked to be led to the sofa. Gerasim, without an effort and without apparent pressure, led him, almost lifting him, to the sofa, and placed him on it.

"Thank you. How easily and well you do it all!"

Gerasim smiled again and turned to leave the room. But Ivan Ilych felt his presence such a comfort that he did not want to let him go.

"One thing more, please move up that chair. No, the other one—under my feet. It is easier for me when my feet are raised."

Gerasim brought the chair, set it down gently in place, and raised Ivan Ilych's legs on to it. It seemed to Ivan Ilych that he felt better while Gerasim was holding up his legs.

"It's better when my legs are higher," he said. "Place that cushion under 205 them."

Gerasim did so. He again lifted the legs and placed them, and again Ivan Ilych felt better while Gerasim held his legs. When he set them down Ivan Ilych fancied he felt worse.

"Gerasim," he said. "Are you busy now?"

"Not at all, sir," said Gerasim, who had learnt from the townsfolk how to speak to gentlefolk.

"What have you still to do?"

"What have I to do? I've done everything except chopping the logs for 210 tomorrow."

"Then hold my legs up a bit higher, can you?"

"Of course I can. Why not?" And Gerasim raised his master's legs higher and Ivan Ilych thought that in that position he did not feel any pain at all.

"And how about the logs?"

"Don't trouble about that, sir. There's plenty of time."

Ivan Ilych told Gerasim to sit down and hold his legs, and began to talk to 215 him. And strange to say it seemed to him that he felt better while Gerasim held his legs up.

After that Ivan Ilych would sometimes call Gerasim and get him to hold his legs on his shoulders, and he liked talking to him. Gerasim did it all easily, willingly, simply, and with a good nature that touched Ivan Ilych. Health, strength, and vitality in other people were offensive to him, but Gerasim's strength and vitality did not mortify but soothed him.

What tormented Ivan Ilych most was the deception, the lie, which for some reason they all accepted, that he was not dying but was simply ill, and that he only need keep quiet and undergo a treatment and then something very good would result. He, however, knew that do what they would nothing would come of it, only still more agonizing suffering and death. This deception tortured him—their not wishing to admit what they all knew and what he knew, but wanting to lie to him concerning his terrible condition, and wishing and forcing him to participate in that lie. Those lies—lies enacted over him on the eve of his death and destined to degrade this awful, solemn act to the level of their visitings, their curtains, their sturgeon for dinner—were a terrible agony for Ivan Ilych. And strangely enough, many times when they were going through their antics over him he had been within a hairbreadth of calling out to them: "Stop lying! You know and I know that I am dying. Then at least stop lying about it!" But he had never had the spirit to do it. The awful, terrible act of his dying was, he could see, reduced by those about him to the level of a casual, unpleasant, and almost indecorous incident (as if someone entered a drawing-room diffusing an unpleasant odor) and this was done by that very decorum which he had served all his life long. He saw that no one felt for him, because no one even wished to grasp his position. Only Gerasim recognized it and pitied him. And so Ivan Ilych felt at ease only with him. He felt comforted when Gerasim supported his legs (sometimes all night long) and refused to go to bed, saying: "Don't you worry, Ivan Ilych. I'll get sleep enough later on," or when he suddenly became familiar and exclaimed: "If you weren't sick it would be another matter, but as it is, why should I grudge a little trouble?" Gerasim alone did not lie; everything showed that he alone understood the facts of the case and did not consider it necessary to disguise them, but simply felt sorry for his emaciated and enfeebled master. Once when Ivan Ilych was sending him away he even said straight out: "We shall all of us die, so why should I grudge a little trouble?"—expressing the fact that he did not think his work burdensome, because he was doing it for a dying man and hoped someone would do the same for him when his time came.

Apart from this lying, or because of it, what most tormented Ivan Ilych was that no one pitied him as he wished to be pitied. At certain moments after prolonged suffering he wished most of all (though he would have been ashamed to confess it) for someone to pity him as a sick child is pitied. He longed to be petted and comforted. He knew he was an important functionary, that he had a beard turning grey, and that therefore what he longed for was impossible, but still he longed for it. And in Gerasim's attitude towards him there was something akin to what he wished for, and so that attitude comforted him. Ivan Ilych wanted to weep, wanted to be petted and cried over, and then his colleague Shebek would come, and instead of weeping and being petted, Ivan Ilych would assume a serious, severe, and profound air, and by force of habit would express his opinion on a decision of the Court of Cassation and would stubbornly insist on that view. This falsity around him and within him did more than anything else to poison his last days.

VIII

It was morning. He knew it was morning because Gerasim had gone, and Peter the footman had come and put out the candles, drawn back one of the curtains, and begun quietly to tidy up. Whether it was morning or evening, Friday or Sunday, made no difference, it was all just the same: the gnawing, unmitigated, agonizing pain, never ceasing for an instant, the consciousness of life inexorably waning but not yet extinguished, the approach of that ever dreaded and hateful Death which was the only reality, and always the same falsity. What were days, weeks, hours, in such a case?

"Will you have some tea, sir?"   220

"He wants things to be regular, and wishes the gentlefolk to drink tea in the morning," thought Ivan Ilych, and only said "No."

"Wouldn't you like to move onto the sofa, sir?"

"He wants to tidy up the room, and I'm in the way. I am uncleanliness and disorder," he thought, and said only:

"No, leave me alone."

The man went on bustling about. Ivan Ilych stretched out his hand. Peter   225
came up, ready to help.

"What is it, sir?"

"My watch."

Peter took the watch which was close at hand and gave it to his master.

"Half-past eight. Are they up?"

"No, sir, except Vasily Ivanovich" (the son) "who has gone to school.   230
Praskovya Fëdorovna ordered me to wake her if you asked for her. Shall I do so?"

"No, there's no need to." "Perhaps I'd better have some tea," he thought, and added aloud: "Yes, bring me some tea."

Peter went to the door, but Ivan Ilych dreaded being left alone. "How can I keep him here? Oh yes, my medicine." "Peter, give me my medicine." "Why not? Perhaps it may still do me some good." He took a spoonful and swallowed it. "No, it won't help. It's all tomfoolery, all deception," he decided as soon as he became aware of the familiar, sickly, hopeless taste. "No, I can't believe in it any longer. But the pain, why this pain? If it would only cease just for a moment!" And he moaned. Peter turned towards him. "It's all right. Go and fetch me some tea."

Peter went out. Left alone Ivan Ilych groaned not so much with pain, terrible though that was, as from mental anguish. Always and forever the same, always these endless days and nights. If only it would come quicker! If only *what* would come quicker? Death, darkness? . . . No, no! Anything rather than death!

When Peter returned with the tea on a tray, Ivan Ilych stared at him for a time in perplexity, not realizing who and what he was. Peter was disconcerted by that look and his embarrassment brought Ivan Ilych to himself.

"Oh, tea! All right, put it down. Only help me to wash and put on a clean shirt."

And Ivan Ilych began to wash. With pauses for rest, he washed his hands and then his face, cleaned his teeth, brushed his hair, and looked in the glass. He was terrified by what he saw, especially by the limp way in which his hair clung to his pallid forehead.

While his shirt was being changed he knew that he would be still more frightened at the sight of his body, so he avoided looking at it. Finally he was ready. He drew on a dressing-gown, wrapped himself in a plaid, and sat down in the armchair to take his tea. For a moment he felt refreshed, but soon as he began to drink the tea he was again aware of the same taste, and the pain also returned. He finished it with an effort, and then lay down stretching out his legs, and dismissed Peter.

Always the same. Now a spark of hope flashes up, then a sea of despair rages, and always pain; always pain, always despair, and always the same. When alone he had a dreadful and distressing desire to call someone, but he knew beforehand that with others present it would be still worse. "Another dose of morphine—to lose consciousness. I will tell him, the doctor, that he must think of something else. It's impossible, impossible, to go on like this."

An hour and another pass like that. But now there is a ring at the door bell. Perhaps it's the doctor? It is. He comes in fresh, hearty, plump, and cheerful, with that look on his face that seems to say: "There now, you're in a panic about something, but we'll arrange it all for you directly!" The doctor knows this expression is out of place here, but he has put it on once for all and can't take it off—like a man who has put on a frock-coat in the morning to pay a round of calls.

The doctor rubs his hands vigorously and reassuringly. 240

"Brr! How cold it is! There's such a sharp frost; just let me warm myself!" he says, as if it were only a matter of waiting till he was warm, and then he would put everything right.

"Well now, how are you?"

Ivan Ilych feels that the doctor would like to say: "Well, how are our affairs?" but that even he feels that this would not do, and says instead: "What sort of a night have you had?"

Ivan Ilych looks at him as much as to say: "Are you really never ashamed of lying?" But the doctor does not wish to understand this question, and Ivan Ilych says: "Just as terrible as ever. The pain never leaves me and never subsides. If only something . . ."

"Yes, you sick people are always like that. . . . There, now I think I am warm 245 enough. Even Praskovya Fëdorovna, who is so particular, could find no fault with my temperature. Well, now I can say good-morning," and the doctor presses his patient's hand.

Then, dropping his former playfulness, he begins with a most serious face to examine the patient, feeling his pulse and taking his temperature, and then begins the sounding and auscultation.

Ivan Ilych knows quite well and definitely that all this is nonsense and pure deception, but when the doctor, getting down on his knee, leans over him, putting his ear first higher then lower, and performs various gymnastic movements over him with a significant expression on his face, Ivan Ilych submits to it all as he used to submit to the speeches of the lawyers, though he knew very well that they were all lying and why they were lying.

The doctor, kneeling on the sofa, is still sounding him when Praskovya Fëdorovna's silk dress rustles at the door and she is heard scolding Peter for not having let her know of the doctor's arrival.

She comes in, kisses her husband, and at once proceeds to prove that she has been up a long time already, and only owing to a misunderstanding failed to be there when the doctor arrived.

Ivan Ilych looks at her, scans her all over, sets against her the whiteness and 250 plumpness and cleanness of her hands and neck, the gloss of her hair, and the sparkle of her vivacious eyes. He hates her with his whole soul. And the thrill of hatred he feels for her makes him suffer from her touch.

Her attitude towards him and his disease is still the same. Just as the doctor had adopted a certain relation to his patient which he could not abandon, so had she formed one towards him—that he was not doing something he ought to do and was himself to blame, and that she reproached him lovingly for this—and she could not now change that attitude.

"You see he doesn't listen to me and doesn't take his medicine at the proper time. And above all he lies in a position that is no doubt bad for him—with his legs up."

She described how he made Gerasim hold his legs up.

The doctor smiled with a contemptuous affability that said: "What's to be done? These sick people do have foolish fancies of that kind, but we must forgive them."

When the examination was over the doctor looked at his watch, and then 255 Praskovya Fëdorovna announced to Ivan Ilych that it was of course as he pleased, but she had sent today for a celebrated specialist who would examine him and have a consultation with Michael Danilovich (their regular doctor).

"Please don't raise any objections. I am doing this for my own sake," she said ironically, letting it be felt that she was doing it all for his sake and only said this to leave him no right to refuse. He remained silent, knitting his brows. He felt that he was so surrounded and involved in a mesh of falsity that it was hard to unravel anything.

Everything she did for him was entirely for her own sake, and she told him she was doing for herself what she actually was doing for herself, as if that was so incredible that he must understand the opposite.

At half-past eleven the celebrated specialist arrived. Again the sounding began and the significant conversations in his presence and in another room, about the kidneys and the appendix, and the questions and answers, with such an air of importance that again, instead of the real question of life and death which now alone confronted him, the question arose of the kidney and appendix which were not behaving as they ought to and would now be attacked by Michael Danilovich and the specialist and forced to amend their ways.

The celebrated specialist took leave of him with a serious though not hopeless look, and in reply to the timid question Ivan Ilych, with eyes glistening with fear and hope, put to him as to whether there was a chance of recovery, said that he could not vouch for it but there was a possibility. The look of hope with which Ivan Ilych watched the doctor out was so pathetic that Praskovya Fëdorovna, seeing it, even wept as she left the room to hand the doctor his fee.

The gleam of hope kindled by the doctor's encouragement did not last long. 260 The same room, the same pictures, curtains, wallpaper, medicine bottles, were all there, and the same aching suffering body, and Ivan Ilych began to moan. They gave him a subcutaneous injection and he sank into oblivion.

It was twilight when he came to. They brought him his dinner and he swallowed some beef tea with difficulty, and then everything was the same again and night was coming on.

After dinner, at seven o'clock, Praskovya Fëdorovna came into the room in evening dress, her full bosom pushed up by her corset, and with traces of powder on her face. She had reminded him in the morning that they were going to the theater. Sarah Bernhardt was visiting the town and they had a box, which he had insisted on their taking. Now he had forgotten about it and her toilet offended him, but he concealed his vexation when he remembered that he had himself insisted on their securing a box and going because it would be an instructive and aesthetic pleasure for the children.

Praskovya Fëdorovna came in, self-satisfied but yet with a rather guilty air. She sat down and asked how he was, but, as he saw, only for the sake of asking and not in order to learn about it, knowing that there was nothing to learn—and then went on to what she really wanted to say: that she would not on any account have gone but that the box had been taken and Helen and their daughter were going, as well as Petrishchev (the examining magistrate, their daughter's fiancé), and that it was out of the question to let them go alone; but that she would have much preferred to sit with him for a while; and he must be sure to follow the doctor's orders while she was away.

"Oh, and Fëdor Petrovich" (the fiancé) "would like to come in. May he? And Lisa?"

"All right." 265

Their daughter came in in full evening dress, her fresh young flesh exposed (making a show of that very flesh which in his own case caused so much suffering), strong, healthy, evidently in love, and impatient with illness, suffering, and death, because they interfered with her happiness.

Fëdor Petrovich came in too, in evening dress, his hair curled à la Capoul, ° a tight stiff collar round his long sinewy neck, an enormous white shirtfront, and narrow black trousers tightly stretched over his strong thighs. He had one white glove tightly drawn on, and was holding his opera hat in his hand.

à la Capoul: imitating the hairdo of Victor Capoul, a contemporary French singer.

Following him the schoolboy crept in unnoticed, in a new uniform, poor little fellow, and wearing gloves. Terribly dark shadows showed under his eyes, the meaning of which Ivan Ilych knew well.

His son had always seemed pathetic to him, and now it was dreadful to see the boy's frightened look of pity. It seemed to Ivan Ilych that Vasya was the only one besides Gerasim who understood and pitied him.

They all sat down and again asked how he was. A silence followed. Lisa asked her mother about the opera-glasses, and there was an altercation between mother and daughter as to who had taken them and where they had been put. This occasioned some unpleasantness. 270

Fëdor Petrovich inquired of Ivan Ilych whether he had ever seen Sarah Bernhardt. Ivan Ilych did not at first catch the question, but then replied: "No, have you seen her before?"

"Yes, in *Adrienne Lecouvreur.*"

Praskovya Fëdorovna mentioned some rôles in which Sarah Bernhardt was particularly good. Her daughter disagreed. Conversation sprang up as to the elegance and realism of her acting—the sort of conversation that is always repeated and is always the same.

In the midst of the conversation Fëdor Petrovich glanced at Ivan Ilych and became silent. The others also looked at him and grew silent. Ivan Ilych was staring with glittering eyes straight before him, evidently indignant with them. This had to be rectified, but it was impossible to do so. The silence had to be broken, but for a time no one dared to break it and they all became afraid that the conventional deception would suddenly become obvious and the truth become plain to all. Lisa was the first to pluck up courage and break that silence, but by trying to hide what everybody was feeling, she betrayed it.

"Well, if we are going it's time to start," she said, looking at her watch, a present from her father, and with a faint and significant smile at Fëdor Petrovich relating to something known only to them. She got up with a rustle of her dress. 275

They all rose, said good-night, and went away.

When they had gone it seemed to Ivan Ilych that he felt better; the falsity had gone with them. But the pain remained—that same pain and that same fear that made everything monotonously alike, nothing harder and nothing easier. Everything was worse.

Again minute followed minute and hour followed hour. Everything remained the same and there was no cessation. And the inevitable end of it all became more and more terrible.

"Yes, send Gerasim here," he replied to a question Peter asked.

IX

His wife returned late at night. She came in on tiptoe, but he heard her, opened his eyes, and made haste to close them again. She wished to send Gerasim away and to sit with him herself, but he opened his eyes and said: "No, go away." 280

"Are you in great pain?"

"Always the same."

"Take some opium."

He agreed and took some. She went away.

Till about three in the morning he was in a state of stupefied misery. It seemed to him that he and his pain were being thrust into a narrow, deep black sack, but though they were pushed further and further in they could not be pushed to the bottom. And this, terrible enough in itself, was accompanied by suffering. He was frightened yet wanted to fall through the sack, he struggled but yet cooperated. And suddenly he broke through, fell, and regained consciousness. Gerasim was sitting at the foot of the bed dozing quietly and patiently, while he himself lay with his emaciated stockinged legs resting on Gerasim's shoulders; the same shaded candle was there and the same unceasing pain.

"Go away, Gerasim," he whispered.

"It's all right, sir. I'll stay a while."

"No. Go away."

He removed his legs from Gerasim's shoulders, turned sideways onto his arm, and felt sorry for himself. He only waited till Gerasim had gone into the next room and then restrained himself no longer but wept like a child. He wept on account of his helplessness, his terrible loneliness, the cruelty of man, the cruelty of God, and the absence of God.

"Why hast Thou done all this? Why hast Thou brought me here? Why, why dost Thou torment me so terribly?"

He did not expect an answer and yet wept because there was no answer and could be none. The pain grew more acute, but he did not stir and did not call. He said to himself: "Go on! Strike me! But what is it for? What have I done to Thee? What is it for?"

Then he grew quiet and not only ceased weeping but even held his breath and became all attention. It was as though he was listening not to an audible voice but to the voice of his soul, to the current of thoughts arising within him.

"What is it you want?" was the first clear conception capable of expression in words, that he heard.

"What do you want? What do you want?" he repeated to himself.

"What do I want? To live and not to suffer," he answered.

And again he listened with such concentrated attention that even his pain did not distract him.

"To live? How?" asked his inner voice.

"Why, to live as I used to—well and pleasantly."

"As you lived before, well and pleasantly?" the voice repeated.

And in imagination he began to recall the best moments of his pleasant life. But strange to say none of those best moments of his pleasant life now seemed at all what they had then seemed—none of them except the first recollections of childhood. There, in childhood, there had been something really pleasant with which it would be possible to live if it could return. But the child who had experienced that happiness existed no longer, it was like a reminiscence of somebody else.

As soon as the period began which had produced the present Ivan Ilych, all that had then seemed joys now melted before his sight and turned into something trivial and often nasty.

And the further he departed from childhood and the nearer he came to the present the more worthless and doubtful were the joys. This began with the School of Law. A little that was really good was still found there—there was lightheartedness, friendship, and hope. But in the upper classes there had already been fewer of such good moments. Then during the first years of his official career, when he was in the service of the Governor, some pleasant moments again occurred: they were the memories of love for a woman. Then all became confused and there was still less of what was good; later on again there was still less that was good, and the further he went the less there was. His marriage, a mere accident, then the disenchantment that followed it, his wife's bad breath and the sensuality and hypocrisy; then the deadly official life and those preoccupations about money, a year of it, and two, and ten, and twenty, and always the same thing. And the longer it lasted the more deadly it became. "It is as if I had been going downhill while I imagined I was going up. And that is really what it was. I was going up in public opinion, but to the same extent life was ebbing away from me. And now it is all done and there is only death."

"Then what does it mean? Why? It can't be that life is so senseless and horrible. But if it really has been so horrible and senseless, why must I die and die in agony? There is something wrong!"

"Maybe I did not live as I ought to have done," it suddenly occurred to him. "But how could that be, when I did everything properly?" he replied, and immediately dismissed from his mind this, the sole solution of all the riddles of life and death, as something quite impossible.

"Then what do you want now? To live? Live how? Live as you lived in the law courts when the usher proclaimed 'The judge is coming!' The judge is coming, the judge!" he repeated to himself. "Here he is, the judge. But I am not guilty!" he exclaimed angrily. "What is it for?" And he ceased crying, but turning his face to the wall continued to ponder on the same question: Why, and for what purpose, is there all this horror? But however much he pondered he found no answer. And whenever the thought occurred to him, as it often did, that it all resulted from his not having lived as he ought to have done, he at once recalled the correctness of his whole life and dismissed so strange an idea.

305

X

Another fortnight passed. Ivan Ilych now no longer left his sofa. He would not lie in bed but lay on the sofa, facing the wall nearly all the time. He suffered ever the same unceasing agonies and in his loneliness pondered always on the same insoluble question: "What is this? Can it be that it is Death?" And the inner voice answered: "Yes, it is Death."

"Why these sufferings?" And the voice answered, "For no reason—they just are so." Beyond and besides this there was nothing.

From the very beginning of his illness, ever since he had first been to see the doctor, Ivan Ilych's life had been divided between two contrary and alternating moods: now it was despair and the expectation of this uncomprehended and terrible death, and now hope and an intently interested observation of the functioning of his organs. Now before his eyes there was only a kidney or an intestine that temporarily evaded its duty, and now only that incomprehensible and dreadful death from which it was impossible to escape.

These two states of mind had alternated from the very beginning of his illness, but the further it progressed the more doubtful and fantastic became the conception of the kidney, and the more real the sense of impending death.

He had but to call to mind what he had been three months before and what he was now, to call to mind with what regularity he had been going downhill, for every possibility of hope to be shattered.

Latterly during that loneliness in which he found himself as he lay facing the back of the sofa, a loneliness in the midst of a populous town and surrounded by numerous acquaintances and relations but that yet could not have been more complete anywhere—either at the bottom of the sea or under the earth—during that terrible loneliness Ivan Ilych had lived only in memories of the past. Pictures of his past rose before him one after another. They always began with what was nearest in time and then went back to what was most remote—to his childhood—and rested there. If he thought of the stewed prunes that had been offered him that day, his mind went back to the raw shrivelled French plums of his childhood, their peculiar flavor and the flow of saliva when he sucked their stones, and along with the memory of that taste came a whole series of memories of those days: his nurse, his brother, and their toys. "No, I mustn't think of that. . . . It is too painful," Ivan Ilych said to himself, and brought himself back to the present—to the button on the back of the sofa and the creases in its morocco. "Morocco is expensive, but it does not wear well: there had been a quarrel about it. It was a different kind of quarrel and a different kind of morocco that time when we tore father's portfolio and were punished, and mamma brought us some tarts. . . ." And again his thoughts dwelt on his childhood, and again it was painful and he tried to banish them and fix his mind on something else.

Then again together with that chain of memories another series passed through his mind—of how his illness had progressed and grown worse. There also the further back he looked the more life there had been. There had been more of what was good in life and more of life itself. The two merged together. "Just as the pain went on getting worse and worse, so my life grew worse and worse," he thought. "There is one bright spot there at the back, at the beginning of life, and afterwards all becomes blacker and blacker and proceeds more and more rapidly—in inverse ratio to the square of the distance from death," thought Ivan Ilych. And the example of a stone falling downwards with increasing velocity entered his mind. Life, a series of increasing sufferings, flies further and further towards its end—the most terrible suffering. "I am flying. . . ." He shuddered, shifted himself, and tried to resist, but was already aware that resistance was impossible, and again, with eyes weary of gazing but unable to cease seeing what was before them, he stared at the back of the sofa and waited—awaiting that dreadful fall and shock and destruction.

"Resistance is impossible!" he said to himself. "If I could only understand what it is all for! But that too is impossible. An explanation would be possible if it could be said that I have not lived as I ought to. But it is impossible to say that," and he remembered all the legality, correctitude, and propriety of his life. "That at any rate can certainly not be admitted," he thought, and his lips smiled ironically as if someone could see that smile and be taken in by it. "There is no explanation! Agony, death. . . . What for?"

XI

Another two weeks went by in this way and during that fortnight an event occurred that Ivan Ilych and his wife had desired. Petrishchev formally proposed. It happened in the evening. The next day Praskovya Fëdorovna came into her husband's room considering how best to inform him of it, but that very night there had been a fresh change for the worse in his condition. She found him still lying on the sofa but in a different position. He lay on his back, groaning and staring fixedly straight in front of him.

She began to remind him of his medicines, but he turned his eyes towards   315
her with such a look that she did not finish what she was saying; so great an animosity, to her in particular, did that look express.

"For Christ's sake let me die in peace!" he said.

She would have gone away, but just then their daughter came in and went up to say good morning. He looked at her as he had done at his wife, and in reply to her inquiry about his health said dryly that he would soon free them all of himself. They were both silent and after sitting with him for a while went away.

"Is it our fault?" Lisa said to her mother. "It's as if we were to blame! I am sorry for papa, but why should we be tortured?"

The doctor came at his usual time. Ivan Ilych answered "Yes" and "No," never taking his angry eyes from him, and at last said: "You know you can do nothing for me, so leave me alone."

"We can ease your sufferings."   320

"You can't even do that. Let me be."

The doctor went into the drawing-room and told Praskovya Fëdorovna that the case was very serious and that the only resource left was opium to allay her husband's sufferings, which must be terrible.

It was true, as the doctor said, that Ivan Ilych's physical sufferings were terrible, but worse than the physical sufferings were his mental sufferings, which were his chief torture.

His mental sufferings were due to the fact that one night, as he looked at Gerasim's sleepy, good-natured face with its prominent cheekbones, the question suddenly occurred to him: "What if my whole life has really been wrong?"

It occurred to him that what had appeared perfectly impossible before, namely that he had not spent his life as he should have done, might after all be true. It occurred to him that his scarcely perceptible attempts to struggle against what was considered good by the most highly placed people, those scarcely noticeable impulses which he had immediately suppressed, might have been the real thing, and all the rest false. And his professional duties and the whole arrangement of his life and of his family, and all his social and official interests, might all have been false. He tried to defend all those things to himself and suddenly felt the weakness of what he was defending. There was nothing to defend.

"But if that is so," he said to himself, "and I am leaving this life with the consciousness that I have lost all that was given me and it is impossible to rectify it—what then?"

He lay on his back and began to pass his life in review in quite a new way. In the morning when he saw first his footman, then his wife, then his daughter, and then the doctor, their every word and movement confirmed to him the awful truth that had been revealed to him during the night. In them he saw himself—all that for which he had lived—and saw clearly that it was not real at all, but a terrible and huge deception which had hidden both life and death. This consciousness intensified his physical suffering tenfold. He groaned and tossed about, and pulled at his clothing which choked and stifled him. And he hated them on that account.

He was given a large dose of opium and became unconscious, but at noon his sufferings began again. He drove everybody away and tossed from side to side.

His wife came to him and said:

"Jean, my dear, do this for me. It can't do any harm and often helps. Healthy people often do it."

He opened his eyes wide.

"What? Take communion? Why? It's unnecessary! However . . ."

She began to cry.

"Yes, do, my dear. I'll send for our priest. He is such a nice man."

"All right. Very well," he muttered.

When the priest came and heard his confession, Ivan Ilych was softened and seemed to feel a relief from his doubts and consequently from his sufferings, and for a moment there came a ray of hope. He again began to think of the vermiform appendix and the possibility of correcting it. He received the sacrament with tears in his eyes.

When they laid him down again afterwards he felt a moment's ease, and the hope that he might live awoke in him again. He began to think of the operation that had been suggested to him. "To live! I want to live!" he said to himself.

His wife came in to congratulate him after his communion, and when uttering the usual conventional words she added:

"You feel better, don't you?"

Without looking at her he said "Yes."

Her dress, her figure, the expression of her face, the tone of her voice, all revealed the same thing. "This is wrong, it is not as it should be. All you have lived for and still live for is falsehood and deception, hiding life and death from you." And as soon as he admitted that thought, his hatred and his agonizing physical suffering again sprang up, and with that suffering a consciousness of the unavoidable, approaching end. And to this was added a new sensation of grinding shooting pain and a feeling of suffocation.

The expression of his face when he uttered that "yes" was dreadful. Having uttered it, he looked her straight in the eyes, turned on his face with a rapidity extraordinary in his weak state and shouted:

"Go away! Go away and leave me alone!"

XII

From that moment the screaming began that continued for three days, and was so terrible that one could not hear it through two closed doors without horror. At the moment he answered his wife he realized that he was lost, that there was no return, that the end had come, the very end, and his doubts were still unsolved and remained doubts.

"Oh! Oh! Oh!" he cried in various intonations. He had begun by screaming "I won't!" and continued screaming on the letter O. 345

For three whole days, during which time did not exist for him, he struggled in that black sack into which he was being thrust by an invisible, resistless force. He struggled as a man condemned to death struggles in the hands of the executioner, knowing that he cannot save himself. And every moment he felt that despite all his efforts he was drawing nearer and nearer to what terrified him. He felt that his agony was due to his being thrust into that black hole and still more to his not being able to get right into it. He was hindered from getting into it by his conviction that his life had been a good one. That very justification of his life held him fast and prevented his moving forward, and it caused him most torment of all.

Suddenly some force struck him in the chest and side, making it still harder to breathe, and he fell through the hole and there at the bottom was a light. What had happened to him was like the sensation one sometimes experiences in a railway carriage when one thinks one is going backwards while one is really going forwards and suddenly becomes aware of the real direction.

"Yes, it was all not the right thing," he said to himself, "but that's no matter. It can be done. But what *is* the right thing?" he asked himself, and suddenly grew quiet.

This occurred at the end of the third day, two hours before his death. Just then his schoolboy son had crept softly in and gone up to the bedside. The dying man was still screaming desperately and waving his arms. His hand fell on the boy's head, and the boy caught it, pressed it to his lips, and began to cry.

At that very moment Ivan Ilych fell through and caught sight of the light, 350 and it was revealed to him that though his life had not been what it should have been, this could still be rectified. He asked himself, "What *is* the right thing?" and grew still, listening. Then he felt that someone was kissing his hand. He opened his eyes, looked at his son, and felt sorry for him. His wife came up to him and he glanced at her. She was gazing at him open-mouthed, with undried tears on her nose and cheek and a despairing look on her face. He felt sorry for her too.

"Yes, I am making them wretched," he thought. "They are sorry, but it will be better for them when I die." He wished to say this but had not the strength to utter it. "Besides, why speak? I must act," he thought. With a look at his wife he indicated his son and said: "Take him away . . . sorry for him . . . sorry for you too. . . ." He tried to add, "Forgive me," but said "forgo" and waved his hand, knowing that He whose understanding mattered would understand.

And suddenly it grew clear to him that what had been oppressing him and would not leave him was all dropping away at once from two sides, from ten sides, and from all sides. He was sorry for them, he must act so as not to hurt them: release them and free himself from these sufferings. "How good and how simple!" he thought. "And the pain?" he asked himself. "What has become of it? Where are you, pain?"

He turned his attention to it.

"Yes, here it is. Well, what of it? Let the pain be."

"And death . . . where is it?"   355

He sought his former accustomed fear of death and did not find it. "Where is it? What death?" There was no fear because there was no death.

In place of death there was light.

"So that's what it is!" he suddenly exclaimed aloud. "What joy!"

To him all this happened in a single instant, and the meaning of that instant did not change. For those present his agony continued for another two hours. Something rattled in his throat, his emaciated body twitched, then the gasping and rattle became less and less frequent.

"It is finished!" said someone near him.   360

He heard these words and repeated them in his soul.

"Death is finished," he said to himself. "It is no more!"

He drew in a breath, stopped in the midst of a sigh, stretched out, and died.

Questions

1. Sum up the reactions of Ivan's colleagues to the news of his death. What is implied in Tolstoy's calling them not friends, but "nearest acquaintances"?
2. What comic elements do you find in the account of the wake that Peter Ivanovich attends?
3. In Tolstoy's description of the corpse and its expression (paragraph 27), what details seem especially revealing and meaningful?
4. Do you think Tolstoy would have improved the story had he placed the events in chronological order? What if the opening scene of Ivan's colleagues at the law courts and the wake scene were to be given last? What would be lost?
5. Would you call Ivan, when we first meet him, a religious man? Sum up his goals in life, his values, and his attitudes.
6. By what "virtues" and abilities does Ivan rise through the ranks? While he continues to succeed in his career, what happens to his marriage?

7. "Every spot on the tablecloth or the upholstery, and every broken window-blind string, irritated him. He had devoted so much trouble to arranging it all that every disturbance of it distressed him" (paragraph 104). What do you make of this passage? What is its tone? Does the narrator sympathize with Ivan's attachment to his possessions?

8. Consider the account of Ivan's routine in paragraph 105 ("he got up at nine . . ."). What elements of a full life, what higher satisfactions, does this routine omit?

9. What caused Ivan's illness? How would it probably be diagnosed today? What is the narrator's attitude toward Ivan's doctors?

10. In what successive stages does Tolstoy depict Ivan's growing isolation as his progressive illness sets him more and more apart?

11. What are we apparently supposed to admire in the character and conduct of the servant Gerasim?

12. What do you understand from the statement that Ivan's justification of his life "prevented his moving forward, and it caused him most torment of all" (paragraph 346)?

13. What is memorable in the character of Ivan's schoolboy son? Why is he crucial to the story? (Suggestion: Look closely at paragraphs 349–350.)

14. What realization allows Ivan to triumph over pain? Why does he die gladly?

15. Henri Troyat has said that through the story of Ivan Ilych we imagine what our own deaths will be. Is it possible to identify with an aging, selfish, worldly, nineteenth-century Russian judge?

Franz Kafka

THE METAMORPHOSIS   1915

TRANSLATED BY JOHN SISCOE

Franz Kafka (1883–1924) was born into a German-speaking Jewish family in Prague, Czechoslovakia (then part of the Austro-Hungarian empire). He was the only surviving son of a domineering, successful father. After earning a law degree, Kafka worked as a claims investigator for the state accident insurance company. He worked on his stories at night, especially during his frequent bouts of insomnia. Despite often tortured relationships with a number of young women, he never married, and lived mostly with his parents. Kafka was such a careful and self-conscious writer that he found it difficult to finish his work and send it out for publication. During his lifetime he published only a few thin volumes of short fiction, most notably The Metamorphosis *(1915) and* In the Penal Colony *(1919). He never finished to his own satisfaction any of his three novels (all published posthumously):* Amerika *(1927),* The Trial *(1925), and* The Castle *(1926). As Kafka was dying of tuberculosis, he begged his friend and literary executor, Max Brod, to burn his uncompleted manuscripts. Brod pondered this request but didn't obey. Kafka's two major novels,* The Trial *and* The Castle, *both depict huge, remote, bumbling, irresponsible bureaucracies in whose power the individual feels helpless and blind. Kafka's works appear startlingly prophetic to readers looking back on them in the later light of Stalinism, World War II, and the Holocaust. His haunting vision of an alienated modern world led the poet W. H. Auden to remark at mid-century, "Had one to name the author who comes nearest to bearing the same kind of relation to our age as Dante, Shakespeare, and Goethe bore to theirs, Kafka is the first one would think of."* The Metamorphosis, *which arguably has the most famous opening sentence in twentieth-century literature, shows Kafka's dreamlike fiction at its most brilliant and most disturbing.*

I

When Gregor Samsa awoke one morning from troubled dreams, he found himself transformed in his bed into a monstrous insect. He was lying on his back, which was hard, as if plated in armor, and when he lifted his head slightly he could see his belly: rounded, brown, and divided into stiff arched segments; on top of it the blanket, about to slip off altogether, still barely clinging. His many legs, which seemed pathetically thin when compared to the rest of his body, flickered helplessly before his eyes.

"What's happened to me?" he thought. It was no dream. His room, a normal though somewhat small human bedroom, lay quietly within its four familiar walls. Above the table on which his unpacked fabric samples were spread— Samsa was a traveling salesman—hung the picture he had recently cut out of an illustrated magazine and had set in a lovely gilt frame. It showed a lady wearing a fur hat and a fur stole, sitting upright, and thrusting out to the viewer a thick fur muff, into which her whole forearm had disappeared.

Gregor's glance then fell on the window, and the overcast sky—one could hear raindrops drumming on the tin sheeting of the windowsill—made him feel profoundly sad. "What if I went back to sleep for a while and forgot all this nonsense," he thought. But that wasn't to be, for he was used to sleeping on his right side and in his present state was unable to get into that position. No matter how hard he threw himself to his right, he would immediately roll onto his back again. He must have tried a hundred times, shutting his eyes so as not to see his wriggling legs, not stopping until he began to feel in his side a slight dull pain that he had never felt before.

"My God," he thought, "what an exhausting job I've chosen! Always on the go, day in and day out. There are far more worries on the road than at the office, what with the constant travel, the nuisance of making your train connections, the wretched meals eaten at odd hours, and the casual acquaintances you meet only in passing, never to see again, never to become intimate friends. To hell with it all!" He felt a slight itch on the surface of his belly. Slowly he shoved himself on his back closer to the bedpost so that he could lift his head more easily. He found the place where it itched. It was covered with small white spots he did not understand. He started to touch it with one of his legs, but pulled back immediately, for the contact sent a cold shiver through him.

He slid back down to his former position. "Getting up this early," he thought, "would turn anyone into an idiot. A man needs his sleep. Other salesmen live like harem women. For example, when I get back to the hotel in the morning to write up the sales I've made, these gentlemen are sitting down to breakfast. If I tried that with my director, I'd be fired on the spot. Actually, that might not be such a bad idea. If I didn't have to curb my tongue because of my parents, I'd have given notice long ago. I'd have gone up to the director and told him from the bottom of my heart exactly what I thought. That would have knocked him from his desk! It's an odd way to run things, this sitting high at a desk and talking down to employees, especially when, since the director is hard of hearing, they have to approach so near. Well, there's hope yet; as soon as I've saved enough money to pay back what my parents owe him—that should take another five or six years—I'll go do it for sure. Then, I'll cut myself completely free. Right now, though, I'd better get up, as my train leaves at five."

He looked at the alarm clock ticking on top of the chest of drawers. "God Almighty!" he thought. It was half-past six and the hands were quietly moving forward, it was later than half-past, it was nearly a quarter to seven. Hadn't the alarm clock gone off? You could see from the bed that it had been correctly set for four o'clock; of course it must have gone off. Yes, but could he really have slept peacefully through that ear-splitting racket? Well, if he hadn't slept peacefully, he'd slept deeply all the same. But what was he to do now? The next train left at seven, to make it he would have to rush like mad, and his samples weren't even packed, and he himself wasn't feeling particularly spry or alert. And even if he were to make the train, there would be no avoiding a scene with the director. The office messenger would've been waiting for the five o'clock train and would've long since reported his not showing up. The messenger, dim-witted and lacking a will of his own, was a tool of the director. Well, what if he were to call in sick? But that would look embarrassing and suspicious since in his five years with the firm Gregor had not been sick once. The director himself was sure to come over with the health insurance doctor, would upbraid his parents for their son's laziness, and would cut short all excuses by deferring to the doctor, who believed that everyone in the world was a perfectly healthy layabout. And really, would he be so wrong in this case? Apart from a drowsiness that was hard to account for after such a long sleep, Gregor really felt quite well, and in fact was exceptionally hungry.

As he was thinking all this at top speed, without being able to make up his mind to get out of bed—the alarm clock had just struck a quarter to seven—a cautious tap sounded on the door behind his head. "Gregor," said a voice—it was his mother—"it's a quarter to seven. Don't you have a train to catch?" That gentle voice! Gregor was shocked when he heard his own voice answering hers; unmistakably his own voice, true, but mixed in with it, like an undertone, a miserable squeaking that allowed the words to be clearly heard only for a moment before rising up, reverberating, to drown out their meaning, so that no one could be sure if he had heard them correctly. Gregor wanted to answer fully and give a complete explanation, but under the circumstances he merely said, "Yes, yes, thank you, Mother, I'm just getting up." Through the wooden door between them the change in Gregor's voice was probably not obvious, for his mother, quietly accepting his words, shuffled away. However, this brief exchange had made the rest of the family aware that Gregor, surprisingly, was still in the house, and already at one of the side doors his father was knocking, softly, yet with his fist. "Gregor, Gregor," he called, "what's the matter?" Before long he called once more in a deeper voice, "Gregor? Gregor?" From the other side door came the sound of his sister's voice, gentle and plaintive. "Gregor, aren't you feeling well? Is there anything I can get you?" Gregor answered the two of them at the same time: "I'm almost ready." He tried hard to keep his voice from sounding strange by enunciating the words with great care, and by inserting long pauses between the words. His father went back to his breakfast but his sister whispered, "Gregor, please, open the door." But Gregor had no intention of opening the door, and was thankful for having formed, while traveling, the prudent habit of keeping all his doors locked at night, even at home.

What he wanted to do now was to get up quietly and calmly, to get dressed, and above all to eat his breakfast. Only then would he think about what to do next, for he understood that mulling things over in bed would lead him nowhere. He remembered how often in the past he had felt some small pain in bed, perhaps caused by lying in an uncomfortable position, which as soon as he had gotten up had proven to be purely imaginary, and he looked forward to seeing how this morning's fancies would gradually fade and disappear. As for the change in his voice, he hadn't the slightest doubt that it was nothing more than the first sign of a severe cold, an occupational hazard of traveling salesmen.

Throwing off the blanket was easy enough; he had only to puff himself up a little and it slipped right off. But the next part was difficult, especially as he was so unusually wide. He would have needed arms and legs to lift himself up; instead he had only these numerous little legs that never stopped moving and over which he had no control at all. As soon as he tried to bend one of them it would straighten itself out, and if he finally succeeded in making it do as he wished, all the others, as if set free, would waggle about in a high degree of painful agitation. "But what's the point of lying uselessly in bed?" Gregor said to himself.

He thought that he might start by easing the lower part of his body out of bed first, but this lower part, which incidentally he hadn't yet seen and of which he couldn't form a clear picture, turned out to be very difficult to budge—it went so slowly. When finally, almost in a frenzy, he gathered his strength and pushed forward desperately, he miscalculated his direction and bumped sharply against the post at the foot of the bed, and the searing pain he felt told him that, for right now at least, it was exactly this lower part of his body that was perhaps the most tender.

So he tried getting the top part of his body out first, and cautiously turned his head towards the side of the bed. This proved easy enough, and eventually, despite its breadth and weight the bulk of his body slowly followed the turning of his head. But when he finally got his head out over the edge of the bed he felt too afraid to go any farther, for if he were to let himself fall from this position only a miracle would prevent him from hurting his head. And it was precisely now, at all costs, that he must not lose consciousness; he would be better off staying in bed.

But when after repeating his efforts he lay, sighing, in his former position, and once more watched his little legs struggling with one another more furiously than ever, if that were possible, and saw no way of bringing calm and order into this mindless confusion, he again told himself that it was impossible to stay in bed and that the wisest course would be to stake everything on the hope, however slight, of getting away from the bed. At the same time he didn't forget to remind himself that the calmest of calm reflection was much better than frantic resolutions. During this time he kept his eyes fixed as firmly as possible on the window, but unfortunately the morning fog, which shrouded even the other side of the narrow street, gave him little comfort and cheer. "Already seven o'clock," he said to himself when the alarm clock chimed again, "already seven and still such a thick fog." And for some time he lay still, breathing quietly, as if in the hope that utter stillness would bring all things back to how they really and normally were.

But then he said to himself: "I must make sure that I'm out of bed before it strikes a quarter past seven. Anyway, by then someone from work will have come to check on me, since the office opens before seven." And he immediately set the whole length of his body rocking with a rhythmic motion in order to swing out of bed. If he tumbled out this way he could prevent his head from being injured by keeping it tilted upward as he fell. His back seemed to be hard; the fall onto the carpet would probably not hurt it. His greatest worry was the thought of the loud crash he was bound to make; it would probably cause anxiety, if not outright fear, on the other side of the doors. Yet he had to take the chance.

When Gregor was already half out of bed—his new technique made it more of a game than a struggle, since all he had to do was to edge himself across by rocking back and forth—it struck him how simple it would be if he could get someone to help him. Two strong people—he thought of his father and the maid—would be more than enough. All they would have to do would be to slip their arms under his curved back, lift him out of bed, bend down with their burden, and then wait patiently while he flipped himself right side up onto the floor, where, one might hope, his little legs would acquire some purpose. Well then, aside from the fact that the doors were locked, wouldn't it be a good idea to call for help? In spite of his misery, he could not help smiling at the thought.

He had reached the point where, if he rocked any harder, he was in danger of losing his balance, and very soon he would have to commit himself, because in five minutes it would be a quarter past seven when the doorbell rang. "It's someone from the office," he said to himself, and almost froze, while his little legs danced even faster. For a moment everything remained quiet. "They won't open the door," Gregor said to himself, clutching at an absurd sort of hope. But then, of course, the maid, as usual, went with her firm tread to the door and opened it. Gregor had only to hear the visitor's first word of greeting to know at once who it was—the office manager himself. Why was Gregor condemned to work for a firm where the most insignificant failure to appear instantly provoked the deepest suspicion? Were the employees, one and all, nothing but scoundrels? Wasn't there among them one man who was true and loyal, who if, one morning, he were to waste an hour or so of the firm's time, would become so conscience-stricken as to be driven out of his mind and actually rendered incapable of leaving his bed? Wouldn't it have been enough to send an office boy to ask—that is, if such prying were necessary at all? Did the office manager have to come

15

in person, and thus demonstrate to an entire family of innocent people that he was the only one wise enough to properly investigate this suspicious affair? And it was more from the anxiety caused by these thoughts than by any act of will that Gregor swung himself out of bed with all his might. There was a loud thump, but not really a crash. The carpet broke his fall somewhat, and his back too was more elastic than he had thought, so there was only a muffled thud that was relatively unobtrusive. However, he had not lifted his head carefully enough and had banged it; he twisted it and rubbed it against the carpet in frustration and pain.

"Something fell down in there," said the office manager in the room on the left. Gregor tried to imagine whether something like what had happened to him today might one day happen to the office manager; really, one had to admit that it was possible. But as if in a blunt reply to this question the office manager took several determined steps in the next room and his patent leather boots creaked. From the room on the right his sister was whispering to let him know what was going on: "Gregor, the office manager is here." "I know," said Gregor to himself, but he didn't dare speak loudly enough for his sister to hear him.

"Gregor," his father now said from the room on the left, "the office manager is here and he wants to know why you weren't on the early train. We don't know what to tell him. Besides he wants to speak to you in person. So please open the door. I'm sure he'll be kind enough to excuse any untidiness in your room." "Good morning, Mr. Samsa," the manager was calling out amiably. "He isn't feeling well," said his mother to the manager, while his father was still speaking at the door. "He's not well, sir, believe me. Why else would Gregor miss his train? The boy thinks of nothing but his work. It nearly drives me to distraction the way he never goes out in the evening; he's been here the last eight days, and every single evening he's stayed at home. He just sits here at the table with us quietly reading the newspapers or looking over train schedules. The only enjoyment he gets is when he's working away with his fretsaw.° For example he spent two or three evenings cutting out a little picture frame, you'd be surprised at how pretty it is, it's hanging in his room, you'll see it in a minute as soon as Gregor opens the door. By the way, I'm glad you've come, Sir, we would've never have gotten him to unlock the door by ourselves, he's so stubborn; and I'm sure he's sick, even though he wouldn't admit it this morning." "I'm coming right now," said Gregor, slowly and carefully and not moving an inch for fear of missing a single word of the conversation. "I can't imagine any other explanation, madam," said the office manager, "I hope it's nothing serious. But on the other hand businessmen such as ourselves—fortunately or unfortunately—very often have to ignore any minor indisposition, since the demands of business come first." "So, can the office manager come in now?" asked Gregor's father impatiently, once more knocking on the door. "No," said Gregor. In the room on the

fretsaw: saw with a long, narrow, fine-toothed blade, for cutting thin wooden boards or metal plates into patterns.

left there was an embarrassed silence; in the room on the right his sister began to sob.

But why didn't his sister go and join the others? Probably because she had just gotten out of bed and hadn't even begun to dress yet. Then why was she crying? Because he was in danger of losing his job, and because the director would start once again dunning his parents for the money they owed him? Yet surely these were matters one didn't need to worry about just now. Gregor was still here, and hadn't the slightest intention of deserting the family. True, at the moment he was lying on the carpet, and no one aware of his condition could seriously expect him to let the office manager in. But this minor discourtesy, for which in good time an appropriate excuse could easily be found, was unlikely to result in Gregor's being fired on the spot. And it seemed to Gregor far more sensible for them now to leave him in peace than to bother him with their tears and entreaties. But the uncertainty that preyed upon them excused their behavior.

"Mr. Samsa," the office manager now called in a louder voice, "what's the matter with you? You've barricaded yourself in your room, giving only yes or no answers, causing your parents a great deal of needless grief and neglecting—I mention this only in passing—neglecting your business responsibilities to an unbelievable degree. I am speaking now in the name of your parents and of your director, and I beg you in all seriousness to give me a complete explanation at once. I'm amazed at you, simply amazed. I took you for a calm and reliable person, and now all at once you seem determined to make a ridiculous spectacle of yourself. Earlier this morning the director did suggest to me a possible explanation for your disappearance—I'm referring to the sums of cash that were recently entrusted to you—but I practically swore on my solemn word of honor that this could not be. However, now when I see how incredibly stubborn you are, I no longer have the slightest desire to defend you. And your position with the firm is by no means secure. I came intending to tell you all this in private, but since you're so pointlessly wasting my time I don't see why your parents shouldn't hear it as well. For some time now your work has left much to be desired. We are aware, of course, that this is not the prime season for doing business; but a season for doing no business at all—that, Mr. Samsa, does not and must not exist."

"But sir," Gregor called out distractedly, forgetting everything else in his excitement, "I'm on the verge of opening the door right now. A slight indisposition, a dizzy spell, has prevented me from getting up. I'm still in bed. But I'm feeling better already. I'm getting up now. Please be patient for just a moment. It seems I'm not quite as well as I thought. But really I'm all right. Something like this can come on so suddenly! Only last night I was feeling fine, as my parents can tell you, or actually I did have a slight premonition. I must have shown some sign of it. Oh, why didn't I report it to the office! But one always thinks one can get better without having to stay at home. Please, sir, have mercy on my parents! None of what you've just accused me of has any basis in fact; no one has even spoken a word to me about it. Perhaps you haven't seen the latest orders I've sent in. Anyway, I can still make the eight o'clock train. Don't let me keep you, sir,

I'll be showing up at the office very soon. Please be kind enough to inform them, and convey my best wishes to the director."

And while hurriedly blurting all this out, hardly knowing what he was saying, Gregor had reached the chest of drawers easily enough, perhaps because of the practice he had already gotten in bed, and was now trying to use it to lift himself upright. For he actually wanted to open the door, actually intended to show himself, and to talk with the manager; he was eager to find out what the others, who now wanted to see him so much, would say at the sight of him. If they recoiled in horror then he would take no further responsibility and could remain peaceably where he was. But if they took it all in stride then he too had no reason to be upset, and, if he hurried, could even get to the station by eight. The first few times, he slipped down the polished surface of the chest, but finally with one last heave he stood upright. He no longer paid attention to the burning pains in his abdomen, no matter how they hurt. Then, allowing himself to fall against the backrest of a nearby chair, he clung to its edges with his little legs. Now he was once more in control of himself; he fell silent, and was able to hear what the manager was saying.

"Did you understand a single word?" the office manager was asking his parents. "He's not trying to make fools of us, is he?" "My God," cried his mother, already in tears, "maybe he's seriously ill and we're tormenting him. Grete! Grete!" she shouted then. "Mother?" called his sister from the other side. They were calling to each other across Gregor's room. "You must go to the doctor at once. Gregor is sick. Go get the doctor now. Did you hear how Gregor was speaking?" "That was the voice of an animal," said the manager in a tone that was noticeably restrained compared to his mother's shrillness. "Anna! Anna!" his father shouted through the hall to the kitchen, clapping his hands, "get a locksmith and hurry!" And the two girls, their skirts rustling, were already running down the hall—how could his sister have gotten dressed so quickly?—and were pulling the front door open. There was no sound of its being shut; evidently they had left it standing open, as is the custom in houses stricken by some great sorrow.

But Gregor now felt much calmer. Though the words he spoke were apparently no longer understandable, they seemed clear enough to him, even clearer than before, perhaps because his hearing had grown accustomed to their sound. In any case, people were now convinced that something was wrong with him, and were ready to help him. The confidence and assurance with which these first measures had been taken comforted him. He felt himself being drawn back into the human circle and hoped for marvelous and astonishing results from both doctor and locksmith, without really drawing a distinction between them. To ready his voice for the crucial discussion that was now almost upon him, to make it sound as clear as possible, he coughed slightly, as quietly as he could, since for all he knew it might sound different from human coughing. Meanwhile in the next room there was utter silence. Perhaps his parents and the manager were sitting at the table, whispering; perhaps they were, all of them, leaning against the door, listening.

Gregor slowly advanced on the door, pushing the chair in front of him. Then he let go of it, grabbed onto the door for support—the pads at the end of his little legs were somewhat sticky—and, leaning against it, rested for a moment after his efforts. Then he started to turn the key in the lock with his mouth. Unfortunately, he didn't really have any teeth—how was he going to grip the key?—but to make up for that he clearly had very powerful jaws; with their help he was in fact able to start turning the key, paying no attention to the fact that he was surely hurting them somehow, for a brown liquid poured out of his mouth, flowed over the key, and dripped onto the floor. "Listen," said the manager on the other side of the door, "he's turning the key." This was a great encouragement to Gregor, but they should all have been cheering him on, his mother and his father too. "Come on, Gregor," they should have been shouting, "keep at it, hold on to that key!" And, imagining that they were all intently following his efforts, he grimly clamped his jaws on the key with all his might. As the key continued to turn he danced around the lock, holding himself by his mouth alone, either hanging onto the key or pressing down on it with the full weight of his body, as the situation required. The sharper sound of the lock as it finally snapped free woke Gregor up completely. With a sigh of relief he said to himself, "So I didn't need the locksmith after all," and he pressed his head down on the handle to open one wing of the double door.

Because he had to pull the wing in towards him, even when it stood wide   25
open he remained hidden from view. He had to edge slowly around this wing and to do it very carefully or he would fall flat on his back as he made his entrance. He was still busy carrying out this maneuver, with no time to notice anything else, when he heard the manager give a loud "Oh!"—it sounded like a gust of wind—and now he could see him, standing closest to the door, his hand over his open mouth, slowly backing away as if propelled by the relentless pressure of some invisible force. His mother—in spite of the manager's presence, she was standing there with her hair still unpinned and sticking out in all directions—first folded her hands and looked at Gregor's father, then took two steps forward and sank to the floor, her skirts billowing out all around her and her face completely buried in her breast. His father, glowering, clenched his fist, as if he intended to drive Gregor back into his room; then he looked around the living room with uncertainty, covered his eyes with his hands, and wept so hard his great chest shook.

Now Gregor made no attempt to enter the living room, but leaned against the locked wing of the double door, so that only half of his body was visible, with his head above it cocked to one side, peering at the others. Meanwhile the daylight had grown much brighter; across the street one could clearly see a section of the endless, dark gray building opposite—it was a hospital—with a row of uniform windows starkly punctuating its facade. The rain was still falling, but only in large, visibly separate drops that looked as though they were being flung, one by one, onto the earth. On the table the breakfast dishes were set out in lavish profusion, for breakfast was the most important meal of the day for Gregor's father, who lingered over it for hours while reading various newspapers. Hanging on the opposite wall was a photograph of Gregor from his army days, showing him as a lieutenant, with his hand on his sword and his carefree smile demanding respect for his bearing and his rank. The door to the hall stood open, and as the front door was open too, one could see the landing beyond and the top of the stairs going down.

"Well," said Gregor, who was perfectly aware that he was the only one who had kept his composure, "I'll go now and get dressed, pack up my samples, and be on my way. You will, you will let me go, won't you? You can see, sir, that I'm not stubborn and I'm willing to work; the life of a traveling salesman is hard, but I couldn't live without it. Where are you going, sir? To the office? You are? Will you give an honest report about all this? A man may be temporarily unable to work, but that's just the time to remember the service he has rendered in the past, and to bear in mind that later on, when the present problem has been resolved, he is sure to work with even more energy and diligence than before. As you know very well, I am deeply obligated to the director. At the same time, I'm responsible for my parents and my sister. I'm in a tight spot right now, but I'll get out of it. Don't make things more difficult for me than they already are. Stand up for me at the office! People don't like traveling salesmen, I know. They think they make scads of money and lead lives of luxury. And there's no compelling reason for them to revise this prejudice. But you sir, have a better understanding of things than the rest of the staff, a better understanding, if I may say so, than even the director himself, who since he is the owner, can be easily swayed against an employee. You also know very well that a traveling salesman, who is away from the office for most of the year, can so easily fall victim to gossip and bad luck and groundless accusations, against which he is powerless to defend himself since he knows nothing about them until, returning home exhausted from his journeys, he suffers personally from evil consequences that can no longer be traced back to their origins. Sir, please don't go away without giving me some word to show that you think that I'm at least partly right!"

But the office manager had turned away at Gregor's first words, and was looking at him now over one twitching shoulder, his mouth agape. And during Gregor's speech he didn't stand still for even a moment, but without once taking his eyes off of him kept edging towards the door, yet very slowly, as if there were some secret injunction against his leaving the room. He was already in the hall, and from the suddenness with which he took his last step out of the living room, one might have thought he had burned the sole of his foot. But once in the hall, he stretched out his right hand as far as possible in the direction of the staircase, as if some supernatural rescuer awaited him there.

Gregor realized that he could not let the manager leave in this frame of mind, or his position with the firm would be in extreme jeopardy. His parents were incapable of clearly grasping this; over the years they had come to believe that Gregor was set for life with this firm, and besides they were now so preoccupied with their immediate problems that they had lost the ability to foresee events. But Gregor had this ability. The manager must be overtaken, calmed, swayed, and finally convinced; the future of Gregor and of his family depended on it! If only his sister were here—she was perceptive; she had already begun to cry while Gregor was still lying calmly on his back. And surely the manager, that ladies' man, would've listened to her; she would've shut the door behind them and in the hall talked him out of his fright. But his sister wasn't there, and he would have to handle this himself. And forgetting that he had no idea what his powers of movement were, and forgetting as well that once again his words would possibly, even probably, be misunderstood, he let go of the door, pushed his way through the opening, and started towards the manager, who by now was on the landing, clinging in a ridiculous manner to the banister with both hands. But as Gregor reached out for support, he immediately fell down with a little cry onto his numerous legs. The moment this happened he felt, for the first time that morning, a sense of physical well-being. His little legs had solid ground under them, and, he noticed with joy, they were at his command, and were even eager to carry him in whatever direction he might desire; and he already felt sure that the final recovery from all his misery was at hand. But at the very moment, as he lay on the floor rocking with suppressed motion, not far from his mother and just opposite her, she, who had seemed so completely overwhelmed, leapt to her feet, stretched her arms out wide, spread her fingers, and cried, "Help! For God's sake, help!" She then craned her neck forward as if to see Gregor better, but at the same time, inconsistently, backed away from him. Forgetting that the table with all its dishes was behind her, she sat down on it, and, as if in a daze when she bumped into it, seemed utterly unaware that the large coffee pot next to her had tipped over and was pouring out a flood of coffee onto the carpet.

"Mother, Mother," said Gregor gently, looking up at her. For the moment 30 he had completely forgotten the office manager; on the other hand, he couldn't resist snapping his jaws a few times at the sight of the streaming coffee. This made his mother scream again; she ran from the table and into the outstretched arms of his father, who came rushing to her. But Gregor had no time now for his parents. The manager had already reached the staircase; with his chin on the banister railing, he was looking back for the last time. Gregor darted forward, to be sure as possible of catching up with him, but the manager must have guessed his intention, for he sprinted down several steps and disappeared. He was still yelling "Oohh!" and the sound echoed throughout the stairwell.

Unfortunately the manager's escape seemed to make his father, who until now had seemed reasonably calm, lose all sense of proportion. Instead of running after the man himself, or at least not interfering with Gregor's pursuit, he grabbed with his right hand the manager's cane, which he had left behind, together with his hat and overcoat, on the chair; with his left hand he snatched up a large newspaper from the table. He began stamping his feet and waving the cane and newspaper in order to drive Gregor back into his room. Nothing Gregor said made any difference, indeed, nothing he said was even understood. No matter how humbly he lowered his head his father only stamped the louder. Behind his father his mother, despite the cold, had flung open a window and was leaning far outside it, her face in her hands. A strong breeze from the street blew across the room to the stairwell, the window curtains billowed inwards, the newspapers fluttered on the table, stray pages skittered across the floor. His father, hissing like a savage, mercilessly drove him back. But as Gregor had had no practice in walking backwards, it was a very slow process. If he had been given a chance to turn around then he would've gotten back into his room at once, but he was afraid that the length of time it would take him to turn around would exasperate his father and that at any moment the cane in his father's hand might deal him a fatal blow on his back or his head. In the end, though, he had no choice, for he noticed to his horror that while moving backwards he couldn't even keep a straight course. And so, looking back anxiously, he began turning around as quickly as possible, which in reality was very slowly. Perhaps his father divined his good intentions, for he did not interfere, and even helped to direct the maneuver from afar with the tip of his cane. If only he would stop that unbearable hissing! It made Gregor completely lose his concentration. He had turned himself almost all the way around when, confused by this hissing, he made a mistake and started turning back the wrong way. But when at last he'd succeeded in getting his head in front of the doorway, he found that his body was too wide to make it through. Of course his father, in the state he was in, couldn't even begin to consider opening the other wing of the door to let Gregor in. His mind was on one thing only: to drive Gregor back into this room as quickly as possible. He would never have permitted the complicated preparations necessary for Gregor to haul himself upright and in that way perhaps slip through. Instead, making even more noise, he urged Gregor forward as if the way were clear. To Gregor the noise behind him no longer sounded like the voice of merely one father; this really wasn't a joke, and Gregor squeezed himself into the doorway, heedless of the consequences. One side of his body lifted up, he was pitched at an angle in the doorway; the other side was scraped raw, ugly blotches stained the white door. Soon he was stuck fast and couldn't have moved any further by himself. On one side his little legs hung trembling in the air, while those on the other were painfully crushed against the floor—when, from behind, his father gave him a hard blow that was truly a deliverance, and bleeding profusely, he flew far into his room. Behind him the door was slammed shut with the cane, and then at last everything was still.

II

It was already dusk when Gregor awoke from a deep, almost comatose sleep. Surely, even if he hadn't been disturbed he would've soon awakened by himself, since he'd rested and slept long enough; yet it seemed to him that he'd been awakened by the sound of hurried steps and the furtive closing of the hallway door. The light from the electric streetlamps cast pale streaks here and there on the ceiling and the upper part of the furniture, but down below, where Gregor was, it was dark. Groping awkwardly with the feelers which he was only now beginning to appreciate, he slowly pushed himself over to the door to see what had been going on there. His left side felt as if it were one long, painfully tightening scar, and he was actually limping on his two rows of legs. One little leg, moreover, had been badly hurt during the morning's events—it was nearly miraculous that only one had been hurt—and it trailed along lifelessly.

Only when he reached the door did he realize what had impelled him forward—the smell of something to eat. For there stood a bowl full of fresh milk, in which floated small slices of white bread. He could almost have laughed for joy, since he was even hungrier now than he'd been during the morning, and he immediately dipped his head into the milk, almost up to his eyes. But he soon drew it back in disappointment; not only did he find it difficult to eat because of the soreness in his left side—and he was capable of eating only if his whole gasping body cooperated—but also because he didn't like the milk at all, although it had once been his favorite drink, which, no doubt, was why his sister had brought it in. In fact, he turned away from the bowl almost in disgust, and crawled back to the middle of the room.

In the living room, as Gregor could see through the crack in the door, the gaslight had been lit. But while this was the hour when his father would usually be reading the afternoon paper in a loud voice to his mother and sometimes to his sister as well, now there wasn't a sound to be heard. Well, perhaps this custom of reading aloud, which his sister was always telling him about or mentioning in her letters, had recently been discontinued. Still, though the apartment was completely silent, it was scarcely deserted. "What a quiet life the family's been leading," said Gregor to himself, and, staring fixedly into the darkness, he felt a genuine pride at having been able to provide his parents and his sister with such a life in such a nice apartment. But what if all this calm, prosperity, and contentment were to end in horror? So as not to give in to such thoughts, Gregor set himself in motion, and he crawled up and down the room.

Once during the long evening first one of the side doors and then the other 35 was opened a crack and then quickly shut. Someone, it seemed, had wanted to come in but then had thought better of it. Gregor now stationed himself so as to somehow get the hesitant visitor to come in or at least to find out who it might be. But the door did not open again and he waited in vain. That morning when the doors had been locked, everyone had wanted to come in, but now after he'd unlocked one of the doors himself—and the others had evidently been unlocked during the day—nobody came in, and the keys, too, were now on the outside.

It was late at night before the light was put out in the living room, and it was easy for Gregor to tell that his parents and sister had stayed up all the while, since he could plainly hear the three of them as they tiptoed away. As it was obvious that no one would be visiting Gregor before morning, he had plenty of time in which to contemplate, undisturbed, how best to rearrange his life. But the open, high-ceilinged room in which he was forced to lie flat on the floor filled him with a dread which he couldn't account for—since it was, after all, the room he had lived in for the past five years. Almost unthinkingly, and not without a faint sense of shame, he scurried under the couch. There, although his back was slightly cramped and he could no longer raise his head, he immediately felt very much at home, and his only regret was that his body was too wide to fit completely under the couch.

There he spent the rest of the night, now in a doze from which hunger pangs kept awakening him with a start, now preoccupied with worries and vague hopes, all of which, however, led to the same conclusion: that for the time being he must remain calm and, by being patient and showing every consideration, try to help his family bear the burdens that his present condition had placed upon them.

Early the next morning—the night was barely over—Gregor got an opportunity to test the strength of his newly-made resolutions, because his sister, who was almost fully dressed, opened the hallway door and looked in expectantly. She didn't see him at first, but when she spotted him underneath the couch—well, my God, he had to be somewhere, he couldn't just fly away—she was so surprised that she lost her self-control and slammed the door shut again. But, as if she felt sorry for her behavior, she opened it again right away and tiptoed in, as if she were in the presence of someone who was very ill, or who was a stranger. Gregor had moved his head forward almost to the edge of the couch and was watching her. Would she notice that he'd let the milk sit there, and not from lack of hunger, and would she bring him some other food that was more to his taste? If she weren't going to do it on her own, he'd sooner starve than call her attention to it, although in fact he was feeling a tremendous urge to dash out from under the couch, fling himself at his sister's feet, and beg her for something good to eat. But his sister immediately noticed to her astonishment that the bowl was still full, with only a little milk spilt around it. She picked up the bowl at once—not, it's true, with her bare hands but using a rag—and carried it out. Gregor was extremely curious to find out what she would bring in its place, and he speculated at length as to what it might be. But he never would have guessed what his sister, in the goodness of her heart, actually did. She brought him a wide range of choices, all spread out on an old newspaper. There were old, half-rotten vegetables; bones left over from dinner, covered with a congealed white sauce; some raisins and almonds; a piece of cheese which Gregor two days ago had declared inedible; a slice of plain bread, a slice of bread and butter, and a slice with butter and salt. In addition to all this she replaced the bowl, now evidently reserved for Gregor, filled this time with water. And out of a sense of delicacy, since she knew that Gregor wouldn't eat in front of her, she left in a hurry, even turning the key in the lock in order that Gregor might know that he was free to make himself as comfortable as possible. Gregor's legs whirred as they propelled him toward the food. Besides, his wounds must have healed completely, for he no longer felt handicapped, which amazed him. He thought of how, a month ago, he'd cut his finger slightly with his knife and how only the day before yesterday that little wound had still hurt. "Am I less sensitive now?" he wondered, greedily sucking on the cheese, to which, above all the other dishes, he was immediately and strongly attracted. Tears of joy welled up in his eyes as he devoured the cheese, the vegetables, and the sauce. The fresh foods, on the other hand, were not to his liking; in fact, he couldn't stand to smell them and he actually dragged the food he wanted to eat a little way off. He'd long since finished eating, and was merely lying lazily in the same spot, when his sister began to slowly turn the key in the lock as a signal for him to withdraw. He got up at once, although he'd almost fallen asleep, and scurried back under the couch. But it took a great deal of self-control for him to remain under the couch even for the brief time his sister was in the room, for his heavy meal had swollen his body to some extent and he could scarcely breathe in that confined space. Between little fits of suffocation he stared with slightly bulging eyes as his unsuspecting sister took a broom and swept away not only the scraps of what he'd eaten, but also the food that he'd left untouched—as if these too were no longer any good—and hurriedly dumped everything into a bucket, which she covered with a wooden lid and carried away. She'd hardly turned her back before Gregor came out from under the couch to stretch and puff himself out.

So this was how Gregor was fed each day, once in the morning when his parents and the maid were still asleep, and again after the family's midday meal, while his parents took another brief nap and his sister could send the maid away on some errand or other. His parents didn't want Gregor to starve any more than his sister did, but perhaps for them to be directly involved in his feeding was more than they could bear, or perhaps his sister wanted to shield them even from what might prove to be no more than a minor discomfort, for they were surely suffering enough as it was.

Gregor was unable to discover what excuses had served to get rid of the doctor and the locksmith that first morning. Since the others couldn't understand what he said it never occurred to them, not even to his sister, that he could understand them, so when his sister was in the room, he had to be satisfied with occasionally hearing her sighs and her appeals to the saints. Only later, after she began to get used to the situation—of course she could never become completely used to it—would Gregor sometimes hear a remark that was intended to be friendly or could be so interpreted. "He really liked it today," she'd say when Gregor had polished off a good portion, and when the opposite was the case, which began to happen more and more often, she'd say almost sadly, "Once again, he didn't touch a thing." 40

But while Gregor wasn't able to get any news directly, he could overhear a considerable amount from the adjoining rooms, and as soon as he would hear the sound of voices he would immediately run to the appropriate door and press his whole body against it. In the early days especially, there wasn't a conversation that didn't in some way, if only indirectly, refer to him. For two whole days, at every meal, the family discussed what they should do, and they kept on doing so between meals as well, for at least two members of the family were now always at home, probably because nobody wanted to be in the apartment alone, and it would be unthinkable to leave it empty. Furthermore, on the very first day the cook—it wasn't completely clear how much she knew of what had happened— had on her knees begged Gregor's mother to dismiss her immediately, and when she said her goodbyes a quarter of an hour later, she thanked them for her dismissal with tears in her eyes, as if this had been the greatest favor ever bestowed on her in the house, and without having to be asked she made a solemn vow never to breathe a word of this to anyone.

So now his sister, together with his mother, had to do all the cooking as well, though in fact this wasn't too much of a chore, since the family ate practically nothing. Gregor kept hearing them vainly urging one another to eat, without receiving any reply except, "No thanks, I've had enough," or some similar remark. They didn't seem to drink anything, either. His sister would often ask his father if he'd like some beer, and would gladly offer to go out and get it herself. When he wouldn't respond she'd say, in order to remove any hesitation on his part, that she could always send the janitor's wife, but at that point the father would finally utter an emphatic "No" and that would be the end of the matter.

It was on the very first day that his father gave a full account, to both mother and sister, of the family's financial situation and prospects. Every now and then he would get up from the table and take a receipt or notebook from out of the small safe he'd salvaged from the collapse of his business five years before. He could be heard opening the complicated lock and then securing it again after taking out whatever he'd been looking for. The account that his father gave, or at least part of it, was the first encouraging news that Gregor had heard since being imprisoned. He'd always had the impression that his father had failed to save a penny from the ruin of his business; at least his father had never told him otherwise, and Gregor, for that matter, had never asked him about it. At that time Gregor's only concern had been to do his utmost to make the family forget as quickly as possible the business failure that had plunged them all into a state of total despair. And so he had set to work with tremendous zeal, and had risen almost overnight from junior clerk to become a traveling salesman, which naturally opened up completely new financial opportunities so that in no time at all his success was instantly translated, by way of commissions, into hard cash, which could be laid out on the table under the eyes of his astonished and delighted family. Those had been wonderful times, and they had never returned, at least not with the same glory, even though later on Gregor had been earning enough to pay the entire family's expenses, and in fact had been doing so. They'd simply gotten used to it, both family and Gregor; they had gratefully accepted the money, and he had given it gladly, but no special warmth went with it. Gregor had remained close only to his sister, and it was his secret plan that she, who unlike Gregor loved music and could play the violin with deep feeling, should next year attend the Conservatory, despite the expense which, great as it was, would have to be met in some way. During Gregor's brief stays in the city the subject of the Conservatory would often come up in his conversations with his sister, but always only as a beautiful dream that wasn't meant to come true. His parents weren't happy to hear even these innocent remarks, but Gregor's ideas on the subject were firm and he intended to make a solemn announcement on Christmas Eve.

Such were the thoughts, so futile in his present condition, that ran through his mind as he stood there, pressed against the door, listening. Sometimes he would grow so thoroughly weary that he couldn't listen any more and would carelessly let his head bump against the door, and though he'd pull it back immediately, even the slight noise he'd made would be heard in the next room, causing everyone to fall silent. "What's he up to now?" his father would say after a pause, obviously looking at the door, and only then would the interrupted conversation gradually be resumed.

Gregor now learned with considerable thoroughness—for his father tended   45
to repeat his explanations several times, partly because he hadn't dealt with
these matters in a long time, and partly because his mother didn't understand
everything the first time through—that despite their catastrophic ruin a certain
amount of capital, a very small amount, it's true, had survived intact from the
old days, and thanks to the interest being untouched had even increased slightly.
And what was more, the money which Gregor had been bringing home every
month—he'd kept only a small sum for himself—hadn't been completely spent
and had grown into a tidy sum. Gregor nodded eagerly behind his door, delighted to hear of this unexpected foresight and thrift. Of course he might have
been able to use this extra money to pay off more of his father's debt to the director, and thus have brought nearer the day when he could quit his current job,
but, given the present circumstances, things were better the way his father had
arranged them.

Now the sum of this money wasn't nearly large enough for the family to
live off the interest; the principal might support them for a year, or two at the
most, but that was all. So this was really only a sum that was not to be
touched, but saved instead for emergencies. As for money to live on—that
would have to be earned. Though Gregor's father was indeed still healthy,
nevertheless he was an old man who hadn't worked for five years and one
from whom not too much should be expected in any case. During those five
years, the first ones of leisure in his hard-working but unsuccessful life, he had
put on a lot of weight and consequently had grown somewhat sluggish. And as
for Gregor's elderly mother, was she supposed to start bringing in money, burdened as she was by her asthma which made it a strain for her to even walk
across the apartment and which kept her gasping for breath every other day
on the couch by the open window? Or should his sister go to work instead—
she who though seventeen was still a child and one moreover whom it would
be cruel to deprive of the life she'd led up until now, a life of wearing pretty
clothes, sleeping late, helping around the house, enjoying a few modest pleasures, and above all playing the violin? At first, whenever their conversation
turned to the need to earn money, Gregor would let go of the door and fling
himself down on the cool leather couch which stood beside it, for he felt hot
with grief and shame.

Often he would lie there all night long, not sleeping a wink, scratching at
the leather couch for hours. Or, undaunted by the great effort it required, he
would push the chair over to the window. Then he would crawl up to the sill
and, propped up by the chair, would lean against the pane, apparently inspired by
some memory of the sense of freedom that gazing out a window used to give him.
For in truth objects only a short distance away were now, each day, becoming
more indistinct; the hospital across the street, which he used to curse because he
could see it all too clearly, was now completely outside his field of vision, and if he
hadn't known for a fact that he lived on Charlotte Street—a quiet but nevertheless urban street—he could have imagined that he was looking out his window at a
wasteland where gray sky and gray earth had indistinguishably merged as one. His
observant sister needed only to notice twice that the armchair had been moved to

the window. From then on, whenever she cleaned the room, she carefully placed the chair back by the window, and even began leaving the inner casement open.

If only Gregor had been able to speak to his sister and thank her for everything she'd had to do for him, he could have borne her kindnesses more easily, but as it was they were painful to him. Of course his sister tried her best to ease the general embarrassment, and naturally as time passed she grew better and better at it. But Gregor too, over time, gained a clearer sense of what was involved. Even the way in which she entered the room was a torture to him. No sooner had she stepped in when—not even pausing to shut the door, despite the care she normally would take in sparing others the sight of Gregor's room—she would run straight over to the window and tear it open with impatient fingers, almost as if she were suffocating, and she would remain for some time by the window, even in the coldest weather, breathing deeply. Twice a day she would terrify Gregor with all this noise and rushing around. He would cower under the couch the entire time, knowing full well that she surely would have spared him this if only she could have stood being in the room with him with the windows closed.

Once, about a month after Gregor's metamorphosis—so there was really no particular reason for his sister to be upset by his appearance—she came in earlier than usual and caught Gregor as he gazed out the window, terrifying in his stillness. It wouldn't have surprised Gregor if she'd decided not to come in, since his position prevented her from opening the window right away, but not only did she not come in, she actually jumped back and shut the door—a stranger might have thought that Gregor had been planning to ambush her and bite her. Of course he immediately hid under the couch, but he had to wait until noon before she came back, and this time she seemed much more nervous than usual. In this way he came to realize that the sight of him disgusted her, and likely would always disgust her, and that she probably had to steel herself not to run away at the sight of even the tiny portion of his body that stuck out from under the couch. So, one day, to spare her even this, he carried the bedsheet on his back over to the couch—it took him four hours—and spread it so that he was completely covered and his sister wouldn't be able to see him even if she bent down. If she felt this sheet wasn't necessary then of course she could remove it, since obviously Gregor wasn't shutting himself away so completely in order to amuse himself. But she left the sheet alone, and Gregor even thought that he caught a look of gratitude when he cautiously lifted the sheet a little with his head in order to see how his sister was taking to this new arrangement.

During the first two weeks, his parents couldn't bring themselves to come in to see him, and he frequently heard them remarking how much they appreciated his sister's efforts, whereas previously they'd often been annoyed with her for being, in their eyes, somewhat useless. But now both father and mother had fallen into the habit of waiting outside Gregor's door while his sister cleaned up the room, and as soon as she emerged she would have to tell them every detail of the room's condition, what Gregor had eaten, how he'd behaved this time, and whether he'd perhaps shown a little improvement. It wasn't long before his mother began to want to visit Gregor, but his father and sister were at first able to dissuade her by rational arguments to which Gregor listened with great care, and with which he thoroughly agreed. But as time went by she had to be re-strained by force, and when she cried out, "Let me go to Gregor, he's my un-happy boy! Don't you understand that I have to go to him?" Gregor began to think that it might be a good idea if his mother did come in after all, not every day, naturally, but say once a week. She was really a much more capable person than his sister, who, for all her courage, was still only a child and had perhaps taken on such a difficult task only out of a childish impulsiveness.

Gregor's wish to see his mother was soon fulfilled. During the day Gregor didn't want to show himself at the window, if only out of consideration for his parents. But his few square meters of floor gave him little room to crawl around in, he found it hard to lie still even at night, and eating soon ceased to give him any pleasure. So in order to distract himself he fell into the habit of crawling all over the walls and the ceiling. He especially enjoyed hanging from the ceiling; it was completely different from lying on the floor. He could breathe more freely, a faint pulsing coursed through his body, and in his state of almost giddy absent-mindedness up there, Gregor would sometimes, to his surprise, lose his grip and tumble onto the floor. But now, of course, since he had much better control over his body, even such a great fall didn't hurt him. His sister noticed right away the new pastime Gregor had discovered for himself—he'd left sticky traces where he'd been crawling—and so she got it into her head to provide Gregor with as much room as possible to crawl around in by removing all the furniture that was in the way—especially the chest of drawers and the desk. But she couldn't manage this by herself; she didn't dare ask her father for help; the maid wouldn't be of any use, for while this girl, who was around sixteen, was brave enough to stay on after the cook had left, she'd asked to be allowed to always keep the kitchen door locked, opening it only when specifically asked to do so. This left his sister with no choice but, one day when her father was out, to ask her mother for help. And indeed, her mother followed her with joyful, excited cries, al-though she fell silent when they reached the door to Gregor's room. Naturally his sister first made sure that everything in the room was as it should be; only then did she let her mother come in. Gregor had hurriedly pulled his sheet even lower and had folded it more tightly and it really did look as if it had been casu-ally tossed over the couch. This time Gregor also refrained from peeking out from under the sheet; he denied himself the pleasure of seeing his mother for now and was simply glad that she'd come after all. "Come on in, he's nowhere in sight," said his sister, apparently leading his mother in by the hand. Now Gregor could hear the two delicate women moving the heavy chest of drawers away from its place, his sister stubbornly insisting on doing the hardest work, ignoring the warnings of her mother, who was afraid her daughter would overstrain her-self. The work took a very long time. After struggling for over a quarter of an hour, his mother suggested that they might leave the chest where it was; in the first place, it was just too heavy, they'd never be done before his father came home and they'd have to leave it in the middle of the room, blocking Gregor's movements in every direction; in the second place, it wasn't at all certain that they were doing Gregor a favor in removing the furniture. It seemed to her that the opposite was true, the sight of the bare walls broke her heart; and why shouldn't Gregor feel the same since he'd been used to this furniture for so long and would feel abandoned in the empty room? "And wouldn't it look as if," his mother concluded very softly—in fact, she'd been almost whispering the entire time, as if she wanted to prevent Gregor, whose exact whereabouts she didn't know, from hearing the sound of her voice (she was convinced that he couldn't understand her words)—"as if by removing his furniture we were telling him that we'd given up all hope of his getting better, and were callously leaving him to his own devices? I think the best course would be to try to keep the room exactly the way it was, so that when Gregor does come back to us he'll find everything the same, making it easier for him to forget what has happened in the meantime."

When he heard his mother's words, Gregor realized that, over the past two months, the lack of having anyone to converse with, together with the monotonous life within the family, must have befuddled his mind; there wasn't any other way he could explain to himself how he could have ever seriously wanted his room cleared out. Did he really want this warm room of his, so comfortably furnished with family heirlooms, transformed into a lair where he'd be perfectly free to crawl around in every direction, but only at the cost of simultaneously forgetting his human past, swiftly and utterly? Just now he'd been on the brink of forgetting, and only his mother's voice, which he hadn't heard for so long, had brought him back. Nothing should be removed; everything must stay. He couldn't do without the furniture's soothing influence on his state of mind, and if the furniture were to impede his senselessly crawling around, that wouldn't be a loss but rather a great advantage.

But unfortunately his sister thought otherwise. She'd become accustomed, and not without some justification, to assume the role of the acknowledged expert whenever she and her parents discussed Gregor's affairs; so her mother's advice was enough for her to insist now not merely on her original plan of moving the chest and the desk, but on the removal of every bit of furniture except for the indispensable couch. Her resolve, to be sure, didn't stem merely from childish stubbornness or from the self-confidence she had recently and unexpectedly gained at such great cost. For in fact she'd noticed that while Gregor needed plenty of room to crawl around in, on the other hand, as far as she could tell, he never used the furniture at all. Perhaps too, the sentimental enthusiasm of girls her age, which they indulge themselves in at every opportunity, now tempted Grete to make Gregor's situation all the more terrifying so that she might be able to do more for him. No one but Grete would ever be likely to enter a room where Gregor ruled the bare walls all alone.

And so she refused to give in to her mother, who in any case, from the sheer anxiety caused by being in Gregor's room, seemed unsure of herself. She soon fell silent and began as best she could to help her daughter remove the chest of drawers. Well, if he must, then Gregor could do without the chest, but the desk had to stay. And no sooner had the two women, groaning and squeezing, gotten the chest out of the room than Gregor poked his head out from under the couch to see how he might intervene as tactfully as possible. But unfortunately it was his mother who came back first, leaving Grete in the next room, gripping the chest with her arms and rocking it back and forth without, of course, being able to budge it from the spot. His mother wasn't used to the sight of him—it might make her sick; so Gregor, frightened, scuttled backwards to the far end of the couch, but he couldn't prevent the front of the sheet from stirring slightly. That was enough to catch his mother's attention. She stopped, stood still for a moment, and then went back to Grete.

Gregor kept telling himself that nothing unusual was happening, that only a 55 few pieces of furniture were being moved around. But he soon had to admit that all this coming and going of the two women, their little calls to one another, the scraping of the furniture across the floor, affected him as if it were some gigantic commotion rushing in on him from every side, and though he tucked in his head and legs and pressed his body against the floor, he had to accept the fact that he wouldn't be able to stand it much longer. They were cleaning out his room, taking away from him everything that he loved; already they'd carried off his chest, where he kept his fretsaw and his other tools; now they were trying to pry his writing desk loose—it was practically embedded in the floor—the same desk where he'd always done his homework when he'd been a student at business school, in high school, and even in elementary school. He really no longer had any time left in which to weigh the good intentions of these two women whose existence, for that matter, he'd almost forgotten, since they were so exhausted by now that they worked in silence, the only sound being that of their weary, plodding steps.

And so, while the women were in the next room, leaning against the desk and trying to catch their breath, he broke out, changing his direction four times—since he really didn't know what to rescue first—when he saw, hanging conspicuously on the otherwise bare wall, the picture of the lady all dressed in furs. He quickly crawled up to it and pressed himself against the glass, which held him fast, soothing his hot belly. Now that Gregor completely covered it, this picture at least wasn't about to be carried away by anyone. He turned his head towards the living room door, so that he could watch the women when they returned.

They hadn't taken much of a rest and were already coming back. Grete had put her arm around her mother and was almost carrying her. "Well, what should we take next?" said Grete, looking around. And then her eyes met Gregor's, looking down at her from the wall. Probably only because her mother was there, she kept her composure, bent her head down to her mother to prevent her from glancing around, and said, though in a hollow, quavering voice: "Come on, let's go back to the living room for a minute." To Gregor, her intentions were obvious: she wanted to get his mother to safety and then chase him down from the wall. Well, just let her try! He clung to his picture and he wasn't going to give it up. He'd rather fly at Grete's face.

But Grete's words had made her mother even more anxious; she stepped aside, glimpsed the huge brown blotch on the flowered wallpaper, and before she fully understood that what she was looking at was Gregor, she cried out, "Oh God, oh God!" in a hoarse scream of a voice, and, as if giving up completely, fell with outstretched arms across the couch, and lay there without moving. "You!

Gregor!" cried his sister, raising her fist and glaring at him. These were the first words she had addressed directly to him since his metamorphosis. She ran into the next room to get some spirits to revive her mother from her faint. Gregor also wanted to help—he could rescue the picture another time—but he was stuck to the glass and had to tear himself free. He then scuttled into the next room as if to give some advice, as he used to, to his sister. Instead he had to stand behind her uselessly while she rummaged among various little bottles. When she turned around she was startled, a bottle fell to the floor, a splinter of glass struck Gregor in the face, some sort of corrosive medicine splashed on him, and Grete, without further delay, grabbing as many of the little bottles as she could carry, ran inside with them to her mother, and slammed the door shut behind her with her foot. Now Gregor was cut off from his mother, who was perhaps near death because of him. He didn't dare open the door for fear of scaring his sister, who had to remain with his mother. There wasn't anything for him to do but wait; and so, tormented by guilt and anxiety, he began crawling. He crawled over everything, walls, furniture, and ceiling, until finally, in despair, the room beginning to spin around him, he collapsed onto the middle of the large table.

A short time passed; Gregor lay there stupefied. Everything was quiet around him; perhaps that was a good sign. Then the doorbell rang. The maid, of course, stayed locked up in her kitchen, so Grete had to answer the door. His father was back. "What's happened?" were his first words. Grete's expression must've told him everything. Her answers came in muffled tones—she was obviously burying her face in her father's chest. "Mother fainted, but she's better now. Gregor's broken loose." "I knew it," her father said. "I told you this would happen, but you women refuse to listen." It was clear to Gregor that his father had put the worst construction on Grete's all too brief account and had assumed that Gregor was guilty of some violent act. That meant that he must calm his father down, since he had neither the time nor the ability to explain things to him. So he fled to the door of his room and pressed himself against it in order that his father might see, as soon as he entered the living room, that Gregor had every intention of returning immediately to his own room and there was no need to force him back. All they had to do was to open the door and he would disappear at once.

But his father wasn't in the mood to notice such subtleties; "Ah!" he roared 60 as he entered, in a voice that sounded at once furious and gleeful. Gregor turned his head from the door and lifted it towards his father. He really hadn't imagined that his father would look the way he did standing before him now; true, Gregor had become too absorbed lately by his new habit of crawling to bother about whatever else might be going on in the apartment, and he should have anticipated that there would be some changes. And yet, and yet, could this really be his father? Was this the same man who used to lie sunk in bed, exhausted, whenever Gregor would set out on one of his business trips; who would greet him upon his return in the evening while sitting in his bathrobe in the armchair; who was hardly capable of getting to his feet, and to show his joy could only lift up his arms; and who, on those rare times when the whole family went out for a walk—

on the occasional Sunday or on a legal holiday—used to painfully shuffle along between Gregor and his mother, who were slow walkers themselves, and yet he was always slightly slower than they, wrapped up in his old overcoat, carefully planting his crook-handled cane before him with every step, and almost invariably stopping and gathering his escort around him whenever he wanted to say something? Now, however, he held himself very erect, dressed up in a closely-fitting blue uniform with gold buttons, of the kind worn by bank messengers. His heavy chin thrust out over the stiff collar of his jacket; his black eyes stared, sharp and bright, from under his bushy eyebrows; his white hair, once so rumpled, was combed flat, it gleamed, and the part was meticulously exact. He tossed his cap—which bore a gold monogram, probably that of some bank—in an arc across the room so that it landed on the couch, and with his hands in his pockets, the tails of his uniform's long jacket flung back, his face grim, he went after Gregor. He probably didn't know himself what he was going to do, but he lifted his feet unusually high, and Gregor was amazed at the immense size of the soles of his boots. However, Gregor didn't dwell on these reflections, for he had known from the very first day of his new life that his father considered only the strictest measures to be appropriate in dealing with him. So he ran ahead of his father, stopped when he stood still, and scurried on again when he made the slightest move. In this way they circled the room several times without anything decisive happening; in fact, their movements, because of their slow tempo, did not suggest those of a chase. So Gregor kept to the floor for the time being, especially since he was afraid that his father might consider any flight to the walls or ceiling to be particularly offensive. All the same, Gregor had to admit that he wouldn't be able to keep up even this pace for long, since whenever his father took a single step, Gregor had to perform an entire series of movements. He was beginning to get winded, since even in his former life his lungs had never been strong. As he kept staggering on like this, so weary he could barely keep his eyes open, since he was saving all his strength for running; not even thinking, dazed as he was, that there might be any other way to escape than by running; having almost forgotten that he was free to use the walls, though against these walls, admittedly, were placed bits of intricately carved furniture, bristling with spikes and sharp corners—suddenly something sailed overhead, hit the floor nearby, and rolled right in front of him. It was an apple; at once a second one came flying after it. Gregor stopped, petrified with fear; it was useless to keep on running, for his father had decided to bombard him. He had filled his pockets with the fruit from the bowl on the sideboard and now he was throwing one apple after another, for now at least without bothering to take good aim. These little red apples, colliding with one another, rolled around on the floor as if electrified. One weakly-thrown apple grazed Gregor's back, rolling off without causing harm. But another one that came flying immediately afterwards actually imbedded itself in Gregor's back. Gregor wanted to drag himself onward, as if this shocking and unbelievable pain might disappear if he could only keep moving, but he felt as if he were nailed to the spot, and he splayed himself out in the utter confusion of his senses. With his last glance he saw the door of his room burst open, and his mother, wearing only her chemise—his sister had removed her dress to help her breathe after she'd fainted—rush out, followed by his screaming sister. He saw his mother run towards his father, her loosened underskirts slipping one by one onto the floor. Stumbling over her skirts she flung herself upon his father, embraced him, was as one with him—but now Gregor's sight grew dim—and with her arms clasped around his father's neck, begged for Gregor's life.

III

Gregor's serious wound, which made him suffer for over a month—the apple remained imbedded in his flesh as a visible reminder, no one having the courage to remove it—seemed to have persuaded even his father that Gregor, despite his present pathetic and disgusting shape, was a member of the family who shouldn't be treated as an enemy. On the contrary, familial duty required them to swallow their disgust and to endure him, to endure him and nothing more.

And though his wound probably had caused Gregor to suffer a permanent loss of mobility, and though it now took him, as if he were some disabled war veteran, many a long minute to creep across his room—crawling above ground level was out of the question—yet in return for this deterioration of his condition he was granted a compensation which satisfied him completely: each day around dusk the living room door—which he was in the habit of watching closely for an hour or two ahead of time—was opened, and lying in the darkness of his room, invisible from the living room, he could see the whole family sitting at the table lit by the lamp and could listen to their conversation as if by general consent, instead of the way he'd done before.

True, these were no longer the lively conversations of old, those upon which Gregor had mused somewhat wistfully as he'd settled wearily into his damp bed in some tiny hotel room. Things were now very quiet for the most part. Soon after dinner his father would fall asleep in his armchair; while his mother and sister would admonish each other to be quiet; his mother, bending forward under the light, would sew fine lingerie for a fashion store; his sister, who had found work as a salesgirl, would study shorthand and French in the evenings, hoping to obtain a better job in the future. Sometimes his father would wake up, as if he hadn't the slightest idea that he'd been asleep, and would say to his mother, "Look how long you've been sewing again today!" and then would fall back to sleep, while his mother and sister would exchange weary smiles.

With a kind of perverse obstinacy his father refused to take off his messenger's uniform even in the apartment; while his robe hung unused on the clothes hook, he would sleep fully dressed in his chair, as if he were always ready for duty and were waiting even here for the voice of his superior. As a result his uniform, which hadn't been new in the first place, began to get dirty in spite of all his mother and sister could do to care for it, and Gregor would often spend entire evenings gazing at this garment covered with stains and with its constantly polished buttons gleaming, in which the old man would sit, upright and uncomfortable, yet peacefully asleep.

As soon as the clock would strike ten, his mother would try to awaken his father with soft words of encouragement and then persuade him to go to bed, for this wasn't any place in which to get a decent night's sleep, and his father badly needed his rest, since he had to be at work at six in the morning. But with the stubbornness that had possessed him ever since he'd become a bank messenger he would insist on staying at the table a little while longer, though he invariably would fall asleep again, and then it was only with the greatest difficulty that he could be persuaded to trade his chair for bed. No matter how much mother and sister would urge him on with little admonishments, he'd keep shaking his head for a good fifteen minutes, his eyes closed, and wouldn't get up. Gregor's mother would tug at his sleeve, whisper sweet words into his ear; and his sister would leave her homework to help her mother, but it was all useless. He only sank deeper into his armchair. Not until the two women would lift him up by the arms would he open his eyes, look now at one, now at the other, and usually say, "What a life. So this is the peace of my old age." And leaning on the two women he would get up laboriously, as if he were his own greatest burden, and would allow the women to lead him to the door, where, waving them aside, he continued on his own, while Gregor's mother abandoned her sewing and her sister her pen so that they might run after his father and continue to look after him.

Who in this overworked and exhausted family had time to worry about Gregor any more than was absolutely necessary? Their resources grew more limited; the maid was now dismissed after all; a gigantic bony cleaning woman with white hair fluttering about her head came in the mornings and evenings to do the roughest work; Gregor's mother took care of everything else, in addition to her sewing. It even happened that certain pieces of family jewelry which his mother and sister had worn with such pleasure at parties and celebrations in days gone by, were sold, as Gregor found out one evening by listening to a general discussion of the prices they'd gone for. But their greatest complaint was that they couldn't give up the apartment, which was too big for their current needs, since no one could figure out how they would move Gregor. But Gregor understood clearly enough that it wasn't simply consideration for him which prevented them moving, since he could have easily been transported in a suitable crate equipped with a few air holes. The main reason preventing them from moving was their utter despair and the feeling that they had been struck by a misfortune far greater than any that had ever visited their friends and relatives. What the world demands of the poor they did to the utmost: his father fetched breakfast for the bank's minor officials, his mother sacrificed herself for the underwear of strangers, his sister ran back and forth behind the counters at the beck and call of customers; but they lacked the strength for anything beyond this. And the wound in Gregor's back began to ache once more when his mother and sister, after putting his father to bed, returned to the room, ignored their work, and sat huddled together cheek to cheek, and his mother said, "Close that door, Grete," so that Gregor was back in the dark, while in the next room the women wept together or simply stared at the table with dry eyes.

Gregor spent the days and nights almost entirely without sleep. Sometimes he imagined that the next time the door opened he would once again assume control of the family's affairs, as he'd done in the old days. Now, after a long absence, there reappeared in his thoughts the director and the manager, the salesmen and the apprentices, the remarkably stupid errand runner, two or three friends from other firms, a chambermaid at one of the provincial hotels—a sweet, fleeting memory—a cashier at a hat store whom he'd courted earnestly but too slowly—they all came to him mixed up with strangers and with people whom he'd already forgotten. But instead of helping him and his family they were all unapproachable, and he was glad when they faded away. At other times he was in no mood to worry about his family; he was utterly filled with rage at how badly he was being treated, and although he couldn't imagine anything that might tempt his appetite, he nevertheless tried to think up ways of getting into the pantry to take what was rightfully his, even if he wasn't hungry. No longer bothering to consider what Gregor might like as a treat, his sister, before she hurried off to work in the morning and after lunch, would shove any sort of food into Gregor's room with her foot. In the evening, regardless of whether the food had been picked at, or—as was more often the case—left completely untouched, she would sweep it out with a swish of the broom. Nowadays she would clean the room in the evening, and she couldn't have done it any faster. Streaks of grime ran along the walls, balls of dust and dirt lay here and there on the floor. At first, whenever his sister would come in, Gregor would station himself in some corner that was particularly objectionable, as if his presence there might serve as a reproach to her. But he probably could have remained there for weeks without her mending her ways; she obviously could see the dirt as clearly as he could, but she'd made up her mind to leave it. At the same time she made certain—with a touchiness that was completely new to her and which indeed was infecting the entire family—that the cleaning of Gregor's room was to remain her prerogative. On one occasion Gregor's mother had subjected his room to a thorough cleaning, which she managed to accomplish only with the aid of several buckets of water—all this dampness being a further annoyance to Gregor, who lay flat, unhappy, and motionless on the couch. But his mother's punishment was not long in coming. For that evening, as soon as Gregor's sister noticed the difference in his room, she ran, deeply insulted, into the living room, and without regard for his mother's uplifted, beseeching hands, burst into a fit of tears. Both parents—the father, naturally, had been startled out of his armchair—at first looked on with helpless amazement, and then they joined in, the father on his right side blaming the mother: she shouldn't have interfered with the sister's cleaning of the room, while on his left side yelling at the sister that she'd never be allowed to clean Gregor's room again. The mother was trying to drag the father, who was half out of his mind, into their bedroom while the sister, shaking with sobs, pounded the table with her little fists, and Gregor hissed loudly with rage because not one of them had thought to close the door and spare him this scene and this commotion.

But even if his sister, worn out by her job at the store, had gotten tired of taking care of Gregor as she once had, it wasn't really necessary for his mother to take her place so that Gregor wouldn't be neglected. For now the cleaning woman was there. This ancient widow, whose powerful bony frame had no doubt helped her through the hard times in her long life, wasn't at all repelled by Gregor. Without being the least bit inquisitive, she had once, by chance, opened the door to Gregor's room and at the sight of Gregor—who, taken completely by surprise, began running back and forth although no one was chasing him—stood there in amazement, her hands folded over her belly. From then on, morning and evening, she never failed to open his door a crack and peek in on him. At first she also would call him to her, using phrases she probably meant to be friendly, such as "Come on over here, you old dung beetle!" or "Just look at that old dung beetle!" Gregor wouldn't respond to such forms of address, but would remain motionless where he was as if the door had never been opened. If only this cleaning woman, instead of pointlessly disturbing him whenever she felt like it, had been given orders to clean his room every day! Once, early in the morning, when a heavy rain, perhaps a sign of the already approaching spring, was beating against the window panes, Gregor became so exasperated when the cleaning woman started in with her phrases that he made as if to attack her, though, of course, in a slow and feeble manner. But instead of being frightened, the cleaning woman simply picked up a chair by the door and, lifting it high in the air, stood there with her mouth wide open. Obviously she didn't plan on shutting it until the chair in her hands had first come crashing down on Gregor's back. "So you're not going through with it?" she asked as Gregor turned back while she calmly set the chair down again in the corner.

By now Gregor was eating next to nothing. Only when he happened to pass by the food set out for him would he take a bite, hold it in his mouth for hours, and then spit most of it out again. At first he imagined that it was his anguish at the state of his room that kept him from eating, but it was those very changes to which he had quickly become accustomed. The family had fallen into the habit of using the room to store things for which there wasn't any place anywhere else, and there were many of these things now, since one room in the apartment had been rented to three boarders. These serious gentlemen—all three of them had full beards, as Gregor once noted, peering through a crack in the door—had a passion for neatness, not only in their room but since they were now settled in as boarders, throughout the entire apartment, and especially in the kitchen. They couldn't abide useless, let alone dirty, junk. Besides, they'd brought most of their own household goods along with them. This meant that many objects were now superfluous, which, while clearly without any resale value, couldn't just be thrown out either. All these things ended up in Gregor's room, and so did the ash bucket and the garbage can from the kitchen. Anything that wasn't being used at the moment was simply tossed into Gregor's room by the cleaning woman, who was always in a tremendous hurry. Fortunately, Gregor generally saw only the object in question and the hand that held it. Perhaps the cleaning woman intended to come back for these things when she had the time, or perhaps she planned on throwing them all out, but in fact there they remained, wherever they'd happened to land, except for Gregor's disturbing them as he squeezed his way through the junk pile. At first he did so simply because he was forced to, since there wasn't any other space to crawl in, but later he took a growing pleasure in these rambles even though they left him dead tired and so sad that he would lie motionless for hours. Since the boarders would sometimes have their dinner at home in the shared living room, on those evenings the door between that room and Gregor's would remain shut. But Gregor didn't experience the door's not being open as a hardship; in fact there had been evenings when he'd ignored the open door and had lain, unnoticed by the family, in the darkest corners of his room. But one time the cleaning woman left the door slightly ajar, and it remained ajar when the boarders came in that evening and the lamp was lit. They sat down at the head of the table, where Gregor, his mother and his father had sat in the old days; they unfolded their napkins, and picked up their knives and forks. At once his mother appeared at the kitchen door carrying a platter of meat and right behind her came his sister carrying a platter piled high with potatoes. The steaming food gave off a thick vapor. The platters were set down in front of the boarders, who bent over them as if to examine them before eating, and in fact the one sitting in the middle, who was apparently looked up to as an authority by the other two, cut into a piece of meat while it was still on the platter, evidently to determine if it was tender enough or whether perhaps it should be sent back to the kitchen. He was satisfied, and both mother and daughter, who'd been watching anxiously, breathed a sigh of relief and began to smile.

The family itself ate in the kitchen. Even so, before going to the kitchen his father came into the living room, bowed once and, cap in hand, walked around the table. The boarders all rose together and mumbled something into their beards. When they were once more alone, they ate in almost complete silence. It seemed strange to Gregor that, out of all the noises produced by eating, he distinctly heard the sound of their teeth chewing; it was as if he were being told you needed teeth in order to eat and that even with the most wonderful toothless jaws, you wouldn't be able to accomplish a thing. "Yes, I'm hungry enough," Gregor told himself sadly, "but not for those things. How well these boarders feed themselves, while I waste away."

That very evening—during this whole time Gregor couldn't once remember hearing the violin—the sound of violin playing came from the kitchen. The boarders had already finished their dinner, the one in the middle had pulled out a newspaper, handed one sheet each to the other two, and now they were leaning back, reading and smoking. When the violin began to play, they noticed it, stood up, and tiptoed to the hall doorway where they stood together in a tight group. They must have been heard in the kitchen for his father called, "Does the playing bother you, gentlemen? We can stop it at once." "On the contrary," said the gentleman in the middle, "wouldn't the young lady like to come and play in here where it's much more roomy and comfortable?" "Why, certainly," called Gregor's father, as if he were the violinist. Soon his father came in carrying the music stand, his mother the sheet music, and his sister the violin. His sister calmly got everything ready for playing; his parents—who had never rented out rooms before and so were overly polite to the boarders—didn't even dare to sit down in their own chairs. His father leaned against the door, slipping his right hand between the buttons of his uniform's jacket, which he'd kept buttoned up; but his mother was offered a chair by one of the gentlemen, and, leaving it where he happened to have placed it, she sat off to one side, in the corner.

His sister began to play; his father and mother, on either side, closely followed the movements of her hands. Gregor, attracted by the playing, had moved a little farther forward and already had his head in the living room. He was hardly surprised that recently he'd shown so little concern for others, although in the past he'd taken pride in being considerate. Now more than ever he had good reason to remain hidden, since he was completely covered with the dust that lay everywhere in his room and was stirred up by the slightest movement. Moreover, threads, hairs, and scraps of food clung to his back and sides, his indifference to everything was much too great for him to have gotten onto his back and rubbed himself clean against the carpet, as he had once done several times a day. And despite his condition he wasn't ashamed to edge his way a little further across the spotless living room floor.

To be sure, no one took any notice of him. The family was completely absorbed by the violin-playing. The boarders, however, who had at first placed themselves, their hands in their pockets, much too close to the music stand—close enough for every one of them to have followed the score, which surely must have flustered his sister—soon retreated to the window, muttering to one another, with their heads lowered. And there they remained while his father watched them anxiously. It seemed all too obvious that they had been disappointed in their hopes of hearing good or entertaining violin-playing; they had had enough of the entire performance, and it was only out of politeness that they continued to let their peace be disturbed. It was especially obvious, by the way they blew their smoke out of their mouths and noses—it floated upwards to the ceiling—just how ill at ease they were. And yet his sister was playing so beautifully. Her face was inclined to one side, and her sad eyes carefully followed the notes of the music. Gregor crawled forward a little farther, keeping his head close to the floor so that their eyes might possibly meet. Was he an animal, that music could move him so? He felt that he was being shown the way to an unknown nourishment he yearned for. He was determined to press on until he reached his sister, to tug at her skirt, and to let her know in this way that she should bring her violin into his room, for no one here would honor her playing as he would. He would never let her out of his room again, at least not for as long as he lived; at last his horrifying appearance would be useful; he would be at every door of his room at once, hissing and spitting at the attackers. His sister, however, wouldn't be forced to remain with him, she would do so of her own free will. She would sit beside him on the couch, leaning towards him and listening as he confided that he had firmly intended to send her to the Conservatory, and if the misfortune hadn't intervened, he would've announced this to everyone last Christmas—for hadn't Christmas come and gone by now?—without paying the slightest attention to any objection. After this declaration his sister would be so moved that she would burst into tears, and Gregor would lift himself up to her shoulder and kiss her on her neck, which, since she had started her job, she had kept bare, without ribbon or collar.

"Mr. Samsa!" cried the middle gentleman to Gregor's father, and without wasting another word pointed with his index finger at Gregor, who was slowly advancing. The violin stopped, the middle gentleman, shaking his head, smiled first at his friend and then looked at Gregor again. Instead of driving Gregor away, his father seemed to think it more important to soothe the boarders, although they weren't upset at all and appeared to consider Gregor more entertaining than the violin-playing. His father rushed over to them and with outstretched arms tried to herd them back into their room and at the same time block their view of Gregor with his body. Now they actually got a little angry—it wasn't clear whether this was due to his father's behavior or to their dawning realization that they had had all along, without knowing it, a next-door neighbor like Gregor. They demanded explanations from his father, raised their own arms now as well, tugged nervously at their beards, and only slowly backed away towards their room. Meanwhile his sister had managed to overcome the bewildered state into which she'd fallen when her playing had been so abruptly interrupted, and after some moments spent holding the violin and bow in her slackly dangling hands and staring at the score as if she were still playing, she suddenly pulled herself together, placed her instrument on her mother's lap—she was still sitting in her chair with her lungs heaving, gasping for breath—and ran into the next room, which the boarders, under pressure from her father, were ever more swiftly approaching. One could see pillows and blankets flying high in the air and then neatly arranging themselves under his sister's practical hands. Before the gentlemen had even reached their room, she had finished making the beds and had slipped out.

Once again a perverse stubbornness seemed to grip Gregor's father, to the extent that he forgot to pay his tenants the respect still due them. He kept on pushing and shoving until the middle gentleman, who was already standing in the room's doorway, brought him up short with a thunderous stamp of his foot. "I hereby declare," he said, raising his hand and looking around for Gregor's mother and sister as well, "that considering the disgusting conditions prevailing in this apartment and in this family"—here he suddenly spat on the floor—"I'm giving immediate notice. Naturally I'm not going to pay a penny for the time I've spent here; on the contrary, I shall be seriously considering bringing some sort of action against you with claims that—I assure you—will be very easy to substantiate." He stopped speaking and stared ahead of him, as if expecting something. And indeed his two friends chimed right in, saying "We're giving immediate notice too." Whereupon he grabbed the doorknob and slammed the door shut with a crash.

Gregor's father, groping his way and staggering forward, collapsed into his armchair; it looked as if he were stretching himself out for his usual evening nap, but his heavily drooping head, looking as if it had lost all means of support, showed that he was anything but asleep. All this time Gregor had lain quietly right where the boarders had first seen him. His disappointment over the failure of his plan, and perhaps also the weakness caused by eating so little for so long, made movement an impossibility. He feared with some degree of certainty that at the very next moment the whole catastrophe would fall on his head, and he waited. He wasn't even startled when the violin slipped from his mother's trembling fingers and fell off her lap with a reverberating clatter.

"Dear parents," said his sister, pounding the table with her hand by way of preamble, "we can't go on like this. Maybe you don't realize it, but I do. I refuse to utter my brother's name in the presence of this monster, and so all I have to say is: we've got to try to get rid of it. We've done everything humanly possible to take care of it and put up with it; I don't think anyone can blame us in the least."

"She's absolutely right," said his father to himself. His mother, still trying to catch her breath, with a wild look in her eyes, began to cough, her cupped hand muffling the sound.

His sister rushed over to his mother and held her forehead. His father seemed to have been led to more definite thoughts by Grete's words; he was sitting up straight and toying with his messenger's cap, which lay on the table among the dishes left over from the boarders' dinner. From time to time he would glance over at Gregor's motionless form.

"We must try to get rid of it," said his sister, speaking only to her father since 80 her mother's coughing was such that she was incapable of hearing a word. "It will be the death of you both. I can see it coming. People who have to work as hard as we do can't stand this constant torture at home. I can't stand it anymore either." And she burst out sobbing so violently that her tears ran down onto her mother's face, where she wiped them away mechanically with her hand.

"But, my child," said her father with compassion and remarkable understanding, "what should we do?"

Gregor's sister could only shrug her shoulder as a sign of the helplessness that had overcome her while she wept, in contrast to her earlier self-confidence.

"If he could understand us," said her father tentatively; Gregor's sister, through her tears, shook her hand violently to indicate how impossible that was.

"If he could understand us," repeated her father, closing his eyes so as to take in his daughter's belief that this was impossible, "then perhaps we might be able to reach some agreement with him, but the way things are—"

"He's got to go," cried Gregor's sister, "it's the only way, Father. You just 85 have to get rid of the idea that this is Gregor. Our real misfortune is having believed it for so long. But how can it be Gregor? If it were, he would've realized a long time ago that it's impossible for human beings to live with a creature like that, and he would've left on his own accord. Then we would've lost a brother, but we'd have been able to go on living and honor his memory. But the way things are, this animal persecutes us, drives away our boarders, obviously it wants to take over the whole apartment and make us sleep in the gutter. Look, Father," she suddenly screamed, "he's at it again!" And in a panic which Gregor found incomprehensible his sister abandoned his mother, and actually pushing herself from the chair as if she would rather sacrifice her mother than remain near Gregor, she rushed behind her father, who, startled by this behavior, got up as well, half raising his arms in front of Grete as if to protect her.

Gregor hadn't the slightest desire to frighten anyone, least of all his sister. He had merely started to turn around in order to go back to his room, a procedure which admittedly looked strange, since, in his weakened condition he had to use his head to help him in this difficult maneuver, several times raising it and then knocking it against the floor. He stopped and looked around. His good intentions seemed to have been understood; the panic had only been temporary. Now, silent and sad, they all looked at him. His mother lay in her armchair with her legs outstretched and pressed together, her eyes almost closed from exhaustion. His father and sister sat side by side, and his sister had put her arm around her father's neck.

"Now maybe they'll let me turn around," thought Gregor, resuming his efforts. He couldn't stop panting from the strain, and he also had to rest from time to time. At least no one harassed him and he was left alone. When he had finished turning around, he immediately began to crawl back in a straight line. He was amazed at the distance between him and his room and couldn't understand how, weak as he was, he'd covered the same stretch of ground only a little while ago almost without being aware of it. Completely intent on crawling rapidly, he scarcely noticed that neither a word nor an exclamation came from his family to interrupt his progress. Only when he reached the doorway did he turn his head; not all the way, for he felt his neck growing stiff, but enough to see that behind him all was as before except that his sister had gotten to her feet. His last glimpse was of his mother, who by now was fast asleep.

He was barely inside the room before the door was slammed shut, bolted, and locked. Gregor was so frightened by the sudden noise behind him that his little legs collapsed underneath him. It was his sister who had been in such a hurry. She'd been standing there, ready and waiting, and then had sprung swiftly forward, before Gregor had even heard her coming. "At last!" she cried to her parents as she turned the key in the lock.

"And now?" Gregor asked himself, looking around in the darkness. He soon discovered that he was no longer able to move. This didn't surprise him; rather it seemed to him strange that until now he'd actually been able to propel himself with these thin little legs. In other respects he felt relatively comfortable. It was true that his entire body ached, but the pain seemed to him to be growing fainter and fainter and soon would go away altogether. The rotten apple in his back and the inflamed area around it, completely covered with fine dust, hardly bothered him anymore. He recalled his family with deep emotion and love. His own belief that he must disappear was, if anything, even firmer than his sister's. He remained in this state of empty and peaceful reflection until the tower clock struck three in the morning. He could still just sense the general brightening outside his window. Then, involuntarily, his head sank all the way down, and from his nostrils came his last feeble breath.

Early that morning, when the cleaning woman appeared—out of sheer en- ergy and impatience she always slammed all the doors, no matter how often she'd been asked not to, so hard that sleep was no longer possible anywhere in the apartment once she'd arrived—she didn't notice anything peculiar when she paid Gregor her usual brief visit. She thought that he was lying there so still on purpose, pretending that his feelings were hurt; she considered him to be very clever. As she happened to be holding a long broom, she tried to tickle Gregor with it from the doorway. When this too had no effect, she became annoyed and jabbed it into Gregor a little, and it was only when she shoved him from his place without meeting resistance that she began to take notice. Quickly realizing how things stood, she opened her eyes wide, gave a soft whistle, and without wasting any time she tore open the bedroom door and yelled at the top of her lungs into the darkness: "Come and look, it's had it, it's lying there, dead and done for."

Mr. and Mrs. Samsa sat up in their marriage bed, trying to absorb the shock the cleaning woman had given them and yet at first unable to comprehend the meaning of her words. Then they quickly climbed out of bed, Mr. Samsa on one side, Mrs. Samsa on the other. Mr. Samsa threw a blanket over his shoulders, Mrs. Samsa wore only her nightgown; dressed in this fashion they entered Gregor's room. Meanwhile the door to the living room, where Grete had been sleeping since the boarders' arrival, opened as well. Grete was fully dressed, as if she'd never gone to bed, and the pallor of her face seemed to confirm this. "Dead?" asked Mrs. Samsa and looked inquiring at the cleaning woman, although she could have checked for herself, or guessed at the truth without having to investigate. "That's for sure," said the cleaning woman, and to prove it she pushed Gregor's corpse a good way to one side with her broom. Mrs. Samsa made a move as if to stop her, then let it go. "Well," said Mr. Samsa, "now thanks be to God." He crossed himself, and the three women followed his example. Grete, who never took her eyes off the corpse, said, "Just look how thin he was. It's been a long time since he's eaten anything. The food came out just as it was when it came in." Indeed, Gregor's body was completely flat and dry; this was only now obvious because the body was no longer raised on its little legs and nothing else distracted the eye.

"Come to our room with us for a little while, Grete," said Mrs. Samsa with a sad smile, and Grete, not without a look back at the corpse, followed her parents into the bedroom. The cleaning woman shut the door and opened the windows wide. Although it was early in the morning, there was a certain mildness in the fresh air. After all, these were the last days of March.

The three boarders came out of their rooms and looked around in amazement for their breakfast; they had been forgotten. "Where's our breakfast?" the middle gentleman asked the cleaning woman in a sour tone. But she put her finger to her lips, and then quickly and quietly beckoned to the gentlemen to enter Gregor's room. So they did, and, with their hands in the pockets of their somewhat threadbare jackets, they stood in a circle around Gregor's corpse in the now sunlit room.

At that point the bedroom door opened and Mr. Samsa, wearing his uniform, appeared with his wife on one arm and his daughter on the other. They all looked a little tearful; from time to time Grete would press her face against her father's sleeve.

"Leave my home at once," Mr. Samsa told the three gentlemen, pointing to the door without letting go of the women. "What do you mean?" said the middle gentleman, who, somewhat taken aback, smiled a sugary smile. The other two held their hands behind their backs, and kept rubbing them together as if cheerfully anticipating a major argument which they were bound to win. "I mean just what I say," replied Mr. Samsa, and advanced in a line with his two companions directly on the middle boarder. At first this gentleman stood still, looking at the floor as if the thoughts inside his head were arranging themselves in a new pattern. "Well, so we'll be off," he then said, looking up at Mr. Samsa as if, suddenly overcome with humility, he was asking permission for even this decision. Mr. Samsa, his eyes glowering, merely gave him a few brief nods. With that the gentleman, taking long strides, actually set off in the direction of the hall; his two friends, who had been listening for some time with their hands quite still, now went hopping right along after him, as if they were afraid that Mr. Samsa might reach the hall before them and cut them off from their leader. Once in the hall the three of them took their hats from the coat rack, pulled their canes from the umbrella stand, bowed silently, and left the apartment. Impelled by a suspicion that would turn out to be utterly groundless, Mr. Samsa led the two women out onto the landing; leaning against the banister railing they watched the three gentlemen as they marched slowly but steadily down the long staircase, disappearing at every floor when the staircase made a turn and then after a few moments reappearing once again. The lower they descended the more the Samsas' interest in them waned; and when a butcher's boy with a basket on his head came proudly up the stairs towards the gentlemen and then swept on past them, Mr. Samsa and the women quickly left the banister and, as if relieved, returned to the apartment.

They decided to spend this day resting and going for a walk; not only did they deserve this break from work, they absolutely needed it. And so they sat down at the table to write their three letters excusing themselves, Mr. Samsa to the bank manager, Mrs. Samsa to her employer, and Grete to the store's owner. While they were writing, the cleaning woman came by to say that she was leaving now, since her morning's work was done. At first the three letter writers merely nodded without looking up, but when the cleaning woman made no move to go, they looked up at her, annoyed. "Well?" asked Mr. Samsa. The cleaning woman stood in the doorway, smiling as if she had some wonderful news for the family, news she wasn't about to share until they came right out and asked her to. The little ostrich feathers in her hat, which stood up nearly straight in the air and which had irritated Mr. Samsa the entire time she had worked for them, swayed gently in every direction. "What can we do for you?" asked Mrs. Samsa, whom the cleaning woman respected the most. "Well," the cleaning woman replied, with such good-humored laughter that she had to pause before continuing, "you don't have to worry about getting rid of that thing in the next room. It's already been taken care of." Mrs. Samsa and Grete bent over their letters as if they intended to keep on writing; Mr. Samsa, who realized that the cleaning woman was about to go into the details, stopped her firmly with an outstretched hand. Seeing that she wasn't going to be allowed to tell her story, she suddenly remembered that she was in a great hurry; clearly insulted, she called out, "Bye, everybody," whirled around wildly, and left the apartment with a terrible slamming of doors.

"She'll be dismissed tonight," said Mr. Samsa, but without getting a reply from his wife or his daughter, for the cleaning woman seemed to have ruined their tenuous peace of mind. They got up, went to the window, and remained there holding each other tightly. Mr. Samsa turned around in his chair towards them and watched them quietly for some time. Then he called out, "Come on now, come over here. Let those old troubles alone. And have a little consideration for me, too." The two women promptly obeyed him, hurried over to him, caressed him, and quickly finished their letters.

Then all three of them left the apartment together, something they hadn't done in months, and took a streetcar out to the open country on the outskirts of the city. Their car, which they had all to themselves, was completely bathed in warm sunlight. Leaning comfortably back in their seats they discussed their prospects for the future, which on closer inspection seemed to be not so bad, since all three of them had jobs which—though they'd never asked one another about them in any detail—were in each case very advantageous and promising. Of course the greatest immediate improvement in their situation would quickly come about when they found a new apartment, one that was smaller, cheaper, and in every way easier to maintain than their current one, which Gregor had chosen for them. As they were talking on in this way, it occurred to both Mr. and Mrs. Samsa, almost simultaneously, as they watched their daughter become more and more vivacious, that in spite of all the recent troubles that had turned her cheeks pale, she had blossomed into a pretty and shapely girl. Growing quieter now, communicating almost unconsciously through glances, they reflected that soon it would be time to find her a good husband. And it was as if in confirmation of their new dreams and good intentions that at the end of their ride their daughter got up first and stretched her young body.

QUESTIONS

1. What was Gregor's occupation before his transformation? How did he come to his particular job? What keeps him working for his firm?
2. When Gregor wakes to discover he has become a gigantic insect, he is mostly intent on the practical implications of his metamorphosis—how to get out of bed, how to get to his job, and so on. He never wonders why or how he has been changed. What does this odd reaction suggest about Gregor?

3. When Gregor's parents first see the gigantic insect (paragraph 25), do they recognize it as their son? What do their initial reactions suggest about their attitude about their son?
4. How does each family member react to Gregor after his transformation? What is different about each reaction? What is similar?
5. What things about Gregor have been changed? What seems to have remained the same? List specific qualities.
6. *The Metamorphosis* takes place entirely in the Samsa family apartment. How does the story's setting shape its themes?
7. What family member first decides that they must "get rid of" the insect? What rationale is given? In what specific ways does the family's decision affect Gregor?
8. How does the family react to Gregor's death?
9. Does Grete change in the course of the story? If so, how does she change?
10. In what ways is Gregor's metamorphosis symbolic?

WRITER'S PERSPECTIVE

Franz Kafka

Franz Kafka on Writing

DISCUSSING *THE METAMORPHOSIS* (c. 1920)

My friend Alfred Kämpf . . . admired Kafka's story *The Metamorphosis*. He described the author as "a new, more profound and therefore more significant Edgar Allan Poe."

During a walk with Franz Kafka on the Altstädter Ring° I told him about this new admirer of his, but aroused neither interest nor understanding. On the contrary, Kafka's expression showed that any discussion of his book was distasteful to him. I, however, was filled with a zeal for discoveries, and so I was tactless.

Altstädter Ring: a major street in Prague.

"The hero of the story is called Samsa," I said. "It sounds like a cryptogram for Kafka. Five letters in each word. The S in the word Samsa has the same position as the K in the word Kafka. The A . . ."

Kafka interrupted me.

"It is not a cryptogram. Samsa is not merely Kafka, and nothing else. *The Metamorphosis* is not a confession, although it is—in a certain sense—an indiscretion."

"I know nothing about that."

"Is it perhaps delicate and discreet to talk about the bugs in one's own family?"

"It isn't usual in good society."

"You see what bad manners I have."

Kafka smiled. He wished to dismiss the subject. But I did not wish to.

"It seems to me that the distinction between good and bad manners hardly applies here," I said. "*The Metamorphosis* is a terrible dream, a terrible conception."

Kafka stood still.

"The dream reveals the reality, which conception lags behind. That is the horror of life—the terror of art. But now I must go home."

. . .

I spent my first week's wages on having Kafka's three stories—*The Metamorphosis*, *The Judgement* and *The Stoker*—bound in a dark brown leather volume, with the name Franz Kafka elegantly tooled in gold lettering.

The book lay in the brief-case on my knee as I told Kafka about the warehouse-cinema [where Janouch worked as a musician]. Then I proudly took the volume out of the case and gave it across the desk to Kafka.

"What is this?" he asked in astonishment.

"It's my first week's wages."

"Isn't that a waste?"

Kafka's eyelids fluttered. His lips were sharply drawn in. For a few seconds he contemplated the name in the gold lettering, hastily thumbed through the pages of the book and—with obvious embarrassment—placed it before me on the desk. I was about to ask why the book offended him, when he began to cough. He took a handkerchief from his pocket, held it to his mouth, replaced it when the attack was over, stood up and went to the small washstand behind his desk and washed his hands, then said as he dried them: "You overrate me. Your trust oppresses me."

He sat himself at his desk and said, with his hands to his temples: "I am no burning bush. I am not a flame."

I interrupted him, "You shouldn't say that. It's not just. To me, for example, you are fire, warmth, and light."

"No, no!" he contradicted me, shaking his head. "You are wrong. My scribbling does not deserve a leather binding. It's only my own personal spectre of horror. It oughtn't to be printed at all. It should be burned and destroyed. It is without meaning. . . ."

I apologized. "Please forgive me, I didn't mean to upset you. I'm stupid."

"No, no—you're not that!" Without removing his hands, he rocked his whole body to and fro. "You are right. You are certainly right. Probably that's why I can't finish anything. I am afraid of the truth. But can one do otherwise?" He took his hands away from his eyes, placed his clenched fists on the table and said in a low, suppressed voice: "One must be silent, if one can't give any help. No one, through his own lack of hope should make the condition of the patient worse. For that reason, all my scribbling is to be destroyed. I am no light. I have merely lost my way among my own thorns. I'm a dead end."

From Conversations with Kafka by Gustav Janouch

◄━━▣►WRITING CRITICALLY◄▣━━►

Leaving Things Out

Perhaps the greatest pleasure in writing a critical essay or research paper—yes, pleasure may be found in the undertaking—is discovering the many ways in which a piece of fiction works. Researching and analyzing a first-rate short story in preparation for writing, we usually notice a wealth of illuminating interconnections of language, image, action, and idea. Sometimes we see so many things unfolding all at once that we get slightly dizzy in the excitement of discovery.

The great frustration in writing a paper, however, is that the researcher must inevitably leave out much of what is discovered. Not every observation—no matter how true or useful—will fit into the final piece. A writer needs to learn that what is omitted is nearly as important as what is included. Leaving things out is never more important than when one writes about a longer work of fiction. There is simply too much to include.

In writing about a long short story or novella, it is essential that you establish what you want to discuss and then leave out observations that are not necessary to your analysis. It sometimes helps to begin with a rough outline—a sort of general chart representing your main ideas. Group individual observations under the major points in your line of argument. Create a special list for ideas that don't fit into your overall scheme. Having somewhere to put them initially will make it easier for you to cut them out eventually. Assure yourself that it is a sign of critical intelligence to know what to omit. As you see how much material there is left to work into your final paper, you may even be relieved to see what you have excluded. Finally, remember that even if you didn't have the pleasure of working every detail into your paper, you still had the private joy of noticing them in the first place.

WRITING ASSIGNMENT—RESEARCH PAPER

Professor Michael Cass of Mercer University gave his students a challenging assignment for their research paper. He asked class members to select the fiction writer on their reading list whose work had seemed most impressive. Then each student had to write a paper defending that author's claim to literary greatness and research the author using at least five different critical sources. The student had to present clear reasons why the author was a major writer and to support the argument with both examples from the writer's work and statements from critics. Choose an author from this book whose greatness you would defend. Here is a short research paper by a student in Professor Cass's class, Stephanie Crowe, who discussed why she believed that Franz Kafka was a great writer.

Stephanie Crowe

Professor Cass

English 120

21 November 20xx

Kafka's Greatness

Although most of his major works remained unfinished
and unpublished at his untimely death in 1924, Franz Kafka
has gradually come to be considered one of the great writers
of the twentieth century. By 1977, well over ten thousand
works of commentary had appeared on Kafka, and many more
have been written since then (Goodden 2). According to
critic Peter Heller, Kafka represents the "mainstream of
German literary and intellectual tradition," a nihilistic
tradition which extends from Goethe and Lessing to the
present (289).

Not only is Kafka generally considered one of the
greatest fiction writers of the modern era, he is also
indisputably one of the most influential. In his 1989 study,
<u>After Kafka</u>, Shimon Sandbank discusses Kafka's influence on
a dozen modern writers, including Sartre, Camus, Beckett,
Borges, and Ionesco. His effects on these writers differ.
Some borrow his understated, almost passive prose style
while others adopt his recurrent images and themes. Whatever
the specific elements they use, however, Kafka's ability to
influence these writers is another measure of his stature.

Great literature often gives us the stories and images
to understand our own age, a process that necessarily
includes understanding our deepest problems. The twentieth
century, to borrow a phrase from W.H. Auden, has mostly been
an "Age of Anxiety." Most modern people are no longer bound
to follow the occupations, behaviors, and beliefs of their
parents, but they gain this newfound freedom at the expense
of a constant, difficult search for identity. The personal
quest for meaningful identity often leads to despair. This

"existential crisis" is the basis for many twentieth-century
problems including the decline of religion, the rise of
totalitarianism, the breakdown of social identity, and the
decay of traditional family structure.

Kafka's works dramatize these problems memorably
because they provide us with myths, images, stories, and
situations that describe the particular dilemmas of the
early twentieth century. When faced with the modern
challenge of not having a predetermined social or religious
identity, Kafka's characters desperately attempt to find
certainty. The problem, however, is that they are usually
afraid to do anything decisive because everything is
uncertain. Auden observed:

> Far from being confident of success, the Kafka
> hero is convinced from the start that he is
> doomed to fail, as he is also doomed, being who
> he is, to make prodigious and unending efforts to
> reach it [the goal]. Indeed, the mere desire to
> reach the goal is itself a proof, not that he is
> one of the elect, but that he is under a special
> curse. (162)

One way that Kafka memorably dramatizes the modern
struggle for identity is by reversing the traditional quest
story. In a quest story, the hero knows the goal that he
wants to achieve and has some confidence that he will be
able to achieve it. As he tries to reach the goals, he must
overcome various enemies and obstacles. "In a typical Kafka
story, on the other hand, the goal is peculiar to the hero
himself: he has no competitors" (Auden 162). His question
then becomes not a practical "Can I succeed?" but instead a
vague and problematic "What should I do?" Unable to answer
this question satisfactorily, the hero becomes increasingly
alienated from his own surroundings. This alienation is yet
another symptom of "the inhumanity of modern society" that
Kafka so memorably portrayed (Kuna 62).

Kafka also distinguishes himself as a great writer because he created a distinctive style that effectively dramatizes twentieth-century problems. Although Kafka's fiction often describes extreme situations, his prose usually seems strangely calm and detached. He uses "clear and simple language" that paints "concrete pictures of human beings, pictures that, in a sense, have to speak for themselves" (Cooper 19). These haunting images (the unreachable castle, the unknown laws, the unspecified trial) dramatize the mysterious struggles of the characters.

Kafka also uses his style to separate himself from his characters, a technique that develops a contrast between the calmness of his style and the nervous desperation of his characters (Heller 237). For example, the opening of Kafka's novella The Metamorphosis, which is perhaps the most famous first sentence in modern fiction, describes an outrageous event--a young man who wakes up transformed into a giant bug--in a strangely matter-of-fact tone. This contrast is important because it reminds us of the desperation of modern man imprisoned in a world he can neither understand nor control.

Perhaps the most interesting feature of Kafka's style is his ability to create works that cannot be explained by a single interpretation. Because he allows his pictures to "speak for themselves," "Kafka's texts have been subject to a variety of widely divergent approaches" (Heller 236). Therefore, no single interpretation of Kafka's texts can adequately explain an entire work. Most interpretations may illuminate particular moments in a work, but inevitably they lead to a dead end when pressed to explain the whole narrative. Whether one is reading on a social, moral, psychological, metaphysical, theological, or existential level, Kafka "tends to suspend all distinction and thus to revert to total ambiguity" (Heller 285). According to

Heller, this characteristic mysteriousness becomes "the epitome of his art" (230).

Auden believed that the impossibility of interpreting Kafka's work is essential in defining him as an important and influential writer. He says that "Kafka is a great, perhaps the greatest, master of the pure parable, a literary genre about which a critic can say very little worth saying" (159). Since the meaning of parables is different for each individual, critics cannot explain them without revealing their own visions and values. Kafka develops stories with important symbols that are easily identified; attempting to interpret these symbols, however, only leads to frustration.

The frustration that comes from trying to interpret Kafka's works exemplifies his recurrent, and particularly twentieth-century, theme, which Peter Heller has described as man's "ever frustrated, ever defeated striving for self-realization in an inhuman human universe in which he is alienated from himself and from the world he lives in" (305). Kafka uses his characteristic difficult symbolism and ambiguity, along with his theme of hopelessness and despair, as a common thread that binds all of his works together.

Kafka's book The Great Wall of China contains several short pieces which have a slightly less desperate tone than the despair of The Metamorphosis. Many of the stories in The Great Wall of China, however, still present the theme of hopelessness. In the reflection entitled "The Problem of Our Laws," Kafka examines the origins and legitimacy of law. This parable begins with the narrator stating, "Our laws are not generally known; they are kept secret by the small group of nobles who rule us" (147). Next the narrator goes through a laborious process of rationally questioning why only the nobility knows the laws, if the laws really exist, and if it will ever be possible for common men to know the laws. He finally concludes that the only way to know the law would be a quiet revolution that ends nobility. But even this solution, he realizes, is futile. The nobility cannot be eliminated because they provide the only order that exists. While this parable makes several interesting points, its structure is essentially static. The narrator ends where he began--trapped in an unknowable world.

One of Kafka's unfinished novels, The Trial, also concentrates on the unknown symbol of the Law. In the novel, Joseph K. is arrested for a crime that no one ever knows. Joseph, like most of Kafka's characters, is a common man with an uneventful life who admits that he knows little of the Law. The drama of the novel is the protagonist's hopeless attempts to master an impossible and unknown situation. Joseph K.'s life itself becomes a trial, although he is never sentenced. Finally, one year after his arrest, two men come and murder him. Instead of trying to understand the Law, "In the end he appears to accept the verdict as a release from the condition of despair," and "dies like an animal, without comprehending the rationale of the Law which condemns him" (Heller 280-81). Like many men, before his death K. is struggling to discover his identity in relation to the Law that governs him; however, K.'s hopeless life ends with a pointless murder.

Kafka's other great, unfinished novel, The Castle, also concentrates on the theme of unknowability and despair. Instead of trying to understand the Law, K. in The Castle has another impossible quest, his attempt to enter the castle of the local ruler to report for duty as a land surveyor. His constant efforts, however, prove futile. Only when K. lies on his deathbed does a call from the castle come, giving him permission to live in the town. Once again, K. suffers hopelessly and dies in despair.

While The Trial emphasizes political and psychological themes characteristic of the twentieth century, The Castle focuses on the religious identity crisis. The Metamorphosis examines similar themes of identity on a personal and family level. All of these works focus on modern humanity's difficult struggle to define its place in existence.

Kafka, through his works, accurately describes the modern condition of many by using memorable images and a distinctive style. This characteristic style has influenced many twentieth-century writers and readers. While difficult and somewhat bleak, Kafka's often ambiguous, yet understated dramatizations of man's condition, along with his lasting influence, form the foundation of his greatness.

Works Cited

Auden, W. H. "The I Without a Self." The Dyer's Hand. New York: Random, 1989. 159-70.

Cooper, Gabriele Bon Natzmer. Kafka and Language: In the Stream of Thoughts and Life. Riverside, CA: Ariadne, 1991.

Goodden, Christina. "Points of Departure." The Kafka Debate: New Perspectives for Our Time. Ed. Angel Flores. New York: Gordian, 1988. 2-9.

Heller, Peter. "Kafka: The Futility of Striving." Dialectics and Nihilism. Massachusetts: U of Massachusetts P, 1966. 227-306.

Kafka, Franz. "The Problem of Our Laws." The Great Wall of China. New York: Schocken, 1946. 147-49.

Kuna, Franz. Franz Kafka: Literature as Corrective Punishment. Bloomington: Indiana UP, 1974.

Sandbank, Shimon. After Kafka: The Influence of Kafka's Fiction. Athens: U of Georgia P, 1989.

FURTHER SUGGESTIONS FOR WRITING

1. In a single, carefully thought-out paragraph, try to sum up what you believe Tolstoy is saying in *The Death of Ivan Ilych*.

2. Compare Tolstoy's short novel with another story of spiritual awakening: Flannery O'Connor's "Revelation" or "A Good Man Is Hard to Find." In each, what brings about the enlightenment of the central character?

3. Compare the last thoughts of Gregor Samsa or Ivan Ilych with the last thoughts of Katherine Anne Porter's Granny Weatherall.

4. Topic for a long term paper: Read either Franz Kafka's *The Trial* or *The Castle* and find a theme that is also important to *The Metamorphosis*.

5. Explore how Gregor Samsa's metamorphosis into a giant insect is symbolic of his earlier life and relations with his family. (For a discussion of literary symbols, see Chapter Seven, "Symbol.")

6. Topic for a medium-length paper (600–1,000 words): Discuss the mixture of comic and tragic elements in Kafka's *The Metamorphosis*. Is everything in the story sad and horrifying, or are there grotesquely funny moments as well?

7. Compare the story of *The Metamorphosis* to the plot of a famous horror film in which the protagonist is accidentally transformed into a monster. Some possible films include David Cronenberg's version of *The Fly* (1986), Neil Jordan's *The Company of Wolves* (1984), Val Lewton's *The Curse of the Cat People* (1944), Brian De Palma's *Carrie* (1976), George Waggner's original *The Wolf Man* (1940), and Jack Arnold's *The Incredible Shrinking Man* (1957). Discuss in which ways the two works are similar, and in which ways they differ. Does Kafka's work compel the reader to explore psychological questions untouched by the film?

8. Read a novel chosen from a list provided by your instructor, or chosen with your instructor's approval. Selecting some element in it that interests you, write an essay in which you demonstrate the importance to the book of that one element. You might write, for instance, on "The Character of the Monster in Mary Shelley's *Frankenstein*"; for an essay on theme, "A Plea for Paganism in D. H. Lawrence's *The Plumed Serpent*"; "Symbolism in *The Scarlet Letter*" (or in *The Great Gatsby*). (Suggestion: You might find it helpful to read the discussion of analysis in "Writing About a Story" at the back of the book.)

10 *Two Critical Casebooks:*
Edgar Allan Poe
and Flannery O'Connor

EDGAR ALLAN POE

Edgar Poe was born in Boston in January 1809, the second son of actors Eliza and David Poe. Edgar inherited his family's legacy of artistic talent, financial instability, and social inferiority (actors were not considered respectable people in the nineteenth century). Although Poe later demonstrated both his mother's expressive gifts and his father's problems with alcohol, he never really knew his parents. His father abandoned the family after the birth of Edgar's little sister Rosalie, and his mother died of tuberculosis in a Richmond, Virginia, boarding house before Edgar turned three.

Eliza Poe's brilliance on stage had earned her many fans and their compassion saved her children. Edgar was taken in by the wealthy John and Frances Allan of Richmond, whose name he added to his own. John Allan educated his foster son at first-rate schools, where the boy excelled in all subjects. Edgar, however, grew from a precocious and charming child into a moody adolescent and his relationship with his foster father deteriorated. His first year at the University of Virginia was marked by scholastic success as well as alcoholic binges and gambling debts. Disgraced, Poe fled to Boston, where he joined the army under the name "Edgar Perry." He performed well as an enlisted man and published his first collection of poetry, Tamerlane and Other Poems, at the age of eighteen.

After an abortive stint at West Point led to a final break with his foster father, Edgar Allan Poe became a full-time writer and editor. Morbidly sensitive to criticism at anytime, and paranoid and belligerent when drunk, Poe left or was fired from every post he held. Nevertheless, he was a respected literary critic and editor and sharply improved both the content and circulation of every magazine with which he was associated. Unfortunately, he was never paid well for his work, either as an editor or a freelance writer. Works such as "The Fall of the House of Usher" and "The Raven," both of which made him famous, earned him almost nothing in his lifetime.

After the break with his foster family, Poe rediscovered his own. From 1831 on, Poe lived with his father's widowed sister, Maria Clemm, and her daughter Virginia. In 1836 Poe married this thirteen-year-old first cousin, and these women provided Poe with much-needed emotional stability. However, like his mother, Virginia died of tuberculosis at age twenty-four, her demise doubtless hastened by poverty.

Poe's life came apart after his wife's death; his drinking intensified, as did his self-destructive tendencies. In October 1849 Edgar Allan Poe died in mysterious circumstances, a few days after being found sick and incoherent on a Baltimore street.

～ STORIES ～

THE TELL-TALE HEART (1843) 1850

True!—nervous—very, very dreadfully nervous I had been and am; but why *will* you say that I am mad? The disease had sharpened my senses—not destroyed—not dulled them. Above all was the sense of hearing acute. I heard all things in the heaven and in the earth. I heard many things in hell. How, then, am I mad? Hearken! and observe how healthily—how calmly I can tell you the whole story.

It is impossible to say how first the idea entered my brain; but once conceived, it haunted me day and night. Object there was none. Passion there was none. I loved the old man. He had never wronged me. He had never given me insult. For his gold I had no desire. I think it was his eye! yes, it was this! One of his eyes resembled that of a vulture—a pale eye, with a film over it. Whenever it fell upon me, my blood ran cold; and so by degrees—very gradually—I made up my mind to take the life of the old man, and thus rid myself of the eye forever.

Now this is the point. You fancy me mad. Madmen know nothing. But you should have seen *me*. You should have seen how wisely I proceeded—with what caution—with what foresight—with what dissimulation I went to work! I was never kinder to the old man than during the whole week before I killed him. And every night, about midnight, I turned the latch of his door and opened it—

oh, so gently! And then, when I had made an opening sufficient for my head, I put in a dark lantern, all closed, closed, so that no light shone out, and then I thrust in my head. Oh, you would have laughed to see how cunningly I thrust it in! I moved it slowly—very, very slowly, so that I might not disturb the old man's sleep. It took me an hour to place my whole head within the opening so far that I could see him as he lay upon his bed. Ha!—would a madman have been so wise as this? And then, when my head was well in the room, I undid the lantern cautiously—oh, so cautiously—cautiously (for the hinges creaked)—I undid it just so much that a single thin ray fell upon the vulture eye. And this I did for seven long nights—every night just at midnight—but I found the eye always closed; and so it was impossible to do the work; for it was not the old man who vexed me, but his Evil Eye. And every morning, when the day broke, I went boldly into the chamber, and spoke courageously to him, calling him by name in a hearty tone, and inquiring how he had passed the night. So you see he would have been a very profound old man, indeed, to suspect that every night, just at twelve, I looked in upon him while he slept.

Upon the eighth night I was more than usually cautious in opening the door. A watch's minute hand moves more quickly than did mine. Never before that night had I *felt* the extent of my own powers—of my sagacity. I could scarcely contain my feelings of triumph. To think that there I was, opening the door, little by little, and he not even to dream of my secret deeds or thoughts. I fairly chuckled at the idea; and perhaps he heard me; for he moved on the bed suddenly, as if startled. Now you may think that I drew back—but no. His room was as black as pitch with the thick darkness (for the shutters were close fastened, through fear of robbers), and so I knew that he could not see the opening of the door, and I kept pushing it on steadily, steadily.

I had my head in, and was about to open the lantern, when my thumb   5
slipped upon the tin fastening, and the old man sprang up in the bed, crying out—"Who's there?"

I kept quite still and said nothing. For a whole hour I did not move a muscle, and in the meantime I did not hear him lie down. He was still sitting up in the bed, listening;—just as I have done, night after night, hearkening to the death watches° in the wall.

Presently I heard a slight groan, and I knew it was the groan of mortal terror. It was not a groan of pain or of grief—oh, no!—it was the low stifled sound that arises from the bottom of the soul when overcharged with awe. I knew the sound very well. Many a night, just at midnight, when all the world slept, it has welled up from my own bosom, deepening, with its dreadful echo, the terrors that distracted me. I say I knew it well. I knew what the old man felt, and pitied him, although I chuckled at heart. I knew that he had been lying awake ever since the first slight noise, when he had turned in the bed. His fears had been ever since growing upon him. He had been trying to fancy them causeless, but could not.

death watches: beetles that infest timbers. Their clicking sound was thought to be an omen of death.

He had been saying to himself—"It is nothing but the wind in the chimney—it is only a mouse crossing the floor," or "it is merely a cricket which has made a single chirp." Yes, he had been trying to comfort himself with these suppositions; but he had found all in vain. *All in vain*; because Death, in approaching him, had stalked with his black shadow before him, and enveloped the victim. And it was the mournful influence of the unperceived shadow that caused him to feel—although he neither saw nor heard—to *feel* the presence of my head within the room.

When I had waited a long time, very patiently, without hearing him lie down, I resolved to open a little—a very, very little crevice in the lantern. So I opened it—you cannot imagine how stealthily, stealthily—until, at length, a single dim ray, like the thread of the spider, shot from out of the crevice and fell upon the vulture eye.

It was open—wide, wide open—and I grew furious as I gazed upon it. I saw it with perfect distinctness—all a dull blue, with a hideous veil over it that chilled the very marrow in my bones; but I could see nothing else of the old man's face or person: for I had directed the ray as if by instinct, precisely upon the damned spot.

And now have I not told you that what you mistake for madness is but over-acuteness of the senses?—now, I say, there came to my ears a low, dull, quick sound, such as a watch makes when enveloped in cotton. I knew *that* sound well, too. It was the beating of the old man's heart. It increased my fury, as the beating of a drum stimulates the soldier into courage.

But even yet I refrained and kept still. I scarcely breathed. I held the lantern motionless. I tried how steadily I could maintain the ray upon the eye. Meantime the hellish tattoo of the heart increased. It grew quicker and quicker, and louder and louder every instant. The old man's terror *must* have been extreme! It grew louder, I say, louder every moment!—do you mark me well? I have told you that I am nervous: so I am. And now at the dead hour of the night, amid the dreadful silence of that old house, so strange a noise as this excited me to uncontrollable terror. Yet, for some minutes longer I refrained and stood still. But the beating grew louder, louder! I thought the heart must burst. And now a new anxiety seized me—the sound would be heard by a neighbor! The old man's hour had come! With a loud yell, I threw open the lantern and leaped into the room. He shrieked once—once only. In an instant I dragged him to the floor, and pulled the heavy bed over him. I then smiled gaily, to find the deed so far done. But, for many minutes, the heart beat on with a muffled sound. This, however, did not vex me; it would not be heard through the wall. At length it ceased. The old man was dead. I removed the bed and examined the corpse. Yes, he was stone, stone dead. I placed my hand upon the heart and held it there many minutes.

If still you think me mad, you will think so no longer when I describe the wise precautions I took for the concealment of the body. The night waned, and I worked hastily, but in silence. First of all I dismembered the corpse. I cut off the head and the arms and the legs.

I then took up three planks from the flooring of the chamber, and deposited all between the scantlings. I then replaced the boards so cleverly, so cunningly,

10

that no human eye—not even *his*—could have detected anything wrong. There was nothing to wash out—no stain of any kind—no bloodspot whatever. I had been too wary for that. A tub had caught all—ha! ha!

When I had made an end of these labors, it was four o'clock—still dark as midnight. As the bell sounded the hour, there came a knocking at the street door. I went down to open it with a light heart,—for what had I *now* to fear? There entered three men, who introduced themselves, with perfect suavity, as officers of the police. A shriek had been heard by a neighbor during the night; suspicion of foul play had been aroused, information had been lodged at the police office, and they (the officers) had been deputed to search the premises.

I smiled,—for *what* had I to fear? I bade the gentlemen welcome. The shriek, 15 I said, was my own in a dream. The old man, I mentioned, was absent in the country. I took my visitors all over the house. I bade them search—search *well*. I led them, at length, to *his* chamber. I showed them his treasures, secure, undisturbed. In the enthusiasm of my confidence, I brought chairs into the room, and desired them *here* to rest from their fatigues, while I myself, in the wild audacity of my perfect triumph, placed my own seat upon the very spot beneath which reposed the corpse of the victim.

The officers were satisfied. My *manner* had convinced them. I was singularly at ease. They sat, and while I answered cheerily, they chatted of familiar things. But, ere long, I felt myself getting pale and wished them gone. My head ached, and I fancied a ringing in my ears: but still they sat and still chatted. The ringing became more distinct:—it continued and became more distinct: I talked more freely to get rid of the feeling: but it continued and gained definitiveness—until, at length, I found that the noise was *not* within my ears.

No doubt I now grew *very* pale:—but I talked more fluently, and with a heightened voice. Yet the sound increased—and what could I do? It was a *low, dull, quick sound—much such a sound as a watch makes when enveloped in cotton.* I gasped for breath—and yet the officers heard it not. I talked more quickly—more vehemently; but the noise steadily increased. I arose and argued about trifles, in a high key and with violent gesticulations; but the noise steadily increased. Why *would* they not be gone? I paced the floor to and fro with heavy strides, as if excited to fury by the observations of the men—but the noise steadily increased. Oh God! what *could* I do? I foamed—I raved—I swore! I swung the chair upon which I had been sitting, and grated it upon the boards, but the noise arose over all and continually increased. It grew louder—louder—*louder!* And still the men chatted pleasantly, and smiled. Was it possible they heard not? Almighty God!—no, no! They heard!—they suspected!—they *knew!*—they were making a mockery of my horror!—this I thought, and this I think. But anything was better than this agony! Anything was more tolerable than this derision! I could bear those hypocritical smiles no longer! I felt that I must scream or die!—and now—again!—hark! louder! louder! louder! *louder!*—

"Villains!" I shrieked, "dissemble no more! I admit the deed!—tear up the planks!—here, here!—it is the beating of his hideous heart!"

QUESTIONS

1. From what point of view is Poe's story told? Why is this point of view particularly effective for "The Tell-Tale Heart"?
2. Point to details in the story that identify its speaker as an unreliable narrator.
3. What do we know about the old man in the story? What motivates the narrator to kill him?
4. In spite of all his precautions, the narrator does not commit the perfect crime. What trips him up?
5. How do you account for the police officers' chatting calmly with the murderer instead of reacting to the sound that stirs the murderer into a frenzy?
6. See the student essays on this story in the chapter "Writing About a Story" later in the book. What do they point out that enlarges your own appreciation of Poe's art?

THE MASQUE OF THE RED DEATH   1842

The "Red Death" had long devastated the country. No pestilence had ever been so fatal, or so hideous. Blood was its Avatar° and its seal—the redness and the horror of blood. There were sharp pains, and sudden dizziness, and then profuse bleeding at the pores, with dissolution. The scarlet stains upon the body and especially upon the face of the victim, were the pest ban which shut him out from the aid and from the sympathy of his fellow-men. And the whole seizure, progress and termination of the disease, were the incidents of half an hour.

But the Prince Prospero was happy and dauntless and sagacious. When his dominions were half depopulated, he summoned to his presence a thousand hale and light-hearted friends from among the knights and dames of his court, and with these retired to the deep seclusion of one of his castellated° abbeys. This was an extensive and magnificent structure, the creation of the prince's own eccentric yet august taste. A strong and lofty wall girdled it in. This wall had gates of iron. The courtiers, having entered, brought furnaces and massy° hammers and welded the bolts. They resolved to leave means neither of ingress or egress to the sudden impulses of despair or of frenzy from within. The abbey was amply provisioned. With such precautions the courtiers might bid defiance to contagion. The external world could take care of itself. In the meantime it was folly to grieve, or to think. The prince had provided all the appliances of pleasure. There were buffoons, there were improvisatori,° there were ballet-dancers, there were musicians, there was Beauty, there was wine. All these and security were within. Without was the "Red Death."

It was toward the close of the fifth or sixth month of his seclusion, and while the pestilence raged most furiously abroad, that the Prince Prospero entertained his thousand friends at a masked ball of the most unusual magnificence.

It was a voluptuous scene, that masquerade. But first let me tell of the rooms in which it was held. There were seven—an imperial suite. In many palaces, however, such suites form a long and straight vista, while the folding doors slide

---

Avatar: earthly embodiment of a deity.   *castellated:* having battlements, like a castle.   *massy:* massive.   *improvisatori:* entertainers who can create theater, poetry, or music extemporaneously.

back nearly to the walls on either hand, so that the view of the whole extent is scarcely impeded. Here the case was very different; as might have been expected from the duke's love of the *bizarre*. The apartments were so irregularly disposed that the vision embraced but little more than one at a time. There was a sharp turn at every twenty or thirty yards, and at each turn a novel effect. To the right and left, in the middle of each wall, a tall and narrow Gothic window looked out upon a closed corridor which pursued the windings of the suite. These windows were of stained glass whose color varied in accordance with the prevailing hue of the decorations of the chamber into which it opened. That at the eastern extremity was hung, for example, in blue—and vividly blue were its windows. The second chamber was purple in its ornaments and tapestries, and here the panes were purple. The third was green throughout, and so were the casements. The fourth was furnished and lighted with orange—the fifth with white—the sixth with violet. The seventh apartment was closely shrouded in black velvet tapestries that hung all over the ceiling and down the walls, falling in heavy folds upon a carpet of the same material and hue. But in this chamber only, the color of the windows failed to correspond with the decorations. The panes here were scarlet—a deep blood color. Now in no one of the seven apartments was there any lamp or candelabrum, amid the profusion of golden ornaments that lay scattered to and fro or depended from the roof. There was no light of any kind emanating from lamp or candle within the suite of chambers. But in the corridors that followed the suite, there stood, opposite to each window, a heavy tripod, bearing a brazier° of fire that projected its rays through the tinted glass and so glaringly illumined the room. And thus were produced a multitude of gaudy and fantastic appearances. But in the western or black chamber the effect of the firelight that streamed upon the dark hangings through the blood-tinted panes, was ghastly in the extreme, and produced so wild a look upon the countenances of those who entered, that there were few of the company bold enough to set foot within its precincts at all.

It was in this apartment, also, that there stood against the western wall, a gigantic clock of ebony. Its pendulum swung to and fro with a dull, heavy, monotonous clang; and when the minute-hand made the circuit of the face, and the hour was to be stricken, there came from the brazen lungs of the clock a sound which was clear and loud and deep and exceedingly musical, but of so peculiar a note and emphasis that, at each lapse of an hour, the musicians of the orchestra were constrained to pause, momentarily, in their performance, to harken to the sound; and thus the waltzers perforce ceased their evolutions; and there was a brief disconcert of the whole gay company; and, while the chimes of the clock yet rang, it was observed that the giddiest grew pale, and the more aged and sedate passed their hands over their brows as if in confused reverie or meditation. But when the echoes had fully ceased, a light laughter at once pervaded the assembly; the musicians looked at each other and smiled as if at their own nervousness and folly, and made whispering vows, each to the other, that the next

brazier: a pan that holds burning coals.

chiming of the clock should produce in them no similar emotion; and then, after the lapse of sixty minutes, (which embrace three thousand and six hundred seconds of the Time that flies,) there came yet another chiming of the clock, and then were the same disconcert and tremulousness and meditation as before.

But, in spite of these things, it was a gay and magnificent revel. The tastes of the duke were peculiar. He had a fine eye for colors and effects. He disregarded the *decora* of mere fashion. His plans were bold and fiery, and his conceptions glowed with barbaric lustre. There are some who would have thought him mad. His followers felt that he was not. It was necessary to hear and see and touch him to be *sure* that he was not.

He had directed, in great part, the moveable embellishments of the seven chambers, upon occasion of this great *fête*; and it was his own guiding taste which had given character to the masqueraders. Be sure they were grotesque. There were much glare and glitter and piquancy and phantasm—much of what has been since seen in "Hernani."° There were arabesque° figures with unsuited limbs and appointments. There were delirious fancies such as the madman fashions. There was much of the beautiful, much of the wanton, much of the *bizarre*, something of the terrible, and not a little of that which might have excited disgust. To and fro in the seven chambers there stalked, in fact, a multitude of dreams. And these—the dreams—writhed in and about, taking hue from the rooms, and causing the wild music of the orchestra to seem as the echo of their steps. And, anon, there strikes the ebony clock which stands in the hall of the velvet. And then, for a moment, all is still, and all is silent save the voice of the clock. The dreams are stiff-frozen as they stand. But the echoes of the chime die away—they have endured but an instant—and a light, half-subdued laughter floats after them as they depart. And now again the music swells, and the dreams live, and writhe to and fro more merrily than ever, taking hue from the many tinted windows through which stream the rays from the tripods. But to the chamber which lies most westwardly of the seven, there are now none of the maskers who venture: for the night is waning away; and there flows a ruddier light through the blood-colored panes; and the blackness of the sable drapery appals; and to him whose foot falls upon the sable carpet, there comes from the near clock of ebony a muffled peal more solemnly emphatic than any which reaches *their* ears who indulge in the more remote gaieties of the other apartments.

But these other apartments were densely crowded, and in them beat feverishly the heart of life. And the revel went whirlingly on, until at length there commenced the sounding of midnight upon the clock. And then the music ceased, as I have told; and the evolutions of the waltzers were quieted; and there was an uneasy cessation of all things as before. But now there were twelve strokes

---

"*Hernani*": tragedy by Victor Hugo in a Gothic, romantic style (later made into an opera). It takes place at the court of Spain, where a young noblewoman is beloved by both the king and her elderly uncle. She, meanwhile, loves Hernani, a bandit. The play features poison, betrayal, and great costumes.   *arabesque*: one of Poe's favorite words, an arabesque is an elaborate, intricate design or pattern of a type that originated in Arabia.

to be sounded by the bell of the clock; and thus it happened, perhaps, that more of thought crept, with more of time, into the meditations of the thoughtful among those who revelled. And thus, too, it happened, perhaps, that before the last echoes of the last chime had utterly sunk into silence, there were many individuals in the crowd who had found leisure to become aware of the presence of a masked figure which had arrested the attention of no single individual before. And the rumor of this new presence having spread itself whisperingly around, there arose at length from the whole company a buzz, or murmur, expressive of disapprobation and surprise—then, finally, of terror, of horror, and of disgust.

In an assembly of phantasms such as I have painted, it may well be supposed that no ordinary appearance could have excited such sensation. In truth the masquerade license of the night was nearly unlimited; but the figure in question had out-Heroded Herod,° and gone beyond the bounds of even the prince's indefinite decorum. There are chords in the hearts of the most reckless which cannot be touched without emotion. Even with the utterly lost, to whom life and death are equally jests, there are matters of which no jest can be made. The whole company, indeed, seemed now deeply to feel that in the costume and bearing of the stranger neither wit nor propriety existed. The figure was tall and gaunt, and shrouded from head to foot in the habiliments° of the grave. The mask which concealed the visage was made so nearly to resemble the countenance of a stiffened corpse that the closest scrutiny must have had difficulty in detecting the cheat. And yet all this might have been endured, if not approved, by the mad revellers around. But the mummer° had gone so far as to assume the type of the Red Death. His vesture was dabbled in *blood*—and his broad brow, with all the features of the face, was besprinkled with the scarlet horror.

When the eye of Prince Prospero fell upon this spectral image (which with a slow and solemn movement, as if more fully to sustain its *rôle*, stalked to and fro among the waltzers) he was seen to be convulsed, in the first moment with a strong shudder either of terror or distaste; but, in the next, his brow reddened with rage.   10

"Who dares?" he demanded hoarsely of the courtiers who stood near him— "who dares insult us with this blasphemous mockery? Seize him and unmask him—that we may know whom we have to hang at sunrise, from the battlements!"

It was in the eastern or blue chamber in which stood the Prince Prospero as he uttered these words. They rang throughout the seven rooms loudly and clearly—for the prince was a bold and robust man, and the music had become hushed at the waving of his hand.

It was in the blue room where stood the prince, with a group of pale courtiers by his side. At first, as he spoke, there was a slight rushing movement of this group in the direction of the intruder, who at the moment was also near at

---

Herod: Biblical king of an opulent court, he so admired the dancing of Salome that he offered her anything she wanted; she wanted the head of John the Baptist and got it.   *habiliments:* refers to clothing.   *mummer:* another way of saying "masker"—a person wearing a mask and costume.

hand, and now, with deliberate and stately step, made closer approach to the speaker. But from a certain nameless awe with which the mad assumptions of the mummer had inspired the whole party, there were found none who put forth hand to seize him; so that, unimpeded, he passed within a yard of the prince's person; and, while the vast assembly, as if with one impulse, shrank from the centers of the rooms to the walls, he made his way uninterruptedly, but with the same solemn and measured step which had distinguished him from the first, through the blue chamber to the purple—through the purple to the green— through the green to the orange—through this again to the white—and even thence to the violet, ere a decided movement had been made to arrest him. It was then, however, that the Prince Prospero, maddening with rage and the shame of his own momentary cowardice, rushed hurriedly through the six chambers, while none followed him on account of a deadly terror that had seized upon all. He bore aloft a drawn dagger, and had approached, in rapid impetuosity, to within three or four feet of the retreating figure, when the latter, having attained the extremity of the velvet apartment, turned suddenly and confronted his pursuer. There was a sharp cry—and the dagger dropped gleaming upon the sable carpet, upon which, instantly afterwards, fell prostrate in death the Prince Prospero. Then, summoning the wild courage of despair, a throng of the revellers at once threw themselves into the black apartment, and, seizing the mummer, whose tall figure stood erect and motionless within the shadow of the ebony clock, gasped in unutterable horror at finding the grave-cerements° and corpselike mask which they handled with so violent a rudeness, untenanted by any tangible form.

And now was acknowledged the presence of the Red Death. He had come like a thief in the night. And one by one dropped the revellers in the blood-bedewed halls of their revel, and died each in the despairing posture of his fall. And the life of the ebony clock went out with that of the last of the gay. And the flames of the tripods expired. And Darkness and Decay and the Red Death held illimitable dominion over all.

QUESTIONS

1. The story begins with a description of the plague known as "the Red Death." Can you think of any global epidemics in your lifetime that "shut [the victims] out from the aid and . . . sympathy" of their fellow humans? What does Prince Prospero's decision to wall himself up in an abbey, away from the pestilence and his people, say about his relationship with his subjects?

2. Prospero retires to a "castellated abbey," in other words, an abbey that is fortified with battlements like a castle. He walls himself and his courtiers in this abbey, sealing the plague and its victims out. What do you make of a structure that is both an abbey and a fortress? Why do you think Poe chose such a building for this story?

3. The story tells us that when the pestilence outside the abbey walls is at its "most furious," the Prince Prospero decides to give "a masked ball of the most unusual magnificence." Why do you suppose the prince chooses this moment to give an opulent party?

grave-cerements: a shroud that a corpse is buried in.

4. Consider the description of the seven rooms where Prospero holds the masked ball. How do they emphasize the prince's "love of the *bizarre*"?
5. Why do you think the masked revellers are afraid of the last chamber?
6. What is the effect of the chiming clock on the party? What role does time play in this story?
7. Although Prospero's friends wear grotesque costumes, "such as the madman fancies," they are nonetheless outraged when they see the figure of the Red Death. Why?
8. Prospero tries to kill the mysterious figure of the Red Death, but dies himself, as does everyone else at the end of the story, and then the clock itself stops and the lights go out. Does this seem a fitting end to the story? If "The Masque of the Red Death" is a parable, as many critics think, what is its moral?

THE FALL OF THE HOUSE OF USHER   1845

Son cœur est un luth suspendu;
Sitôt qu'on le touche il résonne.°
                    —De Béranger

During the whole of a dull, dark, and soundless day in the autumn of the year, when the clouds hung oppressively low in the heavens, I had been passing alone, on horseback, through a singularly dreary tract of country; and at length found myself, as the shades of the evening drew on, within view of the melancholy House of Usher. I know not how it was—but, with the first glimpse of the building, a sense of insufferable gloom pervaded my spirit. I say insufferable; for the feeling was unrelieved by any of that half-pleasurable, because poetic, senti-ment, with which the mind usually received even the sternest natural images of the desolate or terrible. I looked upon the scene before me—upon the mere house, and the simple landscape features of the domain—upon the bleak walls—upon the vacant eyelike windows—upon a few rank sedges—and upon a few white trunks of decayed trees—with an utter depression of soul which I can compare to no earthly sensation more properly than to the after-dream of the reveler upon opium—the bitter lapse into every-day life—the hideous dropping off of the veil. There was an iciness, a sinking, sickening of the heart—an unredeemed dreariness of thought which no goading of the imagination could torture into aught of the sublime. What was it—I paused to think—what was it that so unnerved me in the contemplation of the House of Usher? It was a mystery all insoluble; nor could I grapple with the shadowy fancies that crowded upon me as I pondered. I was forced to fall back upon the unsatisfactory conclusion, that while, beyond doubt, there *are* combinations of very simple natural objects which have the power of thus affecting us, still the analysis of this power lies among considerations beyond our depth. It was possible, I reflected, that a mere different arrangement of the par-ticulars of the scene, of the details of the picture, would be sufficient to modify, or perhaps to annihilate its capacity for sorrowful impression; and acting upon this idea, I reined my horse to the precipitous brink of a black and lurid tarn° that lay

Son . . . résonne: Poe has adapted two famous lines from the French poet Pierre-Jean de Béranger (1780–1857). They translate as "His heart is a tightly strung lute; / As soon as one touches it, it resounds." Béranger's original reads "My heart. . . ."   *tarn:* a small mountain lake or pool.

in unruffled luster by the dwelling, and gazed down—but with a shudder even more thrilling than before—upon the remodelled and inverted images of the gray sedge, and the ghastly tree-stems, and the vacant and eye-like windows.

Nevertheless, in this mansion of gloom I now proposed to myself a sojourn of some weeks. Its proprietor, Roderick Usher, had been one of my boon companions in boyhood; but many years had elapsed since our last meeting. A letter, however, had lately reached me in a distant part of the country—a letter from him—which, in its wildly importunate nature, had admitted of no other than a personal reply. The MS.° gave evidence of nervous agitation. The writer spoke of acute bodily illness—of a mental disorder which oppressed him—and of an earnest desire to see me, as his best, and indeed his only personal friend, with a view of attempting, by the cheerfulness of my society, some alleviation of his malady. It was the manner in which all this, and much more, was said—it was the apparent *heart* that went with his request—which allowed me no room for hesitation; and I accordingly obeyed forthwith what I still considered a very singular summons.

Although, as boys, we had been even intimate associates, yet I really knew little of my friend. His reserve had been always excessive and habitual. I was aware, however, that his very ancient family had been noted, time out of mind, for a peculiar sensibility of temperament, displaying itself, through long ages, in many works of exalted art, and manifested, of late, in repeated deeds of munificent yet unobtrusive charity, as well as in a passionate devotion to the intricacies, perhaps even more than to the orthodox and easily recognizable beauties, of musical science. I had learned, too, the very remarkable fact, that the stem of the Usher race, all time-honored as it was, had put forth, at no period, any enduring branch; in other words, that the entire family lay in the direct line of descent, and had always, with very trifling and very temporary variation, so lain. It was this deficiency, I considered, while running over in thought the perfect keeping of the character of the premises with the accredited character of the people, and while speculating upon the possible influence which the one, in the long lapse of centuries, might have exercised upon the other—it was this deficiency, perhaps, of collateral issue, and the consequent undeviating transmission, from sire to son, of the patrimony with the name, which had, at length, so identified the two as to merge the original title of the estate in the quaint and equivocal appellation of the "House of Usher"—an appellation which seemed to include, in the minds of the peasantry who used it, both the family and the family mansion.

I have said that the sole effect of my somewhat childish experiment—that of looking down within the tarn—had been to deepen the first singular impression. There can be no doubt that the consciousness of the rapid increase of my superstition—for why should I not so term it?—served mainly to accelerate the increase itself. Such, I have long known, is the paradoxical law of all sentiments having terror as a basis. And it might have been for this reason only, that, when I again uplifted my eyes to the house itself, from its image in the pool, there grew in my mind a strange fancy—a fancy so ridiculous, indeed, that I but mention it

MS.: manuscript.

to show the vivid force of the sensations which oppressed me. I had so worked upon my imagination as really to believe that about the whole mansion and domain there hung an atmosphere peculiar to themselves and their immediate vicinity—an atmosphere which had no affinity with the air of heaven, but which had reeked up from the decayed trees, and the gray wall, and the silent tarn—a pestilent and mystic vapor, dull sluggish, faintly discernible, and leaden-hued.

Shaking off from my spirit what *must* have been a dream, I scanned more narrowly the real aspect of the building. Its principal feature seemed to be that of an excessive antiquity. The discoloration of ages had been great. Minute fungi overspread the whole exterior, hanging in a fine tangled web-work from the eaves. Yet all this was apart from any extraordinary dilapidation. No portion of the masonry had fallen; and there appeared to be a wild inconsistency between its still perfect adaptation of parts, and the crumbling condition of the individual stones. In this there was much that reminded me of the specious totality of old woodwork which has rotted for long years in some neglected vault, with no disturbance from the breath of the external air. Beyond this indication of extensive decay, however, the fabric gave little token of instability. Perhaps the eye of a scrutinizing observer might have discovered a barely perceptible fissure, which, extending from the roof of the building in front, made its way down the wall in a zigzag direction, until it became lost in the sullen waters of the tarn.

Noticing these things, I rode over a short causeway to the house. A servant in waiting took my horse, and I entered the Gothic archway of the hall. A valet, of stealthy step, thence conducted me, in silence, through many dark and intricate passages in my progress to the *studio* of his master. Much that I encountered on the way contributed, I know not how, to heighten the vague sentiments of which I have already spoken. While the objects around me—while the carvings of the ceilings, the somber tapestries of the walls, the ebon blackness of the floors, and the phantasmagoric armorial trophies which rattled as I strode, were but matters to which, or to such as which, I had been accustomed from my infancy—while I hesitated not to acknowledge how familiar was all this—I still wondered to find how unfamiliar were the fancies which ordinary images were stirring up. On one of the staircases, I met the physician of the family. His countenance, I thought, wore a mingled expression of low cunning and perplexity. He accosted me with trepidation and passed on. The valet now threw open a door and ushered me into the presence of his master.

The room in which I found myself was very large and lofty. The windows were long, narrow, and pointed, and at so vast a distance from the black oaken floor as to be altogether inaccessible from within. Feeble gleams of encrimsoned light made their way through the trellised panes, and served to render sufficiently distinct the more prominent objects around; the eye, however, struggled in vain to reach the remoter angles of the chamber, or the recesses of the vaulted and fretted ceiling. Dark draperies hung upon the walls. The general furniture was profuse, comfortless, antique, and tattered. Many books and musical instruments lay scattered about, but failed to give any vitality to the scene. I felt that I breathed an atmosphere of sorrow. An air of stern, deep, and irredeemable gloom hung over and pervaded all.

Upon my entrance, Usher arose from a sofa on which he had been lying at full length, and greeted me with a vivacious warmth which had much in it, I at first thought, of an overdone cordiality—of the constrained effort of the *ennuyé*° man of the world. A glance, however, at his countenance, convinced me of his perfect sincerity. We sat down; and for some moments, while he spoke not, I gazed upon him with a feeling half of pity, half of awe. Surely, man had never before so terribly altered, in so brief a period, as had Roderick Usher! It was with difficulty that I could bring myself to admit the identity of the wan being before me with the companion of my early boyhood. Yet the character of his face had been at all times remarkable. A cadaverousness of complexion; an eye large, liquid, and luminous beyond comparison; lips somewhat thin and very pallid, but of a surpassingly beautiful curve; a nose of a delicate Hebrew model, but with a breadth of nostril unusual in similar formations; a finely molded chin, speaking, in its want of prominence, of a want of moral energy; hair of a more than web-like softness and tenuity; these features, with an inordinate expansion above the regions of the temple, made up altogether a countenance not easily to be forgotten. And now in the mere exaggeration of the prevailing character of these features, and of the expression they were wont to convey, lay so much of change that I doubted to whom I spoke. The now ghastly pallor of the skin, and the now miraculous luster of the eye, above all things startled and even awed me. The silken hair, too, had been suffered to grow all unheeded, and as, in its wild gossamer texture, it floated rather than fell about the face, I could not, even with effort, connect its Arabesque° expression with any idea of simple humanity.

In the manner of my friend I was at once struck with an incoherence—an inconsistency; and I soon found this to arise from a series of feeble and futile struggles to overcome an habitual trepidancy—an excessive nervous agitation. For something of this nature I had indeed been prepared, no less by his letter, than by reminiscences of certain boyish traits, and by conclusions deduced from his peculiar physical conformation and temperament. His action was alternately vivacious and sullen. His voice varied rapidly from a tremulous indecision (when the animal spirits seemed utterly in abeyance) to that species of energetic concision—that abrupt, weighty, unhurried, and hollow-sounding enunciation—the leaden, self-balanced and perfectly modulated guttural utterance, which may be observed in the lost drunkard, or the irreclaimable eater of opium, during the periods of his most intense excitement.

It was thus that he spoke of the object of my visit, of his earnest desire to see   10
me, and of the solace he expected me to afford him. He entered, at some length, into what he conceived to be the nature of his malady. It was, he said, a constitutional and a family evil, and one for which he despaired to find a remedy—a mere nervous affection, he immediately added, which would undoubtedly soon pass off. It displayed itself in a host of unnatural sensations. Some of these, as he detailed them, interested and bewildered me; although, perhaps, the terms and the general manner of the narration had their weight. He suffered much from a

ennuyé: bored. *Arabesque*: fantastic and complex design.

morbid acuteness of the senses; the most insipid food was alone endurable; he could wear only garments of certain texture; the odors of all flowers were oppressive; his eyes were tortured by even a faint light; and there were but peculiar sounds, and these from stringed instruments, which did not inspire him with horror.

To an anomalous species of terror I found him a bounden slave. "I shall perish," said he, "I *must* perish in this deplorable folly. Thus, thus, and not otherwise, shall I be lost. I dread the events of the future, not in themselves, but in their results. I shudder at the thought of any, even the most trivial, incident, which may operate upon this intolerable agitation of soul. I have, indeed, no abhorrence of danger, except in its absolute effect—in terror. In this unnerved—in this pitiable condition—I feel that the period will sooner or later arrive when I must abandon life and reason together, in some struggle with the grim phantasm, FEAR."

I learned, moreover, at intervals, and through broken and equivocal hints, another singular feature of his mental condition. He was enchained by certain superstitious impressions in regard to the dwelling which he tenanted, and whence, for many years, he had never ventured forth—in regard to an influence whose suppositious force was conveyed in terms too shadowy here to be restated—an influence which some peculiarities in the mere form and substance of his family mansion, had, by dint of long sufferance, he said, obtained over his spirit—an effect which the *physique* of the gray walls and turrets, and of the dim tarn into which they all looked down, had, at length, brought about upon the *morale* of his existence.

He admitted, however, although with hesitation, that much of the peculiar gloom which thus afflicted him could be traced to a more natural and far more palpable origin—to the severe and long-continued illness—indeed to the evidently approaching dissolution—of a tenderly beloved sister—his sole companion for long years—his last and only relative on earth. "Her decease," he said, with a bitterness which I can never forget, "would leave him (him the hopeless and the frail) the last of the ancient race of the Ushers." While he spoke, the lady Madeline (for so was she called) passed slowly through a remote portion of the apartment, and, without having noticed my presence, disappeared. I regarded her with an utter astonishment not unmingled with dread—and yet I found it impossible to account for such feelings. A sensation of stupor oppressed me, as my eyes followed her retreating steps. When a door, at length, closed upon her, my glance sought instinctively and eagerly the countenance of the brother—but he had buried his face in his hands, and I could only perceive that a far more than ordinary wanness had overspread the emaciated fingers through which trickled many passionate tears.

The disease of the lady Madeline had long baffled the skill of her physicians. A settled apathy, a gradual wasting away of the person, and frequent although transient affections of a partially cataleptical character, were the unusual diagnosis. Hitherto she had steadily borne up against the pressure of her malady, and had not betaken herself finally to bed; but, on the closing in of the evening of my arrival at the house, she succumbed (as her brother told me at night with inexpressible agitation) to the prostrating power of the destroyer; and I learned that the glimpse I had obtained of her person would thus probably be the last I should obtain—that the lady, at least while living, would be seen by me no more.

For several days ensuing, her name was unmentioned by either Usher or myself: and during this period I was busied in earnest endeavors to alleviate the melancholy of my friend. We painted and read together; or I listened, as if in a dream, to the wild improvisations of his speaking guitar. And thus, as a closer and still closer intimacy admitted me more unreservedly into the recesses of his spirit, the more bitterly did I perceive the futility of all attempt at cheering a mind from which darkness, as if an inherent positive quality, poured forth upon all objects of the moral and physical universe, in one unceasing radiation of gloom. 15

I shall ever bear about me a memory of the many solemn hours I thus spent alone with the master of the House of Usher. Yet I should fail in any attempt to convey an idea of the exact character of the studies, or of the occupations, in which he involved me, or led me the way. An excited and highly distempered ideality threw a sulphureous luster over all. His long improvised dirges will ring forever in my ears. Among other things, I hold painfully in mind a certain singular perversion and amplification of the wild air of the last waltz of Von Weber.° From the paintings over which his elaborate fancy brooded, and which grew, touch by touch, into vaguenesses at which I shuddered the more thrillingly, because I shuddered knowing not why;—from these paintings (vivid as their images now are before me) I would in vain endeavor to educe more than a small portion which should lie within the compass of merely written words. By the utter simplicity, by the nakedness of his designs, he arrested and overawed attention. If ever mortal painted an idea, that mortal was Roderick Usher. For me at least—in the circumstances then surrounding me—these arose out of the pure abstractions which the hypochondriac contrived to throw upon his canvas, an intensity of intolerable awe, no shadow of which felt I ever yet in the contemplation of the certainly glowing yet too concrete reveries of Fuseli.°

One of the phantasmagoric conceptions of my friend, partaking not so rigidly of the spirit of abstraction, may be shadowed forth, although feebly, in words. A small picture presented the interior of an immensely long and rectangular vault or tunnel, with low walls, smooth, white, and without interruption or device. Certain accessory points of the design served well to convey the idea that this excavation lay at an exceeding depth below the surface of the earth. No outlet was observed in any portion of its vast extent, and no torch, or other artificial source of light was discernible; yet a flood of intense rays rolled throughout, and bathed the whole in a ghastly and inappropriate splendor.

last waltz of Von Weber: a romantic waltz composed by Karl Gottlieb Reissiger (1798–1859) in honor of the composer, Carl Maria von Weber (1786–1826). _Fuseli:_ Henry Fuseli (1742–1825), a Swiss-born artist, who spent most of his career working in England. Fuseli was an associate of William Blake, and his work reflected the nightmarish and fantastic side of Romanticism.

I have just spoken of that morbid condition of the auditory nerve which rendered all music intolerable to the sufferer, with the exception of certain effects of stringed instruments. It was, perhaps, the narrow limits to which he thus confined himself upon the guitar, which gave birth, in great measure, to the fantastic character of his performances. But the fervid *facility* of his *impromptus* could not be so accounted for. They must have been, and were, in the notes, as well as in the words of his wild fantasias (for he not unfrequently accompanied himself with rhymed verbal improvisations), the result of that intense mental collectedness and concentration to which I have previously alluded as observable only in particular moments of the highest artificial excitement. The words of one of these rhapsodies I have easily remembered. I was, perhaps, the more forcibly impressed with it, as he gave it, because in the under or mystic current of its meaning, I fancied that I perceived, and for the first time, a full consciousness on the part of Usher, of the tottering of his lofty reason upon her throne. The verses, which were entitled "The Haunted Palace," ran very nearly, if not accurately, thus:

I.
In the greenest of our valleys,
    By good angels tenanted,
Once a fair and stately palace—
    Radiant palace—reared its head.
In the monarch Thought's dominion—
    It stood there!
Never seraph spread a pinion
    Over fabric half so fair.

II.
Banners yellow, glorious, golden,
    On its roof did float and flow;
(This—all this—was in the olden
    Time long ago)
And every gentle air that dallied,
    In that sweet day,
Along the ramparts plumed and pallid,
    A winged odor went away.

III.
Wanderers in that happy valley
    Through two luminous windows saw
Spirits moving musically
    To a lute's well-tunèd law,
Round about a throne, where sitting

(Porphyrogene!)°
In state his glory well befitting,
  The ruler of the realm was seen.

IV.
And all with pearl and ruby glowing
  Was the fair palace door,
Through which came flowing, flowing, flowing
  And sparkling evermore,
A troop of Echoes whose sweet duty
  Was but to sing,
In voices of surpassing beauty,
  The wit and wisdom of their king.

V.
But evil things, in robes of sorrow,
  Assailed the monarch's high estate;
(Ah, let us mourn, for never morrow
  Shall dawn upon him, desolate!)
And, round about his home, the glory
  That blushed and bloomed
Is but a dim-remembered story
  Of the old time entombed.

VI.
And travelers now within that valley,
  Through the red-litten windows, see
Vast forms that move fantastically
  To a discordant melody;
While, like a rapid ghastly river,
  Through the pale door,
A hideous throng rush out forever,
  And laugh—but smile no more.

I well remember that suggestions arising from this ballad, led us into a train
of thought wherein there became manifest an opinion of Usher's which I mention not so much on account of its novelty, (for other men° have thought thus,)
as on account of the pertinacity with which he maintained it. This opinion, in

---

Porphyrogene: "born to the purple." In ancient Rome purple robes were worn only by kings,
magistrates, senators, generals, and especially the emperor; the phrase means, therefore, of aristocratic or royal lineage. other men: Watson, Dr. Percival, Spallanzani, and especially the
Bishop of Landaff.—See "Chemical Essays," vol. v. [Poe's note.] The names Poe lists in his
note were eighteenth-century scientists.

its general form, was that of the sentience of all vegetable things. But, in his disordered fancy, the idea had assumed a more daring character, and trespassed, under certain conditions, upon the kingdom of inorganization. I lack words to express the full extent, or the earnest *abandon* of his persuasion. The belief, however, was connected (as I have previously hinted) with the gray stones of the home of his forefathers. The conditions of the sentience had been here, he imagined, fulfilled in the method of collocation of these stones—in the order of their arrangement, as well as in that of the many *fungi* which overspread them, and of the decayed trees which stood around—above all, in the long undisturbed endurance of this arrangement, and in its reduplication in the still waters of the tarn. Its evidence—the evidence of the sentience—was to be seen, he said, (and I here started as he spoke,) in the gradual yet certain condensation of an atmosphere of their own about the waters and the walls. The result was discoverable, he added, in that silent, yet importunate and terrible influence which for centuries had molded the destinies of his family, and which made *him* what I now saw him—what he was. Such opinions need no comment, and I will make none.

Our books—the books which, for years, had formed no small portion of the mental existence of the invalid—were, as might be supposed, in strict keeping with this character of phantasm. We pored together over such works as the Ververt et Chartreuse of Gresset; the Belphegor of Machiavelli; the Heaven and Hell of Swedenborg; the Subterranean Voyage of Nicholas Klimm by Holberg; the Chiromancy of Robert Flud, of Jean D'Indaginé, and of De la Chambre; the Journey into the Blue Distance of Tieck; and the City of the Sun of Campanella. One favorite volume was a small octavo edition of the *Directorium Inquisitorum*, by the Dominican Eymeric de Gironne; and there were passages in Pomponius Mela, about the old African Satyrs and Ægipans, over which Usher would sit dreaming for hours. His chief delight, however, was found in the perusal of an exceedingly rare and curious book in quarto Gothic—the manual of a forgotten church—the *Vigiliae Mortuorum secundum Chorum Ecclesiae Maguntinae*.°

I could not help thinking of the wild ritual of this work, and of its probable influence upon the hypochondriac, when, one evening, having informed me abruptly that the lady Madeline was no more, he stated his intention of preserving her corpse for a fortnight, (previously to its final interment,) in one of the numerous vaults within the main walls of the building. The worldly reason, however, assigned for this singular proceeding, was one which I did not feel at liberty to dispute. The brother had been led to his resolution (so he told me) by consideration of the unusual character of the malady of the deceased, of certain obtrusive and eager inquiries on the part of her medical men, and of the remote and exposed situation of the burial-ground of the family. I will not deny that when I called to mind the sinister countenance of the person whom I met upon the staircase, on the day of my arrival at the house, I had no desire to oppose what I regarded as at best but a harmless, and by no means an unnatural, precaution.

We pored together over . . . Maguntinae: Usher's book collection is a diverse assembly of occult lore and supernatural tales drawn from across two millennia. All the titles and authors are real.

At the request of Usher, I personally aided him in the arrangements for the temporary entombment. The body having been encoffined, we two alone bore it to its rest. The vault in which we placed it (and which had been so long unopened that our torches, half smothered in its oppressive atmosphere, gave us little opportunity for investigation) was small, damp, and entirely without means of admission for light; lying, at great depth, immediately beneath that portion of the building in which was my own sleeping apartment. It had been used, apparently, in remote feudal times, for the worst purposes of a donjon-keep, and, in later days, as a place of deposit for powder, or some other highly combustible substance, as a portion of its floor, and the whole interior of a long archway through which we reached it, were carefully sheathed with copper. The door, of massive iron, had been, also, similarly protected. Its immense weight caused an unusually sharp grating sound, as it moved upon its hinges.

Having deposited our mournful burden upon tressels within this region of horror, we partially turned aside the yet unscrewed lid of the coffin, and looked upon the face of the tenant. A striking similitude between the brother and sister now first arrested my attention; and Usher, divining, perhaps, my thoughts, murmured out some few words from which I learned that the deceased and himself had been twins, and that sympathies of a scarcely intelligible nature had always existed between them. Our glances, however, rested not long upon the dead—for we could not regard her unawed. The disease which had thus entombed the lady in the maturity of youth, had left, as usual in all maladies of a strictly cataleptical character, the mockery of a faint blush upon the bosom and the face, and that suspiciously lingering smile upon the lip which is so terrible in death. We replaced and screwed down the lid, and, having secured the door of iron, made our way, with toil, into the scarcely less gloomy apartments of the upper portion of the house.

And now, some days of bitter grief having elapsed, an observable change came over the features of the mental disorder of my friend. His ordinary manner had vanished. His ordinary occupations were neglected or forgotten. He roamed from chamber to chamber with hurried, unequal, and objectless step. The pallor of his countenance had assumed, if possible, a more ghastly hue—but the luminousness of his eye had utterly gone out. The once occasional huskiness of his tone was heard no more; and a tremulous quaver, as if of extreme terror, habitually characterized his utterance. There were times, indeed, when I thought his unceasingly agitated mind was laboring with some oppressive secret, to divulge which he struggled for the necessary courage. At times, again, I was obliged to resolve all into the mere inexplicable vagaries of madness, for I beheld him gazing upon vacancy for long hours, in an attitude of the profoundest attention as if listening to some imaginary sound. It was no wonder that his condition terrified—that it infected me. I felt creeping upon me, by slow yet certain degrees, the wild influences of his own fantastic yet impressive superstitions.

It was, especially, upon retiring to bed late in the night of the seventh or eighth day after the placing of the lady Madeline within the donjon, that I experienced the full power of such feelings. Sleep came not near my couch—while the hours waned and waned away. I struggled to reason off the nervousness which had dominion over me. I endeavored to believe that much, if not all of what I felt, was due to the bewildering influence of the gloomy furniture of the room—of the dark and tattered draperies, which, tortured into motion by the breath of a rising tempest, swayed fitfully to and fro upon the walls, and rustled uneasily about the decorations of the bed. But my efforts were fruitless. An irrepressible tremor gradually pervaded my frame; and, at length, there sat upon my very heart an incubus of utterly causeless alarm. Shaking this off with a gasp and a struggle, I uplifted myself upon the pillows, and, peering earnestly within the intense darkness of the chamber, hearkened—I know not why, except that an instinctive spirit prompted me—to certain low and indefinite sounds which came, through the pauses of the storm, at long intervals, I knew not whence. Overpowered by an intense sentiment of horror, unaccountable yet unendurable, I threw on my clothes with haste (for I felt that I should sleep no more during the night), and endeavored to arouse myself from the pitiable condition into which I had fallen, by pacing rapidly to and fro through the apartment.

I had taken but few turns in this manner, when a light step on an adjoining staircase arrested my attention. I presently recognized it as that of Usher. In an instant afterward he rapped, with a gentle touch, at my door, and entered, bearing a lamp. His countenance was, as usual, cadaverously wan—but, moreover, there was a species of mad hilarity in his eyes—an evidently restrained *hysteria* in his whole demeanor. His air appalled me—but anything was preferable to the solitude which I had so long endured, and I even welcomed his presence as a relief.

"And you have not seen it?" he said abruptly, after having stared about him for some moments in silence—"you have not then seen it?—but, stay! you shall." Thus speaking, and having carefully shaded his lamp, he hurried to one of the casements, and threw it freely open to the storm.

The impetuous fury of the entering gust nearly lifted us from our feet. It was, indeed, a tempestuous yet sternly beautiful night, and one wildly singular in its terror and its beauty. A whirlwind had apparently collected its force in our vicinity; for there were frequent and violent alterations in the direction of the wind; and the exceeding density of the clouds (which hung so low as to press upon the turrets of the house) did not prevent our perceiving the life-like velocity with which they flew careering from all points against each other, without passing away into the distance. I say that even their exceeding density did not prevent our perceiving this—yet we had no glimpse of the moon or stars—nor was there any flashing forth of the lightning. But the under surfaces of the huge masses of agitated vapor, as well as all terrestrial objects immediately around us, were glowing in the unnatural light of a faintly luminous and distinctly visible gaseous exhalation which hung about and enshrouded the mansion.

"You must not—you shall not behold this!" said I, shudderingly, to Usher, as I led him, with a gentle violence, from the window to a seat. "These appearances, which bewilder you, are merely electrical phenomena not uncommon—or it may be that they have their ghastly origin in the rank miasma of the tarn. Let us close this casement;—the air is chilling and dangerous to your frame. Here is one of your favorite romances. I will read, and you shall listen;—and so we will pass away this terrible night together."

The antique volume which I had taken up was the "Mad Trist" of Sir 30
Launcelot Canning,° but I had called it a favorite of Usher's more in sad jest
than in earnest; for, in truth, there is little in its uncouth and unimaginative pro-
lixity which could have had interest for the lofty and spiritual ideality of my
friend. It was, however, the only book immediately at hand; and I indulged a
vague hope that the excitement which now agitated the hypochondriac, might
find relief (for the history of mental disorder is full of similar anomalies) even in
the extremeness of the folly which I should read. Could I have judged, indeed, by
the wild over-strained air of vivacity with which he hearkened, or apparently
hearkened, to the words of the tale, I might well have congratulated myself upon
the success of my design.

I had arrived at that well-known portion of the story where Ethelred, the
hero of the Trist, having sought in vain for peaceable admission into the
dwelling of the hermit, proceeds to make good an entrance by force. Here, it will
be remembered, the words of the narrative run thus:

"And Ethelred, who was by nature of a doughty heart, and who was now
mighty withal, on account of the powerfulness of the wine which he had drunken,
waited no longer to hold parley with the hermit, who, in sooth, was of an obstinate
and maliceful turn, but, feeling the rain upon his shoulders, and fearing the rising of
the tempest, uplifted his mace outright, and, with blows, made quickly room in the
plankings of the door for his gauntleted hand; and now pulling therewith sturdily,
he so cracked, and ripped, and tore all asunder, that the noise of the dry and hollow-
sounding wood alarumed and reverberated throughout the forest."

At the termination of this sentence I started, and for a moment, paused; for
it appeared to me (although I at once concluded that my excited fancy had deceived me)—it appeared to me that, from some very remote portion of the mansion, there came, indistinctly, to my ears, what might have been, in its exact
similarity of character, the echo (but a stifled and dull one certainly) of the very
cracking and ripping sound which Sir Launcelot had so particularly described. It
was, beyond doubt, the coincidence alone which had arrested my attention; for,
amid the rattling of the sashes of the casements, and the ordinary commingled
noises of the still increasing storm, the sound, in itself, had nothing, surely,
which should have interested or disturbed me. I continued the story:

"But the good champion Ethelred, now entering within the door, was sore
enraged and amazed to perceive no signal of the maliceful hermit; but, in the
stead thereof, a dragon of a scaly and prodigious demeanor, and of a fiery tongue,
which sate in guard before a palace of gold, with a floor of silver; and upon the
wall there hung a shield of shining brass with this legend enwritten—

Who entereth herein, a conqueror hath bin;
Who slayeth the dragon, the shield he shall win;

"Mad Trist" of Sir Launcelot Canning: a fictitious tale and author fabricated by Poe. The tryst alluded to in the title, however, is an ironic foreshadowing of the meeting about to occur.

And Ethelred uplifted his mace, and struck upon the head of the dragon, which fell before him, and gave up his pesty breath, with a shriek so horrid and harsh, and withal so piercing, that Ethelred had fain to close his ears with his hands against the dreadful noise of it, the like whereof was never before heard."

Here again I paused abruptly, and now with a feeling of wild amazement— ³⁵ for there could be no doubt whatever that, in this instance, I did actually hear (although from what direction it proceeded I found it impossible to say) a low and apparently distant, but harsh, protracted, and most unusual screaming or grating sound—the exact counterpart of what my fancy had already conjured up for the dragon's unnatural shriek as described by the romancer.

Oppressed, as I certainly was, upon the occurrence of the second and most extraordinary coincidence, by a thousand conflicting sensations, in which wonder and extreme terror were predominant, I still retained sufficient presence of mind to avoid exciting, by any observation, the sensitive nervousness of my companion. I was by no means certain that he had noticed the sounds in question; although, assuredly, a strange alteration had, during the last few minutes, taken place in his demeanor. From a position fronting my own, he had gradually brought round his chair, so as to sit with his face to the door of the chamber; and thus I could but partially perceive his features, although I saw that his lips trembled as if he were murmuring inaudibly. His head had dropped upon his breast— yet I knew that he was not asleep, from the wide and rigid opening of the eye as I caught a glance of it in profile. The motion of his body, too, was at variance with this idea—for he rocked from side to side with a gentle yet constant and uniform sway. Having rapidly taken notice of all this, I resumed the narrative of Sir Launcelot, which thus proceeded:

"And now, the champion, having escaped from the terrible fury of the dragon, bethinking himself of the brazen shield, and of the breaking up of the enchantment which was upon it, removed the carcass from out of the way before him, and approached valorously over the silver pavement of the castle to where the shield was upon the wall; which in sooth tarried not for his full coming, but fell down at his feet upon the silver floor, with a mighty great and terrible ringing sound."

No sooner had these syllables passed my lips, than—as if a shield of brass had indeed, at the moment, fallen heavily upon a floor of silver—I became aware of a distinct, hollow, metallic, and clangorous, yet apparently muffled reverberation. Completely unnerved, I leaped to my feet; but the measured rocking movement of Usher was undisturbed. I rushed to the chair in which he sat. His eyes were bent fixedly before him, and throughout his whole countenance there reigned a stony rigidity. But, as I placed my hand upon his shoulder, there came a strong shudder over his whole person; a sickly smile quivered about his lips; and I saw that he spoke in a low, hurried, and gibbering murmur, as if unconscious of my presence. Bending closely over him, I at length drank in the hideous import of his words.

"Not hear it?—yes, I hear it, and *have* heard it. Long—long—long—many minutes, many hours, many days, have I heard it—yet I dared not—oh, pity me, miserable wretch that I am!—I dared not—I *dared* not speak! *We have put her living in the tomb!* Said I not that my senses were acute? I *now* tell you that I heard her first feeble movements in the hollow coffin. I heard them—many,

many days ago—yet I dared not—*I dared not speak!* And now—to-night—Ethelred—ha! ha!—the breaking of the hermit's door, and the death-cry of the dragon, and the clangor of the shield! say, rather, the rending of her coffin, and the grating of the iron hinges of her prison, and her struggles within the coppered archway of the vault! Oh whither shall I fly? Will she not be here anon? Is she not hurrying to upbraid me for my haste? Have I not heard her footstep on the stair? Do I not distinguish that heavy and horrible beating of her heart? *Madman!*" here he sprang furiously to his feet, and shrieked out his syllables, as if in the effort he were giving up his soul—"*Madman! I tell you that she now stands without the door!*"

As if in the superhuman energy of his utterance there had been found the   40
potency of a spell—the huge antique panels to which the speaker pointed, threw slowly back, upon the instant, their ponderous and ebony jaws. It was the work of the rushing gust—but then without those doors there *did* stand the lofty and enshrouded figure of the lady Madeline of Usher. There was blood upon her white robes, and the evidence of some bitter struggle upon every portion of her emaciated frame. For a moment she remained trembling and reeling to and fro upon the threshold, then, with a low moaning cry, fell heavily inward upon the person of her brother, and in her violent and now final death-agonies, bore him to the floor a corpse, and a victim to the terrors he had anticipated.

From that chamber, and from that mansion, I fled aghast. The storm was still abroad in all its wrath as I found myself crossing the old causeway. Suddenly there shot along the path a wild light, and I turned to see whence a gleam so unusual could have issued; for the vast house and its shadows were alone behind me. The radiance was that of the full, setting, and blood-red moon which now shone vividly through that once barely-discernible fissure of which I have before spoken as extending from the roof of the building, in a zigzag direction, to the base. While I gazed, this fissure rapidly widened—there came a fierce breath of the whirlwind—the entire orb of the satellite burst at once upon my sight—my brain reeled as I saw the mighty walls rushing asunder—there was a long tumultuous shouting sound like the voice of a thousand waters—and the deep and dank tarn at my feet closed sullenly and silently over the fragments of the "*House of Usher.*"

QUESTIONS

1. Study the first sentence of the story. What words and stylistic devices set the tone of the story? Can you discern, in that very first sentence, a foreshadowing of the story's end?
2. The Usher mansion is described in great detail. What does it look like, inside and out? How is the appearance of the manor related to its inhabitants?
3. Why does the narrator come to visit Usher? How are the narrator and Usher similar; in what ways are they different?
4. Describe Roderick Usher's artistic creations. What do they tell us about him, and how do they reinforce the main theme of this story?
5. What is the nature of Roderick Usher's relationship with his sister Madeline?
6. What do you think Madeline's "malady" is, based on the various references in the story?
7. Why do you think Roderick immured his living sister in a tomb? Can you find evidence in the story to support your answer?

Illustration for "The Fall of the House of Usher" by Arthur Rackham from Poe's Tales of Mystery & Imagination (1935).

THE TALE AND ITS EFFECT   1842

Were we called upon, however, to designate that class of composition which, next to [a short lyric poem], should best fulfill the demands of high genius—should offer it the most advantageous field of exertion—we should unhesitatingly speak of the prose tale, as Mr. Hawthorne has here exemplified it. We allude to the short prose narrative, requiring from a half-hour to one or two hours in its perusal. The ordinary novel is objectionable, from its length, for reasons already stated in substance. As it cannot be read at one sitting, it deprives itself, of course, of the immense force derivable from *totality*. Worldly interests intervening during the pauses of perusal, modify, annul, or counteract, in a greater or less degree, the impressions of the book. But simple cessation in reading would, of itself, be sufficient to destroy the true unity. In the brief tale, however, the author is enabled to carry out the fullness of his intention, be it what it may. During the hour of perusal the soul of the reader is at the writer's control. There are no external or extrinsic influences—resulting from weariness or interruption.

A skillful literary artist has constructed a tale. If wise, he has not fashioned his thoughts to accommodate his incidents; but having conceived, with deliberate care, a certain unique or single *effect* to be wrought out, he then invents such incidents—he then combines such events as may best aid him in establishing this preconceived effect. If his very initial sentence tend not to the out-bringing of this effect, then he has failed in his first step. In the whole composition there should be no word written, of which the tendency, direct or indirect, is not to the one pre-established design. And by such means, with such care and skill, a picture is at length painted which leaves in the mind of him who contemplates it with a kindred art, a sense of the fullest satisfaction. The idea of the tale has been presented unblemished, because undisturbed; and this is an end unattainable by the novel. Undue brevity is just as exceptionable here as in the poem; but undue length is yet more to be avoided.

From a review of *Twice-Told Tales* by Nathaniel Hawthorne

ON IMAGINATION   1849

The *pure Imagination* chooses, from *either Beauty or Deformity*, only the most combinable things hitherto uncombined; the compound, as a general rule, partaking, in character, of beauty, or sublimity, in the ratio of the respective beauty or sublimity of the things combined—which are themselves still to be considered as atomic—that is to say, as previous combinations. But, as often analogously happens in physical chemistry, so not infrequently does it occur in this chemistry of the intellect, that the admixture of two elements results in a something that has nothing of the qualities of one of them, or even nothing of the qualities of either. . . . Thus, the range of Imagination is unlimited. Its materials extend throughout the universe. Even out of deformities it fabricates that *Beauty* which is at once its sole object and its inevitable test. But, in general, the richness or force of the matters combined; the facility for discovering combinable novelties worth combining; and, especially the absolute "chemical combination" of the completed mass—are the particulars to be regarded in our estimate of Imagination. It is this thorough harmony of an imaginative work which so often causes it to be undervalued by the thoughtless, through the character of *obviousness* which is superinduced. We are apt to find ourselves asking *why* it is that these combinations have never been imagined before.

From "Marginalia," *Southern Literary Messenger*

Nothing is more clear than that every plot, worth the name, must be elaborated to its denouement before anything be attempted with the pen. It is only with the denouement constantly in view that we can give a plot its indispensable air of consequence, or causation, by making the incidents, and especially the tone at all points, tend to the development of the intention.

There is a radical error, I think, in the usual mode of constructing a story. Either history affords a thesis—or one is suggested by an incident of the day—or, at best, the author sets himself to work in the combination of striking events to form merely the basis of his narrative—designing, generally, to fill in with description, dialogue, or autorial comment, whatever crevices of fact, or action, may, from page to page, render themselves apparent.

I prefer commencing with the consideration of an effect. Keeping originality always in view—for he is false to himself who ventures to dispense with so obvious and so easily attainable a source of interest—I say to myself, in the first place, "Of the innumerable effects, or impressions, of which the heart, the intellect, or (more generally) the soul is susceptible, what one shall I, on the present occasion, select?" Having chosen a novel, first, and secondly a vivid effect, I consider whether it can be best wrought by incident or tone—whether by ordinary incidents and peculiar tone, or the converse, or by peculiarity both of incident and tone—afterward looking about me (or rather within) for such combinations of event, or tone, as shall best aid me in the construction of the effect.

From "The Philosophy of Composition"

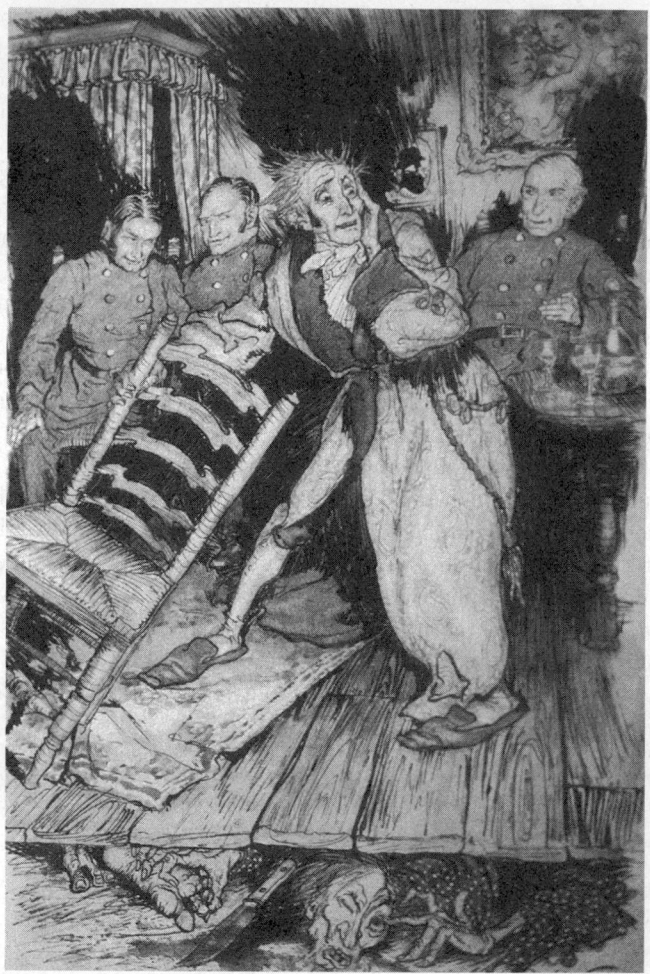

Illustration for "The Tell-Tale Heart" by Arthur Rackham from Poe's Tales of Mystery & Imagaination *(1935).*

Daniel Hoffman (b. 1923)

THE FATHER-FIGURE IN "THE TELL-TALE HEART"   1972

There are no parents in the tales of Edgar Poe, nary a Mum nor a Dad. Instead all is symbol. And what does this total repression of both sonhood and parenthood signify but that to acknowledge such relationships is to venture into territory too dangerous, too terrifying, for specificity. Desire and hatred are alike insatiable and unallayed. But the terrible war of superego upon the id, the endless battle between conscience and impulse, the unsleeping enmity of the self and its Imp of the Perverse—these struggles are enacted and reenacted in Poe's work, but always in disguise.

Take "The Tell-Tale Heart," surely one of his nearly perfect tales. It's only four pages long, a triumph of the art of economy:

> How, then, am I mad? Hearken! and observe how healthily—how calmly I can tell you the whole story.

When a narrator commences in *this* vein, we know him to be mad already. But we also know his author to be sane. For with such precision to portray the methodicalness of a madman is the work not of a madman but of a man who truly understands what it is to be mad. Artistic control is the warrant of auctorial sanity. It is axiomatic in the psychiatric practice of our century that self-knowledge is a necessary condition for the therapeutic process. Never using the language of the modern diagnostician— which was unavailable to him in the first place, and which in any case he didn't need—Poe demonstrates the extent of his self-knowledge in his manipulation of symbolic objects and actions toward ends which his tales embody.

The events are few, the action brief. "I" (in the story) believes himself sane because he is so calm, so methodical, so fully aware and in control of his purpose. Of course his knowledge of that purpose is limited, while his recital thereof endows the reader with a greater knowledge than his own. "The disease," he says right at the start, "had sharpened my senses. . . . Above all was the sense of hearing acute. I heard all things in the heavens and in the earth. I heard many things in hell." Now of whom can this be said but a delusional person? At the same time, mad as he is, this narrator is *the hero of sensibility*. His heightened senses bring close both heaven and hell.

His plot is motiveless. "Object there was none. Passion there was none. I loved the old man. He had never wronged me. He had never given me insult. For his gold I had no desire." The crime he is about to commit will be all the more terrible because apparently gratuitous. But let us not be lulled by this narrator's lack of admitted motive. He may have a motive—one which he cannot admit, even to himself.

Nowhere does this narrator explain what relationship, if any, exists between him and the possessor of the Evil Eye. We do, however, learn from his tale that he and the old man live under the same roof—apparently alone together, for there's no evidence of anyone else's being in the house. Is the young man the old man's servant? Odd that he would not say so. Perhaps the youth is the old man's son. Quite natural that he should not say so. "I loved the old man. He had never wronged me. . . . I was never kinder to the old man than during the whole week before I killed him." Such the aggressive revulsion caused by the old man's Evil Eye!

What can this be all about? The Evil Eye is a belief as old and as dire as any in man's superstitious memory, and it usually signifies the attribution to another of a power wished for by the self. In this particular case there are other vibrations emanating from the vulture-like eye of the benign old man. Insofar as we have warrant— which I think we do—to take him as a father-figure, his Eye becomes the all-seeing surveillance of the child by the father, even by The Father. This surveillance is of course the origin of the child's conscience, the inculcation into his soul of the paternal principles of right and wrong. As such, the old man's eye becomes a ray to be feared. For if the boy deviates ever so little from the strict paths of rectitude, *it will find him out.*

. . . . .

Could he but rid himself of its all-seeing scrutiny, he would then be free of his subjection to time.

All the more so if the father-figure in this tale be, in one of his aspects, a Father-Figure. As, to an infant, his own natural father doubtless is. As, to the baby Eddie, his foster-father may have been. Perhaps he had even a subliminal memory of his natural father, who so early deserted him, eye and all, to the hard knocks experience held in store. So, the evil in that Evil Eye is likely a mingling of the stern reproaches of conscience with the reminder of his own subjection to time, age, and death.

From *Poe Poe Poe Poe Poe Poe Poe*

Marie Bonaparte (1882–1962)

A Psychoanalytic Reading of "The Masque of the Red Death"   1933

Translated by Susan Balée

More than any other story by Edgar Allan Poe, "The Masque of the Red Death" wallows in blood. The tale begins with the description of the "Red Death": "Blood was its Avatar and its seal—the redness and the horror of blood."

The coughing up of blood, its secretion from every pore, does not last long in those afflicted with the disease. After it subsides, the tell-tale scarlet stain appears on victims, "especially" on the face. Death is swift. Despite this plague in his kingdom, Prince Prospero "was happy and dauntless and sagacious." He assembles his favorite courtiers and retreats to one of his castellated abbeys. Provisioned with delectable food and diverted by various entertainments, the prince and his friends lock themselves in the abbey while "without was the 'Red Death.'"

Several months of seclusion pass, at which point "the pestilence raged most furiously abroad" and the prince decides to give a magnificent masked ball. The omniscient narrator tells us, "It was a voluptuous scene, that masquerade." Well, it's quite a strange conception of a "voluptuous scene" that Edgar Poe shows us. The phrase itself suggests the introduction of naked women by the licentious Prospero but, on the contrary, everyone here is fully clothed with the additional cover of a mask. Further, at this sumptuous masked ball, there is "wine," but otherwise not a single lascivious element. Chastity reigns at Prince Prospero's party. Prospero's sense of voluptuousness, like that of his creator, is not expressed sexually.

Soon enough, however, we see what Poe means by "voluptuous," when a series of rooms in the abbey are described minutely. There are seven of these rooms, "irregularly disposed," running from east to west. Stained glass windows color each room successively, in blue, purple, green, orange, white, and violet.

The seventh chamber, the room that is farthest to the west, is described in the most lavish detail. It is shrouded in black hangings and lit by blood-red stained glass. One feels suffocated simply reading this description. There's no air, nothing but windows give onto the corridor; there's no light, only that which filters sluggishly through the stained glass. The rooms meander, one obliquely into another, with no outside exits. This is the interior of a nightmare and it is what, for Poe, counts as "voluptuous."

Remember, however, that in dreams (and nightmares), dwellings of all kinds are symbols. They represent transferences from the primal dwelling place where we originally resided: our mother's body. Poe uses this symbol in a variety of stories, perhaps most notably in "The Fall of the House of Usher" where the sinister mansion is practically a character in its own right. In "The Masque of the Red Death," the symbol of the fortified abbey is equally clear: Prince Prospero, threatened by the "Red Death"—a terrible personification of the criminal father—takes refuge in his abbey. In reality, this abbey is his mother's womb.

. . .

Unfortunately for him, Prince Prospero's womb-like refuge is not completely safe, a fact that the giant clock continues to remind him and the other revelers. Clocks play a large role in Poe's tales, and always the same role. In this tale, the gigantic clock is like a living thing with its beating heart and its "brazen lungs." The huge clock is Father Time and he's a sinister figure as well as a potent one. He represents the father's virility through the powerful male tick-tock of his heart. Even in the abbey-womb, the deepest recesses of the mother's body, Prospero and his friends are not safe from the primal castrator and killer, the avenging father, who has made his presence known. . . . At last, midnight rings out on the clock and suddenly a new masker appears in the crowd. This mummer wears a corpse's shroud and his face is a death mask, one that resembles the dead faces of those who have succumbed to the Red Death. His face is marked with the scarlet stain, his shroud similarly spattered with blood.

Despite Prospero's alarmed order to seize the masker, no one dares to lay a hand on him. Instead, "with deliberate and stately step," the mask of Red Death passes near the prince. Exasperated, the prince attacks the fearsome figure. He cries out and then falls to the ground dead before he can stab the Red Death masker. The throng springs to life then, seizes the mummer, and then all proceed to die of the Red Death in all its gore and agony. "And the life of the ebony clock went out with the last of the gay."

. . .

In "The Masque of the Red Death," we see the criminal father return as an avenger. This masker, sower of death, can be no other. The son, Prince Prospero, has committed a crime. Showing no mercy for his subjects dying in an epidemic, he entrenches himself in his abbey and leads a life of feasts and fun. Believing he's safe, he indulges himself in various revels. These revels, or orgies, lack explicit sexual lust and yet the rape of the mother is written all over them. One only misses it because it is writ so large, just as one sometimes misses the names of continents on a map, because the letters are so large and spaced so widely on the page.

If this fantasy of Prospero's abbey refuge constitutes his mother's body, his possession of it is the equivalent of incest, at least as a child in a pre-genital stage would envision it. In any event, that is how the vanquished father interprets the situation, returning as the "masked avenger" to punish the son in his own refuge. The punishment is two-part, just as the crime was: the son is killed in retaliation for parricide, and castrated, in retaliation for incest. At the moment the prince raises his dagger to strike the figure of Red Death, that being turns. Then there is a cry, the dagger falls to the ground, and then the prince follows, dead.

Death in that scene is artistically but realistically represented; castration can only be symbolically represented by the dagger, which falls at the mere glance of the father and leaves the son disarmed.

Once his vengeance is accomplished, the father himself ceases to be. The clock stops and the tale closes with an end of the world fantasy in which the father, a bloody castrator and killer, represents a God terrible and eternal, reigning solitary over a void.

"And Darkness and Decay and the Red Death held illimitable dominion over all." *Vengeance is mine . . . saith the Lord.*

From *Edgar Poe*, Book III: "Tales of the Father"

Charles Baudelaire (1821–1867)

ON POE'S GENIUS   1856

TRANSLATED BY JOAN F. MELE

[Poe] will win the admiration of thinking people . . . by his love of the Beautiful, by his knowledge of the harmonic conditions of beauty, by his profound and plaintive poetry, carefully worked, correct and as transparent as a crystal jewel—by his admirable style, pure and bizarre—as closely woven as the mesh of armor—complaisant and meticulous, whose slightest intention serves to lead the reader gently toward the desired effect—finally and above all by his very special genius, by the unique temperament which allowed him to paint and to explain, in an impeccable, gripping and terrible manner, *the exception in the moral order*. Diderot,[1] to take one example among a hundred, is a sanguine author; Poe is a writer who is all nerves, and even something more—and the best one I know.

In his case every introductory passage quietly draws you in like a whirlpool. His solemnity takes the reader by surprise and keeps his mind on the alert. Immediately he feels that something serious is involved. And slowly, little by little, a story unfolds in which all interest depends on an imperceptible intellectual deviation on a bold hypothesis, on an imprudent dose of Nature in the amalgam of faculties. The reader, seized by a kind of vertigo, is constrained to follow the author through his compelling deductions.

No man, I repeat, has told about the *exceptions* in human life and in nature with more magic—the enthusiastic curiosities of convalescence, the dying seasons charged with enervating splendors, hot, humid and misty weather when the south wind softens and relaxes one's nerves like the strings of an instrument, when one's eyes fill with tears which do not come from the heart—hallucinations first seeming doubtful, then as con-

[1] Baudelaire compares Poe with Denis Diderot, eighteenth-century French philosopher and art critic whose Enlightenment views stressed the rational order of nature. [Translator's note.]

vincing and as rational as a book—the absurd establishing itself in one's mind and controlling it with a frightful logic—hysteria usurping the place of the will, contradiction set up between the nerves and the mind, and personality so dissonant that it expresses sorrow with laughter. He analyzes whatever is most fleeting, he weighs the imponderable and describes in a meticulous and scientific manner, the effects of which are terrible, all the imaginary world which floats around a very nervous man and leads him into evil.

Poe's Characters

The characters in Poe, or rather the character in Poe, the man with extremely acute faculties, the man with relaxed nerves, the man whose patient and ardent will hurls defiance at difficulties, he whose gaze is fixed as straight as a sword on objects which increase in importance as he stares at them—this man is Poe himself. And his women, all luminous and sickly, dying of strange diseases and speaking with a voice which is like music, they too are Poe; or at least, through their strange aspirations, through their knowledge, through their incurable melancholy, they strongly share the nature of their creator. As for his ideal woman, she is revealed in different portraits scattered through his scant collection of poems, portraits, or rather ways of feeling beauty, which the temperament of the author joins together and blends in a vague but sensible unity, and in which exists perhaps more delicately than elsewhere that insatiable love of the Beautiful, which is his great title, that is to say the summation of his claims on the affection and admiration of poets.

From preface to *Histoires Extraordinaires*

James Tuttleton (1934–1998)

POE'S QUEST FOR SUPERNAL BEAUTY   1998

Edgar Poe's critical observations—scattered throughout his essays, reviews, and letters—established him as one of the foremost romantic literary theorists of his time. His emphasis on pleasure rather than on truth in art, on the indefinite image rather than on the discursive statement, on the priority of music and sound over sense—all of these *obiter dicta*,° however unoriginal, inspired his work, dazzled his contemporaries, and helped to lay the groundwork for aestheticism, surrealism, and symbolism in the *fin de siècle*.° In emphasizing mood and feeling, especially melancholy and pathos, he touched the nerve of his century. Even in our era of polemical feminism, it is not difficult for many people to regard "the death of the beautiful young woman" as that artistic subject "which most induces the pleasurable excitement of melancholy." Thus readers still seek in him the affective states that Poe cited as the end of art. Nor can there be any doubt that the preoccupation today with the lyric form owes much

---

obiter dicta: Latin for "incidental remarks," those tossed off while the speaker is actually discussing something else.   *fin de siècle*: French for "end of the century." The phrase refers specifically to the 1890s, or end of the nineteenth century, a decade notable for its emphasis on art for art's sake over the Victorian emphasis on literature with a moral. Poe had embraced the art-for-art's-sake belief fifty years ahead of his time and was a much celebrated writer among French poets of the 1890s in consequence.

to his theory that true poetry inheres in a pleasurable excitement of the soul, or the intensity of an emotional affect, that can be achieved only in a brief lyric. He thought a rhymed poem, not an hour in length, was about all the excitement one could take in a single sitting. And his formalist insistence on a preconceived unity of effect in art has been one of the foundations of the New Criticism as practiced by Ransom, Tate, Brooks, and Warren.° Poe's was essentially a jerry-built aesthetic, manufactured from piecemeal and not always fully understood reading, but in the era of Longfellow's pious moralizing and Emerson's didactic meter-making arguments in verse, it had the impact in America of a revelation of genius.

. . .

The protagonists of Poe's art are men of imagination, exiles from a primal Paradise, voyagers in a strange land—this disease of our material existence. They have their real being in an Ideal World marked by a Unity and Oneness occurring in some primordial far-off antiquity. Thus there is next to no social context in Poe's tales and poems.

Although he lived at a particularly turbulent time in America—while the westering movement was afoot, immigration was constant, urbanization was dawning, abolitionism and slavery were gearing up for the Civil War—Poe was never interested in giving reportorial or journalistic accounts of the sociological features of American life. For Poe, the artistic vision that might capture an intuition of paradise was the only thing that mattered. It was his passionate means of trying to unify the fragmented world of fallen reality, to recover from the primal alienation produced by the creation itself. He therefore trafficked in the nostalgia of loss, in an ideality known only in dreams, his substitute for the horrifying actuality of the quotidian life. "Israfel," "Ligeia," "The Fall of the House of Usher," *Pym*, "Annabelle Lee," and "Lenore" all allegorize a longing for immortality, for this lost world of Ideal Existence before birth. Accompanying this nostalgia is a concomitant fear of death and annihilation, with obsessive brooding about physical and psychological decay—the grim phantasm of fear afflicting the reason and bringing it to the point of madness, a fear reflected in his characters' preoccupation with dreams, trances, hypnosis, catalepsy, and metempsychosis. Above all, he longed for a love that survives death, bodily dissolution, and the grave. Art, whether created or appreciated, was a means of transcending the paltry circumstances of the actual and attaining the effect of an intimation of immortality.

From "Poe: The Quest For Supernal Beauty"

Ransom, Tate, Brooks, and Warren: John Crowe Ransom (1888–1974), Allen Tate (1899–1979), Cleanth Brooks (1906–1994), and Robert Penn Warren (1905–1989) were Southern poets who became professors in the 1930s and '40s. After World War II, the G.I. Bill permitted thousands of veterans who had never studied literature before to attend college. With this in mind, Ransom, Tate, Brooks, and Warren developed a "New Criticism," a formalist approach to literature that did not require any knowledge of the author's biography, other literary texts or movements, or cultural history. All it needed was close attention to the work itself. How well that given piece of work (and this criticism worked best for short works, e.g., poems) projected a sense of itself as whole and complete, it accomplished the aim of all well-wrought art: a "unity of effect." New Criticism is also known as Formalism and some further statements on it may be found in the chapter "Critical Approaches to Literature."

FLANNERY O'CONNOR

Mary Flannery O'Connor (1925–1964) was born in Savannah, Georgia, but spent most of her life in the small town of Milledgeville. While attending Georgia State College for Women, she won a local reputation for her fledgling stories and satiric cartoons. After graduating in 1945, she went on to study at the University of Iowa, where she earned an M.F.A. in 1947. Diagnosed in 1950 with disseminated lupus, the same incurable illness that had killed her father, O'Connor returned home and spent the last decade of her life living with her mother in Milledgeville. Back on the family dairy farm, she wrote, maintained an extensive literary correspondence, raised peacocks, and underwent medical treatment. When her illness occasionally went into a period of remission, she made trips to lecture and read her stories to college audiences. Her health declined rapidly after surgery early in 1964 for an unrelated complaint. She died at thirty-nine.

O'Connor is unusual among modern American writers in the depth of her Christian vision. A devout Roman Catholic, she attended mass daily while growing up and living in the largely Protestant South. As a latter-day satirist in the manner of Jonathan Swift, O'Connor levels the eye of an uncompromising moralist on the violence and spiritual disorder of the modern world, focusing on what she calls "the action of grace in territory held largely by the devil." She is sometimes called a "Southern Gothic" writer because of her fascination with grotesque incidents and characters. Throughout her career she depicted the South as a troubled region in which the social, racial, and religious status quo that had existed since before the Civil War was coming to a violent end. Despite the inherent seriousness of her religious and social themes, O'Connor's mordant and frequently outrageous humor is everywhere apparent. Her combination of profound vision and dark comedy is the distinguishing characteristic of her literary sensibilities.

O'Connor's published work includes two short novels, Wise Blood (1952) and The Violent Bear It Away (1960), and two collections of short stories, A Good Man Is Hard to Find (1955) and Everything That Rises Must Converge, published posthumously in 1965. A collection of essays and miscellaneous prose, Mystery and Manners (1969), and her selected letters, The Habit of Being (1979), reveal an innate cheerfulness and engaging personal warmth that are not always apparent in her fiction. The Complete Stories of Flannery O'Connor *was posthumously awarded the National Book Award in 1971.*

~ STORIES ~

GOOD COUNTRY PEOPLE   1955

Besides the neutral expression that she wore when she was alone, Mrs. Freeman had two others, forward and reverse, that she used for all her human dealings. Her forward expression was steady and driving like the advance of a heavy truck. Her eyes never swerved to left or right but turned as the story turned as if they followed a yellow line down the center of it. She seldom used the other expression because it was not often necessary for her to retract a statement, but when she did, her face came to a complete stop, there was an almost imperceptible movement of her black eyes, during which they seemed to be receding, and then the observer would see that Mrs. Freeman, though she might stand there as real as several grain sacks thrown on top of each other, was no longer there in spirit. As for getting anything across to her when this was the case, Mrs. Hopewell had given it up. She might talk her head off. Mrs. Freeman could never be brought to admit herself wrong on any point. She would stand there and if she could be brought to say anything, it was something like, "Well, I wouldn't of said it was and I wouldn't of said it wasn't," or letting her gaze range over the top kitchen shelf where there was an assortment of dusty bottles, she might remark, "I see you ain't ate many of them figs you put up last summer."

They carried on their most important business in the kitchen at breakfast. Every morning Mrs. Hopewell got up at seven o'clock and lit her gas heater and Joy's. Joy was her daughter, a large blonde girl who had an artificial leg. Mrs. Hopewell thought of her as a child though she was thirty-two years old and highly educated. Joy would get up while her mother was eating and lumber into the bathroom and slam the door, and before long, Mrs. Freeman would arrive at the back door. Joy would hear her mother call, "Come on in," and then they would talk for a while in low voices that were indistinguishable in the bathroom. By the time Joy came in, they had usually finished the weather report and were on one or the other of Mrs. Freeman's daughters, Glynese or Carramae, Joy called them Glycerin and Caramel. Glynese, a redhead, was eighteen and had many admirers; Carramae, a blonde, was only fifteen but already married and pregnant. She could not keep anything on her stomach. Every morning Mrs. Freeman told Mrs. Hopewell how many times she had vomited since the last report.

Mrs. Hopewell liked to tell people that Glynese and Carramae were two of the finest girls she knew and that Mrs. Freeman was a *lady* and that she was never ashamed to take her anywhere or introduce her to anybody they might meet. Then she would tell how she had happened to hire the Freemans in the first place and how they were a godsend to her and how she had had them four years. The reason for her keeping them so long was that they were not trash. They were good country people. She had telephoned the man whose name they had given as a reference and he had told her that Mr. Freeman was a good farmer but that his wife was the nosiest woman ever to walk the earth. "She's got to be into everything," the man said. "If she don't get there before the dust settles, you can bet she's dead, that's all. She'll want to know all your business. I can stand him real good," he had said, "but me nor my wife neither could have stood that woman one more minute on this place." That had put Mrs. Hopewell off for a few days.

She had hired them in the end because there were no other applicants but she had made up her mind beforehand exactly how she would handle the woman. Since she was the type who had to be into everything, then, Mrs. Hopewell had decided, she would not only let her be into everything, she would *see to it* that she was into everything—she would give her the responsibility of everything, she would put her in charge. Mrs. Hopewell had no bad qualities of her own but she was able to use other people's in such a constructive way that she never felt the lack. She had hired the Freemans and she had kept them four years.

Nothing is perfect. This was one of Mrs. Hopewell's favorite sayings. Another was: that is life! And still another, the most important, was: well, other people have their opinions too. She would make these statements, usually at the table, in a tone of gentle insistence as if no one held them but her, and the large hulking Joy, whose constant outrage had obliterated every expression from her face, would stare just a little to the side of her, her eyes icy blue, with the look of someone who has achieved blindness by an act of will and means to keep it.

When Mrs. Hopewell said to Mrs. Freeman that life was like that, Mrs. Freeman would say, "I always said so myself." Nothing had been arrived at by anyone that had not first been arrived at by her. She was quicker than Mr. Freeman. When Mrs. Hopewell said to her after they had been on the place a while, "You know, you're the wheel behind the wheel," and winked, Mrs. Freeman had said, "I know it. I've always been quick. It's some that are quicker than others."

"Everybody is different," Mrs. Hopewell said.

"Yes, most people is," Mrs. Freeman said.

"It takes all kinds to make the world."

"I always said it did myself."

The girl was used to this kind of dialogue for breakfast and more of it for dinner; sometimes they had it for supper too. When they had no guest they ate in the kitchen because that was easier. Mrs. Freeman always managed to arrive at some point during the meal and to watch them finish it. She would stand in the doorway if it were summer but in the winter she would stand with one elbow on top of the refrigerator and look down on them, or she would stand by the gas heater, lifting the back of her skirt slightly. Occasionally she would stand against the wall and roll her head from side to side. At no time was she in any hurry to leave. All this was very trying on Mrs. Hopewell but she was a woman of great

5

10

patience. She realized that nothing is perfect and that in the Freemans she had good country people and that if, in this day and age, you get good country people, you had better hang onto them.

She had had plenty of experience with trash. Before the Freemans she had averaged one tenant family a year. The wives of these farmers were not the kind you would want to be around you for very long. Mrs. Hopewell, who had divorced her husband long ago, needed someone to walk over the fields with her; and when Joy had to be impressed for these services, her remarks were usually so ugly and her face so glum that Mrs. Hopewell would say, "If you can't come pleasantly, I don't want you at all," to which the girl, standing square and rigid-shouldered with her neck thrust slightly forward, would reply, "If you want me, here I am—LIKE I AM."

Mrs. Hopewell excused this attitude because of the leg (which had been shot off in a hunting accident when Joy was ten). It was hard for Mrs. Hopewell to realize that her child was thirty-two now and that for more than twenty years she had had only one leg. She thought of her still as a child because it tore her heart to think instead of the poor stout girl in her thirties who had never danced a step or had any *normal* good times. Her name was really Joy but as soon as she was twenty-one and away from home, she had had it legally changed. Mrs. Hopewell was certain that she had thought and thought until she had hit upon the ugliest name in any language. Then she had gone and had the beautiful name, Joy, changed without telling her mother until after she had done it. Her legal name was Hulga.

When Mrs. Hopewell thought the name, Hulga, she thought of the broad blank hull of a battleship. She would not use it. She continued to call her Joy to which the girl responded but in a purely mechanical way.

Hulga had learned to tolerate Mrs. Freeman who saved her from taking walks with her mother. Even Glynese and Carramae were useful when they occupied attention that might otherwise have been directed at her. At first she had thought she could not stand Mrs. Freeman for she had found that it was not possible to be rude to her. Mrs. Freeman would take on strange resentments and for days together she would be sullen but the source of her displeasure was always obscure; a direct attack, a positive leer, blatant ugliness to her face—these never touched her. And without warning one day, she began calling her Hulga.

She did not call her that in front of Mrs. Hopewell who would have been incensed but when she and the girl happened to be out of the house together, she would say something and add the name Hulga to the end of it, and the big spectacled Joy-Hulga would scowl and redden as if her privacy had been intruded upon. She considered the name her personal affair. She had arrived at it first purely on the basis of its ugly sound and then the full genius of its fitness had struck her. She had a vision of the name working like the ugly sweating Vulcan who stayed in the furnace and to whom, presumably, the goddess had to come when called. She saw it as the name of her highest creative act. One of her major triumphs was that her mother had not been able to turn her dust into Joy, but the greater one was that she had been able to turn it herself into Hulga. However, Mrs. Freeman's relish for using the name only irritated her. It was as if Mrs. Freeman's beady steel-pointed eyes had penetrated far enough behind her face to reach some secret fact. Something about her seemed to fascinate Mrs. Freeman and then one day Hulga realized that it was the artificial leg. Mrs. Freeman had a special fondness for the details of secret infections, hidden deformities, assaults upon children. Of diseases, she preferred the lingering or incurable. Hulga had heard Mrs. Hopewell give her the details of the hunting accident, how the leg had been literally blasted off, how she had never lost consciousness. Mrs. Freeman could listen to it any time as if it had happened an hour ago.

When Hulga stumped into the kitchen in the morning (she could walk without making the awful noise but she made it—Mrs. Hopewell was certain—because it was ugly-sounding), she glanced at them and did not speak. Mrs. Hopewell would be in her red kimono with her hair tied around her head in rags. She would be sitting at the table, finishing her breakfast and Mrs. Freeman would be hanging by her elbow outward from the refrigerator, looking down at the table. Hulga always put her eggs on the stove to boil and then stood over them with her arms folded, and Mrs. Hopewell would look at her—a kind of indirect gaze divided between her and Mrs. Freeman—and would think that if she would only keep herself up a little, she wouldn't be so bad looking. There was nothing wrong with her face that a pleasant expression wouldn't help. Mrs. Hopewell said that people who looked on the bright side of things would be beautiful even if they were not.

Whenever she looked at Joy this way, she could not help but feel that it would have been better if the child had not taken the Ph.D. It had certainly not brought her out any and now that she had it, there was no more excuse for her to go to school again. Mrs. Hopewell thought it was nice for girls to go to school to have a good time but Joy had "gone through." Anyhow, she would not have been strong enough to go again. The doctors had told Mrs. Hopewell that with the best of care, Joy might see forty-five. She had a weak heart. Joy had made it plain that if it had not been for this condition, she would be far from these red hills and good country people. She would be in a university lecturing to people who knew what she was talking about. And Mrs. Hopewell could very well picture her there, looking like a scarecrow and lecturing to more of the same. Here she went about all day in a six-year-old skirt and a yellow sweat shirt with a faded cowboy on a horse embossed on it. She thought this was funny; Mrs. Hopewell thought it was idiotic and showed simply that she was still a child. She was brilliant but she didn't have a grain of sense. It seemed to Mrs. Hopewell that every year she grew less like other people and more like herself—bloated, rude, and squint-eyed. And she said such strange things! To her own mother she had said—without warning, without excuse, standing up in the middle of a meal with her face purple and her mouth half full—"Woman! do you ever look inside? Do you ever look inside and see what you are *not*? God!" she had cried sinking down again and staring at her plate, "Malebranche was right: we are not our own light. We are not our own light!" Mrs. Hopewell had no idea to this day what brought that on. She had only made the remark, hoping Joy would take it in, that a smile never hurt anyone.

The girl had taken the Ph.D. in philosophy and this left Mrs. Hopewell at a complete loss. You could say, "My daughter is a nurse," or "My daughter is a schoolteacher," or even, "My daughter is a chemical engineer." You could not say, "My daughter is a philosopher." That was something that had ended with the Greeks and Romans. All day Joy sat on her neck in a deep chair, reading. Sometimes she went for walks but she didn't like dogs or cats or birds or flowers or nature or nice young men. She looked at nice young men as if she could smell their stupidity.

One day Mrs. Hopewell had picked up one of the books the girl had just put 20 down and opening it at random, she read, "Science, on the other hand, has to assert its soberness and seriousness afresh and declare that it is concerned solely with what-is. Nothing—how can it be for science anything but a horror and a phantasm? If science is right, then one thing stands firm: science wishes to know nothing of nothing. Such is after all the strictly scientific approach to Nothing. We know it by wishing to know nothing of Nothing." These words had been underlined with a blue pencil and they worked on Mrs. Hopewell like some evil incantation in gibberish. She shut the book quickly and went out of the room as if she were having a chill.

This morning when the girl came in, Mrs. Freeman was on Carramae. "She thrown up four times after supper," she said, "and was up twict in the night after three o'clock. Yesterday she didn't do nothing but ramble in the bureau drawer. All she did. Stand up there and see what she could run up on."

"She's got to eat," Mrs. Hopewell muttered, sipping her coffee, while she watched Joy's back at the stove. She was wondering what the child had said to the Bible salesman. She could not imagine what kind of a conversation she could possibly have had with him.

He was a tall gaunt hatless youth who had called yesterday to sell them a Bible. He had appeared at the door, carrying a large black suitcase that weighted him so heavily on one side that he had to brace himself against the door facing. He seemed on the point of collapse but he said in a cheerful voice, "Good morning, Mrs. Cedars!" and set the suitcase down on the mat. He was not a bad-looking young man though he had on a bright blue suit and yellow socks that were not pulled up far enough. He had prominent face bones and a streak of sticky-looking brown hair falling across his forehead.

"I'm Mrs. Hopewell," she said.

"Oh!" he said, pretending to look puzzled but with his eyes sparkling, "I saw 25 it said 'The Cedars' on the mailbox so I thought you was Mrs. Cedars!" and he burst out in a pleasant laugh. He picked up the satchel and under cover of a pant, he fell forward into her hall. It was rather as if the suitcase had moved first, jerking him after it. "Mrs. Hopewell!" he said and grabbed her hand. "I hope you are well!" and he laughed again and then all at once his face sobered completely. He paused and gave her a straight earnest look and said, "Lady, I've come to speak of serious things."

"Well, come in," she muttered, none too pleased because her dinner was almost ready. He came into the parlor and sat down on the edge of a straight chair and put the suitcase between his feet and glanced around the room as if he were sizing her up by it. Her silver gleamed on the two sideboards; she decided he had never been in a room as elegant as this.

"Mrs. Hopewell," he began, using her name in a way that sounded almost intimate, "I know you believe in Chrustian service."

"Well yes," she murmured.

"I know," he said and paused, looking very wise with his head cocked on one side, "that you're a good woman. Friends have told me."

Mrs. Hopewell never liked to be taken for a fool. "What are you selling?" she   30 asked.

"Bibles," the young man said and his eye raced around the room before he added, "I see you have no family Bible in your parlor, I see that is the one lack you got!"

Mrs. Hopewell could not say, "My daughter is an atheist and won't let me keep the Bible in the parlor." She said, stiffening slightly, "I keep my Bible by my bedside." This was not the truth. It was in the attic somewhere.

"Lady," he said, "the word of God ought to be in the parlor."

"Well, I think that's a matter of taste," she began. "I think . . ."

"Lady," he said, "for a Chrustian, the word of God ought to be in every room   35 in the house besides in his heart. I know you're a Chrustian because I can see it in every line of your face."

She stood up and said, "Well, young man, I don't want to buy a Bible and I smell my dinner burning."

He didn't get up. He began to twist his hands and looking down at them, he said softly, "Well lady, I'll tell you the truth—not many people want to buy one nowadays and besides, I know I'm real simple. I don't know how to say a thing but to say it. I'm just a country boy." He glanced up into her unfriendly face. "People like you don't like to fool with country people like me!"

"Why!" she cried, "good country people are the salt of the earth! Besides, we all have different ways of doing, it takes all kinds to make the world go 'round. That's life!"

"You said a mouthful," he said.

"Why, I think there aren't enough good country people in the world!" she   40 said, stirred. "I think that's what's wrong with it!"

His face had brightened. "I didn't inraduce myself," he said. "I'm Manley Pointer from out in the country around Willohobie, not even from a place, just from near a place."

"You wait a minute," she said. "I have to see about my dinner." She went out to the kitchen and found Joy standing near the door where she had been listening.

"Get rid of the salt of the earth," she said, "and let's eat."

Mrs. Hopewell gave her a pained look and turned the heat down under the vegetables. "I can't be rude to anybody," she murmured and went back into the parlor.

He had opened the suitcase and was sitting with a Bible on each knee.   45

"You might as well put those up," she told him. "I don't want one."

"I appreciate your honesty," he said. "You don't see any more real honest people unless you go way out in the country."

"I know," she said, "real genuine folks!" Through the crack in the door she heard a groan.

"I guess a lot of boys come telling you they're working their way through college," he said, "but I'm not going to tell you that. Somehow," he said, "I don't want to go to college. I want to devote my live to Chrustian service. See," he said, lowering his voice, "I got this heart condition. I may not live long. When you know it's something wrong with you and you may not live long, well then, lady . . ." He paused, with his mouth open, and stared at her.

He and Joy had the same condition! She knew that her eyes were filling with tears but she collected herself quickly and murmured, "Won't you stay for dinner? We'd love to have you!" and was sorry the instant she heard herself say it.

"Yes mam," he said in an abashed voice, "I would sher love to do that!"

Joy had given him one look on being introduced to him and then throughout the meal had not glanced at him again. He had addressed several remarks to her, which she had pretended not to hear. Mrs. Hopewell could not understand deliberate rudeness, although she lived with it, and she felt she had always to overflow with hospitality to make up for Joy's lack of courtesy. She urged him to talk about himself and he did. He said he was the seventh child of twelve and that his father had been crushed under a tree when he himself was eight year old. He had been crushed very badly, in fact, almost cut in two and was practically not recognizable. His mother had got along the best she could by hard working and she had always seen that her children went to Sunday School and that they read the Bible every evening. He was now nineteen year old and he had been selling Bibles for four months. In that time he had sold seventy-seven Bibles and had the promise of two more sales. He wanted to become a missionary because he thought that was the way you could do most for people. "He who losest his life shall find it," he said simply and he was so sincere, so genuine and earnest that Mrs. Hopewell would not for the world have smiled. He prevented his peas from sliding onto the table by blocking them with a piece of bread which he later cleaned his plate with. She could see Joy observing sidewise how he handled his knife and fork and she saw too that every few minutes, the boy would dart a keen appraising glance at the girl as if he were trying to attract her attention.

After dinner Joy cleared the dishes off the table and disappeared and Mrs. Hopewell was left to talk with him. He told her again about his childhood and his father's accident and about various things that had happened to him. Every five minutes or so she would stifle a yawn. He sat for two hours until finally she told him she must go because she had an appointment in town. He packed his Bibles and thanked her and prepared to leave, but in the doorway he stopped and wrung her hand and said that not on any of his trips had he met a lady as nice as her and he asked if he could come again. She had said she would always be happy to see him.

50

Joy had been standing in the road, apparently looking at something in the distance, when he came down the steps toward her, bent to the side with his heavy valise. He stopped where she was standing and confronted her directly. Mrs. Hopewell could not hear what he said but she trembled to think what Joy would say to him. She could see that after a minute Joy said something and that then the boy began to speak again, making an excited gesture with his free hand. After a minute Joy said something else at which the boy began to speak once more. Then to her amazement, Mrs. Hopewell saw the two of them walk off together, toward the gate. Joy had walked all the way to the gate with him and Mrs. Hopewell could not imagine what they had said to each other, and she had not yet dared to ask.

Mrs. Freeman was insisting upon her attention. She had moved from the refrigerator to the heater so that Mrs. Hopewell had to turn and face her in order to seem to be listening. "Glynese gone out with Harvey Hill again last night," she said. "She had this sty."

"Hill," Mrs. Hopewell said absently, "is that the one who works in the garage?"

"Nome, he's the one that goes to chiropracter school," Mrs. Freeman said. "She had this sty. Been had it two days. So she says when he brought her in the other night he says, 'Lemme get rid of that sty for you,' and she says, 'How?' and he says, 'You just lay yourself down acrost the seat of that car and I'll show you.' So she done it and he popped her neck. Kept on a-popping it several times until she made him quit. This morning," Mrs. Freeman said, "she ain't got no sty. She ain't got no traces of a sty."

"I never heard of that before," Mrs. Hopewell said.

"He ast her to marry him before the Ordinary," Mrs. Freeman went on, "and she told him she wasn't going to be married in no *office*."

"Well, Glynese is a fine girl," Mrs. Hopewell said. "Glynese and Carramae are both fine girls."

"Carramae said when her and Lyman was married Lyman said it sure felt sacred to him. She said he said he wouldn't take five hundred dollars for being married by a preacher."

"How much would he take?" the girl asked from the stove.

"He said he wouldn't take five hundred dollars," Mrs. Freeman repeated.

"Well we all have work to do," Mrs. Hopewell said.

"Lyman said it just felt more sacred to him," Mrs. Freeman said. "The doctor wants Carramae to eat prunes. Says instead of medicine. Says them cramps is coming from pressure. You know where I think it is?"

"She'll be better in a few weeks," Mrs. Hopewell said.

"In the tube," Mrs. Freeman said. "Else she wouldn't be as sick as she is."

Hulga had cracked her two eggs into a saucer and was bringing them to the table along with a cup of coffee that she had filled too full. She sat down carefully and began to eat, meaning to keep Mrs. Freeman there by questions if for any reason she showed an inclination to leave. She could perceive her mother's eye on her. The first round-about question would be about the Bible salesman and she did not wish to bring it on. "How did he pop her neck?" she asked.

Mrs. Freeman went into a description of how he had popped her neck. She said he owned a '55 Mercury but that Glynese said she would rather marry a man with only a '36 Plymouth who would be married by a preacher. The girl asked what if he had a '32 Plymouth and Mrs. Freeman said what Glynese had said was a '36 Plymouth.

Mrs. Hopewell said there were not many girls with Glynese's common sense. 70 She said what she admired in those girls was their common sense. She said that reminded her that they had had a nice visitor yesterday, a young man selling Bibles. "Lord," she said, "he bored me to death but he was so sincere and genuine I couldn't be rude to him. He was just good country people, you know," she said, "—just the salt of the earth."

"I seen him walk up," Mrs. Freeman said, "and then later—I seen him walk off," and Hulga could feel the slight shift in her voice, the slight insinuation, that he had not walked off alone, had he? Her face remained expressionless but the color rose into her neck and she seemed to swallow it down with the next spoonful of egg. Mrs. Freeman was looking at her as if they had a secret together.

"Well, it takes all kinds of people to make the world go 'round," Mrs. Hopewell said. "It's very good we aren't all alike."

"Some people are more alike than others," Mrs. Freeman said.

Hulga got up and stumped, with about twice the noise that was necessary, into her room and locked the door. She was to meet the Bible salesman at ten o'clock at the gate. She had thought about it half the night. She had started thinking of it as a great joke and then she had begun to see profound implications in it. She had lain in bed imagining dialogues for them that were insane on the surface but that reached below to depths that no Bible salesman would be aware of. Their conversation yesterday had been of this kind.

He had stopped in front of her and had simply stood there. His face was 75 bony and sweaty and bright, with a little pointed nose in the center of it, and his look was different from what it had been at the dinner table. He was gazing at her with open curiosity, with fascination, like a child watching a new fantastic animal at the zoo, and he was breathing as if he had run a great distance to reach her. His gaze seemed somehow familiar but she could not think where she had been regarded with it before. For almost a minute he didn't say anything. Then on what seemed an insuck of breath, he whispered, "You ever ate a chicken that was two days old?"

The girl looked at him stonily. He might have just put this question up for consideration at the meeting of a philosophical association. "Yes," she presently replied as if she had considered it from all angles.

"It must have been mighty small!" he said triumphantly and shook all over with little nervous giggles, getting very red in the face, and subsiding finally into his gaze of complete admiration, while the girl's expression remained exactly the same.

"How old are you?" he asked softly.

She waited sometime before she answered. Then in a flat voice she said, "Seventeen."

His smiles came in succession like waves breaking on the surface of a little lake. "I see you got a wooden leg," he said. "I think you're brave. I think you're real sweet."

The girl stood blank and solid and silent.

"Walk to the gate with me," he said. "You're a brave sweet little thing and I liked you the minute I seen you walk in the door."

Hulga began to move forward.

"What's your name?" he asked, smiling down on the top of her head.

"Hulga," she said.

"Hulga," he murmured, "Hulga. Hulga. I never heard of anybody name Hulga before. You're shy, aren't you, Hulga?" he asked.

She nodded, watching his large red hand on the handle of the giant valise.

"I like girls that wear glasses," he said. "I think a lot. I'm not like these people that a serious thought don't ever enter their heads. It's because I may die."

"I may die too," she said suddenly and looked up at him. His eyes were very small and brown, glittering feverishly.

"Listen," he said, "don't you think some people was meant to meet on account of what all they got in common and all? Like they both think serious thoughts and all?" He shifted the valise to his other hand so that the hand nearest her was free. He caught hold of her elbow and shook it a little. "I don't work on Saturday," he said. "I like to walk in the woods and see what Mother Nature is wearing. O'er the hills and far away. Pic-nics and things. Couldn't we go on a pic-nic tomorrow? Say yes, Hulga," he said and gave her a dying look as if he felt his insides about to drop out of him. He had even seemed to sway slightly toward her.

During the night she had imagined that she seduced him. She imagined that the two of them walked on the place until they came to the storage barn beyond the two back fields and there, she imagined, that things came to such a pass that she very easily seduced him and that then, of course, she had to reckon with his remorse. True genius can get an idea across even to an inferior mind. She imagined that she took his remorse in hand and changed it into a deeper understanding of life. She took all his shame away and turned it into something useful.

She set off for the gate at exactly ten o'clock, escaping without drawing Mrs. Hopewell's attention. She didn't take anything to eat, forgetting that food is usually taken on a pic-nic. She wore a pair of slacks and a dirty white shirt, and as an afterthought, she had put some Vapex on the collar of it since she did not own any perfume. When she reached the gate no one was there.

She looked up and down the empty highway and had the furious feeling that she had been tricked, that he had only meant to make her walk to the gate after the idea of him. Then suddenly he stood up, very tall, from behind a bush on the opposite embankment. Smiling, he lifted his hat which was new and wide-brimmed. He had not worn it yesterday and she wondered if he had bought it for the occasion. It was toast-colored with a red and white band around it and was slightly too large for him. He stepped from behind the bush still carrying the black valise. He had on the same suit and the same yellow socks sucked down in his shoes from walking. He crossed the highway and said, "I knew you'd come!"

The girl wondered acidly how he had known this. She pointed to the valise and asked, "Why did you bring your Bibles?"

He took her elbow, smiling down on her as if he could not stop. "You can never tell when you'll need the word of God, Hulga," he said. She had a moment in which she doubted that this was actually happening and then they began to climb the embankment. They went down into the pasture toward the woods. The boy walked lightly by her side, bouncing on his toes. The valise did not seem to be heavy today; he even swung it. They crossed half the pasture without saying anything and then, putting his hand easily on the small of her back, he asked softly, "Where does your wooden leg join on?"

She turned an ugly red and glared at him and for an instant the boy looked abashed. "I didn't mean you no harm," he said. "I only meant you're so brave and all. I guess God takes care of you."

"No," she said, looking forward and walking fast, "I don't even believe in God."

At this he stopped and whistled. "No!" he exclaimed as if he were too aston-ished to say anything else.

She walked on and in a second he was bouncing at her side, fanning with his hat. "That's very unusual for a girl," he remarked, watching her out of the corner of his eye. When they reached the edge of the wood, he put his hand on her back again and drew her against him without a word and kissed her heavily.

The kiss, which had more pressure than feeling behind it, produced that extra surge of adrenaline in the girl that enables one to carry a packed trunk out of a burning house, but in her, the power went at once to the brain. Even before he released her, her mind, clear and detached and ironic anyway, was regarding him from a great distance, with amusement but with pity. She had never been kissed before and she was pleased to discover that it was an unexceptional expe-rience and all a matter of the mind's control. Some people might enjoy drain water if they were told it was vodka. When the boy, looking expectant but un-certain, pushed her gently away, she turned and walked on, saying nothing as if such business, for her, were common enough.

He came along panting at her side, trying to help her when he saw a root that she might trip over. He caught and held back the long swaying blades of thorn vine until she had passed beyond them. She led the way and he came breathing heavily behind her. Then they came out on a sunlit hillside, sloping softly into another one a little smaller. Beyond, they could see the rusted top of the old barn where the extra hay was stored.

The hill was sprinkled with small pink weeds. "Then you ain't saved?" he asked suddenly, stopping.

The girl smiled. It was the first time she had smiled at him at all. "In my economy," she said, "I'm saved and you are damned but I told you I didn't be-lieve in God."

Nothing seemed to destroy the boy's look of admiration. He gazed at her now as if the fantastic animal at the zoo had put its paw through the bars and given him a loving poke. She thought he looked as if he wanted to kiss her again and she walked on before he had the chance.

"Ain't there somewhere we can sit down sometime?" he murmured, his 105 voice softening toward the end of the sentence.

"In that barn," she said.

They made for it rapidly as if it might slide away like a train. It was a large two-story barn, cool and dark inside. The boy pointed up the ladder that led into the loft and said, "It's too bad we can't go up there."

"Why can't we?" she asked.

"Yer leg," he said reverently.

The girl gave him a contemptuous look and putting both hands on the 110 ladder, she climbed it while he stood below, apparently awestruck. She pulled herself expertly through the opening and then looked down at him and said, "Well, come on if you're coming," and he began to climb the ladder, awkwardly bringing the suitcase with him.

"We won't need the Bible," she observed.

"You never can tell," he said, panting. After he had got into the loft, he was a few seconds catching his breath. She had sat down in a pile of straw. A wide sheath of sunlight, filled with dust particles, slanted over her. She lay back against a bale, her face turned away, looking out the front opening of the barn where hay was thrown from a wagon into the loft. The two pink-speckled hillsides lay back against a dark ridge of woods. The sky was cloudless and cold blue. The boy dropped down by her side and put one arm under her and the other over her and began methodically kissing her face, making little noises like a fish. He did not remove his hat but it was pushed far enough back not to interfere. When her glasses got in his way, he took them off of her and slipped them into his pocket.

The girl at first did not return any of the kisses but presently she began to and after she had put several on his cheek, she reached his lips and remained there, kissing him again and again as if she were trying to draw all the breath out of him. His breath was clear and sweet like a child's and the kisses were sticky like a child's. He mumbled about loving her and about knowing when he first seen her that he loved her, but the mumbling was like the sleepy fretting of a child being put to sleep by his mother. Her mind, throughout this, never stopped or lost itself for a second to her feelings. "You ain't said you loved me none," he whispered finally, pulling back from her. "You got to say that."

She looked away from him off into the hollow sky and then down at a black ridge and then down farther into what appeared to be two green swelling lakes. She didn't realize he had taken her glasses but this landscape could not seem exceptional to her for she seldom paid any close attention to her surroundings.

"You got to say it," he repeated. "You got to say you love me." 115

She was always careful how she committed herself. "In a sense," she began, "if you use the word loosely, you might say that. But it's not a word I use. I don't have illusions. I'm one of those people who see through to nothing."

The boy was frowning. "You got to say it. I said it and you got to say it," he said.

The girl looked at him almost tenderly. "You poor baby," she murmured. "It's just as well you don't understand," and she pulled him by the neck, face-down, against her. "We are all damned," she said, "but some of us have taken off our blindfolds and see that there's nothing to see. It's a kind of salvation."

The boy's astonished eyes looked blankly through the ends of her hair. "Okay," he almost whined, "but do you love me or don'tcher?"

"Yes," she said and added, "in a sense. But I must tell you something. There mustn't be anything dishonest between us." She lifted his head and looked him in the eye. "I am thirty years old," she said. "I have a number of degrees." 120

The boy's look was irritated but dogged. "I don't care," he said. "I don't care a thing about what all you done. I just want to know if you love me or don'tcher?" and he caught her to him and wildly planted her face with kisses until she said, "Yes, yes."

"Okay then," he said, letting her go. "Prove it."

She smiled, looking dreamily out on the shifty landscape. She had seduced him without even making up her mind to try. "How?" she asked, feeling that he should be delayed a little.

He leaned over and put his lips to her ear. "Show me where your wooden leg joins on," he whispered.

The girl uttered a sharp little cry and her face instantly drained of color. 125 The obscenity of the suggestion was not what shocked her. As a child she had sometimes been subject to feelings of shame but education had removed the last traces of that as a good surgeon scrapes for cancer; she would no more have felt it over what he was asking than she would have believed in his Bible. But she was as sensitive about the artificial leg as a peacock about his tail. No one ever touched it but her. She took care of it as someone else would his soul, in private and almost with her own eyes turned away. "No," she said.

"I known it," he muttered, sitting up. "You're just playing me for a sucker."

"Oh no no!" she cried. "It joins on at the knee. Only at the knee. Why do you want to see it?"

The boy gave her a long penetrating look. "Because," he said, "it's what makes you different. You ain't like anybody else."

She sat staring at him. There was nothing about her face or her round freezing-blue eyes to indicate that this had moved her; but she felt as if her heart had stopped and left her mind to pump her blood. She decided that for the first time in her life she was face to face with real innocence. This boy, with an in-stinct that came from beyond wisdom, had touched the truth about her. When after a minute, she said in a hoarse high voice, "All right," it was like surren-dering to him completely. It was like losing her own life and finding it again, miraculously, in his.

Very gently he began to roll the slack leg up. The artificial limb, in a white 130 sock and brown flat shoe, was bound in a heavy material like canvas and ended in an ugly jointure where it was attached to the stump. The boy's face and his voice were entirely reverent as he uncovered it and said, "Now show me how to take it off and on."

She took it off for him and put it back on again and then he took it off himself, handling it as tenderly as if it were a real one. "See!" he said with a delighted child's face. "Now I can do it myself!"

"Put it back on," she said. She was thinking that she would run away with him and that every night he would take the leg off and every morning put it back on again. "Put it back on," she said.

"Not yet," he murmured, setting it on its foot out of her reach. "Leave it off for a while. You got me instead."

She gave a little cry of alarm but he pushed her down and began to kiss her again. Without the leg she felt entirely dependent on him. Her brain seemed to have stopped thinking altogether and to be about some other function that it was not very good at. Different expressions raced back and forth over her face. Every now and then the boy, his eyes like two steel spikes, would glance behind him where the leg stood. Finally she pushed him off and said, "Put it back on me now."

"Wait," he said. He leaned the other way and pulled the valise toward him 135 and opened it. It had a pale blue spotted lining and there were only two Bibles in it. He took one of these out and opened the cover of it. It was hollow and contained a pocket flask of whiskey, a pack of cards, and a small blue box with printing on it. He laid these out in front of her one at a time in an evenly-spaced row, like one presenting offerings at the shrine of a goddess. He put the blue box in her hand. THIS PRODUCT TO BE USED ONLY FOR THE PREVENTION OF DISEASE, she read, and dropped it. The boy was unscrewing the top of the flask. He stopped and pointed, with a smile, to the deck of cards. It was not an ordinary deck but one with an obscene picture on the back of each card. "Take a swig," he said, offering her the bottle first. He held it in front of her, but like one mesmerized, she did not move.

Her voice when she spoke had an almost pleading sound. "Aren't you," she murmured, "aren't you just good country people?"

The boy cocked his head. He looked as if he were just beginning to understand that she might be trying to insult him. "Yeah," he said, curling his lip slightly, "but it ain't held me back none. I'm as good as you any day in the week."

"Give me my leg," she said.

He pushed it farther away with his foot. "Come on now, let's begin to have us a good time," he said coaxingly. "We ain't got to know one another good yet."

"Give me my leg!" she screamed and tried to lunge for it but he pushed her 140 down easily.

"What's the matter with you all of a sudden?" he asked, frowning as he screwed the top of the flask and put it quickly back inside the Bible. "You just a while ago said you didn't believe in nothing. I thought you was some girl!"

Her face was almost purple. "You're a Christian!" she hissed. "You're a fine Christian! You're just like them all—say one thing and do another. You're a perfect Christian, you're . . ."

The boy's mouth was set angrily. "I hope you don't think," he said in a lofty indignant tone, "that I believe in that crap! I may sell Bibles but I know which end is up and I wasn't born yesterday and I know where I'm going!"

"Give me my leg!" she screeched. He jumped up so quickly that she barely saw him sweep the cards and the blue box into the Bible and throw the Bible into the valise. She saw him grab the leg and then she saw it for an instant slanted forlornly across the inside of the suitcase with a Bible at either side of its opposite ends. He slammed the lid shut and snatched up the valise and swung it down the hole and then stepped through himself.

When all of him had passed but his head, he turned and regarded her with a 145 look that no longer had any admiration in it. "I've gotten a lot of interesting things," he said. "One time I got a woman's glass eye this way. And you needn't to think you'll catch me because Pointer ain't really my name. I use a different name at every house I call at and don't stay nowhere long. And I'll tell you another thing, Hulga," he said, using the name as if he didn't think much of it, "you ain't so smart. I been believing in nothing ever since I was born!" and then the toast-colored hat disappeared down the hole and the girl was left, sitting on the straw in the dusty sunlight. When she turned her churning face toward the opening, she saw his blue figure struggling successfully over the green speckled lake.

Mrs. Hopewell and Mrs. Freeman, who were in the back pasture, digging up onions, saw him emerge a little later from the woods and head across the meadow toward the highway. "Why, that looks like that nice dull young man that tried to sell me a Bible yesterday," Mrs. Hopewell said, squinting. "He must have been selling them to the Negroes back in there. He was so simple," she said, "but I guess the world would be better off if we were all that simple."

Mrs. Freeman's gaze drove forward and just touched him before he disappeared under the hill. Then she returned her attention to the evil-smelling onion shoot she was lifting from the ground. "Some can't be that simple," she said. "I know I never could."

QUESTIONS

1. How significant are the names O'Connor gives her characters in "Good Country People"? Do the names Mrs. Freeman, Mrs. Hopewell, Joy Hopewell, and Manley Pointer suggest—literally or ironically—something about the characters?
2. Why does Joy privately rename herself Hulga?
3. What does Mrs. Hopewell mean by her phrase "good country people," which O'Connor uses as the story's title? Does the significance of this phrase change for the reader by the end of the story?
4. During their brief conversation in front of her house, how many lies does Joy-Hulga tell Manley? What seems to be her motivation in trying to deceive him?
5. How many lies does Manley tell to Joy-Hulga and her mother? What is his motivation in these deceptions?
6. Why does Manley Pointer want to steal something as seemingly useless to him as Joy-Hulga's artificial leg?
7. O'Connor does not describe Joy-Hulga's deeper reaction to the events in "Good Country People." Is it possible to construe the long-term effect Manley's betrayal and final humiliation will have on her?

8. Mrs. Freeman has no direct role in the central plot of "Good Country People." What does her presence add to the story?
9. Critics often describe "Good Country People" as a story full of irony. What ironic elements can you identify?

A GOOD MAN IS HARD TO FIND

The grandmother didn't want to go to Florida. She wanted to visit some of her connections in east Tennessee and she was seizing at every chance to change Bailey's mind. Bailey was the son she lived with, her only boy. He was sitting on the edge of his chair at the table, bent over the orange sports section of the *Journal*. "Now look here, Bailey," she said, "see here, read this," and she stood with one hand on her thin hip and the other rattling the newspaper at his bald head. "Here this fellow that calls himself The Misfit is aloose from the Federal Pen and headed toward Florida and you read here what it says he did to these people. Just you read it. I wouldn't take my children in any direction with a criminal like that aloose in it. I couldn't answer to my conscience if I did."

Bailey didn't look up from his reading so she wheeled around then and faced the children's mother, a young woman in slacks, whose face was as broad and innocent as a cabbage and was tied around with a green head-kerchief that had two points on the top like rabbit's ears. She was sitting on the sofa, feeding the baby his apricots out of a jar. "The children have been to Florida before," the old lady said. "You all ought to take them somewhere else for a change so they would see different parts of the world and be broad. They never have been to east Tennessee."

The children's mother didn't seem to hear her but the eight-year-old boy, John Wesley, a stocky child with glasses, said, "If you don't want to go to Florida, why dontcha stay at home?" He and the little girl, June Star, were reading the funny papers on the floor.

"She wouldn't stay at home to be queen for a day," June Star said without raising her yellow head.

"Yes and what would you do if this fellow, The Misfit, caught you?" the grandmother said.   5

"I'd smack his face," John Wesley said.

"She wouldn't stay at home for a million bucks," June Star said. "Afraid she'd miss something. She has to go everywhere we go."

"All right, Miss," the grandmother said. "Just remember that the next time you want me to curl your hair."

June Star said her hair was naturally curly.

The next morning the grandmother was the first one in the car, ready to go.   10
She had her big black valise that looked like the head of a hippopotamus in one corner, and underneath it she was hiding a basket with Pitty Sing, the cat, in it. She didn't intend for the cat to be left alone in the house for three days because he would miss her too much and she was afraid he might brush against one of the gas burners and accidentally asphyxiate himself. Her son, Bailey, didn't like to arrive at a motel with a cat.

She sat in the middle of the back seat with John Wesley and June Star on either side of her. Bailey and the children's mother and the baby sat in front and they left Atlanta at eight forty-five with the mileage on the car at 55890. The grandmother wrote this down because she thought it would be interesting to say how many miles they had been when they got back. It took them twenty minutes to reach the outskirts of the city.

The old lady settled herself comfortably, removing her white cotton gloves and putting them up with her purse on the shelf in front of the back window. The children's mother still had on slacks and still had her hair tied up in a green kerchief, but the grandmother had on a navy blue straw sailor hat with a bunch of white violets on the brim and a navy blue dress with a small white dot in the print. Her collars and cuffs were white organdy trimmed with lace and at her neckline she had pinned a purple spray of cloth violets containing a sachet. In case of an accident, anyone seeing her dead on the highway would know at once that she was a lady.

She said she thought it was going to be a good day for driving, neither too hot nor too cold, and she cautioned Bailey that the speed limit was fifty-five miles an hour and that the patrolmen hid themselves behind billboards and small clumps of trees and sped out after you before you had a chance to slow down. She pointed out interesting details of the scenery: Stone Mountain; the blue granite that in some places came up to both sides of the highway; the brilliant red clay banks slightly streaked with purple; and the various crops that made rows of green lace-work on the ground. The trees were full of silver-white sunlight and the meanest of them sparkled. The children were reading comic magazines and their mother had gone back to sleep.

"Let's go through Georgia fast so we won't have to look at it much," John Wesley said.

"If I were a little boy," said the grandmother, "I wouldn't talk about my native state that way. Tennessee has the mountains and Georgia has the hills."   15

"Tennessee is just a hillbilly dumping ground," John Wesley said, "and Georgia is a lousy state too."

"You said it," June Star said.

"In my time," said the grandmother, folding her thin veined fingers, "children were more respectful of their native states and their parents and everything else. People did right then. Oh look at the cute little pickaninny!" she said and pointed to a Negro child standing in the door of a shack. "Wouldn't that make a picture, now?" she asked and they all turned and looked at the little Negro out of the back window. He waved.

"He didn't have any britches on," June Star said.

"He probably didn't have any," the grandmother explained. "Little niggers   20
in the country don't have things like we do. If I could paint, I'd paint that picture," she said.

The children exchanged comic books.

The grandmother offered to hold the baby and the children's mother passed him over the front seat to her. She set him on her knee and bounced him and told him about the things they were passing. She rolled her eyes and screwed up her mouth and stuck her leathery thin face into his smooth bland one. Occasionally he gave her a faraway smile. They passed a large cotton field with five or six graves fenced in the middle of it, like a small island. "Look at the graveyard!" the grandmother said, pointing it out. "That was the old family burying ground. That belonged to the plantation."

"Where's the plantation?" John Wesley asked.

"Gone With the Wind," said the grandmother. "Ha. Ha."

When the children finished all the comic books they had brought, they   25
opened the lunch and ate it. The grandmother ate a peanut butter sandwich and an olive and would not let the children throw the box and the paper napkins out the window. When there was nothing else to do they played a game by choosing a cloud and making the other two guess what shape it suggested. John Wesley took one the shape of a cow and June Star guessed a cow and John Wesley said, no, an automobile, and June Star said he didn't play fair, and they began to slap each other over the grandmother.

The grandmother said she would tell them a story if they would keep quiet. When she told a story, she rolled her eyes and waved her head and was very dramatic. She said once when she was a maiden lady she had been courted by a Mr. Edgar Atkins Teagarden from Jasper, Georgia. She said he was a very good-looking man and a gentleman and that he brought her a watermelon every Saturday afternoon with his initials cut in it, E. A. T. Well, one Saturday, she said, Mr. Teagarden brought the watermelon and there was nobody at home and he left it on the front porch and returned in his buggy to Jasper, but she never got the watermelon, she said, because a nigger boy ate it when he saw the initials, E. A. T.!

This story tickled John Wesley's funny bone and he giggled and giggled but June Star didn't think it was any good. She said she wouldn't marry a man that just brought her a watermelon on Saturday. The grandmother said she would have done well to marry Mr. Teagarden because he was a gentleman and had bought Coca-Cola stock when it first came out and that he had died only a few years ago, a very wealthy man.

They stopped at The Tower for barbecued sandwiches. The Tower was a part stucco and part wood filling station and dance hall set in a clearing outside of Timothy. A fat man named Red Sammy Butts ran it and there were signs stuck here and there on the building and for miles up and down the highway saying, TRY RED SAMMY'S FAMOUS BARBECUE. NONE LIKE FAMOUS RED SAMMY'S! RED SAM! THE FAT BOY WITH THE HAPPY LAUGH. A VETERAN! RED SAMMY'S YOUR MAN!

Red Sammy was lying on the bare ground outside The Tower with his head under a truck while a gray monkey about a foot high, chained to a small chinaberry tree, chattered nearby. The monkey sprang back into the tree and got on the highest limb as soon as he saw the children jump out of the car and run toward him.

Inside, The Tower was a long dark room with a counter at one end and ta-   30
bles at the other and dancing space in the middle. They all sat down at a board

table next to the nickelodeon and Red Sam's wife, a tall burnt-brown woman with hair and eyes lighter than her skin, came and took their order. The children's mother put a dime in the machine and played "The Tennessee Waltz," and the grandmother said that tune always made her want to dance. She asked Bailey if he would like to dance but he only glared at her. He didn't have a naturally sunny disposition like she did and trips made him nervous. The grandmother's brown eyes were very bright. She swayed her head from side to side and pretended she was dancing in her chair. June Star said play something she could tap to so the children's mother put in another dime and played a fast number and June Star stepped out onto the dance floor and did her tap routine.

"Ain't she cute?" Red Sam's wife said, leaning over the counter. "Would you like to come be my little girl?"

"No I certainly wouldn't," June Star said. "I wouldn't live in a broken-down place like this for a million bucks!" and she ran back to the table.

"Ain't she cute?" the woman repeated, stretching her mouth politely.

"Arn't you ashamed?" hissed the grandmother.

Red Sam came in and told his wife to quit lounging on the counter and 35
hurry up with these people's order. His khaki trousers reached just to his hip bones and his stomach hung over them like a sack of meal swaying under his shirt. He came over and sat down at a table nearby and let out a combination sigh and yodel. "You can't win," he said. "You can't win," and he wiped his sweating red face off with a gray handkerchief. "These days you don't know who to trust," he said. "Ain't that the truth?"

"People are certainly not nice like they used to be," said the grandmother.

"Two fellers come in here last week," Red Sammy said, "driving a Chrysler. It was a old beat-up car but it was a good one and these boys looked all right to me. Said they worked at the mill and you know I let them fellers charge the gas they bought? Now why did I do that?"

"Because you're a good man!" the grandmother said at once.

"Yes'm, I suppose so," Red Sam said as if he were struck with this answer.

His wife brought the orders, carrying the five plates all at once without a 40
tray, two in each hand and one balanced on her arm. "It isn't a soul in this green world of God's that you can trust," she said. "And I don't count nobody out of that, not nobody," she repeated, looking at Red Sammy.

"Did you read about that criminal, The Misfit, that's escaped?" asked the grandmother.

"I wouldn't be a bit surprised if he didn't attact this place right here," said the woman. "If he hears about it being here, I wouldn't be none surprised to see him. If he hears it's two cent in the cash register, I wouldn't be a-tall surprised if he . . . ."

"That'll do," Red Sam said. "Go bring these people their Co'-Colas," and the woman went off to get the rest of the order.

"A good man is hard to find," Red Sammy said. "Everything is getting terrible. I remember the day you could go off and leave your screen door unlatched. Not no more."

He and the grandmother discussed better times. The old lady said that in 45
her opinion Europe was entirely to blame for the way things were now. She said
the way Europe acted you would think we were made of money and Red Sam
said it was no use talking about it, she was exactly right. The children ran outside into the white sunlight and looked at the monkey in the lacy chinaberry
tree. He was busy catching fleas on himself and biting each one carefully between his teeth as if it were a delicacy.

They drove off again into the hot afternoon. The grandmother took cat
naps and woke up every five minutes with her own snoring. Outside of Toombs-
boro she woke up and recalled an old plantation that she had visited in this
neighborhood once when she was a young lady. She said the house had six white
columns across the front and that there was an avenue of oaks leading up to it
and two little wooden trellis arbors on either side in front where you sat down
with your suitor after a stroll in the garden. She recalled exactly which road to
turn off to get to it. She knew that Bailey would not be willing to lose any time
looking at an old house, but the more she talked about it, the more she wanted
to see it once again and find out if the little twin arbors were still standing.
"There was a secret panel in this house," she said craftily, not telling the truth
but wishing that she were, "and the story went that all the family silver was
hidden in it when Sherman° came through but it was never found . . ."

"Hey!" John Wesley said. "Let's go see it! We'll find it! We'll poke all the
woodwork and find it! Who lives there? Where do you turn off at? Hey, Pop,
can't we turn off there?"

"We never have seen a house with a secret panel!" June Star shrieked. "Let's
go to the house with the secret panel! Hey Pop, can't we go see the house with
the secret panel!"

"It's not far from here, I know," the grandmother said. "It wouldn't take over
twenty minutes."

Bailey was looking straight ahead. His jaw was as rigid as a horseshoe. "No," 50
he said.

The children began to yell and scream that they wanted to see the house
with the secret panel. John Wesley kicked the back of the front seat and June
Star hung over her mother's shoulder and whined desperately into her ear that
they never had any fun even on their vacation, that they could never do what
THEY wanted to do. The baby began to scream and John Wesley kicked the
back of the seat so hard that his father could feel the blows in his kidney.

"All right!" he shouted and drew the car to a stop at the side of the road.
"Will you all shut up? Will you all just shut up for one second? If you don't shut
up, we won't go anywhere."

"It would be very educational for them," the grandmother murmured.

Sherman: General William Tecumseh Sherman, Union commander, whose troops burned Atlanta in 1864, then made a devastating march to the sea.

"All right," Bailey said, "but get this: this is the only time we're going to stop for anything like this. This is the one and only time."

"The dirt road that you have to turn down is about a mile back," the grandmother directed. "I marked it when we passed." 55

"A dirt road," Bailey groaned.

After they had turned around and were headed toward the dirt road, the grandmother recalled other points about the house, the beautiful glass over the front doorway and the candle-lamp in the hall. John Wesley said that the secret panel was probably in the fireplace.

"You can't go inside this house," Bailey said. "You don't know who lives there."

"While you all talk to the people in front, I'll run around behind and get in a window," John Wesley suggested.

"We'll all stay in the car," his mother said. 60

They turned onto the dirt road and the car raced roughly along in a swirl of pink dust. The grandmother recalled the times when there were no paved roads and thirty miles was a day's journey. The dirt road was hilly and there were sudden washes in it and sharp curves on dangerous embankments. All at once they would be on a hill, looking down over the blue tops of trees for miles around, then the next minute, they would be in a red depression with the dust-coated trees looking down on them.

"This place had better turn up in a minute," Bailey said, "or I'm going to turn around."

The road looked as if no one had traveled on it for months.

"It's not much farther," the grandmother said and just as she said it, a horrible thought came to her. The thought was so embarrassing that she turned red in the face and her eyes dilated and her feet jumped up, upsetting her valise in the corner. The instant the valise moved, the newspaper top she had over the basket under it rose with a snarl and Pitty Sing, the cat, sprang onto Bailey's shoulder.

The children were thrown to the floor and their mother, clutching the baby, was thrown out the door onto the ground; the old lady was thrown into the front seat. The car turned over once and landed right-side-up in a gulch off the side of the road. Bailey remained in the driver's seat with the cat—gray-striped with a broad white face and an orange nose—clinging to his neck like a caterpillar. 65

As soon as the children saw they could move their arms and legs, they scrambled out of the car, shouting, "We've had an ACCIDENT!" The grandmother was curled up under the dashboard, hoping she was injured so that Bailey's wrath would not come down on her all at once. The horrible thought she had had before the accident was that the house she had remembered so vividly was not in Georgia but in Tennessee.

Bailey removed the cat from his neck with both hands and flung it out the window against the side of a pine tree. Then he got out of the car and started looking for the children's mother. She was sitting against the side of the red gutted ditch, holding the screaming baby, but she only had a cut down her face and a broken shoulder. "We've had an ACCIDENT!" the children screamed in a frenzy of delight.

"But nobody's killed," June Star said with disappointment as the grandmother limped out of the car, her hat still pinned to her head but the broken front brim standing up at a jaunty angle and the violet spray hanging off the side. They all sat down in the ditch, except the children, to recover from the shock. They were all shaking.

"Maybe a car will come along," said the children's mother hoarsely.

"I believe I have injured an organ," said the grandmother, pressing her side, but no one answered her. Bailey's teeth were clattering. He had on a yellow sport shirt with bright blue parrots designed in it and his face was as yellow as the shirt. The grandmother decided that she would not mention that the house was in Tennessee.

The road was about ten feet above and they could see only the tops of the trees on the other side of it. Behind the ditch they were sitting in there were more woods, tall and dark and deep. In a few minutes they saw a car some distance away on top of a hill, coming slowly as if the occupants were watching them. The grandmother stood up and waved both her arms dramatically to attract their attention. The car continued to come on slowly, disappeared around a bend and appeared again, moving even slower, on top of the hill they had gone over. It was a big black battered hearse-like automobile. There were three men in it.

It came to a stop just over them and for some minutes, the driver looked down with a steady expressionless gaze to where they were sitting, and didn't speak. Then he turned his head and muttered something to the other two and they got out. One was a fat boy in black trousers and a red sweat shirt with a silver stallion embossed on the front of it. He moved around on the right side of them and stood staring, his mouth partly open in a kind of loose grin. The other had on khaki pants and a blue striped coat and a gray hat pulled down very low, hiding most of his face. He came around slowly on the left side. Neither spoke.

The driver got out of the car and stood by the side of it, looking down at them. He was an older man than the other two. His hair was just beginning to gray and he wore silver-rimmed spectacles that gave him a scholarly look. He had a long creased face and didn't have on any shirt or undershirt. He had on blue jeans that were too tight for him and was holding a black hat and a gun. The two boys also had guns.

"We've had an ACCIDENT!" the children screamed.

The grandmother had the peculiar feeling that the bespectacled man was someone she knew. His face was as familiar to her as if she had known him all her life but she could not recall who he was. He moved away from the car and began to come down the embankment, placing his feet carefully so that he wouldn't slip. He had on tan and white shoes and no socks, and his ankles were red and thin. "Good afternoon," he said. "I see you all had you a little spill."

70

75

"We turned over twice!" said the grandmother.

"Oncet," he corrected. "We seen it happen. Try their car and see will it run, Hiram," he said quietly to the boy with the gray hat.

"What you got that gun for?" John Wesley asked. "Whatcha gonna do with that gun?"

"Lady," the man said to the children's mother, "would you mind calling them children to sit down by you? Children make me nervous. I want all you all to sit down right together there where you're at."

"What are you telling US what to do for?" June Star asked.

80

Behind them the line of woods gaped like a dark open mouth. "Come here," said their mother.

"Look here now," Bailey began suddenly, "we're in a predicament! We're in . . ."

The grandmother shrieked. She scrambled to her feet and stood staring. "You're The Misfit!" she said. "I recognized you at once!"

"Yes'm," the man said, smiling slightly as if he were pleased in spite of himself to be known, "but it would have been better for all of you, lady, if you hadn't of reckernized me."

Bailey turned his head sharply and said something to his mother that shocked even the children. The old lady began to cry and The Misfit reddened.

85

"Lady," he said, "don't you get upset. Sometimes a man says things he don't mean. I don't reckon he meant to talk to you thataway."

"You wouldn't shoot a lady, would you?" the grandmother said and removed a clean handkerchief from her cuff and began to slap at her eyes with it.

The Misfit pointed the toe of his shoe into the ground and made a little hole and then covered it up again. "I would hate to have to," he said.

"Listen," the grandmother almost screamed, "I know you're a good man. You don't look a bit like you have common blood. I know you must come from nice people!"

"Yes mam," he said, "finest people in the world." When he smiled he showed a row of strong white teeth. "God never made a finer woman than my mother and my daddy's heart was pure gold," he said. The boy with the red sweat shirt had come around behind them and was standing with his gun at his hip. The Misfit squatted down on the ground. "Watch them children, Bobby Lee," he said. "You know they make me nervous." He looked at the six of them huddled together in front of him and he seemed to be embarrassed as if he couldn't think of anything to say. "Ain't a cloud in the sky," he remarked, looking up at it. "Don't see no sun but don't see no cloud neither."

90

"Yes, it's a beautiful day," said the grandmother. "Listen," she said, "you shouldn't call yourself The Misfit because I know you're a good man at heart. I can just look at you and tell."

"Hush!" Bailey yelled. "Hush! Everybody shut up and let me handle this!" He was squatting in the position of a runner about to sprint forward but he didn't move.

"I pre-chate that, lady," The Misfit said and drew a little circle in the ground with the butt of his gun.

"It'll take a half a hour to fix this here car," Hiram called, looking over the raised hood of it.

"Well, first you and Bobby Lee get him and that little boy to step over yonder with you," The Misfit said, pointing to Bailey and John Wesley. "The boys want to ast you something," he said to Bailey. "Would you mind stepping back in them woods there with them?"

"Listen," Bailey began, "we're in a terrible predicament! Nobody realizes what this is," and his voice cracked. His eyes were as blue and intense as the parrots in his shirt and he remained perfectly still.

The grandmother reached up to adjust her hat brim as if she were going to the woods with him but it came off in her hand. She stood staring at it and after a second she let it fall on the ground. Hiram pulled Bailey up by the arm as if he were assisting an old man. John Wesley caught hold of his father's hand and Bobby Lee followed. They went off toward the woods and just as they reached the dark edge, Bailey turned and supporting himself against a gray naked pine trunk, he shouted, "I'll be back in a minute, Mamma, wait on me!"

"Come back this instant!" his mother shrilled but they all disappeared into the woods.

"Bailey Boy!" the grandmother called in a tragic voice but she found she was looking at The Misfit squatting on the ground in front of her. "I just know you're a good man," she said desperately. "You're not a bit common!"

"Nome, I ain't a good man," The Misfit said after a second as if he had considered her statement carefully, "but I ain't the worst in the world neither. My daddy said I was a different breed of dog from my brothers and sisters. 'You know,' Daddy said, 'it's some that can live their whole life out without asking about it and it's others has to know why it is, and this boy is one of the latters. He's going to be into everything!'" He put on his black hat and looked up suddenly and then away deep into the woods as if he were embarrassed again. "I'm sorry I don't have on a shirt before you ladies," he said, hunching his shoulders slightly. "We buried our clothes that we had on when we escaped and we're just making do until we can get better. We borrowed these from some folks we met," he explained.

"That's perfectly all right," the grandmother said. "Maybe Bailey has an extra shirt in his suitcase."

"I'll look and see terrectly," The Misfit said.

"Where are they taking him?" the children's mother screamed.

"Daddy was a card himself," The Misfit said. "You couldn't put anything over on him. He never got in trouble with the Authorities though. Just had the knack of handling them."

"You could be honest too if you'd only try," said the grandmother. "Think how wonderful it would be to settle down and live a comfortable life and not have to think about somebody chasing you all the time."

The Misfit kept scratching in the ground with the butt of his gun as if he were thinking about it. "Yes'm, somebody is always after you," he murmured.

The grandmother noticed how thin his shoulder blades were just behind his hat because she was standing up looking down on him. "Do you ever pray?" she asked.

He shook his head. All she saw was the black hat wiggle between his shoulder blades. "Nome," he said.

There was a pistol shot from the woods, followed closely by another. Then silence. The old lady's head jerked around. She could hear the wind move through the tree tops like a long satisfied insuck of breath. "Bailey Boy!" she called.

"I was a gospel singer for a while," The Misfit said. "I been most everything.   110
Been in the arm service, both land and sea, at home and abroad, been twict married, been an undertaker, been with the railroads, plowed Mother Earth, been in a tornado, seen a man burnt alive oncet," and he looked up at the children's mother and the little girl who were sitting close together, their faces white and their eyes glassy; "I even seen a woman flogged," he said.

"Pray, pray," the grandmother began, "pray, pray . . ."

"I never was a bad boy that I remember of," The Misfit said in an almost dreamy voice, "but somewheres along the line I done something wrong and got sent to the penitentiary. I was buried alive," and he looked up and held her attention to him by a steady stare.

"That's when you should have started to pray," she said. "What did you do to get sent to the penitentiary that first time?"

"Turn to the right, it was a wall," The Misfit said, looking up again at the cloudless sky. "Turn to the left, it was a wall. Look up it was a ceiling, look down it was a floor. I forget what I done, lady. I set there and set there, trying to remember what it was I done and I ain't recalled it to this day. Oncet in a while, I would think it was coming to me, but it never come."

"Maybe they put you in by mistake," the old lady said vaguely.   115

"Nome," he said. "It wasn't no mistake. They had the papers on me."

"You must have stolen something," she said.

The Misfit sneered slightly. "Nobody had nothing I wanted," he said. "It was a head-doctor at the penitentiary said what I had done was kill my daddy but I known that for a lie. My daddy died in nineteen ought nineteen of the epidemic flu and I never had a thing to do with it. He was buried in the Mount Hopewell Baptist churchyard and you can go there and see for yourself."

"If you would pray," the old lady said, "Jesus would help you."

"That's right," The Misfit said.   120

"Well then, why don't you pray?" she asked trembling with delight suddenly.

"I don't want no hep," he said. "I'm doing all right by myself."

Bobby Lee and Hiram came ambling back from the woods. Bobby Lee was dragging a yellow shirt with bright blue parrots in it.

"Thow me that shirt, Bobby Lee," The Misfit said. The shirt came flying at him and landed on his shoulder and he put it on. The grandmother couldn't name what the shirt reminded her of. "No, lady," The Misfit said while he was buttoning it up, "I found out the crime don't matter. You can do one thing or you can do another, kill a man or take a tire off his car, because sooner or later you're going to forget what it was you done and just be punished for it."

The children's mother had begun to make heaving noises as if she couldn't 125 get her breath. "Lady," he asked, "would you and that little girl like to step off yonder with Bobby Lee and Hiram and join your husband?"

"Yes, thank you," the mother said faintly. Her left arm dangled helplessly and she was holding the baby, who had gone to sleep, in the other. "Hep that lady up, Hiram," The Misfit said as she struggled to climb out of the ditch, "and Bobby Lee, you hold onto that little girl's hand."

"I don't want to hold hands with him," June Star said. "He reminds me of a pig."

The fat boy blushed and laughed and caught her by the arm and pulled her off into the woods after Hiram and her mother.

Alone with The Misfit, the grandmother found that she had lost her voice. There was not a cloud in the sky nor any sun. There was nothing around her but woods. She wanted to tell him that he must pray. She opened and closed her mouth several times before anything came out. Finally she found herself saying, "Jesus. Jesus," meaning, Jesus will help you, but the way she was saying it, it sounded as if she might be cursing.

"Yes'm," The Misfit said as if he agreed. "Jesus thown everything off balance. 130 It was the same case with Him as with me except He hadn't committed any crime and they could prove I had committed one because they had the papers on me. Of course," he said, "they never shown me my papers. That's why I sign myself now. I said long ago, you get you a signature and sign everything you do and keep a copy of it. Then you'll know what you done and you can hold up the crime to the punishment and see do they match and in the end you'll have something to prove you ain't been treated right. I call myself The Misfit," he said, "because I can't make what all I done wrong fit what all I gone through in punishment."

There was a piercing scream from the woods, followed closely by a pistol report. "Does it seem right to you, lady, that one is punished a heap and another ain't punished at all?"

"Jesus!" the old lady cried. "You've got good blood! I know you wouldn't shoot a lady! I know you come from nice people! Pray! Jesus, you ought not to shoot a lady. I'll give you all the money I've got!"

"Lady," The Misfit said, looking beyond her far into the woods, "there never was a body that give the undertaker a tip."

There were two more pistol reports and the grandmother raised her head like a parched old turkey hen crying for water and called, "Bailey Boy, Bailey Boy!" as if her heart would break.

"Jesus was the only One that ever raised the dead," The Misfit continued, 135 "and He shouldn't have done it. He thown everything off balance. If He did what He said, then it's nothing for you to do but thow away everything and follow Him, and if He didn't, then it's nothing for you to do but enjoy the few minutes you got left the best way you can—by killing somebody or burning down his house or doing some other meanness to him. No pleasure but meanness," he said and his voice had become almost a snarl.

"Maybe He didn't raise the dead," the old lady mumbled, not knowing what she was saying and feeling so dizzy that she sank down in the ditch with her legs twisted under her.

"I wasn't there so I can't say He didn't," The Misfit said. "I wisht I had of been there," he said, hitting the ground with his fist. "It ain't right I wasn't there because if I had of been there I would of known. Listen lady," he said in a high voice, "if I had of been there I would of known and I wouldn't be like I am now." His voice seemed about to crack and the grandmother's head cleared for an instant. She saw the man's face twisted close to her own as if he were going to cry and she murmured, "Why you're one of my babies. You're one of my own children!" She reached out and touched him on the shoulder. The Misfit sprang back as if a snake had bitten him and shot her three times through the chest. Then he put his gun down on the ground and took off his glasses and began to clean them.

Hiram and Bobby Lee returned from the woods and stood over the ditch, looking down at the grandmother who half sat and half lay in a puddle of blood with her legs crossed under her like a child's and her face smiling up at the cloudless sky.

Without his glasses, The Misfit's eyes were red-rimmed and pale and defenseless-looking. "Take her off and thow her where you thown the others," he said, picking up the cat that was rubbing itself against his leg.

"She was a talker, wasn't she?" Bobby Lee said, sliding down the ditch with a 140 yodel.

"She would of been a good woman," The Misfit said, "if it had been somebody there to shoot her every minute of her life."

"Some fun!" Bobby Lee said.

"Shut up, Bobby Lee," The Misfit said. "It's no real pleasure in life."

QUESTIONS

1. How early in the story does O'Connor foreshadow what will happen in the end? What further hints does she give us along the way? How does the scene at Red Sammy's Barbecue advance the story toward its conclusion?

2. When we first meet the grandmother, what kind of person is she? What do her various remarks reveal about her? Does she remain a static character, or does she in any way change as the story goes on?

3. When the grandmother's head clears for an instant (paragraph 137), what does she suddenly understand? Reread this passage carefully and prepare to discuss what it means.

4. What do we learn from the conversation between The Misfit and the grandmother while the others go out to the woods? How would you describe The Misfit's outlook on the world? Compare it with the author's, from whatever you know about Flannery O'Connor and from the story itself.

5. How would you respond to a reader who complained, "The title of this story is just an obvious platitude"?

The doctor's waiting room, which was very small, was almost full when the Turpins entered and Mrs. Turpin, who was very large, made it look even smaller by her presence. She stood looming at the head of the magazine table set in the center of it, a living demonstration that the room was inadequate and ridiculous. Her little bright black eyes took in all the patients as she sized up the seating situation. There was one vacant chair and a place on a sofa occupied by a blond child in a dirty blue romper who should have been told to move over and make room for the lady. He was five or six, but Mrs. Turpin saw at once that no one was going to tell him to move over. He was slumped down in the seat, his arms idle at his sides and his eyes idle in his head; his nose ran unchecked.

Mrs. Turpin put a firm hand on Claud's shoulder and said in a voice that included anyone who wanted to listen, "Claud, you sit in that chair there," and gave him a push down into the vacant one. Claud was florid and bald and sturdy, somewhat shorter than Mrs. Turpin, but he sat down as if he were accustomed to doing what she told him to.

Mrs. Turpin remained standing. The only man in the room besides Claud was a lean stringy old fellow with a rusty hand spread out on each knee, whose eyes were closed as if he were asleep or dead or pretending to be so as not to get up and offer her his seat. Her gaze settled agreeably on a well-dressed grey-haired lady whose eyes met hers and whose expression said: if that child belonged to me, he would have some manners and move over—there's plenty of room there for you and him too.

Claud looked up with a sigh and made as if to rise.

"Sit down," Mrs. Turpin said. "You know you're not supposed to stand on   5
that leg. He has an ulcer on his leg," she explained.

Claud lifted his foot onto the magazine table and rolled his trouser leg up to reveal a purple swelling on a plump marble-white calf.

"My!" the pleasant lady said. "How did you do that?"

"A cow kicked him," Mrs. Turpin said.

"Goodness!" said the lady.

Claud rolled his trouser leg down.   10

"Maybe the little boy would move over," the lady suggested, but the child did not stir.

"Somebody will be leaving in a minute," Mrs. Turpin said. She could not understand why a doctor—with as much money as they made charging five dollars a day to just stick their head in the hospital door and look at you—couldn't afford a decent-sized waiting room. This one was hardly bigger than a garage. The table was cluttered with limp-looking magazines and at one end of it there was a big green glass ash tray full of cigaret butts and cotton wads with little blood spots on them. If she had had anything to do with the running of the place, that would have been emptied every so often. There were no chairs against the wall at the head of the room. It had a rectangular-shaped panel in it that permitted a view of the office where the nurse came and went and the secretary listened to the radio. A plastic fern in a gold pot sat in the opening and trailed its fronds down almost to the floor. The radio was softly playing gospel music.

Just then the inner door opened and a nurse with the highest stack of yellow hair Mrs. Turpin had ever seen put her face in the crack and called for the next patient. The woman sitting beside Claud grasped the two arms of her chair and hoisted herself up; she pulled her dress free from her legs and lumbered through the door where the nurse had disappeared.

Mrs. Turpin eased into the vacant chair, which held her tight as a corset. "I wish I could reduce," she said, and rolled her eyes and gave a comic sigh.

"Oh, *you* aren't fat," the stylish lady said.   15

"Ooooo I am too," Mrs. Turpin said. "Claud he eats all he wants to and never weighs over one hundred and seventy-five pounds, but me I just look at something good to eat and I gain some weight," and her stomach and shoulders shook with laughter. "You can eat all you want to, can't you, Claud?" she asked, turning to him.

Claud only grinned.

"Well, as long as you have such a good disposition," the stylish lady said, "I don't think it makes a bit of difference what size you are. You just can't beat a good disposition."

Next to her was a fat girl of eighteen or nineteen, scowling into a thick blue book which Mrs. Turpin saw was entitled *Human Development*. The girl raised her head and directed her scowl at Mrs. Turpin as if she did not like her looks. She appeared annoyed that anyone should speak while she tried to read. The poor girl's face was blue with acne and Mrs. Turpin thought how pitiful it was to have a face like that at that age. She gave the girl a friendly smile but the girl only scowled the harder. Mrs. Turpin herself was fat but she had always had good skin, and, though she was forty-seven years old, there was not a wrinkle in her face except around her eyes from laughing too much.

Next to the ugly girl was the child, still in exactly the same position, and   20
next to him was a thin leathery old woman in a cotton print dress. She and Claud had three sacks of chicken feed in their pump house that was in the same print. She had seen from the first that the child belonged with the old woman. She could tell by the way they sat—kind of vacant and white-trashy, as if they would sit there until Doomsday if nobody called and told them to get up. And at right angles but next to the well-dressed pleasant lady was a lank-faced woman who was certainly the child's mother. She had on a yellow sweat shirt and wine-colored slacks, both gritty-looking, and the rims of her lips were stained with snuff. Her dirty yellow hair was tied behind with a little piece of red paper ribbon. Worse than niggers any day, Mrs. Turpin thought.

The gospel hymn playing was, "When I looked up and He looked down," and Mrs. Turpin, who knew it, supplied the last line mentally, "And wona these days I know I'll we-eara crown."

Without appearing to, Mrs. Turpin always noticed people's feet. The well-dressed lady had on red and grey suede shoes to match her dress. Mrs. Turpin had on her good black patent leather pumps. The ugly girl had on Girl Scout shoes and heavy socks. The old woman had on tennis shoes and the white-trashy mother had on what appeared to be bedroom slippers, black straw with gold braid threaded through them—exactly what you would have expected her to have on.

Sometimes at night when she couldn't go to sleep, Mrs. Turpin would occupy herself with the question of who she would have chosen to be if she couldn't have been herself. If Jesus had said to her before he made her, "There's only two places available for you. You can either be a nigger or white-trash," what would she have said? "Please, Jesus, please," she would have said, "just let me wait until there's another place available," and he would have said, "No, you have to go right now and I have only those two places so make up your mind." She would have wiggled and squirmed and begged and pleaded but it would have been no use and finally she would have said, "All right, make me a nigger then—but that don't mean a trashy one." And he would have made her a neat clean respectable Negro-woman, herself but black.

Next to the child's mother was a red-headed youngish woman, reading one of the magazines and working a piece of chewing gum, hell for leather, as Claud would say. Mrs. Turpin could not see the woman's feet. She was not white-trash, just common. Sometimes Mrs. Turpin occupied herself at night naming the classes of people. On the bottom of the heap were most colored people, not the kind she would have been if she had been one, but most of them; then next to them—not above, just away from—were the white-trash; then above them were the home-owners, and above them the home-and-land owners, to which she and Claud belonged. Above she and Claud were people with a lot of money and much bigger houses and much more land. But here the complexity of it would begin to bear in on her, for some of the people with a lot of money were common and ought to be below she and Claud and some of the people who had good blood had lost their money and had to rent and then there were colored people who owned their homes and land as well. There was a colored dentist in town who had two red Lincolns and a swimming pool and a farm with registered white-face cattle on it. Usually by the time she had fallen asleep all the classes of people were moiling and roiling around in her head, and she would dream they were all crammed in together in a box car, being ridden off to be put in a gas oven.

"That's a beautiful clock," she said and nodded to her right. It was a big wall clock, the face encased in a brass sunburst.

"Yes, it's very pretty," the stylish lady said agreeably. "And right on the dot too," she added, glancing at her watch.

The ugly girl beside her cast an eye upward at the clock, smirked, then looked directly at Mrs. Turpin and smirked again. Then she returned her eyes to her book. She was obviously the lady's daughter because, although they didn't look anything alike as to disposition, they both had the same shape of face and

25

the same blue eyes. On the lady they sparkled pleasantly but in the girl's seared face they appeared alternately to smolder and to blaze.

What if Jesus had said, "All right, you can be white-trash or a nigger or ugly"!

Mrs. Turpin felt an awful pity for the girl, though she thought it was one thing to be ugly and another to act ugly.

The woman with the snuff-stained lips turned around in her chair and looked up at the clock. Then she turned back and appeared to look a little to the side of Mrs. Turpin. There was a cast in one of her eyes. "You want to know wher you can get you one of them ther clocks?" she asked in a loud voice. 30

"No, I already have a nice clock," Mrs. Turpin said. Once somebody like her got a leg in the conversation, she would be all over it.

"You can get you one with green stamps," the woman said. "That's most likely wher he got hisn. Save you up enough, you can get you most anythang. I got me some joo'ry."

Ought to have got you a wash rag and some soap, Mrs. Turpin thought.

"I get contour sheets with mine," the pleasant lady said.

The daughter slammed her book shut. She looked straight in front of her, directly through Mrs. Turpin and on through the yellow curtain and the plate glass window which made the wall behind her. The girl's eyes seemed lit all of a sudden with a peculiar light, an unnatural light like night road signs give. Mrs. Turpin turned her head to see if there was anything going on outside that she should see, but she could not see anything. Figures passing cast only a pale shadow through the curtain. There was no reason the girl should single her out for her ugly looks. 35

"Miss Finley," the nurse said, cracking the door. The gum-chewing woman got up and passed in front of her and Claud and went into the office. She had on red high-heeled shoes.

Directly across the table, the ugly girl's eyes were fixed on Mrs. Turpin as if she had some very special reason for disliking her.

"This is wonderful weather, isn't it?" the girl's mother said.

"It's good weather for cotton if you can get the niggers to pick it," Mrs. Turpin said, "but niggers don't want to pick cotton any more. You can't get the white folks to pick it and now you can't get the niggers—because they got to be right up there with the white folks."

"They gonna *try* anyways," the white-trash woman said, leaning forward. 40

"Do you have one of those cotton-picking machines?" the pleasant lady asked.

"No," Mrs. Turpin said, "they leave half the cotton in the field. We don't have much cotton anyway. If you want to make it farming now, you have to have a little of everything. We got a couple of acres of cotton and a few hogs and chickens and just enough white-face that Claud can look after them himself."

"One thang I don't want," the white-trash woman said, wiping her mouth with the back of her hands. "Hogs. Nasty stinking things, a-gruntin and a-rootin all over the place."

Mrs. Turpin gave her the merest edge of her attention. "Our hogs are not dirty and they don't stink," she said. "They're cleaner than some children I've seen. Their feet never touch the ground. We have a pig-parlor—that's where you raise them on concrete," she explained to the pleasant lady, "and Claud scoots them down with the hose every afternoon and washes off the floor." Cleaner by far than that child right there, she thought. Poor nasty little thing. He had not moved except to put the thumb of his dirty hand into his mouth.

The woman turned her face away from Mrs. Turpin. "I know I wouldn't 45 scoot down no hog with no hose," she said to the wall.

You wouldn't have no hog to scoot down, Mrs. Turpin said to herself.

"A-gruntin and a-rootin and a-groanin," the woman muttered.

"We got a little of everything," Mrs. Turpin said to the pleasant lady. "It's no use in having more than you can handle yourself with help like it is. We found enough niggers to pick our cotton this year but Claud he has to go after them and take them home again in the evening. They can't walk that half a mile. No they can't. I tell you," she said and laughed merrily, "I sure am tired of buttering up niggers, but you got to love em if you want em to work for you. When they come in the morning, I run out and I say, 'Hi yawl this morning?' and when Claud drives them off to the field I just wave to beat the band and they just wave back." And she waved her hand rapidly to illustrate.

"Like you read out of the same book," the lady said, showing she understood perfectly.

"Child, yes," Mrs. Turpin said. "And when they come in from the field, I run 50 out with a bucket of icewater. That's the way it's going to be from now on," she said. "You may as well face it."

"One thang I know," the white-trash woman said. "Two thangs I ain't going to do: love no niggers or scoot down no hog with no hose." And she let out a bark of contempt.

The look that Mrs. Turpin and the pleasant lady exchanged indicated they both understood that you had to *have* certain things before you could *know* certain things. But every time Mrs. Turpin exchanged a look with the lady, she was aware that the ugly girl's peculiar eyes were still on her, and she had trouble bringing her attention back to the conversation.

"When you got something," she said, "you got to look after it." And when you ain't got a thing but breath and britches, she added to herself, you can afford to come to town every morning and just sit on the Court House coping and spit.

A grotesque revolving shadow passed across the curtain behind her and was thrown palely on the opposite wall. Then a bicycle clattered down against the outside of the building. The door opened and a colored boy glided in with a tray from the drug store. It had two large red and white paper cups on it with tops on them. He was a tall, very black boy in discolored white pants and a green nylon shirt. He was chewing gum slowly, as if to music. He set the tray down in the office opening next to the fern and stuck his head through to look for the secretary. She was not in there. He rested his arms on the ledge and waited, his narrow bottom stuck out, swaying slowly to the left and right. He raised a hand over his head and scratched the base of his skull.

"You see that button there, boy?" Mrs. Turpin said. "You can punch that 55 and she'll come. She's probably in the back somewhere."

"Is thas right?" the boy said agreeably, as if he had never seen the button before. He leaned to the right and put his finger on it. "She sometime out," he said and twisted around to face his audience, his elbows behind him on the counter. The nurse appeared and he twisted back again. She handed him a dollar and he rooted in his pocket and made the change and counted it out to her. She gave him fifteen cents for a tip and he went out with the empty tray. The heavy door swung to slowly and closed at length with the sound of suction. For a moment no one spoke.

"They ought to send all them niggers back to Africa," the white-trash woman said. "That's wher they come from in the first place."

"Oh, I couldn't do without my good colored friends," the pleasant lady said.

"There's a heap of things worse than a nigger," Mrs. Turpin agreed. "It's all kinds of them just like it's all kinds of us."

"Yes, and it takes all kinds to make the world go round," the lady said in her 60 musical voice.

As she said it, the raw-complexioned girl snapped her teeth together. Her lower lip turned downwards and inside out, revealing the pale pink inside of her mouth. After a second it rolled back up. It was the ugliest face Mrs. Turpin had ever seen anyone make and for a moment she was certain that the girl had made it at her. She was looking at her as if she had known and disliked her all her life—all of Mrs. Turpin's life, it seemed too, not just all the girl's life. Why, girl, I don't even know you, Mrs. Turpin said silently.

She forced her attention back to the discussion. "It wouldn't be practical to send them back to Africa," she said. "They wouldn't want to go. They got it too good here."

"Wouldn't be what they wanted—if I had anythang to do with it," the woman said.

"It wouldn't be a way in the world you could get all the niggers back over there," Mrs. Turpin said. "They'd be hiding out and lying down and turning sick on you and wailing and hollering and raring and pitching. It wouldn't be a way in the world to get them over there."

"They got over here," the trashy woman said. "Get back like they got over." 65

"It wasn't so many of them then," Mrs. Turpin explained.

The woman looked at Mrs. Turpin as if here was an idiot indeed but Mrs. Turpin was not bothered by the look, considering where it came from.

"Nooo," she said, "they're going to stay here where they can go to New York and marry white folks and improve their color. That's what they all want to do, every one of them, improve their color."

"You know what comes of that, don't you?" Claud asked.

"No, Claud, what?" Mrs. Turpin said. 70

Claud's eyes twinkled. "White-faced niggers," he said with never a smile.

Everybody in the office laughed except the white-trash and the ugly girl. The girl gripped the book in her lap with white fingers. The trashy woman looked around her from face to face as if she thought they were all idiots. The old woman in the feed sack dress continued to gaze expressionless across the floor at the hightop shoes of the man opposite her, the one who had been pretending to be asleep when the Turpins came in. He was laughing heartily, his hands still spread out on his knees. The child had fallen to the side and was lying now almost face down in the old woman's lap.

While they recovered from their laughter, the nasal chorus on the radio kept the room from silence.

> "You go to blank blank
> And I'll go to mine
> But we'll all blank along
> To-geth-ther,
> And all along the blank
> We'll hep each other out
> Smile-ling in any kind of
> Weath-ther!"

Mrs. Turpin didn't catch every word but she caught enough to agree with the spirit of the song and it turned her thoughts sober. To help anybody out that needed it was her philosophy of life. She never spared herself when she found somebody in need, whether they were white or black, trash or decent. And of all she had to be thankful for, she was most thankful that this was so. If Jesus had said, "You can be high society and have all the money you want and be thin and svelte-like, but you can't be a good woman with it," she would have had to say, "Well don't make me that then. Make me a good woman and it don't matter what else, how fat or how ugly or how poor!" Her heart rose. He had not made her a nigger or white-trash or ugly! He had made her herself and given her a little of everything. Jesus, thank you! she said. Thank you thank you thank you! Whenever she counted her blessings she felt as buoyant as if she weighed one hundred and twenty-five pounds instead of one hundred and eighty.

"What's wrong with your little boy?" the pleasant lady asked the white-trashy woman.

"He has a ulcer," the woman said proudly. "He ain't give me a minute's peace since he was born. Him and her are just alike," she said, nodding at the old woman, who was running her leathery fingers through the child's pale hair. "Look like I can't get nothing down them two but Co' Cola and candy."

That's all you try to get down em, Mrs. Turpin said to herself. Too lazy to light the fire. There was nothing you could tell her about people like them that she didn't know already. And it was not just that they didn't have anything. Because if you gave them everything, in two weeks it would all be broken or filthy or they would have chopped it up for lightwood. She knew all this from her own experience. Help them you must, but help them you couldn't.

All at once the ugly girl turned her lips inside out again. Her eyes were fixed like two drills on Mrs. Turpin. This time there was no mistaking that there was something urgent behind them.

75

Girl, Mrs. Turpin exclaimed silently, I haven't done a thing to you! The girl   80
might be confusing her with somebody else. There was no need to sit by and let
herself be intimidated. "You must be in college," she said boldly, looking directly
at the girl. "I see you reading a book there."

The girl continued to stare and pointedly did not answer.

Her mother blushed at this rudeness. "The lady asked you a question, Mary
Grace," she said under her breath.

"I have ears," Mary Grace said.

The poor mother blushed again. "Mary Grace goes to Wellesley College,"
she explained. She twisted one of the buttons on her dress. "In Massachusetts,"
she added with a grimace. "And in the summer she just keeps right on studying.
Just reads all the time, a real book worm. She's done real well at Wellesley; she's
taking English and Math and History and Psychology and Social Studies," she
rattled on, "and I think it's too much. I think she ought to get out and have fun."

The girl looked as if she would like to hurl them all through the plate glass   85
window.

"Way up north," Mrs. Turpin murmured and thought, well, it hasn't done
much for her manners.

"I'd almost rather to have him sick," the white-trash woman said, wrenching
the attention back to herself. "He's so mean when he ain't. Look like some children just take natural to meanness. It's some gets bad when they get sick but he
was the opposite. Took sick and turned good. He don't give me no trouble now.
It's me waitin to see the doctor," she said.

If I was going to send anybody back to Africa, Mrs. Turpin thought, it would
be your kind, woman. "Yes, indeed," she said aloud, but looking up at the ceiling,
"it's a heap of things worse than a nigger." And dirtier than a hog, she added to
herself.

"I think people with bad dispositions are more to be pitied than anyone on
earth," the pleasant lady said in a voice that was decidedly thin.

"I thank the Lord he has blessed me with a good one," Mrs. Turpin said.   90
"The day has never dawned that I couldn't find something to laugh at."

"Not since she married me anyways," Claud said with a comical straight face.

Everybody laughed except the girl and the white-trash.

Mrs. Turpin's stomach shook. "He's such a caution," she said, "that I can't
help but laugh at him."

The girl made a loud ugly noise through her teeth.

Her mother's mouth grew thin and straight. "I think the worst thing in the   95
world," she said, "is an ungrateful person. To have everything and not appreciate
it. I know a girl," she said, "who has parents who would give her anything, a little
brother who loves her dearly, who is getting a good education, who wears the
best clothes, but who can never say a kind word to anyone, who never smiles,
who just criticizes and complains all day long."

"Is she too old to paddle?" Claud asked.

The girl's face was almost purple.

"Yes," the lady said, "I'm afraid there's nothing to do but leave her to her folly. Some day she'll wake up and it'll be too late."

"It never hurt anyone to smile," Mrs. Turpin said. "It just makes you feel better all over."

"Of course," the lady said sadly, "but there are just some people you can't tell anything to. They can't take criticism." 100

"If it's one thing I am," Mrs. Turpin said with feeling, "it's grateful. When I think who all I could have been besides myself and what all I got, a little of everything, and a good disposition besides, I just feel like shouting, 'Thank you, Jesus, for making everything the way it is!' It could have been different!" For one thing, somebody else could have got Claud. At the thought of this, she was flooded with gratitude and a terrible pang of joy ran through her. "Oh thank you, Jesus, Jesus, thank you!" she cried aloud.

The book struck her directly over her left eye. It struck almost at the same instant that she realized the girl was about to hurl it. Before she could utter a sound, the raw face came crashing across the table toward her, howling. The girl's fingers sank like clamps into the soft flesh of her neck. She heard the mother cry out and Claud shout, "Whoa!" There was an instant when she was certain that she was about to be in an earthquake.

All at once her vision narrowed and she saw everything as if it were happening in a small room far away, or as if she were looking at it through the wrong end of a telescope. Claud's face crumpled and fell out of sight. The nurse ran in, then out, then in again. Then the gangling figure of the doctor rushed out of the inner door. Magazines flew this way and that as the table turned over. The girl fell with a thud and Mrs. Turpin's vision suddenly reversed itself and she saw everything large instead of small. The eyes of the white-trashy woman were staring hugely at the floor. There the girl, held down on one side by the nurse and on the other by her mother, was wrenching and turning in their grasp. The doctor was kneeling astride her, trying to hold her arm down. He managed after a second to sink a long needle into it.

Mrs. Turpin felt entirely hollow except for her heart which swung from side to side as if it were agitated in a great empty drum of flesh.

"Somebody that's not busy call for the ambulance," the doctor said in the 105 off-hand voice young doctors adopt for terrible occasions.

Mrs. Turpin could not have moved a finger. The old man who had been sitting next to her skipped nimbly into the office and made the call, for the secretary still seemed to be gone.

"Claud!" Mrs. Turpin called.

He was not in his chair. She knew she must jump up and find him but she felt like some one trying to catch a train in a dream, when everything moves in slow motion and the faster you try to run the slower you go.

"Here I am," a suffocated voice, very unlike Claud's, said.

He was doubled up in the corner on the floor, pale as paper, holding his leg. 110 She wanted to get up and go to him but she could not move. Instead, her gaze was drawn slowly downward to the churning face on the floor, which she could see over the doctor's shoulder.

The girl's eyes stopped rolling and focused on her. They seemed a much lighter blue than before, as if a door that had been tightly closed behind them was now open to admit light and air.

Mrs. Turpin's head cleared and her power of motion returned. She leaned forward until she was looking directly into the fierce brilliant eyes. There was no doubt in her mind that the girl did know her, knew her in some intense and personal way, beyond time and place and condition. "What you got to say to me?" she asked hoarsely and held her breath, waiting, as for a revelation.

The girl raised her head. Her gaze locked with Mrs. Turpin's. "Go back to hell where you came from, you old wart hog," she whispered. Her voice was low but clear. Her eyes burned for a moment as if she saw with pleasure that her message had struck its target.

Mrs. Turpin sank back in her chair.

After a moment the girl's eyes closed and she turned her head wearily to the side.   115

The doctor rose and handed the nurse the empty syringe. He leaned over and put both hands for a moment on the mother's shoulders, which were shaking. She was sitting on the floor, her lips pressed together, holding Mary Grace's hand in her lap. The girl's fingers were gripped like a baby's around her thumb. "Go on to the hospital," he said. "I'll call and make the arrangements."

"Now let's see that neck," he said in a jovial voice to Mrs. Turpin. He began to inspect her neck with his first two fingers. Two little moon-shaped lines like pink fish bones were indented over her windpipe. There was the beginning of an angry red swelling above her eye. His fingers passed over this also.

"Lea'me be," she said thickly and shook him off. "See about Claud. She kicked him."

"I'll see about him in a minute," he said and felt her pulse. He was a thin gray-haired man, given to pleasantries. "Go home and have yourself a vacation the rest of the day," he said and patted her on the shoulder.

Quit your pattin me, Mrs. Turpin growled to herself.   120

"And put an ice pack over that eye," he said. Then he went and squatted down beside Claud and looked at his leg. After a moment he pulled him up and Claud limped after him into the office.

Until the ambulance came, the only sounds in the room were the tremulous moans of the girl's mother, who continued to sit on the floor. The white-trash woman did not take her eyes off the girl. Mrs. Turpin looked straight ahead at nothing. Presently the ambulance drew up, a long dark shadow, behind the curtain. The attendants came in and set the stretcher down beside the girl and lifted her expertly onto it and carried her out. The nurse helped the mother gather up her things. The shadow of the ambulance moved silently away and the nurse came back in the office.

"That ther girl is going to be a lunatic, ain't she?" the white-trash woman asked the nurse, but the nurse kept on to the back and never answered her.

"Yes, she's going to be a lunatic," the white-trash woman said to the rest of them.

"Po' critter," the old woman murmured. The child's face was still in her lap. 125
His eyes looked idly out over her knees. He had not moved during the disturbance except to draw one leg up under him.

"I thank Gawd," the white-trash woman said fervently, "I ain't a lunatic."

Claud came limping out and the Turpins went home.

As their pick-up truck turned into their own dirt road and made the crest of the hill, Mrs. Turpin gripped the window ledge and looked out suspiciously. The land sloped gracefully down through a field dotted with lavender weeds and at the start of the rise their small yellow frame house, with its little flower beds spread out around it like a fancy apron, sat primly in its accustomed place between two giant hickory trees. She would not have been startled to see a burnt wound between two blackened chimneys.

Neither of them felt like eating so they put on their house clothes and lowered the shade in the bedroom and lay down, Claud with his leg on a pillow and herself with a damp washcloth over her eye. The instant she was flat on her back, the image of a razor-backed hog with warts on its face and horns coming out behind its ears snorted into her head. She moaned, a low quiet moan.

"I am not," she said tearfully, "a wart hog. From hell." But the denial had 130
no force. The girl's eyes and her words, even the tone of her voice, low but clear, directed only to her, brooked no repudiation. She had been singled out for the message, though there was trash in the room to whom it might justly have been applied. The full force of this fact struck her only now. There was a woman there who was neglecting her own child but she had been overlooked. The message had been given to Ruby Turpin, a respectable, hard-working, church-going woman. The tears dried. Her eyes began to burn instead with wrath.

She rose on her elbow and the washcloth fell into her hand. Claud was lying on his back, snoring. She wanted to tell him what the girl had said. At the same time, she did not wish to put the image of herself as a wart hog from hell into his mind.

"Hey, Claud," she muttered and pushed his shoulder.

Claud opened one pale baby blue eye.

She looked into it warily. He did not think about anything. He just went his way.

"Wha, whasit?" he said and closed the eye again. 135

"Nothing," she said. "Does your leg pain you?"

"Hurts like hell," Claud said.

"It'll quit terreckly," she said and lay back down. In a moment Claud was snoring again. For the rest of the afternoon they lay there. Claud slept. She scowled at the ceiling. Occasionally she raised her fist and made a small stabbing motion over her chest as if she was defending her innocence to invisible guests who were like the comforters of Job, reasonable-seeming but wrong.

About five-thirty Claud stirred. "Got to go after those niggers," he sighed, not moving.

She was looking straight up as if there were unintelligible handwriting on the ceiling. The protuberance over her eye had turned a greenish-blue. "Listen here," she said.

"What?"

"Kiss me."

Claud leaned over and kissed her loudly on the mouth. He pinched her side and their hands interlocked. Her expression of ferocious concentration did not change. Claud got up, groaning and growling, and limped off. She continued to study the ceiling.

She did not get up until she heard the pick-up truck coming back with the Negroes. Then she rose and thrust her feet in her brown oxfords, which she did not bother to lace, and stumped out onto the back porch and got her red plastic bucket. She emptied a tray of ice cubes into it and filled it half full of water and went out into the back yard. Every afternoon after Claud brought the hands in, one of the boys helped him put out hay and the rest waited in the back of the truck until he was ready to take them home. The truck was parked in the shade under one of the hickory trees.

"Hi yawl this evening?" Mrs. Turpin asked grimly, appearing with the bucket and the dipper. There were three women and a boy in the truck.

"Us doin nicely," the oldest woman said. "Hi you doin?" and her gaze stuck immediately on the dark lump on Mrs. Turpin's forehead. "You done fell down, ain't you?" she asked in a solicitous voice. The old woman was dark and almost toothless. She had on an old felt hat of Claud's set back on her head. The other two women were younger and lighter and they both had new bright green sun hats. One of them had hers on her head; the other had taken hers off and the boy was grinning beneath it.

Mrs. Turpin set the bucket down on the floor of the truck. "Yawl hep your-selves," she said. She looked around to make sure Claud had gone. "No. I didn't fall down," she said, folding her arms. "It was something worse than that."

"Ain't nothing bad happen to you!" the old woman said. She said it as if they all knew Mrs. Turpin was protected in some special way by Divine Provi-dence. "You just had you a little fall."

"We were in town at the doctor's office for where the cow kicked Mr. Turpin," Mrs. Turpin said in a flat tone that indicated they could leave off their foolishness. "And there was this girl there. A big fat girl with her face all broke out. I could look at that girl and tell she was peculiar but I couldn't tell how. And me and her mama were just talking and going along and all of a sudden WHAM! She throws this big book she reading at me and . . ."

"Naw!" the old woman cried out.

"And then she jumps over the table and commences to choke me."

"Naw!" they all exclaimed, "naw!"

"Hi come she do that?" the old woman asked. "What ail her?"

Mrs. Turpin only glared in front of her.

"Something ail her," the old woman said.

"They carried her off in an ambulance," Mrs. Turpin continued, "but before she went she was rolling on the floor and they were trying to hold her down to give her a shot and she said something to me." She paused. "You know what she said to me?"

"What she say?" they asked.

"She said," Mrs. Turpin began, and stopped, her face very dark and heavy. The sun was getting whiter and whiter, blanching the sky overhead so that the leaves of the hickory tree were black in the face of it. She could not bring forth the words. "Something real ugly," she muttered.

"She sho shouldn't said nothin ugly to you," the old woman said. "You so sweet. You the sweetest lady I know."

"She pretty too," the one with the hat on said.

"And stout," the other one said. "I never knowed no sweeter white lady."

"That's the truth befo' Jesus," the old woman said. "Amen! You des as sweet and pretty as you can be."

Mrs. Turpin knew just exactly how much Negro flattery was worth and it added to her rage. "She said," she began again and finished this time with a fierce rush of breath, "that I was an old wart hog from hell."

There was an astounded silence.

"Where she at?" the youngest woman cried in a piercing voice.

"Lemme see her. I'll kill her!"

"I'll kill her with you!" the other one cried.

"She b'long in the sylum," the old woman said emphatically. "You the sweetest white lady I know."

"She pretty too," the other two said. "Stout as she can be and sweet. Jesus satisfied with her!"

"Deed he is," the old woman declared.

Idiots! Mrs. Turpin growled to herself. You could never say anything intelligent to a nigger. You could talk at them but not with them. "Yawl ain't drunk your water," she said shortly. "Leave the bucket in the truck when you're finished with it. I got more to do than just stand around and pass the time of day," and she moved off and into the house.

She stood for a moment in the middle of the kitchen. The dark protuberance over her eye looked like a miniature tornado cloud which might any moment sweep across the horizon of her brow. Her lower lip protruded dangerously. She squared her massive shoulders. Then she marched into the front of the house and out the side door and started down the road to the pig parlor. She had the look of a woman going single-handed, weaponless, into battle.

The sun was a deep yellow now like a harvest moon and was riding westward very fast over the far tree line as if it meant to reach the hogs before she did. The road was rutted and she kicked several good-sized stones out of her path as she strode along. The pig parlor was on a little knoll at the end of a lane that ran off from the side of the barn. It was a square of concrete as large as a small room, with a board fence about four feet high around it. The concrete floor sloped slightly so that the hog wash could drain off into a trench where it was carried to the field for fertilizer. Claud was standing on the outside, on the edge of the concrete, hanging onto the top board, hosing down the floor inside. The hose was connected to the faucet of a water trough nearby.

Mrs. Turpin climbed up beside him and glowered down at the hogs inside. There were seven long-snouted bristly shoats in it—tan with liver-colored spots—and an old sow a few weeks off from farrowing. She was lying on her side grunting. The shoats were running about shaking themselves like idiot children, their little slit pig eyes searching the floor for anything left. She had read that pigs were the most intelligent animal. She doubted it. They were supposed to be smarter than dogs. There had even been a pig astronaut. He had performed his assignment perfectly but died of a heart attack afterwards because they left him in his electric suit, sitting upright throughout his examination when naturally a hog should be on all fours.

A-gruntin and a-rootin and a-groanin.   175

"Gimme that hose," she said, yanking it away from Claud. "Go on and carry them niggers home and then get off that leg."

"You look like you might have swallowed a mad dog," Claud observed, but he got down and limped off. He paid no attention to her humors.

Until he was out of earshot, Mrs. Turpin stood on the side of the pen, holding the hose and pointing the stream of water at the hind quarters of any shoat that looked as if it might try to lie down. When he had had time to get over the hill, she turned her head slightly and her wrathful eyes scanned the path. He was nowhere in sight. She turned back again and seemed to gather herself up. Her shoulders rose and she drew in her breath.

"What do you send me a message like that for?" she said in a low fierce voice, barely above a whisper but with the force of a shout in its concentrated fury. "How am I a hog and me both? How am I saved and from hell too?" Her free fist was knotted and with the other she gripped the hose, blindly pointing the stream of water in and out of the eye of the old sow whose outraged squeal she did not hear.

The pig parlor commanded a view of the back pasture where their twenty   180
beef cows were gathered around the hay-bales Claud and the boy had put out. The freshly cut pasture sloped down to the highway. Across it was their cotton field and beyond that a dark green dusty wood which they owned as well. The sun was behind the wood, very red, looking over the paling of trees like a farmer inspecting his own hogs.

"Why me?" she rumbled. "It's no trash around here, black or white, that I haven't given to. And break my back to the bone every day working. And do for the church."

She appeared to be the right size woman to command the arena before her. "How am I a hog?" she demanded. "Exactly how am I like them?" and she jabbed the stream of water at the shoats. "There was plenty of trash there. It didn't have to be me."

"If you like trash better, go get yourself some trash then," she railed. "You could have made me trash. Or a nigger. If trash is what you wanted why didn't you make me trash?" She shook her fist with the hose in it and a watery snake appeared momentarily in the air. "I could quit working and take it easy and be filthy," she growled. "Lounge about the sidewalks all day drinking root beer. Dip snuff and spit in every puddle and have it all over my face. I could be nasty.

"Or you could have made me a nigger. It's too late for me to be a nigger," she said with deep sarcasm, "but I could act like one. Lay down in the middle of the road and stop traffic. Roll on the ground."

In the deepening light everything was taking on a mysterious hue. The pasture was growing a peculiar glassy green and the streak of highway had turned lavender. She braced herself for a final assault and this time her voice rolled out over the pasture. "Go on," she yelled, "call me a hog! Call me a hog again. From hell. Call me a wart hog from hell. Put that bottom rail on top. There'll still be a top and bottom!"

A garbled echo returned to her.

A final surge of fury shook her and she roared, "Who do you think you are?"

The color of everything, field and crimson sky, burned for a moment with a transparent intensity. The question carried over the pasture and across the highway and the cotton field and returned to her clearly like an answer from beyond the wood.

She opened her mouth but no sound came out of it.

A tiny truck, Claud's, appeared on the highway, heading rapidly out of sight. Its gears scraped thinly. It looked like a child's toy. At any moment a bigger truck might smash into it and scatter Claud's and the niggers' brains all over the road.

Mrs. Turpin stood there, her gaze fixed on the highway, all her muscles rigid, until in five or six minutes the truck reappeared, returning. She waited until it had had time to turn into their own road. Then like a monumental statue coming to life, she bent her head slowly and gazed, as if through the very heart of mystery, down into the pig parlor at the hogs. They had settled all in one corner around the old sow who was grunting softly. A red glow suffused them. They appeared to pant with a secret life.

Until the sun slipped finally behind the tree line, Mrs. Turpin remained there with her gaze bent to them as if she were absorbing some abysmal life-giving knowledge. At last she lifted her head. There was only a purple streak in the sky, cutting through a field of crimson and leading, like an extension of the highway, into the descending dusk. She raised her hands from the side of the pen in a gesture hieratic and profound. A visionary light settled in her eyes. She saw the streak as a vast swinging bridge extending upward from the earth through a field of living fire. Upon it a vast horde of souls were rumbling toward heaven. There were whole companies of white-trash, clean for the first time in their lives, and bands of black niggers in white robes, and battalions of freaks and lunatics shouting and clapping and leaping like frogs. And bringing up the end of the procession was a tribe of people whom she recognized at once as those who, like herself and Claud, had always had a little of everything and the God-given wit to use it right. She leaned forward to observe them closer. They were marching behind the others with great dignity, accountable as they had always been for good order and common sense and respectable behavior. They alone were on key. Yet she could see by their shocked and altered faces that even their virtues were being burned away. She lowered her hands and gripped the rail of the hog pen, her eyes small but fixed unblinkingly on what lay ahead. In a moment the vision faded but she remained where she was, immobile.

At length she got down and turned off the faucet and made her slow way on the darkening path to the house. In the woods around her the invisible cricket choruses had struck up, but what she heard were the voices of the souls climbing upward into the starry field and shouting hallelujah.

QUESTIONS

1. How does Mrs. Turpin see herself before Mary Grace calls her a wart hog?
2. What is the narrator's attitude toward Mrs. Turpin in the beginning of the story? How can you tell? Does this attitude change, or stay the same, at the end?
3. Describe the relationship between Mary Grace and her mother. What annoying platitudes does the mother mouth? Which of Mrs. Turpin's opinions seem especially to anger Mary Grace?
4. Sketch the plot of the story. What moment or event do you take to be the crisis, or turning point? What is the climax? What is the conclusion?
5. What do you infer from Mrs. Turpin's conversation with the black farm workers? Is she their friend? Why does she now find their flattery unacceptable ("Jesus satisfied with her")?
6. When, near the end of the story, Mrs. Turpin roars, "Who do you think you are?" an echo "returned to her clearly like an answer from beyond the wood" (paragraph 188). Explain.
7. What is the final revelation given to Mrs. Turpin? (To state it is to state the theme of the story.) What new attitude does the revelation impart? (How is Mrs. Turpin left with a new vision of humanity?)
8. Other stories in this book contain revelations: "Young Goodman Brown," "The Gospel According to Mark," "Angel Levine." If you have read them, try to sum up the supernatural revelation made to the central character in each story. In each, is the revelation the same as a statement of the story's main theme?

Flannery O'Connor at her mother's Georgia farm where she raised peacocks, c. 1962.

EXCERPT FROM "ON HER OWN WORK": THE ELEMENT OF SUSPENSE IN "A GOOD MAN IS HARD TO FIND"   1963

A story really isn't any good unless it successfully resists paraphrase, unless it hangs on and expands in the mind. Properly, you analyze to enjoy, but it's equally true that to analyze with any discrimination, you have to have enjoyed already, and I think that the best reason to hear a story read is that it should stimulate that primary enjoyment.

I don't have any pretensions to being an Aeschylus or Sophocles and providing you in this story with a cathartic experience out of your mythic background, though this story I'm going to read certainly calls up a good deal of the South's mythic background, and it should elicit from you a degree of pity and terror, even though its way of being serious is a comic one. I do think, though, that like the Greeks you should know what is going to happen in this story so that any element of suspense in it will be transferred from its surface to its interior.

I would be most happy if you had already read it, happier still if you knew it well, but since experience has taught me to keep my expectations along these lines modest, I'll tell you that this is the story of a family of six which, on its way driving to

Florida, gets wiped out by an escaped convict who calls himself the Misfit. The family is made up of the Grandmother and her son, Bailey, and his children, John Wesley and June Star and the baby, and there is also the cat and the children's mother. The cat is named Pitty Sing, and the Grandmother is taking him with them, hidden in a basket.

Now I think it behooves me to try to establish with you the basis on which reason operates in this story. Much of my fiction takes its character from a reasonable use of the unreasonable, though the reasonableness of my use of it may not always be apparent. The assumptions that underlie this use of it, however, are those of the central Christian mysteries. These are assumptions to which a large part of the modern audience takes exception. About this I can only say that there are perhaps other ways than my own in which this story could be read, but none other by which it could have been written. Belief, in my own case anyway, is the engine that makes perception operate.

The heroine of this story, the Grandmother, is in the most significant position life offers the Christian. She is facing death. And to all appearances she, like the rest of us, is not too well prepared for it. She would like to see the event postponed. Indefinitely.

I've talked to a number of teachers who use this story in class and who tell their students that the Grandmother is evil, that in fact, she's a witch, even down to the cat. One of these teachers told me that his students, and particularly his Southern students, resisted this interpretation with a certain bemused vigor, and he didn't understand why. I had to tell him that they resisted it because they all had grandmothers or great-aunts just like her at home, and they knew, from personal experience, that the old lady lacked comprehension, but that she had a good heart. The Southerner is usually tolerant of those weaknesses that proceed from innocence, and he knows that a taste for self-preservation can be readily combined with the missionary spirit.

This same teacher was telling his students that morally the Misfit was several cuts above the Grandmother. He had a really sentimental attachment to the Misfit. But then a prophet gone wrong is almost always more interesting than your grandmother, and you have to let people take their pleasures where they find them.

It is true that the old lady is a hypocritical old soul; her wits are no match for the Misfit's, nor is her capacity for grace equal to his; yet I think the unprejudiced reader will feel that the Grandmother has a special kind of triumph in this story which instinctively we do not allow to someone altogether bad.

I often ask myself what makes a story work, and what makes it hold up as a story, and I have decided that it is probably some action, some gesture of a character that is unlike any other in the story, one which indicates where the real heart of the story lies. This would have to be an action or a gesture which was both totally right and totally unexpected; it would have to be one that was both in character and beyond character; it would have to suggest both the world and eternity. The action or gesture I'm talking about would have to be on the anagogical level, that is, the level which has to do with the Divine life and our participation in it. It would be a gesture that transcended any neat allegory that might have been intended or any pat moral categories a reader could make. It would be a gesture which somehow made contact with mystery.

There is a point in this story where such a gesture occurs. The Grandmother is at last alone, facing the Misfit. Her head clears for an instant and she realizes, even in her limited way, that she is responsible for the man before her and joined to him by ties of kinship which have their roots deep in the mystery she has been merely prattling about so far. And at this point, she does the right thing, she makes the right gesture.

I find that students are often puzzled by what she says and does here, but I think myself that if I took out this gesture and what she says with it, I would have no story. What was left would not be worth your attention. Our age not only does not have a very sharp eye for the almost imperceptible intrusions of grace, it no longer has much feeling for the nature of the violences which precede and follow them. The devil's greatest wile, Baudelaire has said, is to convince us that he does not exist.

I suppose the reasons for the use of so much violence in modern fiction will differ with each writer who uses it, but in my own stories I have found that violence is strangely capable of returning my characters to reality and preparing them to accept their moment of grace. Their heads are so hard that almost nothing else will do the work. This idea, that reality is something to which we must be returned at considerable cost, is one which is seldom understood by the casual reader, but it is one which is implicit in the Christian view of the world.

I don't want to equate the Misfit with the devil. I prefer to think that, however unlikely this may seem, the old lady's gesture, like the mustard-seed, will grow to be a great crow-filled tree in the Misfit's heart, and will be enough of a pain to him there to turn him into the prophet he was meant to become. But that's another story.

This story has been called grotesque, but I prefer to call it literal. A good story is literal in the same sense that a child's drawing is literal. When a child draws, he doesn't intend to distort but to set down exactly what he sees, and as his gaze is direct, he sees the lines that create motion. Now the lines of motion that interest the writer are usually invisible. They are lines of spiritual motion. And in this story you should be on the lookout for such things as the action of grace in the Grandmother's soul, and not for the dead bodies.

We hear many complaints about the prevalence of violence in modern fiction, and it is always assumed that this violence is a bad thing and meant to be an end in itself. With the serious writer, violence is never an end in itself. It is the extreme situation that best reveals what we are essentially, and I believe these are times when writers are more interested in what we are essentially than in the tenor of our daily lives. Violence is a force which can be used for good or evil, and among other things taken by it is the kingdom of heaven. But regardless of what can be taken by it, the man in the violent situation reveals those qualities least dispensable in his personality, those qualities which are all he will have to take into eternity with him; and since the characters in this story are all on the verge of eternity, it is appropriate to think of what they take with them. In any case, I hope that if you consider these points in connection with the story, you will come to see it as something more than an account of a family murdered on the way to Florida.

From "On Her Own Work"

I write the way I do because (not though) I am a Catholic. This is a fact and nothing covers it like the bald statement. However, I am a Catholic peculiarly possessed of the modern consciousness, the thing Jung describes as unhistorical, solitary, and guilty. To possess this within the Church is to bear a burden, the necessary burden for the conscious Catholic. It's to feel the contemporary situation at the ultimate level. I think that the Church is the only thing that is going to make the terrible world we are coming to endurable; the only thing that makes the Church endurable is that it is somehow the body of Christ and that on this we are fed. It seems to be a fact that you suffer as much from the Church as for it but if you believe in the divinity of Christ, you have to cherish the world at the same time that you struggle to endure it. This may explain the lack of bitterness in the stories.

From a letter (July 20, 1955) in *The Habit of Being*

EXCERPT FROM "THE GROTESQUE IN SOUTHERN FICTION": THE SERIOUS WRITER AND THE TIRED READER 1960

Those writers who speak for and with their age are able to do so with a great deal more ease and grace than those who speak counter to prevailing attitudes. I once received a letter from an old lady in California who informed me that when the tired reader comes home at night, he wishes to read something that will lift up his heart. And it seems her heart had not been lifted up by anything of mine she had read. I think that if her heart had been in the right place, it would have been lifted up.

You may say that the serious writer doesn't have to bother about the tired reader, but he does, because they are all tired. One old lady who wants her heart lifted up wouldn't be so bad, but you multiply her two hundred and fifty thousand times and what you get is a book club. I used to think it should be possible to write for some supposed elite, for the people who attend the universities and sometimes know how to read, but I have since found that though you may publish your stories in *Botteghe Oscure*, ° if they are any good at all, you are eventually going to get a letter from some old lady in California, or some inmate of the Federal Penitentiary or the state insane asylum or the local poorhouse, telling you where you have failed to meet his needs.

And his need, of course, is to be lifted up. There is something in us, as storytellers and as listeners to stories, that demands the redemptive act, that demands that what falls at least be offered the chance to be restored. The reader of today looks for this motion, and rightly so, but what he has forgotten is the cost of it. His sense of evil is diluted or lacking altogether and so he has forgotten the price of restoration. When he reads a novel, he wants either his senses tormented or his spirits raised. He wants to be transported, instantly, either to a mock damnation or a mock innocence.

I am often told that the model of balance for the novelist should be Dante, who divided his territory up pretty evenly between hell, purgatory, and paradise. There

Botteghe Oscure: a distinguished and expensive literary magazine published in Rome from 1949 to 1960 by the Princess Marguerite Caetani for a small, sophisticated audience.

can be no objection to this, but also there can be no reason to assume that the result of doing it in these times will give us the balanced picture that it gave in Dante's. Dante lived in the 13th century when that balance was achieved in the faith of his age. We live now in an age which doubts both fact and value, which is swept this way and that by momentary convictions. Instead of reflecting a balance from the world around him, the novelist now has to achieve one from a felt balance inside himself. There are ages when it is possible to woo the reader; there are others when something more drastic is necessary.

There is no literary orthodoxy that can be prescribed as settled for the fiction writer, not even that of Henry James who balanced the elements of traditional realism and romance so admirably within each of his novels. But this much can be said. The great novels we get in the future are not going to be those that the public thinks it wants, or those that critics demand. They are going to be the kind of novels that interest the novelist. And the novels that interest the novelist are those that have not already been written. They are those that put the greatest demands on him, that require him to operate at the maximum of his intelligence and his talents, and to be true to the particularities of his own vocation. The direction of many of us will be toward concentration and the distortion that is necessary to get our vision across; it will be more toward poetry than toward the traditional novel.

The problem for such a novelist will be to know how far he can distort without destroying, and in order not to destroy, he will have to descend far enough into himself to reach those underground springs that give life to his work. This descent into himself will, at the same time, be a descent into his region. It will be a descent through the darkness of the familiar into a world where, like the blind man cured in the gospels, he sees men as if they were trees, but walking. This is the beginning of vision, and I feel it is a vision which we in the South must at least try to understand if we want to participate in the continuance of a vital Southern literature. I hate to think that in twenty years Southern writers too may be writing about men in grey flannel suits and may have lost their ability to see that these gentlemen are even greater freaks than what we are writing about now. I hate to think of the day when the Southern writer will satisfy the tired reader.

From "The Grotesque in Southern Fiction"

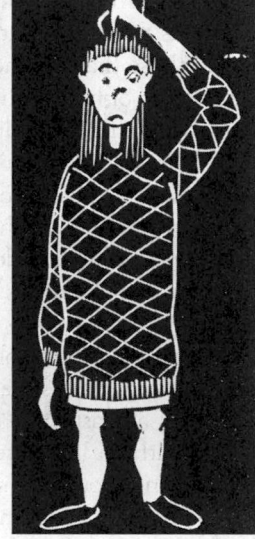

Untitled linoleum block cartoons by O'Connor for the yearbook at Georgia State College.

Robert H. Brinkmeyer Jr. (b. 1951)

FLANNERY O'CONNOR AND HER READERS   1989

As her letters and essays clearly indicate, O'Connor was very much concerned with her reading audience. Her comments on her audience and how it affected her as an artist, however, were not entirely consistent, and it seems clear that O'Connor was of two minds on the subject. One part of O'Connor downplayed the significance of the audience, saying that artists should be concerned with one thing—their art—and that they bear no responsibility to the audience. By this line of thinking writers concentrate on making their fiction—the characters and their worlds—come alive, and they make sure that the story works as a story and not as a medium for expressing an abstract statement. The meaning of a piece of fiction, O'Connor insisted, was the entire experience one has with it and was not a statement imposed on it that could then later be extracted and held up as its "message." Such thinking was central to the advice she wrote (December 11, 1956) to A. about writing fiction. O'Connor wrote that a writer should merely "start simply with a character or anything that you can make come alive." She continued, "When you have a character he will create his own situation and his situation will suggest some kind of resolution as you get into it. Wouldn't it be better to discover a meaning in what you write than to impose one?" (HB, 188).

. . . .

Catholic writers, in O'Connor's eyes, were particularly prone to distort their fiction for utilitarian purposes—to make it do something rather than be something. Particularly disturbing to her were those writers, in part goaded by the Catholic press, who wrote in pious language about the pieties of the Church. O'Connor's attitude toward this type of fiction was sharp: "As for the fiction," she wrote (February 19, 1956) to John Lynch, "the motto of the Catholic press should be: We guarantee to corrupt nothing but your taste" (HB, 138). In ignoring the realities of the here and now outside the Church, such fiction was for O'Connor little more than religious propaganda, the stuff one expects to find in the vestibules of churches but not in bookstores. These writers, she believed, were too concerned with presenting the Church in a favorable light and tending to their readership's spiritual needs; O'Connor's answer to them was that in writing fiction the Catholic writer "does not decide what would be good for the Christian body and proceed to deliver it" (MM, 183). Instead, as we have seen O'Connor stressing, writers must work within the limitations of their vocation to create the best story—not tract—possible. "The writer is only free when he can tell the reader to go jump in the lake," O'Connor said in one of her interviews, stressing the artist's independence from the audience. She added that though the writer of course wants to communicate a personal vision, "whether [the reader] likes it or not is no concern of the writer" (CFO, 39).

If in this way O'Connor downplayed the significance of the audience, she also frequently said something quite different. She argued that the audience played a crucial role in artistic creation and that writers always had to be aware of, and to take account of, their audience. She spoke of this connection in "Catholic Novelists and Their Readers," saying that "it takes readers as well as writers to make literature," and she added in "The Catholic Novelist in the Protestant South" that "it is what writer, character, and reader share that makes it possible to write fiction at all." Elsewhere (in "Novelist and Believer") O'Connor wrote that fiction was ultimately an attempt at communication; successful writing, she added, was not merely a rendering of the artist's vision but a rendering of it in such a way that the reader could understand it. "The novelist doesn't write to express himself, he doesn't write simply to render a vision he believes true, rather he renders his vision so it can be transferred, as nearly whole as possible, to his reader," she wrote. "You can safely ignore the reader's taste, but you can't ignore his nature, you can't ignore his limited patience. Your problem is going to be difficult in direct proportion as your beliefs depart from his." She echoes this observation in "Some Aspects of the Grotesque in Southern Fiction," saying that the writer's vision "has to be transmitted and that the limitations and blind spots of his audience will very definitely affect the way he is able to show what he sees" (MM, 182, 204–205, 162, 47).

When speaking of her own audience, O'Connor almost always stressed the great distance she felt between herself and her readers and pointed to the ways this gulf pressured and limited her as a writer. She believed that she and other American Catholic writers lacked a significant and responsive audience, and that this situation stifled imaginative growth and artistic expression. O'Connor found several reasons for this development. Central to the Catholic writer's plight, O'Connor believed, was the fact that in America Catholic writers lacked a distinctive social and cultural heritage based on religious identity. In "The Catholic Novelist in the Protestant South" she asserts that "the writer whose themes are religious particularly needs a region where these themes find a response in the life of the people." She then adds: "The American Catholic is short on places that reflect his particular religious life and his particular problems. This country isn't exactly cut in his image." She goes on to say that even in areas where there are large numbers of Catholics, Catholic life there lacks "the significant features that result in a high degree of regional self-consciousness" and so offers the Catholic writer few "exploitable benefits." O'Connor's analysis of Catholic writers continues: "They have no great geographical extent, they have no particularly significant history, certainly no history of defeat; they have no real peasant class, and no cultural unity of the kind you find in the South." She adds that Catholics usually "blend almost imperceptively into the general materialistic background." This lack of a strong cultural tradition and a supportive audience greatly burdens Catholic writers, impoverishing their imaginative life and art. "If the Catholic faith were central to life in America, Catholic fiction would fare better, but the Church is not central to this society." O'Connor continues: "The things that bind us together as Catholics are known only to ourselves. A secular society understands us less and less. It becomes more and more difficult in America to make belief believable" (MM, 200, 201).

Given these trends and developments, O'Connor saw her own position, as well as that of almost all American Catholic writers, as being particularly precarious in terms of communicating with her readership. O'Connor frequently asserted in her letters that she could consistently count on only a handful of informed readers—an assertion largely borne out by the number of vicious and misinformed readings her work received, particularly early on—and that she had to make these readers go a long way in her life as an author. O'Connor knew hers was not the type of fiction that most Catholic readers yearned to read—not, in other words, fiction that was thoroughly positive and that went out of its way to celebrate the life of the Church. She characterized the general Catholic reader as unthinking, and she said that this reader "is so busy looking for something that fits his needs, and shows him in the best possible light, that he will find suspect anything that doesn't serve such purpose" (MM, 182). Elsewhere, in a letter (May 4, 1963) to Sister Mariella Gable, she wrote that those Catholic readers who demand that the writer make Christianity look desirable are asking the writer to describe Christianity's essence and not what the writer actually sees. "Ideal Christianity doesn't exist, because anything the human being touches, even Christian truth, he deforms slightly in his own image," she wrote, adding a bit later that the tendency of the Catholic readers she had been discussing "is always toward the abstract and therefore toward allegory, thinness, and ultimately what they are looking for is apologetic fiction. The best of them think: make it look desirable because it is desirable. And the rest of them think: make it look desirable so I won't look like a fool for holding it" (HB, 516). Such readers would find little to like in O'Connor's fiction and in all likelihood would see it as a good deal more than suspect—subversive, probably.

O'Connor of course felt an even greater distance from what she saw as the thoroughly secular and unbelieving general reader, the reader to whom she claimed she primarily wrote. In "The Catholic Novelists and Their Readers" she said that Catholic readers make a great mistake in supposing that Catholic writers write exclusively for them. "Occasionally this may happen," she wrote, "but generally it is not happening today" (MM, 185), and O'Connor made it clear elsewhere that it was not happening in her fiction. To A., O'Connor wrote (August 2, 1955) of the audience she perceived, saying that "one of the awful things about writing when you are a Christian is that for you the ultimate reality is the Incarnation, the present reality is the Incarnation, and nobody believes in the Incarnation; that is, nobody in your audience. My audience are the people who think God is dead. At least these are the people I am conscious of writing for" (HB, 92). Trying to bridge this gap between believing author and unbelieving audience was a terrible burden for O'Connor, and one that haunted her throughout her career.

Abbreviations
Abbreviations of works by Flannery O'Connor used in the Brinkmeyer text refer to:

CFO   *Conversations with Flannery O'Connor*. Edited by Rosemary M. Magee. Jackson, Miss., 1987.

HB   *The Habit of Being: Letters*. Edited by Sally Fitzgerald. New York, 1969.

MM   *Mystery and Manners: Occasional Prose*. Edited by Sally Fitzgerald and Robert Fitzgerald. New York, 1969.

From "Flannery O'Connor and Her Readers"

J. O. Tate

A GOOD SOURCE IS NOT SO HARD TO FIND: THE REAL LIFE MISFIT

1980

The mounting evidence of O'Connor's use of items from the Milledgeville and Atlanta newspapers will interest those who realize that these sources, in and of themselves, have nothing to do with the Gothic, the grotesque, the American Romance tradition, Southwestern humor, Southern literature, adolescent aggression, the New Hermeneutics, the anxiety of influence, structuralism, pentecostal Gnosticism, medieval theology, Christian humanism, existentialism, or the Roman Catholic Church.

I. On "The Misfit" as Name and Word

The text of an Atlanta *Constitution* article of November 6, 1952, p. 29, identifies for us the source of a celebrated sobriquet. This newspaper reference was reprinted in *The Flannery O'Connor Bulletin*, Volume III, Autumn 1974. The headline says enough: "'The Misfit' Robs Office, Escapes With $150." Flannery O'Connor took a forgotten criminal's alias and used it for larger purposes: *her* Misfit was out of place in a grander way than the original. But we should not forget O'Connor's credentials as "a literalist of the imagination." There is always "a little lower layer." She meant to mock pop psychology by exploiting the original Misfit's exploitation of a socio-psychological "excuse" for aberrant behavior. But even a little lower: the original meaning of the word "misfit" has to do with clothing. We should not fail, therefore, to note that The Misfit's "borrowed" blue jeans are too tight. He leaves the story, of course, wearing Bailey's shirt.

II. On the Identity and Destiny of the Original Misfit

By November 15, 1952, The Misfit had been apprehended; he had also advanced himself to page three of the Atlanta *Journal*. The Misfit was a twenty-five-year old named James C. Yancey. He "was found to be of unsound mind" and committed to the state mental hospital at—Milledgeville. Where else?

'The Misfit' Robs Office, Escapes With $150

A bandit who told his victims he was "The Misfit," held up the Atlanta Federal Savings and Loan Association office at 22 Marietta St., N. W., and escaped with $150 cash in a daring daylight raid Wednesday afternoon.

The man was described as being 30 years old, six feet tall and 175 pounds in weight. He carried a nickel-steel .32-caliber revolver, according to J. F. Clemmer, assistant vice-president of the company.

Clemmer told Det. Y. H. Allen the man shoved an envelope through the window where a cashier, Mrs. Beverly Bradshaw of 1919 Sylvan Ridge Dr., S. W., was at work. A crudely lettered message on the envelope read:

"Put $150 in here and don't say anything. I have a gun, and I am 'The Misfit.'"

Mrs. Bradshaw ducked behind the counter. Clemmer said. Clemmer told another cashier to "do whatever the man wanted." Then he told the robber he'd "better go—we're protected by the FBI." The bandit then fled on Marietta St.

Detectives said the description of the man tallied with that of one who Tuesday night held up a hotel clerk at 97 Harris St., N. W., and fled with $50. FBI agents joined Atlanta police in a search.

The article in the Atlanta CONSTITUTION, *November 6, 1952, provided Flannery O'Connor with the criminal nickname "The Misfit."*

III. On The Misfit's Notoriety, Peregrinations, Good Manners, Eye-glasses, Companions, and Mental Hygiene

The original Misfit was, as criminals go, small potatoes. He was an unambitious thief, no more. O'Connor took nothing from him but his imposing signature. But it just so happens that there was another well-publicized criminal aloose in Tennessee and Georgia just before the time that O'Connor appropriated the Misfit's name. This other hold-up artist had four important qualities in common with *her* Misfit. First, he inspired a certain amount of terror through several states. Second, he had, or claimed to have, a certain *politesse*. Third, he wore spectacles. Fourth, he had two accomplices, in more than one account.

James Francis ("Three-Gun") Hill, the sinister celebrity of the front pages, much more closely resembles the object of the grandmother's warnings than the original Misfit. Various articles tell of "a fantastic record of 26 kidnappings in four states, as many robberies, 10 car thefts, and a climactic freeing of four Florida convicts from a prison gang—all in two kaleidoscopic weeks." He had advanced "from an obscure hoodlum to top billing as a public enemy" (The Atlanta *Constitution*, November 1, p. 1). Such headlines as the grandmother had in mind screamed of Hill (though not in the sports section that Bailey was reading): "Maniac's Gang Terrorizes Hills" (*Constitution*, October 24, p. 2, from Sparta, Tenn.); "Search for Kidnap-Robbery Trio Centers in Atlanta and Vicinity" (October 25, p. 1, from Atlanta); "Chattanooga Is Focal Point for Manhunt" (October 27, p. 26); "2nd of Terror Gang Seized In Florida/Pal Said Still In Atlanta Area" (October 29, p. 32); "Self-Styled 3-Gun Maniac Frees 4 Road Gang Convicts at Gunpoint" (October 31, p. 1, from Bartow, Florida). It is quite clear that O'Connor, imagining through the grandmother's point of view, was, like the newspapers, assuming an Atlanta locale and orientation. The southward trip was in the same direction as Hill's last run.

The article of October 24 gives us a bit of color: "A fantastic band of highwaymen, led by a self-styled 'maniac' who laughed weirdly while he looted his victims, spread terror through the Cumberland hills today. . . . [The leader] boasted that he had escaped from the Utah State Prison and 'killed two people' . . . 'They call me a three-gun maniac, and brother, they got the picture straight,' the head bandit was quoted by victims." The October 31 article hints at the rustic setting of O'Connor's story: "The escapees and Hill . . . drove up a dead-end road and abandoned the car. They fled into thick woods on foot. . . ."

The *Constitution* of November 1 speaks of Hill on the front page as "the bespectacled, shrunken-cheeked highwayman." A later article gives us, as it gave O'Connor, a clue to her Misfit's respectful modes of address ("Good afternoon . . . I pre-chate that, lady . . . Nome . . . I'm sorry I don't have on a shirt before you ladies . . . Yes'm . . ."): We read of the trial of "Accused kidnapper, James Francis (Three-Gun) Hill, who says he's a 'gentleman-bandit' because 'I didn't cuss in front of ladies. . . .'" This Associated Press wire story from Chattanooga was on page 26 of the November 13 Atlanta *Journal*.

The *Constitution* of the same date says "Hearing Delayed for 'Maniac' Hill and 2 Cronies," and goes on to mention "James Francis Hill, self-styled 'three-gun maniac.'" We may observe that both Yancey and Hill were referred to in the newspapers as "self-styled," an arresting phrase perhaps to an author attuned to extravagances of self. I think we may also recognize here the genesis of Hiram and Bobby Lee.

The result of Hill's plea of guilty was perhaps not as forthright as his intention: "'Maniac' Hill Is Adjudged Incompetent" (*Constitution*, November 18). Like Yancey, The Misfit, Hill was sent to a mental institution—in Tennessee, this time. (His cronies were sentenced to jail.) The diagnosis of both Yancey and Hill as mentally ill may have suggested O'Connor's Misfit's experiences with the "head-doctor."

IV. On the Misfit, Memory, and Guilt

The fictional Misfit was not easily freudened: he knew perfectly well that he had not killed his daddy. Yet he insisted there was no balance between guilt and punishment—if memory served.

The issues of accuracy of memory, consciousness of guilt, and conscience were also raised in an odd "human-interest" story that was published in those same days when O'Connor was gathering so much material from the newspapers. The Misfit's claim that he was punished for crimes he did not remember may have been inspired by this account of a man who was *not* punished for a crime he *did* remember—but remembered wrongly.

The *Journal* of November 5, 1952 carried the article, written from Brookhaven, New York, on page 12: " 'Murder' Didn't Happen, House Painter Free." Louis Roberts had shot a policeman in 1928; he assumed he had killed him. Over twenty years later, his conscience finally forced him to confess. When his tale was investigated, it was discovered that the policeman had survived after all. There was no prosecution for, as an authority was quoted as saying, "His conscience has punished him enough."

From "A Good Source Is Not So Hard to Find"

Mary Jane Schenck (b. 1944)

DECONSTRUCTING "A GOOD MAN IS HARD TO FIND"   1988

"A Good Man Is Hard to Find" presents a masterful portrait of a woman who creates a self and a world through language. From the outset, the grandmother relies on "texts" to structure her reality. The newspaper article about The Misfit mentioned in the opening paragraph of the story is a written text which has a particular status in the narrative. It refers to events outside and prior to the primary *récit*, but it stands as an unrecognized prophecy of the events which occur at the end. For Bailey, the newspaper story is not important or meaningful, and for the grandmother it does not represent a real threat but is part of a ploy to get her own way. It is thus the first one of her "fictions," one which ironically comes true. The grandmother's whole personality is built upon the fictions she tells herself and her family. Although she knows Bailey would object if she brought her cat on the trip, the grandmother sneaks the cat into the car, justifying her behavior by imagining "he would miss her too much and she was afraid he might brush himself against one of the gas burners and accidentally asphyxiate himself." She also carefully cultivates a fiction about the past when people were good and when "children were more respectful of their native states and their parents and everything else." As she tells Red Sam at the Tower when they stop to eat, "People are certainly not nice like they used to be."

The grandmother reads fictional stories to the children, tells them ostensibly true stories, and provides a continual gloss on the physical world they are passing. "Little niggers in the country don't have things like we do. If I could paint, I'd paint that picture." Lacking that skill, the grandmother nevertheless verbally "creates" a whole universe as they ride along. "'Look at the graveyard!' the grandmother said, pointing it out. 'That was the old family burying ground. That belonged to the plantation.'" She creates the stories behind the visual phenomena she sees and explains relationships between events or her own actions which have no logic other than that which she lends them.

Her most important fiction is, of course, the story of the old plantation house which becomes more of an imperative as she tells it. The more she talks about it, the more she wants to see it again, so she does not hesitate to self-consciously lie about it. "'There was a secret panel in this house,' she said craftily, not telling the truth but wishing she were." At this point we see clearly the performative quality of the grandmother's language. At first it motivates her own desire, then spills over onto the children, finally culminating in their violent outburst of screaming and kicking to get their father to stop the car. The performative quality of her language becomes even more crucial when she realizes that she has fantasized the location of the house. She does not admit it, but her thoughts manifest themselves physically: "The thought was so embarrassing that she turned red in the face and her eyes dilated and her feet jumped up, upsetting her valise in the corner." Of course, it is her physical action which frees the cat and causes the accident. After the accident, she again fictionalizes about her condition, hoping she is injured so she can deflect Bailey's anger, and she cannot even manage to tell the truth about the details of the accident.

The scene with The Misfit is the apogee of the grandmother's use of "fictions" to explain and control reality, attempts that are thwarted by her encounter with a character who understands there is no reality behind her words. When the grandmother recognizes The Misfit, he tells her it would have been better if she hadn't, but she has *named* him, thus forcing him to become what is behind his self-selected name. In a desperate attempt to cope with the threat posed by the murderer, the grandmother runs through her litany of convenient fictions. She believes that there are class distinctions ("I know you're a good man. You don't look a bit like you have common blood"), that appearance reflects reality ("You shouldn't call yourself The Misfit because I know you're a good man at heart. I can just look at you and tell"), that redemption can be achieved through work ("You could be honest too if you'd only try. . . . Think how wonderful it would be to settle down . . ."), and finally, that prayer will change him ("'Pray, pray,' she commanded him").

From "Deconstructing Meaning
in Two Short Stories by Flannery O'Connor"

Kathleen Feeley (b. 1929)

COMIC PERVERSION IN "GOOD COUNTRY PEOPLE"   1972

Comic perversion is a key concept in "Good Country People." Both the girl Joy-Hulga and the Bible salesman have perverted their true selves, and each is revealed in his falsity after the word of God is perverted during a seduction scene—itself a perversion of love. Even the structure of the story appears to be a perversion of a traditional short-story form. Two-thirds of the story elapse before the initial meeting of Joy-Hulga and Manley Pointer, the Bible salesman, occurs. In the first section, Flannery O'Connor sets up a relationship between Mrs. Freeman, the hired man's wife, and Mrs. Hopewell, her employer, and between each of these women and the one-legged protagonist, Joy-Hulga. These relationships structure the story. . . . From Manley Pointer's opening question ("You ever ate a chicken that was two days old?") to his final assertion ("I been believing in nothing since I was born") the story moves "like the advance of a heavy truck" to its moment of truth.

That the salesman is peddling Bibles is the central perversion of the story. Flannery O'Connor believed in the power of the word of God. The Bible was for her, as it is for Jews and for Scripture-oriented Christians, the power of God and the wisdom of God. God's scriptural word is not a dead letter; it is a living presence. Reading it does more than enlighten the intellect; it unleashes power that moves the spirit. As a perversion of Christianity has driven Joy to become Hulga, so a perversion of the meaning of Scripture jolts her into self-recognition. In her raging accusation of the deceitful salesman—"You're a fine Christian! You're just like them all—say one thing and do another"—Hulga identifies Christianity with hypocrisy. She adds another indication of the emptiness of the Christianity she sees when, earlier in the story, she cries out to her mother: "Woman, do you ever look inside and see what you are not?" The obvious disparity between what Christians should be and what marks the Christians she knows moves Hulga to embrace Heidegger's emphasis on "being" and his consequent agnosticism. The Bible salesman quoted one verse of Scripture—"He who losest his life shall find it"—to emphasize his desire to be a missionary (one sent). In the climactic scene, this verse is rephrased when Hulga assents to showing Manley Pointer (almost too suggestive a name) her wooden leg. ". . . It was like surrendering to him completely. It was like losing her own life and finding it again, miraculously, in his." This perverse application of Scripture holds an ironic truth: Hulga does lose her life—her self-created being, symbolized by her wooden leg and her new name—by the salesman's deception. Given the structure of the story, there emerges the strong possibility that, having lost her false life, she will see herself (as her cliché-prone mother would say) "without a leg to stand on" and she will hobble toward "home."

From *Flannery O'Connor: Voice of the Peacock*

How One Story Illuminates Another

The more often we meet someone, the better we know the person. Observing behavior on one occasion, we usually gain perspective on that person's actions on another occasion. Even though we know most authors only on the printed page, our experience with them is similar: the more we read their work, the better we understand them. Reading several short stories by the same writer, we almost inevitably notice similarities—some obvious, others subtle—among the different works. Often a writer whom we find challenging on first encounter (such as Joyce or Borges) becomes more accessible as we read more widely in their work. Each new story throws light on the earlier ones, and knowing the earlier work helps us understand the new one more easily.

It always helps to read an author in depth before writing on his or her work. Characteristic themes emerge. Central ideas become evident. The writer's style grows familiar. Before choosing a topic on a particular writer you have read in depth, you might consider the following questions:

- Do similar or identical themes reappear in different stories?
- Do certain ideas emerge repeatedly in the work?
- Does a particular type of character (for example, a domineering mother, a weak husband, and so forth) appear in different stories?
- Do the stories share any obvious elements of style (for example, simple diction, complex sentences, lots of dialogue, and so forth)?
- Is there anything obviously unusual about the author's subject, setting, or characters?
- Does the author have an identifiable literary personality (a characteristic tone, style, subject, or thematic concern)?

You need not ask every question, but considering such straightforward issues will help clarify your ideas about a writer and also help define a useful topic for your paper.

WRITING ASSIGNMENT

After reading the stories by Edgar Allan Poe or Flannery O'Connor in this chapter (or three stories by any other writer in the book), write an essay identifying a characteristic theme or concern. Support your assertion with evidence from at least three different stories.

FURTHER SUGGESTIONS FOR WRITING ON EDGAR ALLAN POE

1. Compare and contrast Poe's use of point of view in these three stories. How would these stories change if, for example, Prince Prospero narrated "The Masque of the Red Death," Usher told his own story in "The Fall of the House of Usher," or an omniscient narrator described the events of "The Tell-Tale Heart"? Explain why Poe employed the points of view he did to achieve the effects of each story.
2. In his essay "The Tale and Its Effect" (page 405), Poe claims that an author's very first sentence must bring out the effect he's trying to produce on the reader, otherwise "he has

failed in his first step." Consider the first sentences of the three Poe stories in this anthology and judge the author by his own criteria.

3. Poe was one of the first Southern writers to employ the "grotesque"—a combination of horror and humor—in his stories. He has many followers in this genre, most notably Flannery O'Connor, who claimed that Poe's short stories were a major influence on her own writing. What examples of the grotesque can you find in the stories by Poe and O'Connor contained in this chapter? Do you see any evidence in O'Connor's work that she was influenced by Poe's stories?

4. Edgar Allan Poe never knew his real father and had a conflicted relationship with his foster father John Allan. Father/son relationships factor in all three of these stories, albeit in disguised form. Once you discern the father/son connection in each story, however, the tales take on added meaning. How do you think Poe feels about the relationship of fathers and sons based on these stories?

FURTHER SUGGESTIONS FOR WRITING ON FLANNERY O'CONNOR

1. How do the stories of Flannery O'Connor make manifest the principles she states in her remarks entitled "Excerpt from 'The Grotesque in Southern Fiction': The Serious Writer and the Tired Reader"?

2. Compare Mrs. Turpin's defiance of God in "Revelation" ("Who do you think you are?" paragraph 187) with the urge of a shipwrecked man in "The Open Boat" to shake his fist at the clouds ("Just you drown me, now, and then hear what I call you!," paragraph 70). Do Flannery O'Connor and Stephen Crane express similar or different concepts of Whoever runs the universe?

3. "In most good stories it is the character's personality that creates the action of the story," O'Connor declares in her essay "Writing Short Stories." "If you start with a real personality, a real character, then something is bound to happen." Discuss this statement as it applies to one or more of the O'Connor stories you have read. Do O'Connor's characters seem to you to be real people, or do you see them as mere vessels for the author's religious views?

4. Compare the woman protagonists in these two stories of Flannery O'Connor: the grandmother who confronts The Misfit and Mrs. Turpin.

5. In 750 to 1,000 words, comment on O'Connor's use of humor. How does comedy help her say what she has to say?

11 Stories for Further Reading

For human intercourse, as soon as we look at it for its own sake and not as a social adjunct, is seen to be haunted by a specter. We cannot understand each other, except in a rough-and-ready way; we cannot reveal ourselves, even when we want to; what we call intimacy is only a makeshift; perfect knowledge is an illusion. But in the novel we can know people perfectly, and, apart from the general pleasure of reading, we can find here a compensation for their dimness in life. In this direction fiction is truer than history, because it goes beyond the evidence, and each of us knows from his own experience that there is something beyond the evidence, and even if the novelist has not got it correctly, well—he has tried.

—E. M. Forster, *Aspects of the Novel*

Chinua Achebe

DEAD MEN'S PATH   (1953) 1972

Chinua Achebe was born in Ogidi, a village in eastern Nigeria, in 1930. His father was a missionary schoolteacher, and Achebe had a devout Christian upbringing. A member of the Ibo tribe, the future writer grew up speaking Igbo, but at the age of eight, he began learning English. He went abroad to study at London University but returned to Africa to complete his B.A. at the University College of Ibadan in 1953. Achebe worked for years in Nigerian radio. Shortly after Nigeria's independence from Great Britain in 1963, civil war broke out, and the new nation split in two. Achebe left his job to join the Ministry of Information for Biafra, the new country created from eastern Nigeria. It was not until 1970 that the bloody civil war ended.

Chinua Achebe

Approximately one million Ibos lay dead from war, disease, and starvation as the defeated Biafrans reunited with Nigeria. Achebe is often considered Africa's premier novelist. His novels include Things Fall Apart *(1958),* No Longer at Ease *(1962),* A Man of the People *(1966), and* Anthills of the Savannah *(1987). His short stories have been collected in* Girls At War *(1972). He has also published poetry, children's stories, and several volumes of essays, the most recent of which is* Home and Exile *(2000). In 1990 Achebe suffered massive injuries in a car accident outside Lagos that left him paralyzed from the waist down. He currently teaches at Bard College in upstate New York. In 1999 he visited Nigeria again after a deliberate nine-year absence to protest government dictatorship, and his homecoming became a national event.*

Michael Obi's hopes were fulfilled much earlier than he had expected. He was appointed headmaster of Ndume Central School in January 1949. It had always been an unprogressive school, so the Mission authorities decided to send a young and energetic man to run it. Obi accepted this responsibility with enthusiasm. He had many wonderful ideas and this was an opportunity to put them into practice. He had had sound secondary school education which designated him a "pivotal teacher" in the official records and set him apart from the other headmasters in the mission field. He was outspoken in his condemnation of the narrow views of these older and often less-educated ones.

"We shall make a good job of it, shan't we?" he asked his young wife when they first heard the joyful news of his promotion.

"We shall do our best," she replied. "We shall have such beautiful gardens and everything will be just *modern* and delightful . . ." In their two years of married life she had become completely infected by his passion for "modern methods" and his denigration of "these old and superannuated people in the teaching field who would be better employed as traders in the Onitsha market." She began to see herself already as the admired wife of the young headmaster, the queen of the school.

The wives of the other teachers would envy her position. She would set the fashion in everything . . . Then, suddenly, it occurred to her that there might not be other wives. Wavering between hope and fear, she asked her husband, looking anxiously at him.

"All our colleagues are young and unmarried," he said with enthusiasm 5 which for once she did not share. "Which is a good thing," he continued.

"Why?"

"Why? They will give all their time and energy to the school."

Nancy was downcast. For a few minutes she became skeptical about the new school; but it was only for a few minutes. Her little personal misfortune could not blind her to her husband's happy prospects. She looked at him as he sat folded up in a chair. He was stoop-shouldered and looked frail. But he sometimes surprised people with sudden bursts of physical energy. In his present posture, however, all his bodily strength seemed to have retired behind his deep-set eyes, giving them an extraordinary power of penetration. He was only twenty-six, but looked thirty or more. On the whole, he was not unhandsome.

"A penny for your thoughts, Mike," said Nancy after a while, imitating the woman's magazine she read.

"I was thinking what a grand opportunity we've got at last to show these   10
people how a school should be run."

Ndume School was backward in every sense of the word. Mr. Obi put his
whole life into the work, and his wife hers too. He had two aims. A high standard of teaching was insisted upon, and the school compound was to be turned
into a place of beauty. Nancy's dream-gardens came to life with the coming of
the rains, and blossomed. Beautiful hibiscus and allamanda hedges in brilliant
red and yellow marked out the carefully tended school compound from the rank
neighborhood bushes.

One evening as Obi was admiring his work he was scandalized to see an old
woman from the village hobble right across the compound, through a marigold
flower-bed and the hedges. On going up there he found faint signs of an almost
disused path from the village across the school compound to the bush on the
other side.

"It amazes me," said Obi to one of his teachers who had been three years in
the school, "that you people allowed the villagers to make use of this footpath. It
is simply incredible." He shook his head.

"The path," said the teacher apologetically, "appears to be very important to
them. Although it is hardly used, it connects the village shrine with their place
of burial."

"And what has that got to do with the school?" asked the headmaster.   15

"Well, I don't know," replied the other with a shrug of the shoulders. "But I
remember there was a big row some time ago when we attempted to close it."

"That was some time ago. But it will not be used now," said Obi as he
walked away. "What will the Government Education Officer think of this when
he comes to inspect the school next week? The villagers might, for all I know,
decide to use the schoolroom for pagan ritual during the inspection."

Heavy sticks were planted closely across the path at the two places where it
entered and left the school premises. These were further strengthened with
barbed wire.

Three days later the village priest of *Ani* called on the headmaster. He was
an old man and walked with a slight stoop. He carried a stout walking-stick
which he usually tapped on the floor, by way of emphasis, each time he made a
new point in his argument.

"I have heard," he said after the usual exchange of cordialities, "that our an-   20
cestral footpath has recently been closed . . ."

"Yes," replied Mr. Obi. "We cannot allow people to make a highway of our
school compound."

"Look here, my son," said the priest bringing down his walking-stick, "this
path was here before you were born and before your father was born. The whole
life of this village depends on it. Our dead relatives depart by it and our ancestors visit us by it. But most important, it is the path of children coming in to be
born . . ."

Mr. Obi listened with a satisfied smile on his face.

"The whole purpose of our school," he said finally, "is to eradicate just such beliefs as that. Dead men do not require footpaths. The whole idea is just fantastic. Our duty is to teach your children to laugh at such ideas."

"What you say may be true," replied the priest, "but we follow the practices 25 of our fathers. If you reopen the path we shall have nothing to quarrel about. What I always say is: let the hawk perch and let the eagle perch." He rose to go.

"I am sorry," said the young headmaster. "But the school compound cannot be a thoroughfare. It is against our regulations. I would suggest your constructing another path, skirting our premises. We can even get our boys to help in building it. I don't suppose the ancestors will find the little detour too burdensome."

"I have no more words to say," said the old priest, already outside.

Two days later a young woman in the village died in childbed. A diviner was immediately consulted and he prescribed heavy sacrifices to propitiate ancestors insulted by the fence.

Obi woke up next morning among the ruins of his work. The beautiful hedges were torn up not just near the path but right round the school, the flowers trampled to death and one of the school buildings pulled down . . . That day, the white Supervisor came to inspect the school and wrote a nasty report on the state of the premises but more seriously about the "tribal-war situation developing between the school and the village, arising in part from the misguided zeal of the new headmaster."

Isabel Allende

THE JUDGE'S WIFE   1988

TRANSLATED BY MARGARET SAYERS PEDEN

Isabel Allende was born in 1942 in Lima, Peru; her father Tomás was a Chilean diplomat and a cousin of Salvador Allende, who would be elected president of Chile in 1970. When Allende was three years old, her parents' marriage ended, and she and her two siblings were raised in Chile by their mother and maternal grandfather. In 1953 her mother married another Chilean diplomat, and the family spent the next five years in Bolivia and Beirut, Lebanon. From 1959 to 1965 Allende worked for the Food and Agriculture Organization of the United Nations in Santiago, Chile. She married Miguel Frías in 1962; their daughter Paula was born in 1963 and their son Nicolas in 1966 (she and Frías divorced in 1987, and she married Willie Gordon the following year). From 1967 to 1975 Allende

Isabel Allende

wrote for magazines and worked for television stations in Chile, but she and her family left the country in 1975 because of the political situation following the rightist coup that had overthrown the Allende government in 1973. They spent the next thirteen years in Venezuela, where Allende continued to work as a journalist and freelance writer. In 1981, upon learning that her ninety-nine-year-old grandfather was dying, she began to write him a letter, which evolved into her first novel, The House of the Spirits. *Published in Spanish in 1982 and in English translation three years later, it became an international best-seller. Her later novels are* Of Love and Shadows *(1987),* Eva Luna *(1988),* The Infinite Plan *(1993),* Daughter of Fortune *(1999), and* Portrait in Sepia *(2000). She has also published* The Stories of Eva Luna *(1991), a collection of short fiction that includes "The Judge's Wife";* Paula *(1995), an autobiography and family history begun during her daughter's ultimately fatal illness;* Aphrodite: A Memoir of the Senses *(1997), a paean to pleasure in all its manifestations;* City of the Beasts *(2002), a novel for young readers; and* My Invented Country: A Nostalgic Journey Through Chile *(2003). Her novels, written in a lyrical style and blending fantasy and legend with family and social history, have made her one of the most prominent practitioners of Magical Realism. Allende lives with her family in San Rafael, California.*

Nicolas Vidal always knew he would lose his head over a woman. So it was foretold on the day of his birth, and later confirmed by the Turkish woman in the corner shop the one time he allowed her to read his fortune in the coffee grounds. Little did he imagine though that it would be on account of Casilda, Judge Hidalgo's wife. It was on her wedding day that he first glimpsed her. He was not impressed, preferring his women dark-haired and brazen. This ethereal slip of a girl in her wedding gown, eyes filled with wonder, and fingers obviously unskilled in the art of rousing a man to pleasure, seemed to him almost ugly. Mindful of his destiny, he had always been wary of any emotional contact with women, hardening his heart and restricting himself to the briefest of encounters whenever the demands of manhood needed satisfying. Casilda, however, appeared so insubstantial, so distant, that he cast aside all precaution and, when the fateful moment arrived, forgot the prediction that usually weighed in all his decisions. From the roof of the bank, where he was crouching with two of his men, Nicolas Vidal peered down at this young lady from the capital. She had a dozen equally pale and dainty relatives with her, who spent the whole of the ceremony fanning themselves with an air of utter bewilderment, then departed straight away, never to return. Along with everyone else in the town, Vidal was convinced the young bride would not withstand the climate, and that within a few months the old women would be dressing her up again, this time for her funeral. Even if she did survive the heat and the dust that filtered in through every pore to lodge itself in the soul, she would be bound to succumb to the fussy habits of her confirmed bachelor of a husband. Judge Hidalgo was twice her age, and had slept alone for so many years he didn't have the slightest notion of how to go about pleasing a woman. The severity and stubbornness with which he executed the law even at the expense of justice had made him feared throughout the province. He refused to apply any common sense in the exercise of his profession, and was equally harsh in his condemnation of the theft of a chicken as of a premeditated murder. He dressed formally in black, and, despite the all-pervading dust in this godforsaken town, his boots always shone with beeswax. A man such as he was never meant to be a husband, and yet not only did the gloomy wedding-day prophecies remain unfulfilled, but Casilda emerged happy and smiling from three pregnancies in rapid succession. Every Sunday at noon she would go to mass with her husband, cool and collected beneath her Spanish mantilla, seemingly untouched by our pitiless summer, as wan and frail-looking as on the day of her arrival: a perfect example of delicacy and refinement. Her loudest words were a soft-spoken greeting; her most expressive gesture was a graceful nod of the head. She was such an airy, diaphanous creature that a moment's carelessness might mean she disappeared altogether. So slight an impression did she make that the changes noticeable in the Judge were all the more remarkable. Though outwardly he remained the same—he still dressed as black as a crow and was as stiff-necked and brusque as ever—his judgments in court altered dramatically. To general amazement, he found the youngster who robbed the Turkish shopkeeper innocent, on the grounds that she had been selling him short for years, and the money he had taken could therefore be seen as compensation. He also refused to punish an adulterous wife, arguing that since her husband himself kept a mistress he did not have the moral authority to demand fidelity. Word in the town had it that the Judge was transformed the minute he crossed the threshold at home: that he flung off his gloomy apparel, rollicked with his children, chuckled as he sat Casilda on his lap. Though no one ever succeeded in confirming these rumors, his wife got the credit for his newfound kindness, and her reputation grew accordingly. None of this was of the slightest interest to Nicolas Vidal, who as a wanted man was sure there would be no mercy shown him the day he was brought in chains before the Judge. He paid no heed to the talk about Doña Casilda, and the rare occasions he glimpsed her from afar only confirmed his first impression of her as a lifeless ghost.

Born thirty years earlier in a windowless room in the town's only brothel, Vidal was the son of Juana the Forlorn and an unknown father. The world had no place for him. His mother knew it, and so tried to wrench him from her womb with sprigs of parsley, candle butts, douches of ashes, and other violent purgatives, but the child clung to life. Once, years later, Juana was looking at her mysterious son and realized that, while all her infallible methods of aborting might have failed to dislodge him, they had none the less tempered his soul to the hardness of iron. As soon as he came into the world, he was lifted in the air by the midwife who examined him by the light of an oil lamp. She saw he had four nipples.

"Poor creature: he'll lose his head over a woman," she predicted, drawing on her wealth of experience.

Her words rested on the boy like a deformity. Perhaps a woman's love would have made his existence less wretched. To atone for all her attempts to kill him before birth, his mother chose him a beautiful first name, and an imposing family name picked at random. But the lofty name of Nicolas Vidal was no protection against the fateful cast of his destiny. His face was scarred from knife fights before he reached his teens, so it came as no surprise to decent folk that he ended up a bandit. By the age of twenty, he had become the leader of a band of desperadoes. The habit of violence toughened his sinews. The solitude he was condemned to for fear of falling prey to a woman lent his face a doleful expression. As soon as they saw him, everyone in the town knew from his eyes, clouded by tears he would never allow to fall, that he was the son of Juana the Forlorn. Whenever there was an outcry after a crime had been committed in the region, the police set out with dogs to track him down, but after scouring the hills invariably returned empty-handed. In all honesty they preferred it that way, because they could never have fought him. His gang gained such a fearsome reputation that the surrounding villages and estates paid to keep them away. This money would have been plenty for his men, but Nicolas Vidal kept them constantly on horseback in a whirlwind of death and destruction so they would not lose their taste for battle. Nobody dared take them on. More than once, Judge Hidalgo had asked the government to send troops to reinforce the police, but after several useless forays the soldiers returned to their barracks and Nicolas Vidal's gang to their exploits. On one occasion only did Vidal come close to falling into the hands of justice, and then he was saved by his hardened heart.

Weary of seeing the laws flouted, Judge Hidalgo resolved to forget his scruples and set a trap for the outlaw. He realized that to defend justice he was committing an injustice, but chose the lesser of two evils. The only bait he could find was Juana the Forlorn, as she was Vidal's sole known relative. He had her dragged from the brothel where by now, since no clients were willing to pay for her exhausted charms, she scrubbed floors and cleaned out the lavatories. He put her in a specially made cage which was set up in the middle of the Plaza de Armas, with only a jug of water to meet her needs.

"As soon as the water's finished, she'll start to squawk. Then her son will come running, and I'll be waiting for him with the soldiers," Judge Hidalgo said.

News of this torture, unheard of since the days of slavery, reached Nicolas Vidal's ears shortly before his mother drank the last of the water. His men watched as he received the report in silence, without so much as a flicker of emotion on his blank lone wolf's face, or a pause in the sharpening of his dagger blade on a leather strap. Though for many years he had had no contact with Juana, and retained few happy childhood memories, this was a question of honor. No man can accept such an insult, his gang reasoned as they got guns and horses ready to rush into the ambush and, if need be, lay down their lives. Their chief showed no sign of being in a hurry. As the hours went by tension mounted in the camp. The perspiring, impatient men stared at each other, not daring to speak. Fretful, they caressed the butts of their revolvers and their horses' manes, or busied themselves coiling their lassos. Night fell. Nicolas Vidal was the only one in the camp who slept. At dawn, opinions were divided. Some of the men reckoned he was even more heartless than they had ever imagined, while others maintained their leader was planning a spectacular ruse to free his mother. The one thing that never crossed any of their minds was that his courage might have failed him, for he had always proved he had more than enough to spare. By noon, they could bear the suspense no longer, and went to ask him what he planned to do.

"I'm not going to fall into his trap like an idiot," he said.

"What about your mother?"

"We'll see who's got more balls, the Judge or me," Nicolas Vidal coolly replied.   10

By the third day, Juana the Forlorn's cries for water had ceased. She lay curled on the cage floor, with wildly staring eyes and swollen lips, moaning softly whenever she regained consciousness, and the rest of the time dreaming she was in hell. Four armed guards stood watch to make sure nobody brought her water. Her groans penetrated the entire town, filtering through closed shutters or being carried by the wind through the cracks in doors. They got stuck in corners, where dogs worried at them, and passed them on in their howls to the newly born, so that whoever heard them was driven to distraction. The Judge couldn't prevent a steady stream of people filing through the square to show their sympathy for the old woman, and was powerless to stop the prostitutes going on a sympathy strike just as the miners' fortnight holiday was beginning. That Saturday, the streets were thronged with lusty workmen desperate to unload their savings, who now found nothing in town apart from the spectacle of the cage and this universal wailing carried mouth to mouth down from the river to the coast road. The priest headed a group of Catholic ladies to plead with Judge Hidalgo for Christian mercy and to beg him to spare the poor old innocent woman such a frightful death, but the man of the law bolted his door and refused to listen to them. It was then they decided to turn to Doña Casilda.

The Judge's wife received them in her shady living room. She listened to their pleas looking, as always, bashfully down at the floor. Her husband had not been home for three days, having locked himself in his office to wait for Nicolas Vidal to fall into his trap. Without so much as glancing out of the window, she was aware of what was going on, for Juana's long-drawn-out agony had forced its way even into the vast rooms of her residence. Doña Casilda waited until her visitors had left, dressed her children in their Sunday best, tied a black ribbon round their arms as a token of mourning, then strode out with them in the direction of the square. She carried a food hamper and a bottle of fresh water for Juana the Forlorn. When the guards spotted her turning the corner, they realized what she was up to, but they had strict orders, and barred her way with their rifles. When, watched now by a small crowd, she persisted, they grabbed her by the arms. Her children began to cry.

Judge Hidalgo sat in his office overlooking the square. He was the only person in the town who had not stuffed wax in his ears, because his mind was intent on the ambush and he was straining to catch the sound of horses' hoofs, the signal for action. For three long days and nights he put up with Juana's groans and the insults of the townspeople gathered outside the courtroom, but when he heard his own children start to wail he knew he had reached the bounds of his endurance. Vanquished, he walked out of the office with his three days' beard, his eyes bloodshot from keeping watch, and the weight of a thousand years on his back. He crossed the street, turned into the square and came face to face with his wife. They gazed at each other sadly. In seven years, this was the first time she had gone against him, and she had chosen to do so in front of the whole town. Easing the hamper and the bottle from Casilda's grasp, Judge Hidalgo himself opened the cage to release the prisoner.

"Didn't I tell you he wouldn't have the balls?" laughed Nicolas Vidal when the news reached him.

His laughter turned sour the next day, when he heard that Juana the Forlorn   15 had hanged herself from the chandelier in the brothel where she had spent her life, overwhelmed by the shame of her only son leaving her to fester in a cage in the middle of the Plaza de Armas.

"That Judge's hour has come," said Vidal.

He planned to take the Judge by surprise, put him to a horrible death, then dump him in the accursed cage for all to see. The Turkish shopkeeper sent him word that the Hidalgo family had left that same night for a seaside resort to rid themselves of the bitter taste of defeat.

The Judge learned he was being pursued when he stopped to rest at a way-side inn. There was little protection for him there until an army patrol could ar-rive, but he had a few hours' start, and his motor car could outrun the gang's horses. He calculated he could make it to the next town and summon help there. He ordered his wife and children into the car, put his foot down on the acceler-ator, and sped off along the road. He ought to have arrived with time to spare, but it had been ordained that Nicolas Vidal was that day to meet the woman who would lead him to his doom.

Overburdened by the sleepless nights, the townspeople's hostility, the blow to his pride, and the stress of this race to save his family, Judge Hidalgo's heart gave a massive jolt, then split like a pomegranate. The car ran out of control, turned several somersaults and finally came to a halt in the ditch. It took Doña Casilda some minutes to work out what had happened. Her husband's ad-vancing years had often led her to think what it would be like to be left a widow, yet she had never imagined he would leave her at the mercy of his ene-mies. She wasted little time dwelling on her situation, knowing she must act at once to get her children to safety. When she gazed around her, she almost burst into tears. There was no sign of life in the vast plain baked by a scorching sun, only barren cliffs beneath an unbounded sky bleached colorless by the fierce light. A second look revealed the dark shadow of a passage or cave on a distant slope, so she ran towards it with two children in her arms and the third clutching her skirts.

One by one she carried her children up the cliff. The cave was a natural one,   20 typical of many in the region. She peered inside to be certain it wasn't the den of some wild animal, sat her children against its back wall, then, dry-eyed, kissed them good-bye.

"The troops will come to find you a few hours from now. Until then, don't for any reason whatsoever come out of here, even if you hear me screaming—do you understand?"

Their mother gave one final glance at the terrified children clinging to each other, then clambered back down to the road. She reached the car, closed her husband's eyes, smoothed back her hair and settled down to wait. She had no idea how many men were in Nicolas Vidal's gang, but prayed there were a lot of them so it would take them all the more time to have their way with her. She gathered strength pondering on how long it would take her to die if she determined to do it as slowly as possible. She willed herself to be desirable, luscious, to create more work for them and thus gain time for her children.

Casilda did not have long to wait. She soon saw a cloud of dust on the horizon and heard the gallop of horses' hoofs. She clenched her teeth. Then, to her astonishment, she saw there was only one rider, who stopped a few yards from her, gun at the ready. By the scar on his face she recognized Nicolas Vidal, who had set out all alone in pursuit of Judge Hidalgo, as this was a private matter between the two men. The Judge's wife understood she was going to have to endure something far worse than a lingering death.

A quick glance at her husband was enough to convince Vidal that the Judge was safely out of his reach in the peaceful sleep of death. But there was his wife, a shimmering presence in the plain's glare. He leapt from his horse and strode over to her. She did not flinch or lower her gaze, and to his amazement he realized that for the first time in his life another person was facing him without fear. For several seconds that stretched to eternity, they sized each other up, trying to gauge the other's strength, and their own powers of resistance. It gradually dawned on both of them that they were up against a formidable opponent. He lowered his gun. She smiled.

Casilda won each moment of the ensuing hours. To all the wiles of seduction known since the beginning of time she added new ones born of necessity to bring this man to the heights of rapture. Not only did she work on his body like an artist, stimulating his every fiber to pleasure, but she brought all the delicacy of her spirit into play on her side. Both knew their lives were at stake, and this added a new and terrifying dimension to their meeting. Nicolas Vidal had fled from love since birth, and knew nothing of intimacy, tenderness, secret laughter, the riot of the senses, the joy of shared passion. Each minute brought the detachment of troops and the noose that much nearer, but he gladly accepted this in return for her prodigious gifts. Casilda was a passive, demure, timid woman who had been married to an austere old man in front of whom she had never even dared appear naked. Not once during that unforgettable afternoon did she forget that her aim was to win time for her children, and yet at some point, marveling at her own possibilities, she gave herself completely, and felt something akin to gratitude towards him. That was why, when she heard the soldiers in the distance, she begged him to flee to the hills. Instead, Nicolas Vidal chose to fold her in a last embrace, thus fulfilling the prophecy that had sealed his fate from the start.

25

Anjana Appachana

THE PROPHECY

1991

Anjana Appachana was born in Mercara, India, in 1956. Her father was an army officer and her mother a schoolteacher. Appachana received her B.A. from Delhi University in 1976 and, two years later, an M.A. from Jawaharal Nehru University. She held several nonliterary jobs in New Delhi, and then moved with her husband and daughter to the United States in the mid-1980s. She taught at Pennsylvania State University and later at Arizona State University in Tempe, where she now lives and writes. Despite her move to the West, her creative focus remains India, and its rich, although never romanticized, culture pervades her fiction.

Anjana Appachana

Prior to the publication of her first book, a collection of short stories entitled Incantations (1991), Appachana's story "Her Mother" won the O. Henry Festival Award in 1989. In this piece, she revealed the intimate relationship between mother and daughter through the mother's act of writing a letter from India to her daughter in the United States. Despite the superficial differences in their lives, the mother comes to realize that the two are more alike in their womanhood than dissimilar in situation. The stories in Incantations are all markedly realistic, with no hint of the Magical Realism or fantasy found in many postcolonial writers. Appachana's characters are plagued by very real concerns, such as the impossible social and moral quandary caused by one man's rape of his brother's bride.

The bond between women and their common oppression in the patriarchal Indian society are recurrent themes in both Appachana's stories and her novel Listening Now (1998). The book is told through the narrative voices of six women, and encompasses a love story in which a pregnant young woman is cruelly abandoned by her lover. Appachana acknowledges that the men in her novel are seen almost exclusively through the eyes of women: "I can't write from a man's point of view. I don't understand how their minds work. But I didn't reason any of this out when I wrote the book. I wrote what came to me and what came to me were the voices of these women. I could barely hear the men's voices!" The women's voices began to "haunt" her in the 1980s, and in 1990 she began to write Listening Now, using the voices as inspiration. As she told an interviewer for the Hindu newspaper, "I've probably listened to these stories all my life. I've listened to the stories of my women friends, the stories of their mothers, my mother, her sisters and their friends."

In addition to the O. Henry Festival prize, Appachana has been awarded a National Endowment for the Arts fellowship and has twice won the Hawthornden Castle fellowship, which awards a writing residency in a manor house in Scotland.

In the end we decided to visit the astrologer before going to the gynecologist. After an hour's wait in the relentless afternoon sun, a scooter finally stopped for us. When we told the scooterwalla° where we wanted to go, he snorted and spat out a copious stream of paan.°

"I don't go such short distances," he said contemptuously. We turned away wearily. "It will be ten rupees!" he shouted.

"Go to hell," said Amrita. "You scooterwallas are all the same."

I dragged her back. "Forget your principles today. We'll both collapse in this heat."

We sat inside the scooter. To the scooterwalla's left was a picture of Goddess Lakshmi with a tinsel garland around it, to his right, one of a film actress, bare-bosomed and smiling. Surveying us through the rear view mirror, the scooterwalla grinned. He lit a beedi° with a flourish and started the scooter. Loudly and at breakneck speed, the scooter weaved its way through the traffic. We clung to the sides and helplessly tried to hold our sarees down.

"Maybe I'll be lucky and have a miscarriage now," gasped Amrita.

"Slow down," I shouted above the noise of the scooter. He accelerated. "Slow down will you!"

He turned to me, grinning. "What did you say?"

I screamed, "Look at the road, don't look at me! Slow down!"

He missed a car by an inch, swerved violently, threw back his head and   10
laughed. "Which college are you from?" We did not answer. He accelerated.

"Slow down! Do you want us to die!"

"Memsahib,"° he said, "death is neither in your hands nor in mine. If we have to die, we will die. It is all written down."

"You die if you want to. At the rate you're going you'll kill us too."

He bounded up and down in his seat gleefully. "Who cares," he sang, "Who cares if I die, who cares if you die, what difference does it make!"

"Stop talking to him," Amrita told me, "he's enjoying it."   15

The scooterwalla accelerated again and looked at me hopefully in the rear view mirror. I looked out at the road. We had passed our destination. "Stop, stop!"

He turned to me again and winked. "What is there to be so scared about? People die all the time."

"Will you please stop, we've passed the place!"

He braked immediately and we almost fell over him. He leered at our bosoms and said, "Madam, you should have warned me. This is how accidents happen."

I thrust a ten rupee note into his outstretched hand. He took it, caressing   20
my hands as he did, smiled slowly and drove off. Shakily we began walking to Chachaji's house. Chachaji, as the astrologer was called, was very popular with the girls in our college. His prophecies came true and he was cheaper than the rest. He could read your minds. One look at you and he knew everything—your past, your present, your future.

---

scooterwalla: the driver of a motor-scooter taxi.   paan: a green leaf chewed in India.   beedi: a flavored cigarette.   Memsahib: a title of respect used for a woman.

His wife opened the door to us and led us to the living room. I could hear the pressure cooker in the kitchen and the house was redolent with the smell of chicken curry. Somewhere inside a baby cried. The smell of incense wafted in and Chachaji entered. Spotless white pyjama-kurta, soft white beard, frail frame, startling eyes . . . mystic . . . ethereal. We stared at him dumbstruck.

He sat opposite us and gazed into our faces. He smiled. "Yes, my children?"

I looked at Amrita. It had been her idea to come here. When she didn't say anything, I spoke. "We wanted to consult you."

"Yes, yes, they all want to consult me." How soft his voice was.

I looked again at Amrita. Her eyes were deep with tears. I knew how she   25
felt. I could have confessed anything to him.

He turned to Amrita. Almost imperceptibly, he shook his head. "Beti, you are in a forest, lost, wandering. You do not know where to go." Dumbly, Amrita nodded. He sighed and closed his eyes. "I see a boy." We started. "I see trouble. It all began with this boy. What is the date, time and place of your birth?" She told him. On a piece of paper he did some rapid calculations. He shook his head. "The stars are not good. The shadow of Shani is falling on you. It is a very un-lucky year for you."

Amrita whispered. "Chachaji, what will happen?"

"Happen? Has it not already happened?"

She flinched and lowered her eyes. Her fingers gathered and ungathered her pleats. "What will I do, Chachaji, what will I do?"

He closed his eyes once again. I was sweating profusely and there were beads   30
of perspiration above Amrita's mouth.

His wife entered with two glasses of water for us. We drank thirstily. She smiled at us. "You are both so pretty." We smiled gratefully. "But you don't know how to wear sarees," she said, clicking her tongue. "Stand up for a moment." We stood up obediently. She bent and pulled our sarees down. "Always wear your sandals before wearing sarees. Or else it'll ride high," she adjusted our pleats, then stood up and surveyed her work with satisfaction.

"Champa's mother," sighed Chachaji, "they have not come here to talk of sarees."

"Oh you," she dismissed him with a gesture. "Don't frighten these children with all your talk." She picked up the glasses, gave us another sunny smile and walked out of the room, her payals tinkling softly.

Apologetically, we looked at Chachaji. He smiled indulgently. "Yes, children, what else do you want to know?"

"What should I do?" asked Amrita.   35

"I will do a puja° for you. It will negate the bad influence of Shani. After six months I will perform a second puja. Your stars will change. The shadow of Shani will no longer envelop you." Worshipfully, we nodded. "For the puja," he continued, his eyes fixed at the wall behind us, "you will have to give a donation."

"How much?" Amrita asked, fumbling in her purse.

puja: a religious ritual.

"Whatever you wish, beti, whatever you wish. With the blessings of God all will be well. I will do a special puja for you."

Amrita gave him twenty rupees. He took it and fingered the notes meditatively. "My child, this will suffice only for a small puja. For you I will have to perform a big puja. Or else the trouble may become worse."

"Chachaji, I have very little money." 40

He shrugged his shoulders. "If that is your wish, then. This may not suffice to negate the evil influence of Shani." I took out ten rupees from my bag and gave it to him. "Chachaji, this is all we have."

He smiled, took the money with one hand, and patted my cheek with the other. "You are a true friend, beti. You are a loyal friend. Your stars are good. You will do an M.A. It is possible that you will work. You will marry a handsome man and have one son, one daughter."

"When will I get married, Chachaji?"

"How old are you?"

"Seventeen." 45

"In six, seven years, beti."

"Will it be arranged?"

"It will be love. You will have a love marriage."

"Will I go abroad, Chachaji?"

"Many times, many, many times." 50

"Thank you, Chachaji," I said, quietly ecstatic.

He turned to Amrita. "After I perform the puja, your stars will change. You will marry a handsome, fair, rich, influential man. You will have two sons who will rise to powerful positions in the government. They will bring you power, fame, respect. And you will also travel abroad, many, many times."

He rose. We folded our hands.

The heat hit us as we stepped out of the house. We walked towards the bus stop.

"Oh no, Patram!" I gasped and pulled Amrita back from the road. In silence, 55 breathing heavily, we stood where we were. A khaki-clad man walked past us. He was not Patram. Feeling foolish, we continued walking.

Patram was the omnipresent, omniscient peon-cum-bodyguard-cum-regulator-of-rules, employed by our college, who watched the boarders like a hawk and reported all our goings-on to the superintendent. He knew who sneaked out of the gates before the rules permitted, who returned after 8 p.m., who smoked, who had a boyfriend. Just last month two girls had been expelled from the hostel after Patram smelt cigarette smoke in the corridor outside their room and informed the superintendent. The case went up to the principal. The girls pleaded with her but she would not budge. She said that she would not have girls of such loose character in her college. They had to leave. If someone decided to sneak out of the college gates and see a 1:30 film show, Patram was sure to know. He was everywhere—in the markets, cinema, theatres, Connaught Place. We lived in dread of the famous khaki dress and cap and the permanent grin on his face.

That morning we had walked out of the college before official going-out time, and there had been no sign of Patram. Dressed in sarees for the first time in an effort to look older, we had walked out of the gates, awkwardly and with trepidation. Still no Patram.

And now, weak with relief at the false alarm, we waited for the bus that would take us to the gynecologist. It arrived almost immediately, and for once, it was not crowded. "Forty rupees," Amrita said as the bus began to move. "We've spent forty rupees today."

I said nothing. We had just a hundred between us. We had no idea how much the gynecologist would take. The previous day, in a desperate bid to make some money, we had gone around the hostel collecting old newspapers, empty jars and bottles. We had fitted these into six polythene bags and trudged to the nearby market, trying to appear oblivious to the noise they made as we walked, praying that the polythene bags would not fall apart. In the market we had squatted before the kabadiwalla° and bargained at length. He had said he would give us twenty rupees for the whole lot. We had asked for thirty. He had refused. We walked away and he had called us back. Twenty-five, he had said. So we struck the bargain. On the way back, overcome by the sight of pastries in the bakery, we had spent most of it on black forests, lemon tarts, chocolate eclairs and chicken patties. And now we had barely enough for the gynecologist, let alone the abortion. Maybe, I thought, she isn't pregnant after all.

The clinic was plush, beautiful and smelt rich. Our hearts sank. We sat at the reception and waited Amrita's turn. There was just one other person there, in a bright pink chiffon saree. She stared at us. We thumbed unseeingly through the magazines. She continued staring.

"She's going to ask questions," Amrita murmured.   60

"Lie."

"What?"

"So," said the woman, "you have come to visit Dr. Kumar?"

We nodded distantly and went back to our magazines.

"How old are you both?"   65

"Twenty," I lied. Beneath my saree my legs began to tremble.

"Acha? You look younger."

Amrita smiled. "That's good."

She continued surveying us and her face grew grim. She drew her palla° over her shoulders. "Are you married?"

"Yes," I said.   70

"No," said Amrita.

"Acha?" She turned a shocked face towards Amrita. "Then what are you doing here?"

"Period problems," said Amrita and went back to her magazine.

"What problems?"

---

kabadiwalla: player of an Indian stick game (here he is also a junk dealer).   palla: veil.

"Irregular," I said.

"Too frequent," said Amrita.

She smiled knowingly. "There seems to be some confusion about the problem, yes?" We did not reply. She turned her gaze on me. "So are you the married one?"

"Yes."

"You don't look married. How old are you?"

"Twenty."

"So what is *your* problem?"

"I'm accompanying my friend."

"Acha! So the married friend is accompanying the unmarried friend to the gynecologist!" She knew, she knew. She fingered her mangalsutra.° "It seems to me that neither of you is married." She waited. "And if that is so, God knows what you are doing here."

The nurse called, "Mrs. Mehta, your turn please."

She rose, exuding a strong whiff of Intimate as she did, and walked in.

"Bitch," said Amrita.

Ten minutes later, Mrs. Mehta emerged, gave us a meaningful look and left. We went in, sat opposite Dr. Kumar and began to cry.

She was wonderful. She spoke to us in low, comforting tones, gave us tissues, got us cold water and had the nurse serve us tea. Finally, red-nosed and swollen-eyed, we were quiet.

She turned to Amrita. "You're pregnant?"

"I think so."

"Let me check you."

I sat in the room while she and Amrita went into the adjoining room. When they emerged, I knew it was confirmed. Amrita sat next to me. She was trembling. I put my hand on her knee.

Dr. Kumar's eyes, brown and gentle, looked troubled. She reminded me of my mother. But I could not tell my mother if I were pregnant.

"How much will an abortion cost?" asked Amrita.

Dr. Kumar rested her face against her hand. "Does the boy know?"

"No. There's no need for him to know."

"So, you don't intend marrying him?"

"No. How much will it cost?"

Dr. Kumar was silent. Finally she said, "It's a thousand rupees in this clinic."
Amrita and I looked at each other in despair. We didn't even have a hundred. Dr. Kumar, her eyes full of compassion, suggested that there were government hospitals where it could be done for about a hundred rupees. She would give us the addresses. Sensing my apprehension, she assured me that they were perfectly safe. As for the abortion—people were having it all the time. She paused, then said, "Amrita, would you like to take your parents into your confidence?" Seeing Amrita's face, she gently continued, "Sometimes, beti, we tend to misjudge our parents. Often they're the best people to turn to at such times."

mangalsutra: a bridal necklace given by the groom at a wedding.

"Last year," Amrita whispered, "our neighbor's daughter got pregnant. She threw herself in front of a passing train. Her parents refused to claim her body. And my father said, that is how it should be."

"Your mother?"

"What could she say? She cried for days. And Ma can't keep anything to herself. She'll tell my father."

Dr. Kumar seemed lost in thought. After some time she sighed and said, "Are you both in the hostel?" We nodded. "So, your parents are not in Delhi?" We shook our heads. "I see." She wrote down a few addresses and gave them to us. We rose to leave. "Wait," she said, and proceeded to give us a fifteen-minute talk on contraception. Wide-eyed and quivering with embarrassment, I listened. I could barely look Dr. Kumar in the eye as she systematically went through it all. How did people ever buy these things? How did they look chemists in the eye? How did they ever get down to it? Amrita looked tired but unembarrassed, nodding from time to time. After Dr. Kumar finished, she said, "Don't be so foolish next time." We got up. She said, "Amrita, you're already two months gone. Don't wait much longer." Amrita nodded.

Dr. Kumar refused to take any money.   105

It was five when we reached the hostel. We changed out of our sarees and looked at each other.

"Marry him, Amrita," I said tentatively.

"Please," Amrita replied, "you'll never understand."

I didn't. I didn't understand at all. I liked Rakesh; he was handsome, bright, fun to be with. He smelt wonderfully of aftershave and had given us our first motorcycle rides. He's so *nice* I had often told Amrita, so *nice*. But she said he had no aesthetic sense. She didn't *want* nice. She didn't *want* to get married after college. She didn't *want* to end up like her parents. She wanted adventure. I, half in love with Rakesh, his aftershave and his motorcycle, was sure he would provide adventure. She scoffed at the very idea.

Often I wondered why Amrita had gone into this strange, loveless relation-   110
ship. Normally so communicative with me, she was unusually reticent about her affair with Rakesh. Was it just the sex? My mind recoiled at the thought. Nevertheless, I wondered. It's nothing so great, she told me once, and I tried to school my expression at this unexpected revelation. She had done it! How often? She looked the same. On our occasional outings together, I watched them covertly. They laughed, talked, ate, drank. I could see no hidden fire in Rakesh's eyes, no answering flame in Amrita's. In my own fantasies, I was beautiful but enigmatic, virginal, but willing to surrender it all to the man I married. If it happened before marriage he would not respect me. I would tame the beast in him. Did Rakesh respect Amrita? Did she drive him crazy with desire? I waited to hear more, but she said nothing. I continued feeding my fantasies of handsome men on motorcycles, smelling of aftershave, with deep voices and British accents. I would happily have settled for one after college, happily married one. He would never tire of me, nor I of him. Marriage would be that wondrous path of rapid heartbeats and unending, intimate discoveries.

Amrita spent the weekends with Rakesh in his hostel. "This bloody college and those frustrated spinsters make me sick," she would tell me every Sunday evening, referring to the superintendent and the principal. "I'll be glad to get out of this hole." Rakesh never seemed to figure in her plans for the future. She wanted to be a journalist and I had no doubt that she would succeed. Not only did she write expressively, but had strong feelings and a strange kind of courage, an indifference to what people thought of her. While I seemed to spend my life looking over my shoulder to see who was watching, starting, for fear someone was listening, always fearful that "they" would know, Amrita, as long as I had known her, had done exactly what she wanted. Now, on Amrita's behalf, it was I who was guilty, scared of discovery, certain that retribution was imminent.

We could not use the hostel phone to fix up the appointment as it was out of order. We began walking towards the gate again since the taxi-stand outside the college had a public phone. But Nemesis in the form of Patram was just behind us. Grinning, he led us to the superintendent's office. He had seen us outside the college gates that morning, he said. The superintendent, sullen, but with a predatory gleam in her eyes, lectured us on our dishonesty, the wickedness of our actions and on our parents' inability to inculcate in us the virtues of restraint and politeness. As she took a deep breath to renew her attack, Amrita told her that she was an ignorant, power-hungry, narrow-minded, perverse woman and stormed out of the room. Weak with shock and fear, I gave the superintendent an ingratiating smile and followed Amrita.

Back in our room, Amrita raged. She damned the college and the authorities. "One day," she fumed, "I'm going to expose this place for what it is. I'll write about it and publish it. No one will want to attend this wretched place." I replied, "It'll have exactly the opposite effect—your article will reassure every middle-class parent like yours and mine."

We were gated for two weeks. But the next week we sneaked out and waited for a scooter or bus that would take us to one of the clinics Dr. Kumar had suggested. Patram's voice called us from across the road, precipitating another return. Once again he escorted us to the superintendent's office. Our gating was extended to four weeks. Two weeks passed, then three weeks. One day someone casually mentioned that her sister had had a miscarriage after eating pickles. That evening I made Amrita eat half a bottle of mango pickle. The room smelled of it for days and she was violently sick, but nothing happened. She said, "If I starve myself maybe it'll die," and didn't eat for three days. She almost collapsed, but nothing happened. I said, "Eat, you'll need your strength for the abortion." "When," she whispered, "when?" As the days passed I felt Amrita's rising fear. The more fearful she was, the quieter she became. Daily I murmured reassurances while unobtrusively examining her stomach. It seemed to grow no bigger. Would an abortion at this stage kill her? I imagined Amrita's prolonged, bloody death at the clinic, with me left behind to break the news to her parents, to the superintendent, to the principal, to my parents. The horror. Would they hold me responsible? And then I was ridden with guilt for thinking such thoughts, for feeling not sorrow, but terror for the seemingly endless repercussions of such a death. My fantasies turned to nightmares.

As our gating entered the fourth week, Amrita fell ill. She refused to let me 115
call a doctor for fear he would find out that she was pregnant. At midnight her
temperature rose to 104 degrees. The superintendent did not take kindly to my
knock at her door at that hour, urging her to call a doctor. This was no time to
come knocking at her door, she snapped, handing me two aspirins and banging
the door on my face. I stood outside her door for a long time. Then I went back
to ours.

Amrita's temperature remained the same the next day. The superintendent
called a doctor. The diagnosis—measles.

"Oh my God, oh my God," said the superintendent wringing her hands.
"Now everyone in the hostel will get it. She had better leave the hostel."

"She has nowhere to go," I said.

She gave me a look of pure hatred and left the room hurriedly. Half an hour
later I was summoned to her office where the principal had joined her. "What is
all this I hear?" the principal asked me.

"All what?" 120

The principal looked at me in amazement and then spoke to me for ten
minutes on the subject of respect for elders. Subsequently she expressed her outrage that Amrita had no local guardians in Delhi who could take her away, and
her deeper outrage that I couldn't ask my local guardians to look after her. She
ordered the superintendent to send a telegram to Amrita's parents in Bangalore.
In the meantime Amrita and I were to have our meals in our room. On no account were we to enter the dining-hall. To attend classes, we were to use the
back door of the hostel. It would be opened especially for us.

The superintendent placed a call to Amrita's parents but could not get
through. She sent a telegram but there was no response. For a week Amrita
stayed confined to our room. I continued attending classes, leaving through the
back door of the hostel. For some unaccountable reason, it did not matter to
them if I infected the others in class, but the dining-room was taboo. Amrita
wept silently throughout, and when she was asleep, I did. Often I would wake up
at night to find Amrita awake, gazing at the ceiling, her face now full of spots, her
large eyes swollen and red. We hardly spoke. Finally the superintendent got
through to Amrita's parents. They said they would fly to Delhi the next day.
Turning to the wall, Amrita said, "This is the end. My father will have nothing to
do with me. Where will I go? Where will I go?" I could offer no comfort, no sanctuary. I kept saying, "He won't do that, he won't do that." Then I said, "Rakesh is
there, he'll see you through, he'll have to." She was silent and then said, "Call
him, tell him."

The hostel phone was out of order again. I asked the superintendent if I
could use hers. She refused. In the end I walked out of the college gates, my
pocket full of fifty paisa coins, while Patram followed me, calling, "Hemlathaji,
come back, come back, I'll report you to the superintendent, I'll tell the principal, you will see what I will do, you will see what happens." He followed me to
the gate and watched me walk to the taxi-stand. The taxiwallas stared at me
while I dialed Rakesh's number at his engineering college. I got a wrong number
the first time. The second time the call got disconnected. The third time I got

through. Rakesh was out, I was told, but would be back in ten minutes. I waited, while the taxiwallas eyed me. One lay down on the charpoi° next to me. "It is so hot," he groaned. He removed his banyan,° lowered his pyjamas and looked at me. I looked away.

It was growing dark and every emerging shadow seemed khaki-clad and wore a wide grin. I walked down the road slowly. Five minutes. A cyclist swerved towards me and I stepped back. He groaned and cycled away rapidly. I walked back and tried the number again. I got through. Rakesh was back. I told him what I could and he said he would be there immediately. I walked a slight distance away from the taxi-stand and waited. "Madam," said a voice behind me. I shuddered and looked back. It was the same taxiwalla. He looked me over and scratched his groin. "Can I help you in any way?" "No," I said and turned away. He remained where he was. "Do you need any fifty paisa coins?" "No," I said, "No." I walked further away. He followed me. I crossed the road. He stood opposite, staring at me. Ten minutes later Rakesh's motorcycle came to a halt beside me. The taxiwalla walked back.

Rakesh was in a state of shock and incomprehension. He would sell his motorcycle and pay for the abortion, he declared hoarsely. He would protect her from her parents. He would leave college. As I tried to calm him down, a familiar khaki-clad apparition emerged silently from the shadows and stood before us, grinning.

For the third time Patram escorted me back to the superintendent's office. The principal was there too. It was girls like me who ruined the reputation of the college—breaking rules, making boyfriends, smoking, she said. I didn't smoke, I replied. The principal snorted. Next I would say I didn't have a boyfriend. She pulled the telephone towards her. She was going to phone my local guardians to take me away. I could start packing my things.

I wish I could say at this point that I had let her phone them. I wish I could say that I had walked out of the room with an appropriate remark. I wish I could say that I had told them what I thought of them. Even today I relive that scene and say all that I did not at that time. I wish I didn't have to say that I began to cry hysterically while they watched me with satisfaction. That I begged them to give me another chance. That I told them my parents would never understand. That I kept repeating, please, please don't expel me, I'll never repeat my mistakes. That the superintendent said she wanted all this in writing. That I gave her a written apology, still sobbing, still begging. They both smiled and shook their heads. And the principal asked the superintendent, "So you think she has realized?" And the superintendent replied, "Who knows with these girls, they are such good actresses." And I said, (oh God), I said, "I will do anything you want me to do, but please don't expel me, please forgive me, please forgive me." And they said, "We cannot give you an answer now, we shall have to think about it. We will watch your behavior and then we will decide." And I thanked them.

The next morning, from our first floor window, I saw Rakesh's figure next to his motorcycle, waiting outside the gate. I sent him a note through my next-door

charpoi: string bed.   _banyan:_ vest.

neighbor, explaining the situation, but he continued waiting in the afternoon sun while I helped Amrita pack her belongings. Her parents arrived in the evening. Her father waited in the superintendent's office while her mother came up to our room and sat next to her daughter, stroking her hair. "My poor baby," she said, "my poor, poor child." And she smiled at me and said, "Hemu, beti, thank you for looking after her all this time. My daughter is lucky to have such a friend." She continued stroking Amrita's hair. "Ma," Amrita said, "Ma, I'm pregnant." Her mother's hands stopped. "Ma," Amrita said, grasping her thigh, "I'm three months pregnant Ma. Ma, where will I go? Where will I go?" Her mother was still, so still. She closed her eyes and whispered, "Bhagwan, hai Bhagwan."°

In the distance a clock struck six. From my position at the window I could see Rakesh outside the gate, waiting.

"Ma!"   130

We started. Amrita's voice sounded strange.

"Ma, I think I'm bleeding."

She was. Slowly, the white sheets were staining. Amrita began to cry, loud, harsh sounds. Fascinated, I watched the white sheets turning red while the room filled with the horrible sound, till I thought it would have to burst open to let out what it could not possibly contain. And then there was a knock on the door and the superintendent entered. I threw a bedcover over Amrita and her sounds stopped abruptly. The superintendent's eyes bulged. "What is the matter?"

Amrita's mother began stroking her hair again. "My daughter is tired. It has been a strain. Please call a taxi. We must leave now." The superintendent eyed us suspiciously. She came closer to Amrita and whipped the bedcover away. Amrita's mother gasped. The superintendent gave a strangled scream. Amrita closed her eyes and the superintendent said, "I should have known."

"Please call a taxi," her mother said.   135

"Taxi—nothing doing, I'm calling the principal." She rushed out of the room and we heard her heavy footsteps echoing down the corridor.

"Beti," her mother's face was distorted, "Please call a taxi."

"I can't, I can't, I'll be expelled. You call one from outside the gate, I'll stay with her."

"Ma, don't leave me," Amrita moaned.

I held her hands tightly. "I'm here."   140

Small, incoherent sounds escaped her mother's throat. She looked at us and then went out rapidly.

I was with Amrita for fifteen minutes while she continued bleeding. I used up all the sheets we had to use below and between her. The blood soaked through them all, right down to the mattress, and the room was heavy with its smell. Amrita moaned and twisted and turned and held on to my hand until I felt I could no longer bear the pain of it all. Then the superintendent entered the room with the principal. The principal took the scene in and hit her forehead with her hand.

"Tell her parents to take her away," she told me. "Tell them she cannot come back to this college. Where are they?"

Bhagwan, hai Bhagwan: a Hindi exclamation equivalent to "Oh, my God!"

"Her mother's gone to get a taxi." I was shivering violently.

I heard footsteps in the corridor and her mother entered the room, panting. 145 She ignored the superintendent and the principal. "Beti," she told me, "help me carry her down."

"And don't bring her back," the principal said, tight-lipped. "We don't want such girls here."

"Madam, madam," the superintendent said hysterically, "it isn't my fault—she broke the rules and got into this mess."

They called Patram to carry her suitcases down, while her mother and I carried Amrita downstairs to the waiting taxi, past the superintendent's room, past her amazed father, followed by the principal and the superintendent. We laid Amrita down on the back seat of the taxi and her mother said to me, "Come with me, beti, please come with me."

"Nothing doing," the principal said, holding my arm. "This girl is going nowhere. We have had enough trouble. Now Amrita is your responsibility." I stood between them, helpless.

"Will someone tell me what is happening?" her father asked. 150

"Yes, I will tell you," the principal said. "Your daughter is pregnant and at this moment she is aborting. You do what you want with her and don't bring her back to this college."

Her father's face seemed to shrink. He shook his head uncomprehendingly. Her mother took his arm gently and opened the door of the taxi. "Get inside," she said, "we have to go to the hospital." She sat at the back with Amrita. Slowly, the taxi drove away.

"So, Hemlathaji," said the superintendent, but I walked away, away from her, away from the hostel, away from it all, towards the college building. I climbed up the stairs to the first floor and sat there, against the wall.

Much later I looked at my watch. It was 9:45 p.m. They would lock the hostel door at 10:00. I walked back slowly and went upstairs to our room. The stench of blood greeted me, and on the bed, an accumulation of sheets, all red and white. I bolted the door and walked to the window. He was still there. I drew the curtains.

The rest, I heard from my mother's sister in Bangalore, who is a good friend 155 of Amrita's mother. She stayed with us for a week and, in the strictest of confidence, gave us a blow-by-blow account of everything. Amrita was in hospital for a day and then flew back with her parents to Bangalore. The following month she was married off. "That is *luck*," my aunt said. "*Such* a nice boy, you cannot imagine. *So* fair, *so* handsome and on top of that, the *only* son. And the wedding . . . what a wedding! She wore a lahenga° studded with *real* pearls." I asked, "Isn't she going to complete her B.A.?" My aunt replied, "What will she do with a B.A. now? And anyway, her father forbade it. He was a broken man. Do you know, his hair turned grey overnight? Poor man," she sighed. My mother turned to me. She said, "I cannot believe you were friendly with a girl like that. You act as though she did nothing wrong. I hope she hasn't influenced you. You'll never under-

lahenga: a wide dancing skirt.

stand what a mother goes through till you become a mother. It is my only prayer to God these days, that you make the correct decisions, that you know right from wrong, that you do not go astray."

Rakesh came to visit me the following term. I told him about Amrita. At the end he said, "I see." That is all.

The rules in the hostel became stricter. Patram kept a strict eye on me. Like the Cheshire cat his grin followed me everywhere.

The year I graduated, Amrita wrote. She had no time for letter-writing, she said, at least not for the kind she wished to write to me. There had been too much to cope with that first year—the abortion, her marriage, her first child. And the second year, her second child. So much for Dr. Kumar's advice on contraception! she said. Her father began speaking to her after her son was born. Her mother never referred to what happened. But she stood by her.

Of course, her husband knew nothing. He's nice, she said, and also tall and fair and by that definition, they say, handsome. He's all set to groom our sons to be good IAS officers like him, extending his dreary dreams of all that is proper, permanent and powerful. Work was taking her husband abroad the following year. She would probably accompany him. She asked if I could come and stay with her for a while, for more than a while, whenever possible. She longed to talk to me, letters were so difficult. And all the interruptions, babies crying, meals to be cooked . . . you know how it can be, she said. Oh, Hemu, no, you cannot know. Not yet, not yet. She asked, remember Chachaji? He got it all right, didn't he? He will always get it right, won't he? For this is how it will always be, yes, this is how it will always be. Oh, Hemu, Hemu, my stars have changed, haven't they?"

And mine, Amrita, and mine. 160

Margaret Atwood

HAPPY ENDINGS 1983

Born in Ottawa, Ontario, in 1939, Margaret Eleanor Atwood was the daughter of an entomologist and spent her childhood summers in the forests of northern Quebec, where her father carried out research. Atwood began writing at the age of five and had already seriously entertained thoughts of becoming a professional writer before she finished high school. She graduated from the University of Toronto in 1961, and later did graduate work at Radcliffe and Harvard. Atwood first gained prominence as a poet. Her first full-length collection of poems, The Circle Game (1966), was awarded a Governor General's Award, Canada's most prestigious literary honor, and she has published nearly twenty

Margaret Atwood

volumes of verse. Atwood also began to write fiction seriously in graduate school, and her short stories were first collected in Dancing Girls *(1977), followed by* Bluebeard's Egg *(1983),* Murder in the Dark *(1983),* Wilderness Tips *(1991), and* Good Bones *(1992). Among her other influential books is* Survival: A Thematic Guide to Canadian Literature *(1972), in which she argued that Canadian writers should turn from British and American models to a fuller utilization of their own cultural heritage.*

A dedicated feminist, Atwood chose the title of Dancing Girls *with care, alluding to women who are forced to move in patterns determined by a patriarchal society. In her later works of fiction Atwood has continued to explore the complex relations between the sexes, most incisively in* The Handmaid's Tale *(1986), a futuristic novel about a world in which gender roles are ruthlessly enforced by a society based on religious fundamentalism. In the same year that* The Handmaid's Tale *appeared, Atwood was named Woman of the Year by* Ms. *magazine. Subsequent novels include* Cat's Eye *(1988),* The Robber Bride *(1993),* The Blind Assassin *(2000), and* Oryx and Crake *(2003). Atwood has served as writer-in-residence at universities in Canada, the United States, and Europe, and she has been widely in demand for appearances at symposia devoted to literature and women's issues.* Negotiating with the Dead: A Writer on Writing *(2002) collects a series of lectures that she delivered at Cambridge University in 2000.*

> John and Mary meet.
> What happens next?
> If you want a happy ending, try A.

A

John and Mary fall in love and get married. They both have worthwhile and remunerative jobs which they find stimulating and challenging. They buy a charming house. Real estate values go up. Eventually, when they can afford live-in help, they have two children, to whom they are devoted. The children turn out well. John and Mary have a stimulating and challenging sex life and worthwhile friends. They go on fun vacations together. They retire. They both have hobbies which they find stimulating and challenging. Eventually they die. This is the end of the story.

B

Mary falls in love with John but John doesn't fall in love with Mary. He merely uses her body for selfish pleasure and ego gratification of a tepid kind. He comes to her apartment twice a week and she cooks him dinner, you'll notice that he doesn't even consider her worth the price of a dinner out, and after he's eaten the dinner he fucks her and after that he falls asleep, while she does the dishes so he won't think she's untidy, having all those dirty dishes lying around, and puts on fresh lipstick so she'll look good when he wakes up, but when he wakes up he doesn't even notice, he puts on his socks and his shorts and his pants and his shirt and his tie and his shoes, the reverse order from the one in which he took them off. He doesn't take off Mary's clothes, she takes them off herself, she acts as if she's dying for it every time, not because she likes sex exactly, she doesn't, but she wants John to think she does because if they do it often enough surely he'll get used to her, he'll come to depend on her and they will get married, but John goes out the door with hardly so much as a good-night and three days later he turns up at six o'clock and they do the whole thing over again.

Mary gets run-down. Crying is bad for your face, everyone knows that and so does Mary but she can't stop. People at work notice. Her friends tell her John is a rat, a pig, a dog, he isn't good enough for her, but she can't believe it. Inside John, she thinks, is another John, who is much nicer. This other John will emerge like a butterfly from a cocoon, a Jack from a box, a pit from a prune, if the first John is only squeezed enough.

One evening John complains about the food. He has never complained about the food before. Mary is hurt.

Her friends tell her they've seen him in a restaurant with another woman, whose name is Madge. It's not even Madge that finally gets to Mary; it's the restaurant. John has never taken Mary to a restaurant. Mary collects all the sleeping pills and aspirins she can find, and takes them and a half a bottle of sherry. You can see what kind of a woman she is by the fact that it's not even whiskey. She leaves a note for John. She hopes he'll discover her and get her to the hospital in time and repent and then they can get married, but this fails to happen and she dies.

John marries Madge and everything continues as in A.

C

John, who is an older man, falls in love with Mary, and Mary, who is only twenty-two, feels sorry for him because he's worried about his hair falling out. She sleeps with him even though she's not in love with him. She met him at work. She's in love with someone called James, who is twenty-two also and not yet ready to settle down.

John on the contrary settled down long ago: this is what is bothering him. John has a steady, respectable job and is getting ahead in his field, but Mary isn't impressed by him, she's impressed by James, who has a motorcycle and a fabulous record collection. But James is often away on his motorcycle, being free. Freedom isn't the same for girls, so in the meantime Mary spends Thursday evenings with John. Thursdays are the only days John can get away.

John is married to a woman called Madge and they have two children, a charming house which they bought just before the real estate values went up, and hobbies which they find stimulating and challenging, when they have the time. John tells Mary how important she is to him, but of course, he can't leave his wife because a commitment is a commitment. He goes on about this more than is necessary and Mary finds it boring, but older men can keep it up longer so on the whole she has a fairly good time.

One day James breezes in on his motorcycle with some top-grade California hybrid and James and Mary get higher than you'd believe possible and they climb into bed. Everything becomes very underwater, but along comes John, who has a key to Mary's apartment. He finds them stoned and entwined. He's hardly in any position to be jealous, considering Madge, but nevertheless he's overcome with despair. Finally he's middle-aged, in two years he'll be bald as an egg and he can't stand it. He purchases a handgun, saying he needs it for target practice—this is the thin part of the plot, but it can be dealt with later—and shoots the two of them and himself.

Madge, after a suitable period of mourning, marries an understanding man called Fred and everything continues as in A, but under different names.

D

Fred and Madge have no problems. They get along exceptionally well and are good at working out any little difficulties that may arise. But their charming house is by the seashore and one day a giant tidal wave approaches. Real estate values go down. The rest of the story is about what caused the tidal wave and how they escape from it. They do, though thousands drown, but Fred and Madge are virtuous and lucky. Finally on high ground they clasp each other, wet and dripping and grateful, and continue as in A.

E

Yes, but Fred has a bad heart. The rest of the story is about how kind and understanding they both are until Fred dies. Then Madge devotes herself to charity work until the end of A. If you like, it can be "Madge," "cancer," "guilty and confused," and "bird watching."

F

If you think this is all too bourgeois, make John a revolutionary and Mary a counterespionage agent and see how far that gets you. Remember, this is Canada. You'll still end up with A, though in between you may get a lustful brawling saga of passionate involvement, a chronicle of our times, sort of.

You'll have to face it, the endings are the same however you slice it. Don't be deluded by any other endings, they're all fake, either deliberately fake, with malicious intent to deceive, or just motivated by excessive optimism if not by downright sentimentality.

The only authentic ending is the one provided here:
John and Mary die. John and Mary die. John and Mary die.

So much for endings. Beginnings are almost more fun. True connoisseurs, however, are known to favor the stretch in between, since it's the hardest to do anything with.

That's about all that can be said for plots, which anyway are just one thing after another, a what and a what and a what.

Now try How and Why.

Ambrose Bierce

AN OCCURRENCE AT OWL CREEK BRIDGE   1891

Ambrose Bierce (1842–1914?) was born in Horse Cave Creek, Ohio, the youngest child of nine in an impoverished farm family. A year at Kentucky Military Academy was his only formal schooling. Enlisting as a drummer boy in the Union Army, Bierce saw action at Shiloh and Chickamauga, took part in Sherman's March to the Sea, and came out of the army a brevet major. Then he became a writer, later an editor, for San Francisco newspapers. For a while Bierce thrived. He and his wife, on her ample dowry, lived five years in London, where Bierce wrote for London papers, honed his style, and culti-vated his wit. But his wife left him, his two sons died (one of gunfire and the other of alcoholism),

Ambrose Bierce

and in late life Bierce came to deserve his nick-name "Bitter Bierce." In 1913, at seventy-one, he trekked off to Mexico and vanished without a trace, although one report had him riding with the forces of revolutionist Pancho Villa. (A 1989 movie, Old Gringo, imagines Bierce's last days.) Bierce, who regarded the novel as "a short story padded," favored shorter lengths: short story, fable, newspaper column, aphorism. Sardonically, in The Devil's Dictionary (1911), he defines diplomacy as "the patriotic art of lying for one's country," and saint as "a dead sinner revised and edited." Master of both realism and the ghost story, he collected his best Civil War fiction, including "An Occurrence at Owl Creek Bridge," in Tales of Soldiers and Civilians (1891), later retitled In the Midst of Life.

I

A man stood upon a railroad bridge in northern Alabama, looking down into the swift water twenty feet below. The man's hands were behind his back, the wrists bound with a cord. A rope closely encircled his neck. It was attached to a stout cross-timber above his head and the slack fell to the level of his knees. Some loose boards laid upon the sleepers supporting the metals of the railway supplied a footing for him and his executioners—two private soldiers of the Fed-eral army, directed by a sergeant who in civil life may have been a deputy sheriff. At a short remove upon the same temporary platform was an officer in the uniform of his rank, armed. He was a captain. A sentinel at each end of the bridge stood with his rifle in the position known as "support," that is to say, vertical in front of the left shoulder, the hammer resting on the forearm thrown straight across the chest—a formal and unnatural position, enforcing an erect carriage of the body. It did not appear to be the duty of these two men to know what was occurring at the center of the bridge; they merely blockaded the two ends of the foot planking that traversed it.

Beyond one of the sentinels nobody was in sight; the railroad ran straight away into a forest for a hundred yards, then, curving, was lost to view. Doubtless there was an outpost farther along. The other bank of the stream was open ground—a gentle acclivity topped with a stockade of vertical tree trunks, loopholed for rifles, with a single embrasure through which protruded the muzzle of a brass cannon commanding the bridge. Midway of the slope between bridge and fort were the spectators—a single company of infantry in line, at "parade rest," the butts of the rifles on the ground, the barrels inclining slightly backward against the right shoulder, the hands crossed upon the stock. A lieutenant stood at the right of the line, the point of his sword upon the ground, his left hand resting upon his right. Excepting the group of four at the center of the bridge, not a man moved. The company faced the bridge, staring stonily, motionless. The sentinels, facing the banks of the stream, might have been statues to adorn the bridge. The captain stood with folded arms, silent, observing the work of his subordinates, but making no sign. Death is a dignitary who when he comes announced is to be received with formal manifestations of respect, even by those most familiar with him. In the code of military etiquette silence and fixity are forms of deference.

The man who was engaged in being hanged was apparently about thirty-five years of age. He was a civilian, if one might judge from his habit, which was that of a planter. His features were good—a straight nose, firm mouth, broad forehead, from which his long, dark hair was combed straight back, falling behind his ears to the collar of his well-fitting frock-coat. He wore a mustache and pointed beard, but no whiskers; his eyes were large and dark gray, and had a kindly expression which one would hardly have expected in one whose neck was in the hemp. Evidently this was no vulgar assassin. The liberal military code makes provision for hanging many kinds of persons, and gentlemen are not excluded.

The preparations being complete, the two private soldiers stepped aside and each drew away the plank upon which he had been standing. The sergeant turned to the captain, saluted and placed himself immediately behind that officer, who in turn moved apart one pace. These movements left the condemned man and the sergeant standing on the two ends of the same plank, which spanned three of the cross-ties of the bridge. The end upon which the civilian stood almost, but not quite, reached a fourth. This plank had been held in place by the weight of the captain; it was now held by that of the sergeant. At a signal from the former the latter would step aside, the plank would tilt and the condemned man go down between two ties. The arrangement commended itself to his judgment as simple and effective. His face had not been covered nor his eyes bandaged. He looked a moment at his "unstead-fast footing," then let his gaze wander to the swirling water of the stream racing madly beneath his feet. A piece of dancing driftwood caught his attention and his eyes followed it down the current. How slowly it appeared to move! What a sluggish stream!

He closed his eyes in order to fix his last thoughts upon his wife and chil-dren. The water, touched to gold by the early sun, the brooding mists under the banks at some distance down the stream, the fort, the soldiers, the piece of drift—all had distracted him. And now he became conscious of a new distur-bance. Striking through the thought of his dear ones was a sound which he could neither ignore nor understand, a sharp, distinct, metallic percussion like the stroke of a blacksmith's hammer upon the anvil; it had the same ringing quality. He wondered what it was, and whether immeasurably distant or near by—it seemed both. Its recurrence was regular, but as slow as the tolling of a death knell. He awaited each stroke with impatience and—he knew not why—appre-hension. The intervals of silence grew progressively longer; the delays became maddening. With their greater infrequency the sounds increased in strength and sharpness. They hurt his ear like the thrust of a knife; he feared he would shriek. What he heard was the ticking of his watch.

He unclosed his eyes and saw again the water below him. "If I could free my hands," he thought, "I might throw off the noose and spring into the stream. By diving I could evade the bullets and, swimming vigorously, reach the bank, take to the woods and get away home. My home, thank God, is as yet outside their lines; my wife and little ones are still beyond the invader's farthest advance."

As these thoughts, which have here to be set down in words, were flashed into the doomed man's brain rather than evolved from it the captain nodded to the sergeant. The sergeant stepped aside.

II

Peyton Farquhar was a well-to-do planter, of an old and highly respected Alabama family. Being a slave owner and like other slave owners a politician he was naturally an original secessionist and ardently devoted to the Southern cause. Circumstances of an imperious nature, which it is unnecessary to relate here, had prevented him from taking service with the gallant army that had fought the disastrous campaigns ending with the fall of Corinth, and he chafed under the inglorious restraint, longing for the release of his energies, the larger life of the soldier, the opportunity for distinction. That opportunity, he felt, would come, as it comes to all in war time. Meanwhile he did what he could. No service was too humble to him to perform in aid of the South, no adventure too perilous for him to undertake if consistent with the character of a civilian who was at heart a soldier, and who in good faith and without too much qualification assented to at least a part of the frankly villainous dictum that all is fair in love and war.

One evening while Farquhar and his wife were sitting on a rustic bench near the entrance to his grounds, a gray-clad soldier rode up to the gate and asked for a drink of water. Mrs. Farquhar was only too happy to serve him with her own white hands. While she was fetching the water her husband approached the dusty horseman and inquired eagerly for news from the front.

"The Yanks are repairing the railroads," said the man, "and are getting ready 10 for another advance. They have reached the Owl Creek bridge, put it in order and built a stockade on the north bank. The commandant has issued an order, which is posted everywhere, declaring that any civilian caught interfering with the railroad, its bridges, tunnels or trains will be summarily hanged. I saw the order."

"How far is it to the Owl Creek bridge?" Farquhar asked.

"About thirty miles."

"Is there no force on this side the creek?"

"Only a picket post half a mile out, on the railroad, and a single sentinel at this end of the bridge."

"Suppose a man—a civilian and student of hanging—should elude the 15 picket post and perhaps get the better of the sentinel," said Farquhar, smiling, "what could he accomplish?"

The soldier reflected. "I was there a month ago," he replied. "I observed that the flood of last winter had lodged a great quantity of driftwood against the wooden pier at this end of the bridge. It is now dry and would burn like tow."

The lady had now brought the water, which the soldier drank. He thanked her ceremoniously, bowed to her husband and rode away. An hour later, after nightfall, he repassed the plantation, going northward in the direction from which he had come. He was a Federal scout.

III

As Peyton Farquhar fell straight downward through the bridge he lost consciousness and was as one already dead. From this state he was awakened—ages later, it seemed to him—by the pain of a sharp pressure upon his throat, followed by a sense of suffocation. Keen, poignant agonies seemed to shoot from his neck downward through every fiber of his body and limbs. These pains appeared to flash along well-defined lines of ramification and to beat with an inconceivably rapid periodicity. They seemed like streams of pulsating fire heating him to an intolerable temperature. As to his head, he was conscious of nothing but a feeling of fulness—of congestion. These sensations were unaccompanied by thought. The intellectual part of his nature was already effaced; he had power only to feel, and feeling was torment. He was conscious of motion. Encompassed in a luminous cloud, of which he was now merely the fiery heart, without material substance, he swung through unthinkable arcs of oscillation, like a vast pendulum. Then all at once, with terrible suddenness, the light about him shot upward with the noise of a loud plash; a frightful roaring was in his ears, and all was cold and dark. The power of thought was restored; he knew that the rope had broken and he had fallen into the stream. There was no additional strangulation; the noose about his neck was already suffocating him and kept the water from his lungs. To die of hanging at the bottom of a river!—the idea seemed to him ludicrous. He opened his eyes in the darkness and saw above him a gleam of light, but how distant, how inaccessible! He was still sinking, for the light became fainter and fainter until it was a mere glimmer. Then it began to grow and brighten, and he knew that he was rising toward the surface—knew it with reluctance, for he was now very comfortable. "To be hanged and drowned," he thought, "that is not so bad; but I do not wish to be shot. No; I will not be shot; that is not fair."

He was not conscious of an effort, but a sharp pain in his wrist apprised him that he was trying to free his hands. He gave the struggle his attention, as an idler might observe the feat of a juggler, without interest in the outcome. What splendid effort!—what magnificent, what superhuman strength! Ah, that was a fine endeavor! Bravo! The cord fell away; his arms parted and floated upward, the hands dimly seen on each side in the growing light. He watched them with a new interest as first one and then the other pounced upon the noose at his neck. They tore it away and thrust it fiercely aside, its undulations resembling those of a water-snake. "Put it back, put it back!" He thought he shouted these words to his hands, for the undoing of the noose had been succeeded by the direst pang that he had yet experienced. His neck ached horribly; his brain was on fire; his heart, which had been fluttering faintly, gave a great leap, trying to force itself out at his mouth. His whole body was racked and wrenched with an insupportable anguish! But his disobedient hands gave no heed to the command. They beat the water vigorously with quick, downward strokes, forcing him to the surface. He felt his head emerge; his eyes were blinded by the sunlight; his chest expanded convulsively, and with a supreme and crowning agony his lungs engulfed a great draught of air, which instantly he expelled in a shriek!

He was now in full possession of his physical senses. They were, indeed, 20 preternaturally keen and alert. Something in the awful disturbance of his organic system had so exalted and refined them that they made record of things never before perceived. He felt the ripples upon his face and heard their separate sounds as they struck. He looked at the forest on the bank of the stream, saw the individual trees, the leaves and the veining of each leaf—saw the very insects upon them: the locusts, the brilliant-bodied flies, the gray spiders stretching their webs from twig to twig. He noted the prismatic colors in all the dewdrops upon a million blades of grass. The humming of the gnats that danced above the eddies of the stream, the beating of the dragon-flies' wings, the strokes of the water-spiders' legs, like oars which had lifted their boat—all these made audible music. A fish slid along beneath his eyes and he heard the rush of its body parting the water.

He had come to the surface facing down the stream; in a moment the visible world seemed to wheel slowly round, himself the pivotal point, and he saw the bridge, the fort, the soldiers upon the bridge, the captain, the sergeant, the two privates, his executioners. They were in silhouette against the blue sky. They shouted and gesticulated, pointing at him. The captain had drawn his pistol, but did not fire; the others were unarmed. Their movements were grotesque and horrible, their forms gigantic.

Suddenly he heard a sharp report and something struck the water smartly within a few inches of his head, spattering his face with spray. He heard a second report, and saw one of the sentinels with his rifle at his shoulder, a light cloud of blue smoke rising from the muzzle. The man in the water saw the eye of the man on the bridge gazing into his own through the sights of the rifle. He observed that it was a gray eye and remembered having read that gray eyes were keenest, and that all famous marksmen had them. Nevertheless, this one had missed.

A counter-swirl had caught Farquhar and turned him half round; he was again looking into the forest on the bank opposite the fort. The sound of a clear, high voice in a monotonous singsong now rang out behind him and came across the water with a distinctness that pierced and subdued all other sounds, even the beating of the ripples in his ears. Although no soldier, he had frequented camps enough to know the dread significance of that deliberate, drawling, aspirated chant; the lieutenant on shore was taking a part in the morning's work. How coldly and pitilessly—with what an even, calm intonation, presaging, and enforcing tranquility in the men—with what accurately measured intervals fell those cruel words:

"Attention, company! . . . Shoulder arms! . . . Ready! . . . Aim! . . . Fire!"

Farquhar dived—dived as deeply as he could. The water roared in his ears 25 like the voice of Niagara, yet he heard the dulled thunder of the volley and, rising again toward the surface, met shining bits of metal, singularly flattened, oscillating slowly downward. Some of them touched him on the face and hands, then fell away, continuing their descent. One lodged between his collar and neck; it was uncomfortably warm and he snatched it out.

As he rose to the surface, gasping for breath, he saw that he had been a long time under water; he was perceptibly farther down stream—nearer to safety. The soldiers had almost finished reloading; the metal ramrods flashed all at once in the sunshine as they were drawn from the barrels, turned in the air, and thrust into their sockets. The two sentinels fired again, independently and ineffectually.

The hunted man saw all this over his shoulder; he was now swimming vigorously with the current. His brain was as energetic as his arms and legs; he thought with the rapidity of lightning.

"The officer," he reasoned, "will not make that martinet's error a second time. It is as easy to dodge a volley as a single shot. He has probably already given the command to fire at will. God help me, I cannot dodge them all!"

An appalling plash within two yards of him was followed by a loud, rushing sound, *diminuendo*,° which seemed to travel back through the air to the fort and died in an explosion which stirred the very river to its deeps! A rising sheet of water curved over him, fell down upon him, blinded him, strangled him! The cannon had taken a hand in the game. As he shook his head free from the commotion of the smitten water he heard the deflected shot humming through the air ahead, and in an instant it was cracking and smashing the branches in the forest beyond.

diminuendo: diminishing (Italian); a term from music indicating a gradual decrease in loudness or force.

"They will not do that again," he thought; "the next time they will use a   30
charge of grape. I must keep my eye upon the gun; the smoke will apprise me—
the report arrives too late; it lags behind the missile. That is a good gun."

Suddenly he felt himself whirled round and round—spinning like a top. The
water, the banks, the forests, the now distant bridge, fort and men—all were
commingled and blurred. Objects were represented by their colors only; circular
horizontal streaks of color—that was all he saw. He had been caught in a vortex
and was being whirled on with a velocity of advance and gyration that made him
giddy and sick. In a few moments he was flung upon the gravel at the foot of the
left bank of the stream—the southern bank—and behind a projecting point
which concealed him from his enemies. The sudden arrest of his motion, the
abrasion of one of his hands on the gravel, restored him, and he wept with delight. He dug his fingers into the sand, threw it over himself in handfuls and au-
dibly blessed it. It looked like diamonds, rubies, emeralds; he could think of
nothing beautiful which it did not resemble. The trees upon the bank were giant
garden plants; he noted a definite order in their arrangement, inhaled the fragrance of their blooms. A strange, roseate light shone through the spaces among
their trunks and the wind made in their branches the music of aeolian harps. He
had no wish to perfect his escape—was content to remain in that enchanting
spot until retaken.

A whiz and rattle of grapeshot among the branches high above his head
roused him from his dream. The baffled cannoneer had fired him a random
farewell. He sprang to his feet, rushed up the sloping bank, and plunged into the
forest.

All that day he traveled, laying his course by the rounding sun. The forest
seemed interminable; nowhere did he discover a break in it, not even a
woodman's road. He had not known that he lived in so wild a region. There was
something uncanny in the revelation.

By nightfall he was fatigued, footsore, famishing. The thought of his wife and
children urged him on. At last he found a road which led him in what he knew to
be the right direction. It was as wide and straight as a city street, yet it seemed untraveled. No fields bordered it, no dwelling anywhere. Not so much as the barking
of a dog suggested human habitation. The black bodies of the trees formed a
straight wall on both sides, terminating on the horizon in a point, like a diagram
in a lesson in perspective. Overhead, as he looked up through this rift in the wood,
shone great golden stars looking unfamiliar and grouped in strange constellations.
He was sure they were arranged in some order which had a secret and malign significance. The wood on either side was full of singular noises, among which—
once, twice, and again—he distinctly heard whispers in an unknown tongue.

His neck was in pain and lifting his hand to it he found it horribly swollen.   35
He knew that it had a circle of black where the rope had bruised it. His eyes felt
congested; he could no longer close them. His tongue was swollen with thirst; he
relieved its fever by thrusting it forward from between his teeth into the cold air.
How softly the turf had carpeted the untraveled avenue—he could no longer feel
the roadway beneath his feet!

Doubtless, despite his suffering, he had fallen asleep while walking, for now he sees another scene—perhaps he has merely recovered from a delirium. He stands at the gate of his own home. All is as he left it, and all bright and beautiful in the morning sunshine. He must have traveled the entire night. As he pushes open the gate and passes up the wide white walk, he sees a flutter of female garments; his wife, looking fresh and cool and sweet, steps down from the veranda to meet him. At the bottom of the steps she stands waiting, with a smile of ineffable joy, an attitude of matchless grace and dignity. Ah, how beautiful she is! He springs forward with extended arms. As he is about to clasp her he feels a stunning blow upon the back of the neck; a blinding white light blazes all about him with a sound like the shock of a cannon—then all is darkness and silence!

Peyton Farquhar was dead; his body, with a broken neck, swung gently from side to side beneath the timbers of the Owl Creek bridge.

Jorge Luis Borges

THE GOSPEL ACCORDING TO MARK   1970

TRANSLATED BY ANDREW HURLEY

Jorge Luis Borges (1899–1986), an outstanding modern writer of Latin America, was born in Buenos Aires into a family prominent in Argentine history. Borges grew up bilingual, learning English from his English grandmother and receiving his early education from an English tutor. Caught in Europe by the outbreak of World War II, Borges lived in Switzerland and later Spain, where he joined the Ultraists, a group of experimental poets who renounced realism. On returning to Argentina, he edited a poetry magazine printed in the form of a poster and affixed to city walls. For his opposition to the regime of Colonel Juan Perón, Borges was forced to resign his post as a librarian and was mockingly offered a job as a chicken inspector. In 1955, after Perón was deposed, Borges became director of the National Library and professor of English literature at the University of Buenos Aires. A sufferer since childhood from poor eyesight, Borges eventually went blind. His eye problems may have encouraged him to work mainly in short, highly crafted forms: stories, essays, fables, and lyric poems full of elaborate music. His short stories, in Ficciones *(1944),* El hacedor *(1960; translated as* Dreamtigers, *1964), and* Labyrinths *(1962), have been admired worldwide.*

Jorge Luis Borges

The incident took place on the Los Alamos ranch, south of the small town of Junín, in late March of 1928. Its protagonist was a medical student named Baltasar Espinosa. We might define him for the moment as a Buenos Aires youth much like many others, with no traits worthier of note than the gift for public speaking that had won him more than one prize at the English school° in Ramos Mejía and an almost unlimited goodness. He didn't like to argue; he preferred that his interlocutor rather than he himself be right. And though he found the chance twists and turns of gambling interesting, he was a poor gambler, because he didn't like to win. He was intelligent and open to learning, but he was lazy; at thirty-three he had not yet completed the last requirements for his degree. (The work he still owed, incidentally, was for his favorite class.) His father, like all the gentlemen of his day a freethinker,° had instructed Espinosa in the doctrines of Herbert Spencer,° but once, before he set off on a trip to Montevideo, his mother had asked him to say the Lord's Prayer every night and make the sign of the cross, and never in all the years that followed did he break that promise. He did not lack courage; one morning, with more indifference than wrath, he had traded two or three blows with some of his classmates that were trying to force him to join a strike at the university. He abounded in debatable habits and opinions, out of a spirit of acquiescence: his country mattered less to him than the danger that people in other countries might think the Argentines still wore feathers; he venerated France but had contempt for the French; he had little respect for Americans but took pride in the fact that there were skyscrapers in Buenos Aires; he thought that the gauchos° of the plains were better horsemen than the gauchos of the mountains. When his cousin Daniel invited him to spend the summer at Los Alamos, he immediately accepted—not because he liked the country but out of a natural desire to please, and because he could find no good reason for saying no.

The main house at the ranch was large and a bit run-down; the quarters for the foreman, a man named Gutre, stood nearby. There were three members of the Gutre family: the father, the son (who was singularly rough and unpolished), and a girl of uncertain paternity. They were tall, strong, and bony, with reddish hair and Indian features. They rarely spoke. The foreman's wife had died years before.

In the country, Espinosa came to learn things he hadn't known, had never even suspected; for example, that when you're approaching a house there's no reason to gallop and that nobody goes out on a horse unless there's a job to be done. As the summer wore on, he learned to distinguish birds by their call.

Within a few days, Daniel had to go to Buenos Aires to close a deal on some livestock. At the most, he said, the trip would take a week. Espinosa, who was

---

English school: a prep school that emphasized English (well-to-do Argentineans of this era wanted their children to learn English).   *freethinker:* person who rejects traditional beliefs, especially religious dogma, in favor of rational inquiry.   *Herbert Spencer:* a British philosopher (1820–1903) who championed the theory of evolution.   *gaucho:* a South American cowboy.

already a little tired of his cousin's *bonnes fortunes* and his indefatigable interest in the vagaries of men's tailoring, stayed behind on the ranch with his textbooks. The heat was oppressive, and not even nightfall brought relief. Then one morning toward dawn, he was awakened by thunder. Wind lashed the casuarina trees. Espinosa heard the first drops of rain and gave thanks to God. Suddenly the wind blew cold. That afternoon, the Salado overflowed.

The next morning, as he stood on the porch looking out over the flooded plains, Baltasar Espinosa realized that the metaphor equating the pampas with the sea was not, at least that morning, an altogether false one, though Hudson° had noted that the sea seems the grander of the two because we view it not from horseback or our own height, but from the deck of a ship. The rain did not let up; the Gutres, helped (or hindered) by the city dweller, saved a good part of the livestock, though many animals were drowned. There were four roads leading to the ranch; all were under water. On the third day, when a leaking roof threatened the foreman's house, Espinosa gave the Gutres a room at the back of the main house, alongside the toolshed. The move brought Espinosa and the Gutres closer, and they began to eat together in the large dining room. Conversation was not easy; the Gutres, who knew so much about things in the country, did not know how to explain them. One night Espinosa asked them if people still remembered anything about the Indian raids, back when the military command for the frontier had been in Junín. They told him they did, but they would have given him the same answer if he had asked them about the day Charles I° had been beheaded. Espinosa recalled that his father used to say that all the cases of longevity that occur in the country are the result of either poor memory or a vague notion of dates—gauchos quite often know neither the year they were born in nor the name of the man that fathered them.

In the entire house, the only reading material to be found were several copies of a farming magazine, a manual of veterinary medicine, a deluxe edition of the romantic verse drama *Tabaré,* a copy of *The History of the Shorthorn in Argentina,* several erotic and detective stories, and a recent novel that Espinosa had not read—*Don Segundo Sombra,* by Ricardo Güiraldes. In order to put some life into the inevitable after-dinner attempt at conversation, Espinosa read a couple of chapters of the novel to the Gutres, who did not know how to read or write. Unfortunately, the foreman had been a cattle drover himself, and he could not be interested in the adventures of another such a one. It was easy work, he said; they always carried along a pack mule with everything they might need. If he had not been a cattle drover, he announced, he'd never have seen Lake Gómez, or the Bragado River, or even the Núñez ranch, in Chacabuco. . . .

In the kitchen there was a guitar; before the incident I am narrating, the laborers would sit in a circle and someone would pick up the guitar and strum it, though never managing actually to play it. That was called "giving it a strum."

W. H. Hudson: an English naturalist and author (1841–1922) who wrote extensively about South America.   *Charles I:* King of England, beheaded in 1649.

Espinosa, who was letting his beard grow out, would stop before the mirror to look at his changed face; he smiled to think that he'd soon be boring the fellows in Buenos Aires with his stories about the Salado overrunning it banks. Curiously, he missed places in the city he never went, and would never go: a street corner on Cabrera where a mailbox stood; two cement lions on a porch on Calle Jujuy a few blocks from the Plaza del Once; a tile-floored corner grocery-store-and-bar (whose location he couldn't quite remember). As for his father and his brothers, by now Daniel would have told them that he had been iso-lated—the word was etymologically precise—by the floodwaters.

Exploring the house still cut off by the high water, he came upon a Bible printed in English. On its last pages the Guthries (for that was their real name) had kept their family history. They had come originally from Inverness° and had arrived in the New World—doubtlessly as peasant laborers—in the early nine-teenth century; they had intermarried with Indians. The chronicle came to an end in the eighteen-seventies; they no longer knew how to write. Within a few generations they had forgotten their English; by the time Espinosa met them, even Spanish gave them some difficulty. They had no faith, though in their veins, alongside the superstitions of the pampas, there still ran a dim current of the Calvinist's harsh fanaticism. Espinosa mentioned his find to them, but they hardly seemed to hear him.

He leafed through the book, and his fingers opened it to the first verses of the Gospel According to St. Mark. To try his hand at translating, and perhaps to see if they might understand a little of it, he decided that that would be the text he read the Gutres after dinner. He was surprised that they listened first at-tentively and then with mute fascination. The presence of gold letters on the binding may have given it increased authority. "It's in their blood," he thought. It also occurred to him that throughout history, humankind has told two stories: the story of a lost ship sailing the Mediterranean seas in quest of a beloved isle, and the story of a god who allows himself to be crucified on Golgotha. He re-called his elocution classes in Ramos Mejía, and he rose to his feet to preach the parables.

In the following days, the Gutres would wolf down the spitted beef and canned sardines in order to arrive sooner at the Gospel.

The girl had a little lamb; it was her pet, and she prettied it with a sky blue ribbon. One day it cut itself on a piece of barbed wire; to stanch the blood, the Gutres were about to put spiderwebs on the wound, but Espinosa treated it with pills. The gratitude awakened by that cure amazed him. At first, he had not trusted the Gutres and had hidden away in one of his books the two hundred forty pesos he'd brought; now, with Daniel gone, he had taken the master's place and begun to give timid orders, which were immediately followed. The Gutres would trail him through the rooms and along the hallway, as though they were

10

Inverness: a county in Scotland.

lost. As he read, he noticed that they would sweep away the crumbs he had left on the table. One afternoon, he surprised them as they were discussing him in brief, respectful words. When he came to the end of the Gospel According to St. Mark, he started to read another of the three remaining gospels, but the father asked him to reread the one he'd just finished, so they could understand it better. Espinosa felt they were like children, who prefer repetition to variety or novelty. One night he dreamed of the Flood (which is not surprising) and was awakened by the hammering of the building of the Ark, but he told himself it was thunder. And in fact the rain, which had let up for a while, had begun again; it was very cold. The Gutres told him the rain had broken through the roof of the toolshed; when they got the beams repaired, they said, they'd show him where. He was no longer a stranger, a foreigner, and they all treated him with respect; he was almost spoiled. None of them liked coffee, but there was always a little cup for him, with spoonfuls of sugar stirred in.

That second storm took place on a Tuesday. Thursday night there was a soft knock on his door; because of his doubts about the Gutres he always locked it. He got up and opened the door; it was the girl. In the darkness he couldn't see her, but he could tell by her footsteps that she was barefoot, and afterward, in the bed, that she was naked—that in fact she had come from the back of the house that way. She did not embrace him, or speak a word; she lay down beside him and she was shivering. It was the first time she had lain with a man. When she left, she did not kiss him; Espinosa realized that he didn't even know her name. Impelled by some sentiment he did not attempt to understand, he swore that when he returned to Buenos Aires, he'd tell no one of the incident.

The next day began like all the others, except that the father spoke to Espinosa to ask whether Christ had allowed himself to be killed in order to save all mankind. Espinosa, who was a freethinker like his father but felt obliged to defend what he had read them, paused.

"Yes," he finally replied. "To save all mankind from hell." 15

"What *is* hell?" Gutre then asked him.

"A place underground where souls will burn in fire forever."

"And those that drove the nails will also be saved?"

"Yes," replied Espinosa, whose theology was a bit shaky. (He had worried that the foreman wanted to have a word with him about what had happened last night with his daughter.)

After lunch they asked him to read the last chapters again. 20

Espinosa had a long siesta that afternoon, although it was a light sleep, interrupted by persistent hammering and vague premonitions. Toward evening he got up and went out into the hall.

"The water's going down," he said, as though thinking out loud. "It won't be long now."

"Not long now," repeated Gutre, like an echo.

The three of them had followed him. Kneeling on the floor, they asked his blessing. Then they cursed him, spat on him, and drove him to the back of the house. The girl was weeping. Espinosa realized what awaited him on the other side of the door. When they opened it, he saw the sky. A bird screamed; *it's a goldfinch*, Espinosa thought. There was no roof on the shed; they had torn down the roof beams to build the Cross.

Willa Cather

PAUL'S CASE   1905

Willa Cather

Willa Cather (1876–1947) was born in Gore, Virginia, but at nine moved to Webster County, Nebraska, where pioneer sod houses still clung to the windswept plains. There, mainly in the town of Red Cloud, she grew up among Scandinavians, Czechs, Bohemians, and other immigrant settlers, for whom she felt a quick kinship: they too had been displaced from their childhood homes. After graduation from the University of Nebraska, Cather went east to spend ten years in Pittsburgh, where the story "Paul's Case" opens. (When she wrote the story, she was a high school teacher of Latin and English and a music critic for a newspaper.) Then, because her early stories had attracted notice, New York beckoned. A job on the staff of McClure's led to her becoming managing editor of that popular magazine. Her early novels of Nebraska won immense popularity: O Pioneers! *(1913),* My Ántonia *(1918), and* A Lost Lady *(1923). In her later novels Cather explores other regions of the North American past: in* Death Comes to the Archbishop *(1927), frontier New Mexico; in* Shadows on the Rock *(1931), seventeenth-century Quebec. She does not romanticize the rugged lives of farm people on the plains, or glamorize village life. Often, as in* The Song of the Lark *(1915), the story of a Colorado girl who becomes an opera singer, she depicts a small town as stifling. With remarkable skill, she may tell a story from a man's point of view, but her favorite characters are likely to be women of strong will who triumph over obstacles.*

It was Paul's afternoon to appear before the faculty of the Pittsburgh High School to account for his various misdemeanors. He had been suspended a week ago, and his father had called at the Principal's office and confessed his perplexity about his son. Paul entered the faculty room suave and smiling. His clothes were a trifle outgrown and the tan velvet on the collar of his open overcoat was frayed and worn; but for all that there was something of the dandy about him, and he wore an opal pin in his neatly knotted black four-in-hand, and a red carnation in his buttonhole. This latter adornment the faculty somehow felt was not properly significant of the contrite spirit befitting a boy under the ban of suspension.

Paul was tall for his age and very thin, with high, cramped shoulders and a narrow chest. His eyes were remarkable for a certain hysterical brilliancy and he continually used them in a conscious, theatrical sort of way, peculiarly offensive in a boy. The pupils were abnormally large, as though he were addicted to belladonna, but there was a glassy glitter about them which that drug does not produce.

When questioned by the Principal as to why he was there, Paul stated, politely enough, that he wanted to come back to school. This was a lie, but Paul was quite accustomed to lying; found it, indeed, indispensable for overcoming friction. His teachers were asked to state their respective charges against him, which they did with such a rancor and aggrievedness as evinced that this was not a usual case. Disorder and impertinence were among the offenses named, yet each of his instructors felt that it was scarcely possible to put into words the real cause of the trouble, which lay in a sort of hysterically defiant manner of the boy's; in the contempt which they all knew he felt for them, and which he seemingly made not the least effort to conceal. Once, when he had been making a synopsis of a paragraph at the blackboard, his English teacher had stepped to his side and attempted to guide his hand. Paul had started back with a shudder and thrust his hands violently behind him. The astonished woman could scarcely have been more hurt and embarrassed had he struck at her. The insult was so involuntary and definitely personal as to be unforgettable. In one way and another, he had made all his teachers, men and women alike, conscious of the same feeling of physical aversion. In one class he habitually sat with his hand shading his eyes; in another he always looked out of the window during the recitation; in another he made a running commentary on the lecture, with humorous intention.

His teachers felt this afternoon that his whole attitude was symbolized by his shrug and his flippantly red carnation flower, and they fell upon him without mercy, his English teacher leading the pack. He stood through it smiling, his pale lips parted over his white teeth. (His lips were continually twitching, and he had a habit of raising his eyebrows that was contemptuous and irritating to the last degree.) Older boys than Paul had broken down and shed tears under that baptism of fire, but his set smile did not once desert him, and his only sign of discomfort was the nervous trembling of the fingers that toyed with the buttons of his overcoat, and an occasional jerking of the other hand that held his hat. Paul was always smiling, always glancing about him, seeming to feel that people might be watching him and trying to detect something. This conscious expression, since it was as far as possible from boyish mirthfulness, was usually attributed to insolence or "smartness."

As the inquisition proceeded, one of his instructors repeated an impertinent remark of the boy's, and the Principal asked him whether he thought that a courteous speech to have made a woman. Paul shrugged his shoulders slightly and his eyebrows twitched. 5

"I don't know," he replied. "I didn't mean to be polite or impolite, either. I guess it's a sort of way I have of saying things regardless."

The Principal, who was a sympathetic man, asked him whether he didn't think that a way it would be well to get rid of. Paul grinned and said he guessed so. When he was told that he could go, he bowed gracefully and went out. His bow was but a repetition of the scandalous red carnation.

His teachers were in despair, and his drawing master voiced the feeling of them all when he declared there was something about the boy which none of them understood. He added: "I don't really believe that smile of his comes altogether from insolence; there's something sort of haunted about it. The boy is not strong, for one thing. I happen to know that he was born in Colorado, only a few months before his mother died out there of a long illness. There is something wrong about the fellow."

The drawing master had come to realize that, in looking at Paul, one saw only his white teeth and the forced animation of his eyes. One warm afternoon the boy had gone to sleep at his drawing-board, and his master had noted with amazement what a white, blue-veined face it was; drawn and wrinkled like an old man's about the eyes, the lips twitching even in his sleep, and stiff with a nervous tension that drew them back from his teeth.

His teachers left the building dissatisfied and unhappy; humiliated to have   10
felt so vindictive toward a mere boy, to have uttered this feeling in cutting terms, and to have set each other on, as it were, in the gruesome game of intemperate reproach. Some of them remembered having seen a miserable street cat set at bay by a ring of tormentors.

As for Paul, he ran down the hill whistling the Soldiers' Chorus from *Faust*, ° looking wildly behind him now and then to see whether some of his teachers were not there to writhe under his light-heartedness. As it was now late in the afternoon and Paul was on duty that evening as usher at Carnegie Hall,° he decided that he would not go home to supper. When he reached the concert hall the doors were not yet open and, as it was chilly outside, he decided to go up into the picture gallery—always deserted at this hour—where there were some of Raffaelli's° gay studies of Paris streets and an airy blue Venetian scene or two that always exhilarated him. He was delighted to find no one in the gallery but the old guard, who sat in one corner, a newspaper on his knee, a black patch over one eye and the other closed. Paul possessed himself of the place and walked confidently up and down, whistling under his breath. After a while he sat down before a blue Rico° and lost himself. When he bethought him to look at his watch, it was after seven o'clock, and he rose with a start and ran downstairs, making a face at Augustus, peering out from the cast-room,° and an evil gesture at the Venus of Milo as he passed her on the stairway.

When Paul reached the ushers' dressing-room half-a-dozen boys were there already, and he began excitedly to tumble into his uniform. It was one of the few

Faust: tragic grand opera (1859) by French composer Charles Gounod.   *Carnegie Hall:* concert hall endowed by Pittsburgh steel manufacturer Andrew Carnegie, not to be confused with the better-known Carnegie Hall in New York City.   *Raffaelli:* Jean-Francois Raffaelli (1850–1921), painter and graphic artist, native and lifelong resident of Paris, attained great popularity for his paintings and drawings of that city.   *Rico:* (flourished 1500–1550), painter of the Byzantine school, a native of Crete.   *Augustus . . . cast-room:* Paul mocks a plaster cast of the Vatican Museum's famous statue of the first Roman emperor (63 B.C.–A.D. 14), whom an unknown sculptor posed sternly pointing an index finger at his beholders.

that at all approached fitting, and Paul thought it very becoming—though he knew that the tight, straight coat accentuated his narrow chest, about which he was exceedingly sensitive. He was always considerably excited while he dressed, twanging all over to the tuning of the strings and the preliminary flourishes of the horns in the music-room; but tonight he seemed quite beside himself, and he teased and plagued the boys until, telling him that he was crazy, they put him down on the floor and sat on him.

Somewhat calmed by his suppression, Paul dashed out to the front of the house to seat the early comers. He was a model usher; gracious and smiling he ran up and down the aisles; nothing was too much trouble for him; he carried messages and brought programmes as though it were his greatest pleasure in life, and all the people in his section thought him a charming boy, feeling that he remembered and admired them. As the house filled, he grew more and more vivacious and animated, and the color came to his cheeks and lips. It was very much as though this were a great reception and Paul were the host. Just as the musicians came out to take their places, his English teacher arrived with checks for the seats which a prominent manufacturer had taken for the season. She betrayed some embarrassment when she handed Paul the tickets, and a hauteur° which subsequently made her feel very foolish. Paul was startled for a moment, and had the feeling of wanting to put her out; what business had she here among all these fine people and gay colors? He looked her over and decided that she was not appropriately dressed and must be a fool to sit downstairs in such togs. The tickets had probably been sent her out of kindness, he reflected as he put down a seat for her, and she had about as much right to sit there as he had.

When the symphony began Paul sank into one of the rear seats with a long sigh of relief, and lost himself as he had done before the Rico. It was not that symphonies, as such, meant anything in particular to Paul, but the first sigh of the instruments seemed to free some hilarious and potent spirit within him; something that struggled there like the Genius° in the bottle found by the Arab fisherman. He felt a sudden zest of life; the lights danced before his eyes and the concert hall blazed into unimaginable splendor. When the soprano soloist came on, Paul forgot even the nastiness of his teacher's being there and gave himself up to the peculiar stimulus such personages always had for him. The soloist chanced to be a German woman, by no means in her first youth, and the mother of many children; but she wore an elaborate gown and a tiara, and above all she had that indefinable air of achievement, that world-shine upon her, which, in Paul's eyes, made her a veritable queen of Romance.

After a concert was over Paul was always irritable and wretched until he got to sleep, and tonight he was even more than usually restless. He had the feeling of not being able to let down, of its being impossible to give up this delicious excitement which was the only thing that could be called living at all. During the last number he withdrew and, after hastily changing his clothes in the dressing-room, slipped out to the side door where the soprano's carriage

15

hauteur: haughtiness.   _Genius_: genie in a tale from _The Arabian Nights_.

stood. Here he began pacing rapidly up and down the walk, waiting to see her come out.

Over yonder the Schenley, in its vacant stretch, loomed big and square through the fine rain, the windows of its twelve stories glowing like those of a lighted cardboard house under a Christmas tree. All the actors and singers of the better class stayed there when they were in the city, and a number of the big manufacturers of the place lived there in the winter. Paul had often hung about the hotel, watching the people go in and out, longing to enter and leave school-masters and dull care behind him forever.

At last the singer came out, accompanied by the conductor, who helped her into her carriage and closed the door with a cordial *auf wiedersehen*° which set Paul to wondering whether she were not an old sweetheart of his. Paul followed the carriage over to the hotel, walking so rapidly as not to be far from the entrance when the singer alighted and disappeared behind the swinging glass doors that were opened by a negro in a tall hat and a long coat. In the moment that the door was ajar it seemed to Paul that he, too, entered. He seemed to feel himself go after her up the steps, into the warm, lighted building, into an exotic, a tropical world of shiny, glistening surfaces and basking ease. He reflected upon the mysterious dishes that were brought into the dining-room, the green bottles in buckets of ice, as he had seen them in the supper party pictures of the *Sunday World* supplement. A quick gust of wind brought the rain down with sudden vehemence, and Paul was startled to find that he was still outside in the slush of the gravel driveway; that his boots were letting in the water and his scanty over-coat was clinging wet about him; that the lights in front of the concert hall were out, and that the rain was driving in sheets between him and the orange glow of the windows above him. There it was, what he wanted—tangibly before him, like the fairy world of a Christmas pantomime, but mocking spirits stood guard at the doors, and, as the rain beat in his face, Paul wondered whether he were destined always to shiver in the black night outside, looking up at it.

He turned and walked reluctantly toward the car tracks. The end had to come sometime; his father in his night-clothes at the top of the stairs, explanations that did not explain, hastily improvised fictions that were forever tripping him up, his upstairs room and its horrible yellow wall-paper, the creaking bureau with the greasy plush collar-box, and over his painted wooden bed the pictures of George Washington and John Calvin,° and the framed motto, "Feed my Lambs," which had been worked in red worsted by his mother.

Half an hour later, Paul alighted from his car and went slowly down one of the side streets off the main thoroughfare. It was a highly respectable street, where all the houses were exactly alike, and where businessmen of moderate means begot and reared large families of children, all of whom went to Sabbath-school and learned the shorter catechism, and were interested in arithmetic; all of whom were as exactly alike as their homes, and of a piece with the monotony

auf wiedersehen: German equivalent of *au revoir*, or "here's to seeing you again." *John Calvin:* French Protestant theologian of the Reformation (1509–1564) whose teachings are the basis of Presbyterianism.

in which they lived. Paul never went up Cordelia Street without a shudder of loathing. His home was next to the house of the Cumberland° minister. He approached it tonight with the nerveless sense of defeat, the hopeless feeling of sinking back forever into ugliness and commonness that he had always had when he came home. The moment he turned into Cordelia Street he felt the waters close above his head. After each of these orgies of living, he experienced all the physical depression which follows a debauch; the loathing of respectable beds, of common food, of a house penetrated by kitchen odors; a shuddering repulsion for the flavorless, colorless mass of every-day existence; a morbid desire for cool things and soft lights and fresh flowers.

The nearer he approached the house, the more absolutely unequal Paul felt   20 to the sight of it all; his ugly sleeping chamber; the cold bathroom with the grimy zinc tub, the cracked mirror, the dripping spigots; his father, at the top of the stairs, his hairy legs sticking out from his night-shirt, his feet thrust into carpet slippers. He was so much later than usual that there would certainly be inquiries and reproaches. Paul stopped short before the door. He felt that he could not be accosted by his father tonight; that he could not toss again on that miserable bed. He would not go in. He would tell his father that he had no car fare, and it was raining so hard he had gone home with one of the boys and stayed all night.

Meanwhile, he was wet and cold. He went around to the back of the house and tried one of the basement windows, found it open, raised it cautiously, and scrambled down the cellar wall to the floor. There he stood, holding his breath, terrified by the noise he had made, but the floor above him was silent, and there was no creak on the stairs. He found a soap-box, and carried it over to the soft ring of light that streamed from the furnace door, and sat down. He was horribly afraid of rats, so he did not try to sleep, but sat looking distrustfully at the dark, still terrified lest he might have awakened his father. In such reactions, after one of the experiences which made days and nights out of the dreary blanks of the calendar, when his senses were deadened, Paul's head was always singularly clear. Suppose his father had heard him getting in at the window and had come down and shot him for a burglar? Then, again, suppose his father had come down, pistol in hand, and he had cried out in time to save himself, and his father had been horrified to think how nearly he had killed him? Then, again, suppose a day should come when his father would remember that night, and wish there had been no warning cry to stay his hand? With this last supposition Paul entertained himself until daybreak.

The following Sunday was fine; the sodden November chill was broken by the last flash of autumnal summer. In the morning Paul had to go to church and Sabbath-school, as always. On seasonable Sunday afternoons the burghers of Cordelia Street always sat out on their front "stoops," and talked to their neighbors on the next stoop, or called to those across the street in neighborly fashion.

Cumberland: The minister, a Cumberland Presbyterian, belongs to a frontier denomination that had splintered away from the Presbyterian Church and whose ministers were ordained after a briefer training.

The men usually sat on gay cushions placed upon the steps that led down to the sidewalk, while the women, in their Sunday "waists," sat in rockers on the cramped porches, pretending to be greatly at their ease. The children played in the streets; there was so many of them that the place resembled the recreation grounds of a kindergarten. The men on the steps—all in their shirt sleeves, their vests unbuttoned—sat with their legs well apart, their stomachs comfortably pro-truding, and talked of the prices of things, or told anecdotes of the sagacity of their various chiefs and overlords. They occasionally looked over the multitude of squabbling children, listened affectionately to their high-pitched, nasal voices, smiling to see their own proclivities reproduced in their offspring, and interspersed their legends of the iron kings with remarks about their sons' progress at school, their grades in arithmetic, and the amounts they had saved in their toy banks.

On this last Sunday of November, Paul sat all the afternoon on the lowest step of his "stoop," staring into the street, while his sisters, in their rockers, were talking to the minister's daughters next door about how many shirt-waists they had made in the last week, and how many waffles some one had eaten at the last church supper. When the weather was warm, and his father was in a particularly jovial frame of mind, the girls made lemonade, which was always brought out in a red-glass pitcher, ornamented with forget-me-nots in blue enamel. This the girls thought very fine, and the neighbors always joked about the suspicious color of the pitcher.

Today Paul's father sat on the top step, talking to a young man who shifted a restless baby from knee to knee. He happened to be the young man who was daily held up to Paul as a model, and after whom it was his father's dearest hope that he would pattern. This young man was of a ruddy complexion, with a com-pressed, red mouth, and faded, near-sighted eyes, over which he wore thick spec-tacles, with gold bows that curved about his ears. He was clerk to one of the magnates of a great steel corporation, and was looked upon in Cordelia Street as a young man with a future. There was a story that, some five years ago—he was now barely twenty-six—he had been a trifle dissipated but in order to curb his appetites and save the loss of time and strength that a sowing of wild oats might have entailed, he had taken his chief's advice oft reiterated to his employees, and at twenty-one had married the first woman whom he could persuade to share his fortunes. She happened to be an angular school-mistress, much older than he, who also wore thick glasses, and who had now borne him four children, all near-sighted, like herself.

The young man was relating how his chief, now cruising in the Mediter- 25 ranean, kept in touch with all the details of the business, arranging his office hours on his yacht just as though he were at home, and "knocking off work enough to keep two stenographers busy." His father told, in turn, the plan his corporation was considering, of putting in an electric railway plant at Cairo. Paul snapped his teeth; he had an awful apprehension that they might spoil it all before he got there. Yet he rather liked to hear these legends of the iron kings, that were told and retold on Sundays and holidays; these stories of palaces in Venice, yachts on the Mediterranean, and high play at Monte Carlo appealed to his fancy, and he was interested in the triumphs of these cash boys who had become famous, though he had no mind for the cash-boy stage.

After supper was over, and he had helped to dry the dishes, Paul nervously asked his father whether he could go to George's to get some help in his geometry, and still more nervously asked for car fare. This latter request he had to repeat, as his father, on principle, did not like to hear requests for money, whether much or little. He asked Paul whether he could not go to some boy who lived nearer, and told him that he ought not to leave his school work until Sunday; but he gave him the dime. He was not a poor man, but he had a worthy ambition to come up in the world. His only reason for allowing Paul to usher was, that he thought a boy ought to be earning a little.

Paul bounded upstairs, scrubbed the greasy odor of the dish-water from his hands with the ill-smelling soap he hated, and then shook over his fingers a few drops of violet water from the bottle he kept hidden in his drawer. He left the house with his geometry conspicuously under his arm, and the moment he got out of Cordelia Street and boarded a downtown car, he shook off the lethargy of two deadening days, and began to live again.

The leading juvenile of the permanent stock company which played at one of the downtown theatres was an acquaintance of Paul's, and the boy had been invited to drop in at the Sunday-night rehearsals whenever he could. For more than a year Paul had spent every available moment loitering about Charley Edwards's dressing-room. He had won a place among Edward's following not only because the young actor, who could not afford to employ a dresser, often found him useful, but because he recognized in Paul something akin to what churchmen term "vocation."

It was at the theatre and at Carnegie Hall that Paul really lived; the rest was but a sleep and a forgetting. This was Paul's fairy tale, and it had for him all the allurement of a secret love. The moment he inhaled the gassy, painty, dusty odor behind the scenes, he breathed like a prisoner set free, and felt within him the possibility of doing or saying splendid, brilliant, poetic things. The moment the cracked orchestra beat out the overture from *Martha*,° or jerked at the serenade from *Rigoletto*,° all stupid and ugly things slid from him, and his senses were deliciously, yet delicately fired.

Perhaps it was because, in Paul's world, the natural nearly always wore the guise of ugliness, that a certain element of artificiality seemed to him necessary in beauty. Perhaps it was because his experience of life elsewhere was so full of Sabbath-school picnics, petty economies, wholesome advice as to how to succeed in life, and the unescapable odors of cooking, that he found this existence so alluring, these smartly-clad men and women so attractive, that he was so moved by these starry apple orchards that bloomed perennially under the limelight.

It would be difficult to put it strongly enough how convincingly the stage entrance of that theatre was for Paul the actual portal of Romance. Certainly

30

Martha: grand opera about romance among English aristocrats (1847) by German composer Friedrich von Flotow.   *Rigoletto*: tragic grand opera (1851) by Italian composer Giuseppe Verdi.

none of the company ever suspected it, least of all Charley Edwards. It was very like the old stories that used to float about London of fabulously rich Jews, who had subterranean halls there, with palms, and fountains, and soft lamps and richly apparelled women who never saw the disenchanting light of London day. So, in the midst of that smoke-palled city, enamored of figures and grimy toil, Paul had his secret temple, his wishing carpet, his bit of blue-and-white Mediterranean shore bathed in perpetual sunshine.

Several of Paul's teachers had a theory that his imagination had been perverted by garish fiction, but the truth was that he scarcely ever read at all. The books at home were not such as would either tempt or corrupt a youthful mind, and as for reading the novels that some of his friends urged upon him—well, he got what he wanted much more quickly from music; any sort of music, from an orchestra to a barrel organ. He needed only the spark, the indescribable thrill that made his imagination master of his senses, and he could make plots and pictures enough of his own. It was equally true that he was not stage struck—not, at any rate, in the usual acceptation of that expression. He had no desire to become an actor, any more than he had to become a musician. He felt no necessity to do any of these things; what he wanted was to see, to be in the atmosphere, float on the wave of it, to be carried out, blue league after blue league, away from everything.

After a night behind the scenes, Paul found the school-room more than ever repulsive; the bare floors and naked walls; the prosy men who never wore frock coats, or violets in their buttonholes; the women with their dull gowns, shrill voices, and pitiful seriousness about prepositions that govern the dative. He could not bear to have the other pupils think, for a moment, that he took these people seriously; he must convey to them that he considered it all trivial, and was there only by way of a jest, anyway. He had autographed pictures of all the members of the stock company which he showed his classmates, telling them the most incredible stories of his familiarity with these people, of his acquaintance with the soloists who came to Carnegie Hall, his suppers with them and the flowers he sent them. When these stories lost their effect, and his audience grew listless, he became desperate and would bid all the boys good-bye, announcing that he was going to travel for a while; going to Naples, to Venice, to Egypt. Then, next Monday, he would slip back, conscious and nervously smiling; his sister was ill, and he should have to defer his voyage until spring.

Matters went steadily worse with Paul at school. In the itch to let his instructors know how heartily he despised them and their homilies, and how thoroughly he was appreciated elsewhere, he mentioned once or twice that he had no time to fool with theorems; adding—with a twitch of the eyebrows and a touch of that nervous bravado which so perplexed them—that he was helping the people down at the stock company; they were old friends of his.

The upshot of the matter was that the Principal went to Paul's father, and Paul was taken out of school and put to work. The manager at Carnegie Hall was told to get another usher in his stead; the door-keeper at the theatre was warned not to admit him to the house; and Charley Edwards remorsefully promised the boy's father not to see him again.

35

The members of the stock company were vastly amused when some of Paul's stories reached them—especially the women. They were hardworking women, most of them supporting indigent husbands or brothers, and they laughed rather bitterly at having stirred the boy to such fervid and florid inventions. They agreed with the faculty and with his father that Paul's was a bad case.

The east-bound train was ploughing through a January snow-storm; the dull dawn was beginning to show gray when the engine whistled a mile out of Newark. Paul started up from the seat where he had lain curled in uneasy slumber, rubbed the breath-misted window glass with his hand, and peered out. The snow was whirling in curling eddies above the white bottom lands, and the drifts lay already deep in the fields and along the fences, while here and there the long dead grass and dried weed stalks protruded black above it. Lights shone from the scattered houses, and a gang of laborers who stood beside the track waved their lanterns.

Paul had slept very little, and he felt grimy and uncomfortable. He had made the all-night journey in a day coach, partly because he was ashamed, dressed as he was, to go into a Pullman, and partly because he was afraid of being seen there by some Pittsburgh businessmen, who might have noticed him in Denny & Carson's office. When the whistle awoke him, he clutched quickly at his breast pocket, glancing about him with an uncertain smile. But the little, clay-bespattered Italians were still sleeping, the slatternly women across the aisle were in open-mouthed oblivion, and even the crumby, crying babies were for the nonce stilled. Paul settled back to struggle with his impatience as best as he could.

When he arrived at the Jersey City station, he hurried through his breakfast, manifestly ill at ease and keeping a sharp eye about him. After he reached the Twenty-third Street station,° he consulted a cabman, and had himself driven to a men's furnishing establishment that was just opening for the day. He spent upward of two hours there, buying with endless reconsidering and great care. His new street suit he put on in the fitting-room; the frock coat and dress clothes he had bundled into the cab with his linen. Then he drove to a hatter's and a shoe house. His next errand was at Tiffany's, where he selected his silver and a new scarf-pin. He would not wait to have his silver marked, he said. Lastly, he stopped at a trunk shop on Broadway, and had his purchases packed into various travelling bags.

It was a little after one-o'clock when he drove up to the Waldorf, and after settling with the cabman, went into the office. He registered from Washington; said his mother and father had been abroad, and that he had come down to await the arrival of their steamer. He told his story plausibly and had no trouble, since he volunteered to pay for them in advance, in engaging his rooms; a sleeping-room, sitting-room and bath. 40

Not once, but a hundred times Paul had planned this entry into New York. He had gone over every detail of it with Charley Edwards, and in his scrap book at home there were pages of description about New York hotels, cut from the

Twenty-third Street station: The scene is now New York City.

Sunday papers. When he was shown to his sitting-room on the eighth floor, he saw at a glance that everything was as it should be; there was but one detail in his mental picture that the place did not realize, so he rang for the bell boy and sent him down for flowers. He moved about nervously until the boy returned, putting away his new linen and fingering it delightedly as he did so. When the flowers came, he put them hastily into water, and then tumbled into a hot bath. Presently he came out of his white bath-room, resplendent in his new silk underwear, and playing with the tassels of his red robe. The snow was whirling so fiercely outside his windows that he could scarcely see across the street, but within the air was deliciously soft and fragrant. He put the violets and jonquils on the taboret beside the couch, and threw himself down, with a long sigh, covering himself with a Roman blanket. He was thoroughly tired; he had been in such haste, he had stood up to such a strain, covered so much ground in the last twenty-four hours, that he wanted to think how it had all come about. Lulled by the sound of the wind, the warm air, and the cool fragrance of the flowers, he sank into deep, drowsy retrospection.

It had been wonderfully simple; when they had shut him out of the theatre and concert hall, when they had taken away his bone, the whole thing was virtually determined. The rest was a mere matter of opportunity. The only thing that at all surprised him was his own courage—for he realized well enough that he had always been tormented by fear, a sort of apprehensive dread that, of late years, as the meshes of the lies he had told closed about him, had been pulling the muscles of his body tighter and tighter. Until now, he could not remember the time when he had not been dreading something. Even when he was a little boy, it was always there—behind him, or before, or on either side. There had always been the shadowed corner, the dark place into which he dared not look, but from which something seemed always to be watching him—and Paul had done things that were not pretty to watch, he knew.

But now he had a curious sense of relief, as though he had at last thrown down the gauntlet to the thing in the corner.

Yet it was but a day since he had been sulking in the traces; but yesterday afternoon that he had been sent to the bank with Denny & Carson's deposit, as usual—but this time he was instructed to leave the book to be balanced. There was above two thousand dollars in checks, and nearly a thousand in the bank notes which he had taken from the book and quietly transferred to his pocket. At the bank he had made out a new deposit slip. His nerves had been steady enough to permit of his returning to the office, where he had finished his work and asked for a full day's holiday tomorrow, Saturday, giving a perfectly reasonable pretext. The bank book, he knew, would not be returned before Monday or Tuesday, and his father would be out of town for the next week. From the time he slipped the bank notes into his pocket until he boarded the night train for New York, he had not known a moment's hesitation. It was not the first time Paul had steered through treacherous waters.

How astonishingly easy it had all been; here he was, the thing done; and this time there would be no awakening, no figure at the top of the stairs. He watched the snow flakes whirling by his window until he fell asleep.

When he awoke, it was three o'clock in the afternoon. He bounded up with a start; half of one of his precious days gone already! He spent more than an hour in dressing, watching every stage of his toilet carefully in the mirror. Everything was quite perfect; he was exactly the kind of boy he had always wanted to be.

When he went downstairs, Paul took a carriage and drove up Fifth Avenue toward the Park. The snow had somewhat abated; carriages and tradesmen's wagons were hurrying soundlessly to and fro in the winter twilight; boys in woollen mufflers were shovelling off the doorsteps; the avenue stages made fine spots of color against the white street. Here and there on the corners were stands, with whole flower gardens blooming under glass cases, against the sides of which the snow flakes stuck and melted; violets, roses, carnations, lilies of the valley—somewhat vastly more lovely and alluring that they blossomed thus unnaturally in the snow. The Park itself was a wonderful stage winterpiece.

When he returned, the pause of the twilight had ceased, and the tune of the streets had changed. The snow was falling faster, lights streamed from the hotels that reared their dozen stories fearlessly up into the storm, defying the raging Atlantic winds. A long, black stream of carriages poured down the avenue, intersected here and there by other streams, tending horizontally. There were a score of cabs about the entrance of his hotel, and his driver had to wait. Boys in livery were running in and out of the awning stretched across the sidewalk, up and down the red velvet carpet laid from the door to the street. Above, about, within it all was the rumble and roar, the hurry and toss of thousands of human beings as hot for pleasure as himself, and on every side of him towered the glaring affirmation of the omnipotence of wealth.

The boy set his teeth and drew his shoulders together in a spasm of realization: the plot of all dramas, the text of all romances, the nerve-stuff of all sensations was whirling about him like the snow flakes. He burnt like a faggot in a tempest.

When Paul went down to dinner, the music of the orchestra came floating up the elevator shaft to greet him. His head whirled as he stepped into the thronged corridor, and he sank back into one of the chairs against the wall to get his breath. The lights, the chatter, the perfumes, the bewildering medley of color—he had, for a moment, the feeling of not being able to stand it. But only for a moment; these were his own people, he told himself. He went slowly about the corridors, through the writing-rooms, smoking-rooms, reception-rooms, as though he were exploring the chambers of an enchanted palace, built and peopled for him alone.

When he reached the dining-room he sat down at a table near a window. The flowers, the white linen, the many-colored wine glasses, the gay toilettes of the women, the low popping of corks, the undulating repetitions of the *Blue Danube* from the orchestra, all flooded Paul's dream with bewildering radiance. When the roseate tinge of his champagne was added—that cold, precious, bubbling stuff that creamed and foamed in his glass—Paul wondered that there were honest men in the world at all. This was what all the world was fighting for, he reflected; this was what all the struggle was about. He doubted the reality of his past. Had he ever known a place called Cordelia Street, a place where fagged-looking businessmen got on the early car; mere rivets in a machine they seemed to Paul—sickening men, with combings of children's hair always hanging to their coats, and the smell of cooking in their clothes. Cordelia Street—Ah! that belonged to another time and country; had he not always been thus, had he not sat here night after night, from as far back as he could remember, looking pensively over just such shimmering textures, and slowly twirling the stem of a glass like this one between his thumb and middle finger? He rather thought he had.

He was not in the least abashed or lonely. He had no especial desire to meet or to know any of these people; all he demanded was the right to look on and conjecture, to watch the pageant. The mere stage properties were all he contended for. Nor was he lonely later in the evening, in his loge at the Metropolitan. He was now entirely rid of his nervous misgivings, of his forced aggressiveness, of the imperative desire to show himself different from his surroundings. He felt now that his surroundings explained him. Nobody questioned the purple; he had only to wear it passively. He had only to glance down at his attire to reassure himself that here it would be impossible for anyone to humiliate him.

He found it hard to leave his beautiful sitting-room to go to bed that night, and sat long watching the raging storm from his turret window. When he went to sleep it was with the lights turned on in his bedroom; partly because of his old timidity, and partly so that, if he should wake in the night, there would be no wretched moment of doubt, no horrible suspicion of yellow wall-paper, or of Washington and Calvin above his bed.

Sunday morning the city was practically snow-bound. Paul breakfasted late, and in the afternoon he fell in with a wild San Francisco boy, a freshman at Yale, who said he had run down for a "little flyer" over Sunday. The young man offered to show Paul the night side of the town, and the two boys went out together after dinner, not returning to the hotel until seven o'clock the next morning. They had started out in the confiding warmth of a champagne friendship, but their parting in the elevator was singularly cool. The freshman pulled himself together to make his train, and Paul went to bed. He awoke at two o'clock in the afternoon, very thirsty and dizzy, and rang for ice-water, coffee, and the Pittsburgh papers.

On the part of the hotel management, Paul excited no suspicion. There was 55 this to be said for him, that he wore his spoils with dignity and in no way made himself conspicuous. Even under the glow of his wine he was never boisterous, though he found the stuff like a magician's wand for wonder-building. His chief greediness lay in his ears and eyes, and his excesses were not offensive ones. His dearest pleasures were the gray winter twilights in his sitting-room; his quiet enjoyment of his flowers, his clothes, his wide divan, his cigarette, and his sense of power. He could not remember a time when he had felt so at peace with himself. The mere release from the necessity of petty lying, lying every day and every day, restored his self-respect. He had never lied for pleasure, even at school; but to be noticed and admired, to assert his difference from other Cordelia Street boys;

and he felt a good deal more manly, more honest, even, now that he had no need for boastful pretensions, now that he could, as his actor friends used to say, "dress the part." It was characteristic that remorse did not occur to him. His golden days went by without a shadow, and he made each as perfect as he could.

On the eighth day after his arrival in New York, he found the whole affair exploited in the Pittsburgh papers, exploited with a wealth of detail which indicated that local news of a sensational nature was at a low ebb. The firm of Denny & Carson announced that the boy's father had refunded the full amount of the theft, and that they had no intention of prosecuting. The Cumberland minister had been interviewed, and expressed his hope of yet reclaiming the motherless lad, and his Sabbath-school teacher declared that she would spare no effort to that end. The rumor had reached Pittsburgh that the boy had been seen in a New York hotel, and his father had gone East to find him and bring him home.

Paul had just come in to dress for dinner; he sank into a chair, weak to the knees, and clasped his head in his hands. It was to be worse than jail, even; the tepid waters of Cordelia Street were to close over him finally and forever. The gray monotony stretched before him in hopeless, unrelieved years; Sabbath-school, Young People's Meeting, the yellow-papered room, the damp dish-towels; it all rushed back upon him with a sickening vividness. He had the old feeling that the orchestra had suddenly stopped, the sinking sensation that the play was over. The sweat broke out on his face, and he sprang to his feet, looked about him with his white, conscious smile, and winked at himself in the mirror. With something of the old childish belief in miracles with which he had so often gone to class, all his lessons unlearned, Paul dressed and dashed whistling down the corridor to the elevator.

He had no sooner entered the dining-room and caught the measure of the music than his remembrance was lightened by his old elastic power of claiming the moment, mounting with it, and finding it all sufficient. The glare and glitter about him, the mere scenic accessories had again, and for the last time, their old potency. He would show himself that he was game, he would finish the thing splendidly. He doubted, more than ever, the existence of Cordelia Street, and for the first time he drank his wine recklessly. Was he not, after all, one of those fortunate beings born to the purple, was he not still himself and in his own place? He drummed a nervous accompaniment to the Pagliacci music and looked about him, telling himself over and over that it had paid.

He reflected drowsily, to the swell of the music and the chill sweetness of his wine, that he might have done it more wisely. He might have caught an outbound steamer and been well out of their clutches before now. But the other side of the world had seemed too far away and too uncertain then; he could not have waited for it; his need had been too sharp. If he had to choose over again, he would do the same thing tomorrow. He looked affectionately about the dining-room, now gilded with a soft mist. Ah, it had paid indeed!

Paul was awakened next morning by a painful throbbing in his head and feet. He had thrown himself across the bed without undressing, and had slept with his shoes on. His limbs and hands were lead heavy, and his tongue and 60 throat were parched and burnt. There came upon him one of those fateful attacks of clear-headedness that never occurred except when he was physically exhausted and his nerves hung loose. He lay still and closed his eyes and let the tide of things wash over him.

His father was in New York; "stopping at some joint or other," he told himself. The memory of successive summers on the front stoop fell upon him like a weight of black water. He had not a hundred dollars left; and he knew now, more than ever, that money was everything, the wall that stood between all he loathed and all he wanted. The thing was winding itself up; he had thought of that on his first glorious day in New York, and had even provided a way to snap the thread. It lay on his dressing-table now; he had got it out last night when he came blindly up from dinner, but the shiny metal hurt his eyes, and he disliked the looks of it.

He rose and moved about with a painful effort, succumbing now and again to attacks of nausea. It was the old depression exaggerated; all the world had become Cordelia Street. Yet somehow he was not afraid of anything, was absolutely calm; perhaps because he had looked into the dark corner at last and knew. It was bad enough, what he saw there, but somehow not so bad as his long fear of it had been. He saw everything clearly now. He had a feeling that he had made the best of it, that he had lived the sort of life he was meant to live, and for half an hour he sat staring at the revolver. But he told himself that was not the way, so he went downstairs and took a cab to the ferry.

When Paul arrived at Newark, he got off the train and took another cab, directing the driver to follow the Pennsylvania tracks out of the town. The snow lay heavy on the roadways and had drifted deep in the open fields. Only here and there the dead grass or dried weed stalks projected, singularly black, above it. Once well into the country, Paul dismissed the carriage and walked, floundering along the tracks, his mind a medley of irrelevant things. He seemed to hold in his brain an actual picture of everything he had seen that morning. He remembered every feature of both his drivers, of the toothless old woman from whom he had bought the red flowers in his coat, the agent from whom he had got his ticket, and all of his fellow-passengers on the ferry. His mind, unable to cope with vital matters near at hand, worked feverishly and deftly at sorting and grouping these images. They made for him a part of the ugliness of the world, of the ache in his head, and the bitter burning on his tongue. He stooped and put a handful of snow into his mouth as he walked, but that, too, seemed hot. When he reached a little hillside, where the tracks ran through a cut some twenty feet below him, he stopped and sat down.

The carnations in his coat were drooping with the cold, he noticed; their red glory all over. It occurred to him that all the flowers he had seen in the glass cases that first night must have gone the same way, long before this. It was only one splendid breath they had, in spite of their brave mockery at the winter outside the glass; and it was a losing game in the end, it seemed, this revolt against the homilies by which the world is run. Paul took one of the blossoms carefully from his coat and scooped a little hole in the snow, where he covered it up.

Then he dozed a while, from his weak condition, seemingly insensible to the cold.

The sound of an approaching train awoke him, and he started to his feet, remembering only his resolution, and afraid lest he should be too late. He stood watching the approaching locomotive, his teeth chattering, his lips drawn away from them in a frightened smile; once or twice he glanced nervously sidewise, as though he were being watched. When the right moment came, he jumped. As he fell, the folly of his haste occurred to him with merciless clearness, the vastness of what he had left undone. There flashed through his brain, clearer than ever before, the blue of Adriatic water, the yellow of Algerian sands.

He felt something strike his chest, and that his body was being thrown swiftly through the air, on and on, immeasurably far and fast, while his limbs were gently relaxed. Then, because the picture making mechanism was crushed, the disturbing visions flashed into black, and Paul dropped back into the immense design of things.

John Cheever

THE FIVE-FORTY-EIGHT   1954

John Cheever (1912–1982) was born in Quincy, Massachusetts. His parents had been modestly prosperous, but their livelihood declined substantially and was finally dashed by the 1929 stock market crash. Cheever was sent away to Thayer Academy, a prep school, where he was a poor student. When he was expelled at eighteen, he wrote a story about the incident that was published in the New Republic *(1930). Cheever never finished high school or attended college, dedicating himself instead to writing. For years he lived in poverty in one tiny room, sustaining himself on "a bread and buttermilk diet." Gradually he became a celebrated writer. Once famous, however, Cheever hid the financial problems of his parents and his youthful poverty with fanciful*

John Cheever

tales of an aristocratic background. Cheever's stories, most of which appeared in the New Yorker, *often deal with the ordinary lives of middle-class characters living in Manhattan or its suburbs.*

Although his stories are realistic in plot and setting, they also often contain an underlying religious vision—exploring themes of guilt, grace, and redemption. Cheever's novels include The Wapshot Chronicle *(1957), which won the National Book Award;* Bullet Park *(1969); and* Falconer *(1977). The Stories of John Cheever (1978), selected works from his five volumes of short fiction, not only won the Pulitzer Prize and National*

Book Critics Circle Award, it also became the first book of short stories in decades to make the best-seller list. After Cheever's death, his notebooks and letters revealed how tortured his life had been by sex and alcohol. While some early reviewers regarded Cheever's popular stories as "New Yorker fiction" (satiric views of middle-class life), critics now see the psychological and religious vision underlying his work. Once undervalued, Cheever is now generally regarded as one of the finest American short-story writers of the century.

When Blake stepped out of the elevator, he saw her. A few people, mostly men waiting for girls, stood in the lobby watching the elevator doors. She was among them. As he saw her, her face took on a look of such loathing and purpose that he realized she had been waiting for him. He did not approach her. She had no legitimate business with him. They had nothing to say. He turned and walked toward the glass doors at the end of the lobby, feeling that faint guilt and bewilderment we experience when we bypass some old friend or classmate who seems threadbare, or sick, or miserable in some other way. It was five-eighteen by the clock in the Western Union office. He could catch the express. As he waited his turn at the revolving doors, he saw that it was still raining. It had been raining all day, and he noticed now how much louder the rain made the noises of the street. Outside, he started walking briskly east toward Madison Avenue. Traffic was tied up, and horns were blowing urgently on a crosstown street in the distance. The sidewalk was crowded. He wondered what she had hoped to gain by a glimpse of him coming out of the office building at the end of the day. Then he wondered if she was following him.

Walking in the city, we seldom turn and look back. The habit restrained Blake. He listened for a minute—foolishly—as he walked, as if he could distinguish her footsteps from the worlds of sound in the city at the end of a rainy day. Then he noticed, ahead of him on the other side of the street, a break in the wall of buildings. Something had been torn down; something was being put up, but the steel structure had only just risen above the sidewalk fence and daylight poured through the gap. Blake stopped opposite here and looked into a store window. It was a decorator's or an auctioneer's. The window was arranged like a room in which people live and entertain their friends. There were cups on the coffee table, magazines to read, and flowers in the vases, but the flowers were dead and the cups were empty and the guests had not come. In the plate glass, Blake saw a clear reflection of himself and the crowds that were passing, like shadows, at his back. Then he saw her image—so close to him that it shocked him. She was standing only a foot or two behind him. He could have turned then and asked her what she wanted, but instead of recognizing her, he shied away abruptly from the reflection of her contorted face and went along the street. She might be meaning to do him harm—she might be meaning to kill him.

The suddenness with which he moved when he saw the reflection of her face tipped the water out of his hat brim in such a way that some of it ran down his neck. It felt unpleasantly like the sweat of fear. Then the cold water falling into his face and onto his bare hands, the rancid smell of the wet gutters and paving, the knowledge that his feet were beginning to get wet and that he might catch cold—all the common discomforts of walking in the rain—seemed to heighten the menace of his pursuer and to give him a morbid consciousness of his own physicalness and of the ease with which he could be hurt. He could see ahead of him the corner of Madison Avenue, where the lights were brighter. He felt that if he could get to Madison Avenue he would be all right. At the corner, there was a bakery shop with two entrances, and he went in by the door on the crosstown street, bought a coffee ring,° like any other commuter, and went out the Madison Avenue door. As he started down Madison Avenue, he saw her waiting for him by a hut where newspapers were sold.

She was not clever. She would be easy to shake. He could get into a taxi by one door and leave by the other. He could speak to a policeman. He could run— although he was afraid that if he did run, it might precipitate the violence he now felt sure she had planned. He was approaching a part of the city that he knew well and where the maze of street-level and underground passages, elevator banks, and crowded lobbies made it easy for a man to lose a pursuer. The thought of this, and a whiff of sugary warmth from the coffee ring, cheered him. It was absurd to imagine being harmed on a crowded street. She was foolish, misled, lonely perhaps—that was all it could amount to. He was an insignificant man, and there was no point in anyone's following him from his office to the station. He knew no secrets of any consequence. The reports in his briefcase had no bearing on war, peace, the dope traffic, the hydrogen bomb, or any of the other international skulduggeries that he associated with pursuers, men in trench coats, and wet sidewalks. Then he saw ahead of him the door of a men's bar. Oh, it was so simple!

He ordered a Gibson° and shouldered his way in between two other men at ₅ the bar, so that if she should be watching from the window she would lose sight of him. The place was crowded with commuters putting down a drink before the ride home. They had brought in on their clothes—on their shoes and umbrellas—the rancid smell of the wet dusk outside, but Blake began to relax as soon as he tasted his Gibson and looked around at the common, mostly notyoung faces that surrounded him and that were worried, if they were worried at all, about tax rates and who would be put in charge of merchandising. He tried to remember her name—Miss Dent, Miss Bent, Miss Lent—and he was surprised to find that he could not remember it, although he was proud of the retentiveness and reach of his memory and it had only been six months ago.

Personnel had sent her up one afternoon—he was looking for a secretary. He saw a dark woman—in her twenties, perhaps—who was slender and shy. Her dress was simple, her figure was not much, one of her stockings was crooked, but her voice was soft and he had been willing to try her out. After she had been working for him a few days, she told him that she had been in the hospital for eight months and that it had been hard after this for her to find work, and she wanted to thank him for giving her a chance. Her hair was dark, her eyes were

---

coffee ring: a sweet roll.   *Gibson:* a dry martini with a small pickled onion instead of an olive.

dark; she left with him a pleasant impression of darkness. As he got to know her better, he felt that she was oversensitive and, as a consequence, lonely. Once, when she was speaking to him of what she imagined his life to be—full of friendships, money, and a large and loving family—he had thought he recognized a peculiar feeling of deprivation. She seemed to imagine the lives of the rest of the world to be more brilliant than they were. Once, she had put a rose on his desk, and he had dropped it into the wastebasket. "I don't like roses," he told her.

She had been competent, punctual, and a good typist, and he had found only one thing in her that he could object to—her handwriting. He could not associate the crudeness of her handwriting with her appearance. He would have expected her to write a rounded backhand, and in her writing there were intermittent traces of this, mixed with clumsy printing. Her writing gave him the feeling that she had been the victim of some inner—some emotional—conflict that had in its violence broken the continuity of the lines she was able to make on paper. When she had been working for him three weeks—no longer—they stayed late one night and he offered, after work, to buy her a drink. "If you really want a drink," she said. "I have some whiskey at my place."

She lived in a room that seemed to him like a closet. There were suit boxes and hatboxes piled in a corner, and although the room seemed hardly big enough to hold the bed, the dresser, and the chair he sat in, there was an upright piano against one wall, with a book of Beethoven sonatas on the rack. She gave him a drink and said that she was going to put on something more comfortable. He urged her to; that was, after all, what he had come for. If he had any qualms, they would have been practical. Her diffidence, the feeling of deprivation in her point of view, promised to protect him from any consequences. Most of the many women he had known had been picked for their lack of self-esteem.

When he put on his clothes again, an hour or so later, she was weeping. He felt too contented and warm and sleepy to worry much about her tears. As he was dressing, he noticed on the dresser a note she had written to a cleaning woman. The only light came from the bathroom—the door was ajar—and in this half light the hideously scrawled letters again seemed entirely wrong for her, and as if they must be the handwriting of some other and very gross woman. The next day, he did what he felt was the only sensible thing. When she was out for lunch, he called personnel and asked them to fire her. Then he took the afternoon off. A few days later, she came to the office, asking to see him. He told the switchboard girl not to let her in. He had not seen her again until this evening.

Blake drank a second Gibson and saw by the clock that he had missed the express. He would get the local—the five-forty-eight. When he left the bar the sky was still light; it was still raining. He looked carefully up and down the street and saw that the poor woman had gone. Once or twice, he looked over his shoulder, walking to the station, but he seemed to be safe. He was still not quite himself, he realized, because he had left his coffee ring at the bar, and he was not a man who forgot things. This lapse of memory pained him.

He bought a paper. The local was only half full when he boarded it, and he got a seat on the river side and took off his raincoat. He was a slender man with brown hair—undistinguished in every way, unless you could have divined in his pallor or his gray eyes his unpleasant tastes. He dressed—like the rest of us—as if he admitted the existence of sumptuary laws.° His raincoat was the pale buff color of a mushroom. His hat was dark brown; so was his suit. Except for the few bright threads in his necktie, there was a scrupulous lack of color in his clothing that seemed protective.

He looked around the car for neighbors. Mrs. Compton was several seats in front of him, to the right. She smiled, but her smile was fleeting. It died swiftly and horribly. Mr. Watkins was directly in front of Blake. Mr. Watkins needed a haircut, and he had broken the sumptuary laws; he was wearing a corduroy jacket. He and Blake had quarreled, so they did not speak.

The swift death of Mrs. Compton's smile did not affect Blake at all. The Comptons lived in the house next to the Blakes, and Mrs. Compton had never understood the importance of minding her own business. Louise Blake took her troubles to Mrs. Compton, Blake knew, and instead of discouraging her crying jags, Mrs. Compton had come to imagine herself a sort of confessor and had developed a lively curiosity about the Blakes' intimate affairs. She had probably been given an account of their most recent quarrel. Blake had come home one night, overworked and tired, and had found that Louise had done nothing about getting supper. He had gone into the kitchen, followed by Louise, and had pointed out to her that the date was the fifth. He had drawn a circle around the date on the kitchen calendar. "One week is the twelfth," he had said. "Two weeks will be the nineteenth." He drew a circle around the nineteenth. "I'm not going to speak to you for two weeks," he had said. "That will be the nineteenth." She had wept, she had protested, but it had been eight or ten years since she had been able to touch him with her entreaties. Louise had got old. Now the lines in her face were ineradicable, and when she clapped her glasses onto her nose to read the evening paper, she looked to him like an unpleasant stranger. The physical charms that had been her only attraction were gone. It had been nine years since Blake had built a bookshelf in the doorway that connected their rooms and had fitted into the bookshelf wooden doors that could be locked, since he did not want the children to see his books. But their prolonged estrangement didn't seem remarkable to Blake. He had quarreled with his wife, but so did every other man born of woman. It was human nature. In any place where you can hear their voices—a hotel courtyard, an air shaft, a street on a summer evening—you will hear harsh words.

The hard feeling between Blake and Mr. Watkins also had to do with Blake's family, but it was not as serious or as troublesome as what lay behind Mrs. Compton's fleeting smile. The Watkinses rented. Mr. Watkins broke the sumptuary laws day after day—he once went to the eight-fourteen in a pair of sandals—and he made his living as a commercial artist. Blake's oldest son—Charlie was fourteen—had made friends with the Watkins boy. He had spent a lot of

---

sumptuary laws: originally, Roman laws regulating the expenditures for clothes that could be worn in public. Cheever uses this term to suggest that most people wear conventional clothes that will not make them appear different from others.

time in the sloppy rented house where the Watkinses lived. The friendship had affected his manners and his neatness. Then he had begun to take some meals with the Watkinses, and to spend Saturday nights there. When he had moved most of his possessions over to the Watkinses' and had begun to spend more than half his nights there, Blake had been forced to act. He had spoken not to Charlie but to Mr. Watkins, and had, of necessity, said a number of things that must have sounded critical. Mr. Watkins' long and dirty hair and his corduroy jacket reassured Blake that he had been in the right.

But Mrs. Compton's dying smile and Mr. Watkins' dirty hair did not lessen   15 the pleasure Blake took in setting himself in an uncomfortable seat on the five-forty-eight deep underground. The coach was old and smelled oddly like a bomb shelter in which whole families had spent the night. The light that spread from the ceiling down onto their heads and shoulders was dim. The filth on the window glass was streaked with rain from some other journey, and clouds of rank pipe and cigarette smoke had begun to rise from behind each newspaper, but it was a scene that meant to Blake that he was on a safe path, and after his brush with danger he even felt a little warmth toward Mrs. Compton and Mr. Watkins.

The train traveled up from underground into the weak daylight, and the slums and the city reminded Blake vaguely of the woman who had followed him. To avoid speculation or remorse about her, he turned his attention to the evening paper. Out of the corner of his eye he could see the landscape. It was industrial and, at that hour, sad. There were machine sheds and warehouses, and above these he saw a break in the clouds—a piece of yellow light. "Mr. Blake," someone said. He looked up. It was she. She was standing there holding one hand on the back of the seat to steady herself in the swaying coach. He remembered her name then—Miss Dent. "Hello, Miss Dent," he said.

"Do you mind if I sit here?"

"I guess not."

"Thank you. It's very kind of you. I don't like to inconvenience you like this. I don't want to . . ." He had been frightened when he looked up and saw her, but her timid voice rapidly reassured him. He shifted his hams—that futile and reflexive gesture of hospitality—and she sat down. She sighed. He smelled her wet clothing. She wore a formless black hat with a cheap crest stitched onto it. Her coat was thin cloth, he saw, and she wore gloves and carried a large pocketbook.

"Are you living out in this direction now, Miss Dent?"   20

"No."

She opened her purse and reached for her handkerchief. She had begun to cry. He turned his head to see if anyone in the car was looking, but no one was. He had sat beside a thousand passengers on the evening train. He had noticed their clothes, the holes in their gloves; and if they fell asleep and mumbled he had wondered what their worries were. He had classified almost all of them briefly before he buried his nose in the paper. He had marked them as rich, poor, brilliant or dull, neighbors or strangers, but no one of the thousand had ever wept. When she opened her purse, he remembered her perfume. It had clung to his skin the night he went to her place for a drink.

"I've been very sick," she said. "This is the first time I've been out of bed in two weeks. I've been terribly sick."

"I'm sorry that you've been sick, Miss Dent," he said in a voice loud enough to be heard by Mr. Watkins and Mrs. Compton. "Where are you working now?"

"What?"   25

"Where are you working now?"

"Oh, don't make me laugh," she said softly.

"I don't understand."

"You poisoned their minds."

He straightened his neck and braced his shoulders. These wrenching move-   30
ments expressed a brief—and hopeless—longing to be in some other place. She meant trouble. He took a breath. He looked with deep feeling at the half-filled, half-lighted coach to affirm his sense of actuality, of a world in which there was not very much bad trouble after all. He was conscious of her heavy breathing and the smell of her rain-soaked coat. The train stopped. A nun and a man in overalls got off. When it started again, Blake put on his hat and reached for his raincoat.

"Where are you going?" she said.

"I'm going to the next car."

"Oh, no," she said. "No, no, no." She put her white face so close to his ear that he could feel her warm breath on his cheek. "Don't do that," she whispered. "Don't try and escape me. I have a pistol and I'll have to kill you and I don't want to. All I want to do is to talk with you. Don't move or I'll kill you. Don't, don't, don't!"

Blake sat back abruptly in his seat. If he had wanted to stand and shout for help, he would not have been able to. His tongue had swelled to twice its size, and when he tried to move it, it stuck horribly to the roof of his mouth. His legs were limp. All he could think of to do then was to wait for his heart to stop its hysterical beating, so that he could judge the extent of his danger. She was sitting a little sidewise, and in her pocketbook was the pistol, aimed at his belly.

"You understand me now, don't you?" she said. "You understand that I'm   35
serious?" He tried to speak but he was still mute. He nodded his head. "Now we'll sit quietly for a little while," she said. "I got so excited that my thoughts are all confused. We'll sit quietly for a little while, until I can get my thoughts in order again."

Help would come, Blake thought. It was only a question of minutes. Someone, noticing the look on his face or her peculiar posture, would stop and interfere, and it would all be over. All he had to do was to wait until someone noticed his predicament. Out of the window he saw the river and the sky. The rain clouds were rolling down like a shutter, and while he watched, a streak of orange light on the horizon became brilliant. Its brilliance spread—he could see it move—across the waves until it raked the banks of the river with a dim fire-light. Then it was put out. Help would come in a minute, he thought. Help would come before they stopped again; but the train stopped, there were some comings and goings, and Blake still lived on, at the mercy of the woman beside him. The possibility that help might not come was one that he could not face. The possibility that his predicament was not noticeable, that Mrs. Compton would guess that he was taking a poor relation out to dinner at Shady Hill, was something he would think about later. Then the saliva came back into his mouth and he was able to speak.

"Miss Dent?"

"Yes."

"What do you want?"

"I want to talk to you."

"You can come to my office."

"Oh, no. I went there every day for two weeks."

"You could make an appointment."

"No," she said. "I think we can talk here. I wrote you a letter but I've been too sick to go out and mail it. I've put down all my thoughts. I like to travel. I like trains. One of my troubles has always been that I could never afford to travel. I suppose you see this scenery every night and don't notice it any more, but it's nice for someone who's been in bed a long time. They say that He's not in the river and the hills but I think He is. 'Where shall wisdom be found?' it says. 'Where is the place of understanding? The depth saith it is not in me; the sea saith it is not with me. Destruction and death say we have heard the force with our ears.'"⁹

"Oh, I know what you're thinking," she said. "You're thinking that I'm ⋅ 45 crazy, and I have been very sick again but I'm going to be better. It's going to make me better to talk with you. I was in the hospital all the time before I came to work for you but they never tried to cure me, they only wanted to take away my self-respect. I haven't had any work now for three months. Even if I did have to kill you, they wouldn't be able to do anything to me except put me back in the hospital, so you see I'm not afraid. But let's sit quietly for a little while longer. I have to be calm."

The train continued its halting progress up the bank of the river, and Blake tried to force himself to make some plans for escape, but the immediate threat to his life made this difficult, and instead of planning sensibly, he thought of the many ways in which he could have avoided her in the first place. As soon as he had felt these regrets, he realized their futility. It was like regretting his lack of suspicion when she first mentioned her months in the hospital. It was like regretting his failure to have been warned by her shyness, her diffidence, and the handwriting that looked like the marks of a claw. There was no way of rectifying his mistakes, and he felt—for perhaps the first time in his mature life—the full force of regret. Out of the window, he saw some men fishing on the nearly dark river, and then a ramshackle boat club that seemed to have

"Where shall wisdom be found?" it says . . . "the force with our ears.": the *it* being in the Bible. Miss Dent is remembering parts of the book of Job (28:12–22). In the Old Testament text, Job, who has suffered terribly, asks where he shall find understanding of God's ways, but he does not find it in the natural world.

been nailed together out of scraps of wood that had been washed up on the shore.

Mr. Watkins had fallen asleep. He was snoring. Mrs. Compton read her paper. The train creaked, slowed, and halted infirmly at another station. Blake could see the southbound platform, where a few passengers were waiting to go into the city. There was a workman with a lunch pail, a dressed-up woman, and a woman with a suitcase. They stood apart from one another. Some advertisements were posted on the wall behind them. There was a picture of a couple drinking a toast in wine, a picture of a Cat's Paw rubber heel, and a picture of a Hawaiian dancer. Their cheerful intent seemed to go no farther than the puddles of water on the platform and to expire there. The platform and the people on it looked lonely. The train drew away from the station into the scattered lights of a slum and then into the darkness of the country and the river.

"I want you to read my letter before we get to Shady Hill," she said. "It's on the seat. Pick it up. I would have mailed it to you, but I've been too sick to go out. I haven't gone out for two weeks. I haven't had any work for three months. I haven't spoken to anybody but the landlady. Please read my letter."

He picked up the letter from the seat where she had put it. The cheap paper felt abhorrent and filthy to his fingers. It was folded and refolded. "Dear Husband," she had written, in that crazy, wandering hand, "they say that human love leads us to divine love, but is this true? I dream about you every night. I have such terrible desires. I have always had a gift for dreams. I dreamed on Tuesday of a volcano erupting with blood. When I was in the hospital they said they wanted to cure me but they only wanted to take away my self-respect. They only wanted me to dream about sewing and basketwork but I protected my gift for dreams. I'm clairvoyant.° I can tell when the telephone is going to ring. I've never had a true friend in my whole life. . . ."

The train stopped again. There was another platform, another picture of the couple drinking a toast, the rubber heel, and the Hawaiian dancer. Suddenly she pressed her face close to Blake's again and whispered in his ear. "I know what you're thinking. I can see it in your face. You're thinking you can get away from me in Shady Hill, aren't you? Oh, I've been planning this for weeks. It's all I've had to think about. I won't harm you if you'll let me talk. I've been thinking about devils. I mean, if there are devils in the world, if there are people in the world who represent evil, is it our duty to exterminate them? I know that you always prey on weak people. I can tell. Oh, sometimes I think I ought to kill you. Sometimes I think you're the only obstacle between me and my happiness. Sometimes . . ."

She touched Blake with the pistol. He felt the muzzle against his belly. The bullet, at that distance, would make a small hole where it entered, but it would rip out of his back a place as big as a soccer ball. He remembered the unburied dead he had seen in the war. The memory came in a rush; entrails, eyes, shattered bone, ordure, and other filth.

clairvoyant: a person who can see the future.

"All I've ever wanted in life is a little love," she said. She lightened the pressure of the gun. Mr. Watkins still slept. Mrs. Compton was sitting calmly with her hands folded in her lap. The coach rocked gently, and the coats and mushroom-colored raincoats that hung between the windows swayed a little as the car moved. Blake's elbow was on the window sill and his left shoe was on the guard above the steampipe. The car smelled like some dismal classroom. The passengers seemed asleep and apart, and Blake felt that he might never escape the smell of heat and wet clothing and the dimness of the light. He tried to summon the calculated self-deceptions with which he sometimes cheered himself, but he was left without any energy for hope of self-deception.

The conductor put his head in the door and said, "Shady Hill, next, Shady Hill."

"Now," she said. "Now you get out ahead of me."

Mr. Watkins waked suddenly, put on his coat and hat, and smiled at Mrs. Compton, who was gathering her parcels to her in a series of maternal gestures. They went to the door. Blake joined them, but neither of them spoke to him or seemed to notice the woman at his back. The conductor threw open the door, and Blake saw on the platform of the next car a few other neighbors who had missed the express, waiting patiently and tiredly in the wan light for their trip to end. He raised his head to see through the open door the abandoned mansion out of town, a NO TRESPASSING sign nailed to a tree, and then the oil tanks. The concrete abutments of the bridge passed, so close to the open door that he could have touched them. Then he saw the first of the lampposts on the northbound platform, the sign SHADY HILL in black and gold, and the little lawn and flower bed kept up by the Improvement Association, and then the cab stand and a corner of the old-fashioned depot. It was raining again; it was pouring. He could hear the splash of water and see the lights reflected in puddles and in the shining pavement, and the idle sound of splashing and dripping formed in his mind a conception of shelter, so light and strange that it seemed to belong to a time of his life that he could not remember.

He went down the steps with her at his back. A dozen or so cars were waiting by the station with their motors running. A few people got off from each of the other coaches; he recognized most of them, but none of them offered to give him a ride. They walked separately or in pairs—purposefully out of the rain to the shelter of the platform, where the car horns called to them. It was time to go home, time for a drink, time for love, time for supper, and he could see the lights on the hill—lights by which children were being bathed, meat cooked, dishes washed—shining in the rain. One by one, the cars picked up the heads of families, until there were only four left. Two of the stranded passengers drove off in the only taxi the village had. "I'm sorry, darling," a woman said tenderly to her husband when she drove up a few minutes later. "All our clocks are slow." The last man looked at his watch, looked at the rain, and then walked off into it, and Blake saw him go as if they had some reason to say goodbye—not as we say goodbye to friends after a party but as we say goodbye when we are faced with an inexorable and unwanted parting of the spirit and the heart. The man's footsteps sounded as he crossed the parking lot to the sidewalk, and then they were lost. In the station, a telephone began to ring. The ringing was loud, evenly spaced, and unanswered. Someone wanted to know about the next train to Albany, but Mr. Flanagan, the stationmaster, had gone home an hour ago. He had turned on all his lights before he went away. They burned in the empty waiting room. They burned, tin-shaded, at intervals up and down the platform and with the peculiar sadness of dim and purposeless lights. They lighted the Hawaiian dancer, the couple drinking a toast, the rubber heel.

"I've never been here before," she said. "I thought it would look different. I didn't think it would look so shabby. Let's get out of the light. Go over there."

His legs felt sore. All his strength was gone. "Go on," she said.

North of the station there were a freight house and a coalyard and an inlet where the butcher and the baker and the man who ran the service station moored the dinghies, from which they fished on Sundays, sunk now to the gunwales with the rain. As he walked toward the freight house, he saw a movement on the ground and heard a scraping sound, and then he saw a rat take its head out of a paper bag and regard him. The rat seized the bag in its teeth and dragged it into a culvert.

"Stop," she said. "Turn around. Oh, I ought to feel sorry for you. Look at 60 your poor face. But you don't know what I've been through. I'm afraid to go out in the daylight. I'm afraid the blue sky will fall down on me. I'm like poor Chicken-Licken. I only feel like myself when it begins to get dark. But still and all I'm better than you. I still have good dreams sometimes. I dream about picnics and heaven and the brotherhood of man, and about castles in the moonlight and a river with willow trees all along the edge of it and foreign cities, and after all I know more about love than you."

He heard from off the dark river the drone of an outboard motor, a sound that drew slowly behind it across the dark water such a burden of clear, sweet memories of gone summers and gone pleasures that it made his flesh crawl, and he thought of dark in the mountains and the children singing. "They never wanted to cure me," she said. "They . . . ." The noise of a train coming down from the north drowned out her voice, but she went on talking. The noise filled his ears, and the windows where people ate, drank, slept, and read flew past. When the train had passed beyond the bridge, the noise grew distant, and he heard her screaming at him, *"Kneel down!* Kneel down! Do what I say. *Kneel down!"*

He got to his knees. He bent his head. "There," she said. "You see, if you do what I say, I won't harm you, because I really don't want to harm you, I want to help you, but when I see your face it sometimes seems to me that I can't help you. Sometimes it seems to me that if I were good and loving and sane—oh, much better than I am—sometimes it seems to me that if I were all these things and young and beautiful, too, and if I called to show you the right way, you wouldn't heed me. Oh, I'm better than you, I'm better than you, and I shouldn't waste my time or spoil my life like this. Put your face in the dirt. *Put your face in the dirt!* Do what I say. Put your face in the dirt."

He fell forward in the filth. The coal skinned his face. He stretched out on the ground, weeping. "Now I feel better," she said. "Now I can wash my hands of you, I can wash my hands of all this, because you see there is some kindness, some saneness in me that I can find and use. I can wash my hands." Then he heard her footsteps go away from him, over the rubble. He heard the clearer and more distant sound they made on the hard surface of the platform. He heard them diminish. He raised his head. He saw her climb the stairs of the wooden footbridge and cross it and go down to the other platform, where her figure in the dim light looked small, common, and harmless. He raised himself out of the dust—warily at first, until he saw by her attitude, her looks, that she had forgotten him; that she had completed what she had wanted to do, and that he was safe. He got to his feet and picked up his hat from the ground where it had fallen and walked home.

Anton Chekhov

THE LADY WITH THE PET DOG   1899

TRANSLATED BY AVRAHM YARMOLINSKY

Anton Chekhov (1860–1904), one of the Russian writers who helped shape modern fiction, is remembered especially for his plays and short stories. Born in the provincial town of Taganrog, the grandson of a serf who had bought his own freedom, Chekhov as a boy worked in his father's general store, a hangout for vodka-drinking storytellers. As a young man, he studied at Moscow University and became a doctor of medicine. To earn money while a medical student, he wrote his first stories for magazines. By 1886 his work had become so celebrated that he gave up medicine for writing, though continuing to treat sick peasants at his home without fee and to work in clinics during times of famine and epidemic. From 1896 to 1904 Chekhov wrote his great

Anton Chekhov

plays for the Moscow Art Theater, where they were directed by the influential director Konstantin Stanislavsky: The Seagull, The Cherry Orchard, Uncle Vanya, and The Three Sisters. Chekhov's last years were brightened by his marriage to Olga Knipper, a star of the theater company. He died at forty-four, after a long struggle against tuberculosis.

I

A new person, it was said, had appeared on the esplanade°: a lady with a pet dog. Dmitry Dmitrich Gurov, who had spent a fortnight at Yalta° and had got used to the place, had also begun to take an interest in new arrivals. As he sat in

---

esplanade: a walkway or promenade along the shore.   Yalta: a port city on the Black Sea, a popular seaside resort for wealthy Russians.

Vernet's confectionery shop, he saw, walking on the esplanade, a fair-haired young woman of medium height, wearing a beret; a white Pomeranian was trotting behind her.

And afterwards he met her in the public garden and in the square several times a day. She walked alone, always wearing the same beret and always with the white dog; no one knew who she was and everyone called her simply "the lady with the pet dog."

"If she is here alone without husband or friends," Gurov reflected, "it wouldn't be a bad thing to make her acquaintance."

He was under forty, but he already had a daughter twelve years old, and two sons at school. They had found a wife for him when he was very young, a student in his second year, and by now she seemed half as old again as he. She was a tall, erect woman with dark eyebrows, stately and dignified and, as she said of herself, intellectual. She read a great deal, used simplified spelling in her letters, called her husband, not Dmitry, but Dimitry, while he privately considered her of limited intelligence, narrow-minded, dowdy, was afraid of her, and did not like to be at home. He had begun being unfaithful to her long ago—had been unfaithful to her often and, probably for that reason, almost always spoke ill of women, and when they were talked of in his presence used to call them "the inferior race."

It seemed to him that he had been sufficiently tutored by bitter experience to call them what he pleased, and yet he could not have lived without "the inferior race" for two days together. In the company of men he was bored and ill at ease, he was chilly and uncommunicative with them; but when he was among women he felt free, and knew what to speak to them about and how to comport himself; and even to be silent with them was no strain on him. In his appearance, in his character, in his whole make-up there was something attractive and elusive that disposed women in his favor and allured them. He knew that, and some force seemed to draw him to them, too.

Oft-repeated and really bitter experience had taught him long ago that with decent people—particularly Moscow people—who are irresolute and slow to move, every affair which at first seems a light and charming adventure inevitably grows into a whole problem of extreme complexity, and in the end a painful situation is created. But at every new meeting with an interesting woman this lesson of experience seemed to slip from his memory, and he was eager for life, and everything seemed so simple and diverting.

One evening while he was dining in the public garden the lady in the beret walked up without haste to take the next table. Her expression, her gait, her dress, and the way she did her hair told him that she belonged to the upper class, that she was married, that she was in Yalta for the first time and alone, and that she was bored there. The stories told of the immorality in Yalta are to a great extent untrue; he despised them, and knew that such stories were made up for the most part by persons who would have been glad to sin themselves if they had had the chance; but when the lady sat down at the next table three paces from him, he recalled these stories of easy conquests, of trips to the mountains, and the tempting thought of a swift, fleeting liaison, a romance with an unknown woman of whose very name he was ignorant suddenly took hold of him.

He beckoned invitingly to the Pomeranian, and when the dog approached him, shook his finger at it. The Pomeranian growled; Gurov threatened it again.

The lady glanced at him and at once dropped her eyes.

"He doesn't bite," she said and blushed.   10

"May I give him a bone?" he asked; and when she nodded he inquired affably, "Have you been in Yalta long?"

"About five days."

"And I am dragging out the second week here."

There was a short silence.

"Time passes quickly, and yet it is so dull here!" she said, not looking at him.   15

"It's only the fashion to say it's dull here. A provincial will live in Belyov or Zhizdra and not be bored, but when he comes here it's 'Oh, the dullness! Oh, the dust!' One would think he came from Granada."

She laughed. Then both continued eating in silence, like strangers, but after dinner they walked together and there sprang up between them the light banter of people who are free and contented, to whom it does not matter where they go or what they talk about. They walked and talked of the strange light on the sea: the water was a soft, warm, lilac color, and there was a golden band of moonlight upon it. They talked of how sultry it was after a hot day. Gurov told her that he was a native of Moscow, that he had studied languages and literature at the university, but had a post in a bank; that at one time he had trained to become an opera singer but had given it up, that he owned two houses in Moscow. And he learned from her that she had grown up in Petersburg, but had lived in S_____ since her marriage two years previously, that she was going to stay in Yalta for about another month, and that her husband, who needed a rest, too, might perhaps come to fetch her. She was not certain whether her husband was a member of a Government Board or served on a Zemstvo Council,° and this amused her. And Gurov learned that her name was Anna Sergeyevna.

Afterwards in his room at the hotel he thought about her—and was certain that he would meet her the next day. It was bound to happen. Getting into bed he recalled that she had been a schoolgirl only recently, doing lessons like his own daughter; he thought how much timidity and angularity there was still in her laugh and her manner of talking with a stranger. It must have been the first time in her life that she was alone in a setting in which she was followed, looked at, and spoken to for one secret purpose alone, which she could hardly fail to guess. He thought of her slim, delicate throat, her lovely gray eyes.

"There's something pathetic about her, though," he thought, and dropped off.

Zemstvo Council: the elected council for local administration in Czarist Russia, the equivalent of a county administration.

II

A week had passed since they had struck up an acquaintance. It was a holiday. It was close indoors, while in the street the wind whirled the dust about
and blew people's hats off. One was thirsty all day, and Gurov often went into
the restaurant and offered Anna Sergeyevna a soft drink or ice cream. One did
not know what to do with oneself.

In the evening when the wind had abated they went out on the pier to
watch the steamer come in. There were a great many people walking about the
dock; they had come to welcome someone and they were carrying bunches of
flowers. And two peculiarities of a festive Yalta crowd stood out: the elderly
ladies were dressed like young ones and there were many generals.

Owing to the choppy sea, the steamer arrived late, after sunset, and it was a
long time tacking about before it put in at the pier. Anna Sergeyevna peered at
the steamer and the passengers through her lorgnette as though looking for acquaintances, and whenever she turned to Gurov her eyes were shining. She
talked a great deal and asked questions jerkily, forgetting the next moment what
she had asked; then she lost her lorgnette in the crush.

The festive crowd began to disperse; it was now too dark to see people's
faces; there was no wind any more, but Gurov and Anna Sergeyevna still stood
as though waiting to see someone else come off the steamer. Anna Sergeyevna
was silent now, and sniffed her flowers without looking at Gurov.

"The weather has improved this evening," he said. "Where shall we go now?
Shall we drive somewhere?"

She did not reply.

Then he looked at her intently, and suddenly embraced her and kissed her
on the lips, and the moist fragrance of her flowers enveloped him; and at once he
looked round him anxiously, wondering if anyone had seen them.

"Let us go to your place," he said softly. And they walked off together
rapidly.

The air in her room was close and there was the smell of the perfume she had
bought at the Japanese shop. Looking at her, Gurov thought: "What encounters life
offers!" From the past he preserved the memory of carefree, good-natured women
whom love made gay and who were grateful to him for the happiness he gave them,
however brief it might be; and of women like his wife who loved without sincerity,
with too many words, affectedly, hysterically, with an expression that it was not
love or passion that engaged them but something more significant; and of two or
three others, very beautiful, frigid women, across whose faces would suddenly flit a
rapacious expression—an obstinate desire to take from life more than it could give,
and these were women no longer young, capricious, unreflecting, domineering, un-
intelligent, and when Gurov grew cold to them their beauty aroused his hatred, and
the lace on their lingerie seemed to him to resemble scales.

But here there was the timidity, the angularity of inexperienced youth, a
feeling of awkwardness; and there was a sense of embarrassment, as though
someone had suddenly knocked at the door. Anna Sergeyevna, "the lady with

the pet dog," treated what had happened in a peculiar way, very seriously, as though it were her fall—so it seemed, and this was odd and inappropriate. Her features drooped and faded, and her long hair hung down sadly on either side of her face; she grew pensive and her dejected pose was that of a Magdalene in a picture by an old master.

"It's not right," she said. "You don't respect me now, you first of all." 30

There was a watermelon on the table. Gurov cut himself a slice and began eating it without haste. They were silent for at least half an hour.

There was something touching about Anna Sergeyevna; she had the purity of a well-bred, naive woman who has seen little of life. The single candle burning on the table barely illuminated her face, yet it was clear that she was unhappy.

"Why should I stop respecting you, darling?" asked Gurov. "You don't know what you're saying."

"God forgive me," she said, and her eyes filled with tears. "It's terrible."

"It's as though you were trying to exonerate yourself." 35

"How can I exonerate myself? No. I am a bad, low woman; I despise myself and I have no thought of exonerating myself. It's not my husband but myself I have deceived. And not only just now; I have been deceiving myself for a long time. My husband may be a good, honest man, but he is a flunkey! I don't know what he does, what his work is, but I know he is a flunkey! I was twenty when I married him. I was tormented by curiosity; I wanted something better. 'There must be a different sort of life,' I said to myself. I wanted to live! To live, to live! Curiosity kept eating at me—you don't understand, but I swear to God I could no longer control myself; something was going on in me; I could not be held back. I told my husband I was ill, and came here. And here I have been walking about as though in a daze, as though I were mad; and now I have become a vulgar, vile woman whom anyone may despise."

Gurov was already bored with her; he was irritated by her naive tone, by her repentance, so unexpected and so out of place, but for the tears in her eyes he might have thought she was joking or play-acting.

"I don't understand, my dear," he said softly. "What do you want?"

She hid her face on his breast and pressed close to him.

"Believe me, believe me, I beg you," she said, "I love honesty and purity, and 40 sin is loathsome to me; I don't know what I'm doing. Simple people say, 'The Evil One has led me astray.' And I may say of myself now that the Evil One has led me astray."

"Quiet, quiet," he murmured.

He looked into her fixed, frightened eyes, kissed her, spoke to her softly and affectionately, and by degrees she calmed down, and her gaiety returned; both began laughing.

Afterwards when they went out there was not a soul on the esplanade. The town with its cypresses looked quite dead, but the sea was still sounding as it broke upon the beach; a single launch was rocking on the waves and on it a lantern was blinking sleepily.

They found a cab and drove to Oreanda.

"I found out your surname in the hall just now; it was written on the 45 board—von Dideritz," said Gurov. "Is your husband German?"

"No; I believe his grandfather was German, but he is Greek Orthodox himself."

At Oreanda they sat on a bench not far from the church, looked down at the sea, and were silent. Yalta was barely visible through the morning mist; white clouds rested motionlessly on the mountaintops. The leaves did not stir on the trees, cicadas twanged, and the monotonous muffled sound of the sea that rose from below spoke of the peace, the eternal sleep awaiting us. So it rumbled below when there was no Yalta, no Oreanda here; so it rumbles now, and it will rumble as indifferently and as hollowly when we are no more. And in this constancy, in this complete indifference to the life and death of each of us, there lies, perhaps, a pledge of our eternal salvation, of the unceasing advance of life upon earth, of unceasing movement towards perfection. Sitting beside a young woman who in the dawn seemed so lovely, Gurov, soothed and spellbound by these magical surroundings—the sea, the mountains, the clouds, the wide sky—thought how everything is really beautiful in this world when one reflects: everything except what we think or do ourselves when we forget the higher aims of life and our own human dignity.

A man strolled up to them—probably a guard—looked at them and walked away. And this detail, too, seemed so mysterious and beautiful. They saw a steamer arrive from Feodosia, its lights extinguished in the glow of dawn.

"There is dew on the grass," said Anna Sergeyevna, after a silence.

"Yes, it's time to go home." 50

They returned to the city.

Then they met every day at twelve o'clock on the esplanade, lunched and dined together, took walks, admired the sea. She complained that she slept badly, that she had palpitations, asked the same questions, troubled now by jealousy and now by the fear that he did not respect her sufficiently. And often in the square or the public garden, when there was no one near them, he suddenly drew her to him and kissed her passionately. Complete idleness, these kisses in broad daylight exchanged furtively in dread of someone's seeing them, the heat, the smell of the sea, and the continual flitting before his eyes of idle, well-dressed, well-fed people, worked a complete change in him; he kept telling Anna Sergeyevna how beautiful she was, how seductive, was urgently passionate; he would not move a step away from her, while she was often pensive and continually pressed him to confess that he did not respect her, did not love her in the least, and saw in her nothing but a common woman. Almost every evening rather late they drove somewhere out of town, to Oreanda or to the waterfall; and the excursion was always a success, the scenery invariably impressed them as beautiful and magnificent.

They were expecting her husband, but a letter came from him saying that he had eye-trouble, and begging his wife to return home as soon as possible. Anna Sergeyevna made haste to go.

"It's a good thing I am leaving," she said to Gurov. "It's the hand of Fate!"

She took a carriage to the railway station, and he went with her. They were 55
driving the whole day. When she had taken her place in the express, and when
the second bell had rung, she said, "Let me look at you once more—let me look
at you again. Like this."

She was not crying but was so sad that she seemed ill and her face was
quivering.

"I shall be thinking of you—remembering you," she said. "God bless you; be
happy. Don't remember evil against me. We are parting forever—it has to be, for
we ought never to have met. Well, God bless you."

The train moved off rapidly, its lights soon vanished, and a minute later
there was no sound of it, as though everything had conspired to end as quickly as
possible that sweet trance, that madness. Left alone on the platform, and gazing
into the dark distance, Gurov listened to the twang of the grasshoppers and the
hum of the telegraph wires, feeling as though he had just waked up. And he reflected, musing, that there had now been another episode or adventure in his
life, and it, too, was at an end, and nothing was left of it but a memory. He was
moved, sad, and slightly remorseful: this young woman whom he would never
meet again had not been happy with him; he had been warm and affectionate
with her, but yet in his manner, his tone, and his caresses there had been a shade
of light irony, the slightly coarse arrogance of a happy male who was, besides, almost twice her age. She had constantly called him kind, exceptional, high-
minded; obviously he had seemed to her different from what he really was, so he
had involuntarily deceived her.

Here at the station there was already a scent of autumn in the air; it was a
chilly evening.

"It is time for me to go north, too," thought Gurov as he left the platform. 60
"High time!"

III

At home in Moscow the winter routine was already established; the stoves
were heated, and in the morning it was still dark when the children were having
breakfast and getting ready for school, and the nurse would light the lamp for a
short time. There were frosts already. When the first snow falls, on the first day
the sleighs are out, it is pleasant to see the white earth, the white roofs; one
draws easy, delicious breaths, and the season brings back the days of one's youth.
The old limes and birches, white with hoar-frost, have a good-natured look; they
are closer to one's heart than cypresses and palms, and near them one no longer
wants to think of mountains and the sea.

Gurov, a native of Moscow, arrived there on a fine frosty day, and when he
put on his fur coat and warm gloves and took a walk along Petrovka, and when
on Saturday night he heard the bells ringing, his recent trip and the places he
had visited lost all charm for him. Little by little he became immersed in

Moscow life, greedily read three newspapers a day, and declared that he did not read the Moscow papers on principle. He already felt a longing for restaurants, clubs, formal dinners, anniversary celebrations, and it flattered him to entertain distinguished lawyers and actors, and to play cards with a professor at the physicians' club. He could eat a whole portion of meat stewed with pickled cabbage and served in a pan, Moscow style.

A month or so would pass and the image of Anna Sergeyevna, it seemed to him, would become misty in his memory, and only from time to time he would dream of her with her touching smile as he dreamed of others. But more than a month went by, winter came into its own, and everything was still clear in his memory as though he had parted from Anna Sergeyevna only yesterday. And his memories glowed more and more vividly. When in the evening stillness the voices of his children preparing their lessons reached his study, or when he listened to a song or to an organ playing in a restaurant, or when the storm howled in the chimney, suddenly everything would rise up in his memory; what had happened on the pier and the early morning with the mist on the mountains, and the steamer coming from Feodosia, and the kisses. He would pace about his room a long time, remembering and smiling; then his memories passed into reveries, and in his imagination the past would mingle with what was to come. He did not dream of Anna Sergeyevna, but she followed him about everywhere and watched him. When he shut his eyes he saw her before him as though she were there in the flesh, and she seemed to him lovelier, younger, tenderer than she had been, and he imagined himself a finer man than he had been in Yalta. Of evenings she peered out at him from the bookcase, from the fireplace, from the corner—he heard her breathing, the caressing rustle of her clothes. In the street he followed the women with his eyes, looking for someone who resembled her.

Already he was tormented by a strong desire to share his memories with someone. But in his home it was impossible to talk of his love, and he had no one to talk to outside; certainly he could not confide in his tenants or in anyone at the bank. And what was there to talk about? He hadn't loved her then, had he? Had there been anything beautiful, poetical, edifying, or simply interesting in his relations with Anna Sergeyevna? And he was forced to talk vaguely of love, of women, and no one guessed what he meant; only his wife would twitch her black eyebrows and say, "The part of a philanderer does not suit you at all, Dimitry."

One evening, coming out of the physicians' club with an official with whom he had been playing cards, he could not resist saying:

"If you only knew what a fascinating woman I became acquainted with at Yalta!"

The official got into his sledge and was driving away, but turned suddenly and shouted:

"Dmitry Dmitrich!"

"What is it?"

"You were right this evening: the sturgeon was a bit high."

These words, so commonplace, for some reason moved Gurov to indignation, and struck him as degrading and unclean. What savage manners, what mugs! What stupid nights, what dull, humdrum days! Frenzied gambling, gluttony, drunkenness, continual talk always about the same thing! Futile pursuits and conversations always about the same topics take up the better part of one's time, the better part of one's strength, and in the end there is left a life clipped and wingless, an absurd mess, and there is no escaping or getting away from it— just as though one were in a madhouse or a prison.

Gurov, boiling with indignation, did not sleep all night. And he had a headache all the next day. And the following nights too he slept badly; he sat up in bed, thinking, or paced up and down his room. He was fed up with his children, fed up with the bank; he had no desire to go anywhere or to talk of anything.

In December during the holidays he prepared to take a trip and told his wife he was going to Petersburg to do what he could for a young friend—and he set off for S_____. What for? He did not know, himself. He wanted to see Anna Sergeyevna and talk with her, to arrange a rendezvous if possible.

He arrived at S_____ in the morning, and at the hotel took the best room, in which the floor was covered with gray army cloth, and on the table there was an inkstand, gray with dust and topped by a figure on horseback, its hat in its raised hand and its head broken off. The porter gave him the necessary information: von Dideritz lived in a house of his own on Staro-Goncharnaya Street, not far from the hotel: he was rich and lived well and kept his own horses; everyone in the town knew him. The porter pronounced the name: "Dridiritz."

Without haste Gurov made his way to Staro-Goncharnaya Street and found the house. Directly opposite the house stretched a long gray fence studded with nails.

"A fence like that would make one run away," thought Gurov, looking now at the fence, now at the windows of the house.

He reflected: this was a holiday, and the husband was apt to be at home. And in any case, it would be tactless to go into the house and disturb her. If he were to send her a note, it might fall into her husband's hands, and that might spoil everything. The best thing was to rely on chance. And he kept walking up and down the street and along the fence, waiting for the chance. He saw a beggar go in at the gate and heard the dogs attack him; then an hour later he heard a piano, and the sound came to him faintly and indistinctly. Probably it was Anna Sergeyevna playing. The front door opened suddenly, and an old woman came out, followed by the familiar white Pomeranian. Gurov was on the point of calling to the dog, but his heart began beating violently, and in his excitement he could not remember the Pomeranian's name.

He kept walking up and down, and hated the gray fence more and more, and by now he thought irritably that Anna Sergeyevna had forgotten him, and was perhaps already diverting herself with another man, and that that was very natural in a young woman who from morning till night had to look at that damn fence. He went back to his hotel room and sat on the couch for a long while, not knowing what to do, then he had dinner and a long nap.

"How stupid and annoying all this is!" he thought when he woke and looked at the dark windows: it was already evening. "Here I've had a good sleep for some reason. What am I going to do at night?"

He sat on the bed, which was covered with a cheap gray blanket of the kind seen in hospitals, and he twitted himself in his vexation: 80

"So there's your lady with the pet dog. There's your adventure. A nice place to cool your heels in."

That morning at the station a playbill in large letters had caught his eye. *The Geisha* was to be given for the first time. He thought of this and drove to the theater.

"It's quite possible that she goes to first nights," he thought.

The theater was full. As in all provincial theaters, there was a haze above the chandelier, the gallery was noisy and restless; in the front row, before the beginning of the performance the local dandies were standing with their hands clasped behind their backs; in the Governor's box the Governor's daughter, wearing a boa, occupied the front seat, while the Governor himself hid modestly behind the portiere and only his hands were visible; the curtain swayed; the orchestra was a long time tuning up. While the audience was coming in and taking their seats, Gurov scanned the faces eagerly.

Anna Sergeyevna, too, came in. She sat down in the third row, and when 85 Gurov looked at her his heart contracted, and he understood clearly that in the whole world there was no human being so near, so precious, and so important to him; she, this little, undistinguished woman, lost in a provincial crowd, with a vulgar lorgnette in her hand, filled his whole life now, was his sorrow and his joy, the only happiness that he now desired for himself, and to the sounds of the bad orchestra, of the miserable local violins, he thought how lovely she was. He thought and dreamed.

A young man with small side-whiskers, very tall and stooped, came in with Anna Sergeyevna and sat down beside her; he nodded his head at every step and seemed to be bowing continually. Probably this was the husband whom at Yalta, in an access of bitter feeling, she had called a flunkey. And there really was in his lanky figure, his side-whiskers, his small bald patch, something of a flunkey's retiring manner; his smile was mawkish, and in his buttonhole there was an academic badge like a waiter's number.

During the first intermission the husband went out to have a smoke; she remained in her seat. Gurov, who was also sitting in the orchestra, went up to her and said in a shaky voice, with a forced smile:

"Good evening!"

She glanced at him and turned pale, then looked at him again in horror, unable to believe her eyes, and gripped the fan and the lorgnette tightly together in her hands, evidently trying to keep herself from fainting. Both were silent. She was sitting, he was standing, frightened by her distress and not daring to take a seat beside her. The violins and the flute that were being tuned up sang out. He suddenly felt frightened: it seemed as if all the people in the boxes were looking at them. She got up and went hurriedly to the exit; he followed her, and both of them walked blindly along the corridors and up and down stairs, and figures in the uniforms prescribed for magistrates, teachers, and officials of the Department of Crown Lands, all wearing badges, flitted before their eyes, as did also ladies, and fur coats on hangers; they were conscious of drafts and the smell of stale tobacco. And Gurov, whose heart was beating violently, thought:

"Oh, Lord! Why are these people here and this orchestra!"   90

And at that instant he suddenly recalled how when he had seen Anna Sergeyevna off at the station he had said to himself that all was over between them and that they would never meet again. But how distant the end still was!

On the narrow, gloomy staircase over which it said "To the Amphitheatre," she stopped.

"How you frightened me!" she said, breathing hard, still pale and stunned. "Oh, how you frightened me! I am barely alive. Why did you come? Why?"

"But do understand, Anna, do understand—" he said hurriedly, under his breath. "I implore you, do understand—"

She looked at him with fear, with entreaty, with love; she looked at him in-   95 tently, to keep his features more distinctly in her memory.

"I suffer so," she went on, not listening to him. "All this time I have been thinking of nothing but you; I live only by the thought of you. And I wanted to forget, to forget; but why, oh, why have you come?"

On the landing above them two high school boys were looking down and smoking, but it was all the same to Gurov; he drew Anna Sergeyevna to him and began kissing her face and hands.

"What are you doing, what are you doing!" she was saying in horror, pushing him away. "We have lost our senses. Go away today; go away at once—I conjure you by all that is sacred, I implore you—People are coming this way!"

Someone was walking up the stairs.

"You must leave," Anna Sergeyevna went on in a whisper. "Do you hear,   100 Dmitry Dmitrich? I will come and see you in Moscow. I have never been happy; I am unhappy now, and I never, never shall be happy, never! So don't make me suffer still more! I swear I'll come to Moscow. But now let us part. My dear, good, precious one, let us part!"

She pressed his hand and walked rapidly downstairs, turning to look round at him, and from her eyes he could see that she really was unhappy. Gurov stood for a while, listening, then when all grew quiet, he found his coat and left the theater.

IV

And Anna Sergeyevna began coming to see him in Moscow. Once every two or three months she left S_____ telling her husband that she was going to consult a doctor about a woman's ailment from which she was suffering—and her husband did and did not believe her. When she arrived in Moscow she would stop at the Slavyansky Bazar Hotel, and at once send a man in a red cap to Gurov. Gurov came to see her, and no one in Moscow knew of it.

Once he was going to see her in this way on a winter morning (the messenger had come the evening before and not found him in). With him walked his daughter, whom he wanted to take to school; it was on the way. Snow was coming down in big wet flakes.

"It's three degrees above zero,° and yet it's snowing," Gurov was saying to his daughter. "But this temperature prevails only on the surface of the earth; in the upper layers of the atmosphere there is quite a different temperature."

"And why doesn't it thunder in winter, papa?"

He explained that, too. He talked, thinking all the while that he was on his way to a rendezvous, and no living soul knew of it, and probably no one would ever know. He had two lives, an open one, seen and known by all who needed to know it, full of conventional truth and conventional falsehood, exactly like the lives of his friends and acquaintances; and another life that went on in secret. And through some strange, perhaps accidental, combination of circumstances, everything that was of interest and importance to him, everything that was essential to him, everything about which he felt sincerely and did not deceive himself, everything that constituted the core of his life, was going on concealed from others; while all that was false, the shell in which he hid to cover the truth—his work at the bank, for instance, his discussions at the club, his references to the "inferior race," his appearances at anniversary celebrations with his wife—all that went on in the open. Judging others by himself, he did not believe what he saw, and always fancied that every man led his real, most interesting life under cover of secrecy as under cover of night. The personal life of every individual is based on secrecy, and perhaps it is partly for that reason that civilized man is so nervously anxious that personal privacy should be respected.

Having taken his daughter to school, Gurov went on to the Slavyansky Bazar Hotel. He took off his fur coat in the lobby, went upstairs, and knocked gently at the door. Anna Sergeyevna, wearing his favorite gray dress, exhausted by the journey and by waiting, had been expecting him since the previous evening. She was pale, and looked at him without a smile, and had hardly entered when she flung herself on his breast. That kiss was a long, lingering one, as though they had not seen one another for two years.

"Well, darling, how are you getting on there?" he asked. "What news?"

"Wait; I'll tell you in a moment—I can't speak."

She could not speak; she was crying. She turned away from him, and pressed her handkerchief to her eyes.

"Let her have her cry; meanwhile I'll sit down," he thought, and he seated himself in an armchair.

Then he rang and ordered tea, and while he was having his tea she remained standing at the window with her back to him. She was crying out of

three degrees above zero: the Russian temperature is measured in Celsius degrees; the Fahrenheit equivalent would be about thirty-seven degrees.

sheer agitation, in the sorrowful consciousness that their life was so sad; that they could only see each other in secret and had to hide from people like thieves! Was it not a broken life?

"Come, stop now, dear!" he said.

It was plain to him that this love of theirs would not be over soon, that the end of it was not in sight. Anna Sergeyevna was growing more and more attached to him. She adored him, and it was unthinkable to tell her that their love was bound to come to an end some day; besides, she would not have believed it!

He went up to her and took her by the shoulders, to fondle her and say something diverting, and at that moment he caught sight of himself in the mirror.

His hair was already beginning to turn gray. And it seemed odd to him that he had grown so much older in the last few years, and lost his looks. The shoulders on which his hands rested were warm and heaving. He felt compassion for this life, still so warm and lovely, but probably already about to begin to fade and wither like his own. Why did she love him so much? He always seemed to women different from what he was, and they loved in him not himself, but the man whom their imagination created and whom they had been eagerly seeking all their lives; and afterwards, when they saw their mistake, they loved him nevertheless. And not one of them had been happy with him. In the past he had met women, come together with them, parted from them, but he had never once loved; it was anything you please, but not love. And only now when his head was gray he had fallen in love, really, truly—for the first time in his life.

Anna Sergeyevna and he loved each other as people do who are very close and intimate, like man and wife, like tender friends; it seemed to them that Fate itself had meant them for one another, and they could not understand why he had a wife and she a husband; and it was as though they were a pair of migratory birds, male and female, caught and forced to live in different cages. They forgave each other what they were ashamed of in their past, they forgave everything in the present, and felt that this love of theirs had altered them both.

Formerly in moments of sadness he had soothed himself with whatever logical arguments came into his head, but now he no longer cared for logic; he felt profound compassion, he wanted to be sincere and tender.

"Give it up now, my darling," he said. "You've had your cry; that's enough. Let us have a talk now, we'll think up something."

Then they spent a long time taking counsel together, they talked of how to avoid the necessity for secrecy, for deception, for living in different cities, and not seeing one another for long stretches of time. How could they free themselves from these intolerable fetters?

"How? How?" he asked, clutching his head. "How?"

And it seemed as though in a little while the solution would be found, and then a new and glorious life would begin; and it was clear to both of them that the end was still far off, and that what was to be most complicated and difficult for them was only just beginning.

Kate Chopin

THE STORY OF AN HOUR

Kate Chopin (1851–1904) demonstrates again, as in "The Storm" in Chapter Four, her ability to write short stories of compressed intensity. For a brief biography and a portrait see page 127.

Knowing that Mrs. Mallard was afflicted with a heart trouble, great care was taken to break to her as gently as possible the news of her husband's death.

It was her sister Josephine who told her, in broken sentences, veiled hints that revealed in half concealing. Her husband's friend Richards was there, too, near her. It was he who had been in the newspaper office when intelligence of the railroad disaster was received, with Brently Mallard's name leading the list of "killed." He had only taken the time to assure himself of its truth by a second telegram, and had hastened to forestall any less careful, less tender friend in bearing the sad message.

She did not hear the story as many women have heard the same, with a paralyzed inability to accept its significance. She wept at once, with sudden, wild abandonment, in her sister's arms. When the storm of grief had spent itself she went away to her room alone. She would have no one follow her.

There stood, facing the open window, a comfortable, roomy armchair. Into this she sank, pressed down by a physical exhaustion that haunted her body and seemed to reach into her soul.

She could see in the open square before her house the tops of trees that were   5
all aquiver with the new spring life. The delicious breath of rain was in the air. In the street below a peddler was crying his wares. The notes of a distant song which some one was singing reached her faintly, and countless sparrows were twittering in the eaves.

There were patches of blue sky showing here and there through the clouds that had met and piled one above the other in the west facing her window.

She sat with her head thrown back upon the cushion of the chair, quite motionless, except when a sob came up into her throat and shook her, as a child who has cried itself to sleep continues to sob in its dreams.

She was young, with a fair, calm face, whose lines bespoke repression and even a certain strength. But now there was a dull stare in her eyes, whose gaze was fixed away off yonder on one of those patches of blue sky. It was not a glance of reflection, but rather indicated a suspension of intelligent thought.

There was something coming to her and she was waiting for it, fearfully. What was it? She did not know; it was too subtle and elusive to name. But she felt it, creeping out of the sky, reaching toward her through the sounds, the scents, the color that filled the air.

Now her bosom rose and fell tumultuously. She was beginning to recognize   10
this thing that was approaching to possess her, and she was striving to beat it back with her will—as powerless as her two white slender hands would have been.

When she abandoned herself a little whispered word escaped her slightly parted lips. She said it over and over under her breath: "Free, free, free!" The vacant stare and the look of terror that had followed it went from her eyes. They stayed keen and bright. Her pulses beat fast, and the coursing blood warmed and relaxed every inch of her body.

She did not stop to ask if it were not a monstrous joy that held her. A clear and exalted perception enabled her to dismiss the suggestion as trivial.

She knew that she would weep again when she saw the kind, tender hands folded in death; the face that had never looked save with love upon her, fixed and gray and dead. But she saw beyond that bitter moment a long procession of years to come that would belong to her absolutely. And she opened and spread her arms out to them in welcome.

There would be no one to live for during those coming years; she would live for herself. There would be no powerful will bending her in that blind persistence with which men and women believe they have a right to impose a private will upon a fellow creature. A kind intention or a cruel intention made the act seem no less a crime as she looked upon it in that brief moment of illumination.

And yet she had loved him—sometimes. Often she had not. What did it matter! What could love, the unsolved mystery, count for in face of this possession of self-assertion which she suddenly recognized as the strongest impulse of her being. 15

"Free! Body and soul free!" she kept whispering.

Josephine was kneeling before the closed door with her lips to the keyhole, imploring for admission. "Louise, open the door! I beg; open the door—you will make yourself ill. What are you doing, Louise? For heaven's sake open the door."

"Go away. I am not making myself ill." No; she was drinking in a very elixir of life through that open window.

Her fancy was running riot along those days ahead of her. Spring days, and summer days, and all sorts of days that would be her own. She breathed a quick prayer that life might be long. It was only yesterday she had thought with a shudder that life might be long.

She arose at length and opened the door to her sister's importunities. There was a feverish triumph in her eyes, and she carried herself unwittingly like a goddess of Victory. She clasped her sister's waist, and together they descended the stairs. Richards stood waiting for them at the bottom. 20

Some one was opening the front door with a latchkey. It was Brently Mallard who entered, a little travel-stained, composedly carrying his gripsack and umbrella. He had been far from the scene of the accident, and did not even know there had been one. He stood amazed at Josephine's piercing cry; at Richards' quick motion to screen him from the view of his wife.

But Richards was too late.

When the doctors came they said she had died of heart disease—of joy that kills.

Sandra Cisneros

THE HOUSE ON MANGO STREET

1984

Sandra Cisneros was born in Chicago in 1954. The daughter of a Mexican father and a Mexican American mother, she was the only daughter in a family of seven children. She attended Loyola University of Chicago and then received a master's degree from the University of Iowa Writers' Workshop. She has instructed high-school dropouts, but more recently she has taught as a visiting writer at numerous universities, including the University of California at Irvine and at Berkeley, and the University of Michigan. Her honors include fellowships from the National Endowment for the Arts and the MacArthur Foundation. Cisneros's first published books were poetry: Bad Boys (1980), My Wicked Wicked Ways (1987), and Loose Woman (1994). Her fiction collections, The House on Mango Street *(1984) and* Women Hollering Creek *(1991), however, earned her a broader audience. She has also published a bilingual children's book,* Hairs: Pelitos *(1994), and a novel,* Caramelo *(2002). Cisneros currently lives in San Antonio, Texas.*

Sandra Cisneros

We didn't always live on Mango Street. Before that we lived on Loomis on the third floor, and before that we lived on Keeler. Before Keeler it was Paulina, and before that I can't remember. But what I remember most is moving a lot. Each time it seemed there'd be one more of us. By the time we got to Mango Street we were six—Mama, Papa, Carlos, Kiki, my sister Nenny, and me.

The house on Mango Street is ours, and we don't have to pay rent to anybody, or share the yard with the people downstairs, or be careful not to make too much noise, and there isn't a landlord banging on the ceiling with a broom. But even so, it's not the house we'd thought we'd get.

We had to leave the flat on Loomis quick. The water pipes broke and the landlord wouldn't fix them because the house was too old. We had to leave fast. We were using the washroom next door and carrying water over in empty milk gallons. That's why Mama and Papa looked for a house, and that's why we moved into the house on Mango Street, far away, on the other side of town.

They always told us that one day we would move into a house, a real house that would be ours for always so we wouldn't have to move each year. And our house would have running water and pipes that worked. And inside it would have real stairs, not hallway stairs, but stairs inside like the houses on T.V. And we'd have a basement and at least three washrooms so when we took a bath we wouldn't have to tell everybody. Our house would be white with trees around it, a great big yard and grass growing without a fence. This was the house Papa talked about when he held a lottery ticket and this was the house Mama dreamed up in the stories she told us before we went to bed.

But the house on Mango Street is not the way they told it at all. It's small 5 and red with tight steps in front and windows so small you'd think they were holding their breath. Bricks are crumbling in places, and the front door is so swollen you have to push hard to get in. There is no front yard, only four little elms the city planted by the curb. Out back is a small garage for the car we don't own yet and a small yard that looks smaller between the two buildings on either side. There are stairs in our house, but they're ordinary hallway stairs, and the house has only one washroom. Everybody has to share a bedroom—Mama and Papa, Carlos and Kiki, me and Nenny.

Once when we were living on Loomis, a nun from my school passed by and saw me playing out front. The laundromat downstairs had been boarded up because it had been robbed two days before and the owner had painted on the wood YES WE'RE OPEN so as not to lose business.

Where do you live? she asked.

There, I said pointing up to the third floor.

You live *there*?

There. I had to look to where she pointed—the third floor, the paint peeling, 10 wooden bars Papa had nailed on the windows so we wouldn't fall out. You live *there*? The way she said it made me feel like nothing. *There.* I lived *there.* I nodded.

I knew then I had to have a house. A real house. One I could point to. But this isn't it. The house on Mango Street isn't it. For the time being, Mama says. Temporary, says Papa. But I know how those things go.

Ralph Ellison

BATTLE ROYAL 1952

Ralph Ellison (1914–1994) was born in Oklahoma City. His father, a small business owner who sold ice and coal, died when the future author was only three. Ellison's mother, a religious woman of strong convictions, worked as a maid to support her two sons. She also stressed the importance of education. Planning to be a composer, Ellison entered the Tuskegee Institute in 1933. Reading T. S. Eliot's poem The Waste Land, however, helped focus his interests on literature. In 1936 he moved to New York to find a summer job to pay for his senior year's tuition. He never left. In Harlem Ellison met many black writers including Langston Hughes and Richard Wright, and he soon began publishing short stories, poems,

Ralph Ellison

and reviews. In 1952 Ellison published his only novel, Invisible Man, *which won the National Book Award for fiction and has gradually come to be recognized as a contemporary American masterpiece. Over the next forty years Ellison tried to finish a second novel, a project that was delayed by both disaster and the author's obsessive drive for perfection. At one point Ellison's house burned down, destroying the draft of the novel. He eventually published eight sections of the novel-in-progress, but it remained unfinished. Ellison completed two books of essays,* Shadow and Act *(1964) and* Going to the Territory *(1986). For years he taught at New York University. Ellison published "Battle Royal" as a short story in 1948. He later revised it as the first chapter of* Invisible Man *(where it is preceded by a short preface).*

It goes a long way back, some twenty years. All my life I had been looking for something, and everywhere I turned someone tried to tell me what it was. I accepted their answers too, though they were often in contradiction and even self-contradictory. I was naïve. I was looking for myself and asking everyone except myself questions which I, and only I, could answer. It took me a long time and much painful boomeranging of my expectations to achieve a realization everyone else appears to have been born with: That I am nobody but myself. But first I had to discover that I am an invisible man!

And yet I am no freak of nature, nor of history. I was in the cards, other things having been equal (or unequal) eighty-five years ago. I am not ashamed of my grandparents for having been slaves. I am only ashamed of myself for having at one time been ashamed. About eighty-five years ago they were told they were free, united with others of our country in everything pertaining to the common good, and, in everything social, separate like the fingers of the hand. And they believed it. They exulted in it. They stayed in their place, worked hard, and brought up my father to do the same. But my grandfather is the one. He was an odd old guy, my grandfather, and I am told I take after him. It was he who caused the trouble. On his deathbed he called my father to him and said, "Son, after I'm gone I want you to keep up the good fight. I never told you, but our life is a war and I have been a traitor all my born days, a spy in the enemy's country ever since I give up my gun back in the Reconstruction. Live with your head in the lion's mouth. I want you to overcome 'em with yeses, undermine 'em with grins, agree 'em to death and destruction, let 'em swoller you till they vomit or bust wide open." They thought the old man had gone out of his mind. He had been the meekest of men. The younger children were rushed from the room, the shades drawn and the flame of the lamp turned so low that it sputtered on the wick like the old man's breathing. "Learn it to the younguns," he whispered fiercely; then he died.

But my folks were more alarmed over his last words than over his dying. It was as though he had not died at all, his words caused so much anxiety. I was warned emphatically to forget what he had said and, indeed, this is the first time it has been mentioned outside the family circle. It had a tremendous effect upon me, however. I could never be sure of what he meant. Grandfather had been a quiet old man who never made any trouble, yet on his deathbed he had called himself a traitor and a spy, and he had spoken of his meekness as a dangerous activity. It became a constant puzzle which lay unanswered in the back of my mind. And whenever things went well for me I remembered my grandfather and felt guilty and uncomfortable. It was as though I was carrying out his advice in spite of myself. And to make it worse, everyone loved me for it. I was praised by the most lily-white men in town. I was considered an example of desirable conduct—just as my grandfather had been. And what puzzled me was that the old man had defined it as *treachery*. When I was praised for my conduct I felt a guilt that in some way I was doing something that was really against the wishes of the white folks, that if they had understood they would have desired me to act just the opposite, that I should have been sulky and mean, and that that really would have been what they wanted, even though they were fooled and thought they wanted me to act as I did. It made me afraid that some day they would look upon me as a traitor and I would be lost. Still I was more afraid to act any other way because they didn't like that at all. The old man's words were like a curse. On my graduation day I delivered an oration in which I showed that humility was the secret, indeed, the very essence of progress. (Not that I believed this—how could I, remembering my grandfather?—I only believed that it worked.) It was a great success. Everyone praised me and I was invited to give the speech at a gathering of the town's leading white citizens. It was a triumph for the whole community.

It was in the main ballroom of the leading hotel. When I got there I discovered that it was on the occasion of a smoker, and I was told that since I was to be there anyway I might as well take part in the battle royal to be fought by some of my schoolmates as part of the entertainment. The battle royal came first.

All of the town's big shots were there in their tuxedoes, wolfing down the buffet foods, drinking beer and whiskey and smoking black cigars. It was a large room with a high ceiling. Chairs were arranged in neat rows around three sides of a portable boxing ring. The fourth side was clear, revealing a gleaming space of polished floor. I had some misgivings over the battle royal, by the way. Not from a distaste for fighting but because I didn't care too much for the other fellows who were to take part. They were tough guys who seemed to have no grandfather's curse worrying their minds. No one could mistake their toughness. And besides, I suspected that fighting a battle royal might detract from the dignity of my speech. In those pre-invisible days I visualized myself as a potential Booker T. Washington. But the other fellows didn't care too much for me either, and there were nine of them. I felt superior to them in my way, and I didn't like the manner in which we were all crowded together in the servants' elevator. Nor did they like my being there. In fact, as the warmly lighted floors flashed past the elevator we had words over the fact that I, by taking part in the fight, had knocked one of their friends out of a night's work.

We were led out of the elevator through a rococo hall into an anteroom and told to get into our fighting togs. Each of us was issued a pair of boxing gloves and ushered out into the big mirrored hall, which we entered looking cautiously about us and whispering, lest we might accidentally be heard above the noise of the room. It was foggy with cigar smoke. And already the whiskey was taking effect. I was shocked to see some of the most important men of the town quite tipsy. They were all there—bankers, lawyers, judges, doctors, fire chiefs, teachers, merchants. Even one of the more fashionable pastors. Something we

5

could not see was going on up front. A clarinet was vibrating sensuously and the men were standing up and moving eagerly forward. We were a small tight group, clustered together, our bare upper bodies touching and shining with anticipatory sweat: while up front the big shots were becoming increasingly excited over something we still could not see. Suddenly I heard the school superintendent, who had told me to come, yell, "Bring up the shines, gentlemen! Bring up the little shines!"

We were rushed up to the front of the ballroom, where it smelled even more strongly of tobacco and whiskey. Then we were pushed into place. I almost wet my pants. A sea of faces, some hostile, some amused, ringed around us, and in the center, facing us, stood a magnificent blonde—stark naked. There was dead silence. I felt a blast of cold air chill me. I tried to back away, but they were behind me and around me. Some of the boys stood with lowered heads, trembling. I felt a wave of irrational guilt and fear. My teeth chattered, my skin turned to goose flesh, my knees knocked. Yet I was strongly attracted and looked in spite of myself. Had the price of looking been blindness, I would have looked. The hair was yellow like that of a circus kewpie doll, the face heavily powdered and rouged, as though to form an abstract mask, the eyes hollow and smeared a cool blue, the color of a baboon's butt. I felt a desire to spit upon her as my eyes brushed slowly over her body. Her breasts were firm and round as the domes of East Indian temples, and I stood so close as to see the fine skin texture and beads of pearly perspiration glistening like dew around the pink and erected buds of her nipples. I wanted at one and the same time to run from the room, to sink through the floor, or go to her and cover her from my eyes and the eyes of the others with my body; to feel the soft thighs, to caress her and destroy her, to love her and to murder her, to hide from her, and yet to stroke where below the small American flag tattooed upon her belly her thighs formed a capital V. I had a notion that of all in the room she saw only me with her impersonal eyes.

And then she began to dance, a slow sensuous movement; the smoke of a hundred cigars clinging to her like the thinnest of veils. She seemed like a fair bird-girl girdled in veils calling to me from the angry surface of some gray and threatening sea. I was transported. Then I became aware of the clarinet playing and the big shots yelling at us. Some threatened us if we looked and others if we did not. On my right I saw one boy faint. And now a man grabbed a silver pitcher from a table and stepped close as he dashed ice water upon him and stood him up and forced two of us to support him as his head hung and moans issued from his thick bluish lips. Another boy began to plead to go home. He was the largest of the group, wearing dark red fighting trunks much too small to conceal the erection which projected from him as though in answer to the insinuating low-registered moaning of the clarinet. He tried to hide himself with his boxing gloves.

And all the while the blonde continued dancing, smiling faintly at the big shots who watched her with fascination, and faintly smiling at our fear. I noticed a certain merchant who followed her hungrily, his lips loose and drooling. He was a large man who wore diamond studs in a shirtfront which swelled with the ample paunch underneath, and each time the blonde swayed her undulating hips he ran his hand through the thin hair of his bald head and, with his arms upheld, his posture clumsy like that of an intoxicated panda, wound his belly in a slow and obscene grind. This creature was completely hypnotized. The music had quickened. As the dancer flung herself about with a detached expression on her face, the men began reaching out to touch her. I could see their beefy fingers sink into her soft flesh. Some of the others tried to stop them and she began to move around the floor in graceful circles, as they gave chase, slipping and sliding over the polished floor. It was mad. Chairs went crashing, drinks were spilt, as they ran laughing and howling after her. They caught her just as she reached a door, raised her from the floor, and tossed her as college boys are tossed at a hazing, and above her red, fixed-smiling lips I saw the terror and disgust in her eyes, almost like my own terror and that which I saw in some of the other boys. As I watched, they tossed her twice and her soft breasts seemed to flatten against the air and her legs flung wildly as she spun. Some of the more sober ones helped her to escape. And I started off the floor, heading for the anteroom with the rest of the boys.

Some were still crying and in hysteria. But as we tried to leave we were 10 stopped and ordered to get into the ring. There was nothing to do but what we were told. All ten of us climbed under the ropes and allowed ourselves to be blindfolded with broad bands of white cloth. One of the men seemed to feel a bit sympathetic and tried to cheer us up as we stood with our backs against the ropes. Some of us tried to grin. "See that boy over there?" one of the men said. "I want you to run across at the bell and give it to him right in the belly. If you don't get him, I'm going to get you. I don't like his looks." Each of us was told the same. The blindfolds were put on. Yet even then I had been going over my speech. In my mind each word was as bright as a flame. I felt the cloth pressed into place, and frowned so that it would be loosened when I relaxed.

But now I felt a sudden fit of blind terror. I was unused to darkness, it was as though I had suddenly found myself in a dark room filled with poisonous cotton-mouths. I could hear the bleary voices yelling insistently for the battle royal to begin.

"Get going in there!"

"Let me at that big nigger!"

I strained to pick up the school superintendent's voice, as though to squeeze some security out of that slightly more familiar sound.

"Let me at those black sonsabitches!" someone yelled. 15

"No, Jackson, no!" another voice yelled. "Here, somebody, help me hold Jack."

"I want to get at that ginger-colored nigger. Tear him limb from limb," the first voice yelled.

I stood against the ropes trembling. For in those days I was what they called ginger-colored, and he sounded as though he might crunch me between his teeth like a crisp ginger cookie.

Quite a struggle was going on. Chairs were being kicked about and I could hear voices grunting as with terrific effort. I wanted to see, to see more desperately than ever before. But the blindfold was as tight as a thick skin-puckering scab and when I raised my gloved hands to push the layers of white aside a voice yelled, "Oh, no you don't, black bastard! Leave that alone!"

"Ring the bell before Jackson kills him a coon!" someone boomed in the sudden silence. And I heard the bell clang and the sound of the feet scuffling forward.

A glove smacked against my head. I pivoted, striking out stiffly as someone went past, and felt the jar ripple along the length of my arm to my shoulder. Then it seemed as though all nine of the boys had turned upon me at once. Blows pounded me from all sides while I struck out as best I could. So many blows landed upon me that I wondered if I were not the only blindfolded fighter in the ring, or if the man called Jackson hadn't succeeded in getting me after all.

Blindfolded, I could no longer control my motions. I had no dignity. I stumbled about like a baby or a drunken man. The smoke had become thicker and with each new blow it seemed to sear and further restrict my lungs. My saliva became like hot bitter glue. A glove connected with my head, filling my mouth with warm blood. It was everywhere. I could not tell if the moisture I felt upon my body was sweat or blood. A blow landed hard against the nape of my neck. I felt myself going over, my head hitting the floor. Streaks of blue light filled the black world behind the blindfold. I lay prone, pretending that I was knocked out, but felt myself seized by hands and yanked to my feet. "Get going, black boy! Mix it up!" My arms were like lead, my head smarting from blows. I managed to feel my way to the ropes and held on, trying to catch my breath. A glove landed in my midsection and I went over again, feeling as though the smoke had become a knife jabbed into my guts. Pushed this way and that by the legs milling around me, I finally pulled erect and discovered that I could see the black, sweat-washed forms weaving in the smoky-blue atmosphere like drunken dancers weaving to the rapid drum-like thuds of blows.

Everyone fought hysterically. It was complete anarchy. Everybody fought everybody else. No group fought together for long. Two, three, four, fought one, then turned to fight each other, were themselves attacked. Blows landed below the belt and in the kidney, with the gloves open as well as closed, and with my eye partly opened now there was not so much terror. I moved carefully, avoiding blows, although not too many to attract attention, fighting group to group. The boys groped about like blind, cautious crabs crouching to protect their midsections, their heads pulled in short against their shoulders, their arms stretched nervously before them, with their fists testing the smoke-filled air like the knobbed feelers of hypersensitive snails. In one corner I glimpsed a boy violently punching the air and heard him scream in pain as he smashed his hand against a ring post. For a second I saw him bent over holding his hand, then going down as a blow caught his unprotected head. I played one group against the other, slipping in and throwing a punch then stepping out of range while pushing the others into the melee to take the blows blindly aimed at me. The smoke was agonizing and there were no rounds, no bells at three minute intervals to relieve our exhaustion. The room spun round me, a swirl of lights, smoke, sweating bodies surrounded by tense white faces. I bled from both nose and mouth, the blood spattering upon my chest.

The men kept yelling, "Slug him, black boy! Knock his guts out!"

"Uppercut him! Kill him! Kill that big boy!"

Taking a fake fall, I saw a boy going down heavily beside me as though we were felled by a single blow, saw a sneaker-clad foot shoot into his groin as the two who had knocked him down stumbled upon him. I rolled out of range, feeling a twinge of nausea.

The harder we fought the more threatening the men became. And yet, I had begun to worry about my speech again. How would it go? Would they recognize my ability? What would they give me?

I was fighting automatically when suddenly I noticed that one after another of the boys was leaving the ring. I was surprised, filled with panic, as though I had been left alone with an unknown danger. Then I understood. The boys had arranged it among themselves. It was the custom for the two men left in the ring to slug it out for the winner's prize. I discovered this too late. When the bell sounded two men in tuxedoes leaped into the ring and removed the blindfold. I found myself facing Tatlock, the biggest of the gang. I felt sick at my stomach. Hardly had the bell stopped ringing in my ears than it clanged again and I saw him moving swiftly toward me. Thinking of nothing else to do I hit him smash on the nose. He kept coming, bringing the rank sharp violence of stale sweat. His face was a black blank of a face, only his eyes alive—with hate of me and aglow with a feverish terror from what had happened to us all. I became anxious. I wanted to deliver my speech and he came at me as though he meant to beat it out of me. I smashed him again and again, taking his blows as they came. Then on a sudden impulse I struck him lightly and we clinched. I whispered, "Fake like I knocked you out, you can have the prize."

"I'll break your behind," he whispered hoarsely.

"For *them*?"

30

"For *me*, sonafabitch!"

They were yelling for us to break it up and Tatlock spun me half around with a blow, and as a joggled camera sweeps in a reeling scene, I saw the howling red faces crouching tense beneath the cloud of blue-gray smoke. For a moment the world wavered, unraveled, flowed, then my head cleared and Tatlock bounced before me. That fluttering shadow before my eyes was his jabbing left hand. Then falling forward, my head against his damp shoulder, I whispered.

"I'll make it five dollars more."

"Go to hell!"

But his muscles relaxed a trifle beneath my pressure and I breathed, "Seven?"

35

"Give it to your ma," he said, ripping me beneath the heart.

And while I still held him I butted him and moved away. I felt myself bombarded with punches. I fought back with hopeless desperation. I wanted to deliver my speech more than anything else in the world, because I felt that only these men could judge truly my ability, and now this stupid clown was ruining my chances. I began fighting carefully now, moving in to punch him and out again with my greater speed. A lucky blow to his chin and I had him going too— until I heard a loud voice yell, "I got my money on the big boy."

Hearing this, I almost dropped my guard. I was confused: Should I try to win against the voice out there? Would not this go against my speech, and was not this a moment for humility, for nonresistance? A blow to my head as I danced about sent my right eye popping like a jack-in-the-box and settled my dilemma. The room went red as I fell. It was a dream fall, my body languid and fastidious as to where to land, until the floor became impatient and smashed up to meet me. A moment later I came to. An hypnotic voice said FIVE emphatically. And I lay there, hazily watching a dark red spot of my own blood shaping itself into a butterfly, glistening and soaking into the soiled gray world of the canvas.

When the voice drawled TEN I was lifted up and dragged to a chair. I sat dazed. My eye pained and swelled with each throb of my pounding heart and I wondered if now I would be allowed to speak. I was wringing wet, my mouth still bleeding. We were grouped along the wall now. The other boys ignored me as they congratulated Tatlock and speculated as to how much they would be paid. One boy whimpered over his smashed hand. Looking up front, I saw attendants in white jackets rolling the portable ring away and placing a small square rug in the vacant space surrounded by chairs. Perhaps, I thought, I will stand on the rug to deliver my speech.

Then the M.C. called to us. "Come on up here boys and get your money." 40

We ran forward to where the men laughed and talked in their chairs, waiting. Everyone seemed friendly now.

"There it is on the rug," the man said. I saw the rug covered with coins of all dimensions and a few crumpled bills. But what excited me, scattered here and there, were the gold pieces.

"Boys, it's all yours," the man said. "You get all you grab."

"That's right, Sambo," a blond man said, winking at me confidentially.

I trembled with excitement, forgetting my pain. I would get the gold and the 45 bills. I thought. I would use both hands. I would throw my body against the boys nearest me to block them from the gold.

"Get down around the rug now," the man commanded, "and don't anyone touch it until I give the signal."

"This ought to be good," I heard.

As told, we got around the square rug on our knees. Slowly the man raised his freckled hand as we followed it upward with our eyes.

I heard, "These niggers look like they're about to pray!"

Then, "Ready," the man said. "Go!" 50

I lunged for a yellow coin lying on the blue design of the carpet, touching it and sending a surprised shriek to join those around me. I tried frantically to remove my hand but could not let go. A hot, violent force tore through my body, shaking me like a wet rat. The rug was electrified. The hair bristled up on my head as I shook myself free. My muscles jumped, my nerves jangled, writhed. But I saw that this was not stopping the other boys. Laughing in fear and embarrassment, some were holding back and scooping up the coins knocked off by the painful contortions of others. The men roared above us as we struggled.

"Pick it up, goddamnit, pick it up!" someone called like a bass-voiced parrot. "Go on, get it!"

I crawled rapidly around the floor, picking up the coins, trying to avoid the coppers and to get greenbacks and the gold. Ignoring the shock by laughing, as I brushed the coins off quickly, I discovered that I could contain the electricity—a contradiction but it works. Then the men began to push us onto the rug. Laughing embarrassedly, we struggled out of their hands and kept after the coins. We were all wet and slippery and hard to hold. Suddenly I saw a boy lifted into the air, glistening with sweat like a circus seal, and dropped, his wet back landing flush upon the charged rug, heard him yell and saw him literally dance upon his back, his elbows beating a frenzied tattoo upon the floor, his muscles twitching like the flesh of a horse stung by many flies. When he finally rolled off, his face was gray and no one stopped him when he ran from the floor amid booming laughter.

"Get the money," the M.C. called. "That's good hard American cash!"

And we snatched and grabbed, snatched and grabbed. I was careful not to   55
come too close to the rug now, and when I felt the hot whiskey breath descend upon me like a cloud of foul air I reached out and grabbed the leg of a chair. It was occupied and I held on desperately.

"Leggo, nigger! Leggo!"

The huge face wavered down to mine as he tried to push me free. But my body was slippery and he was too drunk. It was Mr. Colcord, who owned a chain of movie houses and "entertainment palaces." Each time he grabbed me I slipped out of his hands. It became a real struggle. I feared the rug more than I did the drunk, so I held on, surprising myself for a moment by trying to topple *him* upon the rug. It was such an enormous idea that I found myself actually carrying it out. I tried not to be obvious, yet when I grabbed his leg, trying to tumble him out of the chair, he raised up roaring with laughter, and, looking at me with soberness dead in the eye, kicked me viciously in the chest. The chair leg flew out of my hand and I felt myself going and rolled. It was as though I had rolled through a bed of hot coals. It seemed a whole century would pass before I would roll free, a century in which I was seared through the deepest levels of my body to the fearful breath within me and the breath seared and heated to the point of explosion. It'll all be over in a flash, I thought as I rolled clear. It'll all be over in a flash.

But not yet, the men on the other side were waiting, red faces swollen as though from apoplexy as they bent forward in their chairs. Seeing their fingers coming toward me I rolled away as a fumbled football rolls off the receiver's fingertips, back into the coals. That time I luckily sent the rug sliding out of place and heard the coins ringing against the floor and the boys scuffling to pick them up and the M.C. calling, "All right, boys, that's all. Go get dressed and get your money."

I was limp as a dish rag. My back felt as though it had been beaten with wires.

When we had dressed the M.C. came in and gave us each five dollars,   60
except Tatlock, who got ten for being the last in the ring. Then he told us to leave. I was not to get a chance to deliver my speech, I thought. I was going out into the dim alley in despair when I was stopped and told to go back. I returned to the ballroom, where the men were pushing back their chairs and gathering in small groups to talk.

The M.C. knocked on a table for quiet. "Gentlemen," he said, "we almost forgot an important part of the program. A most serious part, gentlemen. This boy was brought here to deliver a speech which he made at his graduation yesterday . . ."

"Bravo!"

"I'm told that he is the smartest boy we've got out there in Greenwood. I'm told that he knows more big words than a pocket-sized dictionary."

Much applause and laughter.

"So now, gentlemen, I want you to give him your attention." 65

There was still laughter as I faced them, my mouth dry, my eyes throbbing. I began slowly, but evidently my throat was tense, because they began shouting. "Louder! Louder!"

"We of the younger generation extol the wisdom of that great leader and educator," I shouted, "who first spoke these flaming words of wisdom: 'A ship lost at sea for many days suddenly sighted a friendly vessel. From the mast of the unfortunate vessel was seen a signal: "Water, water; we die of thirst!" The answer from the friendly vessel came back: "Cast down your bucket where you are." The captain of the distressed vessel, at last heeding the injunction, cast down his bucket, and it came up full of fresh sparkling water from the mouth of the Amazon River.' And like him I say, and in his words, 'To those of my race who depend upon bettering their condition in a foreign land, or who underestimate the importance of cultivating friendly relations with the Southern white man, who is his next-door neighbor, I would say: "Cast down your bucket where you are"—cast it down in making friends in every manly way of the people of all races by whom we are surrounded . . .'"

I spoke automatically and with such fervor that I did not realize that the men were still talking and laughing until my dry mouth, filling up with blood from the cut, almost strangled me. I coughed, wanting to stop and go to one of the tall brass, sand-filled spittoons to relieve myself, but a few of the men, especially the superintendent, were listening and I was afraid. So I gulped it down, blood, saliva and all, and continued. (What powers of endurance I had during those days! What enthusiasm! What a belief in the rightness of things!) I spoke even louder in spite of the pain. But still they talked and still they laughed, as though deaf with cotton in dirty ears. So I spoke with greater emotional emphasis. I closed my ears and swallowed blood until I was nauseated. The speech seemed a hundred times as long as before, but I could not leave out a single word. All had to be said, each memorized nuance considered, rendered. Nor was that all. Whenever I uttered a word of three or more syllables a group of voices would yell for me to repeat it. I used the phrase "social responsibility" and they yelled:

"What's the word you say, boy?"

"Social responsibility," I said. 70

"What?"

"Social . . ."

"Louder."

". . . responsibility."

"More!"

"Respon—" 75

"Repeat!"

"—sibility."

The room filled with the uproar of laughter until, no doubt, distracted by having to gulp down my blood, I made a mistake and yelled a phrase I had often seen denounced in newspaper editorials, heard debated in private.

"Social . . ."

"What?" they yelled.

". . . equality—"

The laughter hung smokelike in the sudden stillness. I opened my eyes, puzzled. Sounds of displeasure filled the room. The M.C. rushed forward. They shouted hostile phrases at me. But I did not understand.

A small dry mustached man in the front row blared out, "Say that slowly, son!"

"What, sir?"

"What you just said!"

"Social responsibility, sir," I said.

"You weren't being smart, were you boy?" he said, not unkindly.

"No, sir!"

"You sure that about 'equality' was a mistake?"

"Oh, yes, sir," I said. "I was swallowing blood."

"Well, you had better speak more slowly so we can understand. We mean to do right by you, but you've got to know your place at all times. All right, now, go on with your speech."

I was afraid. I wanted to leave but I wanted also to speak and I was afraid they'd snatch me down.

"Thank you, sir," I said, beginning where I had left off, and having them ignore me as before.

Yet when I finished there was a thunderous applause. I was surprised to see the superintendent come forth with a package wrapped in white tissue paper, and, gesturing for quiet, address the men.

"Gentlemen, you see that I did not overpraise the boy. He makes a good speech and some day he'll lead his people in the proper paths. And I don't have to tell you that this is important in these days and times. This is a good, smart boy, and so to encourage him in the right direction, in the name of the Board of Education I wish to present him a prize in the form of this . . ."

He paused, removing the tissue paper and revealing a gleaming calfskin briefcase.

". . . in the form of this first-class article from Shad Whitmore's shop."

"Boy," he said, addressing me, "take this prize and keep it well. Consider it a badge of office. Prize it. Keep developing as you are and some day it will be filled with important papers that will help shape the destiny of your people."

I was so moved that I could hardly express my thanks. A rope of bloody saliva forming a shape like an undiscovered continent drooled upon the leather and I wiped it quickly away. I felt an importance that I had never dreamed.

"Open it and see what's inside," I was told.

My fingers a-tremble, I complied, smelling fresh leather and finding an official-looking document inside. It was a scholarship to the state college for Negroes. My eyes filled with tears and I ran awkwardly off the floor.

I was overjoyed; I did not even mind when I discovered the gold pieces I had scrambled for were brass pocket tokens advertising a certain make of automobile.

When I reached home everyone was excited. Next day the neighbors came to congratulate me. I even felt safe from grandfather, whose deathbed curse usually spoiled my triumphs. I stood beneath his photograph with my briefcase in hand and smiled triumphantly into his stolid black peasant's face. It was a face that fascinated me. The eyes seemed to follow everywhere I went.

That night I dreamed I was at a circus with him and that he refused to laugh at the clowns no matter what they did. Then later he told me to open my briefcase and read what was inside and I did, finding an official envelope stamped with the state seal: and inside the envelope I found another and another, endlessly, and I thought I would fall of weariness. "Them's years," he said. "Now open that one." And I did and in it I found an engraved stamp containing a short message in letters of gold. "Read it," my grandfather said. "Out loud."

"To Whom It May Concern," I intoned. "Keep This Nigger-Boy Running."

I awoke with the old man's laughter ringing in my ears.

Gabriel García Márquez

THE HANDSOMEST DROWNED MAN IN THE WORLD   1968

TRANSLATED BY GREGORY RABASSA

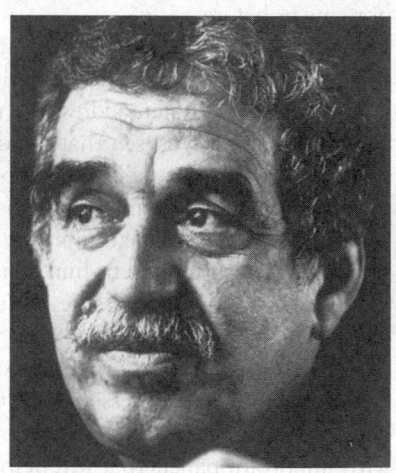

Gabriel García Márquez, among the most eminent of living Latin American writers, was born in 1928 in Aracataca, a Caribbean port in Colombia, one of sixteen children of an impoverished telegraph operator. For a time he studied law in Bogotá, then became a newspaper reporter. Although he never joined the Communist Party, García Márquez outspokenly advocated many left-wing proposals for reform. In 1954, despairing of any prospect for political change, he left Colombia to live in Mexico City. Though at nineteen he had already completed a book of short stories, La hojorasca *(Leaf Storm), he waited until 1955 to publish it. Soon he began to build a*   Gabriel García Márquez *towering reputation among readers of Spanish.*

His celebrated novel Cien años de soledad *(1967), published in English as* One Hundred Years of Solitude *(1969), traces the history of a Colombian family through six generations. Called by Chilean poet Pablo Neruda "the greatest revelation in the Spanish language since* Don Quixote," *the book has sold more than twelve million copies in thirty languages. In 1982 García Márquez was awarded the Nobel Prize for literature. His fiction, rich in myth and invention, has reminded American readers of the work of William Faulkner, another explorer of his native ground; indeed, García Márquez has called Faulkner "my master."*

His later novels include Love in the Time of Cholera *(1988),* The General in His Labyrinth *(1990), and* Of Love and Other Demons *(1995). His* Collected Stories *was published in 1994. García Márquez returned to his journalistic roots with* News of a Kidnapping *(1997), a vivid account of a Colombian drug lord who abducted ten leading journalists and politicians to prevent his extradition to the United States. A* Country for Children *(1998) explores Colombia's potential for a positive future. Living to Tell the Tale *(2003), the first volume of an autobiographical trilogy, traces the author's life up to the beginning of his journalistic career, and offers many insights into the sources and techniques of his works of fiction. The author still lives in Mexico City.*

A TALE FOR CHILDREN

The first children who saw the dark and slinky bulge approaching through the sea let themselves think it was an empty ship. Then they saw it had no flags or masts and they thought it was a whale. But when it washed up on the beach, they removed the clumps of seaweed, the jellyfish tentacles, and the remains of fish and flotsam, and only then did they see that it was a drowned man.

They had been playing with him all afternoon, burying him in the sand and digging him up again, when someone chanced to see them and spread the alarm in the village. The men who carried him to the nearest house noticed that he weighed more than any dead man they had ever known, almost as much as a horse, and they said to each other that maybe he'd been floating too long and the water had got into his bones. When they laid him on the floor they said he'd been taller than all the other men because there was barely enough room for him in the house, but they thought that maybe the ability to keep on growing after death was part of the nature of certain drowned men. He had the smell of the sea about him and only his shape gave one to suppose that it was the corpse of a human being, because the skin was covered with a crust of mud and scales.

They did not even have to clean off his face to know that the dead man was a stranger. The village was made up of only twenty-odd wooden houses that had stone courtyards with no flowers and which were spread about on the end of a desertlike cape. There was so little land that mothers always went about with the fear that the wind would carry off their children and the few dead that the years had caused among them had to be thrown off the cliffs. But the sea was calm and bountiful and all the men fit into seven boats. So when they found the drowned man they simply had to look at one another to see that they were all there. That night they did not go out to work at sea. While the men went to find out if anyone was missing in neighboring villages, the women stayed behind to care for the drowned man. They took the mud off with grass swabs, they removed the underwater stones entangled in his hair, and they scraped the crust off with tools used for scaling fish. As they were doing that they noticed that the vegetation on him came from faraway oceans and deep water and that his clothes were in tatters, as if he had sailed through labyrinths of coral. They noticed too that he bore his death with pride, for he did not have the lonely look of other drowned men who came out of the sea or that haggard, needy look of men who drowned in rivers. But only when they finished cleaning him off did they become aware of the kind of man he was and it left them breathless. Not only was he the tallest, strongest, most virile, and best built man they had ever seen, but even though they were looking at him there was no room for him in their imagination.

They could not find a bed in the village large enough to lay him on nor was there a table solid enough to use for his wake. The tallest men's holiday pants would not fit him, nor the fattest ones' Sunday shirts, nor the shoes of the one with the biggest feet. Fascinated by his huge size and his beauty, the women then decided to make him some pants from a large piece of sail and a shirt from some bridal brabant linen so that he could continue through his death with dignity. As they sewed, sitting in a circle and gazing at the corpse between stitches, it seemed to them that the wind had never been so steady nor the sea so restless as on that night and they supposed that the change had something to do with the dead man. They thought that if that magnificent man had lived in the village, his house would have had the widest doors, the highest ceiling, and the strongest floor, his bedstead would have been made from a midship frame held together by iron bolts, and his wife would have been the happiest woman. They thought that he would have had so much authority that he could have drawn fish out of the sea simply by calling their names and that he would have put so much work into his land that springs would have burst forth from among the rocks so that he would have been able to plant flowers on the cliffs. They secretly compared him to their own men, thinking that for all their lives theirs were incapable of doing what he could do in one night, and they ended up dismissing them deep in their hearts as the weakest, meanest, and most useless creatures on earth. They were wandering through the maze of fantasy when the oldest woman, who as the oldest had looked upon the drowned man with more compassion than passion, sighed:

"He has the face of someone called Esteban."

It was true. Most of them had only to take another look at him to see that he could not have any other name. The more stubborn among them, who were the youngest, still lived for a few hours with the illusion that when they put his clothes on and he lay among the flowers in patent leather shoes his name might be Lautaro. But it was a vain illusion. There had not been enough canvas, the poorly cut and worse sewn pants were too tight, and the hidden strength of his heart popped the buttons on his shirt. After midnight the whistling of the wind died down and the sea fell into its Wednesday drowsiness. The silence put an end to any last doubts: he was Esteban. The women who had dressed him, who had combed his hair, had cut his nails and shaved him were unable to hold back a shudder of pity when they had to resign themselves to his being dragged along the ground. It was then that they understood how unhappy he must have been with that huge body since it bothered him even after death. They could see him in life, condemned to going through doors sideways, cracking his head on crossbeams, remaining on his feet during

5

visits, not knowing what to do with his soft, pink, sea lion hands while the lady of the house looked for her most resistant chair and begged him, frightened to death, sit here, Esteban, please, and he, leaning against the wall, smiling, don't bother, ma'am, I'm fine where I am, his heels raw and his back roasted from having done the same thing so many times whenever he paid a visit, don't bother, ma'am, I'm fine where I am, just to avoid the embarrassment of breaking up the chair, and never knowing perhaps that the ones who said don't go, Esteban, at least wait till the coffee's ready, were the ones who later on would whisper the big boob finally left, how nice, the handsome fool has gone. That was what the women were thinking beside the body a little before dawn. Later, when they covered his face with a handkerchief so that the light would not bother him, he looked so forever dead, so defenseless, so much like their men that the first furrows of tears opened in their hearts. It was one of the younger ones who began the weeping. The others, coming to, went from sighs to wails, and the more they sobbed the more they felt like weeping, because the drowned man was becoming all the more Esteban for them, and so they wept so much, for he was the most destitute, most peaceful, and most obliging man on earth, poor Esteban. So when the men returned with the news that the drowned man was not from the neighboring villages either, the women felt an opening of jubilation in the midst of their tears.

"Praise the Lord," they sighed, "he's ours!"

The men thought the fuss was only womanish frivolity. Fatigued because of the difficult nighttime inquiries, all they wanted was to get rid of the bother of the newcomer once and for all before the sun grew strong on that arid, windless day. They improvised a litter with the remains of foremasts and gaffs, tying it together with rigging so that it would bear the weight of the body until they reached the cliffs. They wanted to tie the anchor from a cargo ship to him so that he would sink easily into the deepest waves, where fish are blind and divers die of nostalgia, and bad currents would not bring him back to shore, as had happened with other bodies. But the more they hurried, the more the women thought of ways to waste time. They walked about like startled hens, pecking with the sea charms on their breasts, some interfering on one side to put a scapular of the good wind on the drowned man, some on the other side to put a wrist compass on him, and after a great deal of *get away from there, woman, stay out of the way, look, you almost made me fall on top of the dead man*, the men began to feel mistrust in their livers and started grumbling about why so many main-altar decorations for a stranger, because no matter how many nails and holy-water jars he had on him, the sharks would chew him all the same, but the women kept piling on their junk relics, running back and forth, stumbling, while they released in sighs what they did not in tears, so that the men finally exploded with *since when has there ever been such a fuss over a drifting corpse, a drowned nobody, a piece of cold Wednesday meat*. One of the women, mortified by so much lack of care, then removed the handkerchief from the dead man's face and the men were left breathless too.

He was Esteban. It was not necessary to repeat it for them to recognize him. If they had been told Sir Walter Raleigh,° even they might have been impressed with his gringo accent, the macaw on his shoulder, his cannibal-killing blunder-buss, but there could be only one Esteban in the world and there he was, stretched out like a sperm whale, shoeless, wearing the pants of an undersized child, and with those stony nails that had to be cut with a knife. They only had to take the handkerchief off his face to see that he was ashamed, that it was not his fault that he was so big or so heavy or so handsome, and if he had known that this was going to happen, he would have looked for a more discreet place to drown in, seriously, I even would have tied the anchor off a galleon around my neck and staggered off a cliff like someone who doesn't like things in order not to be upsetting people now with this Wednesday dead body, as you people say, in order not to be bothering anyone with this filthy piece of cold meat that doesn't have anything to do with me. There was so much truth in his manner that even the most mistrustful men, the ones who felt the bitterness of endless nights at sea fearing that their women would tire of dreaming about them and begin to dream of drowned men, even they and others who were harder still shuddered in the marrow of their bones at Esteban's sincerity.

That was how they came to hold the most splendid funeral they could   10
conceive of for an abandoned drowned man. Some women who had gone to get flowers in the neighboring villages returned with other women who could not believe what they had been told, and those women went back for more flowers when they saw the dead man, and they brought more and more until there were so many flowers and so many people that it was hard to walk about. At the final moment it pained them to return him to the waters as an orphan and they chose a father and mother from among the best people, and aunts and uncles and cousins, so that through him all the inhabitants of the village became kinsmen. Some sailors who heard weeping from a distance went off course and people heard of one who had himself tied to the mainmast, remembering ancient fables about sirens. While they fought for the privilege of carrying him on their shoulders along the steep escarpment by the cliffs, men and women became aware for the first time of the desolation of their streets, the dryness of their courtyards, the nar-rowness of their dreams as they faced the splendor and beauty of their drowned man. They let him go without an anchor so that he could come back if he wished and whenever he wished, and they all held their breath for the fraction of cen-turies the body took to fall into the abyss. They did not need to look at one an-other to realize that they were no longer all present, that they would never be. But they also knew that everything would be different from then on, that their houses would have wider doors, higher ceilings, and stronger floors so that Esteban's memory could go everywhere without bumping into beams and so that no one in the future would dare whisper the big boob finally died, too bad, the

Sir Walter Raleigh: Elizabethan explorer and statesman (1552–1618).

handsome fool has finally died, because they were going to paint their house fronts gay colors to make Esteban's memory eternal and they were going to break their backs digging for springs among the stones and planting flowers on the cliffs so that in future years at dawn the passengers on great liners would awaken, suffocated by the smell of gardens on the high seas, and the captain would have to come down from the bridge in his dress uniform, with his astrolabe, his pole star, and his row of war medals and, pointing to the promontory of roses on the horizon, he would say in fourteen languages, look there, where the wind is so peaceful now that it's gone to sleep beneath the beds, over there, where the sun's so bright that the sunflowers don't know which way to turn, yes, that's Esteban's village.

Charlotte Perkins Gilman

THE YELLOW WALLPAPER   1892

Charlotte Perkins Gilman (1860–1935) was born in Hartford, Connecticut. Her father was the writer Frederick Beecher Perkins (a nephew of reformer-novelist Harriet Beecher Stowe, author of Uncle Tom's Cabin, *and abolitionist minister Henry Ward Beecher), but he abandoned the family shortly after his daughter's birth. Raised in meager surroundings, the young Gilman adopted her intellectual Beecher aunts as role models. Because she and her mother moved from one relation to another, Gilman's early education was neglected—at fifteen, she had had only four years of schooling. In 1878 she studied commercial art at the Rhode Island School of Design. In 1884 she married Walter* Charlotte Perkins Gilman
Stetson, an artist. After the birth of her one daughter, she experienced a severe depression. The rest cure her doctor prescribed became the basis of her most famous story, "The Yellow Wallpaper." This tale combines standard elements of Gothic fiction (the isolated country mansion, the brooding atmosphere of the room, the aloof but dominating husband) with the fresh clarity of Gilman's feminist perspective. Gilman's first marriage ended in an amicable divorce. A celebrated essayist and public speaker, Gilman became an important early figure in American feminism. Her study Women and Economics *(1898) stressed the importance of both sexes having a place in the working world. Her feminist-Utopian novel* Herland *(1915) describes a thriving nation of women without men. In 1900 Gilman married a second time—this time, more happily—to her cousin George Houghton Gilman. Following his sudden death in 1934, Gilman discovered she had inoperable breast cancer. After finishing her autobiography, she killed herself with chloroform in Pasadena, California.*

It is very seldom that mere ordinary people like John and myself secure ancestral halls for the summer.

A colonial mansion, a hereditary estate, I would say a haunted house and reach the height of romantic felicity—but that would be asking too much of fate!

Still I will proudly declare that there is something queer about it.

Else, why should it be let so cheaply? And why have stood so long untenanted?

John laughs at me, of course, but one expects that.   5

John is practical in the extreme. He has no patience with faith, an intense horror of superstition, and he scoffs openly at any talk of things not to be felt and seen and put down in figures.

John is a physician, and *perhaps*—(I would not say it to a living soul, of course, but this is dead paper and a great relief to my mind)—*perhaps* that is one reason I do not get well faster.

You see, he does not believe I am sick! And what can one do?

If a physician of high standing, and one's own husband, assures friends and relatives that there is really nothing the matter with one but temporary nervous depression—a slight hysterical tendency—what is one to do?

My brother is also a physician, and also of high standing, and he says the   10
same thing.

So I take phosphates or phosphites—whichever it is—and tonics, and air and exercise, and journeys, and am absolutely forbidden to "work" until I am well again.

Personally, I disagree with their ideas.

Personally, I believe that congenial work, with excitement and change, would do me good.

But what is one to do?

I did write for a while in spite of them; but it *does* exhaust me a good deal—   15
having to be so sly about it, or else meet with heavy opposition.

I sometimes fancy that in my condition, if I had less opposition and more society and stimulus—but John says the very worst thing I can do is to think about my condition, and I confess it always makes me feel bad.

So I will let it alone and talk about the house.

The most beautiful place! It is quite alone, standing well back from the road, quite three miles from the village. It makes me think of English places that you read about, for there are hedges and walls and gates that lock, and lots of separate little houses for the gardeners and people.

There is a *delicious* garden! I never saw such a garden—large and shady, full of box-bordered paths, and lined with long grape-covered arbors with seats under them.

There were greenhouses, but they are all broken now.   20

There was some legal trouble, I believe, something about the heirs and coheirs; anyhow, the place has been empty for years.

That spoils my ghostliness, I am afraid, but I don't care—there is something strange about the house—I can feel it.

I even said so to John one moonlight evening, but he said what I felt was a *draught*, and shut the window.

I get unreasonably angry with John sometimes. I'm sure I never used to be so sensitive. I think it is due to this nervous condition.

But John says if I feel so I shall neglect proper self-control; so I take pains to control myself—before him, at least, and that makes me very tired. 25

I don't like our room a bit. I wanted one downstairs that opened onto the piazza and had roses all over the window, and such pretty old-fashioned chintz hangings! But John would not hear of it.

He said there was only one window and not room for two beds, and no near room for him if he took another.

He is very careful and loving, and hardly lets me stir without special direction.

I have a schedule prescription for each hour in the day; he takes all care from me, and so I feel basely ungrateful not to value it more.

He said he came here solely on my account, that I was to have perfect rest and all the air I could get. "Your exercise depends on your strength, my dear," said he, "and your food somewhat on your appetite; but air you can absorb all the time." So we took the nursery at the top of the house. 30

It is a big, airy room, the whole floor nearly, with windows that look all ways, and air and sunshine galore. It was a nursery first, and then playroom and gymnasium, I should judge, for the windows are barred for little children, and there are rings and things in the walls.

The paint and paper look as if a boys' school had used it. It is stripped off—the paper—in great patches all around the head of my bed, about as far as I can reach, and in a great place on the other side of the room low down. I never saw a worse paper in my life. One of those sprawling, flamboyant patterns committing every artistic sin.

It is dull enough to confuse the eye in following, pronounced enough constantly to irritate and provoke study, and when you follow the lame uncertain curves for a little distance they suddenly commit suicide—plunge off at outrageous angles, destroy themselves in unheard-of contradictions.

The color is repellent, almost revolting: a smouldering unclean yellow, strangely faded by the slow-turning sunlight. It is a dull yet lurid orange in some places, a sickly sulphur tint in others.

No wonder the children hated it! I should hate it myself if I had to live in this room long. 35

There comes John, and I must put this away—he hates to have me write a word.

We have been here two weeks, and I haven't felt like writing before, since that first day.

I am sitting by the window now, up in this atrocious nursery, and there is nothing to hinder my writing as much as I please, save lack of strength.

John is away all day, and even some nights when his cases are serious.

I am glad my case is not serious! 40

But these nervous troubles are dreadfully depressing.

John does not know how much I really suffer. He knows there is no *reason* to suffer, and that satisfies him.

Of course it is only nervousness. It does weigh on me so not to do my duty in any way!

I meant to be such a help to John, such a real rest and comfort, and here I am a comparative burden already!

Nobody would believe what an effort it is to do what little I am able—to   45
dress and entertain, and order things.

It is fortunate Mary is so good with the baby. Such a dear baby!

And yet I *cannot* be with him, it makes me so nervous.

I suppose John never was nervous in his life. He laughs at me so about this wallpaper!

At first he meant to repaper the room, but afterward he said that I was letting it get the better of me, and that nothing was worse for a nervous patient than to give way to such fancies.

He said that after the wallpaper was changed it would be the heavy bed-   50
stead, and then the barred windows, and then that gate at the head of the stairs, and so on.

"You know the place is doing you good," he said, "and really, dear, I don't care to renovate the house just for a three months' rental."

"Then do let us go downstairs," I said. "There are such pretty rooms there."

Then he took me in his arms and called me a blessed little goose, and said he would go down to the cellar, if I wished, and have it whitewashed into the bargain.

But he is right enough about the beds and windows and things.

It is as airy and comfortable a room as anyone need wish, and, of course, I   55
would not be so silly as to make him uncomfortable just for a whim.

I'm really getting quite fond of the big room, all but that horrid paper.

Out of one window I can see the garden—those mysterious deep-shaded arbors, the riotous old-fashioned flowers, and bushes and gnarly trees.

Out of another I get a lovely view of the bay and a little private wharf belonging to the estate. There is a beautiful shaded lane that runs down there from the house. I always fancy I see people walking in these numerous paths and arbors, but John has cautioned me not to give way to fancy in the least. He says that with my imaginative power and habit of storymaking, a nervous weakness like mine is sure to lead to all manner of excited fancies, and that I ought to use my will and good sense to check the tendency. So I try.

I think sometimes that if I were only well enough to write a little it would relieve the press of ideas and rest me.

But I find I get pretty tired when I try.   60

It is so discouraging not to have any advice and companionship about my work. When I get really well, John says we will ask Cousin Henry and Julia down for a long visit; but he says he would as soon put fireworks in my pillow-case as to let me have those stimulating people about now.

I wish I could get well faster.

But I must not think about that. This paper looks to me as if it *knew* what a vicious influence it had!

There is a recurrent spot where the pattern lolls like a broken neck and two bulbous eyes stare at you upside down.

I get positively angry with the impertinence of it and the everlastingness. 65 Up and down and sideways they crawl, and those absurd unblinking eyes are everywhere. There is one place where two breadths didn't match, and the eyes go all up and down the line, one a little higher than the other.

I never saw so much expression in an inanimate thing before, and we all know how much expression they have! I used to lie awake as a child and get more entertainment and terror out of blank walls and plain furniture than most children could find in a toy-store.

I remember what a kindly wink the knobs of our big old bureau used to have, and there was one chair that always seemed like a strong friend.

I used to feel that if any of the other things looked too fierce I could always hop into that chair and be safe.

The furniture in this room is no worse than inharmonious, however, for we had to bring it all from downstairs. I suppose when this was used as a playroom they had to take the nursery things out, and no wonder! I never saw such ravages as the children have made here.

The wallpaper, as I said before, is torn off in spots, and it sticketh closer 70 than a brother—they must have had perseverance as well as hatred.

Then the floor is scratched and gouged and splintered, the plaster itself is dug out here and there, and this great heavy bed, which is all we found in the room, looks as if it had been through the wars.

But I don't mind it a bit—only the paper.

There comes John's sister. Such a dear girl as she is, and so careful of me! I must not let her find me writing.

She is a perfect and enthusiastic housekeeper, and hopes for no better profession. I verily believe she thinks it is the writing which made me sick!

But I can write when she is out, and see her a long way off from these windows. 75

There is one that commands the road, a lovely shaded winding road, and one that just looks off over the country. A lovely country, too, full of great elms and velvet meadows.

This wallpaper has a kind of subpattern in a different shade, a particularly irritating one, for you can only see it in certain lights, and not clearly then.

But in the places where it isn't faded and where the sun is just so—I can see a strange, provoking, formless sort of figure that seems to skulk about behind that silly and conspicuous front design.

There's sister on the stairs!

Well, the Fourth of July is over! The people are all gone, and I am tired out. 80 John thought it might do me good to see a little company, so we just had Mother and Nellie and the children down for a week.

Of course I didn't do a thing. Jennie sees to everything now.

But it tired me all the same.

John says if I don't pick up faster he shall send me to Weir Mitchell° in the fall.

But I don't want to go there at all. I had a friend who was in his hands once, and she says he is just like John and my brother, only more so!

Besides, it is such an undertaking to go so far.   85

I don't feel as if it was worthwhile to turn my hand over for anything, and I'm getting dreadfully fretful and querulous.

I cry at nothing, and cry most of the time.

Of course I don't when John is here, or anybody else, but when I am alone.

And I am alone a good deal just now. John is kept in town very often by serious cases, and Jennie is good and lets me alone when I want her to.

So I walk a little in the garden or down that lovely lane, sit on the porch   90
under the roses, and lie down up here a good deal.

I'm getting really fond of the room in spite of the wallpaper. Perhaps *because* of the wallpaper.

It dwells in my mind so!

I lie here on this great immovable bed—it is nailed down, I believe—and follow that pattern about by the hour. It is as good as gymnastics, I assure you. I start, we'll say, at the bottom, down in the corner over there where it has not been touched, and I determine for the thousandth time that I *will* follow that pointless pattern to some sort of a conclusion.

I know a little of the principle of design, and I know this thing was not arranged on any laws of radiation,° or alternation, or repetition, or symmetry, or anything else that I ever heard of.

It is repeated, of course, by the breadths, but not otherwise.   95

Looked at in one way, each breadth stands alone; the bloated curves and flourishes—a kind of "debased Romanesque" with *delirium tremens*—go waddling up and down in isolated columns of fatuity.

But, on the other hand, they connect diagonally, and the sprawling outlines run off in great slanting waves of optic horror, like a lot of wallowing sea-weeds in full chase.

The whole thing goes horizontally, too, at least it seems so, and I exhaust myself trying to distinguish the order of its going in that direction.

They have used a horizontal breadth for a frieze, and that adds wonderfully to the confusion.

There is one end of the room where it is almost intact, and there, when the   100
crosslights fade and the low sun shines directly upon it, I can almost fancy radia-

Weir Mitchell (1829–1914): famed nerve specialist who actually treated the author, Charlotte Perkins Gilman, for nervous prostration with his well-known "rest cure." (The cure was not successful.) Also the author of *Diseases of the Nervous System, Especially of Women* (1881). *laws of radiation*: a principle of design in which all elements are arranged in some circular pattern around a center.

tion after all—the interminable grotesque seems to form around a common center and rush off in headlong plunges of equal distraction.

It makes me tired to follow it. I will take a nap, I guess.

I don't know why I should write this.

I don't want to.

I don't feel able.

And I know John would think it absurd. But I *must* say what I feel and think   105
in some way—it is such a relief!

But the effort is getting to be greater than the relief.

Half the time now I am awfully lazy, and lie down ever so much. John says I mustn't lose my strength, and has me take cod liver oil and lots of tonics and things, to say nothing of ale and wines and rare meat.

Dear John! He loves me very dearly, and hates to have me sick. I tried to have a real earnest reasonable talk with him the other day, and tell him how I wish he would let me go and make a visit to Cousin Henry and Julia.

But he said I wasn't able to go, nor able to stand it after I got there; and I did not make out a very good case for myself, for I was crying before I had finished.

It is getting to be a great effort for me to think straight. Just this nervous   110
weakness, I suppose.

And dear John gathered me up in his arms, and just carried me upstairs and laid me on the bed, and sat by me and read to me till it tired my head.

He said I was his darling and his comfort and all he had, and that I must take care of myself for his sake, and keep well.

He says no one but myself can help me out of it, that I must use my will and self-control and not let any silly fancies run away with me.

There's one comfort—the baby is well and happy, and does not have to occupy this nursery with the horrid wallpaper.

If we had not used it, that blessed child would have! What a fortunate   115
escape! Why, I wouldn't have a child of mine, an impressionable little thing, live in such a room for worlds.

I never thought of it before, but it is lucky that John kept me here after all; I can stand it so much easier than a baby, you see.

Of course I never mention it to them any more—I am too wise—but I keep watch for it all the same.

There are things in the wallpaper that nobody knows about but me, or ever will.

Behind that outside pattern the dim shapes get clearer every day.

It is always the same shape, only very numerous.   120

And it is like a woman stooping down and creeping about behind that pattern. I don't like it a bit. I wonder—I begin to think—I wish John would take me away from here!

It is so hard to talk with John about my case, because he is so wise, and because he loves me so.

But I tried it last night.

It was moonlight. The moon shines in all around just as the sun does.

I hate to see it sometimes, it creeps so slowly, and always comes in by one   125
window or another.

John was asleep and I hated to waken him, so I kept still and watched the
moonlight on that undulating wallpaper till I felt creepy.

The faint figure behind seemed to shake the pattern, just as if she wanted to
get out.

I got up softly and went to feel and see if the paper *did* move, and when I
came back John was awake.

"What is it, little girl?" he said. "Don't go walking about like that—you'll
get cold."

I thought it was a good time to talk, so I told him that I really was not   130
gaining here, and that I wished he would take me away.

"Why, darling!" said he. "Our lease will be up in three weeks, and I can't see
how to leave before.

"The repairs are not done at home, and I cannot possibly leave town just
now. Of course, if you were in any danger, I could and would, but you really are
better, dear, whether you can see it or not. I am a doctor, dear, and I know. You
are gaining flesh and color, your appetite is better, I feel really much easier about
you."

"I don't weigh a bit more," said I, "nor as much; and my appetite may be
better in the evening when you are here but it is worse in the morning when you
are away!"

"Bless her little heart!" said he with a big hug. "She shall be as sick as she
pleases! But now let's improve the shining hours by going to sleep, and talk
about it in the morning!"

"And you won't go away?" I asked gloomily.   135

"Why, how can I, dear? It is only three weeks more and then we will take a
nice little trip for a few days while Jennie is getting the house ready. Really, dear,
you are better!"

"Better in body perhaps—" I began, and stopped short, for he sat up straight
and looked at me with such a stern, reproachful look that I could not say another
word.

"My darling," said he, "I beg you, for my sake and for our child's sake, as well
as for your own, that you will never for one instant let that idea enter your
mind! There is nothing so dangerous, so fascinating, to a temperament like
yours. It is a false and foolish fancy. Can you trust me as a physician when I tell
you so?"

So of course I said no more on that score, and we went to sleep before long.
He thought I was asleep first, but I wasn't, and lay there for hours trying to decide whether that front pattern and the back pattern really did move together or
separately.

On a pattern like this, by daylight, there is a lack of sequence, a defiance of   140
law, that is a constant irritant to a normal mind.

The color is hideous enough, and unreliable enough, and infuriating enough, but the pattern is torturing.

You think you have mastered it, but just as you get well under way in following, it turns a back-somersault and there you are. It slaps you in the face, knocks you down, and tramples upon you. It is like a bad dream.

The outside pattern is a florid arabesque,° reminding one of a fungus. If you can imagine a toadstool in joints, an interminable string of toadstools, budding and sprouting in endless convolutions—why, that is something like it.

That is, sometimes!

There is one marked peculiarity about this paper, a thing nobody seems to   145
notice but myself, and that is that it changes as the light changes.

When the sun shoots in through the east window—I always watch for that first long, straight ray—it changes so quickly that I never can quite believe it.

That is why I watch it always.

By moonlight—the moon shines in all night when there is a moon—I wouldn't know it was the same paper.

At night in any kind of light, in twilight, candlelight, lamplight, and worst of all by moonlight, it becomes bars! The outside pattern, I mean, and the woman behind it is as plain as can be.

I didn't realize for a long time what the thing was that showed behind, that   150
dim subpattern, but now I am quite sure it is a woman.

By daylight she is subdued, quiet. I fancy it is the pattern that keeps her so still. It is so puzzling. It keeps me quiet by the hour.

I lie down ever so much now. John says it is good for me, and to sleep all I can.

Indeed he started the habit by making me lie down for an hour after each meal.

It is a very bad habit, I am convinced, for you see, I don't sleep.

And that cultivates deceit, for I don't tell them I'm awake—oh, no!   155

The fact is I am getting a little afraid of John.

He seems very queer sometimes, and even Jennie has an inexplicable look.

It strikes me occasionally, just as a scientific hypothesis, that perhaps it is the paper!

I have watched John when he did not know I was looking, and come into the room suddenly on the most innocent excuses, and I've caught him several times *looking at the paper!* And Jennie too. I caught Jennie with her hand on it once.

She didn't know I was in the room, and when I asked her in a quiet, a very   160
quiet voice, with the most restrained manner possible, what she was doing with the paper, she turned around as if she had been caught stealing, and looked quite angry—asked me why I should frighten her so!

arabesque: a type of ornamental style (Arabic in origin) that uses flowers, foliage, fruit, or other figures to create an intricate pattern of interlocking shapes and lines.

Then she said that the paper stained everything it touched, that she had found yellow smooches° on all my clothes and John's and she wished we would be more careful!

Did not that sound innocent? But I know she was studying that pattern, and I am determined that nobody shall find it out but myself!

Life is very much more exciting now than it used to be. You see, I have something more to expect, to look forward to, to watch. I really do eat better, and am more quiet than I was.

John is so pleased to see me improve! He laughed a little the other day, and said I seemed to be flourishing in spite of my wallpaper.

I turned it off with a laugh. I had no intention of telling him it was *because* of 165
the wallpaper—he would make fun of me. He might even want to take me away.

I don't want to leave now until I have found it out. There is a week more, and I think that will be enough.

I'm feeling so much better!

I don't sleep much at night, for it is so interesting to watch developments; but I sleep a good deal during the daytime.

In the daytime it is tiresome and perplexing.

There are always new shoots on the fungus, and new shades of yellow all 170
over it. I cannot keep count of them, though I have tried conscientiously.

It is the strangest yellow, that wallpaper! It makes me think of all the yellow things I ever saw—not beautiful ones like buttercups, but old, foul, bad yellow things.

But there is something else about that paper—the smell! I noticed it the moment we came into the room, but with so much air and sun it was not bad. Now we have had a week of fog and rain, and whether the windows are open or not, the smell is here.

It creeps all over the house.

I find it hovering in the dining-room, skulking in the parlor, hiding in the hall, lying in wait for me on the stairs.

It gets into my hair. 175

Even when I go to ride, if I turn my head suddenly and surprise it—there is that smell!

Such a peculiar odor, too! I have spent hours in trying to analyze it, to find what it smelled like.

It is not bad—at first—and very gentle, but quite the subtlest, most enduring odor I ever met.

In this damp weather it is awful. I wake up in the night and find it hanging over me.

It used to disturb me at first. I thought seriously of burning the house—to 180
reach the smell.

smooches: smudges or smears.

But now I am used to it. The only thing I can think of that it is like is the *color* of the paper! A yellow smell.

There is a very funny mark on this wall, low down, near the mopboard. A streak that runs round the room. It goes behind every piece of furniture, except the bed, a long, straight, even *smooch,* as if it had been rubbed over and over.

I wonder how it was done and who did it, and what they did it for. Round and round and round—round and round and round—it makes me dizzy!

I really have discovered something at last.

Through watching so much at night, when it changes so, I have finally found out.

The front pattern *does* move—and no wonder! The woman behind shakes it!

Sometimes I think there are a great many women behind, and sometimes only one, and she crawls around fast, and her crawling shakes it all over.

Then in the very bright spots she keeps still, and in the very shady spots she just takes hold of the bars and shakes them hard.

And she is all the time trying to climb through. But nobody could climb through that pattern—it strangles so; I think that is why it has so many heads.

They get through and then the pattern strangles them off and turns them upside down, and makes their eyes white!

If those heads were covered or taken off it would not be half so bad.

I think that woman gets out in the daytime!

And I'll tell you why—privately—I've seen her!

I can see her out of every one of my windows!

It is the same woman, I know, for she is always creeping, and most women do not creep by daylight.

I see her in that long shaded lane, creeping up and down. I see her in those dark grape arbors, creeping all round the garden.

I see her on that long road under the trees, creeping along, and when a carriage comes she hides under the blackberry vines.

I don't blame her a bit. It must be very humiliating to be caught creeping by daylight!

I always lock the door when I creep by daylight. I can't do it at night, for I know John would suspect something at once.

And John is so queer now that I don't want to irritate him. I wish he would take another room! Besides, I don't want anybody to get that woman out at night but myself.

I often wonder if I could see her out of all the windows at once.

But, turn as fast as I can, I can only see out of one at one time.

And though I always see her, she *may* be able to creep faster than I can turn! I have watched her sometimes away off in the open country, creeping as fast as a cloud shadow in a wind.

If only that top pattern could be gotten off from the under one! I mean to try it, little by little.

I have found out another funny thing, but I shan't tell it this time! It does not do to trust people too much.

There are only two more days to get this paper off, and I believe John is beginning to notice. I don't like the look in his eyes.

And I heard him ask Jennie a lot of professional questions about me. She had a very good report to give.

She said I slept a good deal in the daytime.

John knows I don't sleep very well at night, for all I'm so quiet!

He asked me all sorts of questions too, and pretended to be very loving and kind.

As if I couldn't see through him!

Still, I don't wonder he acts so, sleeping under this paper for three months.

It only interests me, but I feel sure John and Jennie are affected by it.

Hurrah! This is the last day, but it is enough. John is to stay in town over night, and won't be out until this evening.

Jennie wanted to sleep with me—the sly thing; but I told her I should undoubtedly rest better for a night all alone.

That was clever, for really I wasn't alone a bit! As soon as it was moonlight and that poor thing began to crawl and shake the pattern, I got up and ran to help her.

I pulled and she shook. I shook and she pulled, and before morning we had peeled off yards of that paper.

A strip about as high as my head and half around the room.

And then when the sun came and that awful pattern began to laugh at me, I declared I would finish it today!

We go away tomorrow, and they are moving all my furniture down again to leave things as they were before.

Jennie looked at the wall in amazement, but I told her merrily that I did it out of pure spite at the vicious thing.

She laughed and said she wouldn't mind doing it herself, but I must not get tired.

How she betrayed herself that time!

But I am here, and no person touches this paper but Me—not *alive!*

She tried to get me out of the room—it was too patent! But I said it was so quiet and empty and clean now that I believed I would lie down again and sleep all I could, and not to wake me even for dinner—I would call when I woke.

So now she is gone, and the servants are gone, and the things are gone, and there is nothing left but that great bedstead nailed down, with the canvas mattress we found on it.

We shall sleep downstairs tonight, and take the boat home tomorrow.

I quite enjoy the room, now it is bare again.

How those children did tear about here!

This bedstead is fairly gnawed!

But I must get to work.

I have locked the door and thrown the key down into the front path.

I don't want to go out, and I don't want to have anybody come in, till John comes.

I want to astonish him.

I've got a rope up here that even Jennie did not find. If that woman does get out, and tries to get away, I can tie her!

But I forgot I could not reach far without anything to stand on!

This bed will *not* move!

I tried to lift and push it until I was lame, and then I got so angry I bit off a little piece at one corner—but it hurt my teeth.

Then I peeled off all the paper I could reach standing on the floor. It sticks horribly and the pattern just enjoys it! All those strangled heads and bulbous eyes and waddling fungus growths just shriek with derision!

I am getting angry enough to do something desperate. To jump out of the window would be admirable exercise, but the bars are too strong even to try.

Besides I wouldn't do it. Of course not. I know well enough that a step like that is improper and might be misconstrued.

I don't like to *look* out of the windows even—there are so many of those creeping women, and they creep so fast.

I wonder if they all come out of that wallpaper as I did!

But I am securely fastened now by my well-hidden rope—you don't get *me* out in the road there!

I suppose I shall have to get back behind the pattern when it comes night, and that is hard!

It is so pleasant to be out in this great room and creep around as I please!

I don't want to go outside. I won't, even if Jennie asks me to.

For outside you have to creep on the ground, and everything is green instead of yellow.

But here I can creep smoothly on the floor, and my shoulder just fits in that long smooch around the wall, so I cannot lose my way.

Why, there's John at the door!

It is no use, young man, you can't open it!

How he does call and pound!

Now he's crying to Jennie for an axe.

It would be a shame to break down that beautiful door!

"John, dear!" said I in the gentlest voice. "The key is down by the front steps, under a plantain leaf!"

That silenced him for a few moments.

Then he said, very quietly indeed, "Open the door, my darling!"

"I can't," said I. "The key is down by the front door under a plantain leaf!" And then I said it again, several times, very gently and slowly, and said it so often that he had to go and see, and he got it of course, and came in. He stopped short by the door.

"What is the matter?" he cried. "For God's sake, what are you doing!"

I kept on creeping just the same, but I looked at him over my shoulder.

"I've got out at last," said I, "in spite of you and Jane. And I've pulled off most of the paper, so you can't put me back!"

Now why should that man have fainted? But he did, and right across my path by the wall, so that I had to creep over him every time!

Nathaniel Hawthorne

YOUNG GOODMAN BROWN
(1829–35)

Nathaniel Hawthorne (1804–1864) was born in the clipper-ship seaport of Salem, Massachusetts, son of a merchant captain and grandson of a judge at the notorious Salem witchcraft trials. Hawthorne takes a keen interest in New England's sin-and-brimstone Puritan past in this and many other of his stories and in The Scarlet Letter *(1848), that enduring novel of a woman taken in adultery. After college, Hawthorne lived at home and trained to be a writer. Only when his first collections* Twice-Told Tales *(1837) made money, did he feel secure enough to marry Sophia Peabody and settle in the Old Manse in Concord, Massachusetts. Three more novels followed* The Scarlet Letter: The House of the Seven Gables *(1851, a story tinged with night-*

Nathaniel Hawthorne

marish humor), The Blithedale Romance *(1852, drawn from his short, disgruntled stay at a Utopian commune, Brook Farm), and* The Marble Faun *(1860, inspired by a stay in Italy). Hawthorne wrote for children, too, retelling classic legends in* The Wonder Book *(1852) and* Tanglewood Tales *(1853). At Bowdoin College, he had been a classmate of Franklin Pierce; later, when Pierce ran for president of the United States, Hawthorne wrote his campaign biography. The victorious Pierce appointed his old friend American consul at Liverpool, England. With his contemporary Edgar Allan Poe, Hawthorne sped the transformation of the American short story from popular magazine filler into a form of art.*

Young Goodman° Brown came forth, at sunset, into the street of Salem village,° but put his head back, after crossing the threshold, to exchange a parting kiss with his young wife. And Faith, as the wife was aptly named, thrust her own pretty head into the street, letting the wind play with the pink ribbons of her cap, while she called to Goodman Brown.

"Dearest heart," whispered she, softly and rather sadly, when her lips were close to his ear, "pray thee, put off your journey until sunrise, and sleep in your

---

Goodman: title given by Puritans to a male head of a household; a farmer or other ordinary citizen.   *Salem village:* in England's Massachusetts Bay Colony.

own bed to-night. A lone woman is troubled with such dreams and such thoughts, that she's afraid of herself, sometimes. Pray, tarry with me this night, dear husband, of all nights in the year!"

"My love and my Faith," replied young Goodman Brown, "of all nights in the year, this one night must I tarry away from thee. My journey, as thou callest it, forth and back again, must needs be done 'twixt now and sunrise. What, my sweet, pretty wife, dost thou doubt me already, and we but three months married!"

"Then, God bless you!" said Faith, with the pink ribbons, "and may you find all well, when you come back."

"Amen!" cried Goodman Brown. "Say thy prayers, dear Faith, and go to bed   5
at dusk, and no harm will come to thee."

So they parted; and the young man pursued his way, until, being about to turn the corner by the meeting-house, he looked back, and saw the head of Faith still peeping after him, with a melancholy air, in spite of her pink ribbons.

"Poor little Faith!" thought he, for his heart smote him. "What a wretch am I, to leave her on such an errand! She talks of dreams, too. Methought, as she spoke, there was trouble in her face, as if a dream had warned her what work is to be done to-night. But, no, no! 'twould kill her to think it. Well; she's a blessed angel on earth; and after this one night, I'll cling to her skirts and follow her to Heaven."

With this excellent resolve for the future, Goodman Brown felt himself justified in making more haste on his present evil purpose. He had taken a dreary road, darkened by all the gloomiest trees of the forest, which barely stood aside to let the narrow path creep through, and closed immediately behind. It was all as lonely as could be; and there is this peculiarity in such a solitude, that the traveller knows not who may be concealed by the innumerable trunks and the thick boughs overhead; so that, with lonely footsteps, he may yet be passing through an unseen multitude.

"There may be a devilish Indian behind every tree," said Goodman Brown, to himself; and he glanced fearfully behind him, as he added, "What if the devil himself should be at my very elbow!"

His head being turned back, he passed a crook of the road, and looking   10
forward again, beheld the figure of a man, in grave and decent attire, seated at the foot of an old tree. He arose, at Goodman Brown's approach, and walked onward, side by side with him.

"You are late, Goodman Brown," said he. "The clock of the Old South was striking as I came through Boston; and that is full fifteen minutes agone."°

"Faith kept me back awhile," replied the young man, with a tremor in his voice, caused by the sudden appearance of his companion, though not wholly unexpected.

It was now deep dusk in the forest, and deepest in that part of it where these two were journeying. As nearly as could be discerned, the second traveller was

full fifteen minutes agone: Apparently this mystery man has traveled in a flash from Boston's Old South Church all the way to the woods beyond Salem—as the crow flies, a good sixteen miles.

about fifty years old, apparently in the same rank of life as Goodman Brown, and bearing a considerable resemblance to him, though perhaps more in expression than features. Still, they might have been taken for father and son. And yet, though the elder person was as simply clad as the younger, and as simple in manner too, he had an indescribable air of one who knew the world, and would not have felt abashed at the governor's dinner-table, or in King William's court,° were it possible that his affairs should call him thither. But the only thing about him, that could be fixed upon as remarkable, was his staff, which bore the likeness of a great black snake, so curiously wrought, that it might almost be seen to twist and wriggle itself, like a living serpent. This, of course, must have been an ocular deception, assisted by the uncertain light.

"Come, Goodman Brown!" cried his fellow-traveller, "this is dull pace for the beginning of a journey. Take my staff, if you are so soon weary."

"Friend," said the other, exchanging his slow pace for a full stop, "having   15
kept covenant by meeting thee here, it is my purpose now to return whence I came. I have scruples, touching the matter thou wot'st° of."

"Sayest thou so?" replied he of the serpent, smiling apart. "Let us walk on, nevertheless, reasoning as we go, and if I convince thee not, thou shalt turn back. We are but a little way in the forest, yet."

"Too far, too far!" exclaimed the goodman, unconsciously resuming his walk. "My father never went into the woods on such an errand, nor his father before him. We have been a race of honest men and good Christians, since the days of the martyrs.° And shall I be the first of the name of Brown, that ever took this path, and kept—"

"Such company, thou wouldst say," observed the elder person, interpreting his pause. "Well said, Goodman Brown! I have been as well acquainted with your family as with ever a one among the Puritans; and that's no trifle to say. I helped your grandfather, the constable, when he lashed the Quaker woman so smartly through the streets of Salem. And it was I that brought your father a pitch-pine knot, kindled at my own hearth, to set fire to an Indian village, in King Philip's war.° They were my good friends, both; and many a pleasant walk have we had along this path, and returned merrily after midnight. I would fain be friends with you, for their sake."

"If it be as thou sayest," replied Goodman Brown, "I marvel they never spoke of these matters. Or, verily, I marvel not, seeing that the least rumor of the sort would have driven them from New England. We are a people of prayer, and good works, to boot, and abide no such wickedness."

King William's court: back in England, where William III reigned from 1689 to 1702.   *wot'st:* know.   *days of the martyrs:* a time when many forebears of the New England Puritans had given their lives for religious convictions—when Mary I (Mary Tudor, nicknamed "Bloody Mary"), queen of England from 1553 to 1558, briefly reestablished the Roman Catholic Church in England and launched a campaign of persecution against Protestants.   *King Philip's war:* Metacomet, or King Philip (as the English called him), chief of the Wampanoag Indians, had led a bitter, widespread uprising of several New England tribes (1675–78). Metacomet died in the war, as did one out of every ten white male colonists.

"Wickedness or not," said the traveller with the twisted staff, "I have a very   20
general acquaintance here in New England. The deacons of many a church
have drunk the communion wine with me; the selectmen, of divers towns, make
me their chairman; and a majority of the Great and General Court are firm sup-
porters of my interest. The governor and I, too—but these are state-secrets."

"Can this be so!" cried Goodman Brown, with a stare of amazement at his
undisturbed companion. "Howbeit, I have nothing to do with the governor and
council; they have their own ways, and are no rule for a simple husbandman, like
me. But, were I to go on with thee, how should I meet the eye of that good old
man, our minister, at Salem village? Oh, his voice would make me tremble, both
Sabbath-day and lecture-day!"°

Thus far, the elder traveller had listened with due gravity, but now burst
into a fit of irrepressible mirth, shaking himself so violently, that his snake-like
staff actually seemed to wriggle in sympathy.

"Ha! ha! ha!" shouted he, again and again; then composing himself, "Well,
go on, Goodman Brown, go on; but pray thee, don't kill me with laughing!"

"Well, then, to end the matter at once," said Goodman Brown, considerably
nettled, "there is my wife, Faith. It would break her dear little heart; and I'd
rather break my own!"

"Nay, if that be the case," answered the other, "e'en go thy ways, Goodman   25
Brown. I would not, for twenty old women like the one hobbling before us, that
Faith should come to any harm."

As he spoke, he pointed his staff at a female figure on the path, in whom
Goodman Brown recognized a very pious and exemplary dame, who had taught
him his catechism, in youth, and was still his moral and spiritual adviser, jointly
with the minister and Deacon Gookin.

"A marvel, truly, that Goody° Cloyse should be so far in the wilderness, at
night-fall!" said he. "But, with your leave, friend, I shall take a cut through the
woods, until we have left this Christian woman behind. Being a stranger to you,
she might ask whom I was consorting with, and whither I was going."

"Be it so," said his fellow-traveller. "Betake you to the woods, and let me
keep the path."

Accordingly, the young man turned aside, but took care to watch his companion, who advanced softly along the road, until he had come within a staff's
length of the old dame. She, meanwhile, was making the best of her way, with
singular speed for so aged a woman, and mumbling some indistinct words, a
prayer, doubtless, as she went. The traveller put forth his staff, and touched her
withered neck with what seemed the serpent's tail.

"The devil!" screamed the pious old lady.   30

---

lecture-day: a weekday when everyone had to go to church to hear a sermon or Bible-reading.
Goody: short for Goodwife, title for a married woman of ordinary station. In his story,
Hawthorne borrows from history the names of two "Goodys"—Goody Cloyse and Goody
Cory—and one unmarried woman, Martha Carrier. In 1692 Hawthorne's great-grandfather,
John Hathorne, a judge in the Salem witchcraft trials, had condemned all three to be hanged.

"Then Goody Cloyse knows her old friend?" observed the traveller, confronting her, and leaning on his writhing stick.

"Ah, forsooth, and is it your worship, indeed?" cried the good dame. "Yea, truly is it, and in the very image of my old gossip,° Goodman Brown, the grandfather of the silly fellow that now is. But—would your worship believe it?—my broomstick hath strangely disappeared, stolen, as I suspect, by that unhanged witch, Goody Cory, and that, too, when I was all anointed with the juice of smallage and cinquefoil and wolf's bane—"°

"Mingled with fine wheat and the fat of a new-born babe," said the shape of old Goodman Brown.

"Ah, your worship knows the receipt," cried the old lady, cackling aloud. "So, as I was saying, being all ready for the meeting, and no horse to ride on, I made up my mind to foot it; for they tell me, there is a nice young man to be taken into communion to-night. But now your good worship will lend me your arm, and we shall be there in a twinkling."

"That can hardly be," answered her friend. "I may not spare you my arm, 35 Goody Cloyse, but here is my staff, if you will."

So saying, he threw it down at her feet, where, perhaps, it assumed life, being one of the rods which its owner had formerly lent to the Egyptian Magi.° Of this fact, however, Goodman Brown could not take cognizance. He had cast up his eyes in astonishment, and looking down again, beheld neither Goody Cloyse nor the serpentine staff, but his fellow-traveller alone, who waited for him as calmly as if nothing had happened.

"That old woman taught me my catechism!" said the young man; and there was a world of meaning in this simple comment.

They continued to walk onward, while the elder traveller exhorted his companion to make good speed and persevere in the path, discoursing so aptly, that his arguments seemed rather to spring up in the bosom of his auditor, than to be suggested by himself. As they went, he plucked a branch of maple, to serve for a walking-stick, and began to strip it of the twigs and little boughs, which were wet with evening dew. The moment his fingers touched them, they became strangely withered and dried up, as with a week's sunshine. Thus the pair proceeded, at a good free pace, until suddenly, in a gloomy hollow of the road, Goodman Brown sat himself down on the stump of a tree, and refused to go any farther.

"Friend," said he, stubbornly, "my mind is made up. Not another step will I budge on this errand. What if a wretched old woman do choose to go to the devil, when I thought she was going to Heaven! Is that any reason why I should quit my dear Faith, and go after her?"

"You will think better of this, by-and-by," said his acquaintance, compos- 40 edly. "Sit here and rest yourself awhile; and when you feel like moving again, there is my staff to help you along."

---

gossip: friend or kinsman.   *smallage and cinquefoil and wolf's bane:* wild plants—here, ingredients for a witch's brew.   *Egyptian Magi:* In the Bible, Pharaoh's wise men and sorcerers who by their magical powers changed their rods into live serpents. (This incident, part of the story of Moses and Aaron, is related in Exodus 7:8–12.)

Without more words, he threw his companion the maple stick, and was as speedily out of sight, as if he had vanished into the deepening gloom. The young man sat a few moments, by the road-side, applauding himself greatly, and thinking with how clear a conscience he should meet the minister, in his morning-walk, nor shrink from the eye of good old Deacon Gookin. And what calm sleep would be his, that very night, which was to have been spent so wickedly, but purely and sweetly now, in the arms of Faith! Amidst these pleasant and praiseworthy meditations, Goodman Brown heard the tramp of horses along the road, and deemed it advisable to conceal himself within the verge of the forest, conscious of the guilty purpose that had brought him thither, though now so happily turned from it.

On came the hoof-tramps and the voices of the riders, two grave old voices, conversing soberly as they drew near. These mingled sounds appeared to pass along the road, within a few yards of the young man's hiding-place; but owing, doubtless, to the depth of the gloom, at that particular spot, neither the travellers nor their steeds were visible. Though their figures brushed the small boughs by the way-side, it could not be seen that they intercepted, even for a moment, the faint gleam from the strip of bright sky, athwart which they must have passed. Goodman Brown alternately crouched and stood on tip-toe, pulling aside the branches, and thrusting forth his head as far as he durst, without discerning so much as a shadow. It vexed him the more, because he could have sworn, were such a thing possible, that he recognized the voices of the minister and Deacon Gookin, jogging along quietly, as they were wont to do, when bound to some ordination or ecclesiastical council. While yet within hearing, one of the riders stopped to pluck a switch.

"Of the two, reverend Sir," said the voice like the deacon's, "I had rather miss an ordination-dinner than to-night's meeting. They tell me that some of our community are to be here from Falmouth and beyond, and others from Connecticut and Rhode Island; besides several of the Indian powows,° who, after their fashion, know almost as much deviltry as the best of us. Moreover, there is a goodly young woman to be taken into communion."

"Mighty well, Deacon Gookin!" replied the solemn old tones of the minister. "Spur up, or we shall be late. Nothing can be done, you know, until I get on the ground."

The hoofs clattered again, and the voices, talking so strangely in the empty 45
air, passed on through the forest, where no church had ever been gathered, nor solitary Christian prayed. Whither, then, could these holy men be journeying, so deep into the heathen wilderness? Young Goodman Brown caught hold of a tree, for support, being ready to sink down on the ground, faint and overburdened with the heavy sickness of his heart. He looked up to the sky, doubting whether there really was a Heaven above him. Yet, there was the blue arch, and the stars brightening in it.

"With Heaven above, and Faith below, I will yet stand firm against the devil!" cried Goodman Brown.

powows: Indian priests or medicine men.

While he still gazed upward, into the deep arch of the firmament, and had lifted his hands to pray, a cloud, though no wind was stirring, hurried across the zenith, and hid the brightening stars. The blue sky was still visible, except directly overhead, where this black mass of cloud was sweeping swiftly northward. Aloft in the air, as if from the depths of the cloud, came a confused and doubtful sound of voices. Once, the listener fancied that he could distinguish the accents of town's-people of his own, men and women, both pious and ungodly, many of whom he had met at the communion-table, and had seen others rioting at the tavern. The next moment, so indistinct were the sounds, he doubted whether he had heard aught but the murmur of the old forest, whispering without a wind. Then came a stronger swell of those familiar tones, heard daily in the sunshine, at Salem village, but never, until now, from a cloud of night. There was one voice, of a young woman, uttering lamentations, yet with an uncertain sorrow, and entreating for some favor, which, perhaps, it would grieve her to obtain. And all the unseen multitude, both saints and sinners, seemed to encourage her onward.

"Faith!" shouted Goodman Brown, in a voice of agony and desperation; and the echoes of the forest mocked him, crying—"Faith! Faith!" as if bewildered wretches were seeking her, all through the wilderness.

The cry of grief, rage, and terror, was yet piercing the night, when the unhappy husband held his breath for a response. There was a scream, drowned immediately in a louder murmur of voices, fading into far-off laughter, as the dark cloud swept away, leaving the clear and silent sky above Goodman Brown. But something fluttered lightly down through the air, and caught on the branch of a tree. The young man seized it, and beheld a pink ribbon.

"My Faith is gone!" cried he, after one stupefied moment. "There is no 50 good on earth; and sin is but a name. Come, devil! for to thee is this world given."

And maddened with despair, so that he laughed loud and long, did Goodman Brown grasp his staff and set forth again, at such a rate, that he seemed to fly along the forest-path, rather than to walk or run. The road grew wilder and drearier, and more faintly traced, and vanished at length, leaving him in the heart of the dark wilderness, still rushing onward, with the instinct that guides mortal man to evil. The whole forest was peopled with frightful sounds; the creaking of the trees, the howling of wild beasts, and the yell of Indians; while, sometimes, the wind tolled like a distant church-bell, and sometimes gave a broad roar around the traveller, as if all Nature were laughing him to scorn. But he was himself the chief horror of the scene, and shrank not from its other horrors.

"Ha! ha! ha!" roared Goodman Brown, when the wind laughed at him. "Let us hear which will laugh loudest! Think not to frighten me with your deviltry! Come witch, come wizard, come Indian powow, come devil himself! and here comes Goodman Brown. You may as well fear him as he fear you!"

In truth, all through the haunted forest, there could be nothing more frightful than the figure of Goodman Brown. On he flew, among the black pines, brandishing his staff with frenzied gestures, now giving vent to an inspiration of horrid blasphemy, and now shouting forth such laughter, as set all the echoes of the forest laughing like demons around him. The fiend in his own shape is less hideous, than when he rages in the breast of man. Thus sped the demoniac on his course, until, quivering among the trees, he saw a red light before him, as when the felled trunks and branches of a clearing have been set on fire, and throw up their lurid blaze against the sky, at the hour of midnight. He paused, in a lull of the tempest that had driven him onward, and heard the swell of what seemed a hymn, rolling solemnly from a distance, with the weight of many voices. He knew the tune; it was a familiar one in the choir of the village meeting-house. The verse died heavily away, and was lengthened by a chorus, not of human voices, but of all the sounds of the benighted wilderness, pealing in awful harmony together. Goodman Brown cried out; and his cry was lost to his own ear, by its unison with the cry of the desert.

In the interval of silence, he stole forward, until the light glared full upon his eyes. At one extremity of an open space, hemmed in by the dark wall of the forest, arose a rock, bearing some rude, natural resemblance either to an altar or a pulpit, and surrounded by four blazing pines, their tops aflame, their stems untouched, like candles at an evening meeting. The mass of foliage, that had overgrown the summit of the rock, was all on fire, blazing high into the night, and fitfully illuminating the whole field. Each pendent twig and leafy festoon was in a blaze. As the red light arose and fell, a numerous congregation alternately shone forth, then disappeared in shadow, and again grew, as it were, out of the darkness, peopling the heart of the solitary woods at once.

"A grave and dark-clad company!" quoth Goodman Brown. 55

In truth, they were such. Among them, quivering to-and-fro, between gloom and splendor, appeared faces that would be seen, next day, at the council-board of the province, and others which, Sabbath after Sabbath, looked devoutly heavenward, and benignantly over the crowded pews, from the holiest pulpits in the land. Some affirm that the lady of the governor was there. At least, there were high dames well known to her, and wives of honored husbands, and widows, a great multitude, and ancient maidens, all of excellent repute, and fair young girls, who trembled, lest their mothers should espy them. Either the sudden gleams of light, flashing over the obscure field, bedazzled Goodman Brown, or he recognized a score of the church-members of Salem village, famous for their especial sanctity. Good old Deacon Gookin had arrived, and waited at the skirts of that venerable saint, his revered pastor. But, irreverently consorting with these grave, reputable, and pious people, these elders of the church, these chaste dames and dewy virgins, there were men of dissolute lives and women of spotted fame, wretches given over to all mean and filthy vice, and suspected even of horrid crimes. It was strange to see, that the good shrank not from the wicked, nor were the sinners abashed by the saints. Scattered, also, among their pale-faced enemies, were the Indian priests, or powows, who had often scared their native forest with more hideous incantations than any known to English witchcraft.

"But, where is Faith?" thought Goodman Brown; and, as hope came into his heart, he trembled.

Another verse of the hymn arose, a slow and mournful strain, such as the pious love, but joined to words which expressed all that our nature can conceive of sin, and darkly hinted at far more. Unfathomable to mere mortals is the lore of fiends. Verse after verse was sung, and still the chorus of the desert swelled between, like the deepest tone of a mighty organ. And, with the final peal of that dreadful anthem, there came a sound, as if the roaring wind, the rushing streams, the howling beasts, and every other voice of the unconverted wilderness, were mingling and according with the voice of guilty man, in homage to the prince of all. The four blazing pines threw up a loftier flame, and obscurely discovered shapes and visages of horror on the smoke-wreaths, above the impious assembly. At the same moment, the fire on the rock shot redly forth, and formed a glowing arch above its base, where now appeared a figure. With reverence be it spoken, the figure bore no slight similitude, both in garb and manner, to some grave divine of the New England churches.

"Bring forth the converts!" cried a voice, that echoed through the field and rolled into the forest.

At the word, Goodman Brown stepped forth from the shadow of the trees, and approached the congregation, with whom he felt a loathful brotherhood, by the sympathy of all that was wicked in his heart. He could have well nigh sworn, that the shape of his own dead father beckoned him to advance, looking downward from a smoke-wreath, while a woman, with dim features of despair, threw out her hand to warn him back. Was it his mother? But he had no power to retreat one step, nor to resist, even in thought, when the minister and good old Deacon Gookin seized his arms, and led him to the blazing rock. Thither came also the slender form of a veiled female, led between Goody Cloyse, that pious teacher of the catechism, and Martha Carrier, who had received the devil's promise to be queen of hell. A rampant hag was she! And there stood the proselytes,° beneath the canopy of fire.

"Welcome, my children," said the dark figure, "to the communion of your race! Ye have found, thus young, your nature and your destiny. My children, look behind you!"

They turned; and flashing forth, as it were, in a sheet of flame, the fiend-worshippers were seen; the smile of welcome gleamed darkly on every visage.

"There," resumed the sable form, "are all whom ye have reverenced from youth. Ye deemed them holier than yourselves, and shrank from your own sin, contrasting it with their lives of righteousness, and prayerful aspirations heavenward. Yet, here are they all, in my worshipping assembly! This night it shall be granted you to know their secret deeds; how hoary-bearded elders of the church have whispered wanton words to the young maids of their households; how many a woman, eager for widow's weeds, has given her husband a drink at bedtime, and let him sleep his last sleep in her bosom; how beardless youths have made haste to inherit their fathers' wealth; and how fair damsels—blush not, sweet ones!—have dug little graves in the garden, and bidden me, the sole guest, to an infant's funeral. By the sympathy of your human hearts for sin, ye shall

proselytes: new converts.

scent out all the places—whether in church, bed-chamber, street, field, or forest—where crime has been committed, and shall exult to behold the whole earth one stain of guilt, one mighty bloodspot. Far more than this! It shall be yours to penetrate, in every bosom, the deep mystery of sin, the fountain of all wicked arts, and which inexhaustibly supplies more evil impulses than human power—than my power, at its utmost!—can make manifest in deeds. And now, my children, look upon each other."

They did so; and, by the blaze of the hell-kindled torches, the wretched man beheld his Faith, and the wife her husband, trembling before that unhallowed altar.

"Lo! there ye stand, my children," said the figure, in a deep and solemn tone, almost sad, with its despairing awfulness, as if his once angelic nature could yet mourn for our miserable race. "Depending upon one another's hearts, ye had still hoped, that virtue were not all a dream. Now are ye undeceived! Evil is the nature of mankind. Evil must be your only happiness. Welcome, again, my children, to the communion of your race!"   65

"Welcome!" repeated the fiend-worshippers, in one cry of despair and triumph.

And there they stood, the only pair, as it seemed, who were yet hesitating on the verge of wickedness, in this dark world. A basin was hollowed, naturally, in the rock. Did it contain water, reddened by the lurid light? or was it blood? or, perchance, a liquid flame? Herein did the Shape of Evil dip his hand, and prepare to lay the mark of baptism upon their foreheads, that they might be partakers of the mystery of sin, more conscious of the secret guilt of others, both in deed and thought, than they could now be of their own. The husband cast one look at his pale wife, and Faith at him. What polluted wretches would the next glance show them to each other, shuddering alike at what they disclosed and what they saw!

"Faith! Faith!" cried the husband. "Look up to Heaven, and resist the Wicked one!"

Whether Faith obeyed, he knew not. Hardly had he spoken, when he found himself amid calm night and solitude, listening to a roar of the wind, which died heavily away through the forest. He staggered against the rock and felt it chill and damp, while a hanging twig, that had been all on fire, besprinkled his cheek with the coldest dew.

The next morning, young Goodman Brown came slowly into the street of   70 Salem village, staring around him like a bewildered man. The good old minister was taking a walk along the grave-yard, to get an appetite for breakfast and meditate his sermon, and bestowed a blessing, as he passed, on Goodman Brown. He shrank from the venerable saint, as if to avoid an anathema.° Old Deacon Goodkin was at domestic worship, and the holy words of his prayer were heard through the open window. "What God doth the wizard pray to?" quoth Goodman Brown. Goody Cloyse, that excellent old Christian, stood in the early

anathema: an official curse, a decree that casts one out of a church and bans him from receiving the sacraments.

sunshine, at her own lattice, catechizing a little girl, who had brought her a pint of morning's milk. Goodman Brown snatched away the child, as from the grasp of the fiend himself. Turning the corner by the meeting-house, he spied the head of Faith, with the pink ribbons, gazing anxiously forth, and bursting into such joy at sight of him, that she skipt along the street, and almost kissed her husband before the whole village. But, Goodman Brown looked sternly and sadly into her face, and passed on without a greeting.

Had Goodman Brown fallen asleep in the forest, and only dreamed a wild dream of a witch-meeting?

Be it so, if you will. But, alas! it was a dream of evil omen for young Goodman Brown. A stern, a sad, a darkly meditative, a distrustful, if not a desperate man, did he become, from the night of that fearful dream. On the Sabbath-day, when the congregation were singing a holy psalm, he could not listen, because an anthem of sin rushed loudly upon his ear, and drowned all the blessed strain. When the minister spoke from the pulpit, with power and fervid eloquence, and, with his hand on the open Bible, of the sacred truths of our religion, and of saint-like lives and triumphant deaths, and of future bliss or misery unutterable, then did Goodman Brown turn pale, dreading, lest the roof should thunder down upon the gray blasphemer and his hearers. Often, awakening suddenly at midnight, he shrank from the bosom of Faith, and at morning or eventide, when the family knelt down at prayer, he scowled, and muttered to himself, and gazed sternly at his wife, and turned away. And when he had lived long, and was borne to his grave, a hoary corpse, followed by Faith, an aged woman, and children and grandchildren, a goodly procession, besides neighbors, not a few, they carved no hopeful verse upon his tombstone; for his dying hour was gloom.

Zora Neale Hurston

SWEAT   1926

Zora Neale Hurston (1901?–1960) was born in Eatonville, Florida, but no record of her actual date of birth exists (best guesses range from 1891 to 1901). Hurston was one of eight children. Her father, a carpenter and Baptist preacher, was also the three-term mayor of Eatonville, the first all-black town incorporated in the United States. When Hurston's mother died in 1912, the father moved the children from one relative to another. Consequently, Hurston never finished grammar school, although in 1918 she began taking classes at Howard University, paying her way through school by working as a manicurist and maid. While at Howard, she published her first story. In early 1925 she moved to New York, arriving with "$1.50, no job, no friends, and a lot of hope." She

Zora Neale Hurston

soon became an important member of the Harlem Renaissance, a group of young black artists (including Langston Hughes, Countee Cullen, Jean Toomer, and Claude McKay) who sought "spiritual emancipation" for African Americans by exploring black heritage and identity in the arts. Hurston eventually became, according to critic Laura Zaidman, "the most prolific black American woman writer of her time." In 1925 she became the first black student at Barnard College, where she completed a B.A. in anthropology. Hurston's most famous story, "Sweat," appeared in the only issue of Fire!!, a 1926 avant-garde Harlem Renaissance magazine edited by Hurston, Hughes, and Wallace Thurman. This powerful story of an unhappy marriage turned murderous was particularly noteworthy for having the characters speak in the black country dialect of Hurston's native Florida. Hurston achieved only modest success during her lifetime, despite the publication of her memorable novel, Their Eyes Were Watching God (1937), and her many contributions to the study of African American folklore. She died, poor and neglected, in a Florida welfare home and was buried in an unmarked grave. In 1973 novelist Alice Walker erected a gravestone for her carved with the words:

Zora Neale Hurston
"A Genius of the South"
1901–1960
Novelist, Folklorist
Anthropologist

I

It was eleven o'clock of a Spring night in Florida. It was Sunday. Any other night, Delia Jones would have been in bed for two hours by this time. But she was a washwoman, and Monday morning meant a great deal to her. So she collected the soiled clothes on Saturday when she returned the clean things. Sunday night after church, she sorted and put the white things to soak. It saved her almost a half-day's start. A great hamper in the bedroom held the clothes that she brought home. It was so much neater than a number of bundles lying around.

She squatted on the kitchen floor beside the great pile of clothes, sorting them into small heaps according to color, and humming a song in a mournful key, but wondering through it all where Sykes, her husband, had gone with her horse and buckboard.°

Just then something long, round, limp, and black fell upon her shoulders and slithered to the floor beside her. A great terror took hold of her. It softened her knees and dried her mouth so that it was a full minute before she could cry out or move. Then she saw that it was the big bull whip her husband liked to carry when he drove.

She lifted her eyes to the door and saw him standing there bent over with laughter at her fright. She screamed at him.

buckboard: a four-wheeled open carriage with the seat resting on a spring platform.

"Sykes, what you throw dat whip on me like dat? You know it would skeer   5
me—looks just like a snake, an' you knows how skeered Ah is of snakes."

"Course Ah knowed it! That's how come Ah done it." He slapped his leg
with his hand and almost rolled on the ground in his mirth. "If you such a big
fool dat you got to have a fit over a earth worm or a string, Ah don't keer how
bad Ah skeer you."

"You ain't got no business doing it. Gawd knows it's a sin. Some day Ah'm
gointuh drop dead from some of yo' foolishness. 'Nother thing, where you been
wid mah rig? Ah feeds dat pony. He ain't fuh you to be drivin' wid no bull whip."

"You sho' is one aggravatin' nigger woman!" he declared and stepped into
the room. She resumed her work and did not answer him at once. "Ah done tole
you time and again to keep them white folks' clothes outa dis house."

He picked up the whip and glared at her. Delia went on with her work. She
went out into the yard and returned with a galvanized tub and set it on the wash-
bench. She saw that Sykes had kicked all of the clothes together again, and now
stood in her way truculently, his whole manner hoping, *praying*, for an argument. But she walked calmly around him and commenced to re-sort the things.

"Next time, Ah'm gointer kick 'em outdoors," he threatened as he struck a   10
match along the leg of his corduroy breeches.

Delia never looked up from her work, and her thin, stooped shoulders
sagged further.

"Ah ain't for no fuss t'night Sykes. Ah just come from taking sacrament at
the church house."

He snorted scornfully. "Yeah, you just come from de church house on a
Sunday night, but heah you is gone to work on them clothes. You ain't nothing
but a hypocrite. One of them amen-corner Christians—sing, whoop, and shout,
then come home and wash white folks' clothes on the Sabbath."

He stepped roughly upon the whitest pile of things, kicking them helter-
skelter as he crossed the room. His wife gave a little scream of dismay, and
quickly gathered them together again.

"Sykes, you quit grindin' dirt into these clothes! How can Ah git through by   15
Sat'day if Ah don't start on Sunday?"

"Ah don't keer if you never git through. Anyhow, Ah done promised Gawd
and a couple of other men, Ah ain't gointer have it in mah house. Don't gimme
no lip neither, else Ah'll throw 'em out and put mah fist up side yo' head to boot."

Delia's habitual meekness seemed to slip from her shoulders like a blown
scarf. She was on her feet; her poor little body, her bare knuckly hands bravely
defying the strapping hulk before her.

"Looka heah, Sykes, you done gone too fur. Ah been married to you fur fifteen years, and Ah been takin' in washin' fur fifteen years. Sweat, sweat, sweat!
Work and sweat, cry and sweat, pray and sweat!"

"What's that got to do with me?" he asked brutally.

"What's it got to do with you, Sykes? Mah tub of suds is filled yo' belly with   20
vittles more times than yo' hands is filled it. Mah sweat is done paid for this
house and Ah reckon Ah kin keep on sweatin' in it."

She seized the iron skillet from the stove and struck a defensive pose, which act surprised him greatly, coming from her. It cowed him and he did not strike her as he usually did.

"Naw you won't," she panted, "that ole snaggle-toothed black woman you runnin' with ain't comin' heah to pile up on *mah* sweat and blood. You ain't paid for nothin' on this place, and Ah'm gointer stay right heah till Ah'm toted out foot foremost."

"Well, you better quit gittin' me riled up, else they'll be totin' you out sooner than you expect. Ah'm so tired of you Ah don't know whut to do. Gawd! How Ah hates skinny wimmen!"

A little awed by this new Delia, he sidled out of the door and slammed the back gate after him. He did not say where he had gone, but she knew too well. She knew very well that he would not return until nearly daybreak also. Her work over, she went on to bed but not to sleep at once. Things had come to a pretty pass!

She lay awake, gazing upon the debris that cluttered their matrimonial trail. Not an image left standing along the way. Anything like flowers had long ago been drowned in the salty stream that had been pressed from her heart. Her tears, her sweat, her blood. She had brought love to the union and he had brought a longing after the flesh. Two months after the wedding, he had given her the first brutal beating. She had the memory of his numerous trips to Orlando with all of his wages when he had returned to her penniless, even before the first year had passed. She was young and soft then, but now she thought of her knotty, muscled limbs, her harsh knuckly hands, and drew herself up into an unhappy little ball in the middle of the big feather bed. Too late now to hope for love, even if it were not Bertha it would be someone else. This case differed from the others only in that she was bolder than the others. Too late for everything except her little home. She had built it for her old days, and planted one by one the trees and flowers there. It was lovely to her, lovely.

Somehow, before sleep came, she found herself saying aloud: "Oh well, whatever goes over the Devil's back, is got to come under his belly. Sometime or ruther, Sykes, like everybody else, is gointer reap his sowing." After that she was able to build a spiritual earthworks° against her husband. His shells could no longer reach her. AMEN. She went to sleep and slept until he announced his presence in bed by kicking her feet and rudely snatching the covers away.

"Gimme some kivah heah, an' git yo' damn foots over on yo' own side! Ah oughter mash you in yo' mouf fuh drawing dat skillet on me."

Delia went clear to the rail without answering him. A triumphant indifference to all that he was or did.

25

spiritual earthworks: earthworks are military fortifications made of earth; here Hurston uses it metaphorically to mean Delia's emotional defenses.

II

The week was full of work for Delia as all other weeks, and Saturday found her behind her little pony, collecting and delivering clothes.

It was a hot, hot day near the end of July. The village men on Joe Clarke's porch even chewed cane listlessly. They did not hurl the cane-knots as usual. They let them dribble over the edge of the porch. Even conversation had collapsed under the heat.

"Heah come Delia Jones," Jim Merchant said, as the shaggy pony came 'round the bend of the road toward them. The rusty buckboard was heaped with baskets of crisp, clean laundry.

"Yep," Joe Lindsay agreed. "Hot or col', rain or shine, jes'ez reg'lar ez de weeks rool roun' Delia carries 'em an' fetches 'em on Sat'day."

"She better if she wanter eat," said Moss. "Syke Jones ain't wuth de shot an' powder hit would tek tuh kill 'em. Not to *huh* he ain't."

"He sho' ain't," Walter Thomas chimed in. "It's too bad, too, cause she wuz a right pretty li'l trick when he got huh. Ah'd uh mah'ied huh mahself if he hadnter beat me to it."

Delia nodded briefly at the men as she drove past.

"Too much knockin' will ruin *any* 'oman. He done beat huh 'nough tuh kill three women, let 'lone change they looks," said Elijah Moseley. "How Syke kin stommuck dat big black greasy Mogul he's layin' roun' wid, gits me. Ah swear dat eight-rock couldn't kiss a sardine can Ah done thowed out de back do' 'way las' yeah."

"Aw, she's fat, thass how come. He's allus been crazy 'bout fat women," put in Merchant. "He'd a' been tied up wid one long time ago if he could a' found one tuh have him. Did Ah tell yuh 'bout him come sidlin' roun' *mah* wife—bringin' her a basket uh peecans outa his yard fuh a present? Yessir, mah wife! She tol' him tuh take 'em right straight back home, 'cause Delia works so hard ovah dat washtub she reckon everything on de place taste lak sweat an' soapsuds. Ah jus' wisht Ah'd a' caught 'im 'roun' dere! Ah'd a' made his hips ketch on fiah down dat shell road."

"Ah know he done it, too. Ah sees 'im grinnin' at every 'oman dat passes," Walter Thomas said. "But even so, he useter eat some mighty big hunks uh humble pie tuh git dat li'l 'oman he got. She wuz ez pritty ez a speckled pup! Dat wuz fifteen years ago. He useter be so skeered uh losin' huh, she could make him do some parts of a husband's duty. Dey never wuz de same in de mind."

"There oughter be a law about him," said Lindsay. "He ain't fit tuh carry guts tuh a bear."

Clarke spoke for the first time. "Tain't no law on earth dat kin make a man be decent if it ain't in 'im. There's plenty men dat takes a wife lak dey do a joint uh sugar-cane. It's round, juicy, an' sweet when dey gits it. But dey squeeze an' grind, squeeze an' grind an' wring tell dey wring every drop uh pleasure dat's in 'em out. When dey's satisfied dat dey is wrung dry, dey treats 'em jes' lak dey do a cane-chew. Dey thows 'em away. Dey knows whut dey is doin' while dey is at it, an' hates theirselves fuh it but they keeps on hangin' after huh tell she's empty. Den dey hates huh fuh bein' a cane-chew an' in de way."

"We oughter take Syke an' dat stray 'oman uh his'n down in Lake Howell swamp an' lay on de rawhide till they cain't say Lawd a' mussy. He allus wuz uh ovahbearin niggah, but since dat white 'oman from up north done teached 'im how to run a automobile, he done got too beggety to live—an' we oughter kill 'im," Old Man Anderson advised.

A grunt of approval went around the porch. But the heat was melting their civic virtue and Elijah Moseley began to bait Joe Clarke.

"Come on, Joe, git a melon outa dere an' slice it up for yo' customers. We'se all sufferin' wid de heat. De bear's done got *me!*"

"Thass right, Joe, a watermelon is jes' whut Ah needs tuh cure de eppizu-dicks," Walter Thomas joined forces with Moseley. "Come on dere, Joe. We all is steady customers an' you ain't set us up in a long time. Ah chooses dat long, bowlegged Floridy favorite."

"A god, an' be dough. You all gimme twenty cents and slice away," Clarke   45
retorted. "Ah needs a col' slice m'self. Heah, everybody chip in. Ah'll lend y'all mah meat knife."

The money was all quickly subscribed and the huge melon brought forth. At that moment, Sykes and Bertha arrived. A determined silence fell on the porch and the melon was put away again.

Merchant snapped down the blade of his jackknife and moved toward the store door.

"Come on in, Joe, an' gimme a slab uh sow belly an' uh pound uh coffee—almost fuhgot 'twas Sat'day. Got to git on home." Most of the men left also.

Just then Delia drove past on her way home, as Sykes was ordering magnifi-cently for Bertha. It pleased him for Delia to see.

"Git whutsoever yo' heart desires, Honey. Wait a minute, Joe. Give huh two   50
bottles uh strawberry soda-water, uh quart parched ground-peas, an' a block uh chewin' gum."

With all this they left the store, with Sykes reminding Bertha that this was his town and she could have it if she wanted it.

The men returned soon after they left, and held their watermelon feast.

"Where did Syke Jones git da 'oman from nohow?" Lindsay asked.

"Ovah Apopka. Guess dey musta been cleanin' out de town when she lef'. She don't look lak a thing but a hunk uh liver wid hair on it."

"Well, she sho' kin squall," Dave Carter contributed. "When she gits ready   55
tuh laff, she jes' opens huh mouf an' latches it back tuh de las' notch. No ole granpa alligator down in Lake Bell ain't got nothin' on huh."

III

Bertha had been in town three months now. Sykes was still paying her room-rent at Della Lewis'—the only house in town that would have taken her in. Sykes took her frequently to Winter Park to "stomps." He still assured her that he was the swellest man in the state.

"Sho' you kin have dat li'l ole house soon's Ah git dat 'oman outadere. Everything b'longs tuh me an' you sho' kin have it. Ah sho' 'bominates uh skinny 'oman. Lawdy, you sho' is got one portly shape on you! You kin git *anything* you wants. Dis is *mah* town an' you sho' kin have it."

Delia's work-worn knees crawled over the earth in Gethsemane° and up the rocks of Calvary° many, many times during these months. She avoided the villagers and meeting places in her efforts to be blind and deaf. But Bertha nullified this to a degree, by coming to Delia's house to call Sykes out to her at the gate.

Delia and Sykes fought all the time now with no peaceful interludes. They slept and ate in silence. Two or three times Delia had attempted a timid friendliness, but she was repulsed each time. It was plain that the breaches must remain agape.

The sun had burned July to August. The heat streamed down like a million 60 hot arrows, smiting all things living upon the earth. Grass withered, leaves browned, snakes went blind in shedding, and men and dogs went mad. Dog days!

Delia came home one day and found Sykes there before her. She wondered, but started to go on into the house without speaking, even though he was standing in the kitchen door and she must either stoop under his arm or ask him to move. He made no room for her. She noticed a soap box beside the steps, but paid no particular attention to it, knowing that he must have brought it there. As she was stooping to pass under his outstretched arm, he suddenly pushed her backward, laughingly.

"Look in de box dere Delia, Ah done brung yuh somethin'!"

She nearly fell upon the box in her stumbling, and when she saw what it held, she all but fainted outright.

"Syke! Syke, mah Gawd! You take dat rattlesnake 'way from heah! You *gottuh*. Oh, Jesus, have mussy!"

"Ah ain't got tuh do nuthin' uh de kin'—fact is Ah ain't got tuh do nothin' 65 but die. Tain't no use uh you puttin' on airs makin' out lak you skeered uh dat snake—he's gointer stay right heah tell he die. He wouldn't bite me cause Ah knows how tuh handle 'im. Nohow he wouldn't risk breakin' out his fangs 'gin *yo* skinny laigs."

"Naw, now Syke, don't keep dat thing 'round tryin' tuh skeer me tuh death. You knows Ah'm even feared uh earth worms. Thass de biggest snake Ah evah did see. Kill 'im Syke, please."

"Doan ast me tuh do nothin' fuh yuh. Goin' 'round tryin' tuh be so damn asterperious.° Naw, Ah ain't gonna kill it. Ah think uh damn sight mo' uh him dan you! Dat's a nice snake an' anybody doan lak 'im kin jes' hit de grit."

The village soon heard that Sykes had the snake, and came to see and ask questions.

Gethsemane: the garden outside Jerusalem that was the scene of Jesus' agony and arrest (see Matthew 26:36–57); hence, a scene of great suffering. Calvary: the hill outside Jerusalem where Jesus was crucified. asterperious: haughty.

"How de hen-fire did you ketch dat six-foot rattler, Syke?" Thomas asked.

"He's full uh frogs so he cain't hardly move, thass how Ah eased up on 'm. But Ah'm a snake charmer an' knows how tuh handle 'em. Shux, dat ain't nothin'. Ah could ketch one eve'y day if Ah so wanted tuh."

"Whut he needs is a heavy hick'ry club leaned real heavy on his head. Dat's de bes' way tuh charm a rattlesnake."

"Naw, Walt, y'all jes' don't understand dese diamon' backs lak Ah do," said Sykes in a superior tone of voice.

The village agreed with Walter, but the snake stayed on. His box remained by the kitchen door with its screen wire covering. Two or three days later it had digested its meal of frogs and literally came to life. It rattled at every movement in the kitchen or the yard. One day as Delia came down the kitchen steps she saw his chalky-white fangs curved like scimitars hung in the wire meshes. This time she did not run away with averted eyes as usual. She stood for a long time in the doorway in a red fury that grew bloodier for every second that she regarded the creature that was her torment.

That night she broached the subject as soon as Sykes sat down to the table.

"Syke, Ah wants you tuh take dat snake 'way fum heah. You done starved me an' Ah put up widcher, you done beat me an Ah took dat, but you done kilt all mah insides bringin' dat varmint heah."

Sykes poured out a saucer full of coffee and drank it deliberately before he answered her.

"A whole lot Ah keer 'bout how you feels inside uh out. Dat snake ain't goin' no damn wheah till Ah gits ready fuh 'im tuh go. So fur as beatin' is concerned, yuh ain't took near all dat you gointer take ef yuh stay 'round *me*."

Delia pushed back her plate and got up from the table. "Ah hates you, Sykes," she said calmly. "Ah hates you tuh de same degree dat Ah useter love yuh. Ah done took an' took till mah belly is full up tuh mah neck. Dat's de reason Ah got mah letter fum de church an' moved mah membership tuh Woodbridge—so Ah don't haftuh take no sacrament wid yuh. Ah don't wantuh see yuh 'round me atall. Lay 'round wid dat 'oman all yuh wants tuh, but gwan 'way fum me an' mah house. Ah hates yuh lak uh suck-egg dog."

Sykes almost let the huge wad of corn bread and collard greens he was chewing fall out of his mouth in amazement. He had a hard time whipping himself up to the proper fury to try to answer Delia.

"Well, Ah'm glad you does hate me. Ah'm sho' tiahed uh you hangin' ontuh me. Ah don't want yuh. Look at yuh stringey ole neck! Yo' rawbony laigs an' arms is enough tuh cut uh man tuh death. You looks jes' lak de devvul's doll-baby tuh *me*. You cain't hate me no worse dan Ah hates you. Ah been hatin' *you* fuh years."

"Yo' ole black hide don't look lak nothin' tuh me, but uh passle uh wrinkled up rubber, wid yo' big ole yeahs flappin' on each side lak uh paih uh buzzard wings. Don't think Ah'm gointuh be run 'way fum mah house neither. Ah'm goin' tuh de white folks 'bout *you*, mah young man, de very nex' time you lay yo' han's on me. Mah cup is done run ovah." Delia said this with no signs of fear and Sykes departed from the house, threatening her, but made not the slightest move to carry out any of them.

601

That night he did not return at all, and the next day being Sunday, Delia was glad she did not have to quarrel before she hitched up her pony and drove the four miles to Woodbridge.

She stayed to the night service—"love feast"—which was very warm and full of spirit. In the emotional winds her domestic trials were borne far and wide so that she sang as she drove homeward,

> Jurden water,° black an' col
> Chills de body, not de soul
> An' Ah wantah cross Jurden in uh calm time.

She came from the barn to the kitchen door and stopped.

"Whut's de mattah, ol' Satan, you ain't kickin' up yo' racket?" She addressed the snake's box. Complete silence. She went on into the house with a new hope in its birth struggles. Perhaps her threat to go to the white folks had frightened Sykes! Perhaps he was sorry! Fifteen years of misery and suppression had brought Delia to the place where she would hope *anything* that looked towards a way over or through her wall of inhibitions.

She felt in the match-safe behind the stove at once for a match. There was 85 only one there.

"Dat niggah wouldn't fetch nothin' heah tuh save his rotten neck, but he kin run thew whut Ah brings quick enough. Now he done toted off nigh on tuh haff uh box uh matches. He done had dat 'oman heah in mah house, too."

Nobody but a woman could tell how she knew this even before she struck the match. But she did and it put her into a new fury.

Presently she brought in the tubs to put the white things to soak. This time she decided she need not bring the hamper out of the bedroom; she would go in there and do the sorting. She picked up the pot-bellied lamp and went in. The room was small and the hamper stood hard by the foot of the white iron bed. She could sit and reach through the bedposts—resting as she worked.

"*Ah wantah cross Jurden in uh calm time.*" She was singing again. The mood of the "love feast" had returned. She threw back the lid of the basket almost gaily. Then, moved by both horror and terror, she sprang back toward the door. *There lay the snake in the basket!* He moved sluggishly at first, but even as she turned round and round, jumped up and down in an insanity of fear, he began to stir vigorously. She saw him pouring his awful beauty from the basket upon the bed, then she seized the lamp and ran as fast as she could to the kitchen. The wind from the open door blew out the light and the darkness added to her terror. She sped to the darkness of the yard, slamming the door after her before she thought to set down the lamp. She did not feel safe even on the ground, so she climbed up in the hay barn.

There for an hour or more she lay sprawled upon the hay a gibbering wreck. 90

Jurden water: black Southern dialect for the River Jordan, which represents the last boundary before entering heaven. It comes from the Old Testament, when the Jews had to cross the River Jordan to reach the Promised Land.

Finally she grew quiet, and after that came coherent thought. With this stalked through her a cold, bloody rage. Hours of this. A period of introspection, a space of retrospection, then a mixture of both. Out of this an awful calm.

"Well, Ah done de bes' Ah could. If things ain't right, Gawd knows tain't mah fault."

She went to sleep—a twitch sleep—and woke up to a faint gray sky. There was a loud hollow sound below. She peered out. Sykes was at the wood-pile, demolishing a wire-covered box.

He hurried to the kitchen door, but hung outside there some minutes before he entered, and stood some minutes more inside before he closed it after him.

The gray in the sky was spreading. Delia descended without fear now, and   95
crouched beneath the low bedroom window. The drawn shade shut out the dawn, shut in the night. But the thin walls held back no sound.

"Dat ol' scratch° is woke up now!" She mused at the tremendous whirr inside, which every woodsman knows, is one of the sound illusions. The rattler is a ventriloquist. His whirr sounds to the right, to the left, straight ahead, behind, close under foot—everywhere but where it is. Woe to him who guesses wrong unless he is prepared to hold up his end of the argument! Sometimes he strikes without rattling at all.

Inside, Sykes heard nothing until he knocked a pot lid off the stove while trying to reach the match-safe in the dark. He had emptied his pockets at Bertha's.

The snake seemed to wake up under the stove and Sykes made a quick leap into the bedroom. In spite of the gin he had had, his head was clearing now.

"Mah Gawd!" he chattered, "ef Ah could on'y strack uh light!"

The rattling ceased for a moment as he stood paralyzed. He waited. It   100
seemed that the snake waited also.

"Oh, fuh de light! Ah thought he'd be too sick"—Sykes was muttering to himself when the whirr began again, closer, right underfoot this time. Long before this, Sykes' ability to think had been flattened down to primitive instinct and he leaped—onto the bed.

Outside Delia heard a cry that might have come from a maddened chimpanzee, a stricken gorilla. All the terror, all the horror, all the rage that man possibly could express, without a recognizable human sound.

A tremendous stir inside there, another series of animal screams, the intermittent whirr of the reptile. The shade torn violently down from the window, letting in the red dawn, a huge brown hand seizing the window stick, great dull blows upon the wooden floor punctuating the gibberish of sound long after the rattle of the snake had abruptly subsided. All this Delia could see and hear from her place beneath the window, and it made her ill. She crept over to the four o'-clocks and stretched herself on the cool earth to recover.

scratch: a folk expression for the devil.

She lay there. "Delia, Delia!" She could hear Sykes calling in a most despairing tone as one who expected no answer. The sun crept on up, and he called. Delia could not move—her legs had gone flabby. She never moved, he called, and the sun kept rising.

"Mah Gawd!" She heard him moan, "Mah Gawd fum Heben!" She heard him stumbling about and got up from her flower-bed. The sun was growing warm. As she approached the door she heard him call out hopefully, "Delia, is dat you Ah heah?"   105

She saw him on his hands and knees as soon as she reached the door. He crept an inch or two toward her—all that he was able, and she saw his horribly swollen neck and his one open eye shining with hope. A surge of pity too strong to support bore her away from that eye that must, could not, fail to see the tubs. He would see the lamp. Orlando with its doctors was too far. She could scarcely reach the chinaberry tree, where she waited in the growing heat while inside she knew the cold river was creeping up and up to extinguish that eye which must know by now that she knew.

Kazuo Ishiguro

A FAMILY SUPPER   1982

Kazuo Ishiguro

Born in Nagasaki, Japan, in 1954, Kazuo Ishiguro moved to England in 1960, while still a child. He completed his education there, graduating from the University of Kent and then receiving an M.A. in creative writing from the University of East Anglia. In his late teens he had the unusual job of grouse-beating for the Queen Mother at Balmoral Castle in Scotland, but after university went on to hone his skill for social observation more directly, as a social worker, first in Scotland and later in West London. Ishiguro became a full-time writer in 1983, following the successful reception of his first novel, A Pale View of Hills *(1982). The book won the Royal Society of Literature's Winifred Holtby Award for the best first novel of the year, and it was soon translated into more than ten languages. It is written in the voice of a Japanese woman living in England, who had given birth to a daughter in Nagasaki following the war. Her recollections of this period are tinged with the bleakness of the postwar years and with the understanding that her own choices and the tragedies attending war were responsible for her daughter's suicide. In a comment that could be applied equally well to Ishiguro's later work, the critic Edith Milton noted, "In this book . . . what is stated is often less important than what is left unsaid." Ishiguro's second novel,* An Artist of the Floating

World (1986), *received a more significant prize, the Whitbread Book of the Year Award (Britain's largest cash prize for literature), but his greatest success came with* The Remains of the Day, *which in 1989 won Great Britain's most prestigious literary award, the Booker Prize, and was made into an Academy Award-winning film in 1993. Ishiguro's two most recent novels are* The Unconsoled (1995) *and* When We Were Orphans (2000).

Ishiguro is not a prolific writer. He has written only five novels in twenty years, along with a handful of short stories, most notably "A Family Supper," which like An Artist of the Floating World, *is set in Japan. "I had very strong emotional relationships in Japan that were broken at a formative age," he has confided. "There's this other life I might have had."*

Fugu is a fish caught off the Pacific shores of Japan. The fish has held a special significance for me ever since my mother died through eating one. The poison resides in the sexual glands of the fish, inside two fragile bags. When preparing the fish, these bags must be removed with caution, for any clumsiness will result in the poison leaking into the veins. Regrettably, it is not easy to tell whether or not this operation has been carried out successfully. The proof is, as it were, in the eating.

Fugu poisoning is hideously painful and almost always fatal. If the fish has been eaten during the evening, the victim is usually overtaken by pain during his sleep. He rolls about in agony for a few hours and is dead by morning. The fish became extremely popular in Japan after the war. Until stricter regulations were imposed, it was all the rage to perform the hazardous gutting operation in one's own kitchen, then to invite neighbors and friends round for the feast.

At the time of my mother's death, I was living in California. My relationship with my parents had become somewhat strained around that period, and consequently I did not learn of the circumstances surrounding her death until I returned to Tokyo two years later. Apparently, my mother had always refused to eat fugu, but on this particular occasion she had made an exception, having been invited by an old schoolfriend whom she was anxious not to offend. It was my father who supplied me with the details as we drove from the airport to his home in the Kamakura district. When we finally arrived, it was nearing the end of a sunny autumn day.

"Did you eat on the plane?" my father asked. We were sitting on the tatami floor of his tea-room.

"They gave me a light snack."   5

"You must be hungry. We'll eat as soon as Kikuko arrives."

My father was a formidable-looking man with a large stony jaw and furious black eyebrows. I think now in retrospect that he much resembled Chou En-lai, although he would not have cherished such a comparison, being particularly proud of the pure samurai blood that ran in the family. His general presence was not one which encouraged relaxed conversation; neither were things helped much by his odd way of stating each remark as if it were the concluding one. In fact, as I sat opposite him that afternoon, a boyhood memory came back to me of the time he had struck me several times around the head for "chattering like an old woman." Inevitably, our conversation since my arrival at the airport had been punctuated by long pauses.

"I'm sorry to hear about the firm," I said when neither of us had spoken for some time. He nodded gravely.

"In fact the story didn't end there," he said. "After the firm's collapse, Watanabe killed himself. He didn't wish to live with the disgrace."

"I see."

"We were partners for seventeen years. A man of principle and honor. I re- 10
spected him very much."

"Will you go into business again?" I said.

"I am—in retirement. I'm too old to involve myself in new ventures now. Business these days has become so different. Dealing with foreigners. Doing things their way. I don't understand how we've come to this. Neither did Watanabe." He sighed. "A fine man. A man of principle."

The tea-room looked out over the garden. From where I sat I could make out the ancient well which as a child I had believed haunted. It was just visible now through the thick foliage. The sun had sunk low and much of the garden had fallen into shadow.

"I'm glad in any case that you've decided to come back," my father said. 15
"More than a short visit, I hope."

"I'm not sure what my plans will be."

"I for one am prepared to forget the past. Your mother too was always ready to welcome you back—upset as she was by your behavior."

"I appreciate your sympathy. As I say, I'm not sure what my plans are."

"I've come to believe now that there were no evil intentions in your mind," my father continued. "You were swayed by certain—influences. Like so many others."

"Perhaps we should forget it, as you suggest."

"As you will. More tea?" 20

Just then, a girl's voice came echoing through the house.

"At last." My father rose to his feet. "Kikuko has arrived."

Despite our difference in years, my sister and I had always been close. Seeing me again seemed to make her excessively excited and for a while she did nothing but giggle nervously. But she calmed down somewhat when my father started to question her about Osaka and the university. She answered him with short formal replies. She in turn asked me a few questions, but she seemed inhibited by the fear that her questions might lead to awkward topics. After a while, the conversation had become even sparser than prior to Kikuko's arrival. Then my father stood up, saying: "I must attend to supper. Please excuse me for being burdened down by such matters. Kikuko will look after you."

My sister relaxed quite visibly once he had left the room. Within a few min- 25
utes, she was chatting freely about her friends in Osaka and about her classes at university. Then quite suddenly she decided we should walk in the garden and went striding out onto the veranda. We put on some straw sandals that had been left along the veranda rail and stepped out into the garden. The daylight had almost gone.

"I've been dying for a smoke for the last half-hour," she said, lighting a cigarette.

"Then why didn't you smoke?"

She made a furtive gesture back toward the house, then grinned mischievously.

"Oh I see," I said.

"Guess what? I've got a boyfriend now."

"Oh yes?"

"Except I'm wondering what to do. I haven't made up my mind yet."

"Quite understandable."

"You see, he's making plans to go to America. He wants me to go with him as soon as I finish studying."

"I see. And you want to go to America?"

"If we go, we're going to hitch-hike." Kikuko waved a thumb in front of my face. "People say it's dangerous, but I've done it in Osaka and it's fine."

"I see. So what is it you're unsure about?"

We were following a narrow path that wound through the shrubs and finished by the old well. As we walked, Kikuko persisted in taking unnecessarily theatrical puffs on her cigarette.

"Well. I've got lots of friends now in Osaka. I like it there. I'm not sure I want to leave them all behind just yet. And Suichi—I like him, but I'm not sure I want to spend so much time with him. Do you understand?"

"Oh perfectly."

She grinned again, then skipped on ahead of me until she reached the well. "Do you remember," she said, as I came walking up to her, "how you used to say this well was haunted?"

"Yes, I remember."

We both peered over the side.

"Mother always told me it was the old woman from the vegetable store you'd seen that night," she said. "But I never believed her and never came out here alone."

"Mother used to tell me that too. She even told me once the old woman had confessed to being the ghost. Apparently she'd been taking a short cut through our garden. I imagine she had some trouble clambering over these walls."

Kikuko gave a giggle. She then turned her back to the well, casting her gaze about the garden.

"Mother never really blamed you, you know," she said, in a new voice. I remained silent. "She always used to say to me how it was their fault, hers and Father's, for not bringing you up correctly. She used to tell me how much more careful they'd been with me, and that's why I was so good." She looked up and the mischievous grin had returned to her face. "Poor Mother," she said.

"Yes. Poor Mother."

"Are you going back to California?"

"I don't know. I'll have to see."

"What happened to—to her? To Vicki?"

"That's all finished with," I said. "There's nothing much left for me now in California."

"Do you think I ought to go there?"

"Why not? I don't know. You'll probably like it." I glanced toward the house. "Perhaps we'd better go in soon. Father might need a hand with the supper."

But my sister was once more peering down into the well. "I can't see any ghosts," she said. Her voice echoed a little.

"Is Father very upset about his firm collapsing?"

"Don't know. You can never tell with Father." Then suddenly she straightened up and turned to me. "Did he tell you about old Watanabe? What he did?"

"I heard he committed suicide."

"Well, that wasn't all. He took his whole family with him. His wife and his two little girls."

"Oh, yes?"

"Those two beautiful little girls. He turned on the gas while they were all asleep. Then he cut his stomach with a meat knife."

"Yes, Father was just telling me how Watanabe was a man of principle."

"Sick." My sister turned back to the well.

"Careful. You'll fall right in."

"I can't see any ghost," she said. "You were lying to me all that time."

"But I never said it lived down the well."

"Where is it, then?"

We both looked around at the trees and shrubs. The light in the garden had grown very dim. Eventually I pointed to a small clearing some ten yards away.

"Just there I saw it. Just there."

We stared at the spot.

"What did it look like?"

"I couldn't see very well. It was dark."

"But you must have seen something."

"It was an old woman. She was just standing there, watching me."

We kept staring at the spot as if mesmerized.

"She was wearing a white kimono," I said. "Some of her hair had come undone. It was blowing around a little."

Kikuko pushed her elbow against my arm. "Oh be quiet. You're trying to frighten me all over again." She trod on the remains of her cigarette, then for a brief moment stood regarding it with a perplexed expression. She kicked some pine needles over it, then once more displayed her grin. "Let's see if supper's ready," she said.

We found my father in the kitchen. He gave us a quick glance, then carried on with what he was doing.

"Father's become quite a chef since he's had to manage on his own," Kikuko said with a laugh. He turned and looked at my sister coldly.

"Hardly a skill I'm proud of," he said. "Kikuko, come here and help."

For some moments my sister did not move. Then she stepped forward and took an apron hanging from a drawer.

"Just these vegetables need cooking now," he said to her. "The rest just needs watching." Then he looked up and regarded me strangely for some seconds. "I expect you want to look around the house," he said eventually. He put down the chopsticks he had been holding. "It's a long time since you've seen it."

As we left the kitchen I glanced back toward Kikuko, but her back was turned.

"She's a good girl," my father said quietly.

I followed my father from room to room. I had forgotten how large the 85
house was. A panel would slide open and another room would appear. But the rooms were all startlingly empty. In one of the rooms the lights did not come on, and we stared at the stark walls and tatami in the pale light that came from the windows.

"This house is too large for a man to live in alone," my father said. "I don't have much use for most of these rooms now."

But eventually my father opened the door to a room packed full of books and papers. There were flowers in vases and pictures on the walls. Then I noticed something on a low table in the corner of the room. I came nearer and saw it was a plastic model of a battleship, the kind constructed by children. It had been placed on some newspaper; scattered around it were assorted pieces of grey plastic.

My father gave a laugh. He came up to the table and picked up the model.

"Since the firm folded," he said, "I have a little more time on my hands." He laughed again, rather strangely. For a moment his face looked almost gentle. "A little more time."

"That seems odd," I said. "You were always so busy." 90

"Too busy perhaps." He looked at me with a small smile. "Perhaps I should have been a more attentive father."

I laughed. He went on contemplating his battleship. Then he looked up. "I hadn't meant to tell you this, but perhaps it's best that I do. It's my belief that your mother's death was no accident. She had many worries. And some disappointments."

We both gazed at the plastic battleship.

"Surely," I said eventually, "my mother didn't expect me to live here for ever."

"Obviously you don't see. You don't see how it is for some parents. Not only 95
must they lose their children, they must lose them to things they don't understand." He spun the battleship in his fingers. "These little gunboats here could have been better glued, don't you think?"

"Perhaps. I think it looks fine."

"During the war I spent some time on a ship rather like this. But my ambition was always the air force. I figured it like this. If your ship was struck by the enemy, all you could do was struggle in the water hoping for a lifeline. But in an aeroplane—well—there was always the final weapon." He put the model back onto the table. "I don't suppose you believe in war."

"Not particularly."

He cast an eye around the room. "Supper should be ready by now," he said. "You must be hungry."

Supper was waiting in a dimly lit room next to the kitchen. The only source 100 of light was a big lantern that hung over the table, casting the rest of the room into shadow. We bowed to each other before starting the meal.

There was little conversation. When I made some polite comment about the food, Kikuko giggled a little. Her earlier nervousness seemed to have returned to her. My father did not speak for several minutes. Finally he said:

"It must feel strange for you, being back in Japan."

"Yes, it is a little strange."

"Already, perhaps, you regret leaving America."

"A little. Not so much. I didn't leave behind much. Just some empty rooms." 105

"I see."

I glanced across the table. My father's face looked stony and forbidding in the half-light. We ate on in silence.

Then my eye caught something at the back of the room. At first I continued eating, then my hands became still. The others noticed and looked at me. I went on gazing into the darkness past my father's shoulder.

"Who is that? In that photograph there?"

"Which photograph?" My father turned slightly, trying to follow my gaze. 110

"The lowest one. The old woman in the white kimono."

My father put down his chopsticks. He looked first at the photograph, then at me.

"Your mother." His voice had become very hard. "Can't you recognize your own mother?"

"My mother. You see, it's dark. I can't see it very well."

No one spoke for a few seconds, then Kikuko rose to her feet. She took the 115 photograph down from the wall, came back to the table and gave it to me.

"She looks a lot older," I said.

"It was taken shortly before her death," said my father.

"It was the dark. I couldn't see very well."

I looked up and noticed my father holding out a hand. I gave him the photograph. He looked at it intently, then held it toward Kikuko. Obediently, my sister rose to her feet once more and returned the picture to the wall.

There was a large pot left unopened at the center of the table. When Kikuko 120 had seated herself again, my father reached forward and lifted the lid. A cloud of steam rose up and curled toward the lantern. He pushed the pot a little toward me.

"You must be hungry," he said. One side of his face had fallen into shadow.

"Thank you." I reached forward with my chopsticks. The steam was almost scalding. "What is it?"

"Fish."

"It smells very good."

In amidst soup were strips of fish that had curled almost into balls. I picked 125
one out and brought it to my bowl.

"Help yourself. There's plenty."

"Thank you." I took a little more, then pushed the pot toward my father. I
watched him take several pieces to his bowl. Then we both watched as Kikuko
served herself.

My father bowed slightly. "You must be hungry," he said again. He took
some fish to his mouth and started to eat. Then I too chose a piece and put it in
my mouth. It felt soft, quite fleshy against my tongue.

"Very good," I said. "What is it?"

"Just fish."   130

"It's very good."

The three of us ate on in silence. Several minutes went by.

"Some more?"

"Is there enough?"

"There's plenty for all of us." My father lifted the lid and once more steam 135
rose up. We all reached forward and helped ourselves.

"Here," I said to my father, "you have the last piece."

"Thank you."

When we had finished the meal, my father stretched out his arms and yawned
with an air of satisfaction. "Kikuko," he said. "Prepare a pot of tea, please."

My sister looked at him, then left the room without comment. My father
stood up.

"Let's retire to the other room. It's rather warm in here."   140

I got to my feet and followed him into the tea-room. The large sliding windows had been left open, bringing in a breeze from the garden. For a while we sat
in silence.

"Father," I said, finally.

"Yes?"

"Kikuko tells me Watanabe-San took his whole family with him."

My father lowered his eyes and nodded. For some moments he seemed deep in 145
thought. "Watanabe was very devoted to his work." He said at last. "The collapse
of the firm was a great blow to him. I fear it must have weakened his judgment."

"You think what he did—it was a mistake?"

"Why, of course. Do you see it otherwise?"

"No, no. Of course not."

"There are other things besides work."

"Yes."   150

We fell silent again. The sound of locusts came in from the garden. I looked
out into the darkness. The well was no longer visible.

"What do you think you will do now?" my father asked. "Will you stay in
Japan for a while?"

"To be honest, I hadn't thought that far ahead."

"If you wish to stay here, I mean here in this house, you would be very welcome. That is, if you don't mind living with an old man."

"Thank you. I'll have to think about it."　155

I gazed out once more into the darkness.

"But of course," said my father, "this house is so dreary now. You'll no doubt return to America before long."

"Perhaps. I don't know yet."

"No doubt you will."

For some time my father seemed to be studying the back of his hands. Then　160
he looked up and sighed.

"Kikuko is due to complete her studies next spring," he said. "Perhaps she will want to come home then. She's a good girl."

"Perhaps she will."

"Things will improve then."

"Yes, I'm sure they will."

We fell silent once more, waiting for Kikuko to bring the tea.　165

James Joyce

ARABY　1914

James Joyce

James Joyce (1884–1941) quit Ireland at twenty to spend his mature life in voluntary exile on the continent, writing of nothing but Dublin, where he was born. In Trieste, Zurich, and Paris, he supported his family with difficulty, sometimes teaching in Berlitz language schools, until his writing won him fame and wealthy patrons. At first Joyce met difficulty in getting his work printed and circulated. Publication of Dubliners (1914), the collection of stories that includes "Araby," was delayed seven years because its prospective Irish publisher feared libel suits. (The book depicts local citizens, some of them recognizable, and views Dubliners mostly as a thwarted, self-deceived lot.) Portrait of the Artist as a Young Man (1916), a novel of thinly veiled autobiography, recounts a young intellectual's breaking away from country, church, and home. Joyce's immense comic novel Ulysses (1922), a parody of the Odyssey, spans eighteen hours in the life of a wandering Jew, a Dublin seller of advertising. Frank about sex but untitillating, the book was banned at one time by the U.S. Post Office. Joyce's later work stepped up its demands on readers. The challenging Finnegans Wake (1939), if read aloud, sounds as though a learned comic poet were sleep-talking, jumbling several languages. Joyce was an innovator whose bold experiments showed many other writers possibilities in fiction that had not earlier been imagined.

North Richmond Street, being blind,° was a quiet street except at the hour when the Christian Brothers' School set the boys free. An uninhabited house of two stories stood at the blind end, detached from its neighbors in a square ground. The other houses of the street, conscious of decent lives within them, gazed at one another with brown imperturbable faces.

The former tenant of our house, a priest, had died in the back drawing-room. Air, musty from having long been enclosed, hung in all the rooms, and the waste room behind the kitchen was littered with old useless papers. Among these I found a few paper-covered books, the pages of which were curled and damp: *The Abbot,* by Walter Scott, *The Devout Communicant* and *The Memoirs of Vidocq.*° I liked the last best because its leaves were yellow. The wild garden behind the house contained a central apple-tree and a few straggling bushes under one of which I found the late tenant's rusty bicycle-pump. He had been a very charitable priest: in his will he had left all his money to institutions and the furniture of his house to his sister.

When the short days of winter came dusk fell before we had well eaten our dinners. When we met in the street the houses had grown somber. The space of sky above us was the color of ever-changing violet and towards it the lamps of the street lifted their feeble lanterns. The cold air stung us and we played till our bodies glowed. Our shouts echoed in the silent street. The career of our play brought us through the dark muddy lanes behind the houses where we ran the gantlet of the rough tribes from the cottages, to the back doors of the dark dripping gardens where odors arose from the ashpits, to the dark odorous stables where a coachman smoothed and combed the horse or shook music from the buckled harness. When we returned to the street light from the kitchen windows had filled the areas. If my uncle was seen turning the corner we hid in the shadow until we had seen him safely housed. Or if Mangan's sister° came out on the doorstep to call her brother in to his tea we watched her from our shadow peer up and down the street. We waited to see whether she would remain or go in and, if she remained, we left our shadow and walked up to Mangan's steps resignedly. She was waiting for us, her figure defined by the light from the half-opened door. Her brother always teased her before he obeyed and I stood by the railings looking at her. Her dress swung as she moved her body and the soft rope of her hair tossed from side to side.

Every morning I lay on the floor in the front parlor watching her door. The blind was pulled down within an inch of the sash so that I could not be seen. When she came out on the doorstep my heart leaped. I ran to the hall, seized my books and followed her. I kept her brown figure always in my eye and, when we came near the point at which our ways diverged, I quickened my pace and passed

---

being blind: being a dead-end street.   *The Abbot . . . Vidocq:* a popular historical romance (1820); a book of pious meditations by an eighteenth-century English Franciscan, Pacificus Baker; and the autobiography of François-Jules Vidocq (1775–1857), a criminal who later turned detective.   *Mangan's sister:* an actual young woman in this story, but the phrase recalls Irish poet James Clarence Mangan (1803–1849) and his best-known poem, "Dark Rosaleen," which personifies Ireland as a beautiful woman for whom the poet yearns.

her. This happened morning after morning. I had never spoken to her, except for a few casual words, and yet her name was like a summons to all my foolish blood.

Her image accompanied me even in places the most hostile to romance. On Saturday evenings when my aunt went marketing I had to go to carry some of the parcels. We walked through the flaring streets, jostled by drunken men and bargaining women, amid the curses of laborers, the shrill litanies of shopboys who stood on guard by the barrels of pigs' cheeks, the nasal chanting of street singers, who sang a *come-all-you* about O'Donovan Rossa,° or a ballad about the troubles in our native land. These noises converged in a single sensation of life for me: I imagined that I bore my chalice safely through the throng of foes. Her name sprang to my lips at moments in strange prayers and praises which I myself did not understand. My eyes were often full of tears (I could not tell why) and at times a flood from my heart seemed to pour itself out into my bosom. I thought little of the future. I did not know whether I would ever speak to her or not or, if I spoke to her, how I could tell her of my confused adoration. But my body was like a harp and her words and gestures were like fingers running upon the wires.

One evening I went into the back drawing-room in which the priest had died. It was a dark rainy evening and there was no sound in the house. Through one of the broken panes I heard the rain impinge upon the earth, the fine incessant needles of water playing in the sodden beds. Some distant lamp or lighted window gleamed below me. I was thankful that I could see so little. All my senses seemed to desire to veil themselves and, feeling that I was about to slip from them, I pressed the palms of my hands together until they trembled, murmuring: *O love! O love!* many times.

At last she spoke to me. When she addressed the first words to me I was so confused that I did not know what to answer. She asked me was I going to *Araby*. I forget whether I answered yes or no. It would be a splendid bazaar, she said; she would love to go.

—And why can't you? I asked.

While she spoke she turned a silver bracelet round and round her wrist. She could not go, she said, because there would be a retreat that week in her convent.° Her brother and two other boys were fighting for their caps and I was alone at the railings. She held one of the spikes, bowing her head towards me. The light from the lamp opposite our door caught the white curve of her neck, lit up her hair that rested there and, falling, lit up the hand upon the railing. It fell over one side of her dress and caught the white border of a petticoat, just visible as she stood at ease.

—It's well for you, she said.

---

come-all-you about O'Donovan Rossa: the street singers earned their living by singing timely songs that usually began, "Come all you gallant Irishmen / And listen to my song." Their subject, also called Dynamite Rossa, was a popular hero jailed by the British for advocating violent rebellion. *a retreat . . . in her convent:* a week devoted to religious observances more intense than usual, at the convent school Miss Mangan attends; probably she will have to listen to a number of hellfire sermons.

—If I go, I said, I will bring you something.

What innumerable follies laid waste my waking and sleeping thoughts after that evening! I wished to annihilate the tedious intervening days. I chafed against the work of school. At night in my bedroom and by day in the classroom her image came between me and the page I strove to read. The syllables of the word *Araby* were called to me through the silence in which my soul luxuriated and cast an Eastern enchantment over me. I asked for leave to go to the bazaar on Saturday night. My aunt was surprised and hoped it was not some Freemason° affair. I answered few questions in class. I watched my master's face pass from amiability to sternness; he hoped I was not beginning to idle. I could not call my wandering thoughts together. I had hardly any patience with the serious work of life which, now that it stood between me and my desire, seemed to me child's play, ugly monotonous child's play.

On Saturday morning I reminded my uncle that I wished to go to the bazaar in the evening. He was fussing at the hall-stand, looking for the hatbrush, and answered me curtly:

—Yes, boy, I know.

As he was in the hall I could not go into the front parlor and lie at the window. I left the house in bad humor and walked slowly towards the school. The air was pitilessly raw and already my heart misgave me.

When I came home to dinner my uncle had not yet been home. Still it was early. I sat staring at the clock for some time and, when its ticking began to irritate me, I left the room. I mounted the staircase and gained the upper part of the house. The high cold empty gloomy rooms liberated me and I went from room to room singing. From the front window I saw my companions playing below in the street. Their cries reached me weakened and indistinct and, leaning my forehead against the cool glass, I looked over at the dark house where she lived. I may have stood there for an hour, seeing nothing but the brown-clad figure cast by my imagination, touched discreetly by the lamplight at the curved neck, at the hand upon the railings and at the border below the dress.

When I came downstairs again I found Mrs. Mercer sitting at the fire. She was an old garrulous woman, a pawnbroker's widow, who collected used stamps for some pious purpose. I had to endure the gossip of the tea-table. The meal was prolonged beyond an hour and still my uncle did not come. Mrs. Mercer stood up to go: she was sorry she couldn't wait any longer, but it was after eight o'clock and she did not like to be out late, as the night air was bad for her. When she had gone I began to walk up and down the room, clenching my fists. My aunt said:

—I'm afraid you may put off your bazaar for this night of Our Lord.

At nine o'clock I heard my uncle's latchkey in the halldoor. I heard him talking to himself and heard the hall-stand rocking when it had received the weight of his overcoat. I could interpret these signs. When he was midway

15

Freemason: Catholics in Ireland viewed the Masonic order as a Protestant conspiracy against them.

through his dinner I asked him to give me the money to go to the bazaar. He had forgotten.

—The people are in bed and after their first sleep now, he said.   20

I did not smile. My aunt said to him energetically:

—Can't you give him the money and let him go? You've kept him late enough as it is.

My uncle said he was very sorry he had forgotten. He said he believed in the old saying: *All work and no play makes Jack a dull boy*. He asked me where I was going and, when I had told him a second time he asked me did I know *The Arab's Farewell to His Steed*.° When I left the kitchen he was about to recite the opening lines of the piece to my aunt.

I held a florin tightly in my hands as I strode down Buckingham Street towards the station. The sight of the streets thronged with buyers and glaring with gas recalled to me the purpose of my journey. I took my seat in a third-class carriage of a deserted train. After an intolerable delay the train moved out of the station slowly. It crept onward among ruinous houses and over the twinkling river. At Westland Row Station a crowd of people pressed to the carriage doors; but the porters moved them back, saying that it was a special train for the bazaar. I remained alone in the bare carriage. In a few minutes the train drew up beside an improvised wooden platform. I passed out on to the road and saw by the lighted dial of a clock that it was ten minutes to ten. In front of me was a large building which displayed the magical name.

I could not find any sixpenny entrance and, fearing that the bazaar would be   25
closed, I passed in quickly through a turnstile, handing a shilling to a weary-looking man. I found myself in a big hall girdled at half its height by a gallery. Nearly all the stalls were closed and the greater part of the hall was in darkness. I recognized a silence like that which pervades a church after a service. I walked into the center of the bazaar timidly. A few people were gathered about the stalls which were still open. Before a curtain, over which the words *Café Chantant*° were written in colored lamps, two men were counting money on a salver.° I listened to the fall of the coins.

Remembering with difficulty why I had come I went over to one of the stalls and examined porcelain vases and flowered tea-sets. At the door of the stall a young lady was talking and laughing with two young gentlemen. I remarked their English accents and listened vaguely to their conversation.

—O, I never said such a thing!

—O, but you did!

—O, but I didn't!

The Arab's Farewell to His Steed: This sentimental ballad by a popular poet, Caroline Norton (1808–1877), tells the story of a nomad of the desert who, in a fit of greed, sells his beloved horse, then regrets the loss, flings away the gold he had received, and takes back his horse. Notice the echo of "Araby" in the song title.   *Café Chantant:* name for a Paris nightspot featuring topical songs.   *salver:* a tray like that used in serving Holy Communion.

—Didn't she say that? 30
—Yes. I heard her.
—O, there's a . . . fib!

Observing me the young lady came over and asked me did I wish to buy anything. The tone of her voice was not encouraging; she seemed to have spoken to me out of a sense of duty. I looked humbly at the great jars that stood like eastern guards at either side of the dark entrance to the stall and murmured:

—No, thank you.

The young lady changed the position of one of the vases and went back to 35 the two young men. They began to talk of the same subject. Once or twice the young lady glanced at me over her shoulder.

I lingered before her stall, though I knew my stay was useless, to make my interest in her wares seem the more real. Then I turned away slowly and walked down the middle of the bazaar. I allowed the two pennies to fall against the sixpence in my pocket. I heard a voice call from one end of the gallery that the light was out. The upper part of the hall was now completely dark.

Gazing up into the darkness I saw myself as a creature driven and derided by vanity; and my eyes burned with anguish and anger.

Jamaica Kincaid

GIRL 1983

Jamaica Kincaid was born Elaine Potter Richardson in 1949 in St. John's, capital of the West Indian island nation of Antigua (she adopted the name Jamaica Kincaid in 1973 because of her family's disapproval of her writing). In 1965 she was sent to Westchester County, New York, to work as an au pair (or "servant," as she prefers to describe it). She attended Franconia College in New Hampshire, but did not complete a degree. Kincaid worked as a staff writer for the New Yorker for nearly twenty years; Talk Stories (2001) is a collection of seventy-seven short pieces that she wrote for the magazine. She won wide attention for At the Bottom of the River (1983), the volume of her stories that includes "Girl." In 1985 she pub-

Jamaica Kincaid

lished Annie John, an interlocking cycle of short stories about growing up in Antigua. Lucy (1990) was her first novel; it was followed by The Autobiography of My Mother (1996) and Mr. Potter (2002), novels inspired by the lives of her parents. Kincaid is also the author of A Small Place (1988), a memoir of her homeland and meditation on the destructiveness of colonialism, and My Brother (1997), a reminiscence of her brother Devon, who died of AIDS at thirty-three. A naturalized U.S. citizen, Kincaid has said of her adopted country: "It's given me a place to be myself—but myself as I was formed somewhere else." She lives in Vermont.

Wash the white clothes on Monday and put them on the stone heap; wash the color clothes on Tuesday and put them on the clothes-line to dry; don't walk barehead in the hot sun; cook pumpkin fritters in very hot sweet oil; soak your little cloths right after you take them off; when buying cotton to make yourself a nice blouse, be sure that it doesn't have gum on it, because that way it won't hold up well after a wash; soak salt fish overnight before you cook it; is it true that you sing benna° in Sunday school?; always eat your food in such a way that it won't turn someone else's stomach; on Sundays try to walk like a lady and not like the slut you are so bent on becoming; don't sing benna in Sunday school; you mustn't speak to wharf-rat boys, not even to give directions; don't eat fruits on the street—flies will follow you; but I don't sing benna on Sundays at all and never in Sunday school; this is how to sew on a button; this is how to make a buttonhole for the button you have just sewed on; this is how to hem a dress when you see the hem coming down and so to prevent yourself from looking like the slut I know you are so bent on becoming; this is how you iron your father's khaki shirt so that it doesn't have a crease; this is how you iron your father's khaki pants so that they don't have a crease; this is how you grow okra—far from the house, because okra tree harbors red ants; when you are growing dasheen, make sure it gets plenty of water or else it makes your throat itch when you are eating it; this is how you sweep a corner; this is how you sweep a whole house; this is how you sweep a yard; this is how you smile to someone you don't like too much; this is how you smile to someone you don't like at all; this is how you smile to someone you like completely; this is how you set a table for tea; this is how you set a table for dinner; this is how you set a table for dinner with an important guest; this is how you set a table for lunch; this is how you set a table for breakfast; this is how to behave in the presence of men who don't know you very well, and this way they won't recognize immediately the slut I have warned you against becoming; be sure to wash every day, even if it is with your own spit; don't squat down to play marbles—you are not a boy, you know; don't pick people's flowers—you might catch something; don't throw stones at blackbirds, because it might not be a blackbird at all; this is how to make a bread pudding; this is how to make doukona; this is how to make pepper pot; this is how to make a good medicine for a cold; this is how to make a good medicine to throw away a child before it even becomes a child; this is how to catch a fish; this is how to throw back a fish you don't like, and that way something bad won't fall on you; this is how to bully a man; this is how a man bullies you; this is how to love a man, and if this doesn't work there are other ways, and if they don't work don't

benna: Kincaid defined this word, for two editors who inquired, as meaning "songs of the sort your parents didn't want you to sing, at first calypso and later rock and roll" (quoted by Sylvan Barnet and Marcia Stubbes, *The Little Brown Reader*, 2nd ed. [Boston: Little, 1980] 74).

feel too bad about giving up; this is how to spit up in the air if you feel like it, and this is how to move quick so that it doesn't fall on you; this is how to make ends meet; always squeeze bread to make sure it's fresh; *but what if the baker won't let me feel the bread?*; you mean to say that after all you are really going to be the kind of woman who the baker won't let near the bread?

D. H. Lawrence

THE ROCKING-HORSE WINNER   1933

David Herbert Lawrence (1885–1930) was born in Nottinghamshire, England, child of a coalminer and a schoolteacher who hated her husband's toil and vowed that her son should escape it. He took up fiction writing, attaining early success. During World War I, Lawrence and his wife were unjustly suspected of treason (he because of his pacifism, she because of her aristocratic German birth). After the armistice they left England and, seeking a climate healthier for Lawrence, who suffered from tuberculosis, wandered in Italy, France, Australia, Mexico, and the American Southwest. Lawrence is an impassioned spokesman for our unconscious instinctive natures, which we moderns (he argues) have neglected in favor of our overweening intellects. In

D. H. Lawrence

Lady Chatterley's Lover (1928), he strove to restore explicit sexuality to English fiction. The book, which today seems tame and repetitious, was long banned in Britain and the United States. Deeper Lawrence novels include Sons and Lovers (1913), a veiled account of his breaking away from his fiercely possessive mother; The Rainbow (1915); Women in Love (1921); and The Plumed Serpent (1926), about a revival of pagan religion in Mexico. Besides fiction, Lawrence left a rich legacy of poetry, essays, criticism (Studies in Classic American Literature, 1923, is especially shrewd and funny), and travel writing. Lawrence exerted deep influence on others, both by the message in his work and by his personal magnetism.

There was a woman who was beautiful, who started with all the advantages, yet she had no luck. She married for love, and the love turned to dust. She had bonny children, yet she felt they had been thrust upon her, and she could not love them. They looked at her coldly, as if they were finding fault with her. And hurriedly she felt she must cover up some fault in herself. Yet what it was that she must cover up she never knew. Nevertheless, when her children were present, she always felt the center of her heart go hard. This troubled her, and in her manner she was all the more gentle and anxious for her children, as if she loved them very much. Only she herself knew that at the center of her heart was a hard little place that could not feel love, no, not for anybody. Everybody else said of her: "She is such a good mother. She adores her children." Only she herself, and her children themselves, knew it was not so. They read it in each other's eyes.

There were a boy and two little girls. They lived in a pleasant house, with a garden, and they had discreet servants, and felt themselves superior to anyone in the neighborhood.

Although they lived in style, they felt always an anxiety in the house. There was never enough money. The mother had a small income, and the father had a small income, but not nearly enough for the social position which they had to keep up. The father went in to town to some office. But though he had good prospects, these prospects never materialized. There was always the grinding sense of the shortage of money, though the style was always kept up.

At last the mother said: "I will see if *I* can't make something." But she did not know where to begin. She racked her brains, and tried this thing and the other, but could not find anything successful. The failure made deep lines come into her face. Her children were growing up, they would have to go to school. There must be more money, there must be more money. The father, who was always very handsome and expensive in his tastes, seemed as if he never *would* be able to do anything worth doing. And the mother, who had a great belief in herself, did not succeed any better, and her tastes were just as expensive.

And so the house came to be haunted by the unspoken phrase: *There must be more money! There must be more money!* The children could hear it all the time, though nobody said it aloud. They heard it at Christmas, when the expensive and splendid toys filled the nursery. Behind the shining modern rocking-horse, behind the smart doll's house, a voice would start whispering: "There *must* be more money! There *must* be more money!" And the children would stop playing, to listen for a moment. They would look into each other's eyes, to see if they had all heard. And each one saw in the eyes of the other two that they too had heard. "There *must* be more money! There *must* be more money!"

It came whispering from the springs of the still-swaying rocking-horse, and even the horse, bending his wooden, champing head, heard it. The big doll, sitting so pink and smirking in her new pram, could hear it quite plainly, and seemed to be smirking all the more self-consciously because of it. The foolish puppy, too, that took the place of the teddy-bear, he was looking so extraordinarily foolish for no other reason but that he heard the secret whisper all over the house: "There *must* be more money!"

Yet nobody ever said it aloud. The whisper was everywhere, and therefore no one spoke it. Just as no one ever says: "We are breathing!" in spite of the fact that breath is coming and going all the time.

"Mother," said the boy Paul one day, "why don't we keep a car of our own? Why do we always use uncle's, or else a taxi?"

"Because we're the poor members of the family," said the mother.

"But why *are* we, mother?"

"Well—I suppose," she said slowly and bitterly, "it's because your father has no luck."

The boy was silent for some time.

"Is luck money, mother?" he asked rather timidly.

"No, Paul. Not quite. It's what causes you to have money."

"Oh!" said Paul vaguely. "I thought when Uncle Oscar said *filthy lucker*, it meant money."

"*Filthy lucre* does mean money," said the mother. "But it's lucre, not luck."

"Oh!" said the boy. "Then what *is* luck, mother?"

"It's what causes you to have money. If you're lucky you have money. That's why it's better to be born lucky than rich. If you're rich, you may lose your money. But if you're lucky, you will always get more money."

"Oh! Will you? And is father not lucky?"

"Very unlucky, I should say," she said bitterly.

The boy watched her with unsure eyes.

"Why?" he asked.

"I don't know. Nobody ever knows why one person is lucky and another unlucky."

"Don't they? Nobody at all? Does *nobody* know?"

"Perhaps God. But He never tells."

"He ought to, then. And aren't you lucky either, mother?"

"I can't be, if I married an unlucky husband."

"But by yourself, aren't you?"

"I used to think I was, before I married. Now I think I am very unlucky indeed."

"Why?"

"Well—never mind! Perhaps I'm not really," she said.

The child looked at her, to see if she meant it. But he saw, by the lines of her mouth, that she was only trying to hide something from him.

"Well, anyhow," he said stoutly, "I'm a lucky person."

"Why?" said his mother, with a sudden laugh.

He stared at her. He didn't even know why he had said it.

"God told me," he asserted, brazening it out.

"I hope He did, dear!" she said, again with a laugh, but rather bitter.

"He did, mother!"

"Excellent!" said the mother, using one of her husband's exclamations.

The boy saw she did not believe him; or, rather, that she paid no attention to his assertion. This angered him somewhat, and made him want to compel her attention.

He went off by himself, vaguely, in a childish way, seeking for the clue to "luck." Absorbed, taking no heed of other people, he went about with a sort of stealth, seeking inwardly for luck. He wanted luck, he wanted it, he wanted it. When the two girls were playing dolls in the nursery, he would sit on his big rocking-horse, charging madly into space, with a frenzy that made the little girls peer at him uneasily. Wildly the horse careered, the waving dark hair of the boy tossed, his eyes had a strange glare in them. The little girls dared not speak to him.

When he had ridden to the end of his mad little journey, he climbed down and stood in front of his rocking-horse, staring fixedly into its lowered face. Its red mouth was slightly open, its big eye was wide and glassy-bright.

"Now!" he would silently command the snorting steed. "Now, take me to where there is luck! Now take me!"

And he would slash the horse on the neck with the little whip he had asked Uncle Oscar for. He *knew* the horse could take him to where there was luck, if only he forced it. So he would mount again, and start on his furious ride, hoping at last to get there. He knew he could get there.

"You'll break your horse, Paul!" said the nurse.   45

"He's always riding like that! I wish he'd leave off!" said his elder sister Joan.

But he only glared down on them in silence. Nurse gave him up. She could make nothing of him. Anyhow he was growing beyond her.

One day his mother and his Uncle Oscar came in when he was on one of his furious rides. He did not speak to them.

"Hallo, you young jockey! Riding a winner?" said his uncle.

"Aren't you growing too big for a rocking-horse? You're not a very little boy   50
any longer, you know," said his mother.

But Paul only gave a blue glare from his big, rather close-set eyes. He would speak to nobody when he was in full tilt. His mother watched him with an anxious expression on her face.

At last he suddenly stopped forcing his horse into the mechanical gallop, and slid down.

"Well, I got there!" he announced fiercely, his blue eyes still flaring, and his sturdy long legs straddling apart.

"Where did you get to?" asked his mother.

"Where I wanted to go," he flared back at her.   55

"That's right, son!" said Uncle Oscar. "Don't you stop till you get there. What's the horse's name?"

"He doesn't have a name," said the boy.

"Gets on without all right?" asked the uncle.

"Well, he has different names. He was called Sansovino last week."

"Sansovino, eh? Won the Ascot. How did you know his name?"   60

"He always talks about horse-races with Bassett," said Joan.

The uncle was delighted to find that his small nephew was posted with all the racing news. Bassett, the young gardener, who had been wounded in the left foot in the war and had got his present job through Oscar Cresswell, whose batman° he had been, was a perfect blade of the "turf." He lived in the racing events, and the small boy lived with him.

Oscar Cresswell got it all from Bassett.

batman: an enlisted man who serves as valet to a cavalry officer.

"Master Paul comes and asks me, so I can't do more than tell him, sir," said Bassett, his face terribly serious, as if he were speaking of religious matters.

"And does he ever put anything on a horse he fancies?"

"Well—I don't want to give him away—he's a young sport, a fine sport, sir. Would you mind asking him himself? He sort of takes a pleasure in it, and perhaps he'd feel I was giving him away, sir, if you don't mind."

Bassett was serious as a church.

The uncle went back to his nephew and took him off for a ride in the car.

"Say, Paul, old man, do you ever put anything on a horse?" the uncle asked.

The boy watched the handsome man closely.

"Why, do you think I oughtn't to?" he parried.

"Not a bit of it. I thought perhaps you might give me a tip for the Lincoln."

The car sped on into the country, going down to Uncle Oscar's place in Hampshire.

"Honor bright?" said the nephew.

"Honor bright, son!" said the uncle.

"Well, then, Daffodil."

"Daffodil! I doubt it, sonny. What about Mirza?"

"I only know the winner," said the boy. "That's Daffodil."

"Daffodil, eh?"

There was a pause. Daffodil was an obscure horse comparatively.

"Uncle!"

"Yes, son?"

"You won't let it go any further, will you? I promised Bassett."

"Bassett be damned, old man! What's he got to do with it?"

"We're partners. We've been partners from the first. Uncle, he lent me my first five shillings, which I lost. I promised him, honor bright, it was only between me and him; only you gave me that ten-shilling note I started winning with, so I thought you were lucky. You won't let it go any further, will you?"

The boy gazed at his uncle from those big, hot, blue eyes, set rather close together. The uncle stirred and laughed uneasily.

"Right you are, son! I'll keep your tip private. Daffodil, eh? How much are you putting on him?"

"All except twenty pounds," said the boy. "I keep that in reserve."

The uncle thought it a good joke.

"You keep twenty pounds in reserve, do you, you young romancer? What are you betting, then?"

"I'm betting three hundred," said the boy gravely. "But it's between you and me, Uncle Oscar! Honor bright?"

The uncle burst into a roar of laughter.

"It's between you and me all right, you young Nat Gould,°" he said, laughing. "But where's your three hundred?"

Nat Gould: celebrated English gambler of the 1920s.

"Bassett keeps it for me. We're partners."

"You are, are you! And what is Bassett putting on Daffodil?" 95

"He won't go quite as high as I do, I expect. Perhaps he'll go a hundred and fifty."

"What, pennies?" laughed the uncle.

"Pounds," said the child, with a surprised look at his uncle. "Bassett keeps a bigger reserve than I do."

Between wonder and amusement Uncle Oscar was silent. He pursued the matter no further, but he determined to take his nephew with him to the Lincoln races.

"Now, son," he said, "I'm putting twenty on Mirza, and I'll put five for you 100 on any horse you fancy. What's your pick?"

"Daffodil, uncle."

"No, not the fiver on Daffodil!"

"I should if it was my own fiver," said the child.

"Good! Good! Right you are! A fiver for me and a fiver for you on Daffodil."

The child had never been to a race-meeting before, and his eyes were blue 105 fire. He pursed his mouth tight, and watched. A Frenchman just in front had put his money on Lancelot. Wild with excitement, he flayed his arms up and down, yelling, "*Lancelot! Lancelot!*" in his French accent.

Daffodil came in first, Lancelot second, Mirza third. The child, flushed and with eyes blazing, was curiously serene. His uncle brought him four five-pound notes, four to one.

"What am I to do with these?" he cried, waving them before the boy's eyes.

"I suppose we'll talk to Bassett," said the boy. "I expect I have fifteen hundred now; and twenty in reserve; and this twenty."

His uncle studied him for some moments.

"Look here, son!" he said. "You're not serious about Bassett and that fifteen 110 hundred, are you?"

"Yes, I am. But it's between you and me, uncle. Honor bright!"

"Honor bright all right, son! But I must talk to Bassett."

"If you'd like to be a partner, uncle, with Bassett and me, we could all be partners. Only, you'd have to promise, honor bright, uncle, not to let it go beyond us three. Bassett and I are lucky, and you must be lucky, because it was your ten shillings I started winning with . . ."

Uncle Oscar took both Bassett and Paul into Richmond Park for an afternoon, and there they talked.

"It's like this, you see, sir," Bassett said. "Master Paul would get me talking 115 about racing events, spinning yarns, you know, sir. And he was always keen on knowing if I'd made or if I'd lost. It's about a year since, now, that I put five shillings on Blush of Dawn for him—and we lost. Then the luck turned, and with that ten shillings he had from you, that we put on Singhalese. And since that time, it's been pretty steady, all things considering. What do you say, Master Paul?"

"We're all right when we're sure," said Paul. "It's when we're not quite sure that we go down."

"Oh, but we're careful then," said Bassett.

"But when are you *sure?*" smiled Uncle Oscar.

"It's Master Paul, sir," said Bassett, in a secret, religious voice. "It's as if he had it from heaven. Like Daffodil, now, for the Lincoln. That was as sure as eggs."

"Did you put anything on Daffodil?" asked Oscar Cresswell. 120

"Yes, sir. I made my bit."

"And my nephew?"

Bassett was obstinately silent, looking at Paul.

"I made twelve hundred, didn't I, Bassett? I told uncle I was putting three hundred on Daffodil."

"That's right," said Bassett, nodding. 125

"But where's the money?" asked the uncle.

"I keep it safe locked up, sir. Master Paul he can have it any minute he likes to ask for it."

"What, fifteen hundred pounds?"

"And twenty! And *forty*, that is, with the twenty he made on the course."

"It's amazing!" said the uncle. 130

"If Master Paul offers you to be partners, sir, I would, if I were you; if you'll excuse me," said Bassett.

Oscar Cresswell thought about it.

"I'll see the money," he said.

They drove home again, and sure enough, Bassett came round to the garden-house with fifteen hundred pounds in notes. The twenty pounds reserve was left with Joe Glee, in the Turf Commission deposit.

"You see, it's all right, uncle, when I'm *sure!* Then we go strong, for all we're 135 worth. Don't we, Bassett!"

"We do that, Master Paul."

"And when are you sure?" said the uncle, laughing.

"Oh, well, sometimes I'm *absolutely* sure, like about Daffodil," said the boy; "and sometimes I have an idea; and sometimes I haven't even an idea, have I, Bassett? Then we're careful, because we mostly go down."

"You do, do you! And when you're sure, like about Daffodil, what makes you sure, sonny?"

"Oh, well, I don't know," said the boy uneasily. "I'm sure, you know, uncle; 140 that's all."

"It's as if he had it from heaven, sir," Bassett reiterated.

"I should say so!" said the uncle.

But he became a partner. And when the Leger was coming on, Paul was "sure" about Lively Spark, which was a quite inconsiderable horse. The boy insisted on putting a thousand on the horse, Bassett went for five hundred, and Oscar Cresswell two hundred. Lively Spark came in first, and the betting had been ten to one against him. Paul had made ten thousand.

"You see," he said, "I was absolutely sure of him."

Even Oscar Cresswell had cleared two thousand. 145

"Look here, son," he said, "this sort of thing makes me nervous."

"It needn't, uncle! Perhaps I shan't be sure again for a long time."

"But what are you going to do with your money?" asked the uncle.

"Of course," said the boy, "I started it for mother. She said she had no luck, because father is unlucky, so I thought if *I* was lucky, it might stop whispering." 150

"What might stop whispering?"

"Our house. I *hate* our house for whispering."

"What does it whisper?"

"Why—why"—the boy fidgeted—"why, I don't know. But it's always short of money, you know, uncle."

"I know it, son, I know it."

"You know people send mother writs, don't you, uncle?" 155

"I'm afraid I do," said the uncle.

"And then the house whispers, like people laughing at you behind your back. It's awful, that is! I thought if I was lucky . . ."

"You might stop it," added the uncle.

The boy watched him with big blue eyes, that had an uncanny cold fire in them, and he said never a word.

"Well, then!" said the uncle. "What are we doing?" 160

"I shouldn't like mother to know I was lucky," said the boy.

"Why not, son?"

"She'd stop me."

"I don't think she would."

"Oh!"—and the boy writhed in an odd way—"I *don't* want her to know, 165 uncle."

"All right, son! We'll manage it without her knowing."

They managed it very easily. Paul, at the other's suggestion, handed over five thousand pounds to his uncle, who deposited it with the family lawyer, who was then to inform Paul's mother that a relative had put five thousand pounds into his hands, which sum was to be paid out a thousand pounds at a time, on the mother's birthday, for the next five years.

"So she'll have a birthday present of a thousand pounds for five successive years," said Uncle Oscar. "I hope it won't make it all the harder for her later."

Paul's mother had her birthday in November. The house had been "whispering" worse than ever lately, and, even in spite of his luck, Paul could not bear up against it. He was very anxious to see the effect of the birthday letter, telling his mother about the thousand pounds.

When there were no visitors, Paul now took his meals with his parents, as 170 he was beyond the nursery control. His mother went into town nearly every day. She had discovered that she had an odd knack of sketching furs and dress materials, so she worked secretly in the studio of a friend who was the chief "artist" for the leading drapers. She drew the figures of ladies in furs and ladies in silk and sequins for the newspaper advertisements. This young woman artist earned several thousand pounds a year, but Paul's mother only made several hundreds, and she was again dissatisfied. She so wanted to be first in something, and she did not succeed, even in making sketches for drapery advertisements.

She was down to breakfast on the morning of her birthday. Paul watched her face as she read the letters. He knew the lawyer's letter. As his mother read it, her face hardened and became more expressionless. Then a cold, determined look came on her mouth. She hid the letter under the pile of others, and said not a word about it.

"Didn't you have anything nice in the post for your birthday, mother?" said Paul.

"Quite moderately nice," she said, her voice cold and absent.

She went away to town without saying more.

But in the afternoon Uncle Oscar appeared. He said Paul's mother had had a long interview with the lawyer, asking if the whole five thousand could not be advanced at once, as she was in debt.

"What do you think, uncle?" said the boy.

"I leave it to you, son."

"Oh, let her have it, then! We can get some more with the other," said the boy.

"A bird in the hand is worth two in the bush, laddie!" said Uncle Oscar.

"But I'm sure to *know* for the Grand National; or the Lincolnshire; or else the Derby. I'm sure to know for *one* of them," said Paul.

So Uncle Oscar signed the agreement, and Paul's mother touched the whole five thousand. Then something very curious happened. The voices in the house suddenly went mad, like a chorus of frogs on a spring evening. There were certain new furnishings, and Paul had a tutor. He was *really* going to Eton, his father's school, in the following autumn. There were flowers in the winter, and a blossoming of the luxury Paul's mother had been used to. And yet the voices in the house, behind the sprays of mimosa and almond blossom, and from under the piles of iridescent cushions, simply trilled and screamed in a sort of ecstasy: "There *must* be more money! Oh-h-h; there *must* be more money. Oh, now, now-w! Now-w-w—there *must* be more money—more than ever! More than ever!"

It frightened Paul terribly. He studied away at his Latin and Greek with his tutors. But his intense hours were spent with Bassett. The Grand National had gone by: he had not "known," and had lost a hundred pounds. Summer was at hand. He was in agony for the Lincoln. But even for the Lincoln he didn't "know," and he lost fifty pounds. He became wild-eyed and strange, as if something were going to explode in him.

"Let it alone, son! Don't you bother about it!" urged Uncle Oscar. But it was as if the boy couldn't really hear what his uncle was saying.

"I've got to know for the Derby! I've got to know for the Derby!" the child reiterated, his big blue eyes blazing with a sort of madness.

His mother noticed how overwrought he was.

"You'd better go to the seaside. Wouldn't you like to go now to the seaside, instead of waiting? I think you'd better," she said, looking down at him anxiously, her heart curiously heavy because of him.

But the child lifted his uncanny blue eyes.

"I couldn't possibly go before the Derby, mother!" he said. "I couldn't possibly!"

"Why not?" she said, her voice becoming heavy when she was opposed. "Why not? You can still go from the seaside to see the Derby with your Uncle Oscar, if that's what you wish. No need for you to wait here. Besides, I think you care too much about these races. It's a bad sign. My family has been a gambling family, and you won't know till you grow up how much damage it has done. But it has done damage. I shall have to send Bassett away, and ask Uncle Oscar not to talk racing to you, unless you promise to be reasonable about it; go away to the seaside and forget it. You're all nerves!"

"I'll do what you like, mother, so long as you don't send me away till after the Derby," the boy said.   190

"Send you away from where? Just from this house?"

"Yes," he said, gazing at her.

"Why, you curious child, what makes you care about this house so much, suddenly? I never knew you loved it."

He gazed at her without speaking. He had a secret within a secret, something he had not divulged, even to Bassett or to his Uncle Oscar.

But his mother, after standing undecided and a little bit sullen for some moments, said: 195

"Very well, then! Don't go to the seaside till after the Derby, if you don't wish it. But promise me you won't let your nerves go to pieces. Promise you won't think so much about horse-racing and *events*, as you call them!"

"Oh, no," said the boy casually. "I won't think much about them, mother. You needn't worry. I wouldn't worry, mother, if I were you."

"If you were me and I were you," said his mother, "I wonder what we *should* do!"

"But you know you needn't worry, mother, don't you?" the boy repeated.

"I should be awfully glad to know it," she said wearily.   200

"Oh, well, you *can*, you know. I mean, you *ought* to know you needn't worry," he insisted.

"Ought I? Then I'll see about it," she said.

Paul's secret of secrets was his wooden horse, that which had no name. Since he was emancipated from a nurse and a nursery-governess, he had had his rocking-horse removed to his own bedroom at the top of the house.

"Surely, you're too big for a rocking-horse!" his mother had remonstrated.

"Well, you see, mother, till I can have a *real* horse, I like to have *some* sort of animal about," had been his quaint answer.   205

"Do you feel he keeps you company?" she laughed.

"Oh, yes! He's very good, he always keeps me company, when I'm there," said Paul.

So the horse, rather shabby, stood in an arrested prance in the boy's bedroom.

The Derby was drawing near, and the boy grew more and more tense. He hardly heard what was spoken to him, he was very frail, and his eyes were really uncanny. His mother had sudden strange seizures of uneasiness about him.

Sometimes, for half-an-hour, she would feel a sudden anxiety about him that was almost anguish. She wanted to rush to him at once, and know he was safe.

Two nights before the Derby, she was at a big party in town, when one of her rushes of anxiety about her boy, her first-born, gripped her heart till she could hardly speak. She fought with the feeling, might and main, for she believed in common-sense. But it was too strong. She had to leave the dance and go downstairs to telephone to the country. The children's nursery-governess was terribly surprised and startled at being rung up in the night.

"Are the children all right, Miss Wilmot?"

"Oh, yes, they are quite all right."

"Master Paul? Is he all right?"

"He went to bed as right as a trivet. Shall I run up and look at him?"

"No," said Paul's mother reluctantly. "No! Don't trouble. It's all right. Don't sit up. We shall be home fairly soon." She did not want her son's privacy intruded upon.

"Very good," said the governess.

It was about one-o'clock when Paul's mother and father drove up to their house. All was still. Paul's mother went to her room and slipped off her white fur cloak. She had told her maid not to wait up for her. She heard her husband downstairs, mixing a whisky-and-soda.

And then, because of the strange anxiety at her heart, she stole upstairs to her son's room. Noiselessly she went along the upper corridor. Was there a faint noise? What was it?

She stood, with arrested muscles, outside his door, listening. There was a strange, heavy, and yet not loud noise. Her heart stood still. It was a soundless noise, yet rushing and powerful. Something huge, in violent, hushed motion. What was it? What in God's name was it? She ought to know. She felt that she knew the noise. She knew what it was.

Yet she could not place it. She couldn't say what it was. And on and on it went, like a madness.

Softly, frozen with anxiety and fear, she turned the door-handle.

The room was dark. Yet in the space near the window, she heard and saw something plunging to and fro. She gazed in fear and amazement.

Then suddenly she switched on the light, and saw her son, in his green pajamas, madly surging on the rocking-horse. The blaze of light suddenly lit him up, as he urged the wooden horse, and lit her up, as she stood, blonde, in her dress of pale green and crystal, in the doorway.

"Paul!" she cried. "Whatever are you doing?"

"It's Malabar!" he screamed, in a powerful, strange voice. "It's Malabar!"

His eyes blazed at her for one strange and senseless second, as he ceased urging his wooden horse. Then he fell with a crash to the ground, and she, all her tormented motherhood flooding upon her, rushed to gather him up.

But he was unconscious, and unconscious he remained, with some brain-fever. He talked and tossed, and his mother sat stonily by his side.

"Malabar! It's Malabar! Bassett, Bassett I *know!* It's Malabar!"

So the child cried, trying to get up and urge the rocking-horse that gave him his inspiration.

"What does he mean by Malabar?" asked the heart-frozen mother.

"I don't know," said the father stonily.

"What does he mean by Malabar?" she asked her brother Oscar.

"It's one of the horses running for the Derby," was the answer.

And, in spite of himself, Oscar Cresswell spoke to Bassett, and himself put a thousand on Malabar: at fourteen to one.

The third day of the illness was critical: they were waiting for a change. The boy, with his rather long, curly hair, was tossing ceaselessly on the pillow. He neither slept nor regained consciousness, and his eyes were like blue stones. His mother sat, feeling her heart had gone, turned actually into a stone.

In the evening, Oscar Cresswell did not come, but Bassett sent a message, saying could he come up for one moment, just one moment? Paul's mother was very angry at the intrusion, but on second thought she agreed. The boy was the same. Perhaps Bassett might bring him to consciousness.

The gardener, a shortish fellow with a little brown moustache, and sharp little brown eyes, tiptoed into the room, touched his imaginary cap to Paul's mother, and stole to the bedside, staring with glittering, smallish eyes, at the tossing, dying child.

"Master Paul!" he whispered. "Master Paul! Malabar came in first all right, a clean win. I did as you told me. You've made over seventy thousand pounds, you have; you've got over eighty thousand. Malabar came in all right, Master Paul."

"Malabar! Malabar! Did I say Malabar, mother? Did I say Malabar? Do you think I'm lucky, mother? I knew Malabar, didn't I? Over eighty thousand pounds! I call that lucky, don't you, mother? Over eighty thousand pounds! I knew, didn't I know I knew? Malabar came in all right. If I ride my horse till I'm sure, then I tell you, Bassett, you can go as high as you like. Did you go for all you were worth, Bassett?"

"I went a thousand on it, Master Paul."

"I never told you, mother, that if I can ride my horse, and *get there*, then I'm absolutely sure—oh, absolutely! Mother, did I ever tell you? I *am* lucky!"

"No, you never did," said the mother.

But the boy died in the night.

And even as he lay dead, his mother heard her brother's voice saying to her: "My God, Hester, you're eighty-odd thousand to the good, and a poor devil of a son to the bad. But, poor devil, poor devil, he's best gone out of a life where he rides his rocking-horse to find a winner."

STORIES FOR FURTHER READING

Bernard Malamud

ANGEL LEVINE

Bernard Malamud

Bernard Malamud (1914–1986) was born in Brooklyn, New York. His parents were Russian Jewish immigrants who ran a small neighborhood grocery store. Having already published his first short stories in a high school literary magazine, Malamud attended the City College of New York and then earned an M.A. in English at Columbia while teaching night-school classes. From 1940 to 1949 he taught English at his former high school, Brooklyn's Erasmus Hall. In 1949 Malamud joined the faculty of Oregon State University where he remained for the next two decades. His first novel, The Natural (1952), tells the mythic story of a baseball player gifted with extraordinary power. (The Natural was made into a film in 1984 starring Robert Redford and Glenn Close.) Malamud's first collection of stories, The Magic Barrel (1958), which contains "Angel Levine," won the first of the author's two National Book Awards. His subsequent novels included The Fixer (1966), which won both the Pulitzer and National Book Award, The Tenants (1971), Dubin's Lives (1979), and God's Grace (1982). Malamud was a central figure in the emergence of Jewish American writers after World War II. His darkly comic but deeply human stories, which often portray the struggles of Jewish immigrants and other minorities, have become classics of modern American literature.

Manischevitz, a tailor, in his fifty-first year suffered many reverses and indignities. Previously a man of comfortable means, he overnight lost all he had, when his establishment caught fire, after a metal container of cleaning fluid exploded, and burned to the ground. Although Manischevitz was insured against fire, damage suits by two customers who had been hurt in the flames deprived him of every penny he had saved. At almost the same time, his son, of much promise, was killed in the war, and his daughter, without so much as a word of warning, married a lout and disappeared with him as off the face of the earth. Thereafter Manischevitz was victimized by excruciating backaches and found himself unable to work even as a presser—the only kind of work available to him—for more than an hour or two daily, because beyond that the pain from standing was maddening. His Fanny, a good wife and mother, who had taken in washing and sewing, began before his eyes to waste away. Suffering shortness of breath, she at last became seriously ill and took to her bed. The doctor, a former customer of Manischevitz, who out of pity treated them, at first had difficulty diagnosing her ailment, but later put it down as hardening of the arteries at an advanced stage. He took Manischevitz aside, prescribed complete rest for her, and in whispers gave him to know there was little hope.

Throughout his trials Manischevitz had remained somewhat stoic, almost unbelieving that all this had descended on his head, as if it were happening, let us say, to an acquaintance or some distant relative; it was in sheer quantity of woe, incomprehensible. It was also ridiculous, unjust, and because he had always been a religious man, an affront to God. Manischevitz believed this in all his suffering. When his burden had grown too crushingly heavy to be borne he prayed in his chair with shut hollow eyes: "My dear God, sweetheart, did I deserve that this should happen to me?" Then recognizing the worthlessness of it, he set aside the complaint and prayed humbly for assistance: "Give Fanny back her health, and to me for myself that I shouldn't feel pain in every step. Help now or to-morrow is too late." And Manischevitz wept.

Manischevitz's flat, which he had moved into after the disastrous fire, was a meager one, furnished with a few sticks of chairs, a table, and bed, in one of the poorer sections of the city. There were three rooms: a small, poorly papered living room; an apology for a kitchen with a wooden icebox; and the comparatively large bedroom where Fanny lay in a sagging secondhand bed, gasping for breath. The bedroom was the warmest room in the house and it was here, after his outburst to God, that Manischevitz, by the light of two small bulbs overhead, sat reading his Jewish newspaper. He was not truly reading because his thoughts were everywhere; however the print offered a convenient resting place for his eyes, and a word or two, when he permitted himself to comprehend them, had the momentary effect of helping him forget his troubles. After a short while he discovered, to his surprise, that he was actively scanning the news, searching for an item of great interest to him. Exactly what he thought he would read he couldn't say—until he realized, with some astonishment, that he was expecting to discover something about himself. Manischevitz put his paper down and looked up with the distinct impression that someone had come into the apartment, though he could not remember having heard the sound of the door opening. He looked around: the room was very still, Fanny sleeping, for once, quietly. Half frightened, he watched her until he was satisfied she wasn't dead; then, still disturbed by the thought of an unannounced visitor, he stumbled into the living room and there had the shock of his life, for at the table sat a black man reading a newspaper he had folded up to fit into one hand.

"What do you want here?" Manischevitz asked in fright.

The Negro put down the paper and glanced up with a gentle expression. 5
"Good evening." He seemed not to be sure of himself, as if he had got into the wrong house. He was a large man, bonily built, with a heavy head covered by a hard derby, which he made no attempt to remove. His eyes seemed sad, but his lips, above which he wore a slight mustache, sought to smile; he was not otherwise prepossessing. The cuffs of his sleeves, Manischevitz noted, were frayed to

the lining, and the dark suit was badly fitted. He had very large feet. Recovering from his fright, Manischevitz guessed he had left the door open and was being visited by a case worker from the Welfare Department—some came at night—for he had recently applied for welfare. Therefore he lowered himself into a chair opposite the Negro, trying, before the man's uncertain smile, to feel comfortable. The former tailor sat stiffly but patiently at the table, waiting for the investigator to take out his pad and pencil and begin asking questions; but before long he became convinced the man intended to do nothing of the sort.

"Who are you?" Manischevitz at last asked uneasily.

"If I may, insofar as one is able to, identify myself, I bear the name of Alexander Levine."

In spite of his troubles Manischevitz felt a smile growing on his lips. "You said Levine?" he politely inquired.

The Negro nodded. "That is exactly right."

Carrying the jest further, Manischevitz asked, "You are maybe Jewish?"   10

"All my life I was, willingly."

The tailor hesitated. He had heard of black Jews but had never met one. It gave an unusual sensation.

Recognizing in afterthought something odd about the tense of Levine's remark, he said doubtfully, "You ain't Jewish any more?"

Levine at this point removed his hat, revealing a very white part in his black hair, but quickly replaced it. He replied, "I have recently been disincarnated into an angel. As such, I offer you my humble assistance, if to offer is within my province and power—in the best sense." He lowered his eyes in apology. "Which calls for added explanation: I am what I am granted to be, and at present the completion is in the future."

"What kind of angel is this?" Manischevitz gravely asked.   15

"A bona fide angel of God, within prescribed limitations," answered Levine, "not to be confused with the members of any particular sect, order, or organization here on earth operating under a similar name."

Manischevitz was thoroughly disturbed. He had been expecting something, but not this. What sort of mockery was it—provided that Levine was an angel— of a faithful servant who had from childhood lived in the synagogues, concerned with the word of God?

To test Levine he asked, "Then where are your wings?"

The Negro blushed as well as he could. Manischevitz understood this from his altered expression. "Under certain circumstances we lose privileges and prerogatives upon returning to earth, no matter for what purpose or endeavoring to assist whomsoever."

"So tell me," Manischevitz said triumphantly, "how did you get here?"   20

"I was translated."

Still troubled, the tailor said, "If you are a Jew, say the blessing for bread."

Levine recited it in sonorous Hebrew.

Although moved by the familiar words Manischevitz still felt doubt he was dealing with an angel.

"If you are an angel," he demanded somewhat angrily, "give me the proof." 25

Levine wet his lips. "Frankly, I cannot perform either miracles or near-miracles, due to the fact that I am in a condition of probation. How long that will persist or even consist depends on the outcome."

Manischevitz racked his brains for some means of causing Levine positively to reveal his true identity, when the Negro spoke again:

"It was given me to understand that both your wife and you require assistance of a salubrious nature?"

The tailor could not rid himself of the feeling that he was the butt of a jokester. Is this what a Jewish angel looks like? he asked himself. This I am not convinced.

He asked a last question. "So if God sends to me an angel, why a black? Why 30 not a white that there are so many of them?"

"It was my turn to go next," Levine explained.

Manischevitz could not be persuaded. "I think you are a faker."

Levine slowly rose. His eyes indicated disappointment and worry. "Mr. Manischevitz," he said tonelessly, "if you should desire me to be of assistance to you any time in the near future, or possibly before, I can be found"—he glanced at his fingernails—"in Harlem."

He was by then gone.

The next day Manischevitz felt some relief from his backache and was able 35 to work four hours at pressing. The day after, he put in six hours; and the third day four again. Fanny sat up a little and asked for some halvah to suck. But after the fourth day the stabbing, breaking ache afflicted his back, and Fanny again lay supine, breathing with blue-lipped difficulty.

Manischevitz was profoundly disappointed at the return of his active pain and suffering. He had hoped for a longer interval of easement, long enough to have a thought other than of himself and his troubles. Day by day, minute after minute, he lived in pain, pain his only memory, questioning the necessity of it, inveighing, though with affection, against God. Why *so much*, Gottenyu? If He wanted to teach His servant a lesson for some reason, some cause—the nature of His nature—to teach him, say, for reasons of his weakness, his pride, perhaps, during his years of prosperity, his frequent neglect of God—to give him a little lesson, why then any of the tragedies that had happened to him, any *one* would have sufficed to chasten him. But *all together*—the loss of both his children, his means of livelihood, Fanny's health and his—that was too much to ask one frail-boned man to endure. Who, after all, was Manischevitz that he had been given so much to suffer? A tailor. Certainly not a man of talent. Upon him suffering was largely wasted. It went nowhere, into nothing: into more suffering. His pain did not earn him bread, nor fill the cracks in the wall, nor lift, in the middle of the night, the kitchen table; only lay upon him, sleepless, so sharply oppressive that he could many times have cried out yet not heard himself this misery.

In this mood he gave no thought to Mr. Alexander Levine, but at moments when the pain wavered, slightly diminishing, he sometimes wondered if he had been mistaken to dismiss him. A black Jew and angel to boot—very hard to believe, but suppose he *had* been sent to succor him, and he, Manischevitz, was in his blindness too blind to understand? It was this thought that put him on the knife-point of agony.

Therefore the tailor, after much self-questioning and continuing doubt, decided he would seek the self-styled angel in Harlem. Of course he had great difficulty because he had not asked for specific directions, and movement was tedious to him. The subway took him to 116th Street, and from there he wandered in the open dark world. It was vast and its lights lit nothing. Everywhere were shadows, often moving. Manischevitz hobbled along with the aid of a cane, and not knowing where to seek in the blackened tenement buildings, would look fruitlessly through store windows. In the stores he saw people and everybody was black. It was an amazing thing to observe. When he was too tired, too unhappy to go farther, Manischevitz stopped in front of a tailor's shop. Out of familiarity with the appearance of it, with some sadness he entered. The tailor, an old skinny man with a mop of woolly gray hair, was sitting cross-legged on his workbench, sewing a pair of tuxedo pants that had a razor slit all the way down the seat.

"You'll excuse me, please, gentleman," said Manischevitz, admiring the tailor's deft thimbled fingerwork, "but you know maybe somebody by the name Alexander Levine?"

The tailor, who, Manischevitz thought, seemed a little antagonistic to him,   40
scratched his scalp.

"Cain't say I ever heared dat name."

"Alex-ander Lev-ine," Manischevitz repeated it.

The man shook his head. "Cain't say I heared."

Manischevitz remembered to say: "He is an angel, maybe."

"Oh *him*," said the tailor, clucking. "He hang out in dat honky-tonk down   45
here a ways." He pointed with his skinny finger and returned to sewing the pants.

Manischevitz crossed the street against a red light and was almost run down by a taxi. On the block after the next, the sixth store from the corner was a cabaret, and the name in sparkling lights was Bella's. Ashamed to go in, Manischevitz gazed through the neon-lit window, and when the dancing couples had parted and drifted away, he discovered at a table on the side, toward the rear, Alexander Levine.

He was sitting alone, a cigarette butt hanging from the corner of his mouth, playing solitaire with a dirty pack of cards, and Manischevitz felt a touch of pity for him, because Levine had deteriorated in appearance. His derby hat was dented and had a gray smudge. His ill-fitting suit was shabbier, as if he had been sleeping in it. His shoes and trouser cuffs were muddy, and his face covered with an impenetrable stubble the color of licorice. Manischevitz, though deeply disappointed, was about to enter, when a big-breasted Negress in a purple evening gown appeared before Levine's table, and with much laughter through many white teeth, broke into a vigorous shimmy. Levine looked at Manischevitz with a haunted expression, but the tailor was too paralyzed to move or acknowledge it. As Bella's gyrations continued Levine rose, his eyes lit in excitement. She embraced him with vigor, both his hands clasped around her restless buttocks, and they tangoed together across the floor, loudly applauded by the customers. She seemed to have lifted Levine off his feet and his large shoes hung limp as they danced. They slid past the windows where Manischevitz, white-faced, stood staring in. Levine winked slyly and the tailor left for home.

Fanny lay at death's door. Through shrunken lips she muttered concerning her childhood, the sorrows of the marriage bed, the loss of her children; yet wept to live. Manischevitz tried not to listen, but even without ears he would have heard. It was not a gift. The doctor panted up the stairs, a broad but bland, unshaven man (it was Sunday), and soon shook his head. A day at most, or two. He left at once to spare himself Manischevitz's multiplied sorrow; the man who never stopped hurting. He would someday get him into a public home.

Manischevitz visited a synagogue and there spoke to God, but God had absented himself. The tailor searched his heart and found no hope. When she died, he would live dead. He considered taking his life although he knew he wouldn't. Yet it was something to consider. Considering, you existed. He railed against God—Can you love a rock, a broom, an emptiness? Baring his chest, he smote the naked bones, cursing himself for having, beyond belief, believed.

Asleep in a chair that afternoon, he dreamed of Levine. He was standing before a faded mirror, preening small decaying opalescent wings. "This means," mumbled Manischevitz, as he broke out of sleep, "that it is possible he could be an angel." Begging a neighbor lady to look in on Fanny and occasionally wet her lips with water, he drew on his thin coat, gripped his walking stick, exchanged some pennies for a subway token, and rode to Harlem. He knew this act was the last desperate one of his woe: to go seeking a black magician to restore his wife to invalidism. Yet if there was no choice, he did at least what was chosen.

He hobbled to Bella's, but the place seemed to have changed hands. It was now, as he breathed, a synagogue in a store. In the front, toward him, were several rows of empty wooden benches. In the rear stood the Ark, its portals of rough wood covered with rainbows of sequins; under it a long table on which lay the sacred scroll unrolled, illuminated by the dim light from a bulb on a chain overhead. Around the table, as if frozen to it and the scroll, which they all touched with their fingers, sat four Negroes wearing skullcaps. Now as they read the Holy Word, Manischevitz could, through the plate-glass window, hear the singsong chant of their voices. One of them was old, with a gray beard. One was bubble-eyed. One was humpbacked. The fourth was a boy, no older than thirteen. Their heads moved in rhythmic swaying. Touched by this sight from his childhood and youth, Manischevitz entered and stood silent in the rear.

"Neshoma," said bubble eyes, pointing to the word with a stubby finger. "Now what dat mean?"

"That's the word that means soul," said the boy. He wore eyeglasses.

"Let's git on wid de commentary," said the old man.

"Ain't necessary," said the humpback. "Souls is immaterial substance. That's all. The soul is derived in that manner. The immateriality is derived from the substance, and they both, causally an' otherwise, derived from the soul. There can be no higher."

"That's the highest."

"Over de top."

"Wait a minute," said bubble eyes. "I don't see what is dat immaterial substance. How come de one gits hitched up to de odder?" He addressed the humpback.

"Ask me somethin' hard. Because it is substanceless immateriality. It couldn't be closer together, like all the parts of the body under one skin—closer."

"Hear now," said the old man.

"All you done is switched de words."

"It's the primum mobile, the substanceless substance from which comes all things that were incepted in the idea—you, me, and everything and -body else."

"Now how did all dat happen? Make it sound simple."

"It de speerit," said the old man. "On de face of de water moved de speerit. An' dat was good. It say so in de Book. From de speerit ariz de man."

"But now listen here. How come it become substance if it all de time a spirit?"

"God alone done dat."

"Holy! Holy! Praise His Name."

"But has dis spirit got some kind of a shade or color?" asked bubble eyes, deadpan.

"Man, of course not. A spirit is a spirit."

"Then how come we is colored?" he said with a triumphant glare.

"Ain't got nothing to do wid dat."

"I still like to know."

"God put the spirit in all things," answered the boy. "He put it in the green leaves and the yellow flowers. He put it with the gold in the fishes and the blue in the sky. That's how come it came to us."

"Amen."

"Praise Lawd and utter loud His speechless Name."

"Blow de bugle till it bust the sky."

They fell silent, intent upon the next word. Manischevitz, with doubt, approached them.

"You'll excuse me," he said. "I am looking for Alexander Levine. You know him maybe?"

"That's the angel," said the boy.

"Oh *him*," snuffed bubble eyes.

"You'll find him at Bella's. It's the establishment right down the street," the humpback said.

Manischevitz said he was sorry that he could not stay, thanked them, and limped across the street. It was already night. The city was dark and he could barely find his way.

But Bella's was bursting with jazz and the blues. Through the window Manischevitz recognized the dancing crowd and among them sought Levine. He was sitting loose-lipped at Bella's side table. They were tippling from an almost empty whiskey fifth. Levine had shed his old clothes, wore a shiny new checkered suit, pearl-gray derby hat, cigar, and big, two-tone, button shoes. To the tailor's dismay, a drunken look had settled upon his formerly dignified face. He leaned toward Bella, tickled her earlobe with his pinky while whispering words that sent her into gales of raucous laughter. She fondled his knee.

Manischevitz, girding himself, pushed open the door and was not welcomed.

"This place reserved." 85

"Beat it, pale puss."

"Exit, Yankel, semitic trash."

But he moved toward the table where Levine sat, the crowd breaking before him as he hobbled forward.

"Mr. Levine," he spoke in a trembly voice. "Is here Manischevitz."

Levine glared blearily. "Speak yo' piece, son." 90

Manischevitz shivered. His back plagued him. Tremors tormented his legs. He looked around, everybody was all ears.

"You'll excuse me. I would like to talk to you in a private place."

"Speak, Ah is a private pusson."

Bella laughed piercingly. "Stop it, boy, you killin' me."

Manischevitz, no end disturbed, considered fleeing but Levine addressed him: 95

"Kindly state the pu'pose of yo' communication with yo's truly."

The tailor wet cracked lips. "You are Jewish. This I am sure."

Levine rose, nostrils flaring. "Anythin' else yo' got to say?"

Manischevitz's tongue lay like a slab of stone.

"Speak now or fo'ever hold off." 100

Tears blinded the tailor's eyes. Was ever man so tried? Should he say he believed a half-drunk Negro was an angel?

The silence slowly petrified.

Manischevitz was recalling scenes of his youth as a wheel in his mind whirred: believe, do not, yes, no, yes, no. The pointer pointed to yes, to between yes and no, to no, no it was yes. He sighed. It moved but one still had to make a choice.

"I think you are an angel from God." He said it in a broken voice, thinking, If you said it it was said. If you believed it you must say it. If you believed, you believed.

The hush broke. Everybody talked but the music began and they went on 105 dancing. Bella, grown bored, picked up the cards and dealt herself a hand.

Levine burst into tears. "How you have humiliated me."

Manischevitz apologized.

"Wait'll I freshen up." Levine went to the men's room and returned in his old suit.

No one said goodbye as they left.

They rode to the flat via subway. As they walked up the stairs Manischevitz 110 pointed with his cane at his door.

"That's all been taken care of," Levine said. "You go in while I take off."

Disappointed that it was so soon over, but torn by curiosity, Manischevitz followed the angel up three flights to the roof. When he got there the door was already padlocked.

Luckily he could see through a small broken window. He heard an odd noise, as though of a whirring of wings, and when he strained for a wider view, could have sworn he saw a dark figure borne aloft on a pair of strong black wings.

A feather drifted down. Manischevitz gasped as it turned white, but it was only snowing.

He rushed downstairs. In the flat Fanny wielded a dust mop under the bed, 115 and then upon the cobwebs on the wall.

"A wonderful thing, Fanny," Manischevitz said. "Believe me, there are Jews everywhere."

Katherine Mansfield

MISS BRILL
1922

Katherine Mansfield

Katherine Mansfield Beauchamp (1888–1923), who shortened her byline, was born into a sedate Victorian family in New Zealand, daughter of a successful businessman. At fifteen, she emigrated to England to attend school and did not ever permanently return Down Under. In 1918, after a time of wild-oat sowing in bohemian London, she married the journalist and critic John Middleton Murray. All at once, Mansfield found herself struggling to define her sexual identity, to earn a living by her pen, to endure World War I (in which her brother was killed in action), and to survive the ravages of tuberculosis. She died at thirty-four, in France, at a spiritualist commune where she had sought to regain her health. Mansfield wrote no novels, but during her brief career concentrated on the short story, in which form of art she has few peers. Bliss (1920) and The Garden-Party and Other Stories (1922) were greeted with an acclaim that has continued; her collected Short Stories was published in 1937. Some of her stories celebrate life, others wryly poke fun at it. Many reveal, in ordinary lives, small incidents that open like doorways into significances.

Although it was so brilliantly fine—the blue sky powdered with gold and great spots of light like white wine splashed over the Jardins Publiques—Miss Brill was glad that she had decided on her fur. The air was motionless, but when you opened your mouth there was just a faint chill, like a chill from a glass of iced water before you sip, and now and again a leaf came drifting—from nowhere, from the sky. Miss Brill put up her hand and touched her fur. Dear little thing! It was nice to feel it again. She had taken it out of its box that afternoon, shaken out the moth-powder, given it a good brush, and rubbed the life back into the dim little eyes. "What has been happening to me?" said the sad little eyes. Oh, how sweet it was to see them snap at her again from the red eiderdown! . . . But the nose, which was of some black composition, wasn't at all firm. It must have had a knock, somehow. Never mind—a little dab of black sealing-wax when the time came—when it was absolutely necessary. . . . Little rogue! Yes, she really felt like that about it. Little rogue biting its tail just by her left ear. She could have taken it off and laid it on her lap and stroked it. She felt a tingling in her hands and arms, but that came from walking, she supposed. And when she breathed, something light and sad—no, not sad, exactly—something gentle seemed to move in her bosom.

There were a number of people out this afternoon, far more than last Sunday. And the band sounded louder and gayer. That was because the Season had begun. For although the band played all year round on Sundays, out of season it was never the same. It was like some one playing with only the family to listen; it didn't care how it played if there weren't any strangers present. Wasn't the conductor wearing a new coat, too? She was sure it was new. He scraped with his foot and flapped his arms like a rooster about to crow, and the bandsmen sitting in the green rotunda blew out their cheeks and glared at the music. Now there came a little "flutey" bit—very pretty!—a little chain of bright drops. She was sure it would be repeated. It was; she lifted her head and smiled.

Only two people shared her "special" seat: a fine old man in a velvet coat, his hands clasped over a huge carved walking-stick, and a big old woman, sitting upright, with a roll of knitting on her embroidered apron. They did not speak. This was disappointing, for Miss Brill always looked forward to the conversation. She had become really quite expert, she thought, at listening as though she didn't listen, at sitting in other people's lives just for a minute while they talked round her.

She glanced, sideways, at the old couple. Perhaps they would go soon. Last Sunday, too, hadn't been as interesting as usual. An Englishman and his wife, he wearing a dreadful Panama hat and she button boots. And she'd gone on the whole time about how she ought to wear spectacles; she knew she needed them; but that it was no good getting any; they'd be sure to break and they'd never keep on. And he'd been so patient. He'd suggested everything—gold rims, the kind that curved round your ears, little pads inside the bridge. No, nothing would please her. "They'll always be sliding down my nose!" Miss Brill wanted to shake her.

The old people sat on the bench, still as statues. Never mind, there was always the crowd to watch. To and fro, in front of the flower-beds and the band rotunda, the couples and groups paraded, stopped to talk, to greet, to buy a handful of flowers from the old beggar who had his tray fixed to the railings. Little chil- 5 dren ran among them, swooping and laughing; little boys with big white silk bows under their chins, little girls, little French dolls, dressed up in velvet and lace. And sometimes a tiny staggerer came suddenly rocking into the open from under the trees, stopped, stared, as suddenly sat down "flop," until its small high-stepping mother, like a young hen, rushed scolding to its rescue. Other people sat on the benches and green chairs, but they were nearly always the same, Sunday after Sunday, and—Miss Brill had often noticed—there was something funny about nearly all of them. They were odd, silent, nearly all old, and from the way they stared they looked as though they'd just come from dark little rooms or even—even cupboards!

Behind the rotunda the slender trees with yellow leaves down drooping, and through them just a line of sea, and beyond the blue sky with gold-veined clouds.

Tum-tum-tum tiddle-um! tiddle-um! tum tiddley-um tum ta! blew the band.

Two young girls in red came by and two young soldiers in blue met them, and they laughed and paired and went off arm-in-arm. Two peasant women with funny straw hats passed, gravely, leading beautiful smoke-colored donkeys. A cold, pale nun hurried by. A beautiful woman came along and dropped her bunch of vi-olets, and a little boy ran after to hand them to her, and she took them and threw them away as if they'd been poisoned. Dear me! Miss Brill didn't know whether to admire that or not! And now an ermine toque and a gentleman in grey met just in front of her. He was tall, stiff, dignified, and she was wearing the ermine toque she'd bought when her hair was yellow. Now everything, her hair, her face, even her eyes, was the same color as the shabby ermine, and her hand, in its cleaned glove, lifted to dab her lips, was a tiny yellowish paw. Oh, she was so pleased to see him—delighted! She rather thought they were going to meet that afternoon. She described where she'd been—everywhere, here, there, along by the sea. The day was so charming—didn't he agree? And wouldn't he, perhaps? . . . But he shook his head, lighted a cigarette, slowly breathed a great deep puff into her face, and, even while she was still talking and laughing, flicked the match away and walked on. The ermine toque was alone; she smiled more brightly than ever. But even the band seemed to know what she was feeling and played more softly, played ten-derly, and the drum beat, "The Brute! The Brute!" over and over. What would she do? What was going to happen now? But as Miss Brill wondered, the ermine toque turned, raised her hand as though she'd seen some one else, much nicer, just over there, and pattered away. And the band changed again and played more quickly, more gaily than ever, and the old couple on Miss Brill's seat got up and marched away, and such a funny old man with long whiskers hobbled along in time to the music and was nearly knocked over by four girls walking abreast.

Oh, how fascinating it was! How she enjoyed it! How she loved sitting here, watching it all! It was like a play. It was exactly like a play. Who could be-lieve the sky at the back wasn't painted? But it wasn't till a little brown dog trotted on solemn and then slowly trotted off, like a little "theatre" dog, a little dog that had been drugged, that Miss Brill discovered what it was that made it so exciting. They were all on the stage. They weren't only the audience, not only looking on; they were acting. Even she had a part and came every Sunday. No doubt somebody would have noticed if she hadn't been there; she was part of the performance after all. How strange she'd never thought of it like that before! And yet it explained why she made such a point of starting from home at just the same time each week—so as not to be late for the performance—and it also explained why she had quite a queer, shy feeling at telling her English pupils how she spent her Sunday afternoons. No wonder! Miss Brill nearly laughed out loud. She was on the stage. She thought of the old invalid gentleman to whom she read the newspaper four afternoons a week while he slept in the garden. She had got quite used to the frail head on the cotton pillow, the hollowed eyes, the open mouth and the high pinched nose. If he'd been dead she mightn't have noticed for weeks; she wouldn't have minded. But suddenly he knew he was having the paper read to him by an actress! "An actress!" The old head lifted; two points of light quivered in the old eyes. "An actress—are ye?" And Miss Brill smoothed the newspaper as though it were the manuscript of her part and said gently: "Yes, I have been an actress for a long time."

The band had been having a rest. Now they started again. And what they played was warm, sunny, yet there was just a faint chill—a something, what was it?—not sadness—no, not sadness—a something that made you want to sing. The tune lifted, lifted, the light shone; and it seemed to Miss Brill that in another moment all of them, all the whole company, would begin singing. The young ones, the laughing ones who were moving together, they would begin, and the men's voices, very resolute and brave, would join them. And then she too, she too, and the others on the benches—they would come in with a kind of accompaniment—something low, that scarcely rose or fell, something so beautiful—moving . . . And Miss Brill's eyes filled with tears and she looked smiling at all the other members of the company. Yes, we understand, we understand, she thought—though what they understood she didn't know.

Just at that moment a boy and a girl came and sat down where the old couple had been. They were beautifully dressed; they were in love. The hero and heroine, of course, just arrived from his father's yacht. And still soundlessly singing, still with that trembling smile, Miss Brill prepared to listen.

"No, not now," said the girl. "Not here, I can't."

"But why? Because of that stupid old thing at the end there?" asked the boy. "Why does she come here at all—who wants her? Why doesn't she keep her silly old mug at home?"

"It's her fu-fur which is so funny," giggled the girl. "It's exactly like a fried whiting."

"Ah, be off with you!" said the boy in an angry whisper. Then: "Tell me, my petite chérie—"

"No, not here," said the girl. "Not yet."

On her way home she usually bought a slice of honeycake at the baker's. It was her Sunday treat. Sometimes there was an almond in her slice, sometimes not. It made a great difference. If there was an almond it was like carrying home a tiny present—a surprise—something that might very well not have been there. She hurried on the almond Sundays and struck the match for the kettle in quite a dashing way.

But to-day she passed the baker's boy, climbed the stairs, went into the little dark room—her room like a cupboard—and sat down on the red eiderdown. She sat there for a long time. The box that the fur came out of was on the bed. She unclasped the necklet quickly; quickly, without looking, laid it inside. But when she put the lid on she thought she heard something crying.

Bobbie Ann Mason

SHILOH   1982

Bobbie Ann Mason, one of the leading voices in the new Southern fiction, was born in 1940 in Mayfield, Kentucky, growing up on a dairy farm in a region of western Kentucky whose people often appear in her stories. After her graduation from the University of Kentucky, she wrote for popular magazines, including Movie Life *and* TV Star Parade, *then began teaching college, taking her Ph.D. at the University of Connecticut and writing the critical studies* Nabokov's Garden *(1974) and* The Girl Sleuth: A Feminist Guide to the Bobbsey Twins, Nancy Drew, and Their Sisters *(1975). Her first fiction collection,* Shiloh and Other Stories *(1982), received wide attention, and with the novels* In Country *(1985),* Spence & Lila *(1988), and*

Bobbie Ann Mason

Feather Crowns *(1993), her audience has continued to grow.* Midnight Magic: Selected Stories of Bobbie Ann Mason *(1998) was followed by the collection* Zigzagging Down a Wild Trail *(2001). Other of her recent books include* Clear Springs *(1999), a family memoir, and* Elvis Presley *(2003), a biography in the Penguin Lives series. Mason has also supplied many unsigned contributions to the "Talk of the Town" feature in the* New Yorker. *She is a professor of English at the University of Kentucky.*

Leroy Moffitt's wife, Norma Jean, is working on her pectorals. She lifts three-pound dumbbells to warm up, then progresses to a twenty-pound barbell. Standing with her legs apart, she reminds Leroy of Wonder Woman.

"I'd give anything if I could just get these muscles to where they're real hard," says Norma Jean. "Feel this arm. It's not as hard as the other one."

"That's 'cause you're right-handed," says Leroy, dodging as she swings the barbell in an arc.

"Do you think so?"

"Sure."

Leroy is a truckdriver. He injured his leg in a highway accident four months ago, and his physical therapy which involves weights and a pulley, prompted Norma Jean to try building herself up. Now she is attending a body-building class. Leroy has been collecting temporary disability since his tractor-trailer jack-knifed in Missouri, badly twisting his left leg in its socket. He has a steel pin in his hip. He will probably not be able to drive his rig again. It sits in the backyard, like a gigantic bird that has flown home to roost. Leroy has been home in Kentucky for three months, and his leg is almost healed, but the accident frightened him and he does not want to drive any more long hauls. He is not sure what to do next. In the meantime, he makes things from craft kits. He started by building a miniature log cabin from notched Popsicle sticks. He varnished it and placed it on the TV set, where it remains. It reminds him of a rustic Nativity scene. Then he tried string art (sailing ships on black velvet), a macrame owl kit, a snap-together B-17 Flying Fortress, and a lamp made out of a model truck, with a light fixture screwed in the top of the cab. At first the kits were diversions, something to kill time, but now he is thinking about building a full-scale log house from a kit. It would be considerably cheaper than building a regular house, and besides, Leroy has grown to appreciate how things are put together. He has begun to realize that in all the years he was on the road he never took time to examine anything. He was always flying past scenery.

"They won't let you build a log cabin in any of the new subdivisions," Norma Jean tells him.

"They will if I tell them it's for you," he says, teasing her. Ever since they were married, he has promised Norma Jean he would build her a new home one day. They have always rented, and the house they live in is small and nondescript. It does not even feel like a home, Leroy realizes now.

Norma Jean works at the Rexall drugstore, and she has acquired an amazing amount of information about cosmetics. When she explains to Leroy the three stages of complexion care, involving creams, toners, and moisturizers, he thinks happily of other petroleum products—axle grease, diesel fuel. This is a connection between him and Norma Jean. Since he has been home, he has felt unusually tender about his wife and guilty over his long absences. But he can't tell what she feels about him. Norma Jean has never complained about his traveling; she has never made hurt remarks, like calling his truck a "widow-maker." He is reasonably certain she has been faithful to him, but he wishes she would celebrate his permanent home-coming more happily. Norma Jean is often startled to find Leroy at home, and he thinks she seems a little disappointed about it. Perhaps he reminds her too much of the early days of their marriage, before he went on the road. They had a child who died as an infant, years ago. They never speak about their memories of Randy, which have almost faded, but now that Leroy is home all the time, they sometimes feel awkward around each other, and Leroy wonders if one of them should mention the child. He has the feeling that they are waking up out of a dream together—that they must create a new marriage, start afresh. They are lucky they are still married. Leroy has read that for most people losing a child destroys the marriage—or else he heard this on *Donahue*. He can't always remember where he learns things anymore.

At Christmas, Leroy bought an electric organ for Norma Jean. She used to   10
play the piano when she was in high school. "It don't leave you," she told him once. "It's like riding a bicycle."

The new instrument had so many keys and buttons that she was bewildered by it at first. She touched the keys tentatively, pushed some buttons, then pecked out "Chopsticks." It came out in an amplified fox-trot rhythm, with marimba sounds.

"It's an orchestra!" she cried.

The organ had a pecan-look finish and eighteen preset chords, with optional flute, violin, trumpet, clarinet, and banjo accompaniments. Norma Jean mastered the organ almost immediately. At first she played Christmas songs. Then she bought *The Sixties Songbook* and learned every tune in it, adding variations to each with the rows of brightly colored buttons.

"I didn't like these old songs back then," she said. "But I have this crazy feeling I missed something."

"You didn't miss a thing," said Leroy.   15

Leroy likes to lie on the couch and smoke a joint and listen to Norma Jean play "Can't Take My Eyes Off You" and "I'll Be Back." He is back again. After fifteen years on the road, he is finally settling down with the woman he loves. She is still pretty. Her skin is flawless. Her frosted curls resemble pencil trimmings.

Now that Leroy has come home to stay, he notices how much the town has changed. Subdivisions are spreading across western Kentucky like an oil slick. The sign at the edge of town says "Pop: 11,500"—only seven hundred more than it said twenty years before. Leroy can't figure out who is living in all the new houses. The farmers who used to gather around the courthouse square on Saturday afternoons to play checkers and spit tobacco juice have gone. It has been years since Leroy has thought about the farmers, and they have disappeared without his noticing.

Leroy meets a kid named Stevie Hamilton in the parking lot at the new shopping center. While they pretend to be strangers meeting over a stalled car, Stevie tosses an ounce of marijuana under the front seat of Leroy's car. Stevie is wearing orange jogging shoes and a T-shirt that says CHATTAHOOCHEE SUPER RAT. His father is a prominent doctor who lives in one of the expensive subdivisions in a new white-columned brick house that looks like a funeral parlor. In the phone book under his name there is a separate number, with the listing "Teenagers."

"Where do you get this stuff?" asks Leroy. "From your pappy?"

"That's for me to know and you to find out," Stevie says. He is slit-eyed and   20
skinny.

"What else you got?"

"What you interested in?"

"Nothing special. Just wondered."

Leroy used to take speed on the road. Now he has to go slowly. He needs to be mellow. He leans back against the car and says, "I'm aiming to build me a log house, soon as I get time. My wife, though, I don't think she likes the idea."

"Well, let me know when you want me again," Stevie says. He has a ciga- 25 rette in his cupped palm, as though sheltering it from the wind. He takes a long drag, then stomps it on the asphalt and slouches away.

Stevie's father was two years ahead of Leroy in high school. Leroy is thirty-four. He married Norma Jean when they were both eighteen, and their child Randy was born a few months later, but he died at the age of four months and three days. He would be about Stevie's age now. Norma Jean and Leroy were at the drive-in, watching a double feature (*Dr. Strangelove* and *Lover Come Back*), and the baby was sleeping in the back seat. When the first movie ended, the baby was dead. It was the sudden infant death syndrome. Leroy remembers handing Randy to a nurse at the emergency room, as though he were offering her a large doll as a present. A dead baby feels like a sack of flour. "It just happens sometimes," said the doctor, in what Leroy always recalls as a nonchalant tone. Leroy can hardly remember the child anymore, but he still sees vividly a scene from *Dr. Strangelove*° in which the President of the United States was talking in a folksy voice on the hot line to the Soviet premier about the bomber acciden-tally headed toward Russia. He was in the War Room, and the world map was lit up. Leroy remembers Norma Jean standing catatonically beside him in the hos-pital and himself thinking: Who is this strange girl? He had forgotten who she was. Now scientists are saying that crib death is caused by a virus. Nobody knows anything, Leroy thinks. The answers are always changing.

When Leroy gets home from the shopping center, Norma Jean's mother, Mabel Beasley, is there. Until this year, Leroy has not realized how much time she spends with Norma Jean. When she visits, she inspects the closets and then the plants, informing Norma Jean when a plant is droopy or yellow. Mabel calls the plants "flowers," although there are never any blooms. She also notices if Norma Jean's laundry is piling up. Mabel is a short, overweight woman whose tight, brown-dyed curls look more like a wig than the actual wig she sometimes wears. Today she has brought Norma Jean an off-white dust ruffle she made for the bed; Mabel works in a custom upholstery shop.

"This is the tenth one I made this year," Mabel says. "I got started and couldn't stop."

"It's real pretty," says Norma Jean.

"Now we can hide things under the bed," says Leroy, who gets along with 30 his mother-in-law primarily by joking with her. Mabel has never really forgiven him for disgracing her by getting Norma Jean pregnant. When the baby died, she said that fate was mocking her.

Dr. Strangelove: Stanley Kubrick's classic 1964 suspense comedy film about a mad U.S. general who launches an unauthorized nuclear attack on Russia.

"What's that thing?" Mabel says to Leroy in a loud voice, pointing to a tangle of yarn on a piece of canvas.

Leroy holds it up for Mabel to see. "It's my needlepoint," he explains. "This is a *Star Trek* pillow cover."

"That's what a woman would do," says Mabel. "Great day in the morning!"

"All the big football players on TV do it," he says.

"Why, Leroy, you're always trying to fool me. I don't believe you for one minute. You don't know what to do with yourself—that's the whole trouble. Sewing!" 35

"I'm aiming to build us a log house," says Leroy. "Soon as my plans come."

"Like *heck* you are," says Norma Jean. She takes Leroy's needlepoint and shoves it into a drawer. "You have to find a job first. Nobody can afford to build now anyway."

Mabel straightens her girdle and says, "I still think before you get tied down y'all ought to take a little run to Shiloh."

"One of these days, Mama," Norma Jean says impatiently.

Mabel is talking about Shiloh, Tennessee. For the past few years, she has been urging Leroy and Norma Jean to visit the Civil War battleground there. Mabel went there on her honeymoon—the only real trip she ever took. Her husband died of a perforated ulcer when Norma Jean was ten, but Mabel, who was accepted into the United Daughters of the Confederacy in 1975, is still preoccupied with going back to Shiloh. 40

"I've been to kingdom come and back in that truck out yonder," Leroy says to Mabel, "but we never yet set foot in that battleground. Ain't that something? How did I miss it?"

"It's not even that far," Mabel says.

After Mabel leaves, Norma Jean reads to Leroy from a list she has made. "Things you could do," she announces. "You could get a job as a guard at Union Carbide, where they'd let you set on a stool. You could get on at the lumberyard. You could do a little carpenter work, if you want to build so bad. You could—"

"I can't do something where I'd have to stand up all day."

"You ought to try standing up all day behind a cosmetics counter. It's amazing that I have strong feet, coming from two parents that never had strong feet at all." At the moment Norma Jean is holding on to the kitchen counter, raising her knees one at a time as she talks. She is wearing two-pound ankle weights. 45

"Don't worry," says Leroy. "I'll do something."

"You could truck calves to slaughter for somebody. You wouldn't have to drive any big old truck for that."

"I'm going to build you this house," says Leroy. "I want to make you a real home."

"I don't want to live in any log cabin."

"It's not a cabin. It's a house."

"I don't care. It looks like a cabin." 50

"You and me together could lift those logs. It's just like lifting weights."

Norma Jean doesn't answer. Under her breath, she is counting. Now she is marching through the kitchen. She is doing goose steps.°

Before his accident, when Leroy came home he used to stay in the house with Norma Jean, watching TV in bed and playing cards. She would cook fried chicken, picnic ham, chocolate pie—all his favorites. Now he is home alone much of the time. In the mornings, Norma Jean disappears, leaving a cooling place in the bed. She eats a cereal called Body Buddies, and she leaves the bowl on the table, with the soggy tan balls floating in a milk puddle. He sees things about Norma Jean that he never realized before. When she chops onions, she stares off into a corner, as if she can't bear to look. She puts on her house slippers almost precisely at nine o'clock every evening and nudges her jogging shoes under the couch. She saves bread heels for the birds. Leroy watches the birds at the feeder. He notices the peculiar way goldfinches fly past the window. They close their wings, then fall, then spread their wings to catch and lift themselves. He wonders if they close their eyes when they fall. Norma Jean closes her eyes when they are in bed. She wants the lights turned out. Even then, he is sure she closes her eyes.

He goes for long drives around town. He tends to drive a car rather care- 55 lessly. Power steering and an automatic shift make a car feel so small and incon-sequential that his body is hardly involved in the driving process. His injured leg stretches out comfortably. Once or twice he has almost hit something, but even the prospect of an accident seems minor in a car. He cruises the new subdivi-sions, feeling like a criminal rehearsing for a robbery. Norma Jean is probably right about a log house being inappropriate here in the new subdivision. All the houses look grand and complicated. They depress him.

One day when Leroy comes home from a drive he finds Norma Jean in tears. She is in the kitchen making a potato and mushroom-soup casserole, with grated cheese topping. She is crying because her mother caught her smoking.

"I didn't hear her coming. I was standing here puffing away pretty as you please," Norma Jean says, wiping her eyes.

"I knew it would happen sooner or later," says Leroy, putting his arm around her.

"She don't know the meaning of the word 'knock,'" says Norma Jean. "It's a wonder she hadn't caught me years ago."

"Think of it this way," Leroy says. "What if she caught me with a joint?" 60

"You better not let her!" Norma Jean shrieks. "I'm warning you, Leroy Moffitt!"

"I'm just kidding. Here, play me a tune. That'll help you relax."

Norma Jean puts the casserole in the oven and sets the timer. Then she plays a ragtime tune, with horns and banjo, as Leroy lights up a joint and lies on the couch, laughing to himself about Mabel's catching him at it. He thinks of Stevie Hamilton—a doctor's son pushing grass. Everything is funny. The whole town

---

goose steps: a stiff-kneed, straight-legged marching step used in military parades. Used here as an exercise routine.

seems crazy and small. He is reminded of Virgil Mathis, a boastful policeman Leroy used to shoot pool with. Virgil recently led a drug bust in a back room at a bowling alley, where he seized ten thousand dollars' worth of marijuana. The newspaper had a picture of him holding up the bags of grass and grinning widely. Right now, Leroy can imagine Virgil breaking down the door and arresting him with a lungful of smoke. Virgil would probably have been alerted to the scene because of all the racket Norma Jean is making. Now she sounds like a hard-rock band. Norma Jean is terrific. When she switches to a Latin-rhythm version of "Sunshine Superman," Leroy hums along. Norma Jean's foot goes up and down, up and down.

"Well, what do you think?" Leroy says, when Norma Jean pauses to search through her music.

"What do I think about what?"   65

His mind has gone blank. Then he says, "I'll sell my rig and build us a house." That wasn't what he wanted to say. He wanted to know what she thought—what she *really* thought—about them.

"Don't start in on that again," says Norma Jean. She begins playing "Who'll Be the Next in Line?"

Leroy used to tell hitchhikers his whole life story—about his travels, his hometown, the baby. He would end with a question: "Well, what do you think?" It was just a rhetorical question. In time, he had the feeling that he'd been telling the same story over and over to the same hitchhikers. He quit talking to hitchhikers when he realized how his voice sounded—whining and self-pitying, like some teenage-tragedy song. Now Leroy has the sudden impulse to tell Norma Jean about himself, as if he had just met her. They have known each other so long they have forgotten a lot about each other. They could become reacquainted. But when the oven timer goes off and she runs to the kitchen, he forgets why he wants to do this.

The next day, Mabel drops by. It is Saturday and Norma Jean is cleaning. Leroy is studying the plans of his log house, which have finally come in the mail. He has them spread out on the table—big sheets of stiff blue paper, with diagrams and numbers printed in white. While Norma Jean runs the vacuum, Mabel drinks coffee. She sets her coffee cup on a blueprint.

"I'm just waiting for time to pass," she says to Leroy, drumming her fingers   70
on the table.

As soon as Norma Jean switches off the vacuum, Mabel says in a loud voice, "Did you hear about the datsun dog that killed the baby?"

Norma Jean says, "The word is 'dachshund.'"

"They put the dog on trial. It chewed the baby's legs off. The mother was in the next room all the time." She raises her voice. "They thought it was neglect."

Norma Jean is holding her ears. Leroy manages to open the refrigerator and get some Diet Pepsi to offer Mabel. Mabel still has some coffee and she waves away the Pepsi.

"Datsuns are like that," Mabel says. "They're jealous dogs. They'll tear a   75
place to pieces if you don't keep an eye on them."

"You better watch out what you're saying, Mabel," says Leroy.

"Well, facts is facts."

Leroy looks out the window at his rig. It is like a huge piece of furniture gathering dust in the backyard. Pretty soon it will be an antique. He hears the vacuum cleaner. Norma Jean seems to be cleaning the living room rug again.

Later, she says to Leroy, "She just said that about the baby because she caught me smoking. She's trying to pay me back."

"What are you talking about?" Leroy says, nervously shuffling blueprints.

80

"You know good and well," Norma Jean says. She is sitting in a kitchen chair with her feet up and her arms wrapped around her knees. She looks small and helpless. She says, "The very idea, her bringing up a subject like that! Saying it was neglect."

"She didn't mean that," Leroy says.

"She might not have *thought* she meant it. She always says things like that. You don't know how she goes on."

"But she didn't really mean it. She was just talking."

Leroy opens a king-sized bottle of beer and pours it into two glasses, dividing it carefully. He hands a glass to Norma Jean and she takes it from him mechanically. For a long time, they sit by the kitchen window watching the birds at the feeder.

85

Something is happening. Norma Jean is going to night school. She has graduated from her six-week body-building course and now she is taking an adult-education course in composition at Paducah Community College. She spends her evenings outlining paragraphs.

"First, you have a topic sentence," she explains to Leroy. "Then you divide it up. Your secondary topic has to be connected to your primary topic."

To Leroy, this sounds intimidating. "I never was any good in English," he says.

"It makes a lot of sense."

"What are you doing this for, anyhow?"

90

She shrugs. "It's something to do." She stands up and lifts her dumbbells a few times.

"Driving a rig, nobody cared about my English."

"I'm not criticizing your English."

Norma Jean used to say, "If I lose ten minutes' sleep, I just drag all day." Now she stays up late, writing compositions. She got a B on her first paper—a how-to theme on soup-based casseroles. Recently Norma Jean has been cooking unusual foods—tacos, lasagna, Bombay chicken. She doesn't play the organ anymore, though her second paper was called "Why Music Is Important to Me." She sits at the kitchen table, concentrating on her outlines, while Leroy plays with his log house plans, practicing with a set of Lincoln Logs. The thought of getting a truckload of notched, numbered logs scares him, and he wants to be prepared. As he and Norma Jean work together at the kitchen table, Leroy has the hopeful thought that they are sharing something, but he knows he is a fool to think this.

Norma Jean is miles away. He knows he is going to lose her. Like Mabel, he is just waiting for time to pass.

One day, Mabel is there before Norma Jean gets home from work, and Leroy 95 finds himself confiding in her. Mabel, he realizes, must know Norma Jean better than he does.

"I don't know what's got into that girl," Mabel says. "She used to go to bed with the chickens. Now you say she's up all hours. Plus her a-smoking. I like to died."

"I want to make her this beautiful home," Leroy says, indicating the Lincoln Logs. "I don't think she even wants it. Maybe she was happier with me gone."

"She don't know what to make of you, coming home like this."

"Is that it?"

Mabel takes the roof off his Lincoln Log cabin. "You couldn't get me in a log 100 cabin," she says. "I was raised in one. It's no picnic, let me tell you."

"They're different now," says Leroy.

"I tell you what," Mabel says, smiling oddly at Leroy.

"What?"

"Take her on down to Shiloh. Y'all need to get out together, stir a little. Her brain's all balled up over them books."

Leroy can see traces of Norma Jean's features in her mother's face. Mabel's 105 worn face has the texture of crinkled cotton, but suddenly she looks pretty. It occurs to Leroy that Mabel has been hinting all along that she wants them to take her with them to Shiloh.

"Let's all go to Shiloh," he says. "You and me and her. Come Sunday."

Mabel throws up her hand in protest. "Oh, no, not me. Young folks want to be by theirselves."

When Norma Jean comes in with groceries, Leroy says excitedly, "Your mama here's been dying to go to Shiloh for thirty-five years. It's about time we went, don't you think?"

"I'm not going to butt in on anybody's second honeymoon," Mabel says.

"Who's going on a honeymoon, for Christ's sake?" Norma Jean says loudly. 110

"I never raised no daughter of mine to talk that-a-way," Mabel says.

"You ain't seen nothing yet," says Norma Jean. She starts putting away boxes and cans, slamming cabinet doors.

"There's a log cabin at Shiloh," Mabel says. "It was there during the battle. There's bullet holes in it."

"When are you going to *shut up* about Shiloh, Mama?" asks Norma Jean.

"I always thought Shiloh was the prettiest place, so full of history," Mabel 115 goes on. "I just hoped y'all could see it once before I die, so you could tell me about it." Later, she whispers to Leroy, "You do what I said. A little change is what she needs."

"Your name means 'the king,'" Norma Jean says to Leroy that evening. He is trying to get her to go to Shiloh, and she is reading a book about another century.

"Well, I reckon I ought to be right proud."

"I guess so."

"Am I still king around here?"

Norma Jean flexes her biceps and feels them for hardness. "I'm not fooling around with anybody, if that's what you mean," she says. 120

"Would you tell me if you were?"

"I don't know."

"What does *your* name mean?"

"It was Marilyn Monroe's real name."

"No kidding!" 125

"Norma comes from the Normans. They were invaders," she says. She closes her book and looks hard at Leroy. "I'll go to Shiloh with you if you'll stop staring at me."

On Sunday, Norma Jean packs a picnic and they go to Shiloh. To Leroy's relief Mabel says she does not want to come with them. Norma Jean drives, and Leroy, sitting beside her, feels like some boring hitchhiker she has picked up. He tries some conversation, but she answers him in monosyllables. At Shiloh, she drives aimlessly through the park, past bluffs and trails and steep ravines. Shiloh is an immense place, and Leroy cannot see it as a battleground. It is not what he expected. He thought it would look like a golf course. Monuments are everywhere, showing through the thick clusters of trees. Norma Jean passes the log cabin Mabel mentioned. It is surrounded by tourists looking for bullet holes.

"That's not the kind of log house I've got in mind," says Leroy apologetically.

"I know *that*."

"This is a pretty place. Your mama was right." 130

"It's O.K.," says Norma Jean. "Well, we've seen it. I hope she's satisfied."

They burst out laughing together.

At the park museum, a movie on Shiloh is shown every half hour, but they decide that they don't want to see it. They buy a souvenir Confederate flag for Mabel, and then they find a picnic spot near the cemetery. Norma Jean has brought a picnic cooler, with pimiento sandwiches, soft drinks, and Yodels. Leroy eats a sandwich and then smokes a joint, hiding it behind the picnic cooler. Norma Jean has quit smoking altogether. She is picking cake crumbs from the cellophane wrapper, like a fussy bird.

Leroy says, "So the boys in gray ended up in Corinth. The Union soldiers zapped 'em finally. April 7, 1862."

They both know that he doesn't know any history. He is just talking about 135 some of the historical plaques they have read. He feels awkward, like a boy on a date with an older girl. They are still just making conversation.

"Corinth is where Mama eloped to," says Norma Jean.

They sit in silence and stare at the cemetery for the Union dead and, beyond, at a tall cluster of trees. Campers are parked nearby, bumper to bumper, and small children in bright clothing are cavorting and squealing. Norma Jean wads up the cake wrapper and squeezes it tightly in her hand. Without looking at Leroy, she says, "I want to leave you."

Leroy takes a bottle of Coke out of the cooler and flips off the cap. He holds the bottle poised near his mouth but cannot remember to take a drink. Finally he says, "No, you don't."

"Yes, I do."

"I won't let you."

"You can't stop me."

"Don't do me that way."

Leroy knows Norma Jean will have her own way. "Didn't I promise to be home from now on?" he says.

"In some ways, a woman prefers a man who wanders," says Norma Jean. "That sounds crazy, I know."

"You're not crazy." Leroy remembers to drink from his Coke. Then he says, "Yes, you *are* crazy. You and me could start all over again. Right back at the beginning."

"We *have* started all over again," says Norma Jean. "And this is how it turned out."

"What did I do wrong?"

"Nothing."

"Is this one of those women's lib things?" Leroy asks.

"Don't be funny."

The cemetery, a green slope dotted with white markers, looks like a subdivision site. Leroy is trying to comprehend that his marriage is breaking up, but for some reason he is wondering about white slabs in a graveyard.

"Everything was fine till Mama caught me smoking," says Norma Jean, standing up. "That set something off."

"What are you talking about?"

"She won't leave me alone—*you* won't leave me alone." Norma Jean seems to be crying, but she is looking away from him. "I feel eighteen again. I can't face that all over again." She starts walking away. "No, it *wasn't* fine. I don't know what I'm saying. Forget it."

Leroy takes a lungful of smoke and closes his eyes as Norma Jean's words sink in. He tries to focus on the fact that thirty-five hundred soldiers died on the grounds around him. He can only think of that war as a board game with plastic soldiers. Leroy almost smiles, as he compares the Confederates' daring attack on the Union camps and Virgil Mathis's raid on the bowling alley. General Grant, drunk and furious, shoved the Southerners back to Corinth, where Mabel and Jet Beasley were married years later, when Mabel was still thin and good-looking. The next day, Mabel and Jet visited the battleground, and then Norma Jean was born, and then she married Leroy and they had a baby, which they lost, and now Leroy and Norma Jean are here at the same battleground. Leroy knows he is leaving out a lot. He is leaving out the insides of history. History was always just names and dates to him. It occurs to him that building a house of logs is similarly empty—too simple. And the real inner workings of a marriage, like most of history, have escaped him. Now he sees that building a log house is the dumbest idea he could have had. It was clumsy of him to think

140

145

150

155

Norma Jean would want a log house. It was a crazy idea. He'll have to think of something else, quickly. He will wad the blueprints into tight balls and fling them into the lake. Then he'll get moving again. He opens his eyes. Norma Jean has moved away and is walking through the cemetery, following a serpentine brick path.

Leroy gets up to follow his wife, but his good leg is asleep and his bad leg still hurts him. Norma Jean is far away, walking rapidly toward the bluff by the river, and he tries to hobble toward her. Some children run past him, screaming noisily. Norma Jean has reached the bluff, and she is looking out over the Tennessee River. Now she turns toward Leroy and waves her arms. Is she beckoning to him? She seems to be doing an exercise for her chest muscles. The sky is unusually pale—the color of the dust ruffle Mabel made for their bed.

Joyce Carol Oates

WHERE ARE YOU GOING, WHERE HAVE YOU BEEN? 1970

Joyce Carol Oates (© Jill Krementz, Inc.)

Joyce Carol Oates was born in 1938 into a blue-collar, Catholic family in Lockport, New York. As an undergraduate at Syracuse University, she won a Mademoiselle *magazine award for fiction. After graduation with top honors, she took a master's degree in English at the University of Wisconsin and went on to teach at several universities: Detroit, Windsor, and Princeton. She now lives in Princeton, New Jersey, where, together with her husband, Raymond Smith, she directs the Ontario Review Press, a small literary publisher. A remarkably prolific writer, Oates has produced more than twenty-five collections of stories and forty novels, including* them, *winner of a National Book Award in 1970,* Because It Is Bitter, and Because It Is My Heart *(1990), and more recently,* Middle Age: A Romance *(2001),* I'll Take You There *(2002), and* The Tattooed Girl *(2003). She also writes poetry, plays, and literary criticism.* Woman Writer: Occasions & Opportunities *(1988) and* The Faith of a Writer: Life, Craft, Art *(2003) are books of varied essays;* On Boxing *(1987) is a nonfiction memoir and study of fighters and fighting.* Foxfire *(1993), her twenty-second novel, is the story of a girl gang in upstate New York. Her 1996 Gothic novella,* First Love, *is a bizarre tale of terror and torture. Violence and the macabre may inhabit her best stories, but Oates has insisted that these elements in her work are never gratuitous. The 1985 film* Smooth Talk, *directed by Joyce Chopra, was based on "Where Are You Going, Where Have You Been?"*

Her name was Connie. She was fifteen and she had a quick nervous giggling habit of craning her neck to glance into mirrors, or checking other people's faces to make sure her own was all right. Her mother, who noticed everything and knew everything and who hadn't much reason any longer to look at her own face, always scolded Connie about it. "Stop gawking at yourself, who are you? You think you're so pretty?" she would say. Connie would raise her eyebrows at these familiar complaints and look right through her mother, into a shadowy vision of herself as she was right at that moment: she knew she was pretty and that was everything. Her mother had been pretty once too, if you could believe those old snapshots in the album, but now her looks were gone and that was why she was always after Connie.

"Why don't you keep your room clean like your sister? How've you got your hair fixed—what the hell stinks? Hair spray? You don't see your sister using that junk."

Her sister June was twenty-four and still lived at home. She was a secretary in the high school Connie attended, and if that wasn't bad enough—with her in the same building—she was so plain and chunky and steady that Connie had to hear her praised all the time by her mother and her mother's sisters. June did this, June did that, she saved money and helped clean the house and cooked and Connie couldn't do a thing, her mind was all filled with trashy daydreams. Their father was away at work most of the time and when he came home he wanted supper and he read the newspaper at supper and after supper he went to bed. He didn't bother talking much to them, but around his bent head Connie's mother kept picking at her until Connie wished her mother was dead and she herself was dead and it was all over. "She makes me want to throw up sometimes," she complained to her friends. She had a high, breathless, amused voice which made everything she said sound a little forced, whether it was sincere or not.

There was one good thing: June went places with girl friends of hers, girls who were just as plain and steady as she, and so when Connie wanted to do that her mother had no objections. The father of Connie's best girl friend drove the girls the three miles to town and left them off at a shopping plaza, so that they could walk through the stores or go to a movie, and when he came to pick them up again at eleven he never bothered to ask what they had done.

They must have been familiar sights, walking around that shopping plaza in their shorts and flat ballerina slippers that always scuffed the sidewalk, with charm bracelets jingling on their thin wrists; they would lean together to whisper and laugh secretly if someone passed by who amused or interested them. Connie had long dark blond hair that drew anyone's eye to it, and she wore part of it pulled up on her head and puffed out and the rest of it she let fall down her back. She wore a pull-over jersey blouse that looked one way when she was at home and another way when she was away from home. Everything about her had two sides to it, one for home and one for anywhere that was not home: her walk that could be childlike and bobbing, or languid enough to make anyone think

5

she was hearing music in her head, her mouth which was pale and smirking most of the time, but bright and pink on these evenings out, her laugh which was cynical and drawling at home—"Ha, ha, very funny"—but high-pitched and nervous anywhere else, like the jingling of the charms on her bracelet.

Sometimes they did go shopping or to a movie, but sometimes they went across the highway, ducking fast across the busy road, to a drive-in restaurant where older kids hung out. The restaurant was shaped like a big bottle, though squatter than a real bottle, and on its cap was a revolving figure of a grinning boy who held a hamburger aloft. One night in mid-summer they ran across, breathless with daring, and right away someone leaned out a car window and invited them over, but it was just a boy from high school they didn't like. It made them feel good to be able to ignore him. They went up through the maze of parked and cruising cars to the bright-lit, fly-infested restaurant, their faces pleased and expectant as if they were entering a sacred building that loomed out of the night to give them what haven and what blessing they yearned for. They sat at the counter and crossed their legs at the ankles, their thin shoulders rigid with excitement, and listened to the music that made everything so good: the music was always in the background like music at a church service, it was something to depend upon.

A boy named Eddie came in to talk with them. He sat backwards on his stool, turning himself jerkily around in semi-circles and then stopping and turning again, and after a while he asked Connie if she would like something to eat. She said she did and so she tapped her friend's arm on her way out—her friend pulled her face up into a brave droll look—and Connie said she would meet her at eleven, across the way. "I just hate to leave her like that," Connie said earnestly, but the boy said that she wouldn't be alone for long. So they went out to his car and on the way Connie couldn't help but let her eyes wander over the windshields and faces all around her, her face gleaming with a joy that had nothing to do with Eddie or even this place; it might have been the music. She drew her shoulders up and sucked in her breath with the pure pleasure of being alive, and just at that moment she happened to glance at a face just a few feet from hers. It was a boy with shaggy black hair, in a convertible jalopy painted gold. He stared at her and then his lips widened into a grin. Connie slit her eyes at him and turned away, but she couldn't help glancing back and there he was still watching her. He wagged a finger and laughed and said, "Gonna get you, baby," and Connie turned away again without Eddie noticing anything.

She spent three hours with him, at the restaurant where they ate hamburgers and drank Cokes in wax cups that were always sweating, and then down an alley a mile or so away, and when he left her off at five to eleven only the movie house was still open at the plaza. Her girl friend was there, talking with a boy. When Connie came up the two girls smiled at each other and Connie said, "How was the movie?" and the girl said, "*You* should know." They rode off with the girl's father, sleepy and pleased, and Connie couldn't help but look at the darkened shopping plaza with its big empty parking lot and its signs that were faded and ghostly now, and over at the drive-in restaurant where cars were still circling tirelessly. She couldn't hear the music at this distance.

Next morning June asked her how the movie was and Connie said, "So-so."

She and that girl and occasionally another girl went out several times a
week that way, and the rest of the time Connie spent around the house—it was summer vacation—getting in her mother's way and thinking, dreaming, about the boys she met. But all the boys fell back and dissolved into a single face that was not even a face, but an idea, a feeling, mixed up with the urgent insistent pounding of the music and the humid night air of July. Connie's mother kept dragging her back to the daylight by finding things for her to do or saying, suddenly, "What's this about the Pettinger girl?"

And Connie would say nervously, "Oh, her. That dope." She always drew thick clear lines between herself and such girls, and her mother was simple and kindly enough to believe her. Her mother was so simple, Connie thought, that it was maybe cruel to fool her so much. Her mother went scuffling around the house in old bedroom slippers and complained over the telephone to one sister about the other, then the other called up and the two of them complained about the third one. If June's name was mentioned her mother's tone was approving, and if Connie's name was mentioned it was disapproving. This did not really mean she disliked Connie and actually Connie thought that her mother preferred her to June because she was prettier, but the two of them kept up a pretense of exasperation, a sense that they were tugging and struggling over something of little value to either of them. Sometimes, over coffee, they were almost friends, but something would come up—some vexation that was like a fly buzzing suddenly around their heads—and their faces went hard with contempt.

One Sunday Connie got up at eleven—none of them bothered with church—and washed her hair so that it could dry all day long, in the sun. Her parents and sister were going to a barbecue at an aunt's house and Connie said no, she wasn't interested, rolling her eyes to let her mother know just what she thought of it. "Stay home alone then," her mother said sharply. Connie sat out back in a lawn chair and watched them drive away, her father quiet and bald, hunched around so that he could back the car out, her mother with a look that was still angry and not at all softened through the windshield, and in the back seat poor old June all dressed up as if she didn't know what a barbecue was, with all the running yelling kids and the flies. Connie sat with her eyes closed in the sun, dreaming and dazed with the warmth about her as if this were a kind of love, the caresses of love, and her mind slipped over onto thoughts of the boy she had been with the night before and how nice he had been, how sweet it always was, not the way someone like June would suppose but sweet, gentle, the way it was in movies and promised in songs; and when she opened her eyes she hardly knew where she was, the back yard ran off into weeds and a fence-line of trees and behind it the sky was perfectly blue and still. The asbestos "ranch house" that was now three years old startled her—it looked small. She shook her head as if to get awake.

It was too hot. She went inside the house and turned on the radio to drown out the quiet. She sat on the edge of her bed, barefoot, and listened for an hour and a half to a program called XYZ Sunday Jamboree, record after record of hard, fast, shrieking songs she sang along with, interspersed by exclamations from

"Bobby King": "An' look here you girls at Napoleon's—Son and Charley want you to pay real close attention to this song coming up!"

And Connie paid close attention herself, bathed in a glow of slow-pulsed joy that seemed to rise mysteriously out of the music itself and lay languidly about the airless little room, breathed in and breathed out with each gentle rise and fall of her chest.

After a while she heard a car coming up the drive. She sat up at once, star- 15 tled, because it couldn't be her father so soon. The gravel kept crunching all the way in from the road—the driveway was long—and Connie ran to the window. It was a car she didn't know. It was an open jalopy, painted a bright gold that caught the sunlight opaquely. Her heart began to pound and her fingers snatched at her hair, checking it, and she whispered "Christ, Christ," wondering how bad she looked. The car came to a stop at the side door and the horn sounded four short taps as if this were a signal Connie knew.

She went into the kitchen and approached the door slowly, then hung out the screen door, her bare toes curling down off the step. There were two boys in the car and now she recognized the driver: he had shaggy, shabby black hair that looked crazy as a wig and he was grinning at her.

"I ain't late, am I?" he said.

"Who the hell do you think you are?" Connie said.

"Toldja I'd be out, didn't I?"

"I don't even know who you are." 20

She spoke sullenly, careful to show no interest or pleasure, and he spoke in a fast bright monotone. Connie looked past him to the other boy, taking her time. He had fair brown hair, with a lock that fell onto his forehead. His sideburns gave him a fierce, embarrassed look, but so far he hadn't even bothered to glance at her. Both boys wore sunglasses. The driver's glasses were metallic and mirrored everything in miniature.

"You wanta come for a ride?" he said.

Connie smirked and let her hair fall loose over one shoulder.

"Don'tcha like my car? New paint job," he said. "Hey."

"What?" 25

"You're cute."

She pretended to fidget, chasing flies away from the door.

"Don'tcha believe me, or what?" he said.

"Look, I don't even know who you are," Connie said in disgust.

"Hey, Ellie's got a radio, see. Mine's broke down." He lifted his friend's arm 30 and showed her the little transistor the boy was holding, and now Connie began to hear the music. It was the same program that was playing inside the house.

"Bobby King?" she said.

"I listen to him all the time. I think he's great."

"He's kind of great," Connie said reluctantly.

"Listen, that guy's *great*. He knows where the action is."

Connie blushed a little, because the glasses made it impossible for her to see 35 just what this boy was looking at. She couldn't decide if she liked him or if he was just a jerk, and so she dawdled in the doorway and wouldn't come down or go back inside. She said, "What's all that stuff painted on your car?"

"Can'tcha read it?" He opened the door very carefully, as if he was afraid it might fall off. He slid out just as carefully, planting his feet firmly on the ground, the tiny metallic world in his glasses slowing down like gelatine hardening and in the midst of it Connie's bright green blouse. "This here is my name, to begin with," he said. ARNOLD FRIEND was written in tarlike black letters on the side, with a drawing of a round grinning face that reminded Connie of a pumpkin, except it wore sunglasses. "I wanta introduce myself, I'm Arnold Friend and that's my real name and I'm gonna be your friend, honey, and inside the car's Ellie Oscar, he's kinda shy." Ellie brought his transistor radio up to his shoulder and balanced it there. "Now these numbers are a secret code, honey," Arnold Friend explained. He read off the numbers 33, 19, 17 and raised his eyebrows at her to see what she thought of that, but she didn't think much of it. The left rear fender had been smashed and around it was written, on the gleaming gold background: DONE BY CRAZY WOMAN DRIVER. Connie had to laugh at that. Arnold Friend was pleased at her laughter and looked up at her. "Around the other side's a lot more—you wanta come and see them?"

"No."

"Why not?"

"Why should I?"

"Don'tcha wanta see what's on the car? Don'tcha wanta go for a ride?"   40

"I don't know."

"Why not?"

"I got things to do."

"Like what?"

"Things."   45

He laughed as if she had said something funny. He slapped his thighs. He was standing in a strange way, leaning back against the car as if he were balancing himself. He wasn't tall, only an inch or so taller than she would be if she came down to him. Connie liked the way he was dressed, which was the way all of them dressed: tight faded jeans stuffed into black, scuffed boots, a belt that pulled his waist in and showed how lean he was, and a white pull-over shirt that was a little soiled and showed the hard small muscles of his arms and shoulders. He looked as if he probably did hard work, lifting and carrying things. Even his neck looked muscular. And his face was a familiar face, somehow: the jaw and chin and cheeks slightly darkened, because he hadn't shaved for a day or two, and the nose long and hawk-like, sniffing as if she were a treat he was going to gobble up and it was all a joke.

"Connie, you ain't telling the truth. This is your day set aside for a ride with me and you know it," he said, still laughing. The way he straightened and recovered from his fit of laughing showed that it had been all fake.

"How do you know what my name is?" she said suspiciously.

"It's Connie."

"Maybe and maybe not."   50

"I know my Connie," he said, wagging his finger. Now she remembered him even better, back at the restaurant, and her cheeks warmed at the thought of how she sucked in her breath just at the moment she passed him—how she must have looked to him. And he had remembered her. "Ellie and I come out here especially for you," he said. "Ellie can sit in back. How about it?"

"Where?"

"Where what?"

"Where're we going?"

He looked at her. He took off the sunglasses and she saw how pale the skin around his eyes was, like holes that were not in shadow but instead in light. His eyes were chips of broken glass that catch the light in an amiable way. He smiled. It was as if the idea of going for a ride somewhere, to some place, was a new idea to him.

"Just for a ride, Connie sweetheart."

"I never said my name was Connie," she said.

"But I know what it is. I know your name and all about you, lots of things," Arnold Friend said. He had not moved yet but stood still leaning back against the side of his jalopy. "I took a special interest in you, such a pretty girl, and found out all about you like I know your parents and sister are gone somewheres and I know where and how long they're going to be gone, and I know who you were with last night, and your best girl friend's name is Betty. Right?"

He spoke in a simple lilting voice, exactly as if he were reciting the words to a song. His smile assured her that everything was fine. In the car Ellie turned up the volume on his radio and did not bother to look around at them.

"Ellie can sit in the back seat," Arnold Friend said. He indicated his friend with a casual jerk of his chin, as if Ellie did not count and she should not bother with him.

"How'd you find out all that stuff?" Connie said.

"Listen: Betty Schultz and Tony Fitch and Jimmy Pettinger and Nancy Pettinger," he said, in a chant. "Raymond Stanley and Bob Hutter—"

"Do you know all those kids?"

"I know everybody."

"Look, you're kidding. You're not from around here."

"Sure."

"But—how come we never saw you before?"

"Sure you saw me before," he said. He looked down at his boots, as if he were a little offended. "You just don't remember."

"I guess I'd remember you," Connie said.

"Yeah?" He looked up at this, beaming. He was pleased. He began to mark time with the music from Ellie's radio, tapping his fists lightly together. Connie looked away from his smile to the car, which was painted so bright it almost hurt her eyes to look at it. She looked at that name, ARNOLD FRIEND. And up at the front fender was an expression that was familiar—MAN THE FLYING SAUCERS. It was an expression kids had used the year before, but didn't use this year. She looked at it for a while as if the words meant something to her that she did not yet know.

"What're you thinking about? Huh?" Arnold Friend demanded. "Not worried about your hair blowing around in the car, are you?"

"No."

"Think I maybe can't drive good?"

"How do I know?"

"You're a hard girl to handle. How come?" he said. "Don't you know I'm your friend? Didn't you see me put my sign in the air when you walked by?" 75

"What sign?"

"My sign." And he drew an X in the air, leaning out toward her. They were maybe ten feet apart. After his hand fell back to his side the X was still in the air, almost visible. Connie let the screen door close and stood perfectly still inside it, listening to the music from her radio and the boy's blend together. She stared at Arnold Friend. He stood there so stiffly relaxed, pretending to be relaxed, with one hand idly on the door handle as if he were keeping himself up that way and had no intention of ever moving again. She recognized most things about him, the tight jeans that showed his thighs and buttocks and the greasy leather boots and the tight shirt, and even that slippery friendly smile of his, that sleepy dreamy smile that all the boys used to get across ideas they didn't want to put into words. She recognized all this and also the singsong way he talked, slightly mocking, kidding, but serious and a little melancholy, and she recognized the way he tapped one fist against the other in homage to the perpetual music behind him. But all these things did not come together.

She said suddenly, "Hey, how old are you?"

His smile faded. She could see then that he wasn't a kid, he was much older—thirty, maybe more. At this knowledge her heart began to pound faster.

"That's a crazy thing to ask. Can'tcha see I'm your own age?" 80

"Like hell you are."

"Or maybe a coupla years older, I'm eighteen."

"Eighteen?" she said doubtfully.

He grinned to reassure her and lines appeared at the corners of his mouth. His teeth were big and white. He grinned so broadly his eyes became slits and she saw how thick the lashes were, thick and black as if painted with a black tar-like material. Then he seemed to become embarrassed, abruptly, and looked over his shoulder at Ellie. "Him, he's crazy," he said. "Ain't he a riot, he's a nut, a real character." Ellie was still listening to the music. His sunglasses told nothing about what he was thinking. He wore a bright orange shirt unbuttoned halfway to show his chest, which was a pale, bluish chest and not muscular like Arnold Friend's. His shirt collar was turned up all around and the very tips of the collar pointed out past his chin as if they were protecting him. He was pressing the transistor radio up against his ear and sat there in a kind of daze, right in the sun.

"He's kinda strange," Connie said. 85

"Hey, she says you're kinda strange! Kinda strange!" Arnold Friend cried. He pounded on the car to get Ellie's attention. Ellie turned for the first time and Connie saw with shock that he wasn't a kid either—he had a fair, hairless face, cheeks reddened slightly as if the veins grew too close to the surface of his skin, the face of a forty-year-old baby. Connie felt a wave of dizziness rise in her at this sight and she stared at him as if waiting for something to change the shock of the moment, make it all right again. Ellie's lips kept shaping words, mumbling along, with the words blasting in his ear.

"Maybe you two better go away," Connie said faintly.

"What? How come?" Arnold Friend cried. "We come out here to take you for a ride. It's Sunday." He had the voice of the man on the radio now. It was the same voice, Connie thought. "Don'tcha know it's Sunday all day and honey, no matter who you were with last night today you're with Arnold Friend and don't you forget it!—Maybe you better step out here," he said, and this last was in a different voice. It was a little flatter, as if the heat was finally getting to him.

"No. I got things to do."

"Hey."   90

"You two better leave."

"We ain't leaving until you come with us."

"Like hell I am—"

"Connie, don't fool around with me. I mean, I mean, don't fool *around*," he said, shaking his head. He laughed incredulously. He placed his sunglasses on top of his head, carefully, as if he were indeed wearing a wig, and brought the stems down behind his ears. Connie stared at him, another wave of dizziness and fear rising in her so that for a moment he wasn't even in focus but was just a blur, standing there against his gold car, and she had the idea that he had driven up the driveway all right but had come from nowhere before that and belonged nowhere and that everything about him and even about the music that was so familiar to her was only half real.

"If my father comes and sees you—"   95

"He ain't coming. He's at the barbecue."

"How do you know that?"

"Aunt Tillie's. Right now they're—uh—they're drinking. Sitting around," he said vaguely, squinting as if he were staring all the way to town and over to Aunt Tillie's backyard. Then the vision seemed to get clear and he nodded energetically. "Yeah. Sitting around. There's your sister in a blue dress, huh? And high heels, the poor sad bitch—nothing like you, sweetheart! And your mother's helping some fat woman with the corn, they're cleaning the corn—husking the corn—"

"What fat woman?" Connie cried.

"How do I know what fat woman. I don't know every goddam fat woman in   100
the world!" Arnold Friend laughed.

"Oh, that's Mrs. Hornby. . . . Who invited her?" Connie said. She felt a little light-headed. Her breath was coming quickly.

"She's too fat. I don't like them fat. I like them the way you are, honey," he said, smiling sleepily at her. They stared at each other for a while, through the screen door. He said softly, "Now what you're going to do is this: you're going to come out that door. You're going to sit up front with me and Ellie's going to sit in the back, the hell with Ellie, right? This isn't Ellie's date. You're my date. I'm your lover, honey."

"What? You're crazy—"

"Yes, I'm your lover. You don't know what that is but you will," he said. "I know that too. I know all about you. But look: it's real nice and you couldn't ask for nobody better than me, or more polite. I always keep my word. I'll tell you how it is, I'm always nice at first, the first time. I'll hold you so tight you won't think you have to try to get away or pretend anything because you'll know you can't. And I'll come inside you where it's all secret and you'll give in to me and you'll love me—"

"Shut up! You're crazy!" Connie said. She backed away from the door. She   105
put her hands against her ears as if she'd heard something terrible, something not meant for her. "People don't talk like that, you're crazy," she muttered. Her heart was almost too big now for her chest and its pumping made sweat break out all over her. She looked out to see Arnold Friend pause and then take a step toward the porch lurching. He almost fell. But, like a clever drunken man, he managed to catch his balance. He wobbled in his high boots and grabbed hold of one of the porch posts.

"Honey?" he said. "You still listening?"

"Get the hell out of here!"

"Be nice, honey. Listen."

"I'm going to call the police—"

He wobbled again and out of the side of his mouth came a fast spat curse, an   110
aside not meant for her to hear. But even this "Christ!" sounded forced. Then he began to smile again. She watched this smile come, awkward as if he were smiling from inside a mask. His whole face was a mask, she thought wildly, tanned down onto his throat but then running out as if he had plastered make-up on his face but had forgotten about his throat.

"Honey—? Listen, here's how it is. I always tell the truth and I promise you this: I ain't coming in that house after you."

"You better not! I'm going to call the police if you—if you don't—"

"Honey," he said, talking right through her voice, "honey, I'm not coming in there but you are coming out here. You know why?"

She was panting. The kitchen looked like a place she had never seen before, some room she had run inside but which wasn't good enough, wasn't going to help her. The kitchen window had never had a curtain, after three years, and there were dishes in the sink for her to do—probably—and if you ran your hand across the table you'd probably feel something sticky there.

"You listening, honey? Hey?"   115

"—going to call the police—"

"Soon as you touch the phone I don't need to keep my promise and can come inside. You won't want that."

She rushed forward and tried to lock the door. Her fingers were shaking. "But why lock it," Arnold Friend said gently, talking right into her face. "It's just a screen door. It's just nothing." One of his boots was at a strange angle, as if his foot wasn't in it. It pointed out to the left, bent at the ankle. "I mean, anybody can break through a screen door and glass and wood and iron or anything else if he needs to, anybody at all and specially Arnold Friend. If the place got lit up with a fire honey you'd come running out into my arms, right into my arms and safe at home—like you knew I was your lover and'd stopped fooling around. I don't mind a nice shy girl but I don't like no fooling around." Part of those words were spoken with a slight rhythmic lilt, and Connie somehow recognized them—the echo of a song from last year, about a girl rushing into her boyfriend's arms and coming home again—

Connie stood barefoot on the linoleum floor, staring at him. "What do you want?" she whispered.

"I want you," he said.   120

"What?"

"Seen you that night and thought, that's the one, yes sir. I never needed to look any more."

"But my father's coming back. He's coming to get me. I had to wash my hair first—" She spoke in a dry, rapid voice, hardly raising it for him to hear.

"No, your daddy is not coming and yes, you had to wash your hair and you washed it for me. It's nice and shining and all for me, I thank you, sweetheart," he said, with a mock bow, but again he almost lost his balance. He had to bend and adjust his boots. Evidently his feet did not go all the way down; the boots must have been stuffed with something so that he would seem taller. Connie stared out at him and behind him Ellie in the car, who seemed to be looking off toward Connie's right, into nothing. This Ellie said, pulling the words out of the air one after another as if he were just discovering them, "You want me to pull out the phone?"

"Shut your mouth and keep it shut," Arnold Friend said, his face red from   125
bending over or maybe from embarrassment because Connie had seen his boots. "This ain't none of your business."

"What—what are you doing? What do you want?" Connie said. "If I call the police they'll get you, they'll arrest you—"

"Promise was not to come in unless you touch that phone, and I'll keep that promise," he said. He resumed his erect position and tried to force his shoulders back. He sounded like a hero in a movie, declaring something important. He spoke too loudly and it was as if he were speaking to someone behind Connie. "I ain't made plans for coming in that house where I don't belong but just for you to come out to me, the way you should. Don't you know who I am?"

"You're crazy," she whispered. She backed away from the door but did not want to go into another part of the house, as if this would give him permission to come through the door. "What do you . . . You're crazy, you . . ."

"Huh? What're you saying, honey?"

Her eyes darted everywhere in the kitchen. She could not remember what it   130
was, this room.

"This is how it is, honey: you come out and we'll drive away, have a nice ride. But if you don't come out we're gonna wait till your people come home and then they're all going to get it."

"You want that telephone pulled out?" Ellie said. He held the radio away from his ear and grimaced, as if without the radio the air was too much for him.

"I toldja shut up, Ellie," Arnold Friend said, "you're deaf, get a hearing aid, right? Fix yourself up. This little girl's no trouble and's gonna be nice to me, so Ellie keep to yourself, this ain't your date—right? Don't hem in on me. Don't hog. Don't crush. Don't bird dog. Don't trail me," he said in a rapid meaningless voice, as if he were running through all the expressions he'd learned but was no longer sure which one of them was in style, then rushing on to new ones, making them up with his eyes closed, "Don't crawl under my fence, don't squeeze in my chipmunk hole, don't sniff my glue, suck my popsicle, keep your own greasy fingers on yourself!" He shaded his eyes and peered in at Connie, who was backed against the kitchen table. "Don't mind him honey he's just a creep. He's a dope. Right? I'm the boy for you and like I said you come out here nice like a lady and give me your hand, and nobody else gets hurt, I mean, your nice old bald-headed daddy and your mummy and your sister in her high heels. Because listen: why bring them in this?"

"Leave me alone," Connie whispered.

"Hey, you know that old woman down the road, the one with the chickens   135
and stuff—you know her?"

"She's dead!"

"Dead? What? You know her?" Arnold Friend said.

"She's dead—"

"Don't you like her?"

"She's dead—she's—she isn't here any more—"   140

"But don't you like her, I mean, you got something against her? Some grudge or something?" Then his voice dipped as if he were conscious of a rudeness. He touched the sunglasses perched on top of his head as if to make sure they were still there. "Now you be a good girl."

"What are you going to do?"

"Just two things, or maybe three," Arnold Friend said. "But I promise it won't last long and you'll like me that way you get to like people you're close to. You will. It's all over for you here, so come on out. You don't want your people in any trouble, do you?"

She turned and bumped against a chair or something, hurting her leg, but she ran into the back room and picked up the telephone. Something roared in her ear, a tiny roaring, and she was so sick with fear that she could do nothing but listen to it—the telephone was clammy and very heavy and her fingers groped down to the dial but were too weak to touch it. She began to scream into the phone, into the roaring. She cried out, she cried for her mother, she felt her breath start jerking back and forth in her lungs as if it were something Arnold Friend were stabbing her with again and again with no tenderness. A noisy sorrowful wailing rose all about her and she was locked inside it the way she was locked inside the house.

After a while she could hear again. She was sitting on the floor with her wet   145
back against the wall.

Arnold Friend was saying from the door, "That's a good girl. Put the phone back."

She kicked the phone away from her.

"No, honey. Pick it up. Put it back right."

She picked it up and put it back. The dial tone stopped.

"That's a good girl. Now come outside." $\qquad$ 150

She was hollow with what had been fear, but what was now just an empti-ness. All that screaming had blasted it out of her. She sat, one leg cramped under her, and deep inside her brain was something like a pinpoint of light that kept going and would not let her relax. She thought, I'm not going to see my mother again. She thought, I'm not going to sleep in my bed again. Her bright green blouse was all wet.

Arnold Friend said, in a gentle-loud voice that was like a stage voice, "The place where you came from ain't there any more, and where you had in mind to go is cancelled out. This place you are now—inside your daddy's house—is nothing but a cardboard box I can knock down any time. You know that and al-ways did know it. You hear me?"

She thought, I have got to think. I have to know what to do.

"We'll go out to a nice field, out in the country here where it smells so nice and it's sunny," Arnold Friend said. "I'll have my arms around you so you won't need to try to get away and I'll show you what love is like, what it does. The hell with this house! It looks solid all right," he said. He ran a fingernail down the screen and the noise did not make Connie shiver, as it would have the day before. "Now put your hand on your heart, honey. Feel that? That feels solid too but we know better, be nice to me, be sweet like you can because what else is there for a girl like you but to be sweet and pretty and give in?—and get away before her people come back?"

She felt her pounding heart. Her hand seemed to enclose it. She thought for $\qquad$ 155 the first time in her life that it was nothing that was hers, that belonged to her, but just a pounding, living thing inside this body that wasn't really hers either.

"You don't want them to get hurt," Arnold Friend went on. "Now get up, honey. Get up all by yourself."

She stood up.

"Now turn this way. That's right. Come over here to me—Ellie, put that away, didn't I tell you? You dope. You miserable creepy dope," Arnold Friend said. His words were not angry but only part of an incantation. The incantation was kindly. "Now come out through the kitchen to me honey and let's see a smile, try it, you're a brave sweet little girl and now they're eating corn and hot-dogs cooked to bursting over an outdoor fire, and they don't know one thing about you and never did and honey you're better than them because not a one of them would have done this for you."

Connie felt the linoleum under her feet; it was cool. She brushed her hair back out of her eyes. Arnold Friend let go of the post tentatively and opened his arms for her, his elbows pointing in toward each other and his wrists limp, to show that this was an embarrassed embrace and a little mocking, he didn't want to make her self-conscious.

She put out her hand against the screen. She watched herself push the door 160 slowly open as if she were safe back somewhere in the other doorway, watching this body and this head of long hair moving out into the sunlight where Arnold Friend waited.

"My sweet little blue-eyed girl," he said, in a half-sung sigh that had nothing to do with her brown eyes but was taken up just the same by the vast sunlit reaches of the land behind him and on all sides of him, so much land that Connie had never seen before and did not recognize except to know that she was going to it.

Tim O'Brien

THE THINGS THEY CARRIED 1990

Tim O'Brien

Tim O'Brien was born in 1946 in Austin, Minnesota. Immediately after graduating summa cum laude from Macalester College in 1968, he was drafted into the U.S. Army. Serving as an infantryman in Vietnam, O'Brien attained the rank of sergeant and won a Purple Heart after being wounded by shrapnel. Upon his discharge in 1970, he began graduate work at Harvard. In 1973 he published If I Die in a Combat Zone, Box Me Up and Ship Me Home, *a mixture of a memoir and fiction about his wartime experiences. His 1978 novel* Going After Cacciato *won the National Book Award, and is considered by some critics to be the best book of American fiction about the Vietnam War. "The Things They Carried" was first published separately in* Esquire *in 1986, but later became the title piece in a book of interlocking short stories published in 1990. His other novels include* The Nuclear Age *(1985),* In the Lake of the Woods *(1994),* Tomcat in Love *(1998) and* July, July *(2002). O'Brien currently lives and teaches in Austin, Texas.*

First Lieutenant Jimmy Cross carried letters from a girl named Martha, a junior at Mount Sebastian College in New Jersey. They were not love letters, but Lieutenant Cross was hoping, so he kept them folded in plastic at the bottom of his rucksack. In the late afternoon, after a day's march, he would dig his foxhole, wash his hands under a canteen, unwrap the letters, hold them with the tips of his fingers, and spend the last hour of light pretending. He would imagine romantic camping trips into the White Mountains in New Hampshire. He would sometimes taste the envelope flaps, knowing her tongue had been there. More than anything, he wanted Martha to love him as he loved her, but the letters were mostly chatty, elusive on the matter of love. She was a virgin, he was almost sure. She was an English major at Mount Sebastian, and she wrote beautifully about her professors and room-mates and midterm exams, about her respect for Chaucer and her great affection for Virginia Woolf. She often quoted lines of poetry; she never mentioned the war, except to say, Jimmy, take care of yourself. The letters weighed 10 ounces. They were signed Love, Martha, but Lieutenant Cross understood that Love was only a way of signing and did not mean what he sometimes pretended it meant. At dusk, he would carefully return the letters to his rucksack. Slowly, a bit distracted, he would get up and move among his men, checking the perimeter; then at full dark he would return to his hold and watch the night and wonder if Martha was a virgin.

The things they carried were largely determined by necessity. Among the necessities or near-necessities were P-38 can openers, pocket knives, heat tabs, wristwatches, dog tags, mosquito repellent, chewing gum, candy, cigarettes, salt tablets, packets of Kool-Aid, lighters, matches, sewing kits, Military Payment Certificates, C rations, and two or three canteens of water. Together, these items weighed between 15 and 20 pounds, depending upon a man's habits or rate of metabolism. Henry Dobbins, who was a big man, carried extra rations; he was especially fond of canned peaches in heavy syrup over pound cake. Dave Jensen, who practiced field hygiene, carried a toothbrush, dental floss, and several hotel-sized bars of soap he'd stolen on R&R° in Sydney, Australia. Ted Lavender, who was scared, carried tranquilizers until he was shot in the head outside the village of Than Khe in mid-April. By necessity, and because it was SOP,° they all carried steel helmets that weighed 5 pounds including the liner and camouflage cover. They carried the standard fatigue jackets and trousers. Very few carried underwear. On their feet they carried jungle boots—2.1 pounds—and Dave Jensen carried three pairs of socks and a can of Dr. Scholl's foot powder as a precaution against trench foot. Until he was shot, Ted Lavender carried six or seven ounces of premium dope, which for him was a necessity. Mitchell Sanders, the RTO,° carried condoms. Norman Bowker carried a diary. Rat Kiley carried comic books. Kiowa, a devout Baptist, carried an illustrated New Testament that had been presented to him by his father, who taught Sunday school in Oklahoma City, Oklahoma. As a hedge against bad times, however, Kiowa also carried his grandmother's distrust of the white man, his grandfather's old hunting hatchet. Necessity dictated. Because the land was mined and booby-trapped, it was SOP for each man to carry a steel-centered, nylon-covered flak jacket, which weighed 6.7 pounds, but which on hot days seemed much heavier. Because you could die so quickly, each man carried at least one large compress bandage, usually in the helmet band for easy access. Because the nights were cold, and because the monsoons were wet, each carried a green plastic poncho that could be used as a raincoat or groundsheet or makeshift tent. With its quilted liner, the poncho weighed almost two pounds, but it was worth every ounce. In April, for instance, when Ted Lavender was shot, they used his poncho to wrap

---

R&R: the military abbreviation for "rest and rehabilitation," a brief vacation from active service.   SOP: standard operating procedure.   RTO: Radio and Telephone Operator.

him up, then to carry him across the paddy, then to lift him into the chopper that took him away.

They were called legs or grunts.

To carry something was to hump it, as when Lieutenant Jimmy Cross humped his love for Martha up the hills and through the swamps. In its intransitive form, to hump meant to walk, or to march, but it implied burdens far beyond the intransitive.

Almost everyone humped photographs. In his wallet, Lieutenant Cross carried two photographs of Martha. The first was a Kodacolor snapshot signed Love, though he knew better. She stood against a brick wall. Her eyes were gray and neutral, her lips slightly open as she stared straight-on at the camera. At night, sometimes, Lieutenant Cross wondered who had taken the picture, because he knew she had boyfriends, because he loved her so much, and because he could see the shadow of the picture-taker spreading out against the brick wall. The second photograph had been clipped from the 1968 Mount Sebastian yearbook. It was an action shot—women's volleyball—and Martha was bent horizontal to the floor, reaching, the palms of her hands in sharp focus, the tongue taut, the expression frank and competitive. There was no visible sweat. She wore white gym shorts. Her legs, he thought, were almost certainly the legs of a virgin, dry and without hair, the left knee cocked and carrying her entire weight, which was just over one hundred pounds. Lieutenant Cross remembered touching that left knee. A dark theater, he remembered, and the movie was *Bonnie and Clyde*, and Martha wore a tweed skirt, and during the final scene, when he touched her knee, she turned and looked at him in a sad, sober way that made him pull his hand back, but he would always remember the feel of the tweed skirt and the knee beneath it and the sound of the gunfire that killed Bonnie and Clyde, how embarrassing it was, how slow and oppressive. He remembered kissing her good night at the dorm door. Right then, he thought, he should've done something brave. He should've carried her up the stairs to her room and tied her to the bed and touched that left knee all night long. He should've risked it. Whenever he looked at the photographs, he thought of new things he should've done.

What they carried was partly a function of rank, partly of field specialty.

As a first lieutenant and platoon leader, Jimmy Cross carried a compass, maps, code books, binoculars, and a .45-caliber pistol that weighed 2.9 pounds fully loaded. He carried a strobe light and the responsibility for the lives of his men.

As an RTO, Mitchell Sanders carried the PRC-25 radio, a killer, 26 pounds with its battery.

As a medic, Rat Kiley carried a canvas satchel filled with morphine and plasma and malaria tablets and surgical tape and comic books and all the things a medic must carry, including M&M's° for especially bad wounds, for a total weight of nearly 20 pounds.

M&M's: comic slang for medical supplies.

As a big man, therefore a machine gunner, Henry Dobbins carried the M-60, which weighed 23 pounds unloaded, but which was almost always loaded. In addition, Dobbins carried between 10 and 15 pounds of ammunition draped in belts across his chest and shoulders.

As PFCs or Spec 4s, most of them were common grunts and carried the standard M-16 gas-operated assault rifle. The weapon weighed 7.5 pounds unloaded, 8.2 pounds with its full 20-round magazine. Depending on numerous factors, such as topography and psychology, the riflemen carried anywhere from 12 to 20 magazines, usually in cloth bandoliers, adding on another 8.4 pounds at minimum, 14 pounds at maximum. When it was available, they also carried M-16 maintenance gear—rods and steel brushes and swabs and tubes of LSA oil—all of which weighed about a pound. Among the grunts, some carried the M-79 grenade launcher, 5.9 pounds unloaded, a reasonably light weapon except for the ammunition, which was heavy. A single round weighed 10 ounces. The typical load was 25 rounds. But Ted Lavender, who was scared, carried 34 rounds when he was shot and killed outside Than Khe, and he went down under an exceptional burden, more than 20 pounds of ammunition, plus the flak jacket and helmet and rations and water and toilet paper and tranquilizers and all the rest, plus the unweighed fear. He was dead weight. There was no twitching or flopping. Kiowa, who saw it happen, said it was like watching a rock fall, or a big sandbag or something—just boom, then down—not like the movies where the dead guy rolls around and does fancy spins and goes ass over teakettle—not like that, Kiowa said, the poor bastard just flat-fuck fell. Boom. Down. Nothing else. It was a bright morning in mid-April. Lieutenant Cross felt the pain. He blamed himself. They stripped off Lavender's canteens and ammo, all the heavy things, and Rat Kiley said the obvious, the guy's dead, and Mitchell Sanders used his radio to report one U.S. KIA° and to request a chopper. Then they wrapped Lavender in his poncho. They carried him out to a dry paddy, established security, and sat smoking the dead man's dope until the chopper came. Lieutenant Cross kept to himself. He pictured Martha's smooth young face, thinking he loved her more than anything, more than his men, and now Ted Lavender was dead because he loved her so much and could not stop thinking about her. When the dustoff arrived, they carried Lavender aboard. Afterward they burned Than Khe. They marched until dusk, then dug their holes, and that night Kiowa kept explaining how you had to be there, how fast it was, how the poor guy just dropped like so much concrete. Boom-down, he said. Like cement.

In addition to the three standard weapons—the M-60, M-16, and M-79—they carried whatever presented itself, or whatever seemed appropriate as a means of killing or staying alive. They carried catch-as-catch-can. At various times, in various situations, they carried M-14s and CAR-15s and Swedish Ks and grease guns and captured AK-47s and Chi-Coms and RPGs and Simonov carbines and black market Uzis and .38-caliber Smith & Wesson handguns and

KIA: killed in action.

66 mm LAWs and shotguns and silencers and blackjacks and bayonets and C-4 plastic explosives. Lee Strunk carried a slingshot; a weapon of last resort, he called it. Mitchell Sanders carried brass knuckles. Kiowa carried his grandfather's feathered hatchet. Every third or fourth man carried a Claymore antipersonnel mine—3.5 pounds with its firing device. They all carried fragmentation grenades—14 ounces each. They all carried at least one M-18 colored smoke grenade—24 ounces. Some carried CS or tear gas grenades. Some carried white phosphorus grenades. They carried all they could bear, and then some, including a silent awe for the terrible power of the things they carried.

In the first week of April, before Lavender died, Lieutenant Jimmy Cross received a good-luck charm from Martha. It was a simple pebble, an ounce at most. Smooth to the touch, it was a milky white color with flecks of orange and violet, oval-shaped, like a miniature egg. In the accompanying letter, Martha wrote that she had found the pebble on the Jersey shoreline, precisely where the land touched water at high tide, where things came together but also separated. It was this separate-but-together quality, she wrote, that had inspired her to pick up the pebble and to carry it in her breast pocket for several days, where it seemed weightless, and then to send it through the mail, by air, as a token of her truest feelings for him. Lieutenant Cross found this romantic. But he wondered what her truest feelings were, exactly, and what she meant by separate-but-together. He wondered how the tides and waves had come into play on that afternoon along the Jersey shoreline when Martha saw the pebble and bent down to rescue it from geology. He imagined bare feet. Martha was a poet, with the poet's sensibilities, and her feet would be brown and bare, the toenails unpainted, the eyes chilly and somber like the ocean in March, and though it was painful, he wondered who had been with her that afternoon. He imagined a pair of shadows moving along the strip of sand where things came together but also separated. It was phantom jealousy, he knew, but he couldn't help himself. He loved her so much. On the march, through the hot days of early April, he carried the pebble in his mouth, turning it with his tongue, tasting sea salt and moisture. His mind wandered. He had difficulty keeping his attention on the war. On occasion he would yell at his men to spread out the column, to keep their eyes open, but then he would slip away into daydreams, just pretending, walking barefoot along the Jersey shore, with Martha, carrying nothing. He would feel himself rising. Sun and waves and gentle winds, all love and lightness.

What they carried varied by mission.

When a mission took them to the mountains, they carried mosquito netting, machetes, canvas tarps, and extra bug juice.   15

If a mission seemed especially hazardous, or if it involved a place they knew to be bad, they carried everything they could. In certain heavily mined AOs,° where the land was dense with Toe Poppers and Bouncing Betties, they took

AOs: areas of operation.

turns humping a 28-pound mine detector. With its headphones and big sensing plate, the equipment was a stress on the lower back and shoulders, awkward to handle, often useless because of the shrapnel in the earth, but they carried it anyway, partly for safety, partly for the illusion of safety.

On ambush, or other night missions, they carried peculiar little odds and ends. Kiowa always took along his New Testament and a pair of moccasins for silence. Dave Jensen carried night-sight vitamins high in carotene. Lee Strunk carried his slingshot; ammo, he claimed, would never be a problem. Rat Kiley carried brandy and M&M's candy. Until he was shot, Ted Lavender carried the starlight scope, which weighed 6.3 pounds with its aluminum carrying case. Henry Dobbins carried his girlfriend's pantyhose wrapped around his neck as a comforter. They all carried ghosts. When dark came, they would move out single file across the meadows and paddies to their ambush coordinates, where they would quietly set up the Claymores and lie down and spend the night waiting.

Other missions were more complicated and required special equipment. In mid-April, it was their mission to search out and destroy the elaborate tunnel complexes in the Than Khe area south of Chu Lai. To blow the tunnels, they carried one-pound blocks of pentrite high explosives, four blocks to a man, 68 pounds in all. They carried wiring, detonators, and battery-powered clackers. Dave Jensen carried earplugs. Most often, before blowing the tunnels, they were ordered by higher command to search them, which was considered bad news, but by and large they just shrugged and carried out orders. Because he was a big man, Henry Dobbins was excused from tunnel duty. The others would draw numbers. Before Lavender died there were 17 men in the platoon, and whoever drew the number 17 would strip off his gear and crawl in headfirst with a flashlight and Lieutenant Cross's .45-caliber pistol. The rest of them would fan out as security. They would sit down or kneel, not facing the hole, listening to the ground beneath them, imagining cobwebs and ghosts, whatever was down there—the tunnel walls squeezing in—how the flashlight seemed impossibly heavy in the hand and how it was tunnel vision in the very strictest sense, compression in all ways, even time, and how you had to wiggle in—ass and elbows—a swallowed-up feeling—and how you found yourself worrying about odd things: Will your flashlight go dead? Do rats carry rabies? If you screamed, how far would the sound carry? Would your buddies hear it? Would they have the courage to drag you out? In some respects, though not many, the waiting was worse than the tunnel itself. Imagination was a killer.

On April 16, when Lee Strunk drew the number 17, he laughed and muttered something and went down quickly. The morning was hot and very still. Not good, Kiowa said. He looked at the tunnel opening, then out across a dry paddy toward the village of Than Khe. Nothing moved. No clouds or birds or people. As they waited, the men smoked and drank Kool-Aid, not talking much, feeling sympathy for Lee Strunk but also feeling the luck of the draw. You win some, you lose some, said Mitchell Sanders, and sometimes you settle for a rain check. It was a tired line and no one laughed.

Henry Dobbins ate a tropical chocolate bar. Ted Lavender popped a tranquilizer and went off to pee.

After five minutes, Lieutenant Jimmy Cross moved to the tunnel, leaned down, and examined the darkness. Trouble, he thought—a cave-in maybe. And then suddenly, without willing it, he was thinking about Martha. The stresses and fractures, the quick collapse, the two of them buried alive under all that weight. Dense, crushing love. Kneeling, watching the hole, he tried to concentrate on Lee Strunk and the war, all the dangers, but his love was too much for him, he felt paralyzed, he wanted to sleep inside her lungs and breathe her blood and be smothered. He wanted her to be a virgin and not a virgin, all at once. He wanted to know her. Intimate secrets: Why poetry? Why so sad? Why that grayness in her eyes? Why so alone? Not lonely, just alone—riding her bike across campus or sitting off by herself in the cafeteria—even dancing, she danced alone—and it was the aloneness that filled him with love. He remembered telling her that one evening. How she nodded and looked away. And how, later, when he kissed her, she received the kiss without returning it, her eyes wide open, not afraid, not a virgin's eyes, just flat and uninvolved.

Lieutenant Cross gazed at the tunnel. But he was not there. He was buried with Martha under the white sand at the Jersey shore. They were pressed together, and the pebble in his mouth was her tongue. He was smiling. Vaguely, he was aware of how quiet the day was, the sullen paddies, yet he could not bring himself to worry about matters of security. He was beyond that. He was just a kid at war, in love. He was twenty-four years old. He couldn't help it.

A few moments later Lee Strunk crawled out of the tunnel. He came up grinning, filthy but alive. Lieutenant Cross nodded and closed his eyes while the others clapped Strunk on the back and made jokes about rising from the dead.

Worms, Rat Kiley said. Right out of the grave. Fuckin' zombie.

The men laughed. They all felt great relief.

Spook city, said Mitchell Sanders.

Lee Strunk made a funny ghost sound, a kind of moaning, yet very happy, and right then, when Strunk made that high happy moaning sound, when he went *Ahhooooo*, right then Ted Lavender was shot in the head on his way back from peeing. He lay with his mouth open. The teeth were broken. There was a swollen black bruise under his left eye. The cheekbone was gone. Oh shit, Rat Kiley said, the guy's dead. The guy's dead, he kept saying, which seemed profound—the guy's dead. I mean really.

The things they carried were determined to some extent by superstition. Lieutenant Cross carried his good-luck pebble. Dave Jensen carried a rabbit's foot. Norman Bowker, otherwise a very gentle person, carried a thumb that had been presented to him as a gift by Mitchell Sanders. The thumb was dark brown, rubbery to the touch, and weighed four ounces at most. It had been cut from a VC corpse, a boy of fifteen or sixteen. They'd found him at the bottom of an irrigation ditch, badly burned, flies in his mouth and eyes. The boy wore black shorts and sandals. At the time of his death he had been carrying a pouch of rice, a rifle, and three magazines of ammunition.

You want my opinion, Mitchell Sanders said, there's a definite moral here.

He put his hand on the dead boy's wrist. He was quiet for a time, as if 30 counting a pulse, then he patted the stomach, almost affectionately, and used Kiowa's hunting hatchet to remove the thumb.

Henry Dobbins asked what the moral was.

Moral?

You know. *Moral*.

Sanders wrapped the thumb in toilet paper and handed it across to Norman Bowker. There was no blood. Smiling, he kicked the boy's head, watched the flies scatter, and said, It's like with that old TV show—Paladin. Have gun, will travel.

Henry Dobbins thought about it. 35

Yeah, well, he finally said. I don't see no moral.

There it *is*, man.

Fuck off.

They carried USO stationery and pencils and pens. They carried Sterno, safety pins, trip flares, signal flares, spools of wire, razor blades, chewing tobacco, liberated joss sticks and statuettes of the smiling Buddha, candles, grease pencils, *The Stars and Stripes*, fingernail clippers, Psy Ops leaflets, bush hats, bolos, and much more. Twice a week, when the resupply choppers came in, they carried hot chow in green mermite cans and large canvas bags filled with iced beer and soda pop. They carried plastic water containers, each with a two-gallon capacity. Mitchell Sanders carried a set of starched tiger fatigues for special occasions. Henry Dobbins carried Black Flag insecticide. Dave Jensen carried empty sandbags that could be filled at night for added protection. Lee Strunk carried tanning lotion. Some things they carried in common. Taking turns, they carried the big PRC-77 scrambler radio, which weighed 30 pounds with its battery. They shared the weight of memory. They took up what others could no longer bear. Often, they carried each other, the wounded or weak. They carried infections. They carried chess sets, basketballs, Vietnamese-English dictionaries, insignia of rank, Bronze Stars and Purple Hearts, plastic cards imprinted with the Code of Conduct. They carried diseases, among them malaria and dysentery. They carried lice and ringworm and leeches and paddy algae and various rots and molds. They carried the land itself—Vietnam, the place, the soil—a powdery orange-red dust that covered their boots and fatigues and faces. They carried the sky. The whole atmosphere, they carried it, the humidity, the monsoons, the stink of fungus and decay, all of it, they carried gravity. They moved like mules. By daylight they took sniper fire, at night they were mortared, but it was not battle, it was just the endless march, village to village, without purpose, nothing won or lost. They marched for the sake of the march. They plodded along slowly, dumbly, leaning forward against the heat, unthinking, all blood and bone, simple grunts, soldiering with their legs, toiling up the hills and down into the paddies and across the rivers and up again and down, just humping, one step and then the next and then another, but no volition, no will, because it was automatic, it was anatomy, and the war was entirely a matter of posture and carriage, the hump was everything, a kind of inertia, a kind of emptiness, a dullness of desire and intellect and conscience and hope and human sensibility. Their principles were in their feet. Their calculations were biological. They had no sense of strategy or mission. They searched the villages without knowing what to look for, not caring, kicking over jars of rice, frisking children and old men, blowing tunnels, sometimes setting fires and sometimes not, then forming up and moving on to the next village, then other villages, where it would always be the same. They carried their own lives. The pressures were enormous. In the heat of early afternoon, they would remove their helmets and flak jackets, walking bare, which was dangerous but which helped ease the strain. They would often discard things along the route of march. Purely for comfort, they would throw away rations, blow their Claymores and grenades, no matter, because by nightfall the resupply choppers would arrive with more of the same, then a day or two later still more, fresh watermelons and crates of ammunition and sunglasses and woolen sweaters—the resources were stunning—sparklers for the Fourth of July, colored eggs for Easter—it was the great American war chest—the fruits of science, the smokestacks, the canneries, the arsenals at Hartford, the Minnesota forests, the machine shops, the vast fields of corn and wheat—they carried like freight trains; they carried it on their backs and shoulders—and for all the ambiguities of Vietnam, all the mysteries and unknowns, there was at least the single abiding certainty that they would never be at a loss for things to carry.

After the chopper took Lavender away, Lieutenant Jimmy Cross led his men 40 into the village of Than Khe. They burned everything. They shot chickens and dogs, they trashed the village well, they called in artillery and watched the wreckage, then they marched for several hours through the hot afternoon, and then at dusk, while Kiowa explained how Lavender died, Lieutenant Cross found himself trembling.

He tried not to cry. With his entrenching tool, which weighed five pounds, he began digging a hole in the earth.

He felt shame. He hated himself. He had loved Martha more than his men, and as a consequence Lavender was now dead, and this was something he would have to carry like a stone in his stomach for the rest of the war.

All he could do was dig. He used his entrenching tool like an ax, slashing, feeling both love and hate, and then later, when it was full dark, he sat at the bottom of his foxhole and wept. It went on for a long while. In part, he was grieving for Ted Lavender, but mostly it was for Martha, and for himself, because she belonged to another world, which was not quite real, and because she was a junior at Mount Sebastian College in New Jersey, a poet and a virgin and uninvolved, and because he realized she did not love him and never would.

Like cement, Kiowa whispered in the dark. I swear to God—boom, down. Not a word.

I've heard this, said Norman Bowker.   45

A pisser, you know? Still zipping himself up. Zapped while zipping.

All right, fine. That's enough.

Yeah, but you had to see it, the guy just—

I *heard,* man. Cement. So why not shut the fuck *up?*

Kiowa shook his head sadly and glanced over at the hole where Lieutenant 50
Jimmy Cross sat watching the night. The air was thick and wet. A warm dense
fog had settled over the paddies and there was the stillness that precedes rain.

After a time Kiowa sighed.

One thing for sure, he said. The lieutenant's in some deep hurt. I mean that
crying jag—the way he was carrying on—it wasn't fake or anything, it was real
heavy-duty hurt. The man cares.

Sure, Norman Bowker said.

Say what you want, the man does care.

We all got problems. 55

Not Lavender.

No, I guess not, Bowker said. Do me a favor, though.

Shut up?

That's a smart Indian. Shut up.

Shrugging, Kiowa pulled off his boots. He wanted to say more, just to lighten 60
up his sleep, but instead he opened his New Testament and arranged it beneath
his head as a pillow. The fog made things seem hollow and unattached. He tried
not to think about Ted Lavender, but then he was thinking how fast it was, no
drama, down and dead, and how it was hard to feel anything except surprise. It
seemed unchristian. He wished he could find some great sadness, or even anger,
but the emotion wasn't there and he couldn't make it happen. Mostly he felt
pleased to be alive. He liked the smell of the New Testament under his cheek,
the leather and ink and paper and glue, whatever the chemicals were. He liked
hearing the sounds of night. Even his fatigue, it felt fine, the stiff muscles and the
prickly awareness of his own body, a floating feeling. He enjoyed not being dead.
Lying there, Kiowa admired Lieutenant Jimmy Cross's capacity for grief. He
wanted to share the man's pain, he wanted to care as Jimmy Cross cared. And yet
when he closed his eyes, all he could think was Boom-down, and all he could feel
was the pleasure of having his boots off and the fog curling in around him and
the damp soil and the Bible smells and the plush comfort of night.

After a moment Norman Bowker sat up in the dark.

What the hell, he said. You want to talk, *talk.* Tell it to me.

Forget it.

No, man, go on. One thing I hate, it's a silent Indian.

For the most part they carried themselves with poise, a kind of dignity. Now 65
and then, however, there were times of panic, when they squealed or wanted to
squeal but couldn't, when they twitched and made moaning sounds and covered
their heads and said Dear Jesus and flopped around on the earth and fired their
weapons blindly and cringed and sobbed and begged for the noise to stop and
went wild and made stupid promises to themselves and to God and to their
mothers and fathers, hoping not to die. In different ways, it happened to all of
them. Afterward, when the firing ended, they would blink and peek up. They
would touch their bodies, feeling shame, then quickly hiding it. They would force
themselves to stand. As if in slow motion, frame by frame, the world would take

on the old logic—absolute silence, then the wind, then sunlight, then voices. It was the burden of being alive. Awkwardly, the men would reassemble themselves, first in private, then in groups, becoming soldiers again. They would repair the leaks in their eyes. They would check for casualties, call in dustoffs, light cigarettes, try to smile, clear their throats and spit and begin cleaning their weapons. After a time someone would shake his head and say, No lie, I almost shit my pants, and someone else would laugh, which meant it was bad, yes, but the guy had obviously not shit his pants, it wasn't that bad, and in any case nobody would ever do such a thing and then go ahead and talk about it. They would squint into the dense, oppressive sunlight. For a few moments, perhaps, they would fall silent, lighting a joint and tracking its passage from man to man, inhaling, holding in the humiliation. Scary stuff, one of them might say. But then someone else would grin or flick his eyebrows and say, Roger-dodger, almost cut me a new asshole, *almost*.

There were numerous such poses. Some carried themselves with a sort of wistful resignation, others with pride or stiff soldierly discipline or good humor or macho zeal. They were afraid of dying but they were even more afraid to show it.

They found jokes to tell.

They used a hard vocabulary to contain the terrible softness. *Greased* they'd say. *Offed, lit up, zapped while zipping.* It wasn't cruelty, just stage presence. They were actors. When someone died, it wasn't quite dying, because in a curious way it seemed scripted, and because they had their lines mostly memorized, irony mixed with tragedy, and because they called it by other names, as if to encyst and destroy the reality of death itself. They kicked corpses. They cut off thumbs. They talked grunt lingo. They told stories about Ted Lavender's supply of tranquilizers, how the poor guy didn't feel a thing, how incredibly tranquil he was.

There's a moral here, said Mitchell Sanders.

They were waiting for Lavender's chopper, smoking the dead man's dope.   70

The moral's pretty obvious, Sanders said, and winked. Stay away from drugs. No joke, they'll ruin your day every time.

Cute, said Henry Dobbins.

Mind blower, get it? Talk about wiggy. Nothing left, just blood and brains.

They made themselves laugh.

There it is, they'd say. Over and over—there it is, my friend, there it is—as   75 if the repetition itself were an act of poise, a balance between crazy and almost crazy, knowing without going, there it is, which meant be cool, let it ride, because Oh yeah, man, you can't change what can't be changed, there it is, there it absolutely and positively and fucking well *is*.

They were tough.

They carried all the emotional baggage of men who might die. Grief, terror, love, longing—these were intangibles, but the intangibles had their own mass and specific gravity, they had tangible weight. They carried shameful memories. They carried the common secret of cowardice barely restrained, the instinct to run or freeze or hide, and in many respects this was the heaviest burden of all, for it could never be put down, it required perfect balance and perfect posture. They carried their reputations. They carried the soldier's greatest fear, which was the fear of blushing. Men killed, and died, because they were embarrassed not to. It was what had brought them to the war in the first place, nothing positive, no dreams of glory or honor, just to avoid the blush of dishonor. They died so as not to die of embarrassment. They crawled into tunnels and walked point and advanced under fire. Each morning, despite the unknowns, they made their legs move. They endured. They kept humping. They did not submit to the obvious alternative, which was simply to close the eyes and fall. So easy, really. Go limp and tumble to the ground and let the muscles unwind and not speak and not budge until your buddies picked you up and lifted you into the chopper that would roar and dip its nose and carry you off to the world. A mere matter of falling, yet no one ever fell. It was not courage, exactly; the object was not valor. Rather, they were too frightened to be cowards.

By and large they carried these things inside, maintaining the masks of composure. They sneered at sick call. They spoke bitterly about guys who had found release by shooting off their own toes or fingers. Pussies, they'd say. Candy-asses. It was fierce, mocking talk, with only a trace of envy or awe, but even so the image played itself out behind their eyes.

They imagined the muzzle against flesh. So easy: squeeze the trigger and blow away a toe. They imagined it. They imagined the quick, sweet pain, then the evacuation to Japan, then a hospital with warm beds and cute geisha nurses.

And they dreamed of freedom birds.   80

At night, on guard, staring into the dark, they were carried away by jumbo jets. They felt the rush of takeoff. *Gone!* they yelled. And then velocity—wings and engines—a smiling stewardess—but it was more than a plane, it was a real bird, a big sleek silver bird with feathers and talons and high screeching. They were flying. The weights fell off; there was nothing to bear. They laughed and held on tight, feeling the cold slap of wind and altitude, soaring, thinking *It's over, I'm gone!* —they were naked, they were light and free—it was all lightness, bright and fast and buoyant, light as light, a helium buzz in the brain, a giddy bubbling in the lungs as they were taken up over the clouds and the war, beyond duty, beyond gravity and mortification and global entanglements—*Sin loi!* ° they yelled. *I'm sorry, mother-fuckers, but I'm out of it, I'm goofed, I'm on a space cruise, I'm gone!* —and it was a restful, unencumbered sensation, just riding the light waves, sailing that big silver freedom bird over the mountains and oceans, over America, over the farms and great sleeping cities and cemeteries and highways and the golden arches of McDonald's, it was flight, a kind of fleeing, a kind of falling, falling higher and higher, spinning off the edge of the earth and beyond the sun and through the vast, silent vacuum where there were no burdens and where everything weighed exactly nothing—*Gone!* they screamed. *I'm sorry but I'm gone!* —and so at night, not quite dreaming, they gave themselves over to lightness, they were carried, they were purely borne.

*

Sin loi: Vietnamese for sorry.

On the morning after Ted Lavender died, First Lieutenant Jimmy Cross crouched at the bottom of his foxhole and burned Martha's letters. Then he burned the two photographs. There was a steady rain falling, which made it difficult, but he used heat tabs and Sterno to build a small fire, screening it with his body, holding the photographs over the tight blue flame with the tips of his fingers.

He realized it was only a gesture. Stupid, he thought. Sentimental, too, but mostly just stupid.

Lavender was dead. You couldn't burn the blame.

Besides, the letters were in his head. And even now, without photographs, Lieutenant Cross could see Martha playing volleyball in her white gym shorts and yellow T-shirt. He could see her moving in the rain.

When the fire died out, Lieutenant Cross pulled his poncho over his shoulders and ate breakfast from a can.

There was no great mystery, he decided.

In those burned letters Martha had never mentioned the war, except to say, Jimmy, take care of yourself. She wasn't involved. She signed the letters Love, but it wasn't love, and all the fine lines and technicalities did not matter. Virginity was no longer an issue. He hated her. Yes, he did. He hated her. Love, too, but it was a hard, hating kind of love.

The morning came up wet and blurry. Everything seemed part of everything else, the fog and Martha and the deepening rain.

He was a soldier, after all.

Half smiling, Lieutenant Jimmy Cross took out his maps. He shook his head hard, as if to clear it, then bent forward and began planning the day's march. In ten minutes, or maybe twenty, he would rouse the men and they would pack up and head west, where the maps showed the country to be green and inviting. They would do what they had always done. The rain might add some weight, but otherwise it would be one more day layered upon all the other days.

He was realistic about it. There was that new hardness in his stomach. He loved her but he hated her.

No more fantasies, he told himself.

Henceforth, when he thought about Martha, it would be only to think that she belonged elsewhere. He would shut down the daydreams. This was not Mount Sebastian, it was another world, where there were no pretty poems or midterm exams, a place where men died because of carelessness and gross stupidity. Kiowa was right. Boom-down, and you were dead, never partly dead.

Briefly, in the rain, Lieutenant Cross saw Martha's gray eyes gazing back at him.

He understood.

It was very sad, he thought. The things men carried inside. The things men did or felt they had to do.

He almost nodded at her, but didn't.

Instead he went back to his maps. He was now determined to perform his duties firmly and without negligence. It wouldn't help Lavender, he knew that, but from this point on he would comport himself as an officer. He would dispose of his good-luck pebble. Swallow it, maybe, or use Lee Strunk's slingshot, or just drop it along the trail. On the march he would impose strict field discipline. He would be careful to send out flank security, to prevent straggling or bunching up, to keep his troops moving at the proper pace and at the proper interval. He would insist on clean weapons. He would confiscate the remainder of Lavender's dope. Later in the day, perhaps, he would call the men together and speak to them plainly. He would accept the blame for what had happened to Ted Lavender. He would be a man about it. He would look them in the eyes, keeping his chin level, and he would issue the new SOPs in a calm, impersonal tone of voice, a lieutenant's voice, leaving no room for argument or discussion. Commencing immediately, he'd tell them, they would no longer abandon equipment along the route of march. They would police up their acts. They would get their shit together, and keep it together, and maintain it neatly and in good working order.

He would not tolerate laxity. He would show strength, distancing himself. 100

Among the men there would be grumbling, of course, and maybe worse, because their days would seem longer and their loads heavier, but Lieutenant Jimmy Cross reminded himself that his obligation was not to be loved but to lead. He would dispense with love; it was not now a factor. And if anyone quarreled or complained, he would simply tighten his lips and arrange his shoulders in the correct command posture. He might give a curt little nod. Or he might not. He might just shrug and say, Carry on, then they would saddle up and form into a column and move out toward the villages west of Than Khe.

Frank O'Connor

FIRST CONFESSION 1952

Frank O'Connor was the pen name that Michael O'Donovan (1903–1966) adopted when he feared that to be known as a writer would hurt his career in civil service. He was born in Cork, Ireland's second city. Desperate poverty forced his parents to take him out of school after he had completed only fourth grade. During the troubles of 1918 through 1921 that led to the new Irish Free State, he served in the Republican Army. After peace came, he worked as a librarian and for several years served as a director of Dublin's influential Abbey Theatre. America offered O'Connor-O'Donovan early hospitality: in 1931 the Atlantic printed his first story. In the 1950s he lived in America, teaching at Northwestern and Harvard. For a time he regularly appeared on

Frank O'Connor

CBS television on Sunday mornings, just sitting and telling stories. Also a fine literary critic, he wrote The Mirror in the Roadway *(1956), a study of the novel, and* The Lonely Voice *(1963), a study of the short story. In* Kings, Lords & Commons *(1959), he proved himself a master translator of Gaelic poetry. O'Connor toiled hard over his stories, trying to polish each to the perfection of a good lyric. "First Confession" appeared in print in three versions because he kept rewriting it. The story is based on his boyhood memories.*

All the trouble began when my grandfather died and my grandmother—my father's mother—came to live with us. Relations in the one house are a strain at the best of times, but, to make matters worse, my grandmother was a real old countrywoman and quite unsuited to the life in town. She had a fat, wrinkled old face, and, to Mother's great indignation, went round the house in bare feet—the boots had her crippled, she said. For dinner she had a jug of porter and a pot of potatoes with—sometimes—a bit of salt fish, and she poured out the potatoes on the table and ate them slowly, with great relish, using her fingers by way of a fork.

Now, girls are supposed to be fastidious, but I was the one who suffered most from this. Nora, my sister, just sucked up to the old woman for the penny she got every Friday out of the old-age pension, a thing I could not do. I was too honest, that was my trouble; and when I was playing with Bill Connell, the sergeant-major's son, and saw my grandmother steering up the path with the jug of porter sticking out from beneath her shawl I was mortified. I made excuses not to let him come into the house, because I could never be sure what she would be up to when we went in.

When Mother was at work and my grandmother made the dinner I wouldn't touch it. Nora once tried to make me, but I hid under the table from her and took the bread-knife with me for protection. Nora let on to be very indignant (she wasn't, of course, but she knew Mother saw through her, so she sided with Gran) and came after me. I lashed out at her with the bread-knife, and after that she left me alone. I stayed there till Mother came in from work and made my dinner, but when Father came in later Nora said in a shocked voice: "Oh, Dadda, do you know what Jackie did at dinnertime?" Then, of course, it all came out; Father gave me a flaking; Mother interfered, and for days after that he didn't speak to me and Mother barely spoke to Nora. And all because of that old woman! God knows, I was heart-scalded.

Then, to crown my misfortunes, I had to make my first confession and communion. It was an old woman called Ryan who prepared us for these. She was about the one age with Gran; she was well-to-do, lived in a big house on Montenotte, wore a black cloak and bonnet, and came every day to school at three o'clock when we should have been going home, and talked to us of hell. She may have mentioned the other place as well, but that could only have been by accident, for hell had the first place in her heart.

She lit a candle, took out a new half-crown, and offered it to the first boy who would hold one finger—only one finger!—in the flame for five minutes by the school clock. Being always very ambitious I was tempted to volunteer, but I thought it might look greedy. Then she asked were we afraid of holding one

5

finger—only one finger!—in a little candle flame for five minutes and not afraid of burning all over in roasting hot furnaces for all eternity. "All eternity! Just think of that! A whole lifetime goes by and it's nothing, not even a drop in the ocean of your sufferings." The woman was really interesting about hell, but my attention was all fixed on the half-crown. At the end of the lesson she put it back in her purse. It was a great disappointment; a religious woman like that, you wouldn't think she'd bother about a thing like a half-crown.

Another day she said she knew a priest who woke one night to find a fellow he didn't recognize leaning over the end of his bed. The priest was a bit frightened—naturally enough—but he asked the fellow what he wanted, and the fellow said in a deep, husky voice that he wanted to go to confession. The priest said it was an awkward time and wouldn't it do in the morning, but the fellow said that last time he went to confession, there was one sin he kept back, being ashamed to mention it, and now it was always on his mind. Then the priest knew it was a bad case, because the fellow was after making a bad confession and committing a mortal sin. He got up to dress, and just then the cock crew in the yard outside, and—lo and behold!—when the priest looked round there was no sign of the fellow, only a smell of burning timber, and when the priest looked at his bed didn't he see the print of two hands burned in it? That was because the fellow had made a bad confession. This story made a shocking impression on me.

But the worst of all was when she showed us how to examine our conscience. Did we take the name of the Lord, our God, in vain? Did we honor our father and our mother? (I asked her did this include grandmothers and she said it did.) Did we love our neighbors as ourselves? Did we covet our neighbor's goods? (I thought of the way I felt about the penny that Nora got every Friday.) I decided that, between one thing and another, I must have broken the whole ten commandments, all on account of that old woman, and so far as I could see, so long as she remained in the house I had no hope of ever doing anything else.

I was scared to death of confession. The day the whole class went I let on to have a toothache, hoping my absence wouldn't be noticed; but at three o'clock, just as I was feeling safe, along comes a chap with a message from Mrs. Ryan that I was to go to confession myself on Saturday and be at the chapel for communion with the rest. To make it worse, Mother couldn't come with me and sent Nora instead.

Now, that girl had ways of tormenting me that Mother never knew of. She held my hand as we went down the hill, smiling sadly and saying how sorry she was for me, as if she were bringing me to the hospital for an operation.

"Oh, God help us!" she moaned. "Isn't it a terrible pity you weren't a good 10 boy? Oh, Jackie, my heart bleeds for you! How will you ever think of all your sins? Don't forget you have to tell him about the time you kicked Gran on the shin."

"Lemme go!" I said, trying to drag myself free of her. "I don't want to go to confession at all."

"But sure, you'll have to go to confession, Jackie," she replied in the same regretful tone. "Sure, if you didn't, the parish priest would be up to the house, looking for you. 'Tisn't, God knows, that I'm not sorry for you. Do you remember the time you tried to kill me with the bread-knife under the table? And the language you used to me? I don't know what he'll do with you at all, Jackie. He might have to send you up to the bishop."

I remember thinking bitterly that she didn't know the half of what I had to tell—if I told it. I knew I couldn't tell it, and understood perfectly why the fellow in Mrs. Ryan's story made a bad confession; it seemed to me a great shame that people wouldn't stop criticizing him. I remember that steep hill down to the church, and the sunlit hillsides beyond the valley of the river, which I saw in the gaps between the houses like Adam's last glimpse of Paradise.

Then, when she had maneuvered me down the long flight of steps to the chapel yard, Nora suddenly changed her tone. She became the raging malicious devil she really was.

"There you are!" she said with a yelp of triumph, hurling me through the church door. "And I hope he'll give you the penitential psalms, you dirty little caffler."° 15

I knew then I was lost, given up to eternal justice. The door with the colored glass panels swung shut behind me, the sunlight went out and gave place to deep shadow, and the wind whistled outside so that the silence within seemed to crackle like ice under my feet. Nora sat in front of me by the confession box. There were a couple of old women ahead of her, and then a miserable-looking poor devil came and wedged me in at the other side, so that I couldn't escape even if I had the courage. He joined his hands and rolled his eyes in the direction of the roof, muttering aspirations in an anguished tone, and I wondered had he a grandmother too. Only a grandmother could account for a fellow behaving in that heartbroken way, but he was better off than I, for he at least could go and confess his sins; while I would make a bad confession and then die in the night and be continually coming back and burning people's furniture.

Nora's turn came, and I heard the sound of something slamming, and then her voice as if butter wouldn't melt in her mouth, and then another slam, and out she came. God, the hypocrisy of women! Her eyes were lowered, her head was bowed, and her hands were joined very low down on her stomach, and she walked up the aisle to the side altar looking like a saint. You never saw such an exhibition of devotion; and I remembered the devilish malice with which she had tormented me all the way from our door, and wondered were all religious people like that, really. It was my turn now. With the fear of damnation in my soul I went in, and the confessional door closed of itself behind me.

It was pitch-dark and I couldn't see priest or anything else. Then I really began to be frightened. In the darkness it was a matter between God and me, and He had all the odds. He knew what my intentions were before I even started; I had no chance. All I had ever been told about confession got mixed up in my mind, and I knelt to one wall and said: "Bless me, father, for I have sinned; this is my first confession." I waited for a few minutes, but nothing happened, so

caffler: scamp, rascal.

I tried it on the other wall. Nothing happened there either. He had me spotted all right.

It must have been then that I noticed the shelf at about one height with my head. It was really a place for grown-up people to rest their elbows, but in my distracted state I thought it was probably the place you were supposed to kneel. Of course, it was on the high side and not very deep, but I was always good at climbing and managed to get up all right. Staying up was the trouble. There was room only for my knees, and nothing you could get a grip on but a sort of wooden moulding a bit above it. I held on to the moulding and repeated the words a little louder, and this time something happened all right. A slide was slammed back; a little light entered the box, and a man's voice said: "Who's there?"

"'Tis me, father," I said for fear he mightn't see me and go away again. I   20
couldn't see him at all. The place the voice came from was under the moulding, about level with my knees, so I took a good grip of the moulding and swung myself down till I saw the astonished face of a young priest looking up at me. He had to put his head on one side to see me, and I had to put mine on one side to see him, so we were more or less talking to one another upside-down. It struck me as a queer way of hearing confessions, but I didn't feel it my place to criticize.

"Bless me, father, for I have sinned; this is my first confession," I rattled off all in one breath, and swung myself down the least shade more to make it easier for him.

"What are you doing up there?" he shouted in an angry voice, and the strain the politeness was putting on my hold of the moulding, and the shock of being addressed in such an uncivil tone, were too much for me. I lost my grip, tumbled, and hit the door an unmerciful wallop before I found myself flat on my back in the middle of the aisle. The people who had been waiting stood up with their mouths open. The priest opened the door of the middle box and came out, pushing his biretta back from his forehead; he looked something terrible. Then Nora came scampering down the aisle.

"Oh, you dirty little caffler!" she said. "I might have known you'd do it. I might have known you'd disgrace me. I can't leave you out of my sight for one minute."

Before I could even get to my feet to defend myself she bent down and gave me a clip across the ear. This reminded me that I was so stunned I had even forgotten to cry, so that people might think I wasn't hurt at all, when in fact I was probably maimed for life. I gave a roar out of me.

"What's all this about?" the priest hissed, getting angrier than ever and   25
pushing Nora off me. "How dare you hit the child like that, you little vixen?"

"But I can't do my penance with him, father," Nora cried, cocking an outraged eye up at him.

"Well, go and do it, or I'll give you some more to do," he said, giving me a hand up. "Was it coming to confession you were, my poor man?" he asked me.

"'Twas, father," said I with a sob.

"Oh," he said respectfully, "a big hefty fellow like you must have terrible sins. Is this your first?"

"'Tis, father," said I.

"Worse and worse," he said gloomily. "The crimes of a life-time. I don't know will I get rid of you at all today. You'd better wait now till I'm finished with these old ones. You can see by the looks of them they haven't much to tell."

"I will, father," I said with something approaching joy.

The relief of it was really enormous. Nora stuck out her tongue at me from behind his back, but I couldn't even be bothered retorting. I knew from the very moment that man opened his mouth that he was intelligent above the ordinary. When I had time to think, I saw how right I was. It only stood to reason that a fellow confessing after seven years would have more to tell than people that went every week. The crimes of a lifetime, exactly as he said. It was only what he expected, and the rest was the cackle of old women and girls with their talk of hell, the bishop, and the penitential psalms. That was all they knew. I started to make my examination of conscience, and barring the one bad business of my grandmother it didn't seem so bad.

The next time, the priest steered me into the confession box himself and left the shutter back the way I could see him get in and sit down at the further side of the grille from me.

"Well, now," he said, "what do they call you?"

"Jackie, father," said I.

"And what's a-trouble to you, Jackie?"

"Father," I said, feeling I might as well get it over while I had him in good humor, "I had it all arranged to kill my grandmother."

He seemed a bit shaken by that, all right, because he said nothing for quite a while.

"My goodness," he said at last, "that'd be a shocking thing to do. What put that into your head?"

"Father," I said, feeling very sorry for myself, "she's an awful woman."

"Is she?" he asked, "What way is she awful?"

"She takes porter, father," I said, knowing well from the way Mother talked of it that this was a mortal sin, and hoping it would make the priest take a more favorable view of my case.

"Oh my!" he said, and I could see he was impressed.

"And snuff, father," said I.

"That's a bad case, sure enough, Jackie," he said.

"And she goes round in her bare feet, father," I went on in a rush of self-pity, "and she knows I don't like her, and she gives pennies to Nora and none to me, and my da sides with her and flakes me, and one night I was so heart-scalded I made up my mind I'd have to kill her."

"And what would you do with the body?" he asked with great interest.

"I was thinking I could chop that up and carry it away in a barrow I have," I said.

"Begor, Jackie," he said, "do you know you're a terrible child?"   50

"I know, father," I said, for I was just thinking the same thing myself. "I tried to kill Nora too with a bread-knife under the table, only I missed her."

"Is that the little girl that was beating you just now?" he asked.

"'Tis, father."

"Someone will go for her with a bread-knife one day, and he won't miss her," he said rather cryptically. "You must have great courage. Between ourselves, there's a lot of people I'd like to do the same to but I'd never have the nerve. Hanging is an awful death."

"Is it, father?" I asked with the deepest interest—I was always very keen on   55
hanging. "Did you ever see a fellow hanged?"

"Dozens of them," he said solemnly. "And they all died roaring."

"Jay!" I said.

"Oh, a horrible death!" he said with great satisfaction. "Lots of the fellows I saw killed their grandmothers too, but they all said 'twas never worth it."

He had me there for a full ten minutes talking, and then walked out the chapel yard with me. I was genuinely sorry to part with him, because he was the most entertaining character I'd ever met in the religious line. Outside, after the shadow of the church, the sunlight was like the roaring of waves on a beach; it dazzled me; and when the frozen silence melted and I heard the screech of trams on the road my heart soared. I knew now I wouldn't die in the night and come back, leaving marks on my mother's furniture. It would be a great worry to her, and the poor soul had enough.

Nora was sitting on the railing, waiting for me, and she put on a very sour   60
puss when she saw the priest with me. She was mad jealous because a priest had never come out of the church with her.

"Well," she asked coldly, after he left me, "what did he give you?"

"Three Hail Marys," I said.

"Three Hail Marys," she repeated incredulously. "You mustn't have told him anything."

"I told him everything," I said confidently.

"About Gran and all?"   65

"About Gran and all."

(All she wanted was to be able to go home and say I'd made a bad confession.)

"Did you tell him you went for me with the bread-knife?" she asked with a frown.

"I did to be sure."

"And he only gave you three Hail Marys?"   70

"That's all."

She slowly got down from the railing with a baffled air. Clearly, this was beyond her. As we mounted the steps back to the main road she looked at me suspiciously.

"What are you sucking?" she asked.

"Bullseyes."

"Was it the priest gave them to you?"

"'Twas."

"Lord God," she wailed bitterly, "some people have all the luck! 'Tis no advantage to anybody trying to be good. I might just as well be a sinner like you."

Tillie Olsen

I STAND HERE IRONING

1961

Tillie Olsen was born in Omaha in 1912, into a family of blue-collar workers who had fled Czarist Russia to escape persecution. Olsen grew up in poverty and quit school in eleventh grade to work. She later declared, "Public libraries were my college." As a member of the Young Communist League, she strove to organize Kansas City meat-packers, and was once thrown into jail. After her first husband deserted her, leaving her with one child, she married a printer and labor activist, Jack Olsen, with whom she had three more children. Although in the 1930s she published fiction in a distinguished little magazine, Partisan Review, *the demands of motherhood, political activity, and fac-tory and office jobs left her scant time to write until 1955. Then her youngest daughter began school and Olsen was awarded a creative writing fellow-*

Tillie Olsen

ship at Stanford University. Long a crusader for causes, she has been active in the feminist movement. "I Stand Here Ironing," from her first book, Tell Me a Riddle *(1961), reads like autobiography. Olsen has since published* Yonnondio *(1974), an unfinished novel begun at age nineteen, and* Silences *(1978), a study of why writers—especially women writers—dry up. She holds several honorary degrees. In 1981 the city of San Francisco, where she has long resided, designated a Tillie Olsen day.*

I stand here ironing, and what you asked me moves tormented back and forth with the iron.

"I wish you would manage the time to come in and talk with me about your daughter. I'm sure you can help me understand her. She's a youngster who needs help and whom I'm deeply interested in helping."

"Who needs help." . . . Even if I came, what good would it do? You think be-cause I am her mother I have a key, or that in some way you could use me as a key? She has lived for nineteen years. There is all that life that has happened outside of me, beyond me.

And when is there time to remember, to sift, to weigh, to estimate, to total? I will start and there will be an interruption and I will have to gather it all together again. Or I will become engulfed with all I did or did not do, with what should have been and what cannot be helped.

She was a beautiful baby. The first and only one of our five that was beautiful at birth. You do not guess how new and uneasy her tenancy in her now-loveliness. You did not know her all those years she was thought homely, or see her poring over her baby pictures, making me tell her over and over how beautiful she had been—and would be, I would tell her—and was now, to the seeing eye. But the seeing eyes were few or nonexistent. Including mine.

I nursed her. They feel that's important nowadays. I nursed all the children, but with her, with all the fierce rigidity of first motherhood, I did like the books then said. Though her cries battered me to trembling and my breasts ached with swollenness, I waited till the clock decreed.

Why do I put that first? I do not even know if it matters, or if it explains anything.

She was a beautiful baby. She blew shining bubbles of sound. She loved motion, loved light, loved color and music and textures. She would lie on the floor in her blue overalls patting the surface so hard in ecstasy her hands and feet would blur. She was a miracle to me, but when she was eight months old I had to leave her daytimes with the woman downstairs to whom she was no miracle at all, for I worked or looked for work and for Emily's father, who "could no longer endure" (he wrote in his good-bye note) "sharing want with us."

I was nineteen. It was the pre-relief, pre-WPA world of the depression. I would start running as soon as I got off the streetcar, running up the stairs, the place smelling sour, and awake or asleep to startle awake, when she saw me she would break into a clogged weeping that could not be comforted, a weeping I can hear yet.

After a while I found a job hashing at night so I could be with her days, and it was better. But it came to where I had to bring her to his family and leave her.

It took a long time to raise the money for her fare back. Then she got chicken pox and I had to wait longer. When she finally came, I hardly knew her, walking quick and nervous like her father, looking like her father, thin, and dressed in a shoddy red that yellowed her skin and glared at the pockmarks. All the baby loveliness gone.

She was two. Old enough for nursery school they said, and I did not know then what I know now—the fatigue of the long day, and the lacerations of group life in the kinds of nurseries that are only parking places for children.

Except that it would have made no difference if I had known. It was the only place there was. It was the only way we could be together, the only way I could hold a job.

And even without knowing, I knew. I knew the teacher that was evil because all these years it has curdled into my memory, the little boy hunched in the corner, her rasp, "why aren't you outside, because Alvin hits you? that's no reason, go out, scaredy." I knew Emily hated it even if she did not clutch and implore "don't go Mommy" like the other children, mornings.

She always had a reason why we should stay home. Momma, you look sick. 15
Momma, I feel sick. Momma, the teachers aren't there today, they're sick.
Momma, we can't go, there was a fire there last night. Momma, it's a holiday
today, no school, they told me.

But never a direct protest, never rebellion. I think of our others in their
three-, four-year-oldness—the explosions, the tempers, the denunciations, the
demands—and I feel suddenly ill. I put the iron down. What in me demanded
that goodness in her? And what was the cost, the cost to her of such goodness?

The old man living in the back once said in his gentle way: "You should
smile at Emily more when you look at her." What *was* in my face when I looked
at her? I loved her. There were all the acts of love.

It was only with the others I remembered what he said, and it was the face of
joy, and not of care or tightness or worry I turned to them—too late for Emily.
She does not smile easily, let alone almost always as her brothers and sisters do.
Her face is closed and somber, but when she wants, how fluid. You must have
seen it in her pantomimes, you spoke of her rare gift for comedy on the stage that
rouses laughter out of the audience so dear they applaud and applaud and do not
want to let her go.

Where does it come from, that comedy? There was none of it in her when she
came back to me that second time, after I had had to send her away again. She had
a new daddy now to learn to love, and I think perhaps it was a better time.

Except when we left her alone nights, telling ourselves she was old enough. 20

"Can't you go some other time, Mommy, like tomorrow?" she would ask.
"Will it be just a little while you'll be gone? Do you promise?"

The time we came back, the front door open, the clock on the floor in the
hall. She rigid awake. "It wasn't just a little while. I didn't cry. Three times I called
you, just three times, and then I ran downstairs to open the door so you could
come faster. The clock talked loud. I threw it away, it scared me what it talked."

She said the clock talked loud again that night I went to the hospital to
have Susan. She was delirious with the fever that comes from red measles, but
she was fully conscious all the week I was gone and the week after we were home
when she could not come near the new baby or me.

She did not get well. She stayed skeleton thin, not wanting to eat, and night
after night she had nightmares. She would call for me, and I would rouse from
exhaustion to sleepily call back: "You're all right, darling, go to sleep, it's just a
dream," and if she still called, in a sterner voice, "now go to sleep, Emily, there's
nothing to hurt you." Twice, only twice, when I had to get up for Susan anyhow,
I went in to sit with her.

Now when it is too late (as if she would let me hold and comfort her like I 25
do the others) I get up and go to her at once at her moan or restless stirring. "Are
you awake, Emily? Can I get you something?" And the answer is always the
same: "No, I'm all right, go back to sleep, Mother."

They persuaded me at the clinic to send her away to a convalescent home in
the country where "she can have the kind of food and care you can't manage for
her, and you'll be free to concentrate on the new baby." They still send children
to that place. I see pictures on the society page of sleek young women planning

affairs to raise money for it, or dancing at the affairs, or decorating Easter eggs or filling Christmas stockings for the children.

They never have a picture of the children so I do not know if the girls still wear those gigantic red bows and the ravaged looks on the every other Sunday when parents can come to visit "unless otherwise notified"—as we were notified the first six weeks.

Oh it is a handsome place, green lawns and tall trees and fluted flower beds. High up on the balconies of each cottage the children stand, the girls in their red bows and white dresses, the boys in white suits and giant red ties. The parents stand below shrieking up to be heard and the children shriek down to be heard, and between them the invisible wall: "Not to Be Contaminated by Parental Germs or Physical Affection."

There was a tiny girl who always stood hand in hand with Emily. Her parents never came. One visit she was gone. "They moved her to Rose Cottage," Emily shouted in explanation. "They don't like you to love anybody here."

She wrote once a week, the labored writing of a seven-year-old. "I am fine.   30
How is the baby. If I write my leter nicly I will have a star. Love." There never was a star. We wrote every other day, letters she could never hold or keep but only hear read—once. "We simply do not have room for children to keep any personal possessions," they patiently explained when we pieced one Sunday's shrieking together to plead how much it would mean to Emily, who loved so to keep things, to be allowed to keep her letters and cards.

Each visit she looked frailer. "She isn't eating," they told us.

(They had runny eggs for breakfast or mush with lumps, Emily said later, I'd hold it in my mouth and not swallow. Nothing ever tasted good, just when they had chicken.)

It took us eight months to get her released home, and only the fact that she gained back so little of her seven lost pounds convinced the social worker.

I used to try to hold and love her after she came back, but her body would stay stiff, and after a while she'd push away. She ate little. Food sickened her, and I think much of life too. Oh she had physical lightness and brightness, twinkling by on skates, bouncing like a ball up and down up and down over the jump rope, skimming over the hill: but these were momentary.

She fretted about her appearance, thin and dark and foreign-looking at a   35
time when every little girl was supposed to look or thought she should look a chubby blonde replica of Shirley Temple. The doorbell sometimes rang for her, but no one seemed to come and play in the house or be a best friend. Maybe because we moved so much.

There was a boy she loved painfully through two school semesters. Months later she told me how she had taken pennies from my purse to buy him candy. "Licorice was his favorite and I brought him some every day, but he still liked Jennifer better'n me. Why, Mommy?" The kind of question for which there is no answer.

School was a worry to her. She was not glib or quick in a world where glibness and quickness were easily confused with ability to learn. To her overworked and exasperated teachers she was an overconscientious "slow learner" who kept trying to catch up and was absent entirely too often.

I let her be absent, though sometimes the illness was imaginary. How different from my now-strictness about attendance with the others. I wasn't working. We had a new baby, I was home anyhow. Sometimes, after Susan grew old enough, I would keep her home from school, too, to have them all together.

Mostly Emily had asthma, and her breathing, harsh and labored, would fill the house with a curiously tranquil sound. I would bring the two old dresser mirrors and her boxes of collections to her bed. She would select beads and single earrings, bottle tops and shells, dried flowers and pebbles, old postcards and scraps, all sorts of oddments; then she and Susan would play Kingdom, setting up landscapes and furniture, peopling them with action.

Those were the only times of peaceful companionship between her and Susan. I have edged away from it, that poisonous feeling between them, that terrible balancing of hurts and needs I had to do between the two, and did so badly, those earlier years.

Oh there are conflicts between the others too, each one human, needing, demanding, hurting, taking—but only between Emily and Susan, no, Emily toward Susan that corroding resentment. It seems so obvious on the surface, yet it is not obvious. Susan, the second child, Susan, golden- and curly-haired and chubby, quick and articulate and assured, everything in appearance and manner Emily was not; Susan, not able to resist Emily's precious things, losing or sometimes clumsily breaking them; Susan telling jokes and riddles to company for applause while Emily sat silent (to say to me later: that was *my* riddle, Mother, I told it to Susan); Susan, who for all the five years' difference in age was just a year behind Emily in developing physically.

I am glad for that slow physical development that widened the difference between her and her contemporaries, though she suffered over it. She was too vulnerable for that terrible world of youthful competition, of preening and parading, of constant measuring of yourself against every other, of envy, "If I had that copper hair," "If I had that skin. . . ." She tormented herself enough about not looking like the others, there was enough of the unsureness, the having to be conscious of words before you speak, the constant caring—what are they thinking of me? without having it all magnified by the merciless physical drives.

Ronnie is calling. He is wet and I change him. It is rare there is such a cry now. That time of motherhood is almost behind me when the ear is not one's own but must always be racked and listening for the child cry, the child call. We sit for a while and I hold him, looking out over the city spread in charcoal with its soft aisles of light. "*Shoogily*," he breathes and curls closer. I carry him back to bed, asleep. *Shoogily*. A funny word, a family word, inherited from Emily, invented by her to say: *comfort*.

In this and other ways she leaves her seal, I say aloud. And startle at my saying it. What do I mean? What did I start to gather together, to try and make coherent? I was at the terrible, growing years. War years. I do not remember them well. I was working, there were four smaller ones now, there was not time for her. She had to help be a mother, and housekeeper, and shopper. She had to set her seal. Mornings of crisis and near hysteria trying to get lunches packed, hair combed, coats and shoes found, everyone to school or Child Care on time, the baby ready for transportation. And always the paper scribbled on by a smaller one, the book looked at by Susan then mislaid, the homework not done. Running out to that huge school where she was one, she was lost, she was a drop; suffering over the unpreparedness, stammering and unsure in her classes.

There was so little time left at night after the kids were bedded down. She 45 would struggle over books, always eating (it was in those years she developed her enormous appetite that is legendary in our family) and I would be ironing, or preparing food for the next day, or writing V-mail to Bill, or tending the baby. Sometimes, to make me laugh, or out of her despair, she would imitate happenings or types at school.

I think I said once: "Why don't you do something like this in the school amateur show?" One morning she phoned me at work, hardly understandable through the weeping: "Mother, I did it. I won, I won; they gave me first prize; they clapped and clapped and wouldn't let me go."

Now suddenly she was Somebody, and as imprisoned in her difference as she had been in anonymity.

She began to be asked to perform at other high schools, even in colleges, then at city and statewide affairs. The first one we went to, I only recognized her that first moment when thin, shy, she almost drowned herself into the curtains. Then: Was this Emily? The control, the command, the convulsing and deadly clowning, the spell, then the roaring, stamping audience, unwilling to let this rare and precious laughter out of their lives.

Afterwards: You ought to do something about her with a gift like that—but without money or knowing how, what does one do? We have left it all to her, and the gift has as often eddied inside, clogged and clotted, as been used and growing.

She is coming. She runs up the stairs two at a time with her light graceful 50 step, and I know she is happy tonight. Whatever it was that occasioned your call did not happen today.

"Aren't you ever going to finish the ironing, Mother? Whistler painted his mother in a rocker. I'd have to paint mine standing over an ironing board." This is one of her communicative nights and she tells me everything and nothing as she fixes herself a plate of food out of the icebox.

She is so lovely. Why did you want me to come in at all? Why were you concerned? She will find her way.

She starts up the stairs to bed. "Don't get me up with the rest in the morning." "But I thought you were having midterms." "Oh, those," she comes back in, kisses me, and says quite lightly, "in a couple of years when we'll all be atom-dead they won't matter a bit."

She has said it before. She *believes* it. But because I have been dredging the past, and all that compounds a human being is so heavy and meaningful in me, I cannot endure it tonight.

I will never total it all. I will never come in to say: She was a child seldom 55
smiled at. Her father left me before she was a year old. I had to work her first six
years when there was work, or I sent her home and to his relatives. There were
years she had care she hated. She was dark and thin and foreign-looking in a world
where the prestige went to blondeness and curly hair and dimples, she was slow
where glibness was prized. She was a child of anxious, not proud, love. We were
poor and could not afford for her the soil of easy growth. I was a young mother, I
was a distracted mother. There were other children pushing up, demanding. Her
younger sister seemed all that she was not. There were years she did not want me
to touch her. She kept too much in herself, her life was such she had to keep too
much in herself. My wisdom came too late. She has much to her and probably
little will come of it. She is a child of her age, of depression, of war, of fear.

Let her be. So all that is in her will not bloom—but in how many does it?
There is still enough left to live by. Only help her to know—help make it so
there is cause for her to know—that she is more than this dress on the ironing
board, helpless before the iron.

Leslie Marmon Silko
THE MAN TO SEND RAIN CLOUDS   1981

*Leslie Marmon Silko was born in Albuquerque,
New Mexico, in 1948. Her mixed ancestry included Laguna Pueblo Indian, Mexican, and
white, but she grew up on the Laguna Pueblo
Reservation, where some part of her family had
lived for generations. After attending Indian
Affairs schools in Laguna Pueblo and Catholic
schools in Albuquerque, Silko graduated from the
University of New Mexico–Albuquerque in
1969. She briefly attended law school before deciding to devote herself full-time to writing. Silko
first became known as a poet with* Laguna
Woman *(1974). Her first novel,* Ceremony,
*was published in 1977 to critical acclaim. Her
second,* Almanac of the Dead, *an apocalyptic
view of the American future, appeared in 1991.*

Leslie Marmon Silko

In her next novel, Gardens in the Dunes *(1999), the author mixed American history,
Christian theology, Southwestern Indian myth, and botany to create an extravagant family
chronicle. Silko has also published* Storyteller *(1981), which includes poetry, short stories,
family history, myths, and photographs, and* Yellow Woman and a Beauty of the Spirit:
Essays on Native American Life Today *(1996). "The Man to Send Rain Clouds" originally appeared in* Storyteller.

They found him under a big cottonwood tree. His Levi jacket and pants were faded light blue so that he had been easy to find. The big cottonwood tree stood apart from a small grove of winterbare cottonwoods which grew in the wide, sandy arroyo. He had been dead for a day or more, and the sheep had wandered and scattered up and down the arroyo. Leon and his brother-in-law, Ken, gathered the sheep and left them in the pen at the sheep camp before they returned to the cottonwood tree. Leon waited under the tree while Ken drove the truck through the deep sand to the edge of the arroyo. He squinted up at the sun and unzipped his jacket—it sure was hot for this time of year. But high and northwest the blue mountains were still in snow. Ken came sliding down the low, crumbling bank about fifty yards down, and he was bringing the red blanket.

Before they wrapped the old man, Leon took a piece of string out of his pocket and tied a small gray feather in the old man's long white hair. Ken gave him the paint. Across the brown wrinkled forehead he drew a streak of white and along the high cheekbones he drew a strip of blue paint. He paused and watched Ken throw pinches of corn meal and pollen into the wind that fluttered the small gray feather. Then Leon painted with yellow under the old man's broad nose, and finally, when he had painted green across the chin, he smiled.

"Send us rain clouds, Grandfather." They laid the bundle in the back of the pickup and covered it with a heavy tarp before they started back to the pueblo.

They turned off the highway onto the sandy pueblo road. Not long after they passed the store and post office they saw Father Paul's car coming toward them. When he recognized their faces he slowed his car and waved for them to stop. The young priest rolled down the car window.

"Did you find old Teofilo?" he asked loudly.   5

Leon stopped the truck. "Good morning, Father. We were just out to the sheep camp. Everything is O.K. now."

"Thank God for that. Teofilo is a very old man. You really shouldn't allow him to stay at the sheep camp alone."

"No, he won't do that any more now."

"Well, I'm glad you understand. I hope I'll be seeing you at Mass this week—we missed you last Sunday. See if you can get old Teofilo to come with you." The priest smiled and waved at them as they drove away.

Louise and Teresa were waiting. The table was set for lunch, and the coffee   10
was boiling on the black iron stove. Leon looked at Louise and then at Teresa.

"We found him under a cottonwood tree in the big arroyo near sheep camp. I guess he sat down to rest in the shade and never got up again." Leon walked toward the old man's bed. The red plaid shawl had been shaken and spread carefully over the bed, and a new brown flannel shirt and pair of stiff new Levi's were arranged neatly beside the pillow. Louise held the screen door open while Leon and Ken carried in the red blanket. He looked small and shriveled, and after they dressed him in the new shirt and pants he seemed more shrunken.

It was noontime now because the church bells rang the Angelus. They ate the beans with hot bread, and nobody said anything until after Teresa poured the coffee.

Ken stood up and put on his jacket. "I'll see about the gravediggers. Only the top layer of soil is frozen. I think it can be ready before dark."

Leon nodded his head and finished his coffee. After Ken had been gone for a while, the neighbors and clanspeople came quietly to embrace Teofilo's family and to leave food on the table because the gravediggers would come to eat when they were finished.

The sky in the west was full of pale yellow light. Louise stood outside with her hands in the pockets of Leon's green army jacket that was too big for her. The funeral was over, and the old men had taken their candles and medicine bags and were gone. She waited until the body was laid into the pickup before she said anything to Leon. She touched his arm, and he noticed that her hands were still dusty from the corn meal that she had sprinkled around the old man. When she spoke, Leon could not hear her.

"What did you say? I didn't hear you."

"I said that I had been thinking about something."

"About what?"

"About the priest sprinkling holy water for Grandpa. So he won't be thirsty."

Leon stared at the new moccasins that Teofilo had made for the ceremonial dances in the summer. They were nearly hidden by the red blanket. It was getting colder, and the wind pushed gray dust down the narrow pueblo road. The sun was approaching the long mesa where it disappeared during the winter. Louise stood there shivering and watching his face. Then he zipped up his jacket and opened the truck door. "I'll see if he's there."

Ken stopped the pickup at the church, and Leon got out; and then Ken drove down the hill to the graveyard where people were waiting. Leon knocked at the old carved door with its symbols of the Lamb. While he waited he looked up at the twin bells from the king of Spain with the last sunlight pouring around them in their tower.

The priest opened the door and smiled when he saw who it was. "Come in! What brings you here this evening?"

The priest walked toward the kitchen, and Leon stood with his cap in his hand, playing with the earflaps and examining the living room—the brown sofa, the green armchair, and the brass lamp that hung down from the ceiling by links of chain. The priest dragged a chair out of the kitchen and offered it to Leon.

"No thank you, Father. I only came to ask you if you would bring your holy water to the graveyard."

The priest turned away from Leon and looked out the window at the patio full of shadows and the dining-room windows of the nuns' cloister across the patio. The curtains were heavy, and the light from within faintly penetrated; it was impossible to see the nuns inside eating supper. "Why didn't you tell me he was dead? I could have brought the Last Rites anyway."

Leon smiled. "It wasn't necessary, Father."

The priest stared down at his scuffed brown loafers and the worn hem of his cassock. "For a Christian burial it was necessary."

His voice was distant, and Leon thought that his blue eyes looked tired.

"It's O.K., Father, we just want him to have plenty of water."

The priest sank down into the green chair and picked up a glossy missionary   30
magazine. He turned the colored pages full of lepers and pagans without looking
at them.

"You know I can't do that, Leon. There should have been the Last Rites and
a funeral Mass at the very least."

Leon put on his green cap and pulled the flaps down over his ears. "It's getting late, Father. I've got to go."

When Leon opened the door Father Paul stood up and said, "Wait." He left
the room and came back wearing a long brown overcoat. He followed Leon out
the door and across the dim churchyard to the adobe steps in front of the church.
They both stooped to fit through the low adobe entrance. And when they started
down the hill to the graveyard only half of the sun was visible above the mesa.

The priest approached the grave slowly, wondering how they had managed
to dig into the frozen ground; and then he remembered that this was New
Mexico, and saw the pile of cold loose sand beside the hole. The people stood
close to each other with little clouds of steam puffing from their faces. The priest
looked at them and saw a pile of jackets, gloves, and scarves in the yellow, dry
tumbleweeds that grew in the graveyard. He looked at the red blanket, not sure
that Teofilo was so small, wondering if it wasn't some perverse Indian trick—
something they did in March to ensure a good harvest—wondering if maybe old
Teofilo was actually at sheep camp corralling the sheep for the night. But there
he was, facing into a cold dry wind and squinting at the last sunlight, ready to
bury a red wool blanket while the faces of his parishioners were in shadow with
the last warmth of the sun on their backs.

His fingers were stiff, and it took him a long time to twist the lid off the   35
holy water. Drops of water fell on the red blanket and soaked into dark icy spots.
He sprinkled the grave and the water disappeared almost before it touched the
dim, cold sand; it reminded him of something—he tried to remember what it
was, because he thought if he could remember he might understand this. He
sprinkled more water; he shook the container until it was empty, and the water
fell through the light from sundown like August rain that fell while the sun was
still shining, almost evaporating before it touched the wilted squash flowers.

The wind pulled at the priest's brown Franciscan robe and swirled away the
corn meal and pollen that had been sprinkled on the blanket. They lowered the
bundle into the ground, and they didn't bother to untie the stiff pieces of new
rope that were tied around the ends of the blanket. The sun was gone, and over
on the highway the eastbound lane was full of headlights. The priest walked
away slowly. Leon watched him climb the hill, and when he had disappeared
within the tall, thick walls, Leon turned to look up at the high blue mountains
in the deep snow that reflected a faint red light from the west. He felt good because it was finished, and he was happy about the sprinkling of the holy water;
now the old man could send them big thunderclouds for sure.

POETRY

Gwendolyn Brooks c. 1950, the year she won the Pulitzer Prize.

TO THE MUSE

Give me leave, Muse, in plain view to array
Your shift and bodice by the light of day.
I would have brought an epic. Be not vexed
Instead to grace a niggling schoolroom text;
Let down your sanction, help me to oblige
Those who would lead fresh devots to your liege,
And at your altar, grant that in a flash
Readers and I know incense from dead ash.

—X. J. K.

What is poetry? Pressed for an answer, Robert Frost made a classic reply: "Poetry is the kind of thing poets write." In all likelihood, Frost was trying not merely to evade the question but to chide his questioner into thinking for himself. A trouble with definitions is that they may stop thought. If Frost had said, "Poetry is a rhythmical composition of words expressing an attitude, designed to surprise and delight, and to arouse an emotional response," the questioner might have settled back in his chair, content to have learned the truth about poetry. He would have learned nothing, or not so much as he might learn by continuing to wonder.

The nature of poetry eludes simple definitions. (In this respect it is rather like jazz. Asked after one of his concerts, "What is jazz?" Louis Armstrong replied, "Man, if you gotta ask, you'll never know.") Definitions will be of little help at first, if we are to know poetry and respond to it. We have to go to it willing to see and hear. For this reason, you are asked in reading this book not to be in any hurry to decide what poetry is, but instead to study poems and to let them grow in your mind. At the end of our discussions of poetry, the problem of definition will be taken up again (for those who may wish to pursue it).

Confronted with a formal introduction to poetry, you may be wondering, "Who needs it?" and you may well be right. It's unlikely that you have avoided meeting poetry before; and perhaps you already have a friendship, or at least a fair acquaintance, with some of the greatest English-speaking poets of all time. What this book provides is an introduction to the *study* of poetry. It tries to help you look at a poem closely, to offer you a wider and more accurate vocabulary with which to express what poems say to you. It will suggest ways to judge for yourself the poems you read. It may set forth some poems new to you.

A frequent objection is that poetry ought not to be studied at all. In this view, a poem is either a series of gorgeous noises to be funneled into one ear and out the other without being allowed to trouble the mind, or an experience so holy that to analyze it in a classroom is as cruel and mechanical as dissecting a hummingbird. To the first view, it might be countered that a good poem has something to say that is well worth listening to. To the second view, it might be argued that poems are much less perishable than hummingbirds, and luckily, we can study them in flight. The risk of a poem's dying from observation is not nearly so great as the risk of not really seeing it at all. It is doubtful that any excellent poem has ever vanished from human memory because people have read it too closely.

That poetry matters to the people who write it has been shown unmistakably by the ordeal of Soviet poet Irina Ratushinskaya. Sentenced to prison for three and a half years, she was given paper and pencil only twice a month to write letters to her husband and her parents and was not allowed to write anything else. Nevertheless, Ratushinskaya composed more than two hundred poems in her cell, engraving them with a burnt match in a bar of soap, then memorizing the lines. "I would read the poem and read it," she said, "until it was committed to memory—then with one washing of my hands, it would be gone."

Good poetry is something that readers can care about. In fact, an ancient persuasion of humankind is that the hearing of a poem, as well as the making of a poem, can be a religious act. Poetry, in speech and song, was part of classic Greek drama, which for playwright, actor, and spectator alike was a holy-day ceremony. The Greeks' belief that a poet writes a poem only by supernatural assistance is clear from the invocations to the Muse that begin the *Iliad* and the *Odyssey* and from the opinion of Socrates (in Plato's *Ion*) that a poet has no powers of invention until divinely inspired. Among the ancient Celts, poets were regarded as magicians and priests, and whoever insulted one of them might expect to receive a curse in rime potent enough to afflict him with boils and to curdle the milk of his cows. Such identifications between the poet and the magician are less common these days, although we know that poetry is involved in the primitive white magic of children, who bring themselves good luck in a game with the charm "Roll, roll, Tootsie-roll! / Roll the marble in the hole!" and who warn against a hex while jumping along a sidewalk: "Step on a crack, / Break your mother's back." To read a poem, we have to be willing to offer it responses *besides* a logical understanding. Whether we attribute the effect of a poem to a divine spirit or to the reactions of our glands and cortexes, we have to take the reading of poetry seriously (not solemnly), if only because—as some of the poems in this book may demonstrate—few other efforts can repay us so generously, both in wisdom and in joy.

If, as we hope you will do, you sometimes browse in the book for fun, you may be annoyed to see so many questions following the poems. Should you feel this way, try reading with a slip of paper to cover up the questions. You will then—if the Muse should inspire you—have paper in hand to write a poem.

12 *Reading a Poem*

How do you read a poem? The literal-minded might say, "Just let your eye light on it"; but there is more to poetry than meets the eye. What Shakespeare called "the mind's eye" also plays a part. Many a reader who has no trouble understanding and enjoying prose finds poetry difficult. This is to be expected. At first glance, a poem usually will make some sense and give some pleasure, but it may not yield everything at once. Sometimes it only hints at meaning still to come if we will keep after it. Poetry is not to be galloped over like the daily news: a poem differs from most prose in that it is to be read slowly, carefully, and attentively. Not all poems are difficult, of course, and some can be understood and enjoyed on first encounter. But good poems yield more if read twice; and the best poems—after ten, twenty, or a hundred readings—still go on yielding.

Approaching a thing written in lines and surrounded with white space, we need not expect it to be a poem just because it is **verse**. (Any composition in lines of more or less regular rhythm, usually ending in rimes, is verse.) Here, for instance, is a specimen of verse that few will call poetry:

> Thirty days hath September,
> April, June, and November;
> All the rest have thirty-one
> Excepting February alone,
> To which we twenty-eight assign
> Till leap year makes it twenty-nine.

To a higher degree than that classic memory-tickler, poetry appeals to the mind and arouses feelings. Poetry may state facts, but, more important, it makes imaginative statements that we may value even if its facts are incorrect. Coleridge's error in placing a star within the horns of the crescent moon in "The Rime of the Ancient Mariner" does not stop the passage from being good poetry, though it is faulty astronomy. According to one poet, Gerard Manley Hopkins, poetry is "to be heard for its own sake and interest even over and above its interest of meaning." There are other elements in a poem besides plain prose sense: sounds, images, rhythms, figures of speech. These may strike us and please us even before we ask, "But what does it all mean?"

This is a truth not readily grasped by anyone who regards a poem as a kind of puzzle written in secret code with a message slyly concealed. The effect of a poem (one's whole mental and emotional response to it) consists of much more than simply a message. By its musical qualities, by its suggestions, it can work on the reader's unconscious. T. S. Eliot put it well when he said in *The Use of Poetry and the Use of Criticism* that the prose sense of a poem is chiefly useful in keeping the reader's mind "diverted and quiet, while the poem does its work upon him." Eliot went on to liken the meaning of a poem to the bit of meat a burglar brings along to throw to the family dog. What is the work of a poem? To touch us, to stir us, to make us glad, and possibly even to tell us something.

How to set about reading a poem? Here are a few suggestions.

To begin with, read the poem once straight through, with no particular expectations; read open-mindedly. Let yourself experience whatever you find, without worrying just yet about the large general and important ideas the poem contains (if indeed it contains any). Don't dwell on a troublesome word or difficult passage—just push on. Some of the difficulties may seem smaller when you read the poem for a second time; at least, they will have become parts of a whole for you.

On the second reading, read for the exact sense of all the words; if there are words you don't understand, look them up in a dictionary. Dwell on any difficult parts as long as you need to.

If you read the poem silently, sound its words in your mind. (This is a technique that will get you nowhere in a speed-reading course, but it may help the poem to do its work on you.) Better still, read the poem aloud, or hear someone else read it. You may discover meanings you didn't perceive in it before. Even if you are no actor, to decide how to speak a poem can be an excellent method of getting to understand it. Some poems, like bells, seem heavy till heard. Listen while reading the following lines from Alexander Pope's *Dunciad*. Attacking the minor poet James Ralph, who had sung the praises of a mistress named Cynthia, Pope makes the goddess of Dullness exclaim:

> "Silence, ye wolves! while Ralph to Cynthia howls,
> And makes night hideous—answer him, ye owls!"

When *ye owls* slide together and become *yowls,* poor Ralph's serenade is turned into the nightly outcry of a cat.

Try to **paraphrase** the poem as a whole, or perhaps just the more difficult lines. In paraphrasing, we put into our own words what we understand the poem to say, restating ideas that seem essential, coming out and stating what the poem may only suggest. This may sound like a heartless thing to do to a poem, but good poems can stand it. In fact, to compare a poem to its paraphrase is a good way to see the distance between poetry and prose. In making a paraphrase, we generally work through a poem or a passage line by line. The statement that results may take as many words as the original, if not more. A paraphrase, then, is ampler than a **summary,** a brief condensation of gist, main idea, or story. (Summary of a horror film in *TV Guide*: "Demented biologist, coveting power over New York, swells sewer rats to hippopotamus-size.") Here is a poem worth considering line by line. The poet writes of an island in a lake in the west of Ireland, in a region where he spent many summers as a boy.

William Butler Yeats (1865–1939)*

THE LAKE ISLE OF INNISFREE 1892

I will arise and go now, and go to Innisfree,
And a small cabin build there, of clay and wattles made:
Nine bean-rows will I have there, a hive for the honey-bee,
And live alone in the bee-loud glade.

And I shall have some peace there, for peace comes dropping slow,   5
Dropping from the veils of the morning to where the cricket sings;
There midnight's all a glimmer, and noon a purple glow,
And evening full of the linnet's wings.

I will arise and go now, for always night and day
I hear lake water lapping with low sounds by the shore;   10
While I stand on the roadway, or on the pavements gray,
I hear it in the deep heart's core.

    Though relatively simple, this poem is far from simple-minded. We need to absorb it slowly and thoughtfully. At the start, for most of us, it raises problems: what are *wattles*, from which the speaker's dream-cabin is to be made? We might guess, but in this case it will help to consult a dictionary: they are "poles interwoven with sticks or branches, formerly used in building as frameworks to support walls or roofs." Evidently, this getaway house will be built in an old-fashioned way: it won't be a prefabricated log cabin or A-frame house, nothing modern or citified. The phrase *bee-loud glade* certainly isn't commonplace language of the sort we find on a cornflakes package, but right away, we can understand it, at least partially: it's a place loud with bees. What is a *glade*? Experience might tell us that it is an open space in woods, but if that word stops us, we can look it up. Although the *linnet* doesn't live in North America, it is a creature with wings—a songbird of the finch family, adds the dictionary. But even if we don't make a special trip to the dictionary to find *linnet*, we probably recognize that the word means "bird," and the line makes sense to us.

*The asterisk indicates a poet who is described in the chapter "Lives of the Poets."

A paraphrase of the whole poem might go something like this (in language easier to forget than that of the original): "I'm going to get up now, go to Innisfree, build a cabin, plant beans, keep bees, and live peacefully by myself amid nature and beautiful light. I want to because I can't forget the sound of that lake water. When I'm in the city, a gray and dingy place, I seem to hear it deep inside me."

These dull remarks, roughly faithful to what Yeats is saying, seem a long way from poetry. Nevertheless, they make certain things clear. For one, they spell out what the poet merely hints at in his choice of the word *gray*: that he finds the city dull and depressing. He stresses the word; instead of saying *gray pavements*, in the usual word order, he turns the phrase around and makes *gray* stand at the end of the line, where it rimes with *day* and so takes extra emphasis. The grayness of the city therefore seems important to the poem, and the paraphrase tries to make its meaning obvious.

Whenever you paraphrase, you stick your neck out. You affirm what the poem gives you to understand. And making a paraphrase can help you see the central thought of the poem, its **theme.** Theme isn't the same as **subject,** the main topic, whatever the poem is "about." In Yeats's poem, the subject is the lake isle of Innisfree, or a wish to retreat to it. But the theme is, "I yearn for an ideal place where I will find perfect peace and happiness." Themes can be stated variously, depending on what you believe most matters in the poem. Taking a different view of the poem, placing more weight on the speaker's wish to escape the city, you might instead state the theme: "This city is getting me down—I want to get back to nature." But after taking a second look at that statement, you might want to sharpen it. After all, this Innisfree seems a special, particular place, where the natural world means more to the poet than just any old trees and birds he might see in a park. Perhaps a stronger statement of theme, one closer to what matters most in the poem, might be: "I want to quit the city for my heaven on earth." That, of course, is saying in an obvious way what Yeats says more subtly, more memorably.

Not all poems clearly assert a proposition, but many do; some even declare their themes in their opening lines: "Gather ye rose-buds while ye may!"—that is, enjoy love before it's too late. This theme, stated in that famous first line of Robert Herrick's "To the Virgins, to Make Much of Time" (page 1191), is so familiar that we give it a name: *carpe diem,* Latin for "seize the day." (For the original *carpe diem* poem, see the Latin poet Horace's ode on page 1028.) Seizing the joys of the present moment is a favorite argument of poets. You will meet it in more than these two poems in this book.

A paraphrase, of course, never tells *all* that a poem contains, nor will every reader agree that a particular paraphrase is accurate. We all make our own interpretations, and sometimes the total meaning of a poem evades even the poet who wrote it. Asked to explain a passage in one of his poems, Robert Browning replied that when he had written the poem, only God and he knew what it meant; but "Now, only God knows." Still, to analyze a poem *as if* we could be certain of its meaning is, in general, more fruitful than to proceed as if no certainty could ever be had. The latter approach is likely to end in complete subjectivity, the attitude of the reader who says, "Yeats's 'Lake Isle of Innisfree' is really about the lost island of Atlantis. It is because I think it is. How can you prove me wrong?" Interpretations can't be proven "wrong." A more fruitful question might be, "What can we understand from the poem's very words?"

All of us bring personal associations to the poems we read. "The Lake Isle of Innisfree" might give you special pleasure if you have ever vacationed on a small island or on the shore of a lake. Such associations are inevitable, even to be welcomed, as long as they don't interfere with our reading the words on the page. We need to distinguish irrelevant responses from those the poem calls for. The reader who can't stand "The Lake Isle of Innisfree" because she is afraid of bees isn't reading a poem by Yeats, but one of her own invention.

Now and again we meet a poem—perhaps startling and memorable—into which the method of paraphrase won't take us far. Some portion of any deep poem resists explanation, but certain poems resist it almost entirely. Many poems by religious mystics seem closer to dream than waking. So do poems that purport to record drug experiences, such as Coleridge's "Kubla Khan" (page 1158), as well as poems that embody some private system of beliefs, such as Blake's "The Sick Rose" (page 1150), or the same poet's lines from *Jerusalem*

> For a Tear is an Intellectual thing,
> And a Sigh is the Sword of an Angel King.

So do nonsense poems, translations of primitive folk songs, and surreal poems.[1] Such poetry may move us and give pleasure (although not, perhaps, the pleasure of intellectual understanding). We do it no harm by trying to paraphrase it, though we may fail. Whether logically clear or strangely opaque, good poems appeal to the intelligence and do not shrink from it.

So far, we have taken for granted that poetry differs from prose; yet all our strategies for reading poetry—plowing straight on through and then going back, isolating difficulties, trying to paraphrase, reading aloud, using a dictionary—are no different from those we might employ in unraveling a complicated piece of prose. Poetry, after all, is similar to prose in most respects. At the very least, it is written in the same language. Like prose, poetry shares knowledge with us. It tells us, for instance, of a beautiful island in Lake Gill, County Sligo, Ireland, and of how one man feels toward it. Maybe the poet knows no more about Innisfree than a writer of a travel guidebook knows. And yet Yeats's poem indicates a kind of knowledge that tourist guidebooks do not ordinarily reveal: that the human heart can yearn for peace and happiness, that the lake isle of Innisfree with its "low sounds by the shore" can echo and reecho in memory forever.

---

[1]The French poet André Breton, founder of **Surrealism,** a movement in art and writing, declared that a higher reality exists, which to mortal eyes looks absurd. To mirror that reality, surrealist poets are fond of bizarre and dreamlike objects such as soluble fish and white-haired revolvers.

LYRIC POETRY

Originally, as its Greek name suggests, a *lyric* was a poem sung to the music of a lyre. This earlier meaning—a poem made for singing—is still current today, when we use *lyrics* to mean the words of a popular song. But the kind of printed poem we now call a *lyric* is usually something else, for over the past five hundred years the nature of lyric poetry has changed greatly. Ever since the invention of the printing press in the fifteenth century, poets have written less often for singers, more often for readers. In general, this tendency has made lyric poems contain less word-music and (since they can be pondered on a page) more thought—and perhaps more complicated feelings.

Here is a rough definition of a **lyric** as it is written today: a short poem expressing the thoughts and feelings of a single speaker. Often a poet will write a lyric in the first person ("I will arise and go now, and go to Innisfree"), but not always. Instead, a lyric might describe an object or recall an experience without the speaker's ever bringing himself or herself into it. (For an example of such a lyric, one in which the poet refrains from saying "I," see William Carlos Williams's "The Red Wheelbarrow" on page 731, Theodore Roethke's "Root Cellar" on page 792, or Gerard Manley Hopkins's "Pied Beauty" on page 797.)

Perhaps because, rightly or wrongly, some people still think of lyrics as lyre-strummings, they expect a lyric to be an outburst of feeling, somewhat resembling a song, at least containing musical elements such as rime, rhythm, or sound effects. Such expectations are fulfilled in "The Lake Isle of Innisfree," that impassioned lyric full of language rich in sound (as you will hear if you'll read it aloud). Many contemporary poets, however, write short poems in which they voice opinions or complicated feelings—poems that no reader would dream of trying to sing. Most people would call such poems lyrics, too; one commentator has argued that a lyric may contain an argument.[2]

But in the sense in which we use it, *lyric* will usually apply to a kind of poem you can easily recognize. Here, for instance, are two lyrics. They differ sharply in subject and theme, but they have traits in common: both are short, and (as you will find) both set forth one speaker's definite, unmistakable feelings.

D. H. Lawrence (1885–1930)*

PIANO   1918

Softly, in the dusk, a woman is singing to me;
Taking me back down the vista of years, till I see
A child sitting under the piano, in the boom of the tingling strings
And pressing the small, poised feet of a mother who smiles as she sings.

---

[2]Jeffrey Walker, "Aristotle's Lyric," *College English* 51 (January 1989) 5–26.

In spite of myself, the insidious mastery of song 5
Betrays me back, till the heart of me weeps to belong
To the old Sunday evenings at home, with winter outside
And hymns in the cozy parlor, the tinkling piano our guide.

So now it is vain for the singer to burst into clamor
With the great black piano appassionato. The glamor 10
Of childish days is upon me, my manhood is cast
Down in the flood of remembrance, I weep like a child for the past.

QUESTIONS

1. Jot down a brief paraphrase of this poem. In your paraphrase, clearly show what the speaker says is happening at present and also what he finds himself remembering. Make clear which seems the more powerful in its effect on him.
2. What are the speaker's various feelings? What do you understand from the words *insidious* and *betrays*?
3. With what specific details does the poem make the past seem real?
4. What is the subject of Lawrence's poem? How would you state its theme?

Adrienne Rich   (b. 1929)*
AUNT JENNIFER'S TIGERS   1951

Aunt Jennifer's tigers prance across a screen,
Bright topaz denizens of a world of green.
They do not fear the men beneath the tree;
They pace in sleek chivalric certainty.

Aunt Jennifer's fingers fluttering through her wool 5
Find even the ivory needle hard to pull.
The massive weight of Uncle's wedding band
Sits heavily upon Aunt Jennifer's hand.

When Aunt is dead, her terrified hands will lie
Still ringed with ordeals she was mastered by. 10
The tigers in the panel that she made
Will go on prancing, proud and unafraid.

COMPARE

"Aunt Jennifer's Tigers" with Adrienne Rich's critical comments on the poem reprinted in the "Writer's Perspective" at the end of this chapter.

NARRATIVE POETRY

Although a lyric sometimes relates an incident, or like "Piano" draws a scene, it does not usually relate a series of events. That happens in a **narrative poem,** one whose main purpose is to tell a story.

In Western literature, narrative poetry dates back to the Babylonian *Epic of Gilgamesh* (composed before 2000 B.C.) and Homer's epics the *Iliad* and the *Odyssey* (composed before 700 B.C.). It may well have originated much earlier. In England and Scotland, storytelling poems have long been popular; in the late Middle Ages, ballads—or storytelling songs—circulated widely. Some, such as "Sir Patrick Spence" and "Bonny Barbara Allan," survive in our day, and folksingers sometimes perform them.

Evidently the art of narrative poetry invites the skills of a writer of fiction: the ability to draw characters and settings briefly, to engage attention, to shape a plot. Needless to say, it calls for all the skills of a poet as well. Here are two narrative poems: one medieval, one modern. How would you paraphrase the stories they tell? How do they hold your attention on their stories?

Anonymous   (traditional Scottish ballad)

SIR PATRICK SPENCE

The king sits in Dumferling toune,
    Drinking the blude-reid wine:
"O whar will I get guid sailor
    To sail this schip of mine?"

Up and spak an eldern knicht,°   *knight* 5
    Sat at the kings richt kne:
"Sir Patrick Spence is the best sailor
    That sails upon the se."

The king has written a braid letter,
    And signed it wi' his hand,   10
And sent it to Sir Patrick Spence,
    Was walking on the sand.

The first line that Sir Patrick red,
    A loud lauch lauchèd he;
The next line that Sir Patrick red,   15
    The teir blinded his ee.

"O wha° is this has don this deid,   *who*
    This ill deid don to me,
To send me out this time o' the yeir,
    To sail upon the se!   20

"Mak haste, mak haste, my mirry men all,
  Our guid schip sails the morne."
"O say na sae,° my master deir,   so
  For I feir a deadlie storme.

"Late late yestreen I saw the new moone,   25
  Wi' the auld moone in hir arme,
And I feir, I feir, my deir master,
  That we will cum to harme."

O our Scots nobles wer richt laith°   loath
  To weet° their cork-heild schoone,°   wet; shoes 30
Bot lang owre° a' the play wer playd,   before
  Their hats they swam aboone.°   above (their heads)

O lang, lang may their ladies sit,
  Wi' their fans into their hand,
Or ere° they se Sir Patrick Spence   long before 35
  Cum sailing to the land.

O lang, lang may the ladies stand,
  Wi' their gold kems° in their hair,   combs
Waiting for their ain° deir lords,   own
  For they'll se thame na mair.   40

Haf owre,° haf owre to Aberdour,   halfway over
  It's fiftie fadom deip,
And thair lies guid Sir Patrick Spence,
  Wi' the Scots lords at his feit.

SIR PATRICK SPENCE. 9 *braid*: Broad, but broad in what sense? Among guesses are *plain-spoken*, *official*, and *on wide paper*.

QUESTIONS

1. That the king drinks "blood-red wine" (line 2)—what meaning do you find in that detail? What does it hint, or foreshadow?
2. What do you make of this king and his motives for sending Spence and the Scots lords into an impending storm? Is he a fool, is he cruel and inconsiderate, is he deliberately trying to drown Sir Patrick and his crew, or is it impossible for us to know? Let your answer depend on the poem alone, not on anything you read into it.
3. Comment on this ballad's methods of storytelling. Is the story told too briefly for us to care what happens to Spence and his men, or are there any means by which the poet makes us feel compassion for them? Do you resent the lack of a detailed account of the shipwreck?
4. Lines 25–28—the new moon with the old moon in her arm—has been much admired as poetry. What does this stanza contribute to the story as well?

Robert Frost   (1874–1963)*

"Out, Out—"   1916

The buzz-saw snarled and rattled in the yard
And made dust and dropped stove-length sticks of wood,
Sweet-scented stuff when the breeze drew across it.
And from there those that lifted eyes could count
Five mountain ranges one behind the other   5
Under the sunset far into Vermont.
And the saw snarled and rattled, snarled and rattled,
As it ran light, or had to bear a load.
And nothing happened: day was all but done.
Call it a day, I wish they might have said   10
To please the boy by giving him the half hour
That a boy counts so much when saved from work.
His sister stood beside them in her apron
To tell them "Supper." At the word, the saw,
As if to prove saws knew what supper meant,   15
Leaped out at the boy's hand, or seemed to leap—
He must have given the hand. However it was,
Neither refused the meeting. But the hand!
The boy's first outcry was a rueful laugh,
As he swung toward them holding up the hand   20
Half in appeal, but half as if to keep
The life from spilling. Then the boy saw all—
Since he was old enough to know, big boy
Doing a man's work, though a child at heart—
He saw all spoiled. "Don't let him cut my hand off—   25
The doctor, when he comes. Don't let him, sister!"
So. But the hand was gone already.
The doctor put him in the dark of ether.
He lay and puffed his lips out with his breath.
And then—the watcher at his pulse took fright.   30
No one believed. They listened at his heart.
Little—less—nothing!—and that ended it.
No more to build on there. And they, since they
Were not the one dead, turned to their affairs.

"Out, Out—" The title of this poem echoes the words of Shakespeare's *Macbeth* on receiving news that his queen is dead: "Out, out, brief candle! / Life's but a walking shadow, a poor player / That struts and frets his hour upon the stage / And then is heard no more. It is a tale / Told by an idiot, full of sound and fury, / Signifying nothing" (*Macbeth* V, v, 23–28).

QUESTIONS

1. How does Frost make the buzz-saw appear sinister? How does he make it seem, in another way, like a friend?
2. What do you make of the people who surround the boy—the "they" of the poem? Who might they be? Do they seem to you concerned and compassionate, cruel, indifferent, or what?
3. What does Frost's reference to *Macbeth* contribute to your understanding of "'Out, Out—'"? How would you state the theme of Frost's poem?
4. Set this poem side by side with "Sir Patrick Spence." How does "'Out, Out—'" resemble that medieval folk ballad in subject, or differ from it? How is Frost's poem similar or different in its way of telling a story?

DRAMATIC POETRY

A third kind of poetry is **dramatic poetry,** which presents the voice of an imaginary character (or characters) speaking directly, without any additional narration by the author. A dramatic poem, according to T. S. Eliot, does not consist of "what the poet would say in his own person, but only what he can say within the limits of one imaginary character addressing another imaginary character." Strictly speaking, the term *dramatic poetry* describes any verse written for the stage (and until a few centuries ago most playwrights, like Shakespeare and Molière, wrote their plays mainly in verse). But the term most often refers to the **dramatic monologue,** a poem written as a speech made by a character (other than the author) at some decisive moment. A dramatic monologue is usually addressed by the speaker to some other character who remains silent. If the listener replies, the poem becomes a dialogue (such as Thomas Hardy's "The Ruined Maid" on page 764) in which the story unfolds in the conversation between two speakers.

The Victorian poet Robert Browning, who developed the form of the dramatic monologue, liked to put words in the mouths of characters who were conspicuously nasty, weak, reckless, or crazy: see, for instance, Browning's "Soliloquy of the Spanish Cloister" (page 1154), in which the speaker is an obsessively proud and jealous monk. The dramatic monologue has been a popular form among American poets, including Edwin Arlington Robinson, Robert Frost, Ezra Pound, Randall Jarrell, and Sylvia Plath. The most famous dramatic monologue ever written is probably Browning's "My Last Duchess," in which the poet creates a Renaissance Italian Duke whose words reveal more about himself than the aristocratic speaker intends.

Robert Browning   (1812–1889)*

MY LAST DUCHESS   1842

Ferrara

That's my last Duchess painted on the wall,
Looking as if she were alive. I call
That piece a wonder, now; Frà Pandolf's hands
Worked busily a day, and there she stands.
Will't please you sit and look at her? I said   5
"Frà Pandolf" by design, for never read
Strangers like you that pictured countenance,
The depth and passion of its earnest glance,
But to myself they turned (since none puts by
The curtain I have drawn for you, but I)   10
And seemed as they would ask me, if they durst,
How such a glance came there; so, not the first
Are you to turn and ask thus. Sir, 'twas not
Her husband's presence only, called that spot
Of joy into the Duchess' cheek; perhaps   15
Frà Pandolf chanced to say, "Her mantle laps
Over my lady's wrist too much," or "Paint
Must never hope to reproduce the faint
Half-flush that dies along her throat." Such stuff
Was courtesy, she thought, and cause enough   20
For calling up that spot of joy. She had
A heart—how shall I say?—too soon made glad,
Too easily impressed; she liked whate'er
She looked on, and her looks went everywhere.
Sir, 'twas all one! My favor at her breast,   25
The dropping of the daylight in the West,
The bough of cherries some officious fool
Broke in the orchard for her, the white mule
She rode with round the terrace—all and each
Would draw from her alike the approving speech,   30
Or blush, at least. She thanked men,—good! but thanked
Somehow—I know not how—as if she ranked
My gift of a nine-hundred-years-old name
With anybody's gift. Who'd stoop to blame
This sort of trifling? Even had you skill   35
In speech—which I have not—to make your will
Quite clear to such an one, and say "Just this
Or that in you disgusts me; here you miss,
Or there exceed the mark"—and if she let
Herself be lessoned so, nor plainly set   40

Her wits to yours, forsooth, and made excuse—
E'en then would be some stooping; and I choose
Never to stoop. Oh, sir, she smiled, no doubt,
Whene'er I passed her; but who passed without
Much the same smile? This grew; I gave commands;   45
Then all smiles stopped together. There she stands
As if alive. Will't please you rise? We'll meet
The company below, then. I repeat,
The Count your master's known munificence
Is ample warrant that no just pretense   50
Of mine for dowry will be disallowed;
Though his fair daughter's self, as I avowed
At starting, is my object. Nay, we'll go
Together down, sir. Notice Neptune, though,
Taming a sea-horse, thought a rarity,   55
Which Claus of Innsbruck cast in bronze for me!

MY LAST DUCHESS. Ferrara, a city in northern Italy, is the scene. Browning may have modeled his speaker after Alonzo, Duke of Ferrara (1533–1598). 3 *Frà Pandolf* and 56 *Claus of Innsbruck:* fictitious names of artists.

QUESTIONS

1. Who is the Duke addressing? What is this person's business in Ferrara?
2. What is the Duke's opinion of his last Duchess's personality? Do we see her character differently?
3. If the Duke was unhappy with the Duchess's behavior, why didn't he make his displeasure known? Cite a specific passage to explain his reticence.
4. How much do we know about the fate of the last Duchess? Would it help our understanding of the poem to know more?
5. Does Browning imply any connection between the Duke's art collection and his attitude toward his wife?

Today, lyrics in the English language seem more plentiful than other kinds of poetry. Although there has recently been a revival of interest in writing narrative poems, they have a far smaller audience today than long verse narratives, such as Henry Wadsworth Longfellow's *Evangeline* and Alfred, Lord Tennyson's *Idylls of the King,* enjoyed in the nineteenth century.

Also more fashionable in former times was a fourth variety of poetry, **didactic poetry:** a poem apparently written to state a message or teach a body of knowledge. In a lyric, a speaker may express sadness; in a didactic poem, he or she may explain that sadness is inherent in life. Poems that impart a body of knowledge, such as Ovid's *Art of Love* and Lucretius's *On the Nature of Things,* are didactic. Such instructive poetry was favored especially by classical Latin poets and by English poets of the eighteenth century. In *The Fleece* (1757), John Dyer celebrated the British woolen industry and included practical advice on raising sheep:

In cold stiff soils the bleaters oft complain
Of gouty ails, by shepherds termed the halt:
Those let the neighboring fold or ready crook
Detain, and pour into their cloven feet
Corrosive drugs, deep-searching arsenic,
Dry alum, verdegris, or vitriol keen.

One might agree with Dr. Johnson's comment on Dyer's effort: "The subject, Sir, cannot be made poetical." But it may be argued that the subject of didactic poetry does not make it any less poetical. Good poems, it seems, can be written about anything under the sun. Like Dyer, John Milton described sick sheep in "Lycidas," a poem few readers have thought unpoetic:

The hungry sheep look up, and are not fed,
But, swoll'n with wind and the rank mist they draw,
Rot inwardly, and foul contagion spread . . .

What makes Milton's lines better poetry than Dyer's is, among other things, a difference in attitude. Sick sheep to Dyer mean the loss of a few shillings and pence; to Milton, whose sheep stand for English Christendom, they mean a moral catastrophe.

WRITER'S PERSPECTIVE

Adrienne Rich

Adrienne Rich on Writing

RECALLING "AUNT JENNIFER'S TIGERS"   1971

I know that my style was formed first by male poets: by the men I was reading as an undergraduate—Frost, Dylan Thomas, Donne, Auden, MacNeice, Stevens, Yeats. What I chiefly learned from them was craft. But poems are like dreams: in them you put what you don't know you know. Looking back at poems I wrote before I was 21, I'm startled because beneath the conscious craft are glimpses of the split I even then experienced between the girl who wrote poems, who defined herself in writing poems, and the girl who was to define herself by her relationships with men. "Aunt Jennifer's Tigers," written while I was a student, looks with deliberate detachment at this split. In writing this poem, composed and apparently cool as it is, I thought I was creating a portrait of an imaginary woman. But this woman suffers from the opposition of her imagination, worked out in tapestry, and her life-style, "ringed with ordeals she was mastered by." It was important to me that Aunt Jennifer was a person as distinct from myself as possible—distanced by the formalism of the poem, by its objective, observant tone—even by putting the woman in a different generation.

In those years formalism was part of the strategy—like asbestos gloves, it allowed me to handle materials I couldn't pick up bare-handed.

From "When We Dead Awaken: Writing as Re-Vision"

◄▬▭▭ WRITING CRITICALLY ▭▭▬►

Can a Poem Be Paraphrased?

Since the full meaning of a poem is so completely wedded to its exact wording, some people maintain that no poem can be truly paraphrased. As we have discussed earlier in the chapter, however, such an opinion misses the point of paraphrasing. A paraphrase doesn't attempt to recreate the full effect of a poem; it only tries to map out clearly the key images, actions, and ideas. A map is no substitute for a landscape, but a good map often helps us find our way through the landscape without getting lost.

Let's look at an example of a paraphrase written, not by a critic, but by an author about one of his own poems. When an editor asked William Stafford if one of his poems could be paraphrased, Stafford responded by providing his own paraphrase of a short poem. Here is the poem he chose, along with his own restatement in prose of what the poem says.

William Stafford (1914–1993)*

ASK ME   1975

Some time when the river is ice ask me
mistakes I have made. Ask me whether
what I have done is my life. Others
have come in their slow way into
my thought, and some have tried to help   5
or to hurt—ask me what difference
their strongest love or hate has made.

I will listen to what you say.
You and I can turn and look
at the silent river and wait. We know   10

the current is there, hidden; and there
are comings and goings from miles away
that hold the stillness exactly before us.
What the river says, that is what I say.

William Stafford   (1914–1993)*

A PARAPHRASE OF "ASK ME"   1977

I think my poem can be paraphrased—and that any poem can be paraphrased. But
every pass through the material, using other words, would have to be achieved at
certain costs, either in momentum, or nuance, or dangerously explicit (and therefore misleading in tone) adjustments. I'll try one such pass through the poem:

> When it's quiet and cold and we have some chance to interchange
> without hurry, confront me if you like with a challenge about
> whether I think I have made mistakes in my life—and ask me, if
> you want to, whether to me my life is actually the sequence of
> events or exploits others would see. Well, those others tag along in
> my living, and some of them in fact have played significant roles in
> the narrative run of my world; they have intended either helping or
> hurting (but by implication in the way I am saying this you will
> know that neither effort is conclusive). So—ask me how important
> their good or bad intentions have been (both intentions get a
> drastic *leveling* judgment from this cool stating of it all). You, too,
> will be entering that realm of maybe-help-maybe-hurt, by entering
> that far into my life by asking this serious question—so: I will stay
> still and consider. Out there will be the world confronting us both;
> we will both know we are surrounded by mystery, tremendous
> things that do not reveal themselves to us. That river, that world—
> and our lives—all share the depth and stillness of much more sig-
> nificance than our talk, or intentions. There is a steadiness and
> somehow a solace in knowing that what is around us so greatly sur-
> passes our human concerns.

From "Ask Me"

WRITING ASSIGNMENT

Write a concise, accurate paraphrase of a short poem from "Poems for Further Reading."
Your instructor may suggest a particular poem or poems. Although your paraphrase should
cover the entire poem, it need not mention everything. Try to include the most vital
points and details and try to state the poem's main thought or theme. Be as specific as possible, but explain the poem in your own words without quoting any original passages.

Be prepared to share your paraphrase with the rest of the class and to compare it with
other paraphrases of the same poem. You may then be able to test yourself as a reader of
poetry. What in the poem whizzed by you that other students noticed? What did you
catch that others ignored?

13 *Listening to a Voice*

TONE

In old Western movies, when one hombre taunts another, it is customary for the second to drawl, "Smile when you say that, pardner" or "Mister, I don't like your tone of voice." Sometimes in reading a poem, although we can neither see a face nor hear a voice, we can infer the poet's attitude from other evidence.

Like tone of voice, **tone** in literature often conveys an attitude toward the person addressed. Like the manner of a person, the manner of a poem may be friendly or belligerent toward its reader, condescending or respectful. Again like tone of voice, the tone of a poem may tell us how the speaker feels about himself or herself: cocksure or humble, sad or glad. But usually when we ask, "What is the tone of a poem?" we mean, "What attitude does the poet take toward a theme or a subject?" Is the poet being affectionate, hostile, earnest, playful, sarcastic, or what? We may never be able to know, of course, the poet's personal feelings. All we need know is how to feel when we read the poem.

Strictly speaking, tone isn't an attitude; it is whatever in the poem makes an attitude clear to us: the choice of certain words instead of others, the picking out of certain details. In A. E. Housman's "Loveliest of trees," for example, the poet communicates his admiration for a cherry tree's beauty by singling out for attention its white blossoms; had he wanted to show his dislike for the tree, he might have concentrated on its broken branches, birdlime, or snails. To perceive the tone of a poem rightly, we need to read the poem carefully, paying attention to whatever suggestions we find in it.

Theodore Roethke   (1908–1963)*

My Papa's Waltz   1948

The whiskey on your breath
Could make a small boy dizzy;
But I hung on like death:
Such waltzing was not easy.

We romped until the pans   5
Slid from the kitchen shelf;
My mother's countenance
Could not unfrown itself.

The hand that held my wrist
Was battered on one knuckle;   10
At every step you missed
My right ear scraped a buckle.

You beat time on my head
With a palm caked hard by dirt,
Then waltzed me off to bed   15
Still clinging to your shirt.

What is the tone of this poem? Most readers find the speaker's attitude toward his father critical, but nonetheless affectionate. They take this recollection
of childhood to be an odd but happy one. Other readers, however, concentrate
on other details, such as the father's rough manners and drunkenness. One
reader has written that "Roethke expresses his resentment for his father, a
drunken brute with dirty hands and whiskey breath who carelessly hurt the
child's ear and manhandled him." Although this reader accurately noticed some
of the events in the poem and perceived that there was something desperate in
the son's hanging onto the father "like death," he simplifies the tone of the poem
and so misses its humorous side.

While "My Papa's Waltz" contains the dark elements of manhandling and
drunkenness, the tone remains grotesquely comic. The rollicking rhythms of the
poem underscore Roethke's complex humor—half loving and half censuring of
the unwashed, intoxicated father. The humor is further reinforced by playful
rimes such as *dizzy* and *easy, knuckle* and *buckle,* as well as the joyful suggestions
of the words *waltz, waltzing,* and *romped.* The scene itself is comic, with kitchen
pans falling due to the father's roughhousing while the mother looks on una-
mused. However much the speaker satirizes the overly rambunctious father, he
does not have the boy identify with the soberly disapproving mother. Not all
comedy is comfortable and reassuring. Certainly, this small boy's family life has
its frightening side, but the last line suggests the boy is *still clinging* to his father
with persistent if also complicated love.

Such a poem, though it includes lifelike details that aren't pretty, has a tone
relatively easy to recognize. So does **satiric poetry,** a kind of comic poetry that

generally conveys a message. Usually its tone is one of detached amusement, withering contempt, and implied superiority. In a satiric poem, the poet ridicules some person or persons (or perhaps some kind of human behavior), examining the victim by the light of certain principles and implying that the reader, too, ought to feel contempt for the victim.

Countee Cullen   (1903–1946)

FOR A LADY I KNOW   1925

She even thinks that up in heaven
   Her class lies late and snores,
While poor black cherubs rise at seven
   To do celestial chores.

QUESTIONS

1. What is Cullen's message?
2. How would you characterize the tone of this poem? Wrathful? Amused?

    In some poems the poet's attitude may be plain enough; while in other poems attitudes may be so mingled that it is hard to describe them tersely without doing injustice to the poem. Does Andrew Marvell in "To His Coy Mistress" (page 1208) take a serious or playful attitude toward the fact that he and his lady are destined to be food for worms? No one-word answer will suffice. And what of T. S. Eliot's "The Love Song of J. Alfred Prufrock" (page 1169)? In his attitude toward his redemption-seeking hero who wades with trousers rolled, Eliot is seriously funny. Such a mingled tone may be seen in the following poem by the wife of a governor of the Massachusetts Bay Colony and the earliest American poet of note. Anne Bradstreet's first book, *The Tenth Muse Lately Sprung Up in America* (1650), had been published in England without her consent. She wrote these lines to preface a second edition:

Anne Bradstreet   (1612?–1672)

THE AUTHOR TO HER BOOK   1678

Thou ill-formed offspring of my feeble brain,
Who after birth did'st by my side remain,
Till snatched from thence by friends, less wise than true,
Who thee abroad exposed to public view;
Made thee in rags, halting, to the press to trudge,   5
Where errors were not lessened, all may judge.
At thy return my blushing was not small,
My rambling brat (in print) should mother call;
I cast thee by as one unfit for light,

Thy visage was so irksome in my sight;   10
Yet being mine own, at length affection would
Thy blemishes amend, if so I could:
I washed thy face, but more defects I saw,
And rubbing off a spot, still made a flaw.
I stretched thy joints to make thee even feet,   15
Yet still thou run'st more hobbling than is meet;
In better dress to trim thee was my mind,
But nought save homespun cloth in the house I find.
In this array, 'mongst vulgars may'st thou roam;
In critics' hands beware thou dost not come;   20
And take thy way where yet thou are not known.
If for thy Father asked, say thou had'st none;
And for thy Mother, she alas is poor,
Which caused her thus to send thee out of door.

In the author's comparison of her book to an illegitimate ragamuffin, we may be struck by the details of scrubbing and dressing a child: details that might well occur to a mother who had scrubbed and dressed many. As she might feel toward such a child, so she feels toward her book. She starts by deploring it but, as the poem goes on, cannot deny it her affection. Humor enters (as in the pun in line 15). She must dress the creature in *homespun cloth*, something both crude and serviceable. By the end of her poem, Bradstreet seems to regard her book-child with tenderness, amusement, and a certain indulgent awareness of its faults. To read this poem is to sense its mingling of several attitudes. A poet can be merry and in earnest at the same time.

Walt Whitman   (1819–1892)*

To a Locomotive in Winter   1881

Thee for my recitative,
Thee in the driving storm even as now, the snow, the winter-day
    declining,
Thee in thy panoply,° thy measur'd dual throbbing and thy beat
    convulsive,   *suit of armor*
Thy black cylindric body, golden brass and silvery steel,
Thy ponderous side-bars, parallel and connecting rods, gyrating,   5
    shuttling at thy sides,
Thy metrical, now swelling pant and roar, now tapering in the distance,
Thy great protruding head-light fix'd in front,
Thy long, pale, floating vapor-pennants, tinged with delicate purple,
The dense and murky clouds out-belching from thy smoke-stack,
Thy knitted frame, thy springs and valves, the tremulous twinkle of thy 10
    wheels,

Thy train of cars behind, obedient, merrily following,
Through gale or calm, now swift, now slack, yet steadily careering;
Type of the modern—emblem of motion and power—pulse of the
    continent,
For once come serve the Muse and merge in verse, even as here I see
    thee,
With storm and buffeting gusts of wind and falling snow,   15
By day thy warning ringing bell to sound its notes,
By night thy silent signal lamps to swing.
Fierce-throated beauty!
Roll through my chant with all thy lawless music, thy swinging lamps
    at night,
Thy madly-whistled laughter, echoing, rumbling like an earthquake,   20
    rousing all,
Law of thyself complete, thine own track firmly holding,
(No sweetness debonair of tearful harp or glib piano thine,)
Thy trills of shrieks by rocks and hills return'd,
Launch'd o'er the prairies wide, across the lakes,
To the free skies unpent and glad and strong.   25

Emily Dickinson (1830–1886)*

I LIKE TO SEE IT LAP THE MILES   (ABOUT 1862)[1]

I like to see it lap the Miles –
And lick the Valleys up –
And stop to feed itself at Tanks –
And then – prodigious step

Around a Pile of Mountains –   5
And supercilious peer
In Shanties – by the sides of Roads –
And then a Quarry pare

To fit its Ribs
And crawl between   10
Complaining all the while
In horrid – hooting stanza –
Then chase itself down Hill –

And neigh like Boanerges –
Then – punctual as a Star   15
Stop – docile and omnipotent
At its own stable door –

---

[1]Parentheses around a date that follows a poem title indicate the poem's date of composition, when it
was composed much earlier than its first publication date.

1. What differences in tone do you find between Whitman's and Dickinson's poems? Point out in each poem whatever contributes to these differences.
2. *Boanerges* in Dickinson's last stanza means "sons of thunder," a name given by Jesus to the disciples John and James (see Mark 3:17). How far should the reader work out the particulars of this comparison? Does it make the tone of the poem serious?
3. In Whitman's opening line, what is a *recitative*? What other specialized terms from the vocabulary of music and poetry does each poem contain? How do they help underscore Whitman's theme?
4. Poets and songwriters probably have regarded the locomotive with more affection than they have shown most other machines. Why do you suppose this is so? Can you think of any other poems or songs as examples?
5. What do these two poems tell you about locomotives that you would not be likely to find in a technical book on railroading?
6. Are the subjects of the two poems identical? Discuss.

Benjamin Alire Sáenz   (b. 1954)

TO THE DESERT   1995

I came to you one rainless August night.
You taught me how to live without the rain.
You are thirst and thirst is all I know.
You are sand, wind, sun, and burning sky,
The hottest blue. You blow a breeze and brand   5
Your breath into my mouth. You reach—then *bend*
Your force, to break, blow, burn, and make me new.
You wrap your name tight around my ribs
And keep me warm. I was born for you.
Above, below, by you, by you surrounded.   10
I wake to you at dawn. Never break your
Knot. Reach, rise, blow, *Sálvame, mi dios,*
Trágame, mi tierra. Salva, traga, Break me,
I am bread. I will be the water for your thirst.

TO THE DESERT. 5–6 *bend . . . make me new:* quoted from John Donne's "Batter my heart" (page 753). 12–13 *Sálvame, mi dios . . . traga:* Spanish for "Save me, my god, / Take me, my land. Save me, take me." (*Trágame* literally means "swallow me.")

QUESTIONS

1. How does the speaker feel about the land being described? What words in the poem suggest or convey those feelings?
2. What effect does the speaker's sudden switch into Spanish create? What is the tone of the Spanish?
3. Of what kind of language do the last few lines of the poem remind you?

Weldon Kees   (1914–1955)

For My Daughter   1940

Looking into my daughter's eyes I read
Beneath the innocence of morning flesh
Concealed, hintings of death she does not heed.
Coldest of winds have blown this hair, and mesh
Of seaweed snarled these miniatures of hands;   5
The night's slow poison, tolerant and bland,
Has moved her blood. Parched years that I have seen
That may be hers appear: foul, lingering
Death in certain war, the slim legs green.
Or, fed on hate, she relishes the sting   10
Of others' agony; perhaps the cruel
Bride of a syphilitic or a fool.
These speculations sour in the sun.
I have no daughter. I desire none.

Questions

1. How does the last line of this sonnet affect the meaning of the poem?
2. "For My Daughter" was first published in 1940. What considerations might a potential American parent have felt at that time? Are these historical concerns mirrored
   in the poem?
3. Donald Justice has said that "Kees is one of the bitterest poets in history." Is bitterness the only attitude the speaker reveals in this poem?

The Person in the Poem

The tone of a poem, we said, is like tone of voice in that both communicate feelings. Still, this comparison raises a question: when we read a poem, whose
"voice" speaks to us?

"The poet's" is one possible answer; and in the case of many a poem that answer may be right. Reading Anne Bradstreet's "The Author to Her Book," we
can be reasonably sure that the poet speaks of her very own book, and of her own
experiences. In order to read a poem, we seldom need to read a poet's biography;
but in truth there are certain poems whose full effect depends upon our knowing
at least a fact or two of the poet's life. Here is one such poem.

Natasha Trethewey (b. 1966)

WHITE LIES
2000

The lies I could tell,
when I was growing up
light-bright, near-white,
high-yellow, red-boned
in a black place,   5
were just white lies.

I could easily tell the white folks
that we lived uptown,
not in that pink and green
shanty-fied shotgun section   10
along the tracks. I could act
like my homemade dresses
came straight out the window
of Maison Blanche. I could even
keep quiet, quiet as kept,   15
like the time a white girl said
(squeezing my hand), *Now
we have three of us in this class.*

But I paid for it every time
Mama found out.   20
She laid her hands on me,
then washed out my mouth
with Ivory soap. *This
is to purify,* she said,
and cleanse your lying tongue.   25
Believing her, I swallowed suds
thinking they'd work
from the inside out.

Through its pattern of vivid color imagery, Trethewey's poem tells of a black child light enough to "pass for white" in a society that was still extremely race-sensitive. But knowing the author's family background gives us a deeper insight into the levels of meaning in the poem. Trethewey was born in Mississippi in 1966, at a time when her parents' interracial marriage was a criminal act in that state. On her birth certificate, her mother's race was given as "colored"; in the box intended to record the race of her father—who was white and had been born in Nova Scotia—appeared the word "Canadian" (although her parents divorced before she began grade school, she remained extremely close to both of them). Trethewey has said of her birth certificate: "Something is left out of the official record that way. The irony isn't lost on me. Even in documenting myself as a person there is a little fiction." "White Lies" succeeds admirably on its own, but these biographical details allow us to read it as an even more complex meditation on issues of racial definition and personal identity in America.

Most of us can tell the difference between a person we meet in life and a person we meet in a work of art—unlike the moviegoer in the Philippines who, watching a villain in an exciting film, pulled out a revolver and peppered the screen. And yet, in reading poems, we are liable to temptation.

When the poet says "I," we may want to assume that he or she is making a personal statement. But reflect: do all poems have to be personal? Here is a brief poem inscribed on the tombstone of an infant in Burial Hill cemetery, Plymouth, Massachusetts:

> Since I have been so quickly done for,
> I wonder what I was begun for.

We do not know who wrote those lines, but it is clear that the poet was not a short-lived infant writing from personal experience. In other poems, the speaker is obviously a **persona,** or fictitious character: not the poet, but the poet's creation. As a grown man, William Blake, a skilled professional engraver, wrote a poem in the voice of a boy, an illiterate chimney sweeper. (The poem appears later in this chapter.)

Let's consider a poem spoken not by a poet, but by a persona—in this case a mysterious one. Edwin Arlington Robinson's "Luke Havergal" is a dramatic monologue, but the identity of the speaker is never clearly stated. Upon first reading the poem in Robinson's *The Children of the Night* (1897), President Theodore Roosevelt was so moved that he wrote a review of the book that made the author famous. Roosevelt, however, admitted that he found the musically seductive poem difficult. "I am not sure I understand 'Luke Havergal,'" he wrote, "but I am entirely sure I like it." Possibly what most puzzled our twenty-sixth president was who was speaking in the poem. How much does Robinson let us know about the voice and the person it addresses?

Edwin Arlington Robinson   (1869–1935)*

Luke Havergal   1897

Go to the western gate, Luke Havergal,
There where the vines cling crimson on the wall,
And in the twilight wait for what will come.
The leaves will whisper there of her, and some,
Like flying words, will strike you as they fall;   5
But go, and if you listen she will call.
Go to the western gate, Luke Havergal—
Luke Havergal.

No, there is not a dawn in eastern skies
To rift the fiery night that's in your eyes;   10

But there, where western glooms are gathering,
The dark will end the dark, if anything:
God slays Himself with every leaf that flies,
And hell is more than half of paradise.
No, there is not a dawn in eastern skies—   15
In eastern skies.

Out of a grave I come to tell you this,
Out of a grave I come to quench the kiss
That flames upon your forehead with a glow
That blinds you to the way that you must go.   20
Yes, there is yet one way to where she is,
Bitter, but one that faith may never miss.
Out of a grave I come to tell you this—
To tell you this.

There is the western gate, Luke Havergal,   25
There are the crimson leaves upon the wall.
Go, for the winds are tearing them away,—
Nor think to riddle the dead words they say,
Nor any more to feel them as they fall;
But go, and if you trust her she will call.   30
There is the western gate, Luke Havergal—
Luke Havergal.

QUESTIONS

1. Who is the speaker of the poem? What specific details does the author reveal about the speaker?
2. What does the speaker ask Luke Havergal to do?
3. What do you understand "the western gate" to be?
4. Would you advise Luke Havergal to follow the speaker's advice? Why or why not?

No literary law decrees that the speaker in a poem even has to be human. Good poems have been uttered by clouds, pebbles, clocks, and cats. Here is a poem spoken by a hawk, a dramatic monologue that expresses the animal's thoughts and attitudes in a way consciously designed to emphasize how different its worldview is from a human perspective.

Ted Hughes   (1930–1998)

HAWK ROOSTING   1960

I sit in the top of the wood, my eyes closed.
Inaction, no falsifying dream
Between my hooked head and hooked feet:
Or in sleep rehearse perfect kills and eat.

The convenience of the high trees!
The air's buoyancy and the sun's ray
Are of advantage to me;
And the earth's face upward for my inspection.

My feet are locked upon the rough bark.
It took the whole of Creation   10
To produce my foot, my each feather:
Now I hold Creation in my foot

Or fly up, and revolve it all slowly—
I kill where I please because it is all mine.
There is no sophistry in my body: 15
My manners are tearing off heads—

The allotment of death.
For the one path of my flight is direct
Through the bones of the living.
No arguments assert my right: 20

The sun is behind me.
Nothing has changed since I began.
My eye has permitted no change.
I am going to keep things like this.

QUESTIONS

1. Find three observations the hawk makes about its world that a human would probably not make. What do these remarks tell us about the bird's character?
2. In what ways does Ted Hughes create an unrealistic portrayal of the hawk's true mental powers? What statements in the poem would an actual hawk be unlikely to make? Do these passages add anything to the poem's impact? What would be lost if they were omitted?

In a famous definition, William Wordsworth calls poetry "the spontaneous overflow of powerful feelings . . . recollected in tranquillity." But in the case of the following poem, Wordsworth's feelings weren't all his; they didn't just overflow spontaneously; and the process of tranquil recollection had to go on for years.

William Wordsworth   (1770–1850)*

I WANDERED LONELY AS A CLOUD   1807

I wandered lonely as a cloud
  That floats on high o'er vales and hills,
When all at once I saw a crowd,
  A host, of golden daffodils,
Beside the lake, beneath the trees,   5
Fluttering and dancing in the breeze.

Continuous as the stars that shine
    And twinkle on the milky way,
They stretched in never-ending line
    Along the margin of a bay:
Ten thousand saw I at a glance,   10
Tossing their heads in sprightly dance.

The waves beside them danced; but they
    Out-did the sparkling waves in glee;
A poet could not but be gay,   15
    In such a jocund company;
I gazed—and gazed—but little thought
What wealth the show to me had brought:

For oft, when on my couch I lie
    In vacant or in pensive mood,   20
They flash upon that inward eye
    Which is the bliss of solitude;
And then my heart with pleasure fills,
And dances with the daffodils.

    Between the first printing of the poem in 1807 and the version of 1815 given here, Wordsworth made several deliberate improvements. He changed *dancing* to *golden* in line 4, *Along* to *Beside* in line 5, *Ten thousand* to *Fluttering and* in line 6, *laughing* to *jocund* in line 16, and he added a whole stanza (the second). In fact, the writing of the poem was unspontaneous enough for Wordsworth, at a loss for lines 21–22, to take them from his wife Mary. It is likely that the experience of daffodil-watching was not entirely his to begin with but was derived in part from the recollections his sister Dorothy Wordsworth had set down in her journal of April 15, 1802, two years before he first drafted his poem.

Dorothy Wordsworth (1771–1855)

JOURNAL ENTRY   1802

When we were in the woods beyond Gowbarrow Park we saw a few daffodils close to the water-side. We fancied that the lake had floated the seeds ashore, and that the little colony had so sprung up. But as we went along there were more and yet more; and at last, under the boughs of the trees, we saw that there was a long belt of them along the shore, about the breadth of a country turnpike road. I never saw daffodils so beautiful. They grew among the mossy stones about and about them; some rested their heads upon these stones as on a pillow for weariness; and the rest tossed and reeled and danced, and seemed as if they verily laughed with the wind, that flew upon them over the Lake; they looked so gay, ever glancing, ever changing. This wind blew directly over the Lake to them. There was here and there a little knot, and a few stragglers a few yards higher up;

but they were so few as not to disturb the simplicity, unity, and life of that one busy highway.

Notice that Wordsworth's poem echoes a few of his sister's observations. Weaving poetry out of their mutual memories, Wordsworth has offered the experience as if altogether his own, made himself lonely, and left Dorothy out. The point is not that Wordsworth is a liar or a plagiarist but that, like any other good poet, he has transformed ordinary life into art. A process of interpreting, shaping, and ordering had to intervene between the experience of looking at daffodils and the finished poem.

We need not deny that a poet's experience can contribute to a poem nor that the emotion in the poem can indeed be the poet's. Still, to write a good poem one has to do more than live and feel. It seems a pity that, as Randall Jarrell has said, a cardinal may write verses worse than his youngest choirboy's. But writing poetry takes skill and imagination—qualities that extensive travel and wide experience do not necessarily give. For much of her life, Emily Dickinson seldom strayed from her family's house and grounds in Amherst, Massachusetts; yet her rimed life studies of a snake, a bee, and a hummingbird contain more poetry than we find in any firsthand description (so far) of the surface of the moon.

James Stephens   (1882–1950)*

A Glass of Beer   1918

The lanky hank of a she in the inn over there
Nearly killed me for asking the loan of a glass of beer;
May the devil grip the whey-faced slut by the hair,
And beat bad manners out of her skin for a year.

That parboiled ape, with the toughest jaw you will see   5
On virtue's path, and a voice that would rasp the dead,
Came roaring and raging the minute she looked at me,
And threw me out of the house on the back of my head!

If I asked her master he'd give me a cask a day;
But she, with the beer at hand, not a gill° would arrange!   *quarter-pint*   10
May she marry a ghost and bear him a kitten, and may
The High King of Glory permit her to get the mange.

Questions

1. Who do you take to be the speaker? Is it the poet? The speaker may be angry, but what is the tone of this poem?
2. Would you agree with a commentator who said, "To berate anyone in truly memorable language is practically a lost art in America"? How well does the speaker (an Irishman) succeed? Which of his epithets and curses strike you as particularly imaginative?

Anne Sexton   (1928–1974)*

HER KIND   1960

I have gone out, a possessed witch,
haunting the black air, braver at night;
dreaming evil, I have done my hitch
over the plain houses, light by light:
lonely thing, twelve-fingered, out of mind.   5
A woman like that is not a woman, quite.
I have been her kind.

I have found the warm caves in the woods,
filled them with skillets, carvings, shelves,
closets, silks, innumerable goods;   10
fixed the suppers for the worms and the elves:
whining, rearranging the disaligned.
A woman like that is misunderstood.
I have been her kind.

I have ridden in your cart, driver,   15
waved my nude arms at villages going by,
learning the last bright routes, survivor
where your flames still bite my thigh
and my ribs crack where your wheels wind.
A woman like that is not ashamed to die.   20
I have been her kind.

QUESTIONS

1. Who is the speaker of this poem? What do we know about her?
2. What does the speaker mean by ending each stanza with the statement, "I have been her kind?"
3. Who are the figures with whom the speaker identifies? What do these figures tell us about the speaker's state of mind?

EXPERIMENT: *Reading with and without Biography*

Read the following poem and state what you understand from it. Then consider the circumstances in which it probably came to be written. (Some information is offered in a note on page 748.) Does the meaning of the poem change? To what extent does an appreciation of the poem need the support of biography?

William Carlos Williams (1883–1963)*

THE RED WHEELBARROW   1923

so much depends
upon

a red wheel
barrow

glazed with rain
water

beside the white
chickens.

IRONY

To see a distinction between the poet and the words of a fictitious character—
between Robert Browning and "My Last Duchess"—is to be aware of **irony:** a
manner of speaking that implies a discrepancy. If the mask says one thing and
we sense that the writer is in fact saying something else, the writer has adopted
an **ironic point of view.** No finer illustration exists in English than Jonathan
Swift's "A Modest Proposal," an essay in which Swift speaks as an earnest, humorless citizen who sets forth his reasonable plan to aid the Irish poor. The
plan is so monstrous no sane reader can assent to it: the poor are to sell their
children as meat for the tables of their landlords. From behind his false face,
Swift is actually recommending not cannibalism but love and Christian
charity.

A poem is often made complicated and more interesting by another kind of
irony. **Verbal irony** occurs whenever words say one thing but mean something
else, usually the opposite. The word *love* means *hate* here: "I just *love* to stay home
and do my hair on a Saturday night!" If the verbal irony is conspicuously bitter,
heavy-handed, and mocking, it is **sarcasm:** "Oh, he's the biggest spender in the
world, all right!" (The sarcasm, if that statement were spoken, would be underscored by the speaker's tone of voice.) A famous instance of sarcasm is Mark
Antony's line in his oration over the body of slain Julius Caesar: "Brutus is an
honorable man." Antony repeats this line until the enraged populace begins
shouting exactly what he means to call Brutus and the other conspirators: traitors, villains, murderers. We had best be alert for irony on the printed page, for if
we miss it, our interpretations of a poem may go wild.

Robert Creeley (b. 1926)

OH NO

1959

If you wander far enough
you will come to it
and when you get there
they will give you a place to sit

for yourself only, in a nice chair, 5
and all your friends will be there
with smiles on their faces
and they will likewise all have places.

    This poem is rich in verbal irony. The title helps point out that between the speaker's words and attitude lie deep differences. In line 2, what is *it?* Old age? The wandering suggests a conventional metaphor: the journey of life. Is *it* literally a rest home for "senior citizens," or perhaps some naïve popular concept of heaven (such as we meet in comic strips: harps, angels with hoops for halos) in which the saved all sit around in a ring, smugly congratulating one another? We can't be sure, but the speaker's attitude toward this final sitting-place is definite. It is a place for the selfish, as we infer from the phrase *for yourself only.* And *smiles on their faces* may hint that the smiles are unchanging and forced. There is a difference between saying "They had smiles on their faces" and "They smiled": the latter suggests that the smiles came from within. The word *nice* is to be regarded with distrust. If we see through this speaker, as Creeley implies we can do, we realize that, while pretending to be sweet-talking us into a seat, actually he is revealing the horror of a little hell. And the title is the poet's reaction to it (or the speaker's unironic, straightforward one): "Oh no! Not *that!*"

    Dramatic irony, like verbal irony, contains an element of contrast, but it usually refers to a situation in a play wherein a character whose knowledge is limited says, does, or encounters something of greater significance than he or she knows. We, the spectators, realize the meaning of this speech or action, for the playwright has afforded us superior knowledge. In Sophocles' *King Oedipus,* when Oedipus vows to punish whomever has brought down a plague upon the city of Thebes, we know—as he does not—that the man he would punish is himself. (Referring to such a situation that precedes the downfall of a hero in a tragedy, some critics speak of **tragic irony** instead of dramatic irony.) Superior knowledge can be enjoyed not only by spectators in a theater but by readers of poetry as well. In *Paradise Lost,* we know in advance that Adam will fall into temptation, and we recognize his overconfidence when he neglects a warning. The situation of Oedipus also contains **cosmic irony,** or **irony of fate:** some Fate with a grim sense of humor seems cruelly to trick a human being. Cosmic irony clearly exists in poems in which fate or the Fates are personified and seen as hostile, as in Thomas Hardy's "The Convergence of the Twain" (page 1182); and it may be said to occur also in Robinson's "Richard Cory" (page 842). Obviously it is a twist of fate for the most envied man in town to kill himself.

To sum up: the effect of irony depends on the reader's noticing some incongruity or discrepancy between two things. In *verbal irony*, there is a contrast between the speaker's words and meaning; in an *ironic point of view*, between the writer's attitude and what is spoken by a fictitious character; in *dramatic irony*, between the limited knowledge of a character and the fuller knowledge of the reader or spectator; in *cosmic irony*, between a character's aspiration and the treatment he or she receives at the hands of Fate. Although, in the work of an inept poet, irony can be crude and obvious sarcasm, it is invaluable to a poet of more complicated mind, who imagines more than one perspective.

W. H. Auden   (1907–1973)*

THE UNKNOWN CITIZEN   1940

(To JS/07/M/378
This Marble Monument
Is Erected by the State)

He was found by the Bureau of Statistics to be
One against whom there was no official complaint,
And all the reports on his conduct agree
That, in the modern sense of an old-fashioned word, he was a saint,
For in everything he did he served the Greater Community.   5
Except for the War till the day he retired
He worked in a factory and never got fired,
But satisfied his employers, Fudge Motors Inc.
Yet he wasn't a scab or odd in his views,
For his Union reports that he paid his dues,   10
(Our report on his Union shows it was sound)
And our Social Psychology workers found
That he was popular with his mates and liked a drink.
The Press are convinced that he bought a paper every day
And that his reactions to advertisements were normal in every way.   15
Policies taken out in his name prove that he was fully insured,
And his Health-card shows he was once in hospital but left it cured.
Both Producers Research and High-Grade Living declare
He was fully sensible to the advantages of the Installment Plan
And had everything necessary to the Modern Man,   20
A phonograph, a radio, a car and a frigidaire.
Our researchers into Public Opinion are content
That he held the proper opinions for the time of year;
When there was peace, he was for peace; when there was war, he went.
He was married and added five children to the population,   25
Which our Eugenist says was the right number for a parent of his
     generation,
And our teachers report that he never interfered with their education.

Was he free? Was he happy? The question is absurd:
Had anything been wrong, we should certainly have heard.

QUESTIONS

1. Read the three-line epitaph at the beginning of the poem as carefully as you read what follows. How does the epitaph help establish the voice by which the rest of the poem is spoken?
2. Who is speaking?
3. What ironic discrepancies do you find between the speaker's attitude toward the subject and that of the poet himself? By what is the poet's attitude made clear?
4. In the phrase "The Unknown Soldier" (of which "The Unknown Citizen" reminds us), what does the word *unknown* mean? What does it mean in the title of Auden's poem?
5. What tendencies in our civilization does Auden satirize?
6. How would you expect the speaker to define a Modern Man, if a CD player, a radio, a car, and a refrigerator are "everything" a Modern Man needs?

Sharon Olds (b. 1942)*

RITES OF PASSAGE

1983

As the guests arrive at my son's party
they gather in the living room—
short men, men in first grade
with smooth jaws and chins.
Hands in pockets, they stand around   5
jostling, jockeying for place, small fights
breaking out and calming. One says to another
How old are you? Six. I'm seven. So?
They eye each other, seeing themselves
tiny in the other's pupils. They clear their   10
throats a lot, a room of small bankers,
they fold their arms and frown. *I could beat you
up*, a seven says to a six,
the dark cake, round and heavy as a
turret, behind them on the table. My son,   15
freckles like specks of nutmeg on his cheeks,
chest narrow as the balsa keel of a
model boat, long hands
cool and thin as the day they guided him
out of me, speaks up as a host   20
for the sake of the group.
We could easily kill a two-year-old,
he says in his clear voice. The other
men agree, they clear their throats
like Generals, they relax and get down to   25
playing war, celebrating my son's life.

1. What is ironic about the way the speaker describes the first-grade boys at her son's birthday party?
2. What other irony does the author underscore in the last two lines?
3. Does this mother sentimentalize her own son by seeing him as better than the other little boys?

John Betjeman   (1906–1984)

IN WESTMINSTER ABBEY   1940

Let me take this other glove off
   As the *vox humana* swells,
And the beauteous fields of Eden
   Bask beneath the Abbey bells.
Here, where England's statesmen lie,   5
Listen to a lady's cry.

Gracious Lord, oh bomb the Germans.
   Spare their women for Thy Sake,
And if that is not too easy
   We will pardon Thy Mistake.   10
But, gracious Lord, whate'er shall be,
Don't let anyone bomb me.

Keep our Empire undismembered,
   Guide our Forces by Thy Hand,
Gallant blacks from far Jamaica,   15
   Honduras and Togoland;
Protect them Lord in all their fights,
And, even more, protect the whites.

Think of what our Nation stands for:
   Books from Boots' and country lanes,   20
Free speech, free passes, class distinction,
   Democracy and proper drains.
Lord, put beneath Thy special care
One-eighty-nine Cadogan Square.

Although dear Lord I am a sinner,   25
   I have done no major crime;
Now I'll come to Evening Service
   Whensoever I have the time.
So, Lord, reserve for me a crown,
And do not let my shares° go down.   *stocks* 30

I will labor for Thy Kingdom,
  Help our lads to win the war,
Send white feathers to the cowards,
  Join the Women's Army Corps,
Then wash the Steps around Thy Throne   35
In the Eternal Safety Zone.

Now I feel a little better,
  What a treat to hear Thy Word,
Where the bones of leading statesmen
  Have so often been interred.   40
And now, dear Lord, I cannot wait
Because I have a luncheon date.

IN WESTMINSTER ABBEY. First printed during World War II. 2 *vox humana*: an organ stop that makes tones similar to those of the human voice. 20 *Boots'*: a chain of pharmacies whose branches had lending libraries.

QUESTIONS

1. Who is the speaker? What do we know about her lifestyle? About her prejudices?
2. Point out some of the places in which she contradicts herself.
3. How would you describe the speaker's attitude toward religion?
4. Through the medium of irony, what positive points do you believe Betjeman makes?

Sarah N. Cleghorn (1876–1959)

THE GOLF LINKS   1917

The golf links lie so near the mill
  That almost every day
The laboring children can look out
  And see the men at play.

QUESTIONS

1. Is this brief poem satiric? Does it contain any verbal irony or is the poet making a matter-of-fact statement in words that mean just what they say?
2. What other kind of irony is present in the poem?
3. Sarah N. Cleghorn's poem dates from before the enactment of legislation against child labor. Is it still a good poem, or is it hopelessly dated?
4. How would you state its theme?
5. Would you call this poem lyric, narrative, or didactic?

Josephine Miles   (1911–1985)

CIVILIAN   1966

The largest stock of armaments allows me
A reason not to kill.
Defense Department does the blasting for me
As soundly as I will.

Indeed, can cover a much wider area   5
Than I will ever score
With a single rifle sent me on approval
From a Sears Roebuck store.

Only the psycho, meaning sick in spirit,
Would aim his personal shot   10
At anybody; he is sick in spirit
As I am not.

QUESTIONS

1. For what reasons does the speaker adopt a position of personal nonviolence?
2. What type of irony is demonstrated in this poem? Explain.

Connie Bensley   (b. 1929)

THE COVETOUS CAT   1994

Because the common is remote
they walk along hand in hand.

On the path ahead of them
some bird-lover has scattered bread

and in the middle of it a plump cat crouches   5
chewing at the crusts.

Cats don't really like bread, the man remarks,
he only wants it because it's someone else's.

Like you, she thinks,
withdrawing her hand slightly.   10

QUESTIONS

1. What is ironic about the man's remark?
2. Is there any hint earlier in the poem about the nature of the couple's relationship?

EXERCISE: *Detecting Irony*

Point out the kinds of irony that occur in the following poem.

Thomas Hardy   (1840–1928)*

THE WORKBOX   1914

"See, here's the workbox, little wife,
    That I made of polished oak."
He was a joiner,° of village life;   carpenter
    She came of borough folk.

He holds the present up to her   5
    As with a smile she nears
And answers to the profferer,
    "'Twill last all my sewing years!"

"I warrant it will. And longer too.
    'Tis a scantling that I got   10
Off poor John Wayward's coffin, who
    Died of they knew not what.

"The shingled pattern that seems to cease
    Against your box's rim
Continues right on in the piece   15
    That's underground with him.

"And while I worked it made me think
    Of timber's varied doom:
One inch where people eat and drink,
    The next inch in a tomb.   20

"But why do you look so white, my dear,
    And turn aside your face?
You knew not that good lad, I fear,
    Though he came from your native place?"

"How could I know that good young man,   25
    Though he came from my native town,
When he must have left far earlier than
    I was a woman grown?"

"Ah, no. I should have understood!
    It shocked you that I gave   30
To you one end of a piece of wood
    Whose other is in a grave?"

"Don't, dear, despise my intellect,
    Mere accidental things
Of that sort never have effect   35
    On my imaginings."

738   LISTENING TO A VOICE

Yet still her lips were limp and wan,
   Her face still held aside,
As if she had known not only John,
   But known of what he died.   40

FOR REVIEW AND FURTHER STUDY

William Blake   (1757–1827)*

THE CHIMNEY SWEEPER   1789

When my mother died I was very young,
And my father sold me while yet my tongue
Could scarcely cry " 'weep! 'weep! 'weep! 'weep!"
So your chimneys I sweep, and in soot I sleep.

There's little Tom Dacre, who cried when his head,   5
That curled like a lamb's back, was shaved: so I said
"Hush, Tom! never mind it, for when your head's bare
You know that the soot cannot spoil your white hair."

And so he was quiet, and that very night,
As Tom was a-sleeping, he had such a sight!   10
That thousands of sweepers, Dick, Joe, Ned, and Jack,
Were all of them locked up in coffins of black.

And by came an Angel who had a bright key,
And he opened the coffins and set them all free;
Then down a green plain leaping, laughing, they run,   15
And wash in a river, and shine in the sun.

Then naked and white, all their bags left behind,
They rise upon clouds and sport in the wind;
And the Angel told Tom, if he'd be a good boy,
He'd have God for his father, and never want° joy.   *lack* 20

And so Tom awoke; and we rose in the dark,
And got with our bags and our brushes to work.
Though the morning was cold, Tom was happy and warm;
So if all do their duty they need not fear harm.

QUESTIONS

1. What does Blake's poem reveal about conditions of life in the London of his day?
2. What does this poem have in common with "The Golf Links" (page 736)?
3. Sum up your impressions of the speaker's character. What does he say and do that displays it to us?
4. What pun do you find in line 3? Is its effect comic or serious?
5. In Tom Dacre's dream (lines 11–20), what wishes come true? Do you understand them to be the wishes of the chimney sweepers, of the poet, or of both?

6. In the last line, what is ironic in the speaker's assurance that the dutiful *need not fear harm*? What irony is there in his urging all to *do their duty*? (Who have failed in their duty to *him*?)
7. What is the tone of Blake's poem? Angry? Hopeful? Sorrowful? Compassionate? (Don't feel obliged to sum it up in a single word.)

Robert McDowell   (b. 1953)

AT HOME WITH DOLLFACE   2002

I stepped down into the little cardboard town.
All day and night we were posing.
I did not need to water or cut
Our plastic lawn, and I gave up shaving because
In my beloved's world no hair or green thing grew.   5
My teeth were exquisitely white,
My body fat absolutely zero.
We dressed from wardrobes without end,
And drove our pink convertible to the river each day.

One might think that we yearned for some controversy,   10
A little spice mixed into the bland stew of our days.
In fact, we were deliriously happy, content with our clothes
And gadgets, determined to look out
At the world's woe through the wise eyes of toys.

QUESTIONS

1. Who is the speaker in this poem?
2. What seems to be the author's attitude toward what he describes? How does his tone help to provide an answer?

William Stafford   (1914–1993)*

AT THE UN-NATIONAL MONUMENT
ALONG THE CANADIAN BORDER   1977

This is the field where the battle did not happen,
where the unknown soldier did not die.
This is the field where grass joined hands,
where no monument stands,
and the only heroic thing is the sky.   5

Birds fly here without any sound,
unfolding their wings across the open.
No people killed—or were killed—on this ground
hallowed by neglect and an air so tame
that people celebrate it by forgetting its name.   10

1. What nonevent does this poem celebrate? What is the speaker's attitude toward it?
2. The speaker describes an empty field. What is odd about the way in which he describes it?
3. What words does the speaker appear to use ironically?

H. L. Hix (b. 1960)

I LOVE THE WORLD, AS DOES ANY DANCER   2000

I love the world, as does any dancer,
with the tips of my toes. I love the world
more than I love my wife, for it contains
more crannies and crevasses, it tenders
more textures to my twenty digits' touch.   5
Lush grass underfoot after April rain,
a pile of petals fallen from a rose,
sun-seared sidewalk in summer, sand, fresh-turned
garden dirt, and, yes, her hummocked ankle
rubbed by the ball of my foot as she sleeps.   10

QUESTIONS

1. This poem describes parts of the world by the way they feel to the speaker's feet. How does that unusual perspective affect the tone of the poem?
2. If you revised the poem to be about the sense of sight rather than touch (for example, "I love the world, as does any painter/with my eyes . . ."), would that shift change the poem's personality?

EXERCISE: *Telling Tone*

Here are two radically different poems on a similar subject. Try stating the theme of each poem in your own words. How is tone (the speaker's attitude) different in the two poems?

Richard Lovelace (1618–1658)

TO LUCASTA   1649

On Going to the Wars

Tell me not, Sweet, I am unkind
    That from the nunnery
Of thy chaste breast and quiet mind,
    To war and arms I fly.

True, a new mistress now I chase,
 The first foe in the field;
And with a stronger faith embrace
 A sword, a horse, a shield.

Yet this inconstancy is such
 As you too shall adore;
I could not love thee, Dear, so much,
 Loved I not Honor more.

Wilfred Owen   (1893–1918)*

DULCE ET DECORUM EST   1920

Bent double, like old beggars under sacks,
Knock-kneed, coughing like hags, we cursed through sludge,
Till on the haunting flares we turned our backs
And towards our distant rest began to trudge.
Men marched asleep. Many had lost their boots
But limped on, blood-shod. All went lame; all blind;
Drunk with fatigue; deaf even to the hoots
Of tired, outstripped Five-Nines that dropped behind.

Gas! Gas! Quick, boys!—An ecstasy of fumbling,
Fitting the clumsy helmets just in time;
But someone still was yelling out and stumbling
And flound'ring like a man in fire or lime . . .
Dim, through the misty panes and thick green light,
As under a green sea, I saw him drowning.

In all my dreams, before my helpless sight,
He plunges at me, guttering, choking, drowning.

If in some smothering dreams you too could pace
Behind the wagon that we flung him in,
And watch the white eyes writhing in his face,
His hanging face, like a devil's sick of sin;
If you could hear, at every jolt, the blood
Come gargling from the froth-corrupted lungs,
Obscene as cancer, bitter as the cud
Of vile, incurable sores on innocent tongues,—
My friend, you would not tell with such high zest
To children ardent for some desperate glory,
The old Lie: Dulce et decorum est
Pro patria mori.

DULCE ET DECORUM EST. 8 *Five-Nines:* German howitzers often used to shoot poison gas shells 17 *you too:* Some manuscript versions of this poem carry the dedication "To Jessie Pope" (a writer of patriotic verse) or "To a certain Poetess." 27–28 *Dulce et . . . mori:* a quotation from the Latin poet Horace, "It is sweet and fitting to die for one's country."

Wilfred Owen

Wilfred Owen was only twenty-one years old when World War I broke out in 1914. Twice wounded in battle, he was rapidly promoted and eventually became a company commander. The shocking violence of modern war summoned up his poetic genius, and in a two-year period he grew from a negligible minor poet into the most important English-language poet of World War I. Owen, however, did not live to see his talent recognized. He was killed one week before the end of the war; he was twenty-five years old. Owen published only four poems during his lifetime. Shortly before his death he drafted a few lines of prose for the preface of a book of poems. (For a short biography of Owen, consult "Lives of the Poets.")

Wilfred Owen on Writing

WAR POETRY   (1917?)

This book is not about heroes. English poetry is not yet fit to speak of them.

Nor is it about deeds, or lands, nor anything about glory, honour, might, majesty, dominion, or power, except War.

Above all I am not concerned with Poetry.

My subject is War, and the pity of War.

The Poetry is in the pity.

Yet these elegies are to this generation in no sense consolatory. They may be to the next. All a poet can do today is warn. That is why the true Poets must be truthful.

From Collected Poems

Paying Attention to the Obvious

If tone is a speaker's attitude toward his or her material, then to understand the tone of a poem, we need mostly just to listen—as we might listen to a real conversation. The key is to hear not only *what* is being said but also *how* it is being said. Does the speaker sound noticeably surprised, angry, nostalgic, tender, or expectant? A common mistake in analyzing poetry is to discuss subtle points of interpretation before you fully understand the *obvious* features of a poem. In critical writing it almost never hurts to begin by asking obvious questions:

1. Does the speaker reveal any obvious emotion or attitude about the subject or the setting of the poem? (When D. H. Lawrence, for example, ends his poem "Piano" on page 706 by saying, "I weep like a child for the past," he makes his nostalgic and tender tone explicit.)

2. If there is an implied listener or listeners to the poem, how does the speaker address them? Is there anything obviously unusual about the tone? (In Betjeman's "In Westminster Abbey," for example, the speaker addresses God with astonishing egocentricity and snooty nonchalance.)

3. Is there any obvious difference between the reaction of the speaker to what is happening in the poem and your own honest reaction? If the gap between the two reactions is large (as it is in Robert Browning's "My Last Duchess," for instance), what does it suggest?

4. If the difference between your honest reaction and the speaker's is enormous, is the poem in some way ironic?

WRITING ASSIGNMENT

Using any poetry selection from this chapter, analyze the speaker's attitude toward the poem's main subject. Support your argument by examining the author's choice of specific words and images to create the particular tone used to convey the speaker's attitudes. (Possible subjects might include Wilfred Owen's attitude toward war in "Dulce et Decorum Est," the tone and imagery of Weldon Kees's "For My Daughter," Ted Hughes's view of the workings of nature in "Hawk Roosting," or Anne Bradstreet's attitude toward her own poetry in "The Author to Her Book.")

Here is an example of an essay written for this assignment by Kim Larsen, a student of Karen Locke at Lane Community College in Eugene, Oregon.

Kim Larsen

Professor Locke

English 110

21 November 20xx

Word Choice, Tone, and Point of View in Roethke's

"My Papa's Waltz"

Some readers may find Theodore Roethke's "My Papa's Waltz" a reminiscence of a happy childhood scene. I believe, however, that the poem depicts a more painful and complicated series of emotions. By examining the choice of words that Roethke uses to convey the tone of his scene, I will demonstrate that beneath the seemingly comic situation of the poem is a darker story. The true point of view of "My Papa's Waltz" is that of a resentful adult reliving his fear of a domineering parent.

The first clue that the dance may not have been a mutually enjoyable experience is in the title itself. The author did not title the poem "Our Waltz" or "Waltzing with My Papa," either of which would set an initial tone for readers to expect a shared, loving sentiment. It does not even have a neutral title, such as "The Waltz." The title specifically implies that the waltz was exclusively the father's. Since a waltz normally involves two people, it can be reasoned that the father dances his waltz without regard for his young partner.

Examining each stanza of the poem offers numerous examples where the choice of words sustains the tone implied in the title. The first line, "The whiskey on your breath," conjures up an olfactory image that most would find unpleasant. The small boy finds it so overpowering he is made "dizzy." This stanza contains the only simile in the poem, "I hung on like death" (3), which creates a ghastly and stark visual image. There are innumerable choices of similes to portray hanging on: a vine, an infant, an animal cub, all of which would have illustrated a lighthearted romp. The choice of "death" was purposefully used to convey an intended image. The first stanza ends by stating the "waltzing was not easy." The definitions of <u>easy</u>, as found in <u>Webster's New Collegiate Dictionary</u>, include "free from pain, annoyance or anxiety," and "not difficult to endure or undergo" ("Easy"). Obviously the speaker did not find those qualities in the waltz.

Further evidence of this harsh and oppressive scene is brought to mind by reckless disregard for "the pans / Slid from the kitchen shelf" (5-6), which the reader can almost hear crashing on the floor in loud cacophony, and the "mother's countenance," which "[c]ould not unfrown itself" (8). If this was only a silly, playful romp between father and son, even a stern, fastidious mother might be expected to at least make an unsuccessful attempt to suppress a grin. Instead, the reader gets a visual image of a silent, unhappy woman, afraid, probably due to past experience, to interfere in the domestic destruction around her. Once more, this detail suggests a domineering father who controls the family.

The third stanza relates the father's "battered" hand holding the boy's wrist. The tactile image of holding a wrist suggests dragging or forcing an unwilling person, not holding hands as would be expected with a mutual dance partner. Further disregard for the son's feelings is displayed by the lines "At every step you missed / My right ear scraped a buckle" (11-12). In each missed step, probably due to his drunkenness, the father causes the boy physical pain.

The tone continues in the final stanza as the speaker recalls "You beat time on my head / With a palm caked hard by dirt" (13-14). The visual and tactile image of a dirt-hardened hand beating on a child's head as if it were a drum is distinctly unpleasant. The last lines "Then waltzed me off to bed / Still clinging to your shirt" (15-16) are the most ambiguous in the poem. It can be reasoned, as X. J. Kennedy and Dana Gioia do, that the lines suggest "the boy is <u>still clinging</u> to his father with persistent if also complicated love" (718). On the other hand, if one notices the earlier dark images, the conclusion could describe a boy clinging out of fear, the physical fear of being dropped by one who is drunk and the emotional fear of not being loved and nurtured as a child needs to be by his father.

It can also be argued that the poem's rollicking rhythm contributes to a sense of fun, and in truth, the poem can be read in that fashion. On the other hand, it can be read in such a way as to deemphasize the rhythm, as the author himself does in his recording of "My Papa's Waltz" (Roethke, <u>Reads</u>). The joyful, rollicking rhythm can be seen as ironic. By reminding readers of a waltzing tempo, it is highlighting the discrepancy of what a waltz should be and the bleak, frightening picture painted in the words.

While "My Papa's Waltz" can be read as a roughhouse comedy, by examining Roethke's title and choice of words closely to interpret the meaning of their images and sounds, it is also plausible to hear an entirely different tone. I believe "My Papa's Waltz" employs the voice of an embittered adult remembering a harsh scene in which both he and his mother were powerless in the presence of a drunk and domineering father.

Works Cited

"Easy." <u>Merriam-Webster's Collegiate Dictionary</u>. 11th ed.
  2003.

Kennedy, X. J., and Dana Gioia, eds. <u>Literature: An
  Introduction to Fiction, Poetry, and Drama</u>. 9th ed. New
  York: Longman, 2005. 718.

Roethke, Theodore. "My Papa's Waltz." <u>Literature: An
  Introduction to Fiction, Poetry, and Drama</u>. Ed. X. J.
  Kennedy and Dana Gioia. 9th ed. New York: Longman,
  2005. 718.

---. <u>Theodore Roethke Reads His Poetry</u>. Audiocassette.
  Caedmon, 1972.

INFORMATION FOR EXPERIMENT: *Reading with and without Biography*

THE RED WHEELBARROW (page 731). Dr. Williams's poem reportedly contains a personal experience: he was gazing from the window of the house where one of his patients, a small girl, lay suspended between life and death. (This account, from the director of the public library in Williams's native Rutherford, N.J., is given by Geri M. Rhodes in "The Paterson Metaphor in William Carlos Williams's *Paterson*," master's essay, Tufts U, 1965.)

FURTHER SUGGESTIONS FOR WRITING

1. Do you think Wilfred Owen's "Dulce et Decorum Est" fulfills his intentions as stated in "War Poetry"? Write a brief essay comparing Owen's poem to his goals as a writer. Cite specific instances of where the poem meets or fails to meet his criteria.
2. In a paragraph, sum up your initial reactions to "The Red Wheelbarrow." Then, taking another look at the poem in light of information noted above, write a second paragraph summing up your further reactions.
3. Write a short essay titled "What Thomas Hardy Leaves Unsaid in 'The Workbox.'"
4. Write a verbal profile or short character sketch of the speaker of John Betjeman's "In Westminster Abbey."
5. In a brief essay, consider the tone of two poems on a similar subject. Compare and contrast Walt Whitman and Emily Dickinson as locomotive-fanciers; or, in the poems by Richard Lovelace and Wilfred Owen, compare and contrast attitudes toward war. (For advice on writing about poetry by the method of comparison and contrast, see "Writing About a Poem.")
6. Rewrite Ted Hughes's "Hawk Roosting" from the perspective of either a pigeon or a turkey. Use either prose or verse for your version.

14 Words

LITERAL MEANING: WHAT A POEM SAYS FIRST

Although successful as a painter, Edgar Degas found poetry discouragingly hard to write. To his friend, the poet Stéphane Mallarmé, he complained, "What a business! My whole day gone on a blasted sonnet, without getting an inch further . . . and it isn't ideas I'm short of . . . I'm full of them, I've got too many . . . "

"But Degas," said Mallarmé, "you can't make a poem with ideas—you make it with *words!*" [1]

Like the celebrated painter, some people assume that all it takes to make a poem is a bright idea. Poems state ideas, to be sure, and sometimes the ideas are invaluable; and yet the most impressive idea in the world will not make a poem, unless its words are selected and arranged with loving art. Some poets take great pains to find the right word. Unable to fill a two-syllable gap in an unfinished line that went, "The seal's wide—gaze toward Paradise," Hart Crane paged through an unabridged dictionary. When he reached S, he found the object of his quest in *spindrift:* "spray skimmed from the sea by a strong wind." The word is exact and memorable. Any word can be the right word, however, if artfully chosen and placed. It may be a word as ordinary as *from.* Consider the difference between "The sedge is withered *on* the lake" (a misquotation of a line by Keats) and "The sedge is withered *from* the lake" (what Keats in fact wrote). Keats's original line suggests, as the altered line doesn't, that because the sedge (a growth of grasslike plants) has withered *from* the lake, it has withdrawn mysteriously.

In reading a poem, some people assume that its words can be skipped over rapidly, and they try to leap at once to the poem's general theme. It is as if they fear being thought clods unless they can find huge ideas in the poem (whether or

[1]Paul Valéry, *Degas . . . Manet . . . Morisot*, translated by David Paul (New York: Pantheon, 1960) 62.

not there are any). Such readers often ignore the literal meanings of words: the ordinary, matter-of-fact sense to be found in a dictionary. (As you will see in the next chapter, "Saying and Suggesting," words possess not only dictionary meanings—denotations—but also many associations and suggestions—connotations.) Consider the following poem and see what you make of it.

William Carlos Williams   (1883–1963)*

THIS IS JUST TO SAY   1934

I have eaten
the plums
that were in
the icebox

and which   5
you were probably
saving
for breakfast

Forgive me
they were delicious   10
so sweet
and so cold

    Some readers distrust a poem so simple and candid. They think, "What's wrong with me? There has to be more to it than this!" But poems seldom are puzzles in need of solutions. We can begin by accepting the poet's statements, without suspecting the poet of trying to hoodwink us. On later reflection, of course, we might possibly decide that the poet is playfully teasing or being ironic; but Williams gives us no reason to think that. There seems no need to look beyond the literal sense of his words, no profit in speculating that the plums symbolize worldly joys and that the icebox stands for the universe. Clearly, a reader who held such a grand theory would have overlooked (in eagerness to find a significant idea) the plain truth that the poet makes clear to us: that ice-cold plums are a joy to taste.

    To be sure, Williams's small poem is simpler than most poems are; and yet in reading any poem, no matter how complicated, you will do well to reach slowly and reluctantly for a theory to explain it by. To find the general theme of a poem, you first need to pay attention to its words. Recall Yeats's "The Lake Isle of Innisfree" (page 703), a poem that makes a statement—crudely summed up, "I yearn to leave the city and retreat to a place of ideal peace and happiness." And yet before we can realize this theme, we have to notice details: nine bean rows, a glade loud with bees, "lake water lapping with low sounds by the shore," the gray of a pavement. These details and not some abstract remark make clear what the poem is saying: that the city is drab, while the island hideaway is sublimely beautiful.

Poets often strive for words that point to physical details and solid objects. They may do so even when speaking of an abstract idea:

> Beauty is but a flower
> Which wrinkles will devour;
> Brightness falls from the air,
> Queens have died young and fair,
> Dust hath closed Helen's eye.
> I am sick, I must die:
>   Lord, have mercy on us!

In these lines by Thomas Nashe, the abstraction *beauty* has grown petals that shrivel. Brightness may be a general name for light, but Nashe succeeds in giving it the weight of a falling body.

If a poem says *daffodils* instead of *plant life*, *diaper years* instead of *infancy*, we call its **diction,** or choice of words, **concrete** rather than **abstract.** Concrete words refer to what we can immediately perceive with our senses: *dog, actor, chemical,* or particular individuals who belong to those general classes: *Bonzo the fox terrier, Clint Eastwood, hydrogen sulfate.* Abstract words express ideas or concepts: *love, time, truth.* In abstracting, we leave out some characteristics found in each individual, and instead observe a quality common to many. The word *beauty,* for instance, denotes what may be observed in numerous persons, places, and things.

Ezra Pound gave a famous piece of advice to his fellow poets: "Go in fear of abstractions." This is not to say that a poet cannot employ abstract words, nor that all poems have to be about physical things. Much of T. S. Eliot's *Four Quartets* is concerned with time, eternity, history, language, reality, and other things that cannot be physically handled. But Eliot, however high he may soar for a larger view, keeps returning to earth. He makes us aware of *things.*

Marianne Moore   (1887–1972)*

SILENCE   1924

My father used to say,
"Superior people never make long visits,
have to be shown Longfellow's grave
or the glass flowers at Harvard.
Self-reliant like the cat—   5
that takes its prey to privacy,
the mouse's limp tail hanging like a shoelace from its mouth—
they sometimes enjoy solitude,

and can be robbed of speech
by speech which has delighted them.   10
The deepest feeling always shows itself in silence;
not in silence, but restraint."
Nor was he insincere in saying, "Make my house your inn."
Inns are not residences.

QUESTIONS

1. Almost all of "Silence" consists of quotation. What are some possible reasons why
   the speaker prefers using another person's words?
2. What are the words the father uses to describe people he admires?
3. The poem makes an important distinction between two similar words (lines 13–14).
   Explain the distinction Moore implies.
4. Why is "Silence" an appropriate title for this poem?

Robert Graves   (1895–1985)*

DOWN, WANTON, DOWN!   1933

Down, wanton, down! Have you no shame
That at the whisper of Love's name,
Or Beauty's, presto! up you raise
Your angry head and stand at gaze?

Poor bombard-captain, sworn to reach   5
The ravelin and effect a breach—
Indifferent what you storm or why,
So be that in the breach you die!

Love may be blind, but Love at least
Knows what is man and what mere beast;   10
Or Beauty wayward, but requires
More delicacy from her squires.

Tell me, my witless, whose one boast
Could be your staunchness at the post,
When were you made a man of parts   15
To think fine and profess the arts?

Will many-gifted Beauty come
Bowing to your bald rule of thumb,
Or Love swear loyalty to your crown?
Be gone, have done! Down, wanton, down!   20

DOWN, WANTON, DOWN! 5 *bombard-captain:* officer in charge of a bombard, an early type of cannon
that hurled stones. 6 *ravelin:* fortification with two faces that meet in a protruding angle. *effect a breach:*
break an opening through (a fortification). 15 *man of parts:* man of talent or ability.

1. How do you define a *wanton?*
2. What wanton does the poet address?
3. Explain the comparison drawn in the second stanza.
4. In line 14, how many meanings do you find in *staunchness at the post?*
5. Explain any other puns you find in lines 15–19.
6. Do you take this to be a cynical poem making fun of Love and Beauty, or is Graves making fun of stupid, animal lust?

John Donne (1572–1631)*

BATTER MY HEART,   (ABOUT 1610)
THREE-PERSONED GOD, FOR YOU

Batter my heart, three-personed God, for You
As yet but knock, breathe, shine, and seek to mend.
That I may rise and stand, o'erthrow me, and bend
Your force to break, blow, burn, and make me new.
I, like an usurped town to another due,   5
Labor to admit You, but Oh! to no end.
Reason, Your viceroy in me, me should defend,
But is captived, and proves weak or untrue.
Yet dearly I love You, and would be lovèd fain,
But am betrothed unto Your enemy;   10
Divorce me, untie or break that knot again;
Take me to You, imprison me, for I,
Except You enthrall me, never shall be free,
Nor ever chaste, except You ravish me.

QUESTIONS

1. In the last line of this sonnet, to what does Donne compare the onslaught of God's love? Do you think the poem is weakened by the poet's comparing a spiritual experience to something so grossly carnal? Discuss.
2. Explain the seeming contradiction in the last line: in what sense can a ravished person be *chaste?* Explain the seeming contradictions in lines 3–4 and 12–13: how can a person thrown down and destroyed be enabled to *rise and stand;* an imprisoned person be *free?*
3. In lines 5–6 the speaker compares himself to a *usurped town* trying to throw off its conqueror by admitting an army of liberation. Who is the "usurper" in this comparison?
4. Explain the comparison of *Reason* to a *viceroy* (lines 7–8).
5. Sum up in your own words the message of Donne's poem. In stating its theme, did you have to read the poem for literal meanings, figurative comparisons, or both?

THE VALUE OF A DICTIONARY

> *Use the dictionary. It's better than the critics.*
> —Elizabeth Bishop to her students

If a poet troubles to seek out the best words available, the least we can do is to find out what the words mean. The dictionary is a firm ally in reading poems; if the poems are more than a century old, it is indispensable. Meanings change. When the Elizabethan poet George Gascoigne wrote, "O Abraham's brats, O brood of blessed seed," the word *brats* implied neither irritation nor contempt. When in the seventeenth century Andrew Marvell imagined two lovers' "vegetable love," he referred to a vegetative or growing love, not one resembling a lettuce. And when Queen Anne, in a famous anecdote, called the just-completed Saint Paul's Cathedral "awful, artificial, and amusing," its architect, Sir Christopher Wren, was overwhelmed with joy and gratidue, for what she had told him was that it was awe-inspiring, artful, and stimulating to contemplate (or *muse* upon).

In reading poetry, there is nothing to be done about the inevitable tendency of language to change except to watch out for it. If you suspect that a word has shifted in meaning over the years, most standard desk dictionaries will be helpful, an unabridged dictionary more helpful still, and most helpful of all the *Oxford English Dictionary (OED)*, which gives, for each definition, successive examples of the word's written use through the past thousand years. You need not feel a grim obligation to keep interrupting a poem in order to rummage in the dictionary; but if the poem is worth reading very closely, you may wish any aid you can find.

One of the valuable services of poetry is to recall for us the concrete, physical sense that certain words once had, but since have lost. As the English critic H. Coombes has remarked in *Literature and Criticism*,

> We use a word like *powerful* without feeling that it is really "powerfull."
> We do not seem today to taste the full flavor of words as we feel that
> Falstaff (and Shakespeare, and probably his audience) tasted them
> when he was applauding the virtues of "good sherris-sack," which makes
> the brain "apprehensive, quick, forgetive, full of nimble, fiery, and delectable shapes." And being less aware of the life and substantiality of
> words, we are probably less aware of the things . . . that these words
> stand for.

"Every word which is used to express a moral or intellectual fact," said Emerson in his study *Nature*, "if traced to its root, is found to be borrowed from some material appearance. *Right* means straight; *wrong* means twisted. *Spirit* primarily means wind; *transgression*, the crossing of a line; *supercilious*, the raising of an eyebrow." Browse in a dictionary and you will discover such original concretenesses. These are revealed in your dictionary's etymologies, or brief notes on the derivation of words, given in most dictionaries near the beginning of an entry on a word; in some dictionaries, at the end of the entry. Look up *squirrel*, for instance, and you will find it comes from two Greek words meaning "shadow-tail." For another example of a common word that originally contained a poetic metaphor, look up the origin of *daisy*.

EXPERIMENT: *Using the Dictionary*

The following short poem seems very simple and straightforward, but much of its total effect depends on the reader knowing the literal meanings of several words. The most crucial word is in the title—*aftermath*. Most readers today will assume that they know what that word means, but in this poem Longfellow uses it in both its current sense and its original, more literal meaning. Read the poem twice—first without a dictionary, then a second time after looking up the meanings of *aftermath, fledged, rowen,* and *mead*. How does knowing the exact meanings of these words add to both your literal and critical reading of the poem?

Henry Wadsworth Longfellow (1807–1882)

AFTERMATH   1873

When the summer fields are mown,
When the birds are fledged and flown,
    And the dry leaves strew the path;
With the falling of the snow,
With the cawing of the crow,   5
Once again the fields we mow
    And gather in the aftermath.

Not the sweet, new grass with flowers
In this harvesting of ours;
    Not the upland clover bloom;   10
But the rowen mixed with weeds,
Tangled tufts from marsh and meads,
Where the poppy drops its seeds
    In the silence and the gloom.

QUESTIONS

1. How does the etymology and meaning of *aftermath* help explain this poem? (Look the word up in your dictionary.)
2. What is the meaning of *fledged* (line 2) and *rowen* (line 11)?
3. Once you understand the literal meaning of the poem, do you think that Longfellow intended any further significance to it?

John Clare   (1793–1864)

Mouse's Nest   (ABOUT 1835)

I found a ball of grass among the hay
And progged it as I passed and went away;
And when I looked I fancied something stirred,
And turned again and hoped to catch the bird—
When out an old mouse bolted in the wheats   5
With all her young ones hanging at her teats;
She looked so odd and so grotesque to me,
I ran and wondered what the thing could be,
And pushed the knapweed bunches where I stood;
Then the mouse hurried from the craking° brood.   *crying*   10
The young ones squeaked, and as I went away
She found her nest again among the hay.
The water o'er the pebbles scarce could run
And broad old cesspools glittered in the sun.

Questions

1. "To prog" (*progged*, line 2) means "to poke about for food, to forage." In what ways does this word fit more exactly here than *prodded*, *touched*, or *searched*?
2. Is *craking* (line 10) better than *crying*? Which word better fits the poem? Why?
3. What connections do you find between the last two lines and the rest of the poem? To what are water that *scarce could run* and *broad old cesspools* (lines 13 and 14) likened?

An **allusion** is an indirect reference to any person, place, or thing—fictitious, historical, or actual. Sometimes, to understand an allusion in a poem, we have to find out something we didn't know before. But usually the poet asks of us only common knowledge. When, in his poem "To Helen," Edgar Allan Poe refers to "the glory that was Greece / And the grandeur that was Rome," he assumes that we have heard of those places. He also expects that we will understand his allusion to the cultural achievements of those ancient nations and perhaps even catch the subtle contrast between those two similar words *glory* and *grandeur*, with its suggestion that, for all its merits, Roman civilization was also more pompous than Greek.

Allusions not only enrich the meaning of a poem, they also save space. In "The Love Song of J. Alfred Prufrock" (page 1169), T. S. Eliot, by giving a brief introductory quotation from the speech of a damned soul in Dante's *Inferno*, is able to suggest that his poem will be the confession of a soul in torment, who sees no chance of escape.

Often in reading a poem, you will meet a name you don't recognize, on which the meaning of a line (or perhaps a whole poem) seems to depend. In this book, most such unfamiliar references and allusions are glossed or footnoted, but when you venture out on your own in reading poems, you may find yourself need-lessly perplexed unless you look up such names, the way you look up any other words. Unless the name is one that the poet made up, you will probably find it in one of the larger desk dictionaries, such as *Webster's Collegiate Dictionary* or the *American Heritage Dictionary*. If you don't solve your problem there, try an ency-clopedia, a world atlas, *The Houghton Mifflin Dictionary of Biography*, or *Brewer's Dictionary of Phrase & Fable*.

Some allusions are quotations from other poems. In R. S. Gwynn's "1-800," the narrator describes an insomniac watching late-night infomercials:

> Credit cards out, pencil and notepad handy,
>   The insomniac sinks deeply in his chair,
> Begging swift needles in his glass of brandy
>   To knit once more the raveled sleeve of care,
> As with control, remotely, in one hand he
>   Summons bright visions from the midnight air:

In addition to some witty wordplay, like the pun on *remote control*, Gwynn borrows a famous line from Shakespeare's *Macbeth*, "Sleep that knits up the raveled sleeve of care," to describe his unsnoozing protagonist. (*To ravel* means the same as *to unravel*—to loosen or disentangle.) Why quote Shakespeare in a poem about watching TV commercials? Partly it is just one poet's delight in replaying another poet's verbal home runs, but well-chosen allusions also pack an extra wallop of meaning into a poem. The line that Gwynn borrows comes from Macbeth's description of a mysterious voice he claims to have heard after murdering Duncan. The voice prophesied that "Macbeth shall sleep no more." Alluding to Shakespeare's line, therefore, Gwynn can summon up all sorts of dark, nocturnal associations that he then turns to satiric ends.

EXERCISE: *Catching Allusions*

From your knowledge, supplemented by a dictionary or other reference work if need be, explain the allusions in the following poems.

J. V. Cunningham   (1911–1985)*

FRIEND, ON THIS SCAFFOLD   1960
THOMAS MORE LIES DEAD

Friend, on this scaffold Thomas More lies dead
Who would not cut the Body from the Head.

Kelly Cherry (b. 1940)

ADVICE TO A FRIEND WHO PAINTS 1975

Consider shy Cezanne,
the lay of the land he loved,
its dumbstruck vanity, polite and brute.
The bather in his sketchy suit.
The skull upon the mute pull of cloth.   5
In your taxing and tearing, tugging at art,
consider shy Cezanne.
His blushing apples.
His love of man.

QUESTIONS

How do you account for the odd combination of images that occur in lines 4–8? What possible connection do a bather, a skull, and an apple share?

Carl Sandburg (1878–1967)*

GRASS 1918

Pile the bodies high at Austerlitz and Waterloo.
Shovel them under and let me work—
          I am the grass; I cover all.

And pile them high at Gettysburg
And pile them high at Ypres and Verdun.   5
Shovel them under and let me work.

Two years, ten years, and passengers ask the conductor:
          What place is this?
          Where are we now?

          I am the grass.   10
          Let me work.

QUESTIONS

1. What do the five proper nouns in Sandburg's poem have in common?
2. How much does the reader need to understand about the allusions in "Grass" to appreciate their importance to the literal meaning of the poem?

WORD CHOICE AND WORD ORDER

Even if Samuel Johnson's famous *Dictionary* of 1755 had been as thick as Webster's unabridged, an eighteenth-century poet searching through it for words to use would have had a narrower choice. For in English literature of the

neoclassical period or **Augustan age**—that period from about 1660 into the late eighteenth century—many poets subscribed to a belief in **poetic diction:** "A system of words," said Dr. Johnson, "refined from the grossness of domestic use." The system admitted into a serious poem only certain words and subjects, excluding others as violations of **decorum** (propriety). Accordingly, such common words as *rat, cheese, big, sneeze,* and *elbow,* although admissible to satire, were thought inconsistent with the loftiness of tragedy, epic, ode, and elegy. Dr. Johnson's biographer, James Boswell, tells how a poet writing an epic reconsidered the word "rats" and instead wrote "the whiskered vermin race." Johnson himself objected to Lady Macbeth's allusion to her "keen knife," saying that "we do not immediately conceive that any crime of importance is to be committed with a knife; or who does not, at last, from the long habit of connecting a knife with sordid offices, feel aversion rather than terror?" Probably Johnson was here the victim of his age, and Shakespeare was right, but Johnson in one of his assumptions was right too: there are inappropriate words as well as appropriate ones.

Neoclassical poets chose their classical models more often from Roman writers than from Greek, as their diction suggests by the frequency of Latin derivatives. For example, a *net,* according to Dr. Johnson's dictionary, is "any thing reticulated or decussated, at equal distances, with interstices between the intersections." In company with Latinate words often appeared fixed combinations of adjective and noun ("finny prey" for "fish"), poetic names (a song to a lady named Molly might rechristen her Parthenia), and allusions to classical mythology. Neoclassical poetic diction was evidently being abused when, instead of saying "uncork the bottle," a poet could write

> Apply thine engine to the spongy door,
> Set *Bacchus* from his glassy prison free,

in some bad lines ridiculed by Alexander Pope in *Peri Bathous, or The Art of Sinking in Poetry.*

Not all poetic diction is excess baggage. To a reader who knew firsthand both living sheep and the pastoral poems of Virgil—as most readers nowadays do not—such a fixed phrase as "the fleecy care," which seems stilted to us, conveyed pleasurable associations. But "fleecy care" was more than a highfalutin way of saying "sheep"; as one scholar has pointed out, "when they wished, our poets could say 'sheep' as clearly and as often as anybody else. In the first place, 'fleecy' drew attention to wool, and demanded the appropriate visual image of sheep; for aural imagery the poets would refer to 'the bleating kind'; it all depended upon what was happening in the poem."[2]

Other poets have found some special kind of poetic language valuable: Old English poets, with their standard figures of speech ("whale-road" for the sea, "ring-giver" for a ruler); makers of folk ballads who, no less than neoclassicists,

---

[2]Bonamy Dobrée, *English Literature in the Early Eighteenth Century, 1700–1740* (New York: Oxford UP, 1959) 161.

love fixed epithet-noun combinations ("milk-white steed," "blood-red wine," "steel-driving man"); and Edmund Spenser, whose example made popular the adjective ending in -y (*fleecy, grassy, milky*).

When Wordsworth, in his Preface to *Lyrical Ballads*, asserted that "the language really spoken by men," especially by humble rustics, is plainer and more emphatic, and conveys "elementary feelings . . . in a state of greater simplicity," he was, in effect, advocating a new poetic diction. Wordsworth's ideas invited freshness into English poetry and, by admitting words that neoclassical poets would have called "low" ("His poor old *ankles* swell"), helped rid poets of the fear of being thought foolish for mentioning a commonplace.

This theory of the superiority of rural diction was, as Coleridge pointed out, hard to adhere to, and, in practice, Wordsworth was occasionally to write a language as Latinate and citified as these lines on yew trees:

> Huge trunks!—and each particular trunk a growth
> Of intertwisted fibers serpentine
> Up-coiling, and inveterately convolved . . .

Language so Latinate sounds pedantic to us, especially the phrase *inveterately convolved*. In fact, some poets, notably Gerard Manley Hopkins, have subscribed to the view that English words derived from Anglo-Saxon (Old English) have more force and flavor than their Latin equivalents. *Kingly*, one may feel, has more power than *regal*. One argument for this view is that so many words of Old English origin—*man, wife, child, house, eat, drink, sleep*—are basic to our living speech. It may be true that a language closer to Old English is particularly fit for rendering abstract notions concretely—as does the memorable title of a medieval work of piety, the *Ayenbite of Inwit* ("again-bite of inner wisdom" or "remorse of conscience"). And yet this view, if accepted at all, must be accepted with reservations. Some words of Latin origin carry meanings both precise and physical. In the King James Bible is the admonition, "See then that ye walk circumspectly, not as fools, but as wise" (Ephesians 5:15). To be *circumspect* (a word from two Latin roots meaning "to look" and "around") is to be watchful on all sides—a meaning altogether lost in a modernized wording of the passage once printed on a subway poster for a Bible society: "Be careful how you live, not thoughtlessly but thoughtfully."

When E. E. Cummings begins a poem, "mr youse needn't be so spry / concernin questions arty," we recognize another kind of diction available to poetry: **vulgate** (speech not much affected by schooling). Handbooks of grammar sometimes distinguish various **levels of diction.** A sort of ladder is imagined, on whose rungs words, phrases, and sentences may be ranked in an ascending order of formality, from the curses of an illiterate thug to the commencement-day address of a doctor of divinity. These levels range from vulgate through **colloquial** (the casual conversation or informal writing of literate people) and **general English** (most literate speech and writing, more studied than colloquial but not pretentious), up to **formal English** (the impersonal language of educated persons, usually only written, possibly spoken on dignified occasions). Recently, however, lexicographers have been shunning such labels. The designation *colloquial* was expelled from *Webster's Third New International Dictionary* on the grounds that "it is impossible to know whether a word out of context is colloquial or not" and that the diction of Americans nowadays is more fluid than the labels suggest. Aware that we are being unscientific, we may find the labels useful. They may help roughly to describe what happens when, as in the following poem, a poet shifts from one level of usage to another.

Robert Herrick   (1591–1674)*

Upon Julia's Clothes   1648

Whenas in silks my Julia goes,
Then, then, methinks, how sweetly flows
That liquefaction of her clothes.

Next, when I cast mine eyes and see
That brave vibration each way free,   5
O how that glittering taketh me!

Even in so short a poem as "Upon Julia's Clothes," we see how a sudden shift in the level of diction can produce a surprising and memorable effect. One word in each stanza—*liquefaction* in the first, *vibration* in the second—stands out from the standard, but not extravagant, language that surrounds it. Try to imagine the entire poem being written in such formal English, in mostly unfamiliar words of several syllables each: the result, in all likelihood, would be merely an oddity, and a turgid one at that. But by using such terms sparingly, Herrick allows them to take on a greater strength and significance through their contrast with the words that surround them. It is *liquefaction* in particular that strikes the reader: like a great catch by an outfielder, it impresses both for its appropriateness in the situation and for its sheer beauty as a demonstration of superior skill. Once we have read the poem, we realize that the effect would be severely compromised, if not ruined, by the substitution of any other word in its place.

At present, most poetry in English avoids elaborate literary expressions such as "fleecy care" in favor of more colloquial language. In many English-speaking areas, such as Scotland, there has even been a movement to write poems in regional dialects. (A **dialect** is a particular variety of language spoken by an identifiable regional group or social class of persons.) Dialect poets frequently try to capture the freshness and authenticity of the language spoken in their immediate locale.

Most Americans know at least part of one Scottish dialect poem by heart— "Auld Lang Syne," the song commonly sung as the clock strikes twelve on New Year's Eve. Although Robert Burns wrote most of the song's stanzas, the poet claimed to have copied down the famous opening stanza (following) from an old man he heard singing. *Auld* is the Scots word for "old"; *lang syne* means "long since." How different the lines would seem if they were standard English.

> Should auld acquaintance be forgot,
> And never brought to mind?
> Should auld acquaintance be forgot
> And days of auld lang syne?
> And days of auld lang syne, my dear,
> And days of auld lang syne,
> Should auld acquaintance be forgot,
> And days of auld lang syne?

Not only the poet's choice of words makes a poem seem more formal, or less, but also the way the words are arranged into sentences. Compare these lines

> Jack and Jill went up the hill
> To fetch a pail of water.
> Jack fell down and broke his crown
> And Jill came tumbling after.

with Milton's account of a more significant downfall:

> Earth trembled from her entrails, as again
> In pangs, and Nature gave a second groan;
> Sky loured, and, muttering thunder, some sad drops
> Wept at completing of the mortal sin
> Original; while Adam took no thought
> Eating his fill, nor Eve to iterate
> Her former trespass feared, the more to soothe
> Him with her loved society, that now
> As with new wine intoxicated both
> They swim in mirth, and fancy that they feel
> Divinity within them breeding wings
> Wherewith to scorn the Earth.

Not all the words in Milton's lines are bookish: indeed, many of them can be found in nursery rimes. What helps, besides diction, to distinguish this account of the Biblical fall from "Jack and Jill" is that Milton's nonstop sentence seems further removed from usual speech in its length (83 words), in its complexity (subordinate clauses), and in its word order ("with new wine intoxicated both" rather than "both intoxicated with new wine"). Should we think less (or more) highly of Milton for choosing a style so elaborate and formal? No judgment need be passed: both Mother Goose and the author of *Paradise Lost* use language appropriate to their purposes.

Among languages, English is by no means the most flexible. English words must be used in fairly definite and inviolable patterns, and whoever departs too far from them will not be understood. In the sentence "Cain slew Abel," if you change the word order, you change the meaning: "Abel slew Cain." Such inflexibility was not true of Latin, in which a poet could lay down words in almost any sequence and, because their endings (inflections) showed what parts of speech they were, could trust that no reader would mistake a subject for an object or a noun for an adjective. (E. E. Cummings has striven, in certain of his poems, for the freedom of Latin. One such poem, "anyone lived in a pretty how town," appears on page 767.)

The rigidity of English word order invites the poet to defy it and to achieve unusual effects by inverting it. It is customary in English to place adjective in front of noun (*a blue mantle, new pastures*). But an unusual emphasis is achieved when Milton ends "Lycidas" by reversing the pattern:

> At last he rose, and twitched his mantle blue:
> Tomorrow to fresh woods, and pastures new.

Perhaps the inversion in *mantle blue* gives more prominence to the color associated with heaven (and in "Lycidas," heaven is of prime importance). Perhaps the inversion in *pastures new*, stressing the *new*, heightens the sense of a rebirth.

Coleridge offered two "homely definitions of prose and poetry; that is, *prose*: words in their best order; *poetry*: the best words in the best order." If all goes well, a poet may fasten the right word into the right place, and the result may be—as T. S. Eliot said in "Little Gidding"—a "complete consort dancing together."

Kay Ryan   (b. 1945)*

BLANDEUR   2000

If it please God,
let less happen.
Even out Earth's
rondure, flatten
Eiger, blanden   5
the Grand Canyon.
Make valleys
slightly higher,
widen fissures
to arable land,   10
remand your
terrible glaciers
and silence
their calving,
halving or doubling   15
all geographical features
toward the mean.
Unlean against our hearts.

Withdraw your grandeur
from these parts.   20

BLANDEUR. 5 *Eiger*: a mountain in the Alps.

QUESTIONS

1. The title of Ryan's poem is a word that she invented. What do you think it means? Explain the reasoning behind your theory.
2. Where else does Ryan use a different form of this new word?
3. What other unusual but real words does the author use?

Thomas Hardy   (1840–1928)*

THE RUINED MAID   1901

"O 'Melia, my dear, this does everything crown!
Who could have supposed I should meet you in Town?
And whence such fair garments, such prosperi-ty?"—
"O didn't you know I'd been ruined?" said she.

—"You left us in tatters, without shoes or socks,   5
Tired of digging potatoes, and spudding up docks°;   *spading up dockweed*
And now you've gay bracelets and bright feathers three!"—
"Yes: that's how we dress when we're ruined," said she.

—"At home in the barton° you said 'thee' and 'thou,'   *farmyard*
And 'thik oon,' and 'theäs oon,' and 't'other'; but now   10
Your talking quite fits 'ee for high compa-ny!"—
"Some polish is gained with one's ruin," said she.

—"Your hands were like paws then, your face blue and bleak
But now I'm bewitched by your delicate cheek,
And your little gloves fit as on any la-dy!"—   15
"We never do work when we're ruined," said she.

—"You used to call home-life a hag-ridden dream,
And you'd sigh, and you'd sock°; but at present you seem   *groan*
To know not of megrims° or melancho-ly!"—   *blues*
"True. One's pretty lively when ruined," said she.   20

—"I wish I had feathers, a fine sweeping gown,
And a delicate face, and could strut about Town!"—
"My dear—a raw country girl, such as you be,
Cannot quite expect that. You ain't ruined," said she.

1. Where does this dialogue take place? Who are the two speakers?
2. Comment on Hardy's use of the word *ruined*. What is the conventional meaning of the word when applied to a woman? As 'Melia applies it to herself, what is its meaning?
3. Sum up the attitude of each speaker toward the other. What details of the new 'Melia does the first speaker most dwell on? Would you expect Hardy to be so impressed by all these details, or is there, between his view of the characters and their view of themselves, any hint of an ironic discrepancy?
4. In losing her country dialect (*thik oon* and *theäs oon* for *this one* and *that one*), 'Melia is presumed to have gained in sophistication. What does Hardy suggest by her *ain't* in the last line?

Richard Eberhart   (b. 1904)

THE FURY OF AERIAL BOMBARDMENT   1947

You would think the fury of aerial bombardment
Would rouse God to relent; the infinite spaces
Are still silent. He looks on shock-pried faces.
History, even, does not know what is meant.

You would feel that after so many centuries   5
God would give man to repent; yet he can kill
As Cain could, but with multitudinous will,
No farther advanced than in his ancient furies.

Was man made stupid to see his own stupidity?
Is God by definition indifferent, beyond us all?   10
Is the eternal truth man's fighting soul
Wherein the Beast ravens in its own avidity?

Of Van Wettering I speak, and Averill,
Names on a list, whose faces I do not recall
But they are gone to early death, who late in school   15
Distinguished the belt feed lever from the belt holding pawl.

QUESTIONS

1. As a naval officer during World War II, Richard Eberhart was assigned for a time as an instructor in a gunnery school. How has this experience apparently contributed to the diction of his poem?
2. In his *Life of John Dryden*, complaining about a description of a sea fight Dryden had filled with nautical language, Samuel Johnson argued that technical terms should be excluded from poetry. Is this criticism applicable to Eberhart's last line? Can a word succeed for us in a poem, even though we may not be able to define it? (For more evidence, see also the technical terms in Henry Reed's "Naming of Parts," page 1229.)

3. Some readers have found a contrast in tone between the first three stanzas of this poem and the last stanza. How would you describe this contrast? What does diction contribute to it?

Wendy Cope (b. 1945)*

LONELY HEARTS   1986

Can someone make my simple wish come true?
Male biker seeks female for touring fun.
Do you live in North London? Is it you?

Gay vegetarian whose friends are few,
I'm into music, Shakespeare and the sun,   5
Can someone make my simple wish come true?

Executive in search of something new—
Perhaps bisexual woman, arty, young.
Do you live in North London? Is it you?

Successful, straight and solvent? I am too—   10
Attractive Jewish lady with a son.
Can someone make my simple wish come true?

I'm Libran, inexperienced and blue—
Need slim non-smoker, under twenty-one.
Do you live in North London? Is it you?   15

Please write (with photo) to Box 152.
Who knows where it may lead once we've begun?
Can someone make my simple wish come true?
Do you live in North London? Is it you?

LONELY HEARTS. This poem has a double form: the rhetorical, a series of "lonely heart" personal ads from a newspaper, and metrical, a **villanelle,** a fixed form developed by French courtly poets in imitation of Italian folk song. For other villanelles, see Elizabeth Bishop's "One Art" (page 1080) and Dylan Thomas's "Do not go gentle into that good night" (page 927). In the villanelle, the first and the third lines are repeated in a set pattern throughout the poem.

QUESTIONS

1. What sort of language does Wendy Cope borrow for this poem?
2. The form of the villanelle requires that the poet end each stanza with one of two repeating lines. What special use does the author make of these mandatory repetitions?
3. How many speakers are there in the poem? Does the author's voice ever enter or is the entire poem spoken by individuals in personal ads?
4. The poem seems to begin satirically. Does the poem ever move beyond the critical, mocking tone typical of satire?

E. E. Cummings   (1894–1962)*

ANYONE LIVED IN A PRETTY HOW TOWN   1940

anyone lived in a pretty how town
(with up so floating many bells down)
spring summer autumn winter
he sang his didn't he danced his did.

Women and men(both little and small)   5
cared for anyone not at all
they sowed their isn't they reaped their same
sun moon stars rain

children guessed(but only a few
and down they forgot as up they grew   10
autumn winter spring summer)
that noone loved him more by more

when by now and tree by leaf
she laughed his joy she cried his grief
bird by snow and stir by still   15
anyone's any was all to her

someones married their everyones
laughed their cryings and did their dance
(sleep wake hope and then)they
said their nevers they slept their dream   20

stars rain sun moon
(and only the snow can begin to explain
how children are apt to forget to remember
with up so floating many bells down)

one day anyone died i guess   25
(and noone stooped to kiss his face)
busy folk buried them side by side
little by little and was by was

all by all and deep by deep
and more by more they dream their sleep   30
noone and anyone earth by april
wish by spirit and if by yes.

Women and men(both dong and ding)
summer autumn winter spring
reaped their sowing and went their came   35
sun moon stars rain

1. Summarize the story told in this poem. Who are the characters?
2. Rearrange the words in the two opening lines into the order you would expect them usually to follow. What effect does Cummings obtain by his unconventional word order?
3. Another of Cummings's strategies is to use one part of speech as if it were another; for instance, in line 4, *didn't* and *did* ordinarily are verbs, but here they are used as nouns. What other words in the poem perform functions other than their expected ones?

Billy Collins (b. 1941)*

THE NAMES   2002

Yesterday, I lay awake in the palm of the night.
A soft rain stole in, unhelped by any breeze,
And when I saw the silver glaze on the windows,
I started with A, with Ackerman, as it happened,
Then Baxter and Calabro,   5
Davis and Eberling, names falling into place
As droplets fell through the dark.

Names printed on the ceiling of the night.
Names slipping around a watery bend.
Twenty-six willows on the banks of a stream.   10

In the morning, I walked out barefoot
Among thousands of flowers
Heavy with dew like the eyes of tears,
And each had a name—
Fiori inscribed on a yellow petal   15
Then Gonzalez and Han, Ishikawa and Jenkins.

Names written in the air
And stitched into the cloth of the day.
A name under a photograph taped to a mailbox.
Monogram on a torn shirt,   20
I see you spelled out on storefront windows
And on the bright unfurled awnings of this city.
I say the syllables as I turn a corner—
Kelly and Lee,
Medina, Nardella, and O'Connor.   25

When I peer into the woods,
I see a thick tangle where letters are hidden
As in a puzzle concocted for children.
Parker and Quigley in the twigs of an ash,

Rizzo, Schubert, Torres, and Upton, 30
Secrets in the boughs of an ancient maple.

Names written in the pale sky.
Names rising in the updraft amid buildings.
Names silent in stone
Or cried out behind a door. 35
Names blown over the earth and out to sea.

In the evening—weakening light, the last swallows.
A boy on a lake lifts his oars.
A woman by a window puts a match to a candle,
And the names are outlined on the rose clouds— 40
Vanacore and Wallace,
(let X stand, if it can, for the ones unfound)
Then Young and Ziminsky, the final jolt of Z.

Names etched on the head of a pin.
One name spanning a bridge, another undergoing a tunnel. 45
A blue name needled into the skin.
Names of citizens, workers, mothers and fathers,
The bright-eyed daughter, the quick son.
Alphabet of names in a green field.
Names in the small tracks of birds. 50
Names lifted from a hat
Or balanced on the tip of the tongue.
Names wheeled into the dim warehouse of memory.
So many names, there is barely room on the walls of the heart.

THE NAMES. This poem originally appeared in the *New York Times* on September 11, 2002. On that same day its author, the Poet Laureate of the United States, read the poem before a joint session of Congress specially convened in New York City to mark the one-year anniversary of the attack on the World Trade Center.

QUESTIONS

1. Occasional poetry—verse written to commemorate a public or historical occasion—is generally held in low esteem because such poems tend to be self-important and overwritten. Does Collins avoid these pitfalls?
2. Discuss the level of diction in "The Names." Is it appropriate to the subject? Explain.

EXERCISE: *Different Kinds of English*

Read the following poems and see what kinds of diction and word order you find in them. Which poems are least formal in their language and which most formal? Is there any use of vulgate English? Any dialect? What does each poem achieve that its own kind of English makes possible?

Anonymous   (American oral verse)

CARNATION MILK   (ABOUT 1900?)

Carnation Milk is the best in the land;
Here I sit with a can in my hand—
No tits to pull, no hay to pitch,
You just punch a hole in the son of a bitch.

CARNATION MILK. "This quatrain is imagined as the caption under a picture of a rugged-looking cowboy seated upon a bale of hay," notes William Harmon in his *Oxford Book of American Light Verse* (New York: Oxford UP, 1979). Possibly the first to print this work was David Ogilvy (1911–1999), who quotes it in his *Confessions of an Advertising Man* (New York: Atheneum, 1963).

William Wordsworth   (1770–1850)*

MY HEART LEAPS UP WHEN I BEHOLD   1807

My heart leaps up when I behold
   A rainbow in the sky:
So was it when my life began;
So is it now I am a man;
So be it when I shall grow old,   5
   Or let me die!
The Child is father of the Man;
And I could wish my days to be
Bound each to each by natural piety.

William Wordsworth   (1770–1850)*

MUTABILITY   1822

From low to high doth dissolution climb,
And sink from high to low, along a scale
Of awful notes, whose concord shall not fail;
A musical but melancholy chime,
Which they can hear who meddle not with crime,   5
Nor avarice, nor over-anxious care.
Truth fails not; but her outward forms that bear
The longest date do melt like frosty rime,°   *frozen dew*
That in the morning whitened hill and plain
And is no more; drop like the tower sublime   10

Of yesterday, which royally did wear
His crown of weeds, but could not even sustain
Some casual shout that broke the silent air,
Or the unimaginable touch of Time.

Anonymous

SCOTTSBORO   1936

Paper come out—done strewed de news
Seven po' chillun moanin' deat' house blues,
Seven po' chillun moanin' deat' house blues.
Seven nappy° heads wit' big shiny eye   *frizzy*
All boun' in jail and framed to die,   5
All boun' in jail and framed to die.

Messin' white woman—snake lyin' tale
Hang and burn and jail wit' no bail.
Dat hang and burn and jail wit' no bail.
Worse ol' crime in white folks' lan'   10
Black skin coverin' po' workin' man,
Black skin coverin' po' workin' man.

Judge and jury—all in de stan'
Lawd, biggety name for same lynchin' ban',
Lawd, biggety name for same lynchin' ban'.   15
White folks and nigger in great co't house
Like cat down cellar wit' nohole mouse.
Like cat down cellar wit' nohole mouse.

SCOTTSBORO. This folk blues, collected by Lawrence Gellert in *Negro Songs of Protest* (New York: Carl Fischer, 1936), is a comment on the Scottsboro case. In 1931 nine black youths were arrested near Scottsboro, Alabama, and charged with the rape of two white women. Though eventually, after several trials, they were found not guilty, some of them at the time this song was composed had been convicted and sentenced to death.

Lewis Carroll
[Charles Lutwidge Dodgson]   (1832–1898)

JABBERWOCKY   1871

'Twas brillig, and the slithy toves
    Did gyre and gimble in the wabe:
All mimsy were the borogoves,
    And the mome raths outgrabe.

"Beware the Jabberwock, my son!   5
    The jaws that bite, the claws that catch!
Beware the Jubjub bird, and shun
    The frumious Bandersnatch!"

He took his vorpal sword in hand;
   Long time the manxome foe he sought— 10
So rested he by the Tumtum tree
   And stood awhile in thought.

And, as in uffish thought he stood,
   The Jabberwock, with eyes of flame,
Came whiffling through the tulgey wood, 15
   And burbled as it came!

One, two! One, two! And through and through
   The vorpal blade went snicker-snack!
He left it dead, and with its head
   He went galumphing back. 20

"And hast thou slain the Jabberwock?
   Come to my arms, my beamish boy!
O frabjous day! Callooh, Callay!"
   He chortled in his joy.

'Twas brillig, and the slithy toves 25
   Did gyre and gimble in the wabe:
All mimsy were the borogoves,
   And the mome raths outgrabe.

JABBERWOCKY. Fussy about pronunciation, Carroll in his preface to *The Hunting of the Snark* declares: "The first 'o' in 'borogoves' is pronounced like the 'o' in 'borrow.' I have heard people try to give it the sound of the 'o' in 'worry.' Such is Human Perversity." *Toves*, he adds, rimes with *groves*.

QUESTIONS

1. Look up *chortled* (line 24) in your dictionary and find out its definition and origin.
2. In *Through the Looking Glass*, Alice seeks the aid of Humpty Dumpty to decipher the meaning of this nonsense poem. "*Brillig*," he explains, "means four o'clock in the afternoon—the time when you begin *broiling* things for dinner." Does *brillig* sound like any other familiar word?
3. "*Slithy*," the explanation goes on, "means 'lithe and slimy.' 'Lithe' is the same as 'active.' You see it's like a portmanteau—there are two meanings packed up into one word." *Mimsy* is supposed to pack together both "flimsy" and "miserable." In the rest of the poem, what other portmanteau—or packed suitcase—words can you find?

Lewis Carroll

Lewis Carroll on Writing

HUMPTY DUMPTY EXPLICATES "JABBERWOCKY"   1871

"You seem very clever at explaining words, sir," said Alice. "Would you kindly tell me the meaning of the poem called 'Jabberwocky'?"

"Let's hear it," said Humpty Dumpty. "I can explain all the poems that ever were invented—and a good many that haven't been invented just yet."

This sounded very hopeful, so Alice repeated the first verse:

> "'Twas brillig, and the slithy toves
>   Did gyre and gimble in the wabe:
> All mimsy were the borogoves,
>   And the mome raths outgrabe."

"That's enough to begin with," Humpty Dumpty interrupted: "there are plenty of hard words there. '*Brillig*' means four o'clock in the afternoon—the time when you begin *broiling* things for dinner."

"That'll do very well," said Alice. "And '*slithy*'?"

"Well, '*slithy*' means 'lithe and slimy.' 'Lithe' is the same as 'active.' You see, it's like a portmanteau—there are two meanings packed up in one word."

"I see it now," Alice remarked thoughtfully. "And what are '*toves*'?"

"Well, '*toves*' are something like badgers—they're something like lizards—and they're something like corkscrews."

"They must be very curious-looking creatures."

"They are that," said Humpty Dumpty, "also they make their nests under sundials—also they live on cheese."

"And what's to '*gyre*' and to '*gimble*'?"

"To '*gyre*' is to go round and round like a gyroscope. To '*gimble*' is to make holes like a gimlet."

"And '*the wabe*' is the grass plot round a sundial, I suppose?" said Alice, surprised at her own ingenuity.

"Of course it is. It's called '*wabe*,' you know, because it goes a long way before it, and a long way behind it."

"And a long way beyond it on each side," Alice added.

"Exactly so. Well, then, '*mimsy*' is flimsy and miserable (there's another portmanteau for you). And a '*borogove*' is a thin, shabby-looking bird with its feathers sticking out all round—something like a live mop."

"And then '*mome raths*'?" said Alice. "I'm afraid I'm giving you a great deal of trouble."

"Well, a '*rath*' is a sort of green pig: but '*mome*' I'm not certain about. I think it's short for 'from home'—meaning that they'd lost their way, you know."

"And what does '*outgrabe*' mean?"

"Well, '*outgribing*' is something between bellowing and whistling, with a kind of sneeze in the middle; however, you'll hear it done, maybe—down in the wood yonder—and when you've once heard it you'll be *quite* content. Who's been repeating all that hard stuff to you?"

"I read it in a book," said Alice.

From Through the Looking Glass

HUMPTY DUMPTY EXPLICATES "JABBERWOCKY." This celebrated passage is the origin of the term *portmanteau word,* an artificial word that combines parts of other words to express some combination of their qualities. (*Brunch*, for example, is a meal that combines aspects of both breakfast and lunch.) A portmanteau is a large suitcase that opens up into two separate compartments.

◄━━━► WRITING CRITICALLY ◄━━━►

How Much Difference Does a Word Make?

Although a poem may contain images and ideas, it is made up of words. Language is the medium of poetry, and the exact wording of a successful poem is the chief source of its power. Writers labor mightily to shape each word and phrase to create particular expressive effects. Changing a single word sometimes ruins a poem's effect, just as changing one number in a combination lock's sequence makes all the other numbers useless.

Before writing about the language of a poem, recruit your intuition into working with your intellect. As you read the poem, ask yourself if there is some particular word or combination of words that gives you particular pleasure or especially intrigues you. Don't worry about why the word or words impress you. Don't even worry about the meaning. Just underline the word or phrase in your book. Then let your analytical powers go to work. Try to determine what makes this part of the poem so intriguing to you. How does it relate to the other lines? What does it contribute to the effect of the poem? In writing about the poem, let that word or phrase be your key into the poem. Often by understanding how a single key word operates in the context of a poem, we gain a special sense of what the whole poem means.

WRITING ASSIGNMENT

In no more than two pages, analyze how a single word or phrase contributes to a poem's total impact. Begin by choosing from any poem in this chapter a line or two that you particularly like. Then, select a key word or phrase and explore how they help shape the poem's total meaning. As part of your analysis rewrite the line by substituting a synonym in place of a single important word. Discuss what is lost by the substitution. A possible topic might be Robert Herrick's line from "Upon Julia's Clothes," "the liquefaction of her clothes." What does the beautiful but unusual word *liquefaction* add to the poem that a synonym would not? Other interesting poems to analyze include Wendy Cope's "Lonely Hearts," Robert Graves's "Down, Wanton, Down," Kay Ryan's "Blandeur," and William Wordsworth's "Mutability."

FURTHER SUGGESTIONS FOR WRITING

1. Choosing a poem that strikes you as particularly inventive or unusual in its language, such as E. E. Cummings's "anyone lived in a pretty how town" (page 767), Gerard Manley Hopkins's "The Windhover" (page 1193), or Wendy Cope's "Lonely Hearts" (page 766), write a brief analysis of it. Concentrate on the diction of the poem and word order. For what possible purposes does the poet depart from standard English or incorporate unusual vocabulary? (For pointers on writing about poetry by the method of analysis, see "Writing About a Poem.")
2. In a short essay, set forth the pleasures of browsing in a dictionary. As you browse, see if you can discover any "found poems."
3. "Printing poetry in dialect, such as 'Scottsboro,' insults the literacy of a people." Think about this critical charge and comment on it.

15 *Saying and Suggesting*

To write so clearly that they might bring "all things as near the mathematical plainness" as possible—that was the goal of scientists, according to Bishop Thomas Sprat, who lived in the seventeenth century. Such an effort would seem bound to fail, because words, unlike numbers, are ambiguous indicators. Although it may have troubled Bishop Sprat, the tendency of a word to have multiplicity of meaning rather than mathematical plainness opens broad avenues to poetry.

Every word has at least one **denotation:** a meaning as defined in a dictionary. But the English language has many a common word with so many denotations that a reader may need to think twice to see what it means in a specific context. The noun *field,* for instance, can denote a piece of ground, a sports arena, the scene of a battle, part of a flag, a profession, and a number system in mathematics. Further, the word can be used as a verb ("he fielded a grounder") or an adjective ("field trip," "field glasses").

A word also has **connotations:** overtones or suggestions of additional meaning that it gains from all the contexts in which we have met it in the past. The word *skeleton,* according to a dictionary, denotes "the bony framework of a human being or other vertebrate animal, which supports the flesh and protects the organs." But by its associations, the word can rouse thoughts of war, of disease and death, or (possibly) of one's plans to go to medical school. Think, too, of the difference between "Old Doc Jones" and "Theodore E. Jones, M.D." In the mind's eye, the former appears in his shirtsleeves; the latter has a gold nameplate on his door. That some words denote the same thing but have sharply different connotations is pointed out in this anonymous Victorian jingle:

> Here's a little ditty that you really ought to know:
> Horses "sweat" and men "perspire," but ladies only "glow."

The terms *druggist, pharmacist,* and *apothecary* all denote the same occupation, but apothecaries lay claim to special distinction.

Poets aren't the only people who care about the connotations of language. Advertisers know that connotations make money. Nowadays many automobile dealers advertise their secondhand cars not as "used" but as "pre-owned," as if fearing that "used car" would connote an old heap with soiled upholstery and mysterious engine troubles. "Pre-owned," however, suggests that the previous owner has taken the trouble of breaking in the car for you. Not long ago prune-packers, alarmed by a slump in sales, sponsored a survey to determine the connotations of prunes in the public consciousness. Asked, "What do you think of when you hear the word *prunes?*" most people replied, "dried up," "wrinkled," or "constipated." Dismayed, the packers hired an advertising agency to create a new image for prunes, in hopes of inducing new connotations. Soon, advertisements began to show prunes in brightly colored settings, in the company of bikinied bathing beauties.

In imaginative writing, connotations are as crucial as they are in advertising. Consider this sentence: "A new brand of journalism is being born, or spawned" (Dwight Macdonald writing in the *New York Review of Books*). The last word, by its associations with fish and crustaceans, suggests that this new journalism is scarcely the product of human beings. And what do we make of Romeo's assertion that Juliet "is the sun"? Surely even a lovesick boy cannot mean that his sweetheart is "the incandescent body of gases about which the earth and other planets revolve" (a dictionary definition). He means, of course, that he thrives in her sight, that he feels warm in her presence or even at the thought of her, that she illumines his world and is the center of his universe. Because in the mind of the hearer these and other suggestions are brought into play, Romeo's statement, literally absurd, makes excellent sense.

Here is a famous poem that groups together things with similar connotations: certain ships and their cargoes. (A *quinquireme*, by the way, was an ancient Assyrian vessel propelled by sails and oars.)

John Masefield (1878–1967)

Cargoes   1902

Quinquireme of Nineveh from distant Ophir,
Rowing home to haven in sunny Palestine,
With a cargo of ivory,
And apes and peacocks,
Sandalwood, cedarwood, and sweet white wine.   5

Stately Spanish galleon coming from the Isthmus,
Dipping through the Tropics by the palm-green shores,
With a cargo of diamonds,

Emeralds, amethysts,
Topazes, and cinnamon, and gold moidores.°   *Portuguese coins*   10

Dirty British coaster with a salt-caked smoke stack,
Butting through the Channel in the mad March days,
With a cargo of Tyne coal,
Road-rails, pig-lead,
Firewood, iron-ware, and cheap tin trays.   15

    To us, as well as to the poet's original readers, the place-names in the first
two stanzas suggest the exotic and faraway. Ophir, a vanished place, may have
been in Arabia; according to the Bible, King Solomon sent expeditions there for
its celebrated pure gold, also for ivory, apes, peacocks, and other luxury items.
(See I Kings 9–10.) In his final stanza, Masefield groups commonplace things
(mostly heavy and metallic), whose suggestions of crudeness, cheapness, and ugliness he deliberately contrasts with those of the precious stuffs he has listed earlier. For British readers, the Tyne is a stodgy and familiar river; the English
Channel in March, choppy and likely to upset a stomach. The quinquireme is
rowing, the galleon is *dipping,* but the dirty British freighter is *butting,* aggressively
pushing. Conceivably, the poet could have described firewood and even coal as
beautiful, but evidently he wants them to convey sharply different suggestions
here, to go along with the rest of the coaster's cargo. In drawing such a sharp
contrast between past and present, Masefield does more than merely draw up
bills-of-lading. Perhaps he even implies a wry and unfavorable comment on life
in the present day. His meaning lies not so much in the dictionary definitions of
his words ("*moidores:* Portuguese gold coins formerly worth approximately five
pounds sterling") as in their rich and vivid connotations.

William Blake   (1757–1827)*

LONDON   1794

I wander through each chartered street,
Near where the chartered Thames does flow,
And mark in every face I meet
Marks of weakness, marks of woe.

In every cry of every man,   5
In every infant's cry of fear,
In every voice, in every ban,
The mind-forged manacles I hear.

How the chimney-sweeper's cry
Every black'ning church appalls   10

And the hapless soldier's sigh
Runs in blood down palace walls.

But most through midnight streets I hear
How the youthful harlot's curse
Blasts the new born infant's tear
And blights with plagues the marriage hearse.

15

Here are only a few of the possible meanings of three of Blake's words:

chartered (lines 1, 2)

> DENOTATIONS: Established by a charter (a written grant or a certificate of incorporation); leased or hired.
>
> CONNOTATIONS: Defined, limited, restricted, channeled, mapped, bound by law; bought and sold (like a slave or an inanimate object); Magna Carta; charters given to crown colonies by the King.
>
> OTHER WORDS IN THE POEM WITH SIMILAR CONNOTATIONS: *Ban,* which can denote (1) a legal prohibition; (2) a churchman's curse or malediction; (3) in medieval times, an order summoning a king's vassals to fight for him. *Manacles,* or shackles, restrain movement. *Chimney-sweeper, soldier,* and *harlot* are all hirelings.
>
> INTERPRETATION OF THE LINES: The street has had mapped out for it the direction in which it must go; the Thames has had laid down to it the course it must follow. Street and river are channeled, imprisoned, enslaved (like every inhabitant of London).

black'ning (line 10)

> DENOTATION: Becoming black.
>
> CONNOTATIONS: The darkening of something once light, the defilement of something once clean, the deepening of guilt, the gathering of darkness at the approach of night.
>
> OTHER WORDS IN THE POEM WITH SIMILAR CONNOTATIONS: Objects becoming marked or smudged (*marks of weakness, marks of woe* in the faces of passers-by; bloodied walls of a palace; marriage blighted with plagues); the word *appalls* (denoting not only "to overcome with horror" but "to make pale" and also "to cast a pall or shroud over"); *midnight streets.*
>
> INTERPRETATION OF THE LINE: Literally, every London church grows black from soot and hires a chimney-sweeper (a small boy) to help clean it. But Blake suggests too that by profiting from the suffering of the child laborer, the church is soiling its original purity.

Blasts, blights (lines 15, 16)

> DENOTATIONS: Both *blast* and *blight* mean "to cause to wither" or "to ruin and destroy." Both are terms from horticulture. Frost *blasts* a bud and kills it; disease *blights* a growing plant.

CONNOTATIONS: Sickness and death; gardens shriveled and dying; gusts of wind and the ravages of insects; things blown to pieces or rotted and warped.

OTHER WORDS IN THE POEM WITH SIMILAR CONNOTATIONS: Faces marked with weakness and woe; the child becomes a chimney-sweep; the soldier killed by war; blackening church and bloodied palace; young girl turned harlot; wedding carriage transformed into a hearse.

INTERPRETATION OF THE LINES: Literally, the harlot spreads the plague of syphilis, which, carried into marriage, can cause a baby to be born blind. In a larger and more meaningful sense, Blake sees the prostitution of even one young girl corrupting the entire institution of matrimony and endangering every child.

Some of these connotations are more to the point than others; the reader of a poem nearly always has the problem of distinguishing relevant associations from irrelevant ones. We need to read a poem in its entirety and, when a word leaves us in doubt, look for other things in the poem to corroborate or refute what we think it means. Relatively simple and direct in its statement, Blake's account of his stroll through the city at night becomes an indictment of a whole social and religious order. The indictment could hardly be this effective if it were "mathematically plain," its every word restricted to one denotation clearly spelled out.

Wallace Stevens   (1879–1955)*

DISILLUSIONMENT OF TEN O'CLOCK   1923

The houses are haunted
By white night-gowns.
None are green,
Or purple with green rings,
Or green with yellow rings,   5
Or yellow with blue rings.
None of them are strange,
With socks of lace
And beaded ceintures.
People are not going   10
To dream of baboons and periwinkles.
Only, here and there, an old sailor,
Drunk and asleep in his boots,
Catches tigers
In red weather.   15

1. What are *beaded ceintures?* What does the phrase suggest?
2. What contrast does Stevens draw between the people who live in these houses and the old sailor? What do the connotations of *white night-gowns* and *sailor* add to this contrast?
3. What is lacking in these people who wear white night-gowns? Why should the poet's view of them be a "disillusionment"?

Gwendolyn Brooks   (1917–2000)*

THE INDEPENDENT MAN   1945

Now who could take you off to tiny life
In one room or in two rooms or in three
And cork you smartly, like the flask of wine
You are? Not any woman. Not a wife.
You'd let her twirl you, give her a good glee   5
Showing your leaping ruby to a friend.
Though twirling would be meek. Since not a cork
Could you allow, for being made so free.

A woman would be wise to think it well
If once a week you only rang the bell.   10

QUESTIONS

1. The poem is addressed to its title character. What can we infer about his personality from the details in lines 1–8?
2. In the last two lines, the poet doesn't explain why "a woman would be wise . . . ," etc. Has she told us enough so that we can supply the explanation ourselves?

Timothy Steele   (b. 1948)*

EPITAPH   1979

Here lies Sir Tact, a diplomatic fellow
Whose silence was not golden, but just yellow.

QUESTIONS

1. To what famous saying does the poet allude?
2. What are the connotations of *golden?* Of *yellow?*

Geoffrey Hill   (b. 1932)

MERLIN   1959

I will consider the outnumbering dead:
For they are the husks of what was rich seed.
Now, should they come together to be fed,
They would outstrip the locusts' covering tide.

Arthur, Elaine, Mordred; they are all gone   5
Among the raftered galleries of bone.
By the long barrows of Logres they are made one,
And over their city stands the pinnacled corn.

MERLIN. In medieval legend, Merlin was a powerful magician and a seer, an aide of King Arthur.
5 *Elaine:* in Arthurian romance, the beloved of Sir Launcelot. *Mordred:* Arthur's treacherous nephew
by whose hand the king died. 7 *barrows:* earthworks for burial of the dead. *Logres:* name of an ancient
British kingdom, according to the twelfth-century historian Geoffrey of Monmouth, who gathered
the legends of King Arthur.

QUESTIONS

1. What does the title "Merlin" contribute to this poem? Do you prefer to read the
   poem as though it is Merlin who speaks to us—or the poet?
2. Line 4 alludes to the plague of locusts that God sent upon Egypt (Exodus 10): "For
   they covered the face of the whole earth, so that the land was darkened . . ." With
   this allusion in mind, explain the comparison of the dead to locusts.
3. Why are the suggestions inherent in the names of *Arthur, Elaine,* and *Mordred* more
   valuable to this poem than those we might find in the names of other dead persons
   called, say, Gus, Tessie, and Butch?
4. Explain the phrase in line 6: *the raftered galleries of bone.*
5. In the last line, what *city* does the poet refer to? Does he mean some particular city,
   or is he making a comparison?
6. What is interesting in the adjective *pinnacled?* How can it be applied to corn?

Walter de la Mare   (1873–1956)

THE LISTENERS   1912

"Is there anybody there?" said the Traveller,
    Knocking on the moonlit door;
And his horse in the silence champed the grasses
    Of the forest's ferny floor:
And a bird flew up out of the turret,   5
    Above the Traveller's head:
And he smote upon the door again a second time;
    "Is there anybody there?" he said.

But no one descended to the Traveller;
    No head from the leaf-fringed sill   10
Leaned over and looked into his gray eyes,
    Where he stood perplexed and still.
But only a host of phantom listeners
    That dwelt in the lone house then
Stood listening in the quiet of the moonlight   15
    To that voice from the world of men:
Stood thronging the faint moonbeams on the dark stair
    That goes down to the empty hall,
Hearkening in an air stirred and shaken
    By the lonely Traveller's call.   20
And he felt in his heart their strangeness,
    Their stillness answering his cry,
While his horse moved, cropping the dark turf,
    'Neath the starred and leafy sky;
For he suddenly smote on the door, even   25
    Louder, and lifted his head:—
"Tell them I came, and no one answered,
    That I kept my word," he said.
Never the least stir made the listeners,
    Though every word he spake   30
Fell echoing through the shadowiness of the still house
    From the one man left awake:
Ay, they heard his foot upon the stirrup,
    And the sound of iron on stone,
And how the silence surged softly backward,   35
    When the plunging hoofs were gone.

QUESTIONS

1. Before you had read this poem, what suggestions did its title bring to mind?
2. Now that you have read the poem, what do you make of these "listeners"? Who or what do you imagine them to be?
3. Why is *the moonlit door* (in line 2) a phrase more valuable to this poem than if the poet had written simply "the door"?
4. What does *turret* (in line 5) suggest?
5. Reconstruct some earlier events that might have preceded the Traveller's visit. Who might this Traveller be? Who are the unnamed persons—"them" (line 27)—for whom the Traveller leaves a message? What promise has he kept? (The poet doesn't tell us; we can only guess.)
6. Do you think this poem any the worse for the fact that its setting, characters, and action are so mysterious? What does "The Listeners" gain from not telling us all?

Robert Frost (1874–1963)*

FIRE AND ICE   1923

Some say the world will end in fire,
Some say in ice.
From what I've tasted of desire
I hold with those who favor fire.
But if it had to perish twice,   5
I think I know enough of hate
To say that for destruction ice
Is also great
And would suffice.

QUESTIONS

1. To whom does Frost refer in line 1? In line 2?
2. What connotations of *fire* and *ice* contribute to the richness of Frost's comparison?

Clare Rossini (b. 1954)

FINAL LOVE NOTE   1997

For months we've been together, hardly wanton,
Never touching. Yet your shade commingled
With my clothes strewn on the floor, and your wind
Moaned over me at night, never tiring
As human lovers do. My lifted garden,   5
Pure-green, wooden-hearted, all your leaves moved
Summer-long, then suddenly caught fire.
In winter I endured your silences,
My sight tangled in your black network
Which trapped whatever moon was on the rise.   10

This summer, the slugs ate the yellow hearts
Right out of my lilies, while you, elm, died on—

Dying as you have for years, leafless branches
Subdividing your shade. Slowly the sun
Found more of my roof, the attic grew hotter.   15
Some nights, the heat would not leave my bed
Until two or three, while I tossed and turned
In my abandonment.

                    This morning,
I hear the chain saw cry out ecstatically.
My heart beats. Then a dull thunder shakes the house.   20

Your many arms are falling. And I must live
More with sky now, that garish blue stretch
Or drafty ceiling harshly lit by stars.

QUESTIONS

1. What do the images of the opening lines suggest about the speaker's feelings toward the elm tree?
2. A factual summary of this poem might state merely that "the speaker misses the shade of a dying elm tree that had to be cut down." What does that summary not suggest about the full effect of the poem?
3. Does the poem become more or less effective because of the equation of the tree with a lost lover? Defend your opinion with lines from the poem that you especially like or dislike.

Alfred, Lord Tennyson   (1809–1892)*

TEARS, IDLE TEARS   1847

Tears, idle tears, I know not what they mean,
Tears from the depth of some divine despair
Rise in the heart, and gather to the eyes,
In looking on the happy autumn-fields,
And thinking of the days that are no more.   5

Fresh as the first beam glittering on a sail,
That brings our friends up from the underworld,
Sad as the last which reddens over one
That sinks with all we love below the verge;
So sad, so fresh, the days that are no more.   10

Ah, sad and strange as in dark summer dawns
The earliest pipe of half-awakened birds
To dying ears, when unto dying eyes
The casement slowly grows a glimmering square;
So sad, so strange, the days that are no more.   15

Dear as remembered kisses after death,
And sweet as those by hopeless fancy feigned
On lips that are for others; deep as love,
Deep as first love, and wild with all regret;
O Death in Life, the days that are no more!   20

Richard Wilbur (b. 1921)*

LOVE CALLS US TO THE THINGS   1956
OF THIS WORLD

The eyes open to a cry of pulleys,
And spirited from sleep, the astounded soul
Hangs for a moment bodiless and simple
As false dawn.
              Outside the open window
The morning air is all awash with angels.   5

Some are in bed-sheets, some are in blouses,
Some are in smocks: but truly there they are.
Now they are rising together in calm swells
Of halcyon feeling, filling whatever they wear
With the deep joy of their impersonal breathing;   10

Now they are flying in place, conveying
The terrible speed of their omnipresence, moving
And staying like white water; and now of a sudden
They swoon down into so rapt a quiet
That nobody seems to be there.
                      The soul shrinks   15

From all that it is about to remember,
From the punctual rape of every blessèd day,
And cries,
        "Oh, let there be nothing on earth but laundry,
Nothing but rosy hands in the rising steam
And clear dances done in the sight of heaven."   20

Yet, as the sun acknowledges
With a warm look the world's hunks and colors,
The soul descends once more in bitter love
To accept the waking body, saying now
In a changed voice as the man yawns and rises,   25

"Bring them down from their ruddy gallows;
Let there be clean linen for the backs of thieves;
Let lovers go fresh and sweet to be undone,
And the heaviest nuns walk in a pure floating
Of dark habits,
              keeping their difficult balance."   30

LOVE CALLS US TO THE THINGS OF THIS WORLD. Wilbur claimed that his title was taken from St. Augustine, but in a recent interview he admitted that neither he nor any critic has ever been able to locate the quotation again. Whatever its source, however, the title establishes the poem's central idea that love allows us to return from the divine world of the spirit to the imperfect world of our everyday lives. Wilbur's own comments on the poem are printed following.

Questions

1. What are the *angels* in line 5? Why does this metaphor seem appropriate to the situation?
2. What is "the punctual rape of every blessed day?" Who is being raped? Who or what commits the rape? Why would Wilbur choose this particular word with all its violent associations?
3. Who or what does the soul love in line 23, and why is that love bitter?
4. Is it merely obesity that make the nuns' balance "difficult" in the two final lines of the poem? What other "balance" does Wilbur's poem suggest?
5. The soul has two speeches in the poem. How do they differ in tone and imagery?
6. The spiritual world is traditionally considered invisible. What concrete images does Wilbur use to express its special character?

WRITER'S PERSPECTIVE

Richard Wilbur

Richard Wilbur *on Writing*

CONCERNING "LOVE CALLS US TO THE THINGS OF THIS WORLD"

1966

If I understand this poem rightly, it has a free and organic rhythm: that is to say, its movement arises naturally from the emotion, and from the things and actions described. At the same time, the lines are metrical and disposed in stanzas. The subject matter is both exalted and vulgar. There is, I should think, sufficient description to satisfy an Imagist, but there is also a certain amount of statement; my hope is that the statement seems to grow inevitably out of the situation described. The language of the poem is at one moment elevated and at the next colloquial or slangy: for example, the imposing word "omnipresence" occurs not far from the undignified word "hunks." A critic would find in this poem certain patterns of sound, but those patterns of sound do not constitute an abstract music; they are meant, at any rate, to be inseparable from what is being said, a subordinate aspect of the poem's meaning.

The title of the poem is a quotation from St. Augustine: "Love Calls Us to the Things of This World." You must imagine the poem as occurring at perhaps seven-thirty in the morning; the scene is a bedroom high up in a city apartment building; outside the bedroom window, the first laundry of the day is being yanked across the sky, and one has been awakened by the squeaking pulleys of the laundry-line.

From "On My Own Work"

═══ WRITING CRITICALLY ═══

The Ways a Poem Suggests

If we open the front door and find a friend standing there in hysterical tears, the person does not need to say "I'm miserable." We see that already. In a like manner, poems suggest some messages so clearly through imagery, tone, and diction that they do not need to declare them overtly. Poetry is a special way of speaking that requires a special way of listening. Poetry does not merely speak to the analytical parts of our minds but to the wholeness of our humanity. A good poem invites us to become fully alive and respond with our intuition, imagination, emotions, and intelligence. It even speaks to our physical bodies through sound, rhythm, and sensory imagery.

Since poems speak to us so completely, they often convey their meaning indirectly. An image may express something so clearly that the poem does not need to repeat it explicitly. In this sense, poems operate no differently from daily life.

In writing about a poem, listen carefully to everything it is telling you. Before beginning your essay, jot down a few key observations both about what the poem tells us and what we might want to know but aren't told. Note anything important to the story or situation of the poem that we have to infer for ourselves. When journalists write a news story, they always try to cover the "five W's" in their opening paragraph—*who, what, where, when, why*. These may be worthwhile questions to ask about a poem. If one or more of them is missing, how does that affect our understanding of the poem?

1. *Who?* Who is the speaker or central figure of the poem? (In Blake's "London," for instance, the speaker is also the protagonist who witnesses the hellish horror of the city.)
2. *What?* What is being seen or presented? Does the poem ever suddenly change its subject? (In Stevens's "Disillusionment at Ten O'Clock," for example, there are essentially two scenes—one dull and proper, the other wild and disreputable. What does that obvious shift suggest about Stevens's meaning?)
3. *Where?* Where is the poem set? Does the setting so clearly suggest something important that the rest of the poem does not need to repeat the message. (The setting of De la Mare's "The Listeners" goes a long way toward creating the mood that the poet wants to evoke.)

4. *When?* When does the poem take place? If a poet explicitly states a time of day or time of year, it is very likely that the *when* of the poem is important. (The fact that Stevens's poem takes place at 10:00 P.M. rather than 2:00 A.M. tells us a great deal about the people it describes.)

5. *Why?* If the poem describes some dramatic action but does not tell us *why* it is being performed, perhaps the author wants us to ponder the situation carefully. (De la Mare's "The Listeners" gains extra mystery by leaving us in the dark about the people involved, and Tennyson's "Tears, Idle Tears" becomes more evocative by not being explicit about why the speaker weeps.)

You don't have to answer all the questions, but it will help to ask them. Remember, it is almost as important to know what a poem doesn't tell us as what it does.

WRITING ASSIGNMENT

In a short essay (750–1000 words) explain why the speaker in Alfred, Lord Tennyson's "Tears, Idle Tears" (page 785) is weeping. Although the speaker claims not to know what the tears mean, the poem's language and imagery suggest some compelling reasons. Support your theory with specific examples. Be sure to differentiate between evidence that the poem explicitly provides and where an idea or event is only suggested. Feel free to extrapolate slightly beyond the limits of the poem, but *state clearly* where your interpretation goes beyond the literal meaning of the words and where it sticks closely to the text.

FURTHER SUGGESTIONS FOR WRITING

1. In a short essay, analyze a poem full of words that radiate suggestions. Looking into "Poems for Further Reading," you might consider T. S. Eliot's "The Love Song of J. Alfred Prufrock," John Keats's "To Autumn," Sylvia Plath's "Daddy," or many others. Focus on particular words: explain their connotations and show how these suggestions are part of the poem's meaning. (For guidelines on writing about poetry by the method of analysis, see "Writing About a Poem.")

2. In a current newspaper or magazine, select an advertisement that tries to surround a product with an aura. A new car, for instance, might be described in terms of some powerful jungle cat ("purring power, ready to spring"). Likely hunting-grounds for such ads are magazines that cater to the affluent (*New Yorker, Vogue,* and others). Clip or photocopy the ad and circle words in it that seem especially suggestive. Then, in an accompanying paper, unfold the suggestions in these words and try to explain the ad's appeal. How is the purpose of connotative language used in advertising copy different from that of such language when used in poetry?

16 *Imagery*

Ezra Pound   (1885–1972)*

IN A STATION OF THE METRO   1916

The apparition of these faces in the crowd;
Petals on a wet, black bough.

    Pound said he wrote this poem to convey an experience: emerging one day from a train in the Paris subway (*Métro*), he beheld "suddenly a beautiful face, and then another and another." Originally he had described his impression in a poem thirty lines long. In this final version, each line contains an image, which, like a picture, may take the place of a thousand words.

    Though the term **image** suggests a thing seen, when speaking of images in poetry, we generally mean *a word or sequence of words that refers to any sensory experience*. Often this experience is a sight (**visual imagery,** as in Pound's poem), but it may be a sound (**auditory imagery**) or a touch (**tactile imagery,** as a perception of roughness or smoothness). It may be an odor or a taste or perhaps a bodily sensation such as pain, the prickling of gooseflesh, the quenching of thirst, or—as in the following brief poem—the perception of something cold.

Taniguchi Buson   (1716–1783)*

THE PIERCING CHILL I FEEL   (ABOUT 1760)

The piercing chill I feel:
   my dead wife's comb, in our bedroom,
     under my heel . . .
         —Translated by Harold G. Henderson

As in this haiku (in Japanese, a poem of about seventeen syllables) an image can convey a flash of understanding. Had he wished, the poet might have spoken of the dead woman, of the contrast between her death and his memory of her, of his feelings toward death in general. But such a discussion would be quite different from the poem he actually wrote. Striking his bare foot against the comb, now cold and motionless but associated with the living wife (perhaps worn in her hair), the widower feels a shock as if he had touched the woman's corpse. A literal, physical sense of death is conveyed; the abstraction "death" is understood through the senses. To render the abstract in concrete terms is what poets often try to do; in this attempt, an image can be valuable.

An image may occur in a single word, a phrase, a sentence, or, as in this case, an entire short poem. To speak of the **imagery** of a poem—all its images taken together—is often more useful than to speak of separate images. To divide Buson's haiku into five images—*chill, wife, comb, bedroom, heel*—is possible, for any noun that refers to a visible object or a sensation is an image, but this is to draw distinctions that in themselves mean little and to disassemble a single experience.

Does an image cause a reader to experience a sense impression? Not quite. Reading the word *petals*, no one literally sees petals; but the occasion is given for imagining them. The image asks to be seen with the mind's eye. And although "In a Station of the Metro" records what Ezra Pound saw, it is of course not necessary for a poet actually to have lived through a sensory experience in order to write of it. Keats may never have seen a newly discovered planet through a telescope, despite the image in his sonnet on Chapman's Homer (page 1199).

It is tempting to think of imagery as mere decoration, particularly when we read Keats, who fills his poems with an abundance of sights, sounds, odors, and tastes. But a successful image is not just a dab of paint or a flashy bauble. When Keats opens "The Eve of St. Agnes" with what have been called the coldest lines in literature, he evokes by a series of images a setting and a mood:

> St. Agnes' eve—Ah, bitter chill it was!
> The owl, for all his feathers, was a-cold;
> The hare limped trembling through the frozen grass,
> And silent was the flock in woolly fold:
> Numb were the Beadsman's fingers, while he told
> His rosary, and while his frosted breath,
> Like pious incense from a censer old,
> Seemed taking flight for heaven, without a death, . . .

Indeed, some literary critics look for much of the meaning of a poem in its imagery, wherein they expect to see the mind of the poet more truly revealed than in whatever the poet explicitly claims to believe. Though Shakespeare's Theseus (in *A Midsummer Night's Dream*) accuses poets of being concerned with "airy nothings," poets are usually very much concerned with what is in front of them. This concern is of use to us. Perhaps, as Alan Watts has remarked, Americans are not the materialists they are sometimes accused of being. How could anyone taking a look at an American city think that its inhabitants deeply cherish material things? Involved in our personal hopes and apprehensions, anticipating the future so hard that much of the time we see the present through a film of thought across our eyes, perhaps we need a poet occasionally to remind us that even the coffee we absentmindedly sip comes in (as Yeats put it) a "heavy spillable cup."

T. S. Eliot   (1888–1965)*

THE WINTER EVENING SETTLES DOWN   1917

The winter evening settles down
With smell of steaks in passageways.
Six o'clock.
The burnt-out ends of smoky days.
And now a gusty shower wraps   5
The grimy scraps
Of withered leaves about your feet
And newspapers from vacant lots;
The showers beat
On broken blinds and chimney-pots,   10
And at the corner of the street
A lonely cab-horse steams and stamps.

And then the lighting of the lamps.

QUESTIONS

1. What mood is evoked by the images in Eliot's poem?
2. What kind of city neighborhood has the poet chosen to describe? How can you tell?

Theodore Roethke   (1908–1963)*

ROOT CELLAR   1948

Nothing would sleep in that cellar, dank as a ditch,
Bulbs broke out of boxes hunting for chinks in the dark,
Shoots dangled and drooped,
Lolling obscenely from mildewed crates,
Hung down long yellow evil necks, like tropical snakes.   5
And what a congress of stinks!—
Roots ripe as old bait,
Pulpy stems, rank, silo-rich,
Leaf-mold, manure, lime, piled against slippery planks.

Nothing would give up life:
Even the dirt kept breathing a small breath.

QUESTIONS

1. As a boy growing up in Saginaw, Michigan, Theodore Roethke spent much of his
   time in a large commercial greenhouse run by his family. What details in his poem
   show more than a passing acquaintance with growing things?
2. What varieties of image does "Root Cellar" contain? Point out examples.
3. What do you understand to be Roethke's attitude toward the root cellar? Does he
   view it as a disgusting chamber of horrors? Pay special attention to the last two lines.

Elizabeth Bishop   (1911–1979)*

THE FISH   1946

I caught a tremendous fish
and held him beside the boat
half out of water, with my hook
fast in a corner of his mouth.
He didn't fight.   5
He hadn't fought at all.
He hung a grunting weight,
battered and venerable
and homely. Here and there
his brown skin hung in strips   10
like ancient wall-paper,
and its pattern of darker brown
was like wall-paper:
shapes like full-blown roses
stained and lost through age.   15
He was speckled with barnacles,
fine rosettes of lime,
and infested
with tiny white sea-lice,
and underneath two or three   20
rags of green weed hung down.
While his gills were breathing in
the terrible oxygen
—the frightening gills,
fresh and crisp with blood,   25
that can cut so badly—
I thought of the coarse white flesh
packed in like feathers,
the big bones and the little bones,
the dramatic reds and blacks   30

of his shiny entrails,
and the pink swim-bladder
like a big peony.
I looked into his eyes
which were far larger than mine
but shallower, and yellowed,
the irises backed and packed
with tarnished tinfoil
seen through the lenses
of old scratched isinglass.
They shifted a little, but not
to return my stare.
—It was more like the tipping
of an object toward the light.
I admired his sullen face,
the mechanism of his jaw,
and then I saw
that from his lower lip
—if you could call it a lip—
grim, wet, and weapon-like,
hung five old pieces of fish-line,
or four and a wire leader
with the swivel still attached,
with all their five big hooks
grown firmly in his mouth.
A green line, frayed at the end
where he broke it, two heavier lines,
and a fine black thread
still crimped from the strain and snap
when it broke and he got away.
Like medals with their ribbons
frayed and wavering,
a five-haired beard of wisdom
trailing from his aching jaw.
I stared and stared
and victory filled up
the little rented boat,
from the pool of bilge
where oil had spread a rainbow
around the rusted engine
to the bailer rusted orange,
the sun-cracked thwarts,
the oarlocks on their strings,
the gunnels—until everything
was rainbow, rainbow, rainbow!
And I let the fish go.

1. How many abstract words does this poem contain? What proportion of the poem is imagery?
2. What is the speaker's attitude toward the fish? Comment in particular on lines 61–64.
3. What attitude do the images of the rainbow of oil (line 69), the orange bailer (bailing bucket, line 71), the *sun-cracked thwarts* (line 72) convey? Does the poet expect us to feel mournful because the boat is in such sorry condition?
4. What is meant by *rainbow, rainbow, rainbow*?
5. How do these images prepare us for the conclusion? Why does the speaker let the fish go?

Anne Stevenson (b. 1933)*

THE VICTORY   1974

I thought you were my victory
though you cut me like a knife
when I brought you out of my body
into your life.

Tiny antagonist, gory,   5
blue as a bruise. The stains
of your cloud of glory
bled from my veins.

How can you dare, blind thing,
blank insect eyes?   10
You barb the air. You sting
with bladed cries.

Snail! Scary knot of desires!
Hungry snarl! Small son.
Why do I have to love you?   15
How have you won?

QUESTIONS

1. Newborn babies are often described as "little angels" or "bundles of joy." How does the speaker of "The Victory" describe her son?
2. Why does the speaker describe the child as an "antagonist" (line 5)?
3. Why is the poem titled "The Victory"?
4. Why is the infant compared to a knife in both lines 2 and 12?

Charles Simic (b. 1938)*

FORK   1969

This strange thing must have crept
Right out of hell.
It resembles a bird's foot
Worn around the cannibal's neck.

As you hold it in your hand,   5
As you stab with it into a piece of meat,
It is possible to imagine the rest of the bird:
Its head which like your fist
Is large, bald, beakless, and blind.

QUESTIONS

1. The title image of this poem is an ordinary and everyday object. What happens to it
   in the first two lines?
2. How does the word *crept* in line 1 change our sense of the fork? How does the author
   develop this new sense later in the poem?

Emily Dickinson (1830–1886)*

A ROUTE OF EVANESCENCE   (1879)

A Route of Evanescence
With a revolving Wheel –
A Resonance of Emerald –
A Rush of Cochineal° –   *red dye*
And every Blossom on the Bush   5
Adjusts its tumbled Head –
The mail from Tunis, probably,
An easy Morning's Ride –

A ROUTE OF EVANESCENCE. Dickinson titled this poem "A Humming-bird" in an 1880 letter to a
friend. 1 *Evanescence*; ornithologist's term for the luminous sheen of certain birds' feathers. 7 *Tunis*:
capital city of Tunisia, North Africa.

QUESTIONS

What is the subject of this poem? How can you tell?

Jean Toomer   (1894–1967)

REAPERS   1923

Black reapers with the sound of steel on stones
Are sharpening scythes. I see them place the hones
In their hip-pockets as a thing that's done,
And start their silent swinging, one by one.
Black horses drive a mower through the weeds,   5
And there, a field rat, startled, squealing bleeds,
His belly close to ground. I see the blade,
Blood-stained, continue cutting weeds and shade.

QUESTIONS

1. Imagine the scene Jean Toomer describes. Which particulars most vividly strike the mind's eye?
2. What kind of image is *silent swinging?*
3. Read the poem aloud. Notice especially the effect of the words *sound of steel on stones* and *field rat, startled, squealing bleeds.* What interesting sounds are present in the very words that contain these images?
4. What feelings do you get from this poem as a whole? Would you agree with someone who said, "This poem gives us a sense of happy, carefree life down on the farm, close to nature"? Exactly what in "Reapers" makes you feel the way you do? Besides appealing to our auditory and visual imagination, what do the images contribute?

Gerard Manley Hopkins   (1844–1889)*

PIED BEAUTY   (1877)

Glory be to God for dappled things—
     For skies of couple-color as a brinded° cow;   streaked
        For rose-moles all in stipple upon trout that swim;
Fresh-firecoal chestnut-falls; finches' wings;
     Landscape plotted and pieced—fold, fallow, and plow;   5
        And áll trádes, their gear and tackle and trim.°   equipment

All things counter, original, spare, strange;
     Whatever is fickle, freckled (who know how?)
        With swift, slow; sweet, sour; adazzle, dim;
He fathers-forth whose beauty is past change: 10
        Praise him.

QUESTIONS

1. What does the word *pied* mean? (Hint: what does a Pied Piper look like?)
2. According to Hopkins, what do *skies, cow, trout, ripe chestnuts, finches' wings,* and *landscapes* all have in common? What landscapes can the poet have in mind? (Have

you ever seen any *dappled* landscape while looking down from an airplane, or from a mountain or high hill?)

3. What do you make of line 6: what can carpenters' saws and ditch-diggers' spades possibly have in common with the dappled things in lines 2–4?

4. Does Hopkins refer only to contrasts that meet the eye? What other kinds of variation interest him?

5. Try to state in your own words the theme of this poem. How essential to our understanding of this theme are Hopkins's images?

ABOUT HAIKU

Arakida Moritake   (1473–1549)

THE FALLING FLOWER

The falling flower
I saw drift back to the branch
Was a butterfly.

—Translated by Babette Deutsch

Haiku means "beginning-verse" in Japanese—perhaps because the form may have originated in a game. Players, given a haiku, were supposed to extend its three lines into a longer poem. Haiku (the word can also be plural) consist mainly of imagery, but as we saw in Buson's lines about the cold comb, their imagery is not always only pictorial; it can also involve any of the five senses. Haiku are so short that they depend on imagery to trigger associations and responses in the reader. A haiku in Japanese is rimeless; its seventeen syllables are traditionally arranged in three lines, usually following a pattern of five, seven, and five syllables. English haiku frequently ignore such a pattern, being rimed or unrimed as the poet prefers. What English haiku do try to preserve is the powerful way Japanese haiku capture the intensity of a particular moment, usually by linking two concrete images. There is little room for abstract thoughts or general observations. The following attempt, though containing seventeen syllables, is far from haiku in spirit:

> Now that our love is gone
> I feel within my soul
> a nagging distress.

Unlike the author of those lines, haiku poets look out upon a literal world, seldom looking inward to *discuss* their feelings. Japanese haiku tend to be seasonal in subject, but because they are so highly compressed, they usually just *imply* a season: a blossom indicates spring; a crow on a branch, autumn; snow, winter. Not just pretty little sketches of nature (as some Westerners think), haiku assume a view of the universe in which observer and nature are not separated.

Haiku emerged in sixteenth-century Japan and soon developed into a deeply esteemed form. Even today, Japanese soldiers, stockbrokers, scientists, schoolchildren, and even the emperor still find occasion to pen haiku. Soon after the form first captured the attention of Western poets at the end of the nineteenth century, it became immensely influential for modern poets such as Ezra Pound, William Carlos Williams, and H. D., as a model for the kind of verse they wanted to write—concise, direct, and imagistic.

The Japanese consider the poems of the "Three Masters"—Basho, Buson, and Issa—to be the pinnacle of the classical haiku. Each poet had his own personality: Basho, the ascetic seeker of Zen enlightenment; Buson, the worldly artist; Issa, the sensitive master of wit and pathos. Here are free translations of poems from each of the "Three Masters."

Matsuo Basho (1644–1694)*

HEAT-LIGHTNING STREAK

Heat-lightning streak—
through darkness pierces
the heron's shriek.

IN THE OLD STONE POOL

In the old stone pool
a frogjump:
splishhhhh.
—*Translations by X. J. Kennedy*

Taniguchi Buson (1716–1783)*

ON THE ONE-TON TEMPLE BELL

On the one-ton temple bell
a moonmoth, folded into sleep,
sits still.
—*Translated by X. J. Kennedy*

I GO

I go,
you stay;
two autumns.
—*Translated by Robert Hass*

Kobayashi Issa (1763–1827)*

ONLY ONE GUY

only one guy and
only one fly trying to
make the guest room do.
—*Translated by Cid Corman*

CRICKET

Cricket, be
careful! I'm rolling
over!
—*Translated by Robert Bly*

Japanese immigrants brought the tradition of haiku-writing to the United States, often forming local clubs to pursue their shared literary interests. During World War II, when Japanese Americans were unjustly considered "enemy aliens" and confined to federal internment camps, these poets continued to write in their bleak new surroundings. Today these haiku provide a vivid picture of the deprivations suffered by the poets, their families, and their fellow internees.

Suiko Matsushita

Rain shower from mountain
quietly soaking
barbed wire fence

Cosmos in bloom
as if no war
were taking place
—*Translations by Violet Kazue de Cristoro*

Neiji Ozawa

War forced us from California
No ripples this day
on desert lake

The war—this year
New Year midnight bell
ringing in the desert
—*Translations by Violet Kazue de Cristoro*

Hakuro Wada

Even the croaking of frogs
comes from outside the barbed wire fence
this is our life
—*Translated by Violet Kazue de Cristoro*

If you care to try your hand at haiku-writing, here are a few suggestions: make every word matter. Include few adjectives, shun needless conjunctions. Set your poem in the present. ("Haiku," said Basho, "is simply what is happening in this place at this moment.") Like many writers of haiku, you may wish to confine your poem to what can be seen, heard, smelled, tasted, or touched. Mere sensory reports, however, will be meaningless unless they make the reader feel something.

Here are seven more recent haiku written in English. (Don't expect them all to observe a strict arrangement of seventeen syllables, however.) Haiku, in any language, is an art of few words, many suggestions. A haiku starts us thinking and telling. "So the reader," Raymond Roseliep wrote, "keeps getting on where the poet got off."

Making jazz swing in
Seventeen syllables AIN'T
No square poet's job.
          —Etheridge Knight

Visitor's Room—
everything bolted down
except my brother.
          — Lee Gurga

broken bowl
the pieces
still rocking.
          —Penny Harter

Born Again
she speaks excitedly
of death.
          —Jennifer Brutschy

THE LAZY MAN'S HAIKU
out in the night
a wheelbarrowful
of moonlight.
> —John Ridland

LAST HAIKU
No, wait a minute,
I can't be old already:
I'm just about to.
> —Connie Bensley

LEARNING TO SHAVE
(FATHER TEACHING SON)
   A nick on the jaw
The razor's edge of manhood
   Along the bloodline.
> — Adelle Foley

FOR REVIEW AND FURTHER STUDY

John Keats   (1795–1821)*

BRIGHT STAR! WOULD I WERE   (1819)
STEADFAST AS THOU ART

Bright star! would I were steadfast as thou art—
   Not in lone splendor hung aloft the night,
And watching, with eternal lids apart,
   Like Nature's patient, sleepless Eremite,°   *hermit*
The moving waters at their priest-like task   5
   Of pure ablution round earth's human shores,
Or gazing on the new soft-fallen mask
   Of snow upon the mountains and the moors—
No—yet still steadfast, still unchangeable,
   Pillowed upon my fair love's ripening breast,   10
To feel for ever its soft fall and swell,
   Awake for ever in a sweet unrest,
Still, still to hear her tender-taken breath,
And so live ever—or else swoon to death.

QUESTIONS

1. Stars are conventional symbols for love and a loved one. (Love, Shakespeare tells us in a sonnet, "is the star to every wandering bark.") In this sonnet, why is it not possible for the star to have this meaning? How does Keats use it?
2. What seems concrete and particular in the speaker's observations?
3. Suppose Keats had said *slow and easy* instead of *tender-taken* in line 13. What would have been lost?

EXPERIMENT: *Writing with Images*

Taking the following poems as examples from which to start rather than as models to be slavishly copied, try to compose a brief poem that consists largely of imagery.

Walt Whitman   (1819–1892)*

THE RUNNER   1867

On a flat road runs the well-train'd runner;
He is lean and sinewy, with muscular legs;
He is thinly clothed—he leans forward as he runs,
With lightly closed fists, and arms partially rais'd.

T. E. Hulme   (1883–1917)

IMAGE   (ABOUT 1910)

Old houses were scaffolding once
                    and workmen whistling.

Chana Bloch   (b. 1940)

TIRED SEX   1998

We're trying to strike a match in a matchbook
that has lain all winter under the woodpile:
damp sulphur
on sodden cardboard.
I catch myself yawning. Through the window   5
I watch that sparrow the cat
keeps batting around.

Like turning the pages of a book the teacher assigned—

You ought to read it, she said.
It's great literature.   10

Robert Bly (b. 1926)*

DRIVING TO TOWN LATE TO MAIL A LETTER   1962

It is a cold and snowy night. The main street is deserted.
The only things moving are swirls of snow.
As I lift the mailbox door, I feel its cold iron.
There is a privacy I love in this snowy night.
Driving around, I will waste more time.   5

Gary Snyder   (b. 1930)

PIUTE CREEK   1965

One granite ridge
A tree, would be enough
Or even a rock, a small creek,
A bark shred in a pool.
Hill beyond hill, folded and twisted   5
Tough trees crammed
In thin stone fractures
A huge moon on it all, is too much.
The mind wanders. A million
Summers, night air still and the rocks   10
Warm.   Sky over endless mountains.
All the junk that goes with being human
Drops away, hard rock wavers
Even the heavy present seems to fail
This bubble of a heart.   15
Words and books
Like a small creek off a high ledge
Gone in the dry air.

A clear, attentive mind
Has no meaning but that   20
Which sees is truly seen.
No one loves rock, yet we are here.
Night chills. A flick
In the moonlight
Slips into Juniper shadow: 25
Back there unseen
Cold proud eyes
Of Cougar or Coyote
Watch me rise and go.

H. D. [Hilda Doolittle]   (1886–1961)*

HEAT   1916

O wind, rend open the heat,
cut apart the heat,
rend it to tatters.

Fruit cannot drop
through this thick air—   5
fruit cannot fall into heat
that presses up and blunts
the points of pears
and rounds the grapes.

Cut the heat—   10
plough through it,
turning it on either side
of your path.

Louise Glück   (b. 1943)

MOCK ORANGE   1985

It is not the moon, I tell you.
It is these flowers
lighting the yard.

I hate them.
I hate them as I hate sex,   5
the man's mouth
sealing my mouth, the man's
paralyzing body—

and the cry that always escapes,
the low, humiliating   10
premise of union—

In my mind tonight
I hear the question and pursuing answer
fused in one sound
that mounts and mounts and then   15
is split into the old selves,
the tired antagonisms. Do you see?
We were made fools of.
And the scent of mock orange
drifts through the window.   20

How can I rest?
How can I be content
when there is still
that odor in the world?

MOCK ORANGE. The mock orange is a flowering shrub with especially fragrant white blossoms and fruit that resemble those of an orange tree.

Billy Collins   (b. 1941)*

EMBRACE   1988

You know the parlor trick.
Wrap your arms around your own body
and from the back it looks like
someone is embracing you,
her hands grasping your shirt,   5
her fingernails teasing your neck.

From the front it is another story.
You never looked so alone,
your crossed elbows and screwy grin.
You could be waiting for a tailor   10
to fit you for a straitjacket,
one that would hold you really tight.

John Haines   (b. 1924)

WINTER NEWS   1966

They say the wells
are freezing
at Northway where
the cold begins.

Oil tins bang   5
as evening comes on,
and clouds of
steaming breath drift
in the street.

Men go out to feed   10
the stiffening dogs,

the voice of the snowman
calls the white-
haired children home.

1. Which of the images in this poem strike you as the most vivid? To which senses do Haines's images appeal?
2. Why are the children described as "white-haired"?

Stevie Smith (1902–1971)*

NOT WAVING BUT DROWNING
1957

Nobody heard him, the dead man,
But still he lay moaning:
I was much further out than you thought
And not waving but drowning.

Poor chap, he always loved larking   5
And now he's dead
It must have been too cold for him his heart gave way,
They said.

Oh, no no no, it was too cold always
(Still the dead one lay moaning)   10
I was much too far out all my life
And not waving but drowning.

Ezra Pound

Ezra Pound on Writing

THE IMAGE   1913

An "Image" is that which presents an intellectual and emotional complex in an instant of time. I use the term "complex" rather in the technical sense employed by the newer psychologists, such as Hart, though we might not agree absolutely in our application.

It is the presentation of such a "complex" instantaneously which gives that sense of sudden liberation; that sense of freedom from time limits and space limits; that sense of sudden growth, which we experience in the presence of the greatest works of art.

It is better to present one Image in a lifetime than to produce voluminous works.

All this, however, some may consider open to debate. The immediate necessity is to tabulate A LIST OF DON'TS for those beginning to write verses. I can not put all of them into Mosaic negative.

Use no superfluous word, no adjective which does not reveal something.

Don't use such an expression as "dim lands *of peace*." It dulls the image. It mixes an abstraction with the concrete. It comes from the writer's not realizing that the natural object is always the *adequate* symbol.

Go in fear of abstractions. Do not retell in mediocre verse what has already been done in good prose. Don't think any intelligent person is going to be deceived when you try to shirk all the difficulties of the unspeakably difficult art of good prose by chopping your composition into line lengths.

From "A Few Don'ts"

Analyzing Images

To help you analyze how the imagery of a poem works, here is a simple exercise: Make a short list of the poem's key images. Be sure to write down the images in the order they appear in the poem, because the sequence of images is often as important as the images themselves. (For example, a poem whose images move from *sunlight* to *darkness* might well signify something different from one that begins with *darkness* and concludes with *sunlight*.) Remember that not all images are visual. Images can draw on any or all of the five senses. In jotting down images, don't omit key adjectives or other qualifying words. Those words are often your best clues to a poem's tone or perspective. (T. E. Hulme's image of "whistling" workmen on page 802, for instance, implies something happier than "sweating" workmen would.)

Let's try this method on a short poem. An initial list of images in Robert Bly's "Driving to Town Late to Mail a Letter" (page 803) might look something like this:

cold and snowy night
deserted main street
mailbox door—cold iron
snowy night (speaker *loves* its privacy)
speaker drives around (to waste time)

Did we forget anything? Yes, the title! Always look to a poem's title for guidance. Bly's title, for instance, contains several crucial images. Let's add them to the top of the list:

driving (to town)
late night
a letter (to be mailed)

Looking at our list, we see how the images provide an outline of the poem's story. We also see how Bly begins the poem without allowing us initially to understand how his speaker views the situation. Is driving to town late on a snowy evening a positive, negative, or neutral experience? By noting where (in line 4) the speaker reveals a subjective response to an image ("There is a privacy I love in this snowy night"), we also begin to grasp the overall emotional structure of the poem. We might also note on our list how the poem begins and ends with the same image (driving), but uses it for different effects at the two places. At the beginning the speaker is driving for the practical purpose of mailing a letter but at the end merely for the pure pleasure of it.

After adding a few notes on our list to capture these insights, we are ready to begin writing our paper. Without realizing it, we have already worked out a rough outline—all on a single sheet of paper or a few inches of computer screen.

WRITING ASSIGNMENT

Examining any poem in this chapter (or in "Poems for Further Reading"), demonstrate how its imagery helps communicate its general theme. Be specific in noting how each key image contributes to the poem's total effect. Feel free to consult criticism on the poem but make sure to credit any observation you borrow exactly from a critical source. (See the chapter "Writing About a Poem" for advice on both writing process and format guidelines.) Here is an essay written in response to this assignment by Becki Woods, a student of Mark Bernier, at Blinn College in Brenham, Texas.

Becki Woods

Professor Bernier

English 220

23 February 20xx

Elizabeth Bishop's Use of Imagery in "The Fish"

Upon first reading, Elizabeth Bishop's "The Fish" appears to be a simple fishing tale. A close investigation of the imagery in Bishop's highly detailed description, however, reveals a different sort of poem. The real theme of Bishop's poem is a compassion and respect for the fish's lifelong struggle to survive. By carefully and effectively describing the captured fish, his reaction to being caught, and the symbols of his past struggles to stay alive, Bishop creates, through her images of beauty, victory, and survival, something more than a simple tale.

The first four lines of the poem are quite ordinary and factual:

> I caught a tremendous fish
> and held him beside the boat
> half out of water, with my hook
> fast in a corner of his mouth. (1-4)

Except for <u>tremendous</u>, Bishop's persona uses no exaggerations--unlike most fishing stories--to set up the situation of catching the fish. The detailed description begins as the speaker recounts the event further, noticing

something signally important about the captive fish: "He
didn't fight" (5). At this point the poem begins to seem
unusual: most fish stories are about how ferociously the
prey resists being captured. The speaker also notes that the
"battered and venerable / and homely" fish offered no
resistance to being caught (8-9). The image of the
submissive attitude of the fish is essential to the theme of
the poem. It is his "utter passivity [that] makes [the
persona's] detailed scrutiny possible" (McNally 192).

Once the image of the passive fish has been
established, the speaker begins an examination of the fish
itself, noting that "Here and there / his brown skin hung in
strips / like ancient wall-paper" (9-11). By comparing the
fish's skin to wallpaper, the persona creates, as Sybil
Estess argues, "implicit suggestions of both artistry and
decay" (713). Images of peeling wallpaper are instantly
brought to mind. The comparison of the fish's skin and
wallpaper, though "helpful in conveying an accurate notion
of the fish's color to anyone with memories of Victorian
parlors and their yellowed wallpaper . . . is," according to
Nancy McNally, "even more useful in evoking the associations
of deterioration which usually surround such memories"
(192). The fish's faded beauty has been hinted at in the
comparison, thereby setting up the detailed imagery that
soon follows:

> He was speckled with barnacles,
> fine rosettes of lime,
> and infested
> with tiny white sea-lice,
> and underneath two or three
> rags of green weed hung down. (16-20)

The persona sees the fish as he is; the infestations
and faults are not left out of the description. Yet, at the

same time, the fisher "express[es] what [he/she] has sensed
of the character of the fish" (Estess 714).

Bishop's persona notices "shapes like full-blown roses
/ stained and lost through age" on the fish's skin (14-15).
The persona's perception of the fish's beauty is revealed
along with a recognition of its faded beauty, which is best
revealed in the description of the fish's being speckled
with barnacles and spotted with lime. However, the fisher
observes these spots and sees them as rosettes--as objects
of beauty, not just ugly brown spots. These images
contribute to the persona's recognition of beauty's having
become faded beauty.

The poem next turns to a description of the fish's
gills. The imagery in "While his gills were breathing in /
the terrible oxygen" (22-23) leads "to the very structure of
the creature" that is now dying (Hopkins 201). The
descriptions of the fish's interior beauty--"the coarse
white flesh / packed in like feathers," the colors "of his
shiny entrails," and his "pink swim-bladder / like a big
peony"--are reminders of the life that seems about to end
(27-28, 31-33).

The composite image of the fish's essential beauty--his
being alive--is developed further in the description of the
five fish hooks that the captive, living fish carries in his
lip:

> grim, wet, and weapon-like
> hung five old pieces of fish-line
> ....
> with all their five big hooks
> grown firmly in his mouth. (50-51, 54-55)

As if fascinated by them, the persona, observing how
the lines must have been broken during struggles to escape,
sees the hooks as "medals with their ribbons / frayed and

wavering, / a five-haired beard of wisdom / trailing from
his aching jaw" (61-64), and the fisher becomes enthralled
by re-created images of the fish's fighting desperately for
his life on at least five separate occasions--and winning.
Crale Hopkins suggests that "[i]n its capability not only
for mere existence, but for action, escaping from previous
anglers, the fish shares the speaker's humanity" (202), thus
revealing the fisher's deepening understanding of how he
must now act. The persona has "all along," notes Estess,
"describe[d] the fish not just with great detail but with an
imaginative empathy for the aquatic creature. In her more-
than-objective description, [the fisher] relates what
[he/she] has seen to be both the pride and poverty of the
fish" (715). It is at this point that the narrator of this
fishing tale has a moment of clarity. Realizing the fish's
history and the glory the fish has achieved in escaping
previous hookings, the speaker sees everything become,
"rainbow, rainbow, rainbow!" (75)--and then unexpectedly
lets the fish go.

　　Bishop's "The Fish" begins by describing an event that
might easily be a conventional story's climax: "I caught a
tremendous fish" (1). The poem, however, develops into a
highly detailed account of a fisher noticing both the age
and the faded beauty of the captive and his present beauty
and past glory as well. The fishing tale is not simply a
recounting of a capture; it is a gradually unfolding
epiphany in which the speaker sees the fish in an entirely
new light. The intensity of this encounter between an
apparently experienced fisher in a rented boat and battle-
hardened fish is delivered through the poet's skillful use
of imagery. It is through the description of the capture of
an aged fish that Bishop offers her audience her theme of
compassion derived from a respect for the struggle for
survival.

Works Cited

Bishop, Elizabeth. "The Fish." Literature:An Introduction to
    Fiction, Poetry, and Drama. Ed. X. J. Kennedy and Dana
    Gioia. 9th ed. New York: Longman, 2005. 793-94.

Estess, Sybil P. "Elizabeth Bishop: The Delicate Art of Map
    Making." Southern Review 13 (1977): 713-17.

Hopkins, Crale D. "Inspiration as Theme: Art and Nature in
    the Poetry of Elizabeth Bishop." Arizona Quarterly 32
    (1976): 200-02.

McNally, Nancy L. "Elizabeth Bishop: The Discipline of
    Description." Twentieth-Century Literature 11 (1966):
    192-94.

FURTHER SUGGESTIONS FOR WRITING

1. Choose, from "Poems for Further Reading," a poem that appeals to you. Then write a brief account of your experience in reading it, paying special attention to its imagery. What images strike you, and why? What do they contribute to the poem as a whole? Poems rich in imagery include Samuel Taylor Coleridge's "Kubla Khan," Robert Frost's "Birches," Charlotte Mew's "The Farmer's Bride," William Carlos Williams's "Spring and All (By the road to the contagious hospital)," and many more.

2. After you have read the haiku and the discussion of haiku-writing in this chapter, write three or four haiku of your own. Then write a brief prose account of your experience in writing them. What, if anything, did you find out?

17 *Figures of Speech*

WHY SPEAK FIGURATIVELY?

"I will speak daggers to her, but use none," says Hamlet, preparing to confront his mother. His statement makes sense only because we realize that *daggers* is to be taken two ways: literally (denoting sharp, pointed weapons) and nonliterally (referring to something that can be used *like* weapons—namely, words). Reading poetry, we often meet comparisons between two things whose similarity we have never noticed before. When Marianne Moore observes that a fir tree has "an emerald turkey-foot at the top," the result is a pleasure that poetry richly affords: the sudden recognition of likenesses.

A treetop like a turkey-foot, words like daggers—such comparisons are called **figures of speech.** In its broadest definition, a figure of speech may be said to occur whenever a speaker or writer, for the sake of freshness or emphasis, departs from the usual denotations of words. Certainly, when Hamlet says he will speak daggers, no one expects him to release pointed weapons from his lips, for *daggers* is not to be read solely for its denotation. Its connotations—sharp, stabbing, piercing, wounding—also come to mind, and we see ways in which words and daggers work alike. (Words too can hurt: by striking through pretenses, possibly, or by wounding their hearer's self-esteem.) In the statement "A razor is sharper than an ax," there is no departure from the usual denotations of *razor* and *ax*, and no figure of speech results. Both objects are of the same class; the comparison is not offensive to logic. But in "How sharper than a serpent's tooth it is to have a thankless child," the objects—snake's tooth (fang) and ungrateful offspring—are so unlike that no reasonable comparison may be made between them. To find similarity, we attend to the connotations of *serpent's tooth*—biting, piercing, venom, pain—rather than to its denotations. If we are aware of the connotations of *red rose* (beauty, softness, freshness, and so forth), then the line "My love is like a red, red rose" need not call to mind a woman with a scarlet face and a thorny neck.

Figures of speech are not devices to state what is demonstrably untrue. Indeed they often state truths that more literal language cannot communicate; they call attention to such truths; they lend them emphasis.

Alfred, Lord Tennyson (1809–1892)*

THE EAGLE   1851

He clasps the crag with crooked hands;
Close to the sun in lonely lands,
Ringed with the azure world, he stands.

The wrinkled sea beneath him crawls;
He watches from his mountain walls,   5
And like a thunderbolt he falls.

This brief poem is rich in figurative language. In the first line, the phrase *crooked hands* may surprise us. An eagle does not have hands, we might protest; but the objection would be a quibble, for evidently Tennyson is indicating exactly how an eagle clasps a crag, in the way that human fingers clasp a thing. By implication, too, the eagle is a person. *Close to the sun,* if taken literally, is an absurd exaggeration, the sun being a mean distance of 93,000,000 miles from the earth. For the eagle to be closer to it by the altitude of a mountain is an approach so small as to be insignificant. But figuratively, Tennyson conveys that the eagle stands above the clouds, perhaps silhouetted against the sun, and for the moment belongs to the heavens rather than to the land and sea. The word *ringed* makes a circle of the whole world's horizons and suggests that we see the world from the eagle's height; the *wrinkled sea* becomes an aged, sluggish animal; *mountain walls,* possibly literal, also suggests a fort or castle; and finally the eagle itself is likened to a thunderbolt in speed and in power, perhaps also in that its beak is—like our abstract conception of a lightning bolt—pointed. How much of the poem can be taken literally? Only *he clasps the crag, he stands, he watches, he falls.* The rest is made of figures of speech. The result is that, reading Tennyson's poem, we gain a bird's-eye view of sun, sea, and land—and even of bird. Like imagery, figurative language refers us to the physical world.

William Shakespeare (1564–1616)*

SHALL I COMPARE THEE TO   1609
A SUMMER'S DAY?

Shall I compare thee to a summer's day?
Thou art more lovely and more temperate.
Rough winds do shake the darling buds of May,
And summer's lease hath all too short a date.

Sometime too hot the eye of heaven shines,   5
And often is his gold complexion dimmed;
And every fair° from fair sometimes declines,   *fair one*
By chance, or nature's changing course, untrimmed.
But thy eternal summer shall not fade,
Nor lose possession of that fair thou ow'st°   *ownest, have*   10
Nor shall death brag thou wand'rest in his shade,
When in eternal lines to time thou grow'st.
    So long as men can breathe or eyes can see,
    So long lives this, and this gives life to thee.

Howard Moss   (1922–1987)

SHALL I COMPARE THEE TO A   1976
SUMMER'S DAY?

Who says you're like one of the dog days?
You're nicer. And better.
Even in May, the weather can be gray,
And a summer sub-let doesn't last forever.
Sometimes the sun's too hot;   5
Sometimes it is not.
Who can stay young forever?
People break their necks or just drop dead!
But you? Never!
If there's just one condensed reader left   10
Who can figure out the abridged alphabet,
    After you're dead and gone,
    In this poem you'll live on!

SHALL I COMPARE THEE TO A SUMMER'S DAY? (MOSS). *Dog days:* the hottest days of summer. The ancient Romans believed that the Dog-star, Sirius, added heat to summer months.

QUESTIONS

1. In Howard Moss's streamlined version of Shakespeare, from a series called "Modified Sonnets (Dedicated to adapters, abridgers, digesters, and condensers everywhere)," to what extent does the poet use figurative language? In Shakespeare's original sonnet, how high a proportion of Shakespeare's language is figurative?
2. Compare some of Moss's lines to the corresponding lines in Shakespeare's sonnet. Why is *Even in May, the weather can be gray* less interesting than the original? In the lines on the sun (5–6 in both versions), what has Moss's modification deliberately left out? Why is Shakespeare's seeing death as a braggart memorable? Why aren't you greatly impressed by Moss's last two lines?

3. Can you explain Shakespeare's play on the word *untrimmed* (line 8)? Evidently the word can mean "divested of trimmings," but what other suggestions do you find in it?
4. How would you answer someone who argued, "Maybe Moss's language isn't as good as Shakespeare's, but the meaning is still there. What's wrong with putting Shakespeare into up-to-date words that can be understood by everybody?"

METAPHOR AND SIMILE

> Life, like a dome of many-colored glass,
> Stains the white radiance of Eternity.

The first of these lines (from Shelley's "Adonais") is a **simile:** a comparison of two things, indicated by some connective, usually *like, as, than,* or a verb such as *resembles.* A simile expresses a similarity. Still, for a simile to exist, the things compared have to be dissimilar in kind. It is no simile to say, "Your fingers are like mine"; it is a literal observation. But to say, "Your fingers are like sausages" is to use a simile. Omit the connective—say, "Your fingers are sausages"—and the result is a **metaphor,** a statement that one thing *is* something else, which, in a literal sense, it is not. In the second of Shelley's lines, it is *assumed* that Eternity is light or radiance, and we have an **implied metaphor,** one that uses neither a connective nor the verb *to be.* Here are examples:

Oh, my love is like a red, red rose.	*Simile*
Oh, my love resembles a red, red rose.	*Simile*
Oh, my love is redder than a rose.	*Simile*
Oh, my love is a red, red rose.	*Metaphor*
Oh, my love has red petals and sharp thorns.	*Implied metaphor*
Oh, I placed my love into a long-stem vase and I bandaged my bleeding thumb.	*Implied metaphor*

Often you can tell a metaphor from a simile by much more than just the presence or absence of a connective. In general, a simile refers to only one characteristic that two things have in common, while a metaphor is not plainly limited in the number of resemblances it may indicate. To use the simile "He eats like a pig" is to compare man and animal in one respect: eating habits. But to say "He's a pig" is to use a metaphor that might involve comparisons of appearance and morality as well.

For scientists as well as poets, the making of metaphors is customary. In 1933 George Lemaitre, the Belgian priest and physicist credited with the Big Bang theory of the origin of the universe, conceived of a primal atom that existed before anything else, which expanded and produced everything. And so, he remarked, making a wonderful metaphor, the evolution of the cosmos as it is today "can be compared to a display of fireworks that has just ended." As astrophysicist and poet Alan Lightman has noted, we can't help envisioning scientific discoveries in terms of things we know from daily life—spinning balls, waves in water, pendulums, weights on springs. "We have no other choice," Lightman reasons. "We cannot avoid forming mental pictures when we try to grasp the meaning of our equations, and how can we picture what we have not seen?"[1] In science as well as in poetry, it would seem, metaphors are necessary instruments of understanding.

In everyday speech, simile and metaphor occur frequently. We use metaphors ("She's a doll") and similes ("The tickets are selling like hotcakes") without being fully conscious of them. If, however, we are aware that words possess literal meanings as well as figurative ones, we do not write *died in the wool* for *dyed in the wool* or *tow the line* for *toe the line*, nor do we use **mixed metaphors** as did the writer who advised, "Water the spark of knowledge and it will bear fruit," or the speaker who urged, "To get ahead, keep your nose to the grindstone, your shoulder to the wheel, your ear to the ground, and your eye on the ball." Perhaps the unintended humor of these statements comes from our seeing that the writer, busy stringing together stale metaphors, was not aware that they had any physical reference.

Unlike a writer who thoughtlessly mixes metaphors, a good poet can join together incongruous things and still keep the reader's respect. In his ballad "Thirty Bob a Week," John Davidson has a British workingman tell how it feels to try to support a large family on small wages:

> It's a naked child against a hungry wolf;
>   It's playing bowls upon a splitting wreck;
> It's walking on a string across a gulf
>   With millstones fore-and-aft about your neck;
> But the thing is daily done by many and many a one;
>   And we fall, face forward, fighting, on the deck.

Like the man with his nose to the grindstone, Davidson's wage earner is in an absurd fix; but his balancing act seems far from merely nonsensical. For every one of the poet's comparisons—of workingman to child, to bowler, to tight rope walker, and to seaman—offers suggestions of a similar kind. All help us see (and imagine) the workingman's hard life: a brave and unyielding struggle against impossible odds.

A poem may make a series of comparisons, like Davidson's, or the whole poem may be one extended comparison:

Emily Dickinson   (1830–1886)*

MY LIFE HAD STOOD –   (ABOUT 1863)
A LOADED GUN

My Life had stood – a Loaded Gun –
In Corners – till a Day
The Owner passed – identified –
And carried Me away –

[1] "Physicists' Use of Metaphor," *The American Scholar* (Winter 1989): 99.

And now We roam in Sovreign Woods –
And now We hunt the Doe –
And every time I speak for Him –
The Mountains straight reply – 5

And do I smile, such cordial light
Upon the Valley glow –
It is as a Vesuvian face
Had let its pleasure through – 10

And when at Night – Our good Day done –
I guard My Master's Head –
'Tis better than the Eider-Duck's 15
Deep Pillow – to have shared –

To foe of His – I'm deadly foe –
None stir the second time –
On whom I lay a Yellow Eye –
Or an emphatic Thumb – 20

Though I than He – may longer live
He longer must – than I –
For I have but the power to kill,
Without – the power to die –

How much life metaphors bring to poetry may be seen by comparing two
poems by Tennyson and Blake.

Alfred, Lord Tennyson   (1809–1892)*

FLOWER IN THE CRANNIED WALL   1869

Flower in the crannied wall,
I pluck you out of the crannies,
I hold you here, root and all, in my hand,
Little flower—but *if* I could understand
What you are, root and all, and all in all, 5
I should know what God and man is.

How many metaphors does this poem contain? None. Compare it with a briefer
poem on a similar theme: the quatrain that begins Blake's "Auguries of Innocence." (We follow here the opinion of W. B. Yeats, who, in editing Blake's
poems, thought the lines ought to be printed separately.)

William Blake (1757–1827)*

TO SEE A WORLD IN A GRAIN (ABOUT 1803)
OF SAND

To see a world in a grain of sand
And a heaven in a wild flower,
Hold infinity in the palm of your hand
And eternity in an hour.

Set beside Blake's poem, Tennyson's—short though it is—seems lengthy. What contributes to the richness of "To see a world in a grain of sand" is Blake's use of a metaphor in every line. And every metaphor is loaded with suggestion. Our world does indeed resemble a grain of sand: in being round, in being stony, in being one of a myriad (the suggestions go on and on). Like Blake's grain of sand, a metaphor holds much, within a small circumference.

Sylvia Plath (1932–1963)*

METAPHORS 1960

I'm a riddle in nine syllables,
An elephant, a ponderous house,
A melon strolling on two tendrils.
O red fruit, ivory, fine timbers!
This loaf's big with its yeasty rising. 5
Money's new-minted in this fat purse.
I'm a means, a stage, a cow in calf.
I've eaten a bag of green apples,
Boarded the train there's no getting off.

QUESTIONS

1. To what central fact do all the metaphors in this poem refer?
2. In the first line, what has the speaker in common with a riddle? Why does she say she has *nine* syllables?

N. Scott Momaday (b. 1934)

SIMILE 1974

What did we say to each other
that now we are as the deer
who walk in single file

with heads high
with ears forward
with eyes watchful
with hooves always placed on firm ground
in whose limbs there is latent flight   5

QUESTIONS

1. Momaday never tells us what was said. Does this omission keep us from understanding the comparison?
2. The comparison is extended with each detail adding some new twist. Explain the implications of the last line.

EXPERIMENT: *Likening*

Write a poem that follows the method of N. Scott Momaday's "Simile," consisting of one
long comparison between two objects. Possible subjects might include: Talking to a loved
one long-distance. What you feel like going to a weekend job. Being on a diet. Not being
noticed by someone you love. Winning a lottery.

Emily Dickinson   (1830–1886)*

IT DROPPED SO LOW –   (ABOUT 1863)
IN MY REGARD

It dropped so low – in my Regard –
I heard it hit the Ground –
And go to pieces on the Stones
At bottom of my Mind –

Yet blamed the Fate that flung it – *less*   5
Than I denounced Myself,
For entertaining Plated Wares
Upon My Silver Shelf –

QUESTIONS

1. What is *it*? What two things are compared?
2. How much of the poem develops and amplifies this comparison?

Craig Raine   (b. 1944)

A MARTIAN SENDS A POSTCARD HOME   1979

Caxtons are mechanical birds with many wings
and some are treasured for their markings—

they cause the eyes to melt
or the body to shriek without pain.

I have never seen one fly, but
sometimes they perch on the hand.

Mist is when the sky is tired of flight
and rests its soft machine on ground:

then the world is dim and bookish
like engravings under tissue paper.

Rain is when the earth is television.
It has the property of making colours darker.

Model T is a room with the lock inside—
a key is turned to free the world

for movement, so quick there is a film
to watch for anything missed.

But time is tied to the wrist
or kept in a box, ticking with impatience.

In homes, a haunted apparatus sleeps,
that snores when you pick it up.

If the ghost cries, they carry it
to their lips and soothe it to sleep

with sounds. And yet, they wake it up
deliberately, by tickling with a finger.

Only the young are allowed to suffer
openly. Adults go to a punishment room

with water but nothing to eat.
They lock the door and suffer the noises

alone. No one is exempt
and everyone's pain has a different smell.

At night, when all the colours die,
they hide in pairs

and read about themselves—
in colour, with their eyelids shut.

A MARTIAN SENDS A POSTCARD HOME. The title of this poem literally describes its contents. A Martian briefly describes everyday objects and activities on earth, but the visitor sees them all from an alien perspective. The Martian/author lacks a complete vocabulary and sometimes describes general categories of things with a proper noun (as in Model T in line 13). 1 *Caxtons*: Books, since William Caxton (c. 1422–1491) was the first person to print books in England.

Can you recognize *everything* the Martian describes and translate it back into Earth-based English?

EXERCISE: *What Is Similar?*

Each of these quotations contains a simile or a metaphor. In each of these figures of speech, what two things is the poet comparing? Try to state exactly what you understand the two things to have in common: the most striking similarity or similarities that the poet sees.

1.   All the world's a stage,
   And all the men and women merely players:
   They have their exits and their entrances,
   And one man in his time plays many parts,
   His acts being seven ages.
                     —William Shakespeare, *As You Like It*

2. When the hounds of spring are on winter's traces . . .
                     —Algernon Charles Swinburne, "Atalanta in Calydon"

3. . . . the sun gnaws the night's bone
   down through the meat and gristle.
                     —John Ridland, "Elegy for My Aunt"

4. Art is long, and Time is fleeting,
   And our hearts, though strong and brave,
   Still, like muffled drums are beating
   Funeral marches to the grave.
                     —Henry Wadsworth Longfellow, "A Psalm of Life"

5. "Hope" is the thing with feathers —
   That perches in the soul —
   And sings the tune without the words —
   And never stops — at all —
                     —Emily Dickinson, an untitled poem

6. Why should I let the toad *work*
      Squat on my life?
   Can't I use my wit as a pitchfork
      And drive the brute off?
                     —Philip Larkin, "Toads"

7. I wear my patience like a light-green dress
   and wear it thin.
                     —Emily Grosholz, "Remembering the Ardèche"

8. a laugh maybe, like glasses on a shelf
    suddenly found by the sun . . .
    —Beth Gylys, "Briefly"

9. Anew electric fence,
    Its five barbed wires tight
    As a steel-stringed banjo.
    —Van K. Brock, "Driving at Dawn"

10. Spring stirs Gossamer Beynon Schoolmistress like a spoon.
    —Dylan Thomas, *Under Milk Wood*

11. Our headlight caught, as in a flashbulb's flare,
    A pair of hitchhikers.
    —Paul Lake, "Two Hitchhikers"

12. My life seems like those country western songs:
    Some man in black keeps walkin' out the door . . .
    —Dessa Crawford, "With Our Boots On"

OTHER FIGURES

When Shakespeare asks, in a sonnet,

> O! how shall summer's honey breath hold out
> Against the wrackful siege of batt'ring days,

it might seem at first that he mixes metaphors. How can a *breath* confront the battering ram of an invading army? But it is summer's breath and, by giving it to summer, Shakespeare makes the season a man or woman. It is as if the fragrance of summer were the breath within a person's body, and winter were the onslaught of old age.

Such is one instance of **personification:** a figure of speech in which a thing, an animal, or an abstract term (*truth, nature*) is made human. A personification extends throughout this whole short poem.

James Stephens (1882–1950)*

THE WIND   1915

The wind stood up and gave a shout.
He whistled on his fingers and

Kicked the withered leaves about
And thumped the branches with his hand

And said he'd kill and kill and kill,   5
And so he will and so he will.

The wind is a wild man, and evidently it is not just any autumn breeze but a
hurricane or at least a stiff gale. In poems that do not work as well as this one,
personification may be employed mechanically. Hollow-eyed personifications
walk the works of lesser English poets of the eighteenth century: Coleridge has
quoted the beginning of one such neoclassical ode, "Inoculation! heavenly Maid,
descend!" It is hard for the contemporary reader to be excited by William
Collins's "The Passions, An Ode for Music" (1747), which personifies, stanza by
stanza, Fear, Anger, Despair, Hope, Revenge, Pity, Jealousy, Love, Hate, Melancholy, and Cheerfulness, and has them listen to Music, until even "Brown Exercise rejoiced to hear, / And Sport leapt up, and seized his beechen spear." Still, in
"Two Sonnets on Fame" John Keats makes an abstraction come alive in seeing
Fame as "a wayward girl."

Hand in hand with personification often goes **apostrophe:** a way of
addressing someone or something invisible or not ordinarily spoken to. In an
apostrophe, a poet (in these examples Wordsworth) may address an inanimate
object ("Spade! with which Wilkinson hath tilled his lands"), some dead or
absent person ("Milton! thou shouldst be living at this hour"), an abstract thing
("Return, Delights!"), or a spirit ("Thou Soul that art the eternity of thought").
More often than not, the poet uses apostrophe to announce a lofty and serious
tone. An "O" may even be put in front of it ("O moon!") since, according to
W. D. Snodgrass, every poet has a right to do so at least once in a lifetime. But
apostrophe doesn't have to be highfalutin. It is a means of giving life to the
inanimate. It is a way of giving body to the intangible, a way of speaking to it
person to person, as in the words of a moving American spiritual: "Death, ain't
you got no shame?"

Most of us, from time to time, emphasize a point with a statement
containing exaggeration: "Faster than greased lightning," "I've told him a
thousand times." We speak, then, not literal truth but use a figure of speech
called **overstatement** (or **hyperbole**). Poets too, being fond of emphasis, often
exaggerate for effect. Instances are Marvell's profession of a love that should
grow "Vaster than empires, and more slow" and John Burgon's description of
Petra: "A rose-red city, half as old as Time." Overstatement can be used also for

humorous purposes, as in a fat woman's boast (from a blues song): "Every time I shake, some skinny gal loses her home."[2] The opposite is **understatement,** implying more than is said. Mark Twain in *Life on the Mississippi* recalls how, as an apprentice steamboat-pilot asleep when supposed to be on watch, he was roused by the pilot and sent clambering to the pilot house: "Mr. Bixby was close behind, commenting." Another example is Robert Frost's line "One could do worse than be a swinger of birches"—the conclusion of a poem that has suggested that to swing on a birch tree is one of the most deeply satisfying activities in the world.

In **metonymy,** the name of a thing is substituted for that of another closely associated with it. For instance, we say "The White House decided," and mean the president did. When John Dyer writes in "Grongar Hill,"

> A little rule, a little sway,
> A sun beam on a winter's day,
> Is all the proud and mighty have
> Between the cradle and the grave,

we recognize that *cradle* and *grave* signify birth and death. A kind of metonymy, **synecdoche** is the use of a part of a thing to stand for the whole of it or vice versa. We say "She lent a hand," and mean that she lent her entire presence. Similarly, Milton in "Lycidas" refers to greedy clergymen as "blind mouths." Another kind of metonymy is the **transferred epithet:** a device of emphasis in which the poet attributes some characteristic of a thing to another thing closely associated with it. When Thomas Gray observes that, in the evening pastures, "drowsy tinklings lull the distant folds," he well knows that sheep's bells do not drowse, but sheep do. When Hart Crane, describing the earth as seen from an airplane, speaks of "nimble blue plateaus," he attributes the airplane's motion to the earth.

Paradox occurs in a statement that at first strikes us as self-contradictory but that on reflection makes some sense. "The peasant," said G. K. Chesterton, "lives in a larger world than the globe-trotter." Here, two different meanings of *larger* are contrasted: "greater in spiritual values" versus "greater in miles." Some paradoxical statements, however, are much more than plays on words. In a moving sonnet, the blind John Milton tells how one night he dreamed he could see his dead wife. The poem ends in a paradox:

> But oh, as to embrace me she inclined,
> I waked, she fled, and day brought back my night.

EXERCISE: *Paradox*

What paradoxes do you find in the following poem? For each, explain the sense that underlies the statement.

---

[2]Quoted by Amiri Baraka [LeRoi Jones] in *Blues People* (New York: Morrow, 1963).

Chidiock Tichborne (1568?–1586)

Elegy, Written with His Own Hand in the Tower Before His Execution   1586

My prime of youth is but a frost of cares,
   My feast of joy is but a dish of pain,
My crop of corn is but a field of tares,°   *weeds*
   And all my good is but vain hope of gain:
The day is past, and yet I saw no sun,   5
And now I live, and now my life is done.

My tale was heard, and yet it was not told,
   My fruit is fall'n, and yet my leaves are green,
My youth is spent, and yet I am not old,
   I saw the world, and yet I was not seen: 10
My thread is cut, and yet it is not spun,
And now I live, and now my life is done.

I sought my death, and found it in my womb,
   I looked for life, and saw it was a shade,
I trod the earth, and knew it was my tomb,   15
   And now I die, and now I was but made:
My glass is full, and now my glass is run,
And now I live, and now my life is done.

Elegy, Written with His Own Hand. Accused of taking part in the Babington Conspiracy, a plot by Roman Catholics against the life of Queen Elizabeth I, eighteen-year-old Chidiock Tichborne was hanged, drawn, and quartered at the Tower of London. That is virtually all we know about him.

Asked to tell the difference between men and women, Samuel Johnson replied, "I can't conceive, madam, can you?" The great dictionary-maker was using a figure of speech known to classical rhetoricians as *paronomasia*, better known to us as a **pun** or play on words. How does a pun operate? It reminds us of another word (or other words) of similar or identical sound but of very different denotation. Although puns at their worst can be mere piddling quibbles, at best they can sharply point to surprising but genuine resemblances. The name of a dentist's country estate, Tooth Acres, is accurate: aching teeth paid for the property. In his novel *Moby-Dick*, Herman Melville takes up questions about whales that had puzzled scientists: for instance, are the whale's spoutings water or gaseous vapor? And when Melville speaks pointedly of the great whale "sprinkling and mistifying the gardens of the deep," we catch his pun, and conclude that the creature both mistifies and mystifies at once.

In poetry, a pun may be facetious, as in Thomas Hood's ballad of "Faithless Nelly Gray":

Ben Battle was a soldier bold,
   And used to war's alarms;

But a cannon-ball took off his legs,
    So he laid down his arms!

Or it may be serious, as in these lines on war by E. E. Cummings:

the bigness of cannon
is skillful,

(*is skillful* becoming *is kill-ful* when read aloud), or perhaps, as in Shakespeare's song in *Cymbeline*, "Fear no more the heat o' th' sun," both facetious and serious at once:

Golden lads and girls all must,
As chimney-sweepers, come to dust.

Poets often make puns on images, thereby combining the sensory force of imagery with the verbal pleasure of wordplay. Find and explain the punning images in these three poems.

Margaret Atwood   (b. 1939)*

You FIT INTO ME   1971

you fit into me
like a hook into an eye

a fish hook
an open eye

John Ashbery   (b. 1927)*

THE CATHEDRAL IS   1979

Slated for demolition

George Herbert   (1593–1633)*

THE PULLEY   1633

    When God at first made man,
Having a glass of blessings standing by—
Let us (said he) pour on him all we can;
Let the world's riches, which dispersèd lie,
    Contract into a span.   5

So strength first made a way,
Then beauty flowed, then wisdom, honor, pleasure:
When almost all was out, God made a stay,
Perceiving that, alone of all His treasure,
    Rest in the bottom lay.   10

    For if I should (said he)
Bestow this jewel also on My creature,
He would adore My gifts instead of Me,
And rest in Nature, not the God of Nature:
    So both should losers be.   15

    Yet let him keep the rest,
But keep them with repining restlessness;
Let him be rich and weary, that at least,
If goodness lead him not, yet weariness
    May toss him to My breast.   20

QUESTIONS

1. What different senses of the word *rest* does Herbert bring into this poem?
2. How do God's words in line 16, *Yet let him keep the rest*, seem paradoxical?
3. What do you feel to be the tone of Herbert's poem? Does the punning make the poem seem comic?
4. Why is the poem called "The Pulley"? What is its implied metaphor?

To sum up: even though figures of speech are not to be taken *only* literally, they refer us to a tangible world. By *personifying* an eagle, Tennyson reminds us that the bird and humankind have certain characteristics in common. Through *metonymy*, a poet can focus our attention on a particular detail in a larger object; through *hyperbole* and *understatement*, make us see the physical actuality in back of words. *Pun* and *paradox* cause us to realize this actuality, too, and probably surprise us enjoyably at the same time. Through *apostrophe*, the poet animates the inanimate and asks it to listen—speaks directly to an immediate god or to the revivified dead. Put to such uses, figures of speech have power. They are more than just ways of playing with words.

Louis MacNeice   (1907–1963)

PLAIN SPEAKING   1941

In the beginning and in the end the only decent
Definition is tautology: man is man,
Woman woman, and tree tree, and world world,
Slippery, self-contained; catch as catch can.

Which when caught between the beginning and end   5
Turn other than themselves, their entities unfurled,
Flapping and overlapping—a tree becomes
A talking tower, and a woman becomes world.

Catch them in nets, but either the thread is thin
Or the mesh too big or, thirdly, the fish die   10
And man from false communion dwindles back
Into a mere man under a mere sky.

But dream was dream and love was love and what
Happened happened—even if the judge said
It should have been otherwise—and glitter glitters   15
And I am I although the dead are dead.

QUESTIONS

1. What figure of speech is used predominantly in this poem? (Look up the definition of *tautology*; does MacNeice use the word in its literal sense, or could its use in the poem also be considered a figure of speech?)
2. Does the poem use any other figures of speech? Give examples.
3. What stages in a person's life does the poet seem to mean by *the beginning, the end*, and the time *between the beginning and end*? According to the text, how does the way we use words at each stage reveal our assumptions and/or expectations at that time of life?
4. Is the mood at the end of the poem one of defeat or affirmation? How does the use of tautologies in the last stanza help provide the answer?

FOR REVIEW AND FURTHER STUDY

Robert Frost   (1874–1963)*

THE SILKEN TENT   1942

She is as in a field a silken tent
At midday when a sunny summer breeze
Has dried the dew and all its ropes relent,
So that in guys° it gently sways at ease,   *attachments that steady it*
And its supporting central cedar pole,   5
That is its pinnacle to heavenward
And signifies the sureness of the soul,
Seems to owe naught to any single cord,
But strictly held by none, is loosely bound
By countless silken ties of love and thought   10
To everything on earth the compass round,
And only by one's going slightly taut
In the capriciousness of summer air
Is of the slightest bondage made aware.

QUESTIONS

1. Is Frost's comparison of a woman and tent a simile or a metaphor?
2. What are the ropes or cords?
3. Does the poet convey any sense of this woman's character? What sort of person do you believe her to be?
4. Paraphrase the poem, trying to state its implied meaning. (If you need to be refreshed about paraphrase, turn back to page 702.) Be sure to include the implications of the last three lines.

Denise Levertov   (1923–1997)*

LEAVING FOREVER   1964

He says the waves in the ship's wake
are like stones rolling away.
I don't see it that way.
But I see the mountain turning,
turning away its face as the ship   5
takes us away.

QUESTIONS

1. What do you understand to be the man's feelings about leaving forever? How does the speaker feel? With what two figures of speech does the poet express these conflicting views?
2. Suppose that this poem had ended in another simile (instead of its three last lines):

> I see the mountain as a suitcase
> left behind on the shore
> as the ship takes us away.

How is Denise Levertov's choice of a figure of speech a much stronger one?

Jane Kenyon   (1947–1995)

THE SUITOR   1978

We lie back to back. Curtains
lift and fall,
like the chest of someone sleeping.
Wind moves the leaves of the box elder;
they show their light undersides,   5
turning all at once
like a school of fish.
Suddenly I understand that I am happy.
For months this feeling
has been coming closer, stopping   10
for short visits, like a timid suitor.

In each simile you find in "The Suitor," exactly what is the similarity?

EXERCISE: *Figures of Speech*

Identify the central figure of speech in the following three short poems.

Robert Frost (1874–1963)*

THE SECRET SITS   1936

We dance round in a ring and suppose,
But the Secret sits in the middle and knows.

H. D. [Hilda Doolittle] (1886–1961)*

LOVE THAT I BEAR   1921

Love that I bear
within my heart, O speak;
tell how beneath the serpent-spotted shell,
the cygnets wait,
how the soft owl   5
opens and flicks with pride,
eye-lids of great bird-eyes,
when underneath its breast
the owlets shrink and turn.

A. R. Ammons (1926–2001)

COWARD   1975

Bravery runs in my family.

Kay Ryan (b. 1945)*

TURTLE   1994

Who would be a turtle who could help it?
A barely mobile hard roll, a four-oared helmet,
she can ill afford the chances she must take
in rowing toward the grasses that she eats.
Her track is graceless, like dragging   5
a packing-case places, and almost any slope

defeats her modest hopes. Even being practical,
she's often stuck up to the axle on her way
to something edible. With everything optimal,
she skirts the ditch which would convert   10
her shell into a serving dish. She lives
below luck-level, never imagining some lottery
will change her load of pottery to wings.
Her only levity is patience,
the sport of truly chastened things.   15

QUESTION

How many metaphors, similes, or implied metaphors can you spot in this poem?

Robinson Jeffers   (1887–1962)*

HANDS   1929

Inside a cave in a narrow canyon near Tassajara
The vault of rock is painted with hands,
A multitude of hands in the twilight, a cloud of men's palms,
      no more,
No other picture. There's no one to say
Whether the brown shy quiet people who are dead intended   5
Religion or magic, or made their tracings
In the idleness of art; but over the division of years these
      careful
Signs-manual are now like a sealed message
Saying: "Look: we also were human; we had hands, not paws.
      All hail
You people with the cleverer hands, our supplanters   10
In the beautiful country; enjoy her a season, her beauty, and
      come down
And be supplanted; for you also are human."

QUESTION

Identify examples of personification and apostrophe in "Hands."

Robert Burns   (1759–1796)*

OH, MY LOVE IS LIKE A RED, RED ROSE   (ABOUT 1788)

Oh, my love is like a red, red rose
   That's newly sprung in June;
My love is like the melody
   That's sweetly played in tune.

So fair art thou, my bonny lass,
    So deep in love am I;
And I will love thee still, my dear,
    Till a' the seas gang° dry.   *go*

Till a' the seas gang dry, my dear,
    And the rocks melt wi' the sun;
And I will love thee still, my dear,   10
    While the sands o' life shall run.

And fare thee weel, my only love!
    And fare thee weel awhile!
And I will come again, my love   15
    Though it were ten thousand mile.

WRITER'S PERSPECTIVE

Robert Frost

Robert Frost on Writing

THE IMPORTANCE OF POETIC METAPHOR   1930

I do not think anybody ever knows the discreet use of metaphors, his own and other peoples, the discreet handling of metaphor, unless he has been properly educated in poetry.

Poetry begins in trivial metaphors, pretty metaphors, "grace" metaphors, and goes on to the profoundest thinking that we have. Poetry provides the one permissible way of saying one thing and meaning another. People say, "Why don't you say what you mean?" We never do that, do we, being all of us too much poets. We like to talk in parables and in hints and in indirections—whether from diffidence or some other instinct.

I have wanted in late years to go further and further in making metaphor the whole of thinking. I find someone now and then to agree with me that all thinking, except mathematical thinking, is metaphorical, or all thinking except scientific thinking. The mathematical might be difficult for me to bring in, but the scientific is easy enough.

What I am pointing out is that unless you are at home in the metaphor, unless you have had your proper poetical education in the metaphor, you are not safe anywhere. Because you are not at ease with figurative values: you don't know the metaphor in its strength and its weakness. You don't know how far you may expect to ride it and when it may break down with you. You are not safe in science; you are not safe in history.

From "Education by Poetry"

◄━━━► WRITING CRITICALLY ◄━━━►

How Metaphors Enlarge a Poem's Meaning

Poems have the particular power of helping us see one thing by pointing out another. One of the most distinctive ways poems manage this feat is by calling a thing by a different name, in other words, by creating a metaphor. Paradoxically, by connecting an object to something else, a metaphor can reveal interesting aspects of the original thing we might either never have noticed or have considered unimportant.

Usually we can see the main point of a good metaphor immediately, but in interpreting a poem, the practical issue sometimes arises on how far to extend a comparison. All readers recognize that metaphors enlarge meaning, but they also know that there is always some limit to the comparison and that in most poems the limit remains unstated. If at the dinner table a big brother calls his kid brother "a pig," he probably does not mean to imply that the child has a snout and a kinky tail. Most metaphors have a finite set of associations—even insults from a big brother.

If you plan an essay on a highly metaphorical poem, it is often useful to examine the key comparison or comparisons in the poem. Jot down the major metaphors (or similes). Under each comparison make a two-column list—one marked "true," the other "false." Now start exploring the connections between the object the poem presents and the thing to which it is being compared. What aspects of the comparison are true? Make this list as long as possible. In the second list write the aspects that the two objects do not truly share; this list soon sets the limits of the metaphorical connections. In poems in which the metaphor is rich and resonant, the "true" list will be much longer than the "false" list. In other poems, those in which the metaphor is narrowly focused on only limited connections between the two objects, the "false" list will quickly outpace the "true" list. Finally, once you have listed the key comparisons in the poem, see if there is any obvious connection between all the metaphors or similes themselves. Do they have something in common? Are all of them threatening? Inviting? Nocturnal? Exaggerated? Their similarities, if any, will almost certainly be significant.

Don't spend more than a few minutes on each list. The object is not to list every possible connection, but only to determine the general scope of the metaphor and its implications. If the poem has a central metaphor, its scope and function should now be clear.

WRITING ASSIGNMENT

In a short essay (approximately 500 words) create your own extended simile or metaphor. Choose something from your life—perhaps a physical possession such as a car or coat, a part of your body such as your face or hair, or even a personal memory or emotion—and compare it to something else. You may begin by comparing what you choose to something it resembles physically, but you are free to use any comparison you find meaningful. Extend the metaphor as far as you can. Use hyperbole or understatement, as appropriate, but keep the metaphorical connection true enough for the reader to see and enjoy some connection. Feel free to be humorous. If you borrow a metaphor from some poem in this chapter, make sure you add an original twist of your own.

FURTHER SUGGESTIONS FOR WRITING

1. Freely using your imagination, write a paragraph in which you make as many hyperbolic statements as possible. Then write another version, changing all your exaggeration to understatement. Then, in a concluding paragraph, sum up what this experiment shows you about figurative language. Some possible topics are "The Most Gratifying (or Terrifying) Moment of My Life," "The Job I Almost Landed," "The Person I Most Admire."
2. Choose a short poem rich in figurative language: Sylvia Plath's "Metaphors," say, or Burns's "Oh, my love is like a red, red rose." Rewrite the poem, taking for your model Howard Moss's deliberately bepiddling version of "Shall I compare thee to a summer's day?" Eliminate every figure of speech. Turn the poem into language as flat and unsuggestive as possible. (Just ignore any rime or rhythm in the original.) Then, in a paragraph, indicate lines in your revised version that seem glaringly worsened. In conclusion, sum up what your barbaric rewrite tells you about the nature of poetry.

18 Song

SINGING AND SAYING

Most poems are more memorable than most ordinary speech, and when music is combined with poetry, the result can be more memorable still. The differences between speech, poetry, and song may appear if we consider, first of all, this fragment of an imaginary conversation between two lovers:

> Let's not drink; let's just sit here and look at each other. Or put a kiss
> inside my goblet and I won't want anything to drink.

Forgettable language, we might think; but let's try to make it a little more interesting:

> Drink to me only with your eyes, and I'll pledge my love to you
> with my eyes;
> Or leave a kiss within the goblet, that's all I'll want to drink.

The passage is closer to poetry, but still has a distance to go. At least we now have a figure of speech—the metaphor that love is wine, implied in the statement that one lover may salute another by lifting an eye as well as by lifting a goblet. But the sound of the words is not yet especially interesting. Here is another try, by Ben Jonson:

> Drink to me only with thine eyes,
>   And I will pledge with mine;
> Or leave a kiss but in the cup,
>   And I'll not ask for wine.

In these opening lines from Jonson's poem "To Celia," the improvement is noticeable. These lines are poetry; their language has become special. For one thing, the lines rime (with an additional rime sound on *thine*). There is interest, too, in the proximity of the words *kiss* and *cup*: the repetition (or alliteration) of the *k* sound. The rhythm of the lines has become regular; generally every other word (or syllable) is stressed:

> DRINK to me ON-ly WITH thine EYES,
>   And I will PLEDGE with MINE;
> Or LEAVE a KISS but IN the CUP,
>   And I'LL not ASK for WINE.

All these devices of sound and rhythm, together with metaphor, produce a pleasing effect—more pleasing than the effect of "Let's not drink; let's look at each other." But the words became more pleasing still when later set to music:

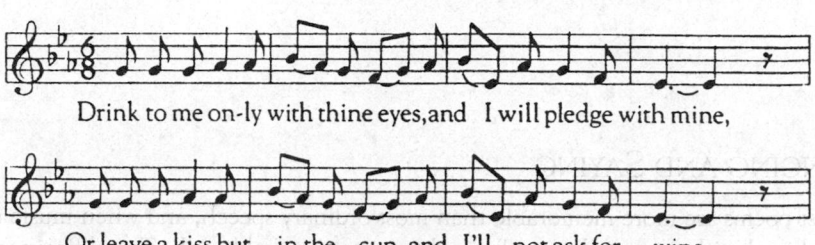

Drink to me on-ly with thine eyes, and   I will pledge with mine,

Or leave a kiss but   in the   cup, and   I'll   not ask for   wine.

In this memorable form, the poem is still alive today.

Ben Jonson   (1573?–1637)*

To Celia   1616

Drink to me only with thine eyes,
   And I will pledge with mine;
Or leave a kiss but in the cup,
   And I'll not ask for wine.
The thirst that from the soul doth rise   5
   Doth ask a drink divine;
But might I of Jove's nectar sup,
   I would not change for thine.

I sent thee late a rosy wreath,
   Not so much honoring thee   10
As giving it a hope that there
   It could not withered be.
But thou thereon didst only breathe,
   And sent'st it back to me;
Since when it grows, and smells, I swear,   15
   Not of itself but thee.

A compliment to a lady has rarely been put in language more graceful, more wealthy with interesting sounds. Other figures of speech besides metaphor make them unforgettable: for example, the hyperbolic tributes to the power of the lady's sweet breath, which can start picked roses growing again, and her kisses, which even surpass the nectar of the gods.

This song falls into stanzas—as many poems that resemble songs also do. A **stanza** (Italian for "stopping-place" or "room") is a group of lines whose pattern is repeated throughout the poem. Most songs have more than one stanza. When printed, the stanzas of songs and poems usually are set off from one another by space. When sung, stanzas of songs are indicated by a pause or by the introduction of a refrain, or chorus (a line or lines repeated). The word **verse,** which strictly refers to one line of a poem, is sometimes loosely used to mean a whole stanza: "All join in and sing the second verse!" In speaking of a stanza, whether sung or read, it is customary to indicate by a convenient algebra its **rime scheme,** the order in which rimed words recur. For instance, the rime scheme of this stanza by Herrick is *a b a b*; the first and third lines rime and so do the second and fourth:

> For shame or pity now incline
>   To play a loving part,
> Either to send me kindly thine
>   Or give me back my heart.

Refrains are words, phrases, or lines repeated at intervals in a song or song-like poem. A refrain usually follows immediately after a stanza, and when it does, it is called **terminal refrain.** A refrain whose words change slightly with each recurrence is called an **incremental refrain.** Sometimes we also hear an **internal refrain:** one that appears within a stanza, generally in a position that stays fixed throughout a poem. Both internal refrains and terminal refrains are used to great effect in the traditional song "The Cruel Mother."

Anonymous   (traditional Scottish ballad)

THE CRUEL MOTHER

She sat down below a thorn,
   Fine flowers in the valley,
And there she has her sweet babe born
   And the green leaves they grow rarely.

"Smile na sae° sweet, my bonny babe,"   *so*   5
   Fine flowers in the valley,
"And° ye smile sae sweet, ye'll smile me dead."   *if*
   And the green leaves they grow rarely.

She's taen out her little pen-knife,
   Fine flowers in the valley,
And twinned° the sweet babe o' its life,   severed
   And the green leaves they grow rarely.

She's howket° a grave by the light of the moon,   dug
   Fine flowers in the valley,
And there she's buried her sweet babe in
   And the green leaves they grow rarely.

As she was going to the church,
   Fine flowers in the valley,
She saw a sweet babe in the porch
   And the green leaves they grow rarely.

"O sweet babe, and thou were mine,"
   Fine flowers in the valley,
"I wad cleed° thee in the silk so fine."   dress
   And the green leaves they grow rarely.

"O mother dear, when I was thine,"
   Fine flowers in the valley,
"You did na prove to me sae kind."
   And the green leaves they grow rarely.

10

15

20

25

Taken by themselves, the refrain lines might seem mere pretty nonsense. But interwoven with the story of the murdered child, they form a terrible counterpoint. What do they come to mean? Possibly that Nature keeps going about her chores, unmindful of sin and suffering. The effect is an ironic contrast. Besides, by hearing the refrain over and over and over, we find it hard to forget.

    We usually meet poems as words on a page, but songs we generally first encounter as sounds in the air. Consequently, songs tend to be written in language simple enough to be understood on first hearing. But some contemporary songwriters have created songs that require listeners to pay close and repeated attention to their words. Beginning in the 1960s with performers like Bob Dylan, Leonard Cohen, Joni Mitchell, and Frank Zappa, some pop songwriters crafted deliberately challenging songs. More recently, Sting, Aimee Mann, Beck, and Suzanne Vega have written complex lyrics, often full of strange, dreamlike imagery. To unravel them, a listener may have to play the recording many times, with the treble turned up all the way. Anyone who feels that literary criticism is solely an academic enterprise should listen to high school and college students discuss the lyrics of their favorite songs.

    Many familiar poems began life as songs, but today, their tunes forgotten, they survive only in poetry anthologies. Shakespeare studded his plays with songs, and many of his contemporaries wrote verses to fit existing tunes. Some poets were themselves musicians (like Thomas Campion), and composed both words and music. In Shakespeare's day, **madrigals,** short secular songs for three or more voices arranged in counterpoint, enjoyed great popularity. A madrigal is always short, usually just one stanza, and rarely exceeds twelve or thirteen lines. Elizabethans loved to sing, and a person was considered a dolt if he or she could not join in a three-part song. Here is a madrigal from one of Shakespeare's comedies.

William Shakespeare   (1564–1616)*

TAKE, O, TAKE THOSE LIPS AWAY   (1604)

Take, O, take those lips away
   That so sweetly were forsworn,
And those eyes, the break of day,
   Lights that do mislead the morn;
But my kisses bring again, bring again,   5
Seals of love, but seal'd in vain, seal'd in vain.

TAKE, O, TAKE THOSE LIPS AWAY. This short song appears in *Measure for Measure*. It is sung by a boy in Act IV, just as we see Mariana, a deserted lover, for the first time.

Some poets who were not composers printed their work in madrigal books for others to set to music. In the seventeenth century, however, poetry and song seem to have fallen away from each other. By the end of the century, much new poetry, other than songs for plays, was written to be printed and to be silently read. Poets who wrote popular songs—like Thomas D'Urfey, compiler of the collection *Pills to Purge Melancholy*—were considered somewhat disreputable. With the notable exceptions of John Gay, who took existing popular tunes for *The Beggar's Opera*, and Robert Burns, who rewrote folk songs or made completely new words for them, few important English poets since Campion have been first-rate songwriters.

Occasionally, a poet has learned a thing or two from music. "But for the opera I could never have written *Leaves of Grass*," said Walt Whitman, who loved the Italian art form for its expansiveness. Coleridge, Hardy, Auden, and many others have learned from folk ballads, and T. S. Eliot patterned his thematically repetitive *Four Quartets* after the structure of a quartet in classical music. "Poetry," said Ezra Pound, "begins to atrophy when it gets too far from music." Still, even in the twentieth century, the poet was more often a corrector of printer's proofs than a tunesmith or performer.

Some people think that to write poems and to travel about singing them, as many rock singer-composers now do, is a return to the venerable tradition of the **troubadours,** minstrels of the late Middle Ages. But there are differences. No doubt the troubadours had to please their patrons, but for better or worse their songs were not affected by a producer's video promotion budget or by the technical resources of a sound studio. Bob Dylan has denied that he is a poet, and Paul Simon once told an interviewer, "If you want poetry read Wallace Stevens."

Nevertheless, many rock lyrics have the verbal intensity of poetry. No rock lyric, however, can be judged independently of its musical accompaniment. A song joins words and music; a great song joins them inseparably. Although the words of a great song cannot stand on their own without their music, they are not invalidated as lyrics. Songwriters rarely create their lyrics to be read on the page. If the words seem rich and interesting in themselves, our enjoyment is only increased. Like most poems and songs of the past, most current songs may end up in the trash can of time. And yet, certain memorable rimed and rhythmic lines may live on, especially if they are expressed in stirring music and have been given wide exposure.

EXERCISE: *Comparing Poem and Song*

Compare the following poem by Edwin Arlington Robinson and a popular song lyric based on it. Notice what Paul Simon had to do to Robinson's original poem in order to make it into a song, and how Simon altered Robinson's conception.

Edwin Arlington Robinson   (1869–1935)*

RICHARD CORY   1897

Whenever Richard Cory went down town,
We people on the pavement looked at him:
He was a gentleman from sole to crown,
Clean favored, and imperially slim.

And he was always quietly arrayed,   5
And he was always human when he talked;
But still he fluttered pulses when he said,
"Good-morning," and he glittered when he walked.

And he was rich—yes, richer than a king—
And admirably schooled in every grace: 10
In fine,° we thought that he was everything   ° *in short*
To make us wish that we were in his place.

So on we worked, and waited for the light,
And went without the meat, and cursed the bread;
And Richard Cory, one calm summer night,   15
Went home and put a bullet through his head.

Paul Simon   (b. 1942)

RICHARD CORY   1966

With Apologies to E. A. Robinson

They say that Richard Cory owns
One half of this old town,
With elliptical connections
To spread his wealth around.
Born into Society,   5
A banker's only child,
He had everything a man could want:
Power, grace and style.

Refrain:

But I, I work in his factory
And I curse the life I'm livin'   10
And I curse my poverty
And I wish that I could be
Oh I wish that I could be
Oh I wish that I could be
Richard Cory.   15

The papers print his picture
Almost everywhere he goes:
Richard Cory at the opera,
Richard Cory at a show
And the rumor of his party   20
And the orgies on his yacht—
Oh he surely must be happy
With everything he's got.   *(Refrain.)*

He freely gave to charity,
He had the common touch,   25
And they were grateful for his patronage
And they thanked him very much,
So my mind was filled with wonder
When the evening headlines read:
"Richard Cory went home last night   30
And put a bullet through his head."   *(Refrain.)*

RICHARD CORY by Paul Simon. If possible, listen to the ballad sung by Simon and Garfunkel on *Sounds of Silence* (Sony, 2001), © 1966 by Paul Simon. Used by permission.

BALLADS

Any narrative song, like Paul Simon's "Richard Cory," may be called a **ballad.** In English, some of the most famous ballads are **folk ballads,** loosely defined as anonymous story-songs transmitted orally before they were ever written down. Sir Walter Scott, a pioneer collector of Scottish folk ballads, drew the ire of an old woman whose songs he had transcribed: "They were made for singing and no' for reading, but ye ha'e broken the charm now and they'll never be sung mair." The old singer had a point. Print freezes songs and tends to hold them fast to a single version. If Scott and others had not written them down, however, many would have been lost.

In his monumental work *The English and Scottish Popular Ballads* (1882–1898), the American scholar Francis J. Child winnowed out 305 folk ballads he considered authentic—that is, creations of illiterate or semiliterate people who had preserved them orally. Child, who worked by insight as well as by learning, did such a good job of telling the difference between folk ballads and other kinds that later scholars have added only about a dozen ballads to his count. Often called **Child ballads,** his texts include "The Three Ravens," "Sir Patrick Spence," "The Twa Corbies," "Edward," "The Cruel Mother," and many others still on the lips of singers. Here is one of the best-known Child ballads.

Anonymous   (traditional Scottish ballad)

BONNY BARBARA ALLAN

It was in and about the Martinmas time,
   When the green leaves were afalling,
That Sir John Graeme, in the West Country,
   Fell in love with Barbara Allan.

He sent his men down through the town,   5
   To the place where she was dwelling;
"O haste and come to my master dear,
   Gin° ye be Barbara Allan."   *if*

O hooly,° hooly rose she up,   *slowly*
   To the place where he was lying,   10
And when she drew the curtain by:
   "Young man, I think you're dying."

"O it's I'm sick, and very, very sick,
   And 'tis a' for Barbara Allan."—
"O the better for me ye's never be,   15
   Tho your heart's blood were aspilling.

"O dinna ye mind,° young man," said she,   *don't you remember*
   "When ye was in the tavern adrinking,

That ye made the health° gae round and round,   *toasts*
    And slighted Barbara Allan?"   20

He turned his face unto the wall,
    And death was with him dealing:
"Adieu, adieu, my dear friends all,
    And be kind to Barbara Allan."

And slowly, slowly raise she up,   25
    And slowly, slowly left him,
And sighing said she could not stay,
    Since death of life had reft him.

She had not gane a mile but twa,
    When she heard the dead-bell ringing,   30
And every jow° that the dead-bell geid,   *stroke*
    It cried, "Woe to Barbara Allan!"

"O mother, mother, make my bed!
    O make it saft and narrow!
Since my love died for me today,   35
    I'll die for him tomorrow."

BONNY BARBARA ALLAN. 1 *Martinmas*: Saint Martin's day, November 11.

QUESTIONS

1. In any line does the Scottish dialect cause difficulty? If so, try reading the line aloud.
2. Without ever coming out and explicitly calling Barbara hard-hearted, this ballad reveals that she is. In which stanza and by what means is her cruelty demonstrated?
3. At what point does Barbara evidently have a change of heart? Again, how does the poem dramatize this change without explicitly talking about it?
4. In many American versions of this ballad, noble knight John Graeme becomes an ordinary citizen. The gist of the story is the same, but at the end are these further stanzas, incorporated from a different ballad:

> They buried Willie in the old churchyard
>   And Barbara in the choir;
> And out of his grave grew a red, red rose,
>   And out of hers a briar.
>
> They grew and grew to the steeple top
>   Till they could grow no higher;
> And there they locked in a true love's knot,
>   The red rose round the briar.

Do you think this appendage heightens or weakens the final impact of the story? Can the American ending be defended as an integral part of a new song? Explain.

5. Paraphrase lines 9, 15–16, 22, 25–28. By putting these lines into prose, what has been lost?

As you can see from "Bonny Barbara Allan," in a traditional English or Scottish folk ballad the storyteller speaks of the lives and feelings of others. Even if the pronoun "I" occurs, it rarely has much personality. Characters often exchange dialogue, but no one character speaks all the way through. Events move rapidly, perhaps because some of the dull transitional stanzas have been forgotten. The events themselves, as ballad scholar Albert B. Friedman has said, are frequently "the stuff of tabloid journalism—sensational tales of lust, revenge and domestic crime. Unwed mothers slay their newborn babes; lovers unwilling to marry their pregnant mistresses brutally murder the poor women, for which, without fail, they are justly punished."[1] There are also many ballads of the supernatural ("The Twa Corbies") and of gallant knights ("Sir Patrick Spence"), and there are a few humorous ballads, usually about unhappy marriages.

A favorite pattern of ballad-makers is the so-called **ballad stanza,** four lines rimed *a b c b*, tending to fall into 8, 6, 8, and 6 syllables:

> Clerk Saunders and Maid Margaret
> Walked owre yon garden green,
> And deep and heavy was the love
> That fell thir twa between.°   *between those two*

Though not the only possible stanza for a ballad, this easily singable quatrain has continued to attract poets since the Middle Ages. Close kin to the ballad stanza is **common meter,** a stanza found in hymns such as "Amazing Grace," by the eighteenth-century English hymnist John Newton:

> Amazing grace! how sweet the sound
> That saved a wretch like me!
> I once was lost, but now am found,
> Was blind, but now I see.

Notice that its pattern is that of the ballad stanza except for its *two* pairs of rimes. That all its lines rime is probably a sign of more literate artistry than we usually hear in folk ballads. Another sign of schoolteachers' influence is that Newton's rimes are exact. (Rimes in folk ballads are often rough-and-ready, as if made by ear, rather than polished and exact, as if the riming words had been matched for their similar spellings. In "Barbara Allan," for instance, the hard-hearted lover's name rimes with *afalling, dwelling, aspilling, dealing,* and even with *ringing* and *adrinking.*) That so many hymns were written in common meter may have been due to convenience. If a congregation didn't know the tune to a hymn in common meter, they readily could sing its words to the tune of another such hymn they knew. Besides hymnists, many poets have favored common meter, among them A. E. Housman and Emily Dickinson.

---

[1] Introduction to *The Viking Book of Folk Ballads of the English-Speaking World,* ed. Albert B. Friedman (New York: Viking, 1956).

Related to traditional folk ballads but displaying characteristics of their own, **broadside ballads** (so called because they were printed on one sheet of paper) often were set to traditional tunes. Most broadside ballads were an early form of journalism made possible by the development of cheap printing and by the growth of audiences who could read, just barely. Sometimes merely humorous or tear-jerking, often they were rimed accounts of sensational news events. That they were widespread and often scorned in Shakespeare's day is attested by the character of Autolycus in *A Winter's Tale*, an itinerant hawker of ballads about sea monsters and strange pregnancies ("a usurer's wife was brought to bed of twenty money-bags"). Although many broadsides tend to be **doggerel** (verse full of irregularities due not to skill but to incompetence), many excellent poets had their work taken up and peddled in the streets—among them Marvell, Swift, and Byron.

Literary ballads, not meant for singing, are written by sophisticated poets for book-educated readers who enjoy being reminded of folk ballads. Literary ballads imitate certain features of folk ballads: they may tell of dramatic conflicts or of mortals who encounter the supernatural; they may use conventional figures of speech or ballad stanzas. Well-known poems of this kind include Keats's "La Belle Dame Sans Merci," Coleridge's "Rime of the Ancient Mariner," and (in our time) Dudley Randall's "Ballad of Birmingham."

Dudley Randall (1914–2000)*

BALLAD OF BIRMINGHAM 1966

(On the Bombing of a Church in Birmingham, Alabama, 1963)

"Mother dear, may I go downtown
Instead of out to play,
And march the streets of Birmingham
In a Freedom March today?"

"No, baby, no, you may not go, 5
For the dogs are fierce and wild,
And clubs and hoses, guns and jail
Aren't good for a little child."

"But, mother, I won't be alone.
Other children will go with me, 10
And march the streets of Birmingham
To make our country free."

"No, baby, no, you may not go,
For I fear those guns will fire.
But you may go to church instead 15
And sing in the children's choir."

She has combed and brushed her night-dark hair,
And bathed rose petal sweet,
And drawn white gloves on her small brown hands,
And white shoes on her feet.   20

The mother smiled to know her child
Was in the sacred place,
But that smile was the last smile
To come upon her face.

For when she heard the explosion,   25
Her eyes grew wet and wild.
She raced through the streets of Birmingham
Calling for her child.

She clawed through bits of glass and brick,
Then lifted out a shoe.   30
"O here's the shoe my baby wore,
But, baby, where are you?"

QUESTIONS

1. This poem, about a dynamite blast set off in an African American church by a racial terrorist (later convicted), delivers a message without preaching. How would you sum up this message, its implied theme?
2. What is ironic in the mother's denying her child permission to take part in a protest march?
3. How does this modern poem resemble a traditional ballad?

EXPERIMENT: *Seeing the Traits of Ballads*

In "Poems for Further Reading" read the Child ballads "The Three Ravens" and "The Twa Corbies" (pages 1138–40). With these ballads in mind, consider one or more of these modern poems:

W. H. Auden, "As I Walked Out One Evening" (page 1144)
William Jay Smith, "American Primitive" (page 1242)
William Butler Yeats, "Crazy Jane Talks with the Bishop" (page 1267)

What characteristics of folk ballads do you find in them? In what ways do these modern poets depart from the traditions of folk ballads of the Middle Ages?

BLUES

Among the many song forms to have shaped the way poetry is written in English, no recent form has been more influential than the blues. Originally a type of folk music developed by black slaves in the South, **blues** songs have both a distinctive form and tone. They traditionally consist of three-line stanzas in which the first two identical lines are followed by a concluding riming third line:

To dream of muddy water—trouble is knocking at your door.
To dream of muddy water—trouble is knocking at your door.
Your man is sure to leave you and never return no more.

Early blues lyrics almost always spoke of some sadness, pain, or deprivation—often the loss of a loved one. The melancholy tone of the lyrics, however, is not only world-weary but also world-wise. The blues expound the hard-
won wisdom of bitter life experience. They frequently create their special mood
through down-to-earth, even gritty, imagery drawn from everyday life. Although blues reach back into the nineteenth century, they were not widely
known outside African American communities before 1920, when the first
commercial recordings appeared. Their influence on both music and song from
that time was rapid and extensive. By 1930 James Weldon Johnson could declare, "It is from the blues that all that may be called American music derives
its most distinctive characteristic." Blues have not only become an enduring
category of popular music, they have also helped shape virtually all the major
styles of contemporary pop—jazz, rap, rock, gospel, country, and of course,
rhythm-and-blues.

The style and structure of blues have also influenced modern poets. Not only
have African American writers like Langston Hughes, Sterling A. Brown,
Etheridge Knight, and Sonia Sanchez written blues poems, but white poets as
dissimilar as W. H. Auden, Elizabeth Bishop, Donald Justice, and Sandra
McPherson have employed the form. The classic touchstones of the blues, however, remain the early singers such as Robert Johnson, Ma Rainey, Blind Lemon
Jefferson, Charley Patton, and—perhaps preeminently—Bessie Smith, "the
Empress of the Blues." Any form that has fascinated Bishop and Auden as well as
B. B. King, Mick Jagger, Tracy Chapman, and Eric Clapton surely deserves special notice. The blues remind us of how closely related song and poetry will al-
ways be. Here are the lyrics of one of Bessie Smith's earliest songs, based on a traditional folk blues, followed by a blues-influenced cabaret song written by W. H.
Auden (with the composer Benjamin Britten) for a night-club singer.

Bessie Smith   (1898?–1937)
with Clarence Williams   (1898–1965)

JAILHOUSE BLUES   1923

Thirty days in jail with my back turned to the wall.
Thirty days in jail with my back turned to the wall.
Look here, Mister Jailkeeper, put another gal in my stall.

I don't mind bein' in jail but I got to stay there so long.
I don't mind bein' in jail but I got to stay there so long.   5
Well, ev'ry friend I had has done shook hands and gone.

You better stop your man from ticklin' me under my chin.
You better stop your man from ticklin' me under my chin.
'Cause if he keep on ticklin' I'm sure gonna take him in.

Good mornin' blues, blues how do you do?   10
Good mornin' blues, blues how do you do?
Well, I just come here to have a few words with you.

W. H. Auden   (1907–1973)*

FUNERAL BLUES   1940

Stop all the clocks, cut off the telephone,
Prevent the dog from barking with a juicy bone,
Silence the pianos and muffled drum
Bring out the coffin, let the mourners come.

Let aeroplanes circle moaning overhead   5
Scribbling on the sky the message He Is Dead,
Tie crepe bows round the white necks of the public doves,
Let the traffic policemen wear black cotton gloves.

He was my North, my South, my East and West,
My working week and my Sunday rest,   10
My noon, my midnight, my talk, my song;
I thought that love would last for ever: I was wrong.

The stars are not wanted now: put out every one,
Pack up the moon and dismantle the sun,
Pour away the ocean and sweep up the woods;   15
For nothing now can ever come to any good.

QUESTIONS

What features of the traditional blues does Auden keep in his song? What features does he discard?

RAP

One of the most interesting musical and literary developments of the 1980s was the emergence of **rap**, a form of popular music in which words are recited to a driving rhythmic beat. It differs from mainstream popular music in several ways, but, most interesting in literary terms, rap lyrics are *spoken* rather than sung. In that sense, rap is a form of popular poetry as well as popular music. In most rap songs, the lead performer or "M.C." talks or recites, usually at top speed, long, rhythmic, four-stress lines that end in rimes. Although today most rap singers and groups use electronic or sampled backgrounds, rap began on city streets in the game of "signifying," in which two poets aim rimed insults at each other, sometimes accompanying their tirades with a beat made by clapping or finger-snapping. This game also includes boasts made by the players on both sides about their own abilities. Rap has developed so rapidly that it now uses a variety of metrical forms, but it is interesting to look more closely at some of the early work that established the genre. Most rap still follows the initial formula of rimed couplets that casually mix full rime with assonance. Here are a few lines from one of the first popular raps:

> I said, "By the way, baby, what's your name?"
> She said, "I go by the name Lois Lane.
> And you can be my boyfriend, you surely can
> Just let me quit my boyfriend, he's called Superman."

> —"Rapper's Delight," Sugarhill Gang, 1979

Rap is not written in the standard meters of English literary verse, but its basic measure does come out of the English tradition. Rap's characteristic four-stress, accentual line has been the most common meter for spoken popular poetry in English from Anglo-Saxon verse and the folk ballads to the work of Robert W. Service and Rudyard Kipling.

> What is a woman that you forsake her,
> And the hearth-fire and the home-acre,
> To go with the old grey Widow-maker?

> —"Harp Song of the Dane Women," Rudyard Kipling, 1906

The four-stress line is also a meter found throughout *Mother Goose*:

> Tom, Tom, the piper's son.
> Stole a pig and away did run
> The pig was eat, and Tom was beat
> Till he run crying down the street.

Rap deliberately makes use of stress-meter's ability to stretch and contract in syllable count. In fact, playing the syllable count against the beat is the basic metrical technique of rap. Like jazz, rap plays off a flexible rhythm against a fixed metrical beat, turning a traditional English folk meter into something distinctively African American. By hitting the beat hard while exploiting other elements of word music, rappers play interesting and elaborate games with the total rhythm of their lines. Here are the lyrics of an early rap recorded by Run D.M.C. that shows a sophisticated understanding of the traditions of English popular poetry (and makes direct references to a number of earlier literary works).

Run D.M.C. [*J. Simmons/D. McDaniels*]

from PETER PIPER   1986

Now Dr. Seuss and Mother Goose both did their thing
But Jam Master's getting loose and D.M.C.'s the king
'Cuz he's the adult entertainer, child educator
Jam Master Jay king of the cross-fader
He's the better of the best, best believe he's the baddest   5
Perfect timing when I'm climbing I'm the rhyming acrobatist
Lotta guts, when he cuts girls move their butts
His name is Jay, here to play, he must be nuts
And on the mix real quick, and I'd like to say
He's not Flash but he's fast and his name is Jay.   10

It goes a one, two, three and . . .
Jay's like King Midas, as I was told,
Everything that he touched turned to gold
He's the greatest of the great get it straight he's great
Claim fame 'cuz his name is known in every state   15
His name is Jay to see him play will make you say
God damn that D.J. made my day
Like the butcher, the baker, the candlestick maker
He's a maker, a breaker, and a title taker
Like the little old lady who lived in a shoe   20
If cuts were kids he would be through
Not lying y'all he's the best I know
And if I lie my nose will grow
Like a little wooden boy named Pinocchio
And you all know how the story go   25
Trix are for kids he plays much gigs
He's the big bad wolf and you're the 3 pigs
He's the big bad wolf in your neighborhood
Not bad meaning bad but bad meaning good . . . There it is!
We're Run D.M.C. got a beef to settle   30
Dee's not Hansel, he's not Gretel
Jay's a winner, not a beginner
His pocket gets fat, others' get thinner
Jump on Jay like cow jumped moon
People chase Jay like dish and spoon   35
And like all fairy tales end
You'll see Jay again my friend, hough!

PETER PIPER. (These lyrics were transcribed from the Run D.M.C. hit.) *2 Jam Master Jay:* the DJ who
provides beats and scratching in the rap group. *4 Cross-fader:* scratching device. *10 Flash:* allusion either to Grandmaster Flash, another DJ, or the comic book superhero Flash; rap critics debate this
point.

FOR REVIEW AND FURTHER STUDY

John Lennon (1940–1980)
Paul McCartney (b. 1942)

ELEANOR RIGBY   1966

Ah, look at all the lonely people!
Ah, look at all the lonely people!

Eleanor Rigby
Picks up the rice in the church where a wedding has been,
Lives in a dream,   5
Waits at the window
Wearing the face that she keeps in a jar by the door.
Who is it for?

All the lonely people,
Where do they all come from?   10
All the lonely people,
Where do they all belong?

Father McKenzie,
Writing the words of a sermon that no one will hear,
No one comes near   15
Look at him working,
Darning his socks in the night when there's nobody there.
What does he care?

All the lonely people
Where do they all come from?   20
All the lonely people
Where do they all belong?

Eleanor Rigby
Died in the church and was buried along with her name.
Nobody came.   25
Father McKenzie,
Wiping the dirt from his hands as he walks from the grave,
No one was saved.

All the lonely people,
Where do they all come from?   30
All the lonely people,
Where do they all belong?

Ah, look at all the lonely people!
Ah, look at all the lonely people!

Is there any reason to call this famous song lyric a ballad? Compare it with a traditional ballad, such as "Bonny Barbara Allan." Do you notice any similarity? What are the differences?

Bob Dylan   (b. 1941)

THE TIMES THEY ARE A-CHANGIN'   1963

Come gather 'round people
Wherever you roam
And admit that the waters
Around you have grown
And accept it that soon   5
You'll be drenched to the bone.
If your time to you
Is worth savin'
Then you better start swimmin'
Or you'll sink like a stone   10
For the times they are a-changin'.

Come writers and critics
Who prophesize with your pen
And keep your eyes wide
The chance won't come again   15
And don't speak too soon
For the wheel's still in spin
And there's no tellin' who
That it's namin'.
For the loser now   20
Will be later to win
For the times they are a-changin'.

Come senators, congressmen
Please heed the call
Don't stand in the doorway   25
Don't block up the hall
For he that gets hurt
Will be he who has stalled
There's a battle outside
And it is ragin'.   30
It'll soon shake your windows
And rattle your walls
For the times they are a-changin'.

Come mothers and fathers
Throughout the land
And don't criticize
What you can't understand
Your sons and your daughters
Are beyond your command
Your old road is
Rapidly agin'.
Please get out of the new one
If you can't lend your hand
For the times they are a-changin'.

The line it is drawn
The curse it is cast
The slow one now
Will later be fast
As the present now
Will later be past
The order is
Rapidly fadin'.
And the first one now
Will later be last
For the times they are a-changin'.

QUESTIONS

1. What features does Dylan keep constant from stanza to stanza? What changes?
2. Who is addressed at the start of each stanza? How do those people affect what is said later in the same stanza?
3. Could the stanzas be sung in a different order without greatly changing the impact of the song? Or would any change undercut the structure of the song?
4. Do the words of this song work well on the page? Or is something essential lost when the music is taken away? Choose and defend one point of view.

Gwendolyn Brooks   (1917–2000)*

QUEEN OF THE BLUES   1945

Mame was singing
At the Midnight Club.
And the place was red
With blues.
She could shake her body   5
Across the floor.
For what did she have
To lose?

She put her mama
Under the ground   10
Two years ago.
(Was it three?)
She covered that grave
With roses and tears.
(A handsome thing   15
To see.)

She didn't have any
Legal pa
To glare at her,
To shame   20
Her off the floor
Of the Midnight Club.
Poor Mame.

She didn't have any
Big brother   25
To shout
"No sister of mine! . . ."
She didn't have any
Small brother
To think she was everything   30
Fine.

She didn't have any
Baby girl
With velvet
Pop-open eyes.   35
She didn't have any
Sonny boy
To tell sweet
Sonny boy lies.

"Show me a man
What will love me
Till I die.
Now show me a man
What will love me
Till I die.   45
Can't find no such man
No matter how hard
You try.
Go 'long, baby.
Ain't a true man left   50
In Chi.

"I loved my daddy.
But what did my daddy
Do?
I loved my daddy.   55
But what did my daddy
Do?
Found him a brown-skin chicken
What's gonna be
Black and blue.   60

"I was good to my daddy.
Gave him all my dough.
I say, I was good to my daddy.
I gave him all of my dough.
Scrubbed hard in them white folks'   65
Kitchens
Till my knees was rusty
And so'."

The M.C. hollered,
"Queen of the blues!
Folks, this is strictly   70
The queen of the blues!"
She snapped her fingers.
She rolled her hips.
What did she have
To lose?   75

But a thought ran through her
Like a fire.
"Men don't tip their
Hats to me.
They pinch my arms   80
And they slap my thighs.

But when has a man
Tipped his hat to me?"

Queen of the blues!
Queen of the blues!   85
Strictly, strictly,
The queen of the blues!

Men are low down
Dirty and mean.   90
Why don't they tip
Their hats to a queen?

QUESTIONS

1. How would you characterize the form of this poem? For what thematic reasons might the poet have chosen this form?
2. Do you think the poem would be more effective, or less so, if it were written in a more conventional "literary" style?

WRITER'S PERSPECTIVE

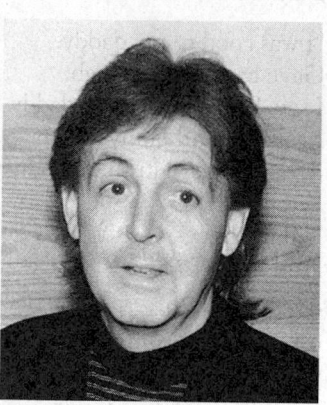

Paul McCartney

Paul McCartney on Writing

CREATING "ELEANOR RIGBY"   1978

Well, that ["Eleanor Rigby"] started off with sitting down at the piano and getting the first line of the melody, and playing around with the words. I think it was "Miss Daisy Hawkins" originally; then it was her picking up the rice in a church after a wedding. That's how nearly all our songs start, with the first line just suggesting itself from books or newspapers.

At first I thought it was a young Miss Daisy Hawkins, a bit like "Annabel Lee," but not so sexy; but then I saw I'd said she was picking up the rice in church, so she had to be a cleaner; she had missed the wedding, and she was suddenly lonely. In fact she had missed it all—she was the spinster type.

Jane° was in a play in Bristol then, and I was walking round the streets waiting for her to finish. I didn't really like "Daisy Hawkins"—I wanted a name that was more real. The thought just came: "Eleanor Rigby picks up the rice and lives in a dream"—so there she was. The next thing was Father McKenzie. It was going to be Father McCartney, but then I thought that was a bit of a hang-up for my Dad, being in this lonely song. So we looked through the phone book. That's the beauty of working at random—it does come up perfectly, much better than if you try to think it with your intellect.

Anyway there was Father McKenzie, and he was just as I had imagined him, lonely, darning his socks. We weren't sure if the song was going to go on. In the next verse we thought of a bin man, an old feller going through dustbins; but it got too involved—embarrassing. John and I wondered whether to have Eleanor Rigby and him have a thing going, but we couldn't really see how. When I played it to John we decided to finish it.

That was the point anyway. She didn't make it, she never made it with anyone, she didn't even look as if she was going to.

From *The Beatles in Their Own Words*

◆─■▭◗ WRITING CRITICALLY ◖▭■─◆

Is There a Difference Between Poetry and Song?

Poetry and song were originally one art, and even today the two forms remain closely related. We celebrate the beauty of a poem by praising its "music" just as we compliment a great song lyric by calling it "poetic." And yet a very simple distinction separates the two arts: in a song, the lyrics combine with music to create a collaborative total work, whereas in a poem the author must create all the effects by words alone.

In analyzing song lyrics as poetry, it is important to separate the words temporarily from their music. Before you transcribe the lyrics onto the page, listen to the song and jot down the three or four moments that affect you most powerfully. After you have transcribed the words, consult your notes and look at the lyrics. Are the effects that moved you in the recorded song still evident in the words alone? Or did they reside mostly in the music? Or did they perhaps originate in some special combination of words and music that is not adequately re-created by the text alone?

A song is no less powerful as a song just because the words don't stand on their own as poetry. A song is meant to be sung—transposing song lyrics onto the page changes their function. This exercise helps you understand lyrics as poetry, but do not scrutinize them unfairly relative to their original purpose.

Jane: refers to Jane Asher, a British actress McCartney was dating at the time.

WRITING ASSIGNMENT

Write a short paper (750–1000 words) in which you analyze the lyrics of a favorite song. Discuss what the words alone provide and what they lack in recreating the total power of the original song. The purpose of the paper is not to justify the song you have chosen as great poetry (though it may perhaps qualify); rather, it is to examine which parts of the song's power come solely from the words and which come from the music or performance. (Don't forget to provide your instructor with an accurate transcription of the song lyrics.)

FURTHER SUGGESTIONS FOR WRITING

1. Write a short study of a lyric (or lyrics) by a recent popular songwriter. Show why you believe the songwriter's work deserves the name of poetry.
2. Compare and contrast the English folk ballad "The Three Ravens" with the Scottish folk ballad "The Twa Corbies" (both in "Poems for Further Reading").
3. Compare the versions of "Richard Cory" by Edwin Arlington Robinson and by Paul Simon. Point out changes Simon apparently made in the poem to render it singable. What other changes did he make? How did he alter Robinson's story and its characters?
4. After listening to some recent examples of rap, compose a short rap lyric of your own, one that tells a story.

19 Sound

SOUND AS MEANING

Isak Dinesen, in a memoir of her life on a plantation in East Africa, tells how some Kikuyu tribesmen reacted to their first hearing of rimed verse:

> The Natives, who have a strong sense of rhythm, know nothing of verse, or at least did not know anything before the times of the schools, where they were taught hymns. One evening out in the maize-field, where we had been harvesting maize, breaking off the cobs and throwing them on to the ox-carts, to amuse myself, I spoke to the field laborers, who were mostly quite young, in Swahili verse. There was no sense in the verses, they were made for the sake of rime—"Ngumbe na-penda chumbe, Malaya mbaya. Wakamba na-kula mamba." The oxen like salt—whores are bad—The Wakamba eat snakes. It caught the interest of the boys, they formed a ring round me. They were quick to understand that meaning in poetry is of no consequence, and they did not question the thesis of the verse, but waited eagerly for the rime, and laughed at it when it came. I tried to make them themselves find the rime and finish the poem when I had begun it, but they could not, or would not, do that, and turned away their heads. As they had become used to the idea of poetry, they begged: "Speak again. Speak like rain." Why they should feel verse to be like rain I do not know. It must have been, however, an expression of applause, since in Africa rain is always longed for and welcomed.[1]

What the tribesmen had discovered is that poetry, like music, appeals to the ear. However limited it may be in comparison with the sound of an orchestra—or a

---

[1] Isak Dinesen, *Out of Africa* (New York: Random, 1972).

tribal drummer—the sound of words in itself gives pleasure. However, we might doubt Isak Dinesen's assumption that "meaning in poetry is of no consequence." "Hey nonny-nonny" and such nonsense has a place in song lyrics and other poems, and we might take pleasure in hearing rimes in Swahili; but most good poetry has meaningful sound as well as musical sound. Certainly the words of a song have an effect different from that of wordless music: they go along with their music and, by making statements, add more meaning. The French poet Isidore Isou, founder of a literary movement called *lettrisme*, maintained that poems can be written not only in words but also in letters (sample lines: *xyl, xyl, / prprali dryl / znglo trpylo pwi*). But the sound of letters alone, without denotation and connotation, has not been enough to make Letterist poems memorable. In the response of the Kikuyu tribesmen, there may have been not only the pleasure of hearing sounds but also the agreeable surprise of finding that things not usually associated had been brought together.

More powerful when in the company of meaning, not apart from it, the sounds of consonants and vowels can contribute greatly to a poem's effect. The sound of *s*, which can suggest the swishing of water, has rarely been used more accurately than in Surrey's line "Calm is the sea, the waves work less and less." When, in a poem, the sound of words working together with meaning pleases mind and ear, the effect is **euphony,** as in the following lines from Tennyson's "Come down, O maid":

> Myriads of rivulets hurrying through the lawn,
> The moan of doves in immemorial elms,
> And murmuring of innumerable bees.

Its opposite is **cacophony:** a harsh, discordant effect. It too is chosen for the sake of meaning. We hear it in Milton's scornful reference in "Lycidas" to corrupt clergymen whose songs "Grate on their scrannel pipes of wretched straw." (Read that line and one of Tennyson's aloud and see which requires lips, teeth, and tongue to do more work.) But note that although Milton's line is harsh in sound, the line (when we meet it in his poem) is pleasing because it is artful. In a famous passage from his *Essay on Criticism*, Pope has illustrated both euphony and cacophony. (Given here as Pope printed it, the passage relies heavily on italics and capital letters, for particular emphasis. If you will read these lines aloud, dwelling a little longer or harder on the words italicized, you will find that Pope has given you very good directions for a meaningful reading.)

Alexander Pope (1688–1744)*

True Ease in Writing comes from Art, not Chance   1711

True Ease in Writing comes from Art, not Chance,
As those move easiest who have learned to dance.
'Tis not enough no Harshness gives Offence,

The *Sound* must seem an *Echo* to the *Sense*.
Soft is the strain when *Zephyr*° gently blows,   *the west wind*   5
And the *smooth Stream* in *smoother Numbers*° flows;   *metrical rhythm*
But when loud Surges lash the sounding Shore,
The *hoarse, rough Verse* should like the *Torrent* roar.
When *Ajax* strives, some Rock's vast Weight to throw,
The Line too *labors,* and the Words move *slow;*   10
Not so, when swift *Camilla* scours the Plain,
Flies o'er th' unbending Corn, and skims along the Main.°   *expanse (of sea)*
Hear how *Timotheus'* varied Lays surprise,
And bid Alternate Passions fall and rise!
While, at each Change, the Son of *Lybian Jove*   15
Now *burns* with Glory, and then *melts* with Love;
Now his *fierce Eyes* with *sparkling Fury* glow;
Now *Sighs* steal out, and *Tears begin to flow:*
Persians and Greeks like *Turns of Nature* found,
And the *World's Victor* stood subdued by *Sound!*   20
The Pow'rs of Music all our Hearts allow;
And what *Timotheus* was, is *Dryden* now.

TRUE EASE IN WRITING COMES FROM ART, NOT CHANCE (*An Essay on Criticism*, lines 362–383).
9 *Ajax:* Greek hero, almost a superman, who in Homer's account of the siege of Troy hurls an enormous rock that momentarily flattens Hector, the Trojan prince (*Iliad* VII, 268–272). 11 *Camilla:* a
kind of Amazon or warrior woman of the Volcians, whose speed and lightness of step are praised by
the Roman poet Virgil: "She could have skimmed across an unmown grainfield / Without so much as
bruising one tender blade; / She could have sped across an ocean's surge / Without so much as wetting her quicksilver soles" (*Aeneid* VII, 808–811). 13 *Timotheus:* favorite musician of Alexander the
Great. In "Alexander's Feast, or The Power of Music," John Dryden imagines him: "Timotheus,
placed on high / Amid the tuneful choir, / With flying fingers touched the lyre: / The trembling notes
ascend the sky, / And heavenly joys inspire." 15 *Lybian Jove:* name for Alexander. A Libyan oracle
had declared the king to be the son of the god Zeus Ammon.

   Notice the pleasing effect of all the *s* sounds in the lines about the west wind
and the stream, and in another meaningful place, the effect of the consonants in
Ajax strives, a phrase that makes our lips work almost as hard as Ajax throwing
the rock.
   Is sound identical with meaning in lines such as these? Not quite. In the passage from Tennyson, for instance, the cooing of doves is not *exactly* a moan. As
John Crowe Ransom pointed out, the sound would be almost the same but the
meaning entirely different in "The murdering of innumerable beeves." While it
is true that the consonant sound *sl-* will often begin a word that conveys ideas of
wetness and smoothness—*slick, slimy, slippery, slush*—we are so used to hearing it
in words that convey nothing of the kind—*slave, slow, sledgehammer*—that it is
doubtful whether, all by itself, the sound communicates anything definite. The
most beautiful phrase in the English language, according to Dorothy Parker, is
cellar door. Another wit once nominated, as our most euphonious word, not
sunrise or *silvery* but *syphilis.*

Relating sound more closely to meaning, the device called **onomatopoeia** is an attempt to represent a thing or action by a word that imitates the sound associated with it: *zoom, whiz, crash, bang, ding-dong, pitter-patter, yakety-yak.* Onomatopoeia is often effective in poetry, as in Emily Dickinson's line about the fly with its "uncertain stumbling Buzz," in which the nasal sounds *n, m, ng* and the sibilants *c, s* help make a droning buzz.

Like the Kikuyu tribesmen, others who care for poetry have discovered in the sound of words something of the refreshment of cool rain. Dylan Thomas, telling how he began to write poetry, said that from early childhood words were to him "as the notes of bells, the sounds of musical instruments, the noises of wind, sea, and rain, the rattle of milkcarts, the clopping of hooves on cobbles, the fingering of branches on the window pane, might be to someone, deaf from birth, who has miraculously found his hearing."[2] For readers, too, the sound of words can have a magical spell, most powerful when it points to meaning. James Weldon Johnson in *God's Trombones* has told of an old-time preacher who began his sermon, "Brothers and sisters, this morning I intend to explain the unexplainable—find out the indefinable—ponder over the imponderable—and unscrew the inscrutable!" The repetition of sound in *unscrew* and *inscrutable* has appeal, but the magic of the words is all the greater if they lead us to imagine the mystery of all Creation as an enormous screw that the preacher's mind, like a screwdriver, will loosen. Though the sound of a word or the meaning of a word may have value all by itself, both become more memorable when taken together.

William Butler Yeats (1865–1939)*

WHO GOES WITH FERGUS? 1892

Who will go drive with Fergus now,
And pierce the deep wood's woven shade,
And dance upon the level shore?
Young man, lift up your russet brow,
And lift your tender eyelids, maid,   5
And brood on hopes and fear no more.

And no more turn aside and brood
Upon love's bitter mystery;
For Fergus rules the brazen cars,°   *chariots*
And rules the shadows of the wood,   10
And the white breast of the dim sea
And all dishevelled wandering stars.

WHO GOES WITH FERGUS? *Fergus:* Irish king who gave up his throne to be a wandering poet.

[2]"Notes on the Art of Poetry," *Modern Poetics*, ed. James Scully (New York: McGraw-Hill, 1965).

QUESTIONS

1. In what lines do you find euphony?
2. In what line do you find cacophony?
3. How do the sounds of these lines stress what is said in them?

EXERCISE: *Listening to Meaning*

Read aloud the following brief poems. In the sounds of which particular words are meanings well captured? In which of the poems below do you find onomatopoeia?

John Updike   (b. 1932)*

RECITAL   1963

> ROGER BOBO GIVES
> RECITAL ON TUBA
> —*Headline in the Times*

Eskimos in Manitoba,
    Barracuda off Aruba,
Cock an ear when Roger Bobo
    Starts to solo on the tuba.

Men of every station—Pooh-Bah,   5
    Nabob, bozo, toff, and hobo—
Cry in unison, "Indubi-
    Tably, there is simply nobo-

Dy who oompahs on the tubo,
Solo, quite like Roger Bubo!"   10

William Wordsworth   (1770–1850)*

A SLUMBER DID MY SPIRIT SEAL   1800

A slumber did my spirit seal;
    I had no human fears—
She seemed a thing that could not feel
    The touch of earthly years

No motion has she now, no force;   5
    She neither hears nor sees;
Rolled round in earth's diurnal course,
    With rocks, and stones, and trees.

Emanuel di Pasquale (b. 1943)

RAIN   1971

Like a drummer's brush,
the rain hushes the surface of tin porches.

Aphra Behn (1640?–1689)

WHEN MAIDENS ARE YOUNG   1687

When maidens are young, and in their spring,
Of pleasure, of pleasure let 'em take their full swing,
  Full swing, full swing,
And love, and dance, and play, and sing,
For Silvia, believe it, when youth is done,   5
There's nought but hum-drum, hum-drum, hum-drum,
There's nought but hum-drum, hum-drum, hum-drum.

ALLITERATION AND ASSONANCE

Listening to a symphony in which themes are repeated throughout each movement, we enjoy both their recurrence and their variation. We take similar pleasure in the repetition of a phrase or a single chord. Something like this pleasure is
afforded us frequently in poetry.

    Analogies between poetry and wordless music, it is true, tend to break down
when carried far, since poetry—to mention a single difference—has denotation.
But like musical compositions, poems have patterns of sounds. Among such patterns long popular in English poetry is **alliteration,** which has been defined as a
succession of similar sounds. Alliteration occurs in the repetition of the same
consonant sound at the beginning of successive words—"round and round the
rugged rocks the ragged rascal ran," or in this delightful stanza by Witter Bynner,
written nearly a century ago as part of an elaborate literary hoax:

> If I were only dafter
>   I might be making hymns
> To the liquor of your laughter
>   Or the lacquer of your limbs.

Or it may occur inside the words, as in Milton's description of the gates of Hell:

>   On a sudden open fly
> With impetuous recoil and jarring sound
> The infernal doors, and on their hinges grate
> Harsh thunder, that the lowest bottom shook
> Of Erebus.

The former kind is called **initial alliteration,** the latter **internal alliteration** or **hidden alliteration.** We recognize alliteration by sound, not by spelling: *know* and *nail* alliterate, *know* and *key* do not. In a line by E. E. Cummings, "colossal hoax of clocks and calendars," the sound of *x* within *hoax* alliterates with the *cks* in *clocks*. Incidentally, the letter *r* does not *always* lend itself to cacophony: elsewhere in *Paradise Lost* Milton said that

> Heaven opened wide
> Her ever-during gates, harmonious sound
> On golden hinges moving . . .

By itself, a letter-sound has no particular meaning. This is a truth forgotten by people who would attribute the effectiveness of Milton's lines on the Heavenly Gates to, say, "the mellow *o*'s and liquid *l* of *harmonious* and *golden*." Mellow *o*'s and liquid *l*'s occur also in the phrase *moldy cold oatmeal*, which may have a quite different effect. Meaning depends on larger units of language than letters of the alphabet.

Poetry formerly contained more alliteration than it usually contains today. In Old English verse, each line was held together by alliteration, a basic pattern still evident in the fourteenth century, as in the following description of the world as a "fair field" in *Piers Plowman:*

> A *f*eir *f*eld *f*ul of *f*olk *f*ond I ther bi-twene,
> Of alle *m*aner of *m*en, the *m*ene and the riche . . .

Most poets nowadays save alliteration for special occasions. They may use it to give emphasis, as Edward Lear does: "Far and few, far and few, / Are the lands where the Jumblies live." With its aid they can point out the relationship between two things placed side by side, as in Pope's line on things of little worth: "The courtier's promises, and sick man's prayers." Alliteration, too, can be a powerful aid to memory. It is hard to forget such tongue twisters as "Peter Piper picked a peck of pickled peppers," or common expressions like "green as grass," "tried and true," and "from stem to stern." In fact, because alliteration directs our attention to something, it had best be used neither thoughtlessly nor merely for decoration, lest it call attention to emptiness. A case in point may be a line by Philip James Bailey, a reaction to a lady's weeping: "I saw, but spared to speak." If the poet chose the word *spared* for any meaningful reason other than that it alliterates with *speak*, the reason is not clear.

As we have seen, to repeat the sound of a consonant is to produce alliteration, but to repeat the sound of a *vowel* is to produce **assonance.** Like alliteration, assonance may occur either initially—"all the *a*wful *a*uguries"[3]—or internally—Edmund Spenser's "Her goodly *eyes* l*i*ke sapph*i*res shining br*i*ght, / Her forehead

[3]Some prefer to call the repetition of an initial vowel-sound by the name of alliteration: "apt alliteration's artful aid."

ivory white . . . " and it can help make common phrases unforgettable: "eager beaver," "holy smoke." Like alliteration, it slows the reader down and focuses attention.

A. E. Housman   (1859–1936)*

Eight O'Clock   1922

He stood, and heard the steeple
    Sprinkle the quarters on the morning town.
One, two, three, four, to market-place and people
    It tossed them down.

Strapped, noosed, nighing his hour,   5
    He stood and counted them and cursed his luck;
And then the clock collected in the tower
    Its strength, and struck.

Questions

1. Why does the protagonist in this brief drama curse his luck? What is his situation?
2. For so short a poem, "Eight O'Clock" carries a great weight of alliteration. What patterns of initial alliteration do you find? What patterns of internal alliteration? What effect is created by all this heavy emphasis?

Robert Herrick   (1591–1674)*

Upon Julia's Voice   1648

So smooth, so sweet, so silv'ry is thy voice,
As, could they hear, the damned would make no noise,
But listen to thee (walking in thy chamber)
Melting melodious words, to lutes of amber.

UPON JULIA'S VOICE. 4 *amber:* either the fossilized resin from which pipestems are sometimes made today, and which might have inlaid the body of a lute; or an alloy of four parts silver and one part gold.

Questions

1. Is Julia speaking or singing? How do we know for sure?
2. In what moments in this brief poem does the sound of words especially help convey meaning?
3. Does Herrick's reference to the *damned* (presumably howling from Hell's torments) seem out of place?

EXPERIMENT: *Reading for Assonance*

Try reading aloud as rapidly as possible the following poem by Tennyson. From the difficulties you encounter, you may be able to sense the slowing effect of assonance. Then read the poem aloud a second time, with consideration.

Alfred, Lord Tennyson (1809–1892)*

THE SPLENDOR FALLS ON CASTLE WALLS   1850

The splendor falls on castle walls
 And snowy summits old in story;
The long light shakes across the lakes,
 And the wild cataract leaps in glory.
Blow, bugle, blow, set the wild echoes flying,   5
Blow, bugle; answer, echoes, dying, dying, dying.

O hark, O hear! how thin and clear,
 And thinner, clearer, farther going!
O sweet and far from cliff and scar°   *jutting rock*
 The horns of Elfland faintly blowing!   10
Blow, let us hear the purple glens replying:
Blow, bugle; answer, echoes, dying, dying, dying.

O love, they die in yon rich sky,
 They faint on hill or field or river;
Our echoes roll from soul to soul,   15
 And grow for ever and for ever.
Blow, bugle, blow, set the wild echoes flying,
And answer, echoes, answer, dying, dying, dying.

RIME

Isak Dinesen's tribesmen, to whom rime was a new phenomenon, recognized at once that rimed language is special language. So do we, for, although much English poetry is unrimed, rime is one means to set poetry apart from ordinary conversation and bring it closer to music. A **rime** (or rhyme), defined most narrowly, occurs when two or more words or phrases contain an identical or similar vowel-sound, usually accented, and the consonant-sounds (if any) that follow the vowel-sound are identical: *hay* and *sleigh, prairie schooner* and *piano tuner*.[4] From these examples it will be seen that rime depends not on spelling but on sound.

Excellent rimes surprise. It is all very well that a reader may anticipate which vowel-sound is coming next, for patterns of rime give pleasure by satisfying expectations; but riming becomes dull clunking if, at the end of each line,

---

[4]Some definitions of *rime* would apply the term to the repetition of any identical or similar sound, not only a vowel-sound. In this sense, assonance is a kind of rime; so is alliteration (called **initial rime**).

the reader can predict the word that will end the next. Hearing many a jukebox song for the first time, a listener can do so: *charms* lead to *arms*, *skies above* to *love*. As Alexander Pope observes of the habits of dull rimesters,

> Where'er you find "the cooling western breeze,"
> In the next line it "whispers through the trees";
> If crystal streams "with pleasing murmurs creep,"
> The reader's threatened (not in vain) with "sleep". . . .

But who—given the opening line of this comic poem—could predict the lines that follow?

William Cole (1919–2000)

ON MY BOAT ON LAKE CAYUGA   1985

On my boat on Lake Cayuga
I have a horn that goes "Ay-oogah!"
I'm not the modern kind of creep
Who has a horn that goes "beep beep."

Robert Herrick, in a more subtle poem, made good use of rime to indicate a startling contrast:

> Then while time serves, and we are but decaying,
> Come, my Corinna, come, let's go a-Maying.

Though good rimes seem fresh, not all will startle, and probably few will call to mind things so unlike as *May* and *decay*, *Cayuga* and *Ay-oogah*. Some masters of rime often link words that, taken out of text, might seem common and unevocative. Here are the opening lines of Rachel Hadas's poem, "Three Silences," which describe an infant feeding at a mother's breast:

> Of all the times when not to speak is best,
> mother's and infant's is the easiest,
> the milky mouth still warm against her breast.

Hadas's rime words are not especially memorable in themselves, and yet these lines are—at least in part because they rime so well. The quiet echo of sound at the end of each line reinforces the intimate tone of the mother's moment with her child. Poetic invention may be driven home without rime, but it is rime sometimes that rings the doorbell. Admittedly, some rimes wear thin from too much use. More difficult to use freshly than before the establishment of Tin Pan Alley, rimes such as *moon*, *June*, *croon* seem leaden and to ring true would need an extremely powerful context. *Death* and *breath* are a rime that poets have used with wearisome frequency; another is *birth*, *earth*, *mirth*. And yet we cannot exclude these from the diction of poetry, for they might be the very words a poet would need in order to say something new and original.

Good poets, said John Dryden, learn to make their rime "so properly a part of the verse, that it should never mislead the sense, but itself be led and governed by it." The comment may remind us that skillful rime—unlike poor rime—is never a distracting ornament. Like other patterns of sound, rime can help a poet to group ideas, emphasize particular words, and weave a poem together. It can start reverberations between words and can point to connections of meaning.

To have an **exact rime,** sounds following the vowel sound have to be the same: *red* and *bread, wealthily* and *stealthily, walk to her* and *talk to her.* If final consonant sounds are the same but the vowel sounds are different, the result is **slant rime,** also called **near rime, off rime,** or **imperfect rime:** *sun* riming with *bone, moon, rain, green, gone, thin.* By not satisfying the reader's expectation of an exact chime, but instead giving a clunk, a slant rime can help a poet say some things in a particular way. It works especially well for disappointed letdowns, negations, and denials, as in Blake's couplet:

> He who the ox to wrath has moved
> Shall never be by woman loved.

Many poets have admired the unexpected and arresting effects of slant rime. One of the first poets to explore the possibilities of rhyming consonants in a consistent way was Wilfred Owen, an English soldier in World War I, who wrote his best poems in the thirteen months before he was killed in action. Seeking a poetic language strong enough to describe the harsh reality of modern war, Owen experimented with matching consonant sounds in striking ways:

> Now men will go content with what we spoiled
> Or, discontent, boil bloody, and be spilled,
> They will be swift with the swiftness of the tigress.
> None will break ranks, though nations trek from progress.
> Courage was mine, and I had mystery,
> Wisdom was mine, and I had mastery:
> To miss the march of this retreating world
> Into vain citadels that are not walled.

Consonance, a kind of slant rime, occurs when the rimed words or phrases have the same beginning and ending consonant sounds but a different vowel, as in *chitter* and *chatter.* Owen rimes *spoiled* and *spilled* in this way. Consonance is used in a traditional nonsense poem, "The Cutty Wren": "'O where are you going?' says *Milder* to *Malder.*" (W. H. Auden wrote a variation on it that begins, "'O where are you going?' said *reader* to *rider,*" thus keeping the consonance.)

End rime, as its name indicates, comes at the ends of lines, **internal rime** within them. Most rime tends to be end rime. Few recent poets have used internal rime so heavily as Wallace Stevens in the beginning of "Bantams in Pine-Woods": "Chieftain Iffucan of Azcan in caftan / Of tan with henna hackles, halt!" (lines also heavy on alliteration). A poet may employ both end rime and internal rime in the same poem, as in Robert Burns's satiric ballad "The Kirk's Alarm":

> Orthodox, Orthodox, wha believe in John Knox,
>   Let me sound an alarm to your conscience:
> There's a heretic blast has been blawn i' the wast,°   *west*
>   "That what is not sense must be nonsense."

Masculine rime is a rime of one-syllable words (*jail, bail*) or (in words of more than one syllable) stressed final syllables: *di-VORCE, re-MORSE,* or *horse, re-MORSE*. **Feminine rime** is a rime of two or more syllables, with stress on a syllable other than the last: *TUR-tle, FER-tile,* or (to take an example from Byron) *in-tel-LECT-u-al, hen-PECKED you all*. Often it lends itself to comic verse, but can occasionally be valuable to serious poems, as in Wordsworth's "Resolution and Independence":

> We poets in our youth begin in gladness,
> But thereof come in the end despondency and madness.

or as in Anne Sexton's seriously witty "Eighteen Days Without You":

> and of course we're not married, we are a pair of scissors
> who come together to cut, without towels saying His. Hers.

Artfully used, feminine rhyme can give a poem a heightened musical effect for the simple reason that it offers the listener twice as many rhyming syllables in each line. In the wrong hands, however, that sonic abundance has the unfortunate ability of making a bad poem twice as painful to endure. Poets can also mix masculine and feminine rhymes, as in the following sonnet by James Reeves.

James Reeves   (1909–1978)

ROUGH WEATHER   1972

To share with you this rough, divisive weather
And not to grieve because we have to share it,
Desire to wear the dark of night together
And feel no colder that we do not wear it,
Because sometimes my sight of you is clearer,   5
The memory not clouded by the sense,
To know that nothing now can make you dearer
Than does the close touch of intelligence,
To be the prisoner of your kindnesses
And tell myself I want you to be free,   10
To wish you here with me despite all this,

To wish you here, knowing you cannot be—
This is a way of love in our rough season,
This side of madness, the other side of reason.

QUESTIONS

Which rhymes in the poem are feminine? Which are masculine?

Serious poems containing feminine rimes of three syllables have been attempted, notably by Thomas Hood in "The Bridge of Sighs":

> Take her up tenderly,
> Lift her with care;
> Fashioned so slenderly,
> Young, and so fair!

But the pattern is hard to sustain without lapsing into unintended comedy, as in the same poem:

> Still, for all slips of hers,
> One of Eve's family—
> Wipe those poor lips of hers,
> Oozing so clammily.

It works better when comedy is wanted.

Hilaire Belloc   (1870–1953)

THE HIPPOPOTAMUS   1896

I shoot the Hippopotamus
  with bullets made of platinum,
Because if I use leaden ones
  his hide is sure to flatten 'em.

In **eye rime,** spellings look alike but pronunciations differ—*rough* and *dough*, *idea* and *flea*, *Venus* and *menus*. Strictly speaking, eye rime is not rime at all.

Rime in American poetry suffered a significant fall from favor in the early 1960s. A new generation of poets took for models the open forms of Whitman, Pound, and William Carlos Williams. In the last few decades, however, some poets have been skillfully using rime again in their work. Often called the **New Formalists,** these poets include Julia Alvarez, Annie Finch, R. S. Gwynn, Rachel Hadas, Mark Jarman, Paul Lake, Charles Martin, Marilyn Nelson, Gjertrud Schnackenberg, and Timothy Steele. Their poems often use rime and meter to present unusual contemporary subjects, but they also sometimes write poems that recollect, converse, and argue with the poetry of the past.

Still, most American poets don't write in rime; some even consider its possibilities exhausted. Such a view may be a reaction against the wearing thin of rimes by overuse or the mechanical and meaningless application of a rime scheme. Yet anyone who listens to children skipping rope in the street, making up rimes to delight themselves as they go along, may doubt that the pleasures of rime are ended; and certainly the practice of Yeats and Emily Dickinson, to name only two, suggests that the possibilities of slant rime may be nearly infinite. If successfully employed, as it has been at times by a majority of English-speaking poets whose work we care to save, rime runs through its poem like a spine: the creature moves by means of it.

William Butler Yeats (1865–1939)*

Leda and the Swan   1924

A sudden blow: the great wings beating still
Above the staggering girl, her thighs caressed
By the dark webs, her nape caught in his bill,
He holds her helpless breast upon his breast.

How can those terrified vague fingers push   5
The feathered glory from her loosening thighs?
And how can body, laid in that white rush,
But feel the strange heart beating where it lies?

A shudder in the loins engenders there
The broken wall, the burning roof and tower   10
And Agamemnon dead.
                    Being so caught up,
So mastered by the brute blood of the air,
Did she put on his knowledge with his power
Before the indifferent beak could let her drop?

Questions

1. According to Greek mythology, the god Zeus in the form of a swan descended on Leda, a Spartan queen. Among Leda's children were Clytemnestra, Agamemnon's unfaithful wife, who conspired in his murder, and Helen, on whose account the Trojan war was fought. What does a knowledge of these allusions contribute to our understanding of the poem's last two lines?
2. The slant rime *up / drop* (lines 11, 14) may seem accidental or inept. Is it? Would this poem have ended nearly so well if Yeats had made an exact rime like *up / cup* or like *stop / drop?*

Gerard Manley Hopkins (1844–1889)*

GOD'S GRANDEUR (1877)

The world is charged with the grandeur of God.
  It will flame out, like shining from shook foil;
  It gathers to a greatness, like the ooze of oil
Crushed. Why do men then now not reck his rod?
Generations have trod, have trod, have trod;   5
  And all is seared with trade; bleared, smeared with toil;
  And wears man's smudge and shares man's smell: the soil
Is bare now, nor can foot feel, being shod.

And for all this, nature is never spent;
  There lives the dearest freshness deep down things;   10
And though the last lights off the black West went
  Oh, morning, at the brown brink eastward, springs—
Because the Holy Ghost over the bent
  World broods with warm breast and with ah! bright wings.

GOD'S GRANDEUR. 1 *charged:* as though with electricity. 3–4 *It gathers . . . Crushed:* The grandeur of God will rise and be manifest, as oil rises and collects from crushed olives or grain. 4 *reck his rod:* heed His law. 10 *deep down things:* Tightly packing the poem, Hopkins omits the preposition *in* or *within* before *things.* 11 *last lights . . . went:* When in 1534 Henry VIII broke ties with the Roman Catholic Church and created the Church of England.

QUESTIONS

1. In a letter Hopkins explained *shook foil* (line 2): "I mean foil in its sense of leaf or tinsel. . . . Shaken goldfoil gives off broad glares like sheet lightning and also, and this is true of nothing else, owing to its zigzag dints and creasings and network of small many cornered facets, a sort of fork lightning too." What do you think he meant by the phrase *ooze of oil* (line 3)? Would you call this phrase an example of alliteration?
2. What instances of internal rime does the poem contain? How would you describe their effects?
3. Point out some of the poet's uses of alliteration and assonance. Do you believe that Hopkins perhaps goes too far in his heavy use of devices of sound, or would you defend his practice?
4. Why do you suppose Hopkins, in the last two lines, says *over the bent / World* instead of (as we might expect) *bent over the world?* How can the world be bent? Can you make any sense out of this wording, or is Hopkins just trying to get his rime scheme to work out?

Fred Chappell (b. 1936)

NARCISSUS AND ECHO 1985

Shall the water not remember   *Ember*
my hand's slow gesture, tracing above   *of*
its mirror my half-imaginary   *airy*

portrait? My only belonging   *longing;*
is my beauty, which I take   *ache*   5
away and then return, as love   *of*
teasing playfully the one being   *unbeing.*
whose gratitude I treasure   *Is your*
moves me. I live apart   *heart*
from myself, yet cannot   *not*   10
live apart. In the water's tone,   *stone?*
that brilliant silence, a flower   *Hour,*
whispers my name with such slight   *light:*
moment, it seems filament of air,   *fare*
the world become cloudswell.   *well.*   15

NARCISSUS AND ECHO. This poem is an example of **Echo Verse**, a form (which dates back to late classical Greek poetry) in which the final syllables of the lines are repeated back as a reply or commentary, often a punning one. *Narcissus:* a beautiful young man, in Greek mythology, who fell in love with his own reflection in the water of a well. He gradually pined away because he could not reach his love; upon dying, he changed into the flower that bears his name. *Echo:* a nymph who, according to Roman tradition, loved Narcissus. When her love was not returned, she pined away until only her voice was left.

QUESTIONS

1. This poem is a dialogue. What is the relation between the two voices? Does the first voice hear the second?
2. How does the meaning of the poem change if we read the speech of each voice separately?
3. Is the echo technique used in this poem a gimmick? Or does it allow the poet to express something he might not be able to in any other way?

Robert Frost   (1874–1963)*

DESERT PLACES   1936

Snow falling and night falling fast, oh, fast
In a field I looked into going past,
And the ground almost covered smooth in snow,
But a few weeds and stubble showing last.

The woods around it have it—it is theirs.   5
All animals are smothered in their lairs,
I am too absent-spirited to count;
The loneliness includes me unawares.

And lonely as it is, that loneliness
Will be more lonely ere it will be less—   10
A blanker whiteness of benighted snow
With no expression, nothing to express.

They cannot scare me with their empty spaces
Between stars—on stars where no human race is.
I have it in me so much nearer home   15
To scare myself with my own desert places.

QUESTIONS

1. What are these desert places that the speaker finds in himself? (More than one theory is possible. What is yours?)
2. Notice how many times, within the short space of lines 8–10, Frost says *lonely* (or *loneliness*). What other words in the poem contain similar sounds that reinforce these words?
3. In the closing stanza, the feminine rimes *spaces*, *race is*, and *places* might well occur in light or comic verse. Does "Desert Places" leave you laughing? If not, what does it make you feel?

READING AND HEARING POEMS ALOUD

Thomas Moore's "The light that lies in women's eyes"—a line rich in internal rime, alliteration, and assonance—is harder to forget than "The light burning in the gaze of a woman." Effective on the page, Moore's line becomes even more striking when heard aloud. Practice reading poetry aloud—there is no better way to understand a poem than to effectively read it aloud. Developing skill at reading poems aloud will not only deepen your understanding of literature, it will also improve your ability to speak in public.

Before trying to read a poem aloud to other people, understand its meaning as thoroughly as possible. If you know what the poet is saying and the poet's attitude toward it, you will be able to find an appropriate tone of voice and to give each part of the poem a proper emphasis.

Except in the most informal situations and in some class exercises, read a poem to yourself before trying it on an audience. No actor goes before the footlights without first having studied the script, and the language of poems usually demands even more consideration than the language of most contemporary plays. Prepare your reading in advance. Check pronunciations you are not sure of. Underline things to be emphasized.

Read more slowly than you would read aloud from a newspaper. Keep in mind that you are saying something to somebody. Don't race through the poem as if you are eager to get it over with.

Don't lapse into singsong. A poem may have a definite swing, but swing should never be exaggerated at the cost of sense. If you understand what the poem is saying and utter the poem as if you do, the temptation to fall into such a mechanical intonation should not occur. Observe the punctuation, making slight pauses for commas, longer pauses for full stops (periods, question marks, exclamation points).

If the poem is rimed, don't raise your voice and make the rimes stand out unnaturally. They should receive no more volume than other words in the poem, though a faint pause at the end of each line will call the listener's attention to them. This advice is contrary to a school that holds that, if a line does not end in any punctuation, one should not pause but run it together with the line following. The trouble is that, from such a reading, a listener may not be able to identify the rimes; besides, the line, that valuable unit of rhythm, is destroyed.

In some older poems rimes that look like slant rimes may have been exact rimes in their day:

> Still so perverse and opposite,
> As if they worshiped God for spite.
>> —Samuel Butler, *Hudibras* (1663)

> Soft yielding minds to water glide away,
> And sip, with nymphs, their elemental tea.
>> —Alexander Pope, "The Rape of the Lock" (1714)

> Tyger! Tyger! burning bright
> In the forests of the night,
> What immortal hand or eye
> Could frame thy fearful symmetry?
>> —William Blake, "The Tyger" (1794)

You may wish to establish a consistent policy toward such shifting usage: is it worthwhile to distort current pronunciation for the sake of the rime?

Listening to a poem, especially if it is unfamiliar, calls for concentration. Merciful people seldom read poetry uninterruptedly to anyone for more than a few minutes at a time. Robert Frost, always kind to his audiences, used to intersperse poems with many silences and seemingly casual remarks—shrewdly giving his hearers a chance to rest from their labors and giving his poems a chance to settle in.

If, in first listening to a poem, you don't take in all its meaning, don't be discouraged. With more practice in listening, your attention span and your ability to understand poems read aloud will increase. Incidentally, following the text of poems in a book while hearing them read aloud may increase your comprehension, but it may not necessarily help you to *listen*. At least some of the time, close your book and let your ears make the poems welcome. That way, their sounds may better work for you.

Hearing recordings of poets reading their work can help both your ability to read aloud and your ability to listen. Not all poets read their poems well, but there is much to be relished in both the highly dramatic reading style of a Dylan Thomas and the quiet underplay of a Robert Frost. You need feel no obligation, of course, to imitate the poet's reading of a poem. You have to feel about the poem in your own way, in order to read it with conviction and naturalness.

Even if you don't have an audience, the act of speaking poetry can have its own rewards. Perhaps that is what Yvor Winters meant when he said that, even though poetry was written for "the mind's ear" as well as the physical ear, "yet the mind's ear can be trained only by way of the other, and the matter, practically considered, comes inescapably back to the reading of poetry aloud."[5]

EXERCISE: *Reading for Sound and Meaning*

Read these brief poems aloud. What devices of sound do you find in each of them? Try to explain what sound contributes to the total effect of the poem and how it reinforces what the poet is saying.

Michael Stillman (b. 1940)

IN MEMORIAM JOHN COLTRANE   1972

Listen to the coal
rolling, rolling through the cold
    steady rain, wheel on

wheel, listen to the
turning of the wheels this night   5
    black as coal dust, steel

on steel, listen to
these cars carry coal, listen
    to the coal train roll.

IN MEMORIAM JOHN COLTRANE. John Coltrane (1926–1967) was a saxophonist whose originality, passion, and technical wizardry have had a deep influence on the history of modern jazz.

William Shakespeare (1564–1616)*

FULL FATHOM FIVE   ABOUT 1611
THY FATHER LIES

Full fathom five thy father lies;
    Of his bones are coral made;
Those are pearls that were his eyes:
    Nothing of him that doth fade,
But doth suffer a sea change   5
Into something rich and strange.
Sea nymphs hourly ring his knell:
    Ding-dong.
Hark! now I hear them—*Ding-dong, bell.*

FULL FATHOM FIVE THY FATHER LIES. The spirit Ariel sings this song in *The Tempest* to Ferdinand, prince of Naples, who mistakenly thinks his father is drowned.

[5]"The Audible Reading of Poetry" (1951), reprinted in *The Function of Criticism* (Denver: Swallow, 1957) 81.

Chryss Yost (b. 1966)

LAI WITH SOUNDS OF SKIN   2000

Shall we dress in skin,
our living linen?
bone weft,
pull of masculine
into feminine,   5
the heft,
the warp, weave and spin
of carded days in

tightly-twisted thin
yarns that we begin—   10
like wool
like *will*, like *has been*,
spoken to silken—
to spool:
thick bolts of linen,   15
skin to skein to skin.

LAI WITH SOUNDS OF SKIN. The *lai* is a French poetic form. Yost uses a version that consists of two, rhymed, eight-line stanzas in an intricate syllabic pattern. Yost's title not only announces the form of the poem but also makes a sexual pun suggesting the poem's subject.

T. S. Eliot (1888–1965)*

VIRGINIA   1934

Red river, red river,
Slow flow heat is silence
No will is still as a river
Still. Will heat move
Only through the mocking-bird   5
Heard once? Still hills
Wait. Gates wait. Purple trees,
White trees, wait, wait,
Delay, decay. Living, living,
Never moving. Ever moving   10
Iron thoughts came with me
And go with me:
Red river, river, river.

VIRGINIA. This poem is one of a series entitled "Landscapes."

T. S. Eliot

T. S. Eliot on Writing

THE MUSIC OF POETRY 1942

I would remind you, first, that the music of poetry is not something which exists apart from the meaning. Otherwise, we could have poetry of great musical beauty which made no sense, and I have never come across such poetry. The apparent exceptions only show a difference of degree: there are poems in which we are moved by the music and take the sense for granted, just as there are poems in which we attend to the sense and are moved by the music without noticing it. Take an apparently extreme example—the non-sense verse of Edward Lear. His non-sense is not vacuity of sense: it is a parody of sense, and that is the sense of it. *The Fumblies* is a poem of adventure, and of nostalgia for the romance of foreign voyage and exploration; *The Yongy-Bongy Bo* and *The Dong with a Luminous Nose* are poems of unrequited passion—"blues" in fact. We enjoy the music, which is of a high order, and we enjoy the feeling of irresponsibility towards the sense. Or take a poem of another type, the *Blue Closet* of William Morris. It is a delightful poem, though I cannot explain what it means and I doubt whether the author could have explained it. It has an effect somewhat like that of a rune or charm, but runes and charms are very practical formulae designed to produce definite results, such as getting a cow out of a bog. But its obvious intention (and I think the author succeeds) is to produce the effect of a dream. It is not necessary, in order to enjoy the poem, to know what the dream means; but human beings have an unshakeable belief that dreams mean something: they used to believe—and many still believe—that dreams disclose the secrets of the future; the orthodox modern faith is that they reveal the secrets—or at least the more horrid secrets—of the past.

So, while poetry attempts to convey something beyond what can be conveyed in prose rhythms, it remains, all the same, one person talking to another; and this is just as true if you sing it, for singing is another way of talking. The immediacy of poetry to conversation is not a matter on which we can lay down exact laws. Every revolution in poetry is apt to be, and sometimes to announce itself to be a return to common speech. . . .

It would be a mistake, however, to assume that all poetry ought to be melodious, or that melody is more than one of the components of the music of words. Some poetry is meant to be sung; most poetry, in modern times, is meant to be spoken—and there are many other things to be spoken of besides the murmur of innumerable bees or the moan of doves in immemorial elms. Dissonance, even cacophony, has its place: just as, in a poem of any length, there must be transitions between passages of greater and less intensity, to give a rhythm of fluctuating emotion essential to the musical structure of the whole; and the passages of less intensity will be, in relation to the level on which the total poem operates, prosaic—so that, in the sense implied by that context, it may be said that no poet can write a poem of amplitude unless he is a master of the prosaic.

From "The Music of Poetry"

━━━◄WRITING CRITICALLY►━━━

Is It Possible to Write About Sound?

Sound represents an essential aspect of most poems, but it can be an elusive element to isolate for analysis. Even professional critics often disagree about the sonic effects of particular poems.

The easiest way to write about the sound of a poem is usually to focus your discussion. Rather than trying to explain every possible auditory element a poem possesses, concentrate on a single, clearly defined aspect that strikes you as especially noteworthy. For example, you might demonstrate how elements of sound in a poem emphasize its literal meaning. Don't look for hidden meanings. Simply try to understand how sound helps communicate the poem's main theme. Here you might examine how certain features (for example, rime, rhythm, meter, alliteration, and so forth) add force to the literal meaning of each line. Or, for ironic poems, you might look at how those same elements undercut and change the surface meaning of the poem.

A good way to begin this sort of writing assignment is to make a list of the main auditory elements you find in the poem. Does it contain rime, meter, alliteration, assonance, euphony, cacophony, repetition, or onomatopoeia? Note each striking instance of the relevant elements. (Remember that in such detailed analysis, it often helps to choose a short poem. If you want to discuss a longer work, focus on a short passage from it.) See if you can find a stylistic pattern in the items you list. Does this poet favor alliteration or repetition? Let your data build up before you force any conclusions on the poem. As your list grows, ideas will probably occur to you that were not apparent earlier.

WRITING ASSIGNMENT

In a short essay, examine how one or two elements of sound strengthen the literal meaning of a short poem. Review the conventional terms for elements of sound found in this chapter (alliteration, assonance, slant rime, euphony, and so on) to make sure you are describing correctly the elements you discuss. Support your argument with specific examples from the poem. Possible topics include "Rime and Repetition in Fred Chappell's 'Narcissus and Echo,'" "Alliteration in Shakespeare's 'Full Fathom Five,'" and "Assonance and Repetition in Tennyson's 'The Splendor Falls on Castle Walls.'"

FURTHER SUGGESTIONS FOR WRITING

1. Write about a personal experience with reading poems aloud.
2. Explain why contemporary poets are right (or wrong) to abandon rime.
3. Consider the verbal music in W. H. Auden's "As I Walked Out One Evening" (or another selection from "Poems for Further Reading"). Analyze the poem for language with ear appeal and show how the poem's sound is of a piece with its meaning.

20 *Rhythm*

STRESSES AND PAUSES

Rhythms affect us powerfully. We are lulled by a hammock's sway, awakened by an alarm clock's repeated yammer. Long after we come home from a beach, the rising and falling of waves and tides continue in memory. How powerfully the rhythms of poetry also move us may be felt in folk songs of railroad workers and chain gangs whose words were chanted in time to the lifting and dropping of a sledgehammer, and in verse that marching soldiers shout, putting a stress on every word that coincides with a footfall:

> Your LEFT! TWO! THREE! FOUR!
> Your LEFT! TWO! THREE! FOUR!
> You LEFT your WIFE and TWEN-ty-one KIDS
> And you LEFT! TWO! THREE! FOUR!
> You'll NEV-er get HOME to-NIGHT!

A rhythm is produced by a series of recurrences: the returns and departures of the seasons, the repetitions of an engine's stroke, the beats of the heart. A rhythm may be produced by the recurrence of a sound (the throb of a drum, a telephone's busy signal), but rhythm and sound are not identical. A totally deaf person at a parade can sense rhythm from the motions of the marchers' arms and feet, from the shaking of the pavement as they tramp. Rhythms inhere in the motions of the moon and stars, even though when they move, we hear no sound.

In poetry, several kinds of recurrent *sound* are possible, including (as we saw in the last chapter) rime, alliteration, and assonance. But most often when we speak of the **rhythm** of a poem, we mean the recurrence of stresses and pauses in it. When we hear a poem read aloud, stresses and pauses are, of course, part of its sound. It is possible to be aware of rhythms in poems read silently, too.

A **stress** (or **accent**) is a greater amount of force given to one syllable in speaking than is given to another. We favor a stressed syllable with a little more breath and emphasis, with the result that it comes out slightly louder, higher in pitch, or longer in duration than other syllables. In this manner we place a stress on the first syllable of words such as *eagle, impact, open,* and *statue,* and on the second syllable in *cigar, mystique, precise,* and *until.* Each word in English carries at least one stress, except (usually) for the articles *a, an,* and *the,* the conjunction *and,* and one-syllable prepositions: *at, by, for, from, of, to, with.* Even these, however, take a stress once in a while: "Get WITH it!" "You're not THE Dolly Parton?" One word by itself is seldom long enough for us to notice a rhythm in it. Usually a sequence of at least a few words is needed for stresses to establish their pattern: a line, a passage, a whole poem. Strong rhythms may be seen in most Mother Goose rimes, to which children have been responding for hundreds of years. This rime is for an adult to chant while jogging a child up and down on a knee:

> Here goes my lord
> A trot, a trot, a trot, a trot!
> Here goes my lady
> A canter, a canter, a canter, a canter!
> Here goes my young master
> Jockey-hitch, jockey-hitch, jockey-hitch, jockey-hitch!
> Here goes my young miss
> An amble, an amble, an amble, an amble!
> The footman lags behind to tipple ale and wine
> And goes gallop, a gallop, a gallop, to make up his time.

More than one rhythm occurs in these lines, as the make-believe horse changes pace. How do these rhythms differ? From one line to the next, the interval between stresses lengthens or grows shorter. In "a TROT a TROT a TROT a TROT," the stress falls on every other syllable. But in the middle of the line "A CAN-ter a CAN-ter a CAN-ter a CAN-ter," the stress falls on every third syllable. When stresses recur at fixed intervals as in these lines, the result is called a **meter.** The line "A trot a trot a trot a trot" is in **iambic meter,** a succession of alternate unstressed and stressed syllables.[1] Of all rhythms in the English language, this one is most familiar; most of our traditional poetry is written in it and ordinary speech tends to resemble it.

Stresses embody meanings. Whenever two or more fall side by side, words gain in emphasis. Consider these hard-hitting lines from John Donne, in which accent marks have been placed, dictionary-fashion, to indicate the stressed syllables:

> Bat·ter my heart, three-per·soned God, for You
> As yet but knock, breathe, shine, and seek to mend.
> That I may rise and stand, o'er throw me, and bend
> Your force to break, blow, burn, and make me new.

---

[1] Another kind of meter is possible, in which the intervals between stresses vary. This is **accentual meter,** not often found in contemporary poetry. It is discussed in the second part of this chapter.

Unstressed (or **slack**) **syllables** also can direct our attention to what the poet means. In a line containing few stresses and a great many unstressed syllables, there can be an effect not of power and force but of hesitation and uncertainty. Yeats asks in "Among School Children" what young mother, if she could see her baby grown to be an old man, would think him:

> A com·pen·sa´tion for the pang of his birth
> Or the un·cer·tain´ty of his set·ting forth?

When unstressed syllables recur in pairs, the result is a rhythm that trips and bounces, as in Robert Service's rollicking line:

> A bunch of the boys were whoop·ing it up in the Ma·la·mute
>   sa·loon . . .

or in Poe's lines—also light but meant to be serious:

> For the moon nev·er beams with·out bring·ing me dreams
> Of the beau·ti·ful An·na·bel Lee.

Apart from the words that convey it, the rhythm of a poem has no meaning. There are no essentially sad rhythms, nor any essentially happy ones. But some rhythms enforce certain meanings better than others do. The bouncing rhythm of Service's line seems fitting for an account of a merry night in a Klondike saloon; but it may be distracting when encountered in Poe's wistful elegy.

The special power of poetry comes from allowing us to hear simultaneously every level of meaning in language—denotation and connotation, image and idea, abstract content and physical sound. Since sound stress is one of the ways that the English language most clearly communicates meaning, any regular rhythmic pattern will affect the poem's effect. Poets learn to use rhythms that reinforce the meaning and the tone of a poem. As film directors know, any movie scene's effect can change dramatically if different background music accompanies the images. Master of the suspense film Alfred Hitchcock, for instance, could fill an ordinary scene with tension or terror just by playing nervous, grating music underneath it. We also often notice the powerful effect rhythm has on meaning when an author goes awry and tries to create a particular mood in a manner that seems to pull us in an opposing direction. In Eliza Cook's "Song of the Sea-Weed," for instance, the poet depicts her grim and ghoulish scene in a bouncy ballad meter that makes the tone unintentionally comic:

> Many a lip is gaping for drink,
>   And madly calling for rain;
> And some hot brains are beginning to think
>   Of a messmate's opened vein.

EXERCISE: *Get with the Beat*

In each of the following passages the author has established a strong rhythm. Describe how the rhythm helps establish the tone and meaning of the poem. How does each poem's beat seem appropriate to the tone and subject?

1. I sprang to the stirrup, and Joris and he;
    I galloped, Dirck galloped, we galloped all three;
    "Good speed," cried the watch as the gatebolts undrew;
    "Speed!" echoed the wall to us galloping through.
    Behind shut the postern, the lights sank to rest,
    And into the midnight we galloped abreast.
                    —Robert Browning, from "How They Brought the Good News
                            from Ghent to Aix"

2. I couldn't be cooler, I come from Missoula,
    And I rope and I chew and I ride.
    But I'm a heroin dealer, and I drive a four-wheeler
    With stereo speakers inside.
    My ol' lady Phoebe's out rippin' off C.B.'s
    From the rigs at the Wagon Wheel Bar,
    Near a Montana truck stop and a shit-outta-luck stop
    For a trucker who's driven too far.
                    —Greg Keeler, from "There Ain't No Such Thing as a Montana
                            Cowboy" (a song lyric)

3. Of all the lives I cannot live,
    I have elected one

    to haunt me till the margins give
    and I am left alone

    One life has sounded in my voice
    and made me like a stone—

    one that the falling leaves can sink
    not over, but upon.
                    —Annie Finch, "Dickinson"

4. Oh newsprint moonprint Marilyn!
    Rub ink from a finger
    to make your beauty mark.
                    —Rachel Eisler, from "Marilyn's Nocturne" (a poem about a
                            newspaper photograph of Marilyn Monroe)

5. The master, the swabber, the boatswain, and I,
    The gunner and his mate
    Loved Moll, Meg, and Marian, and Margery,
    But none of us cared for Kate;
    For she had a tongue with a tang
    Would cry to a sailor "go hang!"—
    She loved not the savor of tar nor of pitch
    Yet a tailor might scratch her where'er she did itch;
    Then to sea, boys, and let her go hang!
                    —William Shakespeare, a song from *The Tempest*

Rhythms in poetry are due not only to stresses but also to pauses. "Every nice ear," observed Alexander Pope (*nice* meaning "finely tuned"), "must, I believe, have observed that in any smooth English verse of ten syllables, there is naturally a pause either at the fourth, fifth, or sixth syllable." Such a light but definite pause within a line is called a **cesura** (or **caesura**), "a cutting." More liberally than Pope, we apply the name to any pause in a line of any length, after any word in the line. In studying a poem, we often indicate a cesura by double lines (||). Usually, a cesura will occur at a mark of punctuation, but there can be a cesura even if no punctuation is present. Sometimes you will find it at the end of a phrase or clause or, as in these lines by William Blake, after an internal rime:

> And priests in black gowns || were walking their rounds
> And binding with briars || my joys and desires.

Lines of ten or twelve syllables (as Pope knew) tend to have just one cesura, though sometimes there are more:

> Cover her face: || mine eyes dazzle: || she died young.

Pauses also tend to recur at more prominent places—namely, after each line. At the end of a verse (from *versus*, "a turning"), the reader's eye, before turning to go on to the next line, makes a pause, however brief. If a line ends in a full pause—usually indicated by some mark of punctuation—we call it **end-stopped.** All the lines in this passage from Christopher Marlowe's *Doctor Faustus* (in which Faustus addresses the apparition of Helen of Troy) are end-stopped:

> Was this the face that launch'd a thousand ships,
> And burnt the topless towers of Ilium?
> Sweet Helen, make me immortal with a kiss.
> Her lips suck forth my soul: see, where it flies!
> Come, Helen, come, give me my soul again.
> Here will I dwell, for heaven is in these lips,
> And all is dross that is not Helena.

A line that does not end in punctuation and that therefore is read with only a slight pause after it is called a **run-on line.** Because a run-on line gives us only part of a phrase, clause, or sentence, we have to read on to the line or lines following, in order to complete a thought. All these lines from Robert Browning's "My Last Duchess" are run-on lines:

> Sir, 'twas not
> Her husband's presence only, called that spot
> Of joy into the Duchess' cheek: perhaps
> Frà Pandolf chanced to say "Her mantle laps
> Over my lady's wrist too much," or "Paint
> Must never hope to reproduce the faint
> Half-flush that dies along her throat." Such stuff
> Was courtesy, she thought . . .[2]

[2]The complete poem, "My Last Duchess," appears on page 712.

A passage in run-on lines has a rhythm different from that of a passage like Marlowe's in end-stopped lines. When emphatic pauses occur in the quotation from Browning, they fall within a line rather than at the end of one. The passage by Marlowe and that by Browning are in lines of the same meter (iambic) and the same length (ten syllables). What makes the big difference in their rhythms is the running on, or lack of it.

To sum up: rhythm is recurrence. In poems, it is made of stresses and pauses. The poet can produce it by doing any of several things: making the intervals between stresses fixed or varied, long or short; indicating pauses (cesuras) within lines; end-stopping lines or running them over; writing in short or long lines. Rhythm in itself cannot convey meaning. And yet if a poet's words have meaning, their rhythm must be one with it.

Gwendolyn Brooks   (1917–2000)*

WE REAL COOL   1960

> The Pool Players.
> Seven at the Golden Shovel.

We real cool. We
Left school. We

Lurk late. We
Strike straight. We

Sing sin. We   5
Thin gin. We

Jazz June. We
Die soon.

QUESTION

Describe the rhythms of this poem. By what techniques are they produced?

Alfred, Lord Tennyson   (1809–1892)*

BREAK, BREAK, BREAK   (1834)

Break, break, break,
    On thy cold gray stones, O Sea!
And I would that my tongue could utter
    The thoughts that arise in me.

O well for the fisherman's boy,   5
    That he shouts with his sister at play!
O well for the sailor lad,
    That he sings in his boat on the bay!

And the stately ships go on
    To their haven under the hill;   10
But O for the touch of a vanish'd hand,
    And the sound of a voice that is still!

Break, break, break,
    At the foot of thy crags, O Sea!
But the tender grace of a day that is dead   15
    Will never come back to me.

QUESTIONS

1. Read the first line aloud. What effect does it create at the beginning of the poem?
2. Is there a regular rhythmic pattern in this poem? If so, how would you describe it?
3. The speaker claims that his or her thoughts are impossible to utter. Using evidence from the poem, can you describe the speaker's thoughts and feelings?

Ben Jonson   (1573–1637)*

SLOW, SLOW, FRESH FOUNT, KEEP TIME   1600
WITH MY SALT TEARS

Slow, slow, fresh fount, keep time with my salt tears;
    Yet slower yet, oh faintly, gentle springs;
List to the heavy part the music bears,
    Woe weeps out her division° when she sings.   *a part in a song*
        Droop herbs and flowers,   5
        Fall grief in showers;
        Our beauties are not ours;
            Oh, I could still,
Like melting snow upon some craggy hill,
    Drop, drop, drop, drop,   10
Since nature's pride is now a withered daffodil.

SLOW, SLOW, FRESH FOUNT. The nymph Echo sings this lament over the youth Narcissus in Jonson's play *Cynthia's Revels*. In mythology, Nemesis, goddess of vengeance, to punish Narcissus for loving his own beauty, caused him to pine away and then transformed him into a narcissus (another name for a *daffodil*, line 11).

QUESTIONS

1. Read the first line aloud rapidly. Why is it difficult to do so?
2. Which lines rely most heavily on stressed syllables?
3. In general, how would you describe the rhythm of this poem? How is it appropriate to what is said?

Alexander Pope   (1688–1744)*

ATTICUS

How did they fume, and stamp, and roar, and chafe?
And swear, not Addison himself was safe.

   Peace to all such! but were there one whose fires
True genius kindles, and fair fame inspires;
Blest with each talent, and each art to please,   5
And born to write, converse, and live with ease,
Should such a man, too fond to rule alone,
Bear, like the Turk, no brother near the throne,
View him with scornful, yet with jealous eyes,
And hate for arts that caused himself to rise;   10
Damn with faint praise, assent with civil leer,
And, without sneering, teach the rest to sneer;
Willing to wound, and yet afraid to strike,
Just hint a fault, and hesitate dislike;
Alike reserved to blame, or to commend,   15
A timorous foe, and a suspicious friend;
Dreading e'en fools, by flatterers besieged,
And so obliging, that he ne'er obliged;
Like Cato, give his little Senate laws,
And sit attentive to his own applause: 20
While wits and Templars every sentence raise,
And wonder with a foolish face of praise—
Who but must laugh, if such a man there be?
Who would not weep, if Atticus were he?

ATTICUS. In this selection from "An Epistle to Dr. Arbuthnot," Pope has been referring to dull versifiers and their angry reception of his satiric thrusts at them. With *Peace to all such!* (line 3) he turns to his celebrated portrait of a rival man of letters, Joseph Addison. 19 *Cato:* Roman senator about whom Addison had written a tragedy. 21 *Templars:* London lawyers who dabbled in literature.

QUESTIONS

1. In these lines—one of the most famous damnations in English poetry—what positive virtues, in Pope's view, does Addison lack?
2. Which lines are end-stopped? What is the effect of these lines on the rhythm of this passage? (Suggestion: read "Atticus" aloud.)

EXERCISE: *Two Kinds of Rhythm*

The following compositions in verse have lines of similar length, yet they differ greatly in rhythm. Explain how they differ and why.

Sir Thomas Wyatt   (1503?–1542)*

WITH SERVING STILL   (1528–1536)

With serving still°   *continually*
  This have I won,
For my goodwill
  To be undone;

And for redress   5
  Of all my pain,
Disdainfulness
  I have again°;   *in return*
And for reward
  Of all my smart   10
Lo, thus unheard,
  I must depart!

Wherefore all ye
  That after shall
By fortune be,   15
  As I am, thrall,

Example take
  What I have won,
Thus for her sake
  To be undone!   20

Dorothy Parker   (1893–1967)

RÉSUMÉ   1926

Razors pain you;
Rivers are damp;
Acids stain you;
And drugs cause cramp.
Guns aren't lawful;   5
Nooses give;
Gas smells awful;
You might as well live.

METER

To enjoy the rhythms of a poem, no special knowledge of meter is necessary. All you need do is pay attention to stresses and where they fall, and you will perceive the basic pattern, if there is any. However, there is nothing occult about the study of meter. Most people find they can master its essentials in no more time than it takes to learn a complicated game such as chess. If you take the time, you will then have the pleasure of knowing what is happening in the rhythms of many a fine poem, and pleasurable knowledge may even deepen your insight into poetry. The following discussion, then, will be of interest only to those who care to go deeper into **prosody,** the study of metrical structures in poetry.

Far from being artificial constructions found only in the minds of poets, meters occur in everyday speech and prose. As the following example will show, they may need only a poet to recognize them. The English satirist Max Beerbohm, after contemplating the title page of his first book, took his pen and added two more lines.

Max Beerbohm (1872–1956)

ON THE IMPRINT OF THE FIRST   (1896)
ENGLISH EDITION OF
THE WORKS OF MAX BEERBOHM

"London: JOHN LANE, *The Bodley Head*
    New York: Charles Scribner's Sons."
This plain announcement, nicely read,
    Iambically runs.

In everyday life, nobody speaks or writes in perfect iambic rhythm, except at moments: "a HAM on RYE and HIT the MUStard HARD!" (As we have seen, iambic rhythm consists of a series of syllables alternately unstressed and stressed.) Poets rarely speak in it for long, either—at least, not with absolute consistency. If you read aloud Max Beerbohm's lines, you'll hear an iambic rhythm, but not an unvarying one. And yet all of us speak with a rising and falling of stress *somewhat like* iambic meter. Perhaps, as the poet and scholar John Thompson has maintained, "The iambic metrical pattern has dominated English verse because it provides the best symbolic model of our language."[3]

To make ourselves aware of a meter, we need only listen to a poem, or sound its words to ourselves. If we care to work out exactly what a poet is doing, we *scan* a line or a poem by indicating the stresses in it. **Scansion,** the art of so doing, is not just a matter of pointing to syllables; it is also a matter of listening to a poem and making sense of it. To scan a poem is one way to indicate how to read it aloud; in order to see where stresses fall, you have to see the places where the poet wishes to put emphasis. That is why, when scanning a poem, you may find yourself suddenly understanding it.

An objection might be raised against scanning: isn't it too simple to pretend that all language (and poetry) can be divided neatly into stressed syllables and

---

[3]*The Founding of English Metre* (New York: Columbia UP, 1966) 12.

unstressed syllables? Indeed it is. As the linguist Otto Jespersen has said, "In reality there are infinite gradations of stress, from the most penetrating scream to the faintest whisper."[4] However, the idea in scanning a poem is not to reproduce the sound of a human voice. For that we would do better to buy a tape recorder. To scan a poem, rather, is to make a diagram of the stresses (and absences of stress) we find in it. Various marks are used in scansion; in this book we use ´ for a stressed syllable and ˘ for an unstressed syllable.

There are four common accentual-syllabic meters in English—iambic, anapestic, trochaic, and dactylic. Each is named for its basic **foot** (usually a unit of two or three syllables that contains one strong stress) or building block. Here are some examples of each meter.

1. **Iambic**—a line made up primarily of **iambs,** an unstressed syllable followed by a stressed syllable, ˘´. The iambic measure is the most common meter in English poetry. Many writers, such as Robert Frost, feel iambs most easily capture the natural rhythms of our speech.

   > But soft, | what light | through yon | der win | dow breaks?
   > —*William Shakespeare*

   > When I | have fears | that I | may cease | to be
   > —*John Keats*

   > If we | had world | e·nough | and time
   > This coy| ness, la | dy, were | no crime
   > —*Andrew Marvell*

   > My life | had stood – | a load | ed Gun
   > —*Emily Dickinson*

2. **Anapestic**—a line made up primarily of **anapests,** two unstressed syllables followed by a stressed syllable, ˘˘´. Anapestic meter resembles iambic but contains an extra unstressed syllable. Totally anapestic lines often start to gallop, so poets sometimes slow them down by substituting an iambic foot (as Poe does in "Annabel Lee").

   > The As·syr | ian came down | like a wolf | on the fold

   > And his co | horts were gleam | ing in pur| ple and gold.

   > And the sheen | of their spears | was like stars | on the sea

   > When the blue | wave rolls night | ly on deep | Gal·i·lee.
   > —*Lord Byron*

[4]"Notes on Metre," (1933), reprinted in *The Structure of Verse: Modern Essays on Prosody*, ed. Harvey Gross, 2nd ed. (New York: Ecco P, 1979).

ᵕ ´ | ᵕ ᵕ ´ | ᵕ ᵕ ´ | ᵕ ᵕ ´ | ᵕ ᵕ ´

Now this | is the Law | of the Jun | gle—as old | and as true

´ | ᵕ ᵕ ´

| as the sky

ᵕ ᵕ ´ | ᵕ ᵕ ´ | ᵕ ᵕ ´ | ᵕ ᵕ ´

And the Wolf | that shall keep | it may pros | per, | but the wolf

ᵕ ᵕ ´ | ᵕ ᵕ ´ | ᵕ ´

| that shall break | it must die.

—*Rudyard Kipling*

ᵕ ᵕ ´ | ᵕ ᵕ ´ | ᵕ ᵕ ´ | ᵕ ᵕ ´

It was ma | ny and ma | ny a year | a·go

ᵕᵕ ´ | ᵕ ´ | ᵕ ´

In a king | dom by | the sea

ᵕ ᵕ ´ | ᵕ ᵕ ´ | ᵕ ᵕ ´ | ᵕ ᵕ ´

That a maid | en there lived | whom you | may know

ᵕ ᵕ ´ | ᵕ ᵕ ´ | ᵕ ᵕ ᵕ ´

By the name | of An | na·bel Lee.

—*Edgar Allan Poe*

3. **Trochaic**—a line made up primarily of **trochees,** a stressed syllable followed by an unstressed syllable, ´ᵕ. The trochaic meter is often associated with songs, chants, and magic spells in English. Trochees make a strong, emphatic meter that is often very mnemonic. Shakespeare and Blake used trochaic meter to exploit its magical associations. Notice how Blake drops the unstressed syllable at the end of his lines from "The Tyger." (The location of a missing syllable in a metrical foot is usually marked with a caret sign, ˅.)

´ ᵕ | ´ ᵕ | ´ ᵕ | ´ ᵕ

Dou·ble, | dou·ble, | toil and | trou·ble

´ᵕ | ´ ᵕ | ´ ᵕ | ´ ᵕ

Fi·re | burn and | caul·dron | bub·ble.

—*Shakespeare*

´ ᵕ | ´ ᵕ | ´ ᵕ | ´ ˅

Ty·ger, | ty·ger, | burn·ing | bright

´ ᵕ | ´ ᵕ | ´ ᵕ | ´ ˅

In the | for·est | of the | night ˅

—*William Blake*

´ ᵕ | ´ ᵕ | ´ ᵕ | ´ ˅

Go and | catch a | fall·ing | star

—*John Donne*

4. **Dactylic**—a line made up primarily of **dactyls,** one stressed syllable followed by two unstressed syllables, ´ᵕᵕ. The dactylic meter is less common in English than in classical languages like Greek or Latin. Used carefully, dactylic meter can sound stately, as in Longfellow's *Evangeline,* but it also easily becomes a prancing, propulsive measure and is often used in comic verse. Poets often drop the unstressed syllables at the end of a dactylic line, the omission usually being noted with a caret sign, ˅.

       ˊ ˘ ˘   ˊ ˘ ˘   ˊ ˘ ˘   ˊ ˘   ˘ ˊ ˘ ˘

This is the | for·est pri | me·val. The | mur·mur·ing | pines and the

      ˊ   ˊ
| hem·lock

—Henry Wadsworth Longfellow

    ˊ ˘ ˘ ˊ   ˘ ˘

Take her up | ten·der·ly

   ˊ ˘   ˘   ˊ ˘

Lift her with | care

  ˊ   ˘   ˘ ˊ ˘ ˘

Fash·ioned so | slen·der·ly

    ˊ   ˘ ˘ ˊ ˘

Young and so | fair.

—Thomas Hood

   ˊ ˘ ˘ ˊ ˘ ˘   ˊ ˘ ˘ ˊ   ˘

Puss·y·cat, | puss·y·cat, | where have you | been?

—Mother Goose

Iambic and anapestic meters are called **rising** meters because their movement rises from an unstressed syllable (or syllables) to stress; trochaic and dactylic meters are called **falling.** In the twentieth century, the bouncing meters—anapestic and dactylic—were used more often for comic verse than for serious poetry. Called feet, though they contain no unaccented syllables, are the **monosyllabic foot** (ˊ) and the **spondee** (ˊˊ). Meters are not ordinarily made up of them; if one were, it would be like the steady impact of nails being hammered into a board— no pleasure to hear or to dance to. But inserted now and then, they can lend emphasis and variety to a meter, as Yeats well knew when he broke up the predominantly iambic rhythm of "Who Goes with Fergus?" (page 864) with the line

   ˘   ˘ ˊ   ˊ ˘ ˘ ˊ ˊ

And the white breast of the dim sea,

in which two spondees occur. Meters are classified also by line lengths: *trochaic monometer,* for instance, is a line one trochee long, as in this anonymous brief comment on microbes:

Adam
Had 'em.

A frequently heard metrical description is **iambic pentameter:** a line of five iambs, a meter especially familiar because it occurs in all blank verse (such as Shakespeare's plays and Milton's *Paradise Lost*), heroic couplets, and sonnets. The commonly used names for line lengths follow:

monometer	one foot
dimeter	two feet
trimeter	three feet
tetrameter	four feet

pentameter	five feet
hexameter	six feet
heptameter	seven feet
octameter	eight feet

Lines of more than eight feet are possible but are rare. They tend to break up into shorter lengths in the listening ear.

When Yeats chose the spondees *white breast* and *dim sea*, he was doing what poets who write in meter do frequently for variety—using a foot other than the expected one. Often such a substitution will be made at the very beginning of a line, as in the third line of this passage from Christopher Marlowe's *Tragical History of Doctor Faustus:*

Was this | the face | that launched | a thou | sand ships
And burnt | the top | less tow'rs | of Il | i·um?
Sweet Hel | en, make | me im·mor | tal with | a kiss.

How, we might wonder, can that last line be called iambic at all? But it is, just as a waltz that includes an extra step or two, or leaves a few steps out, remains a waltz. In the preceding lines the basic iambic pentameter is established, and though in the third line the regularity is varied from, it does not altogether disappear. It continues for a while to run on in the reader's mind, where (if the poet does not stay away from it for too long) the meter will be when the poem comes back to it.

Like a basic dance step, a meter is not to be slavishly adhered to. The fun in reading a metrical poem often comes from watching the poet continually departing from perfect regularity, giving a few heel-kicks to display a bit of joy or ingenuity, then easing back into the basic step again. Because meter is orderly and the rhythms of living speech are unruly, poets can play one against the other, in a sort of counterpoint. Robert Frost, a master at pitting a line of iambs against a very natural-sounding and irregular sentence, declared, "I am never more pleased than when I can get these into strained relation. I like to drag and break the intonation across the meter as waves first comb and then break stumbling on a shingle."[5]

Evidently Frost's skilled effects would be lost to a reader who, scanning a Frost poem or reading it aloud, distorted its rhythms to fit the words exactly to the meter. With rare exceptions, a good poem can be read and scanned the way we would speak its sentences if they were ours. This, for example, is an unreal scansion:

That's my last Duch·ess paint·ed on the wall.

—because no speaker of English would say that sentence in that way. We are likely to stress *That's* and *last.*

[5]Letter to John Cournos in 1914, in *Selected Letters of Robert Frost*, ed. Lawrance Thompson (New York: Holt, 1964) 128.

Although in good poetry we seldom meet a very long passage of absolute metrical regularity, we sometimes find (in a line or so) a monotonous rhythm that is effective. Words fall meaningfully in Macbeth's famous statement of world-weariness: "Tomorrow and tomorrow and tomorrow . . ." and in the opening lines of Thomas Gray's "Elegy":

> The cur·few tolls the knell of part·ing day,
> The low·ing herd wind slow·ly o'er the lea,
> The plow·man home·ward plods his wear·y way,
> And leaves the world to dark·ness and to me.

Although certain unstressed syllables in these lines seem to call for more emphasis than others—you might, for instance, care to throw a little more weight on the second syllable of *curfew* in the opening line—we can still say that the lines are notably iambic. Their almost unvarying rhythm seems just right to convey the tolling of a bell and the weary setting down of one foot after the other.

Besides the two rising meters (iambic, anapestic) and the two falling meters (trochaic, dactylic), English poets have another valuable meter. It is **accentual meter,** in which the poet does not write in feet (as in the other meters) but instead counts accents (stresses). The idea is to have the same number of stresses in every line. The poet may place them anywhere in the line and may include practically any number of unstressed syllables, which do not count. In "Christabel," for instance, Coleridge keeps four stresses to a line, though the first line has only eight syllables and the last line has eleven:

> There is not wind e·nough to twirl
> The one red leaf, the last of its clan,
> That dan·ces as of·ten as dance it can,
> Hang·ing so light, and hang·ing so high,
> On the top-most twig that looks up at the sky.

The history of accentual meter is long and honorable. Old English poetry was written in a kind of accentual meter, but its line was more rule-bound than Coleridge's: four stresses arranged two on either side of a cesura, plus alliteration of three of the stressed syllables. In "Junk," Richard Wilbur revives the pattern:

> An axe an·gles ‖ from my neigh·bor's ash·can . . .

Many poets, from the authors of Mother Goose rimes to Gerard Manley Hopkins, have sometimes found accentual meters congenial. Recently, accentual meter has enjoyed huge popularity through rap poetry, which usually employs a four-stress line (see page 850 for further discussion of rap).

It has been charged that the importation of Greek names for meters and of the classical notion of feet was an unsuccessful attempt to make a Parthenon out of English wattles. The charge is open to debate, but at least it is certain that Greek names for feet cannot mean to us what they meant to Aristotle. Greek and Latin poetry is measured not by stressed and unstressed syllables, but by long and short vowel sounds. An iamb in classical verse is one short syllable followed by a long syllable. Such a meter constructed on the principle of vowel length is called a **quantitative meter.** Campion's "Rose-cheeked Laura" was an attempt to demonstrate it in English, but probably we enjoy the rhythm of the poem's well-placed stresses whether or not we notice its vowel sounds.

Thomas Campion   (1567–1620)

ROSE-CHEEKED LAURA, COME   1602

Rose-cheeked Laura, come,
Sing thou smoothly with thy beauty's
Silent music, either other
    Sweetly gracing.

Lovely forms do flow   5
From concent° divinely framèd;   *harmony*
Heav'n is music, and thy beauty's
    Birth is heavenly.

These dull notes we sing
Discords need for helps to grace them;   10
Only beauty purely loving
    Knows no discord,

But still moves delight,
Like clear springs renewed by flowing,
Ever perfect, ever in them-   15
    Selves eternal.

Although less popular among poets today than formerly, meter endures. Major poets from Shakespeare through Yeats have fashioned their work by it, and if we are to read their poems with full enjoyment, we need to be aware of it. To enjoy metrical poetry—even to write it—you do not have to slice lines into feet; you do need to recognize when a meter is present in a line, and when the line departs from it. An argument in favor of meter is that it reminds us of body rhythms such as breathing, walking, the beating of the heart. In an effective metrical poem, these rhythms cannot be separated from what the poet is saying—or, in the words of an old jazz song of Duke Ellington, "It don't mean a thing if you ain't got that swing." As critic Paul Fussell has put it: "No element of a poem is more basic—and I mean physical—in its effect upon the reader than the metrical element, and perhaps no technical triumphs reveal more readily than the metrical the poet's sympathy with that universal human nature . . . which exists outside his own."[6]

Vachel Lindsay   (1879–1931)

FACTORY WINDOWS ARE ALWAYS BROKEN   1914

Factory windows are always broken.
Somebody's always throwing bricks,
Somebody's always heaving cinders,
Playing ugly Yahoo tricks.

Factory windows are always broken.   5
Other windows are let alone.
No one throws through the chapel-window
The bitter, snarling derisive stone.

Factory windows are always broken.
Something or other is going wrong.   10
Something is rotten—I think, in Denmark.
End of the factory-window song.

FACTORY WINDOWS ARE ALWAYS BROKEN. 4 *Yahoo:* a brutish uncivilized person (adopted from Jonathan Swift's *Gulliver's Travels.* 11 *Something is rotten . . . :* an allusion to a line from William Shakespeare's *Hamlet,* "Something is rotten in the state of Denmark."

QUESTIONS

1. Is the rhythm regular or irregular in this poem? If it is regular, how many strong beats are in each line?
2. What other devices of sound are in the poem?
3. What is the effect of the unusual last line? Does it change the tone of the poem, or is it in keeping with the earlier lines?

EXERCISE: *Meaningful Variation*

At what place or places in each of these passages does the poet depart from basic iambic meter? How does each departure help underscore the meaning?

1. Shadwell alone of all my sons is he
   Who stands confirmed in full stupidity.
   The rest to some faint meaning make pretense,
   But Shadwell never deviates into sense.
                    —John Dryden, "Mac Flecknoe" (speech of Flecknoe, prince of
                    Nonsense, referring to Thomas Shadwell, poet and playwright)

[6]*Poetic Meter and Poetic Form* (New York: Random, 1965) 110.

2. A needless Alexandrine ends the song
   That, like a wounded snake, drags its slow length along.
   —Alexander Pope, from *An Essay on Criticism*

3. Roll on, thou deep and dark blue Ocean—roll!
   Ten thousand fleets sweep over thee in vain;
   Man marks the earth with ruin—his control
   Stops with the shore; upon the watery plain
   The wrecks are all thy deed, nor doth remain
   A shadow of man's ravage, save his own,
   When, for a moment, like a drop of rain,
   He sinks into thy depths with bubbling groan,
   Without a grave, unknell'd, uncoffin'd, and unknown.
   —George Gordon, Lord Byron, *Childe Harold's Pilgrimage*

4. Deer walk upon our mountains, and the quail
   Whistle about us their spontaneous cries;
   Sweet berries ripen in the wilderness;
   And, in the isolation of the sky,
   At evening, casual flocks of pigeons make
   Ambiguous undulations as they sink,
   Downward to darkness, on extended wings.
   —Wallace Stevens, "Sunday Morning"

EXERCISE: *Recognizing Rhythms*

Which of the following poems contain predominant meters? Which poems are not wholly metrical, but are metrical in certain lines? Point out any such lines. What reasons do you see, in such places, for the poet's seeking a metrical effect?

Edna St. Vincent Millay (1892–1950)*

COUNTING-OUT RHYME   1928

Silver bark of beech, and sallow
Bark of yellow birch and yellow
    Twig of willow.

Stripe of green in moosewood maple,
Color seen in leaf of apple,   5
    Bark of popple.

Wood of popple pale as moonbeam,
Wood of oak for yoke and barn-beam,
    Wood of hornbeam.

Silver bark of beech, and hollow   10
Stem of elder, tall and yellow
    Twig of willow.

A. E. Housman   (1859–1936)*

WHEN I WAS ONE-AND-TWENTY   1896

When I was one-and-twenty
  I heard a wise man say,
"Give crowns and pounds and guineas
  But not your heart away;
Give pearls away and rubies   5
  But keep your fancy free."
But I was one-and-twenty,
  No use to talk to me.

When I was one-and-twenty
  I heard him say again,   10
"The heart out of the bosom
  Was never given in vain;
'Tis paid with sighs a plenty
  And sold for endless rue."
And I am two-and-twenty,   15
  And oh, 'tis true, 'tis true.

William Carlos Williams   (1883–1963)*

HEEL & TOE TO THE END   1962

Gagarin says, in ecstasy,
he could have
gone on forever

he floated
ate and sang   5
and when he emerged from that

one hundred eight minutes off
the surface of
the earth he was smiling

Then he returned   10
to take his place
among the rest of us

from all that division and
subtraction a measure
toe and heel   15

heel and toe he felt
as if he had
been dancing

HEEL & TOE TO THE END. 1 *Gagarin*: On April 12, 1961, Soviet cosmonaut Yuri Gagarin (1934–1968) became the first person ever to orbit the earth.

Walt Whitman (1819–1892)*

BEAT! BEAT! DRUMS! (1861)

Beat! beat! drums!—blow! bugles! blow!
Through the windows—through doors—burst like a ruthless force,
Into the solemn church, and scatter the congregation,
Into the school where the scholar is studying;
Leave not the bridegroom quiet—no happiness must he have now with 5
    his bride,
Nor the peaceful farmer any peace, ploughing his field or gathering his
    grain,
So fierce you whirr and pound you drums—so shrill you bugles blow.

Beat! beat! drums!—blow! bugles! blow!
Over the traffic of cities—over the rumble of wheels in the streets;
Are beds prepared for sleepers at night in the houses? no sleepers must 10
    sleep in those beds,
No bargainer's bargains by day—no brokers or speculators—would they
    continue?
Would the talkers be talking? would the singer attempt to sing?
Would the lawyer rise in the court to state his case before the judge?
Then rattle quicker, heavier drums—you bugles wilder blow.

Beat! beat! drums!—blow! bugles! blow! 15
Make no parley—stop for no expostulation,
Mind not the timid—mind not the weeper or prayer,
Mind not the old man beseeching the young man,
Let not the child's voice be heard, nor the mother's entreaties,
Make even the trestles to shake the dead where they lie awaiting the 20
    hearses.
So strong you thump O terrible drums—so loud you bugles blow.

David Mason   (b. 1954)

SONG OF THE POWERS   1996

Mine, said the stone,
mine is the hour.
I crush the scissors,
such is my power.
Stronger than wishes,   5
my power, alone.

Mine, said the paper,
mine are the words
that smother the stone
with imagined birds,   10
reams of them, flown
from the mind of the shaper.

Mine, said the scissors,
mine all the knives
gashing through paper's   15
ethereal lives;
nothing's so proper
as tattering wishes.

As stone crushes scissors,
as paper snuffs stone   20
and scissors cut paper,
all end alone.
So heap up your paper
and scissor your wishes
and uproot the stone   25
from the top of the hill.
They all end alone
as you will, you will.

SONG OF THE POWERS. The three key images of this poem are drawn from the children's game of Scissors, Paper, Stone. In this game each object has a specific power: Scissors cuts paper, paper covers stone, and stone crushes scissors.

Langston Hughes   (1902–1967)*

DREAM BOOGIE   1951

Good morning, daddy!
Ain't you heard
The boogie-woogie rumble
Of a dream deferred?

Listen closely:
You'll hear their feet
Beating out and beating out a— 5

You think
It's a happy beat?

Listen to it closely:
Ain't you heard
something underneath 10
like a—

What did I say?

Sure,
I'm happy!
Take it away! 15

Hey, pop!
Re-bop!
Mop! 20

    Y-e-a-h!

WRITER'S PERSPECTIVE

Gwendolyn Brooks

Gwendolyn Brooks on Writing

HEARING "WE REAL COOL" 1969

STAVROS: How about the seven pool players in the poem "We Real Cool"?

BROOKS: They have no pretensions to any glamor. They are supposedly dropouts, or at least they're in the poolroom when they should be possibly in school, since they're probably young enough or at least those I saw were when I looked in a poolroom, and they. . . . First of all, let me tell you how that's supposed to be said, because there's a reason why I set it out as I did. These are people who are essentially saying, "Kilroy is here. We *are*." But they're a little uncertain of the strength of their identity. The "We"—you're supposed to stop after the "We" and think about *validity*; of course, there's no way for you to tell whether it should be said softly or not, I suppose, but I say it rather softly because I want to represent their basic uncertainty, which they don't bother to question every day, of course.

STAVROS: Are you saying that the form of this poem, then, was determined by the colloquial rhythm you were trying to catch?

BROOKS: No, determined by my feelings about these boys, these young men.

From "On 'We Real Cool'"

◄━━► WRITING CRITICALLY ◄━━━►

Freeze-Framing the Sound

If you plan to write about the rhythm of a poem, the best way to begin is nearly always by scanning. Although scansion may seem a bit intimidating at first, it is really not difficult; it is just a way of notating how to read the poem aloud. A scansion gives us a freeze-frame of the poem's most important sound patterns. And since stress reinforces meaning, it also helps us understand a poem better. Here is a simple way to get started:

1. Copy down the passage you want to analyze.
2. Mark the syllables on which the main speech stresses fall. (When in doubt, just read the line aloud several different ways and try to detect which way seems most natural.)
3. You might also want to make a few notes in the margin about other things that you notice. Are there rimes? How many syllables in each line? Are there any other recurring patterns of sound worth noting?

A simple scansion of the opening of Tennyson's poem "Break, Break, Break" (on page 889) might look like this in your notes:

Break, break, break	(3 syllables)
On thy cold gray stones, o sea	(7 syllables)/rime
And I would that my tongue could utter	(9 syllables)
The thoughts that arise in me.	(7 syllables)/rime

By now some basic organizing principles of the poem have become clear. The lines are rimed *a b c b*, but they contain an irregular number of syllables. The number of strong stresses, however, seems to be constant, at least in the opening stanza. Now that you have a visual diagram of the poem's sound, the rhythm will be much easier to write about.

WRITING ASSIGNMENT

Analyze the rhythm of a key passage from any poem in this chapter. Discuss how the poem uses rhythm to create certain effects. Incorporate into your analysis a scansion of the passage in question. (Your scansion need not identify every element of the poem's sound, but have it show all the elements you discuss.)

FURTHER SUGGESTIONS FOR WRITING

1. When has a rhythm of any kind (whether in poetry or not) stirred you, picked you up, and carried you along with it? Write an account of your experience.
2. The fact that most contemporary poets have given up meter, in the view of Stanley Kunitz, has made poetry "easier to write, but harder to remember." Why so? Comment on Kunitz's remark, or quarrel with it, in two or three paragraphs.
3. Robert Frost once claimed he tried to make poetry out of the "sound of sense." Writing to a friend, Frost discussed his notion that "the simple declarative sentence" in English often contained an abstract sound that helped communicate its meaning. "The best place to get the abstract sound of sense," wrote Frost, "is from voices behind a door that cuts off the words." Ask yourself how these sentences of dialogue would sound without the words in which they are embodied:

    You mean to tell me you can't read?
    I said no such thing.
    Well read then.
    You're not my teacher.

    Frost went on to say that "The reader must be at no loss to give his voice the posture proper to the sentence." Thinking about Frost's theory, can you see how it throws any light on one of his poems? In two or three paragraphs, discuss how Frost uses the "simple declarative sentence" as a distinctive rhythmic feature in his poetry.

21 *Closed Form*

Form, as a general idea, is the design of a thing as a whole, the configuration of all its parts. No poem can escape having some kind of form, whether its lines are as various in length as broomstraws or all in hexameter. To put this point in another way: if you were to listen to a poem read aloud in a language unknown to you, or if you saw the poem printed in that foreign language, whatever in the poem you could see or hear would be the form of it.[1]

Writing in **closed form,** a poet follows (or finds) some sort of pattern, such as that of a sonnet with its rime scheme and its fourteen lines of iambic pentameter. On a page, poems in closed form tend to look regular and symmetrical, often falling into stanzas that indicate groups of rimes. Along with William Butler Yeats, who held that a successful poem will "come shut with a click, like a closing box," the poet who writes in closed form apparently strives for a kind of perfection—seeking, perhaps, to lodge words so securely in place that no word can be budged without a worsening. For the sake of meaning, though, a competent poet often will depart from a symmetrical pattern. As Robert Frost observed, there is satisfaction to be found in things not mechanically regular: "We enjoy the straight crookedness of a good walking stick."

The poet who writes in **open form** usually seeks no final click. Often, such a poet views the writing of a poem as a process, rather than a quest for an absolute. Free to use white space for emphasis, able to shorten or lengthen lines as the sense seems to require, the poet lets the poem discover its shape as it goes along, moving as water flows downhill, adjusting to its terrain, engulfing obstacles. (Open form will provide the focus of the next chapter.)

---

[1]For a good summary of the uses of the term *form* in criticism of poetry, see the article "Form" by G. N. G. Orsini in *Princeton Encyclopedia of Poetry and Poetics,* 2nd ed., ed. Preminger, Warnke, and Hardison (Princeton: Princeton UP, 1975).

Most poetry of the past is in closed form, exhibiting at least a pattern of rime or meter, but since the early 1960s the majority of American poets have preferred forms that stay open. Lately, the situation has been changing yet again, with closed form reappearing in much recent poetry. Whatever the fashion of the moment, the reader who seeks a wide understanding of poetry of both the present and the past will need to know both the closed and open varieties.

Closed form gives some poems a valuable advantage: it makes them more easily memorable. The **epic** poems of nations—long narratives tracing the adventures of popular heroes: the Greek *Iliad* and *Odyssey*, the French *Song of Roland*, the Spanish *Cid*—tend to occur in patterns of fairly consistent line length or number of stresses because these works were sometimes transmitted orally. Sung to the music of a lyre or chanted to a drumbeat, they may have been easier to memorize because of their patterns. If a singer forgot something, the song would have a noticeable hole in it, so rime or fixed meter probably helped prevent an epic from deteriorating when passed along from one singer to another. It is no coincidence that so many English playwrights of Shakespeare's day favored iambic pentameter. Companies of actors, often called on to perform a different play each day, could count on a fixed line length to aid their burdened memories.

Some poets complain that closed form is a straitjacket, a limit to free expression. Other poets, however, feel that, like fires held fast in a narrow space, thoughts stated in a tightly binding form may take on a heightened intensity. "Limitation makes for power," according to one contemporary practitioner of closed form, Richard Wilbur; "the strength of the genie comes of his being confined in a bottle." Compelled by some strict pattern to arrange and rearrange words, delete, and exchange them, poets must focus on them the keenest attention. Often they stand a chance of discovering words more meaningful than the ones they started out with. And at times, in obedience to a rime scheme, the poet may be surprised by saying something quite unexpected. With the conscious portion of the mind, the poet may wish to express what seems to be a good idea. But a line ending in *year* must be followed by another ending in *atmosphere, beer, bier, bombardier, cashier, deer, friction-gear, frontier,* or some other rime word that otherwise might not have entered the poem. That is why rime schemes and stanza patterns can be mighty allies and valuable disturbers of the unconscious. As Rolfe Humphries has said about strict form: "It makes you think of better things than you would all by yourself."

FORMAL PATTERNS

The best-known one-line pattern for a poem in English is **blank verse:** unrimed iambic pentameter. (This pattern is not a stanza: stanzas have more than one line.) Most portions of Shakespeare's plays are in blank verse, and so are Milton's *Paradise Lost*, Tennyson's "Ulysses," certain dramatic monologues of Browning and Frost, and thousands of other poems. Here is a poem in blank verse that startles us by dropping out of its pattern in the final line. Keats appears to have written it late in his life to his fiancée Fanny Brawne.

John Keats (1795–1821)*

THIS LIVING HAND, NOW WARM AND CAPABLE (1819?)

This living hand, now warm and capable
Of earnest grasping, would, if it were cold
And in the icy silence of the tomb,
So haunt thy days and chill thy dreaming nights
That thou wouldst wish thine own heart dry of blood   5
So in my veins red life might stream again,
And thou be conscience-calmed—see here it is—
I hold it towards you.

The **couplet** is a two-line stanza, usually rimed. Its lines often tend to be equal in length, whether short or long. Here are two examples:

Blow,
Snow!

As I in hoary winter's night stood shivering in the snow,
Surprised I was with sudden heat which made my heart to glow.

Actually, any pair of rimed lines that contains a complete thought is called a couplet, even if it is not a stanza, such as the couplet that ends a sonnet by Shakespeare. Unlike other stanzas, couplets are often printed solid, one couplet not separated from the next by white space. This practice is usual in printing the **heroic couplet**—or **closed couplet**—two rimed lines of iambic pentameter, the first ending in a light pause, the second more heavily end-stopped. George Crabbe, in *The Parish Register*, described a shotgun wedding:

Next at our altar stood a luckless pair,
Brought by strong passions and a warrant there:
By long rent cloak, hung loosely, strove the bride,
From every eye, what all perceived, to hide;
While the boy bridegroom, shuffling in his place,
Now hid awhile and then exposed his face.
As shame alternately with anger strove
The brain confused with muddy ale to move,
In haste and stammering he performed his part,
And looked the rage that rankled in his heart.

Though employed by Chaucer, the heroic couplet was named from its later use by Dryden and others in poems, translations of classical epics, and verse plays of epic heroes. It continued in favor through most of the eighteenth century. Much of our pleasure in reading good heroic couplets comes from the seemingly easy precision with which a skilled poet unites statements and strict pattern. In doing so, the poet may place a pair of words, phrases, clauses, or sentences side by side in agreement or similarity, forming a **parallel,** or in contrast and opposition, forming an **antithesis.** The effect is neat. For such skill in manipulating parallels and antitheses, John Denham's lines on the river Thames were much admired:

> O could I flow like thee, and make thy stream
> My great example, as it is my theme!
> Though deep, yet clear; though gentle, yet not dull;
> Strong without rage, without o'erflowing full.

These lines were echoed by Pope, ridiculing a poetaster, in two heroic couplets in *The Dunciad:*

> Flow, Welsted, flow! like thine inspirer, Beer:
> Though stale, not ripe; though thin, yet never clear;
> So sweetly mawkish, and so smoothly dull;
> Heady, not strong; o'erflowing, though not full.

Reading long poems in so exact a form, one may feel like a spectator at a Ping-Pong match, unless the poet skillfully keeps varying rhythms. One way of escaping such metronome-like monotony is to keep the cesura (see page 888) shifting about from place to place—now happening early in a line, now happening late—and at times unexpectedly to hurl in a second or third cesura. This skill, among other things, distinguishes the work of Dryden and Pope. If you care to see it in action, try working through Dryden's elegy for Oldham (page 1166) or Pope's acid portrait of Atticus (page 891), noticing where the cesuras fall. You'll find that the pauses skip around with lively variety.

A **tercet** is a group of three lines. If rimed, they usually keep to one rime sound, as in this anonymous English children's jingle:

> Julius Caesar,
> The Roman geezer,
> Squashed his wife with a lemon-squeezer.

(That, by the way, is a great demonstration of surprising and unpredictable rimes.) *Terza rima,* the form Dante employs in *The Divine Comedy,* is made of tercets linked together by the rime scheme *a b a, b c b, c d c, d e d, e f e,* and so on. Harder to do in English than in Italian—with its greater resources of riming words—the form nevertheless has been managed by Shelley in "Ode to the West Wind" (with the aid of some slant rimes):

> Make me thy lyre, even as the forest is:
> What if my leaves are falling like its own!
> The tumult of thy mighty harmonies

> Will take from both a deep, autumnal tone,
> Sweet though in sadness. Be thou, spirit fierce,
> My spirit! Be thou me, impetuous one!

The workhorse of English poetry is the **quatrain,** a stanza consisting of four lines. Quatrains are used in more rimed poems than any other form.

Robert Graves   (1895–1985)*

COUNTING THE BEATS   1959

You, love, and I,
(He whispers) you and I,
And if no more than only you and I
What care you or I?

Counting the beats,   5
Counting the slow heart beats,
The bleeding to death of time in slow heart beats,
Wakeful they lie.

Cloudless day,
Night, and a cloudless day,   10
Yet the huge storm will burst upon their heads one day
From a bitter sky.

Where shall we be,
(She whispers) where shall we be,
When death strikes home, O where then shall we be   15
Who were you and I?

Not there but here,
(He whispers) only here,
As we are, here, together, now and here,
Always you and I.   20

Counting the beats,
Counting the slow heart beats,
The bleeding to death of time in slow heart beats,
Wakeful they lie.

QUESTION

What elements of sound and rhythm are consistent from stanza to stanza? Do any features change unpredictably from stanza to stanza?

Quatrains come in many line lengths, and sometimes contain lines of varying length, as in the ballad stanza (see page 846). Most often, poets rime the second and fourth lines of quatrains, as in the ballad, but the rimes can occur in any combination the poet chooses. Here are two quatrains from Tennyson's long, elegiac poem, *In Memoriam*. The poem's form—quatrains of iambic tetrameter with the unusual rime scheme *a b b a*—became so celebrated that this pattern is now called the "*In Memoriam* stanza":

Be near me when my light is low,
    When the blood creeps, and the nerves prick
    And tingle; and the heart is sick,
And all the wheels of being slow.

Be near me when the sensuous frame
    Is rack'd with pangs that conquer trust;
    And Time, a maniac scattering dust,
And Life, a Fury slinging flame.

Longer and more complicated stanzas are, of course, possible, but couplet, tercet, and quatrain have been called the building blocks of our poetry because most longer stanzas are made up of them. What short stanzas does John Donne mortar together to make the longer stanza of his "Song"?

John Donne   (1572–1631)*

SONG   1633

Go and catch a falling star,
    Get with child a mandrake root,
Tell me where all past years are,
    Or who cleft the Devil's foot,
Teach me to hear mermaids singing,   5
    Or to keep off envy's stinging,
        And find
        What wind
Serves to advance an honest mind.

If thou be'st borne to strange sights,   10
    Things invisible to see,
Ride ten thousand days and nights,
    Till age snow white hairs on thee,
Thou, when thou return'st, wilt tell me
    All strange wonders that befell thee,   15
        And swear
        Nowhere
Lives a woman true, and fair.

If thou findst one, let me know,
    Such a pilgrimage were sweet—   20
Yet do not, I would not go,
    Though at next door we might meet;
Though she were true, when you met her,
    And last, till you write your letter,
        Yet she   25
        Will be
False, ere I come, to two, or three.

Recently in vogue is a form known as **syllabic verse,** in which the poet establishes a pattern of a certain number of syllables to a line. Either rimed or rimeless but usually stanzaic, syllabic verse has been hailed as a way for poets to escape "the tyranny of the iamb" and discover less conventional rhythms, since, if they take as their line length an *odd* number of syllables, then iambs, being feet of *two* syllables, cannot fit perfectly into it. Offbeat victories have been scored in syllabics by such poets as W. H. Auden, W. D. Snodgrass, Donald Hall, Thom Gunn, and Marianne Moore. A well-known syllabic poem is Dylan Thomas's "Fern Hill" (page 1252). Notice its shape on the page, count the syllables in its lines, and you'll perceive its perfect symmetry. Although it is like playing a game, the writing of such a poem is apparently more than finger exercise: the discipline can help a poet to sing well, though (with Thomas) singing "in . . . chains like the sea."

Poets who write in demanding forms seem to enjoy taking on an arbitrary task for the fun of it, as ballet dancers do, or weightlifters. Much of our pleasure in reading such poems comes from watching words fall into a shape. It is the pleasure of seeing any hard thing done skillfully—a leap executed in a dance, a basketball swished through a basket. Still, to be excellent, a poem needs more than skill; and to enjoy a poem it isn't always necessary for the reader to be aware of the skill that went into it. Unknowingly, the editors of the *New Yorker* once printed an **acrostic**—a poem in which the initial letter of each line, read downward, spells out a word or words—that named (and insulted) a well-known anthologist. Evidently, besides being ingenious, the acrostic was a printable poem. In the Old Testament book of Lamentations, profoundly moving songs tell of the sufferings of the Jews after the destruction of Jerusalem. Four of the songs are written as an alphabetical acrostic, every stanza beginning with a letter of the Hebrew alphabet. However ingenious, such sublime poetry cannot be dismissed as merely witty; nor can it be charged that a poet who writes in such a form does not express deep feeling.

Phillis Levin   (b. 1954)

BRIEF BIO   1995

Bearer of no news
Under the sun, except
The spring, I quicken
Time, drawing you to see
Earth's lightest pamphlet,   5
Reeling mosaic of rainbow dust,
Filament hinging a new set of wings,
Lord of no land, subject to flowers and wind,
Yesterday born in a palace that hangs by a thread.

QUESTIONS

1. What does the poem describe? (How can we know for sure if we have guessed the
correct answer to the poem's riddle?)

2. What is the form of the poem?
3. How does the title relate to the rest of the poem?
4. Does the visual shape of the poem on the page suggest any image from the poem itself?

Patterns of sound and rhythm can, however, be striven after in a dull mechanical way, for which reason many poets today think them dangerous. Swinburne, who loved alliterations and tripping meters, had enough detachment to poke fun at his own excessive patterning:

> From the depth of the dreamy decline of the dawn through a
> notable nimbus of nebulous noonshine,
> Pallid and pink as the palm of the flag-flower that flickers with
> fear of the flies as they float,
> Are the looks of our lovers that lustrously lean from a marvel of
> mystic miraculous moonshine,
> These that we feel in the blood of our blushes that thicken and
> threaten with throbs through the throat?

This is bad, but bad deliberately. Viewed mechanically, as so many empty boxes somehow to be filled up, stanzas can impose the most hollow sort of discipline. If any good at all, a poem in a fixed pattern, such as a sonnet, is created not only by the craftsman's chipping away at it, but by the explosion of a sonnet-shaped *idea*.

Ronald Gross (b. 1935)

Yield   1967

Yield.
No Parking.
Unlawful to Pass.
Wait for Green Light.
Yield.   5

Stop.
Narrow Bridge.
Merging Traffic Ahead.
Yield.

Yield.   10

QUESTIONS

1. This poem by Ronald Gross is a "found poem." After reading it, how would you define **found poetry**?
2. Does "Yield" have a theme? If so, how would you state it?
3. What makes "Yield" mean more than traffic signs ordinarily mean to us?

Ronald Gross, who produces his "found poetry" by arranging prose from such unlikely places as traffic signs and news stories into poem-like lines, has told of making a discovery:

> As I worked with labels, tax forms, commercials, contracts, pin-up captions, obituaries, and the like, I soon found myself rediscovering all the traditional verse forms in found materials: ode, sonnet, epigram, haiku, free verse. Such finds made me realize that these forms are not mere artifices, but shapes that language naturally takes when carrying powerful thoughts or feelings.[2]

It is fun to see words tumble gracefully into such a shape. Consider, for instance, one famous "found poem," a sentence discovered in a physics textbook: "And so no force, however great, can stretch a cord, however fine, into a horizontal line which shall be absolutely straight."[3] What a good clear sentence containing effective parallels ("however great . . . however fine"), you might say, taking pleasure in it. Yet this plain statement gives extra pleasure if arranged like this:

> And so no force, however great,
>   Can stretch a cord, however fine,
>   Into a horizontal line
> Which shall be absolutely straight.

So spaced, in lines that reveal its built-in rimes and rhythms, the sentence would seem one of those "shapes that language naturally takes" that Ronald Gross finds everywhere. (It is possible, of course, that the textbook writer was gleefully planting a quatrain for someone to find; but perhaps it is more likely that he knew much rimed, metrical poetry by heart and couldn't help writing it unconsciously.) Inspired by pop artists who reveal fresh vistas in Brillo boxes and comic strips, found poetry has had a recent flurry of activity. Earlier practitioners include William Carlos Williams, whose long poem *Paterson* quotes historical documents and statistics. Prose, wrote Williams, can be a "laboratory" for poetry: "It throws up jewels which may be cleaned and grouped."

EXPERIMENT: *Finding a Poem*

In a newspaper, magazine, catalogue, textbook, or advertising throwaway, find a sentence or passage that (with a little artistic manipulation on your part) shows promise of becoming a poem. Copy it into lines like poetry, being careful to place what seem to be the most interesting words at the ends of lines to give them greatest emphasis. According to the rules of found poetry, you may excerpt, delete, repeat, and rearrange elements but not add anything. What does this experiment tell you about poetic form? About ordinary prose?

[2]"Speaking of Books: Found Poetry," *New York Times Book Review*, 11 June 1967. See also Gross's *Pop Poems* (New York: Simon, 1967).
[3]William Whewell, *Elementary Treatise on Mechanics* (Cambridge, England, 1819).

THE SONNET

When we speak, with Ronald Gross, of "traditional verse forms," we usually mean **fixed forms.** If written in a fixed form, a poem inherits from other poems certain familiar elements of structure: an unvarying number of lines, say, or a stanza pattern. In addition, it may display certain **conventions:** expected features such as themes, subjects, attitudes, or figures of speech. In medieval folk ballads a "milk-white steed" is a conventional figure of speech; and if its rider be a cruel and beautiful witch who kidnaps mortals, she is a conventional character. (*Conventional* doesn't necessarily mean uninteresting.)

In the poetry of western Europe and America, the **sonnet** is the fixed form that has attracted for the longest time the largest number of noteworthy practitioners. Originally an Italian form (*sonnetto:* "little song"), the sonnet owes much of its prestige to Petrarch (1304–1374), who wrote in it of his love for the unattainable Laura. So great was the vogue for sonnets in England at the end of the sixteenth century that a gentleman might have been thought a boor if he couldn't turn out a decent one. Not content to adopt merely the sonnet's fourteen-line pattern, English poets also tried on its conventional mask of the tormented lover. They borrowed some of Petrarch's similes (a lover's heart, for instance, is like a storm-tossed boat) and invented others. (If you would like more illustrations of Petrarchan conventions, see Shakespeare's sonnet on page 1238.)

Soon after English poets imported the sonnet in the middle of the sixteenth century, they worked out their own rime scheme—one easier for them to follow than Petrarch's, which calls for a greater number of riming words than English can readily provide. (In Italian, according to an exaggerated report, practically everything rimes.) In the following **English sonnet,** sometimes called a **Shakespearean sonnet,** the rimes cohere in four clusters: *a b a b, c d c d, e f e f, g g.* Because a rime scheme tends to shape the poet's statements to it, the English sonnet has three places where the procession of thought is likely to turn in another direction. Within its form, a poet may pursue one idea throughout the three quatrains and then in the couplet end with a surprise.

William Shakespeare   (1564–1616)*

LET ME NOT TO THE MARRIAGE OF TRUE MINDS

1609

Let me not to the marriage of true minds
Admit impediments; love is not love
Which alters when it alteration finds,
Or bends with the remover to remove.
O, no, it is an ever-fixèd mark   5
That looks on tempests and is never shaken;

It is the star to every wand'ring bark,
Whose worth's unknown, although his height be taken.
Love's not Time's fool, though rosy lips and cheeks
Within his bending sickle's compass° come;   *range*   10
Love alters not with his° brief hours and weeks   *Time's*
But bears° it out even to the edge of doom.   *endures*

    If this be error and upon me proved,
    I never writ, nor no man ever loved.

LET ME NOT TO THE MARRIAGE OF TRUE MINDS. 5 *ever-fixèd mark:* a sea-mark like a beacon or a lighthouse that provides mariners with safe bearings. 7 *the star:* presumably the North Star, which gave
sailors the most dependable bearing at sea. 12 *edge of doom:* either the brink of death or—taken more
generally—Judgment Day.

Michael Drayton   (1563–1631)

SINCE THERE'S NO HELP,   1619
COME LET US KISS AND PART

Since there's no help, come let us kiss and part;
Nay, I have done, you get no more of me,
And I am glad, yea, glad with all my heart
That thus so cleanly I myself can free;
Shake hands for ever, cancel all our vows,   5
And when we meet at any time again,
Be it not seen in either of our brows
That we one jot of former love retain.
Now at the last gasp of Love's latest breath,
When, his pulse failing, Passion speechless lies,   10
When Faith is kneeling by his bed of death,
And Innocence is closing up his eyes,
    Now if thou wouldst, when all have given him over,
    From death to life thou mightst him yet recover.

    Less frequently met in English poetry, the **Italian sonnet,** or **Petrarchan
sonnet,** follows the rime scheme *a b b a, a b b a* in its first eight lines, the **octave,**
and then adds new rime sounds in the last six lines, the **sestet.** The sestet may
rime *c d c d c d, c d e c d e, c d c c d c,* or in almost any other variation that doesn't
end in a couplet. This organization into two parts sometimes helps arrange the
poet's thoughts. In the octave, the poet may state a problem, and then, in the
sestet, may offer a resolution. A lover, for example, may lament all octave long
that a loved one is neglectful, then in line 9 begin to foresee some outcome: the
speaker will die, or accept unhappiness, or trust that the beloved will have a
change of heart.

Edna St. Vincent Millay (1892–1950)*

WHAT LIPS MY LIPS HAVE KISSED,   1923
AND WHERE, AND WHY

What lips my lips have kissed, and where, and why,
I have forgotten, and what arms have lain
Under my head till morning; but the rain
Is full of ghosts tonight, that tap and sigh
Upon the glass and listen for reply,   5
And in my heart there sits a quiet pain
For unremembered lads that not again
Will turn to me at midnight with a cry.
Thus in the winter stands the lonely tree,
Nor knows what birds have vanished one by one,   10
Yet knows its boughs more silent than before:
I cannot say what loves have come and gone,
I only know that summer sang in me
A little while, that in me sings no more.

    In this Italian sonnet, the turn of thought comes at the traditional point—
the beginning of the ninth line. Many English-speaking poets, however, feel free
to vary its placement. In John Milton's commanding sonnet on his blindness
("When I consider how my light is spent" on page 1212), the turn comes
midway through line 8, and no one has ever thought the worse of it for bending
the rules.
    When we hear the terms *closed form* or *fixed form*, we imagine traditional po-
etic forms as a series of immutable rules. But, in the hands of the best poets, metrical forms are fluid concepts that change to suit the occasion. Here, for example,
is a haunting poem by Robert Frost that simultaneously fulfills the rules of two
traditional forms. Is it an innovative sonnet or a poem in *terza rima*? (See page
911 for a discussion of *terza rima*.) Frost combined the features of both forms to
create a compressed and powerfully lyric poem.

Robert Frost (1874–1963)*

ACQUAINTED WITH THE NIGHT   1928

I have been one acquainted with the night.
I have walked out in rain—and back in rain.
I have outwalked the furthest city light.

I have looked down the saddest city lane.
I have passed by the watchman on his beat   5
And dropped my eyes, unwilling to explain.

I have stood still and stopped the sound of feet
When far away an interrupted cry
Came over houses from another street,

But not to call me back or say good-bye;   10
And further still at an unearthly height,
One luminary clock against the sky

Proclaimed the time was neither wrong nor right
I have been one acquainted with the night.

"The sonnet," quipped Robert Bly, a contemporary poet-critic, "is where old professors go to die." And certainly in the hands of an unskilled practitioner, the form can seem moribund. Considering the impressive number of powerful sonnets by modern poets such as Yeats, Frost, Auden, Millay, Cummings, Kees, and Heaney, however, the form hardly appears to be exhausted. Like the hero of the popular ballad "Finnegan's Wake," literary forms (though not professors) declared dead have a startling habit of springing up again. No law compels sonnets to adopt an exalted tone, or confines them to an Elizabethan vocabulary. To see some of the surprising shapes contemporary sonnets take, read this selection of five recent examples.

Kim Addonizio   (b. 1954)

FIRST POEM FOR YOU   1994

I like to touch your tattoos in complete
darkness, when I can't see them. I'm sure of
where they are, know by heart the neat
lines of lightning pulsing just above
your nipple, can find, as if by instinct, the blue   5
swirls of water on your shoulder where a serpent
twists, facing a dragon. When I pull you
to me, taking you until we're spent
and quiet on the sheets, I love to kiss
the pictures in your skin. They'll last until   10
you're seared to ashes; whatever persists
or turns to pain between us, they will still
be there. Such permanence is terrifying.
So I touch them in the dark; but touch them, trying.

Mark Jarman   (b. 1952)

UNHOLY SONNET: AFTER THE PRAYING   1997

After the praying, after the hymn-singing,
After the sermon's trenchant commentary

On the world's ills, which make ours secondary,
After communion, after the hand-wringing,
And after peace descends upon us, bringing   5
Our eyes up to regard the sanctuary
And how the light swords through it, and how, scary
In their sheer numbers, motes of dust ride, clinging—
There is, as doctors say about some pain,
Discomfort knowing that despite your prayers,   10
Your listening and rejoicing, your small part
In this communal stab at coming clean,
There is one stubborn remnant of your cares
Intact. There is still murder in your heart.

QUESTIONS

1. What kind of sonnet is "Unholy Sonnet," English or Italian?
2. Does the poem have a turn of thought? If so, point out where it occurs and describe it.

R. S. Gwynn (b. 1948)

SCENES FROM THE PLAYROOM   1986

Now Lucy with her family of dolls
Disfigures Mother with an emery board,
While Charles, with match and rubbing alcohol,
Readies the struggling cat, for Chuck is bored.

The young ones pour more ink into the water   5
Through which the latest goldfish gamely swims,
Laughing, pointing at naked, neutered Father.
The toy chest is a Buchenwald of limbs.

Mother is so lovely; Father, so late.
The cook is off, yet dinner must go on   10
With onions as her only cause for tears
She hacks the red meat from the slippery bone,
Setting the table, where the children wait,
Her grinning babies, clean behind the ears.

QUESTIONS

1. Explain the allusion to Buchenwald in line 8.
2. What do we know about this family and their lifestyle? What is revealed by the word *latest* (line 6)?
3. What do you think of these children and their parents? What does the poet think of them? By what details is his attitude made clear?

Timothy Steele   (b. 1948)*

SUMMER
1986

Voluptuous in plenty, summer is
Neglectful of the earnest ones who've sought her.
She best resides with what she images:
Lakes windless with profound sun-shafted water;
Dense orchards in which high-grassed heat grows thick;   5
The one-lane country road where, on his knees,
A boy initials soft tar with a stick;
Slow creeks which bear flecked light through depths of trees.

And he alone is summer's who relents
In his poor enterprisings; who can sense,   10
In alleys petal-blown, the wealth of chance;
Or can, supine in a deep meadow, pass
Warm hours beneath a moving sky's expanse,
Chewing the sweetness from long stalks of grass.

QUESTIONS

1. Define *voluptuous*. How does this word prepare us for the images to follow?
2. How many of the senses does this poem evoke?
3. What would be lost in the impact of line 5 if *dense* were omitted?
4. What images does the poem use to evoke the slow, heavy feeling of summer?

A. E. Stallings   (b. 1968)

SINE QUA NON
2002

Your absence, father, is nothing. It is nought—
The factor by which nothing will multiply,
The gap of a dropped stitch, the needle's eye
Weeping its black thread. It is the spot
Blindly spreading behind the looking glass.   5
It is the startled silences that come
When the refrigerator stops its hum,
And crickets pause to let the winter pass.

Your absence, father, is nothing—for it is
Omega's long last O, memory's elision,   10
The fraction of impossible division,
The element I move through, emptiness,
The void stars hang in, the interstice of lace,
The zero that still holds the sum in place.

SINE QUA NON. *Sine qua non* is from Latin, meaning literally, "without which not." Used to describe
something that is indispensable, an essential part, a prerequisite.

922   CLOSED FORM

The Epigram

Oscar Wilde said that a cynic is "a man who knows the price of everything and the value of nothing." Such a terse, pointed statement is called an epigram. In poetry, however, an **epigram** is a form: "A short poem ending in a witty or ingenious turn of thought, to which the rest of the composition is intended to lead up" (according to the *Oxford English Dictionary*). Often it is a malicious gibe with an unexpected stinger in the final line—perhaps in the very last word.

Alexander Pope   (1688–1744)*

Epigram Engraved on the Collar of a Dog Which I Gave to His Royal Highness
1738

I am his Highness' dog at Kew;
Pray tell me, sir, whose dog are you?

Sir John Harrington   (1561?–1612)

Of Treason
1618

Treason doth never prosper; what's the reason?
For if it prosper, none dare call it treason.

Robert Herrick   (1591–1674)*

Moderation
1648

In things a moderation keep,
Kings ought to shear, not skin their sheep.

William Blake   (1757–1827)*

Her whole life is an epigram
(1793)

Her whole life is an epigram: smack smooth,° and neatly   *perfectly smooth*
    penned,
Platted° quite neat to catch applause, with a sliding noose   *plaited, woven*
    at the end.

E. E. Cummings   (1894–1962)*

A politician
1944

a politician is an arse upon
which everyone has sat except a man

Langston Hughes   (1902–1967)*

PRAYER   1955

Oh, God of dust and rainbows, help us see
That without dust the rainbow would not be.

J. V. Cunningham   (1911–1985)*

THIS *Humanist* WHOM NO BELIEFS   1947
CONSTRAINED

This *Humanist* whom no beliefs constrained
Grew so broad-minded he was scatter-brained.

John Frederick Nims   (1913–1999)

CONTEMPLATION   1967

"I'm Mark's alone!" you swore. Given cause to doubt you,
I think less of you, dear. But more about you.

Stevie Smith   (1902–1971)

THIS ENGLISHWOMAN   1937

This Englishwoman is so refined
She has no bosom and no behind.

Brad Leithauser   (b. 1953)

A VENUS FLYTRAP   1982

The humming fly is turned to carrion.
This vegetable's no vegetarian.

Dick Davis   (b. 1945)

FATHERHOOD   1991

O my children, whom I love,
Whom I snap at and reprove—
Bide your time and we shall see
Love and rage snap back at me.

Anonymous

EPITAPH ON A DENTIST

Stranger, approach this spot with gravity;
John Brown is filling his last cavity.

Hilaire Belloc   (1870–1956)

FATIGUE   1923

I'm tired of Love: I'm still more tired of Rhyme.
But Money gives me pleasure all the time.

Wendy Cope   (b. 1945)*

VARIATION ON BELLOC'S "FATIGUE"   1992

I hardly ever tire of love or rhyme—
That's why I'm poor and have a rotten time.

EXPERIMENT: *Expanding an Epigram*

Rewrite any of the preceding epigrams, taking them out of rime and adding a few more words to them. See if your revisions have nearly the same effect as the originals.

In English the only other fixed form to rival the sonnet and the epigram in favor is the **limerick:** five anapestic lines usually riming *a a b b a*. The limerick was made popular by Edward Lear (1812–1888), English painter and author of such nonsense poems as "The Owl and the Pussycat." Here is a sample, attributed to President Woodrow Wilson (1856–1924):

> I sat next to the Duchess at tea;
> It was just as I feared it would be:
>   Her rumblings abdominal
>   Were truly phenomenal
> And everyone thought it was me!

EXPERIMENT: *Contriving a Clerihew*

The **clerihew,** a fixed form named for its inventor, Edmund Clerihew Bentley (1875–1956), has straggled behind the limerick in popularity. Here are three examples: How would you define the form and what are its rules? Who or what is its conventional subject matter? Try writing your own example.

> James Watt
> Was the hard-boiled kind of Scot:
> He thought any dream
> Sheer waste of steam.
> —W. H. Auden

Sir Christopher Wren
Said, "I am going to dine with some men.
If anybody calls
Say I am designing St. Paul's."
                    —Edmund Clerihew Bentley

Etienne de Silhouette
(It's a good bet)
Has the shadiest claim
To fame.
                    —Cornelius J. Ter Maat

OTHER FORMS

There are many other verse forms used in English. Some forms, like the villanelle and sestina (discussed below), come from other European literatures. But English has borrowed fixed forms from an astonishing variety of sources. The rubaiyat stanza (see pages 1030–31), for instance, comes from Persian poetry; the haiku (see page 798) and tanka originated in Japan. Other borrowed forms include the ghazal (Arabic), pantoum (Malay), and sapphics (Greek). Even blank verse (see page 909), which seems as English as the royal family, began as an attempt by Elizabethan poets to copy an Italian eleven-syllable line. To conclude this chapter, here are poems in three widely used closed forms—the villanelle, triolet, and sestina. Their patterns, which are sometimes called "French forms," have been particularly fascinating to English-language poets because they do not merely require the repetition of rime sounds; instead, they demand more elaborate echoing, involving the repetition of either full words or whole lines of verse. Sometimes difficult to master, these forms can create a powerful musical effect unlike ordinary riming.

But first let's look at a recent poem in an unusual pattern to see how an unexpected form can suggest surprising images and ideas.

Robert Pinsky (b. 1940)

ABC

2000

Any body can die, evidently. Few
Go happily, irradiating joy,

Knowledge, love. Many
Need oblivion, painkillers,
Quickest respite.

Sweet time unafflicted,
Various world:

X = your zenith.

5

1. What is the form of this poem?
2. If you rewrote the poem keeping all the ideas and images the same but changing the form, how much would that shift affect the poem's impact?

Dylan Thomas   (1914–1953)*

DO NOT GO GENTLE INTO THAT GOOD NIGHT   1952

Do not go gentle into that good night,
Old age should burn and rave at close of day;
Rage, rage against the dying of the light.

Though wise men at their end know dark is right,
Because their words had forked no lightning they   5
Do not go gentle into that good night.

Good men, the last wave by, crying how bright
Their frail deeds might have danced in a green bay,
Rage, rage against the dying of the light.

Wild men who caught and sang the sun in flight,   10
And learn, too late, they grieved it on its way,
Do not go gentle into that good night.

Grave men, near death, who see with blinding sight
Blind eyes could blaze like meteors and be gay,
Rage, rage against the dying of the light.   15

And you, my father, there on the sad height,
Curse, bless, me now with your fierce tears, I pray,
Do not go gentle into that good night.
Rage, rage against the dying of the light.

QUESTIONS

1. "Do not go gentle into that good night" is a **villanelle:** a fixed form originated by French courtly poets of the Middle Ages. What are its rules?
2. Whom does the poem address? What is the speaker saying?
3. Villanelles are sometimes criticized as elaborate exercises in trivial wordplay. How would you defend Thomas's poem against this charge?

Robert Bridges (1844–1930)

TRIOLET

1879

When first we met we did not guess
That Love would prove so hard a master;
Of more than common friendliness
When first we met we did not guess.
Who could foretell this sore distress,   5
This irretrievable disaster
When first we met—We did not guess
That Love would prove so hard a master.

TRIOLET. The **triolet** is a short lyric form borrowed from the French; its two opening lines are
repeated according to a set pattern, as Bridges's poem illustrates. The triolet is often used for light
verse, but Bridges's poem demonstrates how it can carry heavier emotional loads, if used with sufficient skill.

QUESTION

How do the first two lines change in meaning when they reappear at the end of the
poem?

Elizabeth Bishop (1911–1979)*

SESTINA

1965

September rain falls on the house.
In the failing light, the old grandmother
sits in the kitchen with the child
beside the Little Marvel Stove,
reading the jokes from the almanac,   5
laughing and talking to hide her tears.

She thinks that her equinoctial tears
and the rain that beats on the roof of the house
were both foretold by the almanac,
but only known to a grandmother.   10
The iron kettle sings on the stove.
She cuts some bread and says to the child,

It's time for tea now; but the child
is watching the teakettle's small hard tears
dance like mad on the hot black stove,   15
the way the rain must dance on the house.
Tidying up, the old grandmother
hangs up the clever almanac

on its string. Birdlike, the almanac
hovers half open above the child,   20
hovers above the old grandmother
and her teacup full of dark brown tears.
She shivers and says she thinks the house
feels chilly, and puts more wood in the stove.

It was to be, says the Marvel Stove.   25
I know what I know, says the almanac.
With crayons the child draws a rigid house
and a winding pathway. Then the child
puts in a man with buttons like tears
and shows it proudly to the grandmother.   30

But secretly, while the grandmother
busies herself about the stove,
the little moons fall down like tears
from between the pages of the almanac
into the flower bed the child   35
has carefully placed in the front of the house.

Time to plant tears, says the almanac.
The grandmother sings to the marvellous stove
and the child draws another inscrutable house.

SESTINA. As its title indicates, this poem is written in the trickiest of medieval fixed forms, that of the **sestina** (or "song of sixes"), said to have been invented in Provence in the thirteenth century by the troubadour poet Arnaut Daniel. In six six-line stanzas, the poet repeats six end-words (in a prescribed order), then reintroduces the six repeated words (in any order) in a closing **envoy** of three lines. Elizabeth Bishop strictly follows the troubadour rules for the order in which the end-words recur. (If you care, you can figure out the formula: in the first stanza, the six words are arranged A B C D E F; in the second, F A E B D C; and so on.) Notable sestinas in English have been written also by Sir Philip Sidney, Algernon Charles Swinburne, and Rudyard Kipling, more recently by Ezra Pound ("Sestina: Altaforte"), W. H. Auden ("Hearing of Harvests Rotting in the Valleys" and others), and by contemporary poets, among them John Ashbery, Tom Disch, Marilyn Hacker, Michael Heffernan, Donald Justice, Peter Klappert, and Mona Van Duyn.

QUESTIONS

1. A perceptive comment from a student: "Something seems to be going on here that the child doesn't understand. Maybe some terrible loss has happened." Test this guess by reading the poem closely.
2. Then consider this possibility. We don't know that "Sestina" is autobiographical; still, does any information about the poet's early life contribute to your reading of the poem? (See the chapter "Lives of the Poets.")
3. In the "little moons" that fall from the almanac (line 33), does the poem introduce dream or fantasy, or do you take these to be small round pieces of paper?
4. What is the tone of this poem—the speaker's apparent attitude toward the scene described?
5. In an essay, "The Sestina," in *A Local Habitation* (U of Michigan P, 1985), John Frederick Nims defends the form against an obvious complaint against it:

A shallow view of the sestina might suggest that the poet writes a stanza, and then is stuck with six words which he has to juggle into the required positions through five more stanzas and an envoy—to the great detriment of what passion and sincerity would have him say. But in a good sestina the poet has six words, six images, six ideas so urgently in his mind that he cannot get away from them; he wants to test them in all possible combinations and come to a conclusion about their relationship.

How well does this description of a good sestina fit "Sestina"?

EXPERIMENT: *Urgent Repetition*

Write a sestina and see what you find out by doing so. (Even if you fail in the attempt, you just might learn something interesting.) To start, pick six words you think are worth repeating six times. This elaborate pattern gives you much help: as John Ashbery has pointed out, writing a sestina is "like riding downhill on a bicycle and having the pedals push your feet." Here is some encouragement from a poet and critic, John Heath-Stubbs: "I have never read a sestina that seemed to me a total failure."

WRITER'S PERSPECTIVE

Robert Graves

Robert Graves on Writing

POETIC INSPIRATION AND POETIC FORM   1956

It is an axiom among poets that if one trusts whole-heartedly to poetic magic, one will be sure to solve any merely verbal problem or else discover that the verbal problem is hiding an imprecision in poetic thought.

I say magic, since the act of composition occurs in a sort of trance, distinguishable from dream only because the critical faculties are not dormant, but on the contrary, more acute than normally. Often a rugger° player is congratulated

rugger: rugby.

on having played the smartest game of his life, but regrets that he cannot remember a single incident after the first five minutes, when he got kicked on the head. It is much the same with a poet when he completes a true poem. But often he wakes from the trance too soon and is tempted to solve the remaining problems intellectually. Few self-styled poets have experienced the trance; but all who have, know that to work out a line by an exercise of reason, rather than by a deep-seated belief in miracle, is highly unprofessional conduct. If a trance has been interrupted, it is just too bad. The poem should be left unfinished, in the hope that suddenly, out of the blue, days or months later, it may start stirring again at the back of the mind, when the remaining problems will solve themselves without difficulty.

· · ·

It is unprofessional conduct to say: "When next I write a poem I shall use the sonnet form"—because the theme is by definition unforeseeable, and theme chooses metre. A poet should not be conscious of the metrical pattern of a poem he is writing until the first three or four lines have appeared; he may even find himself in the eleventh line of fourteen before realizing that a sonnet is on the way. Besides, metre is only a frame; the atmospheres of two sonnets can be so different that they will not be recognized as having the same form except by a careful count of lines and feet. Theme chooses metre; what is more, theme decides what rhythmic variations should be made on metre. The theory that all poems must be equally rich in sound is an un-English one, borrowed from Virgil. Rainbow-like passages are delightful every now and then, but they match a rare mood of opulence and exaltation which soon fatigues. The riches of *Paradise Lost* fatigue, and even oppress, all but musicians. Rainbows should make their appearances only when the moment has come to disclose the riches of the heart, or soul, or imagination; they testify to passing storms and are short-lived.

From "Harp, Anvil, Oar"

WRITING CRITICALLY

Turning Points

One possible definition of the sonnet might be a fourteen-line poem divided into two unequal parts. Italian sonnets divide their parts into the octave and the sestet, while the English sonnet is more lopsided, with a final couplet balanced against the first twelve lines. Some sonnets use less traditional arrangements, but generally poets build sonnets in which the unequal sections strongly contrast in tone, mood, theme, or point of view.

The moment when a sonnet changes its direction is commonly called "the turn." In a Shakespearean sonnet, the turn usually—but not always—comes in the final couplet. In modern sonnets, the turn is often less overt, but identifying the moment when the poem shifts will usually help you better understand both its theme and structure.

But how do you find the moment when a sonnet turns? Study the poem, latch on to the mood and manner of its opening lines. Is the feeling joyful or sad, loving or angry? Read the poem from this opening perspective until you feel it tug strongly in another direction. Sometimes the second part of a sonnet will directly contradict the opening. More often it explains, augments, or qualifies the opening.

WRITING ASSIGNMENT

Using any sonnet in the book, analyze and explain how the two parts of the poem combine to create a total effect neither part could achieve independently. In discussing the sonnet, identify the turning point and paraphrase what each of the poem's two sections say. In addition to the sonnets in this chapter, you might consider any of the following from "Poems for Further Reading": Elizabeth Barrett Browning's "How Do I Love Thee?"; Gerard Manley Hopkins's "The Windhover"; John Keats's "When I have fears that I may cease to be"; John Milton's "When I consider how my light is spent"; Wilfred Owen's "Anthem for Doomed Youth"; William Shakespeare's "When, in disgrace with Fortune and men's eyes"; or William Wordsworth's "Composed upon Westminster Bridge."

FURTHER SUGGESTIONS FOR WRITING

1. William Carlos Williams, in an interview, delivered this blast:

   > Forcing twentieth-century America into a sonnet—gosh, how I hate sonnets— is like putting a crab into a square box. You've got to cut his legs off to make him fit. When you get through, you don't have a crab any more.

   In a two-page essay, defend the modern American sonnet against Williams's charge. Or instead, open fire on it, using Williams's view for ammunition. Some sonnets to consider: R. S. Gwynn's "Scenes from the Playroom," Julia Alvarez's "The women on my mother's side were known" (page 1006), and Kim Addonizio's "First Poem for You."
2. Write an unserious argument for or against the abolition of limericks. Give illustrations of limericks you think worthy of abolition (or preservation).
3. Compare Dylan Thomas's "Do not go gentle into that good night" with Wendy Cope's "Lonely Hearts" (page 766). Discuss how it is possible for the same form to be used to create such different kinds of poems.

22 *Open Form*

Writing in **open form,** a poet seeks to discover a fresh and individual arrangement for words in every poem. Such a poem, generally speaking, has neither a rime scheme nor a basic meter informing the whole of it. Doing without those powerful (some would say hypnotic) elements, the poet who writes in open form relies on other means to engage and to sustain the reader's attention. Novice poets often think that open form looks easy, not nearly so hard as riming everything; but in truth, formally open poems are easy to write only if written carelessly. To compose lines with keen awareness of open form's demands, and of its infinite possibilities, calls for skill: at least as much as that needed to write in meter and rime, if not more. Should the poet succeed, then the discovered arrangement will seem exactly right for what the poem is saying.

Denise Levertov (1923–1997)*

ANCIENT STAIRWAY   1999

Footsteps like water hollow
the broad curves of stone
ascending, descending
century by century.
Who can say if the last   5
to climb these stairs
will be journeying
downward or upward?

Open form, in this brief poem, affords Denise Levertov certain advantages. Able to break off a line at whatever point she likes (a privilege not available to the poet writing, say, a conventional sonnet, who has to break off each line after its tenth syllable), she selects her pauses artfully. Line breaks lend emphasis: a word or phrase at the end of a line takes a little more stress (and receives a little more attention), because the ending of the line compels the reader to make a slight pause, if only for the brief moment it takes to sling back one's eyes and fix them on the line following. Slight pauses, then, follow the words and phrases *hollow* / *stone* / *descending* / *century* / *last* / *stairs* / *journeying* / *upward*— all these being elements that apparently the poet wishes to call our attention to. (The pause after a line break also casts a little more weight on the *first* word or phrase of each succeeding line.) Levertov makes the most of white space—another means of calling attention to things, as any good picture-framer knows. She has greater control over the shape of the poem, its look on the page, than would be allowed by the demands of meter; she uses that control to stack on top of one another lines that are (roughly) equivalent in width, like the steps of a staircase. The opening line with its quick stresses might suggest to us the many feet passing over the steps. From there, Levertov slows the rhythm to the heavy beats of lines 3–4, which could communicate a sense of repeated trudging up and down the stairs (in a particularly effective touch, all four of the stressed syllables in these two lines make the same sound), a sense that is reinforced by the poem's last line, which echoes the rhythm of line 3. Note too how, without being restricted by the need of a rime, she can order the terms in that last line according to her intended thematic emphasis. In all likelihood, we perceive these effects instinctively, not consciously (which may also be the way the author created them), but no matter how we apprehend them, they serve to deepen our understanding of and pleasure in the text.

Poetry in open form used to be called **free verse** (from the French ***vers libre***), suggesting a kind of verse liberated from the shackles of rime and meter. "Writing free verse," said Robert Frost, who wasn't interested in it, "is like playing tennis with the net down." And yet, as Denise Levertov and many other poets demonstrate, high scores can be made in such an unconventional game, provided it doesn't straggle all over the court. For a successful poem in open form, the term *free verse* seems inaccurate. "Being an art form," said William Carlos Williams, "verse cannot be 'free' in the sense of having *no* limitations or guiding principles."[1] Various substitute names have been suggested: organic poetry, composition by field, raw (as against cooked) poetry, open form poetry. "But what does it matter what you call it?" remark the editors of a 1969 anthology called *Naked Poetry*. "The best poems of the last thirty years don't rhyme (usually) and don't move on feet of more or less equal duration (usually). That nondescription moves toward the only technical principle they all have in common."[2]

And yet many poems in open form have much more in common than absences and lacks. One positive principle has been Ezra Pound's famous suggestion

---

[1]"Free Verse," *Princeton Encyclopedia of Poetry and Poetics,* 2nd ed., 1975.
[2]Stephen Berg and Robert Mezey, eds., foreword, *Naked Poetry: Recent American Poetry in Open Forms* (Indianapolis: Bobbs, 1969).

that poets "compose in the sequence of the musical phrase, not in the sequence of the metronome"—good advice, perhaps, even for poets who write inside fixed forms. In Charles Olson's influential theory of **projective verse,** poets compose by listening to their own breathing. On paper, they indicate the rhythms of a poem by using a little white space or a lot, a slight indentation or a deep one, depending on whether a short pause or a long one is intended. Words can be grouped in clusters on the page (usually no more words than a lungful of air can accommodate). Heavy cesuras are sometimes shown by breaking a line in two and lowering the second part of it.[3]

To the poet working in open form, no less than to the poet writing a sonnet, line length can be valuable. Walt Whitman, who loved to expand vast sentences for line after line, knew well that an impressive rhythm can accumulate if the poet will keep long lines approximately the same length, causing a pause to recur at about the same interval after every line. Sometimes, too, Whitman repeats the same words at each line's opening. An instance is the masterly sixth section of "When Lilacs Last in the Dooryard Bloom'd," an elegy for Abraham Lincoln:

> Coffin that passes through lanes and streets,
> Through day and night with the great cloud darkening the land,
> With the pomp of the inloop'd flags with the cities draped in
> black,
> With the show of the States themselves as of crape-veil'd women
> standing,
> With processions long and winding and the flambeaus of the night,
> With the countless torches lit, with the silent sea of faces and the
> unbared heads,
> With the waiting depot, the arriving coffin, and the somber faces,
> With dirges through the night, with the thousand voices rising
> strong and solemn,
> With all the mournful voices of the dirges pour'd around the
> coffin,
> The dim-lit churches and the shuddering organs—where amid
> these you journey,
> With the tolling tolling bells' perpetual clang,
> Here, coffin that slowly passes,
> I give you my sprig of lilac.

There is music in such solemn, operatic arias. Whitman's lines echo another model: the Hebrew **psalms,** or sacred songs, as translated in the King James Version of the Bible. In Psalm 150, repetition also occurs inside of lines:

> Praise ye the Lord. Praise God in his sanctuary: praise him in the
> firmament of his power.

[3]See Olson's essays "Projective Verse" and "Letter to Elaine Feinstein" in *Selected Writings*, edited by Robert Creeley (New York: New Directions, 1966). Olson's letters to Cid Corman are fascinating: *Letters for Origin, 1950–1955*, edited by Albert Glover (New York: Grossman, 1970).

Praise him for his mighty acts: praise him according to his excel-
  lent greatness.
Praise him with the sound of the trumpet: praise him with the
  psaltery and harp.
Praise him with the timbrel and dance: praise him with stringed
  instruments and organs.
Praise him upon the loud cymbals: praise him upon the high
  sounding cymbals.
Let every thing that hath breath praise the Lord. Praise ye the
  Lord.

In Biblical Psalms, we are in the presence of (as Robert Lowell has said) "supreme poems, written when their translators merely intended prose and were forced by the structure of their originals to write poetry."[4]

Whitman was a more deliberate craftsman than he let his readers think, and to anyone interested in writing in open form, his work will repay close study. He knew that repetitions of any kind often make memorable rhythms, as in this pas-sage from "Song of Myself," with every line ending on an *-ing* word (a stressed syllable followed by an unstressed syllable):

Here and there with dimes on the eyes walking,
To feed the greed of the belly the brains liberally spooning,
Tickets buying, taking, selling, but in to the feast never once
  going,
Many sweating, ploughing, thrashing, and then the chaff for
  payment receiving,
A few idly owning, and they the wheat continually claiming.

Much more than simply repetition, of course, went into the music of those lines—the internal rime *feed*, *greed*, the use of assonance, the trochees that begin the third and fourth lines, whether or not they were calculated.

In such classics of open form poetry, sound and rhythm are positive forces. When speaking a poem in open form, you often may find that it makes a differ-ence for the better if you pause at the end of each line. Try pausing there, how-ever briefly; but don't allow your voice to drop. Read just as you would normally read a sentence in prose (except for the pauses, of course). Why do the pauses matter? Open form poetry usually has no meter to lend it rhythm. *Some* lines in an open form poem, as we have seen in Whitman's "dimes on the eyes" passage, do fall into metrical feet; sometimes the whole poem does. Usually lacking meter's aid, however, open form, in order to have more and more noticeable rhythms, has need of all the recurring pauses it can get. When reading their own work aloud, open form poets such as Robert Creeley and Allen Ginsberg often pause very definitely at each line break.

[4]"On Freedom in Poetry," in Berg and Mezey, *Naked Poetry*.

Some poems, to be sure, seem more widely open in form than others. A poet, for instance, may employ rime, but have the rimes recur at various intervals; or perhaps rime lines of various lengths. (See T. S. Eliot's famous "The Love Song of J. Alfred Prufrock" on page 1169. Is it a closed poem left ajar or an open poem trying to slam itself?) No law requires a poet to split thoughts into verse lines at all. Charles Baudelaire, Rainer Maria Rilke, Jorge Luis Borges, Alexander Solzhenitsyn, T. S. Eliot, and many others have written **prose poems,** in which, without caring that eye appeal and some of the rhythm of a line structure may be lost, the poet prints words in a block like a prose paragraph. For an example of a contemporary prose poem, see Carolyn Forché's "The Colonel" on page 944.

"Farewell, stale pale skunky pentameters (the only honest English meter, gloop! gloop!)," Kenneth Koch exulted, suggesting that it was high time to junk such stale conventions. Many poets who agree with him believe that it is wrong to fit words into any pattern that already exists, and instead believe in letting a poem seek its own shape as it goes along. (Traditionalists might say that that is what all good poems do anyway: sonnets rarely know they are going to be sonnets until the third line has been written. However, there is no doubt that the sonnet form already exists, at least in the back of the head of any poet who has ever read sonnets.) Some open form poets offer a historical motive: they want to reflect the nervous, staccato, disconnected pace of our bumper-to-bumper society. Others see open form as an attempt to suit thoughts and words to a more spontaneous order than the traditional verse forms allow. "Better," says Gary Snyder, quoting from Zen, "the perfect, easy discipline of the swallow's dip and swoop, 'without east or west.'"[5]

At the moment, much exciting new poetry is being written in both open form and closed. Today, a number of poets (labeled New Formalists) have taken up rime and meter and are writing sonnets, epigrams, and poems in rimed stanzas, giving "pale skunky pentameters" a fresh lease on life.[6] Meanwhile most younger poets continue to explore a wide range of open forms from conventional and conversational free verse to wildly challenging experimental styles. One West Coast poet, Jack Foley, often writes long free verse poems that involve two voices speaking simultaneously, which makes for exciting if also dizzying poetry readings. The contemporary American determination to play every possible trick that both written and spoken language allows is at least partially inspired by the early Modernist master E. E. Cummings, the smiling godfather of poetic experimentalists everywhere.

[5]"Some Yips & Barks in the Dark," in Berg and Mezey, *Naked Poetry.*
[6]For more samples of recent formal poetry than this book provides, see *Rebel Angels*, ed. Mark Jarman and David Mason (Brownsville: Story Line, 1996); *The Direction of Poetry*, ed. Robert Richman (Boston: Houghton, 1988); and *Ecstatic Occasions, Expedient Forms*, ed. David Lehman (Ann Arbor: U of Michigan P, 1996).

E. E. Cummings   (1894–1962)*

Buffalo Bill 's   1923

Buffalo Bill 's
defunct
    who used to
    ride a watersmooth-silver
                         stallion   5
and break onetwothreefourfive pigeonsjustlikethat
                             Jesus
he was a handsome man
               and what i want to know is
how do you like your blueeyed boy   10
Mister Death

QUESTION

Cummings's poem would look like this if given conventional punctuation and set in a
solid block like prose:

> Buffalo Bill's defunct, who used to ride a water-smooth silver stallion and break one,
> two, three, four, five pigeons just like that. Jesus, he was a handsome man. And what
> I want to know is: "How do you like your blue-eyed boy, Mister Death?"

If this were done, by what characteristics would it still be recognizable as poetry? But what
would be lost?

W. S. Merwin   (b. 1927)

FOR THE ANNIVERSARY OF MY DEATH   1967

Every year without knowing it I have passed the day
When the last fires will wave to me
And the silence will set out
Tireless traveler
Like the beam of a lightless star   5

Then I will no longer
Find myself in life as in a strange garment
Surprised at the earth
And the love of one woman
And the shamelessness of men   10
As today writing after three days of rain
Hearing the wren sing and the falling cease
And bowing not knowing to what

QUESTIONS

1. Read the poem aloud. Try pausing for a fraction of a second at the end of every line. Is there a justification for each line break?
2. The poem is divided into two asymmetrical sections. Does this formal division reflect some change or difference of meaning between the two sections?

William Carlos Williams   (1883–1963)*

THE DANCE   1944

In Breughel's great picture, The Kermess,
the dancers go round, they go round and
around, the squeal and the blare and the
tweedle of bagpipes, a bugle and fiddles
tipping their bellies (round as the thick-   5
sided glasses whose wash they impound)
their hips and their bellies off balance
to turn them. Kicking and rolling about
the Fair Grounds, swinging their butts, those
shanks must be sound to bear up under such   10
rollicking measures, prance as they dance
in Breughel's great picture, The Kermess.

DETAIL. The Kermess *or Peasant Dance by Pieter Breughel the Elder (1520?–1569).*

THE DANCE. Breughel, a Flemish painter known for his scenes of peasant activities, represented in *The Kermess* a celebration on the feast day of a local patron saint.

QUESTIONS

1. Scan this poem and try to describe the effect of its rhythms.
2. Williams, widely admired for his free verse, insisted for many years that what he sought was a form not in the least bit free. What effect does he achieve by ending lines on such weak words as the articles *and* and *the*? By splitting *thick- / sided*? By splitting a prepositional phrase with the break at the end of line 8? By using line breaks to split *those* and *such* from what they modify? What do you think he is trying to convey?
3. Is there any point in his making line 12 a repetition of the opening line?
4. Look at the reproduction of Breughel's painting *The Kermess* (also called *Peasant Dance*). Aware that the rhythms of dancers, the rhythms of a painting, and the rhythms of a poem are not all the same, can you put in your own words what Breughel's dancing figures have in common with Williams's descriptions of them?
5. Compare with "The Dance" another poem that refers to a Breughel painting: W. H. Auden's "Museé des Beaux Arts" on page 1146. What seems to be each poet's main concern: to convey in words a sense of the painting, or to visualize the painting in order to state some theme?

Stephen Crane   (1871–1900)

THE HEART   1895

In the desert
I saw a creature, naked, bestial,
Who, squatting upon the ground,
Held his heart in his hands,
And ate of it.   5

I said, "Is it good, friend?"
"It is bitter—bitter," he answered;
"But I like it
Because it is bitter,
And because it is my heart."   10

Walt Whitman   (1819–1892)*

CAVALRY CROSSING A FORD   1865

A line in long array where they wind betwixt green islands,
They take a serpentine course, their arms flash in the sun—hark to the
    musical clank,
Behold the silvery river, in it the splashing horses loitering stop to drink,
Behold the brown-faced men, each group, each person a picture, the
    negligent rest on the saddles,
Some emerge on the opposite bank, others are just entering the   5
    ford—while,
Scarlet and blue and snowy white,
The guidon flags flutter gayly in the wind.

The following nit-picking questions are intended to help you see exactly what makes these two open form poems by Crane and Whitman so different in their music.

1. What devices of sound occur in Whitman's phrase *silvery river* (line 3)? Where else in his poem do you find these devices?
2. Does Crane use any such devices?
3. In number of syllables, Whitman's poem is almost twice as long as Crane's. Which poem has more pauses in it? (Count pauses at the ends of lines, at marks of punctuation.)
4. Read the two poems aloud. In general, how would you describe the effect of their sounds and rhythms? Is Crane's poem necessarily an inferior poem for having less music?

Ezra Pound   (1885–1972)*

THE GARRET   1915

Come, let us pity those who are better off than we are.
Come, my friend, and remember
      that the rich have butlers and no friends,
And we have friends and no butlers.
Come, let us pity the married and the unmarried.   5

Dawn enters with little feet
      like a gilded Pavlova,
And I am near my desire.
Nor has life in it aught better
Than this hour of clear coolness,   10
      the hour of waking together.

THE GARRET. 7 *Pavlova*: Anna Pavlova (1885–1931) was a celebrated Russian ballerina.

Wallace Stevens   (1879–1955)*

THIRTEEN WAYS OF LOOKING   1923
AT A BLACKBIRD

I

Among twenty snowy mountains,
The only moving thing
Was the eye of the blackbird.

II

I was of three minds,
Like a tree   5
In which there are three blackbirds.

III

The blackbird whirled in the autumn winds.
It was a small part of the pantomime.

IV

A man and a woman
Are one.
A man and a woman and a blackbird
Are one.   10

V

I do not know which to prefer,
The beauty of inflections
Or the beauty of innuendoes,   15
The blackbird whistling
Or just after.

VI

Icicles filled the long window
With barbaric glass.
The shadow of the blackbird   20
Crossed it, to and fro.
The mood
Traced in the shadow
An indecipherable cause.

VII

O thin men of Haddam,   25
Why do you imagine golden birds?
Do you not see how the blackbird
Walks around the feet
Of the women about you?

VIII

I know noble accents   30
And lucid, inescapable rhythms;
But I know, too,
That the blackbird is involved
In what I know.

IX

When the blackbird flew out of sight,   35
It marked the edge
Of one of many circles.

X

At the sight of blackbirds
Flying in a green light,
Even the bawds of euphony   40
Would cry out sharply.

XI

He rode over Connecticut
In a glass coach.
Once, a fear pierced him,
In that he mistook   45
The shadow of his equipage
For blackbirds.

XII

The river is moving.
The blackbird must be flying.

XIII

It was evening all afternoon.   50
It was snowing
And it was going to snow.
The blackbird sat
In the cedar-limbs.

THIRTEEN WAYS OF LOOKING AT A BLACKBIRD.   25 *Haddam:* This biblical-sounding name is that of a town in Connecticut.

QUESTIONS

1. What is the speaker's attitude toward the men of Haddam? What attitude toward this world does he suggest they lack? What is implied by calling them *thin* (line 25)?
2. What do the landscapes of winter contribute to the poem's effectiveness? If Stevens had chosen images of summer lawns, what would have been lost?
3. In which sections of the poem does Stevens suggest that a unity exists between human being and blackbird, between blackbird and the entire natural world? Can we say that Stevens "philosophizes"? What role does imagery play in Stevens's statement of his ideas?
4. What sense can you make of Part X? Make an enlightened guess.
5. Consider any one of the thirteen parts. What patterns of sound and rhythm do you find in it? What kind of structure does it have?
6. If the thirteen parts were arranged in some different order, would the poem be just as good? Or can we find a justification for its beginning with Part I and ending with Part XIII?
7. Does the poem seem an arbitrary combination of thirteen separate poems? Or is there any reason to call it a whole?

Carolyn Forché   (b. 1950)

THE COLONEL   1982

What you have heard is true. I was in his house. His wife carried a tray of
coffee and sugar. His daughter filed her nails, his son went out for the night.
There were daily papers, pet dogs, a pistol on the cushion beside him. The
moon swung bare on its black cord over the house. On the television was a
cop show. It was in English. Broken bottles were embedded in the walls
around the house to scoop the kneecaps from a man's legs or cut his hands to
lace. On the windows there were gratings like those in liquor stores. We had
dinner, rack of lamb, good wine, a gold bell was on the table for calling the
maid. The maid brought green mangoes, salt, a type of bread. I was asked
how I enjoyed the country. There was a brief commercial in Spanish. His
wife took everything away. There was some talk then of how difficult it had
become to govern. The parrot said hello on the terrace. The colonel told it
to shut up, and pushed himself from the table. My friend said to me with his
eyes: say nothing. The colonel returned with a sack used to bring groceries
home. He spilled many human ears on the table. They were like dried peach
halves. There is no other way to say this. He took one of them in his hands,
shook it in our faces, dropped it into a water glass. It came alive there. I am
tired of fooling around he said. As for the rights of anyone, tell your people
they can go fuck themselves. He swept the ears to the floor with his arm and
held the last of his wine in the air. Something for your poetry, no? he said.
Some of the ears on the floor caught this scrap of his voice. Some of the ears
on the floor were pressed to the ground.

May 1978

QUESTIONS

1. Should we consider "The Colonel" a prose poem or a very short piece of prose? If it is
   poetry, what features distinguish it from prose? If it should be considered prose, what
   essential features of poetry does it lack?
2. Forché begins "The Colonel" by saying "What you have heard is true." Who is the
   you? Does she assume a specific person?
3. Should we believe that this story is true? If so, what leads us to believe its veracity?
4. Why does the author end "The Colonel" by giving a date?

VISUAL POETRY

Let's look at a famous poem with a distinctive visible shape. In the seventeenth
century, ingenious poets trimmed their lines into the silhouettes of altars and
crosses, pillars and pyramids. Here is one. Is it anything more than a demonstration of ingenuity?

EASTER WINGS 1633

Lord, who createdst man in wealth and store,
Though foolishly he lost the same,
Decaying more and more,
Till he became
Most poor;
With thee
Oh, let me rise
As larks, harmoniously,
And sing this day thy victories;
Then shall the fall further the flight in me.

My tender age in sorrow did begin;
And still with sicknesses and shame
Thou didst so punish sin,
That I became
Most thin.
With thee
Let me combine,
And feel this day thy victory;
For if I imp my wing on thine,
Affliction shall advance the flight in me.

In the next-to-last line, *imp* is a term from falconry meaning to repair the wing of an injured bird by grafting feathers into it.

If we see it merely as a picture, we will have to admit that Herbert's word design does not go far. It renders with difficulty shapes that a sketcher's pencil could set down in a flash, in more detail, more accurately. Was Herbert's effort wasted? It might have been, were there not more to his poem than meets the eye. The mind, too, is engaged by the visual pattern, by the realization that the words *most thin* are given emphasis by their narrow form. Here, visual pattern points out meaning. Heard aloud, too, "Easter Wings" gives further pleasure. Its rimes, its rhythm are perceptible.

Ever since George Herbert's day, poets have continued to experiment with the looks of printed poetry. Notable efforts to entertain the eye are Lewis Carroll's rimed mouse's tail in *Alice in Wonderland;* and the *Calligrammes* of Guillaume Apollinaire, who arranged words in the shapes of a necktie, of the Eiffel Tower, of spears of falling rain. Here is a bird-shaped poem of more recent inspiration than Herbert's. What does its visual form have to do with what the poet is saying?

John Hollander (b. 1929)

SWAN AND SHADOW   1969

                              Dusk
                           Above the
                        water hang the
                              loud
                              flies
                             Here
                             O so
                          gray
                          then
                       What   A pale signal will appear
                       When   Soon before its shadow fades
                       Where   Here in this pool of opened eye
                    In us   No Upon us As at the very edges
                    of where we take shape in the dark air
                       this object bares its image awakening
                          ripples of recognition that will
                           brush darkness up into light
     even after this bird this hour both drift by atop the perfect sad instant now
                            already passing out of sight
                        toward yet-untroubled reflection
                       this image bears its object darkening
                       into memorial shades Scattered bits of
                    light   No of water Or something across
                    water   Breaking up No Being regathered
                    soon   Yet by then a swan will have
                    gone   Yet out of mind into what
                       vast
                         pale
                          hush
                           of a
                           place
                            past
                    sudden dark as
                       if a swan
                          sang

A whole poem doesn't need to be such a verbal silhouette, of course, for its appearance on the page to seem meaningful. In some lines of a longer poem, William Carlos Williams has conveyed the way an energetic bellhop (or hotel porter) runs downstairs:

```
       ta tuck a
          ta tuck a
             ta tuck a
                ta tuck a
                   ta tuck a
```

This is not only good onomatopoeia and an accurate description of a rhythm; the steplike appearance of the lines goes together with their meaning.

At least some of our pleasure in silently reading a poem derives from the way it looks upon its page. A poem in an open form can engage the eye with snow-fields of white space and thickets of close-set words. A poem in stanzas can please us by its visual symmetry. And, far from being merely decorative, the visual devices of a poem can be meaningful, too. White space—as poets who work in open forms demonstrate—can indicate pauses. If white space entirely surrounds a word or phrase or line, then that portion of the poem obviously takes special emphasis. Typographical devices such as capital letters and italics also can lay stress upon words. In most traditional poems, a capital letter at the beginning of each new line helps indicate the importance the poet places on line-divisions, whose regular intervals make a rhythm out of pauses. And the poet may be trying to show us that certain lines rime by indenting them.

Some contemporary poets have taken advantage of the computer's ability to mix words and images. They use visual images as integral parts of their poems to explore possibilities beyond traditional prosody. Ezra Pound did similar things in his modernist epic, *The Cantos*, by incorporating Chinese ideograms, musical notations, and marginal notes into the text of the poem. More recently Terry Ehret created a sequence of poems that used ancient Egyptian hieroglyphics to prompt lyric meditations that are half translation and half free association. Here is one section from her poem sequence "Papyrus." (Note how Ehret uses a hieroglyph, a pictorial character used in ancient Egyptian writing, as the title of her short prose poem.)

Terry Ehret   (b. 1955)

from PAPYRUS   1992

A lake. A night without moon. Distant memory of what the sun looks like rising. The darkness blows across the water like a wind. Passions that cool with age.

In recent decades, a movement called **concrete poetry** has traveled far and wide. Though practitioners of the art disagree over its definition, what most concretists seem to do is make designs out of letters and words. Other concrete poets wield typography like a brush dipped in paint, using such techniques as blow-up, montage, and superimposed elements (the same words printed many times on top of the same impression, so that the result is blurriness). They may even keep words in a usual order, perhaps employing white space as freely as any writer of open form verse. (More freely sometimes—Aram Saroyan has a concrete poem that consists of a page blank except for the word *oxygen*.) Poet Richard Kostelanetz has suggested that a more accurate name for concrete poetry might be "word-imagery." He sees it occupying an area somewhere between conventional poetry and visual art.

Admittedly, some concrete poems mean less than meets the eye. That many pretentious doodlers have taken up concretism may have caused a *Time* writer to sneer: did Joyce Kilmer miss all that much by never having seen a poem lovely as a

t

ttt

rrrrr

rrrrrrr

eeeeeeeee

???

Like other structures of language, however, concrete poems evidently can have the effect of poetry, if written by poets. Whether or not it ought to be dubbed "poetry," this art can do what poems traditionally have done: use language in delightful ways that reveal meanings to us.

Dorthi Charles (b. 1963)

Concrete Cat 1971

QUESTIONS

1. What does this writer indicate by capitalizing the *a* in *ear*? The *y* in *eye*? The *u* in *mouth*? By using spaces between the letters in the word *tail*?
2. Why is the word *mouse* upside down?
3. What possible pun might be seen in the cat's middle stripe?
4. What is the tone of "Concrete Cat"? How is it made evident?
5. Do these words seem chosen for their connotations or only for their denotations? Would you call this work of art a poem?

EXPERIMENT: *Do It Yourself*

Make a concrete poem of your own. If you need inspiration, pick some familiar object or animal and try to find words that look like it. For more ideas, study the typography of a magazine or newspaper; cut out interesting letters and numerals and try pasting them into arrangements. What (if anything) do your experiments tell you about familiar letters and words?

FURTHER SUGGESTIONS FOR WRITING

1. Consider whether concrete poetry is a vital art form or merely visual trivia.
2. Should a poem be illustrated, or is it better left to the mind's eye? Discuss this question in a brief essay. You might care to consider the illustrations in a collection of poems for children.

SEEING THE LOGIC OF OPEN FORM VERSE

Read the following poems in open form silently to yourself, noticing what each poet does with white space, repetitions, line breaks, and indentations. Then read the poems aloud, trying to indicate by slight pauses where lines end and also pausing slightly at any space inside a line. Can you see any reasons for the poet's placing his or her words in this arrangement rather than in a prose paragraph? Do any of these poets seem to care also about visual effect? (As with other kinds of poetry, there may not be any obvious logical reason for everything that happens in these poems.)

E. E. Cummings   (1894–1962)*

IN JUST-   1923

in Just-
spring   when the world is mud-
luscious the little
lame balloonman

whistles   far   and wee   5

and eddieandbill come
running from marbles and
piracies and it's
spring

when the world is puddle-wonderful   10

the queer

old balloonman whistles

far   and   wee

and bettyandisbel come dancing

from hop-scotch and jump-rope and   15

it's
spring
and
  the
       goat-footed   20

balloonMan   whistles
far
and
wee

Lucille Clifton   (b. 1936)

HOMAGE TO MY HIPS   1991

these hips are big hips.
they need space to
move around in.
they don't fit into little
petty places, these hips   5
are free hips.
they don't like to be held back.
these hips have never been enslaved,
they go where they want to go
they do what they want to do.   10
these hips are mighty hips.
these hips are magic hips.
i have known them
to put a spell on a man and
spin him like a top!   15

Carole Satyamurti   (b. 1939)

I SHALL PAINT MY NAILS RED   1990

Because a bit of colour is a public service.

Because I am proud of my hands.

Because it will remind me I'm a woman.

Because I will look like a survivor.

Because I can admire them in traffic jams.   5

Because my daughter will say ugh.

Because my lover will be surprised.

Because it is quicker than dyeing my hair.

Because it is a ten-minute moratorium.

Because it is reversible.   10

QUESTION

"I Shall Paint My Nails Red" is written in free verse, but the poem has several organizing principles. How many can you discover?

Alice Fulton   (b. 1952)

WHAT I LIKE   1983

Friend—the face I wallow toward
through a scrimmage of shut faces.
Arms like towropes to haul me home, aide-
memoire, my lost childhood docks, a bottled ark
in harbor. Friend—I can't forget   5
how even the word contains an end.
We circle each other in a scared bolero,
imagining stratagems: postures and imposters.
Cold convictions keep us solo. I ahem
and hedge my affections. Who'll blow the first kiss,   10
land it like the lifeforces we feel
tickling at each wrist? It should be easy
easy to take your hand, whisper down this distance
labeled hers or his: what I like about you is

QUESTION

Does this poem have an ending? Does it need to have an ending to be a successful poem?

Walt Whitman

Walt Whitman on Writing

THE POETRY OF THE FUTURE   1876

The poetry of the future, (a phrase open to sharp criticism, and not satisfactory to me, but significant, and I will use it)—the poetry of the future aims at the free expression of emotion, (which means far, far more than appears at first,) and to arouse and initiate, more than to define or finish. Like all modern tendencies, it has direct or indirect reference continually to the reader, to you or me, to the central identity of everything, the mighty Ego. (Byron's was a vehement dash, with plenty of impatient democracy, but lurid and introverted amid all its magnetism; not at all the fitting, lasting song of a grand, secure, free, sunny race.) It is more akin, likewise, to outside life and landscape, (returning mainly to the antique feeling,) real sun and gale, and woods and shores—to the elements themselves—not sitting at ease in parlor or library listening to a good tale of them, told in good rhyme. Character, a feature far above style or polish—a feature not absent at any time, but now first brought to the fore—gives predominant stamp to advancing poetry. . . .

Is there not even now, indeed, an evolution, a departure from the masters? Venerable and unsurpassable after their kind as are the old works, and always unspeakably precious as studies, (for Americans more than any other people,) is it too much to say that by the shifted combinations of the modern mind the whole underlying theory of first-class verse has changed?

From preface to the centennial edition of *Leaves of Grass*

Lining Up for Free Verse

"That's not poetry! It's just chopped-up prose." So runs one old-fashioned complaint about free verse. Such criticism may be true of inept poems, but in the best free verse the line endings transform language in ways beyond the possibilities of prose.

To understand the special effect of free verse, start by paying special attention to the line breaks. Look especially at the word at the end of each line, which receives special emphasis by its position. (In prose, we might easily pass over the word since in prose we read sentence by sentence.) Free verse almost always invites us to read more slowly and carefully than we would the same passage printed as prose. Look at how Wallace Stevens's lineation in "Thirteen Ways of Looking at a Blackbird" allows us not only to see but also to savor the implications of the ideas and images.

> I was of three minds,
> Like a tree
> In which there are three blackbirds.

On a purely semantic level, these lines may mean the same as the prose statement, "I was of three minds like a tree in which there are three blackbirds," but Stevens's arrangement into verse adds decisive emphasis at several points. Each of his three lines isolates and presents a separate image (the speaker, the tree, and the blackbirds). The placement of *three* at the same position at the end of the opening and closing line helps us feel the similar nature of the two statements. The short middle line allows us to see the image of the tree before we fully understand why it is parallel to the divided mind—thus adding a touch of suspense not in the prose. Ending each line with a key noun and image also gives the poem a concrete feel not altogether evident in the prose.

Even a short passage like Stevens's three lines suggests how powerfully the visual arrangement and rhythmic emphasis of free verse can amplify and transform the prose meaning of words.

WRITING ASSIGNMENT

Take any free verse poem and retype it as prose (adding conventional prose punctuation and capitalization, if necessary). Then compare the prose version to the original poem and discuss how the two passages differ in tone, rhythm, emphasis, or effect. Also acknowledge in what ways the two texts remain similar. Use any poem from this chapter or consider any of the following from "Poems for Further Reading": T. S. Eliot's "Journey of the Magi"; Ezra Pound's "The River Merchant's Wife: a Letter"; Theodore Roethke's "Elegy for Jane"; William Carlos Williams's "To Waken an Old Lady"; or James Wright's "A Blessing."

FURTHER SUGGESTIONS FOR WRITING

1. Compare any poem in this chapter or in "Poems for Further Reading" with a poem in rime and meter. Discuss several key features that they have in common despite their apparent differences in style. Features it might be useful to compare include imagery, tone, figures of speech, and word choice.
2. Is "free verse" totally free? Discuss this question in a short essay, drawing evidence from specific open form poems that you found interesting.

23 Symbol

The national flag is supposed to stir our patriotic feelings. When a black cat crosses his path, a superstitious man shivers, foreseeing bad luck. To each of these, by custom, our society expects a standard response. A flag, a black cat crossing one's path—each is a **symbol:** a visible object or action that suggests some further meaning in addition to itself. In literature, a symbol might be the word *flag* or the words *a black cat crossed his path* or every description of flag or cat in an entire novel, story, play, or poem.

A flag and the crossing of a black cat may be called **conventional symbols,** since they can have a conventional or customary effect on us. Conventional symbols are also part of the language of poetry, as we know when we meet the red rose, emblem of love, in a lyric, or the Christian cross in the devotional poems of George Herbert. More often, however, symbols in literature have no conventional, long-established meaning, but particular meanings of their own. In Melville's novel *Moby-Dick,* to take a rich example, whatever we associate with the great white whale is *not* attached unmistakably to white whales by custom. Though Melville tells us that men have long regarded whales with awe and relates Moby Dick to the celebrated fish that swallowed Jonah, the reader's response is to one particular whale, the creature of Herman Melville. Only the experience of reading the novel in its entirety can give Moby Dick his particular meaning.

We should say *meanings,* for as Eudora Welty has observed, it is a good thing Melville made Moby Dick a whale, a creature large enough to contain all that critics have found in him. A symbol in literature, if not conventional, has more than just one meaning. In "The Raven," by Edgar Allan Poe, the appearance of a strange black bird in the narrator's study is sinister; and indeed, if we take the poem seriously, we may even respond with a sympathetic shiver of dread. Does the bird mean death, fate, melancholy, the loss of a loved one, knowledge in the service of evil? All these, perhaps. Like any well-chosen symbol, Poe's raven sets going within the reader an unending train of feelings and associations.

We miss the value of a symbol, however, if we think it can mean absolutely anything we wish. If a poet has any control over our reactions, the poem will guide our responses in a certain direction.

T. S. Eliot (1888–1965)*

THE *BOSTON EVENING TRANSCRIPT*   1917

The readers of the *Boston Evening Transcript*
Sway in the wind like a field of ripe corn.

When evening quickens faintly in the street,
Wakening the appetites of life in some
And to others bringing the *Boston Evening Transcript,*   5
I mount the steps and ring the bell, turning
Wearily, as one would turn to nod good-bye to La Rochefoucauld,
If the street were time and he at the end of the street,
And I say, "Cousin Harriet, here is the *Boston Evening Transcript.*"

The newspaper, whose name Eliot purposely repeats so monotonously, indicates what this poem is about. Now defunct, the *Transcript* covered in detail the slightest activity of Boston's leading families and was noted for the great length of its obituaries. Eliot, then, uses the newspaper as a symbol for an existence of boredom, fatigue (*Wearily*), petty and unvarying routine (since an evening newspaper, like night, arrives on schedule). The *Transcript* evokes a way of life without zest or passion, for, opposed to people who read it, Eliot sets people who do not: those whose desires revive, not expire, when the working day is through. Suggestions abound in the ironic comparison of the *Transcript*'s readers to a cornfield late in summer. To mention only a few: the readers sway because they are sleepy; they vegetate; they are drying up; each makes a rattling sound when turning a page. It is not necessary that we know the remote and similarly disillusioned friend to whom the speaker might nod: La Rochefoucauld, whose cynical *Maxims* entertained Parisian society under Louis XIV (sample: "All of us have enough strength to endure the misfortunes of others"). We understand that the nod is symbolic of an immense weariness of spirit. We know nothing about Cousin Harriet, whom the speaker addresses, but imagine from the greeting she inspires that she is probably a bore.

If Eliot wishes to say that certain Bostonians lead lives of sterile boredom, why does he couch his meaning in symbols? Why doesn't he tell us directly what he means? These questions imply two assumptions not necessarily true: first, that Eliot has a message to impart; second, that he is concealing it. We have reason to think that Eliot did not usually have a message in mind when beginning a poem, for as he once told a critic: "The conscious problems with which one is concerned in the actual writing are more those of a quasi-musical nature . . . than of a conscious exposition of ideas." Poets sometimes discover what they have to say while in the act of saying it. And it may be that in his *Transcript* poem, Eliot is saying exactly what he means. By communicating his meaning through symbols instead of statements, he may be choosing the only kind of language appropriate to an idea of great subtlety and complexity. (The paraphrase "Certain Bostonians are bored" hardly begins to describe the poem in all its possible meaning.) And by his use of symbolism, Eliot affords us the pleasure of finding our own entrances to his poem.

This power of suggestion that a symbol contains is, perhaps, its greatest advantage. Sometimes, as in the following poem by Emily Dickinson, a symbol will lead us from a visible object to something too vast to be perceived.

Emily Dickinson   (1830–1886)*

THE LIGHTNING IS A YELLOW FORK   (ABOUT 1870)

The Lightning is a yellow Fork
From Tables in the sky
By inadvertent fingers dropt
The awful Cutlery

Of mansions never quite disclosed   5
And never quite concealed
The Apparatus of the Dark
To ignorance revealed.

If the lightning is a fork, then whose are the fingers that drop it, the table from which it slips, the household to which it belongs? The poem implies this question without giving an answer. An obvious answer is "God," but can we be sure? We wonder, too, about these partially lighted mansions: if our vision were clearer, what would we behold?[1]

"But how am I supposed to know a symbol when I see one?" The best approach is to read poems closely, taking comfort in the likelihood that it is better not to notice symbols at all than to find significance in every literal stone and huge meanings in every thing. In looking for the symbols in a poem, pick out all

---

[1] In its suggestion of an infinite realm that mortal eyes cannot quite see, but whose nature can be perceived fleetingly through things visible, Emily Dickinson's poem, by coincidence, resembles the work of late-nineteenth-century French poets called **Symbolists.** To a symbolist the shirt-tail of Truth is continually seen disappearing around a corner. With their Neoplatonic view of ideal realities existing in a great beyond, whose corresponding symbols are the perceptible cats that bite us and tangible stones we stumble over, French poets such as Charles Baudelaire, Jules Laforgue, and Stéphane Mallarmé profoundly affected poets writing in English, notably Yeats (who said a poem "entangles . . . a part of the Divine essence") and Eliot. But in this chapter we consider symbolism as an element in certain poems, not Symbolism, the literary movement.

the references to concrete objects—newspapers, black cats, twisted pins. Consider these with special care. Notice any that the poet emphasizes by detailed description, by repetition, or by placing it at the very beginning or end of the poem. Ask: What is the poem about, what does it add up to? If, when the poem is paraphrased, the paraphrase depends primarily on the meaning of certain concrete objects, these richly suggestive objects may be the symbols.

There are some things a literary symbol usually is *not*. A symbol is not an abstraction. Such terms as *truth, death, love,* and *justice* cannot work as symbols (unless personified, as in the traditional figure of Justice holding a scale). Most often, a symbol is something we can see in the mind's eye: a newspaper, a lightning bolt, a gesture of nodding good-bye.

In narratives, a well-developed character who speaks much dialogue and is not the least bit mysterious is usually not a symbol. But watch out for an executioner in a black hood; a character, named for a Biblical prophet, who does little but utter a prophecy; a trio of old women who resemble the Three Fates. (It has been argued, with good reason, that Milton's fully rounded character of Satan in *Paradise Lost* is a symbol embodying evil and human pride, but a narrower definition of symbol is more frequently useful.) A symbol *may* be a part of a person's body (the baleful eye of the murder victim in Poe's story "The Tell-Tale Heart") or a look, a voice, or a mannerism.

A symbol usually is not the second term of a metaphor. In the line "The Lightning is a yellow Fork," the symbol is the lightning, not the fork.

Sometimes a symbol addresses a sense other than sight: the sound of a mysterious snapping string at the end of Chekhov's play *The Cherry Orchard;* or, in William Faulkner's tale "A Rose for Emily," the odor of decay that surrounds the house of the last survivor of a town's leading family—suggesting not only physical dissolution but also the decay of a social order. A symbol is a special kind of image, for it exceeds the usual image in the richness of its connotations. The dead wife's cold comb in the haiku of Buson (discussed on page 791) works symbolically, suggesting among other things the chill of the grave, the contrast between the living and the dead.

Holding a narrower definition than that used in this book, some readers of poetry prefer to say that a symbol is always a concrete object, never an act. They would deny the label "symbol" to Ahab's breaking his tobacco pipe before setting out to pursue Moby Dick (suggesting, perhaps, his determination to allow no pleasure to distract him from the chase) or to any large motion (as Ahab's whole quest). This distinction, while confining, does have the merit of sparing one from seeing all motion to be possibly symbolic. Some would call Ahab's gesture not a symbol but a **symbolic act.**

To sum up: a symbol radiates hints or casts long shadows (to use Henry James's metaphor). We are unable to say it "stands for" or "represents" a meaning. It evokes, it suggests, it manifests. It demands no single necessary interpretation, such as the interpretation a driver gives to a red traffic light. Rather, like Emily Dickinson's lightning bolt, it points toward an indefinite meaning, which may lie in part beyond the reach of words. In a symbol, as Thomas Carlyle said in *Sartor Resartus*, "the Infinite is made to blend with the Finite, to stand visible, and as it were, attainable there."

Thomas Hardy   (1840–1928)*

NEUTRAL TONES   1898

We stood by a pond that winter day,
And the sun was white, as though chidden of° God,   *rebuked by*
And a few leaves lay on the starving sod;
   —They had fallen from an ash, and were gray.

Your eyes on me were as eyes that rove   5
Over tedious riddles of years ago;
And some words played between us to and fro
   On which lost the more by our love.

The smile on your mouth was the deadest thing
Alive enough to have strength to die;   10
And a grin of bitterness swept thereby
   Like an ominous bird a-wing. . . .

Since then, keen lessons that love deceives,
And wrings with wrong, have shaped to me
Your face, and the God-curst sun, and a tree,   15
   And a pond edged with grayish leaves.

QUESTIONS

1. Sum up the story told in this poem. In lines 1–12, what is the dramatic situation?
   What has happened in the interval between the experience related in these lines and
   the reflection in the last stanza?
2. What meanings do you find in the title?
3. Explain in your own words the metaphor in line 2.
4. What connotations appropriate to this poem does the *ash* (line 4) have that *oak* or
   maple would lack?
5. What visible objects in the poem function symbolically? What actions or gestures?

   If we read of a ship, its captain, its sailors, and the rough seas, and we realize
we are reading about a commonwealth and how its rulers and workers keep it
going even in difficult times, then we are reading an **allegory.** Closely akin to symbolism, allegory is a description—usually narrative—in which persons, places, and
things are employed in a continuous and consistent system of equivalents.
   Although more strictly limited in its suggestions than symbolism, allegory
need not be thought inferior. Few poems continue to interest readers more than
Dante's allegorical *Divine Comedy*. Sublime evidence of the appeal of allegory
may be found in Christ's use of the **parable:** a brief narrative—usually allegorical
but sometimes not—that teaches a moral.

Matthew 13:24–30 (King James Version, 1611)

The Parable of the Good Seed

The kingdom of heaven is likened unto a man which sowed good seed
    in his field:
But while men slept, his enemy came and sowed tares among the
    wheat, and went his way.
But when the blade was sprung up, and brought forth fruit, then
    appeared the tares also.
So the servants of the householder came and said unto him, Sir, didst
    not thou sow good seed in thy field? From whence then hath it tares?
He said unto them, An enemy hath done this. The servants said unto   5
    him, Wilt thou then that we go and gather them up?
But he said, Nay; lest while ye gather up the tares, ye root up also the
    wheat with them.
Let both grow together until the harvest: and in the time of harvest I
    will say to the reapers, Gather ye together first the tares, and bind
    them in bundles to burn them: but gather the wheat into my barn.

The sower is the Son of man, the field is the world, the good seed are the children of the Kingdom, the tares are the children of the wicked one, the enemy is
the devil, the harvest is the end of the world, the reapers are angels. "As therefore the tares are gathered and burned in the fire; so shall it be in the end of this
world" (Matthew 13:36–42).

Usually, as in this parable, the meanings of an allegory are plainly labeled or
thinly disguised. In John Bunyan's allegorical narrative *The Pilgrim's Progress*, it is
clear that the hero Christian, on his journey through places with such pointed
names as Vanity Fair, the Valley of the Shadow of Death, and Doubting Castle, is
the soul, traveling the road of life on the way toward Heaven. An allegory, when
carefully built, is systematic. It makes one principal comparison, the working out of
whose details may lead to further comparisons, then still further comparisons: Christian, thrown by Giant Despair into the dungeon of Doubting Castle, escapes by
means of a key called Promise. Such a complicated design may take great length to
unfold, as in Spenser's *Faerie Queene*; but the method may be seen in a short poem.

George Herbert   (1593–1633)*

The World   1633

Love built a stately house; where *Fortune* came,
And spinning phansies, she was heard to say,
That her fine cobwebs did support the frame,
Whereas they were supported by the same:
But *Wisdome* quickly swept them all away.   5

Then *Pleasure* came, who, liking not the fashion,
Began to make *Balcones, Terraces,*

Till she had weakened all by alteration:
But rev'rend *laws*, and many a *proclamation*
Reformed all at length with menaces.   10

The enter'd *Sinne* and with that Sycomore,
Whose leaves first sheltered man from drought & dew,
Working and winding slily evermore,
The inward walls and sommers cleft and tore:
But *Grace* shor'd these, and cut that as it grew.   15

Then *Sinne* combin'd with *Death* in a firm band
To raze the building to the very floore:
Which they effected, none could them withstand.
But *Love* and *Grace* took *Glorie* by the hand,
And built a braver Palace then before.   20

The World. 2 *phansies*: fancies. 10 *menaces*: threats. 14 *sommers*: summers: that is, beams or girders. 20 *then*: than.

Questions

1. What is the controlling image of this poem? What is that image an allegory of?
2. In each stanza of the poem, a similar pattern of action is repeated. What is that pattern, and how does it illuminate the poem's larger theme?
3. What is the "braver Palace" of the last line?

An object in allegory is like a bird whose cage is clearly lettered with its identity—"RAVEN, *Corvus corax*; habitat of specimen, Maine." A symbol, by contrast, is a bird with piercing eyes that mysteriously appears one evening in your library. It is there; you can touch it. But what does it mean? You look at it. It continues to look at you.

John Ciardi   (1916–1986)

Most Like an Arch This Marriage   1958

Most like an arch—an entrance which upholds
and shores the stone-crush up the air like lace.
Mass made idea, and idea held in place.
A lock in time. Inside half-heaven unfolds.

Most like an arch—two weaknesses that lean   5
into a strength. Two fallings become firm.
Two joined abeyances become a term
naming the fact that teaches fact to mean.

Not quite that? Not much less. World as it is,
what's strong and separate falters. All I do   10
at piling stone on stone apart from you
is roofless around nothing. Till we kiss

I am no more than upright and unset.
It is by falling in and in we make
the all-bearing point, for one another's sake,   15
in faultless failing, raised by our own weight.

QUESTION

Is this poem an allegory or merely a poem with a strong central symbol? (For the definition of allegory, see the Glossary of Literary Terms.)

   Whether an object in literature is a symbol, part of an allegory, or no such
thing at all, it has at least one sure meaning. Moby Dick is first a whale and the
Boston Evening Transcript is a newspaper. Besides deriving a multitude of intangible suggestions from the title symbol in Eliot's long poem The Waste Land, its
readers cannot fail to carry away a sense of the land's physical appearance: a river
choked with sandwich papers and cigarette ends, London Bridge "under the
brown fog of a winter dawn." A virtue of The Pilgrim's Progress is that its walking
abstractions are no mere abstractions but are also human: Giant Despair is a hen-
pecked husband. The most vital element of a literary work may pass us by, unless
before seeking further depths in a thing, we look to the thing itself.

Robert Frost   (1874–1963)*

THE ROAD NOT TAKEN   1916

Two roads diverged in a yellow wood,
And sorry I could not travel both
And be one traveler, long I stood
And looked down one as far as I could
To where it bent in the undergrowth;   5

Then took the other, as just as fair,
And having perhaps the better claim,
Because it was grassy and wanted wear;
Though as for that the passing there
Had worn them really about the same,   10

And both that morning equally lay
In leaves no step had trodden black.
Oh, I kept the first for another day!
Yet knowing how way leads on to way,
I doubted if I should ever come back.   15

I shall be telling this with a sigh
Somewhere ages and ages hence:
Two roads diverged in a wood, and I—
I took the one less traveled by,
And that has made all the difference.   20

QUESTION

What symbolism do you find in this poem, if any? Back up your claim with evidence.

Christina Rossetti   (1830–1894)

UPHILL   1862

Does the road wind uphill all the way?
   Yes, to the very end.
Will the day's journey take the whole long day?
   From morn to night, my friend.

But is there for the night a resting-place?   5
   A roof for when the slow dark hours begin.
May not the darkness hide it from my face?
   You cannot miss that inn.

Shall I meet other wayfarers at night?
   Those who have gone before.   10
Then must I knock, or call when just in sight?
   They will not keep you standing at that door.

Shall I find comfort, travel-sore and weak?
   Of labor you shall find the sum.
Will there be beds for me and all who seek?   15
   Yea, beds for all who come.

QUESTIONS

1. In reading this poem, at what line did you realize that the poet is building an allegory?
2. For what does each thing stand?
3. What does the title of the poem suggest to you?
4. Recast the meaning of line 14, a knotty line, in your own words.
5. Discuss the possible identities of the two speakers—the apprehensive traveler and the character with all the answers. Are they specific individuals? Allegorical figures?
6. Compare "Uphill" with Robert Creeley's "Oh No" (page 732). What striking similarities do you find in these two dissimilar poems?

Gjertrud Schnackenberg   (b. 1953)

SUPERNATURAL LOVE   1985

My father at the dictionary-stand
Touches the page to fully understand
The lamplit answer, tilting in his hand

His slowly scanning magnifying lens,
A blurry, glistening circle he suspends   5
Above the word "Carnation." Then he bends

So near his eyes are magnified and blurred,
One finger on the miniature word,
As if he touched a single key and heard

A distant, plucked, infinitesimal string,   10
"The obligation due to every thing
That's smaller than the universe." I bring

My sewing needle close enough that I
Can watch my father through the needle's eye,
As through a lens ground for a butterfly   15

Who peers down flower-hallways toward a room
Shadowed and fathomed as this study's gloom
Where, as a scholar bends above a tomb

To read what's buried there, he bends to pore
Over the Latin blossom. I am four,   20
I spill my pins and needles on the floor

Trying to stitch "Beloved" X by X.
My dangerous, bright needle's point connects
Myself illiterate to this perfect text

I cannot read. My father puzzles why   25
It is my habit to identify
Carnations as "Christ's flowers," knowing I

Can give no explanation but "Because."
Word-roots blossom in speechless messages
The way the thread behind my sampler does   30

Where following each X I awkward move
My needle through the word whose root is love.
He reads, "A pink variety of Clove,

Carnatio, the Latin, meaning flesh."
As if the bud's essential oils brush   35
Christ's fragrance through the room, the iron-fresh

Odor carnations have floats up to me,
A drifted, secret, bitter ecstasy,
The stems squeak in my scissors, *Child, it's me,*

He turns the page to "Clove" and reads aloud: 40
"The clove, a spice, dried from a flower-bud."
Then twice, as if he hasn't understood,

He reads, "From French, for *clou*, meaning a nail."
He gazes, motionless. "Meaning a nail."
The incarnation blossoms, flesh and nail,   45

I twist my threads like stems into a knot
And smooth "Beloved," but my needle caught
Within the threads, *Thy blood so dearly bought,*

The needle strikes my finger to the bone.
I lift my hand, it is myself I've sewn,   50
The flesh laid bare, the threads of blood my own,

I lift my hand in startled agony
And call upon his name, "Daddy Daddy"—
My father's hand touches the injury

As lightly as he touched the page before,   55
Where incarnation bloomed from roots that bore
The flowers I called Christ's when I was four.

QUESTIONS

1. To understand this poem more fully, one would do well to emulate the speaker's father and consult the dictionary. Look up "incarnation": how do its various meanings help to illuminate the text?
2. Does the father's "magnifying lens" in line 4 seem to have any symbolic function? Explain.
3. What does X represent on the poem's literal level? What does it represent symbolically?
4. Why do you think the poet, instead of using three different riming words, ends all three lines of the fifteenth stanza with the word *nail*?
5. Words *as words* take on more than usual significance in this poem. Trace and discuss the occurrences of two of its key terms, *blossom* and *thread*.
6. What is the significance of the title?

FOR REVIEW AND FURTHER STUDY

Robinson Jeffers   (1887–1962)*

THE BEAKS OF EAGLES   1937

An eagle's nest on the head of an old redwood on one of the precipice-
      footed ridges
Above Ventana Creek, that jagged country which nothing but a falling
      meteor will ever plow; no horseman
Will ever ride there, no hunter cross this ridge but the winged ones, no
      one will steal the eggs from this fortress.
The she-eagle is old, her mate was shot long ago, she is now mated
      with a son of hers.
When lightning blasted her nest she built it again on the same tree, in   5
      the splinters of the thunderbolt.
The she-eagle is older than I; she was here when the fires of eighty-five
      raged on these ridges,

She was lately fledged and dared not hunt ahead of them but ate
   scorched meat. The world has changed in her time;
Humanity has multiplied, but not here; men's hopes and thoughts and
   customs have changed, their powers are enlarged,
Their powers and their follies have become fantastic,
The unstable animal never has been changed so rapidly. The motor   10
   and the plane and the great war have gone over him,
And Lenin has lived and Jehovah died: while the mother-eagle
Hunts her same hills, crying the same beautiful and lonely cry and is
   never tired; dreams the same dreams,
And hears at night the rock-slides rattle and thunder in the throats of
   these living mountains.
                     It is good for man
To try all changes, progress and corruption, powers, peace and anguish,   15
   not to go down the dinosaur's way
Until all his capacities have been explored: and it is good for him
To know that his needs and nature are no more changed in fact in ten
   thousand years than the beaks of eagles.

THE BEAKS OF EAGLES. 2 *Ventana Creek:* an isolated creek near Carmel, California. 10 *the great war:*
World War I (1914–18). 11 *Lenin:* Vladimir Ilyich Lenin (1870–1924), the leader of the Russian
Communist Revolution.

QUESTIONS

1. What does the speaker tell us about the eagle's habitat?
2. What do we know about the age of the eagle? What events have happened in her
   lifetime, both to her and to the outer world?
3. To what other creature is the eagle repeatedly compared?
4. What does the eagle come to symbolize by the end of the poem?
5. Would the meaning of the last line change significantly if the phrase *the beaks of
   eagles* became merely *eagles*? If so, how would it change?

Sara Teasdale   (1884–1933)

THE FLIGHT   1926

We are two eagles
Flying together,
Under the heavens,
Over the mountains,
Stretched on the wind.   5
Sunlight heartens us,
Blind snow baffles us,
Clouds wheel after us,
Raveled and thinned.

We are like eagles;
But when Death harries us,
Human and humbled
When one of us goes,
Let the other follow—
Let the flight be ended,
Let the fire blacken,
Let the book close.

QUESTIONS

1. What do the two eagles experience together? What must they experience separately?
2. In the first stanza, the eagles are a metaphor. In the second stanza, the eagles become a simile. Does this change in the figure of speech have any significance?
3. What new metaphors are introduced in the second stanza?
4. What do the two eagles come to symbolize in this poem?

EXERCISE: *Symbol Hunting*

After you have read each of these poems, decide which description best suits it:

1. The poem has a central symbol.
2. The poem contains no symbolism, but is to be taken literally.

William Carlos Williams   (1883–1963)*

THE TERM   1937

A rumpled sheet
of brown paper
about the length

and apparent bulk
of a man was   5
rolling with the

wind slowly over
and over in
the street as

a car drove down   10
upon it and
crushed it to

the ground. Unlike
a man it rose
again rolling   15

with the wind over
and over to be as
it was before.

Ted Kooser   (b. 1939)*

CARRIE   1979

"There's never an end to dust
and dusting," my aunt would say
as her rag, like a thunderhead,
scudded across the yellow oak
of her little house. There she lived   5
seventy years with a ball
of compulsion closed in her fist,
and an elbow that creaked and popped
like a branch in a storm. Now dust
is her hands and dust her heart.   10
There is never an end to it.

Rafael Campo   (b. 1964)

WHAT THE BODY TOLD   1996

Not long ago, I studied medicine.
It was terrible, what the body told.
I'd look inside another person's mouth
And see the desolation of the world.
I'd see his genitals and think of sin.   5

Because my body speaks the stranger's language,
I've never understood those nods and stares.
My parents held me in their arms, and still
I think I've disappointed them; they care
And stare, they nod, they make their pilgrimage   10

To somewhere distant in my heart, they cry.
I look inside their other-person's mouths
And see the sleek interior of souls.
It's warm and red in there—like love, with teeth.
I've studied medicine until I cried   15

All night. Through certain books, a truth unfolds.
Anatomy and physiology,
The tiny sensing organs of the tongue—
Each nameless cell contributing its needs.
It was fabulous, what the body told.   20

Jon Stallworthy (b. 1935)

AN EVENING WALK   1969

Taking my evening walk
where flats like liners ride
at anchor on a dark
phosphorus-rippled tide
of traffic, ebbing, flowing,   5
I heard from a kiosk
a telephone ringing;
from an empty kiosk.

Its dark voice welling up
out of the earth or air   10
for a moment made me stop,
listen, and consider
whether to break in
on its animal grief.
I could imagine   15
torrents of relief,

anger, explanation—
"*Oh for God's sake*"—but I'd
troubles of my own,
and passed on the other side.   20
All the same I wondered,
with every step I took,
what I would have heard
lifting it from the hook.

As I was returning   25
after the pubs were shut,
I found the bulb still burning
in the kiosk, but
the dark voice from the dark
had done with ringing: 30
the phone was off the hook
like a hanged man swinging.

Lorine Niedecker (1903–1970)*

POPCORN-CAN COVER   (ABOUT 1959)

Popcorn-can cover
screwed to the wall
over a hole
    so the cold
can't mouse in   5

Wallace Stevens (1879–1955)*

ANECDOTE OF THE JAR   1923

I placed a jar in Tennessee,
And round it was, upon a hill.
It made the slovenly wilderness
Surround that hill.

The wilderness rose up to it,   5
And sprawled around, no longer wild.
The jar was round upon the ground
And tall and of a port in air.

It took dominion everywhere.
The jar was gray and bare.   10
It did not give of bird or bush,
Like nothing else in Tennessee.

William Butler Yeats

William Butler Yeats on Writing

POETIC SYMBOLS   1901

Any one who has any experience of any mystical state of the soul knows how there float up in the mind profound symbols, whose meaning, if indeed they do not delude one into the dream that they are meaningless, one does not perhaps understand for years. Nor I think has any one, who has known that experience with any constancy, failed to find some day, in some old book or on some old monument, a strange or intricate image that had floated up before him, and to grow perhaps dizzy with the sudden conviction that our little memories are but a part of some great Memory that renews the world and men's thoughts age after age, and that our thoughts are not, as we suppose, the deep, but a little foam upon the deep.

It is only by ancient symbols, by symbols that have numberless meanings besides the one or two the writer lays an emphasis upon, or the half-score he knows of, that any highly subjective art can escape from the barrenness and shallowness of a too conscious arrangement, into the abundance and depth of Nature. The poet of essences and pure ideas must seek in the half-lights that glimmer from symbol to symbol as if to the ends of the earth, all that the epic and dramatic poet finds of mystery and shadow in the accidental circumstances of life.

From "The Philosophy of Shelley's Poetry"

How to Read a Symbol

A symbol, to use poet John Drury's concise definition, is "an image that radiates meanings." Exactly what those meanings will be, however, often differs from poem to poem. In one poem snow may be a reassuring symbol of sleep and forgetfulness, while in another it becomes a chilling symbol of death. Both meanings easily connect to the natural image of snow, but in each poem, the author has nudged that image in a different direction.

The way a symbol has been used by earlier writers affects the way we grasp the image today. It would be difficult, for example, to put a great white whale in a contemporary poem without summoning up the symbolic association of Melville's Moby Dick. No matter how the poet chooses to handle it, the association will be there as a starting point.

Sometimes a poet gladly adopts the traditional symbolism of an image. In "Go, Lovely Rose" (page 1258) Edmund Waller masterfully employs the image of the rose with all its conventional associations as a symbol of the transience of human beauty. William Butler Yeats believed that poetic symbols acquired their special power by thousands of years of use. Poets, therefore, had to employ symbols consistent with their ancient meanings. Contemporary poets, on the other hand, often enjoy turning traditional symbols upside down. In her poem, "The Victory" (page 795), Anne Stevenson presents the newborn child not as a conventional little angel or bundle of joy, but as a frightening, inhuman antagonist.

The same image, therefore, can often convey divergent meanings in different poems—even when the poems are written by contemporaries. Sara Teasdale and Robinson Jeffers, for example, were born only three years apart, and they often published poems in the same journals. Both employed the eagle as the central image of a poem (Teasdale's "The Flight" and Jeffers's "The Beaks of Eagles"), but the image came to symbolize different things in each poem.

When writing about the meaning (or meanings) of a symbol, follow the image through the poem and give it time to establish its own pattern of associations. Don't jump to quick conclusions. If the symbol is a traditional one (the cross, a rose, a reaper and so on), is it being used in the expected way? Or is the poet playing with its associations? And finally, if the image doesn't seem to radiate meanings above and beyond its literal sense, don't feel you have failed as a critic. Not everything is a symbol. As Sigmund Freud once commented about symbol-hunting, "Sometimes a cigar is just a cigar."

WRITING ASSIGNMENT

Compare the use of the eagle as a symbol in Sara Teasdale's "The Flight" and Robinson Jeffers's "The Beaks of Eagles." What does the central image of the eagle suggest in each poem? How does the symbolism differ in each? Are there any meaningful similarities between the two?

FURTHER SUGGESTIONS FOR WRITING

1. Discuss the symbolism in a poem in "Poems for Further Reading." Likely poems to study (among many) are T. S. Eliot's "The Love Song of J. Alfred Prufrock," Robert Lowell's "Skunk Hour," Gerard Manley Hopkins's "The Windhover," and Mary Jo Salter's "Welcome to Hiroshima."

2. Take a relatively simple, straightforward poem, such as William Carlos Williams's "This Is Just to Say" (page 750), and write a burlesque critical interpretation of it. Claim to discover symbols that the poem doesn't contain. While running wild with your "reading into" the poem, don't invent anything that you can't somehow support from the text of the poem itself. At the end of your burlesque, sum up in a paragraph what this exercise taught you about how to read poems, or how not to.

24 Myth and Narrative

Poets have long been fond of retelling **myths,** narrowly defined as traditional stories about the exploits of immortal beings. Such stories taken collectively may also be called **myth** or **mythology.** In one of the most celebrated collections of myth ever assembled, the *Metamorphoses,* the Roman poet Ovid told—to take one example from many—how Phaeton, child of the sun god, rashly tried to drive his father's fiery chariot on its daily round, lost control of the horses, and caused disaster both to himself and to the world. Our use of the term *myth* in discussing poetry, then, differs from its use in expressions such as "the myth of communism" and "the myth of democracy." In these examples, myth is used broadly to represent any idea people believe in, whether true or false. Nor do we mean—to take another familiar use of the word—a cock-and-bull story: "Judge Rapp doesn't roast speeders alive; that's just a *myth.*" In the following discussion, *myth* will mean a kind of story—either from ancient or modern sources—whose actions implicitly symbolize some profound truth about human or natural existence.

Traditional myths tell us stories of gods or heroes—their battles, their lives, their loves, and often their suffering—all on a scale of magnificence larger than our life. These exciting stories usually reveal part of a culture's worldview. Myths often try to explain universal natural phenomena, like the phases of the moon or the turning of the seasons. But some myths tell the stories of purely local phenomena; one Greek legend, for example, recounts how grief-stricken King Aegeus threw himself into the sea when he mistakenly believed his son, Theseus, had been killed; consequently, the body of water between Greece and Turkey was called the Aegean Sea.

Modern psychologists, such as Sigmund Freud and Carl Jung, have been fascinated by myth and legend, since they believe these stories symbolically enact deep truths about human nature. Our myths, psychologists believe, express our wishes, dreams, and nightmares. Whether or not we believe myths, we recognize their psychological power. Even in the first century B.C., Roman poet Ovid did not believe in the literal truth of the legends he so suavely retold; he confessed, "I prate of ancient poets' monstrous lies."

And yet it is characteristic of a myth that it *can* be believed. Throughout history, myths have accompanied religious doctrines and rituals. They have helped sanction or recall the reasons for religious observances. A sublime instance is the New Testament account of the Last Supper. Because of its record of the words of Jesus, "Do this in remembrance of Me," Christians have continued to re-enact the offering and partaking of the body and blood of their Lord, under the appearances of bread and wine. It is essential to recall that, just because a myth narrates the acts of a god, we do not necessarily mean by the term a false or fictitious narrative. When we speak of the "myth of Islam" or "the Christian myth," we do so without implying either belief or disbelief.

Myths can also help sanction customs and institutions other than religious ones. At the same time that the baking of bread was introduced to ancient Greece—one theory goes—the myth of Demeter, goddess of grain, appeared. Demeter was a kindly deity who sent her emissary to teach humankind the valuable art of baking—thus helping to persuade the distrustful that bread was a good thing. Some myths seem designed to divert and regale, not to sanction anything. Such may be the story of the sculptor Pygmalion, who fell in love with the statue he had carved of a beautiful woman; so exquisite was his work, so deep was his feeling, that Aphrodite, the goddess of Love, brought the statue to life. And yet perhaps the story goes deeper than mere diversion: perhaps it is a way of saying that works of art achieve a reality of their own, that love can transform or animate its object.

How does a myth begin? Several theories have been proposed, none universally accepted. One is that a myth is a way to explain some natural phenomenon. Winter comes and the vegetation perishes because Persephone, child of Demeter, must return to the underworld for several months every year. This theory, as classical scholar Edith Hamilton has pointed out, may lead us to think incorrectly that Greek mythology was the creation of a primitive people. Tales of the gods of Mount Olympus may reflect an earlier inheritance, but the Greek myths known to us were transcribed in an era of high civilization. Anthropologists have questioned whether primitive people generally find beauty in the mysteries of nature. Many anthropologists emphasize the practical function of myth; in his influential work of comparative mythology, *The Golden Bough*, Sir James Frazer argued that most myths were originally expressions of human hope that nature would be fertile. Still another theory maintains that many myths began as real events; mythic heroes were real human beings whose deeds have been changed and exaggerated by posterity. Most present-day myth historians would say that different myths probably have different origins.

Poets have many coherent mythologies on which to draw; perhaps those most frequently consulted by British and American poets are the classical, the Christian, the Norse, the Native American, and the folk tales of the American frontier (embodying the deeds of superhuman characters such as Paul Bunyan). Some poets have taken inspiration from other myths as well: T. S. Eliot's *The Waste Land*, for example, is enriched by allusions to Buddhism and to pagan vegetation-cults. Robert Bly borrowed the terrifying Death Goddess of Aztec, Hindu, and Balinese mythology to make her the climactic figure of his long poem "The Teeth Mother Naked at Last."

A tour through any good art museum will demonstrate how thoroughly myth pervades the painting and sculpture of nearly every civilization. In literature, one evidence of its continuing value to recent poets and storytellers is how frequently ancient myths are retold. Even in modern society, writers often turn to myth when they try to tell stories of deep significance. Mythic structures still touch a powerful and primal part of the human imagination. William Faulkner's story "The Bear" recalls tales of Indian totem animals; John Updike's novel *The Centaur* presents the horse-man Chiron as a modern high-school teacher; James Joyce's *Ulysses* retells the *Odyssey* in modern Dublin; Rita Dove's play *The Darker Face of the Earth* recasts the story of Oedipus in the slave-era South; Bernard Shaw retells the story of Pygmalion in his popular Edwardian social comedy *Pygmalion*, later the basis of the hit musical *My Fair Lady*; Jean Cocteau's film *Orphée* shows us Eurydice riding to the underworld with an escort of motorcycles. Popular interest in such works may testify to the profound appeal myths continue to hold for us. Like other varieties of poetry, myth is a kind of knowledge, not at odds with scientific knowledge but existing in addition to it.

Robert Frost (1874–1963)*
NOTHING GOLD CAN STAY   1923

Nature's first green is gold,
Her hardest hue to hold.
Her early leaf's a flower;
But only so an hour.
Then leaf subsides to leaf.   5
So Eden sank to grief,
So dawn goes down to day.
Nothing gold can stay.

QUESTIONS

1. To what myth does this poem allude? Does Frost sound as though he believes in the myth or as though he rejects it?
2. When Frost says, "Nature's first green is gold," he is describing how many leaves first appear as tiny yellow buds and blossoms. But what else does this line imply?
3. What would happen to the poem's meaning if line 6 were omitted?

D. H. Lawrence   (1885–1930)*

BAVARIAN GENTIANS   1932

Not every man has gentians in his house
in soft September, at slow, sad Michaelmas.

Bavarian gentians, big and dark, only dark
darkening the daytime, torch-like with the smoking blueness of Pluto's
    gloom,
ribbed and torch-like, with their blaze of darkness spread blue   5
down flattening into points, flattened under the sweep of white day
torch-flower of the blue-smoking darkness, Pluto's dark-blue daze,
black lamps from the halls of Dis, burning dark blue,
giving off darkness, blue darkness, as Demeter's pale lamps give off
    light,
lead me then, lead the way.   10

Reach me a gentian, give me a torch!
let me guide myself with the blue, forked torch of this flower
down the darker and darker stairs, where blue is darkened on blueness
even where Persephone goes, just now, from the frosted September
to the sightless realm where darkness is awake upon the dark   15
and Persephone herself is but a voice
or a darkness invisible enfolded in the deeper dark
of the arms Plutonic, and pierced with the passion of dense gloom,
among the splendor of torches of darkness, shedding darkness on the
    lost bride and her groom.

BAVARIAN GENTIANS. 2 *Michaelmas:* The feast of St. Michael (September 29). 4 *Pluto:* Roman name
for Hades, in Greek mythology the ruler of the underworld, who abducted Persephone to be his bride.
Each spring Persephone returns to earth and is welcomed by her mother Demeter, goddess of fruitfulness; each winter she departs again, to dwell with her husband below. 8 *Dis:* Pluto's realm.

QUESTIONS

1. Read this poem aloud. What devices of sound do you hear in it?
2. What characteristics of gentians appear to remind Lawrence of the story of Persephone? What significance do you attach to the poem's being set in September? How
   does the fact of autumn matter to the gentians and to Persephone?

Thomas Hardy   (1840–1928)*

THE OXEN   1915

Christmas Eve, and twelve of the clock.
    "Now they are all on their knees,"

An elder said as we sat in a flock
    By the embers in hearthside ease.

We pictured the meek mild creatures where   5
    They dwelt in their strawy pen,
Nor did it occur to one of us there
    To doubt they were kneeling then.

So fair a fancy few would weave
    In these years! Yet, I feel,   10
If someone said on Christmas Eve,
    "Come; see the oxen kneel

"In the lonely barton° by yonder coomb°   *farmyard; a hollow*
    Our childhood used to know,"
I should go with him in the gloom,   15
    Hoping it might be so.

THE OXEN. This ancient belief has had wide currency among peasants and farmers of Western Europe. Some also say that on Christmas Eve the beasts can speak.

QUESTIONS

1. What body of myth is Hardy's subject and what are his speaker's attitudes toward it? Perhaps, in Hardy's view, the pious report about oxen is only part of it.
2. Read this poem aloud and notice its sound and imagery. What contrast do you find between the sounds of the first stanza and those of the last stanza? Which words make the difference? What images enforce a contrast in tone between the beginning of the poem and its ending?
3. G. K. Chesterton, writing as a defender of Christian faith, called Hardy's writings "the mutterings of the village atheist." See other poems by Hardy in "Poems for Further Reading." What do you think Chesterton might have meant? Can "The Oxen" be called a hostile mutter?

William Wordsworth   (1770–1850)*

THE WORLD IS TOO MUCH WITH US   1807

The world is too much with us; late and soon,
Getting and spending, we lay waste our powers;
Little we see in Nature that is ours;
We have given our hearts away, a sordid boon!
This Sea that bares her bosom to the moon;   5
The winds that will be howling at all hours,
And are up-gathered now like sleeping flowers;
For this, for everything, we are out of tune;
It moves us not. Great God! I'd rather be
A Pagan suckled in a creed outworn;   10

So might I, standing on this pleasant lea,
Have glimpses that would make me less forlorn;
Have sight of Proteus rising from the sea;
Or hear old Triton blow his wreathèd horn.

QUESTIONS

1. In this sonnet by Wordsworth what condition does the poet complain about? To what does he attribute this condition?
2. How does it affect him as an individual?

H. D. [Hilda Doolittle]   (1886–1961)*

HELEN   1924

All Greece hates
the still eyes in the white face,
the lustre as of olives
where she stands,
and the white hands.   5

All Greece reviles
the wan face when she smiles,
hating it deeper still
when it grows wan and white,
remembering past enchantments   10
and past ills.

Greece sees unmoved,
God's daughter, born of love,
the beauty of cool feet
and slenderest knees,   15
could love indeed the maid,
only if she were laid,
white ash amid funereal cypresses.

HELEN. In Greek mythology, Helen, most beautiful of all women, was the daughter of a mortal, Leda, by the god Zeus. Her abduction set off the long and devastating Trojan War. While married to Menelaus, king of the Greek city-state of Sparta, Helen was carried off by Paris, prince of Troy. Menelaus and his brother Agamemnon raised an army, besieged Troy for ten years, and eventually recaptured her. One episode of the Trojan War is related in the *Iliad*, Homer's epic poem, composed before 700 B.C.

ARCHETYPE

An important concept in understanding myth is the **archetype**, a basic image, character, situation, or symbol that appears so often in literature and legend that it evokes a deep universal response. (The Greek root of *archetype* means "original pattern.") The term was borrowed by literary critics from the writings of the Swiss psychologist Carl Jung, a serious scholar of myth and religion, who formulated a theory of the "collective unconscious," a set of primal memories common to the entire human race. Archetypal patterns emerged, he speculated, in prerational thought and often reflect key primordial experiences such as birth, growth, sexual awakening, family, generational struggle, and death, as well as primal elements such as fire, sun, moon, blood, and water. Jung also believed that these situations, images, and figures had actually been genetically coded into the human brain and are passed down to successive generations, but no one has ever been able to prove a biological base for the undeniable phenomenon of similar characters, stories, and symbols appearing across widely separated and diverse cultures.

Whatever their origin, archetypal images do seem verbally coded in most myths, legends, and traditional tales. One sees enough recurring patterns and figures from Greek myth to *Star Wars*, from Hindu epic to Marvel superhero comics, to strongly suggest that there is some common psychic force at work. Typical archetypal figures include the trickster, the cruel stepmother, the rebellious young man, the beautiful but destructive woman, and the stupid youngest son who succeeds through simple goodness. Any one of these figures can be traced from culture to culture. The trickster, for instance, appears in American Indian coyote tales, Norse myths about the fire god Loki, Marx Brothers films, and *Batman* comic books and cartoons featuring the Joker. Archetypal myths are the basic conventions of human storytelling, which we learn without necessarily being aware of the process. The patterns we absorb in our first nursery rhymes and fairy tales, as mythological critic Northrop Frye has demonstrated, underlie—though often very subtly—the most sophisticated poems and novels. One powerful archetype seen across many cultures is the demon-goddess who immobilizes men by locking them into a deathly trance or—in the most primitive forms of the myth—turning them to stone. Here is a modern version of this ancient myth in the following poem by Louise Bogan.

Louise Bogan   (1897–1970)*

MEDUSA   1923

I had come to the house, in a cave of trees,
Facing a sheer sky.
Everything moved,—a bell hung ready to strike,
Sun and reflection wheeled by.

When the bare eyes were before me   5
And the hissing hair,
Held up at a window, seen through a door.
The stiff bald eyes, the serpents on the forehead
Formed in the air.

This is a dead scene forever now.
Nothing will ever stir.
The end will never brighten it more than this,
Nor the rain blur.

The water will always fall, and will not fall,
And the tipped bell make no sound.   15
The grass will always be growing for hay
Deep on the ground.

And I shall stand here like a shadow
Under the great balanced day,
My eyes on the yellow dust, that was lifting in the wind,   20
And does not drift away.

MEDUSA. Medusa was one of the Gorgons of Greek mythology. Hideously ugly with snakes for hair, Medusa turned those who looked upon her face into stone.

QUESTIONS

1. Who is the speaker of the poem?
2. Why are the first two stanzas spoken in the past tense while the final three are mainly in the future tense?
3. What is the speaker's attitude toward Medusa? Is there anything surprising about his or her reaction to being transformed into stone?
4. Does Bogan merely dramatize an incident from classical mythology, or does the poem suggest other interpretations as well?

PERSONAL MYTH

Sometimes poets have been inspired to make up myths of their own, to embody their own visions of life. "I must create a system or be enslaved by another man's," said William Blake, who in his "prophetic books" peopled the cosmos with supernatural beings having names such as Los, Urizen, and Vala (side by side with recognizable figures from the Old Testament and New Testament). This kind of system-making probably has advantages and drawbacks. T. S. Eliot, in his essay on Blake, wishes that the author of *The Four Zoas* had accepted traditional myths, and he compares Blake's thinking to a piece of home-made furniture whose construction diverted valuable energy from the writing of poems. Others have found Blake's untraditional cosmos an achievement—notably William Butler Yeats, himself the author of an elaborate personal mythology. Although we need not know all of Yeats's mythology to enjoy his poems, to know of its existence can make a few great poems deeper for us and less difficult.

William Butler Yeats   (1865–1939)*

THE SECOND COMING   1921

Turning and turning in the widening gyre°   *spiral*
The falcon cannot hear the falconer;
Things fall apart; the center cannot hold;
Mere anarchy is loosed upon the world,
The blood-dimmed tide is loosed, and everywhere   5
The ceremony of innocence is drowned;
The best lack all conviction, while the worst
Are full of passionate intensity.

Surely some revelation is at hand;
Surely the Second Coming is at hand;   10
The Second Coming! Hardly are those words out
When a vast image out of *Spiritus Mundi*
Troubles my sight: somewhere in sands of the desert
A shape with lion body and the head of a man,
A gaze blank and pitiless as the sun,   15
Is moving its slow thighs, while all about it
Reel shadows of the indignant desert birds.
The darkness drops again; but now I know
That twenty centuries of stony sleep
Were vexed to nightmare by a rocking cradle,   20
And what rough beast, its hour come round at last,
Slouches towards Bethlehem to be born?

What kind of Second Coming does Yeats expect? Evidently it is not to be a
Christian one. Yeats saw human history as governed by the turning of a Great
Wheel, whose phases influence events and determine human personalities—
rather like the signs of the Zodiac in astrology. Every two thousand years comes a
horrendous moment: the Wheel completes a turn; one civilization ends and another begins. Strangely, a new age is always announced by birds and by acts of violence. Thus the Greek-Roman world arrives with the descent of Zeus in swan's
form and the burning of Troy, the Christian era with the descent of the Holy
Spirit—traditionally depicted as a dove—and the Crucifixion. In 1919 when
Yeats wrote "The Second Coming," his Ireland was in the midst of turmoil and
bloodshed; the Western Hemisphere had been severely shaken by World War I
and the Russian Revolution. A new millennium seemed imminent. What
sphinxlike, savage deity would next appear on earth, with birds proclaiming it
angrily? Yeats imagines it emerging from *Spiritus Mundi*, Soul of the World, a collective unconscious from which a human being (since the individual soul
touches it) receives dreams, nightmares, and racial memories.[1]

[1]Yeats fully explains his system in *A Vision* (1938; reprinted New York: Macmillan, 1956).

It is hard to say whether a poet who discovers a personal myth does so to have something to live by or to have something to write about. Robert Graves, who professed his belief in a White Goddess ("Mother of All Living, the ancient power of love and terror"), declared that he wrote his poetry in a trance, inspired by his Goddess-Muse.[2] Luckily, we do not have to know a poet's religious affiliation before we can read his or her poems. Perhaps most personal myths that enter poems are not acts of faith but works of art: stories that resemble traditional mythology.

Jonathan Holden (b. 1941)

THE NAMES OF THE RAPIDS   1985

Snaggle-Tooth, Maytag, Taylor Falls—
long before we measured with our eyes
the true size of each monstrosity
its name, downriver, was famous to us.
It lay in wait, something to be slain   5
while our raft, errant, eddied
among glancing pinpricks of sun
and every bend giving way to bend
seemed a last reprieve.
But common terror has a raw taste.   10
It's all banality, as when
you stare straight into a bad cut—
this sense of being slightly more
awake than you might like.
When the raft pitches sideways off   15
a ledge, what you land on is less
than its name. It's a mechanism. None
of the demented expressions
that the fleshly water forms
over that stone profile   20
is more than another collision,
a fleeting logic lost and
forming, now lost in the melee.
When the world is most serious
we approach it with wholly open eyes   25
even as we start the plunge
and the stone explanation.

[2]See Graves's *The White Goddess*, rev. ed. (New York: Farrar, 1966), or for a terser statement of his position, see his lecture "The Personal Muse" in *On Poetry: Collected Talks and Essays* (New York: Doubleday, 1969).

1. From the names of the three rapids mentioned in line 1, describe what you think each one would probably be like.
2. How does personal myth function in this poem?

James Dickey (1923–1997)

THE HEAVEN OF ANIMALS 1962

Here they are. The soft eyes open.
If they have lived in a wood
It is a wood.
If they have lived on plains
It is grass rolling   5
Under their feet forever.

Having no souls, they have come,
Anyway, beyond their knowing.
Their instincts wholly bloom
And they rise.   10
The soft eyes open.

To match them, the landscape flowers,
Outdoing, desperately
Outdoing what is required:
The richest wood,   15
The deepest field.

For some of these,
It could not be the place
It is, without blood.
These hunt, as they have done,
But with claws and teeth grown perfect,   20

More deadly than they can believe.
They stalk more silently,
And crouch on the limbs of trees,
And their descent
Upon the bright backs of their prey   25

May take years
In a sovereign floating of joy.
And those that are hunted
Know this as their life,
Their reward: to walk   30

Under such trees in full knowledge
Of what is in glory above them,

And to feel no fear,
But acceptance, compliance.
Fulfilling themselves without pain   35

At the cycle's center,
They tremble, they walk
Under the tree,
They fall, they are torn,   40
They rise, they walk again.

QUESTIONS

1. In what ways does Dickey's animal heaven resemble the traditional Christian afterlife? In what ways does it differ?
2. How does the poem reconcile the carnivores' need to hunt with the well-being of the
   hunted animals?
3. Does the final stanza of the poem allude to any other part of the Christian mythos?

Diane Thiel (b. 1967)

MEMENTO MORI IN MIDDLE SCHOOL   2000

When I was twelve, I chose Dante's *Inferno*
in gifted class—an oral presentation
with visual aids. My brother, *il miglior fabbro*,

said he would draw the tortures. We used ten
red posterboards. That day, for school, I dressed   5
in pilgrim black, left earlier to hang them

around the class. The students were impressed.
The teacher, too. She acted quite amused
and peered too long at all the punishments.

We knew by reputation she was cruel.   10
The class could see a hint of twisted forms
and asked to be allowed to round the room

as I went through my final presentation.
We passed the first one, full of poets cut
out of a special issue of *Horizon*.   15

The class thought these were such a boring set,
they probably deserved their tedious fates.
They liked the next, though—bodies blown about,

the lovers kept outside the tinfoil gates.
We had a new boy in our class named Paolo   20
and when I noted Paolo's wind-blown state

and pointed out Francesca, people howled.
I knew that more than one of us not-so-
covertly liked him. It seemed like hours

before we moved on to the gluttons, though,   25
where they could hold the cool fistfuls of slime
I brought from home. An extra touch. It sold

in canisters at toy stores at the time.
The students recognized the River Styx,
the logo of a favorite band of mine.   30

We moved downriver to the town of Dis,
which someone loudly re-named Dis and Dat.
And for the looming harpies and the furies,

who shrieked and tore things up, I had clipped out
the shrillest, most deserving teacher's heads   35
from our school paper, then thought better of it.

At the wood of suicides, we quieted.
Though no one in the room would say a word,
I know we couldn't help but think of Fred.

His name was in the news, though we had heard   40
he might have just been playing with the gun.
We moved on quickly by that huge, dark bird

and rode the flying monster, Geryon,
to reach the counselors, each wicked face,
again, I had resisted pasting in.   45

To represent the ice in that last place,
where Satan chewed the traitors' frozen heads,
my mother had insisted that I take

an ice-chest full of popsicles—to end
my gruesome project on a lighter note.   50
"It *is* a comedy, isn't it," she said.

She hadn't read the poem, or seen our art,
but asked me what had happened to the sweet,
angelic poems I once read and wrote.

The class, though, was delighted by the treat,   55
and at the last round, they all pushed to choose
their colors quickly, so they wouldn't melt.

The bell rang. Everyone ran out of school,
as always, yelling at the top of their lungs,
The *Inferno* fast forgotten, but their howls   60

showed off their darkened red and purple tongues.

MEMENTO MORI IN MIDDLE SCHOOL. *Memento Mori:* Latin for "Remember you must die," the phrase now means any reminder of human mortality and the need to lead a virtuous life. 1 *Dante's* Inferno: The late medieval epic poem by the Italian poet Dante Alighieri decribes a Christian soul's journey through hell. (*Inferno* means "hell" in Italian.) 3 *il miglior fabbro:* the better craftsman—Dante's term for fellow poet Arnaut Daniel, which T. S. Eliot later famously quoted to praise Ezra Pound. 15 *Horizon:* a magazine of art and culture. 20–23: *Paolo . . . Francesca:* two lovers in Dante's *Inferno* who have been damned for their adultery. 29 *River Styx:* the sacred river that flows around hell to mark its boundary. 31 *Dis:* the main city of hell named after its ruler, Dis (Pluto). 43 *Geryon:* a mythical three-headed, three-bodied monster Dante places in his *Inferno*.

MYTH AND POPULAR CULTURE

If one can find myths in an art museum, one can also find them abundantly in popular culture. Movies and comic books, for example, are full of myths in modern guise. What is Superman, if not a mythic hero who has adapted himself to modern urban life? Marvel Comics even made the Norse thunder god, Thor, into a superhero, although they initially obliged him, like Clark Kent, to get a job. We also see myths retold on the technicolor screen. Sometimes Hollywood presents the traditional story directly, as in Walt Disney's *Cinderella;* more often the ancient tales acquire contemporary settings, as in another celluloid Cinderella story, *Pretty Woman.* (See how Anne Sexton has retold the Cinderella story from a feminist perspective, later in this chapter, or find a recording of Dana Dane's Brooklyn housing project version of the fairy tale done from a masculine perspective in his underground rap hit "Cinderfella.") George Lucas's *Star Wars* trilogy borrowed the structure of medieval quest legends. In quest stories, young knights pursued their destiny, often by seeking the Holy Grail, the cup Christ used at the Last Supper; in *Star Wars*, Luke Skywalker searched for his own parentage and identity, but his interstellar quest brought him to a surprisingly similar cast of knights, monsters, princesses, and wizards. Medieval Grail romances, which influenced Eliot's *The Waste Land,* also shaped films such as *The Fisher King* and *Brazil.* Science fiction also commonly uses myth to novel effect. Extraterrestrial visitors usually appear as either munificent mythic gods or nightmarish demons. Steven Spielberg's *E.T.,* for example, revealed a gentle, Christ-like alien recognized by innocent children, but persecuted by adults. E.T. even healed the sick, fell into a deathlike coma, and was resurrected.

It hardly matters whether the popular audience recognizes the literal source of a myth; the viewers intuitively understand the structure of the story and feel its deep imaginative resonance. That is why poets retell these myths; they are powerful sources of collective psychic energy, waiting to be tapped. Just as Hollywood screenwriters have learned that often the most potent way to use a myth is to disguise it, poets sometimes borrow the forms of popular culture to retell their myths. Here is a contemporary narrative poem that borrows imagery from motion pictures to reenact a story that not only predates cinema but, most probably, stretches back before the invention of writing itself.

Charles Martin (b. 1942)

TAKEN UP
1978

Tired of earth, they dwindled on their hill,
Watching and waiting in the moonlight until
The aspens' leaves quite suddenly grew still,

No longer quaking as the disc descended,
That glowing wheel of lights whose coming ended   5
All waiting and watching. When it landed

The ones within it one by one came forth,
Stalking out awkwardly upon the earth,
And those who watched them were confirmed in faith:

Mysterious voyagers from outer space,   10
Attenuated, golden—shreds of lace
Spun into seeds of the sunflower's spinning face—

Light was their speech, spanning mind to mind:
We come here not believing what we find—
Can it be your desire to leave behind   15

The earth, which those called angels bless,
Exchanging amplitude for emptiness?
And in a single voice they answered *Yes,*

Discord of human melodies all blent
To the unearthly strain of their assent.   20
Come then, the Strangers said, and those that were taken, went.

QUESTIONS

1. What myths does this poem recall?
2. This poem was written about the same time that Steven Spielberg's film *Close Encounters of the Third Kind* (1977) appeared. If you recall the movie, compare its ending with the ending of the poem. Martin had not seen the film before writing "Taken Up." How can we account for the similarity?

Why do poets retell myths? Why don't they just make up their own stories? First, using myth allows poets to be concise. By alluding to stories that their audiences know, they can draw on powerful associations with just a few words. If someone describes an acquaintance, "He thinks he's James Bond," that one allusion speaks volumes. Likewise, when Robert Frost inserts the single line, "So Eden sank to grief," in "Nothing Gold Can Stay," those five words summon up a wealth of associations. They tie the perishable quality of spring's beauty to the equally transient nature of human youth. They also suggest that everything in the human world is subject to time's ravages, that perfection is impossible for us to maintain, just as it was for Adam and Eve.

Second, poets know that many stories fall into familiar mythic patterns, and that the most powerful stories of human existence tend to be the same, generation after generation. Sometimes using an old story allows a writer to describe a new situation in a fresh and surprising way. Novels often try to capture the exact texture of a social situation; they need to present the everyday details to evoke the world in which their characters live. Myths tend to tell their stories more quickly and in more general terms. They give just the essential actions and leave out everything else. Narrative poems also work best when they focus on just the essential elements. Here are two modern narrative poems that retell traditional myths to make modern interpretations.

A. D. Hope   (1907–2000)

IMPERIAL ADAM   1952

Imperial Adam, naked in the dew,
Felt his brown flanks and found the rib was gone.
Puzzled he turned and saw where, two and two,
The mighty spoor of Jahweh marked the lawn.

Then he remembered through mysterious sleep   5
The surgeon fingers probing at the bone,
The voice so far away, so rich and deep:
"It is not good for him to live alone."

Turning once more he found Man's counterpart
In tender parody breathing at his side.   10
He knew her at first sight, he knew by heart
Her allegory of sense unsatisfied.

The pawpaw drooped its golden breasts above
Less generous than the honey of her flesh;
The innocent sunlight showed the place of love;   15
The dew on its dark hairs winked crisp and fresh.

This plump gourd severed from his virile root,
She promised on the turf of Paradise
Delicious pulp of the forbidden fruit;
Sly as the snake she loosed her sinuous thighs,   20

And waking, smiled up at him from the grass;
Her breasts rose softly and he heard her sigh—
From all the beasts whose pleasant task it was
In Eden to increase and multiply

Adam had learned the jolly deed of kind: 25
He took her in his arms and there and then,
Like the clean beasts, embracing from behind,
Began in joy to found the breed of men.

Then from the spurt of seed within her broke
Her terrible and triumphant female cry,   30
Split upward by the sexual lightning stroke.
It was the beasts now who stood watching by:

The gravid elephant, the calving hind,
The breeding bitch, the she-ape big with young
Were the first gentle midwives of mankind;   35
The teeming lioness rasped her with her tongue;

The proud vicuña nuzzled her as she slept
Lax on the grass; and Adam watching too
Saw how her dumb breasts at their ripening wept,
The great pod of her belly swelled and grew,   40

And saw its water break, and saw, in fear,
Its quaking muscles in the act of birth,
Between her legs a pigmy face appear,
And the first murderer lay upon the earth.

IMPERIAL ADAM. Hope's poem retells the story of Adam and Eve. For the Biblical version, see Genesis
2:18–4:1. 4 *Jahweh:* the Lord of the Old Testament. The Hebrew name of God was written as JHVH,
but it was considered too sacred to say aloud. Yahweh and Jehovah are the other most common
versions of the vowel-less Hebrew name. 25 *deed of kind:* the act of procreation. This particular
expression is usually used to describe the mating of animals. 44 *the first murderer:* Cain, Adam and
Eve's first child, who murdered his brother, Abel. See Genesis 4:1–16.

QUESTIONS

1. Why is Adam called "imperial" What empire does he command?
2. What does Hope imply in lines 18–20, when he describes Eve's sexuality?
3. There is no serpent in Hope's version of the Adam and Eve story. And yet by the end
   of the poem, evil has entered Paradise. What has introduced it?
4. How does the last line of "Imperial Adam" affect the meaning of the poem?

Anne Sexton   (1928–1974)*

CINDERELLA   1971

You always read about it:
the plumber with twelve children
who wins the Irish Sweepstakes.
From toilets to riches.
That story.   5

Or the nursemaid,
some luscious sweet from Denmark
who captures the oldest son's heart.
From diapers to Dior.
That story.

Or a milkman who serves the wealthy,
eggs, cream, butter, yogurt, milk,
the white truck like an ambulance   10
who goes into real estate
and makes a pile.   15
From homogenized to martinis at lunch.

Or the charwoman
who is on the bus when it cracks up
and collects enough from the insurance.
From mops to Bonwit Teller.   20
That story.

Once
the wife of a rich man was on her deathbed
and she said to her daughter Cinderella:
Be devout. Be good. Then I will smile   25
down from heaven in the seam of a cloud.
The man took another wife who had
two daughters, pretty enough
but with hearts like blackjacks.
Cinderella was their maid.   30
She slept on the sooty hearth each night
and walked around looking like Al Jolson.
Her father brought presents home from town,
jewels and gowns for the other women
but the twig of a tree for Cinderella.   35
She planted that twig on her mother's grave
and it grew to a tree where a white dove sat.
Whenever she wished for anything the dove
would drop it like an egg upon the ground.
The bird is important, my dears, so heed him.   40

Next came the ball, as you all know.
It was a marriage market.
The prince was looking for a wife.
All but Cinderella were preparing
and gussying up for the big event.   45
Cinderella begged to go too.

Her stepmother threw a dish of lentils
into the cinders and said: Pick them
up in an hour and you shall go.
The white dove brought all his friends;   50
all the warm wings of the fatherland came,
and picked up the lentils in a jiffy.
No, Cinderella, said the stepmother,
you have no clothes and cannot dance.
That's the way with stepmothers.   55

Cinderella went to the tree at the grave
and cried forth like a gospel singer:
Mama! Mama! My turtledove,
send me to the prince's ball!
The bird dropped down a golden dress   60
and delicate little gold slippers.
Rather a large package for a simple bird.
So she went. Which is no surprise.
Her stepmother and sisters didn't
recognize her without her cinder face   65
and the prince took her hand on the spot
and danced with no other the whole day.

As nightfall came she thought she'd better
get home. The prince walked her home
and she disappeared into the pigeon house   70
and although the prince took an axe and broke
it open she was gone. Back to her cinders.

These events repeated themselves for three days.
However on the third day the prince
covered the palace steps with cobbler's wax   75
and Cinderella's gold shoe stuck upon it.
Now he would find whom the shoe fit
and find his strange dancing girl for keeps.
He went to their house and the two sisters
were delighted because they had lovely feet.   80
The eldest went into a room to try the slipper on
but her big toe got in the way so she simply
sliced it off and put on the slipper.
The prince rode away with her until the white dove
told him to look at the blood pouring forth.   85
That is the way with amputations.
They don't just heal up like a wish.
The other sister cut off her heel
but the blood told as blood will.
The prince was getting tired.   90

He began to feel like a shoe salesman.
But he gave it one last try.
This time Cinderella fit into the shoe
like a love letter into its envelope.

At the wedding ceremony   95
the two sisters came to curry favor
and the white dove pecked their eyes out.
Two hollow spots were left
like soup spoons.

Cinderella and the prince   100
lived, they say, happily ever after,
like two dolls in a museum case
never bothered by diapers or dust,
never arguing over the timing of an egg,
never telling the same story twice,   105
never getting a middle-aged spread,
their darling smiles pasted on for eternity.
Regular Bobbsey Twins.
That story.

CINDERELLA. 32 *Al Jolson:* Extremely popular American entertainer (1886–1950) who frequently
performed in blackface.

QUESTIONS

1. Most of Sexton's "Cinderella" straightforwardly retells a version of the famous fairy
   tale. But in the beginning and ending of the poem, how does Sexton change the
   story?
2. How does Sexton's refrain of "That story" alter the meaning of the episodes it describes? What is the tone of this poem (the poet's attitude toward her material)?
3. What does Sexton's final stanza suggest about the way fairy tales usually end?

Anne Sexton

Anne Sexton on Writing

TRANSFORMING FAIRY TALES   1970

[To Paul Brooks°]

October 14, 1970

Dear Paul,

I wanted to let some time elapse before I answered you so that I could think carefully about what you had to say. I've written seventeen "Transformations."° My goal was twenty, but I may have to make do with seventeen. Seventeen would be a nice book anyway, but I will wait a couple of months and see what comes. I am in the process of typing up the manuscript to submit to you.

But back to your comments. I realize that the "Transformations" are a departure from my usual style. I would say that they lack the intensity and perhaps some of the confessional force of my previous work. I wrote them because I had to . . . because I wanted to . . . because it made me happy. I would want to publish them for the same reason. I would like my readers to see this side of me, and it is not in every case the lighter side. Some of the poems are grim. In fact I don't know how to typify them except to agree that I have made them very contemporary. It would further be a lie to say that they weren't about me, because they are just as much about me as my other poetry.

I look at my work in stages, and each new book is a kind of growth and reaching outward and as always backward. Perhaps the critics will be unhappy with this book and some of my readers maybe will not like it either. I feel I will gain new readers and critics who have always disliked my work (and too true, the critics are not always kind to me) may come around. I have found the people I've shown them to apathetic in some cases and wildly excited in others. It often depends on their own feelings about Grimms' fairy tales.

[*To Kurt Vonnegut, Jr.°*]

November 17, 1970

Dear Kurt,

I meant to write you a postcard before your dentist appointment, but I was away at the time I should have sent it. Sorry. Your graph for "Cinderella" is right over my desk.

The enclosed manuscript is of my new book of poems. I've taken Grimms' Fairy Tales and "Transformed" them into something all of my own. The better books of fairy tales have introductions telling the value of these old fables. I feel my *Transformations* needs an introduction telling of the value of my (one could say) rape of them. Maybe that's an incorrect phrase. I do something very modern to them (have you ever tried to describe your own work? I find I am tongue-tied). They are small, funny and horrifying. Without quite meaning to I have joined the black humorists. I don't know if you know my other work, but humor was never a very prominent feature . . . terror, deformity, madness and torture were my bag. But this little universe of Grimm is not that far away. I think they end up being as wholly personal as my most intimate poems, in a different language, a different rhythm, but coming strangely, for all their story sound, from as deep a place.

From *Anne Sexton: A Self-Portrait in Letters*

Paul Brooks: Sexton's editor at Houghton Mifflin. He initially had reservations about Sexton's fairy tale poems. "*Transformations:*" title of Sexton's 1971 volume of poems that contained "Cinderella." *Kurt Vonnegut, Jr.:* popular author of *Cat's Cradle* (1963) and other novels.

⊰⊹⊱ **WRITING CRITICALLY** ⊰⊹⊱

Demystifying Myth

Myth often seems like an intimidating term. Asked to consider the mythic aspects of a poem, we often begin to worry about how well we remember the original story. Sometimes the version of the myth that we remember from a book or movie seems different from the story being referred to. Or one we have never before encountered feels oddly familiar. Myths often appear elusive because they are stories that lend themselves to adaptation. Two Greek versions of the same story will almost always differ widely in detail: new episodes appear, minor characters change names or vanish. What usually remains fixed, however, is the basic pattern. Orpheus always descends to the Underworld but is never able to rescue his beloved Eurydice. Superhuman Hercules inevitably goes mad and slaughters his wife and sons. Oedipus is always doomed to kill his father and unwittingly marry his widowed mother.

If the artistry of myth is in the details of the tale, the deeper psychological meaning is contained in its permanent underlying structure. In writing about myth, therefore, try to find the underlying pattern of the narrative in question. Does the basic shape of the poem's story seem familiar? Does that story have some recognizable source in myth or legend? If the poem has no obvious narrative line, does its movement call to mind other stories? In "Cinderella" Anne Sexton deliberately reminds us of the mythic patterns of her material ("the plumber with twelve children / who wins the Irish Sweepstakes. / From toilets to riches. / That story"). Although not all poems are conventional narratives, and few authors delight in leaving as many clues as Sexton, most authors do insert some luminous clues in their poems. Why? They want readers to hear the echoes of their sources, because writers understand the resonance of myth. "So Eden sank to grief," confides Frost in "Nothing Gold Can Stay," to let readers know that the poem is not only about spring. His reference to Eden encourages us to see the poem as a universal narrative rather than merely elegant natural description.

Once you have linked the poem to its mythic source, notice what new details the author has added. What do they tell us about his or her attitude toward the original source? Are important elements of the original discarded? What does their absence suggest about the author's primary focus? You can refresh your memory of the original myth by looking it up in a reference work such as *Brewer's Dictionary of Phrase and Fable*, but the essential thing is to recognize the basic narrative underlying the poem and to see how it shapes the new work's meaning. For a helpful overview of how critics analyze myth in literature, see the section "Mythological Criticism" in the chapter "Critical Approaches to Literature."

WRITING ASSIGNMENT

Provide a close reading of any poem from this book that uses a traditional myth or legend. In the course of your analysis, demonstrate how the author borrows or changes certain details of the myth to emphasize his or her meaning. In addition to the poems in this chapter, some selections to consider include: Fred Chappell's "Narcissus and Echo," T. S. Eliot's "Journey of the Magi," Anthony Hecht's "Adam," and William Butler Yeats's "The Magi" or "Leda and the Swan."

Here is an example of an essay on this assignment written by Heather Burke when she was a sophomore at Wesleyan University in Middletown, Connecticut.

Heather Burke

Professor Greene

English 150

18 January 20xx

The Bonds Between Love and Hatred in H.D.'s "Helen"

In her poem "Helen," H.D. examines the close connection between the emotions of love and hatred as embodied in the figure of Helen of Troy. Helen was the cause of the long and bloody Trojan War, and her homecoming is tainted by the memory of the suffering this war caused. As in many Imagist poems, the title is essential to the poem's meaning; it gives the reader both a specific mythic context and a particular subject. Without the title, it would be virtually impossible to understand the poem fully since Helen's name appears nowhere else in the text. The reader familiar with Greek myth knows that Helen, who was the wife of Menelaus, ran away with Paris. Their adultery provoked the Trojan War, which lasted for ten years and resulted in the destruction of Troy.

What is unusual about the poem is H.D.'s perspective on Helen of Troy. The poem refuses to romanticize Helen's story, but its stark new version is easy for a reader to accept. After suffering so much for the sake of one adulterous woman, how could the Greeks not resent her? Rather than idealizing the situation, H.D. describes the enmity which defiles Helen's homecoming and explores the irony of the hatred which "All Greece" feels for her.

The opening line of the poem sets its tone and introduces its central theme--hatred. Helen's beauty required thousands of men to face death in battle, but it cannot assuage the emotional aftermath of the war. Even though Helen is described as "God's daughter, born of love" (13), all she inspires now is resentment, and the poem explores the ways in which these two emotions are closely related.

In the first stanza, the poet uses the color white, as well as the radiance or luster connected with it, in her description of Helen, and this color will be associated with her throughout the poem:

> the still eyes in the white face,
> the lustre as of olives
> where she stands,
> and the white hands. (2-5)

As one of the foundations of agriculture and civilization, the olive was a crucial symbol in Greek culture. Helen's beauty is compared to the "lustre" of this olive. This word presumably refers to the radiance or light which the whiteness of her face reflects, but Helen's identification with this fruit also has an ironic connotation. The olive branch is a traditional symbol of peace, but the woman it is compared to was the cause of a bitter war.

The majority of the imagery in the poem is connected with the color white. H.D. uses white to describe Helen's skin; white would have been seen as the appropriate color for a rich and beautiful woman's skin in pre-twentieth century poetry. This color also has several connotations, all of which operate simultaneously in the poem. The color white has a connection to Helen's paternity; her immortal father Zeus took the form of a white swan when he made love to her mortal mother Leda. At the same time, whiteness suggests a certain chilliness, as with snow or frost. In the third stanza, H.D. makes this suggestion explicit with her use of the phrase "the beauty of cool feet" (14). This image also suggests the barrenness connected with such frigidity. In this sense, it is a very accurate representation of Helen, because in <u>The Odyssey</u> Homer tells us that ". . . the gods had never after granted Helen / a child to bring into the sunlit world / after the first, rose-lipped Hermoine"

(4.13-15). Helen is returned to her rightful husband, but after her adulterous actions, she is unable to bear him any more children. She is a woman who is renowned for exciting passion in legions of men, but that passion is now sterile.

Another traditional connotation of the color white is purity, but this comparison only accentuates Helen's sexual transgressions; she is hardly pure. H.D. emphasizes her lasciviousness through the use of irony. In the third stanza, she refers to Helen as a "maid." A maid is a virgin, but Helen is most definitely not virginal in any sense. In the following line, the poet rhymes "maid" with the word "laid," which refers to the placement of Helen's body on the funeral pyre. This particular word, however, deliberately emphasized by the rhyme, also carries slangy associations with the act of sexual intercourse. This connotation presents another ironic contrast with the word "maid."

The first line of the second stanza is almost identical to that of the first, and again we are reminded of the intense animosity that Helen's presence inspires. This hatred is now made more explicit. The word <u>revile</u> is defined by the <u>American Heritage College Dictionary</u> as "to denounce with abusive language" ("Revile"). Helen is a queen, but she is subjected to the insults of her subjects as well as the rest of Greece.

Helen's homecoming is not joyous, but a time of exile and penance. The war is over, but no one, especially Helen, can forget the past. Her memories seem to cause her wanness, which the dictionary defines as "indicating weariness, illness, or unhappiness" ("Wan"). Her face now ". . . grows wan and white, / remembering past enchantments / and past ills" (9-11). The enchantment she remembers is that of Aphrodite, the goddess who lured her from her husband and home to Paris's bed. The "ills" which Helen remembers can be seen as both her sexual offenses and the human losses sustained in the Trojan War. The use of the word <u>ills</u> works in conjunction with the word <u>wan</u> to demonstrate Helen's spiritual sickness; she is plagued by regret.

As the opening of the third stanza shows, the woman who was famous for her beauty and perfection now leaves Greece "unmoved." This opening may not echo the sharpness of those of the first two stanzas, but it picks up on the theme of Helen as a devalued prize. In the eyes of the Greeks, she is not the beauty who called two armies to battle but merely an unfaithful wife for whom many died needlessly.

The final lines of the poem reveal the one condition which could turn the people's hatred into love again. They "could love indeed the maid, / only if she were laid, / white ash amid funereal cypresses" (16-19). The Greeks can only forgive Helen once her body has been burned on the funeral pyre. These disturbing lines illustrate the destructive power of hatred; it can only be conquered by death. These lines also reveal the final significance of the color white. It suggests Helen's death. As Helen's face is pale and white in life, so her ashes will be in death. The flames of the funeral pyre are the only way to purify the flesh which was tainted by the figurative flames of passion. Death is the only way to restore Helen's beauty and make it immortal. While she is alive, her beauty is only a reminder of lost fathers, sons, and brothers. The people of Greece can only despise her while she is living, but they can love and revere the memory of her beauty once she is dead.

Works Cited

H. D. "Helen." <u>Literature: An Introduction to Fiction,
    Poetry, and Drama</u>. Ed. X. J. Kennedy and Dana Gioia.
    9th ed. New York: Longman, 2005. 979.

Homer. <u>The Odyssey</u>. Trans. Robert Fitzgerald. New York:
    Noonday P, 1998.

"Revile." <u>American Heritage College Dictionary</u>. 4th ed. 2002.

"Wan." <u>American Heritage College Dictionary</u>. 4th ed. 2002.

FURTHER SUGGESTIONS FOR WRITING

1. Read the original version of either the story of Adam and Eve (the first four chapters of Genesis) or "Cinderella" (in Charles Perrault's *Mother Goose Tales*) and compare it to the corresponding poem in this chapter. Which elements in the myth does the poet change and which does he or she retain?
2. Write an explication of D. H. Lawrence's "Bavarian Gentians" or Thomas Hardy's "The Oxen." (For hints on writing about poetry by the method of explication, see the chapter "Writing About a Poem.")
3. Take any famous myth or fairy tale and retell it to reflect your personal philosophy.

25 *Poetry and Personal Identity*

Only a naive reader assumes that all poems directly reflect the personal experience of their authors. That would be like believing that a TV sitcom actually describes the real family life of its cast. As you will recall if you read "The Person in the Poem" (page 723), poets often speak in voices other than their own. These voices may be borrowed or imaginary. Stevie Smith appropriates the voice of a dead swimmer in her poem, "Not Waving but Drowning" (page 806), and Ted Hughes imagines a nonhuman voice in "Hawk Roosting" (page 726). Some poets also try to give their personal poems a universal feeling. Edna St. Vincent Millay's emotion-charged sonnet "Well, I Have Lost You; and I Lost You Fairly" describes the end of a difficult love affair with a younger man, but she dramatizes the situation in such a way that it seems deliberately independent of any particular time and place. Even her lover remains shadowy and nameless. No one has ever been able to identify the characters in Shakespeare's sonnets with actual people, but that fact does not diminish our pleasure in them as poems.

And yet there are times when poets try to speak openly in their own voices. What could be a more natural subject for a poet than examining his or her own life? The autobiographical elements in a poem may be indirect, as in Chidiock Tichborne's elegy, written before his execution for treason in 1586 (page 827), or it may form the central subject, as in Sylvia Plath's "Lady Lazarus," which discusses her suicide attempts. In either case, the poem's autobiographical stance affects a reader's response. Although we respond to a poem's formal elements, we cannot also help reacting to what we know about its human origins. To learn that the elegant elegy we have just read was written by an eighteen-year-old boy, who would soon be horribly executed, adds a special poignancy to the poem's content. Likewise, to read Plath's chilling exploration of her death wish, while knowing that within a few months the poet would kill herself, we receive an extra jolt of emotion. In a good autobiographical poem, that shock of veracity adds to the poem's power. In an unsuccessful poem, the autobiographical facts become a substitute for emotions not credibly conveyed by the words themselves.

One literary movement, **Confessional poetry,** has made such frank self-definition its main purpose. As the name implies, Confessional poetry renders personal experience as candidly as possible, even sharing confidences that may violate social conventions or propriety. Confessional poets sometimes shock their readers with admissions of experiences so intimate and painful—adultery, family violence, suicide attempts—that most people would try to suppress them, or at least not proclaim them to the world.

Some Confessional poets, such as Anne Sexton, W. D. Snodgrass, and Robert Lowell, underwent psychoanalysis, and at times their poems sound like patients telling their analysts every detail of their personal lives. For this reason, Confessional poems run the danger of being more interesting to their authors than to their readers. But when a poet successfully frames his or her personal experience so that the reader can feel an extreme emotion from the inside, the result can be powerful. Here is a chilling poem that takes us within the troubled psyche of a poet who contemplates suicide.

Sylvia Plath   (1932–1963)*

LADY LAZARUS   (1962) 1965

I have done it again.
One year in every ten
I manage it—

A sort of walking miracle, my skin
Bright as a Nazi lampshade,   5
My right foot

A paperweight,
My face a featureless, fine
Jew linen.

Peel off the napkin   10
O my enemy.
Do I terrify?—

The nose, the eye pits, the full set of teeth?
The sour breath
Will vanish in a day.   15

Soon, soon the flesh
The grave cave ate will be
At home on me

And I a smiling woman.
I am only thirty.   20
And like the cat I have nine times to die.

This is Number Three.
What a trash
To annihilate each decade.

What a million filaments.
The peanut-crunching crowd
Shoves in to see

Them unwrap me hand and foot—
The big strip tease.
Gentleman, ladies,

These are my hands,
My knees.
I may be skin and bone,

Nevertheless, I am the same, identical woman.
The first time it happened I was ten.
It was an accident.

The second time I meant
To last it out and not come back at all.
I rocked shut

As a seashell.
They had to call and call
And pick the worms off me like sticky pearls.

Dying
Is an art, like everything else.
I do it exceptionally well.

I do it so it feels like hell.
I do it so it feels real.
I guess you could say I've a call.

It's easy enough to do it in a cell.
It's easy enough to do it and stay put.
It's the theatrical

Comeback in broad day
To the same place, the same face, the same brute
Amused shout:

"A miracle!"
That knocks me out.
There is a charge

For the eyeing of my scars, there is a charge
For the hearing of my heart—
It really goes.

And there is a charge, a very large charge,
For the word or a touch
Or a bit of blood

Or a piece of my hair or my clothes.
So, so, Herr Doktor.   65
So, Herr Enemy.

I am your opus,°   work, work of art
I am your valuable,
The pure gold baby

That melts to a shriek.   70
I turn and burn.
Do not think I underestimate your great concern.

Ash, ash—
You poke and stir.
Flesh, bone, there is nothing there—   75

A cake of soap,
A wedding ring,
A gold filling,

Herr God, Herr Lucifer,
Beware   80
Beware.

Out of the ash
I rise with my red hair.
And I eat men like air.

QUESTIONS

1. Although the poem is openly autobiographical, Plath uses certain symbols to represent herself (Lady Lazarus, a Jew murdered in a concentration camp, a cat with nine lives, and so on.). What do these symbols tell us about Plath's attitude toward herself and the world around her?
2. In her biography of Plath, *Bitter Fame,* the poet Anne Stevenson says that this poem penetrates "the furthest reaches of disdain and rage . . . bereft of all 'normal' human feelings." What do you think Stevenson means? Does anything in the poem strike you as particularly chilling?
3. The speaker in "Lady Lazarus" says, "Dying / Is an art, like everything else" (lines 43–44). What sense do you make of this metaphor?
4. Does the ending of "Lady Lazarus" imply that the speaker assumes that she will outlive her suicide attempts? Set forth your final understanding of the poem.

Not all autobiographical poetry needs to shock the reader, as Plath overtly does in "Lady Lazarus." Poets can also try to share the special moments that illuminate their day-to-day lives, as Elizabeth Bishop does in "Filling Station," when she describes a roadside gas station whose shabby bric-a-brac she saw as symbols of love. But when poets attempt to place their own lives under scrutiny, they face certain difficulties. Honest, thorough self-examination isn't as easy as it might seem. It is one thing to examine oneself in the mirror; it is quite another to sketch accurately what one sees there. Even if we have the skill to describe ourselves in words (or in paint) so that a stranger would recognize the self-portrait, there is the challenge of honesty. Drawing or writing our own self-portrait, most of us yield, often unconsciously, to the temptation of making ourselves a little nobler or better-looking than we really are. The best self-portraits, like Rembrandt's unflattering self-examinations, are usually critical. No one enjoys watching someone else preen in front of a dressing mirror, unless the intention is satiric.

Autobiographical poetry requires a hunger for honest self-examination. Many poets find that, in order to understand themselves and who they are, they must scrutinize more than the self in isolation. Other forces may shape their identities: their ethnic background, their families, their race, their gender, their religion, their economic status, and their age. Aware of these elements, many recent poets have written memorable personal poems. The Dominican American poet Julia Alvarez wrote an autobiographical sequence of thirty-three sonnets as she turned thirty-three. These poems frankly explore her conflicting identities as daughter, sister, divorcee, lover, writer, Dominican, and American. They earn the reader's trust by being open and self-critical. The subject of one sonnet is Alvarez's admission that she is not as beautiful as either her mother or her sister. Reading that admission, we instinctively sympathize with the author.

Julia Alvarez   (b. 1950)

THE WOMEN ON MY MOTHER'S SIDE   1984
WERE KNOWN (FROM "33")

The women on my mother's side were known
for beauty and were given lovely names
passed down for generations. I knew them
as my pretty aunts: Laura, who could turn
any head once, and Ada, whose husband   5
was so devoted he would lay his hand-
kerchief on seats for her and when she rose
thank her; there was Rosa, who got divorced
twice, her dark eyes and thick hair were to blame;
and my mother Julia, who was a catch   10
and looks it in her wedding photographs.
My sister got her looks, I got her name,
and it suits me that between resemblance
and words, I got the right inheritance.

CULTURE, RACE, AND ETHNICITY

One of the personal issues Julia Alvarez faces in "33" is her dual identity as Dominican and American. The daughter of immigrants, she was born in New York but spent her childhood in the Dominican Republic. Consequently, self-definition for her has meant resolving the claims of two potentially contradictory cultures. In this sonnet, Alvarez talks about inheriting two kinds of beauty from her mother's side of the family. First, there is the beauty of the flesh, which has been passed onto Alvarez's sister. Second, there is a poetic impulse to create beauty with words, fulfilled by the family names, which Alvarez herself has inherited. Here Alvarez touches on the central issue facing the autobiographical poet—using *words* to embody experience. For a writer, the gift of words is "the right inheritance," even if those words are, for an immigrant poet, sometimes in a different language from that of one's parents. American poetry is rich in immigrant cultures, as shown in the work of both first-generation writers such as Alvarez or John Ciardi and foreign-born authors such as Joseph Brodsky (Russia), Nina Cassian (Romania), Claude McKay (Jamaica), Eamon Grennan (Ireland), Thom Gunn (England), Shirley Geok-lin Lim (Malaysia), Emanuel di Pasquale (Italy), José Emilio Pacheco (Mexico), Herberto Padilla (Cuba), and Derek Walcott (St. Lucia). Some literary immigrants, such as the late Russian novelist and poet Vladimir Nabokov, make the difficult transition to writing in English. Others such as Cassian or Pacheco continue to write in their native languages. A few such as Brodsky write bilingually. Such texts often remind us of the multicultural nature of American poetry. Here is a poem by one literary immigrant that raises some important issues of personal identity.

Claude McKay   (1890–1948)

AMERICA   1922

Although she feeds me bread of bitterness,
And sinks into my throat her tiger's tooth,
Stealing my breath of life, I will confess
I love this cultured hell that tests my youth.
Her vigor flows like tides into my blood,   5
Giving me strength erect against her hate,
Her bigness sweeps my being like a flood.
Yet, as a rebel fronts a king in state,
I stand within her walls with not a shred
Of terror, malice, not a word of jeer.   10
Darkly I gaze into the days ahead,
And see her might and granite wonders there,
Beneath the touch of Time's unerring hand,
Like priceless treasures sinking in the sand.

1. Is "America" written in a personal or public voice? What specific elements seem personal? What elements seem public?
2. McKay was a black immigrant from Jamaica, but he does not mention either his race or national origin in the poem. Is his personal background important to understanding "America"?
3. "America" is written in a traditional form. How does the poem's form contribute to its impact?

Claude McKay's "America" raises the question of how an author's race and ethnic identity influence the poetry he or she writes. In the 1920s, for instance, there was an ongoing discussion among black poets as to whether their poetry should deal specifically with the African American experience. Did black poetry exist apart from the rest of American poetry or was it, as Robert Hayden would later suggest, "shaped over some three centuries by social, moral, and literary forces essentially American"? Should black authors primarily address a black audience or should they try to engage a broader literary public? Should black poetry focus on specifically black subjects, forms, and idioms or should it rely mainly on the traditions of English literature? Black poets divided into two camps. Claude McKay and Countee Cullen were among the writers who favored universal themes. (Cullen, for example, insisted he be called a "poet," not a "Negro poet.") Langston Hughes and Jean Toomer were among the "new" poets who felt that black poetry must reflect racial themes. They believed, as James Weldon Johnson had once said, that race was "perforce the thing that the American Negro Poet knows best." Writers on both sides of the debate produced excellent poems, but their work has a very different character. Compare McKay's "America" to a recent poem by Rhina Espaillat, which also examines the American experience from the viewpoint of individuals half inside and half outside mainstream society. Espaillat's poem also adds a new human dimension, the generation gap—familiar to anyone raised in an immigrant home—between those raised in "the old country" and those growing up (and feeling at home) in America.

Rhina Espaillat   (b. 1932)

BILINGUAL/BILINGÜE   1998

My father liked them separate, one there,
one here (allá y aquí), as if aware

that words might cut in two his daughter's heart
(el corazón) and lock the alien part

to what he was—his memory, his name   5
(su nombre)—with a key he could not claim.

"English outside this door, Spanish inside,"
he said, "y basta." But who can divide

the world, the word (mundo y palabra) from
any child? I knew how to be dumb   10

and stubborn (testaruda); late, in bed,
I hoarded secret syllables I read

until my tongue (mi lengua) learned to run
where his stumbled. And still the heart was one.

I like to think he knew that, even when,   15
proud (orgulloso) of his daughter's pen,

he stood outside mis versos, half in fear
of words he loved but wanted not to hear.

Questions

1. Espaillat's poem is full of Spanish words and phrases. (Even the title is given in both languages.) What does the Spanish add to the poem? Could we remove the phrases without changing the poem?
2. How does the father want to divide his daughter's world, at least in terms of language? Does his request suggest any other divisions he hopes to enforce in her life?
3. How does the daughter respond to her father's request to leave English outside their home?
4. "And still the heart was one," states the speaker of the poem. Should we take her statement at face value or do we sense a cost of her bilingual existence? Agree or disagree with the daughter's statement but state the reasons for your opinion.

The debate between ethnicity and universality has echoed among American writers of every racial and religious minority. Today, we find the same issues being discussed by Arab, Asian, Hispanic, Italian, Jewish, and Native American authors. There is, ultimately, no one correct answer to the questions of identity, for individual artists need the freedom to pursue their own imaginative vision. But considering the issues of race and ethnicity does help a poet think through the artist's sometimes conflicting responsibilities between group and personal identity. Even in poets who have pursued their individual vision, we often see how unmistakably they write from their racial, social, and cultural background. There may seem to be little overtly Hispanic content in Julia Alvarez's sonnet, but her poem implicitly reflects the close extended family structure of Latin cultures. Alvarez's poem also points out that we inherit our bodies as well as our cultures. Our body represents our genetic inheritance that goes back to the beginning of time. Sometimes a poet's ethnic background becomes part of his or her private mythology. In the following poem, Samuel Menashe talks about how his physical body is the center of his Jewish identity.

Samuel Menashe   (b. 1925)

THE SHRINE WHOSE SHAPE I AM   1961

The shrine whose shape I am
Has a fringe of fire
Flames skirt my skin

There is no Jerusalem but this
Breathed in flesh by shameless love   5
Built high upon the tides of blood
I believe the Prophets and Blake
And like David I bless myself
With all my might

I know many hills were holy once   10
But now in the level lands to live
Zion ground down must become marrow
Thus in my bones I am the King's son
And through death's domain I go
Making my own procession   15

QUESTIONS

1. What does the poem tell you about the race and religion of the author? How is this
   information conveyed? Point to specific lines.
2. The ancient Jews located the center of Judaism at the Temple of Jerusalem, destroyed by the Romans in 70 A.D. When Menashe declares "There is no Jerusalem
   but this," what does he mean? What is he specifically referring to?
3. What does this poem imply about the nature of ethnic identity?

Francisco X. Alarcón   (b. 1954)

THE X IN MY NAME   1993

the poor
signature
of my illiterate
and peasant
self   5
giving away
all rights
in a deceiving
contract for life

QUESTION

What does the speaker imply the X in his name signifies?

Wendy Rose (b. 1948)

FOR THE WHITE POETS WHO WOULD BE INDIAN

1977

just once
just long enough
to snap up the words
fish-hooked
from our tongues.   5
You think of us now
when you kneel
on the earth,
turn holy
in a temporary tourism   10
of our souls.
With words
you paint your faces.
chew your doeskin,
touch breast to tree   15
as if sharing a mother
were all it takes,
could bring
instant and primal
knowledge.   20
You think of us only
when your voice
wants for roots,
when you have sat back
on your heels   25
and become primitive.
You finish your poem
and go back.

QUESTIONS

1. Who is the speaker of the poem? What is the speaker's attitude toward the persons
   addressed?
2. What does the speaker mean in line 16 by "sharing a mother"? Who or what is this
   "mother"?
3. Where do the "white poets" "go back" to in the last line?
4. Why does the speaker believe that "white poets" will always remain outside the
   American Indian's experience?

Sherman Alexie (b. 1966)

INDIAN BOY LOVE SONG (#1)   1992

Everyone I have lost
in the closing of a door
the click of the lock

is not forgotten, they   5
do not die but remain
within the soft edges
of the earth, the ash

of house fires and cancer
in sin and forgiveness
huddled under old blankets   10

dreaming their way into
my hands, my heart
closing tight like fists.

QUESTIONS

1. What is the significance of the simile that concludes the poem?
2. How does the poem's title affect your interpretation of the text? Explain.

Yusef Komunyakaa (b. 1947)

FACING IT   1988

My black face fades,
hiding inside the black granite.
I said I wouldn't,
dammit: No tears.
I'm stone. I'm flesh.   5
My clouded reflection eyes me
like a bird of prey, the profile of night
slanted against morning. I turn
this way—the stone lets me go.
I turn that way—I'm inside   10
the Vietnam Veterans Memorial
again, depending on the light
to make a difference.
I go down the 58,022 names,
half-expecting to find   15
my own in letters like smoke.
I touch the name Andrew Johnson;
I see the booby trap's white flash.
Names shimmer on a woman's blouse

but when she walks away
the names stay on the wall.
Brushstrokes flash, a red bird's
wings cutting across my stare.
The sky. A plane in the sky.
A white vet's image floats   25
closer to me, then his pale eyes
look through mine. I'm a window.
He's lost his right arm
inside the stone. In the black mirror
a woman's trying to erase names: 30
No, she's brushing a boy's hair.

QUESTIONS

1. How does the title of "Facing It" relate to the poem? Does it have more than one meaning?
2. The narrator describes the people around him by their reflections on the polished granite rather than by looking at them directly. What does this indirect way of scrutinizing contribute to the poem?
3. This poem comes out of the life experience of a black Vietnam veteran. Is Komunyakaa's writing closer to McKay's "universal" method or closer to Toomer's "ethnic" style?

GENDER

In her celebrated study *You Just Don't Understand: Women and Men in Conversation* (1990), Georgetown University linguist Deborah Tannen explored how men and women use language differently. Tannen compared many everyday conversations between husbands and wives to "cross-cultural communications," as if people from separate worlds lived under the same roof. (Denise Levertov's "Leaving Forever," on page 831, describes the same situation quite vividly.) While analyzing the divergent ways in which women and men converse, Tannen carefully emphasizes that neither linguistic style is superior, only different.

While it would be simplistic to assume that all poems reveal the sex of their authors, many poems do become both richer and clearer when we examine their gender assumptions. Theodore Roethke's "My Papa's Waltz" (page 718) is hardly a macho poem, but it does reflect the complicated mix of love, authority, and violent horseplay that exists in many father-son relationships. By contrast, Sylvia Plath's "Metaphors" (page 820), which describes her own pregnancy through a series of images, deals with an experience that, by biological definition, only a woman can know first-hand. Feminist criticism has shown us how gender influences literary texts in subtler ways. (See "Critical Approaches to Literature" for a discussion of feminist theory.) The central insight of feminist criticism seems inarguable—our sex does often influence how we speak, write, and interpret language. But that insight need not be intimidating. It can also invite us to bring our whole life experience, as women or men, to reading a poem. It reminds us that poetry, the act of using language with the greatest clarity and specificity, is a means to see the world through the eyes of the opposite sex. Sometimes the messages we get from this exchange aren't pleasant, but at least they may shock us into better understanding.

Anne Stevenson   (b. 1933)*

SOUS-ENTENDU   1969

Don't think

that I don't know
that as you talk to me
the hand of your mind
is inconspicuously   5
taking off my stocking,
moving in resourceful blindness
up along my thigh.

Don't think
that I don't know   10
that you know
everything I say
is a garment.

SOUS-ENTENDU. The title is a French expression for "hidden meaning" or "implication." It describes something left unsaid but assumed to be understood.

QUESTIONS

1. What is left unsaid but assumed to be understood between the two people in this poem?
2. Could this poem have been written by a man? If so, under what circumstances? If not, why not?

Emily Grosholz   (b. 1950)

LISTENING   1992

Words in my ear, and someone still unseen
not yet quite viable, but quietly
astir inside my body;
not yet quite named, and yet
I weave a birthplace for him out of words.   5

Part of the world persists
distinct from what we say, but part will stay
only if we keep talking: only speech
can re-create the gardens of the world.

Not the rose itself,
but the School of Night assembled at its side
arguing, praising, whom we now recall.

A rose can sow its seed
alone, but poets need their auditors
and mothers need their language for a cradle.   15

My son still on his stalk
rides between the silence of the flowers
and conversation offered by his parents,
wise and foolish talk, to draw him out.

QUESTIONS

1. Who is the one listening in this poem? Who is the speaker?
2. What images does the speaker use to describe the person being addressed? What do these metaphors suggest about the relationship between speaker and listener?
3. How does the speaker compare the poet to the rose? How is this comparison relevant to the poem?

EXERCISE

Rewrite either of the following poems from the perspective of the opposite sex. Then evaluate in what ways the new poem has changed the original's meaning and in what ways the original poem comes through more or less unaltered.

Donald Justice   (b. 1925)*

MEN AT FORTY   1967

Men at forty
Learn to close softly
The doors to rooms they will not be
Coming back to.

At rest on a stair landing,   5
They feel it
Moving beneath them now like the deck of a ship,
Though the swell is gentle.

And deep in mirrors
They rediscover   10
The face of the boy as he practices tying
His father's tie there in secret

And the face of that father,
Still warm with the mystery of lather.
They are more fathers than sons themselves now.   15
Something is filling them, something

That is like the twilight sound
Of the crickets, immense,
Filling the woods at the foot of the slope
Behind their mortgaged houses.   20

Adrienne Rich   (b. 1929)*

WOMEN   1968

My three sisters are sitting
on rocks of black obsidian.
For the first time, in this light, I can see who they are.

My first sister is sewing her costume for the procession.
She is going as the Transparent Lady   5
and all her nerves will be visible.

My second sister is also sewing,
at the seam over her heart which has never healed entirely,
At last, she hopes, this tightness in her chest will ease.

My third sister is gazing   10
at a dark-red crust spreading westward far out on the sea.
Her stockings are torn but she is beautiful.

FOR REVIEW AND FURTHER STUDY

Shirley Geok-lin Lim   (b. 1944)

LEARNING TO LOVE AMERICA   1998

because it has no pure products

because the Pacific Ocean sweeps along the coastline
because the water of the ocean is cold
and because land is better than ocean

because I say we rather than they   5

because I live in California
I have eaten fresh artichokes
and jacarandas bloom in April and May

because my senses have caught up with my body
my breath with the air it swallows   10
my hunger with my mouth

because I walk barefoot in my house

because I have nursed my son at my breast
because he is a strong American boy
because I have seen his eyes redden when he is asked who he is   15
because he answers I don't know

because to have a son is to have a country
because my son will bury me here
because countries are in our blood and we bleed them

because it is late and too late to change my mind   20
because it is time.

LEARNING TO LOVE AMERICA. 1 *pure products*: an allusion to poem XVIII of *Spring and All* (1923) by
William Carlos Williams, which begins: "The pure products of America / go crazy—."

QUESTION

Do the reasons given in the poem suggest that the speaker really does love America?

Andrew Hudgins   (b. 1951)

ELEGY FOR MY FATHER, WHO IS NOT DEAD   1991

One day I'll lift the telephone
and be told my father's dead. He's ready.
In the sureness of his faith, he talks
about the world beyond this world
as though his reservations have   5
been made. I think he wants to go,
a little bit—a new desire
to travel building up, an itch
to see fresh worlds. Or older ones.
He thinks that when I follow him   10
he'll wrap me in his arms and laugh,
the way he did when I arrived
on earth. I do not think he's right.
He's ready. I am not. I can't
just say good-bye as cheerfully   15
as if he were embarking on a trip
to make my later trip go well.
I see myself on deck, convinced
his ship's gone down, while he's convinced
I'll see him standing on the dock   20
and waving, shouting, *Welcome back.*

QUESTIONS

1. The speaker describes his father's view of the afterlife in this poem. What image does he use to describe his father's vision of life after death?
2. What metaphor does the poet use to describe his own religious uncertainty?

Judith Ortiz Cofer   (b. 1952)

QUINCEAÑERA   1987

My dolls have been put away like dead
children in a chest I will carry
with me when I marry.
I reach under my skirt to feel
a satin slip bought for this day. It is soft   5
as the inside of my thighs. My hair
has been nailed back with my mother's
black hairpins to my skull. Her hands
stretched my eyes open as she twisted
braids into a tight circle at the nape   10
of my neck. I am to wash my own clothes
and sheets from this day on, as if
the fluids of my body were poison, as if
the little trickle of blood I believe
travels from my heart to the world were   15
shameful. Is not the blood of saints and
men in battle beautiful? Do Christ's hands
not bleed into your eyes from His cross?
At night I hear myself growing and wake
to find my hands drifting of their own will   20
to soothe skin stretched tight
over my bones.
I am wound like the guts of a clock,
waiting for each hour to release me.

QUINCEAÑERA. *Quinceañera:* a fifteen-year-old girl's coming-out party in Latin cultures.

QUESTIONS

1. What items and actions are associated with the speaker's new life? What items are put away?
2. What is the speaker waiting to release in the final two lines?
3. If the poem's title were changed to "Fifteen-Year-Old Girl," what would the poem lose in meaning?

Alastair Reid   (b. 1926)*

SPEAKING A FOREIGN LANGUAGE   1963

How clumsy on the tongue, these acquired idioms,
after the innuendos of our own. How far
we are from foreigners, what faith
we rest in one sentence, hoping a smile will follow
on the appropriate face, always wallowing   5
between what we long to say and what we can,
trusting the phrase is suitable to the occasion,
the accent passable, the smile real,
always asking the traveller's fearful question—
what is being lost in translation?   10
Something, to be sure. And yet, to hear
the stumbling of foreign friends, how little we care
for the wreckage of word or tense. How endearing they are,
and how our speech reaches out, like a helping hand,
or limps in sympathy. East to understand,   15
through the tangle of language, the heart behind
groping toward us, to make the translation of
syntax into love.

COMPARE

Compare Alastair Reid's poem to Rhina Espaillat's "Bilingual/Bilingüe." How does the
view of language differ in each poem? How is it similar?

Philip Larkin   (1922–1985)*

AUBADE   1977

I work all day, and get half-drunk at night.
Waking at four to soundless dark, I stare.
In time the curtain-edges will grow light.
Till then I see what's really always there:
Unresting death, a whole day nearer now,   5
Making all thought impossible but how
And where and when I shall myself die.
Arid interrogation: yet the dread
Of dying, and being dead,
Flashes afresh to hold and horrify.   10

The mind blanks at the glare. Not in remorse
—The good not done, the love not given, time
Torn off unused—nor wretchedly because
An only life can take so long to climb

Clear of its wrong beginnings, and may never;   15
But at the total emptiness for ever,
The sure extinction that we travel to
And shall be lost in always. Not to be here,
Not to be anywhere,
And soon; nothing more terrible, nothing more true.   20

This is a special way of being afraid.
No trick dispels. Religion used to try,
That vast moth-eaten musical brocade
Created to pretend we never die,
And specious stuff that says *No rational being*   25
Can fear a thing it will not feel, not seeing
That this is what we fear—no sight, no sound,
No touch or taste or smell, nothing to think with,
Nothing to love or link with,
The anaesthetic from which none come round.   30

And so it stays just on the edge of vision,
A small unfocused blur, a standing chill
That slows each impulse down to indecision.
Most things may never happen: this one will,
And realisation of it rages out   35
In furnace-fear when we are caught without
People or drink. Courage is no good:
It means not scaring others. Being brave
Lets no one off the grave.
Death is no different whined at than withstood.   40

Slowly light strengthens, and the room takes shape.
It stands plain as a wardrobe, what we know,
Have always known, known that we can't escape,
Yet can't accept. One side will have to go.
Meanwhile telephones crouch, getting ready to ring   45
In locked-up offices, and all the uncaring
Intricate rented world begins to rouse.
The sky is white as clay, with no sun.
Work has to be done.
Postmen like doctors go from house to house.   50

QUESTIONS

1. Is "Aubade" a Confessional poem? If so, what social taboo does it violate?
2. What embarrassing facts about the narrator does the poem reveal? Do these confessions lead us to trust or distrust him?
3. The narrator says that "Courage is no good" (stanza 4). How might he defend this statement?
4. Would a twenty-year-old reader respond differently to this poem than a seventy-year-old one? Would a devout Christian respond differently to the poem than an atheist?

Rhina Espaillat

Rhina Espaillat on Writing

BEING A BILINGUAL WRITER   1998

Recent interest in the phenomenon known as "Spanglish" has led me to reexamine my own experience as a writer who works chiefly in her second language,
and especially to recall my father's inflexible rule against the mixing of languages.
In fact, no English was allowed in that midtown Manhattan apartment that became home after my arrival in New York in 1939. My father read the daily paper
in English, taught himself to follow disturbing events in Europe through the
medium of English-language radio, and even taught me to read the daily comic
strips, in an effort to speed my learning of the language he knew I would need. But
that necessary language was banished from family conversation: it was the medium
of the outer world, beyond the door; inside, among ourselves, only Spanish was
permitted, and it had to be pure, grammatical, unadulterated Spanish.

At the age of seven, however, nothing seems more important than communicating with classmates and neighborhood children. For my mother, too, the
new language was a way out of isolation, a means to deal with the larger world
and with those American women for whom she sewed. But my father, a political
exile waiting for changes in our native country, had different priorities; he lived
in the hope of return, and believed that the new home, the new speech, were
temporary. His theory was simple: if it could be said at all, it could be said best in
the language of those authors whose words were the core of his education. But
his insistence on pure Spanish made it difficult, sometimes impossible, to bring
home and share the jokes of friends, puns, pop lyrics, and other staples of seven-
year-old conversation. Table talk sometimes ended with tears or sullen silence.

And yet, despite the friction it caused from time to time, my native language
was also a source of comfort—the reading that I loved, intimacy within the
family, and a peculiar auditory delight best described as echoes in the mind. I

learned early to relish words as counters in a game that could turn suddenly serious without losing the quality of play, and to value their sound as a meaning behind their meaning.

Nostalgia, a confusion of identity, the fear that if the native language is lost the self will somehow be altered forever; all are part of the subtle flavor of immigrant life, as well as the awareness that one owes gratitude to strangers for acts of communication that used to be simple and once imposed no such debt.

Memory, folklore, and food all become part of the receding landscape that language sets out to preserve. Guilt, too, adds to the mix, the suspicion that to love the second language too much is to betray those ancestors who spoke the first and could not communicate with us in the vocabulary of our education, our new thoughts. And finally, a sense of grievance and loss may spur hostility toward the new language and those who speak it, as if the common speech of the perceived majority could weld together a disparate population into a huge, monolithic, and threatening Other. That Other is then assigned traits and habits that preclude sympathy and mold "Us" into a unity whose cohesiveness gives comfort.

Luckily, there is another side to bilingualism: curiosity about the Other may be as natural and pervasive as group loyalty. If it weren't, travel, foreign residence, and intermarriage would be less common than they are. For some bilingual writers, the Other—and the language he speaks—are appealing. Some acknowledge and celebrate the tendency of languages to borrow from each other and produce something different in the process.

From afterword to Where Horizons Go

⇒⇒⇒ WRITING CRITICALLY ⇐⇐⇐

Poetic Voice and Personal Identity

The poet Julia Alvarez has written about the fear, excitement, and surprise she felt coming home late one night to find copies of her first book of poems, *Homecoming* (1984), waiting by her front door. Reading her own poems in a printed book for the first time, she remarked, "What shocked me that midnight was that I heard my own voice loud and clear." Alvarez is not talking about hearing her physical voice, but about recognizing for the first time the specific personality that had emerged from her poems. She was surprised by the ways in which her verbal creation both resembled and differed from her actual self.

When critics discuss poetic voice, they often focus on matters of style—characteristic tone, word choice, figures of speech, and rhythms. An author's *personal* voice, however, encompasses more than style; it also includes characteristic themes and subjects. A recognizable poetic voice usually emerges only when a writer finds the right way of presenting the right subjects.

Finding an authentic voice has long been a central issue among women and minority poets. In exploring their subjects, which often lie outside existing traditions, these writers sometimes need to find innovative forms of expression. Edna

St. Vincent Millay, for instance, had to invent a new female voice to write the love poems that made her famous. Although her metrics were traditional, Millay's authoritative tone, self-assured manner, and sexual candor were revolutionary for her time. Sometimes a single word announces a new sort of voice; in Judith Ortiz Cofer's "*Quinceañera*," the title is a Spanish noun for which there is no one-word English equivalent. That one word suggests that we will be hearing a new voice.

When writing about voice in poetry, you will often find it illuminating to consider race, gender, age, ethnicity, and religious belief. Is the poem's perspective shaped by any of those elements of the author's identity? Don't limit the poem's meanings to those categories, but see if considering those concepts helps you understand the work better. Pay special attention to the way the poem's personal perspective is reflected in its formal aspects (imagery, tone, metaphor, and sound). Observing how formal aspects embody the author's special themes and subjects will be central to appreciating his or her voice. For further examination of these issues, you may want to read "Gender Criticism" in "Critical Approaches to Literature." Although that section discusses only one aspect of identity, the general principles it explores are relevant to the broader questions of how an author's life experience may influence the kinds of poetry he or she creates.

WRITING ASSIGNMENT

Analyze any poem in this chapter from the perspective of an author's race, gender, ethnicity, age, or religious beliefs. Describe how that perspective illuminates the meaning of the poem. Use whatever biographical research you can find, but make sure all of your arguments are specifically based on the poem itself and not merely on biographical data. For examples of similar analyses, see Darryl Pinckney's "Black Identity in Langston Hughes" (page 1131) and Brett C. Millier's "On Elizabeth Bishop's 'One Art'" in the chapter "Critical Approaches to Literature." Short biographies of many of the poets in this book can be found in the chapter "Lives of the Poets."

FURTHER SUGGESTIONS FOR WRITING

1. Find another poem in "Poems for Further Reading" in which the poet, like Julia Alvarez, considers his or her own family. Tell in a paragraph or two what the poem reveals about the author.
2. Compare Larkin's "Aubade" with another poem about old age and death, such as William Butler Yeats's "Sailing to Byzantium" (page 1075), Dylan Thomas's "Do not go gentle into that good night" (page 927), or William Shakespeare's "That time of year thou mayst in me behold" (page 1238).

26 Translation

IS POETIC TRANSLATION POSSIBLE?

Poetry, said Robert Frost, is what gets lost in translation. If absolutely true, the comment is bad news for most of us, who have to depend on translations for our only knowledge of great poems in many other languages. However, some translators seem able to save a part of their originals and bring it across the language gap. At times they may even add more poetry of their own, as if to try to compensate for what is lost.

Unlike the writer of an original poem, the translator begins with a meaning that already exists. To convey it, the translator may decide to stick closely to the denotations of the original words or else to depart from them, more or less freely, to pursue something he or she values more. The latter aim is evident in the *Imitations* of Robert Lowell, who said he had been "reckless with literal meaning" and instead had "labored hard to get the tone." Particularly defiant of translation are poems in dialect, uneducated speech, and slang: what can be used for English equivalents? Ezra Pound, in a bold move, translates the song of a Chinese peasant in *The Classic Anthology Defined by Confucius*:

> Yaller bird, let my corn alone,
> Yaller bird, let my crawps alone,
> These folks here won't let me eat,
> I wanna go back whaar I can meet
> the folks I used to know at home,
>   I got a home an' I wanna' git goin'.

Here, it is our purpose to judge a translation not by its fidelity to its original, but by the same standards we apply to any other poem written in English. To do so may be another way to see the difference between appropriate and inappropriate words.

Rainer Maria Rilke   (1875–1926)

Eingang   1902

Wer du auch seist: Am Abend tritt hinaus
aus deiner Stube, drin du alles weißt;
als letztes vor der Ferne liegt dein Haus:
Wer du auch seist.
Mit deinen Augen, welche müde kaum   5
von der verbrauchten Schwelle sich befrein,
hebst du ganz langsam einen schwarzen Baum
und stellst ihn vor den Himmel: schlank, allein.
Und hast die Welt gemacht. Und sie ist groß
und win ein Wort, das noch im Schweigen reift.   10
Und wie dein Wille ihren Sinn begreift,
lassen sie deine Augen zärtlich los . . .

Entrance   2001

Whoever you are: step out of doors tonight,
Out of the room that lets you feel secure.
Infinity is open to your sight.
Whoever you are.
With eyes that have forgotten how to see   5
From viewing things already too well-known,
Lift up into the dark a huge, black tree
And put it in the heavens: tall, alone.
And you have made the world and all you see.
It ripens like the words still in your mouth.   10
And when at last you comprehend its truth,
Then close your eyes and gently set it free.

—Translated by Dana Gioia

Questions

1. How well does the translation convey the poem's *poetry*? From what you can discern of
   the original (even if you do not understand German, you can note some of the poem's
   characteristics by studying its appearance on the page and, perhaps, hearing it read
   aloud), how does the translation convey the poem's formal characteristics and tone?
2. Note the title: what is it that the speaker is asking us to leave, and what does he
   desire us to enter into?

World Poetry

English boasts one of the greatest poetic traditions in the world, with over six centuries of continuous literary culture from Geoffrey Chaucer to the present. It is the
language of Shakespeare, Milton, Pope, Keats, Tennyson, Dickinson, Whitman,
Frost, and Yeats. The primary language of over 400 million people, English is

spoken from London to San Francisco, Capetown to Sydney, Vancouver to Nassau. Yet English is the first language of only seven percent of the people of the globe. Mandarin Chinese has almost twice as many native speakers, and two other languages—Hindi and Spanish—have nearly as many speakers as English. Needless to say, all these tongues have rich and ancient literary traditions. To know only the poetry of English, therefore, is to experience a small fraction of world poetry.

Poetry is a universal human phenomenon. Every culture and every language group shape language into verse. To explore the poetry of other languages and cultures is a way of broadening one's vision of humanity. No one, of course, can ever master the whole field of human achievement in poetry, even in translation, but to know a few high spots from poets greatly esteemed by other nations can enlarge our notion of the art as well as enhance our sense of the world.

To gain some perspective on English poetry, one need only look at Chinese literature. China has the oldest uninterrupted literary tradition in the world, dating back at least 3400 years, and poetry has always been its central enterprise. Over a billion people speak one of the dialects of Chinese and all read the same written language. To give a taste of this unparalleled tradition, here is Li Po's "Drinking Alone Beneath the Moon," a classic of Chinese poetry, presented in four ways. First, the poem appears in its original Chinese characters; a phonetic transcription follows, along with a word-for-word literal translation into English. Finally, Li Po's poem is given in a poetic translation.

Li Po (701–762)*

DRINKING ALONE BENEATH THE MOON (ABOUT 750)

月 下 獨 酌

花 間 一 壺 酒
獨 酌 無 相 親
舉 杯 邀 明 月
對 影 成 三 人
月 既 不 解 飲
影 徒 隨 我 身
暫 伴 月 將 影
行 樂 須 及 春
我 歌 月 徘 徊
我 舞 影 零 亂
醒 時 同 交 歡
醉 後 各 分 散
永 結 無 情 遊
相 期 邈 雲 漢

Yueh Hsia Tu Cho
MOON-BENEATH ALONE DRINK (ABOUT 750)

Hua chien yi hu chiu
Flowers-among one pot wine
Tu cho wu hsiang ch'in (ts'ien)
Alone drink no mutual dear
Chü pei yueh ming yueh
Lift cup invite bright moon
Tuei ying ch'eng san jen (nzien)
Face shadow become three men
Yueh chi pu chieh yin
Moon not-only not understand drink   5
Ying t'u suei wo shen (sien)
Shadow in-vain follow my body
Chan pan yueh chiang ying
Temporarily accompany moon with shadow
Hsing lo hsü chi ch'un (ts'iuen)
Practice pleasure must catch spring
Wo ko yueh p' ai-huai
I sing moon linger-to-and-fro
Wo wu ying ling luan (luan)
I dance shadow scatter disorderly   10
Hsing shih t'ung chiao huan
Wake time together exchange joy
Tsui hou ko fen san (san)
Rapt-after each separate disperse
Yung chieh wu-ch'ing yu
Always tie no-passion friendship
Hsiang ch'i miao yun-han (xan)
Mutual expect distant Cloud-river

DRINKING ALONE BY MOONLIGHT   1919

A cup of wine, under the flowering trees;
I drink alone, for no friend is near.
Raising my cup I beckon the bright moon,
For he, with my shadow, will make three men.
The moon, alas, is no drinker of wine;   5
Listless, my shadow creeps about at my side.
Yet with the moon as friend and the shadow as slave
I must make merry before the Spring is spent.
To the songs I sing the moon flickers her beams;

In the dance I weave my shadow tangles and breaks.   10
While we were sober, three shared the fun;
Now we are drunk, each goes his way.
May we long share our odd, inanimate feast,
And meet at last on the Cloudy River of the sky.

—*Translated by Arthur Waley*

DRINKING ALONE BY MOONLIGHT. 14 *the Cloudy River of the sky:* the Milky Way.

QUESTIONS

1. Judging from the literal translation of Li Po's poem, discuss which aspects of the original seem to come across vividly in Arthur Waley's English version.
2. Which aspects change or disappear in Waley's version?
3. Take a line from Waley's version (perhaps one you don't especially like) and use the literal translation to offer a different translation.

EXERCISE: *Comparing Translations*

Which English translation of each of the following poems is the best poetry? The originals may be of interest to some. For those who do not know the foreign language, the editor's line-by-line prose paraphrases may help indicate what the translator had to work with and how much of the translation is the translator's own idea. In which do you find the diction most felicitous? In which do pattern and structure best move as one? What differences in tone are apparent? It is doubtful that any one translation will surpass the others in every detail.

Our verb *translate* is derived from the Latin word *translatus*, the past participle of "to transfer" or "to carry across." The first set of translations tries to carry across into English one of the most influential short poems ever written. Horace's ode, which ends with the advice, *carpe diem* ("seize the day"), has left its mark on countless poems. One even sees its imprint on contemporary novels (such as Saul Bellow's *Seize the Day*) and films (such as *Dead Poets Society*) that echo Horace's command to live in the present moment because no one knows what the future will bring.

Horace   (65–8 B.C.)

ODES I (11)   (ABOUT 20 B.C.)

Tu ne quaesieris—scire nefas—quem mihi, quem tibi   1
finem di dederint, Leuconoe, nec Babylonios   2
temptaris numeros. Ut melius, quicquid erit, pati!   3
seu plures hiemes, seu tribuit Iuppiter ultimam,   4
quae nunc oppositis debilitat pumicibus mare   5

Tyrrhenum. Sapias, vina liques, et spatio brevi   6
spem longam reseces. Dum loquimur, fugerit invida   7
aetas: carpe diem, quam minimum credula postero.   8

ODES I (11). Prose translation: (1,2) Do not ask, Leuconoe—to know is not permitted—what end the gods have given to you and me, do not (3) consult Babylonian horoscopes. It will be better to endure whatever comes, (4) whether Jupiter grants us more winters or whether this is the last one, (5) which now against the opposite cliffs wears out (6) the Tuscan sea. Be wise, decant the wine, and since our space is brief, (7) cut back your far-reaching hope. Even while we talk, envious time has fled away: (8) seize the day, put little trust in what is to come.

HORACE TO LEUCONOE   1891

I pray you not, Leuconoe, to pore
With unpermitted eyes on what may be
Appointed by the gods for you and me,
Nor on Chaldean figures any more.
'T were infinitely better to implore   5
The present only:—whether Jove decree
More winters yet to come, or whether he
Make even this, whose hard, wave-eaten shore
Shatters the Tuscan seas to-day, the last—
Be wise withal, and rack your wine, nor fill   10
Your bosom with large hopes; for while I sing,
The envious close of time is narrowing;—
So seize the day, or ever it be past,
And let the morrow come for what it will.
                        —*Translated by Edwin Arlington Robinson*[*]

DON'T ASK   1963

Don't ask (we may not know), Leuconoe,
    What the gods plan for you or me.
        Leave the Chaldees to parse
        The sentence of the stars.

Better to bear the outcome, good or bad,   5
    Whether Jove purposes to add
        Fresh winters to the past
        Or to make this the last

Which now tires out the Tuscan sea and mocks
    Its strength with barricades of rocks.   10

Be wise, strain clear the wine
  And prune the rambling vine

Of expectation. Life's short. Even while
  We talk Time, hateful, runs a mile.
    Don't trust tomorrow's bough   15
    For fruit. Pluck this, here, now.

—Translated by James Michie

A New Year's Toast   2000

Blanche—don't ask—it isn't right for us to know what ends
Fate may have in store for us. Don't dial up Psychic Friends.
Isn't it better just to take whatever the future sends,
Whether the new millennium goes off without a hitch
Or World War III is triggered by an old computer glitch?   5
Wise up. Have a drink. Keep plans to a modest pitch.
Even as we're talking here, we spend the time we borrow.
Seize Today—trust nothing to that sly old cheat, Tomorrow.

—Translated by A. E. Stallings

Questions

1. Which translation seems closest to the literal meaning of the Latin? Does that
   fidelity help or hinder its impact as a new poem in English?
2. In her translation, A. E. Stallings modernizes most of the images and allusions. What
   does this add to the translation's impact? Does it change the meaning of the original?
3. Which translation do you personally respond to most strongly? While recognizing
   the subjective nature of your preference, explain what aspects of the version appeal
   to you.

The next set of translations tries to recreate a short lyric by the classical Persian poet Omar Khayyam, the master of the *rubai*, a four-line stanza rimed *a a b a*. This Persian form was introduced into English by Edward FitzGerald (1809–1883) in his hugely popular translation, *The Rubaiyat of Omar Khayyam* (rubaiyat is the plural of rubai). In FitzGerald's Victorian version, Omar Khayyam became one of the most frequently quoted poets in English. Eugene O'Neill borrowed the title of his play *Ah, Wilderness!* from the *Rubaiyat* and expected his audience to catch the allusion. TV buffs may remember hearing Khayyam's poetry quoted habitually by the SWAT-team commander Howard Hunter on the classic series *Hill Street Blues*. Here are three poetic translations of a famous *rubai*. Which qualities of the original does each translation seem to capture?

Omar Khayyam   (1048–1131)

RUBAI   (ABOUT 1100)

Tongi-ye may-e la'l kh'aham o divani   1
   Sadd-e ramaghi bayad o nesf-e nani   2
Vangah man o to neshasteh dar virani   3
   Khoshtar bovad as mamlekat-e soltani.   4

RUBAI. Prose translation: (1) I want a jug of ruby wine and a book of poems. (2) There must be something to stop my breath from departing, and a half loaf of bread. (3) Then you and I sitting in some deserted ruin. (4) Would be sweeter than the realm of a sultan.

A BOOK OF VERSES UNDERNEATH   1879
THE BOUGH

A Book of Verses underneath the Bough,
A Jug of Wine, a Loaf of Bread—and Thou
   Beside me singing in the Wilderness—
Oh, Wilderness were Paradise enow°!   enough
                                   —*Translated by Edward FitzGerald**

OUR DAY'S PORTION   1968

Should our day's portion be one mancel loaf,
A haunch of mutton and a gourd of wine
Set for us two alone on the wide plain,
No Sultan's bounty could evoke such joy.
                    —*Translated by Robert Graves* and Omar Ali-Shah*

I NEED A BARE SUFFICIENCY   1992

I need a bare sufficiency—red wine,
   Some poems, half a loaf on which to dine
With you beside me in some ruined shrine:
   A king's state then is not as sweet as mine!
                                          —*Translated by Dick Davis*

EXERCISE: *Persian Versions*

Write a *rubai* of your own on any topic. Some possible subjects include: what you plan to do next weekend to relax; advice to a friend to stop worrying; an invitation to a loved one; a four-line *carpe diem* ode. For your inspiration, here are a few more *rubaiyat* from Edward FitzGerald's celebrated translation.

> Wake! For the Sun who scattered into flight
> The Stars before him from the Field of Night,
>   Drives Night along with them from Heaven, and strikes
> The Sultan's Turret with a Shaft of Light.
>
> * * * *
>
> Come, fill the Cup, and in the Fire of Spring
> Your Winter-garment of Repentence fling:
>   The Bird of Time has but a little way
> To flutter—and the Bird is on the Wing.
>
> * * * *
>
> Some for the Glories of this World; and some
> Sigh for the Prophet's Paradise to come;
>   Ah, take the Cash, and let the Credit go,
> Nor heed the rumble of a Distant Drum!
>
> * * * *
>
> The Moving Finger writes; and, having writ,
> Moves on: nor all your Piety nor Wit
>   Shall lure it back to cancel half a Line
> Nor all your Tears wash out a Word of it.
>
> * * * *
>
> Ah Love! could you and I with Him conspire
> To grasp this sorry Scheme of Things entire,
>   Would we not shatter it to bits—and then
> Remould it nearer to the Heart's desire.

PARODY

There is another literary mode that is related to translation—namely, **parody**—in which one writer imitates another writer or work, usually for the purpose of poking fun. Parody can be considered an irreverent form of translation in which one poem is changed into another written in the same language but with a different effect (usually slipping from serious to silly). When one writer parodies another writer's work, it does not necessarily mean that the original poem is without merit. "Most parodies are written out of admiration rather than contempt," claimed critic Dwight Macdonald, who edited the anthology *Parodies* (1960), because there needs to be enough common sympathy between poet and parodist for the poem's essence not to be lost in the translation. It takes a fine poem to support an even passable parody. "Nobody is going to parody you if you haven't a style," remarked British critic Geoffrey Grigson.

What a parody mostly reveals is that any good poem becomes funny if you change one or more of the assumptions behind it. Gene Fehler, for example, takes Richard Lovelace's lover-soldier in "To Lucasta" (page 741) and turns him into a major league baseball player changing teams; what this new warrior loves, we soon discover, is neither honor nor his lady but a fat salary. Far from ridiculing Lovelace's original, Fehler's parody demonstrates that the poem is strong enough to support a comic translation into contemporary images.

Parodies remind us how much fun poetry can be—an aspect of the art sometimes forgotten during end-of-term exams and research papers. These comic transformations also teach us something essential about the original poems. Parodies are, as Dwight Macdonald said, "an intuitive kind of literary criticism, shorthand for what 'serious' critics must write out at length." If you try your hand at writing a parody, you will soon discover how deeply you need to understand the original work in order to reproduce its style and manner. You will also learn how much easier it is to parody a poem you really love.

Anonymous

WE FOUR LADS FROM   (ABOUT 1963)
LIVERPOOL ARE

We four lads from Liverpool are—
Paul in a taxi, John in a car,
George on a scooter, tootin' his hooter,
Following Ringo Starr.

Skillfully written, parody can be a devastating form of literary criticism. Rather than merely flinging abuse, the wise parodist imitates with understanding, even with sympathy. The many crude parodies of T. S. Eliot's difficult poem *The Waste Land* show parodists mocking what they cannot fathom, with the result that, instead of illuminating the original, they belittle it (and themselves). Good parodists have an ear for the sounds and rhythms of their originals, as does James Camp, who echoes Walt Whitman's stately "Out of the Cradle Endlessly Rocking" in his line "Out of the crock endlessly ladling" (what a weary teacher feels he is doing). Parody can be aimed at poems good or bad; yet there are poems of such splendor and dignity that no parodist seems able to touch them without looking like a small dog defiling a cathedral, and others so illiterate that good parody would be squandered on them. Sometimes parodies are even an odd form of flattery; poets poke fun at poems they simply can't get out of their heads any other way except by rewriting, as in the following parody, in which Wendy Cope delightfully imagines a rustic encounter like those in such classic Wordsworth poems as "We Are Seven" and "Resolution and Independence."

Wendy Cope   (b. 1945)*

A Nursery Rhyme (as it might have   1986
been written by William Wordsworth)

The skylark and the jay sang loud and long,
The sun was calm and bright, the air was sweet,
When all at once I heard above the throng
Of jocund birds a single plaintive bleat.

And, turning, saw, as one sees in a dream,   5
It was a Sheep had broke the moorland peace
With his sad cry, a creature who did seem
The blackest thing that ever wore a fleece.

I walked towards him on the stony track
And, pausing for a while between two crags,   10
I asked him, "Have you wool upon your back?"
Thus he bespake, "Enough to fill three bags."

Most courteously, in measured tones, he told
Who would receive each bag and where they dwelt;
And oft, now years have passed and I am old,   15
I recollect with joy that inky pelt.

Questions

1. What characteristics of Wordsworth's poetry is Cope parodying here?
2. How would you describe the relationship between Cope's diction and the subject matter of the poem? Do they seem appropriate to one another or not?

Hugh Kingsmill
[Hugh Kingsmill Lunn]   (1889–1949)

What, still alive at   (about 1920)
twenty-two?

What, still alive at twenty-two,
A clean, upstanding chap like you?
Sure, if your throat 'tis hard to slit,
Slit your girl's, and swing for it.

Like enough, you won't be glad   5
When they come to hang you, lad:
But bacon's not the only thing
That's cured by hanging from a string.

So, when the spilt ink of the night
Spreads o'er the blotting-pad of light   10
Lads whose job is still to do
Shall whet their knives, and think of you.

QUESTIONS

1. A. E. Housman considered this the best of many parodies of his poetry. Read his poems in this book, particularly "Eight O'Clock" (page 868), "When I was one-and-twenty" (page 902), and "To an Athlete Dying Young" (page 1194). What characteristics of theme, form, and language does Hugh Kingsmill's parody convey?
2. What does Kingsmill exaggerate?

Bruce Bennett   (b. 1940)

THE LADY SPEAKS AGAIN   1992

"I lift my lamp beside the golden door."
More golden now than ever; don't ask why.
Just list your assets, where you can get more,
and who you know. No others need apply.

QUESTIONS

1. Who is the "lady" speaking? What poem is echoed in Bennett's parody?
2. Is Bennett making fun of the original poem (page 1087)? Or is there another object for his satire?

Gene Fehler   (b. 1940)

IF RICHARD LOVELACE BECAME   1984
A FREE AGENT

Tell me not, fans, I am unkind
    For saying my good-bye
And leaving your kind cheers behind
    While I to new fans fly.

Now, I will leave without a trace   5
    And choose a rival's field;
For I have viewed the market place
    And seen what it can yield.

Though my disloyalty is such   10
    That all you fans abhor,
It's not that I don't love you much:
    I just love money more.

1. After comparing this parody to Richard Lovelace's "To Lucasta" (page 741), list the elements that Fehler keeps from the original and those he adds.
2. What ideals motivate the speaker of Lovelace's poem? What ideals motivate Fehler's free agent?

Aaron Abeyta   (b. 1971)

THIRTEEN WAYS OF LOOKING AT A TORTILLA   2001

i.
among twenty different tortillas
the only thing moving
was the mouth of the niño

ii.
i was of three cultures
like a tortilla
for which there are three bolios   5

iii.
the tortilla grew on the wooden table
it was a small part of the earth

iv.
a house and a tortilla
are one   10
a man a woman and a tortilla
are one

v.
i do not know which to prefer
the beauty of the red wall
or the beauty of the green wall   15
the tortilla fresh
or just after

vi.
tortillas filled the small kitchen
with ancient shadows
the shadow of Maclovia   20
cooking long ago
the tortilla
rolled from the shadow
the innate roundness

vii.
o thin viejos of chimayo   25
why do you imagine biscuits
do you not see how the tortilla
lives with the hands
of the women about you

viii.
i know soft corn   30
and beautiful inescapable sopapillas
but i know too
that the tortilla
has taught me what I know

ix.
when the tortilla is gone   35
it marks the end
of one of many tortillas

x.
at the sight of tortillas
browning on a black comal
even the pachucos of española   40
would cry out sharply

xi.
he rode over new mexico
in a pearl low rider
once he got a flat
in that he mistook   45
the shadow of his spare
for a tortilla

xii.
the abuelitas are moving
the tortilla must be baking

xiii.
it was cinco de mayo all year   50
it was warm
and it was going to get warmer
the tortilla sat
on the frijolito plate

WRITING EXERCISE

Try your hand at a parody of Wallace Stevens's "Thirteen Ways of Looking at a Black-bird" (page 941). Take any three or four stanzas from Stevens's poem and change the central image (as Aaron Abeyta did). If you are feeling ambitious, you might even try to parody all thirteen sections.

WRITER'S PERSPECTIVE

Arthur Waley

Arthur Waley on Writing

THE METHOD OF TRANSLATION   1919

It is commonly asserted that poetry, when literally translated, ceases to be poetry. This is often true, and I have for that reason not attempted to translate many poems which in the original have pleased me quite as much as those I have selected. But I present the ones I have chosen in the belief that they still retain the essential characteristics of poetry.

I have aimed at literal translation, not paraphrase. It may be perfectly legitimate for a poet to borrow foreign themes or material, but this should not be called translation.

Above all, considering imagery to be the soul of poetry, I have avoided either adding images of my own or suppressing those of the original.

Any literal translation of Chinese poetry is bound to be to some extent rhythmical, for the rhythm of the original obtrudes itself. Translating literally, without thinking about the meter of the version, one finds that about two lines out of three have a very definite swing similar to that of the Chinese lines. The remaining lines are just too short or too long, a circumstance very irritating to the reader, whose ear expects the rhythm to continue. I have therefore tried to produce regular rhythmic effects similar to those of the original. . . . In a few instances where the English insisted on being shorter than the Chinese, I have preferred to vary the meter of my version, rather than pad out the line with unnecessary verbiage.

I have not used rhyme because it is impossible to produce in English rhyme-effects at all similar to those of the original, where the same rhyme sometimes runs through a whole poem. Also, because the restrictions of rhyme necessarily injure either the vigor of one's language or the literalness of one's version. I do not, at any rate, know of any example to the contrary. What is generally known as "blank verse" is the worst medium for translating Chinese poetry, because the essence of blank verse is that it varies the position of its pauses, whereas in Chinese the stop always comes at the end of the couplet.

From A Hundred and Seventy Chinese Poems

◄━━►WRITING CRITICALLY◄━━►

Parody Is the Sincerest Form of Flattery

When Elizabeth Bishop taught at Harvard, a surprising question appeared on her take-home final exam. She asked students to write parodies of the three poets they had studied during the semester. This assignment was not for a creative writing class, but in her literature course on modern poetry. Bishop believed that in order to write a good parody one had to understand the original poem deeply. W. H. Auden went even further in declaring the value of parody. In designing his ideal college for aspiring poets, he declared that writing parodies would be the only authorized critical exercise in the curriculum.

Before writing a parody, select two or three poems by an author that seem characteristic of his or her style and concerns. Type out or photocopy the poems and then underline phrases or lines that represent the poet's particular sound. You might also make a short list of typical images, words, or even punctuation that the poet frequently uses. Now select one poem and start to imagine it in a different time or setting (as in Gene Fehler's "If Richard Lovelace Became a Free Agent"). Or conceive of the same ideas spoken by an altogether different person (as in Aaron Abeyta's "thirteen ways of looking at a tortilla"). Create a transposition that strikes you as potentially funny but still illuminates some aspect of the original. Try to keep your parody as close to the original poem as possible in terms of length, form, and syntax. You will be surprised by how much strength of expression you'll gain from the poet's line and sentence structure. Finally, have fun. If you don't enjoy your new poem, neither will a reader.

WRITING ASSIGNMENT

Write a parody of any poem in the book. (Remember, it will probably be funnier to your fellow students if it is one you have all studied.) Do your parody in either prose or verse, and make it follow the structure of the original as closely as possible. If you choose to write in verse, stick to the line structure of the original. It may be helpful to choose a model that isn't too difficult to copy (to parody a sonnet would require at least some command of rime and meter). Bring your parody to class and read it aloud.

Further Suggestions for Writing

1. Write your own version of Horace's "Carpe Diem" ode. Follow the original line by line but reset the poem in your home town (not ancient Tuscany) and address it to your best friend (not long-dead Leuconoe). Advise your friend in your new images to "seize the day."

2. Write a serious poem in the manner of Emily Dickinson, William Carlos Williams, E. E. Cummings, or any other modern poet whose work interests you and which you feel able to imitate. Try to make it good enough to slip into the poet's *Collected Poems* without anyone being the wiser. Read all the poet's poems in this book, or you can consult a larger selection or collection of the poet's work. Though it may be simplest to choose a particular poem as your model, you may echo any number of poems, if you like. It is probably a good idea to pick a subject or theme characteristic of the poet. This is a difficult project, but if you can do it even fairly well, you will know a great deal more about poetry and your poet.

27 Critical Casebook: Latin American Poetry

Most Americans experience poetry in only one language—English. Because English is a world language, with its native speakers spread across every continent, it is easy for us to underestimate the significance of poetry written in other tongues. Why is it important to experience poetry in a different language or translation? It matters because such poetry represents and illuminates a different cultural experience. Exposure to different cultures enriches our perspectives and challenges assumptions; it also helps us to understand our own culture better.

Latin American poetry is particularly relevant to the English speaker in the United States or Canada because of the long interconnected history of the Americas. Spanish is also an important world language—spoken by over 350 million people and the primary language in over twenty countries. The vast spread of Spanish has created an enormous and prominent body of literature, an international tradition in which Latin America has gradually replaced Spain as the center. Poetry occupies a very significant place in Latin American culture—a more public place than in the United States. Poetry even plays an important part of the popular culture in Latin America where the average person is able to name his or her favorite poets and can often recite some of their works from memory.

The tradition of Latin American poetry is long and rich. Many poets and scholars consider Sor Juana, a Catholic nun who lived in Mexico during the seventeenth century, to be the mother of Latin American poetry. Mexico's Nobel Laureate poet, Octavio Paz, acknowledges this lineage in his critical work on Sor Juana, *Traps of Faith* (1988), a quintessential book about her life and work. Sor Juana's writing was groundbreaking, not just in the context of Latin American poetry, but truly in the context of world literature, as she was the first writer in Latin America (and one of very few in her era) to address the rights of women to study and write. Her poems are also harbingers of important tendencies in Latin American poetry because of their heightened lyricism.

This lyrical quality finds new form and vitality in the works of the most widely known poets of Latin America—including César Vallejo, Pablo Neruda, Jorge Luis Borges, and Octavio Paz. Each of these poets addresses questions of cultural and personal identity in his work. Events of the twentieth century had great impact on both the subject matter and style of Latin American poets. The Spanish Civil War (1936–1939) sent many poets who had been living in Europe back to the Americas, conscious of the political and social values being tried and tested in Europe at the time.

Latin American women poets have carried on themes introduced by Sor Juana centuries earlier, often linking gender discrimination to other injustices. There is an acknowledged *"peso ancestral"* ("ancestral burden"), to quote Argentinian poet Alfonsina Storni, with which one must struggle. Storni's various struggles with such burdens throughout her life are a focus of her poetry. She filled her later poems with images of the sea and of release, and ended her life in 1938 by tragically walking into the sea. Storni's work is also characteristic of broader themes in Latin American poetry in that it takes on large social issues of the modern era, but does so through a unique and personal perspective.

Latin American poetry, particularly in the twentieth century, is marked by a recognition of the region as a unique blending of different cultures, European and indigenous, among others. It is also marked by a variety of artistic and political movements, of which surrealism is perhaps the most influential. The works of artists such as Mexican painter Frida Kahlo coincided with a body of new writing that emphasized a blurring of fantasy and reality. Some writers, such as Vallejo and Olga Orozco, became most well-known for their surrealist writing, while other poets, such as Neruda and Paz, incorporated some of the elements of the movement into their styles.

A number of Latin American poets were awarded the Nobel Prize in literature in the latter part of the twentieth century, including Paz, Neruda, and Gabriela Mistral. (Borges, to the astonishment of many critics, never won the award, though he captured nearly every other major international literary honor.) The importance of Spanish as a global language and in literature is reflected in the recognition of the stature of Latin American writers in the world. Even when decidedly political, Latin American poetry is known for its focus on the personal experience. One does not love one's country as a symbol, José Emilio Pacheco claims; rather one loves its people, its mountains, and three or four of its rivers.

SOR JUANA

FILL...

Portrait of Sister Juana Inés de la Cruz
*by unknown Mexican artist, eighteenth
century*

Sor Juana Inés de la Cruz is said to have been born in Nepantla, Mexico, somewhere
between 1648 and 1651. Very little is known about "Sister" Juana's life, since church
records were destroyed during the Mexican Revolution. Passages from her famous
Reply to Sor Philothea *allow a glimpse into her early life, such as her desire, at the age
of six or seven, to wear boy's clothing and to study at the University in Mexico City.
She also talks about cutting off her own hair in self-punishment for not having learned
something she had set for herself as a task, saying "there was no cause for a head to be
adorned with hair and naked of learning."*

In 1667 Sor Juana entered the convent of the "barefoot Carmelites," so-named
because of the austere way of life they adopted, going either barefoot or wearing rope
sandals. In 1669 she moved to the convent of San Jerónimo, where she studied and
wrote until 1691. In her Reply, *she states that she chose the convent because it offered
her more possibilities for engaging in her intellectual pursuits, which the restrictions of
marriage at that time would not allow. The baroque period during which Sor Juana
wrote required tight form and rime schemes. Though some of Sor Juana's poetry was
commissioned, there are many poems in which we can see the poet's true spirit, especially in her love poems, which often transcend time in their intensity. In 1691 Sor
Juana wrote the* Reply, *the first document in the Americas to argue for a woman's right
to study and to write. The Church responded by demanding she give up her books and
her instruments of writing. She renewed her vows to the Church, signing documents in
her own blood. Sor Juana died during a devastating plague in 1695, after having given
aid to a great number of the ill. Her famous* Reply *was first published, posthumously,
in 1700.*

Asegura la Confianza de que Ocultará de todo un Secreto 1689

El paje os dirá, discreto,
como, luego que leí,
vuestro secreto rompí
por no romper el secreto.
Y aun hice más, os prometo:
los fragmentos, sin desdén,
del papel, tragué también;
que secretos que venero.
Aun en pedazos no quiero
que fuera del pecho estén.

She Promises to Hold a Secret in Confidence
2004

This page, discreetly, will convey
how, on the moment that I read it,
I tore apart your secret
not to let it be torn away
from me—and I will further say   5
what firm insurance followed:
those paper fragments, I also swallowed.
This secret, so dearly read—
I wouldn't want one shred
out of my chest, to be hollowed.   10

—*Translated by Diane Thiel*

Presente en que el Cariño Hace Regalo la Llaneza   1689

Lysi: a tus manos divinas
doy castañas espinosas,
porque donde sobran rosas
no pueden faltar espinas.
Si a su aspereza te inclinas
y con eso el gusto engañas,
perdona las malas mañas
de quien tal regalo te hizo;
perdona, pues que un erizo
sólo puede dar castañas.

A Simple Gift Made Rich by Affection
2004

Lysi, I give to your divine hand
these chestnuts in their thorny guise
because where velvet roses rise,
thorns also grow unchecked, unplanned.
If you're inclined toward their barbed brand   5
and with this choice, betray your taste,
forgive the ill-bred lack of taste
of one who sends you such a missive—
Forgive me, only this husk can give
the chestnut, in its thorns embraced.   10

—*Translated by Diane Thiel*

Questions

1. What literally is being described in "She Promises to Hold a Secret in Confidence"? Provide a paraphrase.
2. What interesting wordplay do you notice in each of these poems? Consider, for example, the use of "tore" and "be torn" in the first poem. Are there any other significant repetitions?
3. What stylistic and thematic similarities do you notice between these two poems?
4. How does the chestnut work as a metaphor in the second poem? What does the thorny husk seem to represent? What does the chestnut represent?
5. Read the excerpt from *Reply* and "Endgames" at the end of the chapter. How do these prose pieces change your reading of the poems?

PABLO NERUDA

Pablo Neruda

Pablo Neruda (1904–1973) was born Neftali Ricardo Reyes Basoalto in Parral, southern Chile. His mother died a month later, a fact which is said to have affected Neruda's choice of imagery throughout his life's work. He began writing poems as a child despite his family's disapproval; this disapproval led him, as a young man, to adopt the "working class" pen name Pablo Neruda. He published his first book, Crepusculario *(Twilight), in 1923 and soon followed with his* Veinte Poemas de Amor y una Canción Desperada *(Twenty Love Poems and a Song of Despair). The book received vast attention, and Neruda decided to devote himself to writing poetry.*

In 1927 Neruda served as a diplomat in Burma, his first in a long line of such diplomatic positions. He lived several years in Spain and chronicled the Spanish Civil War. Neruda journeyed home to Chile in 1938, then served as consul to Mexico, and returned again to Chile in 1943. When the Chilean government moved to the right, Neruda, who was a communist, went into hiding. During this time, he wrote his famous long sequence Canto General, *which includes his "Alturas de Macchu Picchu" ("Heights of Macchu Picchu"), often considered the single most important modern Latin American poem.*

In 1952, when the Chilean government ceased its persecution of leftist writers, Neruda returned to his native land and married his third wife, Matilde Urrutia. (His first two marriages had ended in divorce.) Neruda's later love poems were addressed to Matilde, including his Cien Sonetos de Amor *(One Hundred Love Sonnets). These later poems bring his work full circle, returning to the themes and image-rich quality of his early* Veinte Poemas de Amor. *In 1970 Neruda was a candidate for the presidency of Chile, but withdrew to support the Socialist candidate, Salvador Allende. In 1973, just twelve days after the fall of Chile's democratic government, Neruda died of cancer in Santiago, Chile.*

De tantos hombres que soy,
   que somos,
no puedo encontrar a ninguno:
se me pierden bajo la ropa,
se fueron a otra ciudad.

Cuando todo está preparado
para mostrarme inteligente
el tonto que llevo escondido
se toma la palabra en mi boca.

Otras veces me duermo en medio
de la sociedad distinguida
y cuando busco en mí al valiente,
un cobarde que no conozco
corre a tomar con mi esqueleto
mil deliciosas precauciones.

Cuando arde una casa estimada
en vez del bombero que llamo
se precipita el incendiario
y ése soy yo. No tengo arreglo.
Qué debo hacer para escogerme?
Cómo puedo rehabilitarme?

Todos los libros que leo
celebran héroes refulgentes
siempre seguros de sí mismos:
me muero de envidia por ellos,
y en los films de vientos y balas
me quedo envidiando al jinete,
me quedo admirando al caballo.

Pero cuando pido al intrépido
me sale el viejo perezoso,
y así yo no sé quién soy,
no sé cuántos soy o seremos.
Me gustaría tocar un timbre
y sacar el mí verdadero
porque si yo me necesito
no debo desaparecerme.

Of the many men who I am, who
   we are,
I can't find a single one;
they disappear among my clothes,
they've left for another city.

When everything seems to be set   5
to show me off as intelligent,
the fool I always keep hidden
takes over all that I say.

At other times, I'm asleep
among distinguished people,   10
and when I look for my brave self,
a coward unknown to me
rushes to cover my skeleton
with a thousand fine excuses.

   15
When a decent house catches fire,
instead of the fireman I summon,
an arsonist bursts on the scene,
and that's me. What can I do?
What can I do to distinguish myself?
How can I pull myself together?   20

All the books I read
are full of dazzling heroes,
always sure of themselves.
I die with envy of them;
and in films full of wind and bullets,   25
I goggle at the cowboys,
I even admire the horses.

But when I call for a hero,
out comes my lazy old self;
so I never know who I am,   30
nor how many I am or will be.
I'd love to be able to touch a bell
and summon the real me,
because if I really need myself,
I mustn't disappear.   35

Mientras escribo estoy ausente
y cuando vuelvo ya he partido:
voy a ver si a las otras gentes
les pasa lo que a mí me pasa,
si son tantos como soy yo,
si se parecen a sí mismos
y cuando lo haya averiguado
voy a aprender tan bien las cosas
que para explicar mis problemas
les hablaré de geografía.

While I am writing, I'm far away;
and when I come back, I've gone.
I would like to know if others
go through the same things that I do,
have as many selves as I have,   40
and see themselves similarly;
and when I've exhausted this problem,
I'm going to study so hard
that when I explain myself,
I'll be talking geography.   45

—Translated by Alastair Reid*

QUESTIONS

1. In line 26, Reid translates Neruda's phrase "me quedo envidiando al jinete" as "I goggle at the cowboys." What does Reid gain or lose with that version? (In Spanish, *jinete* means *horseman* or *rider* but not specifically *cowboy*, which is *vaquero* or even— thanks to Hollywood— *cowboy*.) Neruda once told Reid, "Alastair, don't just translate my poems. I want you to improve them." Is this line an improvement?
2. How many men are in the speaker of the poem? What seems to be their relationship to one another?

CIEN SONETOS DE AMOR (V)   1959

No te toque la noche ni el aire ni la aurora,
sólo la tierra, la virtud de los racimos,
las manzanas que crecen oyendo el agua pura,
el barro y las resinas de tu país fragante.

Desde Quinchamalí donde hicieron tus ojos   5
hasta tus pies creados para mí en la Frontera
eres la greda oscura que conozco:
en tus caderas toco de nuevo todo el trigo.

Tal vez tú no sabías, aracuana,
que cuando antes de amarte me olvidé de tus besos   10
mi corazón quedó recordando tu boca

y fui como un herido por las calles
hasta que comprendí que había encontrado,
amor, mi territorio de besos y volcanes.

I did not touch your night, or your air, or dawn:
only the earth, the truth of the fruit in clusters,
the apples that swell as they drink the sweet water,
the clay and the resins of your sweet-smelling land.

From Quinchamalí where your eyes began,   5
to the Frontera where your feet were made for me,
you are my dark familiar clay: touching your hips,
I touch the wheat in its fields again.

Woman from Arauco, maybe you didn't know
how before I loved you I forgot your kisses.   10
But my heart went on, remembering your mouth—and I went on

and on through the streets like a man wounded,
until I understood, Love: I had found
my place, a land of kisses and volcanoes.

—Translated by Stephen Tapscott

One Hundred Love Sonnets.   5 *Quinchamalí*: small mountain town south of Santiago, Chile.
6 *Frontera*: frontier, border.   9 *Aruaco*: port city south of Santiago.

Questions

1. In Neruda's love sonnet, what extended metaphor does the speaker use to describe
   his love?
2. How does the direct address affect the immediacy of the poem? Does the "you" keep
   the reader out, or draw the reader in?

JORGE LUIS BORGES

Jorge Luis Borges

Jorge Luis Borges (1899–1986), a blind librarian who became one of the most influential writers ever to emerge from Latin America, was born in Buenos Aires. Borges's Protestant father and Catholic mother reflected Argentina's diverse background; their ancestry included Spanish, English, Italian, Portugese, and Indian blood. Borges's British grandmother lived with them, so "Georgie" and his younger sister were raised speaking both English and Spanish. Borges was taught at home by a British governess, until he went to school at the age of nine. The author later commented, "If I were asked to name the chief event in my life, I should say my father's library."

Caught in Europe by the outbreak of World War I, Borges lived in Switzerland and later Spain, where he joined the Ultraists, a group of experimental poets who renounced realism. Borges believed strongly in the power of the image and symbol, as opposed to the ornate, musical quality of fellow poets such as Ruben Darío. On returning to Argentina in 1921, he edited a poetry magazine printed in the form of a poster and affixed to city walls. In 1937, to help support his mother and dying father, the thirty-seven-year-old Borges (who still lived at home) got his first job as an assistant librarian. He had already published seven books of poetry and criticism, and had just begun writing short stories. Over the next fifteen years he published many of the stories that would earn him international acclaim.

During this decisive period, Borges encountered political trouble. For his opposition to the regime of Colonel Juan Perón, in 1946 Borges was forced to resign his post as a librarian and was mockingly offered a job as a chicken inspector. He refused the position and supported his mother and himself on his meager literary earnings. In 1955, after Perón was deposed, Borges became director of the National Library and a professor of English literature at the University of Buenos Aires. Suffering from poor eyesight since childhood, Borges eventually went blind. His eye problems may have encouraged him to work mainly in short, highly crafted forms in both prose and verse—brief stories, essays, and fables, as well as lyric poems full of elaborate music. In international terms, Borges is probably the most influential short story writer of the last half-century. Borges, however, considered himself first and foremost a poet.

Ni la intimidad de tu frente clara como una fiesta
ni la costumbre de tu cuerpo, aún misterioso y tácito y de niña,
ni la sucesión de tu vida asumiendo palabras o silencios
serán favor tan misterioso
como mirar tu sueño implicado   5
en la vigilia de mis brazos.
Virgen milagrosamente otra vez por la virtud absolutoria del sueño,
quieta y resplandeciente como una dicha que la memoria elige,
me darás esa orilla de tu vida que tú misma no tienes.
Arrojado a quietud,   10
divisaré esa playa última de tu ser
y te veré por vez primera, quizá,
como Dios ha de verte,
desbaratada la ficción del Tiempo,
sin el amor, sin mí.   15

ANTICIPATION OF LOVE   1972

Neither the intimacy of your look, your brow fair as a feast day,
not the favor of your body, still mysterious, reserved, and childlike,
nor what comes to me of your life, settling in words or silence,
will be so mysterious a gift
as the sight of your sleep, enfolded   5
in the vigil of my arms.
Virgin again, miraculously, by the absolving power of sleep,
quiet and luminous like some happy thing recovered by memory,
you will give me that shore of your life that you yourself do not own.
Cast up into silence   10
I shall discern that ultimate beach of your being
and see you for the first time, perhaps,
as God must see you—
the fiction of Time destroyed,
free from love, from me.   15

—*Translated by Robert Fitzgerald*

QUESTIONS

1. In "Anticipation of Love," note the translator's choice in line 4 to translate the
   Spanish "*favor*" (which translates more directly to "favor") to "gift." What do you
   think such a choice adds to the poem in English?
2. Why is the sleeping woman described as "virgin again"?
3. Does this poem describe a real event or only an imaginary one?

Yo que soy el que ahora está cantando
Seré mañana el misterioso, el muerto,
El morador de un mágico y desierto
Orbe sin antes ni después ni cuando.
Así afirma la mística. Me creo   5
Indigno del Infierno o de la Gloria,
Pero nada predigo. Nuestra historia
Cambia como las formas de Proteo.
¡Qué errante laberinto, qué blancura
Ciega de resplandor será mi suerte,   10
Cuando me entregue el fin de esta aventura
La curiosa experiencia de la muerte?
Quiero beber su cristalino Olvido.
Ser para siempre; pero no haber sido.

The Enigmas   1972

I who am singing these lines today
Will be tomorrow the enigmatic corpse
Who dwells in a realm, magical and barren,
Without a before or an after or a when.
So say the mystics. I say I believe   5
Myself undeserving of Heaven or of Hell,
But make no predictions. Each man's tale
Shifts like the watery forms of Proteus.
What errant labyrinth, what blinding flash
Of splendor and glory shall become my fate   10
When the end of this adventure presents me with
The curious experience of death?
I want to drink its crystal-pure oblivion,
To be forever; but never to have been.

*—Translated by John Updike**

THE ENIGMAS.   8 *Proteus*: Minor Greek god who had the ability to change form.

Questions

1. What is the speaker's most pressing question about his own future?
2. What is the main enigma or puzzle presented in "The Enigmas"?
3. What is the form of this poem?

OCTAVIO PAZ

Octavio Paz

Octavio Paz (1914–1998), the only Mexican author to win the Nobel Prize in literature, was born in Mexico City. Paz once commented that he came from "a typical Mexican family" because it combined European and Indian ancestors, but his background was quite distinguished. His father was a lawyer who had fought for the Mexican Revolution and served as secretary to guerilla leader, Emiliano Zapata. Paz's father retired and eventually went into exile in the United States after Zapata's 1919 assassination. "Impoverished by the revolution and civil war" his family lived in his grandfather's huge house in Mixoac, a suburb of Mexico City. "The house," he told an interviewer, "gradually crumbled around us," and the family abandoned rooms one by one as the roof collapsed. His grandfather had a library containing over six thousand books ("an enchanted cave," Paz later called it) where the young author immersed himself. Joining his father in exile, the young Paz lived for two years in Los Angeles. He then entered the National University of Mexico, but left in 1937 because he wanted to be a poet rather than a lawyer. Paz went to Spain to fight in the Spanish Civil War in 1937, but the Loyalist army refused to accept him because he didn't belong to the Communist Party (or any other political party). Paz refused to limit his political opinions to those of the two forces—military dictatorship or Marxist revolution— but worked toward democracy, "the mystery of freedom" as he called it in an early poem.

In 1945 Paz became a diplomat, spending years in San Francisco, New York, Geneva, and Delhi. In 1968 he resigned his post as ambassador to India in protest of the Mexican government's massacre of student demonstrators shortly before the Mexico City Olympic games. Paz then taught abroad at Cambridge University, the University of Texas, Harvard University, and other schools, but he always returned to Mexico City.

Paz's study of Mexican culture and national character, The Labyrinth of Solitude (1950), is a Latin American classic. Although deeply rooted in Mexican history and myth, the multilingual Paz was a true cosmopolitan. His study of the poetic process, The Bow and the Lyre (1956), ranged across world literature from Homer and Virgil to Whitman and Neruda. His Nobel Prize acceptance speech, published as "In Search of the Present" (1990), is a brilliant exploration of the cultural and imaginative relationship between the Old and New Worlds.

CON LOS OJOS		WITH OUR EYES SHUT
CERRADOS	1968	

Con los ojos cerrados	With your eyes shut
Te iluminas por dentro	You light up from within
Ertes la piedra ciega	You are blind stone
Noche a noche te labro	Night by night I carve you
Con los ojos cerrados	With my eyes shut 5
Eres la piedra franca	You are clear stone
Nos volvemos inmensos	We become immense
Sólo por conocernos	Just knowing each other
Con los ojos cerrados	With our eyes shut
	—*Translated by John Felstiner*

QUESTIONS

How do the refrains contribute to the musical quality of "With Our Eyes Shut"? What effects do the slight changes in phrasing this refrain create?

CERTEZA	1961	CERTAINTY	1968

Si es real la luz blanca	If it is real the white
de esta lámpara, real	light from this lamp, real
la mano que escribe, ¿son reales	the writing hand, are they
los ojos que miran lo escrito?	real, the eyes looking at what I write?
De una palabra a la otra	From one word to the other 5
lo que digo se desvanece.	what I say vanishes.
Yo sé que estoy vivo	I know that I am alive
entre dos paréntesis.	between two parentheses.
	—*Translated by Charles Tomlinson*

QUESTIONS

In what ways is "Certainty" an *ars poetica* (poem about writing poetry)? What does the poem say about communication?

SURREALISM IN LATIN AMERICAN POETRY

Surrealism was one of the great artistic revolutions of the twentieth century. It first arose in the mockingly named "Dada" movement during World War I. (*Dada* is the French children's word for "hobbyhorse.") Dadaism was a radical rejection of the insanity perpetrated by the self-proclaimed "rational" world of the turbulent modern era. The approach was an attempt to shock the world out of its terrible self-destructive traditions. "The only way for Dada to continue," proclaimed poet André Breton, "is for it to cease to exist." Sure enough, the movement soon fell apart through its own excesses of energy and irreverence. In 1922 surrealism emerged as the successor to Dada, first as a literary movement, soon to spread to the visual arts, promoting the creation of fantastic, dreamlike works that reflected the unconscious mind. Fusing fact and myths, the movement sought to free art from the bounds of rationality. Not every modern writer embraced surrealism. Wallace Stevens referred mockingly to surrealism's dreamlike mixing of images as the act of making a "clam play an accordion."

Surrealism emphasized spontaneity rather than craft as the essential element in literary creation. Not all surrealist art, however, was spontaneous. Bretón, for instance, spent six months on a poem of thirty words, in order to achieve what looked like spontaneity. And many surrealist visual artists would do several versions of the same "automatic drawing" in pursuit of the effect of immediacy. Breton's famous "Manifesto of Surrealism" (1924) launched a movement that continues to influence a great number of writers and artists around the world.

The early surrealists showed as much genius for absurd humor as for art, and their works often tried to shock and amuse. Marcel Duchamp once exhibited a huge printed reproduction of the *Mona Lisa* on which he had painted a large mustache. Louis Aragon's poem "Suicide?" consisted only of the letters of the alphabet, and Bretón once published a poem made up of names and numbers copied from the telephone directory. Is it any wonder that the surrealist motto was, "The approval of the public must be shunned at all cost"?

Surrealism's greatest international literary influence was on Latin American poetry. In the early twentieth century Latin America was much influenced by French culture, and literary innovations in Paris were quickly imported to Mexico City, Buenos Aires, and other New World capitals. In Latin America, however, surrealism lost much of the playfulness it exhibited in Europe, and the movement often took on a darker and more explicitly political quality. Surrealism also had a powerful effect on Latin American art. A tradition of surrealist painting emerged parallel to the movement in literature. One of the best known surrealist painters is the Mexican artist Frida Kahlo, whose work often created dreamlike visions of the human body, especially her own. In the *Two Fridas*, for example, she presents a frightening image of the body's interior exposed and mirrored. Kahlo's paintings are simultaneously personal and political—surrealistically portraying her own trauma, as well as the schism in her native country.

Many Latin American poets had periods that were strongly influenced by surrealism. César Vallejo, for instance, best known for the surrealist vanguardism of his second book, moved toward a more lyrical, inclusive style in his later work. Olga Orozco, as a translator of Breton, Paul Éluard, and other French surrealists, was strongly influenced by Parisian avant-garde poetry. Her work has a mysterious, dreamlike quality, as in the juxtapositions of "Reality and Desire." The repressiveness of Argentinian politics from the 1950s to the 1980s might have had an effect on her style as well, much in the way Dadaism emerged in Europe earlier in the century, as a response to violence. According to Octavio Paz, many poets, such as himself and Pablo Neruda, adopted surrealist processes, and their creative developments often coincided with the movement, although their work is not usually considered "surrealist."

Frida Kahlo   (1907–1957)

THE TWO FRIDAS   1939

The Two Fridas *by Frida Kahlo, c. 1939*

César Vallejo   (1892?–1938)

LA CÓLERA QUE QUIEBRA   (1937) 1939
AL HOMBRE EN NIÑOS

La cólera que quiebra al hombre en niños,
que quiebra al niño, en pájaros iguales,
y al pájaro, después, en huevecillos;
la cólera del pobre
tiene un aceite contra dos vinagres.   5

La cólera que el árbol quiebra en hojas,
a la hoja en botones desiguales
y al botón, en ranuras telescópicas;
la cólera del pobre
tiene dos ríos contra muchos mares.   10

La cólera que quiebra al bien en dudas,
a la duda, en tres arcos semejantes
y al arco, luego, en tumbas imprevistas;

la cólera del pobre
tiene un acero contra dos puñales.   15

   La cólera que quiebra el alma en cuerpos,
al cuerpo en órganos desemejantes
y al órgano, en octavos pensamientos;
la cólera del pobre
tiene un fuego central contra dos cráteres.   20

ANGER   1977

Anger which breaks a man into children,
Which breaks the child into two equal birds,
And after that the bird into a pair of little eggs:
The poor man's anger
Has one oil against two vinegars.   5

Anger which breaks a tree into leaves
And the leaf into unequal buds
And the bud into telescopic grooves;
The poor man's anger
Has two rivers against many seas.   10

Anger which breaks good into doubts
And doubt into three similar arcs
And then the arc into unexpected tombs;
The poor man's anger
Has one steel against two daggers.   15

Anger which breaks the soul into bodies
And the body into dissimilar organs
And the organ into octave thoughts;
The poor man's anger
Has one central fire against two craters.   20

—Translated by Thomas Merton

Olga Orozco (b. 1920)

LA REALIDAD Y EL DESEO   1979

   A Luis Cernada

La realidad, sí, la realidad,
ese relámpago de lo invisible
que revela en nosotros la soledad de Dios.

Es este cielo que huye.
Es este territorio engalanado por las burbujas de la muerte.   5

Es esta larga mesa a la deriva
donde los comensales persisten ataviados por el prestigio de no estar.

A cada cual su copa
para medir el vino que se acaba donde empieza la sed.
Y cada cual su plato   10
para encerrar el hambre que se extingue sin saciarse jamás.
Y cada dos la división del pan:
el milagro al revés, la comunión tan sólo en lo imposible.
Y en medio del amor,
entre uno y otro cuerpo la caída,   15
algo que se asemeja al latido sombrío de unas alas que vuelven desde la
        eternidad,
al pulso del adiós debajo de la tierra.

La realidad, sí, la realidad:
un sello de clausura sobre todas las puertas del deseo.

REALITY AND DESIRE   1993

For Luis Cernada

Reality, yes, reality,
is the lightning-bolt of the invisible
that reveals in us the solitude of God.

This is the sky that escapes.
This is the territory adorned with the bubbles of death.   5
This is the big floating table
where the dinner-guests stay seated, wearing the prestige of
        not-being-there.

Each one has his goblet
to weigh the wine that ends where thirst begins.
Each one has his plate   10
that holds the hunger that ends but is never satisfied.
And for each pair their share of bread:
the miracle in reverse, solitary communion with the impossible.
And in the middle of love,
between one body and another, the fall,   15
something that seems like the shadowy throb of wings flying toward
        eternity,
to a pulse of farewell in the earth.

Reality, yes, reality:
the seal of cloister on all the gates of desire.

                                —Translated by Stephen Tapscott

POEMS FOR FURTHER READING

Alfonsina Storni   (1892–1938)

PESO ANCESTRAL   1919

Tú me dijiste: no lloró mi padre;
tú me dijiste: no lloró mi abuelo;
no han llorado los hombres de mi raza,
eran de acero.

Así diciendo te brotó una lágrima   5
y me cayó en la boca . . . más veneno
yo no he bebido nunca en otro vaso
así pequeño.

Débil mujer, pobre mujer que entiende,
dolor de siglos conocí al beberlo: 10
oh, el alma mía soportar no puede
todo su peso.

ANCESTRAL BURDEN   2004

You told me my father never cried
You told me my grandfather never cried.
The men of my lineage never cried
They were steel inside.

As you were saying this, you dropped a tear   5
that fell into my mouth—such poison
I have never drunk from any other cup
than this small one.

Weak woman, poor woman who understands
the ache of centuries I knew as I swallowed.   10
Oh, my spirit cannot carry all of its load.

—*Translated by Diane Thiel*

José Emilio Pacheco   (b. 1939)

ALTA TRAICIÓN   1969

No amo mi Patria. Su fulgor abstracto
es inasible.
Pero (aunque suene mal) daría la vida
por diez lugares suyos, cierta gente.
Puertos, bosques de piños, fortalezas,   5
una ciudad deshecha, gris, monstruosa,

varias figuras de su historia,
montañas
(y tres o cuatro ríos)

HIGH TREASON

1978

I do not love my country. Its abstract lustre
is beyond my grasp.
But (although it sounds bad) I would give my life
for ten places in it, for certain people,
seaports, pinewoods, fortresses,
a run-down city, gray, grotesque,
various figures from its history,
mountains
(And three or four rivers).

—*Translated by Alastair Reid**

QUESTIONS

1. What surreal effects do you find in Vallejo's and Orozco's poems? In other included poems? How is the Kahlo painting a quintessential example of surrealism?
2. How does the rhythm of Storni's poem (with its three longer lines and one shorter) contribute to the lyrical quality of the poem?

~ LATIN AMERICAN POETS ON POETRY ~

Sor Juana

REPLY TO SOR PHILOTHEA

(1691) 1700

TRANSLATED BY ALAN TRUEBLOOD

This was successful in one instance involving a very holy and very ingenuous prelate who thought studying was something for the Inquisition and ordered me to cease. I obeyed her (for the three months her right to so order me lasted) as regarded not taking a book in hand, but as to ceasing study altogether, it not being in my power, I could not carry it out. For, although I did not study from books, I did from everything God has created, all of it being my letters, and all this universal chain of being my book. I saw nothing without reflecting on it; I heard nothing without wondering at it—not even the tiniest, most material thing. For, as there is no created thing, no matter how lowly, in which one cannot recognize *me fecit Deus* [God made me], there is none that does not confound the mind once it stops to consider it. Thus, I repeat, I looked and marveled at all of them, so much so that simply from the person with whom I spoke, and from what that person said to me, countless reflections arose in my mind. What could be the origin of so great a variety of characters and minds, when all belonged to one species? Which humors and hidden qualities could bring this about? If I saw a figure, I at once fell to working out the relationship of its lines, measuring it with my mind and recasting it along different ones. Sometimes I would walk back and forth across the front of a sleeping-room of ours—a very large one—and observe how, though the lines of its two sides were parallel and its ceiling horizontal, one's vision made it appear as if the lines inclined toward each other and the ceiling were lower at the far end, from which I inferred that visual lines run straight but not parallel, tending rather toward a pyramidal figure. And I asked myself whether this could be the reason the ancients questioned whether the world was spherical or not. Because, although it appears to be, this could be an optical illusion, and show concavities where there might in fact be none.

This type of observation would occur to me about everything and still does, without my having any say in the matter; indeed, it continually irritates me because it tires my mind. I thought the same thing occurred in everyone's case, and with writing verse as well, until experience proved me wrong. This turn, or habit, of mind is so strong that I can look upon nothing without reflecting on it.

From *A Sor Juana Anthology*

Pablo Neruda

TOWARDS THE SPLENDID CITY   1971

I did not learn from books any recipe for writing a poem, and I, in my turn, will avoid giving any advice on mode or style which might give the new poets even a drop of supposed insight. When I am recounting in this speech something about past events, when reliving on this occasion a never-forgotten occurrence, in this place which is so different from what that was, it is because in the course of my life I have always found somewhere the necessary support, the formula which had been waiting for me not in order to be petrified in my words but in order to explain me to myself.

During this long journey I found the necessary components for the making of the poem. There I received contributions from the earth and from the soul. And I believe that poetry is an action, ephemeral or solemn, in which there enter as equal partners solitude and solidarity, emotion and action, the nearness to oneself, the nearness to mankind and to the secret manifestations of nature. And no less strongly I think that all this is sustained—man and his shadow, man and his conduct, man and his poetry—by an ever-wider sense of community, by an effort which will forever bring together the reality and the dreams in us because it is precisely in this way that poetry unites and mingles them. And therefore I say that I do not know, after so many years, whether the lessons I learned when I crossed a daunting river, when I danced around the skull of an ox, when I bathed my body in the cleansing water from the topmost heights—I do not know whether these lessons welled forth from me in order to be imparted to many others or whether it was all a message which was sent to me by others as a demand or an accusation. I do not know whether I experienced this or created it, I do not know whether it was truth or poetry, something passing or permanent, the poems I experienced in this hour, the experiences which I later put into verse.

From all this, my friends, there arises an insight which the poet must learn through other people. There is no insurmountable solitude. All paths lead to the same goal: to convey to others what we are. And we must pass through solitude and difficulty, isolation and silence in order to reach forth to the enchanted place where we can dance our clumsy dance and sing our sorrowful song—but in this dance or in this song there are fulfilled the most ancient rites of our conscience in the awareness of being human and of believing in a common destiny.

From Neruda's Nobel Prize lecture

Jorge Luis Borges

THE RIDDLE OF POETRY   1967

At the outset, I would like to give you fair warning of what to expect—or rather, of what not to expect—from me. I find that I have made a slip in the very title of my first lecture. The title is, if we are not mistaken, "The Riddle of Poetry," and the stress of course is on the first word, "riddle." So you may think the riddle is all-important. Or, what might be still worse, you may think I have deluded myself into believing that I have somehow discovered the true reading of the riddle. The truth is that I have no revelations to offer. I have spent my life reading, analyzing, writing (or trying my hand at writing), and enjoying. I found the last to be the most important thing of all. "Drinking in" poetry, I have come to a final conclusion about it. Indeed, every time I am faced with a blank page, I feel that I have to rediscover literature for myself. But the past is of no avail whatever to me. So, as I have said, I have only my perplexities to offer you. I am nearing seventy. I have given the major part of my life to literature, and I can offer you only doubts. . . .

For example, if I have to define poetry, and if I feel rather shaky about it, if I'm not too sure about it, I say something like: "Poetry is the expression of the beautiful through the medium of words artfully woven together." This definition may be good enough for a dictionary or a textbook, but we all feel that it is rather feeble. There is something far more important—something that may encourage us to go on not only trying our hand at writing poetry, but enjoying it and feeling that we know all about it.

This is that we *know* what poetry is. We know it so well that we cannot define it in other words, even as we cannot define the taste of coffee, the color red or yellow, or the meaning of anger, of love, of hatred, of the sunrise, of the sunset, or of our love for our country. These things are so deep in us that they can be expressed only by those common symbols that we share. So why should we need other words?

From *This Craft of Verse*

In Search of the Present   1990

Languages are vast realities that transcend those political and historical entities we call nations. The European languages we speak in the Americas illustrate this. The special position of our literatures when compared to those of England, Spain, Portugal and France depends precisely on this fundamental fact: they are literatures written in transplanted tongues. Languages are born and grow from the native soil, nourished by a common history. The European languages were rooted out from their native soil and their own tradition, and then planted in an unknown and unnamed world: they took root in the new lands and, as they grew within the societies of America, they were transformed. They are the same plant yet also a different plant. Our literatures did not passively accept the changing fortunes of the transplanted languages: they participated in the process and even accelerated it. They very soon ceased to be mere transatlantic reflections: at times they have been the negation of the literatures of Europe; more often, they have been a reply.

In spite of these oscillations the link has never been broken. My classics are those of my language and I consider myself to be a descendant of Lope and Quevedo,° as any Spanish writer would . . . yet I am not a Spaniard. I think that most writers of Spanish America, as well as those from the United States, Brazil and Canada, would say the same as regards the English, Portuguese and French traditions. To understand more clearly the special position of writers in the Americas, we should think of the dialogue maintained by Japanese, Chinese or Arabic writers with the different literatures of Europe. It is a dialogue that cuts across multiple languages and civilizations. Our dialogue, on the other hand, takes place within the same language. We are Europeans yet we are not Europeans. What are we then? It is difficult to define what we are, but our works speak for us.

From Paz's Nobel Prize lecture

∾ Critics on Latin American Poetry ∾

Stephanie Merrim   (b. 1951)

Endgames: Sor Juana Inés de la Cruz   1999

Why did Sor Juana write so much love poetry? Not only was it untoward for a nun, but love is a topic and emotion that seems to inspire true repugnance in Sor Juana. Consider the title of the following poems that revile love: "Which describes the catastrophe of the joys and desires of lovers," "Which resolves the question of which is more troublesome in conflicting emotions [*encontradas correspondencias*]:

Lope and Quevedo: Lope de Vega (1562–1635) was a major Spanish dramatist and poet; Francisco Gomez de Quevedo (1580–1645) was a major Spanish novelist and poet. Their literary era is often referred to as the Golden Age.

to love or hate," "On a reasonable reflection which allays the pain of a passion," "Which offers a means to love without much grief." Sor Juana, as the titles suggest, is hardly a woman happy with love, an entranced woman in love. Happy or not, the sheer abundance of Sor Juana's love poetry—nearly fifty poems, about one-fifth of her poetry—has provoked scores of commentators to speculate about her motivation in writing it. Did Sor Juana write her amatory poetry in wake of a lost love? Conversely, was it a mere exercise, yet another of her experiments with a literary tradition, of her literary academy-inspired attempts to try her hand at them all? For to be a lyric poet was to be a love poet; love was poetry and poetry love (Frederick Luciani, *The Courtly Love Tradition in the Poetry of Sor Juana Inés de la Cruz*). Or, as Irving Leonard's influential interpretation would have it, did Sor Juana cipher into some of the love poetry an allegorical meaning, using the conventionalized forms of love poetry covertly to express the struggle between her love for church and for knowledge? Or was Sor Juana burdened less with abstract than with emotional struggles, with a melancholy for which the consecrated and depersonalized topics of courtly love provided an acceptable outlet?

From *Early Modern Women's Writing and Sor Juana Inés de la Cruz*

Alastair Reid (b. 1926)*

Translating Neruda   1996

Translating someone's work, poetry in particular, has something about it akin to being possessed, haunted. Translating a poem means not only reading it deeply and deciphering it, but clambering about backstage among the props and the scaffolding. I found I could no longer read a poem of Neruda's simply as words on a page without hearing behind them that languid, caressing voice. Most important to me in translating these two writers [Neruda and Borges] was the sound of their voices in my memory, for it very much helped in finding the English appropriate to those voices. I found that if I learned poems of Neruda's by heart I could replay them at odd moments, on buses, at wakeful times in the night, until, at a certain point, the translation would somehow set. The voice was the clue: I felt that all Neruda's poems were fundamentally vocative—spoken poems, poems of direct address—and that Neruda's voice was in a sense the instrument for which he wrote. He once made a tape for me, reading pieces of different poems, in different tones and rhythms. I played it over so many times that I can hear it in my head at will. Two lines of his I used to repeat like a Zen koan, for they seemed to apply particularly to translating:

in this net it's not just the strings that count
but also the air that escapes through the meshes.

He often wrote of himself as having many selves, just as he had left behind him several very different poetic manners and voices.

From "Neruda and Borges"

Emir Rodríguez Monegal   (1921–1985)

BORGES AND PAZ   1973

There are few more tantalizing names in contemporary culture than Jorge Luis
Borges and Octavio Paz. Both men have for a number of years transcended the
somewhat parochial limits of their respective regions and have directed their
work toward America (Latin or non-Latin) and Europe. To mention Paz or
Borges in an international context today is to speak of writers who can demonstrate the intuition with which *El laberinto de la soledad* ends: today we Latin
Americans are "for the first time in our history the contemporaries of all men."
The frequency with which the works of Paz or Borges are quoted or alluded to in
French or American, English or German criticism is sufficient proof of that con-
temporaneity, achieved with such difficulty by a culture which until very re-
cently had been considered marginal, peripheral and merely colonial. . . .

In the context of present-day Spanish-American culture the names of Borges
and Paz have even greater importance. In more than one sense they embody certain traits that should be taken into account before passing on to a more detailed
analysis of them and their work. They share a certain intellectual attitude toward
the esthetic phenomenon: an attitude which of course does not offer identical solutions to the same problems. Neither Paz nor Borges are disdainful of the day-to-
day exercise of intelligence and erudition. They are highly educated poets, even
in their impulsive or anguished moments. Lucid intelligence and intellectual enlightenment pervade their works and those works can sustain critical, profoundly
personal meditation. Neither Paz nor Borges have renounced intellectuality: they
realize that a poet cannot maintain an attitude of ignorance before the problems
of language, esthetic phenomena and rhetorical speculation. As critics, they have
both analyzed foreign works as well as their own; they have submitted the (ultimately unexplainable) phenomenon of poetic creation to tireless scrutiny.

To say this is not to assert, as some pretend to believe, that Paz and Borges are
unaware of or hold in disdain the other faculties without which poetic creation or
criticism is impossible. Paz's lyrical work begins with lucidity in order to reach the
blinding glare of ecstasy; that of Borges makes use of the intellect in order to undermine and definitively destroy its own arrogance. Overwhelming intuition, the
electric spark that leaps between two distant poles, the ability to seize by oblique
methods the elusive core of reality are also characteristic of Paz's and Borges's
works. But if their intelligence does not function in a vacuum, it is certainly the
conducting medium of that poetic or critical charge both of their works contain.

They also share a deliberate, conscious and programmatic acceptance of a
cultural tradition that comes to us from the West and transforms our literary task
into the renewed construction and destruction of a dialogue begun many centuries ago on the shores of the Mediterranean. In both writers Americanism does
not exclude but embodies that Mediterranean tradition. Too brilliant to ignore
the fact that they are using a European verbal instrument, both look at reality
from their respective Americas with the discipline they have acquired in vast
multilingual libraries. Their Americanism is open.

From *The Perpetual Present*

QUESTIONS

1. Do the opening details included in Sor Juana's *Reply* surprise you? How does it change your reading of her poetry to know that the very act of writing was one of rebellion?
2. Consider the Nobel lectures of Paz and Neruda, and "The Riddle of Poetry" by Borges. What assertions do they make about "defining" poetry? Consider their included poems in terms of their prose comments.

SUGGESTIONS FOR WRITING

1. Consider Alfonsina Storni's "Ancestral Burden" and the two poems by Sor Juana. Discuss how each of the poems explores the experience and concerns of Latin American women. Use Sor Juana's prose piece *Reply* to inform your discussion of the poems.
2. Compare the love poems of Sor Juana, Pablo Neruda, and Jorge Luis Borges. In Stephanie Merrim's critical piece, she suggests some contradictory reasons for Sor Juana's many love poems. Use one of these reasons to support your assertions about love poetry.
3. Consider the surreal effects in Vallejo's and Orozco's poems, as well as in Frida Kahlo's painting, *The Two Fridas*. Examine other included poems for their surrealist techniques.
4. Consider the way personal and political themes merge in some of these poems. Compare Pacheco's "High Treason," Vallejo's "Anger," and Storni's "Ancestral Burden." Incorporate the prose pieces in your discussion. Paz speaks of language and identity in his Nobel acceptance speech. Use the prose comments by and about Paz and Borges to support your discussion of how the personal and political intersect in the poems.

28 *Recognizing Excellence*

Why do we call some poems "bad"? We are talking not about their moral implications. Rather, we mean that, for one or more of many possible reasons, the poem has failed to move us or to engage our sympathies. Instead, it has made us doubt that the poet is in control of language and vision; perhaps it has aroused our antipathies or unwittingly appealed to our sense of the comic, though the poet is serious. Some poems can be said to succeed despite burdensome faults. But in general such faults are symptoms of deeper malady: some weakness in a poem's basic conception or in the poet's competence.

Nearly always, a bad poem reveals only a dim and distorted awareness of its probable effect on its audience. Perhaps the sound of words may clash with what a poem is saying, as in the jarring last word of this opening line of a tender lyric (author unknown, quoted by Richard Wilbur): "Come into the tent, my love, and close the flap." A bad poem usually overshoots or falls short of its mark by the poet's thinking too little or too much. Thinking too much, a poet contrives an excess of ingenuity like that quoted by Alexander Pope in *Peri Bathous, or The Art of Sinking in Poetry:* a hounded stag who "Hears his own feet, and thinks they sound like more; / And fears the hind feet will o'ertake the fore." Thinking too little, a poet writes redundantly, as Wordsworth in "The Thorn": "And they had fixed the wedding-day, / The morning that must wed them both."

In a poem that has a rime scheme or a set line length, when all is well, pattern and structure move inseparably with the rest of the poem, the way a tiger's skin and bones move with the tiger. But sometimes, in a poem that fails, the poet evidently has had difficulty in fitting the statements into a formal pattern. English poets have long felt free to invert word order for a special effect (Milton: "ye myrtles brown"), but the poet having trouble keeping to a rime scheme may invert words for no apparent reason but convenience. Needing a rime for *barge* may lead to ending a line with *a police dog large* instead of *a large police dog.* Another sign of trouble is a profusion of adjectives. If a line of iambic pentameter reads,

"Her lovely skin, like dear sweet white old silk," we suspect the poet of stuffing the line to make it long enough.

Even great poets write awful poems, and after their deaths, their worst efforts are collected with their masterpieces with no consumer warning labels to inform the reader. Some lines in the canon of celebrated bards make us wonder, "How could they have written this?" Wordsworth, Shelley, Whitman, and Browning are among the great whose failures can be painful, and sometimes an excellent poem will have a bad spot in it. To be unwilling to read them, though, would be as ill advised as to refuse to see Venice just because the Grand Canal is said to contain impurities. The seasoned reader of poetry thinks no less of Tennyson for having written, "Form, Form, Riflemen Form! . . . Look to your butts, and take good aims!" The collected works of a duller poet may contain no such lines of unconscious double meaning, but neither do they contain any poem as good as "Ulysses." If the duller poet never had a spectacular failure, it may be because of a failure to take risks. "In poetry," said Ronsard, "the greatest vice is mediocrity."

Often, inept poems fall into familiar categories. At one extreme is the poem written entirely in conventional diction, dimly echoing Shakespeare, Wordsworth, and the Bible, but garbling them. Couched in a rhythm that ticks along like a metronome, this kind of poem shows no sign that its author has ever taken a hard look at anything that can be tasted, handled, or felt. It employs loosely and thoughtlessly the most abstract of words: *love, beauty, life, death, time, eternity*. Littered with old-fashioned contractions (*'tis, o'er, where'er*), it may end in a simple preachment or platitude. George Orwell's complaint against much contemporary writing (not only poetry) is applicable: "As soon as certain topics are raised"—and one thinks of such standard topics for poetry as spring, a first kiss, and stars—"the concrete melts into the abstract and no one seems able to think of turns of speech that are not hackneyed." Writers, Orwell charged, too often make their sentences out of tacked-together phrases "like the sections of a prefabricated hen-house."[1] Versifiers often do likewise.

At the opposite extreme is the poem that displays no acquaintance with poetry of the past but manages, instead, to fabricate its own clichés. Slightly paraphrased, a manuscript once submitted to the *Paris Review* began:

> Vile
> rottenflush
>
> o   —screaming—
>   f CORPSEBLOOD!!   ooze
> STRANGLE my
>   eyes . . .
>
>   HELL's
>   O, ghastly   stench**!!!

[1]George Orwell, "Politics and the English Language," *Shooting an Elephant and Other Essays* (New York: Harcourt, 1945).

At most, such a work has only a private value. The writer has vented personal frustrations upon words, instead of kicking stray dogs. In its way, "Vile Rotten-flush" is as self-indulgent as the oldfangled "first kiss in spring" kind of poem. "I dislike," said John Livingston Lowes, "poems that black your eyes, or put up their mouths to be kissed."

As jewelers tell which of two diamonds is fine by seeing which scratches the other, two poems may be tested by comparing them. This method works only on poems similar in length and kind: an epigram cannot be held up to test an epic. Most poems we meet are neither sheer trash nor obvious masterpieces. Because good diamonds to be proven need softer ones to scratch, in this chapter you will find a few clear-cut gems and a few clinkers.

Anonymous (English)

O MOON, WHEN I GAZE ON THY BEAUTIFUL FACE (ABOUT 1900)

O Moon, when I gaze on thy beautiful face,
Careering along through the boundaries of space,
The thought has often come into my mind
If I ever shall see thy glorious behind.

O MOON. Sir Edmund Gosse, the English critic (1849–1928), offered this quatrain as the work of his servant, but there is reason to suspect him of having written it.

QUESTIONS

1. To what fact of astronomy does the last line refer?
2. Which words seem chosen with too little awareness of their denotations and connotations?
3. Even if you did not know that these lines probably were deliberately bad, how would you argue with someone who maintained that the opening O in the poem was admirable as a bit of concrete poetry?

Grace Treasone

LIFE (ABOUT 1963)

Life is like a jagged tooth
that cuts into your heart;
fix the tooth and save the root,
and laughs, not tears, will start.

QUESTIONS

1. Try to paraphrase this poem. What is the poet saying?
2. How consistent is the working out of the comparison of life to a tooth?

Emily Dickinson (1830–1886)*

A Dying Tiger – moaned for Drink (about 1862)

A Dying Tiger – moaned for Drink –
I hunted all the Sand –
I caught the Dripping of a Rock
And bore it in my Hand –

His Mighty Balls – in death were thick –   5
But searching – I could see
A Vision on the Retina
Of Water – and of me –

'Twas not my blame – who sped too slow –
'Twas not his blame – who died   10
While I was reaching him –
But 'twas – the fact that He was dead –

Questions

How does this poem compare in success with other poems of Emily Dickinson that you
know? Justify your opinion by pointing to some of this poem's particulars.

Exercise: *Ten Terrible Moments in Poetry*

Here is a small anthology of bad moments in poetry.

For what reasons does each selection fail?

In which passages do you attribute the failure

    to inappropriate sound or diction?

    to awkward word order?

    to inaccurate metaphor?

    to excessive overstatement?

    to forced rime?

    to monotonous rhythm?

    to redundancy?

    to simple-mindedness or excessive ingenuity?

1. Last lines of *Enoch Arden* by Alfred, Lord Tennyson:

   So passed the strong heroic soul away.
   And when they buried him, the little port
   Had seldom seen a costlier funeral.

2. From *Purely Original Verse* (1891) by J. Gordon Coogler (1865–1901), of Columbia,
   South Carolina:

   Alas for the South, her books have grown fewer—
   She never was much given to literature.

3. From "Lines Written to a Friend on the Death of His Brother, Caused by a Railway Train Running Over Him Whilst He Was in a State of Inebriation" by James Henry Powell:

> Thy mangled corpse upon the rails in frightful shape was found.
> The ponderous train had killed thee as its heavy wheels went round,
> And thus in dreadful form thou met'st a drunkard's awful death
> And I, thy brother, mourn thy fate, and breathe a purer breath.

4. From *Dolce Far Niente* by the American poet Francis Saltus Saltus, who flourished in the 1890s:

> Her laugh is like sunshine, full of glee,
> And her sweet breath smells like fresh-made tea.

5. From another gem by Francis Saltus Saltus, "The Spider":

> Then all thy feculent majesty recalls
>   The nauseous mustiness of forsaken bowers,
> The leprous nudity of deserted halls—
>   The positive nastiness of sullied flowers.
>
> And I mark the colours yellow and black
>   That fresco thy lithe, dictatorial thighs,
> I dream and wonder on my drunken back
>   How God could possibly have created flies!

6. From "Song to the Suliotes" by George Gordon, Lord Byron:

> Up to battle! Sons of Suli
> Up, and do your duty duly!
> There the wall—and there the moat is:
> Bouwah! Bouwah! Suliotes,
> There is booty—there is beauty!
> Up my boys and do your duty!

7. From a juvenile poem of John Dryden, "Upon the Death of the Lord Hastings" (a victim of smallpox):

> Each little pimple had a tear in it,
> To wail the fault its rising did commit . . .

8. From "The Abbey Mason" by Thomas Hardy:

> When longer yet dank death had wormed
> The brain wherein the style had germed
>
> From Gloucester church it flew afar—
> The style called Perpendicular.—
>
> To Winton and to Westminster
> It ranged, and grew still beautifuller . . .

9. A metaphor from "The Crucible of Life" by the once-popular American newspaper poet Edgar A. Guest:

> Sacred and sweet is the joy that must come
> From the furnace of life when you've poured off the scum.

10. From an elegy for Queen Victoria by one of her subjects:

> Dust to dust, and ashes to ashes,
> Into the tomb the Great Queen dashes.

Sentimentality is a failure of writers who seem to feel a great emotion but who fail to give us sufficient grounds for sharing it. The emotion may be an anger greater than its object seems to call for, as in these lines to a girl who caused scandal (the exact nature of her act never being specified): "The gossip in each hall / Will curse your name . . . / Go! better cast yourself right down the falls!"[2] Or it may be an enthusiasm quite unwarranted by its subject: in *The Fleece* John Dyer temptingly describes the pleasures of life in a workhouse for the poor. The sentimental poet is especially prone to tenderness. Great tears fill his eyes at a glimpse of an aged grandmother sitting by a hearth. For all the poet knows, she may be the manager of a casino in Las Vegas who would be startled to find herself an object of pity, but the sentimentalist doesn't care to know about the woman herself. She is a general excuse for feeling maudlin. Any other conventional object will serve as well: a faded valentine, the strains of an old song, a baby's cast-off pacifier. An instance of such emotional self-indulgence is "The Old Oaken Bucket," by Samuel Woodworth, a stanza of which goes:

> How sweet from the green, mossy brim to receive it,
>   As, poised on the curb, it inclined to my lips!
> Not a full-flushing goblet could tempt me to leave it,
>   Tho' filled with the nectar that Jupiter sips.
> And now, far removed from the loved habitation,
>   The tear of regret will intrusively swell,
> As fancy reverts to my father's plantation,
>   And sighs for the bucket that hung in the well.

The staleness of the phrasing and imagery (Jove's nectar, *tear of regret*) suggests that the speaker is not even seeing the actual physical bucket, and the tripping meter of the lines is inappropriate to an expression of tearful regret. Perhaps the poet's nostalgia is genuine. Indeed, as Keith Waldrop has put it, "a bad poem is always sincere." However sincere in their feelings, sentimental poets fail as artists because they cannot separate their own emotional responses from those of the disinterested reader. Wet-eyed and sighing for a bucket, Woodworth achieves not pathos but **bathos**: a description that can move us to laughter instead of tears.[3] Tears, of course, can be shed for good reason. A piece of sentimentality is not to be confused with a well-wrought poem whose tone is tenderness.

---

[2]Ali. S. Hilmi, "The Preacher's Sermon," *Verse at Random* (Larnaca, Cyprus: Ohanian Press, 1953).
[3]*Bathos* in poetry can also mean an abrupt fall from the sublime to the trivial or incongruous. A sample, from Nicholas Rowe's play *The Fair Penitent:* "Is it the voice of thunder, or my father?" Another, from John Close, a minor Victorian: "Around their heads a dazzling halo shone, / No need of mortal robes, or any hat." When, however, such a letdown is used for a *desirable* effect of humor or contrast, it is usually called an **anticlimax:** as in Alexander Pope's lines on the queen's palace, "Here thou, great Anna! whom three realms obey, / Dost sometimes counsel take—and sometimes tea."

Rod McKuen (b. 1933)

THOUGHTS ON CAPITAL PUNISHMENT   1954

There ought to be capital punishment for cars
that run over rabbits and drive into dogs
and commit the unspeakable, unpardonable crime
of killing a kitty cat still in his prime.

Purgatory, at the very least   5
                should await the driver
   driving over a beast.

Those hurrying headlights coming out of the dark
that scatter the scampering squirrels in the park
should await the best jury that one might compose   10
of fatherless chipmunks and husbandless does.

And then found guilty, after too fair a trial
should be caged in a cage with a hyena's smile
or maybe an elephant with an elephant gun
should shoot out his eyes when the verdict is done.   15

There ought to be something, something that's fair
to avenge Mrs. Badger as she waits in her lair
for her husband who lies with his guts spilling out
cause he didn't know what automobiles are about.

Hell on the highway, at the very least   20
                should await the driver
   driving over a beast.

Who kills a man kills a bit of himself
But a cat too is an extension of God.

William Stafford (1914–1993)*

TRAVELING THROUGH THE DARK   1962

Traveling through the dark I found a deer
dead on the edge of the Wilson River road.
It is usually best to roll them into the canyon:
that road is narrow; to swerve might make more dead.

By glow of the tail-light I stumbled back of the car   5
and stood by the heap, a doe, a recent killing;
she had stiffened already, almost cold.
I dragged her off; she was large in the belly.

My fingers touching her side brought me the reason—
her side was warm; her fawn lay there waiting,   10
alive, still, never to be born.
Beside that mountain road I hesitated.

The car aimed ahead its lowered parking lights;
under the hood purred the steady engine.
I stood in the glare of the warm exhaust turning red;   15
around our group I could hear the wilderness listen.

I thought hard for us all—my only swerving—
then pushed her over the edge into the river.

QUESTIONS

1. Compare these poems by Rod McKuen and William Stafford. How are they similar?
2. Explain Stafford's title. Who are all those traveling through the dark?
3. Comment on McKuen's use of language. Consider especially: *unspeakable, unpardonable crime* (line 3), *kitty cat* (4), *scatter the scampering squirrels* (9), and *cause he didn't know* (19).
4. Compare the meaning of Stafford's last two lines and McKuen's last two. Does either poem have a moral? Can either poem be said to moralize?
5. Which poem might be open to the charge of sentimentality? Why?

In recent years, the belief that poetry cannot be popular has been shaken by practitioners of **cowboy poetry,** verse about life on the range, written by people who know that life firsthand. Usually realistic, riming and metrical, cowboy poetry is designed to be read aloud or recited to audiences such as the large throng that assembles each January at the Cowboy Poetry Gathering in Elko, Nevada. This kind of folk poetry "has its own criteria of good and bad," insists Gibbs Smith, publisher of two best-selling cowboy poetry anthologies; "it has its own rules; its own tradition, and we should respect that."[4] Devotees of cowboy poetry regard the following poem as a classic. Read it and see if you agree.

Wallace McRae   (b. 1936)

REINCARNATION   1980

"What does reincarnation mean?"
A cowpoke ast his friend.
His pal replied, "It happens when
Yer life has reached its end.
They comb yer hair, and warsh yer neck,   5

[4]Quoted by Sara Terry, "Poem on the Range," *Boston Globe Magazine,* Jan. 19, 1992. The anthologies, edited by Hal Cannon, are *Cowboy Poetry: A Gathering* and *New Cowboy Poetry* (Salt Lake City: Gibbs M. Smith, 1985 and 1990).

And clean yer fingernails,
And lay you in a padded box
Away from life's travails.

"The box and you goes in a hole,
That's been dug into the ground.   10
Reincarnation starts in when
Yore planted 'neath a mound.
Them clods melt down, just like yer box,
And you who is inside.
And then yore just beginnin's on   15
Yer transformation ride.

"In a while the grass'll grow
Upon yer rendered mound.
Till some day on yer moldered grave
A lonely flower is found.   20
And say a hoss should wander by
And graze upon this flower
That once wuz you, but now's become
Yer vegetative bower.

"The posey that the hoss done ate   25
Up, with his other feed,
Makes bone, and fat, and muscle
Essential to the steed.
But some is left that he can't use
And so it passes through,   30
And finally lays upon the ground.
This thing, that once wuz you.

"Then say, by chance, I wanders by
And sees this upon the ground,
And I ponders, and I wonders at,   35
This object that I found.
I thinks of reincarnation,
Of life, and death, and such,
And come away concludin': Slim,
You ain't changed, all that much."   40

QUESTIONS

1. If you were Slim, how would you react to that last line?
2. Discuss this harsh judgment: "This isn't much of a poem. The poet is only playing an elaborate joke on Slim and on the rest of us."
3. In general, do you believe that a poem is any the worse for a lack of total seriousness?
4. Take a close look at the poem's language. Which words or phrases seem unschooled cowboy speech? Which might be criticized as stilted or bookish? How do you account for this discrepancy?

5. Compare the poem's central idea with a similar notion advanced by Shakespeare's *Hamlet, Prince of Denmark:*

> *Hamlet:* A man may fish with the worm that hath eat of a king, and eat of the fish that hath fed of that worm.
> *King:* What dost thou mean by this?
> *Hamlet:* Nothing but to show you how a king may go to progress through the guts of a beggar. (4.3.27-32)

Notice that Hamlet, like Slim's friend, also puts his listener on the receiving end of an insult. But how might it be claimed that Shakespeare makes a simple idea rich and complicated?

6. Do you agree with Gibbs Smith that we should judge cowboy poetry only by its own rules (not oblige it to live up to standards we might apply to a passage of Shakespeare or a poem by Robert Frost)?

RECOGNIZING EXCELLENCE

How can we tell an excellent poem from any other? To give reasons for excellence in poetry is harder than to give reasons for failure in poetry (so often due to familiar kinds of imprecision and sentimentality). A bad poem tends to be stereotyped, an excellent poem unique. In judging either, we can have no absolute specifications. A poem is not like an electric toaster that an inspector can test using a check-off list. It has to be judged on the basis of what it is trying to be and how well it succeeds in the effort.

To judge a poem, we first have to understand it. At least, we need to understand it *almost* all the way; there are, to be sure, poems such as Hopkins's "The Windhover" (page 1193), which most readers probably would call excellent even though its meaning is still being debated. Although it is a good idea to give a poem at least a couple of considerate readings before judging it, sometimes our first encounter starts turning into an act of evaluation. Moving along into the poem, becoming more deeply involved in it, we may begin forming an opinion. In general, the more a poem contains for us to understand, the more rewarding we are likely to find it. Of course, an obscure and highly demanding poem is not always to be preferred to a relatively simple one. Difficult poems can be pretentious and incoherent; still, there is something to be said for the poem complicated enough to leave us something to discover on our fifteenth reading (unlike most limericks, which yield their all at a look). Here is such a poem, one not readily fathomed and exhausted.

William Butler Yeats (1865–1939)*

SAILING TO BYZANTIUM   1927

That is no country for old men. The young
In one another's arms, birds in the trees
—Those dying generations—at their song,

The salmon-falls, the mackerel-crowded seas,
Fish, flesh, or fowl, commend all summer long   5
Whatever is begotten, born, and dies.
Caught in that sensual music all neglect
Monuments of unaging intellect.

An aged man is but a paltry thing,
A tattered coat upon a stick, unless   10
Soul clap its hands and sing, and louder sing
For every tatter in its mortal dress,
Nor is there singing school but studying
Monuments of its own magnificence;
And therefore I have sailed the seas and come   15
To the holy city of Byzantium.

O sages standing in God's holy fire
As in the gold mosaic of a wall,
Come from the holy fire, perne in a gyre,°   *spin down a spiral*
And be the singing-masters of my soul.   20
Consume my heart away; sick with desire
And fastened to a dying animal
It knows not what it is; and gather me
Into the artifice of eternity.

Once out of nature I shall never take   25
My bodily form from any natural thing,
But such a form as Grecian goldsmiths make
Of hammered gold and gold enameling
To keep a drowsy Emperor awake;
Or set upon a golden bough to sing   30
To lords and ladies of Byzantium
Of what is past, or passing, or to come.

SAILING TO BYZANTIUM. Byzantium was the capital of the Byzantine Empire, the city now called
Istanbul. Yeats means, though, not merely the physical city. Byzantium is also a name for his conception of paradise.

Though *salmon-falls* (line 4) suggests Yeats's native Ireland, the poem, as we
find out in line 25, is about escaping from the entire natural world. If the poet desires this escape, then probably the *country* mentioned in the opening line is no political nation but the cycle of birth and death in which human beings are trapped;
and, indeed, the poet says his heart is "fastened to a dying animal." Imaginary landscapes, it would seem, are merging with the historical Byzantium. Lines 17–18 refer
to mosaic images, adornments of the Byzantine cathedral of St. Sophia, in which
the figures of saints are inlaid against backgrounds of gold. The clockwork bird of
the last stanza is also a reference to something actual. Yeats noted: "I have read
somewhere that in the Emperor's palace at Byzantium was a tree made of gold and

silver, and artificial birds that sang." This description of the role the poet would seek—that of a changeless, immortal singer—directs us back to the earlier references to music and singing. Taken all together, they point toward the central metaphor of the poem: the craft of poetry can be a kind of singing. One kind of everlasting monument is a great poem. To study masterpieces of poetry is the only "singing school"—the only way to learn to write a poem.

We have no more than skimmed through a few of this poem's suggestions, enough to show that, out of allusion and imagery, Yeats has woven at least one elaborate metaphor. Surely one thing the poem achieves is that, far from merely puzzling us, it makes us aware of relationships between what a person can imagine and the physical world. There is the statement that a human heart is bound to the body that perishes, and yet it is possible to see consciousness for a moment independent of flesh, to sing with joy at the very fact that the body is crumbling away. Much of the power of Yeats's poem comes from the physical terms with which he states the ancient quarrel between body and spirit, body being a "tattered coat upon a stick." There is all the difference in the world between the work of the poet like Yeats whose eye is on the living thing and whose mind is awake and passionate, and that of the slovenly poet whose dull eye and sleepy mind focus on nothing more than some book read hastily long ago. The former writes a poem out of compelling need, the latter as if it seems a nice idea to write something.

Yeats's poem has the three qualities essential to beauty, according to the definition of Thomas Aquinas: wholeness, harmony, and radiance. The poem is all one; its parts move in peace with one another; it shines with emotional intensity. There is an orderly progression going on in it: from the speaker's statement of his discontent with the world of "sensual music," to his statement that he is quitting this world, to his prayer that the sages will take him in, and his vision of future immortality. And the images of the poem relate to one another—*dying generations* (line 3), *dying animal* (line 22), and the undying golden bird (lines 27–32)—to mention just one series of related things. "Sailing to Byzantium" is not the kind of poem that has, in Pope's words, "One simile, that solitary shines / In the dry desert of a thousand lines." Rich in figurative language, Yeats's whole poem develops a metaphor, with further metaphors as its tributaries.

"Sailing to Byzantium" has a theme that matters to us. What human being does not long, at times, to shed timid, imperfect flesh, to live in a state of absolute joy, unperishing? Being human, perhaps we too are stirred by Yeats's prayer: "Consume my heart away, sick with desire / And fastened to a dying animal. . . ." If it is true that in poetry, as Ezra Pound declared, "only emotion endures," then Yeats's poem ought to endure. (If you happen not to feel moved by this poem, try another—but come back to "Sailing to Byzantium" after a while.)

Most excellent poems, it might be argued, contain significant themes, as does "Sailing to Byzantium." But the presence of such a theme is not enough to render a poem excellent. Not theme alone makes an excellent poem, but how well a theme is stated.

Yeats's poem, some would say, is a match for any lyric in our language. Some might call it inferior to an epic (to Milton's *Paradise Lost*, say, or to the *Iliad*), but to make this claim is to lead us into a different argument: whether certain genres are innately better than others. Such an argument usually leads to a dead end. Evidently, *Paradise Lost* has greater range, variety, matter, length, and ambitiousness. But any poem—whether an epic or an epigram—may be judged by how well it fulfills the design it undertakes. God, who created both fleas and whales, pronounced all good. Fleas, like epigrams, have no reason to feel inferior.

EXERCISE: *Two Poems to Compare*

Here are two poems with a similar theme. Which contains more qualities of excellent poetry? Decide whether the other is bad or whether it may be praised for achieving something different.

Arthur Guiterman (1871–1943)

ON THE VANITY OF EARTHLY GREATNESS   1936

The tusks that clashed in mighty brawls
Of mastodons, are billiard balls.

The sword of Charlemagne the Just
Is ferric oxide, known as rust.

The grizzly bear whose potent hug   5
Was feared by all, is now a rug.

Great Caesar's bust is on the shelf,
And I don't feel so well myself.

Percy Bysshe Shelley (1792–1822)

OZYMANDIAS   1818

I met a traveler from an antique land
Who said: Two vast and trunkless legs of stone
Stand in the desert. Near them, on the sand,
Half sunk, a shattered visage lies, whose frown,
And wrinkled lip, and sneer of cold command,   5
Tell that its sculptor well those passions read
Which yet survive, stamped on these lifeless things,
The hand that mocked° them and the heart that fed;   *imitated*
And on the pedestal these words appear:
"My name is Ozymandias, king of kings: 10
Look on my works, ye Mighty, and despair!"
Nothing beside remains. Round the decay
Of that colossal wreck, boundless and bare
The lone and level sands stretch far away.

Some excellent poems of the past will remain sealed to us unless we are willing to sympathize with their conventions. Pastoral poetry, for instance—Marlowe's "Passionate Shepherd" and Milton's "Lycidas"—asks us to accept certain conventions and situations that may seem old-fashioned: idle swains, oaten flutes. We are under no grim duty, of course, to admire poems whose conventions do not appeal to us. But there is no point in blaming a poet for playing a particular game or for observing its rules.

Bad poems, of course, can be woven together out of conventions, like patchwork quilts made of old unwanted words. In Shakespeare's England, poets were busily imitating the sonnets of Petrarch, the Italian poet whose praise of his beloved Laura had become well known. The result of their industry was a surplus of Petrarchan **conceits,** or elaborate comparisons (from the Italian *concetto:* concept, bright idea). In a famous sonnet ("My mistress' eyes are nothing like the sun," page 1238), Shakespeare, who at times helped himself generously from the Petrarchan stockpile, pokes fun at poets who thoughtlessly use such handed-down figures of speech.

There is no predictable pattern for poetic excellence. A reader needs to remain open to surprise and innovation. Remember, too, that a superb poem is not necessarily an uplifting one—full of noble sentiments and inspiring ideas. Some powerful poems deal with difficult and even unpleasant subjects. What matters is the compelling quality of the presentation, the evocative power of the language, and the depth of feeling and perception achieved by the total work. William Trevor once defined the short story as "an explosion of truth"; the same notion applies to poetry, with a special reminder that not all truths are pleasant. Robert Hayden's "The Whipping," for example, is a memorable but disturbing poem on a difficult subject, child abuse. Notice how Hayden refuses to sensationalize the topic into sociological clichés but instead reaches for its deeper human significance—not only for the victim, but also for the victimizer and even the observer.

Robert Hayden   (1913–1980)*

THE WHIPPING   1970

The old woman across the way
   is whipping the boy again
and shouting to the neighborhood
   her goodness and his wrongs.

Wildly he crashes through elephant ears,   5
   pleads in dusty zinnias,
while she in spite of crippling fat
   pursues and corners him.

She strikes and strikes the shrilly circling
    boy till the stick breaks   10
in her hand. His tears are rainy weather
    to woundlike memories:

My head gripped in bony vise
    of knees, the writhing struggle
to wrench free, the blows, the fear   15
    worse than blows that hateful

Words could bring, the face that I
    no longer knew or loved. . . .
Well, it is over now, it is over
    and the boy sobs in his room,   20

And the woman leans muttering against
    a tree, exhausted, purged—
avenged in part for lifelong hidings
    she has had to bear.

QUESTIONS

1. Who is the speaker of the poem? What is the speaker's relation to the people he observes in the opening stanza?
2. How does the scene being depicted change in the fourth stanza? Who are the people depicted here?
3. What reason does the speaker give for the old woman's violence? Does the speaker feel her reason is adequate to excuse her behavior?
4. How would you summarize the theme of this poem?

Sometimes poets use conventions in an innovative way, stretching the rules for new expressive ends. Here Elizabeth Bishop takes the form of the villanelle and bends the rules to give her poem a heartbreaking effect.

Elizabeth Bishop   (1911–1979)*

ONE ART   1976

The art of losing isn't hard to master;
so many things seem filled with the intent
to be lost that their loss is no disaster.

Lose something every day. Accept the fluster
of lost door keys, the hour badly spent.   5
The art of losing isn't hard to master.

Then practice losing farther, losing faster:
places, and names, and where it was you meant
to travel. None of these will bring disaster.

I lost my mother's watch. And look! my last, or   10
next-to-last, of three loved houses went.
The art of losing isn't hard to master.

I lost two cities, lovely ones. And, vaster,
some realms I owned, two rivers, a continent.
I miss them, but it wasn't a disaster.   15

—Even losing you (the joking voice, a gesture
I love) I shan't have lied. It's evident
the art of losing's not too hard to master
though it may look like (*Write* it!) like disaster.

QUESTIONS

1. What things has the speaker lost? Put together a complete list in the order she reveals them. What does the list suggest about her experience with loss?
2. Bishop varies the repeated lines that end with the word *disaster*. Look only at those lines: what do they suggest about the story being unfolded in the poem?
3. What effect does the parenthetical comment in the poem's last line create? Would the poem be different if it were omitted?
4. Compare this poem to other villanelles in this book, such as Dylan Thomas's "Do not go gentle into that good night" (page 927) and Wendy Cope's "Lonely Hearts" (page 766). In what ways does Bishop bend the rules of the form?

Like "One Art," many great poems engage our personal feelings and private concerns. Others explore larger historical issues and our relationship to them. The following poem, which is set in New York City on the day that Hitler invaded Poland and World War II started, was widely circulated in the weeks following the terrorist attacks of September 11, 2001.

W. H. Auden   (1907–1973)*

SEPTEMBER 1, 1939   1940

I sit in one of the dives
On Fifty-Second Street
Uncertain and afraid
As the clever hopes expire
Of a low dishonest decade: 5
Waves of anger and fear
Circulate over the bright
And darkened lands of the earth,
Obsessing our private lives;
The unmentionable odour of death   10
Offends the September night.

Accurate scholarship can
Unearth the whole offence
From Luther until now
That has driven a culture mad,
Find what occurred at Linz,
What huge imago made
A psychopathic god:
I and the public know
What all schoolchildren learn,
Those to whom evil is done
Do evil in return.

Exiled Thucydides knew
All that a speech can say
About Democracy,
And what dictators do,
The elderly rubbish they talk
To an apathetic grave;
Analysed all in his book,
The enlightenment driven away,
The habit-forming pain,
Mismanagement and grief:
We must suffer them all again.

Into this neutral air
Where blind skyscrapers use
Their full height to proclaim
The strength of Collective Man,
Each language pours its vain
Competitive excuse:
But who can live for long
In an euphoric dream;
Out of the mirror they stare,
Imperialism's face
And the international wrong.

Faces along the bar
Cling to their average day:
The lights must never go out,
The music must always play,
All the conventions conspire
To make this fort assume
The furniture of home;
Lest we should see where we are,
Lost in a haunted wood,

Children afraid of the night
Who have never been happy or good.

The windiest militant trash
Important Persons shout
Is not so crude as our wish:
What mad Nijinsky wrote
About Diaghilev
Is true of the normal heart;
For the error bred in the bone
Of each woman and each man
Craves what it cannot have,
Not universal love
But to be loved alone.

From the conservative dark
Into the ethical life
The dense commuters come,
Repeating their morning vow,
"I *will* be true to the wife,
I'll concentrate more on my work,"
And helpless governors wake
To resume their compulsory game:
Who can release them now,
Who can reach the deaf,
Who can speak for the dumb?

All I have is a voice
To undo the folded lie,
The romantic lie in the brain
Of the sensual man-in-the-street
And the lie of Authority
Whose buildings grope the sky:
There is no such thing as the State
And no one exists alone;
Hunger allows no choice
To the citizen or the police;
We must love one another or die.

Defenseless under the night
Our world in stupor lies;
Yet, dotted everywhere,
Ironic points of light
Flash out wherever the Just
Exchange their messages:

55

60

65

70

75

80

85

90

May I, composed like them
Of Eros and of dust,
Beleaguered by the same   95
Negation and despair,
Show an affirming flame.

SEPTEMBER 1, 1939. *2 Fifty-Second Street;* in New York City.   *14 Luther:* German priest Martin
Luther (1483–1546), whose 95 Theses (1517) ignited the Protestant Reformation.   *16 Linz:* town in
Austria where Adolf Hitler was raised.   *23 Thucydides:* Greek historian of the fifth century B.C.,
whose *History of the Peloponnesian War* contains the famous oration by Pericles commemorating the
Athenian war dead.   *59–60 What mad Nijinsky wrote / About Diaghilev:* Russian dancer Vaslav Nijinsky (1890–1960) wrote in his diary of the impresario Sergei Diaghilev (1872–1929): "Some politicians are hypocrites like Diaghilev, who does not want universal love, but to be loved alone. I want
universal love."

QUESTIONS

1. How do the last two lines of the second stanza relate to the specific political and historical situation that the poem addresses? How valid do you find them as a description of human behavior in general?
2. What attitude does the poem take, especially in the third stanza, toward the use of
   patriotic appeals by heads of state to build support for war?
3. In the context of the poem's larger themes, why is it an "error" to desire "to be loved
   alone" (lines 62–66)?
4. What does Auden mean by "There is no such thing as the State" (line 84)?
5. Is this poem relevant to our times? Refer to particular situations and events to back
   up your response.

Excellent poetry might be easier to recognize if each poet had a fixed position on the slopes of Mount Parnassus, but, from one century to the next, the
reputations of some poets have taken humiliating slides, or made impressive
clambers. We decide for ourselves which poems to call excellent, but readers of
the future may reverse our opinions. Most of us no longer would share this popular view of Walt Whitman held by one of his contemporaries:

> Walt Whitman (1819–1892), by some regarded as a great poet; by others,
> as no poet at all. Most of his so-called poems are mere catalogues of things,
> without meter or rime, but in a few more regular poems and in lines here
> and there he is grandly poetical, as in "O Captain! My Captain!"[5]

Walt Whitman   (1819–1892)*

O CAPTAIN! MY CAPTAIN!   1865

O Captain! my Captain! our fearful trip is done,
The ship has weather'd every rack, the prize we sought is won,
The port is near, the bells I hear, the people all exulting,

[5]J. Willis Westlake, A. M., *Common-school Literature, English and American, with Several Hundred
Extracts to be Memorized* (Philadelphia, 1898).

While follow eyes the steady keel, the vessel grim and daring;
　　But O heart! heart! heart!
　　　　O the bleeding drops of red,
　　　　　　Where on the deck my Captain lies,
　　　　　　　　Fallen cold and dead.   5

O Captain! my Captain! rise up and hear the bells;
Rise up—for you the flag is flung—for you the bugle trills,   10
For you bouquets and ribbon'd wreaths—for you the shores a-crowding,
For you they call, the swaying mass, their eager faces turning;
　　Here Captain! dear father!
　　　　This arm beneath your head!
　　　　　　It is some dream that on the deck,   15
　　　　　　　　You've fallen cold and dead.

My Captain does not answer, his lips are pale and still,
My father does not feel my arm, he has no pulse nor will,
The ship is anchor'd safe and sound, its voyage closed and done,
From fearful trip the victor ship comes in with object won;   20
　　Exult O shores, and ring O bells!
　　　　But I with mournful tread,
　　　　　　Walk the deck my Captain lies,
　　　　　　　　Fallen cold and dead.

O CAPTAIN! MY CAPTAIN! Written soon after the death of Abraham Lincoln, this was, in Whitman's lifetime, by far the most popular of his poems.

QUESTIONS

1. Compare this with other Whitman poems. In what ways is "O Captain! My Captain!" uncharacteristic of his works? Do you agree with J. Willis Westlake that this is one of the few occasions on which Whitman is "grandly poetical?"
2. Comment on the appropriateness of the poem's rhythms to its subject.
3. Do you find any evidence in this poem that an excellent poet wrote it?

In a sense, all readers of poetry are constantly reexamining the judgments of the past by choosing those poems they care to go on reading. In the end, we have to admit that the critical principles set forth in this chapter are all very well for admiring excellent poetry we already know, but they cannot be carried like a yardstick in the hand, to go out looking for it. As Ezra Pound said in his *ABC of Reading*, "A classic is classic not because it conforms to certain structural rules, or fits certain definitions (of which its author had quite probably never heard). It is classic because of a certain eternal and irrepressible freshness."

The best poems, like "Sailing to Byzantium," may offer a kind of religious experience. At the beginning of the twenty-first century, some of us rarely set foot outside an artificial environment. Whizzing down four-lane superhighways, we observe lakes and trees in the distance. In a way our cities are to us as anthills are to ants: no less than anthills, they are "natural" structures. But the "unnatural" world of school or business is, as Wordsworth says, too much with us. Locked in the shells of our ambitions, our self-esteem, we forget our kinship to earth and sea. We fabricate self-justifications. But a great poem shocks us into another order of perception. It points beyond language to something still more essential. It ushers us into an experience so moving and true that we feel (to quote King Lear) "cut to the brain." In bad or indifferent poetry, words are all there is.

Carl Sandburg (1878–1967)*

FOG   1916

The fog comes
on little cat feet.

It sits looking
over harbor and city
on silent haunches   5
and then moves on.

QUESTION

In lines 15–22 of "The Love Song of J. Alfred Prufrock" (page 1169), T. S. Eliot also likens fog to a cat. Compare Sandburg's lines and Eliot's. Which passage tells us more about fogs and cats?

EXERCISE: *Reevaluating Popular Classics*

In this exercise you will read two of the most popular American poems of the nineteenth century. In their time, not only were these poems considered classics by serious critics, but thousands of ordinary readers knew them by heart. Recently, however, they have fallen out of critical favor.

Your assignment is to read these poems carefully and make your own personal, tentative evaluation of each poem's merit. Here are some questions you might ask yourself, as you consider them.

- Do these poems engage your sympathies? Do they stir you and touch your feelings?
- What, if anything, might make them memorable? Do they have any vivid images? Any metaphors, understatement, overstatement, or other figures of speech? Do these poems appeal to the ear?
- Do the poems exhibit any wild incompetence? Do you find any forced rimes, inappropriate words, or other unintentionally comic features? Can the poems be accused of bathos or sentimentality, or do you trust the poet to report honest feelings?
- How well does the poet seem in control of language? Does the poet's language reflect in any detail the physical world we know?
- Do these poems seem entirely drawn from other poetry of the past, or do you have a sense that the poet is thinking and feeling on her (or his) own? Does the poet show any evidence of having read other poets' poetry?
- What is the poet trying to do in each poem? How successful, in your opinion, is the attempt?

Try setting these poems next to similar poems you know and admire. (You might try comparing Emma Lazarus's "The New Colossus" to Percy Bysshe Shelley's "Ozymandias," found in this chapter; both are sonnets, and their subjects have interesting similarities and contrasts. Or compare Edgar Allan Poe's "Annabel Lee" to A. E. Housman's "To an Athlete Dying Young," found in "Poems for Further Reading.")

Are these poems sufficiently rich and interesting to repay more than one reading?

Do you think that these poems still deserve to be considered classics? Or do they no longer speak powerfully to a contemporary audience?

Emma Lazarus   (1849–1887)

THE NEW COLOSSUS   1883

Not like the brazen giant of Greek fame,
With conquering limbs astride from land to land;
Here at our sea-washed, sunset gates shall stand
A mighty woman with a torch, whose flame
Is the imprisoned lightning, and her name   5
Mother of Exiles. From her beacon-hand
Glows world-wide welcome; her mild eyes command
The air-bridged harbor that twin cities frame.
"Keep, ancient lands, your storied pomp!" cries she
With silent lips. "Give me your tired, your poor,   10
Your huddled masses yearning to breathe free,
The wretched refuse of your teeming shore.
Send these, the homeless, tempest-tost to me,
I lift my lamp beside the golden door!"

THE NEW COLOSSUS. In 1883, a committee formed to raise funds to build a pedestal for what would be the largest statue in the world, "Liberty Enlightening the World" by Fréderic-Auguste Bartholdi, which was a gift from the French people to celebrate America's centennial. American authors were asked to donate manuscripts for a fund-raising auction. The young poet Emma Lazarus, whose parents had come to America as immigrants, sent in this sonnet composed for the occasion. When President Grover Cleveland unveiled the Statue of Liberty in October 1886, Lazarus's sonnet was read at the ceremony. In 1903, the poem was carved on the statue's pedestal. The reference in the opening line to "the brazen giant of Greek fame" is to the famous Colossus of Rhodes, a huge bronze statue that once stood in the harbor on the Aegean island of Rhodes. Built to commemorate a military victory, it was one of the so-called Seven Wonders of the World.

Edgar Allan Poe   (1809–1849)*

ANNABEL LEE   1849

It was many and many a year ago,
   In a kingdom by the sea,
That a maiden there lived whom you may know
   By the name of Annabel Lee;
And this maiden she lived with no other thought   5
   Than to love and be loved by me.

I was a child and she was a child,
   In this kingdom by the sea,
But we loved with a love that was more than love—
   I and my Annabel Lee—   10
With a love that the wingéd seraphs of Heaven
   Coveted her and me.

And this was the reason that, long ago,
   In this kingdom by the sea,
A wind blew out of a cloud, chilling   15
   My beautiful Annabel Lee;
So that her highborn kinsmen came
   And bore her away from me,
To shut her up in a sepulchre
   In this kingdom by the sea.   20

The angels, not half so happy in Heaven,
   Went envying her and me:—
Yes!—that was the reason (as all men know,
   In this kingdom by the sea)
That the wind came out of the cloud by night,   25
   Chilling and killing my Annabel Lee.

But our love it was stronger by far than the love
   Of those who were older than we—
   Of many far wiser than we—
And neither the angels in Heaven above,   30
   Nor the demons down under the sea,
Can ever dissever my soul from the soul
   Of the beautiful Annabel Lee:—

For the moon never beams, without bringing me dreams
   Of the beautiful Annabel Lee;   35
And the stars never rise, but I feel the bright eyes
   Of the beautiful Annabel Lee:
And so, all the night-tide, I lie down by the side
Of my darling—my darling—my life and my bride,
   In the sepulchre there by the sea—   40
   In her tomb by the sounding sea.

Edgar Allan Poe

Edgar Allan Poe on Writing

A LONG POEM DOES NOT EXIST   1848

I hold that a long poem does not exist. I maintain that the phrase, "a long poem," is simply a flat contradiction in terms.

I need scarcely observe that a poem deserves its title only inasmuch as it excites, by elevating the soul. The value of the poem is in the ratio of its elevative excitement. But all excitements are, through a psychal necessity, transient. That degree of excitement which would entitle a poem to be so called at all cannot be sustained throughout a composition of any great length. After the lapse of half an hour, at the very utmost, it flags—fails—a revulsion ensues—and then the poem is in effect, and in fact, no longer such.

From "The Poetic Principle"

⚫▬▬◻ WRITING CRITICALLY ◻▬▬⚫

How to Begin Evaluating a Poem

Evaluation is both the easiest and the hardest part of literary criticism. It is easy because we almost always have some immediate reaction to the poem or story we are reading. We like it or dislike it—sometimes passionately so. While that initial, unrehearsed response will often become part of our ultimate judgment, it will usually end up being no more than a departure point. Literary evaluation is also hard because we must balance this subjective response against the need to view the poem in an informed perspective. The question is not merely, does the work please or move us, but how well does it manage the literary tasks it sets out to perform? Not all good performances will necessarily be to our own taste. A good critic is willing both to admire a strong poem that he or she doesn't like and to admit that a personal favorite might not really be all that good.

Fair evaluation is so difficult that many contemporary theorists have declared it impossible. They maintain that some external factor—personal or ideological—will always get in the way of disinterested judgment. Some theorists even say that the very notion of disinterested evaluation is illusory: to judge one work of art better than another is always to impose a set of values on it. Although the issues raised by these critics are genuine, there are still both theoretical and practical reasons to evaluate literary works. First, some works of art set out very explicit generic expectations of how they wish to be judged. An epigram, for instance, usually seeks to be witty and concise. If it proves tiresome and verbose, it can fairly be said to fail. Second, there is a strong case to be made for the idea that it is also illusory to pretend we can refrain from judging works of art. Since quality is almost always implicitly evaluated, it may be more useful to make those judgments clear and explicit. Finally, there is the practical issue of time. No one can read (or reread) every work ever written. We need open and informed critical guidance on where best to focus our finite attention.

To begin evaluating a poem, first try to understand your own subjective response—don't pretend it doesn't exist. Admit, at least to yourself, whether the poem delights, moves, bores, or annoys you. Then try to determine what the poem seems designed to make you think and feel. Does it belong to some identifiable form or genre? (Is it, for instance, a love sonnet, narrative ballad, satire, or elegy?) How does its performance stack up against the expectations it creates? Considering those questions will give you some larger sense of perspective from which to evaluate the poem.

Next, move on to specific elements in the poem. How well do its language, imagery, symbols, and figures of speech work in communicating its meaning? Are the metaphors or similes effective? Is the imagery fresh and precise? Is the language ever unnecessarily vague or verbose? Does the poem ever fall into clichés or platitudes? (Although there are dozens of such questions to ask, focus on the specific questions that seem relevant to the particular poem. Finally, once you've examined the details of the poem critically, go back and reread it again—preferably aloud. Does the poem seem better or worse than it did initially? Try to base your final evaluation on your own honest reaction, but make sure you have nourished that personal response with careful critical examination so that your evaluation has grown into an informed judgment. (For further tips on the process of evaluation, read the checklist of critical questions found on page 1086 under "Exercise: Reevaluating Popular Classics.")

WRITING ASSIGNMENT

Choose a short poem from this book that you particularly enjoy and write a defense of its excellence. In making your case, first set up the terms by which you will judge the poem and then demonstrate why such criteria are appropriate to this particular text. Finally, show specifically how the poem succeeds according to those standards.

FURTHER SUGGESTIONS FOR WRITING

1. Write a brief evaluation of either "The New Colossus" by Emma Lazarus or "Annabel Lee" by Edgar Allan Poe.
2. Concoct the worst poem you can possibly write and, in a brief accompanying essay, recount the difficulties you met and overcame in writing it. Quote, for example, any lines you wrote but had to discard for not being bad enough.
3. In "Poems for Further Reading," find a poem you particularly admire or dislike. In a brief essay (300–500 words), evaluate it. Refer to particulars in the poem to support your opinion of it.

29 *What Is Poetry?*

Archibald MacLeish   (1892–1982)

ARS POETICA   1926

A poem should be palpable and mute
As a globed fruit,

Dumb
As old medallions to the thumb,

Silent as the sleeve-worn stone   5
Of casement ledges where the moss has grown—

A poem should be wordless
As the flight of birds.

A poem should be motionless in time
As the moon climbs,   10

Leaving, as the moon releases
Twig by twig the night-entangled trees,

Leaving, as the moon behind the winter leaves,
Memory by memory the mind—

A poem should be motionless in time   15
As the moon climbs.

A poem should be equal to:
Not true.

For all the history of grief
An empty doorway and a maple leaf.   20

For love
The leaning grasses and two lights above the sea—

A poem should not mean
But be.

The title of Archibald MacLeish's provocative poem is Latin for "the poetic art" or "the art of poetry," and it is not unusual for poets to speculate in verse about their art. MacLeish, in fact, borrowed his title from the Roman poet Horace, who wrote a brilliant verse epistle on the subject during the reign of Caesar Augustus. In the two thousand years since then, there has been no shortage of opinions from fellow poets. There is something alluring and mysterious about poetry, even to its practitioners.

What, then, is poetry? By now, perhaps, you have formed your own idea, whether or not you can define it. Robert Frost made a try at a definition: "A poem is an idea caught in the act of dawning." Just in case further efforts at definition may be useful, here are a few memorable ones (including, for a second look, some given earlier):

things that are true expressed in words that are beautiful.
　　　　—Dante

the art of uniting pleasure with truth by calling imagination to the help
　　of reason.
　　　　—Samuel Johnson

the best words in the best order.
　　　　—Samuel Taylor Coleridge

the spontaneous overflow of powerful feelings.
　　　　—William Wordsworth

musical thought.
　　　　—Thomas Carlyle

emotion put into measure.
　　　　—Thomas Hardy

If I feel physically as if the top of my head were taken off, I know *that* is
　　poetry.
　　　　—Emily Dickinson

speech framed . . . to be heard for its own sake and interest even over
　　and above its interest of meaning.
　　　　—Gerard Manley Hopkins

a way of remembering what it would impoverish us to forget.
　　　　—Robert Frost

a revelation in words by means of the words.
　　　　—Wallace Stevens

Poetry is prose bewitched.
        —*Mina Loy*

not the assertion that something is true, but the making of that truth
        more fully real to us.
        —*T. S. Eliot*

the clear expression of mixed feelings.
        —*W. H. Auden*

the body of linguistic constructions that men usually refer to as poems.
        —*J. V. Cunningham*

hundreds of things coming together at the right moment.
        —*Elizabeth Bishop*

Verse should have two obligations: to communicate a precise instance
        and to touch us physically, as the presence of the sea does.
        —*Jorge Luis Borges*

Reduced to its simplest and most essential form, the poem is a song.
        Song is neither discourse nor explanation.
        —*Octavio Paz*

anything said in such a way, or put on the page in such a way, as to
        invite from the hearer or the reader a certain kind of attention.
        —*William Stafford*

Poetry is life distilled.
        —*Gwendolyn Brooks*

A poem is something that penetrates for an instant into the unconscious.
        —*Robert Bly*

A poem differs from most prose in several ways. For one, both writer and
reader tend to regard it differently. The poet's attitude is something like this: I
offer this piece of writing to be read not as prose but as a poem—that is, more
perceptively, thoughtfully, and considerately, with more attention to sounds and
connotations. This is a great deal to expect, but in return, the reader, too, has a
right to certain expectations. Approaching the poem in the anticipation of out-
of-the-ordinary knowledge and pleasure, the reader assumes that the poem may
use certain enjoyable devices not available to prose: rime, alliteration, meter,
and rhythms—definite, various, or emphatic. (The poet may not *always* decide to
use these things.) The reader expects the poet to make greater use, perhaps, of resources of meaning such as figurative language, allusion, symbol, and imagery. As
readers of prose, we might seek no more than meaning: no more than what could
be paraphrased without serious loss. Meeting any figurative language or graceful
turns of word order, we think them pleasant extras. But in poetry all these "extras" matter as much as the paraphraseable content, if not more. For, when we
finish reading a good poem, we cannot explain precisely to ourselves what we

have experienced—without repeating, word for word, the language of the poem itself. Archibald MacLeish makes this point memorably in "*Ars Poetica*":

> A poem should not mean
> But be.

"Poetry is to prose as dancing is to walking," remarked Paul Valéry. It is doubtful, however, that anyone can draw an immovable boundary between poetry and prose. Certain prose needs only to be arranged in lines to be seen as poetry—especially prose that conveys strong emotion in vivid, physical imagery and in terse, figurative, rhythmical language. Even in translation the words of Chief Joseph of the Nez Percé tribe, at the moment of his surrender to the U.S. Army in 1877, still move us and are memorable:

> Hear me, my warriors, my heart is sick and sad:
> Our chiefs are killed,
> The old men all are dead,
> It is cold and we have no blankets.
>
> The little children freeze to death.
>
> Hear me, my warriors, my heart is sick and sad:
> From where the sun now stands I will fight no more forever.

It may be that a poem can point beyond words to something still more essential. Language has its limits, and probably Edgar Allan Poe was the only poet ever to claim he could always find words for whatever he wished to express. For, of all a human being can experience and imagine, words say only part. "Human speech," said Flaubert, who strove after the best of it, "is like a cracked kettle on which we hammer out tunes to make bears dance, when what we long for is the compassion of the stars."

Like Yeats's chestnut-tree in "Among School Children" (which, when asked whether it is leaf, blossom, or bole, has no answer), a poem is to be seen not as a confederation of form, rime, image, metaphor, tone, and theme, but as a whole. We study a poem one element at a time because the intellect best comprehends what it can separate. But only our total attention, involving the participation of our blood and marrow, can see all elements in a poem fused, all dancing together. Yeats knew how to make poems and how to read them:

> God guard me from those thoughts men think
> In the mind alone;
> He that sings a lasting song
> Thinks in a marrow-bone.

Throughout this book, we have been working on the assumption that the patient and conscious explication of poems will sharpen unconscious perceptions. We can only hope that it will; the final test lies in whether you care to go on by yourself, reading other poems, finding in them pleasure and enlightenment. Pedagogy must have a stop; so too must the viewing of poems as if their elements fell into

chapters. For the total experience of reading a poem surpasses the mind's categories. The wind in the grass, says a proverb, cannot be taken into the house.

Ha Jin   (b. 1956)

MISSED TIME   2000

My notebook has remained blank for months
thanks to the light you shower
around me. I have no use
for my pen, which lies
languorously without grief.   5

Nothing is better than to live
a storyless life that needs
no writing for meaning—
when I am gone, let others say
they lost a happy man,   10
though no one can tell how happy I was.

30 *Two Critical Casebooks: Emily Dickinson and Langston Hughes*

EMILY DICKINSON

Amherst College Archives and Special Collections.

Emily Dickinson (1830–1886) spent virtually all her life in her family home in Amherst, Massachusetts. Her father Edward Dickinson was a prominent lawyer who ranked as Amherst's leading citizen. (He even served a term in the U.S. Congress.) Dickinson attended one year of college at Mount Holyoke Female Seminary in South Hadley. She proved to be a good student, but, suffering from homesickness and poor health, she did not return for the second year. This brief period of study and a few trips to Boston, Philadelphia, and Washington, D.C., were the only occasions she left home in her fifty-five-year life. As the years passed, Dickinson became more reclusive. She stopped attending church (and refused to endorse the orthodox Congregationalist creed). She also spent increasing time alone in her room—often writing poems. Dickinson never married, but she had a significant romantic relationship with at least one unidentified man. Although scholars have suggested several likely candidates, the historical object of Dickinson's affections will likely never be known. What survives unmistakably, however, is the intensely passionate poetry written out of these private circumstances. By the end of her life, Dickinson had become a locally famous recluse; she rarely left home. She would greet visitors from her own upstairs room, clearly heard but never seen. In 1886 she was buried, according to her own instructions, within sight of the family home. Although Dickinson composed 1,775 known poems, she published only seven in her lifetime. She often, however, sent copies of poems to friends in letters, but only after her death would the full extent of her writings become known when a cache of manuscripts was discovered in a trunk in the homestead attic—handwritten little booklets of poems sewn together by the poet with needle and thread. From 1890 until the mid-twentieth century, nine posthumous collections of her poems were published by friends and relatives, some of whom rewrote her work and changed her idiosyncratic punctuation to make it more conventional. Thomas H. Johnson's three-volume edition of the Poems (1955) established a more accurate text. In relatively few and simple forms clearly indebted to the hymns she heard in church, Dickinson succeeded in being a true visionary and a poet of colossal originality.

∼ POEMS ∼

SUCCESS IS COUNTED
SWEETEST   (1859) PUBLISHED 1878

Success is counted sweetest
By those who ne'er succeed.
To comprehend a nectar
Requires sorest need.

Not one of all the purple Host°   an army   5
Who took the Flag today
Can tell the definition
So clear of Victory

As he defeated – dying –
On whose forbidden ear   10
The distant strains of triumph
Burst agonized and clear!

WILD NIGHTS – WILD NIGHTS!   (ABOUT 1861)

Wild Nights – Wild Nights!
Were I with thee
Wild Nights should be
Our luxury!

Futile – the Winds –
To a Heart in port –
Done with the Compass –
Done with the Chart!

Rowing in Eden –
Ah, the Sea!
Might I but moor – Tonight –
In Thee!

THERE'S A CERTAIN SLANT OF LIGHT   (ABOUT 1861)

There's a certain Slant of light,
Winter Afternoons –
That oppresses, like the Heft
Of Cathedral Tunes –

Heavenly Hurt, it gives us –   5
We can find no scar,
But internal difference,
Where the Meanings, are –

None may teach it – Any –
'Tis the Seal Despair –   10
An imperial affliction
Sent us of the Air –

When it comes, the landscape listens –
Shadows – hold their breath –
When it goes, 'tis like the Distance   15
On the look of Death –

I FELT A FUNERAL, IN MY BRAIN   (ABOUT 1861)

I felt a Funeral, in my Brain,
And Mourners to and fro
Kept treading – treading – till it seemed
That Sense was breaking through –

And when they all were seated,   5
A Service, like a Drum –
Kept beating – beating – till I thought
My Mind was going numb –

And then I heard them lift a Box
And creak across my Soul   10
With those same Boots of Lead, again,
Then Space – began to toll,

As all the Heavens were a Bell,
And Being, but an Ear,
And I, and Silence, some strange Race   15
Wrecked, solitary, here –

And then a Plank in Reason, broke,
And I dropped down, and down –
And hit a World, at every plunge,
And Finished knowing – then –   20

I'M NOBODY! WHO ARE YOU?   (ABOUT 1861)

I'm Nobody! Who are you?
Are you – Nobody – too?
Then there's a pair of us!
Don't tell! they'd banish us – you know!

How dreary – to be – Somebody!   5
How public – like a Frog –
To tell your name – the livelong June –
To an admiring Bog!

THE SOUL SELECTS
HER OWN SOCIETY   (ABOUT 1862)

The Soul selects her own Society –
Then – shuts the Door –
To her divine Majority –
Present no more –

Unmoved – she notes the Chariots – pausing –   5
At her low Gate –
Unmoved – an Emperor be kneeling
Upon her Mat –

I've known her – from an ample nation –
Choose One –   10
Then – close the Valves of her attention –
Like Stone –

SOME KEEP THE SABBATH GOING TO CHURCH

(1862) PUBLISHED 1864

Some keep the Sabbath going to Church –
I keep it, staying at Home –
With a Bobolink for a Chorister –
And an Orchard, for a Dome –

Some keep the Sabbath in Surplice –   5
I just wear my Wings –
And instead of tolling the Bell, for Church,
Our little Sexton – sings.

God preaches, a noted Clergyman –
And the sermon is never long,   10
So instead of getting to Heaven, at last –
I'm going, all along.

AFTER GREAT PAIN, A FORMAL FEELING COMES

(1862)

After great pain, a formal feeling comes –
The Nerves sit ceremonious, like Tombs –
The stiff Heart questions was it He, that bore,
And Yesterday, or Centuries before?

The Feet, mechanical, go round –   5
Of Ground, or Air, or Ought –
A Wooden way
Regardless grown,
A Quartz contentment, like a stone –

This is the Hour of Lead –   10
Remembered, if outlived,
As Freezing persons, recollect the Snow –
First – Chill – then Stupor – then the letting go –

MUCH MADNESS IS DIVINEST SENSE

(ABOUT 1862)

Much Madness is divinest Sense –
To a discerning Eye –
Much Sense – the starkest Madness –
'Tis the Majority
In this, as All, prevail –   5
Assent – and you are sane –
Demur – you're straightway dangerous –
And handled with a Chain

THIS IS MY LETTER TO THE WORLD (1862)

This is my letter to the World
That never wrote to Me –
The simple News that Nature told –
With tender Majesty

Her Message is committed   5
To Hands I cannot see –
For love of Her – Sweet – countrymen –
Judge tenderly – of Me

I HEARD A FLY BUZZ – WHEN I DIED (ABOUT 1862)

I heard a Fly buzz – when I died –
The Stillness in the Room
Was like the Stillness in the Air –
Between the Heaves of Storm –

The Eyes around – had wrung them dry –   5
And Breaths were gathering firm
For that last Onset – when the King
Be witnessed – in the Room –

I willed my Keepsakes – Signed away
What portion of me be   10
Assignable – and then it was
There interposed a Fly –

With Blue – uncertain stumbling Buzz –
Between the light – and me –
And then the Windows failed – and then   15
I could not see to see –

I STARTED EARLY – TOOK MY DOG (ABOUT 1862)

I started Early – Took my Dog –
And visited the Sea –
The Mermaids in the Basement
Came out to look at me –

And Frigates – in the Upper Floor   5
Extended Hempen Hands –
Presuming Me to be a Mouse –
Aground – upon the Sands –

But no Man moved Me – till the Tide
Went past my simple Shoe –   10
And past my Apron – and my Belt
And past my Bodice – too –

And made as He would eat me up –
As wholly as a Dew
Upon a Dandelion's Sleeve – 15
And then – I started – too –

And He – He followed – close behind –
I felt His Silver Heel
Upon my Ankle – Then my Shoes
Would overflow with Pearl – 20

Until We met the Solid Town –
No One He seemed to know –
And bowing – with a Mighty look –
At me – The Sea withdrew –

BECAUSE I COULD NOT STOP
FOR DEATH (ABOUT 1863)

Because I could not stop for Death –
He kindly stopped for me –
The Carriage held but just Ourselves –
And Immortality.

We slowly drove – He knew no haste
And I had put away
My labor and my leisure too,
For His Civility – 5

We passed the School, where Children strove
At Recess – in the Ring – 10
We passed the Fields of Gazing Grain –
We passed the Setting Sun –

Or rather – He passed Us –
The Dews drew quivering and chill –
For only Gossamer, my Gown – 15
My Tippet° – only Tulle – *cape*

We passed before a House that seemed
A Swelling of the Ground –
The Roof was scarcely visible –
The Cornice – in the Ground – 20

Since then – 'tis Centuries – and yet
Feels shorter than the Day
I first surmised the Horses Heads
Were toward Eternity –

THE BUSTLE IN A HOUSE   (1866)

The Bustle in a House
The Morning after Death
Is solemnest of industries
Enacted upon Earth –

The Sweeping up the Heart   5
And putting Love away
We shall not want to use again
Until Eternity

TELL ALL THE TRUTH BUT
TELL IT SLANT   (ABOUT 1868)

Tell all the Truth but tell it slant –
Success in Circuit lies
Too bright for our infirm Delight
The Truth's superb surprise
As Lightning to the Children eased   5
With explanation kind
The Truth must dazzle gradually
Or every man be blind –

COMPARE

More poems by Emily Dickinson that are found in this book:

    A Dying Tiger – moaned for Drink (page 1069)
    I like to see it lap the Miles (page 721)
    It dropped so low – in my Regard (page 821)
    The Lightning is a yellow Fork (page 957)
    My Life had stood – a Loaded Gun (page 818)
    A Route of Evanescence (page 796)

Emily Dickinson's room in Amherst, Massachusetts.

RECOGNIZING POETRY   (1870)

If I read a book [and] it makes my whole body so cold no fire ever can warm me I know *that* is poetry. If I feel physically as if the top of my head were taken off, I know *that* is poetry. These are the only ways I know it. Is there any other way.

How do most people live without any thoughts. There are many people in the world (you must have noticed them in the street) How do they live. How do they get strength to put on their clothes in the morning.

When I lost the use of my Eyes it was a comfort to think there were so few real *books* that I could easily find some one to read me all of them.

Truth is such a *rare* thing it is delightful to tell it.

I find ecstasy in living – the mere sense of living is joy enough.

From a conversation with Thomas Wentworth Higginson

COMPARE

Dickinson's famous comments on the nature of poetry, which are often quoted out of context, with their original source, a letter—not by the poet herself but by a visiting editor. (See the editor's letter that follows on page 1108.)

25 April 1862

Mr. Higginson,

Your kindness claimed earlier gratitude – but I was ill – and write today, from my pillow.

Thank you for the surgery – it was not so painful as I supposed. I bring you others – as you ask – though they might not differ –

While my thought is undressed – I can make the distinction, but when I put them in the Gown – they look alike, and numb.

You asked how old I was? I made no verse – but one or two – until this winter
– Sir –

I had a terror – since September – I could tell to none – and so I sing, as the Boy does by the Burying Ground – because I am afraid – You inquire my Books – For Poets – I have Keats – and Mr and Mrs Browning. For Prose – Mr Ruskin – Sir Thomas Browne – and the Revelations.° I went to school – but in your manner of the phrase – had no education. When a little Girl, I had a friend, who taught me Immortality – but venturing too near, himself – he never returned – Soon after, my Tutor, died – and for several years, my Lexicon – was my only companion – Then I found one more – but he was not contented I be his scholar – so he left the Land.

You ask of my Companions Hills – Sir – and the Sundown – and a Dog – large as myself, that my Father bought me – They are better than Beings – because they know – but do not tell – and the noise in the Pool, at Noon – excels my Piano. I have a Brother and Sister – My Mother does not care for thought – and Father, too busy with his Briefs° – to notice what we do – He buys me many Books – but begs me not to read them – because he fears they joggle the Mind. They are religious – except me – and address an Eclipse, every morning – whom they call their "Father." But I fear my story fatigues you – I would like to learn – Could you tell me how to grow – or is it unconveyed – like Melody – or Witch-craft?

You speak of Mr Whitman – I never read his Book° – but was told that he was disgraceful –

I read Miss Prescott's "Circumstance,"° but it followed me, in the Dark – so I avoided her –

Two Editors of Journals came to my Father's House, this winter – and asked me for my Mind – and when I asked them "Why," they said I was penurious – and they, would use it for the World –

I could not weigh myself – Myself –

My size felt small – to me – I read your Chapters in the Atlantic – and experienced honor for you – I was sure you would not reject a confiding question –

Is this – Sir – what you asked me to tell you?

Your friend,

E – Dickinson

From a letter to Thomas Wentworth Higginson

SELF-DESCRIPTION. Emily Dickinson's letter was written to Thomas Wentworth Higginson, a noted writer. Dickinson had read his article of advice to young writers in the *Atlantic Monthly*. She sent him four poems and a letter asking if her verse was "alive." When he responded with comments and suggestions (the "surgery" Dickinson mentions in the second paragraph), she wrote him this letter about herself. *Mr Ruskin . . . Revelations:* in listing her favorite prose authors Dickinson chose John Ruskin (1819–1900), an English art critic and essayist, Sir Thomas Browne (1605–1682), a doctor and philosopher with a magnificent prose style, and the final book of the New Testament. *Briefs:* legal papers (her father was a lawyer). *Whitman . . . book: Leaves of Grass* (1855) by Walt Whitman was considered an improper book for women at this time because of the volume's sexual candor. *Miss Prescott's "Circumstance":* a story, also published in the *Atlantic Monthly*, that was full of violence.

Facsimile manuscript of "Some keep the Sabbath going to Church," printed on page 1101.

CRITICS ON EMILY DICKINSON

Thomas Wentworth Higginson (1823–1911)

MEETING EMILY DICKINSON 1870

A large county lawyer's house, brown brick, with great trees & a garden—I sent up my card. A parlor dark & cool & stiffish, a few books & engravings & an open piano. . . .

A step like a pattering child's in entry & in glided a little plain woman with two smooth bands of reddish hair & a face a little like Belle Dove's; not plainer—with no good feature—in a very plain & exquisitely clean white pique & a blue net worsted shawl. She came to me with two day lilies which she put in a sort of childlike way into my hand & said "These are my introduction" in a soft frightened breathless childlike voice—& added under her breath Forgive me if I am frightened; I never see strangers & hardly know what I say—but she talked soon & thenceforward continuously—& deferentially—sometimes stopping to ask me to talk instead of her—but readily recommencing . . . thoroughly ingenuous & simple . . . & saying many things which you would have thought foolish & I wise—& some things you wd. hv. liked. I add a few over the page. . . .

"Women talk; men are silent; that is why I dread women."

"My father only reads on Sunday—he reads *lonely* & *rigorous* books."

"If I read a book [and] it makes my whole body so cold no fire ever can warm me I know *that* is poetry. If I feel physically as if the top of my head were taken off, I know *that* is poetry. These are the only ways I know it. Is there any other way."

"How do most people live without any thoughts. There are many people in the world (you must have noticed them in the street) How do they live. How do they get strength to put on their clothes in the morning"

"When I lost the use of my Eyes it was a comfort to think there were so few real *books* that I could easily find some one to read me all of them"

"Truth is such a *rare* thing it is delightful to tell it."

"I find ecstasy in living—the mere sense of living is joy enough"

I asked if she never felt want of employment, never going off the place & never seeing any visitor "I never thought of conceiving that I could ever have the slightest approach to such a want in all future time" (& added) "I feel that I have not expressed myself strongly enough."

She makes all the bread for her father only likes hers & says "& people must have puddings" this *very* dreamily, as if they were comets—so she makes them.

. . . .

E D again

"Could you tell me what home is"

"I never had a mother. I suppose a mother is one to whom you hurry when you are troubled."

1108   TWO CRITICAL CASEBOOKS: DICKINSON AND HUGHES

"I never knew how to tell time by the clock till I was 15. My father thought he had taught me but I did not understand & I was afraid to say I did not & afraid to ask any one else lest he should know."

Her father was not severe I should think but remote. He did not wish them to read anything but the Bible. One day her brother brought home Kavanagh° hid it under the piano cover & made signs to her & they read it: her father at last found it & was displeased. Perhaps it was before this that a student of his was amazed that they had never heard of Mrs. [Lydia Maria] Child° & used to bring them books & hide in a bush by the door. They were then little things in short dresses with their feet on the rungs of the chair. After the first book she thought in ecstasy "This then is a book! And there are more of them!"

"Is it oblivion or absorption when things pass from our minds?"

Major Hunt interested her more than any man she ever saw. She remembered two things he said—that her great dog "understood gravitation" & when he said he should come again "in a year. If I say a shorter time it will be longer."

When I said I would come again *some time* she said "Say in a long time, that will be nearer. Some time is nothing."

After long disuse of her eyes she read Shakespeare & thought why is any other book needed.

I never was with any one who drained my nerve power so much. Without touching her, she drew from me. I am glad not to live near her. She often thought me *tired* & seemed very thoughtful of others.

From a letter to his wife, August 16–17, 1870

Thomas H. Johnson   (1902–1985)

THE DISCOVERY OF EMILY DICKINSON'S MANUSCRIPTS   1955

Shortly after Emily Dickinson's death on May fifteenth, 1886, her sister Lavinia discovered a locked box in which Emily had placed her poems. Lavinia's amazement seems to have been genuine. Though the sisters had lived intimately together under the same roof all their lives, and though Lavinia had always been aware that her sister wrote poems, she had not the faintest concept of the great number of them. The story of Lavinia's willingness to spare them because she found no instructions specifying that they be destroyed, and her search for an editor and a publisher to give them to the world has already been told in some detail.

Lavinia first consulted the two people most interested in Emily's poetry, her sister-in-law Susan Dickinson, and Mrs. Todd. David Peck Todd, a graduate of Amherst College in 1875, returned to Amherst with his young bride in 1881 as director of the college observatory and soon became professor of Astronomy and Navigation. These were the months shortly before Mrs. Edward Dickinson's death, when neighbors were especially thoughtful. Mrs. Todd endeared herself to

---

Kavanagh: Kavanagh: A Tale (1849), an utterly innocuous work of fiction by the poet Henry Wadsworth Longfellow.   *Mrs. [Lydia Maria] Child*: anti-slavery writer and author (1802–1880) of didactic novels.

Emily and Lavinia by small but understanding attentions, in return for which Emily sent Mrs. Todd copies of her poems. At first approach neither Susan Dickinson nor Mrs. Todd felt qualified for the editorial task which they both were hesitant to undertake. Mrs. Todd says of Lavinia's discovery: "She showed me the manuscripts and there were over sixty little 'volumes,' each composed of four or five sheets of note paper tied together with twine. In this box she discovered eight or nine hundred poems tied up in this way."

. . .

As the story can be reconstructed, at some time during the year 1858 Emily Dickinson began assembling her poems into packets. Always in ink, they are gatherings of four, five, or six sheets of letter paper usually folded once but sometimes single. They are loosely held together by thread looped through them at the spine at two points equidistant from the top and bottom. When opened up they may be read like a small book, a fact that explains why Emily's sister Lavinia, when she discovered them after Emily's death, referred to them as "volumes." All of the packet poems are either fair copies or semifinal drafts, and they constitute two-thirds of the entire body of her poetry.

For the most part the poems in a given packet seem to have been written and assembled as a unit. Since rough drafts of packet poems are almost totally lacking, one concludes that they were systematically discarded. If the poems were in fact composed at the time the copies were made, as the evidence now seems to point, one concludes that nearly two-thirds of her poems were created in the brief span of eight years, centering on her early thirties. Her interest in the packet method of assembling the verses thus coincides with the years of fullest productivity. In 1858 she gathered some fifty poems into packets. There are nearly one hundred so transcribed in 1859, some sixty-five in 1860, and in 1861 more than eighty. By 1862 the creative drive must have been almost frightening; during that year she transcribed into packets no fewer than three hundred and sixty-six poems, the greater part of them complete and final texts.

Whether this incredible number was in fact composed in that year or represents a transcription of earlier worksheet drafts can never be established by direct evidence. But the pattern established during the preceding four years reveals a gathering momentum, and the quality of tenseness and prosodic skill uniformly present in the poems of 1861–1862 bears scant likeness to the conventionality of theme and treatment in the poems of 1858–1859. Excepting a half dozen occasional verses written in the early fifties, there is not a single scrap of poetry that can be dated earlier than 1858.

From *The Poems of Emily Dickinson*

Richard Wilbur   (b. 1921)*

THE THREE PRIVATIONS OF EMILY DICKINSON   1959

Emily Dickinson never lets us forget for very long that in some respects life gave her short measure; and indeed it is possible to see the greater part of her poetry as an effort to cope with her sense of privation. I think that for her there were three major privations: she was deprived of an orthodox and steady religious faith; she was deprived of love; she was deprived of literary recognition.

At the age of seventeen, after a series of revival meetings at Mount Holyoke Seminary, Emily Dickinson found that she must refuse to become a professing Christian. To some modern minds this may seem to have been a sensible and necessary step; and surely it was a step toward becoming such a poet as she became. But for her, no pleasure in her own integrity could then eradicate the feeling that she had betrayed a deficiency, a want of grace. In her letters to Abiah Root she tells of the enhancing effect of conversion on her fellow-students, and says of herself in a famous passage:

> I am one of the lingering bad ones, and so do I slink away, and pause and ponder, and ponder and pause, and do work without knowing why, not surely for this brief world, and more sure it is not for heaven, and I ask what this message *means* that they ask for so very eagerly: *you* know of this depth and fulness, will you try to tell me about it?

There is humor in that, and stubbornness, and a bit of characteristic lurking pride: but there is also an anguished sense of having separated herself, through some dry incapacity, from spiritual community, from purpose, and from magnitude of life. As a child of evangelical Amherst, she inevitably thought of purposive, heroic life as requiring a vigorous faith. Out of such a thought she later wrote:

> The abdication of Belief
> Makes the Behavior small –
> Better an ignis fatuus
> Than no illume at all –

That hers *was* a species of religious personality goes without saying; but by her refusal of such ideas as original sin, redemption, hell, and election, she made it impossible for herself—as Whicher observed—"to share the religious life of her generation." She became an unsteady congregation of one.

Her second privation, the privation of love, is one with which her poems and her biographies have made us exceedingly familiar, though some biographical facts remain conjectural. She had the good fortune, at least once, to bestow her heart on another; but she seems to have found her life, in great part, a history of loneliness, separation, and bereavement.

As for literary fame, some will deny that Emily Dickinson ever greatly desired it, and certainly there is evidence, mostly from her latter years, to support such a view. She *did* write that "Publication is the auction / Of the mind of man." And she *did* say to Helen Hunt Jackson, "How can you print a piece of your soul?" But earlier, in 1861, she had frankly expressed to Sue Dickinson the hope that "sometime" she might make her kinfolk proud of her. The truth is, I think, that Emily Dickinson knew she was good, and began her career with a normal appetite for recognition. I think that she later came, with some reason, to despair of being understood or properly valued, and so directed against her hopes of fame what was by then a well-developed disposition to renounce. That she wrote a good number of poems about fame supports my view: the subjects to which a poet returns are those which vex him.

What did Emily Dickinson do, as a poet, with her sense of privation? One thing she quite often did was to pose as the laureate and attorney of the empty-handed, and question God about the economy of His creation. Why, she asked, is a fatherly God so sparing of His presence? Why is there never a sign that prayers are heard? Why does Nature tell us no comforting news of its Maker? Why do some receive a whole load, while others must starve on a crumb? Where is the benevolence in shipwreck and earthquake? By asking such questions as these, she turned complaint into critique, and used her own sufferings as experiential evidence about the nature of the deity. The God who emerges from these poems is a God who does not answer, an unrevealed God whom one cannot confidently approach through Nature or through doctrine.

From "Sumptuous Destitution"

Cynthia Griffin Wolff (b. 1935)

DICKINSON AND DEATH 1993

(A Reading of "Because I could not stop for Death")

Modern readers are apt to comment upon the frequency with which Dickinson returns to this subject of death—"How morbid," people say. Perhaps. But if Dickinson was morbid, so was everyone else in her culture. Poe's aestheticizing of death (along with the proliferation of Gothic fiction and poetry) reflects a pervasive real-world concern: in mid-nineteenth-century America death rates were high. It was a truism that men had three wives (two of them having predeceased the spouse); infant mortality was so common that parents often gave several of their children the same name so that at least one "John" or "Lavinia" might survive to adulthood; rapid urbanization had intensified the threat of certain diseases—cholera, typhoid, and tuberculosis.

Poe and the Gothic tradition were one response to society's anxiety about death. Another came from the pulpit: mid-nineteenth-century sermons took death as their almost constant subject. Somewhat later in the century, preachers would embrace a doctrine of consolation: God would be figured as a loving parent—almost motherly—who had prepared a home in heaven for us all, and ministers would tell the members of their congregation that they need not be apprehensive. However, stern traces of Puritanism still tinctured the religious discourse of Dickinson's young womanhood, and members of the Amherst congregation were regularly exhorted with blood-stirring urgency to reflect upon the imminence of their own demise. Repeatedly, then, in attempting to comprehend Dickinson's work, a reader must return to the fundamental tenets of Protestant Christianity, for her poetry echoes the Bible more often than any other single work or author.

In part this preoccupation with the doctrines of her day reflected a more general concern with the essential questions of human existence they addressed. In a letter to Higginson she once said, "To live is so startling, it leaves but little room for other occupations." And to her friend Mrs. Holland she wrote, "All this and more, though *is* there more? More than Love and Death? Then tell me its name." The religious thought and language of the culture was important to her poetry because it comprised the semiotic system that her society employed to discuss the mysteries of life and death. If she wished to contemplate these, what other language was there to employ?

In part, however, conventional Christianity—especially the latter-day Puritanism of Dickinson's New England—represented for Dickinson an ultimate expression of patriarchal power. Rebelling against its rule, upbraiding a "Father" in Heaven who required absolute "faith" from his followers, but gave no discernible response, became a way of attacking the very essence of unjust authority, especially male authority.

. . .

It is true that the stern doctrines of New England Protestantism offered hope for a life after death; yet in Dickinson's estimation, the trope that was used for this "salvation" revealed some of the most repellent features of God's power, for the invitation to accept "faith" had been issued in the context of a courtship with a macabre, sexual component. It was promised that those who had faith would be carried to Heaven by the "Bridegroom" Christ. "Blessed are they which are called unto the marriage supper of the Lamb" (Revelation 19:9). Nor did it escape Dickinson's notice that the perverse prurience of Poe's notions were essentially similar to this Christian idea of Christ's "love" for a "bride" which promised a reunion that must be "consummated" through death. Thus the poem that is, perhaps, the apotheosis of that distinctive Dickinson voice, "the speaking dead," offers an astonishing combination: this conventional promise of Christianity suffused with the tonalities of the Gothic tradition.

[Griffin quotes the entire text of "Because I could not stop for Death" found on page 1103.]

The speaker is a beautiful woman (already dead!), and like some spectral Cinderella, she is dressed to go to a ball: "For only Gossamer, my Gown – / My Tippet – only Tulle –." Her escort recalls both the lover of Poe's configuration and the "Bridegroom" that had been promised in the Bible: "We slowly drove – He knew no haste / And I had put away / My labor and my leisure too, / For His Civility –". Their "Carriage" hovers in some surrealistic state that is exterior to both time and place: they are no longer earth-bound, not quite dead (or at least still possessed of consciousness), but they have not yet achieved the celebration that awaits them, the "marriage supper of the Lamb."

Yet the ultimate implication of this work turns precisely upon the *poet's* capacity to explode the finite temporal boundaries that generally define our existence, for there is a third member of the party—also exterior to time and location—and that is "Immortality." *True* immortality, the verse suggests, comes neither from the confabulations of a male lover nor from God's intangible Heaven. Irrefutable "Immortality" resides in the work of art itself, the creation of an empowered woman poet that continues to captivate readers more than one hundred years after her death. And this much-read, often-cited poem stands as patent proof upon the page of its own argument!

From "Emily Dickinson"

Judith Farr (b. 1937)

A Reading of "My Life had stood – a Loaded Gun"[1]   1992

One of the notable qualities of this poem is its formidable directness of statement. Both the substance and the shape of the rhetoric seem straightforward. The ideas of guns and killing are not, superficially, invested by the speaker with negative properties. Far from it. The speaker recounts life with her master in tones of heady confidence and pleasure. If we did not know that this poem had been written by a woman—perhaps especially by "Miss Emily"—some of its presumed complexity and ominousness would be reduced. Let us say that Emily "when a Boy" is speaking; then it may be easier to credit the open delight of the speaker. Liberated from corners in the poem, he/she is freed into a grown-up gunman's life of authority and power, and she likes the idea exceedingly. All the piled-up, dynamic "And"s tell us so.

Or, if we cast her as a woman, she is what has been called "a man's woman"; everything he likes, *she* likes. She likes hunting, and her instincts are not pacifist or nurturing—no ducks and does for her. She smiles at her work of killing; Nature smiles with her (the firing of the gun makes a glow like Vesuvius); and at night she can pronounce the day good. (Hunting is, after all, not always a selfish sport; often it is a protective measure. "Sovereign Woods," of course, suggests a royal preserve, an unfair advantage for the hunter.) Because of her identification with the man, she is nearly human, but with a "Yellow Eye"—the color of explosion in an oval gunbarrel—and "emphatic Thumb." The American hunting pictures of Dickinson's day, like the landscapes of Bowles's favorite painter, Sanford Gifford, present hunting scenes like Dickinson's. Her buoyancy of tone accords with them, depicting easy days roaming in the open air, taking from an apparently complaisant nature all that the Master wants. If we imagine the speaker as a boy with his designated sponsor or master, then she is—up to the last qua-

---

[1]The full text of Dickinson's "My Life had stood – a Loaded Gun" appears on page 818.

train—learning how to be a man in the rustic world dreamed up by Fenimore Cooper.

"Owner," however, suggests sexual love, and to anyone versed in the language of Emily Dickinson, it inflects one of her central themes:

'Twas my one glory –
Let it be
Remembered
I was owned of thee –

For that reason, and because there is such heroic intimacy between the gun and Master, one can see this as a poem of sexual love that emphasizes comradery, robust equality. It may be considered part of the Master cycle and related to "He touched me," where the speaker begins to "live" when Master touches her or carries her away. Although she is a woman, because the two are one in love she imagines herself like him; like him, empowered. . . . Here the speaker appropriates Master's masculinity; she is a loaded gun. Together they become one person, one royal We in a happy life of power. The speaker has always wanted to exercise her stored-up bullets or faculties; now she can. In a letter to her cousin Louise Norcross in 1880, Dickinson used these same images: "what is each instant but a gun, harmless because 'unloaded,' but that touched 'goes off'?" Although she omits one step, loading the gun, she is describing in her letter what she may be describing in her poem: love, "touching," as a means of being empowered.

There remains the final quatrain. It reads as a tightly wrought riddle, inviting explication. In one way, the stanza points up the incontrovertible difference between the mechanical gun and the human owner. He is the complete being, having both the power to die and the power to kill (even without her help). For all her fusion with him in their acts of love and death, she must still depend on him; she must be "carried." Thus this poem is often read—and read brilliantly—as a revelation of the limitations experienced by women under patriarchy, or even of the dependency of the female artist who needs male masters like Higginson to help her exercise her powers.

In reading this poem, however, I think that emphasis should always be placed on the pleasure the speaker experiences. The Master may be carrying her, but she is also speaking for him. He cannot do without her. That the gun's firing is compared to the pleasure of "a Vesuvian face" accents destruction, certainly; and it is hard to exempt this use of Vesuvius from all the others, always destructive, in the Dickinson canon. But the speaker seems to welcome her own destructiveness. She has been waiting a long time in many "corners" until the right lover lets her speak. For Dickinson, love is always the muse. Her variant for "the *power* to kill" in the penultimate line is *art*—which could make others die, from love or from aesthetic rapture. She herself—the gun, the artist—can never "die" like a real woman, however. She is but the arresting voice that speaks to and for the Master.

From *The Passion of Emily Dickinson*

LANGSTON HUGHES

Langston Hughes was born in Joplin, Missouri, in 1902. After his parents separated during his early years, he and his mother often lived a life of itinerant poverty, mostly in Kansas. Hughes attended high school in Cleveland, where as a senior he wrote "The Negro Speaks of Rivers." Reluctantly supported by his father, he attended Columbia University for a year before withdrawing. After a series of menial jobs, Hughes became a merchant seaman in 1923 and visited the ports of West Africa. For a time he lived in Paris, Genoa, and Rome, before returning to the United States. The publication of The Weary Blues (1926) earned him immediate fame, which he solidified a few months later with his pioneering essay "The Negro Artist and the Racial Mountain." In 1926 he also entered Lincoln University in Pennsylvania, from which he graduated in 1929. By then Hughes was already one of the central figures of the Harlem Renaissance, the flowering of African American arts and literature in the Harlem neighborhood of Upper Manhattan in New York City during the 1920s. A strikingly versatile author, Hughes worked in fiction, drama, translation, criticism, opera libretti, memoir, cinema, and songwriting, as well as poetry. He also became a tireless promoter of African American culture, crisscrossing the United States on speaking tours as well as compiling twenty-eight anthologies of African American folklore and poetry. His newspaper columns, which often reported conversations with an imaginary Harlem friend named Jesse B. Semple, nicknamed "Simple," attracted an especially large following. During the 1930s Hughes became involved in radical politics and traveled to the Soviet Union, but after World War II he gradually shifted to mainstream progressive politics. In his last years he became a spokesman for the moderate wing of the civil rights movement. He died in Harlem in 1967.

THE NEGRO SPEAKS OF RIVERS   (1921) 1926

I've known rivers:
I've known rivers ancient as the world and older than the flow of
    human blood in human veins.

My soul has grown deep like the rivers.

I bathed in the Euphrates when dawns were young.
I built my hut near the Congo and it lulled me to sleep.   5
I looked upon the Nile and raised the pyramids above it.
I heard the singing of the Mississippi when Abe Lincoln went down to
    New Orleans, and I've seen its muddy bosom turn all golden in the
    sunset.

I've known rivers:
Ancient, dusky rivers.

My soul has grown deep like the rivers.   10

MOTHER TO SON   (1922) 1932

Well, son, I'll tell you:
Life for me ain't been no crystal stair.
It's had tacks in it,
And splinters,
And boards torn up,   5
And places with no carpet on the floor—
Bare.
But all the time
I'se been a-climbin' on,
And reachin' landin's,   10
And turnin' corners,
And sometimes goin' in the dark
Where there ain't been no light.
So boy, don't you turn back.
Don't you set down on the steps   15
'Cause you finds it's kinder hard.
Don't you fall now—
For I'se still goin', honey,
I'se still climbin',
And life for me ain't been no crystal stair.   20

To fling my arms wide
In some place of the sun,
To whirl and to dance
Till the white day is done.
Then rest at cool evening   5
Beneath a tall tree
While night comes on gently,
    Dark like me—
That is my dream!

To fling my arms wide
In the face of the sun,
Dance! Whirl! Whirl!   10
Till the quick day is done.
Rest at pale evening . . .
A tall, slim tree . . .   15
Night coming tenderly
    Black like me.

I, Too   1926

I, too, sing America.

I am the darker brother.
They send me to eat in the kitchen
When company comes,
But I laugh,   5
And eat well,
And grow strong.

Tomorrow,
I'll be at the table
When company comes.   10
Nobody'll dare
Say to me,
"Eat in the kitchen,"
Then.

Besides,   15
They'll see how beautiful I am
And be ashamed—

I, too, am America.

Droning a drowsy syncopated tune,
Rocking back and forth to a mellow croon,
    I heard a Negro play.
Down on Lenox Avenue the other night
By the pale dull pallor of an old gas light   5
    He did a lazy sway. . . .
    He did a lazy sway. . . .
To the tune o' those Weary Blues.
With his ebony hands on each ivory key
He made that poor piano moan with melody.   10
    O Blues!
Swaying to and fro on his rickety stool
He played that sad raggy tune like a musical fool.
    Sweet Blues!
Coming from a black man's soul.   15
    O Blues!
In a deep song voice with a melancholy tone
I heard that Negro sing, that old piano moan—
    "Ain't got nobody in all this world,
      Ain't got nobody but ma self.   20
      I's gwine to quit ma frownin'
      And put ma troubles on the shelf."

Thump, thump, thump, went his foot on the floor.
He played a few chords then he sang some more—
    "I got the Weary Blues   25
      And I can't be satisfied.
    Got the Weary Blues
      And can't be satisfied—
    I ain't happy no mo'
      And I wish that I had died."   30
And far into the night he crooned that tune.
The stars went out and so did the moon.
The singer stopped playing and went to bed
While the Weary Blues echoed through his head.
He slept like a rock or a man that's dead.   35

THE WEARY BLUES. This poem quotes the first blues song Hughes had ever heard, "The Weary Blues," which begins, "I got de weary blues / And I can't be satisfied / . . . I ain't happy no mo' / And I wish that I had died."

Way Down South in Dixie
    (Break the heart of me)
They hung my black young lover
    To a cross roads tree.

Way Down South in Dixie
    (Bruised body high in air)   5
I asked the white Lord Jesus
    What was the use of prayer.

Way Down South in Dixie
    (Break the heart of me)
Love is a naked shadow   10
    On a gnarled and naked tree.

DESIRE   (1927) 1947

Desire to us
Was like a double death,
Swift dying
Of our mingled breath,
Evaporation   5
Of an unknown strange perfume
Between us quickly
In a naked
Room.

PRAYER   (1931) 1947

Gather up
In the arms of your pity
The sick, the depraved.
The desperate, the tired,
All the scum   5
Of our weary city

Gather up
In the arms of your pity
Gather up
In the arms of your love—   10
Those who expect
No love from above.

Landlord, landlord,
My roof has sprung a leak.
Don't you 'member I told you about it
Way last week?

Landlord, landlord,
These steps is broken down.   5
When you come up yourself
It's a wonder you don't fall down.

Ten Bucks you say I owe you?
Ten Bucks you say is due?
Well, that's Ten Bucks more'n I'll pay you   10
Till you fix this house up new.

What? You gonna get eviction orders?
You gonna cut off my heat?
You gonna take my furniture and   15
Throw it in the street?

Um-huh! You talking high and mighty.
Talk on—till you get through.
You ain't gonna be able to say a word
If I land my fist on you.   20

Police! Police!
Come and get this man!
He's trying to ruin the government
And overturn the land!

Copper's whistle!   25
Patrol bell!
Arrest.

Precinct Station.
Iron cell.
Headlines in press: 30

MAN THREATENS LANDLORD

• •

TENANT HELD NO BAIL

• •

JUDGE GIVES NEGRO 90 DAYS IN COUNTY JAIL

END   1947

There are
No clocks on the wall,
And no time,
No shadows that move
From dawn to dusk   5
Across the floor.

There is neither light
Nor dark
Outside the door.

There is no door!   10

ISLAND   (1950) 1959

Wave of sorrow,
Do not drown me now:

I see the island
Still ahead somehow.

I see the island   5
And its sands are fair:

Wave of sorrow,
Take me there.

THEME FOR ENGLISH B   1951

The instructor said,

> *Go home and write*
> *a page tonight.*
> *And let that page come out of you—*
> *Then, it will be true.*   5

I wonder if it's that simple?
I am twenty-two, colored, born in Winston-Salem.
I went to school there, then Durham, then here
to this college on the hill above Harlem.
I am the only colored student in my class.   10
The steps from the hill lead down into Harlem,
through a park, then I cross St. Nicholas,
Eighth Avenue, Seventh, and I come to the Y,
the Harlem Branch Y, where I take the elevator
up to my room, sit down, and write this page: 15

It's not easy to know what is true for you and me
at twenty-two, my age. But I guess I'm what
I feel and see and hear, Harlem, I hear you:
hear you, hear me—we two—you, me, talk on this page.
(I hear New York, too.) Me—who?   20
Well, I like to eat, sleep, drink, and be in love.
I like to work, read, learn, and understand life.
I like a pipe for a Christmas present,
or records—Bessie, bop, or Bach.
I guess being colored doesn't make me not like   25
the same things other folks like who are other races.
So will my page be colored that I write?
Being me, it will not be white.

But it will be
a part of you, instructor.   30
You are white—
yet a part of me, as I am a part of you.
That's American.
Sometimes perhaps you don't want to be a part of me.
Nor do I often want to be a part of you.   35
But we are, that's true!
As I learn from you,
I guess you learn from me—
although you're older—and white—
and somewhat more free.   40

This is my page for English B.

THEME FOR ENGLISH B.   *9 College on the hill above Harlem:* Columbia University, where Hughes was
briefly a student. (Please note, however, that this poem is not autobiographical. The young speaker is
a character invented by the middle-aged author.)   *24 Bessie:* Bessie Smith (1898?–1937) was a popular blues singer often called the "Empress of the Blues." The lyrics to Smith's "Jailhouse Blues"
appear on page 849.

SUBWAY RUSH HOUR   1951

Mingled
breath and smell
so close
mingled
black and white   5
so near
no room for fear.

SLIVER   1951

Cheap little rhymes
A cheap little tune
Are sometimes as dangerous
As a sliver of the moon.
A cheap little tune   5
To cheap little rhymes
Can cut a man's
Throat sometimes.

HARLEM [DREAM DEFERRED]   1951

What happens to a dream deferred?

    Does it dry up
    like a raisin in the sun?
    Or fester like a sore—
    And then run?
    Does it stink like rotten meat?   5
    Or crust and sugar over—
    like a syrupy sweet?

    Maybe it just sags
    like a heavy load.   10

    Or does it explode?

HARLEM. This famous poem appeared under two titles in the author's lifetime. Both titles appear above.

COMPARE

More poems by Langston Hughes that are found in this book:
Dream Boogie (page 904)
Prayer (page 924)

Lenox Avenue, Harlem, in 1925.

THE NEGRO ARTIST AND THE RACIAL MOUNTAIN   1926

Most of my own poems are racial in theme and treatment, derived from the life I know. In many of them I try to grasp and hold some of the meanings and rhythms of jazz. I am as sincere as I know how to be in these poems and yet after every reading I answer questions like these from my own people: Do you think Negroes should always write about Negroes? I wish you wouldn't read some of your poems to white folks. How do you find anything interesting in a place like a cabaret? Why do you write about black people? You aren't black. What makes you do so many jazz poems?

But jazz to me is one of the inherent expressions of Negro life in America; the eternal tom-tom beating in the Negro soul—the tom-tom of revolt against weariness in a white world, a world of subway trains, and work, work, work; the tom-tom of joy and laughter, and pain swallowed in a smile. Yet the Philadelphia clubwoman is ashamed to say that her race created it and she does not like me to write about it. The old subconscious "white is best" runs through her mind. Years of study under white teachers, a lifetime of white books, pictures, and papers, and white manners, morals, and Puritan standards made her dislike the spirituals. And now she turns up her nose at jazz and all its manifestations—likewise almost everything else distinctly racial. She doesn't care for the Winold Reiss portraits of Negroes because they are "too Negro." She does not want a true picture of herself from anybody. She wants the artist to flatter her, to make the white world believe that all Negroes are as smug and as near white in soul as she wants to be. But, to my mind, it is the duty of the younger Negro artist, if he accepts any duties at all from outsiders, to change through the force of his art that old whispering "I want to be white," hidden in the aspirations of his people, to "Why should I want to be white? I am a Negro—and beautiful."

So I am ashamed for the black poet who says, "I want to be a poet, not a Negro poet," as though his own racial world were not as interesting as any other world. I am ashamed, too, for the colored artist who runs from the painting of Negro faces to the painting of sunsets after the manner of the academicians because he fears the strange un-whiteness of his own features. An artist must be free to choose what he does, certainly, but he must also never be afraid to do what he might choose.

From "The Negro Artist and the Racial Mountain"

COMPARE

Hughes's comments on the African American artist with Darryl Pinckney's critical observations on Langston Hughes's public identity as a black poet (page 1131).

THE HARLEM RENAISSANCE   1940

White people began to come to Harlem in droves. For several years they packed the expensive Cotton Club on Lenox Avenue. But I was never there, because the Cotton Club was a Jim Crow club for gangsters and monied whites. They were not cordial to Negro patronage, unless you were a celebrity like Bojangles.° So Harlem Negroes did not like the Cotton Club and never appreciated its Jim Crow policy in the very heart of their dark community. Nor did ordinary Negroes like the growing influx of whites toward Harlem after sundown, flooding the little cabarets and bars where formerly only colored people laughed and sang, and where now the strangers were given the best ringside tables to sit and stare at the Negro customers—like amusing animals in a zoo.

The Negroes said: "We can't go downtown and sit and stare at you in your clubs. You won't even let us in your clubs." But they didn't say it out loud—for Negroes are practically never rude to white people. So thousands of whites came to Harlem night after night, thinking the Negroes loved to have them there, and firmly believing that all Harlemites left their houses at sundown to sing and dance in cabarets, because most of the whites saw nothing but the cabarets, not the houses.

Some of the owners of Harlem clubs, delighted at the flood of white patronage, made the grievous error of barring their own race, after the manner of the famous Cotton Club. But most of these quickly lost business and folded up, because they failed to realize that a large part of the Harlem attraction for

Bojangles: Bill "Bojangles" Robinson (1876–1949), dancer.

downtown New Yorkers lay in simply watching the colored customers amuse themselves. And the smaller clubs, of course, had no big floor shows or a name band like the Cotton Club, where Duke Ellington usually held forth, so, without black patronage, they were not amusing at all.

Some of the small clubs, however, had people like Gladys Bentley, who was something worth discovering in those days, before she got famous, acquired an accompanist, specially written material, and conscious vulgarity. But for two or three amazing years, Miss Bentley sat, and played a big piano all night long, literally all night, without stopping—singing songs like "The St. James Infirmary," from ten in the evening until dawn, with scarcely a break between the notes, sliding from one song to another, with a powerful and continuous underbeat of jungle rhythm. Miss Bentley was an amazing exhibition of musical energy—a large, dark, masculine lady, whose feet pounded the floor while her fingers pounded the keyboard—a perfect piece of African sculpture, animated by her own rhythm.

But when the place where she played became too well known, she began to sing with an accompanist, became a star, moved to a larger place, then downtown, and is now in Hollywood. The old magic of the woman and the piano and

The first and only issue of Fire!! *(1926), an influential journal of the Harlem Renaissance.*

the night and the rhythm being one is gone. But everything goes, one way or another. The '20's are gone and lots of fine things in Harlem night life have disappeared like snow in the sun—since it became utterly commercial, planned for the downtown tourist trade, and therefore dull.

The lindy-hoppers at the Savoy even began to practice acrobatic routines, and to do absurd things for the entertainment of the whites, that probably never would have entered their heads to attempt merely for their own effortless amusement. Some of the lindy-hoppers had cards printed with their names on them and became dance professors teaching the tourists. Then Harlem nights became show nights for the Nordics.

Some critics say that that is what happened to certain Negro writers, too— that they ceased to write to amuse themselves and began to write to amuse and entertain white people, and in so doing distorted and overcolored their material, and left out a great many things they thought would offend their American brothers of a lighter complexion. Maybe—since Negroes have writer-racketeers, as has any other race. But I have known almost all of them, and most of the good ones have tried to be honest, write honestly, and express their world as they saw it.

From *The Big Sea*

~ CRITICS ON LANGSTON HUGHES ~

Arnold Rampersad   (b. 1941)

HUGHES AS AN EXPERIMENTALIST   1991

From his first publication of verse in the *Crisis*, Hughes had reflected his admiration for Sandburg and Whitman by experimenting with free verse as opposed to committing himself conservatively to rhyme. Even when he employed rhyme in his verse, as he often did, Hughes composed with relative casualness—unlike other major black poets of the day, such as Countee Cullen and Claude McKay, with their highly wrought stanzas. He seemed to prefer, as Whitman and Sandburg had preferred, to write lines that captured the cadences of common American speech, with his ear always especially attuned to the variety of black American language. This last aspect was only a token of his emotional and aesthetic involvement in black American culture, which he increasingly saw as his prime source of inspiration, even as he regarded black Americans ("Loud laughers in the hands of Fate— / My People") as his only indispensable audience.

Early poems captured some of the sights and sounds of ecstatic black church worship ("Glory! Hallelujah!"), but Hughes's greatest technical accomplishment as a poet was in his fusing of the rhythms of blues and jazz with traditional poetry. This technique, which he employed his entire life, surfaced in his art around 1923 with the landmark poem "The Weary Blues," in which the persona recalls hearing a blues singer and piano player ("Sweet Blues! / Coming from a black man's soul") performing in what most likely is a speakeasy in Harlem. The persona recalls the plaintive verse intoned by the singer ("Ain't got nobody in all this world, / Ain't got nobody but ma self") but finally surrenders to the mystery and magic of the blues singer's art. In the process, Hughes had taken an indigenous African American art form, perhaps the most vivid and commanding of all, and preserved its authenticity even as he formally enshrined it in the midst of a poem in traditional European form.

"The Weary Blues," a work virtually unprecedented in American poetry in its blending of black and white rhythms and forms, won Hughes the first prize for poetry in May 1925 in the epochal literary contest sponsored by *Opportunity* magazine, which marked the first high point of the Harlem Renaissance. The work also confirmed his leadership, along with Countee Cullen, of all the younger poets of the burgeoning movement. For Hughes, it was only the first step in his poetical tribute to blues and jazz. By the time of his second volume of verse, *Fine Clothes to the Jew* (1927), he was writing blues poems without either apology or framing devices taken from the traditional world of poetry. He was also delving into the basic subject matters of the blues—love and raw sexuality, deep sorrow and sudden violence, poverty and heartbreak. These subjects, treated with sympathy for the poor and dispossessed, and without false piety, made him easily the most controversial black poet of his time.

From "Langston Hughes"

Rita Dove (b. 1952)* and *Marilyn Nelson* (b. 1946)*

Langston Hughes and Harlem   1998

Affectionately known for most of his life as "The Poet Laureate of Harlem," Langston Hughes was born in Missouri and raised in the Midwest, moving to Harlem only as a young man. There he discovered his spiritual home, in Harlem's heart of Blackness finding both his vocation—"to explain and illuminate the Negro condition in America"—and the proletarian voice of most of his best work. If Johnson was the Renaissance man of the Harlem Renaissance, Hughes was its greatest man of letters; he saw through publication more than a dozen collections of poems, ten plays, two novels, several collections of short fiction, one historical study, two autobiographical works, several anthologies, and many books for children. His essay, "The Negro Artist and the Racial Mountain," provided a personal credo and statement of direction for the poets of his generation, who, he says, "intend to express our individual dark-skinned selves without fear or shame . . . We know we are beautiful. And ugly too." His forthright commitment to the Negro people led him to explore with great authenticity the frustrated dreams of the Black masses and to experiment with diction, rhythm, and musical forms.

Hughes was ever quick to confess the influences of Whitman and Sandburg on his work, and his best poetry also reflects the influence of Sherwood Anderson's *Winesburg, Ohio*. Like these poets, Hughes collected individual voices; his work is a notebook of life-studies. In his best poems Hughes the man remains masked; his voices are the voices of the Negro race as a whole, or of individual Negro speakers. "The Negro Speaks of Rivers," a widely anthologized poem from his first book, *The Weary Blues* (1926), is a case in point. Here Hughes is visible only as spokesman for the race as he proclaims "I bathed in the Euphrates when dawns were young. / I built my hut near the Congo and it lulled me to sleep." Poems frequently present anonymous Black personae, each of whom shares a painful heritage and an ironic pride. As one humorous character announces:

> I do cooking,
> Day's work, too!
> Alberta K. Johnson
> *Madam* to you.

Hughes took poetry out of what Cullen called "the dark tower"—which was, and even during the Harlem Renaissance, ivy-covered and distant and took it directly to the people. His blues and jazz experiments described and addressed an audience for which music was a central experience; he became a spokesman for their troubles, as in "Po' Boy Blues":

> When I was home de
> Sunshine seemed like gold.
> When I was home de
> Sunshine seemed like gold.
> Since I come up North de
> Whole damn world's turned cold.

American democracy appears frequently in Hughes's work as the unfulfilled but potentially realizable dream of the Negro, who says in "Let America Be America Again":

> O, yes,
> I say it plain,
> America never was America *to* me
> And yet I swear this oath—America will be!

There are many fine poems in the Hughes canon, but the strongest single work is *Montage of a Dream Deferred* (1951), a collection of sketches, captured voices, and individual lives unified by the jazzlike improvisations on the central theme of "a dream deferred." Like many of his individual poems, this work is intended for performance: think of it as a Harlem *Under Milk Wood*. Hughes moves rapidly from one voice or scene to the next; from the person in "Blues in Dawn" who says "I don't dare start thinking in the morning," to, in "Dime," a snatch of conversation: "Chile, these steps is hard to climb. / Grandma, lend me a dime."

The moods of the poems are as varied as their voices, for Hughes includes the daylight hours as well as the night. There are the bitter jump-rope rhymes of disillusioned children, the naive exclamations of young lovers, the gossip of friends. A college freshman writes in his "Theme for English B": "I guess being colored doesn't make me not like / the same things other folks like who are other races." A jaded woman offers in "Advice" the observation that "birthing is hard / and dying is mean," and advises youth to "get yourself / a little loving / in between." "Hope" is a miniature vignette in which a dying man asks for fish, and "His wife looked it up in her dream book / and played it." The changing voices, moods, and rhythms of this collection are, as Hughes wrote in a preface, "Like be-bop . . . marked by conflicting change, sudden nuances. . . ." We are reminded throughout that we should be hearing the poem as music; as boogie-woogie, as blues, as bass, as saxophone. Against the eighty-odd dreams collected here, the refrain insists that these frustrated dreams are potentially dangerous:

What happens to a dream deferred?

Does it dry up
like a raisin in the sun?
Or fester like a sore—
And then run?
Does it stink like rotten meat?
Or crust and sugar over—
like a syrupy sweet?

Maybe it just sags
like a heavy load.

Or does it explode?

More than any other Black poet, Langston Hughes spoke for the Negro people. Most of those after him have emulated his ascent of the Racial Mountain, his painfully joyous declaration of pride and commonality. His work offers white readers a glimpse into the social and the personal lives of Black America; Black readers recognize a proud affirmation of self.

From "A Black Rainbow: Modern Afro-American Poetry"

Darryl Pinckney (b. 1953)

BLACK IDENTITY IN LANGSTON HUGHES   1989

Fierce identification with the sorrows and pleasures of the poor black—"I myself belong to that class"—propelled Hughes toward the voice of the black Everyman. He made a distinction between his lyric and his social poetry, the private and the public. In the best of his social poetry he turned himself into a transmitter of messages and made the "I" a collective "I":

I've known rivers:
I've known rivers ancient as the world and older than the flow of
     human blood in human veins.

My soul has grown deep like the rivers.

I bathed in the Euphrates when dawns were young.
I built my hut near the Congo and it lulled me to sleep.

I looked upon the Nile and raised the pyramids above it.
I heard the singing of the Mississippi when Abe Lincoln went down to
    New Orleans, and I've seen its muddy bosom turn all golden in the
    sunset.
                              ("The Negro Speaks of Rivers")

The medium conveys a singleness of intention: to make the black known.
The straightforward, declarative style doesn't call attention to itself. Nothing dis-
tracts from forceful statement, as if the shadowy characters Sandburg wrote about
in, say, "When Mammy Hums" had at last their chance to come forward and testify. Poems like "Aunt Sue's Stories" reflect the folk ideal of black women as
repositories of racial lore. The story told in dramatic monologues like "The Negro
Mother" or "Mother to Son" is one of survival—life "ain't been no crystal stair."
The emphasis is on the capacity of black people to endure, which is why Hughes's
social poetry, though not strictly protest writing, indicts white America, even
taunts it with the steady belief that blacks will overcome simply by "keeping on":

I, too, sing America.

I am the darker brother.
They send me to the kitchen
When company comes,
But I laugh,
And eat well,
And grow strong.   ("I, Too")

Whites were not the only ones who could be made uneasy by Hughes's attempts to boldly connect past and future. The use of "black" and the invocation
of Africa were defiant gestures back in the days when many blacks described
themselves as brown. When Hughes answered Sandburg's "Nigger" ("I am the
nigger, / Singer of Songs . . .") with "I am a Negro, / Black as the night is black, /
Black like the depths of my Africa" ("Negro") he challenged the black middle
class with his absorption in slave heritage.

                                        From "Suitcase in Harlem"

Peter Townsend (b. 1948)

LANGSTON HUGHES AND JAZZ   2000

Hughes's engagement with jazz was close and long-lived, from his "Weary Blues"
of 1926 up to the time of his death in 1967. Jazz crops naturally out of the landscape of Hughes's poetry, which is largely that of the black communities of
Harlem and Chicago, and it remains fluid in its significance. Hughes's earliest
references to jazz, in poems like "Jazzonia" and "Jazz Band in a Parisian Cabaret,"
acknowledge the exoticism which was customary in the presentation of jazz in
the 1920s, and the novelty which the music still possessed for Hughes himself:

In a Harlem cabaret
Six long-headed jazzers play
A dancing girl whose eyes are bold
Lifts high a dress of silken gold.   ("Jazzonia")

This novelty is compounded by a further level of exoticism for the white visitors to the black cabarets who figure frequently in Hughes's jazz world. "Jazz Band in a Parisian Cabaret," for instance, has the band

Play it for the lords and ladies
For the dukes and counts
For the whores and gigolos
For the American millionaires

and "Harlem Night Club" pictures "dark brown girls / In blond men's arms." In Hughes's more politically barbed poetry of the 1930s these comments on white voyeurism harden into his attitude in "Visitors to the Black Belt":

You can say
Jazz on the South Side—
To me it's hell
On the South Side.

At the same time, jazz is one of the threads that make up the fabric of urban life in the "Harlem Renaissance" period. In a poem entitled "Heart of Harlem" Hughes places jazz musicians such as Earl Hines and Billie Holiday alongside individuals of the stature of Adam Clayton Powell, Joe Louis and W. E. B. Dubois. Hughes's continuous awareness of the place of jazz in his community enables him to record its scenes and its changes across the decades. "Lincoln Theatre," a poem published in a collection in 1949, gives a memorably exact rendering of the sort of Swing Era performance, in a Harlem theater, that was discussed [earlier]:

The movies end. The lights flash gaily on.
The band down in the pit bursts into jazz.
The crowd applauds a plump brown-skin bleached blonde
Who sings the troubles every woman has.

Hughes responded with particular sympathy to jazz of the bebop period, which he saw as having great political significance. *Montage of a Dream Deferred*, published in 1951, is one of Hughes's most substantial sequences of poems, and it is shot through with references to jazz. His editorial note to the sequence explains the stylistic influence of bebop on its composition:

This poem on contemporary Harlem, like bebop, is marked by conflicting changes, sudden nuances, sharp and impudent interjections, and passages sometimes in the manner of the jam session, sometimes the popular song, punctuated by the riffs, runs, breaks and distortions of the music of a community in transition.

As Hughes made clear in other places, he heard bebop as an expression of a dissi-
dent spirit within the younger black community:

> Little cullud boys with fears
> frantic, kick their draftee years
> into flatted fifths and flatter beers . . .

and "Dream Boogie" resounds with suggestions, threatening or impudent, that
well up in the music, the "boogie-woogie rumble":

> Listen to it closely
> Ain't you heard
> something underneath.

Bebop affected the forms of Hughes's poetry at the higher architectural
levels, dictating the structural rhythm of longer works like "Dream Deferred,"
but otherwise he employed a small range of simple verse forms that originate in
earlier styles of black music. A particular favourite was a two-stress line rhymed
in quatrains, derived from spirituals, and he also frequently used a looser form
drawn from the 12-bar blues. The first of these Hughes was able to use with remarkable flexibility, considering its brevity. The form is often used for aphoristic
effect, as in "Motto":

> I play it cool
> And dig all jive.
> That's the reason
> I stay alive.

or in "Sliver," a comment on the form itself:

> A cheap little tune
> To cheap little rhymes
> Can cut a man's
> Throat sometimes.

What is even more remarkable is the naturalness of its effect in these diverse
contexts. Hughes makes the form serve the purposes of narrative and description
just as flexibly as that of comment. It gives Hughes's verse its idiomatic flavor, so
that even where the subject is not jazz or even music, the verse is still permeated
with the qualities of black musical culture.

From Jazz in American Culture

Onwuchekwa Jemie (b. 1940)

A READING OF "DREAM DEFERRED"   1976

The deferred dream is examined through a variety of human agencies, of interlocking and recurring voices and motifs fragmented and scattered throughout the

six sections of the poem. Much as in bebop, the pattern is one of constant reversals and contrasts. Frequently the poems are placed in thematic clusters, with poems within the cluster arranged in contrasting pairs. *Montage [of a Dream Deferred]* does not move in a straight line; its component poems move off in invisible directions, reappear and touch, creating a complex tapestry or mosaic.

The dream theme itself is carried in the musical motifs. It is especially characterized by the rumble ("The boogie-woogie ramble / Of a dream deferred")— that rapid thumping and tumbling of notes which so powerfully drives to the bottom of the emotions, stirring feelings too deep to be touched by the normal successions of notes and common rhythms. The rumble is an atomic explosion of musical energy, an articulate confusion, a moment of epiphany, a flash of blinding light in which all things are suddenly made clear. The theme is sounded at strategic times, culminating in the final section. . . .

The poet has taken us on a guided tour of microcosmic Harlem, day and night, past and present. And as a new day dawns and the poem moves into a summing up in the final section, he again poses the question and examines the possibilities:

> What happens to a dream deferred?

> > Does it dry up
> > like a raisin in the sun?
> > Or fester like a sore—
> > And then run?
> > Does it stink like rotten meat?
> > Or crust and sugar over—
> > like a syrupy sweet?

> > Maybe it just sags
> > like a heavy load.

> *Or does it explode?*

The images are sensory, domestic, earthy, like blues images. The stress is on deterioration—drying, rotting, festering, souring—on loss of essential natural quality. The raisin has fallen from a fresh, juicy grape to a dehydrated but still edible raisin to a sun-baked and inedible dead bone of itself. The Afro-American is not unlike the raisin, for he is in a sense a dessicated trunk of his original African self, used and abandoned in the American wilderness with the stipulation that he rot and disappear. Like the raisin lying neglected in the scorching sun, the black man is treated as a thing of no consequence. But the raisin refuses the fate assigned to it, metamorphoses instead into a malignant living sore that will not heal or disappear. Like the raisin, a sore is but a little thing, inconsequential on the surface but in fact symptomatic of a serious disorder. Its stink is like the stink of the rotten meat sold to black folks in so many ghetto groceries; meat no longer suitable for human use, deathly. And while a syrupy sweet is not central to the diet as meat might be, still it is a rounding-off final pleasure (dessert) at the end of a meal, or a delicious surprise that a child looks forward to at Halloween or

Christmas. But that final pleasure turns out to be a pain. Aged, spoiled candy leaves a sickly taste in the mouth; sweetness gone bad turns a treat into a trick.

The elements of the deferred dream are, like the raisin, sore, meat, and candy, little things of no great consequence in themselves. But their unrelieved accretion packs together considerable pressure. Their combined weight becomes too great to carry about indefinitely: not only does the weight increase from continued accumulation, but the longer it is carried the heavier it feels. The load sags from its own weight, and the carrier sags with it; and if he should drop it, it just might explode from all its strange, tortured, and compressed energies.

In short, a dream deferred can be a terrifying thing. Its greatest threat is its unpredictability, and for this reason the question format is especially fitting. Questions demand the reader's participation, corner and sweep him headlong to the final, inescapable conclusion.

From Langston Hughes: An Introduction to the Poetry

FOR FURTHER READING

You can study several other poets in depth in this book. The following writers are represented at length and also have short biographies in "Lives of the Poets."

> Robert Frost—13 poems (plus Writer's Perspective)
> William Shakespeare—9 poems
> William Butler Yeats—8 poems (plus Writer's Perspective)
> Thomas Hardy—7 poems
> William Carlos Williams—7 poems
> William Blake—6 poems

See the Index for specific details.

SUGGESTIONS FOR WRITING

1. Focusing on one or two poems, demonstrate how Dickinson's idiosyncratic capitalization and punctuation add special impact to her work.
2. How do the poems by Dickinson in this chapter and elsewhere in the book illustrate her statement (in "Recognizing Poetry" on page 1105) that "I find ecstasy in living—the mere sense of living is joy enough"?
3. Compare and contrast the use of first-person voices in two poems by Langston Hughes (such as "I, Too" and "Theme for English B" or "Mother to Son" and "Island"). In what ways does the speaker's "I" differ in each poem and in what ways is it similar?
4. Discussing a single poem by Hughes, examine how musical forms (such as jazz, blues, or popular song) help shape the effect of the work.

31 Poems for Further Reading

The manuscript of John Donne's sonnet, "Death be not proud" (page 1162).

Anonymous   (traditional Scottish ballad)

Lord Randall

"O where ha you been, Lord Randal, my son?
And where ha you been, my handsome young man?"
"I ha been at the greenwood; mother, mak my bed soon,
For I'm wearied wi hunting, and fain wad lie down."

"An wha° met ye there, Lord Randal, my son?   *who*   5
An wha met you there, my handsome young man?"
"O I met wi my true-love; mother, mak my bed soon,
For I'm wearied wi hunting, and fain wad lie down."

"And what did she give you, Lord Randal, my son?
And what did she give you, my handsome young man?"   10
"Eels fried in a pan; mother, mak my bed soon,
For I'm wearied with hunting, and fain wad lie down."

"And wha gat° your leavins,° Lord Randal, my son?   *got; leftovers*
And wha gat your leavins, my handsome young man?"
"My hawks and my hounds; mother, mak my bed soon,   15
For I'm wearied wi hunting, and fain wad lie down."

"And what becam of them, Lord Randall, my son?
And what becam of them, my handsome young man?"
"They stretched their legs out an died; mother, mak my bed soon,
For I'm wearied wi hunting, and fain wad lie down."   20

"O I fear you are poisoned, Lord Randal, my son!
I fear you are poisoned, my handsome young man!"
"O yes, I am poisoned; mother, mak my bed soon,
For I'm sick at the heart, and I fain wad lie down."

"What d' ye leave to your mother, Lord Randal, my son?   25
What d' ye leave to your mother, my handsome young man?"
"Four and twenty milk kye°; mother, mak my bed soon,   *cow*
For I'm sick at the heart, and I fain wad lie down."

"What d' ye leave to your sister, Lord Randal, my son?
What d' ye leave to your sister, my handsome young man?"   30
"My gold and my silver; mother, mak my bed soon,
For I'm sick at the heart, and I fain wad lie down."

"What d' ye leave to your brother, Lord Randal, my son?
What d' ye leave to your brother, my handsome young man?"
"My house and my lands; mother, mak my bed soon,   35
For I'm sick at the heart, and I fain wad lie down."

"What d' ye leave to your true-love, Lord Randal, my son?
What d' ye leave to your true-love, my handsome young man?"
"I leave her hell and fire; mother, mak my bed soon,
For I'm sick at the heart, and I fain wad lie down."   40

COMPARE

"Lord Randall" with a modern ballad such as "Ballad of Birmingham" by Dudley Randall
(page 847).

Anonymous   (traditional English ballad)

THE THREE RAVENS

There were three ravens sat on a tree,
   Down a down, hay down, hay down,
There were three ravens sat on a tree,
   With a down,
There were three ravens sat on a tree,   5
They were as black as they might be.
   With a down derry, derry, derry, down, down.

The one of them said to his mate,
"Where shall we our breakfast take?"

"Down in yonder greene field,   10
There lies a knight slain under his shield.

"His hounds they lie down at his feet,
So well they can their master keep.

"His hawks they fly so eagerly,
There's no fowl dare him come nigh."   15

Down there comes a fallow doe,
As great with young as she might go.

She lift up his bloody head,
And kist his wounds that were so red.

She got him up upon her back,   20
And carried him to earthen lake.°   *the grave*

She buried him before the prime,°   *dawn*
She was dead herself ere evensong time.

God send every gentleman
Such hawks, such hounds, and such a leman.°   *lover*   25

THE THREE RAVENS. The lines of refrain are repeated in each stanza. "Perhaps in the folk mind the
doe is the form the soul of a human mistress, now dead, has taken," Albert B. Friedman has suggested
(in *The Viking Book of Folk Ballads*). "Most probably the knight's beloved was understood to be an enchanted woman who was metamorphosed at certain times into an animal." In lines 22 and 23, *prime*
and *evensong* are two of the canonical hours set aside for prayer and worship. Prime is at dawn, evensong at dusk.

Anonymous   (traditional Scottish ballad)

THE TWA CORBIES

As I was walking all alane,
I heard twa corbies° making a mane;°   *ravens; moan*
The tane° unto the t'other say,   *one*
"Where sall we gang° and dine today?"   *go*

"In behint yon auld fail dyke,°   *turf wall*   5
I wot° there lies a new slain knight;   *know*
And naebody kens° that he lies there,   *knows*
But his hawk, his hound, and lady fair.

"His hound is to the hunting gane,
His hawk to fetch the wild-fowl hame,   10
His lady's ta'en another mate,
So we may mak our dinner sweet.

"Ye'll sit on his white hause-bane,°   *neck bone*
And I'll pike out his bonny blue een;
Wi' ae° lock o' his gowden hair   *one*   15
We'll theek° our nest when it grows bare.   *thatch*

"Mony a one for him makes mane,
But nane sall ken where he is gane;
O'er his white banes, when they are bare,
The wind sall blaw for evermair."   20

THE TWA CORBIES. Sir Walter Scott, the first to print this ballad in his *Minstrelsy of the Scottish Border*
(1802–1803), calls it "rather a counterpart than a copy" of "The Three Ravens." M. J. C. Hodgart
and other scholars think he may have written most of it himself.

Anonymous   (English lyric)

WESTERN WIND   (ABOUT 1500)

Western wind, when wilt thou blow,
The° small rain down can rain?   *(so that) the*
Christ, if my love were in my arms,
And I in my bed again!

COMPARE

"Western Wind" with "The River-Merchant's Wife: a Letter" by Ezra Pound (page 1226).

Anonymous   (Navajo mountain chant)

LAST WORDS OF THE PROPHET

Farewell, my younger brother!
From the holy places the gods come for me.
You will never see me again; but when the showers pass and the
    thunders peal,
"There," you will say, "is the voice of my elder brother."
And when the harvest comes, of the beautiful birds and grasshoppers   5
    you will say,
"There is the ordering of my elder brother!"
           —*Translated by Washington Matthews*

COMPARE

"Last Words of the Prophet" with "A Slumber Did My Spirit Seal" by William
Wordsworth (page 865).

Matthew Arnold   (1822–1888)

DOVER BEACH   1867

The sea is calm tonight.
The tide is full, the moon lies fair
Upon the straits;—on the French coast the light
Gleams and is gone; the° cliffs of England stand,
Glimmering and vast, out in the tranquil bay.   5
Come to the window, sweet is the night-air!
Only, from the long line of spray
Where the sea meets the moon-blanched land,
Listen! you hear the grating roar
Of pebbles which the waves draw back, and fling,   10
At their return, up the high strand,
Begin, and cease, and then again begin,

With tremulous cadence slow, and bring
The eternal note of sadness in.

Sophocles long ago   15
Heard it on the Aegean, and it brought
Into his mind the turbid ebb and flow
Of human misery; we
Find also in the sound a thought,
Hearing it by this distant northern sea.   20

The Sea of Faith
Was once, too, at the full, and round earth's shore
Lay like the folds of a bright girdle furled.
But now I only hear
Its melancholy, long, withdrawing roar,   25
Retreating, to the breath
Of the night-wind, down the vast edges drear
And naked shingles° of the world.   *gravel beaches*

Ah, love, let us be true
To one another! for the world, which seems   30
To lie before us like a land of dreams,
So various, so beautiful, so new,
Hath really neither joy, nor love, nor light,
Nor certitude, nor peace, nor help for pain;
And we are here as on a darkling° plain   *darkened or darkening*   35
Swept with confused alarms of struggle and flight,
Where ignorant armies clash by night.

COMPARE

"Dover Beach" with "Hap" by Thomas Hardy (page 1184).

John Ashbery   (b. 1927)*

AT NORTH FARM   1984

Somewhere someone is traveling furiously toward you,
At incredible speed, traveling day and night,
Through blizzards and desert heat, across torrents, through narrow
     passes.
But will he know where to find you,
Recognize you when he sees you,   5
Give you the thing he has for you?

Hardly anything grows here,
Yet the granaries are bursting with meal,

The sacks of meal piled to the rafters.
The streams run with sweetness, fattening fish;   10
Birds darken the sky. Is it enough
That the dish of milk is set out at night,
That we think of him sometimes,
Sometimes and always, with mixed feelings?

COMPARE

"At North Farm" with "Uphill" by Christina Rossetti (page 963).

Margaret Atwood   (b. 1939)*

ROMANTIC   1995

Men and their mournful romanticisms
that can't get the dishes done—
that's freedom, that broken wineglass
in the cold fireplace.

When women wash underpants, it's a chore.   5
When men do it, an intriguing affliction.
How plangent, the damp socks flapping on the line,
how lost and single in the orphaning air . . .

She cherishes that sadness,
tells him to lie down on the grass,   10
closes each of his eyes with a finger,
applies her body like a poultice.

You poor thing, said the Australian woman
while he held our baby—
as if I had forced him to do it,   15
as if I had my high heel in his face.

Still, who's taken in?
Every time?
Us, and our empty hands, the hands
of starving nurses.   20

It's bullet holes we want to see in their skin,
scars, and the chance to touch them.

COMPARE

"Romantic" with "Power" by Adrienne Rich (page 1231).

W. H. Auden

W. H. Auden   (1907–1973)*

AS I WALKED OUT ONE EVENING   1940

As I walked out one evening,
    Walking down Bristol Street,
The crowds upon the pavement
    Were fields of harvest wheat.

And down by the brimming river   5
    I heard a lover sing
Under an arch of the railway:
    "Love has no ending.

"I'll love you, dear, I'll love you
    Till China and Africa meet,   10
And the river jumps over the mountain
    And the salmon sing in the street,

"I'll love you till the ocean
    Is folded and hung up to dry
And the seven stars go squawking   15
    Like geese about the sky.

"The years shall run like rabbits,
    For in my arms I hold
The Flower of the Ages,
    And the first love of the world."   20

But all the clocks in the city
    Began to whirr and chime:

"O let not Time deceive you,
    You cannot conquer Time.

"In the burrows of the Nightmare   25
    Where Justice naked is,
Time watches from the shadow
    And coughs when you would kiss.

"In headaches and in worry
    Vaguely life leaks away,   30
And Time will have his fancy
    Tomorrow or today.

"Into many a green valley
    Drifts the appalling snow;
Time breaks the threaded dances   35
    And the diver's brilliant bow.

"O plunge your hands in water,
    Plunge them in up to the wrist;
Stare, stare in the basin
    And wonder what you've missed.   40

"The glacier knocks in the cupboard,
    The desert sighs in the bed,
And the crack in the teacup opens
    A lane to the land of the dead.

"Where the beggars raffle the banknotes   45
    And the Giant is enchanting to Jack,
And the Lily-white Boy is a Roarer,
    And Jill goes down on her back.

"O look, look in the mirror,
    O look in your distress;   50
Life remains a blessing
    Although you cannot bless.

"O stand, stand at the window
    As the tears scald and start;
You shall love your crooked neighbor   55
    With your crooked heart."

It was late, late in the evening,
    The lovers they were gone;
The clocks had ceased their chiming,
    And the deep river ran on.   60

COMPARE

"As I Walked Out One Evening" with "Dover Beach" by Matthew Arnold (page 1141) and "anyone lived in a pretty how town" by E. E. Cummings (page 767).

W. H. Auden   (1907–1973)*

MUSÉE DES BEAUX ARTS   1940

About suffering they were never wrong,
The Old Masters: how well they understood
Its human position; how it takes place
While someone else is eating or opening a window or just walking
    dully along;
How, when the aged are reverently, passionately waiting   5
For the miraculous birth, there always must be
Children who did not specially want it to happen, skating
On a pond at the edge of the wood:
They never forgot
That even the dreadful martyrdom must run its course   10
Anyhow in a corner, some untidy spot
Where the dogs go on with their doggy life and the torturer's horse
Scratches its innocent behind on a tree.

The Fall of Icarus *by Pieter Breughel the Elder (1520?–1569).*

In Brueghel's *Icarus*, for instance: how everything turns away
Quite leisurely from the disaster; the ploughman may   15
Have heard the splash, the forsaken cry,
But for him it was not an important failure; the sun shone
As it had to on the white legs disappearing into the green
Water; and the expensive delicate ship that must have seen
Something amazing, a boy falling out of the sky,   20
Had somewhere to get to and sailed calmly on.

COMPARE

"Musée des Beaux Arts" with "The Dance" by William Carlos Williams (page 939) and
the painting by Pieter Breughel to which each poem refers.

Elizabeth Bishop

Elizabeth Bishop   (1911–1979)*

FILLING STATION   1965

Oh, but it is dirty!
—this little filling station,
oil-soaked, oil-permeated
to a disturbing, over-all
black translucency.   5
Be careful with that match!

Father wears a dirty,
oil-soaked monkey suit
that cuts him under the arms,
and several quick and saucy   10
and greasy sons assist him

(it's a family filling station),
all quite thoroughly dirty.

Do they live in the station?
It has a cement porch
behind the pumps, and on it   15
a set of crushed and grease-
impregnated wickerwork;
on the wicker sofa
a dirty dog, quite comfy.   20

Some comic books provide
the only note of color—
of certain color. They lie
upon a big dim doily
draping a taboret°   *stool*   25
(part of the set), beside
a big hirsute begonia.

Why the extraneous plant?
Why the taboret?
Why, oh why, the doily?   30
(Embroidered in daisy stitch
with marguerites, I think,
and heavy with gray crochet.)

Somebody embroidered the doily.
Somebody waters the plant,   35
or oils it, maybe. Somebody
arranges the rows of cans
so that they softly say:
ESSO—SO—SO—SO
to high-strung automobiles.   40
Somebody loves us all.

COMPARE

"Filling Station" with "California Hills in August" by Dana Gioia (page 1179) or "The splendor falls on castle walls" by Alfred, Lord Tennyson (page 869).

Detail of William Blake's The Tyger.

William Blake   (1757–1827)*

THE TYGER   1794

Tyger! Tyger! burning bright
In the forests of the night,
What immortal hand or eye
Could frame thy fearful symmetry?

In what distant deeps or skies   5
Burnt the fire of thine eyes?
On what wings dare he aspire?
What the hand dare seize the fire?

And what shoulder, and what art,
Could twist the sinews of thy heart?   10
And when thy heart began to beat,
What dread hand? and what dread feet?

What the hammer? what the chain?
In what furnace was thy brain?
What the anvil? what dread grasp   15
Dare its deadly terrors clasp?

When the stars threw down their spears,
And watered heaven with their tears,
Did he smile his work to see?
Did he who made the Lamb make thee?   20

Tyger! Tyger! burning bright
In the forests of the night,
What immortal hand or eye
Dare frame thy fearful symmetry?

COMPARE

"The Tyger" with "The Windhover" by Gerard Manley Hopkins (page 1193).

William Blake

William Blake (1757–1827)*

THE SICK ROSE   1794

O Rose, thou art sick!
The invisible worm
That flies in the night,
In the howling storm,

Has found out thy bed   5
Of crimson joy,
And his dark secret love
Does thy life destroy.

COMPARE

"The Sick Rose" with "The Man with Night Sweats" by Thom Gunn (page 1180).

Eavan Boland (b. 1944)

ANOREXIC   1980

Flesh is heretic.
My body is a witch.
I am burning it.

Yes I am torching
her curves and paps and wiles.   5
They scorch in my self denials.

How she meshed my head
in the half-truths
of her fevers

till I renounced   10
milk and honey
and the taste of lunch.

I vomited
her hungers.
Now the bitch is burning.   15

I am starved and curveless.
I am skin and bone.
She has learned her lesson.

Thin as a rib
I turn in sleep.   20
My dreams probe

a claustrophobia
a sensuous enclosure.
How warm it was and wide

once by a warm drum,   25
once by the song of his breath
and in his sleeping side.

Only a little more,
only a few more days
sinless, foodless,   30

I will slip
back into him again
as if I had never been away.

Caged so
I will grow   35
angular and holy

past pain,
keeping his heart
such company

as will make me forget   40
in a small space
the fall

into forked dark,
into python needs
heaving to hips and breasts   45
and lips and heat
and sweat and fat and greed.

COMPARE

"Anorexic" with "Her Kind" by Anne Sexton (page 730).

Gwendolyn Brooks   (1917–2000)*
THE MOTHER   1945

Abortions will not let you forget.
You remember the children you got that you did not get,
The damp small pulps with a little or with no hair,
The singers and workers that never handled the air.
You will never neglect or beat   5
Them, or silence or buy with a sweet.
You will never wind up the sucking-thumb
Or scuttle off ghosts that come.
You will never leave them, controlling your luscious sigh,
Return for a snack of them, with gobbling mother-eye.   10
I have heard in the voices of the wind the voices of my dim killed
      children.
I have contracted. I have eased
My dim dears at the breasts they could never suck.
I have said, Sweets, if I sinned, if I seized
Your luck   15
And your lives from your unfinished reach,
If I stole your births and your names,
Your straight baby tears and your games,
Your stilted or lovely loves, your tumults, your marriages, aches, and
      your deaths,

If I poisoned the beginnings of your breaths,   20
Believe that even in my deliberateness I was not deliberate.
Though why should I whine,
Whine that the crime was other than mine?—
Since anyhow you are dead.
Or rather, or instead,   25
You were never made.
But that too, I am afraid,
Is faulty: oh, what shall I say, how is the truth to be said?
You were born, you had body, you died.
It is just that you never giggled or planned or cried.   30

Believe me, I loved you all.
Believe me, I knew you, though faintly, and I loved, I loved you all.

COMPARE

"The Mother" with "Metaphors" by Sylvia Plath (page 820), and "The Victory" by Anne
Stevenson (page 795).

Gwendolyn Brooks   (1917–2000)*

THE PREACHER RUMINATES: 1945
BEHIND THE SERMON

I think it must be lonely to be God.
Nobody loves a master. No. Despite
The bright hosannas, bright dear-Lords, and bright
Determined reverence of Sunday eyes.

Picture Jehovah striding through the hall   5
Of His importance, creatures running out
From servant-corners to acclaim, to shout
Appreciation of His merit's glare.

But who walks with Him?—dares to take His arm,
To slap Him on the shoulder, tweak His ear,   10
Buy Him a Coca-Cola or a beer,
Pooh-pooh His politics, call Him a fool?

Perhaps—who knows?—He tires of looking down.
Those eyes are never lifted. Never straight.
Perhaps sometimes He tires of being great   15
In solitude. Without a hand to hold.

COMPARE

"the preacher ruminates: behind the sermon" with "Death be not proud" by John Donne
(page 1162).

Elizabeth Barrett Browning   (1806–1861)*

HOW DO I LOVE THEE?   1850
LET ME COUNT THE WAYS

How do I love thee? Let me count the ways.
I love thee to the depth and breadth and height
My soul can reach, when feeling out of sight
For the ends of being and ideal grace.
I love thee to the level of every day's   5
Most quiet need, by sun and candle-light.
I love thee freely, as men strive for right.
I love thee purely, as they turn from praise.
I love thee with the passion put to use
In my old griefs, and with my childhood's faith.   10
I love thee with a love I seemed to lose
With my lost saints. I love thee with the breath,
Smiles, tears, of all my life; and, if God choose,
I shall but love thee better after death.

COMPARE

"How Do I Love Thee?" with "What lips my lips have kissed" by Edna St. Vincent Millay
(page 919).

Robert Browning   (1812–1889)*

SOLILOQUY OF THE SPANISH CLOISTER   1842

Gr-r-r—there go, my heart's abhorrence!
    Water your damned flower-pots, do!
If hate killed men, Brother Lawrence,
    God's blood, would not mine kill you!
What? your myrtle-bush wants trimming?   5
    Oh, that rose has prior claims—
Needs its leaden vase filled brimming?
    Hell dry you up with its flames!

At the meal we sit together;
    Salve tibi! ° I must hear   *Hail to thee!*   10
Wise talk of the kind of weather,
    Sort of season, time of year:
Not a plenteous cork-crop: scarcely
    Dare we hope oak-galls, I doubt;
What's the Latin name for "parsley"?   15
    What's the Greek name for "swine's snout"?

Whew! We'll have our platter burnished,
  Laid with care on our own shelf!
With a fire-new spoon we're furnished,
  And a goblet for ourself,   20
Rinsed like something sacrificial
  Ere 'tis fit to touch our chaps—
Marked with L. for our initial!
  (He-he! There his lily snaps!)

Saint, forsooth! While Brown Dolores   25
  Squats outside the Convent bank
With Sanchicha, telling stories,
  Steeping tresses in the tank,
Blue-black, lustrous, thick like horsehairs,
  —Can't I see his dead eye glow,   30
Bright as 'twere a Barbary corsair's?
  (That is, if he'd let it show!)

When he finishes refection,
  Knife and fork he never lays
Cross-wise, to my recollection,   35
  As I do, in Jesu's praise.
I the Trinity illustrate,
  Drinking watered orange-pulp—
In three sips the Arian frustrate;
  While he drains his at one gulp!   40

Oh, those melons! if he's able
  We're to have a feast; so nice!
One goes to the Abbot's table,
  All of us get each a slice.
How go on your flowers? None double?   45
  Not one fruit-sort can you spy?
Strange!—And I, too, at such trouble,
  Keep them close-nipped on the sly!

There's a great text in Galatians,
  Once you trip on it, entails   50
Twenty-nine distinct damnations,
  One sure, if another fails;
If I trip him just a-dying,
  Sure of heaven as sure can be,
Spin him round and send him flying   55
  Off to hell, a Manichee?

Or, my scrofulous French novel
    On grey paper with blunt type!
Simply glance at it, you grovel
    Hand and foot in Belial's gripe;   60
If I double down its pages
    At the woeful sixteenth print,
When he gathers his greengages,
    Ope a sieve and slip it in't?

Or, there's Satan!—one might venture   65
    Pledge one's soul to him, yet leave
Such a flaw in the indenture
    As he'd miss till, past retrieve,
Blasted lay that rose-acacia
    We're so proud of! *Hy, Zy, Hine.* . . .   70
'St, there's Vespers! *Plena gratia*
    Ave, Virgo!° Gr-r-r—you swine!   *Hail, Virgin, full of grace!*

SOLILOQUY OF THE SPANISH CLOISTER.   3 *Brother Lawrence:* one of the speaker's fellow monks. 31
Barbary corsair: a pirate operating off the Barbary coast of Africa. 39 *Arian:* a follower of Arius,
heretic who denied the doctrine of the Trinity. 49 *a great text in Galatians:* a difficult verse in this
book of the Bible. Brother Lawrence will be damned as a heretic if he wrongly interprets it. 56
Manichee: another kind of heretic, one who (after the Persian philosopher Mani) sees in the world a
constant struggle between good and evil, neither able to win. 60 *Belial:* here, not specifically Satan
but (as used in the Old Testament) a name for wickedness. 70 *Hy, Zy, Hine:* possibly the sound of a
bell to announce evening devotions.

COMPARE

"Soliloquy of the Spanish Cloister" with "In Westminster Abbey" by John Betjeman
(page 735).

Geoffrey Chaucer   (1340?–1400)

MERCILESS BEAUTY   (LATE 14TH CENTURY)

Your ÿen° two wol slee° me sodenly;   *eyes; slay*
I may the beautee of hem° not sustene,°   *them; resist*
So woundeth hit thourghout my herte kene.

And but° your word wol helen° hastily   *unless; heal*
My hertes wounde, while that hit is grene,°   *new*   5
    Your ÿen two wol slee me sodenly;
    I may the beautee of hem not sustene.

Upon my trouthe° I sey you feithfully   *word*
That ye ben of my lyf and deeth the quene;
For with my deeth the trouthe° shal be sene.   *truth*   10
    Your ÿen two wol slee me sodenly;
    I may the beautee of hem not sustene,
    So woundeth it thourghout my herte kene.

MERCILESS BEAUTY. This poem is one of a group of three roundels, collectively titled "Merciles Beaute." A **roundel** (or **rondel**) is an English form consisting of 11 lines in 3 stanzas rimed with a refrain. 3 *So woundeth . . . kene:* "So deeply does it wound me through the heart."

COMPARE

"Merciless Beauty" with "My mistress' eyes are nothing like the sun" by William Shakespeare (page 1238).

G. K. Chesterton   (1874–1936)

THE DONKEY   1900

When fishes flew and forests walked
    And figs grew upon thorn,
Some moment when the moon was blood
    Then surely I was born;

With monstrous head and sickening cry   5
    And ears like errant wings,
The devil's walking parody
    On all four-footed things.

The tattered outlaw of the earth,
    Of ancient crooked will;   10
Starve, scourge, deride me: I am dumb,
    I keep my secret still.

Fools! For I also had my hour;
    One far fierce hour and sweet:
There was a shout about my ears,   15
    And palms before my feet.

THE DONKEY. For more details of the donkey's hour of triumph see Matthew 21:1–8.

COMPARE

"The Donkey" with "The Tyger" by William Blake (page 1149).

Samuel Taylor Coleridge   (1772–1834)

Kubla Khan   (1797–1798)

Or, a Vision in a Dream. A Fragment.

In Xanadu did Kubla Khan
A stately pleasure-dome decree:
Where Alph, the sacred river, ran
Through caverns measureless to man
　　Down to a sunless sea.   5
So twice five miles of fertile ground
With walls and towers were girdled round;
And there were gardens bright with sinuous rills,
Where blossomed many an incense-bearing tree;
And here were forests ancient as the hills,   10
Enfolding sunny spots of greenery.

But oh! that deep romantic chasm which slanted
Down the green hill athwart a cedarn cover!
A savage place! as holy and enchanted
As e'er beneath a waning moon was haunted   15
By woman wailing for her demon-lover!
And from this chasm, with ceaseless turmoil seething,
As if this earth in fast thick pants were breathing,
A mighty fountain momently was forced:
Amid whose swift half-intermitted burst   20
Huge fragments vaulted like rebounding hail,
Or chaffy grain beneath the thresher's flail:
And 'mid these dancing rocks at once and ever
It flung up momently the sacred river.
Five miles meandering with a mazy motion   25
Through wood and dale the sacred river ran,
Then reached the caverns measureless to man,
And sank in tumult to a lifeless ocean:
And 'mid this tumult Kubla heard from far
Ancestral voices prophesying war!   30

　　The shadow of the dome of pleasure
　　Floated midway on the waves;
　　Where was heard the mingled measure
　　From the fountain and the caves.
It was a miracle of rare device,   35
A sunny pleasure-dome with caves of ice!

A damsel with a dulcimer
In a vision once I saw:
It was an Abyssinian maid,
And on her dulcimer she played,
Singing of Mount Abora.   40
Could I revive within me
Her symphony and song,
To such a deep delight 'twould win me,
That with music loud and long,   45
I would build that dome in air,
That sunny dome! those caves of ice!
And all who heard should see them there,
And all should cry, Beware! Beware!
His flashing eyes, his floating hair!   50
Weave a circle round him thrice,
And close your eyes with holy dread,
For he on honey-dew hath fed,
And drunk the milk of Paradise.

KUBLA KHAN. There was an actual Kublai Khan, a thirteenth-century Mongol emperor, and a Chinese city of Xanadu; but Coleridge's dream vision also borrows from travelers' descriptions of such other exotic places as Abyssinia and America. 51 *circle:* a magic circle drawn to keep away evil spirits.

COMPARE

"Kubla Khan" with "The Second Coming" by William Butler Yeats (page 982).

Billy Collins (b. 1941)*

CARE AND FEEDING   2003

Because I will turn 420 tomorrow
in dog years
I will take myself for a long walk
along the green shore of the lake,

and when I walk in the door,   5
I will jump up on my chest
and lick my nose and ears and eyelids
while I tell myself again and again to get down.

I will fill my metal bowl at the sink
with cold fresh water,
and lift a biscuit from the jar
and hold it gingerly with my teeth.

Then I will make three circles
and lie down at my feet on the wood floor
and close my eyes
while I type all morning and into the afternoon,

checking every once in a while
to make sure I am still there,
reaching down
to stroke my furry, venerable head.

COMPARE

"Care and Feeding" with "For the Anniversary of My Death" by W. S. Merwin (page 938).

Hart Crane   (1899–1932)

MY GRANDMOTHER'S LOVE LETTERS   1926

There are no stars tonight
But those of memory.
Yet how much room for memory there is
In the loose girdle of soft rain.

There is even room enough
For the letters of my mother's mother,
Elizabeth,
That have been pressed so long
Into a corner of the roof
That they are brown and soft,
And liable to melt as snow.

Over the greatness of such space
Steps must be gentle.
It is all hung by an invisible white hair.
It trembles as birch limbs webbing the air.

And I ask myself:

"Are your fingers long enough to play
Old keys that are but echoes:
Is the silence strong enough
To carry back the music to its source

And back to you again
As though to her?"

Yet I would lead my grandmother by the hand
Through much of what she would not understand;
And so I stumble. And the rain continues on the roof   25
With such a sound of gently pitying laughter.

COMPARE

"My Grandmother's Love Letters" with "When You Are Old" by William Butler Yeats
(page 1268).

E. E. Cummings   (1894–1962)*

SOMEWHERE I HAVE NEVER TRAVELLED,   1931
GLADLY BEYOND

somewhere i have never travelled,gladly beyond
any experience,your eyes have their silence:
in your most frail gesture are things which enclose me,
or which i cannot touch because they are too near

your slightest look easily will unclose me   5
though i have closed myself as fingers,
you open always petal by petal myself as Spring opens
(touching skilfully,mysteriously)her first rose

or if your wish be to close me,i and
my life will shut very beautifully,suddenly,   10
as when the heart of this flower imagines
the snow carefully everywhere descending;

nothing which we are to perceive in this world equals
the power of your intense fragility:whose texture
compels me with the colour of its countries,   15
rendering death and forever with each breathing

(i do not know what it is about you that closes
and opens;only something in me understands
the voice of your eyes is deeper than all roses)
nobody,not even the rain,has such small hands   20

COMPARE

"somewhere i have never travelled,gladly beyond" with "Merciless Beauty" by Geoffrey
Chaucer (page 1157) or "Elegy for Jane" by Theodore Roethke (page 1233).

John Donne

John Donne (1572–1631)*

DEATH BE NOT PROUD (ABOUT 1610)

Death be not proud, though some have callèd thee
Mighty and dreadful, for thou art not so;
For those whom thou think'st thou dost overthrow
Die not, poor death, nor yet canst thou kill me.
From rest and sleep, which but thy pictures be, 5
Much pleasure, then from thee much more must flow,
And soonest our best men with thee do go,
Rest of their bones, and soul's delivery.
Thou art slave to fate, chance, kings, and desperate men,
And dost with poison, war, and sickness dwell, 10
And poppy, or charms can make us sleep as well,
And better than thy stroke; why swell'st thou then?
One short sleep past, we wake eternally,
And death shall be no more; death, thou shalt die.

COMPARE

Compare Donne's personification of Death in "Death be not proud" with Emily Dickinson's in "Because I could not stop for Death" (page 1103).

John Donne   (1572–1631)*

THE FLEA   1633

Mark but this flea, and mark in this
How little that which thou deny'st me is;
It sucked me first, and now sucks thee,
And in this flea our two bloods mingled be;
Thou know'st that this cannot be said   5
A sin, nor shame, nor loss of maidenhead,
   Yet this enjoys before it woo,
    And pampered swells with one blood made of two,
   And this, alas, is more than we would do.

Oh stay, three lives in one flea spare,   10
Where we almost, yea more than married are.
This flea is you and I, and this
Our marriage bed, and marriage temple is;
Though parents grudge, and you, we're met
And cloistered in these living walls of jet.   15
   Though use° make you apt to kill me,   *custom*
   Let not to that, self-murder added be,
   And sacrilege, three sins in killing three.

Cruel and sudden, hast thou since
Purpled thy nail in blood of innocence?   20
Wherein could this flea guilty be,
Except in that drop it sucked from thee?
Yet thou triumph'st, and say'st that thou
Find'st not thyself, nor me, the weaker now;
   'Tis true; then learn how false, fears be;   25
   Just so much honor, when thou yield'st to me,
   Will waste, as this flea's death took life from thee.

COMPARE

"The Flea" with "To His Coy Mistress" by Andrew Marvell (page 1208).

John Donne   (1572–1631)*

A Valediction: Forbidding Mourning   (1611)

As virtuous men pass mildly away,
    And whisper to their souls to go,
Whilst some of their sad friends do say
    The breath goes now, and some say no:

So let us melt, and make no noise,   5
    No tear-floods, nor sigh-tempests move;
'Twere profanation of our joys
    To tell the laity° our love.   *common people*

Moving of th' earth° brings harms and fears;   *earthquake*
    Men reckon what it did and meant;   10
But trepidation of the spheres,
    Though greater far, is innocent.°   *harmless*

Dull sublunary lovers' love
    (Whose soul is sense) cannot admit
Absence, because it doth remove   15
    Those things which elemented° it.   *constituted*

But we, by a love so much refined
    That ourselves know not what it is,
Inter-assurèd of the mind,
    Care less, eyes, lips, and hands to miss.   20

Our two souls, therefore, which are one,
    Though I must go, endure not yet
A breach, but an expansiòn,
    Like gold to airy thinness beat.

If they be two, they are two so   25
    As stiff twin compasses are two:
Thy soul, the fixed foot, makes no show
    To move, but doth, if th' other do.

And though it in the center sit,
    Yet when the other far doth roam,   30
It leans and harkens after it,
    And grows erect as that comes home.

Such wilt thou be to me, who must,
   Like th' other foot, obliquely run;
Thy firmness makes my circle just,°   *perfect*   35
   And makes me end where I begun.

A VALEDICTION: FORBIDDING MOURNING. According to Donne's biographer Izaak Walton, Donne's wife received this poem as a gift before the poet departed on a journey to France. 11 *spheres*: in Ptolemaic astronomy, the concentric spheres surrounding the earth. The trepidation or motion of the ninth sphere was thought to change the date of the equinox. 19 *Inter-assurèd of the mind*: each sure in mind that the other is faithful. 24 *gold to airy thinness*: gold is so malleable that, if beaten to the thickness of gold leaf (1/250,000 of one inch), one ounce of gold would cover 250 square feet.

COMPARE

"A Valediction: Forbidding Mourning" with "To Lucasta" by Richard Lovelace (page 741).

Rita Dove

Rita Dove   (b. 1952)*

SUMMIT BEACH, 1921   1989

The Negro beach jumped to the twitch
of an oil drum tattoo and a mandolin,
sweaters flying off the finest brown shoulders
this side of the world.

She sat by the fire, shawl moored   5
by a single fake cameo. She was cold,
thank you, she did not care to dance—
the scar on her knee winking
with the evening chill.

Papa had said don't be so fast,   10
you're all you've got. So she refused

to cut the wing, though she let the boys
bring her sassafras tea and drank it down
neat as a dropped hankie.

Her knee had itched in the cast   15
till she grew mean from bravery.
She could wait, she was gold.
When the right man smiled it would be
music skittering up her calf

like a chuckle. She could feel   20
the breeze in her ears like water,
like the air as a child when
she climbed Papa's shed and stepped off
the tin roof into blue,

with her parasol and invisible wings.   25

COMPARE

"Summit Beach, 1921" with "Kite Poem" by James Merrill (page 1209).

John Dryden   (1631–1700)

TO THE MEMORY OF MR. OLDHAM   1684

Farewell, too little and too lately known,
Whom I began to think and call my own;
For sure our souls were near allied, and thine
Cast in the same poetic mold with mine.
One common note on either lyre did strike,   5
And knaves and fools we both abhorred alike.
To the same goal did both our studies drive:
The last set out the soonest did arrive.
Thus Nissus fell upon the slippery place,
While his young friend performed and won the race.   10
O early ripe! to thy abundant store
What could advancing age have added more?
It might (what Nature never gives the young)
Have taught the numbers° of thy native tongue.   *meters*
But satire needs not those, and wit will shine   15
Through the harsh cadence of a rugged line.
A noble error, and but seldom made,
When poets are by too much force betrayed.
Thy gen'rous fruits, though gathered ere their prime,
Still showed a quickness; and maturing time   20
But mellows what we write to the dull sweets of rhyme.

Once more, hail, and farewell! farewell, thou young
But ah! too short, Marcellus of our tongue!
Thy brows with ivy and with laurels bound;
But fate and gloomy night encompass thee around.   25

To the Memory of Mr. Oldham. John Oldham, poet best remembered for his *Satires upon the Je-suits*, had died at thirty. 9–10 *Nissus; his young friend:* these two close friends, as Virgil tells us in the *Aeneid*, ran a race for the prize of an olive crown. 23 *Marcellus:* had he not died in his twentieth year, he would have succeeded the Roman emperor Augustus. 25 This line echoes the *Aeneid* (VI, 886), in which Marcellus is seen walking under the black cloud of his impending doom.

Compare

"To the Memory of Mr. Oldham" with "Elegy for Jane" by Theodore Roethke (page 1233).

T. S. Eliot   (1888–1965)*

Journey of the Magi   1927

"A cold coming we had of it,
Just the worst time of the year
For a journey, and such a long journey:
The ways deep and the weather sharp,
The very dead of winter."   5
And the camels galled, sore-footed, refractory,
Lying down in the melting snow.
There were times we regretted
The summer palaces on slopes, the terraces,
And the silken girls bringing sherbet.   10
Then the camel men cursing and grumbling
And running away, and wanting their liquor and women,
And the night-fires going out, and the lack of shelters,
And the cities hostile and the towns unfriendly
And the villages dirty and charging high prices: 15
A hard time we had of it.
At the end we preferred to travel all night,
Sleeping in snatches,
With the voices singing in our ears, saying
That this was all folly.   20

Then at dawn we came down to a temperate valley,
Wet, below the snow line, smelling of vegetation;
With a running stream and a water-mill beating the darkness,
And three trees on the low sky,

And an old white horse galloped away in the meadow.   25
Then we came to a tavern with vine-leaves over the lintel,
Six hands at an open door dicing for pieces of silver,
And feet kicking the empty wine-skins.
But there was no information, and so we continued
And arrived at evening, not a moment too soon   30
Finding the place; it was (you may say) satisfactory.

All this was a long time ago, I remember,
And I would do it again, but set down
This set down
This: were we led all that way for   35
Birth or Death? There was a Birth, certainly,
We had evidence and no doubt. I had seen birth and death,
But had thought they were different; this Birth was
Hard and bitter agony for us, like Death, our death.
We returned to our places, these Kingdoms,   40
But no longer at ease here, in the old dispensation,
With an alien people clutching their gods.
I should be glad of another death.

JOURNEY OF THE MAGI. The story of the Magi, the three wise men who traveled to Bethlehem to behold the baby Jesus, is told in Matthew 2:1–12. That the three were kings is a later tradition. 1–5 A cold coming . . . winter: Eliot quotes with slight changes from a sermon preached on Christmas Day, 1622, by Bishop Lancelot Andrewes. 24 three trees: foreshadowing the three crosses on Calvary (see Luke 23:32–33). 25 white horse: perhaps the steed that carried the conquering Christ in the vision of St. John the Divine (Revelation 19:11–16). 41 old dispensation: older, pagan religion about to be displaced by Christianity.

COMPARE

"Journey of the Magi" with "The Magi" by William Butler Yeats (page 1268).

T. S. Eliot

T. S. Eliot   (1888–1965)*

THE LOVE SONG OF J. ALFRED PRUFROCK   1917

*S'io credessi che mia risposta fosse
A persona che mai tornasse al mondo,
Questa fiamma staria senza piu scosse.
Ma perciocche giammai di questo fondo
Non tornò vivo alcun, s'i'odo il vero,
Senza tema d'infamia ti rispondo.*

Let us go then, you and I,
When the evening is spread out against the sky
Like a patient etherized upon a table;
Let us go, through certain half-deserted streets,
The muttering retreats   5
Of restless nights in one-night cheap hotels
And sawdust restaurants with oyster-shells:
Streets that follow like a tedious argument
Of insidious intent
To lead you to an overwhelming question . . .   10
Oh, do not ask, "What is it?"
Let us go and make our visit.

In the room the women come and go
Talking of Michelangelo.
                                                                              15
The yellow fog that rubs its back upon the window-panes,
The yellow smoke that rubs its muzzle on the window-panes,
Licked its tongue into the corners of the evening,
Lingered upon the pools that stand in drains,
Let fall upon its back the soot that falls from chimneys,
Slipped by the terrace, made a sudden leap,   20

And seeing that it was a soft October night,
Curled once about the house, and fell asleep.

    And indeed there will be time
For the yellow smoke that slides along the street
Rubbing its back upon the window-panes;
There will be time, there will be time   25
To prepare a face to meet the faces that you meet;
There will be time to murder and create,
And time for all the works and days of hands
That lift and drop a question on your plate;   30
Time for you and time for me,
And time yet for a hundred indecisions,
And for a hundred visions and revisions,
Before the taking of a toast and tea.

    In the room the women come and go   35
Talking of Michelangelo.

    And indeed there will be time
To wonder, "Do I dare?" and, "Do I dare?"
Time to turn back and descend the stair,
With a bald spot in the middle of my hair—   40
(They will say: "How his hair is growing thin!")
My morning coat, my collar mounting firmly to the chin,
My necktie rich and modest, but asserted by a simple pin—
(They will say: "But how his arms and legs are thin!")
Do I dare   45
Disturb the universe?
In a minute there is time
For decisions and revisions which a minute will reverse.

    For I have known them all already, known them all—
Have known the evenings, mornings, afternoons,   50
I have measured out my life with coffee spoons;
I know the voices dying with a dying fall
Beneath the music from a farther room.
    So how should I presume?

    And I have known the eyes already, known them all—   55
The eyes that fix you in a formulated phrase,
And when I am formulated, sprawling on a pin,
When I am pinned and wriggling on the wall,
Then how should I begin
To spit out all the butt-ends of my days and ways?   60
    And how should I presume?

    And I have known the arms already, known them all—
Arms that are braceleted and white and bare

(But in the lamplight, downed with light brown hair!)
Is it perfume from a dress   65
That makes me so digress?
Arms that lie along a table, or wrap about a shawl.
    And should I then presume?
    And how should I begin?

     . . . . .

Shall I say, I have gone at dusk through narrow streets   70
And watched the smoke that rises from the pipes
Of lonely men in shirt-sleeves, leaning out of windows? . . .

   I should have been a pair of ragged claws
Scuttling across the floors of silent seas.

     . . . . .

And the afternoon, the evening, sleeps so peacefully!   75
Smoothed by long fingers,
Asleep . . . tired . . . or it malingers,
Stretched on the floor, here beside you and me.
Should I, after tea and cakes and ices,
Have the strength to force the moment to its crisis?   80
But though I have wept and fasted, wept and prayed,
Though I have seen my head (grown slightly bald) brought in upon a
    platter,
I am no prophet—and here's no great matter;
I have seen the moment of my greatness flicker,
And I have seen the eternal Footman hold my coat, and snicker,   85
And in short, I was afraid.

   And would it have been worth it, after all,
After the cups, the marmalade, the tea,
Among the porcelain, among some talk of you and me,
Would it have been worth while,   90
To have bitten off the matter with a smile,
To have squeezed the universe into a ball
To roll it towards some overwhelming question,
To say: "I am Lazarus, come from the dead,
Come back to tell you all, I shall tell you all"—   95
If one, settling a pillow by her head,
    Should say: "That is not what I meant at all.
    That is not it, at all."

   And would it have been worth it, after all,
Would it have been worth while,   100
After the sunsets and the dooryards and the sprinkled streets,
After the novels, after the teacups, after the skirts that trail along the
    floor—
And this, and so much more?—

It is impossible to say just what I mean!
But as if a magic lantern threw the nerves in patterns on a screen: 105
Would it have been worth while
If one, settling a pillow or throwing off a shawl,
And turning toward the window, should say:
  "That is not it at all,
  That is not what I meant, at all."   110

. . . . .

No! I am not Prince Hamlet, nor was meant to be;
Am an attendant lord, one that will do
To swell a progress, start a scene or two,
Advise the prince; no doubt, an easy tool,
Deferential, glad to be of use,   115
Politic, cautious, and meticulous;
Full of high sentence, but a bit obtuse;
At times, indeed, almost ridiculous—
Almost, at times, the Fool.

  I grow old . . . I grow old . . .   120
I shall wear the bottoms of my trousers rolled.

  Shall I part my hair behind? Do I dare to eat a peach?
I shall wear white flannel trousers, and walk upon the beach.
I have heard the mermaids singing, each to each.

  I do not think that they will sing to me.   125

  I have seen them riding seaward on the waves
Combing the white hair of the waves blown back
When the wind blows the water white and black.

  We have lingered in the chambers of the sea
By sea-girls wreathed with seaweed red and brown   130
Till human voices wake us, and we drown.

THE LOVE SONG OF J. ALFRED PRUFROCK. The epigraph, from Dante's *Inferno*, is the speech of one
dead and damned, who thinks that his hearer also is going to remain in Hell. Count Guido da Monte-
feltro, whose sin has been to give false counsel after a corrupt prelate had offered him prior absolution
and whose punishment is to be wrapped in a constantly burning flame, offers to tell Dante his story: "If
I thought my reply were to someone who could ever return to the world, this flame would waver no
more. But since, I'm told, nobody ever escapes from this pit, I'll tell you without fear of ill fame." 29
works and days: title of a poem by Hesiod (eighth century B.C.), depicting his life as a hard-working
Greek farmer and exhorting his brother to be like him. 82 *head . . . platter*: like that of John the Baptist,
prophet and praiser of chastity, whom King Herod beheaded at the demand of Herodias, his unlawfully
wedded wife (see Mark 6:17–28). 92–93 *squeezed . . . To roll it*: an echo from Marvell's "To His Coy
Mistress," lines 41–42. 94 *Lazarus*: probably the Lazarus whom Jesus called forth from the tomb (John
11:1–44), but possibly the beggar seen in Heaven by the rich man in Hell (Luke 16:19–25).

COMPARE

"The Love Song of J. Alfred Prufrock" with "Acquainted with the Night" by Robert Frost
(page 919).

Louise Erdrich

Louise Erdrich (b. 1954)

INDIAN BOARDING SCHOOL: THE RUNAWAYS   1984

Home's the place we head for in our sleep.
Boxcars stumbling north in dreams
don't wait for us. We catch them on the run.
The rails, old lacerations that we love,
shoot parallel across the face and break   5
just under Turtle Mountains. Riding scars
you can't get lost. Home is the place they cross.

The lame guard strikes a match and makes the dark
less tolerant. We watch through cracks in boards
as the land starts rolling, rolling till it hurts   10
to be here, cold in regulation clothes.
We know the sheriff's waiting at midrun
to take us back. His car is dumb and warm.
The highway doesn't rock, it only hums
like a wing of long insults. The worn-down welts   15
of ancient punishments lead back and forth.

All runaways wear dresses, long green ones,
the color you would think shame was. We scrub
the sidewalks down because it's shameful work.
Our brushes cut the stone in watered arcs   20
and in the soak frail outlines shiver clear
a moment, things us kids pressed on the dark
face before it hardened, pale, remembering
delicate old injuries, the spines of names and leaves.

INDIAN BOARDING SCHOOL: THE RUNAWAYS. 6. *Turtle Mountains:* in North Dakota and Manitoba.
The poet, of German and Native American descent, belongs to the Turtle Mountain Band of the
Chippewa.

"Indian Boarding School: The Runaways" with "For the White Poets Who Would Be Indian" by Wendy Rose (page 1011).

B. H. Fairchild (b. 1945)

A STARLIT NIGHT   2002

All over America at this hour men are standing
by an open closet door, slacks slung over one arm,
staring at wire hangers, thinking of taxes
or a broken faucet or their first sex: the smell
of back-seat Naugahyde, the hush of a maize field   5
like breathing, the stars rushing, rushing away.

And a woman lies in an unmade bed watching
the man she has known twenty-one, no,
could it be? twenty-two years, and she is listening
to the polonaise climbing up through radio static   10
from the kitchen where dishes are piled
and the linoleum floor is a great, gray sea.

It's the A-flat polonaise she practiced endlessly,
never quite getting it right, though her father,
calling from the darkened TV room, always said,   15
"Beautiful, kiddo!" and the moon would slide across
the lacquered piano top as if it were something
that lived underwater, something from far below.

They both came from houses with photographs,
the smell of camphor in closets, board games   20
with missing pieces, sunburst clocks in the kitchen
that made them, each morning, a little sad.
They didn't know what they wanted, every night,
every starlit night of their lives, and now they have it.

COMPARE

"A Starlit Night" with Wallace Stevens's "Disillusionment of Ten O'Clock" (page 780).

Robert Frost   (1874–1963)*

BIRCHES   1916

When I see birches bend to left and right
Across the lines of straighter darker trees,
I like to think some boy's been swinging them.
But swinging doesn't bend them down to stay
As ice storms do. Often you must have seen them   5
Loaded with ice a sunny winter morning
After a rain. They click upon themselves
As the breeze rises, and turn many-colored
As the stir cracks and crazes their enamel.
Soon the sun's warmth makes them shed crystal shells   10
Shattering and avalanching on the snow crust—
Such heaps of broken glass to sweep away
You'd think the inner dome of heaven had fallen.
They are dragged to the withered bracken by the load,
And they seem not to break; though once they are bowed   15
So low for long, they never right themselves:
You may see their trunks arching in the woods
Years afterwards, trailing their leaves on the ground
Like girls on hands and knees that throw their hair
Before them over their heads to dry in the sun.   20
But I was going to say when Truth broke in
With all her matter of fact about the ice storm
I should prefer to have some boy bend them
As he went out and in to fetch the cows—
Some boy too far from town to learn baseball,   25
Whose only play was what he found himself,
Summer or winter, and could play alone.
One by one he subdued his father's trees
By riding them down over and over again
Until he took the stiffness out of them,   30
And not one but hung limp, not one was left
For him to conquer. He learned all there was
To learn about not launching out too soon
And so not carrying the tree away
Clear to the ground. He always kept his poise   35
To the top branches, climbing carefully
With the same pains you use to fill a cup
Up to the brim, and even above the brim.
Then he flung outward, feet first, with a swish,
Kicking his way down through the air to the ground.   40
So was I once myself a swinger of birches.

And so I dream of going back to be.
It's when I'm weary of considerations,
And life is too much like a pathless wood
Where your face burns and tickles with the cobwebs   45
Broken across it, and one eye is weeping
From a twig's having lashed across it open.
I'd like to get away from earth awhile
And then come back to it and begin over.
May no fate willfully misunderstand me   50
And half grant what I wish and snatch me away
Not to return. Earth's the right place for love:
I don't know where it's likely to go better.
I'd like to go by climbing a birch tree,
And climb black branches up a snow-white trunk   55
Toward heaven, till the tree could bear no more,
But dipped its top and set me down again.
That would be good both going and coming back.
One could do worse than be a swinger of birches.

COMPARE

"Birches" with "Sailing to Byzantium" by William Butler Yeats (page 1075).

Robert Frost   (1874–1963)*
MENDING WALL   1914

Something there is that doesn't love a wall,
That sends the frozen-ground-swell under it,
And spills the upper boulders in the sun;
And makes gaps even two can pass abreast.
The work of hunters is another thing: 5
I have come after them and made repair
Where they have left not one stone on a stone,
But they would have the rabbit out of hiding,
To please the yelping dogs. The gaps I mean,
No one has seen them made or heard them made,   10
But at spring mending-time we find them there.
I let my neighbor know beyond the hill;
And on a day we meet to walk the line
And set the wall between us once again.
We keep the wall between us as we go.   15
To each the boulders that have fallen to each.
And some are loaves and some so nearly balls
We have to use a spell to make them balance:

"Stay where you are until our backs are turned!"
We wear our fingers rough with handling them.   20
Oh, just another kind of outdoor game,
One on a side. It comes to little more:
There where it is we do not need the wall:
He is all pine and I am apple orchard.
My apple trees will never get across   25
And eat the cones under his pines, I tell him.
He only says, "Good fences make good neighbors."
Spring is the mischief in me, and I wonder
If I could put a notion in his head:
"*Why* do they make good neighbors? Isn't it   30
Where there are cows? But here there are no cows.
Before I built a wall I'd ask to know
What I was walling in or walling out,
And to whom I was like to give offence.
Something there is that doesn't love a wall,   35
That wants it down." I could say "Elves" to him,
But it's not elves exactly, and I'd rather
He said it for himself. I see him there
Bringing a stone grasped firmly by the top
In each hand, like an old-stone savage armed.   40
He moves in darkness as it seems to me,
Not of woods only and the shade of trees.
He will not go behind his father's saying,
And he likes having thought of it so well
He says again, "Good fences make good neighbors."   45

COMPARE

"Mending Wall" with "Digging" by Seamus Heaney (page 1186).

Robert Frost   (1874–1963)*

STOPPING BY WOODS ON A   1923
SNOWY EVENING

Whose woods these are I think I know.
His house is in the village though;
He will not see me stopping here
To watch his woods fill up with snow.

My little horse must think it queer   5
To stop without a farmhouse near
Between the woods and frozen lake
The darkest evening of the year.

He gives his harness bells a shake
To ask if there is some mistake.
The only other sound's the sweep
Of easy wind and downy flake.

The woods are lovely, dark and deep,
But I have promises to keep,
And miles to go before I sleep,
And miles to go before I sleep.

COMPARE

"Stopping by Woods on a Snowy Evening" with "Desert Places" by Robert Frost (page 876).

Allen Ginsberg (1926–1997)

A SUPERMARKET IN CALIFORNIA   1956

What thoughts I have of you tonight, Walt Whitman, for I walked
down the sidestreets under the trees with a headache self-conscious
looking at the full moon.
In my hungry fatigue, and shopping for images, I went into the neon
fruit supermarket, dreaming of your enumerations!
What peaches and what penumbras! Whole families shopping at
night! Aisles full of husbands! Wives in the avocados, babies in the
tomatoes!—and you, García Lorca, what were you doing down by the
watermelons?

I saw you, Walt Whitman, childless, lonely old grubber, poking
among the meats in the refrigerator and eyeing the grocery boys.
I heard you asking questions of each: Who killed the pork chops?
What price bananas? Are you my Angel?
I wandered in and out of the brilliant stacks of cans following you,
and followed in my imagination by the store detective.
We strode down the open corridors together in our solitary fancy
tasting artichokes, possessing every frozen delicacy, and never passing
the cashier.

Where are we going, Walt Whitman? The doors close in an hour.
Which way does your beard point tonight?
(I touch your book and dream of our odyssey in the supermarket and
feel absurd.)
Will we walk all night through solitary streets? The trees add shade
to shade, lights out in the houses, we'll both be lonely.
Will we stroll dreaming of the lost America of love past blue auto-
mobiles in driveways, home to our silent cottage?

Ah, dear father, graybeard, lonely old courage-teacher, what
America did you have when Charon quit poling his ferry and you got
out on a smoking bank and stood watching the boat disappear on the
black waters of Lethe?

A SUPERMARKET IN CALIFORNIA. *2 enumerations:* many of Whitman's poems contain lists of observed details. *3 García Lorca:* modern Spanish poet who wrote an "Ode to Walt Whitman" in his book-length sequence *Poet in New York. 12 Charon . . . Lethe:* Is the poet confusing two underworld rivers? Charon, in Greek and Roman mythology, is the boatman who ferries the souls of the dead across the River Styx. The River Lethe also flows through Hades, and a drink of its waters makes the dead lose their painful memories of loved ones they have left behind.

COMPARE

"A Supermarket in California" with Walt Whitman's "To a Locomotive in Winter" (page 720).

Dana Gioia (b. 1950)

CALIFORNIA HILLS IN AUGUST   1982

I can imagine someone who found
these fields unbearable, who climbed
the hillside in the heat, cursing the dust,
cracking the brittle weeds underfoot,
wishing a few more trees for shade.   5

An Easterner especially, who would scorn
the meagerness of summer, the dry
twisted shapes of black elm,
scrub oak, and chaparral—a landscape
August has already drained of green.   10

One who would hurry over the clinging
thistle, foxtail, golden poppy,
knowing everything was just a weed,
unable to conceive that these trees
and sparse brown bushes were alive.   15

And hate the bright stillness of the noon,
without wind, without motion,
the only other living thing
a hawk, hungry for prey, suspended
in the blinding, sunlit blue.   20

And yet how gentle it seems to someone
raised in a landscape short of rain—

the skyline of a hill broken by no more
trees than one can count, the grass,
the empty sky, the wish for water.   25

COMPARE

"California Hills in August" with "To see a world in a grain of sand" by William Blake
(page 820).

Thom Gunn   (b. 1929)

THE MAN WITH NIGHT SWEATS   1992

I wake up cold, I who
Prospered through dreams of heat
Wake to their residue,
Sweat, and a clinging sheet.

My flesh was its own shield: 5
Where it was gashed, it healed.

I grew as I explored
The body I could trust
Even while I adored
The risk that made robust,   10

A world of wonders in
Each challenge to the skin.

I cannot but be sorry
The given shield was cracked,
My mind reduced to hurry,   15
My flesh reduced and wrecked.

I have to change the bed,
But catch myself instead

Stopped upright where I am
Hugging my body to me   20
As if to shield it from
The pains that will go through me,

As if hands were enough
To hold an avalanche off.

COMPARE

"The Man with Night Sweats" with "When I have fears that I may cease to be" by John
Keats (page 1200).

1180   POEMS FOR FURTHER READING

Donald Hall (b. 1928)

NAMES OF HORSES   1978

All winter your brute shoulders strained against collars, padding
and steerhide over the ash hames, to haul
sledges of cordwood for drying through spring and summer,
for the Glenwood stove next winter, and for the simmering range.

In April you pulled cartloads of manure to spread on the fields,   5
dark manure of Holsteins, and knobs of your own clustered with oats.
All summer you mowed the grass in meadow and hayfield, the mowing
     machine
clacketing beside you, while the sun walked high in the morning;

and after noon's heat, you pulled a clawed rake through the same acres,
gathering stacks, and dragged the wagon from stack to stack,   10
and the built hayrack back, uphill to the chaffy barn,
three loads of hay a day from standing grass in the morning.

Sundays you trotted the two miles to church with the light load
of a leather quartertop buggy, and grazed in the sound of hymns.
Generation on generation, your neck rubbed the windowsill   15
of the stall, smoothing the wood as the sea smooths glass.

When you were old and lame, when your shoulders hurt bending to
     graze,
one October the man, who fed you and kept you, and harnessed you
     every morning,
led you through corn stubble to sandy ground above Eagle Pond,
and dug a hole beside you where you stood shuddering in your skin,   20

and lay the shotgun's muzzle in the boneless hollow behind your ear,
and fired the slug into your brain, and felled you into your grave,
shoveling sand to cover you, setting goldenrod upright above you,
where by next summer a dent in the ground made your monument.

For a hundred and fifty years, in the pasture of dead horses,   25
roots of pine trees pushed through the pale curves of your ribs,
yellow blossoms flourished above you in autumn, and in winter
frost heaved your bones in the ground—old toilers, soil makers:

O Roger, Mackerel, Riley, Ned, Nellie, Chester, Lady Ghost.

COMPARE

"Names of Horses" with "The Bull Calf" by Irving Layton (page 1204).

Thomas Hardy   (1840–1928)*

THE CONVERGENCE OF THE TWAIN   1912

Lines on the Loss of the "Titanic"

I

In a solitude of the sea
Deep from human vanity,
And the Pride of Life that planned her, stilly couches she.

II

Steel chambers, late the pyres
Of her salamandrine fires,   5
Cold currents third,° and turn to rhythmic tidal lyres.   *thread*

III

Over the mirrors meant
To glass the opulent
The sea-worm crawls—grotesque, slimed, dumb, indifferent.

IV

Jewels in joy designed
To ravish the sensuous mind   10
Lie lightless, all their sparkles bleared and black and blind.

V

Dim moon-eyed fishes near
Gaze at the gilded gear
And query: "What does this vaingloriousness down here?"   15

VI

Well: while was fashioning
This creature of cleaving wing,
The Immanent Will that stirs and urges everything

VII

Prepared a sinister mate
For her—so gaily great—   20
A Shape of Ice, for the time far and dissociate.

VIII

And as the smart ship grew
In stature, grace, and hue,
In shadowy silent distance grew the Iceberg too.

IX

Alien they seemed to be:
No mortal eye could see
The intimate welding of their later history,

X

Or sign that they were bent
By paths coincident
On being anon twin halves of one august event,

XI

Till the Spinner of the Years
Said "Now!" And each one hears,
And consummation comes, and jars two hemispheres.

THE CONVERGENCE OF THE TWAIN. The luxury liner *Titanic*, supposedly unsinkable, went down in 1912 after striking an iceberg on its first Atlantic voyage. 5 *salamandrine*: like the salamander, a lizard that supposedly thrives in fires, or like a spirit of the same name that inhabits fire (according to alchemists).

COMPARE

"The Convergence of the Twain" with "Titanic" by David R. Slavitt (page 1239).

Thomas Hardy

Thomas Hardy   (1840–1928)*

THE DARKLING THRUSH   1900

I leant upon a coppice gate
  When Frost was spectre-gray,
And Winter's dregs made desolate
  The weakening eye of day.

The tangled bine-stems scored the sky 5
  Like strings of broken lyres,
And all mankind that haunted nigh
  Had sought their household fires.

The land's sharp features seemed to be
  The Century's corpse outleant, 10
His crypt the cloudy canopy,
  The wind his death-lament.
The ancient pulse of germ and birth
  Was shrunken hard and dry,
And every spirit upon earth 15
  Seemed fervourless as I.

At once a voice arose among
  The bleak twigs overhead
In a full-hearted evensong
  Of joy illimited; 20
An aged thrush, frail, gaunt, and small,
  In blast-beruffled plume,
Had chosen thus to fling his soul
  Upon the growing gloom.

So little cause for carolings
  Of such ecstatic sound 25
Was written on terrestial things
  Afar or nigh around,
That I could think there trembled through
  His happy good-night air
Some blessed Hope, whereof he knew 30
  And I was unaware.

THE DARKLING THRUSH. Hardy set this poem on December 31, 1900, the last day of the nineteenth
century.

COMPARE

"The Darkling Thrush" with "I Wandered Lonely as a Cloud" by William Wordsworth
(page 727).

Thomas Hardy (1840–1928)*

HAP 1866

If but some vengeful god would call to me
From up the sky, and laugh: "Thou suffering thing,
Know that thy sorrow is my ecstasy,
That thy love's loss is my hate's profiting!"

Then would I bear it, clench myself, and die,   5
Steeled by the sense of ire unmerited;
Half-eased in that a Powerfuller than I
Had willed and meted me the tears I shed.

But not so. How arrives it joy lies slain,
And why unblooms the best hope ever sown?   10
—Crass Casualty obstructs the sun and rain,
And dicing Time for gladness casts a moan . . .
These purblind Doomsters had as readily strown
Blisses about my pilgrimage as pain.

COMPARE

"Hap" with the Roman poet Horace's *carpe diem* ode on pages 1029–30. Choose any of the three translations there of Horace's work or use the literal translation provided below the Latin original.

Robert Hayden

Robert Hayden   (1913–1980)*

THOSE WINTER SUNDAYS   1962

Sundays too my father got up early
and put his clothes on in the blueblack cold,
then with cracked hands that ached
from labor in the weekday weather made
banked fires blaze. No one ever thanked him.   5

I'd wake and hear the cold splintering, breaking.
When the rooms were warm, he'd call,
and slowly I would rise and dress,
fearing the chronic angers of that house,

Speaking indifferently to him,   10
who had driven out the cold
and polished my good shoes as well.
What did I know, what did I know
of love's austere and lonely offices?

COMPARE

"Those Winter Sundays" with "Daddy" by Sylvia Plath (page 1222).

Seamus Heaney   (b. 1939)*

DIGGING   1966

Between my finger and my thumb
The squat pen rests; snug as a gun.

Under my window, a clean rasping sound
When the spade sinks into gravelly ground.
My father, digging. I look down   5

Till his straining rump among the flowerbeds
Bends low, comes up twenty years away
Stooping in rhythm through potato drills
Where he was digging.

The coarse boot nestled on the lug, the shaft   10
Against the inside knee was levered firmly.
He rooted out tall tops, buried the bright edge deep
To scatter new potatoes that we picked
Loving their cool hardness in our hands.

By God, the old man could handle a spade.   15
Just like his old man.

My grandfather cut more turf in a day
Than any other man on Toner's bog.
Once I carried him milk in a bottle
Corked sloppily with paper. He straightened up   20
To drink it, then fell to right away

Nicking and slicing neatly, heaving sods
Over his shoulder, going down and down
For the good turf. Digging.

The cold smell of potato mould, the squelch and slap   25
Of soggy peat, the curt cuts of an edge
Through living roots awaken in my head.
But I've no spade to follow men like them.

Between my finger and my thumb
The squat pen rests.
I'll dig with it.

COMPARE

"Digging" with "The Writer" by Richard Wilbur (page 1260).

Seamus Heaney   (b. 1939)*

MOTHER OF THE GROOM   1972

What she remembers
Is his glistening back
In the bath, his small boots
In the ring of boots at her feet.

Hands in her voided lap,   5
She hears a daughter welcomed.
It's as if he kicked when lifted
And slipped her soapy hold.

Once soap would ease off
The wedding ring   10
That's bedded forever now
In her clapping hand.

COMPARE

"Mother of the Groom" with "Most Like an Arch This Marriage" by John Ciardi (page 961) and "The River Merchant's Wife: a Letter" by Ezra Pound (page 1226).

Anthony Hecht

Anthony Hecht   (b. 1923)

ADAM   1967

> *Hath the rain a father? or who hath begotten the drops of dew?*

"Adam, my child, my son,
These very words you hear
Compose the fish and starlight
Of your untroubled dream.
When you awake, my child,   5
It shall all come true.
Know that it was for you
That all things were begun."

Adam, my child, my son,
Thus spoke Our Father in heaven   10
To his first, fabled child,
The father of us all.
And I, your father, tell
The words over again
As innumerable men   15
From ancient times have done.

Tell them again in pain,
And to the empty air.
Where you are men speak
A different mother tongue.   20
Will you forget our games,
Our hide-and-seek and song?
Child, it will be long
Before I see you again.

Adam, there will be
Many hard hours,
As an old poem says,
Hours of loneliness.
I cannot ease them for you;   30
They are our common lot.
During them, like as not,
You will dream of me.

When you are crouched away
In a strange clothes closet
Hiding from one who's "It"   35
And the dark crowds in,
Do not be afraid—
O, if you can, believe
In a father's love
That you shall know some day.   40

Think of the summer rain
Or seedpearls of the mist;
Seeing the beaded leaf,
Try to remember me.
From far away   45
I send my blessing out
To circle the great globe.
It shall reach you yet.

ADAM. According to Genesis 2:6–7, God created Adam, the first man, from the dust of the earth;
Adam is also the name of Anthony Hecht's first son. *Epigraph: "Hath the rain a father . . . ?":* These
words are spoken to Job by the voice of God in Job 38:28.

COMPARE

"Adam" with "Imperial Adam" by A. D. Hope (page 989).

George Herbert

George Herbert   (1593–1633)*

LOVE   1633

Love bade me welcome; yet my soul drew back,
    Guilty of dust and sin.
But quick-eyed Love, observing me grow slack
    From my first entrance in,
Drew nearer to me, sweetly questioning   5
    If I lacked anything.

"A guest," I answered, "worthy to be here";
    Love said, "You shall be he."
"I, the unkind, ungrateful? Ah, my dear,
    I cannot look on Thee."   10
Love took my hand, and smiling did reply,
    "Who made the eyes but I?"

"Truth, Lord, but I have marred them; let my shame
    Go where it doth deserve."
"And know you not," says Love, "who bore the blame?"   15
    "My dear, then I will serve."
"You must sit down," says Love, "and taste My meat."
    So I did sit and eat.

COMPARE

"Love" with "Batter my heart, three-personed God" by John Donne (page 753).

Robert Herrick   (1591–1674)*

TO THE VIRGINS, TO MAKE MUCH OF TIME   1648

Gather ye rose-buds while ye may,
    Old Time is still a-flying;
And this same flower that smiles today,
    Tomorrow will be dying.

The glorious lamp of heaven, the sun,   5
    The higher he's a-getting,
The sooner will his race be run,
    And nearer he's to setting.

That age is best which is the first,
    When youth and blood are warmer;   10
But being spent, the worse, and worst
    Times still succeed the former.

Then be not coy, but use your time,
    And while ye may, go marry;
For having lost but once your prime,   15
    You may for ever tarry.

COMPARE

"To the Virgins, to Make Much of Time" with "To His Coy Mistress" by Andrew Marvell (page 1208) and "Go, Lovely Rose" by Edmund Waller (page 1258).

Gerard Manley Hopkins   (1844–1889)*

SPRING AND FALL   (1880)

    To a young child

Márgarét, áre you gríeving
Over Goldengrove unleaving°   *shedding its leaves*
Leáves, líke the things of man, you
With your fresh thoughts care for, can you?
Áh! ás the heart grows older   5
It will come to such sights colder
By and by, nor spare a sigh
Though worlds of wanwood leafmeal lie;
And yet you *will* weep and know why.
Now no matter, child, the name: 10
Sórrow's spríngs áre the same.
Nor mouth had, no nor mind, expressed
What heart heard of, ghost° guessed: *spirit*

It ís the blight man was born for,
It is Margaret you mourn for.   15

COMPARE

"Spring and Fall" with "Aftermath" by Henry Wadsworth Longfellow (page 755).

Gerard Manley Hopkins

Gerard Manley Hopkins (1844–1889)*

NO WORST, THERE IS NONE   (1884–1885)

No worst, there is none. Pitched past pitch of grief,
More pangs will, schooled at forepangs, wilder wring.
Comforter, where, where is your comforting?
Mary, mother of us, where is your relief?
My cries heave, herds-long; huddle in a main, a chief-   5
woe, world-sorrow; on an age-old anvil wince and sing—
Then lull, then leave off. Fury had shrieked "No ling-
ering! Let me be fell: force I must be brief."
O the mind, mind has mountains; cliffs of fall
Frightful, sheer, no-man-fathomed. Hold them cheap   10
May who ne'er hung there. Nor does long our small
Durance deal with that steep or deep. Here! creep,
Wretch, under a comfort serves in a whirlwind: all
Life death does end and each day dies with sleep.

COMPARE

"No worst, there is none" with "Hap" by Thomas Hardy (page 1184).

Gerard Manley Hopkins   (1844–1889)*

THE WINDHOVER   (1877)

To Christ Our Lord

I caught this morning morning's minion, king-
    dom of daylight's dauphin, dapple-dawn-drawn Falcon, in his riding
    Of the rolling level underneath him steady air, and striding
High there, how he rung upon the rein of a wimpling wing
In his ecstasy! then off, off forth on swing,   5
    As a skate's heel sweeps smooth on a bow-bend: the hurl and gliding
    Rebuffed the big wind. My heart in hiding
Stirred for a bird, —the achieve of, the mastery of the thing!

Brute beauty and valor and act, oh, air, pride, plume, here
    Buckle! AND the fire that breaks from thee then, a billion   10
Times told lovelier, more dangerous, O my chevalier!

    No wonder of it: shéer plód makes plow down sillion°   *furrow*
Shine, and blue-bleak embers, ah my dear,
    Fall, gall themselves, and gash gold-vermilion.

THE WINDHOVER. A windhover is a kestrel, or small falcon, so called because it can hover upon the
wind. 4 *rung . . . wing*: A horse is "rung upon the rein" when its trainer holds the end of a long rein
and has the horse circle him. The possible meanings of *wimpling* include: (1) curving; (2) pleated,
arranged in many little folds one on top of another; (3) rippling or undulating like the surface of a
flowing stream.

COMPARE

"The Windhover" with "Batter my heart, three-personed God" by John Donne (page 753)
and "Easter Wings" by George Herbert (page 945).

A. E. Housman   (1859–1936)*

LOVELIEST OF TREES, THE CHERRY NOW   1896

Loveliest of trees, the cherry now
Is hung with bloom along the bough,
And stands about the woodland ride°   *path*
Wearing white for Eastertide.

Now, of my threescore years and ten,   5
Twenty will not come again,
And take from seventy springs a score,
It only leaves me fifty more.

And since to look at things in bloom
Fifty springs are little room,
About the woodlands I will go
To see the cherry hung with snow.   10

COMPARE

"Loveliest of trees, the cherry now" with "To the Virgins, to Make Much of Time" by
Robert Herrick (page 1191) and "Spring and Fall" by Gerard Manley Hopkins (page
1191).

A. E. *Housman*   (1859–1936)*

TO AN ATHLETE DYING YOUNG   1896

The time you won your town the race
We chaired you through the market-place;
Man and boy stood cheering by,
And home we brought you shoulder-high.

Today, the road all runners come,   5
Shoulder-high we bring you home,
And set you at your threshold down,
Townsman of a stiller town.

Smart lad, to slip betimes away
From fields where glory does not stay,   10
And early though the laurel grows
It withers quicker than the rose.

Eyes the shady night has shut
Cannot see the record cut,
And silence sounds no worse than cheers   15
After earth has stopped the ears.

Now you will not swell the rout
Of lads that wore their honors out,
Runners whom renown outran
And the name died before the man.   20

So set, before its echoes fade,
The fleet foot on the sill of shade,
And hold to the low lintel up
The still-defended challenge-cup.

And round that early-laureled head   25
Will flock to gaze the strengthless dead,
And find unwithered on its curls
The garland briefer than a girl's.

COMPARE

"To an Athlete Dying Young" with "Ex-Basketball Player" by John Updike (page 1253).

Randall Jarrell

Randall Jarrell   (1914–1965)

THE DEATH OF THE BALL TURRET GUNNER   1945

From my mother's sleep I fell into the State
And I hunched in its belly till my wet fur froze.
Six miles from earth, loosed from its dream of life,
I woke to black flak and the nightmare fighters.
When I died they washed me out of the turret with a hose.

THE DEATH OF THE BALL TURRET GUNNER. Jarrell has written: "A ball turret was a plexiglass sphere set into the belly of a B-17 or B-24, and inhabited by two .50 caliber machine-guns and one man, a short small man. When this gunner tracked with his machine-guns a fighter attacking his bomber from below, he revolved with the turret; hunched in his little sphere, he looked like the fetus in the womb. The fighters which attacked him were armed with cannon firing explosive shells. The hose was a steam hose."

COMPARE

"The Death of the Ball Turret Gunner" with "Dulce et Decorum Est" by Wilfred Owen (page 742).

Robinson Jeffers (1887–1962)*

TO THE STONE-CUTTERS   1925

Stone-cutters fighting time with marble, you foredefeated
Challengers of oblivion
Eat cynical earnings, knowing rock splits, records fall down,
The square-limbed Roman letters
Scale in the thaws, wear in the rain. The poet as well   5
Builds his monument mockingly;
For man will be blotted out, the blithe earth die, the brave sun
Die blind, his heart blackening:
Yet stones have stood for a thousand years, and pained thoughts found
The honey peace in old poems.   10

COMPARE

"To the Stone-cutters" with "Not marble nor the gilded monuments" by William Shakespeare (page 1237).

Ben Jonson (1573?–1637)*

ON MY FIRST SON   (1603)

Farewell, thou child of my right hand, and joy.
My sin was too much hope of thee, loved boy;
Seven years thou wert lent to me, and I thee pay,
Exacted by thy fate, on the just day.
Oh, could I lose all father° now. For why   *fatherhood*   5
Will man lament the state he should envy̶—
To have so soon 'scaped world's and flesh's rage,
And, if no other misery, yet age.
Rest in soft peace, and asked, say, "Here doth lie
Ben Jonson his best piece of poetry,"   10
For whose sake henceforth all his vows be such
As what he loves may never like° too much.   *thrive*

ON MY FIRST SON. 1 *child of my right hand:* Jonson's son was named Benjamin; this phrase translates the Hebrew name. 4 *the just day:* the very day. The boy had died on his seventh birthday. 10 *poetry:* Jonson uses the word *poetry* here reflecting its Greek root *poiesis,* which means *creation.*

COMPARE

"On My First Son" with "'Out, Out—'" by Robert Frost (page 710).

Donald Justice   (b. 1925)*

COUNTING THE MAD   1960

This one was put in a jacket,
This one was sent home,
This one was given bread and meat
But would eat none,
And this one cried No No No No   5
All day long.

This one looked at the window
As though it were a wall,
This one saw things that were not there,
This one things that were,   10
And this one cried No No No No
All day long.

This one thought himself a bird,
This one a dog,
And this one thought himself a man,   15
An ordinary man,
And cried and cried No No No No
All day long.

COMPARE

"Counting the Mad" with "Embrace" by Billy Collins (page 805) and "Not Waving but Drowning" by Stevie Smith (page 806).

John Keats   (1795–1821)*

ODE ON A GRECIAN URN   1820

Thou still unravished bride of quietness,
    Thou foster-child of silence and slow time,
Sylvan historian, who canst thus express
    A flowery tale more sweetly than our rhyme:
What leaf-fringed legend haunts about thy shape   5
    Of deities or mortals, or of both,
        In Tempe or the dales of Arcady?
    What men or gods are these? What maidens loth?
What mad pursuit? What struggle to escape?
        What pipes and timbrels? What wild ecstasy?   10

Heard melodies are sweet, but those unheard
  Are sweeter; therefore, ye soft pipes, play on;
Not to the sensual° ear, but, more endeared,   *physical*
  Pipe to the spirit ditties of no tone:
Fair youth, beneath the trees, thou canst not leave   15
  Thy song, nor ever can those trees be bare;
    Bold Lover, never, never canst thou kiss,
Though winning near the goal—yet, do not grieve;
    She cannot fade, though thou hast not thy bliss,
  For ever wilt thou love, and she be fair!   20

Ah, happy, happy boughs! that cannot shed
  Your leaves, nor ever bid the Spring adieu;
And, happy melodist, unweari èd,
  For ever piping songs for ever new;
More happy love! more happy, happy love!   25
  For ever warm and still to be enjoyed,
    For ever panting, and for ever young;
All breathing human passion far above,
  That leaves a heart high-sorrowful and cloyed,
    A burning forehead, and a parching tongue.   30

Who are these coming to the sacrifice?
  To what green altar, O mysterious priest,
Lead'st thou that heifer lowing at the skies,
  And all her silken flanks with garlands drest?
What little town by river or sea shore,   35
  Or mountain-built with peaceful citadel,
    Is emptied of this folk, this pious morn?
And, little town, the streets for evermore
  Will silent be; and not a soul to tell
    Why thou art desolate, can e'er return.   40

O Attic shape! Fair attitude! with brede°   *design*
  Of marble men and maidens overwrought,
With forest branches and the trodden weed;
  Thou, silent form, dost tease us out of thought
As doth Eternity: Cold Pastoral!   45
  When old age shall this generation waste,
    Thou shalt remain, in midst of other woe
Than ours, a friend to man, to whom thou say'st,
Beauty is truth, truth beauty,—that is all
  Ye know on earth, and all ye need to know.   50

ODE ON A GRECIAN URN. *7 Tempe, dales of Arcady:* valleys in Greece. *41 Attic:* Athenian, possessing a classical simplicity and grace. *49–50:* if Keats had put the urn's words in quotation marks,
critics might have been spared much ink. Does the urn say just "beauty is truth, truth beauty," or does
its statement take in the whole of the last two lines?

COMPARE

"Ode on a Grecian Urn" with "Musée des Beaux Arts" by W. H. Auden (page 1146).

John Keats   (1795–1821)*

ON FIRST LOOKING INTO   1816
CHAPMAN'S HOMER

Much have I traveled in the realms of gold,
   And many goodly states and kingdoms seen;
   Round many western islands have I been
Which bards in fealty to Apollo hold.
Oft of one wide expanse had I been told   5
   That deep-browed Homer ruled as his demesne,°   *domain*
   Yet did I never breathe its pure serene
Till I heard Chapman speak out loud and bold.
Then felt I like some watcher of the skies
   When a new planet swims into his ken;   10
Or like stout Cortez when with eagle eyes
   He stared at the Pacific—and all his men
Looked at each other with a wild surmise—
   Silent, upon a peak in Darien.

ON FIRST LOOKING INTO CHAPMAN'S HOMER. When one evening in October 1816 Keats's friend and former teacher Cowden Clarke introduced the young poet to George Chapman's vigorous Elizabethan translations of the *Iliad* and the *Odyssey*, Keats stayed up all night reading and discussing them in high excitement, then went home at dawn to compose this sonnet, which Clarke received at his breakfast table. 4 *fealty:* in feudalism, the loyalty of a vassal to his lord; *Apollo:* classical god of poetic inspiration. 11 *stout Cortez:* the best-known howler in English poetry. (What Spanish explorer *was* the first European to view the Pacific?) 14 *Darien:* old name for the Isthmus of Panama

COMPARE

"On First Looking into Chapman's Homer" with "The Master" by Frederick Morgan (page 1214) and "To the Stone-cutters" by Robinson Jeffers (page 1196).

John Keats

John Keats (1795–1821)*

WHEN I HAVE FEARS THAT I MAY CEASE TO BE   (1818)

When I have fears that I may cease to be
  Before my pen has gleaned my teeming brain,
Before high-pilèd books, in charact'ry,°   *written language*
  Hold like rich garners° the full-ripened grain;   *storehouses*
When I behold, upon the night's starred face,   5
  Huge cloudy symbols of a high romance,
And think that I may never live to trace
  Their shadows with the magic hand of chance;
And when I feel, fair creature of an hour,
  That I shall never look upon thee more,   10
Never have relish in the fairy° power   *supernatural*
  Of unreflecting love—then on the shore
Of the wide world I stand alone, and think
  Till love and fame to nothingness do sink.

WHEN I HAVE FEARS THAT I MAY CEASE TO BE.   12 *unreflecting:* thoughtless and spontaneous, rather than deliberate.

COMPARE

"When I have fears that I may cease to be" with any of the three translations of Horace's *Carpe Diem* ode (pages 1029–30) or Philip Larkin's "Aubade" (page 1019).

John Keats   (1795–1821)*

To Autumn   1820

I

Season of mists and mellow fruitfulness,
  Close bosom-friend of the maturing sun;
Conspiring with him how to load and bless
  With fruit the vines that round the thatch-eaves run;
To bend with apples the mossed cottage-trees,   5
  And fill all fruit with ripeness to the core;
    To swell the gourd, and plump the hazel shells
  With a sweet kernel; to set budding more,
  And still more, later flowers for the bees,
  Until they think warm days will never cease,   10
    For Summer has o'er-brimmed their clammy cells.

II

Who hath not seen thee oft amid thy store?
  Sometimes whoever seeks abroad may find
Thee sitting careless on a granary floor,
  Thy hair soft-lifted by the winnowing wind;   15
Or on a half-reaped furrow sound asleep,
  Drowsed with the fume of poppies, while thy hook°   *sickle*
    Spares the next swath and all its twinèd flowers:
And sometimes like a gleaner thou dost keep
  Steady thy laden head across a brook;   20
  Or by a cider-press, with patient look,
    Thou watchest the last oozings hours by hours.

III

Where are the songs of Spring? Ay, where are they?
  Think not of them, thou hast thy music too,—
While barrèd clouds bloom the soft-dying day,   25
  And touch the stubble-plains with rosy hue;
Then in a wailful choir the small gnats mourn
  Among the river sallows,° borne aloft   *willows*
    Or sinking as the light wind lives or dies;
And full-grown lambs loud bleat from hilly bourn;   30
Hedge-crickets sing; and now with treble soft
The red-breast whistles from a garden-croft°   *garden plot*
  And gathering swallows twitter in the skies.

TO AUTUMN 12 *thee:* Autumn personified. 15 *Thy hair . . . winnowing wind:* Autumn's hair is a billowing cloud of straw. In winnowing, whole blades of grain were laid on a granary floor and beaten with wooden flails, then the beaten mass was tossed in a blanket until the yellow straw (or *chaff*) drifted away on the air, leaving kernels of grain. 30 *bourn*: perhaps meaning a brook. In current English, the word is a cousin of burn, as in the first line of Gerard Manley Hopkins's "Inversnaid"; but in archaic English, which Keats sometimes liked to use, a *bourn* can also be a boundary, or a destination. What possible meaning makes most sense to you?

COMPARE

"To Autumn" with "Spring and Fall" by Gerard Manley Hopkins (page 1191).

Philip Larkin

Philip Larkin   (1922–1985)*

HOME IS SO SAD   1964

Home is so sad. It stays as it was left,
Shaped to the comfort of the last to go
As if to win them back. Instead, bereft
Of anyone to please, it withers so,
Having no heart to put aside the theft   5

And turn again to what it started as,
A joyous shot at how things ought to be,
Long fallen wide. You can see how it was:
Look at the pictures and the cutlery.
The music in the piano stool. That vase.   10

COMPARE

"Home is so Sad" with "Dark house, by which once more I stand" by Alfred, Lord Tennyson (page 1249) and "Piano" by D. H. Lawrence (page 706).

Philip Larkin   (1922–1985)*

POETRY OF DEPARTURES   1955

Sometimes you hear, fifth-hand,
As epitaph:
He chucked up everything
And just cleared off,
And always the voice will sound   5
Certain you approve
This audacious, purifying,
Elemental move.

And they are right, I think.
We all hate home   10
And having to be there:
I detest my room,
Its specially-chosen junk,
The good books, the good bed,
And my life, in perfect order: 15
So to hear it said

He walked out on the whole crowd
Leaves me flushed and stirred,
Like *Then she undid her dress*
Or *Take that you bastard;*   20
Surely I can, if he did?
And that helps me stay
Sober and industrious.
But I'd go today,

Yes, swagger the nut-strewn roads,   25
Crouch in the fo'c'sle
Stubbly with goodness, if
It weren't so artificial,
Such a deliberate step backwards
To create an object: 30
Books; china; a life
Reprehensibly perfect.

COMPARE

"Poetry of Departures" with "I started Early – Took my Dog" by Emily Dickinson (page
1102).

Irving Layton (b. 1912)

THE BULL CALF   1959

The thing could barely stand. Yet taken
from his mother and the barn smells
he still impressed with his pride,
with the promise of sovereignty in the way
his head moved to take us in.   5
The fierce sunlight tugging the maize from the ground
licked at his shapely flanks.
He was too young for all that pride.
I thought of the deposed Richard II.

"No money in bull calves," Freeman had said.   10
The visiting clergyman rubbed the nostrils
now snuffing pathetically at the windless day.
"A pity," he sighed.
My gaze slipped off his hat toward the empty sky
that circled over the black knot of men,   15
over us and the calf waiting for the first blow.

Struck,
the bull calf drew in his thin forelegs
as if gathering strength for a mad rush . . .
tottered . . . raised his darkening eyes to us,   20
and I saw we were at the far end
of his frightened look, growing smaller and smaller
till we were only the ponderous mallet
that flicked his bleeding ear
and pushed him over on his side, stiffly,   25
like a block of wood.

Below the hill's crest
the river snuffled on the improvised beach.
We dug a deep pit and threw the dead calf into it.
It made a wet sound, a sepulchral gurgle,   30
as the warm sides bulged and flattened.
Settled, the bull calf lay as if asleep,
one foreleg over the other,
bereft of pride and so beautiful now,
without movement, perfectly still in the cool pit,   35
I turned away and wept.

COMPARE

"The Bull Calf" with "Names of Horses" by Donald Hall (page 1181).

Philip Levine   (b. 1928)

THEY FEED THEY LION   1972

Out of burlap sacks, out of bearing butter,
Out of black bean and wet slate bread,
Out of the acids of rage, the candor of tar,
Out of creosote, gasoline, drive shafts, wooden dollies,
They Lion grow.   5

          Out of the grey hills
Of industrial barns, out of rain, out of bus ride,
West Virginia to Kiss My Ass, out of buried aunties,
Mothers hardening like pounded stumps, out of stumps,
Out of the bones' need to sharpen and the muscles' to stretch,   10
They Lion grow.

          Earth is eating trees, fence posts,
Gutted cars, earth is calling her little ones,
"Come home, Come home!" From pig balls,
From the ferocity of pig driven to holiness,   15
From the furred ear and the full jowl come
The repose of the hung belly, from the purpose
They Lion grow.

          From the sweet glues of the trotters°   *cooked pigs feet*
Come the sweet kinks of the fist, from the full flower   20
Of the hams the thorax of caves,
From "Bow Down" come "Rise Up,"
Come they Lion from the reeds of shovels,
The grained arm that pulls the hands,
They Lion grow.   25

          From my five arms and all my hands,
From all my white sins forgiven, they feed,
From my car passing under the stars,
They Lion, from my children inherit,
From the oak turned to a wall, they Lion,   30
From they sack and they belly opened
And all that was hidden burning on the oil-stained earth
They feed they Lion and he comes.

COMPARE

"They Feed They Lion" with "Autumn Begins in Martins Ferry, Ohio" by James Wright
(page 1265).

Adrian Louis   (b. 1946)

LOOKING FOR JUDAS   1995

Weathered gray, the wooden walls
of the old barn soak in the bright
sparkling blood of the five-point mule
deer I hang there in the moonlight.
Gutted, skinned, and shimmering in eternal   5
nakedness, the glint in its eyes could
be stolen from the dry hills of Jerusalem.
They say before the white man
brought us Jesus, we had honor.
They say when we killed the Deer People,   10
we told them their spirits
would live in our flesh.
We used bows of ash, no spotlights, no rifles,
and their holy blood became ours.
Or something like that.   15

COMPARE

"Looking for Judas" with "The Negro Speaks of Rivers" (page 1117) and "Song for a Dark
Girl" (page 1120) by Langston Hughes.

Robert Lowell   (1917–1977)

SKUNK HOUR   1959

For Elizabeth Bishop

Nautilus Island's hermit
heiress still lives through winters in her Spartan cottage;
her sheep still graze above the sea.
Her son's a bishop. Her farmer
is first selectman in our village;   5
she's in her dotage.

Thirsting for
the hierarchic privacy
of Queen Victoria's century,
she buys up all   10
the eyesores facing her shore,
and lets them fall.

The season's ill—
we've lost our summer millionaire,
who seemed to leap from an L. L. Bean   15
catalogue. His nine-knot yawl
was auctioned off to lobstermen.
A red fox stain covers Blue Hill.

And now our fairy
decorator brightens his shop for fall;   20
his fishnet's filled with orange cork,
orange, his cobbler's bench and awl;
there is no money in his work,
he'd rather marry.

One dark night,   25
my Tudor Ford climbed the hill's skull;
I watched for love-cars. Lights turned down,
they lay together, hull to hull,
where the graveyard shelves on the town. . . .
My mind's not right.   30

A car radio bleats,
"Love, O careless Love. . . . " I hear
my ill-spirit sob in each blood cell,
as if my hand were at its throat. . . .
I myself am hell;   35
nobody's here—

only skunks, that search
in the moonlight for a bite to eat.
They march on their soles up Main Street:
white stripes, moonstruck eyes' red fire   40
under the chalk-dry and spar spire
of the Trinitarian Church.

I stand on top
of our back steps and breathe the rich air—
a mother skunk with her column of kittens swills the garbage pail.   45
She jabs her wedge-head in a cup
of sour cream, drops her ostrich tail,
and will not scare.

COMPARE

"Skunk Hour" with "Desert Places" by Robert Frost (page 876).

Andrew Marvell   (1621–1678)

To His Coy Mistress   1681

Had we but world enough and time,
This coyness,° lady, were no crime.   *modesty, reluctance*
We would sit down and think which way
To walk, and pass our long love's day.
Thou by the Indian Ganges' side   5
Should'st rubies find; I by the tide
Of Humber would complain.° I would   *sing sad songs*
Love you ten years before the Flood,
And you should, if you please, refuse
Till the conversion of the Jews.   10
My vegetable° love should grow   *vegetative, flourishing*
Vaster than empires, and more slow.
An hundred years should go to praise
Thine eyes, and on thy forehead gaze,
Two hundred to adore each breast,   15
But thirty thousand to the rest.
An age at least to every part,
And the last age should show your heart.
For, lady, you deserve this state,°   *pomp, ceremony*
Nor would I love at lower rate.   20
     But at my back I always hear
Time's wingèd chariot hurrying near,
And yonder all before us lie
Deserts of vast eternity.
Thy beauty shall no more be found,   25
Nor in thy marble vault shall sound
My echoing song; then worms shall try
That long preserved virginity,
And your quaint honor turn to dust,
And into ashes all my lust.   30
The grave's a fine and private place,
But none, I think, do there embrace.
     Now therefore, while the youthful hue
Sits on thy skin like morning glew°   *glow*
And while thy willing soul transpires   35
At every pore with instant° fires,   *eager*
Now let us sport us while we may;
And now, like amorous birds of prey,
Rather at once our time devour
Than languish in his slow-chapped° power.   *slow-jawed*   40
Let us roll all our strength and all

Our sweetness up into one ball
And tear our pleasures with rough strife
Thorough° the iron gates of life.   *through*
Thus, though we cannot make our sun   45
Stand still, yet we will make him run.

TO HIS COY MISTRESS. *7 Humber:* a river that flows by Marvell's town of Hull (on the side of the
world opposite from the Ganges). *10 conversion of the Jews:* an event that, according to St. John the
Divine, is to take place just before the end of the world. *35 transpires:* exudes, as a membrane lets fluid
or vapor pass through it.

COMPARE

"To His Coy Mistress" with "To the Virgins, to Make Much of Time" by Robert Herrick
(page 1191).

James Merrill   (1926–1995)

KITE POEM   1951

"One is reminded of a certain person,"
Continued the parson, settling back in his chair
With a glass of port, "who sought to emulate
The sport of birds (it was something of a chore)
By climbing up on a kite. They found his coat   5
Two counties away; the man himself was missing."

His daughters tittered: it was meant to be a lesson
To them—they had been caught kissing, or some such nonsense,
The night before, under the crescent moon.
So, finishing his pheasant, their father began   10
This thirty-minute discourse, ending with
A story improbable from the start. He paused for breath,

Having shown but a few of the dangers. However, the wind
Blew out the candles and the moon wrought changes
Which the daughters felt along their stockings. Then,   15
Thus persuaded, they fled to their young men
Waiting in the sweet night by the raspberry bed,
And kissed and kissed, as though to escape on a kite.

COMPARE

"Kite Poem" with "To the Virgins, to Make Much of Time" by Robert Herrick (page
1191).

Charlotte Mew   (1869–1928)

THE FARMER'S BRIDE   1916

Three Summers since I chose a maid,
Too young maybe—but more's to do
At harvest-time than bide and woo.
   When us was wed she turned afraid
Of love and me and all things human;   5
Like the shut of a winter's day.
Her smile went out, and 'twasn't a woman—
   More like a little frightened fay.°   *elf*
      One night, in the Fall, she runned away.

"Out 'mong the sheep, her be," they said,   10
'Should properly have been abed;
But sure enough she wasn't there
Lying awake with her wide brown stare.
So over seven-acre field and up-along across the down
We chased her, flying like a hare   15
Before our lanterns. To Church-Town
   All in a shiver and a scare
We caught her, fetched her home at last
   And turned the key upon her, fast.

She does the work about the house   20
As well as most, but like a mouse:
   Happy enough to chat and play
   With birds and rabbits and such as they,
   So long as men-folk keep away.
"Not near, not near!" her eyes beseech   25
When one of us comes within reach.
   The women say that beasts in stall
   Look round like children at her call.
   I've hardly heard her speak at all.

Shy as a leveret,° swift as he,   *hare* 30
Straight and slight as a young larch tree,
Sweet as the first wild violets, she,
To her wild self. But what to me?

The short days shorten and the oaks are brown,
   The blue smoke rises to the low gray sky,   35
One leaf in the still air falls slowly down,
   A magpie's spotted feathers lie
On the black earth spread white with rime,°   *frost*
The berries redden up to Christmas-time.
   What's Christmas-time without there be   40
   Some other in the house than we!

She sleeps up in the attic there
   Alone, poor maid. 'Tis but a stair
Betwixt us. Oh! my God! the down,
   The soft young down of her, the brown,   45
The brown of her—her eyes, her hair, her hair!

COMPARE

"The Farmer's Bride" with "Cinderella" by Anne Sexton (page 990).

Edna St. Vincent Millay

Edna St. Vincent Millay   (1892–1950)*

RECUERDO   1920

We were very tired, we were very merry—
We had gone back and forth all night on the ferry.
It was bare and bright, and smelled like a stable—
But we looked into a fire, we leaned across a table,
We lay on a hill-top underneath the moon;   5
And the whistles kept blowing, and the dawn came soon.

We were very tired, we were very merry—
We had gone back and forth all night on the ferry;
And you ate an apple, and I ate a pear,
From a dozen of each we had bought somewhere;   10
And the sky went wan, and the wind came cold,
And the sun rose dripping, a bucketful of gold.

We were very tired, we were very merry,
We had gone back and forth all night on the ferry.
We hailed, "Good morrow, mother!" to a shawl-covered head,   15
And bought a morning paper, which neither of us read;

And she wept, "God bless you!" for the apples and pears,
And we gave her all our money but our subway fares.

RECUERDO. The Spanish title means "a recollection" or "a memory."

COMPARE

"Recuerdo" with "A Blessing" by James Wright (page 1264).

John Milton   (1608–1674)*

HOW SOON HATH TIME   1632

How soon hath time, the subtle thief of youth,
  Stol'n on his wing my three and twentieth year!
  My hasting days fly on with full career,
  But my late spring no bud or blossom show'th.
Perhaps my semblance might deceive the truth,   5
  That I to manhood am arriv'd so near,
  And inward ripeness doth much less appear,
  That some more timely-happy spirits endu'th.°   *endows*
Yet be it less or more, or soon or slow,
  It shall be still I strictest measure ev'n   10
  To that same lot, however mean or high,
Toward which Time leads me, and the will of Heav'n;
  All is, if I have grace to use it so,
  As ever in my great task-Master's eye.

COMPARE

"How soon hath time" with "When I have fears that I may cease to be" by John Keats
(page 1200).

John Milton   (1608–1674)*

WHEN I CONSIDER HOW MY LIGHT IS SPENT   (1655?)

When I consider how my light is spent,
  Ere half my days in this dark world and wide,
  And that one talent which is death to hide
Lodged with me useless, though my soul more bent
To serve therewith my Maker, and present   5
  My true account, lest He returning chide;
  "Doth God exact day-labor, light denied?"
I fondly° ask. But Patience, to prevent   *foolishly*

That murmur, soon replies, "God doth not need
 Either man's work or His own gifts. Who best   10
 Bear His mild yoke, they serve Him best. His state
Is kingly: thousands at His bidding speed,
 And post o'er land and ocean without rest;
 They also serve who only stand and wait."

WHEN I CONSIDER HOW MY LIGHT IS SPENT. 1 *my light is spent:* Milton had become blind. 3 *that one talent:* For Jesus' parable of the talents (measures of money), see Matthew 25:14–30.

COMPARE

"When I consider how my light is spent" with "Batter my heart" by John Donne (page 753).

Marianne Moore

Marianne Moore (1887–1972)*

POETRY   1921

I too, dislike it: there are things that are important beyond all this
      fiddle.
 Reading it, however, with a perfect contempt for it, one discovers
      that there is in
it after all, a place for the genuine.
 Hands that can grasp, eyes
  that can dilate, hair that can rise   5
   if it must, these things are important not because a
high sounding interpretation can be put upon them but because they
      are
 useful; when they become so derivative as to become
      unintelligible, the

same thing may be said for all of us—that we
    do not admire what
    we cannot understand. The bat,
        holding on upside down or in quest of something to

eat, elephants pushing, a wild horse taking a roll, a tireless wolf under
    a tree, the immovable critic twinkling his skin like a horse that
        feels a flea, the base-
    ball fan, the statistician—case after case
    could be cited did
    one wish it; nor is it valid
        to discriminate against "business documents and

school-books"; all these phenomena are important. One must make a
        distinction
    however: when dragged into prominence by half poets, the result
        is not poetry,
    nor till the autocrats among us can be
      "literalists of
      the imagination"—above
        insolence and triviality and can present

for inspection, imaginary gardens with real toads in them, shall we
        have
    it. In the meantime, if you demand on one hand, in defiance of
        their opinion—
    the raw material of poetry in
      all its rawness and
      that which is, on the other hand,
        genuine then you are interested in poetry.

10

15

20

25

30

COMPARE

Compare "Poetry" with "*Ars Poetica*" by Archibald MacLeish (page 1092).

Frederick Morgan   (b. 1922)

THE MASTER   1982

When Han Kan was summoned
to the imperial capital
it was suggested he sit at the feet of
the illustrious senior court painter
to learn from him the refinements of the art.

"No, thank you," he replied,
"I shall apprentice myself to the stables."

5

And he installed himself and his brushes amid the dung and the flies,
and studied the horses—their bodies' keen alertness—
eye-sparkle of one, another's sensitive stance, 10
the way a third moved graceful in his bulk—
and painted at last the emperor's favorite,
the charger named "Nightshining White,"

whose likeness after centuries still dazzles.

COMPARE

"The Master" with "Advice to a Friend Who Paints" by Kelly Cherry (page 758).

Marilyn Nelson

Marilyn Nelson   (b. 1946)*

A STRANGE BEAUTIFUL WOMAN   1985

A strange beautiful woman
met me in the mirror
the other night.
Hey,
I said, 5
what you doing here?
She asked me
the same thing.

COMPARE

Compare "A Strange Beautiful Woman" with "Embrace" by Billy Collins (page 805).

Howard Nemerov   (1920–1991)

THE WAR IN THE AIR   1987

For a saving grace, we didn't see our dead,
Who rarely bothered coming home to die
But simply stayed away out there
In the clean war, the war in the air.

Seldom the ghosts came back bearing their tales   5
Of hitting the earth, the incompressible sea,
But stayed up there in the relative wind,
Shades fading in the mind,

Who had no graves but only epitaphs
Where never so many spoke for never so few: 10
Per ardua, said the partisans of Mars,
Per aspera, to the stars.

That was the good war, the war we won
As if there were no death, for goodness' sake,
With the help of the losers we left out there   15
In the air, in the empty air.

THE WAR IN THE AIR.   11–12 *Per ardua . . . Per aspera:* allusion to the English Royal Air Force's
motto *"Per ardua ad astra,"* Latin for "through difficult things to the stars."

COMPARE

"The War in the Air" with "The Death of the Ball Turret Gunner" by Randall Jarrell
(page 1195) and "The Fury of Aerial Bombardment" by Richard Eberhart (page 765).

Lorine Niedecker

Lorine Niedecker (1903–1970)*

SORROW MOVES IN WIDE WAVES (ABOUT 1950)

Sorrow moves in wide waves,
    it passes, lets us be.
It uses us, we use it,
    it's blind while we see.

Consciousness is illimitable,   5
    too good to forsake
tho what we feel be misery
    and we know will break.

Old Mother turns blue and from us,
    "Don't let my head drop to the earth.   10
I'm blind and deaf." Death from the heart,
    a thimble in her purse.

"It's a long day since last night.
    Give me space. I need
floors. Wash the floors, Lorine!   15
    Wash clothes! Weed!"

COMPARE

"Sorrow Moves in Wide Waves" with "One Art" by Elizabeth Bishop (page 1080).

Yone Noguchi   (1875–1947)

A Selection of Hokku   1920

Leaves blown,
Birds flown away.

I wander in and out the Hall of Autumn.

    *   *

Are the fallen stars
Returning up the sky?—
The dews on the grass.

    *   *

Like a cobweb hung upon the tree,
A prey to wind and sunlight!
Who will say that we are safe and strong?

    *   *

Oh, How cool—
The sound of the bell
That leaves the bell itself.

HOKKU. *hokku* is an alternate form of the word *haiku*.

COMPARE

Compare Yone Noguchi's four hokku with any of the haiku by the "Three Masters," Basho, Buson, and Issa (page 799).

Sharon Olds

Sharon Olds (b. 1942)*

The One Girl at the Boys' Party   1983

When I take my girl to the swimming party
I set her down among the boys. They tower and
bristle, she stands there smooth and sleek,
her math scores unfolding in the air around her.
They will strip to their suits, her body hard and   5
indivisible as a prime number,
they'll plunge in the deep end, she'll subtract
her height from ten feet, divide it into
hundreds of gallons of water, the numbers
bouncing in her mind like molecules of chlorine   10
in the bright blue pool. When they climb out,
her ponytail will hang its pencil lead
down her back, her narrow silk suit
with hamburgers and french fries printed on it
will glisten in the brilliant air, and they will   15
see her sweet face, solemn and
sealed, a factor of one, and she will
see their eyes, two each,
their legs, two each, and the curves of their sexes,
one each, and in her head she'll be doing her   20
wild multiplying, as the drops
sparkle and fall to the power of a thousand from her body.

Compare

"The One Girl at the Boys' Party" with "My Papa's Waltz" by Theodore Roethke (page
718).

Wilfred Owen   (1893–1918)*

ANTHEM FOR DOOMED YOUTH   (1917?)

What passing-bells for these who die as cattle?
    Only the monstrous anger of the guns.
    Only the stuttering rifles' rapid rattle
Can patter out their hasty orisons.

No mockeries now for them; no prayers nor bells,   5
    Nor any voice of mourning save the choirs,—
The shrill, demented choirs of wailing shells;
    And bugles calling for them from sad shires.°   *counties*

What candles may be held to speed them all?
    Not in the hands of boys, but in their eyes   10
    Shall shine the holy glimmers of good-byes.
The pallor of girls' brows shall be their pall;
Their flowers the tenderness of patient minds,
And each slow dusk a drawing-down of blinds.

COMPARE

"Anthem for Doomed Youth" with "Facing It" by Yusef Komunyakaa (page 1012).

Linda Pastan

Linda Pastan   (b. 1932)

ETHICS   1981

In ethics class so many years ago
our teacher asked this question every fall:
if there were a fire in a museum
which would you save, a Rembrandt painting

or an old woman who hadn't many   5
years left anyhow? Restless on hard chairs
caring little for pictures or old age
we'd opt one year for life, the next for art
and always half-heartedly. Sometimes
the woman borrowed my grandmother's face   10
leaving her usual kitchen to wander
some drafty, half imagined museum.
One year, feeling clever, I replied
why not let the woman decide herself?
Linda, the teacher would report, eschews   15
the burdens of responsibility.
This fall in a real museum I stand
before a real Rembrandt, old woman,
or nearly so, myself. The colors
within this frame are darker than autumn,   20
darker even than winter—the browns of earth,
though earth's most radiant elements burn
through the canvas. I know now that woman
and painting and season are almost one
and all beyond saving by children.   25

COMPARE

"Ethics" with "Welcome to Hiroshima" by Mary Jo Salter (page 1234).

Robert Phillips (b. 1938)

RUNNING ON EMPTY   1981

As a teenager I would drive Father's
Chevrolet cross-county, given me

reluctantly: "Always keep the tank
half full, boy, half full, ya hear?"

The fuel gauge dipping, dipping   5
toward Empty, hitting Empty, then

—thrilling!—'way below Empty,
myself driving cross-county

mile after mile, faster and faster,
all night long, this crazy kid driving   10

the earth's rolling surface,
against all laws, defying chemistry,

rules, and time, riding on nothing
but fumes, pushing luck harder

than anyone pushed before, the wind
screaming past like the Furies . . .

I stranded myself only once, a white
night with no gas station open, ninety miles

from nowhere. Panicked for a while,
at standstill, myself stalled.

At dawn the car and I both refilled. But,
Father, I am running on empty still.

15

20

RUNNING ON EMPTY. 16 *Furies:* In Greek mythology, deities who pursue and torment evildoers.

COMPARE

"Running on Empty" with "Those Winter Sundays" by Robert Hayden (page 1185) and
"My Papa's Waltz" by Theodore Roethke (page 718).

Sylvia Plath

Sylvia Plath (1932–1963)*

DADDY

(1962) 1965

You do not do, you do not do
Any more, black shoe
In which I have lived like a foot
For thirty years, poor and white,
Barely daring to breathe or Achoo.

5

Daddy, I have had to kill you.
You died before I had time—
Marble-heavy, a bag full of God,
Ghastly statue with one grey toe
Big as a Frisco seal   10

And a head in the freakish Atlantic
Where it pours bean green over blue
In the waters off beautiful Nauset.
I used to pray to recover you.
Ach, du.   15

In the German tongue, in the Polish town
Scraped flat by the roller
Of wars, wars, wars.
But the name of the town is common.
My Polack friend   20

Says there are a dozen or two.
So I never could tell where you
Put your foot, your root,
I never could talk to you.
The tongue stuck in my jaw.   25

It stuck in a barb wire snare.
Ich, ich, ich, ich,
I could hardly speak.
I thought every German was you.
And the language obscene   30

An engine, an engine
Chuffing me off like a Jew.
A Jew to Dachau, Auschwitz, Belsen.
I began to talk like a Jew.
I think I may well be a Jew.   35

The snows of the Tyrol, the clear beer of Vienna
Are not very pure or true.
With my gypsy ancestress and my weird luck
And my Taroc pack and my Taroc pack
I may be a bit of a Jew.   40

I have always been scared of you,
With your Luftwaffe, your gobbledygoo.
And your neat moustache
And your Aryan eye, bright blue.
Panzer-man, panzer-man, O You—   45

Not God but a swastika
So black no sky could squeak through.
Every woman adores a Fascist,
The boot in the face, the brute
Brute heart of a brute like you.   50

You stand at the blackboard, daddy,
In the picture I have of you,
A cleft in your chin instead of your foot
But no less a devil for that, no not
Any less the black man who   55

Bit my pretty red heart in two.
I was ten when they buried you.
At twenty I tried to die
And get back, back, back to you.
I thought even the bones would do.   60

But they pulled me out of the sack,
And they stuck me together with glue.
And then I knew what to do.
I made a model of you,
A man in black with a Meinkampf look   65

And a love of the rack and the screw.
And I said I do, I do.
So daddy, I'm finally through.
The black telephone's off at the root,
The voices just can't worm through.   70

If I've killed one man, I've killed two—
The vampire who said he was you
And drank my blood for a year,
Seven years, if you want to know.
Daddy, you can lie back now.   75

There's a stake in your fat black heart
And the villagers never liked you.
They are dancing and stamping on you.
They always *knew* it was you.
Daddy, daddy, you bastard, I'm through.   80

DADDY. Introducing this poem in a reading, Sylvia Plath remarked:

> The poem is spoken by a girl with an Electra complex. Her father died while she thought
> he was God. Her case is complicated by the fact that her father was also a Nazi and her
> mother very possibly part Jewish. In the daughter the two strains marry and paralyze each
> other—she has to act out the awful little allegory before she is free of it.

(Quoted by A. Alvarez, *Beyond All This Fiddle* [New York: Random, 1968].

In some details "Daddy" is autobiography: the poet's father Otto Plath, a German, had come to the United States from Grabow, Poland. He had died following the amputation of a gangrened foot and leg when Sylvia was eight years old. Politically, Otto Plath was a Republican, not a Nazi, but was apparently a somewhat domineering head of the household. (See the recollections of the poet's mother Aurelia Schober Plath in her edition of *Letters Home* by Sylvia Plath [New York: Harper, 1975].

15 *Ach, du:* Oh, you. 27 *Ich, ich, ich, ich:* I, I, I, I. 51 *blackboard:* Otto Plath had been a professor of biology at Boston University. 65 *Meinkampf:* Adolf Hitler entitled his autobiography *Mein Kampf* ("My Struggle").

COMPARE

"Daddy" with "American Primitive" by William Jay Smith (page 1242).

Edgar Allan Poe   (1809–1849)*

A DREAM WITHIN A DREAM   1849

Take this kiss upon the brow!
And, in parting from you now,
Thus much let me avow—
You are not wrong, who deem
That my days have been a dream;   5
Yet if Hope has flown away
In a night, or in a day,
In a vision, or in none,
Is it therefore the less *gone?*
All that we see or seem   10
Is but a dream within a dream.

I stand amid the roar
Of a surf-tormented shore,
And I hold within my hand
Grains of the golden sand—   15
How few! yet how they creep
Through my fingers to the deep,
While I weep—while I weep!
O God! can I not grasp
Them with a tighter clasp?   20
O God! can I not save
One from the pitiless wave?
Is *all* that we see or seem
But a dream within a dream?

COMPARE

"A Dream within a Dream" with "Dover Beach" by Matthew Arnold (page 1141).

Alexander Pope (1688–1744)*

A LITTLE LEARNING IS A DANG'ROUS THING (FROM AN ESSAY ON CRITICISM)   1711

A *little Learning* is a dang'rous Thing;
Drink deep, or taste not the *Pierian* Spring:
There *shallow Draughts* intoxicate the Brain,
And drinking *largely* sobers us again.
Fir'd at first Sight with what the *Muse* imparts,   5
In *fearless Youth* we tempt the Heights of Arts,
While from the bounded *Level* of our Mind,
Short Views we take, nor see the *Lengths behind*,
But *more advanc'd*, behold with strange Surprize
New, distant Scenes of *endless* Science rise!   10
So pleas'd at first, the towring *Alps* we try,
Mount o'er the Vales, and seem to tread the Sky;
Th' Eternal Snows appear already past,
And the first *Clouds* and *Mountains* seem the last:
But *those attain'd*, we tremble to survey   15
The growing Labours of the lengthen'd Way,
Th' *increasing* Prospect *tires* our wandring Eyes,
Hills peep o'er Hills, and *Alps* on *Alps* arise!

A LITTLE LEARNING IS A DANG'ROUS THING.   2 *Pierian Spring:* the spring of the Muses.

COMPARE

"A little Learning is a dang'rous Thing" with "The Writer" by Richard Wilbur (page 1260).

Ezra Pound (1885–1972)*

THE RIVER-MERCHANT'S WIFE: A LETTER   1915

While my hair was still cut straight across my forehead
I played about the front gate, pulling flowers.
You came by on bamboo stilts, playing horse,
You walked about my seat, playing with blue plums.
And we went on living in the village of Chokan: 5
Two small people, without dislike or suspicion.

At fourteen I married My Lord you.
I never laughed, being bashful.
Lowering my head, I looked at the wall.
Called to, a thousand times, I never looked back.   10

At fifteen I stopped scowling,

I desired my dust to be mingled with yours
Forever and forever and forever.
Why should I climb the lookout?

At sixteen you departed,   15
You went into far Ku-to-yen, by the river of swirling eddies,
And you have been gone five months.
The monkeys make sorrowful noise overhead.

You dragged your feet when you went out.
By the gate now, the moss is grown, the different mosses,   20
Too deep to clear them away!
The leaves fall early this autumn, in wind.
The paired butterflies are already yellow with August
Over the grass in the West garden;
They hurt me. I grow older.   25
If you are coming down through the narrows of the river Kiang,
Please let me know before hand,
And I will come out to meet you
     As far as Cho-fu-sa.

THE RIVER-MERCHANT'S WIFE: A LETTER. A free translation from the Chinese poet Li Po (eighth century).

COMPARE

"The River-Merchant's Wife: a Letter" with "A Valediction: Forbidding Mourning" by John Donne (page 1164).

Dudley Randall

Dudley Randall (1914–2000)*

A DIFFERENT IMAGE   1968

The age
requires this task:
create
a different image;
re-animate   5
the mask.
Shatter the icons of slavery and fear.
Replace
the leer
of the minstrel's burnt-cork face   10
with a proud, serene
and classic bronze of Benin.

COMPARE

"A Different Image" with "The Negro Speaks of Rivers" by Langston Hughes (page 1117).

John Crowe Ransom   (1888–1974)

PIAZZA PIECE   1927

—I am a gentleman in a dustcoat trying
To make you hear. Your ears are soft and small
And listen to an old man not at all,
They want the young men's whispering and sighing.
But see the roses on your trellis dying   5
And hear the spectral singing of the moon;
For I must have my lovely lady soon,
I am a gentleman in a dustcoat trying.

—I am a lady young in beauty waiting
Until my truelove comes, and then we kiss.   10
But what grey man among the vines is this
Whose words are dry and faint as in a dream?
Back from my trellis, Sir, before I scream!
I am a lady young in beauty waiting.

COMPARE

Compare "Piazza Piece" with "To His Coy Mistress" by Andrew Marvell (page 1208).

Henry Reed   (1914–1986)

NAMING OF PARTS   1946

Today we have naming of parts. Yesterday,
We had daily cleaning. And tomorrow morning,
We shall have what to do after firing. But today,
Today we have naming of parts. Japonica
Glistens like coral in all of the neighboring gardens,   5
        And today we have naming of parts.

This is the lower sling swivel. And this
Is the upper sling swivel, whose use you will see,
When you are given your slings. And this is the piling swivel,
Which in your case you have not got. The branches   10
Hold in the gardens their silent, eloquent gestures,
        Which in our case we have not got.

This is the safety-catch, which is always released
With an easy flick of the thumb. And please do not let me
See anyone using his finger. You can do it quite easy   15
If you have any strength in your thumb. The blossoms
Are fragile and motionless, never letting anyone see
        Any of them using their finger.

And this you can see is the bolt. The purpose of this
Is to open the breech, as you see. We can slide it   20
Rapidly backwards and forwards: we call this
Easing the spring. And rapidly backwards and forwards
The early bees are assaulting and fumbling the flowers:
    They call it easing the Spring.

They call it easing the Spring: it is perfectly easy   25
If you have any strength in your thumb: like the bolt,
And the breech, and the cocking-piece, and the point of balance,
Which in our case we have not got; and the almond-blossom
Silent in all of the gardens and the bees going backwards and forwards,
    For today we have naming of parts.   30

COMPARE

"Naming of Parts" with "The Fury of Aerial Bombardment" by Richard Eberhart (page
765).

Adrienne Rich   (b. 1929)*

LIVING IN SIN   1955

She had thought the studio would keep itself;
no dust upon the furniture of love.
Half heresy, to wish the taps less vocal,
the panes relieved of grime. A plate of pears,
a piano with a Persian shawl, a cat   5
stalking the picturesque amusing mouse
had risen at his urging.
Not that at five each separate stair would writhe
under the milkman's tramp; that morning light
so coldly would delineate the scraps   10
of last night's cheese and three sepulchral bottles;
that on the kitchen shelf among the saucers
a pair of beetle-eyes would fix her own—
envoy from some village in the moldings . . .
Meanwhile, he, with a yawn,   15
sounded a dozen notes upon the keyboard,
declared it out of tune, shrugged at the mirror,
rubbed at his beard, went out for cigarettes;
while she, jeered by the minor demons,
pulled back the sheets and made the bed and found   20
a towel to dust the table-top,
and let the coffee-pot boil over on the stove.
By evening she was back in love again,

though not so wholly but throughout the night
she woke sometimes to feel the daylight coming   25
like a relentless milkman up the stairs.

COMPARE

Compare and contrast "Living in Sin" with "Let me not to the marriage of true minds" by
William Shakespeare (page 917).

Adrienne Rich   (b. 1929)*

POWER   1978

Living   in the earth-deposits   of our history

Today a backhoe divulged   out of a crumbling flank of earth
one bottle   amber   perfect   a hundred-year-old
cure for fever   or melancholy   a tonic
for living on this earth   in the winters of this climate   5

Today I was reading about Marie Curie:
she must have known she suffered   from radiation sickness
her body bombarded for years   by the element
she had purified
It seems she denied to the end   10
the source of the cataracts on her eyes
the cracked and suppurating skin   of her finger-ends
till she could no longer hold   a test-tube or a pencil

She died   a famous woman   denying
her wounds   15
denying
her wounds   came   from the same source as her power

POWER. 6 *Marie Curie:* the Polish scientist (1867–1934) who helped discover polonium and
radium. She was the first person to win two Nobel Prizes.

COMPARE

"Power" with "Ethics" by Linda Pastan (page 1220).

Edwin Arlington Robinson

Edwin Arlington Robinson   (1869–1935)*

MINIVER CHEEVY   1910

Miniver Cheevy, child of scorn,
    Grew lean while he assailed the seasons;
He wept that he was ever born,
    And he had reasons.

Miniver loved the days of old   5
    When swords were bright and steeds were prancing;
The vision of a warrior bold
    Would set him dancing.

Miniver sighed for what was not,
    And dreamed, and rested from his labors;   10
He dreamed of Thebes and Camelot,
    And Priam's neighbors.

Miniver mourned the ripe renown
    That made so many a name so fragrant;
He mourned Romance, now on the town,   15
    And Art, a vagrant.

Miniver loved the Medici,
    Albeit he had never seen one;
He would have sinned incessantly
    Could he have been one.   20

Miniver cursed the commonplace
    And eyed a khaki suit with loathing;
He missed the medieval grace
    Of iron clothing.

Miniver scorned the gold he sought,   25
    But sore annoyed was he without it;
Miniver thought, and thought, and thought,
    And thought about it.

Miniver Cheevy, born too late,
    Scratched his head and kept on thinking;   30
Miniver coughed, and called it fate,
    And kept on drinking.

MINIVER CHEEVY.   11 *Thebes:* a city in ancient Greece and the setting of many famous Greek myths;
Camelot: the legendary site of King Arthur's Court. 12 *Priam:* the last king of Troy; his "neighbors"
would have included Helen of Troy, Aeneas, and other famous figures. 17 *the Medici:* the ruling
family of Florence during the high Renaissance, the Medici were renowned patrons of the arts.

COMPARE

"Miniver Cheevy" with "Ulysses" by Alfred, Lord Tennyson (page 1250).

Theodore Roethke

Theodore Roethke   (1908–1963)*

ELEGY FOR JANE   1953

> *My Student, Thrown by a Horse*

I remember the neckcurls, limp and damp as tendrils;
And her quick look, a sidelong pickerel smile;
And how, once startled into talk, the light syllables leaped for her,
And she balanced in the delight of her thought,
A wren, happy, tail into the wind,   5
Her song trembling the twigs and small branches.
The shade sang with her;

The leaves, their whispers turned to kissing;
And the mold sang in the bleached valleys under the rose.

Oh, when she was sad, she cast herself down into such a pure depth,   10
Even a father could not find her:
Scraping her cheek against straw;
Stirring the clearest water.

My sparrow, you are not here,
Waiting like a fern, making a spiny shadow.   15
The sides of wet stones cannot console me,
Nor the moss, wound with the last light.

If only I could nudge you from this sleep,
My maimed darling, my skittery pigeon.
Over this damp grave I speak the words of my love: 20
I, with no rights in this matter,
Neither father nor lover.

COMPARE

"Elegy for Jane" with "Annabel Lee" by Edgar Allan Poe (page 1088).

Mary Jo Salter

Mary Jo Salter   (b. 1954)

WELCOME TO HIROSHIMA   1984

is what you first see, stepping off the train:
a billboard brought to you in living English
by Toshiba Electric. While a channel
silent in the TV of the brain

projects those flickering re-runs of a cloud   5
that brims its risen columnful like beer
and, spilling over, hangs its foamy head,
you feel a thirst for history: what year

it started to be safe to breathe the air,
and when to drink the blood and scum afloat   10
on the Ohta River. But no, the water's clear,
they pour it for your morning cup of tea

in one of the countless sunny coffee shops
whose plastic dioramas advertise
mutations of cuisine behind the glass: 15
a pancake sandwich; a pizza someone tops

with a maraschino cherry. Passing by
the Peace Park's floral hypocenter (where
how bravely, or with what mistaken cheer,
humanity erased its own erasure),   20

you enter the memorial museum
and through more glass are served, as on a dish
of blistered grass, three mannequins. Like gloves
a mother clips to coatsleeves, strings of flesh

hang from their fingertips; or as if tied   25
to recall a duty for us, *Reverence
the dead whose mourners too shall soon be dead,*
but all commemoration's swallowed up

in questions of bad taste, how re-created
horror mocks the grim original,   30
and thinking at last *They should have left it all*
you stop. This is the wristwatch of a child.

Jammed on the moment's impact, resolute
to communicate some message, although mute,
it gestures with its hands at eight-fifteen   35
and eight-fifteen and eight-fifteen again

while tables of statistics on the wall
update the news by calling on a roll
of tape, death gummed on death, and in the case
adjacent, an exhibit under glass   40

is glass itself: a shard the bomb slammed in
a woman's arm at eight-fifteen, but some
three decades on—as if to make it plain
hope's only as renewable as pain,

and as if all the unsung
debasements of the past may one day come
rising to the surface once again—
worked its filthy way out like a tongue.

45

COMPARE

"Welcome to Hiroshima" with "Ethics" by Linda Pastan (page 1220) and "Ballad of Birmingham" by Dudley Randall (page 847).

William Shakespeare

William Shakespeare   (1564–1616)*

WHEN, IN DISGRACE WITH FORTUNE AND MEN'S EYES   1609

When, in disgrace with Fortune and men's eyes,
I all alone beweep my outcast state,
And trouble deaf heaven with my bootless° cries,   *futile*
And look upon myself and curse my fate,
Wishing me like to one more rich in hope,   5
Featured like him, like him with friends possessed,
Desiring this man's art, and that man's scope,
With what I most enjoy contented least,
Yet in these thoughts myself almost despising,
Haply° I think on thee, and then my state,   *luckily*   10
Like to the lark at break of day arising
From sullen earth, sings hymns at heaven's gate;
    For thy sweet love rememb'red such wealth brings
    That then I scorn to change my state with kings.

COMPARE

"When, in disgrace with Fortune and men's eyes" with "When I have fears that I may cease to be" by John Keats (page 1200).

William Shakespeare   (1564–1616)*

NOT MARBLE NOR THE GILDED MONUMENTS   1609

Not marble, nor the gilded monuments
Of princes, shall outlive this powerful rhyme;
But you shall shine more bright in these contents
Than unswept stone, besmeared with sluttish time.
When wasteful war shall statues overturn,   5
And broils root out the work of masonry,
Nor Mars his sword nor war's quick fire shall burn
The living record of your memory.
'Gainst death and all-oblivious enmity
Shall you pace forth; your praise shall still find room   10
Even in the eyes of all posterity
That wear this world out to the ending doom.
 So, till the judgment that yourself arise,
 You live in this, and dwell in lovers' eyes.

COMPARE

"Not marble nor the gilded monuments" with "To the Stone-cutters" by Robinson Jeffers
(page 1196).

William Shakespeare   (1564–1616)*

WEARY WITH TOIL, I HASTE ME TO MY BED   1609

Weary with toil, I haste me to my bed,
The dear repose for limbs with travel tired;
But then begins a journey in my head,
To work my mind when body's work's expired:
For then my thoughts, from far where I abide,   5
Intend a zealous pilgrimage to thee,
And keep my drooping eyelids open wide,
Looking on darkness which the blind do see;
Save that my soul's imaginary sight
Presents thy shadow to my sightless view,   10
Which, like a jewel hung in ghastly night,
Makes black night beauteous, and her old face new.
 Lo, thus by day my limbs, by night my mind,
 For thee and for myself no quiet find.

COMPARE

"Weary with toil" with "What lips my lips have kissed, and where, and why" by Edna St.
Vincent Millay (page 919) and "First Poem for You" by Kim Addonizio (page 920).

William Shakespeare (1564–1616)*

THAT TIME OF YEAR THOU MAYST IN ME BEHOLD 1609

That time of year thou mayst in me behold
When yellow leaves, or none, or few, do hang
Upon those boughs which shake against the cold,
Bare ruined choirs where late the sweet birds sang.
In me thou see'st the twilight of such day   5
As after sunset fadeth in the west,
Which by-and-by black night doth take away,
Death's second self that seals up all in rest.
In me thou see'st the glowing of such fire
That on the ashes of his youth doth lie,   10
As the deathbed whereon it must expire,
Consumed with that which it was nourished by.
　　This thou perceiv'st, which makes thy love more strong,
　　To love that well which thou must leave ere long.

COMPARE

"That time of year thou mayst in me behold" with "anyone lived in a pretty how town" by
E. E. Cummings (page 767).

William Shakespeare (1564–1616)*

MY MISTRESS' EYES ARE NOTHING LIKE THE SUN 1609

My mistress' eyes are nothing like the sun;
Coral is far more red than her lips' red;
If snow be white, why then her breasts are dun;
If hairs be wires, black wires grow on her head.
I have seen roses damasked red and white,   5
But no such roses see I in her cheeks;
And in some perfumes is there more delight
Than in the breath that from my mistress reeks.
I love to hear her speak, yet well I know
That music hath a far more pleasing sound;   10
I grant I never saw a goddess go:
My mistress, when she walks, treads on the ground.
　　And yet, by heaven, I think my love as rare
　　As any she,° belied with false compare.   *woman*

COMPARE

"My mistress' eyes are nothing like the sun" with "Homage to my hips" by Lucille Clifton (page 950) and "Crazy Jane Talks with the Bishop" by William Butler Yeats (page 1267).

Louis Simpson (b. 1923)

AMERICAN POETRY   1963

Whatever it is, it must have
A stomach that can digest
Rubber, coal, uranium, moons, poems.

Like the shark, it contains a shoe.
It must swim for miles through the desert   5
Uttering cries that are almost human.

COMPARE

"American Poetry" with *Ars Poetica* by Archibald MacLeish (page 1092).

David R. Slavitt (b. 1935)

TITANIC   1983

Who does not love the *Titanic?*
If they sold passage tomorrow for that same crossing,
who would not buy?

To go down . . . We all go down, mostly
alone. But with crowds of people, friends, servants,   5
well fed, with music, with lights! Ah!

And the world, shocked, mourns, as it ought to do
and almost never does. There will be the books and movies
to remind our grandchildren who we were
and how we died, and give them a good cry.   10

Not so bad, after all. The cold
water is anaesthetic and very quick.
The cries on all sides must be a comfort.

We all go: only a few, first-class.

COMPARE

"Titanic" with "The Convergence of the Twain" by Thomas Hardy (page 1182).

Christopher Smart   (1722–1771)

FOR I WILL CONSIDER MY CAT JEOFFRY   (1759–1763)

For I will consider my Cat Jeoffry.

For he is the servant of the Living God, duly and daily serving him.

For at the first glance of the glory of God in the East he worships in his
    way.

For is this done by wreathing his body seven times round with elegant
    quickness.

For then he leaps up to catch the musk,° which is the   *catnip*   5
    blessing of God upon his prayer.

For he rolls upon prank to work it in.

For having done duty and received blessing he begins to consider
    himself.

For this he performs in ten degrees.

For first he looks upon his fore-paws to see if they are clean.

For secondly he kicks up behind to clear away there.   10

For thirdly he works it upon stretch° with   *he works his muscles, stretching*
    the fore-paws extended.

For fourthly he sharpens his paws by wood.

For fifthly he washes himself.

For sixthly he rolls upon wash.

For seventhly he fleas himself, that he may not be interrupted   15
    upon the beat.°   *his patrol*

For eighthly he rubs himself against a post.

For ninthly he looks up for his instructions.

For tenthly he goes in quest of food.

For having considered God and himself he will consider his neighbor.

For if he meets another cat he will kiss her in kindness.   20

For when he takes his prey he plays with it to give it a chance.

For one mouse in seven escapes by his dallying.

For when his day's work is done his business more properly begins.

For he keeps the Lord's watch in the night against the Adversary.

For he counteracts the powers of darkness by his electrical skin
    and glaring eyes.
        25

For he counteracts the Devil, who is death, by brisking about the life.

For in his morning orisons he loves the sun and the sun loves him.

For he is of the tribe of Tiger.

For the Cherub Cat is a term of the Angel Tiger.

For he has the subtlety and hissing of a serpent, which in goodness he   30
    suppresses.

For he will not do destruction if he is well-fed, neither will he spit
    without provocation.

For he purrs in thankfulness when God tells him he's a good Cat.

For he is an instrument for the children to learn benevolence upon.

For every house is incomplete without him, and a blessing is lacking in
    the spirit.
For the Lord commanded Moses concerning the cats at the departure of   35
    the Children of Israel from Egypt.
For every family had one cat at least in the bag.
For the English cats are the best in Europe.
For he is the cleanest in the use of his fore-paws of any quadruped.
For the dexterity of his defense is an instance of the love of God to him
    exceedingly.
For he is the quickest to his mark of any creature.   40
For he is tenacious of his point.
For he is a mixture of gravity and waggery.
For he knows that God is his Savior.
For there is nothing sweeter than his peace when at rest.
For there is nothing brisker than his life when in motion.   45
For he is of the Lord's poor, and so indeed is he called by benevolence
    perpetually—Poor Jeoffry! poor Jeoffry! the rat has bit thy throat.
For I bless the name of the Lord Jesus that Jeoffry is better.
For the divine spirit comes about his body to sustain it in complete cat.
For his tongue is exceeding pure so that it has in purity what it wants
    in music.
For he is docile and can learn certain things.   50
For he can sit up with gravity which is patience upon approbation.
For he can fetch and carry, which is patience in employment.
For he can jump over a stick which is patience upon proof positive.
For he can spraggle upon waggle at the word of command.
For he can jump from an eminence into his master's bosom.   55
For he can catch the cork and toss it again.
For he is hated by the hypocrite and miser.
For the former is afraid of detection.
For the latter refuses the charge.
For he camels his back to bear the first notion of business.   60
For he is good to think on, if a man would express himself neatly.
For he made a great figure in Egypt for his signal services.
For he killed the Icneumon-rat, very pernicious by land.
For his ears are so acute that they sting again.
For from this proceeds the passing quickness of his attention.   65
For by stroking of him I have found out electricity.
For I perceived God's light about him both wax and fire.
For the electrical fire is the spiritual substance which God sends from
    heaven to sustain the bodies both of man and beast.
For God has blessed him in the variety of his movements.
For, though he cannot fly, he is an excellent clamberer.   70
For his motions upon the face of the earth are more than any other
    quadruped.

For he can tread to all the measures upon the music.
For he can swim for life.
For he can creep.

FOR I WILL CONSIDER MY CAT JEOFFRY. This is a self-contained extract from Smart's long poem *Lord commanded Moses concerning the cats:* No such command is mentioned in Scripture. 54 *spraggle upon waggle:* W. F. Stead, in his edition of Smart's poem, suggests that this means Jeoffry will sprawl when his master waggles a finger or a stick. 59 *the charge:* perhaps the cost of feeding a cat.

COMPARE

"For I will consider my Cat Jeoffry" with "The Tyger" by William Blake (page 1149).

William Jay Smith   (b. 1918)

AMERICAN PRIMITIVE   1957

Look at him there in his stovepipe hat,
His high-top shoes, and his handsome collar;
Only my Daddy could look like that,
And I love my Daddy like he loves his Dollar.

The screen door bangs, and it sounds so funny—   5
There he is in a shower of gold;
His pockets are stuffed with folding money,
His lips are blue, and his hands feel cold.

He hangs in the hall by his black cravat,
The ladies faint, and the children holler: 10
Only my Daddy could look like that,
And I love my Daddy like he loves his Dollar.

COMPARE

"American Primitive" with "Daddy" by Sylvia Plath (page 1222).

Cathy Song

Cathy Song (b. 1955)

STAMP COLLECTING   1988

The poorest countries
have the prettiest stamps
as if impracticality were a major export
shipped with the bananas, t-shirts, and coconuts.
Take Tonga, where the tourists,   5
expecting a dramatic waterfall replete with birdcalls,
are taken to see the island's peculiar mystery:
hanging bats with collapsible wings
like black umbrellas swing upside down from fruit trees.
The Tongan stamp is a fruit.   10
The banana stamp is scalloped like a butter-varnished seashell.
The pineapple resembles a volcano, a spout of green on top,
and the papaya, a tarnished goat skull.

They look impressive,
these stamps of countries without a thing to sell   15
except for what is scraped, uprooted and hulled
from their mule-scratched hills.
They believe in postcards,
in portraits of progress: the new dam;
a team of young native doctors   20
wearing stethoscopes like exotic ornaments;
the recently constructed "Facultad de Medicina,"
a building as lack-lustre as an American motel.

The stamps of others are predictable.
Lucky is the country that possesses indigenous beauty.   25
Say a tiger or a queen.
The Japanese can display to the world
their blossoms: a spray of pink on green.
Like pollen, they drift, airborne.
But pity the country that is bleak and stark.   30

Beauty and whimsey are discouraged as indiscreet.
Unbreakable as their climate, a monument of ice,
they issue serious statements, commemorating
factories, tramways and aeroplanes;
athletes marbled into statues.   35
They turn their noses upon the world, these countries,
and offer this: an unrelenting procession
of a grim, historic profile.

COMPARE

"Stamp Collecting" with "The Virgins" by Derek Walcott (page 1257).

William Stafford   (1914–1993)*

THE FARM ON THE GREAT PLAINS   1960

A telephone line goes cold;
birds tread it wherever it goes.
A farm back of a great plain
tugs an end of the line.

I call that farm every year,   5
ringing it, listening, still;
no one is home at the farm,
the line gives only a hum.

Some year I will ring the line
on a night at last the right one,   10
and with an eye tapered for braille
from the phone on the wall

I will see the tenant who waits—
the last one left at the place;
through the dark my braille eye   15
will lovingly touch his face.

"Hello, is Mother at home?"
No one is home today.
"But Father—he should be there."
No one—no one is here.   20

"But you—are you the one . . . ?"
Then the line will be gone
because both ends will be home:
no space, no birds, no farm.

My self will be the plain,   25
wise as winter is gray,
pure as cold posts go
pacing toward what I know.

COMPARE

"The Farm on the Great Plains" with "Piano" by D. H. Lawrence (page 706) and "Dark
house, by which once more I stand" by Alfred, Lord Tennyson (page 1249).

Wallace Stevens

Wallace Stevens (1879–1955)*
PETER QUINCE AT THE CLAVIER   1923

I

Just as my fingers on these keys
Make music, so the selfsame sounds
On my spirit make a music, too.

Music is feeling, then, not sound;
And thus it is that what I feel,   5
Here in this room, desiring you,

Thinking of your blue-shadowed silk,
Is music. It is like the strain
Waked in the elders by Susanna.

Of a green evening, clear and warm,
She bathed in her still garden, while
The red-eyed elders watching, felt

The basses of their beings throb
In witching chords, and their thin blood
Pulse pizzicati of Hosanna.

II

In the green water, clear and warm,
Susanna lay.
She searched
The touch of springs,
And found
Concealed imaginings.
She sighed,
For so much melody.

Upon the bank, she stood
In the cool
Of spent emotions.
She felt, among the leaves,
The dew
Of old devotions.

She walked upon the grass,
Still quavering.
The winds were like her maids,
On timid feet,
Fetching her woven scarves,
Yet wavering.

A breath upon her hand
Muted the night.
She turned—
A cymbal crashed,
And roaring horns.

III

Soon, with a noise like tambourines,
Came her attendant Byzantines.
They wondered why Susanna cried
Against the elders by her side;

And as they whispered, the refrain
Was like a willow swept by rain.

Anon, their lamps' uplifted flame
Revealed Susanna and her shame.

And then, the simpering Byzantines
Fled, with a noise like tambourines.

IV

Beauty is momentary in the mind—
The fitful tracing of a portal;
But in the flesh it is immortal.

The body dies; the body's beauty lives.
So evenings die, in their green going,   55
A wave, interminably flowing.
So gardens die, their meek breath scenting
The cowl of winter, done repenting.
So maidens die, to the auroral
Celebration of a maiden's choral.   60

Susanna's music touched the bawdy strings
Of those white elders; but, escaping,
Left only Death's ironic scraping.
Now, in its immortality, it plays
On the clear viol of her memory,   65
And makes a constant sacrament of praise.

PETER QUINCE AT THE CLAVIER. In Shakespeare's *Midsummer Night's Dream,* Peter Quince is a
clownish carpenter who stages a mock-tragic play. 9 *Susanna:* In the Book of Susanna in the Apoc-
rypha, two lustful elders who covet Susanna, a virtuous married woman, hide in her garden, spy on
her as she bathes, then threaten to make false accusations against her unless she submits to them.
When she refuses, they cry out, and her servants come running. All ends well when the prophet
Daniel cross-examines the elders and proves them liars. 15 *pizzicati:* thin notes made by plucking a
stringed instrument. 42 *Byzantines:* Susanna's maidservants.

COMPARE

"Peter Quince at the Clavier" with "Ode on a Grecian Urn" by John Keats (page 1197) or
"Sailing to Byzantium" by William Butler Yeats (page 1075).

Wallace Stevens   (1879–1955)*

THE EMPEROR OF ICE-CREAM   1923

Call the roller of big cigars,
The muscular one, and bid him whip
In kitchen cups concupiscent curds.
Let the wenches dawdle in such dress
As they are used to wear, and let the boys   5
Bring flowers in last month's newspapers.
Let be be finale of seem.
The only emperor is the emperor of ice-cream.

Take from the dresser of deal,
Lacking the three glass knobs, that sheet
On which she embroidered fantails once
And spread it so as to cover her face.
If her horny feet protrude, they come
To show how cold she is, and dumb.
Let the lamp affix its beam.
The only emperor is the emperor of ice-cream.

THE EMPEROR OF ICE-CREAM.   9 *deal:* fir or pine wood used to make cheap furniture.

COMPARE

"The Emperor of Ice-Cream" with "This living hand, now warm and capable" by John Keats (page 910) and "A Slumber Did My Spirit Seal" by William Wordsworth (page 865).

Ruth Stone   (b. 1915)

SECOND HAND COAT   1982

I feel
in her pockets; she wore nice cotton gloves,
kept a handkerchief box, washed her undies,
ate at the Holiday Inn, had a basement freezer,
belonged to a bridge club.   5
I think when I wake in the morning
that I have turned into her.
She hangs in the hall downstairs,
a shadow with pulled threads.
I slip her over my arms, skin of a matron.   10
Where are you? I say to myself, to the orphaned body,
and her coat says,
Get your purse, have you got your keys?

COMPARE

"Second Hand Coat" with "Home is so Sad" by Philip Larkin (page 1202).

Jonathan Swift   (1667–1745)

A DESCRIPTION OF THE MORNING   1711

Now hardly here and there an hackney-coach,°   *horse-drawn cab*
Appearing, showed the ruddy morn's approach.
Now Betty from her master's bed had flown

And softly stole to discompose her own.
The slipshod 'prentice from his master's door   5
Had pared the dirt, and sprinkled round the floor.
Now Moll had whirled her mop with dextrous airs,
Prepared to scrub the entry and the stairs.
The youth with broomy stumps began to trace
The kennel°-edge, where wheels had worn the place.   gutter   10
The small-coal man was heard with cadence deep
Till drowned in shriller notes of chimneysweep,
Duns° at his lordship's gate began to meet,   bill-collectors
And Brickdust Moll had screamed through half the street.
The turnkey° now his flock returning sees,   jailkeeper   15
Duly let out a-nights to steal for fees;
The watchful bailiffs° take their silent stands;   constables
And schoolboys lag with satchels in their hands.

A DESCRIPTION OF THE MORNING. 9 *youth with broomy stumps:* a young man sweeping the gutter's
edge with worn-out brooms, looking for old nails fallen from wagonwheels, which were valuable. 14
Brickdust Moll: woman selling brickdust to be used for scouring.

COMPARE

"A Description of the Morning" with "London" by William Blake (page 778).

Alfred, Lord Tennyson   (1809–1892)*

DARK HOUSE, BY WHICH ONCE   1850
MORE I STAND

Dark house, by which once more I stand
   Here in the long unlovely street,
   Doors, where my heart was used to beat
So quickly, waiting for a hand,

A hand that can be clasped no more—   5
   Behold me, for I cannot sleep,
   And like a guilty thing I creep
At earliest morning to the door.

He is not here; but far away
   The noise of life begins again,   10
   And ghastly through the drizzling rain
On the bald street breaks the blank day.

DARK HOUSE. This poem is one part of the series *In Memoriam*, an elegy for Tennyson's friend Arthur
Henry Hallam.

COMPARE

"Dark house, by which once more I stand" with "The piercing chill I feel" by Taniguchi
Buson (page 790) and "Home is so Sad" by Philip Larkin (page 1202).

Alfred, Lord Tennyson

Alfred, Lord Tennyson   (1809–1892)*

ULYSSES   (1833)

It little profits that an idle king,
By this still hearth, among these barren crags,
Matched with an agèd wife, I mete and dole
Unequal laws unto a savage race
That hoard, and sleep, and feed, and know not me.   5
I cannot rest from travel; I will drink
Life to the lees. All times I have enjoyed
Greatly, have suffered greatly, both with those
That loved me, and alone; on shore, and when
Through scudding drifts the rainy Hyades   10
Vexed the dim sea. I am become a name;
For always roaming with a hungry heart
Much have I seen and known—cities of men
And manners, climates, councils, governments,
Myself not least, but honored of them all—   15
And drunk delight of battle with my peers,
Far on the ringing plains of windy Troy.
I am a part of all that I have met;
Yet all experience is an arch wherethrough
Gleams that untraveled world whose margin fades   20
Forever and forever when I move.
How dull it is to pause, to make an end,

To rust unburnished, not to shine in use!
As though to breathe were life! Life piled on life
Were all too little, and of one to me   25
Little remains; but every hour is saved
From that eternal silence, something more,
A bringer of new things; and vile it were
For some three suns to store and hoard myself,
And this grey spirit yearning in desire   30
To follow knowledge like a sinking star,
Beyond the utmost bound of human thought.
    This is my son, mine own Telemachus,
To whom I leave the scepter and the isle—
Well-loved of me, discerning to fulfill   35
This labor, by slow prudence to make mild
A rugged people, and through soft degrees
Subdue them to the useful and the good.
Most blameless is he, centered in the sphere
Of common duties, decent not to fail   40
In offices of tenderness, and pay
Meet adoration to my household gods,
When I am gone. He works his work, I mine.
    There lies the port; the vessel puffs her sail;
There gloom the dark, broad seas. My mariners,   45
Souls that have toiled, and wrought, and thought with me—
That ever with a frolic welcome took
The thunder and the sunshine, and opposed
Free hearts, free foreheads—you and I are old;
Old age hath yet his honor and his toil.   50
Death closes all; but something ere the end,
Some work of noble note, may yet be done,
Not unbecoming men that strove with Gods.
The lights begin to twinkle from the rocks;
The long day wanes; the low moon climbs; the deep   55
Moans round with many voices. Come, my friends,
'Tis not too late to seek a newer world.
Push off, and sitting well in order smite
The sounding furrows; for my purpose holds
To sail beyond the sunset, and the baths   60
Of all the western stars, until I die.
It may be that the gulfs will wash us down;
It may be we shall touch the Happy Isles,
And see the great Achilles, whom we knew.
Though much is taken, much abides; and though   65
We are not now that strength which in old days
Moved earth and heaven, that which we are, we are—

One equal temper of heroic hearts,
Made weak by time and fate, but strong in will
To strive, to seek, to find, and not to yield.   70

ULYSSES. 10 *Hyades:* daughters of Atlas, who were transformed into a group of stars. Their rising with
the sun was thought to be a sign of rain. 63 *Happy Isles:* Elysium, a paradise believed to be attainable
by sailing west.

COMPARE

"Ulysses" with "Sir Patrick Spence" (page 708).

Dylan Thomas (1914–1953)*

FERN HILL   1946

Now as I was young and easy under the apple boughs
About the lilting house and happy as the grass was green,
     The night above the dingle° starry,   *wooded valley*
       Time let me hail and climb
      Golden in the heydays of his eyes,   5
And honored among wagons I was prince of the apple towns
And once below a time I lordly had the trees and leaves
       Trail with daisies and barley
     Down the rivers of the windfall light.

And as I was green and carefree, famous among the barns   10
About the happy yard and singing as the farm was home,
     In the sun that is young once only,
      Time let me play and be
     Golden in the mercy of his means,
And green and golden I was huntsman and herdsman, the calves   15
Sang to my horn, the foxes on the hills barked clear and cold,
      And the sabbath rang slowly
     In the pebbles of the holy streams.

All the sun long it was running, it was lovely, the hay
Fields high as the house, the tunes from the chimneys, it was air   20
     And playing, lovely and watery
      And fire green as grass.
     And nightly under the simple stars
As I rode to sleep the owls were bearing the farm away,
All the moon long I heard, blessed among stables, the nightjars   25
     Flying with the ricks, and the horses
      Flashing into the dark.

And then to awake, and the farm, like a wanderer white
With the dew, come back, the cock on his shoulder: it was all
      Shining, it was Adam and maiden,   30
          The sky gathered again
        And the sun grew round that very day.
So it must have been after the birth of the simple light
In the first, spinning place, the spellbound horses walking warm
        Out of the whinnying green stable   35
          On to the fields of praise.

And honored among foxes and pheasants by the gay house
Under the new made clouds and happy as the heart was long,
        In the sun born over and over,
           I ran my heedless ways,   40
            My wishes raced through the house high hay
And nothing I cared, at my sky blue trades, that time allows
In all his tuneful turning so few and such morning songs
        Before the children green and golden
           Follow him out of grace,   45

Nothing I cared, in the lamb white days, that time would take me
Up to the swallow thronged loft by the shadow of my hand,
        In the moon that is always rising,
          Nor that riding to sleep
      I should hear him fly with the high fields   50
And wake to the farm forever fled from the childless land.
Oh as I was young and easy in the mercy of his means,
        Time held me green and dying
      Though I sang in my chains like the sea.

COMPARE

"Fern Hill" with "in Just-" by E. E. Cummings (page 949) and "The World Is Too Much
with Us" by William Wordsworth (page 978).

John Updike   (b. 1932)*

Ex-Basketball Player   1958

Pearl Avenue runs past the high-school lot,
Bends with the trolley tracks, and stops, cut off
Before it has a chance to go two blocks,
At Colonel McComsky Plaza. Berth's Garage
Is on the corner facing west, and there,   5
Most days, you'll find Flick Webb, who helps Berth out.

Flick stands tall among the idiot pumps—
Five on a side, the old bubble-head style,
Their rubber elbows hanging loose and low.
One's nostrils are two S's, and his eyes
An E and O. And one is squat, without   10
A head at all—more of a football type.

Once Flick played for the high-school team, the Wizards.
He was good: in fact, the best. In '46
He bucketed three hundred ninety points,
A county record still. The ball loved Flick.   15
I saw him rack up thirty-eight or forty
In one home game. His hands were like wild birds.

He never learned a trade, he just sells gas,
Checks oil, and changes flats. Once in a while,
As a gag, he dribbles an inner tube,   20
But most of us remember anyway.
His hands are fine and nervous on the lug wrench.
It makes no difference to the lug wrench, though.

Off work, he hangs around Mae's luncheonette.
Grease-gray and kind of coiled, he plays pinball, 25
Smokes those thin cigars, nurses lemon phosphates.
Flick seldom says a word to Mae, just nods
Beyond her face toward bright applauding tiers
Of Necco Wafers, Nibs, and Juju Beads.   30

COMPARE

"Ex-Basketball Player" with "To an Athlete Dying Young" by A. E. Housman (page 1194).

Amy Uyematsu

Amy Uyematsu   (b. 1947)

THE TEN MILLION FLAMES OF LOS ANGELES   1998

>   *A New Year's Poem, 1994*

I've always been afraid of death by fire,
I am eight or nine when I see the remnants of a cross
burning on the Jacobs' front lawn,
seventeen when Watts explodes in '65,
forty-four when Watts blazes again in 1992.   5
For days the sky scatters soot and ash which cling to my skin,
the smell of burning metal everywhere. And I recall
James Baldwin's warning about the fire next time.

>   *Fires keep burning in my city of the angels,*
>   *from South Central to Hollywood,*   10
>   *burn, baby, burn.*

In '93 LA's Santana winds incinerate Laguna and Malibu.
Once the firestorm begins, wind and heat regenerate
on their own, unleashing a fury so unforgiving
it must be a warning from the gods.   15

>   *Fires keep burning in my city of the angels,*
>   *how many does it take,*
>   *burn, LA, burn.*

Everybody says we're all going to hell.
No home safe   20
from any tagger, gangster, carjacker, neighbor.
LA gets meaner by the minute
as we turn our backs

on another generation of young men,
become too used to this condition   25
of children killing children.
I wonder who to fear more.

　　Fires keep burning in my city of angels,
　　but I hear someone whisper,
　　"Mi angelita, come closer."   30

Though I ready myself for the next conflagration,
I feel myself giving in to something I can't name.
I smile more at strangers, leave big tips to waitresses,
laugh when I'm stuck on the freeway, content
just listening to B.B. King's "Why I Sing the Blues."   35

　　"Mi angelita, mi angelita."

I'm starting to believe in a flame
which tries to breathe in each of us.
I see young Chicanos fasting one more day
in a hunger strike for education,   40
read about gang members preaching peace in the 'hood,
hear Reginald Denny forgiving the men
who nearly beat him to death.
I look at people I know, as if for the first time,
sure that some are angels. I like the unlikeliness   45
of this unhandsome crew—the men losing their hair,
needing a shave, those with dark shining
eyes, and the grey-haired women, rage
and grace in each sturdy step.
What is this fire I feel, this fire which breathes freely   50
inside without burning them alive?

　　Fires keep burning in my city of angels,
　　but someone calls to me.
　　"Angelita, do not run from the flame."

THE TEN MILLION FLAMES OF LOS ANGELES: 4 *Watts:* African American neighborhood in Los Angeles, scene of race riots in 1965 and again in 1992 (following the acquittal of four white Los Angeles
police officers who were caught on videotape beating Rodney King, a black motorist who had been
stopped for speeding). 8 *James Baldwin:* writer and civil rights activist, author of two important books
that were influential in the civil rights movement, *Go Tell It on the Mountain* (1953) and *Notes of a
Native Son* (1955). 42 *Reginald Denny:* white truck-driver beaten by Watts rioters in 1992.

COMPARE

"The Ten Million Flames of Los Angeles" with "The Second Coming" by William Butler
Yeats (page 982).

Derek Walcott

Derek Walcott (b. 1930)

THE VIRGINS 1976

Down the dead streets of sun-stoned Frederiksted,
the first free port to die for tourism,
strolling at funeral pace, I am reminded
of life not lost to the American dream;
but my small-islander's simplicities 5
can't better our new empire's civilized
exchange of cameras, watches, perfumes, brandies
for the good life, so cheaply underpriced
that only the crime rate is on the rise
in streets blighted with sun, stone arches 10
and plazas blown dry by the hysteria
of rumour. A condominium drowns
in vacancy; its bargains are dusted,
but only a jewelled housefly drones
over the bargains. The roulettes spin 15
rustily to the wind—the vigorous trade
that every morning would begin afresh
by revving up green water round the pierhead
heading for where the banks of silver thresh.

THE VIRGINS. The title of this poem refers to the Virgin Islands, a group of 100 small islands in the Caribbean. 1 *Frederiksted:* the biggest seaport in St. Croix, the largest of the American Virgin Islands. 2 *free port:* a port city where goods can be bought and sold without paying customs taxes. 5 *small-islander's:* Walcott was born on St. Lucia, another island in the West Indies. 16 *trade:* trade winds.

COMPARE

"The Virgins" with "London" by William Blake (page 778).

Edmund Waller (1606–1687)

Go, Lovely Rose   1645

  Go, lovely rose,
Tell her that wastes her time and me
  That now she knows,
When I resemble° her to thee,   *compare*
How sweet and fair she seems to be.   5

  Tell her that's young
And shuns to have her graces spied,
  That hadst thou sprung
In deserts where no men abide,
Thou must have uncommended died.   10

  Small is the worth
Of beauty from the light retired:
  Bid her come forth,
Suffer herself to be desired,
And not blush so to be admired.   15

  Then die, that she
The common fate of all things rare
  May read in thee,
How small a part of time they share
That are so wondrous sweet and fair.   20

COMPARE

"Go, Lovely Rose" with "To the Virgins, to Make Much of Time" by Robert Herrick
(page 1191) and "To His Coy Mistress" by Andrew Marvell (page 1208).

Walt Whitman (1819–1892)*

A Noiseless Patient Spider   (1876)

A noiseless patient spider,
I mark'd where on a little promontory it stood isolated,
Mark'd how to explore the vacant vast surrounding,
It launch'd forth filament, filament, filament, out of itself,
Ever unreeling them, ever tirelessly speeding them.   5
And you O my soul where you stand,
Surrounded, detached, in measureless oceans of space,
Ceaselessly musing, venturing, throwing, seeking the spheres to
      connect them,
Till the bridge you will need be form'd, till the ductile anchor hold,
Till the gossamer thread you fling catch somewhere, O my soul.   10

COMPARE

"A Noiseless Patient Spider" with "Ulysses" by Alfred, Lord Tennyson (page 1250) or "The Eagle" by Alfred, Lord Tennyson (page 815).

Walt Whitman

Walt Whitman   (1819–1892)*

I HEAR AMERICA SINGING   1860

I hear America singing, the varied carols I hear,
Those of mechanics, each one singing his as it should be blithe and
    strong,
The carpenter singing his as he measures his plank or beam,
The mason singing his as he makes ready for work, or leaves off work,
The boatman singing what belongs to him in his boat, the deckhand   5
    singing on the steamboat deck,
The shoemaker singing as he sits on his bench, the hatter singing as he
    stands,
The wood-cutter's song, the ploughboy's on his way in the morning, or
    at noon intermission or at sundown,
The delicious singing of the mother, or of the young wife at work, or of
    the girl sewing or washing,
Each singing what belongs to him or her and to none else,
The day what belongs to the day—at night the party of young fellows,   10
    robust, friendly,
Singing with open mouths their strong melodious songs.

COMPARE

"I Hear America Singing" with "I, Too" by Langston Hughes (page 1118).

Richard Wilbur (b. 1921)*

THE WRITER   1976

In her room at the prow of the house
Where light breaks, and the windows are tossed with linden,
My daughter is writing a story.

I pause in the stairwell, hearing
From her shut door a commotion of typewriter-keys   5
Like a chain hauled over a gunwale.

Young as she is, the stuff
Of her life is a great cargo, and some of it heavy:
I wish her a lucky passage.

But now it is she who pauses,   10
As if to reject my thought and its easy figure.
A stillness greatens, in which

The whole house seems to be thinking,
And then she is at it again with a bunched clamor
Of strokes, and again is silent.   15

I remember the dazed starling
Which was trapped in that very room, two years ago;
How we stole in, lifted a sash

And retreated, not to affright it;
And how for a helpless hour, through the crack of the door, 20
We watched the sleek, wild, dark

And iridescent creature
Batter against the brilliance, drop like a glove
To the hard floor, or the desk-top.

And wait then, humped and bloody,   25
For the wits to try it again; and how our spirits
Rose when, suddenly sure,

It lifted off from a chair-back,
Beating a smooth course for the right window
And clearing the sill of the world.   30

It is always a matter, my darling,
Of life or death, as I had forgotten. I wish
What I wished you before, but harder.

COMPARE

"The Writer" with "Digging" by Seamus Heaney (page 1186).

C. K. Williams (b. 1936)

ELMS   1987

All morning the tree men have been taking down the stricken elms
    skirting the broad sidewalks.
The pitiless electric chain saws whine tirelessly up and down their
    piercing, operatic scales
and the diesel choppers in the street shredding the debris chug
    feverishly, incessantly,
packing truckload after truckload with the feathery, homogenized, inert
    remains of heartwood,
twig and leaf and soon the block is stripped, it is as though illusions of   5
    reality were stripped:
the rows of naked facing buildings stare and think, their divagations
    more urgent than they were.
"The winds of time," they think, the mystery charged with fearful
    clarity: "The winds of time . . ."
All afternoon, on to the unhealing evening, minds racing, "Insolent,
    unconscionable, the winds of time . . ."

COMPARE

"Elms" With "Mutability" by William Wordsworth (page 770) and "Final Love Note" by
Clare Rossini (page 784).

William Carlos Williams (1883–1963)*

SPRING AND ALL   1923

By the road to the contagious hospital
under the surge of the blue
mottled clouds driven from the
northeast—a cold wind. Beyond, the
waste of broad, muddy fields   5
brown with dried weeds, standing and fallen

patches of standing water
the scattering of tall trees

All along the road the reddish
purplish, forked, upstanding, twiggy   10
stuff of bushes and small trees
with dead, brown leaves under them
leafless vines—

Lifeless in appearance, sluggish
dazed spring approaches—   15

They enter the new world naked,
cold, uncertain of all
save that they enter. All about them
the cold, familiar wind—

Now the grass, tomorrow   20
the stiff curl of wildcarrot leaf
One by one objects are defined—
It quickens: clarity, outline of leaf

But now the stark dignity of
entrance—Still, the profound change   25
has come upon them: rooted, they
grip down and begin to awaken

COMPARE

"Spring and All" with "in Just-" by E. E. Cummings (page 949) and "Root Cellar" by
Theodore Roethke (page 792).

William Carlos Williams

William Carlos Williams   (1883–1963)*

To Waken an Old Lady   1921

Old age is
a flight of small
cheeping birds
skimming
bare trees
above a snow glaze.
Gaining and failing
they are buffeted

by a dark wind—
But what?
On harsh weedstalks
the flock has rested,
the snow
is covered with broken
seedhusks   15
and the wind tempered
by a shrill
piping of plenty.

COMPARE

"To Waken an Old Lady" with "Sorrow Moves in Wide Waves" by Lorine Niedecker
(page 1217).

William Wordsworth

William Wordsworth   (1770–1850)*

COMPOSED UPON WESTMINSTER BRIDGE   1807

Earth has not anything to show more fair:
Dull would he be of soul who could pass by
A sight so touching in its majesty:
This City now doth, like a garment, wear
The beauty of the morning; silent, bare,   5
Ships, towers, domes, theatres, and temples lie
Open unto the fields, and to the sky;
All bright and glittering in the smokeless air.
Never did sun more beautifully steep
In his first splendor, valley, rock, or hill;   10
Ne'er saw I, never felt, a calm so deep!

The river glideth at his own sweet will:
Dear God! the very houses seem asleep;
And all that mighty heart is lying still!

COMPARE

"Composed upon Westminster Bridge" with "London" by William Blake (page 778).

James Wright   (1927–1980)*

A BLESSING   1961

Just off the highway to Rochester, Minnesota,
Twilight bounds softly forth on the grass.
And the eyes of those two Indian ponies
Darken with kindness.
They have come gladly out of the willows   5
To welcome my friend and me.
We step over the barbed wire into the pasture
Where they have been grazing all day, alone.
They ripple tensely, they can hardly contain their happiness
That we have come.   10
They bow shyly as wet swans. They love each other.
There is no loneliness like theirs.
At home once more,
They begin munching the young tufts of spring in the darkness.
I would like to hold the slenderer one in my arms,   15
For she has walked over to me
And nuzzled my left hand.
She is black and white,
Her mane falls wild on her forehead,
And the light breeze moves me to caress her long ear   20
That is delicate as the skin over a girl's wrist.
Suddenly I realize
That if I stepped out of my body I would break
Into blossom.

COMPARE

"A Blessing" with "God's Grandeur" by Gerard Manley Hopkins (page 875).

James Wright (1927–1980)*

AUTUMN BEGINS IN MARTINS FERRY, OHIO 1963

In the Shreve High football stadium,
I think of Polacks nursing long beers in Tiltonsville,
And gray faces of Negroes in the blast furnace at Benwood,
And the ruptured night watchman of Wheeling Steel,
Dreaming of heroes.   5

All the proud fathers are ashamed to go home.
Their women cluck like starved pullets,
Dying for love.

Therefore,
Their sons grow suicidally beautiful   10
At the beginning of October,
And gallop terribly against each other's bodies.

COMPARE

"Autumn Begins in Martin's Ferry, Ohio" with "Ex-Basketball Player" by John Updike
(page 1253).

Mary Sidney Wroth (1587?–1623?)

IN THIS STRANGE LABYRINTH   1621

In this strange labyrinth how shall I turn?
Ways are on all sides while the way I miss:
If to the right hand, there in love I burn;
Let me go forward, therein danger is;
If to the left, suspicion hinders bliss,   5
Let me turn back, shame cries I ought return
Nor faint though crosses with my fortunes kiss.
Stand still is harder, although sure to mourn;
Thus let me take the right, or left hand way;
Go forward, or stand still, or back retire;   10
I must these doubts endure without allay
Or help, but travail find for my best hire;
Yet that which most my troubled sense doth move
Is to leave all, and take the thread of love.

IN THIS STRANGE LABYRINTH. This sonnet comes from Wroth's *Urania* (1621), the first significant
sonnet sequence by a woman. Wroth was the niece of Sir Philip Sidney and of the countess of Pem-
broke as well as a distant relation of Sir Walter Raleigh. The *Labyrinth* of the title was the maze built
by Minos to trap the young men and women sacrificed to the Minotaur. King Minos's daughter Ariadne saved her beloved Theseus by giving him a skein of thread to guide his way through the
Labyrinth. (See the final line of the sonnet.)

COMPARE

"In this strange labyrinth" with "Let me not to the marriage of true minds" by William Shakespeare (page 917).

Sir Thomas Wyatt   (1503?–1542)*

THEY FLEE FROM ME THAT   (ABOUT 1535)
SOMETIME DID ME SEKË

They flee from me that sometime did me sekë
    With naked fotë° stalking in my chamber.   foot
I have seen them gentle, tame and mekë
    That now are wild, and do not remember
    That sometime they put themself in danger   5
To take bread at my hand; and now they range
Busily seeking with a continual change.

Thankèd be fortune, it hath been otherwise
    Twenty times better; but once in speciàll,
In thin array, after a pleasant guise,   10
    When her loose gown from her shoulders did fall,
    And she me caught in her armës long and small,
Therëwith all sweetly did me kiss,
And softly said, *Dear heart, how like you this?*

It was no dremë: I lay broadë waking.   15
    But all is turned thorough° my gentleness   through
Into a strangë fashion of forsaking;
    And I have leave to go of her goodness,
    And she also to use newfangleness.°   to seek novelty
But since that I so kindëly am served   20
I would fain knowë what she hath deserved.

THEY FLEE FROM ME THAT SOMETIME DID ME SEKË. Some latter-day critics have called Sir Thomas Wyatt a careless poet because some of his lines appear faltering and metrically inconsistent; others have thought he knew what he was doing. It is uncertain whether the final *e*'s in English spelling were still pronounced in Wyatt's day as they were in Chaucer's, but if they were, perhaps Wyatt has been unjustly blamed. In this text, spellings have been modernized except in words where the final *e* would make a difference in rhythm. To sense how it matters, try reading the poem aloud leaving out the *e*'s and then putting them in wherever indicated. Sound them like the *a* in *sofa*. 20 *kindëly*: according to my kind (or hers); that is, as befits the nature of man (or woman). Perhaps there is also irony here, and the word means "unkindly."

COMPARE

"They flee from me that sometimes did me sekë" with "When, in disgrace with Fortune and men's eyes" by William Shakespeare (page 1236).

William Butler Yeats

William Butler Yeats   (1865–1939)*

CRAZY JANE TALKS WITH THE BISHOP   1933

I met the Bishop on the road
And much said he and I.
"Those breasts are flat and fallen now,
Those veins must soon be dry;
Live in a heavenly mansion,   5
Not in some foul sty."

"Fair and foul are near of kin,
And fair needs foul," I cried.
"My friends are gone, but that's a truth
Nor° grave nor bed denied,   *neither*   10
Learned in bodily lowliness
And in the heart's pride.

"A woman can be proud and stiff
When on love intent;
But Love has pitched his mansion in   15
The place of excrement;
For nothing can be sole or whole
That has not been rent."

COMPARE

"Crazy Jane Talks with the Bishop" with "The Flea" by John Donne (page 1163) or
"Down, Wanton, Down!" by Robert Graves (page 752).

William Butler Yeats   (1865–1939)*

THE MAGI   1914

Now as at all times I can see in the mind's eye,
In their stiff, painted clothes, the pale unsatisfied ones
Appear and disappear in the blue depth of the sky
With all their ancient faces like rain-beaten stones,
And all their helms of silver hovering side by side,   5
And all their eyes still fixed, hoping to find once more,
Being by Calvary's turbulence unsatisfied,
The uncontrollable mystery on the bestial floor.

COMPARE

"The Magi" with "Journey of the Magi" by T. S. Eliot (page 1167).

William Butler Yeats   (1865–1939)*

WHEN YOU ARE OLD   1893

When you are old and grey and full of sleep,
And nodding by the fire, take down this book,
And slowly read, and dream of the soft look
Your eyes had once, and of their shadows deep;

How many loved your moments of glad grace,   5
And loved your beauty with love false or true,
But one man loved the pilgrim soul in you,
And loved the sorrows of your changing face;

And bending down beside the glowing bars,
Murmur, a little sadly, how Love fled   10
And paced upon the mountains overhead
And hid his face amid a crowd of stars.

COMPARE

"When You Are Old" with "Not marble nor the gilded monuments" by William
Shakespeare (page 1237).

32 Lives of the Poets

Here you will find a brief biographical note for each poet represented in the book by more than one selection.

John Ashbery

John Ashbery, born in Rochester, New York, in 1927, was educated at Deerfield Academy, Harvard, and Columbia. In 1960 he became an art critic in Paris for the *New York Herald Tribune*, and from 1966 to 1972 served as executive editor of the magazine *Art News* in New York. His first full collection of poetry, *Some Trees* (1956), was chosen by W. H. Auden for publication in the Yale Series of Younger Poets; his *Self-Portrait in a Convex Mirror* (1976) garnered praise and three leading literary prizes, and sold well for a book of serious poetry. Ashbery has written plays and a novel (with James Schuyler), *A Nest of Ninnies* (1969). Some critics have speculated that Ashbery's experience as an art critic has tinged his poetry: that he performs in words what an abstract expressionist performs on canvas in oils.

His work can annoy readers who expect poems to make clear statements to be taken in only one way; others think him the foremost living American poet and major heir to the tradition of Wallace Stevens—that is, to the art of suggesting rather than depicting, of arranging words primarily for their own sake.

Margaret Atwood

Margaret Atwood, born in Ottawa in 1939, is a staunchly Canadian poet, short story writer, and novelist whose literary reputation has extended well beyond the borders of her native country. She published her first book of poems, *Double Persephone*, in 1962, the same year she graduated from the University of Toronto. She went on to earn a master's degree at Radcliffe and to study Victorian fantasy at Harvard. She has advanced her country's cultural identity by publishing *Survival* (1972), a book about Canadian literature, and by editing *The Oxford Book of Canadian Verse* (1982). Her fiction and poetry, at once comic and grim, often deal with alienation and the destructive nature of human relationships. Her novel *Cat's Eye* (1989) won attention on both sides of the Canadian border. The cream of her poetry has been skimmed in *Eating Fire: Selected Poems 1965–1995* (1998).

W. H. Auden

Wystan Hugh Auden (1907–1973), born in York, England, as a young man in the 1930s became the acknowledged spokesman for a generation of English poets that included Stephen Spender, C. Day Lewis, and Louis MacNeice. His early work was characterized by blithe wit, a Marxist outlook, and a knowledge of Freudian psychology; in later life, he professed Christianity and (in his views of poetry) increasing conservatism. In 1939 Auden emigrated to America, and in 1946 became a United States citizen. A prolific editor, anthologist, and translator of poetry, he collaborated on verse plays, travel memoirs, and (with his longtime companion Chester Kallman) librettos for operas, including Igor Stravinsky's *The Rake's Progress* (1951). He wrote influential criticism, notably that collected in *The Dyer's Hand* (1962). Auden divided his last years among England, Italy, Austria, and New York.

Matsuo Basho

Matsuo Basho (1644–1694) was born in Ueno, about thirty miles southwest of Kyoto, which was then the imperial capital of Japan. Basho's father was a samurai-class farmer with considerable land. Basho began writing poetry in adolescence, and he worked variously as a teacher, a waterworks official, and possibly even as a ninja spy. He eventually shaved his head and became a lay monk. In 1689 he and a friend took a five-month journey across Japan in which they covered 1233 miles by foot. *Narrow Road to the Far North*, his account of that trip (written in both verse and prose), is one of the classics of Japanese literature.

Elizabeth Bishop

Elizabeth Bishop (1911–1979) was born in Worcester, Massachusetts. After her father died (in her first year) and her mother was stricken with mental illness, she lived until age six with her grandmother in a coastal village in Nova Scotia. Because she suffered from asthma, Bishop received scant elementary schooling, but she read widely and deeply at home. At sixteen, she entered Walnut Hill, a boarding school, and later graduated from Vassar Collage. Her undergraduate poems won her the friendship of the poet Marianne Moore, who persuaded her not to go on to medical school, but instead to write. Fond of travel and flower-filled climates, Bishop lived for nine years in Key West, Florida, then for fifteen years in Brazil, dividing her time between the mountains and Rio de Janeiro. In 1966 she returned to the United States to teach: first at the University of Washington, then at Harvard from 1969 until 1977, when she retired. Most of her sparely disciplined work is contained in two volumes: *Complete Poems 1927–1979* (1983) and *Collected Prose* (1984). Her sharp-eyed poems, full of vivid images and apt metaphors, have influenced the work of other poets, among them her friends Randall Jarrell and Robert Lowell.

William Blake

William Blake (1757–1827), poet, painter, and visionary, was born in the Soho district of London and early in life was apprenticed to an engraver. Becoming a skilled craftsman, he earned his living illustrating books, among them Dante's *Divine Comedy*, Milton's poems, and the Book of Job. A remarkable and original graphic artist whose only formal training came from a few months at the Royal Academy, Blake published his own poems, engraving them in a careful script embellished with hand-colored illustrations and decorations. His wife Catherine Boucher, whom he taught to read and write, shared his visions and helped him do the coloring. *Songs of Innocence* (1789) and *Songs of Experience* (1794), brief lyrics written from a child's point of view, are easy to enjoy; but anyone deeply interested in Blake copes also with the longer, more demanding "Prophetic Books," among them *The Book of Thel* (1789), *The Marriage of Heaven and Hell* (1790), and *Jerusalem* (1804–1820). In these later works, out of his readings in alchemy, the Bible, and the works of Plato and Swedenborg, Blake derived support for his lifelong hatred of scientific rationalism and created his own mythology, complete with devils and deities. A sympathizer with both the American and French revolutions, Blake was once accused of sedition, but the charges were dismissed. In his lifetime, Wordsworth and Coleridge were among the few admirers of his short lyrics; his "Prophetic Books" had to wait until the twentieth century for sympathetic readers.

Robert Bly

Robert Bly was born on a farm in Madison, Minnesota, in 1926, and continued to live there for most of his life. He graduated from Harvard, where he began studies in mathematics before deciding to devote his life to poetry. Rather than teaching, Bly has preferred to support himself and his family by giving poetry readings and by translating books and poems from Scandinavian and other languages. In 1958 he launched a poetry magazine, *The Fifties* (later renamed, as decades went by, *The Sixties* and *The Seventies*). In it he spoofed academic critics, urged American poets to open their work to dream and surrealism, and introduced in translation the work of important poets of Europe and Latin America. Bly has vitally influenced the work of James Wright, Donald Hall, and many younger poets. His readings, in which he sometimes chants and dons primitive masks, have drawn throngs. In the 1960s he organized (with David Ray) American Writers Against the Vietnam War, and over the years has championed many causes, usually pacifist and antinuclear. Lately he has been leading retreats for men, trying to help them understand their male natures. In 1990 Bly's *Iron John*, a book on contemporary male identity, became a national best-seller.

Louise Bogan

Louise Bogan (1897–1970) was born in Maine to parents of Irish descent. She spent her early years in several New England mill towns. Although she won a scholarship to Radcliffe, she left college to marry an army officer. Her husband's sudden death in 1920 left her alone with a small daughter. She boldly moved to Manhattan and began a literary career. Publishing her first book, *Body of This Death*, in 1923, Bogan developed an austere but emotional style of formal lyric that she continued to use until her final collection *The Blue Estuaries* in 1968. For nearly forty years Bogan reviewed poetry for the *New Yorker*. Underappreciated in their own time, Bogan's quiet poems have steadily risen in critical esteem since her death.

Jorge Luis Borges

See biographical note on page 1049.

Gwendolyn Brooks

Gwendolyn Brooks (1917–2000), born in Topeka, Kansas, moved early in life to Chicago's South Side, whose people she has commemorated in her poetry and in a novel, *Maud Martha* (1953). Recipient of the Pulitzer Prize for poetry in 1950, for *Annie Allen,* Brooks has long been recognized as a leading voice in modern American letters. She combined several teaching positions with raising two children. From 1967, when she took part in a conference for black writers at Fisk University and was impressed with young black poets' views, she was increasingly an activist, teaching teenage black writers in Chicago and addressing her work especially to black audiences. Instead of continuing to publish with a mainstream New York publishing house, she switched her work to Broadside, a small literary press in Detroit founded by black poet Dudley Randall. Her memoir *Report from Part One* (1972) discusses her altered outlook. In 1985 she was named consultant in poetry to the Library of Congress (the position now known as poet laureate of the United States). Her goals in life, she declared, were "to be clean of heart, clear of mind, and claiming of what is right and just."

Elizabeth Barrett Browning

Elizabeth Barrett (1806–1861) was born in a large country house outside Durham, England. The eldest of twelve children, she was raised in a close, affectionate family ruled by her possessive father. Ill health kept her at home as an adult, but she nonetheless achieved literary fame and corresponded with many famous writers. The day after she met one correspondent, Robert Browning, in 1845, he sent her a declaration of love, which she insisted he withdraw if he ever wanted to visit again. Gradually, however, she fell in love with her devoted visitor, but the courtship was conducted in secret, since her father had forbidden his children to marry. In 1846 she and Browning eloped to Italy, where the couple lived happily until her death in 1861. When

William Wordsworth died in 1850, Mrs. Browning was considered for the position of poet laureate (which eventually went to Tennyson). She was the most highly regarded woman poet of the nineteenth century, and her work was immensely popular with both critics and general readers.

Robert Browning

Robert Browning (1812–1889), born in a suburb of London, was educated mainly in his father's six-thousand-volume library. With *Pauline* (1833), he began to print his poetry. After the death of his wife Elizabeth Barrett Browning, with whom he had lived in Italy, he returned to England to become (Henry James wrote) an "accomplished, saturated, sane, sound man of the London world." There, as he neared sixty, he enjoyed late but loud applause and the adulation of the Browning Society: faithful readers whose local groups met over their teacups to explicate his work. Readers have most greatly favored Browning's story-poems in a form he perfected, the dramatic monologue—such as "My Last Duchess" and "Soliloquy of the Spanish Cloister"—in which he brings to life persons from the past (some of them famous), and has them speak their innermost thoughts and reveal their characters. His masterpiece, *The Ring and the Book* (1868–1869), is a long narrative poem in twelve monologues, based on a seventeenth-century Roman murder trial. Browning also wrote several plays, among them *A Blot in the 'Scutcheon* (1842). Through the praise and emulation of his later admirers Ezra Pound and T. S. Eliot, Browning has profoundly af-

fected modern poetry. A formal experimenter, he speaks to us in energetic, punchy words—and like many later poets, he introduces learning into his poems without apology. More important, Browning is among the great yea-sayers in English poetry: an affirmer and celebrant of life.

Robert Burns

Robert Burns (1759–1796), the preeminent poet of Scotland, was born in a two-room farm cottage in Alloway, a hamlet on the River Doon, the son of a farmer who worked himself to death. For most of his days Burns too struggled to farm poor soil. Though his schooling lasted only three years, he eagerly read Shakespeare and Pope as a boy and let poetry pour from his own pen. Only in 1786, when he felt he needed money to emigrate to Jamaica, did he publish his *Poems, Chiefly in the Scottish Dialect*, depicting Scottish rural life with warm humor, tender compassion, and rugged exuberance. The book scored an immediate hit and Burns remained in Scotland for the rest of his days. After Edinburgh's stylish society, which had lionized him for a time, dropped him, he returned to his plough, married Jean Armour (who earlier had borne him two sets of twins), and continued to farm until 1791, when he retired to the easier life of a tax official. But, worn from toil, hardship, and poverty, Burns died at thirty-seven. Among his legacies are songs, such as "Flow Gently, Sweet Afton," "Comin' Through the Rye," and a song still heard in this country each New Year's Eve, "Auld Lang Syne." Like Hugh MacDiarmid, Burns wrote poetry in both standard English and Scots dialect—in the latter whenever, as in "The Jolly Beggars" and "Address to the Unco Guid," he expressed defiantly unconventional views.

Taniguchi Buson

Taniguchi Buson (1716–1783) was born on the outskirts of Osaka. Little is known about his childhood, but as a young man, he went to Edo (later called Tokyo) to study both painting and poetry. He soon became a celebrated painter as well as one of the "Three Masters" of classic haiku. Buson studied Buddhism for many years and may have considered becoming a priest. At forty-five, a prosperous artist, he married Tomo, who was also a poet. He lived a comfortable later life as an artist and teacher.

Billy Collins

Billy Collins was born in New York City in 1941. He graduated from Holy Cross College in 1963 and earned a Ph.D. in Romantic poetry from the University of California at Riverside in 1971. He has received fellowships from the New York Foundation for the Arts, the National Endowment for the Arts, and the Guggenheim Foundation, and was appointed Poet Laureate of the United States in 2001. Written in a witty and accessible style, his poems often begin with ordinary domestic situations and take them in some very surprising directions (although, as he demonstrates in "The Names," he is also capable of writing with great seriousness and power). His collections, including *Sailing Alone Around the Room: New and Selected*

Poems (2001) and *Nine Horses* (2002), have achieved phenomenal sales for books of poetry. Collins is a professor of English at Lehman College, City University of New York. He lives in Somers, New York.

Wendy Cope

Wendy Cope was born in Kent, England, in 1945. Her father, who was nearly sixty when she was born, was a poetry enthusiast of Victorian sensibilities, who often recited Tennyson and Fitzgerald's *Rubaiyat* to the family. After leaving school, she became a primary-school music teacher. Cope claims she "forgot about poetry for more than ten years." Her father's death in 1971, however, triggered a depression that eventually led her to seek psychological help. As she regained her self-esteem, Cope began reading poetry again and soon started writing. She first gained notice for her brilliant parodies of famous poems (which include a retelling of T. S. Eliot's *The Waste Land* in five limericks), but gradually her bittersweet and incisive love poems have become equally prized. Her three collections, *Making Cocoa for Kingsley Amis* (1986), *Serious Concerns*, (1992) and *If I Don't Know* (2001), have become bestsellers in England. In a 1998 BBC Radio 4 poll following the death of Ted Hughes, she was the respondents' first choice to succeed him as poet laureate.

E. E. Cummings

Edward Estlin Cummings (1894–1962) was born in Cambridge, Massachusetts, the son of a minister. As a young man at Harvard, he studied

Greek and Latin. In World War I, while serving as an ambulance driver, he was mistakenly arrested and confined to a French prison—an experience that gave rise to a novel filled with vivid portraits of his fellow prisoners, *The Enormous Room* (1922). Off and on throughout the 1920s, Cummings lived in Paris. In *Eimi* (1933) he scathingly and satirically reported on a trip to the Soviet Union. Although many of his lyric poems revel in typographical experiment, in theme and sentiment they are often more conventional than they appear. Besides poetry Cummings wrote essays, plays—including *Him* (1927) and *Santa Claus* (1946)—the ballet *Tom* (1935), and produced substantial work as a painter and a graphic artist. Throughout his career, he upheld simple themes: love is good, pomp is silly, one individual is worth a thousand faceless societies.

J. V. Cunningham

James Vincent Cunningham (1911–1985) was born in Maryland, but spent his early life in Montana. A Shakespeare scholar with a Stanford Ph.D., Cunningham taught English at Brandeis for many years (1953–1980) and for eight years served as chairman of the department. A reader of Latin and Greek, he became the modern master of the terse, pithy English verse epigram in the classical manner. All his poems have a similar brevity, firm control, and a cold, hardboiled manner. "Poetry is what looks like poetry, what sounds like poetry," he stated. "It is metrical composition." His relatively slim *Collected Poems and Epigrams* (1971) gathers most of his work in

verse; his *Collected Essays* (1976), most of his work in prose, including an earlier study, *Woe and Wonder: The Emotional Effect of Shakespearean Tragedy*. In a late critical work, *Dickinson: Lyric and Legend* (1980), Cunningham took a withering look at the bard of Amherst.

Emily Dickinson

See biographical note on page 1097.

John Donne

John Donne (1572–1631), English poet and divine, wrote his subtle, worldly love lyrics as a young man in the court of Queen Elizabeth I. At the time, he came to be known in London as (wrote his contemporary, Richard Baker) "a great visitor of ladies, a great frequenter of plays, a great writer of conceited verses." The poems of his *Songs and Sonets* were first circulated in manuscript form, for in his lifetime Donne printed little. When in 1601 he married without the consent of his bride's father, he was dismissed from his secretarial post at court. For several years he endured poverty. His longer poems, *The First Anniversary* and *The Second Anniversary* (1611, 1612), suffused with gloom, see the order of the universe shaken by science and doubt. In 1615 Donne—apparently with some reluctance, for he had been raised a Catholic—became a priest of the Anglican church. From 1621 until his death, he was dean of St. Paul's Cathedral in London, where he preached sermons known for their eloquence. His "Holy Sonnets" date from later life. Almost forgotten for two centuries, Donne's work has had much influence in our time. H. J. C. Grierson published a great scholarly edition of it in 1912; shortly thereafter it was championed by T. S. Eliot.

Rita Dove

Rita Dove was born in Akron, Ohio, in 1952. She received her B.A. from Miami University of Ohio and her M.F.A. from the University of Iowa, and was a Fulbright scholar at the Universität Tübingen in Germany. From 1993 to 1995 she served as Poet Laureate of the United States. Her third book of poems, *Thomas and Beulah* (1986), was awarded the Pulitzer Prize. More recent collections include *Selected Poems* (1993), *Mother Love* (1995), and *On the Bus with Rosa Parks* (1999). She has also published a novel, a book of short stories, and a verse play, *The Darker Face of the Earth* (1994), which recasts the Oedipus myth in a drama set on a plantation in pre-Civil War Virginia. Dove's poetry often deals with themes of family, both present-day and historical, in a style that is concentrated and carefully wrought. She is Commonwealth Professor of English at the University of Virginia in Charlottesville, where she lives with her husband and daughter.

T. S. Eliot

Thomas Stearns Eliot (1888–1965) was born of a New England family that had moved to St. Louis. After study at Harvard, Eliot emigrated to London, and worked as a bank clerk and later an influential editor for the publishing house of Faber. In 1927 he became a British citizen and joined the Church of England. During the fire bombings of London in World War II, he served as an air-raid warden. Although Eliot strove to keep his private life private, biographer Peter Ackroyd in *T. S. Eliot* (1984) threw light upon his troubled early marriage. Early poems such as "The Love Song of J. Alfred Prufrock" (1917) and *The Waste Land* (1922), an allusive and seemingly disconnected complaint about the sterility of contemporary city life, enormously influenced young poets. Eliot was mainly responsible for bringing French symbolism into English poetry, and as a critic, he helped revive interest in John Donne and other Metaphysical poets. In an early essay, "Tradition and the Individual Talent" (1919), he finds a necessary continuity in Western civilization. *Four Quartets*, completed in 1943, was Eliot's last major work of poetry: an attempt to structure a long thematic poem like a work of music. In later years he devoted himself to writing verse plays for the London stage; the best received was *The Cocktail Party* (1950), in which Alec Guinness played a psychiatrist. In 1948 Eliot received the Nobel Prize in literature.

Robert Frost

Robert Frost (1874–1963), though born in San Francisco, came to be popularly known as a spokesman for rural New England. In periods of farming, teaching school, and raising chickens and writing for poultry journals, Frost struggled until his late thirties to support his family and to publish his poems, with little success. Moving to England to write and farm in 1912, he had his first two books published in London: *A Boy's Will*

(1913) and *North of Boston* (1914). Returning to America in 1915, he settled in New Hampshire, later teaching for many years (in a casual way) at Amherst College in Massachusetts. Audiences responded warmly to the poet's public readings; he was awarded four Pulitzer Prizes. In his later years the white-haired Frost became a sort of elder statesman and poet laureate of the John F. Kennedy administration, invited to read a poem at President Kennedy's inauguration and dispatched to Russia as a cultural emissary. Frost is sometimes admired for putting colloquial Yankee speech into poetry—and he did, but more essentially he mastered the art of laying conversational American speech along a metrical line. In a three-volume biography (1966–1976), Lawrance Thompson made Frost out to be an overweening egotist who tormented his family, and it has taken us decades to reestablish a more balanced—and properly admiring—view of him.

Robert Graves

Robert von Ranke Graves (1895–1985), one of the most prolifically talented writers of the twentieth century, was born in Wimbledon, England. His father Alfred Perceval Graves was a popular poet. During World War I, Graves enlisted in the Royal Welsh Fusiliers, a unit that saw ferocious combat. Wounded and mistakenly declared dead, Graves was demobilized with shell-shock. His youthful autobiography, *Goodbye to All That* (1929), ranks as the classic British memoir of World War I, and its stark accounts of the despair and brutality of trench warfare are still shocking today.

Moving to Majorca, Spain, in 1929, Graves wrote a series of best-selling historical novels, most famously *I, Claudius* and *Claudius the God* (both 1934). He later wrote an influential study of poetic mythology, *The White Goddess* (1948), which claims the matriarchal Moon Goddess as the true source of poetic inspiration. Graves's vast poetic output covers many subjects, but he is best remembered as a love poet, an area in which he has few modern equals.

Thomas Hardy

Thomas Hardy (1840–1928) was both a major Victorian novelist and a great poet of the twentieth century. After his novel *Jude the Obscure* (1896) was trounced by critics who objected to its dismal morbidity, Hardy, who by then had made a modest fortune from his fiction, switched exclusively to his first love, poetry. Hardy was born in the English county of Dorsetshire ("Wessex" in his fiction and poetry), and, as a young man, he worked as an architect. Determined to be a novelist, he first won success with *Far from the Madding Crowd* (1874), followed by *The Return of the Native* (1878), *The Mayor of Casterbridge* (1886), and his masterpiece, *Tess of the D'Urbervilles* (1891). After the death of his first wife Emma, with whom he appears to have had a rather cold and troubled relationship, Hardy was inspired to write a great spate of love poems in her memory. In old age he wrote a two-volume autobiography and charged his second wife, Florence, to publish it after his death under her own name. In both fiction and poetry, Hardy's view of the universe is somber: God appears to have forgotten us, and happiness usually arrives too late. *The Dynasts* (1903–1908), a long dramatic poem, makes amused gods sneer down on the Napoleonic wars. Many modern poets have credited Hardy with teaching them a good deal (probably about irony and the use of spoken language), among them W. H. Auden, Philip Larkin, Dylan Thomas, and W. D. Snodgrass.

Robert Hayden

Robert Hayden (1913–1980) was born in Detroit, Michigan. He attended Detroit City College (now called Wayne State University) and the University of Michigan, where he studied with W. H. Auden. In 1946 he began teaching at Fisk University in pre-civil-rights-era Nashville, where Hayden, an African American, experienced racial segregation for the first time. Although he lived in Nashville until 1968, he eventually sent his wife and daughter to New York, where schools were integrated. In 1941 he became a convert to the Baha'i faith, a universalist religion that emphasizes charity, tolerance, and equality; his poetry reflects the compassionate moral courage of that creed. Hayden edited the influential 1967 anthology *Kaleidoscope: Poems by American Negro Poets*. In 1976 he was appointed the Consultant in Poetry at the Library of Congress, the first African American to hold that influential office.

H. D. (Hilda Doolittle)

Hilda Doolittle (1886–1961), daughter of a Moravian mother and a professor of mathematics and astronomy, spent her first eight years in Bethlehem, Pennsylvania. At Bryn Mawr,

she failed English and suffered a nervous collapse. By 1911 she had become a confirmed expatriate, living in London. At one time she was engaged to Ezra Pound, who submitted her early poems to Harriet Monroe's magazine *Poetry* and signed them "H. D. Imagiste." In 1913 she married poet and translator Richard Aldington, and in 1916 published *Sea Garden*, her first book of poems. During World War I, H. D. went through a marital breakup and a number of misfortunes, recalled in her novel *Palimpsest* (1926). Alone and in poor health, she was rescued by Winifred Ellerman, a writer signing herself Bryher, who adopted the poet's daughter by Cecil Gray and befriended H. D. for life. During 1933 and 1934, H. D. was a patient of Sigmund Freud, an experience she recalls in *Tribute to Freud* (1956). After World War II, the poet moved to Switzerland. Her last works of poetry were epic-long: *Trilogy* (1944–1946) and the dramatic monologue *Helen in Egypt* (1961). Her earlier poems are available in *Collected Poems 1912–1944* (1983), edited by Louis L. Martz. In 1960, back in the United States for the last time, H. D. received the American Academy of Arts and Letters Award of Merit for Poetry.

Seamus Heaney

Seamus Heaney, the best-known living Irish poet, was born on a farm in County Derry, Northern Ireland, in 1939. He taught at Queens University, Belfast, before leaving Northern Ireland in 1972 to make his home in Dublin. A guest lecturer at the University of California in Berkeley during the 1971–1972 academic year, he now divides his time between

Dublin and America, where he teaches at Harvard. Among his recent books of verse are *The Spirit Level* (1996), *Opened Ground* (1999), and a translation of the Anglo-Saxon epic *Beowulf* (2000). Rich with images of love and loss, Heaney's poetry draws inventively on the history of Ireland and the Irish from ancient times to the violent present. In 1995 he became the first Irish poet since W. B. Yeats to win the Nobel Prize in literature.

George Herbert

George Herbert (1593–1633), English devotional poet, the son of an aristocratic family, began writing poems as an undergraduate at Cambridge University. After dabbling for a time in worldly affairs, he entered the priesthood of the Church of England, to live out his days in a country parish. Herbert's poems have many references to music; according to his contemporary John Aubrey, he "had a very good hand on the lute, and set [to music] his own lyrics and sacred poems." Herbert did not publish his poems, but after his death friends collected them in *The Temple* (1633). The book is said to have stimulated Henry Vaughan to follow in Herbert's footsteps as a poet. Herbert makes the religious experience personal, definite, and familiar. For his use of startling "metaphysical" figures of speech, he has been compared with John Donne; but a rare sweetness and plain-spokenness make him unique among poets in English.

Robert Herrick

Robert Herrick (1591–1674), after serving as a goldsmith's apprentice, entered Cambridge University at twenty-two. For nine years he seems to have lived in London, consorting with a group of poets and wits whose chief was Ben Jonson. In 1629 he became parish priest in Dean Prior in rural Devonshire, where he lived out his days, sometimes chafing about the boorishness of his parishioners. When in 1647 the Puritans temporarily ousted him from his pulpit, Herrick returned to London. There at fifty-six, he published his first book, *Noble Numbers* (1647), all pious poems; he then reprinted them together with five times as many sportive, secular poems in *Hesperides* (1648). Unluckily, the books came too late to cause a stir, Herrick's early fame as a poet having withered and the vogue for chiseled classical lyrics having gone by. Like his master Jonson, Herrick writes song-like poems inspired by Greek and Latin pastoral (or shepherd-and-shepherdess) poetry. We go to him not for profound ideas, but for fresh, tough speech and resonant music. Herrick, who remained a bachelor, probably imagined the mistresses he praised. He declared in *Hesperides*, "To his book's end this last line he'd have placed: / Jocund his Muse was, but his life was chaste."

Gerard Manley Hopkins

Gerard Manley Hopkins (1844–1889), born in Essex, England, was, like Emily Dickinson, a major nineteenth-century poet not known until the following century. At twenty, a student at Oxford, he converted to Roman Catholicism and was received into that church by Cardinal Newman. Ordained a Jesuit, Hopkins at first served as a parish priest and teacher in working-class sections of large cities

(London, Glasgow, Liverpool, Manchester), where poverty and suffering distressed him. But his sermons were reportedly so strange (in one, he likened the church to a cow we milk and whose moo we follow) that his superiors removed him from public view, making him Professor of Greek at University College, Dublin. He died of typhoid fever at forty-four. Nearly thirty years after Hopkins's death, his friend Robert Bridges published his *Poems* (1918), having thought them too demanding for earlier readers. That much of Hopkins's work sounds odd to us may be due to the poet's admiration for Old English, with its gutsy monosyllables, and for Welsh poetry, rich in patterns of sound. Hopkins developed his own theory of versification, "sprung rhythm"—in brief, a kind of accentual verse. Though on entering the priesthood he had renounced poetry, he welcomed the suggestion of a superior that he contribute to a Jesuit magazine a poem on the drowning of five Franciscan nuns. The result, "The Wreck of the *Deutschland*," received a rejection slip. This challenging poem has been called "the dragon guarding the door to Hopkins's poetry," but most readers have gone in by the back door of his more quickly accessible nature poems. In these, the sensuous world bursts forth in irrepressible testimony to its Maker's glory.

A. E. Housman

A. E. Housman (1859–1936), English poet and professor of Latin, was born in a village in rural Shropshire, England. Although as a student at Oxford he distinguished himself as a promising scholar of the classics, he failed his exams, apparently because of some inner crisis precipitated by his love for a fellow male student. Determined to overcome this setback, Housman, while working as a clerk in the British patent office, at night wrote scholarly articles. Within ten years these academic writings, bristling with cold sarcasms and scathing putdowns of rival scholars, had won him such high repute that he was invited to be professor of Latin at the University of London. Later he moved on to the more prestigious Cambridge University, to spend the rest of his days living a retiring academic life befitting his shy temperament. Though Housman published only two slim collections of poems—the instantly and enormously popular *A Shropshire Lad* (1898) and the conclusively titled *Last Poems* (1922)—his place as a minor master of the English lyric seems unshakable. Like many Latin poets he admired, he insists in well-turned lines that life is short and comes to a bad end.

Langston Hughes

See biographical note on page 1116.

Kobayashi Issa

Issa (1763–1827) was born Yataro Kobayashi in Kashiwabara, a mountain village in central Japan. His father was an educated farmer; his mother died when he was only two years old, and he was raised by his grandmother. At fifteen, he became an apprentice in Edo (now Tokyo). His father, who loved poetry, supported his writing. On his father's death, however, Issa's relatives disputed the will. The settlement required the poet to share the family house with his wrangling clan—by dividing it down the middle.

His final years were scarred by the deaths of his first wife and infant children. The poet's pen name, Issa, means "cup of tea."

Robinson Jeffers

John Robinson Jeffers (1887–1962) was born in Pittsburgh, but completed part of his early education in European boarding schools. In 1903 Jeffers's family moved to Southern California, where he entered Occidental College. Graduating at nineteen, he studied medicine, forestry, and literature on a graduate level before devoting his life to poetry. In 1906 he met Una Kuster, who was married to an attorney. Their tempestuous love affair eventually led, in 1913, to their marriage. In 1914 the couple visited Carmel, California, and Jeffers knew that it was his "inevitable place"—he would spend his remaining fifty-eight years there. With the help of a local stonemason, he built his own house on the edge of the Pacific, quarrying stone from the beach. Jeffers's poetry reflects the closeness to nature that made up his daily life. His philosophy of "inhumanism" refused to put mankind above the rest of nature; he demanded that humanity see itself as part of the vast interdependent reality of nature— a message that has made his poetry esteemed by environmentalists. Jeffers's Tor House in Carmel is now a national historic monument.

Ben Jonson

Ben Jonson (1573?–1637), posthumous son of a Scottish minister, was a native Londoner. As a boy, he received a firm grounding in Latin and Greek at Westminster School, but instead of enrolling in a university, took up bricklaying, then served as a soldier in Flanders. Home from the wars, he married and became an actor and playwright in London. Although a coolly rational classicist by persuasion, Jonson seems to have been an outspoken hothead, given to quarrels and brawls. In 1598 he killed a fellow actor in a duel and escaped the gallows only by claiming an ancient law that forbade hanging anyone who could read. From about 1606, Jonson frequented the Mermaid Tavern in London's Fleet Street, a favorite hangout of writers and actors. There, on the first Friday of each month, he presided over famed literary discussions; according to one report, his friend Shakespeare would take part at times and match wits with him. Later changing pubs (to the Devil and St. Dunstan), Jonson and his circle became known as the "Tribe of Ben"; Thomas Carew and Robert Herrick were younger members. Later Jonson became the leading writer of masques, elaborate plays with music and dancing produced at Court. As a poet, Jonson, in his precise Latinate lyrics, odes, and epigrams, helped get rid of worn-out Petrarchan conventions (those that Shakespeare mocks in "My mistress' eyes are nothing like the sun"). As a playwright, he excelled; his comedies, especially *Volpone, or The Fox* (1606) and *The Alchemist* (1610), are among the crown jewels of the English stage.

Donald Justice

Donald Justice was born in Miami, Florida, in 1925. He attended public schools, hoping at first to become a composer, but gradually his interests turned toward literature. After graduating from the University of Miami in

1945, he did graduate work at both the University of North Carolina and Stanford University before finishing a Ph.D. at the University of Iowa. Having spent four decades as a professor of creative writing, Justice is widely regarded as the most influential poetry teacher of his generation. His presence in the Iowa Writers' Workshops from 1957 to 1982 helped build it into national prominence. He later taught at the University of Florida in Gainesville. Justice's first book, *The Summer Anniversaries* (1960), won the Lamont Award, and over the course of his career, virtually every other prominent poetry prize has followed, most notably the Pulitzer and Bollingen Prizes. Retired from teaching, Justice lives in Iowa City. His *New and Selected Poems* was published in 1995.

John Keats

John Keats (1795–1821), son of a London stable-keeper, studied to become a physician and served as a surgeon's apprentice before deciding on poetry as a career. In 1817 he published his first book, *Poems,* which included "On First Looking into Chapman's Homer." Despite critics' hostility to his narrative poem *Endymion* (1818), Keats persisted. In 1818 he fell in love with sixteen-year-old Fanny Brawne, but, stricken with tuberculosis, he postponed plans for marriage. In 1820, shortly after the publication of his third and last book, Keats went to Italy in hopes of regaining his health, but his poetry soon slowed to a stop. In the following year, at twenty-five, he died in Rome and was buried there beneath the epitaph he wrote for himself: "Here lies one whose name was writ in water." His name, how-ever, has continued to endure. No English poet wrote poems richer in sensuous imagery (as in his great odes, among them "Ode on Melancholy" and "To Autumn"), nor quite so beautifully reimagined the Middle Ages (in poems such as "La Belle Dame sans Merci" and "The Eve of St. Agnes"). He wrote several of the finest sonnets in the language; an unfinished epic of great interest, *Hyperion;* hilarious light verse; and scores of superb letters.

Ted Kooser

Ted Kooser, born in Ames, Iowa, in 1939, attended Iowa State University and then received a master's degree at the University of Nebraska in Lincoln. After teaching high school for one year, he took a job in the insurance industry in 1965 and has remained there ever since. Kooser's career, like his employment, has been unusual for an American poet. Although his early work gained little attention, his short, understated poems—many published by small presses—attracted a growing following. Kooser's poems are unmistakable. Brief, imagistic, and accessible, they usually describe a small everyday scene from American life in the Great Plains states, but midway there is almost always some unexpected but magical turn of imagination. Kooser lives on a small farm in Garland, Nebraska. His most recent book is *Braided Creek: A Conversation in Poetry* (2003), a collaboration with Jim Harrison.

Philip Larkin

Philip Larkin (1922–1985), born in Coventry, England, has been called the most influential British poet since

World War II. After studies at Oxford, he drifted into work as a librarian, and for many years was head librarian for the University of Hull. Early in his career Larkin wrote two novels, *Jill* (1946) and *A Girl in Winter* (1947). He also reviewed jazz recordings for a London newspaper. A self-declared foe of modernism in music, art, and literature, he published only four slim volumes of poems, traditional in form. The earliest collection was heavily indebted to Yeats: *The North Ship* (1945, which the author reissued in 1966 with a preface making fun of it). With *The Less Deceived* (1955), Larkin hit his characteristic stride, writing most of the poems in the voice of a tough-minded, disillusioned, self-deprecating man facing a dreary urban landscape of quiet frustration. This voice drew an immediate—and enduring—response from readers in postwar England.

D. H. Lawrence

David Herbert Lawrence (1885–1930) was born in Nottinghamshire, England, child of a coal-miner and a schoolteacher who hated her husband's toil and vowed that her son should escape it. He took up fiction writing, attaining early success. During World War I, Lawrence and his wife were unjustly suspected of treason (he because of his pacifism, she because of her aristocratic German birth). After the armistice they left England and, seeking a healthier climate for Lawrence, who suffered from tuberculosis, wandered in Italy, France, Australia, Mexico, and the American Southwest. Lawrence is an impassioned spokesman for our unconscious,

instinctive natures, which we moderns (he argues) have neglected in favor of our overweening intellects. In *Lady Chatterley's Lover* (1928), he strove to restore explicit sexuality to English fiction. The book, which today seems tame and repetitious, was long banned in Britain and the United States. Deeper Lawrence novels include *Sons and Lovers* (1913), a veiled account of his breaking away from his fiercely possessive mother; *The Rainbow* (1915); *Women in Love* (1921); and *The Plumed Serpent* (1926), about a revival of pagan religion in Mexico. Besides fiction, Lawrence left a rich legacy of poetry, essays, criticism (*Studies in Classic American Literature*, 1923, is especially shrewd and funny), and travel writing. Lawrence exerted deep influence on others, both by the message in his work and by his personal magnetism.

Denise Levertov

Denise Levertov (1923–1997) was born in Essex, England, daughter of a Welsh mother and a Russian Jewish-born priest of the Anglican church. She was educated at home, reading in her father's library. She served as a nurse in World War II. In 1947 she married an American novelist, Mitchell Goodman, and in the following year came to the United States. Her first book, published in England, had observed traditional poetic conventions (including rime and meter), but in America she discovered the work of William Carlos Williams and other open-form poets, and began to write in a different, freer mode. With Robert Creeley and others of the

Black Mountain group, she exerted much influence among younger poets. Her critical essays have been collected in *The Poet in the World* (1973) and *Light Up the Cave* (1981). Levertov was a tireless political activist, prominent in peace movements of the 1960s, 1970s, and 1980s.

Li Po

Very little is known with certainty about the life of Li Po (701–762), who is traditionally honored (with Tu Fu) as one of China's two greatest poets. He was probably born beyond the western borders of China in present-day Asiatic Russia. Having become famous in his youth for his poetry, he spent most of his later life wandering. His contemporaries considered his talent virtually supernatural, calling him the "Banished Immortal," a heavenly spirit who has been sent to earth as punishment for misbehavior, and Li Po was notorious for his heavy drinking. He was also careless about preserving his work, and the majority of his poems, which were sung or chanted, have been lost. Li Po died by drowning after falling into a river in a drunken attempt to embrace the moon's reflection.

Edna St. Vincent Millay

Edna St. Vincent Millay (1892–1950), born in Rockland, Maine, was the eldest of three daughters. When she was twelve, her father deserted the family. At twenty, she had already published "Renascence," one of her most celebrated poems. In 1917 she graduated from Vassar College and settled in Greenwich Village, where she became

as famous for her vivacious personality, her bohemian life-style, her acting and playwriting, and her feminism, as for her verse. Even as she wrote *The Harp Weaver,* a serious volume of verse that won her a Pulitzer Prize in 1923, Millay did hack writing to pay her bills. Among other work for which she is known are verse dramas such as *Aria da Capo* (1920) and the sonnet cycle *Fatal Interview* (1931). In 1923 she married Eugen Jan Boissevain, Dutch businessman and widower of feminist Inez Milholland. In 1927 Millay's political activism expressed itself in poems about Sacco and Vanzetti, two anarchists convicted of murder, and involved her in an unsuccessful campaign to prevent their execution. Though she kept writing poetry well into the 1940s and received several honorary degrees, her reputation waned. Depressed after a nervous breakdown in 1944, she was troubled by a growing sense that the public had deserted her. Millay's life ended with a heart attack at the age of fifty-eight.

John Milton

John Milton (1608–1674), author of *Paradise Lost*, the greatest English epic, was born in London, the son of a scrivener who composed music. His mother early began schooling him to be a minister. He studied zealously. As he later recalled: "From my twelfth year I scarcely ever went to bed before midnight, which was the first cause of injury to my eyes." After he received his B.A. from Cambridge University in 1629, his father supported him through eight years of further study.

"Lycidas" (1638), a poem of this period, shows his deepening seriousness about religion and his growing resentment of corruption within the church, which were to lead him to the Puritan cause. Milton wrote much prose in the service of causes. In *Areopagitica* (1644), he argues for freedom of the press and opposes the strict censorship that had been imposed by Parliament. His unhappy marriage to Mary Powell led him to write tracts in favor of divorce. When Oliver Cromwell and the Puritans ousted King Charles and declared England a commonwealth, Milton's writings were remembered, and earned him a post as Cromwell's foreign secretary. His eyesight strained by years of hard study, Milton went blind and had to dictate his correspondence (in Latin) to clerks, one of whom was fellow poet Andrew Marvell. With the Restoration of Charles II in 1660, Milton's world came crashing down. In retirement, at last he turned to a project he had planned as a young man: his major heroic poem, *Paradise Lost* (1667), about Satan's rebellion and the Fall of Adam and Eve. This epic was followed by *Paradise Regained* (1671) and a verse drama modeled on a Greek tragedy, *Samson Agonistes* (1671).

Marianne Moore

Marianne Moore (1887–1972), whose poems earned praise from fellow poets as dissimilar as William Carlos Williams and T. S. Eliot, was born in Kirkwood, Missouri, a suburb of St. Louis. Her father abandoned the family in 1894, and Moore moved to Pennsylvania. In 1909 she graduated from Bryn Mawr, where a classmate was the poet H. D. For a time, Moore taught business courses at the U.S. Indian School in Carlisle, Pennsylvania, where the athlete Jim Thorpe was among her students. By 1915 her poems—witty, satirical, intellectual, disruptive, and innovative—had begun to appear in *Poetry* magazine. Until her mother died in 1947, Moore, a dutiful daughter, lived with her in Brooklyn, supporting herself by a series of conventional jobs. From 1925 to 1929 she edited the *Dial*, a literary magazine in whose pages she published many of the best poets of her day. Besides poems, Moore wrote essays, reviews, and translations, including *The Fables of La Fontaine* (1945). For her *Collected Poems* (1951), she won a Pulitzer Prize, the Bollingen Prize, and a National Book Award; her *Complete Poems* appeared in 1967. Late in life, Moore became a media figure for her fondness for the Brooklyn Dodgers and her penchant for three-cornered hats. She stayed in Brooklyn, writing and rewriting, through an active and vigorous old age.

Marilyn Nelson

Born in Cleveland, Ohio, in 1946, Marilyn Nelson was the daughter of a U.S. Air Force serviceman. Raised on one military base after another, she attended the University of California at Davis for her B.A. and completed a Ph.D. at the University of Minnesota. She is also a seminary-trained Lutheran lay minister. Two of her books, *The Homeplace* (1990) and *The*

Fields of Praise: New and Selected Poems (1997), have been finalists for the National Book Award. She currently teaches at the University of Delaware.

Pablo Neruda

See biographical note on page 1045.

Lorine Niedecker

Lorine Niedecker (1903–1970) spent nearly all her life on Blackhawk Island near Fort Atkinson, Wisconsin, where her father worked as a carp fisherman. After two years at Beloit College, she returned home to care for her ailing mother. Following a brief marriage in 1928, Niedecker held jobs as a proofreader, librarian's assistant, and cleaning worker in a hospital. After her remarriage in 1963, she lived in Milwaukee, but on her husband's retirement the couple moved into a house they had built by the Rock River, and the poet returned to her native grounds. Although she lived an outwardly quiet life remote from publishing centers, Niedecker read widely and maintained a vigorous life of the mind. In the early 1930s she struck up a correspondence with poet and teacher Louis Zukofsky, who encouraged her poetry. In the 1950s poet Cid Corman printed her work in his avant-garde little magazine *Origin*. During her lifetime she published sparingly, but *From This Condensery: The Complete Writing of Lorine Niedecker* (1985) contains a large body of poems, as well as critical essays, experimental prose, and five radio plays. Her life and work are the subject of Kristine Thatcher's play *Niedecker*, given an off-Broadway production in 1989.

Sharon Olds

Sharon Olds was born in San Francisco in 1942 and attended Stanford University. After graduation in 1964, she moved East and eventually took a Ph.D. from Columbia University in 1972. Her first collection of poems, *Satan Says* (1980), was well received, but her second volume, *The Dead and the Living* (1984), scored a major critical success by winning both the Lamont Award and National Book Critics Circle Award. Olds's work often graphically depicts the passions, joys, and pain of family life. She currently teaches at New York University.

Wilfred Owen

Wilfred Owen (1893–1918) was, like A. E. Housman, a native of Shropshire, England. He attended London University and for a time served as lay assistant to a minister, helping the sick and poor. In 1916, during World War I, he enlisted in the British army, became a company commander, and in less than two years wrote all his famous antiwar poems of life in the trenches. The army seems suddenly to have changed Owen from a competent minor poet with little to say into a powerful voice of pacifism. At age twenty-five, while trying to get his men across a canal under enemy fire on the French front, he was killed in action only a week before the war ended. Though Owen published only four poems, after his death a collection of his work was edited by another front-line war poet, Siegfried Sassoon (1920). Owen is preeminent among English poets who wrote of that conflict, and the reputation of his work has continued to grow.

Octavio Paz

See biographical note on page 1052.

Sylvia Plath

Sylvia Plath (1932–1963), one of the most remarkable poets in English of the past half-century, was born in Boston, the daughter of German immigrants who both taught at Boston University. The death of her father when the poet was eight was a trauma from which she seems never quite to have recovered. As a scholarship-winning student at Smith College, Plath revealed early promise, and her work soon received publication. Like Esther Greenwood, protagonist of her one novel The Bell Jar (1963), Plath won a student contest that sent her to work in New York for a national magazine, and struggled with a year-long siege of mental illness for which she underwent shock treatments. Returning to Smith, she graduated with top honors. Later she studied at Cambridge University in England, where she met and in 1956 married the poet Ted Hughes. Estranged from her husband, she committed suicide in London, leaving two children and, in manuscript form, the intense, powerful poems that went into her posthumous, highly acclaimed collection, Ariel (1965).

Edgar Allan Poe

Edgar Allan Poe (1809–1849) was born in Boston, the son of itinerant actors. He lost his father in 1810 and his mother the next year. Taken in by a well-to-do Richmond merchant, Poe was given an excellent education, but he eventually dropped out of both the University of Virginia and West Point. He became a celebrated journalist, and he edited major journals such as Southern Literary Messenger, Burton's Gentleman's Magazine, and Broadway Journal, to which he contributed stories, poems, articles, and reviews. His romantic idealism, argumentative personality, heavy drinking, and difficult personal life, however, kept him from achieving financial security. After the death of his wife in 1847, Poe began drinking more heavily, and his mental and physical health deteriorated. He was only forty years old when he died in Baltimore on October 7, 1849. The exact circumstances of his death have never been adequately explained.

Alexander Pope

Alexander Pope (1688–1744), the leading English poet of the early eighteenth century, was born in London, son of a Roman Catholic linen merchant. A sickly, stunted, pockmarked child, he suffered from weak health and continual exhaustion throughout his life, and was said to have worn padded clothes to disguise his misshapen frame. Pope excelled early as a poet, composing his *Pastorals* (1709) at age sixteen. His rimed translations of the *Iliad* (1720) and the *Odyssey* (1725–1726) and his edition of Shakespeare (1725), best-sellers in their day, made him independently wealthy, and he was able to buy an estate at Twickenham and live in style. Pope did not write an epic, but instead translated epics and wrote great mock epics: *The Rape of the Lock* (1714), in which he voices compassion for women transformed into wives, and *The Dunciad* (1728–1743), in which he mocks his many literary enemies. He was a master satirist and splendid craftsman of the heroic couplet. Romantic critics generally think him no poet at all, but G. K. Chesterton remarked, "If Pope be not a poet, then who is?"

Ezra Pound

Ezra Pound (1885–1972), among the most influential (and still controversial) modern poets, was born in Hailey, Idaho. He readied himself for a teaching career, but when in 1907 he lost his job at Wabash College for sheltering a penniless prostitute, he left America. Settling in England and later in Paris, he wielded influence on the work of T. S. Eliot, whose long poem *The Waste Land* he edited; W. B. Yeats, whom he served as secretary and critic; and James Joyce. Pound was perpetually championing writers then unknown, such as Robert Frost. In 1924 Pound settled permanently in Italy, where he came to admire Mussolini's economic policies. During World War II he made broadcasts to America by Italian radio, deemed treasonous. When American armed forces

arrested him in 1945, Pound spent three weeks in a cage in an army camp in Pisa. Flown to the United States to stand trial, he was declared incompetent and for twelve years was confined in St. Elizabeths in Washington, a hospital for the criminally insane. In 1958, upon the intervention of Robert Frost, Archibald MacLeish, and other old friends, he was pronounced incurable and allowed to return to Italy to spend his last, increasingly silent years. In his prime, Pound was a swaggeringly confident critic, a berater of smugness and mediocrity, a delectable humorist. Among his lasting books are *Personae* (enlarged edition, 1949), short poems; *ABC of Reading* (1934), an introduction to poetry; and *Literary Essays* (1954). His *Cantos,* a vast poem woven of historical themes and published in installments over forty years, was never finished. Pound was a great translator of poetry from Italian, Provençal, Chinese, and other languages. Pare away his delusions, and a remarkable human being and splendid poet remains.

Dudley Randall

Dudley Randall (1914–2000) was born in Washington, D.C. He graduated from Wayne State University and the University of Michigan, and worked as librarian and poet-in-residence at the University of Detroit. A pioneer in the modern movement to publish the work of black writers, Randall founded what has been called the most influential small publishing house in America, Broadside Press. He also edited an important anthology, *The Black Poets* (1971). Randall's *A Litany of Friends: New and Selected Poems* was published in 1981.

Alastair Reid

Alastair Reid was born in Whithorn, Scotland, in 1926. His college work at St. Andrews was interrupted by service in the Royal Navy during World War II, but he eventually graduated with a degree in classics. After teaching for a few years in America, Reid began to spend part of each year in Majorca with Robert Graves, with whom he collaborated on translations and an opera libretto. Soon Reid became one of the most admired translators of Spanish-language poetry; his versions of the poetry of Pablo Neruda and Jorge Luis Borges are particularly noteworthy. His own poetry, collected in *Weatherings* (1978), is rich and arresting. For years Reid wrote for the *New Yorker*. Married twice, he has one son. He currently lives in the Dominican Republic.

Andrienne Rich

Adrienne Rich was born in Baltimore in 1929. Since the selection of her first volume by W. H. Auden for the Yale Series of Younger Poets in 1951, her work has continually broken new ground, moving from closed forms to feminist poetics and radical politics. A selection of her poems is collected in *The Fact of a Doorframe: Poems 1950–2001* (2002). Her prose works include *On Lies, Secrets, and Silence* (1979), *Blood, Bread, and Poetry* (1986), and *What Is Found There* (1993). Her work has received many awards—most notably the Lenore Marshall / Nation Award, the Lambda

Literary Award, the Frost Medal from the Poetry Society of America, the Wallace Stevens Award of the Academy of American Poets, the Lannan Foundation Lifetime Achievement Award, and the Bollingen Prize.

Edwin Arlington Robinson

Edwin Arlington Robinson (1869–1935) was raised in Gardiner, Maine, the model for Tilbury Town, the setting for many of his poems. After a stint at Harvard, Robinson moved to New York City. Initially, he published three books, but slowly sank into poverty and alcoholism. In 1902 President Theodore Roosevelt discovered Robinson's work and obtained for him a government position with virtually no duties. Robinson used this fortunate intercession to embark on a series of literary projects, and he gradually became the most widely esteemed American poet of the early twentieth century. He won the Pulitzer Prize three times in seven years, and his long poem *Tristram* (1927) became a best-seller. Although Robinson's work has suffered from critical neglect in recent years, he remains an important American poet. His austere style, penetrating psychology, and bitter realism represent a turning point in American poetry from nineteenth-century romanticism to the threshold of modernism. His work decisively influenced the poetry of Robert Frost.

Theodore Roethke

Theodore Roethke (1908–1963) was born in Saginaw, Michigan, where his family ran a large greenhouse. (No poet seems wealthier in his knowledge of vegetation.) He went to the University of Michigan and (for a year) to Harvard. As a young poet teaching college at a time when creative writing teachers without Ph.D.s were suspect, Roethke held impermanent jobs before coming to rest at the University of Washington in Seattle. There, from 1947 until his death, he was an influential teacher of poetry and poetry writing; among his students were Carolyn Kizer, David Wagoner, and James Wright. Roethke was a large, heavyset man light on his feet (he once coached varsity tennis at Lafayette), and would sometimes prepare for a poetry reading by pacing the stage like an athlete warming up. His poetry developed from rather conventional and imitative lyrics through a phase of disconnected stream of consciousness into (at the end) a meditative poetry reminiscent in its open lines of Walt Whitman's.

Kay Ryan

Kay Ryan was born in San Jose, California, in 1945 and was raised in the dry landscapes of the San Joaquin Valley and Mojave Desert. She studied literature in college but never took a writing course. For the past twenty years she has taught remedial English at the College of Marin, a two-year public college, and has also taught writing at San Quentin Prison. Ryan's literary career was slow in building. Her first book was privately printed, but her short and evocatively compressed poetry has slowly gained her a significant reputation. Her recent books include *Elephant Rocks* (1996) and *Say Uncle* (2000). She lives in Fairfax, California.

Carl Sandburg

The first important American poet to be raised in a home where English was a second language, Carl Sandburg (1878–1967) was born in Galesburg, Illinois, the oldest of seven children of poor Swedish immigrants. Leaving school after the eighth grade, he had many jobs, including milkman, bricklayer, and farm laborer. After serving in the Spanish-American War, he paid his way through college by working as a fireman. Sandburg achieved fame with the publication of *Chicago Poems* (1916), which established him as the leading populist in Modernist American poetry. A handsome, charismatic man, he toured the nation reciting his poems and singing folksongs. He won the Pulitzer Prize not only in poetry but also in history, for his multivolume biography of Abraham Lincoln.

Anne Sexton

Anne Sexton (1928–1974) was born in Newton, Massachusetts, to an old and prominent New England family. She attended boarding school and finishing school, but never went on to college. In 1948 she eloped with Alfred Sexton (always known as "Kayo" to his wife and family). Beautiful, elegant, and commanding, Sexton dreamed of becoming a model, but shortly after the birth of her second daughter she suffered the first of many nervous breakdowns. Her fragile mental health would take her in and out of hospitals for the rest of her life. After watching a television program on "How to Write a Sonnet" in 1956, Sexton, encouraged by her psychiatrist, began composing poetry. Dedicating herself to writing, she made astonishing progress and soon published her work in leading journals and magazines such as the *Hudson Review* and the *New Yorker*. Her strongly emotional and confessional poems earned her wide acclaim, and her third volume, *Live or Die* (1967), won the Pulitzer Prize. Fame, however, could not assuage the pain of her troubled psyche or the increasing disorder of her personal life. In October 1974 Sexton committed suicide. She was only forty-five years old.

William Shakespeare

William Shakespeare (1564–1616), the supreme writer of English, was born, baptized, and buried in the market town of Stratford-on-Avon, eighty miles from London. Son of a glovemaker and merchant who was high bailiff (or mayor) of the town, he probably attended grammar school and learned to read Latin authors in the original. At eighteen, he married Anne Hathaway, twenty-six, by whom he had three children, including twins. By 1592 he had become well known and envied as an actor and playwright in London. From 1594 until he retired, he belonged to the same theatrical company, the Lord Chamberlain's Men (later renamed the King's Men in honor of their patron, James I), for whom he wrote thirty-six plays—some of them, such as *Hamlet* and *King Lear*, profound reworkings of old plays. As an actor, Shakespeare is believed to have played supporting roles, such as the ghost of Hamlet's father. The company prospered, moved into the Globe in 1599, and in 1608 bought the fashionable Blackfriars as well; Shakespeare owned an interest in both theaters. When plagues shut down the theaters from 1592 to 1594, Shakespeare turned to poetry; his great *Sonnets* (not published until 1609) probably date from the 1590s. Plays were regarded as entertainments of little literary merit, like comic books today, and Shakespeare did not bother to supervise their publication. He did, however, carefully see through press his sonnets and the narrative poems *Venus and Adonis* (1593) and *The Rape of Lucrece* (1594).

Stevie Smith

Stevie Smith (1902–1971) was born in Hull, Yorkshire, christened Florence Margaret Smith. Being wiry and short, she acquired her nickname from a popular jockey, Stevie Donahue. For more than sixty years, beginning at age three, Smith lived with her aunt in Palmers Green, a suburb of London, and worked for thirty years as a publisher's secretary. *Novel on Yellow Paper* (1936) is the best known of her three novels. Her poetry readings, in public and on BBC radio, widened her audience. *Collected Poems* (1976) is illustrated with her own witty, slapdash, and rakishly charming drawings. *Me Again: Uncollected Writings* (1982) contains poems, stories, essays, and a play for radio. In the film *Stevie* (1978), based on a stage play by Hugh Whitemore, Glenda Jackson plays the poet with keen insight and power.

Sor Juana

See biographical note on page 1043.

William Stafford

William Stafford (1914–1993), born in Hutchinson, Kansas, graduated from the University of Kansas and later took a doctorate at the University of Iowa. During World War II he was interned as a conscientious objector, an experience he recalls in his prose memoir *Down in My Heart* (1947). For many years he taught at Lewis and Clark College in Portland, Oregon, and in 1970 and 1971 he served as Consultant in Poetry for the Library of Congress. *Traveling Through the Dark* (1962) won the National Book Award, and in 1977 Stafford published a large volume of his collected poems, *Stories That Could Be True*. In much of his work he traced the landscapes of the Midwest and of the Pacific Northwest, where he long lived. He described his poetry as "much like talk, with some enhancement." Shortly before his death in 1993, Stafford was chosen in a national poll of American writers as the poet most highly regarded by his peers.

Timothy Steele

Timothy Steele was born in Burlington, Vermont, in 1948. He did his undergraduate work at Stanford. After taking his doctorate in English at Brandeis, where he studied with J. V. Cunningham, Steele returned to California, where he has taught ever since. His first book of poems, *Uncertainties and Rest*, appeared in 1979 and has been followed by two other collections. His study *Missing Measures: Modern Poetry and the Revolt Against Meter* (1990) has been one of the most influential books of literary history of recent years. Steele writes exclusively in traditional forms. His work is characterized by a Yankee reticence and a precise but understated style that holds considerable power within these strict limits. He currently teaches at California State University, Los Angeles.

James Stephens

James Stephens (1882–1950), born in Dublin, Ireland, was a famous member of the Irish Literary Renaissance, a movement early in the century that included William Butler Yeats and the playwrights Lady Gregory, J. M. Synge, and Sean O'Casey. As a young man, Stephens took a job as a typist in a lawyer's office, where access to a typewriter started him writing fantastic fiction, some of it based on Irish folklore, such as his most popular novel, *The Crock of Gold* (1912). Other imaginative novels followed, including *The Demi-Gods* (1914) and *Deirdre* (1923). *Irish Fairy Tales* (1920) retells classic legends for young readers. Although best remembered for such books, Stephens was a considerable poet as well. His first collection appeared in 1909, and in 1926 he published his *Collected Poems*. Some of his poems are actually free translations from the Irish: "A Glass of Beer," for instance, is a version of a seventeenth-century poem by Dáibhí Ó Bruadair.

Wallace Stevens

Wallace Stevens (1879–1955) was born in Reading, Pennsylvania; his father was a successful lawyer; his mother, a former schoolteacher. As a special student at Harvard, he became president of the student literary magazine, the *Harvard Advocate*, but he did not want a liberal arts degree. Instead, he became a lawyer in New York City, and in 1916 joined the legal staff of the Hartford Accident and Indemnity Company. In 1936 he was elected a vice president. Stevens, who would write poems in his head while walking to work and then dictate them to his secretary, was a leading expert on surety claims. Once asked how he was able to combine poetry and insurance, he replied that the two occupations had an element in common: "calculated risk." As a young man in New York, Stevens made lasting friendships with the poets Marianne Moore and William Carlos Williams, but he did not seek literary society. Though his poems are full of references to Europe and remote places, his only travels were annual vacation trips to Key West. He printed his early poems in *Poetry* magazine, but did not publish a book until *Harmonium* appeared in 1923, when he was forty-four. Living quietly in Hartford, Connecticut, Stevens sought to discover order in a chaotic world with his subtle and exotic imagination. His critical essays, collected in *The Necessary Angel* (1951), and his *Letters* (1966), edited by his daughter Holly Stevens, reveal a penetrating, philosophic mind. His *Collected Poems* (1954), published on his seventy-fifth birthday, garnered important prizes and belated recognition for Stevens as a major American poet.

Anne Stevenson

Anne Stevenson is the quintessential transatlantic poet. Born in England in 1933 of American parents, she was educated in the United States. After graduating from the University of Michigan, she returned to England. She has taught in both countries and now lives in Durham, England. Combining two cultures in her background, Stevenson has also combined the careers of scholar and poet. In 1966 she published the first full-length study of Elizabeth Bishop, and in 1989 she released *Bitter Fame: A Life of Sylvia Plath*, a controversial but authoritative biography. Stevenson's *Collected Poems* appeared in 1996. Gathering poems from her ten previous books of verse, this substantial volume confirmed her position as a major contemporary poet.

Alfred, Lord Tennyson

Alfred Tennyson (1809–1892) was born in Lincolnshire, England, the son of an alcoholic rural minister. When Queen Victoria made him a baron in 1883 (at seventy-five), he added the "Lord" to his byline. A precocious poet, Tennyson began writing verse at five, and while still in his teens collaborated with his brother Charles on *Poems by Two Brothers* (1827). As a student at Cambridge, he was unusual: he kept a snake for a pet, won a medal for poetry, and left without earning a degree. But in college he made influential friendships, especially that of Arthur Hallam, whose death in 1833 inspired Tennyson's *In Memoriam* (1850), the elegiac sequence that contains "Dark house by which once more I stand." The year 1850 was a banner one for Tennyson in other ways: he at last felt prosperous enough to marry Emily Sellwood, who had remained engaged to him for fourteen years, and Queen Victoria named him poet laureate, in which capacity he served for four decades, writing poems for state occasions. Between 1859 and 1888 Tennyson completed *Idylls of the King*, a twelve-part narrative poem about Arthur and his Round Table. In his mid-sixties he wrote several plays. A spokesman for the Victorian age and its militant colonialism, Tennyson is still respected as a poet of varied assets, including an excellent ear.

Dylan Thomas

Dylan Thomas (1914–1953) was born in the coastal town of Swansea, Wales, the son of a teacher of English. Much of Thomas's life was a bitter struggle to support his wife and children, a struggle intensified by his fondness for spending freely. Lacking a university education, Thomas found most paying literary work barred to him in Britain, although late in life he received many assignments to write film and radio scripts. A resonant reader-aloud of poetry, he made broadcasts for BBC radio and undertook several immensely popular reading tours of America, preceded by a reputation for heavy drinking and gustatorial lovemaking. He died in a hospital in New York City after drinking a procession of straight whiskeys, apparently courting the end. Thomas wrote not only poems (in the early ones he brought surrealism into English poetry), but also remarkable stories and a "play for voices," *Under Milk Wood* (1954), based on memories of his home town in Wales.

John Updike

John Updike, born in Pennsylvania in 1932, is primarily regarded as a novelist. But his first book was verse, *The Carpentered Hen* (1954), from which we take "Ex-Basketball Player"; and ever since, he has continued to produce verse both light and serious. He received his B.A. from Harvard, then went to Oxford to study drawing and fine art. From 1955 to 1957 he worked on the staff of the *New Yorker*. Though he left the magazine to write full-time, he has continued to supply it with bright stories and searching book reviews. Updike has published nearly fifty books. His *Collected Poems* was published in 1993. His most recent volume of verse is *Americana* (2001).

Walt Whitman

Walt Whitman (1819–1892) was born on Long Island, son of an impoverished farmer. He spent his early years as a school teacher, a temperance propagandist, a carpenter, a printer, and a newspaper editor on the Brooklyn *Eagle*. He began writing poetry in his youth, sometimes declaiming his lines above the crash of waves on New York beaches. Apparently he was also inspired to write wide, spacious, confident lines by attending performances of Italian opera. His self-published *Leaves of Grass* (1855) won praise from Ralph Waldo Emerson and gained Whitman readers in England. For the rest of his life, he kept revising and enlarging it, ceasing only with a ninth or "deathbed edition" in 1891–1892. Americans at first were slow to accept Whitman's unconventionally open verse forms, his sexual frankness, and his gregarious egoism. The poet of boundless faith in American democracy, Whitman tempered his vision by his experiences as a volunteer hospital nurse during the Civil War (described in his poems *Drum-Taps* and his wartime letters). After the war, he held secretarial jobs to support himself, and lost one such job when his employer's scandalized eye fell upon the *Leaves*. In old age, a semi-invalid after a stroke, Whitman made his home in Camden, New Jersey. Before he died, he saw his work finally winning respect and worldwide acceptance. Whitman's influence on later American poetry has been profound, both by the example of his open forms and by his bold encompassing of subject matter that had formerly been considered unpoetic. (In "Song of the Exposition," read aloud at an industrial show in New York, the poet exclaims of his Muse: "She's here, install'd amid the kitchen ware!")

Richard Wilbur

Richard Wilbur, born in 1921 in New York City, graduated from Amherst College, then served in the army during World War II. He has taught English at Harvard, Wellesley, Wesleyan, and Smith. With his first two collections, *The Beautiful Changes* (1947) and *Ceremony* (1950), Wilbur acquired a high reputation for a poetry of sensitivity, wit, grace, and command of traditional forms. Besides writing poetry, for which he has received many prizes, including two Pulitzer Prizes and a National Book Award, he has edited the poetry of Shakespeare and Poe. He has written song lyrics for *Candide*, a Broadway musical by Lillian Hellman and Leonard Bernstein (1956); *Loudmouse*, a story for children (1963); *Responses*, literary criticism (1976); and he has translated plays of Molière and Racine into wonderfully skillful English verse. He divides his time between Cummington, Massachusetts, where he has a home adjacent to an apple orchard, and Key West, Florida. In 1987 he was named United States poet laureate by the Library of Congress. His *New and Collected Poems* (1988) gathers most of his original work in poetry.

William Carlos Williams

William Carlos Williams (1883–1963) was born in Rutherford, New Jersey, where he remained in later life as a practicing pediatrician. While studying for his M.D. degree at the University of Pennsylvania, he made friends with the poets Ezra Pound and H. D. (Hilda Doolittle). Surprisingly prolific for a busy doctor, Williams wrote (besides poetry) novels and short stories, plays, criticism, and essays in history (*In the American Grain*, 1939). He kept a fliptop desk in his office and between patients would haul out his typewriter and dash off poems. His encouragement of younger poets, among them Allen Ginsberg (whose doctor he was when Ginsberg was a baby), and the long-sustained example of his formally open poetry made him an appealing father figure to the generation of the Beat poets and the Black Mountain poets—Ginsberg, Gary Snyder, and Robert Creeley. But he also had great influence on Robert Lowell, and on an entire younger generation of American poets in our day. Williams believed in truth-telling about ordinary life, championed plain speech "out of the mouths of Polish mothers," and insisted that there can be "no ideas but in things." Combining poetry with prose (including documents and statistics), his long poem in five parts, *Paterson* (1946–1958), explores the past, present, and future of the New Jersey industrial city near which Williams lived for most of his days.

William Wordsworth

William Wordsworth (1770–1850) was born in England's Lake District, whose landscapes and people were to inform many of his poems. As a young man, he visited France, sympathized with the Revolution, and met a young Frenchwoman who bore him a child. The Reign of Terror prevented him from returning to France, and he and Annette Vallon never married. With his sister Dorothy (1771–1855), his lifelong intellectual companion and the author of remarkable journals, he settled in Dorsetshire. Later they moved to Grasmere, in the Lake District, where Wordsworth lived the rest of his life. In 1798 his friendship with Samuel Taylor Coleridge resulted in their joint publication of *Lyrical Ballads*, a book credited with introducing Romanticism to English poetry. (Wordsworth contributed "Tintern Abbey" and other poems.) To the second edition of 1800, Wordsworth supplied a preface calling for a poetry written "in the real language of men." Time brought him a small official job, a marriage, a swing from left to right in his political sentiments, and appointment as poet laureate. Although he kept on writing, readers have generally preferred his earlier poems. *The Prelude*, a long poem-memoir completed in 1805, did not appear until after the poet's death. One of the most original of writers, Wordsworth—especially for his poems of nature and simple rustics—occupies a popular place in English poetry, much like that of Robert Frost in America.

James Wright

James Wright (1927–1980) was born in Martins Ferry, Ohio. After taking his doctorate at the University of Washington, where he studied with Theodore Roethke, he taught at the University of Minnesota, Macalester College, and Hunter College in New York. His first book *A Green Wall* (1957), in the Yale Series of Younger Poets, established him as a traditional formalist of great skill. With Robert Bly, by whom he was persuaded to branch out of traditional forms, he translated the poems of César Vallejo, Pablo Neruda, and Georg Trakl. In 1972 he received the Pulitzer Prize for his *Collected Poems*. Wright was a memorable teacher, a great quoter of poetry from memory, and a fine critic. "I try and say how I love my country and how I despise the way it is treated," he declared. "I try and speak of the beauty and again of the ugliness in the lives of the poor and neglected."

Sir Thomas Wyatt

Sir Thomas Wyatt (1503?–1542) was both poet and man of action: diplomat, soldier, and courtier. He was born in his father's castle in Kent, England, and, as a boy, he was sent to Court. In 1516 he entered St. John's College, Cambridge. Wyatt twice saw the inside of prison when he slipped from the favor of King Henry VIII. He is thought to have been a lover of Anne Boleyn, later the king's wife, a fact that perhaps affects some of his remarkable love lyrics. A prominent man in Tudor England, Wyatt carried out diplomatic missions, served as ambassador to Spain, was a member of Parliament and the king's privy council, and was Commander of the Fleet. His mission to Italy in 1527 had great consequence for English poetry, for he brought back knowledge of the works of Petrarch and other Italian love poets. In imitation of them, Wyatt wrote some of the first sonnets in our language—also lyrics, rondels, satires, and psalms.

William Butler Yeats

William Butler Yeats (1865–1939), poet and playwright, an Irishman of English ancestry, was born in Dublin, the son of painter John Butler Yeats. For a time he studied art himself and was irregularly schooled in Dublin and in London. Early in life Yeats sought to transform Irish folklore and legend into mellifluous poems. He overcame shyness to take an active part in cataclysmic events: he became involved in the movement for an Irish nation (partly drawn into it by his unrequited love for Maud Gonne, a crusading nationalist) and in founding the Irish Literary Theatre (1898) and the Irish National Theatre, which in 1904 moved to the renowned Abbey Theatre in Dublin. Dublin audiences were difficult: in 1899 they jeered Yeats's first play, *The Countess Cathleen,* for portraying a woman who, defying the church, sells her soul to the devil to buy bread for starving peasants. Eventually Yeats retired from the fray, to write plays presented in drawing rooms, such as *Purgatory.* After the establishment of the Irish Free State, Yeats served as a senator (1922–1928). His lifelong interest in the occult culminated in his writing of *A Vision* (1925), a view of history as governed by the phases of the moon; Yeats believed the book was inspired by spirit masters who dictated communications to his wife Georgie Hyde-Lees. Had Yeats stopped writing in 1900, he would be remembered as an outstanding minor Victorian. Instead, he went on to become one of the most influential poets of the twentieth century.

DRAMA

Tennessee Williams in Key West, Florida, January 1, 1970.

Drama is life with the dull bits left out.
—Alfred Hitchcock

Unlike a short story or a novel, a **play** is a work of storytelling in which actors represent the characters. In another essential, a play differs from a work of fiction: it is addressed not to readers but to spectators.

To be part of an audience in a theater is an experience far different from reading a story in solitude. Expectant as the house lights dim and the curtain rises, we become members of a community. The responses of people around us affect our own responses. We, too, contribute to the community's response whenever we laugh, sigh, applaud, murmur in surprise, or catch our breath in excitement. In contrast, when we watch a movie by ourselves in our living room—say, a slapstick comedy—we probably laugh less often than if we were watching the same film in a theater, surrounded by a roaring crowd. Of course, no one is spilling popcorn down the back of our necks. Each kind of theatrical experience, to be sure, has its advantages.

A theater of live actors has another advantage: a sensitive give-and-take between actors and audience. Such rapport, of course, depends on the actors being skilled and the audience being perceptive. Although professional actors may try to give a first-rate performance on all occasions, it is natural for them to feel more keenly inspired by a lively, appreciative audience than by a dull, lethargic one. No doubt a large turnout of spectators also helps draw the best from performers on stage: the *Othello* you get may be somewhat less inspired if there are more people in the cast than the audience. At any rate, as veteran playgoers well know, something unique and wonderful can happen when good actors and a good audience respond to each other.

In another sense, a play is more than actors and audience. Like a short story or a poem, a play is a work of art made of words. The playwright devoted thought and care and skill to the selection and arrangement of language. Watching a play, of course, we do not notice the playwright standing between us and the characters.[1] If the play is absorbing, it flows before our eyes. In a silent reading, the usual play consists mainly of **dialogue,**[2] exchanges of speech, punctuated by stage directions. In performance, though, stage directions vanish. And although the thoughtful efforts of perhaps a hundred people—actors, director, producer, stage designer, costumer, makeup artist, technicians—may have gone into a production, a successful play makes us forget its artifice. We may even forget that the play is literature, for its gestures, facial expressions, bodily stances, lighting, and special effects are as much a part of it as the playwright's written words. Even though words are not all there is to

---

[1] The word *playwright*, by the way, invites misspelling. Notice that it is not *playwrite*. The suffix *-wright* (from Old English) means "one who makes"—such as a *boatwright*, a worker in a trade.
[2] Not all plays employ dialogue. There is also **pantomime**—generally, a play without words (sometimes also called a **dumb show**). Originally, in ancient Rome, a pantomime meant an actor who single-handedly played all the parts. An eminent modern pantomime (or **mime**) was French stage and screen actor Marcel Marceau.

a living play, they are its bones. And the whole play, the finished production, is the total of whatever takes place on stage.

The sense of immediacy we derive from **drama** is suggested by the root of the word. *Drama* means "action" or "deed" (from the Greek *dran*, "to do"). We use *drama* as a synonym for *plays*, but the word has several meanings. Sometimes it refers to one play ("a stirring drama"); or to the work of a playwright, or **dramatist** ("Ibsen's drama"); or perhaps to a body of plays written in a particular time or place ("Elizabethan drama," "French drama of the seventeenth century"). In yet another familiar sense, *drama* often means events that elicit high excitement: "A real-life drama," a news story might begin, "was enacted today before lunchtime crowds in downtown Manhattan as firefighters battled to free two children trapped on the sixteenth floor of a burning building." In this sense, whatever is "dramatic" implies suspense, tension, or conflict. Plays, as we shall see, frequently contain such "dramatic" chains of events; and yet, if we expect all plays to be crackling with suspense or conflict, we may be disappointed. "Good drama," said critic George Jean Nathan, "is anything that interests an intelligently emotional group of persons assembled together in an illuminated hall."

In partaking of the nature of ritual—something to be repeated in front of an audience on a special occasion—drama is akin to a festival (whether a religious festival or a rock festival) or a church service. Twice in the history of Europe, drama has sprung forth as a part of worship: when, in ancient Greece, plays were performed on feast days; and when, in the Christian church of the Middle Ages, a play was introduced as an adjunct to the Easter mass with the enactment of the meeting between the three Marys and the angel at Jesus' empty tomb. Evidently, something in drama remains constant over the years—something as old, perhaps, as the deepest desires and highest aspirations of humanity.

33 *Reading a Play*

Most plays are written not to be read in books but to be performed. Finding plays in a literature anthology, the student may well ask: isn't there something wrong with the idea of reading plays on the printed page? Isn't that a perversion of their nature?

True, plays are meant to be seen on stage, but equally true, reading a play may afford advantages. One is that it is better to know some masterpieces by reading them than never to know them at all. Even if you live in a large city with many theaters, even if you attend a college with many theatrical productions, to succeed in your lifetime in witnessing, say, all the plays of Shakespeare might well be impossible. In print, they are as near to hand as a book on a shelf, ready to be enacted (if you like) on the stage of the mind.

After all, a play is literature before it comes alive in a theater, and it might be argued that when we read an unfamiliar play, we meet it in the same form in which it first appears to its actors and its director. If a play is rich and complex or if it dates from the remote past and contains difficulties of language and allusion, to read it on the page enables us to study it at our leisure and return to the parts that demand greater scrutiny.

Let us admit, by the way, that some plays, whatever the intentions of their authors, are destined to be read more often than they are acted. Such a play is sometimes called a **closet drama**—*closet* meaning "a small, private room." Percy Bysshe Shelley's neo-Shakespearean tragedy *The Cenci* (1819) has seldom escaped from its closet, even though Shelley tried without luck to have it performed on the London stage. Perhaps too rich in talk to please an audience or too sparse in opportunities for actors to use their bodies, such works nevertheless may lead long, respectable lives on their own, solely as literature.

But even if a play may be seen in a theater, sometimes to read it in print may be our way of knowing it as the author wrote it in its entirety. Far from regarding Shakespeare's words as holy writ, producers of *Hamlet, King Lear, Othello,* and other masterpieces often leave out whole speeches and scenes, or shorten them. Besides, the nature of the play, as far as you can tell from a stage production, may depend on decisions of the director. Shall Othello dress as a Renaissance Moor or as a modern general? Every actor who plays Iago in *Othello* makes his own interpretation of this knotty character. Some see Iago as a figure of pure evil; others, as a madman; still others, as a suffering human being consumed by hatred, jealousy, and pride. What do you think Shakespeare meant? You can always read the play and decide for yourself. If every stage production of a play is a fresh interpretation, so, too, is every reader's reading of it.

Some readers, when silently reading a play to themselves, try to visualize a stage, imagining the characters in costume and under lights. If such a reader is an actor or a director and is reading the play with an eye toward staging it, then he or she may try to imagine every detail of a possible production, even shades of makeup and the loudness of sound effects. But the nonprofessional reader, who regards the play as literature, need not attempt such exhaustive imagining. Although some readers find it enjoyable to imagine the play taking place on a stage, others prefer to imagine the people and events that the play brings vividly to mind. Sympathetically following the tangled life of Nora in *A Doll's House* by Henrik Ibsen, we forget that we are reading printed stage directions and instead find ourselves in the presence of human conflict. Thus regarded, a play becomes a form of storytelling, and the playwright's instructions to the actors and the director become a conventional mode of narrative that we accept much as we accept the methods of a novel or short story. If we read *A Doll's House* caring more about Nora's fate than the imagined appearance of an actress portraying her, we speed through an ordinary passage such as this (from a scene in which Nora's husband hears the approach of an unwanted caller, Dr. Rank):

> Helmer (*with quiet irritation*): Oh, what does he want now? (*Aloud.*) Hold on.
> (*Goes and opens the door.*) Oh, how nice that you didn't just pass us by!

We read the passage, if the story absorbs us, as though we were reading a novel whose author, employing the conventional devices for recording speech in fiction, might have written:

> "Oh, what does he want now?" said Helmer under his breath, in annoyance. Aloud, he called, "Hold on." Then he walked to the door and opened it and greeted Rank with all the cheer he could muster—"Oh, how nice that you didn't just pass us by!"

Such is the power of an excellent play to make us ignore the playwright's artistry that it becomes a window through which the reader's gaze, given focus, encompasses more than language and typography and beholds a scene of imagined life.

Most plays, whether seen in a theater or in print, employ *some* **conventions:** customary methods of presenting an action, usual and recognizable devices that an audience is willing to accept. In reading a great play from the past, such as *Oedipus the King* or *Othello,* it will help if we know some of the conventions of the classical Greek theater or the Elizabethan theater. When in *Oedipus the King* we encounter a character called the Chorus, it may be useful to be aware that this is a group of citizens who stand to one side of the action, conversing with the principal character and commenting. In *Othello,* when the sinister Iago, left on stage alone, begins to speak (at the end of Act I, Scene 3, we recognize the conventional device of a **soliloquy,** a dramatic monologue in which we seem to overhear the character's inmost thoughts uttered aloud. Like conventions in poetry, such familiar methods of staging a narrative afford us a happy shock of recognition. Often, as in these examples, they are ways of making clear to us exactly what the playwright would have us know.

A PLAY IN ITS ELEMENTS

When we read a play on the printed page and find ourselves swept forward by the motion of its story, we need not wonder how—and from what ingredients—the playwright put it together. Still, to analyze the structure of a play is one way to understand and appreciate a playwright's art. Analysis is complicated, however, because in an excellent play the elements (including plot, theme, and characters) do not stand in isolation. Often, deeds clearly follow from the kinds of people the characters are, and from those deeds it is left to the reader to infer the **theme** of the play—the general point or truth about human beings that may be drawn from it. Perhaps the most meaningful way to study the elements of a play (and certainly the most enjoyable) is to consider a play in its entirety.

Here is a short, famous one-act play worth reading for the boldness of its elements—and for its own sake. *Trifles* tells the story of a murder. As you will discover, the "trifles" mentioned in its title are not of trifling stature. In reading the play, you will probably find yourself imagining what you might see on stage if you were in a theater. You may also care to imagine what took place in the lives of the characters before the curtain rose. All this imagining may sound like a tall order, but don't worry. Just read the play for enjoyment the first time through, and then we will consider what makes it effective.

Susan Glaspell

TRIFLES   1916

Susan Glaspell (1882–1948) grew up in her native Davenport, Iowa, daughter of a grain dealer. After four years at Drake University and a reporting job in Des Moines, she settled in New York's Greenwich Village. In 1915, with her husband George Cram Cook, a theatrical director, she founded the Provincetown Players, the first influential noncommercial theater troupe in America. Summers, in a makeshift playhouse on a Cape Cod pier, the Players staged the earliest plays of Eugene O'Neill and works by John Reed, Edna St. Vincent Millay, and Glaspell herself. (Later transplanting the company to New York, Glaspell and Cook renamed it the Playwrights' Theater.) Glaspell wrote several still-remembered plays, among them a pioneering work of feminist drama, The Verge (1921), and the Pulitzer Prize-winning Alison's House (1930), about the family of a reclusive poet like Emily Dickinson who, after her death, squabble over the right to publish her poems. First widely known for her fiction with an Iowa background, Glaspell wrote ten novels, including Fidelity *(1915) and* The Morning Is Near Us *(1939). Shortly after writing the play* Trifles, *she rewrote it as a short story, "A Jury of Her Peers."*

Characters

George Henderson, county attorney
Henry Peters, sheriff
Lewis Hale, a neighboring farmer
Mrs. Peters
Mrs. Hale

Scene. *The kitchen in the now abandoned farmhouse of John Wright, a gloomy kitchen, and left without having been put in order—unwashed pans under the sink, a loaf of bread outside the breadbox, a dish towel on the table—other signs of incompleted work. At the rear the outer door opens and the Sheriff comes in followed by the County Attorney and Hale. The Sheriff and Hale are men in middle life, the County Attorney is a young man; all are much bundled up and go at once to the stove. They are followed by two women—the Sheriff's wife first; she is a slight wiry woman, a thin nervous face. Mrs. Hale is larger and would ordinarily be called more comfortable looking, but she is disturbed now and looks fearfully about as she enters. The women have come in slowly, and stand close together near the door.*

County Attorney: [*Rubbing his hands.*] This feels good. Come up to the fire, ladies.
Mrs. Peters: [*After taking a step forward.*] I'm not—cold.
Sheriff: [*Unbuttoning his overcoat and stepping away from the stove as if to mark the beginning of official business.*] Now, Mr. Hale, before we move things about, you explain to Mr. Henderson just what you saw when you came here yesterday morning.
County Attorney: By the way, has anything been moved? Are things just as you left them yesterday?
Sheriff: [*Looking about.*] It's just the same. When it dropped below zero last night I thought I'd better send Frank out this morning to make a fire for us—no use getting pneumonia with a big case on, but I told him not to touch anything except the stove—and you know Frank.
County Attorney: Somebody should have been left here yesterday.
Sheriff: Oh—yesterday. When I had to send Frank to Morris Center for that man who went crazy—I want you to know I had my hands full yesterday, I knew you could get back from Omaha by today and as long as I went over everything here myself—
County Attorney: Well, Mr. Hale, tell just what happened when you came here yesterday morning.
Hale: Harry and I had started to town with a load of potatoes. We came along the road from my place and as I got here I said, "I'm going to see if I can't get

John Wright to go in with me on a party telephone." I spoke to Wright about it once before and he put me off, saying folks talked too much anyway, and all he asked was peace and quiet—I guess you know about how much he talked himself; but I thought maybe if I went to the house and talked about it before his wife, though I said to Harry that I didn't know as what his wife wanted made much difference to John—

County Attorney: Let's talk about that later, Mr. Hale. I do want to talk about that, but tell now just what happened when you got to the house.

Hale: I didn't hear or see anything; I knocked at the door, and still it was all quiet inside. I knew they must be up, it was past eight o'clock. So I knocked again, and I thought I heard somebody say, "Come in." I wasn't sure, I'm not sure yet, but I opened the door—this door [Indicating the door by which the two women are still standing] and there in that rocker—[Pointing to it] sat Mrs. Wright.

[They all look at the rocker.]

County Attorney: What—was she doing?

Hale: She was rockin' back and forth. She had her apron in her hand and was kind of—pleating it.

County Attorney: And how did she—look?

Hale: Well, she looked queer.

County Attorney: How do you mean—queer?

Hale: Well, as if she didn't know what she was going to do next. And kind of done up.

County Attorney: How did she seem to feel about your coming?

Hale: Why, I don't think she minded—one way or other. She didn't pay much attention. I said, "How do, Mrs. Wright, it's cold, ain't it?" And she said, "Is it?"—and went on kind of pleating at her apron. Well, I was surprised; she didn't ask me to come up to the stove, or to set down, but just sat there, not even looking at me, so I said, "I want to see John." And then she—laughed. I guess you would call it a laugh. I thought of Harry and the team outside, so I said a little sharp: "Can't I see John?" "No," she says, kind o' dull like. "Ain't he home?" says I. "Yes," says she, "he's home." "Then why can't I see him?" I asked her, out of patience. " 'Cause he's dead," says she. "Dead?" says I. She just nodded her head, not getting a bit excited, but rockin' back and forth. "Why—where is he?" says I, not knowing what to say. She just pointed upstairs—like that [Himself pointing to the room above.] I got up, with the idea of going up there. I walked from there to here—then I says, "Why, what did he die of?" "He died of a rope round his neck," says she, and just went on pleatin' at her apron. Well, I went out and called Harry. I thought I might—need help. We went upstairs and there he was lyin'—

County Attorney: I think I'd rather have you go into that upstairs, where you can point it all out. Just go on now with the rest of the story.

Hale: Well, my first thought was to get that rope off. It looked . . . [Stops, his face twitches] . . . but Harry, he went up to him, and he said, "No, he's dead all right, and we'd better not touch anything." So we went back down stairs. She was still sitting that same way. "Has anybody been notified?" I asked. "No," says she, unconcerned. "Who did this, Mrs. Wright?" said Harry. He said it businesslike—and she stopped pleatin' of her apron. "I don't know," she says. "You don't *know*?" says Harry. "No," says she. "Weren't you sleepin' in the bed with him?" says Harry. "Yes," says she, "but I was on the inside." "Somebody slipped a rope round his neck and strangled him and you didn't wake up?" says Harry. "I didn't wake up," she said after him. We must 'a looked as if we didn't see how that could be, for after a minute she said, "I sleep sound." Harry was going to ask her more questions but I said maybe we ought to let her tell her story first to the coroner, or the sheriff, so Harry went fast as he could to Rivers' place, where there's a telephone.

County Attorney: And what did Mrs. Wright do when she knew that you had gone for the coroner?

Hale: She moved from that chair to this one over here [*Pointing to a small chair in the corner*] and just sat there with her hands held together and looking down. I got a feeling that I ought to make some conversation, so I said I had come in to see if John wanted to put in a telephone, and at that she started to laugh, and then she stopped and looked at me—scared. [*The County Attorney, who has had his notebook out, makes a note.*] I dunno, maybe it wasn't scared. I wouldn't like to say it was. Soon Harry got back, and then Dr. Lloyd came, and you, Mr. Peters, and so I guess that's all I know that you don't.

County Attorney: [*Looking around.*] I guess we'll go upstairs first—and then out to the barn and around there. [*To the Sheriff*] You're convinced that there was nothing important here—nothing that would point to any motive.

Sheriff: Nothing here but kitchen things.

[*The County Attorney, after again looking around the kitchen, opens the door of a cupboard closet. He gets up on a chair and looks on a shelf. Pulls his hand away, sticky.*]

County Attorney: Here's a nice mess.

[*The women draw nearer.*]

Mrs. Peters: [*To the other woman.*] Oh, her fruit; it did freeze. [*To the County Attorney*] She worried about that when it turned so cold. She said the fire'd go out and her jars would break.

Sheriff: Well, can you beat the women! Held for murder and worryin' about her preserves.

County Attorney: I guess before we're through she may have something more serious than preserves to worry about.

Hale: Well, women are used to worrying over trifles.

[*The two women move a little closer together.*]

County Attorney: [*With the gallantry of a young politician.*] And yet, for all their worries, what would we do without the ladies? [*The women do not unbend.*

He goes to the sink, takes a dipperful of water from the pail and pouring it into a basin, washes his hands. Starts to wipe them on the roller towel, turns it for a cleaner place.] Dirty towels! *[Kicks his foot against the pans under the sink.]* Not much of a housekeeper, would you say, ladies?

Mrs. Hale: *[Stiffly.]* There's a great deal of work to be done on a farm.

County Attorney: To be sure. And yet *[With a little bow to her]* I know there are some Dickson county farmhouses which do not have such roller towels.

[He gives it a pull to expose its full length again.]

Mrs. Hale: Those towels get dirty awful quick. Men's hands aren't always as clean as they might be.

County Attorney: Ah, loyal to your sex, I see. But you and Mrs. Wright were neighbors. I suppose you were friends, too.

Mrs. Hale: *[Shaking her head.]* I've not seen much of her of late years. I've not been in this house—it's more than a year.

County Attorney: And why was that? You didn't like her?

Mrs. Hale: I liked her all well enough. Farmers' wives have their hands full, Mr. Henderson. And then—

County Attorney: Yes—?

Mrs. Hale: *[Looking about.]* It never seemed a very cheerful place.

County Attorney: No—it's not cheerful. I shouldn't say she had the home-making instinct.

Mrs. Hale: Well, I don't know as Wright had, either.

County Attorney: You mean that they didn't get on very well?

Mrs. Hale: No, I don't mean anything. But I don't think a place'd be any cheer-fuller for John Wright's being in it.

County Attorney: I'd like to talk more of that a little later. I want to get the lay of things upstairs now.

[He goes to the left, where three steps lead to a stair door.]

Sheriff: I suppose anything Mrs. Peters does'll be all right. She was to take in some clothes for her, you know, and a few little things. We left in such a hurry yesterday.

County Attorney: Yes, but I would like to see what you take, Mrs. Peters, and keep an eye out for anything that might be of use to us.

Mrs. Peters: Yes, Mr. Henderson.

[The women listen to the men's steps on the stairs, then look about the kitchen.]

Mrs. Hale: I'd hate to have men coming into my kitchen, snooping around and criticizing.

[She arranges the pans under sink which the County Attorney had shoved out of place.]

Mrs. Peters: Of course it's no more than their duty.

Mrs. Hale: Duty's all right, but I guess that deputy sheriff that came out to make the fire might have got a little of this on. *[Gives the roller towel a pull.]* Wish

I'd thought of that sooner. Seems mean to talk about her for not having things slicked up when she had to come away in such a hurry.

Mrs. Peters: [*Who has gone to a small table in the left rear corner of the room, and lifted one end of a towel that covers a pan.*] She had bread set.

[*Stands still.*]

Mrs. Hale: [*Eyes fixed on a loaf of bread beside the breadbox, which is on a low shelf at the other side of the room. Moves slowly toward it.*] She was going to put this in there. [*Picks up loaf, then abruptly drops it. In a manner of returning to familiar things.*] It's a shame about her fruit. I wonder if it's all gone. [*Gets up on the chair and looks.*] I think there's some here that's all right, Mrs. Peters. Yes—here; [*Holding it toward the window*] this is cherries, too. [*Looking again.*] I declare I believe that's the only one. [*Gets down, bottle in her hand. Goes to the sink and wipes it off on the outside.*] She'll feel awful bad after all her hard work in the hot weather. I remember the afternoon I put up my cherries last summer.

[*She puts the bottle on the big kitchen table, center of the room. With a sigh, is about to sit down in the rocking-chair. Before she is seated realizes what chair it is; with a slow look at it, steps back. The chair which she has touched rocks back and forth.*]

Mrs. Peters: Well, I must get those things from the front room closet. [*She goes to the door at the right, but after looking into the other room, steps back.*] You coming with me, Mrs. Hale? You could help me carry them.

[*They go in the other room; reappear, Mrs. Peters carrying a dress and skirt, Mrs. Hale following with a pair of shoes.*]

Mrs. Peters: My, it's cold in there.

[*She puts the clothes on the big table, and hurries to the stove.*]

Mrs. Hale: [*Examining her skirt.*] Wright was close. I think maybe that's why she kept so much to herself. She didn't even belong to the Ladies Aid. I suppose she felt she couldn't do her part, and then you don't enjoy things when you feel shabby. She used to wear pretty clothes and be lively, when she was Minnie Foster, one of the town girls singing in the choir. But that—oh, that was thirty years ago. This all you was to take in?

Mrs. Peters: She said she wanted an apron. Funny thing to want, for there isn't much to get you dirty in jail, goodness knows. But I suppose just to make her feel more natural. She said they was in the top drawer in this cupboard. Yes, here. And then her little shawl that always hung behind the door. [*Opens stair door and looks.*] Yes, here it is.

[*Quickly shuts door leading upstairs.*]

Mrs. Hale: [*Abruptly moving toward her.*] Mrs. Peters?
Mrs. Peters: Yes, Mrs. Hale?

Mrs. Hale: Do you think she did it?

Mrs. Peters: [In a frightened voice.] Oh, I don't know.

Mrs. Hale: Well, I don't think she did. Asking for an apron and her little shawl. Worrying about her fruit.

Mrs. Peters: [Starts to speak, glances up, where footsteps are heard in the room above. In a low voice.] Mr. Peters says it looks bad for her. Mr. Henderson is awful sarcastic in a speech and he'll make fun of her sayin' she didn't wake up.

Mrs. Hale: Well, I guess John Wright didn't wake when they was slipping that rope under his neck.

Mrs. Peters: No, it's strange. It must have been done awful crafty and still. They say it was such a—funny way to kill a man, rigging it all up like that.

Mrs. Hale: That's just what Mr. Hale said. There was a gun in the house. He says that's what he can't understand.

Mrs. Peters: Mr. Henderson said coming out that what was needed for the case was a motive; something to show anger, or—sudden feeling.

Mrs. Hale: [Who is standing by the table.] Well, I don't see any signs of anger around here. [She puts her hand on the dish towel which lies on the table, stands looking down at table, one half of which is clean, the other half messy.] It's wiped to here. [Makes a move as if to finish work, then turns and looks at loaf of bread outside the breadbox. Drops towel. In that voice of coming back to familiar things.] Wonder how they are finding things upstairs. I hope she had it a little more red-up° up there. You know, it seems kind of sneaking. Locking her up in town and then coming out here and trying to get her own house to turn against her!

Mrs. Peters: But Mrs. Hale, the law is the law.

Mrs. Hale: I s'pose 'tis. [Unbuttoning her coat.] Better loosen up your things, Mrs. Peters. You won't feel them when you go out.

[Mrs. Peters takes off her fur tippet, goes to hang it on hook at back of room, stands looking at the under part of the small corner table.]

Mrs. Peters: She was piecing a quilt.

[She brings the large sewing basket and they look at the bright pieces.]

Mrs. Hale: It's a log cabin pattern. Pretty, isn't it? I wonder if she was goin' to quilt it or just knot it?

[Footsteps have been heard coming down the stairs. The Sheriff enters followed by Hale and the County Attorney.]

Sheriff: They wonder if she was going to quilt it or just knot it!

[The men laugh; the women look abashed.]

red-up: (slang) readied up, ready to be seen.

County Attorney: [*Rubbing his hands over the stove.*] Frank's fire didn't do much up there, did it? Well, let's go out to the barn and get that cleared up.

[*The men go outside.*]

Mrs. Hale: [*Resentfully.*] I don't know as there's anything so strange, our takin' up our time with little things while we're waiting for them to get the evidence. [*She sits down at the big table smoothing out a block with decision.*] I don't see as it's anything to laugh about.

Mrs. Peters: [*Apologetically.*] Of course they've got awful important things on their minds.

[*Pulls up a chair and joins Mrs. Hale at the table.*]

Mrs. Hale: [*Examining another block.*] Mrs. Peters, look at this one. Here, this is the one she was working on, and look at the sewing! All the rest of it has been so nice and even. And look at this! It's all over the place! Why, it looks as if she didn't know what she was about!

[*After she has said this they look at each, then start to glance back at the door. After an instant Mrs. Hale has pulled at a knot and ripped the sewing.*]

Mrs. Peters: Oh, what are you doing, Mrs. Hale?

Mrs. Hale: [*Mildly.*] Just pulling out a stitch or two that's not sewed very good. [*Threading a needle.*] Bad sewing always made me fidgety.

Mrs. Peters: [*Nervously.*] I don't think we ought to touch things.

Mrs. Hale: I'll just finish up this end. [*Suddenly stopping and leaning forward.*] Mrs. Peters?

Mrs. Peters: Yes, Mrs. Hale?

Mrs. Hale: What do you suppose she was so nervous about?

Mrs. Peters: Oh—I don't know. I don't know as she was nervous. I sometimes sew awful queer when I'm just tired. [*Mrs. Hale starts to say something, looks at Mrs. Peters, then goes on sewing.*] Well, I must get these things wrapped up. They may be through sooner than we think. [*Putting apron and other things together.*] I wonder where I can find a piece of paper, and string.

Mrs. Hale: In that cupboard, maybe.

Mrs. Peters: [*Looking in cupboard.*] Why, here's a birdcage. [*Holds it up.*] Did she have a bird, Mrs. Hale?

Mrs. Hale: Why, I don't know whether she did or not—I've not been here for so long. There was a man around last year selling canaries cheap, but I don't know as she took one; maybe she did. She used to sing real pretty herself.

Mrs. Peters: [*Glancing around.*] Seems funny to think of a bird here. But she must have had one, or why would she have a cage? I wonder what happened to it.

Mrs. Hale: I s'pose maybe the cat got it.

Mrs. Peters: No, she didn't have a cat. She's got that feeling some people have about cats—being afraid of them. My cat got in her room and she was real upset and asked me to take it out.

Mrs. *Hale:* My sister Bessie was like that. Queer, ain't it?

Mrs. *Peters:* [*Examining the cage.*] Why, look at this door. It's broke. One hinge is pulled apart.

Mrs. *Hale:* [*Looking too.*] Looks as if someone must have been rough with it.

Mrs. *Peters:* Why, yes.

[*She brings the cage forward and puts it on the table.*]

Mrs. *Hale:* I wish if they're going to find any evidence they'd be about it. I don't like this place.

Mrs. *Peters:* But I'm awful glad you came with me, Mrs. Hale. It would be lonesome for me sitting here alone.

Mrs. *Hale:* It would, wouldn't it? [*Dropping her sewing.*] But I tell you what I do wish, Mrs. Peters. I wish I had come over sometimes when *she* was here. I— [*Looking around the room.*]—wish I had.

Mrs. *Peters:* But of course you were awful busy, Mrs. Hale—your house and your children.

Mrs. *Hale:* I could've come. I stayed away because it weren't cheerful—and that's why I ought to have come. I—I've never liked this place. Maybe because it's down in a hollow and you don't see the road. I dunno what it is but it's a lonesome place and always was. I wish I had come over to see Minnie Foster sometimes. I can see now—

[*Shakes her head.*]

Mrs. *Peters:* Well, you mustn't reproach yourself, Mrs. Hale. Somehow we just don't see how it is with other folks until—something comes up.

Mrs. *Hale:* Not having children makes less work—but it makes a quiet house, and Wright out to work all day, and no company when he did come in. Did you know John Wright, Mrs. Peters?

Mrs. *Peters:* Not to know him; I've seen him in town. They say he was a good man.

Mrs. *Hale:* Yes—good; he didn't drink, and kept his word as well as most, I guess, and paid his debts. But he was a hard man, Mrs. Peters. Just to pass the time of day with him—[*Shivers.*] Like a raw wind that gets to the bone. [*Pauses, her eye falling on the cage.*] I should think she would'a wanted a bird. But what do you suppose went with it?

Mrs. *Peters:* I don't know, unless it got sick and died.

[*She reaches over and swings the broken door, swings it again. Both women watch it.*]

Mrs. *Hale:* You weren't raised round here, were you? [*Mrs. Peters shakes her head.*] You didn't know—her?

Mrs. *Peters:* Not till they brought her yesterday.

Mrs. *Hale:* She—come to think of it, she was kind of like a bird herself—real sweet and pretty, but kind of timid and—fluttery. How—she—did—change. [*Silence; then as if struck by a happy thought and relieved to get back to everyday things*.] Tell you what, Mrs. Peters, why don't you take the quilt in with you? It might take up her mind.

Mrs. Peters: Why, I think that's a real nice idea, Mrs. Hale. There couldn't possibly be any objection to it, could there? Now, just what would I take? I wonder if her patches are in here—and her things.

[*They look in the sewing basket.*]

Mrs. Hale: Here's some red. I expect this has got sewing things in it. [*Brings out a fancy box.*] What a pretty box. Looks like something somebody would give you. Maybe her scissors are in here. [*Opens box. Suddenly puts her hand to her nose.*] Why—[*Mrs. Peters bends nearer, then turns her face away.*] There's something wrapped up in this piece of silk.

Mrs. Peters: Why, this isn't her scissors.

Mrs. Hale: [*Lifting the silk.*] Oh, Mrs. Peters—it's—

[*Mrs. Peters bends closer.*]

Mrs. Peters: It's the bird.

Mrs. Hale: [*Jumping up.*] But, Mrs. Peters—look at it! Its neck! Look at its neck! It's all—other side *too*.

Mrs. Peters: Somebody—wrung—its—neck.

[*Their eyes meet. A look of growing comprehension, of horror. Steps are heard outside. Mrs. Hale slips box under quilt pieces, and sinks into her chair. Enter Sheriff and County Attorney. Mrs. Peters rises.*]

County Attorney: [*As one turning from serious things to little pleasantries.*] Well, ladies, have you decided whether she was going to quilt it or knot it?

Mrs. Peters: We think she was going to—knot it.

County Attorney: Well, that's interesting, I'm sure. [*Seeing the birdcage.*] Has the bird flown?

Mrs. Hale: [*Putting more quilt pieces over the box.*] We think the—cat got it.

County Attorney: [*Preoccupied.*] Is there a cat?

[*Mrs. Hale glances in a quick covert way at Mrs. Peters.*]

Mrs. Peters: Well, not *now*. They're superstitious, you know. They leave.

County Attorney: [*To Sheriff Peters, continuing an interrupted conversation.*] No sign at all of anyone having come from the outside. Their own rope. Now let's go up again and go over it piece by piece. [*They start upstairs.*] It would have to have been someone who knew just the—

[*Mrs. Peters sits down. The two women sit there not looking at one another, but as if peering into something and at the same time holding back. When they talk now it is in the manner of feeling their way over strange ground, as if afraid of what they are saying, but as if they cannot help saying it.*]

Mrs. *Hale:* She liked the bird. She was going to bury it in that pretty box.

Mrs. *Peters:* [*In a whisper.*] When I was a girl—my kitten—there was a boy took a hatchet, and before my eyes—and before I could get there—[*Covers her face an instant.*] If they hadn't held me back I would have—[*Catches herself, looks upstairs where steps are heard, falters weakly*]—hurt him.

Mrs. *Hale:* [*With a slow look around her.*] I wonder how it would seem never to have had any children around. [*Pause.*] No, Wright wouldn't like the bird—a thing that sang. She used to sing. He killed that, too.

Mrs. *Peters:* [*Moving uneasily.*] We don't know who killed the bird.

Mrs. *Hale:* I knew John Wright.

Mrs. *Peters:* It was an awful thing was done in this house that night, Mrs. Hale. Killing a man while he slept, slipping a rope around his neck that choked the life out of him.

Mrs. *Hale:* His neck. Choked the life out of him.

[*Her hand goes out and rests on the birdcage.*]

Mrs. *Peters:* [*With rising voice.*] We don't know who killed him. We don't *know*.

Mrs. *Hale:* [*Her own feeling not interrupted.*] If there'd been years and years of nothing, then a bird to sing to you, it would be awful—still, after the bird was still.

Mrs. *Peters:* [*Something within her speaking.*] I know what stillness is. When we homesteaded in Dakota, and my first baby died—after he was two years old, and me with no other then—

Mrs. *Hale:* [*Moving.*] How soon do you suppose they'll be through looking for the evidence?

Mrs. *Peters:* I know what stillness is. [*Pulling herself back.*] The law has got to punish crime, Mrs. Hale.

Mrs. *Hale:* [*Not as if answering that.*] I wish you'd seen Minnie Foster when she wore a white dress with blue ribbons and stood up there in the choir and sang. [*A look around the room.*] Oh, I wish I'd come over here once in a while! That was a crime! That was a crime! Who's going to punish that?

Mrs. *Peters:* [*Looking upstairs.*] We mustn't—take on.

Mrs. *Hale:* I might have known she needed help! I know how things can be—for women. I tell you, it's queer, Mrs. Peters. We live close together and we live far apart. We all go through the same things—it's all just a different kind of the same thing. [*Brushes her eyes; noticing the bottle of fruit, reaches out for it.*] If I was you I wouldn't tell her her fruit was gone. Tell her it *ain't.* Tell her it's all right. Take this in to prove it to her. She—she may never know whether it was broke or not.

Mrs. *Peters:* [*Takes the bottle, looks about for something to wrap it in; takes petticoat from the clothes brought from the other room, very nervously begins winding this around the bottle. In a false voice.*] My, it's a good thing the men couldn't hear us. Wouldn't they just laugh! Getting all stirred up over a little thing like a—dead canary. As if that could have anything to do with—with—wouldn't they *laugh*!

[*The men are heard coming down stairs.*]

Mrs. Hale: [*Under her breath.*] Maybe they would—maybe they wouldn't.

County Attorney: No, Peters, it's all perfectly clear except a reason for doing it. But you know juries when it comes to women. If there was some definite thing. Something to show—something to make a story about—a thing that would connect up with this strange way of doing it—

[*The women's eyes meet for an instant. Enter Hale from outer door.*]

Hale: Well, I've got the team around. Pretty cold out there.

County Attorney: I'm going to stay here a while by myself. [*To the Sheriff.*] You can send Frank out for me, can't you? I want to go over everything. I'm not satisfied that we can't do better.

Sheriff: Do you want to see what Mrs. Peters is going to take in?

[*The County Attorney goes to the table, picks up the apron, laughs.*]

County Attorney: Oh, I guess they're not very dangerous things the ladies have picked out. [*Moves a few things about, disturbing the quilt pieces which cover the box. Steps back.*] No, Mrs. Peters doesn't need supervising. For that matter, a sheriff's wife is married to the law. Ever think of it that way, Mrs. Peters?

Mrs. Peters: Not—just that way.

Sheriff: [*Chuckling.*] Married to the law. [*Moves toward the other room.*] I just want you to come in here a minute, George. We ought to take a look at these windows.

County Attorney: [*Scoffingly.*] Oh, windows!

Sheriff: We'll be right out, Mr. Hale.

[*Hale goes outside. The Sheriff follows the County Attorney into the other room. Then Mrs. Hale rises, hands tight together, looking intensely at Mrs. Peters, whose eyes make a slow turn, finally meeting Mrs. Hale's. A moment Mrs. Hale holds her, then her own eyes point the way to where the box is concealed. Suddenly Mrs. Peters throws back quilt pieces and tries to put the box in the bag she is wearing. It is too big. She opens box, starts to take bird out, cannot touch it, goes to pieces, stands there helpless. Sound of a knob turning in the other room. Mrs. Hale snatches the box and puts it in the pocket of her big coat. Enter County Attorney and Sheriff.*]

County Attorney: [*Facetiously.*] Well, Henry, at least we found out that she was not going to quilt it. She was going to—what is it you call it, ladies?

Mrs. Hale: [*Her hand against her pocket.*] We call it—knot it, Mr. Henderson.

CURTAIN

QUESTIONS

1. What attitudes toward women do the Sheriff and the County Attorney express? How do Mrs. Hale and Mrs. Peters react to these sentiments?
2. Why does the County Attorney care so much about discovering a motive for the killing?
3. What does Glaspell show us about the position of women in this early twentieth-century community?
4. What do we learn about the married life of the Wrights? By what means is this knowledge revealed to us?
5. What is the setting of this play, and how does it help us to understand Mrs. Wright's deed?
6. What do you infer from the wildly stitched block in Minnie's quilt? Why does Mrs. Hale rip out the crazy stitches?
7. What is so suggestive in the ruined birdcage and the dead canary wrapped in silk? What do these objects have to do with Minnie Foster Wright? What similarity do you notice between the way the canary died and John Wright's own death?
8. What thoughts and memories confirm Mrs. Peters and Mrs. Hale in their decision to help Minnie beat the murder rap?
9. In what places does Mrs. Peters show that she is trying to be a loyal, law-abiding sheriff's wife? How do she and Mrs. Hale differ in background and temperament?
10. What ironies does the play contain? Comment on Mrs. Hale's closing speech: "We call it—knot it, Mr. Henderson." Why is that little hesitation before "knot it" such a meaningful pause?
11. Point out some moments in the play when the playwright conveys much to the audience without needing dialogue.
12. How would you sum up the play's major theme?
13. How does this play, first produced in 1916, show its age? In what ways does it seem still remarkably new?
14. "*Trifles* is a lousy mystery. All the action took place before the curtain went up. Almost in the beginning, on the third page, we find out 'who done it.' So there isn't really much reason for us to sit through the rest of the play." Discuss this view.

Some plays endure, perhaps because (among other reasons) actors take pleasure in performing them. *Trifles* is such a play, a showcase for the skills of its two principals. While the men importantly bumble about, trying to discover a motive, Mrs. Peters and Mrs. Hale solve the case right under their dull noses. The two players in these leading roles face a challenging task: to show both characters growing onstage before us. Discovering a secret that binds them, the two must realize painful truths in their own lives, become aware of all they have in common with Minnie Wright, and gradually resolve to side with the accused against the men. That *Trifles* has enjoyed a revival of attention may reflect its evident feminist views, its convincing portrait of two women forced reluctantly to arrive at a moral judgment and to make a defiant move.

Some critics say that the essence of drama is conflict. Evidently, Glaspell's play is rich in this essential, even though its most violent conflict—the war between John and Minnie Wright—takes place earlier, off scene. Right away, when the menfolk barge through the door into the warm room, letting the women trail in after them; right away, when the sheriff makes fun of Minnie for worrying about "trifles" and the county attorney (that slick politician) starts crudely trying to flatter the "ladies," we sense a conflict between officious, self-important men and the women they expect to wait on them. What is the play's *theme?* Surely the title points to it: women, who men say worry over trifles, can find in those little things large meanings.

Like a carefully constructed traditional short story, *Trifles* has a **plot,** a term sometimes taken to mean whatever happens in a story, but more exactly referring to the unique arrangement of events that the author has made. (For more about plot in a story, see Chapter One.) If Glaspell had elected to tell the story of John and Minnie Wright in chronological order, the sequence in which events took place in time, she might have written a much longer play, opening perhaps with a scene of Minnie's buying her canary and John's cold complaint, "That damned bird keeps twittering all day long!" She might have included scenes showing John strangling the canary and swearing when it beaks him; the Wrights in their loveless bed while Minnie knots her noose; and farmer Hale's entrance after the murder, with Minnie rocking. Only at the end would she have shown us what happened after the crime. That arrangement of events would have made for a quite different play than the short, tight one Glaspell wrote. By telling of events in retrospect, by having the women detectives piece together what happened, Glaspell leads us to focus not only on the murder but, more importantly, on the developing bond between the two women and their growing compassion for the accused.

If *Trifles* may be said to have a **protagonist,** a leading character—a word we usually save for the primary figure of a larger and more eventful play such as *Othello* or *Death of a Salesman*—then you would call the two women dual protagonists. Both act in unison to make the plot unfold. Or you could argue that Mrs. Hale, because she destroys the wild stitching in the quilt; because she finds the dead canary; because she invents a cat to catch the bird (thus deceiving the county attorney); and because in the end when Mrs. Peters helplessly "goes to pieces" it is she who takes the initiative and seizes the evidence, deserves to be called the protagonist. More than anyone else in the play, you could claim, the more decisive Mrs. Hale makes things happen.

A vital part in most plays is an **exposition,** the part in which we first meet the characters, learn what happened before the curtain rose, and find out what is happening now. For a one-act play, *Trifles* has a fairly long exposition, extending from the opening of the kitchen door through the end of farmer Hale's story. Clearly, this substantial exposition is necessary to set the situation and to fill in the facts of the crime. By comparison, Shakespeare's far longer *Tragedy of Richard III* begins almost abruptly, with its protagonist, a duke who yearns to be king, summing up history in an opening speech and revealing his evil character: "And therefore, since I cannot prove a lover . . . I am determined to prove a villain." But Glaspell, too, knows her craft. In the exposition, we are given a **foreshadowing** (or hint of what is to come) in Hale's dry remark, "I didn't know as what his wife wanted made much difference to John." The remark announces the play's theme that men often ignore women's feelings, and it hints at Minnie Wright's motive, later to be revealed. The county attorney, failing to pick up a valuable clue, tables the discussion. (Still another foreshadowing occurs in Mrs. Hale's ripping out the wild, panicky stitches in Minnie's quilt. In the end, Mrs. Hale will make a similar final move to conceal the evidence.)

With the county attorney's speech to the sheriff, "You're convinced that there was nothing important here—nothing that would point to any motive," we begin to understand what he seeks. As he will make even clearer later, the attorney needs a motive in order to convict the accused wife of murder in the first degree. Will

Minnie's motive in killing her husband be discovered? Through the first two-thirds of *Trifles*, this is the play's **dramatic question.** Whether or not we state such a question in our minds (and it is doubtful that we do), our interest quickens as we sense that here is a problem to be solved, an uncertainty to be dissipated. When Mrs. Hale and Mrs. Peters find the dead canary with the twisted neck, the question is answered. We know that Minnie killed John to repay him for his act of gross cruelty. The playwright, however, now raises a *new* dramatic question. Having discovered Minnie's motive, will the women reveal it to the lawmen? Alternatively (if you care to phrase the new question differently), what will they do with the incriminating evidence? We keep reading, or stay clamped to our theater seats, because we want that question answered. We share the women's secret now, and we want to see what they will do with it.

Tightly packed, the one-act *Trifles* contains but one plot: the story of how two women discover evidence that might hang another woman and then hide it. Some plays, usually longer ones, may be more complicated. They may contain a **double plot** (or **subplot**), a secondary arrangement of incidents, involving not the protagonist but someone less important. In Henrik Ibsen's *A Doll's House*, the main plot involves a woman and her husband; they are joined by a second couple, whose fortunes we also follow with interest and whose futures pose another dramatic question.

Step by step, *Trifles* builds to a **climax:** a moment, usually coming late in a play, when tension reaches its greatest height. At such a moment, we sense that the play's dramatic question (or its final dramatic question, if the writer has posed more than one) is about to be answered. In *Trifles* this climax occurs when Mrs. Peters finds herself torn between her desire to save Minnie and her duty to the law. "It was an awful thing was done in this house that night," she reminds herself in one speech, suggesting that Minnie deserves to be punished; then in the next speech she insists, "We don't know who killed him. We don't *know*." Shortly after that, in one speech she voices two warring attitudes. Remembering the loss of her first child, she sympathizes with Minnie: "I know what stillness is." But in her next breath she recalls once more her duty to be a loyal sheriff's wife: "The law has got to punish crime, Mrs. Hale." For a moment, she is placed in conflict with Mrs. Hale, who knew Minnie personally. The two now stand on the edge of a fateful brink. Which way will they decide?[1]

From this moment of climax, the play, like its protagonist (or if you like, protagonists), will make a final move. Mrs. Peters takes her stand. Mrs. Hale, too, decides. She owes Minnie something to make up for her own "crime"—her failure to visit the desperate woman. The plot now charges ahead to its outcome or **resolution,** also called the **conclusion** or **dénouement** (French for "untying of a knot"). The two women act: they scoop up the damaging evidence. Seconds before the very end, Glaspell heightens the **suspense,** our enjoyable anxiety, by making Mrs. Peters

[1]You will sometimes hear *climax* used in a different sense to mean any **crisis**—that is, a moment of tension when one or another outcome is possible. What *crisis* means will be easy to remember if you think of a crisis in medicine: the turning point in a disease when it becomes clear that a patient will either die or recover. In talking about plays, you will probably find both *crisis* and *climax* useful. You can say that a play has more than one crisis, perhaps several. In such a play, the last and most decisive crisis is the climax. A play has only one climax.

fumble with the incriminating box as the sheriff and the county attorney draw near. Mrs. Hale's swift grab for the evidence saves the day and presumably saves Minnie's life. The sound of the doorknob turning in the next room, as the lawmen return, is a small but effective bit of **stage business**—any nonverbal action that engages the attention of an audience. Earlier, when Mrs. Hale almost sits down in Minnie's place, the empty chair that ominously starts rocking is another brilliant piece of stage business. Not only does it give us something interesting to watch, but it also gives us something to think about.

Some critics maintain that events in a plot can be arranged in the outline of a pyramid.[2] In this view, a play begins with a **rising action,** that part of the story (including the exposition) in which events start moving toward a climax. After the climax, the story tapers off in a **falling action,** that is, the subsequent events, including a resolution. In a tragedy, this falling action usually is recognizable: the protagonist's fortunes proceed downhill to an inexorable end.

Some plays indeed have demonstrable pyramids. In *Trifles*, we might claim that in the first two-thirds of the play a rising action builds in intensity. It proceeds through each main incident: the finding of the crazily stitched quilt, Mrs. Hale's ripping out the evidence, the discovery of the bird cage, then the bird itself, and Mrs. Hale's concealing it. At the climax, the peak of the pyramid, the two women seem about to clash as Mrs. Peters wavers uncertainly. The action then falls to a swift resolution. If you outlined that pyramid on paper, however, it would look lopsided—a long rise and a short, steep fall. The pyramid metaphor seems more meaningfully to fit longer plays, among them some classic tragedies. Try it on *Oedipus the King* or, for an even neater fit, on Shakespeare's *Julius Caesar*—an unusual play in that its climax, the assassination of Caesar, occurs exactly in the middle (Act III, Scene 1), right where a good pyramid's point ought to be. Nevertheless, in most other plays, it is hard to find a symmetrical pyramid. (For a demonstration of another, quite different way to outline *Trifles*, see "Writing a Card Report" on page 2172.)

Because its action occurs all at one time and in one place, *Trifles* happens to observe the **unities,** certain principles of good drama laid down by Italian literary critics in the sixteenth century. Interpreting the theories of Aristotle as binding laws, these critics set down three basic principles: a good play, they maintained, should display unity of *action*, unity of *time*, and unity of *place*. In practical terms, this theory maintained that a play must represent a single series of interrelated actions that take place within twenty-four hours in a single location. Furthermore, they insisted, to have true unity of action, a play had to be entirely serious or entirely funny. Mixing tragic and comic elements was not allowed. That Glaspell consciously strove to obey those critics is doubtful, and certainly many great plays, such as Shakespeare's *Othello*, defy such arbitrary rules. Still, it is at least arguable that some of the power of *Trifles* (or Sophocles' *Oedipus the King*) comes from the intensity of the playwright's concentration on what happens in one place, in one short expanse of time.

---

[2]The metaphor of a play as a pyramid was invented by German critic Gustav Freytag, in his *Techniques of the Drama*, 1904, reprint ed. (New York: Arno, 1968).

Brief though it is, *Trifles* has main elements you will find in much longer, more complicated plays. It even has **symbols,** things that hint at large meanings—for example, the broken bird cage and the dead canary, both suggesting the music and the joy that John Wright stifled in Minnie and the terrible stillness that followed his killing the one thing she loved. Perhaps the lone remaining jar of cherries, too, radiates suggestions: it is the one bright, cheerful thing poor Minnie has to show for a whole summer of toil. Symbols in drama may be as big as a house—the home in Ibsen's *A Doll's House,* for instance—or they may appear to be trifles. In Glaspell's rich art, such trifles aren't trifling at all.[3]

TRAGEDY

By **tragedy,** generally speaking, we mean a play that portrays a conflict between human beings and some superior, overwhelming force. It ends sorrowfully and disastrously, and this outcome seems inevitable. Few spectators of *Oedipus the King* wonder how the play will turn out or wish for a happy ending. "In a tragedy," French playwright Jean Anouilh has remarked, "nothing is in doubt and everyone's destiny is known. . . . Tragedy is restful, and the reason is that hope, that foul, deceitful thing, has no part in it. There isn't any hope. You're trapped. The whole sky has fallen on you, and all you can do about it is shout."[4]

Many of our ideas of tragedy go back to ancient Athens; the plays of the Greek dramatists Sophocles, Aeschylus, and Euripides exemplify the art of tragedy. In the fourth century B.C., the philosopher Aristotle described Sophocles' *Oedipus the King* and other tragedies he had seen, analyzing their elements and trying to account for their power over our emotions. Aristotle's observations will make more sense after you read *Oedipus the King,* so let us save discussion of them for the next chapter. For now, to understand something of the nature of tragedy, we suggest you begin by reading not a classic Greek tragedy but a gripping modern tragedy by the Irish poet and playwright John Millington Synge.

The people of Synge's play are simple fisherfolk who live in the Aran Islands, outposts of barren rock washed by the stormy North Atlantic. They are speakers of Gaelic, the old Irish language. Living in their midst, Synge studied their plain, colorful speech and tried to convey a sense of it in the English of this play. Notice how slowly and quietly the tragedy begins. Gradually, disturbing facts fit into place until we know the whole story of a family that has long struggled with the sea, a dangerous and demanding friend, a relentless enemy.

---

[3]Plays can also contain symbolic characters (generally flat ones such as a prophet who croaks, "Beware the ides of March"), symbolic settings, and symbolic gestures. For more about symbolism, see Chapters Seven and Twenty-three.
[4]Preface to *Antigonê,* translated by Louis Galantière (New York: Random, 1946).

John Millington Synge

RIDERS TO THE SEA°

John Millington Synge (pronounced "Sing," 1871–1909), a leading figure in the Irish literary revival at the turn of this century, was born near Dublin, where he died. After graduation from Dublin's Trinity College, he studied music in Germany, Italy, and France. In 1899 he struck up a friendship with poet and playwright William Butler Yeats, who advised him to go to the Aran Islands off Ireland's west coast, listen to the spoken language, and observe the life of the islanders. For Synge, this advice bore fruit in his plays The Shadow of the Glen *(1903) and* Riders to the Sea *(1904), and in a book of impressions,* The Aran Islands *(1907). When first performed at the Abbey Theater in Dublin in 1907, Synge's dark*

John Millington Synge

comedy The Playboy of the Western World *caused a riot. Some in the audience objected to its unflattering, satiric view of rural Irish womanhood. Later its Irish American audiences rioted in Boston, Philadelphia, and New York. A considerable poet as well as a playwright, Synge struggled for years against lymphatic sarcoma, a disease that curtailed his life. His unfinished tragedy* Deirdre of the Sorrows *was produced after his death.*

Characters

Maurya, an old woman
Bartley, her son
Cathleen, her daughter
Nora, a younger daughter
Men and Women

Scene. An Island off the West of Ireland.
Cottage kitchen, with nets, oil-skins, spinning-wheel, some new boards standing by the wall, etc. Cathleen, a girl of about twenty, finishes kneading cake, and puts it down in the pot-oven by the fire; then wipes her hands, and begins to spin at the wheel. Nora, a young girl, puts her head in at the door.

RIDERS TO THE SEA: The title alludes to a well-known Bible story. After Moses opens a corridor in the sea for the children of Israel to pass through, he obeys the Lord and lets the waters "come again upon the Egyptians, upon their chariots, and upon their horsemen." Then he and the Israelites "sing unto the Lord, for he has triumphed gloriously: the horse and his rider hath he thrown into the sea" (Exodus 14:21–31, 15:1–5).

Nora (in a low voice): Where is she?

Cathleen: She's lying down, God help her, and may be sleeping, if she's able.

Nora comes in softly, and takes a bundle from under her shawl.

Cathleen (spinning the wheel rapidly): What is it you have?

Nora: The young priest is after bringing them.° It's a shirt and a plain stocking were got off a drowned man in Donegal.

Cathleen stops her wheel with a sudden movement, and leans out to listen.

Nora: We're to find out if it's Michael's they are, some time herself will be down looking by the sea.

Cathleen: How would they be Michael's, Nora? How would he go the length of that way to the far north?

Nora: The young priest says he's known the like of it. "If it's Michael's they are," says he, "you can tell yourself he's got a clean burial by the grace of God, and if they're not his, let no one say a word about them, for she'll be getting her death," says he, "with crying and lamenting."

The door which Nora half-closed is blown open by a gust of wind.

Cathleen (looking out anxiously): Did you ask him would he stop Bartley going this day with the horses to the Galway fair?

Nora: "I won't stop him," says he, "but let you not be afraid. Herself does be saying prayers half through the night, and the Almighty God won't leave her destitute," says he, "with no son living."

Cathleen: Is the sea bad by the white rocks, Nora?

Nora: Middling bad, God help us. There's a great roaring in the west, and it's worse it'll be getting when the tide's turned to the wind.

She goes over to the table with the bundle.

Shall I open it now?

Cathleen: Maybe she'd wake up on us, and come in before we'd done. (*Coming to the table.*) It's a long time we'll be, and the two of us crying.

Nora (goes to the inner door and listens): She's moving about on the bed. She'll be coming in a minute.

Cathleen: Give me the ladder, and I'll put them up in the turf-loft, the way she won't know of them at all, and maybe when the tide turns she'll be going down to see would he be floating from the east.

They put the ladder against the gable of the chimney; Cathleen goes up a few steps and hides the bundle in the turf-loft. Maurya comes from the inner room.

Maurya (looking up at Cathleen and speaking querulously): Isn't it turf enough you have for this day and evening?

is after bringing them: has just brought them.

Cathleen: There's a cake baking at the fire for a short space (*throwing down the turf*) and Bartley will want it when the tide turns if he goes to Connemara.

Nora picks up the turf and puts it round the pot-oven.

Maurya (*sitting down on a stool at the fire*): He won't go this day with the wind rising from the south and west. He won't go this day, for the young priest will stop him surely.

Nora: He'll not stop him, mother, and I heard Eamon Simon and Stephen Pheety and Colum Shawn saying he would go.

Maurya: Where is he itself?

Nora: He went down to see would there be another boat sailing in the week, and I'm thinking it won't be long till he's here now, for the tide's turning at the green head, and the hooker's° tacking from the east.

Cathleen: I hear some one passing the big stones.

Nora (*looking out*): He's coming now, and he in a hurry.

Bartley (*comes in and looks round the room. Speaking sadly and quietly*): Where is the bit of new rope, Cathleen, was bought in Connemara?

Cathleen (*coming down*): Give it to him, Nora; it's on a nail by the white boards. I hung it up this morning, for the pig with the black feet was eating it.

Nora (*giving him a rope*): Is that it, Bartley?

Maurya: You'd do right to leave that rope, Bartley, hanging by the boards. (*Bartley takes the rope.*) It will be wanting in this place. I'm telling you, if Michael is washed up to-morrow morning, or the next morning, or any morning in the week, for it's a deep grave we'll make him by the grace of God.

Bartley (*beginning to work with the rope*): I've no halter the way I can ride down on the mare, and I must go now quickly. This is the one boat going for two weeks or beyond it, and the fair will be a good fair for horses I heard them saying below.

Maurya: It's a hard thing they'll be saying below if the body is washed up and there's no man in it to make the coffin, and I after giving a big price for the finest white boards you'd find in Connemara.

She looks round at the boards.

Bartley: How would it be washed up, and we after looking each day for nine days, and a strong wind blowing a while back from the west and south?

Maurya: If it wasn't found itself, that wind is raising the sea, and there was a star up against the moon, and it rising in the night. If it was a hundred horses, or a thousand horses you had itself, what is the price of a thousand horses against a son where there is one son only?

Bartley (*working at the halter, to Cathleen*): Let you go down each day, and see the sheep aren't jumping in on the rye, and if the jobber comes you can sell the pig with the black feet if there is a good price going.

Maurya: How would the like of her get a good price for a pig?

---

hooker: a one-masted fishing boat.

Bartley (to Cathleen): If the west wind holds with the last bit of the moon let you and Nora get up weed enough for another cock for the kelp.° It's hard set we'll be from this day with no one in it but one man to work.

Maurya: It's hard set we'll be surely the day you're drownd'd with the rest. What way will I live and the girls with me, and I an old woman looking for the grave?

Bartley lays down the halter, takes off his old coat, and puts on a newer one of the same flannel.

Bartley (to Nora): Is she coming to the pier?

Nora (looking out): She's passing the green head and letting fall her sails.

Bartley (getting his purse and tobacco): I'll have half an hour to go down, and you'll see me coming again in two days, or in three days, or maybe in four days if the wind is bad.

Maurya (turning round to the fire, and putting her shawl over her head): Isn't it a hard and cruel man won't hear a word from an old woman, and she holding him from the sea?

Cathleen: It's the life of a young man to be going on the sea, and who would listen to an old woman with one thing and she saying it over?

Bartley (taking the halter): I must go now quickly. I'll ride down on the red mare, and the gray pony'll run behind me. . . . The blessing of God on you.

He goes out.

Maurya (crying out as he is in the door): He's gone now, God spare us, and we'll not see him again. He's gone now, and when the black night is falling I'll have no son left me in the world.

Cathleen: Why wouldn't you give him your blessing and he looking round in the door? Isn't it sorrow enough is on every one in this house without your sending him out with an unlucky word behind him, and a hard word in his ear?

Maurya takes up the tongs and begins raking the fire aimlessly without looking round.

Nora (turning towards her): You're taking away the turf from the cake.

Cathleen (crying out): The Son of God forgive us, Nora, we're after forgetting his bit of bread.

She comes over to the fire.

Nora: And it's destroyed he'll be going till dark night, and he after eating nothing since the sun went up.

Cathleen (turning the cake out of the oven): It's destroyed he'll be, surely. There's no sense left on any person in a house where an old woman will be talking for ever.

another cock for the kelp: another pile of seaweed. The islanders harvest the weed to fertilize their sparse, rocky soil.

Maurya sways herself on her stool.

Cathleen (*cutting off some of the bread and rolling it in a cloth; to Maurya*): Let you go down now to the spring well and give him this and he passing. You'll see him then and the dark word will be broken, and you can say "God speed you," the way he'll be easy in his mind.

Maurya (*taking the bread*): Will I be in it as soon as himself?

Cathleen: If you go now quickly.

Maurya (*standing up unsteadily*): It's hard set I am to walk.

Cathleen (*looking at her anxiously*): Give her the stick, Nora, or maybe she'll slip on the big stones.

Nora: What stick?

Cathleen: The stick Michael brought from Connemara.

Maurya (*taking a stick Nora gives her*): In the big world the old people do be leaving things after them for their sons and children, but in this place it is the young men do be leaving things behind for them that do be old.

She goes out slowly. Nora goes over to the ladder.

Cathleen: Wait, Nora, maybe she'd turn back quickly. She's that sorry, God help her, you wouldn't know the thing she'd do.

Nora: Is she gone around by the bush?

Cathleen (*looking out*): She's gone now. Throw it down quickly, for the Lord knows when she'll be out of it again.

Nora (*getting the bundle from the loft*): The young priest said he'd be passing to-morrow, and we might go down and speak to him below if it's Michael's they are surely.

Cathleen (*taking the bundle*): Did he say what way they were found?

Nora (*coming down*): "There were two men," says he, "and they rowing round with poteen before the cocks crowed,° and the oar of one of them caught the body, and they passing the black cliffs of the north."

Cathleen (*trying to open the bundle*): Give me a knife, Nora, the strings perished with the salt water, and there's a black knot on it you wouldn't loosen in a week.

Nora (*giving her a knife*): I've heard tell it was a long way to Donegal.

Cathleen (*cutting the string*): It is surely. There was a man in here a while ago—the man sold us that knife—and he said if you set off walking from the rock beyond, it would be seven days you'd be in Donegal.

Nora: And what time would a man take, and he floating?

Cathleen opens the bundle and takes out a bit of a stocking. They look at them eagerly.

Cathleen (*in a low voice*): The Lord spare us, Nora! Isn't it a queer hard thing to say if it's his they are surely?

---

rowing round with poteen . . . . crowed: transporting moonshine whiskey under cover of darkness.

Nora: I'll get his shirt off the hook the way we can put the one flannel on the other. (*She looks through some clothes hanging in the corner.*) It's not with them, Cathleen, and where will it be?

Cathleen: I'm thinking Bartley put it on him in the morning, for his own shirt was heavy with the salt in it. (*Pointing to the corner.*) There's a bit of a sleeve was of the same stuff. Give me that and it will do.

Nora brings it to her and they compare the flannel.

Cathleen: It's the same stuff, Nora; but if it is itself aren't there great rolls of it in the shops of Galway, and isn't it many another man may have a shirt of it as well as Michael himself?

Nora (*who has taken up the stocking and counted the stitches, crying out*): It's Michael, Cathleen, it's Michael; God spare his soul, and what will herself say when she hears this story, and Bartley on the sea?

Cathleen (*taking the stocking*): It's a plain stocking.

Nora: It's the second one of the third pair I knitted, and I put up three score stitches, and I dropped four of them.

Cathleen (*counts the stitches*): It's that number is in it. (*Crying out.*) Ah, Nora, isn't it a bitter thing to think of him floating that way to the far north, and no one to keen° him but the black hags that do be flying on the sea?

Nora (*swinging herself round, and throwing out her arms on the clothes*): And isn't it a pitiful thing when there is nothing left of a man who was a great rower and fisher, but a bit of an old shirt and a plain stocking?

Cathleen (*after an instant*): Tell me is herself coming, Nora? I hear a little sound on the path.

Nora (*looking out*): She is, Cathleen. She's coming up to the door.

Cathleen: Put these things away before she'll come in. Maybe it's easier she'll be after giving her blessing to Bartley, and we won't let on we've heard anything the time he's on the sea.

Nora (*helping Cathleen to close the bundle*): We'll put them here in the corner.

They put them into a hole in the chimney corner. Cathleen goes back to the spinning-wheel.

Nora: Will she see it was crying I was?

Cathleen: Keep your back to the door the way the light'll not be on you.

Nora sits down at the chimney corner, with her back to the door. Maurya comes in very slowly, without looking at the girls, and goes over to her stool at the other side of the fire. The cloth with the bread is still in her hand. The girls look at each other, and Nora points to the bundle of bread.

Cathleen (*after spinning for a moment*): You didn't give him his bit of bread?

Maurya begins to keen softly, without turning round.

keen: weep and wail.

Cathleen: Did you see him riding down?

Maurya goes on keening.

Cathleen (a little impatiently): God forgive you; isn't it a better thing to raise your voice and tell what you seen, than to be making lamentation for a thing that's done? Did you see Bartley, I'm saying to you.

Maurya (with a weak voice): My heart's broken from this day.

Cathleen (as before): Did you see Bartley?

Maurya: I seen the fearfulest thing.

Cathleen (leaves her wheel and looks out): God forgive you; he's riding the mare now over the green head, and the gray pony behind him.

Maurya (starts, so that her shawl falls back from her head and shows her white tossed hair. With a frightened voice): The gray pony behind him.

Cathleen (coming to the fire): What is it ails you, at all?

Maurya (speaking very slowly): I've seen the fearfulest thing any person has seen, since the day Bride Dara seen the dead man with the child in his arms.

Cathleen and Nora: Uah.°

They crouch down in front of the old woman at the fire.

Nora: Tell us what it is you seen.

Maurya: I went down to the spring well, and I stood there saying a prayer to myself. Then Bartley came along, and he riding on the red mare with the gray pony behind him. (*She puts up her hands, as if to hide something from her eyes.*) The Son of God spare us, Nora!

Cathleen: What is it you seen?

Maurya: I seen Michael himself.

Cathleen (speaking softly): You did not Mother; it wasn't Michael you seen, for his body is after being found in the far north, and he's got a clean burial by the grace of God.

Maurya (a little defiantly): I'm after seeing him this day, and he riding and galloping. Bartley came first on the red mare; and I tried to say "God speed you," but something choked the words in my throat. He went by quickly; and "the blessing of God on you," says he, and I could say nothing. I looked up then, and I crying, at the gray pony, and there was Michael upon it— with fine clothes on him, and new shoes on his feet.

Cathleen (begins to keen): It's destroyed we are from this day. It's destroyed, surely.

Nora: Didn't the young priest say the Almighty God wouldn't leave her destitute with no son living?

Maurya (in a low voice, but clearly): It's little the like of him knows of the sea. . . . Bartley will be lost now, and let you call in Eamon and make me a good coffin out of the white boards, for I won't live after them. I've had a husband, and a husband's father, and six sons in this house—six fine men,

Uah: exclamation of horror and surprise.

though it was a hard birth I had with every one of them and they coming to the world—and some of them were found and some of them were not found, but they're gone now the lot of them. . . . There were Stephen, and Shawn, were lost in the great wind, and found after in the Bay of Gregory of the Golden Mouth, and carried up the two of them on the one plank, and in by that door.

She pauses for a moment, the girls start as if they heard something through the door that is half open behind them.

Nora (*in a whisper*): Did you hear that, Cathleen? Did you hear a noise in the north-east?

Cathleen (*in a whisper*): There's some one after crying out by the seashore.

Maurya (*continues without hearing anything*): There was Sheamus and his father, and his own father again, were lost in a dark night, and not a stick or sign was seen of them when the sun went up. There was Patch after was drowned out of a curagh° that turned over. I was sitting here with Bartley, and he a baby, lying on my two knees, and I seen two women, and three women, and four women coming in, and they crossing themselves, and not saying a word. I looked out then, and there were men coming after them, and they holding a thing in the half of a red sail, and water dripping out of it—it was a dry day, Nora—and leaving a track to the door.

She pauses again with her hand stretched out towards the door. It opens softly and old women begin to come in, crossing themselves on the threshold, and kneeling down in front of the stage with red petticoats over their heads.

Maurya (*half in a dream, to Cathleen*): Is it Patch, or Michael, or what is it at all?

Cathleen: Michael is after being found in the far north, and when he is found there how could he be here in this place?

Maurya: There does be a power of young men floating round in the sea, and what way would they know if it was Michael they had, or another man like him, for when a man is nine days in the sea, and the wind blowing, it's hard set his own mother would be to say what man was it.

Cathleen: It's Michael, God spare him, for they're after sending us a bit of his clothes from the far north.

She reaches out and hands Maurya the clothes that belonged to Michael. Maurya stands up slowly and takes them in her hand. Nora looks out.

Nora: They're carrying a thing among them and there's water dripping out of it and leaving a track by the big stones.

Cathleen (*in a whisper to the women who have come in*): Is it Bartley it is?

One of the Women: It is surely, God rest his soul.

Two younger women come in and pull out the table. Then men carry in the body of Bartley, laid on a plank, with a bit of sail over it, and lay it on the table.

curagh: a canvas-bottomed boat.

Cathleen (*to the women, as they are doing so*): What way was he drowned?

One of the Women: The gray pony knocked him into the sea, and he was washed out where there is a great surf on the white rocks.

Maurya has gone over and knelt down at the head of the table. The women are keening softly and swaying themselves with a slow movement. Cathleen and Nora kneel at the other end of the table. The men kneel near the door.

Maurya (*raising her head and speaking as if she did not see the people around her*): They're all gone now, and there isn't anything more the sea can do to me. . . . I'll have no call now to be up crying and praying when the wind breaks from the south and you can hear the surf is in the east, and the surf is in the west, making a great stir with the two noises, and they hitting one on the other. I'll have no call now to be going down and getting Holy Water in the dark nights after Samhain,° and I won't care what way the sea is when the other women will be keening. (*To Nora*) Give me the Holy Water, Nora, there's a small cup still on the dresser.

Nora gives it to her.

Maurya (*drops Michael's clothes across Bartley's feet, and sprinkles the Holy Water over him.*): It isn't that I haven't prayed for you, Bartley, to the Almighty God. It isn't that I haven't said prayers in the dark night till you wouldn't know what I'd be saying; but it's a great rest I'll have now, and it's time surely. It's a great rest I'll have now, and great sleeping in the long nights after Samhain, if it's only a bit of wet flour we do have to eat, and maybe a fish that would be stinking.

She kneels down again, crossing herself, and saying prayers under her breath.

Cathleen (*to an old man*): Maybe yourself and Eamon would make a coffin when the sun rises. We have fine white boards herself bought, God help her, thinking Michael would be found, and I have a new cake you can eat while you'll be working.

The Old Man (*looking at the boards*): Are there nails with them?

Cathleen: There are not, Colum; we didn't think of the nails.

Another Man: It's a great wonder she wouldn't think of the nails, and all the coffins she's been made already.

Cathleen: It's getting old she is, and broken.

Maurya stands up again very slowly and spreads out the pieces of Michael's clothes beside the body, sprinkling them with the last of the Holy Water.

Nora (*in a whisper to Cathleen*): She's quiet now and easy; but the day Michael was drowned you could hear her crying out from this to the spring well. It's fonder she was of Michael, and would any one have thought that?

Samhain: All Saints' Day.

Cathleen (*slowly and clearly*): An old woman will be soon tired with anything she will do, and isn't it nine days herself is after crying and keening, and making great sorrow in the house?

Maurya (*puts the empty cup mouth downwards on the table, and lays her hands together on Bartley's feet*): They're all together this time, and the end is come. May the Almighty God have mercy on Bartley's soul, and on Michael's soul, and on the souls of Sheamus and Patch, and Stephen and Shawn (*bending her head*); and may He have mercy on my soul, Nora, and on the soul of every one is left living in the world.

She pauses, and the keen rises a little more loudly from the women, then sinks away.

Maurya (*continuing*): Michael has a clean burial in the far north, by the grace of the Almighty God. Bartley will have a fine coffin out of the white boards, and a deep grave surely. What more can we want than that? No man at all can be living for ever, and we must be satisfied.

She kneels down again and the curtain falls slowly.

QUESTIONS

1. What is the situation at the start of *Riders to the Sea?* What motivates Cathleen and Nora to hide Michael's clothes from their mother?
2. What suggestions of deeper meaning do you find in the abruptness with which Cathleen stops her spinning wheel at Nora's mention of the clothes that have been found? in the gust of wind that opens the half-closed door?
3. What motivates the priest not to interfere with Bartley's plan to take the horses to the Galway fair? Why does his mother want him to stay home? How do Cathleen, Nora, and Bartley react to their mother's request?
4. What does Maurya see when she goes to the spring well to give Bartley his bread? What is there about her account of it that makes Cathleen say, "It's destroyed we are from this day. It's destroyed, surely"?
5. How does Bartley die? At what moment is his death foreshadowed?
6. Do you agree with Cathleen's observation at the end of the play that Maurya is "broken"? Explain.
7. Does *Riders to the Sea* have any protagonist? If so, which character has this central role?

COMEDY

Comedy, from the Greek *komos*, "a revel," is thought to have originated in festivities to celebrate spring, ritual performances in praise of Dionysus, god of fertility and wine. In drama, comedy may be broadly defined as whatever makes us laugh. A comedy may be a name for one entire play, or we may say that there is comedy in only part of a play—as in a comic character or a comic situation.

The best-known traditional emblem of drama—a pair of masks, one sorrowful (representing tragedy) and one smiling (representing comedy)—suggests that tragedy and comedy, although opposites, are close relatives. Often, comedy shows people getting into trouble through error or weakness; in this respect it is akin to tragedy. An important difference between comedy and tragedy lies in the attitude toward human failing that is expected of us. When a main character in a comedy suffers from over-weening pride, as does Oedipus, or if he fails to recognize that his bride-to-be is actually his mother, we laugh—something we would never do in watching a competent performance of *Oedipus the King*.

Many theories have been propounded to explain why we laugh; most of these notions fall into a few familiar types. One school, exemplified by French philosopher Henri Bergson, sees laughter as a form of ridicule, implying a feeling of disinterested superiority; all jokes are *on* somebody. Bergson suggests that laughter springs from situations in which we sense a conflict between some mechanical or rigid pattern of behavior and our sense of a more natural or "organic" kind of behavior that is possible.[5] An example occurs in Buster Keaton's comic film *The Boat*. Having launched a little boat that springs a leak, Keaton rigidly goes down with it, with frozen face. (The more natural and organic thing to do would be to swim for shore.) Other thinkers view laughter as our response to expectations fulfilled or to expectations set up but then suddenly frustrated. Some hold it to be the expression of our delight in seeing our suppressed urges acted out (as when a comedian hurls an egg at a pompous stuffed shirt); some, to be our defensive reaction to a painful and disturbing truth.

Derisive humor is basic to **satiric comedy,** in which human weakness or folly is ridiculed from a vantage point of supposedly enlightened superiority. Satiric comedy may be coolly malicious and gently biting, but it tends to be critical of people, their manners, and their morals. It is at least as old as the comedies of Aristophanes, who thrived in the fifth century B.C. In *Lysistrata*, the satirist shows how the women of two warring cities speedily halt a war by agreeing to deny themselves to their husbands. (The satirist's target is men so proud that they go to war rather than make the slightest concession.)

Comedy is often divided into two varieties—"high" and "low." **High comedy** relies more on wit and wordplay than on physical action for its humor. It tries to address the audience's intelligence by pointing out the pretension and hypocrisy of human behavior. High comedy also generally avoids derisive humor. Jokes about physical appearance would, for example, be avoided. One technique it employs to appeal to a sophisticated, verbal audience is use of the **epigram,** a brief and witty statement that memorably expresses some truth, large or small. Oscar Wilde's plays such as *The Importance of Being Earnest* (1895) and *Lady Windermere's Fan* (1892) sparkle with such brilliant epigrams as: "I can resist everything except temptation"; "Experience is the name everyone gives to their mistakes"; "There is only one thing worse than being talked about, and that is not being talked about." A type of high comedy is the **comedy of manners,** a witty satire set in elite or fashionable society. The comedy of manners was especially popular in the **Restoration period** (the period after 1660 when Charles II, restored to the English throne, reopened the London playhouses, which had been closed by the Puritans, who considered theater

---

[5]See Bergson's essay "Le Rire" (1990), translated as "Laughter" in *Comedy*, ed. Wylie Sypher (New York: Anchor, 1956).

immoral). The great Restoration playwrights such as William Congreve and George Farquhar especially excelled at comedies of manners. In the modern period splendid comedies of manners continue to be written. Bernard Shaw's *Pygmalion* (1913), which eventually became the musical *My Fair Lady*, contrasts life in the streets of London with that in aristocratic drawing rooms. Contemporary playwrights such as Tom Stoppard, Michael Frayn, Tina Howe, John Guare, and the late Joe Orton have all created memorable comedies of manners.

Low comedy explores the opposite extreme of humor. It places greater emphasis on physical action and visual gags, and its verbal jokes do not require much intellect to appreciate (as in Groucho Marx's pithy put-down to his brother Chico, "You have the brain of a five-year-old, and I bet he was glad to get rid of it!"). Low comedy does not avoid derisive humor; rather it revels in making fun of whatever will get a good laugh. Drunkenness, stupidity, lust, senility, trickery, insult, and clumsiness are inexhaustible staples of this style of comedy. Although it is all too easy for critics to dismiss low comedy, like high comedy it also serves a valuable purpose in satirizing human failings. Shakespeare indulged in coarse humor in some of his noblest plays. Low comedy is usually the preferred style of popular culture, and it has inspired many incisive satires on modern life—from the classic films of W. C. Fields and the Marx Brothers to the weekly TV antics of *Monty Python's Flying Circus* and Matt Groening's *The Simpsons*.

Low comedy includes several distinct types. One is the **burlesque,** a broadly humorous parody or travesty of another play or kind of play. (In the United States, *burlesque* is something else: a once-popular form of show business featuring stripteases interspersed with bits of ribald low comedy.) Another valuable type of low comedy is the **farce,** a broadly humorous play whose action is usually fast-moving and improbable. The farce is a descendant of the Italian *commedia dell'arte* ("artistic comedy") of the late Renaissance, a kind of theater developed by comedians who traveled from town to town, regaling crowds at country fairs and in marketplaces. This popular art featured familiar stock characters in masks or whiteface: Harlequin, a clown; Columbine, his peppery sweetheart; and Pantaloon, a doddering duffer. Lately making a comeback, the more modern farces of French playwright Georges Feydeau (1862–1891) are practically all plot, with only the flattest of characters, mindless ninnies who play frantic games of hide-and-seek in order to deceive their spouses. **Slapstick comedy** (such as that of the Three Stooges) is a kind of farce. Featuring pratfalls, pie-throwing, fisticuffs, and other violent action, it takes its name from a circus clown's device—a bat with two boards that loudly clap together when one clown swats another.

Romantic comedy, another traditional sort of comedy, is subtler. Its main characters are generally lovers, and its plot unfolds their ultimately successful strivings to be united. Unlike satiric comedy, romantic comedy portrays its characters not with withering contempt but with kindly indulgence. It may take place in the everyday world, or perhaps in some never-never land, such as the forest of Arden in Shakespeare's *As You Like It*.

Here is a short contemporary comedy by one of America's most ingenious playwrights.

David Ives

SURE THING

1988

David Ives (b. 1950) grew up on the South Side of Chicago. He attended Catholic schools before entering Northwestern University. Later Ives studied at the Yale Drama School—"a blissful time for me," he recalls, "in spite of the fact that there is slush on the ground in New Haven 238 days a year." Ives received his first professional production in Los Angeles at the age of twenty-one "at America's smallest, and possibly worst theater, in a storefront that had a pillar dead center in the middle of the stage." He continued writing for the theater while working as an editor at Foreign Affairs, and gradually achieved a reputation in theatrical circles for his wildly original and brilliantly written short comic plays. His public breakthrough came in 1993 with the New York staging of All in

David Ives

the Timing, which presented six short comedies, including Sure Thing. This production earned ecstatic reviews and a busy box office. In the 1995–1996 season, All in the Timing was the most widely performed play in America (except for the works of Shakespeare). Ives followed with Don Juan in Chicago (1994), Ancient History (1996), and Polish Joke (2001). In 1997 a second group of one-act comedies, Mere Mortals, was produced with great success in New York City; it was published with Lives of the Saints, another cycle of his one-act plays, in the volume Time Flies (2001). Ives also writes short stories and screenplays for both motion pictures and television. He lives in New York City.

Characters

Betty
Bill

Scene. A café. Betty, a woman in her late twenties, is reading at a café table. An empty chair is opposite her. Bill, same age, enters.

Bill: Excuse me. Is this chair taken?
Betty: Excuse me?
Bill: Is this taken?
Betty: Yes it is.
Bill: Oh. Sorry.
Betty: Sure thing.

    (A bell rings softly.)

Bill: Excuse me. Is this chair taken?
Betty: Excuse me?
Bill: Is this taken?
Betty: No, but I'm expecting somebody in a minute.
Bill: Oh. Thanks anyway.
Betty: Sure thing.

(A bell rings softly.)

Bill: Excuse me. Is this chair taken?
Betty: No, but I'm expecting somebody very shortly.
Bill: Would you mind if I sit here till he or she or it comes?
Betty (glances at her watch): They do seem to be pretty late. . . .
Bill: You never know who you might be turning down.
Betty: Sorry. Nice try, though.
Bill: Sure thing.

(Bell.)

Is this seat taken?
Betty: No it's not.
Bill: Would you mind if I sit here?
Betty: Yes I would.
Bill: Oh.

(Bell.)

Is this chair taken?
Betty: No it's not.
Bill: Would you mind if I sit here?
Betty: No. Go ahead.
Bill: Thanks. (He sits. She continues reading.) Everyplace else seems to be taken.
Betty: Mm-hm.
Bill: Great place.
Betty: Mm-hm.
Bill: What's the book?
Betty: I just wanted to read in quiet, if you don't mind.
Bill: No. Sure thing.

(Bell.)

Everyplace else seems to be taken.
Betty: Mm-hm.
Bill: Great place for reading.
Betty: Yes, I like it.
Bill: What's the book?
Betty: The Sound and the Fury.
Bill: Oh. Hemingway.

(Bell.)

What's the book?

Betty: *The Sound and the Fury.*

Bill: Oh. Faulkner.

Betty: Have you read it?

Bill: Not . . . actually. I've sure read *about* it, though. It's supposed to be great.

Betty: It is great.

Bill: I hear it's great. (*Small pause.*) Waiter?

   (*Bell.*)

What's the book?

Betty: *The Sound and the Fury.*

Bill: Oh. Faulkner.

Betty: Have you read it?

Bill: I'm a Mets fan, myself.

   (*Bell.*)

Betty: Have you read it?

Bill: Yeah, I read it in college.

Betty: Where was college?

Bill: I went to Oral Roberts University.

   (*Bell.*)

Betty: Where was college?

Bill: I was lying. I never really went to college. I just like to party.

   (*Bell.*)

Betty: Where was college?

Bill: Harvard.

Betty: Do you like Faulkner?

Bill: I love Faulkner. I spent a whole winter reading him once.

Betty: I've just started.

Bill: I was so excited after ten pages that I went out and bought everything else he wrote. One of the greatest reading experiences of my life. I mean, all that incredible psychological understanding. Page after page of gorgeous prose. His profound grasp of the mystery of time and human existence. The smells of the earth . . . What do you think?

Betty: I think it's pretty boring.

   (*Bell.*)

Bill: What's the book?

Betty: *The Sound and the Fury.*

Bill: Oh! Faulkner!

Betty: Do you like Faulkner?

Bill: I love Faulkner.

Betty: He's incredible.

Bill: I spent a whole winter reading him once.

Betty: I was so excited after ten pages that I went out and bought everything else he wrote.

Bill: All that incredible psychological understanding.

Betty: And the prose is so gorgeous.

Bill: And the way he's grasped the mystery of time—

Betty: —and human existence. I can't believe I've waited this long to read him.

Bill: You never know. You might not have liked him before.

Betty: That's true.

Bill: You might not have been ready for him. You have to hit these things at the right moment or it's no good.

Betty: That's happened to me.

Bill: It's all in the timing. (*Small pause.*) My name's Bill, by the way.

Betty: I'm Betty.

Bill: Hi.

Betty: Hi. (*Small pause.*)

Bill: Yes I thought reading Faulkner was . . . a great experience.

Betty: Yes. (*Small pause.*)

Bill: *The Sound and the Fury.* . . . (*Another small pause.*)

Betty: Well. Onwards and upwards. (*She goes back to her book.*)

Bill: Waiter—?

(*Bell.*)

You have to hit these things at the right moment or it's no good.

Betty: That's happened to me.

Bill: It's all in the timing. My name's Bill, by the way.

Betty: I'm Betty.

Bill: Hi.

Betty: Hi.

Bill: Do you come in here a lot?

Betty: Actually I'm just in town for two days from Pakistan.

Bill: Oh. Pakistan.

(*Bell.*)

My name's Bill, by the way.

Betty: I'm Betty.

Bill: Hi.

Betty: Hi.

Bill: Do you come in here a lot?

Betty: Every once in a while. Do you?

Bill: Not so much anymore. Not as much as I used to. Before my nervous breakdown.

(*Bell.*)

Do you come in here a lot?

Betty: Why are you asking?

Bill: Just interested.

Betty: Are you really interested, or do you just want to pick me up?

Bill: No, I'm really interested.

Betty: Why would you be interested in whether I come in here a lot?

Bill: I'm just . . . getting acquainted.

Betty: Maybe you're only interested for the sake of making small talk long enough to ask me back to your place to listen to some music, or because you've just rented this great tape for your VCR, or because you've got some terrific unknown Django Reinhardt record, only all you really want to do is fuck—which you won't do very well—after which you'll go into the bathroom and pee very loudly, then pad into the kitchen and get yourself a beer from the refrigerator without asking me whether I'd like anything, and then you'll proceed to lie back down beside me and confess that you've got a girlfriend named Stephanie who's away at medical school in Belgium for a year, and that you've been involved with her—*off and on*—in what you'll call a very "intricate" relationship, for the past *seven* YEARS. None of which *interests* me, mister!

Bill: Okay.

(*Bell.*)

Do you come in here a lot?

Betty: Every other day, I think.

Bill: I come in here quite a lot and I don't remember seeing you.

Betty: I guess we must be on different schedules.

Bill: Missed connections.

Betty: Yes. Different time zones.

Bill: Amazing how you can live right next door to somebody in this town and never even know it.

Betty: I know.

Bill: City life.

Betty: It's crazy.

Bill: We probably pass each other in the street every day. Right in front of this place, probably.

Betty: Yep.

Bill (*looks around*): Well the waiters here sure seem to be in some different time zone. I can't seem to locate one anywhere. . . . Waiter! (*He looks back.*) So what do you—(*He sees that she's gone back to her book.*)

Betty: I beg pardon?

Bill: Nothing. Sorry.

(*Bell.*)

Betty: I guess we must be on different schedules.

Bill: Missed connections.

Betty: Yes. Different time zones.

Bill: Amazing how you can live right next door to somebody in this town and never even know it.

Betty: I know.

Bill: City life.

Betty: It's crazy.

Bill: You weren't waiting for somebody when I came in, were you?

Betty: Actually I was.

Bill: Oh. Boyfriend?

Betty: Sort of.

Bill: What's a sort-of boyfriend?

Betty: My husband.

Bill: Ah-ha.

(*Bell.*)

You weren't waiting for somebody when I came in, were you?

Betty: Actually I was.

Bill: Oh. Boyfriend?

Betty: Sort of.

Bill: What's a sort-of boyfriend?

Betty: We were meeting here to break up.

Bill: Mm-hm . . .

(*Bell.*)

What's a sort-of boyfriend?

Betty: My lover. Here she comes right now!

(*Bell.*)

Bill: You weren't waiting for somebody when I came in, were you?

Betty: No, just reading.

Bill: Sort of a sad occupation for a Friday night, isn't it? Reading here, all by yourself?

Betty: Do you think so?

Bill: Well sure. I mean, what's a good-looking woman like you doing out alone on a Friday night?

Betty: Trying to keep away from lines like that.

Bill: No, listen—

(*Bell.*)

You weren't waiting for somebody when I came in, were you?

Betty: No, just reading.

Bill: Sort of a sad occupation for a Friday night, isn't it? Reading here all by yourself?

Betty: I guess it is, in a way.

Bill: What's a good-looking woman like you doing out alone on a Friday night anyway? No offense, but . . .

Betty: I'm out alone on a Friday night for the first time in a very long time.

Bill: Oh.

Betty: You see, I just recently ended a relationship.

Bill: Oh.

Betty: Of rather long standing.

Bill: I'm sorry. (*Small pause.*) Well listen, since reading by yourself *is* such a sad occupation for a Friday night, would you like to go elsewhere?

Betty: No . . .

Bill: Do something else?

Betty: No thanks.

Bill: I was headed out to the movies in a while anyway.

Betty: I don't think so.

Bill: Big chance to let Faulkner catch his breath. All those long sentences get him pretty tired.

Betty: Thanks anyway.

Bill: Okay.

Betty: I appreciate the invitation.

Bill: Sure thing.

(*Bell.*)

You weren't waiting for somebody when I came in, were you?

Betty: No, just reading.

Bill: Sort of a sad occupation for a Friday night, isn't it? Reading here all by yourself?

Betty: I guess I was trying to think of it as existentially romantic. You know— cappuccino, great literature, rainy night . . .

Bill: That only works in Paris. We *could* hop the late plane to Paris. Get on a Concorde. Find a café . . .

Betty: I'm a little short on plane fare tonight.

Bill: Darn it, so am I.

Betty: To tell you the truth, I was headed to the movies after I finished this section. Would you like to come along? Since you can't locate a waiter?

Bill: That's a very nice offer, but . . .

Betty: Uh-huh. Girlfriend?

Bill: Two, actually. One of them's pregnant, and Stephanie—

(*Bell.*)

Betty: Girlfriend?

Bill: No, I don't have a girlfriend. Not if you mean the castrating bitch I dumped last night.

(*Bell.*)

Betty: Girlfriend?

Bill: Sort of. Sort of.

Betty: What's a sort-of girlfriend?

Bill: My mother.

(Bell.)

I just ended a relationship, actually.

Betty: Oh.

Bill: Of rather long standing.

Betty: I'm sorry to hear it.

Bill: This is my first night out alone in a long time. I feel a little bit at sea, to tell you the truth.

Betty: So you didn't stop to talk because you're a Moonie, or you have some weird political affiliation—?

Bill: Nope. Straight-down-the-ticket Republican.

(Bell.)

Straight-down-the-ticket Democrat.

(Bell.)

Can I tell you something about politics?

(Bell.)

I like to think of myself as a citizen of the universe.

(Bell.)

I'm unaffiliated.

Betty: That's a relief. So am I.

Bill: I vote my beliefs.

Betty: Labels are not important.

Bill: Labels are not important, exactly. Take me, for example. I mean, what does it matter if I had a two-point at—

(Bell.)

three-point at—

(Bell.)

four-point at college? Or if I did come from Pittsburgh—

(Bell.)

Cleveland—

(Bell.)

Westchester County?

Betty: Sure.

Bill: I believe that a man is what he is.

(Bell.)

A person is what he is.

(Bell.)

A person is . . . what they are.

Betty: I think so too.

Bill: So what if I admire Trotsky?

(*Bell.*)

So what if I once had a total-body liposuction?

(*Bell.*)

So what if I don't have a penis?

(*Bell.*)

So what if I spent a year in the Peace Corps? I was acting on my convictions.

Betty: Sure.

Bill: You just can't hang a sign on a person.

Betty: Absolutely. I'll bet you're a Scorpio.

(*Many bells ring.*)

Listen, I was headed to the movies after I finished this section. Would you like to come along?

Bill: That sounds like fun. What's playing?

Betty: A couple of the really early Woody Allen movies.

Bill: Oh.

Betty: You don't like Woody Allen?

Bill: Sure. I like Woody Allen.

Betty: But you're not crazy about Woody Allen.

Bill: Those early ones kind of get on my nerves.

Betty: Uh-huh.

(*Bell.*)

Bill: Y'know I was headed to the—

Betty (*simultaneously*): I was thinking about—

Bill: I'm sorry.

Betty: No, go ahead.

Bill: I was going to say that I was headed to the movies in a little while, and . . .

Betty: So was I.

Bill: The Woody Allen festival?

Betty: Just up the street.

Bill: Do you like the early ones?

Betty: I think anybody who doesn't ought to be run off the planet.

Bill: How many times have you seen *Bananas*?

Betty: Eight times.

Bill: Twelve. So are you still interested? (*Long pause.*)

Betty: Do you like Entenmann's crumb cake. . . .

Bill: Last night I went out at two in the morning to get one. Did you have an Etch-a-Sketch as a child?

Betty: Yes! And do you like Brussels sprouts? (*Pause.*)
Bill: No, I think they're disgusting.
Betty: They *are* disgusting!
Bill: Do you still believe in marriage in spite of current sentiments against it?
Betty: Yes.
Bill: And children?
Betty: Three of them.
Bill: Two girls and a boy.
Betty: Harvard, Vassar, and Brown.
Bill: And will you love me?
Betty: Yes.
Bill: And cherish me forever?
Betty: Yes.
Bill: Do you still want to go to the movies?
Betty: Sure thing.
Bill and Betty (together): Waiter!

BLACKOUT

QUESTIONS

1. Ives originally planned to set *Sure Thing* at a bus stop. What does its current setting in a café suggest about the characters?
2. What happens on stage when the bell rings?
3. Who is the protagonist? What does the protagonist want?
4. Does the play have a dramatic question?
5. When does the climax of the play occur?
6. Is *Sure Thing* a romantic comedy or a farce? (See pages 1331–33 for a discussion of these types of comedy.)
7. "*Sure Thing* was not a funny play because it isn't realistic. Conversations just don't happen this way." Discuss that opinion. Do you agree or disagree?

Here is another one-act comedy by a contemporary American playwright that—like David Ives's *Sure Thing*—also deals with such issues as how we see ourselves, how we present ourselves to others, and what we want out of our relationships. Notice how the author combines some very up-to-date references with a very old fictional device, the wish-granting genie in the magic lamp, to achieve a striking blend of satire and insight.

Jane Martin

BEAUTY   2001

The identity of Jane Martin is a closely guarded secret. No biographical details, public state-ments, or photographs of this Kentucky-based playwright have been published, nor has she given any interviews or made any public appearances. Martin first came to public notice in 1981 for Talking With, *a collection of monologues that received a number of productions* *worldwide and won a Best Foreign Play of the Year award in Germany. Of Martin's many plays, others include* What Mama Don't Know *(1988),* Cementville *(1991),* Keely and Du *(which was a finalist for the 1993 Pulitzer Prize),* Middle-Aged White Guys *(1995),* Jack and Jill *(1996),* Mr. Bundy *(1998),* Anton in Show Business *(2000),* Flaming Guns of the Purple Sage *(2001), and* Good Boys *(2002).**

Characters

Carla
Bethany

Scene. *An apartment. Minimalist set. A young woman, Carla, on the phone.*

Carla: In love with me? You're in love with me? Could you describe yourself again? Uh-huh. Uh-huh. And you spoke to me? (*A knock at the door.*) Listen, I always hate to interrupt a marriage proposal, but . . . could you possibly hold that thought? (*Puts phone down and goes to door. Bethany, the same age as Carla and a friend, is there. She carries the sort of mid-eastern lamp we know of from Aladdin.*)

Bethany: Thank God you were home. I mean, you're not going to believe this!

Carla: Somebody on the phone. (*Goes back to it.*)

Bethany: I mean, I just had a beach urge, so I told them at work my uncle was dying . . .

Carla (*Motions to Bethany for quiet.*): And you were the one in the leather jacket with the tattoo? What was the tattoo? (*Carla again asks Bethany, who is gesturing wildly that she should hang up, to cool it.*) Look, a screaming eagle from shoulder to shoulder, maybe. There were a lot of people in the bar.

Bethany (*Gesturing and mouthing.*): I have to get back to work.

Carla (*On phone.*): See, the thing is, I'm probably not going to marry someone I can't remember . . . particularly when I don't drink. Sorry. Sorry. Sorry. (*She hangs up.*) Madness.

Bethany: So I ran out to the beach . . .

Carla: This was some guy I never met who apparently offered me a beer . . .

Bethany: . . . low tide and this . . . (*The lamp.*) . . . was just sitting there, lying there . . .

Carla: . . . and he tracks me down . . .

Bethany: . . . on the beach, and I lift this lid thing . . .

Carla: . . . and seriously proposes marriage.

Bethany: . . . and a genie comes out.

Carla: I mean, that's twice in a . . . what?

Bethany: A genie comes out of this thing.

Carla: A genie?

*Please see the Caution Notice in the Acknowledgments, page A.15, that gives important information about using this play in performance.

Bethany: I'm not kidding, the whole Disney kind of thing, swirling smoke, and then this twenty-foot-high, see-through guy in like an Arabian outfit.

Carla: Very funny.

Bethany: Yes, funny, but twenty feet high! I look up and down the beach, I'm alone. I don't have my pepper spray or my hand alarm. You know me, when I'm petrified I joke. I say his voice is too high for Robin Williams, and he says he's a castrati. Naturally. Who else would I meet?

Carla: What's a castrati?

Bethany: You know . . .

(*The appropriate gesture.*)

Carla: Bethany, dear one, I have three modeling calls. I am meeting Ralph Lauren!

Bethany: Okay, good. Ralph Lauren. Look, I am not kidding!

Carla: You're not kidding what?!

Bethany: There is a genie in this thingamajig.

Carla: Uh-huh. I'll be back around eight.

Bethany: And he offered me *wishes!*

Carla: Is this some elaborate practical joke because it's my birthday?

Bethany: No, happy birthday, but I'm like crazed because I'm on this deserted beach with a twenty-foot-high, see-through genie, so like sarcastically . . . you know how I need a new car . . . I said fine, gimme 25,000 dollars . . .

Carla: On the beach with the genie?

Bethany: Yeah, right, exactly, and it rains down out of the sky.

Carla: Oh sure.

Bethany (*Pulling a wad out of her purse.*): Count it, those are thousands. I lost one in the surf.

(*Carla sees the top bill. Looks at Bethany, who nods encouragement. Carla thumbs through them.*)

Carla: These look real.

Bethany: Yeah.

Carla: And they rained down out of the sky?

Bethany: Yeah.

Carla: You've been really strange lately, are you dealing?

Bethany: Dealing what, I've even given up chocolate.

Carla: Let me see the genie.

Bethany: Wait, wait.

Carla: Bethany, I don't have time to screw around. Let me see the genie or let me go on my appointments.

Bethany: Wait! So I pick up the money . . . see, there's sand on the money . . . and I'm like nuts so I say, you know, "Okay, look, ummm, big guy, my uncle is in the hospital" . . . because as you know when I said to the people at work my uncle was dying, I was on one level telling the truth although it had nothing to do with the beach, but he was in Intensive Care after the accident, and that's on my mind, so I say, okay, Genie, heal my uncle . . . which is like impossible given he was hit by two trucks, and the genie says, "Yes, Master" . . . like they're supposed to say, and he goes into this like kind of whirlwind, kicking up sand and stuff, and I'm like, "Oh my God!" and the air clears, and he bows, you know, and says, "It is done, Master," and I say, "Okay, whatever-you-are, I'm calling on my cell phone," and I get it out and I get this doctor who is like dumbstruck who says my uncle came to, walked out of Intensive Care and left the hospital! I'm not kidding, Carla.

Carla: On your mother's grave?

Bethany: On my mother's grave.

(*They look at each other.*)

Carla: Let me see the genie.

Bethany: No, no, look, that's the whole thing . . . I was just, like, reacting, you know, responding, and that's already two wishes . . . although I'm really pleased about my uncle, the $25,000 thing, I could have asked for $10 million, and there is only one wish left.

Carla: So ask for $10 million.

Bethany: I don't think so. I don't think so. I mean, I gotta focus in here. Do you have a sparkling water?

Carla: No. Bethany, I'm missing Ralph Lauren now. Very possibly my one chance to go from catalogue model to the very, very big time, so, if you are joking, stop joking.

Bethany: Not joking. See, see, the thing is, I know what I want. In my guts. Yes. Underneath my entire bitch of a life is this unspoken, ferocious, all-consuming urge . . .

Carla (*Trying to get her to move this along.*): Ferocious, all-consuming urge . . .

Bethany: I want to be like you.

Carla: Me?

Bethany: Yes.

Carla: Half the time you don't even like me.

Bethany: Jealous. The ogre of jealousy.

Carla: You're the one with the $40,000 job straight out of school. You're the one who has published short stories. I'm the one hanging on by her finger-nails in modeling. The one who has creeps calling her on the phone. The one who had to have a nose job.

Bethany: I want to be beautiful.

Carla: You are beautiful.

Bethany: Carla, I'm not beautiful.

Carla: You have charm. You have personality. You know perfectly well you're pretty.

Bethany: "Pretty," see, that's it. Pretty is the minor leagues of beautiful. Pretty is what people discover about you after they know you. Beautiful is what knocks them out across the room. Pretty, you get called a couple of times a year; *beautiful* is 24 hours a day.

Carla: Yeah? So?

Bethany: So?! We're talking *beauty* here. Don't say "So?" Beauty is the real deal. You are the center of any moment of your life. People stare. Men flock. I've seen you get offered discounts on makeup for no reason. Parents treat beautiful children better. Studies show your income goes up. You can have sex anytime you want it. Men have to know me. That takes up to a year. I'm continually horny.

Carla: Bethany, I don't even like sex. I can't have a conversation without men coming on to me. I have no privacy. I get hassled on the street. They start pressuring me from the beginning. Half the time, it never occurs to them to start with a conversation. Smart guys like you. You've had three long-term relationships, and you're only twenty-three. I haven't had one. The good guys, the smart guys are scared to death of me. I'm surrounded by male bimbos who think a preposition is when you go to school away from home. I have no woman friends except you. I don't even want to talk about this!

Bethany: I knew you'd say something like this. See, you're "in the club" so you can say this. It's the way beauty functions as an elite. You're trying to keep it all for yourself.

Carla: I'm trying to tell you it's no picnic.

Bethany: But it's what everybody wants. It's the nasty secret at large in the world. It's the unspoken tidal desire in every room and on every street. It's the unspoken, the soundless whisper . . . millions upon millions of people longing hopelessly and forever to stop being whatever they are and be beautiful, but the difference between those ardent multitudes and me is that I have a goddamn genie and one more wish!

Carla: Well, it's not what I want. This is me, Carla. I have never read a whole book. Page 6, I can't remember page 4. The last thing I read was "The Complete Idiot's Guide to WordPerfect." I leave dinner parties right after the dessert because I'm out of conversation. You know the dumb blond joke about on the application where it says, "Sign here," she put Sagittarius? I've done that. Only beautiful guys approach me, and that's because they want to borrow my eye shadow. I barely exist outside a mirror! You don't want to *be* me.

Bethany: None of you tell the truth. That's why you have no friends. We can all see you're just trying to make us feel better because we aren't in your league. This only proves to me it should be my third wish. Money can only buy things. Beauty makes you the center of the universe.

(*Bethany picks up the lamp.*)

Carla: Don't do it. Bethany, don't wish it! I am telling you you'll regret it.

(*Bethany lifts the lid. There is a tremendous crash, and the lights go out. Then they flicker and come back up, revealing Bethany, and Carla on the floor where they have been thrown by the explosion. We don't realize it at first, but they have exchanged places.*)

Carla/Bethany: Oh God.

Bethany/Carla: Oh God.

Carla/Bethany: Am I bleeding? Am I dying?

Bethany/Carla: I'm so dizzy. You're not bleeding.

Carla/Bethany: Neither are you.

Bethany/Carla: I feel so weired.

Carla/Bethany: Me too. I feel . . . (*Looking at her hands.*) Oh, my God, I'm wearing your jewelry. I'm wearing your nail polish.

Bethany/Carla: I know I'm over here, but I can see myself over there.

Carla/Bethany: I'm wearing your dress. I have your legs!!

Bethany/Carla: These aren't my shoes. I can't meet Ralph Lauren wearing these
shoes!

Carla/Bethany: I wanted to be beautiful, but I didn't want to be you.

Bethany/Carla: Thanks a lot!!

Carla/Bethany: I've got to go. I want to pick someone out and get laid.

Bethany/Carla: You can't just walk out of here in my body!

Carla/Bethany: Wait a minute. Wait a minute. What's eleven eighteenths of
1,726?

Bethany/Carla: Why?

Carla/Bethany: I'm a public accountant. I want to know if you have my brain.

Bethany/Carla: One hundred thirty-two and a half.

Carla/Bethany: You have my brain.

Bethany/Carla: What shade of Rubenstein lipstick does Cindy Crawford wear
with teal blue?

Carla/Bethany: Raging Storm.

Carla/Bethany: You have my brain. You poor bastard.

Carla/Bethany: I don't care. Don't you see?

Bethany/Carla: See what?

Carla/Bethany: We both have the one thing, the one and only thing everybody
wants.

Bethany/Carla: What is that?

Carla/Bethany: It's better than beauty for me; it's better than brains for you.

Bethany/Carla: What? What?!

Carla/Bethany: Different problems.

BLACKOUT

QUESTIONS

1. Reread the discussion of *high* and *low comedy* on pages 1332–33. Which of the two terms,
   in your view, better applies to *Beauty*? Explain and support your choice.
2. Much of the point of the play depends on Carla and Bethany seeing one another as opposites. But do they also have any important traits in common?
3. Is Bethany's unhappiness with herself a demonstration of her own superficiality, or is it a
   commentary on the superficiality of our culture? Can it be both at the same time?
4. Do Carla's claims of unhappiness with her appearance and her life seem genuine, or are
   they more accurately described by Bethany's reactions to them?

5. Reread Bethany's speech beginning "But it's what everybody wants," just before she makes her final wish. How validly, in your view, does she speak for "everybody" here?
6. What elements of tone and characterization help make *Beauty* an effective comedy?

WRITER'S PERSPECTIVE

Susan Glaspell

Susan Glaspell on Drama

CREATING *TRIFLES*   1927

We went to the theater, and for the most part we came away wishing we had gone somewhere else. Those were the days when Broadway flourished almost unchallenged. Plays, like magazine stories, were patterned. They might be pretty good within themselves, seldom did they open out to—where it surprised or thrilled your spirit to follow. They didn't ask much of *you*, those plays. Having paid for your seat, the thing was all done for you, and your mind came out where it went in, only tireder. An audience, Jig° said, had imagination. What was this "Broadway," which could make a thing as interesting as life into a thing as dull as a Broadway play?

There was a meeting at the Liberal Club—Eddie Goodman, Phil Moeller, Ida Rauh, the Boni brothers, exciting talk about starting a theater.

. . .

He [Jig] wrote a letter to the people who had seen the plays, asking if they cared to become associate members of the Provincetown Players. The purpose was to give American playwrights of sincere purpose a chance to work out their ideas in freedom,

Jig: the nickname of George Cram Cook (1873–1924), Glaspell's husband, who was the central founder and director of the Provincetown Players, perhaps the most influential theater company in the history of American drama. *Wharf Theater*: the makeshift theater that Cook created from an old fish-house at the end of a Provincetown wharf.

to give all who worked with the plays their opportunity as artists. Were they interested in this? One dollar for the three remaining bills.

The response paid for seats and stage, and for sets. A production need not cost a lot of money, Jig would say. The most expensive set at the Wharf Theater° cost thirteen dollars. There were sets at the Provincetown Playhouse which cost little more. . . .

"Now, Susan," he [Jig] said to me, briskly, "I have announced a play of yours for the next bill."

"But I have no play!"

"Then you will have to sit down to-morrow and begin one."

I protested. I did not know how to write a play. I had never "studied it."

"Nonsense," said Jig. "You've got a stage, haven't you?"

So I went out on the wharf, sat alone on one of our wooden benches without a back, and looked a long time at that bare little stage. After a time the stage became a kitchen—a kitchen there all by itself. I saw just where the stove was, the table, and the steps going upstairs. Then the door at the back opened, and people all bundled up came in—two or three men, I wasn't sure which, but sure enough about the two women, who hung back, reluctant to enter that kitchen. When I was a newspaper reporter out in Iowa, I was sent down-state to do a murder trial, and I never forgot going into the kitchen of a woman locked up in town. I had meant to do it as a short story, but the stage took it for its own, so I hurried in from the wharf to write down what I had seen. Whenever I got stuck, I would run across the street to the old wharf, sit in that leaning little theater under which the sea sounded, until the play was ready to continue. Sometimes things written in my room would not form on the stage, and I must go home and cross them out. "What playwrights need is a stage," said Jig, "their own stage."

Ten days after the director said he had announced my play, there was a reading at Mary Heaton Vorse's. I was late to the meeting, home revising the play. But when I got there the crowd liked "Trifles," and voted to put it in rehearsal next day.

From *The Road to the Temple*

◄══ WRITING CRITICALLY ══►

Conflict Resolution

A good play almost always presents a **conflict.** One or more characters want to accomplish something, but another person or thing stands in their way. The central action of the play is how those two opposing forces resolve the conflict.

Reading a play, you will understand it better if you can identify the central dramatic conflict. Who is the protagonist? What does he or she want? Who opposes the protagonist? If you can answer those basic questions, the overall design of the plot will usually become obvious. Remember that many full-length plays (or films) have a double plot (or subplot). In such a case, there will be a secondary set of characters with their own conflicts.

To begin writing about a play, you might start by listing the major characters. (It usually suffices to list only the three or four most important people.) Then after each name, write down what that character wants most at the beginning of the play. If you can't figure out a single, compelling motive for each character, write down several things that they want. You can decide later what motive is most important.

Now look at the list, and decide what character is the protagonist, or hero. What does he or she want, and who opposes that ambition? Then notice how the motivations of the other characters fit into the central conflict.

WRITING ASSIGNMENT

Select any short play in this chapter, and write a brief essay identifying the protagonist, central conflict, and dramatic question.

Here is a paper by Tara Mazzucca, a student of Beverly Schneller at Millersville University, that examines and compares the protagonists and dramatic question of two short plays by Susan Glaspell.

Mazzucca 1

Tara Mazzucca

Professor Schneller

English 102

29 April 20xx

Outside <u>Trifles</u>

Susan Glaspell was one of America's first feminist playwrights. A founder of the non-commercial Provincetown Players, she used this experimental company to present plays that realistically explored the lives of women. I would like to examine and compare two of Glaspell's early one-act plays, <u>Trifles</u> (1916) and <u>The Outside</u> (1917). I will discuss how they present women who are forced to survive in a world where men make most of the rules.

Both plays focus on female protagonists, and both realistically present the emotional hardships these women endure in their daily lives. Both plays had contemporary settings; they take place in the early twentieth century. Both plays present women who are isolated from society--Mrs. Wright in <u>Trifles</u> and the two protagonists of <u>The Outside</u>.

And in both plays a pair of female characters work together to solve the central dramatic question.

In *Trifles* Glaspell ironically places two wives, one married to a farmer and the other to the sheriff, at the scene of a mysterious murder case. The play takes place entirely in familiar territory for women in the early 1900s--a kitchen. The kitchen becomes a symbol for the game of hot and cold that the characters unwittingly play. In the kitchen where it is hot, the women find all the clues necessary to solve the case. Meanwhile the men search the rest of the cold house and find nothing to suggest a motive for the crime.

The two wives soon recognize the story behind the murder by observing small details in the house. They see clues in what the men pass over as mere trifles. When the women mention the ruined fruit preserves in the kitchen, Mr. Hale dismisses the potential importance of housekeeping details and comments, "Well, women are used to worrying over trifles" (1308). The two women, however, understand that small things can affect a person deeply.

The two women also recognize the importance of singing in Mrs. Wright's life. Singing was something she was known for when she was younger, only to have it taken away from her when she married John Wright. Doing housework alone all day in silence, Mrs. Wright became a different person. The stress of loneliness and depression finally got to Mrs. Wright. She bought a canary for company and enjoyment. She loved the singing bird, but her husband killed it. In desperation the woman decided to live without her husband.

Mrs. Hale and Mrs. Peters instinctively understand Mrs. Wright's worries. Their perspective gives them an advantage over their male counterparts. The women must work together, because if they did not, each would break under the pressure of the cold treatment they receive from their husbands--break like the glass canned fruit Mrs. Wright stores away in her cabinet.

The plot of <u>The Outside</u> is relatively simple. The widowed Mrs. Patrick lives in a remote building that was once a life-saving station. Mrs. Patrick employs another widow, Allie Mayo, to help her with housekeeping. They lead lives of almost total isolation. One day three life-savers bring in the body of a drowned sailor and attempt unsuccessfully to revive him. Mrs. Patrick is furious that they have used her house as a rescue station and demands that they leave. Her behavior so upsets the usually silent Allie that the servant confronts Mrs. Patrick with a passionate speech about the futility of renouncing life.

Allie also keeps to herself from grief. As a girl, she was talkative, but after her young husband vanished at sea, she resolved never to say an unnecessary word. Now twenty years later, she is notorious for her silence. The two women share a common grief of having lost the husbands they loved. Losing a husband changed each woman. Allie chose silence. Mrs. Patrick left society.

When the men bring the drowned young man into the former life-saving station, the incident upsets Mrs. Patrick, and she explodes with anger. This incident disturbs Allie in a different way. She realizes how isolated they have become. She knows that if they do not change, they will die without anyone caring. Deeply disturbed, Allie breaks her silence and argues with her employer. Mrs. Patrick initially resists Allie's remarks because she still has not come to terms with life without her husband. Allie resembles Mrs. Wright in <u>Trifles</u>. Both women keep quiet for years and do what they're told, until they reach a breaking point. A critical event forces each of them to take dramatic action. Allie violently argues with her employer; Mrs. Wright decides to murder her husband.

Mrs. Hale and Mrs. Peters resemble Mrs. Patrick from <u>The Outside</u>. Throughout the play Mrs. Hale and Mrs. Peters try to understand why Mrs. Wright killed her husband. In the end, they recognize that their lives have much in common

with that of the murderer. Their actions show their
confusion about their own values. They do things that hinder
the sheriff's investigation to protect an oppressed woman.
First, Mrs. Hale rips out Mrs. Wright's erratic stitching so
the men will not notice her nervous condition. Second, Mrs.
Peters, who is--ironically--the sheriff's wife, hides the
strangled bird from her husband and the other men. The women
see a new side of Mrs. Wright's marriage and sympathize with
her pathetic situation. By the end of The Outside Mrs.
Patrick also sees a new side of Allie. Allie's outburst
forces Mrs. Patrick to consider changing her life and
reconsider her ideas.

   Mrs. Patrick of The Outside and Mrs. Wright of Trifles
are also alike because they are now isolated from the world
they used to enjoy. One stopped living because of a harsh
husband, the other because of a dead husband. Mrs. Hale and
Allie also resemble one another because they both waited too
late to understand the depression of their neighbor or
living companion. In Trifles, Mrs. Hale decides to help her
neighbor even though it means protecting a criminal. Allie
speaks truthfully even though it might jeopardize her job.
In the end, the actions Allie and Mrs. Hale take are
helpful. The men never find a motive for the murder. Mrs.
Patrick finally considers changing her way of life in The
Outside . In the end each woman has found something new
inside of her.

   Mrs. Hale and Mrs. Peters both realize the secret they
must keep to protect Mrs. Wright. They also realize the
injustices women go through to be accepted in society. Mrs.
Hale says:

          I might have known she needed help! I know how
          things can be--for women. I tell you, it's queer,
          Mrs. Peters. We live close together and we live
          far apart. We all go through the same things--it's

all just a different kind of the same thing.
(1315)

In <u>The Outside</u>, the women don't feel socially
oppressed by men, but they cannot define their lives except
in relation to their husbands. When they become widows, they
lose their reason to live. Allie realizes that their grief
has gone too far. She finds her voice to say that life must
be lived. Mrs. Patrick listens enough to feel uncertainty
about her life of loneliness and isolation. Each play deals
with death and its effects on the survivors.

A major difference between the two plays is found in
the way the central female characters treat one another. In
<u>Trifles</u> the women work together to solve the mystery, but in
<u>The Outside</u> the women clash and refuse to help one another.
Glaspell did not have only one idealized image of female
behavior. She realized that different women behave
differently. Each play presents different ways women in the
early twentieth century used to survive in a man's world.
Trapped in the trifles of everyday life, many women felt as
if they were living on the outside of the world.

Works Cited

Glaspell, Susan. <u>The Outside</u>. <u>A Century of Plays by American</u>
    <u>Women</u>. Ed. Rachel France. New York: Rosen, 1979. 48-54.
Glaspell, Susan. <u>Trifles</u>. <u>Literature: An Introduction to</u>
    <u>Fiction, Poetry, and Drama</u>. Ed. X. J. Kennedy and Dana
    Gioia. 9th ed. New York: Longman, 2005. 1305-16.

FURTHER SUGGESTIONS FOR WRITING

1. Write an account of the *Trifles* case—the discovery of the murder and the arrest of Mrs. Wright—as a newspaper might have reported it. Then, in a separate paragraph or two, sum up the important facts that a reporter couldn't know, but that Susan Glaspell makes clear to us.

2. Write an essay in praise of the language spoken by the characters in *Riders to the Sea*. Arrive at some generalizations about it. (One suggestion is to turn back to Chapter Seventeen to refresh your acquaintance with metaphors and other figures of speech.)

3. Write an essay titled "Comedy on Campus" or "Comedy in Everyday Life." This essay might depend on what you have lately observed, heard reported in conversation, or noticed in current news media. Give an array of examples.

4. Write an alternate version of *Sure Thing* in which you present a couple in a different setting—a fast-food restaurant, a school library, or a mall. Change the dialogue and the characters to reflect the new setting.

5. Keeping the basic plot (the genie, the wishes, etc.), rewrite—and retitle—*Beauty* with two men as the characters. Instead of simply changing the details from, say, lipstick to cologne, reimagine the entire situation from a male perspective.

34 *Critical Casebook: Sophocles*

THE THEATER OF SOPHOCLES

For the citizens of Athens in the fifth century B.C. theater was both a religious and a civic occasion. Plays were presented only twice a year at religious festivals—both associated with Dionysius, the god of wine and crops. In January there was the Lenaea, the festival of the winepress, when plays, especially comedies, were performed. But the major theatrical event of the year came in March at the Great Dionysia, a citywide celebration that included sacrifices, prize ceremonies, and spectacular processions as well as three days of drama.

Each day at dawn a different author presented a trilogy of tragic plays—three interrelated dramas that portrayed an important mythic or legendary event. Each intense tragic trilogy was followed by a **satyr play,** an obscene parody of a mythic story, performed with the chorus dressed as satyrs, unruly mythic attendants of Dionysius who were half goat or horse and half human.

The Greeks loved competition and believed it fostered excellence. Even theater was a competitive event—not unlike the Olympic games. A panel of five judges voted each year at the Great Dionysia for the best dramatic presentation, and a substantial cash prize was given to the winning poet-playwright (all plays were written in verse). Any aspiring writer who has ever lost a literary contest may be comforted to learn that Sophocles, who triumphed in the competition twenty-four times, seems not to have won the annual prize for *Oedipus the King*. Although this play ultimately proved to be the most celebrated Greek tragedy ever written, it lost the award to a revival of a popular trilogy by Aeschylus, who had recently died.

STAGING

Seated in the open air in a hillside amphitheater, as many as 17,000 spectators could watch a performance that must have somewhat resembled an opera or musical. The

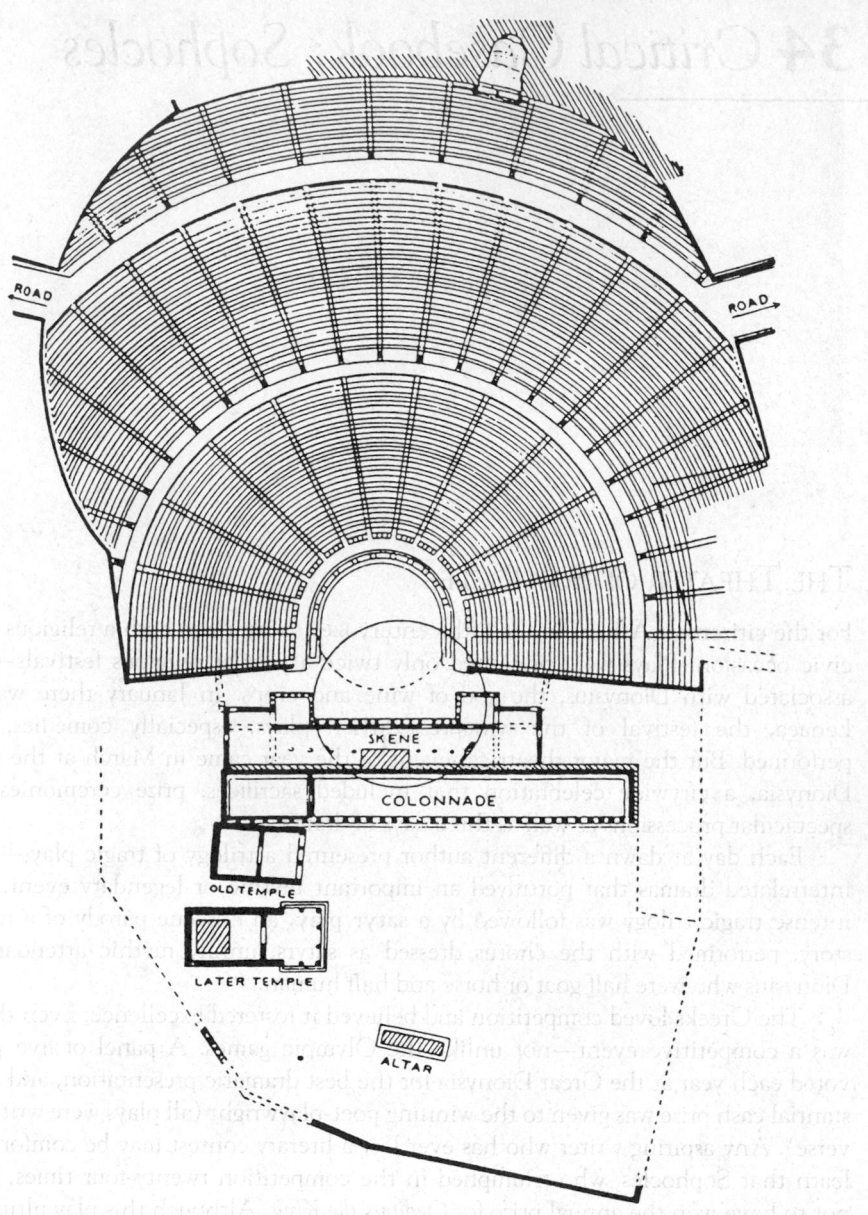

The theater of Dionysus at Athens in the time of Sophocles; a modern drawing based on scholarly guesswork. From R. C. Flickinger, The Greek Theater and Its Drama (1918).

A modern reconstruction of a classical Athenian theater. Note that the chorus performs in the circular orchestra while the actors stand on the raised stage behind.

audience was arranged in rows, with the Athenian governing council and young military cadets seated in the middle sections. Priests, priestesses, and foreign dignitaries were given special places of honor in the front rows. The performance space they watched was divided into two parts—the **orchestra,** a level circular "dancing space" (at the base of the amphitheater), and a slightly raised stage built in front of the *skene* or stage house, originally a canvas or wooden hut for costume changes.

The actors spoke and performed primarily on the stage, and the chorus sang and danced in the orchestra. The *skene* served as a general set or backdrop—the exterior of a palace, a temple, a cave, or a military tent, depending on the action of the play. The *skene* had a large door at its center that served as the major entrance for principal characters. When opened wide, the door could be used to frame a striking tableau, as when the body of Eurydice is displayed at the end of Sophocles' play *Antigone.*

By Sophocles' time, the tragedy had a conventional structure understood by most of the citizens sitting in the audience. No more than three actors were allowed on stage at any one time, along with a chorus of fifteen (the number was fixed by Sophocles himself). The actors' spoken monologue and dialogue alternated with the chorus' singing and dancing. Each tragedy began with a **prologue,** a preparatory scene. In *Oedipus the King,* for example, the play begins with Oedipus asking the suppliants why they have come and the Priest telling him about the plague ravaging Thebes. Next came the **párados,** the song for the entrance of the chorus. Then the action was enacted in **episodes,** like the acts or scenes in modern plays; the episodes were separated by danced choral songs or odes. Finally, there was a closing **éxodos,** the last scene, in which the characters and chorus concluded the action and departed.

What did the actors look like? They wore **masks** (*personae*, the source of our word *person*, "a thing through which sound comes"): some of these masks had exaggerated mouthpieces, possibly designed to project speech across the open air. Certainly, the masks, each of which covered an actor's entire head, helped spectators far away recognize the chief characters. The masks often represented certain conventional types of characters: the old king, the young soldier, the shepherd, the beautiful girl (women's parts were played by male actors). Perhaps in order to gain in both increased dignity and visibility, actors in the Greek theater eventually came to wear **cothurni**, high, thick-soled elevator shoes that made them appear taller than ordinary men. All this equipment must have given the actors a slightly inhuman yet very imposing appearance, but we may infer that the spectators accepted such conventions as easily as opera lovers accept an opera's special artifice. Today's football fans, for instance, hardly think twice about the elaborate helmets, shoulderpads, kneepads, and garishly colored uniforms worn by their favorite teams.

Rehearsal of a satyr play. Mosaic from the House of the Tragic Poet, Pompeii. Late first century.

THE CIVIC ROLE OF GREEK DRAMA

Athenian drama was supported and financed by the state. Administration of the Great Dionysia fell to the head civil magistrate. He annually appointed three wealthy citizens to serve as *choregoi*, or producers, for the competing plays. Each producer had to equip the chorus and rent the rehearsal space in which the poet-playwright would prepare the new work for the festival. The state covered the expenses of the theater, actors, and prizes (which went to author, actors, and *choregos* alike). Theater tickets were distributed free to citizens, which meant that every registered Athenian, even the poorest, could participate. The playwrights therefore addressed themselves to every element of the Athenian democracy. Only the size of the amphitheater limited the attendance. Holding between 14,000 and 17,000 spectators, it could hold slightly less than half of Athens' 40,000 citizens.

Greek theater was directed at the moral and political education of the community. The poet's role was the improvement of the *polis* or city-state (made up of a town and its surrounding countryside). Greek city-states traditionally sponsored public contests between *rhapsodes* (professional poetry performers) reciting stories from Homer's epics, the *Iliad* and *Odyssey*. As Greek society developed and urbanized, however, the competitive and individualized heroism of the Homeric epics had to be tempered with the values of cooperation and compromise necessary to a democracy. Civic theater provided the ideal medium to address these cultural needs.

As a public art form, tragedy was not simply a stage for political propaganda to promote the status quo. Nor was it exclusively a celebration of idealized heroes nobly enduring the blows of harsh circumstance and misfortune. Tragedy often enabled its audience to reflect on personal values that might be in conflict with civic ideals, on the claims of minorities that it neglected or excluded from public life, on its own irrational prejudices toward the foreign or the unknown. Frequently a play challenged its audience to feel sympathy for a vanquished enemy (as in Euripides' *Trojan Women*, the greatest antiwar play of the period, which dramatizes the horrible fate of captured women). Some plays explored the problems facing members of the politically powerless groups that made up nearly three-fourths of the Athenian population—women, children, resident aliens, and slaves. A largely male audience also frequently watched male performers enact stories of the power and anger of women, such as Euripides' *Medea*, which made their tragic violence understandable (if not entirely pardonable) to an audience not particularly disposed to treat them sympathetically. Other plays such as Sophocles' *Oedipus the King* or Euripides' *Herakles* depicted powerful men undone by misfortune, their own bad judgment, or hubris, and thrown into defeat and exile.

Such tragic stories required performers and audience to put themselves in the places of persons quite unlike themselves, in situations that might engulf any unlucky citizen—war, political upheaval, betrayal, domestic crisis. The release of the powerful emotions of pity and fear through a carefully crafted plot in the orderly context of highly conventionalized performance accounts for the paradox of tragic drama—how a viewer takes aesthetic pleasure in witnessing the sufferings of others. That tragedy served to enlarge humane empathy is best demonstrated in the conditions of performance. Male citizens acted principal roles, including not only idealized heroes, gods, and their antagonists, but also goddesses, heroines, and slaves. Many of the choruses in surviving plays are made up of female slaves or war captives. Plato in the *Republic* was particularly scandalized that male citizens played at being women gripped by irrational passions such as love, jealousy, grief, or vengeful wrath. Poet-playwrights such as Sophocles, however, understood that the impersonations necessary to theater did not degrade the actors and audience, but expanded their humanity in ways that philosophy alone could not equal.

ARISTOTLE'S CONCEPT OF TRAGEDY

> Tragedy is an imitation of an action of high importance, complete and of some amplitude; in language enhanced by distinct and varying beauties; acted not narrated; by means of pity and fear effecting its purgation of these emotions.
>
> —Aristotle, *Poetics*, Chapter VI

Aristotle's famous definition of tragedy, constructed in the fourth century B.C., is the testimony of one who probably saw many classical tragedies performed. In making his observations, Aristotle does not seem to be laying down laws for what a tragedy ought to be. More likely, he is drawing—from tragedies he has seen or read—a general description of them.

Aristotle observes that the protagonist, the hero or chief character of a tragedy, is a person of "high estate," apparently a king or queen or other member of a royal family. In thus being as keenly interested as contemporary dramatists in the private lives of the powerful, Greek dramatists need not be accused of snobbery. It is the nature of tragedy that the protagonist must fall from power and from happiness; his high estate gives him a place of dignity to fall from and perhaps makes his fall seem all the more a calamity in that it involves an entire nation or people. Nor is the protagonist extraordinary merely in his position in society. Oedipus is not only a king but also a noble soul who suffers profoundly and who employs splendid speech to express his suffering.

The tragic hero, however, is not a superman; he is fallible. The hero's downfall is the result, as Aristotle said, of his **hamartia:** his error or transgression or (as some translators would have it) his flaw or weakness of character. The notion that a tragic hero has such a **tragic flaw** has often been attributed to Aristotle, but it is by no means clear that Aristotle meant just that. According to this interpretation, every tragic hero has some fatal weakness, some moral Achilles' heel, that brings him to a bad end. In some classical tragedies, his transgression is a weakness the Greeks called **hubris**—extreme pride, leading to overconfidence.

Whatever Aristotle had in mind, however, many later critics find value in the idea of the tragic flaw. In this view, the downfall of a hero follows from his very nature. Whatever view we take—whether we find the hero's sufferings due to a flaw of character or to an error of judgment—we will probably find that his downfall results from acts for which he himself is responsible. In a Greek tragedy, the hero is a character amply capable of making choices—capable, too, of accepting the consequences.

It may be useful to take another look at Aristotle's definition of *tragedy*, with which we began. By **purgation** (or *katharsis*), did the ancient theorist mean that after witnessing a tragedy we feel relief, having released our pent-up emotions? Or did he mean that our feelings are purified, refined into something more ennobling? Scholars continue to argue. Whatever his exact meaning, clearly Aristotle implies that after witnessing a tragedy we feel better, not worse—not depressed, but somehow elated. We take a kind of pleasure in the spectacle of a noble man being abased, but surely this pleasure is a legitimate one. Part of that catharsis may also be based in our feeling of the "rightness" or accuracy of what we have just witnessed. The terrible but undeniable truth of the tragic vision of life is that blind overreaching and the destruction of hopes and dreams are very much a part of what really happens in the world. For tragedy, Edith Hamilton wrote, affects us as "pain transmuted into exaltation by the alchemy of poetry."[1]

Aristotle, in describing the workings of this inexorable force in *Oedipus the King*, uses terms that later critics have found valuable. One is **recognition,** or discovery (*anagnorisis*): the revelation of some fact not known before or some person's true identity. Oedipus makes such a discovery: he recognizes that he himself was the child whom his mother had given over to be destroyed. Such a recognition also occurs in Shakespeare's *Macbeth* when Macduff reveals himself to have been "from his mother's womb / Untimely ripped," thus disclosing a double meaning in the witches' prophecy that Macbeth could be harmed by "none of woman born," and sweeping aside Macbeth's last shred of belief that he is infallible. Modern critics have taken the term to mean also the terrible enlightenment that accompanies such a recognition. "To see things plain—that is *anagnorisis*," Clifford Leech observes, "and it is the ultimate experience we shall have if we have leisure at the point of death . . . It is what tragedy ultimately is about: the realization of the unthinkable."[2]

Having made his discovery, Oedipus suffers a reversal in his fortunes; he goes off into exile, blinded and dethroned. Such a fall from happiness seems intrinsic to tragedy, but we should know that Aristotle has a more particular meaning for his term **reversal** (*peripeteia*, anglicized as **peripety**). He means an action that turns out to have the opposite effect from the one its doer had intended. One of his illustrations of such an ironic reversal is from *Oedipus the King*. The first messenger intends to cheer Oedipus with the partially good news that, contrary to the prophecy that Oedipus would kill his father, his father has died of old age. The reversal is in the fact that, when the messenger further reveals that old Polybus was Oedipus' father only by adoption, the king, instead of having his fears allayed, is stirred to new dread.

We are not altogether sorry, perhaps, to see an arrogant man such as Oedipus humbled, and yet it is difficult not to feel that the punishment of Oedipus is greater than he deserves. Possibly this feeling is what Aristotle meant in his observation that a tragedy arouses our pity and our fear—our compassion for Oedipus and our terror as we sense the remorselessness of a universe in which a man is doomed. Notice, however, that at the end of the play Oedipus does not curse God and die. Although such a complex play is open to many interpretations, it is probably safe to say that the play is not a bitter complaint against the universe. At last, Oedipus accepts the divine will, prays for blessings upon his children, and prepares to endure his exile—fallen from high estate but uplifted in moral dignity.

[1]"The Idea of Tragedy," *The Greek Way to Western Civilization* (New York: Norton, 1942).
[2]*Tragedy* (London: Methuen, 1969) 65.

SOPHOCLES

Sophocles (496?–406 B.C.) tragic dramatist, priest, for a time one of ten Athenian generals, was one of the three great ancient Greek writers of tragedy. (The other two were his contemporaries: Aeschylus, his senior, and Euripides, his junior.) Sophocles won his first victory in the Athenian spring drama competition in 468 B.C., when a tragedy he had written defeated one by Aeschylus. He went on to win many prizes, writing more than 120 plays, of which only seven have survived in their entirety—Ajax, Antigone, Oedipus the King, Electra, Philoctetes, The Trachinian Women, and Oedipus at Colonus. (Of the lost plays, about a thousand fragments remain.) In his long life, Sophocles saw Greece rise to supremacy over the Persian Empire. He enjoyed the favor of the statesman Pericles, who, making peace with enemy Sparta, ruled Athens during a Golden Age (461–429 B.C.), during which the Parthenon was built and music, art, drama, and philosophy flourished. The playwright lived on to see his native city-state in decline, its strength drained by the disastrous Peloponnesian War. His last play, Oedipus at Colonus, set twenty years after the events of Oedipus the King, shows the former king in old age, ragged and blind, cast into exile by his sons, but still accompanied by his faithful daughter Antigone. It was written when Sophocles was nearly ninety. Oedipus the King is believed to have been first produced in 425 B.C., five years after the plague had broken out in Athens.

~ PLAYS ~

THE ORIGINS OF OEDIPUS THE KING

On a Great Dionysia feast day within several years after Athens had survived a devastating plague, the audience turned out to watch a tragedy by Sophocles, set in the city of Thebes at the moment of another terrible plague. This timely play was *Oedipus*, later given the name (in Greek) *Oedipus Tyrannos* to distinguish it from Sophocles' last Oedipus play, *Oedipus at Colonus*, written many years later when the author was ninety. A folktale figure, Oedipus gets his name through a complex pun.

Oida means "to know" (from the root *vid-*, "see"), pointing to the tale's contrasting themes of sight and blindness, wisdom and ignorance. *Oedipus* also means "swollen foot" or "clubfoot," pointing to the injury sustained in the title character's infancy, when his ankles were pinioned together like a goat's. Oedipus is the man who comes to knowledge of his true parentage through the evidence of his feet and his old injury. The term *tyrannos*, in the context of the play, simply means a man who comes to rule through his own intelligence and merit, though not related to the ruling family. The traditional Greek title might be translated, therefore, as *Clubfoot the Ruler*. (*Oedipus Rex*, which means "Oedipus the King," is the conventional Latin title for the play.)

Presumably the audience already knew this old tale referred to in Homer's *Odyssey*. They would have known that because a prophecy had foretold that Oedipus would grow up to slay his father, he had been taken out as a newborn to perish in the wilderness of Mount Cithaeron outside Thebes. (Exposure was the common fate of unwanted children in ancient Greece, though only in the most extraordinary circumstance would a royal heir be exposed.) The audience would also have known that before being left to die the baby's feet had been pinned together. And they would also have known that later, adopted by King Polybus and Queen Merope of Corinth and grown to maturity, Oedipus won both the throne and the recently widowed queen of Thebes as a reward for ridding the city of the Sphinx, a winged, woman-headed lion. All who approached the Sphinx were asked a riddle, and failure to solve it meant death. Her lethal riddle was: "What goes on four legs in the morning, two at noon, and three at evening?" Oedipus correctly answered, "Man." (As a baby he crawls on all fours, then as a man he walks erect, then as an old man he uses a cane.) Chagrined and outwitted, the Sphinx leaped from her rocky perch and dashed herself to death. Familiarity with all these events is necessary to understand *Oedipus the King*, which begins years later, after the title character has long been established as ruler of Thebes.

OEDIPUS THE KING

425 B.C.?

TRANSLATED BY ROBERT FAGLES

Characters

Oedipus, king of Thebes
A *Priest of Zeus*
Creon, brother of Jocasta
A *Chorus* of Theban citizens and their *Leader*
Tiresias, a blind prophet
Jocasta, the queen, wife of Oedipus
A *Messenger* from Corinth
A *Shepherd*
A *Messenger* from inside the palace
Antigone, *Ismene*, daughters of Oedipus and Jocasta
Guards and *Attendants*
Priests of Thebes

Laurence Olivier in Oedipus Rex.

Time and Scene: *The royal house of Thebes. Double doors dominate the façade; a stone altar stands at the center of the stage.*

Many years have passed since Oedipus solved the riddle of the Sphinx and ascended the throne of Thebes, and now a plague has struck the city. A procession of priests enters; suppliants,° broken and despondent, they carry branches wound in wool and lay them on the altar.

The doors open. Guards assemble. Oedipus comes forward, majestic but for a telltale limp, and slowly views the condition of his people.

Oedipus:
Oh my children, the new blood of ancient Thebes,
why are you here? Huddling at my altar,
praying before me, your branches wound in wool.
Our city reeks with the smoke of burning incense,
rings with cries for the Healer° and wailing for the dead.   5
I thought it wrong, my children, to hear the truth
from others, messengers. Here I am myself—

---

suppliants: persons who come to ask some favor of the king.   5 *the Healer:* Apollo, god of music, poetry, and prophecy.

you all know me, the world knows my fame:
I am Oedipus.

[*Helping a Priest to his feet.*]

                 Speak up, old man. Your years,
your dignity—you should speak for the others.   10
Why here and kneeling, what preys upon you so?
Some sudden fear? some strong desire?
You can trust me. I am ready to help,
I'll do anything. I would be blind to misery
not to pity my people kneeling at my feet.   15

Priest:
Oh Oedipus, king of the land, our greatest power!
You see us before you now, men of all ages
clinging to your altars. Here are boys,
still too weak to fly from the nest,
and here the old, bowed down with the years,   20
the holy ones—a priest of Zeus° myself—and here
the picked, unmarried men, the young hope of Thebes.
And all the rest, your great family gathers now,
branches wreathed, massing in the squares,
kneeling before the two temples of queen Athena°   25
or the river-shrine where the embers glow and die
and Apollo sees the future in the ashes.°
                        Our city—
look around you, see with your own eyes—
our ship pitches wildly, cannot lift her head
from the depths, the red waves of death . . .   30
Thebes is dying. A blight on the fresh crops
and the rich pastures, cattle sicken and die,
and the women die in labor, children stillborn,
and the plague, the fiery god of fever hurls down
on the city, his lightning slashing through us—   35
raging plague in all its vengeance, devastating
the house of Cadmus!° And black Death luxuriates
in the raw, wailing miseries of Thebes.

---

21 *Zeus:* lord of the Gods.   25 *Athena:* goddess of wisdom.   27 *Apollo . . . ashes:* At Apollo's
shrine near Thebes, the ashes of fire were used to divine the future.   37 *Cadmus:* according to
legend, the city of Thebes, where the play takes place, had been founded by the hero Cadmus.

Now we pray to you. You cannot equal the gods,
your children know that, bending at your altar.
But we do rate you first of men,
both in the common crises of our lives
and face-to-face encounters with the gods.
You freed us from the Sphinx, you came to Thebes
and cut us loose from the bloody tribute we had paid
that harsh, brutal singer. We taught you nothing,
no skill, no extra knowledge, still you triumphed.
A god was with you, so they say, and we believe it—
you lifted up our lives.

          So now again,
Oedipus, king, we bend to you, your power—
we implore you, all of us on our knees:
find us strength, rescue! Perhaps you've heard
the voice of a god or something from other men,
Oedipus . . . what do you know?
The man of experience—you see it every day—
his plans will work in a crisis, his first of all.

Act now—we beg you, best of men, raise up our city!
Act, defend yourself, your former glory!
Your country calls you savior now
for your zeal, your action years ago.
Never let us remember of your reign:
you helped us stand, only to fall once more.
Oh raise up our city, set us on our feet.
The omens were good that day you brought us joy—
be the same man today!
Rule our land, you know you have the power,
but rule a land of the living, not a wasteland.
Ship and towered city are nothing, stripped of men
alive within it, living all as one.

Oedipus:

                  My children,
I pity you. I see—how could I fail to see
what longings bring you here? Well I know
you are sick to death, all of you,
but sick as you are, not one is sick as I.
Your pain strikes each of you alone, each
in the confines of himself, no other. But my spirit
grieves for the city, for myself and all of you.
I wasn't asleep, dreaming. You haven't wakened me—

40

45

50

55

60

65

70

75

I've wept through the nights, you must know that,
groping, laboring over many paths of thought.
After a painful search I found one cure: 80
I acted at once. I sent Creon,
my wife's own brother, to Delphi°—
Apollo the Prophet's oracle—to learn
what I might do or say to save our city.

Today's the day. When I count the days gone by   85
it torments me . . . what is he doing?
Strange, he's late, he's gone too long.
But once he returns, then, then I'll be a traitor
if I do not do all the god makes clear.

Priest:
Timely words. The men over there   90
are signaling—Creon's just arriving.

Oedipus:
      [Sighting Creon, then turning to the altar.]
                              Lord Apollo,
let him come with a lucky word of rescue,
shining like his eyes!

Priest:
Welcome news, I think—he's crowned, look,
and the laurel wreath is bright with berries.   95

Oedipus:
We'll soon see. He's close enough to hear—

      [Enter Creon from the side; his face is shaded with a wreath.]

Creon, prince, my kinsman, what do you bring us?
What message from the god?

Creon:
                        Good news.
I tell you even the hardest things to bear,
if they should turn out well, all would be well.   100

---

82 *Delphi:* In the temple of Delphi at the foot of Mount Parnassus, a priestess of Dionysus,
while in an ecstatic trance, would speak the wine god's words. Such a priestess was called an
oracle; the word can also mean "a message from the god."

Oedipus:
Of course, but what were the god's *words*? There's no hope
and nothing to fear in what you've said so far.

Creon:
If you want my report in the presence of these . . .

[*Pointing to the Priests while drawing Oedipus toward the palace.*]

I'm ready now, or we might go inside.

Oedipus:
                                    Speak out,
speak to us all. I grieve for these, my people,   105
far more than I fear for my own life.

Creon:
                                    Very well,
I will tell you what I heard from the god.
Apollo commands us—he was quite clear—
"Drive the corruption from the land,
don't harbor it any longer, past all cure,   110
don't nurse it in your soil—root it out!"

Oedipus:
How can we cleanse ourselves—what rites?
What's the source of the trouble?

Creon:
Banish the man, or pay back blood with blood.
Murder sets the plague-storm on the city.

Oedipus:
                                    Whose murder?   115
Whose fate does Apollo bring to light?

Creon:
                                    Our leader,
my lord, was once a man named Laius,
before you came and put us straight on course.

Oedipus:
                                    I know—
or so I've heard. I never saw the man myself.

Creon:
Well, he was killed, and Apollo commands us now—   120
he could not be more clear,
"Pay the killers back—whoever is responsible."

Oedipus:
Where on earth are they? Where to find it now,
the trail of the ancient guilt so hard to trace?

Creon:
"Here in Thebes," he said.   125
Whatever is sought for can be caught, you know,
whatever is neglected slips away.

Oedipus:
                              But where,
in the palace, the fields or foreign soil,
where did Laius meet his bloody death?

Creon:
He went to consult an oracle, Apollo said,   130
and he set out and never came home again.

Oedipus:
No messenger, no fellow-traveler saw what happened?
Someone to cross-examine?

Creon:
                              No,
they were all killed but one. He escaped,
terrified, he could tell us nothing clearly,   135
nothing of what he saw—just one thing.

Oedipus:
                              What's that?
one thing could hold the key to it all,
a small beginning give us grounds for hope.

Creon:
He said thieves attacked them—a whole band,
not single-handed, cut King Laius down.

Oedipus:
                              A thief,   140
so daring, so wild, he'd kill a king? Impossible,
unless conspirators paid him off in Thebes.

Creon:
We suspected as much. But with Laius dead
no leader appeared to help us in our troubles.

Oedipus:
Trouble? Your *king* was murdered—royal blood!   145
What stopped you from tracking down the killer
then and there?

Creon:
                    The singing, riddling Sphinx.
She . . . persuaded us to let the mystery go
and concentrate on what lay at our feet.

Oedipus:
                                No,
I'll start again—I'll bring it all to light myself!   150
Apollo is right, and so are you, Creon,
to turn our attention back to the murdered man.
Now you have *me* to fight for you, you'll see:
I am the land's avenger by all rights,
and Apollo's champion too.   155
But not to assist some distant kinsman, no,
for my own sake I'll rid us of this corruption.
Whoever killed the king may decide to kill me too,
with the same violent hand—by avenging Laius
I defend myself.

        [*To the Priests.*]

                    Quickly, my children.   160
Up from the steps, take up your branches now.

        [*To the Guards.*]

One of you summon the city here before us,
tell them I'll do everything. God help us,
we will see our triumph—or our fall.

        [*Oedipus and Creon enter the palace, followed by the guards.*]

Priest:
Rise, my sons. The kindness we came for   165
Oedipus volunteers himself.
Apollo has sent his word, his oracle—
Come down, Apollo, save us, stop the plague.

[The Priests rise, remove their branches and exit to the side. Enter a
Chorus, the citizens of Thebes, who have not heard the news that
Creon brings. They march around the altar, chanting.]

Chorus:
                                                              Zeus!

Great welcome voice of Zeus, what do you bring?
What word from the gold vaults of Delphi   170
comes to brilliant Thebes? Racked with terror—
        terror shakes my heart
and I cry your wild cries, Apollo, Healer of Delos°
I worship you in dread . . . what now, what is your price?
some new sacrifice? some ancient rite from the past   175
come round again each spring?—
              what will you bring to birth?
Tell me, child of golden Hope
        warm voice that never dies!

You are the first I call, daughter of Zeus   180
deathless Athena—I call your sister Artemis,°
heart of the market place enthroned in glory,
                    guardian of our earth—
I call Apollo, Archer astride the thunderheads of heaven—
O triple shield against death, shine before me now!   185
If ever, once in the past, you stopped some ruin
launched against our walls
        you hurled the flame of pain
far, far from Thebes—you gods
    come now, come down once more!
                        No, no   190
the miseries numberless, grief on grief, no end—
too much to bear, we are all dying
O my people . . .
    Thebes like a great army dying
and there is no sword of thought to save us, no   195
and the fruits of our famous earth, they will not ripen
no and the women cannot scream their pangs to birth—
screams for the Healer, children dead in the womb

---

173 *Delos:* island where Apollo was born.   181 *Artemis:* twin sister of Apollo, daughter of
Zeus; goddess of hunting, the moon, and protector of nature.

and life on life goes down
                    you can watch them go
       like seabirds winging west, outracing the day's fire   200
down the horizon, irresistibly
                    streaking on to the shores of Evening
                                             Death
so many deaths, numberless deaths on deaths, no end—
Thebes is dying, look, her children   205
stripped of pity . . .
          generations strewn on the ground
unburied, unwept, the dead spreading death
and the young wives and gray-haired mothers with them
cling to the altars, trailing in from all over the city—   210
Thebes, city of death, one long cortege
             and the suffering rises
                    wails for mercy rise
     and the wild hymn for the Healer blazes out
clashing with our sobs our cries of mourning—   215
       O golden daughter of god,° send rescue
       radiant as the kindness in your eyes!
Drive him back!—the fever, the god of death
                    that raging god of war
not armored in bronze, not shielded now, he burns me,   220
battle cries in the onslaught burning on—
O rout him from our borders!
Sail him, blast him out to the Sea-queen's chamber
                    the black Atlantic gulfs
       or the northern harbor, death to all   225
where the Thracian surf comes crashing.
Now what the night spares he comes by day and kills—
the god of death.

             O lord of the stormcloud,
you who twirl the lightning, Zeus, Father,
thunder Death to nothing!   230

Apollo, lord of the light, I beg you—
     whip your longbow's golden cord
showering arrows on our enemies—shafts of power
champions strong before us rushing on!

216 *golden daughter of god*: Athena.

Artemis, Huntress,
torches flaring over the eastern ridges—
                    ride Death down in pain!
God of the headdress gleaming gold, I cry to you—
your name and ours are one, Dionysus°—
        come with your face aflame with wine   240
                    your raving women's cries
        your army on the march! Come with the lightning
come with torches blazing, eyes ablaze with glory!
Burn that god of death that all gods hate!

[Oedipus enters from the palace to address the Chorus, as if addressing
the entire city of Thebes.]

Oedipus:
You pray to the gods? Let me grant your prayers.   245
Come, listen to me—do what the plague demands:
you'll find relief and lift your head from the depths.

I will speak out now as a stranger to the story,
a stranger to the crime. If I'd been present then,
there would have been no mystery, no long hunt   250
without a clue in hand. So now, counted
a native Theban years after the murder,
to all of Thebes I make this proclamation:
if any one of you knows who murdered Laius,
the son of Labdacus, I order him to reveal   255
the whole truth to me. Nothing to fear,
even if he must denounce himself,
let him speak up
and so escape the brunt of the charge—
he will suffer no unbearable punishment,   260
nothing worse than exile, totally unharmed.

[Oedipus pauses, waiting for a reply.]

                            Next,
if anyone knows the murderer is a stranger,
a man from alien soil, come, speak up.
I will give him a handsome reward, and lay up   265
gratitude in my heart for him besides.

[Silence again, no reply.]

239–41 *Dionysus . . . raving women's cries.* God of wine with his attendant girl revelers.

But if you keep silent, if anyone panicking,
trying to shield himself or friend or kin,
rejects my offer, then hear what I will do.
I order you, every citizen of the state
where I hold throne and power: banish this man— 270
whoever he may be—never shelter him, never
speak a word to him, never make him partner
to your prayers, your victims burned to the gods.
Never let the holy water touch his hands.
Drive him out, each of you, from every home. 275
He is the plague, the heart of our corruption,
as Apollo's oracle has just revealed to me.
So I honor my obligations:
I fight for the god and for the murdered man.

Now my curse on the murderer. Whoever he is, 280
a lone man unknown in his crime
or one among many, let that man drag out
his life in agony, step by painful step—
I curse myself as well . . . if by any chance
he proves to be an intimate of our house, 285
here at my hearth, with my full knowledge,
may the curse I just called down on him strike me!

These are your orders: perform them to the last.
I command you, for my sake, for Apollo's, for this country
blasted root and branch by the angry heavens. 290
Even if god had never urged you on to act,
how could you leave the crime uncleansed so long?
A man so noble—your king, brought down in blood—
you should have searched. But I am the king now,
I hold the throne that he held then, possess his bed 295
and a wife who shares our seed . . . why, our seed
might be the same, children born of the same mother
might have created blood-bonds between us
if his hope of offspring hadn't met disaster—
but fate swooped at his head and cut him short. 300
So I will fight for him as if he were my father,
stop at nothing, search the world
to lay my hands on the man who shed his blood,
the son of Labdacus descended of Polydorus,
Cadmus of old and Agenor, founder of the line: 305
their power and mine are one.
                                         Oh dear gods,
my curse on those who disobey these orders!

Let no crops grow out of the earth for them—
shrivel their women, kill their sons,
burn them to nothing in this plague   310
that hits us now, or something even worse.
But you, loyal men of Thebes who approve my actions,
may our champion, Justice, may all the gods
be with us, fight beside us to the end!

Leader:
In the grip of your curse, my king, I swear   315
I'm not the murderer, I cannot point him out.
As for the search, Apollo pressed it on us—
he should name the killer.

Oedipus:
                        Quite right,
but to force the gods to act against their will—
no man has the power.

Leader:
                        Then if I might mention   320
the next best thing . . .

Oedipus:
                        The third best too—
don't hold back, say it.

Leader:
                        I still believe . . .
Lord Tiresias sees with the eyes of Lord Apollo.
Anyone searching for the truth, my king,
might learn it from the prophet, clear as day.   325

Oedipus:
I've not been slow with that. On Creon's cue
I sent the escorts, twice, within the hour.
I'm surprised he isn't here.

Leader:
                        We need him—
without him we have nothing but old, useless rumors.

Oedipus:
Which rumors? I'll search out every word.   330

Leader:
Laius was killed, they say, by certain travelers.

Oedipus:
I know—but no one can find the murderer.

Leader:
If the man has a trace of fear in him
he won't stay silent long,
not with your curses ringing in his ears.   335

Oedipus:
He didn't flinch at murder,
he'll never flinch at words.

> [*Enter Tiresias, the blind prophet, led by a boy with escorts in
> attendance. He remains at a distance.*]

Leader:
Here is the one who will convict him, look,
they bring him on at last, the seer, the man of god.
The truth lives inside him, him alone.

Oedipus:

                    O Tiresias,   340
master of all the mysteries of our life,
all you teach and all you dare not tell,
signs in the heavens, signs that walk the earth!
Blind as you are, you can feel all the more
what sickness haunts our city. You, my lord,   345
are the one shield, the one savior we can find.

We asked Apollo—perhaps the messengers
haven't told you—he sent his answer back:
"Relief from the plague can only come one way.
Uncover the murderers of Laius,   350
put them to death or drive them into exile."
So I beg you, grudge us nothing now, no voice,
no message plucked from the birds, the embers
or the other mantic ways within your grasp.
Rescue yourself, your city, rescue me—   355
rescue everything infected by the dead.
We are in your hands. For a man to help others
with all his gifts and native strength:
that is the noblest work.

Tiresias:

　　　　　　How terrible—to see the truth
when the truth is only pain to him who sees!
I knew it well, but I put it from my mind,
else I never would have come.

Oedipus:
What's this? Why so grim, so dire?

Tiresias:
Just send me home. You bear your burdens,
I'll bear mine. It's better that way,
please believe me.

Oedipus:

　　　　　　Strange response . . . unlawful,
unfriendly too to the state that bred and reared you—
you withhold the word of god.

Tiresias:

　　　　　　　　　I fail to see
that your own words are so well-timed.
I'd rather not have the same thing said of me . . . .

Oedipus:
For the love of god, don't turn away,
not if you know something. We beg you,
all of us on our knees.

Tiresias:

　　　　　　None of you knows—
and I will never reveal my dreadful secrets,
not to say your own.

Oedipus:
What? You know and you won't tell?
You're bent on betraying us, destroying Thebes?

Tiresias:
I'd rather not cause pain for you or me.
So why this . . . useless interrogation?
You'll get nothing from me.

360

365

370

375

Oedipus:

Nothing! You, 380
you scum of the earth, you'd enrage a heart of stone!
You won't talk? Nothing moves you?
Out with it, once and for all!

Tiresias:

You criticize my temper . . . unaware
of the one *you* live with, you revile me. 385

Oedipus:

Who could restrain his anger hearing you?
What outrage—you spurn the city!

Tiresias:

What will come will come.
Even if I shroud it all in silence.

Oedipus:

What will come? You're bound to *tell* me that. 390

Tiresias:

I will say no more. Do as you like, build your anger
to whatever pitch you please, rage your worst—

Oedipus:

Oh I'll let loose, I have such fury in me—
now I see it all. You helped hatch the plot,
you did the work, yes, short of killing him
with your own hands—and given eyes I'd say 395
you did the killing single-handed!

Tiresias:

Is that so!
I charge you, then, submit to that decree
you just laid down: from this day onward
speak to no one, not these citizens, not myself. 400
You are the curse, the corruption of the land!

Oedipus:

You, shameless—
aren't you appalled to start up such a story?
You think you can get away with this?

Tiresias:
                              I have already.
The truth with all its power lives inside me.   405

Oedipus:
Who primed you for this? Not your prophet's trade.

Tiresias:
You did, you forced me, twisted it out of me.

Oedipus:
What? Say it again—I'll understand it better.

Tiresias:
Didn't you understand, just now?
Or are you tempting me to talk?   410

Oedipus:
No, I can't say I grasped your meaning.
Out with it, again!

Tiresias:
I say you are the murderer you hunt.

Oedipus:
That obscenity, twice—by god, you'll pay.

Tiresias:
Shall I say more, so you can really rage?   415

Oedipus:
Much as you want. Your words are nothing—
futile.

Tiresias:
       You cannot imagine . . . I tell you,
you and your loved ones live together in infamy,
you cannot see how far you've gone in guilt.

Oedipus:
You think you can keep this up and never suffer?   420

Tiresias:
Indeed, if the truth has any power.

Oedipus:

It does
but not for you, old man. You've lost your power,
stone-blind, stone-deaf—senses, eyes blind as stone!

Tiresias:
I pity you, flinging at me the very insults
each man here will fling at you so soon.

Oedipus:

Blind,   425
lost in the night, endless night that nursed you!
You can't hurt me or anyone else who sees the light—
you can never touch me.

Tiresias:

True, it is not your fate
to fall at my hands. Apollo is quite enough,
and he will take some pains to work this out.   430

Oedipus:
Creon! Is this conspiracy his or yours?

Tiresias:
Creon is not your downfall, no, you are your own.

Oedipus:

O power—
wealth and empire, skill outstripping skill
in the heady rivalries of life,
what envy lurks inside you! Just for this,   435
the crown the city gave me—I never sought it,
they laid it in my hands—for this alone, Creon,
the soul of trust, my loyal friend from the start
steals against me . . . so hungry to overthrow me
he sets this wizard on me, this scheming quack,   440
this fortune-teller peddling lies, eyes peeled
for his own profit—seer blind in his craft!

Come here, you pious fraud. Tell me,
when did you ever prove yourself a prophet?
When the Sphinx, that chanting Fury kept her deathwatch here, 445
why silent then, not a word to set our people free?
There was a riddle, not for some passer-by to solve—
it cried out for a prophet. Where were you?

Did you rise to the crisis? Not a word,
you and your birds, your gods—nothing.
No, but I came by, Oedipus the ignorant,
I stopped the Sphinx! With no help from the birds,
the flight of my own intelligence hit the mark.

And this is the man you'd try to overthrow?
You think you'll stand by Creon when he's king?
You and the great mastermind—
you'll pay in tears, I promise you, for this,
this witch-hunt. If you didn't look so senile
the lash would teach you what your scheming means!

Leader:
I would suggest his words were spoken in anger,
Oedipus . . . yours too, and it isn't what we need.
The best solution to the oracle, the riddle
posed by god—we should look for that.

Tiresias:
You are the king no doubt, but in one respect,
at least, I am your equal: the right to reply.
I claim that privilege too.
I am not your slave. I serve Apollo.
I don't need Creon to speak for me in public.
So,
you mock my blindness? Let me tell you this.
You with your precious eyes,
you're blind to the corruption of your life,
to the house you live in, those you live with—
who *are* your parents? Do you know? All unknowing
you are the scourge of your own flesh and blood,
the dead below the earth and the living here above,
and the double lash of your mother and your father's curse
will whip you from this land one day, their footfall
treading you down in terror, darkness shrouding
your eyes that now can see the light!
Soon, soon
you'll scream aloud—what haven won't reverberate?
What rock of Cithaeron won't scream back in echo?
That day you learn the truth about your marriage,
the wedding-march that sang you into your halls,
the lusty voyage home to the fatal harbor!
And a crowd of other horrors you'd never dream
will level you with yourself and all your children.

450

455

460

465

470

475

480

485

There. Now smear us with insults—Creon, myself
and every word I've said. No man will ever
be rooted from the earth as brutally as you.

Oedipus:

Enough! Such filth from him? Insufferable—   490
what, still alive? Get out—
faster, back where you came from—vanish!

Tiresias:

I would never have come if you hadn't called me here.

Oedipus:

If I thought you would blurt out such absurdities,
you'd have died waiting before I'd had you summoned.   495

Tiresias:

Absurd, am I! To you, not to your parents:
the ones who bore you found me sane enough.

Oedipus:

Parents—who? Wait . . . who is my father?

Tiresias:

This day will bring your birth and your destruction.

Oedipus:

Riddles—all you can say are riddles, murk and darkness.   500

Tiresias:

Ah, but aren't you the best man alive at solving riddles?

Oedipus:

Mock me for that, go on, and you'll reveal my greatness.

Tiresias:

Your great good fortune, true, it was your ruin.

Oedipus:

Not if I saved the city—what do I care?

Tiresias:

Well then, I'll be going.

[*To his attendant.*]

Take me home, boy. 505

Oedipus:
Yes, take him away. You're a nuisance here.
Out of the way, the irritation's gone.

[*Turning his back on Tiresias, moving toward the palace.*]

Tiresias:
I will go,
once I have said what I came here to say.
I'll never shrink from the anger in your eyes—
you can't destroy me. Listen to me closely: 510
the man you've sought so long, proclaiming,
cursing up and down, the murderer of Laius—
he is here. A stranger.
you may think, who lives among you,
he soon will be revealed a native Theban 515
but he will take no joy in the revelation.
Blind who now has eyes, beggar who now is rich,
he will grope his way toward a foreign soil,
a stick tapping before him step by step.

[*Oedipus enters the palace.*]

Revealed at last, brother and father both 520
to the children he embraces; to his mother
son and husband both—he sowed the loins
his father sowed, he spilled his father's blood!

Go in and reflect on that, solve that.
And if you find I've lied 525
from this day onward call the prophet blind,

[*Tiresias and the boy exit to the side.*]

Chorus:
Who—
who is the man the voice of god denounces
resounding out of the rocky gorge of Delphi?
The horror too dark to tell,
whose ruthless bloody hands have done the work? 530

His time has come to fly
    to outrace the stallions of the storm
            his feet a streak of speed—
Cased in armor, Apollo son of the Father
lunges on him, lightning-bolts afire!   535
And the grim unerring Furies°
             closing for the kill.
                          Look,
the word of god has just come blazing
flashing off Parnassus' snowy heights!
    That man who left no trace—   540
after him, hunt him down with all our strength!
Now under bristling timber
    up through rocks and caves he stalks
            like the wild mountain bull—
cut off from men, each step an agony, frenzied, racing blind   545
but he cannot outrace the dread voices of Delphi
ringing out of the heart of Earth,
    the dark wings beating around him shrieking doom
          the doom that never dies, the terror—
                        550

The skilled prophet scans the birds and shatters me with terror!
I can't accept him, can't deny him, don't know what to say,
I'm lost, and the wings of dark foreboding beating—
I cannot see what's come, what's still to come . . .
and what could breed a blood feud between
    Laius' house° and the son of Polybus?°   555
I know of nothing, not in the past and not now,
no charge to bring against our king, no cause
to attack his fame that rings throughout Thebes—
    not without proof—not for the ghost of Laius,   560
    not to avenge a murder gone without a trace.

Zeus and Apollo know, they know, the great masters
    of all the dark and depth of human life.
But whether a mere man can know the truth,
whether a seer can fathom more than I—
there is no test, no certain proof   565
    though matching skill for skill
a man can outstrip a rival. No, not till I see
these charges proved will I side with his accusers.

536 *Furies:* three horrific female spirits whose task was to seek out and punish evildoers.   555
Laius' house: descendants of Laius (true father of Oedipus, although the chorus does not know
it). *Polybus:* king who adopted the child Oedipus.

We saw him then, when the she-hawk° swept against him,
saw with our own eyes his skill, his brilliant triumph—   570
    there was the test—he was the joy of Thebes!
    Never will I convict my king, never in my heart.

    [*Enter Creon from the side.*]

Creon:
My fellow-citizens, I hear King Oedipus
levels terrible charges at me. I had to come.
I resent it deeply. If, in the present crisis   575
he thinks he suffers any abuse from me,
anything I've done or said that offers him
the slightest injury, why, I've no desire
to linger out this life, my reputation in ruins.
The damage I'd face from such an accusation   580
is nothing simple. No, there's nothing worse:
branded a traitor in the city, a traitor
to all of you and my good friends.

Leader:
                             True,
but a slur might have been forced out of him,
by anger perhaps, not any firm conviction.   585

Creon:
The charge was made in public, wasn't it?
I put the prophet up to spreading lies?

Leader:
Such things were said . . .
I don't know with what intent, if any.

Creon:
Was his glance steady, his mind right   590
when the charge was brought against me?

Leader:
I really couldn't say. I never look
to judge the ones in power.

    [*The doors open. Oedipus enters.*]
                    Wait,
here's Oedipus now.

569 *she-hawk:* the Sphinx.

Oedipus:

You—here? You have the gall
to show your face before the palace gates?   595
You, plotting to kill me, kill the king—
I see it all, the marauding thief himself
scheming to steal my crown and power!

Tell me,
in god's name, what did you take me for,
coward or fool, when you spun out your plot?   600
Your treachery—you think I'd never detect it
creeping against me in the dark? Or sensing it,
not defend myself? Aren't you the fool,
you and your high adventure. Lacking numbers,
powerful friends, out for the big game of empire— 605
you need riches, armies to bring that quarry down!

Creon:

Are you quite finished? It's your turn to listen
for just as long as you've . . . instructed me.
Hear me out, then judge me on the facts.

Oedipus:

You've a wicked way with words, Creon,   610
but I'll be slow to learn—from you.
I find you a menace, a great burden to me.

Creon:

Just one thing, hear me out in this.

Oedipus:

Just one thing,
don't tell *me* you're not the enemy, the traitor.

Creon:

Look, if you think crude, mindless stubbornness   615
such a gift, you've lost your sense of balance.

Oedipus:

If you think you can abuse a kinsman,
then escape the penalty, you're insane.

Creon:

Fair enough, I grant you. But this injury
you say I've done you, what is it?   620

Oedipus:
Did you induce me, yes or no,
to send for that sanctimonious prophet?

Creon:
I did. And I'd do the same again.

Oedipus:
All right then, tell me, how long is it now
since Laius . . .

Creon:
              Laius—what did *he* do?

Oedipus:
                                Vanished,   625
swept from sight, murdered in his tracks.

Creon:
The count of the years would run you far back . . .

Oedipus:
And that far back, was the prophet at his trade?

Creon:
Skilled as he is today, and just as honored.

Oedipus:
Did he ever refer to me then, at that time?

Creon:
                        No,   630
never, at least, when I was in his presence.

Oedipus:
But you did investigate the murder, didn't you?

Creon:
We did our best, of course, discovered nothing.

Oedipus:
But the great seer never accused me then—why not?

Creon:
I don't know. And when I don't, *I* keep quiet.   635

Oedipus:
You do know this, you'd tell it too—
if you had a shred of decency.

Creon:
                              What?
If I know, I won't hold back.

Oedipus:
                         Simply this:
if the two of you had never put heads together,
we would never have heard about *my* killing Laius.   640

Creon:
If that's what he says . . . well, you know best.
But now I have a right to learn from you
as you just learned from me.

Oedipus:
                          Learn your fill,
you never will convict me of the murder.

Creon:
Tell me, you're married to my sister, aren't you?   645

Oedipus:
A genuine discovery—there's no denying that.

Creon:
And you rule the land with her, with equal power?

Oedipus:
She receives from me whatever she desires.

Creon:
And I am the third, all of us are equals?

Oedipus:
Yes, and it's there you show your stripes—   650
you betray a kinsman.

Creon:
                    Not at all.
Not if you see things calmly, rationally,

as I do. Look at it this way first:
who in his right mind would rather rule
and live in anxiety than sleep in peace?   655
Particularly if he enjoys the same authority.
Not I, I'm not the man to yearn for kingship,
not with a king's power in my hands. Who would?
No one with any sense of self-control.
Now, as it is, you offer me all I need,   660
there'd be many painful duties to perform,
hardly to my taste.
                          How could kingship
please me more than influence, power
without a qualm? I'm not that deluded yet,   665
to reach for anything but privilege outright,
profit free and clear.
Now all men sing my praises, all salute me,
now all who request your favors curry mine.
I am their best hope: success rests in me.   670
Why give up that, I ask you, and borrow trouble?
A man of sense, someone who sees things clearly
would never resort to treason.
No, I have no lust for conspiracy in me,   675
nor could I ever suffer one who does.

Do you want proof? Go to Delphi yourself,
examine the oracle and see if I've reported
the message word-for-word. This too:
if you detect that I and the clairvoyant
have plotted anything in common, arrest me,   680
execute me. Not on the strength of one vote,
two in this case, mine as well as yours.
But don't convict me on sheer unverified surmise.
How wrong it is to take the good for bad,
purely at random, or take the bad for good.   685
But reject a friend, a kinsman? I would as soon
tear out the life within us, priceless life itself.
You'll learn this well, without fail, in time.
Time alone can bring the just man to light—
the criminal you can spot in one short day.

Leader:

                          Good advice,   690
my lord, for anyone who wants to avoid disaster.
Those who jump to conclusions may go wrong.

Oedipus:
When my enemy moves against me quickly,
plots in secret, I move quickly too, I must,
I plot and pay him back. Relax my guard a moment,   695
waiting his next move—he wins his objective,
I lose mine.

Creon:
                    What do you want?
You want me banished?

Oedipus:
                              No, I want you dead.

Creon:
Just to show how ugly a grudge can . . .

Oedipus:
                                        So,
still stubborn? you don't think I'm serious?   700

Creon:
I think you're insane.

Oedipus:
                    Quite sane—in my behalf.

Creon:
Not just as much in mine?

Oedipus:
                              You—my mortal enemy?

Creon:
What if you're wholly wrong?

Oedipus:
                              No matter—I must rule.

Creon:
Not if you rule unjustly.

Oedipus:
                              Hear him, Thebes, my city!

Creon:
My city too, not yours alone!   705

Leader:
Please, my lords.

    [Enter Jocasta from the palace.]

              Look, Jocasta's coming,
and just in time too. With her help
you must put this fighting of yours to rest.

Jocasta:
Have you no sense? Poor misguided men,
such shouting—why this public outburst?   710
Aren't you ashamed, with the land so sick,
to stir up private quarrels?

    [To Oedipus.]

Into the palace now. And Creon, you go home.
Why make such a furor over nothing?

Creon:
My sister, it's dreadful . . . Oedipus, your husband,   715
he's bent on a choice of punishments for me,
banishment from the fatherland or death.

Oedipus:
Precisely. I caught him in the act, Jocasta,
plotting, about to stab me in the back.

Creon:
Never—curse me, let me die and be damned   720
if I've done you any wrong you charge me with.

Jocasta:
Oh god, believe it, Oedipus,
honor the solemn oath he swears to heaven.
Do it for me, for the sake of all your people.

    [The Chorus begins to chant.]

Chorus:
    Believe it, be sensible   725
      give way, my king, I beg you!

Oedipus:
What do you want from me, concessions?

Chorus:
Respect him—he's been no fool in the past
and now he's strong with the oath he swears to god.

Oedipus:
You know what you're asking?

Chorus:
                                    I do.

Oedipus:
                                    Then out with it!   730

Chorus:
The man's your friend, your kin, he's under oath—
don't cast him out, disgraced
branded with guilt on the strength of hearsay only.

Oedipus:
Know full well, if that is what you want
you want me dead or banished from the land.

Chorus:
                                    Never—   735
no, by the blazing Sun, first god of the heavens!
    Stripped of the gods, stripped of loved ones,
let me die by inches if that ever crossed my mind.
But the heart inside me sickens, dies as the land dies
and now on top of the old griefs you pile this,   740
your fury—both of you!

Oedipus:
                                    Then let him go,
even if it does lead to my ruin, my death
or my disgrace, driven from Thebes for life.
It's you, not him I pity—your words move me.
He, wherever he goes, my hate goes with him.   745

Creon:
Look at you, sullen in yielding, brutal in your rage—
you will go too far. It's perfect justice:
natures like yours are hardest on themselves.

Oedipus:
Then leave me alone—get out!

Creon:
I'm going.
You're wrong, so wrong. These men know I'm right.   750

[*Exit to the side. The Chorus turns to Jocasta.*]

Chorus:
Why do you hesitate, my lady
    why not help him in?

Jocasta:
Tell me what's happened first.

Chorus:
Loose, ignorant talk started dark suspicions
and a sense of injustice cut deeply too.   755

Jocasta:
On both sides?

Chorus:
Oh yes.

Jocasta:
What did they say?

Chorus:
Enough, please, enough! The land's so racked already
or so it seems to me . . .
End the trouble here, just where they left it.

Oedipus:
You see what comes of your good intentions now?   760
And all because you tried to blunt my anger.

Chorus:
My king,
I've said it once, I'll say it time and again—
    I'd be insane, you know it,
senseless, ever to turn my back on you.
You who set our beloved land—storm-tossed, shattered—   765

straight on course. Now again, good helmsman,
steer us through the storm!

[*The Chorus draws away, leaving Oedipus and Jocasta
side by side.*]

Jocasta:
                                     For the love of god,
Oedipus, tell me too, what is it?
Why this rage? You're so unbending.

Oedipus:
I will tell you. I respect you, Jocasta,   770
much more than these men here . . .

        [*Glancing at the Chorus.*]

Creon's to blame, Creon schemes against me.

Jocasta:
Tell me clearly, how did the quarrel start?

Oedipus:
He says I murdered Laius—I am guilty.

Jocasta:
How does he know? Some secret knowledge   775
or simple hearsay?

Oedipus:
                         Oh, he sent his prophet in
to do his dirty work. You know Creon,
Creon keeps his own lips clean.

Jocasta:
                              A prophet?
Well then, free yourself of every charge!
Listen to me and learn some peace of mind: 780
no skill in the world,
nothing human can penetrate the future.
Here is proof, quick and to the point.

An oracle came to Laius one fine day
(I won't say from Apollo himself   785
but his underlings, his priests) and it declared

that doom would strike him down at the hands of a son,
our son, to be born of our own flesh and blood. But Laius,
so the report goes at least, was killed by strangers,
thieves, at a place where three roads meet . . . my son—   790
he wasn't three days old and the boy's father
fastened his ankles, had a henchman fling him away
on a barren, trackless mountain.
                                There, you see?
Apollo brought neither thing to pass. My baby
no more murdered his father than Laius suffered—   795
his wildest fear—death at his own son's hands.
That's how the seers and all their revelations
mapped out the future. Brush them from your mind.
Whatever the god needs and seeks
he'll bring to light himself, with ease.

Oedipus:
                              Strange,   800
hearing you just now . . . my mind wandered,
my thoughts racing back and forth.

Jocasta:
What do you mean? Why so anxious, startled?

Oedipus:
I thought I heard you say that Laius
was cut down at a place where three roads meet.   805

Jocasta:
That was the story. It hasn't died out yet.

Oedipus:
Where did this thing happen? Be precise.

Jocasta:
A place called Phocis, where two branching roads,
one from Daulia, one from Delphi,
come together—a crossroads.   810

Oedipus:
When? How long ago?

Jocasta:
The heralds no sooner reported Laius dead
than you appeared and they hailed you king of Thebes.

Oedipus:

My god, my god—what have you planned to do to me?

Jocasta:

What, Oedipus? What haunts you so?

Oedipus:

                                    Not yet.   815
Laius—how did he look? Describe him.
Had he reached his prime?

Jocasta:

                          He was swarthy,
and the gray had just begun to streak his temples,
and his build . . . wasn't far from yours.

Oedipus:

                                    Oh no no,
I think I've just called down a dreadful curse   820
upon myself—I simply didn't know!

Jocasta:

What are you saying? I shudder to look at you.

Oedipus:

I have a terrible fear the blind seer can see.
I'll know in a moment. One thing more—

Jocasta:

                                    Anything,
afraid as I am—ask, I'll answer, all I can.   825

Oedipus:

Did he go with a light or heavy escort,
several men-at-arms, like a lord, a king?

Jocasta:

There were five in the party, a herald among them,
and a single wagon carrying Laius.

Oedipus:

                          Ai—
now I can see it all, clear as day.   830
Who told you all this at the time, Jocasta?

Jocasta:
A servant who reached home, the lone survivor.

Oedipus:
So, could he still be in the palace—even now?

Jocasta:
No indeed. Soon as he returned from the scene
and saw you on the throne with Laius dead and gone,   835
he knelt and clutched my hand, pleading with me
to send him into the hinterlands, to pasture,
far as possible, out of sight of Thebes.
I sent him away. Slave though he was,
he'd earned that favor—and much more.   840

Oedipus:
Can we bring him back, quickly?

Jocasta:
Easily. Why do you want him so?

Oedipus:
                              I'm afraid,
Jocasta, I have said too much already.
That man—I've got to see him.

Jocasta:
                              Then he'll come.
But even I have a right, I'd like to think,   845
to know what's torturing you, my lord.

Oedipus:
And so you shall—I can hold nothing back from you,
now I've reached this pitch of dark foreboding.
Who means more to me than you? Tell me,
whom would I turn toward but you   850
as I go through all this?

My father was Polybus, king of Corinth.
My mother, a Dorian, Merope. And I was held
the prince of the realm among the people there,
till something struck me out of nowhere,   855
something strange . . . worth remarking perhaps,
hardly worth the anxiety I gave it.
Some man at a banquet who had drunk too much
shouted out—he was far gone, mind you—

that I am not my father's son. Fighting words! 860
I barely restrained myself that day
but early the next I went to mother and father,
questioned them closely, and they were enraged
at the accusation and the fool who let it fly.
So as for my parents I was satisfied, 865
but still this thing kept gnawing at me,
the slander spread—I had to make my move.
                                        And so,
unknown to mother and father I set out for Delphi,
and the god Apollo spurned me, sent me away
denied the facts I came for, 870
but first he flashed before my eyes a future
great with pain, terror, disaster—I can hear him cry,
"You are fated to couple with your mother, you will bring
a breed of children into the light no man can bear to see—
you will kill your father, the one who gave you life!" 875
I heard all that and ran. I abandoned Corinth,
from that day on I gauged its landfall only
by the stars, running, always running
toward some place where I would never see
the shame of all those oracles come true. 880
And as I fled I reached that very spot
where the great king, you say, met his death.

Now, Jocasta, I will tell you all.
Making my way toward this triple crossroad
I began to see a herald, then a brace of colts 885
drawing a wagon, and mounted on the bench . . . a man,
just as you've described him, coming face-to-face,
and the one in the lead and the old man himself
were about to thrust me off the road—brute force—
and the one shouldering me aside, the driver, 890
I strike him in anger!—and the old man, watching me
coming up along his wheels—he brings down
his prod, two prongs straight at my head!
I paid him back with interest!
Short work, by god—with one blow of the staff 895
in this right hand I knock him out of his high seat,
roll him out of the wagon, sprawling headlong—
I killed them all—every mother's son!

Oh, but if there is any blood-tie
between Laius and this stranger . . . 900

what man alive more miserable than I?
More hated by the gods? I am the man
no alien, no citizen welcomes to his house,
law forbids it—not a word to me in public,
driven out of every hearth and home.   905
And all these curses I—no one but I
brought down these piling curses on myself!
And you, his wife, I've touched your body with these,
the hands that killed your husband cover you with blood.

Wasn't I born for torment? Look me in the eyes!   910
I am abomination—heart and soul!
I must be exiled, and even in exile
never see my parents, never set foot
on native ground again. Else I am doomed
to couple with my mother and cut my father down . . .   915
Polybus who reared me, gave me life.
                                    But why, why?
Wouldn't a man of judgment say—and wouldn't he be right—
some savage power has brought this down upon my head?

Oh no, not that, you pure and awesome gods,
never let me see that day! Let me slip   920
from the world of men, vanish without a trace
before I see myself stained with such corruption,
stained to the heart.

Leader:
My lord, you fill our hearts with fear.
But at least until you question the witness,   925
do take hope.

Oedipus:
                    Exactly. He is my last hope—
I am waiting for the shepherd. He is crucial.

Jocasta:
And once he appears, what then? Why so urgent?

Oedipus:
I will tell you. If it turns out that his story
matches yours, I've escaped the worst.   930

Jocasta:
What did I say? What struck you so?

Oedipus:

                    You said *thieves*—
he told you a whole band of them murdered Laius.
So, if he still holds to the same number,
I cannot be the killer. One can't equal many.
But if he refers to one man, one alone,   935
clearly the scales come down on me:
I am guilty.

Jocasta:

                    Impossible. Trust me,
I told you precisely what he said,
and he can't retract it now;
the whole city heard it, not just I.   940
And even if he should vary his first report
by one man more or less, still, my lord,
he could never make the murder of Laius
truly fit the prophecy. Apollo was explicit:
my son was doomed to kill my husband . . . my son,   945
poor defenseless thing, he never had a chance
to kill his father. They destroyed him first.

So much for prophecy. It's neither here nor there.
From this day on, I wouldn't look right or left.

Oedipus:

True, true. Still, that shepherd,   950
someone fetch him—now!

Jocasta:

I'll send at once. But do let's go inside.
I'd never displease you, least of all in this.

        [*Oedipus and Jocasta enter the palace.*]

Chorus:

        Destiny guide me always
        Destiny find me filled with reverence   955
            pure in word and deed.
        Great laws tower above us, reared on high
        born for the brilliant vault of heaven—
            Olympian Sky their only father,
        nothing mortal, no man gave them birth,   960

their memory deathless, never lost in sleep:
within them lives a mighty god, the god does not
      grow old.

Pride breeds the tyrant
violent pride, gorging, crammed to bursting
    with all that is overripe and rich with ruin—   965
clawing up to the heights, headlong pride
crashes down the abyss—sheer doom!
    No footing helps, all foothold lost and gone.
But the healthy strife that makes the city strong—
I pray that god will never end that wrestling: 970
god, my champion, I will never let you go.

But if any man comes striding, high and mighty
    in all he says and does,
no fear of justice, no reverence
for the temples of the gods—   975
    let a rough doom tear him down,
repay his pride, breakneck, ruinous pride!
If he cannot reap his profits fairly
    cannot restrain himself from outrage—
mad, laying hands on the holy things untouchable!   980

        Can such a man, so desperate, still boast
        he can save his life from the flashing bolts of god?
            If all such violence goes with honor now
                why join the sacred dance?   985

Never again will I go reverent to Delphi,
    the inviolate heart of Earth
or Apollo's ancient oracle at Abae
or Olympia of the fires—
    unless these prophecies all come true
for all mankind to point toward in wonder.   990
King of kings, if you deserve your titles
    Zeus, remember, never forget!
You and your deathless, everlasting reign.

        They are dying, the old oracles sent to Laius,
        now our masters strike them off the rolls.   995

Nowhere Apollo's golden glory now—
the gods, the gods go down.

[Enter Jocasta from the palace, carrying a suppliant's branch wound
in wool.]

Jocasta:
Lords of the realm, it occurred to me,
just now, to visit the temples of the gods,
so I have my branch in hand and incense too.   1000

Oedipus is beside himself. Racked with anguish,
no longer a man of sense, he won't admit
the latest prophecies are hollow as the old—
he's at the mercy of every passing voice
if the voice tells of terror.   1005
I urge him gently, nothing seems to help,
so I turn to you, Apollo, you are nearest.

[Placing her branch on the altar, while an old herdsman enters from
the side, not the one just summoned by the King but an unexpected
Messenger from Corinth.]

I come with prayers and offerings . . . I beg you,
cleanse us, set us free of defilement!
Look at us, passengers in the grip of fear,   1010
watching the pilot of the vessel go to pieces.

Messenger:

[Approaching Jocasta and the Chorus.]

Strangers, please, I wonder if you could lead us
to the palace of the king . . . I think it's Oedipus.
Better, the man himself—you know where he is?

Leader:
This is his palace, stranger. He's inside.   1015
But here is his queen, his wife and mother
of his children.

Messenger:
                 Blessings on you, noble queen,
queen of Oedipus crowned with all your family—
blessings on you always!

Jocasta:
nd the same to you, stranger, you deserve it . . .   1020
uch a greeting. But what have you come for?
Have you brought us news?

Messenger:
                    Wonderful news—
for the house, my lady, for your husband too.

Jocasta:
Really, what? Who sent you?

Messenger:
                    Corinth.
I'll give you the message in a moment.   1025
You'll be glad of it—how could you help it?—
though it costs a little sorrow in the bargain.

Jocasta:
What can it be, with such a double edge?

Messenger:
The people there, they want to make your Oedipus
king of Corinth, so they're saying now.   1030

Jocasta:
Why? Isn't old Polybus still in power?

Messenger:
No more. Death has got him in the tomb.

Jocasta:
What are you saying? Polybus, dead?—dead?

Messenger:
                              If not,
if I'm not telling the truth, strike me dead too.

Jocasta:

    [To a servant.]

Quickly, go to your master, tell him this!   1035

You prophecies of the gods, where are you now?
This is the man that Oedipus feared for years,

he fled him, not to kill him—and now he's dead,
quite by chance, a normal, natural death,
not murdered by his son.

Oedipus:

    [Emerging from the palace.]

                          Dearest,   1040
what now? Why call me from the palace?

Jocasta:

    [Bringing the Messenger closer.]

Listen to *him*, see for yourself what all
those awful prophecies of god have come to.

Oedipus:
And who is he? What can he have for me?

Jocasta:
He's from Corinth, he's come to tell you   1045
your father is no more—Polybus—he's dead!

Oedipus:

    [Wheeling on the Messenger.]

What? Let me have it from your lips.

Messenger:

                          Well,
if that's what you want first, then here it is:
make no mistake, Polybus is dead and gone.

Oedipus:
How—murder? sickness?—what? what killed him?   1050

Messenger:
A light tip of the scales put old bones to rest.

Oedipus:
Sickness then—poor man, it wore him down.

Messenger:

                          That,
and the long count of years he'd measured out.

Oedipus:

So!

Jocasta, why, why look to the Prophet's hearth,°
the fires of the future? Why scan the birds   1055
that scream above our heads? They winged me on
to the murder of my father, did they? That was my doom?
Well look, he's dead and buried, hidden under the earth,
and here I am in Thebes, I never put hand to sword—
unless some longing for me wasted him away,   1060
then in a sense you'd say I caused his death.
But now, all those prophecies I feared—Polybus
packs them off to sleep with him in hell!
They're nothing, worthless.

Jocasta:

There.

Didn't I tell you from the start?   1065

Oedipus:
So you did. I was lost in fear.

Jocasta:
No more, sweep it from your mind forever.

Oedipus:
But my mother's bed, surely I must fear—

Jocasta:

Fear?

What should a man fear? It's all chance,
chance rules our lives. Not a man on earth   1070
can see a day ahead, groping through the dark.
Better to live at random, best we can.
And as for this marriage with your mother—
have no fear. Many a man before you,
in his dreams, has shared his mother's bed.   1075
Take such things for shadows, nothing at all—
Live, Oedipus,
as if there's no tomorrow!

1054 *Prophet's hearth:* reference to the shrine at Delphi, whose priestess was famous for her prophecies.

Oedipus:
                    Brave words,
and you'd persuade me if mother weren't alive.
But mother lives, so for all your reassurances   1080
I live in fear, I must.

Jocasta:
                    But your father's death,
that, at least, is a great blessing, joy to the eyes!

Oedipus:
Great, I know . . . but I fear *her*—she's still alive.

Messenger:
Wait, who is this woman, makes you so afraid?

Oedipus:
Merope, old man. The wife of Polybus.   1085

Messenger:
The queen? What's there to fear in her?

Oedipus:
A dreadful prophecy, stranger, sent by the gods.

Messenger:
Tell me, could you? Unless it's forbidden
other ears to hear.

Oedipus:
                    Not at all.
Apollo told me once—it is my fate—   1090
I must make love with my own mother,
shed my father's blood with my own hands.
So for years I've given Corinth a wide berth,
and it's been my good fortune too. But still,
to see one's parents and look into their eyes   1095
is the greatest joy I know.

Messenger:
                    You're afraid of that?
That kept you out of Corinth?

Oedipus:

      My *father*, old man—
so I wouldn't kill my father.

Messenger:

      So that's it.
Well then, seeing I came with such good will, my king,
why don't I rid you of that old worry now?   1100

Oedipus:
What a rich reward you'd have for that!

Messenger:
What do you think I came for, majesty?
So you'd come home and I'd be better off.

Oedipus:
Never, I will never go near my parents.

Messenger:
My boy, it's clear, you don't know what you're doing.   1105

Oedipus:
What do you mean, old man? For god's sake, explain.

Messenger:
If you ran from *them*, always dodging home . . .

Oedipus:
Always, terrified Apollo's oracle might come true—

Messenger:
And you'd be covered with guilt, from both your parents.

Oedipus:
That's right, old man, that fear is always with me.   1110

Messenger:
Don't you know? You've really nothing to fear.

Oedipus:
But why? If I'm their son—Merope, Polybus?

Messenger:
Polybus was nothing to you, that's why, not in blood.

Oedipus:
What are you saying—Polybus was not my father?

Messenger:
No more than I am. He and I are equals.

Oedipus:
                                    My father—   1115
how can my father equal nothing? You're nothing to me!

Messenger:
Neither was he, no more your father than I am.

Oedipus:
Then why did he call me his son?

Messenger:
                         You were a gift,
years ago—know for a fact he took you
from my hands.

Oedipus:
            No, from another's hands?   1120
Then how could he love me so? He loved me, deeply . . .

Messenger:
True, and his early years without a child
made him love you all the more.

Oedipus:
                    And you, did you . . .
buy me? find me by accident?

Messenger:
                    I stumbled on you,
down the woody flanks of Mount Cithaeron.

Oedipus:
                              So close,   1125
what were you doing here, just passing through?

Messenger:
Watching over my flocks, grazing them on the slopes.

Oedipus:
A herdsman, were you? A vagabond, scraping for wages?

Messenger:
Your savior too, my son, in your worst hour.

Oedipus:
                                            Oh—
when you picked me up, was I in pain? What exactly?   1130

Messenger:
Your ankles . . . they tell the story. Look at them.

Oedipus:
Why remind me of that, that old affliction?

Messenger:
Your ankles were pinned together. I set you free.

Oedipus:
That dreadful mark—I've had it from the cradle.

Messenger:
And you got your name from that misfortune too,   1135
the name's still with you.

Oedipus:
                            Dear god, who did it?—
mother? father? Tell me.

Messenger:
                        I don't know.
The one who gave you to me, he'd know more.

Oedipus:
What? You took me from someone else?
You didn't find me yourself?

Messenger:
                    No sir,   1140
another shepherd passed you on to me.

Oedipus:
Who? Do you know? Describe him.

Messenger:
He called himself a servant of . . .
if I remember rightly—Laius.

[*Jocasta turns sharply.*]

Oedipus:
The king of the land who ruled here long ago?   1145

Messenger:
That's the one. That herdsman was *his* man.

Oedipus:
Is he still alive? Can I see him?

Messenger:
They'd know best, the people of these parts.

[*Oedipus and the Messenger turn to the Chorus.*]

Oedipus:
Does anyone know that herdsman,
the one he mentioned? Anyone seen him   1150
in the fields, in the city? Out with it!
The time has come to reveal this once for all.

Leader:
I think he's the very shepherd you wanted to see,
a moment ago. But the queen, Jocasta,
she's the one to say.

Oedipus:
                Jocasta,   1155
you remember the man we just sent for?
Is *that* the one he means?

Jocasta:
                That man . . .
why ask? Old shepherd, talk, empty nonsense,

don't give it another thought, don't even think—

Oedipus:
What—give up now, with a clue like this?
Fail to solve the mystery of my birth?
Not for all the world!

Jocasta:
                    Stop—in the name of god,
if you love your own life, call off this search!
My suffering is enough.

Oedipus:
                    Courage!
Even if my mother turns out to be a slave,
and I a slave, three generations back,
you would not seem common.

Jocasta:
                    Oh no,
listen to me, I beg you, don't do this.

Oedipus:
Listen to you? No more. I must know it all,
must see the truth at last.

Jocasta:
                    No, please—
for your sake—I want the best for you!

Oedipus:
Your best is more than I can bear.

Jocasta:
                    You're doomed—
may you never fathom who you are!

Oedipus.

    [To a servant.]

Hurry, fetch me the herdsman, now!
Leave her to glory in her royal birth.

1160

1165

1170

1175

Jocasta:
Aieeeeee—
          man of agony—
that is the only name I have for you,
that, no other—ever, ever, ever!

[Flinging through the palace doors. A long, tense silence follows.]

Leader:
Where's she gone, Oedipus?
Rushing off, such wild grief . . .
I'm afraid that from this silence
something monstrous may come bursting forth.

Oedipus:
Let it burst! Whatever will, whatever must!
I must know my birth, no matter how common
it may be—I must see my origins face-to-face.   1185
She perhaps, she with her woman's pride
may well be mortified by my birth,
but I, I count myself the son of Chance,
the great goddess, giver of all good things—
I'll never see myself disgraced. She is my mother!   1190
And the moons have marked me out, my blood-brothers,
one moon on the wane, the next moon great with power.
That is my blood, my nature—I will never betray it,
never fail to search and learn my birth!

Chorus:
Yes—if I am a true prophet
     if I can grasp the truth,   1195
   by the boundless skies of Olympus,
at the full moon of tomorrow, Mount Cithaeron
you will know how Oedipus glories in you—
you, his birthplace, nurse, his mountain-mother!   1200
And we will sing you, dancing out your praise—
you lift our monarch's heart!
   Apollo, Apollo, god of the wild cry
               may our dancing please you!
                              Oedipus—
          son, dear child, who bore you?   1205
Who of the nymphs who seem to live forever
mated with Pan, the mountain-striding Father?

Who was your mother? who, some bride of Apollo
the god who loves the pastures spreading toward the sun?
   Or was it Hermes, king of the lightning ridges?   1210
Or Dionysus, lord of frenzy, lord of the barren peaks—
did he seize you in his hands, dearest of all his lucky finds?—
   found by the nymphs, their warm eyes dancing, gift
to the lord who loves them dancing out his joy!

   [*Oedipus strains to see a figure coming from the distance.
   Attended by Palace Guards, an old Shepherd enters slowly,
   reluctant to approach the King.*]

Oedipus:
I never met the man, my friends . . . still,   1215
if I had to guess, I'd say that's the shepherd,
the very one we've looked for all along.
Brothers in old age, two of a kind,
he and our guest here. At any rate
the ones who bring him in are my own men,   1220
I recognize them.

      [*Turning to the Leader.*]

               But you know more than I,
you should, you've seen the man before.

Leader:
I know him, definitely. One of Laius' men,
a trusty shepherd, if there ever was one.

Oedipus:
You, I ask you first, stranger,   1225
you from Corinth—is this the one you mean?

Messenger:
You're looking at him. He's your man.

Oedipus:

   [*To the Shepherd.*]

You, old man, come over here—
look at me. Answer all my questions.
Did you ever serve King Laius?

Shepherd:

                So I did . . .   1230
a slave, not bought on the block though,
born and reared in the palace.

Oedipus:
Your duties, your kind of work?

Shepherd:
Herding the flocks, the better part of my life.

Oedipus:
Where, mostly? Where did you do your grazing?

Shepherd:

                                 Well,   1235
Cithaeron sometimes, or the foothills round about.

Oedipus:
This man—you know him? ever see him there?

Shepherd:

    [*Confused, glancing from the Messenger to the King.*]

Doing what?—what man do you mean?

Oedipus:

    [*Pointing to the Messenger.*]

This one here—ever have dealings with him?

Shepherd:
Not so I could say, but give me a chance,   1240
my memory's bad . . .

Messenger:
No wonder he doesn't know me, master.
But let me refresh his memory for him.
I'm sure he recalls old times we had
on the slopes of Mount Cithaeron;   1245
he and I, grazing our flocks, he with two
and I with one—we both struck up together,
three whole seasons, six months at a stretch

from spring to the rising of Arcturus° in the fall,
then with winter coming on I'd drive my herds   1250
to my own pens, and back he'd go with his
to Laius' folds.

> [*To the Shepherd.*]

                  Now that's how it was,
wasn't it—yes or no?

Shepherd:
                Yes, I suppose . . .
it's all so long ago.

Messenger:
              Come, tell me,
you gave me a child back then, a boy, remember?   1255
A little fellow to rear, my very own.

Shepherd:
What? Why rake up that again?

Messenger:
Look, here he is, my fine old friend—
the same man who was just a baby then.

Shepherd:
Damn you, shut your mouth—quiet!   1260

Oedipus:
Don't lash out at him, old man—
you need lashing more than he does.

Shepherd:
                   Why,
master, majesty—what have I done wrong?

Oedipus:
You won't answer his question about the boy.

Shepherd:
He's talking nonsense, wasting his breath.   1265

1249 *Arcturus:* star that rose at the end of the summer season.

Oedipus:
So, you won't talk willingly—
then you'll talk with pain.

[*The guards seize the Shepherd.*]

Shepherd:
No, dear god, don't torture an old man!

Oedipus:
Twist his arms back, quickly!

Shepherd:
God help us, why?—
what more do you need to know?   1270

Oedipus:
Did you give him that child? He's asking.

Shepherd:
I did . . . I wish to god I'd died that day.

Oedipus:
You've got your wish if you don't tell the truth.

Shepherd:
The more I tell, the worse the death I'll die.

Oedipus:
Our friend here wants to stretch things out, does he?   1275

[*Motioning to his men for torture.*]

Shepherd:
No, no, I gave it to him—I just said so.

Oedipus:
Where did you get it? Your house? Someone else's?

Shepherd:
It wasn't mine, no. I got it from . . . someone.

Oedipus:
Which one of them?

    [*Looking at the citizens.*]

              Whose house?

Shepherd:
                            No—
god's sake, master, no more questions!   1280

Oedipus:
You're a dead man if I have to ask again.

Shepherd:
Then—the child came from the house . . .
of Laius.

Oedipus:
       A slave? or born of his own blood?

Shepherd:
                       Oh no,
I'm right at the edge, the horrible truth—I've got to say it!

Oedipus:
And I'm at the edge of hearing horrors, yes, but I must hear!   1285

Shepherd:
All right! His son, they said it was—his son!
But the one inside, your wife,
she'd tell it best.

Oedipus:
My wife—
she gave it to you?   1290

Shepherd:
Yes, yes, my king.

Oedipus:
Why, what for?

Shepherd:
To kill it.

Oedipus:
Her own child,
how could she?   1295

Shepherd:
She was afraid—
frightening prophecies.

Oedipus:
What?

Shepherd:
          They said—
he'd kill his parents.

Oedipus:
But you gave him to this old man—why?   1300

Shepherd:
I pitied the little baby, master,
hoped he'd take him off to his own country,
far away, but he saved him for this, this fate.
If you are the man he says you are, believe me,
you were born for pain.

Oedipus:
                         O god—   1305
all come true, all burst to light!
O light—now let me look my last on you!
I stand revealed at last—
cursed in my birth, cursed in marriage,   1310
cursed in the lives I cut down with these hands!

          [Rushing through the doors with a great cry. The Corinthian
          Messenger, the Shepherd and attendants exit slowly to the side.]

Chorus:
     O the generations of men
the dying generations—adding the total
of all your lives I find they come to nothing . . .
          does there exist, is there a man on earth
who seizes more joy than just a dream, a vision?   1315
And the vision no sooner dawns than dies
blazing into oblivion.

You are my great example, you, your life
your destiny, Oedipus, man of misery—
I count no man blest.

                  You outranged all men!   1320
        Bending your bow to the breaking-point
you captured priceless glory, O dear god,
and the Sphinx came crashing down,
              the virgin, claws hooked
like a bird of omen singing, shrieking death—   1325
like a fortress reared in the face of death
you rose and saved our land.

From that day on we called you king
we crowned you with honors, Oedipus, towering over all—
mighty king of the seven gates of Thebes.   1330

But now to hear your story—is there a man more agonized?
More wed to pain and frenzy? Not a man on earth,
the joy of your life ground down to nothing
O Oedipus, name for the ages—
        one and the same wide harbor served you   1335
                  son and father both
son and father came to rest in the same bridal chamber.
How, how could the furrows your father plowed
bear you, your agony, harrowing on
in silence O so long?

                But now for all your power   1340
Time, all-seeing Time has dragged you to the light,
judged your marriage monstrous from the start—
the son and the father tangling, both one—
O child of Laius, would to god
        I'd never seen you, never never!   1345
        Now I weep like a man who wails the dead
and the dirge comes pouring forth with all my heart!
I tell you the truth, you gave me life
my breath leapt up in you
and now you bring down the night upon my eyes.   1350

    [Enter a Messenger from the palace.]

Messenger:
Men of Thebes, always first in honor,

what horrors you will hear, what you will see,
what a heavy weight of sorrow you will shoulder . . .
if you are true to your birth, if you still have
some feeling for the royal house of Thebes.   1355
I tell you neither the waters of the Danube
nor the Nile can wash this palace clean.
Such things it hides, it soon will bring to light—
terrible things, and none done blindly now,
all done with a will. The pains   1360
we inflict upon ourselves hurt most of all.

Leader:
God knows we have pains enough already.
What can you add to them?

Messenger:
The queen is dead.

Leader:
                          Poor lady—how?

Messenger:
By her own hand. But you are spared the worst,   1365
you never had to watch . . . I saw it all,
and with all the memory that's in me
you will learn what that poor woman suffered.

Once she'd broken in through the gates,
dashing past us, frantic, whipped to fury,   1370
ripping her hair out with both hands—
straight to her rooms she rushed, flinging herself
across the bridal-bed, doors slamming behind her—
once inside, she wailed for Laius, dead so long,
remembering how she bore his child long ago,   1375
the life that rose up to destroy him, leaving
its mother to mother living creatures
with the very son she'd borne.
Oh how she wept, mourning the marriage-bed
where she let loose that double brood—monsters—   1380
husband by her husband, children by her child.
                                   And then—
but how she died is more than I can say. Suddenly
Oedipus burst in, screaming, he stunned us so
we couldn't watch her agony to the end,
our eyes were fixed on him. Circling   1385

like a maddened beast, stalking, here, there,
crying out to us—
                    Give him a sword! His wife,
no wife, his mother, where can he find the mother earth
that cropped two crops at once, himself and all his children?
He was raging—one of the dark powers pointing the way,   1390
none of us mortals crowding around him, no,
with a great shattering cry—someone, something leading him on—
he hurled at the twin doors and bending the bolts back
out of their sockets, crashed through the chamber.
And there we saw the woman hanging by the neck,   1395
cradled high in a woven noose, spinning,
swinging back and forth. And when he saw her,
giving a low, wrenching sob that broke our hearts,
slipping the halter from her throat, he eased her down,
in a slow embrace he laid her down, poor thing . . .   1400
then, what came next, what horror we beheld!

He rips off her brooches, the long gold pins
holding her robes—and lifting them high,
looking straight up into the points,
he digs them down the sockets of his eyes, crying, "You,   1405
you'll see no more the pain I suffered, all the pain I caused!
Too long you looked on the ones you never should have seen,
blind to the ones you longed to see, to know! Blind
from this hour on! Blind in the darkness—blind!"
His voice like a dirge, rising, over and over   1410
raising the pins, raking them down his eyes.
And at each stroke blood spurts from the roots,
splashing his beard, a swirl of it, nerves and clots—
black hail of blood pulsing, gushing down.

These are the griefs that burst upon them both,   1415
coupling man and woman. The joy they had so lately,
the fortune of their old ancestral house
was deep joy indeed. Now, in this one day,
wailing, madness and doom, death, disgrace,
all the griefs in the world that you can name,   1420
all are theirs forever.

Leader:
                    Oh poor man, the misery—
has he any rest from pain now?

    [A voice within, in torment.]

Messenger:

                                    He's shouting,
"Loose the bolts, someone, show me to all of Thebes!
My father's murderer, my mother's—"
No, I can't repeat it, it's unholy.
Now he'll tear himself from his native earth,   1425
not linger, curse the house with his own curse.
But he needs strength, and a guide to lead him on.
This is sickness more than he can bear.

    [*The palace doors open.*]

                                    Look,
he'll show you himself. The great doors are opening—   1430
you are about to see a sight, a horror
even his mortal enemy would pity.

    [*Enter Oedipus, blinded, led by a boy. He stands at the palace steps,
    as if surveying his people once again.*]

Chorus:

                                    O the terror—
    the suffering, for all the world to see,
    the worst terror that ever met my eyes.
    What madness swept over you? What god,   1435
    what dark power leapt beyond all bounds,
    beyond belief, to crush your wretched life?—
    godforsaken, cursed by the gods!
    I pity you but I can't bear to look.
    I've much to ask, so much to learn,   1440
    so much fascinates my eyes,
    but you . . . I shudder at the sight.

Oedipus:

                                    Oh, Ohh—
    the agony! I am agony—
    where am I going? where on earth?
      where does all this agony hurl me?   1445
    where's my voice?—
      winging, swept away on a dark tide—
    My destiny, my dark power, what a leap you made!

Chorus:
To the depths of terror, too dark to hear, to see.

Oedipus:

>   Dark, horror of darkness
>   my darkness, drowning, swirling around me
>   crashing wave on wave—unspeakable, irresistible
>   headwind, fatal harbor! Oh again,
>   the misery, all at once, over and over
>   the stabbing daggers, stab of memory
> raking me insane.

Chorus:

>   No wonder you suffer
> twice over, the pain of your wounds,
> the lasting grief of pain.

Oedipus:

>   Dear friend, still here?
>   Standing by me, still with a care for me,
>   the blind man? Such compassion,
>   loyal to the last. Oh it's you,
>   I know you're here, dark as it is
>   I'd know you anywhere, your voice—
> it's yours, clearly yours.

Chorus:

>   Dreadful, what you've done . . .
> how could you bear it, gouging out your eyes?
> What superhuman power drove you on?

Oedipus:

>   Apollo, friends, Apollo—
> he ordained my agonies—these, my pains on pains!
>   But the hand that struck my eyes was mine,
>   mine alone—no one else—
>   I did it all myself!
>   What good were eyes to me?
>   Nothing I could see could bring me joy.

Chorus:

No, no, exactly as you say.

Oedipus:

>   What can I ever see?
>   What love, what call of the heart
> can touch my ears with joy? Nothing, friends.

1450

1455

1460

1465

1470

1475

Take me away, far, far from Thebes,
    quickly, cast me away, my friends—
this great murderous ruin, this man cursed to heaven,
    the man the deathless gods hate most of all!

Chorus:
Pitiful, you suffer so, you understand so much . . .
I wish you'd never known.

Oedipus:
                    Die, die—
    whoever he was that day in the wilds
who cut my ankles free of the ruthless pins,
    he pulled me clear of death, he saved my life   1485
    for this, this kindness—
                    Curse him, kill him!
If I'd died then, I'd never have dragged myself,
    my loved ones through such hell.

Chorus:
Oh if only . . . would to god.

Oedipus:
                    I'd never have come to this,   1490
    my father's murderer—never been branded
    mother's husband, all men see me now! Now,
        loathed by the gods, son of the mother I defiled
        coupling in my father's bed, spawning lives in the loins
that spawned my wretched life. What grief can crown this grief?   1495
        It's mine alone, my destiny—I am Oedipus!

Chorus:
How can I say you've chosen for the best?
Better to die than be alive and blind.

Oedipus:
What I did was best—don't lecture me,
no more advice. I, with my eyes,   1500
how could I look my father in the eyes
when I go down to death? Or mother, so abused . . .
I have done such things to the two of them,
crimes too huge for hanging.
                    Worse yet,
the sight of my children, born as they were born,   1505

how could I long to look into their eyes?
No, not with these eyes of mine, never.
Not this city either, her high towers,
the sacred glittering images of her gods—
I am misery! I, her best son, reared   1510
as no other son of Thebes was ever reared,
I've stripped myself, I gave the command myself.
All men must cast away the great blasphemer,
the curse now brought to light by the gods,
the son of Laius—I, my father's son!   1515

Now I've exposed my guilt, horrendous guilt,
could I train a level glance on you, my countrymen?
Impossible! No, if I could just block off my ears,
the springs of hearing, I would stop at nothing—
I'd wall up my loathsome body like a prison,   1520
blind to the sound of life, not just the sight.
Oblivion—what a blessing . . .
for the mind to dwell a world away from pain.

O Cithaeron, why did you give me shelter?
Why didn't you take me, crush my life out on the spot?   1525
I'd never have revealed my birth to all mankind.

O Polybus, Corinth, the old house of my fathers,
so I believed—what a handsome prince you raised—
under the skin, what sickness to the core.
Look at me! Born of outrage, outrage to the core.   1530

O triple roads—it all comes back, the secret,
dark ravine, and the oaks closing in
where the three roads join . . .
You drank my father's blood, my own blood
spilled by my own hands—you still remember me?   1535
What things you saw me do? Then I came here
and did them all once more!
                        Marriages! O marriage,
you gave me birth, and once you brought me into the world
you brought my sperm rising back, springing to light
fathers, brothers, sons—one murderous breed—   1540
brides, wives, mothers. The blackest things
a man can do, I have done them all!
                        No more—
it's wrong to name what's wrong to do. Quickly,

for the love of god, hide me somewhere,
kill me, hurl me into the sea   1545
where you can never look on me again.

[*Beckoning to the Chorus as they shrink away.*]

Closer,
it's all right. Touch the man of grief.
Do. Don't be afraid. My troubles are mine
and I am the only man alive who can sustain them.

[*Enter Creon from the palace, attended by Palace Guards.*]

Leader:
Put your requests to Creon. Here he is,   1550
just when we need him. He'll have a plan, he'll act.
Now that he's the sole defense of the country
in your place.

Oedipus:
                 Oh no, what can I say to him?
How can I ever hope to win his trust?
I wronged him so, just now, in every way.   1555
You must see that—I was so wrong, so wrong.

Creon:
I haven't come to mock you, Oedipus,
or to criticize your former failings.

[*Turning to the Guards.*]

                                   You there,
have you lost all respect for human feelings?
At least revere the Sun, the holy fire   1560
that keeps us all alive. Never expose a thing
of guilt and holy dread so great it appalls
the earth, the rain from heaven, the light of day!
Get him into the halls—quickly as you can.
Piety demands no less. Kindred alone   1565
should see a kinsman's shame. This is obscene.

Oedipus:
Please, in god's name . . . you wipe my fears away,
coming so generously to me, the worst of men.
Do one thing more, for your sake, not mine.

Creon:

What do you want? Why so insistent?   1570

Oedipus:

Drive me out of the land at once, far from sight,
where I can never hear a human voice.

Creon:

I'd have done that already, I promise you.
First I wanted the god to clarify my duties.

Oedipus:

The god? His command was clear, every word: 1575
death for the father-killer, the curse—
he said destroy me!

Creon:

So he did. Still, in such a crisis
it's better to ask precisely what to do.

Oedipus:

                        So miserable—
you would consult the god about a man like me?   1580

Creon:

By all means. And this time, I assume,
even you will obey the god's decrees.

Oedipus:

                        I will,
I will. And you, I command you—I beg you . . .
the woman inside, bury her as you see fit.
It's the only decent thing,   1585
to give your own the last rites. As for me,
never condemn the city of my fathers
to house my body, not while I'm alive, no,
let me live on the mountains, on Cithaeron,
my favorite haunt, I have made it famous.   1590
Mother and father marked out that rock
to be my everlasting tomb—buried alive.
Let me die there, where they tried to kill me.

Oh but this I know: no sickness can destroy me,
nothing can. I would never have been saved   1595
from death—I have been saved

for something great and terrible, something strange.
Well let my destiny come and take me on its way!

About my children, Creon, the boys at least,
don't burden yourself. They're men,   1600
wherever they go, they'll find the means to live.
But my two daughters, my poor helpless girls,
clustering at our table, never without me
hovering near them . . . whatever I touched,
they always had their share. Take care of them,   1605
I beg you. Wait, better—permit me, would you?
Just to touch them with my hands and take
our fill of tears. Please . . . my king.
Grant it, with all your noble heart.
If I could hold them, just once, I'd think   1610
I had them with me, like the early days
when I could see their eyes.

> [Antigone and Ismene, two small children, are led in from the palace
> by a nurse.]

                            What's that
O god! Do I really hear you sobbing?—
my two children. Creon, you've pitied me?
Sent me my darling girls, my own flesh and blood!   1615
Am I right?

Creon:
                    Yes, it's my doing.
I know the joy they gave you all these years,
the joy you must feel now.

Oedipus:
                    Bless you, Creon!
May god watch over you for this kindness,
better than he ever guarded me.

                            Children, where are you?   1620
Here, come quickly—

> [Groping for Antigone and Ismene, who approach their father
> cautiously, then embrace him.]

                    Come to these hands of mine,
your brother's hands, your own father's hands
that served his once bright eyes so well—

that made them blind. Seeing nothing, children,
knowing nothing, I became your father,
I fathered you in the soil that gave me life.

How I weep for you—I cannot see you now . . .
just thinking of all your days to come, the bitterness,
the life that rough mankind will thrust upon you.
Where are the public gatherings you can join,   1630
the banquets of the clans? Home you'll come,
in tears, cut off from the sight of it all,
the brilliant rites unfinished.
And when you reach perfection, ripe for marriage,
who will he be, my dear ones? Risking all   1635
to shoulder the curse that weighs down my parents,
yes and you too—that wounds us all together.
What more misery could you want?
Your father killed his father, sowed his mother,
one, one and the selfsame womb sprang you—   1640
he cropped the very roots of his existence.

Such disgrace, and you must bear it all!
Who will marry you then? Not a man on earth.
Your doom is clear: you'll wither away to nothing,
single, without a child.

      [*Turning to Creon.*]

                              Oh Creon,   1645
you are the only father they have now . . .
we who brought them into the world
are gone, both gone at a stroke—
Don't let them go begging, abandoned,
women without men. Your own flesh and blood!   1650
Never bring them down to the level of my pains.
Pity them. Look at them, so young, so vulnerable,
shorn of everything—you're their only hope.
Promise me, noble Creon, touch my hand!

      [*Reaching toward Creon, who draws back.*]

You, little ones, if you were old enough   1655
to understand, there is much I'd tell you.
Now, as it is, I'd have you say a prayer.
Pray for life, my children,
live where you are free to grow and season.

Pray god you find a better life than mine,   1660
the father who begot you.

Creon:

                                    Enough.
You've wept enough. Into the palace now.

Oedipus:
I must, but I find it very hard.

Creon:
Time is the great healer, you will see.

Oedipus:
I am going—you know on what condition?   1665

Creon:
Tell me. I'm listening.

Oedipus:
Drive me out of Thebes, in exile.

Creon:
Not I. Only the gods can give you that.

Oedipus:
Surely the gods hate me so much—

Creon:
You'll get your wish at once.

Oedipus:

                                    You consent?   1670

Creon:
I try to say what I mean; it's my habit.

Oedipus:
Then take me away. It's time.

Creon:
Come along, let go of the children.

Oedipus:

No—

don't take them away from me, not now! No no no!

[*Clutching his daughters as the guards wrench them loose and take
them through the palace doors.*]

Creon:

Still the king, the master of all things?   1675
No more: here your power ends.
None of your power follows you through life.

[*Exit Oedipus and Creon to the palace. The Chorus comes forward to
address the audience directly.*]

Chorus:

People of Thebes, my countrymen, look on Oedipus.
He solved the famous riddle with his brilliance,
he rose to power, a man beyond all power.   1680
Who could behold his greatness without envy?
Now what a black sea of terror has overwhelmed him.
Now as we keep our watch and wait the final day,
count no man happy till he dies, free of pain at last.

[*Exit in procession.*]

QUESTIONS

1. How explicitly does the prophet Tiresias reveal the guilt of Oedipus? Does it seem to you
   stupidity on the part of Oedipus or a defect in Sophocles' play that the king takes so long
   to recognize his guilt and to admit to it?
2. How does Oedipus exhibit weakness of character? Point to lines that reveal him as imperfectly noble in his words, deeds, or treatment of others.
3. "Oedipus is punished not for any fault in himself, but for his ignorance. Not knowing his
   family history, unable to recognize his parents on sight, he is blameless; and in slaying his
   father and marrying his mother, he behaves as any sensible person might behave in the
   same circumstances." Do you agree with this interpretation?
4. Besides the predictions of Tiresias, what other foreshadowings of the shepherd's revelation does the play contain?
5. Consider the character of Jocasta. Is she a "flat" character—a generalized queen figure—
   or an individual with distinctive traits of personality? Point to speeches or details in the
   play to back up your opinion.
6. What is dramatic irony? Besides the example given on page 732, what other instances of
   dramatic irony do you find in *Oedipus the King*? What do they contribute to the effectiveness of the play?

7. In the drama of Sophocles, violence and bloodshed take place offstage; thus, the suicide of Jocasta is only reported to us. Nor do we witness Oedipus' removal of his eyes; this horror is only given in the report by the second messenger. Of what advantage or disadvantage to the play is this limitation?

8. For what reason does Oedipus blind himself? What meaning, if any, do you find in his choice of a surgical instrument?

9. What are your feelings toward him as the play ends?

10. Read the famous interpretation of this play offered by Sigmund Freud (page 1491). How well does Freud explain why the play moves you?

11. With what attitude toward the gods does the play leave you? By inflicting a plague on Thebes, by causing barrenness, by cursing both the people and their king, do the gods seem cruel, unjust, or tyrannical? Does the play show any reverence toward them?

12. Does this play end in total gloom?

THE BACKGROUND OF ANTIGONE

Although *Antigone* tells a later part of the Oedipus story, it was not part of the trilogy that originally contained *Oedipus the King* (the other plays in that trilogy have been lost). *Antigone* was written in 441 B.C., over twenty years before the author took up the story of Oedipus himself. In *Antigone* duties to family and duties to the state are pitted against one another in a story that has Creon, now king of Thebes many years after Oedipus' exile and death, refusing burial to the body of Oedipus' son (and brother) Polynices, who has led an army against the city to claim the throne from his brother. His sister Antigone (Oedipus' daughter and sister) resists Creon's unjust edict in the name of family loyalty, a defiance both noble and potentially threatening to political stability in a time of crisis. Though the gods approve of her action, she dies a victim of Creon's hubris. (Or perhaps, as Patricia Lines suggests on page 1495, Antigone's own hubris is her downfall.) Creon suffers the death (by suicide) of his son and his wife as a result. Antigone's claim is especially compelling when we imagine her played by a mature male actor who in his public life, as a citizen, must know both how to rule and how to be ruled, how to submit to legitimate authority when he steps down from office.

Antigone: *Martha Henry in the 1971 Lincoln Center Repertory production.*

ANTIGONE

441 B.C.

TRANSLATED BY ROBERT FAGLES

Characters

Antigone, daughter of Oedipus and Jocasta
Ismene, sister of Antigone
A *Chorus*, of old Theban citizens and their *Leader*
Creon, king of Thebes, uncle of Antigone and Ismene
A *Sentry*
Haemon, son of Creon and Eurydice
Tiresias, a blind prophet
A *Messenger*
Eurydice, wife of Creon
Guards, attendants, and a Boy

Time and Scene: *The royal house of Thebes. It is still night, and the invading armies of Argos have just been driven from the city. Fighting on opposite sides, the sons of Oedipus, Eteocles and Polynices, have killed each other in combat. Their uncle, Creon, is now king of Thebes.*

Enter Antigone, slipping through the central doors of the palace. She motions to her sister, Ismene, who follows her cautiously toward an altar at the center of the stage.

Antigone:
My own flesh and blood—dear sister, dear Ismene,
how many griefs our father Oedipus handed down!°
Do you know one, I ask you, one grief
that Zeus will not perfect for the two of us
while we still live and breathe! There's nothing,   5
no pain—our lives are pain—no private shame,
no public disgrace, nothing I haven't seen
in your griefs and mine. And now this:
an emergency decree, they say, the Commander
has just declared for all of Thebes.   10
What, haven't you heard? Don't you see?
The doom reserved for enemies
marches on the ones we love the most.

Ismene:
Not I, I haven't heard a word, Antigone.
Nothing of loved ones,   15
no joy or pain has come my way, not since
the two of us were robbed of our two brothers,
both gone in a day, a double blow—
not since the armies of Argos vanished,
just this very night. I know nothing more,   20
whether our luck's improved or ruin's still to come.

---

2 *griefs our father Oedipus handed down:* As Sophocles tells in *Oedipus the King,* the King of Thebes discovered that he had lived his life under a curse. Unknowingly, he had slain his father and married his mother. On realizing this terrible truth, Oedipus put out his own eyes and departed into exile. Now, years later, as *Antigone* opens, Antigone and Ismene, daughters of Oedipus, are recalling how their two brothers died. After the abdication of their father, the brothers had ruled Thebes together. But they fell to quarreling. When Eteocles expelled Polynices, the latter returned with an army and attacked the city. The two brothers killed each other in combat, leaving the throne to Creon. The new king of Thebes has buried Eteocles with full honors, but, calling Polynices a traitor, has decreed that his body shall be left to the crows—an especially terrible decree, for a rotting corpse might offend Zeus; bring down plague, blight, and barrenness upon Thebes; and prevent the soul of a dead hero from entering the Elysian Fields, abode of those favored by the gods.

Antigone:
I thought so. That's why I brought you out here,
past the gates, so you could hear in private.

Ismene:
What's the matter? Trouble, clearly . . .
you sound so dark, so grim.   25

Antigone:
Why not? Our own brothers' burial!
Hasn't Creon graced one with all the rites,
disgraced the other? Eteocles, they say,
has been given full military honors,
rightly so—Creon's laid him in the earth   30
and he goes with glory down among the dead.
But the body of Polynices, who died miserably—
why, a city-wide proclamation, rumor has it,
forbids anyone to bury him, even mourn him.
He's to be left unwept, unburied, a lovely treasure   35
for birds that scan the field and feast to their heart's content.

Such, I hear, is the martial law our good Creon
lays down for you and me—yes, me, I tell you—
and he's coming here to alert the uninformed
in no uncertain terms,   40
and he won't treat the matter lightly. Whoever
disobeys in the least will die, his doom is sealed:
stoning to death inside the city walls!

There you have it. You'll soon show what you are,
worth your breeding, Ismene, or a coward—   45
for all your royal blood.

Ismene:
My poor sister, if things have come to this,
who am I to make or mend them, tell me,
what good am I to you?

Antigone:
                    Decide.
Will you share the labor, share the work?   50

Ismene:
What work, what's the risk? What do you mean?

Antigone.

[*Raising her hands.*]

Will you lift up his body with these bare hands
and lower it with me?

Ismene:

What? You'd bury him—
when a law forbids the city?

Antigone:

Yes!
He is my brother and—deny it as you will—
your brother too.
No one will ever convict me for a traitor.

Ismene:
So desperate, and Creon has expressly—

Antigone:

No,
he has no right to keep me from my own.

Ismene:
Oh my sister, think—
think how our own father died, hated,
his reputation in ruins, driven on
by the crimes he brought to light himself
to gouge out his eyes with his own hands—
then mother . . . his mother and wife, both in one,   65
mutilating her life in the twisted noose—
and last, our two brothers dead in a single day,
both shedding their own blood, poor suffering boys,
battling out their common destiny hand-to-hand.

Now look at the two of us, left so alone . . .   70
think what a death we'll die, the worst of all
if we violate the laws and override
the fixed decree of the throne, its power—
we must be sensible. Remember we are women,
we're not born to contend with men. Then too,   75
we're underlings, ruled by much stronger hands,
so we must submit in this, and things still worse.

I, for one, I'll beg the dead to forgive me—
I'm forced, I have no choice—I must obey
the ones who stand in power. Why rush to extremes?   80
It's madness, madness.

Antigone:
                    I won't insist,
no, even if you should have a change of heart,
I'd never welcome you in the labor, not with me.
So, do as you like, whatever suits you best—
I'll bury him myself.   85
And even if I die in the act, that death will be a glory.
I'll lie with the one I love and loved by him—
an outrage sacred to the gods! I have longer
to please the dead than please the living here:
in the kingdom down below I'll lie forever.   90
Do as you like, dishonor the laws
the gods hold in honor.

Ismene:
                    I'd do them no dishonor . . .
but defy the city? I have no strength for that.

Antigone:
You have your excuses. I am on my way,
I'll raise a mound for him, for my dear brother.   95

Ismene:
Oh Antigone, you're so rash—I'm so afraid for you!

Antigone:
Don't fear for me. Set your own life in order.

Ismene:
Then don't, at least, blurt this out to anyone.
Keep it a secret. I'll join you in that, I promise.

Antigone:
Dear god, shout it from the rooftops. I'll hate you   100
all the more for silence—tell the world!

Ismene:
So fiery—and it ought to chill your heart.

Antigone:
I know I please where I must please the most.

Ismene:
Yes, if you can, but you're in love with impossibility.

Antigone:
Very well then, once my strength gives out   105
I will be done at last.

Ismene:
                                    You're wrong from the start,
you're off on a hopeless quest.

Antigone:
If you say so, you will make me hate you,
and the hatred of the dead, by all rights,
will haunt you night and day.   110
But leave me to my own absurdity, leave me
to suffer this—dreadful thing. I'll suffer
nothing as great as death without glory.

　　　　[*Exit to the side.*]

Ismene:
Then go if you must, but rest assured,
wild, irrational as you are, my sister,   115
you are truly dear to the ones who love you.

　　　　[*Withdrawing to the palace. Enter a Chorus, the old citizens of Thebes,
　　　　chanting as the sun begins to rise.*]

Chorus:
Glory!—great beam of sun, brightest of all
that ever rose on the seven gates of Thebes,
　　　you burn through night at last!
　　　　　　Great eye of the golden day,   120
mounting the Dirce's banks° you throw him back—
the enemy out of Argos, the white shield, the man of bronze—
he's flying headlong now
　　　　　　the bridle of fate stampeding him with pain!

121 *Dirce's banks:* banks of the River Dirce, near Thebes.

And he had driven against our borders,
launched by the warring claims of Polynices— 125
like an eagle screaming, winging havoc
over the land, wings of armor
shielded white as snow,
a huge army massing, 130
crested helmets bristling for assault.

He hovered above our roofs, his vast maw gaping
closing down around our seven gates,
   his spears thirsting for the kill
         but now he's gone, look, 135
before he could glut his jaws with Theban blood
or the god of fire put our crown of towers to the torch.
He grappled the Dragon none can master—Thebes—
      the clang of our arms like thunder at his back!

   Zeus hates with a vengeance all bravado, 140
   the mighty boasts of men. He watched them
   coming on in a rising flood, the pride
   of their golden armor ringing shrill—
   and brandishing his lightning
   blasted the fighter just at the goal, 145
   rushing to shout his triumph from our walls.

Down from the heights he crashed, pounding down on the earth!
And a moment ago, blazing torch in hand—
      mad for attack, ecstatic
he breathed his rage, the storm 150
  of his fury hurling at our heads!
But now his high hopes have laid him low
and down the enemy ranks the iron god of war
   deals his rewards, his stunning blows—Ares°
   rapture of battle, our right arm in the crisis. 155

   Seven captains marshaled at seven gates
   seven against their equals, gave
   their brazen trophies up to Zeus,
   god of the breaking rout of battle,
   all but two: those blood brothers, 160
   one father, one mother—matched in rage,
   spears matched for the twin conquest—
   clashed and won the common prize of death.

154 *Ares:* god of war.

But now for Victory! Glorious in the morning,
joy in her eyes to meet our joy   165
      she is winging down to Thebes,
our fleets of chariots wheeling in her wake—
    Now let us win oblivion from the wars,
thronging the temples of the gods
in singing, dancing choirs through the night!   170
      Lord Dionysus,° god of the dance
      that shakes the land of Thebes, now lead the way!

    [Enter Creon from the palace, attended by his guard.]

    But look, the king of the realm is coming,
    Creon, the new man for the new day,
    whatever the gods are sending now . . .   175
    what new plan will he launch?
    Why this, this special session?
    Why this sudden call to the old men
    summoned at one command?

Creon:

                              My countrymen,
the ship of state is safe. The gods who rocked her,   180
after a long, merciless pounding in the storm,
have righted her once more.
                      Out of the whole city
I have called you here alone. Well I know,
first, your undeviating respect
for the throne and royal power of King Laius.   185
Next, while Oedipus steered the land of Thebes,
and even after he died, your loyalty was unshakable,
you still stood by their children. Now then,
since the two sons are dead—two blows of fate
in the same day, cut down by each other's hands,   190
both killers, both brothers stained with blood—
as I am next in kin to the dead,
I now possess the throne and all its powers.

Of course you cannot know a man completely,
his character, his principles, sense of judgment,   195
not till he's shown his colors, ruling the people,
making laws. Experience, there's the test.
As I see it, whoever assumes the task,

171 *Dionysus:* god of wine and fertility.

the awesome task of setting the city's course,
and refuses to adopt the soundest policies   200
but fearing someone, keeps his lips locked tight,
he's utterly worthless. So I rate him now,
I always have. And whoever places a friend
above the good of his own country, he is nothing:
I have no use for him. Zeus my witness,   205
Zeus who sees all things, always—

I could never stand by silent, watching destruction
march against our city, putting safety to rout,
nor could I ever make that man a friend of mine
who menaces our country. Remember this: 210
our country *is* our safety.
Only while she voyages true on course
can we establish friendships, truer than blood itself.
Such are my standards. They make our city great.

Closely akin to them I have proclaimed,   215
just now, the following decree to our people
concerning the two sons of Oedipus.
Eteocles, who died fighting for Thebes,
excelling all in arms: he shall be buried,
crowned with a hero's honors, the cups we pour   220
to soak the earth and reach the famous dead.

But as for his blood brother, Polynices,
who returned from exile, home to his father-city
and the gods of his race, consumed with one desire—
to burn them roof to roots—who thirsted to drink   225
his kinsmen's blood and sell the rest to slavery:
that man—a proclamation has forbidden the city
to dignify him with burial, mourn him at all.
No, he must be left unburied, his corpse
carrion for the birds and dogs to tear,   230
an obscenity for the citizens to behold!

These are my principles. Never at my hands
will the traitor be honored above the patriot.
But whoever proves his loyalty to the state—
I'll prize that man in death as well as life.   235

Leader:
If this is your pleasure, Creon, treating
our city's enemy and our friend this way . . .

The power is yours, I suppose, to enforce it
with the laws, both for the dead and all of us,
the living.

Creon:
                    Follow my orders closely then,   240
be on your guard.

Leader:
                    We are too old.
Lay that burden on younger shoulders.

Creon:
                                        No, no,
I don't mean the body—I've posted guards already.

Leader:
What commands for us then? What other service?

Creon:
See that you never side with those who break my orders.   245

Leader:
Never. Only a fool could be in love with death.

Creon:
Death is the price—you're right. But all too often
the mere hope of money has ruined many men.

        [A Sentry enters from the side.]

Sentry:
                                        My lord,
I can't say I'm winded from running, or set out
with any spring in my legs either—no sir,   250
I was lost in thought, and it made me stop, often,
dead in my tracks, wheeling, turning back,
and all the time a voice inside me muttering,
"Idiot, why? You're going straight to your death."
Then muttering, "Stopped again, poor fool?   255
If somebody gets the news to Creon first,
what's to save your neck?"
                            And so,
mulling it over, on I trudged, dragging my feet,
you can make a short road take forever . . .

but at last, look, common sense won out,
I'm here, and I'm all yours,
and even though I come empty-handed
I'll tell my story just the same, because
I've come with a good grip on one hope,
what will come will come, whatever fate—   265

Creon:
Come to the point!
What's wrong—why so afraid?

Sentry:
First, myself, I've got to tell you,
I didn't do it, didn't see who did—
Be fair, don't take it out on me.   270

Creon:
You're playing it safe, soldier,
barricading yourself from any trouble.
It's obvious, you've something strange to tell.

Sentry:
Dangerous too, and danger makes you delay
for all you're worth.   275

Creon:
Out with it—then dismiss!

Sentry:
All right, here it comes. The body—
someone's just buried it, then run off . . .
sprinkled some dry dust on the flesh,
given it proper rites.

Creon:
                                    What?   280
What man alive would dare—

Sentry:
                                    I've no idea, I swear it.
There was no mark of a spade, no pickaxe there,
no earth turned up, the ground packed hard and dry,
unbroken, no tracks, no wheelruts, nothing,
the workman left no trace. Just at sunup   285
the first watch of the day points it out—

it was a wonder! We were stunned . . .
a terrific burden too, for all of us, listen:
you can't see the corpse, not that it's buried,
really, just a light cover of road-dust on it,   290
as if someone meant to lay the dead to rest
and keep from getting cursed.
Not a sign in sight that dogs or wild beasts
had worried the body, even torn the skin.

But what came next! Rough talk flew thick and fast,   295
guard grilling guard—we'd have come to blows
at last, nothing to stop it; each man for himself
and each the culprit, no one caught red-handed,
all of us pleading ignorance, dodging the charges,
ready to take up red-hot iron in our fists,   300
go through fire, swear oaths to the gods—
"I didn't do it, I had no hand in it either,
not in the plotting, not in the work itself!"

Finally, after all this wrangling came to nothing,
one man spoke out and made us stare at the ground,   305
hanging our heads in fear. No way to counter him,
no way to take his advice and come through
safe and sound. Here's what he said:
"Look, we've got to report the facts to Creon,
we can't keep this hidden." Well, that won out,   310
and the lot fell to me, condemned me,
unlucky as ever, I got the prize. So here I am,
against my will and yours too, well I know—
no one wants the man who brings bad news.

Leader:
                                                  My king,
ever since he began I've been debating in my mind,   315
could this possibly be the work of the gods?

Creon:
                                                  Stop—
before you make me choke with anger—the gods!
You, you're senile, must you be insane?
You say—why it's intolerable—say the gods
could have the slightest concern for that corpse?   320
Tell me, was it for meritorious service
they proceeded to bury him, prized him so? The hero
who came to burn their temples ringed with pillars,
their golden treasures—scorch their hallowed earth

and fling their laws to the winds.
Exactly when did you last see the gods
celebrating traitors? Inconceivable!

No, from the first there were certain citizens
who could hardly stand the spirit of my regime,
grumbling against me in the dark, heads together,
tossing wildly, never keeping their necks beneath
the yoke, loyally submitting to their king.
These are the instigators, I'm convinced—
they've perverted my own guard, bribed them
to do their work.
                    Money! Nothing worse
in our lives, so current, rampant, so corrupting.
Money—you demolish cities, root men from their homes,
you train and twist good minds and set them on
to the most atrocious schemes. No limit,
you make them adept at every kind of outrage,
every godless crime—money!
                            Everyone—
the whole crew bribed to commit this crime,
they've made one thing sure at least:
sooner or later they will pay the price.

   [*Wheeling on the Sentry.*]

                        You—
I swear to Zeus as I still believe in Zeus,
if you don't find the man who buried that corpse,
the very man, and produce him before my eyes,
simple death won't be enough for you,
not till we string you up alive
and wring the immorality out of you.
Then you can steal the rest of your days,
better informed about where to make a killing.
You'll have learned, at last, it doesn't pay
to itch for rewards from every hand that beckons.
Filthy profits wreck most men, you'll see—
they'll never save your life.

Sentry:
                    Please,
may I say a word or two, or just turn and go?

Creon:
Can't you tell? Everything you say offends me.

Sentry:
Where does it hurt you, in the ears or in the heart?

Creon:
And who are you to pinpoint my displeasure?   360

Sentry:
The culprit grates on your feelings,
I just annoy your ears.

Creon:
                    Still talking?
You talk too much! A born nuisance—

Sentry:
                            Maybe so,
but I never did this thing, so help me!

Creon:
                            Yes you did—
what's more, you squandered your life for silver!   365

Sentry:
Oh it's terrible when the one who does the judging
judges things all wrong.

Creon:
                      Well now,
you just be clever about your judgments—
if you fail to produce the criminals for me,
you'll swear your dirty money brought you pain.   370

    [*Turning sharply, reentering the palace.*]

Sentry:
I hope he's found. Best thing by far.
But caught or not, that's in the lap of fortune:
I'll never come back, you've seen the last of me.
I'm saved, even now, and I never thought,
I never hoped—   375
dear gods, I owe you all my thanks!

    [*Rushing out.*]

Chorus:

Numberless wonders
terrible wonders walk the world but none the match for man—
that great wonder crossing the heaving gray sea,
                    driven on by the blasts of winter
on through breakers crashing left and right,   380
    holds his steady course
and the oldest of the gods he wears away—
the Earth, the immortal, the inexhaustible—
as his plows go back and forth, year in, year out
    with the breed of stallions turning up the furrows.   385

And the blithe, lightheaded race of birds he snares,
the tribes of savage beasts, the life that swarms the depths—
                    with one fling of his nets
woven and coiled tight, he takes them all,
    man the skilled, the brilliant!   390
He conquers all, taming with his techniques
the prey that roams the cliffs and wild lairs,
training the stallion, clamping the yoke across
    his shaggy neck, and the tireless mountain bull.

And speech and thought, quick as the wind   395
and the mood and mind for law that rules the city—
    all these he has taught himself
and shelter from the arrows of the frost
when there's rough lodging under the cold clear sky
and the shafts of lashing rain—   400
        ready, resourceful man!
            Never without resources
never an impasse as he marches on the future—
only Death, from Death alone he will find no rescue
but from desperate plagues he has plotted his escapes.   405

Man the master, ingenious past all measure
past all dreams, the skills within his grasp—
    he forges on, now to destruction
now again to greatness. When he weaves in
the laws of the land, and the justice of the gods   410
that binds his oaths together
        he and his city rise high—
            but the city casts out
that man who weds himself to inhumanity
thanks to reckless daring. Never share my hearth   415
never think my thoughts, whoever does such things.

[*Enter Antigone from the side, accompanied by the Sentry.*]

> Here is a dark sign from the gods—
> what to make of this? I know her,
> how can I deny it? That young girl's Antigone!
> Wretched, child of a wretched father,   420
> Oedipus. Look, is it possible?
> They bring you in like a prisoner—
> why? did you break the king's laws?
> Did they take you in some act of mad defiance?

Sentry:
She's the one, she did it single-handed—   425
we caught her burying the body. Where's Creon?

[*Enter Creon from the palace.*]

Leader:
Back again, just in time when you need him.

Creon:
In time for what? What is it?

Sentry:
                My king,
there's nothing you can swear you'll never do—
second thoughts make liars of us all.
I could have sworn I wouldn't hurry back   430
(what with your threats, the buffeting I just took),
but a stroke of luck beyond our wildest hopes,
what a joy, there's nothing like it. So,
back I've come, breaking my oath, who cares?   435
I'm bringing in our prisoner—this young girl—
we took her giving the dead the last rites.
But no casting lots this time, this is *my* luck,
my prize, no one else's.
                Now, my lord,
here she is. Take her, question her,   440
cross-examine her to your heart's content.
But set me free, it's only right—
I'm rid of this dreadful business once for all.

Creon:
Prisoner! Her? You took her—where, doing what?

Sentry:
Burying the man. That's the whole story.

Creon:

                   What?   445
You mean what you say, you're telling me the truth?

Sentry:
She's the one. With my own eyes I saw her
bury the body, just what you've forbidden.
There. Is that plain and clear?

Creon:
What did you see? Did you catch her in the act?   450

Sentry:
Here's what happened. We went back to our post,
those threats of yours breathing down our necks—
we brushed the corpse clean of the dust that covered it,
stripped it bare . . . it was slimy, going soft,
and we took to high ground, backs to the wind   455
so the stink of him couldn't hit us;
jostling, baiting each other to keep awake,
shouting back and forth—no napping on the job,
not this time. And so the hours dragged by
until the sun stood dead above our heads,   460
a huge white ball in the noon sky, beating,
blazing down, and then it happened—
suddenly, a whirlwind!
Twisting a great dust-storm up from the earth,
a black plague of the heavens, filling the plain,   465
ripping the leaves off every tree in sight,
choking the air and sky. We squinted hard
and took our whipping from the gods.

And after the storm passed—it seemed endless—
there, we saw the girl!   470
And she cried out a sharp, piercing cry,
like a bird come back to an empty nest,
peering into its bed, and all the babies gone . . .
Just so, when she sees the corpse bare
she bursts into a long, shattering wail   475
and calls down withering curses on the heads
of all who did the work. And she scoops up dry dust,
handfuls, quickly, and lifting a fine bronze urn,

lifting it high and pouring, she crowns the dead
with three full libations.
                          Soon as we saw   480
we rushed her, closed on the kill like hunters,
and she, she didn't flinch. We interrogated her,
charging her with offenses past and present—
she stood up to it all, denied nothing. I tell you,
it made me ache and laugh in the same breath.   485
It's pure joy to escape the worst yourself,
it hurts a man to bring down his friends.
But all that, I'm afraid, means less to me
than my own skin. That's the way I'm made.

Creon:

[Wheeling on Antigone.]

                                          You,
with your eyes fixed on the ground—speak up.   490
Do you deny you did this, yes or no?

Antigone:
I did it. I don't deny a thing.

Creon:

[To the Sentry.]

You, get out, wherever you please—
you're clear of a very heavy charge.

[He leaves; Creon turns back to Antigone.]

You, tell me briefly, no long speeches—   495
were you aware a decree had forbidden this?

Antigone:
Well aware. How could I avoid it? It was public.

Creon:
And still you had the gall to break this law?

Antigone:
Of course I did. It wasn't Zeus, not in the least,
who made this proclamation—not to me.   500
Nor did that Justice, dwelling with the gods
beneath the earth, ordain such laws for men.

Nor did I think your edict had such force
that you, a mere mortal, could override the gods,
the great unwritten, unshakable traditions.   505
They are alive, not just today or yesterday:
they live forever, from the first of time,
and no one knows when they first saw the light.

These laws—I was not about to break them,
not out of fear of some man's wounded pride,   510
and face the retribution of the gods.
Die I must, I've known it all my life—
how could I keep from knowing?—even without
your death-sentence ringing in my ears.
And if I am to die before my time   515
I consider that a gain. Who on earth,
alive in the midst of so much grief as I,
could fail to find his death a rich reward?
So for me, at least, to meet this doom of yours
is precious little pain. But if I had allowed   520
my own mother's son to rot, an unburied corpse—
that would have been an agony! This is nothing.
And if my present actions strike you as foolish,
let's just say I've been accused of folly
by a fool.

Leader:
              Like father like daughter,   525
passionate, wild . . .
she hasn't learned to bend before adversity.

Creon:
No? Believe me, the stiffest stubborn wills
fall the hardest; the toughest iron,
tempered strong in the white-hot fire,   530
you'll see it crack and shatter first of all.
And I've known spirited horses you can break
with a light bit—proud, rebellious horses.
There's no room for pride, not in a slave
not with the lord and master standing by.   535

This girl was an old hand at insolence
when she overrode the edicts we made public.
But once she had done it—the insolence,
twice over—to glory in it, laughing,
mocking us to our face with what she'd done.   540

I'm not the man, not now: she is the man
if this victory goes to her and she goes free.

Never! Sister's child or closer in blood
than all my family clustered at my altar
worshiping Guardian Zeus—she'll never escape,   545
she and her blood sister, the most barbaric death.
Yes, I accuse her sister of an equal part
in scheming this, this burial.

     [*To his Attendants.*]

                                Bring her here!
I just saw her inside, hysterical, gone to pieces.
It never fails: the mind convicts itself   550
in advance, when scoundrels are up to no good,
plotting in the dark. Oh but I hate it more
when a traitor, caught red-handed,
tries to glorify his crimes.

Antigone:
Creon, what more do you want
than my arrest and execution?   555

Creon:
Nothing. Then I have it all.

Antigone:
Then why delay? Your moralizing repels me,
every word you say—pray god it always will.
So naturally all I say repels you too.
                        Enough.   560
Give me glory! What greater glory could I win
than to give my own brother decent burial?
These citizens here would all agree,

     [*To the Chorus.*]

they'd praise me too   565
if their lips weren't locked in fear.

     [*Pointing to Creon.*]

Lucky tyrants—the perquisites of power!
Ruthless power to do and say whatever pleases *them*.

Creon:
You alone, of all the people in Thebes,
see things that way.

Antigone:
                    They see it just that way
but defer to you and keep their tongues in leash.   570

Creon:
And you, aren't you ashamed to differ so from them?
So disloyal!

Antigone:
                    Not ashamed for a moment,
not to honor my brother, my own flesh and blood.

Creon:
Wasn't Eteocles a brother too—cut down, facing him?

Antigone:
Brother, yes, by the same mother, the same father.   575

Creon:
Then how can you render his enemy such honors,
such impieties in his eyes?

Antigone:
He'll never testify to that,
Eteocles dead and buried.

Creon:
                    He will—
if you honor the traitor just as much as him.   580

Antigone:
But it was his brother, not some slave that died—

Creon:
Ravaging our country!—
but Eteocles died fighting in our behalf.

Antigone:
No matter—Death longs for the same rites for all.

Creon:
Never the same for the patriot and the traitor.   585

Antigone:
Who, Creon, who on earth can say the ones below
don't find this pure and uncorrupt?

Creon:
Never. Once an enemy, never a friend,
not even after death.

Antigone:
I was born to join in love, not hate—   590
that is my nature.

Creon:
               Go down below and love,
if love you must—love the dead! While I'm alive,
no woman is going to lord it over me.

     [Enter Ismene from the palace, under guard.]

Chorus:
                                          Look,
Ismene's coming, weeping a sister's tears,
loving sister, under a cloud . . .   595
her face is flushed, her cheeks streaming.
Sorrow puts her lovely radiance in the dark.

Creon:
                                        You—
in my house, you viper, slinking undetected,
sucking my life-blood! I never knew
I was breeding twin disasters, the two of you   600
rising up against my throne. Come, tell me,
will you confess your part in the crime or not?
Answer me. Swear to me.

Ismene:
                         I did it, yes—
if only she consents—I share the guilt,
the consequences too.

Antigone:
                              No,
Justice will never suffer that—not you,
you were unwilling. I never brought you in.

Ismene:
But now you face such dangers . . . I'm not ashamed
to sail through trouble with you,
make your troubles mine.

Antigone:
                              Who did the work?   610
Let the dead and the god of death bear witness!
I've no love for a friend who loves in words alone.

Ismene:
Oh no, my sister, don't reject me, please,
let me die beside you, consecrating
the dead together.

Antigone:
                              Never share my dying,   615
don't lay claim to what you never touched.
My death will be enough.

Ismene:
What do I care for life, cut off from you?

Antigone:
Ask Creon. Your concern is all for him.

Ismene:
Why abuse me so? It doesn't help you now.

Antigone:
                              You're right—   620
if I mock you, I get no pleasure from it,
only pain.

Ismene:
              Tell me, dear one,
what can I do to help you, even now?

Antigone:
Save yourself. I don't grudge you your survival.

Ismene:
Oh no, no, denied my portion in your death?   625

Antigone:
You chose to live, I chose to die.

Ismene:
                                        Not, at least,
without every kind of caution I could voice.

Antigone:
Your wisdom appealed to one world—mine, another.

Ismene:
But look, we're both guilty, both condemned to death.

Antigone:
Courage! Live your life. I gave myself to death,   630
long ago, so I might serve the dead.

Creon:
They're both mad, I tell you, the two of them.
One's just shown it, the other's been that way
since she was born.

Ismene:
                                        True, my king,
the sense we were born with cannot last forever . . .   635
commit cruelty on a person long enough
and the mind begins to go.

Creon:
                                        Yours did,
when you chose to commit your crimes with her.

Ismene:
How can I live alone, without her?

Creon:
                                        Her?
Don't even mention her—she no longer exists.   640

Ismene:
What? You'd kill your own son's bride?

Creon:

Absolutely:

there are other fields for him to plow.

Ismene:

Perhaps,

but never as true, as close a bond as theirs.

Creon:

A worthless woman for my son? It repels me.

Ismene:

Dearest Haemon, your father wrongs you so!   645

Creon:

Enough, enough—you and your talk of marriage!

Ismene:

Creon—you're really going to rob your son of Antigone?

Creon:

Death will do it for me—break their marriage off.

Leader:

So, it's settled then? Antigone must die?

Creon:

Settled, yes—we both know that.   650

[To the Guards.]

Stop wasting time. Take them in.
From now on they'll act like women.
Tie them up, no more running loose;
even the bravest will cut and run,   655
once they see Death coming for their lives.

[The Guards escort Antigone and Ismene into the palace.
Creon remains while the old citizens form their Chorus.]

Chorus:

Blest, they are truly blest who all their lives
have never tasted devastation. For others, once
the gods have rocked a house to its foundations
    the ruin will never cease, cresting on and on

from one generation on throughout the race— 660
like a great mounting tide
driven on by savage northern gales,
     surging over the dead black depths
roiling up from the bottom dark heaves of sand
and the headlands, taking the storm's onslaught full-force, 665
roar, and the low moaning
                 echoes on and on
                     and now
as in ancient times I see the sorrows of the house,
the living heirs of the old ancestral kings,
piling on the sorrows of the dead
     and one generation cannot free the next— 670
some god will bring them crashing down,
the race finds no release.
And now the light, the hope
     springing up from the late last root
in the house of Oedipus, that hope's cut down in turn 675
by the long, bloody knife swung by the gods of death
by a senseless word
          by fury at the heart.
                    Zeus,
yours is the power, Zeus, what man on earth
can override it, who can hold it back?
Power that neither Sleep, the all-ensnaring 680
     no, nor the tireless months of heaven
can ever overmaster—young through all time,
mighty lord of power, you hold fast
     the dazzling crystal mansions of Olympus.
And throughout the future, late and soon 685
as through the past, your law prevails:
no towering form of greatness
     enters into the lives of mortals
               free and clear of ruin.
                    True,
our dreams, our high hopes voyaging far and wide 690
bring sheer delight to many, to many others
     delusion, blithe, mindless lusts
and the fraud steals on one slowly . . . unaware
till he trips and puts his foot into the fire.
     He was a wise old man who coined 695
the famous saying: "Sooner or later
foul is fair, fair is foul
to the man the gods will ruin"—

He goes his way for a moment only
                         free of blinding ruin.

[*Enter Haemon from the palace.*]

Here's Haemon now, the last of all your sons.
Does he come in tears for his bride,
his doomed bride, Antigone—
bitter at being cheated of their marriage?

Creon:
We'll soon know, better than seers could tell us.   705

[*Turning to Haemon.*]

Son, you've heard the final verdict on your bride?
Are you coming now, raving against your father?
Or do you love me, no matter what I do?

Haemon:
Father, I'm your *son* . . . you in your wisdom
set my bearings for me—I obey you.   710
No marriage could ever mean more to me than you,
whatever good direction you may offer.

Creon:
                                    Fine, Haemon.
That's how you ought to feel within your heart,
subordinate to your father's will in every way.
That's what a man prays for: to produce good sons—   715
a household full of them, dutiful and attentive,
so they can pay his enemy back with interest
and match the respect their father shows his friend.
But the man who rears a brood of useless children,
what has he brought into the world, I ask you?   720
Nothing but trouble for himself, and mockery
from his enemies laughing in his face.
                                    Oh Haemon,
never lose your sense of judgment over a woman.
The warmth, the rush of pleasure, it all goes cold
in your arms, I warn you . . , a worthless woman   725
in your house, a misery in your bed.
What wound cuts deeper than a loved one
turned against you? Spit her out,
like a mortal enemy—let the girl go.
Let her find a husband down among the dead.   730

Imagine it: I caught her in naked rebellion,
the traitor, the only one in the whole city.
I'm not about to prove myself a liar,
not to my people, no, I'm going to kill her!
That's right—so let her cry for mercy, sing her hymns   735
to Zeus who defends all bonds of kindred blood.
Why, if I bring up my own kin to be rebels,
think what I'd suffer from the world at large.
Show me the man who rules his household well:
I'll show you someone fit to rule the state.   740
That good man, my son,
I have every confidence he and he alone
can give commands and take them too. Staunch
in the storm of spears he'll stand his ground,
a loyal, unflinching comrade at your side.   745

But whoever steps out of line, violates the laws
or presumes to hand out orders to his superiors,
he'll win no praise from me. But that man
the city places in authority, his orders
must be obeyed, large and small,   750
right and wrong.
                    Anarchy—
show me a greater crime in all the earth!
She, she destroys cities, rips up houses,
breaks the ranks of spearmen into headlong rout.
But the ones who last it out, the great mass of them   755
owe their lives to discipline. Therefore
we must defend the men who live by law,
never let some woman triumph over us.
Better to fall from power, if fall we must,
at the hands of a man—never be rated   760
inferior to a woman, never.

Leader:

                 To us,
unless old age has robbed us of our wits,
you seem to say what you have to say with sense.

Haemon:
Father, only the gods endow a man with reason,
the finest of all their gifts, a treasure.   765
Far be it from me—I haven't the skill,
and certainly no desire, to tell you when,
if ever, you make a slip in speech . . . though
someone else might have a good suggestion.

Of course it's not for you,   770
in the normal run of things, to watch
whatever men say or do, or find to criticize.
The man in the street, you know, dreads your glance,
he'd never say anything displeasing to your face.
But it's for me to catch the murmurs in the dark,   775
the way the city mourns for this young girl.
"No woman," they say, "ever deserved death less,
and such a brutal death for such a glorious action.
She, with her own dear brother lying in his blood—
she couldn't bear to leave him dead, unburied,   780
food for the wild dogs or wheeling vultures.
Death? She deserves a glowing crown of gold!"
So they say, and the rumor spreads in secret,
darkly . . .
                    I rejoice in your success, father—
nothing more precious to me in the world.   785
What medal of honor brighter to his children
than a father's growing glory? Or a child's
to his proud father? Now don't, please,
be quite so single-minded, self-involved,
or assume the world is wrong and you are right.   790
Whoever thinks that he alone possesses intelligence,
the gift of eloquence, he and no one else,
and character too . . . such men, I tell you,
spread them open—you will find them empty.

                                        No,
it's no disgrace for a man, even a wise man,   795
to learn many things and not to be too rigid.
You've seen trees by a raging winter torrent,
how many sway with the flood and salvage every twig,
but not the stubborn—they're ripped out, roots and all.
Bend or break. The same when a man is sailing: 800
haul your sheets too taut, never give an inch,
you'll capsize, and go the rest of the voyage
keel up and the rowing-benches under.

Oh give way. Relax your anger—change!
I'm young, I know, but let me offer this: 805
it would be best by far, I admit,
if a man were born infallible, right by nature.
If not—and things don't often go that way,
it's best to learn from those with good advice.

Leader:
You'd do well, my lord, if he's speaking to the point,   810
to learn from him.

     [Turning to Haemon.]

                and you, my boy, from him.
You both are talking sense.

Creon:
                        So,
men our age, we're to be lectured, are we?—
schooled by a boy his age?

Haemon:
Only in what is right. But if I seem young,   815
look less to my years and more to what I do.

Creon:
Do? Is admiring rebels an achievement?

Haemon:
I'd never suggest that you admire treason.

Creon:
                         Oh?—
isn't that just the sickness that's attacked her?

Haemon:
The whole city of Thebes denies it, to a man.   820

Creon:
And is Thebes about to tell me how to rule?

Haemon:
Now, you see? Who's talking like a child?

Creon:
Am I to rule this land for others—or myself?

Haemon:
It's no city at all, owned by one man alone.

Creon:
What? The city *is* the king's—that's the law!   825

Haemon:
What a splendid king you'd make of a desert island—
you and you alone.

Creon:

[*To the Chorus.*]

This boy, I do believe,
is fighting on her side, the woman's side.

Haemon:
If you are a woman, yes;
my concern is all for you.   830

Creon:
Why, you degenerate—bandying accusations,
threatening me with justice, your own father!

Haemon:
I see my father offending justice—wrong.

Creon:
                              Wrong?
To protect my royal rights?

Haemon:
                    Protect your rights?
When you trample down the honors of the gods?   835

Creon:
You, you soul of corruption, rotten through—
woman's accomplice!

Haemon:
                    That may be,
but you'll never find me accomplice to a criminal.

Creon:
That's what *she* is,
and every word you say is a blatant appeal for her—   840

Haemon:
And you, and me, and the gods beneath the earth.

Creon:
You will never marry her, not while she's alive.

Haemon:
Then she will die . . . but her death will kill another.

Creon:
What, brazen threats? You go too far!

Haemon:
                                        What threat?
Combating your empty, mindless judgments with a word?   845

Creon:
You'll suffer for your sermons, you and your empty wisdom!

Haemon:
If you weren't my father, I'd say you were insane.

Creon:
Don't flatter me with Father—you woman's slave!

Haemon:
You really expect to fling abuse at me
and not receive the same?

Creon:
                                        Is that so!   850
Now, by heaven, I promise you, you'll pay—
taunting, insulting me! Bring her out,
that hateful—she'll die now, here,
in front of his eyes, beside her groom!

Haemon:
No, no, she will never die beside me—   855
don't delude yourself. And you will never
see me, never set eyes on my face again.
Rage your heart out, rage with friends
who can stand the sight of you.

    [*Rushing out.*]

Leader:
Gone, my king, in a burst of anger.   860
A temper young as his . . . hurt him once,
he may do something violent.

Creon:

                Let him do—
dream up something desperate, past all human limit!
Good riddance. Rest assured,
he'll never save those two young girls from death.   865

Leader:
Both of them, you really intend to kill them both?

Creon:
No, not her, the one whose hands are clean—
you're quite right.

Leader:
                But Antigone—
what sort of death do you have in mind for her?

Creon:
I'll take her down some wild, desolate path   870
never trod by men, and wall her up alive
in a rocky vault, and set out short rations,
just the measure piety demands
to keep the entire city free of defilement.
There let her pray to the one god she worships: 875
Death—who knows?—may just reprieve her from death.
Or she may learn at last, better late than never,
what a waste of breath it is to worship Death.

    [Exit to the palace.]

Chorus:
Love, never conquered in battle
Love the plunderer laying waste the rich!   880
Love standing the night-watch
                guarding a girl's soft cheek,
you range the seas, the shepherds' steadings off in the wilds—
not even the deathless gods can flee your onset,
nothing human born for a day—   885
whoever feels your grip is driven mad.
                        Love!—
you wrench the minds of the righteous into outrage,
swerve them to their ruin—you have ignited this,
this kindred strife, father and son at war

and Love alone the victor—   890
warm glance of the bride triumphant, burning with desire!
Throned in power, side-by-side with the mighty laws!
Irresistible Aphrodite,° never conquered—
Love, you mock us for your sport.

    [*Antigone is brought from the palace under guard.*]

        But now, even I would rebel against the king,   895
        I would break all bounds when I see this—
        I fill with tears, I cannot hold them back,
        not any more . . . I see Antigone make her way
        to the bridal vault where all are laid to rest.

Antigone:
Look at me, men of my fatherland,   900
    setting out on the last road
looking into the last light of day
the last I will ever see . . .
the god of death who puts us all to bed
takes me down to the banks of Acheron° alive—   905
    denied my part in the wedding-songs,
no wedding-song in the dusk has crowned my marriage—
I go to wed the lord of the dark waters.

Chorus:
        Not crowned with glory or with a dirge,
        you leave for the deep pit of the dead.   910
        No withering illness laid you low,
        no strokes of the sword—a law to yourself,
        alone, no mortal like you, ever, you go down
        to the halls of Death alive and breathing.

Antigone:
But think of Niobe°—well I know her story—   915
    think what a living death she died,
Tantalus' daughter, stranger queen from the east:
there on the mountain heights, growing stone
binding as ivy, slowly walled her round
and the rains will never cease, the legends say   920
the snows will never leave her . . .

893 *Aphrodite:* goddess of love and beauty.   905 *Acheron:* river in Hades, domain of the dead.
915 *Niobe:* a Theban queen whose fourteen children were slain. She wept so copiously she was
transformed to a stone on Mount Sipylos, and her tears became the mountain's streams.

wasting away, under her brows the tears
showering down her breasting ridge and slopes—
a rocky death like hers puts me to sleep.

Chorus:

> But she was a god, born of gods,   925
> and we are only mortals born to die.
> And yet, of course, it's a great thing
> for a dying girl to hear, even to hear
> she shares a destiny equal to the gods,
> during life and later, once she's dead.

Antigone:

                                    O you mock me!   930
Why, in the name of all my fathers' gods
why can't you wait till I am gone—
     must you abuse me to my face?
O my city, all your fine rich sons!
And you, you springs of the Dirce,   935
holy grove of Thebes where the chariots gather,
     you at least, you'll bear me witness, look,
unmourned by friends and forced by such crude laws
I go to my rockbound prison, strange new tomb—
     always a stranger, O dear god,   940
     I have no home on earth and none below,
          not with the living, not with the breathless dead.

Chorus:

> You went too far, the last limits of daring—
> smashing against the high throne of Justice!
>   Your life's in ruins, child—I wonder . . .   945
> do you pay for your father's terrible ordeal?

Antigone:

There—at last you've touched it, the worst pain
the worst anguish! Raking up the grief for father
     three times over, for all the doom
that's struck us down, the brilliant house of Laius.   950
O mother, your marriage-bed
the coiling horrors, the coupling there—
     you with your own son, my father—doomstruck mother!
Such, such were my parents, and I their wretched child.
I go to them now, cursed, unwed, to share their home—   955
     I am a stranger! O dear brother, doomed

in your marriage—your marriage murders mine,
your dying drags me down to death alive!

[Enter Creon.]

Chorus:
Reverence asks some reverence in return—
but attacks on power never go unchecked,   960
    not by the man who holds the reins of power.
Your own blind will, your passion has destroyed you.

Antigone:
No one to weep for me, my friends,
no wedding-song—they take me away
in all my pain . . . the road lies open, waiting.   965
Never again, the law forbids me to see
the sacred eye of day. I am agony!
No tears for the destiny that's mine,
no loved one mourns my death.

Creon:
                                    Can't you see?
If a man could wail his own dirge *before* he dies,   970
he'd never finish.

    [To the Guards.]

                        Take her away, quickly!
Wall her up in the tomb, you have your orders.
Abandon her there, alone, and let her choose—
death or a buried life with a good roof for shelter.
As for myself, my hands are clean. This young girl—   975
dead or alive, she will be stripped of her rights,
her stranger's rights, here in the world above.

Antigone:
O tomb, my bridal-bed—my house, my prison
cut in the hollow rock, my everlasting watch!
I'll soon be there, soon embrace my own,   980
the great growing family of our dead
Persephone° has received among her ghosts.
                                    I,
the last of them all, the most reviled by far,
go down before my destined time's run out.

982 Persephone: woman whom Pluto, god of the underworld, abducted to be his queen.

But still I go, cherishing one good hope: 985
my arrival may be dear to father,
dear to you, my mother,
dear to you, my loving brother, Eteocles—
When you died I washed you with my hands,
I dressed you all, I poured the sacred cups   990
across your tombs. But now, Polynices,
because I laid your body out as well,
this, this is my reward. Nevertheless
I honored you—the decent will admit it—
well and wisely too.
                              Never, I tell you,   995
if I had been the mother of children
or if my husband died, exposed and rotting—
I'd never have taken this ordeal upon myself,
never defied our people's will. What law,
you ask, do I satisfy with what I say?   1000
A husband dead, there might have been another.
A child by another too, if I had lost the first.
But mother and father both lost in the halls of Death,
no brother could ever spring to light again.
                                                                         1005
For this law alone I held you first in honor.
For this, Creon, the king, judges me a criminal
guilty of dreadful outrage, my dear brother!
And now he leads me off, a captive in his hands,
with no part in the bridal-song, the bridal-bed,
denied all joy of marriage, raising children—   1010
deserted so by loved ones, struck by fate,
I descend alive to the caverns of the dead.

What law of the mighty gods have I transgressed?
Why look to the heavens any more, tormented as I am?
Whom to call, what comrades now? Just think,   1015
my reverence only brands me for irreverence!
Very well: if this is the pleasure of the gods,
once I suffer I will know that I was wrong.
But if these men are wrong, let them suffer
nothing worse than they mete out to me—   1020
these masters of injustice!

Leader:
Still the same rough winds, the wild passion
raging through the girl.

Creon:

[To the Guards.]

Take her away.
You're wasting time—you'll pay for it too.

Antigone:
Oh god, the voice of death. It's come, it's here.   1025

Creon:
True. Not a word of hope—your doom is sealed.

Antigone:
　　　　Land of Thebes, city of all my fathers—
　　　　O you gods, the first gods of the race!
　　　　They drag me away, now, no more delay.
　　　　Look on me, you noble sons of Thebes—   1030
　　　　the last of a great line of kings,
　　　　I alone, see what I suffer now
　　　　at the hands of what breed of men—
　　　　all for reverence, my reverence for the gods!

[She leaves under guard; the Chorus gathers.]

Chorus:
　　　　Danaë,° Danaë—   1035
even she endured a fate like yours,
　　in all her lovely strength she traded
the light of day for the bolted brazen vault—
buried within her tomb, her bridal-chamber,
wed to the yoke and broken.   1040
　　　　But she was of glorious birth
　　　　　　　　　　my child, my child
and treasured the seed of Zeus within her womb,
the cloudburst streaming gold!
　　　　The power of fate is a wonder,   1045
　　　　dark, terrible wonder—
　　　　neither wealth nor armies
　　　　towered walls nor ships

1035 Danaë: In legend, when an oracle told Acrisius, king of Argos, that his daughter Danaë
would bear a son who would grow up to slay him, he locked the princess into a chamber made
of bronze, lest any man impregnate her. But Zeus, father of the gods, entered Danaë's prison in
a shower of gold. The resultant child, the hero Perseus, was accidentally to fulfill the prophecy
by killing Acrisius with an ill-aimed discus throw.

black hulls lashed by the salt
    can save us from that force.   1050

The yoke tamed him too
    young Lycurgus° flaming in anger
king of Edonia, all for his mad taunts
Dionysus clamped him down, encased
in the chain-mail of rock   1055
    and there his rage
            his terrible flowering rage burst—
sobbing, dying away . . . at last that madman
came to know his god—
    the power he mocked, the power   1060
    he taunted in all his frenzy
    trying to stamp out
    the women strong with the god—
    the torch, the raving sacred cries—
    enraging the Muses° who adore the flute.   1065

And far north where the Black Rocks
    cut the sea in half
and murderous straits
split the coast of Thrace
    a forbidding city stands   1070
where once, hard by the walls
the savage Ares° thrilled to watch
a king's new queen, a Fury rearing in rage
    against his two royal sons—
        her bloody hands, her dagger-shuttle   1075
stabbing out their eyes—cursed, blinding wounds—
their eyes blind sockets screaming for revenge!

They wailed in agony, cries echoing cries
    the princes doomed at birth . . .°
and their mother doomed to chains,   1080
walled up in a tomb of stone—
    but she traced her own birth back
to a proud Athenian line and the high gods
and off in caverns half the world away,

1052 *Lycurgus:* King of Thrace, whom Dionysus, god of wine, caused to be stricken with madness.   1065 *Muses:* nine sister goddesses who presided over poetry, music, arts, and sciences.
1072 *savage Ares:* god of war, said to gloat over bloodshed.   1079 *the princes doomed at birth . . . :*
As the Chorus recalls in the rest of this song, the point of this tale is that being nobly born will
not save one from disaster. King Phineas cast off his first wife Cleopatra (not the later Egyptian
queen, but the daughter of Boreas, god of the north wind) and imprisoned her in a cave. Out of
hatred for Cleopatra, the cruel Eidothea, second wife of the king, blinded her stepsons.

born of the wild North Wind
   she sprang on her father's gales,
     racing stallions up the leaping cliffs—
child of the heavens. But even on her the Fates
the gray everlasting Fates rode hard
my child, my child.

    [Enter Tiresias, the blind prophet, led by a Boy.]

Tiresias:
                    Lords of Thebes,
I and the boy have come together,
hand in hand. Two see with the eyes of one . . .
so the blind must go, with a guide to lead the way.

Creon:
What is it, old Tiresias? What news now?

Tiresias:
I will teach you. And you obey the seer.

Creon:
                           I will,
I've never wavered from your advice before.

Tiresias:
And so you kept the city straight on course.

Creon:
I owe you a great deal, I swear to that.

Tiresias:
Then reflect, my son: you are poised,
once more, on the razor-edge of fate.

Creon:
What is it? I shudder to hear you.

Tiresias:
                    You will learn
when you listen to the warnings of my craft.
As I sat on the ancient seat of augury,
in the sanctuary where every bird I know

1085

1090

1095

1100

will hover at my hands—suddenly I heard it,
a strange voice in the wingbeats, unintelligible,
barbaric, a mad scream! Talons flashing, ripping,
they were killing each other—that much I knew—
the murderous fury whirring in those wings
made that much clear!
                    I was afraid, 1110
I turned quickly, tested the burnt-sacrifice,
ignited the altar at all points—but no fire,
the god in the fire never blazed.
Not from those offerings . . . over the embers
slid a heavy ooze from the long thighbones, 1115
smoking, sputtering out, and the bladder
puffed and burst—spraying gall into the air—
and the fat wrapping the bones slithered off
and left them glistening white. No fire!
The rites failed that might have blazed the future 1120
with a sign. So I learned from the boy here:
he is my guide, as I am guide to others.
                        And it's you—
your high resolve that sets this plague on Thebes.
The public altars and sacred hearths are fouled,
one and all, by the birds and dogs with carrion 1125
torn from the corpse, the doomstruck son of Oedipus!
And so the gods are deaf to our prayers, they spurn
the offerings in our hands, the flame of holy flesh.
No birds cry out an omen clear and true—
they're gorged with the murdered victim's blood and fat. 1130

Take these things to heart, my son, I warn you.
All men make mistakes, it is only human.
But once the wrong is done, a man
can turn his back on folly, misfortune too,
if he tries to make amends, however low he's fallen, 1135
and stops his bullnecked ways. Stubbornness
brands you for stupidity—pride is a crime.
No, yield to the dead!
Never stab the fighter when he's down.
Where's the glory, killing the dead twice over? 1140

I mean you well. I give you sound advice.
It's best to learn from a good adviser
when he speaks for your own good:
it's pure gain.

Creon:
                    Old man—all of you! So,
you shoot your arrows at my head like archers at the target—   1145
I even have *him* loosed on me, this fortune-teller.
Oh his ilk has tried to sell me short
and ship me off for years. Well,
drive your bargains, traffic—much as you like—
in the gold of India, silver-gold of Sardis.   1150
You'll never bury that body in the grave,
not even if Zeus's eagles rip the corpse
and wing their rotten pickings off to the throne of god!
Never, not even in fear of such defilement
will I tolerate his burial, that traitor.   1155
Well I know, we can't defile the gods—
no mortal has the power.
                    No,
reverend old Tiresias, all men fall,
it's only human, but the wisest fall obscenely
when they glorify obscene advice with rhetoric—   1160
all for their own gain.

Tiresias:
Oh god, is there a man alive
who knows, who actually believes . . .

Creon:
                              What now?
What earth-shattering truth are you about to utter?

Tiresias:
. . . just how much a sense of judgment, wisdom   1165
is the greatest gift we have?

Creon:
                        Just as much, I'd say,
as a twisted mind is the worst affliction known.

Tiresias:
You are the one who's sick, Creon, sick to death.

Creon:
I am in no mood to trade insults with a seer.

Tiresias:
You have already, calling my prophecies a lie.

Creon:
                                        Why not?   1170
You and the whole breed of seers are mad for money!

Tiresias:
And the whole race of tyrants lusts for filthy gain.

Creon:
This slander of yours—
are you aware you're speaking to the king?

Tiresias:
Well aware. Who helped you save the city?

Creon:
                                        You—   1175
you have your skills, old seer, but you lust for injustice!

Tiresias:
You will drive me to utter the dreadful secret in my heart.

Creon:
Spit it out! Just don't speak it out for profit.

Tiresias:
Profit? No, not a bit of profit, not for you.

Creon:
Know full well, you'll never buy off my resolve.   1180

Tiresias:
Then know this too, learn this by heart!
The chariot of the sun will not race through
so many circuits more, before you have surrendered
one born of your own loins, your own flesh and blood,
a corpse for corpses given in return, since you have thrust   1185
to the world below a child sprung from the world above,
ruthlessly lodged a living soul within the grave—
then you've robbed the gods below the earth,
keeping a dead body here in the bright air,
unburied, unsung, unhallowed by the rites.   1190

You, you have no business with the dead,
nor do the gods above—this is violence
you have forced upon the heavens.

And so the avengers, the dark destroyers late
but true to the mark, now lie in wait for you,   1195
the Furies sent by the gods and the god of death
to strike you down with the pains that you perfected!

There. Reflect on that, tell me I've been bribed.
The day comes soon, no long test of time, not now,
when the mourning cries for men and women break   1200
Great hatred rises against you—throughout your halls.
cities in tumult, all whose mutilated sons
the dogs have graced with burial, or the wild beasts
or a wheeling crow that wings the ungodly stench of carrion
back to each city, each warrior's heart and home.   1205

These arrows for your heart! Since you've raked me
I loose them like an archer in my anger,
arrows deadly true. You'll never escape
their burning, searing force.

     [*Motioning to his escort.*]

Come, boy, take me home.   1210
So he can vent his rage on younger men,
and learn to keep a gentler tongue in his head
and better sense than what he carries now.

     [*Exit to the side.*]

Leader:
The old man's gone, my king—
terrible prophecies. Well I know,   1215
since the hair on this old head went gray,
he's never lied to Thebes.

Creon:
I know it myself—I'm shaken, torn.
It's a dreadful thing to yield . . . but resist now?
Lay my pride bare to the blows of ruin?   1220
That's dreadful too.

Leader:
            But good advice,
Creon, take it now, you must.

Creon:
What should I do? Tell me . . . I'll obey.

Leader:

Go! Free the girl from the rocky vault
and raise a mound for the body you exposed.   1225

Creon:

That's your advice? You think I should give in?

Leader:

Yes, my king, quickly. Disasters sent by the gods
cut short our follies in a flash.

Creon:

                              Oh it's hard,
giving up the heart's desire . . . but I will do it—
no more fighting a losing battle with necessity.   1230

Leader:

Do it now, go, don't leave it to others.

Creon:

Now—I'm on my way! Come, each of you,
take up axes, make for the high ground,
over there, quickly! I and my better judgment
have come round to this—I shackled her,   1235
I'll set her free myself. I am afraid . . .
it's best to keep the established laws
to the very day we die.

> [*Rushing out, followed by his entourage. The Chorus clusters
> around the altar.*]

Chorus:

God of a hundred names!
                    Great Dionysus° —
        Son and glory of Semele! Pride of Thebes—   1240
Child of Zeus whose thunder rocks the clouds—
Lord of the famous lands of evening—

1239–1272 a song of praise or prayer to Dionysus, god of wine. 1239–1248 *God of a hundred names . . . Dragon's teeth:* Dionysus had many names, one of which was Bacchus. "King of Eleusis" is another name for Dionysus, honored in secret rites at Eleusis, a town northwest of Athens. He was the son of Zeus and Semele, daughter of Cadmus, legendary founder of Thebes. Cadmus, so the story goes, sowed dragon's teeth in a field beside the river Ismenus. Up sprang a crop of fierce warriors who fought among themselves until only five remained. These victors became the first Thebans.

King of the Mysteries!
                        King of Eleusis, Demeter's plain°
her breasting hills that welcome in the world—
Great Dionysus!
                        Bacchus, living in Thebes   1245
the mother-city of all your frenzied women°—
                                        Bacchus
        living along the Ismenus'° rippling waters
standing over the field sown with the Dragons' teeth!°

You—we have seen you through the flaring smoky fires,
        your torches blazing over the twin peaks   1250
where nymphs of the hallowed cave climb onward
                        fired with you, your sacred rage—
we have seen you at Castalia's running spring°
and down from the heights of Nysa° crowned with ivy
the greening shore rioting vines and grapes   1255
        down you come in your storm of wild women
                ecstatic, mystic cries—
                        Dionysus—
down to watch and ward the roads of Thebes!
First of all cities, Thebes you honor first
you and your mother, bride of the lightning—   1260
come, Dionysus! now your people lie
in the iron grip of plague,
come in your racing, healing stride
                down Parnassus' slopes
or across the moaning straits.
                        Lord of the dancing—   1265
dance, dance the constellations breathing fire!
Great master of the voices of the night!
Child of Zeus, God's offspring, come, come forth!
Lord, king, dance with your nymphs, swirling, raving
arm-in-arm in frenzy through the night   1270
        they dance you, Iacchus°—
                Dance, Dionysus
giver of all good things!

1243 *Demeter's plain:* Demeter, goddess of grain, was also worshipped at Eleusis. 1245–1246
Bacchus . . . frenzied women: the women of Thebes said to worship Dionysus with wild orgiastic
rites.   1253 *Castalia's running spring:* a spring on Mount Parnassus, named for a maiden who
drowned herself in it to avoid rape by the god Apollo. She became a nymph, or nature spirit,
dwelling in its waters. In the temple of Delphi, at the mountain's foot, priestesses of Dionysus
used the spring's waters in rites of purification.   1254 *Nysa:* mountain, important place of
worship of Dionysus.   1271 *Iacchus:* another name for Dionysus.

[*Enter a Messenger from the side.*]

Messenger:
                  Neighbors,
friends of the house of Cadmus and the kings,
there's not a thing in this mortal life of ours
I'd praise or blame as settled once for all.   1275
Fortune lifts and Fortune fells the lucky
and unlucky every day. No prophet on earth
can tell a man his fate. Take Creon:
there was a man to rouse your envy once,
as I see it. He saved the realm from enemies;   1280
taking power, he alone, the lord of the fatherland,
he set us true on course—flourished like a tree
with the noble line of sons he bred and reared . . .
and now it's lost, all gone.
                     Believe me,
when a man has squandered his true joys,   1285
he's good as dead, I tell you, a living corpse.
Pile up riches in your house, as much as you like—
live like a king with a huge show of pomp,
but if real delight is missing from the lot,
I wouldn't give you a wisp of smoke for it,   1290
not compared with joy.

Leader:
                  What now?
What new grief do you bring the house of kings?

Messenger:
Dead, dead—and the living are guilty of their death!

Leader:
Who's the murderer? Who is dead? Tell us.

Messenger:
Haemon's gone, his blood spilled by the very hand—   1295

Leader:
His father's or his own?

Messenger:
                His own . . .
raging mad with his father for the death—

Leader:
                                   Oh great seer,
you saw it all, you brought your word to birth!

Messenger:
Those are the facts. Deal with them as you will.

[*As he turns to go, Eurydice enters from the palace.*]

Leader:
Look, Eurydice. Poor woman, Creon's wife,   1300
so close at hand. By chance perhaps,
unless she's heard the news about her son.

Eurydice:
                                   My countrymen,
all of you—I caught the sound of your words
as I was leaving to do my part,
to appeal to queen Athena with my prayers.   1305
I was just loosing the bolts, opening the doors,
when a voice filled with sorrow, family sorrow,
struck my ears, and I fell back, terrified,
into the women's arms—everything went black.
Tell me the news, again, whatever it is . . .   1310
sorrow and I are hardly strangers;
I can bear the worst.

Messenger:
                         I—dear lady,
I'll speak as an eye-witness. I was there.
And I won't pass over one word of the truth.
Why should I try to soothe you with a story,   1315
only to prove a liar in a moment?
Truth is always best.
                         So,
I escorted your lord, I guided him
to the edge of the plain where the body lay,
Polynices, torn by the dogs and still unmourned.   1320
And saying a prayer to Hecate of the Crossroads,
Pluto° too, to hold their anger and be kind,

1321–1322 *Hecate . . . Pluto:* two fearful divinities—the goddess of witchcraft and sorcery and
the King of Hades, underworld of the dead.

we washed the dead in a bath of holy water
and plucking some fresh branches, gathering . . .
what was left of him, we burned them all together   1325
and raised a high mound of native earth, and then
we turned and made for that rocky vault of hers,
the hollow, empty bed of the bride of Death.
And far off, one of us heard a voice,
a long wail rising, echoing   1330
out of that unhallowed wedding-chamber;
he ran to alert the master and Creon pressed on,
closer—the strange, inscrutable cry came sharper,
throbbing around him now, and he let loose
a cry of his own, enough to wrench the heart,   1335
"Oh god, am I the prophet now? going down
the darkest road I've ever gone? My son—
it's *his* dear voice, he greets me! Go, men,
closer, quickly! Go through the gap,
the rocks are dragged back—   1340
right to the tomb's very mouth—and look,
see if it's Haemon's voice I think I hear,
or the gods have robbed me of my senses."

The king was shattered. We took his orders,
went and searched, and there in the deepest,   1345
dark recesses of the tomb we found her . . .
hanged by the neck in a fine linen noose,
strangled in her veils—and the boy,
his arms flung around her waist,
clinging to her, wailing for his bride,   1350
dead and down below, for his father's crimes
and the bed of his marriage blighted by misfortune.
When Creon saw him, he gave a deep sob,
he ran in, shouting, crying out to him,
"Oh my child—what have you done? what seized you,   1355
what insanity? what disaster drove you mad?
Come out, my son! I beg you on my knees!"
But the boy gave him a wild burning glance,
spat in his face, not a word in reply,
he drew his sword—his father rushed out,   1360
running as Haemon lunged and missed!—
and then, doomed, desperate with himself,
suddenly leaning his full weight on the blade,
he buried it in his body, halfway to the hilt.
And still in his senses, pouring his arms around her,   1365
he embraced the girl and breathing hard,

released a quick rush of blood,
bright red on her cheek glistening white.
And there he lies, body enfolding body . . .
he has won his bride at last, poor boy,
not here but in the houses of the dead.

Creon shows the world that of all the ills
afflicting men the worst is lack of judgment.

    [*Eurydice turns and reenters the palace.*]

Leader:
What do you make of that? The lady's gone,
without a word, good or bad.

Messenger:
                    I'm alarmed too
but here's my hope—faced with her son's death,
she finds it unbecoming to mourn in public.
Inside, under her roof, she'll set her women
to the task and wail the sorrow of the house.
She's too discreet. She won't do something rash.

Leader:
I'm not so sure. To me, at least,
a long heavy silence promises danger,
just as much as a lot of empty outcries.

Messenger:
We'll see if she's holding something back,
hiding some passion in her heart.
I'm going in. You may be right—who knows?
Even too much silence has its dangers.

    [*Exit to the palace. Enter Creon from the side, escorted by
    attendants carrying Haemon's body on a bier.*]

Leader:
    The king himself! Coming toward us,
    look, holding the boy's head in his hands.
    Clear, damning proof, if it's right to say so—
    proof of his own madness, no one else's,
      no, his own blind wrongs.

1370

1375

1380

1385

1390

Creon:

                  Ohhh,
so senseless, so insane . . . my crimes,
my stubborn, deadly—
Look at us, the killer, the killed,   1395
father and son, the same blood—the misery!
My plans, my mad fanatic heart,
my son, cut off so young!
Ai, dead, lost to the world,
not through your stupidity, no, my own.

Leader:

                       Too late,   1400
too late, you see what justice means.

Creon:

                 Oh I've learned
through blood and tears! Then, it was then,
when the god came down and struck me—a great weight
shattering, driving me down that wild savage path,
ruining, trampling down my joy. Oh the agony,   1405
   the heartbreaking agonies of our lives.

[*Enter the Messenger from the palace.*]

Messenger:

                    Master,
what a hoard of grief you have, and you'll have more.
The grief that lies to hand you've brought yourself—

   [*Pointing to Haemon's body.*]

the rest, in the house, you'll see it all too soon.

Creon:
What now? What's worse than this?

Messenger:

                The queen is dead.   1410
The mother of this dead boy . . . mother to the end—
poor thing, her wounds are fresh.

Creon:

              No, no,
harbor of Death, so choked, so hard to cleanse!—

why me? why are you killing me?
Herald of pain, more words, more grief?   1415
I died once, you kill me again and again!
What's the report, boy . . . some news for me?
My wife dead? O dear god!
Slaughter heaped on slaughter?

[*The doors open; the body of Eurydice is brought out on her bier.*]

Messenger:
                                    See for yourself:
now they bring her body from the palace.

Creon:
                                    Oh no,   1420
another, a second loss to break the heart.
What next, what fate still waits for me?
I just held my son in my arms and now,
look, a new corpse rising before my eyes—
    wretched, helpless mother—O my son!   1425

Messenger:
She stabbed herself at the altar,
then her eyes went dark, after she'd raised
a cry for the noble fate of Megareus,° the hero
killed in the first assault, then for Haemon,
then with her dying breath she called down   1430
torments on your head—you killed her sons.

Creon:
                                    Oh the dread,
I shudder with dread! Why not kill me too?—
run me through with a good sharp sword?
Oh god, the misery, anguish—
I, I'm churning with it, going under.   1435

Messenger:
Yes, and the dead, the woman lying there,
piles the guilt of all their deaths on you.

1428 *Megareus:* son of Creon and brother of Haemon, Megareus was slain in the unsuccessful
attack on Thebes.

Creon:
How did she end her life, what bloody stroke?

Messenger:
She drove home to the heart with her own hand,
once she learned her son was dead . . . that agony.   1440

Creon:
And the guilt is all mine—
can never be fixed on another man,
no escape for me. I killed you,
I, god help me, I admit it all!

[To his Attendants.]

Take me away, quickly, out of sight.   1445
I don't even exist—I'm no one. Nothing.

Leader:
Good advice, if there's any good in suffering.
Quickest is best when troubles block the way.

Creon:

[Kneeling in prayer.]

Come, let it come!—that best of fates for me
that brings the final day, best fate of all.   1450
Oh quickly, now—
so I never have to see another sunrise.

Leader:
That will come when it comes;
we must deal with all that lies before us.
The future rests with the ones who tend the future.   1455

Creon:
That prayer—I poured my heart into that prayer!

Leader:
No more prayers now. For mortal men
there is no escape from the doom we must endure.

Creon:
Take me away, I beg you, out of sight.
A rash, indiscriminate fool!   1460

I murdered you, my son, against my will—
you too, my wife . . .
                    Wailing wreck of a man,
whom to look to? where to lean for support?

[*Desperately turning from Haemon to Eurydice on their biers.*]

Whatever I touch goes wrong—once more   1465
a crushing fate's come down upon my head.

[*The Messenger and attendants lead Creon into the palace.*]

Chorus:
        Wisdom is by far the greatest part of joy,
        and reverence toward the gods must be safeguarded.
        The mighty words of the proud are paid in full
        with mighty blows of fate, and at long last   1470
        those blows will teach us wisdom.

[*The old citizens exit to the side.*]

QUESTIONS

1. What is Creon's motivation for forbidding the burial of his own nephew Polynices? Why would he issue an edict that runs so contrary to his family obligations?
2. What are Antigone's reasons for performing funeral rites on her brother's corpse in direct violation of Creon's edict?
3. What are the larger issues behind the conflicting positions of both Creon and Antigone? Is either person or position clearly wrong?
4. Does the chorus take a position in the argument between Creon and Antigone?
5. If Antigone is a tragic heroine, what is her tragic flaw? Does she have any particular *hubris* or excess of virtue that dooms her?
6. Can a modern reader discern Sophocles' own position on the debate between civic responsibility (Creon's edict) and family duty (Antigone's defiance)? Are his authorial sympathies anywhere evident in the play?
7. What is the role of Eurydice? Is her presence essential to the story? What would be the effect of removing her from the drama?
8. Can you imagine a modern setting in which a new production of Antigone might be staged? Describe your idea in terms of sets, costumes, and staging.

Robert Fitzgerald

TRANSLATING SOPHOCLES   1941

The style of Sophocles was smooth. It has been likened by a modern critic to a molten flow of language, fitting and revealing every contour of the meaning, with no words wasted and no words poured on for effect. To approximate such purity I have sought a spare but felicitous manner of speech, not common and not "elevated" either, except by force of natural eloquence. The Greek writer did not disdain plainness when plainness was appropriate—appropriate, that is, both dramatically and within a context of verse very brilliant, mellifluous and powerful. As in every highly inflected language, the Greek order of words was controlled, by its masters, for special purposes of emphasis and even of meaning; and such of these as I have been acute enough to grasp I have tried to bring out by a comparable phrasing or rhythm in English. This I hold to be part of the business of "literal" rendering.

The difficulties involved in translating Greek dialogue are easily tripled when it comes to translating a chorus. Here the ellipses and compressions possible to the inflected idiom are particularly in evidence; and in the chorus, too, the poet concentrates his allusive power. For the modern reader, who has very little "literature" in the sense in which Samuel Johnson° used the term, two out of three allusions in the Greek odes will be meaningless. This is neither surprising nor deplorable. The Roman writer, Ennius,° translating Euripides for a Latin audience two centuries after the Periclean period, found it advisable to omit many place names and to omit or explain many mythological references; and his public had greater reason to be familiar with such things than we have.

From Sophocles, The Oedipus Cycle

Samuel Johnson: Johnson (1709–1784) was the great eighteenth-century critic, lexicographer, poet, and conversationalist. His definition of *literature* would have referred mostly to the Greek and Latin classics.   *Ennius:* Quintus Ennius (239–169 B.C.) was an early Latin epic poet and tragedian. He created Latin versions of the Greek tragic plays, especially those of Euripides.

Aristotle   (384–322 B.C.)

DEFINING TRAGEDY   330 B.C.?

TRANSLATED BY L. J. POTTS

Tragedy is an imitation of an action of high importance, complete and of some amplitude; in language enhanced by distinct and varying beauties; acted not narrated;
by means of pity and fear effecting its purgation of these emotions. By the beauties
enhancing the language I mean rhythm and melody; by "distinct and varying" I mean
that some are produced by meter alone, and others at another time by melody.

. . .

What will produce the tragic effect? Since, then, tragedy, to be at its finest, requires a complex, not a simple, structure, and its structure should also imitate fearful
and pitiful events (for that is the peculiarity of this sort of imitation), it is clear: first,
that decent people must not be shown passing from good fortune to misfortune (for
that is not fearful or pitiful but disgusting); again, vicious people must not be shown
passing from misfortune to good fortune (for that is the most untragic situation possible—it has none of the requisites, it is neither humane, nor pitiful, nor fearful); nor
again should an utterly evil man fall from good fortune into misfortune (for though a
plot of that kind would be humane, it would not induce pity or fear—pity is induced
by undeserved misfortune, and fear by the misfortunes of normal people, so that this
situation will be neither pitiful nor fearful). So we are left with the man between
these extremes: that is to say, the kind of man who neither is distinguished for excellence and virtue, nor comes to grief on account of baseness and vice, but on account
of some error; a man of great reputation and prosperity, like Oedipus and Thyestes
and conspicuous people of such families as theirs. So, to be well formed, a fable must
be single rather than (as some say) double—there must be no change from misfortune to good fortune, but only the opposite, from good fortune to misfortune; the
cause must not be vice, but a great error; and the man must be either of the type specified or better, rather than worse. This is borne out by the practice of poets; at first
they picked a fable at random and made an inventory of its contents, but now the
finest tragedies are plotted, and concern a few families—for example, the tragedies
about Alcmeon, Oedipus, Orestes, Meleager, Thyestes, Telephus, and any others
whose lives were attended by terrible experiences or doings.

This is the plot that will produce the technically finest tragedy. Those critics are
therefore wrong who censure Euripides on this very ground—because he does this in
his tragedies, and many of them end in misfortune; for it is, as I have said, the right
thing to do. This is clearly demonstrated on the stage in the competitions, where
such plays, if they succeed, are the most tragic, and Euripides, even if he is inefficient
in every other respect, still shows himself the most tragic of our poets. The next best
plot, which is said by some people to be the best, is the tragedy with a double plot,
like the *Odyssey*, ending in one way for the better people and in the opposite way for
the worse. But it is the weakness of theatrical performances that gives priority to this

kind; when poets write what the audience would like to happen, they are in leading strings.° This is not the pleasure proper to tragedy, but rather to comedy, where the greatest enemies in the fable, say Orestes and Aegisthus, make friends and go off at the end, and nobody is killed by anybody.

The pity and fear can be brought about by the *mise en scène°*; but they can also come from the mere plotting of the incidents, which is preferable, and better poetry. For, without seeing anything, the fable ought to have been so plotted that if one heard the bare facts, the chain of circumstances would make one shudder and pity. That would happen to any one who heard the fable of the *Oedipus*. To produce this effect by the *mise en scène* is less artistic and puts one at the mercy of the technician; and those who use it not to frighten but merely to startle have lost touch with tragedy altogether. We should not try to get all sorts of pleasure from tragedy, but the particular tragic pleasure. And clearly, since this pleasure coming from pity and fear has to be produced by imitation, it is by his handling of the incidents that the poet must create it.

. . .

And in the characterization, as in the plotting of the incidents, the aim should always be either necessity or probability: so that they say or do such things as it is necessary or probable that they would, being what they are; and that for this to follow that is either necessary or probable. (Thus it is clear that the untying of the fable should follow on the circumstances of the fable itself, and not be done *ex machina*, as it is in the *Medea*, or in Book Two of Homer. But the *deus ex machina°* should be used for matters outside the drama—either things that happened before and that man could not know, or future events that need to be announced prophetically; for we allow the gods to see everything. As for extravagant incidents, there should be none in the story, or if there are they should be kept outside the tragedy, as is the one in the *Oedipus* of Sophocles.)

Since tragedy is an imitation of people above the normal, we must be like good portrait-painters, who follow the original model closely, but refine on it; in the same way the poet, in imitating people whose character is choleric or phlegmatic, and so forth, must keep them as they are and at the same time make them attractive. So Homer made Achilles noble, as well as a pattern of obstinacy.

From *Poetics*, VI, XIII–XV

Sigmund Freud (1856–1939)

The Destiny of Oedipus   1900

Translated by James Strachey

If *Oedipus the King* moves a modern audience no less than it did the contemporary Greek one, the explanation can only be that its effect does not lie in the contrast between destiny and human will, but is to be looked for in the particular nature of the

---

in leading strings: each is led, by a string, wherever the audience wills. *mise en scène:* arrangement of actors and scenery. *deus ex machina:* "god out of the machine," or an arbitrary way of concluding a play. See Glossary of Literary Terms for further discussion.

material on which that contrast is exemplified. There must be something which makes a voice within us ready to recognize the compelling force of destiny in the *Oedipus*, while we can dismiss as merely arbitrary such dispositions as are laid down in *Die Ahnfrau*° or other modern tragedies of destiny. And a factor of this kind is in fact involved in the story of King Oedipus. His destiny moves us only because it might have been ours—because the oracle laid the same curse upon us before our birth as upon him. It is the fate of all of us, perhaps, to direct our first sexual impulse towards our mother and our first hatred and our first murderous wish against our father. Our dreams convince us that that is so. King Oedipus, who slew his father Laius and married his mother Jocasta, merely shows us the fulfillment of our own childhood wishes. But, more fortunate than he, we have meanwhile succeeded, insofar as we have not become psychoneurotics, in detaching our sexual impulses from our mothers and in forgetting our jealousy of our fathers. Here is one in whom these primeval wishes of our childhood have been fulfilled, and we shrink back from him with the whole force of the repression by which those wishes have since that time been held down within us. While the poet, as he unravels the past, brings to light the guilt of Oedipus, he is at the same time compelling us to recognize our own inner minds, in which those same impulses, though suppressed, are still to be found. The contrast with which the closing Chorus leaves us confronted—

> look upon Oedipus.
> This is the king who solved the famous riddle
> And towered up, most powerful of men.
> No mortal eyes but looked on him with envy,
> Yet in the end ruin swept over him.

—strikes as a warning at ourselves and our pride, at us who since our childhood have grown so wise and so mighty in our own eyes. Like Oedipus, we live in ignorance of these wishes, repugnant to morality, which have been forced upon us by Nature, and after their revelation we may all of us well seek to close our eyes to the scenes of our childhood.

From *The Interpretation of Dreams*

E. R. Dodds (1893–1979)

ON MISUNDERSTANDING OEDIPUS   1966

Some readers of the *Oedipus Rex* have told me that they find its atmosphere stifling and oppressive: they miss the tragic exaltation that one gets from the *Antigone* or the *Prometheus Vinctus*. And I fear that what I have said here has done nothing to remove that feeling. Yet it is not a feeling which I share myself. Certainly the *Oedipus Rex* is a play about the blindness of man and the desperate insecurity of the human condition: in a sense every man must grope in the dark as Oedipus gropes, not knowing who he is or what he has to suffer; we all live in a world of appearance which hides from us who-

---

Die Ahnfrau: "The Foremother," a verse play by Franz Grillparzer (1791–1872), Austrian dramatist and poet.

knows-what dreadful reality. But surely the *Oedipus Rex* is also a play about human greatness. Oedipus is great, not in virtue of a great worldly position—for his worldly position is an illusion which will vanish like a dream—but in virtue of his inner strength: strength to pursue the truth at whatever personal cost, and strength to accept and endure it when found. "This horror is mine," he cries, "and none but I is *strong* enough to bear it." Oedipus is great because he accepts the responsibility for *all* his acts, including those which are objectively most horrible, though subjectively innocent.

To me personally Oedipus is a kind of symbol of the human intelligence which cannot rest until it has solved all the riddles—even the last riddle, to which the answer is that human happiness is built on an illusion. I do not know how far Sophocles intended that. But certainly in the last lines of the play (which I firmly believe to be genuine) he does generalize the case, does appear to suggest that in some sense Oedipus is every man and every man is potentially Oedipus. Freud felt this (he was not insensitive to poetry), but as we all know he understood it in a specific psychological sense. "Oedipus' fate," he says, "moves us only because it might have been our own, because the oracle laid upon us before birth is the very curse which rested upon him. It may be that we were all destined to direct our first sexual impulses towards our mothers, and our first impulses of hatred and violence towards our fathers; our dreams convince us that we were." Perhaps they do; but Freud did not ascribe his interpretation of the myth to Sophocles, and it is not the interpretation I have in mind. Is there not in the poet's view a much wider sense in which every man is Oedipus? If every man could tear away the last veils of illusion, if he could see human life as time and the gods see it, would he not see that against that tremendous background all the generations of men are as if they had not been, *isa kai to mēden zōsas*? That was how Odysseus saw it when he had conversed with Athena, the embodiment of divine wisdom. "In Ajax' condition," he says, "I recognize my own: I perceive that all men living are but appearance or unsubstantial shadow."

From "On Misunderstanding the *Oedipus Rex*"

A. E. *Haigh*   (1855–1905)

THE IRONY OF SOPHOCLES   1896

The use of "tragic irony," as it has been called, is a favorite device in all dramatic literature. It is mostly employed when some catastrophe is about to happen, which is known and foreseen by the spectators, but concealed either from all, or from some, of the actors in the drama. In such cases the dialogue may be couched in terms which, though perfectly harmless upon the surface, carry an ominous significance to the initiated, and point suggestively to what is about to happen; and the contrast between the outer and the inner meaning of the language produces a deep effect upon the stage. Examples of this "irony" are to be found in most tragic writers, but especially in those of Greece, who use it with far greater frequency than the moderns; the reason being that, as the subjects of Greek tragedy were taken from the old legends with which every one was familiar, it was far easier for the ancient dramatist to indulge in those ambiguous allusions which presuppose a certain knowledge on the part of the spectators. Sophocles, however, is distinguished even among the Greek poets for his predilection for this form of speech, and his "irony" has become proverbial. It figures so prominently in his dramas, and goes so far to determine their general tone, that a detailed consideration of the matter will not be out of place.

Tragic irony may be divided into two kinds, the conscious and the unconscious. Conscious irony occurs in those cases where the speaker is not himself the victim of any illusion, but foresees the calamity that is about to fall on others, and exults in the prospect. His language, though equivocal, is easily intelligible to the audience, and to those actors who are acquainted with the facts; and its dark humor adds to the horror of the situation. This kind of irony is the one more commonly met with in the modern drama.

But in Sophocles the examples of such irony are far more numerous and more subtle than in the other poets, his love of intricate and allusive phraseology causing him to take especial delight in these ambiguities. Ajax, when he has once resolved upon self-destruction, continues in speech after speech to beguile his wife and the chorus by the sinister obscurity of his language, inducing them to believe that he will soon be "delivered from all evil." And in the *Electra*, when Clytaemnestra has been slain, and Aegisthus comes hastening back in triumph to the palace, thinking that the corpse is that of his enemy Orestes, the dialogue which ensues between himself and Electra is one long series of bitter equivocations, of which he alone fails to perceive the significance.

The other kind of irony, the unconscious, is perhaps the more impressive of the two. Here the sufferer is himself the spokesman. Utterly blind as to the doom which overhangs him, he uses words which, to the mind of the audience, have an ominous suggestiveness, and without knowing it, probes his own wounds to the bottom. Such irony is not confined merely to the language, but runs through the whole situation; and the contrast between the cheerful heedlessness of the victim, and the dark shadows which surround him, produces an impression more terrible than that which any form of speech could convey. Scenes of this kind had a peculiar fascination for the ancients. The fear of a sudden reverse of fortune, and of some fatal Nemesis which waits upon pride and boastfulness, was of all ideas the one most deeply impressed upon the mind of antiquity. Hence the popularity upon the stage of those thrilling spectacles, in which confidence and presumption were seen advancing blindfold to destruction, and the bitterness of the doom was intensified by the unconscious utterances of the victim.

The greatest example of all is the *Oedipus Rex*, the masterpiece of Sophocles, and the most typical of all Greek tragedies. The irony of destiny is here exhibited with unexampled force. In the opening scene Oedipus is depicted in the height of his prosperity, renowned and venerated, and surrounded by his suppliant countrymen; and the priest addresses him as the "wisest of men in dealing with life's chances and with the visitations of heaven." To the audience who know that within a few short hours the wrath of heaven will have crushed and shattered him, the pathetic meaning of these words is indescribable. From this first scene until the final catastrophe the speeches of

Oedipus are all full of the same tragic allusiveness. He can scarcely open his lips without touching unconsciously on his own approaching fate. When he insists upon the fact that his search for the assassin is "not on behalf of strangers, but in his own cause," and when he cautiously warns Jocasta that, as his mother still lives, the guilt of incest is not yet an impossibility, every word that he utters has a concealed barb. Perhaps the most tragic passage of all is that in which, while cursing the murderer of Laius, he prounounces his own doom. "As for the man who did the deed of guilt, whether alone he lurks, or in league with others, I pray that he may waste his life away in suffering, perishing vilely for his vile actions. And if he should become a dweller in my house, I knowing it, may every curse I utter fall on my own head."

From *The Tragic Drama of the Greeks*

Patricia M. Lines (b. 1938)

ANTIGONE'S FLAW   1999

Antigone does not seem to fit the Aristotelian formula. Aristotle himself did not seem to know what to make of it. In the *Poetica*'s sole reference to the play Aristotle offers *Antigone* as an example of a poor plot for a tragedy. The least tragic plot, he avers, involves a character who resolves to do a fearful deed and does not do it. His example is Haemon who seems ready to slay his father, Creon, and does not. This may be one of those rare cases where Aristotle misses the point. First, after more than two millennia of experience with drama, one can imagine a situation where delay in doing the dread deed makes the tragedy. Nor is it clear that Haemon had resolved to kill his father; his veiled threat may have been to kill himself, an action which he finally takes. Most important, the conflict between Haemon and his father does not stir our emotions as much as the conflict swirling around Antigone.

The play strikes us as a fine one—Hegel thought it was the supreme example of tragedy, prompting him to pose a different theory for the form. Hegel sees a dialectical clash between two ideals of justice. A noble and wise Antigone fights for the justice of traditional belief, while a tyrannical Creon fights for a right based on might. Irving Babbitt has suggested a more subtle variation of dialectic theory, hailing Antigone as the "perfect example of the ethical imagination" in contrast to her sister, Ismene, who knows merely "the law of the community." Both Antigone and Ismene are ethical, but Ismene lacks ethical imagination. As Babbitt sees it:

> This law, the convention of a particular place and time, is always but a very imperfect image, a mere shadow indeed of the unwritten law which being above the ordinary rational level is . . . infinite and incapable of final formulation.

While such interpretations no doubt are true—with each uncovering layers of meaning—alone they reduce *Antigone* to a morality play. Such interpretations fail to explain the play's more complex and turbulent moods.

The suggestion that Sophocles intended to present a flawed Antigone rubs against the grain. She is the paragon. The religion of the Greeks, like virtually all religions, required burial of the dead—even the enemy dead. The ancient tales in the *Iliad*, the bible to the Greeks, warn of the anger of the gods upon a failure to honor the dead. Besides, the restless shades of the unburied could cause trouble. Antigone stands for all that is right and for the opposition to tyranny. Thus, we have only a play about Creon's excessive harshness and his tragically delayed conversion. Yet, Sophocles provides a fair amount of evidence that he intended to create something more complex than a morality play.

Consider first the parallels between *Antigone* and *Oedipus Rex*. Both stories begin with a problem facing family and polis, and with the central character resolving to make things right. Antigone proceeds with unswerving resolution in her judgment of the situation. She possesses complete confidence in her ability to choose and execute a just action. She does not see the full situation; she is blind to key elements of the problem. She is like her father in most respects. Both Antigone and Oedipus claim to know justice with the certainty of a god. Oedipus believes most in his cunning and strength, Antigone in her goodness.

The flaw of hubris is easy to spot in Oedipus, but Antigone's brilliance is so dazzling that we overlook her flaw. After all, she has formulated a great and noble truth and maintains it with courage. She asserts God's law over man's law. Especially in our own time, where we formally recognize the superiority, within specified spheres, of individual right over the demands of overly broad laws, Antigone seems a genius beyond her time.

Creon, by contrast, understands the needs of the polis. Following a civil war, he has placed a premium on order. He will do whatever is necessary, including the stern enforcement of harsh rules. He faces another dilemma in his role as leader: he forbade the burial of Polynices and decreed this harsh punishment before he was aware of Antigone's guilt. To pardon his future daughter-in-law as his first serious act as ruler of Thebes would compromise all future claims to fairness in his rule. Yet Creon listens to the chorus of old men; he listens to the blind seer. After struggling with the issue, he reconsiders his judgment; he determines to bury the body of Polynices and to unbury Antigone with his own hands.

Antigone, on the other hand, recognizes the demands of true justice and champions it. She spurns Ismene, who initially hesitated to assist her but soon after wished to share in her sister's punishment and death. Antigone refuses the offer. When Ismene asks whether her sister has cast her aside, Antigone's answer ignores Ismene's change of heart: "Yes. For you chose to live when I chose death." Antigone seems to speak not to spare Ismene, but to wound her to the quick. Antigone leaves Haemon, her betrothed, in the cold, as she left Ismene. She never seeks him out, nor even mentions his name. Yet Haemon is ready to defy his father for Antigone's sake, and he refuses to live without her. Ironically, this may be what he must do to win her affection, for Antigone reveals no tenderness for anyone except those already dead.

Despite the solicitous love of Ismene and the fierce love of Haemon, Antigone complains of being alone and friendless:

I call upon Thebes' grove in the armored plain, to be my witnesses, how with no friend's mourning, by what decree I go to the fresh-made prison-tomb.

She compares her fate to Niobe's—alluding to the stone image weeping on a cliff near Thebes. Significantly, Antigone overlooks the fact that hubris destroyed Niobe.

Niobe had boasted that her six (in some versions seven) sons and six (or seven) daughters made her the equal of the goddess Leto, mother of Apollo and Artemis. Apollo and Artemis took offense on hearing of this interesting assertion of quantity over quality. They resolved the issue by killing the hapless children and turning Niobe to stone.

The chorus, often the truth-sayer for Sophocles, provides more clues. Of Antigone, they tell us:

> The girl is bitter. She's her father's child.
> She cannot yield to trouble; nor could he.

In perhaps the most revealing exchange, the chorus turns to Antigone and tells her, plainly:

> You showed respect for the dead.
> So we for you: but power
> is not to be thwarted so.
> Your self-sufficiency has brought you down.

The last line is key: "σε δ αυτογνωτος ωλεσ οργα." The above quotation is from Wyckoff's translation. But all translations seem to head in the same direction: "A self-determined impulse hath undone thee" (Campbell). "You were self-willed. That has been your undoing" (Townsend). "And thee, thy stubborne mood, self-chosen, layeth low" (students of the University of Notre Dame, 1983)[1]. In any translation, it seems the chorus has identified Antigone's flaw. She follows a truth that springs only from her self: It is αυτογνωτος, or autognotos. She will not consult with others. We could call it self-certainty or, perhaps even better, self-righteousness. It is a form of hubris.

At another point, the chorus tells Antigone she is autonomos. Literally, this means "a law unto yourself." The English word autonomy does not convey quite the right meaning, as individual autonomy was a condition the Greeks viewed with discomfort and suspicion. The autonomous being is either beast or god, living only within the horizons of its own laws.

From "Antigone's Flaw"

━━▸ WRITING CRITICALLY ◂━━

Some Things Change, Some Things Don't

Reading an ancient work of literature, such as Sophocles' *Oedipus the King* or *Antigone*, a modern student will often have two contradictory reactions. On the one hand, the student will note how differently people thought, spoke, and conducted themselves in the ancient world. The past will seem in many respects like an alien world. On the other hand, the student will recognize how many things about humanity remain constant across the ages. These presumably mythic characters are recognizably human.

---

[1]This is line 962 of Robert Fagles's translation: "Your own blind will, your passion has destroyed you."

Writing about a classical tragedy, you should stay alert to both impulses. Be open to the play's universal appeal, but never forget its foreignness. Understand in specific detail the basic beliefs and values that the characters hold that are different from your own. How do those elements influence their actions and motivations?

In making notes for your paper, jot down something about each major character that seems odd or exotic to you. Don't worry about being too basic. They don't represent your finished essay, just a starting place. Furthermore, no one will see the notes but you. You might observe, for example, that Oedipus and Jocasta both believe in the power of prophecy. They also believe that Apollo and the gods would punish the city with a plague for an unsolved crime committed twenty years earlier. These are certainly not mainstream modern beliefs.

You do not need to understand the historical origins or cultural context of the differences you note. You can safely leave those things to scholars. What you want to observe are the differences themselves—at least a few important ones—so that you don't automatically make modern assumptions about the characters. Keeping those differences in mind will give you greater insight into the characters.

WRITING ASSIGNMENT

Write a brief personality profile (two or three pages) of any major character in *Oedipus the King* or *Antigone*. Describe the character's age, social position, family background, personality, and beliefs. What is his or her major motivation in the play? In what ways does the character resemble his or her modern equivalent? In what way do they differ?

FURTHER SUGGESTIONS FOR WRITING

1. Suppose you face the task of directing and producing a new stage production of *Oedipus the King*. Decide how you would go about it. Would you use masks? How would you render the chorus? Would you set the play in contemporary North America? Justify your decisions by referring to the play itself.
2. Write a brief comment on the play under the title, "Does Sophocles' Oedipus Have an Oedipus Complex?" Consider psychiatrist Sigmund Freud's famous observations (quoted on page 1491). Your comment can be either serious or light.
3. Compare the version of *Oedipus the King* given in this book with a different English translation of the play. You might use, for instance, any of the versions by Robert Fitzgerald and Dudley Fitts; Gilbert Murray, J. T. Sheppard, and H. D. F. Kitto; by Paul Roche (in a Signet paperback); by William Butler Yeats (in his *Collected Plays*); by David Grene (University of Chicago Press, 1942); or by Stephen Berg and Diskin Clay (Oxford UP, 1978). Point to significant differences between the two texts. What decisions did the translators have to make? Which version do you prefer? Why?
4. Compare *Oedipus the King* to *Antigone* in terms of their characterizations of their respective protagonists. In what ways does Antigone resemble Oedipus and in what ways does she differ?
5. John Millington Synge's *Riders to the Sea* has been called the closest approximation to a Greek tragedy in English. Does Synge's play resemble a tragedy of Sophocles in any ways? How does it noticeably differ?
6. Taking the protagonist of either play by Sophocles, write an essay explaining how he or she exemplifies or refutes Aristotle's definition of a tragic hero.

35 *Critical Casebook: Shakespeare*

THE THEATER OF SHAKESPEARE

Compared with the technical resources of a theater of today, those of a London public theater in the time of Queen Elizabeth I seem hopelessly limited. Plays had to be performed by daylight, and scenery had to be kept simple: a table, a chair, a throne, perhaps an artificial tree or two to suggest a forest. But these limitations were, in a sense, advantages. What the theater of today can spell out for us realistically, with massive scenery and electric lighting, Elizabethan playgoers had to imagine and the playwright had to make vivid for them by means of language. Not having a lighting technician to work a panel, Shakespeare had to indicate the dawn by having Horatio, in *Hamlet*, say in a speech rich in metaphor and descriptive detail:

> But look, the morn in russet mantle clad
> Walks o'er the dew of yon high eastward hill.

And yet the theater of Shakespeare was not bare, for the playwright did have *some* valuable technical resources. Costumes could be elaborate, and apparently some costumes conveyed recognized meanings: one theater manager's inventory included "a robe for to go invisible in." There could be musical accompaniment and sound effects such as gunpowder explosions and the beating of a pan to simulate thunder.

The stage itself was remarkably versatile. At its back were doors for exits and entrances and a curtained booth or alcove useful for hiding inside. Above the stage was a higher acting area—perhaps a porch or balcony—useful for a Juliet to stand upon and for a Romeo to raise his eyes to. In the stage floor was a trapdoor leading to a "hell" or cellar, especially useful for ghosts or devils who had to appear or disappear. The stage itself was a rectangular platform that projected into a yard enclosed by three-storied galleries.

The building was round or octagonal. In *Henry V*, Shakespeare calls it a "wooden O." The audience sat in these galleries or else stood in the yard in front of the stage and at its sides. A roof or awning protected the stage and the high-priced gallery seats, but in a sudden rain, the *groundlings*, who paid a penny to stand in the yard, must have been dampened.

The newly reconstructed Globe Theatre in today's London—built as an exact replica of the original theater.

Built by the theatrical company to which Shakespeare belonged, the Globe, most celebrated of Elizabethan theaters, was not in the city of London itself but on the south bank of the Thames River. This location had been chosen because earlier, in 1574, public plays had been banished from the city by an ordinance that blamed them for "corruptions of youth and other enormities" (such as providing opportunities for prostitutes and pick pockets.).

A playwright had to please all members of the audience, not only the mannered and educated. This obligation may help to explain the wide range of matter and tone in an Elizabethan play: passages of subtle poetry, of deep philosophy, of coarse bawdry; scenes of sensational violence and of quiet psychological conflict (not that most members of the audience did not enjoy all these elements). Because he was an actor as well as a playwright, Shakespeare well knew what his company could do and what his audience wanted. In devising a play, he could write a part to take advantage of some actor's specific skills, or he could avoid straining the company's resources (some of his plays have few female parts, perhaps because of a shortage of competent boy actors). The company might offer as many as thirty plays in a season, customarily changing the program daily. The actors thus had to hold many parts in their heads, which may account for Elizabethan playwrights' fondness for blank verse. Lines of fixed length were easier for actors to commit to memory.

WILLIAM SHAKESPEARE

William Shakespeare (1564–1616), the supreme writer of English, was born, baptized, and buried in the market town of Stratford-on-Avon, eighty miles from London. Son of a glove maker and merchant who was high bailiff (or mayor) of the town, he probably attended grammar school and learned to read Latin authors in the original. At eighteen, he married Anne Hathaway, twenty-six, by whom he had three children, including twins. By 1592 he had become well known and envied as an actor and playwright in London. From 1594 until he retired, he belonged to the same theatrical company, the Lord Chamberlain's Men (later renamed the King's Men in honor of their patron, James I), for whom he wrote thirty-six plays—some of them, such as Hamlet and King Lear, profound reworkings of old plays. As an actor, Shakespeare is believed to have played supporting roles, such as the ghost of Hamlet's father. The company prospered, moved into the Globe in 1599, and in 1608 bought the fashionable Blackfriars as well; Shakespeare owned an interest in both theaters. When plagues shut down the theaters from 1592 to 1594, Shakespeare turned to story poems; his great Sonnets (published only in 1609) probably also date from the 1590s. Plays were regarded as entertainments of little literary merit, like comic books today, and Shakespeare did not bother to supervise their publication. After writing The Tempest (1611), the last play entirely from his hand, he retired to Stratford, where since 1597 he had owned the second largest house in town. Most critics agree that when he wrote Othello, about 1604, Shakespeare was at the height of his powers.

∽ PLAYS ∽

A NOTE ON OTHELLO

Othello, the Moor of Venice, here offered for study, may be (if you are fortunate) new to you. It is seldom taught in high school, for it is ablaze with passion and violence. Even if you already know the play, we trust that you (like your instructor and your editors) still have much more to learn from it. Following his usual practice, Shakespeare based the play on a story he had appropriated—from a tale, "Of the Unfaithfulness of Husbands and Wives," by a sixteenth-century Italian writer, Giraldi Cinthio. As he could not help but do, Shakespeare freely transformed his source material. In the original tale, the heroine Disdemona (whose name Shakespeare so hugely improved) is beaten to death with a stocking full of sand—a shoddier death than the bard imagined for her.

Surely no character in literature can touch us more than Desdemona; no character can shock and disgust us more than Iago. Between these two extremes stands Othello, a black man of courage and dignity—and yet insecure, capable of being fooled, a pushover for bad advice. Besides breathing life into these characters and a host of others, Shakespeare—as brilliant a writer as any the world has known—enables them to speak poetry.

James Earl Jones as Othello

Sometimes this poetry seems splendid and rich in imagery; at other times quiet and understated. Always, it seems to grow naturally from the nature of Shakespeare's characters and from their situations. *Othello, the Moor of Venice* has never ceased to grip readers and beholders alike. It is a safe bet that it will triumphantly live as long as fathers dislike whomever their daughters marry, as long as husbands suspect their wives of cheating, as long as blacks remember slavery, and as long as the ambitious court favor and the jealous practice deceit. The play may well make sense as long as public officials connive behind smiling faces, and it may even endure as long as the world makes room for the kind, the true, the beautiful—the blessed pure in heart.

OTHELLO, THE MOOR OF VENICE
1604?

EDITED BY DAVID BEVINGTON

The Names of the Actors

Othello, the Moor
Brabantio, [a senator,] father to Desdemona
Cassio, an honorable lieutenant [to Othello]
Iago, [Othello's ancient,] a villain
Roderigo, a gulled gentleman
Duke of Venice

NOTE ON THE TEXT: This text of *Othello* is based on that of the First Folio, or large collection, of Shakespeare's plays (1623). But there are many differences between the Folio text and that of the play's first printing in the Quarto, or small volume, of 1621 (eighteen or nineteen years after the play's first performance). Some readings from the Quarto are included. For the reader's convenience, some material has been added by the editor, David Bevington (some indications of scene, some stage directions). Such additions are enclosed in brackets. Mr. Bevington's text and notes were prepared for his book, *The Complete Works of Shakespeare*, updated 4th ed. (New York: Longman, 1997).

Senators [of Venice]
Montano, governor of Cyprus
Gentlemen of Cyprus
Lodovico and Gratiano, [kinsmen to Brabantio,] two noble Venetians
Sailors
Clown
Desdemona, [daughter to Brabantio and] wife to Othello
Emilia, wife to Iago
Bianca, a courtesan [and mistress to Cassio]
[A Messenger
A Herald
A Musician
Servants, Attendants, Officers, Senators, Musicians, Gentlemen

Scene. Venice; a seaport in Cyprus]

ACT I

Scene I [Venice. A Street.]

Enter Roderigo and Iago.

Roderigo: Tush, never tell me!° I take it much unkindly
    That thou, Iago, who hast had my purse
    As if the strings were thine, shouldst know of this.°
Iago: 'Sblood,° but you'll not hear me.
    If ever I did dream of such a matter,   5
    Abhor me.
Roderigo: Thou toldst me thou didst hold him in thy hate.
Iago: Despise me
    If I do not. Three great ones of the city,
    In personal suit to make me his lieutenant,   10
    Off-capped to him;° and by the faith of man,
    I know my price, I am worth no worse a place.
    But he, as loving his own pride and purposes,
    Evades them with a bombast circumstance°
    Horribly stuffed with epithets of war,°   15
    And, in conclusion,
    Nonsuits° my mediators. For, "Certes,"° says he,
    "I have already chose my officer."
    And what was he?
    Forsooth, a great arithmetician,°   20

1 *never tell me* (An expression of incredulity, like "tell me another one.")   3 *this* i.e., Desdemona's elopement   4 *'Sblood* by His (Christ's) blood   11 *him* i.e., Othello   14 *bombast circumstance* wordy evasion. (Bombast is cotton padding.)   15 *epithets of war* military expressions 17 *Nonsuits* rejects the petition of. *Certes* certainly   20 *arithmetician* i.e., a man whose military knowledge is merely theoretical, based on books of tactics

One Michael Cassio, a Florentine,
A fellow almost damned in a fair wife,°
That never set a squadron in the field
Nor the division of a battle° knows
More than a spinster°—unless the bookish theoric,°   25
Wherein the togaed° consuls° can propose°
As masterly as he. Mere prattle without practice
Is all his soldiership. But he, sir, had th' election;
And I, of whom his° eyes had seen the proof
At Rhodes, at Cyprus, and on other grounds   30
Christened° and heathen, must be beleed and calmed°
By debitor and creditor.° This countercaster,°
He, in good time,° must his lieutenant be,
And I—God bless the mark!°—his Moorship's ancient.°
Roderigo: By heaven, I rather would have been his hangman.°   35
Iago: Why, there's no remedy. 'Tis the curse of service;
Preferment° goes by letter and affection,°
And not by old gradation,° where each second
Stood heir to th' first. Now, sir, be judge yourself
Whether I in any just term° am affined°   40
To love the Moor.
Roderigo: I would not follow him then.
Iago: O sir, content you.°
I follow him to serve my turn upon him.
We cannot all be masters, nor all masters
Cannot be truly° followed. You shall mark   45
Many a duteous and knee-crooking knave
That, doting on his own obsequious bondage,
Wears out his time, much like his master's ass,
For naught but provender, and when he's old, cashiered.°   50
Whip me° such honest knaves. Others there are
Who, trimmed in forms and visages of duty,°
Keep yet their hearts attending on themselves,

22 A . . . wife (Cassio does not seem to be married, but his counterpart in Shakespeare's source does have a woman in his house. See also Act IV, Scene i, line 127.)   24 division of a battle disposition of a military unit   25 a spinster i.e., a housewife, one whose regular occupation is spinning. theoric theory   26 togaed wearing the toga. consuls counselors, senators. propose discuss   29 his i.e., Othello's   31 Christened Christian. beleed and calmed left to leeward without wind, becalmed. (A sailing metaphor.)   32 debitor and creditor (A name for a system of bookkeeping, here used as a contemptuous nickname for Cassio.)   countercaster i.e., bookkeeper, one who tallies with counters, or "metal disks." (Said contemptuously.)   33 in good time opportunely, i.e., forsooth   34 God bless the mark (Perhaps originally a formula to ward off evil; here an expression of impatience.)   ancient standard-bearer, ensign   35 his hangman the executioner of him   37 Preferment promotion.   letter and affection personal influence and favoritism   38 old gradation step-by-step seniority, the traditional way   40 term respect.   affined bound   43 content you don't you worry about that   46 truly faithfully   50 cashiered dismissed from service   51 Whip me whip, as far as I'm concerned   52 trimmed . . . duty dressed up in the mere form and show of dutifulness

And, throwing but shows of service on their lords,
Do well thrive by them, and when they have lined their coats,° 55
Do themselves homage.° These fellows have some soul,
And such a one do I profess myself. For, sir,
It is as sure as you are Roderigo,
Were I the Moor I would not be Iago.°
In following him, I follow but myself— 60
Heaven is my judge, not I for love and duty,
But seeming so for my peculiar° end.
For when my outward action doth demonstrate
The native° act and figure° of my heart
In compliment extern,° 'tis not long after 65
But I will wear my heart upon my sleeve
For daws° to peck at. I am not what I am.°
Roderigo: What a full° fortune does the thick-lips° owe°
If he can carry 't thus!°
Iago: Call up her father.
Rouse him, make after him, poison his delight, 70
Proclaim him in the streets; incense her kinsmen,
And, though he in a fertile climate dwell,
Plague him with flies.° Though that his joy be joy,°
Yet throw such changes of vexation° on 't
As it may° lose some color.° 75
Roderigo: Here is her father's house. I'll call aloud.
Iago: Do, with like timorous° accent and dire yell
As when, by night and negligence,° the fire
Is spied in populous cities.
Roderigo: What ho, Brabantio! Signor Brabantio, ho! 80
Iago: Awake! What ho, Brabantio! Thieves, thieves, thieves!
Look to your house, your daughter, and your bags!
Thieves, thieves!

Brabantio [enters] above [at a window].°

55 *lined their coats* i.e., stuffed their purses   56 *Do themselves homage* i.e., attend to self-interest
solely   59 *Were . . . Iago* i.e., if I were able to assume command, I certainly would not choose
to remain a subordinate, or, I would keep a suspicious eye on a flattering subordinate   62
peculiar particular, personal   64 *native* innate.   *figure* shape, intent   65 *compliment extern* outward show. (Conforming in this case to the inner workings and intention of the heart.)   67
daws small crowlike birds, proverbially stupid and avaricious.   *I am not what I am* i.e., I am not
one who wears his heart on his sleeve   68 *full* swelling.   *thick-lips* (Elizabethans often applied
the term "Moor" to Negroes.)   *owe* own   69 *carry 't thus* carry this off   72–73 *though . . . flies*
though he seems prosperous and happy now, vex him with misery   73 *Though . . . be joy* although he seems fortunate and happy. (Repeats the idea of line 72.)   74 *changes of vexation*
vexing changes   75 *As it may* that may cause it to.   *some color* some of its fresh gloss   77
timorous frightening   78 *and negligence* i.e., by negligence   83 s.d. *at a window* (This stage direction, from the Quarto, probably calls for an appearance on the gallery above and rearstage.)

Brabantio: What is the reason of this terrible summons?
    What is the matter° there?   85
Roderigo: Signor, is all your family within?
Iago: Are your doors locked?
Brabantio: Why, wherefore ask you this?
Iago: Zounds,° sir, you're robbed. For shame, put on your gown!
    Your heart is burst; you have lost half your soul.
    Even now, now, very now, an old black ram   90
    Is tupping° your white ewe. Arise, arise!
    Awake the snorting° citizens with the bell,
    Or else the devil° will make a grandsire of you.
    Arise, I say!
Brabantio: What, have you lost your wits?
Roderigo: Most reverend signor, do you know my voice?   95
Brabantio: Not I. What are you?
Roderigo: My name is Roderigo.
Brabantio: The worser welcome.
    I have charged thee not to haunt about my doors.
    In honest plainness thou hast heard me say   100
    My daughter is not for thee; and now, in madness,
    Being full of supper and distempering° drafts,
    Upon malicious bravery° dost thou come
    To start° my quiet.
Roderigo: Sir, sir, sir—
Brabantio: But thou must needs be sure   105
    My spirits and my place° have in° their power
    To make this bitter to thee.
Roderigo: Patience, good sir.
Brabantio: What tell'st thou me of robbing? This is Venice;
    My house is not a grange.°
Roderigo: Most grave Brabantio,
    In simple° and pure soul I come to you.   110
Iago: Zounds, sir, you are one of those that will not serve God if the devil bid you.
    Because we come to do you service and you think we are ruffians, you'll have
    your daughter covered with a Barbary° horse; you'll have your nephews°
    neigh to you; you'll have coursers° for cousins° and jennets° for germans.°
Brabantio: What profane wretch art thou?
Iago: I am one, sir, that comes to tell you your daughter and the Moor are now
    making the beast with two backs.

---

85 *the matter* your business   88 *Zounds* by His (Christ's) wounds   91 *tupping* covering, copulating
with. (Said of sheep.)   92 *snorting* snoring   93 *the devil* (The devil was conventionally pictured
as black.)   102 *distempering* intoxicating   103 *Upon malicious bravery* with hostile intent to defy
me   104 *start* startle, disrupt   106 *My spirits and my place* my temperament and my authority of
office. *have in* have it in   109 *grange* isolated country house   110 *simple* sincere   113 *Barbary*
from northern Africa (and hence associated with Othello). *nephews* i.e., grandsons   114
coursers powerful horses. *cousins* kinsmen. *jennets* small Spanish horses. *germans* near relatives

Brabantio: Thou art a villain.

Iago: You are—a senator.°

Brabantio: This thou shalt answer.° I know thee, Roderigo.

Roderigo: Sir, I will answer anything. But I beseech you,   120
     If't be your pleasure and most wise° consent—
     As partly I find it is—that your fair daughter,
     At this odd-even° and dull watch o' the night,
     Transported with° no worse nor better guard
     But with a knave° of common hire, a gondolier,   125
     To the gross clasps of a lascivious Moor—
     If this be known to you and your allowance°
     We then have done you bold and saucy° wrongs.
     But if you know not this, my manners tell me
     We have your wrong rebuke. Do not believe   130
     That, from° the sense of all civility,°
     I thus would play and trifle with your reverence.°
     Your daughter, if you have not given her leave,
     I say again, hath made a gross revolt,
     Tying her duty, beauty, wit,° and fortunes   135
     In an extravagant° and wheeling° stranger°
     Of here and everywhere. Straight° satisfy yourself.
     If she be in her chamber or your house,
     Let loose on me the justice of the state
     For thus deluding you.   140

Brabantio: Strike on the tinder,° ho!
     Give me a taper! Call up all my people!
     This accident° is not unlike my dream.
     Belief of it oppresses me already.
     Light, I say, light!   *Exit [above].*

Iago: Farewell, for I must leave you.   145
     It seems not meet° nor wholesome to my place°
     To be producted°—as, if I stay, I shall—
     Against the Moor. For I do know the state,
     However this may gall° him with some check,°
     Cannot with safety cast° him, for he's embarked°   150
     With such loud reason° to the Cyprus wars,

---

118 *a senator* (Said with mock politeness, as though the word itself were an insult.)   119 *answer* be held accountable for   121 *wise* well-informed   123 *odd-even* between one day and the next, i.e., about midnight   124 *with* by   125 *But with a knave* than by a low fellow, a servant   127 *allowance* permission   128 *saucy* insolent   131 *from* contrary to. *civility* good manners, decency   132 *your reverence* the respect due to you   135 *wit* intelligence   136 *extravagant* expatriate, wandering far from home. *wheeling* roving about, vagabond. *stranger* foreigner   137 *Straight* straightway   141 *tinder* charred linen ignited by a spark from flint and steel, used to light torches or *tapers* (lines 142, 167)   143 *accident* occurrence, event   146 *meet* fitting. *place* position (as ensign)   147 *producted* produced (as a witness)   149 *gall* rub; oppress. *check* rebuke   150 *cast* dismiss. *embarked* engaged   151 *loud reason* unanimous shout of confirmation (in the Senate)

Which even now stands in act,° that, for their souls,°
Another of his fathom° they have none
To lead their business; in which regard,°
Though I do hate him as I do hell pains,   155
Yet for necessity of present life°
I must show out a flag and sign of love,
Which is indeed but sign. That you shall surely find him,
Lead to the Sagittary° the raisèd search,°
And there will I be with him. So farewell.   *Exit.*   160

Enter [below] Brabantio [in his nightgown°] with servants and torches.

Brabantio: It is too true an evil. Gone she is;
    And what's to come of my despisèd time°
    Is naught but bitterness. Now, Roderigo,
    Where didst thou see her?—O unhappy girl!—
    With the Moor, sayst thou?—Who would be a father!—   165
    How didst thou know 'twas she?—O, she deceives me
    Past thought!—What said she to you?—Get more tapers.
    Raise all my kindred.—Are they married, think you?
Roderigo: Truly, I think they are.
Brabantio: O heaven! How got she out? O treason of the blood!   170
    Fathers, from hence trust not your daughters' minds
    By what you see them act. Is there not charms°
    By which the property° of youth and maidhood
    May be abused?° Have you not read, Roderigo,
    Of some such thing?
Roderigo: Yes, sir, I have indeed.   175
Brabantio: Call up my brother.—O, would you had had her!—
    Some one way, some another.—Do you know
    Where we may apprehend her and the Moor?
Roderigo: I think I can discover° him, if you please
    To get good guard and go along with me.   180
Brabantio: Pray you, lead on. At every house I'll call;
    I may command° at most.—Get weapons, ho!
    And raise some special officers of night.—
    On, good Roderigo. I will deserve° your pains.

    Exeunt.

152 *stands in act* are going on.   *for their souls* to save themselves   153 *fathom* i.e., ability, depth
of experience   154 *in which regard* out of regard for which   156 *life* livelihood   159 *Sagittary*
(An inn or house where Othello and Desdemona are staying, named for its sign of Sagittarius,
or Centaur.)   *raisèd search* search party roused out of sleep   160 s.d. *nightgown* dressing gown.
(This costuming is specified in the Quarto text.)   162 *time* i.e., remainder of life   172 *charms*
spells   173 *property* special quality, nature   174 *abused* deceived   179 *discover* reveal, uncover   182 *command* demand assistance   184 *deserve* show gratitude for

Scene II [Venice. Another Street, Before Othello's Lodgings.]

Enter Othello, Iago, attendants with torches.

Iago: Though in the trade of war I have slain men,
　　　Yet do I hold it very stuff° o' the conscience
　　　To do no contrived° murder. I lack iniquity
　　　Sometimes to do me service. Nine or ten times
　　　I had thought t' have yerked° him° here under the ribs.　　5
Othello: 'Tis better as it is.
Iago:　　　　　　　　Nay, but he prated,
　　　And spoke such scurvy and provoking terms
　　　Against your honor
　　　That, with the little godliness I have,
　　　I did full hard forbear him.° But, I pray you, sir,　　10
　　　Are you fast married? Be assured of this,
　　　That the magnifico° is much beloved,
　　　And hath in his effect° a voice potential°
　　　As double as the Duke's. He will divorce you,
　　　Or put upon you what restraint or grievance　　15
　　　The law, with all his might to enforce it on,
　　　Will give him cable.°
Othello:　　　　　　Let him do his spite.
　　　My services which I have done the seigniory°
　　　Shall out-tongue his complaints. 'Tis yet to know°—
　　　Which, when I know that boasting is an honor,　　20
　　　I shall promulgate—I fetch my life and being
　　　From men of royal siege,° and my demerits°
　　　May speak unbonneted° to as proud a fortune
　　　As this that I have reached. For know, Iago,
　　　But that I love the gentle Desdemona,　　25
　　　I would not my unhousèd° free condition
　　　Put into circumscription and confine°
　　　For the sea's worth.° But look, what lights come yond?

Enter Cassio [and certain officers°] with torches.

---

2 *very stuff* essence, basic material (continuing the metaphor of *trade* from line 1)　3 *contrived* premeditated　5 *yerked* stabbed. *him* i.e., Roderigo　10 *I . . . him* I restrained myself with great difficulty from assaulting him　12 *magnifico* Venetian grandee, i.e., Brabantio　13 *in his effect* at his command. *potential* powerful　17 *cable* i.e., scope　18 *seigniory* Venetian government　19 *yet to know* not yet widely known　22 *siege* i.e., rank. (Literally, a seat used by a person of distinction.) *demerits* deserts　23 *unbonneted* without removing the hat, i.e., on equal terms (?) (Or "with hat off," "in all due modesty.")　26 *unhousèd* unconfined, undomesticated　27 *circumscription and confine* restriction and confinement　28 *the sea's worth* all the riches at the bottom of the sea.　s.d. *officers* (The Quarto text calls for "Cassio with lights, officers with torches.")

Iago: Those are the raisèd father and his friends.
     You were best go in.
Othello: Not I. I must be found.   30
     My parts, my title, and my perfect soul°
     Shall manifest me rightly. Is it they?
Iago: By Janus,° I think no.
Othello: The servants of the Duke? And my lieutenant?
     The goodness of the night upon you, friends!   35
     What is the news?
Cassio: The Duke does greet you, General,
     And he requires your haste-post-haste appearance
     Even on the instant.
Othello: What is the matter,° think you?
Cassio: Something from Cyprus, as I may divine.°
     It is a business of some heat.° The galleys   40
     Have sent a dozen sequent° messengers
     This very night at one another's heels,
     And many of the consuls,° raised and met,
     Are at the Duke's already. You have been hotly called for;
     When, being not at your lodging to be found,   45
     The Senate hath sent about° three several° quests
     To search you out.
Othello: 'Tis well I am found by you.
     I will but spend a word here in the house
     And go with you.   [*Exit.*]
Cassio: Ancient, what makes° he here?
Iago: Faith, he tonight hath boarded° a land carrack.°   50
     If it prove lawful prize,° he's made forever.
Cassio: I do not understand.
Iago: He's married.
Cassio: To who?

     [*Enter Othello.*]

Iago: Marry,° to—Come, Captain, will you go?
Othello: Have with you.°
Cassio: Here comes another troop to seek for you.   55

     Enter Brabantio, Roderigo, with officers and torches.°

31 *My . . . soul* my natural gifts, my position or reputation, and my unflawed conscience   33
Janus Roman two-faced god of beginnings   38 *matter* business   39 *divine* guess   40 *heat* urgency   41 *sequent* successive   43 *consuls* senators   46 *about* all over the city.   *several* separate   49 *makes* does   50 *boarded* gone aboard and seized as an act of piracy (with sexual suggestion).   *carrack* large merchant ship   51 *prize* booty   53 *Marry* (An oath, originally "by the
Virgin Mary"; here used with wordplay on *married*.)   54 *Have with you* i.e., let's go   55 s.d.
officers and torches (The Quarto text calls for "others with lights and weapons.")

Iago: It is Brabantio. General, be advised.°
     He comes to bad intent.
Othello: Holla! Stand there!
Roderigo: Signor, it is the Moor.
Brabantio: Down with him, thief!

[*They draw on both sides.*]

Iago: You, Roderigo! Come, sir, I am for you.
Othello: Keep up° your bright swords, for the dew will rust them.   60
     Good signor, you shall more command with years
     Than with your weapons.
Brabantio: O thou foul thief, where hast thou stowed my daughter?
     Damned as thou art, thou hast enchanted her!
     For I'll refer me° to all things of sense,°   65
     If she in chains of magic were not bound
     Whether a maid so tender, fair, and happy,
     So opposite to marriage that she shunned
     The wealthy curlèd darlings of our nation,
     Would ever have, t' incur a general mock,   70
     Run from her guardage° to the sooty bosom
     Of such a thing as thou—to fear, not to delight.
     Judge me the world if 'tis not gross in sense°
     That thou hast practiced on her with foul charms,
     Abused her delicate youth with drugs or minerals°   75
     That weakens motion.° I'll have 't disputed on;°
     'Tis probable and palpable to thinking.
     I therefore apprehend and do attach° thee
     For an abuser of the world, a practicer
     Of arts inhibited° and out of warrant.°—   80
     Lay hold upon him! If he do resist,
     Subdue him at his peril.
Othello: Hold your hands,
     Both you of my inclining° and the rest.
     Were it my cue to fight, I should have known it
     Without a prompter.—Whither will you that I go   85
     To answer this your charge?
Brabantio: To prison, till fit time
     Of law and course of direct session°
     Call thee to answer.

56 *be advised* be on your guard   60 *Keep up* keep in the sheath   65 *refer me* submit my case.
things of sense commonsense understandings, or, creatures possessing common sense   71 *her
guardage* my guardianship of her   73 *gross in sense* obvious   75 *minerals* i.e., poisons   76 *weakens
motion* impair the vital faculties.   *disputed on* argued in court by professional counsel, debated by
experts   78 *attach* arrest   80 *arts inhibited* prohibited arts, black magic.   *out of warrant* illegal   83
inclining following, party   88 *course of direct session* regular or specially convened legal proceedings

Othello: What if I do obey?
How may the Duke be therewith satisfied,   90
Whose messengers are here about my side
Upon some present business of the state
To bring me to him?
Officer: 'Tis true, most worthy signor.
The Duke's in council, and your noble self,
I am sure, is sent for.
Brabantio: How? The Duke in council?   95
In this time of the night? Bring him away.°
Mine's not an idle° cause. The Duke himself,
Or any of my brothers of the state,
Cannot but feel this wrong as 'twere their own;
For if such actions may have passage free,°   100
Bondslaves and pagans shall our statesmen be.

Exeunt.

Scene III [Venice. A Council Chamber.]

*Enter Duke [and] Senators [and sit at a table, with lights], and Officers.° [The
Duke and Senators are reading dispatches.]*

Duke: There is no composition° in these news
That gives them credit.
First Senator: Indeed, they are disproportioned.°
My letters say a hundred and seven galleys.
Duke: And mine, a hundred forty.
Second Senator: And mine, two hundred.   5
But though they jump° not on a just° account—
As in these cases, where the aim° reports
'Tis oft with difference—yet do they all confirm
A Turkish fleet, and bearing up to Cyprus.
Duke: Nay, it is possible enough to judgment.   10
I do not so secure me in the error
But the main article I do approve°
In fearful sense.
Sailor (within):   What ho, what ho, what ho!

Enter Sailor.

Officer: A messenger from the galleys.

96 *away* right along   97 *idle* trifling   100 *have passage free* are allowed to go unchecked
s.d. *Enter . . . Officers* (The Quarto text calls for the Duke and senators to "sit at a table with lights
and attendants.")   1 *composition* consistency   3 *disproportioned* inconsistent   6 *jump* agree.   *just*
exact   7 *the aim* conjecture   11–12 *I do not . . . approve* I do not take such (false) comfort in the
discrepancies that I fail to perceive the main point, i.e., that the Turkish fleet is threatening

Duke: Now, what's the business?

Sailor: The Turkish preparation° makes for Rhodes. 15
 So was I bid report here to the state
 By Signor Angelo.

Duke: How say you by° this change?

First Senator: This cannot be
 By no assay° of reason. 'Tis a pageant° 20
 To keep us in false gaze.° When we consider
 Th' importancy of Cyprus to the Turk,
 And let ourselves again but understand
 That, as it more concerns the Turk than Rhodes,
 So may he with more facile question bear it,° 25
 For that° it stands not in such warlike brace,°
 But altogether lacks th' abilities°
 That Rhodes is dressed in°—if we make thought of this,
 We must not think the Turk is so unskillful°
 To leave that latest° which concerns him first, 30
 Neglecting an attempt of ease and gain
 To wake° and wage° a danger profitless.

Duke: Nay, in all confidence, he's not for Rhodes.

Officer: Here is more news.

 Enter a Messenger.

Messenger: The Ottomites, reverend and gracious, 35
 Steering with due course toward the isle of Rhodes,
 Have there injointed them° with an after° fleet.

First Senator: Ay, so I thought. How many, as you guess?

Messenger: Of thirty sail; and now they do restem
 Their backward course,° bearing with frank appearance° 40
 Their purposes toward Cyprus. Signor Montano,
 Your trusty and most valiant servitor,°
 With his free duty° recommends° you thus,
 And prays you to believe him.

Duke: 'Tis certain then for Cyprus. 45
 Marcus Luccicos, is not he in town?

First Senator: He's now in Florence.

Duke: Write from us to him, post-post-haste. Dispatch.

First Senator: Here comes Brabantio and the valiant Moor.

16 *preparation* fleet prepared for battle   19 *by* about   20 *assay* test.   *pageant* mere show   21 *in false gaze* looking the wrong way   25 *So may . . . it* so also he (the Turk) can more easily capture it (Cyprus)   26 *For that* since.   *brace* state of defense   27 *abilities* means of self-defense   28 *dressed in* equipped with   29 *unskillful* deficient in judgment   30 *latest* last   32 *wake* stir up.   *wage* risk   37 *injointed them* joined themselves.   *after* second, following   39–40 *restem . . . course* retrace their original course   40 *frank appearance* undisguised intent   42 *servitor* officer under your command   43 *free duty* freely given and loyal service.   *recommends* commends himself and reports to

Enter Brabantio, Othello, Cassio, Iago, Roderigo, and officers.

Duke: Valiant Othello, we must straight° employ you 50
    Against the general enemy° Ottoman.
    [*To Brabantio.*] I did not see you; welcome, gentle° signor.
    We lacked your counsel and your help tonight.

Brabantio: So did I yours. Good Your Grace, pardon me;
    Neither my place° nor aught I heard of business 55
    Hath raised me from my bed, nor doth the general care
    Take hold on me, for my particular° grief
    Is of so floodgate° and o'erbearing nature
    That it engluts° and swallows other sorrows
    And it is still itself.°

Duke: Why, what's the matter? 60

Brabantio: My daughter! O, my daughter!

Duke and Senators: Dead?

Brabantio: Ay, to me.
    She is abused,° stol'n from me, and corrupted
    By spells and medicines bought of mountebanks;
    For nature so preposterously to err,
    Being not deficient,° blind, or lame of sense,° 65
    Sans° witchcraft could not.

Duke: Whoe'er he be that in this foul proceeding
    Hath thus beguiled your daughter of herself,
    And you of her, the bloody book of law
    You shall yourself read in the bitter letter 70
    After your own sense°—yea, though our proper° son
    Stood in your action.°

Brabantio: Humbly I thank Your Grace.
    Here is the man, this Moor, whom now it seems
    Your special mandate for the state affairs
    Hath hither brought.

All: We are very sorry for 't. 75

Duke [*to Othello*]: What, in your own part, can you say to this?

Brabantio: Nothing, but this is so.

Othello: Most potent, grave, and reverend signors,
    My very noble and approved° good masters:
    That I have ta'en away this old man's daughter, 80
    It is most true; true, I have married her.
    The very head and front° of my offending

50 *straight* straightway   51 *general enemy* universal enemy to all Christendom   52 *gentle* noble
55 *place* official position   57 *particular* personal   58 *floodgate* i.e., overwhelming (as when
floodgates are opened)   59 *engluts* engulfs   60 *is still itself* remains undiminished   62 *abused* deceived   65 *deficient* defective. *lame of sense* deficient in sensory perception   66 *Sans* without
71 *After . . . sense* according to your own interpretation. *our proper* my own   72 *Stood . . .
action* were under your accusation   79 *approved* proved, esteemed   82 *head and front* height and
breadth, entire extent

Hath this extent, no more. Rude° am I in my speech,
And little blessed with the soft phrase of peace;
For since these arms of mine had seven years' pith,°   85
Till now some nine moons wasted,° they have used
Their dearest° action in the tented field;
And little of this great world can I speak
More than pertains to feats of broils and battle,
And therefore little shall I grace my cause   90
In speaking for myself. Yet, by your gracious patience,
I will a round° unvarnished tale deliver
Of my whole course of love—what drugs, what charms,
What conjuration, and what mighty magic,
For such proceeding I am charged withal,°   95
I won his daughter.
Brabantio: A maiden never bold;
Of spirit so still and quiet that her motion
Blushed at herself;° and she, in spite of nature,
Of years,° of country, credit,° everything,
To fall in love with what she feared to look on!   100
It is a judgment maimed and most imperfect
That will confess° perfection so could err
Against all rules of nature, and must be driven
To find out practices° of cunning hell
Why this should be. I therefore vouch° again   105
That with some mixtures powerful o'er the blood,°
Or with some dram conjured to this effect,°
He wrought upon her.
Duke: To vouch this is no proof,
Without more wider° and more overt test°
Than these thin habits° and poor likelihoods°   110
Of modern seeming° do prefer° against him.
First Senator: But Othello, speak.
Did you by indirect and forcèd courses°
Subdue and poison this young maid's affections?
Or came it by request and such fair question°   115
As soul to soul affordeth?

83 *Rude* unpolished   85 *since . . . pith* i.e., since I was seven.   *pith* strength, vigor   86 *Till . . . wasted* until some nine months ago (since when Othello has evidently not been on active duty, but in Venice)   87 *dearest* most valuable   92 *round* plain   95 *withal* with   97–98 *her . . . herself* i.e., she blushed easily at herself. (*Motion* can suggest the impulse of the soul or of the emotions, or physical movement.)   99 *years* i.e., difference in age.   *credit* virtuous reputation   102 *confess* concede (that)   104 *practices* plots   105 *vouch* assert   106 *blood* passions   107 *dram . . . effect* dose made by magical spells to have this effect   109 *more wider* fuller.   *test* testimony   110 *habits* garments, i.e., appearances.   *poor likelihoods* weak inferences   111 *modern seeming* commonplace assumption.   *prefer* bring forth   113 *forcèd courses* means used against her will   115 *question* conversation

Othello: I do beseech you,
  Send for the lady to the Sagittary
  And let her speak of me before her father.
  If you do find me foul in her report,
  The trust, the office I do hold of you   120
  Not only take away, but let your sentence
  Even fall upon my life.
Duke: Fetch Desdemona hither.
Othello: Ancient, conduct them. You best know the place.

  [*Exeunt Iago and attendants.*]

  And, till she come, as truly as to heaven
  I do confess the vices of my blood,°   125
  So justly° to your grave ears I'll present
  How I did thrive in this fair lady's love,
  And she in mine.
Duke: Say it, Othello.
Othello: Her father loved me, oft invited me,   130
  Still° questioned me the story of my life
  From year to year—the battles, sieges, fortunes
  That I have passed.
  I ran it through, even from my boyish days
  To th' very moment that he bade me tell it,   135
  Wherein I spoke of most disastrous chances,
  Of moving accidents° by flood and field,
  Of hairbreadth scapes i' th' imminent deadly breach,°
  Of being taken by the insolent foe
  And sold to slavery, of my redemption thence,   140
  And portance° in my travels' history,
  Wherein of antres° vast and deserts idle,°
  Rough quarries,° rocks, and hills whose heads touch heaven,
  It was my hint° to speak—such was my process—
  And of the Cannibals that each other eat,   145
  The Anthropophagi,° and men whose heads
  Do grow beneath their shoulders. These things to hear
  Would Desdemona seriously incline;
  But still the house affairs would draw her thence,
  Which ever as she could with haste dispatch   150
  She'd come again, and with a greedy ear

125 *blood* passions, human nature   126 *justly* truthfully, accurately   131 *Still* continually
137 *moving accidents* stirring happenings   138 *imminent . . . breach* death-threatening gaps
made in a fortification   141 *portance* conduct   142 *antres* caverns.   *idle* barren, desolate
143 *Rough quarries* rugged rock formations   144 *hint* occasion, opportunity   146 *Anthropophagi* man-eaters. (A term from Pliny's *Natural History*.)

Devour up my discourse. Which I, observing,
Took once a pliant° hour, and found good means
To draw from her a prayer of earnest heart
That I would all my pilgrimage dilate,° 155
Whereof by parcels° she had something heard,
But not intentively.° I did consent,
And often did beguile her of her tears,
When I did speak of some distressful stroke
That my youth suffered. My story being done, 160
She gave me for my pains a world of sighs.
She swore, in faith, 'twas strange, 'twas passing° strange,
'Twas pitiful, 'twas wondrous pitiful.
She wished she had not heard it, yet she wished
That heaven had made her° such a man. She thanked me, 165
And bade me, if I had a friend that loved her,
I should but teach him how to tell my story,
And that would woo her. Upon this hint° I spake.
She loved me for the dangers I had passed,
And I loved her that she did pity them. 170
This only is the witchcraft I have used.
Here comes the lady. Let her witness it.

Enter Desdemona, Iago, [and] attendants.

Duke: I think this tale would win my daughter too.
  Good Brabantio,
  Take up this mangled matter at the best.° 175
  Men do their broken weapons rather use
  Than their bare hands.
Brabantio: I pray you, hear her speak.
  If she confess that she was half the wooer,
  Destruction on my head if my bad blame
  Light on the man!—Come hither, gentle mistress. 180
  Do you perceive in all this noble company
  Where most you owe obedience?
Desdemona: My noble Father,
  I do perceive here a divided duty.
  To you I am bound for life and education;°
  My life and education both do learn° me 185
  How to respect you. You are the lord of duty;°

---

153 *pliant* well-suiting   155 *dilate* relate in detail   156 *by parcels* piecemeal   157 *intentively*
with full attention, continuously   162 *passing* exceedingly   165 *made her* created her to be
168 *hint* opportunity. (Othello does not mean that she was dropping hints.)   175 *Take . . .*
best make the best of a bad bargain   184 *education* upbringing   185 *learn* teach   186 *of duty*
to whom duty is due

I am hitherto your daughter. But here's my husband,
And so much duty as my mother showed
To you, preferring you before her father,
So much I challenge° that I may profess   190
Due to the Moor my lord.
Brabantio: God be with you! I have done.
Please it Your Grace, on to the state affairs.
I had rather to adopt a child than get° it.
Come hither, Moor.   *[He joins the hands of Othello and Desdemona.]* 195
I here do give thee that with all my heart°
Which, but thou hast already, with all my heart°
I would keep from thee.—For your sake,° jewel,
I am glad at soul I have no other child,
For thy escape° would teach me tyranny,   200
To hang clogs° on them.—I have done, my lord.
Duke: Let me speak like yourself,° and lay a sentence°
Which, as a grece° or step, may help these lovers
Into your favor.
When remedies° are past, the griefs are ended   205
By seeing the worst, which late on hopes depended.°
To mourn a mischief° that is past and gone
Is the next° way to draw new mischief on.
What° cannot be preserved when fortune takes,
Patience her injury a mockery makes.°   210
The robbed that smiles steals something from the thief;
He robs himself that spends a bootless grief.°
Brabantio: So let the Turk of Cyprus us beguile,
We lose it not, so long as we can smile.
He bears the sentence well that nothing bears°   215
But the free comfort which from thence he hears,
But he bears both the sentence and the sorrow
That, to pay grief, must of poor patience borrow.°
These sentences, to sugar or to gall,

190 *challenge* claim   194 *get* beget   196 *with all my heart* wherein my whole affection has been
engaged   197 *with all my heart* willingly, gladly   198 *For your sake* on your account   200
escape elopement   201 *clogs* (Literally, blocks of wood fastened to the legs of criminals or convicts to inhibit escape.)   202 *like yourself* i.e., as you would, in your proper temper.   *lay a sentence* apply a maxim   203 *grece* step   205 *remedies* hopes of remedy   206 *which . . . depended*
which griefs were sustained until recently by hopeful anticipation   207 *mischief* misfortune, injury   208 *next* nearest   209 *What* whatever   210 *Patience . . . makes* patience laughs at the
injury inflicted by fortune (and thus eases the pain)   212 *spends a bootless grief* indulges in unavailing grief   215–218 *He bears . . . borrow* a person well bears out your maxim who can
enjoy its platitudinous comfort, free of all genuine sorrow, but anyone whose grief bankrupts
his poor patience is left with your saying and his sorrow, too. (*Bears the sentence* also plays on
the meaning, "receives judicial sentence.")

Being strong on both sides, are equivocal.° 220
But words are words. I never yet did hear
That the bruised heart was piercèd through the ear.°
I humbly beseech you, proceed to th' affairs of state.

Duke: The Turk with a most mighty preparation makes for Cyprus. Othello, the
fortitude° of the place is best known to you; and though we have there a
substitute° of most allowed° sufficiency, yet opinion, a sovereign mistress of
effects, throws a more safer voice on you.° You must therefore be content to
slubber° the gloss of your new fortunes with this more stubborn° and boisterous expedition.

Othello: The tyrant custom, most grave senators, 230
Hath made the flinty and steel couch of war
My thrice-driven° bed of down. I do agnize°
A natural and prompt alacrity
I find in hardness,° and do undertake
These present wars against the Ottomites. 235
Most humbly therefore bending to your state,°
I crave fit disposition for my wife,
Due reference of place and exhibition,°
With such accommodation° and besort°
As levels° with her breeding.° 240

Duke: Why, at her father's.

Brabantio: I will not have it so.

Othello: Nor I.

Desdemona: Nor I. I would not there reside,
To put my father in impatient thoughts
By being in his eye. Most gracious Duke,
To my unfolding° lend your prosperous° ear, 245
And let me find a charter° in your voice,
T' assist my simpleness.

Duke: What would you, Desdemona?

Desdemona: That I did love the Moor to live with him,
My downright violence and storm of fortunes° 250
May trumpet to the world. My heart's subdued

219–220 *These . . . equivocal* these fine maxims are equivocal, either sweet or bitter in their application 222 *piercèd . . . ear* i.e., surgically lanced and cured by mere words of advice 225
fortitude strength 226 *substitute* deputy. *allowed* acknowledged 226–227 *opinion . . . on you*
general opinion, an important determiner of affairs, chooses you as the best man 228 *slubber*
soil, sully. *stubborn* harsh, rough 232 *thrice-driven* thrice sifted, winnowed. *agnize* know in
myself, acknowledge 234 *hardness* hardship 236 *bending . . . state* bowing or kneeling to
your authority 238 *reference . . . exhibition* provision of appropriate place to live and allowance of money 239 *accommodation* suitable provision. *besort* attendance 240 *levels*
equals, suits. *breeding* social position, upbringing 245 *unfolding* explanation, proposal.
prosperous propitious 246 *charter* privilege, authorization 250 *My . . . fortunes* my plain
and total breach of social custom, taking my future by storm and disrupting my whole life

Even to the very quality of my lord.°
I saw Othello's visage in his mind,
And to his honors and his valiant parts°
Did I my soul and fortunes consecrate.   255
So that, dear lords, if I be left behind
A moth° of peace, and he go to the war,
The rites° for why I love him are bereft me,
And I a heavy interim shall support
By his dear° absence. Let me go with him.   260

Othello: Let her have your voice.°
Vouch with me, heaven, I therefor beg it not
To please the palate of my appetite,
Nor to comply with heat°—the young affects°
In me defunct—and proper° satisfaction,   265
But to be free° and bounteous to her mind.
And heaven defend° your good souls that you think°
I will your serious and great business scant
When she is with me. No, when light-winged toys
Of feathered Cupid seel° with wanton dullness   270
My speculative and officed instruments,°
That° my disports° corrupt and taint° my business,
Let huswives make a skillet of my helm,
And all indign° and base adversities
Make head° against my estimation!°   275

Duke: Be it as you shall privately determine,
Either for her stay or going. Th' affair cries haste,
And speed must answer it.

A Senator: You must away tonight.

Desdemona: Tonight, my lord?

Duke: This night.

Othello: With all my heart.

Duke: At nine i' the morning here we'll meet again.   280
Othello, leave some officer behind,
And he shall our commission bring to you,
With such things else of quality and respect°
As doth import° you.

Othello: So please Your Grace, my ancient;

251–252 *My heart's . . . lord* my heart is brought wholly into accord with Othello's virtues; I love
him for his virtues   254 *parts* qualities   257 *moth* i.e., one who consumes merely   258 *rites* rites
of love (with a suggestion, too, of "rights," sharing)   260 *dear* (1) heartfelt (2) costly   261 *voice*
consent   264 *heat* sexual passion.   *young affects* passions of youth, desires   265 *proper* personal
266 *free* generous   267 *defend* forbid.   *think* should think   270 *seel* i.e., make blind (as in falconry, by sewing up the eyes of the hawk during training)   271 *speculative . . . instruments* eyes
and other faculties used in the performance of duty   272 *That* so that.   *disports* sexual pastimes.
taint impair   274 *indign* unworthy, shameful   275 *Make head* raise an army.   *estimation* reputation   283 *of quality and respect* of importance and relevance   284 *import* concern

A man he is of honesty and trust.   285
To his conveyance I assign my wife,
With what else needful Your Good Grace shall think
To be sent after me.
Duke: Let it be so.
Good night to everyone. [*To Brabantio.*] And, noble signor,
If virtue no delighted° beauty lack,   290
Your son-in-law is far more fair than black.
First Senator: Adieu, brave Moor. Use Desdemona well.
Brabantio: Look to her, Moor, if thou hast eyes to see.
She has deceived her father, and may thee.
            Exeunt [Duke, Brabantio, Cassio, Senators, and officers].
Othello: My life upon her faith! Honest Iago,   295
My Desdemona must I leave to thee.
I prithee, let thy wife attend on her,
And bring them after in the best advantage.°
Come, Desdemona. I have but an hour
Of love, of worldly matters and direction,°   300
To spend with thee. We must obey the time.°
                                        Exit [with Desdemona].
Roderigo: Iago—
Iago: What sayst thou, noble heart?
Roderigo: What will I do, think'st thou?
Iago: Why, go to bed and sleep.   305
Roderigo: I will incontinently° drown myself.
Iago: If thou dost, I shall never love thee after. Why, thou silly gentleman?
Roderigo: It is silliness to live when to live is torment; and then have we a pre-
    scription° to die when death is our physician.
Iago: O villainous!° I have looked upon the world for four times seven years,   310
    and, since I could distinguish betwixt a benefit and an injury, I never found
    man that knew how to love himself. Ere I would say I would drown myself
    for the love of a guinea hen,° I would change my humanity with a baboon.
Roderigo: What should I do? I confess it is my shame to be so fond,° but it is not
    in my virtue° to amend it.   315
Iago: Virtue? A fig!° 'Tis in ourselves that we are thus or thus. Our bodies are
    our gardens, to the which our wills are gardeners; so that if we will plant net-
    tles or sow lettuce, set hyssop° and weed up thyme, supply it with one
    gender° of herbs or distract it with° many, either to have it sterile with idle-

290 *delighted* capable of delighting   298 *in . . . advantage* at the most favorable opportunity
300 *direction* instructions   301 *the time* the urgency of the present crisis   306 *incontinently* immediately, without self-restraint   308–309 *prescription* (1) right based on long-established
custom (2) doctor's prescription   310 *villainous* i.e., what perfect nonsense   313 *guinea hen* (A
slang term for a prostitute.)   314 *fond* infatuated   315 *virtue* strength, nature   316 *fig* (To give
a fig is to thrust the thumb between the first and second fingers in a vulgar and insulting gesture.)
318 *hyssop* an herb of the mint family   319 *gender* kind.   *distract it with* divide it among

ness° or manured with industry—why, the power and corrigible authority° 320
of this lies in our wills. If the beam° of our lives had not one scale of reason
to poise° another of sensuality, the blood° and baseness of our natures would
conduct us to most preposterous conclusions. But we have reason to cool
our raging motions,° our carnal stings, our unbitted° lusts, whereof I take
this that you call love to be a sect or scion.° 325

Roderigo: It cannot be.

Iago: It is merely a lust of the blood and a permission of the will. Come, be a
man. Drown thyself? Drown cats and blind puppies. I have professed me thy
friend, and I confess me knit to thy deserving with cables of perdurable°
toughness. I could never better stead° thee than now. Put money in thy 330
purse. Follow thou the wars; defeat thy favor° with an usurped° beard. I say,
put money in thy purse. It cannot be long that Desdemona should continue
her love to the Moor—put money in thy purse—nor he his to her. It was a
violent commencement in her, and thou shalt see an answerable sequestra-
tion°—put but money in thy purse. These Moors are changeable in their 335
wills°—fill thy purse with money. The food that to him now is as luscious as
locusts° shall be to him shortly as bitter as coloquintida.° She must change
for youth; when she is sated with his body, she will find the error of her
choice. She must have change, she must. Therefore put money in thy purse.
If thou wilt needs damn thyself, do it a more delicate way than drowning. 340
Make° all the money thou canst. If sanctimony° and a frail vow betwixt an
erring° barbarian and a supersubtle Venetian be not too hard for my wits
and all the tribe of hell, thou shalt enjoy her. Therefore make money. A pox
of drowning thyself! It is clean out of the way.° Seek thou rather to be
hanged in compassing° thy joy than to be drowned and go without her. 345

Roderigo: Wilt thou be fast° to my hopes if I depend on the issue?°

Iago: Thou art sure of me. Go, make money. I have told thee often, and I retell
thee again and again, I hate the Moor. My cause is hearted;° thine hath no
less reason. Let us be conjunctive° in our revenge against him. If thou canst
cuckold him, thou dost thyself a pleasure, me a sport. There are many events 350
in the womb of time which will be delivered. Traverse,° go, provide thy
money. We will have more of this tomorrow. Adieu.

Roderigo: Where shall we meet i' the morning?

Iago: At my lodging.

319–320 *idleness* want of cultivation. *corrigible authority* power to correct 321 *beam* balance
322 *poise* counterbalance. *blood* natural passions 324 *motions* appetites. *unbitted* unbridled,
uncontrolled 325 *sect or scion* cutting or offshoot 329 *perdurable* very durable 330 *stead* assist 331 *defeat thy favor* disguise your face. *usurped* (The suggestion is that Roderigo is not
man enough to have a beard of his own.) 334–335 *an answerable sequestration* a corresponding
separation or estrangement 336 *wills* carnal appetites 337 *locusts* fruit of the carob tree (see
Matthew 3:4), or perhaps honeysuckle. *coloquintida* colocynth or bitter apple, a purgative
341 *Make* raise, collect. *sanctimony* sacred ceremony 342 *erring* wandering, vagabond, unsteady 344 *clean . . . way* entirely unsuitable as a course of action 345 *compassing* encompassing, embracing 346 *fast* true. *issue* (successful) outcome 348 *hearted* fixed in the heart,
heartfelt 349 *conjunctive* united 351 *Traverse* (A military marching term.)

Roderigo: I'll be with thee betimes.°   *[He starts to leave.]*   355

Iago: Go to, farewell.—Do you hear, Roderigo?

Roderigo: What say you?

Iago: No more of drowning, do you hear?

Roderigo: I am changed.

Iago: Go to, farewell. Put money enough in your purse.   360

Roderigo: I'll sell all my land.   *Exit.*

Iago: Thus do I ever make my fool my purse;
    For I mine own gained knowledge should profane
    If I would time expend with such a snipe°
    But for my sport and profit. I hate the Moor;   365
    And it is thought abroad° that twixt my sheets
    He's done my office.° I know not if 't be true;
    But I, for mere suspicion in that kind,
    Will do as if for surety.° He holds me well;°
    The better shall my purpose work on him.   370
    Cassio's a proper° man. Let me see now:
    To get his place and to plume up° my will
    In double knavery—How, how?—Let's see:
    After some time, to abuse° Othello's ear
    That he° is too familiar with his wife.   375
    He hath a person and a smooth dispose°
    To be suspected, framed to make women false.
    The Moor is of a free° and open° nature,
    That thinks men honest that but seem to be so,
    And will as tenderly° be led by the nose   380
    As asses are.
    I have 't. It is engendered. Hell and night
    Must bring this monstrous birth to the world's light.

    [Exit.]

Act II

Scene I [A Seaport in Cyprus. An Open Place Near the Quay.]

    Enter Montano and two Gentlemen.

Montano: What from the cape can you discern at sea?

First Gentleman: Nothing at all. It is a high-wrought flood.°
    I cannot, twixt the heaven and the main,°
    Descry a sail.

---

355 *betimes* early   364 *snipe* woodcock, i.e., fool   366 *it is thought abroad* it is rumored   367 *my office* i.e., my sexual function as husband   369 *do . . . surety* act as if on certain knowledge. *holds me well* regards me favorably   371 *proper* handsome   372 *plume up* put a feather in the cap of, i.e., glorify, gratify   374 *abuse* deceive   375 *he* i.e., Cassio   376 *dispose* disposition   378 *free* frank, generous. *open* unsuspicious   380 *tenderly* readily   2 *high-wrought flood* very agitated sea   3 *main* ocean (also at line 41)

A scene from Oliver Parker's 1995 film version of Othello—(left to right) Kenneth Branagh as Iago, Laurence Fishburne as Othello, and Nathaniel Parker as Cassio.

Montano: Methinks the wind hath spoke aloud at land; 5
    A fuller blast ne'er shook our battlements.
    If it hath ruffianed° so upon the sea,
    What ribs of oak, when mountains° melt on them,
    Can hold the mortise?° What shall we hear of this?
Second Gentleman: A segregation° of the Turkish fleet. 10
    For do but stand upon the foaming shore,
    The chidden° billow seems to pelt the clouds;
    The wind-shaked surge, with high and monstrous mane,°
    Seems to cast water on the burning Bear°
    And quench the guards of th' ever-fixèd pole. 15
    I never did like molestation° view
    On the enchafèd° flood.
Montano: If that° the Turkish fleet
    Be not ensheltered and embayed,° they are drowned;
    It is impossible to bear it out.° 20

7 *ruffianed* raged 8 *mountains* i.e., of water 9 *hold the mortise* hold their joints together. (A *mortise* is the socket hollowed out in fitting timbers.) 10 *segregation* dispersal 12 *chidden* i.e., rebuked, repelled (by the shore), and thus shot into the air 13 *monstrous mane* (The surf is like the mane of a wild beast.) 14 *the burning Bear* i.e., the constellation Ursa Minor or the Little Bear, which includes the polestar (and hence regarded as the *guards of th' ever-fixèd pole* in the next line; sometimes the term *guards* is applied to the two "pointers" of the Big Bear or Dipper, which may be intended here). 16 *like molestation* comparable disturbance 17 *enchafèd* angry 18 *If that* if 19 *embayed* sheltered by a bay 20 *bear it out* survive, weather the storm

Enter a [Third] Gentleman.

Third Gentleman: News, lads! Our wars are done.
    The desperate tempest hath so banged the Turks
    That their designment° halts.° A noble ship of Venice
    Hath seen a grievous wreck° and sufferance°
    On most part of their fleet.   25
Montano: How? Is this true?
Third Gentleman: The ship is here put in,
    A Veronesa;° Michael Cassio,
    Lieutenant to the warlike Moor Othello,
    Is come on shore; the Moor himself at sea,   30
    And is in full commission here for Cyprus.
Montano: I am glad on 't. 'Tis a worthy governor.
Third Gentleman: But this same Cassio, though he speak of comfort
    Touching the Turkish loss, yet he looks sadly°
    And prays the Moor be safe, for they were parted   35
    With foul and violent tempest.
Montano: Pray heaven he be,
    For I have served him, and the man commands
    Like a full° soldier. Let's to the seaside, ho!
    As well to see the vessel that's come in
    As to throw out our eyes for brave Othello,   40
    Even till we make the main and th' aerial blue°
    An indistinct regard.°
Third Gentleman: Come, let's do so,
    For every minute is expectancy°
    Of more arrivance.°

    Enter Cassio.

Cassio: Thanks, you the valiant of this warlike isle,   45
    That so approve° the Moor! O, let the heavens
    Give him defense against the elements,
    For I have lost him on a dangerous sea.
Montano: Is he well shipped?
Cassio: His bark is stoutly timbered, and his pilot   50
    Of very expert and approved allowance;°
    Therefore my hopes, not surfeited to death,°
    Stand in bold cure.°

23 *designment* design, enterprise. *halts* is lame   24 *wreck* shipwreck. *sufferance* damage, disaster   28 *Veronesa* i.e., fitted out in Verona for Venetian service, or possibly *Verennessa* (the Folio spelling), i.e., *verrinessa*, a cutter (from *verrinare*, "to cut through")   34 *sadly* gravely   38 *full* perfect   41 *the main . . . blue* the sea and the sky   42 *An indistinct regard* indistinguishable in our view   43 *is expectancy* gives expectation   44 *arrivance* arrival   46 *approve* admire, honor   51 *approved allowance* tested reputation   52 *surfeited to death* i.e., overextended, worn thin through repeated application or delayed fulfillment   53 *in bold cure* in strong hopes of fulfillment

[A cry] *within:*   "A sail, a sail, a sail!"

Cassio: What noise?

A Gentleman: The town is empty. On the brow o' the sea°   55
    Stand ranks of people, and they cry "A sail!"

Cassio: My hopes do shape him for° the governor.

    [A *shot within.*]

Second Gentleman: They do discharge their shot of courtesy;°
    Our friends at least.

Cassio: I pray you, sir, go forth,
    And give us truth who 'tis that is arrived.   60

Second Gentleman: I shall.   *Exit.*

Montano: But, good Lieutenant, is your general wived?

Cassio: Most fortunately. He hath achieved a maid
    That paragons° description and wild fame,°
    One that excels the quirks° of blazoning° pens,   65
    And in th' essential vesture of creation
    Does tire the enginer.°

    Enter [Second] Gentleman.°

                    How now? Who has put in?°

Second Gentleman: 'Tis one Iago, ancient to the General.

Cassio: He's had most favorable and happy speed.
    Tempests themselves, high seas, and howling winds,   70
    The guttered° rocks and congregated sands—
    Traitors ensteeped° to clog the guiltless keel—
    As° having sense of beauty, do omit°
    Their mortal° natures, letting go safely by
    The divine Desdemona.

Montano: What is she?   75

Cassio: She that I spake of, our great captain's captain,
    Left in the conduct of the bold Iago,
    Whose footing° here anticipates our thoughts
    A sennight's° speed. Great Jove, Othello guard,
    And swell his sail with thine own powerful breath,   80
    That he may bless this bay with his tall° ship,
    Make love's quick pants in Desdemona's arms,

---

55 *brow o' the sea* cliff-edge   57 *My . . . for* I hope it is   58 *discharge . . . courtesy* fire a salute in token of respect and courtesy   64 *paragons* surpasses.   *wild fame* extravagant report   65 *quirks* witty conceits.   *blazoning* setting forth as though in heraldic language   66–67 *in . . . enginer* in her real, God-given, beauty, (she) defeats any attempt to praise her.   *enginer* engineer, i.e., poet, one who devises.   s.d. *[Second] Gentleman* (So identified in the Quarto text here and in lines 58, 61, 68, and 96; the Folio calls him a gentleman.)   67 *put in* i.e., to harbor   71 *guttered* jagged, trenched   72 *ensteeped* lying under water   73 *As* as if.   *omit* forbear to exercise   74 *mortal* deadly   78 *footing* landing   79 *sennight's* week's   81 *tall* splendid, gallant

Give renewed fire to our extincted spirits,
And bring all Cyprus comfort!

Enter Desdemona, Iago, Roderigo, and Emilia.

                        O, behold,
The riches of the ship is come on shore!   85
You men of Cyprus, let her have your knees.

[The gentlemen make curtsy to Desdemona.]

Hail to thee, lady! And the grace of heaven
Before, behind thee, and on every hand
Enwheel thee round!
Desdemona: I thank you, valiant Cassio.
What tidings can you tell me of my lord?   90
Cassio: He is not yet arrived, nor know I aught
But that he's well and will be shortly here.
Desdemona: O, but I fear—How lost you company?
Cassio: The great contention of the sea and skies
Parted our fellowship.

(Within)   "A sail, a sail!" *[A shot.]*
                        But hark. A sail!   95
Second Gentleman: They give their greeting to the citadel.
This likewise is a friend.
Cassio: See for the news.

[Exit Second Gentleman.]

Good Ancient, you are welcome. *[Kissing Emilia.]* Welcome, mistress.
Let it not gall your patience, good Iago,
That I extend° my manners; 'tis my breeding°   100
That gives me this bold show of courtesy.
Iago: Sir, would she give you so much of her lips
As of her tongue she oft bestows on me,
You would have enough.
Desdemona: Alas, she has no speech!°   105
Iago: In faith, too much.
I find it still,° when I have list° to sleep.
Marry, before your ladyship, I grant,
She puts her tongue a little in her heart
And chides with thinking.°
Emilia: You have little cause to say so.   110
Iago: Come on, come on. You are pictures out of doors,°

---

100 *extend* give scope to. *breeding* training in the niceties of etiquette 105 *she has no speech*
i.e., she's not a chatterbox, as you allege 107 *still* always. *list* desire 110 *with thinking* i.e., in
her thoughts only 111 *pictures out of doors* i.e., silent and well-behaved in public

Bells° in your parlors, wildcats in your kitchens,°
Saints° in your injuries, devils being offended,
Players° in your huswifery,° and huswives° in your beds.
Desdemona: O, fie upon thee, slanderer!   115
Iago: Nay, it is true, or else I am a Turk.°
    You rise to play, and go to bed to work.
Emilia: You shall not write my praise.
Iago: No, let me not.
Desdemona: What wouldst write of me, if thou shouldst praise me?
Iago: O gentle lady, do not put me to 't,   120
    For I am nothing if not critical.°
Desdemona: Come on, essay.°—There's one gone to the harbor?
Iago: Ay, madam.
Desdemona: I am not merry, but I do beguile
    The thing I am° by seeming otherwise.   125
    Come, how wouldst thou praise me?
Iago: I am about it, but indeed my invention
    Comes from my pate as birdlime° does from frieze°—
    It plucks out brains and all. But my Muse labors,°
    And thus she is delivered: 130
    If she be fair and wise, fairness and wit,
    The one's for use, the other useth it.°
Desdemona: Well praised! How if she be black° and witty?
Iago: If she be black, and thereto have a wit,
    She'll find a white° that shall her blackness fit.°   135
Desdemona: Worse and worse.
Emilia: How if fair and foolish?
Iago: She never yet was foolish that was fair,
    For even her folly° helped her to an heir.°
Desdemona: These are old fond° paradoxes to make fools laugh i' th' alehouse.
    What miserable praise hast thou for her that's foul and foolish?   140
Iago: There's none so foul° and foolish thereunto,°
    But does foul° pranks which fair and wise ones do.
Desdemona: O heavy ignorance! Thou praisest the worst best. But what praise
    couldst thou bestow on a deserving woman indeed, one that, in the
    authority of her merit, did justly put on the vouch° of very malice itself?   145

112 *Bells* i.e., jangling, noisy, and brazen.   *in your kitchens* i.e., in domestic affairs. (Ladies would
not do the cooking.)   113 *Saints* martyrs   114 *Players* idlers, triflers, or deceivers.   *huswifery*
housekeeping.   *huswives* hussies (i.e., women are "busy" in bed, or unduly thrifty in dispensing
sexual favors)   116 *a Turk* an infidel, not to be believed   121 *critical* censorious   122 *essay* try
125 *The thing I am* i.e., my anxious self   128 *birdlime* sticky substance used to catch small birds.
frieze coarse woolen cloth   129 *labors* (1) exerts herself (2) prepares to deliver a child (with a
following pun on *delivered* in line 130)   132 *The one's . . . it* i.e., her cleverness will make use of
her beauty   133 *black* dark-complexioned, brunette   135 *a white* a fair person (with word-play
on "wight," a person).   *fit* (with sexual suggestion of mating)   138 *folly* (with added meaning
of "lechery, wantonness").   *to an heir* i.e., to bear a child   139 *fond* foolish   141 *foul* ugly.
thereunto in addition   142 *foul* sluttish   145 *put . . . vouch* compel the approval

Iago: She that was ever fair, and never proud,
    Had tongue at will, and yet was never loud,
    Never lacked gold and yet went never gay,°
    Fled from her wish, and yet said, "Now I may,"°
    She that being angered, her revenge being nigh,   150
    Bade her wrong stay° and her displeasure fly,
    She that in wisdom never was so frail
    To change the cod's head for the salmon's tail,°
    She that could think and ne'er disclose her mind,
    See suitors following and not look behind,   155
    She was a wight, if ever such wight were—
Desdemona: To do what?
Iago: To suckle fools° and chronicle small beer.°
Desdemona: O most lame and impotent conclusion! Do not learn of him, Emilia, though he be thy husband. How say you, Cassio? Is he not a most 160 profane° and liberal° counselor?
Cassio: He speaks home,° madam. You may relish° him more in° the soldier than in the scholar.

[*Cassio and Desdemona stand together, conversing intimately.*]

Iago [aside]: He takes her by the palm. Ay, well said,° whisper. With as little a web as this will I ensnare as great a fly as Cassio. Ay, smile upon her, do; I 165 will gyve° thee in thine own courtship.° You say true;° 'tis so, indeed. If such tricks as these strip you out of your lieutenantry, it had been better you had not kissed your three fingers so oft, which now again you are most apt to play the sir° in. Very good; well kissed! An excellent courtesy! 'Tis so, indeed. Yet again your fingers to your lips? Would they were clyster pipes° 170 for your sake! [*Trumpet within.*] The Moor! I know his trumpet.
Cassio: 'Tis truly so.
Desdemona: Let's meet him and receive him.
Cassio: Lo, where he comes!

    Enter Othello and attendants.

Othello: O my fair warrior!
Desdemona: My dear Othello!   175
Othello: It gives me wonder great as my content
    To see you here before me. O my soul's joy,

---

148 *gay* extravagantly clothed   149 *Fled . . . may* avoided temptation where the choice was hers   151 *Bade . . . stay* i.e., resolved to put up with her injury patiently   153 *To . . . tail* i.e., to exchange a lackluster husband for a sexy lover (?) (*Cod's head* is slang for "penis," and *tail*, for "pudendum.")   158 *suckle fools* breastfeed babies. *chronicle small beer* i.e., keep petty household accounts, keep track of trivial matters   161 *profane* irreverent, ribald. *liberal* licentious, free-spoken   162 *home* right to the target. (A term from fencing.) *relish* appreciate *in* in the character of   164 *well said* well done   166 *gyve* fetter, shackle. *courtship* courtesy, show of courtly manners.   *You say true* i.e., that's right, go ahead   169 *the sir* i.e., the fine gentleman   170 *clyster pipes* tubes used for enemas and douches

If after every tempest come such calms,
May the winds blow till they have wakened death,
And let the laboring bark climb hills of seas   180
Olympus-high, and duck again as low
As hell's from heaven! If it were now to die,
'Twere now to be most happy, for I fear
My soul hath her content so absolute
That not another comfort like to this   185
Succeeds in unknown fate.°
Desdemona: The heavens forbid
But that our loves and comforts should increase
Even as our days do grow!
Othello: Amen to that, sweet powers!
I cannot speak enough of this content.   190
It stops me here; it is too much of joy.
And this, and this, the greatest discords be

[*They kiss.*]°

That e'er our hearts shall make!
Iago [*aside*]: O, you are well tuned now!
But I'll set down° the pegs that make this music,   195
As honest as I am.°
Othello: Come, let us to the castle.
News, friends! Our wars are done, the Turks are drowned.
How does my old acquaintance of this isle?—
Honey, you shall be well desired° in Cyprus;   200
I have found great love amongst them. O my sweet,
I prattle out of fashion,° and I dote
In mine own comforts.—I prithee, good Iago,
Go to the bay and disembark my coffers.°
Bring thou the master° to the citadel;   205
He is a good one, and his worthiness
Does challenge° much respect.—Come, Desdemona.—
Once more, well met at Cyprus!

Exeunt Othello and Desdemona [and all but Iago and Roderigo].

Iago [*to an attendant*]: Do thou meet me presently at the harbor. [*To Roderigo.*]
Come hither. If thou be'st valiant—as, they say, base men° being in love   210
have then a nobility in their natures more than is native to them—list° me.

---

186 *Succeeds . . . fate* i.e., can follow in the unknown future   192 s.d. *They kiss* (The direction
is from the Quarto.)   195 *set down* loosen (and hence untune the instrument)   196 *As . . . I
am* for all my supposed honesty   200 *desired* welcomed   202 *out of fashion* irrelevantly, inco-
herently (?)   204 *coffers* chests, baggage   205 *master* ship's captain   207 *challenge* lay claim
to, deserve   210 *base men* even lowly born men   211 *list* listen to

The Lieutenant tonight watches on the court of guard.° First, I must tell
thee this: Desdemona is directly in love with him.

Roderigo: With him? Why, 'tis not possible.

Iago: Lay thy finger thus,° and let thy soul be instructed. Mark me with what vi-   215
olence she first loved the Moor, but° for bragging and telling her fantastical
lies. To love him still for prating? Let not thy discreet heart think it. Her eye
must be fed; and what delight shall she have to look on the devil? When the
blood is made dull with the act of sport,° there should be, again to inflame it
and to give satiety a fresh appetite, loveliness in favor,° sympathy° in years,   220
manners, and beauties—all which the Moor is defective in. Now, for want
of these required conveniences,° her delicate tenderness will find itself
abused,° begin to heave the gorge,° disrelish and abhor the Moor. Very
nature° will instruct her in it and compel her to some second choice. Now,
sir, this granted—as it is a most pregnant° and unforced position—who   225
stands so eminent in the degree of° this fortune as Cassio does? A knave
very voluble,° no further conscionable° than in putting on the mere form of
civil and humane° seeming for the better compassing of his salt° and most
hidden loose affection.° Why, none, why, none. A slipper° and subtle
knave, a finder out of occasions, that has an eye can stamp° and counterfeit   230
advantages,° though true advantage never present itself; a devilish knave.
Besides, the knave is handsome, young, and hath all those requisites in him
that folly° and green° minds look after. A pestilent complete knave, and the
woman hath found him° already.

Roderigo: I cannot believe that in her. She's full of most blessed condition.°   235

Iago: Blessed fig's end!° The wine she drinks is made of grapes. If she had been
blessed, she would never have loved the Moor. Blessed pudding!° Didst thou
not see her paddle with the palm of his hand? Didst not mark that?

Roderigo: Yes, that I did; but that was but courtesy.

Iago: Lechery, by this hand. An index° and obscure° prologue to the history of   240
lust and foul thoughts. They met so near with their lips that their breaths
embraced together. Villainous thoughts, Roderigo! When these
mutualities° so marshal the way, hard at hand° comes the master and main
exercise, th' incorporate° conclusion. Pish! But, sir, be you ruled by me. I
have brought you from Venice. Watch you° tonight; for the command, I'll   245

---

212 *court of guard* guardhouse. (Cassio is in charge of the watch.)   215 *thus* i.e., on your lips
216 *but* only   219 *the act of sport* sex   220 *favor* appearance.   *sympathy* correspondence, similarity   222 *required conveniences* things conducive to sexual compatibility   223 *abused* cheated,
revolted.   *heave the gorge* experience nausea   223–224 *Very nature* her very instincts   225
pregnant evident, cogent   226 *in . . . of* as next in line for   227 *voluble* facile, glib.   *conscionable*
conscientious, conscience-bound   228 *humane* polite, courteous.   *salt* licentious   229 *affection*
passion.   *slipper* slippery   230 *an eye can stamp* an eye that can coin, create   231 *advantages* favorable opportunities   233 *folly* wantonness.   *green* immature   234 *found him* sized him up,
perceived his intent   235 *condition* disposition   236 *fig's end* (See Act I, Scene iii, line 316 for
the vulgar gesture of the fig.)   237 *pudding* sausage   240 *index* table of contents.   *obscure* (i.e.,
the *lust and foul thoughts* in line   241 are secret, hidden from view)   243 *mutualities* exchanges,
intimacies.   *hard at hand* closely following   244 *incorporate* carnal   245 *Watch you* stand watch

lay 't upon you.° Cassio knows you not. I'll not be far from you. Do you find some occasion to anger Cassio, either by speaking too loud, or tainting° his discipline, or from what other course you please, which the time shall more favorably minister.°

Roderigo: Well.   250

Iago: Sir, he's rash and very sudden in choler,° and haply° may strike at you. Provoke him that he may, for even out of that will I cause these of Cyprus to mutiny,° whose qualification° shall come into no true taste° again but by the displanting of Cassio. So shall you have a shorter journey to your desires by the means I shall then have to prefer° them, and the impediment most   255 profitably removed, without the which there were no expectation of our prosperity.

Roderigo: I will do this, if you can bring it to any opportunity.

Iago: I warrant° thee. Meet me by and by° at the citadel. I must fetch his neces- saries ashore. Farewell.   260

Roderigo: Adieu.   *Exit.*

Iago: That Cassio loves her, I do well believe 't;
That she loves him, 'tis apt° and of great credit.°
The Moor, howbeit that I endure him not,
Is of a constant, loving, noble nature,   265
And I dare think he'll prove to Desdemona
A most dear husband. Now, I do love her too,
Not out of absolute lust—though peradventure
I stand accountant° for as great a sin—
But partly led to diet° my revenge   270
For that I do suspect the lusty Moor
Hath leaped into my seat, the thought whereof
Doth, like a poisonous mineral, gnaw my innards;
And nothing can or shall content my soul
Till I am evened with him, wife for wife,   275
Or failing so, yet that I put the Moor
At least into a jealousy so strong
That judgment cannot cure. Which thing to do,
If this poor trash of Venice, whom I trace°
For° his quick hunting, stand the putting on,°   280
I'll have our Michael Cassio on the hip,°
Abuse° him to the Moor in the rank garb°—

245–246 *for the command . . . you* I'll arrange for you to be appointed, given orders   247 *tainting* disparaging   249 *minister* provide   251 *choler* wrath.   *haply* perhaps   253 *mutiny* riot.   *quali- fication* appeasement.   *true taste* i.e., acceptable state   255 *prefer* advance   259 *warrant* assure. *by and by* immediately   263 *apt* probable.   *credit* credibility   269 *accountant* accountable 270 *diet* feed   279 *trace* i.e., train, or follow (?), or perhaps *trash*, a hunting term, meaning to put weights on a hunting dog in order to slow him down   280 *For* to make more eager.   *stand . . . on* respond properly when I incite him to quarrel   281 *on the hip* at my mercy, where I can throw him. (A wrestling term.)   282 *Abuse* slander.   *rank garb* coarse manner, gross fashion

For I fear Cassio with my nightcap° too—
Make the Moor thank me, love me, and reward me
For making him egregiously an ass   285
And practicing upon° his peace and quiet
Even to madness. 'Tis here, but yet confused.
Knavery's plain face is never seen till used.   *Exit.*

Scene II [Cyprus. A Street.]

Enter Othello's Herald with a proclamation.

Herald: It is Othello's pleasure, our noble and valiant general, that, upon certain
tidings now arrived, importing the mere perdition° of the Turkish fleet,
every man put himself into triumph:° some to dance, some to make bonfires,
each man to what sport and revels his addiction° leads him. For, besides
these beneficial news, it is the celebration of his nuptial. So much was his   5
pleasure should be proclaimed. All offices° are open, and there is full liberty
of feasting from this present hour of five till the bell have told eleven.
Heaven bless the isle of Cyprus and our noble general Othello!

Exit.

Scene III [Cyprus. The Citadel.]

Enter Othello, Desdemona, Cassio, and attendants.

Othello: Good Michael, look you to the guard tonight.
Let's teach ourselves that honorable stop°
Not to outsport° discretion.
Cassio: Iago hath direction what to do,
But notwithstanding, with my personal eye   5
Will I look to 't.
Othello: Iago is most honest.
Michael, good night. Tomorrow with your earliest°
Let me have speech with you. [*To Desdemona.*]
                            Come, my dear love,
The purchase made, the fruits are to ensue;
That profit's yet to come 'tween me and you.°—   10
Good night.

Exit [Othello, with Desdemona and attendants].

Enter Iago.

Cassio: Welcome, Iago. We must to the watch.

283 *with my nightcap* i.e., as a rival in my bed, as one who gives me cuckold's horns   286
practicing upon plotting against   2 *mere perdition* complete destruction   3 *triumph* public celebration   4 *addiction* inclination   6 *offices* rooms where food and drink are kept   2 *stop* restraint   3 *outsport* celebrate beyond the bounds of   7 *with your earliest* at your earliest convenience   9–10 *The purchase . . . you* i.e., though married, we haven't yet consummated our love

Iago: Not this hour,° Lieutenant; 'tis not yet ten o' the clock. Our general cast°
us thus early for the love of his Desdemona; who° let us not therefore blame.
He hath not yet made wanton the night with her, and she is sport for Jove. 15

Cassio: She's a most exquisite lady.

Iago: And, I'll warrant her, full of game.

Cassio: Indeed, she's a most fresh and delicate creature.

Iago: What an eye she has! Methinks it sounds a parley° to provocation.

Cassio: An inviting eye, and yet methinks right modest. 20

Iago: And when she speaks, is it not an alarum° to love?

Cassio: She is indeed perfection.

Iago: Well, happiness to their sheets! Come, Lieutenant, I have a stoup° of
wine, and here without° are a brace° of Cyprus gallants that would fain have
a measure° to the health of black Othello. 25

Cassio: Not tonight, good Iago. I have very poor and unhappy brains for drinking.
I could well wish courtesy would invent some other custom of entertainment.

Iago: O, they are our friends. But one cup! I'll drink for you.°

Cassio: I have drunk but one cup tonight, and that was craftily qualified° too,
and behold what innovation° it makes here.° I am unfortunate in the infir- 30
mity and dare not task my weakness with any more.

Iago: What, man? 'Tis a night of revels. The gallants desire it.

Cassio: Where are they?

Iago: Here at the door. I pray you, call them in.

Cassio: I'll do 't, but it dislikes me.°   *Exit.* 35

Iago: If I can fasten but one cup upon him,
With that which he hath drunk tonight already,
He'll be as full of quarrel and offense°
As my young mistress' dog. Now, my sick fool Roderigo,
Whom love hath turned almost the wrong side out, 40
To Desdemona hath tonight caroused°
Potations pottle-deep;° and he's to watch.°
Three lads of Cyprus—noble swelling° spirits,
That hold their honors in a wary distance,°
The very elements° of this warlike isle— 45
Have I tonight flustered with flowing cups,
And they watch° too. Now, 'mongst this flock of drunkards
Am I to put our Cassio in some action
That may offend the isle.—But here they come.

---

13 *Not this hour* not for an hour yet.   *cast* dismissed   14 *who* i.e., Othello   19 *sounds a parley*
calls for a conference, issues an invitation   21 *alarum* signal calling men to arms (continuing the
military metaphor of *parley*, line 19)   23 *stoup* measure of liquor, two quarts   24 *without* outside.
brace pair   24–25 *fain have a measure* gladly drink a toast   28 *for you* in your place. (Iago will do
the steady drinking to keep the gallants company while Cassio has only one cup.)   29 *qualified* diluted   30 *innovation* disturbance, insurrection.   *here* i.e., in my head   35 *it dislikes me* i.e., I'm reluctant   38 *offense* readiness to take offense   41 *caroused* drunk off   42 *pottle-deep* to the bottom
of the tankard.   *watch* stand watch   43 *swelling* proud   44 *hold . . . distance* i.e., are extremely
sensitive of their honor   45 *very elements* typical sort   47 *watch* are members of the guard

Enter Cassio, Montano, and gentlemen; [servants following with wine].

If consequence do but approve my dream,°   50
My boat sails freely both with wind and stream.°
Cassio: 'Fore God, they have given me a rouse° already.
Montano: Good faith, a little one; not past a pint, as I am a soldier.
Iago: Some wine, ho! [*He sings.*]

       55
     "And let me the cannikin° clink, clink,
     And let me the cannikin clink.
     A soldier's a man,
     O, man's life's but a span;°
     Why, then, let a soldier drink."

     Some wine, boys!   60
Cassio: 'Fore God, an excellent song.
Iago: I learned it in England, where indeed they are most potent in potting.°
     Your Dane, your German, and your swag-bellied Hollander—drink, ho!—
     are nothing to your English.
Cassio: Is your Englishman so exquisite in his drinking?   65
Iago: Why, he drinks you,° with facility, your Dane° dead drunk; he sweats not°
     to overthrow your Almain;° he gives your Hollander a vomit ere the next
     pottle can be filled.
Cassio: To the health of our general!
Montano: I am for it, Lieutenant, and I'll do you justice.°   70
Iago: O sweet England! [*He sings.*]

     "King Stephen was and-a worthy peer,
     His breeches cost him but a crown;
     He held them sixpence all too dear,
     With that he called the tailor lown.°   75

     He was a wight of high renown,
     And thou art but of low degree.
     'Tis pride° that pulls the country down;
     Then take thy auld° cloak about thee."

     Some wine, ho!   80
Cassio: 'Fore God, this is a more exquisite song than the other.
Iago: Will you hear 't again?
Cassio: No, for I hold him to be unworthy of his place that does those things.
     Well, God's above all; and there be souls must be saved, and there be souls
     must not be saved.   85

---

50 *If . . . dream* if subsequent events will only substantiate my scheme   51 *stream* current   52 *rouse* full draft of liquor   55 *cannikin* small drinking vessel   58 *span* brief span of time. (Compare Psalm 39:6 as rendered in the 1928 Book of Common Prayer: "Thou hast made my days as it were a span long.")   62 *potting* drinking   66 *drinks you* drinks.   *your Dane* your typical Dane. *sweats not* i.e., need not exert himself   67 *Almain* German   70 *I'll . . . justice* i.e., I'll drink as much as you   75 *lown* lout, rascal   78 *pride* i.e., extravagance in dress   79 *auld* old

Iago: It's true, good Lieutenant.

Cassio: For mine own part—no offense to the General, nor any man of quality°—I hope to be saved.

Iago: And so do I too, Lieutenant.

Cassio: Ay, but, by your leave, not before me; the lieutenant is to be saved be- 90
fore the ancient. Let's have no more of this; let's to our affairs.—God forgive
us our sins!—Gentlemen, let's look to our business. Do not think, gentlemen, I am drunk. This is my ancient; this is my right hand, and this is my
left. I am not drunk now. I can stand well enough, and speak well enough.

Gentlemen: Excellent well. 95

Cassio: Why, very well then; you must not think then that I am drunk.   *Exit.*

Montano: To th' platform, masters. Come, let's set the watch.°

　　[*Exeunt Gentlemen.*]

Iago: You see this fellow that is gone before.
　　He's a soldier fit to stand by Caesar
　　And give direction; and do but see his vice. 100
　　'Tis to his virtue a just equinox,°
　　The one as long as th' other. 'Tis pity of him.
　　I fear the trust Othello puts him in,
　　On some odd time of his infirmity,
　　Will shake this island.

Montano:　　　　　　　But is he often thus? 105

Iago: 'Tis evermore the prologue to his sleep.
　　He'll watch the horologe a double set,°
　　If drink rock not his cradle.

Montano:　　　　　　　　　It were well
　　The General were put in mind of it.
　　Perhaps he sees it not, or his good nature 110
　　Prizes the virtue that appears in Cassio
　　And looks not on his evils. Is not this true?

　　Enter Roderigo.

Iago [aside to him]: How now, Roderigo?
　　I pray you, after the Lieutenant; go.　　　　　　　　[*Exit Roderigo.*]

Montano: And 'tis great pity that the noble Moor 115
　　Should hazard such a place as his own second
　　With° one of an engraffed° infirmity.
　　It were an honest action to say so
　　To the Moor.

88 *quality* rank   97 *set the watch* mount the guard   101 *just equinox* exact counterpart.
(*Equinox* is an equal length of days and nights.)   107 *watch . . . set* stay awake twice around
the clock or *horologe*   116–117 *hazard . . . With* risk giving such an important position as his
second in command to   117 *engraffed* engrafted, inveterate

Iago: Not I, for this fair island.
    I do love Cassio well and would do much   120
    To cure him of this evil.   [*Cry within:* "Help! Help!"]
            But, hark! What noise?

    Enter Cassio, pursuing° Roderigo.

Cassio: Zounds, you rogue! You rascal!
Montano: What's the matter, Lieutenant?
Cassio: A knave teach me my duty? I'll beat the knave into a twiggen° bottle.
Roderigo: Beat me?   125
Cassio: Dost thou prate, rogue?   [*He strikes Roderigo.*]
Montano: Nay, good Lieutenant. [*Restraining him.*] I pray you, sir, hold your hand.
Cassio: Let me go, sir, or I'll knock you o'er the mazard.°
Montano: Come, come, you're drunk.
Cassio: Drunk?   [*They fight.*]   130
Iago [*aside to Roderigo*]: Away, I say. Go out and cry a mutiny.°

    [*Exit Roderigo.*]

    Nay, good Lieutenant—God's will, gentlemen—
    Help, ho!—Lieutenant—sir—Montano—sir—
    Help, masters!°—Here's a goodly watch indeed!

    [*A bell rings.*]°

    Who's that which rings the bell?—Diablo,° ho!   135
    The town will rise.° God's will, Lieutenant, hold!
    You'll be ashamed forever.

    Enter Othello and attendants [*with weapons*].

Othello: What is the matter here?
Montano: Zounds, I bleed still.
    I am hurt to th' death. He dies!   [*He thrusts at Cassio.*]
Othello: Hold, for your lives!
Iago: Hold, ho! Lieutenant—sir—Montano—gentlemen—   140
    Have you forgot all sense of place and duty?
    Hold! The General speaks to you. Hold, for shame!
Othello: Why, how now, ho! From whence ariseth this?
    Are we turned Turks, and to ourselves do that
    Which heaven hath forbid the Ottomites?°   145

---

121 s.d. *pursuing* (The Quarto text reads, "driving in.")   124 *twiggen* wicker-covered. (Cassio
vows to assail Roderigo until his skin resembles wickerwork or until he has driven Roderigo
through the holes in a wickerwork.)   128 *mazard* i.e., head. (Literally, a drinking vessel.)
131 *mutiny* riot   134 *masters* sirs.   s.d. *A bell rings* (This direction is from the Quarto, as are
Exit Roderigo at line 114, *They fight* at line 130, and *with weapons* at line 137.)   135 *Diablo* the
devil   136 *rise* grow riotous   144–145 *to ourselves . . . Ottomites* inflict on ourselves the harm
that heaven has prevented the Turks from doing (by destroying their fleet)

For Christian shame, put by this barbarous brawl!
He that stirs next to carve for° his own rage
Holds his soul light;° he dies upon his motion.°
Silence that dreadful bell. It frights the isle
From her propriety.° What is the matter, masters?   150
Honest Iago, that looks dead with grieving,
Speak. Who began this? On thy love, I charge thee.

Iago: I do not know. Friends all but now, even now,
In quarter° and in terms° like bride and groom
Devesting them° for bed; and then, but now—   155
As if some planet had unwitted men—
Swords out, and tilting one at others' breasts
In opposition bloody. I cannot speak°
Any beginning to this peevish odds;°
And would in action glorious I had lost   160
Those legs that brought me to a part of it!

Othello: How comes it, Michael, you are thus forgot?°

Cassio: I pray you, pardon me. I cannot speak.

Othello: Worthy Montano, you were wont be° civil;
The gravity and stillness° of your youth   165
The world hath noted, and your name is great
In mouths of wisest censure.° What's the matter
That you unlace° your reputation thus
And spend your rich opinion° for the name
Of a night-brawler? Give me answer to it.   170

Montano: Worthy Othello, I am hurt to danger.
Your officer, Iago, can inform you—
While I spare speech, which something° now offends° me—
Of all that I do know; nor know I aught
By me that's said or done amiss this night,   175
Unless self-charity be sometimes a vice,
And to defend ourselves it be a sin
When violence assails us.

Othello: Now, by heaven,
My blood° begins my safer guides° to rule,
And passion, having my best judgment collied,°   180
Essays° to lead the way. Zounds, if I stir,
Or do but lift this arm, the best of you

---

147 *carve for* i.e., indulge, satisfy with his sword   148 *Holds . . . light* i.e., places little value on his life.   *upon his motion* if he moves   150 *propriety* proper state or condition   154 *In quarter* in friendly conduct, within bounds.   *in terms* on good terms   155 *Devesting them* undressing themselves   158 *speak* explain   159 *peevish odds* childish quarrel   162 *are thus forgot* have forgotten yourself thus   164 *wont be* accustomed to be   165 *stillness* sobriety   167 *censure* judgment   168 *unlace* undo, lay open (as one might loose the strings of a purse containing reputation)   169 *opinion* reputation   173 *something* somewhat.   *offends* pains   179 *blood* passion (of anger).   *guides* i.e., reason   180 *collied* darkened   181 *Essays* undertakes

Shall sink in my rebuke. Give me to know
How this foul rout° began, who set it on;
And he that is approved in° this offense,   185
Though he had twinned with me, both at a birth,
Shall lose me. What? In a town of° war
Yet wild, the people's hearts brim full of fear,
To manage° private and domestic quarrel?
In night, and on the court and guard of safety?°   190
'Tis monstrous. Iago, who began 't?
Montano [to Iago]: If partially affined,° or leagued in office,°
Thou dost deliver more or less than truth,
Thou art no soldier.
Iago: Touch me not so near.
I had rather have this tongue cut from my mouth   195
Than it should do offense to Michael Cassio;
Yet, I persuade myself, to speak the truth
Shall nothing wrong him. Thus it is, General.
Montano and myself being in speech,
There comes a fellow crying out for help,   200
And Cassio following him with determined sword
To execute° upon him. Sir, this gentleman

[indicating Montano]

Steps in to Cassio and entreats his pause.°
Myself the crying fellow did pursue,
Lest by his clamor—as it so fell out—   205
The town might fall in fright. He, swift of foot,
Outran my purpose, and I returned, the rather°
For that I heard the clink and fall of swords
And Cassio high in oath, which till tonight
I ne'er might say before. When I came back—   210
For this was brief—I found them close together
At blow and thrust, even as again they were
When you yourself did part them.
More of this matter cannot I report.
But men are men; the best sometimes forget.°   215
Though Cassio did some little wrong to him,
As men in rage strike those that wish them best,°
Yet surely Cassio, I believe, received

---

184 *rout* riot   185 *approved in* found guilty of   187 *town of* town garrisoned for   189 *manage* undertake   190 *on . . . safety* at the main guardhouse or headquarters and on watch   192 *partially affined* made partial by some personal relationship.   *leagued in office* in league as fellow officers   202 *execute* give effect to (his anger)   203 *his pause* him to stop   207 *rather* sooner   215 *forget* forget themselves   217 *those . . . best* i.e., even those who are well disposed

From him that fled some strange indignity,
Which patience could not pass.°

Othello: I know, Iago,   220
Thy honesty and love doth mince this matter,
Making it light to Cassio. Cassio, I love thee,
But nevermore be officer of mine.

Enter Desdemona, attended.

Look if my gentle love be not raised up.
I'll make thee an example.   225

Desdemona: What is the matter, dear?

Othello: All's well now, sweeting;
Come away to bed. [*To Montano.*] Sir, for your hurts,
Myself will be your surgeon.°—Lead him off.

[*Montano is led off.*]

Iago, look with care about the town
And silence those whom this vile brawl distracted.   230
Come, Desdemona. 'Tis the soldiers' life
To have their balmy slumbers waked with strife.

Exit [with all but Iago and Cassio].

Iago: What, are you hurt, Lieutenant?

Cassio: Ay, past all surgery.

Iago: Marry, God forbid!   235

Cassio: Reputation, reputation, reputation! O, I have lost my reputation! I have
lost the immortal part of myself, and what remains is bestial. My reputation,
Iago, my reputation!

Iago: As I am an honest man, I thought you had received some bodily wound;
there is more sense in that than in reputation. Reputation is an idle and   240
most false imposition,° oft got without merit and lost without deserving.
You have lost no reputation at all, unless you repute yourself such a loser.
What, man, there are more ways to recover° the General again. You are but
now cast in his mood°—a punishment more in policy° than in malice, even
so as one would beat his offenseless dog to affright an imperious lion.°   245
Sue° to him again and he's yours.

Cassio: I will rather sue to be despised than to deceive so good a commander
with so slight,° so drunken, and so indiscreet an officer. Drunk? And speak
parrot?° And squabble? Swagger? Swear? And discourse fustian with one's

220 *pass* pass over, overlook   228 *be your surgeon* i.e., make sure you receive medical attention
241 *false imposition* thing artificially imposed and of no real value   243 *recover* regain favor
with   244 *cast in his mood* dismissed in a moment of anger.   *in policy* done for expediency's
sake and as a public gesture   245 *would . . . lion* i.e., would make an example of a minor offender in order to deter more important and dangerous offenders   246 *Sue* petition   248 *slight*
worthless   248–249 *speak parrot* talk nonsense, rant

own shadow? O thou invisible spirit of wine, if thou hast no name to be 250
known by, let us call thee devil!

Iago: What was he that you followed with your sword? What had he done to you?

Cassio: I know not.

Iago: Is 't possible?

Cassio: I remember a mass of things, but nothing distinctly; a quarrel, but 255
nothing wherefore.° O God, that men should put an enemy in their mouths
to steal away their brains! That we should, with joy, pleasance, revel, and
applause° transform ourselves into beasts!

Iago: Why, but you are now well enough. How came you thus recovered?

Cassio: It hath pleased the devil drunkenness to give place to the devil wrath. 260
One unperfectness shows me another, to make me frankly despise myself.

Iago: Come, you are too severe a moraler.° As the time, the place, and the condition of this country stands, I could heartily wish this had not befallen; but
since it is as it is, mend it for your own good.

Cassio: I will ask him for my place again; he shall tell me I am a drunkard. Had I 265
as many mouths as Hydra,° such an answer would stop them all. To be now
a sensible man, by and by a fool, and presently a beast! O, strange! Every inordinate cup is unblessed, and the ingredient is a devil.

Iago: Come, come, good wine is a good familiar creature, if it be well used.
Exclaim no more against it. And, good Lieutenant, I think you think I love 270
you.

Cassio: I have well approved° it, sir. I drunk!

Iago: You or any man living may be drunk at a time,° man. I'll tell you what you
shall do. Our general's wife is now the general—I may say so in this respect,
for that° he hath devoted and given up himself to the contemplation, mark, 275
and denotement° of her parts° and graces. Confess yourself freely to her; im-
portune her help to put you in your place again. She is of so free,° so kind, so
apt, so blessed a disposition, she holds it a vice in her goodness not to do
more than she is requested. This broken joint between you and her husband
entreat her to splinter;° and, my fortunes against any lay° worth naming, 280
this crack of your love shall grow stronger than it was before.

Cassio: You advise me well.

Iago: I protest,° in the sincerity of love and honest kindness.

Cassio: I think it freely;° and betimes in the morning I will beseech the virtuous
Desdemona to undertake for me. I am desperate of my fortunes if they 285
check° me here.

Iago: You are in the right. Good night, Lieutenant. I must to the watch.

256 *wherefore* why   258 *applause* desire for applause   262 *moraler* moralizer   266 *Hydra* the Ler-
naean Hydra, a monster with many heads and the ability to grow two heads when one was cut off,
slain by Hercules as the second of his twelve labors   272 *approved* proved   273 *at a time* at one
time or another   274–275 *in . . . that* in view of this fact, that   275–276 *mark, and denotement*
(Both words mean "observation.")   276 *parts* qualities   277 *free* generous   280 *splinter* bind with
splints.   *lay* stake, wager   283 *protest* insist, declare   284 *freely* unreservedly   286 *check* repulse

Cassio: Good night, honest Iago.   *Exit Cassio.*
Iago: And what's he then that says I play the villain,
    When this advice is free° I give, and honest,   290
    Probal° to thinking, and indeed the course
    To win the Moor again? For 'tis most easy
    Th' inclining° Desdemona to subdue°
    In any honest suit; she's framed as fruitful°
    As the free elements.° And then for her   295
    To win the Moor—were 't to renounce his baptism,
    All seals and symbols of redeemèd sin—
    His soul is so enfettered to her love
    That she may make, unmake, do what she list,
    Even as her appetite° shall play the god   300
    With his weak function.° How am I then a villain,
    To counsel Cassio to this parallel° course
    Directly to his good? Divinity of hell!°
    When devils will the blackest sins put on,°
    They do suggest° at first with heavenly shows,   305
    As I do now. For whiles this honest fool
    Plies Desdemona to repair his fortune,
    And she for him pleads strongly to the Moor,
    I'll pour this pestilence into his ear,
    That she repeals him° for her body's lust;   310
    And by how much she strives to do him good,
    She shall undo her credit with the Moor.
    So will I turn her virtue into pitch,°
    And out of her own goodness make the net
    That shall enmesh them all.

    Enter Roderigo.

                         How now, Roderigo?   315
Roderigo: I do follow here in the chase, not like a hound that hunts, but one that
    fills up the cry.° My money is almost spent; I have been tonight exceedingly
    well cudgeled; and I think the issue will be I shall have so much° experience
    for my pains, and so, with no money at all and a little more wit, return again
    to Venice.   320

290 *free* (1) free from guile (2) freely given   291 *Probal* probable, reasonable   293 *inclining* favorably disposed.   *subdue* persuade   294 *framed as fruitful* created as generous   295 *free elements* i.e., earth, air, fire, and water, unrestrained and spontaneous   300 *her appetite* her desire, or, perhaps, his desire for her   301 *function* exercise of faculties (weakened by his fondness for her)   302 *parallel* corresponding to these facts and to his best interests   303 *Divinity of hell* inverted theology of hell (which seduces the soul to its damnation)   304 *put on* further, instigate   305 *suggest* tempt   310 *repeals him* attempts to get him restored   313 *pitch* i.e., (1) foul blackness (2) a snaring substance   317 *fills up the cry* merely takes part as one of the pack   318 *so much* just so much and no more

Iago: How poor are they that have not patience!
    What wound did ever heal but by degrees?
    Thou know'st we work by wit, and not by witchcraft,
    And wit depends on dilatory time.
    Does 't not go well? Cassio hath beaten thee,   325
    And thou, by that small hurt, hast cashiered° Cassio.
    Though other things grow fair against the sun,
    Yet fruits that blossom first will first be ripe.°
    Content thyself awhile. By the Mass, 'tis morning!
    Pleasure and action make the hours seem short.   330
    Retire thee; go where thou art billeted.
    Away, I say! Thou shalt know more hereafter.
    Nay, get thee gone.   *Exit Roderigo.*
                            Two things are to be done.
    My wife must move° for Cassio to her mistress;
    I'll set her on;   335
    Myself the while to draw the Moor apart
    And bring him jump° when he may Cassio find
    Soliciting his wife. Ay, that's the way.
    Dull not device° by coldness° and delay.   *Exit.*

Act III

Scene I [Before the Chamber of Othello and Desdemona.]

Enter Cassio [and] Musicians.

Cassio: Masters, play here—I will content your pains°—
    Something that's brief, and bid "Good morrow, General."   [*They play.*]

    [*Enter*] *Clown.*

Clown: Why, masters, have your instruments been in Naples, that they speak i'
    the nose° thus?
A Musician: How, sir, how?   5
Clown: Are these, I pray you, wind instruments?
A Musician: Ay, marry, are they, sir.
Clown: O, thereby hangs a tail.
A Musician: Whereby hangs a tale, sir?

---

326 *cashiered* dismissed from service   327–328 *Though . . . ripe* i.e., plans that are well prepared
and set expeditiously in motion will soonest ripen into success   334 *move* plead   337 *jump*
precisely   339 *device* plot.   *coldness* lack of zeal   1 *content your pains* reward your efforts   3–4
speak i' the nose (1) sound nasal (2) sound like one whose nose has been attacked by syphilis.
(Naples was popularly supposed to have a high incidence of venereal disease.)

Clown: Marry, sir, by many a wind instrument° that I know. But, masters, here's   10
money for you. [*He gives money.*] And the General so likes your music that
he desires you, for love's sake,° to make no more noise with it.
A Musician: Well, sir, we will not.
Clown: If you have any music that may not° be heard, to 't again; but, as they
say, to hear music the General does not greatly care.   15
A Musician: We have none such, sir.
Clown: Then put up your pipes in your bag, for I'll away.° Go, vanish into air,
away!   *Exeunt Musicians.*
Cassio: Dost thou hear, mine honest friend?
Clown: No, I hear not your honest friend; I hear you.   20
Cassio: Prithee, keep up° thy quillets.° There's a poor piece of gold for thee. [*He
gives money.*] If the gentle-woman that attends the General's wife be stirring,
tell her there's one Cassio entreats her a little favor of speech.° Wilt thou do
this?
Clown: She is stirring, sir. If she will stir° hither, I shall seem° to notify unto her.   25
Cassio: Do, good my friend.   *Exit Clown.*

    Enter Iago.

                    In happy time,° Iago.
Iago: You have not been abed, then?
Cassio: Why, no. The day had broke
Before we parted. I have made bold, Iago,
To send in to your wife. My suit to her   30
Is that she will to virtuous Desdemona
Procure me some access.
Iago: I'll send her to you presently;
And I'll devise a means to draw the Moor
Out of the way, that your converse and business   35
May be more free.
Cassio: I humbly thank you for 't.   *Exit [Iago].*
                  I never knew
A Florentine° more kind and honest.

    Enter Emilia.

Emilia: Good morrow, good Lieutenant. I am sorry
For your displeasure;° but all will sure be well.   40
The General and his wife are talking of it,

---

10 *wind instrument* (With a joke on flatulence.   The *tail*, line 8, that hangs nearby the *wind instrument* suggests the penis.)   12 *for love's sake* (1) out of friendship and affection (2) for the sake
of lovemaking in Othello's marriage   14 *may not* cannot   17 *I'll away* (Possibly a misprint, or a
snatch of song?)   21 *keep up* do not bring out, do not use.   *quillets* quibbles, puns   23 *a little . . .
speech* the favor of a brief talk   25 *stir* bestir herself (with a play on *stirring,* "rousing herself from
rest")   *seem* deem it good, think fit   26 *In happy time* i.e., well met   38 *Florentine* i.e., even a
fellow Florentine. (Iago is a Venetian; Cassio is a Florentine.)   40 *displeasure* fall from favor

And she speaks for you stoutly.° The Moor replies
That he you hurt is of great fame° in Cyprus
And great affinity,° and that in wholesome wisdom
He might not but refuse you; but he protests° he loves you   45
And needs no other suitor but his likings
To take the safest occasion by the front°
To bring you in again.
Cassio: Yet I beseech you,
  If you think fit, or that it may be done,
  Give me advantage of some brief discourse   50
  With Desdemona alone.
Emilia: Pray you, come in.
                         I will bestow you where you shall have time
  To speak your bosom° freely.
Cassio: I am much bound to you.   [Exeunt.]

Scene II [The Citadel.]

Enter Othello, Iago, and Gentlemen.

Othello [*giving letters*]: These letters give, Iago, to the pilot,
  And by him do my duties° to the Senate.
  That done, I will be walking on the works;°
  Repair° there to me.
Iago: Well, my good lord, I'll do 't.
Othello: This fortification, gentlemen, shall we see 't?   5
Gentlemen: We'll wait upon° your lordship.   *Exeunt.*

Scene III [The Garden of the Citadel.]

Enter Desdemona, Cassio, and Emilia.

Desdemona: Be thou assured, good Cassio, I will do
  All my abilities in thy behalf.
Emilia: Good madam, do. I warrant it grieves my husband
  As if the cause were his.
Desdemona: O, that's an honest fellow. Do not doubt, Cassio,   5
  But I will have my lord and you again
  As friendly as you were.
Cassio: Bounteous madam,
  Whatever shall become of Michael Cassio,
  He's never anything but your true servant.

---

42 *stoutly* spiritedly   43 *fame* reputation, importance   44 *affinity* kindred, family connection
45 *protests* insists   47 *occasion . . . front* opportunity by the forelock   53 *bosom* inmost
thoughts   2 *do my duties* convey my respects   3 *works* breastworks, fortifications   4 *Repair* return, come   6 *wait upon* attend

Desdemona: I know 't. I thank you. You do love my lord;   10
　　　You have known him long, and be you well assured
　　　He shall in strangeness° stand no farther off
　　　Than in a politic° distance.
Cassio:　　　　　　　　　　　Ay, but, lady,
　　　That policy may either last so long,
　　　Or feed upon such nice and waterish diet,°   15
　　　Or breed itself so out of circumstance,°
　　　That, I being absent and my place supplied,°
　　　My general will forget my love and service.
Desdemona: Do not doubt° that. Before Emilia here
　　　I give thee warrant° of thy place. Assure thee,   20
　　　If I do vow a friendship I'll perform it
　　　To the last article. My lord shall never rest.
　　　I'll watch him tame° and talk him out of patience;°
　　　His bed shall seem a school, his board° a shrift;°
　　　I'll intermingle everything he does   25
　　　With Cassio's suit. Therefore be merry, Cassio,
　　　For thy solicitor° shall rather die
　　　Than give thy cause away.°

　　　Enter Othello and Iago [at a distance].

Emilia: Madam, here comes my lord.
Cassio: Madam, I'll take my leave.
Desdemona: Why, stay, and hear me speak.   30
Cassio: Madam, not now. I am very ill at ease,
　　　Unfit for mine own purposes.
Desdemona: Well, do your discretion.°   *Exit Cassio.*
Iago: Ha? I like not that.   35
Othello: What dost thou say?
Iago: Nothing, my lord; or if—I know not what.
Othello: Was not that Cassio parted from my wife?
Iago: Cassio, my lord? No, sure, I cannot think it,
　　　That he would steal away so guiltylike,   40
　　　Seeing you coming.
Othello: I do believe 'twas he.
Desdemona: How now, my lord?
　　　I have been talking with a suitor here,

---

12 *strangeness* aloofness   13 *politic* required by wise policy   15 *Or* . . . *diet* or sustain itself at
length upon such trivial and meager technicalities   16 *breed* . . . *circumstance* continually
renew itself so out of chance events, or yield so few chances for my being pardoned   17
supplied filled by another person   19 *doubt* fear   20 *warrant* guarantee   23 *watch him tame*
tame him by keeping him from sleeping. (A term from falconry.)   *out of patience* past his endurance   24 *board* dining table.   *shrift* confessional   27 *solicitor* advocate   28 *away* up   34
do your discretion act according to your own discretion

A man that languishes in your displeasure.   45

Othello: Who is 't you mean?

Desdemona: Why, your lieutenant, Cassio. Good my lord,
    If I have any grace or power to move you,
    His present reconciliation take;°
    For if he be not one that truly loves you,   50
    That errs in ignorance and not in cunning,°
    I have no judgment in an honest face.
    I prithee, call him back.

Othello: Went he hence now?

Desdemona: Yes, faith, so humbled   55
    That he hath left part of his grief with me
    To suffer with him. Good love, call him back.

Othello: Not now, sweet Desdemon. Some other time.

Desdemona: But shall 't be shortly?

Othello: The sooner, sweet, for you.   60

Desdemona: Shall 't be tonight at supper?

Othello: No, not tonight.

Desdemona: Tomorrow dinner,° then?

Othello: I shall not dine at home.
    I meet the captains at the citadel.   65

Desdemona: Why, then, tomorrow night, or Tuesday morn,
    On Tuesday noon, or night, on Wednesday morn.
    I prithee, name the time, but let it not
    Exceed three days. In faith, he's penitent;
    And yet his trespass, in our common reason°—   70
    Save that, they say, the wars must make example
    Out of her best°—is not almost° a fault
    T' incur a private check.° When shall he come?
    Tell me, Othello. I wonder in my soul
    What you would ask me that I should deny,   75
    Or stand so mammering on.° What? Michael Cassio,
    That came a-wooing with you, and so many a time,
    When I have spoke of you dispraisingly,
    Hath ta'en your part—to have so much to do
    To bring him in!° By 'r Lady, I could do much—   80

Othello: Prithee, no more. Let him come when he will;
    I will deny thee nothing.

Desdemona: Why, this is not a boon.
    'Tis as I should entreat you wear your gloves,

49 *His . . . take* let him be reconciled to you right away   51 *in cunning* wittingly   63 *dinner* (The noontime meal.)   70 *common reason* everyday judgments   71–72 *Save . . . best* were it not that, as the saying goes, military discipline requires making an example of the very best men. (Her refers to *wars* as a singular concept.)   72 *not almost* scarcely   73 *private check* even a private reprimand   76 *mammering on* wavering about   80 *bring him in* restore him to favor

Or feed on nourishing dishes, or keep you warm,   85
Or sue to you to do a peculiar° profit
To your own person. Nay, when I have a suit
Wherein I mean to touch° your love indeed,
It shall be full of poise° and difficult weight,
And fearful to be granted.   90
Othello: I will deny thee nothing.
Whereon,° I do beseech thee, grant me this,
To leave me but a little to myself.
Desdemona: Shall I deny you? No. Farewell, my lord.
Othello: Farewell, my Desdemona. I'll come to thee straight.°   95
Desdemona: Emilia, come.—Be as your fancies° teach you;
Whate'er you be, I am obedient.   *Exit [with Emilia].*
Othello: Excellent wretch!° Perdition catch my soul
But I do love thee! And when I love thee not,
Chaos is come again.°   100
Iago: My noble lord—
Othello: What dost thou say, Iago?
Iago: Did Michael Cassio, when you wooed my lady,
Know of your love?
Othello: He did, from first to last. Why dost thou ask?   105
Iago: But for a satisfaction of my thought;
No further harm.
Othello: Why of thy thought, Iago?
Iago: I did not think he had been acquainted with her.
Othello: O, yes, and went between us very oft.
Iago: Indeed?   110
Othello: Indeed? Ay, indeed. Discern'st thou aught in that?
Is he not honest?
Iago: Honest, my lord?
Othello: Honest. Ay, honest.
Iago: My lord, for aught I know.   115
Othello: What dost thou think?
Iago: Think, my lord?
Othello: "Think, my lord?" By heaven, thou echo'st me,
As if there were some monster in thy thought
Too hideous to be shown. Thou dost mean something.   120
I heard thee say even now, thou lik'st not that,
When Cassio left my wife. What didst not like?

---

86 *peculiar* particular, personal   88 *touch* test   89 *poise* weight, heaviness; or equipoise, delicate balance involving hard choice   92 *Whereon* in return for which   95 *straight* straightway
96 *fancies* inclinations   98 *wretch* (A term of affectionate endearment.)   99–100 *And . . .
again* i.e., my love for you will last forever, until the end of time when chaos will return. (But
with an unconscious, ironic suggestion that, if anything should induce Othello to cease loving
Desdemona, the result would be chaos.)

And when I told thee he was of my counsel°
In my whole course of wooing, thou criedst "Indeed?"
And didst contract and purse° thy brow together   125
As if thou then hadst shut up in thy brain
Some horrible conceit.° If thou dost love me,
Show me thy thought.

Iago: My lord, you know I love you.

Othello: I think thou dost;   130
And, for° I know thou'rt full of love and honesty,
And weigh'st thy words before thou giv'st them breath,
Therefore these stops° of thine fright me the more;
For such things in a false disloyal knave
Are tricks of custom,° but in a man that's just   135
They're close dilations,° working from the heart
That passion cannot rule.°

Iago: For° Michael Cassio,
I dare be sworn I think that he is honest.

Othello: I think so too.

Iago: Men should be what they seem;
Or those that be not, would they might seem none!°   140

Othello: Certain, men should be what they seem.

Iago: Why, then, I think Cassio's an honest man.

Othello: Nay, yet there's more in this.
I prithee, speak to me as to thy thinkings,
As thou dost ruminate, and give thy worst of thoughts   145
The worst of words.

Iago: Good my lord, pardon me.
Though I am bound to every act of duty,
I am not bound to that° all slaves are free to.°
Utter my thoughts? Why, say they are vile and false,
As where's the palace whereinto foul things   150
Sometimes intrude not? Who has that breast so pure
But some uncleanly apprehensions
Keep leets and law days,° and in sessions sit
With° meditations lawful?°

Othello: Thou dost conspire against thy friend,° Iago,   155
If thou but think'st him wronged and mak'st his ear
A stranger to thy thoughts.

---

123 *of my counsel* in my confidence   125 *purse* knit   127 *conceit* fancy   131 *for* because   133
stops pauses   135 *of custom* customary   136 *close dilations* secret or involuntary expressions or
delays   137 *That passion cannot rule* i.e., that are too passionately strong to be restrained (referring to the workings), or that cannot rule its own passions (referring to the heart).   137 *For* as
for   140 *none* i.e., not to be men, or not seem to be honest   148 *that* that which. *free to* free
with respect to   153 *Keep leets and law days* i.e., hold court, set up their authority in one's
heart. (*Leets* are a kind of manor court; *law days* are the days courts sit in session, or those sessions.)   154 *With* along with. *lawful* innocent   155 *thy friend* i.e., Othello

Iago: I do beseech you,
    Though I perchance am vicious° in my guess—
    As I confess it is my nature's plague
    To spy into abuses, and oft my jealousy°   160
    Shapes faults that are not—that your wisdom then,°
    From one° that so imperfectly conceits,°
    Would take no notice, nor build yourself a trouble
    Out of his scattering° and unsure observance.
    It were not for your quiet nor your good,   165
    Nor for my manhood, honesty, and wisdom,
    To let you know my thoughts.
Othello: What dost thou mean?
Iago: Good name in man and woman, dear my lord,
    Is the immediate° jewel of their souls.
    Who steals my purse steals trash; 'tis something, nothing; 170
    'Twas mine, 'tis his, and has been slave to thousands;
    But he that filches from me my good name
    Robs me of that which not enriches him
    And makes me poor indeed.
Othello: By heaven, I'll know thy thoughts.   175
Iago: You cannot, if° my heart were in your hand,
    Nor shall not, whilst 'tis in my custody.
Othello: Ha?
Iago: O, beware, my lord, of jealousy.
    It is the green-eyed monster which doth mock
    The meat it feeds on.° That cuckold lives in bliss   180
    Who, certain of his fate, loves not his wronger;°
    But O, what damnèd minutes tells° he o'er
    Who dotes, yet doubts, suspects, yet fondly loves!
Othello: O misery!
Iago: Poor and content is rich, and rich enough,°   185
    But riches fineless° is as poor as winter
    To him that ever fears he shall be poor.
    Good God, the souls of all my tribe defend
    From jealousy!
Othello: Why, why is this?   190
    Think'st thou I'd make a life of jealousy,
    To follow still the changes of the moon

---

158 *vicious* wrong   160 *jealousy* suspicious nature   161 *then* on that account   162 *one* i.e.,
myself, Iago.   *conceits* judges, conjectures   164 *scattering* random   169 *immediate* essential,
most precious   176 *if* even if   179–180 *doth mock . . . on* mocks and torments the heart of its
victim, the man who suffers jealousy   181 *his wronger* i.e., his faithless wife. (The unsuspecting
cuckold is spared the misery of loving his wife only to discover she is cheating on him.)   182
tells counts   185 *Poor . . . enough* to be content with what little one has is the greatest wealth
of all. (Proverbial.)   186 *fineless* boundless

With fresh suspicions?° No! To be once in doubt
Is once° to be resolved.° Exchange me for a goat
When I shall turn the business of my soul   195
To such exsufflicate and blown° surmises
Matching thy inference.° 'Tis not to make me jealous
To say my wife is fair, feeds well, loves company,
Is free of speech, sings, plays, and dances well;
Where virtue is, these are more virtuous.   200
Nor from mine own weak merits will I draw
The smallest fear or doubt of her revolt,°
For she had eyes, and chose me. No, Iago,
I'll see before I doubt; when I doubt, prove;
And on the proof, there is no more but this—   205
Away at once with love or jealousy.

Iago: I am glad of this, for now I shall have reason
To show the love and duty that I bear you
With franker spirit. Therefore, as I am bound,
Receive it from me. I speak not yet of proof.   210
Look to your wife; observe her well with Cassio.
Wear your eyes thus, not° jealous nor secure.°
I would not have your free and noble nature,
Out of self-bounty,° be abused.° Look to 't.
I know our country disposition well;   215
In Venice they do let God see the pranks
They dare not show their husbands; their best conscience
Is not to leave 't undone, but keep 't unknown.

Othello: Dost thou say so?

Iago: She did deceive her father, marrying you;   220
And when she seemed to shake and fear your looks,
She loved them most.

Othello: And so she did.

Iago: Why, go to,° then!
She that, so young, could give out such a seeming,°
To seel° her father's eyes up close as oak,°
He thought 'twas witchcraft! But I am much to blame.   225
I humbly do beseech you of your pardon
For too much loving you.

192–193 _To follow . . . suspicions_ to be constantly imagining new causes for suspicion, changing
incessantly like the moon   194 _once_ once and for all.   _resolved_ free of doubt, having settled
the matter   196 _exsufflicate and blown_ inflated and blown up, rumored about, or, spat out and fly-
blown, hence, loathsome, disgusting   197 _inference_ description or allegation   202 _doubt . . ._
revolt fear of her unfaithfulness   212 _not_ neither.   _secure_ free from uncertainty   214 _self-_
bounty inherent or natural goodness and generosity.   _abused_ deceived   222 _go to_ (An expression of impatience.)   223 _seeming_ false appearance   224 _seel_ blind. (A term from falconry.)
oak (A close-grained wood.)

Othello: I am bound° to thee forever.
Iago: I see this hath a little dashed your spirits.
Othello: Not a jot, not a jot.
Iago: I' faith, I fear it has.   230
    I hope you will consider what is spoke
    Comes from my love. But I do see you're moved.
    I am to pray you not to strain my speech
    To grosser issues° nor to larger reach°
    Than to suspicion.   235
Othello: I will not.
Iago: Should you do so, my lord,
    My speech should fall into such vile success°
    Which my thoughts aimed not. Cassio's my worthy friend.
    My lord, I see you're moved.
Othello: No, not much moved.   240
    I do not think but Desdemona's honest.°
Iago: Long live she so! And long live you to think so!
Othello: And yet, how nature erring from itself—
Iago: Ay, there's the point! As—to be bold with you—
    Not to affect° many proposèd matches   245
    Of her own clime, complexion, and degree,°
    Whereto we see in all things nature tends—
    Foh! One may smell in such a will° most rank,
    Foul disproportion,° thoughts unnatural.
    But pardon me. I do not in position°   250
    Distinctly speak of her, though I may fear
    Her will, recoiling° to her better° judgment,
    May fall to match you with her country forms°
    And happily° repent.
Othello: Farewell, farewell!
    If more thou dost perceive, let me know more.   255
    Set on thy wife to observe. Leave me, Iago.
Iago [going]: My lord, I take my leave.
Othello: Why did I marry? This honest creature doubtless
    Sees and knows more, much more, than he unfolds.
Iago [returning]: My Lord, I would I might entreat your honor   260
    To scan° this thing no farther. Leave it to time.

228 *bound* indebted (but perhaps with ironic sense of "tied")   234 *issues* significances.   *reach* meaning, scope   238 *success* effect, result   241 *honest* chaste   245 *affect* prefer, desire   246 *clime . . . degree* country, color, and social position   248 *will* sensuality, appetite   249 *disproportion* abnormality   250 *position* argument, proposition   252 *recoiling* reverting.   *better* i.e., more natural and reconsidered   253 *fall . . . forms* undertake to compare you with Venetian norms of handsomeness   254 *happily repent* haply repent her marriage   261 *scan* scrutinize

Although 'tis fit that Cassio have his place—
For, sure, he fills it up with great ability—
Yet, if you please to hold him off awhile,
You shall by that perceive him and his means.° 265
Note if your lady strain his entertainment°
With any strong or vehement importunity;
Much will be seen in that. In the meantime,
Let me be thought too busy° in my fears—
As worthy cause I have to fear I am— 270
And hold her free,° I do beseech your honor.
Othello: Fear not my government.°
Iago: I once more take my leave. *Exit.*
Othello: This fellow's of exceeding honesty,
And knows all qualities,° with a learnèd spirit, 275
Of human dealings. If I do prove her haggard,°
Though that her jesses° were my dear heartstrings,
I'd whistle her off and let her down the wind°
To prey at fortune.° Haply, for° I am black
And have not those soft parts of conversation° 280
That chamberers° have, or for I am declined
Into the vale of years—yet that's not much—
She's gone. I am abused,° and my relief
Must be to loathe her. O curse of marriage,
That we can call these delicate creatures ours 285
And not their appetites! I had rather be a toad
And live upon the vapor of a dungeon
Than keep a corner in the thing I love
For others' uses. Yet, 'tis the plague of great ones;
Prerogatived° are they less than the base.° 290
'Tis destiny unshunnable, like death.
Even then this forkèd° plague is fated to us
When we do quicken.° Look where she comes.

---

265 *his means* the method he uses (to regain his post)   266 *strain his entertainment* urge his re-instatement   269 *busy* interfering   271 *hold her free* regard her as innocent   272 *government* self-control, conduct   275 *qualities* natures, types   276 *haggard* wild (like a wild female hawk)   277 *jesses* straps fastened around the legs of a trained hawk   278 *I'd . . . wind* i.e., I'd let her go forever. (To release a hawk downwind was to invite it not to return.)   279 *prey at fortune* fend for herself in the wild.   *Haply, for* perhaps because   280 *soft . . . conversation* pleasing graces of social behavior   281 *chamberers* gallants   283 *abused* deceived   290 *Prerogatived* privi-leged (to have honest wives).   *the base* ordinary citizens. (Socially prominent men are espe-cially prone to the unavoidable destiny of being cuckolded and to the public shame that goes with it.)   292 *forkèd* (An allusion to the horns of the cuckold.)   293 *quicken* receive life. (Quicken may also mean to swarm with maggots as the body festers, as in Act IV, Scene ii, line 69, in which case lines 292–293 suggest that *even then*, in death, we are cuckolded by *forkèd* worms.)

Enter Desdemona and Emilia.

　　If she be false, O, then heaven mocks itself!
　　I'll not believe 't.
Desdemona:　　　　　How now, my dear Othello?
　　Your dinner, and the generous° islanders
　　By you invited, do attend° your presence.
Othello: I am to blame.
Desdemona:　　　　　Why do you speak so faintly?
　　Are you not well?
Othello: I have a pain upon my forehead here.
Desdemona: Faith, that's with watching.° 'Twill away again.

　　　　[*She offers her handkerchief.*]

　　Let me but bind it hard, within this hour
　　It will be well.
Othello:　　　　　Your napkin° is too little.
　　Let it alone.° Come, I'll go in with you.

　　　　[*He puts the handkerchief from him, and it drops.*]

Desdemona: I am very sorry that you are not well.

　　　　Exit [*with Othello*].

Emilia [*picking up the handkerchief*]: I am glad I have found this napkin.
　　This was her first remembrance from the Moor.
　　My wayward° husband hath a hundred times
　　Wooed me to steal it, but she so loves the token—
　　For he conjured her she should ever keep it—
　　That she reserves it evermore about her
　　To kiss and talk to. I'll have the work ta'en out,°
　　And give 't Iago. What he will do with it
　　Heaven knows, not I;
　　I nothing but to please his fantasy.°

　　　　Enter Iago.

Iago: How now? What do you here alone?
Emilia: Do not you chide. I have a thing for you.
Iago: You have a thing for me? It is a common thing°—
Emilia: Ha?
Iago: To have a foolish wife.
Emilia: O, is that all? What will you give me now

295

300

305

310

315

320

296 *generous* noble　297 *attend* await　301 *watching* too little sleep　303 *napkin* handkerchief
304 *Let it alone* i.e., never mind　308 *wayward* capricious　312 *work ta'en out* design of the
embroidery copied　315 *fantasy* whim　318 *common thing* (With bawdy suggestion; *common*
suggests coarseness and availability to all comers, and *thing* is a slang term for the pudendum.)

For that same handkerchief?

Iago: What handkerchief?

Emilia: What handkerchief?
Why, that the Moor first gave to Desdemona;   325
That which so often you did bid me steal.

Iago: Hast stolen it from her?

Emilia: No, faith. She let it drop by negligence,
And to th' advantage° I, being here, took 't up.
Look, here 'tis.

Iago: A good wench! Give it me.   330

Emilia: What will you do with 't, that you have been so earnest
To have me filch it?

Iago [*snatching it*]:   Why, what is that to you?

Emilia: If it be not for some purpose of import,
Give 't me again. Poor lady, she'll run mad
When she shall lack° it.

Iago: Be not acknown on 't.°   335
I have use for it. Go, leave me.   *Exit Emilia.*
I will in Cassio's lodging lose° this napkin
And let him find it. Trifles light as air
Are to the jealous confirmations strong
As proofs of Holy Writ. This may do something.   340
The Moor already changes with my poison.
Dangerous conceits° are in their natures poisons,
Which at the first are scarce found to distaste,°
But with a little act° upon the blood
Burn like the mines of sulfur.

Enter Othello.

                    I did say so.   345
Look where he comes! Not poppy nor mandragora°
Nor all the drowsy syrups of the world
Shall ever medicine thee to that sweet sleep
Which thou owedst° yesterday.

Othello: Ha, ha, false to me?

Iago: Why, how now, General? No more of that.   350

Othello: Avaunt! Begone! Thou hast set me on the rack.
I swear 'tis better to be much abused
Than but to know 't a little.

Iago: How now, my lord?

Othello: What sense had I of her stolen hours of lust?

---

329 *to th' advantage* taking the opportunity   335 *lack* miss.   *Be . . . on 't* do not confess knowledge of it   337 *lose* (The Folio spelling, *loose*, is a normal spelling for "lose," but it may also contain the idea of "let go," "release.")   342 *conceits* fancies, ideas   343 *distaste* be distasteful   344 *act* action, working   346 *mandragora* an opiate made of the mandrake root   349 *thou owedst* you did own

I saw 't not, thought it not, it harmed not me.   355
I slept the next night well, fed well, was free° and merry;
I found not Cassio's kisses on her lips.
He that is robbed, not wanting° what is stolen,
Let him not know 't and he's not robbed at all.
Iago: I am sorry to hear this.   360
Othello: I had been happy if the general camp,
    Pioners° and all, had tasted her sweet body,
    So° I had nothing known. O, now, forever
    Farewell the tranquil mind! Farewell content!
    Farewell the plumèd troops and the big° wars   365
    That makes ambition virtue! O, farewell!
    Farewell the neighing steed and the shrill trump,
    The spirit-stirring drum, th' ear-piercing fife,
    The royal banner, and all quality,°
    Pride,° pomp, and circumstance° of glorious war!   370
    And O, you mortal engines,° whose rude throats
    Th' immortal Jove's dread clamors° counterfeit,
    Farewell! Othello's occupation's gone.
Iago: Is 't possible, my lord?
Othello: Villain, be sure thou prove my love a whore!   375
    Be sure of it. Give me the ocular proof,
    Or, by the worth of mine eternal soul,
    Thou hadst been better have been born a dog
    Than answer my waked wrath!
Iago: Is 't come to this?
Othello: Make me to see 't, or at the least so prove it   380
    That the probation° bear no hinge nor loop
    To hang a doubt on, or woe upon thy life!
Iago: My noble lord—
Othello: If thou dost slander her and torture me,
    Never pray more; abandon all remorse;°   385
    On horror's head horrors accumulate;°
    Do deeds to make heaven weep, all earth amazed;°
    For nothing canst thou to damnation add
    Greater than that.
Iago: O grace! O heaven forgive me!
    Are you a man? Have you a soul or sense?   390
    God b' wi' you; take mine office. O wretched fool,°

356 *free* carefree   358 *wanting* missing   362 *Pioners* diggers of mines, the lowest grade of soldiers   363 *So* provided   365 *big* stately   369 *quality* character, essential nature   370 *Pride* rich display. *circumstance* pageantry   371 *mortal engines* i.e., cannon. (*Mortal* means "deadly.") 372 *Jove's dread clamors* i.e., thunder   381 *probation* proof   385 *remorse* pity, penitent hope for salvation   386 *horrors accumulate* add still more horrors   387 *amazed* confounded with horror 391 *O wretched fool* (Iago addresses himself as a fool for having carried honesty too far.)

That lov'st to make thine honesty a vice!°
O monstrous world! Take note, take note, O world,
To be direct and honest is not safe.
I thank you for this profit,° and from hence°   395
I'll love no friend, sith° love breeds such offense.°
Othello: Nay, stay. Thou shouldst be° honest.
Iago: I should be wise, for honesty's a fool
And loses that° it works for.
Othello: By the world,
I think my wife be honest and think she is not;   400
I think that thou art just and think thou art not.
I'll have some proof. My name, that was as fresh
As Dian's° visage, is now begrimed and black
As mine own face. If there be cords, or knives,
Poison, or fire, or suffocating streams,   405
I'll not endure it. Would I were satisfied!
Iago: I see, sir, you are eaten up with passion.
I do repent me that I put it to you.
You would be satisfied?
Othello: Would? Nay, and I will.
Iago: And may; but how? How satisfied, my lord?   410
Would you, the supervisor,° grossly gape on?
Behold her topped?
Othello: Death and damnation! O!
Iago: It were a tedious difficulty, I think,
To bring them to that prospect. Damn them then,°
If ever mortal eyes do see them bolster°   415
More° than their own.° What then? How then?
What shall I say? Where's satisfaction?
It is impossible you should see this,
Were they as prime° as goats, as hot as monkeys,
As salt° as wolves in pride,° and fools as gross   420
As ignorance made drunk. But yet I say,
If imputation and strong circumstances°
Which lead directly to the door of truth
Will give you satisfaction, you might have 't.
Othello: Give me a living reason she's disloyal.   425
Iago: I do not like the office.

392 *vice* failing, something overdone   395 *profit* profitable instruction.   *hence* henceforth
396 *sith* since.   *offense* i.e., harm to the one who offers help and friendship   397 *Thou shouldst
be* it appears that you are. (But Iago replies in the sense of "ought to be.")   399 *that* what   403
Dian Diana, goddess of the moon and of chastity   411 *supervisor* onlooker   414 *Damn them
then* i.e., they would have to be really incorrigible   415 *bolster* go to bed together, share a bolster   416 *More* other.   *own* own eyes   419 *prime* lustful   420 *salt* wanton, sensual.   *pride*
heat   422 *imputation . . . circumstances* strong circumstantial evidence

But sith° I am entered in this cause so far,
Pricked° to 't by foolish honesty and love,
I will go on. I lay with Cassio lately,
And being troubled with a raging tooth   430
I could not sleep. There are a kind of men
So loose of soul that in their sleeps will mutter
Their affairs. One of this kind is Cassio.
In sleep I heard him say, "Sweet Desdemona,
Let us be wary, let us hide our loves!"   435
And then, sir, would he grip and wring my hand,
Cry "O sweet creature!", then kiss me hard,
As if he plucked up kisses by the roots
That grew upon my lips; then laid his leg
Over my thigh, and sighed, and kissed, and then   440
Cried, "Cursèd fate that gave thee to the Moor!"
Othello: O monstrous! Monstrous!
Iago: Nay, this was but his dream.
Othello: But this denoted a foregone conclusion.°
'Tis a shrewd doubt,° though it be but a dream.
Iago: And this may help to thicken other proofs   445
That do demonstrate thinly.
Othello: I'll tear her all to pieces.
Iago: Nay, but be wise. Yet we see nothing done;
She may be honest yet. Tell me but this:
Have you not sometimes seen a handkerchief
Spotted with strawberries° in your wife's hand?   450
Othello: I gave her such a one. 'Twas my first gift.
Iago: I know not that; but such a handkerchief—
I am sure it was your wife's—did I today
See Cassio wipe his beard with.
Othello: If it be that—
Iago: If it be that, or any that was hers,   455
It speaks against her with the other proofs.
Othello: O, that the slave° had forty thousand lives!
One is too poor, too weak for my revenge.
Now do I see 'tis true. Look here, Iago,
All my fond° love thus do I blow to heaven.   460
'Tis gone.
Arise, black vengeance, from the hollow hell!
Yield up, O love, thy crown and hearted° throne

427 *sith* since   428 *Pricked* spurred   443 *foregone conclusion* concluded experience or action
444 *shrewd doubt* suspicious circumstance   450 *Spotted with strawberries* embroidered with a
strawberry pattern   457 *the slave* i.e., Cassio   460 *fond* foolish (but also suggesting "affectionate")   463 *hearted* fixed in the heart

To tyrannous hate! Swell, bosom, with thy freight,°
    For 'tis of aspics'° tongues!   465

Iago: Yet be content.°

Othello: O, blood, blood, blood!

Iago: Patience, I say. Your mind perhaps may change.

Othello: Never, Iago. Like to the Pontic Sea,°
    Whose icy current and compulsive course   470
    Ne'er feels retiring ebb, but keeps due on
    To the Propontic° and the Hellespont,°
    Even so my bloody thoughts with violent pace
    Shall ne'er look back, ne'er ebb to humble love,
    Till that a capable° and wide revenge   475
    Swallow them up. Now, by yond marble° heaven,
    [*Kneeling*] In the due reverence of a sacred vow
    I here engage my words.

Iago: Do not rise yet.
    [*He kneels.*]° Witness, you ever-burning lights above,
    You elements that clip° us round about,   480
    Witness that here Iago doth give up
    The execution° of his wit,° hands, heart,
    To wronged Othello's service. Let him command,
    And to obey shall be in me remorse,°
    What bloody business ever.°   [*They rise.*]

Othello: I greet thy love,   485
    Not with vain thanks, but with acceptance bounteous,
    And will upon the instant put thee to 't.°
    Within these three days let me hear thee say
    That Cassio's not alive.

Iago: My friend is dead;
    'Tis done at your request. But let her live.   490

Othello: Damn her, lewd minx!° O, damn her, damn her!
    Come, go with me apart. I will withdraw
    To furnish me with some swift means of death
    For the fair devil. Now art thou my lieutenant.

Iago: I am your own forever.   *Exeunt.* 495

---

464 *freight* burden   465 *aspics'* venomous serpents'   466 *content* calm   469 *Pontic Sea* Black Sea   472 *Propontic* Sea of Marmara, between the Black Sea and the Aegean. *Hellespont* Dardanelles, straits where the Sea of Marmara joins with the Aegean   475 *capable* ample, comprehensive   476 *marble* i.e., gleaming like marble and unrelenting   479 s.d. *He kneels* (In the Quarto text, Iago kneels here after Othello has knelt at line 477.)   480 *clip* encompass   482 *execution* exercise, action. *wit* mind   484 *remorse* pity (for Othello's wrongs)   485 *ever soever*   487 *to 't* to the proof   491 *minx* wanton

Scene IV [Before the Citadel.]

Enter Desdemona, Emilia, and Clown.

Desdemona: Do you know, sirrah,° where Lieutenant Cassio lies?°
Clown: I dare not say he lies anywhere.
Desdemona: Why, man?
Clown: He's a soldier, and for me to say a soldier lies, 'tis stabbing.
Desdemona: Go to. Where lodges he?   5
Clown: To tell you where he lodges is to tell you where I lie.
Desdemona: Can anything be made of this?
Clown: I know not where he lodges, and for me to devise a lodging and say he
        lies here, or he lies there, were to lie in mine own throat.°
Desdemona: Can you inquire him out, and be edified by report?   10
Clown: I will catechize the world for him; that is, make questions, and by them
        answer.
Desdemona: Seek him, bid him come hither. Tell him I have moved° my lord on
        his behalf and hope all will be well.
Clown: To do this is within the compass of man's wit, and therefore I will
        attempt the doing it.   *Exit Clown.*
Desdemona: Where should I lose that handkerchief, Emilia?
Emilia: I know not, madam.
Desdemona: Believe me, I had rather have lost my purse
        Full of crusadoes;° and but my noble Moor   20
        Is true of mind and made of no such baseness
        As jealous creatures are, it were enough
        To put him to ill thinking.
Emilia: Is he not jealous?
Desdemona: Who, he? I think the sun where he was born
        Drew all such humors° from him.
Emilia: Look where he comes.   25

        Enter Othello.

Desdemona: I will not leave him now till Cassio
        Be called to him.—How is 't with you, my lord?
Othello: Well, my good lady. [*Aside.*] O, hardness to dissemble!—
        How do you, Desdemona?
Desdemona: Well, my good lord.
Othello: Give me your hand. [*She gives her hand.*] This hand is moist, my lady.   30
Desdemona: It yet hath felt no age nor known no sorrow.
Othello: This argues° fruitfulness° and liberal° heart.

---

1 *sirrah* (A form of address to an inferior.)   *lies* lodges. (But the Clown makes the obvious
pun.)   9 *lie . . . throat* (1) lie egregiously and deliberately (2) use the windpipe to speak a lie
13 *moved* petitioned   20 *crusadoes* Portuguese gold coins   25 *humors* (Refers to the four bodily
fluids thought to determine temperament.)   32 *argues* gives evidence of.   *fruitfulness* generosity, amorousness, and fecundity.   *liberal* generous and sexually free

Hot, hot, and moist. This hand of yours requires
A sequester° from liberty, fasting and prayer,
Much castigation,° exercise devout;°   35
For here's a young and sweating devil here
That commonly rebels. 'Tis a good hand,
A frank° one.
Desdemona: You may indeed say so,
For 'twas that hand that gave away my heart.
Othello: A liberal hand. The hearts of old gave hands,°   40
But our new heraldry is hands, not hearts.°
Desdemona: I cannot speak of this. Come now, your promise.
Othello: What promise, chuck?°
Desdemona: I have sent to bid Cassio come speak with you.
Othello: I have a salt and sorry rheum° offends me;   45
Lend me thy handkerchief.
Desdemona: Here, my lord.   [*She offers a handkerchief.*]
Othello: That which I gave you.
Desdemona: I have it not about me.
Othello: Not?
Desdemona: No, faith, my lord.   50
Othello: That's a fault. That handkerchief
Did an Egyptian to my mother give.
She was a charmer,° and could almost read
The thoughts of people. She told her, while she kept it
'Twould make her amiable° and subdue my father   55
Entirely to her love, but if she lost it
Or made a gift of it, my father's eye
Should hold her loathèd and his spirits should hunt
After new fancies.° She, dying, gave it me,
And bid me, when my fate would have me wived,   60
To give it her.° I did so; and take heed on 't;
Make it a darling like your precious eye.
To lose 't or give 't away were such perdition°
As nothing else could match.
Desdemona: Is 't possible?
Othello: 'Tis true. There's magic in the web° of it.   65
A sibyl, that had numbered in the world
The sun to course two hundred compasses,°

---

34 *sequester* separation, sequestration   35 *castigation* corrective discipline. *exercise devout* i.e.,
prayer, religious meditation, etc.   38 *frank* generous, open (with sexual suggestion)   40 *The
hearts . . . hands* i.e., in former times, people would give their hearts when they gave their
hands to something   41 *But . . . hearts* i.e., in our decadent times, the joining of hands is no
longer a badge to signify the giving of hearts   43 *chuck* (A term of endearment.)   45 *salt . . .
rheum* distressful head cold or watering of the eyes   53 *charmer* sorceress   55 *amiable* desirable
59 *fancies* loves   61 *her* i.e., to my wife   63 *perdition* loss   65 *web* fabric, weaving   67
compasses annual circlings. (The *sibyl*, or prophetess, was two hundred years old.)

In her prophetic fury° sewed the work;°
The worms were hallowed that did breed the silk,
And it was dyed in mummy° which the skillful   70
Conserved of° maidens' hearts.
Desdemona: I' faith! Is 't true?
Othello: Most veritable. Therefore look to 't well.
Desdemona: Then would to God that I had never seen 't!
Othello: Ha? Wherefore?
Desdemona: Why do you speak so startingly and rash?°   75
Othello: Is 't lost? Is 't gone? Speak, is 't out o' the way?°
Desdemona: Heaven bless us!
Othello: Say you?
Desdemona: It is not lost; but what an if° it were?
Othello: How?   80
Desdemona: I say it is not lost.
Othello: Fetch 't, let me see 't.
Desdemona: Why, so I can, sir, but I will not now.
This is a trick to put me from my suit.
Pray you, let Cassio be received again.
Othello: Fetch me the handkerchief! My mind misgives.   85
Desdemona: Come, come,
You'll never meet a more sufficient° man.
Othello: The handkerchief!
Desdemona: I pray, talk° me of Cassio.
Othello: The handkerchief!
Desdemona: A man that all his time°
Hath founded his good fortunes on your love,   90
Shared dangers with you—
Othello: The handkerchief!
Desdemona: I' faith, you are to blame.
Othello: Zounds!   *Exit Othello.*
Emilia: Is not this man jealous?   95
Desdemona: I ne'er saw this before.
Sure, there's some wonder in this handkerchief.
I am most unhappy in the loss of it.
Emilia: 'Tis not a year or two shows us a man.°
They are all but stomachs, and we all but° food;   100
They eat us hungerly,° and when they are full
They belch us.

---

68 *prophetic fury* frenzy of prophetic inspiration.   *work* embroidered pattern   70 *mummy* medicinal or magical preparation drained from mummified bodies   71 *Conserved of* prepared or preserved out of   75 *startingly and rash* disjointedly and impetuously, excitedly   76 *out o' the way* lost, misplaced   79 *an if* if   87 *sufficient* able, complete   88 *talk* talk to   89 *all his time* throughout his career   99 *'Tis . . . man* i.e., you can't really know a man even in a year or two of experience (?), or, real men come along seldom (?)   100 *but* nothing but   101 *hungerly* hungrily

Enter Iago and Cassio.

                    Look you, Cassio and my husband.

Iago [to Cassio]: There is no other way; 'tis she must do 't.
    And, lo, the happiness!° Go and importune her.
Desdemona: How now, good Cassio? What's the news with you?   105
Cassio: Madam, my former suit. I do beseech you
    That by your virtuous° means I may again
    Exist and be a member of his love
    Whom I, with all the office° of my heart,
    Entirely honor. I would not be delayed.   110
    If my offense be of such mortal° kind
    That nor my service past, nor° present sorrows,
    Nor purposed merit in futurity
    Can ransom me into his love again,
    But to know so must be my benefit;°   115
    So shall I clothe me in a forced content,
    And shut myself up in° some other course,
    To fortune's alms.°
Desdemona: Alas, thrice-gentle Cassio,
    My advocation° is not now in tune.
    My lord is not my lord; nor should I know him,   120
    Were he in favor° as in humor° altered.
    So help me every spirit sanctified
    As I have spoken for you all my best
    And stood within the blank° of his displeasure
    For my free speech! You must awhile be patient.   125
    What I can do I will, and more I will
    Than for myself I dare. Let that suffice you.
Iago: Is my lord angry?
Emilia: He went hence but now,
    And certainly in strange unquietness.
Iago: Can he be angry? I have seen the cannon   130
    When it hath blown his ranks into the air,
    And like the devil from his very arm
    Puffed his own brother—and is he angry?
    Something of moment° then. I will go meet him.
    There's matter in 't indeed, if he be angry.   135

---

104 *the happiness* in happy time, fortunately met   107 *virtuous* efficacious   109 *office* loyal service   111 *mortal* fatal   112 *nor . . . nor* neither . . . nor   115 *But . . . benefit* merely to know
that my case is hopeless will have to content me (and will be better than uncertainty)   117
shut . . . in confine myself to   118 *To fortune's alms* throwing myself on the mercy of fortune
119 *advocation* advocacy   121 *favor* appearance. *humor* mood   124 *within the blank* within
point-blank range. (The *blank* is the center of the target.)   134 *of moment* of immediate importance, momentous

Desdemona: I prithee, do so.   *Exit [Iago].*
                            Something, sure, of state,°
    Either from Venice, or some unhatched practice°
    Made demonstrable here in Cyprus to him,
    Hath puddled° his clear spirit; and in such cases
    Men's natures wrangle with inferior things,   140
    Though great ones are their object. 'Tis even so;
    For let our finger ache, and it indues°
    Our other, healthful members even to a sense
    Of pain. Nay, we must think men are not gods,
    Nor of them look for such observancy°   145
    As fits the bridal.° Beshrew me° much, Emilia,
    I was, unhandsome° warrior as I am,
    Arraigning his unkindness with° my soul;
    But now I find I had suborned the witness,°
    And he's indicted falsely.
Emilia: Pray heaven it be   150
    State matters, as you think, and no conception
    Nor no jealous toy° concerning you.
Desdemona: Alas the day! I never gave him cause.
Emilia: But jealous souls will not be answered so;
    They are not ever jealous for the cause,   155
    But jealous for° they're jealous. It is a monster
    Begot upon itself,° born on itself.
Desdemona: Heaven keep that monster from Othello's mind!
Emilia: Lady, amen.
Desdemona: I will go seek him. Cassio, walk hereabout.   160
    If I do find him fit, I'll move your suit
    And seek to effect it to my uttermost.
Cassio: I humbly thank your ladyship.

    Exit [Desdemona with Emilia].

    Enter Bianca.

Bianca: Save° you, friend Cassio!
Cassio: What make° you from home?
    How is 't with you, my most fair Bianca?   165
    I' faith, sweet love, I was coming to your house.

---

136 *of state* concerning state affairs   137 *unhatched practice* as yet unexecuted or undiscovered
plot   139 *puddled* muddied   142 *indues* brings to the same condition   145 *observancy* atten-
tiveness   146 *bridal* wedding (when a bridegroom is newly attentive to his bride). *Beshrew
me* (A mild oath.)   147 *unhandsome* insufficient, unskillful   148 *with* before the bar of   149
suborned the witness induced the witness to give false testimony   152 *toy* fancy   156 *for* because   157 *Begot upon itself* generated solely from itself   164 *Save* God save.   *make* do

Bianca: And I was going to your lodging, Cassio.
      What, keep a week away? Seven days and nights?
      Eightscore-eight° hours? And lovers' absent hours
      More tedious than the dial° eightscore times?   170
      O weary reckoning!
Cassio: Pardon me, Bianca.
      I have this while with leaden thoughts been pressed;
      But I shall, in a more continuate° time,
      Strike off this score° of absence. Sweet Bianca,

      [*giving her Desdemona's handkerchief*]

      Take me this work out.°
Bianca: O Cassio, whence came this?   175
      This is some token from a newer friend.°
      To the felt absence now I feel a cause.
      Is 't come to this? Well, well.
Cassio: Go to, woman!
      Throw your vile guesses in the devil's teeth,
      From whence you have them. You are jealous now   180
      That this is from some mistress, some remembrance.
      No, by my faith, Bianca.
Bianca: Why, whose is it?
Cassio: I know not, neither. I found it in my chamber.
      I like the work well. Ere it be demanded°—
      As like° enough it will—I would have it copied.   185
      Take it and do 't, and leave me for this time.
Bianca: Leave you? Wherefore?
Cassio: I do attend here on the General,
      And think it no addition,° nor my wish,
      To have him see me womaned.   190
Bianca: Why, I pray you?
Cassio: Not that I love you not.
Bianca: But that you do not love me.
      I pray you, bring° me on the way a little,
      And say if I shall see you soon at night.   195
Cassio: 'Tis but a little way that I can bring you,
      For I attend here; but I'll see you soon.
Bianca: 'Tis very good. I must be circumstanced.°

      Exeunt omnes.

169 *Eightscore-eight* one hundred sixty-eight, the number of hours in a week   170 *the dial* a
complete revolution of the clock   173 *continuate* uninterrupted   174 *Strike . . . score* settle
this account   175 *Take . . . out* copy this embroidery for me   176 *friend* mistress   184
demanded inquired for   185 *like* likely   189 *addition* i.e., addition to my reputation   194 *bring*
accompany   198 *be circumstanced* be governed by circumstance, yield to your conditions

Laurence Fishburne as Othello and Kenneth Branagh as Iago in the 1995 film.

ACT IV

Scene I [Before the Citadel.]

Enter Othello and Iago.

Iago: Will you think so?
Othello: Think so, Iago?
Iago: What,
    To kiss in private?
Othello: An unauthorized kiss!
Iago: Or to be naked with her friend in bed
    An hour or more, not meaning any harm?
Othello: Naked in bed, Iago, and not mean harm?   5
    It is hypocrisy against the devil.
    They that mean virtuously and yet do so,
    The devil their virtue tempts, and they tempt heaven.
Iago: If they do nothing, 'tis a venial° slip.
    But if I give my wife a handkerchief—   10
Othello: What then?
Iago: Why then, 'tis hers, my lord, and being hers,
    She may, I think, bestow 't on any man.
Othello: She is protectress of her honor too.
    May she give that?   15

9 *venial* pardonable

Iago: Her honor is an essence that's not seen;
    They have it° very oft that have it not.
    But, for the handkerchief—
Othello: By heaven, I would most gladly have forgot it.
    Thou saidst—O, it comes o'er my memory   20
    As doth the raven o'er the infectious house,°
    Boding to all—he had my handkerchief.
Iago: Ay, what of that?
Othello: That's not so good now.
Iago: What
    If I had said I had seen him do you wrong?
    Or heard him say—as knaves be such abroad,°   25
    Who having, by their own importunate suit,
    Or voluntary dotage° of some mistress,
    Convincèd or supplied° them, cannot choose
    But they must blab—
Othello: Hath he said anything?
Iago: He hath, my lord; but, be you well assured,   30
    No more than he'll unswear.
Othello: What hath he said?
Iago: Faith, that he did—I know not what he did.
Othello: What? What?
Iago: Lie—
Othello: With her?
Iago: With her, on her; what you will.
Othello: Lie with her? Lie on her? We say "lie on her" when they belie° her. Lie   35
    with her? Zounds, that's fulsome.°—Handkerchief—confessions—handker-
    chief!—To confess and be hanged for his labor—first to be hanged and then
    to confess.°—I tremble at it. Nature would not invest herself in such shad-
    owing passion without some instruction.° It is not words° that shakes me
    thus. Pish! Noses, ears, and lips.—Is 't possible?—Confess—handker-   40
    chief!—O devil!

    Falls in a trance.

Iago: Work on,
    My medicine, work! Thus credulous fools are caught,
    And many worthy and chaste dames even thus,

17 *They have it* i.e., they enjoy a reputation for it   21 *raven . . . house* (Allusion to the belief
that the raven hovered over a house of sickness or infection, such as one visited by the plague.)
25 *abroad* around about   27 *voluntary dotage* willing infatuation   28 *Convincèd or supplied*
seduced or sexually gratified   35 *belie* slander   36 *fulsome* foul   37–38 *first . . . to confess*
(Othello reverses the proverbial *confess* and *be hanged*; Cassio is to be given no time to confess
before he dies.)   38–39 *Nature . . . instruction* i.e., without some foundation in fact, nature
would not have dressed herself in such an overwhelming passion that comes over me now and
fills my mind with images, or in such a lifelike fantasy as Cassio had in his dream of lying with
Desdemona   39 *words* mere words

All guiltless, meet reproach.—What, ho! My lord!   45
My lord, I say! Othello!

Enter Cassio.

                              How now, Cassio?
Cassio: What's the matter?
Iago: My lord is fall'n into an epilepsy.
    This is his second fit. He had one yesterday.
Cassio: Rub him about the temples.
Iago: No, forbear.   50
    The lethargy° must have his° quiet course.
    If not, he foams at mouth, and by and by
    Breaks out to savage madness. Look, he stirs.
    Do you withdraw yourself a little while.
    He will recover straight. When he is gone,   55
    I would on great occasion° speak with you.

    [*Exit Cassio.*]

    How is it, General? Have you not hurt your head?
Othello: Dost thou mock me?°
Iago: I mock you not, by heaven.
    Would you would bear your fortune like a man!
Othello: A hornèd man's a monster and a beast.   60
Iago: There's many a beast then in a populous city,
    And many a civil° monster.
Othello: Did he confess it?
Iago: Good sir, be a man.
    Think every bearded fellow that's but yoked°   65
    May draw with you.° There's millions now alive
    That nightly lie in those unproper° beds
    Which they dare swear peculiar.° Your case is better.°
    O, 'tis the spite of hell, the fiend's arch-mock,
    To lip° a wanton in a secure° couch   70
    And to suppose her chaste! No, let me know,
    And knowing what I am,° I know what she shall be.°
Othello: O, thou art wise. 'Tis certain.
Iago: Stand you awhile apart;
    Confine yourself but in a patient list.°   75
    Whilst you were here o'erwhelmèd with your grief—

---

51 *lethargy* coma.   *his* its   56 *on great occasion* on a matter of great importance   58 *mock me*
(Othello takes Iago's question about hurting his head to be a mocking reference to the
cuckold's horns.)   62 *civil* i.e., dwelling in a city   65 *yoked* (1) married (2) put into the yoke
of infamy and cuckoldry   66 *draw with you* pull as you do, like oxen who are yoked, i.e., share
your fate as cuckold   67 *unproper* not exclusively their own   68 *peculiar* private, their own.
better i.e., because you know the truth   70 *lip* kiss.   *secure* free from suspicion   72 *what I am*
i.e., a cuckold.   *she shall be* will happen to her   75 *in . . . list* within the bounds of patience

A passion most unsuiting such a man—
Cassio came hither. I shifted him away,°
And laid good 'scuse upon your ecstasy,°
Bade him anon return and here speak with me,   80
The which he promised. Do but encave° yourself
And mark the fleers,° the gibes, and notable° scorns
That dwell in every region of his face;
For I will make him tell the tale anew,
Where, how, how oft, how long ago, and when   85
He hath and is again to cope° your wife.
I say, but mark his gesture. Marry, patience!
Or I shall say you're all-in-all in spleen,°
And nothing of a man.

Othello: Dost thou hear, Iago?
I will be found most cunning in my patience;   90
But—dost thou hear?—most bloody.

Iago: That's not amiss;
But yet keep time° in all. Will you withdraw?

[*Othello stands apart.*]

Now will I question Cassio of Bianca,
A huswife° that by selling her desires
Buys herself bread and clothes. It is a creature   95
That dotes on Cassio—as 'tis the strumpet's plague
To beguile many and be beguiled by one.
He, when he hears of her, cannot restrain°
From the excess of laughter. Here he comes.

Enter Cassio.

As he shall smile, Othello shall go mad;   100
And his unbookish° jealousy must conster°
Poor Cassio's smiles, gestures, and light behaviors
Quite in the wrong.—How do you now, Lieutenant?

Cassio: The worser that you give me the addition°
Whose want° even kills me.   105

Iago: Ply Desdemona well and you are sure on 't.
[*Speaking lower.*] Now, if this suit lay in Bianca's power,
How quickly should you speed!

Cassio [*laughing*]: Alas, poor caitiff!°

Othello [*aside*]: Look how he laughs already!   110

---

78 *shifted him away* used a dodge to get rid of him   79 *ecstasy* trance   81 *encave* conceal   82
fleers sneers.   *notable* obvious   86 *cope* encounter with, have sex with   88 *all-in-all in spleen*
utterly governed by passionate impulses   92 *keep time* keep yourself steady (as in music)   94
huswife hussy   98 *restrain* refrain   101 *unbookish* uninstructed.   *conster* construe   104
addition title   105 *Whose want* the lack of which   109 *caitiff* wretch

Iago: I never knew a woman love man so.

Cassio: Alas, poor rogue! I think, i' faith, she loves me.

Othello: Now he denies it faintly, and laughs it out.

Iago: Do you hear, Cassio?

Othello: Now he importunes him
    To tell it o'er. Go to!° Well said,° well said.   115

Iago: She gives it out that you shall marry her.
    Do you intend it?

Cassio: Ha, ha, ha!

Othello: Do you triumph, Roman?° Do you triumph?

Cassio: I marry her? What? A customer?° Prithee, bear some charity to my wit;°   120
    do not think it so unwholesome. Ha, ha, ha!

Othello: So, so, so, so! They laugh that win.°

Iago: Faith, the cry° goes that you shall marry her.

Cassio: Prithee, say true.

Iago: I am a very villain else.°   125

Othello: Have you scored me?° Well.

Cassio: This is the monkey's own giving out. She is persuaded I will marry her
    out of her own love and flattery,° not out of my promise.

Othello: Iago beckons me.° Now he begins the story.

Cassio: She was here even now; she haunts me in every place. I was the other   130
    day talking on the seabank° with certain Venetians, and thither comes the
    bauble,° and, by this hand,° she falls me thus about my neck—

    [*He embraces Iago.*]

Othello: Crying, "O dear Cassio!" as it were; his gesture imports it.

Cassio: So hangs and lolls and weep upon me, so shakes and pulls me. Ha, ha, ha!

Othello: Now he tells how she plucked him to my chamber. O, I see that nose of   135
    yours, but not that dog I shall throw it to.°

Cassio: Well, I must leave her company.

Iago: Before me,° look where she comes.

    Enter Bianca [*with Othello's handkerchief*].

Cassio: 'Tis such another fitchew!° Marry, a perfumed one.—What do you
    mean by this haunting of me?   140

---

115 *Go to* (An expression of remonstrance.)   *Well said* well done   119 *Roman* (The Romans were noted for their *triumphs* or triumphal processions.)   120 *customer* i.e., prostitute.   *bear . . . wit* be more charitable to my judgment   122 *They . . . win* i.e., they that laugh last laugh best   123 *cry* rumor   125 *I . . . else* call me a complete rogue if I'm not telling the truth   126 *scored me* scored off me, beaten me, made up my reckoning, branded me   128 *flattery* self-flattery, self-deception   129 *beckons* signals   131 *seabank* seashore   132 *bauble* plaything.   *by this hand* I make my vow   136 *not . . . to* (Othello imagines himself cutting off Cassio's nose and throwing it to a dog.)   138 *Before me* i.e., on my soul   139 *'Tis . . . fitchew* what a polecat she is! Just like all the others. (Polecats were often compared with prostitutes because of their rank smell and presumed lechery.)

Bianca: Let the devil and his dam° haunt you! What did you mean by that same handkerchief you gave me even now? I was a fine fool to take it. I must take out the work? A likely piece of work,° that you should find it in your chamber and know not who left it there! This is some minx's token, and I must take out the work? There; give it your hobbyhorse.° [*She gives him the* 145 *handkerchief.*] Wheresoever you had it, I'll take out no work on 't.

Cassio: How now, my sweet Bianca? How now? How now?

Othello: By heaven, that should be° my handkerchief!

Bianca: If you'll come to supper tonight, you may; if you will not, come when you are next prepared for.° *Exit.* 150

Iago: After her, after her.

Cassio: Faith, I must. She'll rail in the streets else.

Iago: Will you sup there?

Cassio: Faith, I intend so.

Iago: Well, I may chance to see you, for I would very fain speak with you. 155

Cassio: Prithee, come. Will you?

Iago: Go to.° Say no more. [*Exit Cassio.*]

Othello [*advancing*]: How shall I murder him, Iago?

Iago: Did you perceive how he laughed at his vice?

Othello: O, Iago! 160

Iago: And did you see the handkerchief?

Othello: Was that mine?

Iago: Yours, by this hand. And to see how he prizes the foolish woman your wife! She gave it him, and he hath given it his whore.

Othello: I would have him nine years a-killing. A fine woman! A fair woman! A 165 sweet woman!

Iago: Nay, you must forget that.

Othello: Ay, let her rot and perish, and be damned tonight, for she shall not live. No, my heart is turned to stone; I strike it, and it hurts my hand. O, the world hath not a sweeter creature! She might lie by an emperor's side and 170 command him tasks.

Iago: Nay, that's not your way.°

Othello: Hang her! I do but say what she is. So delicate with her needle! An admirable musician! O, she will sing the savageness out of a bear. Of so high and plenteous wit and invention!° 175

Iago: She's the worse for all this.

Othello: O, a thousand, a thousand times! And then, of so gentle a condition!°

Iago: Ay, too gentle.°

Othello: Nay, that's certain. But yet the pity of it, Iago! O, Iago, the pity of it, Iago! 180

---

141 *dam* mother   143 *A likely . . . work* a fine story   145 *hobbyhorse* harlot   148 *should be* must be   149–150 *when . . . for* when I'm ready for you (i.e., never)   157 *Go to* (An expression of remonstrance.)   172 *your way* i.e., the way you should think of her   175 *invention* imagination   177 *gentle a condition* wellborn and well-bred   178 *gentle* generous, yielding (to other men)

Iago: If you are so fond° over her iniquity, give her patent° to offend, for if it touch not you it comes near nobody.

Othello: I will chop her into messes.° Cuckold me?

Iago: O, 'tis foul in her.

Othello: With mine officer?   185

Iago: That's fouler.

Othello: Get me some poison, Iago, this night. I'll not expostulate with her, lest her body and beauty unprovide° my mind again. This night, Iago.

Iago: Do it not with poison. Strangle her in her bed, even the bed she hath contaminated.   190

Othello: Good, good! The justice of it pleases. Very good.

Iago: And for Cassio, let me be his undertaker.° You shall hear more by midnight.

Othello: Excellent good. [*A trumpet within.*] What trumpet is that same?

Iago: I warrant, something from Venice.

Enter Lodovico, Desdemona, and attendants.

'Tis Lodovico. This comes from the Duke.   195
See, your wife's with him.

Lodovico: God save you, worthy General!

Othello: With all my heart,° sir.

Lodovico [*giving him a letter*]: The Duke and the senators of Venice greet you.

Othello: I kiss the instrument of their pleasures.

[*He opens the letter, and reads.*]

Desdemona: And what's the news, good cousin Lodovico?   200

Iago: I am very glad to see you, signor.
Welcome to Cyprus.

Lodovico: I thank you. How does Lieutenant Cassio?

Iago: Lives, sir.

Desdemona: Cousin, there's fall'n between him and my lord   205
An unkind° breach; but you shall make all well.

Othello: Are you sure of that?

Desdemona: My lord?

Othello [*reads*]: "This fail you not to do, as you will—"

Lodovico: He did not call; he's busy in the paper.   210
Is there division twixt my lord and Cassio?

Desdemona: A most unhappy one. I would do much
T' atone° them, for the love I bear to Cassio.

Othello: Fire and brimstone!

181 *fond* foolish. *patent* license 183 *messes* portions of meat, i.e., bits 188 *unprovide* weaken, render unfit 192 *be his undertaker* undertake to dispatch him 197 *With all my heart* i.e., I thank you most heartily 206 *unkind* unnatural, contrary to their natures; hurtful 213 *atone* reconcile

Desdemona: My lord?

Othello: Are you wise?

Desdemona: What, is he angry?

Lodovico: Maybe the letter moved him;
    For, as I think, they do command him home,
    Deputing Cassio in his government.°

Desdemona: By my troth, I am glad on 't.°   220

Othello: Indeed?

Desdemona: My lord?

Othello: I am glad to see you mad.°

Desdemona: Why, sweet Othello—

Othello [striking her]: Devil!   225

Desdemona: I have not deserved this.

Lodovico: My lord, this would not be believed in Venice,
    Though I should swear I saw 't. 'Tis very much.°
    Make her amends; she weeps.

Othello: O devil, devil!
    If that the earth could teem° with woman's tears,   230
    Each drop she falls would prove a crocodile.°
    Out of my sight!

Desdemona: I will not stay to offend you. [*Going.*]

Lodovico: Truly, an obedient lady.
    I do beseech your lordship, call her back.

Othello: Mistress!   235

Desdemona [returning]: My lord?

Othello: What would you with her, sir?°

Lodovico: Who, I, my lord?

Othello: Ay, you did wish that I would make her turn.
    Sir, she can turn, and turn, and yet go on   240
    And turn again; and she can weep, sir, weep;
    And she's obedient,° as you say, obedient,
    Very obedient.—Proceed you in your tears.—
    Concerning this, sir—O well-painted passion!°—
    I am commanded home.—Get you away;   245
    I'll send for you anon.—Sir, I obey the mandate
    And will return to Venice.—Hence, avaunt!

    [*Exit Desdemona.*]

219 *government* office   220 *on 't* of it   223 *I am . . . mad* i.e., I am glad to see that you are insane enough to rejoice in Cassio's promotion (?) (Othello bitterly plays on Desdemona's *I am glad.*) 228 *very much* too much, outrageous   230 *teem* breed, be impregnated   231 *falls . . . crocodile* (Crocodiles were supposed to weep hypocritical tears for their victims.) 237 *What . . . sir* (Othello implies that Desdemona is pliant and will do a *turn*, lines 239–241, for any man.)   242 *obedient* (With much the same sexual connotation as *turn* in lines 239–241.)   244 *passion* i.e., grief

Cassio shall have my place. And, sir, tonight
I do entreat that we may sup together.
You are welcome, sir, to Cyprus.—Goats and monkeys!°   *Exit.* 250
Lodovico: Is this the noble Moor whom our full Senate
Call all in all sufficient? Is this the nature
Whom passion could not shake? Whose solid virtue
The shot of accident nor dart of chance
Could neither graze nor pierce?
Iago: He is much changed.   255
Lodovico: Are his wits safe? Is he not light of brain?
Iago: He's that he is. I may not breathe my censure
What he might be. If what he might he is not,
I would to heaven he were!°
Lodovico: What, strike his wife?
Iago: Faith, that was not so well; yet would I knew   260
That stroke would prove the worst!
Lodovico: Is it his use?°
Or did the letters work upon his blood°
And new-create his fault?
Iago: Alas, alas!
It is not honesty in me to speak
What I have seen and known. You shall observe him,   265
And his own courses will denote° him so
That I may save my speech. Do but go after,
And mark how he continues.
Lodovico: I am sorry that I am deceived in him.   *Exeunt.*

Scene II [The Citadel.]

Enter Othello and Emilia.

Othello: You have seen nothing then?
Emilia: Nor ever heard, nor ever did suspect.
Othello: Yes, you have seen Cassio and she together.
Emilia: But then I saw no harm, and then I heard
Each syllable that breath made up between them.   5
Othello: What, did they never whisper?
Emilia: Never, my lord.
Othello: Nor send you out o' the way?
Emilia: Never.
Othello: To fetch her fan, her gloves, her mask, nor nothing?   10
Emilia: Never, my lord.
Othello: That's strange.

---

250 *Goats and monkeys* (See Act III, Scene iii, line 419.)   257–259 *I may . . . were* i.e., I dare
not venture an opinion as to whether he's of unsound mind, as you suggest, but, if he isn't, then
it might be better to wish he were in fact insane, since only that could excuse his wild behavior
261 *use* custom   262 *blood* passions   266 *courses will denote* actions will reveal

Emilia: I durst, my lord, to wager she is honest,
    Lay down my soul at stake.° If you think other,
    Remove your thought; it doth abuse your bosom.°   15
    If any wretch have put this in your head,
    Let heaven requite it with the serpent's curse!°
    For if she be not honest, chaste, and true,
    There's no man happy; the purest of their wives
    Is foul as slander.
Othello: Bid her come hither. Go.   20

    Exit Emilia.

    She says enough; yet she's a simple bawd
    That cannot say as much.° This° is a subtle whore,
    A closet lock and key° of villainous secrets.
    And yet she'll kneel and pray; I have seen her do 't.

    Enter Desdemona and Emilia.

Desdemona: My lord, what is your will?   25
Othello: Pray you, chuck, come hither.
Desdemona: What is your pleasure?
Othello: Let me see your eyes.
    Look in my face.
Desdemona: What horrible fancy's this?
Othello [to Emilia]: Some of your function,° mistress.
    Leave procreants° alone and shut the door;   30
    Cough or cry "hem" if anybody come.
    Your mystery, your mystery!° Nay, dispatch.

    Exit Emilia.

Desdemona [kneeling]: Upon my knees, what doth your speech import?
    I understand a fury in your words,
    But not the words.   35
Othello: Why, what art thou?
Desdemona: Your wife, my lord, your true
    And loyal wife.
Othello: Come, swear it, damn thyself,
    Lest, being like one of heaven,° the devils themselves
    Should fear to seize thee. Therefore be double damned:
    Swear thou art honest.

---

14 *at stake* as the wager   15 *abuse your bosom* deceive you   17 *the serpent's curse* the curse pronounced by God on the serpent for deceiving Eve, just as some man has done to Othello and Desdemona. (See Genesis 3:14.)   21–22 *she's . . . much* i.e., any procuress or go-between who couldn't make up as plausible a story as Emilia's would have to be pretty stupid   22 *This* i.e., Desdemona   23 *closet lock and key* i.e., concealer   29 *Some . . . function* i.e., practice your chosen profession, that of bawd (by guarding the door)   30 *procreants* mating couples   32 *mystery* trade, occupation   38 *being . . . heaven* looking like an angel

Desdemona: Heaven doth truly know it.   40
Othello: Heaven truly knows that thou art false as hell.
Desdemona: To whom, my lord? With whom? How am I false?
Othello [*weeping*]: Ah, Desdemon! Away, away, away!
Desdemona: Alas the heavy day! Why do you weep?
  Am I the motive° of these tears, my lord?   45
  If haply you my father do suspect
  An instrument of this your calling back,
  Lay not your blame on me. If you have lost him,
  I have lost him too.
Othello: Had it pleased heaven
  To try me with affliction, had they° rained   50
  All kinds of sores and shames on my bare head,
  Steeped me in poverty to the very lips,
  Given to captivity me and my utmost hopes,
  I should have found in some place of my soul
  A drop of patience. But, alas, to make me   55
  A fixèd figure for the time of scorn°
  To point his° slow and moving finger° at!
  Yet could I bear that too, well, very well.
  But there where I have garnered° up my heart,
  Where either I must live or bear no life,   60
  The fountain° from the which my current runs
  Or else dries up—to be discarded thence!
  Or keep it as a cistern° for foul toads
  To knot° and gender° in! Turn thy complexion there,°
  Patience, thou young and rose-lipped cherubin—   65
  Ay, there look grim as hell!°
Desdemona: I hope my noble lord esteems me honest.°
Othello: O, ay, as summer flies are in the shambles,°
  That quicken° even with blowing.° O thou weed,
  Who art so lovely fair and smell'st so sweet   70
  That the sense aches at thee, would thou hadst ne'er been born!
Desdemona: Alas, what ignorant° sin have I committed?
Othello: Was this fair paper, this most goodly book,
  Made to write "whore" upon? What committed?
  Committed? O thou public commoner!°   75

45 *motive* cause   50 *they* i.e., heavenly powers   56 *time of scorn* i.e., scornful world   57 *his* its.
slow and moving finger i.e., hour hand of the clock, moving so slowly it seems hardly to move at
all. (Othello envisages himself as being eternally pointed at by the scornful world as the numbers on a clock are pointed at by the hour hand.)   59 *garnered* stored   61 *fountain* spring   63
cistern cesspool   64 *knot* couple.   *gender* engender.   *Turn . . . there* change your color, grow
pale, at such a sight   65–66 *Patience . . . hell* (Even Patience, that rose-lipped cherub, will look
grim and pale at this spectacle.)   67 *honest* chaste   68 *shambles* slaughterhouse   69 *quicken*
come to life.   *with blowing* i.e., with the puffing up of something rotten in which maggots are
breeding   72 *ignorant sin* sin in ignorance   75 *commoner* prostitute

I should make very forges of my cheeks,
That would to cinders burn up modesty,
Did I but speak thy deeds. What committed?
Heaven stops the nose at it and the moon winks;°
The bawdy° wind, that kisses all it meets,   80
Is hushed within the hollow mine° of earth
And will not hear 't. What committed?
Impudent strumpet!

Desdemona: By heaven, you do me wrong.

Othello: Are not you a strumpet?

Desdemona: No, as I am a Christian.   85
  If to preserve this vessel° for my lord
  From any other foul unlawful touch
  Be not to be a strumpet, I am none.

Othello: What, not a whore?

Desdemona: No, as I shall be saved.   90

Othello: Is 't possible?

Desdemona: O, heaven forgive us!

Othello: I cry you mercy,° then.
  I took you for that cunning whore of Venice
  That married with Othello. [*Calling out.*] You, mistress,
  That have the office opposite to Saint Peter   95
  And keep the gate of hell!

  Enter Emilia.

                    You, you, ay, you!
  We have done our course.° There's money for your pains. [*He gives money.*]
  I pray you, turn the key and keep our counsel.   *Exit.*

Emilia: Alas, what does this gentleman conceive?°
  How do you, madam? How do you, my good lady?   100

Desdemona: Faith, half asleep.°

Emilia: Good madam, what's the matter with my lord?

Desdemona: With who?

Emilia: Why, with my lord, madam.

Desdemona: Who is thy lord?

Emilia: He that is yours, sweet lady.   105

Desdemona: I have none. Do not talk to me, Emilia.
  I cannot weep, nor answers have I none
  But what should go by water.° Prithee, tonight
  Lay on my bed my wedding sheets, remember;
  And call thy husband hither.   110

---

79 *winks* closes her eyes. (The moon symbolizes chastity.) 80 *bawdy* kissing one and all 81 *mine*
cave (where the winds were thought to dwell) 86 *vessel* body 92 *cry you mercy* beg your pardon
97 *course* business (with an indecent suggestion of "trick," turn at sex) 99 *conceive* suppose,
think 101 *half asleep* i.e., dazed 108 *go by water* be expressed by tears

Emilia: Here's a change indeed!   *Exit.*

Desdemona: 'Tis meet I should be used so, very meet.°
     How have I been behaved, that he might stick°
     The small'st opinion° on my least misuse?°

Enter Iago and Emilia.

Iago: What is your pleasure, madam? How is 't with you?   115
Desdemona: I cannot tell. Those that do teach young babes
     Do it with gentle means and easy tasks.
     He might have chid me so, for, in good faith,
     I am a child to chiding.
Iago: What is the matter, lady?   120
Emilia: Alas, Iago, my lord hath so bewhored her,
     Thrown such despite and heavy terms upon her,
     That true hearts cannot bear it.
Desdemona: Am I that name, Iago?
Iago: What name, fair lady?   125
Desdemona: Such as she said my lord did say I was.
Emilia: He called her whore. A beggar in his drink
     Could not have laid such terms upon his callet.°
Iago: Why did he so?
Desdemona [weeping]:
     I do not know. I am sure I am none such.   130
Iago: Do not weep, do not weep. Alas the day!
Emilia: Hath she forsook so many noble matches,
     Her father and her country and her friends,
     To be called whore? Would it not make one weep?
Desdemona: It is my wretched fortune.
Iago: Beshrew° him for 't!   135
     How comes this trick° upon him?
Desdemona: Nay, heaven doth know.
Emilia: I will be hanged if some eternal° villain,
     Some busy and insinuating° rogue,
     Some cogging,° cozening° slave, to get some office,
     Have not devised this slander. I will be hanged else.   140
Iago: Fie, there is no such man. It is impossible.
Desdemona: If any such there be, heaven pardon him!
Emilia: A halter° pardon him! And hell gnaw his bones!
     Why should he call her whore? Who keeps her company?
     What place? What time? What form?° What likelihood?   145

---

112 *meet* fitting   113 *stick* attach   114 *opinion* censure.   *least misuse* slightest misconduct
128 *callet* whore   135 *Beshrew* curse   136 *trick* strange behavior, delusion   137 *eternal* inveterate   138 *insinuating* ingratiating, fawning, wheedling   139 *cogging* cheating.   *cozening* de-
frauding   143 *halter* hangman's noose   145 *form* appearance, circumstance

The Moor's abused by some most villainous knave,
Some base notorious knave, some scurvy fellow.
O heaven, that° such companions° thou'dst unfold,°
And put in every honest hand a whip
To lash the rascals naked through the world   150
Even from the east to th' west!

Iago: Speak within door.°

Emilia: O, fie upon them! Some such squire° he was
That turned your wit the seamy side without°
And made you to suspect me with the Moor.

Iago: You are a fool. Go to.°

Desdemona: Alas, Iago,   155
What shall I do to win my lord again?
Good friend, go to him; for, by this light of heaven,
I know not how I lost him. Here I kneel. [*She kneels.*]
If e'er my will did trespass 'gainst his love,
Either in discourse of thought° or actual deed,   160
Or that° mine eyes, mine ears, or any sense
Delighted them° in any other form;
Or that I do not yet,° and ever did,
And ever will—though he do shake me off
To beggarly divorcement—love him dearly,   165
Comfort forswear° me! Unkindness may do much,
And his unkindness may defeat° my life,
But never taint my love. I cannot say "whore."
It does abhor° me now I speak the word;
To do the act that might the addition° earn   170
Not the world's mass of vanity° could make me.

[*She rises.*]

Iago: I pray you, be content. 'Tis but his humor.°
The business of the state does him offense,
And he does chide with you.

Desdemona: If 'twere no other—   175

Iago: It is but so, I warrant.   [*Trumpets within.*]
Hark, how these instruments summon you to supper!
The messengers of Venice stays the meat.°
Go in, and weep not. All things shall be well.

---

148 *that* would that. *companions* fellows. *unfold* expose   151 *within door* i.e., not so loud
152 *squire* fellow   153 *seamy side without* wrong side out   155 *Go to* i.e., that's enough   160
discourse of thought process of thinking   161 *that* if. (Also in line 163.)   162 *Delighted them*
took delight   163 *yet* still   166 *Comfort forswear* may heavenly comfort forsake   167 *defeat*
destroy   169 *abhor* (1) fill me with abhorrence (2) make me whorelike   170 *addition* title
171 *vanity* showy splendor   172 *humor* mood   178 *stays the meat* are waiting to dine

Exeunt Desdemona and Emilia.

Enter Roderigo.

How now, Roderigo?   180
Roderigo: I do not find that thou deal'st justly with me.
Iago: What in the contrary?
Roderigo: Every day thou daff'st me° with some device,° Iago, and rather, as it
    seems to me now, keep'st from me all conveniency° than suppliest me with
    the least advantage° of hope. I will indeed no longer endure it, nor am I yet   185
    persuaded to put up° in peace what already I have foolishly suffered.
Iago: Will you hear me, Roderigo?
Roderigo: Faith, I have heard too much, for your words and performances are no
    kin together.
Iago: You charge me most unjustly.   190
Roderigo: With naught but truth. I have wasted myself out of my means. The
    jewels you have had from me to deliver° Desdemona would half have cor-
    rupted a votarist.° You have told me she hath received them and returned
    me expectations and comforts of sudden respect° and acquaintance, but I
    find none.   195
Iago: Well, go to, very well.
Roderigo: "Very well"! "Go to"! I cannot go to,° man, nor 'tis not very well. By
    this hand, I think it is scurvy, and begin to find myself fopped° in it.
Iago: Very well.
Roderigo: I tell you 'tis not very well.° I will make myself known to Desdemona.   200
    If she will return me my jewels, I will give over my suit and repent my un-
    lawful solicitation; if not, assure yourself I will seek satisfaction° of you.
Iago: You have said now?°
Roderigo: Ay, and said nothing but what I protest intendment° of doing.
Iago: Why, now I see there's mettle in thee, and even from this instant do build   205
    on thee a better opinion than ever before. Give me thy hand, Roderigo.
    Thou hast taken against me a most just exception; but yet I protest I have
    dealt most directly in thy affair.
Roderigo: It hath not appeared.
Iago: I grant indeed it hath not appeared, and your suspicion is not without wit   210
    and judgment. But, Roderigo, if thou hast that in thee indeed which I have
    greater reason to believe now than ever—I mean purpose, courage, and
    valor—this night show it. If thou the next night following enjoy not

183 *thou daff'st me* you put me off. *device* excuse, trick   184 *conveniency* advantage, opportunity 185 *advantage* increase 186 *put up* submit to, tolerate 192 *deliver* deliver to   193
votarist nun 194 *sudden respect* immediate consideration 197 *I cannot go to* (Roderigo
changes Iago's *go to,* an expression urging patience, to *I cannot go to,* "I have no opportunity for
success in wooing.") 198 *fopped* fooled, duped 200 *not very well* (Roderigo changes Iago's
very well, "all right, then," to *not very well,* "not at all good.") 202 *satisfaction* repayment.
(The term normally means settling of accounts in a duel.) 203 *You . . . now* have you finished? 204 *intendment* intention

Desdemona, take me from this world with treachery and devise engines for° my life. 215

Roderigo: Well, what is it? Is it within reason and compass?

Iago: Sir, there is especial commission come from Venice to depute Cassio in Othello's place.

Roderigo: Is that true? Why, then Othello and Desdemona return again to Venice. 220

Iago: O, no; he goes into Mauritania and takes away with him the fair Desdemona, unless his abode be lingered here by some accident; wherein none can be so determinate° as the removing of Cassio.

Roderigo: How do you mean, removing of him?

Iago: Why, by making him uncapable of Othello's place—knocking out his 225 brains.

Roderigo: And that you would have me to do?

Iago: Ay, if you dare do yourself a profit and a right. He sups tonight with a harlotry,° and thither will I go to him. He knows not yet of his honorable fortune. If you will watch his going thence, which I will fashion to fall out° 230 between twelve and one, you may take him at your pleasure. I will be near to second your attempt, and he shall fall between us. Come, stand not amazed at it, but go along with me. I will show you such a necessity in his death that you shall think yourself bound to put it on him. It is now high° suppertime, and the night grows to waste.° About it. 235

Roderigo: I will hear further reason for this.

Iago: And you shall be satisfied. *Exeunt.*

Scene III [The Citadel.]

Enter Othello, Lodovico, Desdemona, Emilia, and attendants.

Lodovico: I do beseech you, sir, trouble yourself no further.

Othello: O, pardon me; 'twill do me good to walk.

Lodovico: Madam, good night. I humbly thank your ladyship.

Desdemona: Your honor is most welcome.

Othello: Will you walk, sir?
   O, Desdemona!   5

Desdemona: My lord?

Othello: Get you to bed on th' instant.
   I will be returned forthwith. Dismiss your attendant there. Look
   't be done.

Desdemona: I will, my lord. 10

Exit [Othello, with Lodovico and attendants].

Emilia: How goes it now? He looks gentler than he did.

214 *engines for* plots against   223 *determinate* conclusive   229 *harlotry* slut   230 *fall out* occur
234 *high* fully   235 *grows to waste* wastes away

Desdemona: He says he will return incontinent,°
   And hath commanded me to go to bed,
   And bid me to dismiss you.
Emilia: Dismiss me?   15
Desdemona: It was his bidding. Therefore, good Emilia,
   Give me my nightly wearing, and adieu.
   We must not now displease him.
Emilia: I would you had never seen him!
Desdemona: So would not I. My love doth so approve him   20
   That even his stubbornness,° his checks,° his frowns—
   Prithee, unpin me—have grace and favor in them.

   [*Emilia prepares Desdemona for bed.*]

Emilia: I have laid those sheets you bade me on the bed.
Desdemona: All's one.° Good faith, how foolish are our minds!
   If I do die before thee, prithee shroud me   25
   In one of these same sheets.
Emilia: Come, come, you talk.°
Desdemona: My mother had a maid called Barbary.
   She was in love, and he she loved proved mad°
   And did forsake her. She had a song of "Willow."
   An old thing 'twas, but it expressed her fortune,   30
   And she died singing it. That song tonight
   Will not go from my mind; I have much to do
   But to go hang° my head all at one side
   And sing it like poor Barbary. Prithee, dispatch.
Emilia: Shall I go fetch your nightgown?°   35
Desdemona: No, unpin me here.
   This Lodovico is a proper° man.
Emilia: A very handsome man.
Desdemona: He speaks well.
Emilia: I know a lady in Venice would have walked barefoot to Palestine for a   40
   touch of his nether lip.
Desdemona [*singing*]:
             "The poor soul sat sighing by a sycamore tree,
             Sing all a green willow;°
             Her hand on her bosom, her head on her knee,
             Sing willow, willow, willow.   45
             The fresh streams ran by her and murmured her moans;
             Sing willow, willow, willow;
             Her salt tears fell from her, and softened the stones—"

12 *incontinent* immediately   21 *stubbornness* roughness.   *checks* rebukes   24 *All's one* all right.
It doesn't really matter   26 *talk* i.e., prattle   28 *mad* wild, i.e., faithless   32–33 *I . . . hang* I
can scarcely keep myself from hanging   35 *nightgown* dressing gown   37 *proper* handsome
43 *willow* (A conventional emblem of disappointed love.)

Lay by these.

        [*Singing.*] "Sing willow, willow, willow—"   50

Prithee, hie thee.° He'll come anon.°

        [*Singing.*] "Sing all a green willow must be my garland.

        Let nobody blame him; his scorn I approve—"

Nay, that's not next.—Hark! Who is 't that knocks?

Emilia: It's the wind.   55

Desdemona [*singing*]:

        "I called my love false love; but what said he then?

        Sing willow, willow, willow;

        If I court more women, you'll couch with more men."

So, get thee gone. Good night. Mine eyes do itch;

Doth that bode weeping?

Emilia: 'Tis neither here nor there.   60

Desdemona: I have heard it said so. O, these men, these men!

Dost thou in conscience think—tell me, Emilia—

That there be women do abuse° their husbands

In such gross kind?

Emilia: There be some such, no question.

Desdemona: Wouldst thou do such a deed for all the world?   65

Emilia: Why, would not you?

Desdemona: No, by this heavenly light!

Emilia: Nor I neither by this heavenly light;

I might do 't as well i' the dark.

Desdemona: Wouldst thou do such a deed for all the world?

Emilia: The world's a huge thing. It is a great price   70

For a small vice.

Desdemona: Good troth, I think thou wouldst not.

Emilia: By my troth, I think I should, and undo 't when I had done. Marry, I would not do such a thing for a joint ring,° nor for measures of lawn,° nor for gowns, petticoats, nor caps, nor any petty exhibition.° But for all the   75 whole world! Uds° pity, who would not make her husband a cuckold to make him a monarch? I should venture purgatory for 't.

Desdemona: Beshrew me if I would do such a wrong

For the whole world.

Emilia: Why, the wrong is but a wrong i' the world, and having the world for   80 your labor, 'tis a wrong in your own world, and you might quickly make it right.

Desdemona: I do not think there is any such woman.

Emilia: Yes, a dozen, and as many

To th' vantage° as would store° the world they played° for.   85

---

51 *hie thee* hurry. *anon* right away   63 *abuse* deceive   74 *joint ring* a ring made in separate halves.   *lawn* fine linen   75 *exhibition* gift   76 *Uds* God's   85 *To th' vantage* in addition, to boot.   *store* populate.   *played* (1) gambled (2) sported sexually

But I do think it is their husbands' faults
If wives do fall. Say that they slack their duties°
And pour our treasures into foreign laps,°
Or else break out in peevish jealousies,
Throwing restraint upon us? Or say they strike us,°   90
Or scant our former having in despite?°
Why, we have galls,° and though we have some grace,
Yet have we some revenge. Let husbands know
Their wives have sense° like them. They see, and smell,
And have their palates both for sweet and sour,   95
As husbands have. What is it that they do
When they change us for others? Is it sport?°
I think it is. And doth affection° breed it?
I think it doth. Is 't frailty that thus errs?
It is so, too. And have not we affections,   100
Desires for sport, and frailty, as men have?
Then let them use us well; else let them know,
The ills we do, their ills instruct us so.
Desdemona: Good night, good night. God me such uses° send
Not to pick bad from bad, but by bad mend!°   105

Exeunt.

Act V

Scene I [A Street in Cyprus.]

Enter Iago and Roderigo.

Iago: Here stand behind this bulk.° Straight will he come.
Wear thy good rapier bare,° and put it home.
Quick, quick! Fear nothing. I'll be at thy elbow.
It makes us or it mars us. Think on that,
And fix most firm thy resolution.   5
Roderigo: Be near at hand. I may miscarry in 't.
Iago: Here, at thy hand. Be bold, and take thy stand.

[*Iago stands aside. Roderigo conceals himself.*]

87 *duties* marital duties   88 *pour . . . laps* i.e., are unfaithful, give what is rightfully ours
(semen) to other women   90 *Throwing . . . us* i.e., jealously restricting our freedom to see
other men   91 *scant . . . despite* reduce our allowance to spite us   92 *have galls* i.e., are capable
of resenting injury and insult   94 *sense* physical sense   97 *sport* sexual pastime   98 *affection*
passion   104 *uses* habit, practice   105 *Not . . . mend* i.e., not to learn bad conduct from
others' badness (as Emilia has suggested women learn from men), but to mend my ways by perceiving what badness is, making spiritual benefit out of evil and adversity   1 *bulk* framework
projecting from the front of a shop   2 *bare* unsheathed

Roderigo: I have no great devotion to the deed;
    And yet he hath given me satisfying reasons.
    'Tis but a man gone. Forth, my sword! He dies.   10

    [*He draws.*]

Iago: I have rubbed this young quat° almost to the sense,°
    And he grows angry. Now, whether he kill Cassio
    Or Cassio him, or each do kill the other,
    Every way makes my gain. Live Roderigo,°
    He calls me to a restitution large   15
    Of gold and jewels that I bobbed° from him
    As gifts to Desdemona.
    It must not be. If Cassio do remain,
    He hath a daily beauty in his life
    That makes me ugly; and besides, the Moor   20
    May unfold° me to him; there stand I in much peril.
    No, he must die. Be 't so. I hear him coming.

    Enter Cassio.

Roderigo [*coming forth*]: I know his gait, 'tis he.—Villain, thou diest!

    [*He attacks Cassio.*]

Cassio: That thrust had been mine enemy indeed,
    But that my coat° is better than thou know'st.   25
    I will make proof° of thine.

    [*He draws, and wounds Roderigo.*]

Roderigo: O, I am slain!   [*He falls.*]

    [*Iago, from behind, wounds Cassio in the leg, and exits.*]

Cassio: I am maimed forever. Help, ho! Murder! Murder!

    Enter Othello.

Othello: The voice of Cassio! Iago keeps his word.
Roderigo: O, villain that I am!
Othello: It is even so.   30
Cassio: O, help, ho! Light! A surgeon!
Othello: 'Tis he. O brave Iago, honest and just,
    That hast such noble sense of thy friend's wrong!
    Thou teachest me. Minion,° your dear lies dead,

---

11 *quat* pimple, pustule.   *to the sense* to the quick   14 *Live Roderigo* if Roderigo lives   16
bobbed swindled   21 *unfold* expose   25 *coat* (Possibly a garment of mail under the outer
clothing, or simply a tougher coat than Roderigo expected.)   26 *proof* a test   34 *Minion* hussy
(i.e., Desdemona)

And your unblest fate hies.° Strumpet, I come.   35
Forth of° my heart those charms, thine eyes, are blotted;
Thy bed, lust-stained, shall with lust's blood be spotted.   *Exit Othello.*

    Enter Lodovico and Gratiano.

Cassio: What ho! No watch? No passage?° Murder! Murder!
Gratiano: 'Tis some mischance. The voice is very direful.
Cassio: O, help!   40
Lodovico: Hark!
Roderigo: O wretched villain!
Lodovico: Two or three groan. 'Tis heavy° night;
    These may be counterfeits. Let's think 't unsafe
    To come in to° the cry without more help.   45

    [They remain near the entrance.]

Roderigo: Nobody come? Then shall I bleed to death.

    Enter Iago [in his shirtsleeves, with a light].

Lodovico: Hark!
Gratiano: Here's one comes in his shirt, with light and weapons.
Iago: Who's there? Whose noise is this that cries on° murder?
Lodovico: We do not know.
Iago: Did not you hear a cry?   50
Cassio: Here, here! For heaven's sake, help me!
Iago: What's the matter?

    [He moves toward Cassio.]

Gratiano [to Lodovico]: This is Othello's ancient, as I take it.
Lodovico [to Gratiano]: The same indeed, a very valiant fellow.
Iago [to Cassio]: What° are you here that cry so grievously?
Cassio: Iago? O, I am spoiled,° undone by villains!   55
    Give me some help.
Iago: O me, Lieutenant! What villains have done this?
Cassio: I think that one of them is hereabout,
    And cannot make° away.
Iago: O treacherous villains!

    [To Lodovico and Gratiano.]

    What are you there? Come in, and give some help.   *[They advance.]*   60
Roderigo: O, help me there!

---

35 *hies* hastens on   36 *Forth of* from out   38 *passage* people passing by   43 *heavy* thick, dark
45 *come in to* approach   49 *cries on* cries out   54 *What* who (also at lines 60 and 66)   55
spoiled ruined, done for   59 *make* get

Cassio: That's one of them.

Iago: O murderous slave! O villain!

   [*He stabs Roderigo.*]

Roderigo: O damned Iago! O inhuman dog!

Iago: Kill men i' the dark?—Where be these bloody thieves?—

   How silent is this town!—Ho! Murder, murder!—   65

   [*To Lodovico and Gratiano.*] What may you be? Are you of good or evil?

Lodovico: As you shall prove us, praise° us.

Iago: Signor Lodovico?

Lodovico: He, sir.

Iago: I cry you mercy.° Here's Cassio hurt by villains.   70

Gratiano: Cassio?

Iago: How is 't, brother?

Cassio: My leg is cut in two.

Iago: Marry, heaven forbid!

   Light, gentlemen! I'll bind it with my shirt.   75

   [*He hands them the light, and tends to Cassio's wound.*]

   Enter Bianca.

Bianca: What is the matter, ho? Who is 't that cried?

Iago: Who is 't that cried?

Bianca: O my dear Cassio!

   My sweet Cassio! O Cassio, Cassio, Cassio!

Iago: O notable strumpet! Cassio, may you suspect

   Who they should be that have thus mangled you?   80

Cassio: No.

Gratiano: I am sorry to find you thus. I have been to seek you.

Iago: Lend me a garter. [*He applies a tourniquet.*] So. —O, for a chair,°

   To bear him easily hence!

Bianca: Alas, he faints! O Cassio, Cassio, Cassio!   85

Iago: Gentlemen all, I do suspect this trash

   To be a party in this injury.—

   Patience awhile, good Cassio.—Come, come;

   Lend me a light.   [*He shines the light on Roderigo.*]

                  Know we this face or no?

   Alas, my friend and my dear countryman   90

   Roderigo! No.—Yes, sure.—O heaven! Roderigo!

Gratiano: What, of Venice?

Iago: Even he, sir. Did you know him?

Gratiano: Know him? Ay.

Iago: Signor Gratiano? I cry your gentle° pardon.   95

---

67 *praise* appraise   70 *I cry you mercy* I beg your pardon   83 *chair* litter   95 *gentle* noble

These bloody accidents° must excuse my manners
That so neglected you.
Gratiano: I am glad to see you.
Iago: How do you, Cassio? O, a chair, a chair!
Gratiano: Roderigo!
Iago: He, he, 'tis he. [*A litter is brought in.*] O, that's well said;° the chair.   100
    Some good man bear him carefully from hence;
    I'll fetch the General's surgeon. [*To Bianca.*] For you, mistress,
    Save you your labor.°—He that lies slain here, Cassio,
    Was my dear friend. What malice° was between you?
Cassio: None in the world, nor do I know the man.   105
Iago [*to Bianca*]: What, look you pale?—O, bear him out o' th' air.°

    [*Cassio and Roderigo are borne off.*]

    Stay you,° good gentlemen.—Look you pale, mistress?—
    Do you perceive the gastness° of her eye?—
    Nay, if you stare,° we shall hear more anon.—
    Behold her well; I pray you, look upon her.   110
    Do you see, gentlemen? Nay, guiltiness
    Will speak, though tongues were out of use.

    [*Enter Emilia.*]

Emilia: 'Las, what's the matter? What's the matter, husband?
Iago: Cassio hath here been set on in the dark
    By Roderigo and fellows that are scaped.   115
    He's almost slain, and Roderigo dead.
Emilia: Alas, good gentleman! Alas, good Cassio!
Iago: This is the fruits of whoring. Prithee, Emilia,
    Go know° of Cassio where he supped tonight.
    [*To Bianca.*] What, do you shake at that?   120
Bianca: He supped at my house, but I therefore shake not.
Iago: O, did he so? I charge you go with me.
Emilia: O, fie upon thee, strumpet!
Bianca: I am no strumpet, but of life as honest°
    As you that thus abuse me.   125
Emilia: As I? Faugh! Fie upon thee!
Iago: Kind gentlemen, let's go see poor Cassio dressed.°—
    Come, mistress, you must tell's another tale.
    Emilia, run you to the citadel

---

96 *accidents* sudden events 100 *well said* well done 103 *Save . . . labor* i.e., never you mind
tending Cassio 104 *malice* enmity 106 *bear . . . air* (Fresh air was thought to be dangerous for
a wound.) 107 *Stay you* (Lodovico and Gratiano are evidently about to leave.) 108 *gastness*
terror 109 *stare* (Iago pretends to interpret Bianca's wild looks as an involuntary confession of
guilt.) 119 *know* learn 124 *honest* chaste 127 *Cassio dressed* Cassio's wounds dressed

And tell my lord and lady what hath happed.—   130
Will you go on afore? [*Aside.*] This is the night
That either makes me or fordoes° me quite.   *Exeunt.*

Scene II [A Bedchamber in the Citadel.]

Enter Othello [with a light], and Desdemona in her bed.°

Othello: It is the cause,° it is the cause, my soul.
    Let me not name it to you, you chaste stars!
    It is the cause. Yet I'll not shed her blood,
    Nor scar that whiter skin of hers than snow,
    And smooth as monumental° alabaster.   5
    Yet she must die, else she'll betray more men.
    Put out the light, and then put out the light.°
    If I quench thee, thou flaming minister,°
    I can again thy former light restore,
    Should I repent me;° but once put out thy light,   10
    Thou cunning'st pattern° of excelling nature,
    I know not where is that Promethean heat°
    That can thy light relume.° When I have plucked thy rose,
    I cannot give it vital growth again;
    It needs must wither. I'll smell thee on the tree.   15

    [*He kisses her.*]

    O balmy breath, that dost almost persuade
    Justice to break her sword! One more, one more.
    Be thus when thou art dead, and I will kill thee,
    And love thee after. One more, and that's the last.

    [*He kisses her.*]

    So sweet was ne'er so fatal. I must weep,   20
    But they are cruel° tears. This sorrow's heavenly;
    It strikes where it doth love.° She wakes.
Desdemona: Who's there? Othello?
Othello: Ay, Desdemona.
Desdemona: Will you come to bed, my lord?   25
Othello: Have you prayed tonight, Desdemon?

132 *fordoes* undoes, ruins   s.d. *in her bed* (Either the curtains are drawn back to reveal the bed in a recessed area backstage, or the bed is "thrust out" onstage as the scene begins.)   1 *cause* i.e., cause of justice, the offense itself, which Othello must correct as an agent of justice   5 *monumental* i.e., used in making tombs and funeral monuments   7 *the light . . . light* the torch or lamp . . . Desdemona's life   8 *flaming minister* torch or lamp that serves me   10 *repent me* change my mind   11 *Thou . . . pattern* you skillfully wrought perfect example   12 *Promethean heat* divine fire. (Alluding to the theft of fire from heaven by Prometheus.)   13 *relume* rekindle   21 *cruel* unrelenting   22 *It . . . love* (Compare Hebrews 12:6: "For whom the Lord loveth he chasteneth.")

Desdemona: Ay, my lord.

Othello: If you bethink yourself of any crime°
    Unreconciled as yet to heaven and grace,
    Solicit° for it straight.°   30

Desdemona: Alack, my lord, what may you mean by that?

Othello: Well, do it, and be brief. I will walk by.
    I would not kill thy unpreparèd spirit.
    No, heaven forfend!° I would not kill thy soul.

Desdemona: Talk you of killing?

Othello: Ay, I do.

Desdemona: Then heaven   35
    Have mercy on me!

Othello: Amen, with all my heart!

Desdemona: If you say so, I hope you will not kill me.

Othello: Humh!

Desdemona: And yet I fear you; for you're fatal then
    When your eyes roll so. Why I should fear I know not,   40
    Since guiltiness I know not; but yet I feel I fear.

Othello: Think on thy sins.

Desdemona: They are loves I bear to you.°

Othello: Ay, and for that thou diest.

Desdemona: That death's unnatural that kills for loving.
    Alas, why gnaw you so your nether lip?   45
    Some bloody passion shakes your very frame.
    These are portents; but yet I hope, I hope,
    They do not point on° me.

Othello: Peace, and be still!

Desdemona: I will so. What's the matter?   50

Othello: That handkerchief which I so loved and gave thee
    Thou gav'st to Cassio.

Desdemona: No, by my life and soul!
    Send for the man and ask him.

Othello: Sweet soul, take heed, take heed of perjury.
    Thou art on thy deathbed.   55

Desdemona: Ay, but not yet to die.

Othello: Yes, presently.°
    Therefore confess thee freely of thy sin;
    For to deny each article with oath
    Cannot° remove nor choke the strong conception°
    That I do groan withal.° Thou art to die.   60

---

28 *crime* sin   30 *Solicit* petition, pray. *straight* immediately   34 *forfend* forbid   42 *They are
. . . you* i.e., if I sinned, it was in loving you more than my father or more than God   48 *point
on* point at, predict what is to happen to   56 *presently* immediately   59 *conception* (1) belief in
your guilt (2) plan in my mind   60 *groan withal* (1) groan at in sorrow (2) as in giving birth

Desdemona: Then Lord have mercy on me!

Othello: I say, amen.

Desdemona: And have you mercy too! I never did
    Offend° you in my life; never loved Cassio
    But with such general warranty° of heaven
    As I might love. I never gave him token.   65

Othello: By heaven, I saw my handkerchief in 's hand.
    O perjured woman! Thou dost stone° my heart,
    And makes me call what I intend to do
    A murder, which I thought a sacrifice.
    I saw the handkerchief.

Desdemona: He found it, then.   70
    I never gave it him. Send for him hither;
    Let him confess a truth.

Othello: He hath confessed.

Desdemona: What, my lord?

Othello: That he hath used thee.

Desdemona: How? Unlawfully?

Othello: Ay.

Desdemona: He will not say so.

Othello: No, his mouth is stopped;   75
    Honest Iago hath ta'en order° for 't.

Desdemona: O, my fear interprets. What, is he dead?

Othello: Had all his hairs been lives, my great revenge
    Had stomach for them all.

Desdemona: Alas, he is betrayed and I undone!   [*She weeps.*]   80

Othello: Out, strumpet! Weep'st thou for him to my face?

Desdemona: O, banish me, my lord, but kill me not!

Othello: Down, strumpet!

Desdemona: Kill me tomorrow; let me live tonight!

Othello: Nay, if you strive—   85

Desdemona: But half an hour!

Othello: Being done,° there is no pause.

Desdemona: But while I say one prayer!

Othello: It is too late.

    Smothers her.

Emilia [*at the door*]: My lord, my lord! What, ho! My lord, my lord!

Othello: What noise is this? Not dead? Not yet quite dead?
    I that am cruel am yet merciful;   90
    I would not have thee linger in thy pain.

---

63 *Offend* wrong   64 *warranty* sanction   67 *stone* turn to stone, harden   76 *ta'en order* taken measures   86 *Being done* i.e., since justice has begun its relentless course

[*He dispatches her.*]

So, so.

Emilia [*within*]: What, ho! My lord, my lord!

Othello: Who's there?

Emilia [*within*]: O, good my lord, I would speak a word with you!

Othello: Yes, 'tis Emilia.—By and by.—She's dead.

'Tis like° she comes to speak of Cassio's death.—   95

The noise was here.° Ha! No more moving?

Still as the grave. Shall she come in? Were 't good?—

I think she stirs again. No. What's best to do?

If she come in, she'll sure speak to my wife.

My wife! My wife! What wife? I have no wife.   100

O, insupportable! O heavy hour!

Methinks it should be now a huge eclipse

Of sun and moon, and that th' affrighted globe

Should yawn° at alteration.°

Emilia [*within*]:   I do beseech you

That I may speak with you, O, good my lord!   105

Othello: I had forgot thee. O, come in, Emilia.—

Soft,° by and by. Let me the curtains draw.—

[*He closes the bed-curtains and opens the door.*]

Where art thou?

Enter Emilia.

                          What's the matter with thee now?

Emilia: O, my good lord, yonder's foul murders done!

Othello: What, now?   110

Emilia: But now, my lord.

Othello: It is the very error° of the moon;

She comes more nearer earth than she was wont,

And makes men mad.

Emilia: Cassio, my lord, hath killed a young Venetian   115

Called Roderigo.

Othello: Roderigo killed?

And Cassio killed?

Emilia: No, Cassio is not killed.

Othello: Not Cassio killed? Then murder's out of tune,

And sweet revenge grows harsh.

95 *like* likely that   96 *here* (The Folio's *high* is possible, suggesting that the commotion of the attack on Cassio was loud.)   104 *yawn* gape in amazement, i.e., move in an earthquake. (According to Pliny, earthquakes often happen during eclipses.)   *at alteration* at these cataclysmic events in nature, well suited to express the horror of Desdemona's death   107 *Soft* wait a minute   112 *error* aberration, irregularity

Desdemona: O, falsely, falsely murdered!   120

Emilia: O Lord, what cry is that?

Othello: That? What?

Emilia: Out° and alas, that was my lady's voice.

> [*She opens the bed-curtains.*]

> Help, help, ho, help! O lady, speak again!
> Sweet Desdemona! O sweet mistress, speak!   125

Desdemona: A guiltless death I die.

Emilia: O, who hath done this deed?

Desdemona: Nobody; I myself. Farewell.
> Commend me to my kind lord. O, farewell!   [*She dies.*]

Othello: Why, how should she be murdered?

Emilia: Alas, who knows?   130

Othello: You heard her say herself it was not I.

Emilia: She said so. I must needs report the truth.

Othello: She's like a liar gone to burning hell!
> 'Twas I that killed her.

Emilia: O, the more angel she,
> And you the blacker devil!   135

Othello: She turned to folly,° and she was a whore.

Emilia: Thou dost belie° her, and thou art a devil.

Othello: She was false as water.

Emilia: Thou art rash as fire to say
> That she was false. O, she was heavenly true!   140

Othello: Cassio did top her. Ask thy husband else.°
> O, I were damned beneath all depth in hell
> But that I did proceed upon just grounds
> To this extremity. Thy husband knew it all.

Emilia: My husband?   145

Othello: Thy husband.

Emilia: That she was false to wedlock?

Othello: Ay, with Cassio. Nay, had she been true,
> If heaven would make me such another world
> Of one entire and perfect chrysolite,°   150
> I'd not have sold her for it.

Emilia: My husband?

Othello: Ay, 'twas he that told me on her first.
> An honest man he is, and hates the slime
> That sticks on filthy deeds.   155

Emilia: My husband?

---

123 *Out* (A cry of dismay, intensifying *alas*.)   136 *folly* i.e., wantonness, fleshly sin   137 *belie* slander   141 *else* i.e., if you don't believe me   150 *chrysolite* precious topaz

Othello: What needs this iterance,° woman? I say thy husband.

Emilia: O mistress, villainy hath made mocks with° love!
My husband say she was false?

Othello: He, woman;
I say thy husband. Dost understand the word?   160
My friend, thy husband, honest, honest Iago.

Emilia: If he say so, may his pernicious soul
Rot half a grain a day! He lies to th' heart.
She was too fond of her most filthy bargain.

Othello: Ha?   [*He draws.*] 165

Emilia: Do thy worst!
This deed of thine is no more worthy heaven
Than thou wast worthy her.

Othello: Peace, you were best.°

Emilia: Thou hast not half that power to do me harm
As I have to be hurt.° O gull!° O dolt!   170
As ignorant as dirt! Thou hast done a deed—
I care not for thy sword; I'll make thee known,
Though I lost twenty lives.—Help! Help, ho, help!
The Moor hath killed my mistress! Murder, murder!

Enter Montano, Gratiano, and Iago.

Montano: What is the matter? How now, General?   175

Emilia: O, are you come, Iago? You have done well,
That men must lay their murders on your neck.

Gratiano: What is the matter?

Emilia [to Iago]: Disprove this villain, if thou be'st a man.
He says thou toldst him that his wife was false.   180
I know thou didst not; thou'rt not such a villain.
Speak, for my heart is full.

Iago: I told him what I thought, and told no more
Than what he found himself was apt° and true.

Emilia: But did you ever tell him she was false?   185

Iago: I did.

Emilia: You told a lie, an odious, damnèd lie!
Upon my soul, a lie, a wicked lie.
She false with Cassio? Did you say with Cassio?

Iago: With Cassio, mistress. Go to, charm° your tongue.   190

Emilia: I will not charm my tongue; I am bound to speak.
My mistress here lies murdered in her bed—

157 *iterance* iteration, repetition   158 *made mocks with* derided, made sport of   168 *you were best* it would be best for you   170 *to be hurt* i.e., to endure hurt. *gull* dupe   184 *apt* plausible   190 *charm* keep silent (as though by a magic spell)

All: O heavens forfend!

Emilia: And your reports have set the murder on.

Othello: Nay, stare not, masters. It is true indeed.   195

Gratiano: 'Tis a strange truth.

Montano: O monstrous act!

Emilia: Villainy, villainy, villainy!
   I think upon 't—I think I smell 't! O villainy!
   I thought so then°—I'll kill myself for grief—
   O villainy, villainy!   200

Iago: What, are you mad? I charge you, get you home.

Emilia: Good gentlemen, let me have leave to speak.
   'Tis proper I obey him, but not now.
   Perchance, Iago, I will ne'er go home.

Othello: O! O! O!   [*Othello falls on the bed.°*]   205

Emilia: Nay, lay thee down and roar,
   For thou hast killed the sweetest innocent
   That e'er did lift up eye.°

Othello [rising]:   O, she was foul!
   I scarce did know you, uncle. There lies your niece,
   Whose breath indeed these hands have newly stopped.
   I know this act shows° horrible and grim.   210

Gratiano: Poor Desdemon! I am glad thy father's dead.
   Thy match was mortal to him, and pure grief
   Shore his old thread° in twain. Did he live now,
   This sight would make him do a desperate turn,°
   Yea, curse his better angel from his side,   215
   And fall to reprobance.°

Othello: 'Tis pitiful. But yet Iago knows
   That she with Cassio hath the act of shame
   A thousand times committed. Cassio confessed it;
   And she did gratify° his amorous works   220
   With that recognizance° and pledge of love
   Which I first gave her. I saw it in his hand;
   It was a handkerchief, an antique token
   My father gave my mother.

Emilia: O God! O heavenly God!   225

Iago: Zounds, hold your peace.

Emilia: 'Twill out, 'twill out! I peace?

---

199 *then* (Perhaps at Act III, Scene iii, lines 331–332 and Act IV, Scene ii, lines 137–154.)
205 s.d. *Othello . . . bed* (This direction is from the Quarto, as also *He kisses her* at line 19 and
She dies at line 129.) 207 *lift up eye* i.e., lift her eyes to heaven 210 *shows* looks 213 *Shore
. . . thread* sheared the thread of his old age (as Atropos, one of the three Fates, was thought to
do) 214 *turn* deed 216 *reprobance* damnation, i.e., suicide 220 *gratify* reward 221 *recognizance* token

No, I will speak as liberal as the north.°
Let heaven and men and devils, let them all,
All, all, cry shame against me, yet I'll speak.
Iago: Be wise, and get you home.
Emilia: I will not.

[*Iago threatens Emilia.*]

Gratiano: Fie   230
Your sword upon a woman?
Emilia: O thou dull Moor! That handkerchief thou speak'st of
I found by fortune and did give my husband;
For often, with a solemn earnestness,
More than indeed belonged° to such a trifle,   235
He begged of me to steal 't.
Iago: Villainous whore!
Emilia: She give it Cassio? No, alas! I found it,
And I did give 't my husband.
Iago: Filth, thou liest!
Emilia: By heaven, I do not, I do not, gentlemen.
O murderous coxcomb!° What should such a fool   240
Do with so good a wife?
Othello: Are there no stones° in heaven
But what serves for the thunder?—Precious° villain!

[*He runs at Iago; Montano disarms Othello. Iago, from behind, stabs Emilia.°*]

Gratiano: The woman falls! Sure he hath killed his wife.
Emilia: Ay, ay. O, lay me by my mistress' side.   245

Exit [*Iago.*]

Gratiano: He's gone, but his wife's killed.
Montano: 'Tis a notorious villain. Take you this weapon,
Which I have here recovered from the Moor.
Come, guard the door without. Let him not pass,
But kill him rather. I'll after that same villain,°   250
For 'tis a damnèd slave.

Exit [*with all but Othello and Emilia, who has been laid by Desdemona's side*].

Othello: I am not valiant neither,
But every puny whipster° gets my sword.

227 *liberal as the north* freely as the north wind (blows)   235 *belonged* was appropriate   240
coxcomb fool. (Addressed to Othello.)   242 *stones* bolts, such as those used for thunderbolts   243
Precious i.e., arrant, utter.   s.d. *He . . . Emilia* (The Quarto text reads, "The Moor runs at Iago.
Iago kills his wife." The Quarto also specifies the exit of Iago at line 245 and the death of Emilia at
line 260.)   253 *whipster* contemptible fellow (one who is always ready to whip out his sword)

But why should honor° outlive honesty?°
Let it go all.
Emilia: What did thy song bode, lady?   255
Hark, canst thou hear me? I will play the swan,
And die in music. [*She sings.*] "Willow, willow, willow."
Moor, she was chaste. She loved thee, cruel Moor.
So come my soul to bliss as I speak true.
So speaking as I think, alas, I die.   [*She dies.*] 260
Othello: I have another weapon in this chamber;
It was a sword of Spain, the ice-brook's temper°—
O, here it is. [*He finds a sword.*] Uncle, I must come forth.
Gratiano [*within*]: If thou attempt it, it will cost thee dear.
Thou hast no weapon, and perforce must suffer.   265
Othello: Look in upon me then and speak with me,
Or, naked° as I am, I will assault thee.

[*Enter Gratiano.*]

Gratiano: What is the matter?
Othello: Behold, I have a weapon;
A better never did itself sustain
Upon a soldier's thigh. I have seen the day   270
That, with this little arm and this good sword,
I have made my way through more impediments
Than twenty times your stop.° But O, vain boast!
Who can control his fate? 'Tis not so now.
Be not afraid, though you do see me weaponed;   275
Here is my journey's end, here is my butt°
And very seamark° of my utmost sail.

[*Gratiano steps back.*]

Do you go back dismayed? 'Tis a lost° fear;
Man but a rush° against Othello's breast
And he retires. Where should Othello go?   280

[*He turns to Desdemona.*]

Now, how dost thou look now? O ill-starred wench!
Pale as thy smock! When we shall meet at compt,°
This look of thine will hurl my soul from heaven,
And fiends will snatch at it. Cold, cold, my girl?

---

254 *honor* i.e., the bravery for which one enjoys a soldier's reputation. *honesty* true integrity
262 *the ice-brook's temper* tempered in ice-cold water   267 *naked* unarmed   273 *stop* power (to
stop)   276 *butt* goal, limit. (An archery term.)   277 *seamark* beacon (marking his destination
or limit)   278 *lost* wasted, unneeded   279 *Man . . . rush* wield no more than a reed   282
compt account, judgment day

Even like thy chastity. O cursèd, cursèd slave!°   285
Whip me, ye devils,
From the possession of this heavenly sight!
Blow me about in winds! Roast me in sulfur!
Wash me in steep-down gulfs of liquid fire!
O Desdemon! Dead, Desdemon! Dead! O! O!   290

*Enter Lodovico, Cassio [carried in a litter°], Montano, and Iago [prisoner], with
officers.*

Lodovico: Where is this rash and most unfortunate man?
Othello: That's he that was Othello. Here I am.
Lodovico: Where is that viper? Bring the villain forth.

    [Iago is led forward.]

Othello: I look down towards his feet;° but that's a fable.
    If that thou be'st a devil, I cannot kill thee.   295

    [He wounds Iago.]

Lodovico: Wrench his sword from him.   *[Othello is disarmed.]*
Iago: I bleed, sir, but not killed.
Othello: I am not sorry neither. I'd have thee live,
    For in my sense° 'tis happiness to die.
Lodovico: O thou Othello, that was once so good,
    Fall'n in the practice° of a cursèd slave,°   300
    What shall be said to thee?
Othello: Why, anything.
    An honorable murderer, if you will,
    For naught I did in hate, but all in honor.
Lodovico: This wretch hath part confessed his villainy.
    Did you and he consent° in Cassio's death?   305
Othello: Ay.
Cassio: Dear General, I never gave you cause.
Othello: I do believe it, and I ask your pardon.
    Will you, I pray, demand that demi-devil
    Why he hath thus ensnared my soul and body?   310
Iago: Demand me nothing. What you know, you know.
    From this time forth I never will speak word.
Lodovico: What, not to pray?
Gratiano: Torments° will ope your lips.
Othello: Well, thou dost best.   315

---

285 *slave* i.e., Othello himself   290 s.d. *in a litter* (The Quarto specifies that Cassio is "in a
chair.")   294 *towards his feet* i.e., to see if they are cloven, as the devil's are fabled to be   298
in my sense to one who feels as I do   300 *in the practice* through the plotting, into the snare.
slave villain   305 *consent* agree   314 *Torments* torture

Lodovico: Sir, you shall understand what hath befall'n,
　　Which, as I think, you know not. Here is a letter
　　Found in the pocket of the slain Roderigo;
　　And here another. [*He produces letters.*] The one of them imports
　　The death of Cassio, to be undertook　　　　　　　　　　　320
　　By Roderigo.
Othello: O villain!
Cassio:　　　　　Most heathenish and most gross!°
Lodovico [*showing another paper*]: Now here's another discontented° paper
　　Found in his pocket too. And this, it seems,
　　Roderigo meant t' have sent this damnèd villain;　　　325
　　But that belike° Iago in the interim
　　Came in and satisfied him.°
Othello: O thou pernicious caitiff!—
　　How came you, Cassio, by that handkerchief
　　That was my wife's?
Cassio:　　　　　　　I found it in my chamber;　　　　330
　　And he himself confessed but even now
　　That there he dropped it for a special purpose
　　Which wrought to his desire.°
Othello:　　　　　　　O fool, fool, fool!
Cassio: There is besides in Roderigo's letter
　　How he upbraids Iago, that he made him　　　　　　　335
　　Brave° me upon the watch, whereon it came°
　　That I was cast;° and even but now he spake,
　　After long seeming dead, Iago hurt him,
　　Iago set him on.
　　Lodovico [*to Othello*]: You must forsake this room and go with us.　340
　　Your power and your command is taken off,°
　　And Cassio rules in Cyprus. For this slave,
　　If there be any cunning cruelty
　　That can torment him much and hold him long,°
　　It shall be his. You shall close prisoner rest°　　　345
　　Till that the nature of your fault be known
　　To the Venetian state.—Come, bring away.
Othello: Soft you;° a word or two before you go.
　　I have done the state some service, and they know 't.
　　No more of that. I pray you, in your letters,　　　　350
　　When you shall these unlucky° deeds relate,
　　Speak of me as I am; nothing extenuate,

322 *gross* monstrous　323 *discontented* full of discontent　326 *belike* most likely　327 *Came . . .
him* interposed and gave him satisfactory explanation　333 *wrought . . . desire* worked out as he
wished, fitted in with his plan　336 *Brave* defy.　*whereon it came* whereof it came about　337
cast dismissed　341 *taken off* taken away　344 *hold him long* keep him alive a long time (during
his torture)　345 *rest* remain　348 *Soft you* one moment　351 *unlucky* unfortunate

Nor set down aught in malice. Then must you speak
Of one that loved not wisely but too well;
Of one not easily jealous but, being wrought,° 355
Perplexed° in the extreme; of one whose hand,
Like the base Indian,° threw a pearl away
Richer than all his tribe; of one whose subdued° eyes,
Albeit unusèd to the melting mood,
Drops tears as fast as the Arabian trees 360
Their medicinable gum.° Set you down this;
And say besides that in Aleppo once,
Where a malignant and a turbaned Turk
Beat a Venetian and traduced the state,
I took by th' throat the circumcisèd dog 365
And smote him, thus. 　　　　　　　　　　　[*He stabs himself.*°]
Lodovico: O bloody period!°
Gratiano: All that is spoke is marred.
Othello: I kissed thee ere I killed thee. No way but this,
Killing myself, to die upon a kiss. 370

[*He kisses Desdemona and dies.*]

Cassio: This did I fear, but thought he had no weapon;
For he was great of heart.
Lodovico [*to Iago*]: 　　　　　　　O Spartan dog,°
More fell° than anguish, hunger, or the sea!
Look on the tragic loading of this bed.
This is thy work. The object poisons sight; 375
Let it be hid.° Gratiano, keep° the house,

[*The bed curtains are drawn*]

And seize upon° the fortunes of the Moor,
For they succeed on° you. [*To Cassio.*] To you, Lord Governor,
Remains the censure° of this hellish villain,
The time, the place, the torture. O, enforce it! 380
Myself will straight aboard, and to the state
This heavy act with heavy heart relate. 　　　　　　　*Exeunt.*

355 *wrought* worked upon, worked into a frenzy   356 *Perplexed* distraught   357 *Indian* (This reading from the Quarto pictures an ignorant savage who cannot recognize the value of a precious jewel. The Folio reading, *Iudean* or *Judean*, i.e., infidel or disbeliever, may refer to Herod, who slew Miriamne in a fit of jealousy, or to Judas Iscariot, the betrayer of Christ.)   358 *subdued* i.e., overcome by grief   361 *gum* i.e., myrrh   366 s.d. *He stabs himself* (This direction is in the Quarto text.)   367 *period* termination, conclusion   372 *Spartan dog* (Spartan dogs were noted for their savagery and silence.)   373 *fell* cruel   376 *Let it be hid* i.e., draw the bed curtains. (No stage direction specifies that the dead are to be carried offstage at the end of the play.)   *keep* remain in   377 *seize upon* take legal possession of   378 *succeed on* pass as though by inheritance to   379 *censure* sentencing

QUESTIONS

ACT I

1. What is Othello's position in society? How is he regarded by those who know him? By his own words, when we first meet him in Scene ii, what traits of character does he manifest?
2. How do you account for Brabantio's dismay on learning of his daughter's marriage, despite the fact that Desdemona has married a man so generally honored and admired?
3. What is Iago's view of human nature? In his fondness for likening men to animals (as in I, i, 49–50; I, i, 90–91; and I, iii, 380–381), what does he tell us about himself?
4. What reasons does Iago give for his hatred of Othello?
5. In Othello's defense before the senators (Scene iii), how does he explain Desdemona's gradual falling in love with him?
6. Is Brabantio's warning to Othello (I, iii, 293–294) an accurate or an inaccurate prophecy?
7. By what strategy does Iago enlist Roderigo in his plot against the Moor? In what lines do we learn Iago's true feelings toward Roderigo?

ACT II

1. What do the Cypriots think of Othello? Do their words (in Scene i) make him seem to us a lesser man or a larger one?
2. What cruelty does Iago display toward Emilia? How well founded is his distrust of his wife's fidelity?
3. In II, iii, 221, Othello speaks of Iago's "honesty and love." How do you account for Othello's being so totally deceived?
4. For what major events does the merrymaking (proclaimed in Scene ii) give opportunity?

ACT III

1. Trace the steps by which Iago rouses Othello to suspicion. Is there anything in Othello's character or circumstances that renders him particularly susceptible to Iago's wiles?
2. In III, iv, 49–98, Emilia knows of Desdemona's distress over the lost handkerchief. At this moment, how do you explain her failure to relieve Desdemona's mind? Is Emilia aware of her husband's villainy?

ACT IV

1. In this act, what circumstantial evidence is added to Othello's case against Desdemona?
2. How plausible do you find Bianca's flinging the handkerchief at Cassio just when Othello is looking on? How important is the handkerchief in this play? What does it represent? What suggestions or hints do you find in it?
3. What prevents Othello from being moved by Desdemona's appeal (IV, ii, 33–92)?
4. When Roderigo grows impatient with Iago (IV, ii, 181–202), how does Iago make use of his fellow plotter's discontent?
5. What does the conversation between Emilia and Desdemona (Scene iii) tell us about the nature of each?
6. In this act, what scenes (or speeches) contain memorable dramatic irony?

ACT V

1. Summarize the events that lead to Iago's unmasking.
2. How does Othello's mistaken belief that Cassio is slain (V, i, 27–34) affect the outcome of the play?
3. What is Iago's motive in stabbing Roderigo?

4. In your interpretation of the play, exactly what impels Othello to kill Desdemona? Jealousy? Desire for revenge? Excess idealism? A wish to be a public avenger who punishes, "else she'll betray more men"?

5. What do you understand by Othello's calling himself "one that loved not wisely but too well" (V, ii, 354)?

6. In your view, does Othello's long speech in V, ii, 348–366 succeed in restoring his original dignity and nobility? Do you agree with Cassio (V, ii, 372) that Othello was "great of heart"?

GENERAL QUESTIONS

1. What motivates Iago to carry out his schemes? Do you find him a devil incarnate, a madman, or a rational human being?

2. Whom besides Othello does Iago deceive? What is Desdemona's opinion of him? Emilia's? Cassio's (before Iago is found out)? To what do you attribute Iago's success as a deceiver?

3. How essential to the play is the fact that Othello is a black man, a Moor, and not a native of Venice?

4. In the introduction to his edition of the play in *The Complete Signet Classic Shakespeare*, Alvin Kernan remarks:

> *Othello* is probably the most neatly, the most formally constructed of Shakespeare's plays. Every character is, for example, balanced by another similar or contrasting character. Desdemona is balanced by her opposite, Iago; love and concern for others at one end of the scale, hatred and concern for self at the other.

Besides Desdemona and Iago, what other pairs of characters strike balances?

5. Consider any passage of the play in which there is a shift from verse to prose, or from prose to verse. What is the effect of this shift?

6. Indicate a passage that you consider memorable for its poetry. Does the passage seem introduced for its own sake? Does it in any way advance the action of the play, express theme, or demonstrate character?

7. Does the play contain any tragic *recognition*—as discussed on page 1363, a moment of terrible enlightenment, a "realization of the unthinkable"?

8. Does the downfall of Othello proceed from any flaw in his nature, or is his downfall entirely the work of Iago?

The Background of Hamlet

William Shakespeare wrote *Hamlet* around 1600. The Hamlet story first appears in the *Danish History* of the twelfth-century writer Saxo Gramaticus, but the tale is probably even older than that. Saxo's version recounts the murder of the king of Denmark by his wicked brother and the brother's marriage to the widowed queen; then Prince Amlethus, the dead king's son, feigns madness, escapes a plot on his life, and eventually gains revenge. There was an earlier English play, also called *Hamlet*, based on this tale. Written in the 1580s, probably by Thomas Kyd, it is now lost. It is believed that Shakespeare based his own play on it. Although he borrowed his story (as he did the basic plot of *Othello*), Shakespeare made it entirely his own and populated it with some of the most memorable characters in English drama. It is usually assumed that *Hamlet* was the earliest of Shakespeare's four great mature tragedies (being written just before *Othello*, *King Lear*, and *Macbeth*). If this speculative dating is true, Hamlet represented something extraordinarily innovative in world drama, especially in respect to the title character—a deeply intelligent and reflective man compelled by justice and filial duty to avenge his father's murder but simultaneously riddled with self-doubt and moral conscience. In the brooding figure of Hamlet, Shakespeare presented both the prince's inner and exterior life with startling immediacy and mysterious depth. For centuries critics have considered *Hamlet* Shakespeare's most philosophical play, yet it does not lack action. *Hamlet* contains a vengeful ghost, two sorts of madness (one tragically genuine, the other comically feigned), a suicide, sword fights, poisonings, incest, and multiple murders. The play provides both the compelling entertainment beloved by Elizabethan audiences and a tragic meditation on human existence that has haunted readers of every subsequent age.

Kevin Kline as Hamlet.

Kenneth Branagh as Hamlet and Kate Winslet as Ophelia

EDITED BY DAVID BEVINGTON

[Dramatis Personae

Ghost of Hamlet, the former King of Denmark
Claudius, King of Denmark, the former King's brother
Gertrude, Queen of Denmark, widow of the former King and now wife of Claudius
Hamlet, Prince of Denmark, son of the late King and of Gertrude
Polonius, councillor to the King
Laertes, his son
Ophelia, his daughter
Reynaldo, his servant
Horatio, Hamlet's friend and fellow student
Voltimand,
Cornelius,
Rosencrantz,
Guildenstern,   } members of the Danish court
Osric,
A Gentleman,
A Lord,
Bernardo,
Francisco,   } officers and soldiers on watch
Marcellus,
Fortinbras, Prince of Norway
Captain in his army
Three or Four Players, taking the roles of *Prologue, Player King, Player Queen,* and
    Lucianus
Two Messengers
First Sailor
Two Clowns, a gravedigger and his companion
Priest
First Ambassador from England
Lords, Soldiers, Attendants, Guards, other Players, Followers of Laertes, other Sailors,
    another Ambassador or Ambassadors from England

Scene. *Denmark*]

ACT I

Scene I [Elsinore Castle. A Guard Platform.]

Enter Bernardo and Francisco, two sentinels, [meeting].

NOTE ON THE TEXT: This text is based primarily on the Second Quarto of 1604–1605.

Bernardo: Who's there?

Francisco: Nay, answer me.° Stand and unfold yourself.°

Bernardo: Long live the King!

Francisco: Bernardo?

Bernardo: He.   5

Francisco: You come most carefully upon your hour.

Bernardo: 'Tis now struck twelve. Get thee to bed, Francisco.

Francisco: For this relief much thanks. 'Tis bitter cold,
    And I am sick at heart.

Bernardo: Have you had quiet guard?   10

Francisco: Not a mouse stirring.

Bernardo: Well, good night.
    If you do meet Horatio and Marcellus,
    The rivals° of my watch, bid them make haste.

    Enter Horatio and Marcellus.

Francisco: I think I hear them.—Stand, ho! Who is there?   15

Horatio: Friends to this ground.°

Marcellus: And liegemen to the Dane.°

Francisco: Give° you good night.

Marcellus: O, farewell, honest soldier. Who hath relieved you?

Francisco: Bernardo hath my place. Give you good night.   20

                                            Exit Francisco.

Marcellus: Holla! Bernardo!

Bernardo: Say, what, is Horatio there?

Horatio: A piece of him.

Bernardo: Welcome, Horatio. Welcome, good Marcellus.

Horatio: What, has this thing appeared again tonight?   25

Bernardo: I have seen nothing.

Marcellus: Horatio says 'tis but our fantasy,°
    And will not let belief take hold of him
    Touching this dreaded sight twice seen of us.
    Therefore I have entreated him along°   30
    With us to watch° the minutes of this night,
    That if again this apparition come
    He may approve° our eyes and speak to it.

Horatio: Tush, tush, 'twill not appear.

Bernardo: Sit down awhile,
    And let us once again assail your ears,   35
    That are so fortified against our story,
    What° we have two nights seen.

2 *me* (Francisco emphasizes that *he* is the sentry currently on watch.)   *unfold yourself* reveal your identity   14 *rivals* partners   16 *ground* country, land   17 *liegemen to the Dane* men sworn to serve the Danish king   18 *Give* i.e., may God give   27 *fantasy* imagination   30 *along* to come along   31 *watch* keep watch during   33 *approve* corroborate   37 *What* with what

Horatio: Well, sit we down,
    And let us hear Bernardo speak of this.

Bernardo: Last night of all,°

    When yond same star that's westward from the pole°   40

    Had made his° course t' illume° that part of heaven

    Where now it burns, Marcellus and myself,

    The bell then beating one—

    Enter Ghost.

Marcellus: Peace, break thee off! Look where it comes again!

Bernardo: In the same figure like the King that's dead.   45

Marcellus: Thou art a scholar.° Speak to it, Horatio.

Bernardo: Looks 'a° not like the King? Mark it, Horatio.

Horatio: Most like. It harrows me with fear and wonder.

Bernardo: It would be spoke to.°

Marcellus: Speak to it, Horatio.

Horatio: What are thou that usurp'st° this time of night,   50

    Together with that fair and warlike form

    In which the majesty of buried Denmark°

    Did sometime° march? By heaven, I charge thee, speak!

Marcellus: It is offended.

Bernardo: See, it stalks away.

Horatio: Stay! Speak, speak! I charge thee, speak!   *Exit Ghost.*   55

Marcellus: 'Tis gone and will not answer.

Bernardo: How now, Horatio? You tremble and look pale.

    Is not this something more than fantasy?

    What think you on 't?°

Horatio: Before my God, I might not this believe   60

    Without the sensible° and true avouch°

    Of mine own eyes.

Marcellus: Is it not like the King?

Horatio: As thou art to thyself.

    Such was the very armor he had on

    When he the ambitious Norway° combated.   65

    So frowned he once when, in an angry parle,°

    He smote the sledded° Polacks° on the ice.

    'Tis strange.

Marcellus: Thus twice before, and jump° at this dead hour,

---

39 *Last . . . all* i.e., this *very* last night (Emphatic.)   40 *pole* polestar, north star   41 *his* its.
illume illuminate   46 *scholar* one learned enough to know how to question a ghost properly
47 *'a* he   49 *It . . . to* (It was commonly believed that a ghost could not speak until spoken to.)
50 *usurp'st* wrongfully takes over   52 *buried Denmark* the buried King of Denmark   53
sometime formerly   59 *on 't* of it   61 *sensible* confirmed by the senses. *avouch* warrant, evidence   65 *Norway* King of Norway   66 *parle* parley   67 *sledded* traveling on sleds. *Polacks*
Poles   69 *jump* exactly

      With martial stalk° hath he gone by our watch.   70

Horatio: In what particular thought to work° I know not,

      But in the gross and scope° of mine opinion

      This bodes some strange eruption to our state.

Marcellus: Good now,° sit down, and tell me, he that knows,

      Why this same strict and most observant watch   75

      So nightly toils° the subject° of the land,

      And why such daily cast° of brazen cannon

      And foreign mart° for implements of war,

      Why such impress° of shipwrights, whose sore task

      Does not divide the Sunday from the week.   80

      What might be toward,° that this sweaty haste

      Doth make the night joint-laborer with the day?

      Who is 't that can inform me?

Horatio: That can I;

      At least, the whisper goes so. Our last king,

      Whose image even but now appeared to us,   85

      Was, as you know, by Fortinbras of Norway,

      Thereto° pricked° on by a most emulate° pride,

      Dared to the combat; in which our valiant Hamlet—

      For so this side of our known world° esteemed him—

      Did slay this Fortinbras; who by a sealed° compact   90

      Well ratified by law and heraldry

      Did forfeit, with his life, all those his lands

      Which he stood seized° of, to the conqueror;

      Against the° which a moiety competent°

      Was gagèd° by our king, which had returned°   95

      To the inheritance° of Fortinbras

      Had he been vanquisher, as, by the same cov'nant°

      And carriage of the article designed,°

      His fell to Hamlet. Now, sir, young Fortinbras,

      Of unimprovèd mettle° hot and full,   100

      Hath in the skirts° of Norway here and there

      Sharked up° a list° of lawless resolutes°

---

70 *stalk* stride   71 *to work* i.e., to collect my thoughts and try to understand this   72 *gross and scope* general drift   74 *Good now* (An expression denoting entreaty or expostulation.)   76 *toils* causes to toil. *subject* subjects   77 *cast* casting   78 *mart* buying and selling   79 *impress* impressment, conscription   81 *toward* in preparation   87 *Thereto . . . pride* (Refers to old Fortinbras, not the Danish King.) *pricked on* incited. *emulate* emulous, ambitious   89 *this . . . world* i.e., all Europe, the Western world   90 *sealed* certified, confirmed   93 *seized* possessed   94 *Against the* in return for. *moiety competent* corresponding portion   95 *gagèd* engaged, pledged. *had returned* would have passed   96 *inheritance* possession   97 *cov'nant* i.e., the *sealed compact* of line 90   98 *carriage . . . designed* carrying out of the article or clause drawn up to cover the point   100 *unimprovèd mettle* untried, undisciplined spirits   101 *skirts* outlying regions, outskirts   102 *Sharked up* gathered up, as a shark takes fish. *list* i.e., troop. *resolutes* desperadoes

For food and diet° to some enterprise
That hath a stomach° in 't, which is no other—
As it doth well appear unto our state—   105
But to recover of us, by strong hand
And terms compulsatory, those foresaid lands
So by his father lost. And this, I take it,
Is the main motive of our preparations,
The source of this our watch, and the chief head°   110
Of this posthaste and rummage° in the land.
Bernardo: I think it be no other but e'en so.
     Well may it sort° that this portentous figure
     Comes armèd through our watch so like the King
     That was and is the question° of these wars.   115
Horatio: A mote° it is to trouble the mind's eye.
     In the most high and palmy° state of Rome,
     A little ere the mightiest Julius fell,
     The graves stood tenantless, and the sheeted° dead
     Did squeak and gibber in the Roman streets;   120
     As° stars with trains° of fire and dews of blood,
     Disasters° in the sun; and the moist star°
     Upon whose influence Neptune's° empire stands°
     Was sick almost to doomsday° with eclipse.
     And even the like precurse° of feared events,   125
     As harbingers° preceding still° the fates
     And prologue to the omen° coming on,
     Have heaven and earth together demonstrated
     Unto our climatures° and countrymen.

     Enter Ghost.

     But soft,° behold! Lo, where it comes again!   130
     I'll cross° it, though it blast° me. (It spreads his° arms.) Stay, illusion!
     If thou hast any sound or use of voice,
     Speak to me!
     If there be any good thing to be done
     That may to thee do ease and grace to me,   135

103 *For food and diet* i.e., they are to serve as *food,* or "means," *to some enterprise;* also they serve in
return for the rations they get   104 *stomach* (1) a spirit of daring (2) an appetite that is fed by the
lawless resolutes   110 *head* source   111 *rummage* bustle, commotion   113 *sort* suit   115 *question*
focus of contention   116 *mote* speck of dust   117 *palmy* flourishing   119 *sheeted* shrouded   121
As (This abrupt transition suggests that matter is possibly omitted between lines 120 and 121.)
trains trails   122 *Disasters* unfavorable signs or aspects.   *moist star* i.e., moon, governing tides
123 *Neptune* god of the sea.   *stands* depends   124 *sick . . . doomsday* (See Matthew 24:29 and
Revelation 6:12.)   125 *precurse* heralding, foreshadowing   126 *harbingers* forerunners.   *still*
continually   127 *omen* calamitous event   129 *climatures* regions   130 *soft* i.e., enough, break
off   131 *cross* stand in its path, confront.   *blast* wither, strike with a curse.   s.d. *his* its

Speak to me!
If thou art privy to° thy country's fate,
Which, happily,° foreknowing may avoid,
O, speak!
Or if thou hast uphoarded in thy life   140
Extorted treasure in the womb of earth,
For which, they say, you spirits oft walk in death,
Speak of it! (*The cock crows.*) Stay and speak!—Stop it, Marcellus.
Marcellus: Shall I strike at it with my partisan?°
Horatio: Do, if it will not stand.   [*They strike at it.*]   145
Bernardo: 'Tis here!
Horatio: 'Tis here!   [*Exit Ghost.*]
Marcellus: 'Tis gone.
    We do it wrong, being so majestical,
    To offer it the show of violence,   150
    For it is as the air invulnerable,
    And our vain blows malicious mockery.
Bernardo: It was about to speak when the cock crew.
Horatio: And then it started like a guilty thing
    Upon a fearful summons. I have heard   155
    The cock, that is the trumpet° to the morn,
    Doth with his lofty and shrill-sounding throat
    Awake the god of day, and at his warning,
    Whether in sea or fire, in earth or air,
    Th' extravagant and erring° spirit hies°   160
    To his confine; and of the truth herein
    This present object made probation.°
Marcellus: It faded on the crowing of the cock.
    Some say that ever 'gainst° that season comes
    Wherein our Savior's birth is celebrated,   165
    This bird of dawning singeth all night long,
    And then, they say, no spirit dare stir abroad;
    The nights are wholesome, then no planets strike,°
    No fairy takes,° nor witch hath power to charm,
    So hallowed and so gracious° is that time.   170
Horatio: So have I heard and do in part believe it.
    But, look, the morn in russet mantle clad
    Walks o'er the dew of yon high eastward hill.
    Break we our watch up, and by my advice
    Let us impart what we have seen tonight   175

137 *privy to* in on the secret of   138 *happily* haply, perchance   144 *partisan* long-handled spear
156 *trumpet* trumpeter   160 *extravagant and erring* wandering beyond bounds. (The words have
similar meaning.)   *hies* hastens   162 *probation* proof   164 *'gainst* just before   168 *strike* destroy by evil influence   169 *takes* bewitches   170 *gracious* full of grace

Unto young Hamlet; for upon my life,
This spirit, dumb to us, will speak to him.
Do you consent we shall acquaint him with it,
As needful in our loves, fitting our duty?

Marcellus: Let's do 't, I pray, and I this morning know   180
Where we shall find him most conveniently.

                                                                    Exeunt.

Scene II [The Castle.]

*Flourish. Enter Claudius, King of Denmark, Gertrude the Queen, [the] Council,
as° Polonius and his son Laertes, Hamlet, cum aliis° [including Voltimand and
Cornelius].*

King: Though yet of Hamlet our° dear brother's death
The memory be green, and that it us befitted
To bear our hearts in grief and our whole kingdom
To be contracted in one brow of woe,
Yet so far hath discretion fought with nature   5
That we with wisest sorrow think on him
Together with remembrance of ourselves.
Therefore our sometime° sister, now our queen,
Th' imperial jointress° to this warlike state,
Have we, as 'twere with a defeated joy—   10
With an auspicious and a dropping eye,°
With mirth in funeral and with dirge in marriage,
In equal scale weighing delight and dole°—
Taken to wife. Nor have we herein barred
Your better wisdoms, which have freely gone   15
With this affair along. For all, our thanks.
Now follows that you know° young Fortinbras,
Holding a weak supposal° of our worth,
Or thinking by our late dear brother's death
Our state to be disjoint and out of frame,   20
Co-leaguèd with° this dream of his advantage,°
He hath not failed to pester us with message
Importing° the surrender of those lands
Lost by his father, with all bonds° of law,
To our most valiant brother. So much for him.   25

s.d. *as* i.e., such as, including. *cum aliis* with others   1 *our* my. (The royal "we"; also in the
following lines.)   8 *sometime* former   9 *jointress* woman possessing property with her husband
11 *With . . . eye* with one eye smiling and the other weeping   13 *dole* grief   17 *that you know*
what you know already, that; or, that you be informed as follows   18 *weak supposal* low estimate   21 *Co-leaguèd with* joined to, allied with.   *dream . . . advantage* illusory hope of having
the advantage. (His only ally is this hope.)   23 *Importing* pertaining to   24 *bonds* contracts

Now for ourself and for this time of meeting.
Thus much the business is: we have here writ
To Norway, uncle of young Fortinbras—
Who, impotent° and bed-rid, scarcely hears
Of this his nephew's purpose—to suppress   30
His° further gait° herein, in that the levies,
The lists, and full proportions are all made
Out of his subject;° and we here dispatch
You, good Cornelius, and you, Voltimand,
For bearers of this greeting to old Norway,   35
Giving to you no further personal power
To business with the King more than the scope
Of these dilated° articles allow.   [*He gives a paper.*]
Farewell, and let your haste commend your duty.°
Cornelius, Voltimand:
    In that, and all things, will we show our duty.   40
King: We doubt it nothing.° Heartily farewell.
                    [*Exeunt Voltimand and Cornelius.*]
    And now, Laertes, what's the news with you?
    You told us of some suit; what is 't, Laertes?
    You cannot speak of reason to the Dane°
    And lose your voice.° What wouldst thou beg, Laertes,   45
    That shall not be my offer, not thy asking?
    The head is not more native° to the heart,
    The hand more instrumental° to the mouth,
    Than is the throne of Denmark to thy father.
    What wouldst thou have, Laertes?
Laertes: My dread lord,   50
    Your leave and favor° to return to France,
    From whence though willingly I came to Denmark
    To show my duty in your coronation,
    Yet now I must confess, that duty done,
    My thoughts and wishes bend again toward France   55
    And bow them to your gracious leave and pardon.°
King: Have you your father's leave? What says Polonius?
Polonius: H'ath,° my lord, wrung from me my slow leave
    By laborsome petition, and at last

Upon his will I sealed° my hard° consent.   60
I do beseech you, give him leave to go.
King: Take thy fair hour,° Laertes. Time be thine,
And thy best graces spend it at thy will!°
But now, my cousin° Hamlet, and my son—
Hamlet: A little more than kin, and less than kind.°   65
King: How is it that the clouds still hang on you?
Hamlet: Not so, my lord. I am too much in the sun.°
Queen: Good Hamlet, cast thy nighted color° off,
And let thine eye look like a friend on Denmark.°
Do not forever with thy vailèd lids°   70
Seek for thy noble father in the dust.
Thou know'st 'tis common,° all that lives must die,
Passing through nature to eternity.
Hamlet: Ay, madam, it is common.
Queen: If it be,
Why seems it so particular° with thee?   75
Hamlet: Seems, madam? Nay, it is. I know not "seems."
'Tis not alone my inky cloak, good Mother,
Nor customary° suits of solemn black,
Nor windy suspiration° of forced breath,
No, nor the fruitful° river in the eye,   80
Nor the dejected havior° of the visage,
Together with all forms, moods,° shapes of grief,
That can denote me truly. These indeed seem,
For they are actions that a man might play.
But I have that within which passes show;   85
These but the trappings and the suits of woe.
King: 'Tis sweet and commendable in your nature, Hamlet,
To give these mourning duties to your father.
But you must know your father lost a father,
That father lost, lost his, and the survivor bound   90
In filial obligation for some term

---

60 *sealed* (as if sealing a legal document). *hard* reluctant   62 *Take thy fair hour* enjoy your time
of youth   63 *And . . . will* and may your finest qualities guide the way you choose to spend your
time   64 *cousin* any kin not of the immediate family   65 *A little . . . kind* i.e., closer than an
ordinary nephew (since I am stepson), and yet more separated in natural feeling (with pun on
kind meaning "affectionate" and "natural," "lawful." This line is often read as an aside, but it
need not be. The King chooses perhaps not to respond to Hamlet's cryptic and bitter remark.)
67 *the sun* i.e., the sunshine of the King's royal favor (with pun on *son*)   68 *nighted color* (1)
mourning garments of black (2) dark melancholy   69 *Denmark* the King of Denmark   70
vailèd lids lowered eyes   72 *common* of universal occurrence. (But Hamlet plays on the sense of
"vulgar" in line 74.)   75 *particular* personal   78 *customary* (1) socially conventional (2) habitual with me   79 *suspiration* sighing   80 *fruitful* abundant   81 *havior* expression   82 *moods*
outward expression of feeling

To do obsequious° sorrow. But to persever°
In obstinate condolement° is a course
Of impious stubbornness. 'Tis unmanly grief.
It shows a will most incorrect to heaven,   95
A heart unfortified,° a mind impatient,
An understanding simple° and unschooled.
For what we know must be and is as common
As any the most vulgar thing to sense,°
Why should we in our peevish opposition   100
Take it to heart? Fie, 'tis a fault to heaven,
A fault against the dead, a fault to nature,
To reason most absurd, whose common theme
Is death of fathers, and who still° hath cried,
From the first corpse° till he that died today,   105
"This must be so." We pray you, throw to earth
This unprevailing° woe and think of us
As of a father; for let the world take note,
You are the most immediate° to our throne,
And with no less nobility of love   110
Than that which dearest father bears his son
Do I impart toward° you. For° your intent
In going back to school° in Wittenberg,°
It is most retrograde° to our desire,
And we beseech you bend you° to remain   115
Here in the cheer and comfort of our eye,
Our chiefest courtier, cousin, and our son.
Queen: Let not thy mother lose her prayers, Hamlet.
    I pray thee, stay with us, go not to Wittenberg.
Hamlet: I shall in all my best° obey you, madam.   120
King: Why, 'tis a loving and a fair reply.
    Be as ourself in Denmark. Madam, come.
    This gentle and unforced accord of Hamlet
    Sits smiling to° my heart, in grace° whereof
    No jocund° health that Denmark drinks today   125
    But the great cannon to the clouds shall tell,
    And the King's rouse° the heaven shall bruit again,°
    Respeaking earthly thunder.° Come away.

92 *obsequious* suited to obsequies or funerals.   *persever* persevere   93 *condolement* sorrowing   96
unfortified i.e., against adversity   97 *simple* ignorant   99 *As . . . sense* as the most ordinary experience   104 *still* always   105 *the first corpse* (Abel's)   107 *unprevailing* unavailing, useless   109 *most
immediate* next in succession   112 *impart toward* i.e., bestow my affection on.   *For* as for   113 *to
school* i.e., to your studies.   *Wittenberg* famous German university founded in 1502   114 *retrograde*
contrary   115 *bend you* incline yourself   120 *in all my best* to the best of my ability   124 *to* i.e., at.
grace thanksgiving   125 *jocund* merry   127 *rouse* drinking of a draft of liquor.   *bruit again* loudly
echo   128 *thunder* i.e., of trumpet and kettledrum, sounded when the King drinks; see 1.4.8–12

Hamlet: O, that this too too sullied° flesh would melt,
    Thaw, and resolve itself into a dew!   130
    Or that the Everlasting had not fixed
    His canon° 'gainst self-slaughter! O God, God,
    How weary, stale, flat, and unprofitable
    Seem to me all the uses° of this world!
    Fie on 't, ah fie! 'Tis an unweeded garden   135
    That grows to seed. Things rank and gross in nature
    Possess it merely.° That it should come to this!
    But two months dead—nay, not so much, not two.
    So excellent a king, that was to° this
    Hyperion° to a satyr,° so loving to my mother   140
    That he might not beteem° the winds of heaven
    Visit her face too roughly. Heaven and earth,
    Must I remember? Why, she would hang on him
    As if increase of appetite had grown
    By what it fed on, and yet within a month—   145
    Let me not think on 't; frailty, thy name is woman!—
    A little month, or ere° those shoes were old
    With which she followed my poor father's body,
    Like Niobe,° all tears, why she, even she—
    O God, a beast, that wants discourse of reason,°   150
    Would have mourned longer—married with my uncle,
    My father's brother, but no more like my father
    Than I to Hercules. Within a month,
    Ere yet the salt of most unrighteous tears
    Had left the flushing in her gallèd° eyes,   155
    She married. O, most wicked speed, to post°
    With such dexterity to incestuous° sheets!
    It is not, nor it cannot come to good.
    But break, my heart, for I must hold my tongue.

    Enter Horatio, Marcellus, and Bernardo.

Horatio: Hail to your lordship!
Hamlet: I am glad to see you well.   160

129 *sullied* defiled. (The early quartos read *sallied;* the Folio, *solid.*)   132 *canon* law   134 *all the uses* the whole routine   137 *merely* completely   139 *to* in comparison to   140 *Hyperion* Titan sun-god, father of Helios. *satyr* a lecherous creature of classical mythology, half-human but with a goat's legs, tail, ears, and horns   141 *beteem* allow   147 *or ere* even before   149 *Niobe* Tantalus' daughter, Queen of Thebes, who boasted that she had more sons and daughters than Leto; for this, Apollo and Artemis, children of Leto, slew her fourteen children. She was turned by Zeus into a stone that continually dropped tears.   150 *wants . . . reason* lacks the faculty of reason   155 *gallèd* irritated, inflamed   156 *post* hasten   157 *incestuous* (In Shakespeare's day, the marriage of a man like Claudius to his deceased brother's wife was considered incestuous.)

Horatio!—or I do forget myself.

Horatio: The same, my lord, and your poor servant ever.

Hamlet: Sir, my good friend; I'll change that name° with you.
And what make you from° Wittenberg, Horatio?
Marcellus.   165

Marcellus: My good lord.

Hamlet: I am very glad to see you. [*To Bernardo.*] Good even, sir.—
But what in faith make you from Wittenberg?

Horatio: A truant disposition, good my lord.

Hamlet: I would not hear your enemy say so,   170
Nor shall you do my ear that violence
To make it truster of your own report
Against yourself. I know you are no truant.
But what is your affair in Elsinore?
We'll teach you to drink deep ere you depart.   175

Horatio: My lord, I came to see your father's funeral.

Hamlet: I prithee, do not mock me, fellow student;
I think it was to see my mother's wedding.

Horatio: Indeed, my lord, it followed hard° upon.

Hamlet: Thrift, thrift, Horatio! The funeral baked meats°   180
Did coldly° furnish forth the marriage tables.
Would I had met my dearest° foe in heaven
Or ever° I had seen that day, Horatio!
My father!—Methinks I see my father.

Horatio: Where, my lord?

Hamlet: In my mind's eye, Horatio.   185

Horatio: I saw him once. 'A° was a goodly king.

Hamlet: 'A was a man. Take him for all in all,
I shall not look upon his like again.

Horatio: My lord, I think I saw him yesternight.

Hamlet: Saw? Who?   190

Horatio: My lord, the King your father.

Hamlet: The King my father?

Horatio: Season your admiration° for a while
With an attent° ear till I may deliver,
Upon the witness of these gentlemen,   195
This marvel to you.

Hamlet: For God's love, let me hear!

Horatio: Two nights together had these gentlemen,
Marcellus and Bernardo, on their watch,

---

163 *change that name* i.e., give and receive reciprocally the name of "friend" (rather than talk of "servant") 164 *make you from* are you doing away from 179 *hard* close 180 *baked meats* meat pies 181 *coldly* i.e., as cold leftovers 182 *dearest* closest (and therefore deadliest) 183 *Or ever* before 186 'A he 193 *Season your admiration* restrain your astonishment 194 *attent* attentive

In the dead waste° and middle of the night,
Been thus encountered. A figure like your father,   200
Armèd at point° exactly, cap-à-pie,°
Appears before them, and with solemn march
Goes slow and stately by them. Thrice he walked
By their oppressed and fear-surprisèd eyes
Within his truncheon's° length, whilst they, distilled°   205
Almost to jelly with the act° of fear,
Stand dumb and speak not to him. This to me
In dreadful° secrecy impart they did,
And I with them the third night kept the watch,
Where, as they had delivered, both in time,   210
Form of the thing, each word made true and good,
The apparition comes. I knew your father;
These hands are not more like.
Hamlet: But where was this?
Marcellus: My lord, upon the platform where we watch.
Hamlet: Did you not speak to it?
Horatio: My lord, I did,   215
But answer made it none. Yet once methought
It lifted up its head and did address
Itself to motion, like as it would speak;°
But even then° the morning cock crew loud,
And at the sound it shrunk in haste away   220
And vanished from our sight.
Hamlet: 'Tis very strange.
Horatio: As I do live, my honored lord, 'tis true,
And we did think it writ down in our duty
To let you know of it.
Hamlet: Indeed, indeed, sirs. But this troubles me.   225
Hold you the watch tonight?
All: We do, my lord.
Hamlet: Armed, say you?
All: Armed, my lord.
Hamlet: From top to toe?
All: My lord, from head to foot.   230
Hamlet: Then saw you not his face?
Horatio: O, yes, my lord, he wore his beaver° up.
Hamlet: What° looked he, frowningly?
Horatio: A countenance more in sorrow than in anger.

199 *dead waste* desolate stillness   201 *at point* correctly in every detail.   *cap-à-pie* from head to
foot   205 *truncheon* officer's staff.   *distilled* dissolved   206 *act* action, operation   208 *dreadful*
full of dread   217–218 *did . . . speak* began to move as though it were about to speak   219
even then at that very instant   232 *beaver* visor on the helmet   233 *What* how

Hamlet: Pale or red?   235

Horatio: Nay, very pale.

Hamlet: And fixed his eyes upon you?

Horatio: Most constantly.

Hamlet: I would I had been there.

Horatio: It would have much amazed you.   240

Hamlet: Very like, very like. Stayed it long?

Horatio: While one with moderate haste might tell° a hundred.

Marcellus, Bernardo: Longer, longer.

Horatio: Not when I saw 't.

Hamlet: His beard was grizzled°—no?   245

Horatio: It was, as I have seen it in his life,
    A sable silvered.°

Hamlet: I will watch tonight.
    Perchance 'twill walk again.

Horatio: I warrant° it will.

Hamlet: If it assume my noble father's person,
    I'll speak to it though hell itself should gape   250
    And bid me hold my peace. I pray you all,
    If you have hitherto concealed this sight,
    Let it be tenable° in your silence still,
    And whatsoever else shall hap tonight,
    Give it an understanding but no tongue.   255
    I will requite your loves. So, fare you well.
    Upon the platform twixt eleven and twelve
    I'll visit you.

All: Our duty to your honor.

Hamlet: Your loves, as mine to you. Farewell.

                              Exeunt [all but Hamlet].

    My father's spirit in arms! All is not well.   260
    I doubt° some foul play. Would the night were come!
    Till then sit still, my soul. Foul deeds will rise,
    Though all the earth o'erwhelm them, to men's eyes.

                                    Exit.

Scene III [Polonius' Chambers.]

Enter Laertes and Ophelia, his sister.

Laertes: My necessaries are embarked. Farewell.
    And, sister, as the winds give benefit

---

242 *tell* count   245 *grizzled* gray   247 *sable silvered* black mixed with white   248 *warrant* assure you   253 *tenable* held   261 *doubt* suspect

And convoy is assistant,° do not sleep
        But let me hear from you.
Ophelia: Do you doubt that?
Laertes: For Hamlet, and the trifling of his favor,   5
        Hold it a fashion and a toy in blood,°
        A violet in the youth of primy° nature,
        Forward,° not permanent, sweet, not lasting,
        The perfume and suppliance° of a minute—
        No more.
Ophelia: No more but so?
Laertes: Think it no more.   10
        For nature crescent° does not grow alone
        In thews° and bulk, but as this temple° waxes
        The inward service of the mind and soul
        Grows wide withal.° Perhaps he loves you now,
        And now no soil° nor cautel° doth besmirch   15
        The virtue of his will;° but you must fear,
        His greatness weighed,° his will is not his own.
        For he himself is subject to his birth.
        He may not, as unvalued persons do,
        Carve° for himself, for on his choice depends   20
        The safety and health of this whole state,
        And therefore must his choice be circumscribed
        Unto the voice and yielding° of that body
        Whereof he is the head. Then if he says he loves you,
        It fits your wisdom so far to believe it   25
        As he in his particular act and place°
        May give his saying deed, which is no further
        Than the main voice° of Denmark goes withal.°
        Then weigh what loss your honor may sustain
        If with too credent° ear you list° his songs,   30
        Or lose your heart, or your chaste treasure open
        To his unmastered importunity.
        Fear it, Ophelia, fear it, my dear sister,
        And keep you in the rear of your affection,°
        Out of the shot and danger of desire.   35
        The chariest° maid is prodigal enough

3 *convoy is assistant* means of conveyance are available   6 *toy in blood* passing amorous fancy   7
primy in its prime, springtime   8 *Forward* precocious   9 *suppliance* supply, filler   11 *crescent*
growing, waxing   12 *thews* bodily strength.   *temple* i.e., body   14 *Grows wide withal* grows
along with it   15 *soil* blemish.   *cautel* deceit   16 *will* desire   17 *His greatness weighed* if you
take into account his high position   20 *Carve* i.e., choose   23 *voice and yielding* assent, approval
26 *in . . . place* in his particular restricted circumstances   28 *main voice* general assent.   *withal*
along with   30 *credent* credulous.   *list* listen to   34 *keep . . . affection* don't advance as far as
your affection might lead you. (A military metaphor.)   36 *chariest* most scrupulously modest

If she unmask° her beauty to the moon.°
Virtue itself scapes not calumnious strokes.
The canker galls° the infants of the spring
Too oft before their buttons° be disclosed,°   40
And in the morn and liquid dew° of youth
Contagious blastments° are most imminent.
Be wary then; best safety lies in fear.
Youth to itself rebels,° though none else near.

Ophelia: I shall the effect of this good lesson keep   45
As watchman to my heart. But, good my brother,
Do not, as some ungracious° pastors do,
Show me the steep and thorny way to heaven,
Whiles like a puffed° and reckless libertine
Himself the primrose path of dalliance treads,   50
And recks° not his own rede.°

Enter Polonius.

Laertes: O, fear me not.°
I stay too long. But here my father comes.
A double° blessing is a double grace;
Occasion smiles upon a second leave.°

Polonius: Yet here, Laertes? Aboard, aboard, for shame!   55
The wind sits in the shoulder of your sail,
And you are stayed for. There—my blessing with thee!
And these few precepts in thy memory
Look° thou character.° Give thy thoughts no tongue,
Nor any unproportioned° thought his° act.   60
Be thou familiar,° but by no means vulgar.°
Those friends thou hast, and their adoption tried,°
Grapple them unto thy soul with hoops of steel,
But do not dull thy palm° with entertainment
Of each new-hatched, unfledged courage.° Beware   65
Of entrance to a quarrel, but being in,
Bear 't that° th' opposèd may beware of thee.

---

37 *If she unmask* if she does no more than show her beauty.   *moon* (Symbol of chastity.)   39
canker galls cankerworm destroys   40 *buttons* buds.   *disclosed* opened   41 *liquid dew* i.e., time
when dew is fresh and bright   42 *blastments* blights   44 *Youth . . . rebels* youth is inherently
rebellious   47 *ungracious* ungodly   49 *puffed* bloated, or swollen with pride   51 *recks* heeds.
rede counsel.   51 *fear me not* don't worry on my account   53 *double* (Laertes has already bid
his father good-bye.)   54 *Occasion . . . leave* happy is the circumstance that provides a second
leave-taking. The goddess Occasion, or Opportunity, smiles.)   59 *Look* be sure that.   *character* inscribe   60 *unproportioned* badly calculated, intemperate.   *his* its   61 *familiar* sociable.
vulgar common   62 *and their adoption tried* and also their suitability for adoption as friends
having been tested   64 *dull thy palm* i.e., shake hands so often as to make the gesture meaningless   65 *courage* young man of spirit   67 *Bear 't that* manage it so that

Give every man thy ear, but few thy voice;
Take each man's censure,° but reserve thy judgment.
Costly thy habit° as thy purse can buy,   70
But not expressed in fancy;° rich, not gaudy,
For the apparel oft proclaims the man,
And they in France of the best rank and station
Are of a most select and generous chief in that.°
Neither a borrower nor a lender be,   75
For loan oft loses both itself and friend,
And borrowing dulleth edge of husbandry.°
This above all: to thine own self be true,
And it must follow, as the night the day,
Thou canst not then be false to any man.   80
Farewell. My blessing season° this in thee!
Laertes: Most humbly do I take my leave, my lord.
Polonius: The time invests° you. Go, your servants tend.°
Laertes: Farewell, Ophelia, and remember well
        What I have said to you.   85
Ophelia: 'Tis in my memory locked,
        And you yourself shall keep the key of it.
Laertes: Farewell.   *Exit Laertes.*
Polonius: What is 't, Ophelia, he hath said to you?
Ophelia: So please you, something touching the Lord Hamlet.   90
Polonius: Marry,° well bethought.
        'Tis told me he hath very oft of late
        Given private time to you, and you yourself
        Have of your audience been most free and bounteous.
        If it be so—as so 'tis put on° me,   95
        And that in way of caution—I must tell you
        You do not understand yourself so clearly
        As it behooves° my daughter and your honor.
        What is between you? Give me up the truth.
Ophelia: He hath, my lord, of late made many tenders°   100
        Of his affection to me.
Polonius: Affection? Pooh! You speak like a green girl,
        Unsifted° in such perilous circumstance.
        Do you believe his tenders, as you call them?
Ophelia: I do not know, my lord, what I should think.   105
Polonius: Marry, I will teach you. Think yourself a baby

---

69 *censure* opinion, judgment 70 *habit* clothing 71 *fancy* excessive ornament, decadent
fashion 74 *Are . . . that* are of a most refined and well-bred preeminence in choosing what to
wear 77 *husbandry* thrift 81 *season* mature 83 *invests* besieges, presses upon. *tend* attend,
wait 91 *Marry* i.e., by the Virgin Mary. (A mild oath.) 95 *put on* impressed on, told to 98
behooves befits 100 *tenders* offers 103 *Unsifted* i.e., untried

That you have ta'en these tenders for true pay
Which are not sterling.° Tender° yourself more dearly,
Or—not to crack the wind° of the poor phrase,
Running it thus—you'll tender me a fool.°   110
Ophelia: My lord, he hath importuned me with love
In honorable fashion.°
Polonius: Ay, fashion you may call it. Go to,° go to.
Ophelia: And hath given countenance° to his speech, my lord,
With almost all the holy vows of heaven.   115
Polonius: Ay, springes° to catch woodcocks.° I do know,
When the blood burns, how prodigal° the soul
Lends the tongue vows. These blazes, daughter,
Giving more light than heat, extinct in both
Even in their promise as it° is a-making,   120
You must not take for fire. From this time
Be something° scanter of your maiden presence.
Set your entreatments° at a higher rate
Than a command to parle.° For Lord Hamlet,
Believe so much in him° that he is young,   125
And with a larger tether may he walk
Than may be given you. In few,° Ophelia,
Do not believe his vows, for they are brokers,°
Not of that dye° which their investments° show,
But mere implorators° of unholy suits,   130
Breathing° like sanctified and pious bawds,
The better to beguile. This is for all:°
I would not, in plain terms, from this time forth
Have you so slander° any moment° leisure
As to give words or talk with the Lord Hamlet.   135
Look to 't, I charge you. Come your ways.°
Ophelia: I shall obey, my lord.   *Exeunt.*

108 *sterling* legal currency.   *Tender* hold, look after, offer   109 *crack the wind* i.e., run it until
it is broken-winded   110 *tender me a fool* (1) show yourself to me as a fool (2) show me up as a
fool (3) present me with a grand-child. (*Fool* was a term of endearment for a child.)   113
fashion mere form, pretense.   *Go to* (An expression of impatience.)   114 *countenance* credit,
confirmation   116 *springes* snares.   *woodcocks* birds easily caught; here used to connote gullibility.   117 *prodigal* prodigally   120 *it* i.e., the promise   122 *something* somewhat   123 *en-
treatments* negotiations for surrender. (A military term.)   124 *parle* discuss terms with the
enemy. (Polonius urges his daughter, in the metaphor of military language, not to meet with
Hamlet and consider giving in to him merely because he requests an interview.)   125 *so . . .
him* this much concerning him   127 *In few* briefly   128 *brokers* go-between, procurers   129
dye color or sort.   *investments* clothes. (The vows are not what they seem.)   130 *mere im-
plorators* out and out solicitors   131 *Breathing* speaking   132 *for all* once for all, in sum   134
slander abuse, misuse.   *moment* moment's   136 *Come your ways* come along

Scene IV [The Guard Platform.]

Enter Hamlet, Horatio, and Marcellus.

Hamlet: The air bites shrewdly;° it is very cold.
Horatio: It is a nipping and an eager° air.
Hamlet: What hour now?
Horatio: I think it lacks of° twelve.
Marcellus: No, it is struck.
Horatio: Indeed? I heard it not.
   It then draws near the season°   5
   Wherein the spirit held his wont° to walk.

A flourish of trumpets, and two pieces° go off [within].

   What does this mean, my lord?
Hamlet: The King doth wake° tonight and takes his rouse,°
   Keeps wassail,° and the swaggering upspring° reels;°
   And as he drains his drafts of Rhenish° down,   10
   The kettledrum and trumpet thus bray out
   The triumph of his pledge.°
Horatio: Is it a custom?
Hamlet: Ay, marry, is 't,
   But to my mind, though I am native here
   And to the manner° born, it is a custom   15
   More honored in the breach than the observance.°
   This heavy-headed revel east and west°
   Makes us traduced and taxed of° other nations.
   They clepe° us drunkards, and with swinish phrase°
   Soil our addition;° and indeed it takes   20
   From our achievements, though performed at height,°
   The pith and marrow of our attribute.°
   So, oft it chances in particular men,
   That for° some vicious mole of nature° in them,
   As in their birth—wherein they are not guilty,   25
   Since nature cannot choose his° origin—
   By their o'ergrowth of some complexion,°

---

1 *shrewdly* keenly, sharply   2 *eager* biting   3 *lacks of* is just short of   5 *season* time   6 *held his wont* was accustomed. s.d. *pieces* i.e., of ordnance, cannon   8 *wake* stay awake and hold revel. *takes his rouse* carouses   9 *wassail* carousal. *upspring* wild German dance. *reels* dances   10 *Rhenish* Rhine wine   12 *The triumph . . . pledge* i.e., his feat in draining the wine in a single draft   15 *manner* custom (of drinking)   16 *More . . . observance* better neglected than followed   17 *east and west* i.e., everywhere   18 *taxed of* censured by   19 *clepe* call. *with swinish phrase* i.e., by calling us swine   20 *addition* reputation   21 *at height* outstandingly   22 *The pith . . . attribute* the essence of the reputation that others attribute to us   24 *for* on account of. *mole of nature* natural blemish in one's constitution   26 *his* its   27 *their o'ergrowth . . . complexion* the excessive growth in individuals of some natural trait

Oft breaking down the pales° and forts of reason,
Or by some habit that too much o'erleavens°
The form of plausive° manners, that these men,   30
Carrying, I say, the stamp of one defect,
Being nature's livery° or fortune's star,°
His virtues else,° be they as pure as grace,
As infinite as man may undergo,°
Shall in the general censure° take corruption   35
From that particular fault. The dram of evil
Doth all the noble substance often dout
To his own scandal.°

Enter Ghost.

Horatio: Look, my lord, it comes!
Hamlet: Angels and ministers of grace° defend us!
Be thou° a spirit of health° or goblin damned,   40
Bring° with thee airs from heaven or blasts from hell,
Be thy intents° wicked or charitable,
Thou com'st in such a questionable° shape
That I will speak to thee. I'll call thee Hamlet,
King, father, royal Dane. O, answer me!   45
Let me not burst in ignorance, but tell
Why thy canonized° bones, hearsèd° in death,
Have burst their cerements;° why the sepulcher
Wherein we saw thee quietly inurned°
Hath oped his ponderous and marble jaws   50
To cast thee up again. What may this mean,
That thou, dead corpse, again in complete steel,°
Revisits thus the glimpses of the moon,°
Making night hideous, and we fools of nature°
So horridly to shake our disposition°   55
With thoughts beyond the reaches of our souls?
Say, why is this? Wherefore? What should we do?

---

28 *pales* palings, fences (as of a fortification)   29 *o'erleavens* induces a change throughout (as yeast works in dough)   30 *plausive* pleasing   32 *nature's livery* sign of one's servitude to nature. *fortune's star* the destiny that chance brings   33 *His virtues else* i.e., the other qualities of *these men* (line 30)   34 *may undergo* can sustain   35 *general censure* general opinion that people have of him   36–38 *The dram . . . scandal* i.e., the small drop of evil blots out or works against the noble substance of the whole and brings it into disrepute. To *dout* is to blot out. (A famous crux.)   39 *ministers of grace* messengers of God   40 *Be thou* whether you are.   *spirit of health* good angel   41 *Bring* whether you bring   42 *Be thy intents* whether your intentions are   43 *questionable* inviting question   47 *canonized* buried according to the canons of the church.   *hearsèd* coffined   48 *cerements* grave clothes   49 *inurned* entombed   52 *complete steel* full armor   53 *glimpses of the moon* pale and uncertain moonlight   54 *fools of nature* mere men, limited to natural knowledge and subject to nature   55 *So . . . disposition* to distress our mental composure so violently

Horatio: It beckons you to go away with it,
    As if it some impartment° did desire
    To you alone.
Marcellus: Look with what courteous action   60
    It wafts you to a more removèd ground.
    But do not go with it.
Horatio: No, by no means.
Hamlet: It will not speak. Then I will follow it.
Horatio: Do not, my lord!
Hamlet: Why, what should be the fear?
    I do not set my life at a pin's fee,°   65
    And for my soul, what can it do to that,
    Being a thing immortal as itself?
    It waves me forth again. I'll follow it.
Horatio: What if it tempt you toward the flood,° my lord,
    Or to the dreadful summit of the cliff   70
    That beetles o'er° his base into the sea,
    And there assume some other horrible form
    Which might deprive your sovereignty of reason°
    And draw you into madness? Think of it.
    The very place puts toys of desperation,°   75
    Without more motive, into every brain
    That looks so many fathoms to the sea
    And hears it roar beneath.
Hamlet: It wafts me still.—Go on, I'll follow thee.
Marcellus: You shall not go, my lord.   *[They try to stop him.]*
Hamlet: Hold off your hands!   80
Horatio: Be ruled. You shall not go.
Hamlet: My fate cries out,°
    And makes each petty° artery° in this body
    As hardy as the Nemean lion's° nerve.°
    Still am I called. Unhand me, gentlemen.
    By heaven, I'll make a ghost of him that lets° me!   85
    I say, away!—Go on, I'll follow thee.

    Exeunt Ghost and Hamlet.

Horatio: He waxes desperate with imagination.

---

59 *impartment* communication   65 *fee* value   69 *flood* sea   71 *beetles o'er* overhangs threateningly (like bushy eyebrows.)   73 *deprive . . . reason* take away the rule of reason over your mind 75 *toys of desperation* fancies of desperate acts, i.e., suicide   81 *My fate cries out* my destiny summons me   82 *petty* weak.   *artery* (through which the vital spirits were thought to have been conveyed)   83 *Nemean lion's* one of the monsters slain by Hercules in his twelve labors. *nerve* sinew   85 *lets* hinders

Marcellus: Let's follow. 'Tis not fit thus to obey him.
Horatio: Have after.° To what issue° will this come?
Marcellus: Something is rotten in the state of Denmark.   90
Horatio: Heaven will direct it.°
Marcellus: Nay, let's follow him.   *Exeunt.*

Scene V [The Battlements of the Castle.]

    Enter Ghost and Hamlet.

Hamlet: Whither wilt thou lead me? Speak. I'll go no further.
Ghost: Mark me.
Hamlet: I will.
Ghost: My hour is almost come,
    When I to sulfurous and tormenting flames
    Must render up myself.
Hamlet: Alas, poor ghost!
Ghost: Pity me not, but lend thy serious hearing   5
    To what I shall unfold.
Hamlet: Speak. I am bound° to hear.
Ghost: So art thou to revenge, when thou shalt hear.
Hamlet: What?
Ghost: I am thy father's spirit,   10
    Doomed for a certain term to walk the night,
    And for the day confined to fast° in fires,
    Till the foul crimes° done in my days of nature°
    Are burnt and purged away. But that° I am forbid
    To tell the secrets of my prison house,   15
    I could a tale unfold whose lightest word
    Would harrow up° thy soul, freeze thy young blood,
    Make thy two eyes like stars start from their spheres,°
    Thy knotted and combinèd locks° to part,
    And each particular hair to stand on end   20
    Like quills upon the fretful porcupine.
    But this eternal blazon° must not be
    To ears of flesh and blood. List, list, O, list!
    If thou didst ever thy dear father love—
Hamlet: O God!   25
Ghost: Revenge his foul and most unnatural murder.
Hamlet: Murder?

89 *Have after* let's go after him. *issue* outcome   91 *it* i.e., the outcome   7 *bound* (1) ready (2) obligated by duty and fate. (The Ghost, in line 8, answers in the second sense.)   12 *fast* do penance by fasting   13 *crimes* sins. *of nature* as a mortal   14 *But that* were it not that   17 *harrow up* lacerate, tear   18 *spheres* i.e., eye-sockets, here compared to the orbits or transparent revolving spheres in which, according to Ptolemaic astronomy, the heavenly bodies were fixed   19 *knotted . . . locks* hair neatly arranged and confined   22 *eternal blazon* revelation of the secrets of eternity

Ghost: Murder most foul, as in the best° it is,
   But this most foul, strange, and unnatural.
Hamlet: Haste me to know 't, that I, with wings as swift   30
   As meditation or the thoughts of love,
   May sweep to my revenge.
Ghost: I find thee apt;
   And duller shouldst thou be° than the fat° weed
   That roots itself in ease on Lethe° wharf,
   Wouldst thou not stir in this. Now, Hamlet, hear.   35
   'Tis given out that, sleeping in my orchard,°
   A serpent stung me. So the whole ear of Denmark
   Is by a forgèd process° of my death
   Rankly abused.° But know, thou noble youth,
   The serpent that did sting thy father's life   40
   Now wears his crown.
Hamlet: O, my prophetic soul! My uncle!
Ghost: Ay, that incestuous, that adulterate° beast,
   With witchcraft of his wit, with traitorous gifts°—
   O wicked wit and gifts, that have the power   45
   So to seduce!—won to his shameful lust
   The will of my most seeming-virtuous queen.
   O Hamlet, what a falling off was there!
   From me, whose love was of that dignity
   That it went hand in hand even with the vow°   50
   I made to her in marriage, and to decline
   Upon a wretch whose natural gifts were poor
   To° those of mine!
   But virtue, as it° never will be moved,
   Though lewdness court it in a shape of heaven,°   55
   So lust, though to a radiant angel linked,
   Will sate itself in a celestial bed°
   And prey on garbage.
   But soft, methinks I scent the morning air.
   Brief let me be. Sleeping within my orchard,   60
   My custom always of the afternoon,
   Upon my secure° hour thy uncle stole,
   With juice of cursèd hebona° in a vial,

---

28 *in the best* even at best   33 *shouldst thou be* you would have to be.   *fat* torpid, lethargic   34
Lethe the river of forgetfulness in Hades   36 *orchard* garden   38 *forgèd process* falsified account
39 *abused* deceived   43 *adulterate* adulterous   44 *gifts* (1) talents (2) presents   50 *even with
the vow* with the very vow   53 *To* compared to   54 *virtue, as it* as virtue   55 *shape of heaven*
heavenly form   57 *sate . . . bed* cease to find sexual pleasure in a virtuously lawful marriage
62 *secure* confident, unsuspicious   63 *hebona* a poison. (The word seems to be a form of *ebony*,
though it is thought perhaps to be related to *henbane,* a poison, or to *ebenus,* "yew.")

And in the porches of my ears° did pour
The leprous distillment,° whose effect   65
Holds such an enmity with blood of man
That swift as quicksilver it courses through
The natural gates and alleys of the body,
And with a sudden vigor it doth posset°
And curd, like eager° droppings into milk,   70
The thin and wholesome blood. So did it mine,
And a most instant tetter° barked° about,
Most lazar-like,° with vile and loathsome crust,
All my smooth body.
Thus was I, sleeping, by a brother's hand   75
Of life, of crown, of queen at once dispatched,°
Cut off even in the blossom of my sin,
Unhouseled,° disappointed,° unaneled,°
No reckoning° made, but sent to my account
With all my imperfections on my head.   80
O, horrible! O, horrible, most horrible!
If thou hast nature° in thee, bear it not.
Let not the royal bed of Denmark be
A couch for luxury° and damnèd incest.
But, howsoever thou pursues this act,   85
Taint not thy mind nor let thy soul contrive
Against thy mother aught. Leave her to heaven
And to those thorns that in her bosom lodge,
To prick and sting her. Fare thee well at once.
The glowworm shows the matin° to be near,   90
And 'gins to pale his° uneffectual fire.
Adieu, adieu, adieu! Remember me.   [Exit.]
Hamlet: O all you host of heaven! O earth! What else?
And shall I couple° hell? O, fie! Hold,° hold, my heart,
And you, my sinews, grow not instant° old,   95
But bear me stiffly up. Remember thee?
Ay, thou poor ghost, whiles memory holds a seat
In this distracted globe.° Remember thee?
Yea, from the table° of my memory
I'll wipe away all trivial fond° records,   100

64 *porches of my ears* ears as a porch or entrance of the body   65 *leprous distillment* distillation
causing leprosylike disfigurement   69 *posset* coagulate, curdle   70 *eager* sour, acid   72 *tetter*
eruption of scabs.   *barked* covered with a rough covering, like bark of a tree   73 *lazar-like* lep-
erlike   76 *dispatched* suddenly deprived   78 *Unhouseled* without having received the Sacrament.   *disappointed* unready (spiritually) for the last journey.   *unaneled* without having received extreme unction   79 *reckoning* settling of accounts   82 *nature* i.e., the promptings of a
son   84 *luxury* lechery   90 *matin* morning   91 *his* its   94 *couple* add.   *Hold* hold together
95 *instant* instantly   98 *globe* (1) head (2) world   99 *table* tablet, slate   100 *fond* foolish

All saws° of books, all forms,° all pressures° past
That youth and observation copied there,
And thy commandment all alone shall live
Within the book and volume of my brain,
Unmixed with baser matter. Yes, by heaven!   105
O most pernicious woman!
O villain, villain, smiling, damnèd villain!
My tables°—meet it is° I set it down
That one may smile, and smile, and be a villain.
At least I am sure it may be so in Denmark.   110

[*Writing.*]

So, uncle, there you are.° Now to my word:
It is "Adieu, adieu! Remember me."
I have sworn 't.

Enter Horatio and Marcellus.

Horatio: My lord, my lord!
Marcellus: Lord Hamlet!   115
Horatio: Heavens secure him!°
Hamlet: So be it.
Marcellus: Hillo, ho, ho, my lord!
Hamlet: Hillo, ho, ho, boy! Come, bird, come.°
Marcellus: How is 't, my noble lord?   120
Horatio: What news, my lord?
Hamlet: O, wonderful!
Horatio: Good my lord, tell it.
Hamlet: No, you will reveal it.
Horatio: Not I, my lord, by heaven.   125
Marcellus: Nor I, my lord.
Hamlet: How say you, then, would heart of man once° think it?
    But you'll be secret?
Horatio, Marcellus: Ay, by heaven, my lord.
Hamlet: There's never a villain dwelling in all Denmark
    But he's an arrant° knave.   130
Horatio: There needs no ghost, my lord, come from the grave
    To tell us this.
Hamlet: Why, right, you are in the right.
    And so, without more circumstance° at all,

101 *saws* wise sayings.   *forms* shapes or images copied onto the slate; general ideas.   *pressures*
impressions stamped   108 *tables* writing tablets.   *meet it is* it is fitting   111 *there you are* i.e.,
there, I've written that down against you   116 *secure him* keep him safe   119 *Hillo . . . come* (A
falconer's call to a hawk in air. Hamlet mocks the hallooing as though it were a part of hawking.)
127 *once* ever   130 *arrant* thoroughgoing   133 *circumstance* ceremony, elaboration

I hold it fit that we shake hands and part,
You as your business and desire shall point you—   135
For every man hath business and desire,
Such as it is—and for my own poor part,
Look you, I'll go pray.

Horatio: These are but wild and whirling words, my lord.

Hamlet: I am sorry they offend you, heartily;   140
Yes, faith, heartily.

Horatio: There's no offense, my lord.

Hamlet: Yes, by Saint Patrick,° but there is, Horatio,
And much offense° too. Touching this vision here,
It is an honest ghost,° that let me tell you.
For your desire to know what is between us,   145
O'ermaster 't as you may. And now, good friends,
As you are friends, scholars, and soldiers,
Give me one poor request.

Horatio: What is 't, my lord? We will.

Hamlet: Never make known what you have seen tonight.   150

Horatio, Marcellus: My lord, we will not.

Hamlet: Nay, but swear 't.

Horatio: In faith, my lord, not I.°

Marcellus: Nor I, my lord, in faith.

Hamlet: Upon my sword.°   [*He holds out his sword.*]   155

Marcellus: We have sworn, my lord, already.°

Hamlet: Indeed, upon my sword, indeed.

Ghost (*cries under the stage*): Swear.

Hamlet: Ha, ha, boy, sayst thou so? Art thou there, truepenny?°
Come on, you hear this fellow in the cellarage.   160
Consent to swear.

Horatio: Propose the oath, my lord.

Hamlet: Never to speak of this that you have seen,
Swear by my sword.

Ghost [*beneath*]: Swear.   [*They swear.*]°

Hamlet: Hic et ubique?° Then we'll shift our ground.   165

                                      [*He moves to another spot.*]

142 *Saint Patrick* (The keeper of Purgatory and patron saint of all blunders and confusion.)
143 *offense* (Hamlet deliberately changes Horatio's "no offense taken" to "an offense against all
decency.")   144 *an honest ghost* i.e., a real ghost and not an evil spirit   153 *In faith . . . I* i.e., I
swear not to tell what I have seen. (Horatio is not refusing to swear.)   155 *sword* i.e., the hilt
in the form of a cross   156 *We . . . already* i.e., we swore in faith   159 *truepenny* honest old
fellow   164 s.d. *They swear* (Seemingly they swear here, and at lines 170 and 190, as they lay
their hands on Hamlet's sword. Triple oaths would have particular force; these three oaths deal
with what they have seen, what they have heard, and what they promise about Hamlet's *antic
disposition.*)   165 *Hic et ubique* here and everywhere. (Latin.)

Come hither, gentlemen,
And lay your hands again upon my sword.
Swear by my sword
Never to speak of this that you have heard.
Ghost [*beneath*]: Swear by his sword.   [*They swear.*]
Hamlet: Well said, old mole. Canst work i' th' earth so fast?
A worthy pioner!°—Once more remove, good friends.

[*He moves again.*]

Horatio: O day and night, but this is wondrous strange!
Hamlet: And therefore as a stranger° give it welcome.
There are more things in heaven and earth, Horatio,   175
Than are dreamt of in your philosophy.°
But come;
Here, as before, never, so help you mercy,°
How strange or odd soe'er I bear myself—
As I perchance hereafter shall think meet   180
To put an antic° disposition on—
That you, at such times seeing me, never shall,
With arms encumbered° thus, or this headshake,
Or by pronouncing of some doubtful phrase
As "Well, we know," or "We could, an if° we would,"   185
Or "If we list° to speak," or "There be, an if they might,"°
Or such ambiguous giving out,° to note°
That you know aught° of me—this do swear,
So grace and mercy at your most need help you.
Ghost [*beneath*]: Swear.   [*They swear.*] 190
Hamlet: Rest, rest, perturbèd spirit! So, gentlemen,
With all my love I do commend me to you;°
And what so poor a man as Hamlet is
May do t' express his love and friending° to you,
God willing, shall not lack.° Let us go in together,   195
And still° your fingers on your lips, I pray.
The time° is out of joint. O cursèd spite°

172 *pioner* foot soldier assigned to dig tunnels and excavations   174 *as a stranger* i.e., needing
your hospitality   176 *your philosophy* this subject called "natural philosophy" or "science" that
people talk about   178 *so help you mercy* as you hope for God's mercy when you are judged
181 *antic* fantastic   183 *encumbered* folded   185 *an if* if   186 *list* wished.   *There . . . might*
i.e., there are people here (we, in fact) who could tell news if we were at liberty to do so   187
giving out intimation.   *note* draw attention to the fact   188 *aught* i.e., something secret   192
do . . . you entrust myself to you   194 *friending* friendliness   195 *lack* be lacking   196 *still* always   197 *The time* the state of affairs.   *spite* i.e., the spite of Fortune

That ever I was born to set it right!

[They wait for him to leave first.]

Nay, come, let's go together.°   *Exeunt.*

ACT II

Scene I [Polonius' Chambers.]

Enter Old Polonius With His Man [Reynaldo].

Polonius: Give him this money and these notes, Reynaldo.

[He gives money and papers.]

Reynaldo: I will, my lord.
Polonius: You shall do marvelous° wisely, good Reynaldo,
    Before you visit him, to make inquire°
    Of his behavior.
Reynaldo: My lord, I did intend it.   5
Polonius: Marry, well said, very well said. Look you, sir,
    Inquire me first what Danskers° are in Paris,
    And how, and who, what means,° and where they keep,°
    What company, at what expense; and finding
    By this encompassment° and drift° of question   10
    That they do know my son, come you more nearer
    Than your particular demands will touch it.°
    Take you,° as 'twere, some distant knowledge of him,
    As thus, "I know his father and his friends,
    And in part him." Do you mark this, Reynaldo?   15
Reynaldo: Ay, very well, my lord.
Polonius: "And in part him, but," you may say, "not well.
    But if 't be he I mean, he's very wild,
    Addicted so and so," and there put on° him
    What forgeries° you please—marry, none so rank°   20
    As may dishonor him, take heed of that,
    But, sir, such wanton,° wild, and usual slips
    As are companions noted and most known
    To youth and liberty.
Reynaldo: As gaming, my lord.   25
Polonius: Ay, or drinking, fencing, swearing,
    Quarreling, drabbing°—you may go so far.

199 *let's go together* (Probably they wait for him to leave first, but he refuses this ceremoniousness.)   3 *marvelous* marvelously   4 *inquire* inquiry   7 *Danskers* Danes   8 *what means* what wealth (they have).   *keep* dwell   10 *encompassment* roundabout talking.   *drift* gradual approach or course   11–12 *come . . . it* you will find out more this way than by asking pointed questions (*particular demands*)   13 *Take you* assume, pretend   19 *put on* impute to   20 *forgeries* invented tales.   *rank* gross   22 *wanton* sportive, unrestrained   27 *drabbing* whoring

Reynaldo: My lord, that would dishonor him.

Polonius: Faith, no, as you may season° it in the charge.

You must not put another scandal on him   30

That he is open to incontinency;°

That's not my meaning. But breathe his faults so quaintly°

That they may seem the taints of liberty,°

The flash and outbreak of a fiery mind,

A savageness in unreclaimèd blood,   35

Of general assault.°

Reynaldo: But, my good lord—

Polonius: Wherefore should you do this?

Reynaldo: Ay, my lord, I would know that.

Polonius: Marry, sir, here's my drift,   40

And I believe it is a fetch of warrant.°

You laying these slight sullies on my son,

As 'twere a thing a little soiled wi' the working,°

Mark you,

Your party in converse,° him you would sound,°   45

Having ever° seen in the prenominate crimes°

The youth you breathe° of guilty, be assured

He closes with you in this consequence:°

"Good sir," or so, or "friend," or "gentleman,"

According to the phrase or the addition°   50

Of man and country.

Reynaldo: Very good, my lord.

Polonius: And then, sir, does 'a this—'a does—

what was I about to say? By the Mass, I was

about to say something. Where did I leave?

Reynaldo: At "closes in the consequence."   55

Polonius: At "closes in the consequence," ay, marry.

He closes thus: "I know the gentleman,

I saw him yesterday," or "th' other day,"

Or then, or then, with such or such, "and as you say,

There was 'a gaming," "there o'ertook in 's rouse,"°   60

"There falling out° at tennis," or perchance

"I saw him enter such a house of sale,"

---

29 *season* temper, soften   31 *incontinency* habitual sexual excess   32 *quaintly* artfully, subtly
33 *taints of liberty* faults resulting from free living   35–36 *A savageness . . . assault* a wildness in
untamed youth that assails all indiscriminately   41 *fetch of warrant* legitimate trick   43 *soiled
wi' the working* soiled by handling while it is being made, i.e., by involvement in the ways of the
world   45 *converse* conversation. *sound* i.e., sound out   46 *Having ever* if he has ever.
prenominate crimes before-mentioned offenses   47 *breathe* speak   48 *closes . . . consequence*
takes you into his confidence in some fashion, as follows   50 *addition* title   60 *o'ertook in 's
rouse* overcome by drink   61 *falling out* quarreling

Videlicet° a brothel, or so forth. See you now,
Your bait of falsehood takes this carp° of truth;
And thus do we of wisdom and of reach,°   65
With windlasses° and with assays of bias,°
By indirections find directions° out.
So by my former lecture and advice
Shall you my son. You have° me, have you not?
Reynaldo: My lord, I have.
Polonius: God b' wi'° ye; fare ye well.   70
Reynaldo: Good my lord.
Polonius: Observe his inclination in yourself.°
Reynaldo: I shall, my lord.
Polonius: And let him ply his music.
Reynaldo: Well, my lord.   75
Polonius: Farewell.   Exit Reynaldo.

        Enter Ophelia.

                        How now, Ophelia, what's the matter?
Ophelia: O my lord, my lord, I have been so affrighted!
Polonius: With what, i' the name of God?
Ophelia: My lord, as I was sewing in my closet,°
        Lord Hamlet, with his doublet° all unbraced,°   80
        No hat upon his head, his stockings fouled,
        Ungartered, and down-gyvèd° to his ankle,
        Pale as his shirt, his knees knocking each other,
        And with a look so piteous in purport°
        As if he had been loosèd out of hell   85
        To speak of horrors—he comes before me.
Polonius: Mad for thy love?
Ophelia: My lord, I do not know,
        But truly I do fear it.
Polonius: What said he?
Ophelia: He took me by the wrist and held me hard.
        Then goes he to the length of all his arm,   90
        And, with his other hand thus o'er his brow
        He falls to such perusal of my face
        As° 'a would draw it. Long stayed he so.
        At last, a little shaking of mine arm

63 *Videlicet* namely   64 *carp* a fish   65 *reach* capacity, ability   66 *windlasses* i.e., circuitous
paths. (Literally, circuits made to head off the game in hunting.)   *assays of bias* attempts
through indirection (like the curving path of the bowling ball, which is biased or weighted to
one side)   67 *directions* i.e., the way things really are   69 *have* understand   70 *b' wi'* be with
72 *in yourself* in your own person (as well as by asking questions)   79 *closet* private chamber
80 *doublet* close-fitting jacket.   *unbraced* unfastened   82 *down-gyvèd* fallen to the ankles (like
gyves or fetters)   84 *in purport* in what it expressed   93 *As* as if (also in line 97)

And thrice his head thus waving up and down,   95
He raised a sigh so piteous and profound
As it did seem to shatter all his bulk°
And end his being. That done, he lets me go,
And with his head over his shoulder turned
He seemed to find his way without his eyes,   100
For out o' doors he went without their helps,
And to the last bended their light on me.

Polonius: Come, go with me. I will go seek the King.
  This is the very ecstasy° of love,
  Whose violent property° fordoes° itself   105
  And leads the will to desperate undertakings
  As oft as any passion under heaven
  That does afflict our natures. I am sorry.
  What, have you given him any hard words of late?

Ophelia: No, my good lord, but as you did command   110
  I did repel his letters and denied
  His access to me.

Polonius: That hath made him mad.
  I am sorry that with better heed and judgment
  I had not quoted° him. I feared he did but trifle
  And meant to wrack° thee. But beshrew my jealousy!°   115
  By heaven, it is as proper to our age°
  To cast beyond° ourselves in our opinions
  As it is common for the younger sort
  To lack discretion. Come, go we to the King.
  This must be known,° which, being kept close,° might move   120
  More grief to hide than hate to utter love.°
  Come.

                                                                   Exeunt.

Scene II [The Castle.]

Flourish. Enter King and Queen, Rosencrantz, and Guildenstern [with others].

King: Welcome, dear Rosencrantz and Guildenstern.
  Moreover that° we much did long to see you,
  The need we have to use you did provoke
  Our hasty sending. Something have you heard
  Of Hamlet's transformation—so call it,   5

97 *bulk* body   104 *ecstasy* madness   105 *property* nature. *fordoes* destroys   114 *quoted* observed   115 *wrack* ruin, seduce. *beshrew my jealousy* a plague upon my suspicious nature   116
proper . . . age characteristic of us (old) men   117 *cast beyond* overshoot, miscalculate. (A
metaphor from hunting.)   120 *known* made known (to the King). *close* secret   120–121
might . . . love i.e., might cause more grief (because of what Hamlet might do) by hiding the
knowledge of Hamlet's strange behavior to Ophelia than unpleasantness by telling it   2
Moreover that besides the fact that

Sith nor° th' exterior nor the inward man
Resembles that° it was. What it should be,
More than his father's death, that thus hath put him
So much from th' understanding of himself,
I cannot dream of. I entreat you both   10
That, being of so young days° brought up with him,
And sith so neighbored to° his youth and havior,°
That you vouchsafe your rest° here in our court
Some little time, so by your companies
To draw him on to pleasures, and to gather   15
So much as from occasion° you may glean,
Whether aught to us unknown afflicts him thus
That, opened,° lies within our remedy.
Queen: Good gentlemen, he hath much talked of you,
And sure I am two men there is not living   20
To whom he more adheres. If it will please you
To show us so much gentry° and good will
As to expend your time with us awhile
For the supply and profit of our hope,°
Your visitation shall receive such thanks   25
As fits a king's remembrance.°
Rosencrantz: Both Your Majesties
Might, by the sovereign power you have of° us,
Put your dread° pleasures more into command
Than to entreaty.
Guildenstern: But we both obey,
And here give up ourselves in the full bent°   30
To lay our service freely at your feet,
To be commanded.
King: Thanks, Rosencrantz and gentle Guildenstern.
Queen: Thanks, Guildenstern and gentle Rosencrantz.
And I beseech you instantly to visit   35
My too much changèd son. Go, some of you,
And bring these gentlemen where Hamlet is.
Guildenstern: Heavens make our presence and our practices°
Pleasant and helpful to him!
Queen: Ay, amen!

Exeunt Rosencrantz and Guildenstern [with some attendants].

6 *Sith nor* since neither   7 *that* what   11 *of . . . days* from such early youth   12 *And sith so
neighbored to* and since you are (or, and since that time you are) intimately acquainted with.
havior demeanor   13 *vouchsafe your rest* please to stay   16 *occasion* opportunity   18 *opened*
being revealed   22 *gentry* courtesy   24 *supply . . . hope* aid and furtherance of what we hope
for   26 *As fits . . . remembrance* as would be a fitting gift of a king who rewards true service
27 *of* over   28 *dread* inspiring awe   30 *in . . . bent* to the utmost degree of our capacity. (An
archery metaphor.)   38 *practices* doings

Enter Polonius.

Polonius: Th' ambassadors from Norway, my good lord,   40
    Are joyfully returned.
King: Thou still° hast been the father of good news.
Polonius: Have I, my lord? I assure my good liege
    I hold° my duty, as° I hold my soul,
    Both to my God and to my gracious king;   45
    And I do think, or else this brain of mine
    Hunts not the trail of policy° so sure
    As it hath used to do, that I have found
    The very cause of Hamlet's lunacy.
King: O, speak of that! That do I long to hear.   50
Polonius: Give first admittance to th' ambassadors.
    My news shall be the fruit° to that great feast.
King: Thyself do grace° to them and bring them in.

                                           [*Exit Polonius.*]

    He tells me, my dear Gertrude, he hath found
    The head and source of all your son's distemper.   55
Queen: I doubt° it is no other but the main,°
    His father's death and our o'erhasty marriage.

Enter Ambassadors [Voltimand and Cornelius, with Polonius].

King: Well, we shall sift him.°—Welcome, my good friends!
    Say, Voltimand, what from our brother° Norway?
Voltimand: Most fair return of greetings and desires.°   60
    Upon our first,° he sent out to suppress
    His nephew's levies, which to him appeared
    To be a preparation 'gainst the Polack,
    But, better looked into, he truly found
    It was against Your Highness. Whereat grieved   65
    That so his sickness, age, and impotence°
    Was falsely borne in hand,° sends out arrests°
    On Fortinbras, which he, in brief, obeys,
    Receives rebuke from Norway, and in fine°
    Makes vow before his uncle never more   70
    To give th' assay° of arms against Your Majesty.
    Whereon old Norway, overcome with joy,

---

42 *still* always   44 *hold* maintain.   *as* as firmly as   47 *policy* sagacity   52 *fruit* dessert   53
grace honor (punning on *grace* said before a *feast*, line 52)   56 *doubt* fear, suspect.   *main* chief
point, principal concern   58 *sift him* question Polonius closely   59 *brother* fellow king   60
desires good wishes   61 *Upon our first* at our first words on the business   66 *impotence* helplessness   67 *borne in hand* deluded, taken advantage of.   *arrests* orders to desist   69 *in fine* in conclusion   71 *give th' assay* make trial of strength, challenge

Gives him three thousand crowns in annual fee
And his commission to employ those soldiers,
So levied as before, against the Polack,   75
With an entreaty, herein further shown,

[giving a paper]

That it might please you to give quiet pass
Through your dominions for this enterprise
On such regards of safety and allowance°
As therein are set down.
King: It likes° us well,   80
And at our more considered° time we'll read,
Answer, and think upon this business.
Meantime we thank you for your well-took labor.
Go to your rest; at night we'll feast together.
Most welcome home!   *Exeunt Ambassadors.*
Polonius: This business is well ended.   85
My liege, and madam, to expostulate°
What majesty should be, what duty is,
Why day is day, night night, and time is time,
Were nothing but to waste night, day, and time.
Therefore, since brevity is the soul of wit,°   90
And tediousness the limbs and outward flourishes,
I will be brief. Your noble son is mad.
Mad call I it, for, to define true madness,
What is 't but to be nothing else but mad?
But let that go.
Queen: More matter, with less art.   95
Polonius: Madam, I swear I use no art at all.
That he's mad, 'tis true; 'tis true 'tis pity,
And pity 'tis 'tis true—a foolish figure,°
But farewell it, for I will use no art.
Mad let us grant him, then, and now remains   100
That we find out the cause of this effect,
Or rather say, the cause of this defect,
For this effect defective comes by cause.°
Thus it remains, and the remainder thus.
Perpend.°   105
I have a daughter—have while she is mine—
Who, in her duty and obedience, mark,

79 *On . . . allowance* i.e., with such considerations for the safety of Denmark and permission for
Fortinbras   80 *likes* pleases   81 *considered* suitable for deliberation   86 *expostulate* expound,
inquire into   90 *wit* sense or judgment   98 *figure* figure of speech   103 *For . . . cause* i.e., for
this defective behavior, this madness, has a cause   105 *Perpend* consider

Hath given me this. Now gather and surmise.°
[*He reads the letter.*] "To the celestial and my soul's idol, the most beautified
Ophelia"—That's an ill phrase, a vile phrase; "beautified" is a vile phrase.   110
But you shall hear. Thus:

[*He reads.*]

"In her excellent white bosom,° these,° etc."
Queen: Came this from Hamlet to her?
Polonius: Good madam, stay° awhile, I will be faithful.°

[*He reads.*]

"Doubt° thou the stars are fire,   115
    Doubt that the sun doth move,
  Doubt truth to be a liar,
    But never doubt I love.

O dear Ophelia, I am ill at these numbers.° I have not art to reckon°
my groans. But that I love thee best, O most best, believe it. Adieu.   120
Thine evermore, most dear lady, whilst this machine° is to him, Hamlet."
This in obedience hath my daughter shown me,
And, more above,° hath his solicitings,
As they fell out° by° time, by means, and place,
All given to mine ear.°
King: But how hath she   125
  Received his love?
Polonius: What do you think of me?
King: As of a man faithful and honorable.
Polonius: I would fain° prove so. But what might you think,
When I had seen this hot love on the wing—
As I perceived it, I must tell you that,   130
Before my daughter told me—what might you,
Or my dear Majesty your queen here, think,
If I had played the desk or table book,°
Or given my heart a winking,° mute and dumb,
Or looked upon this love with idle sight?°   135
What might you think? No, I went round° to work,
And my young mistress thus I did bespeak:°
"Lord Hamlet is a prince out of thy star;°
This must not be." And then I prescripts° gave her,

108 *gather and surmise* draw your own conclusions   112 *In . . . bosom* (The letter is poetically
addressed to her heart.)   *these* i.e., the letter   114 *stay* wait.   *faithful* i.e., in reading the letter
accurately   115 *Doubt* suspect   119 *ill . . . numbers* unskilled at writing verses.   *reckon* (1)
count (2) number metrically, scan   121 *machine* i.e., body   123 *more above* moreover   124
fell out occurred.   *by* according to   125 *given . . . ear* i.e., told me about   128 *fain* gladly
133 *played . . . table book* i.e., remained shut up, concealing the information   134 *given . . .
winking* closed the eyes of my heart to this   135 *with idle sight* complacently or incomprehend-
ingly   136 *round* roundly, plainly   137 *bespeak* address   138 *out of thy star* above your sphere,
position   139 *prescripts* orders

That she should lock herself from his resort,°   140
Admit no messengers, receive no tokens.
Which done, she took the fruits of my advice;
And he, repellèd—a short tale to make—
Fell into a sadness, then into a fast,
Thence to a watch,° thence into a weakness,   145
Thence to a lightness,° and by this declension°
Into the madness wherein now he raves,
And all we° mourn for.
King [*to the Queen*]:   Do you think 'tis this?
Queen: It may be, very like.
Polonius: Hath there been such a time—I would fain know that—   150
    That I have positively said " 'Tis so,"
    When it proved otherwise?
King: Not that I know.
Polonius: Take this from this,° if this be otherwise.
    If circumstances lead me, I will find
    Where truth is hid, though it were hid indeed   155
    Within the center.°
King: How may we try° it further?
Polonius: You know sometimes he walks four hours together
    Here in the lobby.
Queen: So he does indeed.
Polonius: At such a time I'll loose° my daughter to him.
    Be you and I behind an arras° then.   160
    Mark the encounter. If he love her not
    And be not from his reason fall'n thereon,°
    Let me be no assistant for a state,
    But keep a farm and carters.°
King: We will try it.

    Enter Hamlet [reading on a book].

Queen: But look where sadly° the poor wretch comes reading.   165
Polonius: Away, I do beseech you both, away.
    I'll board° him presently.° O, give me leave.°

                      Exeunt King and Queen [with attendants].

    How does my good Lord Hamlet?

140 *his resort* his visits   145 *watch* state of sleeplessness   146 *lightness* lightheadedness.
declension decline, deterioration (with a pun on the grammatical sense)   148 *all we* all of us,
or, into everything that we   153 *Take this from this* (The actor probably gestures, indicating
that he means his head from his shoulders, or his staff of office or chain from his hands or neck,
or something similar.)   156 *center* middle point of the earth (which is also the center of the
Ptolemaic universe).   *try* test, judge   159 *loose* (as one might release an animal that is being
mated)   160 *arras* hanging, tapestry   162 *thereon* on that account   164 *carters* wagon drivers
165 *sadly* seriously   167 *board* accost. *presently* at once. *give me leave* i.e., excuse me, leave
me alone. (Said to those he hurries offstage, including the King and Queen.)

Hamlet: Well, God-a-mercy.°

Polonius: Do you know me, my lord?

Hamlet: Excellent well. You are a fishmonger.°   170

Polonius: Not I, my lord.

Hamlet: Then I would you were so honest a man.

Polonius: Honest, my lord?

Hamlet: Ay, sir. To be honest, as this world goes, is to be one man picked   175
out of ten thousand.

Polonius: That's very true, my lord.

Hamlet: For if the sun breed maggots in a dead dog, being a good kissing
carrion°—Have you a daughter?

Polonius: I have, my lord.   180

Hamlet: Let her not walk i' the sun.° Conception° is a blessing, but as your
daughter may conceive, friend, look to 't.

Polonius [*aside*]: How say you by that? Still harping on my daughter. Yet he knew
me not at first; 'a° said I was a fishmonger. 'A is far gone. And truly in my
youth I suffered much extremity for love, very near this. I'll speak to him   185
again.—What do you read, my lord?

Hamlet: Words, words, words.

Polonius: What is the matter,° my lord?

Hamlet: Between who?

Polonius: I mean, the matter that you read, my lord.   190

Hamlet: Slanders, sir; for the satirical rogue says here that old men have gray
beards, that their faces are wrinkled, their eyes purging° thick amber° and
plum-tree gum, and that they have a plentiful lack of wit,° together with
most weak hams. All which, sir, though I most powerfully and potently
believe, yet I hold it not honesty° to have it thus set down, for yourself, sir,   195
shall grow old° as I am, if like a crab you could go backward.

Polonius [*aside*]: Though this be madness, yet there is method in 't.—Will you
walk out of the air,° my lord?

Hamlet: Into my grave.

Polonius: Indeed, that's out of the air. [*Aside.*] How pregnant° sometimes his   200
replies are! A happiness° that often madness hits on, which reason and
sanity could not so prosperously° be delivered of. I will leave him and
suddenly° contrive the means of meeting between him and my daughter.—
My honorable lord, I will most humbly take my leave of you.

---

169 *God-a-mercy* God have mercy, i.e., thank you   171 *fishmonger* fish merchant   178–179 *a
good kissing carrion* i.e., a good piece of flesh for kissing, or for the sun to kiss   181 *i' the sun* in
public (with additional implication of the sunshine of princely favors).   *Conception* (1) understanding (2) pregnancy   184 *'a* he   188 *matter* substance. (But Hamlet plays on the sense of
"basis for a dispute.")   192 *purging* discharging.   *amber* i.e., resin, like the resinous *plum-tree gum*
193 *wit* understanding   195 *honesty* decency, decorum   196 *old* as old   198 *out of the air* (The
open air was considered dangerous for sick people.)   200 *pregnant* quick-witted, full of meaning
201 *happiness* felicity of expression   202 *prosperously* successfully   203 *suddenly* immediately

Hamlet: You cannot, sir, take from me anything that I will more willingly part 205
withal°—except my life, except my life, except my life.

Enter Guildenstern and Rosencrantz.

Polonius: Fare you well, my lord.
Hamlet: These tedious old fools!°
Polonius: You go to seek the Lord Hamlet. There he is.
Rosencrantz [to Polonius]: God save you, sir! 210

[*Exit Polonius.*]

Guildenstern: My honored lord!
Rosencrantz: My most dear lord!
Hamlet: My excellent good friends! How dost thou, Guildenstern? Ah,
Rosencrantz! Good lads, how do you both?
Rosencrantz: As the indifferent° children of the earth. 215
Guildenstern: Happy in that we are not overhappy.
On Fortune's cap we are not the very button.
Hamlet: Nor the soles of her shoe?
Rosencrantz: Neither, my lord.
Hamlet: Then you live about her waist, or in the middle of her favors?° 220
Guildenstern: Faith, her privates we.°
Hamlet: In the secret parts of Fortune? O, most true, she is a strumpet.° What
news?
Rosencrantz: None, my lord, but the world's grown honest.
Hamlet: Then is doomsday near. But your news is not true. Let me question 225
more in particular. What have you, my good friends, deserved at the hands
of fortune that she sends you to prison hither?
Guildenstern: Prison, my lord?
Hamlet: Denmark's a prison.
Rosencrantz: Then is the world one. 230
Hamlet: A goodly one, in which there are many confines,° wards,° and
dungeons, Denmark being one o' the worst.
Rosencrantz: We think not so, my lord.
Hamlet: Why then 'tis none to you, for there is nothing either good or bad but
thinking makes it so. To me it is a prison. 235
Rosencrantz: Why then, your ambition makes it one. 'Tis too narrow for your
mind.
Hamlet: O God, I could be bounded in a nutshell and count myself a king of
infinite space, were it not that I have bad dreams.

206 *withal* with   208 *old fools* i.e., old men like Polonius   215 *indifferent* ordinary, at neither
extreme of fortune or misfortune   220 *favors* i.e., sexual favors   221 *her privates we* i.e., (1) we
are sexually intimate with Fortune, the fickle goddess who bestows her favors indiscriminately
(2) we are her private citizens   222 *strumpet* prostitute. (A common epithet for indiscriminate
Fortune; see line 430.)   231 *confines* places of confinement.   *wards* cells

Guildenstern: Which dreams indeed are ambition, for the very substance of the 240
ambitious° is merely the shadow of a dream.

Hamlet: A dream itself is but a shadow.

Rosencrantz: Truly, and I hold ambition of so airy and light a quality that it is
but a shadow's shadow.

Hamlet: Then are our beggars bodies,° and our monarchs and outstretched° heroes 245
the beggars' shadows. Shall we to the court? For, by my fay,° I cannot reason.

Rosencrantz, Guildenstern: We'll wait upon° you.

Hamlet: No such matter. I will not sort° you with the rest of my servants, for, to
speak to you like an honest man, I am most dreadfully attended.° But, in the
beaten way° of friendship, what make° you at Elsinore? 250

Rosencrantz: To visit you, my lord, no other occasion.

Hamlet: Beggar that I am, I am even poor in thanks; but I thank you, and sure,
dear friends, my thanks are too dear a halfpenny.° Were you not sent for? Is
it your own inclining? Is it a free° visitation? Come, come, deal justly with
me. Come, come. Nay, speak. 255

Guildenstern: What should we say, my lord?

Hamlet: Anything but to the purpose.° You were sent for, and there is a kind of
confession in your looks which your modesties° have not craft enough to
color.° I know the good King and Queen have sent for you.

Rosencrantz: To what end, my lord? 260

Hamlet: That you must teach me. But let me conjure° you, by the rights of our
fellowship, by the consonancy of our youth,° by the obligation of our ever-
preserved love, and by what more dear a better° prosper could charge° you
withal, be even° and direct with me whether you were sent for or no.

Rosencrantz [aside to Guildenstern]: What say you? 265

Hamlet [aside]: Nay, then, I have an eye of° you.—If you love me, hold not off.°

Guildenstern: My lord, we were sent for.

Hamlet: I will tell you why; so shall my anticipation prevent your discovery,°
and your secrecy to the King and Queen molt no feather.° I have of late—
but wherefore I know not—lost all my mirth, forgone all custom of exer- 270
cises; and indeed it goes so heavily with my disposition that this goodly
frame, the earth, seems to me a sterile promontory; this most excellent

240–241 *the very . . . ambitious* that seemingly very substantial thing that the ambitious pursue
245 *bodies* i.e., solid substances rather than shadows (since beggars are not ambitious).
outstretched (1) far-reaching in their ambition (2) elongated as shadows   246 *fay* faith   247
wait upon accompany, attend. (But Hamlet uses the phrase in the sense of providing menial
service.)   248 *sort* class, categorize   249 *dreadfully attended* waited upon in slovenly fashion
250 *beaten way* familiar path, tried-and-true course.   *make* do   253 *too dear a halfpenny* (1) too
expensive at even a halfpenny, i.e., of little worth (2) too expensive by a halfpenny in return
for worthless kindness   254 *free* voluntary   257 *Anything but to the purpose* anything except a
straightforward answer. (Said ironically.)   258 *modesties* sense of shame   259 *color* disguise
261 *conjure* adjure, entreat   262 *the consonancy of our youth* our closeness in our younger days
263 *better* more skillful.   *charge* urge   264 *even* straight, honest   266 *of* on. *hold not off* don't
hold back   268 *so . . . discovery* in that way my saying it first will spare you from revealing the
truth   269 *molt no feather* i.e., not diminish in the least

canopy, the air, look you, this brave° o'erhanging firmament, this majestical
roof fretted° with golden fire, why, it appeareth nothing to me but a foul and
pestilent congregation° of vapors. What a piece of work° is a man! How   275
noble in reason, how infinite in faculties, in form and moving how express°
and admirable, in action how like an angel, in apprehension° how like a
god! The beauty of the world, the paragon of animals! And yet, to me, what
is this quintessence° of dust? Man delights not me—no, nor woman neither,
though by your smiling you seem to say so.   280

Rosencrantz: My lord, there was no such stuff in my thoughts.

Hamlet: Why did you laugh, then, when I said man delights not me?

Rosencrantz: To think, my lord, if you delight not in man, what Lenten enter-
tainment° the players shall receive from you. We coted° them on the way,
and hither are they coming to offer you service.   285

Hamlet: He that plays the king shall be welcome; His Majesty shall have
tribute° of° me. The adventurous knight shall use his foil and target,° the
lover shall not sigh gratis,° the humorous man° shall end his part in peace,°
the clown shall make those laugh whose lungs are tickle o' the sear,° and the
lady shall say her mind freely, or the blank verse shall halt° for 't. What   290
players are they?

Rosencrantz: Even those you were wont to take such delight in, the tragedians°
of the city.

Hamlet: How chances it they travel? Their residence,° both in reputation and
profit, was better both ways.   295

Rosencrantz: I think their inhibition° comes by the means of the late° innovation.°

Hamlet: Do they hold the same estimation they did when I was in the city? Are
they so followed?

Rosencrantz: No, indeed are they not.

Hamlet: How° comes it? Do they grow rusty?   300

Rosencrantz: Nay, their endcavor keeps° in the wonted° pace. But there is, sir,
an aerie° of children, little eyases,° that cry out on the top of question° and

273 *brave* splendid 274 *fretted* adorned (with fretwork, as in a vaulted ceiling) 275
congregation mass. *piece of work* masterpiece 276 *express* well-framed, exact, expressive 277
apprehension power of comprehending 279 *quintessence* the fifth essence of ancient philosophy, beyond earth, water, air, and fire, supposed to be the substance of the heavenly bodies
and to be latent in all things 283–284 *Lenten entertainment* meager reception (appropriate to
Lent) 284 *coted* overtook and passed by 287 *tribute* (1) applause (2) homage paid in money.
of from. *foil and target* sword and shield 288 *gratis* for nothing. *humorous man* eccentric
character, dominated by one trait or "humor." *in peace* i.e., with full license 289 *tickle o' the
sear* easy on the trigger, ready to laugh easily. (A *sear* is part of a gunlock.) 290 *halt* limp 292
tragedians actors 294 *residence* remaining in their usual place, i.e., in the city 296 *inhibition*
formal prohibition (from acting plays in the city). *late* recent. *innovation* i.e., the new
fashion in satirical plays performed by boy actors in the "private" theaters; or possibly a political uprising; or the strict limitations set on the theaters in London in 1600 300–317 *How . . .
load too* (The passage, omitted from the early quartos, alludes to the so-called War of the Theaters, 1599–1602, the rivalry between the children's companies and the adult actors.) 301
keeps continues. *wonted* usual 302 *aerie* nest. *eyases* young hawks. *cry . . . question* speak
shrilly, dominating the controversy (in decrying the public theaters)

are most tyrannically° clapped for 't. These are now the fashion, and so be-
rattle° the common stages°—so they call them—that many wearing rapiers°
are afraid of goose quills° and dare scarce come thither.   305

Hamlet: What, are they children? Who maintains 'em? How are they escoted?°
Will they pursue the quality° no longer than they can sing?° Will they not
say afterwards, if they should grow themselves to common° players—as it is
most like,° if their means are no better°—their writers do them wrong to
make them exclaim against their own succession?°   310

Rosencrantz: Faith, there has been much to-do° on both sides, and the nation
holds it no sin to tar° them to controversy. There was for a while no money
bid for argument unless the poet and the player went to cuffs in the question.°

Hamlet: Is 't possible?

Guildenstern: O, there has been much throwing about of brains.   315

Hamlet: Do the boys carry it away?°

Rosencrantz: Ay, that they do, my lord—Hercules and his load° too.

Hamlet: It is not very strange; for my uncle is King of Denmark, and those that
would make mouths° at him while my father lived give twenty, forty, fifty, a
hundred ducats° apiece for his picture in little.° 'Sblood,° there is something 320
in this more than natural, if philosophy° could find it out.

                              A flourish [of trumpets within].

Guildenstern: There are the players.

Hamlet [to Rosenkrantz and Guildenstern]: Gentlemen, you are welcome to Elsinore. Your hands, come then. Th' appurtenance° of welcome is fashion and
ceremony. Let me comply° with you in this garb,° lest my extent° to the   325
players, which, I tell you, must show fairly outwards,° should more appear
like entertainment° than yours. You are welcome. But my uncle-father and
aunt-mother are deceived.

Guildenstern: In what, my dear lord?

---

303 *tyrannically* outrageously   304 *berattle* berate, clamor against.   *common stages* public theaters.   *many wearing rapiers* i.e., many men of fashion, afraid to patronize the common players
for fear of being satirized by the poets writing for the boy actors   305 *goose quills* i.e., pens of
satirists   306 *escoted* maintained   307 *quality* (acting) profession.   *no longer . . . sing* i.e., only
until their voices change   308 *common* regular, adult   309 *like* likely.   *if . . . better* if they
find no better way to support themselves   310 *succession* i.e., future careers   311 *to-do* ado
312 *tar* set on (as dogs)   312–313 *There . . . question* i.e., for a while, no money was offered by
the acting companies to playwrights for the plot to a play unless the satirical poets who wrote
for the boys and the adult actors came to blows in the play itself   316 *carry it away* i.e., win the
day   317 *Hercules . . . load* (Thought to be an allusion to the sign of the Globe Theatre, which
was Hercules bearing the world on his shoulders.)   319 *mouths* faces   320 *ducats* gold coins.
in little in miniature. *'Sblood* by God's (Christ's) blood   321 *philosophy* i.e., scientific inquiry
324 *appurtenance* proper accompaniment   325 *comply* observe the formalities of courtesy.
garb i.e., manner.   *my extent* that which I extend, i.e., my polite behavior   326–327 *show
fairly outwards* show every evidence of cordiality   327 *entertainment* a (warm) reception

Hamlet: I am but mad north-north-west.° When the wind is southerly I know a   330
  hawk° from a handsaw.

  Enter Polonius.

Polonius: Well be with you, gentlemen!
Hamlet: Hark you, Guildenstern, and you too; at each ear a hearer. That great
  baby you see there is not yet out of his swaddling clouts.°
Rosencrantz: Haply° he is the second time come to them, for they say an old
  man is twice a child.   335
Hamlet: I will prophesy he comes to tell me of the players. Mark it.—You say
  right, sir, o' Monday morning, 'twas then indeed.
Polonius: My lord, I have news to tell you.
Hamlet: My lord, I have news to tell you. When Roscius° was an actor in Rome—   340
Polonius: The actors are come hither, my lord.
Hamlet: Buzz,° buzz!
Polonius: Upon my honor—
Hamlet: Then came each actor on his ass.
Polonius: The best actors in the world, either for tragedy, comedy, history,   345
  pastoral, pastoral-comical, historical-pastoral, tragical-historical, tragical-
  comical-historical-pastoral, scene individable,° or poem unlimited.°
  Seneca° cannot be too heavy, nor Plautus° too light. For the law of writ and
  the liberty,° these° are the only men.
Hamlet: O Jephthah, judge of Israel,° what a treasure hadst thou!   350
Polonius: What a treasure had he, my lord?
Hamlet: Why,
      "One fair daughter, and no more,
      The which he lovèd passing° well."
Polonius [aside]: Still on my daughter.   355
Hamlet: Am I not i' the right, old Jephthah?
Polonius: If you call me Jephthah, my lord, I have a daughter that I love passing
  well.
Hamlet: Nay, that follows not.
Polonius: What follows then, my lord?   360
Hamlet: Why,
      "As by lot,° God wot,"°

---

330 *north-north-west* just off true north, only partly   331 *hawk, handsaw* i.e., two very different
things, though also perhaps meaning a mattock (or *hack*) and a carpenter's cutting tool, respectively; also birds, with a play on *hernshaw*, or heron   °334 *swaddling clouts* cloths in which to wrap
a newborn baby   335 *Haply* perhaps   340 *Roscius* a famous Roman actor who died in 62 B.C.
342 *Buzz* (An interjection used to denote stale news.)   347 *scene individable* a play observing the
unity of place; or perhaps one that is unclassifiable, or performed without intermission.   *poem
unlimited* a play disregarding the unities of time and place; one that is all-inclusive.   348 *Seneca*
writer of Latin tragedies.   *Plautus* writer of Latin comedy   348–349 *law . . . liberty* dramatic
composition both according to the rules and disregarding the rules   349 *these* i.e., the actors
350 *Jephthah . . . Israel* (Jephthah had to sacrifice his daughter; see Judges 11. Hamlet goes on to
quote from a ballad on the theme.)   354 *passing* surpassingly   362 *lot* chance.   *wot* knows

and then, you know,

"It came to pass, as most like° it was"—

the first row° of the pious chanson° will show you more, for look where my   365
abridgement° comes.

Enter the Players.

You are welcome, masters; welcome, all. I am glad to see thee well. Welcome, good friends. O, old friend! Why, thy face is valanced° since I saw
thee last. Com'st thou to beard° me in Denmark? What, my young lady° and
mistress! By 'r Lady,° your ladyship is nearer to heaven than when I saw you   370
last, by the altitude of a chopine.° Pray God your voice, like a piece of uncur-
rent° gold, be not cracked within the ring.° Masters, you are all welcome.
We'll e'en to 't° like French falconers, fly at anything we see. We'll have a
speech straight.° Come, give us a taste of your quality.° Come, a passionate
speech.   375

First Player: What speech, my good lord?

Hamlet: I heard thee speak me a speech once, but it was never acted, or if it was,
not above once, for the play, I remember, pleased not the million; 'twas caviar
to the general.° But it was—as I received it, and others, whose judgments
in such matters cried in the top of° mine—an excellent play, well digested°   380
in the scenes, set down with as much modesty° as cunning.° I remember one
said there were no sallets° in the lines to make the matter savory, nor no
matter in the phrase that might indict° the author of affectation, but called it
an honest method, as wholesome as sweet, and by very much more hand-
some° than fine.° One speech in 't I chiefly loved: 'twas Aeneas' tale to Dido,   385
and there-about of it especially when he speaks of Priam's slaughter.° If it live
in your memory, begin at this line: let me see, let me see—
"The rugged Pyrrhus,° like th' Hyrcanian beast"°—
'Tis not so. It begins with Pyrrhus:

364 *like* likely, probable   365 *row* stanza.   *chanson* ballad, song   365–366 *my abridgment* something that cuts short my conversation; also, a diversion   368 *valanced* fringed (with a beard)   369
beard confront, challenge (with obvious pun).   *young lady* i.e., boy playing women's parts   370
By 'r Lady by Our Lady   371 *chopine* thick-soled shoe of Italian fashion   371–372 *uncurrent* not
passable as lawful coinage.   *cracked . . . ring* i.e., changed from adolescent to male voice, no longer
suitable for women's roles. (Coins featured rings enclosing the sovereign's head; if the coin was
cracked within this ring, it was unfit for currency.)   373 *e'en to 't* go at it   374 *straight* at once.
quality professional skill   378–379 *caviar to the general* caviar to the multitude, i.e., a choice dish
too elegant for coarse tastes   380 *cried in the top of* i.e., spoke with greater authority than.   *digested*
arranged, ordered   381 *modesty* moderation, restraint.   *cunning* skill   382 *sallets* i.e., something
savory, spicy improprieties   383 *indict* convict   384–385 *handsome* well-proportioned.   *fine* elab-
orately ornamented, showy   386 *Priam's slaughter* the slaying of the ruler of Troy, when the
Greeks finally took the city   388 *Pyrrhus* a Greek hero in the Trojan War, also known as Neop-
tolemus, son of Achilles—another avenging son.   *Hyrcanian beast* i.e., tiger. (On the death of
Priam, see Virgil, *Aeneid,* 2.506 ff.; compare the whole speech with Marlowe's *Dido Queen of
Carthage,* 2.1.214 ff. On the *Hyrcanian* tiger, see *Aeneid,* 4.366–367. Hyrcania is on the Caspian Sea.)

"The rugged° Pyrrhus, he whose sable° arms,   390
Black as his purpose, did the night resemble
When he lay couchèd° in the ominous horse,°
Hath now this dread and black complexion smeared
With heraldry more dismal.° Head to foot
Now is he total gules,° horridly tricked°   395
With blood of fathers, mothers, daughters, sons,
Baked and impasted° with the parching streets,°
That lend a tyrannous° and a damnèd light
To their lord's° murder. Roasted in wrath and fire,
And thus o'ersizèd° with coagulate gore,   400
With eyes like carbuncles,° the hellish Pyrrhus
Old grandsire Priam seeks."
So proceed you.

Polonius: 'Fore God, my lord, well spoken, with good
accent and good discretion.

First Player: "Anon he finds him   405
Striking too short at Greeks. His antique° sword,
Rebellious to his arm, lies where it falls,
Repugnant° to command. Unequal matched,
Pyrrhus at Priam drives, in rage strikes wide,
But with the whiff and wind of his fell° sword   410
Th' unnervèd° father falls. Then senseless Ilium,°
Seeming to feel this blow, with flaming top
Stoops to his° base, and with a hideous crash
Takes prisoner Pyrrhus' ear. For, lo! His sword,
Which was declining° on the milky° head   415
Of reverend Priam, seemed i' th' air to stick.
So as a painted° tyrant Pyrrhus stood,
And, like a neutral to his will and matter,°
Did nothing.
But as we often see against° some storm   420
A silence in the heavens, the rack° stand still,
The bold winds speechless, and the orb° below

390 *rugged* shaggy, savage. *sable* black (for reasons of camouflage during the episode of the Trojan horse) 392 *couchèd* concealed. *ominous horse* fateful Trojan horse, by which the Greeks gained access to Troy 394 *dismal* ill-omened 395 *total gules* entirely red. (A heraldic term.) *tricked* spotted and smeared. (Heraldic.) 397 *impasted* crusted, like a thick paste. *with . . . streets* by the parching heat of the streets (because of the fires everywhere) 398 *tyrannous* cruel 399 *their lord's* i.e., Priam's 400 *o'ersizèd* covered as with size or glue 401 *carbuncles* large fiery-red precious stones thought to emit their own light 406 *antique* ancient, long-used 408 *Repugnant* disobedient, resistant 410 *fell* cruel 411 *unnervèd* strengthless. *senseless Ilium* inanimate citadel of Troy 413 *his* its 415 *declining* descending. *milky* white-haired 417 *painted* i.e., painted in a picture 418 *like . . . matter* i.e., as though suspended between his intention and its fulfillment 420 *against* just before 421 *rack* mass of clouds 422 *orb* globe, earth

As hush as death, anon the dreadful thunder
Doth rend the region,° so, after Pyrrhus' pause,
A rousèd vengeance sets him new a-work,   425
And never did the Cyclops'° hammers fall
On Mars's armor forged for proof eterne°
With less remorse° than Pyrrhus' bleeding sword
Now falls on Priam.
        Out, out, thou strumpet Fortune! All you gods   430
In general synod° take away her power!
Break all the spokes and fellies° from her wheel,
And bowl the round nave° down the hill of heaven°
As low as to the fiends!"

Polonius: This is too long.   435

Hamlet: It shall to the barber's with your beard.—Prithee, say on. He's for
     a jig° or a tale of bawdry, or he sleeps. Say on; come to Hecuba.°

First Player: "But who, ah woe! had° seen the moblèd° queen"—

Hamlet: "The moblèd queen?"

Polonius: That's good. "Moblèd queen" is good.   440

First Player: "Run barefoot up and down, threat'ning the flames°
     With bisson rheum,° a clout° upon that head
     Where late° the diadem stood, and, for a robe,
     About her lank and all o'erteemèd° loins
     A blanket, in the alarm of fear caught up—   445
     Who this had seen, with tongue in venom steeped,
     'Gainst Fortune's state° would treason have pronounced.°
     But if the gods themselves did see her then
     When she saw Pyrrhus make malicious sport
     In mincing with his sword her husband's limbs,   450
     The instant burst of clamor that she made,
     Unless things mortal move them not at all,
     Would have made milch° the burning eyes of heaven,°
     And passion° in the gods."

Polonius: Look whe'er° he has not turned his color and has tears in 's eyes. 455
     Prithee, no more.

---

424 *region* sky   426 *Cyclops* giant armor makers in the smithy of Vulcan   427 *proof eterne*
eternal resistance to assault   428 *remorse* pity   431 *synod* assembly   432 *fellies* pieces of wood
forming the rim of a wheel   433 *nave* hub. *hill of heaven* Mount Olympus   437 *jig* comic
song and dance often given at the end of a play. *Hecuba* wife of Priam   438 *who . . . had*
anyone who had (also in line 446). *moblèd* muffled   441 *threat'ning the flames* i.e., weeping
hard enough to dampen the flames   442 *bisson rheum* blinding tears. *clout* cloth   443 *late*
lately   444 *all o'erteemèd* utterly worn out with bearing children   447 *state* rule, managing.
pronounced proclaimed   453 *milch* milky, moist with tears. *burning eyes of heaven* i.e., heavenly bodies   454 *passion* overpowering emotion   455 *whe'er* whether

Hamlet: 'Tis well; I'll have thee speak out the rest of this soon.—Good my lord, will you see the players well bestowed?° Do you hear, let them be well used, for they are the abstract° and brief chronicles of the time. After your death you were better have a bad epitaph than their ill report while you live.   460

Polonius: My lord, I will use them according to their desert.

Hamlet: God's bodikin,° man, much better. Use every man after° his desert, and who shall scape whipping? Use them after your own honor and dignity. The less they deserve, the more merit is in your bounty. Take them in.

Polonius: Come, sirs.   [*Exit.*]   465

Hamlet: Follow him, friends. We'll hear a play tomorrow. [*As they start to leave, Hamlet detains the First Player.*] Dost thou hear me, old friend? Can you play *The Murder of Gonzago?*

First Player: Ay, my lord.

Hamlet: We'll ha 't° tomorrow night. You could, for a need, study° a speech of some   470
dozen or sixteen lines which I would set down and insert in 't, could you not?

First Player: Ay, my lord.

Hamlet: Very well. Follow that lord, and look you mock him not.
                                                                            (*Exeunt Players.*)

My good friends, I'll leave you till night. You are welcome to Elsinore.

Rosencrantz: Good my lord!   475
                                        Exeunt [*Rosencrantz and Guildenstern*].

Hamlet: Ay, so, goodbye to you.—Now I am alone.
O, what a rogue and peasant slave am I!
Is it not monstrous that this player here,
But° in a fiction, in a dream of passion,
Could force his soul so to his own conceit°   480
That from her working° all his visage wanned,°
Tears in his eyes, distraction in his aspect,°
A broken voice, and his whole function suiting
With forms to his conceit?° And all for nothing!
For Hecuba!   485
What's Hecuba to him, or he to Hecuba,
That he should weep for her? What would he do
Had he the motive and the cue for passion
That I have? He would drown the stage with tears
And cleave the general ear° with horrid° speech,   490
Make mad the guilty and appall° the free,°

---

458 *bestowed* lodged   459 *abstract* summary account   462 *God's bodikin* by God's (Christ's) little body, *bodykin.* (Not to be confused with *bodkin,* "dagger."). *after* according to   470 *ha 't* have it.   *study* memorize   479 *But* merely   480 *force . . . conceit* bring his innermost being so entirely into accord with his conception (of the role)   481 *from her working* as a result of, or in response to, his soul's activity.   *wanned* grew pale   482 *aspect* look, glance   483–484 *his whole . . . conceit* all his bodily powers responding with actions to suit his thought   490 *the general ear* everyone's ear.   *horrid* horrible   491 *appall* (Literally, make pale.)   *free* innocent

Confound the ignorant,° and amaze° indeed
The very faculties of eyes and ears. Yet I,
A dull and muddy-mettled° rascal, peak°
Like John-a-dreams,° unpregnant° of my cause,   495
And can say nothing—no, not for a king
Upon whose property° and most dear life
A damned defeat° was made. Am I a coward?
Who calls me villain? Breaks my pate° across?
Plucks off my beard and blows it in my face?   500
Tweaks me by the nose? Gives me the lie i' the throat°
As deep as to the lungs? Who does me this?
Ha, 'swounds,° I should take it; for it cannot be
But I am pigeon-livered° and lack gall
To make oppression bitter,° or ere this   505
I should ha' fatted all the region kites°
With this slave's offal.° Bloody, bawdy villain!
Remorseless,° treacherous, lecherous, kindless° villain!
O, vengeance!
Why, what an ass am I! This is most brave,°   510
That I, the son of a dear father murdered,
Prompted to my revenge by heaven and hell,
Must like a whore unpack my heart with words
And fall a-cursing, like a very drab,°
A scullion!° Fie upon 't, foh! About,° my brains!   515
Hum, I have heard
That guilty creatures sitting at a play
Have by the very cunning° of the scene°
Been struck so to the soul that presently°
They have proclaimed their malefactions;   520
For murder, though it have no tongue, will speak
With most miraculous organ. I'll have these players
Play something like the murder of my father
Before mine uncle. I'll observe his looks;
I'll tent° him to the quick.° If 'a do blench,°   525

492 *Confound the ignorant* i.e., dumbfound those who know nothing of the crime that has been committed. *amaze* stun   494 *muddy-mettled* dull-spirited. *peak* mope, pine   495 *John-a-dreams* a sleepy, dreaming idler.   *unpregnant of* not quickened by   497 *property* i.e., the crown; also character, quality   498 *damned defeat* damnable act of destruction   499 *pate* head   501 *Gives . . . throat* calls me an out-and-out liar   503 *'swounds* by his (Christ's) wounds   504 *pigeon-livered* (The pigeon or dove was popularly supposed to be mild because it secreted no gall.)   505 *bitter* i.e., bitter to me   506 *region kites* kites (birds of prey) of the air   507 *offal* entrails   508 *Remorseless* pitiless.   *kindless* unnatural   510 *brave* fine, admirable. (Said ironically.)   514 *drab* whore   515 *scullion* menial kitchen servant (apt to be foul-mouthed). *About* about it, to work   518 *cunning* art, skill.   *scene* dramatic presentation   519 *presently* at once   525 *tent* probe.   *the quick* the tender part of a wound, the core.   *blench* quail, flinch

I know my course. The spirit that I have seen
May be the devil, and the devil hath power
T' assume a pleasing shape; yea, and perhaps,
Out of my weakness and my melancholy,
As he is very potent with such spirits,°   530
Abuses° me to damn me. I'll have grounds
More relative° than this. The play's the thing
Wherein I'll catch the conscience of the King.   *Exit.*

ACT III

Scene I [The Castle.]

Enter King, Queen, Polonius, Ophelia, Rosencrantz, Guildenstern, lords.

King: And can you by no drift of conference°
    Get from him why he puts on this confusion,
    Grating so harshly all his days of quiet
    With turbulent and dangerous lunacy?
Rosencrantz: He does confess he feels himself distracted,   5
    But from what cause 'a will by no means speak.
Guildenstern: Nor do we find him forward° to be sounded,°
    But with a crafty madness keeps aloof
    When we would bring him on to some confession
    Of his true state.
Queen: Did he receive you well?   10
Rosencrantz: Most like a gentleman.
Guildenstern: But with much forcing of his disposition.°
Rosencrantz: Niggard° of question,° but of our demands
    Most free in his reply.
Queen: Did you assay° him
    To any pastime?   15
Rosencrantz: Madam, it so fell out that certain players
    We o'erraught° on the way. Of these we told him,
    And there did seem in him a kind of joy
    To hear of it. They are here about the court,
    And, as I think, they have already order   20
    This night to play before him.
Polonius: 'Tis most true,
    And he beseeched me to entreat Your Majesties
    To hear and see the matter.
King: With all my heart, and it doth much content me

530 *spirits* humors (of melancholy)   531 *Abuses* deludes   532 *relative* cogent, pertinent   1 *drift of
conference* directing of conversation   7 *forward* willing.   *sounded* questioned   12 *disposition* inclination   13 *Niggard* stingy.   *question* conversation   14 *assay* try to win   17 *o'erraught* overtook

      To hear him so inclined.
      Good gentlemen, give him a further edge°   25
      And drive his purpose into these delights.
Rosencrantz: We shall, my lord.

                                                        Exeunt Rosencrantz and Guildenstern.
  King: Sweet Gertrude, leave us too,
      For we have closely° sent for Hamlet hither,
      That he, as 'twere by accident, may here   30
      Affront° Ophelia.
      Her father and myself, lawful espials,°
      Will so bestow ourselves that seeing, unseen,
      We may of their encounter frankly judge,
      And gather by him, as he is behaved,   35
      If 't be th' affliction of his love or no
      That thus he suffers for.
  Queen: I shall obey you.
      And for your part, Ophelia, I do wish
      That your good beauties be the happy cause
      Of Hamlet's wildness. So shall I hope your virtues   40
      Will bring him to his wonted° way again,
      To both your honors.
  Ophelia: Madam, I wish it may.

                                                                          [*Exit Queen.*]

  Polonius: Ophelia, walk you here.—Gracious,° so please you,
      We will bestow° ourselves. [*To Ophelia.*] Read on this book, [*giving her a book*]
      That show of such an exercise° may color°   45
      Your loneliness.° We are oft to blame in this—
      'Tis too much proved°—that with devotion's visage
      And pious action we do sugar o'er
      The devil himself.
  King [*aside*]: O, 'tis too true!   50
      How smart a lash that speech doth give my conscience!
      The harlot's cheek, beautied with plastering art,
      Is not more ugly to° the thing° that helps it
      Than is my deed to my most painted word.
      O heavy burden!   55
  Polonius: I hear him coming. Let's withdraw, my lord.

                                                          [*The King and Polonius withdraw.°*]

---

26 *edge* incitement   29 *closely* privately   31 *Affront* confront, meet   32 *espials* spies   41
wonted accustomed   43 *Gracious* Your Grace (i.e., the King)   44 *bestow* conceal   45 *exercise*
religious exercise. (The book she reads is one of devotion.)   *color* give a plausible appearance
to   46 *loneliness* being alone   47 *too much proved* too often shown to be true, too often practiced   53 *to* compared to.   *the thing* i.e., the cosmetic   56 s.d. *withdraw* (The King and Polonius may retire behind an arras. The stage directions specify that they "enter" again near the
end of the scene.)

Enter Hamlet. [Ophelia pretends to read a book.]

Hamlet: To be, or not to be, that is the question:
    Whether 'tis nobler in the mind to suffer
    The slings° and arrows of outrageous fortune,
    Or to take arms against a sea of troubles   60
    And by opposing end them. To die, to sleep—
    No more—and by a sleep to say we end
    The heartache and the thousand natural shocks
    That flesh is heir to. 'Tis a consummation
    Devoutly to be wished. To die, to sleep;   65
    To sleep, perchance to dream. Ay, there's the rub,°
    For in that sleep of death what dreams may come,
    When we have shuffled° off this mortal coil,°
    Must give us pause. There's the respect°
    That makes calamity of so long life.°   70
    For who would bear the whips and scorns of time,
    Th' oppressor's wrong, the proud man's contumely,°
    The pangs of disprized° love, the law's delay,
    The insolence of office,° and the spurns°
    That patient merit of th' unworthy takes,°   75
    When he himself might his quietus° make
    With a bare bodkin?° Who would fardels° bear,
    To grunt and sweat under a weary life,
    But that the dread of something after death,
    The undiscovered country from whose bourn°   80
    No traveler returns, puzzles the will,
    And makes us rather bear those ills we have
    Than fly to others that we know not of?
    Thus conscience does make cowards of us all;
    And thus the native hue° of resolution   85
    Is sicklied o'er with the pale cast° of thought,
    And enterprises of great pitch° and moment°
    With this regard° their currents° turn awry
    And lose the name of action.—Soft you° now,
    The fair Ophelia. Nymph, in thy orisons°   90
    Be all my sins remembered.

59 *slings* missiles   66 *rub* (Literally, an obstacle in the game of bowls.)   68 *shuffled* sloughed, cast. *coil* turmoil   69 *respect* consideration   70 *of . . . life* so long-lived, something we willingly endure for so long (also suggesting that long life is itself a calamity)   72 *contumely* insolent abuse   73 *disprized* unvalued   74 *office* officialdom. *spurns* insults   75 *of . . . takes* receives from unworthy persons   76 *quietus* acquitance; here, death   77 *a bare bodkin* a mere dagger, unsheathed. *fardels* burdens   80 *bourn* frontier, boundary   85 *native hue* natural color, complexion   86 *cast* tinge, shade of color   87 *pitch* height (as of a falcon's flight). *moment* importance   88 *regard* respect, consideration. *currents* courses   89 *Soft you* i.e., wait a minute, gently   90 *orisons* prayers

Ophelia: Good my lord,
   How does your honor for this many a day?
Hamlet: I humbly thank you; well, well, well.
Ophelia: My lord, I have remembrances of yours,
   That I have longèd long to redeliver.   95
   I pray you, now receive them.   *[She offers tokens.]*
Hamlet: No, not I, I never gave you aught.
Ophelia: My honored lord, you know right well you did,
   And with them words of so sweet breath composed
   As made the things more rich. Their perfume lost,   100
   Take these again, for to the noble mind
   Rich gifts wax poor when givers prove unkind.
   There, my lord.   *[She gives tokens.]*
Hamlet: Ha, ha! Are you honest?°
Ophelia: My lord?   105
Hamlet: Are you fair?°
Ophelia: What means your lordship?
Hamlet: That if you be honest and fair, your honesty° should admit no discourse
   to° your beauty.
Ophelia: Could beauty, my lord, have better commerce° than with honesty?   110
Hamlet: Ay, truly, for the power of beauty will sooner transform honesty from
   what it is to a bawd than the force of honesty can translate beauty into his°
   likeness. This was sometime° a paradox,° but now the time° gives it proof. I
   did love you once.
Ophelia: Indeed, my lord, you made me believe so.   115
Hamlet: You should not have believed me, for virtue cannot so inoculate° our
   old stock but we shall relish of it.° I loved you not.
Ophelia: I was the more deceived.
Hamlet: Get thee to a nunnery.° Why wouldst thou be a breeder of sinners? I am
   myself indifferent honest,° but yet I could accuse me of such things that it   120
   were better my mother had not borne me: I am very proud, revengeful, ambitious, with more offenses at my beck° than I have thoughts to put them in,
   imagination to give them shape, or time to act them in. What should such
   fellows as I do crawling between earth and heaven? We are arrant knaves all;
   believe none of us. Go thy ways to a nunnery. Where's your father?   125
Ophelia: At home, my lord.

---

104 *honest* (1) truthful (2) chaste   106 *fair* (1) beautiful (2) just, honorable   108 *your honesty*
your chastity   108–109 *discourse to* familiar dealings with   110 *commerce* dealings, intercourse
112 *his* its   113 *sometime* formerly.   *a paradox* a view opposite to commonly held opinion.
the time the present age   116 *inoculate* graft, be engrafted to   117 *but . . . it* that we do not still
have about us a taste of the old stock, i.e., retain our sinfulness   119 *nunnery* convent (with
possibly an awareness that the word was also used derisively to denote a brothel)   120 *indifferent honest* reasonably virtuous   122 *beck* command

Hamlet: Let the doors be shut upon him, that he may play the fool nowhere but in 's own house. Farewell.

Ophelia: O, help him, you sweet heavens!

Hamlet: If thou dost marry, I'll give thee this plague for thy dowry: be thou as 130
    chaste as ice, as pure as snow, thou shalt not escape calumny. Get thee to a
    nunnery, farewell. Or, if thou wilt needs marry, marry a fool, for wise men
    know well enough what monsters° you° make of them. To a nunnery, go,
    and quickly too. Farewell.

Ophelia: Heavenly powers, restore him! 135

Hamlet: I have heard of your paintings too, well enough. God hath given you one
    face, and you make yourselves another. You jig,° you amble,° and you lisp,
    you nickname God's creatures,° and make your wantonness your ignorance.°
    Go to, I'll no more on 't;° it hath made me mad. I say we will have no more
    marriage. Those that are married already—all but one—shall live. The rest 140
    shall keep as they are. To a nunnery, go.   *Exit.*

Ophelia: O, what a noble mind is here o'erthrown!
    The courtier's, soldier's, scholar's, eye, tongue, sword,
    Th' expectancy° and rose° of the fair state,
    The glass of fashion and the mold of form,° 145
    Th' observed of all observers,° quite, quite down!
    And I, of ladies most deject and wretched,
    That sucked the honey of his music° vows,
    Now see that noble and most sovereign reason
    Like sweet bells jangled out of tune and harsh, 150
    That unmatched form and feature of blown° youth
    Blasted° with ecstasy.° O, woe is me,
    T' have seen what I have seen, see what I see!

    Enter King and Polonius.

King: Love? His affections° do not that way tend;
    Nor what he spake, though it lacked form a little, 155
    Was not like madness. There's something in his soul
    O'er which his melancholy sits on brood,°
    And I do doubt° the hatch and the disclose°
    Will be some danger; which for to prevent,
    I have in quick determination 160

---

133 *monsters* (An illusion to the horns of a cuckold.)   *you* i.e., you women   137 *jig* dance. *amble* move coyly   138 *you nickname . . . creatures* i.e., you give trendy names to things in place of their God-given names. *make . . . ignorance* i.e., excuse your affectation on the grounds of pretended ignorance   139 *on 't* of it   144 *expectancy* hope. *rose* ornament   145 *The glass . . . form* the mirror of true self-fashioning and the pattern of courtly behavior   146 *Th' observed . . . observers* i.e., the center of attention and honor in the court   148 *music* musical, sweetly uttered   151 *blown* blooming   152 *Blasted* withered. *ecstasy* madness   154 *affections* emotions, feelings   157 *sits on brood* sits like a bird on a nest, about to *hatch* mischief (line 158)   158 *doubt* fear. *disclose* disclosure, hatching

Thus set it down:° he shall with speed to England
For the demand of° our neglected tribute.
Haply the seas and countries different
With variable objects° shall expel
This something-settled matter in his heart,°   165
Whereon his brains still° beating puts him thus
From fashion of himself.° What think you on 't?
Polonius: It shall do well. But yet do I believe
The origin and commencement of his grief
Sprung from neglected love.—How now, Ophelia?   170
You need not tell us what Lord Hamlet said;
We heard it all.—My lord, do as you please,
But, if you hold it fit, after the play
Let his queen-mother° all alone entreat him
To show his grief. Let her be round° with him;   175
And I'll be placed, so please you, in the ear
Of all their conference. If she find him not,°
To England send him, or confine him where
Your wisdom best shall think.
King: It shall be so.
Madness in great ones must not unwatched go.   180

Exeunt.

Scene II [The Castle.]

Enter Hamlet and three of the Players.

Hamlet: Speak the speech, I pray you, as I pronounced it to you, trippingly on
the tongue. But if you mouth it, as many of our players° do, I had as lief° the
town crier spoke my lines. Nor do not saw the air too much with your hand,
thus, but use all gently; for in the very torrent, tempest, and, as I may say,
whirlwind of your passion, you must acquire and beget a temperance that   5
may give it smoothness. O, it offends me to the soul to hear a robustious°
periwig-pated° fellow tear a passion to tatters, to very rags, to split the ears
of the groundlings,° who for the most part are capable of° nothing but inex-

---

161 *set it down* resolved   162 *For . . . of* to demand   164 *variable objects* various sights and surroundings to divert him   165 *This something . . . heart* the strange matter settled in his heart
166 *still* continually   167 *From . . . himself* out of his natural manner   174 *queen-mother* queen
and mother   175 *round* blunt   177 *find him not* fails to discover what is troubling him   2 *our
players* players nowadays.   *I had as lief* I would just as soon   6 *robustious* violent, boisterous   7
periwig-pated wearing a wig   8 *groundlings* spectators who paid least and stood in the yard of the
theater.   *capable of* able to understand

plicable dumb shows° and noise. I would have such a fellow whipped for
o'erdoing Termagant.° It out-Herods Herod.° Pray you, avoid it.   10
First Player: I warrant your honor.
Hamlet: Be not too tame neither, but let your own discretion be your tutor. Suit
the action to the word, the word to the action, with this special observance,
that you o'erstep not the modesty° of nature. For anything so o'erdone is
from° the purpose of playing, whose end, both at the first and now, was and   15
is to hold as 't were the mirror up to nature, to show virtue her feature,
scorn° her own image, and the very age and body of the time° his° form and
pressure.° Now this overdone or come tardy off,° though it makes the un-
skillful° laugh, cannot but make the judicious grieve, the censure of the
which one° must in your allowance° o'erweigh a whole theater of others. O,   20
there be players that I have seen play, and heard others praise, and that
highly, not to speak it profanely,° that, neither having th' accent of Chris-
tians° nor the gait of Christian, pagan, nor man,° have so strutted and bellowed that I have thought some of nature's journeymen° had made men and
not made them well, they imitated humanity so abominably.°   25
First Player: I hope we have reformed that indifferently° with us, sir.
Hamlet: O, reform it altogether. And let those that play your clowns speak no
more than is set down for them; for there be of them° that will themselves
laugh, to set on some quantity of barren° spectators to laugh too, though in
the meantime some necessary question of the play be then to be considered.   30
That's villainous, and shows a most pitiful ambition in the fool that uses it.
Go make you ready.   [*Exeunt Players.*]

Enter Polonius, Guildenstern, and Rosencrantz.

How now, my lord, will the King hear this piece of work?
Polonius: And the Queen too, and that presently.°
Hamlet: Bid the players make haste.   [*Exit Polonius.*]   35
Will you two help to hasten them?
Rosencrantz: Ay, my lord.   *Exeunt they two.*

9 *dumb shows* mimed performances, often used before Shakespeare's time to precede a play or
each act   10 *Termagant* a supposed deity of the Mohammedans, not found in any English medieval play but elsewhere portrayed as violent and blustering.   *Herod* Herod of Jewry. (A character in *The Slaughter of the Innocents* and other cycle plays. The part was played with great
noise and fury.)   14 *modesty* restraint, moderation   15 *from* contrary to   17 *scorn* i.e., something foolish and deserving of scorn.   *the very . . . time* i.e., the present state of affairs.   *his* its
18 *pressure* stamp, impressed character.   *come tardy off* inadequately done   18–19 *the unskillful*
those lacking in judgment   19–20 *the censure . . . one* the judgment of even one of whom   20
your allowance your scale of values   22 *not . . . profanely* (Hamlet anticipates his idea in lines
24–25 that some men were not made by God at all.)   22–23 *Christians* i.e., ordinary decent
folk   23 *nor man* i.e., nor any human being at all   24 *journeymen* laborers who are not yet
masters in their trade   25 *abominably* (Shakespeare's usual spelling, abhominably, suggests a
literal though etymologically incorrect meaning, "removed from human nature.")   26 *indifferently* tolerably   28 *of them* some among them   29 *barren* i.e., of wit   34 *presently* at once

Hamlet:	What ho, Horatio!

Enter Horatio.

Horatio:	Here, sweet lord, at your service.
Hamlet:	Horatio, thou art e'en as just a man
	As e'er my conversation coped withal.°	40
Horatio:	O, my dear lord—
Hamlet:	Nay, do not think I flatter,

For what advancement may I hope from thee
That no revenue hast but thy good spirits
To feed and clothe thee? Why should the poor be flattered?
No, let the candied° tongue lick absurd pomp,   45
And crook the pregnant° hinges of the knee
Where thrift° may follow fawning. Dost thou hear?
Since my dear soul was mistress of her choice
And could of men distinguish her election,°
Sh' hath sealed thee° for herself, for thou hast been   50
As one, in suffering all, that suffers nothing,
A man that Fortune's buffets and rewards
Hast ta'en with equal thanks; and blest are those
Whose blood° and judgment are so well commeddled°
That they are not a pipe for Fortune's finger   55
To sound what stop° she please. Give me that man
That is not passion's slave, and I will wear him
In my heart's core, ay, in my heart of heart,
As I do thee.—Something too much of this.—
There is a play tonight before the King.   60
One scene of it comes near the circumstance
Which I have told thee of my father's death.
I prithee, when thou seest that act afoot,
Even with the very comment of thy soul°
Observe my uncle. If his occulted° guilt   65
Do not itself unkennel° in one speech,
It is a damnèd° ghost that we have seen,
And my imaginations are as foul
As Vulcan's stithy.° Give him heedful note,
For I mine eyes will rivet to his face,   70

40 *my . . . withal* my dealings encountered   45 *candied* sugared, flattering   46 *pregnant* compliant   47 *thrift* profit   49 *could . . . election* could make distinguishing choices among persons   50 *sealed thee* (Literally, as one would seal a legal document to mark possession.)   54 *blood* passion.   *commeddled* commingled   56 *stop* hole in a wind instrument for controlling the sound   64 *very . . . soul* your most penetrating observation and consideration   65 *occulted* hidden   66 *unkennel* (As one would say of a fox driven from its lair.)   67 *damnèd* in league with Satan   69 *stithy* smithy, place of stiths (anvils)

And after we will both our judgments join
In censure of his seeming.°
Horatio: Well, my lord.
If 'a steal aught° the whilst this play is playing
And scape detecting, I will pay the theft.

[Flourish.] Enter trumpets and kettledrums, King,

Queen, Polonius, Ophelia, [Rosencrantz, Guildenstern, and other lords, with
guards carrying torches].
Hamlet: They are coming to the play. I must be idle.° Get you a place.   75

[The King, Queen, and courtiers sit.]

King: How fares our cousin° Hamlet?
Hamlet: Excellent, i' faith, of the chameleon's dish:° I eat the air, promise-
  crammed. You cannot feed capons° so.
King: I have nothing with° this answer, Hamlet. These words are not mine.°
Hamlet: No, nor mine now.° [To Polonius.] My lord, you played once i' th'   80
  university, you say?
Polonius: That did I, my lord, and was accounted a good actor.
Hamlet: What did you enact?
Polonius: I did enact Julius Caesar. I was killed i' the Capitol; Brutus killed me.
Hamlet: It was a brute° part° of him to kill so capital a calf° there.—Be the   85
  players ready?
Rosencrantz: Ay, my lord. They stay upon° your patience.
Queen: Come hither, my dear Hamlet, sit by me.
Hamlet: No, good Mother, here's metal° more attractive.
Polonius [to the King]: O, ho, do you mark that?   90
Hamlet: Lady, shall I lie in your lap?

                                                     [Lying down at Ophelia's feet.]

Ophelia: No, my lord.
Hamlet: I mean, my head upon your lap?
Ophelia: Ay, my lord.
Hamlet: Do you think I meant country matters?°   95

72 censure of his seeming judgment of his appearance or behavior   73 If 'a steal aught if he gets
away with anything   75 idle (1) unoccupied (2) mad   76 cousin i.e., close relative   77
chameleon's dish (Chameleons were supposed to feed on air. Hamlet deliberately misinterprets
the King's fares as "feeds." By his phrase eat the air, he also plays on the idea of feeding himself
with the promise of succession, of being the heir.)   78 capons roosters castrated and crammed
with feed to make them succulent   79 have . . . with make nothing of, or gain nothing from.
are not mine do not respond to what I asked   80 nor mine now (Once spoken, words are proverbially no longer the speaker's own—and hence should be uttered warily.)   85 brute (The Latin
meaning of brutus, "stupid," was often used punningly with the name Brutus.)   part (1) deed
(2) role.   calf fool   87 stay upon await   89 metal substance that is attractive, i.e., magnetic,
but with suggestion also of mettle, "disposition"   95 country matters sexual intercourse (making
a bawdy pun on the first syllable of country)

Ophelia: I think nothing, my lord.

Hamlet: That's a fair thought to lie between maids' legs.

Ophelia: What is, my lord?

Hamlet: Nothing.°

Ophelia: You are merry, my lord.   100

Hamlet: Who, I?

Ophelia: Ay, my lord.

Hamlet: O God, your only jig maker.° What should a man do but be merry? For look you how cheerfully my mother looks, and my father died within 's° two hours.   105

Ophelia: Nay, 'tis twice two months, my lord.

Hamlet: So long? Nay then, let the devil wear black, for I'll have a suit of sables.° O heavens! Die two months ago, and not forgotten yet? Then there's hope a great man's memory may outlive his life half a year. But, by'r Lady, 'a must build churches, then, or else shall 'a suffer not thinking on,° with the hobby-   110 horse, whose epitaph is "For O, for O, the hobbyhorse is forgot."°

The trumpets sound. Dumb show follows.

Enter a King and a Queen [very lovingly]; the Queen embracing him, and he her. [She kneels, and makes show of protestation unto him.] He takes her up, and declines his head upon her neck. He lies him down upon a bank of flowers. She, seeing him asleep, leaves him. Anon comes in another man, takes off his crown, kisses it, pours poison in the sleeper's ears, and leaves him. The Queen returns, finds the King dead, makes passionate action. The Poisoner with some three or four come in again, seem to condole with her. The dead body is carried away. The Poisoner woos the Queen with gifts; she seems harsh awhile, but in the end accepts love.

[Exeunt players.]

Ophelia: What means this, my lord?

Hamlet: Marry, this' miching mallico;° it means mischief.

Ophelia: Belike° this show imports the argument° of the play.

Enter Prologue.

Hamlet: We shall know by this fellow. The players cannot keep counsel;° they'll   115 tell all.

99 *Nothing* the figure zero or naught, suggesting the female sexual anatomy. (*Thing* not infrequently has a bawdy connotation of male or female anatomy, and the reference here could be male.)   103 *only jig maker* very best composer of jigs, i.e., pointless merriment. (Hamlet replies sardonically to Ophelia's observation that he is merry by saying, "If you're looking for someone who is really merry, you've come to the right person.")   104 *within 's* within this (i.e., these)   107 *suit of sables* garments trimmed with the fur of the sable and hence suited for a wealthy person, not a mourner (but with a pun on *sable*, "black," ironically suggesting mourning once again)   110 *suffer . . . on* undergo oblivion   111 *For . . . forgot* (Verse of a song occurring also in *Love's Labor's Lost*, 3.1.27–28. The hobbyhorse was a character made up to resemble a horse and rider, appearing in the morris dance and such May-game sports. This song laments the disappearance of such customs under pressure from the Puritans.)   113 *this' miching mallico* this is sneaking mischief   114 *Belike* probably.   *argument* plot   115 *counsel* secret

Ophelia: Will 'a tell us what this show meant?

Hamlet: Ay, or any show that you will show him. Be not you° ashamed to show,
   he'll not shame to tell you what it means.

Ophelia: You are naught, you are naught.° I'll mark the play.   120

Prologue: For us, and for our tragedy,
   Here stooping° to your clemency,
   We beg your hearing patiently.   *[Exit.]*

Hamlet: Is this a prologue, or the posy of a ring?°

Ophelia: 'Tis brief, my lord.   125

Hamlet: As woman's love.

     Enter [two Players as] King and Queen.

Player King: Full thirty times hath Phoebus' cart° gone round
   Neptune's salt wash° and Tellus'° orbèd ground,
   And thirty dozen moons with borrowed° sheen
   About the world have times twelve thirties been,   130
   Since love our hearts and Hymen° did our hands
   Unite commutual° in most sacred bands.°

Player Queen: So many journeys may the sun and moon
   Make us again count o'er ere love be done!
   But, woe is me, you are so sick of late,   135
   So far from cheer and from your former state,
   That I distrust° you. Yet, though I distrust,
   Discomfort° you, my lord, it nothing° must.
   For women's fear and love hold quantity;°
   In neither aught, or in extremity.°   140
   Now, what my love is, proof° hath made you know,
   And as my love is sized,° my fear is so.
   Where love is great, the littlest doubts are fear;
   Where little fears grow great, great love grows there.

Player King: Faith, I must leave thee, love, and shortly too;   145
   My operant powers° their functions leave to do.°
   And thou shalt live in this fair world behind,°
   Honored, beloved; and haply one as kind
   For husband shalt thou—

118 *Be not you* provided you are not   120 *naught* indecent. (Ophelia is reacting to Hamlet's
pointed remarks about not being ashamed to show all.)   122 *stooping* bowing   124 *posy* . . .
ring brief motto in verse inscribed in a ring   127 *Phoebus' cart* the sun-god's chariot, making its
yearly cycle   128 *salt wash* the sea. *Tellus* goddess of the earth, of the *orbèd ground*   129
borrowed i.e., reflected   131 *Hymen* god of matrimony   132 *commutual* mutually. *bands*
bonds   137 *distrust* am anxious about   138 *Discomfort* distress. *nothing* not at all   139 *hold
quantity* keep proportion with one another   140 *In* . . . *extremity* i.e., women fear and love either too little or too much, but the two, fear and love, are equal in either case   141 *proof* experience   142 *sized* in size   146 *operant powers* vital functions. *leave to do* cease to perform
147 *behind* after I have gone

Player Queen: O, confound the rest!

    Such love must needs be treason in my breast.   150

    In second husband let me be accurst!

    None° wed the second but who° killed the first.

Hamlet: Wormwood,° wormwood.

Player Queen: The instances° that second marriage move°

    Are base respects of thrift,° but none of love.   155

    A second time I kill my husband dead

    When second husband kisses me in bed.

Player King: I do believe you think what now you speak,

    But what we do determine oft we break.

    Purpose is but the slave to memory,°   160

    Of violent birth, but poor validity,°

    Which° now, like fruit unripe, sticks on the tree,

    But fall unshaken when they mellow be.

    Most necessary 'tis that we forget

    To pay ourselves what to ourselves is debt.°   165

    What to ourselves in passion we purpose,

    The passion ending, doth the purpose lose.

    The violence of either grief or joy

    Their own enactures° with themselves destroy.

    Where joy most revels, grief doth most lament;   170

    Grief joys, joy grieves, on slender accident.°

    This world is not for aye,° nor 'tis not strange

    That even our loves should with our fortunes change;

    For 'tis a question left us yet to prove,

    Whether love lead fortune, or else fortune love.   175

    The great man down,° you mark his favorite flies;

    The poor advanced makes friends of enemies.°

    And hitherto° doth love on fortune tend;°

    For who not needs° shall never lack a friend,

    And who in want° a hollow friend doth try°   180

    Directly seasons him° his enemy.

    But, orderly to end where I begun,

---

152 *None* i.e., let no woman. *but who* except the one who   153 *Wormwood* i.e., how bitter.
(Literally, a bitter-tasting plant.)   154 *instances* motives. *move* motivate   155 *base . . . thrift*
ignoble considerations of material prosperity   160 *Purpose . . . memory* our good intentions are
subject to forgetfulness   161 *validity* strength, durability   162 *Which* i.e., purpose   164–165
Most . . . debt it's inevitable that in time we forget the obligations we have imposed on ourselves   169 *enactures* fulfillments   170–171 *Where . . . accident* the capacity for extreme joy
and grief go together, and often one extreme is instantly changed into its opposite on the
slightest provocation   172 *aye* ever   176 *down* fallen in fortune   177 *The poor . . . enemies*
when one of humble station is promoted, you see his enemies suddenly becoming his friends
178 *hitherto* up to this point in the argument, or, to this extent. *tend* attend   179 *who not
needs* he who is not in need (of wealth)   180 *who in want* he who, being in need. *try* test (his
generosity)   181 *seasons him* ripens him into

Our wills and fates do so contrary run°
That our devices still° are overthrown;
Our thoughts are ours, their ends° none of our own.   185
So think thou wilt no second husband wed,
But die thy thoughts when thy first lord is dead.
Player Queen: Nor° earth to me give food, nor heaven light,
    Sport and repose lock from me day and night,°
    To desperation turn my trust and hope,   190
    An anchor's cheer° in prison be my scope!°
    Each° opposite that blanks° the face of joy
    Meet what I would have well and it destroy!
    Both here and hence° pursue me lasting strife
    If, once a widow, ever I be wife!   195
Hamlet: If she should break it now!
Player King: 'Tis deeply sworn. Sweet, leave me here awhile;
    My spirits° grow dull, and fain I would beguile
    The tedious day with sleep.
Player Queen: Sleep rock thy brain,
    And never come mischance between us twain!   200
                          [*He sleeps.*] *Exit* [*Player Queen*].

Hamlet: Madam, how like you this play?
Queen: The lady doth protest too much,° methinks.
Hamlet: O, but she'll keep her word.
King: Have you heard the argument?° Is there no offense° in 't?
Hamlet: No, no, they do but jest,° poison in jest. No offense i' the world.   205
King: What do you call the play?
Hamlet: *The Mousetrap.* Marry, how? Tropically.° This play is the image of a
    murder done in Vienna. Gonzago is the Duke's° name, his wife, Baptista.
    You shall see anon. 'Tis a knavish piece of work, but what of that? Your
    Majesty, and we that have free° souls, it touches us not. Let the galled jade°   210
    wince, our withers° are unwrung.°

    Enter Lucianus.

    This is one Lucianus, nephew to the King.

183 *Our . . . run* what we want and what we get go so contrarily   184 *devices still* intentions
continually   185 *ends* results   188 *Nor* let neither   189 *Sport . . . night* may day deny me its
pastimes and night its repose   191 *anchor's cheer* anchorite's or hermit's fare.   *my scope* the
extent of my happiness   192–193 *Each . . . destroy* may every adverse thing that causes the
face of joy to turn pale meet and destroy everything that I desire to see prosper.   192 *blanks*
causes to blanch or grow pale   194 *hence* in the life hereafter   198 *spirits* vital spirits   202
doth . . . much makes too many promises and protestations   204 *argument* plot   204–205
offense . . . offense cause for objection . . . actual injury, crime   205 *jest* make believe   207
Tropically figuratively. (The First Quarto reading, *trapically,* suggests a pun on *trap* in
Mousetrap.)   208 *Duke's* i.e., King's. (A slip that may be due to Shakespeare's possible source,
the alleged murder of the Duke of Urbino by Luigi Gonzaga in 1538.)   210 *free* guiltless.
galled jade horse whose hide is rubbed by saddle or harness.   211 *withers* the part between the
horse's shoulder blades   *unwrung* not rubbed sore

Ophelia: You are as good as a chorus,° my lord.

Hamlet: I could interpret° between you and your love, if I could see the puppets dallying.°

215

Ophelia: You are keen, my lord, you are keen.°

Hamlet: It would cost you a groaning to take off mine edge.

Ophelia: Still better, and worse.°

Hamlet: So° you mis-take° your husbands. Begin, murderer; leave thy damnable faces and begin. Come, the croaking raven doth bellow for revenge.

220

Lucianus: Thoughts black, hands apt, drugs fit, and time agreeing,

Confederate season,° else° no creature seeing,°

Thou mixture rank, of midnight weeds collected,

With Hecate's ban° thrice blasted, thrice infected,

Thy natural magic and dire property°

225

On wholesome life usurp immediately.

[*He pours the poison into the sleeper's ear.*]

Hamlet: 'A poison him i' the garden for his estate.° His° name's Gonzago. The story is extant, and written in very choice Italian. You shall see anon how the murderer gets the love of Gonzago's wife.

[*Claudius rises.*]

Ophelia: The King rises.

230

Hamlet: What, frighted with false fire?°

Queen: How fares my lord?

Polonius: Give o'er the play.

King: Give me some light. Away!

Polonius: Lights, lights, lights!

235

Exeunt all but Hamlet and Horatio.

Hamlet:

"Why,° let the strucken deer go weep,
The hart ungallèd° play.

213 *chorus* (In many Elizabethan plays, the forthcoming action was explained by an actor known as the "chorus"; at a puppet show, the actor who spoke the dialogue was known as an "interpreter," as indicated by the lines following.) 214 *interpret* (1) ventriloquize the dialogue, as in puppet show (2) act as pander 214–215 *puppets dallying* (With suggestion of sexual play, continued in lines 216–218: *keen,* "sexually aroused," *groaning,* "moaning in pregnancy," and *edge,* "sexual desire" or "impetuosity.") 216 *keen* sharp, bitter 218 *Still . . . worse* more keen, always *bettering* what other people say with witty wordplay, but at the same time more offensive 219 *So* even thus (in marriage). *mis-take* take falseheartedly and cheat on. (The marriage vows say "for better, for worse.") 222 *Confederate season* the time and occasion conspiring (to assist the murderer). *else* otherwise. *seeing* seeing me 224 *Hecate's ban* the curse of Hecate, the goddess of witchcraft 225 *dire property* baleful quality 227 *estate* i.e., the kingship. *His* i.e., the King's 231 *false fire* the blank discharge of a gun loaded with powder but no shot 236–239 *Why . . . away* (Probably from an old ballad, with allusion to the popular belief that a wounded deer retires to weep and die; compare with *As You Like It,* Act II, Scene i, lines 33–66.) 237 *ungallèd* unafflicted

> For some must watch,° while some must sleep;
> Thus runs the world away."°

Would not this,° sir, and a forest of feathers°—if the rest of my fortunes 240
turn Turk with° me—with two Provincial roses° on my razed° shoes, get me
a fellowship° in a cry° of players?

Horatio: Half a share.

Hamlet: A whole one, I.

> "For thou dost know, O Damon° dear, 245
> This° realm dismantled° was
> Of Jove himself, and now reigns here
> A very, very—pajock."

Horatio: You might have rhymed.

Hamlet: O good Horatio, I'll take the ghost's word for a thousand pound. Didst 250
perceive?

Horatio: Very well, my lord.

Hamlet: Upon the talk of the poisoning?

Horatio: I did very well note him.

Enter Rosencrantz and Guildenstern.

Hamlet: Aha! Come, some music! Come, the recorders.° 255

> "For if the King like not the comedy,
> Why then, belike, he likes it not, perdy."°

Come, some music.

Guildenstern: Good my lord, vouchsafe me a word with you.

Hamlet: Sir, a whole history. 260

Guildenstern: The King, sir—

Hamlet: Ay, sir, what of him?

Guildenstern: Is in his retirement° marvelous distempered.°

Hamlet: With drink, sir?

Guildenstern: No, my lord, with choler. 265

---

238 *watch* remain awake   239 *Thus . . . away* thus the world goes   240 *this* i.e., the play.
feathers (Allusion to the plumes that Elizabethan actors were fond of wearing.)   241 *turn Turk*
with turn renegade against, go back on   241 *Provincial roses* rosettes of ribbon, named for roses
grown in a part of France.   *razed* with ornamental slashing.   242 *fellowship . . . players* partnership in a theatrical company.   *cry* pack (of hounds)   245 *Damon* the friend of Pythias, as
Horatio is friend of Hamlet; or, a traditional pastoral name   246–248 *This realm*
. . . pajock i.e., Jove, representing divine authority and justice, has abandoned this realm to its
own devices, leaving in his stead only a peacock or vain pretender to virtue (though the
rhyme-word expected in place of *pajock* or "peacock" suggests that the realm is now ruled over
by an "ass").   246 *dismantled* stripped, divested   255 *recorders* wind instruments of the flute
kind   257 *perdy* (A corruption of the French *par dieu*, "by God.")   263 *retirement* withdrawal
to his chambers.   *distempered* out of humor. (But Hamlet deliberately plays on the wider application to any illness of mind or body, especially to drunkenness.)

Hamlet: Your wisdom should show itself more richer to signify this to the doctor, for for me to put him to his purgation° would perhaps plunge him into more choler.°

Guildenstern: Good my lord, put your discourse into some frame° and start° not so wildly from my affair. 270

Hamlet: I am tame, sir. Pronounce.

Guildenstern: The Queen, your mother, in most great affliction of spirit, hath sent me to you.

Hamlet: You are welcome.

Guildenstern: Nay, good my lord, this courtesy is not of the right breed.° If it 275 shall please you to make me a wholesome answer, I will do your mother's commandment; if not, your pardon° and my return shall be the end of my business.

Hamlet: Sir, I cannot.

Rosencrantz: What, my lord? 280

Hamlet: Make you a wholesome answer; my wit's diseased. But, sir, such answer as I can make, you shall command, or rather, as you say, my mother. There-fore no more, but to the matter. My mother, you say—

Rosencrantz: Then thus she says: your behavior hath struck her into amazement and admiration.° 285

Hamlet: O wonderful son, that can so stonish a mother! But is there no sequel at the heels of this mother's admiration? Impart.

Rosencrantz: She desires to speak with you in her closet° ere you go to bed.

Hamlet: We shall obey, were she ten times our mother. Have you any further trade with us? 290

Rosencrantz: My lord, you once did love me.

Hamlet: And do still, by these pickers and stealers.°

Rosencrantz: Good my lord, what is your cause of distemper? You do surely bar the door upon your own liberty° if you deny° your griefs to your friend.

Hamlet: Sir, I lack advancement. 295

Rosencrantz: How can that be, when you have the voice of the King himself for your succession in Denmark?

Hamlet: Ay, sir, but "While the grass grows"°—the proverb is something° musty.

Enter the Players° with recorders.

---

267 *purgation* (Hamlet hints at something going beyond medical treatment to blood-letting and the extraction of confession.)   268 *choler* anger. (But Hamlet takes the word in its more basic humoral sense of "bilious disorder.")   269 *frame* order.   *start* shy or jump away (like a horse; the opposite of *tame* in line 271)   275 *breed* (1) kind (2) breeding, manners   277 *pardon* permission to depart   285 *admiration* bewilderment   288 *closet* private chamber   292 *pickers and stealers* i.e., hands. (So called from the catechism, "to keep my hands from picking and stealing.")   294 *liberty* i.e., being freed from *distemper*, line 293; but perhaps with a veiled threat as well.   *deny* refuse to share   298 *While . . . grows* (The rest of the proverb is "the silly horse starves"; Hamlet may not live long enough to succeed to the kingdom.)   *something* somewhat.   s.d. *Players* actors

O, the recorders. Let me see one. [*He takes a recorder.*] To withdraw° with
you: why do you go about to recover the wind° of me, as if you would drive   300
me into a toil?°
Guildenstern: O, my lord, if my duty be too bold, my love is too unmannerly.°
Hamlet: I do not well understand that.° Will you play upon this pipe?
Guildenstern: My lord, I cannot.
Hamlet: I pray you.   305
Guildenstern: Believe me, I cannot.
Hamlet: I do beseech you.
Guildenstern: I know no touch of it, my lord.
Hamlet: It is as easy as lying. Govern these ventages° with your fingers and
thumb, give it breath with your mouth, and it will discourse most eloquent   310
music. Look you, these are the stops.
Guildenstern: But these cannot I command to any utterance of harmony. I have
not the skill.
Hamlet: Why, look you now, how unworthy a thing you make of me! You would
play upon me, you would seem to know my stops, you would pluck out the   315
heart of my mystery, you would sound° me from my lowest note to the top of
my compass,° and there is much music, excellent voice, in this little organ,°
yet cannot you make it speak. 'Sblood, do you think I am easier to be played
on than a pipe? Call me what instrument you will, though you can fret° me,
you cannot play upon me.   320

Enter Polonius.

God bless you, sir!
Polonius: My lord, the Queen would speak with you, and presently.°
Hamlet: Do you see yonder cloud that's almost in shape of a camel?
Polonius: By the Mass and 'tis, like a camel indeed.
Hamlet: Methinks it is like a weasel.   325
Polonius: It is backed like a weasel.
Hamlet: Or like a whale.
Polonius: Very like a whale
Hamlet: Then I will come to my mother by and by.° [*Aside.*] They fool me° to
the top of my bent.°—I will come by and by.   330
Polonius: I will say so.   [*Exit.*]
Hamlet: "By and by" is easily said. Leave me, friends.

299 *withdraw* speak privately   300 *recover the wind* get to the windward side (thus driving the
game into the *toil,* or "net")   301 *toil* snare   302 *if . . . unmannerly* if I am using an unmannerly boldness, it is my love that occasions it   303 *I . . . that* i.e., I don't understand how genuine love can be unmannerly   309 *ventages* finger-holes or *stops* (line 315) of the recorder
316 *sound* (1) fathom (2) produce sound in   317 *compass* range (of voice).   *organ* musical instrument   319 *fret* irritate (with a quibble on *fret,* meaning the piece of wood, gut, or metal
that regulates the fingering on an instrument)   322 *presently* at once   329 *by and by* quite
soon.   *fool me* trifle with me, humor my fooling   330 *top of my bent* limit of my ability or endurance. (Literally, the extent to which a bow may be bent.)

'Tis now the very witching time° of night,
When churchyards yawn and hell itself breathes out
Contagion to this world. Now could I drink hot blood   335
And do such bitter business as the day
Would quake to look on. Soft, now to my mother.
O heart, lose not thy nature!° Let not ever
The soul of Nero° enter this firm bosom.
Let me be cruel, not unnatural;   340
I will speak daggers to her, but use none.
My tongue and soul in this be hypocrites:
How in my words soever° she be shent,°
To give them seals° never my soul consent!   *Exit.*

Scene III [The Castle.]

Enter King, Rosencrantz, and Guildenstern.

King: I like him° not, nor stands it safe with us
    To let his madness range. Therefore prepare you.
    I your commission will forthwith dispatch,°
    And he to England shall along with you.
    The terms of our estate° may not endure   5
    Hazard so near 's as doth hourly grow
    Out of his brows.°
Guildenstern: We will ourselves provide.
    Most holy and religious fear° it is
    To keep those many many bodies safe
    That live and feed upon Your Majesty.   10
Rosencrantz: The single and peculiar° life is bound
    With all the strength and armor of the mind
    To keep itself from noyance,° but much more
    That spirit upon whose weal depends and rests
    The lives of many. The cess° of majesty   15
    Dies not alone, but like a gulf° doth draw
    What's near it with it; or it is a massy° wheel
    Fixed on the summit of the highest mount,
    To whose huge spokes ten thousand lesser things

333 *witching time* time when spells are cast and evil is abroad   338 *nature* natural feeling   339
Nero murderer of his mother, Agrippina   343 *How . . . soever* however much by my words.
shent rebuked   344 *give them seals* i.e., confirm them with deeds   1 *him* i.e., his behavior   3
dispatch prepare, cause to be drawn up   5 *terms of our estate* circumstances of my royal position
7 *Out of his brows* i.e., from his brain, in the form of plots and threats   8 *religious fear* sacred
concern   11 *single and peculiar* individual and private   13 *noyance* harm   15 *cess* decrease,
cessation   16 *gulf* whirlpool   17 *massy* massive

Are mortised° and adjoined, which, when it falls,°   20
Each small annexment, petty consequence,°
Attends° the boisterous ruin. Never alone
Did the King sigh, but with a general groan.
King: Arm° you, I pray you, to this speedy voyage,
For we will fetters put about this fear,   25
Which now goes too free-footed.
Rosencrantz: We will haste us.
                    Exeunt gentlemen [Rosencrantz and Guildenstern].

    Enter Polonius.

Polonius: My lord, he's going to his mother's closet.
Behind the arras° I'll convey myself
To hear the process.° I'll warrant she'll tax him home,°
And, as you said—and wisely was it said—   30
'Tis meet° that some more audience than a mother,
Since nature makes them partial, should o'erhear
The speech, of vantage.° Fare you well, my liege.
I'll call upon you ere you go to bed
And tell you what I know.
King: Thanks, dear my lord.   35
                                                      Exit [Polonius].

O, my offense is rank! It smells to heaven.
It hath the primal eldest curse° upon 't,
A brother's murder. Pray can I not,
Though inclination be as sharp as will;°
My stronger guilt defeats my strong intent,   40
And like a man to double business bound°
I stand in pause where I shall first begin,
And both neglect. What if this cursèd hand
Were thicker than itself with brother's blood,
Is there not rain enough in the sweet heavens   45
To wash it white as snow? Whereto serves mercy
But to confront the visage of offense?°
And what's in prayer but this twofold force,

---

20 *mortised* fastened (as with a fitted joint).   *when it falls* i.e., when it descends, like the wheel of
Fortune, bringing a king down with it   21 *Each . . . consequence* i.e., every hanger-on and unimportant person or thing connected with the King   22 *Attends* participates in   24 *Arm* prepare
28 *arras* screen of tapestry placed around the walls of household apartments. (On the Elizabethan
stage, the arras was presumably over a door or discovery space in the tiring-house facade.)   29
process proceedings.   *tax him home* reprove him severely   31 *meet* fitting   33 *of vantage* from an
advantageous place, or, in addition   37 *the primal eldest curse* the curse of Cain, the first murderer;
he killed his brother Abel   39 *Though . . . will* though my desire is as strong as my determination
41 *bound* (1) destined (2) obliged. (The King wants to repent and still enjoy what he has gained.)
46–47 *Whereto . . . offense* what function does mercy serve other than to meet sin face to face?

To be forestallèd° ere we come to fall,
Or pardoned being down? Then I'll look up.   50
My fault is past. But O, what form of prayer
Can serve my turn? "Forgive me my foul murder"?
That cannot be, since I am still possessed
Of those effects for which I did the murder:
My crown, mine own ambition, and my queen.   55
May one be pardoned and retain th' offense?°
In the corrupted currents° of this world
Offense's gilded hand° may shove° by justice,
And oft 'tis seen the wicked prize° itself
Buys out the law. But 'tis not so above.   60
There° is no shuffling,° there the action lies°
In his° true nature, and we ourselves compelled,
Even to the teeth and forehead° of our faults,
To give in° evidence. What then? What rests?°
Try what repentance can. What can it not?   65
Yet what can it, when one cannot repent?
O wretched state, O bosom black as death,
O limèd° soul that, struggling to be free,
Art more engaged!° Help, angels! Make assay.°
Bow, stubborn knees, and heart with strings of steel,   70
Be soft as sinews of the newborn babe!
All may be well.   [He kneels.]

Enter Hamlet.

Hamlet: Now might I do it pat,° now 'a is a-praying;
And now I'll do 't. [He draws his sword.] And so 'a goes to heaven,
And so am I revenged. That would be scanned:°   75
A villain kills my father, and for that,
I, his sole son, do this same villain send
To heaven.
Why, this is hire and salary, not revenge.
'A took my father grossly, full of bread,°   80
With all his crimes broad blown,° as flush° as May;

---

49 *forestallèd* prevented (from sinning)   56 *th' offense* the thing for which one offended   57
currents courses   58 *gilded hand* hand offering gold as a bribe.   *shove by* thrust aside   59 *wicked
prize* prize won by wickedness   61 *There* i.e., in heaven.   *shuffling* escape by trickery.   *the action lies* the accusation is made manifest. (A legal metaphor.)   62 *his* its   63 *to the teeth and
forehead* face to face, concealing nothing   64 *give in* provide.   *rests* remains   68 *limèd* caught
as with birdlime, a sticky substance used to ensnare birds   69 *engaged* entangled.   *assay* trial.
(Said to himself.)   73 *pat* opportunely   75 *would be scanned* needs to be looked into, or, would
be interpreted as follows   80 *grossly, full of bread* i.e., enjoying his worldly pleasures rather than
fasting. (See Ezekiel 16:49.)   81 *crimes broad blown* sins in full bloom.   *flush* vigorous

And how his audit° stands who knows save° heaven?
But in our circumstance and course of thought°
'Tis heavy with him. And am I then revenged,
To take him in the purging of his soul,   85
When he is fit and seasoned° for his passage?
No!
Up, sword, and know° thou a more horrid hent.°

[He puts up his sword.]

When he is drunk asleep, or in his rage,°
Or in th' incestuous pleasure of his bed,   90
At game,° a-swearing, or about some act
That has no relish° of salvation in 't—
Then trip him, that his heels may kick at heaven,
And that his soul may be as damned and black
As hell, whereto it goes. My mother stays.°   95
This physic° but prolongs thy sickly days.   *Exit.*
King: My words fly up, my thoughts remain below.
Words without thoughts never to heaven go.   *Exit.*

Scene IV [The Queen's Private Chamber.]

Enter [Queen] Gertrude and Polonius.

Polonius: 'A will come straight. Look you lay home° to him.
    Tell him his pranks have been too broad° to bear with,
    And that Your Grace hath screened and stood between
    Much heat° and him. I'll shroud° me even here.
    Pray you, be round° with him.   5
Hamlet (*within*): Mother, Mother, Mother!
Queen: I'll warrant you, fear me not.
    Withdraw, I hear him coming.

[*Polonius hides behind the arras.*]

Enter Hamlet.

Hamlet: Now, Mother, what's the matter?
Queen: Hamlet, thou hast thy father° much offended.   10
Hamlet: Mother, you have my father much offended.

---

82 *audit* account. *save* except for 83 *in . . . thought* as we see it from our mortal perspective
86 *seasoned* matured, readied 88 *know . . . hent* await to be grasped by me on a more horrid
occasion. *hent* act of seizing 89 *drunk . . . rage* dead drunk, or in a fit of sexual passion 91
game gambling 92 *relish* trace, savor 95 *stays* awaits (me) 96 *physic* purging (by prayer), or,
Hamlet's postponement of the killing 1 *lay home* thrust to the heart, reprove him soundly 2
broad unrestrained 4 *Much heat* i.e., the King's anger. *shroud* conceal (with ironic fitness to
Polonius' imminent death. The word is only in the First Quarto; the Second Quarto and the
Folio read "silence.") 5 *round* blunt 10 *thy father* i.e., your stepfather, Claudius

Queen: Come, come, you answer with an idle° tongue.
Hamlet: Go, go, you question with a wicked tongue.
Queen: Why, how now, Hamlet?
Hamlet: What's the matter now?
Queen: Have you forgot me?°
Hamlet: No, by the rood,° not so: 15
   You are the Queen, your husband's brother's wife,
   And—would it were not so!—you are my mother.
Queen: Nay, then, I'll set those to you that can speak.°
Hamlet: Come, come, and sit you down; you shall not budge.
   You go not till I set you up a glass   20
   Where you may see the inmost part of you.
Queen: What wilt thou do? Thou wilt not murder me?
   Help, ho!
Polonius [behind the arras]: What ho! Help!
Hamlet [drawing]: How now? A rat? Dead for a ducat,° dead!   25
                          [He thrusts his rapier through the arras.]
Polonius [behind the arras]: O, I am slain!   [He falls and dies.]
Queen: O me, what has thou done?
Hamlet: Nay, I know not. Is it the King?
Queen: O, what a rash and bloody deed is this!
Hamlet: A bloody deed—almost as bad, good Mother,
   As kill a king, and marry with his brother.   30
Queen: As kill a king!
Hamlet: Ay, lady, it was my word.
                          [He parts the arras and discovers Polonius.]
   Thou wretched, rash, intruding fool, farewell!
   I took thee for thy better. Take thy fortune.
   Thou find'st to be too busy° is some danger.—
   Leave wringing of your hands. Peace, sit you down,   35
   And let me wring your heart, for so I shall,
   If it be made of penetrable stuff,
   If damnèd custom° have not brazed° it so
   That it be proof° and bulwark against sense.°
Queen: What have I done, that thou dar'st wag thy tongue   40
   In noise so rude against me?
Hamlet: Such an act
   That blurs the grace and blush of modesty,
   Calls virtue hypocrite, takes off the rose
   From the fair forehead of an innocent love

12 *idle* foolish   15 *forgot me* i.e., forgotten that I am your mother.   *rood* cross of Christ   18
speak i.e., to someone so rude   25 *Dead for a ducat* i.e., I bet a ducat he's dead; or, a ducat is his
life's fee   34 *busy* nosey   38 *damnèd custom* habitual wickedness.   *brazed* brazened, hardened
39 *proof* armor.   *sense* feeling

And sets a blister° there, makes marriage vows 45
As false as dicers' oaths. O, such a deed
As from the body of contraction° plucks
The very soul, and sweet religion makes°
A rhapsody° of words. Heaven's face does glow
O'er this solidity and compound mass 50
With tristful visage, as against the doom,
Is thought-sick at the act.°

Queen: Ay me, what act,
That roars so loud and thunders in the index?°

Hamlet [*showing her two likenesses*]: Look here upon this picture, and on this,
The counterfeit presentment° of two brothers. 55
See what a grace was seated on this brow:
Hyperion's° curls, the front° of Jove himself,
An eye like Mars° to threaten and command,
A station° like the herald Mercury°
New-lighted° on a heaven-kissing hill— 60
A combination and a form indeed
Where every god did seem to set his seal°
To give the world assurance of a man.
This was your husband. Look you now what follows:
Here is your husband, like a mildewed ear,° 65
Blasting° his wholesome brother. Have you eyes?
Could you on this fair mountain leave° to feed
And batten° on this moor?° Ha, have you eyes?
You cannot call it love, for at your age
The heyday° in the blood° is tame, it's humble, 70
And waits upon the judgment, and what judgment
Would step from this to this? Sense,° sure, you have,
Else could you not have motion, but sure that sense
Is apoplexed,° for madness would not err,°

45 *sets a blister* i.e., brands as a harlot   47 *contraction* the marriage contract   48 *sweet religion makes* i.e., makes marriage vows   49 *rhapsody* senseless string   49–52 *Heaven's . . . act* heaven's face blushes at this solid world compounded of the various elements, with sorrowful face as though the day of doom were near, and is sick with horror at the deed (i.e., Gertrude's marriage)   53 *index* table of contents, prelude or preface   55 *counterfeit presentment* portrayed representation   57 *Hyperion's* the sun-god's.   *front* brow   58 *Mars* god of war   59 *station* manner of standing.   *Mercury* winged messenger of the gods   60 *New-lighted* newly alighted   62 *set his seal* i.e., affix his approval   65 *ear* i.e., of grain   66 *Blasting* blighting   67 *leave* cease   68 *batten* gorge.   *moor* barren or marshy ground (suggesting also "dark-skinned")   70 *heyday* state of excitement.   *blood* passion   72 *Sense* perception through the five senses (the functions of the middle or sensible soul)   74 *apoplexed* paralyzed. (Hamlet goes on to explain that, without such a paralysis of will, mere madness would not so err, nor would the five senses so enthrall themselves to *ecstasy* or lunacy; even such deranged states of mind would be able to make the obvious choice between Hamlet Senior and Claudius.)   *err* so err

Nor sense to ecstasy was ne'er so thralled,   75
But° it reserved some quantity of choice
To serve in such a difference.° What devil was 't
That thus hath cozened° you at hoodman-blind?°
Eyes without feeling, feeling without sight,
Ears without hands or eyes, smelling sans° all,   80
Or but a sickly part of one true sense
Could not so mope.° O shame, where is thy blush?
Rebellious hell,
If thou canst mutine° in a matron's bones,
To flaming youth let virtue be as wax   85
And melt in her own fire.° Proclaim no shame
When the compulsive ardor gives the charge,
Since frost itself as actively doth burn,
And reason panders will.°

Queen: O Hamlet, speak no more!   90
Thou turn'st mine eyes into my very soul,
And there I see such black and grainèd° spots
As will not leave their tinct.°

Hamlet: Nay, but to live
In the rank sweat of an enseamèd° bed,
Stewed° in corruption, honeying and making love   95
Over the nasty sty!

Queen: O, speak to me no more!
These words like daggers enter in my ears.
No more, sweet Hamlet!

Hamlet: A murderer and a villain,
A slave that is not twentieth part the tithe°   100
Of your precedent lord,° a vice° of kings,
A cutpurse of the empire and the rule,
That from a shelf the precious diadem stole
And put it in his pocket!

Queen: No more!   105

    Enter Ghost.

76 But but that   77 To . . . difference to help in making a choice between two such men   78
cozened cheated.   hoodman-blind blindman's buff. (In this game, says Hamlet, the devil must
have pushed Claudius toward Gertrude while she was blindfolded.)   80 sans without   82 mope
be dazed, act aimlessly   84 mutine incite mutiny   85–86 be as wax . . . fire melt like a candle or
stick of sealing wax held over the candle flame   86–89 Proclaim . . . will call it no shameful
business when the compelling ardor of youth delivers the attack, i.e., commits lechery, since
the frost of advanced age burns with as active a fire of lust and reason perverts itself by fo-
menting lust rather than restraining it   92 grainèd dyed in grain, indelible   93 leave their tinct
surrender their color   94 enseamèd saturated in the grease and filth of passionate lovemaking
95 Stewed soaked, bathed (with a suggestion of "stew," brothel)   100 tithe tenth part   101
precedent lord former husband.   vice buffoon. (A reference to the Vice of the morality plays.)

Hamlet: A king of shreds and patches°—
 Save me, and hover o'er me with your wings,
 You heavenly guards! What would your gracious figure?
Queen: Alas, he's mad!
Hamlet: Do you not come your tardy son to chide,   110
 That, lapsed° in time and passion, lets go by
 Th' important° acting of your dread command?
 O, say!
Ghost: Do not forget. This visitation
 Is but to whet thy almost blunted purpose.   115
 But look, amazement° on thy mother sits.
 O, step between her and her fighting soul!
 Conceit° in weakest bodies strongest works.
 Speak to her, Hamlet.
Hamlet: How is it with you, lady?
Queen: Alas, how is 't with you,   120
 That you do bend your eye on vacancy,
 And with th' incorporal° air do hold discourse?
 Forth at your eyes your spirits wildly peep,
 And, as the sleeping soldiers in th' alarm,°
 Your bedded° hair, like life in excrements,°   125
 Start up and stand on end. O gentle son,
 Upon the heat and flame of thy distemper°
 Sprinkle cool patience. Whereon do you look?
Hamlet: On him, on him! Look you how pale he glares!
 His form and cause conjoined,° preaching to stones,   130
 Would make them capable.°—Do not look upon me,
 Lest with this piteous action you convert
 My stern effects.° Then what I have to do
 Will want true color—tears perchance for blood.°
Queen: To whom do you speak this?   135
Hamlet: Do you see nothing there?
Queen: Nothing at all, yet all that is I see.
Hamlet: Nor did you nothing hear?
Queen: No, nothing but ourselves.
Hamlet: Why, look you there, look how it steals away!   140

---

106 *shreds and patches* i.e., motley, the traditional costume of the clown or fool 111 *lapsed* delaying 112 *important* importunate, urgent 116 *amazement* distraction 118 *Conceit* imagination 122 *incorporal* immaterial 124 *as . . . alarm* like soldiers called out of sleep by an alarm 125 *bedded* laid flat. *like life in excrements* i.e., as though hair, an outgrowth of the body, had a life of its own. (Hair was thought to be lifeless because it lacks sensation, and so its standing on end would be unnatural and ominous.) 127 *distemper* disorder 130 *His . . . conjoined* his appearance joined to his cause for speaking 131 *capable* receptive 132–133 *convert . . . effects* divert me from my stern duty 134 *want . . . blood* lack plausibility so that (with a play on the normal sense of *color*) I shall shed colorless tears instead of blood

My father, in his habit° as° he lived!
Look where he goes even now out at the portal!

Exit Ghost.

Queen: This is the very° coinage of your brain.
    This bodiless creation ecstasy
    Is very cunning in.°   145
Hamlet: Ecstasy?
    My pulse as yours doth temperately keep time,
    And makes as healthful music. It is not madness
    That I have uttered. Bring me to the test,
    And I the matter will reword,° which madness   150
    Would gambol° from. Mother, for love of grace,
    Lay not that flattering unction° to your soul
    That not your trespass but my madness speaks.
    It will but skin° and film the ulcerous place,
    Whiles rank corruption, mining° all within,   155
    Infects unseen. Confess yourself to heaven,
    Repent what's past, avoid what is to come,
    And do not spread the compost° on the weeds
    To make them ranker. Forgive me this my virtue;°
    For in the fatness° of these pursy° times   160
    Virtue itself of vice must pardon beg,
    Yea, curb° and woo for leave° to do him good.
Queen: O Hamlet, thou hast cleft my heart in twain.
Hamlet: O, throw away the worser part of it,
    And live the purer with the other half.   165
    Good night. But go not to my uncle's bed;
    Assume a virtue, if you have it not.
    That monster, custom, who all sense doth eat,°
    Of habits devil,° is angel yet in this,
    That to the use of actions fair and good   170
    He likewise gives a frock or livery°
    That aptly° is put on. Refrain tonight,
    And that shall lend a kind of easiness
    To the next abstinence; the next more easy;
    For use° almost can change the stamp of nature,°   175

141 *habit* clothes. *as* as when   143 *very* mere   144–145 *This . . . in* madness is skillful in creating this kind of hallucination   150 *reword* repeat word for word   151 *gambol* skip away
152 *unction* ointment   154 *skin* grow a skin for   155 *mining* working under the surface   158
compost manure   159 *this my virtue* my virtuous talk in reproving you   160 *fatness* grossness.
pursy flabby, out of shape   162 *curb* bow, bend the knee. *leave* permission   168 *who . . . eat*
which consumes all proper or natural feeling, all sensibility   169 *Of habits devil* devillike in
prompting evil habits   171 *livery* an outer appearance, a customary garb (and hence a predis-
position easily assumed in time of stress)   172 *aptly* readily   175 *use* habit. *the stamp of nature* our inborn traits

And either° . . . the devil, or throw him out
With wondrous potency. Once more, good night;
And when you are desirous to be blest,
I'll blessing beg of you.° For this same lord,

                                        [*pointing to Polonius*]

I do repent; but heaven hath pleased it so   180
To punish me with this, and this with me,
That I must be their scourge and minister.°
I will bestow° him, and will answer° well
The death I gave him. So, again, good night.
I must be cruel only to be kind.   185
This° bad begins, and worse remains behind.°
One word more, good lady.
Queen: What shall I do?
Hamlet: Not this by no means that I bid you do:
Let the bloat° king tempt you again to bed,
Pinch wanton° on your cheek, call you his mouse,   190
And let him, for a pair of reechy° kisses,
Or paddling° in your neck with his damned fingers,
Make you to ravel all this matter out°
That I essentially am not in madness,
But mad in craft.° 'Twere good° you let him know,   195
For who that's but a queen, fair, sober, wise,
Would from a paddock,° from a bat, a gib,°
Such dear concernings° hide? Who would do so?
No, in despite of sense and secrecy,°
Unpeg the basket° on the house's top,   200
Let the birds fly, and like the famous ape,°
To try conclusions,° in the basket creep
And break your own neck down.°
Queen: Be thou assured, if words be made of breath,

176 *And either* (A defective line, usually emended by inserting the word *master* after *either*, following the Fourth Quarto and early editors.)   178–179 *when . . . you* i.e., when you are ready
to be penitent and seek God's blessing, I will ask your blessing as a dutiful son should   182
their scourge and minister i.e., agent of heavenly retribution. (By *scourge*, Hamlet also suggests
that he himself will eventually suffer punishment in the process of fulfilling heaven's will.)
183 *bestow* stow, dispose of.   *answer* account or pay for   186 *This* i.e., the killing of Polonius.
behind to come   189 *bloat* bloated   190 *Pinch wanton* i.e., leave his love pinches on your
cheeks, branding you as wanton   191 *reechy* dirty, filthy   192 *paddling* fingering amorously
193 *ravel . . . out* unravel, disclose   195 *in craft* by cunning.   *good* (Said sarcastically; also the
following eight lines.)   197 *paddock* toad.   *gib* tomcat   198 *dear concernings* important affairs
199 *sense and secrecy* secrecy that common sense requires   200 *Unpeg the basket* open the cage,
i.e., let out the secret   201 *famous ape* (In a story now lost.)   202 *try conclusions* test the outcome (in which the ape apparently enters a cage from which birds have been released and then
tries to fly out of the cage as they have done, falling to its death)   203 *down* in the fall: utterly

And breath of life, I have no life to breathe   205
    What thou hast said to me.
Hamlet: I must to England. You know that?
Queen: Alack,
    I had forgot. 'Tis so concluded on.
Hamlet: There's letters sealed, and my two schoolfellows,
    Whom I will trust as I will adders fanged,   210
    They bear the mandate; they must sweep my way
    And marshal me to knavery.° Let it work.°
    For 'tis the sport to have the enginer°
    Hoist with° his own petard,° and 't shall go hard
    But I will° delve one yard below their mines°   215
    And blow them at the moon. O, 'tis most sweet
    When in one line° two crafts° directly meet.
    This man shall set me packing.°
    I'll lug the guts into the neighbor room.
    Mother, good night indeed. This counselor   220
    Is now most still, most secret, and most grave,
    Who was in life a foolish prating knave.—
    Come, sir, to draw toward an end° with you.—
    Good night, Mother.

                        Exeunt [separately, Hamlet dragging in Polonius].

ACT IV

Scene I [The Castle.]

Enter King and Queen,° with Rosencrantz and Guildenstern.

King: There's matter° in these sighs, these profound heaves.°
    You must translate; 'tis fit we understand them.
    Where is your son?
Queen: Bestow this place on us a little while.

211–212 *sweep . . . knavery* sweep a path before me and conduct me to some *knavery* or
treachery prepared for me   212 *work* proceed   213 *enginer* maker of military contrivances
214 *Hoist with* blown up by.   *petard* an explosive used to blow in a door or make a breach
214–215 *'t shall . . . will* unless luck is against me, I will   215 *mines* tunnels used in warfare to
undermine the enemy's emplacements: Hamlet will countermine by going under their mines
217 *in one line* i.e., mines and countermines on a collision course, or the countermines directly
below the mines.   *crafts* acts of guile, plots   218 *set me packing* set me to making schemes, and
set me to lugging (him), and, also, send me off in a hurry   223 *draw . . . end* finish up (with a
pun on *draw*, "pull")   s.d. *Enter . . . Queen* (Some editors argue that Gertrude never exits in
Act III, Scene iv, and that the scene is continuous here, as suggested in the Folio, but the
Second Quarto marks an entrance for her and at line 35 Claudius speaks of Gertrude's *closet* as
though it were elsewhere. A short time has elapsed, during which the King has become aware
of her highly wrought emotional state.)   1 *matter* significance.   *heaves* heavy sighs

Ah, mine own lord, what have I seen tonight!   5

King: What, Gertrude? How does Hamlet?

Queen: Mad as the sea and wind when both contend
Which is the mightier. In his lawless fit,
Behind the arras hearing something stir,
Whips out his rapier, cries, "A rat, a rat!"   10
And in this brainish apprehension° kills
The unseen good old man.

King: O heavy° deed!
It had been so with us,° had we been there.
His liberty is full of threats to all—
To you yourself, to us, to everyone.   15
Alas, how shall this bloody deed be answered?°
It will be laid to us, whose providence°
Should have kept short,° restrained, and out of haunt°
This mad young man. But so much was our love,
We would not understand what was most fit,   20
But, like the owner of a foul disease,
To keep it from divulging,° let it feed
Even on the pith of life. Where is he gone?

Queen: To draw apart the body he hath killed,
O'er whom his very madness, like some ore°   25
Among a mineral° of metals base,
Shows itself pure: 'a weeps for what is done.

King: O Gertrude, come away!
The sun no sooner shall the mountains touch
But we will ship him hence, and this vile deed   30
We must with all our majesty and skill
Both countenance° and excuse.—Ho, Guildenstern!

Enter Rosencrantz and Guildenstern.

Friends both, go join you with some further aid.
Hamlet in madness hath Polonius slain,
And from his mother's closet hath he dragged him.   35
Go seek him out, speak fair, and bring the body
Into the chapel. I pray you, haste in this.
                              [Exeunt Rosencrantz and Guildenstern.]
Come, Gertrude, we'll call up our wisest friends

---

11 *brainish apprehension* headstrong conception   12 *heavy* grievous   13 *us* i.e., me. (The royal
"we"; also in line 15.)   16 *answered* explained   17 *providence* foresight   18 *short* i.e., on a
short tether.   *out of haunt* ecluded   22 *divulging* becoming evident   25 *ore* vein of gold   26
mineral mine   32 *countenance* put the best face on

And let them know both what we mean to do
And what's untimely done.........°   40
Whose whisper o'er the world's diameter,°
As level° as the cannon to his blank,°
Transports his poisoned shot, may miss our name
And hit the woundless° air. O, come away!
My soul is full of discord and dismay.   *Exeunt.*   45

Scene II [The Castle.]

Enter Hamlet.

Hamlet: Safely stowed.
Rosencrantz, Guildenstern (*within*): Hamlet! Lord Hamlet!
Hamlet: But soft, what noise? Who calls on Hamlet? O, here they come.

Enter Rosencrantz and Guildenstern.

Rosencrantz: What have you done, my lord, with the dead body?
Hamlet: Compounded it with dust, whereto 'tis kin.   5
Rosencrantz: Tell us where 'tis, that we may take it thence
  And bear it to the chapel.
Hamlet: Do not believe it.
Rosencrantz: Believe what?
Hamlet: That I can keep your counsel and not mine own.° Besides, to be de-   10
  manded of° a sponge, what replication° should be made by the son of a king?
Rosencrantz: Take you me for a sponge, my lord?
Hamlet: Ay, sir, that soaks up the King's countenance,° his rewards, his authori-
  ties.° But such officers do the King best service in the end. He keeps them,
  like an ape, an apple, in the corner of his jaw, first mouthed to be last swal- 15
  lowed. When he needs what you have gleaned, it is but squeezing you, and,
  sponge, you shall be dry again.
Rosencrantz: I understand you not, my lord.
Hamlet: I am glad of it. A knavish speech sleeps in° a foolish ear.
Rosencrantz: My lord, you must tell us where the body is and go with us to the   20
  King.

---

40 *And . . . done* (A defective line: conjectures as to the missing words include *So, haply, slander* [Capell and others]; *For, haply, slander* [Theobald and others]; and *So envious slander* [Jenkins].)   41 *diameter* extent from side to side   42 *As level* with as direct aim.   *his blank* its target at point-blank range   44 *woundless* invulnerable   10 *That . . . own* i.e., that I can follow your advice (by telling where the body is) and still keep my own secret   10–11 *demanded of* questioned by   11 *replication* reply   13 *countenance* favor.   13–14 *authorities* delegated power, influence   19 *sleeps in* has no meaning to

Hamlet: The body is with the King, but the King is not with the body.° The
King is a thing—
Guildenstern: A thing, my lord?
Hamlet: Of nothing.° Bring me to him. Hide fox, and all after!° *Exeunt [running].*   25

Scene III [The Castle.]

Enter King, and two or three.

King: I have sent to seek him, and to find the body.
How dangerous is it that this man goes loose!
Yet must not we put the strong law on him.
He's loved of° the distracted° multitude,
Who like not in their judgment, but their eyes,°   5
And where 'tis so, th' offender's scourge° is weighed,°
But never the offense. To bear all smooth and even,°
This sudden sending him away must seem
Deliberate pause.° Diseases desperate grown
By desperate appliance° are relieved,   10
Or not at all.

Enter Rosencrantz, [Guildenstern,] and all the rest.

              How now, what hath befall'n?
Rosencrantz: Where the dead body is bestowed, my lord,
We cannot get from him.
King: But where is he?
Rosencrantz: Without, my lord; guarded, to know your pleasure.
King: Bring him before us.
Rosencrantz: Ho! Bring in the lord.   15

They enter [with Hamlet].

King: Now, Hamlet, where's Polonius?
Hamlet: At supper.
King: At supper? Where?

---

22 *The . . . body* (Perhaps alludes to the legal commonplace of "the king's two bodies," which
drew a distinction between the sacred office of kingship and the particular mortal who possessed it at any given time. Hence, although Claudius' body is necessarily a part of him, true
kingship is not contained in it. Similarly, Claudius will have Polonius' body when it is found,
but there is no kingship in this business either.)   25 *Of nothing* (1) of no account (2) lacking
the essence of kingship, as in line 22 and note.   *Hide . . . after* (An old signal cry in the game
of hide-and-seek, suggesting that Hamlet now runs away from them.)   4 *of* by.   *distracted*
fickle, unstable   5 *Who . . . eyes* who choose not by judgment but by appearance   6 *scourge*
punishment. (Literally, blow with a whip.)   *weighed* sympathetically considered   7 *To . . .
even* to manage the business in an unprovocative way   9 *Deliberate pause* carefully considered
action   10 *appliance* remedies

Hamlet: Not where he eats, but where 'a is eaten. A certain convocation of
politic worms° are e'en° at him. Your worm° is your only emperor for diet.°   20
We fat all creatures else to fat us, and we fat ourselves for maggots. Your fat
king and your lean beggar is but variable service°—two dishes, but to one
table. That's the end.

King: Alas, alas!

Hamlet: A man may fish with the worm that hath eat° of a king, and eat of the   25
fish that hath fed of that worm.

King: What dost thou mean by this?

Hamlet: Nothing but to show you how a king may go a progress° through the
guts of a beggar.

King: Where is Polonius?   30

Hamlet: In heaven. Send thither to see. If your messenger find him not there,
seek him i' th' other place yourself. But if indeed you find him not within
this month, you shall nose him as you go up the stairs into the lobby.

King [*to some attendants*]: Go seek him there.

Hamlet: 'A will stay till you come.   [*Exeunt attendants.*]   35

King: Hamlet, this deed, for thine especial safety—
    Which we do tender,° as we dearly° grieve
    For that which thou hast done—must send thee hence
    With fiery quickness. Therefore prepare thyself.
    The bark° is ready, and the wind at help,   40
    Th' associates tend,° and everything is bent°
    For England.

Hamlet: For England!

King: Ay, Hamlet.

Hamlet: Good.   45

King: So is it, if thou knew'st our purposes.

Hamlet: I see a cherub° that sees them. But come, for England! Farewell, dear
mother.

King: Thy loving father, Hamlet.

Hamlet: My mother. Father and mother is man and wife, man and wife is one   50
flesh, and so, my mother. Come, for England!   *Exit.*

King: Follow him at foot;° tempt him with speed aboard.
    Delay it not. I'll have him hence tonight.
    Away! For everything is sealed and done
    That else leans on° th' affair. Pray you, make haste.   55

                              [*Exeunt all but the King.*]

20 *politic worms* crafty worms (suited to a master spy like Polonius). *e'en* even now. *Your
worm* your average worm (Compare *your fat king* and *your lean beggar* in lines 21–22) *diet*
food, eating (with a punning reference to the Diet of Worms, a famous *convocation* held in
1521) 22 *variable service* different courses of a single meal 25 *eat* eaten. (Pronounced *et.*)
28 *progress* royal journey of state 37 *tender* regard, hold dear. *dearly* intensely 40 *bark* sailing
vessel 41 *tend* wait. *bent* in readiness 47 *cherub* (Cherubim are angels of knowledge.
Hamlet hints that both he and heaven are onto Claudius' tricks.) 52 *at foot* close behind, at
heel 55 *leans on* bears upon, is related to

And, England,° if my love thou hold'st at aught—°
As my great power thereof may give thee sense,°
Since yet thy cicatrice° looks raw and red
After the Danish sword, and thy free awe°
Pays homage to us—thou mayst not coldly set°   60
Our sovereign process,° which imports at full,°
By letters congruing° to that effect,
The present° death of Hamlet. Do it, England,
For like the hectic° in my blood he rages,
And thou must cure me. Till I know 'tis done,   65
Howe'er my haps,° my joys were ne'er begun.   *Exit.*

Scene IV [The Coast of Denmark.]

Enter Fortinbras with his army over the stage.

Fortinbras: Go, Captain, from me greet the Danish king.
    Tell him that by his license° Fortinbras
    Craves the conveyance of° a promised march
    Over his kingdom. You know the rendezvous.
    If that His Majesty would aught with us,   5
    We shall express our duty° in his eye;°
    And let him know so.
Captain: I will do 't, my lord.
Fortinbras: Go softly° on. [*Exeunt all but the Captain.*]

    Enter Hamlet, Rosencrantz, [Guildenstern,] etc.

Hamlet: Good sir, whose powers° are these?   10
Captain: They are of Norway, sir.
Hamlet: How purposed, sir, I pray you?
Captain: Against some part of Poland.
Hamlet: Who commands them, sir?
Captain: The nephew to old Norway, Fortinbras.   15
Hamlet: Goes it against the main° of Poland, sir,
    Or for some frontier?
Captain: Truly to speak, and with no addition,°
    We go to gain a little patch of ground
    That hath in it no profit but the name.   20
    To pay° five ducats, five, I would not farm it;°

56 *England* i.e., King of England. *at aught* at any value   57 *As . . . sense* for so my great power
may give you a just appreciation of the importance of valuing my love   58 *cicatrice* scar   59
free awe voluntary show of respect   60 *coldly set* regard with indifference   61 *process* command. *imports at full* conveys specific directions for   62 *congruing* agreeing   63 *present* immediate   64 *hectic* persistent fever   66 *haps* fortunes   2 *license* permission   3 *the conveyance of*
escort during   6 *duty* respect. *eye* presence   9 *softly* slowly, circumspectly   10 *powers* forces
16 *main* main part   18 *addition* exaggeration   21 *To pay* i.e., for a yearly rental of. *farm it*
take a lease of it

Nor will it yield to Norway or the Pole
A ranker° rate, should it be sold in fee.°
Hamlet: Why, then the Polack never will defend it.
Captain: Yes, it is already garrisoned.   25
Hamlet: Two thousand souls and twenty thousand ducats
Will not debate the question of this straw.°
This is th' impostume° of much wealth and peace,
That inward breaks, and shows no cause without
Why the man dies. I humbly thank you, sir.   30
Captain: God b' wi' you, sir.

[Exit.]

Rosencrantz: Will 't please you go, my lord?
Hamlet: I'll be with you straight. Go a little before.

                                                [Exeunt all except Hamlet.]

How all occasions do inform against° me
And spur my dull revenge! What is a man,
If his chief good and market of° his time   35
Be but to sleep and feed? A beast, no more.
Sure he that made us with such large discourse,°
Looking before and after,° gave us not
That capability and godlike reason
To fust° in us unused. Now, whether it be   40
Bestial oblivion,° or some craven° scruple
Of thinking too precisely° on th' event—°
A thought which, quartered, hath but one part wisdom
And ever three parts coward—I do not know
Why yet I live to say "This thing's to do,"   45
Sith° I have cause, and will, and strength, and means
To do 't. Examples gross° as earth exhort me:
Witness this army of such mass and charge,°
Led by a delicate and tender° prince,
Whose spirit with divine ambition puffed
Makes mouths° at the invisible event,°   50
Exposing what is mortal and unsure
To all that fortune, death, and danger dare,°

23 ranker higher. in fee fee simple, outright 27 debate . . . straw settle this trifling matter
28 impostume abscess 33 inform against denounce, betray: take shape against 35 market of
profit of, compensation for 37 discourse power of reasoning 38 Looking before and after able
to review past events and anticipate the future 40 fust grow moldy 41 oblivion forgetfulness.
craven cowardly 42 precisely scrupulously. event outcome 46 Sith since 47 gross obvious
48 charge expense 49 delicate and tender of fine and youthful qualities 51 Makes mouths
makes scornful faces. invisible event unforeseeable outcome 53 dare could do (to him)

Even for an eggshell. Rightly° to be great
Is not to stir without great argument,   55
But greatly to find quarrel in a straw
When honor's at the stake.° How stand I, then,
That have a father killed, a mother stained,
Excitements of° my reason and my blood,
And let all sleep, while to my shame I see   60
The imminent death of twenty thousand men
That for a fantasy° and trick° of fame
Go to their graves like beds, fight for a plot°
Whereon the numbers cannot try the cause,°
Which is not tomb enough and continent°   65
To hide the slain? O, from this time forth
My thoughts be bloody or be nothing worth!   *Exit.*

Scene V [The Castle.]

Enter Horatio, [Queen] Gertrude, and a Gentleman.

Queen: I will not speak with her.
Gentleman: She is importunate,
   Indeed distract.° Her mood will needs be pitied.
Queen: What would she have?
Gentleman: She speaks much of her father, says she hears
   There's tricks° i' the world, and hems,° and beats her heart,°   5
   Spurns enviously at straws,° speaks things in doubt°
   That carry but half sense. Her speech is nothing,
   Yet the unshapèd use° of it doth move
   The hearers to collection;° they yawn° at it,
   And botch° the words up fit to their own thoughts,   10
   Which,° as her winks and nods and gestures yield° them,
   Indeed would make one think there might be thought,°
   Though nothing sure, yet much unhappily.°
Horatio: 'Twere good she were spoken with, for she may strew
   Dangerous conjectures in ill-breeding° minds.   15

54–57 *Rightly . . . stake* true greatness does not normally consist of rushing into action over some
trivial provocation: however, when one's honor is involved, even a trifling insult requires that one
respond greatly (?)   57 *at the stake* (A metaphor from gambling or bear-baiting.)   59 *Excitements
of* promptings by   62 *fantasy* fanciful caprice, illusion. *trick* trifle, deceit   63 *plot* plot of ground
64 *Whereon . . . . cause* on which there is insufficient room for the soldiers needed to engage in a
military contest   65 *continent* receptacle, container   2 *distract* distracted   5 *tricks* deceptions.
hems makes "hmm" sounds.   *heart* i.e., breast   6 *Spurns . . . straws* kicks spitefully, takes offense at
trifles.   *in doubt* obscurely   8 *unshapèd use* incoherent manner   9 *collection* inference, a guess at
some sort of meaning.   *yawn* gape, wonder; grasp. (The Folio reading, *aim*, is possible.)   10 *botch*
patch   11 *Which* which words.   *yield* deliver, represent   12 *thought* intended   13 *unhappily* unpleasantly near the truth, shrewdly   15 *ill-breeding* prone to suspect the worst and to make mischief

Queen: Let her come in.   [*Exit Gentleman.*]

   [*Aside.*] To my sick soul, as sin's true nature is,
   Each toy° seems prologue to some great amiss.°
   So full of artless jealousy is guilt,
   It spills itself in fearing to be spilt.°   20

   Enter Ophelia° [*distracted*].

Ophelia: Where is the beauteous majesty of Denmark?
Queen: How now, Ophelia?
Ophelia (*she sings*):
       "How should I your true love know
       From another one?
       By his cockle hat° and staff,   25
       And his sandal shoon.°"
Queen: Alas, sweet lady, what imports this song?
Ophelia: Say you? Nay, pray you, mark.
       "He is dead and gone, lady,   (*Song.*)
       He is dead and gone;   30
       At his head a grass-green turf,
       At his heels a stone."
   O, ho!
Queen: Nay, but Ophelia—
Ophelia: Pray you, mark. [*Sings.*]   35
       "White his shroud as the mountain snow"—

   Enter King.

Queen: Alas, look here, my lord.
Ophelia:
       "Larded° with sweet flowers;   (*Song.*)
       Which bewept to the ground did not go
       With true-love showers.°"   40
King: How do you, pretty lady?
Ophelia: Well, God 'ild° you! They say the owl° was a baker's daughter. Lord,
   we know what we are, but know not what we may be. God be at your table!
King: Conceit° upon her father.
Ophelia: Pray let's have no words of this; but when they ask you what it means,   45
   say you this:

18 *toy* trifle. *amiss* calamity   19–20 *So . . . split* guilt is so full of suspicion that it unskillfully
betrays itself in fearing betrayal   20 s.d *Enter Ophelia* (In the First Quarto, Ophelia enters,
"playing on a lute, and her hair down, singing.")   25 *cockle hat* hat with cockleshell stuck in it
as a sign that the wearer had been a pilgrim to the shrine of Saint James of Compostella in
Spain   26 *shoon* shoes   38 *Larded* decorated   40 *showers* i.e., tears   42 *God 'ild* God yield or
reward.   *owl* (Refers to a legend about a baker's daughter who was turned into an owl for being
ungenerous when Jesus begged a loaf of bread.)   44 *Conceit* brooding

    "Tomorrow is Saint Valentine's day,   *(Song.)*
    All in the morning betime,°
    And I a maid at your window,
    To be your Valentine.   50
    Then up he rose, and donned his clothes,
    And dupped° the chamber door,
    Let in the maid, that out a maid
    Never departed more."

King: Pretty Ophelia—   55

Ophelia: Indeed, la, without an oath, I'll make an end on 't:
    "By Gis° and by Saint Charity,
    Alack, and he for shame!
    Young men will do 't, if they come to 't;
    By Cock,° they are to blame.   60
    Quoth she, 'Before you tumbled me,
    You promised me to wed.'"

He answers:
    "'So would I ha' done, by yonder sun,
    An° thou hadst not come to my bed.'"   65

King: How long hath she been thus?

Ophelia: I hope all will be well. We must be patient, but I cannot choose but weep to think they would lay him i' the cold ground. My brother shall know of it. And so I thank you for your good counsel. Come, my coach! Good night, ladies, good night, sweet ladies, good night, good night.   *[Exit.]*   70

King [to Horatio]: Follow her close. Give her good watch, I pray you.
                                      [Exit Horatio.]

  O, this is the poison of deep grief; it springs
  All from her father's death—and now behold!
  O Gertrude, Gertrude,
  When sorrows come, they come not single spies,°   75
  But in battalions. First, her father slain;
  Next, your son gone, and he most violent author
  Of his own just remove;° the people muddied,°
  Thick and unwholesome in their thoughts and whispers
  For good Polonius' death—and we have done but greenly,°   80
  In hugger-mugger° to inter him; poor Ophelia
  Divided from herself and her fair judgment,
  Without the which we are pictures or mere beasts;
  Last, and as much containing° as all these,

---

48 *betime* early   52 *dupped* did up, opened   57 *Gis* Jesus   60 *Cock* (A perversion of "God" in oaths; here also with a quibble on the slang word for penis.)   65 An if   75 *spies* scouts sent in advance of the main force   78 *remove* removal.   *muddied* stirred up, confused   80 *greenly* in an inexperienced way, foolishly   81 *hugger-mugger* secret haste   84 *as much containing* as full of serious matter

Her brother is in secret come from France, 85
Feeds on this wonder, keeps himself in clouds,°
And wants° not buzzers° to infect his ear
With pestilent speeches of his father's death,
Wherein necessity,° of matter beggared,°
Will nothing stick our person to arraign 90
In ear and ear.° O my dear Gertrude, this,
Like to a murdering piece,° in many places
Gives me superfluous death.°   *A noise within.*
Queen: Alack, what noise is this?
King: Attend!° 95
Where is my Switzers?° Let them guard the door.

Enter a Messenger.

What is the matter?
Messenger: Save yourself, my lord!
The ocean, overpeering of his list,°
Eats not the flats° with more impetuous° haste
Than young Laertes, in a riotous head,° 100
O'erbears your officers. The rabble call him lord,
And, as° the world were now but to begin,
Antiquity forgot, custom not known,
The ratifiers and props of every word,°
They cry, "Choose we! Laertes shall be king!" 105
Caps,° hands, and tongues applaud it to the clouds,
"Laertes shall be king, Laertes king!"
Queen: How cheerfully on the false trail they cry!   *A noise within.*
O, this is counter,° you false Danish dogs!

Enter Laertes with others.

King: The doors are broke. 110
Laertes: Where is this King?—Sirs, stand you all without.
All: No, let's come in.
Laertes: I pray you, give me leave.

---

86 *Feeds . . . clouds* feeds his resentment or shocked grievance, holds himself inscrutable and
aloof amid all this rumor   87 *wants* lacks. *buzzers* gossipers, informers   89 *necessity* i.e., the
need to invent some plausible explanation. *of matter beggared* unprovided with facts   90–91
Will . . . ear will not hesitate to accuse my (royal) person in everybody's ears   92 *murdering
piece* cannon loaded so as to scatter its shot   93 *Gives . . . death* kills me over and over   95
Attend i.e., guard me   96 *Switzers* Swiss guards, mercenaries   98 *overpeering of his list* over-
flowing its shore, boundary   99 *flats* i.e., flatlands near shore. *impetuous* violent (perhaps also
with the meaning of impiteous [*impitious, Second Quarto*], "pitiless")   100 *head* insurrection
102 *as* as if   104 *The ratifiers . . . word* i.e., *antiquity* (or tradition) and *custom* ought to confirm
(*ratify*) and underprop our every word or promise   106 *Caps* (The caps are thrown in the air.)
109 *counter* (A hunting term, meaning to follow the trail in a direction opposite to that which
the game has taken.)

All: We will, we will.

Laertes: I thank you. Keep the door. [*Exeunt followers.*]
                       O thou vile king, Give me my father!   115

Queen [restraining him]: Calmly, good Laertes.

Laertes: That drop of blood that's calm proclaims me bastard,
     Cries cuckold to my father, brands the harlot
     Even here, between° the chaste unsmirchèd brow
     Of my true mother.

King: What is the cause, Laertes,   120
     That thy rebellion looks so giantlike?
     Let him go, Gertrude. Do not fear our° person.
     There's such divinity doth hedge° a king
     That treason can but peep to what it would,°
     Acts little of his will.° Tell me, Laertes,   125
     Why thou art thus incensed. Let him go, Gertrude.
     Speak, man.

Laertes: Where is my father?

King: Dead.

Queen: But not by him.

King: Let him demand his fill.

Laertes: How came he dead? I'll not be juggled with.°
     To hell, allegiance! Vows, to the blackest devil!   130
     Conscience and grace, to the profoundest pit!
     I dare damnation. To this point I stand,°
     That both the worlds I give to negligence,°
     Let come what comes, only I'll be revenged
     Most throughly° for my father.   135

King: Who shall stay you?

Laertes: My will, not all the world's.°
     And for° my means, I'll husband them so well
     They shall go far with little.

King: Good Laertes,
     If you desire to know the certainty   140
     Of your dear father, is 't writ in your revenge
     That, swoopstake,° you will draw both friend and foe,
     Winner and loser?

Laertes: None but his enemies.

---

119 *between* in the middle of   122 *fear our* fear for my   123 *hedge* protect, as with a surrounding barrier   124 *can . . . would* can only peep furtively, as through a barrier at what it would intend   125 *Acts . . . will* (but) performs little of what it intends   129 *juggled with* cheated, deceived   132 *To . . . stand* I am resolved in this   133 *both . . . negligence* i.e., both this world and the next are of no consequence to me   135 *throughly* thoroughly   137 *My will . . . world's* I'll stop (*stay*) when my will is accomplished, not for anyone else's.   138 *for* as for 142 *swoopstake* i.e., indiscriminately. (Literally taking all stakes on the gambling table at once. *Draw* is also a gambling term meaning "take from.")

King: Will you know them, then?   145

Laertes: To his good friends thus wide I'll ope my arms,
   And like the kind life-rendering pelican°
   Repast° them with my blood.

King: Why, now you speak
   Like a good child and a true gentleman.
   That I am guiltless of your father's death,   150
   And am most sensibly° in grief for it,
   It shall as level° to your judgment 'pear
   As day does to your eye.   *A noise within.*

Laertes: How now, what noise is that?

   Enter Ophelia.

King: Let her come in.

Laertes: O heat, dry up my brains! Tears seven times salt   155
   Burn out the sense and virtue° of mine eye!
   By heaven, thy madness shall be paid with weight°
   Till our scale turn the beam.° O rose of May!
   Dear maid, kind sister, sweet Ophelia!
   O heavens, is 't possible a young maid's wits   160
   Should be as mortal as an old man's life?
   Nature is fine in° love, and where 'tis fine
   It sends some precious instance° of itself
   After the thing it loves.°

Ophelia:
      "They bore him barefaced on the bier,   *(Song.)* 165
      Hey non nonny, nonny, hey nonny,
      And in his grave rained many a tear—"
   Fare you well, my dove!

Laertes: Hadst thou thy wits and didst persuade° revenge,
   It could not move thus.   170

Ophelia: You must sing "A-down a-down," and you "call him a-down-a.°" O, how the
   wheel° becomes it! It is the false steward° that stole his master's daughter.

Laertes: This nothing's more than matter.°

---

147 *pelican* (Refers to the belief that the female pelican fed its young with its own blood.)   148
Repast feed   151 *sensibly* feelingly   152 *level* plain   156 *virtue* faculty, power   157 *paid with
weight* repaid, avenged equally or more   158 *beam* crossbar of a balance   162 *fine in* refined by
163 *instance* token   164 *After . . . loves* i.e., into the grave, along with Polonius   169 *persuade*
argue cogently for   171 *You . . . a-down a* (Ophelia assigns the singing of refrains, like her own
"Hey non nonny," to others present.)   172 *wheel* spinning wheel as accompaniment to the
song, or refrain.   *false steward* (The story is unknown.)   173 *This . . . matter* this seeming
nonsense is more eloquent than sane utterance

Ophelia: There's rosemary,° that's for remembrance; pray you, love, remember. And there is pansies;° that's for thoughts. 175

Laertes: A document° in madness, thoughts and remembrance fitted.

Ophelia: There's fennel° for you, and columbines.° There's rue° for you, and here's some for me; we may call it herb of grace o' Sundays. You must wear your rue with a difference.° There's a daisy.° I would give you some violets,° but they withered all when my father died. They say 'a made a good end— 180 [*Sings.*]

        "For bonny sweet Robin is all my joy."

Laertes: Thought° and affliction, passion,° hell itself, She turns to favor° and to prettiness.

Ophelia:

    "And will 'a not come again?   (*Song.*)
    And will 'a not come again? 185
    No, no, he is dead.
    Go to thy deathbed,
    He never will come again.
    "His beard was as white as snow,
    All flaxen was his poll.° 190
    He is gone, he is gone,
    And we cast away moan.
    God ha' mercy on his soul!"
And of all Christian souls, I pray God. God b' wi' you.

                        [*Exit, followed by Gertrude.*]

Laertes: Do you see this, O God? 195

King: Laertes, I must commune with your grief,
Or you deny me right. Go but apart,
Make choice of whom° your wisest friends you will,
And they shall hear and judge twixt you and me.
If by direct or by collateral hand° 200
They find us touched,° we will our kingdom give,
Our crown, our life, and all that we call ours
To you in satisfaction; but if not,
Be you content to lend your patience to us,

---

174 *rosemary* (Used as a symbol of remembrance both at weddings and at funerals.) 175 *pansies* (Emblems of love and courtship; perhaps from French *pensées*, "thoughts.") 176 *document* instruction, lesson 177 *fennel* (Emblem of flattery.) *columbines* (Emblems of unchastity or ingratitude.) *rue* (Emblem of repentance—a signification that is evident in its popular name, *herb of grace.*) 179 *with a difference* (A device used in heraldry to distinguish one family from another on the coat of arms, here suggesting that Ophelia and the others have different causes of sorrow and repentance; perhaps with a play on *rue* in the sense of "ruth," "pity.") *daisy* (Emblem of dissembling, faithlessness.) *violets* (Emblems of faithfulness.) 182 *Thought* melancholy. *passion* suffering 183 *favor* grace, beauty 190 *poll* head 198 *whom* whichever of 200 *collateral hand* indirect agency 201 *us touched* be implicated

And we shall jointly labor with your soul   205
    To give it due content.
Laertes: Let this be so.
    His means of death, his obscure funeral—
    No trophy,° sword, nor hatchment° o'er his bones,
    No noble rite, nor formal ostentation°—
    Cry to be heard, as 'twere from heaven to earth,   210
    That° I must call 't in question.°
King: So you shall,
    And where th' offense is, let the great ax fall.
    I pray you, go with me.   *Exeunt.*

Scene VI [The Castle.]

Enter Horatio and others.

Horatio: What are they that would speak with me?
Gentleman: Seafaring men, sir. They say they have letters for you.
Horatio: Let them come in.   [*Exit Gentleman.*]
    I do not know from what part of the world
    I should be greeted, if not from Lord Hamlet.   5

Enter Sailors.

First Sailor: God bless you, sir.
Horatio: Let him bless thee too.
First Sailor: 'A shall, sir, an 't° please him. There's a letter for you, sir—it came
    from th' ambassador° that was bound for England—if your name be Horatio,
    as I am let to know it is.   [*He gives a letter.*]   10
Horatio [*reads*]: "Horatio, when thou shalt have overlooked° this, give these fel-
    lows some means° to the King; they have letters for him. Ere we were two
    days old at sea, a pirate of very warlike appointment° gave us chase. Finding
    ourselves too slow of sail, we put on a compelled valor, and in the grapple I
    boarded them. On the instant they got clear of our ship, so I alone became   15
    their prisoner. They have dealt with me like thieves of mercy,° but they
    knew what they did: I am to do a good turn for them. Let the King have the
    letters I have sent, and repair° thou to me with as much speed as thou
    wouldest fly death. I have words to speak in thine ear will make thee dumb,
    yet are they much too light for the bore° of the matter. These good fellows   20
    will bring thee where I am. Rosencrantz and Guildenstern hold their course
    for England. Of them I have much to tell thee. Farewell.

208 *trophy* memorial. *hatchment* tablet displaying the armorial bearings of a deceased person
209 *ostentation* ceremony   211 *That* so that. *call 't in question* demand an explanation   8 *an
't* if it   9 *th' ambassador* (Evidently Hamlet. The sailor is being circumspect.)   11 *overlooked*
looked over   12 *means* means of access   13 *appointment* equipage   16 *thieves of mercy* merciful thieves   18 *repair* come   20 *bore* caliber, i.e., importance

He that thou knowest thine, Hamlet."
Come, I will give you way° for these your letters,
And do 't the speedier that you may direct me   25
To him from whom you brought them.   *Exeunt.*

Scene VII [The Castle.]

Enter King and Laertes.

King: Now must your conscience my acquittance seal,°
       And you must put me in your heart for friend,
       Sith° you have heard, and with a knowing ear,
       That he which hath your noble father slain
       Pursued my life.
Laertes: It well appears. But tell me   5
       Why you proceeded not against these feats°
       So crimeful and so capital° in nature,
       As by your safety, greatness, wisdom, all things else,
       You mainly° were stirred up.
King: O, for two special reasons,   10
       Which may to you perhaps seem much unsinewed,°
       But yet to me they're strong. The Queen his mother
       Lives almost by his looks, and for myself—
       My virtue or my plague, be it either which—
       She is so conjunctive° to my life and soul   15
       That, as the star moves not but in his° sphere,°
       I could not but by her. The other motive
       Why to a public count° I might not go
       Is the great love the general gender° bear him,
       Who, dipping all his faults in their affection,   20
       Work° like the spring° that turneth wood to stone,
       Convert his gyves° to graces, so that my arrows,
       Too slightly timbered° for so loud° a wind,
       Would have reverted° to my bow again
       But not where I had aimed them.   25
Laertes: And so have I a noble father lost,
       A sister driven into desperate terms,°

24 *way* means of access   1 *my acquittance seal* confirm or acknowledge my innocence   3 *Sith* since   6 *feats* acts   7 *capital* punishable by death   9 *mainly* greatly   11 *unsinewed* weak   15 *conjunctive* closely united. (An astronomical metaphor.)   16 *his* its.   *sphere* one of the hollow spheres in which, according to Ptolemaic astronomy, the planets were supposed to move   18 *count* account, reckoning, indictment   19 *general gender* common people   21 *Work* operate, act.   *spring* i.e., a spring with such a concentration of lime that it coats a piece of wood with limestone, in effect gilding and petrifying it   22 *gyves* fetters (which, gilded by the people's praise, would look like badges of honor)   23 *slightly timbered* light.   *loud* (suggesting public outcry on Hamlet's behalf)   24 *reverted* returned   27 *terms* state, condition

Whose worth, if praises may go back° again,
Stood challenger on mount° of all the age
For her perfections. But my revenge will come.   30

King: Break not your sleeps for that. You must not think
  That we are made of stuff so flat and dull
  That we can let our beard be shook with danger
  And think it pastime. You shortly shall hear more.
  I loved your father, and we love ourself;   35
  And that, I hope, will teach you to imagine—

Enter a Messenger with letters.

  How now? What news?
Messenger: Letters, my lord, from Hamlet:
  This to Your Majesty, this to the Queen.

                                                [He gives letters.]

King: From Hamlet? Who brought them?
Messenger: Sailors, my lord, they say. I saw them not.   40
  They were given me by Claudio. He received them
  Of him that brought them.
King: Laertes, you shall hear them.—
  Leave us.   *[Exit Messenger.]*
  [He reads.] "High and mighty, you shall know I am set naked° on your
  kingdom. Tomorrow shall I beg leave to see your kingly eyes, when I shall,   45
  first asking your pardon,° thereunto recount the occasion of my sudden and
  more strange return.   Hamlet."
  What should this mean? Are all the rest come back? Or is it some abuse,°
  and no such thing?°
Laertes: Know you the hand?
King: 'Tis Hamlet's character.° "Naked!"   50
  And in a postscript here he says "alone."
  Can you devise° me?
Laertes: I am lost in it, my lord. But let him come.
  It warms the very sickness in my heart
  That I shall live and tell him to his teeth,   55
  "Thus didst thou.°"
King: If it be so, Laertes—
  As how should it be so? How otherwise?°—
  Will you be ruled by me?
Laertes: Ay, my lord,

---

28 *go back* i.e., recall what she was   29 *on mount* set up on high   44 *naked* destitute, unarmed,
without following   46 *pardon* permission   49 *abuse* deceit.   *no such thing* not what it appears
50 *character* handwriting   52 *devise* explain to   56 *Thus didst thou* i.e., here's for what you did
to my father   57 *As . . . otherwise* how can this (Hamlet's return) be true? Yet how otherwise
than true (since we have the evidence of his letter)?

So° you will not o'errule me to a peace.

King: To thine own peace. If he be now returned,   60
  As checking at° his voyage, and that° he means
  No more to undertake it, I will work him
  To an exploit, now ripe in my device,°
  Under the which he shall not choose but fall;
  And for his death no wind of blame shall breathe,   65
  But even his mother shall uncharge the practice°
  And call it accident.

Laertes: My lord, I will be ruled,
  The rather if you could devise it so
  That I might be the organ.°

King: It falls right.
  You have been talked of since your travel much,   70
  And that in Hamlet's hearing, for a quality
  Wherein they say you shine. Your sum of parts°
  Did not together pluck such envy from him
  As did that one, and that, in my regard,
  Of the unworthiest siege.°   75

Laertes: What part is that, my lord?

King: A very ribbon in the cap of youth,
  Yet needful too, for youth no less becomes°
  The light and careless livery that it wears
  Than settled age his sables° and his weeds°   80
  Importing health and graveness.° Two months since
  Here was a gentleman of Normandy.
  I have seen myself, and served against, the French,
  And they can well° on horseback, but this gallant
  Had witchcraft in 't; he grew unto his seat,   85
  And to such wondrous doing brought his horse
  As had he been incorpsed and demi-natured°
  With the brave beast. So far he topped° my thought
  That I in forgery° of shapes and tricks
  Come short of what he did.

Laertes: A Norman was 't?   90

King: A Norman.

Laertes: Upon my life, Lamord.

59 *So* provided that   61 *checking at* i.e., turning aside from (like a falcon leaving the quarry to fly at a chance bird).   *that* if   63 *device* devising, invention   66 *uncharge the practice* acquit the stratagem of being a plot   69 *organ* agent, instrument   72 *Your . . . parts* i.e., all your other virtues   75 *unworthiest siege* least important rank   78 *no less becomes* is no less suited by 80 *his sables* its rich robes furred with sable.   *weeds* garments   81 *Importing . . . graveness* signifying a concern for health and dignified prosperity; also, giving an impression of comfortable prosperity   84 *can well* are skilled   87 *As . . . demi-natured* as if he had been of one body and nearly of one nature (like the centaur)   88 *topped* surpassed   89 *forgery* imagining

King: The very same.

Laertes: I know him well. He is the brooch° indeed
        And gem of all the nation.

King: He made confession° of you.   95
        And gave you such a masterly report
        For art and exercise in your defense,°
        And for your rapier most especial,
        That he cried out 'twould be a sight indeed
        If one could match you. Th' escrimers° of their nation,   100
        He swore, had neither motion, guard, nor eye
        If you opposed them. Sir, this report of his
        Did Hamlet so envenom with his envy
        That he could nothing do but wish and beg
        Your sudden° coming o'er, to play° with you.   105
        Now, out of this—

Laertes: What out of this, my lord?

King: Laertes, was your father dear to you?
        Or are you like the painting of a sorrow,
        A face without a heart?

Laertes: Why ask you this?

King: Not that I think you did not love your father,   110
        But that I know love is begun by time,°
        And that I see, in passages of proof,°
        Time qualifies° the spark and fire of it.
        There lives within the very flame of love
        A kind of wick or snuff° that will abate it,   115
        And nothing° is at a like goodness still,
        For goodness, growing to a pleurisy,°
        Dies in his own too much.° That° we would do,
        We should do when we would; for this "would" changes
        And hath abatements° and delays as many   120
        As there are tongues, are hands, are accidents,°
        And then this "should" is like a spendthrift sigh,°
        That hurts by easing.° But, to the quick o' th' ulcer:°

---

93 *brooch* ornament   95 *confession* testimonial, admission of superiority   97 *For . . . defense*
with respect to your skill and practice with your weapon   100 *escrimers* fencers   105 *sudden*
immediate.   *play* fence   111 *begun by time* i.e., created by the right circumstance and hence
subject to change   112 *passages of proof* actual instances that prove it   113 *qualifies* weakens,
moderates   115 *snuff* the charred part of a candlewick   116 *nothing . . . still* nothing remains at
a constant level of perfection   117 *pleurisy* excess, plethora. (Literally, a chest inflammation.)
118 *in . . . much* of its own excess.   *That* that which   120 *abatements* diminutions   121 *As . . .
accidents* as there are tongues to dissuade, hands to prevent, and chance events to intervene
122 *spendthrift sigh* (An allusion to the belief that sighs draw blood from the heart.)   123 *hurts
by easing* i.e., costs the heart blood and wastes precious opportunity even while it affords emotional relief.   *quick o' th' ulcer* i.e., heart of the matter

Hamlet comes back. What would you undertake
To show yourself in deed your father's son   125
More than in words?
Laertes: To cut his throat i' the church.
King: No place, indeed, should murder sanctuarize;°
Revenge should have no bounds. But good Laertes,
Will you do this,° keep close within your chamber.
Hamlet returned shall know you are come home.   130
We'll put on those shall° praise your excellence
And set a double varnish on the fame
The Frenchman gave you, bring you in fine° together,
And wager on your heads. He, being remiss,°
Most generous,° and free from all contriving,   135
Will not peruse the foils, so that with ease,
Or with a little shuffling, you may choose
A sword unbated,° and in a pass of practice°
Requite him for your father.
Laertes: I will do 't,
And for that purpose I'll anoint my sword.   140
I bought an unction° of a mountebank°
So mortal that, but dip a knife in it,
Where it draws blood no cataplasm° so rare,
Collected from all simples° that have virtue°
Under the moon,° can save the thing from death   145
That is but scratched withal. I'll touch my point
With this contagion, that if I gall° him slightly,
It may be death.
King: Let's further think of this,
Weigh what convenience both of time and means
May fit us to our shape.° If this should fail,   150
And that our drift look through our bad performance,°
'Twere better not assayed. Therefore this project
Should have a back or second, that might hold
If this did blast in proof.° Soft, let me see.
We'll make a solemn wager on your cunnings°—   155
I ha 't!

127 *sanctuarize* protect from punishment. (Alludes to the right of sanctuary with which certain religious places were invested.)   129 *Will you do this* if you wish to do this   131 *put on those shall* arrange for some to   133 *in fine* finally   134 *remiss* negligently unsuspicious   135 *generous* noble-minded   138 *unbated* not blunted, having no button.   *pass of practice* treacherous thrust   141 *unction* ointment.   *mountebank* quack doctor   143 *cataplasm* plaster or poultice   144 *simples* herbs.   *virtue* potency   145 *Under the moon* i.e., anywhere (with reference perhaps to the belief that herbs gathered at night had a special power)   147 *gall* graze, wound   150 *shape* part we propose to act   151 *drift . . . performance* intention should be made visible by our bungling   154 *blast in proof* burst in the test (like a cannon)   155 *cunnings* respective skills

When in your motion you are hot and dry—
As° make your bouts more violent to that end—
And that he calls for drink, I'll have prepared him
A chalice for the nonce,° whereon but sipping,   160
If he by chance escape your venomed stuck,°
Our purpose may hold there. [*A cry within.*] But stay, what noise?

Enter Queen.

Queen: One woe doth tread upon another's heel,
    So fast they follow. Your sister's drowned, Laertes.
Laertes: Drowned! O, where?   165
Queen: There is a willow grows askant° the brook,
    That shows his hoar leaves° in the glassy stream;
    Therewith fantastic garlands did she make
    Of crowflowers, nettles, daisies, and long purples,°
    That liberal° shepherds give a grosser name,°   170
    But our cold° maids do dead men's fingers call them.
    There on the pendent° boughs her crownet° weeds
    Clamb'ring to hang, an envious sliver° broke,
    When down her weedy° trophies and herself
    Fell in the weeping brook. Her clothes spread wide,   175
    And mermaidlike awhile they bore her up,
    Which time she chanted snatches of old lauds,°
    As one incapable of° her own distress,
    Or like a creature native and endued°
    Unto that element. But long it could not be   180
    Till that her garments, heavy with their drink,
    Pulled the poor wretch from her melodious lay
    To muddy death.
Laertes: Alas, then she is drowned?
Queen: Drowned, drowned.
Laertes: Too much of water hast thou, poor Ophelia,   185
    And therefore I forbid my tears. But yet
    It is our trick;° nature her custom holds.
    Let shame say what it will. [*He weeps.*] When these are gone,
    The woman will be out.° Adieu, my lord.

158 *As* i.e., and you should   160 *nonce* occasion   161 *stuck* thrust. (From *stoccado*; a fencing
term.)   166 *askant* aslant   167 *hoar leaves* white or gray undersides of the leaves   169 *long
purples* early purple orchids   170 *liberal* free-spoken.   *a grosser name* (The testicle-resembling
tubers of the orchid, which also in some cases resemble *dead men's fingers*, have earned various
slang names like "dogstones" and "cullions.")   171 *cold* chaste   172 *pendent* overhanging.
crownet made into a chaplet or coronet   173 *envious sliver* malicious branch   174 *weedy* i.e.,
of plants   177 *lauds* hymns   178 *incapable of* lacking capacity to apprehend   179 *endued*
adapted by nature   187 *It is our trick* i.e., weeping is our natural way (when sad)   188–189
When . . . out when my tears are all shed, the woman in me will be expended, satisfied

I have a speech of fire that fain would blaze,
But that this folly douts° it.   *Exit.*   190

King: Let's follow, Gertrude.
How much I had to do to calm his rage!
Now fear I this will give it start again;
Therefore let's follow.   *Exeunt.*

Act V

Scene I [A Churchyard.]

Enter two Clowns° [with spades and mattocks].

First Clown: Is she to be buried in Christian burial, when she willfully seeks her
     own salvation?°

Second Clown: I tell thee she is; therefore make her grave straight.° The
     crowner° hath sat on her,° and finds it° Christian burial.

First Clown: How can that be, unless she drowned herself in her own defense?   5

Second Clown: Why, 'tis found so.°

First Clown: It must be *se offendendo*,° it cannot be else. For here lies the point:
     if I drown myself wittingly, it argues an act, and an act hath three
     branches—it is to act, to do, and to perform. Argal,° she drowned herself
     wittingly.   10

Second Clown: Nay, but hear you, goodman° delver—

First Clown: Give me leave. Here lies the water; good. Here stands the man;
     good. If the man go to this water and drown himself, it is, will he, nill he,°
     he goes, mark you that. But if the water come to him and drown him, he
     drowns not himself. Argal, he that is not guilty of his own death shortens   15
     not his own life.

Second Clown: But is this law?

First Clown: Ay, marry, is 't—crowner's quest law.

Second Clown: Will you ha' the truth on 't? If this had not been a gentlewoman,
     she should have been buried out o' Christian burial.   20

First Clown: Why, there thou sayst.° And the more pity that great folk should
     have countenance° in this world to drown or hang themselves, more than

191 *douts* extinguishes. (The Second Quarto reads "drowns.")   s.d. *Clowns* rustics   2 *salvation*
(A blunder for "damnation," or perhaps a suggestion that Ophelia was taking her own shortcut
to heaven.)   3 *straight* straightway, immediately. (But with a pun on *strait*, "narrow.")   4
crowner coroner.   *sat on her* conducted an inquest on her case.   *finds it* gives his official verdict that her means of death was consistent with   6 *found so* determined so in the coroner's
verdict   7 *se offendendo* (A comic mistake for *se defendendo*, a term used in verdicts of justifi-
able homicide.   9 *Argal* (Corruption of *ergo*, "therefore.")   11 *goodman* (An honorific title
often used with the name of a profession or craft.)   13 *will he, nill he* whether he will or no,
willy-nilly   21 *there thou sayst*, i.e., that's right   22 *countenance* privilege

their even-Christian.° Come, my spade. There is no ancient° gentlemen but
gardeners, ditchers, and grave makers. They hold up° Adam's profession.

Second Clown: Was he a gentleman?   25

First Clown: 'A was the first that ever bore arms.°

Second Clown: Why, he had none.

First Clown: What, art a heathen? How dost thou understand the Scripture?
The Scripture says Adam digged. Could he dig without arms?° I'll put another
question to thee. If thou answerest me not to the purpose, confess thyself°—   30

Second Clown: Go to.

First Clown: What is he that builds stronger than either the mason, the shipwright, or the carpenter?

Second Clown: The gallows maker, for that frame° outlives a thousand tenants.   35

First Clown: I like thy wit well, in good faith. The gallows does well.° But how
does it well? It does well to those that do ill. Now thou dost ill to say the gallows is built stronger than the church. Argal, the gallows may do well to
thee. To 't again, come.

Second Clown: "Who builds stronger than a mason, a shipwright, or a   40
carpenter?"

First Clown: Ay, tell me that, and unyoke.°

Second Clown: Marry, now I can tell.

First Clown: To 't.

Second Clown: Mass,° I cannot tell.   45

Enter Hamlet and Horatio [at a distance].

First Clown: Cudgel thy brains no more about it, for your dull ass will not mend
his pace with beating; and when you are asked this question next, say "a
grave maker." The houses he makes lasts till doomsday. Go get thee in and
fetch me a stoup° of liquor.

> *[Exit Second Clown. First Clown digs.]*
> *Song.*

> "In youth, when I did love, did love,°   50
> Methought it was very sweet,
> To contract—O—the time for—a—my behove,°
> O, methought there—a—was nothing—a—meet.°"

23 *even-Christian* fellow Christians.   *ancient* going back to ancient times   24 *hold up* maintain
26 *bore arms* (To be entitled to bear a coat of arms would make Adam a gentleman, but as one
who bore a spade, our common ancestor was an ordinary delver in the earth.)   29 *arms* i.e.,
the arms of the body   30–31 *confess thyself* (The saying continues, "and be hanged.")   35
frame (1) gallows (2) structure   36 *does well* (1) is an apt answer (2) does a good turn   42
unyoke i.e., after this great effort, you may unharness the team of your wits   45 *Mass* by the
Mass   49 *stoup* two-quart measure   50 *In . . . love* (This and the two following stanzas, with
nonsensical variations, are from a poem attributed to Lord Vaux and printed in *Tottel's Miscel-
lany,* 1557. The O and *a* [for "ah"] seemingly are the grunts of the digger.)   52 *To contract . . .
behove* i.e., to shorten the time for my own advantage. (Perhaps he means to *prolong* it.)   53
meet suitable, i.e., more suitable

Hamlet: Has this fellow no feeling of his business, 'a° sings in grave-making?

Horatio: Custom hath made it in him a property of easiness.° 55

Hamlet: 'Tis e'en so. The hand of little employment hath the daintier sense.°

First Clown: Song.

> "But age with his stealing steps
> Hath clawed me in his clutch,
> And hath shipped me into the land,°
> As if I had never been such." 60

[*He throws up a skull.*]

Hamlet: That skull had a tongue in it and could sing once. How the knave jowls° it to the ground, as if 'twere Cain's jawbone, that did the first murder! This might be the pate of a politician,° which this ass now o'erreaches,° one that would circumvent God, might it not?

Horatio: It might, my lord. 65

Hamlet: Or of a courtier, which could say, "Good morrow, sweet lord! How dost thou, sweet lord?" This might be my Lord Such-a-one, that praised my Lord Such-a-one's horse when 'a meant to beg it, might it not?

Horatio: Ay, my lord.

Hamlet: Why, e'en so, and now my Lady Worm's, chapless,° and knocked about 70 the mazard° with a sexton's spade. Here's fine revolution,° an° we had the trick to see° 't. Did these bones cost no more the breeding but° to play at loggets° with them? Mine ache to think on 't.

First Clown: Song.

> "A pickax and a spade, a spade,
> For and° a shrouding sheet; 75
> O, a pit of clay for to be made
> For such a guest is meet."

[*He throws up another skull.*]

Hamlet: There's another. Why may not that be the skull of a lawyer? Where be his quiddities° now, his quillities,° his cases, his tenures,° and his tricks? Why does he suffer this mad knave now to knock him about the sconce° 80 with a dirty shovel, and will not tell him of his action of battery?° Hum, this fellow might be in 's time a great buyer of land, with his statutes, his recog-

---

54 *'a* that he   55 *property of easiness* something he can do easily and indifferently   56 *daintier sense* more delicate sense of feeling   59 *into the land* i.e., toward my grave (?) (But note the lack of rhyme in *steps, land.*)   62 *jowls* dashes (with a pun on *jowl,* "jawbone")   63 *politician* schemer, plotter.   *o'erreaches* circumvents, gets the better of (with a quibble on the literal sense)   70 *chapless* having no lower jaw.   71 *mazard* i.e., head. (Literally, a drinking vessel.) *revolution* turn of Fortune's wheel, change.   *an* if   72 *trick to see* knack of seeing.   *cost . . . but* involve so little expense and care in upbringing that we may.   73 *loggets* a game in which pieces of hard wood shaped like Indian clubs or bowling pins are thrown to lie as near as possible to a stake   75 *For and* and moreover   79 *quiddities* subtleties, quibbles. (From Latin *quid,* "a thing.")   *quillities* verbal niceties, subtle distinctions. (Variation of *quiddities*.)   *tenures* the holding of a piece of property or office, or the conditions or period of such holding   80 *sconce* head   81 *action of battery* lawsuit about physical assault

nizances,° his fines,° his double° vouchers° his recoveries.° Is this the fine of
his fines and the recovery of his recoveries, to have his fine pate full of fine
dirt?° Will his vouchers vouch him no more of his purchases, and double   85
ones too, than the length and breadth of a pair of indentures?° The very
conveyances° of his lands will scarcely lie in this box,° and must th'
inheritor° himself have no more, ha?

Horatio: Not a jot more, my lord.

Hamlet: Is not parchment made of sheepskins?   90

Horatio: Ay, my lord, and of calves' skins too.

Hamlet: They are sheep and calves which seek out assurance in that.° I will
speak to this fellow.—Whose grave's this, sirrah?°

First Clown: Mine, sir. [*Sings.*]

"O, pit of clay for to be made   95
For such a guest is meet."

Hamlet: I think it be thine, indeed, for thou liest in 't.

First Clown: You lie out on 't, sir, and therefore 'tis not yours. For my part, I do
not lie in 't, yet it is mine.

Hamlet: Thou dost lie in 't, to be in 't and say it is thine. 'Tis for the dead, not   100
for the quick;° therefore thou liest.

First Clown: 'Tis a quick lie, sir; 'twill away again from me to you.

Hamlet: What man dost thou dig it for?

First Clown: For no man, sir.

Hamlet: What woman, then?   105

First Clown: For none, neither.

Hamlet: Who is to be buried in 't?

First Clown: One that was a woman, sir, but, rest her soul, she's dead.

Hamlet: How absolute° the knave is! We must speak by the card,° or equivoca-
tion° will undo us. By the Lord, Horatio, this three years I have took° note   110
of it: the age is grown so picked° that the toe of the peasant comes so near
the heel of the courtier, he galls his kibe.°—How long hast thou been grave
maker?

First Clown: Of all the days i' the year, I came to 't that day that our last king
Hamlet overcame Fortinbras.   115

Hamlet: How long is that since?

82–83 *statutes, his recognizances* legal documents guaranteeing a debt by attaching land and
property   83 *fines, recoveries* ways of converting entailed estates into "fee simple" or freehold.
double signed by two signatories.   *vouchers* guarantees of the legality of a title to real estate
83–85 *fine of his fines . . . fine pate . . . fine dirt* end of his legal maneuvers . . . elegant head . . .
minutely sifted dirt   86 *pair of indentures* legal document drawn up in duplicate on a single
sheet and then cut apart on a zigzag line so that each pair was uniquely matched. (Hamlet may
refer to two rows of teeth or dentures.)   87 *conveyances* deeds.   *box* (1) deed box   (2) coffin.
("Skull" has been suggested.)   88 *inheritor* possessor, owner   92 *assurance in that* safety in legal
parchments   93 *sirrah* (A term of address to inferiors.)   101 *quick* living   109 *absolute* strict,
precise.   *by the card* i.e., with precision. (Literally, by the mariner's compass-card, on which
the points of the compass were marked.)   109–110 *equivocation* ambiguity in the use of terms
110 *took* taken   111 *picked* refined, fastidious   112 *galls his kibe* chafes the courtier's chilblain

First Clown: Cannot you tell that? Every fool can tell that. It was that very day
  that young Hamlet was born—he that is mad and sent into England.

Hamlet: Ay, marry, why was he sent into England?

First Clown: Why, because 'a was mad. 'A shall recover his wits there, or if 'a do   120
  not, 'tis no great matter there.

Hamlet: Why?

First Clown: 'Twill not be seen in him there. There the men are as mad as he.

Hamlet: How came he mad?

First Clown: Very strangely, they say.   125

Hamlet: How strangely?

First Clown: Faith, e'en with losing his wits.

Hamlet: Upon what ground?°

First Clown: Why, here in Denmark. I have been sexton here, man and boy,
  thirty years.   130

Hamlet: How long will a man lie i' th' earth ere he rot?

First Clown: Faith, if 'a be not rotten before 'a die—as we have many pocky°
  corpses nowadays, that will scarce hold the laying in°—'a will last you°
  some eight year or nine year. A tanner will last you nine year.

Hamlet: Why he more than another?   135

First Clown: Why, sir, his hide is so tanned with his trade that 'a will keep out
  water a great while, and your water is a sore° decaver of your whoreson°
  dead body. [*He picks up a skull.*] Here's a skull now hath lien you° i' th' earth
  three-and-twenty years.

Hamlet: Whose was it?   140

First Clown: A whoreson mad fellow's it was. Whose do you think it was?

Hamlet: Nay, I know not.

First Clown: A pestilence on him for a mad rogue! 'A poured a flagon of
  Rhenish° on my head once. This same skull, sir, was, sir, Yorick's skull, the
  King's jester.   145

Hamlet: This?

First Clown: E'en that.

Hamlet: Let me see. [*He takes the skull.*] Alas, poor Yorick! I knew him, Horatio,
  a fellow of infinite jest, of most excellent fancy. He hath bore° me on his
  back a thousand times, and now how abhorred in my imagination it is! My   150
  gorge rises° at it. Here hung those lips that I have kissed I know not how oft.
  Where be your gibes now? Your gambols, your songs, your flashes of merri-

---

128 *ground* cause. (But, in the next line, the gravedigger takes the word in the sense of "land,"
"country.")   132 *pocky* rotten, diseased. (Literally, with the pox, or syphilis.)   133 *hold the
laying in* hold together long enough to be interred.   *last you* last. (*You* is used colloquially here
and in the following lines.)   137 *sore* i.e., terrible, great.   *whoreson* i.e., vile, scurvy   138 *lien
you* lain. (See the note at line 133.)   144 *Rhenish* Rhine wine   149 *bore* borne   150–151 *My
gorge rises* i.e., I feel nauseated

ment that were wont° to set the table on a roar? Not one now, to mock your own grinning?° Quite chopfallen?° Now get you to my lady's chamber and tell her, let her paint an inch thick, to this favor° she must come. Make her 155 laugh at that. Prithee, Horatio, tell me one thing.

Horatio: What's that, my lord?

Hamlet: Dost thou think Alexander looked o' this fashion i' th' earth?

Horatio: E'en so.

Hamlet: And smelt so? Pah! [*He throws down the skull.*] 160

Horatio: E'en so, my lord.

Hamlet: To what base uses we may return, Horatio! Why may not imagination trace the noble dust of Alexander till 'a find it stopping a bunghole?°

Horatio: 'Twere to consider too curiously° to consider so.

Hamlet: No, faith, not a jot, but to follow him thither with modesty° enough, 165 and likelihood to lead it. As thus: Alexander died, Alexander was buried, Alexander returneth to dust, the dust is earth, of earth we make loam,° and why of that loam whereto he was converted might they not stop a beer barrel?
Imperious° Caesar, dead and turned to clay, 170
Might stop a hole to keep the wind away.
O, that that earth which kept the world in awe
Should patch a wall t' expel the winter's flaw!°

Enter King, Queen, Laertes, and the corpse [of Ophelia, in procession, with Priest, lords, etc.].

But soft,° but soft awhile! Here comes the King,
The Queen, the courtiers. Who is this they follow? 175
And with such maimèd° rites? This doth betoken
The corpse they follow did with desperate hand
Fordo° its own life. 'Twas of some estate.°
Couch we° awhile and mark.
    [*He and Horatio conceal themselves. Ophelia's body is taken to the grave.*]

Laertes: What ceremony else? 180

Hamlet [to Horatio]: That is Laertes, a very noble youth. Mark.

Laertes: What ceremony else?

Priest: Her obsequies have been as far enlarged
As we have warranty.° Her death was doubtful,
And but that great command o'ersways the order° 185

---

153 *were wont* used   153–154 *mock your own grinning* mock at the way your skull seems to be grinning (just as you used to mock at yourself and those who grinned at you)   154 *chopfallen* (1) lacking the lower jaw (2) dejected   155 *favor* aspect, appearance   163 *bunghole* hole for filling or emptying a cask   164 *curiously* minutely   165 *modesty* plausible moderation   167 *loam* mortar consisting chiefly of moistened clay and straw   170 *Imperious* imperial   173 *flaw* gust of wind   174 *soft* i.e., wait, be careful   176 *maimèd* mutilated, incomplete   178 *Fordo* destroy.   *estate* rank   179 *Couch we* let's hide, lie low   184 *warranty* i.e., ecclesiastical authority   185 *great . . . order* orders from on high overrule the prescribed procedures

She should in ground unsanctified been lodged°
Till the last trumpet. For° charitable prayers,
Shards,° flints, and pebbles should be thrown on her.
Yet here she is allowed her virgin crants,°
Her maiden strewments,° and the bringing home   190
Of bell and burial.°

Laertes: Must there no more be done?

Priest: No more be done.
We should profane the service of the dead
To sing a requiem and such rest° to her
As to peace-parted souls.°

Laertes: Lay her i' th' earth,   195
And from her fair and unpolluted flesh
May violets spring! I tell thee, churlish priest,
A ministering angel shall my sister be
When thou liest howling.°

Hamlet [to Horatio]:   What, the fair Ophelia!

Queen [scattering flowers]: Sweets to the sweet! Farewell.   200
I hoped thou shouldst have been my Hamlet's wife.
I thought thy bride-bed to have decked, sweet maid,
And not t' have strewed thy grave.

Laertes: O, treble woe
Fall ten times treble on that cursèd head
Whose wicked deed thy most ingenious sense°   205
Deprived thee of! Hold off the earth awhile,
Till I have caught her once more in mine arms.
          [*He leaps into the grave and embraces Ophelia.*]
Now pile your dust upon the quick and dead,
Till of this flat a mountain you have made
T' o'ertop old Pelion or the skyish head   210
Of blue Olympus.°

Hamlet [coming forward]: What is he whose grief
Bears such an emphasis,° whose phrase of sorrow
Conjures the wandering stars° and makes them stand
Like wonder-wounded° hearers? This is I,
Hamlet the Dane.°   215

---

186 *She should . . . lodged* she should have been buried in unsanctified ground   187 *For* in
place of   188 *Shards* broken bits of pottery   189 *crants* garlands betokening maidenhood
190 *strewments* flowers strewn on a coffin   190–191 *bringing . . . burial* laying the body to rest,
to the sound of the bell   194 *such rest* i.e., to pray for such rest   195 *peace-parted souls* those
who have died at peace with God   199 *howling* i.e., in hell   205 *ingenious sense* a mind that is
quick, alert, of fine qualities   210–211 *Pelion, Olympus* sacred mountains in the north of Thessaly   212 *emphasis* i.e., rhetorical and florid emphasis. (*Phrase* has a similar rhetorical connotation.)   213 *wandering stars* planets   214 *wonder-wounded* struck with amazement   215 *the
Dane* (This title normally signifies the King; see Act I, Scene i, line 17 and note.)

Laertes [*grappling with him°*]: The devil take thy soul!

Hamlet: Thou pray'st not well.
    I prithee, take thy fingers from my throat,
    For though I am not splenitive° and rash,
    Yet have I in me something dangerous,   220
    Which let thy wisdom fear. Hold off thy hand.

King: Pluck them asunder.

Queen: Hamlet, Hamlet!

All: Gentlemen!

Horatio: Good my lord, be quiet.   225

                    [*Hamlet and Laertes are parted.*]

Hamlet: Why, I will fight with him upon this theme
    Until my eyelids will no longer wag.°

Queen: O my son, what theme?

Hamlet: I loved Ophelia. Forty thousand brothers
    Could not with all their quantity of love   230
    Make up my sum. What wilt thou do for her?

King: O, he is mad, Laertes.

Queen: For love of God, forbear him.°

Hamlet: 'Swounds,° show me what thou'lt do.
    Woo't° weep? Woo't fight? Woo't fast? Woo't tear thyself?   235
    Woo't drink up° eisel?° Eat a crocodile?°
    I'll do 't. Dost come here to whine?
    To outface me with leaping in her grave?
    Be buried quick° with her, and so will I.
    And if thou prate of mountains, let them throw   240
    Millions of acres on us, till our ground,
    Singeing his pate° against the burning zone,°
    Make Ossa° like a wart! Nay, an° thou'lt mouth,°
    I'll rant as well as thou.

Queen: This is mere° madness,
    And thus awhile the fit will work on him;   245

---

216 s.d. *grappling with him* The testimony of the First Quarto that "*Hamlet leaps in after Laertes*" and the "Elegy on Burbage" ("Oft have I seen him leap into the grave") seem to indicate one way in which this fight was staged; however, the difficulty of fitting two contenders and Ophelia's body into a confined space (probably the trapdoor) suggests to many editors the alternative, that Laertes jumps out of the grave to attack Hamlet.)   219 *splenitive* quick-tempered 227 *wag* move. (A fluttering eyelid is a conventional sign that life has not yet gone.)   233 *forbear him* leave him alone   234 *'Swounds* by His (Christ's) wounds   235 *Woo't* wilt thou 236 *drink up* drink deeply. *eisel* vinegar. *crocodile* (Crocodiles were tough and dangerous, and were supposed to shed hypocritical tears.)   239 *quick* alive   242 *his pate* its head, i.e., top. *burning zone* zone in the celestial sphere containing the sun's orbit, between the tropics of Cancer and Capricorn   243 *Ossa* another mountain in Thessaly. (In their war against the Olympian gods, the giants attempted to heap Ossa on Pelion to scale Olympus.) *an if.* *mouth* i.e., rant   244 *mere* utter

Anon, as patient as the female dove
When that her golden couplets° are disclosed,°
His silence will sit drooping.
Hamlet: Hear you, sir.
    What is the reason that you use me thus?
    I loved you ever. But it is no matter.   250
    Let Hercules himself do what he may,
    The cat will mew, and dog will have his day.°

                                                        Exit Hamlet.

King: I pray thee, good Horatio, wait upon him.

                                                        [Exit] Horatio.

    [*To Laertes.*] Strengthen your patience in° our last night's speech;
    We'll put the matter to the present push.°—   255
    Good Gertrude, set some watch over your son.—
    This grave shall have a living° monument.
    An hour of quiet° shortly shall we see;
    Till then, in patience our proceeding be.   *Exeunt.*

Scene II [The Castle.]

Enter Hamlet and Horatio.

Hamlet: So much for this, sir; now shall you see the other.°
    You do remember all the circumstance?
Horatio: Remember it, my lord!
Hamlet: Sir, in my heart there was a kind of fighting
    That would not let me sleep. Methought I lay   5
    Worse than the mutines° in the bilboes.° Rashly,°
    And praised be rashness for it—let us know°
    Our indiscretion° sometimes serves us well
    When our deep plots do pall,° and that should learn° us
    There's a divinity that shapes our ends,   10
    Rough-hew° them how we will—
Horatio: That is most certain.
Hamlet: Up from my cabin,
    My sea-gown° scarfed° about me, in the dark

247 *golden couplets* two baby pigeons, covered with yellow down.   *disclosed* hatched   251–252 *Let . . . day* i.e., (1) even Hercules couldn't stop Laertes' theatrical rant (2) I, too, will have my turn; i.e., despite any blustering attempts at interference, every person will sooner or later do what he or she must do   254 *in* i.e., by recalling   255 *present push* immediate test   257 *living* lasting. (For Laertes' private understanding, Claudius also hints that Hamlet's death will serve as such a monument.)   258 *hour of quiet* time free of conflict   1 *see the other* hear the other news   6 *mutines* mutineers.   *bilboes* shackles.   *Rashly* on impulse. (This adverb goes with lines 12 ff.)   7 *know* acknowledge   8 *indiscretion* lack of foresight and judgment (not an indiscreet act)   9 *pall* fail, falter, go stale.   *learn* teach   11 *Rough-hew* shape roughly   13 *sea-gown* seaman's coat.   *scarfed* loosely wrapped

Groped I to find out them,° had my desire,
Fingered° their packet, and in fine° withdrew   15
To mine own room again, making so bold,
My fears forgetting manners, to unseal
Their grand commission; where I found, Horatio—
Ah, royal knavery!—an exact command,
Larded° with many several° sorts of reasons   20
Importing° Denmark's health and England's too,
With, ho! such bugs° and goblins in my life,°
That on the supervise,° no leisure bated,°
No, not to stay° the grinding of the ax,
My head should be struck off.

Horatio: Is 't possible?   25

Hamlet [*giving a document*]: Here's the commission. Read it at more leisure.
    But wilt thou hear now how I did proceed?

Horatio: I beseech you.

Hamlet: Being thus benetted round with villainies—
    Ere I could make a prologue to my brains,   30
    They had begun the play°—I sat me down,
    Devised a new commission, wrote it fair.°
    I once did hold it, as our statists° do,
    A baseness° to write fair, and labored much
    How to forget that learning, but, sir, now   35
    It did me yeoman's° service. Wilt thou know
    Th' effect° of what I wrote?

Horatio: Ay, good my lord.

Hamlet: An earnest conjuration° from the King,
    As England was his faithful tributary,
    As love between them like the palm° might flourish,   40
    As peace should still° her wheaten garland° wear
    And stand a comma° 'tween their amities,
    And many suchlike "as"es° of great charge,°
    That on the view and knowing of these contents,
    Without debatement further more or less,   45
    He should those bearers put to sudden death,
    Not shriving time° allowed.

14 *them* i.e., Rosencrantz and Guildenstern   15 *Fingered* pilfered, pinched.   *in fine* finally, in
conclusion   20 *Larded* garnished.   *several* different   21 *Importing* relating to   22 *bugs* bug-
bears, hobgoblins.   *in my life* i.e., to be feared if I were allowed to live   23 *supervise* reading.
leisure bated delay allowed   24 *stay* await   30–31 *Ere . . . play* before I could consciously turn
my brain to the matter, it had started working on a plan   32 *fair* in a clear hand   33 *statists*
statesmen   34 *baseness* i.e., lower-class trait   36 *yeoman's* i.e., substantial, faithful, loyal   37
effect purport   38 *conjuration* entreaty   40 *palm* (An image of health; see Psalm 92:12.)   41 *still*
always. *wheaten garland* (Symbolic of fruitful agriculture, of peace and plenty.)   42 *comma* (Indicating continuity, link.)   43 *"as"es* (1) the "whereases" of a formal document (2) asses.   *charge*
(1) import (2) burden (appropriate to asses)   47 *shriving time* time for confession and absolution

Horatio: How was this sealed?

Hamlet: Why, even in that was heaven ordinant.°
    I had my father's signet° in my purse,
    Which was the model° of that Danish seal;   50
    Folded the writ° up in the form of th' other,
    Subscribed° it, gave 't th' impression,° placed it safely,
    The changeling° never known. Now, the next day
    Was our sea fight, and what to this was sequent°
    Thou knowest already.   55

Horatio: So Guildenstern and Rosencrantz go to 't.

Hamlet: Why, man, they did make love to this employment.
    They are not near my conscience. Their defeat°
    Does by their own insinuation° grow.
    'Tis dangerous when the baser° nature comes   60
    Between the pass° and fell° incensed points
    Of mighty opposites.°

Horatio: Why, what a king is this!

Hamlet: Does it not, think thee, stand me now upon°—
    He that hath killed my king and whored my mother,
    Popped in between th' election° and my hopes,   65
    Thrown out his angle° for my proper° life,
    And with such cozenage°—is 't not perfect conscience
    To quit° him with this arm? And is 't not to be damned
    To let this canker° of our nature come
    In° further evil?   70

Horatio: It must be shortly known to him from England
    What is the issue of the business there.

Hamlet: It will be short. The interim is mine,
    And a man's life's no more than to say "one."°
    But I am very sorry, good Horatio,   75
    That to Laertes I forgot myself.
    For by the image of my cause I see
    The portraiture of his. I'll court his favors.
    But, sure, the bravery° of his grief did put me
    Into a tow'ring passion.

48 *ordinant* directing   49 *signet* small seal   50 *model* replica   51 *writ* writing   52 *Subscribed* signed (with forged signature).   *impression* i.e., with a wax seal   53 *changeling* i.e., substituted letter. (Literally, a fairy child substituted for a human one.)   54 *was sequent* followed   58 *defeat* destruction   59 *insinuation* intrusive intervention, sticking their noses in my business   60 *baser* of lower social station   61 *pass* thrust.   *fell* fierce   62 *opposites* antagonists   63 *stand me now upon* become incumbent on me now   65 *election* (The Danish monarch was "elected" by a small number of high-ranking electors.)   66 *angle* fishhook.   *proper* very   67 *cozenage* trickery   68 *quit* requite, pay back   69 *canker* ulcer   69–70 *come in* grow into   74 *a man's . . . "one"* one's whole life occupies such a short time, only as long as it takes to count to 1   79 *bravery* bravado

Horatio: Peace, who comes here?   80

Enter a Courtier [Osric].

Osric: Your lordship is right welcome back to Denmark.
Hamlet: I humbly thank you, sir. [*To Horatio.*] Dost know this water fly?
Horatio: No, my good lord.
Hamlet: Thy state is the more gracious, for 'tis a vice to know him. He hath much
      land, and fertile. Let a beast be lord of beasts, and his crib° shall stand at the   85
      King's mess.° 'Tis a chuff,° but, as I say, spacious in the possession of dirt.
Osric: Sweet lord, if your lordship were at leisure, I should impart a thing to you
      from His Majesty.
Hamlet: I will receive it, sir, with all diligence of spirit.
      Put your bonnet° to his° right use; 'tis for the head.   90
Osric: I thank your lordship, it is very hot.
Hamlet: No, believe me, 'tis very cold. The wind is northerly.
Osric: It is indifferent° cold, my lord, indeed.
Hamlet: But yet methinks it is very sultry and hot for my complexion.°
Osric: Exceedingly, my lord. It is very sultry, as 'twere—I cannot tell how. My   95
      lord, His Majesty bade me signify to you that 'a has laid a great wager on
      your head. Sir, this is the matter—
Hamlet: I beseech you, remember.

                                   [*Hamlet moves him to put on his hat.*]

Osric: Nay, good my lord; for my ease,° in good faith. Sir, here is newly come to
      court Laertes—believe me, an absolute° gentleman, full of most excellent   100
      differences,° of very soft society° and great showing.° Indeed, to speak feel-
      ingly° of him, he is the card° or calendar° of gentry,° for you shall find in
      him the continent of what part a gentleman would see.°
Hamlet: Sir, his definement° suffers no perdition° in you,° though I know to di-
      vide him inventorially° would dozy° th' arithmetic of memory, and yet but   105
      yaw° neither° in respect of° his quick sail. But, in the verity of extolment,° I
      take him to be a soul of great article,° and his infusion° of such dearth and

85–86 *Let . . . mess* i.e., if a man, no matter how beastlike, is as rich in livestock and possessions
as Osric, he may eat at the King's table   85 *crib* manger   86 *chuff* boor, churl. (The Second
Quarto spelling, *chough*, is a variant spelling that also suggests the meaning here of "chattering
jackdaw.")   90 *bonnet* any kind of cap or hat. *his* its   93 *indifferent* somewhat   94
complexion temperament   99 *for my ease* (A conventional reply declining the invitation to put
his hat back on.)   100 *absolute* perfect   101 *differences* special qualities. *soft society* agreeable
manners. *great showing* distinguished appearance   101–102 *feelingly* with just perception
102 *card* chart, map. *calendar* guide. *gentry* good breeding   103 *the continent . . . see* one
who contains in him all the qualities a gentleman would like to see. (A *continent* is that which
contains.)   104 *definement* definition. (Hamlet proceeds to mock Osric by throwing his lofty
diction back at him.) *perdition* loss, diminution. *you* your description   104–105 *divide him
inventorially* enumerate his graces. *dozy* dizzy.   106 *yaw* swing unsteadily off course. (Said of a
ship.) *neither* for all that. *in respect of* in comparison with. *in . . . extolment* in true praise
(of him)   107 *of great article* one with many articles in his inventory. *infusion* essence, character infused into him by nature

rareness° as, to make true diction° of him, his semblable° is his mirror and
who else would trace° him his umbrage,° nothing more.

Osric: Your lordship speaks most infallibly of him.   110

Hamlet: The concernancy,° sir? Why do we wrap the gentleman in our more
rawer breath?°

Osric: Sir?

Horatio: Is 't not possible to understand in another tongue?° You will do 't,° sir,
really.   115

Hamlet: What imports the nomination of this gentleman?

Osric: Of Laertes?

Horatio [to Hamlet]: His purse is empty already; all 's golden words are spent.

Hamlet: Of him, sir.

Osric: I know you are not ignorant—   120

Hamlet: I would you did, sir. Yet in faith if you did, it would not much approve°
me. Well, sir?

Osric: You are not ignorant of what excellence Laertes is—

Hamlet: I dare not confess that, lest I should compare with him in excellence.
But to know a man well were to know himself.°   125

Osric: I mean, sir, for° his weapon; but in the imputation laid on him by them,°
in his meed° he's unfellowed.°

Hamlet: What's his weapon?

Osric: Rapier and dagger.

Hamlet: That's two of his weapons—but well.°   130

Osric: The King, sir, hath wagered with him six Barbary horses, against the
which he° has impawned,° as I take it, six French rapiers and poniards,°
with their assigns,° as girdle, hangers,° and so.° Three of the carriages,° in
faith, are very dear to fancy,° very responsive° to the hilts, most delicate°
carriages, and of very liberal conceit.°   135

Hamlet: What call you the carriages?

Horatio [to Hamlet]: I knew you must be edified by the margent° ere you had done.

107–108 *dearth and rareness* rarity   108 *make true diction* speak truly.   *semblable* only true likeness   109 *who . . . trace* any other person who would wish to follow.   *umbrage* shadow   111
concernancy import, relevance   112 *rawer breath* unrefined speech that can only come short in
praising him   114 *to understand . . . tongue* i.e., for you, Osric, to understand when someone else
speaks your language. (Horatio twits Osric for not being able to understand the kind of flowery
speech he himself uses, when Hamlet speaks in such a vein. Alternatively, all this could be said
to Hamlet.)   *You will do 't* i.e., you can if you try, or, you may well have to try (to speak plainly)
121 *approve* commend   124–125 *I dare . . . himself* I dare not boast of knowing Laertes' excellence lest I seem to imply a comparable excellence in myself. Certainly to know another person
well, one must know oneself   126 *for* i.e., with.   *imputation . . . them* reputation given him by
others   127 *meed* merit.   *unfellowed* unmatched   130 *but well* but never mind   132 *he* i.e.,
Laertes.   *impawned* staked, wagered.   *poniards* daggers   133 *assigns* appurtenances.   *hangers*
straps on the sword belt (*girdle*), from which the sword hung.   *and so* and so on.   *carriages* (An
affected way of saying *hangers*; literally, gun carriages.)   134 *dear to fancy* delightful to the fancy.
responsive corresponding closely, matching or well-adjusted.   *delicate* (i.e., in workmanship)
135 *liberal conceit* elaborate design   137 *margent* margin of a book, place for explanatory notes

Osric: The carriages, sir, are the hangers.

Hamlet: The phrase would be more germane to the matter if we could carry a cannon by our sides; I would it might be hangers till then. But, on: six 140 Barbary horses against six French swords, their assigns, and three liberal— conceited carriages; that's the French bet against the Danish. Why is this impawned, as you call it?

Osric: The King, sir, hath laid,° sir, that in a dozen passes° between yourself and him, he shall not exceed you three hits. He hath laid on twelve for nine, 145 and it would come to immediate trial, if your lordship would vouchsafe the answer.°

Hamlet: How if I answer no?

Osric: I mean, my lord, the opposition of your person in trial.

Hamlet: Sir, I will walk here in the hall. If it please His Majesty, it is the 150 breathing time° of day with me. Let° the foils be brought, the gentleman willing, and the King hold his purpose, I will win for him an I can; if not, I will gain nothing but my shame and the odd hits.

Osric: Shall I deliver you° so?

Hamlet: To this effect, sir—after what flourish your nature will. 155

Osric: I commend° my duty to your lordship.

Hamlet: Yours, yours. [*Exit Osric.*] 'A does well to commend it himself; there are no tongues else for 's turn.°

Horatio: This lapwing° runs away with the shell on his head.

Hamlet: 'A did comply with his dug° before 'a sucked it. Thus has he—and many 160 more of the same breed that I know the drossy° age dotes on—only got the tune° of the time and, out of an habit of encounter,° a kind of yeasty° collec- tion,° which carries them through and through the most fanned and win- nowed opinions;° and do° but blow them to their trial, the bubbles are out.°

---

144 *laid* wagered. *passes* bouts. (The odds of the betting are hard to explain. Possibly the King bets that Hamlet will win at least five out of twelve, at which point Laertes raises the odds against himself by betting he will win nine.) 146–147 *vouchsafe the answer* be so good as to accept the challenge. (Hamlet deliberately takes the phrase in its literal sense of replying.) 151 *breathing time* exercise period. *Let* i.e., if 154 *deliver you* report what you say 156 *commend* commit to your favor. (A conventional salutation, but Hamlet wryly uses a more lit- eral meaning, "recommend," "praise," in line 157.) 158 *for 's turn* for his purposes, i.e., to do it for him 159 *lapwing* (A proverbial type of youthful forwardness. Also, a bird that draws in- truders away from its nest and was thought to run about with its head in the shell when newly hatched; a seeming reference to Osric's hat.) 160 *comply . . . dug* observe ceremonious for- mality toward his nurse's or mother's teat 161 *drossy* laden with scum and impurities, frivo- lous 162 *tune* temper, mood, manner of speech. *an habit of encounter* a demeanor in con- versing (with courtiers of his own kind). *yeasty* frothy 162–163 *collection* i.e., of current phrases 163–164 *carries . . . opinions* sustains them right through the scrutiny of persons whose opinions are select and refined. (Literally, like grain separated from its chaff. Osric is both the chaff and the bubbly froth on the surface of the liquor that is soon blown away.) 164 *and do* yet do. *blow . . . out* test them by merely blowing on them, and their bubbles burst

Enter a Lord.

Lord:

My lord, His Majesty commended him to you by young Osric, who brings 165
back to him that you attend him in the hall. He sends to know if your pleasure hold to play with Laertes, or that you will take longer time.

Hamlet: I am constant to my purposes; they follow the King's pleasure. If his fitness speaks, mine is ready;° now or whensoever, provided I be so able as
now. 170

Lord: The King and Queen and all are coming down.

Hamlet: In happy time.°

Lord: The Queen desires you to use some gentle entertainment° to Laertes before you fall to play.

Hamlet: She well instructs me. [*Exit Lord.*] 175

Horatio: You will lose, my lord.

Hamlet: I do not think so. Since he went into France, I have been in continual
practice; I shall win at the odds. But thou wouldst not think how ill all's
here about my heart; but it is no matter.

Horatio: Nay, good my lord— 180

Hamlet: It is but foolery, but it is such a kind of gaingiving° as would perhaps
trouble a woman.

Horatio: If your mind dislike anything, obey it. I will forestall their repair°
hither and say you are not fit.

Hamlet: Not a whit, we defy augury. There is special providence in the fall of a 185
sparrow. If it be now, 'tis not to come; if it be not to come, it will be now; if
it be not now; yet it will come. The readiness is all. Since no man of aught
he leaves knows, what is 't to leave betimes? Let be.°

*A table prepared. [Enter] trumpets, drums, and officers with cushions; King,
Queen, [Osric,] and all the state; foils, daggers, [and wine borne in;] and Laertes.*

King: Come, Hamlet, come and take this hand from me.

[*The King puts Laertes' hand into Hamlet's.*]

Hamlet [to Laertes]: Give me your pardon, sir. I have done you wrong, 190
But pardon 't as you are a gentleman.
This presence° knows,
And you must needs have heard, how I am punished°
With a sore distraction. What I have done
That might your nature, honor, and exception° 195
Roughly awake, I here proclaim was madness.

168–169 *If . . . ready* if he declares his readiness, my convenience waits on his   172 *In happy
time* (A phrase of courtesy indicating that the time is convenient.)   173 *entertainment* greeting
181 *gaingiving* misgiving   183 *repair* coming   187–188 *Since . . . Let be* since no one has
knowledge of what he is leaving behind, what does an early death matter after all? Enough;
don't struggle against it.   192 *presence* royal assembly   193 *punished* afflicted   195 *exception*
disapproval

Was 't Hamlet wronged Laertes? Never Hamlet.
If Hamlet from himself be ta'en away,
And when he's not himself does wrong Laertes,
Then Hamlet does it not, Hamlet denies it.   200
Who does it, then? His madness. If 't be so,
Hamlet is of the faction° that is wronged;
His madness is poor Hamlet's enemy.
Sir, in this audience
Let my disclaiming from a purposed evil   205
Free me so far in your most generous thoughts
That I have° shot my arrow o'er the house
And hurt my brother.
Laertes: I am satisfied in nature,°
Whose motive° in this case should stir me most
To my revenge. But in my terms of honor   210
I stand aloof, and will no reconcilement
Till by some elder masters of known honor
I have a voice° and precedent of peace°
To keep my name ungored.° But till that time
I do receive your offered love like love,   215
And will not wrong it.
Hamlet: I embrace it freely,
And will this brother's wager frankly° play.—
Give us the foils. Come on.
Laertes: Come, one for me.
Hamlet: I'll be your foil,° Laertes. In mine ignorance
Your skill shall, like a star i' the darkest night,   220
Stick fiery off° indeed.
Laertes: You mock me, sir.
Hamlet: No, by this hand.
King: Give them the foils, young Osric. Cousin Hamlet,
You know the wager?
Hamlet: Very well, my lord.
Your Grace has laid the odds o'° the weaker side.   225
King: I do not fear it; I have seen you both.
But since he is bettered,° we have therefore odds.
Laertes: This is too heavy. Let me see another.

[*He exchanges his foil for another.*]

202 *faction* party   207 *That I have as* if I had   208 *in nature* i.e., as to my personal feelings
209 *motive* prompting   213 *voice* authoritative pronouncement.   *of peace* for reconciliation
214 *name ungored* reputation unwounded   217 *frankly* without ill feeling or the burden of
rancor   219 *foil* thin metal background that sets a jewel off (with pun on the blunted rapier for
fencing)   221 *Stick fiery off* stand out brilliantly   225 *laid the odds o'* bet on, backed   227 *is
bettered* has improved; is the odds-on favorite. (Laertes' handicap is the "three hits" specified in
line 145.)

Hamlet: This likes me° well. These foils have all a length?

[*They prepare to play.*]

Osric: Ay, my good lord.

King: Set me the stoups of wine upon that table.   230
    If Hamlet give the first or second hit,
    Or quit in answer of the third exchange,°
    Let all the battlements their ordnance fire.
    The King shall drink to Hamlet's better breath,°   235
    And in the cup an union° shall he throw
    Richer than that which four successive kings
    In Denmark's crown have worn. Give me the cups,
    And let the kettle° to the trumpet speak,
    The trumpet to the cannoneer without,   240
    The cannons to the heavens, the heaven to earth,
    "Now the King drinks to Hamlet." Come, begin.

Trumpets the while.

    And you, the judges, bear a wary eye.

Hamlet: Come on, sir.

Laertes: Come, my lord. [*They play. Hamlet scores a hit.*]   245

Hamlet: One.

Laertes: No.

Hamlet: Judgment.

Osric: A hit, a very palpable hit.

Drum, trumpets, and shot. Flourish.
A piece goes off.

Laertes: Well, again.

King: Stay, give me drink. Hamlet, this pearl is thine.   250

[*He drinks, and throws a pearl in Hamlet's cup.*]

    Here's to thy health. Give him the cup.

Hamlet: I'll play this bout first. Set it by awhile.
    Come. [*They play.*] Another hit; what say you?

Laertes: A touch, a touch, I do confess 't.

King: Our son shall win.

Queen: He's fat° and scant of breath.   255
    Here, Hamlet, take my napkin,° rub thy brows.
    The Queen carouses° to thy fortune, Hamlet.

Hamlet: Good madam!

King: Gertrude, do not drink.

Queen: I will, my lord, I pray you pardon me.   [*She drinks.*]   260

---

229 *likes me* pleases me   233 *Or . . . exchange* i.e., or requites Laertes in the third bout for
having won the first two   235 *better breath* improved vigor   236 *union* pearl. (So called, according to Pliny's *Natural History,* 9, because pearls are *unique,* never identical.)   239 *kettle*
kettledrum   255 *fat* not physically fit, out of training   256 *napkin* handkerchief   257 *carouses*
drinks a toast

King [*aside*]: It is the poisoned cup. It is too late.
Hamlet: I dare not drink yet, madam; by and by.
Queen: Come, let me wipe thy face.
Laertes [*to King*]: My lord, I'll hit him now.
King: I do not think 't.
Laertes [*aside*]: And yet it is almost against my conscience.   265
Hamlet: Come, for the third, Laertes. You do but dally.
    I pray you, pass° with your best violence;
    I am afeard you make a wanton of me.°
Laertes: Say you so? Come on.   [*They play.*]
Osric: Nothing neither way.   270
Laertes: Have at you now!

    [*Laertes wounds Hamlet; then, in scuffling, they change rapiers,° and Hamlet
                                   wounds Laertes.*]

King: Part them! They are incensed.
Hamlet: Nay, come, again.   [*The Queen falls.*]
Osric: Look to the Queen there, ho!
Horatio: They bleed on both sides. How is it, my lord?
Osric: How is 't, Laertes?
Laertes: Why, as a woodcock° to mine own springe,° Osric;   275
    I am justly killed with mine own treachery.
Hamlet: How does the Queen?
King: She swoons to see them bleed.
Queen: No, no, the drink, the drink—O my dear Hamlet—
    The drink, the drink! I am poisoned.   [*She dies.*]
Hamlet: O villainy! Ho, let the door be locked!   280
    Treachery! Seek it out.   [*Laertes falls. Exit Osric.*]
Laertes: It is here, Hamlet. Hamlet, thou art slain.
    No med'cine in the world can do thee good;
    In thee there is not half an hour's life.
    The treacherous instrument is in thy hand,   285
    Unbated° and envenomed. The foul practice°
    Hath turned itself on me. Lo, here I lie,
    Never to rise again. Thy mother's poisoned.
    I can no more. The King, the King's to blame.
Hamlet: The point envenomed too? Then, venom, to thy work.   290
                                   [*He stabs the King.*]

267 *pass* thrust   268 *make . . . me* i.e., treat me like a spoiled child, trifle with me   271 s.d. *in scuffling, they change rapiers* (This stage direction occurs in the Folio. According to a widespread stage tradition, Hamlet receives a scratch, realizes that Laertes' sword is unbated, and accordingly forces an exchange.)   275 *woodcock* a bird, a type of stupidity or as a decoy.   *springe* trap, snare   286 *Unbated* not blunted with a button.   *practice* plot

All: Treason! Treason!

King: O, yet defend me, friends! I am but hurt.

Hamlet [*forcing the King to drink*]:
 Here, thou incestuous, murderous, damnèd Dane,
 Drink off this potion. Is thy union° here?
 Follow my mother.   [*The King dies.*]

Laertes: He is justly served.   295
 It is a poison tempered° by himself.
 Exchange forgiveness with me, noble Hamlet.
 Mine and my father's death come not upon thee,
 Nor thine on me!   [*He dies.*]

Hamlet: Heaven make thee free of it! I follow thee.   300
 I am dead, Horatio. Wretched Queen, adieu!
 You that look pale and tremble at this chance,°
 That are but mutes° or audience to this act,
 Had I but time—as this fell° sergeant,° Death,
 Is strict° in his arrest°—O, I could tell you—   305
 But let it be. Horatio, I am dead;
 Thou livest. Report me and my cause aright
 To the unsatisfied.

Horatio: Never believe it.
 I am more an antique Roman° than a Dane.
 Here's yet some liquor left.

[*He attempts to drink from the poisoned cup. Hamlet prevents him.*]

Hamlet: As thou'rt a man,   310
 Give me the cup! Let go! By heaven, I'll ha 't.
 O God, Horatio, what a wounded name,
 Things standing thus unknown, shall I leave behind me!
 If thou didst ever hold me in thy heart,
 Absent thee from felicity awhile,   315
 And in this harsh world draw thy breath in pain
 To tell my story. A *march afar off* [*and a volley within*]. What warlike noise is
  this?

 Enter Osric.

Osric: Young Fortinbras, with conquest come from Poland,
 To th' ambassadors of England gives
 This warlike volley.

---

294 *union* pearl. (See line 236; with grim puns on the word's other meanings: marriage, shared death.) 296 *tempered* mixed 302 *chance* mischance 303 *mutes* silent observers. (Literally, actors with nonspeaking parts.) 304 *fell* cruel. *sergeant* sheriff's officer 305 *strict* (1) severely just (2) unavoidable. *arrest* (1) taking into custody (2) stopping my speech 309 *Roman* (Suicide was an honorable choice for many Romans as an alternative to a dishonorable life.)

Hamlet: O, I die, Horatio!   320
    The potent poison quite o'ercrows° my spirit.
    I cannot live to hear the news from England,
    But I do prophesy th' election lights
    On Fortinbras. He has my dying voice.°
    So tell him, with th' occurrents° more and less   325
    Which have solicited°—the rest is silence.   [He dies.]
Horatio: Now cracks a noble heart. Good night, sweet prince,
    And flights of angels sing thee to thy rest!

    [March within.]

    Why does the drum come hither?

    Enter Fortinbras, with the [English] Ambassadors [with drum, colors, and atten-
    dants].

Fortinbras: Where is this sight?
Horatio: What is it you would see?   330
    If aught of woe or wonder, cease your search.
Fortinbras: This quarry° cries on havoc.° O proud Death,
    What feast° is toward° in thine eternal cell,
    That thou so many princes at a shot
    So bloodily hast struck?
First Ambassador: The sight is dismal,   335
    And our affairs from England come too late.
    The ears are senseless that should give us hearing,
    To tell him his commandment is fulfilled,
    That Rosencrantz and Guildenstern are dead.
    Where should we have our thanks?
Horatio: Not from his° mouth,   340
    Had it th' ability of life to thank you.
    He never gave commandment for their death.
    But since, so jump° upon this bloody question,°
    You from the Polack wars, and you from England,
    Are here arrived, give order that these bodies   345
    High on a stage° be placèd to the view,
    And let me speak to th' yet unknowing world
    How these things came about. So shall you hear
    Of carnal, bloody, and unnatural acts,

321 o'ercrows triumphs over (like the winner in a cockfight)   324 voice vote   325 occurrents
events, incidents   326 solicited moved, urged. (Hamlet doesn't finish saying what the events
have prompted—presumably, his acts of vengeance, or his reporting of those events to Fortinbras.)   332 quarry heap of dead.   cries on havoc proclaims a general slaughter   333 feast i.e.,
Death feasting on those who have fallen.   toward in preparation   340 his i.e., Claudius'   343
jump precisely, immediately.   question dispute, affair   346 stage platform

Of accidental judgments,° casual° slaughters,   350
Of deaths put on° by cunning and forced cause,°
And, in this upshot, purposes mistook
Fall'n on th' inventors' heads. All this can I
Truly deliver.
Fortinbras: Let us haste to hear it,
And call the noblest to the audience.   355
For me, with sorrow I embrace my fortune.
I have some rights of memory° in this kingdom,
Which now to claim my vantage° doth invite me.
Horatio: Of that I shall have also cause to speak,
And from his mouth whose voice will draw on more.°   360
But let this same be presently° performed,
Even while men's minds are wild, lest more mischance
On° plots and errors happen.
Fortinbras: Let four captains
Bear Hamlet, like a soldier, to the stage,
For he was likely, had he been put on,°   365
To have proved most royal; and for his passage,°
The soldiers' music and the rite of war
Speak° loudly for him.
Take up the bodies. Such a sight as this
Becomes the field,° but here shows much amiss.   370
Go bid the soldiers shoot.

Exeunt [marching, bearing off the dead bodies; a peal of ordnance is shot off].

QUESTIONS

ACT I

1. By what means does Shakespeare build suspense before the Ghost's appearances? What
   disturbing political events happen in the background of the first act?
2. Why is Hamlet so unwilling to trust what the Ghost tells him? What precisely does the
   Ghost instruct him to do? (What does the Ghost command him not to do?) Why does
   Hamlet not immediately obey the Ghost's orders?
3. What is Hamlet's relationship to Horatio at the beginning of the play (ii, 160–188)? How
   does their relationship change in the course of the play?
4. How does Claudius appear in his first scene (ii, 1–128)? Does he betray any evidence of
   guilt?

350 *judgments* retributions. *casual* occurring by chance   351 *put on* instigated. *forced cause*
contrivance   357 *of memory* traditional, remembered, unforgotten   358 *vantage* favorable opportunity   360 *voice . . . more* vote will influence still others   361 *presently* immediately   363
On on the basis of; on top of   365 *put on* i.e., invested in royal office and so put to the test
366 *passage* i.e., from life to death   368 *Speak* (let them) speak   370 *Becomes the field* suits the
field of battle

5. Hamlet's first soliloquy (ii, 129–159) occurs before Horatio reports the Ghost's appearance. What does this speech reveal about the Prince's state of mind? What specific things trouble him?
6. Is the advice Polonius offers Laertes trustworthy? As the play continues, Polonius often appears humbling and self-deluded. Does his opening speech (iii, 58–80) offer good or bad advice?
7. What does Polonius tell Ophelia about Hamlet's declarations of affection(iii, 102–136)? What do his remarks reveal about his opinion of Ophelia?

ACT II

1. How does Polonius's conversation with Reynaldo change our opinion of the old counselor? What verbal mannerisms does Shakespeare give to Polonius that now make him appear comic? What precisely does Polonius ask Reynaldo to do in Paris?
2. When Ophelia tells her father about Hamlet's frightening visit to her room (i, 77–102), how does Polonius interpret the event? What does the audience know that might lead them to analyze the Prince's visit differently?
3. When Polonius announces his theory of Hamlet's madness to the King, the counselor indulges in wordplay and metaphor (ii, 86–91). What does his performance suggest about his personality?
4. Is Polonius entirely foolish? Is he capable of genuine insight? Give a specific example of a wise and a deluded judgment by Polonius.
5. Polonius observes "there is method" in Hamlet's madness (ii, 197). Give an example of something important that Hamlet utters under the guise of madness that he probably would not say openly in a more rational way.
6. What does Hamlet imply about Polonius in his remark "That great baby you see there is not yet out of his swaddling clouts" (ii, 333–334)? Does Rosenkrantz understand the Prince's joke (335–336)?
7. What does Hamlet's request to hear a recitation from the players about Pyrrhus's bloody slaughter at Troy suggest about the Prince's state of mind? What specific actions by Pyrrhus are the most suggestive of Hamlet's own plans?

ACT III

1. In his most famous soliloquy (i, 57–91), what course of action does Hamlet contemplate? How does he resolve his internal argument?
2. How guilty is Gertrude? With what offenses does Hamlet charge her (Scene iv)? Is our attitude toward her the same as Hamlet's or different? Does our sympathy for her grow or diminish as the play continues?
3. What is odd about the Ghost's appearance to Hamlet in the Queen's bedroom (iv, 106–142)?
4. From the play-within-a-play (Scene ii) and from Hamlet's remarks on acting, what do we learn about the Elizabethan theater? How do Hamlet's remarks also serve to advance the story?
5. Discuss Hamlet's treatment of Ophelia (see especially Scene i). Does his behavior seem cruel, in conflict with his supposed nobility and sensitivity?

ACT IV

1. When Claudius demands that the Queen explain her son's behavior, Gertrude claims that the Prince is insane (i, 1–27). Does she truly believe Hamlet is mad or is she trying to protect him from Claudius?
2. What events cause Ophelia to go mad? Cite specific lines or events in the play for your interpretation.

3. Discuss how Shakespeare differently portrays Hamlet's feigned madness and Ophelia's real madness. State some specific differences in Shakespeare's presentation.
4. When Laertes returns to avenge his father's death, does he appear heroic or confused? How does his behavior compare with Hamlet's strategy for revenge?

ACT V

1. The final act of *Hamlet* begins with a long comic scene featuring two gravediggers. This episode has little direct bearing on the plot, and the two gravediggers never reappear. What does this comic interlude add to the tragedy? Would the play be more focused and forceful without this humorous scene?
2. *Hamlet* ends with the arrival of Fortinbras. If someone suggested that Fortinbras be cut from the play, what reasons would you offer for his inclusion?

GENERAL QUESTIONS

1. What is the play's major dramatic question? (For a discussion of this term, see page 1319.) At what point is the question formulated? Does this play have a crisis, or turning point?
2. How early in the play, and from what passages, do you perceive that Claudius is a villain?
3. What comic elements does the play contain—what scenes, what characters, what exchanges of dialogue? What is their value to a play that, as a whole, is a tragedy?
4. A familiar kind of behavior is showing one face to the world and another to oneself. What characters in *Hamlet* do so? Is their deception ever justified?
5. Is Laertes a villain like Claudius, or is there reason to feel that his contrived duel with Hamlet is justified?
6. How is Hamlet shown to be a noble and extraordinary person, not merely by birth, but by nature? See Ophelia's praise of Hamlet as "The glass of fashion, and the mold of form" (III, i, 142–153). Are we to take Ophelia's speech as the prejudiced view of a lover, or does Shakespeare demonstrate that her opinion of Hamlet is trustworthy?
7. If the characters of Rosencrantz or Guildenstern are cut from the play, as is the case in some productions, what is lost?

The Background of A Midsummer Night's Dream

The theme in A *Midsummer Night's Dream* of love being best fulfilled in marital union suggests that the play may have originally been written for performance at an aristocratic wedding. The work is certainly Shakespeare's most lyrical and romantic comedy, full of reflections on fantasy, dreaming, and desire, set mostly amid festive palaces and moonlit woods filled with fairies. In the Renaissance there were two major varieties of comedy—both borrowed from Greek and Roman drama. The first was satiric comedy, which usually poked bitter fun at human folly. Shakespeare generally avoided this mode, which was very well practiced by his friend Ben Jonson. Instead, Shakespeare preferred the second type, romantic comedy, which he had discovered as a schoolboy reading the Latin plays of Terence and Plautus. Romantic comedy is less concerned with correcting misdeeds and folly than with following the delightful and embarrassing behavior of imperfect but mostly likeable characters. Always ending in the happy marriage (or marriages) of young lovers who have overcome considerable obstacles to unite, romantic comedy also encourages the viewer to accept and forgive human faults and frailties.

A *Midsummer Night's Dream* also demonstrates Shakespeare's particular genius for plotting, a necessary skill for comic theater. Although Shakespeare often borrowed (and usually greatly improved) the stories of his plays from various sources, the plot of A *Midsummer Night's Dream* appears to be original, though he took individual characters like Theseus and Titania from classical mythology. The comedy has a delightfully complex structure combining four different plots—all romantic in different ways from young love to marital reconciliation. The play presents five different sets of lovers. The general action is framed around the wedding of the first set of lovers, King Theseus and the Amazon Queen Hippolyta, whom he has conquered in war and taken as his wife. Both a personal and public union, their marriage will end the enmity between their nations. More complicated are the love affairs of the second group, the young aristocrats—Helena, Lysander, Hermia, and Demetrius. The adventures of these two passionately mismatched couples, who ultimately find happy marriages, form the main plot of the comedy. The third set of lovers is a supernatural couple, Oberon and Titania, the King and Queen of the fairy realm, who are in the midst of a bitter marital dispute. Then, there is a group of rustic workmen led by Nick Bottom, a weaver with theatrical aspirations. While this group does not initially seem to contain any lovers, Bottom eventually becomes entangled in a series of enchantments that transforms him into Titania's ass-eared darling for a single night. Finally, at the play's end the rustics perform a burlesque of tragic love that presents a fifth, imaginary set of lovers, Pyramus and Thisbe. Their tale of "tragical mirth" subtly comments on the consequences of doomed romance. No other comedy by Shakespeare focuses so single-mindedly or happily on sexual love and marriage. No wonder A *Midsummer Night's Dream* has been popular for centuries, not only in English-speaking countries but around the world.

Edited by David Bevington

Titania and Oberon: John Gielgud and Peggy Ashcroft, 1945 production of A Midsummer Night's Dream.

[Dramatis Personae

Theseus, Duke of Athens
Hippolyta, Queen of the Amazons, betrothed to Theseus
Philostrate, Master of the Revels
Egeus, father of Hermia

NOTE ON THE TEXT: This text of A Midsummer Night's Dream is taken from the First Quarto of 1600.

Hermia, daughter of Egeus, in love with Lysander
Lysander, in love with Hermia
Demetrius, in love with Hermia and favored by Egeus
Helena, in love with Demetrius

Oberon, King of the Fairies
Titania, Queen of the Fairies
Puck, or Robin Goodfellow
Peaseblossom, ⎫
Cobweb,   ⎪
Mote,   ⎬ fairies attending Titania
Mustardseed,   ⎭
Other fairies attending

Peter Quince, a carpenter,   ⎫   Prologue
Nick Bottom, a weaver,   ⎪   Pyramus
Francis Flute, a bellows mender,   ⎬ representing Thisbe
Tom Snout, a tinker,   ⎪   Wall
Snug, a joiner,   ⎪   Lion
Robin Starveling, a tailor,   ⎭   Moonshine
Lords and Attendants on Theseus and Hippolyta

Scene. Athens, and a wood near it]

ACT I

Scene I [Athens. Theseus' Court.]

Enter Theseus, Hippolyta, [and Philostrate,] with others.

Theseus: Now, fair Hippolyta, our nuptial hour
    Draws on apace. Four happy days bring in
    Another moon; but, O, methinks, how slow
    This old moon wanes! She lingers° my desires,
    Like to a stepdame° or a dowager°   5
    Long withering out° a young man's revenue.
Hippolyta: Four days will quickly steep themselves° in night;
    Four nights will quickly dream away the time;
    And then the moon, like to a silver bow
    New bent in heaven, shall behold the night   10
    Of our solemnities.°

---

4 *lingers* postpones, delays the fulfillment of   5 *stepdame* stepmother.   *a dowager* i.e., a widow (whose right of inheritance from her dead husband is eating into her son's estate)   6 *withering out* causing to dwindle   7 *steep themselves* saturate themselves, be absorbed in   11 *solemnities* festive ceremonies of marriage

Theseus: Go, Philostrate,
    Stir up the Athenian youth to merriments.
    Awake the pert and nimble spirit of mirth.
    Turn melancholy forth to funerals;
    The pale companion° is not for our pomp.°   [*Exit Philostrate.*]   15
    Hippolyta, I wooed thee with my sword°
    And won thy love doing thee injuries;
    But I will wed thee in another key,
    With pomp, with triumph,° and with reveling.

Enter Egeus and his daughter Hermia, and Lysander, and Demetrius.

Egeus: Happy be Theseus, our renownèd duke!   20
Theseus: Thanks, good Egeus. What's the news with thee?
Egeus: Full of vexation come I, with complaint
    Against my child, my daughter Hermia.—
    Stand forth, Demetrius.—My noble lord,
    This man hath my consent to marry her.—   25
    Stand forth, Lysander.—And, my gracious Duke,
    This man hath bewitched the bosom of my child.
    Thou, thou Lysander, thou hast given her rhymes
    And interchanged love tokens with my child.
    Thou hast by moonlight at her window sung   30
    With feigning° voice verses of feigning° love,
    And stol'n the impression of her fantasy°
    With bracelets of thy hair, rings, gauds,° conceits,°
    Knacks,° trifles, nosegays, sweetmeats—messengers
    Of strong prevailment in° unhardened youth.   35
    With cunning hast thou filched my daughter's heart,
    Turned her obedience, which is due to me,
    To stubborn harshness. And, my gracious Duke,
    Be it so° she will not here before Your Grace
    Consent to marry with Demetrius,   40
    I beg the ancient privilege of Athens:
    As she is mine, I may dispose of her,
    Which shall be either to this gentleman
    Or to her death, according to our law
    Immediately° provided in that case.   45
Theseus: What say you, Hermia? Be advised, fair maid.

15 *companion* fellow. *pomp* ceremonial magnificence   16 *with my sword* i.e., in a military engagement against the Amazons, when Hippolyta was taken captive   19 *triumph* public festivity
31 *feigning* (1) counterfeiting (2) faining, desirous   32 *And . . . fantasy* and made her fall in love with you (imprinting your image on her imagination) by stealthy and dishonest means
33 *gauds* playthings. *conceits* fanciful trifles   34 *Knacks* knickknacks   35 *prevailment in* influence on   39 *Be it so* if   45 *Immediately* directly, with nothing intervening

To you your father should be as a god—
One that composed your beauties, yea, and one
To whom you are but as a form in wax
By him imprinted, and within his power   50
To leave° the figure or disfigure° it.
Demetrius is a worthy gentleman.

Hermia: So is Lysander.

Theseus: In himself he is;
But in this kind,° wanting° your father's voice,°
The other must be held the worthier.   55

Hermia: I would my father looked but with my eyes.

Theseus: Rather your eyes must with his judgment look.

Hermia: I do entreat Your Grace to pardon me.
I know not by what power I am made bold,
Nor how it may concern° my modesty   60
In such a presence here to plead my thoughts;
But I beseech Your Grace that I may know
The worst that may befall me in this case
If I refuse to wed Demetrius.

Theseus: Either to die the death° or to abjure   65
Forever the society of men.
Therefore, fair Hermia, question your desires,
Know of your youth, examine well your blood,°
Whether, if you yield not to your father's choice,
You can endure the livery° of a nun,   70
For aye° to be in shady cloister mewed,°
To live a barren sister all your life,
Chanting faint hymns to the cold fruitless moon.
Thrice blessèd they that master so their blood
To undergo such maiden pilgrimage;   75
But earthlier happy° is the rose distilled°
Than that which, withering on the virgin thorn,
Grows, lives, and dies in single blessedness.

Hermia: So will I grow, so live, so die, my lord,
Ere I will yield my virgin patent° up   80
Unto his lordship, whose unwishèd yoke
My soul consents not to give sovereignty.

Theseus: Take time to pause, and by the next new moon—
The sealing day betwixt my love and me
For everlasting bond of fellowship—   85

---

51 *leave* i.e., leave unaltered.   *disfigure* obliterate   54 *kind* respect.   *wanting* lacking.   *voice* approval   60 *concern* befit   65 *die the death* be executed by legal process   68 *blood* passions   70 *livery* habit, costume   71 *aye* ever.   *mewed* shut in. (Said of a hawk, poultry, etc.)   76 *earthlier happy* happier as respects this world.   *distilled* i.e., to make perfume   80 *patent* privilege

Upon that day either prepare to die
For disobedience to your father's will,
Or° else to wed Demetrius, as he would,
Or on Diana's altar to protest°
For aye austerity and single life.   90
Demetrius: Relent, sweet Hermia, and, Lysander, yield
Thy crazèd° title to my certain right.
Lysander: You have her father's love, Demetrius;
Let me have Hermia's. Do you marry him.
Egeus: Scornful Lysander! True, he hath my love,   95
And what is mine my love shall render him.
And she is mine, and all my right of her
I do estate unto° Demetrius:
Lysander: I am, my lord, as well derived° as he,
As well possessed;° my love is more than his;   100
My fortunes every way as fairly° ranked,
If not with vantage,° as Demetrius';
And, which is more than all these boasts can be,
I am beloved of beauteous Hermia.
Why should not I then prosecute my right?   105
Demetrius, I'll avouch it to his head,°
Made love to Nedar's daughter, Helena,
And won her soul; and she, sweet lady, dotes,
Devoutly dotes, dotes in idolatry
Upon this spotted° and inconstant man.   110
Theseus: I must confess that I have heard so much,
And with Demetrius thought to have spoke thereof;
But, being overfull of self-affairs,°
My mind did lose it. But, Demetrius, come,
And come, Egeus, you shall go with me;   115
I have some private schooling° for you both.
For you, fair Hermia, look you arm° yourself
To fit your fancies° to your father's will,
Or else the law of Athens yields you up—
Which by no means we may extenuate°—   120
To death or to a vow of single life.
Come, my Hippolyta. What cheer, my love?
Demetrius and Egeus, go° along.

88 *Or* either   89 *protest* vow   92 *crazèd* cracked, unsound   98 *estate unto* settle or bestow
upon   99 *as well derived* as well born and descended   100 *possessed* endowed with wealth
101 *fairly* handsomely   102 *vantage* superiority   106 *head* i.e., face   110 *spotted* i.e., morally
stained   113 *self-affairs* my own concerns   116 *schooling* admonition   117 *look you arm* take
care you prepare   118 *fancies* likings, thoughts of love   120 *extenuate* mitigate, relax   123 *go*
i.e., come

I must employ you in some business
Against° our nuptial, and confer with you   125
Of something nearly that° concerns yourselves.
Egeus: With duty and desire we follow you.

                                        Exeunt [all but Lysander and Hermia].
Lysander: How now, my love, why is your cheek so pale?
    How chance the roses there do fade so fast?
Hermia: Belike° for want of rain, which I could well   130
    Beteem° them from the tempest of my eyes.
Lysander: Ay me! For aught that I could ever read,
    Could ever hear by tale or history,
    The course of true love never did run smooth;
    But either it was different in blood°—   135
Hermia: O cross!° Too high to be enthralled to low.
Lysander: Or else misgrafted° in respect of years—
Hermia: O spite! Too old to be engaged to young.
Lysander: Or else it stood upon the choice of friends°—
Hermia: O hell, to choose love by another's eyes!   140
Lysander: Or if there were a sympathy° in choice,
    War, death, or sickness did lay siege to it,
    Making it momentany° as a sound,
    Swift as a shadow, short as any dream,
    Brief as the lightning in the collied° night   145
    That in a spleen° unfolds° both heaven and earth,
    And ere a man hath power to say "Behold!"
    The jaws of darkness do devour it up.
    So quick° bright things come to confusion.°
Hermia: If then true lovers have been ever crossed,°   150
    It stands as an edict in destiny.
    Then let us teach our trial patience,°
    Because it is a customary cross,
    As due to love as thoughts, and dreams, and sighs,
    Wishes, and tears, poor fancy's° followers.   155
Lysander: A good persuasion.° Therefore, hear me, Hermia:
    I have a widow aunt, a dowager
    Of great revenue, and she hath no child.
    From Athens is her house remote seven leagues;

---

125 *Against* in preparation for   126 *nearly that* that closely   130 *Belike* very likely   131
Beteem grant, afford   135 *blood* hereditary station   136 *cross* vexation   137 *misgrafted* ill
grafted, badly matched   139 *friends* relatives   141 *sympathy* agreement   143 *momentany*
lasting but a moment   145 *collied* blackened (as with coal dust), darkened   146 *in a spleen* in a
swift impulse, in a violent flash.   *unfolds* reveals   149 *quick* quickly; also, living, alive.   *confusion* ruin   150 *ever crossed* always thwarted   152 *teach . . . patience* i.e., teach ourselves patience in this trial   155 *fancy's* amorous passion's   156 *persuasion* doctrine

And she respects° me as her only son.   160
There, gentle Hermia, may I marry thee,
And to that place the sharp Athenian law
Cannot pursue us. If thou lovest me, then,
Steal forth thy father's house tomorrow night;
And in the wood, a league without° the town,   165
Where I did meet thee once with Helena
To do observance to a morn of May,°
There will I stay for thee.
Hermia: My good Lysander!
I swear to thee by Cupid's strongest bow,
By his best arrow° with the golden head,   170
By the simplicity° of Venus' doves,°
By that which knitteth souls and prospers loves,
And by that fire which burned the Carthage queen°
When the false Trojan° under sail was seen,
By all the vows that ever men have broke,   175
In number more than ever women spoke,
In that same place thou hast appointed me
Tomorrow truly will I meet with thee.
Lysander: Keep promise, love. Look, here comes Helena.

   Enter Helena.

Hermia: God speed, fair° Helena! Whither away?   180
Helena: Call you me fair? That "fair" again unsay.
Demetrius loves your fair.° O happy fair!°
Your eyes are lodestars,° and your tongue's sweet air°
More tunable° than lark to shepherd's ear
When wheat is green, when hawthorn buds appear.   185
Sickness is catching. O, were favor° so,
Yours would I catch, fair Hermia, ere I go;
My ear should catch your voice, my eye your eye,
My tongue should catch your tongue's sweet melody.
Were the world mine, Demetrius being bated,°   190
The rest I'd give to be to you translated.°

---

160 *respects* regards   165 *without* outside   167 *do . . . May* perform the ceremonies of May
Day   170 *best arrow* (Cupid's best gold-pointed arrows were supposed to induce love; his blunt
leaden arrows, aversion.)   171 *simplicity* innocence. *doves* i.e., those that drew Venus' chariot
173, 174 *Carthage queen, false Trojan* (Dido, Queen of Carthage, immolated herself on a funeral
pyre after having been deserted by the Trojan hero Aeneas.)   180 *fair* fair-complexioned
(generally regarded by the Elizabethans as more beautiful than a dark complexion)   182 *your
fair* your beauty (even though Hermia is dark-complexioned). *happy fair* lucky fair one   183
lodestars guiding stars. *air* music   184 *tunable* tuneful, melodious   186 *favor* appearance,
looks   190 *bated* excepted   191 *translated* transformed

O, teach me how you look and with what art
You sway° the motion° of Demetrius' heart.
Hermia: I frown upon him, yet he loves me still.
Helena: O, that your frowns would teach my smiles such skill!   195
Hermia: I give him curses, yet he gives me love.
Helena: O, that my prayers could such affection° move!°
Hermia: The more I hate, the more he follows me.
Helena: The more I love, the more he hateth me.
Hermia: His folly, Helena, is no fault of mine.   200
Helena: None, but your beauty. Would that fault were mine!
Hermia: Take comfort. He no more shall see my face.
    Lysander and myself will fly this place.
    Before the time I did Lysander see
    Seemed Athens as a paradise to me.°   205
    O, then, what graces in my love do dwell,
    That he hath turned a heaven unto a hell?
Lysander: Helen, to you our minds we will unfold.
    Tomorrow night, when Phoebe° doth behold
    Her silver visage in the watery glass,°   210
    Decking with liquid pearl the bladed grass,
    A time that lovers' flights doth still° conceal,
    Through Athens' gates have we devised to steal.
Hermia: And in the wood, where often you and I
    Upon faint° primrose beds were wont to lie,   215
    Emptying our bosoms of their counsel° sweet,
    There my Lysander and myself shall meet,
    And thence from Athens turn away our eyes
    To seek new friends and stranger companies.°
    Farewell, sweet playfellow. Pray thou for us,   220
    And good luck grant thee thy Demetrius!
    Keep word, Lysander: We must starve our sight
    From lovers' food till morrow deep midnight.
Lysander: I will, my Hermia. *(Exit Hermia.)* Helena, adieu.
    As you on him, Demetrius dote on you!   225

                                                        Exit Lysander.

Helena: How happy some o'er other some can be!°
    Through Athens I am thought as fair as she.
    But what of that? Demetrius thinks not so;
    He will not know what all but he do know.

---

193 *sway* control. *motion* impulse   197 *affection* passion. *move* arouse   204–205 *Before . . .
to me* (Hermia seemingly means that love has led to complications and jealousies, making
Athens hell for her.)   209 *Phoebe* Diana, the moon   210 *glass* mirror   212 *still* always   215
faint pale   216 *counsel* secret thought   219 *stranger companies* the company of strangers   226
o'er . . . can be can be in comparison to some others

And as he errs, doting on Hermia's eyes,   230
So I, admiring of° his qualities.
Things base and vile, holding no quantity,°
Love can transpose to form and dignity.
Love looks not with the eyes, but with the mind,
And therefore is winged Cupid painted blind.   235
Nor hath Love's mind of any judgment taste;°
Wings and no eyes figure° unheedy haste.
And therefore is Love said to be a child,
Because in choice° he is so oft beguiled.°
As waggish° boys in game° themselves forswear,   240
So the boy Love is perjured everywhere.
For ere Demetrius looked on Hermia's eyne,°
He hailed down oaths that he was only mine;
And when this hail some heat from Hermia felt,
So he dissolved, and showers of oaths did melt.   245
I will go tell him of fair Hermia's flight.
Then to the wood will he tomorrow night
Pursue her; and for this intelligence°
If I have thanks, it is a dear expense.°
But herein mean I to enrich my pain,   250
To have his sight thither and back again.

                                                          Exit.

Scene II [Athens.]

*Enter Quince the carpenter, and Snug the joiner, and Bottom the weaver, and
Flute the bellows mender, and Snout the tinker, and Starveling the tailor.*

Quince: Is all our company here?
Bottom: You were best to call them generally,° man by man, according to the scrip.°
Quince: Here is the scroll of every man's name which is thought fit, through all
 Athens, to play in our interlude° before the Duke and the Duchess on his
 wedding day at night.   5
Bottom: First, good Peter Quince, say what the play treats on, then read the
 names of the actors, and so grow to° a point.

---

231 *admiring of* wondering at 232 *holding no quantity* i.e., unsubstantial, unshapely 236 *Nor
. . . taste* i.e., nor has Love, which dwells in the fancy or imagination, any *taste* or least bit of
judgment or reason 237 *figure* are a symbol of 239 *in choice* in choosing. *beguiled* self-
deluded, making unaccountable choices 240 *waggish* playful, mischievous. *game* sport, jest
242 *eyne* eyes. (Old form of plural.) 248 *intelligence* information 249 *a dear expense* i.e., a
trouble worth taking on my part, or a begrudging effort on his part. *dear* costly 2 *generally*
(Bottom's blunder for "individually."). *scrip* scrap (Bottom's error for "script.") 4 *interlude*
play 7 *grow to* come to

Quince: Marry,° our play is "The most lamentable comedy and most cruel death of Pyramus and Thisbe."

Bottom: A very good piece of work, I assure you, and a merry. Now, good Peter 10
Quince, call forth your actors by the scroll. Masters, spread yourselves.

Quince: Answer as I call you. Nick Bottom,° the weaver.

Bottom: Ready. Name what part I am for, and proceed.

Quince: You, Nick Bottom, are set down for Pyramus.

Bottom: What is Pyramus? A lover or a tyrant? 15

Quince: A lover, that kills himself most gallant for love.

Bottom: That will ask some tears in the true performing of it. If I do it, let the
audience look to their eyes. I will move storms; I will condole° in some measure. To the rest—yet my chief humor° is for a tyrant. I could play Ercles°
rarely, or a part to tear a cat° in, to make all split.° 20

      "The raging rocks
      And shivering shocks
      Shall break the locks
      Of prison gates;
      And Phibbus' car° 25
      Shall shine from far
      And make and mar
      The foolish Fates."

This was lofty! Now name the rest of the players. This is Ercles' vein, a
tyrant's vein. A lover is more condoling. 30

Quince: Francis Flute, the bellows mender.

Flute: Here, Peter Quince.

Quince: Flute, you must take Thisbe on you.

Flute: What is Thisbe? A wandering knight?

Quince: It is the lady that Pyramus must love. 35

Flute: Nay, faith, let not me play a woman. I have a beard coming.

Quince: That's all one.° You shall play it in a mask, and you may speak as small°
as you will.

Bottom: An° I may hide my face, let me play Thisbe too. I'll speak in a monstrous little voice, "Thisne, Thisne!" "Ah Pyramus, my lover dear! Thy 40
Thisbe dear, and lady dear!"

Quince: No, no, you must play Pyramus, and Flute, you Thisbe.

Bottom: Well, proceed.

Quince: Robin Starveling, the tailor.

Starveling: Here, Peter Quince. 45

Quince: Robin Starveling, you must play Thisbe's mother. Tom Snout,
the tinker.

8 *Marry* (A mild oath; originally the name of the Virgin Mary.)   12 *Bottom* (As a weaver's
term, a *bottom* was an object around which thread was wound.)   18 *condole* lament, arouse pity
19 *humor* inclination, whim.   *Ercles* Hercules (The tradition of ranting came from Seneca's
Hercules Furens.)   20 *tear a cat* i.e., rant.   *make all split* i.e., cause a stir, bring the house down
25 *Phibbus' car* Phoebus', the sun god's, chariot   37 *That's all one* it makes no difference.
small high-pitched   39 *An* if (also at line 57)

Snout: Here, Peter Quince.

Quince: You, Pyramus' father; myself, Thisbe's father; Snug, the joiner, you, the lion's part, and I hope here is a play fitted. 50

Snug: Have you the lion's part written? Pray you, if it be, give it me, for I am slow of study.

Quince: You may do it extempore, for it is nothing but roaring.

Bottom: Let me play the lion too. I will roar that I will do any man's heart good to hear me. I will roar that I will make the Duke say, "Let him roar again, let 55 him roar again."

Quince: An you should do it too terribly, you would fright the Duchess and the ladies, that they would shriek; and that were enough to hang us all.

All: That would hang us, every mother's son.

Bottom: I grant you, friends, if you should fright the ladies out of their wits, they 60 would have no more discretion but to hang us; but I will aggravate° my voice so that I will roar you° as gently as any sucking dove;° I will roar you an 'twere° any nightingale.

Quince: You can play no part but Pyramus; for Pyramus is a sweet-faced man, a proper° man as one shall see in a summer's day, a most lovely gentlemanlike 65 man. Therefore you must needs play Pyramus.

Bottom: Well, I will undertake it. What beard were I best to play it in?

Quince: Why, what you will.

Bottom: I will discharge° it in either your° straw-color beard, your orange-tawny beard, your purple-in-grain° beard, or your French-crown-color° beard, your 70 perfect yellow.

Quince: Some of your French crowns° have no hair at all, and then you will play barefaced. But, masters, here are your parts. [*He distributes parts.*] And I am to entreat you, request you, and desire you to con° them by tomorrow night, and meet me in the palace wood, a mile without the town, by moonlight. 75 There will we rehearse; for if we meet in the city, we shall be dogged with company, and our devices° known. In the meantime I will draw a bill° of properties, such as our play wants. I pray you, fail me not.

Bottom: We will meet, and there we may rehearse most obscenely° and coura- geously. Take pains, be perfect.° Adieu. 80

Quince: At the Duke's oak we meet.

Bottom: Enough. Hold, or cut bowstrings.° *Exeunt.*

---

61 *aggravate* (Bottom's blunder for "moderate.") 62 *roar you* i.e., roar for you. *sucking dove* (Bottom conflates *sitting dove* and *sucking lamb*, two proverbial images of innocence.) 63 *an 'twere* as if it were 65 *proper* handsome 69 *discharge* perform. *your* i.e., you know the kind I mean 70 *purple-in-grain* dyed a very deep red. (From *grain*, the name applied to the dried in- sect used to make the dye.) *French-crown-color* i.e., color of a French crown, a gold coin 72 *crowns* heads bald from syphilis, the "French disease" 74 *con* learn by heart 77 *devices* plans. *draw a bill* draw up a list 79 *obscenely* (An unintentionally funny blunder, whatever Bottom meant to say.) 80 *perfect* i.e., letter-perfect in memorizing your parts 82 *Hold . . . bowstrings* (An archer's expression, not definitely explained, but probably meaning here "keep your prom- ises, or give up the play.")

ACT II

Scene I [A Wood Near Athens.]

Enter a Fairy at one door, and Robin Goodfellow [Puck] at another.

Puck: How now, spirit, whither wander you?
Fairy:

> Over hill, over dale,
> Thorough° bush, thorough brier,
> Over park, over pale,°
> Thorough flood, thorough fire,   5
> I do wander everywhere,
> Swifter than the moon's sphere;°
> And I serve the Fairy Queen,
> To dew° her orbs° upon the green.
> The cowslips tall her pensioners° be.   10
> In their gold coats spots you see;
> Those be rubies, fairy favors;°
> In those freckles live their savors.°

I must go seek some dewdrops here
And hang a pearl in every cowslip's ear.   15
Farewell, thou lob° of spirits; I'll be gone.
Our Queen and all her elves come here anon.°
Puck: The King doth keep his revels here tonight.
Take heed the Queen come not within his sight.
For Oberon is passing fell° and wrath,°   20
Because that she as her attendant hath
A lovely boy, stolen from an Indian king;
She never had so sweet a changeling.°
And jealous Oberon would have the child
Knight of his train, to trace° the forests wild.   25
But she perforce° withholds the lovèd boy,
Crowns him with flowers, and makes him all her joy.
And now they never meet in grove or green,
By fountain° clear, or spangled starlight sheen,°
But they do square,° that all their elves for fear   30
Creep into acorn cups and hide them there.

---

3 *Thorough* through   4 *pale* enclosure   7 *sphere* orbit   9 *dew* sprinkle with dew.   *orbs* circles, i.e., fairy rings (circular bands of grass, darker than the surrounding area, caused by fungi enriching the soil)   10 *pensioners* retainers, members of the royal bodyguard   12 *favors* love tokens   13 *savors* sweet smells   16 *lob* country bumpkin   17 *anon* at once   20 *passing fell* exceedingly angry.   *wrath* wrathful   23 *changeling* child exchanged for another by the fairies   25 *trace* range through   26 *perforce* forcibly   29 *fountain* spring.   *starlight sheen* shining starlight   30 *square* quarrel

Fairy: Either I mistake your shape and making quite,
Or else you are that shrewd° and knavish sprite°
Called Robin Goodfellow. Are not you he
That frights the maidens of the villagery,° 35
Skim milk,° and sometimes labor in the quern,°
And bootless° make the breathless huswife° churn,
And sometimes make the drink to bear no barm,°
Mislead night wanderers,° laughing at their harm?
Those that "Hobgoblin" call you, and "Sweet Puck,"° 40
You do their work, and they shall have good luck.
Are you not he?

Puck: Thou speakest aright;
I am that merry wanderer of the night.
I jest to Oberon and make him smile
When I a fat and bean-fed° horse beguile, 45
Neighing in likeness of a filly foal;
And sometimes lurk I in a gossip's° bowl
In very likeness of a roasted crab,°
And when she drinks, against her lips I bob
And on her withered dewlap° pour the ale. 50
The wisest aunt,° telling the saddest° tale,
Sometimes for three-foot stool mistaketh me;
Then slip I from her bum, down topples she,
And "Tailor"° cries, and falls into a cough;
And then the whole choir° hold their hips and laugh, 55
And waxen° in their mirth, and neeze,° and swear
A merrier hour was never wasted° there.
But, room,° fairy! Here comes Oberon.

Fairy: And here my mistress. Would that he were gone!

Enter [Oberon] the King of Fairies at one door, with his train, and [Titania] the Queen at another, with hers.

Oberon: Ill met by moonlight, proud Titania. 60
Titania: What, jealous Oberon? Fairies, skip hence.
I have forsworn his bed and company.

---

33 *shrewd* mischievous. *sprite* spirit 35 *villagery* village population 36 *Skim milk* i.e., steal the cream. *quern* hand mill (where Puck presumably hampers the grinding of grain) 37 *bootless* in vain (Puck prevents the cream from turning to butter.) *huswife* housewife 38 *barm* head on the ale (Puck prevents the barm or yeast from producing fermentation.) 39 *Mislead night wanderers* i.e., mislead with false fire those who walk abroad at night (hence earning Puck his other names of Jack o' Lantern and Will o' the Wisp) 40 *Those . . . Puck* i.e., those who call you by the names you favor rather than those denoting the mischief you do. 45 *bean-fed* well fed on field beans 47 *gossip's* old woman's 48 *crab* crab apple 50 *dewlap* loose skin on neck 51 *aunt* old woman. *saddest* most serious 54 *Tailor* (possibly because she ends up sitting cross-legged on the floor, looking like a tailor, or else referring to the *tail* or buttocks.) 55 *choir* company 56 *waxen* increase. *neeze* sneeze 57 *wasted* spent 58 *room* stand aside, make room

Oberon: Tarry, rash wanton.° Am not I thy lord?
Titania: Then I must be thy lady; but I know
 When thou hast stolen away from Fairyland   65
 And in the shape of Corin° sat all day,
 Playing on pipes of corn° and versing love
 To amorous Phillida.° Why art thou here
 Come from the farthest step° of India,
 But that, forsooth, the bouncing Amazon,   70
 Your buskined° mistress and your warrior love,
 To Theseus must be wedded, and you come
 To give their bed joy and prosperity.
Oberon: How canst thou thus for shame, Titania,
 Glance at my credit with Hippolyta,°   75
 Knowing I know thy love to Theseus?
 Didst not thou lead him through the glimmering night
 From Perigenia,° whom he ravishèd?
 And make him with fair Aegles° break his faith,
 With Ariadne° and Antiopa?°   80
Titania: These are the forgeries of jealousy;
 And never, since the middle summer's spring,°
 Met we on hill, in dale, forest, or mead,°
 By pavèd° fountain or by rushy° brook,
 Or in° the beachèd margent° of the sea,   85
 To dance our ringlets° to° the whistling wind,
 But with thy brawls thou hast disturbed our sport.
 Therefore the winds, piping to us in vain,
 As in revenge, have sucked up from the sea
 Contagious° fogs which, falling in the land,   90
 Hath every pelting° river made so proud
 That they have overborne their continents.°
 The ox hath therefore stretched his yoke° in vain,

---

63 *wanton* headstrong creature   66, 68 *Corin, Phillida* (Conventional names of pastoral lovers.)   67 *corn* (Here, oat stalks.)   69 *step* farthest limit of travel, or, perhaps, *steep,* "mountain range"   71 *buskined* wearing half-boots called buskins   75 *Glance . . . Hippolyta* make insinuations about my favored relationship with Hippolyta   78 *Perigenia* i.e., Perigouna, one of Theseus's conquests. (This and the following women are named in Thomas North's translation of Plutarch's "Life of Theseus.")   79 *Aegles* i.e., Aegle, for whom Theseus deserted Ariadne according to some accounts   80 *Ariadne* the daughter of Minos, King of Crete, who helped Theseus to escape the labyrinth after killing the Minotaur; later she was abandoned by Theseus. *Antiopa* Queen of the Amazons and wife of Theseus; elsewhere identified with Hippolyta, but here thought of as a separate woman   82 *middle summer's spring* beginning of midsummer   83 *mead* meadow   84 *pavèd* with pebbled bottom. *rushy* bordered with rushes   85 *in* on. *margent* edge, border   86 *ringlets* dances in a ring. (See *orbs* in line 9.)   *to* to the sound of   90 *Contagious* noxious   91 *pelting* paltry   92 *continents* banks that contain them   93 *stretched his yoke* i.e., pulled at his yoke in plowing

The plowman lost his sweat, and the green corn°
Hath rotted ere his youth attained a beard;   95
The fold° stands empty in the drownèd field,
And crows are fatted with the murrain° flock;
The nine-men's morris° is filled up with mud,
And the quaint mazes° in the wanton° green
For lack of tread are undistinguishable.   100
The human mortals want° their winter° here;
No night is now with hymn or carol blessed.
Therefore° the moon, the governess of floods,
Pale in her anger, washes° all the air,
That rheumatic diseases° do abound.   105
And thorough this distemperature° we see
The seasons alter: hoary-headed frosts
Fall in the fresh lap of the crimson rose,
And on old Hiems'° thin and icy crown
An odorous chaplet of sweet summer buds   110
Is, as in mockery, set. The spring, the summer,
The childing° autumn, angry winter, change
Their wonted liveries,° and the mazèd° world
By their increase° now knows not which is which.
And this same progeny of evils comes   115
From our debate,° from our dissension.
We are their parents and original.°
Oberon: Do you amend it, then. It lies in you.
        Why should Titania cross her Oberon?
        I do but beg a little changeling boy   120
        To be my henchman.°
Titania: Set your heart at rest.
        The fairy land buys not the child of me.
        His mother was a vot'ress of my order,°
        And in the spicèd Indian air by night
        Full often hath she gossiped by my side   125
        And sat with me on Neptune's yellow sands,

94 corn grain of any kind   96 fold pen for sheep or cattle   97 murrain having died of the
plague   98 nine-men's morris i.e., portion of the village green marked out in a square for a game
played with nine pebbles or pegs   99 quaint mazes i.e., intricate paths marked out on the village green to be followed rapidly on foot as a kind of contest.   wanton luxuriant   101 want
lack.   winter i.e., regular winter season; or, proper observances of winter, such as the hymn or
carol in the next line (?)   103 Therefore i.e., as a result of our quarrel   104 washes saturates
with moisture   105 rheumatic diseases colds, flu, and other respiratory infections   106 distem-
perature disturbance in nature   109 Hiems' the winter god's   112 childing fruitful, pregnant
113 wonted liveries usual apparel.   mazèd bewildered   114 their increase their yield, what they
produce   116 debate quarrel   117 original origin   121 henchman attendant, page   123 was . . .
order had taken a vow to serve me

Marking th' embarkèd traders° on the flood,°
When we have laughed to see the sails conceive
And grow big-bellied with the wanton° wind;
Which she, with pretty and with swimming° gait,   130
Following—her womb then rich with my young squire—
Would imitate, and sail upon the land
To fetch me trifles, and return again
As from a voyage, rich with merchandise.
But she, being mortal, of that boy did die;   135
And for her sake do I rear up her boy,
And for her sake I will not part with him.
Oberon: How long within this wood intend you stay?
Titania: Perchance till after Theseus' wedding day.
   If you will patiently dance in our round°   140
   And see our moonlight revels, go with us;
   If not, shun me, and I will spare° your haunts.
Oberon: Give me that boy, and I will go with thee.
Titania: Not for thy fairy kingdom. Fairies, away!
   We shall chide downright, if I longer stay.   145

                               Exeunt [Titania with her train].

Oberon: Well, go thy way. Thou shalt not from° this grove
   Till I torment thee for this injury.
   My gentle Puck, come hither. Thou rememb'rest
   Since° once I sat upon a promontory,
   And heard a mermaid on a dolphin's back   150
   Uttering such dulcet° and harmonious breath°
   That the rude° sea grew civil at her song,
   And certain stars shot madly from their spheres
   To hear the sea-maid's music?
Puck: I remember.
Oberon: That very time I saw, but thou couldst not,   155
   Flying between the cold moon and the earth
   Cupid, all° armed. A certain° aim he took
   At a fair vestal° thronèd by° the west,
   And loosed° his love shaft smartly from his bow
   As° it should pierce a hundred thousand hearts;   160
   But I might° see young Cupid's fiery shaft
   Quenched in the chaste beams of the watery moon,

127 *traders* trading vessels.   *flood* flood tide   129 *wanton* (1) playful (2) amorous   130 *swimming* smooth, gliding   140 *round* circular dance   142 *spare* shun   146 *from* go from   149 *Since* when   151 *dulcet* sweet.   *breath* voice, song   152 *rude* rough   157 *all* fully.   *certain* sure   158 *vestal* vestal virgin. (Contains a complimentary allusion to Queen Elizabeth as a votaress of Diana and probably refers to an actual entertainment in her honor at Elvetham in 1591.)   *by* in the region of   159 *loosed* released   160 *As* as if   161 *might* could

And the imperial vot'ress passèd on,
In maiden meditation, fancy-free.°
Yet marked I where the bolt° of Cupid fell: 165
It fell upon a little western flower,
Before milk-white, now purple with love's wound,
And maidens call it love-in-idleness.°
Fetch me that flower; the herb I showed thee once.
The juice of it on sleeping eyelids laid   170
Will make or man or° woman madly dote
Upon the next live creature that it sees.
Fetch me this herb, and be thou here again
Ere the leviathan° can swim a league.

Puck: I'll put a girdle round about the earth   175
    In forty° minutes.   [*Exit.*]

Oberon: Having once this juice,
    I'll watch Titania when she is asleep
    And drop the liquor of it in her eyes.
    The next thing then she waking looks upon,
    Be it on lion, bear, or wolf, or bull,   180
    On meddling monkey, or on busy ape,
    She shall pursue it with the soul of love.
    And ere I take this charm from off her sight,
    As I can take it with another herb,
    I'll make her render up her page to me.   185
    But who comes here? I am invisible,
    And I will overhear their conference.

Enter Demetrius, Helena following him.

Demetrius: I love thee not; therefore pursue me not.
    Where is Lysander and fair Hermia?
    The one I'll slay; the other slayeth me.   190
    Thou toldst me they were stol'n unto this wood;
    And here am I, and wood° within this wood
    Because I cannot meet my Hermia.
    Hence, get thee gone, and follow me no more.

Helena: You draw me, you hardhearted adamant!°   195
    But yet you draw not iron, for my heart
    Is true as steel. Leave you° your power to draw,
    And I shall have no power to follow you.

164 *fancy-free* free of love's spell 165 *bolt* arrow 168 *love-in-idleness* pansy, heartsease 171
or . . . or either . . . or 174 *leviathan* sea monster, whale 176 *forty* (Used indefinitely.) 192
and wood and mad, frantic (with an obvious word play on *wood*, meaning "woods") 195
adamant lodestone, magnet (with pun on *hardhearted*, since adamant was also thought to be the
hardest of all stones and was confused with the diamond) 197 *Leave you* give up

Demetrius: Do I entice you? Do I speak you fair?°
    Or rather do I not in plainest truth   200
    Tell you I do not nor I cannot love you?
Helena: And even for that do I love you the more.
    I am your spaniel; and, Demetrius,
    The more you beat me I will fawn on you.
    Use me but as your spaniel, spurn me, strike me,   205
    Neglect me, lose me; only give me leave,
    Unworthy as I am, to follow you.
    What worser place can I beg in your love—
    And yet a place of high respect with me—
    Than to be usèd as you use your dog?   210
Demetrius: Tempt not too much the hatred of my spirit,
    For I am sick when I do look on thee.
Helena: And I am sick when I look not on you.
Demetrius: You do impeach° your modesty too much
    To leave° the city and commit yourself   215
    Into the hands of one that loves you not,
    To trust the opportunity of night
    And the ill counsel of a desert° place
    With the rich worth of your virginity.
Helena: Your virtue° is my privilege.° For that°   220
    It is not night when I do see your face,
    Therefore I think I am not in the night;
    Nor doth this wood lack worlds of company,
    For you, in my respect,° are all the world.
    Then how can it be said I am alone   225
    When all the world is here to look on me?
Demetrius: I'll run from thee and hide me in the brakes,°
    And leave thee to the mercy of wild beasts.
Helena: The wildest hath not such a heart as you.
    Run when you will. The story shall be changed: 230
    Apollo flies and Daphne holds the chase,°
    The dove pursues the griffin,° the mild hind°
    Makes speed to catch the tiger—bootless° speed,
    When cowardice pursues and valor flies!
Demetrius: I will not stay° thy questions.° Let me go!   235

199 *speak you fair* speak courteously to you   214 *impeach* call into question   215 *To leave* by leaving   218 *desert* deserted   220 *virtue* goodness or power to attract. *privilege* safeguard, warrant. *For that* because   224 *in my respect* as far as I am concerned, in my esteem   227 *brakes* thickets   231 *Apollo . . . chase* (In the ancient myth, Daphne fled from Apollo and was saved from rape by being transformed into a laurel tree; here it is the female who *holds the chase*, or pursues, instead of the male.)   232 *griffin* a fabulous monster with the head and wings of an eagle and the body of a lion. *hind* female deer   233 *bootless* fruitless   235 *stay* wait for, put up with. *questions* talk or argument

Or if thou follow me, do not believe
But I shall do thee mischief in the wood.
Helena: Ay, in the temple, in the town, the field,
You do me mischief. Fie, Demetrius!
Your wrongs do set a scandal on my sex.°   240
We cannot fight for love, as men may do;
We should be wooed and were not made to woo.

                                                                    [*Exit Demetrius.*]

I'll follow thee and make a heaven of hell,
To die upon° the hand I love so well.   [*Exit.*]
Oberon: Fare thee well, nymph. Ere he do leave this grove.   245
Thou shalt fly him, and he shall seek thy love.

Enter Puck.

Hast thou the flower there? Welcome, wanderer.
Puck: Ay, there it is.   [*He offers the flower.*]
Oberon: I pray thee, give it me.
I know a bank where the wild thyme blows,°
Where oxlips° and the nodding violet grows,   250
Quite overcanopied with luscious woodbine,°
With sweet muskroses° and with eglantine.°
There sleeps Titania sometimes of° the night,
Lulled in these flowers with dances and delight;
And there the snake throws° her enameled skin,   255
Weed° wide enough to wrap a fairy in.
And with the juice of this I'll streak° her eyes
And make her full of hateful fantasies.
Take thou some of it, and seek through this grove.

                                                            [*He gives some love juice.*]
A sweet Athenian lady is in love   260
With a disdainful youth. Anoint his eyes,
But do it when the next thing he espies
May be the lady. Thou shalt know the man
By the Athenian garments he hath on.
Effect it with some care, that he may prove   265
More fond on° her than she upon her love;
And look thou meet me ere the first cock crow.
Puck: Fear not, my lord, your servant shall do so.

                                                            Exeunt [*separately*].

240 *Your . . . sex* i.e., the wrongs that you do me cause me to act in a manner that disgraces my
sex   244 *upon* by   249 *blows* blooms   250 *oxlips* flowers resembling cowslip and primrose
251   *woodbine* honeysuckle   252 *muskroses* a kind of large, sweet-scented rose. *eglantine*
sweetbrier, another kind of rose   253 *sometimes of* for part of   255 *throws* sloughs off, sheds
256 *Weed* garment   257 *streak* anoint, touch gently   266 *fond on* doting on

Scene II [The Wood.]

Enter Titania, Queen of Fairies, with her train.

Titania: Come, now a roundel° and a fairy song;
　　Then, for the third part of a minute,° hence—
　　Some to kill cankers° in the muskrose buds,
　　Some war with reremice° for their leathern wings
　　To make my small elves coats, and some keep back　　　　　5
　　The clamorous owl, that nightly hoots and wonders
　　At our quaint° spirits. Sing me now asleep.
　　Then to your offices, and let me rest.

Fairies sing.

First Fairy:　　You spotted snakes with double° tongue,
　　　　Thorny hedgehogs, be not seen;　　　　　　　　　　10
　　　　Newts° and blindworms, do no wrong;
　　　　Come not near our Fairy Queen.
Chorus [dancing]:　　Philomel,° with melody
　　　　Sing in our sweet lullaby;
　　　　Lulla, lulla, lullaby, lulla, lulla, lullaby.　　　　　　15
　　　　Never harm
　　　　Nor spell nor charm
　　　　Come our lovely lady nigh.
　　　　So good night, with lullaby.
First Fairy:　　Weaving spiders, come not here;　　　　　　　20
　　　　Hence, you long-legged spinners, hence!
　　　　Beetles black, approach not near;
　　　　Worm nor snail, do no offense.°
Chorus [dancing.]:　　Philomel, with melody
　　　　Sing in our sweet lullaby;　　　　　　　　　　　　25
　　　　Lulla, lulla, lullaby, lulla, lulla, lullaby.
　　　　Never harm
　　　　Nor spell nor charm
　　　　Come our lovely lady nigh.
　　　　So good night, with lullaby.　　　　　　　　　　　30

　　　　　　　　　　　　　　　　　　　　[Titania sleeps.]

Second Fairy: Hence, away! Now all is well.
　　One aloof stand sentinel.°

1 *roundel* dance in a ring　2 *the third . . . minute* (Indicative of the fairies' quickness.)　3 *cankers* cankerworms (i.e., caterpillars or grubs)　4 *reremice* bats　7 *quaint* dainty　9 *double* forked　11 *Newts* water lizards (considered poisonous, as were *blindworms*—small snakes with tiny eyes—and spiders)　13 *Philomel* the nightingale. (Philomela, daughter of King Pandion, was transformed into a nightingale, according to Ovid's *Metamorphoses* 6, after she had been raped by her sister Procne's husband, Tereus.)　23 *offense* harm　32 *sentinel* (Presumably Oberon is able to outwit or intimidate this guard.)

[Exeunt Fairies, leaving one sentinel.]

Enter Oberon [and squeezes the flower on Titania's eyelids].

Oberon: What thou seest when thou dost wake,
            Do it for thy true love take;
            Love and languish for his sake.   35
            Be it ounce,° or cat, or bear,
            Pard,° or boar with bristled hair,
            In thy eye that shall appear
            When thou wak'st, it is thy dear.
            Wake when some vile thing is near.   *[Exit.]*   40

        Enter Lysander and Hermia.

Lysander: Fair love, you faint with wandering in the wood;
           And to speak truth, I have forgot our way.
           We'll rest us, Hermia, if you think it good,
           And tarry for the comfort of the day.
Hermia: Be it so, Lysander. Find you out a bed,   45
           For I upon this bank will rest my head.
Lysander: One turf shall serve as pillow for us both;
           One heart, one bed, two bosoms, and one troth.°
Hermia: Nay, good Lysander, for my sake, my dear,
           Lie further off yet. Do not lie so near.   50
Lysander: O, take the sense, sweet, of my innocence!°
           Love takes the meaning in love's conference.°
           I mean that my heart unto yours is knit,
           So that but one heart we can make of it;
           Two bosoms interchainèd with an oath—   55
           So then two bosoms and a single troth.
           Then by your side no bed-room me deny,
           For lying so, Hermia, I do not lie.°
Hermia: Lysander riddles very prettily.
           Now much beshrew° my manners and my pride   60
           If Hermia meant to say Lysander lied.
           But, gentle friend, for love and courtesy
           Lie further off, in human° modesty.
           Such separation as may well be said
           Becomes a virtuous bachelor and a maid,   65
           So far be distant; and good night, sweet friend.
           Thy love ne'er alter till thy sweet life end!

36 *ounce* lynx   37 *Pard* leopard   48 *troth* faith, trothplight   51 *take . . . innocence* i.e., interpret my intention as innocent   52 *Love . . . conference* i.e., when lovers confer, love teaches
each lover to interpret the other's meaning lovingly   58 *lie* tell a falsehood (with a riddling
pun on *lie*, "recline")   60 *beshrew* curse. (But mildly meant.)   63 *human* courteous (and perhaps suggesting "humane," the Quarto spelling)

Lysander: Amen, amen, to that fair prayer, say I,
    And then end life when I end loyalty!
    Here is my bed. Sleep give thee all his rest!   70
Hermia: With half that wish the wisher's eyes be pressed!°

                                    [*They sleep, separated by a short distance.*]

    Enter Puck:

Puck: Through the forest have I gone,
                But Athenian found I none
                On whose eyes I might approve°
                This flower's force in stirring love.   75
                Night and silence.—Who is here?
                Weeds of Athens he doth wear.
                This is he, my master said,
                Despisèd the Athenian maid;
                And here the maiden, sleeping sound,   80
                On the dank and dirty ground.
                Pretty soul, she durst not lie
                Near this lack-love, this kill-courtesy.
                Churl, upon thy eyes I throw
                All the power this charm doth owe.°   85

                                    [*He applies the love juice.*]

                When thou wak'st, let love forbid
                Sleep his seat on thy eyelid.
                So awake when I am gone,
                For I must now to Oberon.   *Exit.*

    Enter Demetrius and Helena, running.

Helena: Stay, though thou kill me, sweet Demetrius!   90
Demetrius: I charge thee, hence, and do not haunt me thus.
Helena: O, wilt thou darkling° leave me? Do not so.
Demetrius: Stay, on thy peril!° I alone will go.   [*Exit.*]
Helena: O, I am out of breath in this fond° chase!
    The more my prayer, the lesser is my grace.°   95
    Happy is Hermia, wheresoe'er she lies,°
    For she hath blessèd and attractive eyes.
    How came her eyes so bright? Not with salt tears;
    If so, my eyes are oftener washed than hers.

71 *With . . . pressed* i.e., may we share your wish, so that your eyes too are *pressed,* closed, in sleep   74 *approve* test   85 *owe* own   92 *darkling* in the dark   93 *on thy peril* i.e., on pain of danger to you if you don't obey me and stay   94 *fond* doting   95 *my grace* the favor I obtain   96 *lies* dwells

No, no, I am as ugly as a bear,   100
For beasts that meet me run away for fear.
Therefore no marvel though Demetrius
Do, as a monster, fly my presence thus.°
What wicked and dissembling glass of mine
Made me compare° with Hermia's sphery eyne?°   105
But who is here? Lysander, on the ground?
Dead, or asleep? I see no blood, no wound.
Lysander, if you live, good sir, awake.

Lysander [*awaking*]: And run through fire I will for thy sweet sake.
Transparent° Helena! Nature shows art,°   110
That through thy bosom makes me see thy heart.
Where is Demetrius? O, how fit a word
Is that vile name to perish on my sword!

Helena: Do not say so, Lysander, say not so.
What though he love your Hermia? Lord, what though?   115
Yet Hermia still loves you. Then be content.

Lysander: Content with Hermia? No! I do repent
The tedious minutes I with her have spent.
Not Hermia but Helena I love.
Who will not change a raven for a dove?   120
The will° of man is by his reason swayed,
And reason says you are the worthier maid.
Things growing are not ripe until their season;
So I, being young, till now ripe not° to reason.
And, touching° now the point° of human skill,°   125
Reason becomes the marshal to my will
And leads me to your eyes, where I o'erlook°
Love's stories written in love's richest book.

Helena: Wherefore° was I to this keen mockery born?
When at your hands did I deserve this scorn?   130
Is 't not enough, is 't not enough, young man,
That I did never—no, nor never can—
Deserve a sweet look from Demetrius' eye,
But you must flout my insufficiency?
Good troth, you do me wrong, good sooth,° you do,   135
In such disdainful manner me to woo.
But fare you well. Perforce I must confess
I thought you lord of° more true gentleness.°

102–103 *no marvel . . . thus* i.e., no wonder that Demetrius flies from me as from a monster
105 *compare* vie. *sphery eyne* eyes as bright as stars in their spheres   110 *Transparent* (1) radiant
(2) able to be seen through, lacking in deceit.   *art* skill, magic power   121 *will* desire   124
ripe not (am) not ripened   125 *touching* reaching.   *point* summit.   *skill* judgment   127
o'erlook read   129 *Wherefore* why   135 *Good troth, good sooth* i.e., indeed, truly   138 *lord of*
i.e., possessor of.   *gentleness* courtesy

O, that a lady, of° one man refused,
Should of another therefore be abused!°   *Exit.* 140
Lysander: She sees not Hermia. Hermia, sleep thou there,
          And never mayst thou come Lysander near!
          For as a surfeit of the sweetest things
          The deepest loathing to the stomach brings,
          Or as the heresies that men do leave   145
          Are hated most of those they did deceive,°
          So thou, my surfeit and my heresy,
          Of all be hated, but the most of° me!
          And, all my powers, address° your love and might
          To honor Helen and to be her knight!   *Exit.* 150
Hermia [*awaking*]: Help me, Lysander, help me! Do thy best
          To pluck this crawling serpent from my breast!
          Ay me, for pity! What a dream was here!
          Lysander, look how I do quake with fear.
          Methought a serpent ate my heart away,   155
          And you sat smiling at his cruel prey.°
          Lysander! What, removed? Lysander! Lord!
          What, out of hearing? Gone? No sound, no word?
          Alack, where are you? Speak, an if° you hear;
          Speak, of all loves!° I swoon almost with fear.   160
          No? Then I well perceive you are not nigh.
          Either death, or you, I'll find immediately.

          Exit. [The sleeping Titania remains.]

ACT III

Scene I [The Action Is Continuous.]

Enter the clowns° [Quince, Snug, Bottom, Flute, Snout, and Starveling].

Bottom: Are we all met?
Quince: Pat,° pat; and here's a marvelous convenient place for our rehearsal.
          This green plot shall be our stage, this hawthorn brake° our tiring-house,°
          and we will do it in action as we will do it before the Duke.
Bottom: Peter Quince?   5
Quince: What sayest thou, bully° Bottom?

---

139 *of* by   140 *abused* ill treated   145–146 *as . . . deceive* as renounced heresies are hated most
by those persons who formerly were deceived by them   148 *Of . . . of* by . . . by   149 *address*
direct, apply   156 *prey* act of preying   159 *an if* if   160 *of all loves* for all love's sake   s.d.
clowns rustics   2 *Pat* on the dot, punctually   3 *brake* thicket. *tiring-house* attiring area, hence
backstage   6 *bully* i.e., worthy, jolly, fine fellow

Bottom: There are things in this comedy of Pyramus and Thisbe that will never please. First, Pyramus must draw a sword to kill himself, which the ladies cannot abide. How answer you that?

Snout: By 'r lakin,° a parlous° fear.

Starveling: I believe we must leave the killing out, when all is done.°

Bottom: Not a whit. I have a device to make all well. Write me° a prologue, and let the prologue seem to say, we will do no harm with our swords, and that Pyramus is not killed indeed; and for the more better assurance, tell them that I, Pyramus, am not Pyramus but Bottom the weaver. This will put them out of fear.

Quince: Well, we will have such a prologue, and it shall be written in eight and six.°

Bottom: No, make it two more: let it be written in eight and eight.

Snout: Will not the ladies be afeard of the lion?

Starveling: I fear it, I promise you.

Bottom: Masters, you ought to consider with yourself, to bring in—God shield us!—a lion among ladies° is a most dreadful thing. For there is not a more fearful° wildfowl than your lion living, and we ought to look to 't.

Snout: Therefore another prologue must tell he is not a lion.

Bottom: Nay, you must name his name, and half his face must be seen through the lion's neck, and he himself must speak through, saying thus or to the same defect:° "Ladies," or "Fair ladies, I would wish you," or "I would request you," or "I would entreat you, not to fear, not to tremble; my life for yours.° If you think I come hither as a lion, it were pity of my life.° No, I am no such thing; I am a man as other men are." And there indeed let him name his name, and tell them plainly he is Snug the joiner.

Quince: Well, it shall be so. But there is two hard things: that is, to bring the moonlight into a chamber; for, you know, Pyramus and Thisbe meet by moonlight.

Snout: Doth the moon shine that night we play our play?

Bottom: A calendar, a calendar! Look in the almanac. Find out moonshine, find out moonshine.

[They consult an almanac.]

Quince: Yes, it doth shine that night.

Bottom: Why then may you leave a casement of the great chamber window where we play open, and the moon may shine in at the casement.

10
15
20
25
30
35
40

10 *By 'r lakin* by our ladykin, i.e., the Virgin Mary. *parlous* perilous, alarming   11 *when all is done* i.e., when all is said and done   12 *Write me* i.e., write at my suggestion (Me is used colloquially.)   17–18 *eight and six* alternate lines of eight and six syllables, a common ballad measure   23 *lion among ladies* (A contemporary pamphlet tells how, at the christening in 1594 of Prince Henry, eldest son of King James VI of Scotland, later James I of England, a "blackamoor" instead of a lion drew the triumphal chariot, since the lion's presence might have "brought some fear to the nearest.")   24 *fearful* fear-inspiring   28 *defect* (Bottom's blunder for "effect.")   29 *my life for yours* i.e., I pledge my life to make your lives safe   30 *it were . . . life* i.e., I should be sorry, by my life; or, my life would be endangered

Quince: Ay; or else one must come in with a bush of thorns° and a lantern and say he comes to disfigure,° or to present,° the person of Moonshine. Then there is another thing: we must have a wall in the great chamber; for Pyramus and Thisbe, says the story, did talk through the chink of a wall.   45

Snout: You can never bring in a wall. What say you, Bottom?

Bottom: Some man or other must present Wall. And let him have some plaster, or some loam, or some roughcast° about him, to signify wall; or let him hold his fingers thus, and through that cranny shall Pyramus and Thisbe whisper.   50

Quince: If that may be, then all is well. Come, sit down, every mother's son, and rehearse your parts. Pyramus, you begin. When you have spoken your speech, enter into that brake, and so everyone according to his cue.

Enter Robin [Puck].

Puck [aside]: What hempen homespuns° have we swaggering here
So near the cradle° of the Fairy Queen?   55
What, a play toward?° I'll be an auditor;
An actor, too, perhaps, if I see cause.

Quince: Speak, Pyramus. Thisbe, stand forth.

Bottom [as Pyramus]: "Thisbe, the flowers of odious savors sweet—"

Quince: Odors, odors.   60

Bottom: "—Odors savors sweet;
So hath thy breath, my dearest Thisbe dear.
But hark, a voice! Stay thou but here awhile,
And by and by I will to thee appear."   *Exit.*

Puck: A stranger Pyramus than e'er played here.°   *[Exit.]*   65

Flute: Must I speak now?

Quince: Ay, marry, must you; for you must understand he goes but to see a noise that he heard, and is to come again.

Flute [as Thisbe]: "Most radiant Pyramus, most lily-white of hue,
Of color like the red rose on triumphant° brier,   70
Most brisky juvenal° and eke° most lovely Jew,°
As true as truest horse that yet would never tire.
I'll meet thee, Pyramus, at Ninny's tomb."

---

42 *bush of thorns* bundle of thornbush faggots (part of the accoutrements of the man in the moon, according to the popular notions of the time, along with his lantern and his dog)   43 *disfigure* (Quince's blunder for "figure.")   *present* represent   48 *roughcast* a mixture of lime and gravel used to plaster the outside of buildings   54 *hempen homespuns* i.e., rustics dressed in clothes woven of coarse, homespun fabric made from hemp   55 *cradle* i.e., Titania's bower   56 *toward* about to take place   65 *A stranger . . . here* (Either Puck refers to an earlier dramatic version played in the same theater, or he has conceived of a plan to present a "stranger" Pyramus than ever seen before.)   70 *triumphant* magnificent   71 *brisky juvenal* lively youth. *eke* also.   *Jew* (An absurd repetition of the first syllable of *juvenal*, and an indication of how desperately Quince searches for his rhymes.)

Quince: "Ninus'° tomb," man. Why, you must not speak that yet. That you an-   75
swer to Pyramus: You speak all your part° at once, cues and all. Pyramus,
enter. Your cue is past; it is "never tire."

Flute: O—"As true as truest horse, that yet would never tire."

[*Enter Puck, and Bottom as Pyramus with the ass head.°*]

Bottom: "If I were fair,° Thisbe, I were° only thine."

Quince: O, monstrous! O, strange! We are haunted. Pray, masters! Fly, masters!
Help!   80

               [*Exeunt Quince, Snug, Flute, Snout, and Starveling.*]

Puck: I'll follow you, I'll lead you about a round,°
Thorough bog, thorough bush, thorough brake, thorough brier.
Sometimes a horse I'll be, sometimes a hound,
A hog, a headless bear, sometimes a fire;°
And neigh, and bark, and grunt, and roar, and burn,   85
Like horse, hound, hog, bear, fire, at every turn.   *Exit.*

Bottom: Why do they run away? This is a knavery of them to make me afeard.

Enter Snout.

Snout: O Bottom, thou art changed! What do I see on thee?

Bottom: What do you see? You see an ass head of your own, do you?
               [*Exit Snout.*]

Enter Quince.

Quince: Bless thee, Bottom, bless thee! Thou art translated.°   *Exit.*   90

Bottom: I see their knavery. This is to make an ass of me, to fright me, if they
could. But I will not stir from this place, do what they can. I will walk up
and down here, and will sing, that they shall hear I am not afraid.
               [*He sings.*]

    The ouzel cock° so black of hue,
        With orange-tawny bill,   95
    The throstle° with his note so true,
        The wren with little quill°—

Titania [*awaking*]: What angel wakes me from my flowery bed?

74 *Ninus* mythical founder of Nineveh (whose wife, Semiramis, was supposed to have built the
walls of Babylon where the story of Pyramus and Thisbe takes place)   75 *part* (An actor's *part*
was a script consisting only of his speeches and their cues.)   s.d. *with the ass head* (This stage
direction, taken from the Folio, presumably refers to a standard stage property.)   78 *fair* handsome.   *were* would be   81 *about a round* roundabout   84 *fire* will-o'-the-wisp   90 *translated*
transformed   94 *ouzel cock* male blackbird   96 *throstle* song thrush   97 *quill* (Literally, a reed
pipe; hence, the bird's piping song.)

Bottom [sings]:
<blockquote>
The finch, the sparrow, and the lark,
    The plainsong° cuckoo gray,   100
Whose note full many a man doth mark,
    And dares not answer nay°—
</blockquote>
For, indeed, who would set his wit to° so foolish a bird? Who would give a
bird the lie,° though he cry "cuckoo" never so?°

Titania: I pray thee, gentle mortal, sing again.   105
Mine ear is much enamored of thy note;
So is mine eye enthrallèd to thy shape;
And thy fair virtue's force° perforce doth move me
On the first view to say, to swear, I love thee.

Bottom: Methinks, mistress, you should have little reason for that. And yet, to 110
say the truth, reason and love keep little company together nowadays—the
more the pity that some honest neighbors will not make them friends. Nay,
I can gleek° upon occasion.

Titania: Thou art as wise as thou art beautiful.

Bottom: Not so, neither. But if I had wit enough to get out of this wood, I have 115
enough to serve mine own turn.°

Titania: Out of this wood do not desire to go.
Thou shalt remain here, whether thou wilt or no.
I am a spirit of no common rate.°
The summer still doth tend upon my state,°   120
And I do love thee. Therefore go with me.
I'll give thee fairies to attend on thee,
And they shall fetch thee jewels from the deep,
And sing while thou on pressèd flowers dost sleep,
And I will purge thy mortal grossness° so   125
That thou shalt like an airy spirit go.
Peaseblossom, Cobweb, Mote,° and Mustardseed!

Enter four Fairies [Peaseblossom, Cobweb, Mote, and Mustardseed].

Peaseblossom: Ready.
Cobweb: And I.
Mote: And I.
Mustardseed: And I.
All: Where shall we go?

---

100 *plainsong* singing a melody without variations   102 *dares . . . nay* i.e., cannot deny that he
is a cuckold   103 *set his wit to* employ his intelligence to answer   103–104 *give . . . lie* call the
bird a liar.   *never so* ever so much   108 *thy . . . force* the power of your unblemished excellence   113 *gleek* jest   116 *serve . . . turn* answer my purpose   119 *rate* rank, value   120 *still
. . . state* always waits upon me as a part of my royal retinue   125 *mortal grossness* materiality
(i.e., the corporeal nature of a mortal being)   127 *Mote* i.e., speck. (The two words *moth* and
mote were pronounced alike, and both meanings may be present.)

Kevin Kline as Bottom and Michelle Pfeiffer as Titania in a 1999 film adaptation of A Midsummer Night's Dream.

Titania: Be kind and courteous to this gentleman.   130
      Hop in his walks and gambol in his eyes;°
      Feed him with apricots and dewberries,°
      With purple grapes, green figs, and mulberries;
      The honey bags steal from the humble-bees,
      And for night tapers crop their waxen thighs   135
      And light them at the fiery glowworms' eyes,
      To have my love to bed and to arise;
      And pluck the wings from painted butterflies
      To fan the moonbeams from his sleeping eyes.
      Nod to him, elves, and do him courtesies.   140

Peaseblossom: Hail, mortal!

Cobweb: Hail!

Mote: Hail!

Mustardseed: Hail!

Bottom: I cry your worships mercy,° heartily. I beseech your worship's name.   145

Cobweb: Cobweb.

Bottom: I shall desire you of more acquaintance,° good Master Cobweb. If I cut
      my finger, I shall make bold with you.°—Your name, honest gentleman?

131 *in his eyes* in his sight (i.e., before him)   132 *dewberries* blackberries   145 *I cry . . . mercy* I beg pardon of your worships (for presuming to ask a question)   147 *I . . . acquaintance* I crave to be better acquainted with you   147–148 *If . . . you* (Cobwebs were used to stanch bleeding.)

Peaseblossom: Peaseblossom.

Bottom: I pray you, commend me to Mistress Squash,° your mother, and to   150
   Master Peascod,° your father. Good Master Peaseblossom, I shall desire you
   of more acquaintance too.—Your name, I beseech you, sir?

Mustardseed: Mustardseed.

Bottom: Good Master Mustardseed, I know your patience° well. That same cowardly, giantlike ox-beef hath devoured many a gentleman of your house. I   155
   promise you, your kindred hath made my eyes water° ere now. I desire you of
   more acquaintance, good Master Mustardseed.

Titania: Come wait upon him; lead him to my bower.
   The moon methinks looks with a watery eye;
   And when she weeps,° weeps every little flower,   160
   Lamenting some enforcèd° chastity.
   Tie up my lover's tongue,° bring him silently.

                                                              [*Exeunt.*]

Scene II [The Wood.]

   Enter [Oberon,] King of Fairies.

Oberon: I wonder if Titania be awaked;
   Then, what it was that next came in her eye,
   Which she must dote on in extremity.

   [*Enter*] *Robin Goodfellow* [*Puck*].

   Here comes my messenger. How now, mad spirit?
   What night-rule° now about this haunted° grove?   5
Puck: My mistress with a monster is in love.
   Near to her close° and consecrated bower,
   While she was in her dull° and sleeping hour,
   A crew of patches,° rude mechanicals,°
   That work for bread upon Athenian stalls,°   10
   Were met together to rehearse a play
   Intended for great Theseus' nuptial day.
   The shallowest thickskin of that barren sort,°
   Who Pyramus presented,° in their sport
   Forsook his scene° and entered in a brake.   15
   When I did him at this advantage take,

150 *Squash* unripe pea pod   151 *Peascod* ripe pea pod   154 *your patience* what you have endured. (Mustard is eaten with beef.)   156 *water* (1) weep for sympathy (2) smart, sting   160
she weeps i.e., she causes dew   161 *enforcèd* forced, violated; or, possibly, constrained (since Titania at this moment is hardly concerned about chastity)   162 *Tie . . . tongue* (Presumably
Bottom is braying like an ass.)   5 *night-rule* diversion or misrule for the night.   *haunted* much
frequented   7 *close* secret, private   8 *dull* drowsy   9 *patches* clowns, fools.   *rude mechanicals*
ignorant artisans   10 *stalls* market booths   13 *barren sort* stupid company or crew   14
presented acted   15 *scene* playing area

An ass's noll° I fixèd on his head.
Anon his Thisbe must be answerèd,
And forth my mimic° comes. When they him spy,
As wild geese that the creeping fowler° eye,   20
Or russet-pated choughs,° many in sort,°
Rising and cawing at the gun's report,
Sever° themselves and madly sweep the sky,
So, at his sight, away his fellows fly;
And, at our stamp, here o'er and o'er one falls;   25
He "Murder!" cries and help from Athens calls.
Their sense thus weak, lost with their fears thus strong,
Made senseless things begin to do them wrong,
For briers and thorns at their apparel snatch;
Some, sleeves—some, hats; from yielders all things catch.°   30
I led them on in this distracted fear
And left sweet Pyramus translated there,
When in that moment, so it came to pass,
Titania waked and straightway loved an ass.
Oberon: This falls out better than I could devise.   35
    But hast thou yet latchèd° the Athenian's eyes
    With the love juice, as I did bid thee do?
Puck: I took him sleeping—that is finished too—
    And the Athenian woman by his side,
    That, when he waked, of force° she must be eyed.   40

    Enter Demetrius and Hermia.

Oberon: Stand close. This is the same Athenian.
Puck: This is the woman, but not this the man.

                                    [They stand aside.]

Demetrius: O, why rebuke you him that loves you so?
    Lay breath so bitter on your bitter foe.
Hermia: Now I but chide; but I should use thee worse,   45
    For thou, I fear, hast given me cause to curse.
    If thou hast slain Lysander in his sleep,
    Being o'er shoes° in blood, plunge in the deep,
    And kill me too.
    The sun was not so true unto the day   50
    As he to me. Would he have stolen away
    From sleeping Hermia? I'll believe as soon
    This whole° earth may be bored, and that the moon

17 *noll* noddle, head   19 *mimic* burlesque actor   20 *fowler* hunter of game birds   21 *russet-pated choughs* reddish brown or gray-headed jackdaws.   *in sort* in a flock   23 *Sever* i.e., scatter   30 *from . . . catch* i.e., everything preys on those who yield to fear   36 *latched* fastened, snared   40 *of force* perforce   48 *Being o'er shoes* having waded in so far   53 *whole* solid

May through the center creep, and so displease
Her brother's° noontide with th' Antipodes.°   55
It cannot be but thou hast murdered him;
So should a murderer look, so dead,° so grim.
Demetrius: So should the murdered look, and so should I,
Pierced through the heart with your stern cruelty.
Yet you, the murderer, look as bright, as clear   60
As yonder Venus in her glimmering sphere.
Hermia: What's this to° my Lysander? Where is he?
Ah, good Demetrius, wilt thou give him me?
Demetrius: I had rather give his carcass to my hounds.
Hermia: Out, dog! Out, cur! Thou driv'st me past the bounds   65
Of maiden's patience. Hast thou slain him, then?
Henceforth be never numbered among men.
O, once° tell true, tell true, even for my sake:
Durst thou have looked upon him being awake?
And hast thou killed him sleeping? O brave touch!°   70
Could not a worm,° an adder, do so much?
An adder did it; for with doubler° tongue
Than thine, thou serpent, never adder stung.
Demetrius: You spend your passion° on a misprised mood.°
I am not guilty of Lysander's blood,   75
Nor is he dead, for aught that I can tell.
Hermia: I pray thee, tell me then that he is well.
Demetrius: And if I could, what should I get therefor?°
Hermia: A privilege never to see me more.
And from thy hated presence part I so.   80
See me no more, whether he be dead or no.   *Exit.*
Demetrius: There is no following her in this fierce vein.
Here therefore for a while I will remain.
So sorrow's heaviness doth heavier° grow
For debt that bankrupt° sleep doth sorrow owe;   85
Which now in some slight measure it will pay,
If for his tender here I make some stay.°   [*He*] *lie*[*s*] *down* [*and sleeps*].
Oberon: What hast thou done? Thou hast mistaken quite
And laid the love juice on some true love's sight.

---

55 *Her brother's* i.e., the sun's.   *th' Antipodes* the people on the opposite side of the earth
(where the moon is imagined bringing night to noontime)   57 *dead* deadly, or deathly pale
62 *to* to do with   68 *once* once and for all   70 *brave touch!* fine stroke! (Said ironically.)   71
worm serpent   72 *doubler* (1) more forked (2) more deceitful   74 *passion* violent feelings.
misprised mood anger based on misconception   78 *therefor* in return for that   84 *heavier* (1)
harder to bear (2) more drowsy   85 *bankrupt* (Demetrius is saying that his sleepiness adds to
the weariness caused by sorrow.)   86–87 *Which . . . stay* i.e., to a small extent, I will be able to
"pay back" and hence find some relief from sorrow, if I pause here awhile (*make some stay*)
while sleep "tenders" or offers itself by way of paying the debt owed to sorrow

Of thy misprision° must perforce ensue   90
Some true love turned, and not a false turned true.
Puck: Then fate o'errules, that, one man holding troth,°
A million fail, confounding oath on oath.°
Oberon: About the wood go swifter than the wind,
And Helena of Athens look° thou find.   95
All fancy-sick° she is and pale of cheer°
With sighs of love, that cost the fresh blood° dear.
By some illusion see thou bring her here.
I'll charm his eyes against she do appear.°
Puck: I go, I go, look how I go,   100
Swifter than arrow from the Tartar's bow.°   [*Exit.*]
Oberon [*applying love juice to Demetrius' eyes*]:
    Flower of this purple dye,
    Hit with Cupid's archery,
    Sink in apple° of his eye.
    When his love he doth espy,   105
    Let her shine as gloriously
    As the Venus of the sky.
    When thou wak'st, if she be by,
    Beg of her for remedy.

  Enter Puck:

Puck: Captain of our fairy band,   110
    Helena is here at hand,
    And the youth, mistook by me,
    Pleading for a lover's fee.°
    Shall we their fond pageant° see?
    Lord, what fools these mortals be!   115
Oberon: Stand aside. The noise they make
    Will cause Demetrius to awake.
Puck: Then will two at once woo one;
    That must needs be sport alone.°
    And those things do best please me   120
    That befall preposterously.°

             [*They stand aside.*]

90 *misprision* mistake 92 *that . . . troth* in that, for each man keeping true faith in love 93 *confounding . . . oath* i.e., breaking oath after oath 95 *look* i.e., be sure 96 *fancy-sick* lovesick. *cheer* face 97 *sighs . . . blood* (An allusion to the physiological theory that each sigh costs the heart a drop of blood.) 99 *against . . . appear* in anticipation of her coming 101 *Tartar's bow* (Tartars were famed for their skill with the bow.) 104 *apple* pupil 113 *fee* privilege, reward 114 *fond pageant* foolish spectacle 119 *alone* unequaled 121 *preposterously* out of the natural order

Enter Lysander and Helena.

Lysander: Why should you think that I should woo in scorn?
    Scorn and derision never come in tears.
    Look when° I vow, I weep; and vows so born,
    In their nativity all truth appears.°
    How can these things in me seem scorn to you,   125
    Bearing the badge° of faith to prove them true?
Helena: You do advance° your cunning more and more.
    When truth kills truth,° O, devilish-holy fray!
    These vows are Hermia's. Will you give her o'er?   130
    Weigh oath with oath, and you will nothing weigh.
    Your vows to her and me, put in two scales,
    Will even weigh, and both as light as tales.°
Lysander: I had no judgment when to her I swore.
Helena: Nor none, in my mind, now you give her o'er.   135
Lysander: Demetrius loves her, and he loves not you.
Demetrius [awaking]: O Helen, goddess, nymph, perfect, divine!
    To what, my love, shall I compare thine eyne?
    Crystal is muddy. O, how ripe in show°
    Thy lips, those kissing cherries, tempting grow!   140
    That pure congealèd white, high Taurus'° snow,
    Fanned with the eastern wind, turns to a crow°
    When thou hold'st up thy hand. O, let me kiss
    This princess of pure white, this seal° of bliss!
Helena: O spite! O hell! I see you all are bent   145
    To set against° me for your merriment.
    If you were civil and knew courtesy,
    You would not do me thus much injury.
    Can you not hate me, as I know you do,
    But you must join in souls° to mock me too?   150
    If you were men, as men you are in show,
    You would not use a gentle lady so—
    To vow, and swear, and superpraise° my parts,°
    When I am sure you hate me with your hearts.
    You both are rivals, and love Hermia,   155
    And now both rivals, to mock Helena.

---

124 *Look when* whenever   124–125 *vows . . . appears* i.e., vows made by one who is weeping
give evidence thereby of their sincerity   127 *badge* identifying device such as that worn on servants' livery (here, his tears)   128 *advance* carry forward, display   129 *truth kills truth* i.e., one
of Lysander's vows must invalidate the other   133 *tales* lies   139 *show* appearance   141
Taurus a lofty mountain range in Asia Minor   142 *turns to a crow* i.e., seems black by contrast
144 *seal* pledge   146 *set against* attack   150 *in souls* i.e., heart and soul   153 *superpraise* overpraise.   *parts* qualities

A trim° exploit, a manly enterprise,
To conjure tears up in a poor maid's eyes
With your derision! None of noble sort°
Would so offend a virgin and extort°   160
A poor soul's patience, all to make you sport.
Lysander: You are unkind, Demetrius. Be not so.
For you love Hermia; this you know I know.
And here, with all good will, with all my heart,
In Hermia's love I yield you up my part;   165
And yours of Helena to me bequeath,
Whom I do love, and will do till my death.
Helena: Never did mockers waste more idle breath.
Demetrius: Lysander, keep thy Hermia; I will none.°
If e'er I loved her, all that love is gone.   170
My heart to her but as guestwise sojourned,°
And now to Helen is it home returned,
There to remain.
Lysander: Helen, it is not so.
Demetrius: Disparage not the faith thou dost not know,
Lest, to thy peril, thou aby° it dear.   175
Look where thy love comes; yonder is thy dear.

    Enter Hermia.

Hermia: Dark night, that from the eye his° function takes,
The ear more quick of apprehension makes;
Wherein it doth impair the seeing sense,
It pays the hearing double recompense.   180
Thou art not by mine eye, Lysander, found;
Mine ear, I thank it, brought me to thy sound.
But why unkindly didst thou leave me so?
Lysander: Why should he stay, whom love doth press to go?
Hermia: What love could press Lysander from my side?   185
Lysander: Lysander's love, that would not let him bide—
Fair Helena, who more engilds° the night
Than all yon fiery oes° and eyes of light.
Why seek'st thou me? Could not this make thee know
The hate I bear thee made me leave thee so?   190
Hermia: You speak not as you think. It cannot be.
Helena: Lo, she is one of this confederacy!
Now I perceive they have conjoined all three

---

157 *trim* pretty, fine (Said ironically.)   159 *sort* character, quality   160 *extort* twist, torture
169 *will none* i.e., want no part of her   171 *to . . . sojourned* only visited with her   175 *aby* pay
for   177 *his* its   187 *engilds* gilds, brightens with a golden light   188 *oes* spangles (here, stars)

To fashion this false sport in spite of me.°
Injurious Hermia, most ungrateful maid!   195
Have you conspired, have you with these contrived°
To bait° me with this foul derision?
Is all the counsel° that we two have shared—
The sisters' vows, the hours that we have spent
When we have chid the hasty-footed time   200
For parting us—O, is all forgot?
All schooldays' friendship, childhood innocence?
We, Hermia, like two artificial° gods,
Have with our needles created both one flower,
Both on one sampler, sitting on one cushion,   205
Both warbling of one song, both in one key,
As if our hands, our sides, voices, and minds
Had been incorporate.° So we grew together,
Like to a double cherry, seeming parted,
But yet an union in partition,   210
Two lovely° berries molded on one stem;
So with two seeming bodies but one heart,
Two of the first, like coats in heraldry,
Due but to one and crownèd with one crest.°
And will you rend our ancient love asunder,   215
To join with men in scorning your poor friend?
It is not friendly, 'tis not maidenly.
Our sex, as well as I, may chide you for it,
Though I alone do feel the injury.
Hermia: I am amazèd at your passionate words.   220
I scorn you not. It seems that you scorn me.
Helena: Have you not set Lysander, as in scorn,
To follow me and praise my eyes and face?
And made your other love, Demetrius,
Who even but now did spurn me with his foot,   225
To call me goddess, nymph, divine, and rare,
Precious, celestial? Wherefore speaks he this
To her he hates? And wherefore doth Lysander
Deny your love, so rich within his soul,
And tender° me, forsooth, affection,   230
But by your setting on, by your consent?
What though I be not so in grace° as you,

194 *in spite of me* to vex me   196 *contrived* plotted   197 *bait* torment, as one sets on dogs to
bait a bear   198 *counsel* confidential talk   203 *artificial* skilled in art or creation   208
incorporate of one body   211 *lovely* loving   213–214 *Two . . . crest* i.e., we have two separate
bodies, just as a coat of arms in heraldry can be represented twice on a shield but surmounted
by a single crest   230 *tender* offer   232 *grace* favor

So hung upon with love, so fortunate,
But miserable most, to love unloved?
This you should pity rather than despise.   235
Hermia: I understand not what you mean by this.
Helena: Ay, do! Persever, counterfeit sad° looks,
   Make mouths° upon° me when I turn my back,
   Wink each at other, hold the sweet jest up.°
   This sport, well carried,° shall be chronicled.   240
   If you have any pity, grace, or manners,
   You would not make me such an argument.°
   But fare ye well. 'Tis partly my own fault,
   Which death, or absence, soon shall remedy.
Lysander: Stay, gentle Helena; hear my excuse,   245
   My love, my life, my soul, fair Helena!
Helena: O excellent!
Hermia [to Lysander]: Sweet, do not scorn her so.
Demetrius [to Lysander]: If she cannot entreat,° I can compel.
Lysander: Thou canst compel no more than she entreat.
   Thy threats have no more strength than her weak prayers.   250
   Helen, I love thee, by my life I do!
   I swear by that which I will lose for thee,
   To prove him false that says I love thee not.
Demetrius [to Helena]:
   I say I love thee more than he can do.
Lysander: If thou say so, withdraw, and prove it too.°   255
Demetrius: Quick, come!
Hermia: Lysander, whereto tends all this?
Lysander: Away, you Ethiope!°

                                   [He tries to break away from Hermia.]

Demetrius: No, no; he'll
   Seem to break loose; take on as° you would follow,
   But yet come not. You are a tame man. Go!
Lysander [to Hermia]: Hang off,° thou cat, thou burr! Vile thing, let loose,   260
   Or I will shake thee from me like a serpent!
Hermia: Why are you grown so rude? What change is this,
   Sweet love?
Lysander: Thy love? Out, tawny Tartar, out!
   Out, loathèd med'cine!° O hated potion, hence!

---

237 *sad* grave, serious   238 *mouths* i.e., mows, faces, grimaces.   *upon* at   239 *hold . . . up* keep
up the joke   240 *carried* managed   242 *argument* subject for a jest   248 *entreat* i.e., succeed by
entreaty   255 *withdraw . . . too* i.e., withdraw with me and prove your claim in a duel. (The
two gentlemen are armed.)   257 *Ethiope* (Referring to Hermia's relatively dark hair and complexion; see also *tawny Tartar* six lines later.)   258 *take on as* act as if, make a fuss as if   260
Hang off let go   264 *med'cine* i.e., poison

Hermia: Do you not jest?

Helena: Yes, sooth,° and so do you.   265

Lysander: Demetrius, I will keep my word with thee.

Demetrius: I would I had your bond, for I perceive

    A weak bond° holds you. I'll not trust your word.

Lysander: What, should I hurt her, strike her, kill her dead?

    Although I hate her, I'll not harm her so.   270

Hermia: What, can you do me greater harm than hate?

    Hate me? Wherefore? O me, what news,° my love?

    Am not I Hermia? Are not you Lysander?

    I am as fair now as I was erewhile.°

    Since night you loved me; yet since night you left me.   275

    Why, then you left me—O, the gods forbid!—

    In earnest, shall I say?

Lysander: Ay, by my life!

    And never did desire to see thee more.

    Therefore be out of hope, of question, of doubt;

    Be certain, nothing truer. 'Tis no jest   280

    That I do hate thee and love Helena.

Hermia [to Helena]: O me! You juggler! You cankerblossom!°

    You thief of love! What, have you come by night

    And stol'n my love's heart from him?

Helena: Fine, i' faith!

    Have you no modesty, no maiden shame,   285

    No touch of bashfulness? What, will you tear

    Impatient answers from my gentle tongue?

    Fie, fie! You counterfeit, you puppet,° you!

Hermia: "Puppet"? Why, so!° Ay, that way goes the game.

    Now I perceive that she hath made compare   290

    Between our statures; she hath urged her height,

    And with her personage, her tall personage,

    Her height, forsooth, she hath prevailed with him.

    And are you grown so high in his esteem

    Because I am so dwarfish and so low?   295

    How low am I, thou painted maypole? Speak!

    How low am I? I am not yet so low

    But that my nails can reach unto thine eyes.

                          [She flails at Helena but is restrained.]

Helena: I pray you, though you mock me, gentlemen,

    Let her not hurt me. I was never curst;°   300

---

265 *sooth* truly   268 *weak bond* i.e., Hermia's arm (with a pun on *bond*, "oath," in the previous line)   272 *what news* what is the matter   274 *erewhile* just now   282 *cankerblossom* worm that destroys the flower bud, or wild rose   288 *puppet* (1) counterfeit (2) dwarfish woman (in reference to Hermia's smaller stature)   289 *Why, so* i.e., Oh, so that's how it is   300 *curst* shrewish

I have no gift at all in shrewishness;
I am a right° maid for my cowardice.
Let her not strike me. You perhaps may think,
Because she is something° lower than myself,
That I can match her.
Hermia: Lower? Hark, again!   305
Helena: Good Hermia, do not be so bitter with me.
I evermore did love you, Hermia,
Did ever keep your counsels, never wronged you,
Save that, in love unto Demetrius,
I told him of your stealth° unto this wood.   310
He followed you; for love I followed him.
But he hath chid me hence° and threatened me
To strike me, spurn me, nay, to kill me too.
And now, so° you will let me quiet go,
To Athens will I bear my folly back   315
And follow you no further. Let me go.
You see how simple and how fond° I am.
Hermia: Why, get you gone. Who is 't that hinders you?
Helena: A foolish heart, that I leave here behind.
Hermia: What, with Lysander?
Helena: With Demetrius.   320
Lysander: Be not afraid; she shall not harm thee, Helena.
Demetrius: No, sir, she shall not, though you take her part.
Helena: O, when she is angry, she is keen° and shrewd.°
She was a vixen when she went to school;
And though she be but little, she is fierce.   325
Hermia: "Little" again? Nothing but "low" and "little"?
Why will you suffer her to flout me thus?
Let me come to her.
Lysander: Get you gone, you dwarf!
You minimus,° of hindering knotgrass° made!
You bead, you acorn!
Demetrius: You are too officious   330
In her behalf that scorns your services.
Let her alone. Speak not of Helena;
Take not her part. For, if thou dost intend°
Never so little show of love to her,
Thou shalt aby° it.
Lysander: Now she holds me not.   335

302 *right* true   304 *something* somewhat   310 *stealth* stealing away   312 *chid me hence* driven
me away with his scolding   314 *so* if only   317 *fond* foolish   323 *keen* fierce, cruel.   *shrewd*
shrewish   329 *minimus* diminutive creature.   *knotgrass* a weed, an infusion of which was
thought to stunt the growth   333 *intend* give sign of   335 *aby* pay for

Now follow, if thou dar'st, to try whose right,
Of thine or mine, is most in Helena.   [*Exit.*]
Demetrius: Follow? Nay, I'll go with thee, cheek by jowl.°

                                 [*Exit, following Lysander.*]

Hermia: You, mistress, all this coil° is 'long of° you.
    Nay, go not back.°
Helena: I will not trust you, I,   340
    Nor longer stay in your curst company.
    Your hands than mine are quicker for a fray;
    My legs are longer, though, to run away.   [*Exit.*]
Hermia: I am amazed and know not what to say.   *Exit.*

    [*Oberon and Puck come forward.*]

Oberon: This is thy negligence. Still thou mistak'st,   345
    Or else committ'st thy knaveries willfully.
Puck: Believe me, king of shadows, I mistook.
    Did not you tell me I should know the man
    By the Athenian garments he had on?
    And so far blameless proves my enterprise   350
    That I have 'nointed an Athenian's eyes;
    And so far° am I glad it so did sort,°
    As° this their jangling I esteem a sport.
Oberon: Thou seest these lovers seek a place to fight.
    Hie° therefore, Robin, overcast the night;   355
    The starry welkin° cover thou anon
    With drooping fog as black as Acheron,°
    And lead these testy rivals so astray
    As° one come not within another's way.
    Like to Lysander sometimes frame thy tongue,   360
    Then stir Demetrius up with bitter wrong;°
    And sometimes rail thou like Demetrius.
    And from each other look thou lead them thus,
    Till o'er their brows death-counterfeiting sleep
    With leaden legs and batty° wings doth creep.   365
    Then crush this herb° into Lysander's eye,   [*giving herb.*]
    Whose liquor hath this virtuous° property,
    To take from thence all error with his° might
    And make his eyeballs roll with wonted° sight.

338 *cheek by jowl* i.e., side by side   339 *coil* turmoil, dissension. *'long of* on account of   340 *go not back* i.e., don't retreat (Hermia is again proposing a fight.)   352 *so far* at least to this extent.   *sort* turn out   353 *As that*   355 *Hie* hasten   356 *welkin* sky   357 *Acheron* river of Hades (here representing Hades itself)   359 *As that*   361 *wrong* insults   365 *batty* batlike   366 *this herb* i.e., the antidote (mentioned in 2.1.184) to love-in-idleness   367 *virtuous* efficacious   368 *his* its   369 *wonted* accustomed

When they next wake, all this derision°
Shall seem a dream and fruitless vision,
And back to Athens shall the lovers wend
With league whose date° till death shall never end.
Whiles I in this affair do thee employ,
I'll to my queen and beg her Indian boy;
And then I will her charmèd eye release
From monster's view, and all things shall be peace.

Puck: My fairy lord, this must be done with haste,
For night's swift dragons° cut the clouds full fast,
And yonder shines Aurora's harbinger,°
At whose approach ghosts, wand'ring here and there,
Troop home to churchyards. Damnèd spirits all,
That in crossways and floods have burial,°
Already to their wormy beds are gone.
For fear lest day should look their shames upon,
They willfully themselves exile from light
And must for aye° consort with black-browed night.

Oberon: But we are spirits of another sort.
I with the Morning's love° have oft made sport,
And, like a forester,° the groves may tread
Even till the eastern gate, all fiery red,
Opening on Neptune with fair blessèd beams,
Turns into yellow gold his salt green streams.
But notwithstanding, haste, make no delay.
We may effect this business yet ere day. *[Exit.]*

Puck:
        Up and down, up and down,
        I will lead them up and down.
        I am feared in field and town.
        Goblin,° lead them up and down.
Here comes one.

        Enter Lysander.

Lysander: Where art thou, proud Demetrius? Speak thou now.
Puck [*mimicking Demetrius*]:
        Here, villain, drawn° and ready. Where art thou?

370
375
380
385
390
395
400

370 *derision* laughable business   373 *date* term of existence   379 *dragons* (Supposed by Shakespeare to be yoked to the car of the goddess of night or the moon.)   380 *Aurora's harbinger* the morning star, precursor of dawn   383 *crossways . . . burial* (Those who had committed suicide were buried at crossways, with a stake driven through them; those who intentionally or accidentally drowned (in floods or deep water), would be condemned to wander disconsolate for lack of burial rites.)   387 *for aye* forever   389 *the Morning's love* Cephalus, a beautiful youth beloved by Aurora; or perhaps the goddess of the dawn herself   390 *forester* keeper of a royal forest   399 *Goblin* Hobgoblin. (Puck refers to himself.)   402 *drawn* with drawn sword

Lysander: I will be with thee straight.°
Puck: Follow me, then,
     To plainer° ground.

                              [Lysander wanders about,° following the voice.]

     Enter Demetrius.

Demetrius: Lysander! Speak again!
     Thou runaway, thou coward, art thou fled?   405
     Speak! In some bush? Where dost thou hide thy head?
Puck [mimicking Lysander]:
     Thou coward, art thou bragging to the stars,
     Telling the bushes that thou look'st for wars,
     And wilt not come? Come, recreant;° come, thou child,
     I'll whip thee with a rod. He is defiled   410
     That draws a sword on thee.
Demetrius: Yea, art thou there?
Puck: Follow my voice. We'll try° no manhood here.

                                                  Exeunt.

     [Lysander returns.]

Lysander: He goes before me and still dares me on.
     When I come where he calls, then he is gone.
     The villain is much lighter-heeled than I.   415
     I followed fast, but faster he did fly,
     That fallen am I in dark uneven way,
     And here will rest me. [He lies down.] Come, thou gentle day!
     For if but once thou show me thy gray light,
     I'll find Demetrius and revenge this spite.   [He sleeps.]   420

     [Enter] Robin [Puck] and Demetrius.

Puck: Ho, ho, ho! Coward, why com'st thou not?
Demetrius: Abide° me, if thou dar'st; for well I wot°
     Thou runn'st before me, shifting every place,
     And dar'st not stand nor look me in the face.
     Where art thou now?
Puck: Come hither. I am here.   425
Demetrius: Nay, then, thou mock'st me. Thou shalt buy° this dear,°
     If ever I thy face by daylight see.
     Now, go thy way. Faintness constraineth me
     To measure out my length on this cold bed.
     By day's approach look to be visited.   430

---

403 straight immediately   404 plainer more open.   s.d. Lysander wanders about (Lysander may
exit here, but perhaps not; neither exit nor reentrance is indicated in the early texts.)   409
recreant cowardly wretch   412 try test   422 Abide confront, face.   wot know   426 buy aby,
pay for.   dear dearly

[He lies down and sleeps.]

Enter Helena.

Helena: O weary night, O long and tedious night,
  Abate° thy hours! Shine comforts from the east,
  That I may back to Athens by daylight
  From these that my poor company detest;
  And sleep, that sometimes shuts up sorrow's eye,   435
  Steal me awhile from mine own company.

            [She lies down and] sleep[s].

Puck: Yet but three? Come one more;
    Two of both kinds makes up four.
    Here she comes, curst° and sad.
    Cupid is a knavish lad,   440
    Thus to make poor females mad.

 [Enter Hermia.]

Hermia: Never so weary, never so in woe,
  Bedabbled with the dew and torn with briers,
  I can no further crawl, no further go;
  My legs can keep no pace with my desires.   445
  Here will I rest me till the break of day.
  Heavens shield Lysander, if they mean a fray!

            [She lies down and sleeps.]

Puck: On the ground
    Sleep sound.
    I'll apply   450
    To your eye,
   Gentle lover, remedy.

  [He squeezes the juice on Lysander's eyes.]

    When thou wak'st,
    Thou tak'st
    True delight   455
    In the sight
  Of thy former lady's eye;
  And the country proverb known,
  That every man should take his own,
  In your waking shall be shown: 460
    Jack shall have Jill;°

432 *Abate* lessen, shorten 439 *curst* ill-tempered 461 *Jack shall have Jill* (Proverbial for "boy gets girl.")

Naught shall go ill;
The man shall have his mare again, and all shall be well.

[Exit. The four sleeping lovers remain.]

ACT IV

Scene I [The Action Is Continuous. The Four Lovers Are Still Asleep° Onstage.]

Enter [Titania,] Queen of Fairies, and [Bottom the] clown, and Fairies; and [Oberon,] the King, behind them.

Titania: Come, sit thee down upon this flowery bed,
While I thy amiable° cheeks do coy,°
And stick muskroses in thy sleek smooth head,
And kiss thy fair large ears, my gentle joy.

[They recline.]

Bottom: Where's Peaseblossom?   5
Peaseblossom: Ready.
Bottom: Scratch my head, Peaseblossom. Where's Monsieur Cobweb?
Cobweb: Ready.
Bottom: Monsieur Cobweb, good monsieur, get you your weapons in your hand,
and kill me a red-hipped humble-bee on the top of a thistle; and, good mon-   10
sieur, bring me the honey bag. Do not fret yourself too much in the action,
monsieur; and, good monsieur, have a care the honey bag break not. I would
be loath to have you overflown with a honey bag, signor. *[Exit Cobweb.]*
Where's Monsieur Mustardseed?
Mustardseed: Ready.   15
Bottom: Give me your neaf,° Monsieur Mustardseed. Pray you, leave your cour-
tesy,° good monsieur.
Mustardseed: What's your will?
Bottom: Nothing, good monsieur, but to help Cavalery° Cobweb° to scratch. I
must to the barber's, monsieur, for methinks I am marvelous hairy about the   20
face; and I am such a tender ass, if my hair do but tickle me I must scratch.
Titania: What, wilt thou hear some music, my sweet love?
Bottom: I have a reasonable good ear in music. Let's have the tongs and the
bones.°

[Music: tongs, rural music.°]

s.d. *still asleep* (Compare with the Folio stage direction: "They sleep all the act.")   2 *amiable*
lovely.   *coy* caress   16 *neaf* fist   16–17 *leave your courtesy* i.e., stop bowing, or put on your hat
19 *Cavalery* cavalier. (Form of address for a gentleman.)   *Cobweb* (Seemingly an error, since
Cobweb has been sent to bring honey, while Peaseblossom has been asked to scratch.)   23–24
tongs . . . bones instruments for rustic music. (The tongs were played like a triangle, whereas
the bones were held between the fingers and used as clappers.)   s.d. *Music . . . music* (This
stage direction is added from the Folio.)

Titania: Or say, sweet love, what thou desirest to eat.   25

Bottom: Truly, a peck of provender.° I could munch your good dry oats. Me-
    thinks I have a great desire to a bottle° of hay. Good hay, sweet hay, hath no
    fellow.°

Titania: I have a venturous fairy that shall seek
    The squirrel's hoard, and fetch thee new nuts.   30

Bottom: I had rather have a handful or two of dried peas. But, I pray you, let
    none of your people stir° me. I have an exposition of° sleep come upon me.

Titania: Sleep thou, and I will wind thee in my arms.
    Fairies, begone, and be all ways° away.

                                                [Exeunt Fairies.]

    So doth the woodbine° the sweet honeysuckle   35
    Gently entwist; the female ivy so
    Enrings the barky fingers of the elm.
    O, how I love thee! How I dote on thee!

                                                      [They sleep.]

      Enter Robin Goodfellow [Puck].

Oberon [coming forward]: Welcome, good Robin. Seest thou this sweet sight?
    Her dotage now I do begin to pity.   40
    For, meeting her of late behind the wood
    Seeking sweet favors° for this hateful fool,
    I did upbraid her and fall out with her.
    For she his hairy temples then had rounded
    With coronet of fresh and fragrant flowers;   45
    And that same dew, which sometime° on the buds
    Was wont to swell like round and orient° pearls,
    Stood now within the pretty flowerets' eyes
    Like tears that did their own disgrace bewail.
    When I had at my pleasure taunted her,   50
    And she in mild terms begged my patience,
    I then did ask of her her changeling child,
    Which straight she gave me, and her fairy sent
    To bear him to my bower in Fairyland.
    And, now I have the boy, I will undo   55
    This hateful imperfection of her eyes.
    And, gentle Puck, take this transformèd scalp
    From off the head of this Athenian swain,
    That he, awaking when the other° do,

26 *peck of provender* one-quarter bushel of grain   27 *bottle* bundle   28 *fellow* equal   32 *stir* disturb.   *exposition of* (Bottom's phrase for "disposition to.")   34 *all ways* in all directions   35
woodbine bindweed, a climbing plant that twines in the opposite direction from that of honeysuckle   42 *favors* i.e., gifts of flowers   46 *sometime* formerly   47 *orient pearls* i.e., the most
beautiful of all pearls, those coming from the Orient   59 *other* others

May all to Athens back again repair,° 60
And think no more of this night's accidents
But as the fierce vexation of a dream.
But first I will release the Fairy Queen.

[*He squeezes an herb on her eyes.*]

    Be as thou wast wont to be;
    See as thou wast wont to see. 65
    Dian's bud° o'er Cupid's flower
    Hath such force and blessèd power.
Now, my Titania, wake you, my sweet queen.
Titania [*waking*]: My Oberon! What visions have I seen!
    Methought I was enamored of an ass. 70
Oberon: There lies your love.
Titania: How came these things to pass?
    O, how mine eyes do loathe his visage now!
Oberon: Silence awhile. Robin, take off this head.
    Titania, music call, and strike more dead
    Than common sleep of all these five° the sense. 75
Titania: Music, ho! Music, such as charmeth° sleep!   [*Music.*]
Puck [*removing the ass head*]:
    Now, when thou wak'st, with thine own fool's eyes peep.
Oberon: Sound, music! Come, my queen, take hands with me,
    And rock the ground whereon these sleepers be.   [*They dance.*]
    Now thou and I are new in amity, 80
    And will tomorrow midnight solemnly°
    Dance in Duke Theseus' house triumphantly,
    And bless it to all fair prosperity.
    There shall the pairs of faithful lovers be
    Wedded, with Theseus, all in jollity. 85
Puck: Fairy King, attend, and mark:
    I do hear the morning lark.
Oberon: Then, my queen, in silence sad,°
    Trip we after night's shade.
    We the globe can compass soon,
    Swifter than the wandering moon. 90
Titania: Come, my lord, and in our flight
    Tell me how it came this night
    That I sleeping here was found
    With these mortals on the ground. 95

---

60 *repair* return   66 *Dian's bud* (Perhaps the flower of the *agnus castus* or chaste-tree, supposed to preserve chastity; or perhaps referring simply to Oberon's herb by which he can undo the effects of "Cupid's flower," the love-in-idleness of 2.1.166–168.)   75 *these five* i.e., the four lovers and Bottom   76 *charmeth* brings about, as though by a charm   81 *solemnly* ceremoniously   88 *sad* sober

Exeunt. [*Oberon, Titania, and Puck*].

Wind horn [*within*].

Enter Theseus and all his train; [*Hippolyta, Egeus*].

Theseus: Go, one of you, find out the forester,
   For now our observation° is performed;
   And since we have the vaward° of the day,
   My love shall hear the music of my hounds.
   Uncouple° in the western valley; let them go.   100
   Dispatch, I say, and find the forester.   [*Exit an Attendant.*]
   We will, fair queen, up to the mountain's top
   And mark the musical confusion
   Of hounds and echo in conjunction.
Hippolyta: I was with Hercules and Cadmus° once,   105
   When in a wood of Crete they bayed° the bear
   With hounds of Sparta.° Never did I hear
   Such gallant chiding;° for, besides the groves,
   The skies, the fountains, every region near
   Seemed all one mutual cry. I never heard   110
   So musical a discord, such sweet thunder.
Theseus: My hounds are bred out of the Spartan kind,°
   So flewed,° so sanded;° and their heads are hung
   With ears that sweep away the morning dew;
   Crook-kneed, and dewlapped° like Thessalian bulls;   115
   Slow in pursuit, but matched in mouth like bells,
   Each under each.° A cry° more tunable°
   Was never holloed to nor cheered° with horn
   In Crete, in Sparta, nor in Thessaly.
   Judge when you hear.   [*He sees the sleepers.*]
            But soft!° What nymphs are these?   120
Egeus: My lord, this is my daughter here asleep,
   And this Lysander; this Demetrius is;
   This Helena, old Nedar's Helena.
   I wonder of° their being here together.
Theseus: No doubt they rose up early to observe   125

97 *observation* i.e., observance to a morn of May (1.1.167)   98 *vaward* vanguard, i.e., earliest part   100 *Uncouple* set free for the hunt   105 *Cadmus* mythical founder of Thebes. (This story about him is unknown.)   106 *bayed* brought to bay   107 *hounds of Sparta* (A breed famous in antiquity for their hunting skill.)   108 *chiding* i.e., yelping   112 *kind* strain, breed 113 *So flewed* similarly having large hanging chaps or fleshy covering of the jaw.   *sanded* of sandy color   115 *dewlapped* having pendulous folds of skin under the neck   116–117 *matched . . . each* i.e., harmoniously matched in their various cries like a set of bells, from treble down to bass   117 *cry* pack of hounds.   *tunable* well tuned, melodious   118 *cheered* encouraged   120 *soft* i.e., gently, wait a minute   124 *wonder of* wonder at

The rite of May, and hearing our intent,
Came here in grace of our solemnity.°
But speak, Egeus. Is not this the day
That Hermia should give answer of her choice?
Egeus: It is, my lord.   130
Theseus: Go, bid the huntsmen wake them with their horns.

                                         [*Exit an Attendant.*]

   Shout within. Wind horns. They all start up.

Good morrow, friends. Saint Valentine° is past.
Begin these woodbirds but to couple now?
Lysander: Pardon, my lord.   [*They kneel.*]
Theseus: I pray you all, stand up.   [*They stand.*]
   I know you two are rival enemies;   135
   How comes this gentle concord in the world,
   That hatred is so far from jealousy°
   To sleep by hate and fear no enmity?
Lysander: My lord, I shall reply amazedly,
   Half sleep, half waking; but as yet, I swear,   140
   I cannot truly say how I came here.
   But, as I think—for truly would I speak,
   And now I do bethink me, so it is—
   I came with Hermia hither. Our intent
   Was to be gone from Athens, where° we might,   145
   Without° the peril of the Athenian law—
Egeus: Enough, enough, my lord; you have enough.
   I beg the law, the law, upon his head.
   They would have stol'n away; they would, Demetrius,
   Thereby to have defeated° you and me,   150
   You of your wife and me of my consent,
   Of my consent that she should be your wife.
Demetrius: My lord, fair Helen told me of their stealth,
   Of this their purpose hither° to this wood,
   And I in fury hither followed them,   155
   Fair Helena in fancy° following me.
   But, my good lord, I wot not by what power—
   But by some power it is—my love to Hermia,
   Melted as the snow, seems to me now
   As the remembrance of an idle gaud°   160
   Which in my childhood I did dote upon;
   And all the faith, the virtue of my heart,

127 *in . . . solemnity* in honor of our wedding ceremony 132 *Saint Valentine* (Birds were supposed to choose their mates on Saint Valentine's Day.) 137 *jealousy* suspicion 145 *where*
wherever; or, to where 146 *Without* outside of, beyond 150 *defeated* defrauded 154 *hither*
in coming hither 156 *in fancy* driven by love 160 *idle gaud* worthless trinket

The object and the pleasure of mine eye,
Is only Helena. To her, my lord,
Was I betrothed ere I saw Hermia,   165
But like a sickness did I loathe this food;
But, as in health, come to my natural taste,
Now I do wish it, love it, long for it,
And will forevermore be true to it.
Theseus: Fair lovers, you are fortunately met.   170
Of this discourse we more will hear anon.
Egeus, I will overbear your will;
For in the temple, by and by, with us
These couples shall eternally be knit.
And, for° the morning now is something° worn,   175
Our purposed hunting shall be set aside.
Away with us to Athens. Three and three,
We'll hold a feast in great solemnity.°
Come, Hippolyta.
                                    [*Exeunt Theseus, Hippolyta, Egeus, and train.*]
Demetrius: These things seem small and undistinguishable,   180
    Like far-off mountains turnèd into clouds.
Hermia: Methinks I see these things with parted° eye,
    When everything seems double.
Helena: So methinks;
    And I have found Demetrius like a jewel,
    Mine own, and not mine own.°
Demetrius: Are you sure   185
    That we are awake? It seems to me
    That yet we sleep, we dream. Do not you think
    The Duke was here, and bid us follow him?
Hermia: Yea, and my father.
Helena: And Hippolyta.
Lysander: And he did bid us follow to the temple.   190
Demetrius: Why, then, we are awake. Let's follow him,
    And by the way let us recount our dreams.   [*Exeunt the lovers.*]
Bottom [*awaking*]: When my cue comes, call me, and I will answer. My next is,
    "Most fair Pyramus." Heigh—ho! Peter Quince! Flute, the bellows mender!
    Snout, the tinker! Starveling! God's° my life, stolen hence and left me   195
    asleep! I have had a most rare vision. I have had a dream, past the wit of
    man to say what dream it was. Man is but an ass if he go about° to expound
    this dream. Methought I was—there is no man can tell what. Methought I

---

175 *for* since. *something* somewhat   178 *in great solemnity* with great ceremony   182 *parted*
i.e., improperly focused   184–185 *like . . . mine own* i.e., like a jewel that one finds by chance
and therefore possesses but cannot certainly consider one's own property   195 *God's* may God
save   197 *go about* attempt

was—and methought I had—but man is but a patched° fool if he will offer°
to say what methought I had. The eye of man hath not heard, the ear of   200
man hath not seen, man's hand is not able to taste, his tongue to conceive,
nor his heart to report,° what my dream was. I will get Peter Quince to write
a ballad° of this dream. It shall be called "Bottom's Dream," because it hath
no bottom;° and I will sing it in the latter end of a play, before the Duke.
Peradventure, to make it the more gracious, I shall sing it at her° death.   205

[*Exit.*]

Scene II [Athens.]

Enter Quince, Flute, [Snout, and Starveling].

Quince: Have you sent to Bottom's house? Is he come home yet?
Starveling: He cannot be heard of. Out of doubt he is transported.°
Flute: If he come not, then the play is marred. It goes not forward. Doth it?
Quince: It is not possible. You have not a man in all Athens able to discharge°
    Pyramus but he.   5
Flute: No, he hath simply the best wit° of any handicraft man in Athens.
Quince: Yea, and the best person° too, and he is a very paramour for a sweet
    voice.
Flute: You must say "paragon." A paramour is, God bless us, a thing of naught.°

Enter Snug the joiner.

Snug: Masters, the Duke is coming from the temple, and there is two or three   10
    lords and ladies more married. If our sport had gone forward, we had all been
    made men.°
Flute: O sweet bully Bottom! Thus hath he lost sixpence a day° during his life;
    he could not have scaped sixpence a day. An the Duke had not given him
    sixpence a day for playing Pyramus, I'll be hanged. He would have deserved   15
    it. Sixpence a day in Pyramus, or nothing.

Enter Bottom.

Bottom: Where are these lads? Where are these hearts?°
Quince: Bottom! O most courageous day! O most happy hour!
Bottom: Masters, I am to discourse wonders.° But ask me not what; for if I tell
    you, I am no true Athenian. I will tell you everything, right as it fell out.   20
Quince: Let us hear, sweet Bottom.

199 *patched* wearing motley, i.e., a dress of various colors.   *offer* venture   200–202 *The eye . . .
report* (Bottom garbles the terms of 1 Corinthians 2:9)   203 *ballad* (The proper medium for relating sensational stories and preposterous events.)   203–204 *hath no bottom* is unfathomable
205 *her* Thisbe's (?)   2 *transported* carried off by fairies; or, possibly, transformed   4 *discharge*
perform   6 *wit* intellect   7 *person* appearance   9 *a . . . naught* a shameful thing   11–12 *we
. . . men* i.e., we would have had our fortunes made   13 *sixpence a day* i.e., as a royal pension
17 *hearts* good fellows   19 *am . . . wonders* have wonders to relate

Bottom: Not a word of° me. All that I will tell you is that the Duke hath dined. Get your apparel together, good strings° to your beards, new ribbons to your pumps;° meet presently° at the palace; every man look o'er his part; for the short and the long is, our play is preferred.° In any case, let Thisbe have clean linen; and let not him that plays the lion pare his nails, for they shall hang out for the lion's claws. And, most dear actors, eat no onions nor garlic, for we are to utter sweet breath; and I do not doubt but to hear them say it is a sweet comedy. No more words. Away! Go, away!

25

[Exeunt.]

Act V

Scene I [Athens. The Palace of Theseus.]

Enter Theseus, Hippolyta, and Philostrate, [lords, and attendants].

Hippolyta: 'Tis strange, my Theseus, that° these lovers speak of.
Theseus: More strange than true. I never may° believe
    These antique° fables nor these fairy toys.°
    Lovers and madmen have such seething brains,
    Such shaping fantasies,° that apprehend°   5
    More than cool reason ever comprehends.°
    The lunatic, the lover, and the poet
    Are of imagination all compact.°
    One sees more devils than vast hell can hold;
    That is the madman. The lover, all as frantic,   10
    Sees Helen's° beauty in a brow of Egypt.°
    The poet's eye, in a fine frenzy rolling,
    Doth glance from heaven to earth, from earth to heaven;
    And as imagination bodies forth
    The forms of things unknown, the poet's pen   15
    Turns them to shapes and gives to airy nothing
    A local habitation and a name.
    Such tricks hath strong imagination
    That, if it would but apprehend some joy,
    It comprehends some bringer° of that joy;   20
    Or in the night, imagining some fear,°
    How easy is a bush supposed a bear!
Hippolyta: But all the story of the night told over,

22 *of* out of   23 *strings* (to attach the beards)   24 *pumps* light shoes or slippers. *presently* immediately   25 *preferred* selected for consideration   1 *that* that which   2 *may* can   3 *antique* old-fashioned (punning too on "*antic,*" "strange," "grotesque"). *fairy toys* trifling stories about fairies   5 *fantasies* imaginations. *apprehend* conceive, imagine   6 *comprehends* understands   8 *compact* formed, composed   11 *Helen's* i.e., of Helen of Troy, pattern of beauty. *brow of Egypt* i.e., face of a gypsy   20 *bringer* i.e., source   21 *fear* object of fear

And all their minds transfigured so together,
More witnesseth than fancy's images° 25
And grows to something of great constancy;°
But, howsoever,° strange and admirable.°

Enter lovers: Lysander, Demetrius, Hermia, and Helena.

Theseus: Here come the lovers, full of joy and mirth.
   Joy, gentle friends! Joy and fresh days of love
   Accompany your hearts!
Lysander: More than to us 30
   Wait in your royal walks, your board, your bed!
Theseus: Come now, what masques,° what dances shall we have,
   To wear away this long age of three hours
   Between our after-supper and bedtime?
   Where is our usual manager of mirth? 35
   What revels are in hand? Is there no play
   To ease the anguish of a torturing hour?
   Call Philostrate.
Philostrate: Here, mighty Theseus.
Theseus: Say, what abridgment° have you for this evening?
   What masque? What music? How shall we beguile 40
   The lazy time, if not with some delight?
Philostrate [giving him a paper]: There is a brief° how many sports are ripe.
   Make choice of which Your Highness will see first.
Theseus [He reads]: "The battle with the Centaurs,° to be sung
   By an Athenian eunuch to the harp"? 45
   We'll none of that. That have I told my love,
   In glory of my kinsman° Hercules.
   [*He reads.*] "The riot of the tipsy Bacchanals,
   Tearing the Thracian singer in their rage"?°
   That is an old device;° and it was played 50
   When I from Thebes came last a conqueror.
   [*He reads.*] "The thrice three Muses mourning for the death
   Of Learning, late deceased in beggary"?°

---

25 *More . . . images* testifies to something more substantial than mere imaginings   26 *constancy* certainty   27 *howsoever* in any case.   *admirable* a source of wonder   32 *masques* courtly entertainments   39 *abridgment* pastime (to abridge or shorten the evening)   42 *brief* short written statement, summary   44 *battle . . . Centaurs* (Probably refers to the battle of the Centaurs and the Lapithae, when the Centaurs attempted to carry off Hippodamia, bride of Theseus' friend Pirothous. The story is told in Ovid's *Metamorphoses* 12.)   47 *kinsman* (Plutarch's "Life of Theseus" states that Hercules and Theseus were near kinsmen. Theseus is referring to a version of the battle of the Centaurs in which Hercules was said to be present.)   48–49 *The riot . . . rage* (This was the story of the death of Orpheus, as told in *Metamorphoses* 11.)   50 *device* show, performance   52–53 *The thrice . . . beggary* (Possibly an allusion to Spenser's *Teares of the Muses*, 1591, though "satires" deploring the neglect of learning and the creative arts were commonplace.)

That is some satire, keen and critical,
Not sorting with° a nuptial ceremony.   55
[*He reads.*] "A tedious brief scene of young Pyramus
And his love Thisbe; very tragical mirth"?
Merry and tragical? Tedious and brief?
That is, hot ice and wondrous strange° snow.
How shall we find the concord of this discord?   60
Philostrate: A play there is, my lord, some ten words long,
   Which is as brief as I have known a play;
   But by ten words, my lord, it is too long,
   Which makes it tedious. For in all the play
   There is not one word apt, one player fitted.   65
   And tragical, my noble lord, it is,
   For Pyramus therein doth kill himself.
   Which, when I saw rehearsed, I must confess,
   Made mine eyes water; but more merry tears
   The passion of loud laughter never shed.   70
Theseus: What are they that do play it?
Philostrate: Hardhanded men that work in Athens here,
   Which never labored in their minds till now,
   And now have toiled° their unbreathed° memories
   With this same play, against° your nuptial.   75
Theseus: And we will hear it.
Philostrate: No, my noble lord,
   It is not for you. I have heard it over,
   And it is nothing, nothing in the world;
   Unless you can find sport in their intents,
   Extremely stretched° and conned° with cruel pain   80
   To do you service.
Theseus: I will hear that play;
   For never anything can be amiss
   When simpleness° and duty tender it.
   Go, bring them in; and take your places, ladies.
                     [*Philostrate goes to summon the players.*]
Hippolyta: I love not to see wretchedness o'ercharged,°   85
   And duty in his service° perishing.
Theseus: Why, gentle sweet, you shall see no such thing.
Hippolyta: He says they can do nothing in this kind.°
Theseus: The kinder we, to give them thanks for nothing.

---

55 *sorting with* befitting   59 *strange* (Sometimes emended to an adjective that would contrast
with *snow*, just as *hot* contrasts with *ice*.)   74 *toiled* taxed. *unbreathed* unexercised   75
against in preparation for   80 *stretched* strained. *conned* memorized   83 *simpleness* simplicity
85 *wretchedness o'ercharged* social or intellectual inferiors overburdened   86 *his service* its attempt to serve   88 *kind* kind of thing

Our sport shall be to take what they mistake;   90
And what poor duty cannot do, noble respect°
Takes it in might, not merit.°
Where I have come, great clerks° have purposèd
To greet me with premeditated welcomes;
Where I have seen them shiver and look pale,   95
Make periods in the midst of sentences,
Throttle their practiced accent° in their fears,
And in conclusion dumbly have broke off,
Not paying me a welcome. Trust me, sweet,
Out of this silence yet I picked a welcome;   100
And in the modesty of fearful duty
I read as much as from the rattling tongue
Of saucy and audacious eloquence.
Love, therefore, and tongue-tied simplicity
In least° speak most, to my capacity.°   105

[*Philostrate returns.*]

Philostrate: So please Your Grace, the Prologue° is addressed.°
Theseus: Let him approach.   [*A flourish of trumpets.*]

    Enter the Prologue [*Quince*].

Prologue: If we offend, it is with our good will.
    That you should think, we come not to offend,
    But with good will. To show our simple skill,   110
    That is the true beginning of our end.
    Consider, then, we come but in despite.
    We do not come, as minding° to content you,
    Our true intent is. All for your delight
    We are not here. That you should here repent you,   115
    The actors are at hand; and, by their show,
    You shall know all that you are like to know.
Theseus: This fellow doth not stand upon points.°
Lysander: He hath rid° his prologue like a rough° colt; he knows not the stop.°
    A good moral, my lord: it is not enough to speak, but to speak true.   120
Hippolyta: Indeed, he hath played on his prologue like a child on a recorder;° a
    sound, but not in government.°

91 *respect* evaluation, consideration   92 *Takes . . . merit* values it for the effort made rather
than for the excellence achieved   93 *clerks* learned men   97 *practiced accent* i.e., rehearsed
speech; or, usual way of speaking   105 *least* i.e., saying least.   *to my capacity* in my judgment
and understanding   106 *Prologue* speaker of the prologue.   *addressed* ready   113 *minding* intending   118 *stand upon points* (1) heed niceties or small points (2) pay attention to punctuation in his reading. (The humor of Quince's speech is in the blunders of its punctuation.)   119
rid ridden.   *rough* unbroken.   *stop* (1) the stopping of a colt by reining it in (2) punctuation
mark   121 *recorder* a wind instrument like a flute   122 *government* control

Theseus: His speech was like a tangled chain: nothing° impaired, but all disordered. Who is next?

*Enter Pyramus [Bottom], and Thisbe [Flute], and Wall [Snout], and Moonshine
[Starveling], and Lion [Snug].*

Prologue:
    Gentles, perchance you wonder at this show;   125
    But wonder on, till truth makes all things plain.
    This man is Pyramus, if you would know;
    This beauteous lady Thisbe is, certain.
    This man with lime and roughcast doth present
    Wall, that vile wall which did these lovers sunder;   130
    And through Wall's chink, poor souls, they are content
    To whisper. At the which let no man wonder.
    This man, with lantern, dog, and bush of thorn,
    Presenteth Moonshine; for, if you will know,
    By moonshine did these lovers think no scorn°   135
    To meet at Ninus' tomb, there, there to woo.
    This grisly beast, which Lion hight° by name,
    The trusty Thisbe coming first by night
    Did scare away, or rather did affright;
    And as she fled, her mantle she did fall,°   140
    Which Lion vile with bloody mouth did stain.
    Anon comes Pyramus, sweet youth and tall,°
    And finds his trusty Thisbe's mantle slain;
    Whereat, with blade, with bloody, blameful blade,
    He bravely broached° his boiling bloody breast.   145
    And Thisbe, tarrying in mulberry shade,
    His dagger drew, and died. For all the rest,
    Let Lion, Moonshine, Wall, and lovers twain
    At large° discourse, while here they do remain.
                            Exeunt Lion, Thisbe, and Moonshine.

Theseus: I wonder if the lion be to speak.   150
Demetrius: No wonder, my lord. One lion may, when many asses do.
Wall: In this same interlude° it doth befall
    That I, one Snout by name, present a wall;
    And such a wall as I would have you think
    That had in it a crannied hole or chink,   155
    Through which the lovers, Pyramus and Thisbe,
    Did whisper often, very secretly.
    This loam, this roughcast, and this stone doth show
    That I am that same wall; the truth is so.

123 *nothing* not at all   135 *think no scorn* think it no disgraceful matter   137 *hight* is called
140 *fall* let fall   142 *tall* courageous   145 *broached* stabbed   149 *At large* in full, at length
152 *interlude* play

And this the cranny is, right and sinister,°   160
Through which the fearful lovers are to whisper.
Theseus: Would you desire lime and hair to speak better?
Demetrius: It is the wittiest partition° that ever I heard discourse, my lord.

   [*Pyramus comes forward.*]

Theseus: Pyramus draws near the wall. Silence!
Pyramus: O grim-looked° night! O night with hue so black!   165
   O night, which ever art when day is not!
   O night, O night! Alack, alack, alack,
   I fear my Thisbe's promise is forgot.
   And thou, O wall, O sweet, O lovely wall,
   That stand'st between her father's ground and mine,   170
   Thou wall, O wall, O sweet and lovely wall,
   Show me thy chink, to blink through with mine eyne.
                                   [*Wall makes a chink with his fingers.*]
   Thanks, courteous wall. Jove shield thee well for this.
   But what see I? No Thisbe do I see.
   O wicked wall, through whom I see no bliss!   175
   Cursed be thy stones for thus deceiving me!
Theseus: The wall, methinks, being sensible,° should curse again.°
Pyramus: No, in truth, sir, he should not. "Deceiving me" is Thisbe's cue: she is
   to enter now, and I am to spy her through the wall. You shall see, it will fall
   pat° as I told you. Yonder she comes.   180

   Enter Thisbe.

Thisbe: O wall, full often hast thou heard my moans
   For parting my fair Pyramus and me.
   My cherry lips have often kissed thy stones,
   Thy stones with lime and hair knit up in thee.
Pyramus: I see a voice. Now will I to the chink,   185
   To spy an° I can hear my Thisbe's face.
   Thisbe!
Thisbe: My love! Thou art my love, I think.
Pyramus: Think what thou wilt, I am thy lover's grace,°
   And like Limander° am I trusty still.
Thisbe: And I like Helen,° till the Fates me kill.   190
Pyramus: Not Shafalus° to Procrus° was so true.
Thisbe: As Shafalus to Procrus, I to you.

---

160 *right and sinister* i.e., the right side of it and the left; or, running from right to left, horizontally   163 *partition* (1) wall (2) section of a learned treatise or oration   165 *grim-looked* grim-
looking   177 *sensible* capable of feeling.   *again* in return   180 *pat* exactly   186 *an* if   188
lover's grace i.e., gracious lover   189, 190 *Limander, Helen* (Blunders for "Leander" and
"Hero.")   191 *Shafalus, Procrus* (Blunders for "Cephalus" and "Procris," also famous lovers.)

Pyramus: O, kiss me through the hole of this vile wall!

Thisbe: I kiss the wall's hole, not your lips at all.

Pyramus: Wilt thou at Ninny's tomb meet me straightway? 195

Thisbe: 'Tide° life, 'tide death, I come without delay.

                                                  [Exeunt Pyramus and Thisbe.]

Wall: Thus have I, Wall, my part dischargèd so;

    And, being done, thus Wall away doth go.   *[Exit.]*

Theseus: Now is the mural down between the two neighbors.

Demetrius: No remedy, my lord, when walls are so willful° to hear without 200 warning.°

Hippolyta: This is the silliest stuff that ever I heard.

Theseus: The best in this kind° are but shadows;° and the worst are no worse, if imagination amend them.

Hippolyta: It must be your imagination then, and not theirs. 205

Theseus: If we imagine no worse of them than they of themselves, they may pass for excellent men. Here come two noble beasts in, a man and a lion.

    Enter Lion and Moonshine.

Lion:

    You, ladies, you, whose gentle hearts do fear

    The smallest monstrous mouse that creeps on floor,

    May now perchance both quake and tremble here,   210

    When lion rough in wildest rage doth roar.

    Then know that I, as Snug the joiner, am

    A lion fell,° nor else no lion's dam;

    For, if I should as lion come in strife

    Into this place, 'twere pity on my life.   215

Theseus: A very gentle beast, and of a good conscience.

Demetrius: The very best at a beast, my lord, that e'er I saw.

Lysander: This lion is a very fox for his valor.°

Theseus: True; and a goose for his discretion.°

Demetrius: Not so, my lord; for his valor cannot carry his discretion, and the fox 220 carries the goose.

Theseus: His discretion, I am sure, cannot carry his valor; for the goose carries not the fox. It is well. Leave it to his discretion, and let us listen to the moon.

Moon: This lanthorn° doth the hornèd moon present—

---

196 *'Tide* betide, come   200 *willful* willing   200–201 *without warning* i.e., without warning the parents (Demetrius makes a joke on the proverb "Walls have ears.")   203 *in this kind* of this sort. *shadows* likenesses, representations   213 *lion fell* fierce lion (with a play on the idea of "lion skin")   218 *is . . . valor* i.e., his valor consists of craftiness and discretion   219 *a goose . . . discretion* i.e., as discreet as a goose, that is, more foolish than discreet   224 *lanthorn* (This original spelling, *lanthorn*, may suggest a play on the *horn* of which lanterns were made, and also on a cuckold's horns; however, the spelling *lanthorn* is not used consistently for comic effect in this play or elsewhere. At 5.1.133, for example, the word is *lantern* in the original.)

Demetrius: He should have worn the horns on his head.°   225
Theseus: He is no crescent,° and his horns are invisible within the circumference.
Moon: This lanthorn doth the hornèd moon present;
    Myself the man i' the moon do seem to be.
Theseus: This is the greatest error of all the rest. The man should be put into the
    lanthorn. How is it else the man i' the moon?   230
Demetrius: He dares not come there for the candle, for° you see it is already in
    snuff.°
Hippolyta: I am aweary of this moon. Would he would change!
Theseus: It appears, by his small light of discretion, that he is in the wane; but
    yet, in courtesy, in all reason, we must stay the time.   235
Lysander: Proceed, Moon.
Moon: All that I have to say is to tell you that the lanthorn is the moon, I, the
    man i' the moon, this thornbush my thornbush, and this dog my dog.
Demetrius: Why, all these should be in the lanthorn, for all these are in the
    moon. But silence! Here comes Thisbe.   240

    Enter Thisbe.

Thisbe: This is old Ninny's tomb. Where is my love?
Lion [roaring]: O!
Demetrius: Well roared, Lion.

                          [Thisbe runs off, dropping her mantle.]

Theseus: Well run, Thisbe.
Hippolyta: Well shone, Moon. Truly, the moon shines with a good grace.   245

                          [The Lion worries Thisbe's mantle.]

Theseus: Well moused,° Lion.

                          [Enter Pyramus; exit Lion.]

Demetrius: And then came Pyramus.
Lysander: And so the lion vanished.
Pyramus: Sweet Moon, I thank thee for thy sunny beams;
    I thank thee, Moon, for shining now so bright;   250
    For, by thy gracious, golden, glittering gleams,
        I trust to take of truest Thisbe sight.
                But stay, O spite!
                But mark, poor knight,
            What dreadful dole° is here?   255
                Eyes, do you see?
                How can it be?

225 *on his head* (as a sign of cuckoldry)   226 *crescent* a waxing moon   231 *for* because of, for
fear of   232 *in snuff* (1) offended (2) in need of snuffing or trimming   246 *moused* shaken,
torn, bitten   255 *dole* grievous event

O dainty duck! O dear!
          Thy mantle good,
          What, stained with blood?   260
      Approach, ye Furies° fell!°
          O Fates,° come, come,
          Cut thread and thrum;°
      Quail,° crush, conclude, and quell!°

Theseus: This passion, and the death of a dear friend, would go near to make a   265
      man look sad.°

Hippolyta: Beshrew my heart, but I pity the man.

Pyramus: O, wherefore, Nature, didst thou lions frame?
      Since lion vile hath here deflowered my dear,
      Which is—no, no, which was—the fairest dame   270
      That lived, that loved, that liked, that looked with cheer.°
              Come, tears, confound,
              Out, sword, and wound
          The pap° of Pyramus;
              Ay, that left pap,   275
              Where heart doth hop.   [*He stabs himself.*]
      Thus die I, thus, thus, thus.
          Now am I dead,
          Now am I fled;
      My soul is in the sky.   280
          Tongue, lose thy light;
          Moon, take thy flight.   [*Exit Moonshine.*]
      Now die, die, die, die, die.   [*Pyramus dies.*]

Demetrius: No die, but an ace,° for him; for he is but one.°

Lysander: Less than an ace, man; for he is dead, he is nothing.   285

Theseus: With the help of a surgeon he might yet recover, and yet prove an ass.°

Hippolyta: How chance Moonshine is gone before Thisbe comes back and finds
      her lover?

Theseus: She will find him by starlight.

      [*Enter Thisbe.*]

      Here she comes, and her passion ends the play.   290

261 *Furies* avenging goddesses of Greek myth. *fell* fierce   262 *Fates* the three goddesses
(Clotho, Lachesis, Atropos) of Greek myth who spun, drew, and cut the thread of human life
263 *thread and thrum* i.e., everything—the good and bad alike; literally, the warp in weaving
and the loose end of the warp   264 *Quail* overpower.   *quell* kill, destroy   265–266 *This . . .
sad* i.e., if one had other reason to grieve, one might be sad, but not from this absurd portrayal
of passion   271 *cheer* countenance   274 *pap* breast   284 *ace* the side of the die featuring the
single pip, or spot (The pun is on *die* as a singular of *dice*; Bottom's performance is not worth a
whole *die* but rather one single face of it, one small portion.).   *one* (1) an individual person (2)
unique   286 *ass* (with a pun on *ace*)

Hippolyta: Methinks she should not use a long one for such a Pyramus. I hope she will be brief.

Demetrius: A mote° will turn the balance, which Pyramus, which° Thisbe, is the better: he for a man, God warrant us; she for a woman, God bless us.

Lysander: She hath spied him already with those sweet eyes.   295

Demetrius: And thus she means,° videlicet:°

Thisbe: Asleep, my love?
              What, dead, my dove?
                 O Pyramus, arise!
                    Speak, speak. Quite dumb?   300
                    Dead, dead? A tomb
                 Must cover thy sweet eyes.
                    These lily lips,
                    This cherry nose,
                 These yellow cowslip cheeks,   305
                    Are gone, are gone!
                    Lovers, make moan.
                 His eyes were green as leeks.
                    O Sisters Three,°
                    Come, come to me,   310
                 With hands as pale as milk;
                    Lay them in gore,
                    Since you have shore°
                 With shears his thread of silk.
                    Tongue, not a word.   315
                    Come, trusty sword,
                 Come, blade, my breast imbrue!°   [*She stabs herself.*]
                    And farewell, friends.
                    Thus Thisbe ends.
                    Adieu, adieu, adieu.   [*She dies.*]   320

Theseus: Moonshine and Lion are left to bury the dead.

Demetrius: Ay, and Wall too.

Bottom [*starting up, as Flute does also*]: No, I assure you, the wall is down that parted their fathers. Will it please you to see the epilogue, or to hear a Bergomask dance° between two of our company?   325

[*The other players enter.*]

Theseus: No epilogue, I pray you; for your play needs no excuse. Never excuse; for when the players are all dead, there need none to be blamed. Marry, if he

---

293 *mote* small particle.   *which . . . which* whether . . . or   296 *means* moans, laments (with a pun on the meaning, "lodge a formal complaint").   *videlicet* to wit   309 *Sisters Three* the Fates   313 *shore* shorn   317 *imbrue* stain with blood   324–325 *Bergomask dance* a rustic dance named from Bergamo, a province in the state of Venice

that writ it had played Pyramus and hanged himself in Thisbe's garter, it
would have been a fine tragedy; and so it is, truly, and very notably dis-
charged. But, come, your Bergomask. Let your epilogue alone.   [*A dance.*]   330
The iron tongue° of midnight hath told° twelve.
Lovers, to bed, 'tis almost fairy time.
I fear we shall outsleep the coming morn
As much as we this night have overwatched.°
This palpable-gross° play hath well beguiled   335
The heavy° gait of night. Sweet friends, to bed.
A fortnight hold we this solemnity,
In nightly revels and new jollity.   *Exeunt.*

Enter Puck [carrying a broom].

Puck: Now the hungry lion roars,
                And the wolf behowls the moon,   340
            Whilst the heavy° plowman snores,
                All with weary task fordone.°
            Now the wasted brands° do glow,
                Whilst the screech owl, screeching loud,
            Puts the wretch that lies in woe   345
                In remembrance of a shroud.
            Now it is the time of night
                That the graves, all gaping wide,
            Every one lets forth his sprite,°
                In the church-way paths to glide.   350
            And we fairies, that do run
                By the triple Hecate's° team
            From the presence of the sun,
                Following darkness like a dream,
            Now are frolic.° Not a mouse   355
                Shall disturb this hallowed house.
            I am sent with broom before,
                To sweep the dust behind° the door.

Enter [Oberon and Titania,] King and Queen of Fairies, with all their train.

Oberon: Through the house give glimmering light,
                By the dead and drowsy fire;   360
            Every elf and fairy sprite

331 *iron tongue* i.e., of a bell.   *told* counted, struck ("tolled")   334 *overwatched* stayed up too late
335 *palpable-gross* palpably gross, obviously crude   336 *heavy* drowsy, dull   341 *heavy* tired
342 *fordone* exhausted   343 *wasted brands* burned-out logs   349 *Every . . . sprite* every grave lets
forth its ghost   352 *triple Hecate's* (Hecate ruled in three capacities: as Luna or Cynthia in
heaven, as Diana on earth, and as Proserpina in hell.)   355 *frolic* merry   358 *behind* from behind, or else like sweeping the dirt under the carpet. (Robin Goodfellow was a household spirit
who helped good housemaids and punished lazy ones, but he could, of course, be mischievous.)

	Hop as light as bird from brier;
	And this ditty, after me,
	Sing, and dance it trippingly.
Titania:	First, rehearse° your song by rote, 365
	To each word a warbling note.
	Hand in hand, with fairy grace,
	Will we sing, and bless this place.

[Song and dance.]

Oberon:	Now, until the break of day,
	Through this house each fairy stray. 370
	To the best bride-bed will we,
	Which by us shall blessèd be;
	And the issue there create°
	Ever shall be fortunate.
	So shall all the couples three 375
	Ever true in loving be;
	And the blots of Nature's hand
	Shall not in their issue stand;
	Never mole, harelip, nor scar,
	Nor mark prodigious,° such as are 380
	Despisèd in nativity,
	Shall upon their children be.
	With this field dew consecrate°
	Every fairy take his gait,°
	And each several° chamber bless, 385
	Through this palace, with sweet peace;
	And the owner of it blest
	Ever shall in safety rest.
	Trip away; make no stay;
	Meet me all by break of day. 390

Exeunt [Oberon, Titania, and train].

Puck [to the audience]:	If we shadows have offended,
	Think but this, and all is mended,
	That you have but slumbered here°
	While these visions did appear.
	And this weak and idle theme, 395
	No more yielding but a dream,°
	Gentles, do not reprehend.

---

365 *rehearse* recite   373 *create* created   380 *prodigious* monstrous, unnatural   383 *consecrate* consecrated   384 *take his gait* go his way   385 *several* separate   393 *That . . . here* i.e., that it is a "midsummer night's dream"   396 *No . . . but* yielding no more than

If you pardon, we will mend.°
And, as I am an honest Puck,
If we have unearnèd luck   400
Now to scape the serpent's tongue,°
We will make amends ere long;
Else the Puck a liar call.
So, good night unto you all.
Give me your hands,° if we be friends,   405
And Robin shall restore amends.°   [*Exit.*]

---

398 *mend* improve   401 *serpent's tongue* i.e., hissing   405 *Give . . . hands* applaud   406 *restore amends* give satisfaction in return

Questions

1. Describe the relationship between King Theseus and Queen Hippolyta in the opening scene. How did they meet? Does their imminent marriage promise to be happy?
2. Describe the personality of each young aristocratic lover. How does Shakespeare differentiate them?
3. Characterize Nick Bottom. What aspects of his personality and behavior make him comic?
4. In what ways does Shakespeare differentiate his rustic tradesmen from the aristocrats?
5. Are the supernatural lovers, Oberon and Titania, characterized differently from their mortal counterparts? How are they similar to the aristocratic lovers and how are they different?
6. In what ways is Puck the unifying character of the play? How do his actions touch on every plot and subplot?
7. The main plot of *A Midsummer Night's Dream* concludes by the end of Act IV. What purpose does the final act serve in the play? Could it be omitted without significant loss?

Shakespeare left no commentary on his own work except for occasional remarks in the plays themselves, but his friend and fellow dramatist Ben Jonson did record a few interesting observations about the elder playwright's methods. Jonson knew Shakespeare well. He had produced several plays with Shakespeare's theatrical company, The Lord Chamberlain's Men, and Shakespeare had acted in those productions. He was genuinely fond of Shakespeare, but he was also clearly jealous of his colleague's immense popularity. Here are a few remarks Jonson made in his old age about his late friend.

Ben Jonson   (1573?–1637)

On His Friend and Rival William Shakespeare   1640

I remember the players have often mentioned it as an honor to Shakespeare, that in his writing (whatsoever he penned) he never blotted out a line. My answer hath been, "Would he had blotted a thousand," which they thought a malevolent speech. I had not told posterity this but for their ignorance who chose that circumstance to commend their friend by wherein he most faulted; and to justify mine own candor, for I loved the man, and do honor his memory on this side idolatry as much as any. He was, indeed, honest, and of an open and free nature; had an excellent phantasy, brave notions, and gentle expressions, wherein he flowed with that facility that sometimes it was necessary he should be stopped. "*Sufflaminandus erat*,"° as Augustus°

Ben Jonson

said of Haterius.° His wit was in his own power; would the rule of it had been so, too! Many times he fell into those things, could not escape laughter, as when he said in the person of Caesar,° one speaking to him, "Caesar, thou dost me wrong." He replied, "Caesar did never wrong but with just cause"; and such like, which were ridiculous. But he redeemed his vices with his virtues. There was ever more in him to be praised than to be pardoned.

From *Discoveries*

Sufflaminandus erat: Latin for "He ought to have been plugged up." *Augustus*: the first emperor of Rome (63 B.C.–14 A.D.) *Haterius*: a very verbose orator of the Augustan age. *Caesar*: Shakespeare's tragedy *Julius Caesar*. Jonson misremembers the quotation, which (in the First Folio) actually reads "Know, Caesar doth not wrong, nor without cause will he be satisfied." (III.i.47)

A. C. *Bradley* (1851–1935)

HAMLET'S MELANCHOLY   1903

That Hamlet was not far from insanity is very probable. His adoption of the pretence of madness may well have been due in part to fear of the reality; to an instinct of self-preservation, a fore-feeling that the pretence would enable him to give some utterance to the load that pressed on his heart and brain, and a fear that he would be unable altogether to repress such utterance. And if the pathologist calls his state melancholia, and even proceeds to determine its species, I see nothing to object to in that; I am grateful to him for emphasizing the fact that Hamlet's melancholy was no mere common depression of spirits; and I have no doubt that many readers of the play would understand it better if they read an account of melancholia in a work on mental diseases. If we like to use the word "disease" loosely, Hamlet's condition may truly be called diseased. No exertion of will could have dispelled it. Even if he had been able at once to do the bidding of the Ghost he would doubtless have still remained for some time under the cloud. It would be absurdly unjust to call *Hamlet* a study of melancholy, but it contains such a study.

But this melancholy is something very different from insanity, in anything like the usual meaning of that word. No doubt it might develop into insanity. The longing for death might become an irresistible impulse to self-destruction; the disorder of feeling and will might extend to sense and intellect; delusions might arise; and the man might become, as we say, incapable and irresponsible. But Hamlet's melancholy is some way from this condition. It is a totally different thing from the madness which he feigns; and he never, when alone or in company with Horatio alone, exhibits the signs of that madness. Nor is the dramatic use of this melancholy, again, open to the objections which would justly be made to the portrayal of an insanity which brought the hero to a tragic end. The man who suffers as Hamlet suffers—and thousands go about their business suffering thus in greater or less degree—is considered irresponsible neither by other people nor by himself: he is only too keenly conscious of his responsibility. He is therefore, so far, quite capable of being a tragic agent, which an insane person, at any rate according to Shakespeare's practice, is not. And, finally, Hamlet's state is not one which a healthy mind is unable sufficiently to imagine. It is probably not further from average experience, nor more difficult to realize, than the great tragic passions of Othello, Antony or Macbeth.

Let me try to show now, briefly, how much this melancholy accounts for.

It accounts for the main fact, Hamlet's inaction. For the *immediate* cause of that is simply that his habitual feeling is one of disgust at life and everything in it, himself included—a disgust which varies in intensity, rising at times into a longing for death, sinking often into weary apathy, but is never dispelled for more than brief intervals. Such a state of feeling is inevitably adverse to *any* kind of decided action; the body is inert, the mind indifferent or worse; its response is, "it does not matter," "it is not worth while," "it is no good." And the action required of Hamlet is very exceptional.

It is violent, dangerous, difficult to accomplish perfectly, on one side repulsive to a man of honor and sensitive feeling, on another side involved in a certain mystery (here come in thus, in their subordinate place, various causes of inaction assigned by various theories). These obstacles would not suffice to prevent Hamlet from acting, if his state were normal; and against them there operate, even in his morbid state, healthy and positive feelings, love of his father, loathing of his uncle, desire of revenge, desire to do duty. But the retarding motives acquire an unnatural strength because they have an ally in something far stronger than themselves, the melancholic disgust and apathy; while the healthy motives, emerging with difficulty from the central mass of diseased feeling, rapidly sink back into it and "lose the name of action."

From *Shakespearean Tragedy*

Rebecca West (1892–1983)

HAMLET AND OPHELIA   1958

There is no more bizarre aspect of the misreading of Hamlet's character than the assumption that his relations with Ophelia were innocent and that Ophelia was a correct and timid virgin of exquisite sensibilities. . . . She was not a chaste young woman. That is shown by her tolerance of Hamlet's obscene conversations, which cannot be explained as consistent with the custom of the time. If that were the reason for it, all the men and women in Shakespeare's plays, Romeo and Juliet, Beatrice and Benedict, Miranda and Ferdinand, Antony and Cleopatra, would have talked obscenely together, which is not the case. "The marriage of true minds" would hardly, even in the most candid age, have expressed itself by this ugly chatter, which Wilson Knight has so justly described as governed by "infra-sexual neurosis." The truth is that Ophelia was a disreputable young woman: not scandalously so, but still disreputable. She was foredoomed to it by her father, whom it is a mistake to regard as a simple platitudinarian. Shakespeare, like all major writers, was never afraid of a good platitude, and he would certainly never have given time to deriding a character because his only attribute was a habit of stating the obvious. Polonius is interesting because he was a cunning old intriguer who, like an iceberg, only showed one-eighth of himself above the surface. The innocuous sort of worldly wisdom that rolled off his tongue in butter balls was a very small part of what he knew. It has been insufficiently noted that Shakespeare would never have held up the action in order that Polonius should give his son advice as to how to conduct himself abroad, unless the scene helped him to develop his theme. But "This above all: to thine own self be true; / And it must follow, as the night the day, / Thou canst not then be false to any man" (1.3.78–80), has considerable contrapuntal value when it is spoken by an old gentleman who is presently going to instruct a servant to spy on his son, and to profess great anxiety about his daughter's morals, when plainly he needed to send her away into the country if he really wanted her to retain any.

There is no mistaking the disingenuousness of his dealings with his daughter. When Ophelia comes to him with her tale of how Hamlet had come to her as she was sewing in her chamber, "with his doublet all unbraced," and had looked madly on her, Polonius eagerly interprets this as "the very ecstasy of love," and asks her

"What, have you given him any hard words of late?" . . . The girl is not to be kept out of harm's way. She is a card that can be played to take several sorts of tricks. She might be Hamlet's mistress; but she might be more honored for resistance. And if Hamlet was himself an enemy of the King, and an entanglement with him had ceased to be a means of winning favor, then she can give a spy's report on him to Claudius. Surely Ophelia is one of the few authentic portraits of that army of not virgin martyrs, the poor little girls who were sacrificed to family ambition in the days when a court was a cat's cradle of conspiracies. Man's persuasion that his honor depends on the chastity of his women folk has always been liable to waste away and perish within sight of a throne. Particularly where monarchy had grown from a yeasty mass of feudalism, few families found themselves able to resist the temptation to hawk any young beauty in their brood, if it seemed likely that she might catch the eye of the king or any man close to the king. Unfortunately the king's true favorite was usually not a woman but an ideology. If royal approval was withdrawn from the religious or political faith held by the family which had hawked the girl, she was as apt to suffer fatality as any of her kinsmen. The axe has never known chivalry. Shakespeare, writing this play only three reigns from Henry the Eighth, had heard of such outrages on half-grown girls from the lips of those who had seen the final bloodletting.

From *The Court and the Castle*

Jan Kott   (1914–2001)

PRODUCING *HAMLET*   1964

There are many subjects in *Hamlet*. There is politics, force opposed to morality; there is discussion of the divergence between theory and practice, of the ultimate purpose of life; there is tragedy of love, as well as family drama; political, eschatological and metaphysical problems are considered. There is everything you want, including deep psychological analysis, a bloody story, a duel, and general slaughter. One can select at will. But one must know what one selects, and why.

   The *Hamlet* produced in Cracow a few weeks after the XXth Congress of the Soviet Communist Party lasted exactly three hours.° It was light and clear, tense and sharp, modern and consistent, limited to one issue only. It was a political drama par excellence. "Something is rotten in the state of Denmark" was the first chord of *Hamlet*'s new meaning. And then the dead sound of the words "Denmark's a prison," three times repeated. Finally the magnificent churchyard scene, with the gravediggers' dialogue rid of metaphysics, brutal and unequivocal. Gravediggers know for whom they dig graves. "The gallows is built stronger than the church," they say.

   "Watch" and "enquire" were the words most commonly heard from the stage. In this performance everybody, without exception, was being constantly watched. Polonius, minister to the royal murderer, sends a man to France even after his own son. Was Shakespeare not a genius for our time? Let us listen to the minister:

The Hamlet *produced . . . hours:* The production of *Hamlet* Kott discusses was staged in Cracow, Poland, in 1956 at the height of Soviet repression in Eastern Europe.

Inquire me first what Danskers are in Paris,
And how, and who, what means, and where they keep,
What company, at what expense; and finding
By this encompassment and drift of question
That they do know my son, come you more nearer
Than your particular demands will touch it.

(II, i, 7–12)

At Elsinore castle someone is hidden behind every curtain. The good minister does not even trust the Queen. Let us listen to him again:

'Tis meet that some more audience than a mother,
Since nature makes them partial, should o'erhear
The speech, of vantage.

(III, iii, 31–33)

Everything at Elsinore has been corroded by fear: marriage, love and friendship. Shakespeare, indeed, must have experienced terrible things at the time of Essex's plot and execution, since he came to learn so well the working of the Grand Mechanism. Let us listen to the King talking to Hamlet's young friends:

. . . I entreat you both
That, being of so young days brought up with him,
And since so neighbour'd to his youth and haviour,
That you vouchsafe your rest here in our court
Some little time; so by your companies
To draw him on to pleasures, and to gather
So much as from occasion you may glean,
Whether aught to us unknown afflicts him thus
That, open'd, lies within our remedy.

(II, ii, 10–18)

The murderous uncle keeps a constant watchful eye on Hamlet. Why does he not want him to leave Denmark? His presence at court is inconvenient, reminding everybody of what they would like to forget. Perhaps he suspects something? Would it not be better not to issue him a passport and keep him at hand? Or does the King wish to get rid of Hamlet as soon as possible, but give way to the Queen, who wants to have her son near her? And the Queen? What does she think about it all? Does she feel guilty? What does the Queen know? She has been through passion, murder and silence. She had to suppress everything inside her. One can sense a volcano under her superficial poise.

Ophelia, too, has been drawn into the big game. They listen in to her conversations, ask questions, read her letters. It is true that she gives them up herself. She is at the same time part of the Mechanism, and its victim. Politics hangs here over every feeling, and there is no getting away from it. All the characters are poisoned by it. The only subject of their conversations is politics. It is a kind of madness.

Hamlet loves Ophelia. But he knows he is being watched; moreover—he has more important matters to attend to. Love is gradually fading away. There is no room for it in this world. Hamlet's dramatic cry: "Get thee to a nunnery!" is addressed not to Ophelia alone, but also to those who are overhearing the two lovers. It is to confirm their impression of his alleged madness. But for Hamlet and for Ophelia it means that in the world where murder holds sway, there is no room for love.

From *Shakespeare: Our Contemporary*

Joel Wingard   (b. 1946)

READER-RESPONSE ISSUES IN *HAMLET*   1996

Hamlet is a long play, one of Shakespeare's longest in terms of lines and scenes (though all his plays are five acts). Like any play on the page and like Shakespeare's especially, it is riddled with gaps. Many of these gaps . . . involve the reader's knowing or unknowing. As you read on through the text, you will fill in some of these gaps easily enough as you find out more through the characters' words and actions. Others will remain open; some that have been identified over the years are still open and always will be, even if one strong reading or another has proposed a way to close them.

One consequence of a reader's identification of gaps in the text is the opportunity to apply consistency building as a reading strategy. As you read, or as you watch a production, you may find yourself trying to explain in some kind of logical or consistent terms why Hamlet does what he does, or why he doesn't do what he's supposed to do—get revenge on Claudius—right away. Indeed the question of Hamlet's "delay" or why he delays exacting revenge has been a significant gap in the text for many readers for the past couple of hundred years, a gap filled in differently by various readers. Many readers also have pondered the question of Hamlet's "madness." After he hears his father's ghost's story in Act 1, Hamlet tells his friend Horatio that he will "put an antic disposition on" in order to disguise his inquiry into what the ghost has told him; in other words, he'll act crazy. But over the years, readers have debated the extent to which Hamlet is in control of his insanity act or whether he goes at least temporarily insane as he plays it out. A reader's decision that Hamlet really *is* mad, for instance, based on the way he behaves in Acts 2–4 and on what other characters say about him, is an instance of consistency building to fill in this gap.

The play affords many opportunities for you to use this reading strategy, but you should also remember before you start to read that consistency building has a complementary reading strategy: what the critic Wolfgang Iser calls "wandering viewpoint." This strategy isn't exactly what it sounds like, so it would probably help if you think of it in contrast to consistency building. If consistency building is filling in gaps or closing down interpretive options as you read (Hamlet delays because he goes insane, for instance), adopting a wandering viewpoint means keeping those gaps or options open, not making up your mind as to, for instance, what makes Hamlet tick.

In an academic context, you are used to engaging in consistency building as you read, even if the term itself is new to you, and you are encouraged to practice it for the sake of writing about literature in papers where you have to argue an interpretation. Reading to come up with a consistent interpretation of a complex character or text seems to be the "natural" way of doing things, but of course it is really a learned procedure. If you find *Hamlet* difficult, apart from the language, it may be because you have trouble building a consistent interpretation with such a contradictory character in such a complex play. So it may just take some of that pressure off you to remember that consistency building is an *optional* reading strategy and that you can also read with a wandering viewpoint and leave your interpretive options open.

From "Reading and Responding: A Shakespearean Tragedy"

W. H. Auden   (1907–1973)

Iago as a Triumphant Villain   1962

Any consideration of the *Tragedy of Othello* must be primarily occupied, not with its official hero but with its villain. I cannot think of any other play in which only one character performs personal actions—all the *deeds* are Iago's—and all the others without exception only exhibit behavior. In marrying each other, Othello and Desdemona have performed a deed, but this took place before the play begins. Nor can I think of another play in which the villain is so completely triumphant: everything Iago sets out to do, he accomplishes—(among his goals, I include his self-destruction). Even Cassio, who survives, is maimed for life.

If *Othello* is a tragedy—and one certainly cannot call it a comedy—it is tragic in a peculiar way. In most tragedies the fall of the hero from glory to misery and death is the work, either of the gods, or of his own freely chosen acts, or, more commonly, a mixture of both. But the fall of Othello is the work of another human being; nothing he says or does originates with himself. In consequence we feel pity for him but no respect; our aesthetic respect is reserved for Iago.

Iago is a wicked man. The wicked man, the stage villain, as a subject of serious dramatic interest does not, so far as I know, appear in the drama of western Europe before the Elizabethans. In the mystery plays, the wicked characters, like Satan or Herod, are treated comically, but the theme of the triumphant villain cannot be treated comically because the suffering he inflicts is real.

From "The Joker in the Pack"

Maud Bodkin   (1875–1967)

Lucifer in Shakespeare's *Othello*   1934

If we attempt to define the devil in psychological terms, regarding him as an archetype, a persistent or recurrent mode of apprehension, we may say that the devil is our tendency to represent in personal form the forces within and without us that threaten our supreme values. When Othello finds those values of confident love, of honor, and pride in soldiership, that made up his purposeful life, falling into ruin, his sense of the devil in all around him becomes acute. Desdemona has become "a fair devil"; he feels "a young and sweating devil" in her hand. The cry "O devil" breaks out among his incoherent words of raving. When Iago's falsehoods are disclosed, and Othello at last, too late, wrenches himself free from the spell of Iago's power over him, his sense of the devil incarnate in Iago's shape before him becomes overwhelming. If those who tell of the devil have failed to describe Iago, they have lied:

> I look down towards his feet; but that's a fable.
> If that thou be'st a devil, I cannot kill thee.

We also, watching or reading the play, experience the archetype. Intellectually aware, as we reflect, of natural forces, within a man himself as well as in society around, that betray or shatter his ideals, we yet feel these forces aptly symbolized for the imagination by such a figure as Iago—a being though personal yet hardly human, concentrated wholly on the hunting to destruction of its destined prey, the proud figure of the hero.

From *Archetypal Patterns in Poetry*

Virginia Mason Vaughan (b. 1947)

BLACK AND WHITE IN *OTHELLO* 1994

If virtue no delighted beauty lack, / Your son-in-law is far more fair than black.
—*Othello* (1.3.290–291)

Black/white oppositions permeate *Othello*. Throughout the play, Shakespeare exploits a discourse of racial difference that by 1604 had become ingrained in the English psyche. From Iago's initial racial epithets at Brabantio's window ("old black ram," "barbary horse") to Emilia's cries of outrage in the final scene ("ignorant as dirt"), Shakespeare shows that the union of a white Venetian maiden and a black Moorish general is from at least one perspective emphatically unnatural. The union is of course a central fact of the play, and to some commentators, the spectacle of the pale-skinned woman caught in Othello's black arms has indeed seemed monstrous. Yet that spectacle is a major source of *Othello*'s emotional power. From Shakespeare's day to the present, the sight has titillated and terrified predominantly white audiences.

The effect of *Othello* depends, in other words, on the essential fact of the hero's darkness, the visual signifier of his Otherness. To Shakespeare's original audience, this chromatic sign was probably dark black, although there were other signifiers as well. Roderigo describes the Moor as having "thick lips," a term many sixteenth-century explorers employed in their descriptions of Africans. But, as historian Winthrop Jordan notes, by the late sixteenth century, "Blackness became so generally associated with Africa that every African seemed a black man[,] . . . the terms *Moor* and *Negro* used almost interchangeably." "Moor" became, G. K. Hunter observes, "a word for 'people not like us,' so signaled by color." Richard Burbage's Othello was probably black. But in any production, whether he appears as a tawny Moor (as nineteenth-century actors preferred) or as a black man of African descent, Othello bears the visual signs of his Otherness, a difference that the play's language insists can never be eradicated.

From Othello: A Contextual History

Anthony Burgess   (1917–1993)

AN ASIAN CULTURE LOOKS AT SHAKESPEARE   1982

Is translation possible? I first found myself asking this question in the Far East, when I was given the task of translating T. S. Eliot's *The Waste Land* into Indonesian. The difficulties began with the first line: "April is the cruellest month . . ." This I rendered as *"Bulan Abril ia-lah bulan yang dzalim sa-kali . . . ."* I had to take *dzalim* from Arabic, since Indonesian did not, at that time, seem to possess a word for *cruel*. The term was accepted, but not the notion that a month, as opposed to a person or institution, could be cruel. Moreover, even if a month could be cruel, how—in the tropics where all the months are the same and the concepts of spring and winter do not exist—can one month be crueller than another? When I came to *forgetful snow*—rendered as *thalji berlupa*—I had to borrow a highly poetical word from the Persian, acceptable as a useful descriptive device for the brown skin of the beloved but not known in terms of a climatic reality. And, again, how could this inanimate substance possess the faculty of forgetting? I gave up the task as hopeless. Evidently the imagery of *The Waste Land* does not relate to a universal experience but applies only to the northern hemisphere, with its temperate climate and tradition of spring and fertility rituals.

As a teacher in Malaysia, I had to consider with a mixed group of Malay, Chinese, Indian, and Eurasian students, seasoned with the odd Buginese, Achinese, and Japanese, a piece of representative postwar British fiction. Although the setting of the book is West Africa, I felt that its story was of universal import. It was a novel by Graham Greene called *The Heart of the Matter*—a tragic story about a police officer named Scobie who is a Catholic convert. He is in love with his wife but falls in love with another woman, discovers that he cannot repent of this adultery, makes a sacrilegious communion so that his very Catholic wife will not suspect that a love affair is in progress, then commits suicide in despair, trusting that God will thrust him into the outer darkness and be no longer agonized by the exploits of sinning Scobie. To us this is a tragic situation. To my Muslim students it was extremely funny. One girl said: "Why cannot this Mr. Scobie become a Muslim? Then he can have four wives and there is no problem."

The only author who seemed to have the quality of universal appeal in Malaysia was William Shakespeare. Despite the problems of translating him, there is always an intelligible residue. I remember seeing in a Borneo kampong the film of *Richard III* made by Laurence Olivier, and the illiterate tribe which surrounded me was most appreciative. They knew nothing here of literary history and nothing of the great world outside this jungle clearing. They took this film about medieval conspiracy and tyranny to be a kind of newsreel representation of contemporary England. They approved the medieval costumes because they resembled their own ceremonial dress.

This story of the assassination of innocents, including children, Machiavellian massacre, and the eventual defeat of a tyrant was typical of their own history, even their contemporary experience, and they accepted Shakespeare as a great poet. Eliot would not have registered with them at all. Translation is not a matter of words only; it is a matter of making intelligible a whole culture. Evidently the Elizabethan culture was still primitive enough to survive transportation over much time and space.

From spoken remarks on the "Importance of Translation"

John Russell Brown (b. 1923)

RECOGNIZING LOVE IN A MIDSUMMER NIGHT'S DREAM 1957

The commonest form in which Shakespeare presents the mutual recognition of two lovers is the realization of each other's beauty. For the young lovers in A *Midsummer Night's Dream*, such realization carries its own conviction of exclusive truth; Hermia will not "choose love by another's eyes" (I.i.140), and when Duke Theseus orders her to marry Demetrius whom her father favors, she answers in a single line:

I would my father looked but with my eyes.

(I.i.56)

Even if a lover is inconstant he will always demand the use of his own eyes, and neither the authority of a father nor the force of general opinion can displace a conviction based on such experience. Some lovers, like Helena, may live by such a "truth" even though they recognize that it is exclusive and irrational:

Things base and vile, holding no quantity,
Love can transpose to form and dignity.
Love looks not with the eyes, but with the mind,
And therefore is winged Cupid painted blind.

(I.i.232–235)

In this comedy the irrationality of love's choice provides sport rather than grief. The action takes place in a wood where moonlight and fairy influence suspend our belief in lasting hardship; sometimes a bush may seem to be a bear, but contrariwise even a bear may seem to have no more awful reality than a shadow and may vanish as easily. Moreover the dialogue of the lovers is light and agile so that we are not allowed to dwell upon frustration or suffering. When the sport natural to blind Cupid is heightened by Oberon's enchantment of the lovers' eyes and when events befall preposterously, we find that, even in the telling of the "saddest tale," a "merrier hour was never wasted" (II.i.51, 57).

But our laughter is not thoughtless, for, by bringing Bottom and his fellows to the wood to rehearse a play for the Duke's nuptials, Shakespeare has contrived a contrast to the lovers' single-minded pursuit of their own visions of beauty. Once more Shakespeare's comic vision is expressed in contrasts and relationships; Bottom is the sober man by whom we judge the intoxicated. When Lysander's eyes have been touched with the magic herb, he rationalizes his new love for Helena in the loftiest terms:

Not Hermia but Helena I love.
Who will not change a raven for a dove?
The will of man is by his *reason* swayed;
And *reason* says you are the worthier maid.

(II.ii.119–122)

Without the agency of magic but simply because Demetrius scorns her, Helena has come to believe that she is as "ugly as a bear" (II.ii.100), and protests, as if it were self-evident:

. . . I did never—no, nor never can—
Deserve a sweet look from Demetrius' eye.

(II.ii.132–133)

Helena rationally judges that Lysander's love is a "flout" for her own "insufficiency." And when, in the next scene, Titania is charmed to love Bottom whom Puck has disfigured with an ass's head, she too declares her love as if she were convinced by the best of reasons:

I pray thee, gentle mortal, sing again.
Mine ear is much enamored of thy note;
So is mine eye enthrallèd to thy shape;
And thy fair virtue's force perforce doth move me
On the first view to say, to swear, I love thee.

(III.i.105–109)

With more modesty in judgment, Bottom answers the other lovers as well as Titania:

Methinks, mistress, you should have little reason for that. And yet, to say
the truth, *reason* and love keep little company together nowadays—the
more the pity that some honest neighbors will not make them friends.

(III.i.110–112)

Bottom's modesty in judgment is well placed, for life makes fewer demands on him— "if I had wit enough to get out of this wood, I have enough to serve mine own turn" (III.i. 115–116)—he is not asked to love and also to be wise; his judgment is not at the mercy of his eyes.

When Oberon's spell is broken, Bottom seems to have had a strange dream, but it does not count for so much as the helpless game the lovers have played; much as he would like to, Bottom dares not tell his dream, but the lovers must tell theirs, even to the skeptical ear of Theseus. As the vagaries of love and enchantment had seemed perfectly reasonable to those who were involved, and unreasonable or ridiculous to those who had only observed, so the whole action in the wood, once the first sight of day has passed, will seem more real or more fantastic.

From *Shakespeare and His Comedies*

Germaine Greer   (b. 1939)

SHAKESPEARE'S "HONEST MIRTH"   1986

The Puritan attack on the acting of plays rested on two assumptions, the first that the imitation of human speech and actions was lying and taught dissimulation, and the second that the dressing of men as women was evil in itself. Shakespeare mocks such ethical conundra in divers ways. In *Love's Labor's Lost* and *A Midsummer Night's Dream*, he goes behind the scenes to show the mounting of theatrical presentations, and deliberately poises the simplicity of the performers against the sophistication of the audience. Theseus's master of the revels warns the noble company (in *A Midsummer Night's Dream*) that they will not enjoy the "tedious brief scene of young Pyramus / And his love Thisbe":

> It is not for you. I have heard it over,
> And it is nothing, nothing in the world;
> Unless you can find sport in their intents,
> Extremely stretched and conned with cruel pain
> To do you service.
>   (V, i, 77–81)

Theseus's description of the importance of the active participation of the audience in creating and maintaining the illusion is a basic tenet of the Shakespearian aesthetic, to which he was to cling despite the gibes of more arrogant poets until the end of his writing career.

> The best in this kind are but shadows; and the worst are no worse, if
> imagination amend them.
>   (V, i, 203–204)

The frantic efforts of the players to reassure their audience that there is no need to be afraid of Snug dressed up as a lion are seen in this context as ridiculous not only because the players are not so expert that they could deceive anybody, but because audiences know that what is being presented is invented. Indeed, the action is taken from a classical source that would be known to all literate people either from their school Latin or from Golding's translation, namely the *Metamorphoses of Ovid*.

From Shakespeare

Linda Bamber   (b. 1945)

FEMALE POWER IN *A MIDSUMMER NIGHT'S DREAM*   1982

The best example of the relationship between male dominance and the status quo comes in *A Midsummer Night's Dream*, which begins with a rebellion of the feminine against the power of masculine authority. Hermia refuses the man both Egeus and

Theseus order her to marry; her refusal sends us off into the forest, beyond the power of the father and the masculine state. Once in the forest, of course, we find the social situation metaphorically repeated in this world of imagination and nature. The fairy king, Oberon, rules the forest. His rule, too, is troubled by the rebellion of the feminine. Titania has refused to give him her page, the child of a human friend who died in child birth. But by the end of the story Titania is conquered, the child relinquished, and order restored. Even here the comic upheavals, whether we see them as May games or bad dreams, are associated with an uprising of women. David P. Young, in *Something of Great Constancy,* has pointed out how firmly this play connects order with masculine dominance and the disruption of order with the rebellion of the feminine:

> It is appropriate that Theseus, as representative of daylight and right reason, should have subdued his bride-to-be to the rule of his masculine will. That is the natural order of things. It is equally appropriate that Oberon, as king of darkness and fantasy, should have lost control of his wife, and that the corresponding natural disorder described by Titania should ensue.

The natural order, the status quo, is for men to rule women. When they fail to do so, we have the exceptional situation, the festive, disruptive, disorderly moment of comedy.

A *Midsummer Night's Dream* is actually an anomaly among the festive comedies. It is unusual for the forces of the green world to be directed, as they are here, by a masculine figure. Because the green world here is a partial reproduction of the social world, the feminine is reduced to a kind of first cause of the action while a masculine power directs it. In the other festive comedies the feminine Other presides. She does not *command* the forces of the alternative world, as Oberon does, but since she acts in harmony with these forces her will and desire often prevail.

Where are we to bestow our sympathies? On the forces that make for the disruption of the status quo and therefore for the plot? Or on the force that asserts itself against the disruption and reestablishes a workable social order? Of course we cannot choose. We can only say that in comedy we owe our holiday to such forces as the tendency of the feminine to rebel, whereas to the successful reassertion of masculine power we owe our everyday order. Shakespearean comedy endorses both sides. Holiday is, of course, the subject and the analogue of each play; but the plays always end in a return to everyday life. The optimistic reading of Shakespearean comedy says that everyday life is clarified and enriched by our holiday from it; according to the pessimistic reading the temporary subversion of the social order has revealed how much that order excludes, how high a price we pay for it. But whether our return to everyday life is a comfortable one or not, the return itself is the inevitable conclusion to the journey out.

From *Comic Women, Tragic Men*

Breaking the Language Barrier

The basic problem a modern reader faces with Shakespeare is language. Shakespeare's English is now four hundred years old, and it differs in innumerable small ways from contemporary American usage. Although his idiom may at first seem daunting, it is easily mastered if you make the effort. There is only one way to grow comfortable with Shakespeare's language: you must immerse yourself in it—a highly pleasurable undertaking.

There is no substitute for hearing Shakespeare's language in performance. He wrote the plays to be heard as spoken language rather than read silently on the page. Let your ears do the work. After reading the play in this book, listen to a recording of it. (This is also an invaluable and enjoyable way to review a play.) Most school libraries have recordings of all the major plays of Shakespeare. Hearing *Othello* or *Hamlet* recited by an accomplished actor will almost always communicate its meaning to you, as well as familiarize you with the bard's Elizabethan idiom. It will also help to watch a video or DVD of the play, although you will need to read it carefully as well since most films cut sections of the original text. The more time you spend listening, the more quickly you will master the nuances of the language.

Before you write about any Shakespeare play, read the text more than once. The first time through an Elizabethan-era text, you will almost certainly miss many things. As you grow more familiar with Shakespeare's language, you will be able to read it with more complete comprehension. If you choose to write about a particular episode or character, carefully study the speeches and dialogue in question (paying special attention to footnotes) so that you understand each word. You can't write about a text you don't know how to read. In your paper, don't hesitate to bring in what you have learned. Discuss how key words you quote had different meanings in Shakespeare's day.

Enjoy yourself. From Peking to Berlin, Buenos Aires to Oslo, Shakespeare is almost universally acknowledged as the world's greatest playwright, a master entertainer as well as a consummate artist. Literature holds few pleasures so consistently delectable.

WRITING ASSIGNMENT

Select any tragedy found in the book (*Othello, Hamlet, Riders to the Sea, Oedipus the King,* or *Antigone*), and analyze it using Aristotle's definition of the form. Does the play measure up to Aristotle's requirements for a tragedy? In what ways does it meet the definition? In what ways does it depart from it? (Be sure to state clearly the Aristotelian rules by which drama is to be judged.)

Here is a paper written in response to this assignment by Janet Housden, a student of Melinda Barth at El Camino College.

Janet Housden
Professor Barth
English 201
3 November 20xx

<u>Othello</u>: Tragedy or Soap Opera?

    When we hear the word "tragedy," we usually think of either a terrible real-life disaster, or a dark and serious drama filled with pain, suffering, and loss that involves the downfall of a powerful person due to some character flaw or error in judgment. William Shakespeare's <u>Othello</u> is such a drama. Set in Venice and Cyprus during the Renaissance, the play tells the story of Othello, a Moorish general in the Venetian army, who has just married Desdemona, the daughter of a Venetian nobleman. Through the plotting of a jealous villain, Iago, Othello is deceived into believing that Desdemona has been unfaithful to him. He murders her in revenge, only to discover too late how he has been tricked. Overcome by shame and grief, Othello kills himself.

    Dealing as it does with jealousy, murder, and suicide, the play is certainly dark, but is <u>Othello</u> a true tragedy? In the fourth century B.C., the Greek philosopher Aristotle proposed a formal definition of tragedy (Kennedy 1362), which only partially fits <u>Othello</u>.

    The first characteristic of tragedy identified by Aristotle is that the protagonist is a person of outstanding quality and high social position. While Othello is not of royal birth as are many tragic heroes and heroines, he does occupy a sufficiently high position to satisfy this part of Aristotle's definition. Although Othello is a foreigner and a soldier by trade, he has risen to the rank of general and has married into a noble family, which is quite an accomplishment for an outsider. Furthermore, Othello is generally liked and respected by those around him. He is often described by others as being "noble," "brave," and "valiant." By virtue of his high rank and the respect he commands from others, Othello would appear to possess the high stature commonly given to the tragic hero in order to make his eventual fall seem all the more tragic.

While Othello displays the nobility and high status commonly associated with the tragic hero, he also possesses another, less admirable characteristic, the flaw or character defect shared by all heroes of classical tragedy. In Othello's case, it is a stunning gullibility, combined with a violent temper that once awakened overcomes all reason. These flaws permit Othello to be easily deceived and manipulated by the villainous Iago and make him easy prey for the "green-eyed monster" (3.3.179).

It is because of this tragic flaw, according to Aristotle, that the hero is at least partially to blame for his own downfall. While Othello's "free and open nature, / That thinks men honest that but seem to be so" (1.3.378–79) is not a fault in itself, it does allow Iago to convince the Moor of his wife's infidelity without one shred of concrete evidence. Furthermore, once Othello has been convinced of Desdemona's guilt, he makes up his mind to take vengeance, and that his "bloody thoughts with violent pace / Shall ne'er look back, ne'er ebb to humble love" (3.3.473–74). He thereby renders himself deaf to the voice of reason, and ignoring Desdemona's protestations of innocence, brutally murders her, only to discover too late that he has made a terrible mistake. Although he is goaded into his crime by Iago, who is a master at manipulating people, it is Othello's own character flaws that lead to his horrible misjudgment.

Aristotle's definition also states that the hero's misfortune is not wholly deserved, that the punishment he receives exceeds his crime. Although it is hard to sympathize with a man as cruel as Othello is to the innocent Desdemona, Othello pays an extremely high price for his sin of gullibility. Othello loses everything--his wife, his position, even his life. Even though it's partially his fault, Othello is not entirely to blame, for without Iago's interference it's highly unlikely that things would turn out as they do. Though it seems incredibly stupid on Othello's part, that a man who has travelled the world and commanded armies should be so easily deceived, there is little evidence that Othello has had much experience with civilian society, and although he is "declined / Into the vale of years" (3.3.281-82) Othello has apparently never been married before. By his own admission, "little of this great world can I speak / More than pertains to feats of broils and battle" (1.3.88-89). Furthermore, Othello has no reason to suspect that "honest Iago" is anything but his loyal friend and supporter.

While it is understandable that Othello could be fooled into believing Desdemona unfaithful, the question remains whether his fate is deserved. In addition to his mistake of believing Iago's lies, Othello commits a more serious error: he lets himself be blinded by anger. Worse yet, in deciding to take vengeance, he also makes up his mind not be swayed from his course, even by his love for Desdemona. In fact, he refuses to listen to her at all, "lest her body and beauty unprovide my mind again" (4.1.187-88), therefore denying her the right to defend herself. Because of his rage and unfairness, perhaps Othello deserves his fate more than Aristotle's ideal tragic hero. Othello's punishment does exceed his crime, but just barely.

According to Aristotle, the tragic hero's fall gives the protagonist deeper understanding and self-awareness. Othello departs from Aristotle's model in that Othello apparently learns nothing from his mistakes. He never realizes that he is partly at fault. He sees himself only as an innocent victim and blames his misfortune on fate rather than accepting responsibility for his actions. To be sure, he realizes he has been tricked and deeply regrets his mistake, but he seems to feel that he was justified under the circumstances, "For naught I did in hate, but all in honor" (5.2.303). Othello sees himself not as someone whose bad judgment and worse temper have resulted in the death of an innocent party, but as one who has "loved not wisely but too well" (5.2.354). This failure to grasp the true nature of his error indicates that Othello hasn't learned his lesson.

Neither accepting responsibility nor learning from his mistakes, Othello fails to fulfill yet another of Aristotle's requirements. Since the protagonist usually gains some understanding along with his defeat, classical tragedy conveys a sense of human greatness and of life's unrealized potentialities--a quality totally absent from Othello. Not only does Othello fail to learn from his mistakes, he never really realizes what those mistakes are, and it apparently never crosses his mind that things could have turned out any differently. "Who can control his fate?" Othello asks (5.2.274), and this defeatist attitude, combined with his failure to salvage any wisdom from his defeat, separates Othello from the tragedy defined by Aristotle.

The last part of Aristotle's definition states that viewing the conclusion of a tragedy should result in catharsis for the audience, and that the audience should be left with a feeling of exaltation rather than depression. Unfortunately, the feeling we are left with after viewing Othello is neither catharsis nor exaltation but rather a feeling of horror, pity, and disgust at the senseless waste of human lives. The deaths of Desdemona and Othello, as well as those of Emilia and Roderigo, serve no purpose whatsoever. They die not in the service of a great cause but because of lies, treachery, jealousy, and spite. Their deaths don't even benefit Iago, who is directly or indirectly responsible for all of them. No lesson is learned, no epiphany is reached, and the audience, instead of experiencing catharsis, is left with its negative feeling unresolved.

Since <u>Othello</u> only partially fits Aristotle's definition of tragedy, it is questionable whether or not it should be classified as one. Though it does involve a great man undone by a defect in his own character, the hero gains neither insight nor understanding from his defeat, and so there can be no inspiration or catharsis for the audience, as there would be in a "true" tragedy. <u>Othello</u> is tragic only in the everyday sense of the word, the way a plane crash or fire is tragic. At least in terms of Aristotle's classic definition, <u>Othello</u> ultimately comes across as more of a melodrama or soap opera than a tragedy.

Works Cited

Kennedy, X. J., and Dana Gioia, eds. <u>Literature: An Introduction to Fiction, Poetry, and Drama</u>. 9th ed. New York: Longman, 2005. 1362–63.

Shakespeare, William. <u>Othello, The Moor of Venice</u>. <u>Literature: An Introduction to Fiction, Poetry, and Drama</u>. Ed. X. J. Kennedy and Dana Gioia. 9th ed. New York: Longman, 2005. 1502–1600.

Further Suggestions for Writing

1. Write a defense of Iago.
2. "Never was any play fraught, like this of Othello, with improbabilities," wrote Thomas Rymer in a famous attack (*A Short View of Tragedy*, 1692). Consider Rymer's objection to the play, either answering it or finding evidence to back him up.
3. Suppose yourself a casting director assigned to a film version of *Othello*. What well-known actors would you cast in the principal roles? Write a report justifying your choices. Don't merely discuss the stars and their qualifications; discuss (with specific reference to the play) what Shakespeare appears to call for.
4. Emilia's long speech at the end of Act IV (iii, 84–103) has been called a Renaissance plea for women's liberation. Do you agree? Write a brief, close analysis of this speech. How timely is it?
5. "The downfall of Oedipus is the work of the gods; the downfall of Othello is self-inflicted." Test this comment with reference to the two plays, and report your findings.
6. In what respects does *Hamlet* resemble a classical tragedy, such as *Oedipus Rex*? In what ways is Shakespeare's play different? Is Hamlet, like Oedipus, driven to his death by some inexorable force (Fate, the gods, the nature of things)?
7. Write a defense of Claudius.
8. "Hamlet is a mentally unstable young man who is obsessed with his father's death. He is angry at his mother for remarrying so quickly. The Ghost is not real. It is only a projection of the Prince's deranged imagination." Write an essay to support or refute this argument. Use specific incidents in the play to back up your position.
9. Suppose you are a casting director assigned to a film version of *Hamlet*. What well-known actors would you cast in the principal roles? Write a report to the producer justifying your choices. Don't merely discuss the stars and their qualifications; discuss how each star possesses specific skills and attributes that Shakespeare calls for.
10. Contrast the palace and the woods as settings in *A Midsummer Night's Dream*.
11. Explain the connection between the comic sketch presented by the rustic tradesmen on Pyramus and Thisbe with the events that occur elsewhere in the play.

REALISM AND NATURALISM

As the twentieth century began, realism in the theaters of Western Europe, England, and America appeared to have won a resounding victory. (**Realism** in drama, like realism in fiction, may be broadly defined as an attempt to reproduce faithfully the surface appearance of life, especially that of ordinary people in everyday situations.) The theater had been slow to admit controversial or unpleasant themes and reluctant to shed its traditional conventions. From Italian playhouses of the sixteenth century, it had inherited the **picture-frame stage:** one that holds the action within a **proscenium arch,** a gateway standing (as the word *proscenium* indicates) "in front of the scenery." This manner of constructing a playhouse in effect divided the actors from their audience; most commercial theaters even today are so constructed. But as the new century began, actors less often declaimed their passions in oratorical style in front of backdrops painted with waterfalls and volcanoes, while stationed exactly at the center of the stage as if to sing "duets meant to bring forth applause" (as Swedish playwright August Strindberg complained). By 1891 even Victorian London had witnessed a production of a play that frankly portrayed a man dying of venereal disease—Henrik Ibsen's *Ghosts.*

In the theater of realism, a room was represented by a **box set**—three walls that joined in two corners and a ceiling that tilted as if seen in perspective—replacing drapery walls that had billowed and doors that had flapped, not slammed. Instead of posing at stage center to deliver key speeches, actors were instructed to speak from wherever the dramatic situation placed them and now and then turn their backs upon the audience. They were to behave as if they were in a room with the fourth wall sliced away, unaware that they had an audience.

This realistic convention is familiar to us today, not only from realistic plays but also from the typical television soap opera or situation comedy that takes place in such a three-walled room, with every cup and spoon revealed by the camera. However, such realism went against a long tradition. Watching a play by Sophocles, the spectators, we may safely assume, had to exert their imaginations. We do not expect an ancient Greek tragedy literally to represent the lives of ordinary people in everyday situations. On the contrary, a tragedy, according to Aristotle, its leading ancient theorist, represents an "action of supreme importance," an extraordinary moment in the life of a king or queen or other person of high estate. An open-air stage, though Sophocles adorned it with painted scenery, could hardly change day into night as lighting technicians commonly do today or aspire to reproduce in detail a whole palace. Such limitations prevailed upon the theater of Shakespeare as well, encouraging the Bard to flesh out his scene with vivid language, making the spectator willing to imagine that the simple stage— the "wooden O"—is a forest, a storm-swept landscape, or a battlefield. In the classic Nō theater of Japan, spectators recognize conventional props. A simple framework is a boat, four posts and a roof are a palace, an actor's fan may be any useful object—a paintbrush, say, or a knife. In such a nonrealistic theater, the playwright, unhampered by stage sets, can shift scenes as rapidly as the audience can imagine.

In the realistic three-walled room, actors could hardly rant (or, Hamlet said, "tear a passion to tatters") without seeming foolish. Another effect of more lifelike direction was to discourage use of such devices as the soliloquy and the **aside** (villain to audience: "Heh! heh! Now she's in my power!"). To encourage actors further to imitate reality, the influential director Constantin Stanislavsky of the Moscow Art Theater developed his famous system to help actors feel at home inside a playwright's characters. One of Stanislavsky's exercises was to have actors search their memories for personal experiences like those of the characters in the play; another was to have them act out things a character did *not* do in the play but might do in life. The system enabled Stanislavsky to bring authenticity to his productions of Chekhov's plays and of Maxim Gorky's *The Lower Depths* (1902), a play that showed the tenants of a sordid lodging house drinking themselves to death (and hanging themselves) in surroundings of realistic squalor.

Gorky's play is a masterpiece of **naturalism,** a kind of realism in fiction and drama dealing with the more brutal or unpleasant aspects of reality. As codified by French novelist and playwright Émile Zola, who influenced Ibsen, naturalism viewed a person as a creature whose acts are determined by heredity and environment; Zola urged writers to study their characters' behavior with the detachment of zoologists studying animals.

No sooner had realism and naturalism won the day than a reaction arose. One opposing force was the **Symbolist movement** in the French theater, most influentially expressed by Belgian playwright Maurice Maeterlinck. Like French Symbolist poets Charles Baudelaire and Stéphane Mallarmé, Maeterlinck assumes that the visible world reflects a spirit world we cannot directly perceive. Accordingly, his plays are filled with hints and portents: suggestive objects (jeweled rings, veils, distant candles), mysterious locales (crumbling castles, dim grottoes), vague sounds from afar, and dialogue rich in silences and unfinished sentences. In *The Intruder* (1890), a blind man sees the approach of Death. In *Pelléas and Mélisande* (1892), a typical bit of Symbolist stage business occurs. A small boy stands on his grandfather's shoulders to peer through a high window and speak of wonders invisible to an audience. (For more about symbolism and Symbolists, see Chapters Seven and Twenty-three.)

Elsewhere, others were working along similar lines. In Russia, Anton Chekhov, whose plays on the surface appeared realistic, created some of his best work around a symbol (*The Seagull, The Cherry Orchard*). In Ireland, poet William Butler Yeats, who in 1899 had helped found the Irish Dramatic Movement, was himself of a different mind from the realistic playwrights whose work he had helped produce in Dublin's Abbey Theater. Drawing on Irish lore and legend, Yeats wrote (among other plays) "plays for dancers" to be performed in drawing rooms, often in friends' homes, with simple costumes and props, a few masked actors, and a very few musicians. In Sweden, August Strindberg, who earlier had won fame as a naturalist, reversed direction and in *The Dream Play* (1902) and *The Ghost Sonata* (1907) introduced characters who change their identities and, ignoring space and time, move across dreamlike landscapes. In these plays Strindberg anticipated the movement called **Expressionism** in German theater after World War I. Delighting in bizarre sets and exaggerated makeup and costuming, expressionist playwrights and producers sought to reflect intense states of emotion and, sometimes, to depict the world through lunatic eyes. A classic example (on film) is *The Cabinet of Dr. Caligari*, made in Berlin in 1919–1920, in which a hypnotist sends forth a subject to murder people. Garbed in jet black, the killer sleepwalks through a town of lopsided houses, twisted streets, and railings that tilt at gravity-defying angles. In expressionist movies and plays, madness is objectified and dreams become realities.

In 1893 Strindberg had complained of producers who represented a kitchen by a drapery painted with pictures of kettles; but by 1900, realistic play production had gone to opposite extremes. In the 1920s the curtain rose upon a Broadway play with a detailed replica of a Schrafft's restaurant, complete to the last fork and folded napkin. (Still, critic George Jean Nathan remarked, no matter how elaborate a stage dinner, the table never seemed to have any butter.) Theaters housed increasingly complicated machines, making it all the easier to present scenes full of realistic detail. Elevators lifted heavy sets swiftly and quietly into place; other sets, at the touch of a button, revolved on giant turntables. Theaters became warehouses for huge ready-made scenery.

Some playwrights fought domination by the painstakingly realistic set. Bertolt Brecht in Germany and Luigi Pirandello in Italy conceived plays to be performed on bare stages—gas pipes and plaster in full view—to remind spectators that they beheld events in a theater, not in the world. In reaction against the traditional picture-frame stage, new kinds of theaters were designed, such as the **arena theater,** or **theater in the round,** in which the audience sits on all four sides of the performing area; and the **flexible theater,** in which the seats are movable. Such theaters usually are not commercial (most of which maintain their traditional picture-frame stages, built decades ago). Rather, the alternative theaters are found in college and civic playhouses, in storefronts, and in converted lofts. Proponents of arena staging claim that it brings actors and audience into greater intimacy; opponents, that it keeps the actors artificially circulating like goldfish in a bowl. Perhaps it is safe to say only that some plays lend themselves to being seen head-on in a picture frame; others, to being surrounded. Ibsen's *A Doll's House*, a pioneering work of realism, is of the former type. The play derives a good deal of its power from our ability to identify with its characters and the lives they live, an identification that Ibsen achieves in part by framing the action with the details of daily existence.

Henrik Ibsen

A DOLL'S HOUSE 1879

TRANSLATED BY JAMES MCFARLANE

Henrik Ibsen

Henrik Ibsen (1828–1906) was born in Skien, a seaport in Norway. When he was six, his father's business losses suddenly reduced his wealthy family to poverty. After a brief attempt to study medicine, young Ibsen worked as a stage manager in provincial Bergen; then, becoming known as a playwright, he moved to Oslo as artistic director of the National Theater—practical experiences that gained him firm grounding in his craft. Discouraged when his theater failed and the king turned down his plea for a grant to enable him to write, Ibsen left Norway and for twenty-seven years lived in Italy and Germany. There, in his middle years (1879–1891), he wrote most of his famed plays about small-town life, among them A Doll's House, Ghosts, An Enemy of the People, The Wild Duck, *and* Hedda Gabler. *Introducing social problems to the stage, these plays aroused storms of controversy. Although best known as a realist, Ibsen early in his career wrote poetic dramas based on Norwegian history and folklore: the tragedy* Brand *(1866) and the powerful, wildly fantastic* Peer Gynt *(1867). He ended as a Symbolist in* John Gabriel Borkman *(1896) and* When We Dead Awaken *(1899), both encompassing huge mountains that heaven-assaulting heroes try to climb. Late in life Ibsen returned to Oslo, honored at last both at home and abroad.*

Characters

Torvald Helmer, a lawyer
Nora, his wife
Dr. Rank
Mrs. Kristine Linde
Nils Krogstad
Anne Marie, the nursemaid
Helene, the maid
The Helmers' three children
A Porter

The action takes place in the Helmers' flat.

ACT I

A pleasant room, tastefully but not expensively furnished. On the back wall, one door on the right leads to the entrance hall, a second door on the left leads to Helmer's study. Between these two doors, a piano. In the middle of the left wall, a door; and downstage from it, a window. Near the window a round table with armchairs and a small sofa. In the right wall, upstage, a door; and on the same wall downstage, a porcelain stove with a couple of armchairs and a rocking chair. Between the stove and the door a small table. Etchings on the walls. A whatnot with china and other small objets d'art; a small bookcase with books in handsome bindings. Carpet on the floor; a fire burns in the stove. A winter's day.

The front door-bell rings in the hall; a moment later, there is the sound of the front door being opened. Nora comes into the room, happily humming to herself. She is dressed in her outdoor things, and is carrying lots of parcels which she then puts down on the table, right. She leaves the door into the hall standing open; a Porter can be seen outside holding a Christmas tree and a basket; he hands them to the Maid who has opened the door for them.

Nora: Hide the Christmas tree away carefully, Helene. The children mustn't see it till this evening when it's decorated. [*To the Porter, taking out her purse.*] How much?

A Doll's House (*The Harvard Theatre Collection, The Houghton Library*)

Porter: Fifty öre.

Nora: There's a crown. Keep the change.

[*The Porter thanks her and goes. Nora shuts the door. She continues to laugh quietly and happily to herself as she takes off her things. She takes a bag of macaroons out of her pocket and eats one or two; then she walks stealthily across and listens at her husband's door.*]

Nora: Yes, he's in.

[*She begins humming again as she walks over to the table, right.*]

Helmer [*in his study*]: Is that my little sky-lark chirruping out there?

Nora [*busy opening some of the parcels*]: Yes, it is.

Helmer: Is that my little squirrel frisking about?

Nora: Yes!

Helmer: When did my little squirrel get home?

Nora: Just this minute. [*She stuffs the bag of macaroons in her pocket and wipes her mouth.*] Come on out, Torvald, and see what I've bought.

Helmer: I don't want to be disturbed! [*A moment later, he opens the door and looks out, his pen in his hand.*] "Bought," did you say? All that? Has my little spendthrift been out squandering money again?

Nora: But, Torvald, surely this year we can spread ourselves just a little. This is the first Christmas we haven't had to go carefully.

Helmer: Ah, but that doesn't mean we can afford to be extravagant, you know.

Nora: Oh yes, Torvald, surely we can afford to be just a little bit extravagant now, can't we? Just a teeny-weeny bit. You are getting quite a good salary now, and you are going to earn lots and lots of money.

Helmer: Yes, after the New Year. But it's going to be three whole months before the first pay cheque comes in.

Nora: Pooh! We can always borrow in the meantime.

Helmer: Nora! [*Crosses to her and takes her playfully by the ear.*] Here we go again, you and your frivolous ideas! Suppose I went and borrowed a thousand crowns today, and you went and spent it all over Christmas, then on New Year's Eve a slate fell and hit me on the head and there I was. . . .

Nora [*putting her hand over his mouth*]: Sh! Don't say such horrid things.

Helmer: Yes, but supposing something like that did happen . . . what then?

Nora: If anything as awful as that did happen, I wouldn't care if I owed anybody anything or not.

Helmer: Yes, but what about the people I'd borrowed from?

Nora: Them? Who cares about them! They are only strangers!

Helmer: Nora, Nora! Just like a woman! Seriously though, Nora, you know what I think about these things. No debts! Never borrow! There's always something inhibited, something unpleasant, about a home built on credit and borrowed money. We two have managed to stick it out so far, and that's the way we'll go on for the little time that remains.

Nora [*walks over to the stove*]: Very well, just as you say, Torvald.

Helmer [*following her*]: There, there! My little singing bird mustn't go drooping her wings, eh? Has it got the sulks, that little squirrel of mine? [*Takes out his wallet.*] Nora, what do you think I've got here?

Nora [*quickly turning round*]: Money!

Helmer: There! [*He hands her some notes*]. Good heavens, I know only too well how Christmas runs away with the housekeeping.

Nora [*counts*]: Ten, twenty, thirty, forty. Oh, thank you, thank you, Torvald! This will see me quite a long way.

Helmer: Yes, it'll have to.

Nora: Yes, yes, I'll see that it does. But come over here, I want to show you all the things I've bought. And so cheap! Look, some new clothes for Ivar . . . and a little sword. There's a horse and a trumpet for Bob. And a doll and a doll's cot for Emmy. They are not very grand but she'll have them all broken before long anyway. And I've got some dress material and some handkerchiefs for the maids. Though, really, dear old Anne Marie should have had something better.

Helmer: And what's in this parcel here?

Nora [*shrieking*]: No, Torvald! You mustn't see that till tonight!

Helmer: All right. But tell me now, what did my little spendthrift fancy for herself?

Nora: For me? Puh, I don't really want anything.

Helmer: Of course you do. Anything reasonable that you think you might like, just tell me.

Nora: Well, I don't really know. As a matter of fact, though, Torvald . . .

Helmer: Well?

Nora [*toying with his coat buttons, and without looking at him*]: If you did want to give me something, you could . . . you could always . . .

Helmer: Well, well, out with it!

Nora [*quickly*]: You could always give me money, Torvald. Only what you think you could spare. And then I could buy myself something with it later on.

Helmer: But Nora. . . .

Nora: Oh, please, Torvald dear! Please! I beg you. Then I'd wrap the money up in some pretty gilt paper and hang it on the Christmas tree. Wouldn't that be fun?

Helmer: What do we call my pretty little pet when it runs away with all the money?

Nora: I know, I know, we call it a spendthrift. But please let's do what I said, Torvald. Then I'll have a bit of time to think about what I need most. Isn't that awfully sensible, now, eh?

Helmer [*smiling*]: Yes, it is indeed—that is, if only you really could hold on to the money I gave you, and really did buy something for yourself with it. But it just gets mixed up with the housekeeping and frittered away on all sorts of useless things, and then I have to dig into my pocket all over again.

Nora: Oh but, Torvald. . . .

Helmer: You can't deny it, Nora dear. [*Puts his arm round her waist.*] My pretty little pet is very sweet, but it runs away with an awful lot of money. It's incredible how expensive it is for a man to keep such a pet.

Nora: For shame! How can you say such a thing? As a matter of fact I save everything I can.

Helmer [*laughs*]: Yes, you are right there. Everything you *can*. But you simply can't.

Nora [*hums and smiles quietly and happily*]: Ah, if you only knew how many expenses the likes of us sky-larks and squirrels have, Torvald!

Helmer: What a funny little one you are! Just like your father. Always on the look-out for money, wherever you can lay your hands on it; but as soon as you've got it, it just seems to slip through your fingers. You never seem to know what you've done with it. Well, one must accept you as you are. It's in the blood. Oh yes, it is, Nora. That sort of thing is hereditary.

Nora: Oh, I only wish I'd inherited a few more of Daddy's qualities.

Helmer: And I wouldn't want my pretty little song-bird to be the least bit different from what she is now. But come to think of it, you look rather . . . rather . . . how shall I put it? . . . rather guilty today. . . .

Nora: Do I?

Helmer: Yes, you do indeed. Look me straight in the eye.

Nora [*looks at him*]: Well?

Helmer [*wagging his finger at her*]: My little sweet-tooth surely didn't forget herself in town today?

Nora: No, whatever makes you think that?

Helmer: She didn't just pop into the confectioner's for a moment?

Nora: No, I assure you, Torvald . . . !

Helmer: Didn't try sampling the preserves?

Nora: No, really I didn't.

Helmer: Didn't go nibbling a macaroon or two?

Nora: No, Torvald, honestly, you must believe me . . . !

Helmer: All right then! It's really just my little joke. . . .

Nora [*crosses to the table*]: I would never dream of doing anything you didn't want me to.

Helmer: Of course not, I know that. And then you've given me your word. . . . [*Crosses to her.*] Well then, Nora dearest, you shall keep your little Christmas secrets. They'll all come out tonight, I dare say, when we light the tree.

Nora: Did you remember to invite Dr. Rank?

Helmer: No. But there's really no need. Of course he'll come and have dinner with us. Anyway, I can ask him when he looks in this morning. I've ordered some good wine. Nora, you can't imagine how I am looking forward to this evening.

Nora: So am I. And won't the children enjoy it, Torvald!

Helmer: Oh, what a glorious feeling it is, knowing you've got a nice, safe job, and a good fat income. Don't you agree? Isn't it wonderful, just thinking about it?

Nora: Oh, it's marvellous!

Helmer: Do you remember last Christmas? Three whole weeks beforehand you shut yourself up every evening till after midnight making flowers for the Christmas tree and all the other splendid things you wanted to surprise us with. Ugh, I never felt so bored in all my life.

Nora: I wasn't the least bit bored.

Helmer [smiling]: But it turned out a bit of an anticlimax, Nora.

Nora: Oh, you are not going to tease me about that again! How was I to know the cat would get in and pull everything to bits?

Helmer: No, of course you weren't. Poor little Nora! All you wanted was for us to have a nice time—and it's the thought behind it that counts, after all. All the same, it's a good thing we've seen the back of those lean times.

Nora: Yes, really it's marvellous.

Helmer: Now there's no need for me to sit here all on my own, bored to tears. And you don't have to strain your dear little eyes, and work those dainty little fingers to the bone. . . .

Nora [clapping her hands]: No, Torvald, I don't, do I? Not any more. Oh, how marvellous it is to hear that! [*Takes his arm.*] Now I want to tell you how I've been thinking we might arrange things, Torvald. As soon as Christmas is over. . . . [*The door-bell rings in the hall.*] Oh, there's the bell. [*Tidies one or two things in the room.*] It's probably a visitor. What a nuisance!

Helmer: Remember I'm not at home to callers.

Maid [in the doorway]: There's a lady to see you, ma'am.

Nora: Show her in, please.

Maid [to Helmer]: And the doctor's just arrived, too, sir.

Helmer: Did he go straight into my room?

Maid: Yes, he did, sir.

[*Helmer goes into his study. The Maid shows in Mrs. Linde, who is in traveling clothes, and closes the door after her.*]

Mrs. Linde [subdued and rather hesitantly]: How do you do, Nora?

Nora [uncertainly]: How do you do?

Mrs. Linde: I'm afraid you don't recognize me.

Nora: No, I don't think I . . . And yet I seem to. . . . [*Bursts out suddenly.*] Why! Kristine! Is it really you?

Mrs. Linde: Yes, it's me.

Nora: Kristine! Fancy not recognizing you again! But how was I to, when . . . [*Gently.*] How you've changed, Kristine!

Mrs. Linde: I dare say I have. In nine . . . ten years. . . .

Nora: Is it so long since we last saw each other? Yes, it must be. Oh, believe me these last eight years have been such a happy time. And now you've come up to town, too? All that long journey in wintertime. That took courage.

Mrs. Linde: I just arrived this morning on the steamer.

Nora: To enjoy yourself over Christmas, of course. How lovely! Oh, we'll have such fun, you'll see. Do take off your things. You are not cold, are you?

[*Helps her.*] There now! Now let's sit down here in comfort beside the stove. No, here, you take the armchair, I'll sit here on the rocking chair. [*Takes her hands.*] Ah, now you look a bit more like your old self again. It was just that when I first saw you. . . . But you are a little paler, Kristine . . . and perhaps even a bit thinner!

Mrs. Linde: And much, much older, Nora.

Nora: Yes, perhaps a little older . . . very, very little, not really very much. [*Stops suddenly and looks serious.*] Oh, what a thoughtless creature I am, sitting here chattering on like this! Dear, sweet Kristine, can you forgive me?

Mrs. Linde: What do you mean, Nora?

Nora [*gently*]: Poor Kristine, of course you're a widow now.

Mrs. Linde: Yes, my husband died three years ago.

Nora: Oh, I remember now. I read about it in the papers. Oh, Kristine, believe me I often thought at the time of writing to you. But I kept putting it off, something always seemed to crop up.

Mrs. Linde: My dear Nora, I understand so well.

Nora: No, it wasn't very nice of me, Kristine. Oh, you poor thing, what you must have gone through. And didn't he leave you anything?

Mrs. Linde: No.

Nora: And no children?

Mrs. Linde: No.

Nora: Absolutely nothing?

Mrs. Linde: Nothing at all . . . not even a broken heart to grieve over.

Nora [*looks at her incredulously*]: But, Kristine, is that possible?

Mrs. Linde [*smiles sadly and strokes Nora's hair*]: Oh, it sometimes happens, Nora.

Nora: So utterly alone. How terribly sad that must be for you. I have three lovely children. You can't see them for the moment, because they're out with their nanny. But now you must tell me all about yourself. . . .

Mrs. Linde: No, no, I want to hear about you.

Nora: No, you start. I won't be selfish today. I must think only about your affairs today. But there's just one thing I really must tell you. Have you heard about the great stroke of luck we've had in the last few days?

Mrs. Linde: No. What is it?

Nora: What do you think? My husband has just been made Bank Manager!

Mrs. Linde: Your husband? How splendid!

Nora: Isn't it tremendous! It's not a very steady way of making a living, you know, being a lawyer, especially if he refuses to take on anything that's the least bit shady—which of course is what Torvald does, and I think he's quite right. You can imagine how pleased we are! He starts at the Bank straight after New Year, and he's getting a big salary and lots of commission. From now on we'll be able to live quite differently . . . we'll do just what we want. Oh, Kristine, I'm so happy and relieved. I must say it's lovely to have plenty of money and not have to worry. Isn't it?

Mrs. Linde: Yes. It must be nice to have enough, at any rate.

Nora: No, not just enough, but pots and pots of money.

Mrs. Linde [*smiles*]: Nora, Nora, haven't you learned any sense yet? At school you used to be an awful spendthrift.

Nora: Yes, Torvald still says I am. [*Wags her finger.*] But little Nora isn't as stupid as everybody thinks. Oh, we haven't really been in a position where I could afford to spend a lot of money. We've both had to work.

Mrs. Linde: You too?

Nora: Yes, odd jobs—sewing, crochet-work, embroidery and things like that. [*Casually.*] And one or two other things, besides. I suppose you know that Torvald left the Ministry when we got married. There weren't any prospects of promotion in his department, and of course he needed to earn more money than he had before. But the first year he wore himself out completely. He had to take on all kinds of extra jobs, you know, and he found himself working all hours of the day and night. But he couldn't go on like that; and he became seriously ill. The doctors said it was essential for him to go South.

Mrs. Linde: Yes, I believe you spent a whole year in Italy, didn't you?

Nora: That's right. It wasn't easy to get away, I can tell you. It was just after I'd had Ivar. But of course we had to go. Oh, it was an absolutely marvellous trip. And it saved Torvald's life. But it cost an awful lot of money, Kristine.

Mrs. Linde: That I can well imagine.

Nora: Twelve hundred dollars. Four thousand eight hundred crowns. That's a lot of money, Kristine.

Mrs. Linde: Yes, but in such circumstances, one is very lucky if one has it.

Nora: Well, we got it from Daddy, you see.

Mrs. Linde: Ah, that was it. It was just about then your father died, I believe, wasn't it?

Nora: Yes, Kristine, just about then. And do you know, I couldn't even go and look after him. Here was I expecting Ivar any day. And I also had poor Torvald, gravely ill, on my hands. Dear, kind Daddy! I never saw him again, Kristine. Oh, that's the saddest thing that has happened to me in all my married life.

Mrs. Linde: I know you were very fond of him. But after that you left for Italy?

Nora: Yes, we had the money then, and the doctors said it was urgent. We left a month later.

Mrs. Linde: And your husband came back completely cured?

Nora: Fit as a fiddle!

Mrs. Linde: But . . . what about the doctor?

Nora: How do you mean?

Mrs. Linde: I thought the maid said something about the gentleman who came at the same time as me being a doctor.

Nora: Yes, that was Dr. Rank. But this isn't a professional visit. He's our best friend and he always looks in at least once a day. No, Torvald has never had a day's illness since. And the children are fit and healthy, and so am I. [*Jumps up and claps her hands.*] Oh God, oh God, isn't it marvellous to be alive, and to be happy, Kristine! . . . Oh, but I ought to be ashamed of myself . . . Here I go on talking about nothing but myself. [*She sits on a low stool near*

Mrs. Linde and lays her arms on her lap.] Oh, please, you mustn't be angry with me! Tell me, is it really true that you didn't love your husband? What made you marry him, then?

Mrs. Linde: My mother was still alive; she was bedridden and helpless. And then I had my two young brothers to look after as well. I didn't think I would be justified in refusing him.

Nora: No, I dare say you are right. I suppose he was fairly wealthy then?

Mrs. Linde: He was quite well off, I believe. But the business was shaky. When he died, it went all to pieces, and there just wasn't anything left.

Nora: What then?

Mrs. Linde: Well, I had to fend for myself, opening a little shop, running a little school, anything I could turn my hand to. These last three years have been one long relentless drudge. But now it's finished, Nora. My poor dear mother doesn't need me any more, she's passed away. Nor the boys either; they're at work now, they can look after themselves.

Nora: What a relief you must find it. . . .

Mrs. Linde: No, Nora! Just unutterably empty. Nobody to live for any more. [*Stands up restlessly.*] That's why I couldn't stand it any longer being cut off up there. Surely it must be a bit easier here to find something to occupy your mind. If only I could manage to find a steady job of some kind, in an office perhaps. . . .

Nora: But, Kristine, that's terribly exhausting; and you look so worn out even before you start. The best thing for you would be a little holiday at some quiet little resort.

Mrs. Linde [*crosses to the window*]: I haven't any father I can fall back on for the money, Nora.

Nora [*rises*]: Oh, please, you mustn't be angry with me!

Mrs. Linde [*goes to her*]: My dear Nora, you mustn't be angry with me either. That's the worst thing about people in my position, they become so bitter. One has nobody to work for, yet one has to be on the look-out all the time. Life has to go on, and one starts thinking only of oneself. Believe it or not, when you told me the good news about your step up, I was pleased not so much for your sake as for mine.

Nora: How do you mean? Ah, I see. You think Torvald might be able to do something for you.

Mrs. Linde: Yes, that's exactly what I thought.

Nora: And so he shall, Kristine. Just leave things to me. I'll bring it up so cleverly . . . I'll think up something to put him in a good mood. Oh, I do so much want to help you.

Mrs. Linde: It is awfully kind of you, Nora, offering to do all this for me, particularly in your case, where you haven't known much trouble or hardship in your own life.

Nora: When I . . . ? I haven't known much . . . ?

Mrs. Linde [*smiling*]: Well, good heavens, a little bit of sewing to do and a few things like that. What a child you are, Nora!

Nora [*tosses her head and walks across the room*]: I wouldn't be too sure of that, if I were you.

Mrs. Linde: Oh?

Nora: You're just like the rest of them. You all think I'm useless when it comes to anything really serious. . . .

Mrs. Linde: Come, come. . . .

Nora: You think I've never had anything much to contend with in this hard world.

Mrs. Linde: Nora dear, you've only just been telling me all the things you've had to put up with.

Nora: Pooh! They were just trivialities! [*Softly.*] I haven't told you about the really big thing.

Mrs. Linde: What big thing? What do you mean?

Nora: I know you rather tend to look down on me, Kristine. But you shouldn't, you know. You are proud of having worked so hard and so long for your mother.

Mrs. Linde: I'm sure I don't look down on anybody. But it's true what you say: I am both proud and happy when I think of how I was able to make Mother's life a little easier towards the end.

Nora: And you are proud when you think of what you have done for your brothers, too.

Mrs. Linde: I think I have every right to be.

Nora: I think so too. But now I'm going to tell you something, Kristine. I too have something to be proud and happy about.

Mrs. Linde: I don't doubt that. But what is it you mean?

Nora: Not so loud. Imagine if Torvald were to hear! He must never on any account . . . nobody must know about it, Kristine, nobody but you.

Mrs. Linde: But what is it?

Nora: Come over here. [*She pulls her down on the sofa beside her.*] Yes, Kristine, I too have something to be proud and happy about. I was the one who saved Torvald's life.

Mrs. Linde: Saved . . . ? How . . . ?

Nora: I told you about our trip to Italy. Torvald would never have recovered but for that. . . .

Mrs. Linde: Well? Your father gave you what money was necessary. . . .

Nora [*smiles*]: That's what Torvald thinks, and everybody else. But . . .

Mrs. Linde: But . . . ?

Nora: Daddy never gave us a penny. I was the one who raised the money.

Mrs. Linde: You? All that money?

Nora: Twelve hundred dollars. Four thousand eight hundred crowns. What do you say to that!

Mrs. Linde: But, Nora, how was it possible? Had you won a sweepstake or something?

Nora [*contemptuously*]: A sweepstake? Pooh! There would have been nothing to it then.

Mrs. Linde: Where did you get it from, then?

Nora [hums and smiles secretively]: H'm, tra-la-la!

Mrs. Linde: Because what you couldn't do was borrow it.

Nora: Oh? Why not?

Mrs. Linde: Well, a wife can't borrow without her husband's consent.

Nora [tossing her head]: Ah, but when it happens to be a wife with a bit of a sense
for business . . . a wife who knows her way about things, then. . . .

Mrs. Linde: But, Nora, I just don't understand. . . .

Nora: You don't have to. I haven't said I did borrow the money. I might have
got it some other way. [Throws herself back on the sofa.] I might even have
got it from some admirer. Anyone as reasonably attractive as I am. . . .

Mrs. Linde: Don't be so silly!

Nora: Now you must be dying of curiosity, Kristine.

Mrs. Linde: Listen to me now, Nora dear—you haven't done anything rash,
have you?

Nora [sitting up again]: Is it rash to save your husband's life?

Mrs. Linde: I think it was rash to do anything without telling him. . . .

Nora: But the whole point was that he mustn't know anything. Good heavens,
can't you see! He wasn't even supposed to know how desperately ill he was.
It was me the doctors came and told his life was in danger, that the only way
to save him was to go South for a while. Do you think I didn't try talking
him into it first? I began dropping hints about how nice it would be if I could
be taken on a little trip abroad, like other young wives. I wept, I pleaded. I
told him he ought to show some consideration for my condition, and let me
have a bit of my own way. And then I suggested he might take out a loan.
But at that he nearly lost his temper, Kristine. He said I was being frivolous,
that it was his duty as a husband not to give in to all these whims and fancies of mine—as I do believe he called them. All right, I thought, somehow
you've got to be saved. And it was then I found a way. . . .

Mrs. Linde: Did your husband never find out from your father that the money
hadn't come from him?

Nora: No, never. It was just about the time Daddy died. I'd intended letting him
into the secret and asking him not to give me away. But when he was so ill
. . . I'm sorry to say it never became necessary.

Mrs. Linde: And you never confided in your husband?

Nora: Good heavens, how could you ever imagine such a thing! When he's so
strict about such matters! Besides, Torvald is a man with a good deal of
pride—it would be terribly embarrassing and humiliating for him if he
thought he owed anything to me. It would spoil everything between us; this
happy home of ours would never be the same again.

Mrs. Linde: Are you never going to tell him?

Nora [reflectively, half-smiling]: Oh yes, some day perhaps . . . in many years time,
when I'm no longer as pretty as I am now. You mustn't laugh! What I mean
of course is when Torvald isn't quite so much in love with me as he is now,
when he's lost interest in watching me dance, or get dressed up, or recite.

Then it might be a good thing to have something in reserve. . . . [*Breaks off.*] What nonsense! That day will never come. Well, what have you got to say to my big secret, Kristine? Still think I'm not much good for anything? One thing, though, it's meant a lot of worry for me, I can tell you. it hasn't always been easy to meet my obligations when the time came. You know in business there is something called quarterly interest, and other things called instalments, and these are always terribly difficult things to cope with. So what I've had to do is save a little here and there, you see, wherever I could. I couldn't really save anything out of the housekeeping, because Torvald has to live in decent style. I couldn't let the children go about badly dressed either—I felt any money I got for them had to go on them alone. Such sweet little things!

Mrs. Linde: Poor Nora! So it had to come out of your own allowance?

Nora: Of course. After all, I was the one it concerned most. Whenever Torvald gave me money for new clothes and such-like, I never spent more than half. And always I bought the simplest and cheapest things. It's a blessing most things look well on me, so Torvald never noticed anything. But sometimes I did feel it was a bit hard, Kristine, because it is nice to be well dressed, isn't it?

Mrs. Linde: Yes, I suppose it is.

Nora: I have had some other sources of income, of course. Last winter I was lucky enough to get quite a bit of copying to do. So I shut myself up every night and sat and wrote through to the small hours of the morning. Oh, sometimes I was so tired, so tired. But it was tremendous fun all the same, sitting there working and earning money like that. It was almost like being a man.

Mrs. Linde: And how much have you been able to pay off like this?

Nora: Well, I can't tell exactly. It's not easy to know where you are with transactions of this kind, you understand. All I know is I've paid off just as much as I could scrape together. Many's the time I was at my wit's end. [*Smiles.*] Then I used to sit here and pretend that some rich old gentleman had fallen in love with me. . . .

Mrs. Linde: What! What gentleman?

Nora: Oh, rubbish! . . . and that now he had died, and when they opened his will, there in big letters were the words: "My entire fortune is to be paid over, immediately and in cash, to charming Mrs. Nora Helmer."

Mrs. Linde: But my dear Nora—who is this man?

Nora: Good heavens, don't you understand? There never was any old gentleman; it was just something I used to sit here pretending, time and time again, when I didn't know where to turn next for money. But it doesn't make very much difference; as far as I'm concerned, the old boy can do what he likes, I'm tired of him; I can't be bothered any more with him or his will. Because now all my worries are over. [*Jumping up.*] Oh God, what a glorious thought, Kristine! No more worries! Just think of being without a care in the world . . . being able to romp with the children, and making the house nice and attractive, and having things just as Torvald likes to have them! And then spring will soon be here, and blue skies. And maybe we can go away somewhere. I might even see something of the sea again. Oh yes! When you're happy, life is a wonderful thing!

[*The door-bell is heard in the hall.*]

Mrs. Linde [*gets up*]: There's the bell. Perhaps I'd better go.

Nora: No, do stay, please. I don't suppose it's for me; it's probably somebody for Torvald. . . .

Maid [*in the doorway*]: Excuse me, ma'am, but there's a gentleman here wants to see Mr. Helmer, and I didn't quite know . . . because the Doctor is in there. . . .

Nora: Who is the gentleman?

Krogstad [*in the doorway*]: It's me, Mrs. Helmer.

[*Mrs. Linde starts, then turns away to the window.*]

Nora [*tense, takes a step towards him and speaks in a low voice*]: You? What is it? What do you want to talk to my husband about?

Krogstad: Bank matters . . . in a manner of speaking. I work at the bank, and I hear your husband is to be the new manager. . . .

Nora: So it's . . .

Krogstad: Just routine business matters, Mrs. Helmer. Absolutely nothing else.

Nora: Well then, please go into his study.

[*She nods impassively and shuts the hall door behind him; then she walks across and sees to the stove.*]

Mrs. Linde: Nora . . . who was that man?

Nora: His name is Krogstad.

Mrs. Linde: So it really was him.

Nora: Do you know the man?

Mrs. Linde: I used to know him . . . a good many years ago. He was a solicitor's clerk in our district for a while.

Nora: Yes, so he was.

Mrs. Linde: How he's changed!

Nora: His marriage wasn't a very happy one, I believe.

Mrs. Linde: He's a widower now, isn't he?

Nora: With a lot of children. There, it'll burn better now.

[*She closes the stove door and moves the rocking chair a little to one side.*]

Mrs. Linde: He does a certain amount of business on the side, they say?

Nora: Oh? Yes, it's always possible. I just don't know. . . . But let's not think about business . . . it's all so dull.

[*Dr. Rank comes in from Helmer's study.*]

Dr. Rank [*still in the doorway*]: No, no, Torvald, I won't intrude. I'll just look in on your wife for a moment. [*Shuts the door and notices Mrs. Linde.*] Oh, I beg your pardon. I'm afraid I'm intruding here as well.

Nora: No, not at all! [*Introduces them.*] Dr. Rank . . . Mrs. Linde.

Rank: Ah! A name I've often heard mentioned in this house. I believe I came past you on the stairs as I came in.

Mrs. Linde: I have to take things slowly going upstairs. I find it rather a trial.

Rank: Ah, some little disability somewhere, eh?

Mrs. Linde: Just a bit run down, I think, actually.

Rank: Is that all? Then I suppose you've come to town for a good rest—doing the rounds of the parties?

Mrs. Linde: I have come to look for work.

Rank: Is that supposed to be some kind of sovereign remedy for being run down?

Mrs. Linde: One must live, Doctor.

Rank: Yes, it's generally thought to be necessary.

Nora: Come, come, Dr. Rank. You are quite as keen to live as anybody.

Rank: Quite keen, yes. Miserable as I am, I'm quite ready to let things drag on as long as possible. All my patients are the same. Even those with a moral affliction are no different. As a matter of fact, there's a bad case of that kind in talking with Helmer at this very moment. . . .

Mrs. Linde [*softly*]: Ah!

Nora: Whom do you mean?

Rank: A person called Krogstad—nobody you would know. He's rotten to the core. But even he began talking about having to *live,* as though it were something terribly important.

Nora: Oh? And what did he want to talk to Torvald about?

Rank: I honestly don't know. All I heard was something about the Bank.

Nora: I didn't know that Krog . . . that this Mr. Krogstad had anything to do with the Bank.

Rank: Oh yes, he's got some kind of job down there. [*To Mrs. Linde.*] I wonder if you've got people in your part of the country too who go rushing round sniffing out cases of moral corruption, and then installing the individuals concerned in nice, well-paid jobs where they can keep them under observation. Sound, decent people have to be content to stay out in the cold.

Mrs. Linde: Yet surely it's the sick who most need to be brought in.

Rank [*shrugs his shoulders*]: Well, there we have it. It's that attitude that's turning society into a clinic.

[*Nora, lost in her own thoughts, breaks into smothered laughter and claps her hands.*]

Rank: Why are you laughing at that? Do you know in fact what society is?

Nora: What do I care about your silly old society? I was laughing about something quite different . . . something frightfully funny. Tell me, Dr. Rank, are all the people who work at the Bank dependent on Torvald now?

Rank: Is that what you find so frightfully funny?

Nora [*smiles and hums*]: Never you mind! Never you mind! [*Walks about the room.*] Yes, it really is terribly amusing to think that we . . . that Torvald now has power over so many people. [*She takes the bag out of her pocket.*] Dr. Rank, what about a little macaroon?

Rank: Look at this, eh? Macaroons. I thought they were forbidden here.

Nora: Yes, but these are some Kristine gave me.

Mrs. Linde: What? I . . . ?

Nora: Now, now, you needn't be alarmed. You weren't to know that Torvald had forbidden them. He's worried in case they ruin my teeth, you know. Still . . . what's it matter once in a while! Don't you think so, Dr. Rank? Here! [*She pops a macaroon into his mouth.*] And you too, Kristine. And I shall have one as well; just a little one . . . or two at the most. [*She walks about the room again.*] Really I am so happy. There's just one little thing I'd love to do now.

Rank: What's that?

Nora: Something I'd love to say in front of Torvald.

Rank: Then why can't you?

Nora: No, I daren't. It's not very nice.

Mrs. Linde: Not very nice?

Rank: Well, in that case it might not be wise. But to us, I don't see why. . . . What is this you would love to say in front of Helmer?

Nora: I would simply love to say: "Damn."

Rank: Are you mad!

Mrs. Linde: Good gracious, Nora . . . !

Rank: Say it! Here he is!

Nora [*hiding the bag of macaroons*]: Sh! Sh!

[*Helmer comes out of his room, his overcoat over his arm and his hat in his hand.*]

Nora [*going over to him*]: Well, Torvald dear, did you get rid of him?

Helmer: Yes, he's just gone.

Nora: Let me introduce you. This is Kristine, who has just arrived in town. . . .

Helmer: Kristine . . . ? You must forgive me, but I don't think I know . . .

Nora: Mrs. Linde, Torvald dear. Kristine Linde.

Helmer: Ah, indeed. A school-friend of my wife's, presumably.

Mrs. Linde: Yes, we were girls together.

Nora: Fancy, Torvald, she's come all this long way just to have a word with you.

Helmer: How is that?

Mrs. Linde: Well, it wasn't really. . . .

Nora: The thing is, Kristine is terribly clever at office work, and she's frightfully keen on finding a job with some efficient man, so that she can learn even more. . . .

Helmer: Very sensible, Mrs. Linde.

Nora: And then when she heard you'd been made Bank Manager—there was a bit in the paper about it—she set off at once. Torvald please! You *will* try and do something for Kristine, won't you? For my sake?

Helmer: Well, that's not altogether impossible. You are a widow, I presume?

Mrs. Linde: Yes.

Helmer: And you've had some experience in business?

Mrs. Linde: A fair amount.

Helmer: Well, it's quite probable I can find you a job, I think. . . .

Nora [*clapping her hands*]: There, you see!

Helmer: You have come at a fortunate moment, Mrs. Linde. . . .

Mrs. Linde: Oh, how can I ever thank you . . . ?

Helmer: Not a bit. [*He puts on his overcoat.*] But for the present I must ask you to excuse me . . . .

Rank: Wait. I'm coming with you.

[*He fetches his fur coat from the hall and warms it at the stove.*]

Nora: Don't be long, Torvald dear.

Helmer: Not more than an hour, that's all.

Nora: Are you leaving too, Kristine?

Mrs. Linde [*putting on her things*]: Yes, I must go and see if I can't find myself a room.

Helmer: Perhaps we can all walk down the road together.

Nora [*helping her*]: What a nuisance we are so limited for space here. I'm afraid it just isn't possible. . . .

Mrs. Linde: Oh, you mustn't dream of it! Goodbye, Nora dear, and thanks for everything.

Nora: Goodbye for the present. But . . . you'll be coming back this evening, of course. And you too, Dr. Rank? What's that? If you are up to it? Of course you'll be up to it. Just wrap yourself up well.

[*They go out, talking, into the hall; children's voices can be heard on the stairs.*]

Nora: Here they are! Here they are! [*She runs to the front door and opens it. Anne Marie, the nursemaid, enters with the children.*] Come in! Come in! [*She bends down and kisses them.*] Ah! my sweet little darlings. . . . You see them, Kristine? Aren't they lovely!

Rank: Don't stand here chattering in this draught!

Helmer: Come along, Mrs. Linde. The place now becomes unbearable for anybody except mothers.

[*Dr. Rank, Helmer and Mrs. Linde go down the stairs: the nursemaid comes into the room with the children, then Nora, shutting the door behind her.*]

Nora: How fresh and bright you look! My, what red cheeks you've got! Like apples and roses. [*During the following, the children keep chattering away to her.*] Have you had a nice time? That's splendid. And you gave Emmy and Bob a ride on your sledge? Did you now! Both together! Fancy that! There's a clever boy, Ivar. Oh, let me take her a little while, Anne Marie. There's my sweet little baby-doll! [*She takes the youngest of the children from the nursemaid and dances with her.*] All right, Mummy will dance with Bobby too. What? You've been throwing snowballs? Oh, I wish I'd been there. No, don't bother, Anne Marie, I'll help them off with their things. No, please, let me—I like doing it. You go on in, you look frozen. You'll find some hot coffee on the stove. [*The nursemaid goes into the room, left. Nora takes off the children's coats and hats and throws them down anywhere, while the children all talk at once.*] Really! A great big dog came running after you? But he didn't bite. No, the doggies wouldn't bite my pretty little dollies. You mustn't touch the parcels, Ivar! What are they? Wouldn't you like to know! No, no, that's nasty. Now? Shall we play something? What shall we play? Hide and seek? Yes, let's play hide and seek. Bob can hide first. Me first? All right, let me hide first.

[*She and the children play, laughing and shrieking, in this room and in the adjacent room on the right. Finally Nora hides under the table; the children come rushing in to look for her but cannot find her; they hear her stifled laughter, rush to the table, lift up the tablecloth and find her. Tremendous shouts of delight. She creeps out and pretends to frighten them. More shouts. Meanwhile there has been a knock at the front door, which nobody has heard. The door half opens, and Krogstad can be seen. He waits a little; the game continues.*]

Krogstad: I beg your pardon, Mrs. Helmer. . . .
Nora [*turns with a stifled cry and half jumps up*]: Ah! What do you want?
Krogstad: Excuse me. The front door was standing open. Somebody must have forgotten to shut it. . . .
Nora [*standing up*]: My husband isn't at home, Mr. Krogstad.
Krogstad: I know.
Nora: Well . . . what are you doing here?
Krogstad: I want a word with you.
Nora: With . . . ? [*Quietly, to the children.*] Go to Anne Marie. What? No, the strange man won't do anything to Mummy. When he's gone we'll have another game. [*She leads the children into the room, left, and shuts the door after them; tense and uneasy.*] You want to speak to me?
Krogstad: Yes, I do.
Nora: Today? But it isn't the first of the month yet. . . .
Krogstad: No, it's Christmas Eve. It depends entirely on you what sort of Christmas you have.
Nora: What do you want? Today I can't possibly . . .
Krogstad: Let's not talk about that for the moment. It's something else. You've got a moment to spare?
Nora: Yes, I suppose so, though . . .
Krogstad: Good. I was sitting in Olsen's café, and I saw your husband go down the road . . .
Nora: Did you?
Krogstad: . . . with a lady.
Nora: Well?
Krogstad: May I be so bold as to ask whether that lady was a Mrs. Linde?
Nora: Yes.
Krogstad: Just arrived in town?
Nora: Yes, today.
Krogstad: And she's a good friend of yours?
Nora: Yes, she is. But I can't see . . .
Krogstad: I also knew her once.

Nora: I know.

Krogstad: Oh? So you know all about it. I thought as much. Well, I want to ask you straight: is Mrs. Linde getting a job in the Bank?

Nora: How dare you cross-examine me like this, Mr. Krogstad? You, one of my husband's subordinates? But since you've asked me, I'll tell you. Yes, Mrs. Linde *has* got a job. And I'm the one who got it for her, Mr. Krogstad. Now you know.

Krogstad: So my guess was right.

Nora [*walking up and down*]: Oh, I think I can say that some of us have a little influence now and again. Just because one happens to be a woman, that doesn't mean. . . . People in subordinate positions, ought to take care they don't offend anybody . . . who . . . hm . . .

Krogstad: . . . has influence?

Nora: Exactly.

Krogstad [*changing his tone*]: Mrs. Helmer, will you have the goodness to use your influence on my behalf?

Nora: What? What do you mean?

Krogstad: Will you be so good as to see that I keep my modest little job at the Bank?

Nora: What do you mean? Who wants to take it away from you?

Krogstad: Oh, you needn't try and pretend to me you don't know. I can quite see that this friend of yours isn't particularly anxious to bump up against me. And I can also see now whom I can thank for being given the sack.

Nora: But I assure you. . . .

Krogstad: All right, all right. But to come to the point: there's still time. And I advise you to use your influence to stop it.

Nora: But, Mr. Krogstad, I *have* no influence.

Krogstad: Haven't you? I thought just now you said yourself . . .

Nora: I didn't mean it that way, of course. Me? What makes you think I've got any influence of that kind over my husband?

Krogstad: I know your husband from our student days. I don't suppose he is any more steadfast than other married men.

Nora: You speak disrespectfully of my husband like that and I'll show you the door.

Krogstad: So the lady's got courage.

Nora: I'm not frightened of you any more. After New Year's I'll soon be finished with the whole business.

Krogstad [*controlling himself*]: Listen to me, Mrs. Helmer. If necessary I shall fight for my little job in the Bank as if I were fighting for my life.

Nora: So it seems.

Krogstad: It's not just for the money, that's the last thing I care about. There's something else . . . well, I might as well out with it. You see it's like this. You know as well as anybody that some years ago I got myself mixed up in a bit of trouble.

Nora: I believe I've heard something of the sort.

Krogstad: It never got as far as the courts; but immediately it was as if all paths were barred to me. So I started going in for the sort of business you know about. I had to do something, and I think I can say I haven't been one of the worst. But now I have to get out of it. My sons are growing up; for their sake I must try and win back what respectability I can. That job in the Bank was like the first step on the ladder for me. And now your husband wants to kick me off the ladder again, back into the mud.

Nora: But in God's name, Mr. Krogstad, it's quite beyond my power to help you.

Krogstad: That's because you haven't the will to help me. But I have ways of making you.

Nora: You wouldn't go and tell my husband I owe you money?

Krogstad: Suppose I did tell him?

Nora: It would be a rotten shame. [*Half choking with tears.*] That secret is all my pride and joy—why should he have to hear about it in this nasty, horrid way . . . hear about it from *you*. You would make things horribly unpleasant for me. . . .

Krogstad: Merely unpleasant?

Nora [*vehemently*]: Go on, do it then! It'll be all the worse for you. Because then my husband will see for himself what a bad man you are, and then you certainly won't be able to keep your job.

Krogstad: I asked whether it was only a bit of domestic unpleasantness you were afraid of?

Nora: If my husband gets to know about it, he'll pay off what's owing at once. And then we'd have nothing more to do with you.

Krogstad [*taking a pace towards her*]: Listen, Mrs. Helmer, either you haven't a very good memory, or else you don't understand much about business. I'd better make the position a little bit clearer for you.

Nora: How do you mean?

Krogstad: When your husband was ill, you came to me for the loan of twelve hundred dollars.

Nora: I didn't know of anybody else.

Krogstad: I promised to find you the money. . . .

Nora: And you did find it.

Krogstad: I promised to find you the money on certain conditions. At the time you were so concerned about your husband's illness, and so anxious to get the money for going away with, that I don't think you paid very much attention to all the incidentals. So there is perhaps some point in reminding you of them. Well, I promised to find you the money against an IOU which I drew up for you.

Nora: Yes, and which I signed.

Krogstad: Very good. But below that I added a few lines, by which your father was to stand security. This your father was to sign.

Nora: Was to . . . ? He did sign it.

Krogstad: I had left the date blank. The idea was that your father was to add the date himself when he signed it. Remember?

Nora: Yes, I think. . . .

Krogstad: I then gave you the IOU to post to your father. Wasn't that so?

Nora: Yes.

Krogstad: Which of course you did at once. Because only about five or six days later you brought it back to me with your father's signature. I then paid out the money.

Nora: Well? Haven't I paid the instalments regularly?

Krogstad: Yes, fairly. But . . . coming back to what we were talking about . . . that was a pretty bad period you were going through then, Mrs. Helmer.

Nora: Yes, it was.

Krogstad: Your father was seriously ill, I believe.

Nora: He was very near the end.

Krogstad: And died shortly afterwards?

Nora: Yes.

Krogstad: Tell me, Mrs. Helmer, do you happen to remember which day your father died? The exact date, I mean.

Nora: Daddy died on 29 September.

Krogstad: Quite correct. I made some inquiries. Which brings up a rather curious point [*takes out a paper*] which I simply cannot explain.

Nora: Curious . . . ? I don't know . . .

Krogstad: The curious thing is, Mrs. Helmer, that your father signed this document three days after his death.

Nora: What? I don't understand. . . .

Krogstad: Your father died on 29 September. But look here. Your father has dated his signature 2 October. Isn't that rather curious, Mrs. Helmer? [*Nora remains silent.*] It's also remarkable that the words "2 October" and the year are not in your father's handwriting, but in a handwriting I rather think I recognize. Well, perhaps that could be explained. Your father might have forgotten to date his signature, and then somebody else might have made a guess at the date later, before the fact of your father's death was known. There is nothing wrong in that. What really matters is the signature. And *that* is of course genuine, Mrs. Helmer? It really was your father who wrote his name here?

Nora [*after a moment's silence, throws her head back and looks at him defiantly*]: No, it wasn't. It was me who signed father's name.

Krogstad: Listen to me. I suppose you realize that that is a very dangerous confession?

Nora: Why? You'll soon have all your money back.

Krogstad: Let me ask you a question: why didn't you send that document to your father?

Nora: It was impossible. Daddy was ill. If I'd asked him for his signature, I'd have to tell him what the money was for. Don't you see, when he was as ill as that I couldn't go and tell him that my husband's life was in danger. It was simply impossible.

Krogstad: It would have been better for you if you had abandoned the whole trip.

Nora: No, that was impossible. This was the thing that was to save my husband's life. I couldn't give it up.

Krogstad: But did it never strike you that this was fraudulent . . . ?

Nora: That wouldn't have meant anything to me. Why should I worry about you? I couldn't stand you, not when you insisted on going through with all those cold-blooded formalities, knowing all the time what a critical state my husband was in.

Krogstad: Mrs. Helmer, it's quite clear you still haven't the faintest idea what it is you've committed. But let me tell you, my own offence was no more and no worse than that, and it ruined my entire reputation.

Nora: You? Are you trying to tell me that you once risked everything to save your wife's life?

Krogstad: The law takes no account of motives.

Nora: Then they must be very bad laws.

Krogstad: Bad or not, if I produce this document in court, you'll be condemned according to them.

Nora: I don't believe it. Isn't a daughter entitled to try and save her father from worry and anxiety on his deathbed? Isn't a wife entitled to save her husband's life? I might not know very much about the law, but I feel sure of one thing: it must say somewhere that things like this are allowed. You mean to say you don't know that—you, when it's your job? You must be a rotten lawyer, Mr. Krogstad.

Krogstad: That may be. But when it comes to business transactions—like the sort between us two—perhaps you'll admit I know something about *them?* Good. Now you must please yourself. But I tell you this: if I'm pitched out a second time, you are going to keep me company.

[*He bows and goes out through the hall.*]

Nora [*stands thoughtfully for a moment, then tosses her head*]: Rubbish! He's just trying to scare me. I'm not such a fool as all that. [*Begins gathering up the children's clothes; after a moment she stops.*] Yet . . . ? No, it's impossible! I did it for love, didn't I?

The Children [*in the doorway, left*]: Mummy, the gentleman's just gone out of the gate.

Nora: Yes, I know. But you mustn't say anything to anybody about that gentleman. You hear? Not even to Daddy!

The Children: All right, Mummy. Are you going to play again?

Nora: No, not just now.

The Children: But Mummy, you promised!

Nora: Yes, but I can't just now. Off you go now, I have a lot to do. Off you go, my darlings. [*She herds them carefully into the other room and shuts the door behind them. She sits down on the sofa, picks up her embroidery and works a few stitches, but soon stops.*] No! [*She flings her work down, stands up, goes to the hall door and calls out.*] Helene! Fetch the tree in for me, please. [*She walks across to the table, left, and opens the drawer; again pauses.*] No, really, it's quite impossible!

Maid [*with the Christmas tree*]: Where shall I put it, ma'am?

Nora: On the floor there, in the middle.

Maid: Anything else you want me to bring?

Nora: No, thank you. I've got what I want.

[*The maid has put the tree down and goes out.*]

Nora [*busy decorating the tree*]: Candles here . . . and flowers here—Revolting man! It's all nonsense! There's nothing to worry about. We'll have a lovely Christmas tree. And I'll do anything you want me to, Torvald; I'll sing for you, dance for you. . . .

[*Helmer, with a bundle of documents under his arm, comes in by the hall door.*]

Nora: Ah, back again already?

Helmer: Yes. Anybody been?

Nora: Here? No.

Helmer: That's funny. I just saw Krogstad leave the house.

Nora: Oh? O yes, that's right. Krogstad was here a minute.

Helmer: Nora, I can tell by your face he's been asking you to put a good word in for him.

Nora: Yes.

Helmer: And you were to pretend it was your own idea? You were to keep quiet about his having been here. He asked you to do that as well, didn't he?

Nora: Yes, Torvald. But . . .

Helmer: Nora, Nora, what possessed you to do a thing like that? Talking to a person like him, making him promises? And then on top of everything, to tell me a lie!

Nora: A lie . . . ?

Helmer: Didn't you say that nobody had been here? [*Wagging his finger at her.*] Never again must my little song-bird do a thing like that! Little song-birds must keep their pretty little beaks out of mischief; no chirruping out of tune! [*Puts his arm round her waist.*] Isn't that the way we want things to be? Yes, of course it is. [*Lets her go.*] So let's say no more about it. [*Sits down by the stove.*] Ah, nice and cosy here!

[*He glances through his papers.*]

Nora [*busy with the Christmas tree, after a short pause*]: Torvald!

Helmer: Yes.

Nora: I'm so looking forward to the fancy dress ball at the Stenborgs on Boxing Day.

Helmer: And I'm terribly curious to see what sort of surprise you've got for me.

Nora: Oh, it's too silly.

Helmer: Oh?

Nora: I just can't think of anything suitable. Everything seems so absurd, so pointless.

Helmer: Has my little Nora come to *that* conclusion?

Nora [*behind his chair, her arms on the chairback*]: Are you very busy, Torvald?

Helmer: Oh. . . .

Nora: What are all those papers?

Helmer: Bank matters.

Nora: Already?

Helmer: I have persuaded the retiring manager to give me authority to make any changes in organisation or personnel I think necessary. I have to work on it over the Christmas week. I want everything straight by the New Year.

Nora: So that was why that poor Krogstad. . . .

Helmer: Hm!

Nora [*still leaning against the back of the chair, running her fingers through his hair*]: If you hadn't been so busy, Torvald, I'd have asked you to do me an awfully big favour.

Helmer: Let me hear it. What's it to be?

Nora: Nobody's got such good taste as you. And the thing is I do so want to look my best at the fancy dress ball. Torvald, couldn't you give me some advice and tell me what you think I ought to go as, and how I should arrange my costume?

Helmer: Aha! So my impulsive little woman is asking for somebody to come to her rescue, eh?

Nora: Please, Torvald, I never get anywhere without your help.

Helmer: Very well, I'll think about it. We'll find something.

Nora: That's sweet of you. [*She goes across to the tree again; pause.*] How pretty these red flowers look.—Tell me, was it really something terribly wrong this man Krogstad did?

Helmer: Forgery. Have you any idea what that means?

Nora: Perhaps circumstances left him no choice?

Helmer: Maybe. Or perhaps, like so many others, he just didn't think. I am not so heartless that I would necessarily want to condemn a man for a single mistake like that.

Nora: Oh no, Torvald, of course not!

Helmer: Many a man might be able to redeem himself, if he honestly confessed his guilt and took his punishment.

Nora: Punishment?

Helmer: But that wasn't the way Krogstad chose. He dodged what was due to him by a cunning trick. And that's what has been the cause of his corruption.

Nora: Do you think it would . . . ?

Helmer: Just think how a man with a thing like that on his conscience will always be having to lie and cheat and dissemble; he can never drop the mask, not even with his own wife and children. And the children—*that's* the most terrible part of it, Nora.

Nora: Why?

Helmer: A fog of lies like that in a household, and it spreads disease and infection to every part of it. Every breath the children take in that kind of house is reeking with evil germs.

Nora [*closer behind him*]: Are you sure of that?

Helmer: My dear Nora, as a lawyer I know what I'm talking about. Practically all juvenile delinquents come from homes where the mother is dishonest.

Nora: Why mothers particularly?

Helmer: It's generally traceable to the mothers, but of course fathers can have the same influence. Every lawyer knows that only too well. And yet there's Krogstad been poisoning his own children for years with lies and deceit. That's the reason I call him morally depraved. [*Holds out his hands to her.*] That's why my sweet little Nora must promise me not to try putting in any more good words for him. Shake hands on it. Well? What's this? Give me your hand. There now! That's settled. I assure you I would have found it impossible to work with him. I quite literally feel physically sick in the presence of such people.

Nora [*draws her hand away and walks over to the other side of the Christmas tree*]: How hot it is in here! And I still have such a lot to do.

Helmer [*stands up and collects his papers together*]: Yes, I'd better think of getting some of this read before dinner. I must also think about your costume. And I might even be able to lay my hands on something to wrap in gold paper and hang on the Christmas tree. [*He lays his hand on her head.*] My precious little singing bird.

[*He goes into his study and shuts the door behind him.*]

Nora [*quietly, after a pause*]: Nonsense! It can't be. It's impossible. It *must* be impossible.

Maid [*in the doorway, left*]: The children keep asking so nicely if they can come in and see Mummy.

Nora: No, no, don't let them in! You stay with them, Anne Marie.

Maid: Very well, ma'am.

[*She shuts the door.*]

Nora [*pale with terror*]: Corrupt my children . . . ! Poison my home? [*Short pause; she throws back her head.*] It's not true! It could never, never be true!

Act II

The same room. In the corner beside the piano stands the Christmas tree, stripped, bedraggled and with its candles burnt out. Nora's outdoor things lie on the sofa. Nora, alone there, walks about restlessly; at last she stops by the sofa and picks up her coat.

Nora [*putting her coat down again*]: Somebody's coming! [*Crosses to the door, listens.*] No, it's nobody. Nobody will come today, of course, Christmas Day— nor tomorrow, either. But perhaps. . . . [*She opens the door and looks out.*] No, nothing in the letter box; quite empty. [*Comes forward.*] Oh, nonsense! He didn't mean it seriously. Things like that *can't* happen. It's impossible. Why, I have three small children.

[*The Nursemaid comes from the room, left, carrying a big cardboard box.*]

Nursemaid: I finally found it, the box with the fancy dress costumes.

Nora: Thank you. Put it on the table, please.

Nursemaid [*does this*]: But I'm afraid they are in an awful mess.

Nora: Oh, if only I could rip them up into a thousand pieces!

Nursemaid: Good heavens, they can be mended all right, with a bit of patience.

Nora: Yes, I'll go over and get Mrs. Linde to help me.

Nursemaid: Out again? In this terrible weather? You'll catch your death of cold, Ma'am.

Nora: Oh, worse things might happen.—How are the children?

Nursemaid: Playing with their Christmas presents, poor little things, but . . .

Nora: Do they keep asking for me?

Nursemaid: They are so used to being with their Mummy.

Nora: Yes, Anne Marie, from now on I can't be with them as often as I was before.

Nursemaid: Ah well, children get used to anything in time.

Nora: Do you think so? Do you think they would forget their Mummy if she went away for good?

Nursemaid: Good gracious—for good?

Nora: Tell me, Anne Marie—I've often wondered—how on earth could you bear to hand your child over to strangers?

Nursemaid: Well, there was nothing else for it when I had to come and nurse my little Nora.

Nora: Yes but . . . how could you *bring* yourself to do it?

Nursemaid: When I had the chance of such a good place? When a poor girl's been in trouble she must make the best of things. Because *he* didn't help, the rotter.

Nora: But your daughter will have forgotten you.

Nursemaid: Oh no, she hasn't. She wrote to me when she got confirmed, and again when she got married.

Nora [*putting her arms round her neck*]: Dear old Anne Marie, you were a good mother to me when I was little.

Nursemaid: My poor little Nora never had any other mother but me.

Nora: And if my little ones only had you, I know you would. . . . Oh, what am I talking about! [*She opens the box.*] Go in to them. I must . . . Tomorrow I'll let you see how pretty I am going to look.

Nursemaid: Ah, there'll be nobody at the ball as pretty as my Nora.

[*She goes into the room, left.*]

Nora [*begins unpacking the box, but soon throws it down*]: Oh, if only I dare go out. If only I could be sure nobody would come. And that nothing would happen in the meantime here at home. Rubbish—nobody's going to come. I mustn't think about it. Brush this muff. Pretty gloves, pretty gloves! I'll put it right out of my mind. One, two, three, four, five, six. . . . [*Screams.*] Ah, they are coming. . . . [*She starts towards the door, but stops irresolute. Mrs. Linde comes from the hall, where she has taken off her things.*] Oh, it's you, Kristine. There's nobody else out there, is there? I'm so glad you've come.

Mrs. Linde: I heard you'd been over looking for me.

Nora: Yes, I was just passing. There's something you must help me with. Come and sit beside me on the sofa here. You see, the Stenborgs are having a fancy dress party upstairs tomorrow evening, and now Torvald wants me to go as a Neapolitan fisher lass and dance the tarantella. I learned it in Capri, you know.

Mrs. Linde: Well, well! So you are going to do a party piece?

Nora: Torvald says I should. Look, here's the costume, Torvald had it made for me down there. But it's got all torn and I simply don't know. . . .

Mrs. Linde: We'll soon have that put right. It's only the trimming come away here and there. Got a needle and thread? Ah, here's what we are after.

Nora: It's awfully kind of you.

Mrs. Linde: So you are going to be all dressed up tomorrow, Nora? Tell you what—I'll pop over for a minute to see you in all your finery. But I'm quite forgetting to thank you for the pleasant time we had last night.

Nora [gets up and walks across the room]: Somehow I didn't think yesterday was as nice as things generally are.—You should have come to town a little earlier, Kristine.—Yes, Torvald certainly knows how to make things pleasant about the place.

Mrs. Linde: You too, I should say. You are not your father's daughter for nothing. But tell me, is Dr. Rank always as depressed as he was last night?

Nora: No, last night it was rather obvious. He's got something seriously wrong with him, you know. Tuberculosis of the spine, poor fellow. His father was a horrible man, who used to have mistresses and things like that. That's why the son was always ailing, right from being a child.

Mrs. Linde [lowering her sewing]: But my dear Nora, how do you come to know about things like that?

Nora [walking about the room]: Huh! When you've got three children, you get these visits from . . . women who have had a certain amount of medical training. And you hear all sorts of things from them.

Mrs. Linde [begins sewing again; short silence]: Does Dr. Rank call in every day?

Nora: Every single day. He was Torvald's best friend as a boy, and he's a good friend of *mine,* too. Dr. Rank is almost like one of the family.

Mrs. Linde: But tell me—is he really genuine? What I mean is: doesn't he sometimes rather turn on the charm?

Nora: No, on the contrary. What makes you think that?

Mrs. Linde: When you introduced me yesterday, he claimed he'd often heard my name in this house. But afterwards I noticed your husband hadn't the faintest idea who I was. Then how is it that Dr. Rank should. . . .

Nora: Oh yes, it was quite right what he said, Kristine. You see Torvald is so terribly in love with me that he says he wants me all to himself. When we were first married, it even used to make him sort of jealous if I only as much as mentioned any of my old friends from back home. So of course I stopped doing it. But I often talk to Dr. Rank about such things. He likes hearing about them.

Mrs. Linde: Listen, Nora! In lots of ways you are still a child. Now, I'm a good deal older than you, and a bit more experienced. I'll tell you something: I think you ought to give up all this business with Dr. Rank.

Nora: Give up what business?

Mrs. Linde: The whole thing, I should say. Weren't you saying yesterday something about a rich admirer who was to provide you with money. . . .

Nora: One who's never existed, I regret to say. But what of it?

Mrs. Linde: Has Dr. Rank money?

Nora: Yes, he has.

Mrs. Linde: And no dependents?

Nora: No, nobody. But . . . ?

Mrs. Linde: And he comes to the house every day?

Nora: Yes, I told you.

Mrs. Linde: But how can a man of his position want to pester you like this?

Nora: I simply don't understand.

Mrs. Linde: Don't pretend, Nora. Do you think I don't see now who you borrowed the twelve hundred from?

Nora: Are you out of your mind? Do you really think that? A friend of ours who comes here every day? The whole situation would have been absolutely intolerable.

Mrs. Linde: It *really* isn't him?

Nora: No, I give you my word. It would never have occurred to me for one moment. . . . Anyway, he didn't have the money to lend then. He didn't inherit it till later.

Mrs. Linde: Just as well for you, I'd say, my dear Nora.

Nora: No, it would never have occurred to me to ask Dr. Rank. . . . All the same I'm pretty certain if I were to ask him . . .

Mrs. Linde: But of course you won't.

Nora: No, of course not. I can't ever imagine it being necessary. But I'm quite certain if ever I were to mention it to Dr. Rank. . . .

Mrs. Linde: Behind your husband's back?

Nora: I have to get myself out of that other business. That's also behind his back. I *must* get myself out of that.

Mrs. Linde: Yes, that's what I said yesterday. But . . .

Nora [walking up and down]: A man's better at coping with these things than a woman. . . .

Mrs. Linde: Your own husband, yes.

Nora: Nonsense! [Stops.] When you've paid everything you owe, you do get your IOU back again, don't you?

Mrs. Linde: Of course.

Nora: And you can tear it up into a thousand pieces and burn it—the nasty, filthy thing!

Mrs. Linde [looking fixedly at her, puts down her sewing and slowly rises]: Nora, you are hiding something from me.

Nora: Is it so obvious?

Mrs. Linde: Something has happened to you since yesterday morning. Nora, what is it?

Nora [*going towards her*]: Kristine! [*Listens.*] Hush! There's Torvald back. Look, you go and sit in there beside the children for the time being. Torvald can't stand the sight of mending lying about. Get Anne Marie to help you.

Mrs. Linde [*gathering a lot of the things together*]: All right, but I'm not leaving until we have thrashed this thing out.

[*She goes into the room, left; at the same time Helmer comes in from the hall.*]

Nora [*goes to meet him*]: I've been longing for you to be back, Torvald, dear.

Helmer: Was that the dressmaker . . . ?

Nora: No, it was Kristine; she's helping me with my costume. I think it's going to look very nice . . .

Helmer: Wasn't that a good idea of mine, now?

Nora: Wonderful! But wasn't it also nice of me to let you have your way?

Helmer [*taking her under the chin*]: Nice of you—because you let your husband have his way? All right, you little rogue, I know you didn't mean it that way. But I don't want to disturb you. You'll be wanting to try the costume on, I suppose.

Nora: And I dare say you've got work to do?

Helmer: Yes. [*Shows her a bundle of papers.*] Look at this. I've been down at the Bank. . . .

[*He turns to go into his study.*]

Nora: Torvald!

Helmer [*stopping*]: Yes.

Nora: If a little squirrel were to ask ever so nicely . . . ?

Helmer: Well?

Nora: Would you do something for it?

Helmer: Naturally I would first have to know what it is.

Nora: Please, if only you would let it have its way, and do what it wants, it'd scamper about and do all sorts of marvellous tricks.

Helmer: What is it?

Nora: And the pretty little sky-lark would sing all day long. . . .

Helmer: Huh! It does that anyway.

Nora: I'd pretend I was an elfin child and dance a moonlight dance for you, Torvald.

Helmer: Nora—I hope it's not that business you started on this morning?

Nora [*coming closer*]: Yes, it is, Torvald. I implore you!

Helmer: You have the nerve to bring that up again?

Nora: Yes, yes, you *must* listen to me. You must let Krogstad keep his job at the Bank.

Helmer: My dear Nora, I'm giving his job to Mrs. Linde.

Nora: Yes, it's awfully sweet of you. But couldn't you get rid of somebody else in the office instead of Krogstad?

Helmer: This really is the most incredible obstinacy! Just because you go and make some thoughtless promise to put in a good word for him, you expect me . . .

Nora: It's not that, Torvald. It's for your own sake. That man writes in all the nastiest papers, you told me that yourself. He can do you no end of harm. He terrifies me to death. . . .

Helmer: Aha, now I see. It's your memories of what happened before that are frightening you.

Nora: What do you mean?

Helmer: It's your father you are thinking of.

Nora: Yes . . . yes, that's right. You remember all the nasty insinuations those wicked people put in the papers about Daddy? I honestly think they would have had him dismissed if the Ministry hadn't sent you down to investigate, and you hadn't been so kind and helpful.

Helmer: My dear little Nora, there is a considerable difference between your father and me. Your father's professional conduct was not entirely above suspicion. Mine is. And I hope it's going to stay that way as long as I hold this position.

Nora: But nobody knows what some of these evil people are capable of. Things could be so nice and pleasant for us here, in the peace and quiet of our home—you and me and the children, Torvald! That's why I implore you. . . .

Helmer: The more you plead for him, the more impossible you make it for me to keep him on. It's already known down at the Bank that I am going to give Krogstad his notice. If it ever got around that the new manager had been talked over by his wife. . . .

Nora: What of it?

Helmer: Oh, nothing! As long as the little woman gets her own stubborn way . . . ! Do you want me to make myself a laughing stock in the office? . . . Give people the idea that I am susceptible to any kind of outside pressure? You can imagine how soon I'd feel the consequences of that! Anyway, there's one other consideration that makes it impossible to have Krogstad in the Bank as long as I am manager.

Nora: What's that?

Helmer: At a pinch I might have overlooked his past lapses. . . .

Nora: Of course you could, Torvald!

Helmer: And I'm told he's not bad at his job, either. But we knew each other rather well when we were younger. It was one of those rather rash friendships that prove embarrassing in later life. There's no reason why you shouldn't know we were once on terms of some familiarity. And he, in his tactless way, makes no attempt to hide the fact, particularly when other people are present. On the contrary, he thinks he has every right to treat me as an equal, with his "Torvald this" and "Torvald that" every time he opens his mouth. I find it extremely irritating, I can tell you. He would make my position at the Bank absolutely intolerable.

Nora: Torvald, surely you aren't serious?

Helmer: Oh? Why not?

Nora: Well, it's all so petty.

Helmer: What's that you say? Petty? Do you think I'm petty?

Nora: No, not at all, Torvald dear! And that's why . . .

Helmer: Doesn't make any difference! . . . You call my motives petty; so I must be petty too. Petty! Indeed! Well, we'll put a stop to that, once and for all. [*He opens the hall door and calls.*] Helene!

Nora: What are you going to do?

Helmer [*searching among his papers*]: Settle things. [*The Maid comes in.*] See this letter? I want you to take it down at once. Get hold of a messenger and get him to deliver it. Quickly. The address is on the outside. There's the money.

Maid: Very good, sir.

[*She goes with the letter.*]

Helmer [*putting his papers together*]: There now, my stubborn little miss.

Nora [*breathless*]: Torvald . . . what was that letter?

Helmer: Krogstad's notice.

Nora: Get it back, Torvald! There's still time! Oh, Torvald, get it back! Please for my sake, for your sake, for the sake of the children! Listen, Torvald, please! You don't realize what it can do to us.

Helmer: Too late.

Nora: Yes, too late.

Helmer: My dear Nora, I forgive you this anxiety of yours, although it is actually a bit of an insult. Oh, but it is, I tell you! It's hardly flattering to suppose that anything this miserable pen-pusher wrote could frighten *me*! But I forgive you all the same, because it is rather a sweet way of showing how much you love me. [*He takes her in his arms.*] This is how things must be, my own darling Nora. When it comes to the point, I've enough strength and enough courage, believe me, for whatever happens. You'll find I'm man enough to take everything on myself.

Nora [*terrified*]: What do you mean?

Helmer: Everything, I said. . . .

Nora [*in command of herself*]: That is something you shall never, never do.

Helmer: All right, then we'll share it, Nora—as man and wife. That's what we'll do. [*Caressing her.*] Does that make you happy now? There, there, don't look at me with those eyes, like a little frightened dove. The whole thing is sheer imagination.—Why don't you run through the tarantella and try out the tambourine? I'll go into my study and shut both the doors, then I won't hear anything. You can make all the noise you want. [*Turns in the doorway.*] And when Rank comes, tell him where he can find me.

[*He nods to her, goes with his papers into his room, and shuts the door behind him.*]

Nora [*wild-eyed with terror, stands as though transfixed*]: He's quite capable of doing it! He would do it! No matter what, he'd do it.—No, never in this world! Anything but that! Help? Some way out . . . . ? [*The door-bell rings in the hall.*] Dr. Rank . . . ! Anything but that, *anything!* [*She brushes her hands over her face, pulls herself together and opens the door into the hall. Dr. Rank is standing outside hanging up his fur coat. During what follows it begins to grow dark.*] Hello, Dr. Rank. I recognized your ring. Do you mind not going in to Torvald just yet, I think he's busy.

Rank: And you?

[*Dr. Rank comes into the room and she closes the door behind him.*]

Nora: Oh, you know very well I've always got time for you.

Rank: Thank you. A privilege I shall take advantage of as long as I am able.

Nora: What do you mean—as long as you are able?

Rank: Does that frighten you?

Nora: Well, it's just that it sounds so strange. Is anything likely to happen?

Rank: Only what I have long expected. But I didn't think it would come quite so soon.

Nora [*catching at his arm*]: What have you found out? Dr. Rank, you must tell me!

Rank: I'm slowly sinking. There's nothing to be done about it.

Nora [*with a sigh of relief*]: Oh, it's *you* you're . . . ?

Rank: Who else? No point in deceiving oneself. I am the most wretched of all my patients, Mrs. Helmer. These last few days I've made a careful analysis of my internal economy. Bankrupt! Within a month I shall probably be lying rotting up there in the churchyard.

Nora: Come now, what a ghastly thing to say!

Rank: The whole damned thing is ghastly. But the worst thing is all the ghastliness that has to be gone through first. I only have one more test to make; and when that's done I'll know pretty well when the final disintegration will start. There's something I want to ask you. Helmer is a sensitive soul; he loathes anything that's ugly. I don't want him visiting me. . . .

Nora: But Dr. Rank. . . .

Rank: On no account must he. I won't have it. I'll lock the door on him.—As soon as I'm absolutely certain of the worst, I'll send you my visiting card with a black cross on it. You'll know then the final horrible disintegration has begun.

Nora: Really, you are being quite absurd today. And here was I hoping you would be in a thoroughly good mood.

Rank: With death staring me in the face? Why should I suffer for another man's sins? What justice is there in that? Somewhere, somehow, every single family must be suffering some such cruel retribution. . . .

Nora [*stopping up her ears*]: Rubbish! Do cheer up!

Rank: Yes, really the whole thing's nothing but a huge joke. My poor innocent spine must do penance for my father's gay subaltern life.

Nora [*by the table, left*]: Wasn't he rather partial to asparagus and *pâté de foie gras?*

Rank: Yes, he was. And truffles.

Nora: Truffles, yes. And oysters, too, I believe?

Rank: Yes, oysters, oysters, of course.

Nora: And all the port and champagne that goes with them. It does seem a pity all these delicious things should attack the spine.

Rank: Especially when they attack a poor spine that never had any fun out of them.

Nora: Yes, that is an awful pity.

Rank [*looks at her sharply*]: Hm. . . .

Nora [*after a pause*]: Why did you smile?

Rank: No, it was you who laughed.

Nora: No, it was you who smiled, Dr. Rank!

Rank [*getting up*]: You are a bigger rascal than I thought you were.

Nora: I feel full of mischief today.

Rank: So it seems.

Nora [*putting her hands on his shoulders*]: Dear, dear Dr. Rank, you mustn't go and die on Torvald and me.

Rank: You wouldn't miss me for long. When you are gone, you are soon forgotten.

Nora [*looking at him anxiously*]: Do you think so?

Rank: People make new contacts, then . . .

Nora: Who make new contacts?

Rank: Both you and Helmer will, when I'm gone. You yourself are already well on the way, it seems to me. What was this Mrs. Linde doing here last night?

Nora: Surely you aren't jealous of poor Kristine?

Rank: Yes, I am. She'll be my successor in this house. When I'm done for, I can see this woman. . . .

Nora: Hush! Don't talk so loud, she's in there.

Rank: Today as well? There you are, you see!

Nora: Just to do some sewing on my dress. Good Lord, how absurd you are! [*She sits down on the sofa.*] Now Dr. Rank, cheer up. You'll see tomorrow how nicely I can dance. And you can pretend I'm doing it just for you—and for Torvald as well, of course. [*She takes various things out of the box.*] Come here, Dr. Rank. I want to show you something.

Rank [*sits*]: What is it?

Nora: Look!

Rank: Silk stockings.

Nora: Flesh-coloured! Aren't they lovely! Of course, it's dark here now, but tomorrow. . . . No, no, no, you can only look at the feet. Oh well, you might as well see a bit higher up, too.

Rank: Hm. . . .

Nora: Why are you looking so critical? Don't you think they'll fit?

Rank: I couldn't possibly offer any informed opinion about that.

Nora [*looks at him for a moment*]: Shame on you. [*Hits him lightly across the ear with the stockings.*] Take that! [*Folds them up again.*]

Rank: And what other delights am I to be allowed to see?

Nora: Not another thing. You are too naughty. [*She hums a little and searches among her things.*]

Rank [*after a short pause*]: Sitting here so intimately like this with you, I can't imagine . . . I simply cannot conceive what would have become of me if I had never come to this house.

Nora [*smiles*]: Yes, I rather think you do enjoy coming here.

Rank [*in a low voice, looking fixedly ahead*]: And the thought of having to leave it all . . .

Nora: Nonsense. You aren't leaving.

Rank [*in the same tone*]: . . . without being able to leave behind even the slightest token of gratitude, hardly a fleeting regret even . . . nothing but an empty place to be filled by the first person that comes along.

Nora: Supposing I were to ask you to . . . ? No . . .

Rank: What?

Nora: . . . to show me the extent of your friendship . . .

Rank: Yes?

Nora: I mean . . . to do me a tremendous favour. . . .

Rank: Would you really, for once, give me that pleasure?

Nora: You have no idea what it is.

Rank: All right, tell me.

Nora: No, really I can't, Dr. Rank. It's altogether too much to ask . . . because I need your advice and help as well. . . .

Rank: The more the better. I cannot imagine what you have in mind. But tell me anyway. You do trust me, don't you?

Nora: Yes, I trust you more than anybody I know. You are my best and my most faithful friend. I know that. So I will tell you. Well then, Dr. Rank, there is something you must help me to prevent. You know how deeply, how passionately Torvald is in love with me. He would never hesitate for a moment to sacrifice his life for my sake.

Rank [*bending towards her*]: Nora . . . do you think he's the only one who . . . ?

Nora [*stiffening slightly*]: Who . . . ?

Rank: Who wouldn't gladly give his life for your sake.

Nora [*sadly*]: Oh!

Rank: I swore to myself you would know before I went. I'll never have a better opportunity. Well, Nora! Now you know. And now you know too that you can confide in me as in nobody else.

Nora [*rises and speaks evenly and calmly*]: Let me past.

Rank [*makes way for her, but remains seated*]: Nora. . . .

Nora [*in the hall doorway*]: Helene, bring the lamp in, please. [*Walks over to the stove.*] Oh, my dear Dr. Rank, that really was rather horrid of you.

Rank [*getting up*]: That I have loved you every bit as much as anybody? Is *that* horrid?

Nora: No, but that you had to go and tell me. When it was all so unnecessary. . . .

Rank: What do you mean? Did you know . . . ?

[*The Maid comes in with the lamp, puts it on the table, and goes out again.*]

Rank: Nora . . . Mrs. Helmer . . . I'm asking you if you knew?

Nora: How can I tell whether I did or didn't. I simply can't tell you. . . . Oh, how could you be so clumsy, Dr. Rank! When everything was so nice.

Rank: Anyway, you know now that I'm at your service, body and soul. So you can speak out.

Nora [*looking at him*]: After this?

Rank: I beg you to tell me what it is.

Nora: I can tell you nothing now.

Rank: You must. You can't torment me like this. Give me a chance—I'll do anything that's humanly possible.

Nora: You can do nothing for me now. Actually, I don't really need any help. It's all just my imagination, really it is. Of course! [*She sits down in the rocking chair, looks at him and smiles.*] I must say, you are a nice one, Dr. Rank! Don't you feel ashamed of yourself, now the lamp's been brought in?

Rank: No, not exactly. But perhaps I ought to go—for good?

Nora: No, you mustn't do that. You must keep coming just as you've always done. You know very well Torvald would miss you terribly.

Rank: And you?

Nora: I always think it's tremendous fun having you.

Rank: That's exactly what gave me wrong ideas. I just can't puzzle you out. I often used to feel you'd just as soon be with me as with Helmer.

Nora: Well, you see, there are those people you love and those people you'd almost rather *be* with.

Rank: Yes, there's something in that.

Nora: When I was a girl at home, I loved Daddy best, of course. But I also thought it great fun if I could slip into the maids' room. For one thing they never preached at me. And they always talked about such exciting things.

Rank: Aha! So it's their role I've taken over!

Nora [*jumps up and crosses to him*]: Oh, my dear, kind Dr. Rank, I didn't mean that at all. But you can see how it's a bit with Torvald as it was with Daddy. . . .

[*The Maid comes in from the hall.*]

Maid: Please, ma'am . . . !

[*She whispers and hands her a card.*]

Nora [*glances at the card*]: Ah!

[*She puts it in her pocket.*]

Rank: Anything wrong?

Nora: No, no, not at all. It's just . . . it's my new costume. . . .

Rank: How is that? There's your costume in there.

Nora: That one, yes. But this is another one. I've ordered it. Torvald mustn't hear about it. . . .

Rank: Ah, so that's the big secret, is it!

Nora: Yes, that's right. Just go in and see him, will you? He's in the study. Keep him occupied for the time being. . . .

Rank: Don't worry. He shan't escape me.

[*He goes into Helmer's study.*]

Nora [*to the maid*]: Is he waiting in the kitchen?

Maid: Yes, he came up the back stairs. . . .

Nora: But didn't you tell him somebody was here?

Maid: Yes, but it was no good.

Nora: Won't he go?

Maid: No, he won't till he's seen you.

Nora: Let him in, then. But quietly. Helene, you mustn't tell anybody about this. It's a surprise for my husband.

Maid: I understand, ma'am. . . .

[*She goes out.*]

Nora: Here it comes! What I've been dreading! No, no, it can't happen, it *can't* happen.

[*She walks over and bolts Helmer's door. The maid opens the hall door for Krogstad and shuts it again behind him. He is wearing a fur coat, over-shoes, and a fur cap.*]

Nora [*goes towards him*]: Keep your voice down, my husband is at home.

Krogstad: What if he is?

Nora: What do you want with me?

Krogstad: To find out something.

Nora: Hurry, then. What is it?

Krogstad: You know I've been given notice.

Nora: I couldn't prevent it, Mr. Krogstad, I did my utmost for you, but it was no use.

Krogstad: Has your husband so little affection for you? He knows what I can do to you, yet he dares . . . .

Nora: You don't imagine he knows about it!

Krogstad: No, I didn't imagine he did. It didn't seem a bit like my good friend Torvald Helmer to show that much courage. . . .

Nora: Mr. Krogstad, I must ask you to show some respect for my husband.

Krogstad: Oh, sure! All due respect! But since you are so anxious to keep this business quiet, Mrs. Helmer, I take it you now have a rather clearer idea of just what it is you've done, than you had yesterday.

Nora: Clearer than *you* could ever have given me.

Krogstad: Yes, being as I am such a rotten lawyer. . . .

Nora: What do you want with me?

Krogstad: I just wanted to see how things stood, Mrs. Helmer. I've been thinking about you all day. Even a mere money-lender, a hack journalist, a—well, even somebody like me has a bit of what you might call feeling.

Nora: Show it then. Think of my little children.

Krogstad: Did you or your husband think of mine? But what does it matter now? There was just one thing I wanted to say: you needn't take this business too seriously. I shan't start any proceedings, for the present.

Nora: Ah, I knew you wouldn't.

Krogstad: The whole thing can be arranged quite amicably. Nobody need know. Just the three of us.

Nora: My husband must never know.

Krogstad: How can you prevent it? Can you pay off the balance?

Nora: No, not immediately.

Krogstad: Perhaps you've some way of getting hold of the money in the next few days.

Nora: None I want to make use of.

Krogstad: Well, it wouldn't have been very much help to you if you had. Even if you stood there with the cash in your hand and to spare, you still wouldn't get your IOU back from me now.

Nora: What are you going to do with it?

Krogstad: Just keep it—have it in my possession. Nobody who isn't implicated need know about it. So if you are thinking of trying any desperate remedies . . .

Nora: Which I am. . . .

Krogstad: . . . if you happen to be thinking of running away . . .

Nora: Which I am!

Krogstad: . . . or anything worse . . .

Nora: How did you know?

Krogstad: . . . forget it!

Nora: How did you know I was thinking of *that*?

Krogstad: Most of us think of *that*, to begin with. I did, too; but I didn't have the courage. . . .

Nora [*tonelessly*]: I haven't either.

Krogstad [*relieved*]: So you haven't the courage either, eh?

Nora: No, I haven't! I haven't!

Krogstad: It would also be very stupid. There'd only be the first domestic storm to get over. . . . I've got a letter to your husband in my pocket here. . . .

Nora: And it's all in there?

Krogstad: In as tactful a way as possible.

Nora [*quickly*]: He must never read that letter. Tear it up. I'll find the money somehow.

Krogstad: Excuse me, Mrs. Helmer, but I've just told you. . . .

Nora: I'm not talking about the money I owe you. I want to know how much you are demanding from my husband, and I'll get the money.

Krogstad: I want no money from your husband.

Nora: What do you want?

Krogstad: I'll tell you. I want to get on my feet again, Mrs. Helmer; I want to get to the top. And your husband is going to help me. For the last eighteen months I've gone straight; all that time it's been hard going; I was content to work my way up, step by step. Now I'm being kicked out, and I won't stand for being taken back again as an act of charity. I'm going to get to the top, I tell you. I'm going back into that Bank—with a better job. Your husband is going to create a new vacancy, just for me. . . .

Nora: He'll never do that!

Krogstad: He will do it. I know him. He'll do it without so much as a whimper. And once I'm in there with him, you'll see what's what. In less than a year I'll be his right-hand man. It'll be Nils Krogstad, not Torvald Helmer, who'll be running that Bank.

Nora: You'll never live to see that day!

Krogstad: You mean you . . . ?

Nora: Now I have the courage.

Krogstad: You can't frighten me! A precious pampered little thing like you. . . .

Nora: I'll show you! I'll show you!

Krogstad: Under the ice, maybe? Down in the cold, black water? Then being washed up in the spring, bloated, hairless, unrecognizable. . . .

Nora: You can't frighten me.

Krogstad: You can't frighten me, either. People don't do that sort of thing, Mrs. Helmer. There wouldn't be any point to it, anyway, I'd still have him right in my pocket.

Nora: Afterwards? When I'm no longer . . .

Krogstad: Aren't you forgetting that your reputation would then be entirely in my hands? [*Nora stands looking at him, speechless.*] Well, I've warned you. Don't do anything silly. When Helmer gets my letter, I expect to hear from him. And don't forget: it's him who is forcing me off the straight and narrow again, your own husband! That's something I'll never forgive him for. Goodbye, Mrs. Helmer.

[*He goes out through the hall. Nora crosses to the door, opens it slightly, and listens.*]

Nora: He's going. He hasn't left the letter. No, no, that would be impossible! [*Opens the door further and further.*] What's he doing? He's stopped outside. He's not going down the stairs. Has he changed his mind? Is he . . . ? [*A letter falls into the letter-box. Then Krogstad's footsteps are heard receding as he walks downstairs. Nora gives a stifled cry, runs across the room to the sofa table; pause.*] In the letter-box! [*She creeps stealthily across to the hall door.*] There it is! Torvald, Torvald! It's hopeless now!

Mrs. Linde [*comes into the room, left, carrying the costume*]: There, I think that's everything. Shall we try it on?

Nora [*in a low, hoarse voice*]: Kristine, come here.

Mrs. Linde [*throws the dress down on the sofa*]: What's wrong with you? You look upset.

Nora: Come here. Do you see that letter? *There,* look! Through the glass in the letter-box.

Mrs. Linde: Yes, yes, I can see it.

Nora: It's a letter from Krogstad.

Mrs. Linde: Nora! It was Krogstad who lent you the money!

Nora: Yes. And now Torvald will get to know everything.

Mrs. Linde: Believe me, Nora, it's best for you both.

Nora: But there's more to it than that. I forged a signature. . . .

Mrs. Linde: Heavens above!

Nora: Listen, I want to tell you something, Kristine, so you can be my witness.

Mrs. Linde: What do you mean "witness"? What do you want me to . . . ?

Nora: If I should go mad . . . which might easily happen. . . .

Mrs. Linde: Nora!

Nora: Or if anything happened to me . . . which meant I couldn't be here. . . .

Mrs. Linde: Nora, Nora! Are you out of your mind?

Nora: And if somebody else wanted to take it all upon himself, the whole blame, you understand. . . .

Mrs. Linde: Yes, yes. But what makes you think. . . .

Nora: Then you must testify that it isn't true, Kristine. I'm not out of my mind; I'm quite sane now. And I tell you this: nobody else knew anything, I alone was responsible for the whole thing. Remember that!

Mrs. Linde: I will. But I don't understand a word of it.

Nora: Why should you? You see something miraculous is going to happen.

Mrs. Linde: Something miraculous?

Nora: Yes, a miracle. But something so terrible as well, Kristine—oh, it must *never* happen, not for anything.

Mrs. Linde: I'm going straight over to talk to Krogstad.

Nora: Don't go. He'll only do you harm.

Mrs. Linde: There was a time when he would have done anything for me.

Nora: Him!

Mrs. Linde: Where does he live?

Nora: How do I know . . . ? Wait a minute. [*She feels in her pocket.*] Here's his card. But the letter, the letter . . . !

Helmer [*from his study, knocking on the door*]: Nora!

Nora [*cries out in terror*]: What's that? What do you want?

Helmer: Don't be frightened. We're not coming in. You've locked the door. Are you trying on?

Nora: Yes, yes, I'm trying on. It looks so nice on me, Torvald.

Mrs. Linde [*who has read the card*]: He lives just round the corner.

Nora: It's no use. It's hopeless. The letter is there in the box.

Mrs. Linde: Your husband keeps the key?

Nora: Always.

Mrs. Linde: Krogstad must ask for his letter back unread, he must find some sort of excuse. . . .

Nora: But this is just the time that Torvald generally . . .

Mrs. Linde: Put him off! Go in and keep him busy. I'll be back as soon as I can.

[*She goes out hastily by the hall door. Nora walks over to Helmer's door, opens it and peeps in.*]

Nora: Torvald!

Helmer [*in the study*]: Well, can a man get into his own living-room again now? Come along, Rank, now we'll see . . . [*In the doorway.*] But what's this?

Nora: What, Torvald dear?

Helmer: Rank led me to expect some kind of marvellous transformation.

Rank [*in the doorway*]: That's what I thought too, but I must have been mistaken.

Nora: I'm not showing myself off to anybody before tomorrow.

Helmer: Nora dear, you look tired. You haven't been practising too hard?

Nora: No, I haven't practised at all yet.

Helmer: You'll have to, though.

Nora: Yes, I certainly must, Torvald. But I just can't get anywhere without your help: I've completely forgotten it.

Helmer: We'll soon polish it up.

Nora: Yes, do help me, Torvald. Promise? I'm so nervous. All those people. . . . You must devote yourself exclusively to me this evening. Pens away! Forget all about the office! Promise me, Torvald dear!

Helmer: I promise. This evening I am wholly and entirely at your service . . . helpless little thing that you are. Oh, but while I remember, I'll just look first . . .

[*He goes towards the hall door.*]

Nora: What do you want out there?

Helmer: Just want to see if there are any letters.

Nora: No, don't, Torvald!

Helmer: Why not?

Nora: Torvald, *please!* There aren't any.

Helmer: Just let me see.

[*He starts to go. Nora, at the piano, plays the opening bars of the tarantella.*]

Helmer [*at the door, stops*]: Aha!

Nora: I shan't be able to dance tomorrow if I don't rehearse it with you.

Helmer [*walks to her*]: Are you really so nervous, Nora dear?

Nora: Terribly nervous. Let me run through it now. There's still time before supper. Come and sit here and play for me, Torvald dear. Tell me what to do, keep me right—as you always do.

Helmer: Certainly, with pleasure, if that's what you want.

[*He sits at the piano. Nora snatches the tambourine out of the box, and also a long gaily-coloured shawl which she drapes round herself, then with a bound she leaps forward.*]

Nora [*shouts*]: Now play for me! Now I'll dance!

[*Helmer plays and Nora dances; Dr. Rank stands at the piano behind Helmer and looks on.*]

Helmer [*playing*]: Not so fast! Not so fast!

Nora: I can't help it.

Helmer: Not so wild, Nora!

Nora: This is how it has to be.

Helmer [*stops*]: No, no, that won't do at all.

Nora [*laughs and swings the tambourine*]: Didn't I tell you?

Rank: Let me play for her.

Helmer [*gets up*]: Yes, do. Then I'll be better able to tell her what to do.

[*Rank sits down at the piano and plays. Nora dances more and more wildly. Helmer stands by the stove giving her repeated directions as she dances; she does not seem to hear them. Her hair comes undone and falls about her shoulders; she pays no attention and goes on dancing. Mrs. Linde enters.*]

Mrs. Linde [*standing as though spellbound in the doorway*]: Ah . . . !

Nora [*dancing*]: See what fun we are having, Kristine.

Helmer: But my dear darling Nora, you are dancing as though your life depended on it.

Nora: It does.

Helmer: Stop, Rank! This is sheer madness. Stop, I say.

[*Rank stops playing and Nora comes to a sudden halt.*]

Helmer [*crosses to her*]: I would never have believed it. You have forgotten everything I ever taught you.

Nora [*throwing away the tambourine*]: There you are, you see.

Helmer: Well, some more instruction is certainly needed there.

Nora: Yes, you see how necessary it is. You must go on coaching me right up to the last minute. Promise me, Torvald?

Helmer: You can rely on me.

Nora: You mustn't think about anything else but me until after tomorrow . . . mustn't open any letters . . . mustn't touch the letter-box.

Helmer: Ah, you are still frightened of what that man might . . .

Nora: Yes, yes, I am.

Helmer: I can see from your face there's already a letter there from him.

Nora: I don't know. I think so. But you mustn't read anything like that now. We don't want anything horrid coming between us until all this is over.

Rank [*softly to Helmer*]: I shouldn't cross her.

Helmer [*puts his arm round her*]: The child must have her way. But tomorrow night, when your dance is done. . . .

Nora: Then you are free.

Maid [*in the doorway, right*]: Dinner is served, madam.

Nora: We'll have champagne, Helene.

Maid: Very good, madam.

[*She goes.*]

Helmer: Aha! It's to be quite a banquet, eh?

Nora: With champagne flowing until dawn. [*Shouts.*] And some macaroons, Helene . . . lots of them, for once in a while.

Helmer [*seizing her hands*]: Now, now, not so wild and excitable! Let me see you being my own little singing bird again.

Nora: Oh yes, I will. And if you'll just go in . . . you, too, Dr. Rank. Kristine, you must help me to do my hair.

Rank [*softly, as they leave*]: There isn't anything . . . anything as it were, impending, is there?

Helmer: No, not at all, my dear fellow. It's nothing but these childish fears I was telling you about.

[*They go out to the right.*]

Nora: Well?

Mrs. Linde: He's left town.

Nora: I saw it in your face.

Mrs. Linde: He's coming back tomorrow evening. I left a note for him.

Nora: You shouldn't have done that. You must let things take their course. Because really it's a case for rejoicing, waiting like this for the miracle.

Mrs. Linde: What is it you are waiting for?

Nora: Oh, you wouldn't understand. Go and join the other two. I'll be there in a minute.

[*Mrs. Linde goes into the dining-room. Nora stands for a moment as though to collect herself, then looks at her watch.*]

Nora: Five. Seven hours to midnight. Then twenty-four hours till the next midnight. Then the tarantella will be over. Twenty-four and seven? Thirty-one hours to live.

Helmer [*in the doorway, right*]: What's happened to our little sky-lark?

Nora [*running towards him with open arms*]: Here she is!

ACT III

The same room. The round table has been moved to the centre of the room, and the chairs placed round it. A lamp is burning on the table. The door to the hall stands open. Dance music can be heard coming from the floor above. Mrs. Linde is sitting by the table, idly turning over the pages of a book; she tries to read, but does not seem able to concentrate. Once or twice she listens, tensely, for a sound at the front door.

Mrs. Linde [*looking at her watch*]: Still not here. There isn't much time left. I only hope he hasn't . . . [*She listens again.*] Ah, there he is. [*She goes out into the hall, and cautiously opens the front door. Soft footsteps can be heard on the stairs. She whispers.*] Come in. There's nobody here.

Krogstad [*in the doorway*]: I found a note from you at home. What does it all mean?

Mrs. Linde: I had to talk to you.

Krogstad: Oh? And did it have to be here, in this house?

Mrs. Linde: It wasn't possible over at my place, it hasn't a separate entrance. Come in. We are quite alone. The maid's asleep and the Helmers are at a party upstairs.

Krogstad [*comes into the room*]: Well, well! So the Helmers are out dancing tonight! Really?

Mrs. Linde: Yes, why not?

Krogstad: Why not indeed!

Mrs. Linde: Well then, Nils. Let's talk.

Krogstad: Have we two anything more to talk about?

Mrs. Linde: We have a great deal to talk about.

Krogstad: I shouldn't have thought so.

Mrs. Linde: That's because you never really understood me.

Krogstad: What else was there to understand, apart from the old, old story? A heartless woman throws a man over the moment something more profitable offers itself.

Mrs. Linde: Do you really think I'm so heartless? Do you think I found it easy to break it off?

Krogstad: Didn't you?

Mrs. Linde: You didn't really believe that?

Krogstad: If that wasn't the case, why did you write to me as you did?

Mrs. Linde: There was nothing else I could do. If I had to make the break, I felt in duty bound to destroy any feeling that you had for me.

Krogstad [*clenching his hands*]: So that's how it was. And all that . . . was for money!

Mrs. Linde: You mustn't forget I had a helpless mother and two young brothers. We couldn't wait for you, Nils. At that time you hadn't much immediate prospect of anything.

Krogstad: That may be. But you had no right to throw me over for somebody else.

Mrs. Linde: Well, I don't know. Many's the time I've asked myself whether I was justified.

Krogstad [*more quietly*]: When I lost you, it was just as if the ground had slipped away from under my feet. Look at me now: a broken man clinging to the wreck of his life.

Mrs. Linde: Help might be near.

Krogstad: It was near. Then you came along and got in the way.

Mrs. Linde: Quite without knowing, Nils. I only heard today it's you I'm supposed to be replacing at the Bank.

Krogstad: If you say so, I believe you. But now you do know, aren't you going to withdraw?

Mrs. Linde: No, that wouldn't benefit you in the slightest.

Krogstad: Benefit, benefit . . . ! I would do it just the same.

Mrs. Linde: I have learned to go carefully. Life and hard, bitter necessity have taught me that.

Krogstad: And life has taught me not to believe in pretty speeches.

Mrs. Linde: Then life has taught you a very sensible thing. But deeds are something you surely must believe in?

Krogstad: How do you mean?

Mrs. Linde: You said you were like a broken man clinging to the wreck of his life.

Krogstad: And I said it with good reason.

Mrs. Linde: And I am like a broken woman clinging to the wreck of her life. Nobody to care about, and nobody to care for.

Krogstad: It was your own choice.

Mrs. Linde: At the time there was no other choice.

Krogstad: Well, what of it?

Mrs. Linde: Nils, what about us two castaways joining forces.

Krogstad: What's that you say?

Mrs. Linde: Two of us on *one* wreck surely stand a better chance than each on his own.

Krogstad: Kristine!

Mrs. Linde: Why do you suppose I came to town?

Krogstad: You mean, you thought of me?

Mrs. Linde: Without work I couldn't live. All my life I have worked, for as long as I can remember; that has always been my one great joy. But now I'm completely alone in the world, and feeling horribly empty and forlorn. There's no pleasure in working only for yourself. Nils, give me somebody and something to work for.

Krogstad: I don't believe all this. It's only a woman's hysteria, wanting to be all magnanimous and self-sacrificing.

Mrs. Linde: Have you ever known me hysterical before?

Krogstad: Would you really do this? Tell me—do you know all about my past?

Mrs. Linde: Yes.

Krogstad: And you know what people think about me?

Mrs. Linde: Just now you hinted you thought you might have been a different person with me.

Krogstad· I'm convinced I would.

Mrs. Linde: Couldn't it still happen?

Krogstad: Kristine! You know what you are saying, don't you! Yes, you do. I can see you do. Have you really the courage . . . ?

Mrs. Linde: I need someone to mother, and your children need a mother. We two need each other. Nils, I have faith in what, deep down, you are. With you I can face anything.

Krogstad [*seizing her hands*]: Thank you, thank you, Kristine. And I'll soon have everybody looking up to me, or I'll know the reason why. Ah, but I was forgetting. . . .

Mrs. Linde: Hush! The tarantella! You must go!

Krogstad: Why? What is it?

Mrs. Linde: You hear that dance upstairs? When it's finished they'll be coming.

Krogstad: Yes, I'll go. It's too late to do anything. Of course, you know nothing about what steps I've taken against the Helmers.

Mrs. Linde: Yes, Nils, I do know.

Krogstad: Yet you still want to go on. . . .

Mrs. Linde: I know how far a man like you can be driven by despair.

Krogstad: Oh, if only I could undo what I've done!

Mrs. Linde: You still can. Your letter is still there in the box.

Krogstad: Are you sure?

Mrs. Linde: Quite sure. But . . .

Krogstad [*regards her searchingly*]: Is that how things are? You want to save your friend at any price? Tell me straight. Is that it?

Mrs. Linde: When you've sold yourself *once* for other people's sake, you don't do it again.

Krogstad: I shall demand my letter back.

Mrs. Linde: No, no.

Krogstad: Of course I will, I'll wait here till Helmer comes. I'll tell him he has to give me my letter back . . . that it's only about my notice . . . that he mustn't read it. . . .

Mrs. Linde: No, Nils, don't ask for it back.

Krogstad: But wasn't that the very reason you got me here?

Mrs. Linde: Yes, that was my first terrified reaction. But that was yesterday, and it's quite incredible the things I've witnessed in this house in the last twenty-four hours. Helmer must know everything. This unhappy secret must come out. Those two must have the whole thing out between them. All this secrecy and deception, it just can't go on.

Krogstad: Well, if you want to risk it. . . . But one thing I can do, and I'll do it at once. . . .

Mrs. Linde [*listening*]: Hurry! Go, go! The dance has stopped. We aren't safe a moment longer.

Krogstad: I'll wait for you downstairs.

Mrs. Linde: Yes, do. You must see me home.

Krogstad: I've never been so incredibly happy before.

[*He goes out by the front door. The door out into the hall remains standing open.*]

Mrs. Linde [*tidies the room a little and gets her hat and coat ready*]: How things change! How things change! Somebody to work for. . . .to live for. A home to bring happiness into. Just let me get down to it. . . . I wish they'd come. . . . [*Listens.*] Ah, there they are. . . . Get my things.

[*She takes her coat and hat. The voices of Helmer and Nora are heard outside. A key is turned and Helmer pushes Nora almost forcibly into the hall. She is dressed in the Italian costume, with a big black shawl over it. He is in evening dress, and over it a black cloak, open.*]

Nora [*still in the doorway, reluctantly*]: No, no, not in here! I want to go back up again. I don't want to leave so early.

Helmer: But my dearest Nora . . .

Nora: Oh, please, Torvald, I beg you. . . . *Please*, just for another hour.

Helmer: Not another minute, Nora my sweet. You remember what we agreed. There now, come along in. You'll catch cold standing there.

[*He leads her, in spite of her resistance, gently but firmly into the room.*]

Mrs. Linde: Good evening.

Nora: Kristine!

Helmer: Why, Mrs. Linde. You here so late?

Mrs. Linde: Yes. You must forgive me but I did so want to see Nora all dressed up.

Nora: Have you been sitting here waiting for me?

Mrs. Linde: Yes, I'm afraid I wasn't in time to catch you before you went up-stairs. And I felt I couldn't leave again without seeing you.

Helmer [removing Nora's shawl]: Well take a good look at her. I think I can say she's worth looking at. Isn't she lovely, Mrs. Linde?

Mrs. Linde: Yes, I must say. . . .

Helmer: Isn't she quite extraordinarily lovely? That's what everybody at the party thought, too. But she's dreadfully stubborn . . . the sweet little thing! And what shall we do about that? Would you believe it, I nearly had to use force to get her away.

Nora: Oh Torvald, you'll be sorry you didn't let me stay, even for half an hour.

Helmer: You hear that, Mrs. Linde? She dances her tarantella, there's wild applause—which was well deserved, although the performance was perhaps rather realistic . . . I mean, rather more so than was strictly necessary from the artistic point of view. But anyway! The main thing is she was a success, a tremendous success. Was I supposed to let her stay after that? Spoil the effect? No thank you! I took my lovely little Capri girl—my capricious little Capri girl, I might say—by the arm, whisked her once round the room, a curtsey all round, and then—as they say in novels—the beautiful vision vanished. An exit should always be effective, Mrs. Linde. But I just can't get Nora to see that. Phew! It's warm in here. [*He throws his cloak over a chair and opens the door to his study.*] What? It's dark. Oh yes, of course. Excuse me. . . .

[*He goes in and lights a few candles.*]

Nora [quickly, in a breathless whisper]: Well?

Mrs. Linde [softly]: I've spoken to him.

Nora: And . . . ?

Mrs. Linde: Nora . . . you must tell your husband everything.

Nora [tonelessly]: I knew it.

Mrs. Linde: You've got nothing to fear from Krogstad. But you must speak.

Nora: I won't.

Mrs. Linde: Then the letter will.

Nora: Thank you, Kristine. Now I know what's to be done. Hush . . . !

Helmer [comes in again]: Well, Mrs. Linde, have you finished admiring her?

Mrs. Linde: Yes. And now I must say good night.

Helmer: Oh, already? Is this yours, this knitting?

Mrs. Linde [takes it]: Yes, thank you. I nearly forgot it.

Helmer: So you knit, eh?

Mrs. Linde: Yes.

Helmer: You should embroider instead, you know.

Mrs. Linde: Oh? Why?

Helmer: So much prettier. Watch! You hold the embroidery like this in the left hand, and then you take the needle in the right hand, like this, and you describe a long, graceful curve. Isn't that right?

Mrs. Linde: Yes, I suppose so. . . .

Helmer: Whereas knitting on the other hand just can't help being ugly. Look! Arms pressed into the sides, the knitting needles going up and down— there's something Chinese about it. . . . Ah, that was marvellous champagne they served tonight.

Mrs. Linde: Well, good night, Nora! And stop being so stubborn.

Helmer: Well said, Mrs. Linde!

Mrs. Linde: Good night, Mr. Helmer.

Helmer [*accompanying her to the door*]: Good night, good night! You'll get home all right, I hope? I'd be only too pleased to. . . . But you haven't far to walk. Good night, good night! [*She goes; he shuts the door behind her and comes in again.*] There we are, got rid of her at last. She's a frightful bore, that woman.

Nora: Aren't you very tired, Torvald?

Helmer: Not in the least.

Nora: Not sleepy?

Helmer: Not at all. On the contrary, I feel extremely lively. What about you? Yes, you look quite tired and sleepy.

Nora: Yes, I'm very tired. I just want to fall straight off to sleep.

Helmer: There you are, you see! Wasn't I right in thinking we shouldn't stay any longer.

Nora: Oh, everything you do is right.

Helmer [*kissing her forehead*]: There's my little sky-lark talking common sense. Did you notice how gay Rank was this evening?

Nora: Oh, was he? I didn't get a chance to talk to him.

Helmer: I hardly did either. But it's a long time since I saw him in such a good mood. [*Looks at Nora for a moment or two, then comes nearer her.*] Ah, it's wonderful to be back in our own home again, and quite alone with you. How irresistibly lovely you are, Nora!

Nora: Don't look at me like that, Torvald!

Helmer: Can't I look at my most treasured possession? At all this loveliness that's mine and mine alone, completely and utterly mine.

Nora [*walks round to the other side of the table*]: You mustn't talk to me like that tonight.

Helmer [*following her*]: You still have the tarantella in your blood, I see. And that makes you even more desirable. Listen! The guests are beginning to leave now. [*Softly.*] Nora . . . soon the whole house will be silent.

Nora: I should hope so.

Helmer: Of course you do, don't you, Nora my darling? You know, whenever I'm out at a party with you . . . do you know why I never talk to you very much, why I always stand away from you and only steal a quick glance at you now and then . . . do you know why I do that? It's because I'm pretending we are secretly in love, secretly engaged and nobody suspects there is anything between us.

Nora: Yes, yes. I know your thoughts are always with me, of course.

Helmer: And when it's time to go, and I lay your shawl round those shapely, young shoulders, round the exquisite curve of your neck . . . I pretend that you are my young bride, that we are just leaving our wedding, that I am taking you to our new home for the first time . . . to be alone with you for the first time . . . quite alone with your young and trembling loveliness! All evening I've been longing for you, and nothing else. And as I watched you darting and swaying in the tarantella, my blood was on fire . . . I couldn't bear it any longer . . . and that's why I brought you down here with me so early. . . .

Nora: Go away, Torvald! Please leave me alone. I won't have it.

Helmer: What's this? It's just your little game isn't it, my little Nora. Won't! Won't! Am I not your husband . . . ?

[*There is a knock on the front door.*]

Nora [*startled*]: Listen . . . !

Helmer [*going towards the hall*]: Who's there?

Rank [*outside*]: It's me. Can I come in for a minute?

Helmer [*in a low voice, annoyed*]: Oh, what does he want now? [*Aloud.*] Wait a moment. [*He walks across and opens the door.*] How nice of you to look in on your way out.

Rank: I fancied I heard your voice and I thought I would just look in. [*He takes a quick glance round.*] Ah yes, this dear, familiar old place! How cosy and comfortable you've got things here, you two.

Helmer: You seemed to be having a pretty good time upstairs yourself.

Rank: Capital! Why shouldn't I? Why not make the most of things in this world? At least as much as one can, and for as long as one can. The wine was excellent. . . .

Helmer: Especially the champagne.

Rank: You noticed that too, did you? It's incredible the amount I was able to put away.

Nora: Torvald also drank a lot of champagne this evening.

Rank: Oh?

Nora: Yes, and that always makes him quite merry.

Rank: Well, why shouldn't a man allow himself a jolly evening after a day well spent?

Helmer: Well spent? I'm afraid I can't exactly claim that.

Rank [*clapping him on the shoulder*]: But I can, you see!

Nora: Dr. Rank, am I right in thinking you carried out a certain laboratory test today?

Rank: Exactly.

Helmer: Look at our little Nora talking about laboratory tests!

Nora: And may I congratulate you on the result?

Rank: You may indeed.

Nora: So it was good?

Rank: The best possible, for both doctor and patient—certainty!

Nora [*quickly and searchingly*]: Certainty?

Rank: Absolute certainty. So why shouldn't I allow myself a jolly evening after that?

Nora: Quite right, Dr. Rank.

Helmer: I quite agree. As long as you don't suffer for it in the morning.

Rank: Well, you never get anything for nothing in this life.

Nora: Dr. Rank . . . you are very fond of masquerades, aren't you?

Rank: Yes, when there are plenty of amusing disguises. . . .

Nora: Tell me, what shall we two go as next time?

Helmer: There's frivolity for you . . . thinking about the next time already!

Rank: We two? I'll tell you. You must go as Lady Luck. . . .

Helmer: Yes, but how do you find a costume to suggest *that*?

Rank: Your wife could simply go in her everyday clothes. . . .

Helmer: That was nicely said. But don't you know what you would be?

Rank: Yes, my dear friend, I know exactly what I shall be.

Helmer: Well?

Rank: At the next masquerade, I shall be invisible.

Helmer: That's a funny idea!

Rank: There's a big black cloak . . . haven't you heard of the cloak of invisibility? That comes right down over you, and then nobody can see you.

Helmer [*suppressing a smile*]: Of course, that's right.

Rank: But I'm clean forgetting what I came for. Helmer, give me a cigar, one of the dark Havanas.

Helmer: With the greatest of pleasure.

[*He offers his case.*]

Rank [*takes one and cuts the end off*]: Thanks.

Nora [*strikes a match*]: Let me give you a light.

Rank: Thank you. [*She holds out the match and he lights his cigar.*] And now, goodbye!

Helmer: Goodbye, goodbye, my dear fellow!

Nora: Sleep well, Dr. Rank.

Rank: Thank you for that wish.

Nora: Wish me the same.

Rank: You? All right, if you want me to. . . . Sleep well. And thanks for the light.

[*He nods to them both, and goes.*]

Helmer [*subdued*]: He's had a lot to drink.

Nora [*absently*]: Very likely.

[*Helmer takes a bunch of keys out of his pocket and goes out into the hall.*]

Nora: Torvald . . . what do you want there?

Helmer: I must empty the letter-box, it's quite full. There'll be no room for the papers in the morning. . . .

Nora: Are you going to work tonight?

Helmer: You know very well I'm not. Hello, what's this? Somebody's been at the lock.

Nora: At the lock?

Helmer: Yes, I'm sure of it. Why should that be? I'd hardly have thought the maids . . . ? Here's a broken hair-pin. Nora, it's one of yours. . . .

Nora [quickly]: It must have been the children. . . .

Helmer: Then you'd better tell them not to. Ah . . . there . . . I've managed to get it open. [*He takes the things out and shouts into the kitchen.*] Helene! . . . Helene, put the light out in the hall. [*He comes into the room again with the letters in his hand and shuts the hall door.*] Look how it all mounts up. [*Runs through them.*] What's this?

Nora: The letter! Oh no, Torvald, no!

Helmer: Two visiting cards . . . from Dr. Rank.

Nora: From Dr. Rank?

Helmer [looking at them]: Dr. Rank, Medical Practitioner. They were on top. He must have put them in as he left.

Nora: Is there anything on them?

Helmer: There's a black cross above his name. Look. What an uncanny idea. It's just as if he were announcing his own death.

Nora: He is.

Helmer: What? What do you know about it? Has he said anything to you?

Nora: Yes. He said when these cards came, he would have taken his last leave of us. He was going to shut himself up and die.

Helmer: Poor fellow! Of course I knew we couldn't keep him with us very long. But so soon. . . . And hiding himself away like a wounded animal.

Nora: When it has to happen, it's best that it should happen without words. Don't you think so, Torvald?

Helmer [walking up and down]: He had grown so close to us. I don't think I can imagine him gone. His suffering and his loneliness seemed almost to provide a background of dark cloud to the sunshine of our lives. Well, perhaps it's all for the best. For him at any rate. [*Pauses.*] And maybe for us as well, Nora. Now there's just the two of us. [*Puts his arms round her.*] Oh, my darling wife, I can't hold you close enough. You know, Nora . . . many's the time I wish you were threatened by some terrible danger so I could risk everything, body and soul, for your sake.

Nora [tears herself free and says firmly and decisively]: Now you must read your letters, Torvald.

Helmer: No, no, not tonight. I want to be with you, my darling wife.

Nora: Knowing all the time your friend is dying . . . ?

Helmer: You are right. It's been a shock to both of us. This ugly thing has come between us . . . thoughts of death and decay. We must try to free ourselves from it. Until then . . . we shall go our separate ways.

Nora [her arms round his neck]: Torvald . . . good night! Good night!

Helmer [*kisses her forehead*]: Goodnight, my little singing bird. Sleep well, Nora, I'll just read through my letters.

[*He takes the letters into his room and shuts the door behind him.*]

Nora [*gropes around her, wild-eyed, seizes Helmer's cloak, wraps it round herself, and whispers quickly, hoarsely, spasmodically*]: Never see him again. Never, never, never. [*Throws her shawl over her head.*] And never see the children again either. Never, never. Oh, that black icy water. Oh, that bottomless . . . ! If only it were all over! He's got it now. Now he's reading it. Oh no, no! Not yet! Torvald, goodbye . . . and my children. . . .

[*She rushes out in the direction of the hall; at the same moment Helmer flings open his door and stands there with an open letter in his hand.*]

Helmer: Nora!

Nora [*shrieks*]: Ah!

Helmer: What is this? Do you know what is in this letter?

Nora: Yes, I know. Let me go! Let me out!

Helmer [*holds her back*]: Where are you going?

Nora [*trying to tear herself free*]: You mustn't try to save me, Torvald!

Helmer [*reels back*]: True! Is it true what he writes? How dreadful! No, no, it can't possibly be true.

Nora: It *is* true. I loved you more than anything else in the world.

Helmer: Don't come to me with a lot of paltry excuses!

Nora [*taking a step towards him*]: Torvald . . . !

Helmer: Miserable woman . . . what is this you have done?

Nora: Let me go. I won't have you taking the blame for me. You mustn't take it on yourself.

Helmer: Stop play-acting! [*Locks the front door.*] You are staying here to give an account of yourself. Do you understand what you have done? Answer me! Do you understand?

Nora [*looking fixedly at him, her face hardening*]: Yes, now I'm really beginning to understand.

Helmer [*walking up and down*]: Oh, what a terrible awakening this is. All these eight years . . . this woman who was my pride and joy . . . a hypocrite, a liar, worse than that, a criminal! Oh, how utterly squalid it all is! Ugh! Ugh! [*Nora remains silent and looks fixedly at him.*] I should have realized something like this would happen. I should have seen it coming. All your father's irresponsible ways. . . . Quiet! All your father's irresponsible ways are coming out in you. No religion, no morals, no sense of duty. . . . Oh, this is my punishment for turning a blind eye to him. It was for your sake I did it, and this is what I get for it.

Nora: Yes, this.

Helmer: Now you have ruined my entire happiness, jeopardized my whole future. It's terrible to think of. Here I am, at the mercy of a thoroughly unscrupulous person; he can do whatever he likes with me, demand anything he wants, order me about just as he chooses . . . and I daren't even whimper. I'm done for, a miserable failure, and it's all the fault of a feather-brained woman!

Nora: When I've left this world behind, you will be free.

Helmer: Oh, stop pretending! Your father was just the same, always ready with fine phrases. What good would it do me if you left this world behind, as you put it? Not the slightest bit of good. He can still let it all come out, if he likes; and if he does, people might even suspect me of being an accomplice in these criminal acts of yours. They might even think I was the one behind it all, that it was I who pushed you into it! And it's you I have to thank for this . . . and when I've taken such good care of you, all our married life. Now do you understand what you have done to me?

Nora [*coldly and calmly*]: Yes.

Helmer: I just can't understand it, it's so incredible. But we must see about putting things right. Take that shawl off. Take it off, I tell you! I must see if I can't find some way or other of appeasing him. The thing must be hushed up at all costs. And as far as you and I are concerned, things must appear to go on exactly as before. But only in the eyes of the world, of course. In other words you'll go on living here; that's understood. But you will not be allowed to bring up the children, I can't trust you with them. . . . Oh, that I should have to say this to the woman I loved so dearly, the woman I still. . . . Well, that must be all over and done with. From now on, there can be no question of happiness. All we can do is save the bits and pieces from the wreck, preserve appearances. . . . [*The front door-bell rings. Helmer gives a start.*] What's that? So late? How terrible, supposing. . . . If he should . . . ? Hide, Nora! Say you are not well.

[*Nora stands motionless. Helmer walks across and opens the door into the hall.*]

Maid [*half dressed, in the hall*]: It's a note for Mrs. Helmer.

Helmer: Give it to me. [*He snatches the note and shuts the door.*] Yes, it's from him. You can't have it. I want to read it myself.

Nora: You read it then.

Helmer [*by the lamp*]: I hardly dare. Perhaps this is the end, for both of us. Well, I must know. [*He opens the note hurriedly, reads a few lines, looks at another enclosed sheet, and gives a cry of joy.*] Nora! [*Nora looks at him inquiringly.*] Nora! I must read it again. Yes, yes, it's true! I am saved! Nora, I am saved!

Nora: And me?

Helmer: You too, of course, we are both saved, you as well as me. Look, he's sent your IOU back. He sends his regrets and apologies for what he has done. . . . His luck has changed. . . . Oh, what does it matter what he says. We are saved, Nora! Nobody can do anything to you now. Oh, Nora, Nora . . . but let's get rid of this disgusting thing first. Let me see. . . . [*He glances at the IOU.*] No, I don't want to see it. I don't want it to be anything but a dream. [*He tears up the IOU and both letters, throws all the pieces into the stove and watches them burn.*] Well, that's the end of that. He said in his note you'd known since Christmas Eve. . . . You must have had three terrible days of it, Nora.

Nora: These three days haven't been easy.

Helmer: The agonies you must have gone through! When the only way out seemed to be. . . . No, let's forget the whole ghastly thing. We can rejoice and say: It's all over! It's all over! Listen to me, Nora! You don't seem to understand: it's all over! Why this grim look on your face? Oh, poor little Nora, of course I understand. You can't bring yourself to believe I've forgiven you. But I have, Nora, I swear it. I forgive you everything. I know you did what you did because you loved me.

Nora: That's true.

Helmer: You loved me as a wife should love her husband. It was simply that you didn't have the experience to judge what was the best way of going about things. But do you think I love you any the less for that; just because you don't know how to act on your own responsibility? No, no, you just lean on me, I shall give you all the advice and guidance you need. I wouldn't be a proper man if I didn't find a woman doubly attractive for being so obviously helpless. You mustn't dwell on the harsh things I said in that first moment of horror, when I thought everything was going to come crashing down about my ears. I have forgiven you, Nora, I swear it! I have forgiven you!

Nora: Thank you for your forgiveness.

[*She goes out through the door, right.*]

Helmer: No, don't go! [*He looks through the doorway.*] What are you doing in the spare room?

Nora: Taking off this fancy dress.

Helmer [*standing at the open door*]: Yes, do. You try and get some rest, and set your mind at peace again, my frightened little song-bird. Have a good long sleep; you know you are safe and sound under my wing. [*Walks up and down near the door.*] What a nice, cosy little home we have here, Nora! Here you can find refuge. Here I shall hold you like a hunted dove I have rescued unscathed from the cruel talons of the hawk, and calm your poor beating heart. And that will come, gradually, Nora, believe me. Tomorrow you'll see everything quite differently. Soon everything will be just as it was before. You won't need me to keep on telling you I've forgiven you; you'll feel convinced of it in your own heart. You don't really imagine me ever thinking of turning you out, or even of reproaching you? Oh, a real man isn't made that way, you know, Nora. For a man, there's something indescribably moving and very satisfying in knowing that he has forgiven his wife—forgiven her, completely and genuinely, from the depths of his heart. It's as though it made her his property in a double sense: he has, as it were, given her a new life, and she becomes in a way both his wife and at the same time his child. That is how you will seem to me after today, helpless, perplexed little thing that you are. Don't you worry your pretty little head about anything, Nora. Just you be frank with me, and I'll take all the decisions for you. . . . What's this? Not in bed? You've changed your things?

Nora [*in her everyday dress*]: Yes, Torvald, I've changed.

Helmer: What for? It's late.

Nora: I shan't sleep tonight.

Helmer: But my dear Nora. . . .

Nora [*looks at her watch*]: It's not so terribly late. Sit down, Torvald. We two have a lot to talk about.

[*She sits down at one side of the table.*]

Helmer: Nora, what is all this? Why so grim?

Nora: Sit down. It'll take some time. I have a lot to say to you.

Helmer [*sits down at the table opposite her*]: You frighten me, Nora. I don't understand you.

Nora: Exactly. You don't understand me. And I have never understood you, either—until tonight. No, don't interrupt. I just want you to listen to what I have to say. We are going to have things out, Torvald.

Helmer: What do you mean?

Nora: Isn't there anything that strikes you about the way we two are sitting here?

Helmer: What's that?

Nora: We have now been married eight years. Hasn't it struck you this is the first time you and I, man and wife, have had a serious talk together?

Helmer: Depends what you mean by "serious."

Nora: Eight whole years—no, more, ever since we first knew each other—and never have we exchanged one serious word about serious things.

Helmer: What did you want me to do? Get you involved in worries that you couldn't possibly help me to bear?

Nora: I'm not talking about worries. I say we've never once sat down together and seriously tried to get to the bottom of anything.

Helmer: But, my dear Nora, would that have been a thing for you?

Nora: That's just it. You have never understood me . . . I've been greatly wronged, Torvald. First by my father, and then by you.

Helmer: What! Us two! The two people who loved you more than anybody?

Nora [*shakes her head*]: You two never loved me. You only thought now nice it was to be in love with me.

Helmer: But, Nora, what's this you are saying?

Nora: It's right, you know, Torvald. At home, Daddy used to tell me what he thought, then I thought the same. And if I thought differently, I kept quiet about it, because he wouldn't have liked it. He used to call me his baby doll, and he played with me as I used to play with my dolls. Then I came to live in your house. . . .

Helmer: What way is that to talk about our marriage?

Nora [*imperturbably*]: What I mean is: I passed out of Daddy's hands into yours. You arranged everything to your tastes, and I acquired the same tastes. Or I pretended to . . . I don't really know . . . I think it was a bit of both, sometimes one thing and sometimes the other. When I look back, it seems to me I have been living here like a beggar, from hand to mouth. I lived by doing tricks for you, Torvald. But that's the way you wanted it. You and Daddy did me a great wrong. It's your fault that I've never made anything of my life.

Helmer: Nora, how unreasonable . . . how ungrateful you are! Haven't you been happy here?

Nora: No, never. I thought I was, but I wasn't really.

Helmer: Not . . . not happy!

Nora: No, just gay. And you've always been so kind to me. But our house has never been anything but a play-room. I have been your doll wife, just as at home I was Daddy's doll child. And the children in turn have been my dolls. I thought it was fun when you came and played with me, just as they thought it was fun when I went and played with them. That's been our marriage, Torvald.

Helmer: There is some truth in what you say, exaggerated and hysterical though it is. But from now on it will be different. Play-time is over; now comes the time for lessons.

Nora: Whose lessons? Mine or the children's?

Helmer: Both yours and the children's, my dear Nora.

Nora: Ah, Torvald, you are not the man to teach me to be a good wife for you.

Helmer: How can you say that?

Nora: And what sort of qualifications have I to teach the children?

Helmer: Nora!

Nora: Didn't you say yourself, a minute or two ago, that you couldn't trust me with that job.

Helmer: In the heat of the moment! You shouldn't pay any attention to that.

Nora: On the contrary, you were quite right. I'm not up to it. There's another problem needs solving first. I must take steps to educate myself. You are not the man to help me there. That's something I must do on my own. That's why I'm leaving you.

Helmer [jumps up]: What did you say?

Nora: If I'm ever to reach any understanding of myself and the things around me, I must learn to stand alone. That's why I can't stay here with you any longer.

Helmer: Nora! Nora!

Nora: I'm leaving here at once. I dare say Kristine will put me up for tonight. . . .

Helmer: You are out of your mind! I won't let you! I forbid you!

Nora: It's no use forbidding me anything now. I'm taking with me my own personal belongings. I don't want anything of yours, either now or later.

Helmer: This is madness!

Nora: Tomorrow I'm going home—to what used to be my home, I mean. It will be easier for me to find something to do there.

Helmer: Oh, you blind, inexperienced . . .

Nora: I must set about getting experience, Torvald.

Helmer: And leave your home, your husband and your children? Don't you care what people will say?

Nora: That's no concern of mine. All I know is that this is necessary for *me*.

Helmer: This is outrageous! You are betraying your most sacred duty.

Nora: And what do you consider to be my most sacred duty?

Helmer: Does it take me to tell you that? Isn't it your duty to your husband and your children?

Nora: I have another duty equally sacred.

Helmer: You have not. What duty might *that* be?

Nora: My duty to myself.

Helmer: First and foremost, you are a wife and mother.

Nora: That I don't believe any more. I believe that first and foremost I am an individual, just as much as you are—or at least I'm going to try to be. I know most people agree with you, Torvald, and that's also what it says in books. But I'm not content any more with what most people say, or with what it says in books. I have to think things out for myself, and get things clear.

Helmer: Surely you are clear about your position in your own home? Haven't you an infallible guide in questions like these? Haven't you your religion?

Nora: Oh, Torvald, I don't really know what religion is.

Helmer: What do you say!

Nora: All I know is what Pastor Hansen said when I was confirmed. He said religion was this, that and the other. When I'm away from all this and on my own, I'll go into that, too. I want to find out whether what Pastor Hansen told me was right—or at least whether it's right for *me*.

Helmer: This is incredible talk from a young woman! But if religion cannot keep you on the right path, let me at least stir your conscience. I suppose you do have some moral sense? Or tell me—perhaps you don't?

Nora: Well, Torvald, that's not easy to say. I simply don't know. I'm really very confused about such things. All I know is my ideas about such things are very different from yours. I've also learnt that the law is different from what I thought; but I simply can't get it into my head that that particular law is right. Apparently a woman has no right to spare her old father on his deathbed, or to save her husband's life, even. I just don't believe it.

Helmer: You are talking like a child. You understand nothing about the society you live in.

Nora: No, I don't. But I shall go into that too. I must try to discover who is right, society or me.

Helmer: You are ill, Nora. You are delirious. I'm half inclined to think you are out of your mind.

Nora: Never have I felt so calm and collected as I do tonight.

Helmer: Calm and collected enough to leave your husband and children?

Nora: Yes.

Helmer: Then only one explanation is possible.

Nora: And that is?

Helmer: You don't love me any more.

Nora: Exactly.

Helmer: Nora! Can you say that!

Nora: I'm desperately sorry, Torvald. Because you have always been so kind to me. But I can't help it. I don't love you any more.

Helmer [*struggling to keep his composure*]: Is that also a "calm and collected" decision you've made?

Nora: Yes, absolutely calm and collected. That's why I don't want to stay here.

Helmer: And can you also account for how I forfeited your love?

Nora: Yes, very easily. It was tonight, when the miracle didn't happen. It was then I realized you weren't the man I thought you were.

Helmer: Explain yourself more clearly. I don't understand.

Nora: For eight years I have been patiently waiting. Because, heavens, I knew miracles didn't happen every day. Then this devastating business started, and I became absolutely convinced the miracle *would* happen. All the time Krogstad's letter lay there, it never so much as crossed my mind that you would ever submit to that man's conditions. I was absolutely convinced you would say to him: Tell the whole wide world if you like. And when that was done . . .

Helmer: Yes, then what? After I had exposed my own wife to dishonour and shame . . . !

Nora: When that was done, I was absolutely convinced you would come forward and take everything on yourself, and say: I am the guilty one.

Helmer: Nora!

Nora: You mean I'd never let you make such a sacrifice for my sake? Of course not. But what would my story have counted for against yours?—That was the miracle I went in hope and dread of. It was to prevent it that I was ready to end my life.

Helmer: I would gladly toil day and night for you, Nora, enduring all manner of sorrow and distress. But nobody sacrifices his *honor* for the one he loves.

Nora: Hundreds and thousands of women have.

Helmer: Oh, you think and talk like a stupid child.

Nora: All right. But you neither think nor talk like the man I would want to share my life with. When you had got over your fright—and you weren't concerned about me but only about what might happen to you—and when all danger was past, you acted as though nothing had happened. I was your little sky-lark again, your little doll, exactly as before; except you would have to protect it twice as carefully as before, now that it had shown itself to be so weak and fragile. [*Rises.*] Torvald, that was the moment I realised that for eight years I'd been living with a stranger, and had borne him three children. . . . Oh, I can't bear to think about it! I could tear myself to shreds.

Helmer [*sadly*]: I see. I see. There is a tremendous gulf dividing us. But, Nora, is there no way we might bridge it?

Nora: As I am now, I am no wife for you.

Helmer: I still have it in me to change.

Nora: Perhaps . . . if you have your doll taken away.

Helmer: And be separated from you! No, no, Nora, the very thought of it is inconceivable.

Nora [goes into the room, right]: All the more reason why it must be done.

[*She comes back with her outdoor things and a small travelling bag which she puts on the chair beside the table.*]

Helmer: Nora, Nora, not now! Wait till the morning.

Nora [putting on her coat]: I can't spend the night in a strange man's room.

Helmer: Couldn't we go on living here like brother and sister . . . ?

Nora [tying on her hat]: You know very well that wouldn't last. [*She draws the shawl round her.*] Goodbye, Torvald. I don't want to see the children. I know they are in better hands than mine. As I am now, I can never be anything to them.

Helmer: But some day, Nora, some day . . . ?

Nora: How should I know? I've no idea what I might turn out to be.

Helmer: But you are my wife, whatever you are.

Nora: Listen, Torvald, from what I've heard, when a wife leaves her husband's house as I am doing now, he is absolved by law of all responsibility for her. I can at any rate free you from all responsibility. You must not feel in any way bound, any more than I shall. There must be full freedom on both sides. Look, here's your ring back. Give me mine.

Helmer: That too?

Nora: That too.

Helmer: There it is.

Nora: Well, that's the end of that. I'll put the keys down here. The maids know where everything is in the house—better than I do, in fact. Kristine will come in the morning after I've left to pack up the few things I brought with me from home. I want them sent on.

Helmer: The end! Nora, will you never think of me?

Nora: I dare say I'll often think about you and the children and this house.

Helmer: May I write to you, Nora?

Nora: No, never. I won't let you.

Helmer: But surely I can send you . . .

Nora: Nothing, nothing.

Helmer: Can't I help you if ever you need it?

Nora: I said 'no.' I don't accept things from strangers.

Helmer: Nora, can I never be anything more to you than a stranger?

Nora [takes her bag]: Ah, Torvald, only by a miracle of miracles. . . .

Helmer: Name it, this miracle of miracles!

Nora: Both you and I would have to change to the point where. . . . Oh, Torvald, I don't believe in miracles any more.

Helmer: But I *will* believe. Name it! Change to the point where . . . ?

Nora: Where we could make a real marriage of our lives together. Goodbye!

[*She goes out through the hall door.*]

Helmer [*sinks down on a chair near the door, and covers his face with his hands*]: Nora! Nora! [*He rises and looks round.*] Empty! She's gone! [*With sudden hope.*] The miracle of miracles . . . ?

[*The heavy sound of a door being slammed is heard from below.*]

QUESTIONS

ACT I

1. From the opening conversation between Helmer and Nora, what are your impressions of him? of her? of their marriage?
2. At what moment in the play do you understand why it is called *A Doll's House*?
3. In what ways does Mrs. Linde provide a contrast for Nora?
4. What in Krogstad's first appearance on stage, and in Dr. Rank's remarks about him, indicates that the bank clerk is a menace?
5. Of what illegal deed is Nora guilty? How does she justify it?
6. When the curtain falls on Act I, what problems now confront Nora?

ACT II

1. As Act II opens, what are your feelings on seeing the stripped, ragged Christmas tree? How is it suggestive?
2. What events that soon occur make Nora's situation even more difficult?
3. How does she try to save herself?
4. Why does Nora fling herself into the wild tarantella?

ACT III

1. For what possible reasons does Mrs. Linde pledge herself to Krogstad?
2. How does Dr. Rank's announcement of his impending death affect Nora and Helmer?
3. What is Helmer's reaction to learning the truth about Nora's misdeed? Why does he blame Nora's father? What is revealing (of Helmer's own character) in his remark, "From now on, there can be no question of happiness. All we can do is save the bits and pieces from the wreck, preserve appearances. . . ."?
4. When Helmer finds that Krogstad has sent back the note, what is his response? How do you feel toward him?
5. How does the character of Nora develop in this act?
6. How do you interpret her final slamming of the door?

GENERAL QUESTIONS

1. In what ways do you find Nora a victim? In what ways at fault?
2. Try to state the theme of the play. Does it involve women's rights? Self-fulfillment?
3. What dramatic question does the play embody? At what moment can this question first be stated?
4. What is the crisis? In what way is this moment or event a "turning point"? (In what new direction does the action turn?)
5. Eric Bentley, in an essay titled "Ibsen, Pro and Con" (*In Search of Theater* [New York: Knopf, 1953]), criticizes the character of Krogstad, calling him "a mere pawn of the plot."

He then adds, "When convenient to Ibsen, he is a blackmailer. When inconvenient, he is converted." Do you agree or disagree?

6. Why is the play considered a work of realism? Is there anything in it that does not seem realistic?

7. In what respects does *A Doll's House* seem to apply to life today? Is it in any way dated? Could there be a Nora in North America today?

WRITER'S PERSPECTIVE

George Bernard Shaw

George Bernard Shaw on Drama

IBSEN AND THE FAMILIAR SITUATION   1913

Up to a certain point in the last act, *A Doll's House* is a play that might be turned into a very ordinary French drama by the excision of a few lines, and the substitution of a sentimental happy ending for the famous last scene: indeed the very first thing the theatrical wiseacres did with it was to effect exactly this transformation, with the result that the play thus pithed° had no success and attracted no notice worth mentioning. But at just that point in the last act, the heroine very unexpectedly (by the wiseacres) stops her emotional acting and says: "We must sit down and discuss all this that has been happening between us." And it was by this new technical feature: this addition of a new movement, as musicians would say, to the dramatic form, that *A Doll's House* conquered Europe and founded a new school of dramatic art.

The drama was born of old from the union of two desires: the desire to have a dance and the desire to hear a story. The dance became a rant: the story became a situation. When Ibsen began to make plays, the art of the dramatist had shrunk into the

pithed: killed (to pith is to kill an animal by severing its spinal cord).

art of contriving a situation. And it was held that the stranger the situation, the better the play. Ibsen saw that, on the contrary, the more familiar the situation, the more interesting the play. Shakespeare had put ourselves on the stage but not our situations. Our uncles seldom murder our fathers, and cannot legally marry our mothers; we do not meet witches; our kings are not as a rule stabbed and succeeded by their stabbers; and when we raise money by bills we do not promise to pay pounds of our flesh. Ibsen supplies the want left by Shakespeare. He gives us not only ourselves, but ourselves in our own situations. The things that happen to his stage figures are things that happen to us. One consequence is that his plays are much more important to us than Shakespeare's. Another is that they are capable both of hurting us cruelly and of filling us with excited hopes of escape from idealistic tyrannies, and with visions of intenser life in the future.

From *The Quintessence of Ibsenism*, 2nd edition

TRAGICOMEDY AND THE ABSURD

One of the more prominent developments in mid-twentieth-century drama was the rise of **tragicomedies,** plays that stir us not only to pity and fear (echoing Aristotle's description of the effect of tragedy) but also to laughter. Although tragicomedy is a kind of drama we think distinctively modern, it is by no means a new invention. The term was used (although jokingly) by the Roman writer of comedy Plautus in about 185 B.C.

Since ancient times, playwrights have mingled laughter and tears, defying the neoclassical doctrine that required strict unity of action and tone (discussed on page 1320) and decreed that a play must be entirely comic or entirely tragic. Shakespeare is fond of tragicomic mingling. For example, in *Hamlet* the prince jokes with a grave-digger, and in *Antony and Cleopatra* the queen commits suicide with a poisonous asp brought to her by a wise cracking clown. Likewise, Shakespeare's darker comedies such as *Measure for Measure* and *The Merchant of Venice* deal so forcefully with such stark themes as lust, greed, racism, revenge, and cruelty, that they often seem like tragedies until their happy endings. In the tragedies of Shakespeare and others, passages of clownish humor are sometimes called **comic relief,** meaning that the section of comedy introduces a sharp contrast in mood. But such passages can do more than provide relief. In *Othello* (III, iv, 1–22) the clown's banter with Desdemona for a moment makes the surrounding tragedy seem, by comparison, more poignant and intense.

No one doubts that *Othello* is a tragedy, but some twentieth-century plays leave us both bemused and confused: should we laugh or cry? One of the most talked-about plays since World War II, Samuel Beckett's *Waiting for Godot* portrays two clownish tramps who mark time in a wasteland, wistfully looking for a savior who never arrives. Modern drama, by the way, has often featured such **antiheroes:** ordinary people, inglorious and inarticulate, who carry on not from bravery but from inertia. (The rise of the antihero in recent fiction is discussed briefly on page 93; those remarks could apply equally well to contemporary drama.) We cannot help laughing, in *Godot*, at the tramps' painful situation; but, turning the idea around, we also feel deeply moved by their ridiculous plight. Perhaps a modern tragicomedy like *Godot* does not show us great souls suffering greatly—as Edith Hamilton has said we observe in a classical tragedy—but Beckett's play nonetheless touches mysteriously on the universal sorrows of human existence.

Perhaps the full effect of such a play takes time to sink in. Contemporary playwright Edward Albee suggests that sometimes the spectator's sense of relief after experiencing pity and fear (Aristotle calls it *katharsis*) may be a delayed reaction: "I don't feel that catharsis in a play necessarily takes place during the course of a play. Often it should take place afterwards."[1] If Albee is right, we may be amused while watching a tragicomedy and then go home and feel deeply stirred by it.

Straddling the fence between tragedy and comedy, the plays of some modern playwrights portray people whose suffering seems ridiculous. These plays belong to the **theater of the absurd:** a general name for a type of play first staged in Paris in the 1950s. "For the modern critical spirit, nothing can be taken entirely seriously, nor entirely lightly," said Eugène Ionesco, one of the movement's leading playwrights. Behind the literary conventions of the theater of the absurd stands a philosophical fear that human existence has no meaning. Every person, such playwrights assume, is a helpless waif alone in a universe full of ridiculous obstacles. In Ionesco's *Amédée* (1953), a couple share an apartment with a gigantic corpse that keeps swelling relentlessly; in his *Rhinoceros* (1958), the human race starts turning into rhinos, except for one man, who remains human and isolated. A favorite theme in the theater of the absurd is that communication between people is impossible. Language is therefore futile. Ionesco's *The Bald Soprano* (1948) accordingly pokes fun at polite social conversation in a scene whose dialogue consists entirely of illogical strings of catchphrases. In *Endgame* (1957), Samuel Beckett dramatizes his vision of mankind's present condition: the main character is blind and paralyzed, and his legless parents live inside two garbage cans. Oddly, the effect of the play isn't total gloom; we leave the theater both amused and bemused by it.[2]

Trends in drama change along with playwrights' convictions, and during the 1970s and 1980s the theater of the absurd no longer seemed the dominant influence on new drama in America. Along with other protests of the 1960s, experimental theater seemed to have spent its force. During the later period most of the critically celebrated new plays were neither absurd nor experimental. David Mamet's *American Buffalo* (1975) realistically portrays three petty thieves in a junk shop as they plot to steal a coin collection. Albert Innaurato's *Gemini* (1977) takes a realistic (and comic) view of family life and sexual awakening in one of Philadelphia's Italian neighborhoods. Beth Henley's 1979 Pulitzer Prize-winning play *Crimes of the Heart* presents an eccentric but still believable group of sisters in a small Southern town. The dialogue in all three plays shows high fidelity to ordinary speech. Meanwhile, many of the most influential plays of **feminist theater,** which explores the lives, problems, and occasional triumphs of contemporary women, were also written in a realistic style. Notable success—with both critics and the ticket-buying public—greeted plays such as Marsha Norman's *'Night, Mother*

---

[1]"The Art of the Theater," interview, *Paris Review* 39 (1996).
[2]For an excellent study of the theater of the absurd, see Martin Esslin, *The Theater of the Absurd*, rev. ed. (New York: Overlook, 1973).

(1983), Tina Howe's *Painting Churches* (1983), and Wendy Wasserstein's *The Heidi Chronicles* (1988).

Some leading critics, among them Richard Gilman, believed that the American theater had entered an era of **new naturalism**.[3] Indeed, many plays of this time subjected the lives of people, especially poor and unhappy people, to a realistic, searching light, showing the forces that shaped them. Sam Shepard in *Buried Child* (1978) explores violence and desperation in a family that dwells on the edge of poverty; while August Wilson in *Joe Turner's Come and Gone* (1988) convincingly portrays life in a Pittsburgh ghetto lodging house. But if these newly established playwrights sometimes showed life as frankly as did the earlier naturalists, both of the plays just mentioned also contain rich and suggestive symbolism.

In the same period, however, experimental drama, greatly influenced by the theater of the absurd, continued to flourish. David Hwang's work (see his one-act play, *The Sound of a Voice,* on page 2044) combines realistic elements with overtly symbolic devices. Caryl Churchill's *Top Girls* (1982) presents a dinner party in which a contemporary woman invites legendary women from history to a dinner party in a restaurant. Although Churchill's play examines serious political issues, her straightforward treatment of an impossible premise owes much to Ionesco and Albee. Tony Kushner's *Angels in America* (1992) also mixes realism and fantasy to dramatize the plight of AIDS. Shel Silverstein, popular author of children's poetry, wrote a raucous one-man play, *The Devil and Bill Markham* (1991), entirely in rime, about a series of fantastic adventures in hell featuring a hard-drinking gambler and the Prince of Darkness. Silverstein's play is simultaneously experimental in form but traditional in content with its homage to American ballads and tall tales.

Experimental theater continues to exert a strong influence on contemporary drama. The following play, Milcha Sanchez-Scott's *The Cuban Swimmer,* deftly assimilates several dramatic styles—symbolism, new naturalism, ethnic drama, theater of the absurd—to create a brilliant original work. The play is simultaneously a family drama, a Latin comedy, a religious parable, and a critique of a media-obsessed American culture.

Milcha Sanchez-Scott

The Cuban Swimmer
1984

Milcha Sanchez-Scott (b. 1955) was born on the island of Bali. Her father was Colombian. Her mother was Chinese, Indonesian, and Dutch. Her father's work as an agronomist required constant travel, so when the young Sanchez-Scott reached school age, she was sent to a convent boarding school near London where she first learned English. Colombia, however, remained the family's one permanent home. Every Christmas and summer vacation was spent on a ranch in San Marta, Colombia, where four generations of family lived together. When she was fourteen, Sanchez-Scott's family moved to California. After attending the University of San Diego, where she majored in literature and philosophy, she worked at the

---

[3]"Out Goes Absurdism—In Comes the New Naturalism," *New York Times Book Review* 19 Mar. 1978.

San Diego Zoo and later at an employment agency in Los Angeles. Her first play, Latina, premiered in 1980 and won seven Drama-Logue awards. Dog Lady and The Cuban Swimmer followed in 1984. Sanchez-Scott then went to New York for a year to work with playwright Irene Fornes, in whose theater workshop she developed Roosters (1988). A feature-film version of Roosters, starring Edward James Olmos, was released in 1995. Her other plays include Evening Star (1989), El Dorado (1990), and The Old Matador (1995). Sanchez-Scott lives in Los Angeles.

Characters

Margarita Suárez, the swimmer
Eduardo Suárez, her father, the coach
Simón Suárez, her brother
Aída Suárez, the mother
Abuela, her grandmother
Voice of Mel Munson
Voice of Mary Beth White
Voice of Radio Operator

Setting. *The Pacific Ocean between San Pedro and Catalina Island.*

Time. *Summer.*

Live conga drums can be used to punctuate the action of the play.

SCENE I

Pacific Ocean. Midday. On the horizon, in perspective, a small boat enters upstage left, crosses to upstage right, and exits. Pause. Lower on the horizon, the same boat, in larger perspective, enters upstage right, crosses and exits upstage left. Blackout.

SCENE II

Pacific Ocean. Midday. The swimmer, Margarita Suárez, is swimming. On the boat following behind her are her father, Eduardo Suárez, holding a megaphone, and Simón, her brother, sitting on top of the cabin with his shirt off, punk sunglasses on, binoculars hanging on his chest.

Eduardo (*Leaning forward, shouting in time to Margarita's swimming.*): Uno, dos, uno, dos. Y uno, dos° . . . keep your shoulders parallel to the water.
Simón: I'm gonna take these glasses off and look straight into the sun.
Eduardo (*Through megaphone.*): Muy bien, muy bien° . . . but punch those arms in, baby.

Uno, dos, uno, dos. Y uno, dos: One, two, one, two. And one, two. *Muy bien, muy bien:* Very good, very good.

Scene from the University of Colorado's production of The Cuban Swimmer

Simón (*Looking directly at the sun through binoculars.*): Come on, come on, zap me. Show me something. (*He looks behind at the shoreline and ahead at the sea.*) Stop! Stop, *Papi!* Stop!

(*Aída Suárez and Abuela, the swimmer's mother and grandmother, enter running from the back of the boat.*)

Aída and Abuela: Qué? Qué es?°
Aída: Es un shark?°

Qué? Qué es?: What? What is it?   *Es un shark?:* Is it a shark?

Eduardo: Eh?

Abuela: Que es un shark dicen?°

(*Eduardo blows whistle. Margarita looks up at the boat.*)

Simón: No, *Papi*, no shark, no shark. We've reached the halfway mark.

Abuela (*Looking into the water.*): *A dónde está?°*

Aída: It's not in the water.

Abuela: Oh, no? Oh, no?

Aída: No! *A poco* do you think they're gonna have signs in the water to say you are halfway to Santa Catalina? No. It's done very scientific. *A ver, hijo,°* explain it to your grandma.

Simón: Well, you see, Abuela—(*He points behind.*) There's San Pedro. (*He points ahead.*) And there's Santa Catalina. Looks halfway to me.

(*Abuela shakes her head and is looking back and forth, trying to make the decision, when suddenly the sound of a helicopter is heard.*)

Abuela (*Looking up.*): *Virgencita de la Caridad del Cobre. Qué es eso?°*

(*Sound of helicopter gets closer. Margarita looks up.*)

Margarita: Papi, Papi!

(*A small commotion on the boat, with everybody pointing at the helicopter above. Shadows of the helicopter fall on the boat. Simón looks up at it through binoculars.*)

Papi—*qué es?* What is it?

Eduardo (*Through megaphone.*): Uh . . . uh . . . uh, *un momentico* . . . *mi hija.°* . . . Your *papi's* got everything under control, understand? Uh . . . you just keep stroking. And stay . . . uh . . . close to the boat.

Simón: Wow, *Papi!* We're on TV, man! Holy Christ, we're all over the fucking U.S.A.! It's Mel Munson and Mary Beth White!

Aída: Por Dios!° Simón, don't swear. And put on your shirt.

(*Aída fluffs her hair, puts on her sunglasses and waves to the helicopter. Simón leans over the side of the boat and yells to Margarita.*)

Simón: Yo, Margo! You're on TV, man.

Eduardo: Leave your sister alone. Turn on the radio.

Margarita: Papi! Qué está pasando?°

Abuela: Que es la televisión dicen? (*She shakes her head.*) *Porque como yo no puedo ver nada sin mis espejuelos.°*

Que es un shark *dicen?*: Did they say a shark?   *A dónde está?*: Where is it?   *A ver, hijo*: Look here, son.   *Virgencita de la Caridad del Cobre. Qué es eso?*: Virgin of Charity! What is that?   *un momentico* . . . *mi hija*: Just a second, my daughter.   *Por Dios!*: For God's Sake!   *Papi! Qué está pasando?*: Dad. What's happening?   *Que es la televisión dicen? Porque como yo no puedo ver nada sin mis espejuelos*: Did they say television? Because I can't see without my glasses.

(Abuela rummages through the boat, looking for her glasses. Voices of Mel Munson and Mary Beth White are heard over the boat's radio.)

Mel's Voice: As we take a closer look at the gallant crew of *La Havana* . . . and there . . . yes, there she is . . . the little Cuban swimmer from Long Beach, California, nineteen-year-old Margarita Suárez. The unknown swimmer is our Cinderella entry . . . a bundle of tenacity, battling her way through the choppy, murky waters of the cold Pacific to reach the Island of Romance . . . Santa Catalina . . . where should she be the first to arrive, two thousand dollars and a gold cup will be waiting for her.

Aída: Doesn't even cover our expenses.

Abuela: Qué dice?

Eduardo: Shhhh!

Mary Beth's Voice: This is really a family effort, Mel, and—

Mel's Voice: Indeed it is. Her trainer, her coach, her mentor, is her father, Eduardo Suárez. Not a swimmer himself, it says here, Mr. Suárez is head usher of the Holy Name Society and the owner-operator of Suárez Treasures of the Sea and Salvage Yard. I guess it's one of those places—

Mary Beth's Voice: If I might interject a fact here, Mel, assisting in this swim is Mrs. Suárez, who is a former Miss Cuba.

Mel's Voice: And a beautiful woman in her own right. Let's try and get a closer look.

(Helicopter sound gets louder. Margarita, frightened, looks up again.)

Margarita: Papi!

Eduardo (Through megaphone.): Mi hija, don't get nervous . . . it's the press. I'm handling it.

Aída: I see how you're handling it.

Eduardo (Through megaphone.): Do you hear? Everything is under control. Get back into your rhythm. Keep your elbows high and kick and kick and kick and kick . . .

Abuela (Finds her glasses and puts them on.): Ay sí, es la televisión . . . *(She points to helicopter.)* Qué lindo mira . . . *(She fluffs her hair, gives a big wave.)* Aló América! Viva mi Margarita, viva todo los Cubanos en los Estados Unidos!°

Aída: Ay por Dios, Cecilia, the man didn't come all this way in his helicopter to look at you jumping up and down, making a fool of yourself.

Abuela: I don't care. I'm proud.

Aída: He can't understand you anyway.

Abuela: Viva . . . *(She stops.)* Simón, cómo se dice viva?°

Simón: Hurray.

Abuela: Hurray for mi Margarita y for all the Cubans living en the United States, y un abrazo . . . Simón, abrazo . . .

Aló América! Viva mi Margarita, viva todo los Cubanos en los Estados Unidos!: Hello America! Hurray for my Margarita, hurray for all the Cubans in the United States!   cómo se dice viva?: How do you say "viva" [in English]?

Simón: A big hug.

Abuela: Sí, a big hug to all my friends in Miami, Long Beach, Union City, except
for my son Carlos, who lives in New York in sin! He lives . . . (*She crosses herself.*) in Brooklyn with a Puerto Rican woman in sin! *No decente* . . .

Simón: Decent.

Abuela: Carlos, *no decente.* This family, *decente.*

Aída: Cecilia, *por Dios.*

Mel's Voice: Look at that enthusiasm. The whole family has turned out to cheer
little Margarita on to victory! I hope they won't be too disappointed.

Mary Beth's Voice: She seems to be making good time, Mel.

Mel's Voice: Yes, it takes all kinds to make a race. And it's a testimonial to the all-
encompassing fairness . . . the greatness of this, the Wrigley Invitational
Women's Swim to Catalina, where among all the professionals there is still
room for the amateurs . . . like these, the simple people we see below us on the
ragtag *La Havana,* taking their long-shot chance to victory. *Vaya con Dios!°*

(*Helicopter sound fading as family, including Margarita, watch silently. Static as
Simón turns radio off. Eduardo walks to bow of boat, looks out on the horizon.*)

Eduardo (*To himself.*): Amateurs.

Aída: Eduardo, that person insulted us. Did you hear, Eduardo? That he called
us a simple people in a ragtag boat? Did you hear . . . ?

Abuela (*Clenching her fist at departing helicopter.*): Mal-Rayo los parta!°

Simón (*Same gesture.*): Asshole!

(*Aída follows Eduardo as he goes to side of boat and stares at Margarita.*)

Aída: This person comes in his helicopter to insult your wife, your family, your
daughter . . .

Margarita (*Pops her head out of the water.*): Papi?

Aída: Do you hear me, Eduardo? I am not simple.

Abuela: Sí.

Aída: I am complicated.

Abuela: Sí, *demasiada complicada.*

Aída: Me and my family are not so simple.

Simón: Mom, the guy's an asshole.

Abuela (*Shaking her fist at helicopter.*): Asshole!

Aída: If my daughter was simple, she would not be in that water swimming.

Margarita: Simple? Papi . . . ?

Aída: Ahora, Eduardo, this is what I want you to do. When we get to Santa
Catalina, I want you to call the TV station and demand an apology.

Eduardo: Cállete mujer! Aquí mando yo.° I will decide what is to be done.

Margarita: Papi, tell me what's going on.

Eduardo: Do you understand what I am saying to you, Aída?

Vaya con Dios!: Go with God. [God bless you.] *Mal-Rayo los parta!:* To hell with you! *Cállete mujer! Aquí mando yo:* Quiet! I'm in charge here.

Simón (*Leaning over side of boat, to Margarita.*): Yo Margo! You know that Mel Munson guy on TV? He called you a simple amateur and said you didn't have a chance.

Abuela (*Leaning directly behind Simón.*): Mi hija, insultó a la familia. Desgraciado!

Aída (*Leaning in behind Abuela.*): He called us peasants! And your father is not doing anything about it. He just knows how to yell at me.

Eduardo (*Through megaphone.*): Shut up! All of you! Do you want to break her concentration? Is that what you are after? Eh?

(*Abuela, Aída and Simón shrink back. Eduardo paces before them.*)

Swimming is rhythm and concentration. You win a race *aquí*. (*Pointing to his head.*) Now . . . (*To Simón.*) you, take care of the boat, Aída y Mama . . . do something. Anything. Something practical.

(*Abuela and Aída get on knees and pray in Spanish.*)

Hija, give it everything, eh? . . . *por la familia. Uno . . . dos. . . .* You must win.

(*Simón goes into cabin. The prayers continue as lights change to indicate bright sunlight, later in the afternoon.*)

SCENE III

Tableau for a couple of beats. Eduardo on bow with timer in one hand as he counts strokes per minute. Simón is in the cabin steering, wearing his sunglasses, baseball cap on backward. Abuela and Aída are at the side of the boat, heads down, hands folded, still muttering prayers in Spanish.

Aída and Abuela (*Crossing themselves.*): En el nombre del Padre, del Hijo y del Espíritu Santo amén.°

Eduardo (*Through megaphone.*): You're stroking seventy-two!

Simón (*Singing.*): Mama's stroking, Mama's stroking seventy-two. . . .

Eduardo (*Through megaphone.*): You comfortable with it?

Simón (*Singing.*): Seventy-two, seventy-two, seventy-two for you.

Aída (*Looking at the heavens.*): Ay, Eduardo, ven acá,° we should be grateful that Nuestro Señor° gave us such a beautiful day.

Abuela (*Crosses herself.*): Sí, gracias a Dios.°

Eduardo: She's stroking seventy-two, with no problem (*He throws a kiss to the sky.*) It's a beautiful day to win.

Aída: Qué hermoso!° So clear and bright. Not a cloud in the sky. Mira! Mira!° Even rainbows on the water . . . a sign from God.

Simón (*Singing.*): Rainbows on the water . . . you in my arms . . .

Abuela and Eduardo (*Looking the wrong way.*): Dónde?

En el nombre del Padre, del Hijo y del Espíritu Santo amén: In the name of the Father, the Son, and the Holy Ghost, Amen.   *ven acá:* Look here.   *Nuestro Señor:* Our father [God].   *Sí, gracias a Dios:* Yes, thanks be to God.   *Qué hermoso!:* How beautiful!   *Mira!:* look.

Aída (*Pointing toward Margarita.*): There, dancing in front of Margarita, leading
her on . . .

Eduardo: Rainbows on . . . Ay coño! It's an oil slick! You . . . you . . . (*To Simón.*)
Stop the boat. (*Runs to bow, yelling.*) Margarita! Margarita!

(*On the next stroke, Margarita comes up all covered in black oil.*)

Margarita: Papi! Papi . . . !

(*Everybody goes to the side and stares at Margarita, who stares back. Eduardo
freezes.*)

Aída: Apúrate,° Eduardo, move . . . what's wrong with you . . . no me oíste, get
my daughter out of the water.

Eduardo (*Softly.*): We can't touch her. If we touch her, she's disqualified.

Aída: But I'm her mother.

Eduardo: Not even by her own mother. Especially by her own mother. . . . You always want the rules to be different for you, you always want to be the exception. (*To Simón.*) And you . . . you didn't see it, eh? You were playing again?

Simón: Papi, I was watching . . .

Aída (*Interrupting.*): Pues, do something Eduardo. You are the big coach, the
monitor.

Simón: Mentor! Mentor!

Eduardo: How can a person think around you? (*He walks off to bow, puts head in
hands.*)

Abuela (*Looking over side.*): Mira como todos los little birds are dead. (*She crosses
herself.*)

Aída: Their little wings are glued to their sides.

Simón: Christ, this is like the La Brea tar pits.

Aída: They can't move their little wings.

Abuela: Esa niña tiene que moverse.°

Simón: Yeah, Margo, you gotta move, man.

(*Abuela and Simón gesture for Margarita to move. Aída gestures for her to
swim.*)

Abuela: Anda niña, muévete.°

Aída: Swim, hija, swim or the aceite° will stick to your wings.

Margarita: Papi?

Abuela (*Taking megaphone.*): Your papi say "move it!"

(*Margarita with difficulty starts moving.*)

Abuela, Aída and Simón (*Laboriously counting.*): Uno, dos . . . uno, dos . . . anda
. . . uno, dos.

Eduardo (*Running to take megaphone from Abuela.*): Uno, dos . . .

Apúrate . . . no me oíste: Finish this! . . . didn't you hear me?   Esa niña tiene que moverse: That
girl has to move.   Anda niña, muévete: Come on, girl, Move!   aceite: oil.

(*Simón races into cabin and starts the engine. Abuela, Aída and Eduardo count together.*)

Simón (*Looking ahead.*): Papi, it's over there!
Eduardo: Eh?
Simón (*Pointing ahead and to the right.*): It's getting clearer over there.
Eduardo (*Through megaphone.*): Now pay attention to me. Go to the right.

(*Simón, Abuela, Aída and Eduardo all lean over side. They point ahead and to the right, except Abuela, who points to the left.*)

Family (*Shouting together.*): Para yá!° Para yá!

(*Lights go down on boat. A special light on Margarita, swimming through the oil, and on Abuela, watching her.*)

Abuela: Sangre de mi sangre,° you will be another to save us. En Bolondron, where your great-grandmother Luz Suárez was born, they say one day it rained blood. All the people, they run into their houses. They cry, they pray, *pero* your great-grandmother Luz she had *cojones* like a man. She run outside. She look straight at the sky. She shake her fist. And she say to the evil one, "Mira . . . (*Beating her chest.*) coño, Diablo, aquí estoy si me quieres."° And she open her mouth, and she drunk the blood.

BLACKOUT.

SCENE IV

Lights up on boat. Aída and Eduardo are on deck watching Margarita swim. We hear the gentle, rhythmic lap, lap, lap of the water, then the sound of inhaling and exhaling as Margarita's breathing becomes louder. Then Margarita's heartbeat is heard, with the lapping of the water and the breathing under it. These sounds continue beneath the dialogue to the end of the scene.

Aída: Dios mío. Look how she moves through the water. . . .
Eduardo: You see, it's very simple. It is a matter of concentration.
Aída: The first time I put her in water she came to life, she grew before my eyes. She moved, she smiled, she loved it more than me. She didn't want my breast any longer. She wanted the water.
Eduardo: And of course, the rhythm. The rhythm takes away the pain and helps the concentration.

(*Pause. Aída and Eduardo watch Margarita.*)

Aída: Is that my child or a seal. . . .
Eduardo: Ah, a seal, the reason for that is that she's keeping her arms very close to her body. She cups her hands, and then she reaches and digs, reaches and digs.

Para yá: over there. *Sangre de mi sangre:* blood of my blood. *Mira . . . coño, Diablo, aquí estoy si me quieres:* Look . . . damn it Devil, here I am if you want me.

Aída: To think that a daughter of mine. . . .

Eduardo: It's the training, the hours in the water. I used to tie weights around her little wrists and ankles.

Aída: A spirit, an ocean spirit, must have entered my body when I was carrying her.

Eduardo (To Margarita.): Your stroke is slowing down.

(*Pause. We hear Margarita's heartbeat with the breathing under, faster now.*)

Aída: Eduardo, that night, the night on the boat . . .

Eduardo: Ah, the night on the boat again . . . the moon was . . .

Aída: The moon was full. We were coming to America. . . . *Qué romantico.*

(*Heartbeat and breathing continue.*)

Eduardo: We were cold, afraid, with no money, and on top of everything, you were hysterical, yelling at me, tearing at me with your nails. (*Opens his shirt, points to the base of his neck.*) Look, I still bear the scars . . . telling me that I didn't know what I was doing . . . saying that we were going to die. . . .

Aída: You took me, you stole me from my home . . . you didn't give me a chance to prepare. You just said we have to go now, now! Now, you said. You didn't let me take anything. I left everything behind. . . . I left everything behind.

Eduardo: Saying that I wasn't good enough, that your father didn't raise you so that I could drown you in the sea.

Aída: You didn't let me say even a good-bye. You took me, you stole me, you tore me from my home.

Eduardo: I took you so we could be married.

Aída: That was in Miami. But that night on the boat, Eduardo. . . . We were not married, that night on the boat.

Eduardo: *No pasó nada!°* Once and for all get it out of your head, it was cold, you hated me, and we were afraid. . . .

Aída: *Mentiroso!°*

Eduardo: A man can't do it when he is afraid.

Aída: Liar! You did it very well.

Eduardo: I did?

Aída: Sí. Gentle. You were so gentle and then strong . . . my passion for you so deep. Standing next to you . . . I would ache . . . looking at your hands I would forget to breathe, you were irresistible.

Eduardo: I was?

Aída: You took me into your arms, you touched my face with your fingertips . . . you kissed my eyes . . . *la esquina de la boca y* . . .

Eduardo: Sí, Sí, and then . . .

Aída: I look at your face on top of mine, and I see the lights of Havana in your eyes. That's when you seduced me.

Eduardo: Shhh, they're gonna hear you.

No pasó nada!: Nothing happened.   *Mentiroso!:* Liar!

(Lights go down. Special on Aída.)

Aída: That was the night. A woman doesn't forget those things . . . and later that night was the dream . . . the dream of a big country with fields of fertile land and big, giant things growing. And there by a green, slimy pond I found a giant pea pod and when I opened it, it was full of little, tiny baby frogs.

(Aída crosses herself as she watches Margarita. We hear louder breathing and heartbeat.)

Margarita: Santa Teresa. Little Flower of God, pray for me. San Martín de Porres, pray for me. Santa Rosa de Lima, *Virgencita de la Caridad del Cobre,* pray for me. . . . Mother pray for me.

SCENE V

Loud howling of wind is heard, as lights change to indicate unstable weather, fog and mist. Family on deck, braced and huddled against the wind. Simón is at the helm.

Aída: Ay Dios mío, qué viento.°
Eduardo (Through megaphone.): Don't drift out . . . that wind is pushing you out.
  (To Simón.) You! Slow down. Can't you see your sister is drifting out?
Simón: It's the wind, *Papi.*
Aída: Baby, don't go so far. . . .
Abuela (To heaven.): Ay Gran Poder de Dios, quita este maldito viento.°
Simón: Margo! Margo! Stay close to the boat.
Eduardo: Dig in. Dig in hard . . . .Reach down from your guts and dig in.
Abuela (To heaven.): Ay Virgen de la Caridad del Cobre, por lo más tú quieres a pararla.
Aída (Putting her hand out, reaching for Margarita.): Baby, don't go far.

(Abuela crosses herself. Action freezes. Lights get dimmer, special on Margarita. She keeps swimming, stops, starts again, stops, then, finally exhausted, stops altogether. The boat stops moving.)

Eduardo: What's going on here? Why are we stopping?
Simón: Papi, she's not moving! Yo Margo!

(The family all run to the side.)

Eduardo: Hija! . . . Hijita! You're tired, eh?
Aída: Por supuesto she's tired. I like to see you get in the water, waving your arms and legs from San Pedro to Santa Catalina. A person isn't a machine, a person has to rest.
Simón: Yo, Mama! Cool out, it ain't fucking brain surgery.
Eduardo (To Simón.): Shut up, you. *(Louder to Margarita.)* I guess your mother's right for once, huh? . . . I guess you had to stop, eh? . . . Give your brother, the idiot . . . a chance to catch up with you.

Ay Dios mío, qué viento: Oh my God, what wind! Ay Gran Poder de Dios, quita este maldito viento: By the great power of God, keep the cursed winds away!

Simón (*Clowning like Mortimer Snerd.*): Dum dee dum dee dum ooops, ah shucks . . .

Eduardo: I don't think he's Cuban.

Simón (*Like Ricky Ricardo.*): Oye, Lucy! I'm home! Ba ba lu!

Eduardo (*Joins in clowning, grabbing Simón in a headlock.*): What am I gonna do
　　with this idiot, eh? I don't understand this idiot. He's not like us, Margarita.
　　(*Laughing.*) You think if we put him into your bathing suit with a cap on his
　　head . . . (*He laughs hysterically.*) You think anyone would know . . . huh? Do
　　you think anyone would know? (*Laughs.*)

Simón (*Vamping.*): Ay, mi amor. Anybody looking for tits would know.

　　(*Eduardo slaps Simón across the face, knocking him down. Aída runs to Simón's
　　aid. Abuela holds Eduardo back.*)

Margarita: Mía culpa!° Mía culpa!

Abuela: Qué dices hija?

Margarita: Papi, it's my fault, it's all my fault. . . . I'm so cold, I can't move. . . . I put
　　my face in the water . . . and I hear them whispering . . . laughing at me. . . .

Aída: Who is laughing at you?

Margarita: The fish are all biting me . . . they hate me . . . they whisper about me.
　　She can't swim, they say. She can't glide. She has no grace. . . . Yellowtails,
　　bonita, tuna, man-o'-war, snub-nose sharks, *los baracudas* . . . they all hate me
　　. . . only the dolphins care . . . and sometimes I hear the whales crying . . . she
　　is lost, she is dead. I'm so numb, I can't feel. Papi! Papi! Am I dead?

Eduardo: Vamos, baby, punch those arms in. Come on . . . do you hear me?

Margarita: Papi . . . Papi . . . forgive me. . . .

　　(*All is silent on the boat. Eduardo drops his megaphone, his head bent down in de-
　　jection. Abuela, Aída, Simón, all leaning over the side of the boat. Simón slowly
　　walks away.*)

Aída: Mi hija, qué tienes?

Simón: Oh, Christ, don't make her say it. Please don't make her say it.

Abuela: Say what? Qué cosa?

Simón: She wants to quit, can't you see she's had enough?

Abuela: Mira, para eso. Esta niña is turning blue.

Aída: Oyeme, mi hija. Do you want to come out of the water?

Margarita: Papi?

Simón (*To Eduardo.*): She won't come out until *you* tell her.

Aída: Eduardo . . . answer your daughter.

Eduardo: Le dije to concentrate . . . concentrate on your rhythm. Then the
　　rhythm would carry her . . . ay, it's a beautiful thing, Aída. It's like yoga, like
　　meditation, the mind over matter . . . the mind controlling the body . . .
　　that's how the great things in the world have been done. I wish you . . . I
　　wish my wife could understand.

Margarita: Papi?

Simón (*To Margarita.*): Forget him.

Mía culpa!: It's my fault.

Aída (*Imploring.*): Eduardo, *por favor.*

Eduardo (*Walking in circles.*): Why didn't you let her concentrate? Don't you understand, the concentration, the rhythm is everything. But no, you wouldn't listen. (*Screaming to the ocean.*) Goddamn Cubans, why, God, why do you make us go everywhere with our families? (*He goes to back of boat.*)

Aída (*Opening her arms.*): Mi hija, ven, come to Mami. (*Rocking.*) Your *mami* knows.

(*Abuela has taken the training bottle, puts it in a net. She and Simón lower it to Margarita.*)

Simón: Take this. Drink it. (*As Margarita drinks, Abuela crosses herself.*)

Abuela: Sangre de mi sangre.

(*Music comes up softly. Margarita drinks, gives the bottle back, stretches out her arms, as if on a cross. Floats on her back. She begins a graceful backstroke. Lights fade on boat as special lights come up on Margarita. She stops. Slowly turns over and starts to swim, gradually picking up speed. Suddenly as if in pain she stops, tries again, then stops in pain again. She becomes disoriented and falls to the bottom of the sea. Special on Margarita at the bottom of the sea.*)

Margarita: *Ya no puedo* . . . I can't. . . . A person isn't a machine . . . *es mi culpa* . . . Father forgive me . . . *Papi! Papi!* One, two. *Uno, dos.* (*Pause.*) *Papi!* A dónde estás? (*Pause.*) One, two, one, two. *Papi! Ay, Papi!* Where are you . . . ? Don't leave me. . . . Why don't you answer me? (*Pause. She starts to swim, slowly.*) *Uno, dos, uno, dos.* Dig in, dig in. (*Stops swimming.*) *Por favor, Papi!* (*Starts to swim again.*) One, two, one, two. Kick from your hip, kick from your hip. (*Stops swimming. Starts to cry.*) Oh God, please. . . . (*Pause.*) Hail Mary, full of grace . . . dig in, dig in . . . the Lord is with thee. . . . (*She swims to the rhythm of her Hail Mary.*) Hail Mary, full of grace . . . dig in, dig in . . . the Lord is with thee . . . dig in, dig in. . . . Blessed art thou among women. . . . *Mami,* it hurts. You let go of my hand. I'm lost. . . . And blessed is the fruit of thy womb, now and at the hour of our death. Amen. I don't want to die, I don't want to die.

(*Margarita is still swimming. Blackout. She is gone.*)

SCENE VI

Lights up on boat, we hear radio static. There is a heavy mist. On deck we see only black outline of Abuela with shawl over her head. We hear the voices of Eduardo, Aída, and Radio Operator.

Eduardo's Voice: *La Havana!* Coming from San Pedro. Over.

Radio Operator's Voice: Right, DT6-6, you say you've lost a swimmer.

Aída's Voice: Our child, our only daughter . . . listen to me. Her name is Margarita Inez Suárez, she is wearing a black one-piece bathing suit cut high in the legs with a white racing stripe down the sides, a white bathing cap with goggles and her whole body covered with a . . . with a . . .

Eduardo's Voice: With lanolin and paraffin.
Aída's Voice: Sí . . . *con lanolin and paraffin.*

(*More radio static. Special on Simón, on the edge of the boat.*)

Simón: Margo! Yo Margo! (*Pause.*) Man don't do this. (*Pause.*) Come on. . . . Come on. . . . (*Pause.*) God, why does everything have to be so hard? (*Pause.*) Stupid. You know you're not supposed to die for this. Stupid. It's his dream and he can't even swim. (*Pause.*) Punch those arms in. Come home. Come home. I'm your little brother. Don't forget what Mama said. You're not supposed to leave me behind. *Vamos,* Margarita, take your little brother, hold his hand tight when you cross the street. He's so little. (*Pause.*) Oh Christ, give us a sign. . . . I know! I know! Margo, I'll send you a message . . . like mental telepathy. I'll hold my breath, close my eyes, and I'll bring you home. (*He takes a deep breath; a few beats.*) This time I'll beep . . . I'll send out sonar signals like a dolphin. (*He imitates dolphin sounds.*)

(*The sound of real dolphins takes over from Simón, then fades into sound of Abuela saying the Hail Mary in Spanish, as full lights come up slowly.*)

SCENE VII

Eduardo coming out of cabin, sobbing, Aída holding him. Simón anxiously scanning the horizon. Abuela looking calmly ahead.

Eduardo: Es mi culpa, sí, es mi culpa.° (*He hits his chest.*)
Aída: Ya, ya viejo.° . . . it was my sin . . . I left my home.
Eduardo: Forgive me, forgive me. I've lost our daughter, our sister, our grand-daughter, *mi carne, mi sangre, mis ilusiones.*° (*To heaven.*) Dios mío, take me . . . take me, I say . . . Goddammit, take me!
Simón: I'm going in.
Aída and Eduardo: No!
Eduardo (*Grabbing and holding Simón, speaking to heaven.*): God, take me, not my children. They are my dreams, my illusions . . . and not this one, this one is my mystery . . . he has my secret dreams. In him are the parts of me I cannot see.

(*Eduardo embraces Simón. Radio static becomes louder.*)

Aída: I . . . I think I see her.
Simón: No, it's just a seal.
Abuela (*Looking out with binoculars.*): Mi nietacita, dónde estás? (*She feels her heart.*) I don't feel the knife in my heart . . . my little fish is not lost.

(*Radio crackles with static. As lights dim on boat, Voices of Mel and Mary Beth are heard over the radio.*)

Es mi culpa, sí, es mi culpa: It's my fault, yes, it's my fault. *Ya, ya viejo:* Yes, yes, old man. *mi carne, mi sangre, mis ilusiones:* My flesh, my blood, my dreams.

Mel's Voice: Tragedy has marred the face of the Wrigley Invitational Women's Race to Catalina. The Cuban swimmer, little Margarita Suárez, has reportedly been lost at sea. Coast Guard and divers are looking for her as we speak. Yet in spite of this tragedy the race must go on because . . .

Mary Beth's Voice (Interrupting loudly.): Mel!

Mel's Voice (Startled.): What!

Mary Beth's Voice: Ah . . . excuse me, Mel . . . we have a winner. We've just received word from Catalina that one of the swimmers is just fifty yards from the breakers . . . it's, oh, it's . . . Margarita Suárez!

(Special on family in cabin listening to radio.)

Mel's Voice: What? I thought she died!

(Special on Margarita, taking off bathing cap, trophy in hand, walking on the water.)

Mary Beth's Voice: Ahh . . . unless . . . unless this is a tragic . . . No . . . there she is, Mel. Margarita Suárez! The only one in the race wearing a black bathing suit cut high in the legs with a racing stripe down the side.

(Family cheering, embracing.)

Simón (Screaming.): Way to go, Margo!

Mel's Voice: This is indeed a miracle! It's a resurrection! Margarita Suárez, with a flotilla of boats to meet her, is now walking on the waters, through the breakers . . . onto the beach, with crowds of people cheering her on. What a jubilation! This is a miracle!

(Sound of crowds cheering. Lights and cheering sounds fade.)

BLACKOUT.

Milcha Sanchez-Scott

Milcha Sanchez-Scott on Drama

WRITING *THE CUBAN SWIMMER*   1989

From these women [recent immigrants Sanchez-Scott met at the employment agency where she worked] I got my material for *Latina*, my first play. I'd never tried to write. I was just collecting stories—for instance, a woman told me her child had died two years previously, and that at the mortuary she had lifted her child and put it across her face to give it a last goodbye. For two years, she said, the whole side of her face and her lips were cold. And being with my cousin again reminded me of the way we say things in Colombia: "Do you remember the summer when all the birds flew into the bedroom?" I was just writing things down.

About this time I was hired by Susan Loewenberg of L.A. Theatre Works to act in a project at the women's prison in Chino. I saw the way Doris Baizley, the writer, had put the women's stories together. When I offered Susan my notes, hoping she could make a piece out of them, she persuaded me to write it myself.

I'd found a channel to get all sorts of things flowing out. I liked controlling my own time, and *making* things—I've always admired architects. Acting seemed very airy to me because I could never take it home and show it to anybody. I had trouble being alone for long periods, but then I would go to the airport or someplace else busy to write. Doris and I used to do things like write under blankets by flashlight, which makes you feel like a little kid with a big secret.

L.A. Theatre Works got a grant and we toured *Latina* up and down the state with ten Latin actresses who were always feuding. We had one who was illegal, and wouldn't perform anyplace she thought Immigration might come, so I had to go on in her place. Then Susan commissioned me to write something else, which turned out to be *Dog Lady* and *Cuban Swimmer*. I saw the long-distance swimmer Diana Nyad on TV and I saw Salazar—the Cuban runner—and started thinking. I wanted to set a play in the water. So I put a family on a boat and a swimmer in the water and said, "Now, *what?*" I happened to be in a church and saw the most beautiful Stations of the Cross. It struck me as a good outline for anybody undertaking an endeavor—there's all this tripping and falling and rising. So that's what I used.

From *On New Ground*

⊰▣⊷ WRITING CRITICALLY ⊷▣⊰

What's So Realistic About Realism?

When you hear the word *realism* used in relation to drama, it often refers to certain ways of writing and performing plays that emerged during the nineteenth century. In drama, realism tries to imitate the texture of everyday life. To understand the conventions of realism, it might help to contrast a play by Henrik Ibsen with one by Sophocles. Ibsen's characters speak in prose, not verse. His settings are drawn from contemporary life, not a legendary past. His characters are ordinary middle-class citizens, not kings, queens, and aristocrats.

Those external characteristics are easy to spot, but you should also notice some less obvious ways that plays of the Realist movement often differ from earlier drama. Realist dramatists like Ibsen and Anton Chekhov try to portray the complexity of human psychology—especially motivation—in a detailed, subtle way. In Shakespeare's *Othello*, the villain Iago announces that he wants revenge on the title character because the Moor has reportedly cuckolded him. This far-fetched assertion is never proved—the facts of the play seem to contradict it everywhere else—and Iago never mentions the motivation again. Shakespeare appears less interested in the reason for Iago's villainy than its consequences. Did Iago have an unhappy childhood or a troubled adolescence? These questions do not greatly matter in Renaissance drama, but to Ibsen they become central. The inner lives, memories, and motivations of the characters now play a crucial role in the dramatic action.

Realist drama does not necessarily come any closer than other dramatic styles to getting at the truths of human existence. *A Doll's House*, for example, does not provide a more profound picture of psychological struggle than *Oedipus the King*. But Ibsen does offer a more detailed view of his protagonist's inner life and her daily routine.

When writing about the protagonist of a realistic play, try to understand not only the motivation of the main character but also where those motives originated. Is there some key event, for example, in the protagonist's past that influences his or her present behavior? Do the characters around the protagonist understand the deeper motivation, or do they see only its outward effects? You may even want to construct a brief biography of the central character to understand how his or her childhood or early adulthood affects his or her current situation.

WRITING ASSIGNMENT

Al Capovilla of Folsom Lake Center College has developed an ingenious assignment based on Ibsen's *A Doll's House* that asks you to combine the skills of a literary critic with those of a lawyer. Here is Professor Capovilla's assignment:

> You are the family lawyer for Torvald and Nora Helmer. The couple comes to you with a request. They want you to listen to an account of their domestic problems and recommend whether they should pursue a divorce or try to reconcile.
>
> You listen to both sides of the argument. (You also know everything that is said by every character.)
>
> Now, it is your task to write a short decision. In stating your opinion, provide a clear and organized explanation of your reasoning. Show both sides of the argument. You may employ as evidence anything said or done in the play.
>
> Conclude your paper with your recommendation. What do you advise under the circumstances—divorce or an attempt at reconciliation?

Here is a paper from Professor Capovilla's course written by Carlota Llarena, a student at Folsom Lake Center College.

Carlota Llarena

Professor Capovilla

English 320

19 April 20xx

Helmer vs. Helmer

In reaching a determination of whether Torvald and Nora Helmer should either get divorced or attempt reconciliation, I have carefully considered the events leading to the breakdown of their marriage in order to decide on an amicable solution to their present predicament. In my belief, marriage is a sacred institution--one that should not be taken lightly. Love and happiness in a marriage should be cultivated by the parties. Obstacles are often found throughout marriage, but in order to overcome those obstacles, a husband and wife should share responsibilities, discuss whatever problems arise, and jointly work on finding solutions to those problems. Based on this belief, I recommend that Torvald and Nora Helmer attempt a reconciliation of the marriage.

In reviewing the testimony provided by both parties, I find it true that Torvald has treated Nora in such a manner as to make her feel she was considered a child rather than an equal partner. Torvald handled all their finances and solely resolved all their problems. Torvald never discussed any of their household problems with Nora or attempted to seek her advice. In that regard, I believe that Torvald treated Nora in that fashion because he felt Nora was incapable of handling these types of situations. Nora's every need had always been looked after by her father. She grew up with nannies, never had to take responsibility for herself, and never had to work to earn money as money was always given to her.

I find it also true, however, that Nora has always acted like a child. She has the tendency to sulk if matters don't go her way, is happy when rewarded with gifts, hides treats (like macaroons) for herself when they are prohibited, and likes to play games. These characteristics are clearly evident in Nora. There are at least six examples of her child-like behaviors in the testimonies. First, Nora denied nibbling on a macaroon or two (1813) as a child would deny any wrongdoing. Second, Nora thought it would be "fun" to hang the bills [money] in pretty gilt paper on the Christmas tree (1812) as a child would enjoy bright and colorful objects. Third, Nora considered it to be "wonderful fun" to sit and work to earn money "almost like being a man" (1820) as a child would pretend and play-act adult roles. Fourth, Nora was excited when she received a gift of money from Torvald (1812) as a child would be excited when she receives a present. Fifth, Nora enjoyed dreaming of a rich old gentleman falling in love with her (1820) as a child would dream of getting married to a rich man who would take complete care of her. And, finally, Nora would "do anything to please . . . I'll sing for you, dance for you" (1830) as a child would always attempt to please her parents.

Unfortunately, Torvald reinforced Nora's child-like characteristics by calling her names such as "my little lark" (1811), "my squirrel" (1811), "my pretty little pet" (1812), and "my little Nora" (1830). These nicknames seem more appropriate for a child than a grown woman. Torvald has also been very protective of Nora--just as a parent would be protective of a child. Torvald claimed that Nora had "precious eyes" and "fair little delicate hands" which indicates his belief that Nora was a fragile person, one who does not know how to take care of herself. Since Nora was treated in that same manner by her father, she has never experienced life in any other fashion other than that of a child.

As a further review of the testimony presented, I opine that Torvald is not solely to be blamed for the predicament at hand. Nora has allowed Torvald to treat her in this manner during the eight years they were married. She never told Torvald that she wanted to be treated as an adult and as his equal or that she wanted to become more involved with family matters to help determine solutions to problems they may have. Nora was also guilty of not confiding in Torvald or discussing her problems with him. Did Nora discuss with Torvald the need for them to live in Italy for a year (1819)? Did she sit with her husband and discuss issues concerning money to make such a trip to Italy feasible and where the money actually came from (1819)? Did Nora ever tell Torvald the truth that she had "borrowed" the money from Krogstad, how she was repaying "the loan" and what she did to secure that loan (1828)? The answer to all these questions is no! Accordingly, it is quite clear that Nora and Torvald are both equally guilty of not discussing problems and issues with one another.

In summation, Nora and Torvald are equally at fault on the following issues. First, Torvald treated Nora as a child, and Nora allowed herself to be treated in that manner. Second, Torvald never confided in Nora regarding matters concerning the family or their finances. Nora, however, also did not confide in Torvald. Now that these issues and concerns are made known to the parties, the parties may work on resolving their differences, share the responsibility of handling both family and financial matters by discussing them with one another and finding amicable solutions, and cultivate the trust and judgment of one another. Accordingly, it is my ruling that Nora and Torvald attempt reconciling

their marriage and forgo divorce as an immediate option. Only
if the parties reach an impasse after an honest and sustained
attempt at reconciliation would I suggest reconsidering the
option of divorce.

Work Cited

Ibsen, Henrik. A Doll's House. Trans. James McFarlane.
   Literature: An Introduction to Fiction, Poetry, and
   Drama. Ed. X. J. Kennedy and Dana Gioia. 9th ed. New
   York: Longman, 2005. 1809-66.

FURTHER SUGGESTIONS FOR WRITING

1. Demonstrate, in a paragraph or two, how Nora in *A Doll's House* resembles or differs from a feminist of today.
2. Placing yourself in the character of Ibsen's Torvald Helmer, write a defense of him and his attitudes as he himself might write it.
3. Choose the play in this chapter that in your opinion might best lend itself to a television production. Then tell your reader how you would go about adapting it. What changes or deletions, if any, would you make? What problems would you expect to meet in transferring it to a different medium?
4. Perform Sanchez-Scott's *The Cuban Swimmer* in class. Use only chairs, desks, and other classroom objects for all the sets and props. After you have performed the play, write a short paper on what the experience of seeing the play produced in this way taught you about the work. What elements came off well in this improvised production? What things were lost? Did the play seem different in the classroom from how it seemed on the page?

37 *Evaluating a Play*

To **evaluate** a play is to decide whether the play is any good or not and, if it is good, how good it is in relation to other plays of its kind. In the theater, evaluation is usually thought to be the task of the play reviewer (or, with nobler connotations, "drama critic"), ordinarily a person who sees a new play on its first night and who then tells us, in print or over the air, what the play is about, how well it is done, and whether or not we ought to go to see it. Enthroned in an excellent free seat, the drama critic apparently plies a glamorous trade. What fun it must be to whittle a nasty epigram, for example, to be able to observe, as did a critic of a faltering production of *Uncle Tom's Cabin*, that "the Siberian wolf hound was weakly supported."

Unless you find a job with a large city newspaper or radio station, write for a college paper, or broadcast on a campus FM station, the opportunities to be a drama critic today are probably few and strictly limited. Much more significant, for most of us, is the task of evaluating for our own satisfaction. We see a play, a film, or a television program, and then we make up our minds about it; we often have to decide whether to recommend it to someone else.

To evaluate new drama isn't easy. (For this discussion, let us define *drama* broadly as including not only plays but also anything that actors perform in the movies or on television, for most of us see more movies and television programs than plays.) By the time we see a production of any kind, at least a part of the process of evaluation has already been accomplished for us. To produce a new play, even in an amateur theater, or to produce a new drama for the movies or for television is complicated and involves large sums of money and the efforts of many people. Sifted from a mountain of submitted scripts, already subjected to long scrutiny and evaluation, a new play or film, whether or not it is of deep interest, arrives with a built-in air of professional competence. It is probably seldom that a dull play written by the producer's relative or friend finds enough financial backers to reach the stage; only on the fictitious Broadway of Mel Brooks's film and hit play *The Producers* could there be a musical comedy as awful as *Springtime for Hitler*. Nor do most college and civic theaters afford us much opportunity to see thoroughly inept plays. Usually they give us new productions of *Oedipus the King* or *Pygmalion* or else (if they are less adventurous) new versions of whatever succeeded on Broadway in the recent past.

And so new plays—the few that we do see—are usually, like television drama, somebody's safe investment. More often than not, our powers of evaluation confront only slick, pleasant, and efficient mediocrity. We owe it to ourselves to discriminate. Life is too short and theater tickets too expensive to spend either on the agreeably second-rate. There are too many marvelous plays we might miss.

<hr>

⬤■▭ WRITING CRITICALLY ▭■⬤

<hr>

Critical Performance

Here are a few suggestions designed to help you tell the difference between an ordinary, run-of-the-reel product and a work of drama that may offer high reward.

1. Discard any inexorable rules you may have collected that affirm what a drama ought to be. (One such rule states that a tragedy is innately superior to a comedy, no matter how deep a truth a comedy may strike.) Don't expect all plays to "observe the unities"—that is, unfold their events in one day and in one place and keep tragedy and comedy strictly apart. (Shakespeare ignores such rules.) There is no sense in damning a play for lacking "realism." (What if it's an expressionist play or a fantasy?)

2. Instead, watch the play (or read it) alertly, with your mind and your senses open wide. Recall that theaters, such as the classic Greek theater of Sophocles, impose conventions. Do not condemn *Oedipus the King* for the reason one spectator gave: "That damned chorus keeps sticking their noses in!" Do not complain that Hamlet utters soliloquies.

3. Ask yourself whether the characters are fully realized. Do their actions follow from the kinds of persons they are, or does the action seem to impose itself upon them, making the play seem falsely contrived? Does the resolution arrive (as in a satisfying play) because of the nature of the characters, or are the characters saved (or destroyed) merely by some *deus ex machina* or nick-of-time arrival of the Marines?

4. Recognize drama that belongs to a family, for example *a farce, a comedy of manners,* or a **melodrama** (a play in which suspense and physical action are the prime ingredients). Recognizing such a familiar type of drama may help make some things clear to you and may save you from attacking a play for being what it is, in fact, supposed to be. After all, there can be satisfying melodramas, and excellent plays may have melodramatic elements. What is wrong with thrillers is not that they have suspense, but that suspense usually is all they have. Awhirl with furious action, they employ stick-figure characters.

5. If there are symbols, ask how well they belong to their surrounding worlds. Do they help to reveal meaning or merely decorate? In Tennessee

Williams's *The Glass Menagerie*, Laura's collection of figurines is much more than simply ornamental.

6. Test the play or film for **sentimentality,** the failure of a dramatist, actor, or director who expects from us a greater emotional response than we are given reason to feel. (For further discussions of sentimentality, see pages 285 and 1071.)

7. Decide what it is that you admire or dislike and, for a play, whether it is the play or the production that you admire or dislike. (It is useful to draw this distinction if you are evaluating the play and not the production.)

8. Ask yourself what the theme is. What does the drama reveal? How far and how deep does its statement go; how readily can we apply it beyond the play to the human world outside? Be slow, of course, to attribute to the play-wright the opinions of the characters.

9. Don't be afraid of stating your own honest reaction (balanced, of course, by the careful considerations listed above). When the playwright Eugène Ionesco states that a "critic should describe, and not prescribe," he does not restrict the critic from trying accurately to describe his or her own response to the work in question. We cannot truthfully judge a work of art without somehow involving our own reactions—simple or complicated—to the ex-perience of it.

Follow all these steps, and you may find that evaluating plays, movies, and tele-vision plays is a richly meaningful activity. It may reveal wisdom and pleasure that had previously bypassed you. It may even help you decide what to watch in the fu-ture, how to choose those works of drama that help you to fulfill—not merely to spend—your waking life.

WRITING ASSIGNMENT

Select any play in this book that is available in performance on tape or DVD. Pretend you are a critic attending the world premiere, and write a 750 to 1,000-word review of the play. In evaluating the play and performance, clearly state your criteria for judgment. (For practical hints on writing a review, see "Reviewing a Play" on page 2174.)

FURTHER SUGGESTIONS FOR WRITING

1. Attend a performance of a play, and write a critical review of it. Consider both the play itself and its production. (For advice on reviewing and a sample review, see page 2174.)

2. Read two celebrated, still much performed plays of the same era, *Death of a Salesman* (1949) and *The Glass Menagerie* (1945), both in "Plays for Further Reading." Then, in an essay of 700 words or more, decide which you consider the finer play. Back up your evalu-ation by referring to both.

3. Read the printed text of a modern or contemporary play not included in this book. (If you can see the play live or in a recorded performance, so much the better.) Then, in an essay of 500 to 750 words, state your considered opinion of it. Among interesting plays to choose from are these:

   The Zoo Story by Edward Albee
   Waiting for Godot by Samuel Beckett

"Master Harold" and the Boys by Athol Fugard
Six Degrees of Separation by John Guare
Hedda Gabler, The Master Builder, or Peer Gynt by Henrik Ibsen
The Bald Soprano or The Chairs by Eugène Ionesco
Words, Words, Words by David Ives
American Buffalo by David Mamet
Joe Egg by Peter Nichols
'Night, Mother by Marsha Norman
Long Day's Journey into Night by Eugene O'Neill
Topdog/Underdog by Suzan-Lori Parks
The Birthday Party or The Caretaker by Harold Pinter
Roosters by Milcha Sanchez-Scott
No Exit by Jean-Paul Sartre
for colored girls who have considered suicide / when the rainbow is enuf
    by Ntozake Shange
Major Barbara or Pygmalion by George Bernard Shaw
Buried Child or True West by Sam Shepard
Rosencrantz and Guildenstern Are Dead by Tom Stoppard
How I Learned to Drive by Paula Vogel
The Heidi Chronicles by Wendy Wasserstein
The Piano Lesson by August Wilson

All the world's a stage,
And all the men and women merely players:
They have their exits and their entrances,
And one man in his time plays many parts,
His acts being seven ages. At first, the infant
Mewling° and puking in the nurse's arms.   *bawling*
Then the whining schoolboy, with his satchel
And shining morning face, creeping like snail
Unwillingly to school. And then the lover,
Sighing like furnace, with a woeful ballad
Made to his mistress' eyebrow. Then a soldier
Full of strange oaths and bearded like the pard,°   *leopard*
Jealous in honor, sudden and quick in quarrel,
Seeking the bubble reputation
Even in the cannon's mouth. And then the justice,
In fair round belly with good capon lined,
With eyes severe and beard of formal cut,
Full of wise saws° and modern instances;°   *sayings; examples*
And so he plays his part. The sixth age shifts
Into the lean and slippered pantaloon,°   *old man (from Pantalone*
With spectacles on nose and pouch on side;   *in the* commedia dell'arte)
His youthful hose, well saved, a world too wide
For his shrunk shank, and his big manly voice
Turning again toward childish treble, pipes
And whistles in his sound. Last scene of all,
That ends this strange eventful history,
Is second childishness and mere oblivion,
Sans teeth, sans eyes, sans taste, sans everything.

    —William Shakespeare, *As You Like It*, II, vii

Arthur Miller

DEATH OF A SALESMAN

1949

Certain Private Conversations in Two Acts and a Requiem

Arthur Miller (b. 1915) was born into a lower-income Jewish family in New York City's Harlem but grew up in Brooklyn. He studied playwriting at the University of Michigan, later wrote radio scripts, and during World War II worked as a steamfitter. When the New York Drama Critics named his All My Sons *best play of 1947, Miller told an interviewer, "I don't see how you can write anything decent without using as your basis the question of right and wrong." (The play is about a guilty manufacturer of defective aircraft parts.) Death of a Salesman (1949) made Miller famous. The Crucible (1953), a dramatic indictment of the Salem witch trials, gained him further attention at a time when Senator Joseph McCarthy was conducting loyalty investigations; in 1996, The Crucible was made into a film staring Daniel Day-Lewis and Winona Ryder. For a while (1956–1961), Miller was the husband of actress Marilyn Monroe, whom the main character of his After the Fall (1964) resembles. Among Miller's other plays are* A View from the Bridge *(1955);* The Price *(1968);* The Creation of the World and Other Businesses *(1972);* Playing for Time *(1980), written for television;* Broken Glass *(1994); and* Mr. Peters' Connections *(1999). He has published an autobiography, several volumes of essays, two collections of short stories, and two novels,* Focus *(1945) and* The Misfits *(1960), drawn from his screenplay for the film starring Monroe. A new production of* Death of a Salesman, *starring Brian Dennehy as Willy Loman, opened on Broadway on February 10, 1999, fifty years to the day after its original premiere.*

Cast

Willy Loman
Linda
Biff
Charley
Uncle Ben
Howard Wagner
Jenny
Happy
Bernard
The Woman
Stanley
Miss Forsythe
Letta

Scene: *The action takes place in Willy Loman's house and yard and in various places he visits in the New York and Boston of today. Throughout the play, in the stage directions, left and right mean stage left and stage right.*

Act I

A melody is heard, played upon a flute. It is small and fine, telling of grass and trees and the horizon. The curtain rises.

Before us is the Salesman's house. We are aware of towering, angular shapes behind it, surrounding it on all sides. Only the blue light of the sky falls upon the house and forestage; the surrounding area shows an angry glow of orange. As more light appears, we see a solid vault of apartment houses around the small, fragile-seeming home. An air of the dream clings to the place, a dream rising out of reality. The kitchen at center seems actual enough, for there is a kitchen table with three chairs, and a refrigerator. But no other fixtures are seen. At the back of the kitchen there is a draped entrance, which leads to the living room. To the right of the kitchen, on a level raised two feet, is a bedroom furnished only with a brass bedstead and a straight chair. On a shelf over the bed a silver athletic trophy stands. A window opens onto the apartment house at the side.

Behind the kitchen, on a level raised six and a half feet, is the boys' bedroom, at present barely visible. Two beds are dimly seen, and at the back of the room a dormer window. (This bedroom is above the unseen living room.) At the left a stairway curves up to it from the kitchen.

The entire setting is wholly or, in some places, partially transparent. The roof-line of the house is one-dimensional; under and over it we see the apartment buildings. Before the house lies an apron, curving beyond the forestage into the orchestra. This forward area serves as the backyard as well as the locale of all Willy's imaginings and of his city scenes. Whenever the action is in the present the actors observe the imaginary wall-lines, entering the house only through the door at the left. But in the scenes of the past these boundaries are broken, and characters enter or leave a room by stepping "through" a wall onto the forestage.

From the right, Willy Loman, the Salesman, enters, carrying two large sample cases. The flute plays on. He hears but is not aware of it. He is past sixty years of age, dressed quietly. Even as he crosses the stage to the doorway of the house, his exhaustion is apparent. He unlocks the door, comes into the kitchen, and thankfully lets his burden down, feeling the soreness of his palms. A word-sigh escapes his lips—it might be, "Oh, boy, oh, boy." He closes the door, then carries his cases out into the living room, through the draped kitchen doorway.

Linda, his wife, has stirred in her bed at the right. She gets out and puts on a robe, listening. Most often jovial, she has developed an iron repression of her exceptions to Willy's behavior—she more than loves him, she admires him, as though his mercurial nature, his temper, his massive dreams and little cruelties, served her only as sharp reminders of the turbulent longings within him, longings which she shares but lacks the temperament to utter and follow to their end.

Linda (*hearing Willy outside the bedroom, calls with some trepidation*): Willy!
Willy: It's all right. I came back.
Linda: Why? What happened? (*Slight pause.*) Did something happen, Willy?
Willy: No, nothing happened.

Linda: You didn't smash the car, did you?

Willy (*with casual irritation*): I said nothing happened. Didn't you hear me?

Linda: Don't you feel well?

Willy: I am tired to the death. (*The flute has faded away. He sits on the bed beside her, a little numb.*) I couldn't make it. I just couldn't make it, Linda.

Linda (*very carefully, delicately*): Where were you all day? You look terrible.

Willy: I got as far as a little above Yonkers. I stopped for a cup of coffee. Maybe it was the coffee.

Linda: What?

Willy (*after a pause*): I suddenly couldn't drive any more. The car kept going onto the shoulder, y'know?

Linda (*helpfully*): Oh. Maybe it was the steering again. I don't think Angelo knows the Studebaker.

Willy: No, it's me, it's me. Suddenly I realize I'm goin' sixty miles an hour and I don't remember the last five minutes. I'm—I can't seem to—keep my mind to it.

Linda: Maybe it's your glasses. You never went for your new glasses.

Willy: No, I see everything. I came back ten miles an hour. It took me nearly four hours from Yonkers.

Linda (*resigned*): Well, you'll just have to take a rest. Willy, you can't continue this way.

Willy: I just got back from Florida.

Linda: But you didn't rest your mind. Your mind is overactive, and the mind is what counts, dear.

Willy: I'll start out in the morning. Maybe I'll feel better in the morning. (*She is taking off his shoes.*) These goddam arch supports are killing me.

Linda: Take an aspirin. Should I get you an aspirin? It'll soothe you.

Willy (*with wonder*): I was driving along, you understand? And I was fine. I was even observing the scenery. You can imagine, me looking at scenery, on the road every week of my life. But it's so beautiful up there, Linda, the trees are so thick, and the sun is warm. I opened the windshield and just let the warm air bathe over me. And then all of a sudden I'm goin' off the road! I'm tellin' ya, I absolutely forgot I was driving. If I'd've gone the other way over the white line I might've killed somebody. So I went on again—and five minutes later I'm dreamin' again, and I nearly—(*He presses two fingers against his eyes.*) I have such thoughts, I have such strange thoughts.

Linda: Willy, dear. Talk to them again. There's no reason why you can't work in New York.

Willy: They don't need me in New York. I'm the New England man. I'm vital in New England.

Linda: But you're sixty years old. They can't expect you to keep traveling every week.

Willy: I'll have to send a wire to Portland. I'm supposed to see Brown and Morrison tomorrow morning at ten o'clock to show the line. Goddammit, I could sell them! (*He starts putting on his jacket.*)

Linda (*taking the jacket from him*): Why don't you go down to the place tomorrow and tell Howard you've simply got to work in New York? You're too accommodating, dear.

Willy: If old man Wagner was alive I'd a been in charge of New York now! That man was a prince, he was a masterful man. But that boy of his, that Howard, he don't appreciate. When I went north the first time, the Wagner Company didn't know where New England was!

Linda: Why don't you tell those things to Howard, dear?

Willy (*encouraged*): I will, I definitely will. Is there any cheese?

Linda: I'll make you a sandwich.

Willy: No, go to sleep. I'll take some milk. I'll be up right away. The boys in?

Linda: They're sleeping. Happy took Biff on a date tonight.

Willy (*interested*): That so?

Linda: It was so nice to see them shaving together, one behind the other, in the bathroom. And going out together. You notice? The whole house smells of shaving lotion.

Willy: Figure it out. Work a lifetime to pay off a house. You finally own it, and there's nobody to live in it.

Linda: Well, dear, life is a casting off. It's always that way.

Willy: No, no, some people—some people accomplish something. Did Biff say anything after I went this morning?

Linda: You shouldn't have criticized him, Willy, especially after he just got off the train. You mustn't lose your temper with him.

Willy: When the hell did I lose my temper? I simply asked him if he was making any money. Is that a criticism?

Linda: But, dear, how could he make any money?

Willy (*worried and angered*): There's such an undercurrent in him. He became a moody man. Did he apologize when I left this morning?

Linda: He was crestfallen, Willy. You know how he admires you. I think if he finds himself, then you'll both be happier and not fight any more.

Willy: How can he find himself on a farm? Is that a life? A farmhand? In the beginning, when he was young, I thought, well, a young man, it's good for him to tramp around, take a lot of different jobs. But it's more than ten years now and he has yet to make thirty-five dollars a week!

Linda: He's finding himself, Willy.

Willy: Not finding yourself at the age of thirty-four is a disgrace!

Linda: Shh!

Willy: The trouble is he's lazy, goddammit!

Linda: Willy, please!

Willy: Biff is a lazy bum.

Linda: They're sleeping. Get something to eat. Go on down.

Willy: Why did he come home? I would like to know what brought him home.

Linda: I don't know. I think he's still lost, Willy. I think he's very lost.

Willy: Biff Loman is lost. In the greatest country in the world a young man with such—personal attractiveness, gets lost. And such a hard worker. There's one thing about Biff—he's not lazy.

Linda: Never.

Willy (with pity and resolve): I'll see him in the morning. I'll have a nice talk with him. I'll get him a job selling. He could be big in no time. My God! Remember how they used to follow him around in high school? When he smiled at one of them their faces lit up. When he walked down the street . . . (*He loses himself in reminiscences.*)

Linda (trying to bring him out of it): Willy, dear, I got a new kind of American-type cheese today. It's whipped.

Willy: Why do you get American when I like Swiss?

Linda: I just thought you'd like a change—

Willy: I don't want a change! I want Swiss cheese. Why am I always being contradicted?

Linda (with a covering laugh): I thought it would be a surprise.

Willy: Why don't you open a window in here, for God's sake?

Linda (with infinite patience): They're all open, dear.

Willy: The way they boxed us in here. Bricks and windows, windows and bricks.

Linda: We should've bought the land next door.

Willy: The street is lined with cars. There's not a breath of fresh air in the neighborhood. The grass don't grow any more, you can't raise a carrot in the back yard. They should've had a law against apartment houses. Remember those two beautiful elm trees out there? When I and Biff hung the swing between them?

Linda: Yeah, like being a million miles from the city.

Willy: They should've arrested the builder for cutting those down. They massacred the neighborhood. (*Lost.*) More and more I think of those days, Linda. This time of year it was lilac and wisteria. And then the peonies would come out, and the daffodils. What fragrance in this room!

Linda: Well, after all, people had to move somewhere.

Willy: No, there's more people now.

Linda: I don't think there's more people. I think—

Willy: There's more people! That's what's ruining this country! Population is getting out of control. The competition is maddening! Smell the stink from that apartment house! And another on the other side . . . How can they whip cheese?

On Willy's last line, Biff and Happy raise themselves up in their beds, listening.

Linda: Go down, try it. And be quiet.

Willy (turning to Linda, guiltily): You're not worried about me, are you, sweetheart?

Biff: What's the matter?

Happy: Listen!

Linda: You've got too much on the ball to worry about.

Willy: You're my foundation and my support, Linda.

Linda: Just try to relax, dear. You make mountains out of molehills.

Willy: I won't fight with him any more. If he wants to go back to Texas, let him go.

Linda: He'll find his way.

Willy: Sure. Certain men just don't get started till later in life. Like Thomas Edison, I think. Or B. F. Goodrich. One of them was deaf. (*He starts for the bedroom doorway.*) I'll put my money on Biff.

Linda: And Willy—if it's warm Sunday we'll drive in the country. And we'll open the windshield, and take lunch.

Willy: No, the windshields don't open on the new cars.

Linda: But you opened it today.

Willy: Me? I didn't. (*He stops.*) Now isn't that peculiar! Isn't that a remark-able—(*He breaks off in amazement and fright as the flute is heard distantly.*)

Linda: What, darling?

Willy: That is the most remarkable thing.

Linda: What, dear?

Willy: I was thinking of the Chevvy. (*Slight pause.*) Nineteen twenty-eight . . . when I had that red Chevvy—(*Breaks off.*) That funny? I coulda sworn I was driving that Chevvy today.

Linda: Well, that's nothing. Something must've reminded you.

Willy: Remarkable. Ts. Remember those days? The way Biff used to simonize that car? The dealer refused to believe there was eighty thousand miles on it. (*He shakes his head.*) Heh! (*To Linda.*) Close your eyes, I'll be right up. (*He walks out of the bedroom.*)

Happy (to Biff): Jesus, maybe he smashed up the car again!

Linda (calling after Willy): Be careful on the stairs, dear! The cheese is on the middle shelf! (*She turns, goes over to the bed, takes his jacket, and goes out of the bedroom.*)

Light has risen on the boys' room. Unseen, Willy is heard talking to himself, "Eighty thousand miles," and a little laugh. Biff gets out of bed, comes downstage a bit, and stands attentively. Biff is two years older than his brother Happy, well built, but in these days bears a worn air and seems less self-assured. He has suc-ceeded less, and his dreams are stronger and less acceptable than Happy's. Happy is tall, powerfully made. Sexuality is like a visible color on him, or a scent that many women have discovered. He, like his brother, is lost, but in a different way, for he has never allowed himself to turn his face toward defeat and is thus more confused and hardskinned, although seemingly more content.

Happy (getting out of bed): He's going to get his license taken away if he keeps that up. I'm getting nervous about him, y'know, Biff?

Biff: His eyes are going.

Happy: No, I've driven with him. He sees all right. He just doesn't keep his mind on it. I drove into the city with him last week. He stops at a green light and then it turns red and he goes. (*He laughs.*)

Biff: Maybe he's color-blind.

Happy: Pop? Why he's got the finest eye for color in the business. You know that.

Biff (sitting down on his bed): I'm going to sleep.

Happy: You're not still sour on Dad, are you, Biff?

Biff: He's all right, I guess.

Willy (underneath them, in the living room): Yes, sir, eighty thousand miles— eighty-two thousand!

Biff: You smoking?

Happy (holding out a pack of cigarettes): Want one?

Biff (taking a cigarette): I can never sleep when I smell it.

Willy: What a simonizing job, heh!

Happy (with deep sentiment): Funny, Biff, y'know? Us sleeping in here again? The old beds. (*He pats his bed affectionately.*) All the talk that went across those two beds, huh? Our whole lives.

Biff: Yeah. Lotta dreams and plans.

Happy (with a deep and masculine laugh): About five hundred women would like to know what was said in this room.

They share a soft laugh.

Biff: Remember that big Betsy something—what the hell was her name—over on Bushwick Avenue?

Happy (combing his hair): With the collie dog!

Biff: That's the one. I got you in there, remember?

Happy: Yeah, that was my first time—I think. Boy, there was a pig! (*They laugh, almost crudely.*) You taught me everything I know about women. Don't forget that.

Biff: I bet you forgot how bashful you used to be. Especially with girls.

Happy: Oh, I still am, Biff.

Biff: Oh, go on.

Happy: I just control it, that's all. I think I got less bashful and you got more so. What happened, Biff? Where's the old humor, the old confidence? (*He shakes Biff's knee. Biff gets up and moves restlessly about the room.*) What's the matter?

Biff: Why does Dad mock me all the time?

Happy: He's not mocking you, he—

Biff: Everything I say there's a twist of mockery on his face. I can't get near him.

Happy: He just wants you to make good, that's all. I wanted to talk to you about Dad for a long time, Biff. Something's—happening to him. He—talks to himself.

Biff: I noticed that this morning. But he always mumbled.

Happy: But not so noticeable. It got so embarrassing I sent him to Florida. And you know something? Most of the time he's talking to you.

Biff: What's he say about me?

Happy: I can't make it out.

Biff: What's he say about me?

Happy: I think the fact that you're not settled, that you're still kind of up in the air . . . .

Biff: There's one or two other things depressing him, Happy.

Happy: What do you mean?

Biff: Never mind. Just don't lay it all on me.

Happy: But I think if you just got started—I mean—is there any future for you out there?

Biff: I tell ya, Hap, I don't know what the future is. I don't know—what I'm supposed to want.

Happy: What do you mean?

Biff: Well, I spent six or seven years after high school trying to work myself up. Shipping clerk, salesman, business of one kind or another. And it's a measly manner of existence. To get on that subway on the hot mornings in summer. To devote your whole life to keeping stock, or making phone calls, or selling or buying. To suffer fifty weeks of the year for the sake of a two-week vacation, when all you really desire is to be outdoors, with your shirt off. And always to have to get ahead of the next fella. And still—that's how you build a future.

Happy: Well, you really enjoy it on a farm? Are you content out there?

Biff (*with rising agitation*): Hap, I've had twenty or thirty different kinds of jobs since I left home before the war, and it always turns out the same. I just realized it lately. In Nebraska when I herded cattle, and the Dakotas, and Arizona, and now in Texas. It's why I came home now, I guess, because I realized it. This farm I work on, it's spring there now, see? And they've got about fifteen new colts. There's nothing more inspiring or—beautiful than the sight of a mare and a new colt. And it's cool there now, see? Texas is cool now, and it's spring. And whenever spring comes to where I am, I suddenly get the feeling, my God, I'm not gettin' anywhere! What the hell am I doing, playing around with horses, twenty-eight dollars a week! I'm thirty-four years old, I oughta be makin' my future. That's when I come running home. And now, I get here, and I don't know what to do with myself. (*After a pause.*) I've always made a point of not wasting my life, and everytime I come back here I know that all I've done is to waste my life.

Happy: You're a poet, you know that, Biff? You're a—you're an idealist!

Biff: No, I'm mixed up very bad. Maybe I oughta get married. Maybe I oughta get stuck into something. Maybe that's my trouble. I'm like a boy. I'm not married, I'm not in business, I just—I'm like a boy. Are you content, Hap? You're a success, aren't you? Are you content?

Happy: Hell, no!

Biff: Why? You're making money, aren't you?

Happy (*moving about with energy, expressiveness*): All I can do now is wait for the merchandise manager to die. And suppose I get to be merchandise manager? He's a good friend of mine, and he just built a terrific estate on Long Island. And he lived there about two months and sold it, and now he's building another one. He can't enjoy it once it's finished. And I know that's just what I would do. I don't know what the hell I'm workin' for. Sometimes I sit in my apartment—all alone. And I think of the rent I'm paying. And it's crazy. But then, it's what I always wanted. My own apartment, a car, and plenty of women. And still, goddammit, I'm lonely.

Biff (*with enthusiasm*): Listen, why don't you come out West with me?

Happy: You and I, heh?

Biff: Sure, maybe we could buy a ranch. Raise cattle, use our muscles. Men built like we are should be working out in the open.

Happy (avidly): The Loman Brothers, heh?

Biff (with vast affection): Sure, we'd be known all over the counties!

Happy (enthralled): That's what I dream about, Biff. Sometimes I want to just rip my clothes off in the middle of the store and outbox that goddam merchandise manager. I mean I can outbox, outrun, and outlift anybody in that store, and I have to take orders from those common, petty sons-of-bitches till I can't stand it any more.

Biff: I'm tellin' you, kid, if you were with me I'd be happy out there.

Happy (enthused): See, Biff, everybody around me is so false that I'm constantly lowering my ideals . . .

Biff: Baby, together we'd stand up for one another, we'd have someone to trust.

Happy: If I were around you—

Biff: Hap, the trouble is we weren't brought up to grub for money. I don't know how to do it.

Happy: Neither can I!

Biff: Then let's go!

Happy: The only thing is—what can you make out there?

Biff: But look at your friend. Builds an estate and then hasn't the peace of mind to live in it.

Happy: Yeah, but when he walks into the store the waves part in front of him. That's fifty-two thousand dollars a year coming through the revolving door, and I got more in my pinky finger than he's got in his head.

Biff: Yeah, but you just said—

Happy: I gotta show some of those pompous, self-important executives over there that Hap Loman can make the grade. I want to walk into the store the way he walks in. Then I'll go with you, Biff. We'll be together yet, I swear. But take those two we had tonight. Now weren't they gorgeous creatures?

Biff: Yeah, yeah, most gorgeous I've had in years.

Happy: I get that any time I want, Biff. Whenever I feel disgusted. The only trouble is, it gets like bowling or something. I just keep knockin' them over and it doesn't mean anything. You still run around a lot?

Biff: Naa. I'd like to find a girl—steady, somebody with substance.

Happy: That's what I long for.

Biff: Go on! You'd never come home.

Happy: I would! Somebody with character, with resistance! Like Mom, y'know? You're gonna call me a bastard when I tell you this. That girl Charlotte I was with tonight is engaged to be married in five weeks. (*He tries on his new hat.*)

Biff: No kiddin'!

Happy: Sure, the guy's in line for the vice-presidency of the store. I don't know what gets into me, maybe I just have an overdeveloped sense of competition or something, but I went and ruined her, and furthermore I can't get rid of her. And he's the third executive I've done that to. Isn't that a crummy characteristic? And to top it all, I go to their weddings! (*Indignantly, but laughing.*) Like I'm not supposed to take bribes. Manufacturers offer me a hundred-dollar bill now and then to throw an order their way. You know how honest I am, but it's like this girl, see. I hate myself for it. Because I don't want the girl, and, still, I take it and—I love it!

Biff: Let's go to sleep.

Happy: I guess we didn't settle anything, heh?

Biff: I just got one idea that I think I'm going to try.

Happy: What's that?

Biff: Remember Bill Oliver?

Happy: Sure, Oliver is very big now. You want to work for him again?

Biff: No, but when I quit he said something to me. He put his arm on my shoulder, and he said, "Biff, if you ever need anything, come to me."

Happy: I remember that. That sounds good.

Biff: I think I'll go to see him. If I could get ten thousand or even seven or eight thousand dollars I could buy a beautiful ranch.

Happy: I bet he'd back you. 'Cause he thought highly of you, Biff. I mean, they all do. You're well liked, Biff. That's why I say to come back here, and we both have the apartment. And I'm tellin' you, Biff, any babe you want . . .

Biff: No, with a ranch I could do the work I like and still be something. I just wonder though. I wonder if Oliver still thinks I stole that carton of basketballs.

Happy: Oh, he probably forgot that long ago. It's almost ten years. You're too sensitive. Anyway, he didn't really fire you.

Biff: Well, I think he was going to. I think that's why I quit. I was never sure whether he knew or not. I know he thought the world of me, though. I was the only one he'd let lock up the place.

Willy (below): You gonna wash the engine, Biff?

Happy: Shh!

Biff looks at Happy, who is gazing down, listening. Willy is mumbling in the parlor.

Happy: You hear that?

They listen. Willy laughs warmly.

Biff (growing angry): Doesn't he know Mom can hear that?

Willy: Don't get your sweater dirty, Biff!

A look of pain crosses Biff's face.

Happy: Isn't that terrible? Don't leave again, will you? You'll find a job here. You gotta stick around. I don't know what to do about him, it's getting embarrassing.

Willy: What a simonizing job!

Biff: Mom's hearing that!

Willy: No kiddin', Biff, you got a date? Wonderful!

Happy: Go on to sleep. But talk to him in the morning, will you?

Biff (*reluctantly getting into bed*): With her in the house. Brother!

Happy (*getting into bed*): I wish you'd have a good talk with him.

> *The light on their room begins to fade.*

Biff (*to himself in bed*): That selfish, stupid . . .

Happy: Sh . . . Sleep, Biff.

> *Their light is out. Well before they have finished speaking, Willy's form is dimly seen below in the darkened kitchen. He opens the refrigerator, searches in there, and takes out a bottle of milk. The apartment houses are fading out, and the entire house and surroundings become covered with leaves. Music insinuates itself as the leaves appear.*

Willy: Just wanna be careful with those girls, Biff, that's all. Don't make any promises. No promises of any kind. Because a girl, y'know, they always believe what you tell 'em, and you're very young, Biff, you're too young to be talking seriously to girls.

> *Light rises on the kitchen. Willy, talking, shuts the refrigerator door and comes downstage to the kitchen table. He pours milk into a glass. He is totally immersed in himself, smiling faintly.*

Willy: Too young entirely, Biff. You want to watch your schooling first. Then when you're all set, there'll be plenty of girls for a boy like you. (*He smiles broadly at a kitchen chair.*) That so? The girls pay for you? (*He laughs.*) Boy, you must really be makin' a hit.

> *Willy is gradually addressing—physically—a point offstage, speaking through the wall of the kitchen, and his voice has been rising in volume to that of a normal conversation.*

Willy: I been wondering why you polish the car so careful. Ha! Don't leave the hubcaps, boys. Get the chamois to the hubcaps. Happy, use newspaper on the windows, it's the easiest thing. Show him how to do it, Biff! You see, Happy? Pad it up, use it like a pad. That's it, that's it, good work. You're doin' all right, Hap. (*He pauses, then nods in approbation for a few seconds, then looks upward.*) Biff, first thing we gotta do when we get time is clip that big branch over the house. Afraid it's gonna fall in a storm and hit the roof. Tell you what. We get a rope and sling her around, and then we climb up there with a couple of saws and take her down. Soon as you finish the car, boys, I wanna see ya. I got a surprise for you, boys.

Biff (*offstage*): Whatta ya got, Dad?

Willy: No, you finish first. Never leave a job till you're finished—remember that. (*Looking toward the "big trees."*) Biff, up in Albany I saw a beautiful hammock. I think I'll buy it next trip, and we'll hang it right between those two elms. Wouldn't that be something? Just swingin' there under those branches. Boy, that would be . . .

Young Biff and Young Happy appear from the direction Willy was addressing. Happy carries rags and a pail of water. Biff, wearing a sweater with a block "S," carries a football.

Biff (*pointing in the direction of the car offstage*): How's that, Pop, professional?
Willy: Terrific. Terrific job, boys. Good work, Biff.
Happy: Where's the surprise, Pop?
Willy: In the back seat of the car.
Happy: Boy! (*He runs off.*)
Biff: What is it, Dad? Tell me, what'd you buy?
Willy (*laughing, cuffs him*): Never mind, something I want you to have.
Biff (*turns and starts off*): What is it, Hap?
Happy (*offstage*): It's a punching bag!
Biff: Oh, Pop!
Willy: It's got Gene Tunney's signature on it.

Happy runs onstage with a punching bag.

Biff: Gee, how'd you know we wanted a punching bag?
Willy: Well, it's the finest thing for the timing.
Happy (*lies down on his back and pedals with his feet*): I'm losing weight, you notice, Pop?
Willy (*to Happy*): Jumping rope is good too.
Biff: Did you see the new football I got?
Willy (*examining the ball*): Where'd you get a new ball?
Biff: The coach told me to practice my passing.
Willy: That so? And he gave you the ball, heh?
Biff: Well, I borrowed it from the locker room. (*He laughs confidentially.*)
Willy (*laughing with him at the theft*): I want you to return that.
Happy: I told you he wouldn't like it!
Biff (*angrily*): Well, I'm bringing it back!
Willy (*stopping the incipient argument, to Happy*): Sure, he's gotta practice with a regulation ball, doesn't he? (*To Biff.*) Coach'll probably congratulate you on your initiative.
Biff: Oh, he keeps congratulating my initiative all the time, Pop.
Willy: That's because he likes you. If somebody else took that ball there'd be an uproar. So what's the report, boys, what's the report?
Biff: Where'd you go this time, Dad? Gee we were lonesome for you.
Willy (*pleased, puts an arm around each boy and they come down to the apron*): Lonesome, heh?
Biff: Missed you every minute.
Willy: Don't say? Tell you a secret, boys. Don't breathe it to a soul. Someday I'll have my own business, and I'll never have to leave home any more.
Happy: Like Uncle Charley, heh?

Willy: Bigger than Uncle Charley! Because Charley is not—liked. He's liked, but he's not—well liked.

Biff: Where'd you go this time, Dad?

Willy: Well, I got on the road, and I went north to Providence. Met the Mayor.

Biff: The Mayor of Providence!

Willy: He was sitting in the hotel lobby.

Biff: What'd he say?

Willy: He said, "Morning!" And I said, "You've got a fine city here, Mayor." And then he had coffee with me. And then I went to Waterbury. Waterbury is a fine city. Big clock city, the famous Waterbury clock. Sold a nice bill there. And then Boston—Boston is the cradle of the Revolution. A fine city. And a couple of other towns in Mass., and on to Portland and Bangor and straight home!

Biff: Gee, I'd love to go with you sometime, Dad.

Willy: Soon as summer comes.

Happy: Promise?

Willy: You and Hap and I, and I'll show you all the towns. America is full of beautiful towns and fine, upstanding people. And they know me, boys, they know me up and down New England. The finest people. And when I bring you fellas up, there'll be open sesame for all of us, 'cause one thing, boys: I have friends. I can park my car in any street in New England, and the cops protect it like their own. This summer, heh?

Biff and Happy(together): Yeah! You bet!

Willy: We'll take our bathing suits.

Happy: We'll carry your bags, Pop!

Willy: Oh, won't that be something! Me comin' into the Boston stores with you boys carryin' my bags. What a sensation!

> *Biff is prancing around, practicing passing the ball.*

Willy: You nervous, Biff, about the game?

Biff: Not if you're gonna be there.

Willy: What do they say about you in school, now that they made you captain?

Happy: There's a crowd of girls behind him everytime the classes change.

Biff (taking Willy's hand): This Saturday, Pop, this Saturday—just for you, I'm going to break through for a touchdown.

Happy: You're supposed to pass.

Biff: I'm takin' one play for Pop. You watch me, Pop, and when I take off my helmet, that means I'm breakin' out. Then you watch me crash through that line!

Willy (kisses Biff): Oh, wait'll I tell this in Boston!

> *Bernard enters in knickers. He is younger than Biff, earnest and loyal, a worried boy.*

Bernard: Biff, where are you? You're supposed to study with me today.

Willy: Hey, looka Bernard. What're you lookin' so anemic about, Bernard?

Bernard: He's gotta study, Uncle Willy. He's got Regents next week.

Happy (tauntingly, spinning Bernard around): Let's box, Bernard!

Bernard: Biff! (*He gets away from Happy.*) Listen, Biff, I heard Mr. Birnbaum say that if you don't start studyin' math he's gonna flunk you, and you won't graduate. I heard him!

Willy: You better study with him, Biff. Go ahead now.

Bernard: I heard him!

Biff: Oh, Pop, you didn't see my sneakers! (*He holds up a foot for Willy to look at.*)

Willy: Hey, that's a beautiful job of printing!

Bernard (wiping his glasses): Just because he printed University of Virginia on his sneakers doesn't mean they've got to graduate him, Uncle Willy!

Willy (angrily): What're you talking about? With scholarships to three universities they're gonna flunk him?

Bernard: But I heard Mr. Birnbaum say—

Willy: Don't be a pest, Bernard! (*To his boys.*) What an anemic!

Bernard: Okay, I'm waiting for you in my house, Biff.

    Bernard goes off. The Lomans laugh.

Willy: Bernard is not well liked, is he?

Biff: He's liked, but he's not well liked.

Happy: That's right, Pop.

Willy: That's just what I mean. Bernard can get the best marks in school, y'understand, but when he gets out in the business world, y'understand, you are going to be five times ahead of him. That's why I thank Almighty God you're both built like Adonises. Because the man who makes an appearance in the business world, the man who creates personal interest, is the man who gets ahead. Be liked and you will never want. You take me, for instance. I never have to wait in line to see a buyer. "Willy Loman is here!" That's all they have to know, and I go right through.

Biff: Did you knock them dead, Pop?

Willy: Knocked 'em cold in Providence, slaughtered 'em in Boston.

Happy (on his back, pedaling again): I'm losing weight, you notice, Pop?

    Linda enters, as of old, a ribbon in her hair, carrying a basket of washing.

Linda (with youthful energy): Hello, dear!

Willy: Sweetheart!

Linda: How'd the Chevvy run?

Willy: Chevrolet, Linda, is the greatest car every built. (*To the boys.*) Since when do you let your mother carry wash up the stairs?

Biff: Grab hold there, boy!

Happy: Where to, Mom?

Linda: Hang them up on the line. And you better go down to your friends, Biff. The cellar is full of boys. They don't know what to do with themselves.

Biff: Ah, when Pop comes home they can wait!

Willy (laughs appreciatively): You better go down and tell them what to do, Biff.

Biff: I think I'll have them sweep out the furnace room.

Willy: Good work, Biff.

Biff (goes through wall-line of kitchen to doorway at back and calls down): Fellas! Everybody sweep out the furnace room! I'll be right down!

Voices: All right! Okay, Biff.

Biff: George and Sam and Frank, come out back! We're hangin' up the wash! Come on, Hap, on the double! (*He and Happy carry out the basket.*)

Linda: The way they obey him!

Willy: Well, that's training, the training. I'm tellin' you, I was sellin' thousands and thousands, but I had to come home.

Linda: Oh, the whole block'll be at that game. Did you sell anything?

Willy: I did five hundred gross in Providence and seven hundred gross in Boston.

Linda: No! Wait a minute, I've got a pencil. (*She pulls pencil and paper out of her apron pocket.*) That makes your commission . . . Two hundred—my God! Two hundred and twelve dollars!

Willy: Well, I didn't figure it yet, but . . .

Linda: How much did you do?

Willy: Well, I—I did—about a hundred and eighty gross in Providence. Well, no—it came to—roughly two hundred gross on the whole trip.

Linda (without hesitation): Two hundred gross. That's . . . (*She figures.*)

Willy: The trouble was that three of the stores were half closed for inventory in Boston. Otherwise I woulda broke records.

Linda: Well, it makes seventy dollars and some pennies. That's very good.

Willy: What do we owe?

Linda: Well, on the first there's sixteen dollars on the refrigerator—

Willy: Why sixteen?

Linda: Well, the fan belt broke, so it was a dollar eighty.

Willy: But it's brand new.

Linda: Well, the man said that's the way it is. Till they work themselves in, y'know.

They move through the wall-line into the kitchen.

Willy: I hope we didn't get stuck on that machine.

Linda: They got the biggest ads of any of them.

Willy: I know, it's a fine machine. What else?

Linda: Well, there's nine-sixty for the washing machine. And for the vacuum cleaner there's three and a half due on the fifteenth. Then the roof, you got twenty-one dollars remaining.

Willy: It don't leak, does it?

Linda: No, they did a wonderful job. Then you owe Frank for the carburetor.

Willy: I'm not going to pay that man! That goddam Chevrolet, they ought to prohibit the manufacture of that car!

Linda: Well, you owe him three and a half. And odds and ends, comes to around a hundred and twenty dollars by the fifteenth.

Willy: A hundred and twenty dollars! My God, if business don't pick up I don't know what I'm gonna do!

Linda: Well, next week you'll do better.

Willy: Oh, I'll knock 'em dead next week. I'll go to Hartford. I'm very well liked in Hartford. You know, the trouble is, Linda, people don't seem to take to me.

They move on the forestage.

Linda: Oh, don't be foolish.

Willy: I know it when I walk in. They seem to laugh at me.

Linda: Why? Why would they laugh at you? Don't talk that way, Willy.

Willy moves to the edge of the stage. Linda goes into the kitchen and starts to darn stockings.

Willy: I don't know the reason for it, but they just pass me by. I'm not noticed.

Linda: But you're doing wonderful, dear. You're making seventy to a hundred dollars a week.

Willy: But I gotta be at it ten, twelve hours a day. Other men—I don't know— they do it easier. I don't know why—I can't stop myself—I talk too much. A man oughta come in with a few words. One thing about Charley. He's a man of few words, and they respect him.

Linda: You don't talk too much, you're just lively.

Willy (smiling): Well, I figure, what the hell, life is short, a couple of jokes. (*To himself.*) I joke too much! (*The smile goes.*)

Linda: Why? You're—

Willy: I'm fat. I'm very—foolish to look at, Linda. I didn't tell you, but Christmas time I happened to be calling on F. H. Stewarts, and a salesman I know, as I was going in to see the buyer I heard him say something about walrus. And I—I cracked him right across the face. I won't take that. I simply will not take that. But they do laugh at me. I know that.

Linda: Darling . . .

Willy: I gotta overcome it. I know I gotta overcome it. I'm not dressing to advantage, maybe.

Linda: Willy, darling, you're the handsomest man in the world—

Willy: Oh, no, Linda.

Linda: To me you are. (*Slight pause.*) The handsomest.

From the darkness is heard the laughter of a woman. Willy doesn't turn to it, but it continues through Linda's lines.

Linda: And the boys, Willy. Few men are idolized by their children the way you are.

Music is heard as behind a scrim, to the left of the house, The Woman, dimly seen, is dressing.

Willy (with great feeling): You're the best there is, Linda, you're a pal, you know that? On the road—on the road I want to grab you sometimes and just kiss the life outa you.

The laughter is loud now, and he moves into a brightening area at the left, where The Woman has come from behind the scrim and is standing, putting on her hat, looking into a "mirror" and laughing.

Willy: 'Cause I get so lonely—especially when business is bad and there's no-body to talk to. I get the feeling that I'll never sell anything again, that I won't make a living for you, or a business, a business for the boys. (*He talks through The Woman's subsiding laughter; The Woman primps at the "mirror."*) There's so much I want to make for—

The Woman: Me? You didn't make me, Willy. I picked you.

Willy (*pleased*): You picked me?

The Woman (*who is quite proper-looking, Willy's age*): I did. I've been sitting at that desk watching all the salesmen go by, day in, day out. But you've got such a sense of humor, and we do have such a good time together, don't we?

Willy: Sure, sure. (*He takes her in his arms.*) Why do you have to go now?

The Woman: It's two o'clock . . .

Willy: No, come on in! (*He pulls her.*)

The Woman: . . . my sisters'll be scandalized. When'll you be back?

Willy: Oh, two weeks about. Will you come up again?

The Woman: Sure thing. You do make me laugh. It's good for me. (*She squeezes his arm, kisses him.*) And I think you're a wonderful man.

Willy: You picked me, heh?

The Woman: Sure. Because you're so sweet. And such a kidder.

Willy: Well, I'll see you next time I'm in Boston.

The Woman: I'll put you right through to the buyers.

Willy (*slapping her bottom*): Right. Well, bottoms up!

The Woman (*slaps him gently and laughs*): You just kill me, Willy. (*He suddenly grabs her and kisses her roughly.*) You kill me. And thanks for the stockings. I love a lot of stockings. Well, good night.

Willy: Good night. And keep your pores open!

The Woman: Oh, Willy!

The Woman bursts out laughing, and Linda's laughter blends in. The Woman dis-appears into the dark. Now the area at the kitchen table brightens. Linda is sitting where she was at the kitchen table, but now is mending a pair of silk stockings.

Linda: You are, Willy. The handsomest man. You've got no reason to feel that—

Willy (*coming out of The Woman's dimming area and going over to Linda*): I'll make it all up to you, Linda, I'll—

Linda: There's nothing to make up, dear. You're doing fine, better than—

Willy (*noticing her mending*): What's that?

Linda: Just mending my stockings. They're so expensive—

Willy (*angrily, taking them from her*): I won't have you mending stockings in this house! Now throw them out!

Linda puts the stockings in her pocket.

Bernard (*entering on the run*): Where is he? If he doesn't study!

Willy (*moving to the forestage, with great agitation*): You'll give him the answers!

Bernard: I do, but I can't on a Regents! That's a state exam! They're liable to arrest me!

Willy: Where is he? I'll whip him, I'll whip him!

Linda: And he'd better give back that football, Willy, it's not nice.

Willy: Biff! Where is he? Why is he taking everything?

Linda: He's too rough with the girls, Willy. All the mothers are afraid of him!

Willy: I'll whip him!

Bernard: He's driving the car without a license!

> *The Woman's laugh is heard.*

Willy: Shut up!

Linda: All the mothers—

Willy: Shut up!

Bernard (*backing quietly away and out*): Mr. Birnbaum says he's stuck up.

Willy: Get outa here!

Bernard: If he doesn't buckle down he'll flunk math! (*He goes off.*)

Linda: He's right, Willy, you've gotta—

Willy (*exploding at her*): There's nothing the matter with him! You want him to be a worm like Bernard? He's got spirit, personality . . .

> *As he speaks, Linda, almost in tears, exits into the living room. Willy is alone in the kitchen, wilting and staring. The leaves are gone. It is night again, and the apartment houses look down from behind.*

Willy: Loaded with it. Loaded! What is he stealing? He's giving it back, isn't he? Why is he stealing? What did I tell him? I never in my life told him anything but decent things.

> *Happy in pajamas has come down the stairs; Willy suddenly becomes aware of Happy's presence.*

Happy: Let's go now, come on.

Willy (*sitting down at the kitchen table*): Huh! Why did she have to wax the floors herself? Everytime she waxes the floors she keels over. She knows that!

Happy: Shh! Take it easy. What brought you back tonight?

Willy: I got an awful scare. Nearly hit a kid in Yonkers. God! Why didn't I go to Alaska with my brother Ben that time! Ben! That man was a genius, that man was success incarnate! What a mistake! He begged me to go.

Happy: Well, there's no use in—

Willy: You guys! There was a man started with the clothes on his back and ended up with diamond mines!

Happy: Boy, someday I'd like to know how he did it.

Willy: What's the mystery? The man knew what he wanted and went out and got it! Walked into a jungle, and comes out, the age of twenty-one, and he's rich! The world is an oyster, but you don't crack it open on a mattress!

Happy: Pop, I told you I'm gonna retire you for life.

Willy: You'll retire me for life on seventy goddam dollars a week? And your women and your car and your apartment, and you'll retire me for life! Christ's sake, I couldn't get past Yonkers today! Where are you guys, where are you? The woods are burning! I can't drive a car!

Charley has appeared in the doorway. He is a large man, slow of speech, laconic, immovable. In all he says, despite what he says, there is pity, and, now, trepidation. He has a robe over his pajamas, slippers on his feet. He enters the kitchen.

Charley: Everything all right?

Happy: Yeah, Charley, everything's . . .

Willy: What's the matter?

Charley: I heard some noise. I thought something happened. Can't we do something about the walls? You sneeze in here, and in my house hats blow off.

Happy: Let's go to bed, Dad. Come on.

Charley signals to Happy to go.

Willy: You go ahead, I'm not tired at the moment.

Happy (to Willy): Take it easy, huh? (*He exits.*)

Willy: What're you doin' up?

Charley (sitting down at the kitchen table opposite Willy): Couldn't sleep good. I had a heartburn.

Willy: Well, you don't know how to eat.

Charley: I eat with my mouth.

Willy: No, you're ignorant. You gotta know about vitamins and things like that.

Charley: Come on, let's shoot. Tire you out a little.

Willy (hesitantly): All right. You got cards?

Charley (taking a deck from his pocket): Yeah, I got them. Someplace. What is it with those vitamins?

Willy (dealing): They build up your bones. Chemistry.

Charley: Yeah, but there's no bones in a heartburn.

Willy: What are you talkin' about? Do you know the first thing about it?

Charley: Don't get insulted.

Willy: Don't talk about something you don't know anything about.

They are playing. Pause.

Charley: What're you doin' home?

Willy: A little trouble with the car.

Charley: Oh. (*Pause.*) I'd like to take a trip to California.

Willy: Don't say.

Charley: You want a job?

Willy: I got a job, I told you that. (*After a slight pause.*) What the hell are you offering me a job for?

Charley: Don't get insulted.

Willy: Don't insult me.

Charley: I don't see no sense in it. You don't have to go on this way.

Willy: I got a good job. (*Slight pause.*) What do you keep comin' in here for?

Charley: You want me to go?

Willy (*after a pause, withering*): I can't understand it. He's going back to Texas again. What the hell is that?

Charley: Let him go.

Willy: I got nothin' to give him, Charley, I'm clean, I'm clean.

Charley: He won't starve. None a them starve. Forget about him.

Willy: Then what have I got to remember?

Charley: You take it too hard. To hell with it. When a deposit bottle is broken you don't get your nickel back.

Willy: That's easy enough for you to say.

Charley: That ain't easy for me to say.

Willy: Did you see the ceiling I put up in the living room?

Charley: Yeah, that's a piece of work. To put up a ceiling is a mystery to me. How do you do it?

Willy: What's the difference?

Charley: Well, talk about it.

Willy: You gonna put up a ceiling?

Charley: How could I put up a ceiling?

Willy: Then what the hell are you bothering me for?

Charley: You're insulted again.

Willy: A man who can't handle tools is not a man. You're disgusting.

Charley: Don't call me disgusting, Willy.

> *Uncle Ben, carrying a valise and an umbrella, enters the forestage from around the right corner of the house. He is a stolid man, in his sixties, with a mustache and an authoritative air. He is utterly certain of his destiny, and there is an aura of far places about him. He enters exactly as Willy speaks.*

Willy: I'm getting awfully tired, Ben.

> *Ben's music is heard. Ben looks around at everything.*

Charley: Good, keep playing; you'll sleep better. Did you call me Ben?

> *Ben looks at his watch.*

Willy: That's funny. For a second there you reminded me of my brother Ben.

Ben: I have only a few minutes. (*He strolls, inspecting the place. Willy and Charley continue playing.*)

Charley: You never heard from him again, heh? Since that time?

Willy: Didn't Linda tell you? Couple of weeks ago we got a letter from his wife in Africa. He died.

Charley: That so.

Ben (*chuckling*): So this is Brooklyn, eh?

Charley: Maybe you're in for some of his money.

Willy: Naa, he had seven sons. There's just one opportunity I had with that man . . .

Ben: I must make a train, William. There are several properties I'm looking at in Alaska.

Willy: Sure, sure! If I'd gone with him to Alaska that time, everything would've been totally different.

Charley: Go on, you'd froze to death up there.

Willy: What're you talking about?

Ben: Opportunity is tremendous in Alaska, William. Surprised you're not up there.

Willy: Sure, tremendous.

Charley: Heh?

Willy: There was the only man I ever met who knew the answers.

Charley: Who?

Ben: How are you all?

Willy (taking a pot, smiling): Fine, fine.

Charley: Pretty sharp tonight.

Ben: Is Mother living with you?

Willy: No, she died a long time ago.

Charley: Who?

Ben: That's too bad. Fine specimen of a lady, Mother.

Willy (to Charley): Heh?

Ben: I'd hoped to see the old girl.

Charley: Who died?

Ben: Heard anything from Father, have you?

Willy (unnerved): What do you mean, who died?

Charley (taking a pot): What're you talkin' about?

Ben (looking at his watch): William, it's half-past eight!

Willy (as though to dispel his confusion he angrily stops Charley's hand): That's my build!

Charley: I put the ace—

Willy: If you don't know how to play the game I'm not gonna throw my money away on you!

Charley (rising): It was my ace, for God's sake!

Willy: I'm through, I'm through!

Ben: When did Mother die?

Willy: Long ago. Since the beginning you never knew how to play cards.

Charley (picks up the cards and goes to the door): All right! Next time I'll bring a deck with five aces.

Willy: I don't play that kind of game!

Charley (turning to him): You ought to be ashamed of yourself!

Willy: Yeah?

Charley: Yeah! (*He goes out.*)

Willy (slamming the door after him): Ignoramus!

Ben (as Willy comes toward him through the wall-line of the kitchen): So you're William.

Willy (shaking Ben's hand): Ben! I've been waiting for you so long! What's the answer? How did you do it?

Ben: Oh, there's a story in that.

Linda enters the forestage, as of old, carrying the wash basket.

Linda: Is this Ben?

Ben (gallantly): How do you do, my dear.

Linda: Where've you been all these years? Willy's always wondered why you—

Willy (pulling Ben away from her impatiently): Where is Dad? Didn't you follow him? How did you get started?

Ben: Well, I don't know how much you remember.

Willy: Well, I was just a baby, of course, only three or four years old—

Ben: Three years and eleven months.

Willy: What a memory, Ben!

Ben: I have many enterprises, William, and I have never kept books.

Willy: I remember I was sitting under the wagon in—was it Nebraska?

Ben: It was South Dakota, and I gave you a bunch of wild flowers.

Willy: I remember you walking away down some open road.

Ben (laughing): I was going to find Father in Alaska.

Willy: Where is he?

Ben: At that age I had a very faulty view of geography, William. I discovered after a few days that I was heading due south, so instead of Alaska, I ended up in Africa.

Linda: Africa!

Willy: The Gold Coast!

Ben: Principally, diamond mines.

Linda: Diamond mines!

Ben: Yes, my dear. But I've only a few minutes—

Willy: No! Boys! Boys! (Young Biff and Happy appear.) Listen to this. This is your Uncle Ben, a great man! Tell my boys, Ben!

Ben: Why, boys, when I was seventeen I walked into the jungle, and when I was twenty-one I walked out. (He laughs.) And by God I was rich.

Willy (to the boys): You see what I been talking about? The greatest things can happen!

Ben (glancing at his watch): I have an appointment in Ketchikan Tuesday week.

Willy: No, Ben! Please tell about Dad. I want my boys to hear. I want them to know the kind of stock they sprang from. All I remember is a man with a big beard, and I was in Mamma's lap, sitting around a fire, and some kind of high music.

Ben: His flute. He played the flute.

Willy: Sure, the flute, that's right!

New music is heard, a high, rollicking tune.

Ben: Father was a very great and a very wild-hearted man. We would start in Boston, and he'd toss the whole family into the wagon, and then he'd drive the team right across the country; through Ohio, and Indiana, Michigan, Illinois, and all the Western states. And we'd stop in the towns and sell the flutes that he'd made on the way. Great inventor, Father. With one gadget he made more in a week than a man like you could make in a lifetime.

Willy: That's just the way I'm bringing them up, Ben—rugged, well-liked, all-around.

Ben: Yeah? (*To Biff.*) Hit that, boy—hard as you can. (*He pounds his stomach.*)

Biff: Oh, no, sir!

Ben (*taking boxing stance*): Come on, get to me! (*He laughs.*)

Willy: Go to it, Biff! Go ahead, show him!

Biff: Okay! (*He cocks his fist and starts in.*)

Linda (*to Willy*): Why must he fight, dear?

Ben (*sparring with Biff*): Good boy! Good boy!

Willy: How's that, Ben, heh?

Happy: Give him the left, Biff!

Linda: Why are you fighting?

Ben: Good boy! (*Suddenly comes in, trips Biff, and stands over him, the point of his umbrella poised over Biff's eye.*)

Linda: Look out, Biff!

Biff: Gee!

Ben (*patting Biff's knee*): Never fight fair with a stranger, boy. You'll never get out of the jungle that way. (*Taking Linda's hand and bowing.*) It was an honor and a pleasure to meet you, Linda.

Linda (*withdrawing her hand coldly, frightened*): Have a nice—trip.

Ben (*to Willy*): And good luck with your—what do you do?

Willy: Selling.

Ben: Yes. Well . . . (*He raises his hand in farewell to all.*)

Willy: No, Ben, I don't want you to think . . . (*He takes Ben's arm to show him.*) It's Brooklyn, I know, but we hunt too.

Ben: Really, now.

Willy: Oh, sure, there's snakes and rabbits and—that's why I moved out here. Why, Biff can fell any one of these trees in no time! Boys! Go right over to where they're building the apartment house and get some sand. We're gonna rebuild the entire front stoop right now! Watch this, Ben!

Biff: Yes, sir! On the double, Hap!

Happy (*as he and Biff run off*): I lost weight, Pop, you notice?

   Charley enters in knickers, even before the boys are gone.

Charley: Listen, if they steal any more from that building the watchman'll put the cops on them!

Linda (*to Willy*): Don't let Biff . . .

   Ben laughs lustily.

Willy: You shoulda seen the lumber they brought home last week. At least a dozen six-by-tens worth all kinds of money.

Charley: Listen, if that watchman—

Willy: I gave them hell, understand. But I got a couple of fearless characters there.

Charley: Willy, the jails are full of fearless characters.

Ben (clapping Willy on the back, with a laugh at Charley): And the stock exchange, friend!

Willy (joining in Ben's laughter): Where are the rest of your pants?

Charley: My wife bought them.

Willy: Now all you need is a golf club and you can go upstairs and go to sleep. (*To Ben.*) Great athlete! Between him and his son Bernard they can't hammer a nail!

Bernard (rushing in): The watchman's chasing Biff!

Willy (angrily): Shut up! He's not stealing anything!

Linda (alarmed, hurrying off left): Where is he? Biff, dear! (*She exits.*)

Willy (moving toward the left, away from Ben): There's nothing wrong. What's the matter with you?

Ben: Nervy boy. Good!

Willy (laughing): Oh, nerves of iron, that Biff!

Charley: Don't know what it is. My New England man comes back and he's bleedin', they murdered him up there.

Willy: It's contacts, Charley, I got important contacts!

Charley (sarcastically): Glad to hear it, Willy. Come in later, we'll shoot a little casino. I'll take some of your Portland money. (*He laughs at Willy and exits.*)

Willy (turning to Ben): Business is bad, it's murderous. But not for me, of course.

Ben: I'll stop by on my way back to Africa.

Willy (longingly): Can't you stay a few days? You're just what I need, Ben, because I—I have a fine position, but I—well, Dad left when I was such a baby and I never had a chance to talk to him and I still feel—kind of temporary about myself.

Ben: I'll be late for my train.

They are at opposite ends of the stage.

Willy: Ben, my boys—can't we talk? They'd go into the jaws of hell for me, see, but I—

Ben: William, you're being first-rate with your boys. Outstanding, manly chaps!

Willy (hanging on to his words): Oh, Ben, that's good to hear! Because sometimes I'm afraid that I'm not teaching them the right kind of—Ben, how should I teach them?

Ben (giving great weight to each word, and with a certain vicious audacity): William, when I walked into the jungle, I was seventeen. When I walked out I was twenty-one. And, by God, I was rich! (*He goes off into darkness around the right corner of the house.*)

Willy: . . . was rich! That's just the spirit I want to imbue them with! To walk into a jungle! I was right! I was right! I was right!

Ben is gone, but Willy is still speaking to him as Linda, in nightgown and robe, enters the kitchen, glances around for Willy, then goes to the door of the house, looks out and sees him. Comes down to his left. He looks at her.

Linda: Willy, dear? Willy?

Willy: I was right!

Linda: Did you have some cheese? (*He can't answer.*) It's very late, darling. Come to bed, heh?

Willy (*looking straight up*): Gotta break your neck to see a star in this yard.

Linda: You coming in?

Willy: What ever happened to that diamond watch fob? Remember? When Ben came from Africa that time? Didn't he give me a watch fob with a diamond in it?

Linda: You pawned it, dear. Twelve, thirteen years ago. For Biff's radio correspondence course.

Willy: Gee, that was a beautiful thing. I'll take a walk.

Linda: But you're in your slippers.

Willy (*starting to go around the house at the left*): I was right! I was! (*Half to Linda, as he goes, shaking his head.*) What a man! There was a man worth talking to. I was right!

Linda (*calling after Willy*): But in your slippers, Willy!

Willy is almost gone when Biff, in his pajamas, comes down the stairs and enters the kitchen.

Biff: What is he doing out there?

Linda: Sh!

Biff: God Almighty, Mom, how long has he been doing this?

Linda: Don't, he'll hear you.

Biff: What the hell is the matter with him?

Linda: It'll pass by morning.

Biff: Shouldn't we do anything?

Linda: Oh, my dear, you should do a lot of things, but there's nothing to do, so go to sleep.

Happy comes down the stairs and sits on the steps.

Happy: I never heard him so loud, Mom.

Linda: Well, come around more often; you'll hear him. (*She sits down at the table and mends the lining of Willy's jacket.*)

Biff: Why didn't you ever write me about this, Mom?

Linda: How would I write to you? For over three months you had no address.

Biff: I was on the move. But you know I thought of you all the time. You know that, don't you, pal?

Linda: I know, dear, I know. But he likes to have a letter. Just to know that there's still a possibility for better things.

Biff: He's not like this all the time, is he?

Linda: It's when you come home he's always the worst.

Biff: When I come home?

Linda: When you write you're coming, he's all smiles, and talks about the future, and—he's just wonderful. And then the closer you seem to come, the more shaky he gets, and then, by the time you get here, he's arguing, and he seems angry at you. I think it's just that maybe he can't bring himself to—to open up to you. Why are you so hateful to each other? Why is that?

Biff (evasively): I'm not hateful, Mom.

Linda: But you no sooner come in the door than you're fighting!

Biff: I don't know why. I mean to change. I'm tryin', Mom, you understand?

Linda: Are you home to stay now?

Biff: I don't know. I want to look around, see what's doin'.

Linda: Biff, you can't look around all your life, can you?

Biff: I just can't take hold, Mom. I can't take hold of some kind of a life.

Linda: Biff, a man is not a bird, to come and go with the springtime.

Biff: Your hair . . . (*He touches her hair.*) Your hair got so gray.

Linda: Oh, it's been gray since you were in high school. I just stopped dyeing it, that's all.

Biff: Dye it again, will ya? I don't want my pal looking old. (*He smiles.*)

Linda: You're such a boy! You think you can go away for a year and . . . . You've got to get it into your head now that one day you'll knock on this door and there'll be strange people here—

Biff: What are you talking about? You're not even sixty, Mom.

Linda: But what about your father?

Biff (lamely): Well, I meant him too.

Happy: He admires Pop.

Linda: Biff dear, if you don't have any feeling for him, then you can't have any feeling for me.

Biff: Sure I can, Mom.

Linda: No. You can't just come to see me, because I love him. (*With a threat, but only a threat, of tears.*) He's the dearest man in the world to me, and I won't have anyone making him feel unwanted and low and blue. You've got to make up your mind now, darling, there's no leeway any more. Either he's your father and you pay him that respect, or else you're not to come here. I know he's not easy to get along with—nobody knows that better than me—but . . .

Willy (from the left, with a laugh): Hey, hey, Biffo!

Biff (starting to go out after Willy): What the hell is the matter with him? (*Happy stops him.*)

Linda: Don't—don't go near him!

Biff: Stop making excuses for him! He always, always wiped the floor with you. Never had an ounce of respect for you.

Happy: He's always had respect for—

Biff: What the hell do you know about it?

Happy (surlily): Just don't call him crazy!

Biff: He's got no character—Charley wouldn't do this. Not in his own house— spewing out that vomit from his mind.

Happy: Charley never had to cope with what he's got to.

Biff: People are worse off than Willy Loman. Believe me, I've seen them!

Linda: Then make Charley your father, Biff. You can't do that, can you? I don't say he's a great man. Willy Loman never made a lot of money. His name was never in the paper. He's not the finest character that ever lived. But he's a human being, and a terrible thing is happening to him. So attention must be paid. He's not to be allowed to fall into his grave like an old dog. Attention, attention must be finally paid to such a person. You called him crazy—

Biff: I didn't mean—

Linda: No, a lot of people think he's lost his—balance. But you don't have to be very smart to know what his trouble is. The man is exhausted.

Happy: Sure!

Linda: A small man can be just as exhausted as a great man. He works for a company thirty-six years this March, opens up unheard-of territories to their trademark, and now in his old age they take his salary away.

Happy (indignantly): I didn't know that, Mom!

Linda: You never asked, my dear! Now that you get your spending money someplace else you don't trouble your mind with him.

Happy: But I gave you money last—

Linda: Christmas time, fifty dollars! To fix the hot water it cost ninety-seven fifty! For five weeks he's been on straight commission, like a beginner, an unknown!

Biff: Those ungrateful bastards!

Linda: Are they any worse than his sons? When he brought them business, when he was young, they were glad to see him. But now his old friends, the old buyers that loved him so and always found some order to hand him in a pinch—they're all dead, retired. He used to be able to make six, seven calls a day in Boston. Now he takes his valises out of the car and puts them back and takes them out again and he's exhausted. Instead of walking he talks now. He drives seven hundred miles, and when he gets there no one knows him any more, no one welcomes him. And what goes through a man's mind, driving seven hundred miles home without having earned a cent? Why shouldn't he talk to himself? Why? When he has to go to Charley and borrow fifty dollars a week and pretend to me that it's his pay? How long can that go on? How long? You see what I'm sitting here and waiting for? And you tell me he has no character? The man who never worked a day but for your benefit? When does he get the medal for that? Is this his reward—to turn around at the age of sixty-three and find his sons, who he loved better than his life, one a philandering bum—

Happy: Mom!

Linda: That's all you are, my baby! (*To Biff.*) And you! What happened to the love you had for him? You were such pals! How you used to talk to him on the phone every night! How lonely he was till he could come home to you!

Biff: All right, Mom. I'll live here in my room, and I'll get a job. I'll keep away from him, that's all.

Linda: No, Biff. You can't stay here and fight all the time.

Biff: He threw me out of this house, remember that.

Linda: Why did he do that? I never knew why.

Biff: Because I know he's a fake and he doesn't like anybody around who knows!

Linda: Why a fake? In what way? What do you mean?

Biff: Just don't lay it all at my feet. It's between me and him—that's all I have to say. I'll chip in from now on. He'll settle for half my pay check. He'll be all right. I'm going to bed. (*He starts for the stairs.*)

Linda: He won't be all right.

Biff (*turning on the stairs, furiously*): I hate this city and I'll stay here. Now what do you want?

Linda: He's dying, Biff.

Happy turns quickly to her, shocked.

Biff (*after a pause*): Why is he dying?

Linda: He's been trying to kill himself.

Biff (*with great horror*): How?

Linda: I live from day to day.

Biff: What're you talking about?

Linda: Remember I wrote you that he smashed up the car again? In February?

Biff: Well?

Linda: The insurance inspector came. He said that they have evidence. That all these accidents in the last year—weren't—weren't—accidents.

Happy: How can they tell that? That's a lie.

Linda: It seems there's a woman . . . (*She takes a breath as—*)

Biff (*sharply but contained*): What woman?

Linda (*simultaneously*): . . . and this woman . . .

Linda: What?

Biff: Nothing. Go ahead.

Linda: What did you say?

Biff: Nothing. I just said what woman?

Happy: What about her?

Linda: Well, it seems she was walking down the road and saw his car. She says that he wasn't driving fast at all, and that he didn't skid. She says he came to that little bridge, and then deliberately smashed into the railing, and it was only the shallowness of the water that saved him.

Biff: Oh, no, he probably just fell asleep again.

Linda: I don't think he fell asleep.

Biff: Why not?

Linda: Last month . . . (*With great difficulty.*) Oh, boys, it's so hard to say a thing like this! He's just a big stupid man to you, but I tell you there's more good in him than in many other people. (*She chokes, wipes her eyes.*) I was looking for a fuse. The lights blew out, and I went down the cellar. And behind the fuse box—it happened to fall out—was a length of rubber pipe—just short.

Happy: No kidding?

Linda: There's a little attachment on the end of it. I knew right away. And sure enough, on the bottom of the water heater there's a new little nipple on the gas pipe.

Happy (angrily): That—jerk.

Biff: Did you have it taken off?

Linda: I'm—I'm ashamed to. How can I mention it to him? Every day I go down and take away that little rubber pipe. But, when he comes home, I put it back where it was. How can I insult him that way? I don't know what to do. I live from day to day, boys. I tell you, I know every thought in his mind. It sounds so old-fashioned and silly, but I tell you he put his whole life into you and you've turned your backs on him. (*She is bent over in the chair, weeping, her face in her hands.*) Biff, I swear to God! Biff, his life is in your hands!

Happy (to Biff): How do you like that damned fool!

Biff (kissing her): All right, pal, all right. It's all settled now. I've been remiss. I know that, Mom. But now I'll stay, and I swear to you, I'll apply myself. (*Kneeling in front of her, in a fever of self-reproach.*) It's just—you see, Mom, I don't fit in business. Not that I won't try. I'll try, and I'll make good.

Happy: Sure you will. The trouble with you in business was you never tried to please people.

Biff: I know, I—

Happy: Like when you worked for Harrison's. Bob Harrison said you were tops, and then you go and do some damn fool thing like whistling whole songs in the elevator like a comedian.

Biff (against Happy): So what? I like to whistle sometimes.

Happy: You don't raise a guy to a responsible job who whistles in the elevator!

Linda: Well, don't argue about it now.

Happy: Like when you'd go off and swim in the middle of the day instead of taking the line around.

Biff (his resentment rising): Well, don't you run off? You take off sometimes, don't you? On a nice summer day?

Happy: Yeah, but I cover myself!

Linda: Boys!

Happy: If I'm going to take a fade the boss can call any number where I'm sup- posed to be and they'll swear to him that I just left. I'll tell you something that I hate to say, Biff, but in the business world some of them think you're crazy.

Biff (Angered): Screw the business world!

Happy: All right, screw it! Great, but cover yourself!

Linda: Hap! Hap!

Biff: I don't care what they think! They've laughed at Dad for years, and you know why? Because we don't belong in this nut-house of a city! We should be mixing cement on some open plain, or—or carpenters. A carpenter is allowed to whistle!

Willy walks in from the entrance of the house, at left.

Willy: Even your grandfather was better than a carpenter. (*Pause. They watch him.*) You never grew up. Bernard does not whistle in the elevator, I assure you.

Biff (as though to laugh Willy out of it): Yeah, but you do, Pop.

Willy: I never in my life whistled in an elevator! And who in the business world thinks I'm crazy?

Biff: I didn't mean it like that, Pop. Now don't make a whole thing out of it, will ya?

Willy: Go back to the West! Be a carpenter, a cowboy, enjoy yourself!

Linda: Willy, he was just saying—

Willy: I heard what he said!

Happy (trying to quiet Willy): Hey, Pop, come on now . . .

Willy (continuing over Happy's line): They laugh at me, heh? Go to Filene's, go to the Hub, go to Slattery's, Boston. Call out the name Willy Loman and see what happens! Big shot!

Biff: All right, Pop.

Willy: Big!

Biff: All right!

Willy: Why do you always insult me?

Biff: I didn't say a word. (*To Linda.*) Did I say a word?

Linda: He didn't say anything, Willy.

Willy (going to the doorway of the living room): All right, good night, good night.

Linda: Willy, dear, he just decided . . .

Willy (to Biff): If you get tired hanging around tomorrow, paint the ceiling I put up in the living room.

Biff: I'm leaving early tomorrow.

Happy: He's going to see Bill Oliver, Pop.

Willy (interestedly): Oliver? For what?

Biff (with reserve, but trying, trying): He always said he'd stake me. I'd like to go into business, so maybe I can take him up on it.

Linda: Isn't that wonderful?

Willy: Don't interrupt. What's wonderful about it? There's fifty men in the City of New York who'd stake him. (*To Biff.*) Sporting goods?

Biff: I guess so. I know something about it and—

Willy: He knows something about it! You know sporting goods better than Spalding, for God's sake! How much is he giving you?

Biff: I don't know, I didn't even see him yet, but—

Willy: Then what're you talkin' about?

Biff (getting angry): Well, all I said was I'm gonna see him, that's all!

Willy (*turning away*): Ah, you're counting your chickens again.

Biff (*starting left for the stairs*): Oh, Jesus, I'm going to sleep!

Willy (*calling after him*): Don't curse in this house!

Biff (*turning*): Since when did you get so clean!

Happy (*trying to stop them*): Wait a . . .

Willy: Don't use that language to me! I won't have it!

Happy (*grabbing Biff, shouts*): Wait a minute! I got an idea. I got a feasible idea. Come here, Biff, let's talk this over now, let's talk some sense here. When I was down in Florida last time, I thought of a great idea to sell sporting goods. It just came back to me. You and I, Biff—we have a line, the Loman Line. We train a couple of weeks, and put on a couple of exhibitions, see?

Willy: That's an idea!

Happy: Wait! We form two basketball teams, see? Two water-polo teams. We play each other. It's a million dollars' worth of publicity. Two brothers, see? The Loman Brothers. Displays in the Royal Palms—all the hotels. And banners over the ring and the basketball court: "Loman Brothers." Baby, we could sell sporting goods!

Willy: That is a one-million-dollar idea.

Linda: Marvelous!

Biff: I'm in great shape as far as that's concerned.

Happy: And the beauty of it is, Biff, it wouldn't be like a business. We'd be out playin' ball again . . .

Biff (*enthused*): Yeah, that's . . .

Willy: Million-dollar . . .

Happy: And you wouldn't get fed up with it, Biff. It'd be the family again. There'd be the old honor, and comradeship, and if you wanted to go off for a swim or somethin'—well, you'd do it! Without some smart cooky gettin' up ahead of you!

Willy: Lick the world! You guys together could absolutely lick the civilized world.

Biff: I'll see Oliver tomorrow. Hap, if we could work that out . . .

Linda: Maybe things are beginning to—

Willy (*wildly enthused, to Linda*): Stop interrupting! (*To Biff.*) But don't wear sport jacket and slacks when you see Oliver.

Biff: No, I'll—

Willy: A business suit, and talk as little as possible, and don't crack any jokes.

Biff: He did like me. Always liked me.

Linda: He loved you!

Willy (*to Linda*): Will you stop! (*To Biff.*) Walk in very serious. You are not applying for a boy's job. Money is to pass. Be quiet, fine, and serious. Everybody likes a kidder, but nobody lends him money.

Happy: I'll try to get some myself, Biff. I'm sure I can.

Willy: I can see great things for you, kids, I think your troubles are over. But remember, start big and you'll end big. Ask for fifteen. How much you gonna ask for?

Biff: Gee, I don't know—

Willy: And don't say "Gee." "Gee" is a boy's word. A man walking in for fifteen thousand dollars does not say "Gee!"

Biff: Ten, I think, would be top though.

Willy: Don't be so modest. You always started too low. Walk in with a big laugh. Don't look worried. Start off with a couple of your good stories to lighten things up. It's not what you say, it's how you say it—because personality always wins the day.

Linda: Oliver always thought the highest of him—

Willy: Will you let me talk?

Biff: Don't yell at her, Pop, will ya?

Willy (angrily): I was talking, wasn't I?

Biff: I don't like you yelling at her all the time, and I'm tellin' you, that's all.

Willy: What're you, takin' over the house?

Linda: Willy—

Willy (turning on her): Don't take his side all the time, goddammit!

Biff (furiously): Stop yelling at her!

Willy (suddenly pulling on his cheek, beaten down, guilt ridden): Give my best to Bill Oliver—he may remember me. (*He exits through the living room doorway.*)

Linda (her voice subdued): What'd you have to start that for? (*Biff turns away.*) You see how sweet he was as soon as you talked hopefully? (*She goes over to Biff.*) Come up and say good night to him. Don't let him go to bed that way.

Happy: Come on, Biff, let's buck him up.

Linda: Please, dear. Just say good night. It takes so little to make him happy. Come. (*She goes through the living room doorway, calling upstairs from within the living room.*) Your pajamas are hanging in the bathroom. Willy!

Happy (looking toward where Linda went out): What a woman! They broke the mold when they made her. You know that, Biff?

Biff: He's off salary. My God, working on commission!

Happy: Well, let's face it: he's no hot-shot selling man. Except that sometimes, you have to admit, he's a sweet personality.

Biff (deciding): Lend me ten bucks, will ya? I want to buy some new ties.

Happy: I'll take you to a place I know. Beautiful stuff. Wear one of my striped shirts tomorrow.

Biff: She got gray. Mom got awful old. Gee, I'm gonna go in to Oliver tomorrow and knock him for a—

Happy: Come on up. Tell that to Dad. Let's give him a whirl. Come on.

Biff (steamed up): You know, with ten thousand bucks, boy!

Happy (as they go into the living room): That's the talk, Biff, that's the first time I've heard the old confidence out of you! (*From within the living room, fading off.*) You're gonna live with me, kid, and any babe you want you just say the word . . . (*The last lines are hardly heard. They are mounting the stairs to their parents' bedroom.*)

Linda (entering her bedroom and addressing Willy, who is in the bathroom. She is straightening the bed for him): Can you do anything about the shower? It drips.

Willy (*from the bathroom*): All of a sudden everything falls to pieces! Goddam plumbing, oughta be sued, those people. I hardly finished putting it in and the thing ... (*His words rumble off.*)

Linda: I'm just wondering if Oliver will remember him. You think he might?

Willy (*coming out of the bathroom in his pajamas*): Remember him? What's the matter with you, you crazy? If he'd've stayed with Oliver he'd be on top by now! Wait'll Oliver gets a look at him. You don't know the average caliber any more. The average young man today—(*he is getting into bed*)—is got a caliber of zero. Greatest thing in the world for him was to bum around.

Biff and Happy enter the bedroom. Slight pause.

Willy (*stops short, looking at Biff*): Glad to hear it, boy.

Happy: He wanted to say good night to you, sport.

Willy (*to Biff*): Yeah. Knock him dead, boy. What'd you want to tell me?

Biff: Just take it easy, Pop. Good night. (*He turns to go.*)

Willy (*unable to resist*): And if anything falls off the desk while you're talking to him—like a package or something—don't you pick it up. They have office boys for that.

Linda: I'll make a big breakfast—

Willy: Will you let me finish? (*To Biff.*) Tell him you were in the business in the West. Not farm work.

Biff: All right, Dad.

Linda: I think everything—

Willy (*going right through her speech*): And don't undersell yourself. No less than fifteen thousand dollars.

Biff (*unable to bear him*): Okay. Good night, Mom. (*He starts moving.*)

Willy: Because you got a greatness in you, Biff, remember that. You got all kinds a greatness ... (*He lies back, exhausted. Biff walks out.*)

Linda (*calling after Biff*): Sleep well, darling!

Happy: I'm gonna get married, Mom. I wanted to tell you.

Linda: Go to sleep, dear.

Happy (*going*): I just wanted to tell you.

Willy: Keep up the good work. (*Happy exits.*) God ... remember that Ebbets Field game? The championship of the city?

Linda: Just rest. Should I sing to you?

Willy: Yeah. Sing to me. (*Linda hums a soft lullaby.*) When that team came out—he was the tallest, remember?

Linda: Oh, yes. And in gold.

Biff enters the darkened kitchen, takes a cigarette, and leaves the house. He comes downstage into a golden pool of light. He smokes, staring at the night.

Willy: Like a young god. Hercules—something like that. And the sun, the sun all around him. Remember how he waved to me? Right up from the field, with the representatives of three colleges standing by? And the buyers I brought, and the cheers when he came out—Loman, Loman, Loman! God

Almighty, he'll be great yet. A star like that, magnificent, can never really fade away!

The light on Willy is fading. The gas heater begins to glow through the kitchen wall, near the stairs, a blue flame beneath red coils.

Linda (*timidly*): Willy, dear, what has he got against you?
Willy: I'm so tired. Don't talk any more.

Biff slowly returns to the kitchen. He stops, stares toward the heater.

Linda: Will you ask Howard to let you work in New York?
Willy: First thing in the morning. Everything'll be all right.

Biff reaches behind the heater and draws out a length of rubber tubing. He is horrified and turns his head toward Willy's room, still dimly lit, from which the strains of Linda's desperate but monotonous humming rise.

Willy (*staring through the window into the moonlight*): Gee, look at the moon moving between the buildings!

Biff wraps the tubing around his hand and quickly goes up the stairs. Curtain.

ACT II

Music is heard, gay and bright. The curtain rises as the music fades away. Willy, in shirt sleeves, is sitting at the kitchen table, sipping coffee, his hat in his lap. Linda is filling his cup when she can.

Willy: Wonderful coffee. Meal in itself.
Linda: Can I make you some eggs?
Willy: No. Take a breath.
Linda: You look so rested, dear.
Willy: I slept like a dead one. First time in months. Imagine, sleeping till ten on a Tuesday morning. Boys left nice and early, heh?
Linda: They were out of here by eight o'clock.
Willy: Good work!
Linda: It was so thrilling to see them leaving together. I can't get over the shaving lotion in this house.
Willy (*smiling*): Mmm—
Linda: Biff was very changed this morning. His whole attitude seemed to be hopeful. He couldn't wait to get downtown to see Oliver.
Willy: He's heading for a change. There's no question, there simply are certain men that take longer to get—solidified. How did he dress?
Linda: His blue suit. He's so handsome in that suit. He could be a—anything in that suit!

Willy gets up from the table. Linda holds his jacket for him.

Willy: There's no question, no question at all. Gee, on the way home tonight I'd like to buy some seeds.

Linda (laughing): That'd be wonderful. But not enough sun gets back there. Nothing'll grow any more.

Willy: You wait, kid, before it's all over we're gonna get a little place out in the country, and I'll raise some vegetables, a couple of chickens . . .

Linda: You'll do it yet, dear.

Willy walks out of his jacket. Linda follows him.

Willy: And they'll get married, and come for a weekend. I'd build a little guest house. 'Cause I got so many fine tools, all I'd need would be a little lumber and some peace of mind.

Linda (Joyfully): I sewed the lining . . .

Willy: I could build two guest houses, so they'd both come. Did he decide how much he's going to ask Oliver for?

Linda (getting him into the jacket): He didn't mention it, but I imagine ten or fifteen thousand. You going to talk to Howard today?

Willy: Yeah. I'll put it to him straight and simple. He'll just have to take me off the road.

Linda: And Willy, don't forget to ask for a little advance, because we've got the insurance premium. It's the grace period now.

Willy: That's a hundred . . . ?

Linda: A hundred and eight, sixty-eight. Because we're a little short again.

Willy: Why are we short?

Linda: Well, you had the motor job on the car . . .

Willy: That goddam Studebaker!

Linda: And you got one more payment on the refrigerator . . .

Willy: But it just broke again!

Linda: Well, it's old, dear.

Willy: I told you we should've bought a well-advertised machine. Charley bought a General Electric and it's twenty years old and it's still good, that son-of-a-bitch.

Linda: But, Willy—

Willy: Whoever heard of a Hastings refrigerator? Once in my life I would like to own something outright before it's broken! I'm always in a race with the junkyard! I just finished paying for the car and it's on its last legs. The refrigerator consumes belts like a goddam maniac. They time those things. They time them so when you finally paid for them, they're used up.

Linda (buttoning up his jacket as he unbuttons it): All told, about two hundred dollars would carry us, dear. But that includes the last payment on the mortgage. After this payment, Willy, the house belongs to us.

Willy: It's twenty-five years!

Linda: Biff was nine years old when we bought it.

Willy: Well, that's a great thing. To weather a twenty-five year mortgage is—

Linda: It's an accomplishment.

Willy: All the cement, the lumber, the reconstruction I put in this house! There ain't a crack to be found in it any more.

Linda: Well, it served its purpose.

Willy: What purpose? Some stranger'll come along, move in, and that's that. If only Biff would take this house, and raise a family . . . (*He starts to go.*) Good-by, I'm late.

Linda (suddenly remembering): Oh, I forgot! You're supposed to meet them for dinner.

Willy: Me?

Linda: At Frank's Chop House on Forty-eighth near Sixth Avenue.

Willy: Is that so! How about you?

Linda: No, just the three of you. They're gonna blow you to a big meal!

Willy: Don't say! Who thought of that?

Linda: Biff came to me this morning, Willy, and he said, "Tell Dad, we want to blow him to a big meal." Be there six o'clock. You and your two boys are going to have dinner.

Willy: Gee whiz! That's really somethin'. I'm gonna knock Howard for a loop, kid. I'll get an advance, and I'll come home with a New York job. Goddammit, now I'm gonna do it!

Linda: Oh, that's the spirit, Willy!

Willy: I will never get behind a wheel the rest of my life!

Linda: It's changing, Willy, I can feel it changing!

Willy: Beyond a question. G'by, I'm late. (*He starts to go again.*)

Linda (calling after him as she runs to the kitchen table for a handkerchief): You got your glasses?

Willy (feels for them, then comes back in): Yeah, yeah, got my glasses.

Linda (giving him the handkerchief): And a handkerchief.

Willy: Yeah, handkerchief.

Linda: And your saccharine?

Willy: Yeah, my saccharine.

Linda: Be careful on the subway stairs.

She kisses him, and a silk stocking is seen hanging from her hand. Willy notices it.

Willy: Will you stop mending stockings? At least while I'm in the house. It gets me nervous. I can't tell you. Please.

Linda hides the stocking in her hand as she follows Willy across the forestage in front of the house.

Linda: Remember, Frank's Chop House.

Willy (passing the apron): Maybe beets would grow out there.

Linda (laughing): But you tried so many times.

Willy: Yeah. Well, don't work hard today. (*He disappears around the right corner of the house.*)

Linda: Be careful!

As Willy vanishes, Linda waves to him. Suddenly the phone rings. She runs across the stage and into the kitchen and lifts it.

Linda: Hello? Oh, Biff! I'm so glad you called, I just . . . Yes, sure, I just told him. Yes, he'll be there for dinner at six o'clock, I didn't forget. Listen, I was just dying to tell you. You know that little rubber pipe I told you about? That he connected to the gas heater? I finally decided to go down the cellar this morning and take it away and destroy it. But it's gone! Imagine? He took it away himself, it isn't there! (*She listens.*) When? Oh, then you took it. Oh—nothing, it's just that I'd hoped he'd taken it away himself. Oh, I'm not worried, darling, because this morning he left in such high spirits, it was like the old days! I'm not afraid any more. Did Mr. Oliver see you? . . . Well, you wait there then. And make a nice impression on him, darling. Just don't perspire too much before you see him. And have a nice time with Dad. He may have big news too! . . . That's right, a New York job. And be sweet to him tonight, dear. Be loving to him. Because he's only a little boat looking for a harbor. (*She is trembling with sorrow and joy.*) Oh, that's wonderful, Biff, you'll save his life. Thanks, darling. Just put your arm around him when he comes into the restaurant. Give him a smile. That's the boy . . . Good-by, dear. . . . You got your comb? . . . That's fine. Good-by, Biff dear.

In the middle of her speech, Howard Wagner, thirty-six, wheels in a small typewriter table on which is a wire-recording machine and proceeds to plug it in. This is on the left forestage. Light slowly fades on Linda as it rises on Howard. Howard is intent on threading the machine and only glances over his shoulder as Willy appears.

Willy: Pst! Pst!

Howard: Hello, Willy, come in.

Willy: Like to have a little talk with you, Howard.

Howard: Sorry to keep you waiting. I'll be with you in a minute.

Willy: What's that, Howard?

Howard: Didn't you ever see one of these? Wire recorder.

Willy: Oh. Can we talk a minute?

Howard: Records things. Just got delivery yesterday. Been driving me crazy, the most terrific machine I ever saw in my life. I was up all night with it.

Willy: What do you do with it?

Howard: I bought it for dictation, but you can do anything with it. Listen to this. I had it home last night. Listen to what I picked up. The first one is my daughter. Get this. (*He flicks the switch and "Roll out the Barrel" is heard being whistled.*) Listen to that kid whistle.

Willy: That is lifelike, isn't it?

Howard: Seven years old. Get that tone.

Willy: Ts, ts. Like to ask a little favor if you . . .

The whistling breaks off, and the voice of Howard's Daughter is heard.

His Daughter: "Now you, Daddy."

Howard: She's crazy for me! (*Again the same song is whistled.*) That's me! Ha! (*He winks.*)

Willy: You're very good!

The whistling breaks off again. The machine runs silent for a moment.

Howard: Sh! Get this now, this is my son.

His Son: "The capital of Alabama is Montgomery; the capital of Arizona is Phoenix; the capital of Arkansas is Little Rock; the capital of California is Sacramento . . ." (*And on, and on.*)

Howard (*holding up five fingers*): Five years old, Willy!

Willy: He'll make an announcer some day!

His Son (*continuing*): "The capital . . ."

Howard: Get that—alphabetical order! (*The machine breaks off suddenly.*) Wait a minute. The maid kicked the plug out.

Willy: It certainly is a—

Howard: Sh, for God's sake!

His son: "It's nine o'clock, Bulova watch time. So I have to go to sleep."

Willy: That really is—

Howard: Wait a minute! The next is my wife.

They wait.

Howard's Voice: "Go on, say something." (*Pause.*) "Well, you gonna talk?"

His Wife: "I can't think of anything."

Howard's Voice: "Well, talk—it's turning."

His Wife (*shyly, beaten*): "Hello." (*Silence.*) "Oh, Howard, I can't talk into this . . ."

Howard (*snapping the machine off*): That was my wife.

Willy: That is a wonderful machine. Can we—

Howard: I tell you, Willy, I'm gonna take my camera, and my bandsaw, and all my hobbies, and out they go. This is the most fascinating relaxation I ever found.

Willy: I think I'll get one myself.

Howard: Sure, they're only a hundred and a half. You can't do without it. Supposing you wanna hear Jack Benny, see? But you can't be at home at that hour. So you tell the maid to turn the radio on when Jack Benny comes on, and this automatically goes on with the radio . . .

Willy: And when you come home you . . .

Howard: You can come home twelve o'clock, one o'clock, any time you like, and you get yourself a Coke and sit yourself down, throw the switch, and there's Jack Benny's program in the middle of the night!

Willy: I'm definitely going to get one. Because lots of times I'm on the road, and I think to myself, what I must be missing on the radio!

Howard: Don't you have a radio in the car?

Willy: Well, yeah, but who ever thinks of turning it on?

Howard: Say, aren't you supposed to be in Boston?

Willy: That's what I want to talk to you about, Howard. You got a minute?

(*He draws a chair in from the wing.*)

Howard: What happened? What're you doing here?

Willy: Well . . .

Howard: You didn't crack up again, did you?

Willy: Oh, no. No . . . .

Howard: Geez, you had me worried there for a minute. What's the trouble?

Willy: Well, to tell you the truth, Howard, I've come to the decision that I'd rather not travel any more.

Howard: Not travel! Well, what'll you do?

Willy: Remember, Christmas time, when you had the party here? You said you'd try to think of some spot for me here in town.

Howard: With us?

Willy: Well, sure.

Howard: Oh, yeah, yeah. I remember. Well, I couldn't think of anything for you, Willy.

Willy: I tell ya, Howard. The kids are all grown up, y'know. I don't need much any more. If I could take home—well, sixty-five dollars a week, I could swing it.

Howard: Yeah, but Willy, see I—

Willy: I tell ya why, Howard. Speaking frankly and between the two of us, y'know—I'm just a little tired.

Howard: Oh, I could understand that, Willy. But you're a road man, Willy, and we do a road business. We've only got a half-dozen salesmen on the floor here.

Willy: God knows, Howard, I never asked a favor of any man. But I was with the firm when your father used to carry you in here in his arms.

Howard: I know that, Willy, but—

Willy: Your father came to me the day you were born and asked me what I thought of the name of Howard, may he rest in peace.

Howard: I appreciate that, Willy, but there just is no spot here for you. If I had a spot I'd slam you right in, but I just don't have a single, solitary spot.

He looks for his lighter. Willy has picked it up and gives it to him. Pause.

Willy (with increasing anger): Howard, all I need to set my table is fifty dollars a week.

Howard: But where am I going to put you, kid?

Willy: Look, it isn't a question of whether I can sell merchandise, is it?

Howard: No, but it's a business, kid, and everybody's gotta pull his own weight.

Willy (desperately): Just let me tell you a story, Howard—

Howard: 'Cause you gotta admit, business is business.

Willy (angrily): Business is definitely business, but just listen for a minute. You don't understand this. When I was a boy—eighteen, nineteen—I was already on the road. And there was a question in my mind as to whether selling had a future for me. Because in those days I had a yearning to go to Alaska. See, there were three gold strikes in one month in Alaska, and I felt like going out. Just for the ride, you might say.

Howard (barely interested): Don't say.

Willy: Oh, yeah, my father lived many years in Alaska. He was an adventurous man. We've got quite a little streak of self-reliance in our family. I thought I'd go out with my older brother and try to locate him, and maybe settle in the North with the old man. And I was almost decided to go, when I met a salesman in the Parker House. His name was Dave Singleman. And he was eighty-four years old, and he'd drummed merchandise in thirty-one states. And old Dave, he'd go up to his room, y'understand, put on his green velvet slippers—I'll never forget—and pick up his phone and call the buyers, and without ever leaving his room, at the age of eighty-four, he made his living. And when I saw that, I realized that selling was the greatest career a man could want. 'Cause what could be more satisfying than to be able to go, at the age of eighty-four, into twenty or thirty different cities, and pick up a phone, and be remembered and loved and helped by so many different people? Do you know? When he died—and by the way he died the death of a salesman, in his green velvet slippers in the smoker of the New York, New Haven and Hartford, going into Boston—when he died, hundreds of salesmen and buyers were at his funeral. Things were sad on a lotta trains for months after that. *(He stands up. Howard has not looked at him.)* In those days there was personality in it, Howard. There was respect, and comradeship, and gratitude in it. Today, it's all cut and dried, and there's no chance for bringing friendship to bear—or personality. You see what I mean? They don't know me any more.

Howard (moving away, to the right): That's just the thing, Willy.

Willy: If I had forty dollars a week—that's all I'd need. Forty dollars, Howard.

Howard: Kid, I can't take blood from a stone, I—

Willy (desperation is on him now): Howard, the year Al Smith was nominated, your father came to me and—

Howard (starting to go off): I've got to see some people, kid.

Willy (stopping him): I'm talking about your father! There were promises made across this desk! You mustn't tell me you've got people to see—I put thirty-four years into this firm, Howard, and now I can't pay my insurance! You can't eat the orange and throw the peel away—a man is not a piece of fruit! *(After a pause.)* Now pay attention. Your father—in 1928 I had a big year. I averaged a hundred and seventy dollars a week in commissions.

Howard (impatiently): Now, Willy, you never averaged—

Willy (banging his hand on the desk): I averaged a hundred and seventy dollars a week in the year of 1928! And your father came to me—or rather, I was in the office here—it was right over this desk—and he put his hand on my shoulder—

Howard (getting up): You'll have to excuse me, Willy, I gotta see some people. Pull yourself together. (*Going out.*) I'll be back in a little while.

On Howard's exit, the light on his chair grows very bright and strange.

Willy: Pull yourself together! What the hell did I say to him? My God, I was yelling at him! How could I! (*Willy breaks off, staring at the light, which occupies the chair, animating it. He approaches this chair, standing across the desk from it.*) Frank, Frank, don't you remember what you told me that time? How you put your hand on my shoulder, and Frank . . . (*He leans on the desk and as he speaks the dead man's name he accidentally switches on the recorder, and instantly—*)

Howard's Son: ". . . of New York is Albany. The capital of Ohio is Cincinnati, the capital of Rhode Island is . . . " (*The recitation continues.*)

Willy (leaping away with fright, shouting): Ha! Howard! Howard! Howard!

Howard (rushing in): What happened?

Willy (pointing at the machine, which continues nasally, childishly, with the capital cities): Shut it off! Shut it off!

Howard (pulling the plug out): Look, Willy . . .

Willy (pressing his hands to his eyes): I gotta get myself some coffee. I'll get some coffee . . .

Willy starts to walk out. Howard stops him.

Howard (rolling up the cord): Willy, look . . .

Willy: I'll go to Boston.

Howard: Willy, you can't go to Boston for us.

Willy: Why can't I go?

Howard: I don't want you to represent us. I've been meaning to tell you for a long time now.

Willy: Howard, are you firing me?

Howard: I think you need a good long rest, Willy.

Willy: Howard—

Howard: And when you feel better, come back, and we'll see if we can work something out.

Willy: But I gotta earn money, Howard. I'm in no position—

Howard: Where are your sons? Why don't your sons give you a hand?

Willy: They're working on a very big deal.

Howard: This is no time for false pride, Willy. You go to your sons and tell them that you're tired. You've got two great boys, haven't you?

Willy: Oh, no question, no question, but in the meantime . . .

Howard: Then that's that, heh?

Willy: All right, I'll go to Boston tomorrow.

Howard: No, no.

Willy: I can't throw myself on my sons. I'm not a cripple!

Howard: Look, kid, I'm busy this morning.

Willy (grasping Howard's arm): Howard, you've got to let me go to Boston!

Howard (*hard, keeping himself under control*): I've got a line of people to see this morning. Sit down, take five minutes, and pull yourself together, and then go home, will ya? I need the office, Willy. (*He starts to go, turns, remembering the recorder, starts to push off the table holding the recorder.*) Oh, yeah. Whenever you can this week, stop by and drop off the samples. You'll feel better, Willy, and then come back and we'll talk. Pull yourself together, kid, there's people outside.

Howard exits, pushing the table off left. Willy stares into space, exhausted. Now the music is heard—Ben's music—first distantly, then closer, closer. As Willy speaks, Ben enters from the right. He carries valise and umbrella.

Willy: Oh, Ben, how did you do it? What is the answer? Did you wind up the Alaska deal already?

Ben: Doesn't take much time if you know what you're doing. Just a short business trip. Boarding ship in an hour. Wanted to say good-by.

Willy: Ben, I've got to talk to you.

Ben (*glancing at his watch*): Haven't the time, William.

Willy (*crossing the apron to Ben*): Ben, nothing's working out. I don't know what to do.

Ben: Now, look here, William. I've bought timberland in Alaska and I need a man to look after things for me.

Willy: God, timberland! Me and my boys in those grand outdoors!

Ben: You've a new continent at your doorstep, William. Get out of these cities, they're full of talk and time payments and courts of law. Screw on your fists and you can fight for a fortune up there.

Willy: Yes, yes! Linda! Linda!

Linda enters as of old, with the wash.

Linda: Oh, you're back?

Ben: I haven't much time.

Willy: No, wait! Linda, he's got a proposition for me in Alaska.

Linda: But you've got—(*To Ben.*) He's got a beautiful job here.

Willy: But in Alaska, kid, I could—

Linda: You're doing well enough, Willy!

Ben (*to Linda*): Enough for what, my dear?

Linda (*frightened of Ben and angry at him*): Don't say those things to him! Enough to be happy right here, right now. (*To Willy, while Ben laughs.*) Why must everybody conquer the world? You're well liked, and the boys love you, and someday—(*to Ben*)—why, old man Wagner told him just the other day that if he keeps it up he'll be a member of the firm, didn't he, Willy?

Willy: Sure, sure. I am building something with this firm, Ben, and if a man is building something he must be on the right track, mustn't he?

Ben: What are you building? Lay your hand on it. Where is it?

Willy (*hesitantly*): That's true, Linda, there's nothing.

Linda: Why? (*To Ben.*) There's a man eighty-four years old—

Willy: That's right, Ben, that's right. When I look at that man I say, what is there to worry about?

Ben: Bah!

Willy: It's true, Ben. All he has to do is go into any city, pick up the phone, and he's making his living and you know why?

Ben (picking up his valise): I've got to go.

Willy (holding Ben back): Look at this boy!

Biff, in his high school sweater, enters carrying suitcase. Happy carries Biff's shoulder guards, gold helmet, and football pants.

Willy: Without a penny to his name, three great universities are begging for him, and from there the sky's the limit, because it's not what you do, Ben. It's who you know and the smile on your face! It's contacts, Ben, contacts! The whole wealth of Alaska passes over the lunch table at the Commodore Hotel, and that's the wonder, the wonder of this country, that a man can end with diamonds here on the basis of being liked! (*He turns to Biff.*) And that's why when you get out on that field today it's important. Because thousands of people will be rooting for you and loving you. (*To Ben, who has again begun to leave.*) And Ben! when he walks into a business office his name will sound out like a bell and all the doors will open to him! I've seen it, Ben, I've seen it a thousand times! You can't feel it with your hand like timber, but it's there!

Ben: Good-by, William.

Willy: Ben, am I right? Don't you think I'm right? I value your advice.

Ben: There's a new continent at your doorstep, William. You could walk out rich. Rich. (*He is gone.*)

Willy: We'll do it here, Ben! You hear me? We're gonna do it here!

Young Bernard rushes in. The gay music of the boys is heard.

Bernard: Oh, gee, I was afraid you left already!

Willy: Why? What time is it?

Bernard: It's half-past one!

Willy: Well, come on, everybody! Ebbets Field next stop! Where's the pennants? (*He rushes through the wall-line of the kitchen and out into the living room.*)

Linda (to Biff): Did you pack fresh underwear?

Biff (who has been limbering up): I want to go!

Bernard: Biff, I'm carrying your helmet, ain't I?

Happy: No, I'm carrying the helmet.

Bernard: Oh, Biff, you promised me.

Happy: I'm carrying the helmet.

Bernard: How am I going to get in the locker room?

Linda: Let him carry the shoulder guards. (*She puts her coat and hat on in the kitchen.*)

Bernard: Can I, Biff? 'Cause I told everybody I'm going to be in the locker room.

Happy: In Ebbets Field it's the clubhouse.
Bernard: I meant the clubhouse. Biff!
Happy: Biff!
Biff (grandly, after a slight pause): Let him carry the shoulder guards.
Happy (as he gives Bernard the shoulder guards): Stay close to us now.

   Willy rushes in with the pennants.

Willy (handing them out): Everybody wave when Biff comes out on the field. (*Happy and Bernard run off.*) You set now, boy?

   The music has died away.

Biff: Ready to go, Pop. Every muscle is ready.
Willy (at the edge of the apron): You realize what this means?
Biff: That's right, Pop.
Willy (feeling Biff's muscles): You're comin' home this afternoon captain of the All-Scholastic Championship Team of the City of New York.
Biff: I got it, Pop. And remember, pal, when I take off my helmet, that touchdown is for you.
Willy: Let's go! (*He is starting out, with his arm around Biff, when Charley enters, as of old, in knickers.*) I got no room for you, Charley.
Charley: Room? For what?
Willy: In the car.
Charley: You goin' for a ride? I wanted to shoot some casino.
Willy (furiously): Casino! (*Incredulously.*) Don't you realize what today is?
Linda: Oh, he knows, Willy. He's just kidding you.
Willy: That's nothing to kid about!
Charley: No, Linda, what's goin' on?
Linda: He's playing in Ebbets Field.
Charley: Baseball in this weather?
Willy: Don't talk to him. Come on, come on! (*He is pushing them out.*)
Charley: Wait a minute, didn't you hear the news?
Willy: What?
Charley: Don't you listen to the radio? Ebbets Field just blew up.
Willy: You go to hell! (*Charley laughs. Pushing them out.*) Come on, come on! We're late.
Charley (as they go): Knock a homer, Biff, knock a homer!
Willy (the last to leave, turning to Charley): I don't think that was funny, Charley. This is the greatest day of his life.
Charley: Willy, when are you going to grow up?
Willy: Yeah, heh? When this game is over, Charley, you'll be laughing out of the other side of your face. They'll be calling him another Red Grange. Twenty-five thousand a year.
Charley (kidding): Is that so?
Willy: Yeah, that's so.
Charley: Well, then, I'm sorry, Willy. But tell me something.

Willy: What?

Charley: Who is Red Grange?

Willy: Put up your hands. Goddam you, put up your hands!

> Charley, chuckling, shakes his head and walks away, around the left corner of the stage. Willy follows him. The music rises to a mocking frenzy.

Willy: Who the hell do you think you are, better than everybody else? You don't know everything, you big, ignorant, stupid . . . Put up your hands!

> Light rises, on the right side of the forestage, on a small table in the reception room of Charley's office. Traffic sounds are heard. Bernard, now mature, sits whistling to himself. A pair of tennis rackets and an overnight bag are on the floor beside him.

Willy (offstage): What are you walking away for? Don't walk away! If you're going to say something say it to my face! I know you laugh at me behind my back. You'll laugh out of the other side of your goddam face after this game. Touchdown! Touchdown! Eighty thousand people! Touchdown! Right between the goal posts.

> Bernard is a quiet, earnest, but self-assured young man. Willy's voice is coming from right upstage now. Bernard lowers his feet off the table and listens. Jenny, his father's secretary, enters.

Jenny (distressed): Say, Bernard, will you go out in the hall?

Bernard: What is that noise? Who is it?

Jenny: Mr. Loman. He just got off the elevator.

Bernard (getting up): Who's he arguing with?

Jenny: Nobody. There's nobody with him. I can't deal with him any more, and your father gets all upset everytime he comes. I've got a lot of typing to do, and your father's waiting to sign it. Will you see him?

Willy (entering): Touchdown! Touch —(He sees Jenny.) Jenny, Jenny, good to see you. How're ya? Workin'? Or still honest?

Jenny: Fine. How've you been feeling?

Willy: Not much any more, Jenny. Ha, ha! (He is surprised to see the rackets.)

Bernard: Hello, Uncle Willy.

Willy (almost shocked): Bernard! Well, look who's here! (He comes quickly, guiltily, to Bernard and warmly shakes his hand.)

Bernard: How are you? Good to see you.

Willy: What are you doing here?

Bernard: Oh, just stopped by to see Pop. Get off my feet till my train leaves. I'm going to Washington in a few minutes.

Willy: Is he in?

Bernard: Yes, he's in his office with the accountant. Sit down.

Willy (sitting down): What're you going to do in Washington?

Bernard: Oh, just a case I've got there, Willy.

Willy: That so? (indicating the rackets.) You going to play tennis there?

Bernard: I'm staying with a friend who's got a court.

Willy: Don't say. His own tennis court. Must be fine people, I bet.

Bernard: They are, very nice. Dad tells me Biff's in town.

Willy (with a big smile): Yeah, Biff's in. Working on a very big deal, Bernard.

Bernard: What's Biff doing?

Willy: Well, he's been doing very big things in the West. But he decided to establish himself here. Very big. We're having dinner. Did I hear your wife had a boy?

Bernard: That's right. Our second.

Willy: Two boys! What do you know!

Bernard: What kind of deal has Biff got?

Willy: Well, Bill Oliver—very big sporting-goods man—he wants Biff very badly. Called him in from the West. Long distance, carte blanche, special deliveries. Your friends have their own private tennis court?

Bernard: You still with the old firm, Willy?

Willy (after a pause): I'm—I'm overjoyed to see how you made the grade, Bernard, overjoyed. It's an encouraging thing to see a young man really— really—Looks very good for Biff—very—(*He breaks off, then.*) Bernard— (*He is so full of emotion, he breaks off again.*)

Bernard: What is it, Willy?

Willy (small and alone): What—what's the secret?

Bernard: What secret?

Willy: How—how did you? Why didn't he ever catch on?

Bernard: I wouldn't know that, Willy.

Willy (confidentially, desperately): You were his friend, his boyhood friend. There's something I don't understand about it. His life ended after that Ebbets Field game. From the age of seventeen nothing good ever happened to him.

Bernard: He never trained himself for anything.

Willy: But he did, he did. After high school he took so many correspondence courses. Radio mechanics; television; God knows what, and never made the slightest mark.

Bernard (taking off his glasses): Willy, do you want to talk candidly?

Willy (rising, faces Bernard): I regard you as a very brilliant man, Bernard. I value your advice.

Bernard: Oh, the hell with the advice, Willy. I couldn't advise you. There's just one thing I've always wanted to ask you. When he was supposed to graduate, and the math teacher flunked him—

Willy: Oh, that son-of-a-bitch ruined his life.

Bernard: Yeah, but, Willy, all he had to do was go to summer school and make up that subject.

Willy: That's right, that's right.

Bernard: Did you tell him not to go to summer school?

Willy: Me? I begged him to go. I ordered him to go!

Bernard: Then why wouldn't he go?

Willy: Why? Why! Bernard, that question has been trailing me like a ghost for the last fifteen years. He flunked the subject, and laid down and died like a hammer hit him!

Bernard: Take it easy, kid.

Willy: Let me talk to you—I got nobody to talk to. Bernard, Bernard, was it my fault? Y'see? It keeps going around in my mind, maybe I did something to him. I got nothing to give him.

Bernard: Don't take it so hard.

Willy: Why did he lay down? What is the story there? You were his friend!

Bernard: Willy, I remember, it was June, and our grades came out. And he'd flunked math.

Willy: That son-of-a-bitch!

Bernard: No, it wasn't right then. Biff just got very angry, I remember, and he was ready to enroll in summer school.

Willy (surprised): He was?

Bernard: He wasn't beaten by it at all. But then, Willy, he disappeared from the block for almost a month. And I got the idea that he'd gone up to New England to see you. Did he have a talk with you then?

Willy stares in silence.

Bernard: Willy?

Willy (with a strong edge of resentment in his voice): Yeah, he came to Boston. What about it?

Bernard: Well, just that when he came back—I'll never forget this, it always mystifies me. Because I'd thought so well of Biff, even though he'd always taken advantage of me. I loved him, Willy, y'know? And he came back after that month and took his sneakers—remember those sneakers with "University of Virginia" printed on them? He was so proud of those, wore them every day. And he took them down in the cellar, and burned them up in the furnace. We had a fist fight. It lasted at least half an hour. Just the two of us, punching each other down the cellar, and crying right through it. I've often thought of how strange it was that I knew he'd given up his life. What happened in Boston, Willy?

Willy looks at him as at an intruder.

Bernard: I just bring it up because you asked me.

Willy (angrily): Nothing. What do you mean, "What happened?" What's that got to do with anything?

Bernard: Well, don't get sore.

Willy: What are you trying to do, blame it on me? If a boy lays down is that my fault?

Bernard: Now, Willy, don't get—

Willy: Well, don't—don't talk to me that way! What does that mean, "What happened?"

Charley enters. He is in his vest, and he carries a bottle of bourbon.

Charley: Hey, you're going to miss that train. (*He waves the bottle.*)

Bernard: Yeah, I'm going. (*He takes the bottle.*) Thanks, Pop. (*He picks up his rackets and bag.*) Good-by, Willy, and don't worry about it. You know, "If at first you don't succeed . . ."

Willy: Yes, I believe in that.

Bernard: But sometimes, Willy, it's better for a man just to walk away.

Willy: Walk away?

Bernard: That's right.

Willy: But if you can't walk away?

Bernard (*after a slight pause*): I guess that's when it's tough. (*Extending his hand.*) Good-by, Willy.

Willy (*shaking Bernard's hand*): Good-by, boy.

Charley (*an arm on Bernard's shoulder*): How do you like this kid? Gonna argue a case in front of the Supreme Court.

Bernard (*protesting*): Pop!

Willy (*genuinely shocked, pained, and happy*): No! The Supreme Court!

Bernard: I gotta run. 'By, Dad!

Charley: Knock 'em dead, Bernard!

Bernard goes off.

Willy (*as Charley takes out his wallet*): The Supreme Court! And he didn't even mention it!

Charley (*counting out money on the desk*): He don't have to—he's gonna do it.

Willy: And you never told him what to do, did you? You never took any interest in him.

Charley: My salvation is that I never took any interest in anything. There's some money—fifty dollars. I got an accountant inside.

Willy: Charley, look . . . (*With difficulty.*) I got my insurance to pay. If you can manage it—I need a hundred and ten dollars.

Charley doesn't reply for a moment; merely stops moving.

Willy: I'd draw it from my bank but Linda would know, and I . . .

Charley: Sit down, Willy.

Willy (*moving toward the chair*): I'm keeping an account of everything, remember. I'll pay every penny back. (*He sits.*)

Charley: Now listen to me, Willy.

Willy: I want you to know I appreciate . . .

Charley (*sitting down on the table*): Willy, what're you doin'? What the hell is goin' on in your head?

Willy: Why? I'm simply . . .

Charley: I offered you a job. You can make fifty dollars a week. And I won't send you on the road.

Willy: I've got a job.

Charley: Without pay? What kind of a job is a job without pay? (*He rises.*) Now, look, kid, enough is enough. I'm no genius but I know when I'm being insulted.

Willy: Insulted!

Charley: Why don't you want to work for me?

Willy: What's the matter with you? I've got a job.

Charley: Then what're you walkin' in here every week for?

Willy (getting up): Well, if you don't want me to walk in here—

Charley: I am offering you a job.

Willy: I don't want your goddam job!

Charley: When the hell are you going to grow up?

Willy (furiously): You big ignoramus, if you say that to me again I'll rap you one! I don't care how big you are! (*He's ready to fight.*)

Pause.

Charley (kindly, going to him): How much do you need, Willy?

Willy: Charley, I'm strapped. I'm strapped. I don't know what to do. I was just fired.

Charley: Howard fired you?

Willy: That snotnose. Imagine that? I named him. I named him Howard.

Charley: Willy, when're you gonna realize that them things don't mean anything? You named him Howard, but you can't sell that. The only thing you got in this world is what you can sell. And the funny thing is that you're a salesman, and you don't know that.

Willy: I've always tried to think otherwise, I guess. I always felt that if a man was impressive, and well liked, that nothing—

Charley: Why must everybody like you? Who liked J. P. Morgan? Was he impressive? In a Turkish bath he'd look like a butcher. But with his pockets on he was very well liked. Now listen, Willy, I know you don't like me, and nobody can say I'm in love with you, but I'll give you a job because—just for the hell of it, put it that way. Now what do you say?

Willy: I—I just can't work for you, Charley.

Charley: What're you, jealous of me?

Willy: I can't work for you, that's all, don't ask me why.

Charley (angered, takes out more bills): You been jealous of me all your life, you damned fool! Here, pay your insurance. (*He puts the money in Willy's hand.*)

Willy: I'm keeping strict accounts.

Charley: I've got some work to do. Take care of yourself. And pay your insurance.

Willy (moving to the right): Funny, y'know? After all the highways, and the trains, and the appointments, and the years, you end up worth more dead than alive.

Charley: Willy, nobody's worth nothin' dead. (*After a slight pause.*) Did you hear what I said?

Willy stands still, dreaming.

Charley: Willy!

Willy: Apologize to Bernard for me when you see him. I didn't mean to argue with him. He's a fine boy. They're all fine boys, and they'll end up big—all of them. Someday they'll all play tennis together. Wish me luck, Charley. He saw Bill Oliver today.

Charley: Good luck.

Willy (on the verge of tears): Charley, you're the only friend I got. Isn't that a remarkable thing? *(He goes out.)*

Charley: Jesus!

Charley stares after him a moment and follows. All light blacks out. Suddenly raucous music is heard, and a red glow rises behind the screen at right. Stanley, a young waiter, appears, carrying a table, followed by Happy, who is carrying two chairs.

Stanley (putting the table down): That's all right, Mr. Loman, I can handle it myself. *(He turns and takes the chairs from Happy and places them at the table.)*

Happy (glancing around): Oh, this is better.

Stanley: Sure, in the front there you're in the middle of all kinds a noise. Whenever you got a party, Mr. Loman, you just tell me and I'll put you back here. Y'know, there's a lotta people they don't like it private, because when they go out they like to see a lotta action around them because they're sick and tired to stay in the house by theirself. But I know you, you ain't from Hackensack. You know what I mean?

Happy (sitting down): So how's it coming, Stanley?

Stanley: Ah, it's a dog's life. I only wish during the war they'd a took me in the Army. I coulda been dead by now.

Happy: My brother's back, Stanley.

Stanley: Oh, he come back, heh? From the Far West.

Happy: Yeah, big cattle man, my brother, so treat him right. And my father's coming too.

Stanley: Oh, your father too!

Happy: You got a couple of nice lobsters?

Stanley: Hundred per cent, big.

Happy: I want them with the claws.

Stanley: Don't worry, I don't give you no mice. *(Happy laughs.)* How about some wine? It'll put a head on the meal.

Happy: No. You remember, Stanley, that recipe I brought you from overseas? With the champagne in it?

Stanley: Oh, yeah, sure. I still got it tacked up yet in the kitchen. But that'll have to cost a buck apiece anyways.

Happy: That's all right.

Stanley: What'd you, hit a number or somethin'?

Happy: No, it's a little celebration. My brother is—I think he pulled off a big deal today. I think we're going into business together.

Stanley: Great! That's the best for you. Because a family business, you know what I mean?—that's the best.

Happy: That's what I think.

Stanley: 'Cause what's the difference? Somebody steals? It's in the family. Know what I mean? (*Sotto voce.*) Like this bartender here. The boss is goin' crazy what kinda leak he's got in the cash register. You put it in but it don't come out.

Happy (*raising his head*): Sh!

Stanley: What?

Happy: You notice I wasn't lookin' right or left, was I?

Stanley: No.

Happy: And my eyes are closed.

Stanley: So what's the—?

Happy: Strudel's comin'.

Stanley (*catching on, looks around*): Ah, no, there's no—

He breaks off as a furred, lavishly dressed Girl enters and sits at the next table. Both follow her with their eyes.

Stanley: Geez, how'd ya know?

Happy: I got radar or something. (*Staring directly at her profile.*) Oooooooo . . . Stanley.

Stanley: I think that's for you, Mr. Loman.

Happy: Look at that mouth. Oh, God. And the binoculars.

Stanley: Geez, you got a life, Mr. Loman.

Happy: Wait on her.

Stanley (*going to The Girl's table*): Would you like a menu, ma'am?

Girl: I'm expecting someone, but I'd like a—

Happy: Why don't you bring her—excuse me, miss, do you mind? I sell champagne, and I'd like you to try my brand. Bring her a champagne, Stanley.

Girl: That's awfully nice of you.

Happy: Don't mention it. It's all company money. (*He laughs.*)

Girl: That's a charming product to be selling, isn't it?

Happy: Oh, gets to be like everything else. Selling is selling, y'know.

Girl: I suppose.

Happy: You don't happen to sell, do you?

Girl: No, I don't sell.

Happy: Would you object to a compliment from a stranger? You ought to be on a magazine cover.

Girl (*looking at him a little archly*): I have been.

Stanley comes in with a glass of champagne.

Happy: What'd I say before, Stanley? You see? She's a cover girl.

Stanley: Oh, I could see, I could see.

Happy (*to The Girl*): What magazine?

Girl: Oh, a lot of them. (*She takes the drink.*) Thank you.

Happy: You know what they say in France, don't you? "Champagne is the drink of the complexion"—Hya, Biff!

Biff has entered and sits with Happy.

Biff: Hello, kid. Sorry I'm late.

Happy: I just got here. Uh, Miss—?

Girl: Forsythe.

Happy: Miss Forsythe, this is my brother.

Biff: Is Dad here?

Happy: His name is Biff. You might've heard of him. Great football player.

Girl: Really? What team?

Happy: Are you familiar with football?

Girl: No, I'm afraid I'm not.

Happy: Biff is quarterback with the New York Giants.

Girl: Well, that is nice, isn't it? (*She drinks.*)

Happy: Good health.

Girl: I'm happy to meet you.

Happy: That's my name. Hap. It's really Harold, but at West Point they called me Happy.

Girl (*now really impressed*): Oh, I see. How do you do? (*She turns her profile.*)

Biff: Isn't Dad coming?

Happy: You want her?

Biff: Oh, I could never make that.

Happy: I remember the time that idea would never come into your head. Where's the old confidence, Biff?

Biff: I just saw Oliver—

Happy: Wait a minute. I've got to see that old confidence again. Do you want her? She's on call.

Biff: Oh, no. (*He turns to look at The Girl.*)

Happy: I'm telling you. Watch this. (*Turning to The Girl.*) Honey? (*She turns to him.*) Are you busy?

Girl: Well, I am . . . but I could make a phone call.

Happy: Do that, will you, honey? And see if you can get a friend. We'll be here for a while. Biff is one of the greatest football players in the country.

Girl (*standing up*): Well, I'm certainly happy to meet you.

Happy: Come back soon.

Girl: I'll try.

Happy: Don't try, honey, try hard.

The Girl exits. Stanley follows, shaking his head in bewildered admiration.

Happy: Isn't that a shame now? A beautiful girl like that? That's why I can't get married. There's not a good woman in a thousand. New York is loaded with them, kid!

Biff: Hap, look—

Happy: I told you she was on call!

Biff (strangely unnerved): Cut it out, will ya? I want to say something to you.

Happy: Did you see Oliver?

Biff: I saw him all right. Now look, I want to tell Dad a couple of things and I want you to help me.

Happy: What? Is he going to back you?

Biff: Are you crazy? You're out of your goddam head, you know that?

Happy: Why? What happened?

Biff (breathlessly): I did a terrible thing today, Hap. It's been the strangest day I ever went through. I'm all numb, I swear.

Happy: You mean he wouldn't see you?

Biff: Well, I waited six hours for him, see? All day. Kept sending my name in. Even tried to date his secretary so she'd get me to him, but no soap.

Happy: Because you're not showin' the old confidence, Biff. He remembered you, didn't he?

Biff (stopping Happy with a gesture): Finally, about five o'clock, he comes out. Didn't remember who I was or anything. I felt like such an idiot, Hap.

Happy: Did you tell him my Florida idea?

Biff: He walked away. I saw him for one minute. I got so mad I could've torn the walls down! How the hell did I ever get the idea I was a salesman there? I even believed myself that I'd been a salesman for him! And then he gave me one look and—I realized what a ridiculous lie my whole life has been! We've been talking in a dream for fifteen years. I was a shipping clerk.

Happy: What'd you do?

Biff (with great tension and wonder): Well, he left, see. And the secretary went out. I was all alone in the waiting-room. I don't know what came over me, Hap. The next thing I know I'm in his office—paneled walls, everything. I can't explain it. I—Hap, I took his fountain pen.

Happy: Geez, did he catch you?

Biff: I ran out. I ran down all eleven flights. I ran and ran and ran.

Happy: That was an awful dumb—what'd you do that for?

Biff (agonized): I don't know, I just—wanted to take something, I don't know. You gotta help me, Hap. I'm gonna tell Pop.

Happy: You crazy? What for?

Biff: Hap, he's got to understand that I'm not the man somebody lends that kind of money to. He thinks I've been spiting him all these years and it's eating him up.

Happy: That's just it. You tell him something nice.

Biff: I can't.

Happy: Say you got a lunch date with Oliver tomorrow.

Biff: So what do I do tomorrow?

Happy: You leave the house tomorrow and come back at night and say Oliver is thinking it over. And he thinks it over for a couple of weeks, and gradually it fades away and nobody's the worse.

Biff: But it'll go on forever!

Happy: Dad is never so happy as when he's looking forward to something!

Willy enters.

Happy: Hello, scout!

Willy: Gee, I haven't been here in years!

Stanley has followed Willy in and sets a chair for him. Stanley starts off but Happy stops him.

Happy: Stanley!

Stanley stands by, waiting for an order.

Biff (going to Willy with guilt, as to an invalid): Sit down, Pop. You want a drink?

Willy: Sure, I don't mind.

Biff: Let's get a load on.

Willy: You look worried.

Biff: N-no. (*To Stanley.*) Scotch all around. Make it doubles.

Stanley: Doubles, right. (*He goes.*)

Willy: You had a couple already, didn't you?

Biff: Just a couple, yeah.

Willy: Well, what happened, boy? (*Nodding affirmatively, with a smile.*) Everything go all right?

Biff (takes a breath, then reaches out and grasps Willy's hand): Pal . . . (*He is smiling bravely, and Willy is smiling too.*) I had an experience today.

Happy: Terrific, Pop.

Willy: That so? What happened?

Biff (high, slightly alcoholic, above the earth): I'm going to tell you everything from first to last. It's been a strange day. (*Silence. He looks around, composes himself as best he can, but his breath keeps breaking the rhythm of his voice.*) I had to wait quite a while for him, and—

Willy: Oliver?

Biff: Yeah, Oliver. All day, as a matter of cold fact. And a lot of—instances— facts, Pop, facts about my life came back to me. Who was it, Pop? Who ever said I was a salesman with Oliver?

Willy: Well, you were.

Biff: No, Dad, I was a shipping clerk.

Willy: But you were practically—

Biff (with determination): Dad, I don't know who said it first, but I was never a salesman for Bill Oliver.

Willy: What're you talking about?

Biff: Let's hold on to the facts tonight, Pop. We're not going to get anywhere bullin' around. I was a shipping clerk.

Willy (angrily): All right, now listen to me—

Biff: Why don't you let me finish?

Willy: I'm not interested in stories about the past or any crap of that kind because the woods are burning, boys, you understand? There's a big blaze going on all around. I was fired today.

Biff (*shocked*): How could you be?

Willy: I was fired, and I'm looking for a little good news to tell your mother, because the woman has waited and the woman has suffered. The gist of it is that I haven't got a story left in my head, Biff. So don't give me a lecture about facts and aspects. I am not interested. Now what've you got to say to me?

Stanley enters with three drinks. They wait until he leaves.

Willy: Did you see Oliver?

Biff: Jesus, Dad!

Willy: You mean you didn't go up there?

Happy: Sure he went up there.

Biff: I did. I—saw him. How could they fire you?

Willy (*on the edge of his chair*): What kind of a welcome did he give you?

Biff: He won't even let you work on commission?

Willy: I'm out! (*Driving.*) So tell me, he gave you a warm welcome?

Happy: Sure, Pop, sure!

Biff (*driven*): Well, it was kind of—

Willy: I was wondering if he'd remember you. (*To Happy.*) Imagine, man doesn't see him for ten, twelve years and gives him that kind of welcome!

Happy: Damn right!

Biff (*trying to return to the offensive*): Pop, look—

Willy: You know why he remembered you, don't you? Because you impressed him in those days.

Biff: Let's talk quietly and get this down to the facts, huh?

Willy (*as though Biff had been interrupting*): Well, what happened? It's great news, Biff. Did he take you into his office or'd you talk in the waiting-room?

Biff: Well, he came in, see, and—

Willy (*with a big smile*): What'd he say? Betcha he threw his arm around you.

Biff: Well, he kinda—

Willy: He's a fine man. (*To Happy.*) Very hard man to see, y'know.

Happy (*agreeing*): Oh, I know.

Willy (*to Biff*): Is that where you had the drinks?

Biff: Yeah, he gave me a couple of—no, no!

Happy (*cutting in*): He told him my Florida idea.

Willy: Don't interrupt. (*To Biff.*) How'd he react to the Florida idea?

Biff: Dad, will you give me a minute to explain?

Willy: I've been waiting for you to explain since I sat down here! What happened? He took you into his office and what?

Biff: Well—I talked. And—and he listened, see.

Willy: Famous for the way he listens, y'know. What was his answer?

Biff: His answer was—(*He breaks off, suddenly angry.*) Dad, you're not letting me tell you what I want to tell you!

Willy (*accusing, angered*): You didn't see him, did you?

Biff: I did see him!

Willy: What'd you insult him or something? You insulted him, didn't you?

Biff: Listen, will you let me out of it, will you just let me out of it!

Happy: What the hell!

Willy: Tell me what happened!

Biff (to Happy): I can't talk to him!

> *A single trumpet note jars the ear. The light of green leaves stains the house, which holds the air of night and a dream. Young Bernard enters and knocks on the door of the house.*

Young Bernard (frantically): Mrs. Loman, Mrs. Loman!

Happy: Tell him what happened!

Biff (to Happy): Shut up and leave me alone!

Willy: No, no! You had to go and flunk math!

Biff: What math? What're you talking about?

Young Bernard: Mrs. Loman, Mrs. Loman!

> *Linda appears in the house, as of old.*

Willy (wildly): Math, math, math!

Biff: Take it easy, Pop.

Young Bernard: Mrs. Loman!

Willy (furiously): If you hadn't flunked you'd've been set by now!

Biff: Now, look, I'm gonna tell you what happened, and you're going to listen to me.

Young Bernard: Mrs. Loman!

Biff: I waited six hours—

Happy: What the hell are you saying?

Biff: I kept sending in my name but he wouldn't see me. So finally he . . . (*He continues unheard as light fades low on the restaurant.*)

Young Bernard: Biff flunked math!

Linda: No!

Young Bernard: Birnbaum flunked him! They won't graduate him!

Linda: But they have to. He's gotta go to the university. Where is he? Biff! Biff!

Young Bernard: No, he left. He went to Grand Central.

Linda: Grand—You mean he went to Boston?

Young Bernard: Is Uncle Willy in Boston?

Linda: Oh, maybe Willy can talk to the teacher. Oh, the poor, poor boy!

> *Light on house area snaps out.*

Biff (at the table, now audible, holding up a gold fountain pen): . . . so I'm washed up with Oliver, you understand? Are you listening to me?

Willy (at a loss): Yeah, sure. If you hadn't flunked—

Biff: Flunked what? What're you talking about?

Willy: Don't blame everything on me! I didn't flunk math—you did! What pen?

Happy: That was awful dumb, Biff, a pen like that is worth—

Willy (seeing the pen for the first time): You took Oliver's pen?

Biff (weakening): Dad, I just explained it to you.

Willy: You stole Bill Oliver's fountain pen!

Biff: I didn't exactly steal it! That's just what I've been explaining to you!

Happy: He had it in his hand and just then Oliver walked in, so he got nervous and stuck it in his pocket!

Willy: My God, Biff!

Biff: I never intended to do it, Dad!

Operator's voice: Standish Arms, good evening!

Willy (shouting): I'm not in my room!

Biff (frightened): Dad, what's the matter? (*He and Happy stand up.*)

Operator: Ringing Mr. Loman for you!

Willy: I'm not there, stop it!

Biff (horrified, gets down on one knee before Willy): Dad, I'll make good, I'll make good. (*Willy tries to get to his feet. Biff holds him down.*) Sit down now.

Willy: No, you're no good, you're no good for anything.

Biff: I am, Dad, I'll find something else, you understand? Now don't worry about anything. (*He holds up Willy's face.*) Talk to me, Dad.

Operator: Mr. Loman does not answer. Shall I page him?

Willy (attempting to stand, as though to rush and silence the Operator): No, no, no!

Happy: He'll strike something, Pop.

Willy: No, no . . .

Biff (desperately, standing over Willy): Pop, listen! Listen to me! I'm telling you something good. Oliver talked to his partner about the Florida idea. You listening? He—he talked to his partner, and he came to me . . . I'm to be all right, you hear? Dad, listen to me, he said it was just a question of the amount!

Willy: Then you . . . got it?

Happy: He's gonna be terrific, Pop!

Willy (trying to stand): Then you got it, haven't you? You got it! You got it!

Biff (agonized, holds Willy down): No, no. Look, Pop. I'm supposed to have lunch with them tomorrow. I'm just telling you this so you'll know that I can still make an impression, Pop. And I'll make good somewhere, but I can't go tomorrow, see?

Willy: Why not? You simply—

Biff: But the pen, Pop!

Willy: You give it to him and tell him it was an oversight!

Happy: Sure, have lunch tomorrow!

Biff: I can't say that—

Willy: You were doing a crossword puzzle and accidentally used his pen!

Biff: Listen, kid, I took those balls years ago, now I walk in with his fountain pen? That clinches it, don't you see? I can't face him like that! I'll try elsewhere.

Page's voice: Paging Mr. Loman!

Willy: Don't you want to be anything?

Biff: Pop, how can I go back?

Willy: You don't want to be anything, is that what's behind it?

Biff (now angry at Willy for not crediting his sympathy): Don't take it that way! You think it was easy walking into that office after what I'd done to him? A team of horses couldn't have dragged me back to Bill Oliver!

Willy: Then why'd you go?

Biff: Why did I go? Why did I go? Look at you! Look at what's become of you!

    Off left, The Woman laughs.

Willy: Biff, you're going to go to that lunch tomorrow, or—

Biff: I can't go. I've got no appointment!

Happy: Biff, for . . . !

Willy: Are you spiting me?

Biff: Don't take it that way! Goddammit!

Willy (strikes Biff and falters away from the table): You rotten little louse! Are you
    spiting me?

The Woman: Someone's at the door, Willy!

Biff: I'm no good, can't you see what I am?

Happy (separating them): Hey, you're in a restaurant! Now cut it out, both of
    you! *(The Girls enter.)* Hello, girls, sit down.

    The Woman laughs, off left.

Miss Forsythe: I guess we might as well. This is Letta.

The Woman: Willy, are you going to wake up?

Biff (ignoring Willy): How're ya, miss, sit down. What do you drink?

Miss Forsythe: Letta might not be able to stay long.

Letta: I gotta get up very early tomorrow. I got jury duty. I'm so excited! Were
    you fellows ever on a jury?

Biff: No, but I been in front of them! *(The Girls laugh.)* This is my father.

Letta: Isn't he cute? Sit down with us, Pop.

Happy: Sit him down, Biff!

Biff (going to him): Come on, slugger, drink us under the table. To hell with it!
    Come on, sit down, pal.

    On Biff's last insistence, Willy is about to sit.

The Woman (now urgently): Willy, are you going to answer the door!

    The Woman's call pulls Willy back. He starts right, befuddled.

Biff: Hey, where are you going?

Willy: Open the door.

Biff: The door?

Willy: The washroom . . . the door . . . where's the door?

Biff (leading Willy to the left): Just go straight down.

    Willy moves left.

The Woman: Willy, Willy, are you going to get up, get up, get up, get up?

    Willy exits left.

Letta: I think it's sweet you bring your daddy along.

Miss Forsythe: Oh, he isn't really your father!

Biff (at left, turning to her resentfully): Miss Forsythe, you've just seen a prince walk by. A fine, troubled prince. A hard-working, unappreciated prince. A pal, you understand? A good companion. Always for his boys.

Letta: That's so sweet.

Happy: Well, girls, what's the program? We're wasting time. Come on, Biff. Gather round. Where would you like to go?

Biff: Why don't you do something for him?

Happy: Me!

Biff: Don't you give a damn for him, Hap?

Happy: What're you talking about? I'm the one who—

Biff: I sense it, you don't give a good goddam about him. (*He takes the rolled-up hose from his pocket and puts it on the table in front of Happy.*) Look what I found in the cellar, for Christ's sake. How can you bear to let it go on?

Happy: Me? Who goes away? Who runs off and—

Biff: Yeah, but he doesn't mean anything to you. You could help him—I can't! Don't you understand what I'm talking about? He's going to kill himself, don't you know that?

Happy: Don't I know it! Me!

Biff: Hap, help him! Jesus . . . Help him . . . Help me, help me, I can't bear to look at his face! (*Ready to weep, he hurries out, up right.*)

Happy (starting after him): Where are you going?

Miss Forsythe: What's he so mad about?

Happy: Come on, girls, we'll catch up with him.

Miss Forsythe (as Happy pushes her out): Say, I don't like that temper of his!

Happy: He's just a little overstrung, he'll be all right!

Willy (off left, as The Woman laughs): Don't answer! Don't answer!

Letta: Don't you want to tell your father—

Happy: No, that's not my father. He's just a guy. Come on, we'll catch Biff, and, honey, we're going to paint this town! Stanley, where's the check? Hey, Stanley!

They exit. Stanley looks toward left.

Stanley (calling to Happy indignantly): Mr. Loman! Mr. Loman!

Stanley picks up a chair and follows them off. Knocking is heard off left. The Woman enters, laughing. Willy follows her. She is in a black slip; he is buttoning his shirt. Raw, sensuous music accompanies their speech.

Willy: Will you stop laughing? Will you stop?

The Woman: Aren't you going to answer the door? He'll wake the whole hotel.

Willy: I'm not expecting anybody.

The Woman: Whyn't you have another drink, honey, and stop being so damn self-centered?

Willy: I'm so lonely.

The Woman: You know you ruined me, Willy? From now on, whenever you come to the office, I'll see that you go right through to the buyers. No waiting at my desk any more, Willy. You ruined me.

Willy: That's nice of you to say that.

The Woman: Gee, you are self-centered! Why so sad? You are the saddest self-centeredest soul I ever did see-saw. (*She laughs. He kisses her.*) Come on inside, drummer boy. It's silly to be dressing in the middle of the night. (*As knocking is heard.*) Aren't you going to answer the door?

Willy: They're knocking on the wrong door.

The Woman: But I felt the knocking. And he heard us talking in here. Maybe the hotel's on fire!

Willy (his terror rising): It's a mistake.

The Woman: Then tell him to go away!

Willy: There's nobody there.

The Woman: It's getting on my nerves, Willy. There's somebody standing out there and it's getting on my nerves!

Willy (pushing her away from him): All right, stay in the bathroom here, and don't come out. I think there's a law in Massachusetts about it, so don't come out. It may be that new room clerk. He looked very mean. So don't come out. It's a mistake, there's no fire.

The knocking is heard again. He takes a few steps away from her, and she vanishes into the wing. The light follows him, and now he is facing Young Biff, who carries a suitcase. Biff steps toward him. The music is gone.

Biff: Why didn't you answer?

Willy: Biff! What are you doing in Boston?

Biff: Why didn't you answer? I've been knocking for five minutes, I called you on the phone—

Willy: I just heard you. I was in the bathroom and had the door shut. Did anything happen at home?

Biff: Dad—I let you down.

Willy: What do you mean?

Biff: Dad . . .

Willy: Biffo, what's this about? (*Putting his arm around Biff.*) Come on, let's go downstairs and get you a malted.

Biff: Dad, I flunked math.

Willy: Not for the term?

Biff: The term. I haven't got enough credits to graduate.

Willy: You mean to say Bernard wouldn't give you the answers?

Biff: He did, he tried, but I only got a sixty-one.

Willy: And they wouldn't give you four points?

Biff: Birnbaum refused absolutely. I begged him, Pop, but he won't give me those points. You gotta talk to him before they close the school. Because if he saw the kind of man you are, and you just talked to him in your way, I'm sure he'd come through for me. The class came right before practice, see, and I didn't go enough. Would you talk to him? He'd like you, Pop. You know the way you could talk.

Willy: You're on. We'll drive right back.

Biff: Oh, Dad, good work! I'm sure he'll change it for you!

Willy: Go downstairs and tell the clerk I'm checkin' out. Go right down.

Biff: Yes, Sir! See, the reason he hates me, Pop—one day he was late for class so I got up at the blackboard and imitated him. I crossed my eyes and talked with a lithp.

Willy (laughing): You did? The kids like it?

Biff: They nearly died laughing!

Willy: Yeah? What'd you do?

Biff: The thquare root of thixthy twee is . . . (*Willy bursts out laughing; Biff joins him.*) And in the middle of it he walked in!

Willy laughs and The Woman joins in offstage.

Willy (without hesitating): Hurry downstairs and—

Biff: Somebody in there?

Willy: No, that was next door.

The Woman laughs offstage.

Biff: Somebody got in your bathroom!

Willy: No, it's the next room, there's a party—

The Woman (enters, laughing. She lisps this): Can I come in? There's something in the bathtub, Willy, and it's moving!

Willy looks at Biff, who is staring open-mouthed and horrified at The Woman.

Willy: Ah—you better go back to your room. They must be finished painting by now. They're painting her room so I let her take a shower here. Go back, go back . . . (*He pushes her.*)

The Woman (resisting): But I've got to get dressed, Willy, I can't—

Willy: Get out of here! Go back, go back . . . (*Suddenly striving for the ordinary.*) This is Miss Francis, Biff, she's a buyer. They're painting her room. Go back, Miss Francis, go back . . .

The Woman: But my clothes, I can't go out naked in the hall!

Willy (pushing her offstage): Get outa here! Go back, go back!

Biff slowly sits down on his suitcase as the argument continues offstage.

The Woman: Where's my stockings? You promised me stockings, Willy!

Willy: I have no stockings here!

The Woman: You had two boxes of size nine sheers for me, and I want them!

Willy: Here, for God's sake, will you get outa here!

The Woman (enters holding a box of stockings): I just hope there's nobody in the hall. That's all I hope. (*To Biff.*) Are you football or baseball?

Biff: Football.

The Woman (*angry, humiliated*): That's me too. G'night. (*She snatches her clothes from Willy, and walks out.*)

Willy (*after a pause*): Well, better get going. I want to get to the school first thing in the morning. Get my suits out of the closet. I'll get my valise. (*Biff doesn't move.*) What's the matter? (*Biff remains motionless, tears falling.*) She's a buyer. Buys for J. H. Simmons. She lives down the hall—they're painting. You don't imagine—(*He breaks off. After a pause.*) Now listen, pal, she's just a buyer. She sees merchandise in her room and they have to keep it looking just so . . . (*Pause. Assuming command.*) All right, get my suits. (*Biff doesn't move.*) Now stop crying and do as I say. I gave you an order. Biff, I gave you an order! Is that what you do when I give you an order? How dare you cry! (*Putting his arm around Biff.*) Now look, Biff, when you grow up you'll understand about these things. You mustn't—you mustn't overemphasize a thing like this. I'll see Birnbaum first thing in the morning.

Biff: Never mind.

Willy (*getting down beside Biff*): Never mind! He's going to give you those points. I'll see to it.

Biff: He wouldn't listen to you.

Willy: He certainly will listen to me. You need those points for the U. of Virginia.

Biff: I'm not going there.

Willy: Heh? If I can't get him to change that mark you'll make it up in summer school. You've got all summer to—

Biff (*his weeping breaking from him*): Dad . . .

Willy (*infected by it*): Oh, my boy . . .

Biff: Dad . . .

Willy: She's nothing to me, Biff. I was lonely, I was terribly lonely.

Biff: You—you gave her Mama's stockings! (*His tears break through and he rises to go.*)

Willy (*grabbing for Biff*): I gave you an order!

Biff: Don't touch me, you—liar!

Willy: Apologize for that!

Biff: You fake! You phony little fake! (*Overcome, he turns quickly and weeping fully goes out with his suitcase. Willy is left on the floor on his knees.*)

Willy: I gave you an order! Biff, come back here or I'll beat you! Come back here! I'll whip you!

Stanley comes quickly in from the right and stands in front of Willy.

Willy (*shouts at Stanley*): I gave you an order . . .

Stanley: Hey, let's pick it up, pick it up, Mr. Loman. (*He helps Willy to his feet.*) Your boys left with the chippies. They said they'll see you at home.

A second waiter watches some distance away.

Willy: But we were supposed to have dinner together.

Music is heard, Willy's theme.

Stanley: Can you make it?

Willy: I'll—sure, I can make it. (*Suddenly concerned about his clothes.*) Do I—I look all right?

Stanley: Sure, you look all right. (*He flicks a speck off Willy's lapel.*)

Willy: Here—here's a dollar.

Stanley: Oh, your son paid me. It's all right.

Willy (*putting it in Stanley's hand*): No, take it. You're a good boy.

Stanley: Oh, no, you don't have to . . .

Willy: Here—here's some more, I don't need it any more. (*After a slight pause.*) Tell me—is there a seed store in the neighborhood?

Stanley: Seeds? You mean like to plant?

As Willy turns, Stanley slips the money back into his jacket pocket.

Willy: Yes. Carrots, peas . . .

Stanley: Well, there's hardware stores on Sixth Avenue, but it may be too late now.

Willy (*anxiously*): Oh, I'd better hurry. I've got to get some seeds. (*He starts off to the right.*) I've got to get some seeds, right away. Nothing's planted. I don't have a thing in the ground.

Willy hurries out as the light goes down. Stanley moves over to the right after him, watches him off. The other waiter has been staring at Willy.

Stanley (*to the waiter*): Well, whatta you looking at?

The waiter picks up the chairs and moves off right. Stanley takes the table and follows him. The light fades on this area. There is a long pause, the sound of the flute coming over. The light gradually rises on the kitchen, which is empty. Happy appears at the door of the house, followed by Biff. Happy is carrying a large bunch of long-stemmed roses. He enters the kitchen, looks around for Linda. Not seeing her, he turns to Biff, who is just outside the house door, and makes a gesture with his hands, indicating "Not here, I guess." He looks into the living room and freezes. Inside, Linda, unseen, is seated, Willy's coat on her lap. She rises ominously and quietly and moves toward Happy, who backs up into the kitchen, afraid.

Happy: Hey, what're you doing up? (*Linda says nothing but moves toward him implacably.*) Where's Pop? (*He keeps backing to the right, and now Linda is in full view in the doorway to the living room.*) Is he sleeping?

Linda: Where were you?

Happy (*trying to laugh it off*): We met two girls, Mom, very fine types. Here, we brought you some flowers. (*Offering them to her.*) Put them in your room, Ma.

She knocks them to the floor at Biff's feet. He has now come inside and closed the door behind him. She stares at Biff, silent.

Happy: Now what'd you do that for? Mom, I want you to have some flowers—

Linda (cutting Happy off, violently to Biff): Don't you care whether he lives or dies?

Happy (going to the stairs): Come upstairs, Biff.

Biff (with a flare of disgust, to Happy): Go away from me! (*To Linda.*) What do you mean, lives or dies? Nobody's dying around here, pal.

Linda: Get out of my sight! Get out of here!

Biff: I wanna see the boss.

Linda: You're not going near him!

Biff: Where is he? (*He moves into the living room and Linda follows.*)

Linda (shouting after Biff): You invite him for dinner. He looks forward to it all day—(*Biff appears in his parents' bedroom, looks around, and exits*)—and then you desert him there. There's no stranger you'd do that to!

Happy: Why? He had a swell time with us. Listen, when I—(*Linda comes back into the kitchen*)—desert him I hope I don't outlive the day!

Linda: Get out of here!

Happy: Now look, Mom . . .

Linda: Did you have to go to women tonight? You and your lousy rotten whores!

Biff re-enters the kitchen.

Happy: Mom, all we did was follow Biff around trying to cheer him up! (*To Biff.*) Boy, what a night you gave me!

Linda: Get out of here, both of you, and don't come back! I don't want you tormenting him anymore. Go on now, get your things together! (*To Biff.*) You can sleep in his apartment. (*She starts to pick up the flowers and stops herself.*) Pick up this stuff, I'm not your maid any more. Pick it up, you bum, you!

Happy turns his back to her in refusal. Biff slowly moves over and gets down on his knees, picking up the flowers.

Linda: You're a pair of animals! Not one, not another living soul would have had the cruelty to walk out on that man in a restaurant!

Biff (not looking at her): Is that what he said?

Linda: He didn't have to say anything. He was so humiliated he nearly limped when he came in.

Happy: But, Mom he had a great time with us—

Biff (cutting him off violently): Shut up!

Without another word, Happy goes upstairs.

Linda: You! You didn't even go in to see if he was all right!

Biff (still on the floor in front of Linda, the flowers in his hand; with self-loathing): No. Didn't. Didn't do a damned thing. How do you like that, heh? Left him babbling in a toilet.

Linda: You louse. You . . .

Biff: Now you hit it on the nose! (*He gets up, throws the flowers in the wastebasket.*) The scum of the earth, and you're looking at him!

Linda: Get out of here!

Biff: I gotta talk to the boss, Mom. Where is he?

Linda: You're not going near him. Get out of this house!

Biff (with absolute assurance, determination): No. We're gonna have an abrupt conversation, him and me.

Linda: You're not talking to him!

> *Hammering is heard from outside the house, off right. Biff turns toward the noise.*

Linda (suddenly pleading): Will you please leave him alone?

Biff: What's he doing out there?

Linda: He's planting the garden!

Biff (quietly): Now? Oh, my God!

> *Biff moves outside, Linda following. The light dies down on them and comes up on the center of the apron as Willy walks into it. He is carrying a flashlight, a hoe and a handful of seed packets. He raps the top of the hoe sharply to fix it firmly, and then moves to the left, measuring off the distance with his foot. He holds the flashlight to look at the seed packets, reading off the instructions. He is in the blue of night.*

Willy: Carrots . . . quarter-inch apart. Rows . . . . one-foot rows. (*He measures it off.*) One foot. (*He puts down a package and measures off.*) Beets. (*He puts down another package and measures again.*) Lettuce. (*He reads the package, puts it down.*) One foot—(*He breaks off as Ben appears at the right and moves slowly down to him.*) What a proposition, ts, ts. Terrific, terrific. 'Cause she's suffered, Ben, the woman has suffered. You understand me? A man can't go out the way he came in, Ben, a man has got to add up to something. You can't, you can't—(*Ben moves toward him as though to interrupt.*) You gotta consider, now. Don't answer so quick. Remember, it's a guaranteed twenty-thousand-dollar proposition. Now look, Ben, I want you to go through the ins and outs of this thing with me. I've got nobody to talk to, Ben, and the woman has suffered, you hear me?

Ben (standing still, considering): What's the proposition?

Willy: It's twenty thousand dollars on the barrelhead. Guaranteed, gilt-edged, you understand?

Ben: You don't want to make a fool of yourself. They might not honor the policy.

Willy: How can they dare refuse? Didn't I work like a coolie to meet every premium on the nose? And now they don't pay off? Impossible!

Ben: It's called a cowardly thing, William.

Willy: Why? Does it take more guts to stand here the rest of my life ringing up a zero?

Ben (yielding): That's a point, William. (*He moves, thinking, turns.*) And twenty thousand—that is something one can feel with the hand, it is there.

Willy (now assured, with rising power): Oh, Ben, that's the whole beauty of it! I see it like a diamond, shining in the dark, hard and rough, that I can pick up and touch in my hand. Not like—like an appointment! This would not be another damned-fool appointment, Ben, and it changes all the aspects. Because he thinks I'm nothing, see, and so he spites me. But the funeral— (*Straightening up.*) Ben, that funeral will be massive! They'll come from Maine, Massachusetts, Vermont, New Hampshire! All the old-timers with the strange license plates—that boy will be thunder-struck, Ben, because he never realized—I am known! Rhode Island, New York, New Jersey—I am known, Ben, and he'll see it with his eyes once and for all. He'll see what I am, Ben! He's in for a shock, that boy!

Ben (*coming down to the edge of the garden*): He'll call you a coward.

Willy (*suddenly fearful*): No, that would be terrible.

Ben: Yes. And a damned fool.

Willy: No, no, he mustn't, I won't have that! (*He is broken and desperate.*)

Ben: He'll hate you, William.

The gay music of the boys is heard.

Willy: Oh, Ben, how do we get back to all the great times? Used to be so full of light, and comradeship, the sleigh-riding in winter, and the ruddiness on his cheeks. And always some kind of good news coming up, always something nice coming up ahead. And never even let me carry the valises in the house, and simonizing, simonizing that little red car! Why, why can't I give him something and not have him hate me?

Ben: Let me think about it. (*He glances at his watch.*) I still have a little time. Remarkable proposition, but you've got to be sure you're not making a fool of yourself.

Ben drifts off upstage and goes out of sight. Biff comes down from the left.

Willy (*suddenly conscious of Biff, turns and looks up at him, then begins picking up the packages of seeds in confusion*): Where the hell is that seed? (*Indignantly.*) You can't see nothing out here! They boxed in the whole goddam neighborhood!

Biff: There are people all around here. Don't you realize that?

Willy: I'm busy. Don't bother me.

Biff (*taking the hoe from Willy*): I'm saying good-by to you, Pop. (*Willy looks at him, silent, unable to move.*) I'm not coming back any more.

Willy: You're not going to see Oliver tomorrow?

Biff: I've got no appointment, Dad.

Willy: He put his arm around you, and you've got no appointment?

Biff: Pop, get this now, will you? Everytime I've left it's been a fight that sent me out of here. Today I realized something about myself and I tried to explain it to you and I—I think I'm just not smart enough to make any sense out of it for you. To hell with whose fault it is or anything like that. (*He takes Willy's arm.*) Let's just wrap it up, heh? Come on in, we'll tell Mom. (*He gently tries to pull Willy to the left.*)

Willy (*frozen, immobile, with guilt in his voice*): No, I don't want to see her.

Biff: Come on! (*He pulls again, and Willy tries to pull away.*)

Willy (*highly nervous*): No, no, I don't want to see her.

Biff (*tries to look into Willy's face, as if to find the answer there*): Why don't you want to see her?

Willy (*more harshly now*): Don't bother me, will you?

Biff: What do you mean, you don't want to see her? You don't want them calling you yellow, do you? This isn't your fault; it's me, I'm a bum. Now come inside! (*Willy strains to get away.*) Did you hear what I said to you?

Willy pulls away and quickly goes by himself into the house. Biff follows.

Linda (*to Willy*): Did you plant, dear?

Biff (*at the door, to Linda*): All right, we had it out. I'm going and I'm not writing any more.

Linda (*going to Willy in the kitchen*): I think that's the best way, dear. 'Cause there's no use drawing it out, you'll just never get along.

Willy doesn't respond.

Biff: People ask where I am and what I'm doing, you don't know, and you don't care. That way it'll be off your mind and you can start brightening up again. All right? That clears it, doesn't it? (*Willy is silent, and Biff goes to him.*) You gonna wish me luck, scout? (*He extends his hand.*) What do you say?

Linda: Shake his hand, Willy.

Willy (*turning to her, seething with hurt*): There's no necessity to mention the pen at all, y'know.

Biff (*gently*): I've got no appointment, Dad.

Willy (*erupting fiercely*): He put his arm around . . . ?

Biff: Dad, you're never going to see what I am, so what's the use of arguing? If I strike oil I'll send you a check. Meantime forget I'm alive.

Willy (*to Linda*): Spite, see?

Biff: Shake hands, Dad.

Willy: Not my hand.

Biff: I was hoping not to go this way.

Willy: Well, this is the way you're going. Good-by.

Biff looks at him a moment, then turns sharply and goes to the stairs.

Willy (*stops him with*): May you rot in hell if you leave this house!

Biff (*turning*): Exactly what is it that you want from me?

Willy: I want you to know, on the train, in the mountains, in the valleys, wherever you go, that you cut down your life for spite!

Biff: No, no.

Willy: Spite, spite, is the word of your undoing! And when you're down and out, remember what did it. When you're rotting somewhere beside the railroad tracks, remember, and don't you dare blame it on me!

Biff: I'm not blaming it on you!

Willy: I won't take the rap for this, you hear?

Happy comes down the stairs and stands on the bottom step, watching.

Biff: That's just what I'm telling you!

Willy (*sinking into a chair at the table, with full accusation*): You're trying to put a knife in me—don't think I don't know what you're doing!

Biff: All right, phony! Then let's lay it on the line. (*He whips the rubber tube out of his pocket and puts it on the table.*)

Happy: You crazy—

Linda: Biff! (*She moves to grab the hose, but Biff holds it down with his hand.*)

Biff: Leave it there! Don't move it!

Willy (*not looking at it*): What is that?

Biff: You know goddam well what that is.

Willy (*caged, wanting to escape*): I never saw that.

Biff: You saw it. The mice didn't bring it into the cellar! What is this supposed to do, make a hero out of you? This supposed to make me sorry for you?

Willy: Never heard of it.

Biff: There'll be no pity for you, you hear? No pity!

Willy (*to Linda*): You hear the spite!

Biff: No, you're going to hear the truth—what you are and what I am!

Linda: Stop it!

Willy: Spite!

Happy (*coming down toward Biff*): You cut it now!

Biff (*to Happy*): The man don't know who we are! The man is gonna know! (*To Willy.*) We never told the truth for ten minutes in this house!

Happy: We always told the truth!

Biff (*turning on him*): You big blow, are you the assistant buyer? You're one of the two assistants to the assistant, aren't you?

Happy: Well, I'm practically—

Biff: You're practically full of it! We all are! And I'm through with it. (*To Willy.*) Now hear this, Willy, this is me.

Willy: I know you!

Biff: You know why I had no address for three months? I stole a suit in Kansas City and I was in jail. (*To Linda, who is sobbing.*) Stop crying. I'm through with it.

Linda *turns away from them, her hands covering her face.*

Willy: I suppose that's my fault!

Biff: I stole myself out of every good job since high school!

Willy: And whose fault is that?

Biff: And I never got anywhere because you blew me so full of hot air I could never stand taking orders from anybody! That's whose fault it is!

Willy: I hear that!

Linda: Don't, Biff!

Biff: It's goddam time you heard that! I had to be boss big shot in two weeks, and I'm through with it!

Willy: Then hang yourself! For spite, hang yourself!

Biff: No! Nobody's hanging himself, Willy! I ran down eleven flights with a pen in my hand today. And suddenly I stopped, you hear me? And in the middle of that office building, do you hear this? I stopped in the middle of that building and I saw—the sky. I saw the things that I love in this world. The work and the food and time to sit and smoke. And I looked at the pen and said to myself, what the hell am I grabbing this for? Why am I trying to become what I don't want to be? What am I doing in an office, making a contemptuous, begging fool of myself, when all I want is out there, waiting for me the minute I say I know who I am! Why can't I say that, Willy? (*He tries to make Willy face him, but Willy pulls away and moves to the left.*)

Willy (*with hatred, threateningly*): The door of your life is wide open!

Biff: Pop! I'm a dime a dozen, and so are you!

Willy (*turning on him now in an uncontrolled outburst*): I am not a dime a dozen! I am Willy Loman, and you are Biff Loman!

Biff starts for Willy, but is blocked by Happy. In his fury, Biff seems on the verge of attacking his father.

Biff: I am not a leader of men, Willy, and neither are you. You were never anything but a hard-working drummer who landed in the ash can like all the rest of them! I'm one dollar an hour, Willy! I tried seven states and couldn't raise it. A buck an hour! Do you gather my meaning? I'm not bringing home any prizes any more, and you're going to stop waiting for me to bring them home!

Willy (*directly to Biff*): You vengeful, spiteful mutt!

Biff breaks from Happy. Willy, in fright, starts up the stairs. Biff grabs him.

Biff (*at the peak of his fury*): Pop, I'm nothing! I'm nothing, Pop. Can't you understand that? There's no spite in it any more. I'm just what I am, that's all.

Biff's fury has spent itself, and he breaks down, sobbing, holding on to Willy, who dumbly fumbles for Biff's face.

Willy (*astonished*): What're you doing? What're you doing? (*To Linda.*) Why is he crying?

Biff (*crying, broken*): Will you let me go, for Christ sake? Will you take that phony dream and burn it before something happens? (*Struggling to contain himself, he pulls away and moves to the stairs.*) I'll go in the morning. Put him—put him to bed. (*Exhausted, Biff moves up the stairs to his room.*)

Willy (*after a long pause, astonished, elevated*): Isn't that remarkable? Biff—he likes me!

Linda: He loves you, Willy!

Happy (*deeply moved*): Always did, Pop.

Willy: Oh, Biff! (*Staring wildly.*) He cried! Cried to me. (*He is choking with his love, and now cries out his promise.*) That boy—that boy is going to be magnificent!

Ben appears in the light just outside the kitchen.

Ben: Yes, outstanding, with twenty thousand behind him.

Linda (*sensing the racing of his mind, fearfully, carefully*): Now come to bed, Willy. It's all settled now.

Willy (finding it difficult not to rush out of the house): Yes, we'll sleep. Come on. Go to sleep, Hap.

Ben: And it does take a great kind of man to crack the jungle.

In accents of dread, Ben's idyllic music starts up.

Happy (his arm around Linda): I'm getting married, Pop, don't forget it. I'm changing everything. I'm gonna run that department before the year is up. You'll see, Mom. (*He kisses her.*)

Ben: The jungle is dark but full of diamonds, Willy.

Willy turns, moves, listening to Ben.

Linda: Be good. You're both good boys, just act that way, that's all.

Happy: 'Night, Pop. (*He goes upstairs.*)

Linda (to Willy): Come, dear.

Ben (with greater force): One must go in to fetch a diamond out.

Willy (to Linda, as he moves slowly along the edge of the kitchen, toward the door): I just want to get settled down, Linda. Let me sit alone for a little.

Linda (almost uttering her fear): I want you upstairs.

Willy (taking her in his arms): In a few minutes, Linda. I couldn't sleep right now. Go on, you look awful tired. (*He kisses her.*)

Ben: Not like an appointment at all. A diamond is rough and hard to the touch.

Willy: Go on now, I'll be right up.

Linda: I think this is the only way, Willy.

Willy: Sure, it's the best thing.

Ben: Best thing!

Willy: The only way. Everything is gonna be—go on, kid, get to bed. You look so tired.

Linda: Come right up.

Willy: Two minutes.

Linda goes into the living room, then reappears in her bedroom. Willy moves just outside the kitchen door.

Willy: Loves me. (*Wonderingly.*) Always loved me. Isn't that a remarkable thing? Ben, he'll worship me for it!

Ben (with promise): It's dark there, but full of diamonds.

Willy: Can you imagine that magnificence with twenty thousand dollars in his pocket?

Linda (calling from her room): Willy! Come up!

Willy (calling from the kitchen): Yes! Yes! Coming! It's very smart, you realize that, don't you, sweetheart? Even Ben sees it. I gotta go, baby. 'By! By! (*Going over to Ben, almost dancing.*) Imagine? When the mail comes he'll be ahead of Bernard again!

Ben: A perfect proposition all around.

Willy: Did you see how he cried to me? Oh, if I could kiss him, Ben!

Ben: Time, William, time!

Willy: Oh, Ben, I always knew one way or another we were gonna make it, Biff and I!

Ben (looking at his watch): The boat. We'll be late. (*He moves slowly off into the darkness.*)

Willy (elegiacally, turning to the house): Now when you kick off, boy, I want a seventy-yard boot, and get right down the field under the ball, and when you hit, hit low and hit hard, because it's important, boy. (*He swings around and faces the audience.*) There's all kinds of important people in the stands, and the first thing you know . . . (*Suddenly realizing he is alone.*) Ben! Ben, where do I . . . ? (*He makes a sudden movement of search.*) Ben, how do I . . . ?

Linda (calling): Willy, you coming up?

Willy (uttering a gasp of fear, whirling about as if to quiet her): Sh! (*He turns around as if to find his way; sounds, faces, voices, seem to be swarming in upon him and he flicks at them, crying.*) Sh! Sh! (*Suddenly music, faint and high, stops him. It rises in intensity, almost to an unbearable scream. He goes up and down on his toes, and rushes off around the house.*) Shhh!

Linda: Willy?

> *There is no answer. Linda waits. Biff gets up off his bed. He is still in his clothes. Happy sits up. Biff stands listening.*

Linda (with real fear): Willy, answer me! Willy!

> *There is the sound of a car starting and moving away at full speed.*

Linda: No!

Biff (rushing down the stairs): Pop!

> *As the car speeds off, the music crashes down in a frenzy of sound, which becomes the soft pulsation of a single cello string. Biff slowly returns to his bedroom. He and Happy gravely don their jackets. Linda slowly walks out of her room. The music has developed into a dead march. The leaves of day are appearing over everything. Charley and Bernard, somberly dressed, appear and knock on the kitchen door. Biff and Happy slowly descend the stairs to the kitchen as Charley and Bernard enter. All stop a moment when Linda, in clothes of mourning, bearing a little bunch of roses, comes through the draped doorway into the kitchen. She goes to Charley and takes his arm. Now all move toward the audience, through the wall-line of the kitchen. At the limit of the apron, Linda lays down the flowers, kneels, and sits back on her heels. All stare down at the grave.*

REQUIEM

Charley: It's getting dark, Linda.

> *Linda doesn't react. She stares at the grave.*

Biff: How about it, Mom? Better get some rest, heh? They'll be closing the gate soon.

Linda makes no move. Pause.

Happy (deeply angered): He had no right to do that! There was no necessity for it. We would've helped him.

Charley (grunting): Hmmm.

Biff: Come along, Mom.

Linda: Why didn't anybody come?

Charley: It was a very nice funeral.

Linda: But where are all the people he knew? Maybe they blame him.

Charley: Naa. It's a rough world, Linda. They wouldn't blame him.

Linda: I can't understand it. At this time especially. First time in thirty-five years we were just about free and clear. He only needed a little salary. He was even finished with the dentist.

Charley: No man only needs a little salary.

Linda: I can't understand it.

Biff: There were a lot of nice days. When he'd come home from a trip; or on Sundays, making the stoop; finishing the cellar; putting on the new porch; when he built the extra bathroom; and put up the garage. You know something, Charley, there's more of him in that front stoop than in all the sales he ever made.

Charley: Yeah. He was a happy man with a batch of cement.

Linda: He was so wonderful with his hands.

Biff: He had the wrong dreams. All, all, wrong.

Happy (almost ready to fight Biff): Don't say that!

Biff: He never knew who he was.

Charley (stopping Happy's movement and reply. To Biff.): Nobody dast blame this man. You don't understand: Willy was a salesman. And for a salesman, there is no rock bottom to the life. He don't put a bolt to a nut, he don't tell you the law or give you medicine. He's a man out there in the blue, riding on a smile and a shoeshine. And when they start not smiling back—that's an earthquake. And then you get yourself a couple of spots on your hat, and you're finished. Nobody dast blame this man. A salesman is got to dream, boy. It comes with the territory.

Biff: Charley, the man didn't know who he was.

Happy (infuriated): Don't say that!

Biff: Why don't you come with me, Happy?

Happy: I'm not licked that easily. I'm staying right in this city, and I'm gonna beat this racket! (*He looks at Biff, his chin set.*) The Loman Brothers!

Biff: I know who I am, kid.

Happy: All right, boy. I'm gonna show you and everybody else that Willy Loman did not die in vain. He had a good dream. It's the only dream you can have—to come out number-one man. He fought it out here, and this is where I'm gonna win it for him.

Biff (with a hopeless glance at Happy, bends toward his mother): Let's go, Mom.

Linda: I'll be with you in a minute. Go on, Charley. (*He hesitates.*) I want to, just for a minute. I never had a chance to say good-by.

Charley moves away, followed by Happy. Biff remains a slight distance up and left of Linda. She sits there, summoning herself. The flute begins, not far away, playing behind her speech.

Linda: Forgive me, dear. I can't cry. I don't know what it is, but I can't cry. I don't understand it. Why did you ever do that? Help me, Willy, I can't cry. It seems to me that you're just on another trip. I keep expecting you. Willy, dear, I can't cry. Why did you do it? I search and search and search, and I can't understand it, Willy. I made the last payment on the house today. Today, dear. And there'll be nobody home. (*A sob rises in her throat.*) We're free and clear. (*Sobbing more fully, released.*) We're free. (*Biff comes slowly toward her.*) We're free . . . We're free . . .

Biff lifts her to her feet and moves out up right with her in his arms. Linda sobs quietly. Bernard and Charley come together and follow them, followed by Happy. Only the music of the flute is left on the darkening stage as over the house the hard towers of the apartment buildings rise into sharp focus, and—

THE CURTAIN FALLS

WRITER'S PERSPECTIVE

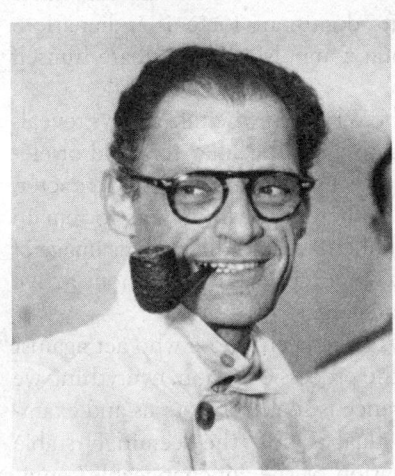

Arthur Miller

Arthur Miller on Drama

TRAGEDY AND THE COMMON MAN°   1949

In this age few tragedies are written. It has often been held that the lack is due to a paucity of heroes among us, or else that modern man has had the blood drawn out of his organs of belief by the skepticism of science, and the heroic attack on life cannot

A complete essay, originally published in the *New York Times*.

feed on an attitude of reserve and circumspection. For one reason or another, we are often held to be below tragedy—or tragedy above us. The inevitable conclusion is, of course, that the tragic mode is archaic, fit only for the very highly placed, the kings or the kingly, and where this admission is not made in so many words it is most often implied.

I believe that the common man is as apt a subject for tragedy in its highest sense as kings were. On the face of it this ought to be obvious in the light of modern psychiatry, which bases its analysis upon classific formulations, such as the Oedipus and Orestes complexes, for instance, which were enacted by royal beings, but which apply to everyone in similar emotional situations.

More simply, when the question of tragedy in art is not at issue, we never hesitate to attribute to the well-placed and the exalted the very same mental processes as the lowly. And finally, if the exaltation of tragic action were truly a property of the high-bred character alone, it is inconceivable that the mass of mankind should cherish tragedy above all other forms, let alone be capable of understanding it.

As a general rule, to which there may be exceptions unknown to me, I think the tragic feeling is evoked in us when we are in the presence of a character who is ready to lay down his life, if need be, to secure one thing—his sense of personal dignity. From Orestes to Hamlet, Medea to Macbeth, the underlying struggle is that of the individual attempting to gain his "rightful" position in his society.

Sometimes he is one who has been displaced from it, sometimes one who seeks to attain it for the first time, but the fateful wound from which the inevitable events spiral is the wound of indignity, and its dominant force is indignation. Tragedy, then, is the consequence of a man's total compulsion to evaluate himself justly.

In the sense of having been initiated by the hero himself, the tale always reveals what has been called his "tragic flaw," a failing that is not peculiar to grand or elevated characters. Nor is it necessarily a weakness. The flaw, or crack in the character, is really nothing—and need be nothing—but his inherent unwillingness to remain passive in the face of what he conceives to be a challenge to his dignity, his image of his rightful status. Only the passive, only those who accept their lot without active retaliation, are "flawless." Most of us are in that category.

But there are among us today, as there always have been, those who act against the scheme of things that degrades them, and in the process of action, everything we have accepted out of fear or insensitivity or ignorance is shaken before us and examined, and from this total onslaught by an individual against the seemingly stable cosmos surrounding us—from this total examination of the "unchangeable" environment—comes the terror and the fear that is classically associated with tragedy.

More important, from this total questioning of what has been previously unquestioned, we learn. And such a process is not beyond the common man. In revolutions around the world, these past thirty years, he has demonstrated again and again this inner dynamic of all tragedy.

Insistence upon the rank of the tragic hero, or the so-called nobility of his character, is really but a clinging to the outward forms of tragedy. If rank or nobility of character was indispensable, then it would follow that the problems of those with rank were the particular problems of tragedy. But surely the right of one monarch to capture the domain from another no longer raises our passions, nor are our concepts of justice what they were to the mind of an Elizabethan king.

The quality in such plays that does shake us, however, derives from the underlying fear of being displaced, the disaster inherent in being torn away from our chosen image of what and who we are in this world. Among us today this fear is as strong, and perhaps stronger, than it ever was. In fact, it is the common man who knows this fear best.

Now, if it is true that tragedy is the consequence of a man's total compulsion to evaluate himself justly, his destruction in the attempt posits a wrong or an evil in his environment. And this is precisely the morality of tragedy and its lesson. The discovery of the moral law, which is what the enlightenment of tragedy consists of, is not the discovery of some abstract or metaphysical quantity.

The tragic right is a condition of life, a condition in which the human personality is able to flower and realize itself. The wrong is the condition which suppresses man, perverts the flowing out of his love and creative instinct. Tragedy enlightens— and it must, in that it points the heroic finger at the enemy of man's freedom. The thrust for freedom is the quality in tragedy which exalts. The revolutionary questioning of the stable environment is what terrifies. In no way is the common man debarred from such thoughts or such actions.

Seen in this light, our lack of tragedy may be partially accounted for by the turn which modern literature has taken toward the purely psychiatric view of life, or the purely sociological. If all our miseries, our indignities, are born and bred within our minds, then all action, let alone the heroic action, is obviously impossible.

And if society alone is responsible for the cramping of our lives, then the protagonist must needs be so pure and faultless as to force us to deny his validity as a character. From neither of these views can tragedy derive, simply because neither represents a balanced concept of life. Above all else, tragedy requires the finest appreciation by the writer of cause and effect.

No tragedy can therefore come about when its author fears to question absolutely everything, when he regards any institution, habit or custom as being either everlasting, immutable or inevitable. In the tragic view the need of man to wholly realize himself is the only fixed star, and whatever it is that hedges his nature and lowers it is ripe for attack and examination. Which is not to say that tragedy must preach revolution.

The Greeks could probe the very heavenly origin of their ways and return to confirm the rightness of laws. And Job could face God in anger, demanding his right, and end in submission. But for a moment everything is in suspension, nothing is accepted, and in this stretching and tearing apart of the cosmos, in the very action of so doing, the character gains "size," the tragic stature which is spuriously attached to the royal or the high born in our minds. The commonest of men may take on that stature to the extent of his willingness to throw all he has into the contest, the battle to secure his rightful place in his world.

There is a misconception of tragedy with which I have been struck in review after review, and in many conversations with writers and readers alike. It is the idea that tragedy is of necessity allied to pessimism. Even the dictionary says nothing more about the word than that it means a story with a sad or unhappy ending. This impression is so firmly fixed that I almost hesitate to claim that in truth tragedy implies more optimism in its author than does comedy, and that its final result ought to be the reinforcement of the onlooker's brightest opinions of the human animal.

For, if it is true to say that in essence the tragic hero is intent upon claiming his whole due as a personality, and if this struggle must be total and without reservation, then it automatically demonstrates the indestructible will of man to achieve his humanity.

The possibility of victory must be there in tragedy. Where pathos rules, where pathos is finally derived, a character has fought a battle he could not possibly have won. The pathetic is achieved when the protagonist is, by virtue of his witlessness, his insensitivity, or the very air he gives off, incapable of grappling with a much superior force.

Pathos truly is the mode for the pessimist. But tragedy requires a nicer balance between what is possible and what is impossible. And it is curious, although edifying, that the plays we revere, century after century, are the tragedies. In them, and in them alone, lies the belief—optimistic, if you will—in the perfectibility of man.

It is time, I think, that we who are without kings took up this bright thread of our history and followed it to the only place it can possibly lead in our time—the heart and spirit of the average man.

From The Theater Essays of Arthur Miller

Tennessee Williams

<table>
<tr><td>THE GLASS MENAGERIE</td><td align="right">1945</td></tr>
</table>

Tennessee Williams (1914–1983) was born Thomas Lanier Williams in Columbus, Mississippi, went to high school in St. Louis, and graduated from the University of Iowa. As an undergraduate, he saw a performance of Ibsen's Ghosts *and decided to become a playwright himself. His family bore a close resemblance to the Wingfields in* The Glass Menagerie: *his mother came from a line of Southern blue bloods (Tennessee pioneers); his sister Rose suffered from incapacitating shyness; and as a young man, Williams himself, like Tom, worked at a job he disliked (in a shoe factory where his father worked), wrote poetry, sought refuge in moviegoing, and finally left home to wander and hold odd jobs. He worked as a bellhop in a New Orleans hotel; a teletype operator in Jacksonville, Florida; an usher and a waiter in New York. In 1945* The Glass Menagerie *scored a success on Broadway, winning a Drama Critics Circle award. Two years later Williams received a Pulitzer Prize for* A Streetcar Named Desire, *a grim, powerful study of a woman's illusions and frustrations, set in New Orleans. In 1955 Williams was awarded another Pulitzer Prize for* Cat on a Hot Tin Roof. *Besides other plays, including* Summer and Smoke (1948), Sweet Bird of Youth (1959), The Night of the Iguana (1961), Small Craft Warnings (1973),

Clothes for a Summer Hotel *(1980), and* A House Not Meant to Stand *(1981),* Williams wrote two novels, poetry, essays, short stories, and Memoirs *(1975)*.

Nobody, not even the rain, has such small hands.
—*E. E. Cummings*

Characters

Amanda Wingfield, the mother. A little woman of great but confused vitality clinging frantically to another time and place. Her characterization must be carefully created, not copied from type. She is not paranoiac, but her life is paranoia. There is much to admire in Amanda, and as much to love and pity as there is to laugh at. Certainly she has endurance and a kind of heroism, and though her foolishness makes her unwittingly cruel at times, there is tenderness in her slight person.

Laura Wingfield, her daughter. Amanda, having failed to establish contact with reality, continues to live vitally in her illusions, but Laura's situation is even

Left to right: Anthony Ross (Jim), Laurette Taylor (Amanda), Eddie Dowling (Tom), and Julie Hayden (Laura) in the 1945 original production of The Glass Menagerie, The Playhouse, *New York.*

graver. A childhood illness has left her crippled, one leg slightly shorter than the other, and held in a brace. This defect need not be more than suggested on the stage. Stemming from this, Laura's separation increases till she is like a piece of her own glass collection, too exquisitely fragile to move from the shelf.

Tom Wingfield, her son. And the narrator of the play. A poet with a job in a warehouse. His nature is not remorseless, but to escape from a trap he has to act without pity.

Jim O'Connor, the gentleman caller. A nice, ordinary, young man.

Scene. *An alley in St. Louis.*

Part I. *Preparation for a Gentleman Caller.*

Part II. *The Gentleman Calls.*

Time. *Now and the Past.*

SCENE I

The Wingfield apartment is in the rear of the building, one of those vast hive-like conglomerations of cellular living-units that flower as warty growths in overcrowded urban centers of lower middle-class population and are symptomatic of the impulse of this largest and fundamentally enslaved section of American society to avoid fluidity and differentiation and to exist and function as one interfused mass of automatism.

The apartment faces an alley and is entered by a fire-escape, a structure whose name is a touch of accidental poetic truth, for all of these huge buildings are always burning with the slow and implacable fires of human desperation. The fire-escape is included in the set—that is, the landing of it and steps descending from it.

The scene is memory and is therefore unrealistic. Memory takes a lot of poetic license. It omits some details; others are exaggerated, according to the emotional value of the articles it touches, for memory is seated predominantly in the heart. The interior is therefore rather dim and poetic.

At the rise of the curtain, the audience is faced with the dark, grim rear wall of the Wingfield tenement. This building, which runs parallel to the footlights, is flanked on both sides by dark, narrow alleys which run into murky canyons of tangled clotheslines, garbage cans, and the sinister latticework of neighboring fire-escapes. It is up and down these side alleys that exterior entrances and exits are made, during the play. At the end of Tom's opening commentary, the dark tenement wall slowly reveals (by means of a transparency) the interior of the ground floor Wingfield apartment.

Downstage is the living room, which also serves as a sleeping room for Laura, the sofa unfolding to make her bed. Upstage, center, and divided by a wide arch or second proscenium with transparent faded portieres (or second curtain), is the dining room. In an old-fashioned what-not in the living room are seen scores of transparent glass animals. A blown-up photograph of the father hangs on the wall of the living room, facing the audience, to the left of the archway. It is the face of a very handsome young man in a doughboy's First World War cap. He is gallantly smiling, ineluctably smiling, as if to say, "I will be smiling forever."

The audience hears and sees the opening scene in the dining room through both the transparent fourth wall of the building and the transparent gauze portieres of the dining room arch. It is during this revealing scene that the fourth wall slowly ascends, out of sight. This transparent exterior wall is not brought down again until the very end of the play, during Tom's final speech.

The narrator is an undisguised convention of the play. He takes whatever license with dramatic convention as is convenient to his purposes.

Tom enters dressed as a merchant sailor from the alley, stage left, and strolls across the front of the stage to the fire-escape. There he stops and lights a cigarette. He addresses the audience.

Tom: Yes, I have tricks in my pocket, I have things up my sleeve. But I am the opposite of a stage magician. He gives you illusion that has the appearance of truth. I give you truth in the pleasant disguise of illusion. To begin with, I turn back time. I reverse it to that quaint period, the thirties, when the huge middle class of America was matriculating in a school for the blind. Their eyes had failed them, or they had failed their eyes, and so they were having their fingers pressed forcibly down on the fiery Braille alphabet of a dissolving economy. In Spain there was revolution. Here there was only shouting and confusion. In Spain there was Guernica. Here there were disturbances of labor, sometimes pretty violent, in otherwise peaceful cities such as Chicago, Cleveland, St. Louis. . . . This is the social background of the play.

(Music.)

The play is memory. Being a memory play, it is dimly lighted, it is senti-mental, it is not realistic. In memory everything seems to happen to music. That explains the fiddle in the wings. I am the narrator of the play, and also a character in it. The other characters are my mother, Amanda, my sister, Laura, and a gentleman caller who appears in the final scenes. He is the most realistic character in the play, being an emissary from a world of reality that we were somehow set apart from. But since I have a poet's weakness for symbols, I am using this character also as a symbol; he is the long delayed but always expected something that we live for. There is a fifth character in the play who doesn't appear except in this larger-than-life photograph over the mantel. This is our father who left us a long time ago. He was a tele-phone man who fell in love with long distances; he gave up his job with the telephone company and skipped the light fantastic out of town. . . . The last we heard of him was a picture post-card from Mazatlan, on the Pacific coast of Mexico, containing a message of two words—"Hello—Good-bye!" and an address. I think the rest of the play will explain itself. . . .

Amanda's voice becomes audible through the portieres.

(Screen Legend: "Où Sont Les Neiges.")°

He divides the portieres and enters the upstage area.

Amanda and Laura are seated at a drop-leaf table. Eating is indicated by gestures without food or utensils. Amanda faces the audience. Tom and Laura are seated in profile.

The interior has lit up softly and through the scrim we see Amanda and Laura seated at the table in the upstage area.

Amanda (*calling*): Tom?

Tom: Yes, Mother.

Amanda: We can't say grace until you come to the table!

Tom: Coming, Mother. (*He bows slightly and withdraws, reappearing a few moments later in his place at the table.*)

Amanda (*to her son*): Honey, don't *push* with your *fingers*. If you have to push with something, the thing to push with is a crust of bread. And chew—chew! Animals have sections in their stomachs which enable them to digest food without mastication, but human beings are supposed to chew their food before they swallow it down. Eat food leisurely, son, and really enjoy it. A well-cooked meal has lots of delicate flavors that have to be held in the mouth for appreciation. So chew your food and give your salivary glands a chance to function!

Tom deliberately lays his imaginary fork down and pushes his chair back from the table.

Tom: I haven't enjoyed one bite of this dinner because of your constant directions on how to eat it. It's you that makes me rush through meals with your hawk-like attention to every bite I take. Sickening—spoils my appetite—all this discussion of animals' secretion—salivary glands—mastication!

Amanda (*lightly*): Temperament like a Metropolitan star! (*He rises and crosses downstage.*) You're not excused from the table.

Tom: I am getting a cigarette.

Amanda: You smoke too much.

Laura rises.

Laura: I'll bring in the blanc mange.

He remains standing with his cigarette by the portieres during the following.

Amanda (*rising*): No, sister, no, sister—you be the lady this time and I'll be the darky.

Laura: I'm already up.

(*Screen Legend . . . Neiges.*"): "Where are the snows (of yesteryear)?" A slide bearing this line by the French poet François Villon is to be projected on a stage wall.

Amanda: Resume your seat, little sister—I want you to stay fresh and pretty— for gentlemen callers!

Laura: I'm not expecting any gentlemen callers.

Amanda (crossing out to kitchenette. Airily): Sometimes they come when they are least expected! Why, I remember one Sunday afternoon in Blue Mountain— *(Enters kitchenette.)*

Tom: I know what's coming!

Laura: Yes. But let her tell it.

Tom: Again?

Laura: She loves to tell it.

Amanda returns with bowl of dessert.

Amanda: One Sunday afternoon in Blue Mountain—your mother received— seventeen!—gentlemen callers! Why, sometimes there weren't chairs enough to accommodate them all. We had to send the nigger over to bring in folding chairs from the parish house.

Tom (remaining at portieres): How did you entertain those gentlemen callers?

Amanda: I understood the art of conversation!

Tom: I bet you could talk.

Amanda: Girls in those days *knew* how to talk, I can tell you.

Tom: Yes?

(Image: Amanda As A Girl On A Porch Greeting Callers.)

Amanda: They knew how to entertain their gentlemen callers. It wasn't enough for a girl to be possessed of a pretty face and a graceful figure—although I wasn't slighted in either respect. She also needed to have a nimble wit and a tongue to meet all occasions.

Tom: What did you talk about?

Amanda: Things of importance going on in the world! Never anything coarse or common or vulgar. *(She addresses Tom as though he were seated in the vacant chair at the table though he remains by portieres. He plays this scene as though he held the book.)* My callers were gentlemen—all! Among my callers were some of the most prominent young planters of the Mississippi Delta— planters and sons of planters!

Tom motions for music and a spot of light on Amanda. Her eyes lift, her face glows, her voice becomes rich and elegiac.

(Screen Legend: "Où Sont Les Neiges.")

There was young Champ Laughlin who later became vice-president of the Delta Planters Bank. Hadley Stevenson who was drowned in Moon Lake and left his widow one hundred and fifty thousand in Government bonds. There were the Cutrere brothers, Wesley and Bates. Bates was one of my bright particular beaux! He got in a quarrel with that wild Wainright boy. They shot it out on the floor of Moon Lake Casino. Bates was shot through the stomach. Died in the ambulance on his way to Memphis. His widow was also well-provided for, came into eight or ten thousand acres, that's all. She married him on the rebound—never loved her—carried my picture on him the night he died! And there was that boy that every girl in the Delta had set her cap for! That beautiful, brilliant young Fitzhugh boy from Green County!

Tom: What did he leave his widow?

Amanda: He never married! Gracious, you talk as though all of my old admirers had turned up their toes to the daisies!

Tom: Isn't this the first you mentioned that still survives?

Amanda: That Fitzhugh boy went North and made a fortune—came to be known as the Wolf of Wall Street! He had the Midas touch, whatever he touched turned to gold! And I could have been Mrs. Duncan J. Fitzhugh, mind you! But—I picked your *father!*

Laura (rising): Mother, let me clear the table.

Amanda: No dear, you go in front and study your typewriter chart. Or practice your shorthand a little. Stay fresh and pretty!—It's almost time for our gentlemen callers to start arriving. (*She flounces girlishly toward the kitchenette.*) How many do you suppose we're going to entertain this afternoon?

Tom throws down the paper and jumps up with a groan.

Laura (alone in the dining room): I don't believe we're going to receive any, Mother.

Amanda (reappearing, airily): What? No one—not one? You must be joking! (*Laura nervously echoes her laugh. She slips in a fugitive manner through the half-open portieres and draws them gently behind her. A shaft of very clear light is thrown on her face against the jaded tapestry of the curtains.*) (**Music: "The Glass Menagerie" Under Faintly.**) (*Lightly.*) Not one gentleman caller? It can't be true! There must be a flood, there must have been a tornado!

Laura: It isn't a flood, it's not a tornado, Mother. I'm just not popular like you were in Blue Mountain. . . . (*Tom utters another groan. Laura glances at him with a faint, apologetic smile. Her voice catching a little.*) Mother's afraid I'm going to be an old maid.

(**The Scene Dims Out With "Glass Menagerie" Music.**)

SCENE II

"Laura, Haven't You Ever Liked Some Boy?"

On the dark stage the screen is lighted with the image of blue roses.

Gradually Laura's figure becomes apparent and the screen goes out.

The music subsides.

Laura is seated in the delicate ivory chair at the small clawfoot table.

She wears a dress of soft violet material for a kimono—her hair tied back from her forehead with a ribbon.

She is washing and polishing her collection of glass.

Amanda appears on the fire-escape steps. At the sound of her ascent, Laura catches her breath, thrusts the bowl of ornaments away and seats herself stiffly before the diagram of the typewriter keyboard as though it held her spellbound. Something has happened to Amanda. It is written in her face as she climbs to the landing: a look that is grim and hopeless and a little absurd.

She has on one of those cheap or imitation velvety-looking cloth coats with imitation fur collar. Her hat is five or six years old, one of those dreadful cloche hats that were worn in the late twenties, and she is clasping an enormous black patent-leather pocketbook with nickel clasp and initials. This is her full-dress outfit, the one she usually wears to the D.A.R.

Before entering she looks through the door.

She purses her lips, opens her eyes wide, rolls them upward and shakes her head.

Then she slowly lets herself in the door. Seeing her mother's expression Laura touches her lips with a nervous gesture.

Laura: Hello, Mother, I was—(She makes a nervous gesture toward the chart on the wall. Amanda leans against the shut door and stares at Laura with a martyred look.)
Amanda: Deception? Deception? (She slowly removes her hat and gloves, continuing the swift suffering stare. She lets the hat and gloves fall on the floor—a bit of acting.)
Laura (shakily): How was the D.A.R. meeting? (Amanda slowly opens her purse and removes a dainty white handkerchief which she shakes out delicately and delicately touches to her lips and nostrils.) Didn't you go to the D.A.R. meeting, Mother?
Amanda (faintly, almost inaudibly): —No.—No. (Then more forcibly.) I did not have the strength—to go to the D.A.R. In fact, I did not have the courage! I wanted to find a hole in the ground and hide myself in it forever! (She crosses slowly to the wall and removes the diagram of the typewriter keyboard. She holds it in front of her for a second, staring at it sweetly and sorrowfully—then bites her lips and tears it in two pieces.)
Laura (faintly): Why did you do that, Mother? (Amanda repeats the same procedure with the chart of the Gregg Alphabet.) Why are you—
Amanda: Why? Why? How old are you, Laura?
Laura: Mother, you know my age.
Amanda: I thought that you were an adult; it seems that I was mistaken. (She crosses slowly to the sofa and sinks down and stares at Laura.)
Laura: Please don't stare at me, Mother.

Amanda closes her eyes and lowers her head. Count ten.

Amanda: What are we going to do, what is going to become of us, what is the future?

Count ten.

Laura: Has something happened, Mother? (*Amanda draws a long breath and takes out the handkerchief again. Dabbing process.*) Mother, has—something happened?

Amanda: I'll be all right in a minute. I'm just bewildered—(*count five*)—by life . . .

Laura: Mother, I wish that you would tell me what's happened.

Amanda: As you know, I was supposed to be inducted into my office at the D.A.R. this afternoon. (**Image: A Swarm of Typewriters.**) But I stopped off at Rubicam's Business College to speak to your teachers about your having a cold and ask them what progress they thought you were making down there.

Laura: Oh . . .

Amanda: I went to the typing instructor and introduced myself as your mother. She didn't know who you were. Wingfield, she said. We don't have any such student enrolled at the school! I assured her she did, that you had been going to classes since early in January. "I wonder," she said, "if you could be talking about that terribly shy little girl who dropped out of school after only a few days' attendance?" "No," I said, "Laura, my daughter, has been going to school every day for the past six weeks!" "Excuse me," she said. She took the attendance book out and there was your name, unmistakably printed, and all the dates you were absent until they decided that you had dropped out of school. I still said, "No, there must have been some mistake! There must have been some mix-up in the records!" And she said, "No—I remember her perfectly now. Her hand shook so that she couldn't hit the right keys! The first time we gave a speed-test, she broke down completely—was sick at the stomach and almost had to be carried into the wash-room! After that morning she never showed up any more. We phoned the house but never got any answer"—while I was working at Famous and Barr, I suppose, demonstrating those—Oh! I felt so weak I could barely keep on my feet. I had to sit down while they got me a glass of water! Fifty dollars' tuition, all of our plans—my hopes and ambitions for you—just gone up the spout, just gone up the spout like that. (*Laura draws a long breath and gets awkwardly to her feet. She crosses to the victrola and winds it up.*) What are you doing?

Laura: Oh! (*She releases the handle and returns to her seat.*)

Amanda: Laura, where have you been going when you've gone out pretending that you were going to business college?

Laura: I've just been going out walking.

Amanda: That's not true.

Laura: It is. I just went walking.

Amanda: Walking? Walking? In winter? Deliberately courting pneumonia in that light coat? Where did you walk to, Laura?

Laura: It was the lesser of two evils, Mother. (**Image: Winter Scene In Park.**) I couldn't go back. I—threw up—on the floor!

Amanda: From half past seven till after five every day you mean to tell me you walked around in the park, because you wanted to make me think that you were still going to Rubicam's Business College?

Laura: It wasn't as bad as it sounds. I went inside places to get warmed up.

Amanda: Inside where?

Laura: I went in the art museum and the bird-houses at the Zoo. I visited the penguins every day! Sometimes I did without lunch and went to the movies. Lately I've been spending most of my afternoons in the Jewel-box, that big glass house where they raise the tropical flowers.

Amanda: You did all this to deceive me, just for the deception? (*Laura looks down.*) Why?

Laura: Mother, when you're disappointed, you get that awful suffering look on your face, like the picture of Jesus' mother in the museum!

Amanda: Hush!

Laura: I couldn't face it.

Pause. A whisper of strings.

(**Legend: "The Crust Of Humility."**)

Amanda (*hopelessly fingering the huge pocketbook*): So what are we going to do the rest of our lives? Stay home and watch the parades go by? Amuse ourselves with the glass menagerie, darling? Eternally play those worn-out phonograph records your father left as a painful reminder of him? We won't have a business career—we've given that up because it gave us nervous indigestion! (*Laughs wearily.*) What is there left but dependence all our lives? I know so well what becomes of unmarried women who aren't prepared to occupy a position. I've seen such pitiful cases in the South— barely tolerated spinsters living upon the grudging patronage of sister's husband or brother's wife!—stuck away in some little mouse-trap of a room—encouraged by one in-law to visit another—little birdlike women without any nest—eating the crust of humility all their life! Is that the future that we've mapped out for ourselves? I swear it's the only alternative I can think of! It isn't a very pleasant alternative, is it? Of course—some girls *do* marry. (*Laura twists her hands nervously.*) Haven't you ever liked some boy?

Laura: Yes I liked one once. (*Rises.*) I came across his picture a while ago.

Amanda (*with some interest*): He gave you his picture?

Laura: No, it's in the year-book.

Amanda (*disappointed*): Oh—a high-school boy.

(**Screen Image: Jim As A High-School Hero Bearing A Silver Cup.**)

Laura: Yes. His name was Jim. (*Laura lifts the heavy annual from the clawfoot table.*) Here he is in *The Pirates of Penzance.*

Amanda (absently): The what?

Laura: The operetta the senior class put on. He had a wonderful voice and we sat across the aisle from each other Mondays, Wednesdays, and Fridays in the Aud. Here he is with the silver cup for debating! See his grin?

Amanda (absently): He must have had a jolly disposition.

Laura: He used to call me—Blue Roses.

(Image: Blue Roses.)

Amanda: Why did he call you such a name as that?

Laura: When I had that attack of pleurosis—he asked me what was the matter when I came back. I said pleurosis—he thought that I said Blue Roses! So that's what he always called me after that. Whenever he saw me, he'd holler, "Hello, Blue Roses!" I didn't care for the girl he went out with. Emily Meisenbach. Emily was the best-dressed girl at Soldan. She never struck me, though, as being sincere . . . It says in the Personal Section—they're engaged. That's—six years ago! They must be married by now.

Amanda: Girls that aren't cut out for business careers usually wind up married to some nice man. *(Gets up with a spark of revival.)* Sister, that's what you'll do!

Laura utters a startled, doubtful laugh. She reaches quickly for a piece of glass.

Laura: But, Mother—

Amanda: Yes? *(Crossing to phonograph.)*

Laura (in a tone of frightened apology): I'm—crippled!

(Image: Screen.)

Amanda: Nonsense! Laura, I've told you never, never to use that word. Why, you're not crippled, you just have a little defect—hardly noticeable, even! When people have some slight disadvantage like that, they cultivate other things to make up for it—develop charm—and vivacity—and—*charm!* That's all you have to do! *(She turns again to the phonograph.)* One thing your father had *plenty of*—was *charm!*

Tom motions to the fiddle in the wings.

(The Scene Fades Out With Music.)

SCENE III

(Legend On The Screen: "After The Fiasco—")

Tom speaks from the fire-escape landing.

Tom: After the fiasco at Rubicam's Business College, the idea of getting a gentleman caller for Laura began to play a more important part in Mother's calculations. It became an obsession. Like some archetype of the universal unconscious, the image of the gentleman caller haunted our small apartment. . . . (**Image: Young Man At Door With Flowers.**) An evening at home rarely passed without some allusion to this image, this spectre, this hope. . . . Even when he wasn't mentioned, his presence hung in Mother's preoccupied look and in my sister's frightened, apologetic manner—hung like a sentence passed upon the Wingfields! Mother was a woman of action as well as words. She began to take logical steps in the planned direction. Late that winter and in the early spring—realizing that extra money would be needed to properly feather the nest and plume the bird—she conducted a vigorous campaign on the telephone, roping in subscribers to one of those magazines for matrons called *The Home-maker's Companion,* the type of journal that features the serialized sublimations of ladies of letters who think in terms of delicate cup-like breasts, slim, tapering waists, rich, creamy thighs, eyes like wood-smoke in autumn, fingers that soothe and caress like strains of music, bodies as powerful as Etruscan sculpture.

(**Screen Image: Glamor Magazine Cover.**)

Amanda enters with phone on long extension cord. She is spotted in the dim stage.

Amanda: Ida Scott? This is Amanda Wingfield! We *missed* you at the D.A.R. last Monday! I said to myself: She's probably suffering with that sinus condition! How is that sinus condition? Horrors! Heaven have mercy!—You're a Christian martyr, yes, that's what you are, a Christian martyr! Well, I just now happened to notice that your subscription to the *Companion's* about to expire! Yes, it expires with the next issue, honey!—just when that wonderful new serial by Bessie Mae Hopper is getting off to such an exciting start. Oh, honey, it's something that you can't miss! You remember how *Gone With the Wind* took everybody by storm? You simply couldn't go out if you hadn't read it. All everybody *talked* was Scarlett O'Hara. Well, this is a book that critics already compare to *Gone With the Wind.* It's the *Gone With the Wind* of the post-World War generation!—What?—Burning?—Oh, honey, don't let them burn, go take a look in the oven and I'll hold the wire! Heavens—I think she's hung up!

(**Dim Out.**)

(**Legend On Screen: "You Think I'm In Love With Continental Shoe-makers?"**)

Before the stage is lighted, the violent voices of Tom and Amanda are heard. They are quarreling behind the portieres. In front of them stands Laura with clenched hands and panicky expression.

A clear pool of light on her figure throughout this scene.

Tom: What in Christ's name am I—
Amanda (*shrilly*): Don't you use that—

Tom: Supposed to do!

Amanda: Expression! Not in my—

Tom: Ohhh!

Amanda: Presence! Have you gone out of your senses?

Tom: I have, that's true, *driven* out!

Amanda: What is the matter with you, you—big—big—IDIOT!

Tom: Look—I've got *no thing*, no single thing—

Amanda: Lower your voice!

Tom: In my life here that I can call my OWN! Everything is—

Amanda: Stop that shouting!

Tom: Yesterday you confiscated my books! You had the nerve to—

Amanda: I took that horrible novel back to the library—yes! That hideous book by that insane Mr. Lawrence. (*Tom laughs wildly.*) I cannot control the output of diseased minds or people who cater to them—(*Tom laughs still more wildly.*) BUT I WON'T ALLOW SUCH FILTH BROUGHT INTO MY HOUSE! No, no, no, no, no!

Tom: House, house! Who pays rent on it, who makes a slave of himself to—

Amanda (*fairly screeching*): Don't you DARE to—

Tom: No, no, I mustn't say things! *I've* got to just—

Amanda: Let me tell you—

Tom: I don't want to hear any more! (*He tears the portieres open. The upstage area is lit with a turgid smoky red glow.*)

Amanda's hair is in metal curlers and she wears a very old bathrobe, much too large for her slight figure, a relic of the faithless Mr. Wingfield.

An upright typewriter and a wild disarray of manuscripts are on the drop-leaf table. The quarrel was probably precipitated by Amanda's interruption of his creative labor. A chair lying overthrown on the floor.

Their gesticulating shadows are cast on the ceiling by the fiery glow.

Amanda: You *will* hear more, you—

Tom: No, I won't hear more, I'm going out!

Amanda: You come right back in—

Tom: Out, out out! Because I'm—

Amanda: Come back here, Tom Wingfield! I'm not through talking to you!

Tom: Oh, go—

Laura (*desperately*): Tom!

Amanda: You're going to listen, and no more insolence from you! I'm at the end of my patience! (*He comes back toward her.*)

Tom: What do you think I'm at? Aren't I supposed to have any patience to reach the end of, Mother? I know, I know. It seems unimportant to you, what I'm *doing*—what *I* want to do—having a little *difference* between them! You don't think that—

Amanda: I think you've been doing things that you're ashamed of. That's why you act like this. I don't believe that you go every night to the movies. Nobody goes to the movies night after night. Nobody in their right minds goes to the movies as often as you pretend to. People don't go to the movies at nearly midnight, and movies don't let out at two A.M. Come in stumbling. Muttering to yourself like a maniac! You get three hours' sleep and then go to work. Oh, I can picture the way you're doing down there. Moping, doping, because you're in no condition.

Tom (wildly): No, I'm in no condition!

Amanda: What right have you got to jeopardize your job? Jeopardize the security of us all? How do you think we'd manage if you were—

Tom: Listen! You think I'm crazy *about* the *warehouse?* (*He bends fiercely toward her slight figure.*) You think I'm in love with the Continental Shoemakers? You think I want to spend fifty-five *years* down there in that—*celotex interior!* with—*fluorescent—tubes!* Look! I'd rather somebody picked up a crowbar and battered out my brains—than go back mornings! I *go!* Every time you come in yelling that God damn *"Rise and Shine!" "Rise and Shine!"* I say to myself "How *lucky dead* people are!" But I get up. I *go!* For sixty-five dollars a month I give up all that I dream of doing and being *ever!* And you say self—*self's* all I ever think of. Why, listen, if self is what I thought of, Mother, I'd be where he is— GONE! (*Pointing to father's picture.*) As far as the system of transportation reaches! (*He starts past her. She grabs his arm.*) Don't grab at me, Mother!

Amanda: Where are you going?

Tom: I'm going to the *movies!*

Amanda: I don't believe that lie!

Tom (crouching toward her, overtowering her tiny figure. She backs away, gasping): I'm going to opium dens! Yes, opium dens, dens of vice and criminals' hang-outs, Mother. I've joined the Hogan gang, I'm a hired assassin, I carry a tommy-gun in a violin case! I run a string of cat-houses in the Valley! They call me Killer, Killer Wingfield, I'm leading a double-life, a simple, honest warehouse worker by day, by night a dynamic *czar* of the *underworld,* Mother. I go to gambling casinos, I spin away fortunes on the roulette table! I wear a patch over one eye and a false mustache, sometimes I put on green whiskers. On those occasions they call me—*El Diablo!* Oh, I could tell you things to make you sleepless! My enemies plan to dynamite this place. They're going to blow us all sky-high some night! I'll be glad, very happy, and so will you! You'll go up, up on a broomstick, over Blue Mountain with seventeen gentlemen callers! You ugly—babbling old—*witch.* . . . (*He goes through a series of violent, clumsy movements, seizing his overcoat, lunging to the door, pulling it fiercely open. The women watch him, aghast. His arm catches in the sleeve of the coat as he struggles to pull it on. For a moment he is pinioned by the bulky garment. With an outraged groan he tears the coat off again, splitting the shoulders of it, and hurls it across the room. It strikes against the shelf of Laura's glass collection, there is a tinkle of shattering glass. Laura cries out as if wounded.*)

(Music Legend: "The Glass Menagerie.")

Laura (shrilly): My glass!—menagerie. . . . (*She covers her face and turns away.*)

But Amanda is still stunned and stupefied by the "ugly witch" so that she barely notices this occurrence. Now she recovers her speech.

Amanda (*in an awful voice*): I won't speak to you—until you apologize! (*She crosses through portieres and draws them together behind her. Tom is left with Laura. Laura clings weakly to the mantel with her face averted. Tom stares at her stupidly for a moment. Then he crosses to shelf. Drops awkwardly to his knees to collect the fallen glass, glancing at Laura as if he would speak but couldn't.*)

("The Glass Menagerie" steals in as the Scene Dims Out.)

SCENE IV

The interior is dark. Faint in the alley.

A deep-voiced bell in a church is tolling the hour of five as the scene commences.

Tom appears at the top of the alley. After each solemn boom of the bell in the tower, he shakes a little noise-maker or rattle as if to express the tiny spasm of man in contrast to the sustained power and dignity of the Almighty. This and the unsteadiness of his advance make it evident that he has been drinking.

As he climbs the few steps to the fire-escape landing light steals up inside. Laura appears in night-dress, observing Tom's empty bed in the front room.

Tom fishes in his pockets for the door-key, removing a motley assortment of articles in the search, including a perfect shower of movie-ticket stubs and an empty bottle. At last he finds the key, but just as he is about to insert it, it slips from his fingers. He strikes a match and crouches below the door.

Tom (*bitterly*): One crack—and it falls through!

(*Laura opens the door.*)

Laura: Tom! Tom, what are you doing?
Tom: Looking for a door-key.
Laura: Where have you been all this time?
Tom: I have been to the movies.
Laura: All this time at the movies?
Tom: There was a very long program. There was a Garbo picture and a Mickey Mouse and a travelogue and a newsreel and a preview of coming attractions. And there was an organ solo and a collection for the milk-fund—simultaneously—which ended up in a terrible fight between a fat lady and an usher!
Laura (*innocently*): Did you have to stay through everything?
Tom: Of course! And, oh, I forgot! There was a big stage show! The headliner on this stage show was Malvolio the Magician. He performed wonderful tricks, many of them, such as pouring water back and forth between pitchers. First it turned to wine and then it turned to beer and then it turned

to whiskey. I know it was whiskey it finally turned into because he needed somebody to come up out of the audience to help him, and I came up—both shows! It was Kentucky Straight Bourbon. A very generous fellow, he gave souvenirs. (*He pulls from his back pocket a shimmering rainbow-colored scarf.*) He gave me this. This is his magic scarf. You can have it, Laura. You wave it over a canary cage and you get a bowl of gold-fish. You wave it over the gold-fish bowl and they fly away canaries. . . . But the wonderfullest trick of all was the coffin trick. We nailed him into a coffin and he got out of the coffin without removing one nail. (*He has come inside.*) There is a trick that would come in handy for me—get me out of this 2 by 4 situation! (*Flops onto bed and starts removing shoes.*)

Laura: Tom—Shhh!

Tom: What're you shushing me for?

Laura: You'll wake up Mother.

Tom: Goody, goody! Pay'er back for all those "Rise an' Shines." (*Lies down, groaning.*) You know it don't take much intelligence to get yourself into a nailed-up coffin, Laura. But who in hell ever got himself out of one without removing one nail?

As if in answer, the father's grinning photograph lights up.

(Scene Dims Out.)

Immediately following: The church bell is heard striking six. At the sixth stroke the alarm clock goes off in Amanda's room, and after a few moments we hear her calling: "Rise and Shine! Rise and Shine! Laura, go tell your brother to rise and shine!"

Tom (sitting up slowly): I'll rise—but I won't shine.

The light increases.

Amanda: Laura, tell your brother his coffee is ready.

Laura slips into front room.

Laura: Tom! it's nearly seven. Don't make Mother nervous. (*He stares at her stupidly. Beseechingly.*) Tom, speak to Mother this morning. Make up with her, apologize, speak to her!

Tom: She won't to me. It's her that started not speaking.

Laura: If you just say you're sorry she'll start speaking.

Tom: Her not speaking—is that such a tragedy?

Laura: Please—please!

Amanda (calling from kitchenette): Laura, are you going to do what I asked you to do, or do I have to get dressed and go out myself?

Laura: Going, going—soon as I get on my coat! (*She pulls on a shapeless felt hat with nervous, jerky movements, pleadingly glancing at Tom. Rushes awkwardly for coat. The coat is one of Amanda's inaccurately made-over, the sleeves too short for Laura.*) Butter and what else?

Amanda (entering upstage): Just butter. Tell them to charge it.

Laura: Mother, they make such faces when I do that.

Amanda: Sticks and stones may break my bones, but the expression on Mr. Garfinkel's face won't harm us! Tell your brother his coffee is getting cold.

Laura (at door): Do what I asked you, will you, will you, Tom?

He looks sullenly away.

Amanda: Laura, go now or just don't go at all!

Laura (rushing out): Going—going! (*A second later she cries out. Tom springs up and crosses to the door. Amanda rushes anxiously in. Tom opens the door.*)

Tom: Laura?

Laura: I'm all right. I slipped, but I'm all right.

Amanda (peering anxiously after her): If anyone breaks a leg on those fire-escape steps, the landlord ought to be sued for every cent he possesses! (*She shuts door. Remembers she isn't speaking and returns to other room.*)

As Tom enters listlessly for his coffee, she turns her back to him and stands rigidly facing the window on the gloomy gray vault of the areaway. Its light on her face with its aged but childish features is cruelly sharp, satirical as a Daumier print.

(Music Under: "Ave Maria.")

Tom glances sheepishly but sullenly at her averted figure and slumps at the table. The coffee is scalding hot; he sips it and gasps and spits it back in the cup. At his gasp, Amanda catches her breath and half turns. Then catches herself and turns back to window.

Tom blows on his coffee, glancing sidewise at his mother. She clears her throat. Tom clears his. He starts to rise. Sinks back down again, scratches his head, clears his throat again. Amanda coughs. Tom raises his cup in both hands to blow on it, his eyes staring over the rim of it at his mother for several moments. Then he slowly sets the cup down and awkwardly and hesitantly rises from the chair.

Tom (hoarsely): Mother. I—I apologize. Mother. (*Amanda draws a quick, shuddering breath. Her face works grotesquely. She breaks into childlike tears.*) I'm sorry for what I said, for everything that I said, I didn't mean it.

Amanda (sobbingly): My devotion has made me a witch and so I make myself hateful to my children!

Tom: No, you *don't.*

Amanda: I worry so much, don't sleep, it makes me nervous!

Tom (gently): I understand that.

Amanda: I've had to put up a solitary battle all these years. But you're my right-hand bower! Don't fall down, don't fail!

Tom (gently): I try, Mother.

Amanda (*with great enthusiasm*): Try and you will SUCCEED! (*The notion makes her breathless.*) Why, you—you're just *full* of natural endowments! Both of my children—they're *unusual* children! Don't you think I know it? I'm so—proud! Happy and—feel I've—so much to be thankful for but—Promise me one thing, son!

Tom: What, Mother?

Amanda: Promise, son you'll—never be a drunkard!

Tom (*turns to her grinning*): I will never be a drunkard, Mother.

Amanda: That's what frightened me so, that you'd be drinking! Eat a bowl of Purina!

Tom: Just coffee, Mother.

Amanda: Shredded wheat biscuit?

Tom: No. No, Mother, just coffee.

Amanda: You can't put in a day's work on an empty stomach. You've got ten minutes—don't gulp! Drinking too-hot liquids makes cancer of the stomach. . . . Put cream in.

Tom: No, thank you.

Amanda: To cool it.

Tom: No! No, thank you, I want it black.

Amanda: I know, but it's not good for you. We have to do all that we can to build ourselves up. In these trying times we live in, all that we have to cling to is—each other. . . . That's why it's so important to—Tom, I—I sent out your sister so I could discuss something with you. If you hadn't spoken I would have spoken to you. (*Sits down.*)

Tom (*gently*): What is it, Mother, that you want to discuss?

Amanda: Laura!

Tom puts his cup down slowly.

(Legend On Screen: "Laura.")

(Music: "The Glass Menagerie.")

Tom: —Oh.—Laura . . .

Amanda (*touching his sleeve*): You know how Laura is. So quiet but—still water runs deep! She notices things and I think she—broods about them. (*Tom looks up.*) A few days ago I came in and she was crying.

Tom: What about?

Amanda: You.

Tom: Me?

Amanda: She has an idea that you're not happy here.

Tom: What gave her that idea?

Amanda: What gives her any idea? However, you do act strangely. I—I'm not criticizing, understand *that*! I know your ambitions do not lie in the warehouse, that like everybody in the whole wide world—you've had to—make sacrifices, but—Tom—Tom—life's not easy, it calls for—Spartan endurance!

There's so many things in my heart that I cannot describe to you! I've never told you but I—*loved* your father. . . .

Tom (*gently*): I know that, Mother.

Amanda: And you—when I see you taking after his ways! Staying out late—and—well, you had been drinking the night you were in that—terrifying condition! Laura says that you hate the apartment and that you go out nights to get away from it! Is that true, Tom?

Tom: No. You say there's so much in your heart that you can't describe to me. That's true of me, too. There's so much in my heart that I can't describe to you! So let's respect each other's—

Amanda: But, why—*why*, Tom—are you always so *restless?* Where do you go to, nights?

Tom: I—go to the movies.

Amanda: Why do you go to the movies so much, Tom?

Tom: I go to the movies because—I like adventure. Adventure is something I don't have much of at work, so I go to the movies.

Amanda: But, Tom, you go to the movies *entirely* too *much!*

Tom: I like a lot of adventure.

> *Amanda looks baffled, then hurt. As the familiar inquisition resumes he becomes hard and impatient again. Amanda slips back into her querulous attitude toward him.*

(Image On Screen: Sailing Vessel With Jolly Roger.)

Amanda: Most young men find adventure in their careers.

Tom: Then most young men are not employed in a warehouse.

Amanda: The world is full of young men employed in warehouses and offices and factories.

Tom: Do all of them find adventure in their careers?

Amanda: They do or they do without it! Not everybody has a craze for adventure.

Tom: Man is by instinct a lover, a hunter, a fighter, and none of those instincts are given much play at the warehouse!

Amanda: Man is by instinct! Don't quote instinct to me! Instinct is something that people have got away from! It belongs to animals! Christian adults don't want it!

Tom: What do Christian adults want, then, Mother?

Amanda: Superior things! Things of the mind and the spirit! Only animals have to satisfy instincts! Surely your aims are somewhat higher than theirs! Than monkeys—pigs—

Tom: I reckon they're not.

Amanda: You're joking. However, that isn't what I wanted to discuss.

Tom (*rising*): I haven't much time.

Amanda (*pushing his shoulder*): Sit down.

Tom: You want me to punch in red at the warehouse, Mother?

Amanda: You have five minutes. I want to talk about Laura.

(Legend: "Plans And Provisions.")

Tom: All right! What about Laura?

Amanda: We have to be making plans and provisions for her. She's older than you, two years, and nothing has happened. She just drifts along doing nothing. It frightens me terribly how she just drifts along.

Tom: I guess she's the type that people call home girls.

Amanda: There's no such type, and if there is, it's a pity! That is unless the home is hers, with a husband!

Tom: What?

Amanda: Oh, I can see the handwriting on the wall as plain as I see the nose in front of my face! It's terrifying! More and more you remind me of your father! He was out all hours without explanation—Then *left!* Goodbye! And me with the bag to hold. I saw that letter you got from the Merchant Marine. I know what you're dreaming of. I'm not standing here blindfolded. Very well, then. Then *do* it! But not till there's somebody to take your place.

Tom: What do you mean?

Amanda: I mean that as soon as Laura has got somebody to take care of her, married, a home of her own, independent—why, then you'll be free to go wherever you please, on land, on sea, whichever way the wind blows! But until that time you've got to look out for your sister. I don't say me because I'm old and don't matter! I say for your sister because she's young and depen-dent. I put her in business college—a dismal failure! Frightened her so it made her sick to her stomach. I took her over to the Young People's League at the church. Another fiasco. She spoke to nobody, nobody spoke to her. Now all she does is fool with those pieces of glass and play those worn-out records. What kind of a life is that for a girl to lead!

Tom: What can I do about it?

Amanda: Overcome selfishness! Self, self, self is all that you ever think of! (*Tom springs up and crosses to get his coat. It is ugly and bulky. He pulls on a cap with earmuffs.*) Where is your muffler? Put your wool muffler on! (*He snatches it angrily from the closet and tosses it around his neck and pulls both ends tight.*) Tom! I haven't said what I had in mind to ask you.

Tom: I'm too late to—

Amanda (*catching his arms—very importunately. Then shyly*): Down at the warehouse, aren't there some—nice young men?

Tom: No!

Amanda: There *must* be—some . . .

Tom: Mother—

Gesture.

Amanda: Find one that's clean-living—doesn't drink and—ask him out for sister!

Tom: What?

Amanda: For *Sister!* To meet! Get *acquainted!*

Tom (stamping to door): Oh, my go-osh!

Amanda: Will you? (*He opens door. Imploringly.*) Will you? (*He starts down.*) Will you? Will, you, dear?

Tom (calling back): YES!

Amanda closes the door hesitantly and with a troubled but faintly hopeful expression.

(Screen Image: Glamor Magazine Cover.)

Spot Amanda at phone.

Amanda: Ella Cartwright? This is Amanda Wingfield! How are you, honey? How is that kidney condition? (*Count five.*) Horrors! (*Count five.*) You're a Christian martyr, yes, honey, that's what you are, a Christian martyr! Well, I just happened to notice in my little red book that your subscription to the *Companion* has just run out! I knew that you wouldn't want to miss out on the wonderful serial starting in this new issue. It's by Bessie Mae Hopper, the first thing she's written since *Honeymoon for Three.* Wasn't that a strange and interesting story? Well, this one is even lovelier, I believe. It has a so-phisticated society background. It's all about the horsey set on Long Island!

(Fade Out.)

Scene V

(Legend On Screen: "Annunciation.") *Fade with music.*

It is early dusk of a spring evening. Supper has just been finished in the Wingfield apart-ment. Amanda and Laura in light colored dresses are removing dishes from the table, in the upstage area, which is shadowy, their movements formalized almost as a dance or ritual, their moving forms as pale and silent as moths.

Tom, in white shirt and trousers, rises from the table and crosses toward the fire-escape.

Amanda (as he passes her): Son, will you do me a favor?

Tom: What?

Amanda: Comb your hair! You look so pretty when your hair is combed! (*Tom slouches on sofa with evening paper. Enormous caption "Franco Triumphs."*) There is only one respect in which I would like you to emulate your father.

Tom: What respect is that?

Amanda: The care he always took of his appearance. He never allowed himself to look untidy. (*He throws down the paper and crosses to fire-escape.*) Where are you going?

Tom: I'm going out to smoke.

Amanda: You smoke too much. A pack a day at fifteen cents a pack. How much would that amount to in a month? Thirty times fifteen is how much, Tom? Figure it out and you will be astounded at what you could save. Enough to give you a night-school course in accounting at Washington U! Just think what a wonderful thing that would be for you, son!

Tom is unmoved by the thought.

Tom: I'd rather smoke. (*He steps out on landing, letting the screen door slam.*)

Amanda (*sharply*): I know! That's the tragedy of it. . . . (*Alone, she turns to look at her husband's picture.*)

(Dance Music: "All The World Is Waiting For The Sunrise.")

Tom (*to the audience*): Across the alley from us was the Paradise Dance Hall. On evenings in spring the windows and doors were open and the music came outdoors. Sometimes the lights were turned out except for a large glass sphere that hung from the ceiling. It would turn slowly about and filter the dusk with delicate rainbow colors. Then the orchestra played a waltz or a tango, something that had a slow and sensuous rhythm. Couples would come outside, to the relative privacy of the alley. You could see them kissing behind ash-pits and telephone poles. This was the compensation for lives that passed like mine, without any change or adventure. Adventure and change were imminent in this year. They were waiting around the corner for all these kids. Suspended in the mist over Berchtesgaden, caught in the folds of Chamberlain's umbrella—In Spain there was Guernica! But here there was only hot swing music and liquor, dance halls, bars, and movies, and sex that hung in the gloom like a chandelier and flooded the world with brief, deceptive rainbows. . . . All the world was waiting for bombardments!

Amanda turns from the picture and comes outside.

Amanda (*sighing*): A fire-escape landing's a poor excuse for a porch. (*She spreads a newspaper on a step and sits down, gracefully and demurely as if she were settling into a swing on a Mississippi veranda.*) What are you looking at?

Tom: The moon.

Amanda: Is there a moon this evening?

Tom: It's rising over Garfinkel's Delicatessen.

Amanda: So it is! A little silver slipper of a moon. Have you made a wish on it yet?

Tom: Um-hum.

Amanda: What did you wish for?

Tom: That's a secret.

Amanda: A secret, huh? Well, I won't tell mine either. I will be just as mysterious as you.

Tom: I bet I can guess what yours is.

Amanda: Is my head so transparent?

Tom: You're not a sphinx.

Amanda: No, I don't have secrets. I'll tell you what I wished for on the moon. Success and happiness for my precious children! I wish for that whenever there's a moon, and when there isn't a moon, I wish for it, too.

Tom: I thought perhaps you wished for a gentleman caller.

Amanda: Why do you say that?

Tom: Don't you remember asking me to fetch one?

Amanda: I remember suggesting that it would be nice for your sister if you brought home some nice young man from the warehouse. I think I've made that suggestion more than once.

Tom: Yes, you have made it repeatedly.

Amanda: Well?

Tom: We are going to have one.

Amanda: What?

Tom: A gentleman caller!

(The Annunciation Is Celebrated With Music.)

Amanda rises.

(Image On Screen: Caller With Bouquet.)

Amanda: You mean you have asked some nice young man to come over?

Tom: Yep. I've asked him to dinner.

Amanda: You really did?

Tom: I did!

Amanda: You did, and did he—*accept?*

Tom: He did!

Amanda: Well, well—well, well! That's—lovely!

Tom: I thought that you would be pleased.

Amanda: It's definite, then?

Tom: Very definite.

Amanda: Soon?

Tom: Very soon.

Amanda: For heaven's sake, stop putting on and tell me some things, will you?

Tom: What things do you want me to tell you?

Amanda: Naturally I would like to know when he's *coming!*

Tom: He's coming tomorrow.

Amanda: Tomorrow?

Tom: Yep. Tomorrow.

Amanda: But, Tom!

Tom: Yes, Mother?

Amanda: Tomorrow gives me no time!

Tom: Time for what?

Amanda: Preparations! Why didn't you phone me at once, as soon as you asked him, the minute that he accepted? Then, don't you see, I could have been getting ready!

Tom: You don't have to make any fuss.

Amanda: Oh, Tom, Tom, Tom, of course I have to make a fuss! I want things nice, not sloppy! Not thrown together. I'll certainly have to do some fast thinking, won't I?

Tom: I don't see why you have to think at all.

Amanda: You just don't know. We can't have a gentleman caller in a pig-sty! All my wedding silver has to be polished, the monogrammed table linen ought to be laundered! The windows have to be washed and fresh curtains put up. And how about clothes? We have to *wear* something, don't we?

Tom: Mother, this boy is no one to make a fuss over!

Amanda: Do you realize he's the first young man we've introduced to your sister? It's terrible, dreadful, disgraceful that poor little sister has never received a single gentleman caller! Tom, come inside! (*She opens the screen door.*)

Tom: What for?

Amanda: I want to ask you some things.

Tom: If you're going to make such a fuss, I'll call it off, I'll tell him not to come.

Amanda: You certainly won't do anything of the kind. Nothing offends people worse than broken engagements. It simply means I'll have to work like a Turk! We won't be brilliant, but we'll pass inspection. Come on inside. (*Tom follows, groaning.*) Sit down.

Tom: Any particular place you would like me to sit?

Amanda: Thank heavens I've got that new sofa! I'm also making payments on a floor lamp I'll have sent out! And put the chintz covers on, they'll brighten things up! Of course I'd hoped to have these walls re-papered. . . . What is the young man's name?

Tom: His name is O'Connor.

Amanda: That, of course, means fish—tomorrow is Friday! I'll have that salmon loaf—with Durkee's dressing! What does he do? He works at the warehouse?

Tom: Of course! How else would I—

Amanda: Tom, he—doesn't drink?

Tom: Why do you ask me that?

Amanda: Your father *did!*

Tom: Don't get started on that!

Amanda: He *does* drink, then?

Tom: Not that I know of!

Amanda: Make sure, be certain! The last thing I want for my daughter's a boy who drinks!

Tom: Aren't you being a little premature? Mr. O'Connor has not yet appeared on the scene!

Amanda: But will tomorrow. To meet your sister, and what do I know about his character? Nothing! Old maids are better off than wives of drunkards!

Tom: Oh, my God!

Amanda: Be still!

Tom (*leaning forward to whisper*): Lots of fellows meet girls whom they don't marry!

Amanda: Oh, talk sensibly, Tom—and don't be sarcastic! (*She has gotten a hair-brush.*)

Tom: What are you doing?

Amanda: I'm brushing that cow-lick down! What is this young man's position at the warehouse?

Tom (*submitting grimly to the brush and the interrogation*): This young man's position is that of a shipping clerk, Mother.

Amanda: Sounds to me like a fairly responsible job, the sort of a job *you* would be in if you just had more *get-up*. What is his salary? Have you got any idea?

Tom: I would judge it to be approximately eighty-five dollars a month.

Amanda: Well—not princely, but—

Tom: Twenty more than I make.

Amanda: Yes, how well I know! But for a family man, eighty-five dollars a month is not much more than you can just get by on. . . .

Tom: Yes, but Mr. O'Connor is not a family man.

Amanda: He might be, mightn't he? Some time in the future?

Tom: I see. Plans and provisions.

Amanda: You are the only young man that I know of who ignores the fact that the future becomes the present, the present the past, and the past turns into everlasting regret if you don't plan for it!

Tom: I will think that over and see what I can make of it!

Amanda: Don't be supercilious with your mother! Tell me some more about this—what do you call him?

Tom: James D. O'Connor. The D. is for Delaney.

Amanda: Irish on *both* sides! *Gracious!* And doesn't drink?

Tom: Shall I call him up and ask him right this minute?

Amanda: The only way to find out about those things is to make discreet inquiries at the proper moment. When I was a girl in Blue Mountain and it was suspected that a young man drank, the girl whose attentions he had been receiving, if any girl *was*, would sometimes speak to the minister of his church, or rather her father would if her father was living, and sort of feel him out on the young man's character. That is the way such things are discreetly handled to keep a young woman from making a tragic mistake!

Tom: Then how did you happen to make a tragic mistake?

Amanda: That innocent look of your father's had everyone fooled! He *smiled*— the world was *enchanted!* No girl can do worse than put herself at the mercy of a handsome appearance! I hope that Mr. O'Connor is not too good-looking.

Tom: No, he's not too good-looking. He's covered with freckles and hasn't too much of a nose.

Amanda: He's not right-down homely, though?

Tom: Not right-down homely. Just medium homely, I'd say.

Amanda: Character's what to look for in a man.

Tom: That's what I've always said, Mother.

Amanda: You've never said anything of the kind and I suspect you would never give it a thought.

Tom: Don't be suspicious of me.

Amanda: At least I hope he's the type that's up and coming.

Tom: I think he really goes in for self-improvement.

Amanda: What reason have you to think so?

Tom: He goes to night school.

Amanda (*beaming*): Splendid! What does he do, I mean study?

Tom: Radio engineering and public speaking!

Amanda: Then he has visions of being advanced in the world! Any young man who studies public speaking is aiming to have an executive job some day! And radio engineering? A thing for the future! Both of these facts are very illuminating. Those are the sort of things that a mother should know concerning any young man who comes to call on her daughter. Seriously or—not.

Tom: One little warning. He doesn't know about Laura. I didn't let on that we had dark ulterior motives. I just said, why don't you come have dinner with us? He said okay and that was the whole conversation.

Amanda: I bet it was! You're eloquent as an oyster. However, he'll know about Laura when he gets here. When he sees how lovely and sweet and pretty she is, he'll thank his lucky stars he was asked to dinner.

Tom: Mother, you mustn't expect too much of Laura.

Amanda: What do you mean?

Tom: Laura seems all those things to you and me because she's ours and we love her. We don't even notice she's crippled any more.

Amanda: Don't say crippled! You know that I never allow that word to be used!

Tom: But face facts, Mother. She is and—that not's all—

Amanda: What do you mean "not all"?

Tom: Laura is very different from other girls.

Amanda: I think the difference is all to her advantage.

Tom: Not quite all—in the eyes of others—strangers—she's terribly shy and lives in a world of her own and those things make her seem a little peculiar to people outside the house.

Amanda: Don't say peculiar.

Tom: Face the facts. She is.

(The Dance-Hall Music Changes To A Tango That Has A Minor And Somewhat Ominous Tone.)

Amanda: In what way is she peculiar—may I ask?

Tom (*gently*): She lives in a world of her own—a world of—little glass ornaments, Mother. . . . (*Gets up. Amanda remains holding brush, looking at him, troubled.*) She plays old phonograph records and—that's about all—(*He glances at himself in the mirror and crosses to door.*)

Amanda (*sharply*): Where are you going?

Tom: I'm going to the movies. (*Out screen door.*)

Amanda: Not to the movies, every night to the movies! (*Follows quickly to screen door.*) I don't believe you always go to the movies! (*He is gone. Amanda looks worriedly after him for a moment. Then vitality and optimism return and she turns from the door. Crossing to portieres.*) Laura! Laura! (*Laura answers from kitchenette.*)

Laura: Yes, Mother.

Amanda: Let those dishes go and come in front! (*Laura appears with dish towel. Gaily.*) Laura, come here and make a wish on the moon!

Laura (entering): Moon—moon?

Amanda: A little silver slipper of a moon. Look over your left shoulder, Laura, and make a wish! (*Laura looks faintly puzzled as if called out of sleep. Amanda seizes her shoulders and turns her at an angle by the door.*) Now! Now, darling, wish!

Laura: What shall I wish for, Mother?

Amanda (her voice trembling and her eyes suddenly filling with tears): Happiness! Good Fortune!

The violin rises and the stage dims out.

SCENE VI

(Image: High-School Hero.)

Tom: And so the following evening I brought him home to dinner. I had known Jim slightly in high school. In high school Jim was a hero. He had tremendous Irish good nature and vitality with the scrubbed and polished look of white chinaware. He seemed to move in a continual spotlight. He was a star in basketball, captain of the debating club, president of the senior class and the glee club and he sang the male lead in the annual light operas. He was always running or bounding, never just walking. He seemed always at the point of defeating the law of gravity. He was shooting with such velocity through his adolescence that you would logically expect him to arrive at nothing short of the White House by the time he was thirty. But Jim apparently ran into more interference after his graduation from Soldan. His speed had definitely slowed. Six years after he left high school he was holding a job that wasn't much better than mine.

(Image: Clerk.)

He was the only one at the warehouse with whom I was on friendly terms. I was valuable to him as someone who could remember his former glory, who had seen him win basketball games and the silver cup in debating. He knew of my secret practice of retiring to a cabinet of the washroom to work on my poems when business was slack in the warehouse. He called me Shakespeare. And while the other boys in the warehouse regarded me with suspicious hostility, Jim took a humorous attitude toward me. Gradually his attitude affected the others, their hostility wore off and they also began to smile at me as people smile at an oddly fashioned dog who trots across their path at some distance.

I knew that Jim and Laura had known each other at Soldan, and I had heard Laura speak admiringly of his voice. I didn't know if Jim remembered her or not. In high school Laura had been as unobtrusive as Jim had been astonishing. If he did remember Laura, it was not as my sister, for when I asked him to dinner, he grinned and said, "You know, Shakespeare, I never thought of you as having folks!"

He was about to discover that I did. . . .

(Light Up Stage.)

(Legend On Screen: "The Accent Of A Coming Foot.")

Friday evening. It is about five o'clock of a late spring evening which comes "scattering poems in the sky."

A delicate lemony light is in the Wingfield apartment.

Amanda has worked like a Turk in preparation for the gentleman caller. The results are astonishing. The new floor lamp with its rose-silk shade is in place, a colored paper lantern conceals the broken light fixture in the ceiling, new billowing white curtains are at the windows, chintz covers are on chairs and sofa, a pair of new sofa pillows make their initial appearance.

Open boxes and tissue paper are scattered on the floor.

Laura stands in the middle with lifted arms while Amanda crouches before her, adjusting the hem of the new dress, devout and ritualistic. The dress is colored and designed by memory. The arrangement of Laura's hair is changed; it is softer and more becoming. A fragile, unearthly prettiness has come out in Laura: she is like a piece of translucent glass touched by light, given a momentary radiance, not actual, not lasting.

Amanda (*impatiently*): Why are you trembling?
Laura: Mother, you've made me so nervous!
Amanda: How have I made you nervous?
Laura: By all this fuss! You make it seem so important!
Amanda: I don't understand you, Laura. You couldn't be satisfied with just sitting home, and yet whenever I try to arrange something for you, you seem to resist it. (*She gets up.*) Now take a look at yourself. No, wait! Wait just a moment—I have an idea!
Laura: What is it now?

Amanda produces two powder puffs which she wraps in handkerchiefs and stuffs in Laura's bosom.

Laura: Mother, what are you doing?
Amanda: They call them "Gay Deceivers"!

Laura: I won't wear them!

Amanda: You will!

Laura: Why should I?

Amanda: Because, to be painfully honest, your chest is flat.

Laura: You make it seem like we were setting a trap.

Amanda: All pretty girls are a trap, a pretty trap, and men expect them to be. **(Legend: "A Pretty Trap.")** Now look at yourself, young lady. This is the prettiest you will ever be! I've got to fix myself now! You're going to be surprised by your mother's appearance! (*She crosses through the portieres, humming gaily.*)

Laura moves slowly to the long mirror and stares solemnly at herself.

A wind blows the white curtains inward in a slow, graceful motion and with a faint, sorrowful sighing.

Amanda (*offstage*): It isn't dark enough yet. (*She turns slowly before the mirror with a troubled look.*)

(Legend On Screen: "This Is My Sister: Celebrate Her With Strings!" Music.)

Amanda (*laughing, off*): I'm going to show you something. I'm going to make a spectacular appearance!

Laura: What is it, Mother?

Amanda: Possess your soul in patience—you will see! Something I've resurrected from that old trunk! Styles haven't changed so terribly much after all. . . . (*She parts the portieres.*) Now just look at your mother! (*She wears a girlish frock of yellowed voile with a blue silk sash. She carries a bunch of jonquils—the legend of her youth is nearly revived. Feverishly.*) This is the dress in which I led the cotillion. Won the cakewalk twice at Sunset Hill, wore one spring to the Governor's ball in Jackson! See how I sashayed around the ballroom, Laura? (*She raises her skirt and does a mincing step around the room.*) I wore it on Sundays for my gentlemen callers! I had it on the day I met your father— I had malaria fever all that spring. The change of climate from East Tennessee to the Delta—weakened resistance—I had a little temperature all the time—not enough to be serious—just enough to make me restless and giddy! Invitations poured in—parties all over the Delta!—"Stay in bed," said Mother, "you have fever!"—but I just wouldn't.—I took quinine but kept on going, going!—Evenings, dances!—Afternoons, long, long rides! Picnics—lovely!—So lovely, that country in May.—All lacy with dogwood, literally flooded with jonquils!—That was the spring I had the craze for jonquils. Jonquils became an absolute obsession. Mother said, "Honey, there's no more room for jonquils." And still I kept bringing in more jonquils. Whenever, wherever I saw them, I'd say, "Stop! Stop! I see jonquils!" I made the young men help me gather the jonquils! It was a joke, Amanda and her jonquils! Finally there were no more vases to hold them, every available space was filled with jonquils. No vases to hold them? All right, I'll hold them myself! And then I—(*She stops in front of the picture.*) (**Music.**) met your father! Malaria fever and jonquils and then—this—boy. . . . (*She switches on the rose-colored lamp.*) I hope they get here before it starts to rain. (*She crosses upstage and places the jonquils in bowl on table.*) I gave your brother a little extra change so he and Mr. O'Connor could take the service car home.

Laura (*with altered look*): What did you say his name was?

Amanda: O'Connor.

Laura: What is his first name?

Amanda: I don't remember. Oh, yes, I do. It was—Jim!

Laura sways slightly and catches hold of a chair.

(Legend On Screen. "Not Jim!")

Laura (*faintly*): Not—Jim!

Amanda: Yes, that was it, it was Jim! I've never known a Jim that wasn't nice!

(Music: Ominous.)

Laura: Are you sure his name is Jim O'Connor?

Amanda: Yes. Why?

Laura: Is he the one that Tom used to know in high school?

Amanda: He didn't say so. I think he just got to know him at the warehouse.

Laura: There was a Jim O'Connor we both knew in high school—(*Then, with effort.*) If that is the one that Tom is bringing to dinner—you'll have to excuse me, I won't come to the table.

Amanda: What sort of nonsense is this?

Laura: You asked me once if I'd ever liked a boy. Don't you remember I showed you this boy's picture?

Amanda: You mean the boy you showed me in the year-book?

Laura: Yes, that boy.

Amanda: Laura, Laura, were you in love with that boy?

Laura: I don't know, Mother. All I know is I couldn't sit at the table if it was him!

Amanda: It won't be him! It isn't the least bit likely. But whether it is or not, you will come to the table. You will not be excused.

Laura: I'll have to be, Mother.

Amanda: I don't intend to humor your silliness, Laura. I've had too much from you and your brother, both! So just sit down and compose yourself till they come. Tom has forgotten his key so you'll have to let them in, when they arrive.

Laura (*panicky*): Oh, Mother—*you* answer the door!

Amanda (*lightly*): I'll be in the kitchen—busy!

Laura: Oh, Mother, please answer the door, don't make me do it!

Amanda (*crossing into kitchenette*): I've got to fix the dressing for the salmon. Fuss, fuss—silliness!—over a gentleman caller!

Door swings shut. Laura is left alone.

(Legend: "Terror!")

She utters a low moan and turns off the lamp—sits stiffly on the edge of the sofa, knotting her fingers together.

(Legend On Screen: "The Opening Of A Door!")

Tom and Jim appear on the fire-escape steps and climb to landing. Hearing their approach, Laura rises with a panicky gesture. She retreats to the portieres.

The doorbell. Laura catches her breath and touches her throat. Low drums.

Amanda (*calling*): Laura, sweetheart! The door!

Laura stares at it without moving.

Jim: I think we just beat the rain.

Tom: Uh-huh. (*He rings again, nervously. Jim whistles and fishes for a cigarette.*)

Amanda (*very, very gaily*): Laura, that is your brother and Mr. O'Connor! Will you let them in, darling?

Laura crosses toward kitchenette door.

Laura (*breathlessly*): Mother—you go to the door!

Amanda steps out of kitchenette and stares furiously at Laura. She points imperiously at the door.

Laura: Please, please!

Amanda (*in a fierce whisper*): What is the matter with you, you silly thing?

Laura (*desperately*): Please, you answer it, *please!*

Amanda: I told you I wasn't going to humor you, Laura. Why have you chosen this moment to lose your mind?

Laura: Please, please, please, you go!

Amanda: You'll have to go to the door because I can't!

Laura (*despairingly*): I can't either!

Amanda: Why?

Laura: I'm *sick!*

Amanda: I'm sick, too—of your nonsense! Why can't you and your brother be normal people? Fantastic whims and behavior! (*Tom gives a long ring.*) Preposterous goings on! Can you give me one reason—(*Calls out lyrically.*) COMING! JUST ONE SECOND!—why should you be afraid to open a door? Now you answer it, Laura!

Laura: Oh, oh, oh . . . (*She returns through the portieres. Darts to the victrola and winds it frantically and turns it on.*)

Amanda: Laura Wingfield, you march right to that door!

Laura: Yes—yes, Mother!

A faraway, scratchy rendition of "Dardanella" softens the air and gives her strength to move through it. She slips to the door and draws it cautiously open. Tom enters with the caller, Jim O'Connor.

Tom: Laura, this is Jim. Jim, this is my sister, Laura.

Jim (stepping inside): I didn't know that Shakespeare had a sister!

Laura (retreating stiff and trembling from the door): How—how do you do?

Jim (heartily extending his hand): Okay!

Laura touches it hesitantly with hers.

Jim: Your hand's *cold,* Laura!

Laura: Yes, well—I've been playing the victrola. . . .

Jim: Must have been playing classical music on it! You ought to play a little hot swing music to warm you up!

Laura: Excuse me—I haven't finished playing the victrola. . . .

She turns awkwardly and hurries into the front room. She pauses a second by the victrola. Then catches her breath and darts through the portieres like a frightened deer.

Jim (grinning): What was the matter?

Tom: Oh—with Laura? Laura is—terribly shy.

Jim: Shy, huh? It's unusual to meet a shy girl nowadays. I don't believe you ever mentioned you had a sister.

Tom: Well, now you know. I have one. Here is the *Post Dispatch.* You want a piece of it?

Jim: Uh-huh.

Tom: What piece? The comics?

Jim: Sports! (*Glances at it.*) Ole Dizzy Dean is on his bad behavior.

Tom (disinterest): Yeah? (*Lights cigarette and crosses back to fire-escape door.*)

Jim: Where are you going?

Tom: I'm going out on the terrace.

Jim (goes after him): You know, Shakespeare—I'm going to sell you a bill of goods!

Tom: What goods?

Jim: A course I'm taking.

Tom: Huh?

Jim: In public speaking! You and me, we're not the warehouse type.

Tom: Thanks—that's good news. But what has public speaking got to do with it?

Jim: It fits you for—executive positions!

Tom: Awww.

Jim: I tell you it's done a helluva lot for me.

(Image: Executive At Desk.)

Tom: In what respect?

Jim: In every! Ask yourself what is the difference between you an' me and men in the office down front? Brains?—No!—Ability?—No! Then what? Just one little thing—

Tom: What is that one little thing?

Jim: Primarily it amounts to—social poise! Being able to square up to people and hold your own on any social level!

Amanda (*offstage*): Tom?

Tom: Yes, Mother?

Amanda: Is that you and Mr. O'Connor?

Tom: Yes, Mother.

Amanda: Well, you just make yourselves comfortable in there.

Tom: Yes, Mother.

Amanda: Ask Mr. O'Connor if he would like to wash his hands.

Jim: Aw—no—thank you—I took care of that at the warehouse. Tom—

Tom: Yes?

Jim: Mr. Mendoza was speaking to me about you.

Tom: Favorably?

Jim: What do you think?

Tom: Well—

Jim: You're going to be out of a job if you don't wake up.

Tom: I am waking up—

Jim: You show no signs.

Tom: The signs are interior.

(Image On Screen: The Sailing Vessel With Jolly Roger Again.)

Tom: I'm planning to change. (*He leans over the rail speaking with quiet exhilaration. The incandescent marquees and signs of the first-run movie houses light his face from across the alley. He looks like a voyager.*) I'm right at the point of committing myself to a future that doesn't include the warehouse and Mr. Mendoza or even a night-school course in public speaking.

Jim: What are you gassing about?

Tom: I'm tired of the movies.

Jim: Movies!

Tom: Yes, movies! Look at them—(*A wave toward the marvels of Grand Avenue.*) All of those glamorous people—having adventures—hogging it all, gobbling the whole thing up! You know what happens? People go to the *movies* instead of *moving!* Hollywood characters are supposed to have all the adventures for everybody in America, while everybody in America sits in a dark room and watches them have them! Yes, until there's a war. That's when adventure becomes available to the masses! *Everyone's* dish, not only Gable's! Then the people in the dark room come out of the dark room to have some adventures themselves—Goody, goody—It's our turn now, to go to the South Sea Island—to make a safari—to be exotic, far-off—But I'm not patient. I don't want to wait till then. I'm tired of the *movies* and I am *about* to move!

Jim (*incredulously*): Move?

Tom: Yes!

Jim: When?

Tom: Soon!

Jim: Where? Where?

> *Theme three music seems to answer the question, while Tom thinks it over. He searches among his pockets.*

Tom: I'm starting to boil inside. I know I seem dreamy, but inside—well, I'm boiling! Whenever I pick up a shoe, I shudder a little thinking how short life is and what I am doing!—Whatever that means. I know it doesn't mean shoes—except as something to wear on a traveler's feet! (*Finds paper.*) Look—

Jim: What?

Tom: I'm a member.

Jim (*reading*): The Union of Merchant Seamen.

Tom: I paid my dues this month, instead of the light bill.

Jim: You will regret it when they turn the lights off.

Tom: I won't be here.

Jim: How about your mother?

Tom: I'm like my father. The bastard son of a bastard! See how he grins? And he's been absent going on sixteen years!

Jim: You're just talking, you drip. How does your mother feel about it?

Tom: Shhh—Here comes Mother! Mother is not acquainted with my plans!

Amanda (*enters portieres*): Where are you all?

Tom: On the terrace, Mother.

> *They start inside. She advances to them. Tom is distinctly shocked at her appearance. Even Jim blinks a little. He is making his first contact with girlish Southern vivacity and in spite of the night-school course in public speaking is somewhat thrown off the beam by the unexpected outlay of social charm.*
>
> *Certain responses are attempted by Jim but are swept aside by Amanda's gay laughter and chatter. Tom is embarrassed but after the first shock Jim reacts very warmly. Grins and chuckles, is altogether won over.*

(Image: Amanda As A Girl.)

Amanda (*coyly smiling, shaking her girlish ringlets*): Well, well, well, so this is Mr. O'Connor. Introductions entirely unnecessary. I've heard so much about you from my boy. I finally said to him, Tom—good gracious!—why don't you bring this paragon to supper? I'd like to meet this nice young man at the warehouse!—Instead of just hearing him sing your praises so much! I don't know why my son is so stand-offish—that's not Southern behavior! Let's sit down and—I think we could stand a little more air in here! Tom, leave the door open. I felt a nice fresh breeze a moment ago. Where has it gone? Mmm, so warm already! And not quite summer, even. We're going to burn up when summer really gets started. However, we're having—we're having a very light supper. I think light things are better fo' this time of year. The same as light clothes are. Light clothes an' light food are what warm weather calls fo'. You know our blood gets so thick during th' winter—it takes a while fo' us to *adjust* ou'selves!—when the season changes . . . It's come so quick this year. I wasn't prepared. All of a sudden—heavens! Already summer!—I ran to the trunk an' pulled out this light dress—Terribly old! Historical almost! But feels so good—so good an' co-ol, y'know. . . .

Tom: Mother—

Amanda: Yes, honey?

Tom: How about—supper?

Amanda: Honey, you go ask Sister if supper is ready! You know that Sister is in full charge of supper! Tell her you hungry boys are waiting for it. (*To Jim.*) Have you met Laura?

Jim: She—

Amanda: Let you in? Oh, good, you've met already! It's rare for a girl as sweet an' pretty as Laura to be domestic! But Laura is, thank heavens, not only pretty but also very domestic. I'm not at all. I never was a bit. I never could make a thing but angel-food cake. Well, in the South we had so many servants. Gone, gone, gone. All vestiges of gracious living! Gone completely! I wasn't prepared for what the future brought me. All of my gentlemen callers were sons of planters and so of course I assumed that I would be married to one and raise my family on a large piece of land with plenty of servants. But man proposes—and woman accepts the proposal!—To vary that old, old saying a little bit—I married no planter! I married a man who worked for the tele-phone company!—that gallantly smiling gentleman over there! (*Points to the picture.*) A telephone man who—fell in love with long-distance!—Now he travels and I don't even know where!—But what am I going on for about my—tribulations? Tell me yours—I hope you don't have any! Tom?

Tom (*returning*): Yes, Mother?

Amanda: Is supper nearly ready?

Tom: It looks to me like supper is on the table.

Amanda: Let me look—(*She rises prettily and looks through portieres.*) Oh, lovely—But where is Sister?

Tom: Laura is not feeling well and she says that she thinks she'd better not come to the table.

Amanda: What?—Nonsense!—Laura? Oh, Laura!

Laura (*offstage, faintly*): Yes, Mother.

Amanda: You really must come to the table. We won't be seated until you come to the table! Come in, Mr. O'Connor. You sit over there and I'll—Laura? Laura Wingfield! You're keeping us waiting, honey! We can't say grace until you come to the table!

The back door is pushed weakly open and Laura comes in. She is obviously quite faint, her lips trembling, her eyes wide and staring. She moves unsteadily toward the table.

(Legend: "Terror!")

Outside a summer storm is coming abruptly. The white curtains billow inward at the windows and there is a sorrowful murmur and deep blue dusk.

Laura suddenly stumbles—She catches at a chair with a faint moan.

Tom: Laura!

Amanda: Laura! (*There is a clap of thunder.*) (**Legend: "Ah!"**) (*Despairingly.*) Why, Laura, you *are* sick, darling! Tom, help your sister into the living room, dear! Sit in the living room, Laura—rest on the sofa. Well! (*To the gentleman caller.*) Standing over the hot stove made her ill!—I told her that it was just too warm this evening, but—(*Tom comes back in. Laura is on the sofa.*) Is Laura all right now?

Tom: Yes.

Amanda: What is that? Rain? A nice cool rain has come up! (*She gives the gentleman caller a frightened look.*) I think we may—have grace—now . . . (*Tom looks at her stupidly.*) Tom, honey—you say grace!

Tom: Oh . . . "For these and all thy mercies—" (*They bow their heads, Amanda stealing a nervous glance at Jim. In the living room Laura, stretched on the sofa, clenches her hand to her lips, to hold back a shuddering sob.*) God's Holy Name be praised—

(The Scene Dims Out.)

SCENE VII

(*A Souvenir.*)

Half an hour later. Dinner is just being finished in the upstage area which is concealed by the drawn portieres.

As the curtain rises Laura is still huddled upon the sofa, her feet drawn under her, her head resting on a pale blue pillow, her eyes wide and mysteriously watchful. The new floor lamp with its shade of rose-colored silk gives a soft, becoming light to her face, bringing out the fragile, unearthly prettiness which usually escapes attention. There is a steady murmur of rain, but it is slackening and stops soon after the scene begins; the air outside becomes pale and luminous as the moon breaks out.

A moment after the curtain rises, the lights in both rooms flicker and go out.

Jim: Hey, there, Mr. Light Bulb!

Amanda laughs nervously.

(Legend: "Suspension Of A Public Service.")

Amanda: Where was Moses when the lights went out? Ha-ha. Do you know the answer to that one, Mr. O'Connor?

Jim: No, Ma'am, what's the answer?

Amanda: In the dark! (*Jim laughs appreciatively.*) Everybody sit still. I'll light the candles. Isn't it lucky we have them on the table? Where's a match? Which of you gentlemen can provide a match?

Jim: Here.

Amanda: Thank you, sir.

Jim: Not at all, Ma'am!

Amanda: I guess the fuse has burnt out. Mr. O'Connor, can you tell a burnt-out fuse? I know I can't and Tom is a total loss when it comes to mechanics. **(Sound: Getting Up: Voices Recede A Little To Kitchenette.)** Oh, be careful you don't bump into something. We don't want our gentleman caller to break his neck. Now wouldn't that be a fine howdy-do?

Jim: Ha-ha! Where is the fuse-box?

Amanda: Right here next to the stove. Can you see anything?

Jim: Just a minute.

Amanda: Isn't electricity a mysterious thing? Wasn't it Benjamin Franklin who tied a key to a kite? We live in such a mysterious universe, don't we? Some people say that science clears up all the mysteries for us. In my opinion it only creates more! Have you found it yet?

Jim: No, Ma'am. All these fuses look okay to me.

Amanda: Tom!

Tom: Yes, Mother?

Amanda: That light bill I gave you several days ago. The one I told you we got the notices about?

Tom: Oh.—Yeah.

(**Legend:** "Ha!")

Amanda: You didn't neglect to pay it by any chance?

Tom: Why, I—

Amanda: Didn't! I might have known it!

Jim: Shakespeare probably wrote a poem on that light bill, Mrs. Wingfield.

Amanda: I might have known better than to trust him with it! There's such a high price for negligence in this world!

Jim: Maybe the poem will win a ten-dollar prize.

Amanda: We'll just have to spend the remainder of the evening in the nineteenth century, before Mr. Edison made the Mazda lamp!

Jim: Candlelight is my favorite kind of light.

Amanda: That shows you're romantic! But that's no excuse for Tom. Well, we got through dinner. Very considerate of them to let us get through dinner before they plunged us into everlasting darkness, wasn't it, Mr. O'Connor?

Jim: Ha-ha!

Amanda: Tom, as a penalty for your carelessness you can help me with the dishes.

Jim: Let me give you a hand.

Amanda: Indeed you will not!

Jim: I ought to be good for something.

Amanda: Good for something? (*Her tone is rhapsodic.*) *You?* Why, Mr. O'Connor, nobody, *nobody's* given me this much entertainment in years—as you have!

Jim: Aw, now, Mrs. Wingfield!

Amanda: I'm not exaggerating, not one bit! But Sister is all by her lonesome. You go keep her company in the parlor! I'll give you this lovely old candelabrum that used to be on the altar at the church of the Heavenly Rest. It was melted a little out of shape when the church burnt down. Lightning struck it one spring. Gypsy Jones was holding a revival at the time and he intimated that the church was destroyed because the Episcopalians gave card parties.

Jim: Ha-ha.

Amanda: And how about coaxing Sister to drink a little wine? I think it would be good for her! Can you carry both at once?

Jim: Sure. I'm Superman!

Amanda: Now, Thomas, get into this apron!

The door of kitchenette swings closed on Amanda's gay laughter; the flickering light approaches the portieres.

Laura sits up nervously as he enters. Her speech at first is low and breathless from the almost intolerable strain of being alone with a stranger.

(The Legend: "I Don't Suppose You Remember Me At All!")

In her first speeches in this scene, before Jim's warmth overcomes her paralyzing shyness, Laura's voice is thin and breathless as though she has run up a steep flight of stairs.

Jim's attitude is gently humorous. In playing this scene it should be stressed that while the incident is apparently unimportant, it is to Laura the climax of her secret life.

Jim: Hello, there, Laura.

Laura (faintly): Hello. (*She clears her throat.*)

Jim: How are you feeling now? Better?

Laura: Yes. Yes, thank you.

Jim: This is for you. A little dandelion wine. (*He extends it toward her with extravagant gallantry.*)

Laura: Thank you.

Jim: Drink it—but don't get drunk! (*He laughs heartily. Laura takes the glass uncertainly; laughs shyly.*) Where shall I set the candles?

Laura: Oh—oh, anywhere . . .

Jim: How about here on the floor? Any objections?

Laura: No.

Jim: I'll spread a newspaper under to catch the drippings. I like to sit on the floor. Mind if I do?

Laura: Oh, no.

Jim: Give me a pillow?

Laura: What?

Jim: A pillow!

Laura: Oh . . . (*Hands him one quickly.*)

Jim: How about you? Don't you like to sit on the floor?

Laura: Oh—yes.

Jim: Why don't you, then?

Laura: I—will.

Jim: Take a pillow! (*Laura does. Sits on the other side of the candelabrum. Jim crosses his legs and smiles engagingly at her.*) I can't hardly see you sitting way over there.

Laura: I can—see you.

Jim: I know, but that's not fair, I'm in the limelight. (*Laura moves her pillow closer.*) Good! Now I can see you! Comfortable?

Laura: Yes.

Jim: So am I. Comfortable as a cow. Will you have some gum?

Laura: No, thank you.

Jim: I think that I will indulge, with your permission. (*Musingly unwraps it and holds it up.*) Think of the fortune made by the guy that invented the first piece of chewing gum. Amazing, huh? The Wrigley Building is one of the sights of Chicago.—I saw it summer before last when I went up to the Century of Progress. Did you take in the Century of Progress?

Laura: No, I didn't.

Jim: Well, it was quite a wonderful exposition. What impressed me most was the Hall of Science. Gives you an idea of what the future will be in America, even more wonderful than the present time is! (*Pause. Smiling at her.*) Your brother tells me you're shy. Is that right, Laura?

Laura: I—don't know.

Jim: I judge you to be an old-fashioned type of girl. Well, I think that's pretty good type to be. Hope you don't think I'm being too personal—do you?

Laura (hastily, out of embarrassment): I believe I *will* take a piece of gum, if you—don't mind. (*Clearing her throat.*) Mr. O'Connor, have you—kept up with your singing?

Jim: Singing? Me?

Laura: Yes. I remember what a beautiful voice you had.

Jim: When did you hear me sing?

(Voice Offstage In The Pause.)

Voice (offstage):
> O blow, ye winds, heigh-ho,
> A-roving I will go!
> I'm off to my love
> With a boxing glove—
> Ten thousand miles away!

Jim: You say you've heard me sing?

Laura: Oh, yes! Yes, very often . . . I—don't suppose you remember me—at all?

Jim (smiling doubtfully): You know I have an idea I've seen you before. I had that idea soon as you opened the door. It seemed almost like I was about to remember your name. But the name that I started to call you—wasn't a name! And so I stopped myself before I said it.

Laura: Wasn't it—Blue Roses?

Jim (springs up, grinning): Blue Roses! My gosh, yes—Blue Roses! That's what I had on my tongue when you opened the door! Isn't it funny what tricks your memory plays? I didn't connect you with the high school somehow or other. But that's where it was; it was high school. I didn't even know you were Shakespeare's sister! Gosh, I'm sorry.

Laura: I didn't expect you to. You—barely knew me!

Jim: But we did have a speaking acquaintance, huh?

Laura: Yes, we—spoke to each other.

Jim: When did you recognize me?

Laura: Oh, right away!

Jim: Soon as I came in the door?

Laura: When I heard your name I thought it was probably you. I knew that Tom used to know you a little in high school. So when you came in the door— Well, then I was—sure.

Jim: Why didn't you say something, then?

Laura (breathlessly): I didn't know what to say, I was—too surprised!

Jim: For goodness sakes! You know, this sure is funny!

Laura: Yes! Yes, isn't it, though . . .

Jim: Didn't we have a class in something together?

Laura: Yes, we did.

Jim: What class was that?

Laura: It was—singing—Chorus!

Jim: Aw!

Laura: I sat across the aisle from you in the Aud.

Jim: Aw.

Laura: Mondays, Wednesdays and Fridays.

Jim: Now I remember—you always came in late.

Laura: Yes, it was so hard for me, getting upstairs. I had that brace on my leg—it clumped so loud!

Jim: I never heard any clumping.

Laura (wincing at the recollection): To me it sounded like thunder!

Jim: Well, well, well. I never even noticed.

Laura: And everybody was seated before I came in. I had to walk in front of all those people. My seat was in the back row. I had to go clumping all the way up the aisle with everyone watching!

Jim: You shouldn't have been self-conscious.

Laura: I know, but I was. It was always such a relief when the singing started.

Jim: Aw, yes, I've placed you now! I used to call you Blue Roses. How was it that I got started calling you that?

Laura: I was out of school a little while with pleurosis. When I came back you asked me what was the matter. I said I had pleurosis—you thought I said Blue Roses. That's what you always called me after that!

Jim: I hope you didn't mind.

Laura: Oh, no—I liked it. You see, I wasn't acquainted with many—people. . . .

Jim: As I remember you sort of stuck by yourself.

Laura: I—I—never had much luck at—making friends.

Jim: I don't see why you wouldn't.

Laura: Well, I—started out badly.

Jim: You mean being—

Laura: Yes, it sort of—stood between me—

Jim: You shouldn't have let it!

Laura: I know, but it did, and—

Jim: You were shy with people!

Laura: I tried not to be but never could—

Jim: Overcome it?

Laura: No, I—I never could!

Jim: I guess being shy is something you have to work out of kind of gradually.

Laura (sorrowfully): Yes—I guess it—

Jim: Takes time!

Laura: Yes—

Jim: People are not so dreadful when you know them. That's what you have to remember! And everybody has problems, not just you, but practically everybody has got some problems. You think of yourself as having the only problems, as being the only one who is disappointed. But just look around you and you will see lots of people as disappointed as you are. For instance, I hoped when I was going to high school that I would be further along at this time, six years later, than I am now—You remember that wonderful write-up I had in *The Torch?*

Laura: Yes! (*She rises and crosses to table.*)

Jim: It said I was bound to succeed in anything I went into! (*Laura returns with the annual.*) Holy Jeez! *The Torch!* (*He accepts it reverently. They smile across it with mutual wonder. Laura crouches beside him and they begin to turn through it. Laura's shyness is dissolving in his warmth.*)

Laura: Here you are in *Pirates of Penzance!*

Jim (wistfully): I sang the baritone lead in that operetta.

Laura (rapidly): So—beautifully!

Jim (protesting): Aw—

Laura: Yes, yes—beautifully—beautifully!

Jim: You heard me?

Laura: All three times!

Jim: No!

Laura: Yes!

Jim: All three performances?

Laura (looking down): Yes.

Jim: Why?

Laura: I—wanted to ask you to—autograph my program.

Jim: Why didn't you ask me to?

Laura: You were always surrounded by your own friends so much that I never had a chance to.

Jim: You should have just—

Laura: Well, I—thought you might think I was—

Jim: Thought I might think you was—what?

Laura: Oh—

Jim (with reflective relish): I was beleaguered by females in those days.

Laura: You were terribly popular!

Jim: Yeah—

Laura: You had such a—friendly way—

Jim: I was spoiled in high school.

Laura: Everybody—liked you!

Jim: Including you?

Laura: I—yes, I—did, too—(*She gently closes the book in her lap.*)

Jim: Well, well, well!—Give me that program, Laura. (*She hands it to him. He signs it with a flourish.*) There you are—better late than never!

Laura: Oh, I—what a—surprise!

Jim: My signature isn't worth very much right now. But some day—maybe—it will increase in value! Being disappointed is one thing and being discouraged is something else. I am disappointed but I'm not discouraged. I'm twenty-three years old. How old are you?

Laura: I'll be twenty-four in June.

Jim: That's not old age!

Laura: No, but—

Jim: You finished high school?

Laura (with difficulty): I didn't go back.

Jim: You mean you dropped out?

Laura: I made bad grades in my final examinations. (*She rises and replaces the book and the program. Her voice strained.*) How is—Emily Meisenbach getting along?

Jim: Oh, that kraut-head!

Laura: Why do you call her that?

Jim: That's what she was.

Laura: You're not still—going with her?

Jim: I never see her.

Laura: It said in the Personal Section that you were— engaged!

Jim: I know, but I wasn't impressed by that—propaganda!

Laura: It wasn't—the truth?

Jim: Only in Emily's optimistic opinion!

Laura: Oh—

(Legend: "What Have You Done Since High School?")

Jim lights a cigarette and leans indolently back on his elbows smiling at Laura with a warmth and charm which light her inwardly with altar candles. She remains by the table and turns in her hands a piece of glass to cover her tumult.

Jim (after several reflective puffs on a cigarette): What have you done since high school? (*She seems not to hear him.*) Huh? (*Laura looks up.*) I said what have you done since high school, Laura?

Laura: Nothing much.

Jim: You must have been doing something these six long years.

Laura: Yes.

Jim: Well, then, such as what?

Laura: I took a business course at business college—

Jim: How did that work out?

Laura: Well, not very—well—I had to drop out, it gave me—indigestion—

> *Jim laughs gently.*

Jim: What are you doing now?

Laura: I don't do anything—much. Oh, please don't think I sit around doing nothing! My glass collection takes up a good deal of my time. Glass is something you have to take good care of.

Jim: What did you say—about glass?

Laura: Collection I said—I have one—(*She clears her throat and turns away again, acutely shy.*)

Jim (abruptly): You know what I judge to be the trouble with you? Inferiority complex! Know what that is? That's what they call it when someone low-rates himself! I understand it because I had it, too. Although my case was not so aggravated as yours seems to be. I had it until I took up public speaking, developed my voice, and learned that I had an aptitude for science. Before that time I never thought of myself as being outstanding in any way whatsoever! Now I've never made a regular study of it, but I have a friend who says I can analyze people better than doctors that make a profession of it. I don't claim that to be necessarily true, but I can sure guess a person's psychology, Laura! (*Takes out his gum.*) Excuse me, Laura. I always take it out when the flavor is gone. I'll use this scrap of paper to wrap it in. I know how it is to get it stuck on a shoe. Yep—that's what I judge to be your principal trouble. A lack of confidence in yourself as a person. You don't have the proper amount of faith in yourself. I'm basing that fact on a number of your remarks and also on certain observations I've made. For instance that clumping you thought was so awful in high school. You say that you even dreaded to walk into class. You see what you did? You dropped out of school, you gave up an education because of a clump, which as far as I know was practically non-existent! A little physical defect is what you have. Hardly noticeable even! Magnified thousands of times by imagination! You know what my strong advice to you is? Think of yourself as *superior* in some way!

Laura: In what way would I think?

Jim: Why, man alive, Laura! Just look about you a little. What do you see? A world full of common people! All of 'em born and all of 'em going to die! Which of them has one-tenth of your good points! Or mine! Or anyone else's, as far as that goes—Gosh! Everybody excels in some one thing. Some in many! (*Unconsciously glances at himself in the mirror.*) All you've got to do is discover in *what*! Take me, for instance. (*He adjusts his tie at the mirror.*) My interest happens to lie in electrodynamics. I'm taking a course in radio engineering at night school, Laura, on top of a fairly responsible job at the warehouse. I'm taking that course and studying public speaking.

Laura: Ohhhh.

Jim: Because I believe in the future of television! (*Turning back to her.*) I wish to be ready to go up right along with it. Therefore I'm planning to get in on the ground floor. In fact, I've already made the right connections and all that remains is for the industry itself to get under way! Full steam—(*His eyes are starry.*) Knowledge—Zzzzzp! Money—Zzzzzp!—Power! That's the cycle democracy is built on! (*His attitude is convincingly dynamic. Laura stares at him, even her shyness eclipsed in her absolute wonder. He suddenly grins.*) I guess you think I think a lot of myself!

Laura: No—o-o-o, I—

Jim: Now how about you? Isn't there something you take more interest in than anything else?

Laura: Well, I do—as I said—have my—glass collection—

A peal of girlish laughter from the kitchen.

Jim: I'm not right sure I know what you're talking about. What kind of glass is it?

Laura: Little articles of it, they're ornaments mostly! Most of them are little animals made out of glass, the tiniest little animals in the world. Mother calls them a glass menagerie! Here's an example of one, if you'd like to see it! This one is one of the oldest. It's nearly thirteen. (*He stretches out his hand.*) **(Music: "The Glass Menagerie.")** Oh, be careful—if you breathe, it breaks!

Jim: I'd better not take it. I'm pretty clumsy with things.

Laura: Go on, I trust you with him! (*Places it in his palm.*) There now—you're holding him gently! Hold him over the light, he loves the light! You see how the light shines through him?

Jim: It sure does shine!

Laura: I shouldn't be partial, but he is my favorite one.

Jim: What kind of a thing is this one supposed to be?

Laura: Haven't you noticed the single horn on his forehead?

Jim: A unicorn, huh?

Laura: Mmm-hmmm!

Jim: Unicorns, aren't they extinct in the modern world?

Laura: I know!

Jim: Poor little fellow, he must feel sort of lonesome.

Laura (smiling): Well, if he does he doesn't complain about it. He stays on a shelf with some horses that don't have horns and all of them seem to get along nicely together.

Jim: How do you know?

Laura (lightly): I haven't heard any arguments among them!

Jim (grinning): No arguments, huh? Well, that's a pretty good sign! Where shall I set him?

Laura: Put him on the table. They all like a change of scenery once in a while!

Jim (stretching): Well, well, well, well—Look how big my shadow is when I stretch!

Laura: Oh, oh, yes—it stretches across the ceiling!

Jim (crossing to door): I think it's stopped raining. (*Opens fire-escape door.*) Where does the music come from?

Laura: From the Paradise Dance Hall across the alley.

Jim: How about cutting the rug a little, Miss Wingfield?

Laura: Oh, I—

Jim: Or is your program filled up? Let me have a look at it. (*Grasps imaginary card.*) Why, every dance is taken! I'll just have to scratch some out. (**Waltz Music: "La Golondrina."**) Ahhh, a waltz! (*He executes some sweeping turns by himself, then holds his arms toward Laura.*)

Laura (*breathlessly*): I—can't dance!

Jim: There you go, that inferiority stuff!

Laura: I've never danced in my life!

Jim: Come on, try!

Laura: Oh, but I'd step on you!

Jim: I'm not made out of glass.

Laura: How—how—how do we start?

Jim: Just leave it to me. You hold your arms out a little.

Laura: Like this?

Jim: A little bit higher. Right. Now don't tighten up, that's the main thing about it—relax.

Laura (*laughing breathlessly*): It's hard not to.

Jim: Okay.

Laura: I'm afraid you can't budge me.

Jim: What do you bet I can't? (*He swings her into motion.*)

Laura: Goodness, yes, you can!

Jim: Let yourself go, now, Laura, just let yourself go.

Laura: I'm—

Jim: Come on!

Laura: Trying!

Jim: Not so stiff—Easy does it!

Laura: I know but I'm—

Jim: Loosen th' backbone! There now, that's a lot better.

Laura: Am I?

Jim: Lots, lots better! (*He moves her about the room in a clumsy waltz.*)

Laura: Oh, my!

Jim: Ha-ha!

Laura: Goodness, yes you can!

Jim: Ha-ha-ha! (*They suddenly bump into the table, Jim stops.*) What did we hit on?

Laura: Table.

Jim: Did something fall off it? I think—

Laura: Yes.

Jim: I hope that it wasn't the little glass horse with the horn!

Laura: Yes.

Jim: Aw, aw, aw. Is it broken?

Laura: Now it is just like all the other horses.

Jim: It's lost its—

Laura: Horn! It doesn't matter. Maybe it's a blessing in disguise.

Jim: You'll never forgive me. I bet that that was your favorite piece of glass.

Laura: I don't have favorites much. It's no tragedy, Freckles. Glass breaks so easily. No matter how careful you are. The traffic jars the shelves and things fall off them.

Jim: Still I'm awfully sorry that I was the cause.

Laura (smiling): I'll just imagine he had an operation. The horn was removed to make him feel less—freakish! (*They both laugh.*) Now he will feel more at home with the other horses, the ones that don't have horns . . .

Jim: Ha-ha, that's very funny! (*Suddenly serious.*) I'm glad to see that you have a sense of humor. You know—you're—well—very different! Surprisingly different from anyone else I know! (*His voice becomes soft and hesitant with a genuine feeling.*) Do you mind me telling you that? (*Laura is abashed beyond speech.*) You make me feel sort of—I don't know how to put it! I'm usually pretty good at expressing things, but—This is something that I don't know how to say! (*Laura touches her throat and clears it—turns the broken unicorn in her hands.*) (*Even softer.*) Has anyone ever told you that you were pretty? **(Pause: Music.)** (*Laura looks up slowly, with wonder, and shakes her head.*) Well, you are! In a very different way from anyone else. And all the nicer because of the difference, too. (*His voice becomes low and husky. Laura turns away, nearly faint with the novelty of her emotions.*) I wish you were my sister. I'd teach you to have some confidence in yourself. The different people are not like other people, but being different is nothing to be ashamed of. Because other people are not such wonderful people. They're one hundred times one thousand. You're one times one! They walk all over the earth. You just stay here. They're common as—weeds, but—you—well, you're—*Blue Roses!*

(Image On Screen: Blue Roses.)

(Music Changes.)

Laura: But blue is wrong for—roses . . .

Jim: It's right for you—You're pretty!

Laura: In what respect am I pretty?

Jim: In all respects—believe me! Your eyes—your hair—are pretty! Your hands are pretty! (*He catches hold of her hand.*) You think I'm making this up because I'm invited to dinner and have to be nice. Oh, I could do that! I could put on an act for you, Laura, and say lots of things without being very sincere. But this time I am. I'm talking to you sincerely. I happened to notice you had this inferiority complex that keeps you from feeling comfortable with people. Somebody needs to build your confidence up and make you proud instead of shy and turning away and—blushing—Somebody ought to—ought to—*kiss* you, Laura! (*His hand slips slowly up her arm to her shoulder.*) **(Music Swells Tumultuously.)** (*He suddenly turns her about and kisses her on the lips. When he releases her Laura sinks on the sofa with a bright, dazed look. Jim backs away and fishes in his pocket for a cigarette.*) (**Legend On Screen: "Souvenir."**) Stumble-john! (*He lights the cigarette, avoiding her look. There is a peal of girlish laughter from Amanda in the kitchen. Laura slowly raises and opens her hand. It still contains the little broken glass animal. She looks* at it with a tender, bewildered expression.) Stumble-john! I shouldn't have done that—That was way off the beam. You don't smoke, do you? (*She looks up, smiling, not hearing the question. He sits beside her a little gingerly. She looks at him speechlessly—waiting. He coughs decorously and moves a little farther aside as he considers the situation and senses her feelings, dimly, with perturbation. Gently.*) Would you—care for a—mint? (*She doesn't seem to hear him but her look grows brighter even.*) Peppermint—Life Saver? My pocket's a regular drug store—wherever I go . . . (*He pops a mint in his mouth. Then gulps and decides to make a clean breast of it. He speaks slowly and gingerly.*) Laura, you know, if I had a sister like you, I'd do the same thing as Tom, I'd bring out fellows—introduce her to them. The right type of boys of a type to—appreciate her. Only—well—he made a mistake about me. Maybe I've got no call to be saying this. That may not have been the idea in having me over. But what if it was? There's nothing wrong about that. The only trouble is that in my case—I'm not in a situation to—do the right thing. I can't take down your number and say I'll phone. I can't call up next week and—ask for a date. I thought I had better explain the situation in case you misunderstood it and—hurt your feelings. . . . (*Pause. Slowly, very slowly, Laura's look changes, her eyes returning slowly from his to the ornament in her palm.*)

Amanda utters another gay laugh in the kitchen.

Laura (*faintly*): You—won't—call again?

Jim: No, Laura, I can't. (*He rises from the sofa.*) As I was just explaining, I've—got strings on me, Laura, I've—been going steady! I go out all the time with a girl named Betty. She's a home-girl like you, and Catholic, and Irish, and in a great many ways we—get along fine. I met her last summer on a moonlight boat trip up the river to Alton, on the *Majestic*. Well—right away from the start it was—love! (**Legend: Love!**) (*Laura sways slightly forward and grips the arm of the sofa. He fails to notice, now enrapt in his own comfortable being.*) Being in love has made a new man of me! (*Leaning stiffly forward, clutching the arm of the sofa, Laura struggles visibly with her storm. But Jim is oblivious, she is a long way off.*) The power of love is really pretty tremendous! Love is something that—changes the whole world, Laura! (*The storm abates a little and Laura leans back. He notices her again.*) It happened that Betty's aunt took sick, she got a wire and had to go to Centralia. So Tom—when he asked me to dinner—I naturally just accepted the invitation, not knowing that you—that he—that I—(*He stops awkwardly.*) Huh—I'm a stumble-john! (*He flops back on the sofa. The holy candles in the altar of Laura's face have been snuffed out! There is a look of almost infinite desolation. Jim glances at her uneasily.*) I wish that you would—say something. (*She bites her lip which was trembling and then bravely smiles. She opens her hand again on the broken glass ornament. Then she gently takes his hand and raises it level with her own. She carefully places the unicorn in the palm of his hand, then pushes his fingers closed upon it.*) What are you—doing that for? You want me to have him?—Laura? (*She nods.*) What for?

Laura: A—souvenir . . .

> *She rises unsteadily and crouches beside the victrola to wind it up.*

(Legend On Screen: "Things Have A Way Of Turning Out So Badly.")

(Or Image: "Gentleman Caller Waving Good-bye!—Gaily.")

At this moment Amanda rushes brightly back in the front room. She bears a pitcher of fruit punch in an old-fashioned cut-glass pitcher and a plate of macaroons. The plate has a gold border and poppies painted on it.

Amanda: Well, well, well! Isn't the air delightful after the shower? I've made you children a little liquid refreshment. (*Turns gaily to the gentleman caller.*) Jim, do you know that song about lemonade?

> "Lemonade, lemonade
> Made in the shade and stirred with a spade—
> Good enough for any old maid!"

Jim (uneasily): Ha-ha! No—I never heard it.

Amanda: Why, Laura! You look so serious!

Jim: We were having a serious conversation.

Amanda: Good! Now you're better acquainted!

Jim (uncertainly): Ha-ha! Yes.

Amanda: You modern young people are much more serious-minded than my generation. I was so gay as a girl!

Jim: You haven't changed, Mrs. Wingfield.

Amanda: Tonight I'm rejuvenated! The gaiety of the occasion, Mr. O'Connor! (*She tosses her head with a peal of laughter. Spills lemonade.*) Oooo! I'm baptizing myself!

Jim: Here—let me—

Amanda (setting the pitcher down): There now. I discovered we had some maraschino cherries. I dumped them in, juice and all!

Jim: You shouldn't have gone to that trouble, Mrs. Wingfield.

Amanda: Trouble, trouble? Why it was loads of fun! Didn't you hear me cutting up in the kitchen? I bet your ears were burning! I told Tom how outdone with him I was for keeping you to himself so long a time! He should have brought you over much, much sooner! Well, now that you've found your way, I want you to be a very frequent caller! Not just occasional but all the time. Oh, we're going to have a lot of gay times together! I see them coming! Mmm, just breathe that air! So fresh, and the moon's so pretty! I'll skip back out—I know where my place is when young folks are having a— serious conversation!

Jim: Oh, don't go out, Mrs. Wingfield. The fact of the matter is I've got to be going.

Amanda: Going, now? You're joking! Why, it's only the shank of the evening, Mr. O'Connor!

Jim: Well, you know how it is.

Amanda: You mean you're a young workingman and have to keep workingmen's hours. We'll let you off early tonight. But only on the condition that next time you stay later. What's the best night for you? Isn't Saturday night the best night for you workingmen?

Jim: I have a couple of time-clocks to punch, Mrs. Wingfield. One at morning, another one at night!

Amanda: My, but you *are* ambitious! You work at night, too?

Jim: No, Ma'am, not work but—Betty! (*He crosses deliberately to pick up his hat. The band at the Paradise Dance Hall goes into a tender waltz.*)

Amanda: Betty? Betty? Who's—Betty? (*There is an ominous cracking sound in the sky.*)

Jim: Oh, just a girl. The girl I go steady with! (*He smiles charmingly. The sky falls.*)

(Legend: "The Sky Falls.")

Amanda (*a long-drawn exhalation*): Ohhhh . . . Is it a serious romance, Mr. O'Connor?

Jim: We're going to be married the second Sunday in June.

Amanda: Ohhhh—how nice! Tom didn't mention that you were engaged to be married.

Jim: The cat's not out of the bag at the warehouse yet. You know how they are. They call you Romeo and stuff like that. (*He stops at the oval mirror to put on his hat. He carefully shapes the brim and the crown to give a discreetly dashing effect.*) It's been a wonderful evening, Mrs. Wingfield. I guess this is what they mean by Southern hospitality.

Amanda: It really wasn't anything at all.

Jim: I hope it don't seem like I'm rushing off. But I promised Betty I'd pick her up at the Wabash depot, an' by the time I get my jalopy down there her train'll be in. Some women are pretty upset if you keep 'em waiting.

Amanda: Yes, I know—The tyranny of women! (*Extends her hand.*) Goodbye, Mr. O'Connor. I wish you luck—and happiness—and success! All three of them, and so does Laura!—Don't you, Laura?

Laura: Yes!

Jim (*taking her hand*): Goodbye, Laura. I'm certainly going to treasure that souvenir. And don't you forget the good advice I gave you. (*Raises his voice to a cheery shout.*) So long, Shakespeare! Thanks again, ladies—Good night!

He grins and ducks jauntily out.

Still bravely grimacing, Amanda closes the door on the gentleman caller. Then she turns back to the room with a puzzled expression. She and Laura don't dare to face each other. Laura crouches beside the victrola to wind it.

Amanda (*faintly*): Things have a way of turning out so badly. I don't believe that I would play the victrola. Well, well—well—Our gentleman caller was engaged to be married! Tom!

Tom (*from back*): Yes, Mother?

Amanda: Come in here a minute. I want to tell you something awfully funny.

Tom (*enters with macaroon and a glass of the lemonade*): Has the gentleman caller gotten away already?

Amanda: The gentleman caller has made an early departure. What a wonderful joke you played on us!

Tom: How do you mean?

Amanda: You didn't mention that he was engaged to be married.

Tom: Jim? Engaged?

Amanda: That's what he just informed us.

Tom: I'll be jiggered! I didn't know about that.

Amanda: That seems very peculiar.

Tom: What's peculiar about it?

Amanda: Didn't you call him your best friend down at the warehouse?

Tom: He is, but how did I know?

Amanda: It seems extremely peculiar that you wouldn't know your best friend was going to be married!

Tom: The warehouse is where I work, not where I know things about people!

Amanda: You don't know things anywhere! You live in a dream; you manufacture illusions! (*He crosses to door.*) Where are you going?

Tom: I'm going to the movies.

Amanda: That's right, now that you've had us make such fools of ourselves. The effort, the preparations, all the expense! The new floor lamp, the rug, the clothes for Laura! All for what? To entertain some other girl's fiancé! Go to the movies, go! Don't think about us, a mother deserted, an unmarried sister who's crippled and has no job! Don't let anything interfere with your selfish pleasure! Just go, go, go—to the movies!

Tom: All right, I will! The more you shout about my selfishness to me the quicker I'll go, and I won't go to the movies!

Amanda: Go, then! Then go to the moon—you selfish dreamer!

Tom smashes his glass on the floor. He plunges out on the fire-escape, slamming the door. Laura screams—cut by door.

Dance-hall music up. Tom goes to the rail and grips it desperately, lifting his face in the chill white moonlight penetrating the narrow abyss of the alley.

(Legend On Screen: "And So Good-bye . . . ")

Tom's closing speech is timed with the interior pantomime. The interior scene is played as though viewed through sound-proof glass. Amanda appears to be making a comforting speech to Laura who is huddled upon the sofa. Now that we cannot hear the mother's speech, her silliness is gone and she has dignity and tragic beauty. Laura's dark hair hides her face until at the end of the speech she lifts it to smile at her mother. Amanda's gestures are slow and graceful, almost dancelike, as she comforts the daughter. At the end of her speech she glances a moment at the father's picture—then withdraws through the portieres. At close of Tom's speech, Laura blows out the candles, ending the play.

Tom: I didn't go to the movies, I went much further—for time is the longest distance between two places—Not long after that I was fired for writing a poem on the lid of a shoe-box. I left Saint Louis. I descended the steps of this fire-escape for a last time and followed, from then on, in my father's footsteps, attempting to find in motion what was lost in space—I traveled around a great deal. The cities swept about me like dead leaves, leaves that were brightly colored but torn away from the branches. I would have stopped, but was pursued by something. It always came upon me unawares, taking me altogether by surprise. Perhaps it was a familiar bit of music. Perhaps it was only a piece of transparent glass. Perhaps I am walking along a street at night, in some strange city, before I have found companions. I pass the lighted window of a shop where perfume is sold. The window is filled with pieces of colored glass, tiny transparent bottles in delicate colors, like bits of a shattered rainbow. Then all at once my sister touches my shoulder. I turn around and look into her eyes . . . Oh, Laura, Laura, I tried to leave you behind me, but I am more faithful than I intended to be! I reach for a cigarette, I cross the street, I run into the movies or a bar, I buy a drink, I speak to the nearest stranger—anything that can blow your candles out! (*Laura bends over the candles.*)—for nowadays the world is lit by lightning! Blow out your candles, Laura—and so good-bye. . . .

She blows the candles out.

(The Scene Dissolves.)

Tennessee Williams

Tennessee Williams on Drama

HOW TO STAGE *THE GLASS MENAGERIE*   1945

Being a "memory play," *The Glass Menagerie* can be presented with unusual freedom of convention. Because of its considerably delicate or tenuous material, atmospheric touches and subtleties of direction play a particularly important part. Expressionism and all other unconventional techniques in drama have only one valid aim, and that is a closer approach to truth. When a play employs unconventional techniques, it is not, or certainly shouldn't be, trying to escape its responsibility of dealing with reality, or interpreting experience, but is actually or should be attempting to find a closer approach, a more penetrating and vivid expression of things as they are. The straight realistic play with its genuine Frigidaire and authentic ice-cubes, its characters that speak exactly as its audience speaks, corresponds to the academic landscape and has the same virtue of a photographic likeness. Everyone should know nowadays the unimportance of the photographic in art: that truth, life, or reality is an organic thing which the poetic imagination can represent or suggest, in essence, only through transformation, through changing into other forms than those which were merely present in appearance.

These remarks are not meant as a preface only to this particular play. They have to do with a conception of a new, plastic theater which must take the place of the exhausted theater of realistic conventions if the theater is to resume vitality as a part of our culture.

THE SCREEN DEVICE. There is *only one important difference between the original and acting version of the play* and that is the *omission* in the latter of the device which I tentatively included in my *original* script. This device was the use of a screen on which were projected magic-lantern slides bearing images or titles. I do not regret the omission of this device from the present Broadway production. The extraordinary power of Miss Taylor's performance° made it suitable to have the utmost simplicity in the physical production. But I think it may be interesting to some readers to see how this device was conceived. So I am putting it into the published manuscript. These images and legends, projected from behind, were cast on a section of wall between the front-room and dining-room areas, which should be indistinguishable from the rest when not in use.

The purpose of this will probably be apparent. It is to give accent to certain values in each case. Each scene contains a particular point (or several) which is structurally the most important. In an episodic play, such as this, the basic structure or narrative line may be obscured from the audience; the effect may seem fragmentary rather than architectural. This may not be the fault of the play so much as a lack of attention in the audience. The legend or image upon the screen will strengthen the effect of what is merely allusion in the writing and allow the primary point to be made more simply and lightly than if the entire responsibility were on the spoken lines. Aside from this structural value, I think the screen will have a definite emotional appeal, less definable but just as important. An imaginative producer or director may invent many other uses for this device than those indicated in the present script. In fact the possibilities of the device seem much larger to me than the instance of this play can possibly utilize.

THE MUSIC. Another extra-literary accent in this play is provided by the use of music. A single recurring tune, "The Glass Menagerie," is used to give emotional emphasis to suitable passages. This tune is like circus music, not when you are on the grounds or in the immediate vicinity of the parade, but when you are at some distance and very likely thinking of something else. It seems under those circumstances to continue almost interminably and it weaves in and out of your preoccupied consciousness; then it is the lightest, most delicate music in the world and perhaps the saddest. It expresses the surface vivacity of life with the underlying strain of immutable and inexpressible sorrow. When you look at a piece of delicately spun glass you think of two things: how beautiful it is and how easily it can be broken. Both of those ideas should be woven into the recurring tune, which dips in and out of the play as if it were carried on a wind that changes. It serves as a thread of connection and allusion between the narrator with his separate point in time and space and the subject of his story. Between each episode it returns as reference to the emotion, nostalgia, which is the first condition of the play. It is primarily Laura's music and therefore comes out most clearly when the play focuses upon her and the lovely fragility of glass which is her image.

THE LIGHTING. The lighting in the play is not realistic. In keeping with the atmosphere of memory, the stage is dim. Shafts of light are focused on selected areas or actors, sometimes in contradistinction to what is the apparent center. For instance, in the quarrel scene between Tom and Amanda, in which Laura has no active part, the clearest pool of light is on her figure. This is also true of the supper

---

Miss Taylor's performance: In the original Broadway production of the play in 1945 (see photograph on page 1973), the role of Amanda Wingfield, the mother, was played by veteran actress Laurette Taylor.

scene, when her silent figure on the sofa should remain the visual center. The light upon Laura should be distinct from the others, having a peculiar pristine clarity such as light used in early religious portraits of female saints or madonnas. A certain correspondence to light in religious paintings, such as El Greco's, where the figures are radiant in atmosphere that is relatively dusky, could be effectively used throughout the play. (It will also permit a more effective use of the screen.) A free, imaginative use of light can be of enormous value in giving a mobile, plastic quality to plays of a more or less static nature.

From the author's production notes for *The Glass Menagerie*

The theater is one of the most useful and expressive instruments for a country's edification, the barometer that registers its greatness or its decline.

—Federico García Lorca

Beth Henley

AM I BLUE   1972

Beth Henley was born in Jackson, Mississippi, in 1952, the second of four daughters of theater-loving parents. Her mother was an actress, her father a lawyer and Mississippi state senator. Henley began writing and performing in plays while still in grade school, and by the time of her high-school graduation she had decided to become an actress herself. In 1972, while a student at Southern Methodist University in Dallas, Henley wrote her first play, Am I Blue, for a playwriting class: it was later produced in New York and selected for inclusion in The Best Short Plays of 1983. *After studying acting at the University of Illinois, Henley moved to Los Angeles in 1976. Finding roles difficult to come by, she began to concentrate on writing.* Crimes of the Heart (1979), *her first full-length play, was produced in Louisville, Kentucky, and New York City in an off-Broadway theater. After it won a Pulitzer Prize, the acclaimed comedy was produced on Broadway. Henley's other plays include* The Miss Firecracker Contest (1980), The Debutante Ball (1985), Control Freaks (1992), Impossible Marriage (1998), *and* Family Week (2000). *She has also written screenplays for a number of films, including* Crimes of the Heart, *(starring Diane Keaton, Jessica Lange, and Sissy Spacek),* Miss Firecracker *(starring Holly Hunter, Tim Robbins, and Mary Steenburgen), and* Nobody's Fool *(starring Rosanna Arquette and Eric Roberts).*

DEDICATED TO STUART WHITE, MY LOVE

Characters

John Polk, 17
Ashbe, 16
Hilda, 35, a waitress
Street Characters: Barker, Whore, Bum, Clareece

The Setting. *A bar, the street, the living room of a run-down apartment.*
The Time. *Fall 1968.*

The scene opens on a street in the New Orleans French Quarter on a rainy blue bourbon night. Various people: a whore, bum, street barker, Clareece appear and disappear along the street. The scene then focuses on a bar where a piano is heard from the back room playing softly and indistinctly "Am I Blue?" The lights go up on John Polk, who sits alone at a table. He is seventeen, a bit overweight and awkward. He wears nice clothes, perhaps a navy sweater with a large white monogram. His navy raincoat is slung over an empty chair. While drinking, John Polk concentrates on the red-and-black card that he holds in his hand. As soon as the scene is established, Ashbe enters from the street. She is sixteen, wears a flowered plastic rain cap, red galoshes, a butterfly barrette, and jeweled cat eyeglasses. She is carrying a bag full of stolen goods. Her hair is very curly. Ashbe makes her way cautiously to John Polk's table. As he sees her coming he puts the card into his pocket. She sits in the empty chair and pulls his raincoat over her head.

Ashbe: Excuse me . . . do you mind if I sit here please?

John Polk (Looks up at her—then down into his glass.): What are you doing hiding under my raincoat? You're getting it all wet.

Ashbe: Well, I'm very sorry, but after all it is a raincoat.

(He tries to pull off coat.)

Ashbe: It was rude of me I know, but look I just don't want them to recognize me.

Adam Smith and Kristen Bonstein in the Drew University Theater Arts Department production of *Am I Blue?, directed by Kirsten Finberg.*

John Polk (Looking about.): Who to recognize you?

Ashbe: Well, I stole these two ashtrays from the Screw Inn, ya know right down the street. (*She pulls out two glass commercial ashtrays from her white plastic bag.*) Anyway, I'm scared the manager saw me. They'll be after me I'm afraid.

John Polk: Well, they should be. Look, do you mind giving me back my raincoat? I don't want to be found protecting any thief.

Ashbe (Coming out from under coat.): Thief—would you call Robin Hood a thief?

John Polk: Christ.

Ashbe (Back under coat.): No, you wouldn't. He was valiant—all the time stealing from the rich and giving to the poor.

John Polk: But your case isn't exactly the same, is it? You're stealing from some crummy little bar and keeping the ashtrays for yourself. Now give me back my coat.

Ashbe (Throws coat at him.): Sure take your old coat. I suppose I should have explained—about Miss Marcey. (*Silence.*) Miss Marcey, this cute old lady with a little hump in her back. I always see her in her sun hat and blue print dress. Miss Marcey lives in the apartment building next to ours. I leave all the stolen goods, as gifts on her front steps.

John Polk: Are you one of those kleptomaniacs? (*He starts checking his wallet.*)

Ashbe: You mean when people all the time steal and they can't help it?

John Polk: Yeah.

Ashbe: Oh, no. I'm not a bit careless. Take my job tonight, my very first night job, if you want to know. Anyway, I've been planning it for two months, trying to decipher which bar most deserved to be stolen from. I finally decided on the Screw Inn. Mainly because of the way they're so mean to Mr. Groves. He works at the magazine rack at Diver's Drugstore and is really very sweet, but he has a drinking problem. I don't think that's fair to be mean to people simply because they have a drinking problem—and, well, anyway, you see I'm not just stealing for personal gain. I mean, I don't even smoke.

John Polk: Yeah, well, most infants don't, but then again, most infants don't hang around bars.

Ashbe: I don't see why not, Toulouse Lautrec did.

John Polk: They'd throw me out.

Ashbe: Oh, they throw me out too, but I don't accept defeat. (*Slowly moves into him.*) Why, it's the very same with my pickpocketing.

(*John Polk sneers, turns away.*)

Ashbe: It's a very hard art to master. Why, every time I've done it I've been caught.

John Polk: That's all I need is to have some slum kid tell me how good it is to steal. Everyone knows it's not.

Ashbe (About his drink.): That looks good. What is it?

John Polk: Hey, would you mind leaving me alone—I just wanted to be alone.

Ashbe: Okay, I'm sorry. How about if I'm quiet?

(*John Polk shrugs. He sips drink, looks around, catches her eye, she smiles and sighs.*)

Ashbe: I was just looking at your pin. What fraternity are you in?

John Polk: S.A.E.

Ashbe: Is it a good fraternity?

John Polk: Sure, it's the greatest.

Ashbe: I bet you have lots of friends.

John Polk: Tons.

Ashbe: Are you being serious?

John Polk: Yes.

Ashbe: Hmm. Do they have parties and all that?

John Polk: Yeah, lots of parties, booze, honking horns, it's exactly what you would expect.

Ashbe: I wouldn't expect anything. Why did you join?

John Polk: I don't know. Well, my brother—I guess it was my brother—he told me how great it was, how the fraternity was supposed to get you dates, make you study, solve all your problems.

Ashbe: Gee, does it?

John Polk: Doesn't help you study.

Ashbe: How about dates? Do they get you a lot of dates?

John Polk: Some.

Ashbe: What were the girls like?

John Polk: I don't know—they were like girls.

Ashbe: Did you have a good time?

John Polk: I had a pretty good time.

Ashbe: Did you make love to any of them?

John Polk (*To self.*): Oh, Christ—

Ashbe: I'm sorry—I just figured that's why you had the appointment with the whore—'cause you didn't have any one else—to make love to.

John Polk: How did you know I had the, ah, the appointment?

Ashbe: I saw you put the red card in your pocket when I came up. Those red cards are pretty familiar around here. The house is only about a block or so away. It's one of the best though really very plush. Only two murders and a knifing in its whole history. Do you go there often?

John Polk: Yeah, I like to give myself a treat.

Ashbe: Who do you have?

John Polk: What do you mean?

Ashbe: I mean which girl.

(*John Polk gazes into his drink.*)

Ashbe: Look, I just thought I might know her is all.

John Polk: Know her, ah, how would you know her?

Ashbe: Well, some of the girls from my high school go there to work when they get out.

John Polk: G. G., her name is G. G.

Ashbe: G. G.—Hmm, well, how does she look?

John Polk: I don't know.

Ashbe: Oh, you've never been with her before?

John Polk: No.

Ashbe (Confidentially.): Are you one of those kinds that likes a lot of variety?

John Polk: Variety? Sure, I guess I like variety.

Ashbe: Oh, yes, now I remember.

John Polk: What?

Ashbe: G. G., that's just her working name. Her real name is Myrtle Reims, she's
Kay Reims' older sister. Kay is in my grade at school.

John Polk: Myrtle? Her name is Myrtle?

Ashbe: I never liked the name either.

John Polk: Myrtle, oh. Christ. Is she pretty?

Ashbe (Matter-of-factly.): Pretty, no she's not real pretty.

John Polk: What does she look like?

Ashbe: Let's see . . . she's, ah, well, Myrtle had acne and there are a few scars left.
It's not bad. I think they sort of give her character. Her hair's red only I
don't think it's really red. It sort of fizzles out all over her head. She's got a
pretty good figure—big top—but the rest of her is kind of skinny.

John Polk: I wonder if she has a good personality.

Ashbe: Well, she was a senior when I was a freshman; so I never really knew her.
I remember she used to paint her fingernails lots of different colors—pink,
orange, purple. I don't know, but she kind of scares me. About the only time
I ever saw her true personality was around a year ago. I was over at Kay's
making a health poster for school. Anyway, Myrtle comes busting in
screaming about how she can't find her spangled bra anywhere. Kay and I
just sat on the floor cutting pictures of food out of magazines while she was
storming about slamming drawers and swearing. Finally, she found it. It was
pretty garish—red with black and gold sequined G.'s on each cup. That's
how I remember the name—G. G.

*(As Ashbe illustrates the placement of the G.'s, she spots Hilda, the waitress, ap-
proaching. Ashbe pulls the raincoat over her head and hides on the floor. Hilda
enters through the beaded curtains spilling her tray. Hilda is a woman of few
words.)*

Hilda: Shit, damn curtain. Nuther drink?

John Polk: Mam?

Hilda (Points to drink.): Vodka coke?

John Polk: No, thank you. I'm not quite finished yet.

Hilda: Napkins clean.

*(Ashbe pulls her bag off the table. Hilda looks at Ashbe then to John Polk. She
walks around the table, as Ashbe is crawling along the floor to escape. Ashbe runs
into Hilda's toes.)*

Ashbe: Are those real gold?

Hilda: You again. Out.

Ashbe: She wants me to leave. Why should a paying customer leave? (*Back to Hilda.*) Now I'll have a mint julep and easy on the mint.

Hilda: This preteen with you?

John Polk: Well—I—No—I—

Hilda: I.D.'s.

Ashbe: Certainly, I always try to cooperate with the management.

Hilda (*Looking at John Polk's I.D.*): I.D., 11-12-50. Date 11-11-68.

John Polk: Yes, but—well, 11-12 is less than two hours away.

Hilda: Back in two hours.

Ashbe: I seem to have left my identification in my gold lamé bag.

Hilda: Well, boo hoo. (*Motions for Ashbe to leave with a minimum of effort. She goes back to table.*) No tip.

Ashbe: You didn't tip her?

John Polk: I figured the drinks were so expensive—I just didn't—

Hilda: No tip!

John Polk: Look, Miss, I'm sorry. (*Going through his pockets.*) Here, would you like a—a nickel—wait, wait, here's a quarter.

Hilda: Just move ass, sonny. You too, Barbie.

Ashbe: Ugh, I hate public rudeness. I'm sure I'll refrain from ever coming here again.

Hilda: Think I'll go in the back room and cry.

(*Ashbe and John Polk exit. Hilda picks up tray and exits through the curtain tripping again.*)

Hilda: Shit. Damn curtain.

(*Ashbe and John Polk are now standing outside under the awning of the bar.*)

Ashbe: Gee, I didn't know it was your birthday tomorrow. Happy birthday! Don't be mad. I thought you were at least twenty or twenty-one, really.

John Polk: It's O.K. Forget it.

(*As they begin walking various blues are heard coming from the nearby bars.*)

Ashbe: It's raining.

John Polk: I know.

Ashbe: Are you going over to the house now?

John Polk: No, not till twelve.

Ashbe: Yeah, the pink and black cards—they mean all night. Midnight till morning.

(*At this point a street barker beckons the couple into his establishment. Perhaps he is accompanied by a whore.*)

Barker: Hey, mister, bring your baby on in, buy her a few drinks, maybe tonight ya get lucky.

Ashbe: Keep walking.

John Polk: What's wrong with the place?

Ashbe: The drinks are watery rot gut and the showgirls are boys.

Barker: Up yours, punk!

John Polk (Who has now sat down on a street bench.): Look, just tell me where a cheap bar is. I've got to stay drunk, but I don't have much money left.

Ashbe: Yikes, there aren't too many cheap bars around here and a lot of them check I.D.'s.

John Polk: Well, do you know of any that don't?

Ashbe: No, not for sure.

John Polk: Oh, God, I need to get drunk.

Ashbe: Aren't you?

John Polk: Some, but I'm losing ground fast.

> *(By this time a bum who has been traveling drunkenly down the street falls near the couple and begins throwing up.)*

Ashbe: Oh, I know! You can come to my apartment. It's just down the block. We keep one bottle of rum around. I'll serve you a grand drink, three or four if you like.

John Polk (Fretfully.): No thanks.

Ashbe: But look, we're getting all wet.

John Polk: Sober too, wet and sober.

Ashbe: Oh, come on! Rain's blurring my glasses.

John Polk: Well, how about your parents? What would they say?

Ashbe: Daddy's out of town and Mama lives in Atlanta; so I'm sure they won't mind. I think we have some cute little marshmallows. *(Pulling on him.)* Won't you really come?

John Polk: You've probably got some gang of muggers waiting to kill me. Oh, alright—what the hell, let's go.

Ashbe: Hurrah! Come on. It's this way. *(She starts across the stage, stops, and picks up an old hat.)* Hey, look at this hat. Isn't it something! Here, wear it to keep off the rain.

John Polk (Throwing hat back onto street): No, thanks, you don't know who's worn it before.

Ashbe (Picking hat back up.): That makes it all the more exciting. Maybe it was a butcher's who slaughtered his wife or a silver pirate with a black bird on his throat. Who do you guess?

John Polk: I don't know. Anyway what's the good of guessing? I mean you'll never really know.

Ashbe (Trying the hat on.): Yeah, probably not. *(At this point, Ashbe and John Polk reach the front door.)* Here we are.

> *(Ashe begins fumbling for her key. Clareece, a teeny-bopper, walks up to John Polk.)*

Clareece: Hey, man, got any spare change?

John Polk (Looking through his pockets.): Let me see—I—

Ashbe (Coming up between them, giving Clareece a shove.): Beat it, Clareece. He's my company.

Clareece (Walks away and sneers.): Oh, shove it, Frizzels.

Ashbe: A lot of jerks live around here. Come on in.

(*She opens the door. Lights go up on the living room of a run-down apartment in a run-down apartment house. Besides being merely run-down the room is a malicious pig sty with colors, paper hats, paper dolls, masks, torn up stuffed animals, dead flowers and leaves, dress up clothes, etc. thrown all about.*)

Ashbe: My bones are cold. Do you want a towel to dry off?

John Polk: Yes, thank you.

Ashbe (She picks a towel up off of the floor and tosses it to him.): Here.

(*He begins drying off, as she takes off her rain things then she begins raking things off the sofa.*)

Ashbe: Please do sit down.

(*He sits.*)

Ashbe: I'm sorry the place is disheveled, but my father's been out of town. I always try to pick up and all before he gets in. Of course he's pretty used to messes. My mother never was too good at keeping things clean.

John Polk: When's he coming back?

Ashbe: Sunday, I believe. Oh, I've been meaning to say—

John Polk: What?

Ashbe: My name's Ashbe Williams.

John Polk: Ashbe?

Ashbe: Yeah, Ashbe.

John Polk: My name's John Polk Richards.

Ashbe: John Polk? They call you John Polk?

John Polk: It's family.

Ashbe (Putting on socks.): These are my favorite socks, the red furry ones. Well, here's some books and magazines to look at while I fix you something to drink. What do you want in your rum?

John Polk: Coke's fine.

Ashbe: I'll see do we have any. I think I'll take some hot Koolade myself. (*She exits to the kitchen.*)

John Polk: Hot Koolade?

Ashbe: It's just Koolade that's been heated, like hot chocolate or hot tea.

John Polk: Sounds great.

Ashbe: Well, I'm used to it. You get so much for your dime it makes it worth your while. I don't buy presweetened, of course, it's better to sugar your own.

John Polk: I remember once I threw up a lot of grape Koolade when I was a kid. I've hated it ever since. Hey, would you check on the time?

Ashbe (She enters carrying a tray with several bottles of food coloring, a bottle of rum, and a huge glass.): I'm sorry we don't have Cokes. I wonder if rum and Koolade is good? Oh, we don't have a clock either. (*She pours a large amount of rum into the large glass.*)

John Polk: I'll just have it with water then.

Ashbe (She finds an almost empty glass of water somewhere in the room and dumps it in with the rum.): Would you like food coloring in the water? It makes a drink all the more aesthetic. Of course, some people don't care for aesthetics.

John Polk: No thank you, just plain water.

Ashbe: Are you sure? The taste is entirely the same. I put it in all my water.

John Polk: Well.

Ashbe: What color do you want?

John Polk: I don't know.

Ashbe: What's your favorite color?

John Polk: Blue, I guess.

(She puts a few blue drops into the glass—as she has nothing to stir with, she blows into the glass turning the water blue.)

John Polk: Thanks.

Ashbe (Exits. She screams from kitchen.): Come on, say come on cat, eat your fresh good milk.

John Polk: You have a cat?

Ashbe (Off.): No.

John Polk: Oh.

Ashbe (She enters carrying a tray with a cup of hot Koolade and Cheerios and colored marshmallows.): Here are some Cheerios and some cute little colored marshmallows to eat with your drink.

John Polk: Thanks.

Ashbe: I one time smashed all the big white marshmallows in the plastic bag at the grocery store.

John Polk: Why did you do that?

Ashbe: I was angry. Do you like ceramics?

John Polk: Yes.

Ashbe: My mother makes them. It's sort of her hobby. She is very talented.

John Polk: My mother never does anything. Well, I guess she can shuffle the bridge deck okay.

Ashbe: Actually, my mother is a dancer. She teaches at a school in Atlanta. She's really very talented.

John Polk (Indicates ceramics.): She must be to do all these.

Ashbe: Well, Madeline, my older sister, did the blue one. Madeline gets to live with Mama.

John Polk: And you live with your father.

Ashbe: Yeah, but I get to go visit them sometimes.

John Polk: You do ceramics too?

Ashbe: No, I never learned . . . but I have this great potholder set. *(Gets up to show him.)* See I make lots of multicolored potholders and send them to Mama and Madeline. I also make paper hats. *(Gets material to show him.)* I guess they're more creative but making potholders is more relaxing. Here would you like to make a hat?

John Polk: I don't know, I'm a little drunk.

Ashbe: It's not hard a bit. (*Hands him material.*) Just draw a real pretty design on the paper. It really doesn't have to be pretty, just whatever you want.

John Polk: It's kind of you to give my creative drives such freedom.

Ashbe: Ha, ha, ha, I'll work on my potholder set a bit.

John Polk: What time is it? I've really got to check on the time.

Ashbe: I know, I'll call the time operator. (*She goes to the phone.*)

John Polk: How do you get along without a clock?

Ashbe: Well, I've been late for school a lot. Daddy has a watch. It's 11:03.

John Polk: I've got a while yet.

(*Ashbe twirls back to her chair, drops, and sighs.*)

John Polk: Are you a dancer too?

Ashbe (*Delighted.*): I can't dance a bit, really. I practice a lot is all, at home in the afternoon. I imagine you go to a lot of dances.

John Polk: Not really, I'm a terrible dancer. I usually get bored or drunk.

Ashbe: You probably drink too much.

John Polk: No, it's just since I've come to college. All you do there is drink more beer and write more papers.

Ashbe: What are you studying for to be?

John Polk: I don't know.

Ashbe: Why don't you become a rancher?

John Polk: Dad wants me to help run his soybean farm.

Ashbe: Soybean farm. Yikes, that's really something. Where is it?

John Polk: Well, I live in the Delta, Hollybluff, Mississippi. Anyway, Dad feels I should go to business school first; you know, so I'll become, well, management-minded. Pass the blue.

Ashbe: Is that what you really want to do?

John Polk: I don't know. It would probably be as good as anything else I could do. Dad makes good money. He can take vacations whenever he wants. Sure it'll be a ball.

Ashbe: I'd hate to have to be management-minded.

(*John Polk shrugs.*)

Ashbe: I don't mean to hurt your feelings but I would really hate to be a management mind. (*She starts walking on her knees, twisting her fists in front of her eyes, and making clicking sounds as a management mind would make.*)

John Polk: Cut it out. Just forget it. The farm could burn down and I wouldn't even have to think about it.

Ashbe (*After a pause.*): Well, what do you want to talk about?

John Polk: I don't know.

Ashbe: When was the last dance you went to?

John Polk: Dances. That's a great subject. Let's see, oh, I don't really remember it was probably some blind date. God, I hate dates.

Ashbe: Why?

John Polk: Well, they always say that they don't want popcorn and they wind up eating all yours.

Ashbe: You mean, you hate dates just because they eat your popcorn? Don't you think that's kind of stingy?

John Polk: It's the principle of the thing. Why can't they just say, yes, I'd like some popcorn when you ask them. But, no, they're always so damn coy.

Ashbe: I'd tell my date if I wanted popcorn. I'm not that immature.

John Polk: Anyway, it's not only the popcorn. It's a lot of little things. I've finished coloring. What do I do now?

Ashbe: Now you have to fold it. Here . . . like this. (*She explains the process with relish.*) Say, that's really something.

John Polk: It's kind of funny looking. (*Putting the hat on.*) Yeah, I like it, but you could never wear it anywhere.

Ashbe: Well, like what anyway?

John Polk: Huh?

Ashbe: The things dates do to you that you don't like, the little things.

John Polk: Oh, well, just the way they wear those false eyelashes and put their hand on your knee when you're trying to parallel park, and keep on giggling and going off to the bathroom with their girlfriends. It's obvious they don't want to go out with me. They just want to go out so that they can wear their new clothes and won't have to sit on their ass in the dormitory. They never want to go out with me. I can never even talk to them.

Ashbe: Well, you can talk to me and I'm a girl.

John Polk: Well, I'm really kind of drunk and you're a stranger . . . well, I probably wouldn't be able to talk to you tomorrow. That makes a difference.

Ashbe: Maybe it does. (*A bit of a pause and then extremely pleased by the idea she says.*) You know we're alike because I don't like dances either.

John Polk: I thought you said you practiced . . . in the afternoons.

Ashbe: Well, I like dancing. I just don't like dances. At least not like—well, not like the one our school was having tonight . . . they're so corny.

John Polk: Yeah, most dances are.

Ashbe: All they serve is potato chips and fruit punch, and then this stupid baby band plays and everybody dances around thinking they're so hot. I frankly wouldn't dance there. I would prefer to wait till I am invited to an exclusive ball. It doesn't really matter which ball, just one where they have huge, golden chandeliers and silver fountains, and serve delicacies of all sorts and bubble blue champagne. I'll arrive in a pink silk cape. (*Laughing.*) I want to dance in pink!

John Polk: You're mixed up. You're probably one of those people that live in a fantasy world.

Ashbe: I do not. I accept reality as well as anyone. Anyway, you can talk to me remember. I know what you mean by the kind of girls it's hard to talk to. There are girls a lot that way in the small clique at my school. Really tacky and mean. They expect everyone to be as stylish as they are and they won't even speak to you in the hall. I don't mind if they don't speak to me, but I really love the orphans and it hurts my feelings when they are so mean to them.

John Polk: What do you mean—they're mean to the orpheens? (*Notices pun and giggles to self.*)

Ashbe: Oh, well, they sometimes snicker at the orphans' dresses. The orphans usually have hand-me down drab ugly dresses. Once Shelly Maxwell wouldn't let Glinda borrow her pencil, even though she had two. It hurt her feelings.

John Polk: Are you best friends with these orphans?

Ashbe: I hardly know them at all. They're really shy. I just like them a lot. They're the reason I put spells on the girls in the clique.

John Polk: Spells, what do you mean, witch spells?

Ashbe: Witch spells? Not really, mostly just voodoo.

John Polk: Are you kidding? Do you really do voodoo?

Ashbe: Sure, here I'll show you my doll. (*Goes to get doll, comes back with straw voodoo doll. Her air as she returns is one of frightening mystery.*) I know a lot about the subject. Cora, she used to wash dishes in the Moonlight Cafe, told me all about voodoo. She's a real expert on the subject, went to all the meetings and everything. Once she caused a man's throat to rot away and turn almost totally black. She's moved to Chicago now.

John Polk: It doesn't really work. Does it?

Ashbe: Well, not always. The thing about voodoo is that both parties have to believe in it for it to work.

John Polk: Do the girls in school believe in it?

Ashbe: Not really, I don't think. That's where my main problem comes in. I have to make the clique believe in it, yet I have to be very subtle. Mainly, I give reports in English class or Speech.

John Polk: Reports?

Ashbe: On voodoo.

John Polk: That's really kind of sick, you know.

Ashbe: Not really. I don't cast spells that'll do any real harm. Mainly, just the kind of thing to make them think—to keep them on their toes.

(*Blue drink intoxication begins to take over and John Polk begins laughing.*)

Ashbe: What's so funny?

John Polk: Nothing. I was just thinking what a mean little person you are.

Ashbe: Mean! I'm not mean a bit.

John Polk: Yes, you are mean—(*Picking up color.*) and green too.

Ashbe: Green?

John Polk: Yes, green with envy of those other girls; so you play all those mean little tricks.

Ashbe: Envious of those other girls, that stupid, close-minded little clique!

John Polk: Green as this marshmallow. (*Eats marshmallow.*)

Ashbe: You think I want to be in some group . . . a sheep like you? A little sheep like you that does everything when he's supposed to do it!

John Polk: Me a sheep—I do what I want!

Ashbe: Ha! I've known you for an hour and already I see you for the sheep you are!

John Polk: Don't take your green meanness out on me.

Ashbe: Not only are you a sheep, you are a NORMAL sheep. Give me back my colors! *(Begins snatching colors away.)*

John Polk (Pushing colors at her.): Green and mean! Green and mean! Green and mean! Etc.

Ashbe (Throwing marshmallows at him.): That's the reason you're in a fraternity and the reason you're going to manage your mind, and dates—you go out on dates merely because it's expected of you even though you have a terrible time. That's the reason you go to the whorehouse to prove you're a normal man. Well, you're much too normal for me.

John Polk: Infant bitch. You think you're really cute.

Ashbe: That really wasn't food coloring in your drink, it was poison!

(She laughs, he picks up his coat to go and she stops throwing marshmallows at him.)

Ashbe: Are you going? I was only kidding. For Christ sake it wasn't really poison. Come on, don't go. Can't you take a little friendly criticism?

John Polk: Look, did you have to bother me tonight? I had enough problems without—

(Phone rings. Both look at phone, it rings for the third time. He stands undecided.)

Ashbe: Look, wait, we'll make it up. *(She goes to answer phone.)* Hello—Daddy. How are you? . . . . I'm fine . . . . Dad, you sound funny . . . what? Come on Daddy, you know she's not here. *(Pause.)* Look, I told you I wouldn't call anymore. You've got her number in Atlanta. *(Pause, as she sinks to the floor.)* Why have you started again? . . . Don't say that. I can tell it. I can. Hey, I have to go to bed now, I don't want to talk anymore, O.K.? *(Hangs up phone, softly to self.)* Goddamnit.

John Polk (He has heard the conversation and is taking off his coat.): Hey, Ashbe—

(She looks at him blankly, her mind far away.)

John Polk: You want to talk?

Ashbe: No. *(Slight pause.)* Why don't you look at my shell collection? I have this special shell collection. *(She shows him collection.)*

John Polk: They're beautiful, I've never seen colors like this.

(Ashbe is silent, he continues to himself.)

John Polk: I used to go to Biloxi a lot when I was a kid . . . one time my brother and I, we camped out on the beach. The sky was purple. I remember it was really purple. We ate pork and beans out of a can. I'd always kinda wanted to do that. Every night for about a week after I got home, I dreamt about these waves foaming over my head and face. It was funny. Did you find these shells or buy them?

Ashbe: Some I found, some I bought. I've been trying to decipher their meaning. Here, listen, do you hear that?

John Polk: Yes.

Ashbe: That's the soul of the sea. *(She listens.)* I'm pretty sure it's the soul of the sea. Just imagine when I decipher the language. I'll know all the secrets of the world.

John Polk: Yeah, probably you will. *(Looking into the shell.)* You know, you were right.

Ashbe: What do you mean?

John Polk: About me, you were right. I am a sheep, a normal one. I've been trying to get out of it, but now I'm as big a sheep as ever.

Ashbe: Oh, it doesn't matter. You're company. It was rude of me to say.

John Polk: No, because it was true. I really didn't want to go into a fraternity, I didn't even want to go to college, and I sure as hell don't want to go back to Hollybluff and work the soybean farm till I'm eighty.

Ashbe: I still say you could work on a ranch.

John Polk: I don't know. I wanted to be a minister or something good, but I don't even know if I believe in God.

Ashbe: Yeah.

John Polk: I never used to worry about being a failure. Now I think about it all the time. It's just I need to do something that's—fulfilling.

Ashbe: Fulfilling, yes, I see what you mean. Well, how about college? Isn't it fulfilling? I mean, you take all those wonderful classes, and you have all your very good friends.

John Polk: Friends, yeah, I have some friends.

Ashbe: What do you mean?

John Polk: Nothing—well, I do mean something. What the hell, let me try to explain. You see it was my "friends," the fraternity guys that set me up with G. G., excuse me Myrtle, as a gift for my eighteenth birthday.

Ashbe: You mean, you didn't want the appointment?

John Polk: No, I didn't want it. Hey, ah, where did my blue drink go?

Ashbe (As she hands him the drink.): They probably thought you really wanted to go.

John Polk: Yeah, I'm sure they gave a damn what I wanted. They never even asked me. Hell, I would have told them a handkerchief, a pair of argyle socks, but, no, they have to get me a whore just because it's a cool ass thing to do. They make me sick. I couldn't even stay at the party they gave. All the sweaty T-shirts, and moron sex stories—I just couldn't take it.

Ashbe: Is that why you were at the Blue Angel so early?

John Polk: Yeah, I needed to get drunk but not with them. They're such creeps.

Ashbe: Gosh, so you really don't want to go to Myrtle's?

John Polk: No, I guess not.

Ashbe: Then are you going?

John Polk (Pause.): Yes.

Ashbe: That's wrong. You shouldn't go just to please them.

John Polk: Oh, that's not the point anymore, maybe at first it was, but it's not anymore. Now I have to go for myself—to prove to myself that I'm not afraid.

Ashbe: Afraid? *(Slowly, as she begins to grasp his meaning.)* You mean, you've never slept with a girl before?

John Polk: Well, I've never been in love.

Ashbe (In amazement.): You're a virgin?

John Polk: Oh, God.

Ashbe: No, don't feel bad, I am too.

John Polk: I thought I should be in love—

Ashbe: Well, you're certainly not in love with Myrtle. I mean, you haven't even met her.

John Polk: I know, but, God, I thought maybe I'd never fall in love. What then? You should experience everything—shouldn't you? Oh, what's it matter, everything's so screwed.

Ashbe: Screwed? Yeah, I guess it is. I mean, I always thought it would be fun to have a lot of friends who gave parties and go to dances all dressed up. Like the dance tonight—it might have been fun.

John Polk: Well, why didn't you go?

Ashbe: I don't know. I'm not sure it would have been fun. Anyway, you can't go—alone.

John Polk: Oh, you need a date?

Ashbe: Yeah, or something.

John Polk: Say, Ashbe, ya wanna dance here?

Ashbe: No, I think we'd better discuss your dilemma.

John Polk: What dilemma?

Ashbe: Myrtle. It doesn't seem right you should—

John Polk: Let's forget Myrtle for now. I've got a while yet. Here, have some more of this blue-moon drink.

Ashbe: You're only trying to escape through artificial means.

John Polk: Yeah, you got it. Now come on. Would you like to dance? Hey, you said you liked to dance.

Ashbe: You're being ridiculous.

John Polk (Winking at her.): Dance?

Ashbe: John Polk, I just thought—

John Polk: Hmm?

Ashbe: How to solve your problem—

John Polk: Well—

Ashbe: Make love to me!

John Polk: What?!

Ashbe: It all seems logical to me. It would prove you weren't scared and you wouldn't be doing it just to impress others.

John Polk: Look, I—I mean I hardly know you—

Ashbe: But we've talked. It's better this way, really. I won't be so apt to point out your mistakes.

John Polk: I'd feel great stripping a twelve-year-old of her virginity.

Ashbe: I'm sixteen! Anyway, I'd be stripping you of yours just as well. I'll go put on some Tiger Claw perfume. (*She runs out.*)

John Polk: Hey, come back! Tiger Claw perfume, Christ.

Ashbe (Entering.): I think one should have different scents for different moods.

John Polk: Hey, stop spraying that! You know I'm not going to—well, you'd get neurotic, or pregnant, or some damn thing. Stop spraying, will you!

Ashbe: Pregnant? You really think I could get pregnant?

John Polk: Sure, it'd be a delightful possibility.

Ashbe: It really wouldn't be bad. Maybe I would get to go to Tokyo for an abortion. I've never been to the Orient.

John Polk: Sure, getting cut on is always a real treat.

Ashbe: Anyway, I might just want to have my dear baby. I could move to Atlanta with Mama and Madeline. It'd be wonderful fun. Why, I could take him to the supermarket, put him in one of those little baby seats to stroll him about. I'd buy peach baby food and feed it to him with a tiny golden spoon. Why, I could take colored pictures of him and send them to you through the mail. Come on— *(Starts putting pillows onto the couch.)* Well, I guess you should kiss me for a start. It's only etiquette, everyone begins with it.

John Polk: I don't think I could even kiss you with a clear conscience. I mean, you're so small with those little cat eyeglasses and curly hair—I couldn't even kiss you.

Ashbe: You couldn't even kiss me? I can't help it if I have to wear glasses. I got the prettiest ones I could find.

John Polk: Your glasses are fine. Let's forget it, O.K.?

Ashbe: I know, my lips are too purple, but if I eat carrots, the dye'll come off and they'll be orange.

John Polk: I didn't say anything about your lips being too purple.

Ashbe: Well, what is it? You're just plain chicken I suppose—

John Polk: Sure, right, I'm chicken, totally chicken. Let's forget it. I don't know how; but, somehow, this is probably all my fault.

Ashbe: You're darn right it's all your fault! I want to have my dear baby or at least get to Japan. I'm so sick of school I could smash every marshmallow in sight! *(She starts smashing.)* Go on to your skinny pimple whore. I hope the skinny whore laughs in your face which she probably will because you have an easy face to laugh in.

John Polk: You're absolutely right, she'll probably hoot and howl her damn fizzle red head off. Maybe you can wait outside the door and hear her, give you lots of pleasure, you sadistic little thief.

Ashbe: Thief—was Robin Hood—oh, what's wrong with this world? I just wasn't made for it is all. I've probably been put in the wrong world, I can see that now.

John Polk: You're fine in this world.

Ashbe: Sure, everyone just views me as an undesirable lump.

John Polk: Who?

Ashbe: You for one.

John Polk (Pause.): You mean because I wouldn't make love to you?

Ashbe: It seems clear to me.

John Polk: But you're wrong, you know.

Ashbe (To self, softly.): Don't pity me.

John Polk: The reason I wouldn't wasn't that—it's just that—well, I like you too much to.

Ashbe: You like me?

John Polk: Undesirable lump, Jesus. Your cheeks, they're—they're—

Ashbe: My cheeks? They're what?

John Polk: They're rosy.

Ashbe: My cheeks are rosy?

John Polk: Yeah, your cheeks, they're really rosy.

Ashbe: Well, they're natural, you know. Say, would you like to dance?

John Polk: Yes.

Ashbe: I'll turn on the radio. *(She turns on radio. Ethel Waters is heard singing "Honey in the Honeycomb." Ashbe begins snapping her fingers.)* Yikes, let's jazz it out.

(They dance.)

John Polk: Hey, I'm not good or anything—

Ashbe: John Polk.

John Polk: Yeah?

Ashbe: Baby, I think you dance fine!

(They dance on, laughing, saying what they want till end of song. Then a radio announcer comes on and says the 12:00 news will be in five minutes. Billie Holiday or Terry Pierce, begins singing, "Am I Blue?")

John Polk: Dance?

Ashbe: News in five minutes.

John Polk: Yeah.

Ashbe: That means five minutes till midnight.

John Polk: Yeah, I know.

Ashbe: Then you're not—

John Polk: Ashbe, I've never danced all night. Wouldn't it be something to—to dance all night and watch the rats come out of the gutter?

Ashbe: Rats?

John Polk: Don't they come out at night? I hear New Orleans has lots of rats.

Ashbe: Yeah, yeah, its got lots of rats.

John Polk: Then let's dance all night and wait for them to come out.

Ashbe: Alright—but, but how about our feet?

John Polk: Feet?

Ashbe: They'll hurt.

John Polk: Yeah.

Ashbe (Smiling.): Okay, then let's dance.

(He takes her hand and they dance as lights black out and the music soars and continues to play.)

END OF PLAY

Beth Henley

Beth Henley on Drama

A PLAYWRIGHT IS BORN   2000

Am I Blue was written for a playwriting class at Southern Methodist University in 1972. Originally it was titled *No, I Don't Have a Cat.* That summer I went to the New Orleans French Quarter and heard the song "Am I Blue?" for the first time. I loved it immediately and helplessly. Whenever the bandleader asked for requests I shouted out "Am I blue?! Am I blue?!" . . .

When *Am I Blue?* was produced as a major production at SMU in 1974, my recently divorced parents came to Dallas to see it. This was the only play of mine my father ever saw. He died in the summer of 1978. He seemed indifferent to the play but gave me an excellent suggestion concerning the title. "There shouldn't be a question mark in the title. Am I blue. It's a statement, it's a fact."

My mother, on the other hand, loved the play and even cried. Her concern was that I had chosen to present the play under the pseudonym "Amy Peach." There was the practical dilemma of taking the program back to friends and relatives in Mississippi and explaining that her daughter, Beth Henley, was now known as Amy Peach. She also feared I had done this in reaction to the divorce and was ashamed to be their child. Although I could not tell her at the time, the pen name was in fact an early nod to nihilism. At fourteen I went unchaperoned with some girlfriends on a trip to Mississippi State College for Women to see the Miss Mississippi Contest. I was delirious with the first smell of freedom and in a fit of pubescent euphoria ran up to a strange college man and said, "One day I am going to be a writer and I will call myself Amy Peach! Remember that name!" He responded with bitter disdain, "Little girl, if you were just half as cute as you think you are, you'd still be ugly." That was my last fearless attempt at flamboyance.

From *Collected Plays, Volume 1: 1980–1989*

David Henry Hwang

THE SOUND OF A VOICE

1983

David Henry Hwang (b. 1957) grew up in San Gabriel, California, the son of first-generation Chinese immigrants. He was born into a family of musicians: his mother was a concert pianist, his sister plays cello in a string quartet, and he studied the violin. In 1979, as a senior at Stanford University, he directed his first play, F. O. B. (an acronym for "fresh off the boat") in a dormitory lounge. F. O. B. was later staged at the New York Shakespeare Festival Public Theater and won a 1981 Obie Award. The Sound of a Voice was also produced at the Public Theater as part of a double bill with another one-act play by Hwang, The House of Sleeping Beauties. Hwang enjoyed his greatest commercial and critical success with M. Butterfly (1988), that won the Tony Award for best play. Among his more recent plays are Face Value (1993) and Golden Child (1997). While some of his plays are realistic in their approach, Hwang has always been fascinated by the possibilities of symbolic drama. In The Sound of a Voice, he creates a timeless, placeless scene in which two characters named Man and Woman act out a story reminiscent of a folk legend or a traditional Japanese Nō drama (a type of symbolic aristocratic drama developed in the fourteenth century in which a ghost recounts the struggles of his or her life for a traveler). Hwang's interest in nonrealistic and experimental drama has also led him to explore opera. He has collaborated with composer Philip Glass on three works: 1000 Airplanes on the Roof (1988), a science-fiction music drama; The Voyage (1992), an allegorical grand opera commissioned by New York's Metropolitan Opera for the 500th anniversary of Christopher Columbus's arrival in America; and The Sound of a Voice (2003), a combined staging of the following play with The House of Sleeping Beauties. Hwang lives in New York City.

Characters

Man, fifties, Japanese
Woman, fifties, Japanese

Setting. *Woman's house, in a remote corner of the forest.*

SCENE I

Woman pours tea for Man. Man rubs himself, trying to get warm.

Man: You're very kind to take me in.
Woman: This is a remote corner of the world. Guests are rare.
Man: The tea—you pour it well.
Woman: No.
Man: The sound it makes—in the cup—very soothing.
Woman: That is the tea's skill, not mine. (*She hands the cup to him.*) May I get you something else? Rice, perhaps?

Man: No.

Woman: And some vegetables?

Man: No, thank you.

Woman: Fish? (*Pause.*) It is at least two days' walk to the nearest village. I saw no horse. You must be very hungry. You would do a great honor to dine with me. Guests are rare.

Man: Thank you.

Woman (*Woman gets up, leaves. Man holds the cup in his hands, using it to warm himself. He gets up, walks around the room. It is sparsely furnished, drab, except for one shelf on which stands a vase of brightly colored flowers. The flowers stand out in sharp contrast to the starkness of the room. Slowly, he reaches out towards them. He touches them. Quickly, he takes one of the flowers from the vase, hides it in his clothes. He returns to where he had sat previously. He waits. Woman re-enters. She carries a tray with food.*): Please. Eat. It will give me great pleasure.

Man: This—this is magnificent.

Woman: Eat.

Man: Thank you. (*He motions for Woman to join him.*)

Woman: No, thank you.

Man: This is wonderful. The best I've tasted.

Woman: You are reckless in your flattery. But anything you say, I will enjoy hearing. It's not even the words. It's the sound of a voice, the way it moves through the air.

Man: How long has it been since you last had a visitor? (*Pause.*)

Woman: I don't know.

Man: Oh?

Woman: I lose track. Perhaps five months ago, perhaps ten years, perhaps yesterday. I don't consider time when there is no voice in the air. It's pointless. Time begins with the entrance of a visitor, and ends with his exit.

Man: And in between? You don't keep track of the days? You can't help but notice—

Woman: Of course I notice.

Man: Oh.

Woman: I notice, but I don't keep track. (*Pause.*) May I bring out more?

Man: More? No. No. This was wonderful.

Woman: I have more.

Man: Really—the best I've had.

Woman: You must be tired. Did you sleep in the forest last night?

Man: Yes.

Woman: Or did you not sleep at all?

Man: I slept.

Woman: Where?

Man: By a waterfall. The sound of the water put me to sleep. It rumbled like the sounds of a city. You see, I can't sleep in too much silence. It scares me. It makes me feel that I have no control over what is about to happen.

Woman: I feel the same way.

Man: But you live here—alone?

Woman: Yes.

Man: It's so quiet here. How can you sleep?

Woman: Tonight, I'll sleep. I'll lie down in the next room, and hear your breathing through the wall, and fall asleep shamelessly. There will be no silence.

Man: You're very kind to let me stay here.

Woman: This is yours. (*She unrolls a mat; there is a beautiful design of a flower on the mat. The flower looks exactly like the flowers in the vase.*)

Man: Did you make it yourself?

Woman: Yes. There is a place to wash outside.

Man: Thank you.

Woman: Goodnight.

Man: Goodnight. (*Man starts to leave.*)

Woman: May I know your name?

Man: No. I mean, I would rather not say. If I gave you a name, it would only be made-up. Why should I deceive you? You are too kind for that.

Woman: Then what should I call you? Perhaps—"Man Who Fears Silence"?

Man: How about, "Man Who Fears Women"?

Woman: That name is much too common.

Man: And you?

Woman: Yokiko.

Man: That's your name?

Woman: It's what you may call me.

Man: Goodnight, Yokiko. You are very kind.

Woman: You are very smart. Goodnight.

> (*Man exits. Hanako° goes to the mat. She tidies it, brushes it off. She goes to the vase. She picks up the flowers, studies them. She carries them out of the room with her. Man re-enters. He takes off his outer clothing. He glimpses the spot where the vase used to sit. He reaches into his clothing, pulls out the stolen flower. He studies it. He puts it underneath his head as he lies down to sleep, like a pillow. He starts to fall asleep. Suddenly, a start. He picks up his head. He listens.*)

SCENE II

Dawn. Man is getting dressed. Woman enters with food.

Woman: Good morning.

Man: Good morning, Yokiko.

Woman: You weren't planning to leave?

Man: I have quite a distance to travel today.

Woman: Please. (*She offers him food.*)

Hanako: The woman.

Man: Thank you.

Woman: May I ask where you're travelling to?

Man: It's far.

Woman: I know this region well.

Man: Oh? Do you leave the house often?

Woman: I used to. I used to travel a great deal. I know the region from those days.

Man: You probably wouldn't know the place I'm headed.

Woman: Why not?

Man: It's new. A new village. It didn't exist in "those days." (*Pause.*)

Woman: I thought you said you wouldn't deceive me.

Man: I didn't. You don't believe me, do you?

Woman: No.

Man: Then I didn't deceive you. I'm travelling. That much is true.

Woman: Are you in such a hurry?

Man: Travelling is a matter of timing. Catching the light. (*Woman exits; Man finishes eating, puts down his bowl. Woman re-enters with the vase of flowers.*) Where did you find those? They don't grow native around these parts, do they?

Woman: No; they've all been brought in. They were brought in by visitors. Such as yourself. They were left here. In my custody.

Man: But—they look so fresh, so alive.

Woman: I take care of them. They remind me of the people and places outside this house.

Man: May I touch them?

Woman: Certainly.

Man: These have just blossomed.

Woman: No; they were in bloom yesterday. If you'd noticed them before, you would know that.

Man: You must have received these very recently. I would guess—within five days.

Woman: I don't know. But I wouldn't trust your estimate. It's all in the amount of care you show to them. I create a world which is outside the realm of what you know.

Man: What do you do?

Woman: I can't explain. Words are too inefficient. It takes hundreds of words to describe a single act of caring. With hundreds of acts, words become irrelevant. (*Pause.*) But perhaps you can stay.

Man: How long?

Woman: As long as you'd like.

Man: Why?

Woman: To see how I care for them.

Man: I am tired.

Woman: Rest.

Man: The light?

Woman: It will return.

Scene III

Man is carrying chopped wood. He is stripped to the waist. Woman enters.

Woman: You're very kind to do that for me.

Man: I enjoy it, you know. Chopping wood. It's clean. No questions. You take your axe, you stand up the log, you aim—pow!—you either hit it or you don't. Success or failure.

Woman: You seem to have been very successful today.

Man: Why shouldn't I be? It's a beautiful day. I can see to those hills. The trees are cool. The sun is gentle. Ideal. If a man can't be successful on a day like this, he might as well kick the dust up into his own face. (*Man notices Woman staring at him. Man pats his belly, looks at her.*) Protection from falls.

Woman: What? (*Man pinches his belly, showing some fat.*) Oh. Don't be silly. (*Man begins slapping the fat on his belly to a rhythm.*)

Man: Listen—I can make music—see?—that wasn't always possible. But now— that I've developed this—whenever I need entertainment.

Woman: You shouldn't make fun of your body.

Man: Why not? I saw you. You were staring.

Woman: I wasn't making fun. (*Man inflates his cheeks.*) I was just—stop that!

Man: Then why were you staring?

Woman: I was—

Man: Laughing?

Woman: No.

Man: Well?

Woman: I was—Your body. It's . . . strong. (*Pause.*)

Man: People say that. But they don't know. I've heard that age brings wisdom. That's a laugh. The years don't accumulate here. They accumulate here. (*Pause; he pinches his belly.*) But today is a day to be happy, right? The woods. The sun. Blue. It's a happy day. I'm going to chop wood.

Woman: There's nothing left to chop. Look.

Man: Oh. I guess . . . that's it.

Woman: Sit. Here.

Man: But—

Woman: There's nothing left. (*Man sits; Woman stares at his belly.*) Learn to love it.

Man: Don't be ridiculous.

Woman: Touch it.

Man: It's flabby.

Woman: It's strong.

Man: It's weak.

Woman: And smooth.

Man: Do you mind if I put on my shirt?

Woman: Of course not. Shall I get it for you?

Man: No. No. Just sit there. (*Man starts to put on his shirt. He pauses, studies his body.*) You think it's cute, huh?

Woman: I think you should learn to love it. (*Man pats his belly, talks to it.*)

Man (To belly): You're okay, sir. You hang onto my body like a great horseman.

Woman: Not like that.

Man (Ibid.): You're also faithful. You'll never leave me for another man.

Woman: No.

Man: What do you want me to say? (*Woman walks over to Man. She touches his belly with her hand. They look at each other.*)

SCENE IV

Night. Man is alone. Flowers are gone from stand. Mat is unrolled. Man lies on it, sleeping. Suddenly, he starts. He lifts up his head. He listens. Silence. He goes back to sleep. Another start. He lifts up his head, strains to hear. Slowly, we begin to make out the strains of a single shakuhachi° playing a haunting line. It is very soft. He strains to hear it. The instrument slowly fades out. He waits for it to return, but it does not. He takes out the stolen flower. He stares into it.

SCENE V

Day. Woman is cleaning, while Man relaxes. She is on her hands and knees, scrubbing. She is dressed in a simple outfit, for working. Her hair is tied back. Man is sweating. He has not, however, removed his shirt.

Man: I heard your playing last night.

Woman: My playing?

Man: Shakuhachi.

Woman: Oh.

Man: You played very softly. I had to strain to hear it. Next time, don't be afraid. Play out. Fully. Clear. It must've been very beautiful, if only I could've heard it clearly. Why don't you play for me sometime?

Woman: I'm very shy about it.

Man: Why?

Woman: I play for my own satisfaction. That's all. It's something I developed on my own. I don't know if it's at all acceptable by outside standards.

Man: Play for me. I'll tell you.

Woman: No; I'm sure you're too knowledgeable in the arts.

Man: Who? Me?

Woman: You being from the city and all.

Man: I'm ignorant, believe me.

Woman: I'd play, and you'd probably bite your cheek.

Man: Ask me a question about music. Any question. I'll answer incorrectly. I guarantee it.

Woman: Look at this.

Man: What?

shakuhachi: A Japanese bamboo flute.

Woman: A stain.

Man: Where?

Woman: Here? See? I can't get it out.

Man: Oh. I hadn't noticed it before.

Woman: I notice it every time I clean.

Man: Here. Let me try.

Woman: Thank you.

Man: Ugh. It's tough.

Woman: I know.

Man: How did it get here?

Woman: It's been there as long as I've lived here.

Man: I hardly stand a chance. (*Pause.*) But I'll try. Uh—one—two—three—four! One—two—three—four! See, you set up . . . gotta set up . . . a rhythm—two—three—four. Like fighting! Like battle! One—two—three—four! Used to practice with a rhythm . . . beat . . . battle! Yes! (*The stain starts to fade away.*) Look—it's—yes!—whoo!—there it goes—got the sides—the edges—yes!—fading quick—fading away—ooo—here we come—towards the center—to the heart—two—three—four—slow—slow death—tough—dead! (*Man rolls over in triumphant laughter.*)

Woman: Dead.

Man: I got it! I got it! Whoo! A little rhythm! All it took! Four! Four!

Woman: Thank you.

Man: I didn't think I could do it—but there—it's gone—I did it!

Woman: Yes. You did.

Man: And you—you were great.

Woman: No—I was carried away.

Man: We were a team! You and me!

Woman: I only provided encouragement.

Man: You were great! You were! (*Man grabs Woman. Pause.*)

Woman: It's gone. Thank you. Would you like to hear me play *shakuhachi*?

Man: Yes I would.

Woman: I don't usually play for visitors. It's so . . . I'm not sure. I developed it—all by myself—in times when I was alone. I heard nothing—no human voice. So I learned to play *shakuhachi*. I tried to make these sounds resemble the human voice. The *shakuhachi* became my weapon. To ward off the air. It kept me from choking on many a silent evening.

Man: I'm here. You can hear my voice.

Woman: Speak again.

Man: I will.

SCENE VI

Night. Man is sleeping. Suddenly, a start. He lifts his head up. He listens. Silence. He strains to hear. The shakuhachi melody rises up once more. This time, however, it becomes louder and more clear than before. He gets up. He cannot tell from what direc-

tion the music is coming. He walks around the room, putting his ear to different places in the wall, but he cannot locate the sound. It seems to come from all directions at once, as omnipresent as the air. Slowly, he moves towards the wall with the sliding panel through which the Woman enters and exits. He puts his ear against it, thinking the music may be coming from there. Slowly, he slides the door open just a crack, ever so carefully. He peeks through the crack. As he peeks through, the Upstage wall of the set becomes transparent, and through the scrim, we are able to see what he sees. Woman is Upstage of the scrim. She is tending a room filled with potted and vased flowers of all variety. The lushness and beauty of the room Upstage of the scrim stands out in stark contrast to the barrenness of the main set. She is also transformed. She is a young woman. She is beautiful. She wears a brightly colored kimono. Man observes this scene for a long time. He then slides the door shut. The scrim returns to opaque. The music continues. He returns to his mat. He picks up the stolen flower. It is brown and wilted, dead. He looks at it. The music slowly fades out.

SCENE VII

Morning. Man is half-dressed. He is practicing sword maneuvers. He practices with the feel of a man whose spirit is willing, but the flesh is inept. He tries to execute deft movements, but is dissatisfied with his efforts. He curses himself, and returns to basic exercises. Suddenly, he feels something buzzing around his neck—a mosquito. He slaps his neck, but misses it. He sees it flying near him. He swipes at it with his sword. He keeps missing. Finally, he thinks he's hit it. He runs over, kneels down to recover the fallen insect. He picks up two halves of a mosquito on two different fingers. Woman enters the room. She looks as she normally does. She is carrying a vase of flowers, which she places on its shelf.

Man: Look.
Woman: I'm sorry?
Man: Look.
Woman: What? (*He brings over the two halves of mosquito to show her.*)
Man: See?
Woman: Oh.
Man: I hit it—chop!
Woman: These are new forms of target practice?
Man: Huh? Well—yes—in a way.
Woman: You seem to do well at it.
Man: Thank you. For last night. I heard your *shakuhachi*. It was very loud, strong—good tone.
Woman: Did you enjoy it? I wanted you to enjoy it. If you wish, I'll play it for you every night.
Man: Every night!
Woman: If you wish.
Man: No—I don't—I don't want you to treat me like a baby.
Woman: What? I'm not.

Man: Oh, yes. Like a baby. Who you must feed in the middle of the night or he cries. Waaah! Waaah!

Woman: Stop that!

Man: You need your sleep.

Woman: I don't mind getting up for you. (*Pause.*) I would enjoy playing for you. Every night. While you sleep. It will make me feel—like I'm shaping your dreams. I go through long stretches when there is no one in my dreams. It's terrible. During those times, I avoid my bed as much as possible. I paint. I weave. I play *shakuhachi.* I sit on mats and rub powder into my face. Anything to keep from facing a bed with no dreams. It is like sleeping on ice.

Man: What do you dream of now?

Woman: Last night—I dreamt of you. I don't remember what happened. But you were very funny. Not in a mocking way. I wasn't laughing at you. But you made me laugh. And you were very warm. I remember that. (*Pause.*) What do you remember about last night?

Man: Just your playing. That's all. I got up, listened to it, and went back to sleep. (*Man gets up, resumes practicing with his sword.*)

Woman: Another mosquito bothering you?

Man: Just practicing. Ah! Weak! Too weak! I tell you, it wasn't always like this. I'm telling you, there were days when I could chop the fruit from a tree without ever taking my eyes off the ground. (*He continues practicing.*) You ever use one of these?

Woman: I've had to pick one up, yes.

Man: Oh?

Woman: You forget—I live alone—out here—there is . . . not much to sustain me but what I manage to learn myself. It wasn't really a matter of choice.

Man: I used to be very good, you know. Perhaps I can give you some pointers.

Woman: I'd really rather not.

Man: C'mon—a woman like you—you're absolutely right. You need to know how to defend yourself.

Woman: As you wish.

Man: Do you have something to practice with?

Woman: Yes. Excuse me. (*She exits. He practices more. She re-enters with two wooden sticks. He takes one of them.*) Will these do?

Man: Nice. Now, show me what you can do.

Woman: I'm sorry?

Man: Run up and hit me.

Woman: Please.

Man: Go on—I'll block it.

Woman: I feel so . . . undignified.

Man: Go on. (*She hits him playfully with stick.*) Not like that!

Woman: I'll try to be gentle.

Man: What?

Woman: I don't want to hurt you.

Man: You won't—Hit me! (*Woman charges at Man, quickly, deftly. She scores a hit.*) Oh!

Woman: Did I hurt you?

Man: No—you were—let's try that again. (*They square off again. Woman rushes forward. She appears to attempt a strike. He blocks that apparent strike, which turns out to be a feint. She scores.*) Huh?

Woman: Did I hurt you? I'm sorry.

Man: No.

Woman: I hurt you.

Man: No.

Woman: Do you wish to hit me?

Man: No.

Woman: Do you want me to try again?

Man: No.

Woman: Thank you.

Man: Just practice there—by yourself—let me see you run through some maneuvers.

Woman: Must I?

Man: Yes! Go! (*She goes to an open area.*) My greatest strength was always as a teacher. (*Woman executes a series of deft movements. Her whole manner is transformed. Man watches with increasing amazement. Her movements end. She regains her submissive manner.*)

Woman: I'm so embarrassed. My skills—they're so—inappropriate. I look like a man.

Man: Where did you learn that?

Woman: There is much time to practice here.

Man: But you—the techniques.

Woman: I don't know what's fashionable in the outside world. (*Pause.*) Are you unhappy?

Man: No.

Woman: Really?

Man: I'm just . . . surprised.

Woman: You think it's unbecoming for a woman.

Man: No, no. Not at all.

Woman: You want to leave.

Man: No!

Woman: All visitors do. I know. I've met many. They say they'll stay. And they do. For a while. Until they see too much. Or they learn something new. There are boundaries outside of which visitors do not want to see me step. Only who knows what those boundaries are? Not I. They change with every visitor. You have to be careful not to cross them, but you never know where they are. And one day, inevitably, you step outside the lines. The visitor knows. You don't. You didn't know that you'd done anything different. You thought it was just another part of you. The visitor sneaks away. The next day, you learn that you had stepped outside his heart. I'm afraid you've seen too much.

Man: There are stories.

Woman: What?

Man: People talk.

Woman: Where? We're two days from the nearest village.

Man: Word travels.

Woman: What are you talking about?

Man: There are stories about you. I heard them. They say that your visitors never leave this house.

Woman: That's what you heard?

Man: They say you imprison them.

Woman: Then you were a fool to come here.

Man: Listen.

Woman: Me? Listen? You. Look! Where are these prisoners? Have you seen any?

Man: They told me you were very beautiful.

Woman: Then they are blind as well as ignorant.

Man: You are.

Woman: What?

Man: Beautiful.

Woman: Stop that! My skin feels like seaweed.

Man: I didn't realize it at first. I must confess—I didn't. But over these few days—your face has changed for me. The shape of it. The feel of it. The color. All changed. I look at you now, and I'm no longer sure you are the same woman who had poured tea for me just a week ago. And because of that I remembered—how little I know about a face that changes in the night. (*Pause.*) Have you heard those stories?

Woman: I don't listen to old wives' tales.

Man: But have you heard them?

Woman: Yes. I've heard them. From other visitors—young—hotblooded—or old—who came here because they were told great glory was to be had by killing the witch in the woods.

Man: I was told that no man could spend time in this house without falling in love.

Woman: Oh? So why did you come? Did you wager gold that you could come out untouched? The outside world is so flattering to me. And you—are you like the rest? Passion passing through your heart so powerfully that you can't hold onto it?

Man: No! I'm afraid!

Woman: Of what?

Man: Sometimes—when I look into the flowers, I think I hear a voice—from inside—a voice beneath the petals. A human voice.

Woman: What does it say? "Let me out"?

Man: No. Listen. It hums. It hums with the peacefulness of one who is completely imprisoned.

Woman: I understand that if you listen closely enough, you can hear the ocean.

Man: No. Wait. Look at it. See the layers? Each petal—hiding the next. Try and see where they end. You can't. Follow them down, further down, around—and as you come down—faster and faster—the breeze picks up. The breeze becomes a wail. And in that rush of air—in the silent midst of it—you can hear a voice.

Woman (*Woman grabs flower from Man.*): So, you believe I water and prune my lovers? How can you be so foolish? (*She snaps the flower in half, at the stem. She throws it to the ground.*) Do you come only to leave again? To take a chunk of my heart, then leave with your booty on your belt, like a prize? You say that I imprison hearts in these flowers? Well, bits of my heart are trapped with travellers across this land. I can't even keep track. So kill me. If you came here to destroy a witch, kill me now. I can't stand to have it happen again.

Man: I won't leave you.

Woman: I believe you. (*She looks at the flower that she has broken, bends to pick it up. He touches her. They embrace.*)

SCENE VIII

Day. Woman wears a simple undergarment, over which she is donning a brightly colored kimono, the same one we saw her wearing Upstage of the scrim. Man stands apart.

Woman: I can't cry. I don't have the capacity. Right from birth, I didn't cry. My mother and father were shocked. They thought they'd given birth to a ghost, a demon. Sometimes I've thought myself that. When great sadness has welled up inside me, I've prayed for a means to release the pain from my body. But my prayers went unanswered. The grief remained inside me. It would sit like water, still. (*Pause; she models her kimono.*) Do you like it?

Man: Yes, it's beautiful.

Woman: I wanted to wear something special today.

Man: It's beautiful. Excuse me. I must practice.

Woman: Shall I get you something?

Man: No.

Woman: Some tea, maybe?

Man: No. (*Man resumes swordplay.*)

Woman: Perhaps later today—perhaps we can go out—just around here. We can look for flowers.

Man: All right.

Woman: We don't have to.

Man: No. Let's.

Woman: I just thought if—

Man: Fine. Where do you want to go?

Woman: There are very few recreational activities around here, I know.

Man: All right. We'll go this afternoon. (*Pause.*)

Woman: Can I get you something?

Man (*Turning around.*): What?

Woman: You might be—

Man: I'm not hungry or thirsty or cold or hot.

Woman: Then what are you?

Man: Practicing. (*Man resumes practicing; Woman exits. As soon as she exits, he rests. He sits down. He examines his sword. He runs his finger along the edge of it. He takes the tip, runs it against the soft skin under his chin. He places the sword on the ground with the tip pointed directly upwards. He keeps it from falling by placing the tip under his chin. He experiments with different degrees of pressure. Woman re-enters. She sees him in this precarious position. She jerks his head upward; the sword falls.)*

Woman: Don't do that!

Man: What?

Woman: You can hurt yourself!

Man: I was practicing!

Woman: You were playing!

Man: I was practicing!

Woman: It's dangerous.

Man: What do you take me for—a child?

Woman: Sometimes wise men do childish things.

Man: I knew what I was doing!

Woman: It scares me.

Man: Don't be ridiculous. (*He reaches for the sword again.*)

Woman: Don't! Don't do that!

Man: Get back! (*He places the sword back in its previous position, suspended between the floor and his chin, upright.*)

Woman: But—

Man: Sssssh!

Woman: I wish—

Man: Listen to me! The slightest shock, you know—the slightest shock—surprise—it might make me jerk or—something—and then . . . so you must be perfectly still and quiet.

Woman: But I—

Man: Sssssh! (*Silence.*) I learned this exercise from a friend—I can't even remember his name—good swordsman—many years ago. He called it his meditation position. He said, like this, he could feel the line between this world and the others because he rested on it. If he saw something in another world that he liked better, all he would have to do is let his head drop, and he'd be there. Simple. No fuss. One day, they found him with the tip of his sword run clean out the back of his neck. He was smiling. I guess he saw something he liked. Or else he'd fallen asleep.

Woman: Stop that.

Man: Stop what?

Woman: Tormenting me.

Man: I'm not.

Woman: Take it away!

Man: You don't have to watch, you know.

Woman: Do you want to die that way—an accident?

Man: I was doing this before you came in.

Woman: If you do, all you need to do is tell me.

Man: What?

Woman: I can walk right over. Lean on the back of your head.

Man: Don't try to threaten—

Woman: Or jerk your sword up.

Man: Or scare me. You can't threaten—

Woman: I'm not. But if that's what you want.

Man: You can't threaten me. You wouldn't do it.

Woman: Oh?

Man: Then I'd be gone. You wouldn't let me leave that easily.

Woman: Yes, I would.

Man: You'd be alone.

Woman: No. I'd follow you. Forever. (*Pause.*) Now, let's stop this nonsense.

Man: No! I can do what I want! Don't come any closer!

Woman: Then release your sword.

Man: Come any closer and I'll drop my head.

Woman (*Woman slowly approaches Man. She grabs the hilt of the sword. She looks into his eyes. She pulls it out from under his chin.*): There will be no more of this. (*She exits with the sword. He starts to follow her, then stops. He touches under his chin. On his finger, he finds a drop of blood.*)

Scene IX

Night. Man is leaving the house. He is just about out, when he hears a shakuhachi playing. He looks around, trying to locate the sound. Woman appears in the doorway to the outside. Shakuhachi slowly fades out.

Woman: It's time for you to go?

Man: Yes. I'm sorry.

Woman: You're just going to sneak out? A thief in the night? A frightened child?

Man: I care about you.

Woman: You express it strangely.

Man: I leave in shame because it is proper. (*Pause.*) I came seeking glory.

Woman: To kill me? You can say it. You'll be surprised at how little I blanche. As if you'd said, "I came for a bowl of rice," or "I came seeking love" or "I came to kill you."

Man: Weakness. All weakness. Too weak to kill you. Too weak to kill myself. Too weak to do anything but sneak away in shame. (*Woman brings out Man's sword.*)

Woman: Were you even planning to leave without this? (*He takes sword.*) Why not stay here?

Man: I can't live with someone who's defeated me.

Woman: I never thought of defeating you. I only wanted to take care of you. To make you happy. Because that made me happy and I was no longer alone.

Man: You defeated me.

Woman: Why do you think that way?

Man: I came here with a purpose. The world was clear. You changed the shape of your face, the shape of my heart—rearranged everything—created a world where I could do nothing.

Woman: I only tried to care for you.

Man: I guess that was all it took. (*Pause.*)

Woman: You still think I'm a witch. Just because old women gossip. You are so cruel. Once you arrived, there were only two possibilities: I would die or you would leave. (*Pause.*) If you believe I'm a witch, then kill me. Rid the province of one more evil.

Man: I can't—

Woman: Why not? If you believe that about me, then it's the right thing to do.

Man: You know I can't.

Woman: Then stay.

Man: Don't try and force me.

Woman: I won't force you to do anything. (*Pause.*) All I wanted was an escape—for both of us. The sound of a human voice—the simplest thing to find, and the hardest to hold onto. This house—my loneliness is etched into the walls. Kill me, but don't leave. Even in death, my spirit would rest here and be comforted by your presence.

Man: Force me to stay.

Woman: I won't. (*Man starts to leave.*) Beware.

Man: What?

Woman: The ground on which you walk is weak. It could give way at any moment. The crevice beneath is dark.

Man: Are you talking about death? I'm ready to die.

Woman: Fear for what is worse than death.

Man: What?

Woman: Falling. Falling through the darkness. Waiting to hit the ground. Picking up speed. Waiting for the ground. Falling faster. Falling alone. Waiting. Falling. Waiting. Falling.

(*Woman wails and runs out through the door to her room. Man stands, confused, not knowing what to do. He starts to follow her, then hesitates, and rushes out the door to the outside. Silence. Slowly, he re-enters from the outside. He looks for her in the main room. He goes slowly towards the panel to her room. He throws down his sword. He opens the panel. He goes inside. He comes out. He unrolls his mat. He sits on it, cross-legged. He looks out into space. He notices near him a shakuhachi. He picks it up. He begins to blow into it. He tries to make sounds. He continues trying through the end of the play. The Upstage scrim lights up. Upstage, we see the Woman. She is young. She is hanging from a rope suspended from the roof. She has hung herself. Around her are scores of vases with flowers in them whose blossoms have been blown off. Only the stems remain in the vases. Around her swirl the thousands of petals from the flowers. They fill the Upstage scrim area like a blizzard of color. Man continues to attempt to play. Lights fade to black.*)

David Henry Hwang

David Henry Hwang on Drama

MULTICULTURAL THEATER   1989

INTERVIEWER: How did you begin . . . exploring your [Chinese American] heritage?

HWANG: A lot of that happened in college. I was in college in the mid-to-late 1970s, and whereas most people seem to associate collegiate life in the seventies with John Travolta, there was at that time a third-world consciousness, a third-world power movement, in the universities, particularly among Hispanics and Asians. The blacks really started it in the late sixties and early seventies, and it took a while to trickle down into the other third-world communities. Asians probably picked it up last. . . . While I was never a very ardent Marxist, I studied the ideas and I was interested in the degree to which we all may have been affected by certain prejudices in the society without having realized it, and to what degree we had incorporated that into our persons by the time we'd reached our early twenties.

The other thing that I think fascinated me about exploring my Chineseness at that time was consistent with my interest in play-writing. I had become very interested in Sam Shepard, particularly in the way in which Shepard likes to create a sort of American mythology. In his case it's the cowboy mythology, but nonetheless it's something that is larger than simply our present-day, fast-food existence. In my context, creating a mythology, creating a past for myself, involved going into Chinese history and Chinese American history. I think the combination of wanting to delve into those things for artistic reasons and being exposed to an active third-world-consciousness movement was what started to get me interested in my roots when I was in college.

INTERVIEWER: I wonder if there will come a time when the expression "ethnic theater" won't have any meaning.

HWANG: I'm hopeful that there will be a time at some point, but I think it's going to be fifty years or so down the road. The whole idea of being ethnic only applies when it's clear what the dominant culture is. Once it becomes less clear and the culture is acknowledged to be more multicultural, then the idea of what's ethnic becomes irrelevant. I think even today we're starting to see that. The monoethnic theaters—that is, the Asian theaters, the black theaters, the Hispanic theaters—are really useful; they serve a purpose. But I think, if we do our jobs correctly, we will phase out our own need for existence, and the future of theaters will be in multicultural theaters, theaters that do a black play and a Jewish play and a classic and whatever . . .

There are so many people now who can't be labeled. I know a couple in which the man is Japanese and Jewish and the woman is Haitian and Filipino. They have a child, and sociologists have told them that a child of that stock probably hasn't existed before. When someone like that becomes a writer, what do we call him? Do we say he's an Asian writer, or what? As those distinctions become increasingly muddled, the whole notion of what is ethnic as opposed to what is mainstream is going to become more and more difficult to define.

From interview in *Contemporary Authors*

Terrence McNally

ANDRE'S MOTHER   1988

Terrence McNally (b. 1939) was born in St. Petersburg, Florida, but he was raised mostly in Corpus Christi, Texas, where his Irish-Catholic father worked as a beer distributor. After attending Columbia University, McNally worked as a theatrical stage manager, magazine editor, and film critic while writing his first plays. A versatile dramatist, he has written plays, musicals, and screenplays. His screwball comedy The Ritz *(1973) became a popular 1976 film, which McNally himself adapted for the screen. He also rewrote his romantic drama* Frankie and Johnny in the Claire de Lune *(1987) for Gary Marshall's film* Frankie and Johnny *(1991), starring Al Pacino and Michelle Pfeiffer. Other notable McNally plays include* The Lisbon Traviata *(1985);* Lips Together, Teeth Apart *(1991); and* A Perfect Ganesh *(1993). In 1995 his play about the opera singer Maria Callas,* Master Class, *became an international success. His work for television includes an adaptation of John Cheever's "The 5:48" (1980). McNally has also written extensively for musical theater, authoring the books for the Broadway productions of* Kiss of the Spider Woman *(1992),* Ragtime *(1997), and* The Full Monty *(2000). He also wrote the libretto for Jake Heggie's opera,* Dead Man Walking *(2000), based on the book by Sister Helen Prejean. McNally's television version of* Andre's Mother *won an Emmy in 1990, but the original stage version—written as one brief and memorable scene—needs no video backup to communicate its troubling message of heartache and loss.*

Characters

Cal, a young man
Arthur, his father
Penny, his sister
Andre's Mother

Time. *Now*

Place. *New York City, Central Park*

Four people—Cal, Arthur, Penny, and Andre's Mother—enter. They are nicely dressed and each carries a white helium-filled balloon on a string.

Cal: You know what's really terrible? I can't think of anything terrific to say. Goodbye. I love you. I'll miss you. And I'm supposed to be so great with words!

Penny: What's that over there?

Arthur: Ask your brother.

Cal: It's a theatre. An outdoor theatre. They do plays there in the summer. Shakespeare's plays. (*To Andre's Mother.*) God, how much he wanted to play Hamlet again. He would have gone to Timbuktu to have another go at that part. The summer he did it in Boston, he was so happy!

Penny: Cal, I don't think she . . . ! It's not the time. Later.

Arthur: Your son was a . . . the Jews have a word for it . . .

Penny (*quietly appalled*): Oh my God!

Arthur: Mensch, I believe it is, and I think I'm using it right. It means warm, solid, the real thing. Correct me if I'm wrong.

Penny: Fine, Dad, fine. Just quit while you're ahead.

Arthur: I won't say he was like a son to me. Even my son isn't always like a son to me. I mean . . . ! In my clumsy way, I'm trying to say how much I liked Andre. And how much he helped me to know my own boy. Cal was always two handsful but Andre and I could talk about anything under the sun. My wife was very fond of him, too.

Penny: Cal, I don't understand about the balloons.

Cal: They represent the soul. When you let go, it means you're letting his soul ascend to Heaven. That you're willing to let go. Breaking the last earthly ties.

Penny: Does the Pope know about this?

Arthur: Penny!

Penny: Andre loved my sense of humor. Listen, you can hear him laughing. (*She lets go of her white balloon.*) So long, you glorious, wonderful, I-know-what-Cal-means-about-words . . . *man!* God forgive me for wishing you were straight every time I laid eyes on you. But if any man was going to have you, I'm glad it was my brother! Look how fast it went up. I bet that means something. Something terrific.

Arthur (*lets his balloon go*): Goodbye. God speed.

Penny: Cal?

Cal: I'm not ready yet.

Penny: Okay. We'll be over there. Come on, Pop, you can buy your little girl a Good Humor.

Arthur: They still make Good Humor?

Penny: Only now they're called Dove Bars and they cost twelve dollars.

(*Penny takes Arthur off. Cal and Andre's Mother stand with their balloons.*)

Cal: I wish I knew what you were thinking. I think it would help me. You know almost nothing about me and I only know what Andre told me about you. I'd always had it in my mind that one day we would be friends, you and me. But if you didn't know about Andre and me . . . If this hadn't happened, I wonder if he would have ever told you. When he was sick, if I asked him once I asked him a thousand times, tell her. She's your mother. She won't mind. But he was so afraid of hurting you and of your disapproval. I don't know which was worse. (*No response. He sighs.*) God, how many of us live in this city because we don't want to hurt our mothers and live in mortal terror of their disapproval. We lose ourselves here. Our lives aren't furtive, just our feelings toward people like you are! A city of fugitives from our parents' scorn or heartbreak. Sometimes he'd seem a little down and I'd say, "What's the matter, babe?" and this funny sweet, sad smile would cross his face and he'd say, "Just a little homesick, Cal, just a little bit." I always accused him of being a country boy just playing at being a hotshot, sophisticated New Yorker. (*He sighs.*)

It's bullshit. It's all bullshit. (*Still no response.*)

Do you remember the comic strip *Little Lulu?* Her mother had no name, she was so remote, so formidable to all the children. She was just Lulu's mother. "Hello, Lulu's Mother," Lulu's friends would say. She was almost anonymous in her remoteness. You remind me of her. Andre's mother. Let me answer the questions you can't ask and then I'll leave you alone and you won't ever have to see me again. Andre died of AIDS. I don't know how he got it. I tested negative. He died bravely. You would have been proud of him. The only thing that frightened him was you. I'll have everything that was his sent to you. I'll pay for it. There isn't much. You should have come up the summer he played Hamlet. He was magnificent. Yes, I'm bitter. I'm bitter I've lost him. I'm bitter what's happening. I'm bitter even now, after all this, I can't reach you. I'm beginning to feel your disapproval and it's making me ill. (*He looks at his balloon.*) Sorry, old friend. I blew it. (*He lets go of the balloon.*)

Good night, sweet prince, and flights of angels sing thee to thy rest! (*Beat.*)

Goodbye, Andre's mother.

(*He goes. Andre's Mother stands alone holding her white balloon. Her lips tremble. She looks on the verge of breaking down. She is about to let go of the balloon when she pulls it down to her. She looks at it awhile before she gently kisses it. She lets go of the balloon. She follows it with her eyes as it rises and rises. The lights are beginning to fade. Andre's Mother's eyes are still on the balloon. The lights fade.*)

Terrence McNally

Terrence McNally on Drama

HOW TO WRITE A PLAY   1995

INTERVIEWER: Could you tell us how you go about writing a play? What is your writing process?

MCNALLY: It's very simple, really. You have to go to the typewriter, that's all you have to do. I have a word processor now, and you turn it on and something happens after a while, and that's all writing is to me. If I don't go to the typewriter I don't write. I'm not being facetious. I think it's a very practical thing, and deadlines help a lot. You realize that *Lips Together* opens April twelfth and it's December twelfth and you haven't written a word of the play. I carry them up in my head for a long time. That process is very hard to talk about. It's partially my unconscious. It's usually a year or two before I sit at the typewriter, but people say, "God, you write plays so quickly." Well, I think walking around with things in your head for two years is not exactly quickly. The typing part is pretty quick, if you really know what you're doing in a play. Once I know what my characters are doing, the play just comes very, very easily.

. . .

INTERVIEWER: Do you write to discover what you feel about something?

MCNALLY: That's not the motive to write something, but I do discover something and how I feel about things while I'm writing a play. But it's not the motive. I don't say, "Well, I'll write a play about suicide so I can see what it would be like to kill myself." Writing a play is not psychotherapy. But I do learn an awful lot about myself, and it makes me more aware of other people. I would like to think that my work is about equal parts autobiographical feeling, imagined feeling, and people I've observed. I've never created a character that I've had no empathy for, and I've never based a character 100 percent on a person I've known in real life. It's a blend, and in the process you learn something about yourself.

From interview with Joy Zinoman,
The Playwright's Art: Conversations with Contemporary American Dramatists

August Wilson

JOE TURNER'S COME AND GONE°   1988

August Wilson (b. 1945) was the eldest son of a German American father and an African American mother. His parents separated early, and the young Wilson was raised on the Hill, a Pittsburgh ghetto neighborhood. Although he quit school in the ninth grade when a teacher wrongly accused him of submitting a ghost-written paper, Wilson continued his education in local libraries, supporting himself by working as a cook and stock clerk. In 1968 he co-founded a community troupe, the Black Horizons Theater, staging plays by LeRoi Jones and other militants; later he moved from Pittsburgh to Saint Paul, Minnesota, where at last he saw a play of his own performed. Jitney, his first effort, won him entry to a 1982 playwrights' conference at the Eugene O'Neill Theater Center. There, Lloyd Richards, dean of Yale University School of Drama, took an interest in Wilson's work and offered to produce his plays at Yale. Ma Rainey's Black Bottom was the first to reach Broadway (in 1985), where it ran for ten months and received a prize from the New York Drama Critics Circle. In 1987 Fences, starring Mary Alice and James Earl Jones, won another Critics Circle Award, as well as a Tony Award and the Pulitzer Prize for best American play of its year. It set a box office record for a Broadway nonmusical. Joe Turner's Come and Gone (1988) also received high acclaim, and in 1990 his fourth major work, The Piano Lesson, won him a second Pulitzer Prize. His recent plays include Two Trains Running (1992), Seven Guitars (1995), King Hedley II (2000), and Gem of the Ocean (2003). These nine plays, each one set in a different decade of the 1900s, all belong to a cycle in which Wilson traces the black experience in America throughout the twentieth century. He is presently at work on its final component, a play set in the 1990s. A published poet, Wilson once told an interviewer, "After writing poetry for twenty-one years, I approach a play the same way. The mental process is poetic: you use metaphor and condense."

Characters

Seth Holly, owner of the boardinghouse
Bertha Holly, his wife
Bynum Walker, a rootworker°
Rutherford Selig, a peddler
Jeremy Furlow, a resident
Herald Loomis, a resident
Zonia Loomis, his daughter
Mattie Campbell, a resident
Reuben Scott, boy who lives next door
Molly Cunningham, a resident
Martha Pentecost, Herald Loomis's wife

Joe Turner's Come and Gone: In Tennessee around the turn of the century, Joe Turner became legendary: a professional bounty hunter, and one who claimed a reward for finding an escaped convict. To increase his profits, Turner impressed not only convicts into a chain gang but innocent men as well.   *rootworker:* a conjure man, or voodoo practitioner.

Setting. *August, 1911. A boardinghouse in Pittsburgh. At right is a kitchen. Two doors open off the kitchen. One leads to the outhouse and Seth's workshop. The other to Seth's and Bertha's bedroom. At left is a parlor. The front door opens into the parlor, which gives access to the stairs leading to the upstairs rooms.*

There is a small outside playing area.

The Play. *It is August in Pittsburgh, 1911. The sun falls out of heaven like a stone. The fires of the steel mill rage with a combined sense of industry and progress. Barges loaded with coal and iron ore trudge up the river to the mill towns that dot the Monongahela and return with fresh, hard, gleaming steel. The city flexes its muscles. Men throw countless bridges across the river, lay roads and carve tunnels through the hills sprouting with houses.*

From the deep and the near South the sons and daughters of newly freed African slaves wander into the city. Isolated, cut off from memory, having forgotten the names of the gods and only guessing at their faces, they arrive dazed and stunned, their heart kicking in their chest with a song worth singing. They arrive carrying Bibles and guitars, their pockets lined with dust and fresh hope, marked men and women seeking to scrape from the narrow, crooked cobbles and the fiery blasts of the coke furnace a way of bludgeoning and shaping the malleable parts of themselves into a new identity as free men of definite and sincere worth.

Foreigners in a strange land, they carry as part and parcel of their baggage a long line of separation and dispersement which informs their sensibilities and marks their conduct as they search for ways to reconnect, to reassemble, to give clear and luminous meaning to the song which is both a wail and a whelp of joy.

ACT I
Scene I

The lights come up on the kitchen. Bertha busies herself with breakfast preparations. Seth stands looking out the window at Bynum in the yard. Seth is in his early fifties. Born of Northern free parents, a skilled craftsman, and owner of the boardinghouse, he has a stability that none of the other characters have. Bertha is five years his junior. Married for over twenty-five years, she has learned how to negotiate around Seth's apparent orneriness.

Seth (*at the window, laughing*): If that ain't the damndest thing I seen. Look here, Bertha.
Bertha: I done seen Bynum out there with them pigeons before.
Seth: Naw . . . naw . . . look at this. That pigeon flopped out of Bynum's hand and he about to have a fit.

(*Bertha crosses over to the window.*)

He down there on his hands and knees behind that bush looking all over for that pigeon and it on the other side of the yard. See it over there?

Bertha: Come on and get your breakfast and leave that man alone.

Seth: Look at him . . . he still looking. He ain't seen it yet. All that old mumbo jumbo nonsense. I don't know why I put up with it.

Bertha: You don't say nothing when he bless the house.

Seth: I just go along with that 'cause of you. You around here sprinkling salt all over the place . . . got pennies lined up across the threshold . . . all that heebie-jeebie stuff. I just put up with that 'cause of you. I don't pay that kind of stuff no mind. And you going down there to the church and wanna come home and sprinkle salt all over the place.

Bertha: It don't hurt none. I can't say if it help . . . but it don't hurt none.

Seth: Look at him. He done found that pigeon and now he's talking to it.

Bertha: These biscuits be ready in a minute.

Seth: He done drew a big circle with that stick and now he's dancing around. I know he'd better not . . .

(*Seth bolts from the window and rushes to the back door.*)

Hey, Bynum! Don't be hopping around stepping in my vegetables. Hey, Bynum . . . Watch where you stepping!

Bertha: Seth, leave that man alone.

Seth (*coming back into the house*): I don't care how much he be dancing around . . . just don't be stepping in my vegetables. Man got my garden all messed up now . . . planting them weeds out there . . . burying them pigeons and whatnot.

Bertha: Bynum don't bother nobody. He ain't even thinking about your vegetables.

Seth: I know he ain't! That's why he out there stepping on them.

Bertha: What Mr. Johnson say down there?

Seth: I told him if I had the tools I could go out here and find me four or five fellows and open up my own shop instead of working for Mr. Olowski. Get me four or five fellows and teach them how to make pots and pans. One man making ten pots is five men making fifty. He told me he'd think about it.

Bertha: Well, maybe he'll come to see it your way.

Seth: He wanted me to sign over the house to him. You know what I thought of that idea.

Bertha: He'll come to see you're right.

Seth: I'm going up and talk to Sam Green. There's more than one way to skin a cat. I'm going up and talk to him. See if he got more sense than Mr. Johnson. I can't get nowhere working for Mr. Olowski and selling Selig five or six pots on the side. I'm going up and see Sam Green. See if he loan me the money.

(*Seth crosses back to the window.*)

Now he got that cup. He done killed that pigeon and now he's putting its blood in that little cup. I believe he drink that blood.

Bertha: Seth Holly, what is wrong with you this morning? Come on and get your breakfast so you can go to bed. You know Bynum don't be drinking no pigeon blood.

Seth: I don't know what he do.

Bertha: Well, watch him, then. He's gonna dig a little hole and bury that pigeon. Then he's gonna pray over that blood . . . pour it on top . . . mark out his circle and come on into the house.

Seth: That's what he doing . . . he pouring that blood on top.

Bertha: When they gonna put you back working daytime? Told me two months ago he was gonna put you back working daytime.

Seth: That's what Mr. Olowski told me. I got to wait till he say when. He tell me what to do. I don't tell him. Drive me crazy to speculate on the man's wishes when he don't know what he want to do himself.

Bertha: Well, I wish he go ahead and put you back working daytime. This working all hours of the night don't make no sense.

Seth: It don't make no sense for that boy to run out of here and get drunk so they lock him up either.

Bertha: Who? Who they got locked up for being drunk?

Seth: That boy that's staying upstairs . . . Jeremy. I stopped down there on Logan Street on my way home from work and one of the fellows told me about it. Say he seen it when they arrested him.

Bertha: I was wondering why I ain't seen him this morning.

Seth: You know I don't put up with that. I told him when he came . . .

(*Bynum enters from the yard carrying some plants. He is a short, round man in his early sixties. A conjure man, or rootworker, he gives the impression of always being in control of everything. Nothing ever bothers him. He seems to be lost in a world of his own making and to swallow any adversity or interference with his grand design.*)

What you doing bringing them weeds in my house? Out there stepping on my vegetables and now wanna carry them weeds in my house.

Bynum: Morning, Seth. Morning, Sister Bertha.

Seth: Messing up my garden growing them things out there. I ought to go out there and pull up all them weeds.

Bertha: Some gal was by here to see you this morning, Bynum. You was out there in the yard . . . I told her to come back later.

Bynum (to Seth): You look sick. What's the matter, you ain't eating right?

Seth: What if I was sick? You ain't getting near me with none of that stuff.

(*Bertha sets a plate of biscuits on the table.*)

Bynum: My . . . my . . . Bertha, your biscuits getting fatter and fatter.

(*Bynum takes a biscuit and begins to eat.*)

Where Jeremy? I don't see him around this morning. He usually be around riffing and raffing on Saturday morning.

Seth: I know where he at. I know just where he at. They got him down there in the jail. Getting drunk and acting a fool. He down there where he belong with all that foolishness.

Bynum: Mr. Piney's boys got him, huh? They ain't gonna do nothing but hold on to him for a little while. He's gonna be back here hungrier than a mule directly.

Seth: I don't go for all that carrying on and such. This is a respectable house. I don't have no drunkards or fools around here.

Bynum: That boy got a lot of country in him. He ain't been up here but two weeks. It's gonna take a while before he can work that country out of him.

Seth: These niggers coming up here with that old backward country style of living. It's hard enough now without all that ignorant kind of acting. Ever since slavery got over with there ain't been nothing but foolish-acting niggers. Word get out they need men to work in the mill and put in these roads . . . and niggers drop everything and head North looking for freedom. They don't know the white fellows looking too. White fellows coming from all over the world. White fellow come over and in six months got more than what I got. But these niggers keep on coming. Walking . . . riding . . . carrying their Bibles. That boy done carried a guitar all the way from North Carolina. What he gonna find out? What he gonna do with that guitar? This the city.

(There is a knock on the door.)

Niggers coming up here from the backwoods . . . coming up here from the country carrying Bibles and guitars looking for freedom. They got a rude awakening.

(Seth goes to answer the door. Rutherford Selig enters. About Seth's age, he is a thin white man with greasy hair. A peddler, he supplies Seth with the raw materials to make pots and pans which he then peddles door to door in the mill towns along the river. He keeps a list of his customers as they move about and is known in the various communities as the People Finder. He carries squares of sheet metal under his arm.)

Ho! Forgot you was coming today. Come on in.

Bynum: If it ain't Rutherford Selig . . . the People Finder himself.

Selig: What say there, Bynum?

Bynum: I say about my shiny man. You got to tell me something. I done give you my dollar . . . I'm looking to get a report.

Selig: I got eight here, Seth.

Seth (taking the sheet metal): What is this? What you giving me here? What I'm gonna do with this?

Selig: I need some dustpans. Everybody asking me about dustpans.

Seth: Gonna cost you fifteen cents apiece. And ten cents to put a handle on them.

Selig: I'll give you twenty cents apiece with the handles.

Seth: Alright. But I ain't gonna give you but fifteen cents for the sheet metal.

Selig: It's twenty-five cents apiece for the metal. That's what we agreed on.

Seth: This low-grade sheet metal. They ain't worth but a dime. I'm doing you a favor giving you fifteen cents. You know this metal ain't worth no twenty-five cents. Don't come talking that twenty-five cent stuff to me over no low-grade sheet metal.

Selig: Alright, fifteen cents apiece. Just make me some dustpans out of them.

(*Seth exits with the sheet metal out the back door.*)

Bertha: Sit on down there, Selig. Get you a cup of coffee and a biscuit.

Bynum: Where you coming from this time?

Selig: I been upriver. All along the Monongahela. Past Rankin and all up around Little Washington.

Bynum: Did you find anybody?

Selig: I found Sadie Jackson up in Braddock. Her mother's staying down there in Scotchbottom say she hadn't heard from her and she didn't know where she was at. I found her up in Braddock on Enoch Street. She bought a frying pan from me.

Bynum: You around here finding everybody how come you ain't found my shiny man?

Selig: The only shiny man I saw was the Nigras working on the road gang with the sweat glistening on them.

Bynum: Naw, you'd be able to tell this fellow. He shine like new money.

Selig: Well, I done told you I can't find nobody without a name.

Bertha: Here go one of these hot biscuits, Selig.

Bynum: This fellow don't have no name. I call him John 'cause it was up around Johnstown where I seen him. I ain't even so sure he's one special fellow. That shine could pass on to anybody. He could be anybody shining.

Selig: Well, what's he look like besides being shiny? There's lots of shiny Nigras.

Bynum: He's just a man I seen out on the road. He ain't had no special look. Just a man walking toward me on the road. He come up and asked me which way the road went. I told him everything I knew about the road, where it went and all, and he asked me did I have anything to eat 'cause he was hungry. Say he ain't had nothing to eat in three days. Well, I never be out there on the road without a piece of dried meat. Or an orange or an apple. So I give this fellow an orange. He take and eat that orange and told me to come and go along the road a little ways with him, that he had something he wanted to show me. He had a look about him made me wanna go with him, see what he gonna show me.

We walked on a bit and it's getting kind of far from where I met him when it come up on me all of a sudden, we wasn't going the way he had come from, we was going back my way. Since he said he ain't knew nothing about the road, I asked him about this. He say he had a voice inside him telling him which way to go and if I come and go along with him he was gonna show me the Secret of Life. Quite naturally I followed him. A fellow that's gonna show you the Secret of Life ain't to be taken lightly. We get near this bend in the road . . .

(*Seth enters with an assortment of pans.*)

Seth: I got six here, Selig.

Selig: Wait a minute, Seth. Bynum's telling me about the secret of life. Go ahead, Bynum. I wanna hear this.

(Seth sets the pots down and exits out the back.)

Bynum: We get near this bend in the road and he told me to hold out my hands. Then he rubbed them together with his and I looked down and see they got blood on them. Told me to take and rub it all over me . . . say that was a way of cleaning myself. Then we went around the bend in that road. Got around that bend and it seem like all of a sudden we ain't in the same place. Turn around that bend and everything look like it was twice as big as it was. The trees and everything bigger than life! Sparrows big as eagles! I turned around to look at this fellow and he had this light coming out of him. I had to cover up my eyes to keep from being blinded. He shining like new money with that light. He shined until all the light seemed like it seeped out of him and then he was gone and I was by myself in this strange place where everything was bigger than life.

I wandered around there looking for that road, trying to find my way back from this big place . . . and I looked over and seen my daddy standing there. He was the same size he always was, except for his hands and his mouth. He had a great big old mouth that look like it took up his whole face and his hands were as big as hams. Look like they was too big to carry around. My daddy called me to him. Said he had been thinking about me and it grieved him to see me in the world carrying other people's songs and not having one of my own. Told me he was gonna show me how to find my song. Then he carried me further into this big place until we come to this ocean. Then he showed me something I ain't got words to tell you. But if you stand to witness it, you done seen something there. I stayed in that place awhile and my daddy taught me the meaning of this thing that I had seen and showed me how to find my song. I asked him about the shiny man and he told me he was the One Who Goes Before and Shows the Way. Said there was lots of shiny men and if I ever saw one again before I died then I would know that my song had been accepted and worked its full power in the world and I could lay down and die a happy man. A man who done left his mark on life. On the way people cling to each other out of the truth they find in themselves. Then he showed me how to get back to the road. I came out where everything was its own size and I had my song. I had the Binding Song. I choose that song because that's what I seen most when I was traveling . . . people walking away and leaving one another. So I takes the power of my song and binds them together.

(Seth enters from the yard carrying cabbages and tomatoes.)

Been binding people ever since. That's why they call me Bynum. Just like glue I sticks people together.

Seth: Maybe they ain't supposed to be stuck sometimes. You ever think of that?

Bynum: Oh, I don't do it lightly. It cost me a piece of myself every time I do. I'm a Binder of What Clings. You got to find out if they cling first. You can't bind what don't cling.

Selig: Well, how is that the Secret of Life? I thought you said he was gonna show you the secret of life. That's what I'm waiting to find out.

Bynum: Oh, he showed me alright. But you still got to figure it out. Can't nobody figure it out for you. You got to come to it on your own. That's why I'm looking for the shiny man.

Selig: Well, I'll keep my eye out for him. What you got there, Seth?

Seth: Here go some cabbage and tomatoes. I got some green beans coming in real nice. I'm gonna take and start me a grapevine out there next year. Butera says he gonna give me a piece of his vine and I'm gonna start that out there.

Selig: How many of them pots you got?

Seth: I got six. That's six dollars minus eight on top of fifteen for the sheet metal come to a dollar twenty out the six dollars leave me four dollars and eighty cents.

Selig (counting out the money): There's four dollars . . . and . . . eighty cents.

Seth: How many of them dustpans you want?

Selig: As many as you can make out them sheets.

Seth: You can use that many? I get to cutting on them sheets figuring how to make them dustpans . . . ain't no telling how many I'm liable to come up with.

Selig: I can use them and you can make me some more next time.

Seth: Alright, I'm gonna hold you to that, now.

Selig: Thanks for the biscuit, Bertha.

Bertha: You know you welcome anytime, Selig.

Seth: Which way you heading?

Selig: Going down to Wheeling. All through West Virginia there. I'll be back Saturday. They putting in new roads down that way. Makes traveling easier.

Seth: That's what I hear. All up around here too. Got a fellow staying here working on that road by the Brady Street Bridge.

Selig: Yeah, it's gonna make traveling real nice. Thanks for the cabbage, Seth. I'll see you on Saturday.

(*Selig exits.*)

Seth (to Bynum): Why you wanna start all that nonsense talk with that man? All that shiny man nonsense.

Bynum: You know it ain't no nonsense. Bertha know it ain't no nonsense. I don't know if Selig know or not.

Bertha: Seth, when you get to making them dustpans make me a coffeepot.

Seth: What's the matter with your coffee? Ain't nothing wrong with your coffee. Don't she make some good coffee, Bynum?

Bynum: I ain't worried about the coffee. I know she makes some good biscuits.

Seth: I ain't studying no coffeepot, woman. You heard me tell the man I was gonna cut as many dustpans as them sheets will make . . . and all of a sudden you want a coffeepot.

Bertha: Man, hush up and go on and make me that coffeepot.

(*Jeremy enters the front door. About twenty-five, he gives the impression that he has the world in his hand, that he can meet life's challenges head on. He smiles a lot. He is a proficient guitar player, though his spirit has yet to be molded into song.*)

Bynum: I hear Mr. Piney's boys had you.

Jeremy: Fined me two dollars for nothing! Ain't done nothing.

Seth: I told you when you come on here everybody know my house. Know these is respectable quarters. I don't put up with no foolishness. Everybody know Seth Holly keep a good house. Was my daddy's house. This house been a decent house for a long time.

Jeremy: I ain't done nothing, Mr. Seth. I stopped by the Workmen's Club and got me a bottle. Me and Roper Lee from Alabama. Had us a half pint. We was fixing to cut that half in two when they came up on us. Asked us if we was working. We told them we was putting in the road over yonder and that it was our payday. They snatched hold of us to get that two dollars. Me and Roper Lee ain't even had a chance to take a drink when they grabbed us.

Seth: I don't go for all that kind of carrying on.

Bertha: Leave the boy alone, Seth. You know the police do that. Figure there's too many people out on the street they take some of them off. You know that.

Seth: I ain't gonna have folks talking.

Bertha: Ain't nobody talking nothing. That's all in your head. You want some grits and biscuits, Jeremy?

Jeremy: Thank you, Miss Bertha. They didn't give us a thing to eat last night. I'll take one of them big bowls if you don't mind.

(*There is a knock at the door. Seth goes to answer it. Enter Herald Loomis and his eleven-year-old daughter, Zonia. Herald Loomis is thirty-two years old. He is at times possessed. A man driven not by the hellhounds that seemingly bay at his heels, but by his search for a world that speaks to something about himself. He is unable to harmonize the forces that swirl around him, and seeks to recreate the world into one that contains his image. He wears a hat and a long wool coat.*)

Loomis: Me and my daughter looking for a place to stay, mister. You got a sign say you got rooms.

(*Seth stares at Loomis, sizing him up.*)

Mister, if you ain't got no rooms we can go somewhere else.

Seth: How long you plan on staying?

Loomis: Don't know. Two weeks or more maybe.

Seth: It's two dollars a week for the room. We serve meals twice a day. It's two dollars for room and board. Pay up in advance.

(Loomis reaches into his pocket.)

It's a dollar extra for the girl.

Loomis: The girl sleep in the same room.

Seth: Well, do she eat off the same plate? We serve meals twice a day. That's a dollar extra for food.

Loomis: Ain't got no extra dollar. I was planning on asking your missus if she could help out with the cooking and cleaning and whatnot.

Seth: Her helping out don't put no food on the table. I need that dollar to buy some food.

Loomis: I'll give you fifty cents extra. She don't eat much.

Seth: Okay . . . but fifty cents don't buy but half a portion.

Bertha: Seth, she can help me out. Let her help me out. I can use some help.

Seth: Well, that's two dollars for the week. Pay up in advance. Saturday to Saturday. You wanna stay on then it's two more come Saturday.

(Loomis pays Seth the money.)

Bertha: My name's Bertha. This my husband, Seth. You got Bynum and Jeremy over there.

Loomis: Ain't nobody else live here?

Bertha: They the only ones live here now. People come and go. They the only ones here now. You want a cup of coffee and a biscuit?

Loomis: We done ate this morning.

Bynum: Where you coming from, Mister . . . I didn't get your name.

Loomis: Name's Herald Loomis. This my daughter, Zonia.

Bynum: Where you coming from?

Loomis: Come from all over. Whicheverway the road take us that's the way we go.

Jeremy: If you looking for a job, I'm working putting in that road down there by the bridge. They can't get enough mens. Always looking to take somebody on.

Loomis: I'm looking for a woman named Martha Loomis. That's my wife. Got married legal with the papers and all.

Seth: I don't know nobody named Loomis. I know some Marthas but I don't know no Loomis.

Bynum: You got to see Rutherford Selig if you wanna find somebody. Selig's the People Finder. Rutherford Selig's a first-class People Finder.

Jeremy: What she look like? Maybe I seen her.

Loomis: She a brownskin woman. Got long pretty hair. About five feet from the ground.

Jeremy: I don't know. I might have seen her.

Bynum: You got to see Rutherford Selig. You give him one dollar to get her name on his list . . . and after she get her name on his list Rutherford Selig will go right on out there and find her. I got him looking for somebody for me.

Loomis: You say he find people. How you find him?

Bynum: You just missed him. He's gone downriver now. You got to wait till Saturday. He's gone downriver with his pots and pans. He come to see Seth on Saturdays. You got to wait till then.

Seth: Come on, I'll show you to your room.

(*Seth, Loomis, and Zonia exit up the stairs.*)

Jeremy: Miss Bertha, I'll take that biscuit you was gonna give that fellow, if you don't mind. Say, Mr. Bynum, they got somebody like that around here sure enough? Somebody that find people?

Bynum: Rutherford Selig. He go around selling pots and pans and every house he come to he write down the name and address of whoever lives there. So if you looking for somebody, quite naturally you go and see him . . . 'cause he's the only one who know where everybody live at.

Jeremy: I ought to have him look for this old gal I used to know. It be nice to see her again.

Bertha (giving Jeremy a biscuit): Jeremy, today's the day for you to pull them sheets off the bed and set them outside your door. I'll set you out some clean ones.

Bynum: Mr. Piney's boys done ruined your good time last night, Jeremy . . . what you planning for tonight?

Jeremy: They got me scared to go out, Mr. Bynum. They might grab me again.

Bynum: You ought to take your guitar and go down to Seefus. Seefus got a gambling place down there on Wylie Avenue. You ought to take your guitar and go down there. They got guitar contest down there.

Jeremy: I don't play no contest, Mr. Bynum. Had one of them white fellows cure me of that. I ain't been nowhere near a contest since.

Bynum: White fellow beat you playing guitar?

Jeremy: Naw, he ain't beat me. I was sitting at home just fixing to sit down and eat when somebody come up to my house and got me. Told me there's a white fellow say he was gonna give a prize to the best guitar player he could find. I take up my guitar and go down there and somebody had gone up and got Bobo Smith and brought him down there. Him and another fellow called Hooter. Old Hooter couldn't play no guitar, he do more hollering than playing, but Bobo could go at it awhile.

This fellow standing there say he the one that was gonna give the prize and me and Bobo started playing for him. Bobo play something and then I'd try to play something better than what he played. Old Hooter, he just holler and bang at the guitar. Man was the worst guitar player I ever seen. So me and Bobo played and after a while I seen where he was getting the attention of this white fellow. He'd play something and while he was playing it he be slapping on the side of the guitar, and that made it sound like he was playing more than he was. So I started doing it too. White fellow ain't knew no difference. He ain't knew as much about guitar playing as Hooter did. After we play awhile, the white fellow called us to him and said he couldn't make up his mind, say all three of us was the best guitar player and we'd have to split the prize between us. Then he give us twenty-five cents. That's eight cents apiece and a penny on the side. That cured me of playing contest to this day.

Bynum: Seefus ain't like that. Seefus give a whole dollar and a drink of whiskey.

Jeremy: What night they be down there?

Bynum: Be down there every night. Music don't know no certain night.

Bertha: You go down to Seefus with them people and you liable to end up in a raid and go to jail sure enough. I don't know why Bynum tell you that.

Bynum: That's where the music at. That's where the people at. The people down there making music and enjoying themselves. Some things is worth taking the chance going to jail about.

Bertha: Jeremy ain't got no business going down there.

Jeremy: They got some women down there, Mr. Bynum?

Bynum: Oh, they got women down there, sure. They got women everywhere. Women be where the men is so they can find each other.

Jeremy: Some of them old gals come out there where we be putting in that road. Hanging around there trying to snatch somebody.

Bynum: How come some of them ain't snatched hold of you?

Jeremy: I don't want them kind. Them desperate kind. Ain't nothing worse than a desperate woman. Tell them you gonna leave them and they get to crying and carrying on. That just make you want to get away quicker. They get to cutting up your clothes and things trying to keep you staying. Desperate women ain't nothing but trouble for a man.

(*Seth enters from the stairs.*)

Seth: Something ain't setting right with that fellow.

Bertha: What's wrong with him? What he say?

Seth: I take him up there and try to talk to him and he ain't for no talking. Say he been traveling . . . coming over from Ohio. Say he a deacon in the church. Say he looking for Martha Pentecost. Talking about that's his wife.

Bertha: How you know it's the same Martha? Could be talking about anybody. Lots of people named Martha.

Seth: You see that little girl? I didn't hook it up till he said it, but that little girl look just like her. Ask Bynum. (*To Bynum.*) Bynum. Don't that little girl look just like Martha Pentecost?

Bertha: I still say he could be talking about anybody.

Seth: The way he described her wasn't no doubt who he was talking about. Described her right down to her toes.

Bertha: What did you tell him?

Seth: I ain't told him nothing. The way that fellow look I wasn't gonna tell him nothing. I don't know what he looking for her for.

Bertha: What else he have to say?

Seth: I told you he wasn't for no talking. I told him where the outhouse was and to keep that gal off the front porch and out of my garden. He asked if you'd mind setting a hot tub for the gal and that was about the gist of it.

Bertha: Well, I wouldn't let it worry me if I was you. Come on get your sleep.

Bynum: He says he looking for Martha and he a deacon in the church.

Seth: That's what he say. Do he look like a deacon to you?

Bertha: He might be, you don't know. Bynum ain't got no special say on whether he a deacon or not.

Seth: Well, if he the deacon I'd sure like to see the preacher.

Bertha: Come on get your sleep. Jeremy, don't forget to set them sheets outside the door like I told you.

(*Bertha exits into the bedroom.*)

Seth: Something ain't setting right with that fellow, Bynum. He's one of them mean-looking niggers look like he done killed somebody gambling over a quarter.

Bynum: He ain't no gambler. Gamblers wear nice shoes. This fellow got on clod-hoppers. He been out there walking up and down them roads.

(*Zonia enters from the stairs and looks around.*)

Bynum: You looking for the back door, sugar? There it is. You can go out there and play. It's alright.

Seth (*showing her the door*): You can go out there and play. Just don't get in my garden. And don't go messing around in my workshed.

(*Seth exits into the bedroom. There is a knock on the door.*)

Jeremy: Somebody at the door.

(*Jeremy goes to answer the door. Enter Mattie Campbell. She is a young woman of twenty-six whose attractiveness is hidden under the weight and concerns of a dissatisfied life. She is a woman in an honest search for love and companionship. She has suffered many defeats in her search, and though not always uncompromising, still believes in the possibility of love.*)

Mattie: I'm looking for a man named Bynum. Lady told me to come back later.

Jeremy: Sure, he here. Mr. Bynum, somebody here to see you.

Bynum: Come to see me, huh?

Mattie: Are you the man they call Bynum? The man folks say can fix things?

Bynum: Depend on what need fixing. I can't make no promises. But I got a powerful song in some matters.

Mattie: Can you fix it so my man come back to me?

Bynum: Come on in . . . have a sit down.

Mattie: You got to help me. I don't know what else to do.

Bynum: Depend on how all the circumstances of the thing come together. How all the pieces fit.

Mattie: I done everything I knowed how to do. You got to make him come back to me.

Bynum: It ain't nothing to make somebody come back. I can fix it so he can't stand to be away from you. I got my roots and powders, I can fix it so wherever he's at this thing will come up on him and he won't be able to sleep for seeing your face. Won't be able to eat for thinking of you.

Mattie: That's what I want. Make him come back.

Bynum: The roots is a powerful thing. I can fix it so one day he'll walk out his front door . . . won't be thinking of nothing. He won't know what it is. All he knows is that a powerful dissatisfaction done set in his bones and can't nothing he do make him feel satisfied. He'll set his foot down on the road and the wind in the trees be talking to him and everywhere he step on the road, that road'll give back your name and something will pull him right up to your doorstep. Now, I can do that. I can take my roots and fix that easy. But maybe he ain't supposed to come back. And if he ain't supposed to come back . . . then he'll be in your bed one morning and it'll come up on him that he's in the wrong place. That he's lost outside of time from his place that he's supposed to be in. Then both of you be lost and trapped outside of life and ain't no way for you to get back into it. 'Cause you lost from yourselves and where the places come together, where you're supposed to be alive, your heart kicking in your chest with a song worth singing.

Mattie: Make him come back to me. Make his feet say my name on the road. I don't care what happens. Make him come back.

Bynum: What's your man's name?

Mattie: He go by Jack Carper. He was born in Alabama then he come to West Texas and find me and we come here. Been here three years before he left. Say I had a curse prayer on me and he started walking down the road and ain't never come back. Somebody told me, say you can fix things like that.

Bynum: He just got up one day, set his feet on the road, and walked away?

Mattie: You got to make him come back, mister.

Bynum: Did he say goodbye?

Mattie: Ain't said nothing. Just started walking. I could see where he disappeared. Didn't look back. Just keep walking. Can't you fix it so he come back? I ain't got no curse prayer on me. I know I ain't.

Bynum: What made him say you had a curse prayer on you?

Mattie: 'Cause the babies died. Me and Jack had two babies. Two little babies that ain't lived two months before they died. He say it's because somebody cursed me not to have babies.

Bynum: He ain't bound to you if the babies died. Look like somebody trying to keep you from being bound up and he's gone on back to whoever it is 'cause he's already bound up to her. Ain't nothing to be done. Somebody else done got a powerful hand in it and ain't nothing to be done to break it. You got to let him go find where he's supposed to be in the world.

Mattie: Jack done gone off and you telling me to forget about him. All my life I been looking for somebody to stop and stay with me. I done already got too many things to forget about. I take Jack Carper's hand and it feel so rough and strong. Seem like he's the strongest man in the world the way he hold me. Like he's bigger than the whole world and can't nothing bad get to me. Even when he act mean sometimes he still make everything seem okay with the world. Like there's part of it that belongs just to you. Now you telling me to forget about him?

Bynum: Jack Carper gone off to where he belong. There's somebody searching for your doorstep right now. Ain't no need you fretting over Jack Carper. Right now he's a strong thought in your mind. But every time you catch yourself fretting over Jack Carper you push that thought away. You push it out your mind and that thought will get weaker and weaker till you wake up one morning and you won't even be able to call him up on your mind.

(Bynum gives her a small cloth packet.)

Take this and sleep with it under your pillow and it'll bring good luck to you. Draw it to you like a magnet. It won't be long before you forget all about Jack Carper.

Mattie: How much . . . do I owe you?

Bynum: Whatever you got there . . . that'll be alright.

(Mattie hands Bynum two quarters. She crosses to the door.)

You sleep with that under your pillow and you'll be alright.

(Mattie opens the door to exit and Jeremy crosses over to her. Bynum overhears the first part of their conversation, then exits out the back.)

Jeremy: I overheard what you told Mr. Bynum. Had me an old gal did that to me. Woke up one morning and she was gone. Just took off to parts unknown. I woke up that morning and the only thing I could do was look around for my shoes. I woke up and got out of there. Found my shoes and took off. That's the only thing I could think of to do.

Mattie: She ain't said nothing?

Jeremy: I just looked around for my shoes and got out of there.

Mattie: Jack ain't said nothing either. He just walked off.

Jeremy: Some mens do that. Womens too. I ain't gone off looking for her. I just let her go. Figure she had a time to come to herself. Wasn't no use of me standing in the way. Where you from?

Mattie: Texas. I was born in Georgia but I went to Texas with my mama. She dead now. Was picking peaches and fell dead away. I come up here with Jack Carper.

Jeremy: I'm from North Carolina. Down around Raleigh where they got all that tobacco. Been up here about two weeks. I likes it fine except I still got to find me a woman. You got a nice look to you. Look like you have mens standing in your door. Is you got mens standing in your door to get a look at you?

Mattie: I ain't got nobody since Jack left.

Jeremy: A woman like you need a man. Maybe you let me be your man. I got a nice way with the women. That's what they tell me.

Mattie: I don't know. Maybe Jack's coming back.

Jeremy: I'll be your man till he come. A woman can't be by her lonesome. Let me be your man till he come.

Mattie: I just can't go through life piecing myself out to different mens. I need a man who wants to stay with me.

Jeremy: I can't say what's gonna happen. Maybe I'll be the man. I don't know. You wanna go along the road a little ways with me?

Mattie: I don't know. Seem like life say it's gonna be one thing and end up being another. I'm tired of going from man to man.

Jeremy: Life is like you got to take a chance. Everybody got to take a chance. Can't nobody say what's gonna be. Come on . . . take a chance with me and see what the year bring. Maybe you let me come and see you. Where you staying?

Mattie: I got me a room up on Bedford. Me and Jack had a room together.

Jeremy: What's the address? I'll come by and get you tonight and we can go down to Seefus. I'm going down there and play my guitar.

Mattie: You play guitar?

Jeremy: I play guitar like I'm born to it.

Mattie: I live at 1727 Bedford Avenue. I'm gonna find out if you can play guitar like you say.

Jeremy: I plays it sugar, and that ain't all I do. I got a ten-pound hammer and I knows how to drive it down. Good god . . . you ought to hear my hammer ring!

Mattie: Go on with that kind of talk, now. If you gonna come by and get me I got to get home and straighten up for you.

Jeremy: I'll be by at eight o'clock. How's eight o'clock? I'm gonna make you forget all about Jack Carper.

Mattie: Go on, now. I got to get home and fix up for you.

Jeremy: Eight o'clock, sugar.

(The lights go down in the parlor and come up on the yard outside. Zonia is singing and playing a game.)

Zonia:
> I went downtown
> To get my grip
> I came back home
> Just a pullin' the skiff
>
> I went upstairs
> To make my bed
> I made a mistake
> And I bumped my head
> Just a pullin' the skiff
>
> I went downstairs
> To milk the cow
> I made a mistake
> And I milked the sow
> Just a pullin' the skiff

Tomorrow, tomorrow
Tomorrow never comes
The marrow the marrow
The marrow in the bone.

(*Reuben enters.*)

Reuben: Hi.

Zonia: Hi.

Reuben: What's your name?

Zonia: Zonia.

Reuben: What kind of name is that?

Zonia: It's what my daddy named me.

Reuben: My name's Reuben. You staying in Mr. Seth's house?

Zonia: Yeah.

Reuben: That your daddy I seen you with this morning?

Zonia: I don't know. Who you see me with?

Reuben: I saw you with some man had on a great big old coat. And you was walking up to Mr. Seth's house. Had on a hat too.

Zonia: Yeah, that's my daddy.

Reuben: You like Mr. Seth?

Zonia: I ain't see him much.

Reuben: My grandpap say he a great big old windbag. How come you living in Mr. Seth's house? Don't you have no house?

Zonia: We going to find my mother.

Reuben: Where she at?

Zonia: I don't know. We got to find her. We just go all over.

Reuben: Why you got to find her? What happened to her?

Zonia: She ran away.

Reuben: Why she run away?

Zonia: I don't know. My daddy say some man named Joe Turner did something bad to him once and that made her run away.

Reuben: Maybe she coming back and you don't have to go looking for her.

Zonia: We ain't there no more.

Reuben: She could have come back when you wasn't there.

Zonia: My daddy said she ran off and left us so we going looking for her.

Reuben: What he gonna do when he find her?

Zonia: He didn't say. He just say he got to find her.

Reuben: Your daddy say how long you staying in Mr. Seth's house?

Zonia: He don't say much. But we never stay too long nowhere. He say we got to keep moving till we find her.

Reuben: Ain't no kids hardly live around here. I had me a friend but he died. He was the best friend I ever had. Me and Eugene used to keep secrets. I still got his pigeons. He told me to let them go when he died. He say, "Reuben, promise me when I die you'll let my pigeons go." But I keep them to remember him by. I ain't never gonna let them go. Even when I get to be grown up. I'm just always gonna have Eugene's pigeons.

(*Pause.*)

Mr. Bynum a conjure man. My grandpap scared of him. He don't like me to come over here too much. I'm scared of him too. My grandpap told me not to let him get close enough to where he can reach out his hand and touch me.

Zonia: He don't seem scary to me.

Reuben: He buys pigeons from me . . . and if you get up early in the morning you can see him out in the yard doing something with them pigeons. My grandpap say he kill them. I sold him one yesterday. I don't know what he do with it. I just hope he don't spook me up.

Zonia: Why you sell him pigeons if he's gonna spook you up?

Reuben: I just do like Eugene do. He used to sell Mr. Bynum pigeons. That's how he got to collecting them to sell to Mr. Bynum. Sometime he give me a nickel and sometime he give me a whole dime.

(*Loomis enters from the house.*)

Loomis: Zonia!

Zonia: Sir?

Loomis: What you doing?

Zonia: Nothing.

Loomis: You stay around this house, you hear? I don't want you wandering off nowhere.

Zonia: I ain't wandering off nowhere.

Loomis: Miss Bertha set that hot tub and you getting a good scrubbing. Get scrubbed up good. You ain't been scrubbing.

Zonia: I been scrubbing.

Loomis: Look at you. You growing too fast. Your bones getting bigger everyday. I don't want you getting grown on me. Don't you get grown on me too soon. We gonna find your mamma. She around here somewhere. I can smell her. You stay on around this house now. Don't you go nowhere.

Zonia: Yes, sir.

(*Loomis exits into the house.*)

Reuben: Wow, your daddy's scary!

Zonia: He is not! I don't know what you talking about.

Reuben: He got them mean-looking eyes!

Zonia: My daddy ain't got no mean-looking eyes!

Reuben: Aw, girl, I was just messing with you. You wanna go see Eugene's pigeons? Got a great big coop out the back of my house. Come on, I'll show you.

(*Reuben and Zonia exit as the lights go down.*)

Scene II

It is Saturday morning, one week later. The lights come up on the kitchen. Bertha is at the stove preparing breakfast while Seth sits at the table.

Seth: Something ain't right about that fellow. I been watching him all week. Something ain't right, I'm telling you.

Bertha: Seth Holly, why don't you hush up about that man this morning?

Seth: I don't like the way he stare at everybody. Don't look at you natural like. He just be staring at you. Like he trying to figure out something about you. Did you see him when he come back in here?

Bertha: That man ain't thinking about you.

Seth: He don't work nowhere. Just go out and come back. Go out and come back.

Bertha: As long as you get your boarding money it ain't your cause about what he do. He don't bother nobody.

Seth: Just go and come back. Going around asking everybody about Martha. Like Henry Allen seen him down at the church last night.

Bertha: The man's allowed to go to church if he want. He say he a deacon. Ain't nothing wrong about him going to church.

Seth: I ain't talking about him going to church. I'm talking about him hanging around *outside* the church.

Bertha: Henry Allen say that?

Seth: Say he be standing around outside the church. Like he be watching it.

Bertha: What on earth he wanna be watching the church for, I wonder?

Seth: That's what I'm trying to figure out. Looks like he fixing to rob it.

Bertha: Seth, now do he look like the kind that would rob the church?

Seth: I ain't saying that. I ain't saying how he look. It's how he do. Anybody liable to do anything as far as I'm concerned. I ain't never thought about how no church robbers look . . . but now that you mention it, I don't see where they look no different than how he look.

Bertha: Herald Loomis ain't the kind of man who would rob no church.

Seth: I ain't even so sure that's his name.

Bertha: Why the man got to lie about his name?

Seth: Anybody can tell anybody anything about what their name is. That's what you call him . . . Herald Loomis. His name is liable to be anything.

Bertha: Well, until he tell me different that's what I'm gonna call him. You just getting yourself all worked up about the man for nothing.

Seth: Talking about Loomis: Martha's name wasn't no Loomis nothing. Martha's name is Pentecost.

Bertha: How you so sure that's her right name? Maybe she changed it.

Seth: Martha's a good Christian woman. This fellow here look like he owe the devil a day's work and he's trying to figure out how he gonna pay him. Martha ain't had a speck of distrust about her the whole time she was living here. They moved the church out there to Rankin and I was sorry to see her go.

Bertha: That's why he be hanging around the church. He looking for her.

Seth: If he looking for her, why don't he go inside and ask? What he doing hanging around outside the church acting sneaky like?

(Bynum enters from the yard.)

Bynum: Morning, Seth. Morning, Sister Bertha.

(Bynum continues through the kitchen and exits up the stairs.)

Bertha: That's who you should be asking the questions. He been out there in that yard all morning. He was out there before the sun come up. He didn't even come in for breakfast. I don't know what he's doing. He had three of them pigeons line up out there. He dance around till he get tired. He sit down awhile then get up and dance some more. He come through here a little while ago looking like he was mad at the world.

Seth: I don't pay Bynum no mind. He don't spook me up with all that stuff.

Bertha: That's how Martha come to be living here. She come to see Bynum. She come to see him when she first left from down South.

Seth: Martha was living here before Bynum. She ain't come on here when she first left from down there. She come on here after she went back to get her little girl. That's when she come on here.

Bertha: Well, where was Bynum? He was here when she came.

Seth: Bynum ain't come till after her. That boy Hiram was staying up there in Bynum's room.

Bertha: Well, how long Bynum been here?

Seth: Bynum ain't been here no longer than three years. That's what I'm trying to tell you. Martha was staying up there and sewing and cleaning for Doc Goldblum when Bynum came. This the longest he ever been in one place.

Bertha: How you know how long the man been in one place?

Seth: I know Bynum. Bynum ain't no mystery to me. I done seen a hundred niggers like him. He's one of them fellows never could stay in one place. He was wandering all around the country till he got old and settled here. The only thing different about Bynum is he bring all this heebie-jeebie stuff with him.

Bertha: I still say he was staying here when she came. That's why she came . . . to see him.

Seth: You can say what you want. I know the facts of it. She come on here four years ago all heartbroken 'cause she couldn't find her little girl. And Bynum wasn't nowhere around. She got mixed up in that old heebie-jeebie nonsense with him after he came.

Bertha: Well, if she came on before Bynum I don't know where she stayed. 'Cause she stayed up there in Hiram's room. Hiram couldn't get along with Bynum and left out of here owing you two dollars. Now, I know you ain't forgot about that!

Seth: Sure did! You know Hiram ain't paid me that two dollars yet. So that's why he be ducking and hiding when he see me down on Logan Street. You right. Martha did come on after Bynum. I forgot that's why Hiram left.

Bertha: Him and Bynum never could see eye to eye. They always rubbed each other the wrong way. Hiram got to thinking that Bynum was trying to put a fix on him and he moved out. Martha came to see Bynum and ended up taking Hiram's room. Now, I know what I'm talking about. She stayed on here three years till they moved the church.

Seth: She out there in Rankin now. I know where she at. I know where they moved the church to. She right out there in Rankin in that place used to be shoe store. Used to be Wolf's shoe store. They moved to a bigger place and they put that church in there. I know where she at. I know just where she at.

Bertha: Why don't you tell the man? You see he looking for her.

Seth: I ain't gonna tell that man where that woman is! What I wanna do that for? I don't know nothing about that man. I don't know why he looking for her. He might wanna do her a harm. I ain't gonna carry that on my hands. He looking for her, he gonna have to find her for himself. I ain't gonna help him. Now, if he had come and presented himself as a gentleman—the way Martha Pentecost's husband would have done—then I would have told him. But I ain't gonna tell this old wild-eyed mean-looking nigger nothing!

Bertha: Well, why don't you get a ride with Selig and go up there and tell her where he is? See if she wanna see him. If that's her little girl . . . you say Martha was looking for her.

Seth: You know me, Bertha. I don't get mixed up in nobody's business.

(*Bynum enters from the stairs.*)

Bynum: Morning, Seth. Morning, Bertha. Can I still get some breakfast? Mr. Loomis been down here this morning?

Seth: He done gone out and come back. He up there now. Left out of here early this morning wearing that coat. Hot as it is, the man wanna walk around wearing a big old heavy coat. He come back in here paid me for another week, sat down there waiting on Selig. Got tired of waiting and went on back upstairs.

Bynum: Where's the little girl?

Seth: She out there in the front. Had to chase her and that Reuben off the front porch. She out there somewhere.

Bynum: Look like if Martha was around here he would have found her by now. My guess is she ain't in the city.

Seth: She ain't! I know where she at. I know just where she at. But I ain't gonna tell him. Not the way he look.

Bertha: Here go your coffee, Bynum.

Bynum: He says he gonna get Selig to find her for him.

Seth: Selig can't find her. He talk all that . . . but unless he get lucky and knock on her door he can't find her. That's the only way he find anybody. He got to get lucky. But I know just where she at.

Bertha: Here go some biscuits, Bynum.

Bynum: What else you got over there, Sister Bertha? You got some grits and gravy over there? I could go for some of that this morning.

Bertha (*sets a bowl on the table*): Seth, come on and help me turn this mattress over. Come on.

Seth: Something ain't right with that fellow, Bynum. I don't like the way he stare at everybody.

Bynum: Mr. Loomis alright, Seth. He just a man got something on his mind. He just got a straightforward mind, that's all.

Seth: What's that fellow that they had around here? Moses, that's Moses Houser. Man went crazy and jumped off the Brady Street Bridge. I told you when I seen him something wasn't right about him. And I'm telling you about this fellow now.

(*There is a knock on the door. Seth goes to answer it. Enter Rutherford Selig.*)

Ho! Come on in, Selig.

Bynum: If it ain't the People Finder himself.

Selig: Bynum, before you start . . . I ain't seen no shiny man now.

Bynum: Who said anything about that? I ain't said nothing about that. I just called you a first-class People Finder.

Selig: How many dustpans you get out of that sheet metal, Seth?

Seth: You walked by them on your way in. They sitting out there on the porch. Got twenty-eight. Got four out of each sheet and made Bertha a coffeepot out the other one. They a little small but they got nice handles.

Selig: That was twenty cents apiece, right? That's what we agreed on.

Seth: That's five dollars and sixty cents. Twenty on top of twenty-eight. How many sheets you bring me?

Selig: I got eight out there. That's a dollar twenty makes me owe you . . .

Seth: Four dollars and forty cents.

Selig (*paying him*): Go on and make me some dustpans. I can use all you can make.

(*Loomis enters from the stairs.*)

Loomis: I been watching for you. He say you find people.

Bynum: Mr. Loomis here wants you to find his wife.

Loomis: He say you find people. Find her for me.

Selig: Well, let see here . . . find somebody, is it?

(*Selig rummages through his pockets. He has several notebooks and he is searching for the right one.*)

Alright now . . . what's the name?

Loomis: Martha Loomis. She my wife. Got married legal with the paper and all.

Selig (*writing*): Martha . . . Loomis. How tall is she?

Loomis: She five feet from the ground.

Selig: Five feet . . . tall. Young or old?

Loomis: She a young woman. Got long pretty hair.

Selig: Young . . . long . . . pretty . . . hair. Where did you last see her?

Loomis: Tennessee. Nearby Memphis.

Selig: When was that?

Loomis: Nineteen hundred and one.

Selig: Nineteen . . . hundred and one. I'll tell you, mister . . . you better off without them. Now you take me . . . old Rutherford Selig could tell you a thing or two about these women. I ain't met one yet I could understand. Now, you take Sally out there. That's all a man needs is a good horse. I say giddup and she go. Say whoa and she stop. I feed her some oats and she carry me wherever I want to go. Ain't had a speck of trouble out of her since I had her. Now, I been married. A long time ago down in Kentucky. I got up one morning and I saw this look on my wife's face. Like way down deep inside her she was wishing I was dead. I walked around that morning and every time I looked at her she had that look on her face. It seem like she knew I could see it on her. Every time I looked at her I got smaller and smaller. Well, I wasn't gonna stay around there and just shrink away. I walked out on the porch and closed the door behind me. When I closed the door she locked it. I went out and bought me a horse. And I ain't been without one since! Martha Loomis, huh? Well, now I'll do the best I can do. That's one dollar.

Loomis (holding out dollar suspiciously): How you find her?

Selig: Well now, it ain't no easy job like you think. You can't just go out there and find them like that. There's a lot of little tricks to it. It's not an easy job keeping up with you Nigras the way you move about so. Now you take this woman you looking for . . . this Martha Loomis. She could be anywhere. Time I find her, if you don't keep your eye on her, she'll be gone off some-place else. You'll be thinking she over here and she'll be over there. But like I say there's lot of little tricks to it.

Loomis: You say you find her.

Selig: I can't promise anything but we been finders in my family for a long time. Bringers and finders. My great-granddaddy used to bring Nigras across the ocean on ships. That's wasn't no easy job either. Sometimes the winds would blow so hard you'd think the hand of God was set against the sails. But it set him well in pay and he settled in this new land and found him a wife of good Christian charity with a mind for kids and the like and well . . . here I am, Rutherford Selig. You're in good hands, mister. Me and my daddy have found plenty Nigras. My daddy, rest his soul, used to find run-away slaves for the plantation bosses. He was the best there was at it. Jonas B. Selig. Had him a reputation stretched clean across the country. After Abraham Lincoln give you all Nigras your freedom papers and with you all looking all over for each other . . . we started finding Nigras for Nigras. Of course, it don't pay as much. But the People Finding business ain't so bad.

Loomis (hands him the dollar): Find her. Martha Loomis. Find her for me.

Selig: Like I say, I can't promise you anything. I'm going back upriver, and if she's around in them parts I'll find her for you. But I can't promise you anything.

Loomis: When you coming back?

Selig: I'll be back on Saturday. I come and see Seth to pick up my order on Saturday.

Bynum: You going upriver, huh? You going up around my way. I used to go all up through there. Blawknox . . . Clairton. Used to go up to Rankin and take that first righthand road. I wore many a pair of shoes out walking around that way. You'd have thought I was a missionary spreading the gospel the way I wandered all around them parts.

Selig: Okay, Bynum. See you on Saturday.

Seth: Here, let me walk out with you. Help you with them dustpans.

(*Seth and Selig exit out the back. Bertha enters from the stairs carrying a bundle of sheets.*)

Bynum: Herald Loomis got the People Finder looking for Martha.

Bertha: You can call him a People Finder if you want to. I know Rutherford Selig carries people away too. He done carried a whole bunch of them away from here. Folks plan on leaving plan by Selig's timing. They wait till he get ready to go, then they hitch a ride on his wagon. Then he charge folks a dollar to tell them where he took them. Now, that's the truth of Rutherford Selig. This old People Finding business is for the birds. He ain't never found nobody he ain't took away. Herald Loomis, you just wasted your dollar.

(*Bertha exits into the bedroom.*)

Loomis: He say he find her. He say he find her by Saturday. I'm gonna wait till Saturday.

(*The lights fade to black.*)

Scene III

It is Sunday morning, the next day. The lights come up on the kitchen. Seth sits talking to Bynum. The breakfast dishes have been cleared away.

Seth: They can't see that. Neither one of them can see that. Now, how much sense it take to see that? All you got to do is be able to count. One man making ten pots is five men making fifty pots. But they can't see that. Asked where I'm gonna get my five men. Hell, I can teach anybody how to make a pot. I can teach you. I can take you out there and get you started right now. Inside of two weeks you'd know how to make a pot. All you got to do is want to do it. I can get five men. I ain't worried about getting no five men.

Bertha (calls from the bedroom): Seth. Come on and get ready now. Reverend Gates ain't gonna be holding up his sermon 'cause you sitting out there talking.

Seth: Now, you take the boy, Jeremy. What he gonna do after he put in that road? He can't do nothing but go put in another one somewhere. Now, if he

let me show him how to make some pots and pans . . . then he'd have something can't nobody take away from him. After a while he could get his own
tools and go off somewhere and make his own pots and pans. Find him
somebody to sell them to. Now, Selig can't make no pots and pans. He can
sell them but he can't make them. I get me five men with some tools and
we'd make him so many pots and pans he'd have to open up a store somewhere. But they can't see that. Neither Mr. Cohen nor Sam Green.

Bertha (calls from the bedroom): Seth . . . time be wasting. Best be getting on.

Seth: I'm coming, woman! (*To Bynum.*) Want me to sign over the house to
borrow five hundred dollars. I ain't that big a fool. That's all I got. Sign it
over to them and then I won't have nothing.

(*Jeremy enters waving a dollar and carrying his guitar.*)

Jeremy: Look here, Mr. Bynum . . . won me another dollar last night down at
Seefus! Me and that Mattie Campbell went down there again and I played
contest. Ain't no guitar players down there. Wasn't even no contest. Say,
Mr. Seth, I asked Mattie Campbell if she wanna come by and have Sunday
dinner with us. Get some fried chicken.

Seth: It's gonna cost you twenty-five cents.

Jeremy: That's alright. I got a whole dollar here. Say Mr. Seth . . . me and Mattie
Campbell talked it over last night and she gonna move in with me. If that's
alright with you.

Seth: Your business is your business . . . but it's gonna cost her a dollar a week for
her board. I can't be feeding nobody for free.

Jeremy: Oh, she know that, Mr. Seth. That's what I told her, say she'd have to
pay for her meals.

Seth: You say you got a whole dollar there . . . turn loose that twenty-five cents.

Jeremy: Suppose she move in today, then that make seventy-five cents more, so
I'll give you the whole dollar for her now till she gets here.

(*Seth pockets the money and exits into the bedroom.*)

Bynum: So you and that Mattie Campbell gonna take up together?

Jeremy: I told her she don't need to be by her lonesome, Mr. Bynum. Don't make
no sense for both of us to be by our lonesome. So she gonna move in with me.

Bynum: Sometimes you got to be where you supposed to be. Sometimes you can
get all mixed up in life and come to the wrong place.

Jeremy: That's just what I told her, Mr. Bynum. It don't make no sense for her to
be all mixed up and lonesome. May as well come here and be with me. She a
fine woman too. Got them long legs. Knows how to treat a fellow too. Treat
you like you wanna be treated.

Bynum: You just can't look at it like that. You got to look at the whole thing.
Now, you take a fellow go out there, grab hold to a woman and think he got
something 'cause she sweet and soft to the touch. Alright. Touching's part
of life. It's in the world like everything else. Touching's nice. It feels good.
But you can lay your hand upside a horse or a cat, and that feels good too.

What's the difference? When you grab hold to a woman, you got something there. You got a whole world there. You got a way of life kicking up under your hand. That woman can take and make you feel like something. I ain't just talking about in the way of jumping off into bed together and rolling around with each other. Anybody can do that. When you grab hold to that woman and look at the whole thing and see what you got . . . why, she can take and make something out of you. Your mother was a woman. That's enough right there to show you what a woman is. Enough to show you what she can do. She made something out of you. Taught you converse, and all about how to take care of yourself, how to see where you at and where you going tomorrow, how to look out to see what's coming in the way of eating, and what to do with yourself when you get lonesome. That's a mighty thing she did. But you just can't look at a woman to jump off into bed with her. That's a foolish thing to ignore a woman like that.

Jeremy: Oh, I ain't ignoring her, Mr. Bynum. It's hard to ignore a woman got legs like she got.

Bynum: Alright. Let's try it this way. Now, you take a ship. Be out there on the water traveling about. You out there on that ship sailing to and from. And then you see some land. Just like you see a woman walking down the street. You see that land and it don't look like nothing but a line out there on the horizon. That's all it is when you first see it. A line that cross your path out there on the horizon. Now, a smart man know when he see that land, it ain't just a line setting out there. He know that if you get off the water to go take a good look . . . why, there's a whole world right there. A whole world with everything imaginable under the sun. Anything you can think of you can find on that land. Same with a woman. A woman is everything a man need. To a smart man she water and berries. And that's all a man need. That's all he need to live on. You give me some water and berries and if there ain't nothing else I can live a hundred years. See, you just like a man looking at the horizon from a ship. You just seeing a part of it. But it's a blessing when you learn to look at a woman and see in maybe just a few strands of her hair, the way her cheek curves . . . to see in that everything there is out of life to be gotten. It's a blessing to see that. You know you done right and proud by your mother to see that. But you got to learn it. My telling you ain't gonna mean nothing. You got to learn how to come to your own time and place with a woman.

Jeremy: What about your woman, Mr. Bynum? I know you done had some woman.

Bynum: Oh, I got them in memory time. That lasts longer than any of them ever stayed with me.

Jeremy: I had me an old gal one time . . .

(There is a knock on the door, Jeremy goes to answer it. Enter Molly Cunningham. She is about twenty-six, the kind of woman that "could break in on a dollar anywhere she goes." She carries a small cardboard suitcase, and wears a colorful dress of the fashion of the day. Jeremy's heart jumps out of his chest when he sees her.)

Molly: You got any rooms here? I'm looking for a room.

Jeremy: Yeah . . . Mr. Seth got rooms. Sure . . . wait till I get Mr. Seth. (*Calls.*) Mr. Seth! Somebody here to see you! (*To Molly.*) Yeah, Mr. Seth got some rooms. Got one right next to me. This is a nice place to stay, too. My name's Jeremy. What's yours?

(*Seth enters dressed in his Sunday clothes.*)

Seth: Ho!

Jeremy: This here woman looking for a place to stay. She say you got any rooms.

Molly: Mister, you got any rooms? I seen your sign say you got rooms.

Seth: How long you plan to staying?

Molly: I ain't gonna be here long. I ain't looking for no home or nothing. I'd be in Cincinnati if I hadn't missed my train.

Seth: Rooms cost two dollars a week.

Molly: Two dollars!

Seth: That includes meals. We serve two meals a day. That's breakfast and dinner.

Molly: I hope it ain't on the third floor.

Seth: That's the only one I got. Third floor to the left. That's pay up in advance week to week.

Molly (*going into her bosom*): I'm gonna pay you for one week. My name's Molly. Molly Cunningham.

Seth: I'm Seth Holly. My wife's name is Bertha. She do the cooking and take care of around here. She got sheets on the bed. Towels twenty-five cents a week extra if you ain't got none. You get breakfast and dinner. We got fried chicken on Sundays.

Molly: That sounds good. Here's two dollars and twenty-five cents. Look here, Mister . . . ?

Seth: Holly. Seth Holly.

Molly: Look here, Mr. Holly. I forgot to tell you. I likes me some company from time to time. I don't like being by myself.

Seth: Your business is your business. I don't meddle in nobody's business. But this is a respectable house. I don't have no riffraff around here. And I don't have no women hauling no men up to their rooms to be making their living. As long as we understand each other then we'll be alright with each other.

Molly: Where's the outhouse?

Seth: Straight through the door over yonder.

Molly: I get my own key to the front door?

Seth: Everybody get their own key. If you come in late just don't be making no whole lot of noise and carrying on. Don't allow no fussing and fighting around here.

Molly: You ain't got to worry about that, mister. Which way you say that out house was again?

Seth: Straight through that door over yonder.

(Molly exits out the back door. Jeremy crosses to watch her.)

Jeremy: Mr. Bynum, you know what? I think I know what you was talking about
now.

(The lights go down on the scene.)

Scene IV

The lights come up on the kitchen. It is later the same evening. Mattie and all the residents of the house, except Loomis, sit around the table. They have finished eating and most of the dishes have been cleared.

Molly: That sure was some good chicken.

Jeremy: That's what I'm talking about. Miss Bertha, you sure can fry some
chicken. I thought my mama could fry some chicken. But she can't do half
as good as you.

Seth: I know it. That's why I married her. She don't know that, though. She
think I married her for something else.

Bertha: I ain't studying you, Seth. Did you get your things moved in alright,
Mattie?

Mattie: I ain't had that much. Jeremy helped me with what I did have.

Bertha: You'll get to know your way around here. If you have any questions
about anything just ask me. You and Molly both. I get along with everybody. You'll find I ain't no trouble to get along with.

Mattie: You need some help with the dishes?

Bertha: I got me a helper. Ain't I, Zonia? Got me a good helper.

Zonia: Yes, ma'am.

Seth: Look at Bynum sitting over there with his belly all poked out. Ain't saying
nothing. Sitting over there half asleep. Ho, Bynum!

Bertha: If Bynum ain't saying nothing what you wanna start him up for?

Seth: Ho, Bynum!

Bynum: What you hollering at me for? I ain't doing nothing.

Seth: Come on, we gonna Juba.

Bynum: You know me, I'm always ready to Juba.

Seth: Well, come on, then.

(Seth pulls out a harmonica and blows a few notes.)

Come on there, Jeremy. Where's your guitar? Go get your guitar. Bynum
says he's ready to Juba.

Jeremy: Don't need no guitar to Juba. Ain't you never Juba without a guitar?

(Jeremy begins to drum on the table.)

Seth: It ain't that. I ain't never Juba with one! Figured to try it and see how it
worked.

Bynum (*drumming on the table*): You don't need no guitar. Look at Molly sitting over there. She don't know we Juba on Sunday. We gonna show you something tonight. You and Mattie Campbell both. Ain't that right, Seth?

Seth: You said it! Come on, Bertha, leave them dishes be for a while. We gonna Juba.

Bynum: Alright. Let's Juba down!

(*The Juba is reminiscent of the Ring Shouts of the African slaves. It is a call and response dance. Bynum sits at the table and drums. He calls the dance as others clap hands, shuffle and stomp around the table. It should be as African as possible, with the performers working themselves up into a near frenzy. The words can be improvised, but should include some mention of the Holy Ghost. In the middle of the dance Herald Loomis enters.*)

Loomis (*in a rage*): Stop it! Stop!

(*They stop and turn to look at him.*)

You all sitting up here singing about the Holy Ghost. What's so holy about the Holy Ghost? You singing and singing. You think the Holy Ghost coming? You singing for the Holy Ghost to come? What he gonna do, huh? He gonna come with tongues of fire to burn up your woolly heads? You gonna tie onto the Holy Ghost and get burned up? What you got then? Why God got to be so big? Why he got to be bigger than me? How much big is there? How much big do you want?

(*Loomis starts to unzip his pants.*)

Seth: Nigger, you crazy!

Loomis: How much big you want?

Seth: You done plumb lost your mind!

(*Loomis begins to speak in tongues and dance around the kitchen. Seth starts after him.*)

Bertha: Leave him alone, Seth. He ain't in his right mind.

Loomis (*stops suddenly*): You all don't know nothing about me. You don't know what I done seen. Herald Loomis done seen some things he ain't got words to tell you.

(*Loomis starts to walk out the front door and is thrown back and collapses, terror-stricken by his vision. Bynum crawls to him.*)

Bynum: What you done seen, Herald Loomis?

Loomis: I done seen bones rise up out the water. Rise up and walk across the water. Bones walking on top of the water.

Bynum: Tell me about them bones, Herald Loomis. Tell me what you seen.

Loomis: I come to this place . . . to this water that was bigger than the whole world. And I looked out . . . and I seen these bones rise up out the water. Rise up and begin to walk on top of it.

Bynum: Wasn't nothing but bones and they walking on top of the water.

Loomis: Walking without sinking down. Walking on top of the water.

Bynum: Just marching in a line.

Loomis: A whole heap of them. They come up out the water and started marching.

Bynum: Wasn't nothing but bones and they walking on top of the water.

Loomis: One after the other. They just come up out the water and start to walking.

Bynum: They walking on the water without sinking down. They just walking and walking. And then . . . what happened, Herald Loomis?

Loomis: They just walking across the water.

Bynum: What happened, Herald Loomis? What happened to the bones?

Loomis: They just walking across the water . . . and then . . . they sunk down.

Bynum: The bones sunk into the water. They all sunk down.

Loomis: All at one time! They just all fell in the water at one time.

Bynum: Sunk down like anybody else.

Loomis: When they sink down they made a big splash and this here wave come up . . .

Bynum: A big wave, Herald Loomis. A big wave washed over the land.

Loomis: It washed them out of the water and up on the land. Only . . . only . . .

Bynum: Only they ain't bones no more.

Loomis: They got flesh on them! Just like you and me!

Bynum: Everywhere you look the waves is washing them up on the land right on top of one another.

Loomis: They black. Just like you and me. Ain't no difference.

Bynum: Then what happened, Herald Loomis?

Loomis: They ain't moved or nothing. They just laying there.

Bynum: You just laying there. What you waiting on, Herald Loomis?

Loomis: I'm laying there . . . waiting.

Bynum: What you waiting on, Herald Loomis?

Loomis: I'm waiting on the breath to get into my body.

Bynum: The breath coming into you, Herald Loomis. What you gonna do now?

Loomis: The wind's blowing the breath into my body. I can feel it. I'm starting to breathe again.

Bynum: What you gonna do, Herald Loomis?

Loomis: I'm gonna stand up. I got to stand up. I can't lay here no more. All the breath coming into my body and I got to stand up.

Bynum: Everybody's standing up at the same time.

Loomis: The ground's starting to shake. There's a great shaking. The world's busting half in two. The sky's splitting open. I got to stand up.

(*Loomis attempts to stand up.*)

My legs . . . my legs won't stand up!

Bynum: Everybody's standing and walking toward the road. What you gonna do, Herald Loomis?

Loomis: My legs won't stand up.

Bynum: They shaking hands and saying goodbye to each other and walking every whichaway down the road.

Loomis: I got to stand up!

Bynum: They walking around here now. Mens. Just like you and me. Come right up out the water.

Loomis: Got to stand up.

Bynum: They walking, Herald Loomis. They walking around here now.

Loomis: I got to stand up. Get up on the road.

Bynum: Come on, Herald Loomis.

(*Loomis tries to stand up.*)

Loomis: My legs won't stand up! My legs won't stand up!

(*Loomis collapses on the floor as the lights go down to black.*)

ACT II

Scene I

The lights come up on the kitchen. Bertha busies herself with breakfast preparations. Seth sits at the table.

Seth: I don't care what his problem is! He's leaving here!

Bertha: You can't put the man out and he got that little girl. Where they gonna go then?

Seth: I don't care where he go. Let him go back where he was before he come here. I ain't asked him to come here. I knew when I first looked at him something wasn't right with him. Dragging that little girl around with him. Looking like he be sleeping in the woods somewhere. I knew all along he wasn't right.

Bertha: A fellow get a little drunk he's liable to say or do anything. He ain't done no big harm.

Seth: I just don't have all that carrying on in my house. When he come down here I'm gonna tell him. He got to leave here. My daddy wouldn't stand for it and I ain't gonna stand for it either.

Bertha: Well, if you put him out you have to put Bynum out too. Bynum right there with him.

Seth: If it wasn't for Bynum ain't no telling what would have happened. Bynum talked to that fellow just as nice and calmed him down. If he wasn't here ain't no telling what would have happened. Bynum ain't done nothing but talk to him and kept him calm. Man acting all crazy with that foolishness. Naw, he's leaving here.

Bertha: What you gonna tell him? How you gonna tell him to leave?

Seth: I'm gonna tell him straight out. Keep it nice and simple. Mister, you got to leave here!

(*Molly enters from the stairs.*)

Molly: Morning.

Bertha: Did you sleep alright in that bed?

Molly: Tired as I was I could have slept anywhere. It's a real nice room, though. This is a nice place.

Seth: I'm sorry you had to put up with all that carrying on last night.

Molly: It don't bother me none. I done seen that kind of stuff before.

Seth: You won't have to see it around here no more.

(*Bynum is heard singing offstage.*)

I don't put up with all that stuff. When that fellow come down here I'm gonna tell him.

Bynum (*singing*):
Soon my work will all be done
Soon my work will all be done
Soon my work will all be done
I'm going to see the king.

Bynum (*enters*): Morning, Seth. Morning, Sister Bertha. I see we got Molly Cunningham down here at breakfast.

Seth: Bynum, I wanna thank you for talking to that fellow last night and calming him down. If you hadn't been here ain't no telling what might have happened.

Bynum: Mr. Loomis alright, Seth. He just got a little excited.

Seth: Well, he can get excited somewhere else 'cause he leaving here.

(*Mattie enters from the stairs.*)

Bynum: Well, there's Mattie Campbell.

Mattie: Good morning.

Bertha: Sit on down there, Mattie. I got some biscuits be ready in a minute. The coffee's hot.

Mattie: Jeremy gone already?

Bynum: Yeah, he leave out of here early. He got to be there when the sun come up. Most working men got to be there when the sun come up. Everybody but Seth. Seth work at night. Mr. Olowski so busy in his shop he got fellows working at night.

(*Loomis enters from the stairs.*)

Seth: Mr. Loomis, now . . . I don't want no trouble. I keeps me a respectable house here. I don't have no carrying on like what went on last night. This has been a respectable house for a long time. I'm gonna have to ask you to leave.

Loomis: You got my two dollars. That two dollars say we stay till Saturday.

(*Loomis and Seth glare at each other.*)

Seth: Alright. Fair enough. You stay till Saturday. But come Saturday you got to leave here.

Loomis (*continues to glare at Seth. He goes to the door and calls*): Zonia. You stay around this house, you hear? Don't you go anywhere.

(*Loomis exits out the front door.*)

Seth: I knew it when I first seen him. I knew something wasn't right with him.

Bertha: Seth, leave the people alone to eat their breakfast. They don't want to hear that. Go on out there and make some pots and pans. That's the only time you satisfied is when you out there. Go on out there and make some pots and pans and leave them people alone.

Seth: I ain't bothering anybody. I'm just stating the facts. I told you, Bynum.

(*Bertha shoos Seth out the back door and exits into the bedroom.*)

Molly (*to Bynum*): You one of them voo-doo people?

Bynum: I got a power to bind folks if that what you talking about.

Molly: I thought so. The way you talked to that man when he started all that spooky stuff. What you say you had the power to do to people? You ain't the cause of him acting like that, is you?

Bynum: I binds them together. Sometimes I help them find each other.

Molly: How do you do that?

Bynum: With a song. My daddy taught me how to do it.

Molly: That's what they say. Most folks be what they daddy is. I wouldn't want to be like my daddy. Nothing ever set right with him. He tried to make the world over. Carry it around with him everywhere he go. I don't want to be like that. I just take life as it come. I don't be trying to make it over.

(*Pause.*)

Your daddy used to do that too, huh? Make people stay together?

Bynum: My daddy used to heal people. He had the Healing Song. I got the Binding Song.

Molly: My mama used to believe in all that stuff. If she got sick she would have gone and saw your daddy. As long as he didn't make her drink nothing. She wouldn't drink nothing nobody give her. She was always afraid somebody was gonna poison her. How your daddy heal people?

Bynum: With a song. He healed people by singing over them. I seen him do it. He sung over this little white girl when she was sick. They made a big to-do about it. They carried the girl's bed out in the yard and had all her kinfolk standing around. The little girl laying up there in the bed. Doctors standing around can't do nothing to help her. And they had my daddy come up and sing his song. It didn't sound no different than any other song. It was just somebody singing. But the song was its own thing and it come out and took upon this little girl with its power and it healed her.

Molly: That's sure something else. I don't understand that kind of thing. I guess if the doctor couldn't make me well I'd try it. But otherwise I don't wanna be bothered with that kind of thing. It's too spooky.

Bynum: Well, let me get on out here and get to work.

(Bynum gets up and heads out the back door.)

Molly: I ain't meant to offend you or nothing. What's your name . . . Bynum? I ain't meant to say nothing to make you feel bad now.

(Bynum exits out the back door.)

(To Mattie.) I hope he don't feel bad. He's a nice man. I don't wanna hurt nobody's feelings or nothing.

Mattie: I got to go on up to Doc Goldblum's and finish this ironing.

Molly: Now, that's something I don't never wanna do. Iron no clothes. Especially somebody else's. That's what I believe killed my mama. Always ironing and working, doing somebody else's work. Not Molly Cunningham.

Mattie: It's the only job I got. I got to make it someway to fend for myself.

Molly: I thought Jeremy was your man. Ain't he working?

Mattie: We just be keeping company till maybe Jack come back.

Molly: I don't trust none of these men. Jack or nobody else. These men liable to do anything. They wait just until they get one woman tied and locked up with them . . . then they look around to see if they can get another one. Molly don't pay them no mind. One's just as good as the other if you ask me. I ain't never met one that meant nobody no good. You got any babies?

Mattie: I had two for my man, Jack Carper. But they both died.

Molly: That be the best. These men make all these babies, then run off and leave you to take care of them. Talking about they wanna see what's on the other side of the hill. I make sure I don't get no babies. My mama taught me how to do that.

Mattie: Don't make me no mind. That be nice to be a mother.

Molly: Yeah? Well, you go on, then. Molly Cunningham ain't gonna be tied down with no babies. Had me a man one time who I thought had some love in him. Come home one day and he was packing his trunk. Told me the time come when even the best of friends must part. Say he was gonna send me a Special Delivery some old day. I watched him out the window when he carried that trunk out and down to the train station. Said if he was gonna send me a Special Delivery I wasn't gonna be there to get it. I done found out the harder you try to hold onto them, the easier it is for some gal to pull them away. Molly done learned that. That's why I don't trust nobody but the good Lord above, and I don't love nobody but my mama.

Mattie: I got to get on. Doc Goldblum gonna be waiting.

(Mattie exits out the front door. Seth enters from his workshop with his apron, gloves, goggles, etc. He carries a bucket and crosses to the sink for water.)

Seth: Everybody gone but you, huh?

Molly: That little shack out there by the outhouse . . . that's where you make them pots and pans and stuff?

Seth: Yeah, that's my workshed. I go out there . . . take these hands and make something out of nothing. Take that metal and bend and twist it whatever way I want. My daddy taught me that. He used to make pots and pans. That's how I learned it.

Molly: I never knew nobody made no pots and pans. My uncle used to shoe horses.

(*Jeremy enters at the front door.*)

Seth: I thought you was working? Ain't you working today?

Jeremy: Naw, they fired me. White fellow come by told me to give him fifty cents if I wanted to keep working. Going around to all the colored making them give him fifty cents to keep hold to their jobs. Them other fellows, they was giving it to him. I kept hold to mine and they fired me.

Seth: Boy, what kind of sense that make? What kind of sense it make to get fired from a job where you making eight dollars a week and all it cost you is fifty cents. That's seven dollars and fifty cents profit! This way you ain't got nothing.

Jeremy: It didn't make no sense to me. I don't make but eight dollars. Why I got to give him fifty cents of it? He go around to all the colored and he got ten dollars extra. That's more than I make for a whole week.

Seth: I see you gonna learn the hard way. You just looking at the facts of it. See, right now, without the job, you ain't got nothing. What you gonna do when you can't keep a roof over your head? Right now, come Saturday, unless you come up with another two dollars, you gonna be out there in the streets. Down up under one of them bridges trying to put some food in your belly and wishing you had given that fellow that fifty cents.

Jeremy: Don't make me no difference. There's a big road out there. I can get my guitar and always find me another place to stay. I ain't planning on staying in one place for too long noway.

Seth: We gonna see if you feel like that come Saturday!

(*Seth exits out the back. Jeremy sees Molly.*)

Jeremy: Molly Cunningham. How you doing today, sugar?

Molly: You can go on back down there tomorrow and go back to work if you want. They won't even know who you is. Won't even know it's you. I had me a fellow did that one time. They just went ahead and signed him up like they never seen him before.

Jeremy: I'm tired of working anyway. I'm glad they fired me. You sure look pretty today.

Molly: Don't come telling me all that pretty stuff. Beauty wanna come in and sit down at your table asking to be fed. I ain't hardly got enough for me.

Jeremy: You know you pretty. Ain't no sense in you saying nothing about that. Why don't you come on and go away with me?

Molly: You tied up with that Mattie Campbell. Now you talking about running away with me.

Jeremy: I was just keeping her company 'cause she lonely. You ain't the lonely kind. You the kind that know what she want and how to get it. I need a woman like you to travel around with. Don't you wanna travel around and look at some places with Jeremy? With a woman like you beside him, a man can make it nice in the world.

Molly: Molly can make it nice by herself too. Molly don't need nobody leave her cold in hand. The world rough enough as it is.

Jeremy: We can make it better together. I got my guitar and I can play. Won me another dollar last night playing guitar. We can go around and I can play at the dances and we can just enjoy life. You can make it by yourself alright, I agrees with that. A woman like you can make it anywhere she go. But you can make it better if you got a man to protect you.

Molly: What places you wanna go around and look at?

Jeremy: All of them! I don't want to miss nothing. I wanna go everywhere and do everything there is to be got out of life. With a woman like you it's like having water and berries. A man got everything he need.

Molly: You got to be doing more than playing that guitar. A dollar a day ain't hardly what Molly got in mind.

Jeremy: I gambles real good. I got a hand for it.

Molly: Molly don't work. And Molly ain't up for sale.

Jeremy: Sure, baby. You ain't got to work with Jeremy.

Molly: There's one more thing.

Jeremy: What's that, sugar?

Molly: Molly ain't going South.

(*The lights go down on the scene.*)

Scene II

The lights come up on the parlor. Seth and Bynum sit playing a game of dominoes. Bynum sings to himself.

Bynum (*singing*):
    They tell me Joe Turner's come and gone
    Ohhh Lordy
    They tell me Joe Turner's come and gone
    Ohhh Lordy
    Got my man and gone

    Come with forty links of chain
    Ohhh Lordy
    Come with forty links of chain
    Ohhh Lordy
    Got my man and gone

Seth: Come on and play if you gonna play.

Bynum: I'm gonna play. Soon as I figure out what to do.

Seth: You can't figure out if you wanna play or you wanna sing.

Bynum: Well sir, I'm gonna do a little bit of both.

(*Playing.*)

There. What you gonna do now?

(*Singing.*)

They tell me Joe Turner's come and gone
Ohhh Lordy
They tell me Joe Turner's come and gone
Ohhh Lordy

Seth: Why don't you hush up that noise.

Bynum: That's a song the women sing down around Memphis. The women down there made up that song. I picked it up down there about fifteen years ago.

(*Loomis enters from the front door.*)

Bynum: Evening, Mr. Loomis.

Seth: Today's Monday, Mr. Loomis. Come Saturday your time is up. We done ate already. My wife roasted up some yams. She got your plate sitting in there on the table. (*To Bynum.*) Whose play is it?

Bynum: Ain't you keeping up with the game? I thought you was a domino player. I just played so it got to be your turn.

(*Loomis goes into the kitchen, where a plate of yams is covered and set on the table. He sits down and begins to eat with his hands.*)

Seth (*plays*): Twenty! Give me twenty! You didn't know I had that ace five. You was trying to play around that. You didn't know I had that lying there for you.

Bynum: You ain't done nothing. I let you have that to get mine.

Seth: Come on and play. You ain't doing nothing but talking. I got a hundred and forty points to your eighty. You ain't doing nothing but talking. Come on and play.

Bynum (*singing*):

They tell me Joe Turner's come and gone
Ohhh Lordy
They tell me Joe Turner's come and gone
Ohhh Lordy
Got my man and gone

He come with forty links of chain
Ohhh Lordy

Loomis: Why you singing that song? Why you singing about Joe Turner?

Bynum: I'm just singing to entertain myself.

Seth: You trying to distract me. That's what you trying to do.

Bynum (singing):

> Come with forty links of chain
> Ohhh Lordy
> Come with forty links of chain
> Ohhh Lordy

Loomis: I don't like you singing that song, mister!

Seth: Now, I ain't gonna have no more disturbance around here, Herald Loomis. You start any more disturbance and you leavin' here, Saturday or no Saturday.

Bynum: The man ain't causing no disturbance, Seth. He just say he don't like the song.

Seth: Well, we all friendly folk. All neighborly like. Don't have no squabbling around here. Don't have no disturbance. You gonna have to take that someplace else.

Bynum: He just say he don't like the song. I done sung a whole lot of songs people don't like. I respect everybody. He here in the house too. If he don't like the song, I'll sing something else. I know lots of songs. You got "I Belong to the Band," "Don't You Leave Me Here." You got "Praying on the Old Campground," "Keep Your Lamp Trimmed and Burning" . . . I know lots of songs. *(Sings.)*

> Boys, I'll be so glad when payday come
> Captain, Captain, when payday comes
> Gonna catch that Illinois Central
> Going to Kankakee

Seth: Why don't you hush up that hollering and come on and play dominoes.

Bynum: You ever been to Johnstown, Herald Loomis? You look like a fellow I seen around there.

Loomis: I don't know no place with that name.

Bynum: That's around where I seen my shiny man. See, you looking for this woman. I'm looking for a shiny man. Seem like everybody looking for something.

Seth: I'm looking for you to come and play these dominoes. That's what I'm looking for.

Bynum: You a farming man, Herald Loomis? You look like you done some farming.

Loomis: Same as everybody. I done farmed some, yeah.

Bynum: I used to work at farming . . . picking cotton. I reckon everybody done picked some cotton.

Seth: I ain't! I ain't never picked no cotton. I was born up here in the North. My daddy was a freedman. I ain't never even seen no cotton!

Bynum: Mr. Loomis done picked some cotton. Ain't you, Herald Loomis? You done picked a bunch of cotton.

Loomis: How you know so much about me? How you know what I done? How much cotton I picked?

Bynum: I can tell from looking at you. My daddy taught me how to do that. Say when you look at a fellow, if you taught yourself to look for it, you can see his song written on him. Tell you what kind of man he is in the world. Now, I can look at you, Mr. Loomis, and see you a man who done forgot his song. Forgot how to sing it. A fellow forget that and he forget who he is. Forget how he's supposed to mark down life. Now, I used to travel all up and down this road and that . . . looking here and there. Searching. Just like you, Mr. Loomis. I didn't know what I was searching for. The only thing I knew was something was keeping me dissatisfied. Something wasn't making my heart smooth and easy. Then one day my daddy gave me a song. That song had a weight to it that was hard to handle. That song was hard to carry. I fought against it. Didn't want to accept that song. I tried to find my daddy to give him back the song. But I found out it wasn't his song. It was my song. It had come from way deep inside me. I looked long back in memory and gathered up pieces and snatches of things to make that song. I was making it up out of myself. And that song helped me on the road. Made it smooth to where my footsteps didn't bite back at me. All the time that song getting bigger and bigger. That song growing with each step of the road. It got so I used all of myself up in the making of that song. Then I was the song in search of itself. That song rattling in my throat and I'm looking for it. See, Mr. Loomis, when a man forgets his song he goes off in search of it . . . till he find out he's got it with him all the time. That's why I can tell you one of Joe Turner's niggers. 'Cause you forgot how to sing your song.

Loomis: You lie! How you see that? I got a mark on me? Joe Turner done marked me to where you can see it? You telling me I'm a marked man. What kind of mark you got on you?

(Bynum begins singing.)

Bynum:

They tell me Joe Turner's come and gone
Ohhh Lordy
They tell me Joe Turner's come and gone
Ohhh Lordy
Got my man and gone

Loomis: Had a whole mess of men he catched. Just go out hunting regular like you go out hunting possum. He catch you and go home to his wife and family. Ain't thought about you going home to yours. Joe Turner catched me when my little girl was born. Wasn't nothing but a little baby sucking on her mama's titty when he catched me. Joe Turner catched me in nineteen hundred and one. Kept me seven years until nineteen hundred and eight. Kept everybody seven years. He'd go out hunting and bring back forty men at a time. And keep them seven years.

I was walking down this road in this little town outside of Memphis. Come up on these fellows gambling. I was a deacon in the Abundant Life Church. I stopped to preach to these fellows to see if maybe I could turn some of them from their sinning when Joe Turner, brother of the Governor of the great sovereign state of Tennessee, swooped down on us and grabbed everybody there. Kept us all seven years.

My wife Martha gone from me after Joe Turner catched me. Got out from under Joe Turner on his birthday. Me and forty other men put in our seven years and he let us go on his birthday. I made it back to Henry Thompson's place where me and Martha was sharecropping and Martha's gone. She taken my little girl and left her with her mama and took off North. We been looking for her ever since. That's been going on four years now we been looking. That's the only thing I know to do. I just wanna see her face so I can get me a starting place in the world. The world got to start somewhere. That's what I been looking for. I been wandering a long time in somebody else's world. When I find my wife that be the making of my own.

Bynum: Joe Turner tell why he caught you? You ever asked him that?

Loomis: I ain't never seen Joe Turner. Seen him to where I could touch him. I asked one of them fellows one time why he catch niggers. Asked him what I got he want? Why don't he keep on to himself? Why he got to catch me going down the road by my lonesome? He told me I was worthless. Worthless is something you throw away. Something you don't bother with. I ain't seen him throw me away. Wouldn't even let me stay away when I was by my lonesome. I ain't tried to catch him when he going down the road. So I must got something he want. What I got?

Seth: He just want you to do his work for him. That's all.

Loomis: I can look at him and see where he big and strong enough to do his own work. So it can't be that. He must want something he ain't got.

Bynum: That ain't hard to figure out. What he wanted was your song. He wanted to have that song to be his. He thought by catching you he could learn that song. Every nigger he catch he's looking for the one he can learn that song from. Now he's got you bound up to where you can't sing your own song. Couldn't sing it them seven years 'cause you was afraid he would snatch it from under you. But you still got it. You just forgot how to sing it.

Loomis (to Bynum): I know who you are. You one of them bones people.

(The lights go down to black.)

Scene III

The lights come up on the kitchen. It is the following morning. Mattie and Bynum sit at the table. Bertha busies herself at the stove.

Bynum: Good luck don't know no special time to come. You sleep with that up under your pillow and good luck can't help but come to you. Sometimes it come and go and you don't even know it's been there.

Bertha: Bynum, why don't you leave that gal alone? She don't wanna be hearing all that. Why don't you go on and get out the way and leave her alone?

Bynum (getting up): Alright, alright. But you mark what I'm saying. It'll draw it to you just like a magnet.

(Bynum exits up the stairs and Loomis enters.)

Bertha: I got some grits here, Mr. Loomis.

(Bertha sets a bowl on the table.)

If I was you, Mattie, I wouldn't go getting all tied up with Bynum in that stuff. That kind of stuff, even if it do work for a while, it don't last. That just get people more mixed up than they is already. And I wouldn't waste my time fretting over Jeremy either. I seen it coming. I seen it when she first come here. She that kind of woman run off with the first man got a dollar to spend on her. Jeremy just young. He don't know what he getting into. That gal don't mean him no good. She's just using him to keep from being by herself. That's the worst use of a man you can have. You ought to be glad to wash him out of your hair. I done seen all kind of men. I done seen them come and go through here. Jeremy ain't had enough to him for you. You need a man who's got some understanding and who willing to work with that understanding to come to the best he can. You got your time coming. You just tries too hard and can't understand why it don't work for you. Trying to figure it out don't do nothing but give you a troubled mind. Don't no man want a woman with a troubled mind.

You get all that trouble off your mind and just when it look like you ain't never gonna find what you want . . . you look up and it's standing right there. That's how I met my Seth. You gonna look up one day and find everything you want standing right in front of you. Been twenty-seven years now since that happened to me. But life ain't no happy-go-lucky time where everything be just like you want it. You got your time coming. You watch what Bertha's saying.

(Seth enters.)

Seth: Ho!

Bertha: What you doing come in here so late?

Seth: I was standing down there on Logan Street talking with the fellows. Henry Allen tried to sell me that old piece of horse he got.

(He sees Loomis.)

Today's Tuesday, Mr. Loomis.

Bertha (pulling him toward the bedroom): Come on in here and leave that man alone to eat his breakfast.

Seth: I ain't bothering nobody. I'm just reminding him what day it is.

(Seth and Bertha exit into the bedroom.)

Loomis: That dress got a color to it.

Mattie: Did you really see them things like you said? Them people come up out the ocean?

Loomis: It happened just like that, yeah.

Mattie: I hope you find your wife. It be good for your little girl for you to find her.

Loomis: Got to find her for myself. Find my starting place in the world. Find me a world I can fit in.

Mattie: I ain't never found no place for me to fit. Seem like all I do is start over. It ain't nothing to find no starting place in the world. You just start from where you find yourself.

Loomis: Got to find my wife. That be my starting place.

Mattie: What if you don't find her? What you gonna do then if you don't find her?

Loomis: She out there somewhere. Ain't no such thing as not finding her.

Mattie: How she got lost from you? Jack just walked away from me.

Loomis: Joe Turner split us up. Joe Turner turned the world upside-down. He bound me on to him for seven years.

Mattie: I hope you find her. It be good for you to find her.

Loomis: I been watching you. I been watching you watch me.

Mattie: I was just trying to figure out if you seen things like you said.

Loomis (getting up): Come here and let me touch you. I been watching you. You a full woman. A man needs a full woman. Come on and be with me.

Mattie: I ain't got enough for you. You'd use me up too fast.

Loomis: Herald Loomis got a mind seem like you a part of it since I first seen you. It's been a long time since I seen a full woman. I can smell you from here. I know you got Herald Loomis on your mind, can't keep him apart from it. Come on and be with Herald Loomis.

(*Loomis has crossed to Mattie. He touches her awkwardly, gently, tenderly. Inside he howls like a lost wolf pup whose hunger is deep. He goes to touch her but finds he cannot.*)

I done forgot how to touch.

(*The lights fade to black.*)

Scene IV

It is early the next morning. The lights come up on Zonia and Reuben in the yard.

Reuben: Something spooky going on around here. Last night Mr. Bynum was out in the yard singing and talking to the wind . . . and the wind it just be talking back to him. Did you hear it?

Zonia: I heard it. I was scared to get up and look. I thought it was a storm.

Reuben: That wasn't no storm. That was Mr. Bynum. First he say something . . . and the wind it say back to him.

Zonia: I heard it. Was you scared? I was scared.

Reuben: And then this morning . . . I seen Miss Mabel!

Zonia: Who Miss Mabel?

Reuben: Mr. Seth's mother. He got her picture hanging up in the house. She been dead.

Zonia: How you seen her if she been dead?

Reuben: Zonia . . . if I tell you something you promise you won't tell anybody?

Zonia: I promise.

Reuben: It was early this morning . . . I went out to the coop to feed the pigeons. I was down on the ground like this to open up the door to the coop . . . when all of a sudden I seen some feets in front of me. I looked up . . . and there was Miss Mabel standing there.

Zonia: Reuben, you better stop telling that! You ain't seen nobody!

Reuben: Naw, it's the truth. I swear! I seen her just like I see you. Look . . . you can see where she hit me with her cane.

Zonia: Hit you? What she hit you for?

Reuben: She says, "Didn't you promise Eugene something?" Then she hit me with her cane. She say, "Let them pigeons go." Then she hit me again. That's what made them marks.

Zonia: Jeez man . . . get away from me. You done see a haunt!

Reuben: Shhhh. You promised, Zonia!

Zonia: You sure it wasn't Miss Bertha come over there and hit you with her hoe?

Reuben: It wasn't no Miss Bertha. I told you it was Miss Mabel. She was standing right there by the coop. She had this light coming out of her and then she just melted away.

Zonia: What she had on?

Reuben: A white dress. Ain't even had no shoes or nothing. Just had on that white dress and them big hands . . . and that cane she hit me with.

Zonia: How you reckon she knew about the pigeons? You reckon Eugene told her?

Reuben: I don't know. I sure ain't asked her none. She say Eugene was waiting on them pigeons. Say he couldn't go back home till I let them go. I couldn't get the door to the coop open fast enough.

Zonia: Maybe she an angel? From the way you say she look with that white dress. Maybe she an angel.

Reuben: Mean as she was . . . how she gonna be an angel? She used to chase us out her yard and frown up and look evil all the time.

Zonia: That don't mean she can't be no angel 'cause of how she looked and 'cause she wouldn't let no kids play in her yard. It go by if you got any spots on your heart and if you pray and go to church.

Reuben: What about she hit me with her cane? An angel wouldn't hit me with her cane.

Zonia: I don't know. She might. I still say she was an angel.

Reuben: You reckon Eugene the one who sent old Miss Mabel?

Zonia: Why he send her? Why he don't come himself?

Reuben: Figured if he send her maybe that'll make me listen. 'Cause she old.

Zonia: What you think it feel like?

Reuben: What?

Zonia: Being dead.

Reuben: Like being sleep only you don't know nothing and can't move no more.

Zonia: If Miss Mabel can come back . . . then maybe Eugene can come back too.

Reuben: We can go down to the hideout like we used to! He could come back everyday! It be just like he ain't dead.

Zonia: Maybe that ain't right for him to come back. Feel kinda funny to be playing games with a haunt.

Reuben: Yeah . . . what if everybody came back? What if Miss Mabel came back just like she ain't dead? Where you and your daddy gonna sleep then?

Zonia: Maybe they go back at night and don't need no place to sleep.

Reuben: It still don't seem right. I'm sure gonna miss Eugene. He's the bestest friend anybody ever had.

Zonia: My daddy say if you miss somebody too much it can kill you. Say he missed me till it liked to killed him.

Reuben: What if your mama's already dead and all the time you looking for her?

Zonia: Naw, she ain't dead. My daddy say he can smell her.

Reuben: You can't smell nobody that ain't here. Maybe he smelling old Miss Bertha. Maybe Miss Bertha your mama?

Zonia: Naw, she ain't. My mama got long pretty hair and she five feet from the ground!

Reuben: Your daddy say when you leaving?

(Zonia doesn't respond.)

Maybe you gonna stay in Mr. Seth's house and don't go looking for your mama no more.

Zonia: He say we got to leave on Saturday.

Reuben: Dag! You just only been here for a little while. Don't seem like nothing ever stay the same.

Zonia: He say he got to find her. Find him a place in the world.

Reuben: He could find him a place in Mr. Seth's house.

Zonia: It don't look like we never gonna find her.

Reuben: Maybe he find her by Saturday then you don't have to go.

Zonia: I don't know.

Reuben: You look like a spider!

Zonia: I ain't no spider!

Reuben: Got them long skinny arms and legs. You look like one of them Black Widows.

Zonia: I ain't no Black Window nothing! My name is Zonia!

Reuben: That's what I'm gonna call you . . . Spider.

Zonia: You can call me that, but I don't have to answer.

Reuben: You know what? I think maybe I be your husband when I grow up.

Zonia: How you know?

Reuben: I ask my grandpap how you know and he say when the moon falls into a girl's eyes that how you know.

Zonia: Did it fall into my eyes?

Reuben: Not that I can tell. Maybe I ain't old enough. Maybe you ain't old enough.

Zonia: So there! I don't know why you telling me that lie!

Reuben: That don't mean nothing 'cause I can't see it. I know it's there. Just the way you look at me sometimes look like the moon might have been in your eyes.

Zonia: That don't mean nothing if you can't see it. You supposed to see it.

Reuben: Shucks, I see it good enough for me. You ever let anybody kiss you?

Zonia: Just my daddy. He kiss me on the cheek.

Reuben: It's better on the lips. Can I kiss you on the lips?

Zonia: I don't know. You ever kiss anybody before?

Reuben: I had a cousin let me kiss her on the lips one time. Can I kiss you?

Zonia: Okay.

(*Reuben kisses her and lays his head against her chest.*)

What you doing?

Reuben: Listening. Your heart singing?

Zonia: It is not.

Reuben: Just beating like a drum. Let's kiss again.

(*They kiss again.*)

Now you mine, Spider. You my girl, okay?

Zonia: Okay.

Reuben: When I get grown, I come looking for you.

Zonia: Okay.

(*The lights fade to black.*)

Scene V

The lights come up on the kitchen. It is Saturday. Bynum, Loomis, and Zonia sit at the table. Bertha prepares breakfast. Zonia has on a white dress.

Bynum: With all this rain we been having he might have ran into some washed-out roads. If that wagon got stuck in the mud he's liable to be still upriver somewhere. If he's upriver then he ain't coming until tomorrow.

Loomis: Today's Saturday. He say he be here on Saturday.

Bertha: Zonia, you gonna eat your breakfast this morning.

Zonia: Yes, ma'am.

Bertha: I don't know how you expect to get any bigger if you don't eat. I ain't never seen a child that didn't eat. You about as skinny as a bean pole.

(*Pause.*)

Mr. Loomis, there's a place down on Wylie. Zeke Mayweather got a house down there. You ought to see if he got any rooms.

(Loomis doesn't respond.)

Well, you're welcome to some breakfast before you move on.

(Mattie enters from the stairs.)

Mattie: Good morning.

Bertha: Morning, Mattie. Sit on down there and get you some breakfast.

Bynum: Well, Mattie Campbell, you been sleeping with that up under your pillow like I told you?

Bertha: Bynum, I done told you to leave that gal alone with all that stuff. You around here meddling in other people's lives. She don't want to hear all that. You ain't doing nothing but confusing her with that stuff.

Mattie *(to Loomis)*: You all fixing to move on?

Loomis: Today's Saturday. I'm paid up till Saturday.

Mattie: Where you going to?

Loomis: Gonna find my wife.

Mattie: You going off to another city?

Loomis: We gonna see where the road take us. Ain't no telling where we wind up.

Mattie: Eleven years is a long time. Your wife . . . she might have taken up with someone else. People do that when they get lost from each other.

Loomis: Zonia. Come on, we gonna find your mama.

(Loomis and Zonia cross to the door.)

Mattie *(to Zonia)*: Zonia, Mattie got a ribbon here match your dress. Want Mattie to fix your hair with her ribbon?

(Zonia nods. Mattie ties the ribbon in her hair.)

There . . . it got a color just like your dress. *(To Loomis.)* I hope you find her. I hope you be happy.

Loomis: A man looking for a woman be lucky to find you. You a good woman, Mattie. Keep a good heart.

(Loomis and Zonia exit.)

Bertha: I been watching that man for two weeks . . . and that's the closest I come to seeing him act civilized. I don't know what's between you all, Mattie . . . but the only thing that man needs is somebody to make him laugh. That's all you need in the world is love and laughter. That's all anybody needs. To have love in one hand and laughter in the other.

(Bertha moves about the kitchen as though blessing it and chasing away the huge sadness that seems to envelop it. It is a dance and demonstration of her own magic, her own remedy that is centuries old and to which she is connected by the muscles of her heart and the blood's memory.)

You hear me, Mattie? I'm talking about laughing. The kind of laugh that comes from way deep inside. To just stand and laugh and let life flow right through you. Just laugh to let yourself know you're alive.

(*She begins to laugh. It is a near-hysterical laughter that is a celebration of life, both its pain and its blessing. Mattie and Bynum join in the laughter. Seth enters from the front door.*)

Seth: Well, I see you all having fun.

(*Seth begins to laugh with them.*)

That Loomis fellow standing up there on the corner watching the house. He standing right up there on Manila Street.

Bertha: Don't you get started on him. The man done left out of here and that's the last I wanna hear of it. You about to drive me crazy with that man.

Seth: I just say he standing up there on the corner. Acting sneaky like he always do. He can stand up there all he want. As long as he don't come back in here.

(*There is a knock on the door. Seth goes to answer it. Enter Martha Loomis [Pentecost]. She is a young woman about twenty-eight. She is dressed as befitting a member of an Evangelist church. Rutherford Selig follows.*)

Seth: Look here, Bertha. It's Martha Pentecost. Come on in, Martha. Who that with you? Oh . . . that's Selig. Come on in, Selig.

Bertha: Come on in, Martha. It's sure good to see you.

Bynum: Rutherford Selig, you a sure enough first-class People Finder!

Selig: She was right out there in Rankin. You take that first righthand road . . . right there at that church on Wooster Street. I started to go right-past and something told me to stop at the church and see if they needed any dust-pans.

Seth: Don't she look good, Bertha.

Bertha: Look all nice and healthy.

Martha: Mr. Bynum . . . Selig told me my little girl was here.

Seth: There's some fellow around here say he your husband. Say his name is Loomis. Say you his wife.

Martha: Is my little girl with him?

Seth: Yeah, he got a little girl with him. I wasn't gonna tell him where you was. Not the way this fellow look. So he got Selig to find you.

Martha: Where they at? They upstairs?

Seth: He was standing right up there on Manila Street. I had to ask him to leave 'cause of how he was carrying on. He come in here one night—

(*The door opens and Loomis and Zonia enter. Martha and Loomis stare at each other.*)

Loomis: Hello, Martha.

Martha: Herald . . . Zonia?

Loomis: You ain't waited for me, Martha. I got out the place looking to see your face. Seven years I waited to see your face.

Martha: Herald, I been looking for you. I wasn't but two months behind you when you went to my mama's and got Zonia. I been looking for you ever since.

Loomis: Joe Turner let me loose and I felt all turned around inside. I just wanted to see your face to know that the world was still there. Make sure everything still in its place so I could reconnect myself together. I got there and you was gone, Martha.

Martha: Herald . . .

Loomis: Left my little girl motherless in the world.

Martha: I didn't leave her motherless, Herald. Reverend Tolliver wanted to move the church up North 'cause of all the trouble the colored folks was having down there. Nobody knew what was gonna happen traveling them roads. We didn't even know if we was gonna make it up here or not. I left her with my mama so she be safe. That was better than dragging her out on the road having to duck and hide from people. Wasn't no telling what was gonna happen to us. I didn't leave her motherless in the world. I been looking for you.

Loomis: I come up on Henry Thompson's place after seven years of living in hell, and all I'm looking to do is see your face.

Martha: Herald, I didn't know if you was ever coming back. They told me Joe Turner had you and my whole world split half in two. My whole life shattered. It was like I had poured it in a cracked jar and it all leaked out the bottom. When it go like that there ain't nothing you can do to put it back together. You talking about Henry Thompson's place like I'm still gonna be working the land by myself. How I'm gonna do that? You wasn't gone but two months and Henry Thompson kicked me off his land and I ain't had no place to go but to my mama's. I stayed and waited there for five years before I woke up one morning and decided that you was dead. Even if you weren't, you was dead to me. I wasn't gonna carry you with me no more. So I killed you in my heart. I buried you. I mourned you. And then I picked up what was left and went on to make life without you. I was a young woman with life at my beckon. I couldn't drag you behind me like a sack of cotton.

Loomis: I just been waiting to look on your face to say my goodbye. That goodbye got so big at times, seem like it was gonna swallow me up. Like Jonah in the whale's belly I sat up in that goodbye for three years. That goodbye kept me out on the road searching. Not looking on women in their houses. It kept me bound up to the road. All the time that goodbye swelling up in my chest till I'm about to bust. Now that I see your face I can say my goodbye and make my own world.

(Loomis takes Zonia's hand and presents her to Martha.)

Martha . . . here go your daughter. I tried to take care of her. See that she had something to eat. See that she was out of the elements. Whatever I know I tried to teach her. Now she need to learn from her mother whatever you got to teach her. That way she won't be no one-sided person.

(*Loomis stoops to Zonia.*)

Zonia, you go live with your mama. She a good woman. You go on with her
and listen to her good. You my daughter and I love you like a daughter. I
hope to see you again in the world somewhere. I'll never forget you.

Zonia (*throws her arms around Loomis in a panic*): I won't get no bigger! My bones
won't get no bigger! They won't! I promise! Take me with you till we keep
searching and never finding. I won't get no bigger! I promise!

Loomis: Go on and do what I told you now.

Martha (*goes to Zonia and comforts her*): It's alright, baby. Mama's here. Mama's
here. Don't worry. Don't cry.

(*Martha turns to Bynum.*)

Mr. Bynum, I don't know how to thank you. God bless you.

Loomis: It was you! All the time it was you that bind me up! You bound me to
the road!

Bynum: I ain't bind you, Herald Loomis. You can't bind what don't cling.

Loomis: Everywhere I go people wanna bind me up. Joe Turner wanna bind me
up! Reverend Tolliver wanna bind me up. You wanna bind me up. Everybody wanna bind me up. Well, Joe Turner's come and gone and Herald
Loomis ain't for no binding. I ain't gonna let nobody bind me up!

(*Loomis pulls out a knife.*)

Bynum: It wasn't you, Herald Loomis. I ain't bound you. I bound the little girl to
her mother. That's who I bound. You binding yourself. You bound onto your
song. All you got to do is stand up and sing it, Herald Loomis. It's right there
kicking at your throat. All you got to do is sing it. Then you be free.

Martha: Herald . . . look at yourself! Standing there with a knife in your hand.
You done gone over to the devil. Come on . . . put down the knife. You got
to look to Jesus. Even if you done fell away from the church you can be
saved again. The Bible say, "The Lord is my shepherd I shall not want. He
maketh me to lie down in green pastures. He leads me beside the still water.
He restoreth my soul. He leads me in the path of righteousness for His
name's sake. Even though I walk through the shadow of death—"

Loomis: That's just where I be walking!

Martha: "I shall fear no evil. For Thou art with me. Thy rod and thy staff, they
comfort me."

Loomis: You can't tell me nothing about no valleys. I done been all across the
valleys and the hills and the mountains and the oceans.

Martha: "Thou preparest a table for me in the presence of my enemies."

Loomis: And all I seen was a bunch of niggers dazed out of their woolly heads.
And Mr. Jesus Christ standing there in the middle of them, grinning.

Martha: "Thou anointest my head with oil, my cup runneth over."

Loomis: He grin that big old grin . . . and niggers wallowing at his feet.

Martha: "Surely goodness and mercy shall follow me all the days of my life, and I shall dwell in the house of the Lord forever."

Loomis: Great big old white man . . . your Mr. Jesus Christ. Standing there with a whip in one hand and tote board in another, and them niggers swimming in a sea of cotton. And he counting. He tallying up the cotton. "Well, Jeremiah . . . what's the matter, you ain't picked but two hundred pounds of cotton today? Got to put you on half rations." And Jeremiah go back and lay up there on his half rations and talk about what a nice man Mr. Jesus Christ is 'cause he give him salvation after he die. Something wrong here. Something don't fit right!

Martha: You got to open up your heart and have faith, Herald. This world is just a trial for the next. Jesus offers you salvation.

Loomis: I been wading in the water. I been walking all over the River Jordan. But what it get me, huh? I done been baptized with blood of the lamb and the fire of the Holy Ghost. But what I got, huh? I got salvation? My enemies all around me picking the flesh from my bones. I'm choking on my own blood and all you got to give me is salvation?

Martha: You got to be clean, Herald. You got to be washed with the blood of the lamb.

Loomis: Blood make you clean? You clean with blood?

Martha: Jesus bled for you. He's the Lamb of God who takest away the sins of the world.

Loomis: I don't need nobody to bleed for me! I can bleed for myself.

Martha: You got to be something, Herald. You just can't be alive. Life don't mean nothing unless it got a meaning.

Loomis: What kind of meaning you got? What kind of clean you got, woman? You want blood? Blood make you clean? You clean with blood?

(*Loomis slashes himself across the chest. He rubs the blood over his face and comes to a realization.*)

I'm standing! I'm standing. My legs stood up! I'm standing now!

(*Having found his song, the song of self-sufficiency, fully resurrected, cleansed and given breath, free from any encumbrance other than the workings of his own heart and the bonds of the flesh, having accepted the responsibility for his own presence in the world, he is free to soar above the environs that weighed and pushed his spirit into terrifying contractions.*)

Goodbye, Martha.

(*Loomis turns and exits, the knife still in his hands. Mattie looks about the room and rushes out after him.*)

Bynum: Herald Loomis, you shining! You shining like new money!

The lights go down to BLACK.

August Wilson

August Wilson on Drama

BLACK EXPERIENCE IN AMERICA 1989

INTERVIEWER: Your plays are set in the past—*Joe Turner's Come and Gone* in 1911, *Ma Rainey's Black Bottom* in 1927, *Fences* in the 1950s. Do you ever consider writing about what's happening today?

WILSON: I suspect eventually I will get to that. Right now I enjoy the benefit of the historical perspective. You can look back to a character in 1936, for instance, and you can see him going down a particular path that you know did not work out for that character. Part of what I'm trying to do is to see some of the choices that we as blacks in America have made. Maybe we have made some incorrect choices. By writing about that, you can illuminate the choices.

INTERVIEWER: Give me an example of a choice that you think may have been the wrong one.

WILSON: I think we should have stayed in the South. We attempted to plant what in essence was an emerging culture, a culture that had grown out of our experience of 200 years as slaves in the South. The cities of the urban North have not been hospitable. If we had stayed in the South, we could have strengthened the culture. . . .

INTERVIEWER: One of your characters has said, "Everyone has to find his own song." How do these people find their song?

WILSON: They have it. They just have to realize that, and then they have to learn how to sing it. In that particular case, in *Joe Turner*, the song was the African identity. It was connecting yourself to that and understanding that this is who you are. Then you can go out in the world and sing your song as an African. . . .

INTERVIEWER: But if blacks keep looking for the African in them, if they keep returning spiritually or emotionally to their roots, can they ever come to terms with living in these two worlds? Aren't they always going to be held by the past in a way that is potentially destructive?

WILSON: It's not potentially destructive at all. To say that I am an African, and I can participate in this society as an African, is to say that I don't have to adopt European values, European aesthetics, and European ways of doing things in order to live in the world. We would not be here had we not learned to adapt to American culture. Blacks know more about whites in the white culture and white life than whites know about blacks. We *have* to know because our survival depends on it. White people's survival does not depend on knowing blacks.

. . .

INTERVIEWER: Don't you grow weary of thinking black, writing black, being asked questions about blacks?

WILSON: How could one grow weary of that? Whites don't get tired of thinking white or being who they are. I'm just who I am. You never transcend who you are. Black is not limiting. There's no idea in the world that is not contained by black life. I could write forever about the black experience in America.

From "August Wilson's America,"
interview with Bill Moyers in American Theatre

WRITING

40 *Writing About Literature*

In the study of literature, common sense (poet Gerard Manley Hopkins assures us) is never out of place. For most of a class hour, a professor once rhapsodized about the arrangement of the contents of W. H. Auden's *Collected Poems*. Auden, he claimed, was a master of thematic continuity, who had brilliantly placed the poems in an order that (to the ingenious mind) best complemented each other. Near the end of the hour, his theories were punctured—with a great inaudible pop—when a student, timidly raising a hand, pointed out that Auden had arranged the poems in the book not by theme but in alphabetical order according to the first word of each poem. The professor's jaw dropped: "Why didn't you say that sooner?" The student was apologetic: "I—I was afraid I'd sound too *ordinary*." Don't be afraid to state a conviction, though it seems obvious. Does it matter that you may be repeating something that, once upon a time or even just the other day, has been said before? There are excellent old ideas as well as new.

BEGINNING

Offered a choice of literary works to write about, you probably will do best if you choose what appeals to you. And how to find out what appeals? Whether you plan to write a short paper that requires no research beyond the story or poem or play itself, or a long paper that will take you to the library or the Internet, the first stage of your project is reading carefully—and taking notes. To focus your attention, one time-honored method is to read with a pencil, marking (if the book is yours) passages that stand out in importance, jotting brief notes in a margin (*"Key symbol— this foreshadows the ending,"* *"Dramatic irony,"* or other possibly useful remarks). In a long story or poem or play, some students asterisk passages that cry for comparison— for instance, all the places in which they find the same theme or symbol. Later, at a glance, they can review the highlights of a work and, when writing a paper about it, quickly refer to evidence. Students who dislike marking up a book may prefer to take notes on looseleaf notebook paper, holding one sheet beside a page in the book and giving it the book's page number. Later, in writing a paper, they can place book page and companion note page together again. This method has the advantage of affording a lot of room for note taking; it is a good one for short poems closely packed with complexities.

KEEPING A JOURNAL

After you have taken some notes, reflect on them. Before you go to the library to consult other people's published thoughts, try to work out your own. There is much to be said for the gut reaction of the first-time reader of a work of literature. That reaction is pure, forceful, and unadulterated by too much outside knowledge. It may contain insights that are unique to the reader, insights that will be lost if not written down immediately and explored by that reader.

To be sure that the power of that initial reaction is not lost, many instructors ask students to keep a journal: a day-to-day account of what they read and how they react to it. A great advantage in keeping a journal is that you can express your thoughts and feelings immediately, in your own words, before they grow cold. You can set down all your miscellaneous reactions to what you read, whether or not they fit into a paper topic. (If you have to write a paper later on, your journal just might suggest topics galore.) Depending on what your instructor thinks is essential, your journal may take in all your reading for the course, or you may concentrate on the work of some writer or writers, or on one kind of story. As you read, you can jot down anything that you wish to remember. Does a theme in a story or a line of dialogue strike you forcefully? Make a note of it. Does something in the story not make sense? Record your bewilderment.

Your journal is personal: a place for you to sound off, to express your feelings. Don't just copy your class notes into it; don't simply quote the stories. The mere length of your entries will not impress your instructor either: try for insights. A paragraph or two will probably suffice to set down your main reactions to most stories. In keeping a journal (a kind of writing primarily for yourself), you don't rewrite; so you need not feel obliged to polish your prose. Your aim is to store information without delay, to wrap words around your reactions and observations.

Keeping a journal will be satisfying only if you keep it up-to-date. Record your feelings and insights while you still have a story freshly in mind. Get weeks behind, and you will have to grind out a journal from scratch, the night before it is due, and the whole project will decay into meaningless drudgery. If you faithfully do a little reading and writing every day or so, you will find yourself keeping track of the life of your mind. When your journal is closed, you will have a lively record not only of the literature you have read but also of your personal involvement with it.

Using Critical Sources
and Maintaining Academic Integrity

Certain literary works, because they offer intriguing difficulties, have attracted professional critics by the score. On library shelves, great phalanxes of critical books now stand at the side of James Joyce's complex novels *Ulysses* and *Finnegans Wake* and T. S. Eliot's allusive poem *The Waste Land*. The student who undertakes to study such works seriously is well advised to profit from the critics' labors. Chances are, too, that even in discussing a relatively uncomplicated work, you will want to seek the aid of some critics. If you quote them, quote them exactly, in quotation marks, and give them credit. When employed in any but the most superlative student paper, a brilliant phrase (or even a not-so-brilliant sentence) from a renowned critic is likely to stand out like a golf ball in a garter snake's midriff, and most English instructors are likely to recognize it. If you rip off the critic's words, then go ahead and steal the whole essay, for good critics write in seamless unities. Then, when apprehended, you can exclaim—like the student whose term paper was found to be the work of a well-known scholar—"I've been robbed! That paper cost me fifty dollars!" This student not only cheated his teacher but himself, having got nothing for his college tuition but a little practice in typing. Giving proper acknowledgment to works and ideas not your own is both a moral and legal obligation. Take it seriously.

A later chapter, "Writing a Research Paper," will discuss the topic of plagiarism and academic integrity in greater depth; for now, students should simply remember that claiming another's work as one's own is the worst offense of the learning community. It negates the very purpose of education, which is to learn to think for oneself. Even if you summarize a critic's idea in your own words rather than quote his or her exact words, you have to give credit to your source. Nothing is cheaper to give than proper credit.

Discovering Essay Ideas

Writing is not likely to proceed in a straight line. Like thought, it often goes by fits and starts, by charges and retreats and mopping-up operations. All the while you read other critics' thoughts and take notes, you discover material to write about; all the while you turn your topic in your mind, you plan your paper. It is the nature of ideas, those headstrong things, to happen in any order they desire. While you continue to plan, while you write a draft, and while you revise, expect to keep discovering new thoughts—perhaps the best thoughts of all. If you do, be sure to invite them in.

Choosing an Appropriate Topic

Choose a topic appropriate to the assigned length of your paper. How do you know the probable length of your discussion until you write it? When in doubt, you are better off to define your topic narrowly. Your paper will be stronger if you go more deeply into your subject than if you choose some gigantic subject and then find yourself able to touch on most aspects of it only superficially. A thorough explication of a short story is hardly possible in a paper of 250 words. There are, in truth, four-line poems whose surface 250 words might only begin to scratch. A profound topic ("The Character of Shakespeare's Hamlet") might overflow a book, but a more focused topic ("Hamlet's Views of Acting" or "Hamlet's Puns") might result in a manageable paper.

Many student writers find it helpful in defining a topic to state an emerging idea for a paper in a provisional **thesis sentence:** a summing-up of the one main idea or argument that the paper will embody. A good statement of a thesis is not just a disembodied subject; it comes with both subject and verb. ("The Downfall of Oedipus Rex" is not yet a complete idea for a paper; "What Caused the Downfall of Oedipus Rex?" is.) "The Isolation of Laura in *The Glass Menagerie*" might be a decent title for a paper, but it isn't a useful thesis because it doesn't indicate what one might say about that isolation (nor what Tennessee Williams is saying about it). It may be obvious that isolation isn't desirable, but a clearer and more workable thesis sentence might be, "In *The Glass Menagerie*, the playwright shows how Laura's isolation leads her to take refuge in a world of dreams."

Think of your thesis sentence as the announcement of the argument you intend to prove. Once you've said what it is, the rest of the paper will be the presentation of the evidence you've gathered from the text or your research to support your argument. If you find you can't support certain aspects of the statement, then refine it so that you can. Until you turn it in, your essay is a work-in-progress. Anything can be changed and should be if it doesn't further the development of the paper's main idea.

Topic in hand (which may get drastically changed as you continue), you begin to sort out your miscellaneous notes, and the thoughts and impressions you recorded in your journal. If you can see that you haven't had enough ideas, you may wish to brainstorm or freewrite—to set yourself, say, fifteen minutes in which to write down as fast as you can all the ideas on your topic that come into your head, without worrying whether they are going to be useful. (You can look over the results and decide that later.) Write rapidly and uncritically, letting your thoughts tumble onto paper as fast as your pen or computer can capture them. This method will often goad the unconscious into coming up with unexpectedly good ideas; at least you will generate more potentially useful raw material.

Outlining

To outline or not to outline? Unless your topic, by its nature, suggests some obvious way to organize your paper ("An Explication of a Wordsworth Sonnet" might mean simply working through the poem line by line), then some kind of outline will probably help. In high school or other prehistoric times, you perhaps learned how to construct a beautiful outline, laid out with Roman numerals, capital letters, Arabic numerals, and lowercase letters. It was a thing of beauty and symmetry, and it possibly even had something to do with paper writing. But if now you are skeptical of the value of outline, reflect: not every outline needs to be detailed and elaborate. Some students, of course, find it helpful to outline in detail—particularly if they are planning a long research paper involving several literary works, comparing and contrasting several aspects of them. For a 500-word analysis of a short story's figures of speech, though, all you might need is a simple list of points to make, scribbled down in the order in which you will make them. This order is probably not, of course, the order in which the points first occurred to you. Thoughts, when they first come to mind, can arrive as a confused rabble.

While granting the need for order in a piece of writing, the present authors confess that they are reluctant outliners. Their tendency (or curse) is to want to keep whatever random thoughts occur to them, to polish their prose right then and there, and finally to try to juggle their disconnected paragraphs into something like logical order. The usual result is that they have large blocks of illogical thought left over. This process is wasteful, and if you can learn to live with an outline, then you belong to the legion of the blessed and will never know the pain of scrapping pages that cost you hours. On the other hand, you will never know the joy of meandering—of bursting into words and surprising yourself. As novelist E. M. Forster remarked, "How do I know what I think until I see what I say?"

An outline, if you use one, is not meant to stand as an achievement in itself. It should—as Ezra Pound said literary criticism ought to do—consume itself and disappear. Here is a once-valuable outline not worth keeping—a very informal one that enabled a student to organize the paper appearing on page 2136, "The Hearer of the Tell-Tale Heart." Before he wrote, the student jotted down the ideas that had occurred to him. Looking them over, he could see that certain ones predominated. Since the aim of his paper was to analyze Poe's story for its point of view, he began with some notes about the narrator of the story. His other leading ideas had emerged as questions: is the story supposed to be a ghost story or an account of a delusion? Can we read the whole thing as a nightmare, having no reality outside the narrator's mind? Having seen that his thoughts weren't a totally disconnected jumble, he drew connections. Going down his list, he numbered with the same numbers those ideas that belonged together.

Point of view

1 Killer is mad--can listen in on Hell.

2 He is obsessed with the Evil Eye.

1 He thinks he is sane, we know he's mad.

  Old man rich--a miser?

  Is this a ghost story? NO! Natural explanations

4   for the heartbeat:

  His mind is playing tricks.

  Hears his _own_ heart (Hoffman's idea).

3 Maybe the whole story is only his dream?

  Poe must have been crazy too.

The numbers now showed him the order in which he planned to take up each of his four chief ideas. Labeling his remarks about the narrator with the number "1," he decided to open his paper with them and to declare at once that they indicated the story's point of view. As you can tell from his finished paper, he discarded two notions that didn't seem to relate to his purpose: the point about the old man's wealth and the speculation (which he realized he couldn't prove) that Poe himself was mad. Having completed this rough outline, he felt encouraged to return to Poe's story and, on rereading it, noticed a few additional points, which you will find in his paper. His outline didn't tell him exactly what to say at every moment, but it was clear and easy to follow.

DRAFTING AND REVISING, OR CREATIVITY VS. ANALYSIS

Seated at last or striking some other businesslike stance,[1] you prepare to write, only to find yourself besieged with petty distractions. All of a sudden you remember a friend you had promised to call, some double-A batteries you were supposed to pick up, a neglected Coke (in another room) growing warmer and flatter by the minute. If your paper is to be written, you have only one course of action: collar these thoughts and for the moment banish them.

When first you draft your paper—that is, when you write it out in the rough— you will probably do best to write rapidly. At this early stage, you don't need to be fussy about spelling, grammar, and punctuation. To be sure, those picayune details matter, but you can worry about them later, when you are **editing** (combing through your draft repairing grammar, cutting excess words, making small verbal improvements) and **proofreading** (going over your finished paper line by line, checking it for typographical or other mistakes). At the moment, you want your creative mind to take charge of the writing process; this part of yourself has the good ideas and the insights; it has the confidence. Indulge your creative mind: get your thoughts down on paper and forget about checking spellings in the dictionary. Your analytical, critical mind can do all that later. Now is the time to forge ahead, to believe in yourself and the force of your ideas. Perhaps when you write your draft, you won't even want to look at all those notes on your reading that you collected so industriously. When you come to a place where a note will fit, you might just insert a reminder to yourself, such as SEE CARD 19 or SEE ARISTOTLE ON COMEDY.

Let us admit that writing about literature is a more formal kind of writing than turning out a narrative essay called, "My Most Exciting Experience." You may need to draft some of your paper slowly and painstakingly. You'll find yourself coping with all sorts of small problems, many of them simple and mechanical. What, for instance, will you call the author whose work you are dealing with? Decide at the outset. Most

---

[1]Vladimir Nabokov, author of *Lolita* and *Pale Fire*, wrote most of his novels on large index cards while standing up—eventually buying a lectern to work on.

critics favor the author's last name alone: "Dickinson implies . . ." ("Miss Dickinson" or "Ms. Dickinson" may sound too fussy, overly polite; "Emily," too chummy.) Will you include footnotes in your paper, and if so, do you know how they work? (Some pointers on handling the pesky things are given in the chapter "Writing a Research Paper.")

Using Literary Terminology

One more word of friendly advice. In this book you are offered a vocabulary with which to discuss literature: a flurry of terms such as *irony*, *symbol*, and *image*, printed in **boldface** when first introduced. (All these boldface words are defined again in the Glossary of Literary Terms found at the end of this book.) In your writing, you may decide to enlist a few of these terms. Literary terminology sometimes sounds so impressive that a beginning critic can be tempted to use it indiscriminately. Nothing is less sophisticated or more opaque, however, than too many technical terms thrown together for grandiose effect: "The mythic *symbolism* of this *archetype* is the *antithesis* of the *dramatic situation*." Far better to choose plain words you're already at ease with. Your instructor has met many a critical term before and is not likely to be impressed by the mere sight of another one. Knowingly selected and placed, a critical term can help sharpen a thought and make it easier to handle. It is less cumbersome, for example, to refer to the *tone* of a story than to say, "the way the author makes you feel that she feels about what she is talking about."

Just remember that even graduate students working toward their doctorates in literature have trouble with the incomprehensibility of some specimens of literary theory. Thus, rather than modeling your writing on the turgid and jargon-filled prose too frequently found in contemporary criticism, aim for intelligent clarity in your own essays. It is, in fact, possible to discuss a complex idea in clear prose. When you use specialized terms, do so to smooth the way for your reader—to make your meaning more precise. They should not serve as stumbling blocks to understanding, or semantic puzzles that your teacher must tease out.

Revising

When you write your first draft, by the way, leave plenty of space between lines and set enormous margins. Then, when later thoughts come to you, you can easily squeeze them in.

Does any writer write with perfection on the first try? Some writers have claimed to do so—among them the English novelist Anthony Trollope, who thought it "unmanly" not to write a thought precisely the first time. Jack Kerouac, leading novelist of the Beat Generation of the 1950s, believed in spontaneous prose. He wrote entire novels on uncut ribbons of teletype paper, thus saving himself the interruption of stopping at the bottom of each page. His specialty, though, was fiction of ecstasy and hallucination, not essays in explication, or comparison and contrast. For most of us, however, good writing is largely a matter of revising—of going back over our first thoughts word by word. Now you can turn on your analytical mind and be as critical of your creativity as the final product warrants. Of course, painstaking revision is more than a matter of tidying up grammar and spelling; in the process of reconsidering our words, we sometimes discover fresher and sharper ideas. "Writing and rewriting," says John Updike, "are a constant search for what one is saying."

To achieve effective writing, you must have the courage to be wild. Aware that no reader need see your rough drafts, you can treat them mercilessly—tear them apart, rearrange their pieces, reassemble them into a stronger order. The art of revising calls for a textbook in itself, but here are a few simple suggestions:

1. Insofar as your deadline allows, be willing to revise as many times as need be.

2. Don't think of revision as the simple chore of fixing up spelling mistakes. That's proofreading, and it comes last. When you revise, be willing to cut and slash, to discover new insights, to move blocks of words around so that they follow in a stronger order. Stand ready to question your whole approach to a work of literature, to entertain the notion of throwing everything you have written into the wastebasket and starting over again.

3. At this stage, you may find it helpful to enlist outside advice—from your instructor, from your roommate or your mate, from any friend who will read your rough draft and give you a reaction. If you can enlist such a willing reader, ask him or her: What isn't clear to you?

4. If you (or your willing reader) should find any places that aren't readily understandable, single them out for rewriting. After all, you don't need to revise a whole draft if only parts of it need work. Try rewriting any troublesome passage or paragraph.

5. Short, skimpy paragraphs of one or two sentences may indicate places that call for more thought or more material. Can you supply them with more evidence, more explanation, more example and illustration?

6. A time-tested method of revising is to lay aside your paper for a while, forget about it, and then after a long interval (the Roman poet Horace recommended nine years, but obviously that's a bit long for most students), go back to it for a fresh look. If you have time, take a nap or a walk, or at least a yawn and a stretch before you take yet another look. Remember that the literal meaning of "revision" is "to see again."

7. When your paper is in a *last* draft—then it's time to edit it. Once you have your ideas in firm shape, you can check those uncertain spellings, look up the agreement of subjects and verbs in a grammar book or handbook, make your pronouns and antecedents agree, cut needless words, pull out a weak word and send in a stronger one. Back when you were drafting, being prematurely fussy about such small things might have frozen you up. But once you feel satisfied that you have made yourself clear, you can be as fussy as you like.

The Form of Your Finished Paper

Now that you have smoothed your final draft as fleck-free as you can, your instructor may have specific advice for the form of your finished paper. If none is forthcoming, follow the guidelines in the *MLA Handbook for Writers of Research Papers*, which you will find more fully described in the chapter "Writing a Research paper." In brief:

1. Choose standard letter-size ($8\frac{1}{2} \times 11$) white paper.

2. Give your name, your instructor's name, the course number, and the date at the top left-hand corner of your first page.

3. Title your paper and make that title reflect your thesis. A title such as "Essay on *The Glass Menagerie*" is not a title at all, but a file folder heading; your final paper requires something far more original. Most writers don't give their work a title until after they've completed it. At that point, you will be able to provide a fresh, focused title.

4. Leave an inch or more of margin on all four sides of each page and a few inches of blank paper or an additional sheet after your conclusion, so that your instructor can offer comments. If you include a Works Cited section, it belongs on a separate page.

5. Double-space, including quotations and notes. Don't forget to double-space the Works Cited page too.

6. Give your last name and the page number in the top right-hand corner of each page, one-half inch from the top.

And what of titles of works discussed: when do you put them in quotation marks and when do you underline them? One rule of thumb is that titles of works shorter than book length rate quotation marks (poems, short stories, articles); but titles of books (including book-length poems such as *The Odyssey*), plays, and periodicals take underlining or italics. (In a manuscript to be typeset, an <u>underline</u> is a signal to the compositor to use *italics*.)

Using Spell-Check and Grammar-Check Programs

Most computers have a program to automatically check spelling. These devices make it much easier to proofread your papers, but they will not catch all errors. It is still crucial that you proofread and correct your papers in the old-fashioned way—read them yourself.

The most common type of error that occurs is when the spell checker approves of a perfectly acceptable word that is incorrect in context. *In* or *it* frequently is mistyped as *is*, for example, and the spell checker won't catch the misspelling. Likewise, *the* is often erroneously keyboarded as *he*. This produces memorable spell-check-approved sentences such as "It Edna St. Vincent Millay's sonnet, we hear he voice of feminist concerns not often found is Modernist poetry." No human reader would ever approve of this pseudosentence, but a computer might.

Another common problem is that the names of most authors, places, and special literary terms won't be in many standard spell-check memories. Unfamiliar words will be identified during the spell-check process, but you still must intervene to correct possible errors made during keyboarding. Check all proper nouns carefully, so that Robert Forst, Gwendolyn Broks, or Emily Dickenson don't make unauthorized appearances midway in your otherwise exemplary paper. As the well-known authors Dina Gioia, Dan Goia, Dana Glola, Dona Diora, and Dana Gioia advise, always check the spelling of all names.

As a final warning about letting your computer write your finished paper, here are some cautionary verses that have circulated over the last few years on the Internet. (Based on a charming piece of light verse by Jerrold H. Zar, "Candidate for a Pullet Surprise," this version reflects additions and revisions by numerous anonymous Internet collaborators.)

A LITTLE POEM REGARDING COMPUTER SPELL CHECKERS   2000?

Eye halve a spelling checker
   It came with my pea sea
It plainly marques four my revue
   Miss steaks eye kin knot sea.

Eye strike a key and type a word   5
   And weight four it two say
Weather eye am wrong oar write
   It shows me strait a weigh.

As soon as a mist ache is made
   It nose bee fore two long   10
And eye can put the error rite
   Its rare lea ever wrong.

Eye have run this poem threw it
   I am shore your pleased two no
Its letter perfect awl the weigh   15
   My checker tolled me sew.

In addition to spell-check programs, most computers also feature grammar checkers. These programs will highlight sentences that have obvious grammatical mistakes: subjects and verbs that don't agree, sentence fragments, dangling modifiers. Unfortunately, if you don't know what is wrong with your sentence in the first place, the grammar program won't tell you. You can try recasting the sentence until the highlighting disappears (indicating that it's now grammatically correct), or you can simply be sure that you have a good grasp of grammar already. Most colleges offer brief refresher courses in grammar, and, of course, writers' handbooks with grammar rules are readily available. Still, the best way to improve your grammar, your spelling, and your general command of language is to read widely and well. To that end, we urge you to read the works of literature collected in this book beyond those texts assigned to you by your teacher. A well-furnished mind is a great place to live, an address you'll want to have forever.

What to do now but hand in your paper? "And good riddance!" you may feel, after such an expenditure of thinking, time, and energy. But a good paper is not only worth submitting, it is also worth keeping. If you return to it after a while, you may find to your surprise that it will preserve and even renew what you have learned.

41 *Writing About a Story*

A good discussion of fiction doesn't just toss forth a random lot of impressions. It makes some point about which the writer feels strongly. In order to write a meaningful paper, then, you need something you *want* to say—a meaningful topic. For suggestions on finding such a topic (also some pointers on organizing, writing, revising, and finishing your paper), please see "Writing About Literature," which begins on page 2119. The advice there may be applied to papers on fiction, poetry, and drama. Some methods especially useful for writing about stories are gathered in the present chapter.

Unlike a brief poem or a painting that you can take in with one long glance, a work of fiction—even a short story—may be too complicated to hold all at once in the mind's eye. Before you can write about it, you may need to give it two or more careful readings, and even then, as you begin to think further about it, you will probably have to thumb through it to reread passages. The first time through, it is best just to read attentively, open to whatever pleasure and wisdom the story may afford. On second look, you may find it useful to read with pencil in hand, either to mark your personal copy or to take notes to jog your memory. To see the design and meaning of a story need not be a boring chore, any more than it is to land a fighting fish and to study it with admiration.

In this chapter all the discussions and examples refer to Edgar Allan Poe's short story "The Tell-Tale Heart" (page 382). If you haven't already read it, you can do so in only a few minutes, so that the rest of this chapter will make more sense to you.

EXPLICATING

Explication is the patient unfolding of meanings in a work of literature. An explication—that is, an essay that follows this method—proceeds carefully through a story, poem, or play, usually interpreting it line by line—perhaps even word by word. A good explication dwells on details, as well as on larger things. It brings them to the attention of a reader who might have missed them (the reader probably hasn't read so closely as the writer of the explication). Alert and willing to take pains, the writer of such an essay notices anything meaningful that isn't obvious, whether it is a colossal theme suggested by a symbol or a little hint contained in a single word.

To write an honest explication of a story takes time and space, probably too much time and space to devote to a long and complex story unless you are writing a long term paper, an honors thesis, or a dissertation. For example, a thorough explication of Nathaniel Hawthorne's "Young Goodman Brown" would be likely to run much longer than the rich and intriguing short story itself. Ordinarily, explication is best suited dealing with a short passage or section of a story: a key scene, a crucial conversation, a statement of theme, or an opening or closing paragraph. Storytellers who are especially fond of language invite closer attention to their words than others do. Edgar Allan Poe, for one, is a poet sensitive to the rhythms of his sentences and a symbolist whose stories abound in potent suggestions. Here is an explication, by a student, of a short but essential passage in "The Tell-Tale Heart." The passage occurs in the third paragraph of the story, and (to help us follow the explication) the student quotes it in full at the beginning of her paper.

Susan Kim

Professor A. M. Lundy

English 100

20 May 20xx

By Lantern Light:

An Explication of a Passage

in Poe's "The Tell-Tale Heart"

> And every night, about midnight, I turned the
> latch of his door and opened it--oh, so gently!
> And then, when I had made an opening sufficient
> for my head, I put in a dark lantern, all closed,
> closed, so that no light shone out, and then I
> thrust in my head. Oh, you would have laughed to
> see how cunningly I thrust it in! I moved it
> slowly--very, very slowly, so that I might not
> disturb the old man's sleep. It took me an hour to
> place my whole head within the opening so far that
> I could see him as he lay upon his bed. Ha!--would
> a madman have been so wise as this? And then, when
> my head was well in the room, I undid the lantern
> cautiously--oh, so cautiously--cautiously (for the
> hinges creaked)--I undid it just so much that a
> single thin ray fell upon the vulture eye. And
> this I did for seven long nights--every night just
> at midnight--but I found the eye always closed;
> and so it was impossible to do the work; for it
> was not the old man who vexed me, but his Evil Eye.
> (382-83)

Although Edgar Allan Poe has suggested in the first
lines of his story "The Tell-Tale Heart" that the person who
addresses us is insane, it is only when we come to the
speaker's account of his preparations for murdering the old
man that we find his madness fully revealed. Even more
convincingly than his earlier words (for we might possibly
think that someone who claims to hear things in heaven and

hell is a religious mystic), these preparations reveal him to be mad. What strikes us is that they are so elaborate and meticulous. A significant detail is the exactness of his schedule for spying: "every night just at midnight." The words with which he describes his motions also convey the most extreme care (and I will indicate them by underlining): "how wisely I proceeded--with what caution," "I turned the latch of his door and opened it--oh, so gently!" "how cunningly I thrust it [my head] in! I moved it slowly--very, very slowly," "I undid the lantern cautiously--oh, so cautiously--cautiously." Taking a whole hour to intrude his head into the room, he asks, "Ha!--would a madman have been so wise as this?" But of course the word wise is unconsciously ironic, for clearly it is not wisdom the speaker displays, but an absurd degree of care, an almost fiendish ingenuity. Such behavior, I understand, is typical of certain mental illnesses. All his careful preparations that he thinks prove him sane only convince us instead that he is mad.

   Obviously his behavior is self-defeating. He wants to catch the "vulture eye" open, and yet he takes all these pains not to disturb the old man's sleep. If he behaved logically, he might go barging into the bedroom with his lantern ablaze, shouting at the top of his voice. And yet, if we can see things his way, there is a strange logic to his reasoning. He regards the eye as a creature in itself, quite apart from its possessor. "It was not," he says, "the old man who vexed me, but his Evil Eye." Apparently, to be inspired to do his deed, the madman needs to behold the eye --at least, this is my understanding of his remark, "I found the eye always closed; and so it was impossible to do the work." Poe's choice of the word work, by the way, is also revealing. Murder is made to seem a duty or a job; and anyone who so regards murder is either extremely cold-blooded, like a hired killer for a gangland assassination, or else deranged. Besides, the word suggests again the

curious sense of detachment that the speaker feels toward
the owner of the eye.

In still another of his assumptions, the speaker shows
that he is madly logical, or operating on the logic of a
dream. There seems a dreamlike relationship between his dark
lantern "all closed, closed, so that no light shone out,"
and the sleeping victim. When the madman opens his lantern
so that it emits a single ray, he is hoping that the eye in
the old man's head will be open too, letting out its
corresponding gleam. The latch that he turns so gently, too,
seems like the eye, whose lid needs to be opened in order
for the murderer to go ahead. It is as though the speaker is
<u>trying</u> to get the eyelid to lift. By taking such great pains
and by going through all this nightly ritual, he is
practicing some kind of magic, whose rules are laid down not
by our logic, but by the logic of dreams.

Work Cited

Poe, Edgar Allan. "The Tell-Tale Heart." Literature: An
    Introduction to Fiction, Poetry, and Drama. Ed. X. J.
    Kennedy and Dana Gioia. 9th ed. New York: Longman,
    2005. 382–85.

An unusually well-written paper, "By Lantern Light" cost the student two or three careful revisions. Rather than attempting to say something about *everything* in the passage from Poe, she selects only the details that strike her as most meaningful. In her very first sentence, she briefly shows us how the passage functions in the context of Poe's story: how it clinches our suspicions that the narrator is mad. In writing her paper, the student went by the following rough, simple outline—nothing more than a list of the points she wanted to express:

1. Speaker's extreme care and exactness--typical of some
   mental illnesses.
2. Speaker doesn't act by usual logic but by a crazy logic.
3. Dreamlike connection between latch and lantern and old
   man's eye.

As she wrote, she followed her brief list, setting forth her ideas one at a time, one idea to a paragraph. There is a different (and still easier) way to organize an explication: just work through the original passage line by line or sentence by sentence. The danger of this procedure, however, is that you may find yourself falling into a boring singsong: "In the first sentence I noticed . . . ," "In the next sentence . . . ," "Now in the third sentence . . . ," "Finally, in the last paragraph." (If you choose to organize an explication in such a way, then boldly vary your transitions.) Notice that the student who wrote "By Lantern Light" doesn't inch through the passage sentence by sentence but freely takes up its details in an order that seems appropriate to her argument.

In a long critical essay in which we don't adhere to one method all the way through, the method of explication may appear from time to time—as when the critic, in discussing a story, stops to unravel a particularly knotty passage. However, useful as it may be to know how to write an explication of fiction, it is probably still more useful (in most literature courses) to know how to write an analysis.

ANALYZING

Assignment: "Write an **analysis** of a story or novel." What do you do? Following the method of analysis (from the Greek: "breaking up"), you separate a story or novel into its components and then (usually) select one part for close study. One likely topic for an analysis might be "The Character of James Baldwin's Sonny," in which the writer would concentrate on showing us Sonny's highly individual features and traits of personality. Other typical analyses might be written about, say, "Gothic Elements in a Story by Joyce Carol Oates" (referring to "Where Are You Going, Where Have You Been?") or "The Unidentified Narrator in 'A Rose for Emily.'"

To be sure, no element of a story dwells in isolation from the story's other elements. In "The Tell-Tale Heart," the madness of the leading character apparently makes it necessary to tell the story from a special point of view and probably helps determine the author's choice of theme, setting, symbolism, tone, style, and ironies. But it would be mind-boggling to try to study all those elements simultaneously. For this reason, when we write an analysis, we generally study just one element, though we may suggest— probably at the start of the essay—its relation to the whole story. Indeed, analysis is the method used in this book, in which, chapter by chapter, we have separated fiction into its components of plot, point of view, character, setting, tone and style, and so on. If you have read the discussion on the plot of "Godfather Death" (page 9) or the attempt to state the theme of Hemingway's "A Clean, Well-Lighted Place" (page 174), then you have already read some brief essays in analysis. Here is a student-written analysis of "The Tell-Tale Heart," dealing with just one element—the story's point of view.

Mike Frederick
Professor Stone
English 110
18 January 20xx

The Hearer of the Tell-Tale Heart

Although there are many things we do not know about
the narrator of Edgar Allan Poe's story "The Tell-Tale
Heart"--is he a son? a servant? a companion?--there is one
thing we are sure of from the start. He is mad. In the
opening paragraph, Poe makes the narrator's condition
unmistakable, not only from his excited and worked-up speech
(full of dashes and exclamation points), but also from his
wild claims. He says it is merely some disease which has
sharpened his senses that has made people call him crazy.
Who but a madman, however, would say, "I heard all things in
the heaven and in the earth," and brag how his ear is a kind
of CB radio, listening in on Hell? Such a statement leaves
no doubt that the point of view in the story is an ironic
one.

Because the participating narrator is telling his
story in the first person, some details in the story stand
out more than others. When the narrator goes on to tell how
he watches the old man sleeping, he rivets his attention on
the old man's "vulture eye." When a ray from his lantern
finds the Evil Eye open, he says, "I could see nothing else
of the old man's face or person" (384). Actually, the reader
can see almost nothing else about the old man anywhere in
the rest of the story. All we are told is that the old man
treated the younger man well, and we gather that the old man
was rich, because his house is full of treasures. We do not
have a clear idea of what the old man looks like, though,
nor do we know how he talks, for we are not given any of his
words. Our knowledge of him is mainly confined to his eye
and its effect on the narrator. This confinement gives that
symbolic eye a lot of importance in the story. The narrator

tells us all we know and directs our attention to parts
of it.

This point of view raises an interesting question.
Since we are dependent on the narrator for all our
information, how do we know the whole story isn't just a
nightmare in his demented mind? We have really no way to be
sure it isn't, as far as I can see. I assume, however, that
there really is a dark shuttered house and an old man and
real policemen who start snooping around when screams are
heard in the neighborhood, because it is a more memorable
story if it is a crazy man's view of reality than if it is
all just a terrible dream. But we can't take stock in the
madman's interpretation of what happens. Poe keeps putting
distances between what the narrator says and what we are
supposed to think, apparently. For instance: the narrator
has boasted that he is calm and clear in the head, but as
soon as he starts trying to explain why he killed the old
man, we gather that he is confused, to say the least (382).
"I think it was his eye!" the narrator exclaims, as if not
quite sure (382). As he goes on to explain how he conducted
the murder, we realize that he is a man with a fixed idea
working with a patience that is certainly mad, almost
diabolical.

Some readers might wonder if "The Tell-Tale Heart" is
a story of the supernatural. Is the heartbeat that the
narrator hears a ghost come back to haunt him? Here, I
think, the point of view is our best guide to what to
believe. The simple explanation for the heartbeat is this:
it is all in the madman's mind. Perhaps he feels such guilt
that he starts hearing things. Another explanation is
possible, one suggested by Daniel Hoffman, a critic who has
discussed the story: the killer hears the sound of his own
heart (227). Hoffman's explanation (which I don't like as
well as mine) also is a natural one, and it fits the story
as a whole. Back when the narrator first entered the old

man's bedroom to kill him, the heartbeat sounded so loud to
him that he was afraid the neighbors would hear it too.
Evidently they didn't, and so Hoffman may be right in
thinking that the sound was only that of his own heart
pounding in his ears. Whichever explanation you take, it is
a more down-to-earth and reasonable explanation than that
(as the narrator believes) the heart is still alive, even
though its owner has been cut to pieces. Then, too, the
police keep chatting. If they heard the heartbeat, wouldn't
they leap to their feet, draw their guns, and look all
around the room? As the author has kept showing us in the
rest of the story, the narrator's view of things is
untrustworthy. You don't kill someone just because you
dislike the look in his eye. You don't think that such a
murder is funny. For all its Gothic atmosphere of the old
dark house with a secret hidden inside, "The Tell-Tale
Heart" is not a ghost story. We have only to see its point
of view to know it is a study in abnormal psychology.

Works Cited

Hoffman, Daniel. Poe Poe Poe Poe Poe Poe Poe. New York:
    Anchor, 1973.

Poe, Edgar Allan. "The Tell-Tale Heart." Literature: An
    Introduction to Fiction, Poetry, and Drama. Ed. X. J.
    Kennedy and Dana Gioia. 9th ed. New York: Longman,
    2005. 382-85.

A temptation in writing an analysis is to include all sorts of insights that the
writer proudly wishes to display, even though they aren't related to the main idea. In
the preceding essay, the student resists this temptation admirably. In fairly plump and
ample paragraphs, he works out his ideas and supports his contentions with specific

references to Poe's story. Although his paper is not brilliantly written and contains no insight so fresh as the suggestion (by the writer of the first paper) that the madman's lantern is like the old man's head, still, it is a good brief analysis. By sticking faithfully to his purpose and by confronting the problems he raises ("how do we know the whole story isn't just a nightmare?"), the writer persuades us that he understands not only the story's point of view but also the story in its entirety.

Our analysis so far deals with one element in Poe's story: point of view. In another type of writing assignment, the **card report,** one is asked to analyze a story into its *several* elements. Usually confined to the front and back of one 5- × 8-inch index card (see the next page for an example), such a report is just as challenging to write as an essay, if not more so. To do the job well, you have to see the story in its elements and then specify them succinctly and accurately. Following is a typical card report listing and detailing the essentials of "The Tell-Tale Heart." In this assignment, the student was asked to include:

1. The title of the story and the date of its original publication.
2. The author's name and dates.
3. The name (if any) of the main character, together with a description of that character's dominant traits or features.
4. Other characters in the story, dealt with in the same fashion.
5. A short description of the setting.
6. The narrator of the story. (To identify him or her is, of course, to define the point of view from which the story is told.)
7. A terse summary of the main events of the story, given in chronological order.
8. A description of the general tone of the story, that is, the author's feelings toward the central character or the main events.
9. Some comments on the style in which the story is written. (Brief illustrative quotations are helpful, insofar as space permits.)
10. Whatever kinds of irony the story contains and what they contribute to the story.
11. The story's main theme in a sentence.
12. Leading symbols (if the story has any), with an educated guess at whatever each symbol suggests.
13. Finally, an evaluation of the story as a whole, concisely setting forth the student's opinion of it. (Some instructors regard this as the most important part of the report, and most students find that, by the time they have so painstakingly separated the ingredients of the story, they have arrived at a definite opinion of it.)

To fit so much on one card may sometimes seem like trying to engrave the Declaration of Independence on the head of a pin. The student who wrote this succinct report had to spoil a few trial cards before he was able to do it. Every word has to count, and making each count is a discipline worthwhile in almost any sort of expository writing. Some students enjoy the challenge. In doing such a report, though you may feel severely limited, you'll probably be surprised at how thoroughly you come to understand a story. Besides, if you care to keep the card for future reference, it won't take much storage room. A longer story, even a novel, may be analyzed in the same way, but insist on taking a second card if you are asked to analyze some especially hefty and complicated novel—say, Leo Tolstoy's panoramic, thousand-page *War and Peace.*

Front of Card

(Student's name)   (Course and section)

<u>Story</u>: "The Tell-Tale Heart," 1850

<u>Author</u>: Edgar Allan Poe (1809-1849)

   <u>Central character</u>: An unnamed younger man whom people call mad, who claims that a nervous disease has greatly sharpened his sense perceptions. He is proud of his own cleverness. <u>Other character</u>: The old man, whose leading feature is one pale blue, filmed eye; said to be rich, kind, and lovable. Also three policemen, not individually described.

   <u>Setting</u>: A shuttered house full of wind, mice, and treasures; pitch dark even in the afternoon.

   <u>Narrator</u>: The madman himself.

   <u>Events in summary</u>: (1) Dreading one vulturelike eye of the old man he shares a house with, a madman determines to kill its owner. (2) Each night he spies on the sleeping old man, but finding the eye shut, he stays his hand. (3) On the eighth night, finding the eye open, he suffocates its owner beneath the mattress and conceals the dismembered body under the floor of the bedchamber. (4) Entertaining some inquiring police officers in the very room where the body lies hidden, the killer again hears (or thinks he hears) the beat of the victim's heart. (5) Terrified, convinced that the police also hear the heartbeat growing louder, the killer confesses.

   <u>Tone</u>: Horror at the events described, skepticism toward the narrator's claims to be sane, detachment from his gaiety and laughter.

Back of Card

Style: Written as if told aloud by a deranged man eager to be believed, the story is punctuated by laughter, interjections ("Hearken!"), nervous halts, and fresh beginnings--indicated by dashes that grow more frequent as the story goes on and the narrator becomes more excited. Poe often relies on general adjectives ("mournful," "hideous," "hellish,") to convey atmosphere; also on exact details (the lantern that emits "a single dim ray, like the thread of a spider").

Irony: The whole story is ironic in its point of view. Presumably the author is not mad, nor does he share the madman's self-admiration. Many of the narrator's statements therefore seem verbal ironies: his account of taking an hour to move his head through the bedroom door.

Theme: Possibly "Murder will out," but I really don't find any theme either stated or clearly implied.

Symbols: The vulture eye, called an Evil Eye (in superstition, one that can implant a curse), perhaps suggesting too the all-seeing eye of God the Father, from whom no guilt can be concealed. The ghostly heartbeat, sound of the victim's coming back to be avenged (or the God who cannot be slain?). Death watches: beetles said to be death omens, whose ticking sound foreshadows the sound of the tell-tale heart "as a watch makes when enveloped in cotton."

Evaluation: Despite the overwrought style (to me slightly comic bookish), a powerful story, admirable for its conclusion and for its memorable portrait of a deranged killer. Poe knows how it is to be mad.

COMPARING AND CONTRASTING

If you were to write on "The Humor of Frank O'Connor's 'First Confession' and Eudora Welty's 'Why I Live at the P. O.,'" you would probably employ one or two other methods. You might use **comparison,** placing the two stories side by side and pointing out their similarities, or you might use **contrast,** pointing out their differences. Most of the time, in dealing with a pair of stories, you will find them similar in some ways and different in others, and so you will be using both methods in writing your paper.

No law requires you to devote equal space to each method. You might have to do more contrasting than comparing, or the other way around. If the stories are obviously similar but subtly different, you will probably compare them briefly, listing the similarities and then, at greater length, contrast them by calling attention to their important differences. If, however, the stories at first glance seem as different as peas and polecats yet are in fact closely related, you'll probably spend most of your time comparing them rather than contrasting them. (You might not just compare and contrast but also analyze, in that you might select one element of the stories for your investigation.) Other topics for papers involving two stories might be "The Experience of Coming of Age in James Joyce's 'Araby' and William Faulkner's 'Barn Burning'"; and "Mother and Daughter Relationships in Alice Walker's 'Everyday Use' and Tillie Olsen's 'I Stand Here Ironing.'"

Your paper, of course, will hang together better if you choose a pair of stories that apparently have much in common than if you choose two as unlike as cow and cantaloupe. Before you start writing, think: do the two stories I've selected throw some light on each other? An essay that likened W. Somerset Maugham's terse, ironic fable "The Appointment in Samarra" with William Faulkner's rich, complex "Barn Burning" just might reveal unexpected similarities. More likely, it would seem strained and pointless.

You can also write an essay in comparison and contrast that deals with just one story. You might consider, for example, the attitudes of the younger waiter and the older waiter in Hemingway's "A Clean, Well-Lighted Place." In Flannery O'Connor's "Revelation," you might contrast Mrs. Turpin's smug view of herself with young Mary Grace's merciless view of her.

If your topic calls for both comparison and contrast and you are dealing with two stories, don't write the first half of your paper all about one story, then pivot and write the second half about the other, never permitting the two to mingle. The result probably would not be a unified essay in contrast and comparison but two separate commentaries yoked together.

One workable way to organize such a paper is to make (before you begin) a brief list of points to look for in each story. Then, as you write, consider each point—first in one story and then in the other. Here is a simple outline for an essay bringing together William Faulkner's "A Rose for Emily" and Flannery O'Connor's "Revelation." The topic is "Two Would-Be Aristocrats: The Characters of Emily Grierson and Mrs. Turpin."

1. Character's view of her own innate superiority
   a. Emily Grierson
   b. Mrs. Turpin
2. Author's evaluation of character's moral worth
   a. Emily Grierson
   b. Mrs. Turpin
3. Character's ability to change
   a. Emily Grierson
   b. Mrs. Turpin

It is best, however, not to follow such an outline in plodding, mechanical fashion ("Well, now it's time to whip over to Mrs. Turpin again"), lest your readers feel they are watching a back-and-forth tennis match. Some points are bound to interest you more than others, and, when they do, you will want to give them greater emphasis.

SUGGESTIONS FOR WRITING

What kinds of topics are likely to result in papers that will reveal something about works of fiction? Here is a list of typical topics, suitable for papers of various lengths, offered in the hope of stimulating your own ideas. For other topics, see Further Suggestions for Writing at the end of most chapters. For specific advice on finding a topic of your own, see "Discovering Essay Ideas," page 2121.

Topics for Brief Papers (250–500 words)

1. Consider a short story in which the central character has to make a decision or must take some decisive step that will alter the rest of his or her life. Faulkner's "Barn Burning" is one such story; another is Updike's "A & P." As concisely and as thoroughly as you can, explain the nature of the character's decision, the reasons for it, and its probable consequences (as suggested by what the author tells us).

2. Write an informal (rather than a complete) explication of the opening paragraph or first few lines of a story. Show how it prepares us for what will happen. (An alternate topic: take instead a closing paragraph and sum up whatever insight it leaves us with.) Don't feel obliged to deal with everything in the passage, as you would do in writing a more complete explication. Within this suggested word length, limit your discussion to whatever strikes you as most essential.

3. Make a card report (see page 2140) on a short story in "Stories for Further Reading" or one suggested by your instructor. Include all the elements in the report illustrated in this chapter (unless your instructor wishes you to emphasize some element or offers other advice).
4. Show how reading a specific short story caused you to change or modify an attitude or opinion you once had.
5. Just for fun, try writing a different ending to one of the short stories in this anthology. What does this exercise suggest about the wisdom of the author in ending things as done in the original? (Try to keep a sense of the author's style.)
6. Another wild idea: write a sequel to one of your favorite short stories—or at least the beginning of a sequel, enough to give your reader a sense of it.
7. Argue from your own experience that a character in any story behaves (or doesn't behave) as people behave in life.

Topics for More Extended Papers (600–1,000 words)

1. Choose a short passage (one of, say, three or four sentences) in a story, a passage that interests you. Perhaps it will contain a decisive movement in a plot, a revealing comment on a character, or a statement of the story's major theme. Then write a reasonably thorough explication. As the writer of the paper "By Lantern Light" did (page 2132), go through the passage in some detail, noticing words that especially convey the author's meanings.
2. Write an analysis of a short story, singling out an element such as the author's voice (tone, style, irony), point of view, character, theme, symbolism, or Gothic elements (if the story has any). Try to show how this element functions in the story as a whole. For a typical paper in response to this assignment, see "The Hearer of the Tell-Tale Heart" (page 2136).
3. Analyze a story in which a character experiences some realization or revelation. How does the writer prepare us for the moment of enlightenment? What is the nature of each realization or revelation? How does it affect the character? Stories to consider might include "Miss Brill," "Greasy Lake," "Araby," "The Chrysanthemums," "Revelation," and "Sonny's Blues."
4. Explore how humor functions in a story. What is funny? How is humor implied by the story's style or tone? Does humor help set forth a theme or reveal character? Any of the following stories deserves exploration: "A & P," "Greasy Lake," "Revelation," "First Confession," or "Angel Levine."
5. For anyone interested in a career in teaching: explain how you would teach a story, either to an imaginary class or to the class you belong to now. Perhaps you might arrange with your instructor to write about a story your class hasn't read yet; and then, after writing your paper, actually to teach the story in class.
6. See whether you can discover a new Stephen Crane—another journalist who brings literary skill to reporting (as Crane does in "The Open Boat"). In an essay, examine some news story, interview, or feature that you think reads like excellent fiction. Point out whatever elements of good storytelling you find in it. (Is there a plot? lively dialogue? suspense? vivid style?

thought-provoking theme? rounded characters, or at least memorable ones? shrewd choice of a point of view?) For such a story, consult your daily newspaper or a weekly news magazine. Supply a clipping or copy of your discovery along with your finished paper.

7. If your daily newspaper lacks literary quality but you'd like to try that last topic, see any of the following books. Each contains some reporting that will show you storytelling art:

Annie Dillard, *For the Time Being* (New York: Knopf, 1999). An account of Dillard's journey through Asia in a search for spiritual enlightenment—a deeply intelligent and very witty treatment of a challenging subject.

Donald Hall, *Life Work* (Boston: Beacon Press, 1993). An inspiring account of the pleasures of working at what one loves, especially good on the joys of writing.

John Hersey, *Hiroshima* (New York: Knopf, 1946). The first atomic holocaust as seen by six survivors.

Garrison Keillor, *Lake Wobegon Days* (New York: Viking, 1985). Gentle comic reports of a practically vanished small-town way of life.

Tracy Kidder, *Among Schoolchildren* (Boston: Houghton, 1989). Close observations of a year in the life of an elementary school teacher.

Lillian Ross, *Reporting* (New York: Dodd, 1981). Seven classic essays in journalism, among them a profile of Ernest Hemingway.

Hunter S. Thompson, *The Great Shark Hunt* (New York: Summit, 1979). Reports of politics, sports, and pleasure seeking in the 1960s and 1970s.

Tom Wolfe, *The Right Stuff* (New York: Farrar, 1979). The story of America's first astronauts.

Topics for Long Papers (1,500 words or more)

1. Selecting a short story from "Stories for Further Reading" in this book or taking one suggested by your instructor, write an informal essay setting forth (as thoroughly as you can) your understanding of it. Point out any difficulties you encountered in first reading the story, for the benefits of other students who might meet the same difficulties. If you find particularly complicated passages, briefly explicate them. An ample statement of the meaning of the story probably will not deal only with plot or only with theme but will also consider how the story is written and structured.

2. Dealing with a single element of fiction, write an analysis of Baldwin's "Sonny's Blues," Kafka's *The Metamorphosis,* or some other long story that your instructor suggests.

3. Select a short story in which most of the events take place in the physical world (rather than inside some character's mind), and translate it into a

one-act play, complete with stage directions. After you have done so, you might present a reading of it with the aid of other members of the class and then perhaps discuss what you had to do to the story to make a play of it.

4. Selecting an author from this book whose work appeals to you, read at least three or four of his or her other stories. Then write an analysis of them, concentrating on an element of fiction that you find present in all.

5. Again going beyond this book if necessary, compare and contrast two writers' handling of a similar theme. Let your essay build to a conclusion in which you state your opinion: which author's expression of theme is deeper or more memorable?

42 *Writing About a Poem*

Assignment: write a paper about a poem. You can approach your paper as a grim duty: any activity can look like a dull obligation. For Don Juan, in Spanish legend, even making love became a chore. But the act of writing, like the act of love, is easier if your feelings take part in it. Write about something you dislike and don't understand, and you not only set for yourself the labors of Hercules, but you also guarantee your reader discouragingly hard labor, too.

To write about a poem well, you need first to experience it. It helps to live with the poem for as long as possible; there is little point in trying to fully understand the poem in a ten-minute tour of inspection on the night before the paper falls due. However challenging, writing about poetry has immediate rewards. To mention just one, the poem you spend time writing about is going to mean much more to you than poems skimmed over ever do.

Most of the problems you will meet in writing about a poem are the same ones you encounter in writing about a play or a story: finding a topic, organizing your thoughts, writing, revising. For general advice on writing papers about any kind of literature, see the earlier chapter, "Writing About Literature," on page 2119. In a few ways, however, a poem requires a different approach. In this chapter we will deal briefly with some of them and will offer a few papers that students have written. We think you will agree that these papers are interesting, and we assure you that most students can write equally good papers.

Briefer than most stories and plays, lyric poems look easier to write about. They call, however, for your keenest attention. You may find that, before you can discuss a short poem, you will have to read it slowly and painstakingly, with your mind (like your pencil) sharp and ready. Unlike a play or a short story, a lyric poem tends to have very little plot, and perhaps you will find little to say about what happens in it. In order to understand a poem, you'll need to notice elements other than narrative: the connotations or suggestions of its words, surely, and the rhythm of phrases and lines. The subtleties of language are so essential to a poem (and so elusive) that Robert Frost was moved to say, "Poetry is what gets lost in translation." Once in a while, of course, you'll read a story whose prose abounds in sounds, rhythms, figures of speech, imagery, and other elements you expect of poetry. Certain novels of Herman Melville and William Faulkner contain paragraphs that, if extracted, seem in themselves prose poems—so lively are they in their wordplay, so rich in metaphor. But such writing is exceptional, and the main business of most fiction is to get a story told. An extreme case of a fiction writer who didn't want his prose to sound poetic is Georges Simenon, best known for his mystery novels, who said that whenever he noticed in his manuscript any word or phrase that called attention to itself, he struck it out. This method of writing would never do for a poet, who revels in words and phrases that fix themselves in memory. It is safe to say that, in order to write well about a poem, you have to read it carefully enough to remember at least part of it word for word.

Let's consider three commonly useful approaches to writing about poetry.

EXPLICATING

In an **explication** (literally, "an unfolding") of a poem, a writer explains the entire poem in detail, unraveling any complexities to be found in it. This method is a valuable one in approaching a lyric poem, especially if the poem is rich in complexities (or in suggestions worth rendering explicit). Most poems that you'll ever be asked to explicate are short enough to discuss thoroughly within a limited time; fully to explicate a long and involved work, such as John Milton's epic *Paradise Lost*, might require a lifetime. (To explicate a short passage of Milton's long poem, however, would be a practical and interesting course assignment.)

The writer of an explication tries to examine and unfold all the details in a poem that a sensitive reader might consider. These might include allusions, the denotations or connotations of words, the possible meanings of symbols, the effects of certain sounds and rhythms and formal elements (rime schemes, for instance), the sense of any statements that contain irony, and other particulars. Not intent on ripping a poem to pieces, the author of a useful explication instead tries to show how each part contributes to the whole.

An explication is easy to organize. You can start with the first line of the poem and keep working straight on through. An explication should not be confused with a paraphrase. A paraphrase simply puts the literal meaning of a poem into plain prose sense: it is a sort of translation that might prove helpful in clarifying a poem's main theme. Perhaps in writing an explication, you will wish to do some paraphrasing, but an explication (unlike a paraphrase) does not simply restate. It explains a poem, in great detail.

Here, for example, is a famous poem by Robert Frost, followed by a student's concise explication. (The assignment was to explain whatever in "Design" seemed most essential, in not more than 750 words.)

Robert Frost   (1874–1963)

DESIGN

1936

I found a dimpled spider, fat and white,
On a white heal-all, holding up a moth
Like a white piece of rigid satin cloth—
Assorted characters of death and blight
Mixed ready to begin the morning right,   5
Like the ingredients of a witches' broth—
A snow-drop spider, a flower like a froth,
And dead wings carried like a paper kite.

What had that flower to do with being white,
The wayside blue and innocent heal-all?   10
What brought the kindred spider to that height,
Then steered the white moth thither in the night?
What but design of darkness to appall?—
If design govern in a thing so small.

Ted Jasper
Professor Hirsch
English 130
21 November 20xx

An Unfolding of Robert Frost's "Design"

"I always wanted to be very observing," Robert Frost
once told an audience, after reading his poem "Design." Then
he added, "But I have always been afraid of my own
observations" (qtd. in Cook 126-27). What could Frost have
observed that could scare him? Let's examine the poem in
question and see what we discover.

Starting with the title, "Design," any reader of this
poem will find it full of meaning. As the Merriam-Webster
Dictionary defines design, the word can denote among other
things a plan, purpose, or intention ("Design"). Some

arguments for the existence of God (I remember from Sunday School) are based on the "argument from design": that because the world shows a systematic order, there must be a Designer who made it. But the word <u>design</u> can also mean "a deliberate undercover project or scheme" such as we attribute to a "designing person" ("Design"). As we shall see, Frost's poem incorporates all of these meanings. His poem raises the old philosophic question of whether there is a Designer, an evil Designer, or no Designer at all.

Like many other sonnets, "Design" is divided into two parts. The first eight lines draw a picture centering on the spider, who at first seems almost jolly. It is <u>dimpled</u> and <u>fat</u> like a baby, or Santa Claus. The spider stands on a wildflower whose name, <u>heal-all</u>, seems ironic: a heal-all is supposed to cure any disease, but this flower has no power to restore life to the dead moth. (Later, in line ten, we learn that the heal-all used to be blue. Presumably, it has died and become bleached-looking.) In the second line we discover, too, that the spider has hold of another creature, a dead moth. We then see the moth described with an odd simile in line three: "Like a white piece of rigid satin cloth." Suddenly, the moth becomes not a creature but a piece of fabric--lifeless and dead--and yet <u>satin</u> has connotations of beauty. Satin is a luxurious material used in rich formal clothing, such as coronation gowns and brides' dresses. Additionally, there is great accuracy in the word: the smooth and slightly plush surface of satin is like the powder-smooth surface of moths' wings. But this "cloth," rigid and white, could be the lining to Dracula's coffin.

In the fifth line an invisible hand enters. The characters are "mixed" like ingredients in an evil potion. Some force doing the mixing is behind the scene. The characters in themselves are innocent enough, but when brought together, their whiteness and look of <u>rigor mortis</u> are overwhelming. There is something diabolical in the spider's feast. The "morning right" echoes the word <u>rite</u>, a ritual--in this case apparently a Black Mass or a Witches' Sabbath. The simile in line seven ("a flower like a froth") is more ambiguous and harder to describe. A froth is white, foamy, and delicate--something found on a brook in the woods or on a beach after a wave recedes. However, in the natural world, froth also can be ugly: the foam on a polluted stream or a rabid dog's mouth. The dualism in nature--its beauty and its horror--is there in that one simile.

So far, the poem has portrayed a small, frozen scene, with the dimpled killer holding its victim as innocently as a boy holds a kite. Already, Frost has hinted that Nature may be, as Radcliffe Squires suggests, "Nothing but an ash-white plain without love or faith or hope, where ignorant appetites cross by chance" (87). Now, in the last six lines of the sonnet, Frost comes out and directly states his theme. What else could bring these deathly pale, stiff things together "but design of darkness to appall?" The question is clearly rhetorical; we are meant to answer, "Yes, there does seem an evil design at work here!" I take the next-to-last line to mean, "What except a design so dark and sinister that we're appalled by it?" "Appall," by the way, is the second pun in the poem: it sounds like <u>a pall</u> or shroud. (The derivation of <u>appall</u>, according to <u>Merriam-Webster</u>, is ultimately from a Latin word meaning "to be pale"--an interesting word choice for a poem full of white pale images ["Appall"].) <u>Steered</u> carries the suggestion of a steering-wheel or rudder that some pilot had to control. Like the word <u>brought</u>, it implies that some invisible force charted the paths of spider, heal-all, and moth, so that they arrived together.

Having suggested that the universe is in the hands of that sinister force (an indifferent God? Fate? the Devil?),

Frost adds a note of doubt. The Bible tells us that "His eye
is on the sparrow," but at the moment the poet doesn't seem
sure. Maybe, he hints, when things in the universe drop
below a certain size, they pass completely out of the
Designer's notice. When creatures are this little, maybe God
doesn't bother to govern them but just lets them run wild.
And possibly the same mindless chance is all that governs
human lives. And because this is even more senseless than
having an angry God intent on punishing us, it is, Frost
suggests, the worst suspicion of all.

Works Cited

"Appall." Merriam-Webster Online. 2004. Merriam-Webster.
    14 Oct. 20xx <http://www.m-w.com/>.
Cook, Reginald. Robert Frost: A Living Voice. Amherst: U of
    Massachusetts P, 1974.
"Design." Merriam-Webster Online. 2004. Merriam-Webster.
    14 Oct. 20xx <http://www.m-w.com/>.
Frost, Robert. "Design." Collected Poems, Prose and Plays.
    New York: Library of America, 1995. 275.
Squires, Radcliffe. The Major Themes of Robert Frost. Ann
    Arbor: U of Michigan P, 1963.

This excellent paper, while finding something worth unfolding in every line in
Frost's poem, does so without seeming mechanical. Notice that, although the student
proceeds sequentially through the poem from the title to the last line, he takes up,
when necessary, some points, out of order. In paragraph two, for example, the writer
looks ahead to the end of the poem and briefly states the poem's main theme. (He
does so in order to relate this theme to the poem's title.) In the third paragraph, he
explicates the poem's *later* image of the heal-all, relating it to the first image. He also

comments on the form of the poem ("Like many other sonnets"), on its similes and puns, and on its denotations and connotations.

This paper also demonstrates good use of manuscript form, following the *MLA Handbook*, 6th ed. Brief references (in parentheses) tell us where the writer found Frost's remarks and give page numbers for his quotation from a book by Radcliffe Squires. At the end of the paper, a list of Works Cited uses the abbreviations for *University* and *Press* that the *MLA Handbook* recommends.

It might seem that to work through a poem line by line is a mechanical task, and yet there can be genuine excitement in doing so. Randall Jarrell once wrote an explication of "Design" in which he managed to convey just such excitement. See if you can sense Jarrell's joy in writing about the poem.

> Frost's details are so diabolically good that it seems criminal to leave some unremarked; but notice how *dimpled, fat,* and *white* (all but one; all but one) come from our regular description of any baby; notice how the *heal-all,* because of its name, is the one flower in all the world picked to be the altar for this Devil's Mass; notice how *holding up* the moth brings something ritual and hieratic, a ghostly, ghastly formality, to this priest and its sacrificial victim; notice how terrible to the fingers, how full of the stilling rigor of death, that *white piece of rigid satin cloth* is. And *assorted characters of death and blight* is, like so many things in this poem, sharply ambiguous: *a mixed bunch of actors* or *diverse representative signs.* The tone of the phrase *assorted characters of death and blight* is beautifully developed in the ironic Breakfast-Club-calisthenics, Radio-Kitchen heartiness of *mixed ready to begin the morning right* (which assures us, so unreassuringly, that this isn't any sort of Strindberg *Spook Sonata,* but hard fact), and concludes in the *ingredients* of the witches' broth, giving the soup a sort of cuddly shimmer that the cauldron in *Macbeth* never had; the *broth,* even, is brought to life—we realize that witches' broth *is* broth, to be supped with a long spoon.[1]

Evidently, Jarrell's cultural interests are broad: ranging from August Strindberg's groundbreaking modern play down to *The Breakfast Club* (a once-popular radio program that cheerfully exhorted its listeners to march around their tables). And yet breadth of knowledge, however much it deepens and enriches Jarrell's writing, isn't all that he brings to the reading of poetry. For him an explication isn't a dull plod, but a voyage of discovery. His prose—full of figures of speech (*diabolically good, cuddly shimmer*)—conveys the apparent delight he takes in showing off his findings. Such a joy, of course, can't be acquired deliberately. But it can grow, the more you read and study poetry.

ANALYZING

An **analysis** of a poem, like a news commentator's analysis of a crisis in the Middle East or a chemist's analysis of an unknown fluid, separates its subject into elements, as a means to understanding that subject—to see what composes it. Usually, the writer of

---

[1] *Poetry and the Age* (New York: Knopf, 1953), 42–43.

such an essay singles out one of these elements for attention: "Imagery of Light and Darkness in Frost's 'Design' "; "The Character of Satan in Milton's *Paradise Lost*."

Like explication, analysis can be particularly useful in dealing with a short poem. Unlike explication (which inches through a poem line by line), analysis often suits a long poem, too, because it allows the writer to discuss just one manageable element in the poem. A good analysis casts intense light on a poem from one direction. If you care enough about a poem and about some perspective on it—its theme, say, or its symbolism or its singability—writing an analysis can enlighten and give pleasure.

In this book you probably have met a few brief analyses: the discussion of connotations in John Masefield's "Cargoes" (page 777), for instance, or the examination of symbols in T. S. Eliot's "The *Boston Evening Transcript*" (page 956). In fact, most of the discussions in this book are analytic. Temporarily, we have separated the whole art of poetry into elements such as tone, irony, literal meaning, suggestions, imagery, figures of speech, sound, rhythm, and so on. No element of a poem, of course, exists apart from all the other elements. Still, by taking a closer look at particular elements, one at a time, we see them more clearly and can more easily study them.

Long analyses of metrical feet, rime schemes, and indentations tend to make ponderous reading. Such formal and technical elements are perhaps the hardest to discuss engagingly. And yet formal analysis (at least a little of it) can be interesting and illuminating; it can measure the very pulse beat of lines. If you do care about the technical side of poetry, then write about it, by all means. You will probably find it helpful to learn the terms for the various meters, stanzas, fixed forms, and other devices, so that you can summon them to your aid with confidence. Here is a short formal analysis of "Design" by a student who evidently cares for technicalities and finds an interesting way to talk about them. Concentrating on Frost's use of the sonnet form in "Design," the student casts light on the entire poem.

Lopez 1

Guadalupe Lopez

Professor Faber

English 210

16 April 20xx

The Design of Robert Frost's "Design"

For "Design" the sonnet form has at least two advantages. As in most Italian sonnets, the poem's argument falls into two parts. In the octave Robert Frost's persona draws a still-life of a spider, a flower, and a moth; then

---

in the sestet he contemplates the meaning of his still-life.
The sestet focuses on a universal: the possible existence of
a vindictive deity who causes the spider to catch the moth
and, no doubt, also causes--when viewed anthropomorphically
--other suffering.

Frost's persona weaves his own little web. The unwary
audience is led through the poem's argument from its opening
"story" to a point at which something must be made of the
story's symbolic significance. Even the rhyme scheme
contributes to the poem's successful leading of the audience
toward the sestet's theological questioning. The word <u>white</u>
ends the first line of the sestet, and the same vowel sound
is echoed in the lines that follow. All in all, half of the
sonnet's lines end in the "ite" sound, as if to render
significant the wh<u>ite</u>ness--the symbolic innocence--of
nature's representation of a greater truth.

A sonnet has a familiar design, and the poem's
classical form points to the thematic concern that there
seems to be an order to the universe that might be perceived
by looking at even seemingly insignificant natural events.
The sonnet must follow certain conventions, and nature,
though not as readily apprehensible as a poetic form, is
apparently governed by a set of laws. There is a ready-made
irony in Frost's choosing such an order-driven form to
meditate on whether or not there is any order in the
universe. However, whether or not his questioning sestet is
actually approaching an answer or, indeed, the answer, Frost
has approached an order that seems to echo a larger order in
his using the sonnet form. An approach through poetic form
and substance is itself significant in Frost's own
estimation, for Frost argues that what a poet achieves in
writing poetry is "a momentary stay against confusion" (777).

Although design clearly governs in this poem--in this
"thing so small"--the design is not entirely predictable.

The poem does start out in the form of an Italian sonnet, relying on only two rhyming sounds. However, unlike an Italian sonnet, one of the octave's rhyming sounds--the "ite"--continues into the sestet. And additionally, "Design" ends in a couplet, much in the manner of the Shakespearean sonnet, which frequently offers, in the final couplet, a summing up of the sonnet's argument. Perhaps not only nature's "story" of the spider, the flower, and the moth but also Frost's poem itself echoes the larger universe. It looks perfectly orderly until the details are given their due.

Work Cited

Frost, Robert. "The Figure a Poem Makes." Collected Poems, Prose and Plays. New York: Library of America, 1995. 776-78.

COMPARING AND CONTRASTING

To write a **comparison** of two poems, you place them side by side and point out their likenesses; to write a **contrast,** you point out their differences. If you wish, you can combine the two methods in the same paper. For example, even though you may emphasize similarities, you may also call attention to significant differences, or vice versa.

Such a paper makes the most sense if you pair two poems that have much in common. It would be possible to compare Wallace McRae's comic cowboy poem "Reincarnation" with Thomas Gray's profoundly elegiac "Elegy Written in a Country Churchyard" but comparison would be difficult, perhaps futile. Though both poems are in English and both deal with the themes of death and transfiguration, the two seem hopelessly remote from each other—in diction, tone, complexity, and scope. Your first task, therefore, is to choose two poems that shed light on one another when they are examined together.

Having found a pair of poems that illuminate each other, you then try to demonstrate in your paper further, unsuspected resemblances—not just those that are obvious ("'Design' and 'Wing-Spread' are both about bugs"). The interesting resemblances are ones that take thinking to discover. Similarly, you may want to show noteworthy differences—besides those your reader will see without any help.

In comparing two poems, you may be tempted to discuss one of them and be done with it, then spend the latter half of your paper discussing the other. This simple way of organizing an essay can be dangerous if it leads you to keep the two poems in total isolation from each other. The whole idea of such an assignment, of course, is to see what can be learned by comparing the two poems. There is nothing wrong in discussing all of poem A first, then discussing poem B—*if* in discussing B, you keep looking back at A. Another procedure is to keep comparing the two poems all the way through your paper—dealing first, let's say, with their themes; then with their central metaphors; and finally, with their respective merits.

More often than not, a comparison is a kind of analysis—a study of a theme common to two poems, for instance, or of two poets' similar fondness for the myth of Eden. You also can evaluate poems by comparing and contrasting them, placing them side by side in order to decide which poet deserves the brighter laurels. Here, for example, is a poem by Abbie Huston Evans, followed by a paper that considers Frost's "Design" and Evans's "Wing-Spread." By comparing and contrasting the two poems for both their language and their themes, this student shows us reasons for his evaluation.

Abbie Huston Evans   (1881–1979)

WING-SPREAD   1938

The midge spins out to safety
Through the spider's rope;
But the moth, less lucky,
Has to grope.

Mired in glue-like cable   5
See him foundered swing
By the gap he opened
With his wing,

Dusty web enlacing
All that blue and beryl.   10
In a netted universe
Wing-spread is peril.

Tom Munjee
Professor Mickey
English 110
21 October 20xx

              "Wing-Spread" Does a Dip

    Abbie Huston Evans's "Wing-Spread" is an effective
short poem, but it lacks the complexity and depth of Robert
Frost's "Design." These two poems were published only two
years apart, and both present a murderous spider and an
unlucky moth, but Frost's treatment differs from Evans's
approach in at least two important ways. First, Frost uses
poetic language more evocatively than Evans. Second,
"Design" digs more deeply into the situation to uncover a
more memorable theme.

      If we compare the language of the two poems, we find
"Design" is full of words and phrases rich with suggestions.
The language of "Wing-Spread," by comparison, seems thinner.
Frost's "dimpled spider, fat and white," for example, is
certainly a more suggestive description. Actually, Evans
does not describe her spider; she just says, "the spider's
rope." (Evans does vividly show the spider and moth in
action. In Frost's poem, they are already dead and
petrified.) In "Design," the spider's dimples show that it
is like a chubby little baby. This seems an odd way to look
at a spider, but it is more original than Evans's
conventional view (although I like her word cable,
suggesting that the spider's web is a kind of high-tech food
trap). Frost's word-choice--his repetition of white--paints
a more striking scene than Evans's slightly vague "All that
blue and beryl." Except for her brief personification of the
moth in the second stanza, Evans hardly uses any figures of
speech, and even this one is not a clear personification--

she simply gives the moth a sex by referring to it as "him."
Frost's striking metaphors, similes, and even puns (right,
appall), show him, as usual, to be a master of figures of
speech. He calls the moth's wings "satin cloth" and "a paper
kite;" Evans just refers in line 8 to a moth's wing. As far
as the language of the two poems goes, we might as well
compare a vase brimming with flowers and a single flower
stuck in a vase. In fairness to Evans, I would say that her
poem, while lacking complexity, still makes its point
effectively. Her poem has powerful sounds: short lines with
the riming words coming at us again and again.

In theme, however, "Wing-Spread" seems much more
narrow than "Design." The first time I read Evans's poem,
all I felt was: Ho hum, the moth's wings were too wide and
got stuck. The second time I read it, I realized that she
was saying something with a universal application. This
message comes out in line 11, in "a netted universe." That
metaphorical phrase is the most interesting part of her
poem. Netted makes me imagine the universe as being full of
nets rigged by someone who is fishing for us. Maybe, like
Frost, Evans sees an evil plan operating. She does not,
though, investigate it. She says that the midge escapes
because it is tiny. On the other hand, things with wide
wing-spreads get stuck. Her theme as I read it is, "Be small
and inconspicuous if you want to survive," or maybe, "Isn't
it too bad that in this world the big beautiful types crack
up and die, while the little puny punks keep sailing?" Now,
this is a valuable idea. I have often thought that very same
thing myself. But Frost's closing note ("If design govern in
a thing so small") is really devastating because it raises a
huge uncertainty. "Wing-Spread" leaves us with not much
besides a moth stuck in a web and a moral. In both language
and theme, "Design" climbs to a higher altitude.

Works Cited

Evans, Abbie Huston. "Wing-Spread." <u>Literature: An</u>
  <u>Introduction to Fiction, Poetry and Drama</u>. Ed. X. J.
  Kennedy and Dana Gioia. 9th ed. New York: Longman,
  2005. 2157.

Frost, Robert. "Design." <u>Collected Poems, Prose and Plays</u>.
  New York: Library of America, 1995. 275.

HOW TO QUOTE A POEM

When you discuss a short poem, you should usually quote the whole text of the poem at the beginning of your paper, with its lines numbered. Then you can refer to it with ease, and your instructor can follow you without having to juggle a book. Ask your instructor, however, whether he or she prefers the full text to be quoted this way. Quoted to illustrate some point, memorable lines can add interest to your paper. Good commentators on poetry tend to be apt quoters, helping their readers to experience a word, a phrase, a line, or a passage that otherwise might be neglected. Quoting poetry accurately, however, raises certain difficulties you don't face in quoting prose.

If you are quoting fewer than four lines of poetry, you should transform the line arrangement into prose form, separating each line by a space, diagonal (/), and a space. The diagonal (/) indicates the writer's respect for where the poet's lines begin and end. Do not change the poet's capitalization or punctuation. Be sure to identify the line numbers you are quoting, as follows:

> The color white preoccupies Frost. The spider is "fat
>
> and white, / On a white heal-all" (1-2), and even the
>
> victim moth is pale, too.

There are also lines to think about—important and meaningful units whose shape you will need to preserve. If you are quoting four or more lines, it is good policy to arrange the lines that you are quoting just as they occur in the poem, white space and all, and to identify the line numbers you are quoting. In general, follow these rules:

1. Indent the quotation one inch, or ten spaces, from the left-hand margin.
2. Double-space between the quoted lines.
3. Type the poem exactly as it appears in the original; you do not need to use quotation marks.
4. Cite the line numbers you are quoting in parentheses.

```
At the outset, the poet tells us of his discovery of

                    a dimpled spider, fat and white,

          On a white heal-all, holding up a moth

          Like a white piece of rigid satin cloth--

          Assorted characters of death and blight (1-4)

     and implies that the small killer is both childlike

     and sinister.
```

When you are beginning the quotation in the middle of a line of verse, position your starting word as closely as possible to where it occurs in the poem (as in the above example)—not at the left-hand margin.

If a line you are quoting is too long to fit on one line, you should indent it one-quarter inch, or three spaces, as follows:

```
          What had that flower to do with being

             white,

          The wayside blue and innocent heal-all?

          What brought the kindred spider to that

             height,

          Then steered the white moth thither in the

             night? (9-12)
```

If you omit words from the lines you quote, indicate the omission with an ellipsis (. . .), as in the following example:

```
     The color white preoccupies Frost in his description

     of the spider "fat and white, / On a white heal-all

     . . . / Like a white piece of rigid satin cloth" (1-3).
```

There's no need for an ellipsis, if the lines you are quoting go right to the end of a sentence in the original, or if it is obvious that only a phrase is being quoted.

```
     The speaker says that he "found a dimpled spider,"

     and he goes on to portray it as a kite-flying boy.
```

If you leave out whole lines of verse, indicate the omission by a line of spaced periods about the length of a line of the poem you are quoting.

Maybe, she hints, when things in the universe drop

below a certain size, they pass completely out of the

Designer's notice:

    The midge spins out to safety

    Through the spider's rope;

    . . . .

    In a netted universe

    Wing-spread is peril. (1-2, 11-12)

BEFORE YOU BEGIN

You will probably already have spent considerable time in reading, thinking, and feeling. Having selected your topic, you will have taken a further look at the poem or poems you have chosen, letting further thoughts and feelings come to you. The quality of your paper will depend, above all, on the quality of your preparation. Now you are ready at last to write.

Try to make the language with which you analyze a poem as fresh and accurate as possible. It is easy to fall into habitual expression—especially to overuse a few convenient words. Mechanical language may tempt you to think of the poem in mechanical terms. Here, for instance, is a plodding discussion of Robert Frost's poem:

The symbols Frost uses in "Design" are very

successful. Frost makes the spider stand for Nature.

He wants us to see nature as blind and cruel. He also

employs good sounds. He uses a lot of i's because he

is trying to make you think of falling rain.

What's wrong with this "analysis"? The underscored words are worth questioning here. While understandable, the words *employs* and *uses* seem to lead the writer to see Frost only as a conscious tool-manipulator. To be sure, Frost in a sense "uses" symbols, but did he grab hold of them and lay them into his poem? For all we know, perhaps the symbols arrived quite unbidden and used the poet. To write a good poem, Frost maintained, a poet himself has to be surprised. (How, by the way, can we hope to know what a poet *wants* to do? And there isn't much point in saying that the poet is *trying* to do something. He has already done it, if he has written a good poem.) At least it is likely that Frost didn't plan to fulfill a certain quota of *i*-sounds. Writing his poem, not by following a blueprint but probably by bringing it slowly to the surface of his mind, Frost no doubt had enough to do without trying to engineer the reactions of his possible audience. Like all true symbols, Frost's spider doesn't *stand for* anything. The writer would be closer to the truth to say that the spider *suggests* or *reminds us* of Nature or of certain forces in the natural world. (Symbols just hint; they don't indicate.)

After the student discussed the paper in a conference with his instructor, he rewrote the two sentences:

```
The symbols in Frost's "Design" are highly effective.
The spider, for instance, suggests the blindness and
cruelty of Nature. Frost's word-sounds, too, are part
of the meaning of his poem, for the i's remind the
reader of falling rain.
```

Not every reader of "Design" will hear rain falling, but the student's revision probably comes closer to describing the experience of the poem most of us know.

In writing about poetry, an occasional note of self-doubt can be useful—now and then a *perhaps* or a *possibly* or an *it seems*. Such qualifying expressions may seem timid shilly-shallying, but at least they keep the writer from thinking, "I know all there is to know about this poem."

Facing the showdown with your empty sheaf of paper or blank computer screen, however, you can't worry forever about your critical vocabulary. To do so is to risk the fate of the centipede in a bit of comic verse, who was running along efficiently until someone asked, "Pray, which leg comes after which?" whereupon "He lay distracted in a ditch / Considering how to run." It is a safe bet that your instructor is human. Your main task as a writer is to communicate to another human being your sensitive reading of a poem.

SUGGESTIONS FOR WRITING

Topics for Brief Papers (250–500 words)

1. Write a concise *explication* of a short poem of your choice or one suggested by your instructor. In a paper this brief, you probably won't have room to explain everything in the poem; explain what you think most needs explaining. (An illustration of an explication appears on page 2149.)

2. Write an *analysis* of a short poem that focuses on how one of its key elements shapes its meaning. (An illustration of an analysis appears on page 2154.) For examples, here are a few specific topics:

    Kinds of Irony in Hardy's "The Workbox"

    The Attitude of the Speaker in Marvell's "To His Coy Mistress"

    The Theme of Pastan's "Ethics"

    The Rhythms of Plath's "Daddy"

    An Extended Metaphor in Yeats's "Long-legged Fly." (Explain the one main comparison that the poem makes and show how the whole poem makes it. Other likely poems for a paper on extended metaphor: Dickinson's "Because I could not stop for Death," Frost's "The Silken Tent," Lowell's "Skunk Hour," Rich's "Aunt Jennifer's Tigers," Stevenson's "The Victory.")

(To locate any of these poems, see the Index of Authors and Titles.)

3. Select a poem in which the main speaker is a character who for any reason interests you. You might consider, for instance, Betjeman's "In Westminster Abbey," Browning's "Soliloquy of the Spanish Cloister," Eliot's "The Love Song of J. Alfred Prufrock," or Rhina Espaillat's "Bilingual/Bilingüe." Then write a brief profile of this character, drawing only on what the poem tells you (or reveals). What is the character's approximate age? Situation in life? Attitude toward self? Attitude toward others? General personality? Do you find this character admirable?

4. Although each of these poems tells a story, what happens in the poem isn't necessarily obvious: Cummings's "anyone lived in a pretty how town," Eliot's "The Love Song of J. Alfred Prufrock," Robinson's "Luke Havergal," Stevenson's "The Victory," Wright's "A Blessing." Choose one of these poems, and in a paragraph sum up what you think happens in it. Then in a second paragraph, ask yourself: what, *besides* the element of story, did you consider in order to understand the poem?

5. Think of someone you know (or someone you can imagine) whose attitude toward poetry in general is one of dislike. Suggest a poem for that person to read—a poem that you like—and, addressing your skeptical reader, point out whatever you find to enjoy in it, something that you think the skeptic just might enjoy too.

Topics for More Extensive Papers (600–1,000 words)

1. Write an explication of a poem short enough for you to work through line by line—for instance, Dickinson's "My Life had stood – a Loaded Gun" or Stevie Smith's "Not Waving But Drowning," or Frost's "Nothing Gold Can Stay." As if offering your reading experience to a friend who hasn't read the poem before, try to point out all the leading difficulties you encountered and set forth in detail your understanding of any lines that contain such difficulties.

2. Write an explication of a longer poem—for instance, Eliot's "The Love Song of J. Alfred Prufrock," Hardy's "The Convergence of the Twain," Plath's "Lady Lazarus," or Stevens's "Peter Quince at the Clavier." Although you will not be able to go through every line of the poem, explain what you think most needs explaining.

3. In this book you will find numerous poems by each of these poets: Auden, Blake, Dickinson, Donne, Eliot, Frost, Hardy, Hopkins, Hughes, Keats, Cummings, Shakespeare, Stevens, Tennyson, Whitman, William Carlos Williams, Wordsworth, and Yeats; and multiple selections for many more. After you read a few poems by a poet who interests you, write an analysis of *more than one* of the poet's poems. To do this, you need to select one characteristic theme (or

other element) to deal with—something typical of the poet's work not found only in a single poem. Here are a few specific topics for such an analysis:

> Love and Loss in Alfred, Lord Tennyson's Poetry
>
> The Cost of Achieving Individual Identity: The Work of Adrienne Rich
>
> How Emily Dickinson's Lyrics Resemble Hymns
>
> The Humor of Robert Frost
>
> Folk Elements in the Poetry of Langston Hughes
>
> John Keats's Sensuous Imagery
>
> The Vocabulary of Music in Poems of Wallace Stevens
>
> Non-free Verse: Patterns of Sound in Three Poems of William Carlos Williams

4. Compare and contrast two poems in order to evaluate them. Which is more satisfying and effective poetry? To make a meaningful comparison, be sure to choose two poems that genuinely have much in common, perhaps a similar theme or subject. (For an illustration of such a paper, see the one given in this chapter. For suggestions of poems to compare, see "Poems for Further Reading.")

5. Evaluate by the method of comparison two versions of a poem, one an early draft and one a late draft, or perhaps two translations from another language. For parallel versions to work on, see Chapter 26, "Translation."

6. If the previous topic appeals to you, consider this. In 1912, twenty-four years before he published "Design," Robert Frost sent a correspondent this early version:

IN WHITE

A dented spider like a snow drop white
On a white Heal-all, holding up a moth
Like a white piece of lifeless satin cloth—
Saw ever curious eye so strange a sight?—
Portent in little, assorted death and blight   5
Like ingredients of a witches' broth?—
The beady spider, the flower like a froth,
And the moth carried like a paper kite.

What had that flower to do with being white,
The blue prunella every child's delight.   10
What brought the kindred spider to that height?
(Make we no thesis of the miller's plight.)
What but design of darkness and of night?
Design, design! Do I use the word aright?

Compare "In White" with "Design." In what respects is the finished poem superior?

Topics for Long Papers (1,500 words or more)

1. Write a line-by-line explication of a poem rich in matters to explain or of a longer poem that offers ample difficulty. While relatively short, Donne's "A Valediction: Forbidding Mourning" or Hopkins's "The Windhover" are poems that will take a good bit of time to explicate. Even a short, apparently simple poem such as Frost's "Stopping by Woods on a Snowy Evening" can provide more than enough to explicate thoughtfully in a longer paper.

2. Write an analysis of the work of one poet (as suggested above, in the third topic for more extensive papers) in which you go beyond this book to read an entire collection of that poet's work.

3. Write an analysis of a certain theme (or other element) that you find in the work of two or more poets. It is probable that in your conclusion you will want to set the poets' work side by side, comparing or contrasting it, and perhaps making some evaluation. Sample topics include:

   Langston Hughes, Gwendolyn Brooks, and Dudley Randall as Prophets of Social Change

   What It Is to Be a Woman: The Special Knowledge of Sylvia Plath, Anne Sexton, and Adrienne Rich

   Popular Culture as Reflected in the Poetry of Wendy Cope, Michael B. Stillman, Gene Fehler, and Charles Martin

   The Complex Relations Between Fathers and Sons in the Poetry of Robert Hayden, Andrew Hudgins, and Robert Phillips

   Making Up New Words for New Meanings: Neologisms in Lewis Carroll and Kay Ryan

4. Select one of the "Writer's Perspectives" that are found at the end of each chapter, and use the ideas it contains to cast light on a poem by the same author. Do Frost's ideas on metaphors seem consistent with his own poetic practice? How do Ezra Pound's comments on imagery help us read his poems?

43 *Writing About a Play*

METHODS

How is writing about a play any different from writing about a short story or a poem? Differences will quickly appear if you are writing about a play you have actually seen performed. Although, like a story or a poem, a play in print is usually the work of one person (and it is relatively fixed and changeless), a play on stage may be the joint effort of seventy or eighty people—actors, director, costumers, set designers, and technicians—and in its many details it may change from season to season, or even from night to night. Later in this chapter, you will find some advice on reviewing a performance of a play, as you might do for a class assignment or for publication in, say, a campus newspaper. But in a literature course, for the most part, you will probably write about the plays you quietly read and behold only in the theater of your mind. At least one advantage in writing about a printed play is that you can always go back and reread it, unlike the reviewer who, unless provided with a script, has nothing but memory to rely on.

Before you begin to write, it makes sense to read the *whole* play—not just the dialogue but also everything in italics: descriptions of scenes, instructions to the actors, and other stage directions. This point may seem obvious, but the meaning of a scene, or even of an entire play, may depend on the tone of voice in which an actor is supposed to deliver a line. At the end of *A Doll's House,* for example, we need to pay attention to what Ibsen tells the actor playing Helmer—*"With sudden hope"*—if we are to understand that, when Nora departs, she ignores Helmer's last desperate hope for a reconciliation and slams the door emphatically. And of course there is a resounding meaning in the final stage direction—*"The heavy sound of a door being slammed is heard from below."*

Taking notes on passages you will want to quote or refer to in your paper, you can use a concise method for keeping track of them. If you are reading a play in verse, jot down the numbers of act, scene, and line—for instance: 1.2.42. Later, when you write, this handy shorthand will save space, and you can use the MLA format to indicate the exact lines you are quoting or referring to:

Iago's hypocrisy, apparent in his famous defense of
his good name (3.3.168-74), is aptly summed up by
Roderigo, who accuses him: "Your words and
performances are no kin together" (4.2.188-89).

Any of the methods frequently applied in writing about fiction and poetry—explication, analysis, comparison and contrast—can serve in writing about a play. All three methods are discussed in "Writing About a Story," and again in "Writing About a Poem." (For student papers that illustrate explication, see pages 2132 and 2149; analysis, pages 2136 and 2154; comparison and contrast, page 2158.) Here are a few suggestions for using these methods to write about plays in particular.

A whole play is too much to cover in an ordinary **explication**—a detailed, line-by-line unfolding of meaning. For example, an explication of *Othello* could take years. A more reasonable class assignment would be to explicate a single key speech or passage from a play, such as Iago's description of a "deserving woman" (*Othello*, II, i, 148–158); or the first chorus in *Oedipus the King*.

If you decide to write an essay by the method of **comparison and contrast** (two methods, actually, but they usually work together), you might set two plays side by side and point out their similarities and differences. Again, watch out: do not bite off more than you can chew. A profound topic—"The Self-Deceptions of Othello and Oedipus"—might do for a three-hundred-page dissertation, but an essay of a mere thousand words could treat it only sketchily. Probably the dual methods of comparison and contrast are most useful for a long term paper on a large but finite topic: "Attitudes Toward Marriage in *A Doll's House* and *Trifles*." In a shorter paper, you might confine your comparing and contrasting to the same play: "Willy's and Biff's Illusions in *Death of a Salesman*."

For writing about drama, **analysis** (a separation into elements) is an especially useful method. You can consider just one element in a play, and so your topic tends to be humanly manageable—"Animal Imagery in Some Speeches from *Othello*," or "The Theme of Fragility in *The Glass Menagerie*." Not all plays, however, contain every element you might find in fiction and poetry. Unlike a short story or a novel, for example, a play does not ordinarily have a narrator. In most plays, the point of view is that of the audience, who sees the events not through some narrator's eyes but through its own.[1] Furthermore, though it is usual for a short story to be written in an all-pervading style, some plays seem written in as many styles as there are speaking

---

[1]Point of view in drama is a study in itself; this mere mention grossly simplifies the matter. Some playwrights attempt to govern what the spectator sees, trying to make the stage become the mind of a character. An obvious example is the classic German film *The Cabinet of Dr. Caligari*, in which the scenery is distorted as though perceived by a lunatic. Some plays contain characters who act as narrators, directly addressing the audience in much the way that first-person narrators in fiction often address the reader. In Tennessee Williams's *The Glass Menagerie*, Tom Wingfield behaves as such a narrator, introducing scenes, commenting on the action. The Stage Manager in Thornton Wilder's *Our Town* (1938) actually addresses the audience directly, but such a character in a play does not alter our angle of vision, our physical point of view.

characters. (You might also argue that in Susan Glaspell's *Trifles* both main characters speak the same language.) Traditional poetic devices, such as rime schemes and metrical patterns, are seldom found in contemporary plays, which tend to sound like ordinary conversation. To be sure, some plays *are* written in poetic forms, for example, the blank verse of the greater portion of *Othello*. Nevertheless, despite whatever some plays may lack, most have more than enough elements for analysis, including characters, themes, tone, irony, imagery, figures of speech, symbols, myths, and conventions.

Ready to begin writing an analysis of a play, you might think at first that one element—the plot—ought to be particularly easy to detach from the rest and write about. But beware. In a good play (as in a good novel or short story), plot and character and theme are likely to be one, not perfectly simple to tell apart. Besides, if in your essay you were to summarize the events in the play and then stop, you wouldn't tell your readers much that they couldn't observe for themselves just by reading the play or by seeing it. In a meaningful, informative analysis, the writer does not merely isolate an element but also shows how it functions within its play and why it is necessary to the whole.

HOW TO QUOTE A PLAY

To quote from a play, you should use the same guidelines as for quoting prose or poetry (see the chapters "Writing About Literature" and "Writing About a Poem"). When you are quoting an extended section or dialogue that involves more than one character, set the passage off from the body of your paper using the following format:

1. Indent one inch (or ten spaces).
2. Type the character's names in all capitals, followed by a period.
3. Indent any additional lines in the same character's speech an additional one-quarter inch (or three spaces on a typewriter).
4. Provide a citation reference (and if the play is written in prose, a page number).

Here is an example of that format:

```
The men never find a motive for the murder because,

ironically, they consider all the real clues

"trifles" that don't warrant their attention:

          SHERIFF. Well, can you beat the women! Held

              for murder and worryin' about her

          preserves.

          COUNTY ATTORNEY. I guess before we're

              through she may have something more

              serious than preserves to worry about.
```

```
                    HALES. Well, women are used to worrying over

                        trifles. (1308)
```

If you are quoting a *verse* play, however, the rules for citing poetry should be observed. Be careful to respect the line breaks. For citation references, use the act, scene, and line numbers. This helps readers find your quotation in any edition of the play. Here is an example of a quotation from Shakespeare's *Othello* using the MLA format:

```
Even before her death, Othello will not confront

Desdemona with his specific suspicions:

        OTHELLO. Think on thy sins.

        DESDEMONA.                    They are loves I bear to you.

        OTHELLO. Ay, and for that thou diest.

        DESDEMONA. That death's unnatural that kills for loving.

          Alas, why gnaw you so your nether lip?

          Some bloody passion shakes your very frame.

          These are portents; but yet I hope, I hope,

          They do not point on me. (5.2.42-48)
```

WRITING A CARD REPORT

Instead of an essay, some instructors like to assign a **card report.** If asked to write a card report on a play, you will find yourself writing a kind of analysis. To do so, you first single out elements of a play and then list them on 5- × 8-inch index cards as concisely as possible. Such an exercise is often assigned in a class studying fiction; and one student's card report on the Edgar Allan Poe story, "The Tell-Tale Heart," appears on page 2140. When you deal with a play, however, you need to include some elements different from those in a short story. And because a full-length play may take more room to summarize than a short story, your instructor may suggest that, if necessary, you take two cards (four sides) for your report. Still, in order to write a good card report, you have to be both brief and specific. Before you start, sort out your impressions of the play and try to decide which characters, scenes, and lines of dialogue are the most important and memorable. Reducing your scattered impressions to essentials, you will have to reexamine what you have read. When you finish, you will know the play much more thoroughly.

Here is an example: a card report on Susan Glaspell's one-act play *Trifles*. (For the play itself, see page 1305.) By including only the elements that seemed most important, the writer managed to analyze the brief play on the front and back of one card. Still, he managed to work in a few pertinent quotations to give a sense of the play's remarkable language. Although the report does not say everything about Glaspell's little masterpiece, an adequate criticism of the play could hardly be much briefer. For this report, the writer was assigned to include:

1. The playwright's name, nationality, and dates.
2. The title of the play and the date of its first performance.
3. The central character or characters, with a brief description that includes leading traits.
4. Other characters, also described.
5. The scene or scenes and, if the play does not take place in the present, the time of its action.
6. The dramatic question. This question is whatever the play leads us to ask ourselves: some conflict whose outcome we wonder about, some uncertainty to whose resolution we look forward. (For a more detailed discussion of dramatic questions, see page 1319.)
7. A brief summary of the play's principal events, in the order in which the playwright presents them. If you are reporting on a play longer than *Trifles*, you may find it simplest to sum up what happens in each act, perhaps in each scene.
8. The tone of the play, as best you can detect it. Try to describe the playwright's apparent feelings toward the characters or what happens to them.
9. The language spoken in the play: try to describe it. Does any character speak with a choice of words or with figures of speech that strike you as unusual, distinctive, poetic—or maybe dull and drab? Does language indicate a character's background or place of birth? Brief quotations, in what space you have, will be valuable.
10. In a sentence, try to sum up the play's central theme. If you find none, say so. Plays often contain more than one theme. Which of them seems most clearly borne out by the main events?
11. Any symbols you notice and believe to matter. Try to state in a few words what each suggests.
12. A concise evaluation of the play: what did you think of it? (For more suggestions on being a drama critic, see "Evaluating a Play.")

The card report on *Trifles* begins on the following page.

Front of Card

Susan Glaspell, American, 1882-1948   <u>Trifles</u>, 1916

    <u>Central characters</u>: Mrs. Peters, the sheriff's nervous wife, dutiful but independent, not "married to the law"-- whose sorrows make her able to sympathize with a woman accused of murder. Mrs. Hale, who knows the accused; more decisive.

    <u>Other characters</u>: The County Attorney, self-important but short-sighted. The Sheriff, a man of only middling intelligence, another sexist. Hale, a farmer, a cautious man. Not seen on stage, two others are central: Minnie (Foster) Wright, the accused, a music lover reduced to near despair by years of grim marriage and isolation; and John Wright, the victim, known for his cruelty.

    <u>Scene</u>: The kitchen of a gloomy farmhouse after the arrest of a wife on suspicion of murder; little things left in disarray.

    <u>Major dramatic question</u>: Why did Minnie Wright kill her husband? When this question is answered, a new major dramatic question is raised: Will Mrs. Peters and Mrs. Hale cover up incriminating evidence?

    <u>Events</u>: In the exposition, Sheriff and C.A., investigating the death of Wright, hear Hale tell how he found the body and a distracted Mrs. Wright. Then (1) C.A. starts looking for a motive. (2) His jeering at Mrs. Wright (and all women) for their concern with "trifles" cause Mrs. Peters and Mrs. Hale to rally to the woman's defense.

[continued on back of card]

[Events, continued] (3) When the two women find evidence that Mrs. Wright had panicked (a patch of wild sewing in a quilt), Mrs. Hale destroys it. (4) Mrs. Peters finds more evidence: a wrecked birdcage. (5) The women find a canary with its neck wrung and realize that Minnie killed her husband in a similar way. (6) The women align themselves with Minnie when Mrs. Peters recalls her own sorrows, and Mrs. Hale decides her own failure to visit Minnie was "a crime." (7) The C.A. unwittingly provides Mrs. Peters with a means to smuggle out the canary. (8) The two women unite to seize the evidence.

Tone: Made clear in the women's dialogue: mingled horror and sadness at what has happened, compassion for a fellow woman, smoldering resentment toward men who crush women.

Language: The plain speech of farm people, with a dash of rural Midwestern slang (red-up for tidy; Hale's remark that the accused was "kind of done up"). Unschooled speech: Mrs. Hale says ain't--and yet her speech rises at moments to simple poetry: "She used to sing. He killed that too." Glaspell hints the self-importance of the County Attorney by his heavy reliance on the first person.

Central theme: Women, in their supposed concern for trifles, see more deeply than men do.

Symbols: The broken birdcage and the dead canary, both suggesting the music and the joy that John Wright stifled in Minnie.

Evaluation: A powerful, successful, realistic play that conveys its theme with great economy--in its views, more than seventy years ahead of its time.

Reviewing a Play

Writing a **play review,** a brief critical account of an actual performance, involves making an evaluation. To do so, you first have to decide what to evaluate: the work of the playwright; the work of the actors, director, and production staff; or the work of both. If the play is some classic of Shakespeare or Ibsen, evidently the more urgent task for a reviewer is not to evaluate the playwright's work but to evaluate the success of the actors, director, and production staff in interpreting it. To be sure, a reviewer's personal feelings toward a play (even a towering classic) may deserve mention. Writing of an Ibsen masterpiece, the critic H. L. Mencken made the memorable comment that, next to being struck down by a taxicab and having his hat smashed, he could think of no worse punishment than going to another production of *Rosmersholm*. However, a newer, less well-known play is probably more in need of evaluation.

To judge a live performance is, in many ways, more of a challenge than to judge a play read in a book. Obviously there is much to consider besides the playwright's script: acting, direction, costumes, sets, lighting, perhaps music, anything else that contributes to one's total experience in the theater. Still, many students find that to write a play review is more stimulating—and even more fun—than most writing assignments. Although the student with experience in acting or in stagecraft may be a more knowing reviewer than the student without such experience, the latter may prove just as capable in responding to a play and in judging it fairly and perceptively.

In the chapter "Evaluating a Play," we assumed that in order to judge a play, one has to understand it and be aware of its conventions. (For a list of things to consider in judging a play, see "Writing Critically" on page 1893.) Some plays evoke a strong positive or negative response in the reviewer, either at once or by the time the final curtain tumbles; others need to be pondered. Incidentally, harsh evaluations sometimes tempt a reviewer to flashes of wit. One celebrated flash is Eugene Field's observation of an actor in a production of *Hamlet*, that "he played the king as though he were in constant fear that somebody else was going to play the ace." The comment isn't merely nasty; it implies that Field had closely watched the actor's performance and had discerned what was wrong with it. Readers, of course, have a right to expect that reviewers do not just sneer (or gush praise) but clearly set forth reasons for their feelings.

Reviewing plays is an act with few fixed rules, but a competent critic usually tries to include at least the following information somewhere in the review:

1. *The basic facts.* Give the play's title and author, the theatrical company producing it, and the theater in which it is performed.
2. *A brief plot summary.* Tell a reader unacquainted with the play what it is generally about.
3. *An evaluation of the chief actors.* Name the actors playing the principal roles, and comment on the quality of their performance.

A good reviewer will, of course, want to go far beyond these few fundamentals. If the play is unfamiliar, it is also helpful to summarize its theme. If the play is familiar and often performed, some comment on the director's whole approach to it may be useful. Is the production exactly what you'd expect, or are there any fresh and apparently original innovations? If the production is fresh, does it achieve its freshness by violating the play? (The director of one college production of *Othello*—a fresh, but not entirely successful, innovation—emphasized the play's being partly set in Venice by staging it in the campus swimming pool, with actors floating about on barges and a homemade gondola.) Does the play seem firmly directed, so that the actors neither lag nor hurry and so that they speak and gesture not in an awkward, stylized manner, but naturally? Are they well cast? Usually, also, a reviewer pays attention to the costumes, sets, and lighting, if these are noteworthy. And if the reviewer has not been making clear an opinion of the play and its production all along, an opinion will probably come in the concluding paragraph.

For further pointers, read a few professional play reviews in magazines such as the *New Yorker, Time, Newsweek*, the *New Criterion, American Theatre*, and others; or on the entertainment pages of a metropolitan newspaper. Here is a good, concise review of an amateur production of *Trifles* as it might be written for a college newspaper. It is similar to what your instructor might ask you to write for a course assignment.

Trifles Scores Mixed Success in Monday Players' Production

Women have come a long way since 1916. At least, that impression was conveyed yesterday when the Monday Players presented Susan Glaspell's classic one-act play Trifles in Alpaugh Theater.

At first, in Glaspell's taut story of two subjugated farm women who figure out why a fellow farm woman strangled her husband, Lloyd Fox and Cal Federicci get to strut around. As a small-town sheriff and a county attorney, they lord it over the womenfolk, making sexist remarks about women in general. Fox and Federicci obviously enjoy themselves as the pompous types that Glaspell means them to be.

But of course it is the women with their keen eyes for small details who prove the superior detectives. In the demanding roles of the two Nebraska Miss Marples, Kathy Betts and Ruth Fine cope as best they can with what is asked of them. Fine is especially convincing. As Mrs. Hale, a friend of the wife accused of the murder, she projects a growing sense of independence. Visibly smarting under the verbal lashes of the menfolk, she seems to straighten her spine inch by inch as the play goes on.

Unluckily for Betts, director Alvin Klein seems determined to view Mrs. Peters as a comedian. Though Glaspell's stage directions call the woman "nervous," I doubt she is supposed to be quite so fidgety as Betts makes her. Betts vibrates like a tuning fork every time a new clue turns up, and when obliged to smell a dead canary bird (another clue), you would think she was whiffing a dead hippopotamus. Mrs. Peters, whose sad past includes a lost baby and a kitten some maniac chopped up with a hatchet, is no figure of fun to my mind. Played for laughs, her character fails to grow visibly on stage, as Fine makes Mrs. Hale grow.

Klein, be it said in his favor, makes the quiet action proceed at a brisk pace. Feminists in the audience must have been a little embarrassed, though, by his having Betts and Fine deliver every speech defending women in an extra-loud voice. After all, Glaspell makes her points clear enough just by showing us what she shows. Not everything is overstated, however. As a farmer who found the murder victim, Cal Valdez acts his part with quiet authority.

Despite flaws in its direction, this powerful play still spellbinds an audience. Anna Winterbright's set, seen last week as a background for _Dracula_ and just slightly touched up, provides appropriate gloom.

SUGGESTIONS FOR WRITING

Finding a topic you care to write about is, of course, the most important step toward writing a valuable paper. (For some general advice on topic finding, see page 2122.) The following list of suggestions is not meant to replace your own ideas but to stimulate them.

Topics for Brief Papers (250–500 words)

1. When the curtain comes down on the conclusion of some plays, the audience is left to decide exactly what finally happened. In a short informal essay, state your interpretation of the conclusion of one of these plays: _The Sound of a Voice, Andre's Mother, The Glass Menagerie, Joe Turner's Come and Gone_. Don't just give a plot summary; tell what you think the conclusion means.

2. Sum up the main suggestions you find in one of these meaningful objects (or actions): the handkerchief in _Othello_; the Christmas tree in _A Doll's House_ (or Nora's doing a wild tarantella); Willy Loman's planting a garden in _Death of a Salesman_; Laura's collection of figurines in _The Glass Menagerie_.

3. Here is an exercise in being terse. Write a card report on a short, one-scene play (other than _Trifles_), and confine your remarks to both sides of one 5- × 8-inch card. (For further instructions see pages 2170–71.) Possible subjects: _Riders to the Sea, The Sound of a Voice, Andre's Mother_.

4. Review a play you have seen within recent memory and have felt strongly about (for or against). Give your opinion of *either* the performance or the playwright's writing, with reasons for your evaluation.
5. Write an essay entitled "Why I Prefer Plays to Films" (or vice versa). Cite some plays and films to support your argument. (If you have never seen any professional plays, pick some other topic.)

Topics for More Extended Papers (600–1,000 words)

1. From a play you have enjoyed, choose a passage that strikes you as difficult, worth reading closely. Try to pick a passage not longer than about 200 words, or twenty lines. Explicate it, working through it sentence by sentence or line by line. For instance, any of these passages might be considered memorable (and essential to their plays):

> Oedipus to Tiresias, speech beginning, "O power—wealth and empire" (*Oedipus the King*, 432–59).
>
> Iago's soliloquy, "Thus do I ever make my fool my purse" (*Othello*, 1.3.362–83).
>
> Tom Wingfield's opening speech, "Yes, I have tricks in my pocket," through "I think the rest of the play will explain itself. . . ." (*The Glass Menagerie*, Scene I).

2. Take just a single line or sentence from a play—one that stands out for some reason as greatly important. Perhaps it states a theme, reveals a character, or serves as a crisis (or turning point). Write an essay demonstrating its importance—how it functions, why it is necessary. Some possible lines include:

> Iago to Roderigo: "I am not what I am" (*Othello*, 1.1.67).
>
> Amanda to Tom: "You live in a dream; you manufacture illusions!" (*The Glass Menagerie*, Scene VII).
>
> Charley to Biff: "A salesman is got to dream, boy. It comes with the territory" (*Death of a Salesman*, the closing Requiem).

3. Write an essay in analysis, in which you single out an element of a play for examination—character, plot, setting, theme, dramatic irony, tone, language, symbolism, conventions, or any other element. Try to relate this element to the play as a whole. Sample topics: "The Function of Tiresias in *Oedipus the King*," "Imagery of Poison in *Othello*," "Irony in *Antigone*," "Williams's Use of Magic-Lantern Slides in *The Glass Menagerie*," "The Theme of Success in *Death of a Salesman*," "Magic in *Joe Turner's Come and Gone*."

4. Compare a character, situation, or theme in a play with a similar element in a short story. For instance: women's role in society as seen in *Trifles* and in Tillie Olsen's "I Stand Here Ironing"; "The Ocean as an Opponent in *Riders to the Sea* and Stephen Crane's 'The Open Boat.'"

5. Imagine a completely different ending for a play you have read, one that especially interests you. Briefly summarize the new resolution you have in

mind. Then, looking back over the play's earlier scenes, tell what would happen to the rest of the play if it were to acquire this new ending. What else would need to be changed? What, if anything, does this exercise reveal?

6. In an essay, consider how you would go about staging a play of Shakespeare, Sophocles, or some other classic, in modern dress, with sets representing the world of today. What problems would you face? Can such an attempt ever succeed?

Topics for Long Papers (1,500 words or more)

1. Choosing any of the works in "New Voices in American Drama" or taking some other modern or contemporary play your instructor suggests, report any difficulties you encountered in reading and responding to it. Explicate any troublesome passages for the benefit of other readers.

2. Compare and contrast two plays—a play in this book and another play by the same author—with attention to one element. For instance: "The Theme of Woman's Independence in Ibsen's *A Doll's House* and *Hedda Gabler*"; "Antirealism in the Stagecraft of Tennessee Williams: *The Glass Menagerie* and *Camino Real*"; or "Christian Symbols and Allusions in Williams's *Menagerie* and *Night of the Iguana*."

3. Compare and contrast in *The Glass Menagerie* and *Death of a Salesman* the elements of dream life and fantasy.

4. For at least a month, keep a journal of your experiences in watching drama on stage, on a movie screen, or on television. Make use of any skills you have learned from your reading and study of plays, and try to demonstrate how you have become a more critical and perceptive member of the viewing audience.

5. If you have ever acted or taken part in staging plays, consult with your instructor and see whether you both find that your experience could enable you to write a substantial paper. With the aid of specific recollections, perhaps, you might sum up what you have learned about the nature of drama or about what makes a play effective.

6. Watch a film version of a play, and then read the original as produced on stage. What differences do you find, and how do you account for them? You might, for instance, compare one of the film versions of *Hamlet* with Shakespeare's original, or Ibsen's *A Doll's House* with any of its movie adaptations.

44 *Writing a Research Paper*

DOING RESEARCH FOR AN ESSAY

For short essays, students are usually asked simply to explore their own responses to a work of literature. This task requires thought and reflection, but doesn't demand research. Many people do their best thinking while walking—in nature, in a park, or even just across campus. Imagine, then, that your initial reaction to a story or poem draws you into the quiet forest of your own deepest insights. That's a valuable place, where epiphanies can occur. Carefully note down those thoughts in your reading journal for they will form the creative core of your essay

Later, when a research paper is assigned, you will need to step from the forest of your own reflections into the clearing where other minds meet. That clearing is usually your school's library, though it may be a virtual space visited via your computer's Internet connection. Once in that place where thoughts are shared via published work, you will need to find, read, and assimilate published material that expands and corroborates some aspect of your gut reaction to a piece of literature.

How to Get Started

Unfortunately for novice researchers, sometimes the first material uncovered in the library or on the Internet isn't the desired evidence needed to support a main idea. Worse, you may find your idea has already been examined a dozen times over. Like Odysseus, tie yourself to the mast so that when you hear the siren voices of published professors, you can listen without abandoning your own point of view. Your idea may have been treated, but not yet by you—your particular take on a topic is bound to be different from someone else's. After all, thousands of books have been written on Shakespeare's plays, and there are still new things to say.

Don't forget that the ideal research paper is still based on your *own* observations and interpretations of a literary text. You come up with the point you want to support with research, and then you find the material that will help you demonstrate its plausibility. Of course, sometimes you will find that certain ideas are unworkable. There may be a flaw in your initial observation based on something you didn't know about the context of the piece or its author. For example, perhaps you read William Butler Yeats's poem "Who Goes With Fergus?" and assumed that "brazen cars" were pink Cadillacs and "the white breast of the dim sea" was that huge, white, gelatinous sea creature recently found off the coast of Chile. Obviously, if you then try to write a paper about Yeats's poem in light of phat rides and freaky sea creatures, you won't get anything for your pains but a hysterically laughing instructor who might give your paper an "F" for "Funny."

In the beginning, your research will show you both where you might have misinterpreted and how others have treated your idea. Of course, it is annoying to find that you may be wrong about something, or that someone else has taken off with what you thought was your original argument, but don't let these discoveries put you off. Now you're getting to the vexed center of your subject, and soon you will be able to compare your own ideas against the others and use some of those seemingly similar arguments to refine your thoughts. It is always a good idea to concede the presence of other ideas as you sharpen your own. For example, you may have noticed something strange about the body of Arnold Friend in Joyce Carol Oates's story "Where Are You Going, Where Have You Been?" Perhaps you noticed he has trouble standing in his shoes and you want to explore that odd detail. If you do some research on this character, you may find Arnold Friend referred to as the devil (who has cloven hoofs and hence might have problems with standard-issue cowboy boots), or as the wolf in "Little Red Riding Hood" (also a character not accustomed to standing on his hind legs in human clothes). At that point you may think, "Okay, my idea is shot. Everyone has written about this aspect of the Oates character." Well, just sharpen your focus. Can you think of other stories that deal with potentially supernatural characters, possibly evil ones? What about "Young Goodman Brown"? Or Flannery O'Connor's "A Good Man Is Hard to Find"? How might you compare Arnold Friend with Hawthorne's devil or O'Connor's Misfit?

Or perhaps it is the general topic of physical abnormalities in literature that really intrigues you. You might explore what descriptions of unusual characteristics have to say about human perception, about outer and inner selves, appearance and reality. Several works in this book treat characters that, in one way or another, are unusual. Compare them to Arnold Friend, or find some articles on typical human responses to physical differences in a few popular psychology journals and see where that takes you. Your initial idea is always the most important one you will have because it is your purest response to the work you have read, but sometimes it is only the jumping-off point to other ideas, an indicator of a more general topic that you will focus on and refine in your paper.

Notecards

Once you have done a little initial research—enough to refine your topic to one that you can usefully pursue in a research paper, start taking notes on everything you are reading that relates to your topic. One method of taking notes is to write on index cards—the 3- × 5-inch kind for brief notes and titles, 5- × 8-inch cards for longer notes. Write on one side only; notes on the back of a card are often later overlooked. Cards are easy to shuffle and order, and will help you better organize your material. To save work, instead of copying on a card the title and author of a book you're taking a note on, just keep a numbered list of the books you're using. Then, when making a note, you need write only the book's identifying number and page references on the card in order to identify your source.

You can organize your notes based on the books you're taking them from, or by the theme you are exploring. However, whichever method you choose, be sure you keep track of the source of all quoted material. Certainly, it is easier to take notes while you read than to have to run back to the library during the final typing. Bear in mind the cautionary tale of historian Doris Kearns Goodwin. She was charged with plagiarizing sections of two of her famous books when her words were found to be jarringly similar to those published in other books. She was forced to admit that the plagiarism occurred because she had not clearly marked on her notecards what were her own ideas and words and what were comments from other sources. Goodwin's once enormous reputation is still suffering from these charges, but you can learn from her mistakes and save your own reputation—and your grades.

Photocopying

As photocopy machines are to be found in practically all libraries, you do not need to spend hours copying by hand whole poems and long prose passages. If accuracy is essential (and surely it is), then copying a long poem or prose passage is worth the small investment. Copyright law permits students and scholars to reproduce a single copy in this fashion; it does not, however, permit making a dozen or more copies for public sale. Of course, it is also helpful to make copies of the critical passages you are using from research articles or books—having material from those texts verbatim will help you to accurately quote and cite your sources.

EVALUATING AND USING INTERNET SOURCES

The Internet can be a valuable tool to student researchers. Not only can students access libraries and universities around the world; they can also access countless online publications and Web sites. But it is important to remember that a Web site can be created by anyone with access to a computer and the Internet—no matter how poorly qualified that person might be. Therefore, students must remain analytical or discerning when they enter the World Wide Web or they may find themselves tangled in the spidery threads of a dubious site.

A good place to begin your search is through your own college library. College libraries subscribe to specialized online or CD-ROM database services covering all academic subjects. When searching for articles and books on literary topics, you can also use the *MLA International Bibliography*. If you are not familiar with how to use your library's database system, ask the reference librarian for help—all too often students ignore this primary source of help and leave the library complaining, "I can't find anything on my topic."

Of course, if you are a bit adventurous and want to navigate the Web on your own, you need to make sure that you find reliable sources. Many Internet search engines (e.g., *Yahoo!*) arrange subject directories in a hierarchy, allowing you to go from very general topic areas into more specific ones (e.g., Path: Humanities; Literature; Literary Criticism); this structure *may* be helpful in trying to find a topic on which to write an essay. Remember that if you use general phrases or terms on one of these search engines (e.g., the author's name and the story title), you most likely will get thousands of hits, but only a few of them will be usable sources for a literary research paper. For example, if you enter the phrase CHARLOTTE PERKINS GILMAN'S THE YELLOW WALLPAPER on the search line, you will get Web sites on which you can buy the book, paper assignments that have been posted for classes that use the Internet as a communication tool, and even some listings for stores that sell yellow wallpaper.

A more efficient way to search is by using KEYWORDS to search a specified topic and use the available "advanced" search options (e.g., *Alta Vista*'s "More Precision" search option). When you search using keywords, the results will contain those keywords (LITERARY CRITICISM ON GILMAN'S THE YELLOW WALLPAPER or SYMBOLISM IN HAWTHORNE'S YOUNG GOODMAN BROWN). However, even a keyword search may not provide you with the reputable sources you need, as anyone with Internet access can post a document on the Web. So how do you unlock the Web and gain access to sites that will truly help you to accomplish your task, namely, to write a well-supported literary research paper?

Using Reliable Web Sites and Metapages

One way to increase the likelihood that you will find useful and reliable material on the Web is to begin searching at a reliable Web site. The Library of Congress is an excellent starting point and you don't have to travel to Washington to use it. There are eight alcoves in the Main Reading Room of the Library of Congress, and in recent years they have added a ninth—a virtual alcove that provides an annotated collection of Web sites in the Humanities and Social Sciences Division. For your purpose—writing a literary research paper—access the Subject Index (http://www.loc.gov/rr/main/alcove9/), select "Literature," and then select "Literary Criticism." You will be given a list of metapages and Web sites with collections of critical and biographical material on authors and their works. (A metapage is a page that provides links to other Web sites.)

There are Web-based libraries that are also useful starting points. The *Internet Public Library* (http://www.ipl.org) allows you to search for literary criticism by author, work, country of origin, or literary period. The University of Michigan School of Information and Library Studies started the Internet Public Library in 1995, and it maintains the site. *Library Spot* (http://www.libraryspot.com) is a portal to over 5,000 libraries around the world, periodicals, online texts, reference works, and links to metapages and Web sites on any topic including literary criticism. It is a carefully maintained library site published by Start Spot Mediaworks, Inc., in the North-western University/Evanston Research Park in Evanston, Illinois.

The *Voice of the Shuttle* (http://www.vos.ucsb.edu/) is another useful Web site for the literary researcher. Here you will find research links in over 25 categories in the Humanities and Social Sciences, including online texts, libraries, academic Web sites, and metapages. The site was developed and is maintained by Dr. Alan Liu of the English Department of the University of California, Santa Barbara.

All the Web sites mentioned here are reliable points from which to begin your research. (You should be aware that some journals and university Web sites might not be fully accessible to you from home and might require access through your college library's Internet database connection.) When you follow the links posted on reliable sites, you should access trustworthy material. Of course the ultimate determination of whether a source is reliable falls to you—and you need to know how to make that determination.

Putting Sources to the Test

When evaluating any Web site, the first thing to look for is AUTHORSHIP or SPONSOR-SHIP of the site. Is the author/sponsor known to you or reputable by association? Is contact information provided on the site? A government or university-sponsored site is considered to be reliable. We can contact them via e-mail, U.S. mail, or telephone. When you access a book excerpt or article in a periodical, you should also look closely at the information provided on the author. Is this someone known for expertise in the field? Are the author's academic or association credentials presented?

DATE OF PUBLICATION could be another important factor to consider when deciding on the suitability of an online document. In some cases you may want to base your essay on the most current literary theory, and so will want to use the most recently published material. Always check for a publication date. If the document lists an edition number, make sure that you are using the latest edition of the material.

When using periodicals, consider the TITLE OF THE MAGAZINE OR JOURNAL. Is it an academic journal or a popular magazine? What type of reputation does it have? Obviously, you do not want to use a magazine that periodically reports on Elvis sightings and alien births. And you most likely will want to limit your use of popular magazines in favor of scholarly journals published to enhance the study of literature.

If you need help in analyzing Internet sources, there are several good Web sites that offer support. Cornell University has two good documents posted: "Critically Analyzing Information Sources" (<http://www.library.cornell.edu> Path: Research & Subject Guides; Critically Analyzing Information Sources) and "Distinguishing Scholarly Journals from Other Periodicals" (<http://www.library.cornell.edu> Path: Research & Subject Guides; Distinguishing Scholarly Journals from Other Periodicals). The UCLA College Library also provides valuable information: "Thinking Critically about World Wide Web Resources" (<http://www.library.ucla.edu/libraries/college/help/critical/index.htm>) and "Thinking Critically about Discipline-Based World Wide Web Resources" (<http://www/library.ucla.edu/libraries/college/help/critical/discipline.htm>).

GUARDING ACADEMIC INTEGRITY

Papers for Sale Are Papers That "F"ail

Do not be seduced by the apparent ease of cheating by computer. Your Internet searches may turn up several sites that offer term papers to download. (Just as you can find pornography; political propaganda, and questionable get-rich-quick schemes!) These sites will often want money for what they offer, but some will not, happy just to strike a blow against the "oppressive" insistence of English teachers that students learn to think and write.

Plagiarized term papers are an old game: the fraternity file and the "research-assistance" service have been around far longer than the computer. It may seem easy enough to download a paper, put your name at the head of it, and turn it in for an easy grade. Such papers usually stick out like a sore thumb, however, as any writing teacher can tell you. The style will be wrong, the work will not be consistent with other work by the same student in any number of ways, and the teacher will sometimes have seen the same phony paper before. The ease with which electronic texts are reproduced makes it even more likely that the same paper will appear again and again. It is far better to take the "C" or "D" you have earned for your own work, no matter how mediocre, than to try and pass off someone else's work as your own. Even if, somehow, your instructor does not recognize your submission as a plagiarized paper, you have diminished your character through dishonesty and lost an opportunity to learn something on your own.

A Final Word of Warning on Internet Plagiarism

The battle against academic dishonesty, moreover, may now have been won by computer program designers. Professors now can use plagiarism detection services to identify plagiarism. Questionable research papers can even be sent to services (e.g., Turnitin.com, EVE2) that will perform complex searches of the Internet to locate sources of plagiarized material. The research paper will be returned with plagiarized sections annotated and the source URLs documented. The end result—a failing grade on the essay, perhaps a failing grade for the course, and, depending on the policies of your university, the very real possibility of expulsion.

ACKNOWLEDGING AND DOCUMENTING SOURCES

Acknowledging Your Sources

It is essential to give credit to any critics who supplied you with ideas, information, or specific phrases, and to do so properly means being painstaking. To paraphrase a critic, you do more than just rearrange the critic's words and phrases; you translate them into language of your own. Suppose you wish to refer to an insight of Randall Jarrell, who commented as follows on the images of spider, flower, and moth in Robert Frost's poem "Design":

> Notice how the *heal-all*, because of its name, is the one flower in all the
> world picked to be the altar for this Devil's Mass; notice how *holding up* the

moth brings something ritual and hieratic, a ghostly, ghastly formality, to this priest and its sacrificial victim.

It would be incorrect to say, without quotation marks:

```
Frost picks the heal-all as the one flower in all the
world to be the altar for this Devil's Mass. There is
a ghostly, ghastly formality to the spider holding up
the moth, like a priest holding a sacrificial victim.
```

This rewording, although not exactly in Jarrell's language, manages to steal his memorable phrases without giving him credit. Nor is it sufficient just to include Jarrell's essay in the Works Cited list at the end of your paper. If you do, you are still a crook; you merely point to the scene of your crime. What is needed, clearly, is to think through Jarrell's words to the point he is making; and if you want to keep any of his striking phrases (and why not?), put them exactly as he wrote them in quotation marks:

```
As Randall Jarrell points out, Frost portrays the
spider as a kind of priest in a Mass, or Black Mass,
elevating the moth like an object for sacrifice, with
"a ghostly, ghastly formality" (42).
```

To be scrupulous in your acknowledgment, tell where you found your quotation from Jarrell, citing the page reference, as detailed in the next section.

Documenting Your Sources

When you quote from other writers, when you borrow their information, or when you summarize or paraphrase their ideas, make sure you give them their due. Document everything you take. Identify the writer by name; cite not only the very book, magazine, newspaper, pamphlet, letter, or other source you are using, but also the page or pages from which you are quoting.

By so doing, you invite your readers to go to your original source and check up on you. Most readers won't bother, of course, but at least your invitation enlists their confidence. Besides, the duty to document keeps you carefully looking at your sources—and so helps keep your writing accurate and responsible. The latest and most efficient way for writers to document their sources is that recommended in the *MLA Handbook for Writers of Research Papers*, 6th ed. (New York: Mod. Lang. Assn., 2003). In the long run, whether you write a long term paper citing dozens of sources or a short paper citing only three or four, the MLA's advice will save you and your reader time and trouble.

These pointers cannot take the place of the *MLA Handbook* itself, but the gist of the method is this: begin by listing your sources—all the works from which you're going to quote, summarize, paraphrase, or take information. Later on, when you key your paper in finished form, you're going to *end* it with a neat copy of this list (once called a "bibliography," now entitled "Works Cited"). Then, in writing your paper, every time you refer to one of these works, you need give only enough information to help a reader locate it under "Works Cited." Usually, you can just give (in parentheses) an author's last name and a page citation. If you were writing, for example, a paper on Weldon Kees's sonnet "For My Daughter" and wanted to include an observation from Samuel Maio's book *Creating Another Self*, you would incorporate the information right in the text of your paper, most often at the end of a sentence:

```
One critic has observed that the distinctive tone of

"For My Daughter" depends on Kees's combination of

personal subject matter with an impersonal voice

(Maio 123).
```

If you wanted to cite *two* books or magazine articles by Maio in your paper, how would the reader tell them apart? In your text, condense the title of each book or article into a word or two. Remember that condensed book titles are also underlined or italicized, and condensed article titles are still placed within quotation marks:

```
One critic has observed that the distinctive tone of

"For My Daughter" depends on Kees's combination of

personal subject matter with an impersonal voice

(Maio, Creating 123).
```

If you have already mentioned the name of the author in your sentence, you need give only the page number when you refer to the source:

```
As Samuel Maio has observed, Kees creates a

distinctive tone in this sonnet by combining a

personal subject with an impersonal voice (123).
```

If you wanted to quote more than four lines, you should set it off from the body of your paper. Start a new line; indent one inch (or ten typewriter spaces); type the quote, double-spaced. After the period at the end of the quotation, put the page reference in parentheses. You do not need to use quotation marks.

Samuel Maio made an astute observation about the
nature of Kees's distinctive tone:

> Kees has therefore combined a personal
> subject matter with an impersonal voice--
> that is, one that is consistent in its tone
> evenly recording the speaker's thoughts
> without showing any emotional intensity
> which might lie behind those thoughts. (123)

The beauty of this documentation method is that you don't have to stop the flow of your thought with a detailed footnote identifying your source. At the end of your paper, in your list of works cited, your reader can find a fuller description of your source—in this case, a critical book:

> Maio, Samuel. *Creating Another Self: Voice in Modern*
> *American Personal Poetry*. Kirksville, MO: Thomas
> Jefferson UP, 1995.

Documentation may seem tedious, but rest assured, your instructor simply wants to smooth the path between your paper and your interested readers. Documenting sources may look arcane, but it is really simple and logical: it's not for your benefit, it's for someone else reading your paper who wants to pursue a topic that you have researched. That interested reader resembles you when you were first in the library searching for material—he or she wants to find all the cited sources that relate to their own particular interest in the subject under scrutiny. Your paper is kindly providing the necessary information for that reader to track down those sources. In the community of researchers, this is not just required—it is common courtesy to one's fellow thinkers.

Works Cited List

At the end of your research paper, you should include a complete list of all the works you have cited. The *MLA Handbook* provides complete instructions for citing a myriad of different types of sources, from books to online databases. Here is a partial checklist of the *Handbook*'s recommendations for presenting such a list.

1. Start a new page for the Works Cited list, and continue the page numbering from the body of your paper.
2. Center the title, "Works Cited," one inch from the top of the page.
3. Double-space between all lines (including after the title and between entries).
4. Type each entry beginning at the left-hand margin. If an entry runs longer than a single line, indent the following lines one-half inch (or five full spaces) from the left-hand margin.

5. Alphabetize each entry according to the author's last name.
6. Include three sections in each entry: author, title, publication or access information. You will, however, give slightly different information for a book, journal article, online source, or other references.

Citing Print Sources

For a book cite:

a. **Author's full name** as it appears on the title page, last name first, followed by a period.

b. **Book's full title** (and subtitle, if it has one, separated by a colon) followed by a period. Remember to underline or italicize the title.

c. **Publication information:** city of publication followed by a colon, the name of the publisher followed by a comma, and the year of publication followed by a period.

(1) **Make your citation of the city of publication brief, but clear.** If the title page lists more than one city, cite only the first. For U.S. cities, you need not provide the state unless the name of the city alone may be confusing or is unfamiliar. For cities outside the United States, add a country abbreviation if the city is unfamiliar. For Canadian cities, use the province abbreviation. (Examples: Rome, GA; Leeds, Eng.; Victoria, BC)

(2) **Shorten the publisher's name.** Eliminate articles (*A, An, The*), business abbreviations (*Co., Corp., Inc., Ltd.*), and descriptive words (*Books, House, Press, Publishers*). The exception is a university press, for which you should use the letters *U* (for University) and *P* (for Press). Use only the first listed *surname* of the publisher. Examples below:

Publisher's Name	Proper Citation
Harvard University Press	Harvard UP
University of Chicago Press	U of Chicago P
Farrar, Straus and Giroux, Inc.	Farrar
Alfred A. Knopf, Inc.	Knopf

The final citation for a book should read:

Author's last name, First name. <u>Book Title</u>. Publication city:
   Publisher, Year.

For a journal article cite:

a. **Author's name,** last name first, followed by a period.

b. **Title of the article,** followed by a period, all within quotation marks.

c. **Publication information:** journal title (underlined or italicized); volume number; the year of publication in parentheses, followed by a colon; and, finally, the inclusive page numbers of the entire article followed by a period.

The final citation for a journal article should read:

```
Author's last name, First name. "Article Title." Journal Volume
     (Year): Pages.
```

If the journal starts the pagination of *each* issue from page one (in contrast to continuous numbering from the previous issue), then you must give both the volume and issue number, with a period between the two. For example, if the article you cite appears in volume 5, issue 2 of such a journal, cite it as 5.2.

```
Author's last name, First name. "Article Title." Journal
     Volume. Issue (Year): Pages.
```

Citing Internet Sources

If you decide to gather source material from the Internet, you must make a careful record of the required bibliographic information for documentation, just as you do for print sources. However, documentation of Internet sources is a bit more complex than it is for print sources. Make a list of the documentation information that you will need *before* you begin your Internet search; recording the information as you go will ensure that you can document a source correctly and find that item on the Web again should you need to do so.

To document an Internet source, you will need the following: author's name when available; title of the document; full information about any previous or simultaneous publication in print form; title of the scholarly project, database, periodical, or professional or personal site; name of the editor of the scholarly project or database; date of electronic publication or last update; name of the institution or organization sponsoring or associated with the site; date when you accessed the source; the Web site address or URL. (Not all the listed information will be available or appropriate for each Internet source—this is a listing of all the possible data you will need for documentation). Many Web sites provide much of this information at the start or end of an article or at the bottom of a Web site home page.

The basic components of any Internet citation are:
    a. **Author's name,** last name first, followed by a period.
    b. **Title of document,** followed by a period, all within quotation marks.
    c. **Print publication information,** if available: title of periodical or book underlined or italicized, volume number and date of publication followed by a period (if page numbers are given, insert a colon followed by the page numbers).

d. **Electronic publication information:** the title of the Web site, underlined or italicized, followed by a period; editor's name or version number if provided, followed by a period; the date of electronic publication or the latest update, followed by a period; the name of any organization or institution sponsoring the site, followed by a period.

e. **Access information:** the date that you viewed the document online, followed by the URL (uniform resource locator) enclosed in angle brackets.

   (1) If the URL is very long and complicated, give the URL for the site's search page. If no specific URL was assigned to the document, give the URL for the site's home page.

   (2) If you accessed a document that does not show a specific URL through a series of links from a Web site's home page, insert the word *Path* followed by a colon after the angle bracket enclosing the URL, and give the title of each link, separating each with a semicolon.

In many cases, not all this information is available for an Internet source. However, when available, the final citation for a document obtained on the Web should read:

```
Author's Last Name, First Name. "Document Title." Print
     Periodical Title Volume (Date of Print Publication): Page
     Numbers. Title of Internet Site. Site Editor. Date of
     Electronic Publication. Web Site Sponsor. Your Access Date
     <URL>.
```

Sample Works Cited List

For a paper on Weldon Kees's "For My Daughter," a student's Works Cited list might look as follows:

```
                          Works Cited
Grosholz, Emily. "The Poetry of Memory." Weldon Kees: A
     Critical Introduction. Ed. Jim Elledge. Metuchen, NJ:
     Scarecrow, 1985. 46-47.
Howard, Ben. "Four Voices." Weldon Kees: A Critical
     Introduction. Ed. Jim Elledge. Metuchen, NJ: Scarecrow,
     1985. 177-79.
Kees, Weldon. The Collected Poems of Weldon Kees. Ed. Donald
     Justice. Lincoln: U of Nebraska P, 1975.
Maio, Samuel. Creating Another Self: Voice in Modern American
     Personal Poetry. Kirksville, MO: Thomas Jefferson UP,
     1995.
```

Nelson, Raymond. "The Fitful Life of Weldon Kees." American
    Literary History 1 (1989): 816-52.
Reidel, James. Vanished Act: The Life and Art of Weldon Kees.
    Lincoln: U of Nebraska P, 2003.
Ross, William T. Weldon Kees. Twayne's US Authors Ser. 484.
    Boston: Twayne, 1985.
Weldon Kees. Ed. James Reidel. 2003. Nebraska Center for
    Writers, Creighton University. 26 Aug. 2004
    <http://mockingbird.creighton.edu/NCW/kees.htm>.
"Weldon Kees." Online Poetry Classroom. 2003. Academy of
    American Poets. 20 Sept. 2004
    <http://www.onlinepoetryclassroom.org/
    poets/poets.cfm?prmID=744>.

See the Reference Guide for Citations at the end of this chapter for additional examples of the types of citations that you are likely to need for your essays or check the 6th edition of the MLA Handbook.

Endnotes and Footnotes

It is imperative to keep the citations and quotations in your text brief and snappy, lest they hinder the flow of your prose. You may wish to append a note supplying a passage of less important (yet possibly valuable) information or making careful qualifying statements ("On the other hand, not every expert agrees. John Binks finds that poets are often a little magazine's only cash customers; while Molly MacGuire maintains that . . ."). If you want to insert such an aside and suspect that you can't put it in your text without awkwardly interrupting your paper, then cast it into an **endnote** (a note placed at the end of a paper), or a **footnote** (a note placed at the bottom of a page).

How do you drop in such notes? The number of each consecutive note comes (following any punctuation) after the last word of a sentence. So that the number will stand out, use the "Insert Footnote" option or create a superscript number from the Font menu in your word-processing program, thus lifting the number slightly above the level of your prose.

as other observers have claimed.[1]

When you use the "Insert Footnote" option in your word-processing program, the formatting and placement of the footnote at the bottom of the page will be done automatically.

[1] John Binks, to name only one such observer,
finds that poets are often . . .

Although now useful mainly for such asides, endnotes and footnotes are time-honored ways to document *all* sources in a research paper. Indeed, some instructors still prefer them to a Works Cited list and ask students to use notes to indicate every writer cited. In a brief paper containing only one or two citations, endnotes or footnotes may be simpler and less showy than a Works Cited list that has only two entries. Once again, always check with your instructor on the preferred style.

The *MLA Handbook* encourages writers to use endnotes rather than footnotes in research papers. Endnotes are listed on a new page at the end of your essay text (number this page in sequence with the previous page). Center the title "Notes" one inch from the top of the page, double-space, and follow this format: indent each entry one-half inch from the left-hand margin, subsequent lines in the entry should begin at the left margin, type the notes consecutively and double-spaced. In notes, the author's first name comes first. (In a list of Works Cited, you put the last name first, so that you can readily arrange your list of authors in alphabetical order.)

An endnote identifying a magazine article looks like this:

16 Louise Horton, "Who Reads Small Literary
Magazines and What Good Do They Do?" Texas Review 9.1
(1984): 108-09.

An endnote referencing a book looks like this:

17 Elizabeth Frank, Louise Bogan: A Portrait (New
York: Knopf, 1985) 59-60.

Should you return later to cite another place in Frank's book, you need not repeat all its information. Just write:

18 Frank 192.

If in your paper you refer to two sources by Elizabeth Frank, give the full title of each in the first note citing it. Then, if you cite it again, use a shortened form of its title:

19 Frank, Bogan 192.

If you do use footnotes to document all your sources, format them as you do endnotes. Begin to type footnotes four lines below the text on your page, *single-spaced*, with the first line indented one-half inch from the left margin and subsequent lines brought to the left margin. Double-space between entries, and indent the first line of each. Two footnotes at the bottom of the page look like this:

[16] Louise Horton, "Who Reads Small Literary Magazines and What Good Do They Do?" Texas Review 9.1 (1984): 108-09.

[17] John Binks, to name only one such observer, finds that poets are often . . .

Sample Student Research Paper—Page 374

Professor Michael Cass of Mercer University asked his class to select the fiction writer on their reading list whose work had seemed most impressive and write a research paper defending that author's claim to literary greatness. See page 374 to read the research essay Stephanie Crowe wrote to fulfill the assignment.

Concluding Thoughts

A well-crafted research essay is a wondrous thing—as delightful, in its own way, as a well-crafted poem or short story or play. Good essays prompt thought and add to knowledge. Writing a research paper sharpens your own mind and exposes you to the honed insights of other thinkers. Think of anything you write as a piece that could be published for the benefit of other people interested in your topic. After all, such a goal is not as far-fetched as it seems: this textbook, for example, features a number of papers written by students. Why shouldn't yours number among them? Aim high.

Reference Guide for Citations

Here is a comprehensive summary of the types of citations you are likely to need for most student papers. The format follows the current MLA standards for Works Cited lists.

Print Publications

Books

No Author Listed

A Keepsake Anthology of the Fiftieth Anniversary Celebration of
    the Consultantship In Poetry. Washington: Library of
    Congress, 1987.

One Author

Middlebrook, Diane Wood. Anne Sexton: A Biography. Boston:
    Houghton, 1991.

Two or Three Authors

Jarman, Mark, and Robert McDowell. The Reaper: Essays.
    Brownsville, OR: Story Line, 1996.

Four or More Authors

Phillips, Rodney, et al. The Hand of the Poet. New York:
    Rizzoli, 1997.

or

Phillips, Rodney, Susan Benesch, Kenneth Benson, and Barbara
    Bergeron. The Hand of the Poet. New York: Rizzoli, 1997.

Two Books by Same Author

Bawer, Bruce. The Aspect of Eternity. St. Paul: Graywolf, 1993.

---. Diminishing Fictions: Essays on the Modern American Novel
    and Its Critics. St. Paul: Graywolf, 1988.

Corporate Author

Poets and Writers. A Writer's Guide to Copyright. New York:
      Poets & Writers, 1979.

Author and Editor

Shakespeare, William. The Sonnets. Ed. G. Blakemore Evans.
      Cambridge, Eng.: Cambridge UP, 1996.

One Editor

Monteiro, George, ed. Conversations with Elizabeth Bishop.
      Jackson: UP of Mississippi, 1996.

Two Editors

Craig, David, and Janet McCann, eds. Odd Angles of Heaven:
      Contemporary Poetry by People of Faith. Wheaton, IL:
      Shaw, 1994.

Translation

Dante Alighieri. Inferno: A New Verse Translation. Trans.
      Michael Palma. New York: Norton, 2002.

Introduction, Preface, Foreword, or Afterword

Thwaite, Anthony, Preface. Contemporary Poets. Ed. Thomas
      Riggs. 6th ed. New York: St. James, 1996. vii-viii.
Lapham, Lewis. Introduction. Understanding Media: The
      Extensions of Man. By Marshall McLuhan. Cambridge: MIT P,
      1994. vi-x.

Work in an Anthology

Allen, Dick. "The Emperor's New Clothes." Poetry After
      Modernism. Ed. Robert McDowell. Brownsville, OR: Story
      Line, 1991. 71-99.

Translation in an Anthology

Neruda, Pablo. "We Are Many." Trans. Alastair Reid. <u>Literature:</u>
    <u>An Introduction to Fiction, Poetry, and Drama</u>. Ed. X. J.
    Kennedy and Dana Gioia. 9th ed. New York: Longman, 2005.
    1046.

Multivolume Work

Wellek, René. <u>A History of Modern Criticism, 1750-1950</u>. 8 vols.
    New Haven: Yale UP, 1955-92.

One Volume of a Multivolume Work

Wellek René. <u>A History of Modern Criticism, 1750-1950</u>. Vol. 7.
    New Haven: Yale UP, 1991.

Book in a Series

Ross, William T. <u>Weldon Kees</u>. Twayne's US Authors Ser. 484.
    Boston: Twayne, 1985.

Republished Book

Ellison, Ralph. <u>Invisible Man</u>. 1952. New York: Vintage, 1995.

Revised or Subsequent Editions

Janouch, Gustav. <u>Conversations with Kafka</u>. Trans. Goronwy Rees.
    Rev. ed. New York: New Directions, 1971.

Reference Books

Signed Article in Reference Book

Cavoto, Janice E. "Harper Lee's <u>To Kill a Mockingbird</u>." <u>The</u>
    <u>Oxford Encyclopedia of American Literature</u>. Ed. Jay
    Parini. Vol. 2. New York: Oxford UP, 2004. 418-21.

Unsigned Encyclopedia Article—Standard Reference Book

"James Dickey." The New Encyclopaedia Britannica: Micropaedia.
    15th ed. 1987.

Dictionary Entry

"Design." Merriam-Webster's Collegiate Dictionary. 11th ed.
    2003.

Periodicals

Journal with Continuous Paging

Balée, Susan. "Flannery O'Connor Resurrected." Hudson Review
    47 (1994): 377-93.

Journal That Pages Each Issue Separately

Salter, Mary Jo. "The Heart Is Slow to Learn." New Criterion
    10.8 (1992): 23-29.

Signed Magazine Article

Gioia, Dana. "Studying with Miss Bishop." New Yorker 5 Sept.
    1986: 90-101.

Unsigned Magazine Article

"The Real Test." New Republic 5 Feb. 2001: 7.

Newspaper Article

Lyall, Sarah. "In Poetry, Ted Hughes Breaks His Silence on
    Sylvia Plath." New York Times 19 Jan. 1998, natl. ed.:
    A1+.

Signed Book Review

Harper, John. "Well-Crafted Tales with Tabloid Titles." Rev. of
    Tabloid Dreams, by Robert Olen Butler. Orlando Sentinel 15
    Dec. 1996: D4.

Unsigned, Untitled Book Review

Rev. of Otherwise: New and Selected Poems, by Jane Kenyon.
    Virginia Quarterly Review 72 (1996): 136.

ELECTRONIC PUBLICATIONS

Online Resources

Web Site

Voice of the Shuttle. Ed. Alan Liu. 2003. U of California,
        Santa Barbara. 17 Oct. 2003 <http://vos.ucsb.edu/>.

Document on a Web Site

"Wallace Stevens." Poetry Exhibits. 31 Jan. 2001. The Academy
        of American Poets. 20 Sept. 2003 <http://www.poets.org/
        poets/poets.cfm?45442B7C000C07070C>.

Document on a Web Site: Citing a Path

"Wallace Stevens." Poetry Exhibits. 31 Jan. 2001. The Academy
        of American Poets. 20 Sept. 2003 <http://www.poets.org>.
        Path: Find a Poet; S; Stevens, Wallace.

Document on a Web Site: Citing a Search Page

"A Hughes Timeline." PBS Online. 2001. Public Broadcasting
        Service. 20 Sept. 2003 <http://www.pbs.org/search>.

An Entire Online Book

Jewett, Sarah Orne. The Country of the Pointed Firs. Boston:
        Houghton, 1910. Bartleby.com:Great Books Online. Ed.
        Steven van Leeuwen. 1999. 10 Oct. 2003
        <http://www.bartleby.com/125/>.

Online Reference Database

Encyclopaedia Britannica Online. 2002. Encyclopaedia
        Britannica. 15 Feb. 2003 <http://www.britannica.com/>.

Article in Online Scholarly Journal

Hoffman, Tyler B. "Emily Dickinson and the Limit of War." Emily
        Dickinson Journal 3.2 (1994). 15 Mar. 2004
        <http://www.colorado.edu/EDIS/journal/articles/
        III.2.Hoffman.html>.

Article from a Scholarly Journal, Part of an Archival Database

Oates, Joyce Carol. "'Soul at the White Heat': The Romance of
    Emily Dickinson's Poetry." Critical Inquiry 13.4 (1987).
    Literary Criticism on the Web. Ed. Randy Souther. 7 July
    2003 <http://start.at/literarycriticism>. Path: D;
    Dickinson; Joyce Carol Oates on Emily Dickinson; "Soul at
    the White Heat."

Article in Online Newspaper

Atwood, Margaret. "The Writer: A New Canadian Life-Form."
    New York Times on the Web 18 May 1997. 20 Aug. 2003
    <http://www.nytimes.com/books/97/05/18/
    bookend/bookend.html>.

Article in Online Magazine

Garner, Dwight. "The Salon Interview: Jamaica Kincaid."
    Salon 13 Jan. 1996. 15 Feb. 2004
    <http://www.salonmagazine.com/05/features/kincaid.html>.

Article Accessed via a Library Subscription Service

Seitler, Dana. "Unnatural Selection: Mothers, Eugenic Feminism,
    and Charlotte Perkins Gilman's Regeneration Narratives."
    American Quarterly 55.1 (2003): 61-87. ProQuest. Arcadia U
    Landman Lib., Glenside, PA. 7 July 2003
    <http://www.il.proquest.com/proquest/>.

Online Posting

Grossenbacher, Laura. "Comments about the Ending Illustration."
    Online Posting. 4 Sept. 1996. The Yellow Wallpaper Site.
    14 Mar. 2001 <http://www.cwrl.utexas.edu/
    ~daniel/amlit/wallpaper/readcomments.html>.

CD-ROM Reference Works

CD-ROM Publication

"Appall." The Oxford English Dictionary. 2nd ed. CD-ROM.
    Oxford: Oxford UP, 1992.

Periodically Published Information, Collected on CD-ROM

Kakutani, Michiko. "Slogging Surreally in the Vietnamese Jungle." Rev. of <u>The Things They Carried</u>, by Tim O'Brien. <u>New York Times Ondisc</u>. CD-ROM. UMI-ProQuest. Oct. 1993.

MISCELLANEOUS SOURCES

Compact Disc (CD)

Shakespeare, William. <u>The Complete Arkangel Shakespeare: 38 Fully-Dramatized Plays</u>. Narr. Eileen Atkins and John Gielgud. Read by Imogen Stubbs, Joseph Fiennes, et al. Audio Partners, 2003.

Audiocassette

Roethke, Theodore. <u>Theodore Roethke Reads His Poetry</u>. Audiocassette. Caedmon, 1972.

Videocassette

<u>Henry V</u>. By William Shakespeare. Dir. Laurence Olivier. Perf. Laurence Olivier. Two Cities Films. 1944. Videocassette. Paramount, 1988.

DVD

<u>Hamlet</u>. By William Shakespeare. Perf. Laurence Olivier, Eileen Herlie, and Basil Sydney. Two Cities Films. 1948. DVD. Criterion, 2000.

Film

<u>Hamlet</u>. By William Shakespeare. Dir. Franco Zeffirelli. Perf. Mel Gibson, Glenn Close, Helena Bonham Carter, Alan Bates, and Paul Scofield. Warner, 1991.

Television or Radio Program

<u>Moby Dick</u>. By Herman Melville. Dir. Franc Roddam. Perf. Patrick Stewart and Gregory Peck. 2 episodes. USA Network. 16-17 Mar. 1998.

45 *Critical Approaches to Literature*

Literary criticism should arise out of a debt of love.
—George Steiner

Literary criticism is not an abstract, intellectual exercise; it is a natural human response to literature. If a friend informs you she is reading a book you have just finished, it would be odd indeed if you did not begin swapping opinions. Literary criticism is nothing more than discourse—spoken or written—about literature. A student who sits quietly in a morning English class, intimidated by the notion of literary criticism, will spend an hour that evening talking animatedly about the meaning of rock lyrics or comparing the relative merits of the *Star Wars* trilogies. It is inevitable that people will ponder, discuss, and analyze the works of art that interest them.

The informal criticism of friends talking about literature tends to be casual, unorganized, and subjective. Since Aristotle, however, philosophers, scholars, and writers have tried to create more precise and disciplined ways of discussing literature. Literary critics have borrowed concepts from other disciplines, such as philosophy, history, linguistics, psychology, and anthropology, to analyze imaginative literature more perceptively. Some critics have found it useful to work in the abstract area of **literary theory,** criticism that tries to formulate general principles rather than discuss specific texts. Mass media critics, such as newspaper reviewers, usually spend their time evaluating works—telling us which books are worth reading, which plays not to bother seeing. But most serious literary criticism is not primarily evaluative; it assumes we know that *Othello* or *The Metamorphosis* is worth reading. Instead, such criticism is analytic; it tries to help us better understand a literary work.

In the following pages you will find overviews of ten critical approaches to literature. While these ten methods do not exhaust the total possibilities of literary criticism, they represent the most widely used contemporary approaches. Although presented separately, the approaches are not necessarily mutually exclusive; many critics mix methods to suit their needs and interests. For example, a historical critic may use formalist techniques to analyze a poem; a biographical critic will frequently use psychological theories to analyze an author. The summaries neither try to provide a history of each approach, nor do they try to present the latest trends in each school.

Their purpose is to give you a practical introduction to each critical method and then provide representative examples of it. If one of these critical methods interests you, why not try to write a class paper using the approach?

FORMALIST CRITICISM

Formalist criticism regards literature as a unique form of human knowledge that needs to be examined on its own terms. "The natural and sensible starting point for work in literary scholarship," René Wellek and Austin Warren wrote in their influential *Theory of Literature*, "is the interpretation and analysis of the works of literature themselves." To a formalist, a poem or story is not primarily a social, historical, or biographical document; it is a literary work that can be understood only by reference to its intrinsic literary features, that is, those elements found in the text itself. To analyze a poem or story, therefore, the formalist critic focuses on the words of the text rather than facts about the author's life or the historical milieu in which it was written. The critic would pay special attention to the formal features of the text—the style, structure, imagery, tone, and genre. These features, however, are usually not examined in isolation, because formalist critics believe that what gives a literary text its special status as art is how all its elements work together to create the reader's total experience. As Robert Penn Warren commented, "Poetry does not inhere in any particular element but depends upon the set of relationships, the structure, which we call the poem."

A key method that formalists use to explore the intense relationships within a poem is **close reading,** a careful step-by-step analysis and explication of a text. (For further discussion of explication, see pages 2130 and 2148.) The purpose of close reading is to understand how various elements in a literary text work together to shape its effects on the reader. Since formalists believe that the various stylistic and thematic elements of literary work influence each other, these critics insist that form and content cannot be meaningfully separated. The complete interdependence of form and content is what makes a text literary. When we extract a work's theme or paraphrase its meaning, we destroy the aesthetic experience of the work.

When Robert Langbaum examines Robert Browning's "My Last Duchess," he uses several techniques of formalist criticism. First, he places the poem in relation to its literary form, the dramatic monologue. Second, he discusses the dramatic structure of the poem—why the duke tells his story, whom he addresses, and the physical circumstances in which he speaks. Third, Langbaum analyzes how the duke tells his story—his tone, manner, even the order in which he makes his disclosures. Langbaum neither introduces facts about Browning's life into his analysis, nor relates the poem to the historical period or social conditions that produced it. He focuses on the text itself to explain how it produces a complex effect on the reader.

Cleanth Brooks   (1906–1994)

THE FORMALIST CRITIC 1951

Here are some articles of faith I could subscribe to:

> That literary criticism is a description and an evaluation of its object.
>
> That the primary concern of criticism is with the problem of unity—the kind of whole which the literary work forms or fails to form, and the relation of the various parts to each other in building up this whole.
>
> That the formal relations in a work of literature may include, but certainly exceed, those of logic.
>
> That in a successful work, form and content cannot be separated.
>
> That form is meaning.
>
> That literature is ultimately metaphorical and symbolic.
>
> That the general and the universal are not seized upon by abstraction, but got at through the concrete and the particular.
>
> That literature is not a surrogate for religion.
>
> That, as Allen Tate says, "specific moral problems" are the subject matter of literature, but that the purpose of literature is not to point a moral.
>
> That the principles of criticism define the area relevant to literary criticism; they do not constitute a method for carrying out the criticism.

. . . .

The formalist critic knows as well as anyone that poems and plays and novels are written by men—that they do not somehow happen—and that they are written as expressions of particular personalities and are written from all sorts of motives—for money, from a desire to express oneself, for the sake of a cause, etc. Moreover, the formalist critic knows as well as anyone that literary works are merely potential until they are read—that is, that they are recreated in the minds of actual readers, who vary enormously in their capabilities, their interests, their prejudices, their ideas. But the formalist critic is concerned primarily with the work itself. Speculation on the mental processes of the author takes the critic away from the work into biography and psychology. There is no reason, of course, why he should not turn away into biography and psychology. Such explorations are very much worth making. But they should not be confused with an account of the work. Such studies describe the process of composition, not the structure of the thing composed, and they may be performed quite as validly for the poor work as for the good one. They may be validly performed for any kind of expression—non-literary as well as literary.

From "The Formalist Critic"

Michael Clark   (b. 1946)

LIGHT AND DARKNESS IN "SONNY'S BLUES"   1985

"Sonny's Blues" by James Baldwin is a sensitive story about the reconciliation of two brothers, but it is much more than that. It is, in addition, an examination of the importance of the black heritage and of the central importance of music in that heritage. Finally, the story probes the central role that art must play in human existence. To examine all of these facets of human existence is a rather formidable undertaking in a short story, even in a longish short story such as this one. Baldwin not only undertakes this task, but he does it superbly. One of the central ways that Baldwin fuses all of these complex elements is by using a metaphor of childhood, which is supported by ancillary images of light and darkness. He does the job so well that the story is a *tour de force*, a penetrating study of American culture.

. . .

Sonny's quest is best described by himself when he writes to the narrator: "I feel like a man who's been trying to climb up out of some deep, real deep and funky hole and just saw the sun up there, outside. I got to get outside." Sonny is a person who finds his life a living hell, but he knows enough to strive for the "light." As it is chronicled in this story, his quest is for regaining something from the past—from his own childhood and from the pasts of all who have come before him. The means for doing this is his music, which is consistently portrayed in terms of light imagery. When Sonny has a discussion with the narrator about the future, the narrator describes Sonny's face as a mixture of concern and hope: "[T]he worry, the thoughtfulness, played on it still, the way shadows play on a face which is staring into the fire." This fire image is reinforced shortly afterward when the narrator describes Sonny's aspirations once more in terms of light: "[I]t was as though he were all wrapped up in some cloud, some fire, some vision all his own." To the narrator and to Isabel's family, the music that Sonny plays is simply "weird and disordered," but to Sonny, the music is seen in starkly positive terms: his failure to master the music will mean "death," while success will mean "life."

The light and dark imagery culminates in the final scene, where the narrator, apparently for the first time, listens to Sonny play the piano. The location is a Greenwich Village club. Appropriately enough, the narrator is seated "in a dark corner." In contrast, the stage is dominated by light, which Baldwin reiterates with a succession of images: "light . . . circle of light . . . light . . . flame . . . light." Although Sonny has a false start, he gradually settles into his playing and ends the first set with some intensity: "Everything had been burned out of [Sonny's face], and at the same time, things usually hidden were being burned in, by the fire and fury of the battle which was occurring in him up there."

The culmination of the set occurs when Creole, the leader of the players, begins to play "Am I Blue." At this point, "something began to happen." Apparently, the narrator at this time realizes that this music *is* important. The music is central to the experience of the black experience, and it is described in terms of light imagery:

Creole began to tell us what the blues were all about. They were not about anything very new. He and his boys up there were keeping it new, at the risk of ruin, destruction, madness, and death, in order to find new ways to make us listen. For, while the tale of how we suffer, and how we are delighted, and how we may triumph is never new, it always must be heard. There isn't any other tale to tell, it's the only light we've got in all this darkness.

From "James Baldwin's 'Sonny's Blues': Childhood, Light, and Art"

Robert Langbaum   (b. 1924)

On Robert Browning's "My Last Duchess"   1957

When we have said all the objective things about Browning's "My Last Duchess," we will not have arrived at the meaning until we point out what can only be substantiated by an appeal to effect—that moral judgment does not figure importantly in our response to the duke, that we even identify ourselves with him. But how is such an effect produced in a poem about a cruel Italian duke of the Renaissance who out of unreasonable jealousy has had his last duchess put to death, and is now about to contract a second marriage for the sake of dowry? Certainly, no summary or paraphrase would indicate that condemnation is not our principal response. The difference must be laid to form, to that extra quantity which makes the difference in artistic discourse between content and meaning.

The objective fact that the poem is made up entirely of the duke's utterance has of course much to do with the final meaning, and it is important to say that the poem is in form a monologue. But much more remains to be said about the way in which the content is laid out, before we can come near accounting for the whole meaning. It is important that the duke tells the story of his kind and generous last duchess to, of all people, the envoy from his prospective duchess. It is important that he tells his story while showing off to the envoy the artistic merits of a portrait of the last duchess. It is above all important that the duke carries off his outrageous indiscretion, proceeding triumphantly in the end downstairs to conclude arrangements for the dowry. All this is important not only as content but also as form, because it establishes a relation between the duke on the one hand, and the portrait and the envoy on the other, which determines the reader's relation to the duke and therefore to the poem—which determines, in other words, the poem's meaning.

The utter outrageousness of the duke's behavior makes condemnation the least interesting response, certainly not the response that can account for the poem's success. What interests us more than the duke's wickedness is his immense attractiveness. His conviction of matchless superiority, his intelligence and bland amorality, his poise, his taste for art, his manners—high-handed aristocratic manners that break the ordinary rules and assert the duke's superiority when he is being most solicitous of the envoy, waiving their difference of rank ("Nay, we'll go / Together down, sir"); these qualities overwhelm the envoy, causing him apparently to suspend judgment of the duke, for he raises no demur. The reader is no less overwhelmed. We suspend moral judgment because we prefer to participate in the duke's power and freedom, in his hard core of character fiercely loyal to itself. Moral judgment is in fact important as the thing to be suspended, as a measure of the price we pay for the privilege of appreciating to the full this extraordinary man.

It is because the duke determines the arrangement and relative subordination of the parts that the poem means what it does. The duchess's goodness shines through the duke's utterance; he makes no attempt to conceal it, so preoccupied is he with his own standard of judgment and so oblivious of the world's. Thus the duchess's case is subordinated to the duke's, the novelty and complexity of which engages our attention. We are busy trying to understand the man who can combine the connoisseur's pride in the lady's beauty with a pride that caused him to murder the lady rather than tell her in what way she displeased him, for in that

> would be some stooping; and I choose
> Never to stoop.
>
> (lines 42–43)

The duke's paradoxical nature is fully revealed when, having boasted how at his command the duchess's life was extinguished, he turns back to the portrait to admire of all things its life-likeness:

> There she stands
> As if alive.
>
> (lines 46–47)

This occurs ten lines from the end, and we might suppose we have by now taken the duke's measure. But the next ten lines produce a series of shocks that outstrip each time our understanding of the duke, and keep us panting after revelation with no opportunity to consolidate our impression of him for moral judgment. For it is at this point that we learn to whom he has been talking; and he goes on to talk about dowry, even allowing himself to murmur the hypocritical assurance that the new bride's self and not the dowry is of course his object. It seems to me that one side of the duke's nature is here stretched as far as it will go; the dazzling figure threatens to decline into paltriness admitting moral judgment, when Browning retrieves it with two brilliant strokes. First, there is the lordly waiving of rank's privilege as the duke and the envoy are about to proceed downstairs, and then there is the perfect all-revealing gesture of the last two and a half lines when the duke stops to show off yet another object in his collection:

> Notice Neptune, though,
> Taming a sea-horse, thought a rarity,
> Which Claus of Innsbruck cast in bronze for me!
>
> (lines 54–56)

The lines bring all the parts of the poem into final combination, with just the relative values that constitute the poem's meaning. The nobleman does not hurry on his way to business, the connoisseur cannot resist showing off yet another precious object, the possessive egotist counts up his possessions even as he moves toward the acquirement of a new possession, a well-dowered bride; and most important, the last duchess is seen in final perspective. She takes her place as one of a line of objects in an art collection; her sad story becomes the *cicerone's* anecdote° lending piquancy to the portrait. The duke has taken from her what he wants, her beauty, and thrown the life away; and we watch with awe as he proceeds to take what he wants from the envoy and by implication from the new duchess. He carries all before him by sheer force of will so undeflected by ordinary compunctions as even, I think, to call into question—the question rushes into place behind the startling illumination of the last lines, and lingers as the poem's haunting afternote—the duke's sanity.

From *The Poetry of Experience*

BIOGRAPHICAL CRITICISM

Biographical criticism begins with the simple but central insight that literature is written by actual people and that understanding an author's life can help readers more thoroughly comprehend the work. Anyone who reads the biography of a writer quickly sees how much an author's experience shapes—both directly and indirectly—what he or she creates. Reading that biography will also change (and usually deepen) our response to the work. Sometimes even knowing a single important fact illuminates our reading of a poem or story. Learning, for example, that poet Josephine Miles was confined to a wheelchair or that Weldon Kees committed suicide at forty-one will certainly make us pay attention to certain aspects of their poems we might otherwise have missed or considered unimportant. A formalist critic might complain that we would also have noticed those things through careful textual analysis, but biographical information provides the practical assistance of underscoring subtle but important meanings in the poems. Though many literary theorists have assailed biographical criticism on philosophical grounds, the biographical approach to literature has never disappeared because of its obvious practical advantage in illuminating literary texts.

It may be helpful here to make a distinction between biography and biographical criticism. **Biography** is, strictly speaking, a branch of history; it provides a written account of a person's life. To establish and interpret the facts of a poet's life, for instance, a biographer would use all the available information—not just personal documents such as letters and diaries but also the poems for the possible light they might shed on the subject's life. A biographical *critic*, however, is not concerned with re-creating the record of an author's life. Biographical criticism focuses on explicating the literary work by using the insight provided by knowledge of the author's life.

cicerone's anecdote: The Duke's tale. (In Italian, a *cicerone* is one who conducts guided tours for sightseers.)

Quite often, biographical critics, such as Brett C. Millier in her discussion of Elizabeth Bishop's "One Art," will examine the drafts of a poem or story to see both how the work came into being and how it might have been changed from its autobiographical origins.

A reader, however, must use biographical interpretations cautiously. Writers are notorious for revising the facts of their own lives; they often delete embarrassments and invent accomplishments while changing the details of real episodes to improve their literary impact. John Cheever, for example, frequently told reporters about his sunny, privileged youth; after the author's death, his biographer Scott Donaldson discovered a childhood scarred by a distant mother; a failed, alcoholic father; and nagging economic uncertainty. Likewise, Cheever's outwardly successful adulthood was plagued by alcoholism, sexual promiscuity, and family tension. The chilling facts of Cheever's life significantly changed the way critics read his stories. The danger in the case of a famous writer (Sylvia Plath and F. Scott Fitzgerald are two modern examples) is that the life story can overwhelm and eventually distort the work. A savvy biographical critic always remembers to base an interpretation on what is in the text itself; biographical data should amplify the meaning of the text, not drown it out with irrelevant material.

Virginia Llewellyn Smith

CHEKHOV'S ATTITUDE TO ROMANTIC LOVE   1973

It has been shown that the theme of love being destroyed by a cruel fate did not always have for Chekhov the appeal of the tragic: that it could also serve him as a good framework on which to build farce. Nor could one claim that the theme of illicit passion found its source in Chekhov's own imagination, let alone experience: Tolstoy's *Anna Karenina*° had been published in the later 1870s, before any of Chekhov's work. None the less the coincidence of plot and emotion found in "About Love" and "The Lady with the Dog," together with the fact that the theme occupied Chekhov chiefly in the 1890s, has given rise to some speculation as to whether in fact Chekhov's own love-life during those years suffered as one critic puts it from the interference of a *force majeure*.° Since in this period Chekhov's private life is no longer a closed book (although many pages are indecipherable) the search for the romantic heroine becomes more complex. It becomes feasible to try to connect with her image certain women whose relations with Chekhov are at least partially illuminated and illuminating. Of Chekhov's female friends three in particular must now claim our attention.

No other single work of Chekhov's fiction constitutes a more meaningful comment on Chekhov's attitude to women and to love than does "The Lady with the Dog." So many threads of Chekhov's thought and experience appear to

Anna Karenina: Leo Tolstoy's novel (1875–1877) dealt explicitly with an adulterous affair.
force majeure: French for an "irresistible force."

have been woven together into this succinct story that it may be regarded as something in the nature of a summary of the entire topic.

Gurov, the hero of the story, may at first appear no more closely identifiable with Chekhov himself than are many other sympathetic male characters in Chekhov's fiction: he has a post in a bank and is a married man with three children. It is because he has this wife and family that his love-affair with Anna Sergeevna leads him into an *impasse*. And the affair itself, involving Gurov's desperate trip to Anna's home town, has no obvious feature in common with anything we know of Chekhov's amorous liaisons.

And yet Chekhov's own attitudes and experience have clearly shaped Gurov's character and fate. The reader is told that Gurov "was not yet forty": Chekhov was thirty-nine when he wrote "The Lady with the Dog." Gurov "was married young" (*ego zhenili rano*): there is a faint implication in the phrase that an element of coercion played some part in his taking this step—a step which Chekhov, when he was young, managed to avoid. As in general with early marriages in Chekhov's fiction, Gurov's has not proved a success. His wife seems "much older than he" and imagines herself to be an intellectual: familiar danger-signals. She is summed-up in three words: "stiff, pompous, dignified" (*pryamaya, vazhnaya, solidnaya*) which epitomize a type of woman (and man) that Chekhov heartily disliked.

.   .   .

Gurov has had, however, liaisons that were, for him, enjoyable—and these we note, were brief: as was Chekhov's liaison with Yavorskaya and indeed, so far as we know, all the sexual relationships that he had before he met Olga Knipper.

"Frequent experience and indeed bitter experience had long since taught [Gurov] that every liaison which to begin with makes such a pleasant change . . . inevitably evolves into a real and extremely complex problem, and the situation eventually becomes a burden." That his friendships with, for instance, Lika and Avilova should evolve into a situation of this kind seems to have been exactly what Chekhov himself feared: he backed out of these friendships as soon as there appeared to be a danger of close involvement.

Gurov cannot do without the company of women, and yet he describes them as an "inferior breed": his experience of intimacy with women is limited to casual affairs and an unsatisfactory marriage. Chekhov also enjoyed the company of women and had many female friends and admirers: but he failed, or was unwilling, to involve himself deeply or lastingly with them. That in his work he should suggest that women are an inferior breed can be to some extent explained by the limited knowledge of women his self-contained attitude brought him—and perhaps, to some extent, by a sense of guilt concerning his inability to feel involved.

Gurov's behaviour to Anna Sergeevna at the beginning of their love-affair is characterized by an absence of emotional involvement, just such as appears in Chekhov's attitude towards certain women. There is a scene in "The Lady with the Dog" where, after they have been to bed together, Gurov eats a watermelon while Anna Sergeevna weeps over her corruption. It is not difficult to imagine

Chekhov doing something similarly prosaic—weeding his garden, perhaps—while Lika poured out her emotional troubles to him.

Gurov's egocentricity is dispelled, however, by the potent influence of love, because Anna Sergeevna turns out to be the ideal type of woman: pitiable, defenseless, childlike, capable of offering Gurov an unquestioning love. Love is seen to operate as a force for good: under its influence Gurov feels revulsion for the philistinism of his normal life and associates.

. . .

Chekhov wrote "The Lady with the Dog" in Yalta in the autumn of 1899, not long after he and Olga were there together (although they were not, as yet, lovers) and had made the trip back to Moscow together. In the Kokkoz valley, it will be remembered, they apparently agreed to marry: and so by then, we may presume, Chekhov knew what it was to love.

From Anton Chekhov and the Lady with the Dog

Brett C. Millier   (b. 1958)

On Elizabeth Bishop's "One Art"   1993

Elizabeth Bishop left seventeen drafts of the poem "One Art" among her papers. In the first draft, she lists all the things she's lost in her life—keys, pens, glasses, cities—and then she writes "One might think this would have prepared me / for losing one average-sized not exceptionally / beautiful or dazzlingly intelligent person . . . / But it doesn't seem to have at all. . . ." By the seventeenth draft, nearly every word has been transformed, but most importantly, Bishop discovered along the way that there might be a way to master this loss.

One way to read Bishop's modulation between the first and last drafts from "the loss of you is impossible to master" to something like "I am still the master of losing even though losing you looks like a disaster" is that in the writing of such a disciplined, demanding poem as this villanelle ("[*Write it!*]") lies the potential mastery of the loss. Working through each of her losses—from the bold, painful catalog of the first draft to the finely-honed and privately meaningful final version—is the way to overcome them or, if not to overcome them, then to see the way in which she might possibly master herself in the face of loss. It is all, perhaps "one art"—writing elegy, mastering loss, mastering grief, self-mastery. Bishop had a precocious familiarity with loss. Her father died before her first birthday, and four years later her mother disappeared into a sanitarium, never to be seen by her daughter again. The losses in the poem are real: time in the form of the "hour badly spent" and, more tellingly for the orphaned Bishop "my mother's watch": the lost houses, in Key West, Petrópolis, and Ouro Prêto, Brazil. The city of Rio de Janeiro and the whole South American continent (where she had lived for nearly two decades) were lost to her with the suicide of her Brazilian companion. And currently, in the fall of 1975, she seemed to have lost her dearest friend and lover, who was trying to end their relationship. But each version of the poem distanced the pain a little more, depersonalized it, moved it away from the tawdry self-pity and "confession" that Bishop disliked in so many of her contemporaries.

Bishop's friends remained for a long time protective of her personal reputation, and unwilling to have her grouped among lesbian poets or even among the other great poets of her generation—Robert Lowell, John Berryman, Theodore Roethke—as they seemed to self-destruct before their readers' eyes. Bishop herself taught them this reticence by keeping her private life to herself, and by investing what "confession" there was in her poems deeply in objects and places, thus deflecting biographical inquiry. In the development of this poem, discretion is both a poetic method, and a part of a process of self-understanding, the seeing of a pattern in her own life.

Adapted by the author from *Elizabeth Bishop: Life and the Memory of It*

Emily Toth (b. 1944)

The Source for Alcée Laballière in "The Storm" 1990

In January 1898, right after Kate Chopin had finished writing her controversial novel *The Awakening*, about one woman's quest for love (and sexual fulfillment) outside of marriage, a St. Louis newspaper asked her to answer the question, "Is Love Divine?"

Chopin's response was telling. She wrote, "I am inclined to think that love springs from animal instinct, and therefore is, in a measure, divine. One can never resolve to love this man, this woman or child, and then carry out the resolution unless one feels irresistibly drawn by an indefinable current of magnetism."

In that case, it was no doubt magnetism that led Kate Chopin to the handsome, wealthy Creole planter Albert Sampité (pronounced "Al-bear Sam-pi-TAY") after the death of her husband Oscar. This may also be why Kate Chopin's widowhood stories emphasize hope, not bereavement; spring, not winter; possibility, not loss. After Oscar died, Kate—who had grown up in a house full of widows who managed their own lives and their own money—decided to run Oscar's businesses herself.

She became an accomplished entrepreneur, a brisk businesswoman during the day who nevertheless kept the dark night as her own, with its prospects for silence and mystery and sin. Men flocked to aid the handsome widow in 1883, but when villagers gossiped generations later about who was "sweet on Kate," one name kept recurring. It was no secret to anyone—including his wife—that Albert Sampité was pursuing Kate Chopin. An examination of Chopin's stories show that the male characters who kindle desire and who devote themselves to sexual pleasure are named Alcée, an abbreviated form of Albert Sampité. Al. S——é and Alcée are both pronounced "Al-say."

It was not unseemly, or even odd, for Monsieur Sampite (his family dropped the accent mark, though they continued to use French pronunciation) to meet with Madame Chopin at the point where their lands intersected. When merchandise arrived for Kate's store, by boat from New Orleans, she had to go down to the landing to get her goods. It was not uncommon for a local planter like Albert Sampite to be at the landing at the same time. Somehow, too, Albert Sampite became involved in Kate Chopin's money matters. Papers that he saved show that Albert was apparently helping Kate to collect money owed her—and he also valued her financial records enough to keep them with his own personal papers.

There were still other ways in which a willing couple could make connections. And in a sudden storm, it was not impossible for two people to take refuge alone together in a house—a sensual scenario Kate Chopin sketched out, years later, in her most explicit short story, "The Storm."

Kate and Albert were discreet about their romance, by the standards of a century later. If anyone wrote down dates and places and eyewitness descriptions, none of those survive—although Cloutierville residents would certainly have been able to recognize him in her writings. But an affair in the 1880s was not simply a matter of physical consummation. Much less than that could be called "making love": flirting, significant glances, stolen kisses, secret silences.

Kate Chopin, in her diary eleven years after the first spring of her widowhood, suggested that more than flirting had gone on in her life: "I had loved— lovers who were not divine," she wrote, and "And then, there are so many ways of saying good night!" And even in her published writings, Kate left proof that her relationship with Albert Sampite was much more than a casual friendship. It shaped what she wrote about women and men, and love and lust and forbidden desires.

Adapted from Kate Chopin

HISTORICAL CRITICISM

Historical criticism seeks to understand a literary work by investigating the social, cultural, and intellectual context that produced it—a context that necessarily includes the artist's biography and milieu. Historical critics are less concerned with explaining a work's literary significance for today's readers than with helping us understand the work by recreating, as nearly as possible, the exact meaning and impact it had on its original audience. A historical reading of a literary work begins by exploring the possible ways in which the meaning of the text has changed over time. An analysis of William Blake's poem "London," for instance, carefully examines how certain words had different connotations for the poem's original readers than they do today. It also explores the probable associations an eighteenth-century English reader would have made with certain images and characters, like the poem's persona, the chimney sweep—a type of exploited child laborer who, fortunately, no longer exists in our society.

Reading ancient literature, no one doubts the value of historical criticism. There have been so many social, cultural, and linguistic changes that some older texts are incomprehensible without scholarly assistance. But historical criticism can even help one better understand modern texts. To return to Weldon Kees's "For My Daughter" for example, one learns a great deal by considering two rudimentary historical facts—the year in which the poem was first published (1940) and the nationality of its author (American)—and then asking how this information has shaped the meaning of the poem. In 1940 war had already broken out in Europe, and most Americans realized that their country, still recovering from the Depression, would soon be drawn into it. For a young man like Kees, the future seemed bleak, uncertain, and personally dangerous. Even this simple historical analysis helps explain at least part of the bitter pessimism of Kees's poem, though a psychological critic would rightly insist that Kees's dark personality also played a crucial role. In writing a paper on a poem, you might explore how the time and place of its creation affect its meaning. For a splendid example of how to recreate the historical context of a poem's genesis, read the following account by Hugh Kenner of Ezra Pound's imagistic "In a Station of the Metro."

Hugh Kenner (1923–2003)

IMAGISM 1971

For it was English post-Symbolist verse that Pound's Imagism set out to reform, by deleting its self-indulgences, intensifying its virtues, and elevating the glimpse into the vision. The most famous of all Imagist poems commenced, like any poem by Arthur Symons,° with an accidental glimpse. Ezra Pound, on a visit to Paris in 1911, got out of the Metro at La Concorde, and "saw suddenly a beautiful face, and then another and another, and then a beautiful child's face, and then another beautiful woman, and I tried all that day to find words for what they had meant to me, and I could not find any words that seemed to me worthy, or as lovely as that sudden emotion."

The oft-told story is worth one more retelling. This was just such an experience as Arthur Symons cultivated, bright unexpected glimpses in a dark setting, instantly to melt into the crowd's kaleidoscope. And a poem would not have given Symons any trouble. But Pound by 1911 was already unwilling to write a Symons poem.

He tells us that he first satisfied his mind when he hit on a wholly abstract vision of colors, splotches on darkness like some canvas of Kandinsky's (whose work he had not then seen). This is a most important fact. Satisfaction lay not in preserving the vision, but in devising with mental effort an abstract equivalent for it, reduced, intensified. He next wrote a 30-line poem and destroyed it; after six months he wrote a shorter poem, also destroyed; and after another year, with, as he tells us, the Japanese *hokku* in mind, he arrived at a poem which needs every one of its 20 words, including the six words of its title:

Arthur Symons: Symons (1865–1945) was a British poet who helped introduce French symbolist verse into English. His own verse was often florid and impressionistic.

In a Station of the Metro

The apparition of these faces in the crowd;
Petals on a wet, black bough.

We need the title so that we can savor that vegetal contrast with the world of machines: this is not any crowd, moreover, but a crowd seen underground, as Odysseus and Orpheus and Koré saw crowds in Hades. And carrying forward the suggestion of wraiths, the word "apparition" detaches these faces from all the crowded faces, and presides over the image that conveys the quality of their separation:

Petals on a wet, black bough.

Flowers, underground; flowers, out of the sun; flowers seen as if against a natural gleam, the bough's wetness gleaming on its darkness, in this place where wheels turn and nothing grows. The mind is touched, it may be, with a memory of Persephone, as we read of her in the 106th Canto,

Dis' bride, Queen over Phlegethon,
girls faint as mist about her.

—the faces of those girls likewise "apparitions."

What is achieved, though it works by way of the visible, is no picture of the thing glimpsed, in the manner of

The light of our cigarettes
Went and came in the gloom.

It is a simile with "like" suppressed: Pound called it an equation, meaning not a redundancy, *a* equals *a,* but a generalization of unexpected exactness. The statements of analytic geometry, he said, "are 'lords' over fact. They are the thrones and dominations that rule over form and recurrence. And in like manner are great works of art lords over fact, over race-long recurrent moods, and over tomorrow." So this tiny poem, drawing on Gauguin and on Japan, on ghosts and on Persephone, on the Underworld and on the Underground, the Metro of Mallarmé's capital and a phrase that names a station of the Metro as it might a station of the Cross, concentrates far more than it need ever specify, and indicates the means of delivering post-Symbolist poetry from its pictorialist impasse. "An 'Image' is that which presents an intellectual and emotional complex in an instant of time": that is the elusive Doctrine of the Image. And, just 20 months later, "The image . . . is a radiant node or cluster; it is what I can, and must perforce, call a VORTEX, from which, and through which, and into which, ideas are constantly rushing." And: "An *image* . . . is real because we know it directly."

From *The Pound Era*

Joseph Moldenhauer   (b. 1934)

"To His Coy Mistress" and the Renaissance Tradition   1968

Obedient to the neoclassical aesthetic which ruled his age, Andrew Marvell strove for excellence within established forms rather than trying to devise unique forms of his own. Like Herrick, Ben Jonson, and Campion, like Milton and the Shakespeare of the sonnets, Marvell was derivative. He held imitation to be no vice; he chose a proven type and exploited it with a professionalism rarely surpassed even in a century and a land as amply provided with verse craftsmen as his. Under a discipline so willingly assumed, Marvell's imagination flourished, producing superb and enduring examples of the verse types he attempted.

. . .

When he undertook to write a *carpe diem* lyric in "To His Coy Mistress," Marvell was working once more within a stylized form, one of the favorite types in the Renaissance lyric catalogue. Again he endowed the familiar model with his own special sensibility, composing what for many readers is the most vital English instance of the *carpe diem* poem. We can return to it often, with undiminished enthusiasm—drawn not by symbolic intricacy, though it contains two or three extraordinary conceits, nor by philosophical depth, though it lends an unusual seriousness to its theme—but drawn rather by its immediacy and concreteness, its sheer dynamism of statement within a controlled structure.

The *carpe diem* poem, whose label comes from a line of Horace and whose archetype for Renaissance poets was a lyric by Catullus, addresses the conflict of beauty and sensual desire on the one hand and the destructive force of time on the other. Its theme is the fleeting nature of life's joys; its counsel, overt or implied, is Horace's "seize the present," or, in the language of Herrick's "To the Virgins,"

> Gather ye Rose-buds while ye may,
> Old Time is still a flying.

It takes rise from that most pervasive and aesthetically viable of all Renaissance preoccupations, man's thralldom to time, the limitations of mortality upon his senses, his pleasures, his aspirations, his intellectual and creative capacities. Over the exuberance of Elizabethan and seventeenth-century poetry the pall of death continually hovers, and the lyrics of the age would supply a handbook of strategies for the circumvention of decay. The birth of an heir, the preservative balm of memory, the refuge of Christian resignation or Platonic ecstasy—these are some solutions which the poets offer. Another is the artist's ability to immortalize this world's values by means of his verse. Shakespeare's nineteenth and fifty-fifth sonnets, for example, employ this stratagem for the frustration of "Devouring Time," as does Michael Drayton's "How Many Paltry, Foolish, Painted Things." In such poems the speaker's praise of the merits of the beloved is coupled with a celebration of his own poetic gift, through which he can eternize those merits as a "pattern" for future men and women.

The *carpe diem* lyric proposes a more direct and immediate, if also more temporary, solution to the overwhelming problem. Whether subdued or gamesome in tone, it appeals to the young and beautiful to make time their own for a while, to indulge in the "harmless folly" of sensual enjoyment. Ordinarily, as in "To His Coy Mistress" and Herrick's "Corrina's Going A-Maying," the poem imitates an express invitation to love, a suitor's immodest proposal to his lady. Such works are both sharply dramatic and vitally rhetorical; to analyze their style and structure is, in effect, to analyze a persuasive appeal.

From "The Voices of Seduction in 'To His Coy Mistress'"

Barbara T. Christian   (1943–2000)

"EVERYDAY USE" AND THE BLACK POWER MOVEMENT   1994

"Everyday Use" is, in part, Alice Walker's response to the concept of heritage as articulated by the black movements of the 1960s. In that period, many African Americans, disappointed by the failure of integration, gravitated to the philosophy of cultural nationalism as the means to achieve liberation. In contrast to the veneration of Western ideas and ideals by many integrationists of the 1950s, Black Power ideologues emphasized the African cultural past as the true heritage of African Americans. The acknowledgment and appreciation of that heritage, which had too often been denigrated by African Americans themselves as well as by Euro-Americans, was a major tenet of the revolutionary movements of the period. Many blacks affirmed their African roots by changing their "slave names" to African names, and by wearing Afro styles and African clothing. Yet, ideologues of the period also lambasted older African Americans, opposing them to the lofty mythical models of the ancient past. These older men and women, they claimed, had become Uncle Toms and Aunt Jemimas who displayed little awareness of their culture and who, as a result of their slave past, had internalized the white man's view of blacks. So while these 1960s ideologues extolled an unknown ancient history, they denigrated the known and recent past. The tendency to idealize an ancient African past while ignoring the recent African American past still persists in the Afrocentric movements of the 1990s.

In contrast to that tendency, Walker's "Everyday Use" is dedicated to "your grandmama." And the story is told by a woman many African Americans would recognize as their grandmama, that supposedly backward Southern ancestor the cultural nationalists of the North probably visited during the summers of their youth and probably considered behind the times. Walker stresses those physical qualities which suggest such a person, qualities often demeaned by cultural nationalists. For this grandmama, like the stereotypical mammy of slavery, is "a large big-boned woman with rough, man-working hands," who wears "flannel nightgowns to bed and overalls during the day," and whose "fat keeps [her] hot in zero weather." Nor is this grandmama politically conscious according to the fashion of the day; she never had an education after the second grade, she knows nothing about African names, and she eats pork. In having the grandmama tell this story,

Walker gives voice to an entire maternal ancestry often silenced by the political rhetoric of the period. Indeed, Walker tells us in "In Search of Our Mothers' Gardens" that her writing is part of her mother's legacy to her, that many of her stories are based on stories *her* mother told her. Thus, Walker's writing is her way of breaking silences and stereotypes about her grandmothers', mothers', sisters' lives. In effect, her work is a literary continuation of a distinctly oral tradition in which African American women have been and still are pivotal participants.

Alice Walker is well aware of the restrictions of the African American Southern past, for she is the eighth child of Georgia sharecroppers. Born in 1944, she grew up during the period when, as she put it, apartheid existed in America. For in the 1940s and 1950s, when segregation was the law of the South, opportunities for economic and social advancement were legally denied to Southern blacks. Walker was fortunate to come to adulthood during the social and political movements of the late fifties and sixties. Of her siblings, only she, and a slightly older sister, Molly, were able even to imagine the possibility of moving beyond the poverty of their parents. It is unlikely that Alice Walker would have been able to go to college—first at Spelman, the African American women's college in Atlanta, and then at Sarah Lawrence, the white women's college near New York City—if it had not been for the changes that came about as a result of the Civil Rights Movement. Nor is it likely that she, a Southern black woman from a poor family, would have been able to become the writer that she did without the changes resulting from the ferment of the Black and Women's Movements of the 1960s and early 1970s.

While Walker was a participant in these movements, she was also one of their most astute critics. As a Southerner, she was aware of the ways in which black Southern culture was often thought of as backward by predominantly Northern Black Power ideologues, even as they proclaimed their love for black people. She was also acutely aware of the ways in which women were oppressed within the Black Power Movement itself, even as the very culture its participants revered was so often passed on by women. Walker had also visited Africa during her junior year of college and had personally experienced the gap between the Black Power advocates' idealization of Africa and the reality of the African societies she visited.

. . .

Names are extremely important in African and African American culture as a means of indicating a person's spirit. During the 1960s Walker criticized the tendency among some African Americans to give up the names their parents gave them—names which embodied the history of their recent past—for African names that did not relate to a single person they knew. Hence the grandmama in "Everyday Use" is amazed that Dee would give up her name for the name Wangero. For Dee was the name of her great-grandmother, a woman who had kept her family together against great odds. Wangero might have sounded authentically African but it had no relationship to a person she knew, nor to the personal history that had sustained her.

In "Everyday Use," by contrasting a sister who has the opportunity to go to college with a sister who stays at home, Walker reminds us of the challenges that contemporary African American women face as they discover what it means to be truly educated. The same concern appears in many of her works. For example, in "For My Sister Molly Who in the Fifties," she explores the conflicts that can result from an education that takes a woman away from her cultural source. Like Molly, Dee/Wangero in "Everyday Use" is embarrassed by her folk. She has been to the North, wears an Afro, and knows the correct political rhetoric of the 1960s, but she has little regard for her relatives who have helped to create that heritage. Thus, she does not know how to quilt and can only conceive of her family's quilts as priceless artifacts, as things, which she intends to hang on her wall as a means of demonstrating to others that she has "heritage." On the other hand, Maggie, the supposedly uneducated sister, who has been nowhere beyond the supposedly uneducated black South, loves and understands her family and can appreciate its history. She knows how to quilt and would put the precious quilts to "everyday use," which is precisely what, Walker suggests, one needs to do with one's heritage. For Maggie, the quilts are an embodiment of the spirit her folks have passed on to her.

Because Walker came from a background of poverty and social restriction, she also experienced first hand those values through which the grandmama and Maggie transformed the little they had into much more, so that they might survive. As important, Walker understood that poor people needed beauty in their lives and went to great lengths to create it. Although Walker's mother worked long hours in the fields and as a domestic, she cultivated beautiful gradens, artfully told stories, and created beautiful, functional quilts out of scraps. In creating beauty in the media available to them, Walker's mother and other "ordinary" African American women not usually considered artists were, in fact, models of creativity for young African American women who now have the opportunity to become artists.

From introduction to Everyday Use

PSYCHOLOGICAL CRITICISM

Modern psychology has had an immense effect on both literature and literary criticism. The psychoanalytic theories of the Austrian neurologist Sigmund Freud changed our notions of human behavior by exploring new or controversial areas such as wish fulfillment, sexuality, the unconscious, and repression. Perhaps Freud's greatest contribution to literary study was his elaborate demonstration of how much human mental process was unconscious. He analyzed language, often in the form of jokes and conversational slips of the tongue (now often called "Freudian slips"), to show how it reflected the speaker's unconscious fears and desires. He also examined symbols not only in art and literature but also in dreams to study how the unconscious mind expressed itself in coded form to avoid the censorship of the conscious mind. His theory of human cognition asserted that much of what we apparently forget is actually stored deep in the subconscious mind, including painful traumatic memories from childhood that have been repressed.

Freud admitted that he himself had learned a great deal about psychology from studying literature. Sophocles, Shakespeare, Goethe, and Dostoyevsky were as important to the development of his ideas as were his clinical studies. Some of Freud's most influential writing was, in a broad sense, literary criticism, such as his psychoanalytic examination of Sophocles' Oedipus in *The Interpretation of Dreams* (1900). In analyzing Sophocles' tragedy, *Oedipus the King,* Freud paid the classical Greek dramatist the considerable compliment that the playwright had such profound insight into human nature that his characters display the depth and complexity of real people. In focusing on literature, Freud and his disciples like Carl Jung, Ernest Jones, Marie Bonaparte, and Bruno Bettelheim endorsed the belief that great literature truthfully reflects life.

Psychological criticism is a diverse category, but it often employs three approaches. First, it investigates the creative process of the arts: what is the nature of literary genius, and how does it relate to normal mental functions? Such analysis may also focus on literature's effects on the reader. How does a particular work register its impact on the reader's mental and sensory faculties? The second approach involves the psychological study of a particular artist. Most modern literary biographers employ psychology to understand their subject's motivations and behavior. One book, Diane Middlebrook's controversial *Anne Sexton: A Biography* (1991), actually used tapes of the poet's sessions with her psychiatrist as material for the study. The third common approach is the analysis of fictional characters. Freud's study of Oedipus is the prototype for this approach, which tries to bring modern insights about human behavior into the study of how fictional people act. While psychological criticism carefully examines the surface of the literary work, it customarily speculates on what lies underneath the text—the unspoken or perhaps even unspeakable memories, motives, and fears that covertly shape the work, especially in fictional characterizations.

Sigmund Freud   (1856–1939)

THE NATURE OF DREAMS   1933

Let us go back once more to the latent dream-thoughts. Their dominating element is the repressed impulse, which has obtained some kind of expression, toned down and disguised though it may be, by associating itself with stimuli which happen to be there and by tacking itself on the residue of the day before. Just like any other impulse this one presses forward toward satisfaction in action, but the path to motor discharge is closed to it on account of the physiological characteristics of the state of sleep, and so it is forced to travel in the retrograde direction to perception, and content itself with an hallucinatory satisfaction. The latent dream-thoughts are therefore turned into a collection of sensory images and visual scenes. As they are travelling in this direction something happens to them which seems to us new and bewildering. All the verbal apparatus by means of which the more subtle thought-relations are expressed, the conjunctions and prepositions, the variations of declension and conjugation, are lacking, because the means of portraying them are absent: just as in primitive, grammarless speech, only the raw material of thought can be expressed, and the abstract is merged again in the concrete from which it sprang. What is left over may very well seem to lack coherence. It is as much the result of the archaic regression in the mental apparatus as of the demands of the censorship that so much use is made of the representation of certain objects and processes by means of symbols which have become strange to conscious thought. But of more far-reaching import are the other alterations to which the elements comprising the dream-thoughts are subjected. Such of them as have any point of contact are *condensed* into new unities. When the thoughts are translated into pictures those forms are indubitably preferred which allow of this kind of telescoping, or condensation; it is as though a force were at work which subjected the material to a process of pressure or squeezing together. As a result of condensation one element in a manifest dream may correspond to a number of elements of the dream-thoughts; but conversely one of the elements from among the dream-thoughts may be represented by a number of pictures in the dream.

From *New Introductory Lectures on Psychoanalysis*

Gretchen Schulz (b. 1943) and **R. J. R. Rockwood**

FAIRY TALE MOTIFS IN "WHERE ARE YOU GOING, WHERE HAVE YOU BEEN?"

1980

In her fiction both short and long Miss Oates makes frequent use of fairy tale material. Again and again she presents characters and situations which parallel corresponding motifs from the world of folk fantasy. And never is this more true than in the present story ["Where Are You Going, Where Have You Been?"]— never in all the novels and collections of short stories which she has written at last count. Woven into the complex texture of "Where Are You Going, Where Have You Been?" are motifs from such tales as "The Spirit in the Bottle," "Snow White," "Cinderella," "Sleeping Beauty," "Rapunzel," "Little Red Riding Hood," and "The Three Little Pigs." *The Pied Piper of Hamelin*, which ends tragically and so according to [Bruno] Bettelheim does not qualify as a proper fairy tale, serves as the "frame device" that contains all the other tales.

There is a terrible irony here, for although the story is full of fairy tales, Connie, its protagonist, is not. Connie represents an entire generation of young people who have grown up—or tried to—without the help of those bedtime stories which not only entertain the child, but also enable him vicariously to experience and work through problems which he will encounter in adolescence. The only "stories" Connie knows are those of the sexually provocative but superficial lyrics of the popular songs she loves or of the equally insubstantial movies she attends. Such songs and movies provide either no models of behavior for her to imitate, or dangerously inappropriate ones. Connie has thus been led to believe that life and, in particular, love will be "sweet, gentle, the way it was in the movies and promised in songs." She has no idea that life actually can be just as grim as in folk fairy tales. The society that is depicted in "Where Are You Going, Where Have You Been?" has failed to make available to children like Connie maps of the unconscious such as fairy tales provide, because it has failed to recognize that in the unconscious past and future coalesce, and that, psychologically, where the child is going is where he has already been. Since Connie has been left—in the words of yet another of the popular songs—to "wander through that wonderland alone"—it is small wonder, considering her lack of spiritual preparation, that Connie's journey there soon becomes a terrifying schizophrenic separation from reality, with prognosis for recovery extremely poor.

• • •

Bettelheim points out that a fairy tale like "Spirit in the Bottle" deals with two problems that confront the child as he struggles to establish a sense of identity: parental belittlement, and integration of a divided personality. In Connie's case, her mother's belittling remarks that "Connie couldn't do a thing, her mind was all filled with trashy daydreams," certainly have contributed to Connie's two-sidedness, with her one personality "for home" and another for "anywhere that was not home," a division also apparent in the relationship between Connie and the "girl friend" who accompanies her to the bottle-shaped restaurant—the two are so poorly differentiated as to suggest a mere *doubling* of Connie, rather than two separate individuals. While such personality division may at first glance seem pathological, it is not, according to Bettelheim, necessarily abnormal, since the "manner in which the child can bring some order into his world view is by dividing everything into opposites," and that "in the late oedipal and post oedipal ages, this splitting extends to the child himself."

• • •

To be assured of safe passage through what Bettelheim terms "that thorniest of thickets, the oedipal period," a child like Connie would need to have absorbed the wisdom of the other fairy tales to which Miss Oates alludes, tales such as "Snow White," "Cinderella," "Rapunzel," and "Little Red Riding Hood." By their applicability to Connie's situation, these tales reveal that at its deepest level Connie's most compelling psychological problem is *unresolved oedipal conflict, aggravated by sibling rivalry.*

Suggestive of "Snow White" is Connie's "habit of craning her neck to glance into mirrors, or checking other people's faces to make sure her own was all right" (as though other people's faces were mirrors, too); and we are told also that her mother, "who noticed everything and knew everything"—as though with the wicked queen's magic power—"hadn't much reason any longer to look at her own face," and so was jealous of her daughter's beauty and "always after Connie." Arnold Friend's sunglasses also mirror everything, which means that, in this instance he personifies the Magic Mirror and, of course, he finds Connie the fairest one of all. In his words, "Seen you that night and thought, that's the one, yes sir, I never needed to look anymore." Though he thus serves as Prince, there is a hint of the dwarf motif in Arnold's short stature and obvious phallicism; and most particularly is this true of his friend, Ellie Oscar, a case of arrested development, whose face is that of a "forty-year-old baby." Connie's "Someday My Prince Will Come" daydreams, plus the many references to how dazed and sleepy she always is, especially the day Arnold comes for her, when she "lay languidly about the airless little room" and "breathed in and breathed out with each gentle rise and fall of her chest"—these too, suggest "Snow White" and, for that matter, "Sleeping Beauty," whose heroine in the Brothers Grimm is, like Connie, fifteen.

The oedipal implications of "Snow White" are evident in the fact that, as Bettelheim points out, the queen's Magic Mirror speaks not with the mother's but the daughter's voice, revealing the jealous child's own sense of inferiority and frustration projected onto her mother. The father's romantic feelings for the daughter are never at issue in such a fairy tale and he is generally depicted as weak, ineffectual, and oblivious to the struggle that issues between mother and daughter—exactly as in Miss Oates's story.

From "In Fairyland Without a Map: Connie's Exploration Inward in Joyce Carol Oates's 'Where Are You Going, Where Have You Been?'"

Harold Bloom   (b. 1930)

Poetic Influence   1975

Let me reduce my argument to the hopelessly simplistic; poems, I am saying, are neither about "subjects" nor about "themselves." They are necessarily about *other poems*; a poem is a response to a poem, as a poet is a response to a poet, or a person to his parent. Trying to write a poem takes the poet back to the origins of what a poem *first was* for him, and so takes the poet back beyond the pleasure principle to the decisive initial encounter and response that began him. We do not think of W. C. Williams as a Keatsian poet, yet he *began and ended as one,* and his late celebration of his Greeny Flower is another response to Keats's odes. *Only a poet challenges a poet as poet,* and so only a poet makes a poet. To the poet-in-a-poet, a poem is always *the other man,* the precursor, and so a poem is always a person, always the father of one's Second Birth. To live, the poet must *misinterpret* the father, by the crucial act of misprision, which is the rewriting of the father.

But who, what is the poetic father? The voice of the other, of the *daimon,* is always speaking in one; the voice that cannot die because already it has survived death—*the dead poet lives in one.* In the last phase of strong poets, they attempt to join the undying *by living in the dead poets* who are already alive in them. This late Return of the Dead recalls us, as readers, to a recognition of the original motive for the catastrophe of poetic incarnation. Vico, who identified the origins of poetry with the impulse towards divination (to foretell, but also to become a god by foretelling), implicitly understood (as did Emerson, and Wordsworth) that a poem is written to escape dying. Literally, poems are refusals of mortality. Every poem therefore has two makers: the precursor, and the ephebe's rejected mortality.

A poet, I argue in consequence, is not so much a man speaking to men as a man rebelling against being spoken to by a dead man (the precursor) outrageously more alive than himself.

From A Map of Misreading

Mythological Criticism

Mythological critics look for the recurrent universal patterns underlying most literary works. **Mythological criticism** is an interdisciplinary approach that combines the insights of anthropology, psychology, history, and comparative religion. If psychological criticism examines the artist as an individual, mythological criticism explores the artist's common humanity by tracing how the individual imagination uses symbols and situations—consciously or unconsciously—in ways that transcend its own historical milieu and resemble the mythology of other cultures or epochs.

A central concept in mythological criticism is the **archetype,** a symbol, character, situation, or image that evokes a deep universal response. The idea of the archetype came into literary criticism from the Swiss psychologist Carl Jung, a lifetime student of myth and religion. Jung believed that all individuals share a "collective unconscious," a set of primal memories common to the human race, existing below each person's conscious mind. Archetypal images (which often relate to experiencing primordial phenomena like the sun, moon, fire, night, and blood), Jung believed, trigger the collective unconscious. We do not need to accept the literal truth of the collective unconscious, however, to endorse the archetype as a helpful critical concept. Northrop Frye defined the archetype in considerably less occult terms as "a symbol, usually an image, which recurs often enough in literature to be recognizable as an element of one's literary experience as a whole."

Identifying archetypal symbols and situations in literary works, mythological critics almost inevitably link the individual text under discussion to a broader context of works that share an underlying pattern. In discussing Shakespeare's *Hamlet,* for instance, a mythological critic might relate Shakespeare's Danish prince to other mythic sons avenging the deaths of their fathers, like Orestes from Greek myth or Sigmund of Norse legend; or, in discussing *Othello,* relate the sinister figure of Iago to the devil in traditional Christian belief. Critic Joseph Campbell took such comparisons even further; his compendious study *The Hero with a Thousand Faces* demonstrates how similar mythic characters appear in virtually every culture on every continent.

Carl G. Jung   (1875–1961)

The Collective Unconscious and Archetypes   1931

Translated by R. F. C. Hull

A more or less superficial layer of the unconscious is undoubtedly personal. I call it the *personal unconscious.* But this personal unconscious rests upon a deeper layer, which does not derive from personal experience and is not a personal acquisition but is inborn. This deeper layer I call the *collective unconscious.* I have

chosen the term "collective" because this part of the unconscious is not individual but universal; in contrast to the personal psyche, it has contents and
modes of behavior that are more or less the same everywhere and in all individuals. It is, in other words, identical in all men and thus constitutes a common
psyche substrate of a suprapersonal nature which is present in every one of us.

Psychic existence can be recognized only by the presence of contents that
are *capable of consciousness*. We can therefore speak of an unconscious only in so
far as we are able to demonstrate its contents. The contents of the personal unconscious are chiefly the *feeling-toned complexes*, as they are called; they constitute the personal and private side of psychic life. The contents of the collective
unconscious, on the other hand, are known as *archetypes*. . . .

For our purposes this term is apposite and helpful, because it tells us that so far
as the collective unconscious contents are concerned we are dealing with archaic
or—I would say—primordial types, that is, with universal images that have existed
since the remotest times. The term "representations collectives," used by Lévy-
Bruhl to denote the symbolic figures in the primitive view of the world, could
easily be applied to unconscious contents as well, since it means practically the
same thing. Primitive tribal lore is concerned with archetypes that have been
modified in a special way. They are no longer contents of the unconscious, but
have already been changed into conscious formulae taught according to tradition,
generally in the form of esoteric teaching. This last is a typical means of expression
for the transmission of collective contents originally derived from the unconscious.

Another well-known expression of the archetypes is myth and fairy tale. But
here too we are dealing with forms that have received a specific stamp and have
been handed down through long periods of time. The term "archetype" thus applies only indirectly to the "representations collectives," since it designates only
those psychic contents which have not yet been submitted to conscious elaboration and are therefore an immediate datum of psychic experience. In this sense
there is a considerable difference between the archetype and the historical formula
that has evolved. Especially on the higher levels of esoteric teaching the archetypes appear in a form that reveals quite unmistakably the critical and evaluating
influence of conscious elaboration. Their immediate manifestation, as we encounter it in dreams and visions, is much more individual, less understandable, and
more naïve than in myths, for example. The archetype is essentially an unconscious content that is altered by becoming conscious and by being perceived, and it
takes its color from the individual consciousness in which it happens to appear.

From *The Collected Works of C. G. Jung*

Northrop Frye   (1912–1991)

MYTHIC ARCHETYPES   1957

We begin our study of archetypes, then, with a world of myth, an abstract or
purely literary world of fictional and thematic design, unaffected by canons of
plausible adaptation to familiar experience. In terms of narrative, myth is the

imitation of actions near or at the conceivable limits of desire. The gods enjoy beautiful women, fight one another with prodigious strength, comfort and assist man, or else watch his miseries from the height of their immortal freedom. The fact that myth operates at the top level of human desire does not mean that it necessarily presents its world as attained or attainable by human beings. . . .

Realism, or the art of verisimilitude, evokes the response "How like that is to what we know!" When what is written is *like* what is known, we have an art of extended or implied simile. And as realism is an art of implicit simile, myth is an art of implicit metaphorical identity. The word "sun-god," with a hyphen used instead of a predicate, is a pure ideogram, in Pound's terminology, or literal metaphor, in ours. In myth we see the structural principles of literature isolated; in realism we see the *same* structural principles (not similar ones) fitting into a context of plausibility. (Similarly in music, a piece by Purcell and a piece by Benjamin Britten may not be in the least *like* each other, but if they are both in D major their tonality will be the same.) The presence of a mythical structure in realistic fiction, however, poses certain technical problems for making it plausible, and the devices used in solving these problems may be given the general name of *displacement*.

Myth, then, is one extreme of literary design; naturalism is the other, and in between lies the whole area of romance, using that term to mean, not the historical mode of the first essay, but the tendency, noted later in the same essay, to displace myth in a human direction and yet, in contrast to "realism," to conventionalize content in an idealized direction. The central principle of displacement is that what can be metaphorically identified in a myth can only be linked in romance by some form of simile: analogy, significant association, incidental accompanying imagery, and the like. In a myth we can have a sun-god or a tree-god; in a romance we may have a person who is significantly associated with the sun or trees.

From *Anatomy of Criticism*

Edmond Volpe   (b. 1922)

Myth in Faulkner's "Barn Burning"   1964

"Barn Burning" however is not really concerned with class conflict. The story is centered upon Sarty's emotional dilemma. His conflict would not have been altered in any way if the person whose barn Ab burns had been a simple poor farmer, rather than an aristocratic plantation owner. The child's tension, in fact, begins to surface during the hearing in which a simple farmer accuses Ab of burning his barn. The moral antagonists mirrored in Sarty's conflict are not sharecropper and aristocrat. They are the father, Ab Snopes, versus the rest of mankind. Major De Spain is not developed as a character; his house is important to Sarty because it represents a totally new and totally different social and moral entity. Within the context of the society Faulkner is dealing with, the gap between the rich aristocrat and the poor sharecropper provides a viable metaphor for dramatizing the crisis Sarty is undergoing. Ab Snopes is by no means a social crusader. The De Spain manor is Sarty's first contact with a rich man's house, though he can recall, in the short span of his life, at least a dozen times the family had to move because Ab burned barns. Ab does not discriminate between rich and poor. For him there are only two categories: blood kin and "they," into which he lumps all the rest of mankind. Ab's division relates to Sarty's crisis and only by defining precisely the nature of the conflict the boy is undergoing can we determine the moral significance Faulkner sees in it. The clue to Sarty's conflict rests in its resolution.

. . .

The boy's anxiety is created by his awakening sense of his own individuality. Torn between strong emotional attachment to the parent and his growing need to assert his own identity, Sarty's crisis is psychological and his battle is being waged far below the level of his intellectual and moral awareness.

Faulkner makes this clear in the opening scene with imagery that might be described as synesthesia. The real smell of cheese is linked with the smell of the hermetic meat in the tin cans with the scarlet devils on the label that his "intestines believed he smelled coming in intermittent gusts momentary and brief between the other constant one, the smell and sense just a little of fear because mostly of despair and grief, the old fierce pull of blood." The smells below the level of the olfactory sense link the devil image and the blood image to identify the anxiety the father creates in the child's psyche. Tension is created by the blood demanding identification with his father against "*our enemy* he thought in that despair; *ourn! mine and hisn both! He's my father!*" Sarty's conflict is played out in terms of identification, not in moral terms. He does not think of his father as bad, his father's enemies as good.

Ab unjustly accuses Sarty of intending to betray him at the hearing, but he correctly recognizes that his son is moving out of childhood, developing a mind and will of his own and is no longer blindly loyal. In instructing the boy that everyone is the enemy and his loyalty belongs to his blood, Ab's phrasing is revealing: "'Don't you know all they wanted was a chance to get at me because they knew I had them beat?'" Ab does not use the plural "us." It is "I" and "they." Blood loyalty means total identification with Ab, and in the ensuing scenes, Snopes attempts to make his son an extension of himself by taking him to the De Spain house, rise up before dawn to be with him when he returns the rug, accompany him to the hearing against De Spain and finally make him an accomplice in the burning of De Spain's barn.

The moral import of Ab's insistence on blood loyalty is fully developed by the satanic imagery Faulkner introduces in the scene at the mansion. As they go up the drive, Sarty follows his father, seeing the stiff black form against the white plantation house. Traditionally the devil casts no shadow, and Ab's figure appears to the child as having "that impervious quality of something cut ruthlessly from tin, depthless, as though sidewise to the sun it would cast no shadow." The cloven hoof of the devil is suggested by Ab's limp upon which the boy's eyes are fixed as the foot unwaveringly comes down into the manure. Sarty's increasing tension resounds in the magnified echo of the limping foot on the porch boards, "a sound out of all proportion to the displacement of the body it bore, as though it had attained to a sort of vicious and ravening minimum not to be dwarfed by anything." At first Sarty thought the house was impervious to his father, but his burgeoning fear of the threat the father poses is reflected in his vision of Ab becoming magnified and monstrous as the black arm reaches up the white door and Sarty sees "the lifted hand like a curled claw."

The satanic images are projected out of the son's nightmarish vision of his father, but they are reinforced by the comments of the adult narrator. Sarty believes Snopes fought bravely in the Civil War, but Ab, we are told, wore no uniform, gave his fealty to no cause, admitted the authority of no man. He went to war for booty. Ab's ego is so great it creates a centripetal force into which everything must flow or be destroyed. The will-less, abject creature who is his wife symbolizes the power of his will. What Ab had done to his wife, he sets out to do to the emerging will of his son. Ab cannot tolerate any entity that challenges the dominance of his will. By allowing his hog to forage in the farmer's corn and by dirtying and ruining De Spain's rug, he deliberately creates a conflict that requires the assertion of primacy. Fire, the element of the devil, is the weapon for the preservation of his dominance. Ab's rage is not fired by social injustice. It is fired by a pride, like Lucifer's, so absolute it can accept no order beyond its own. In the satanic myth, Lucifer asserts his will against the divine order and is cast out of heaven. The angels who fall with Lucifer become extensions of his will. In the same way, Ab is an outcast and pariah among men. He accepts no order that is not of his blood.

From "'Barn Burning': A Definition of Evil"

SOCIOLOGICAL CRITICISM

Sociological criticism examines literature in the cultural, economic, and political context in which it is written or received. "Art is not created in a vacuum," critic Wilbur Scott observed, "it is the work not simply of a person, but of an author fixed in time and space, answering a community of which he is an important, because articulate part." Sociological criticism explores the relationships between the artist and society. Sometimes it looks at the sociological status of the author to evaluate how the profession of the writer in a particular milieu affected what was written. Sociological criticism also analyzes the social content of literary works—what cultural, economic, or political values a particular text implicitly or explicitly promotes. Finally, sociological criticism examines the role the audience has in shaping literature. A sociological view of Shakespeare, for example, might look at the economic position of Elizabethan playwrights and actors; it might also study the political ideas expressed in the plays or discuss how the nature of an Elizabethan theatrical audience (which was usually all male unless the play was produced at court) helped determine the subject, tone, and language of the plays.

An influential type of sociological criticism has been Marxist criticism, which focuses on the economic and political elements of art. Marxist criticism, like the work of the Hungarian philosopher Georg Lukacs, often explores the ideological content of literature. Whereas a formalist critic would maintain that form and content are inextricably blended, Lukacs believed that content determines form and that, therefore, all art is political. Even if a work of art ignores political issues, it makes a political statement, Marxist critics believe, because it endorses the economic and political status quo. Consequently, Marxist criticism is frequently evaluative and judges some literary work better than others on an ideological basis; this tendency can lead to reductive judgment, as when Soviet critics rated Jack London a novelist superior to William Faulkner, Ernest Hemingway, Edith Wharton, and Henry James, because he illustrated the principles of class struggle more clearly. London was America's first major working-class writer. To examine the political ideas and observations found in his fiction can be illuminating, but to fault other authors for lacking his instincts and ideas is not necessarily helpful in understanding their particular qualities. There is always a danger in sociological criticism—Marxist or otherwise— of imposing the critic's personal politics on the work in question and then evaluating it according to how closely it endorses that ideology. As an analytical tool, however, Marxist criticism and sociological methods can illuminate political and economic dimensions of literature that other approaches overlook.

Georg Lukacs   (1885–1971)

CONTENT DETERMINES FORM   1962

What determines the style of a given work of art? How does the intention determine the form? (We are concerned here, of course, with the intention realized in the work; it need not coincide with the writer's conscious intention.) The distinctions that concern us are not those between stylistic "techniques" in the formalistic sense. It is the view of the world, the ideology or *Weltanschauung*° underlying a writer's work, that counts. And it is the writer's attempt to reproduce this view of the world which constitutes his "intention" and is the formative principle underlying the style of a given piece of writing. Looked at in this way, style ceases to be a formalistic category. Rather, it is rooted in content; it is the specific form of a specific content.

Content determines form. But there is no content of which Man himself is not the focal point. However various the *données*° of literature (a particular experience, a didactic purpose), the basic question is, and will remain: what is Man?

Here is a point of division: if we put the question in abstract, philosophical terms, leaving aside all formal considerations, we arrive—for the realist school— at the traditional Aristotelian dictum (which was also reached by other than purely aesthetic considerations): Man is *zoon politikon*,° a social animal. The Aristotelian dictum is applicable to all great realistic literature. Achilles and Werther, Oedipus and Tom Jones, Antigone and Anna Karenina: their individual existence—their *Sein an sich*,° in the Hegelian terminology; their "ontological being,"

Weltanschauung: German for "world view," an outlook on life.   *données* French for "given"; it means the materials a writer uses to create his or her work or the subject or purpose of a literary work.   *zoon politikon:* Greek for "political animal."   *Sein an sich:* the German philosopher G. W. F. Hegel's term for "pure existence."

as a more fashionable terminology has it—cannot be distinguished from their social and historical environment. Their human significance, their specific individuality cannot be separated from the context in which they were created.

From *Realism in Our Time*

Daniel P. Watkins (b. 1952)

Money and Labor in "The Rocking-Horse Winner" 1987

It is a commonplace that D. H. Lawrence's "The Rocking-Horse Winner" is a story about the devastating effect that money can have on a family, and, further, that Lawrence's specific objections in the story are not to money abstractly conceived but to money as it is understood and valued by capitalist culture. This is one of Lawrence's most savage and compact critiques of what he elsewhere calls "the god-damn bourgeoisie" and of individuals who, despite their natural or potential goodness, "swallow the culture bait" and hence become victims to the world they (wrongly) believe holds the key to human happiness.

. . .

The class nature of labor under capital is presented symbolically in the story in terms of the adult and non-adult worlds. That is, social reality is controlled by parents whose primary concern is to bring in money sufficient to "the social position which they (have) to keep up." While they have a small income, and while "The father went in to town to some office," they never are really seen to work actively and productively. Rather, they set a tone of need in their world that generates intense and pervasive anxiety, which then is passed down to their children, who interiorize the values and attitudes of the adult world and set about (as best they can) to satisfy the demands of that world. Even when money is produced, however, the demands of the adult world are never fully met, but, quite the reverse, intensify further, so that more labor is necessary. In this context, work is not a means of meeting basic human needs, but rather only a way of producing greater sums of money, and thus it is clearly socially unproductive. Seen from this perspective, it is not important that the parents are not capitalists in the crudest sense (that is, they are not drawn as investors of money); what is important is that they both set the tone (economic scarcity) and determine the values (consumerism) of the world they inhabit, and in addition expropriate the wealth that others produce for their own private consumption.

Young Paul exemplifies vividly the sort of work that arises under capital. Simply put, he is a laborer for his mother, to whom he gives all of his money, only to find that the more he gives the more she needs. It is true, of course, that as a handicapper he invests money, betting on a profitable return on his investment, and that in this sense he is a sort of capitalist; indeed, it is his betting that is the literal sign of the economic relations controlling the world of the story. But at the same time his character is made to carry a much larger symbolic significance, for what he is investing, in real terms, is himself, selling his skills to generate wealth that he is not free to possess, but that is necessary to the maintenance of existing social relations. As his mother touches the money he earns, she uses it not to satisfy family needs—it has little or no *use* value—but to extend her social position and social power, and the process of extension of course is never ending, requiring ever greater sums of money: "There were certain new furnishings, and Paul had a tutor. He was *really* going to Eton, his father's school, in the following autumn. There were flowers in the winter, and a blossoming of the luxury Paul's mother had been used to. And yet the voices in the house, behind the sprays of mimosa and almond-blossom, and from under the piles of iridescent cushions, simply trilled and screamed in a sort of ecstasy: 'There *must* be more money!'" This passage clearly focuses the priority of money over commodity and the relentlessness with which the power associated with money controls even the most personal dimension of life.

The work itself that Paul performs cannot, under such conditions, be personally satisfying, and this is shown powerfully by the sort of work he does. The rocking horse is a brilliant symbol of non-productive labor, for even while it moves it remains stationary: even while Paul is magically (humanly) creative, producing untold wealth for his mother, he does not advance in the least, and in fact becomes increasingly isolated and fearful that even the abilities he now possesses will be taken from him. The labor, which drives him to "a sort of madness," that consumes him to an ever greater degree, leaves him nothing for himself, driving him down a terrible path to emotional and then physical distress. He is never satisfied with what he produces because it in no way relieves the pressure that his world places on him, and thus his anxiety and alienation grow to the point of destroying any sense of real personal worth and removing him literally from all meaningful social exchange, as when he takes his rocking horse to his bedroom and rides alone late into the night trying to find the key to wealth.

From "Labor and Religion in D. H. Lawrence's 'The Rocking-Horse Winner'"

Alfred Kazin (1915–1998)

WALT WHITMAN AND ABRAHAM LINCOLN   1984

In Lincoln's lifetime Whitman was the only major writer to describe him with love. Whitman identified Lincoln with himself in the worshipful fashion that became standard after Lincoln's death. That Lincoln was a class issue says a good deal about the prejudices of American society in the East. A leading New Yorker, George Templeton Strong, noted in his diary that while he never disavowed the "lank and hard featured man," Lincoln was "despised and rejected by a third of the community, and only tolerated by the other two-thirds." Whitman the professional man of the people had complicated reasons for loving Lincoln. The uneasiness about him among America's elite was based on the fear that this unknown, untried man, elected without administrative experience (and without a majority) might not be up to his "fearful task."

. . .

Whitman related himself to the popular passion released by war and gave himself to this passion as a political cause. He understood popular opinion in a way that Emerson, Thoreau, and Hawthorne did not attempt to understand it. Emerson said, like any conventional New England clergyman, that the war was holy. He could not speak for the masses who bore the brunt of the war. Whitman was able to get so much out of the war, to create a lasting image of it, because he knew what people were feeling. He was not above the battle like Thoreau and Hawthorne, not suspicious of the majority like his fellow New Yorker Herman Melville, who in "The House-top," the most personal poem in *Battle-Pieces*, denounced the "ship-rats" who had taken over the city in the anti-draft riots of 1863.

Despite Whitman's elusiveness—he made a career out of longings it would have ended that career to fulfill—he genuinely felt at home with soldiers and other "ordinary" people who were inarticulate by the standards of men "from the schools." He was always present, if far from available, presenting the picture of a nobly accessible and social creature. He certainly got on better with omnibus drivers, workingmen, and now "simple" soldiers (especially when they were wounded and open to his ministrations) than he did with "scribblers." By the time Whitman went down after Fredericksburg to look for brother George, the war was becoming a revolution of sorts and Whitman's old radical politics were becoming "the nation." This made him adore Lincoln as the symbol of the nation's unity. An essential quality of Whitman's Civil War "memoranda" is Whitman's libidinous urge to associate himself with the great, growing, ever more powerful federal cause. Whitman's characteristic lifelong urge to join, to combine, to see life as movement, unity, totality, became during the Civil War an actively loving association with the broad masses of the people and *their* war. In his cult of the Civil War, Whitman allies himself with a heroic and creative energy which sees itself spreading out from the people and their representative men, Lincoln and Whitman.

Hawthorne's and Thoreau's horror of America as the Big State did not reflect Whitman's image of the Union. His passion for the "cause" reflected his intense faith in democracy at a juncture when the United States at war represented the revolutionary principle to Marx, the young Ibsen, Mill, Browning, Tolstoy. Whitman's deepest feeling was that his own rise from the city streets, his future as a poet of democracy, was tied up with the Northern armies.

From *An American Procession*

GENDER CRITICISM

Gender criticism examines how sexual identity influences the creation and reception of literary works. Gender studies began with the feminist movement and were influenced by such works as Simone de Beauvoir's *The Second Sex* (1949) and Kate Millett's *Sexual Politics* (1970) as well as sociology, psychology, and anthropology. Feminist critics believe that culture has been so completely dominated by men that literature is full of unexamined "male-produced" assumptions. They see their criticism correcting this imbalance by analyzing and combatting patriarchal attitudes.

Feminist criticism has explored how an author's gender influences—consciously or unconsciously—his or her writing. While a formalist critic like Allen Tate emphasized the universality of Emily Dickinson's poetry by demonstrating how powerfully the language, imagery, and mythmaking of her poems combine to affect a generalized reader, Sandra M. Gilbert, a leading feminist critic, has identified attitudes and assumptions in Dickinson's poetry that she believes are essentially female. Another important theme in feminist criticism is analyzing how sexual identity influences the reader of a text. If Tate's hypothetical reader was deliberately sexless, Gilbert's reader sees a text through the eyes of his or her sex. Finally, feminist critics carefully examine how the images of men and women in imaginative literature reflect or reject the social forces that have historically kept the sexes from achieving total equality.

Recently, gender criticism has expanded beyond its original feminist perspective. Critics have explored the impact of different sexual orientations on literary creation and reception. A men's movement has also emerged in response to feminism, seeking not to reject feminism but to rediscover masculine identity in an authentic, contemporary way. Led by poet Robert Bly, the men's movement has paid special attention to interpreting poetry and fables as myths of psychic growth and sexual identity.

Elaine Showalter   (b. 1941)

TOWARD A FEMINIST POETICS   1979

Feminist criticism can be divided into two distinct varieties. The first type is concerned with *woman as reader*—with woman as the consumer of male-produced literature, and with the way in which the hypothesis of a female reader changes our apprehension of a given text, awakening us to the significance of its sexual codes. I shall call this kind of analysis the *feminist critique*, and like other kinds of critique it is a historically grounded inquiry which probes the ideological assumptions of literary phenomena. Its subjects include the images and stereotypes of women in literature, the omissions of and misconceptions about women in criticism, and the fissures in male-constructed literary history. It is also concerned with the exploitation and manipulation of the female audience, especially in popular culture and film; and with the analysis of woman-as-sign in semiotic systems. The second type of feminist criticism is concerned with *woman as writer*—with woman as the producer of textual meaning, with the history, themes, genres, and structures of literature by women. Its subjects include the psychodynamics of female creativity; linguistics and the problem of a female language; the trajectory of the individual or collective female literary career; literary history; and, of course, studies of particular writers and works. No term exists in English for such a specialized discourse, and so I have adapted the French term *la gynocritique*: "gynocritics" (although the significance of the male pseudonym in the history of women's writing also suggested the term "georgics").

The feminist critique is essentially political and polemical, with theoretical affiliations to Marxist sociology and aesthetics; gynocritics is more self-contained and experimental, with connections to other modes of new feminist research. In a dialogue between these two positions, Carolyn Heilbrun, the writer, and Catharine Stimpson, editor of the journal *Signs: Women in Culture and Society*, compare the feminist critique to the Old Testament, "looking for the sins and errors of the past," and gynocritics to the New Testament, seeking "the grace of imagination." Both kinds are necessary, they explain, for only the Jeremiahs of the feminist critique can lead us out of the "Egypt of female servitude" to the promised land of the feminist vision. That the discussion makes use of these Biblical metaphors points to the connections between feminist consciousness and conversion narratives which often appear in women's literature; Carolyn Heilbrun comments on her own text, "When I talk about feminist criticism, I am amazed at how high a moral tone I take."

From "Toward a Feminist Poetics"

Juliann Fleenor   (b. 1942)

Gender and Pathology in "The Yellow Wallpaper"   1983

Although it is not generally known, Gilman wrote at least two other Gothic stories around the same time as "The Yellow Wallpaper." All three were published in the *New England Magazine*. At the time that "The Rocking Chair" and "The Giant Wistaria" were written, Gilman and her young daughter, Katherine, were living in the warmth of Pasadena, separated from her husband, Charles Walter Stetson. Gilman later noted in her papers: "'The Yellow Wallpaper' was written in two days, with the thermometer at one hundred and three in Pasadena, Ca." Her husband was living on the east coast, and, perhaps coincidentally, all three stories appear to be set in a nameless eastern setting, one urban and two rural. All three display similar themes, and all three are evidence that the conflict, central to Gilman's Gothic fiction and later to her autobiography, was a conflict with the mother, with motherhood, and with creation.

In all three stories women are confined within the home; it is their prison, their insane asylum, even their tomb. A sense of the female isolation which Gilman felt, of exclusion from the public world of work and of men, is contained in the anecdote related by Zona Gale in her introduction to Gilman's autobiography. After watching the approach of several locomotives to a train platform in a small town in Wisconsin, Gilman said, "'All that, . . . and women have no part in it. Everything done by men, working together, while women worked on alone within their four walls!'" Female exclusion, women denied the opportunity to work, or their imprisonment behind four walls, led to madness. Her image, interestingly, does not suggest a female subculture of women working together; Gilman was working against her own culture's definition of women, and her primary antagonists were women like her own mother.

Diseased maternity is explicit in Gilman's third Gothic story. The yellow wallpaper symbolizes more than confinement, victimization, and the inability to write. It suggests a disease within the female self. When the narrator peels the wallpaper off, "It sticks horribly and the pattern just enjoys it! All those strangled heads and bulbous eyes and the waddling fungus growths just shriek with derision." This passage describes more than the peeling of wallpaper: the "strangled heads and bulbous eyes and waddling fungus" imply something strange and terrible about birth and death conjoined, about female procreation, and about female physiology. Nature is perverted here, too. The narrator thinks of "old foul, bad yellow things." The smell "creeps all over the house." She finds it "hovering in the dining-room, skulking in the parlor, hiding in the hall, lying in wait for me on the stairs." Finally, "it gets into my hair."

The paper stains the house in a way that suggests the effect of afterbirth. The house, specifically this room, becomes more than a symbol of a repressive society; it represents the physical self of the narrator as well. She is disgusted, perhaps awed, perhaps frightened of her own bodily processes. The story establishes a sense of fear and disgust, the skin crawls and grows clammy with the sense of physiological fear that Ellen Moers refers to as the Female Gothic.

My contention that one of the major themes in the story, punishment for becoming a mother (as well as punishment for being female), is supported by the absence of the child. The child is taken away from the mother, almost in punishment, as was the child in "The Giant Wistaria." This differs from Gilman's experience; she had been told to keep her child with her at all times. In both the story and in Gilman's life, a breakdown occurs directly after the birth of a child. The narrator is confined as if she had committed a crime. Maternity—the creation of a child—is combined with writing—the creation of writing—in a way that suggests they are interrelated and perhaps symbiotic, as are the strange toadstools behind the wallpaper.

The pathological nature of both experiences is not surprising, given the treatment Gilman received, and given the fact that maternity reduced women to mothers and not writers. Childbirth has long been a rite of passage for women. But the question is, where does that passage lead? Becoming a mother leads to a child-like state. The narrator becomes the absent child.

From "The Gothic Prism"

Sandra M. Gilbert (b. 1936)
and Susan Gubar (b. 1944)

THE FREEDOM OF EMILY DICKINSON 1985

[Emily Dickinson] defined herself as a *woman* writer, reading the works of female precursors with special care, attending to the implications of novels like Charlotte Brontë's *Jane Eyre*, Emily Brontë's *Wuthering Heights*, and George Eliot's *Middlemarch* with the same absorbed delight that characterized her devotion to Elizabeth Barrett Browning's *Aurora Leigh*. Finally, then, the key to her enigmatic identity as a "supposed person" who was called the "Myth of Amherst" may rest, not in investigations of her questionable romance, but in studies of her unquestionably serious reading as well as in analyses of her disquietingly powerful writing. Elliptically phrased, intensely compressed, her poems are more linguistically innovative than any other nineteenth-century verses, with the possible exception of some works by Walt Whitman and Gerard Manley Hopkins, her two most radical male contemporaries. Throughout her largely secret but always brilliant career, moreover, she confronted precisely the questions about the individual and society, time and death, flesh and spirit, that major precursors from Milton to Keats had faced. Dreaming of "Amplitude and Awe," she recorded sometimes vengeful, sometimes mystical visions of social and personal transformation in poems as inventively phrased and imaginatively constructed as any in the English language.

Clearly such accomplishments required not only extraordinary talent but also some measure of freedom. Yet because she was the unmarried daughter of conservative New Englanders, Dickinson was obliged to take on many household tasks; as a nineteenth-century New England wife, she would have had the same number of obligations, if not more. Some of these she performed with pleasure; in 1856, for instance, she was judge of a bread-baking contest, and in 1857 she won a prize in that contest. But as Higginson's "scholar," as a voracious reader and an ambitious writer, Dickinson had to win herself time for "Amplitude and Awe," and it is increasingly clear that she did so through a strategic withdrawal from her ordinary world. A story related by her niece Martha Dickinson Bianchi reveals that the poet herself knew from the first what both the price and the prize might be: on one occasion, said Mrs. Bianchi, Dickinson took her up to the room in which she regularly sequestered herself, and, mimicking locking herself in, "thumb and forefinger closed on an imaginary key," said "with a quick turn of her wrist, 'It's just a turn—and freedom, Matty!'"

In the freedom of her solitary, but not lonely, room, Dickinson may have become what her Amherst neighbors saw as a bewildering "myth." Yet there, too, she created myths of her own. Reading the Brontës and Barrett Browning, studying Transcendentalism and the Bible, she contrived a theology which is powerfully expressed in many of her poems. That it was at its most hopeful a female-centered theology is revealed in verses like those she wrote about the women artists she admired, as well as in more general works like her gravely pantheistic address to the "Sweet Mountains" who "tell me no lie," with its definition of the hills around Amherst as "strong Madonnas" and its description of the writer herself as "The Wayward Nun – beneath the Hill – / Whose service is to You – ." As Dickinson's admirer and descendant Adrienne Rich has accurately observed, this passionate poet consistently chose to confront her society—to "have it out"—"on her own premises."

From introduction to Emily Dickinson,
The Norton Anthology of Literature by Women

READER-RESPONSE CRITICISM

Reader-response criticism attempts to describe what happens in the reader's mind while interpreting a text. If traditional criticism assumes that imaginative writing is a creative act, reader-response theory recognizes that reading is also a creative process. Reader-response critics believe that no text provides self-contained meaning; literary texts do not exist independently of readers' interpretations. A text, according to this critical school, is not finished until it is read and interpreted. As Oscar Wilde remarked in the preface to his novel *The Picture of Dorian Gray* (1891), "It is the spectator, and not life that art really mirrors." The practical problem then arises, however, that no two individuals necessarily read a text in exactly the same way. Rather than declare one interpretation correct and the other mistaken, reader-response criticism recognizes the inevitable plurality of readings. Instead of trying to ignore or reconcile the contradictions inherent in this situation, it explores them.

The easiest way to explain reader-response criticism is to relate it to the common experience of rereading a favorite book after many years. Rereading a novel as an adult, for example, that "changed your life" as an adolescent, is often a shocking experience. The book may seem substantially different. The character you remembered liking most now seems less admirable, and another character you disliked now seems more sympathetic. Has the book changed? Very unlikely, but *you* certainly have in the intervening years. Reader-response criticism explores how the different individuals (or classes of individuals) see the same text differently. It emphasizes how religious, cultural, and social values affect readings; it also overlaps with gender criticism in exploring how men and women read the same text with different assumptions.

While reader-response criticism rejects the notion that there can be a single correct reading for a literary text, it doesn't consider all readings permissible. Each text creates limits to its possible interpretations. As Stanley Fish admits in the following critical selection, we cannot arbitrarily place an Eskimo in William Faulkner's story "A Rose for Emily" (though Professor Fish does ingeniously imagine a hypothetical situation where this bizarre interpretation might actually be possible).

Stanley Fish   (b. 1938)

An Eskimo "A Rose for Emily"   1980

The fact that it remains easy to think of a reading that most of us would dismiss out of hand does not mean that the text excludes it but that there is as yet no elaborated interpretive procedure for producing that text. . . . Norman Holland's analysis of Faulkner's "A Rose for Emily" is a case in point. Holland is arguing for a kind of psychoanalytic pluralism. The text, he declares, is "at most a matrix of psychological possibilities for its readers," but, he insists, "only some possibilities . . . truly fit the matrix": "One would not say, for example, that a reader of . . . 'A Rose for Emily' who thought the 'tableau' [of Emily and her father in the doorway] described an Eskimo was really responding to the story at all—only pursuing some mysterious inner exploration."

Holland is making two arguments: first, that anyone who proposes an Eskimo reading of "A Rose for Emily" will not find a hearing in the literary community. And that, I think, is right. ("We are right to rule out at least some readings.") His second argument is that the unacceptability of the Eskimo reading is a function of the text, of what he calls its "sharable promptuary," the public "store of structured language" that sets limits to the interpretations the words can accommodate. And that, I think, is wrong. The Eskimo reading is unacceptable because there is at present no interpretive strategy for producing it, no way of "looking" or reading (and remember, all acts of looking or reading are "ways") that would result in the emergence of obviously Eskimo meanings. This does not mean, however, that no such strategy could ever come into play, and it is not difficult to imagine the circumstances under which it would establish itself. One such circumstance would be the discovery of a letter in which Faulkner confides that he has always believed himself to be an Eskimo changeling. (The example is absurd only if one forgets Yeats's *Vision* or Blake's Swedenborgianism° or James Miller's recent elaboration of a homosexual reading of *The Waste Land*.) Immediately the workers in the Faulkner industry would begin to reinterpret the canon in the light of this newly revealed "belief" and the work of reinterpretation would involve the elaboration of a symbolic or allusive system (not unlike mythological or typological criticism) whose application would immediately transform the text into one informed everywhere by Eskimo meanings. It might seem that I am admitting that there is a text to be transformed, but the object of transformation would be the text (or texts) given by whatever interpretive strategies the Eskimo strategy was in the process of dislodging or expanding. The result would be that whereas we now have a Freudian "A Rose for Emily," a mythological "A Rose for Emily," a Christological "A Rose for Emily," a regional "A Rose for Emily," a sociological "A Rose for Emily," a linguistic "A Rose for Emily," we would in addition have an Eskimo "A Rose for Emily," existing in some relation of compatibility or incompatibility with the others.

Again the point is that while there are always mechanisms for ruling out readings, their source is not the text but the presently recognized interpretive strategies for producing the text. It follows, then, that no reading, however outlandish it might appear, is inherently an impossible one.

From *Is There a Text in This Class?*

Robert Scholes   (b. 1929)

"How Do We Make a Poem?"   1982

Let us begin with one of the shortest poetic texts in the English language, "Elegy" by W. S. Merwin:

Who would I show it to

One line, one sentence, unpunctuated, but proclaimed an interrogative by its grammar and syntax—what makes it a poem? Certainly without its title it would not be a poem; but neither would the title alone constitute a poetic text. Nor do

---

Yeats's Vision *or Blake's Swedenborgianism:* Irish poet William Butler Yeats and Swedish mystical writer Emanuel Swedenborg both claimed to have received revelations from the spirit world; some of Swedenborg's ideas are embodied in the long poems of William Blake.

the two together simply make a poem by themselves. Given the title and the text, the *reader* is encouraged to make a poem. He is not forced to do so, but there is not much else he can do with this material, and certainly nothing else so rewarding. (I will use the masculine pronoun here to refer to the reader, not because all readers are male but because I am, and my hypothetical reader is not a pure construct but an idealized version of myself.)

How do we make a poem out of this text? There are only two things to work on, the title and the question posed by the single, colloquial line. The line is not simply colloquial, it is prosaic; with no words of more than one syllable, concluded by a preposition, it is within the utterance range of every speaker of English. It is, in a sense, completely intelligible. But in another sense it is opaque, mysterious. Its three pronouns—who, I, it—pose problems of reference. Its conditional verb phrase—would . . . show to—poses a problem of situation. The context that would supply the information required to make that simple sentence meaningful as well as intelligible is not there. It must be supplied by the reader.

To make a poem of this text the reader must not only know English, he must know a poetic code as well: the code of the funeral elegy, as practiced in English from the Renaissance to the present time. The "words on the page" do not constitute a poetic "work," complete and self-sufficient, but a "text," a sketch or outline that must be completed by the active participation of a reader equipped with the right sort of information. In this case part of that information consists of an acquaintance with the elegiac tradition: its procedures, assumptions, devices, and values. One needs to know works like Milton's "Lycidas," Shelley's "Adonais," Tennyson's "In Memoriam," Whitman's "When Lilacs Last in the Dooryard Bloomed," Thomas's "Refusal to Mourn the Death by Fire of a Child in London," and so on, in order to "read" this simple poem properly. In fact, it could be argued that the more elegies one can bring to bear on a reading of this one, the better, richer poem this one becomes. I would go even further, suggesting that a knowledge of the critical tradition—of Dr. Johnson's objections to "Lycidas," for instance, or Wordsworth's critique of poetic diction—will also enhance one's reading of this poem. For the poem is, of course, an anti-elegy, a refusal not simply to mourn, but to write a sonorous, eloquent, mournful, but finally acquiescent, accepting—in a word, "elegiac"—poem at all.

Reading the poem involves, then, a special knowledge of its tradition. It also involves a special interpretive skill. The forms of the short, written poem as they have developed in English over the past few centuries can be usefully seen as compressed, truncated, or fragmented imitations of other verbal forms, especially the play, story, public oration, and personal essay. The reasons for this are too complicated for consideration here, but the fact will be apparent to all who reflect upon the matter. Our short poems are almost always elliptical versions of what can easily be conceived of as dramatic, narrative, oratorical, or meditative texts. Often, they are combinations of these and other modes of address. To take an obvious example, the dramatic monologue in the hands of Robert Browning is like a speech from a play (though usually more elongated than most such speeches). But to "read" such a monologue we must imagine the setting, the situation, the context, and so on. The dramatic monologue is "like" a play but gives us less information of certain sorts than a play would, requiring us to provide that information by decoding the clues in the monologue itself in the light of our understanding of the generic model. Most short poems work this way. They require both special knowledge and special skills to be "read."

To understand "Elegy" we must construct a situation out of the clues provided. The "it" in "Who would I show it to" is of course the elegy itself. The "I" is the potential writer of the elegy. The "Who" is the audience for the poem. But the verb phrase "would . . . show to" indicates a condition contrary to fact. Who would I show it to *if* I were to write it? This implies in turn that for the potential elegiac poet there is one person whose appreciation means more than that of all the rest of the potential audience for the poem he might write, and it further implies that the death of this particular person is the one imagined in the poem. If this person were dead, the poet suggests, so would his inspiration be dead. With no one to write for, no poem would be forthcoming. This poem is not only a "refusal to mourn," like that of Dylan Thomas, it is a refusal to elegize. The whole elegiac tradition, like its cousin the funeral oration, turns finally away from mourning toward acceptance, revival, renewal, a return to the concerns of life, symbolized by the very writing of the poem. Life goes on; there *is* an audience; and the mourned person will live through accomplishments, influence, descendants, and also (not least) in the elegiac poem itself. Merwin rejects all that. *If* I wrote an elegy for X, the person for whom I have always written, X would not be alive to read it; therefore, there is no reason to write an elegy for the one person in my life who most deserves one; therefore, there is no reason to write any elegy, anymore, ever. Finally, and of course, this poem called "Elegy" is not an elegy.

From *Semiotics and Interpretation*

Michael J. Colacurcio (b. 1936)

THE END OF YOUNG GOODMAN BROWN 1995

Having begun by assuming that all visible sanctity was real sanctity and by presuming his own final perseverance in faith, having next despaired of *all* virtue, he [Goodman Brown] ends by doubting the existence of any unblighted goodness but his own. There is simply no other way to account for the way Goodman Brown spends the rest of his life. Evidently he clings to the precious knowledge that he, at least, resisted the wicked one's final invitation to diabolical communion; accordingly, the lurid satisfactions of Satan's anti-covenant are not available to him. But neither are the sweet delights of the Communion of the Saints. He knows he resisted the "last, last crime" of witchcraft, but his deepest suspicion seems to be that Faith did not resist. Or if that seems too strong a formulation for tender-minded readers, he cannot make his faith in Faith prevail. Without such a prevailing faith, he is left outside the bounds of all communion: his own unbartered soul is the only certain locus of goodness in a world otherwise altogether blasted.

It would be easy enough to praise Young Goodman Brown for his recovery from the blasphemous nihilism of his mid-forest rage against the universe; for his refusal to translate his cosmic paranoia into an Ahabian plan of counterattack. Or, from another point of view, it would even be possible to suggest that if the Devil's proffered community of evil is the only community possible, perhaps he should have accepted membership instead of protecting the insular sacredness of his own separate and too precious soul. Perhaps salvation is not worth having— perhaps it is meaningless—in a universe where depravity has undone so many. But both of these moral prescriptions miss Hawthorne's principal emphasis, which, as I read the tale, is on the problem of faith and evidence; on that peculiar kind of "doubt" (in epistemological essence, really a kind of negative faith) which follows from a discrediting of evidences formerly trusted. Brown is damned to stony moral isolation because his "evidential" Puritan biases have led him all un-prepared into a terrifying betrayal of Faith. He believes the Devil's spectral sug-gestions not merely because he is naive, though he is that; and not merely because he is incapable of the sort of evidential subtlety by which John Cotton instructed the very first members of those newly purified New England churches in the art of separating sheep and goats, or by which the Mathers sermonized the court of Oyer and Terminer on the occult art of the distinguishing of spirits. Brown believes the Devil because, at one level, the projected guilt of a man in bad faith *is* specter ev-idence and because, even more fundamentally, absolute moral quality is related to outward appearance as a real person is to his specter.

In short, Hawthorne suggests, one had better not raise such ultimate ques-tions at all: to do so is to risk the appearance-and-reality question in its most per-nicious, even "paranoic" form. At best one would be accepting the deceptive ap-pearances of sanctity, as Goodman Brown evidently continued to be accepted at the communion table of a community which never suspected his presumption, de-spair, blasphemy, and his near approach to witchcraft; . . . And at worst, if one is already in bad faith, his penetrating glimpses into the "reality" behind the appear-ances will be no more than spectral projections of his own guilty wishes; . . . The truly naive will simply accept the smiling light of daytime, church-day appear-ances; the already compromised will "see" in others (as irrevocable commitment) what already pre-exists in themselves (as fantasy, wish, desire, or momentary in-tention). The only alternative would seem to be the acceptance of some ultimate and fundamental equality in a common moral struggle; a healthy skepticism about all moral appearances, firmly wedded to the faith that, whatever men may fanta-size, or however they may fall, they generally love the good and hate the evil.

From *The Province of Piety: Moral History in Hawthorne's Early Tales*

DECONSTRUCTIONIST CRITICISM

Deconstructionist criticism rejects the traditional assumption that language can accu-rately represent reality. Language, according to deconstructionists, is a fundamentally unstable medium; consequently, literary texts, which are made up of words, have no fixed, single meaning. Deconstructionists insist, according to critic Paul de Man, on "the impossibility of making the actual expression coincide with what has to be expressed, of making the actual signs coincide with what is signified." Since they believe that literature cannot definitively express its subject matter, deconstructionists tend to shift their attention away from *what* is being said to *how* language is being used in a text.

Paradoxically, deconstructionist criticism often resembles formalist criticism; both methods usually involve close reading. But while a formalist usually tries to demonstrate how the diverse elements of a text cohere into meaning, the deconstructionist approach attempts to show how the text "deconstructs," that is, how it can be broken down—by a skeptical critic—into mutually irreconcilable positions. A biographical or historical critic might seek to establish the author's intention as a means to interpreting a literary work, but deconstructionists reject the notion that the critic should endorse the myth of authorial control over language. Deconstructionist critics like Roland Barthes and Michel Foucault have therefore called for "the death of the author," that is, the rejection of the assumption that the author, no matter how ingenious, can fully control the meaning of a text. They have also announced the death of literature as a special category of writing. In their view, poems and novels are merely words on a page that deserve no privileged status as art; all texts are created equal—equally untrustworthy, that is.

Deconstructionists focus on how language is used to achieve power. Since they believe, in the words of critic David Lehman, that "there are no truths, only rival interpretations," deconstructionists try to understand how some "interpretations" come to be regarded as truth. A major goal of deconstruction is to demonstrate how those supposed truths are at best provisional and at worst contradictory.

Deconstruction, as you may have inferred, calls for intellectual subtlety and skill. If you pursue your literary studies beyond the introductory stage, you will want to become more familiar with its assumptions. Deconstruction may strike you as a negative, even destructive, critical approach, and yet its best practitioners are adept at exposing the inadequacy of much conventional criticism. By patient analysis, they can sometimes open up the most familiar text and find unexpected significance.

Roland Barthes (1915–1980)

THE DEATH OF THE AUTHOR   1968

TRANSLATED BY STEPHEN HEATH

Succeeding the Author, the scriptor no longer bears within him passions, humours, feelings, impressions, but rather this immense dictionary from which he draws a writing that can know no halt: life never does more than imitate the book, and the book itself is only a tissue of signs, an imitation that is lost, infinitely deferred.

Once the Author is removed, the claim to decipher a text becomes quite futile. To give a text an Author is to impose a limit on that text, to furnish it with a final signified, to close the writing. Such a conception suits criticism very well, the latter then allotting itself the important task of discovering the Author (or its hypostases: society, history, psyché, liberty) beneath the work: when the Author has been found, the text is "explained"—victory to the critic. Hence there is no surprise in the fact that, historically, the reign of the Author has also been that of the Critic, nor again in the fact that criticism (be it new) is today undermined along with the Author. In the multiplicity of writing, everything is to be *disentangled,* nothing *deciphered;* the structure can be followed, "run" (like the thread of a stocking) at every point and at every level, but there is nothing beneath: the space of writing is to be ranged over, not pierced; writing ceaselessly posits meaning ceaselessly to evaporate it, carrying out a systematic exemption of meaning. In precisely this way literature (it would be better from now on to say *writing*), by refusing to assign a "secret," an ultimate meaning, to the text (and to the world as text), liberates what may be called an anti-theological activity, an activity that is truly revolutionary since to refuse to fix meaning is, in the end, to refuse God and his hypostases—reason, science, law.

From "The Death of the Author"

Barbara Johnson   (b. 1947)

Rigorous Unreliability

1987

As a critique of a certain Western conception of the nature of signification, deconstruction focuses on the functioning of claim-making and claim-subverting structures within texts. A deconstructive reading is an attempt to show how the conspicuously foregrounded statements in a text are systematically related to discordant signifying elements that the text has thrown into its shadows or margins, an attempt both to recover what is lost and to analyze what happens when a text is read solely in function of intentionality, meaningfulness, and representativity. Deconstruction thus confers a new kind of readability on those elements in a text that readers have traditionally been trained to disregard, overcome, explain away, or edit out—contradictions, obscurities, ambiguities, incoherences, discontinuities, ellipses, interruptions, repetitions, and plays of the signifier. In this sense it involves a reversal of values, a revaluation of the signifying function of everything that, in a signified-based theory of meaning, would constitute "noise." Derrida° has chosen to speak of the values involved in this reversal in terms of "speech" and "writing," in which "speech" stands for the privilege accorded to meaning as immediacy, unity, identity, truth, and presence, while "writing" stands for the devalued functions of distance, difference, dissimulation, and deferment.

This transvaluation has a number of consequences for the appreciation of literature. By shifting the attention from intentional meaning to writing as such, deconstruction has enabled readers to become sensitive to a number of recurrent literary topoi° in a new way.

· · ·

In addition, by seeing interpretation itself as a fiction-making activity, deconstruction has both reversed and displaced the narrative categories of "showing" and "telling," mimesis and diegesis.° Instead of according moments of tex-

---

Derrida: Jacques Derrida (b. 1930), French philosopher active in the development of deconstructionism.   *topoi:* the plural of the Greek *topos,* for "place"; it means a commonly used literary device.   *diegesis:* the main events of a story, the basic plot, as distinct from the narration.

tual self-interpretation an authoritative metalinguistic status, deconstruction considers anything the text says about itself to be another fiction, an allegory of the reading process. Hence, the privilege traditionally granted to showing over telling is reversed: "telling" becomes a more sophisticated form of "showing," in which what is "shown" is the breakdown of the show/tell distinction. Far from doing the reader's work for her, the text's self-commentary only gives the reader more to do. Indeed, it is the way in which a text subverts the possibility of any authoritative reading by inscribing the reader's strategies into its own structures that often, for de Man, ends up being constitutive of literature as such.

Deconstructors, therefore, tend to privilege texts that are self-reflexive in interestingly and rigorously unreliable ways. Since self-reflexive texts often explicitly posit themselves as belated or revolutionary with respect to a tradition on which they comment, deconstruction can both reinstate the self-consciously outmoded or overwritten (such as Melville's *Pierre*°) and canonize the experimental or avant-garde. But because deconstruction has focused on the ways in which the Western white male philosophico-literary tradition subverts itself *from within*, it has often tended to remain within the confines of the established literary and philosophical canon. . . . If it has questioned the boundary lines of literature, it has done so not with respect to the noncanonical but with respect to the line between literature and philosophy or between literature and criticism. It is as a rethinking of those distinctions that deconstruction most radically displaces certain traditional evaluative assumptions.

From *A World of Difference*

Geoffrey Hartman   (b. 1929)

ON WORDSWORTH'S "A SLUMBER DID MY SPIRIT SEAL"   1987

Take Wordsworth's well-known lyric of eight lines, one of the "Lucy" poems, which has been explicated so many times without its meaning being fully determined:

> A slumber did my spirit seal;
>   I had no human fears:
> She seemed a thing that could not feel
>   The touch of earthly years.
>
> No motion has she now, no force;
>   She neither hears nor sees;
> Rolled round in earth's diurnal course,
>   With rocks, and stones, and trees.

It does not matter whether you interpret the second stanza (especially its last line) as tending toward affirmation, or resignation, or a grief verging on bitterness. The tonal assignment of one rather than another possible meaning, to

---

Pierre: Pierre, or the Ambiguities (1852), a complex novel by Herman Melville, was a failure during the author's lifetime; it was not widely read until the mid-twentieth century.

repeat Susanne Langer° on musical form, is curiously open or beside the point. Yet the lyric does not quite support Langer's general position, that "Articulation is its life, but not assertion," because the poem is composed of a series of short and definitive statements, very like assertions. You could still claim that the poem's life is not in the assertions but somewhere else: but where then? What would articulation mean in that case? Articulation is not anti-assertive here; indeed the sense of closure is so strong that it thematizes itself in the very first line.

Nevertheless, is not the harmony or aesthetic effect of the poem greater than this local conciseness; is not the sense of closure broader and deeper than our admiration for a perfect technical construct? The poem is surely something else than a fine box, a well-wrought coffin.

That it is a kind of epitaph is relevant, of course. We recognize, even if genre is not insisted on, that Wordsworth's style is laconic, even lapidary. There may be a mimetic or formal motive related to the ideal of epitaphic poetry. But the motive may also be, in a precise way, meta-epitaphic. The poem, first of all, marks the closure of a life that has never opened up: Lucy is likened in other poems to a hidden flower or the evening star. Setting overshadows rising, and her mode of existence is inherently inward, westering. I will suppose then, that Wordsworth was at some level giving expression to the traditional epitaphic wish: Let the earth rest lightly on the deceased. If so, his conversion of this epitaphic formula is so complete that to trace the process of conversion might seem gratuitous. The formula, a trite if deeply grounded figure of speech, has been catalyzed out of existence. Here it is formula itself, or better, the adjusted words of the mourner that lie lightly on the girl and everyone who is a mourner.

I come back, then, to the "aesthetic" sense of a burden lifted, rather than denied. A heavy element is made lighter. One may still feel that the term "elation" is inappropriate in this context; yet elation is, as a mood, the very subject of the first stanza. For the mood described is love or desire when it *eternizes* the loved person, when it makes her a star-like being that "could not feel / The touch of earthly years." This *naive* elation, this spontaneous movement of the spirit upward, is reversed in the downturn or catastrophe of the second stanza. Yet this stanza does not close out the illusion; it preserves it within the elegiac form. The illusion is elated, in our use of the word: *aufgehoben*° seems the proper term. For the girl is still, and all the more, what she seemed to be: beyond touch, like a star, if the earth in its daily motion is a planetary and erring rather than a fixed star, and if all on this star of earth must partake of its sublunar, mortal, temporal nature.

. . .

To sum up: In Wordsworth's lyric the specific gravity of words is weighed in the balance of each stanza; and this balance is as much a judgment on speech in the context of our mortality as it is a meaningful response to the individual

Susanne Langer: Langer (1895–1985) was an American philosopher who discussed the relationship between aesthetics and artistic form.   *aufgehoben:* German for "taken up" or "lifted up," but this term can also mean "canceled" or "nullified." Hartman uses the term for its double meaning.

death. At the limit of the medium of words, and close to silence, what has been purged is not concreteness, or the empirical sphere of the emotions—shock, disillusion, trauma, recognition, grief, atonement—what has been purged is a series of flashy schematisms and false or partial mediations: artificial plot, inflated consolatory rhetoric, the coercive absolutes of logic or faith.

From "Elation in Hegel and Wordsworth"

CULTURAL STUDIES

Unlike the other critical approaches discussed in this chapter, cultural criticism (or **cultural studies**) does not offer a single way of analyzing literature. No central methodology is associated with cultural studies. Nor is cultural criticism solely, or even mainly, concerned with literary texts in the conventional sense. Instead, the term *cultural studies* refers to a relatively recent interdisciplinary field of academic inquiry. This field borrows methodologies from other approaches to analyze a wide range of cultural products and practice.

To understand cultural studies, it helps to know a bit about its origins. In the English-speaking world, the field was first defined at the Centre for Contemporary Cultural Studies of Birmingham University in Britain. Founded in 1964, this graduate program tried to expand the range of literary study beyond traditional approaches to canonic literature in order to explore a broader spectrum of historical, cultural, and political issues. The most influential teacher at the Birmingham Centre was Raymond Williams (1921–1983), a Welsh socialist with wide intellectual interests. Williams argued that scholars should not study culture as a canon of great works by individual artists but rather examine it as an evolutionary process that involves the entire society. "We cannot separate literature and art," Williams said, "from other kinds of social practice." The cultural critic, therefore, does not study fixed aesthetic objects as much as dynamic social processes. The critic's challenge is to identify and understand the complex forms and effects of the process of culture.

A Marxist intellectual, Williams called his approach cultural materialism (a reference to the Marxist doctrine of dialectical materialism), but later scholars soon discarded that name for two broader and more neutral terms, cultural criticism and cultural studies. From the start, this interdisciplinary field relied heavily on literary theory, especially Marxist and feminist criticism. It also employed the documentary techniques of historical criticism combined with political analysis focused on issues of social class, race, and gender. (This approach flourished in the United States, where it is called New Historicism.) Cultural studies is also deeply antiformalist, since the field concerns itself with investigating the complex relationship among history, politics, and literature. Cultural studies rejects the notion that literature exists in an aesthetic realm separate from ethical and political categories.

A chief goal of cultural studies is to understand the nature of social power as reflected in "texts." For example, if the object of analysis were a sonnet by Shakespeare, the cultural studies adherent might investigate the moral, psychological, and political assumptions reflected in the poem and then deconstruct them to see what individuals, social classes, or gender might benefit from having those assumptions perceived as true. The relevant mission of cultural studies is to identify both the overt and covert values reflected in a cultural practice. The cultural studies critic also tries to trace out and understand the structures of meaning that hold those assumptions in place and give them the appearance of objective representation. Any analytical technique that helps illuminate these issues is employed.

In theory, a cultural studies critic might employ any methodology. In practice, however, he or she will most often borrow concepts from deconstruction, Marxist analysis, gender criticism, race theory, and psychology. Each of these earlier methodologies provides particular analytical tools that cultural critics find useful. What cultural studies borrows from deconstructionism is its emphasis on uncovering conflict, dissent, and contradiction in the works under analysis. Whereas traditional critical approaches often sought to demonstrate the unity of a literary work, cultural studies often seeks to portray social, political, and psychological conflicts it masks. What cultural studies borrows from Marxist analysis is an attention to the ongoing struggle between social classes, each seeking economic (and therefore political) advantage. Cultural studies often asks questions about what social class created a work of art and what class (or classes) served as its audience. Among the many things that cultural studies borrowed from gender criticism and race theory is a concern with social inequality between the sexes and races. It seeks to investigate how these inequities have been reflected in the texts of a historical period or a society. Cultural studies is, above all, a political enterprise that views literary analysis as a means of furthering social justice.

Since cultural studies does not adhere to any single methodology (or even a consistent set of methodologies), it is impossible to characterize the field briefly, because there are exceptions to every generalization offered. What one sees most clearly are characteristic tendencies, especially the commitment to examining issues of class, race, and gender. There is also the insistence on expanding the focus of critical inquiry beyond traditional high literary culture. British cultural studies guru Anthony Easthope can, for example, analyze with equal aplomb Gerard Manley Hopkins's "The Windhover," Edgar Rice Burrough's *Tarzan of the Apes,* a Benson and Hedges's cigarette advertisement, and Sean Connery's eyebrows. Cultural studies is infamous—even among its practitioners—for its habitual use of literary jargon. It is also notorious for its complex intellectual analysis of mundane materials such as Easthope's analysis of a cigarette ad, which may be interesting in its own right but remote from most readers' literary experience. Some scholars, such as Heather Glen, however, use the principles of cultural studies to provide new social, political, and historical insights on canonic texts such as William Blake's "London." Omnivorous, iconoclastic, and relentlessly analytic, cultural criticism has become a major presence in contemporary literary studies.

Vincent B. Leitch   (b. 1944)

POSTSTRUCTURALIST CULTURAL CRITIQUE   1992

Whereas a major goal of New Criticism and much other modern formalistic criticism is aesthetic evaluation of freestanding texts, a primary objective of cultural criticism is cultural critique, which entails investigation and assessment of ruling and oppositional beliefs, categories, practices, and representations, inquiring into the causes, constitutions, and consequences as well as the modes of circulation and consumption of linguistic, social, economic, political, historical, ethical, religious, legal, scientific, philosophical, educational, familial, and aesthetic discourses and institutions. In rendering a judgment on an aesthetic artifact, a New Critic privileges such key things as textual coherence and unity, intricacy and complexity, ambiguity and irony, tension and balance, economy and autonomy, literariness and spatial form. In mounting a critique of a cultural "text," an advocate of poststructuralist cultural criticism evaluates such things as degrees of exclusion and inclusion, of complicity and resistance, of domination and letting-be, of abstraction and situatedness, of violence and tolerance, of monologue and polylogue, of quietism and activism, of sameness and otherness, of oppression and emancipation, of centralization and decentralization. Just as the aforementioned system of evaluative criteria underlies the exegetical and judgmental labor of New Criticism, so too does the above named set of commitments undergird the work of poststructuralist cultural critique.

Given its commitments, poststructuralist cultural criticism is, as I have suggested, suspicious of literary formalism. Specifically, the trouble with New Criticism is its inclination to advocate a combination of quietism and asceticism, connoisseurship and exclusiveness, aestheticism and apoliticism. . . . The monotonous practical effect of New Critical reading is to illustrate the subservience of each textual element to a higher, overarching, economical poetic structure without remainders. What should be evident here is that the project of poststructuralist cultural criticism possesses a set of commitments and criteria that enable it to engage in the enterprise of cultural critique. It should also be evident that the cultural ethicopolitics of this enterprise is best characterized, using current terminology, as "liberal" or "leftist," meaning congruent with certain socialist, anarchist, and libertarian ideals, none of which, incidentally, are necessarily Marxian. Such congruence, derived from extrapolating a generalized stance for poststructuralism, constitutes neither a party platform nor an observable course of practical action; avowed tendencies often account for little in the unfolding of practical engagements.

From *Cultural Criticism, Literary Theory, Poststructuralism*

Mark Bauerlein   (b. 1959)

WHAT IS CULTURAL STUDIES?   1997

Traditionally, disciplines naturally fell into acknowledged subdivisions, for example, as literary criticism broke up into formalist literary criticism, philological criticism, narratological analysis, and other methodologically distinguished pursuits, all of which remained comfortably within the category "literary criticism." But cultural studies eschews such institutional disjunctions and will not let any straitening adjective precede the "cultural studies" heading. There is no distinct formalist cultural studies or historicist cultural studies, but only cultural studies.

(Feminist cultural studies may be one exception.) Cultural studies is a field that will not be parceled out to the available disciplines. It spans culture at large, not this or that institutionally separated element of culture. To guarantee this transcendence of disciplinary institutions, cultural studies must select a name for itself that has no specificity, that has too great an extension to mark off any expedient boundaries for itself. "Cultural studies" serves well because, apart from distinguishing between "physical science" and "cultural analysis," the term provides no indication of where any other boundaries lie.

This is exactly the point. To blur disciplinary boundaries and frustrate the intellectual investments that go along with them is a fundamental motive for cultural studies practice, one that justifies the vagueness of the titular term. This explains why the related label "cultural criticism," so much in vogue in 1988, has declined. The term "criticism" has a narrower extension than does "studies," ruling out some empirical forms of inquiry (like field work) that "studies" admits. "Studies" preserves a methodological openness that "criticism" closes. Since such closures have suspect political intentions behind them, cultural studies maintains its institutional purity by disdaining disciplinary identity and methodological uniformity.

. . .

A single approach will miss too much, will overlook important aspects of culture not perceptible to that particular angle of vision. A multitude of approaches will pick up an insight here and a piece of knowledge there and more of culture will enter into the inquiry. A diversity of methods will match the diversity of culture, thereby sheltering the true nature of culture from the reductive appropriations of formal disciplines.

But how do cultural critics bring all these methods together into a coherent inquiry? Are there any established rules of incorporating "important insights and knowledge" coming out of different methods into a coherent scholarly project of cultural studies? How might a scholar use both phonemic analysis and deconstruction in a single inquiry when deconstructionist arguments call into question the basic premises of phonetics? What scholar has the competence to handle materials from so many disciplines in a rigorous and knowing manner? Does cultural criticism as a "studies" practice offer any transdisciplinary evaluative standards to apply to individual pieces of cultural criticism? If not, if there is no clear methodological procedures or evaluative principles in cultural studies, it is hard to see how one might popularize it, teach it, make it into a recognized scholarly activity. In practical terms, one does not know how to communicate it to others or show students how to do it when it assumes so many different methodological forms. How does one create an academic department out of an outspokenly antidisciplinary practice? What criteria can faculty members jointly invoke when they are trying to make curricular and personnel decisions?

Once again, this is precisely the point. One reason for the generality of the term is to render such institutional questions unanswerable. Cultural studies practice mingles methods from a variety of fields, jumps from one cultural subject matter to another, simultaneously proclaims superiority to other institutionalized inquiries (on a correspondence to culture basis) and renounces its own institutionalization—gestures that strategically forestall disciplinary standards being applied to it. By studying culture in heterogenous ways, by clumping texts, events, persons, objects, and ideologies into a cultural whole (which, cultural critics say, is reality) and bringing a melange of logical argument, speculative propositions, empirical data, and political outlooks to bear upon it, cultural critics invent a new kind of investigation immune to methodological attack.

From *Literary Criticism: An Autopsy*

Heather Glen

THE STANCE OF OBSERVATION IN
WILLIAM BLAKE'S "LONDON"

1983

In choosing to present his vision of social disaster thus, Blake was engaging with a familiar literary mode. The assumption of a stance of "observation," freely passing judgment on that which is before it, is common to much eighteenth-century literature: "There mark what ills the scholar's life assail".[1] But nowhere is it more prominent than in that which attempts to describe London, a place of bewildering diversity, changing and growing rapidly, in which a new kind of anonymity and alienation was becoming a remarked-upon fact of life. Indeed, it seems that in the literature of London the implications of this state were beginning to become an explicit preoccupation. Thus, Ben Sedgly in 1751:

> No man can take survey of this opulent city, without meeting in his way, many melancholy instances resulting from this consumption of spirituous liquors: poverty, diseases, misery and wickedness, are the daily observations to be made in every part of this great metropolis: whoever passes along the streets, may find numbers of abandoned wretches stretched upon the cold pavement, motionless and insensible, removed only by the charity of passengers from the danger of being crushed by carriages, trampled by horses, or strangled with filth in the common sewers.

"Take survey of," "meeting in his way," "observations to be made," "whoever passes along the streets may find"—the sense throughout is of an anonymous and freely observing stranger, rather than of a member of a society who sees himself as shaped by it and interacting with others within it. Perhaps such a perspective is natural in a documentary work such as Sedgly's. But this sense of the self in the city is central, too, to much of the most powerful imaginative literature of the century, literature which is after all not merely a description of or meditation upon the world, but the recreation of a certain mode of being within it. It is a sense that informs the novels of Defoe: the figures of Roxana and

[1] Johnson, "The Vanity of Human Wishes," I. 159. The opening lines of this poem are perhaps the dramatization *par excellence* of this stance: "Let observation with extensive view, / Survey mankind, from China to Peru; / Remark each anxious toil, each eager strife, / And watch the busy scenes of crouded life."

Colonel Jack and Moll Flanders move through the streets from adventure to adventure with a freedom from social constraint which is only possible because of the nature of London life. It is to be found in Gay's *Trivia* and *The Beggar's Opera*; in Boswell's *Journal*; in Johnson's *London*, and even in those of his essays which seem to have nothing to do with London at all:

> He that considers how little he dwells upon the condition of others, will learn how little the attention of others is attracted by himself. While we see multitudes passing before us, of whom perhaps not one appears to deserve our notice, or excites our sympathy, we should remember, that we likewise are lost in the same throng, that eye which happens to glance upon us is turned in a moment on him that follows us, and that the utmost which we can reasonably hope or fear is to fill a vacant hour with prattle, and be forgotten.[2]

Here, the tone is one of judicious moralizing. But the imagery is that of the confusing eighteenth-century London street, in which relations with one's fellow beings involve attracting attention, deserving notice, glancing and turning, even *exciting* sympathy: in which the other is the object of observation rather than one with whom one interacts. And the supposedly free individual who sees those who pass before him as a mighty spectacle is himself "lost in the same throng."

The eighteenth-century London street was not, then, merely a place where suffering and distress could be seen on a hitherto unprecedented scale: it was also a place where that sense of the other as object—often as feeble and wretched object—which Blake exposes in "The Human Abstract" ("we . . . make somebody Poor") was the dominant mode of relationship. And it is a sense which is an ironic point of reference in "London." For this poem begins with a speaker who seems to be a detached observer, who wanders "thro'" the streets of the city and "marks" the sights before him. Yet his is not the lively and distinctive London of Defoe or Gay or Johnson: what he records is not variety, but sameness. To him, both streets and river are simply "charter'd": the different faces which pass all bear the same message, "Marks of weakness, marks of woe." And the tight quatrain with its present indicative tense conveys not flexible responsiveness to constantly changing possibilities, but entrapment. What this speaker sees is fatally linked to the way in which he sees it. In the notebook draft, the second word of the third line was "see": Blake's alteration limits any incipient sense of freedom. The triple beat of "mark"—an active verb materializing into two plural nouns—registers a new consciousness of this "I"'s implication in the world "thro'" which he wanders. What he observes is the objectification of his own activity.

"Mark" is not the only change which Blake made in this stanza. In the notebook draft, the first two lines read:

I wander thro' each dirty street,
Near where the dirty Thames does flow.

[2]Samuel Johnson, *The Rambler*, 159.

The substitution, in the engraved version, of "charter'd," signals a complex process of poetic thought. For "charter'd" in 1793 was a word at the centre of political debate: a word whose accepted meaning of "granted privileges or rights" had been challenged by Paine a year earlier, in a book whose sales had by now reached 200,000:

> It is a perversion of terms to say, that a charter gives rights. It operates by a contrary effect, that of taking rights away. Rights are inherently in all the inhabitants; but charters, by annulling those rights in the majority, leave the right by exclusion in the hands of a few . . . all charters have no other than an indirect negative operation. They do not give rights to A, but they make a difference in favour of A by taking away the right of B, and consequently are instruments of injustice.[3]

No contemporary of Blake's could have read the two altered opening lines of his poem as an objective description of the trading organization of the city. Their repetition of "charter'd" forces into prominence the newly, ironically recognized sense that the very language of "objective" description may be riddled with ideological significance: that beneath the assurance of polite usage may lurk another, "cheating" meaning. And this sense informs the stanza in a peculiar way. It is as though beneath the polite surface—the observer in London wandering the streets of a city whose "charter'd" organization he notes, as the guidebooks noted its commercial organization, and whose manifestations of distress and depravity he, like hundreds of other eighteenth-century writers, remarks—there is another set of meanings, which are the *reverse* of those such description could customarily bear. They are not meanings private to Blake: and they are meanings which focus in those sound-linked and repeated words, "mark" and "charter'd."

From Vision and Disenchantment

---

[3]Paine, *Rights of Man*, ed. Henry Collins (Harmondsworth: Penguin, 1969), 242–43.

Glossary of Literary Terms

Abstract diction *See* **Diction.**

Accent An emphasis or stress placed on a syllable in speech. Clear pronunciation of polysyllabic words almost always depends on correct placement of their accents (e.g., *de*-sert and de-*sert* are two different words and parts of speech, depending on their accent). Accent or speech stress is the basis of most meters in English. (*See also* **Accentual meter, Meter.**)

Accentual meter A meter that uses a consistent number of strong speech stresses per line. The number of unstressed syllables may vary, as long as the accented syllables do not. Much popular poetry, such as rap and nursery rhymes, is written in accentual meter.

Acrostic A poem in which the initial letters of each line, when read downward, spell out a hidden word or words (often the name of a beloved person). Acrostics date back as far as the Hebrew Bible and classical Greek poetry.

Allegory A narrative in verse or prose in which the literal events (persons, places, and things) consistently point to a parallel sequence of symbolic ideas. This narrative strategy is often used to dramatize abstract ideas, historical events, religious systems, or political issues. An allegory has two levels of meaning: a literal level that tells a surface story and a symbolic level in which the abstract ideas unfold. The names of allegorical characters often hint at their symbolic roles. For example, in Nathaniel Hawthorne's "Young Goodman Brown," Faith is not only the name of the protagonist's wife but also a symbol of the protagonist's religious faith.

Alliteration The repetition of two or more consonant sounds in successive words in a line of verse or prose. Alliteration can be used at the beginning of words ("cool cats"—**initial alliteration**) or internally on stressed syllables ("In kitchen cups concupiscent curds"—which combines initial and **internal alliteration**). Alliteration was a central feature of Anglo-Saxon poetry and is still used by contemporary writers.

All-knowing narrator *See* **Omniscient narrator.**

Allusion A brief (and sometimes indirect) reference in a text to a person, place, or thing—fictitious or actual. An allusion may appear in a literary work as an initial quotation, a passing mention of a name, or as a phrase borrowed from another writer—often carrying the meanings and implications of the original. Allusions imply a common set of knowledge between reader and writer and operate as a literary shorthand to enrich the meaning of a text.

Analysis The examination of a piece of literature as a means of understanding its subject or structure. An effective analysis often clarifies a work by focusing on a single element such as tone, irony, symbolism, imagery, or rhythm in a way that enhances the reader's understanding of the whole. *Analysis* comes from the Greek word meaning to "undo," to "loosen."

Anapest A metrical foot in verse in which two unstressed syllables are followed by a stressed syllable, as in "on a *boat*" or "in a *slump*." (*See also* **Meter**.)

Anecdote A short narrative usually consisting of a single incident or episode. Often humorous, anecdotes can be real or fictional. When they appear within a larger narrative as a brief story told by one character to another, the author usually employs them to reveal something significant to the larger narrative.

Antagonist The most significant character or force that opposes the protagonist in a narrative or drama. The antagonist may be another character, society itself, a force of nature, or even—in modern literature—conflicting impulses within the protagonist.

Anticlimax An unsatisfying and trivial turn of events in a literary work that occurs in place of a genuine climax. An anticlimax often involves a surprising shift in tone from the lofty or serious into the petty or ridiculous. The term is often used negatively to denote a feeble moment in a plot in which an author fails to create an intended effect. Anticlimax, however, can also be a strong dramatic device when a writer uses it for humorous or ironic effect.

Antihero A protagonist who is lacking in one or more of the conventional qualities attributed to a hero. Instead of being dignified, brave, idealistic, or purposeful, for instance, the antihero may be buffoonish, cowardly, self-interested, or weak. The antihero is often considered an essentially modern form of characterization, a satiric or frankly realistic commentary on traditional portrayals of idealized heroes or heroines. Modern examples range from Kafka's many protagonists to Beckett's tramps in *Waiting for Godot*.

Antithesis Words, phrases, clauses, or sentences set in deliberate contrast to one another. Antithesis balances opposing ideas, tones, or structures, usually to heighten the effect of a statement.

Apostrophe A direct address to someone or something. In poetry an apostrophe often addresses something not ordinarily spoken to (e.g., "O mountain!"). In an apostrophe, a speaker may address an inanimate object, a dead or absent person, an abstract thing, or a spirit. Apostrophe is often used to provide a speaker with means to articulate thoughts aloud.

Apprenticeship novel *See* **Bildungsroman**.

Archetype A recurring symbol, character, landscape, or event found in myth and literature across different cultures and eras. The idea of the archetype came into literary criticism from the Swiss psychologist Carl Jung who believed that all individuals share a "collective unconscious," a set of primal memories common to the human race that exists in our subconscious. An example of an archetypal character is the devil who may appear in pure mythic form (as in John Milton's *Paradise Lost*) but occurs more often in a disguised form like Fagin in Charles Dickens's *Oliver Twist* or Abner Snopes in William Faulkner's "Barn Burning."

Arena theater A modern, nontraditional performance space in which the audience surrounds the stage on four sides. The stage can be circular, square, rectangular, or ellipsoidal. In contrast to the **picture-frame stage**, with its privileged single point of view from the center of the orchestra seats, arena staging favors no one portion of the audience.

Aside In drama a few words or short passage spoken in an undertone or to the audience. By convention, other characters onstage are deaf to the aside.

Assonance The repetition of two or more vowel sounds in successive words, which creates a kind of rhyme. Like alliteration, the assonance may occur initially ("*all the awful auguries*") or internally ("*white lilacs*"). Assonance may be used to focus attention on key words or concepts. Assonance also helps make a phrase or line more memorable.

Atmosphere The dominant mood or feeling that pervades all or part of a literary work. Atmosphere is the total effect conveyed by the author's use of language, images, and physical setting. Atmosphere is often used to foreshadow the ultimate climax in a narrative.

Auditory imagery A word or sequence of words that refers to the sense of hearing. (*See also* **Imagery**.)

Augustan age This term has two related meanings. First, it originally referred to the greatest period of Roman literature under the Emperor Augustus (27 B.C.–14 A.D.) in which Virgil, Horace, and Ovid wrote. Second, it refers to the early eighteenth century in English literature, a neoclassical period dominated by Alexander Pope, Thomas Gray, and Jonathan Swift. English Augustan poetry was characteristically formal in both structure and diction.

Authorial intrusion *See* **Editorial point of view**.

Ballad Traditionally, a song that tells a story. The ballad was originally an oral verse form—sung or recited and transmitted from performer to performer without being written down. Ballads are characteristically compressed, dramatic, and objective in their narrative style. There are many variations to the ballad form, most consisting of quatrains (made up of lines of three or four metrical feet) in a simple rhyme scheme. (*See also* **Ballad stanza**.)

Ballad stanza The most common pattern of ballad makers consists of four lines rhymed *abcb*, in which the first and third lines have four metrical feet and the second and fourth lines have three feet (4, 3, 4, 3).

Bathos In poetry, an unintentional lapse from the sublime to the ridiculous or trivial. Bathos differs from anticlimax, in that the latter is a deliberate effect, often for the purpose of humor or contrast, whereas bathos occurs through failure.

Bildungsroman German for "novel of growth and development." Sometimes called an **apprenticeship novel**, this genre depicts a youth who struggles toward maturity, forming a worldview or philosophy of life. Dickens's *David Copperfield* and Joyce's *Portrait of the Artist as a Young Man* are classic examples of the genre.

Biographical criticism The practice of analyzing a literary work by using knowledge of the author's life to gain insight.

Biography A factual account of a person's life, examining all available information or texts relevant to the subject.

Blank verse The most common and well-known meter of unrhymed poetry in English. Blank verse contains five iambic feet per line and is never rhymed. (*Blank* means "unrhymed.") Many literary works have been written in blank verse, including Tennyson's "Ulysses" and Frost's "The Mending Wall." Shakespeare's plays are written primarily in blank verse. (*See also* **Iambic pentameter**.)

Blues A type of folk music originally developed by African Americans in the South, often about some pain or loss. Blues lyrics traditionally consist of three-line stanzas in which the first two identical lines are followed by a third concluding, rhyming line. The influence of the blues is fundamental in virtually all styles of contemporary pop—jazz, rap, rock, gospel, country, and rhythm and blues.

Box set The illusion of scenic realism for interior rooms was achieved in the early nineteenth century with the development of the box set, consisting of three walls that joined in two corners and a ceiling that tilted as if seen in perspective. The "fourth wall," invisible, ran parallel to the proscenium arch. By the middle of the nineteenth century, the addition of realistic props and furnishings made it possible for actors to behave onstage as if they inhabited private space, oblivious to the presence of an audience, even turning their backs to the audience if the dramatic situation required it.

Broadside ballads Poems printed on a single sheet of paper, often set to traditional tunes. Most broadside ballads, which originated in the late sixteenth century, were an early form of verse journalism, cheap to print, and widely circulated. Often they were humorous or pathetic accounts of sensational news events.

Burlesque Incongruous imitation of either the style or subject matter of a serious genre, humorous due to the disparity between the treatment and the subject. On the nineteenth-century English stage, the burlesque was a broad caricature, parody, travesty, or take-off of popular plays, opera, or current events. Gilbert and Sullivan's Victorian operettas, for example, burlesqued grand opera.

Cacophony A harsh, discordant sound often mirroring the meaning of the context in which it is used. For example, "Grate on the scrannel pipes of wretched straw" (Milton's "Lycidas"). The opposite of cacophony is **euphony**.

Caesura, cesura A pause within a line of verse. Traditionally, caesuras appear near the middle of a line, but their placement may be varied to create expressive rhythmic effects. A caesura will usually occur at a mark of punctuation, but there can be a caesura even if no punctuation is present.

Carpe diem Latin for "seize the day." Originally said in Horace's famous "Odes I (11)," this phrase has been applied to characterize much lyric poetry concerned with human mortality and the passing of time.

Central intelligence The character through whose sensibility and mind a story is told. Henry James developed this term to describe a narrator—not the author—whose perceptions shape the way a story is presented. (*See also* **Narrator.**)

Character An imagined figure inhabiting a narrative or drama. By convention, the reader or spectator endows the fictional character with moral, dispositional, and emotional qualities expressed in what the character says—the dialogue—and by what he or she does—the action. What a character says and does in any particular situation is motivated by his or her desires, temperament, and moral nature. (*See also* **Dynamic character** and **Flat character.**)

Character development The process in which a character is introduced, advanced, and possibly transformed in a story. This development can prove to be either static (the character's personality is unchanging throughout the narrative) or dynamic (the character's personality undergoes some meaningful change during the course of the narrative). (*See also* **Dynamic character.**)

Characterization The techniques a writer uses to create, reveal, or develop the characters in a narrative. (*See also* **Character.**)

Child ballads American scholar Francis J. Child compiled a collection of over three hundred authentic ballads in his book *The English and Scottish Popular Ballads* (1882–1898). He demonstrated that these ballads were the creations of oral folk culture. These works have come to be called Child ballads.

Clerihew A comic verse form named for its inventor, Edmund Clerihew Bentley. A clerihew begins with the name of a person and consists of two metrically awkward, rhymed couplets. Humorous and often insulting, clerihews serve as ridiculous biographies, usually of famous people.

Climax The moment of greatest intensity in a story, which almost inevitably occurs toward the end of the work. The climax often takes the form of a decisive confrontation between the protagonist and antagonist. In a conventional story, the climax is followed by the **resolution** or **dénouement** in which the effects and results of the climactic action are presented. (*See also* **Falling action, Rising action.**)

Closed couplet Two rhymed lines that contain an independent and complete thought or statement. The closed couplet usually pauses lightly at the end of the first line; the second is more heavily end-stopped, or "closed." When such couplets are written in rhymed iambic pentameter, they are called **heroic couplets.** (*See also* **Couplet.**)

Closed dénouement One of two types of conventional dénouement or resolution in a narrative. In closed dénouement, the author ties everything up at the end of the story so that little is left unresolved. (*See also* **Open dénouement.**)

Closed form A generic term that describes poetry written in some preexisting pattern of meter, rhyme, line, or stanza. A closed form produces a prescribed structure as in the triolet, with a set rhyme scheme and line length. Closed forms include the sonnet, sestina, villanelle, ballade, and rondeau.

Close reading A method of analysis involving careful step-by-step explication of a poem in order to understand how various elements work together. Close reading is a common practice of formalist critics in the study of a text.

Closet drama A play or dramatic poem designed to be read aloud rather than performed. Many post-Renaissance verse dramas like Milton's *Samson Agonistes* (1671) or Byron's *Manfred* (1817) are examples of closet drama.

Colloquial English The casual or informal but correct language of ordinary native speakers, which may include contractions, slang, and shifts in grammar, vocabulary, and diction. Wordsworth helped introduce colloquialism into English poetry, challenging the past constraints of highly formal language in verse and calling for the poet to become "a man speaking to men." Conversational in tone, *colloquial* is derived from the Latin *colloquium*, "speaking together." (*See also* **Diction, Levels of diction.**)

Comedy A literary work aimed at amusing an audience. Comedy is one of the basic modes of storytelling and can be adapted to most literary forms—from poetry to film. In traditional comic plotting, the action often involves the adventures of young lovers, who face obstacles and complications that threaten disaster but are overturned at the last moment to produce a happy ending. Comic situations or comic characters can provide humor in tragicomedy and even in tragedies (the gravediggers in *Hamlet*).

Comedy of manners A realistic form of comic drama that flourished with seventeenth-century playwrights such as Molière and English Restoration dramatists. It deals with the social relations and sexual intrigues of sophisticated, intelligent, upper-class men and women, whose verbal fencing and witty repartee produce the principal comic effects. Stereotyped characters from contemporary life, such as would-be wits, jealous husbands, conniving rivals, country bumpkins, and foppish dandies, reveal by their deviations from the norm the decorum and conventional behaviors expected in polite society. William Congreve's *The Way of the World* (1700) is considered the finest example of Restoration comedy of manners. Modern examples include G. B. Shaw (*Arms and the Man*), Noel Coward (*Private Lives*), or Tom Stoppard (*Arcadia*).

Comic relief The appearance of a comic situation, character, or clownish humor in the midst of a serious action that introduces a sharp contrast in mood. The drunken porter in *Macbeth*, who imagines himself the doorkeeper of Hell, not only provides comic relief but intensifies the horror of Macbeth's murder of King Duncan.

Coming-of-age story *See* **Initiation story**.

Commedia dell'arte A form of comic drama developed by guilds of professional Italian actors in the mid-sixteenth century. Playing stock characters, masked *commedia* players improvised dialogue around a given scenario (a brief outline marking entrances of characters and the main course of action). In a typical play a pair of young lovers (played without masks), aided by a clever servant (Harlequin), outwit older masked characters.

Common meter A highly regular form of ballad meter with two sets of rhymes—*abab*. "Amazing Grace" and many other hymns are in common meter. (*See also* **Ballad stanza**.)

Comparison In the analysis or criticism of literature, one may place two works side-by-side to point out their similarities. The product of this, a comparison, may be more meaningful when paired with its counterpart, a **contrast**.

Complication The introduction of a significant development in the central conflict in a drama or narrative between characters (or between a character and his or her situation). Traditionally, a complication begins the rising action of a story's plot. Dramatic conflict (motivation versus obstacle) during the complication is the force that drives a literary work from action to action. Complications may be *external* or *internal* or a combination of the two. A fateful blow such as an illness or an accident that affects a character is a typical example of an *external* complication—a problem the characters cannot turn away from. An *internal* complication, in contrast, might not be immediately apparent, such as the result of some important aspect of a character's values or personality.

Conceit A poetic device using elaborate comparisons, such as equating a loved one with the graces and beauties of the world. Most notably used by the Italian poet Petrarch in praise of his beloved Laura, *conceit* comes from the Italian *concetto*, "concept" or "idea."

Conclusion In plotting, the logical end or outcome of a unified plot, shortly following the climax. Also called **resolution** or **dénouement** ("the untying of the knot"), as in resolving or untying the knots created by plot complications during the rising action. The action or intrigue ends in success or failure for the protagonist, the mystery is solved, or misunderstandings are dispelled. Sometimes a conclusion is ambiguous; at the climax of the story the characters are changed, but the conclusion suggests different possibilities for what that change is or means.

Concrete diction *See* **Diction**.

Concrete poetry A visual poetry composed exclusively for the page in which a picture or image is made of printed letters and words. Concrete poetry attempts to blur the line between language and visual art. Concrete poetry was especially popular as an experimental movement in the 1960s.

Confessional poetry A poetic genre emerging in the 1950s and 1960s primarily concerned with autobiography and the unexpurgated exposure of the poet's personal life. Notable practitioners included Robert Lowell, W. D. Snodgrass, and Anne Sexton.

Conflict In Greek, *agon,* or contest. The central struggle between two or more forces in a story. Conflict generally occurs when some person or thing prevents the protagonist from achieving his or her intended goal. Opposition can arise from another character, external events, preexisting situations, fate, or even some aspect of the main character's own personality. Conflict is the basic material out of which most plots are made. (*See also* **Antagonist, Character, Complication, Rising action**.)

Connotation An association or additional meaning that a word, image, or phrase may carry, apart from its literal denotation or dictionary definition. A word picks up connotations from all the uses to which it has been put in the past. For example, an owl in literature is not merely the literal bird. It also carries the many associations (connotations, that is) attached to it.

Consonance Also called **Slant rhyme**. A kind of rhyme in which the linked words share similar consonant sounds but different vowel sounds, as in *reason* and *raisin, mink* and *monk*. Sometimes only the final consonant sound is identical, as in *fame* and *room, crack* and *truck*. Used mostly by modern poets, consonance often registers more subtly than exact rhyme, lending itself to special poetic effects.

Contrast A contrast of two works of literature is developed by placing them side-by-side to point out their differences. This method of analysis works well with its opposite, a **comparison**, which focuses on likenesses.

Convention Any established feature or technique in literature that is commonly understood by both authors and readers. A convention is something generally agreed on to be appropriate for its customary uses, such as the sonnet form for a love poem or the opening "Once upon a time" for a fairy tale.

Conventional symbols Literary symbols that have a conventional or customary effect on most readers. We would respond similarly to a black cat crossing our path or a young bride in a white dress. These are conventional symbols because they carry recognizable connotations and suggestions.

Cosmic irony Also called **irony of fate**, it is the irony that exists between a character's aspiration and the treatment he or she receives at the hands of fate. Oedipus's ill-destined relationship with his parents is an example of cosmic irony.

Cothurni High thick-soled boots worn by Greek and Roman tragic actors in late classical times to make them appear taller than ordinary men. (Earlier, in the fifth-century classical Athenian theater, actors wore soft shoes or boots or went barefoot.)

Couplet A two-line stanza in poetry, usually rhymed, which tends to have lines of equal length. Shakespeare's sonnets were famous for ending with a summarizing, rhymed couplet: "Give my love fame faster than Time wastes life; / So thou prevent'st his scythe and crookèd knife." (*See also* **Closed couplet**.)

Cowboy poetry A contemporary genre of folk poetry written by people with firsthand experience in the life of horse, trail, and ranch. Plainspoken and often humorous, cowboy poetry is usually composed in rhymed ballad stanzas and meant to be recited aloud.

Crisis The point in a drama when the crucial action, decision, or realization must be made, marking the turning point or reversal of the protagonist's fortunes. From the Greek word *krisis*, meaning "decision." For example, Hamlet's decision to refrain from killing Claudius while the guilty king is praying is a crisis that leads directly to his accidental murder of Polonius, pointing forward to the catastrophe of Act V. Typically, the crisis inaugurates the falling action (after Hamlet's murder of Polonius, Claudius controls the events) until the catastrophe (or conclusion), which is decided by the death of the hero, King Claudius, Queen Gertrude, and Laertes. In *Oedipus*, the crisis occurs as the hero presses forward to the horrible truth, to realize he is an incestuous parricide and to take responsibility by blinding himself.

Cultural studies A contemporary interdisciplinary field of academic study that focuses on understanding the social power encoded in "texts." Cultural studies defines "texts" more broadly than literary works; they include any analyzable phenomenon from a traditional poem to an advertising image or an actor's face. Cultural studies has no central critical methodology but uses whatever intellectual tools are appropriate to the analysis at hand.

Dactyl A metrical foot of verse in which one stressed syllable is followed by two unstressed syllables (*bat*-ter-y or *par*-a-mour). The dactylic meter is less common to English than it was to classical Greek and Latin verse. Longfellow's *Evangeline* is the most famous English-language long dactylic poem.

Deconstructionist criticism A school of criticism that rejects the traditional assumption that language can accurately represent reality. Deconstructionists believe that literary texts can have no single meaning; therefore, they concentrate their attentions on *how* language is being used in a text, rather than on *what* is being said.

Decorum Propriety or appropriateness. In poetry, decorum usually refers to a level of diction that is proper to use in a certain occasion. Decorum can also apply to characters, setting, and the harmony that exists between the elements in a poem. For example, aged nuns speaking inner-city jive might violate decorum.

Denotation The literal, dictionary meaning of a word. (*See also* **Connotation**.)

Dénouement The resolution or conclusion of a literary work as plot complications are unraveled after the climax. In French, *dénouement* means "unknotting" or "untying." (*See also* **Closed dénouement, Conclusion, Open dénouement**.)

Deus ex machina Latin for "a god from a machine." The phrase refers to the Greek playwrights' frequent use of a god, mechanically lowered to the stage from the skene roof, to resolve human conflict with judgments and commands. Conventionally, the phrase now refers to any forced or improbable device in plot resolution.

Dialect A particular variety of language spoken by an identifiable regional group or social class of persons. Dialects are often used in literature in an attempt to present a character more realistically and to express significant differences in class or background.

Dialogue The direct representation of the conversation between two or more characters. (*See also* **Monologue**.)

Diction Word choice or vocabulary. Diction refers to the class of words that an author decides is appropriate to use in a particular work. Literary history is the story of diction being challenged, upheld, and reinvented. **Concrete diction** involves a highly specific word choice in the naming of something or someone. **Abstract diction** contains words that express more general ideas or concepts. More concrete diction would offer *boxer puppy* rather than *young canine*, *Lake Ontario* rather than *body of fresh water*. Concrete words refer to what we can immediately perceive with our senses. (*See also* **Levels of diction**.)

Didactic fiction A narrative that intends to teach a specific moral lesson or provide a model for proper behavior. This term is now often used pejoratively to describe a story in which the events seem manipulated in order to convey an uplifting idea, but much classic fiction has been written in the didactic mode—Aesop's *Fables*, John Bunyan's *The Pilgrim's Progress*, and Harriet Beecher Stowe's *Uncle Tom's Cabin*.

Didactic poetry Kind of poetry intended to teach the reader a moral lesson or impart a body of knowledge. Poetry that aims for education over art.

Dimeter A verse meter consisting of two metrical feet, or two primary stresses, per line.

Doggerel Verse full of irregularities often due to the poet's incompetence. Doggerel is crude verse that brims with cliché, obvious rhyme, and inept rhythm.

Double plot Also called **subplot**. Familiar in Elizabethan drama, a second story or plotline that is complete and interesting in its own right, often doubling or inverting the main plot. By analogy or counterpoint, a skillful subplot broadens perspective on the main plot to enhance rather than dilute its effect. In Shakespeare's *Othello*, for instance, Iago's duping of Rodrigo reflects the main plot of Iago's treachery to Othello.

Drama Derived from the Greek *dran*, "to do," *drama* means "action" or "deed." Drama is the form of literary composition designed for performance in the theater, in which actors take the roles of the characters, perform the indicated action, and speak the written dialogue. In the *Poetics*, Aristotle described tragedy or dramatic enactment as the most fully evolved form of the impulse to imitate or make works of art.

Dramatic irony A special kind of suspenseful expectation, when the audience or reader understands the implication and meaning of a situation onstage and foresees the oncoming disaster (in tragedy) or triumph (in comedy) but the character does not. The irony forms between the contrasting levels of knowledge of the character and the audience. Dramatic irony is pervasive throughout Sophocles' *Oedipus*, for example, because we know from the beginning what Oedipus does not. We watch with dread and fascination the spectacle of a morally good man, committed to the salvation of his city, unwittingly preparing undeserved suffering for himself.

Dramatic monologue A poem written as a speech made by a character at some decisive moment. The speaker is usually addressing a silent listener as in T. S. Eliot's "The Love Song of J. Alfred Prufrock" or Robert Browning's "My Last Duchess."

Dramatic poetry Any verse written for the stage, as in the plays of classical Greece, the Renaissance (Shakespeare), and neoclassical periods (Molière, Racine). Also a kind of poetry that presents the voice of an imaginary character (or characters) speaking directly, without any additional narration by the author. In poetry, the term usually refers to the dramatic monologue, a lyric poem written as a speech made by a character at some decisive moment, such as Lord, Alfred Tennyson's "Ulysses." (*See also* **Dramatic monologue**.)

Dramatic point of view A point of view in which the narrator merely reports dialogue and action with minimal interpretation or access to the characters' minds. The dramatic point of view, as the name implies, uses prose fiction to approximate the method of plays (where readers are provided only with set descriptions, stage directions, and dialogue, and thus must supply motivations based solely on this external evidence).

Dramatic question The primary unresolved issue in a drama as it unfolds. The dramatic question is the result of artful plotting, raising suspense and expectation in a play's action as it moves toward its outcome. Will the Prince in *Hamlet*, for example, achieve what he has been instructed to do and what he intends to do?

Dramatic situation The basic conflict that initiates a work or establishes a scene. It usually describes both a protagonist's motivation and the forces that oppose its realization. (*See also* **Antagonist, Character, Complication, Plot, Rising action**.)

Dumb show In Renaissance theater, a mimed dramatic performance whose purpose is to prepare the audience for the main action of the play to follow. Jacobean playwrights like John Webster used it to show violent events that occur some distance from the play's locale. The most famous Renaissance example is the dumb show preceding the presentation of "The Murder of Gonzago" in *Hamlet*.

Dynamic character A character who, during the course of the narrative, grows or changes in some significant way. (*See also* **Character development**.)

Echo verse A poetic form in which the final syllables of the lines are repeated back as a reply or commentary, often using puns. Echo verse dates back to late classical Greek poetry. Fred Chappell's "Narcissus and Echo" is a contemporary example of this form.

Editing The act of rereading a draft in order to correct mistakes, cut excess words, and make improvements.

Editorial omniscience When an omniscient narrator goes beyond reporting the thoughts of his or her characters to make a critical judgment or commentary, making explicit the narrator's own thoughts or philosophies.

Editorial point of view Also called **Authorial intrusion**. The effect that occurs when a third-person narrator adds his or her own comments (which presumably represent the ideas and opinions of the author) into the narrative.

Elegy A lament or a sadly meditative poem, often written on the occasion of a death or other solemn theme. An elegy is usually a sustained poem in a formal style.

Endnote An additional piece of information that the author includes in a note at the end of a paper. Endnotes usually contain information that the author feels is important to convey but not appropriate to fit into the main body of text. (*See also* **Footnote**.)

End rhyme Rhyme that occurs at the ends of lines, rather than within them (as internal rhyme does). End rhyme is the most common kind of rhyme in English-language poetry.

End-stopped line A line of verse that ends in a full pause, usually indicated by a mark of punctuation.

English sonnet Also called **Shakespearean sonnet**. The English sonnet has a rhyme scheme organized into three quatrains with a final couplet: *abab cdcd efef gg*. The poem may turn, that is, shift in mood or tone, between any of the quatrains (although it usually occurs on the ninth line). (*See also* **Sonnet**.)

Envoy A short, often summarizing stanza that appears at the end of certain poetic forms (most notably the sestina, chant royal, and the French ballade). The envoy contains the poet's parting words. The word comes from the French *envoi*, meaning "sending forth."

Epic A long narrative poem usually composed in an elevated style tracing the adventures of a legendary or mythic hero. Epics are usually written in a consistent form and meter throughout. Famous epics include Homer's *Iliad* and *Odyssey*, Virgil's *Aeneid*, and Milton's *Paradise Lost*.

Epigram A very short poem, often comic, usually ending with some sharp turn of wit or meaning.

Epigraph A brief quotation preceding a story or other literary work. An epigraph usually suggests the subject, theme, or atmosphere the story will explore.

Epiphany A moment of insight, discovery, or revelation by which a character's life is greatly altered. An epiphany generally occurs near the end of a story. The term, which means "showing forth" in Greek, was first used in Christian theology to signify the manifestation of God's presence in the world. This theological idea was first borrowed by James Joyce to refer to a heightened moment of secular revelation.

Episode An incident in a large narrative that has unity in itself. An episode may bear close relation to the central narrative, but it can also be a digression.

Episodic plot, episodic structure A form of plotting where the individual scenes and events are presented chronologically without any profound sense of cause-and-effect relationship. In an episodic narrative the placement of many scenes could be changed without greatly altering the overall effect of the work.

Epistolary novel Novel in which the story is told by way of letters written by one or more of the characters. This form often lends an authenticity to the story, a sense that the author may have discovered these letters; but in fact they are a product of the author's invention.

Euphony The harmonious effect when the sounds of the words connect with the meaning in a way pleasing to the ear and mind. An example is found in Tennyson's lines, "The moan of doves in immemorial elms, / And murmuring of innumerable bees." The opposite of euphony is **cacophony**.

Exact rhyme A full rhyme in which the sounds following the initial letters of the words are identical in sound, as in *follow* and *hollow*, *go* and *slow*, *disband* and *this hand*.

Explication Literally, an "unfolding." In an explication an entire poem is explained in detail, addressing every element and unraveling any complexities as a means of analysis.

Exposition The opening portion of a narrative or drama. In the exposition, the scene is set, the protagonist is introduced, and the author discloses any other background information necessary to allow the reader to understand and relate to the events that are to follow.

Expressionism A dramatic style developed between 1910 and 1924 in Germany in reaction against realism's focus on surface details and external reality. To draw an audience into a dreamlike subjective realm, expressionistic artistic styles used episodic plots, distorted lines, exaggerated shapes, abnormally intense coloring, mechanical physical movement, and telegraphic speech (the broken syntax of a disordered psyche). Staging the contents of the unconscious, expressionist plays ranged from utopian visions of a fallen, materialistic world redeemed by the spirituality of "new men" to pessimistic nightmare visions of universal catastrophe.

Eye rhyme Rhyme in which the spelling of the words appears alike, but the pronunciations differ, as in *laughter* and *daughter*, *idea* and *flea*.

Fable A brief, often humorous narrative told to illustrate a moral. The characters in fables are traditionally animals whose personality traits symbolize human traits. Particular animals have conventionally come to represent specific human qualities or values. For example, the ant represents industry, the fox craftiness, and the lion nobility. A fable often concludes by summarizing its moral message in abstract terms. For example, Aesop's fable "The North Wind and the Sun" concludes with the moral "Persuasion is better than force." (*See also* **Allegory**.)

Fairy tale A traditional form of short narrative folklore, originally transmitted orally, that features supernatural characters such as witches, giants, fairies, or animals with human personality traits. Fairy tales often feature a hero or heroine who seems destined to achieve some desirable fate—such as marrying a prince or princess, becoming wealthy, or destroying an enemy.

Falling action The events in a narrative that follow the climax and bring the story to its conclusion, or dénouement.

Falling meter Trochaic and dactylic meters are called falling meters because their first syllable is accented, followed by one or more unaccented syllables. A foot of falling meter falls in its level of stress, as in the words *co*-medy or *aw*-ful.

Fantasy A narrative that depicts events, characters, or places that could not exist in the real world. Fantasy has limited interest in portraying experience realistically. Instead, it freely pursues the possibilities of the imagination. Fantasy usually includes elements of magic or the supernatural. Sometimes it is used to illustrate a moral message as in fables. Fantasy is a type of romance that emphasizes wish fulfillment (or nightmare fulfillment) instead of verisimilitude.

Farce A type of comedy featuring exaggerated character types in ludicrous and improbable situations, provoking belly laughs with sexual mix-ups, crude verbal jokes, pratfalls, and knockabout horseplay (like the comic violence of the Punch and Judy show).

Feminine rhyme A rhyme of two or more syllables with a stress on a syllable other than the last, as in *tur*-tle and *fer*-tile. (*See also* **Masculine rhyme, Rhyme.**)

Feminist criticism *See* **Gender criticism**.

Fiction From the Latin *ficio*, "act of fashioning, a shaping, a making." Fiction refers to any literary work that—although it might contain factual information—is not bound by factual accuracy, but creates a narrative shaped or made up by the author's imagination. Drama and poetry (especially narrative poetry) can be considered works of fiction, but the term now usually refers more specifically to prose stories and novels. Historical and other factual writing also requires shaping and making, but it is distinct from fiction because it is not free to invent people, places, and events; forays from documented fact must identify themselves as conjecture or hypothesis. Nonfiction, as the name suggests, is a category conventionally separate from fiction. Certainly an essay or work of literary journalism is "a made thing," and writers of nonfiction routinely employ the techniques used by fiction writers (moving forward and backward in time, reporting the inner thoughts of characters, etc.), but works of nonfiction must be not only true but factual. The truth of a work of fiction depends not on facts, but on how convincingly the writer creates the world of the story.

Figure of speech An expression or comparison that relies not on its literal meaning, but rather on its connotations and suggestions. For example, "He's dumber than dirt" is not literally true; it is a figure of speech. Major figures of speech include **metaphor, metonymy, simile,** and **synecdoche.**

First-person narrator A story in which the narrator is a participant in the action. Such a narrator refers to himself or herself as "I" and may be a major or minor character in the story. His or her attitude and understanding of characters and events shapes the reader's perception of the story being told.

Fixed form A traditional verse form requiring certain predetermined elements of structure, for example, a stanza pattern, set meter, or predetermined line length. A fixed form like the sonnet, for instance, must have no more or less than fourteen lines, rhymed according to certain conventional patterns. (*See also* **Closed form.**)

Flashback A scene relived in a character's memory. Flashbacks can be related by the narrator in a summary or they can be experienced by the characters themselves. Flashbacks allow the author to include events that occurred before the opening of the story, which may show the reader something significant that happened in the character's past or give an indication of what kind of person the character used to be.

Flat character A term coined by English novelist E. M. Forster to describe a character with only one outstanding trait. Flat characters are rarely the central characters in a narrative and are often based on **stock characters**. Flat characters stay the same throughout a story. (*See also* **Dynamic character.**)

Flexible theater Also called **black box** or **experimental theater space**. A modern, nontraditional performance space in which actor-audience relationships can be flexibly configured, with movable seating platforms. Usually seating anywhere from 100 to 250 spectators, black box theaters can accommodate staging in the round, thrust staging, tennis court staging, and even temporary proscenium arch (fourth wall) staging.

Folk ballads Anonymous narrative songs, usually in ballad meter, that were originally transmitted orally. Although most well-known ballads have been transcribed and published in order to protect them from being lost, they were originally created for oral performance, often resulting in many versions of a single ballad.

Folk epic Also called **Traditional epic**. A long narrative poem that traces the adventures of a tribe or nation's popular heroes. Some examples of epics are the *Iliad* and the *Odyssey* (Greek), *The Song of Roland* (French), and *The Cid* (Spanish). A folk epic originates in an oral tradition as opposed to a literary epic, which is written by an individual author consciously emulating earlier epic poetry.

Folklore The body of traditional wisdom and customs—including songs, stories, myths, and proverbs—of a people as collected and continued through oral tradition.

Folktale A short narrative drawn from folklore that has been passed down through an oral tradition. (*See also* **Fairy tale, Legend.**)

Foot The unit of measurement in metrical poetry. Different meters are identified by the pattern and order of stressed and unstressed syllables in their foot, usually containing two or three syllables, with one syllable accented.

Footnote An additional piece of information that the author includes at the bottom of a page, usually noted by a small reference number in the main text. A footnote might supply the reader with brief facts about a related historical figure or event, the definition of a foreign word or phrase, or any other relevant information that may help in understanding the text. (*See also* **Endnote.**)

Foreshadowing In plot construction, the technique of arranging events and information in such a way that later events are prepared for, or shadowed, beforehand. The author may introduce specific words, images, or actions in order to suggest significant later events. The effective use of foreshadowing by an author may prevent a story's outcome from seeming haphazard or contrived.

Form The means by which a literary work conveys its meaning. Traditionally, form refers to the way in which an artist expresses meaning rather than the content of that meaning, but it is now commonplace to note that form and content are inextricably related. Form, therefore, is more than the external framework of a literary work. It includes the totality of ways in which it unfolds and coheres as a structure of meaning and expression.

Formal English The heightened, impersonal language of educated persons, usually only written, although possibly spoken on dignified occasions. (*See also* **Levels of diction.**)

Formalist criticism A school of criticism which argues that literature may only be discussed on its own terms; that is, without outside influences or information. A key method that formalists use is close reading, a step-by-step analysis of the elements in a text.

Found poetry Poetry constructed by arranging bits of "found" prose. A found poem is a literary work made up of nonliterary language arranged for expressive effect.

Free verse From the French *vers libre*. Free verse describes poetry that organizes its lines without meter. It may be rhymed (as in some poems by H. D.), but it usually is not. There is no one means of organizing free verse, and different authors have used irreconcilable systems. What unites the two approaches is a freedom from metrical regularity. (*See also* **Open form.**)

Gender criticism Gender criticism examines how sexual identity influences the creation, interpretation, and evaluation of literary works. This critical approach began with feminist criticism in the 1960s and 1970s which stated that literary study had been so dominated by men that it contained many unexamined "male-produced" assumptions. Feminist criticism sought to address this imbalance in two ways: first in insisting that sexless interpretation was impossible, and second by articulating responses to the texts that were explicitly male or female. More recently, gender criticism has focused on gay and lesbian literary identity as interpretive strategies.

General English The ordinary speech of educated native speakers. Most literate speech and writing is general English. Its diction is more educated than **colloquial English**, yet not as elevated as **formal English**. (*See also* **Levels of diction.**)

Genre A conventional combination of literary form and subject matter, usually aimed at creating certain effects. A genre implies a preexisting understanding between the artist and the reader about the purpose and rules of the work. A horror story, for example, combines the form of the short story with certain conventional subjects, style, and theme with the expectation of frightening the reader. Major short story genres include science fiction, gothic, horror, and detective tales.

Gothic fiction A genre that creates terror and suspense, usually set in an isolated castle, mansion, or monastery populated by mysterious or threatening individuals. The Gothic form, invented by Horace Walpole in *The Castle of Otranto* (1764), has flourished in one form or another ever since. The term *Gothic* is also applied to medieval architecture, and Gothic fiction almost inevitably exploits claustrophobic interior architecture in its plotting—often featuring dungeons, crypts, torture chambers, locked rooms, and secret passageways. In the nineteenth century, writers such as Nathaniel Hawthorne, Edgar Allan Poe, and Charlotte Perkins Gilman brought the genre into the mainstream of American fiction.

Haiku A Japanese verse form that has three unrhymed lines of five, seven, and five syllables. Traditional haiku is often serious and spiritual in tone, relying mostly on imagery, and usually set in one of the four seasons.

Hamartia Greek for "error." An offense committed in ignorance of some material fact (without deliberate criminal intent) and therefore free of blameworthiness. A big mistake unintentionally made as a result of an intellectual error (not vice or criminal wickedness) by a morally good person, usually involving the identity of a blood relation. The *hamartia* of Oedipus, quite simply, is based on his ignorance of his true parentage; inadvertently and unwittingly, then, he commits the *hamartia* of patricide and incest. (*See also* **Recognition**.)

Heptameter A verse meter consisting of seven metrical feet, or seven primary stresses, per line.

Hero The central character in a narrative. The term is derived from the Greek epic tradition, in which *heroes* were the leading warriors among the princes. By extension, *hero* and *heroine* have come to mean the principal male and female figures in a narrative or dramatic literary work, although many today call protagonists of either gender *heroes*. When a critic terms the protagonist a *hero*, the choice of words often implies a positive moral assessment of the character. (*See also* **Antihero**.)

Heroic couplet *See* **Closed couplet**.

Hexameter A verse meter consisting of six metrical feet, or six primary stresses, per line.

High comedy A comic genre evoking so-called intellectual or thoughtful laughter from an audience that remains emotionally detached from the play's depiction of the folly, pretense, and incongruity of human behavior. The French playwright Molière and the English dramatists of the Restoration period developed a special form of high comedy in the **comedy of manners**, focused on the social relations and amorous intrigues of sophisticated upper-class men and women, conducted through witty repartee and verbal combat.

Historical criticism The practice of analyzing a literary work by investigating the social, cultural, and intellectual context that produced it—a context that necessarily includes the artist's biography and milieu. Historical critics strive to recreate the exact meaning and impact a work had on its original audience.

Historical fiction A type of fiction in which the narrative is set in another time or place. In historical fiction, the author usually attempts to recreate a faithful picture of daily life during the period. For example, Robert Graves's *I, Claudius* depicts the lives of the ancient Roman ruling class in the early Imperial age. Historical fiction sometimes introduces well-known figures from the past. More often it places imaginary characters in a carefully reconstructed version of a particular historical era.

Hubris Overweening pride, outrageous behavior, or the insolence that leads to ruin, *hubris* was in the Greek moral vocabulary the antithesis of moderation or rectitude. Creon, in Sophocles' *Antigone*, is a good example of a character brought down by his *hubris*.

Hyperbole *See* **Overstatement**.

Iamb A metrical foot in verse in which an unaccented syllable is followed by an accented one, as in "ca-*ress*" or "a *cat*" (⌣ ′). The iambic measure is the most common meter used in English poetry.

Iambic meter A verse meter consisting of a specific recurring number of iambic feet per line. (*See also* **Iamb, Iambic pentameter.**)

Iambic pentameter The most common meter in English verse—five iambic feet per line. Many fixed forms, such as the sonnet and heroic couplets, are written in iambic pentameter. Unrhymed iambic pentameter is called **blank verse**.

Image A word or series of words that refers to any sensory experience (usually sight, although also sound, smell, touch, or taste). An image is a direct or literal recreation of physical experience and adds immediacy to literary language.

Imagery The collective set of images in a poem or other literary work.

Impartial omniscience Refers to an omniscient narrator who, although he or she presents the thoughts and actions of the characters, does not judge them or comment on them. (Contrasts with **Editorial omniscience**.)

Implied metaphor A metaphor that uses neither connectives nor the verb *to be*. If we say, "John crowed over his victory," we imply metaphorically that John is a rooster but do not say so specifically. (*See also* **Metaphor**.)

Impressionism In fiction, a style of writing that emphasizes external events less than the impression those events make on the narrator or protagonist. Impressionist short stories, like Katherine Mansfield's "Miss Brill," usually center the narrative on the chief characters' mental lives rather than the reality around them.

Incremental refrain A refrain whose words change slightly with each recurrence. (*See also* **Refrain**.)

Initial alliteration *See* **Alliteration**.

Initiation story Also called **Coming-of-age story**. A narrative in which the main character, usually a child or adolescent, undergoes an important experience or rite of passage—often a difficult or disillusioning one—that prepares him or her for adulthood. James Joyce's "Araby" is a classic example of an initiation story.

In medias res A Latin phrase meaning "in the midst of things" that refers to a narrative device of beginning a story midway in the events it depicts (usually at an exciting or significant moment) before explaining the context or preceding actions. Epic poems such as Virgil's *Aeneid* or John Milton's *Paradise Lost* commonly begin *in medias res*, but the technique is also found in modern fiction.

Innocent narrator Also called **naive narrator**. A character who fails to understand all the implications of the story he or she tells. Of course, virtually any narrator has some degree of innocence or naiveté, but the innocent narrator—often a child or childlike adult—is used by an author trying to generate irony, sympathy, or pity by creating a gap between what the narrator knows and what the reader knows. Mark Twain's Huckleberry Finn—despite his mischievous nature—is an example of an innocent narrator.

Interior monologue An extended presentation of a character's thoughts in a narrative. Usually written in the present tense and printed without quotation marks, an interior monologue reads as if the character was speaking aloud to himself or herself, for the reader to overhear. A famous example of interior monologue comes at the end of *Ulysses* when Joyce gives us the rambling memories and reflections of Molly Bloom.

Internal alliteration *See* **Alliteration**.

Internal refrain A refrain that appears within a stanza, generally in a position that stays fixed throughout a poem. (*See also* **Refrain**.)

Internal rhyme Rhyme that occurs within a line of poetry, as opposed to **end rhyme**. Read aloud, these Wallace Stevens lines are rich in internal rhyme: "Chieftain Iffucan of Azcan in caftan / Of tan with henna hackles, halt!" (from "Bantams in Pine-Woods").

Ironic point of view The perspective of a character or narrator whose voice or position is rich in ironic contradictions. (*See also* **Irony**.)

Irony A literary device in which a discrepancy of meaning is masked beneath the surface of the language. Irony is present when a writer says one thing but means something quite the opposite. There are many kinds of irony, but the two major varieties are **verbal irony** (in which the discrepancy is contained in words) and **situational irony** (in which the discrepancy exists when something is about to happen to a character or characters who expect the opposite outcome). (*See also* **Cosmic irony, Irony of fate, Sarcasm, Verbal irony**.)

Irony of fate A type of situational irony that can be used for either tragic or comic purposes. Irony of fate is the discrepancy between actions and their results, between what characters deserve and what they get, between appearance and reality. In Sophocles' tragedy, for instance, Oedipus unwittingly fulfills the prophecy even as he takes the actions a morally good man would take to avoid it. (*See also* **Cosmic irony**.)

Italian sonnet Also called **Petrarchan sonnet**, a sonnet with the following rhyme pattern for the first eight lines (the **octave**): *abba, abba*; the final six lines (the **sestet**) may follow any pattern of rhymes, as long as it does not end in a couplet. The poem traditionally turns, or shifts in mood or tone, after the octave. (*See also* **Sonnet**.)

Katharsis, **catharsis** Often translated as purgation or purification, the term is drawn from the last element of Aristotle's definition of tragedy, relating to the final cause or purpose of tragic art. Catharsis generally refers to the feeling of emotional release or calm the spectator feels at the end of tragedy. In Aristotle *katharsis* is the final effect of the playwright's skillful use of plotting, character, and poetry to elicit pity and fear from the audience. Through *katharsis,* drama taught the audience compassion for the vulnerabilities of others and schooled it in justice and other civic virtues.

Legend A traditional narrative handed down through popular oral tradition to illustrate and celebrate a remarkable character, an important event, or to explain the unexplainable. Legends, unlike other folktales, claim to be true and usually take place in real locations, often with genuine historical figures.

Levels of diction In English, there are conventionally four basic levels of formality in word choice, or four levels of diction. From the least formal to the most elevated they are **vulgate, colloquial English, general English**, and **formal English**. (*See also* **Diction**.)

Limerick A short and usually comic verse form of five anapestic lines usually rhyming *aabba*. The first, second, and fifth lines traditionally have three stressed syllables each; the third and fourth have two stresses each (3, 3, 2, 2, 3).

Limited omniscience Also called third-person limited point of view. A type of point of view in which the narrator sees into the minds of some but not all of the characters. Most typically, limited omniscience sees through the eyes of one major or minor character. In limited omniscience, the author can compromise between the immediacy of first-person narration and the mobility of third person.

Literary ballad Ballad not meant for singing, written for literate readers by sophisticated poets rather than arising from the anonymous oral tradition. (*See also* **Ballad**.)

Literary epic A crafted imitation of the oral folk epic written by an author living in a society where writing has been invented. Examples of the literary epic are *The Aeneid* by Virgil and *The Divine Comedy* by Dante Alighieri. (*See also* **Folk epic**.)

Literary genre *See* **Genre**.

Literary theory Literary criticism that tries to formulate general principles rather than discuss specific texts. Theory operates at a high level of abstraction and often focuses on understanding basic issues of language, communication, art, interpretation, culture, and ideological content.

Local color The use of specific regional material—unique customs, dress, habits, and speech patterns of ordinary people—to create atmosphere or realism in a literary work.

Locale The location where a story takes place.

Low comedy A comic style arousing laughter through jokes, slapstick humor, sight gags, and boisterous clowning. Unlike **high comedy**, it has little intellectual appeal. (*See also* **Comedy**.)

Lyric A short poem expressing the thoughts and feelings of a single speaker. Often written in the first person, lyric poetry traditionally has a songlike immediacy and emotional force.

Madrigal A short secular song for three or more voices arranged in counterpoint. The madrigal is often about love or pastoral themes. It originated in Italy in the fourteenth century and enjoyed great success during the Elizabethan Age.

Magic realism Also called **Magical realism**. A type of contemporary narrative in which the magical and the mundane are mixed in an overall context of realistic storytelling. The term was coined by Cuban novelist Alejo Carpentier in 1949 to describe the matter-of-fact combination of the fantastic and everyday in Latin American fiction. Magic realism has become the standard name for an international trend in contemporary fiction such as Gabriel García Márquez's *One Hundred Years of Solitude*.

Masculine rhyme Either a rhyme of one syllable words (as in *fox* and *socks*) or—in polysyllabic words—a rhyme on the stressed final syllables: con-*trive* and sur-*vive*. (*See also* **Feminine rhyme**.)

Masks In Latin, *personae*. In classical Greek theater, full facial masks made of leather, linen, or light wood, with headdress, allowed male actors to embody the conventionalized characters (or *dramatis personae*) of the tragic and comic stage. Later, in the seventeenth and eighteenth centuries, stock characters of the ***commedia dell' arte*** wore characteristic half masks made of leather. (*See also* **Persona**.)

Melodrama Originally a stage play featuring background music and sometimes songs to underscore the emotional mood of each scene. Melodramas were notoriously weak in characterization and motivation but famously strong on action, suspense, and passion. Melodramatic characters were stereotyped villains, heroes, and young lovers. When the term *melodrama* is applied to fiction, it is almost inevitably a negative criticism implying that the author has sacrificed psychological depth and credibility for emotional excitement and adventurous plotting.

Metafiction Fiction that consciously explores its own nature as a literary creation. The Greek word *meta* means "upon"; metafiction consequently is a mode of narrative that does not try to create the illusion of verisimilitude but delights in its own fictional nature, often by speculating on the story it is telling. The term is usually associated with late-twentieth-century writers like John Barth, Italo Calvino, and Jorge Luis Borges.

Metaphor A statement that one thing *is* something else, which, in a literal sense, it is not. By asserting that a thing is something else, a metaphor creates a close association between the two entities and usually underscores some important similarity between them. An example of metaphor is "Richard is a pig."

Meter A recurrent, regular, rhythmic pattern in verse. When stresses recur at fixed intervals, the result is meter. Traditionally, meter has been the basic organizational device of world poetry. There are many existing meters, each identified by the different patterns of recurring sounds. In English most common meters involve the arrangement of stressed and unstressed syllables.

Metonymy Figure of speech in which the name of a thing is substituted for that of another closely associated with it. For instance, in saying "The White House decided," one could mean that the president decided.

Microcosm The small world as created by a poem, play, or story that reflects the tensions of the larger world beyond. In some sense, most successful literary works offer a microcosm that illuminates the greater world around it.

Mime Either a play or sketch without words, or the performer. (*See also* **Pantomime**.)

Minimalist fiction Contemporary fiction written in a deliberately flat, unemotional tone and an appropriately unadorned style. Minimalist fiction often relies more on dramatic action, scene, and dialogue than complex narration or authorial summary. Examples of minimalist fiction can be found in the short stories of Raymond Carver and Bobbie Ann Mason.

Mixed metaphor A metaphor that trips over another metaphor—usually unconsciously—already in the statement. Mixed metaphors are the result of combining two or more incompatible metaphors resulting in ridiculousness or nonsense. For example, "Mary was such a tower of strength that she breezed her way through all the work" ("towers" do not "breeze").

Monologue An extended speech by a single character. The term originated in drama, where it describes a solo speech that has listeners (as opposed to a **soliloquy**, where the character speaks only to himself or herself). A short story or even a novel can be written in monologue form if it is an unbroken speech by one character to another silent character or characters.

Monometer A verse meter consisting of one metrical foot, or one primary stress, per line.

Monosyllabic Foot A foot, or unit of meter, that contains only one syllable.

Moral A paraphrasable message or lesson implied or directly stated in a literary work. Commonly, a moral is stated at the end of a fable.

Motif An element that recurs significantly throughout a narrative. A motif can be an image, idea, theme, situation, or action (and was first commonly used as a musical term for a recurring melody or melodic fragment). A motif can also refer to an element that recurs across many literary works like a beautiful lady in medieval romances who turns out to be an evil fairy or three questions that are asked a protagonist to test his or her wisdom.

Motivation What a character in a story or drama wants. The reasons an author provides for a character's actions. Motivation can be either *explicit* (in which reasons are specifically stated in a story) or *implicit* (in which the reasons are only hinted at or partially revealed).

Myth A traditional narrative of anonymous authorship that arises out of a culture's oral tradition. The characters in traditional myths are usually gods or heroic figures. Myths characteristically explain the origins of things—gods, people, places, plants, animals, and natural events—usually from a cosmic view. A culture's values and belief systems are traditionally passed from generation to generation in myth. In literature, myth may also refer to boldly imagined narratives that embody primal truths about life. Myth is usually differentiated from legend, which has a specific historical base.

Mythological criticism The practice of analyzing a literary work by looking for recurrent universal patterns. Mythological criticism explores the artist's common humanity by tracing how the individual imagination uses myths and symbols that are shared by different cultures and epochs.

Naive narrator *See* **Innocent narrator**.

Narrative poem A poem that tells a story. Narrative is one of the four traditional modes of poetry, along with lyric, dramatic, and didactic. **Ballads** and **epics** are two common forms of narrative poetry.

Narrator A voice or character that provides the reader with information and insight about the characters and incidents in a narrative. A narrator's perspective and personality can greatly affect how a story is told. (*See also* **Omniscient narrator**, **Point of view**.)

Naturalism A type of fiction or drama in which the characters are presented as products or victims of environment and heredity. Naturalism, considered an extreme form of realism, customarily depicts the social, psychological, and economic milieu of the primary characters. Naturalism was first formally developed by French novelist Émile Zola in the 1870s. In promoting naturalism as a theory of animal behavior, Zola urged the modeling of naturalist literature and drama on the scientific case study. The writer, like the scientist, was to record objective reality with detachment; events onstage should be reproduced with sufficient exactness to demonstrate the strict laws of material causality. Important American Naturalists include Jack London, Theodore Dreiser, and Stephen Crane. (*See also* **Realism**.)

Neoclassical period *See* **Augustan age**.

New Formalism A term for a recent literary movement (begun around 1980) in which young poets began using rhyme, meter, and narrative again. New Formalists attempt to write poetry that appeals to an audience beyond academia. Timothy Steele, Gertrude Schnackenberg, R. S. Gwynn, David Mason, and Marilyn Nelson are poets commonly associated with the movement.

New naturalism A term describing some American plays of the 1970s and 1980s, frankly showing the internal and external forces that shape the lives of unhappy, alienated, dehumanized, and often impoverished characters. Examples include the plays of Sam Shepard, August Wilson, and David Mamet.

Nonfiction novel A genre in which actual events are presented as a novel-length story, using the techniques of fiction (flashback, interior monologues, etc.). Truman Capote's *In Cold Blood* (1966), which depicts a multiple murder and subsequent trial in Kansas, is a classic example of this modern genre.

Nonparticipant narrator A narrator who does not appear in the story as a character but is capable of revealing the thoughts and motives of one or more characters. A nonparticipant narrator is also capable of moving from place to place in order to describe action and report dialogue. (*See also* **Omniscient narrator**.)

Nouvelle The French term for the short prose tale (called **novella** by Italian Renaissance writers) that usually depicted in relatively realistic terms illicit love, ingenious trickery, and sensational adventure, often with an underlying moral. Margarite de Navarre's *Heptameron* is a classic collection of *nouvelle*.

Novel An extended work of fictional prose narrative. The term *novel* usually implies a book-length narrative (as compared to more compact forms of prose fiction like the short story). Because of its extended length, a novel usually has more characters, more varied scenes, and a broader coverage of time than a short story.

Novella In modern terms, a prose narrative longer than a short story but shorter than a novel (approximately 30,000 to 50,000 words). Unlike a short story, a novella is long enough to be published independently as a brief book. Classic modern novellas include Franz Kafka's *The Metamorphosis*, Joseph Conrad's *Heart of Darkness*, and Thomas Mann's *Death in Venice*. During the Renaissance, however, the term *novella* originally referred to short prose narratives such as those found in Giovanni Boccaccio's *Decameron*.

Objective point of view *See* **Dramatic point of view**.

Observer A type of first-person narrator who is relatively detached from or plays only a minor role in the events described.

Octameter A verse meter consisting of eight metrical feet, or eight primary stresses, per line.

Octave A stanza of eight lines. *Octave* is a term usually used when speaking of sonnets to indicate the first eight-line section of the poem, as distinct from the *sestet* (the final six lines). Some poets also use octaves as separate stanzas as in W. B. Yeats's "Sailing to Byzantium," which employs the *ottava rima* ("eighth rhyme") stanza—*abababcc*.

Off rhyme *See* **Slant rhyme**.

O. Henry ending *See* **Trick ending**.

Omniscient narrator Also called **all-knowing narrator**. A narrator who has the ability to move freely through the consciousness of any character. The omniscient narrator also has complete knowledge of all of the external events in a story. (*See also* **Nonparticipant narrator**.)

Onomatopoeia A literary device that attempts to represent a thing or action by the word that imitates the sound associated with it (e.g., *crash, bang, pitter-patter*).

Open dénouement One of the two conventional types of dénouement or resolution. In open dénouement, the author ends a narrative with a few loose ends, or unresolved matters, on which the reader is left to speculate. (*See also* **Closed dénouement**.)

Open form Verse that has no set formal scheme—no meter, rhyme, or even set stanzaic pattern. Open form is always in free verse. (*See also* **Free verse**.)

Oral tradition The tradition within a culture that transmits narratives by word of mouth from one generation to another. Fables, folktales, ballads, and songs are examples of some types of narratives found originally in an oral tradition.

Orchestra In classical Greek theater architecture, "the place for dancing," a circular, level performance space at the base of a horseshoe-shaped amphitheater, where twelve, then later (in Sophocles' plays) fifteen, young, masked, male chorus members sang and danced the odes interspersed between dramatic episodes making up the classical Greek play. Today the orchestra refers to the ground floor seats in a theater or concert hall.

Overstatement Also called **hyperbole**. Exaggeration used to emphasize a point.

Pantomime Acting on the stage without speech, using only posture, gesture, bodily movement, and exaggerated facial expressions to mimic a character's actions and express feelings. Originally, in ancient Rome, a pantomime was a performer who played all the parts single-handedly. (*See also* **Mime**.)

Parable A brief, usually allegorical narrative that teaches a moral. The parables found in Christian literature, such as "The Parable of the Prodigal Son" (Luke 15:11–32), are classic examples of the form. In parables, unlike fables (where the moral is explicitly stated within the narrative), the moral themes are implicit and can often be interpreted in several ways. Modern parables can be found in the works of Franz Kafka and Jorge Luis Borges.

Paradox A statement that at first strikes one as self-contradictory, but that on reflection reveals some deeper sense. Paradox is often achieved by a play on words.

Parallelism An arrangement of words, phrases, clauses, or sentences side-by-side in a similar grammatical or structural way. Parallelism organizes ideas in a way that demonstrates their coordination to the reader.

Paraphrase The restatement in one's own words of what we understand a literary work to say. A paraphrase is similar to a summary, although not as brief or simple.

Parody A mocking imitation of a literary work or individual author's style, usually for comic effect. A parody typically exaggerates distinctive features of the original for humorous purposes.

Participant narrator A narrator that participates as a character within a story. (*See also* **First-person narrator**.)

Pentameter A verse meter consisting of five metrical feet, or five primary stresses, per line. In English, the most common form of pentameter is iambic.

Peripeteia Anglicized as *peripety*, Greek for "sudden change." Reversal of fortune. In a play's plotting, a sudden change of circumstance affecting the protagonist, often also including a reversal of intent on the protagonist's part. The play's peripety occurs usually when a certain result is expected and instead its opposite effect is produced. For example, at the beginning of *Oedipus*, the protagonist expects to discover the identity of the murderer of Laius. However, after the Corinthian messenger informs Oedipus that he was adopted, the hero's intent changes to encompass the search for his true parentage. A comedy's peripety restores a character to good fortune, when a moment in which the worst can happen is suddenly turned into happy circumstance.

Persona Latin for "mask." A fictitious character created by an author to be the speaker of a poem, story, or novel. A persona is always the narrator of the work and not merely a character in it.

Personification A figure of speech in which a thing, an animal, or an abstract term is endowed with human characteristics. Personification allows an author to dramatize the nonhuman world in tangibly human terms.

Petrarchan sonnet *See* **Italian sonnet**.

Picaresque A type of narrative, usually a novel, that presents the life of a likable scoundrel who is at odds with respectable society. The narrator of a picaresque was originally a *picaro* (Spanish for "rascal" or "rogue") who recounts his adventures tricking the rich and gullible. This type of narrative rarely has a tight plot, and the episodes or adventures follow in a loose chronological order.

Picture-frame stage Developed in sixteenth-century Italian playhouses, the picture-frame stage held the action within a proscenium arch, a gateway standing "in front of the scenery" (as the word *proscenium* indicates). The proscenium framed painted scene panels (receding into the middle distance) designed to give the illusion of three-dimensional perspective. Only one seat in the auditorium, reserved for the theater's royal patron or sponsor, enjoyed the complete perspectivist illusion. The raised and framed stage separated actors from the audience and the world of the play from the real world of the auditorium. Picture-frame stages became the norm throughout Europe and England up into the twentieth century.

Play *See* **Drama**.

Play review A critical account of a performance, providing the basic facts of the production, a brief plot summary, and an evaluation (with adequate rationale) of the chief elements of performance, including the acting, the direction, scene and light design, and the script, especially if the play is new or unfamiliar.

Plot The particular arrangement of actions, events, and situations that unfold in a narrative. A plot is not merely the general story of a narrative but the author's artistic pattern made from the parts of the narrative, including the exposition, complications, climax, and dénouement. How an author chooses to construct the plot determines the way the reader experiences the story. Manipulating a plot, therefore, can be the author's most important expressive device when writing a story. More than just a story made up of episodes or a bare synopsis of the temporal order of events, the plotting is the particular embodiment of an action that allows the audience to see the causal relationship between the parts of the action. (*See also* **Climax**, **Falling action**, **Rising action**.)

Poetic diction Strictly speaking, *poetic diction* means any language deemed suitable for verse, but the term generally refers to elevated language intended for poetry rather than common use. Poetic diction often refers to the ornate language used in literary periods such as the Augustan age, when authors employed a highly specialized vocabulary for their verse. (*See also* **Diction**.)

Point of view The perspective from which a story is told. There are many types of point of view, including first-person narrator (a story in which the narrator is a participant in the action) and third-person narrator (a type of narration in which the narrator is a nonparticipant).

Portmanteau word An artificial word that combines parts of other words to express some combination of their qualities. Sometimes portmanteau words prove so useful that they become part of the standard language. For example, *smog* from *smoke* and *fog*; or *brunch* from *breakfast* and *lunch*.

Print culture A culture that depends primarily on the printed word—in books, magazines, and newspapers—to distribute and preserve information. In recent decades the electronic media have taken over much of this role from print.

Projective verse Charles Olson's theory that poets compose by listening to their own breathing and using it as a rhythmic guide rather than poetic meter or form. (*See also* **Open form.**)

Proscenium arch Separating the auditorium from the raised stage and the world of the play, the architectural picture frame or gateway "standing in front of the scenery" (as the word *proscenium* indicates) in traditional European theaters from the sixteenth century on.

Prose poem Poetic language printed in prose paragraphs, but displaying the careful attention to sound, imagery, and figurative language characteristic of poetry.

Prosody The study of metrical structures in poetry. (*See also* **Scansion.**)

Protagonist The central character in a literary work. The protagonist usually initiates the main action of the story, often in conflict with the antagonist. (*See also* **Antagonist.**)

Psalms Sacred songs, usually referring to the 150 Hebrew poems collected in the Old Testament.

Psychological criticism The practice of analyzing a literary work through investigating three major areas: the nature of literary genius, the psychological study of a particular artist, and the analysis of fictional characters. This methodology uses the analytical tools of psychology and psychoanalysis to understand the underlying motivations and meanings of a literary work.

Pulp fiction A type of formulaic and quickly written fiction originally produced for cheap mass circulation magazines. The term *pulp* refers to the inexpensive woodpulp paper developed in the mid-nineteenth century on which these magazines were printed. Most pulp fiction journals printed only melodramatic genre work—westerns, science fiction, romance, horror, adventure tales, or crime stories.

Pun A play on words in which one word is substituted for another similar or identical sound, but of very different meaning.

Purgation *See Katharsis.*

Quantitative meter A meter constructed on the principle of vowel length. Such quantities are difficult to hear in English, so this meter remains slightly foreign to our language. Classical Greek and Latin poetry were written in quantitative meters.

Quatrain A stanza consisting of four lines. Quatrains are the most common stanza used in English-language poetry.

Rap A popular style of music that emerged in the 1980s in which lyrics are spoken or chanted over a steady beat, usually sampled or prerecorded. Rap lyrics are almost always rhymed and very rhythmic—syncopating a heavy metrical beat in a manner similar to jazz. Originally an African American form, rap is now international. In that way, rap can be seen as a form of popular poetry.

Reader-response criticism The practice of analyzing a literary work by describing what happens in the reader's mind while interpreting the text. Reader-response critics believe that no literary text exists independently of readers' interpretations and that there is no single fixed interpretation of any literary work.

Realism An attempt to reproduce faithfully the surface appearance of life, especially that of ordinary people in everyday situations. As a literary term, *realism* has two meanings—one general, the other historical. In a general sense, realism refers to the representation of characters, events, and settings in ways that the spectator will consider plausible, based on consistency and likeness to type. This sort of realism does not necessarily depend on elaborate factual description or documentation but more on the author's ability to draft plots and characters within a conventional framework of social, economic, and psychological reality. In a historical sense, Realism (usually capitalized) refers to a movement in nineteenth-century European literature and theater that rejected the idealism, elitism, and romanticism of earlier verse dramas and prose fiction in an attempt to represent life truthfully. Realist literature customarily focused on the middle class (and occasionally the working class) rather than the aristocracy, and it used social and economic detail to create an accurate account of human behavior. Realism began in France with Honoré de Balzac, Gustave Flaubert, and Guy de Maupassant and then moved internationally. Other major Realists include Leo Tolstoy, Henry James, Anton Chekhov, and Edith Wharton.

Recognition In tragic plotting, the moment of recognition occurs when ignorance gives way to knowledge, illusion to disillusion. In Aristotle's *Poetics*, this is usually a recognition of blood ties or kinship between the persons involved in grave actions involving suffering. According to Aristotle, the ideal moment of recognition coincides with *peripeteia* or reversal of fortune. The classic example is in *Oedipus* when Oedipus discovers that he had unwittingly and inadvertently killed his own father when defending himself at the crossroads and later married his own mother when assuming the Theban throne. (*See also* **Hamartia, Katharsis, Peripeteia**.)

Refrain A word, phrase, line, or stanza repeated at intervals in a song or poem. The repeated chorus of a song is a refrain.

Regionalism The literary representation of a specific locale that consciously uses the particulars of geography, custom, history, folklore, or speech. In regional narratives, the locale plays a crucial role in the presentation and progression of a story that could not be moved to another setting without artistic loss. Usually, regional narratives take place at some distance from the literary capital of a culture, often in small towns or rural areas. Examples of American regionalism can be found in the writing of Willa Cather, Kate Chopin, William Faulkner, and Eudora Welty.

Resolution The final part of a narrative, the concluding action or actions that follow the climax. (*See also* **Conclusion, Dénouement**.)

Restoration period In England, the period following the restoration of Charles II to the throne in 1660, extending to 1700. King Charles reopened the theaters that had been closed by the Puritans as sinful institutions. The Restoration period reintroduced a strong secular and urbane element back into English literature.

Retrospect *See* **Flashback**.

Reversal *See* **Peripeteia**.

Rhyme, Rime Two or more words that contain an identical or similar vowel sound, usually accented, with following consonant sounds (if any) identical as well: *queue* and *stew*, *prairie schooner* and *piano tuner*. (*See also* **Consonance, Exact rhyme**.)

Rhyme scheme, Rime scheme Any recurrent pattern of rhyme within an individual poem or fixed form. A rhyme scheme is usually described by using small letters to represent each end rhyme—*a* for the first rhyme, *b* for the second, and so on. The rhyme scheme of a stanza of **common meter** or hymn meter, for example, would be notated as *abab*.

Rhythm The pattern of stresses and pauses in a poem. A fixed and recurring rhythm in a poem is called **meter**.

Rising action That part of the play or narrative, including the exposition, in which events start moving toward a climax. In the rising action the protagonist usually faces the complications of the plot to reach his or her goal. In *Hamlet*, the rising action develops the conflict between Hamlet and Claudius, with Hamlet succeeding in controlling the course of events. Because the mainspring of the play's first half is the mystery of Claudius's guilt, the rising action reaches a climax when Hamlet proves the king's guilt by the device of the play within a play (3.2—the "mousetrap" scene), when Hamlet as heroic avenger has positive proof of Claudius's guilt.

Rising meter A meter whose movement rises from an unstressed syllable (or syllables) to a stressed syllable (for-*get*, in De-*troit*). Iambic and anapestic are examples of rising meter.

Romance In general terms, romance is a narrative mode that employs exotic adventure and idealized emotion rather than realistic depiction of character and action. In the romantic mode—out of which most popular genre fictions develop—people, actions, and events are depicted more as we wish them to be (heroes are very brave, villains are very bad) rather than the complex ways they usually are. Medieval romances (in both prose and verse) presented chivalric tales of kings, knights, and aristocratic ladies. Modern romances, emerging in the nineteenth century, were represented by adventure novels like Sir Walter Scott's *Ivanhoe* or Nathaniel Hawthorne's *The House of the Seven Gables*, which embodied the symbolic quests and idealized characters of earlier, chivalric tales in slightly more realistic terms, a tradition carried on in contemporary popular works like the *Star Wars* and James Bond films.

Romantic comedy A form of comic drama in which the plot focuses on one or more pairs of young lovers who overcome difficulties to achieve a happy ending (usually marriage). Shakespeare's *A Midsummer Night's Dream* is a classic example of the genre.

Rondel A thirteen-line English verse form consisting of three stanzas rhymed with a refrain.

Round character A term coined by English novelist E. M. Forster to describe a complex character who is presented in depth and detail in a narrative. Round characters are those who change significantly during the course of a narrative. Most often, round characters are the central characters in a narrative. (*See also* **Flat character**.)

Run-on line A line of verse that does not end in punctuation, but carries on grammatically to the next line. Such lines are read aloud with only a slight pause at the end. A run-on line is also called *enjambment*.

Sarcasm A conspicuously bitter form of irony in which the ironic statement is designed to hurt or mock its target. (*See also* **Irony**.)

Satiric comedy A genre using derisive humor to ridicule human weakness and folly or attack political injustices and incompetence. Satiric comedy often focuses on ridiculing characters or killjoys, who resist the festive mood of comedy. Such characters, called humors, are often characterized by one dominant personality trait or ruling obsession.

Satiric poetry Poetry that blends criticism with humor to convey a message. Satire characteristically uses irony to make its points. Usually, its tone is one of detached amusement, withering contempt, and implied superiority.

Satyr play A type of Greek comic play that was performed after the tragedies at the City Dionysia, the principal civic and religious festival of Athens. The playwrights winning the right to perform their works in the festival wrote three tragedies and one satyr play to form the traditional tetralogy, or group of four. The structure of a satyr play was similar to tragedy's. Its subject matter, treated in burlesque, was drawn from myth or the epic cycles. Its chorus was composed of satyrs (half human and half horse or goat) under the leadership of Silenus, the adoptive father of Dionysius. Rascals and revelers, satyrs represented wild versions of humanity, opposing the values of civilized men. Euripides' *Cyclops* is the only complete surviving example of the genre.

Scansion A practice used to describe rhythmic patterns in a poem by separating the metrical feet, counting the syllables, marking the accents, and indicating the pauses. Scansion can be very useful in analyzing the sound of a poem and how it should be read aloud.

Scene In drama, the scene is a division of the action in an act of the play. There is no universal convention as to what constitutes a scene, and the practice differs by playwright and period. Usually, a scene represents a single dramatic action that builds to a climax (often ending in the entrance or exit of a major character). In this last sense of a vivid and unified action, the term can be applied to fiction.

Selective omniscience The point of view that sees the events of a narrative through the eyes of a single character. The selectively omniscient narrator is usually a nonparticipant narrator.

Sentimentality A usually pejorative description of the quality of a literary work that tries to convey great emotion but fails to give the reader sufficient grounds for sharing it.

Sestet A poem or stanza of six lines. *Sestet* is a term usually used when speaking of sonnets, to indicate the final six-line section of the poem, as distinct from the octave (the first eight lines). (*See also* **Sonnet.**)

Sestina A complex verse form ("song of sixes") in which six end words are repeated in a prescribed order through six stanzas. A sestina ends with an **envoy** of three lines in which all six words appear—for a total of thirty-nine lines. Originally used by French and Italian poets, the sestina has become a popular modern form in English.

Setting The time and place of a literary work. The setting may also include the climate and even the social, psychological, or spiritual state of the participants.

Shakespearean sonnet *See* **English sonnet.**

Short Story A prose narrative too brief to be published in a separate volume—as novellas and novels frequently are. The short story is usually a focused narrative that presents one or two main characters involved in a single compelling action.

Simile A comparison of two things, indicated by some connective, usually *like, as, than,* or a verb such as *resembles.* A simile usually compares two things that initially seem unlike but are shown to have a significant resemblance. "Cool as a cucumber" and "My love is like a red, red rose" are examples of similes.

Situational Irony *See* **Irony.**

Skene In classical Greek staging of the fifth century B.C., the temporary wooden stage building in which actors changed masks and costumes when changing roles. Its facade, with double center doors and possibly two side doors, served as the setting for action taking place before a palace, temple, cave, or other interior space.

Sketch A short, static, descriptive composition. Literary sketches can be either fiction or nonfiction. A sketch usually focuses on describing a person or place without providing a narrative.

Slack syllable An unstressed syllable in a line of verse.

Slant rhyme A rhyme in which the final consonant sounds are the same but the vowel sounds are different, as in letter and litter, bone and bean. Slant rhyme may also be called *near rhyme, off rhyme,* or *imperfect rhyme.* (*See also* **Consonance.**)

Slapstick comedy A kind of farce, featuring pratfalls, pie throwing, fisticuffs, and other violent action. It takes its name originally from the slapstick carried by the *commedia dell'arte*'s main servant type, Harlequin.

Sociological criticism The practice of analyzing a literary work by examining the cultural, economic, and political context in which it was written or received. Sociological criticism primarily explores the relationship between the artist and society.

Soliloquy In drama, a speech by a character alone onstage in which he or she utters his or her thoughts aloud. The soliloquy is important in drama because it gives the audience insight into a character's inner life, private motivations, and uncertainties.

Sonnet From the Italian *sonnetto*: "little song." A traditional and widely used verse form, especially popular for love poetry. The sonnet is a fixed form of fourteen lines, traditionally written in iambic pentameter, usually made up of an **octave** (the first eight lines) and a concluding **sestet** (six lines). There are, however, several variations, most conspicuously the Shakespearean, or English sonnet, which consists of three quatrains and a concluding couplet. Most sonnets turn, or shift in tone or focus, after the eight lines, although the placement may vary. (*See also* **English sonnet, Italian sonnet.**)

Spondee A metrical foot of verse containing two stressed syllables (′ ′) often substituted into a meter to create extra emphasis.

Stage business Nonverbal action that engages the attention of an audience. Expressing what cannot be said, stage business became a particularly important means of revealing the inner thoughts and feelings of a character in the development of Realism.

Stanza From the Italian, meaning "stopping-place" or "room." A recurring pattern of two or more lines of verse, poetry's equivalent to the paragraph in prose. The stanza is the basic organizational principle of most formal poetry.

Static character *See* **Flat character**.

Stock character A common or stereotypical character that occurs frequently in literature. Examples of stock characters are the mad scientist, the battle-scarred veteran, or the strong-but-silent cowboy. (*See also* **Archetype**.)

Stream of consciousness Not a specific technique, but a type of modern narration that uses various literary devices, especially interior monologue, in an attempt to duplicate the subjective and associative nature of human consciousness. Stream of consciousness often focuses on imagistic perception in order to capture the preverbal level of consciousness.

Stress An emphasis or accent placed on a syllable in speech. Clear pronunciation of polysyllabic words almost always depends on correct placement of their stress. (For instance, *de*-sert and de-*sert* are two different words and parts of speech, depending on their stress.) Stress is the basic principle of most English-language meter.

Style All the distinctive ways in which an author, genre, movement, or historical period uses language to create a literary work. An author's style depends on his or her characteristic use of diction, imagery, tone, syntax, and figurative language. Even sentence structure and punctuation can play a role in an author's style.

Subject The main topic of a poem, story, or play.

Subplot *See* **Double plot**.

Summary A brief condensation of the main idea or story of a literary work. A summary is similar to a paraphrase, but less detailed.

Surrealism A modernist movement in art and literature that tries to organize art according to the irrational dictates of the unconscious mind. Founded by the French poet André Breton, Surrealism sought to reach a higher plane of reality by abandoning logic for the seemingly absurd connections made in dreams and other unconscious mental activities.

Suspense Enjoyable anxiety created in the reader by the author's handling of plot. When the outcome of events is unclear, the author's suspension of resolution intensifies the reader's interest—particularly if the plot involves characters to whom the reader or audience is sympathetic. Suspense is also created when the fate of a character is clear to the audience, but not to the character. The suspense results from the audience's anticipation of how and when the character will meet his or her inevitable fate.

Syllabic verse A verse form in which the poet establishes a pattern of a certain number of syllables to a line. Syllabic verse is the most common meter in most Romance languages such as Italian, French, and Spanish; it is less common in English because it is difficult to hear syllable count. Syllabic verse was used by several Modernist poets, most conspicuously Marianne Moore.

Symbol A person, place, or thing in a narrative that suggests meanings beyond its literal sense. Symbol is related to allegory, but it works more complexly. In an allegory an object has a single additional significance. By contrast, a symbol usually contains multiple meanings and associations. In Herman Melville's *Moby-Dick*, for example, the great white whale does not have just a single significance but accrues powerful associations as the narrative progresses.

Symbolic act An action whose significance goes well beyond its literal meaning. In literature, symbolic acts usually involve some conscious or unconscious ritual element like rebirth, purification, forgiveness, vengeance, or initiation.

Symbolist movement An international literary movement that originated with nineteenth-century French poets such as Charles Baudelaire, Arthur Rimbaud, and Paul Verlaine. Symbolists aspired to make literature resemble music. They avoided direct statement and exposition for powerful evocation and suggestion. Symbolists also considered the poet as a seer who could look beyond the mundane aspects of the everyday world to capture visions of a higher reality.

Symbolists Members of the Symbolist movement.

Synecdoche The use of a significant part of a thing to stand for the whole of it or vice versa. To say *wheels* for *car* or *rhyme* for *poetry* are examples of synecdoche. (*See also* **Metonymy**.)

Synopsis A brief summary or outline of a story or dramatic work.

Tactile imagery A word or sequence of words that refers to the sense of touch. (*See also* **Imagery**.)

Tale A short narrative without a complex plot, the word originating from the Old English *talu*, or "speech." Tales are an ancient form of narrative found in folklore, and traditional tales often contain supernatural elements. A tale differs from a short story by its tendency toward lesser developed characters and linear plotting. British writer A. E. Coppard characterized the underlying difference by claiming that a story is something that is written and a tale is something that is told. The ambition of a tale is usually similar to that of a yarn: revelation of the marvelous rather than illumination of the everyday world.

Tall tale A humorous short narrative that provides a wildly exaggerated version of events. Originally an oral form, the tall tale assumes that its audience knows the narrator is distorting the events. The form is often associated with the American frontier.

Tercet A group of three lines of verse, usually all ending in the same rhyme. (*See also* **Terza rima**.)

Terminal refrain A refrain that appears at the end of each stanza in a song or poem. (*See also* **Refrain**.)

Terza rima A verse form made up of three-line stanzas that are connected by an overlapping rhyme scheme (*aba, bcb, cdc, ded,* etc.). Dante employs *terza rima* in *The Divine Comedy*.

Tetrameter A verse meter consisting of four metrical feet, or four primary stresses, per line.

Theater of the absurd Post World War II European genre depicting the grotesquely comic plight of human beings thrown by accident into an irrational and meaningless world. The critic Martin Esslin coined the term to characterize plays by writers such as Samuel Beckett, Jean Genet, and Eugene Ionesco. Samuel Beckett's *Waiting for Godot* (1955), considered to be the greatest example of the absurd, features in two nearly identical acts two tramps waiting almost without hope on a country road for an unidentified person, Godot. "Nothing happens, nobody comes, nobody goes, it's awful," one of them cries, perhaps echoing the unspoken thoughts of an audience confronted by a play that refuses to do anything.

Theme A generally recurring subject or idea conspicuously evident in a literary work. A short didactic work like a fable may have a single obvious theme, but longer works can contain multiple themes. Not all subjects in a work can be considered themes, only the central subject or subjects.

Thesis sentence A summing-up of the one main idea or argument that an essay or critical paper will embody.

Third-person narrator A type of narration in which the narrator is a nonparticipant. In a third-person narrative the characters are referred to as "he," "she," or "they." Third-person narrators are most commonly omniscient, but the level of their knowledge may vary from total omniscience (the narrator knows everything about the characters and their lives) to limited omniscience (the narrator is limited to the perceptions of a single character).

Tone The attitude toward a subject conveyed in a literary work. No single stylistic device creates tone; it is the net result of the various elements an author brings to creating the works, feeling, and manner. Tone may be playful, sarcastic, ironic, sad, solemn, or any other possible attitude. A writer's tone plays an important role in establishing the reader's relationship to the characters or ideas presented in a literary work.

Total omniscience A type of point of view in which the narrator knows everything about all of the characters and events in a story. A narrator with total omniscience can also move freely from one character to another. Generally, a totally omniscient narrative is written in the third person.

Traditional epic *See* **Folk epic**.

Tragedy The representation of serious and important actions that lead to a disastrous end for the protagonist. The final purpose of tragedy in Aristotle's formulation is to evoke *katharsis* by means of events involving pity and fear. A unified tragic action, from beginning to end, brings a morally good but not perfect tragic hero from happiness to unhappiness because of a mistaken act, to which he or she is led by a *hamartia*, an error in judgment. Tragic heroes move us to pity because their misfortunes are greater than they deserve, because they are not evil, having committed the fateful deed or deeds unwittingly and involuntarily. They also move us to fear, because we recognize in ourselves similar possibilities of error. We share with the tragic hero a common world of mischance. (*See also* **Tragic flaw**.)

Tragic flaw A fatal weakness or moral flaw in the protagonist that brings him or her to a bad end, for example, Creon in *Antigone* or Macbeth. Sometimes offered as an alternative translation of **hamartia,** in contrast to the idea that the tragic hero's catastrophe is caused by an error in judgment, the idea of a protagonist ruined by a tragic flaw makes more sense in relation to the Greek idea of **hubris**, commonly translated as "outrage," involving deliberate transgressions against moral or divine law.

Tragic irony A form of **dramatic irony** that ultimately arrives at some tragedy.

Tragicomedy A type of drama that combines elements of both tragedy and comedy. Usually, it creates potentially tragic situations that bring the protagonists to the brink of disaster but then ends happily. Tragicomedy can be traced as far back as the Renaissance (in plays like Shakespeare's *Measure for Measure*), but it also refers to modern plays like Chekhov's *Cherry Orchard* and Beckett's *Waiting for Godot.*

Transferred epithet A figure of speech in which the poet attributes some characteristic of a thing to another thing closely associated with it. Transferred epithet is a kind of metonymy. It usually places an adjective next to a noun in which the connection is not strictly logical (Milton's phrase "blind mouths" or Hart Crane's "nimble blue plateaus") but has expressive power.

Trick ending A surprising climax that depends on a quick reversal of the situation from an unexpected source. The success of a trick ending is relative to the degree in which the reader is surprised but not left incredulous when it occurs. The American writer O. Henry popularized this type of ending.

Trimeter A verse meter consisting of three metrical feet, or three primary stresses, per line.

Triolet A short lyric form of eight rhymed lines borrowed from the French. The two opening lines are repeated according to a set pattern. Triolets are often playful, but dark lyric poems like Robert Bridge's "Triolet" demonstrate the form's flexibility.

Trochaic, trochee A metrical foot in which a stressed syllable is followed by an unstressed syllable (′ ◡) as in the words *sum*-mer and *chor*-us. The trochaic meter is often associated with songs, chants, and magic spells in English.

Troubadours The minstrels of the late Middle Ages. Originally, troubadours were lyric poets living in southern France and northern Italy who sang to aristocratic audiences mostly of chivalry and love.

Understatement An ironic figure of speech that deliberately describes something in a way that is less than the true case.

Unities The three formal qualities recommended by Italian Renaissance literary critics to unify a plot in order to give it a cohesive and complete integrity. Traditionally, good plots honored the three unities—of action, time, and place. The action in neoclassical drama, therefore, was patterned by cause and effect to occur within a 24-hour period. The setting took place in one unchanging locale. In the *Poetics*, Aristotle urged only the requirement of unity of plot, with events patterned in a cause-and-effect relationship from beginning through middle to the end of the single action imitated.

Unreliable narrator A narrator who—intentionally or unintentionally—relates events in a subjective or distorted manner. The author usually provides some indication early on in such stories that the narrator is not to be completely trusted.

Verbal irony A statement in which the speaker or writer says the opposite of what is really meant. For example, a friend might comment, "How graceful you are!" after you trip clumsily on a stair.

Verisimilitude The quality in a literary work of appearing true to life. In fiction, verisimilitude is usually achieved by careful use of realistic detail in description, characterization, and dialogue. (*See also* **Realism**.)

Verse From the Latin *versum*, "to turn." Verse has two major meanings. First, it refers to any single line of poetry. Second, it refers to any composition in lines of more or less regular rhythm—in contrast to prose.

Vers libre *See* **Free verse**.

Villanelle A fixed form developed by French courtly poets of the Middle Ages in imitation of Italian folk song. A villanelle consists of six rhymed stanzas in which two lines are repeated in a prescribed pattern.

Visual imagery A word or sequence of words that refers to the sense of sight or presents something one may see.

Vulgate From the Latin word *vulgus*, "mob" or "common people." The lowest level of formality in language, vulgate is the diction of the common people with no pretensions at refinement or elevation. The vulgate is not necessarily vulgar in the sense of containing foul or inappropriate language; it refers simply to unschooled, everyday language.

Literary Acknowledgments

FICTION

Chinua Achebe: "Dead Men's Path" from *Girls at War and Other Stories* by Chinua Achebe, copyright © 1972, 1973 by Chinua Achebe. Used by permission of Doubleday, a division of Random House, Inc. and Harold Ober Associates.

Isabel Allende: "The Judge's Wife" reprinted with the permission of Scribner, an imprint of Simon & Schuster Adult Publishing Group, from *The Stories of Eva Luna* by Isabel Allende, translated from the Spanish by Margaret Sayers Peden. Copyright © 1989 by Isabel Allende. English translation copyright © 1991 by Macmillan Publishing Company.

Anjana Appachana: "The Prophecy" from *Incantations and Other Stories* by Anjana Appachana, Virago Press 1991. Reprinted by permission of the author.

Margaret Atwood: "Happy Endings" from *Good Bones and Simple Murders* by Margaret Atwood, copyright © 1983, 1992, 1994 by O. W. Toad Ltd. A Nan A. Talese Book. Used by permission of Doubleday, a division of Random House, Inc.

James Baldwin: "Sonny's Blues," © 1957 by James Baldwin, was originally published in *Partisan Review*. Copyright renewed. Collected in *Going to Meet the Man*, published by Vintage Books. Reprinted by arrangement with the James Baldwin Estate. Pages 3–8 from *Notes of a Native Son* by James Baldwin, copyright © 1955, renewed 1983 by James Baldwin. Reprinted by permission of Beacon Press, Boston.

Mark Bauerlein: From *Literary Criticism: An Autopsy* by Mark Bauerlein. Copyright © 1997 University of Pennsylvania Press. Reprinted by permission.

Bidpai: "The Camel and His Friends" by Bidpai, retold in English by Arundhati Khanwalkar, from *The Panchatantra*. (The Association of Grandparents of Indian Immigrants).

Marie Bonaparte: Excerpt from *The Life and Works of Edgar Allan Poe: A Psychoanalytic Interpretation* by Marie Bonaparte, translated by Susan Balée. Used by permission.

Jorge Luis Borges: "The Gospel According to Mark" from *Collected Fiction* by Jorge Luis Borges, translated by Andrew Hurley. Copyright © 1998 by Maria Kodama; translation copyright © 1998 by Penguin Putnam Inc. Used by permission of Viking Penguin, a division of Penguin Group (USA) Inc.

T. Coraghessan Boyle: "Greasy Lake" from *Greasy Lake and Other Stories* by T. Coraghessan Boyle. Copyright © 1979, 1981, 1982, 1983, 1984, 1985 by T. Coraghessan Boyle. Used by permission of Viking Penguin, a division of Penguin Group (USA) Inc.

Robert Brinkmeyer, Jr.: "Flannery O'Connor and Her Readers" from *The Art and Vision of Flannery O'Connor* by Robert H. Brinkmeyer, Jr. Copyright © 1989 by Louisiana State University Press. Reprinted by permission of Louisiana State University Press.

Raymond Carver: "Cathedral" from *Cathedral* by Raymond Carver, copyright © 1983 by Raymond Carver. Used by permission of Alfred A. Knopf, a division of Random House, Inc. Excerpt from "On Writing" from *Fires: Essays, Poems, Stories by Raymond Carver*, Vintage Press, copyright by Raymond Carver, 1983, 1988; copyright by Tess Gallagher, 1989, 2001, 2003. Reprinted by permission of Tess Gallagher.

John Cheever: "The Five-Forty-Eight" from *The Stories of John Cheever* by John Cheever, copyright © 1978 by John Cheever. Used by permission of Alfred A. Knopf, a division of Random House, Inc.

Anton Chekhov: "The Lady with the Peg Dog," translated by Avrahm Yarmolinsky, from *The Portable Chekhov* by Anton Chekhov, edited by Avrahm Yarmolinsky, copyright 1947, © 1968 by Viking Penguin, Inc. Renewed © 1975 by Avrahm Yarmolinsky. Used by permission of Viking Penguin, a division of Penguin Group (USA) Inc.

Barbara T. Christian: Excerpt from Introduction to "Everyday Use" by Alice Walker from *The Women Writers: Text and Contexts Series*. Copyright © 1994. Reprinted by permission of Rutgers University Press.

Sandra Cisneros: "The House on Mango Street" from *The House On Mango Street*. Copyright © 1984 by Sandra Cisneros. Published by Vintage Books, a division of Random House, Inc., and in hardcover by Alfred A. Knopf in 1994. Reprinted by permission of Susan

Vincent B. Leitch: Excerpt from *Cultural Criticism, Literary Theory, Poststructuralism* by Vincent B. Leitch. Copyright © 1992, Columbia University Press. Reprinted by permission of the author.

Bernard Malamud: "Angel Levine" from *The Stories of Bernard Malamud*. Copyright © 1983 by Bernard Malamud. All rights reserved. Reprinted by permission of Farrar, Straus and Giroux LLC.

Katherine Mansfield: "Miss Brill" from *The Short Stories of Katherine Mansfield* by Katherine Mansfield, copyright 1923 by Alfred A. Knopf, a division of Random House, Inc. and renewed 1951 by John Middleton Murry. Used by permission of Alfred A. Knopf, a division of Random House, Inc.

Bobbie Ann Mason: "Shiloh" from *Shiloh and Other Stories* by Bobbie Ann Mason. Reprinted by permission of International Creative Management, Inc. Copyright © 1982 by Bobbie Ann Mason.

W. Somerset Maugham: "An Appointment in Samarra" from *Sheppey* by W. Somerset Maugham, copyright 1933 by W. Somerset Maugham. Used by permission of Doubleday, a division of Random House, Inc. and A. P. Watt Ltd. on behalf of the Royal Literary Fund.

Alice Munro: "Day of the Butterfly" from *Dance of the Happy Shades and Other Stories*. Copyright © Alice Munro. Reprinted by permission of the William Morris Agency and McGraw-Hill Ryerson Limited.

Tim O'Brien: "The Things They Carried" from *The Things They Carried* by Tim O'Brien. Copyright © 1990 by Tim O'Brien. Reprinted by permission of Houghton Mifflin Company. All rights reserved.

Flannery O'Connor: "A Good Man Is Hard to Find," copyright © 1953 by Flannery O'Connor and renewed 1981 by Regina O'Connor. "Good Country People," copyright © 1955 by Flannery O'Connor and renewed 1983 by Regina O'Connor. Both from *A Good Man Is Hard to Find and Other Stories*. Reprinted by permission of Harcourt, Inc. Excerpt from letter "To 'A'" 20 July 1955 from *The Habit of Being: Letters of Flannery O'Connor*, edited by Sally Fitzgerald. Copyright © 1979 by Regina O'Connor. Excerpts from "Some Aspects of the Grotesque in Southern Fiction" and "A Reasonable Use of the Unreasonable" from "On Her Own Work" in *Mystery and Manners* by Flannery O'Connor. Copyright © 1967, 1979, by The Estate of Mary Flannery O'Connor. Reprinted by permission of Farrar, Straus & Giroux, LLC. "Revelation" from *Everything That Rises Must Converge* by Flannery O'Connor. Copyright © 1961, 1965 by the Estate of Mary Flannery O'Connor. Reprinted with permission of Farrar, Straus and Giroux, LLC.

Frank O'Connor: "First Confession" from *The Collected Stories of Frank O'Connor* by Frank O'Connor, copyright © 1981 by Harriet O'Donovan Sheehy, Executrix of the Estate of Frank O'Connor. Used by permission of Alfred A. Knopf, a division of Random House, Inc.

Joyce Carol Oates: "Where Are You Going, Where Have You Been?" by Joyce Carol Oates, published in *The Wheel of Love and Other Stories* in 1970 by Vanguard. Copyright © by *Ontario Review*, 1970. Reprinted by permission of John Hawkins & Associates, Inc.

Tillie Olsen: "I Stand Here Ironing," copyright © 1956, 1957, 1960, 1961 by Tillie Olsen, from *Tell Me A Riddle* by Tillie Olsen. Introduction by John Leonard. Used by permission of Dell Publishing, a division of Random House, Inc.

Katherine Anne Porter: "The Jilting of Granny Weatherall" from *Flowering Judas and Other Stories*, copyright 1930 and renewed 1958 by Katherine Anne Porter. Reprinted by permission of Harcourt, Inc.

Mary Jane Schenck: "Deconstructed Meaning in Two Short Stories by Flannery O'Connor" in *Ambiguities in Literature and Film*, edited by Hans Braendlin. Florida State University Press, 1988. Courtesy of the University Press of Florida.

Gretchen Schulz and R. J. R. Rockwood: "In Fairyland Without a Map: Connie's Exploration Inward in Joyce Carol Oates' 'Where Are You Going, Where Have You Been?'" Copyright © 1980 by Gretchen E. Schulz and R. J. R. Rockwood. Reprinted by permission.

Leslie Marmon Silko: "The Man to Send Rain Clouds," copyright © 1981 by Leslie Marmon Silko. Reprinted from *Storyteller* by Leslie Marmon Silko, published by Seaver Books, New York, New York.

Virginia Llewellyn Smith: "Chekhov's Attitude to Romantic Love" from *Anton Chekhov and the Lady with the Dog* by Virginia Llewellyn Smith. Reprinted by permission of Oxford University Press.

John Steinbeck: "Chrysanthemums," copyright 1937, renewed 1965 by John Steinbeck, from *The Long Valley* by John Steinbeck. Used by permission of Viking Penguin, a division of Penguin Group (USA) Inc.

Elizabeth Tallent: "No One's a Mystery" from *Time with Children* by Elizabeth Tallent. Copyright © 1986 by Elizabeth Tallent. Reprinted with the permission of The Wylie Agency, Inc.

Amy Tan: "A Pair of Tickets" from *The Joy Luck Club* by Amy Tan. Copyright © 1989 by Amy

Tan. Used by permission of G. P. Putnam's Sons, a division of Penguin Group (USA) Inc. "Setting the Voice" excerpted from "Mother Tongue," copyright © 1990 by Amy Tan. First appeared in the *Threepenny Review*. Reprinted by permission of the author and the Sandra Dijkstra Literary Agency.

J. O. Tate: "A Good Source Is Not So Hard to Find" by J. O. Tate from *The Flannery O'Connor Bulletin* 9 (1980): pp. 98–103. Reprinted by permission of The Flannery O'Connor Bulletin.

Emily Toth: "The Source for Alcée LaBallière in 'The Storm'" adapted from *Kate Chopin: A Life of the Author of The Awakening* by Emily Toth. Reprinted by permission of the author.

James W. Tuttleton: "Poe: The Quest for Supernal Beauty," excerpted from pages 34–52 of *A Fine Silver Thread: Essays on American Writing and Criticism*. Copyright © 1998 by James W. Tuttleton, by permission of Ivan R. Dee, Publisher.

John Updike: "A & P" from *Pigeon Feathers and Other Stories* by John Updike, copyright © 1962 and renewed 1990 by John Updike. "Why Write?" from *Picked-Up Pieces* by John Updike, copyright © 1975 by John Updike. Used by permission of Alfred A. Knopf, a division of Random House, Inc.

Edmond L. Volpe: "'Barn Burning': A Definition of Evil" from *Faulkner, The Unappeased Imagination: A Collection of Critical Essays*, edited by Glen O. Carey.

Kurt Vonnegut, Jr.: "Harrison Bergeron" by Kurt Vonnegut from *Welcome to the Monkey House* by Kurt Vonnegut, Jr., copyright © 1961 by Kurt Vonnegut, Jr. Used by permission of Dell Publishing, a division of Random House, Inc. "The Themes of Science Fiction" from *Meangin Quarterly*, 30, Autumn 1971.

Alice Walker: "Everyday Use" from *In Love & Trouble: Stories of Black Women*, copyright © 1973 by Alice Walker, reprinted by permission of Harcourt, Inc.

Daniel P. Watkins: Excerpt from "Labor and Religion in D. H. Lawrence's 'The Rocking-Horse Winner'" from *Studies in Short Fiction*, Volume 24, No. 3, Summer, 1987. Reprinted by permission of the author.

Eudora Welty: "Why I Live at the P.O." from *A Curtain of Green and Other Stories*, copyright 1941 and renewed 1969 by Eudora Welty, reprinted by permission of Harcourt, Inc.

POETRY

Aaron Abeyta: "thirteen ways of looking at a tortilla" from *Colcha* by Aaron Abeyta. Copyright © 2000. Reprinted by permission of the University Press of Colorado.

Kim Addonizio: "First Poem for You," copyright © 1994 by Kim Addonizio. Reprinted from *The Philosopher's Club* by Kim Addonizio, with the permission of BOA Editions, Ltd., Rochester, NY.

Francisco X. Alarcón: "The X in My Name" from *No Golden Gate for Us* by Francisco X. Alarcón. Copyright © 1993 by Francisco X. Alarcón. Reprinted by permission of Pennywhistle Press, Tesuque, NM 87574.

Sherman Alexie: "Indian Boy Love Song (#1)" reprinted from *The Business of Fancy Dancing*, © 1992 by Sherman Alexie, by permission of Hanging Loose Press.

Julia Alvarez: "The Women On My Mother's Side Were Known" from *Homecoming*. Copyright © 1984, 1996 by Julia Alvarez. Published by Plume, an imprint of The Penguin Group; originally published by Grove Press. Reprinted by permission of Susan Bergholz Literary Services, New York. All rights reserved.

A. R. Ammons: "Coward" reprinted by permission of the author.

John Ashbery: "At North Farm" from *A Wave* by John Ashbery. Copyright © 1981, 1982, 1983, 1984 by John Ashbery. "The Cathedral Is" from *As We Know* by John Ashbery. Copyright © 1979 by John Ashbery. Reprinted by permission of Georges Borchardt, Inc. for the author.

Margaret Atwood: "Romantic" from *Morning in the Burned House* by Margaret Atwood. Copyright © 1995 by Margaret Atwood. Reprinted by permission of Houghton Mifflin Company. All rights reserved. "You fit into me" from *Power Politics* by Margaret Atwood. Copyright © 1971 by Margaret Atwood. (House of Anansi Press Ltd.) Reprinted by permission.

W. H. Auden: "James Watt" from *Academic Graffiti* by W. H. Auden and Sanjust Filippo (illustrator), copyright © 1972 by W. H. Auden. Illustration copyright © 1972 by Sanjust Filippo. "Funeral Blues," copyright 1940 and renewed 1968 by W. H. Auden, "Musée des Beaux Arts," copyright 1940 and renewed 1968 by W. H. Auden, "The Unknown Citizen," copyright 1940 and renewed 1968 by W. H. Auden, "As I Walked Out One Evening," copyright 1940 and renewed 1968 by W. H. Auden, "September 1, 1939," copyright 1940 and renewed 1968 by W. H. Auden. All from *Collected Poems* by W. H. Auden. Used by permission of Random House, Inc. and Faber and Faber Ltd.

Roland Barthes: "The Death of the Author" from *Image/Music/Text*, translated by Stephen Heath. Reprinted by permission of Farrar, Straus & Giroux, LLC.

Max Beerbohm: "On the imprint of the first English edition of The Works of Max Beerbohm." Final two lines inscribed by Max Beerbohm in a presentation copy of his book. Used by permission of Sir. Geoffrey Keynes.

Hilaire Belloc: "The Hippopotamus" from *Cautionary Verses* by Hilaire Belloc. Reprinted by permission of Peters Fraser & Dunlop.

Bruce Bennett: "The Lady Speaks Again" from *Taking Off* by Bruce Bennett (Orchises Press). Copyright © 1992 by Bruce Bennett. Reprinted by permission of the author.

Connie Bensley: "Last Haiku" and "The Covetous Cat" from *Choosing to Be a Swan*, Bloodaxe Books, 1994. Reprinted by permission of the publisher.

John Betjeman: "In Westminster Abbey" from *Collected Poems* by John Betjeman. Reprinted by permission of John Murray, London.

Elizabeth Bishop: "The Fish," "Filling Station," "One Art" and "Sestina" from *The Complete Poems 1927–1979* by Elizabeth Bishop. Copyright © 1979, 1983 by Alice Helen Methfessel. Reprinted by permission of Farrar, Straus and Giroux, LLC.

Chana Bloch: "Tired Sex" from *Mrs. Dumpty*, © 1998. Reprinted by permission of The University of Wisconsin Press.

Harold Bloom: "Poetic Influence" from *A Map of Misreading* by Harold Bloom. Copyright © 1975 by Oxford University Press. Used by permission of Oxford University Press, Inc.

Robert Bly: "Driving to Town Late to Mail a Letter" from *Silence in the Snow Fields* by Robert Bly, Wesleyan University Press. Copyright © 1959, 1960, 1961, 1962, by Robert Bly. Reprinted by permission of the author.

Eavan Boland: "Anorexic" from *An Origin Like Water: Collected Poems 1967–1987* by Eavan Boland. Copyright © 1996 by Eavan Boland. Used by permission of W. W. Norton & Company, Inc.

Jorge Luis Borges: "The Enigmas" translated by John Updike, copyright © 1999 by Maria Kodama; translation copyright © 1999 by John Updike from *Selected Poems* by Jorge Borges, edited by Alexander Coleman. Used by permission of Viking Penguin, a division of Penguin Group (USA) Inc. "Los Enigmas" by Jorge Borges reprinted by permission of Emece Editores S. A. "Amarosa Anticipación (Anticipation of Love)" translated by Robert Fitzgerald from *Jorge Luis Borges: Selected Poems 1923–1967* by Jorge Luis Borges, copyright © 1968, 1969, 1970, 1971, 1972 by Jorge Luis Borges, Emece Editores, S. A. and Norman Thomas Di Giovanni. Used by permission of Dell Publishing, a division of Random House, Inc. Excerpt from *This Craft of Verse:The Charles Eliot Norton Lectures 1967–1968* by Jorge Luis Borges, edited by

Calin-Andrei Mihailescu, pp. 1–2, 17–18, Cambridge, Mass: Harvard University Press, copyright © 2000 by the President and Fellows of Harvard College. Reprinted by permission of the publisher.

Cleanth Brooks: Excerpts from "The Formalist Critic," copyright 1951 by Cleanth Brooks. Originally appeared in *The Kenyon Review*. Reprinted by permission of Patricia Sue Brooks.

Gwendolyn Brooks: "Queen of the Blues," "The Independent Man" "The Preacher Ruminates: Behind the Sermon" from *Blacks*. Reprinted by consent of Brooks Permissions. "The Mother" and "We Real Cool" from *Blacks*. Reprinted by permission of the author. Excerpt entitled "On 'We Real Cool'" from *Part One* by Gwendolyn Brooks. Reprinted by permission of the author.

Jennifer Brutschy: "Born Again" from *The San Francisco Haiku Anthology*, edited by J. Ball. Reprinted by permission of the author.

Buson: "The piercing chill I feel" from *An Introduction to Haiku* by Harold G. Henderson, copyright © 1958 by Harold G. Henderson. Used by permission of Doubleday, a division of Random House. "I Go" from *The Essential Haiku: Versions of Basho, Buson & Issa*, edited and with an Introduction by Robert Hass. Introduction and selection copyright © 1994 by Robert Hass. Unless otherwise noted, all translations copyright © 1994 by Robert Hass. Reprinted by permission of HarperCollins Publishers, Inc.

Rafael Campo: "What the Body Told" from *What the Body Told*, by Rafael Campo. Copyright © 1996 by Rafael Campo. Reprinted by permission of Georges Borchardt, Inc. for the author.

Fred Chappell: "Narcissus and Echo" reprinted by permission of Louisiana State University Press from *Source: Poems by Fred Chappell*. Copyright © 1985 by Fred Chappell.

Dorothi Charles: "Concrete Cat" reprinted by permission of the author.

Kelly Cherry: "Advice to a Friend Who Paints" from *Lovers and Agnostics* by Kelly Cherry. Reprinted by permission of the author.

John Ciardi: "Most Like an Arch This Marriage," copyright © 1958 by John Ciardi. Reprinted from *Collected Poems* by John Ciardi. Reprinted by permission from the University of Arkansas Press.

Lucille Clifton: "Homage to my hips" first published in *Two-headed Woman*, copyright © 1980 by The University of Massachusetts Press, published by The University of Massachusetts Press. Now appears in *Good Woman: Poems and a Memoir 1969-1980*, copyright © 1987 by Lucille Clifton, published by BOA

Editions Ltd. Reprinted by permission of Curtis Brown, Ltd.

Judith Ortiz Cofer: "Quinceañera" is reprinted with permission from the publisher of *Terms of Survival* (Houston: Arte Publico Press-University of Houston, 1987).

William Cole: "On my boat on Lake Cayuga" reprinted by permission.

Billy Collins: "The Names" was read at a special joint session of Congress held in New York City, September 9, 2002. "Care and Feeding" first appeared in *Five Points*, March 2003. Both poems are reprinted by permission of the author. "Embrace" from *The Apple That Astonished Paris*. Copyright © 1988 by Billy Collins. Reprinted by permission of the University of Arkansas Press.

Wendy Cope: "Lonely Hearts" and "A Nursery Rhyme (as it might have been written by William Wordsworth)" from *Making Cocoa for Kingsley Amis*. © Wendy Cope 1986. Reprinted by permission of Faber and Faber Ltd. "Variations on Belloc's 'Fatigue'" from *Serious Concerns* by Wendy Cope. Reprinted by permission of Faber and Faber and Peters, Fraser & Dunlop.

Robert Creeley: "Oh No" from *The Collected Poems of Robert Creeley, 1945–1975*. Copyright © 1983 by The Regents of the University of California. Reprinted by permission of the University of California Press.

Countee Cullen: "For a Lady I Know" reprinted from *Color* by Countee Cullen. Copyright 1925 by Harper & Brothers; copyright renewed 1953 by Ida M. Cullen. Reprinted by permission of Thompson & Thompson.

E. E. Cummings: "a politician is an arse upon," copyright 1944 © 1972, 1991 by the Trustees for the E. E. Cummings Trust. "anyone lived in a pretty how town," copyright 1940, © 1968, 1991 by the Trustees for the E. E. Cummings Trust. "somewhere i have never travelled,gladly beyond," copyright 1931 © 1959, 1991 by the Trustees for the E. E. Cummings Trust. Copyright © 1979 by George James Firmage. "in Just-," copyright 1923, 1951, © 1991 by the Trustees for the E. E. Cummings Trust. Copyright © 1976 by George James Firmage. "Buffalo Bill 's," copyright 1923, 1951 © 1991 by the Trustees for the E. E. Cummings Trust. Copyright © 1976 by George James Firmage, from *Complete Poems: 1904–1962* by E. E. Cummings, edited by George J. Firmage. Used by permission of Liveright Publishing Corporation.

J. V. Cunningham: "Friend, on this scaffold Thomas More lies dead. . ." from *Poems of J.V. Cunningham* (Swallow Press/Ohio University Press, Athens, 1997). Reprinted with the permission of Swallow Press/Ohio University Press, Athens, Ohio. "This Humanist whom no beliefs constrained" reprinted by permission of the author.

H. D. (Hilda Doolittle) "Helen" from *Collected Poems, 1912–1944*, copyright © 1982 by The Estate of Hilda Doolittle. Reprinted by permission of New Directions Publishing Corp.

Dick Davis: "Fatherhood" reprinted by permission of the author.

Emanuel di Pasquale: "Rain" reprinted by permission of the author.

James Dickey: "The Heaven of Animals" from *Poems, 1957–1967*. Copyright © by James Dickey. Reprinted by permission of Wesleyan University Press.

Emily Dickinson: "I like to see it lap the Miles," "A Route of Evanescence," "My Life had stood – a Loaded Gun," "It dropped so low – in my Regard," "The Lightning is a yellow Fork," "A Dying Tiger – moaned for Drink," "Success is counted sweetest," "Wild Nights – Wild Nights!," "I Felt a Funeral, in my Brain," "I'm Nobody! Who are you?," "The Soul selects her own Society," "After great pain, a formal feeling comes," "This is my letter to the World," "I heard a Fly buzz – when I died," "I started Early – Took my Dog," "There's a certain slant of light," "Much Madness is divinest sense," "Because I could not stop for Death," "Some keep the Sabbath going to Church," "The Bustle in a House," "Tell all the Truth but tell it slant" reprinted by permission of the publishers and the Trustees of Amherst College from *The Poems of Emily Dickinson*, Thomas H. Johnson, ed., Cambridge, Mass.: The Belknap Press of Harvard University Press, Copyright © 1951, 1955, 1979 by the President and Fellows of Harvard College.

Rita Dove: "Summit Beach, 1921" from *Grace Notes* by Rita Dove. Copyright © 1989 by Rita Dove. Used by permission of the author and Rita Dove. Rita Dove and Marilyn Nelson: "Langston Hughes and Harlem" from "A Black Rainbow: Modern Afro-American Poetry" in *Poetry After Modernism*, edited by Robert McDowell. Reprinted by permission of the authors and Story Line Press.

Bob Dylan: "The Times They Are a Changin'," copyright © 1985 by Special Rider Music. All rights reserved. International copyright secured. Reprinted by permission.

Richard Eberhart: "The Fury of Aerial Bombardment from *Collected Poems 1930–1976* by Richard Eberhart. Copyright © 1976 by Richard Eberhart. Used by permission of Oxford University Press, Inc.

Terry Ehret: "A lake. A night without a moon" from *Lost Body*. Copyright © 1992 by Terry Ehret. Reprinted with the permission of

Copper Canyon Press, P.O. Box 271, Port Townsend, WA 98368-0271.

T. S. Eliot "Journey of the Magi" and "Virginia" from *Collected Poems 1909–1962* by T. S. Eliot, copyright 1936 by Harcourt, Inc., copyright © 1964, 1963 by T. S. Eliot, reprinted by permission of Harcourt, Inc. and Faber and Faber Ltd. "The Love Song of J. Alfred Prufrock" from *Prufrock and Other Observations*. Reprinted by permission of Faber and Faber Ltd. "The Music of Poetry" from *On Poetry and Poets* by T. S. Eliot. Copyright © 1957 by T. S. Eliot. Copyright © renewed 1985 by Valerie Eliot. Reprinted by permission of Farrar, Straus and Giroux, Inc. and Faber and Faber Ltd.

Louise Erdrich: "Indian Boarding School: The Runaways" from *Jacklight* by Louise Erdrich. © 1984 by Louise Erdrich. Reprinted by permission of Henry Holt and Company, LLC.

Rhina P. Espaillat: "Bilingual/ Bilingüe" and an excerpt from "Afterword" in *Where Horizons Go* by Rhina P. Espaillat, published by Truman State University Press. Copyright © 1998. Reprinted by permission of the author.

Abbie Huston Evans: "Wing-Spread" reprinted from *Collected Poems* by Abbie Huston Evans, by permission of the University of Pittsburgh Press. Copyright 1950 by Abbie Huston Evans.

B. H. Fairchild: "A Starlit Night" from *Early Occult Memory System of the Lower Midwest* by B. H. Fairchild. Copyright © 2003 by B. H. Fairchild. Used by permission of W. W. Norton & Company.

Judith Farr: Excerpt from pages 241–244 of *The Passion of Emily Dickinson* by Judith Farr, reprinted by permission of the publisher. Cambridge, Mass.: Harvard University Press, Copyright © 1992 by the President and Fellows of Harvard College.

Gene Fehler: "If Richard Lovelace Became a Free Agent" reprinted by permission of the author.

Adelle Foley: "Learning to Shave (Father Teaching Son)," copyright © 2001 by Adelle Foley. Reprinted by permission.

Carolyn Forche: "The Colonel" from *The Country Between Us* by Carolyn Forche. Copyright © 1981 by Carolyn Forche. Originally appeared in Women's International Resource Exchange. Reprinted by permission of HarperCollins Publishers, Inc.

Robert Frost: "The Silken Tent," "The Secret Sits," "Desert Places," "Acquainted with the Night," "Fire and Ice," "Design," "Stopping by Woods on a Snowy Evening" from *The Poetry of Robert Frost*, edited by Edward Connery Lathem. Copyright 1922, 1923, © 1969 by Henry Holt and Company, copyright 1936, 1951 by Robert Frost, © 1964 by Lesley Frost Ballantine. "In White" the earlier version of "Design" first appeared in *The Dimensions of Robert Frost* by Reginald L. Cook, © 1958 by Reginald L. Cook. Reprinted by permission of Henry Holt and Company, LLC.

Northrup Frye: "Mythic Archetypes" from *Anatomy of Criticism*. Copyright © 1957, renewed 1985 by Princeton University Press. Reprinted by permission of Princeton University Press.

Alice Fulton: "What I Like" from *Dance Script with Electric Ballerina: Poems*. Copyright © 1983 by Alice Fulton. Used with permission of the poet and the University of Illinois Press.

Shirley Geok-lin Lim: "Learning to Love America" from *What the Fortune Teller Didn't Say*. Copyright © 1998 by Shirley Geok-lin Lim. Reprinted with the permission of West End Press, Albuquerque, NM.

Sandra Gilbert and Susan Gubar: "Editor's Introduction to Emily Dickinson" from *The Norton Anthology of Literature by Women: The Tradition in English* by Sandra M. Gilbert and Susan Gubar. Copyright © 1985 by Sandra M. Gilbert aand Susan Gubar. Used by permission of W. W. Norton & Company, Inc.

Allen Ginsberg: "A Supermarket in California" from *Collected Poems 1947–1980* by Allen Ginsberg. Copyright © 1955 by Allen Ginsberg. Reprinted by permission of HarperCollins Publishers, Inc.

Dana Gioia: "California Hills in August," copyright © 1986 by Dana Gioia. Reprinted from *Daily Horoscope*. "Entrance (After Rilke)," copyright © 2001 by Dana Gioia. Reprinted from *Interrogations at Noon*. Both poems reprinted with the permission of Graywolf Press, Saint Paul, Minnesota.

Heather Glen: Excerpt from *Vision and Disenchantment: Blake's "Songs" and Wordsworth's "Lyrical Ballads"* reprinted by permission of Cambridge University Press.

Louise Glück "Mock Orange" from *The First Four Books of Poems* by Louise Glück. Copyright 1968, 1971, 1973, 1973, 1974, 1975, 1976, 1977, 1978, 1979, 1980, 1985, 1995 by Louise Glück. Ecco Press. Reprinted by permission of HarperCollins Inc.

Robert Graves: "Down, Wanton, Down!" and "Counting the Beats" from *Complete Poems* by Robert Graves. Excerpt from *The Crowning Privilege* by Robert Graves copyright © 1955 by Robert Graves, renewed. Reprinted by permission of Carcanet Press Limited.

Emily Grosholz: "Listening" from *Eden*, p. 73, © 1992. Reprinted with permission of The Johns Hopkins University Press.

Ronald Gross: "Yield" reprinted with permission of Simon & Schuster from *Pop Poems* by Ronald Gross. Copyright © 1967 by Ronald

(Gnomon Press, 1984). Reprinted by permission of the publisher and the author. "Cricket" translated by Robert Bly. Reprinted from *Ten Poems by Issa*, English versions by Robert Bly, Floating Island, 1992. Copyright 1972, 1992 by Robert Bly. Reprinted with permission.

Mark Jarman: "Unholy Sonnet: After the Praying" reprinted by permission of the author.

Randall Jarrell: "The Death of the Ball Turret Gunner" from *The Complete Poems by Randall Jarrell*. Copyright © 1969, renewed 1997 by Mary von S. Jarrell. Reprinted by permission of Farrar, Straus and Giroux LLC.

Robinson Jeffers: "Hands" and "The Beaks of Eagles" from *The Collected Poetry of Robinson Jeffers, Volume 2, 1928–1938*, edited by Tim Hunt. Reprinted with the permission of the publishers, Stanford University Press www.sup.org. Copyright 1938, renewed 1966 by Donnan Jeffers and Garth Jeffers. "To the Stone-cutters" copyright 1924 and renewed 1952 by Robinson Jeffers from *Selected Poetry of Robinson Jeffers* by Robinson Jeffers. Used by permission of Random House, Inc.

Onwuchekwa Jemie: "A Dream Deferred" from *Langston Hughes: An Introduction to Poetry* by Onwuchekwa Jemie. Copyright © 1976 by Onwuchekwa Jemie. Published by Columbia University Press.

Thomas H. Johnson: "The Discovery of Emily Dickinson's Manuscripts" reprinted by permission of the publishers and the Trustees of Amherst College from *The Poems of Emily Dickinson*, Thomas H. Johnson, ed., Cambridge, Mass.: The Belknap Press of Harvard University Press. Copyright © 1951, 1955, 1979 by the President and Fellows of Harvard College.

Donald Justice: "Men at Forty" and "Counting the Mad" from *New and Selected Poems* by Donald Justice, copyright © 1995 by Donald Justice. Used by permission of Alfred A. Knopf, a division of Random House, Inc.

Alfred Kazin: Excerpt from *An American Procession* by Alfred Kazin, copyright © 1984 by Alfred Kazin. Used by permission of Alfred A. Knopf, a division of Random House, Inc.

Weldon Kees: "For My Daughter" reprinted from *The Collected Poems of Weldon Kees*, edited by Donald Justice, by permission of the University of Nebraska Press. Copyright 1975 by the University of Nebraska Press.

Hugh Kenner: "Imagism" from *The Pound Era* by Hugh Kenner. Copyright © 1971 by Hugh Kenner. Reprinted by permission of the University of California Press.

Jane Kenyon: "The Suitor" from *From Room to Room*. © 1978 by Jane Kenyon. Reprinted courtesy of Alice James Books, 33 Richdale Avenue, Cambridge, MA 02138.

Omar Khayyam: "Rubai" translated by Dick Davis. Reprinted by permission. "Rubai" translated by Robert Graves and Omar Ali-Shah from *The Rubaiayt of Omar Khayyam*. Reprinted by permission of Carcanet Press.

Hugh Kingsmill: "What, still alive at twenty-two?" from *The Best of Hugh Kingsmill*. Reprinted by permission of Victor Gollancz Ltd.

Etheridge Knight: "Making jazz swing in" is from *The Essential Etheridge Knight* by Etheridge Knight © 1986. Reprinted by permission of the University of Pittsburgh Press.

Yusef Komunyakaa: "Facing It" from *Dien Kai Dau*. Copyright © 1988 by Yusef Komunyakaa. Reprinted by permission of Wesleyan University Press.

Ted Kooser: "Carrie" from *Sure Signs: New and Selected Poems* by Ted Kooser. © 1980 by Ted Kooser. Reprinted by permission of the University of Pittsburgh Press.

Robert Langbaum: "On Robert Browning's 'My Last Duchess'" from *The Poetry of Experience* by Robert Langbaum. Copyright © 1957, 1986 by Robert Langbaum. Reprinted by permission of the author.

Philip Larkin: "Aubade," "Home is so Sad," and "Poetry of Departures" from *Collected Poems* by Philip Larkin, edited by Anthony Twait. Copyright © 1988, 1989 by the Estate of Philip Larkin. Reprinted by permission of Farrar, Straus and Giroux and the Marvell Press.

D. H. Lawrence: "Bavarian Gentians" by D. H. Lawrence from *The Complete Poems of D. H. Lawrence*, edited by V. de Sola Pinto and F. W. Roberts. Copyright © 1964, 1971 by Angelo Ravagli and C. M. Weekley, Executors of the Estate of Frieda Lawrence Ravagli. Used by permission of Viking Penguin, a Division of Penguin (USA).

Irving Layton: "The Bull Calf" from *A Red Carpet for the Sun* (McClelland & Stewart). Reprinted by permission of the author.

Brad Leithauser Brad: "A Venus Flytrap" from *Hundreds of Fireflies* by Brad Leithauser. Copyright © 1981 by Brad Leithauser. Used by permission of Alfred A. Knopf, a division of Random House, Inc.

John Lennon and Paul McCartney: "Eleanor Rigby," words and music by John Lennon and Paul McCartney. Copyright © 1966 Sony/ATV Tunes LLC (Renewed). All rights administered by Sony/ATV Music Publishing, 8 Music Square West, Nashville, TN 37203. All rights reserved. Used by permission.

Denise Levertov: "Leaving Forever" from *Poems 1960–1967*, copyright © 1966 by Denise Levertov. "Ancient Stairway" from *This Great Unknowing: Last Poems*, copyright © 1998 by The Denise Levertov Literary Trust, Paul A.

Lacey and Valerie Trueblood Rapport, Co-Trustees. Reprinted by permission of New Directions Publishing Corp.

Phillis Levin: "Brief Bio" from *The Afterimage*. Reprinted by permission of Copper Beach Press.

Philip Levine: "They Feed They Lion" from *They Feed They Lion and the Names of the Lost* by Philip Levine, copyright © 1968, 1969, 1970, 1971, 1972 by Philip Levine. *The Names of the Lost*, copyright © 1976 by Philip Levine. Used by permission of Alfred A. Knopf, a division of Random House, Inc.

Li Po: "Drinking Alone by Moonlight" by Li Po from *Liu, The Art of Chinese Poetry*. Reprinted by permission of the University of Chicago Press and Routledge.

Adrian Louis: "Looking for Judas" from *Vortex of Indian Fevers*. Evanston: TriQuarterly Books/Northwestern University Press, 1995, p. 25. Reprinted by permission of Northwestern University Press.

Robert Lowell: "Skunk Hour" from *Life Studies* by Robert Lowell. Copyright © 1959 by Robert Lowell. Copyright renewed © 1987 by Harriet Lowell, Sheridan Lowell and Caroline Lowell. Reprinted by permission of Farrar, Straus and Giroux, LLC.

Archibald MacLeish: "Ars Poetica" from *Collected Poems 1917–1982* by Archibald MacLeish. Copyright © 1985 by The Estate of Archibald MacLeish. Reprinted by permission of Houghton Mifflin Company. All rights reserved.

Louis MacNeice: "Plain Speaking" from *Collected Poems of Louis MacNeice*, edited by E. R. Dodds. Reprinted by permission of Faber and Faber Ltd.

Charles Martin: "Taken Up" from *Room for Error* (University of Georgia Press, 1978). Reprinted by permission of the author.

David Mason: "Song of the Powers" from *The Country I Remember*. Reprinted by permission of the author and Story Line Press.

Sukio Matsushita: "Rain shower from mountain," "Cosmos in bloom" from *May Sky: There is Always Tomorrow*. Translated by Violet Kazue de Cristoforo. Sun & Moon Press. Reprinted by permission.

Paul McCartney: "Creating 'Eleanor Rigby'" from *The Beatles, In Their Own Words* by Miles. Used by permission of the publisher, Omnibus Press, 8/9 Frith Street, London W1V 5TZ.

Robert McDowell: "At Home with Dollface" from *On Foot, In Flames* by Robert McDowell, © 2002. Reprinted by permission of the University of Pittsburgh Press.

Rod McKuen: "Thoughts on Capital Punishment" from *Stanyan Street and Other Sorrows* by Rod McKuen, copyright 1954, 1960, 1961, 1962, 1963, 1964, 1965, 1966 by Rod McKuen. Used by permission of Random House, Inc.

Wallace McRae: "Reincarnation" from *Cowboy Curmudgeon and Other Poems*. Reprinted by permission of the author.

Samuel Menashe: "The Shrine Whose Shape I Am" from *Collected Poems* by Samuel Menashe. Copyright © 1986 by Samuel Menashe. Reprinted by permission of the National Poetry Foundation.

James Merril: "Kite Poem" from *Collected Poems* by James Merrill and J. D. McClatchy and Stephen Yenser, editors, copyright © 2001 by the Literary Estate of James Merrill at Washington University. Used by permission of Alfred A. Knopf, a division of Random House, Inc.

Stephanie Merrim: "Endgames: Sor Juana Ines de la Cruz" from *Early Modern Women's Writing and Sor Juana Ines de la Cruz*. Reprinted by permission of Vanderbilt University Press.

W. S. Merwin: "For the Anniversary of My Death," copyright © 1967 by W. S. Merwin from *Poems, Selections, The Second Four Books of Poems*. Reprinted with the permission of The Wylie Agency, Inc.

Josephine Miles: "Civilian" from *Collected Poems, 1930–1983*. Copyright © 1983 by Josephine Miles. Used with permission of the University of Illinois Press.

Edna St. Vincent Millay: "Counting-out Rhyme" from *Collected Poems*, HarperCollins Publishers, Inc. Copyright © 1928, 1955 by Edna St. Vincent Millay and Norma Millay Ellis. All rights reserved. Reprinted by permission of Elizabeth Barnett, literary executor.

Brett C. Millier: "On Elizabeth Bishop's 'One Art,'" copyright © 1993 by Brett C. Millier. Used by permission of the author. A fuller treatment of the subject appears in *Elizabeth Bishop: Life and the Memory of It* by Brett C. Millier (University of California Press, 1993). Lines from the first draft of "One Art" are quoted by permission of the Special Collections of the Vassar College Libraries and Elizabeth Bishop's literary executor, Alice H. Methfessell.

Joseph Moldenhauer: "'To His Coy Mistress' and the Renaissance Tradition" from "The Voices of Seduction in 'To His Coy Mistress.'" Reprinted by permission of Joseph Moldenhauer.

N. Scott Momaday: "Simile" from *Angle of Geese and Other Poems* by Scott Momaday. Reprinted by permission of David R. Godine, Publisher, Inc. Copyright © 1972 by Scott Momaday.

Emir Rodriguez Monegal: "Borges and Paz" from the *Perpetual Present: The Poetry and Prose of Octavio Paz*, edited by Ivar Ivask. Reprinted by permission of the University of Oklahoma Press.

Marianne Moore: "Silence" is reprinted with permission of Scribner, an imprint of Simon & Schuster Adult Publishing Group from *The Collected Poems of Marianne Moore*. Copyright 1935 by Marianne Moore. Copyright renewed © 1963 by Marianne Moore and T. S. Eliot.

Frederick Morgan: "The Master" from *Poems: New and Selected*. Copyright © 1987 by Frederick Morgan. Used with permission of the poet and the University of Illinois Press.

Howard Moss: "Shall I Compare Thee to a Summer's Day?" from *A Swim off the Rocks*. Copyright © 1976 by Howard Moss. Reprinted by permission of Richard Evans.

Marilyn Nelson: "A Strange Beautiful Woman" reprinted by permission of Louisiana State University Press from *The Fields of Praise* by Marilyn Nelson. Copyright © 1997 by Marilyn Nelson.

Howard Nemerov: "The War in the Air" from *Trying Conclusions* by Howard Nemerov. Reprinted by permission of Margaret Nemerov.

Pablo Neruda: "Muchos Somos" ("We Are Many") from *Estravagario* by Pablo Neruda. Translated by Alastair Reid. Translation copyright © 1974 by Alastair Reid. Reprinted by permission of Farrar, Straus and Giroux LLC. "Sonnet V" from *100 Love Sonnets: Cien Sonetos de Amor* by Pablo Neruda, translated by Stephen Tapscott. Copyright © Pablo Neruda 1959 and Fundacion Pablo Neruda, copyright © 1986 by the University of Texas Press. Reprinted by permission of the University of Texas Press. "Towards the Splendid City," © The Nobel Foundation 1971. Reprinted by permission.

Lorine Niedecker: "Sorrow Moves in Wide Waves" from *Lorine Niedecker: Collected Works*, edited by Jenny Lynn Pemberthy. Copyright © 2002 by the Regents of the University of California. Reprinted by permission of the University of California Press. "Pop-corn-can cover" from *From This Condensery: The Complete Writings of Lorine Niedecker*, edited by Robert J. Bertolf. Copyright © Cid Corman, Literary Executor of the Lorine Niedecker Estate. Reprinted by permission.

John Frederick Nims: "Contemplation" reprinted by permission.

Sharon Olds: "Rites of Passage" and "The One Girl at the Boys' Party" from *The Dead and the Living* by Sharon Olds, copyright © 1987 by Sharon Olds. Used by permission of Alfred A. Knopf, a division of Random House, Inc.

Olga Orozco: "La Realidad y el Deseo" ("Reality and Desire") translated by Stephen Tapscott, from *Museo Salvaje*. Copyright © Stephen Tapscott. Reprinted by permission.

Neiji Ozawa: "War forced us from California" and "The war" from *May Sky: There Is Always Tomorrow: An Anthology of Japanese American Concentration Camp Kaiko Haiku*, compiled, translated, and prefaced by Violet Kazue de Cristoforo. Copyright © 1997 by Violet Kazue de Cristoforo. Reprinted by permission of Sun & Moon Press.

José Emilio Pacheco: "Alta Traición" ("High Treason") translated by Alastair Reid, from *Don't Ask Me How the Time Goes By*. Reprinted by permission of Columbia University Press.

Dorothy Parker: "Résumé," copyright 1926, 1928, renewed 1954, © 1956 by Dorothy Parker from *The Portable Dorothy Parker* by Dorothy Parker. Used by permission of Viking Penguin, a division of Penguin USA.

Linda Pastan: "Ethics" from *Waiting for My Life* by Linda Pastan. Copyright © 1981 by Linda Pastan. Used by permission of W. W. Norton & Company, Inc.

Octavio Paz: "With Our Eyes Shut" by Octavio Paz, translated by Eliot Weinberger, from *Collected Poems 1957–1987*, copyright © 1986 by Octavio Paz and Eliot Weinberger. "Certainty" by Octavio Paz, translated by Charles Tomlinson, from *Collected Poems 1957–1987*, copyright © 1968 by Octavio Paz and Charles Tomlinson. Reprinted by permission of New Directions Publishing Corp. "In Search of the Present" © The Nobel Foundation 1990. Reprinted by permission.

Robert Phillips: "Running on Empty" from *Personal Accounts: New and Selected Poems 1966–1986* (Princeton: Ontario Review Press, 1986). Copyright © 1981, 1986 by Robert Phillips. Reprinted by permission.

Darryl Pinckney: "Black Identity in Langston Hughes" from "Suitcase in Harlem" by Darryl Pinckney in the *New York Review of Books*, February 16, 1989. Reprinted with permission from the *New York Review of Books*. Copyright © 1989 by NYREV, Inc.

Robert Pinsky: "ABC" from *Jersey Rain* by Robert Pinsky. Copyright © 2000 by Robert Pinsky. Reprinted by permission of Farrar, Straus and Giroux LLC.

Sylvia Plath: "Metaphors" from *Crossing the Water* by Sylvia Plath. Copyright © 1960 by Ted Hughes. "Lady Lazarus" and "Daddy" from *Ariel* by Sylvia Plath. Copyright © 1963 by Ted Hughes. Reprinted by permission of HarperCollins Publishers, Inc. and Faber and Faber Ltd.

Craig Raine: "A Martian Sends a Postcard Home" from *A Martian Sends a Postcard Home* by Craig Raine. Reprinted by permission of David Godwin Associates.

Arnold Rampersad: "Hughes as an Experimentalist" from *African American Writers,* edited by Smith, Bacchler & Litz. Reprinted by permission of The Gale Group.

Dudley Randall: "A Different Image" from *Cities Burning* (Broadside Press) Copyright © 1966 by Dudley Randall. Reprinted by permission of Broadside Press. "Ballad of Birmingham" from *Cities Burning.* Reprinted by permission of the author.

John Crowe Ransom: "Piazza Piece" from *Selected Poems,* Third Edition, Revised and Enlarged by John Crowe Ransom, copyright 1924, 1927 by Alfred A. Knopf, Inc. and renewed 1952, 1955 by John Crowe Ransom. Used by permission of Alfred A. Knopf, a division of Random House, Inc.

Henry Reed: "Naming of Parts" from *A Map of Verona* by Henry Reed. © 1946 The executor of the Estate of Henry Reed. Reprinted by permission of John Tydeman.

James Reeves: "Rough Weather" reprinted by permission of The Estate of the Late James Reeves.

Alastair Reid: "High Treason," "Speaking a Foreign Language" and excerpt from "Neruda and Borges" reprinted by permission. © 1996 Alastair Reid. Originally in the *New Yorker.* All rights reserved.

Adrienne Rich: "Aunt Jennifer's Tigers," copyright © 2002, 1951 by Adrienne Rich, "Living in Sin," copyright © 2002, 1955 by Adrienne Rich, "Power," Copyright © 2002 by Adrienne Rich. From *The Fact of a Doorframe: Selected Poems 1950–2001* by Adrienne Rich, copyright © 1978 by W. W. Norton & Company, Inc. "Women," Copyright © 1993 by Adrienne Rich. From *Collected Early Poems: 1950–1970* by Adrienne Rich, copyright © 1969 by W. W. Norton & Company, Inc. Used by permission of the author and W. W. Norton & Company, Inc.

John Ridland: "The Lazy Man's Haiku" Reprinted by permission of the author.

Ranier Maria Rilke "Entrance (After Rilke)," copyright © 2001 by Dana Gioia. Reprinted from *Interrogations at Noon* with the permission of Graywolf Press, Saint Paul, Minnesota.

Theodore Roethke: "My Papa's Waltz," copyright 1942 by Hearst Magazines, Inc., "Root Cellar," copyright 1943 by Modern Poetry Association, Inc., "Elegy for Jane," copyright 1950 by Theodore Roethke, from *The Collected Poems of Theodore Roethke* by Theodore Roethke. Used by permission of Doubleday, a division of Random House, Inc.

Wendy Rose: "For the White Poets Who Would Be Indian" from *Bone Dance: New and Selected Poems 1965–1993. Sun Tracks,* Vol. 27. © 1994 by University of Arizona Press.

Clare Rossini: "Final Love Note" from *Winter Morning with Crow* by Clare Rossini. Reprinted by permission of the University of Akron Press.

Run D.M.C.: "Peter Piper" by Joseph W. Simmons and Darryl M. McDaniels © 1986 Rabasse Music Ltd. And Rush Groove Music (ASCAP). All rights administered by WB Music Corp. (ASCAP) All Rights Reserved. Used by permission. Warner Bros. Publications U.S. Inc., Miami, FL 33014.

Kay Ryan: "Turtle" from *Flamingo Watching.* Reprinted by permission of Copper Beach Press. "Blandeur" from *Say Uncle* by Kay Ryan. Copyright © 2000 by Kay Ryan. Used by permission of Grove/Atlantic, Inc.

Benjamin Alire Saenz: "To the Desert" from *Dark and Perfect Angels* by Benjamin Alire Saenz, 1995. Used by permission of the publisher, Cinco Puntos Press.

Mary Jo Salter: "Welcome to Hiroshima" from *Henry Purcell in Japan* by Mary Jo Salter, copyright © 1984 by Mary Jo Salter. Used by permission of Alfred A. Knopf, a division of Random House, Inc.

Carole Satyamurti: "I Shall Paint My Nails Red" © 1990 by Carole Satyamurti. Reprinted by permission of Bloodaxe Books Ltd.

Gjertrud Schnackenberg: "Supernatural Love" from *Supernatural Love: Poems 1976–1992,* copyright © 2000 by Gjertrud Schnackenberg. Reprinted by permission of Farrar, Straus and Giroux, LLC.

Robert Scholes: "How Do We Make a Poem?" excerpt from *Semiotics and Interpretation* by Robert Scholes. Copyright © 1982 by Yale University. Reprinted by permission of Yale University Press.

Anne Sexton: "Her Kind" from *To Bedlam and Part Way Back* by Anne Sexton. Copyright © 1960 by Anne Sexton, © renewed 1988 by Linda G. Sexton. "Cinderella" from *Transformations* by Anne Sexton. Copyright © 1971 by Anne Sexton. Letter, from *Anne Sexton: A Self Portrait in Letters,* edited by Linda Gray Sexton and Lois Ames. Copyright © 1977 by Linda Gray Sexton and Loring Conant, Jr., executors of the will of Anne Sexton. All reprinted by permission of Houghton Mifflin Company. All rights reserved.

Elaine Showalter: Excerpt from "Toward a Feminist Criticism," copyright © 1979 by Elaine Showalter. From Elaine Showalter, ed., *Feminist Criticism: Essays on Women, Literature, and Theory* (Pantheon, 1985). Reprinted by permission of the author.

Charles Simic: "Fork" from *Somewhere Among Us a Stone is Taking Notes,* first published in

Kayak 1969, from *Charles Simic: Selected Early Poems*, published by George Braziller.

Louis Simpson: "American Poetry" from *A Poetry Collection*. Reprinted by permission of the author and Story Line Press.

David R. Slavitt: "Titanic" reprinted by permission of Louisiana State University Press from *Big Nose: Poems* by David R. Slavitt. Copyright © 1983 by David R. Slavitt.

Stevie Smith: "Not Waving But Drowning" and "This Englishwoman" by Stevie Smith from *Collected Poems of Stevie Smith*, copyright © 1972 by Stevie Smith. Reprinted by permission of New Directions Publishing Corp.

William Jay Smith: "American Primitive" from *The World Below the Window: Poems 1937–1997*, pp. 91 © 1998. Reprinted with permission of The Johns Hopkins University Press.

Gary Snyder: "Piute Creek" from *Riprap & Cold Mountain Poems*. Reprinted by permission.

Cathy Song: "Stamp Collecting" from *Frameless Windows, Squares of Light: Poems* by Cathy Song. Copyright © 1988 by Cathy Song. Used by permission of W. W. Norton & Company, Inc.

Sor Juana: Excerpt reprinted by permission of the publisher from *A Sor Juana Anthology*, translated by Alan S. Trueblood, pp. 224–225, Cambridge, Mass.: Harvard University Press, copyright © 1988 by the President and Fellows of Harvard College. "Asegura la Confianza de que Oculturö de Todo un Secreto" (She Promises to Hold a Secret in Confidence) and "Presente En qu el Cario Hace Regalo la Llaneza" (A Simple Gift Made Rich by Affection) both translated by Diane Thiel. Reprinted by permission.

William Stafford: "Farm on the Great Plains," "Traveling Through the Dark," "Ask Me," copyright © 1959, 1962, 1977, 1988 by the Estate of William Stafford. Reprinted from *The Way It Is: New & Selected Poems* with the permission of Graywolf Press, Saint Paul, Minnesota. "At the Un-National Monument Along the Canadian Border" reprinted by permission of the author.

A. E. Stallings: "Sine Qua Non" first appeared in *Poetry*, October–November 2002. Copyright © 2002 by The Poetry Foundation. Reprinted by permission of the Editor of *Poetry* and the author. "A New Year's Toast" (translation of Horace *Odes*, Book 1, Ode XI) by A. E. Stallings. First appeared in *Light*. Reprinted by permission of the author.

Jon Stallworthy: "An Evening Walk" from *Rounding the Horn* reprinted by permission of Carcanet Press Limited.

Timothy Steele: "Epitaph" from *Uncertainties and Rest* by Timothy Steele. Copyright © 1979. "Summer" from *Sapphics Against Anger and Other Poems* Random House, 1986. Copyright © 1986 by Timothy Steele. Reprinted by permission of the author.

Anne Stevenson: "Sous-Entendu" and "The Victory" from *The Collected Poems 1955–1985* (Bloodaxe Books, 2000). Reprinted by permission of the publisher.

Michael Stillman: "In Memoriam John Coltrane" from *Occident*, Fall, 1971. Copyright © 1976 by Michael Stillman. Reprinted by permission of the author.

Ruth Stone: "Second Hand Coat" from *The Iowa Review*, Volume 12: 2/3, Spring/Summer 1981. Reprinted by permission of the author.

Alfonsina Storni: "Peso Ancestral" from *Obras completas*, copyright 1964 by Ed. Aguilar. Translated by Diane Thiel. Reprinted by permission.

Sara Teasdale: "The Flight" reprinted with the permission of Scribner, an imprint of Simon & Schuster Adult Publishing group, from *The Collected Poems of Sara Teasdale* by Sara Teasdale. Copyright © 1926 by The Macmillan Company; copyright renewed © 1954 by Mamie T. Wheless.

Cornelius J. Ter Maat: "Etienne de Silhouette" reprinted by permission of the author.

Diane Thiel: "Memento Mori in Middle School" from *Echolocations*. Copyright © 2000. Reprinted by permission of the author and Story Line Press.

Dylan Thomas: "Fern Hill," copyright © 1945 by The Trustees for the Copyrights of Dylan Thomas and "Do Not Go Gentle Into That Good Night," copyright © 1952 by Dylan Thomas. Both from *The Poems of Dylan Thomas*. Reprinted by permission of New Directions Publishing Corp. and David Higham Associates.

Peter Townsend: Excerpt from "Langston Hughes and Jazz" from *Jazz in American Culture* by Peter Townsend. Copyright © 2000. Reprinted by permission of Edinburgh University Press.

Natasha Trethewey: "White Lies," copyright © 2000 by Natasha Trethewey. Reprinted from *Domestic Work* with the permission of Graywolf Press, Saint Paul, Minnesota.

John Updike: "Recital" from *Telephone Poles & Other Poems* by John Updike, coypright © 1959 by John Updike. "Ex-Basketball Player" from *The Carpentered Hen and Other Tame Creatures* by John Updike, copyright © 1982 by John Updike. Used by permission of Alfred A. Knopf, a division of Random House, Inc.

Amy Uyematsu: "The Ten Million Flames of Los Angeles" from *Nights of Fire, Nights of Rain*. Reprinted by permission of the author and Story Line Press.

DRAMA

"How to Write a Play" from *The Playwright's Art: Conversations with Contemporary American Dramatists*, edited by Jackson R. Bryer. Copyright © 1995 by Rutgers, The State University. Reprinted by permission of Rutgers University Press.

Arthur Miller: *Death of a Salesman* from *Death of a Salesman* by Arthur Miller. Copyright 1949, renewed © 1977 by Arthur Miller. Used by permission of Viking Penguin, a division of Penguin Group (USA) Inc. "Tragedy and the Common Man," copyright 1949, renewed © 1977 by Arthur Miller from *The Theater Essays of Arthur Miller*, edited by Robert A. Martin. Reprinted by permission of Viking Penguin, a division of Penguin Group (USA) Inc.

Bill Moyers: August Wilson, "Black Experience in America" from *Bill Moyers: A World of Ideas* by Bill Moyers, copyright © 1989 by Public Affairs Television, Inc. Used by permission of Doubleday, a division of Random House, Inc.

Milcha Sanchez-Scott: *The Cuban Swimmer*, copyright © 1984, 1988 by Milcha Sanchez-Scott. Reprinted by permission of William Morris Agency, Inc. on behalf of the author. CAUTION: Professionals and amateurs are hereby warned that *The Cuban Swimmer* is subject to a royalty. It is fully protected under the copyright laws of the United States of America and of all countries covered by the International Copyright Union (including the Dominion of Canada and the rest of the British Commonwealth), the Berne Convention, the Pan-American Copyright Convention and the Universal Copyright Convention as well as all countries with which the United States has reciprocal copyright relations. All rights, including professional/amateur stage rights, motion picture, recitation, lecturing, public reading, radio broadcasting, television, video or sound recording, all other forms of mechanical or electronic reproduction, such as CD-ROM, CD-I, information storage and retrieval systems and photocopying, and the rights of translation into foreign languages, are strictly reserved. Particular emphasis is laid upon the matter of readings, permission for which must be secured from the Author's agent in writing. Inquiries concerning rights should be addressed to: William Morris Agency, Inc. 1325 Avenue of the Americas, New York, NY 10019, Attn: Jeremy Katz. Originally produced in New York City by INTAR Hispanic American Arts Center.

William Shakespeare: Notes to *Hamlet* and *Othello* from *The Complete Works of Shakespeare*, 4th edition, by David Bevington. Copyright © 1997 by Addison-Wesley Educational Publishers, Inc. Reprinted by permission of Pearson Education.

Sophocles: *Antigone* by Sophocles, *Oedipus the King* by Sophocles from *Three Theban Plays by Sophocles,* translated by Robert Fagles, copyright © 1982 by Robert Fagles. Used by permission of Viking Penguin, a division of Penguin Group (USA) Inc.

Rebecca West: Excerpt from "The Court and the Castle" by Rebecca West. Copyright © 1958 by Yale University Press. Reprinted by permission.

Tennessee Williams: From *The Glass Menagerie* by Tennessee Williams, copyright 1945 by Tennessee Williams and Edwina D. Williams; copyright renewed 1973 by Tennessee Williams. Used by permission of Random House, Inc.

Joel Wingard: Excerpt from *Literature* by Joel Wingard. Reprinted by permission of Pearson Education Inc.

Photo Acknowledgments

FICTION

1: Robert Capa/Magnum Photos, Inc.; 9: Brown Brothers; 20: Bettmann/CORBIS; 29: Bettmann/CORBIS; 37: Marion Ettlinger; 77: AP/Wide World Photos; 87: Bettmann/CORBIS; 94: © Jill Krementz, Inc.; 102: AP/Wide World Photos; 121: Scott, Foresman and Company; 127: Missouri Historical Society, St. Louis. Photograph by J. A. Scholten, 1870; 132: Bettmann/CORBIS; 143: © Nancy Crampton; 167: © Nancy Crampton; 193: Hulton I Archive/Getty Images; 200: Jerry Bauer; 209: Bettmann/CORBIS; 215: Courtesy of the Newark Public Library; 234: Jerry Bauer; 248: © Nancy Crampton; 253: Scott, Foresman and Company; 262: Erich Hartmann/Magnum Photos, Inc.; 269: © Nancy Crampton; 278: Marian Wood Kolisch; 294: Bettmann/CORBIS; 371: AP/Wide World Photos; 381: Bettmann/CORBIS; 405: © Courtesy of the family of Arthur Rackham/The Bridgeman Art Library; 408: © Courtesy of the family of Arthur Rackham/The Bridgeman Art Library; 415: AP/Wide World Photos; 459: Joe McTyre/*Atlanta Constitution*; 464: Flannery O'Connor Collection, Ina Dillard Russell Library, Georgia College & State University. © 1944 by Flannery O'Connor. Reprinted by permission of the Harold Matson Co., Inc.; 468: © 2002 *The Atlanta Journal-Constitution*. Reprinted with permission from *The Atlanta Journal-Constitution*; 475: AP/Wide World Photos; 478: Steve Allen/Getty Images; 485: Courtesy of Anjana Appachana; 497: Laurence Acland; 501: Bettmann/CORBIS; 508: Bettmann /CORBIS; 513: Nebraska State Historical Society, Willa Cather Pioneer Memorial Collection; 528: Bettmann/CORBIS; 539: Bettmann/CORBIS; 554: Rubén Guzmán; 555: © Nancy Crampton; 566: AP/Wide World Photos; 571: Bettmann/CORBIS; 584: Photograph courtesy Peabody Essex Museum, Image ID No. : 14,509; 594: Scott, Foresman and Company; 604: © Nancy Crampton; 612: © Berenice Abbott/Commerce Graphics Ltd, Inc., NYC; 617: Sigrid Estrada; 619: Bettmann/CORBIS; 631: David Lees/Hulton I Archive/Getty Images; 639: Courtesy Alfred A. Knopf, Inc.; 643: Jerry Bauer; 654: © Jill Krementz, Inc.; 667: Jerry Bauer; 680: Elliot Erwitt/Magnum Photos, Inc.; 687: AP/Wide World Photos; 693: © Nancy Crampton

POETRY

697: The Granger Collection, New York; 714: Ed Souza/Stanford News Service; 743: Used with the permission of The Trustees of the Imperial War Museum, London; 773: Brown Brothers; 787: Bettmann/CORBIS; 807: Courtesy of New Directions; 834: Brown Brothers; 858: Bettmann/CORBIS; 881: AP/Wide World Photos; 905: Bettmann/CORBIS; 930: Bettmann/CORBIS; 939: Kunsthistorisches Museum, Vienna; 952: Gabriel Harrison/Library of Congress; 971: Culver Pictures, Inc.; 994: Bettmann/CORBIS; 1021: Brian Eaton, courtesy of *The Daily News*; 1038: Copyright estate of Pamela Chandler/National Portrait Gallery, London; 1043: Philadelphia Museum of Art: The Robert H. Lamborn Collection, 1903 (Accession #1903-918). Photograph by Graydon Wood, 2001; 1045: RDA/Hulton I Archive Photos/Getty Images; 1049: Bettmann/CORBIS; 1052: William Coupon/Getty Images; 1055: © 2003 Banco de México Diego Rivera & Frida Kahlo Museums Trust. Av. Cinco de Mayo No. 2, Col. Centro Del. Cuauhtémoc 06059, Mexico, D.F. Photograph: Bob Schalkwijk/Art Resource, NY; 1089: Scott, Foresman and Company; 1097: By permission of the Trustees of Amherst College; 1105: Courtesy the Emily Dickinson Museum: The Homestead and The Evergreens; 1107: By permission of the Houghton Library, Harvard University (MS Am 1118.3 (84)). © The President and Fellows of Harvard College; 1116: Henri Cartier-Bresson/Magnum Photos, Inc.; 1125: Underwood & Underwood/CORBIS; 1127: Courtesy Aaron and Alta Sawyer Douglas Foundation. Private Collection; 1137: Private Collection; 1144: Bettmann/CORBIS; 1146: Musées Royaux des Beaux-Arts de Belgique; 1147: Thomas Victor; 1149: Berg Collection of English and American Literature, The New York Public Library, Astor, Lenox, and Tilden Foundations/Art Resource, NY; 1150: Private Collection; 1162: By courtesy of the National Portrait Gallery, London, and the Marquess of Lothian; 1165: Photograph of Rita Dove © by Fred Viebahn; 1169: By permission of the Houghton Library, Harvard University (AC9.E1464.Zzx Box 2, env.13a); 1173: © Nancy Crampton; 1183: By courtesy of the National Portrait Gallery, London; 1185: Scott, Foresman and Company; 1188: Dorothy Alexander; 1190: Bettmann/CORBIS; 1192: Brown Brothers; 1195: Ted Russell; 1200: By courtesy of the National Portrait Gallery, London; 1202: Fay Godwin/Network Photographers/CORBIS SABA; 1211: Brown Brothers; 1213: AP/Wide World Photos; 1215: Dorothy Alexander; 1217: Gail and Bonnie Roub; 1219: © Nancy Crampton; 1220: Dorothy Alexander; 1222: Bettmann/CORBIS; 1228: Willie Williams, courtesy Broadside Press; 1232: Bettmann/CORBIS; 1233: Photograph by Imogen Cunningham © 1978 The Imogen Cunningham Trust; 1234: Jerry Bauer; 1236: By courtesy of the National Portrait Gallery, London; 1243: Reprinted from School Figures, by Cathy Song, © 1994, by permission of the University of Pittsburgh Press; 1245: Bettmann/CORBIS; 1250: By courtesy of the National Portrait Gallery, London; 1255: Amy Uyematsu, courtesy Story Line Press; 1257: Bettmann/CORBIS; 1259: Gabriel Harrison/Library of Congress; 1262: Courtesy of New Directions; 1263: By courtesy of the National Portrait Gallery, London; 1267: The Royal Photographic Society

DRAMA

1299: John Van Hasselt/CORBIS SYGMA; 1322: Bettmann/CORBIS; 1334: Courtesy Writers & Artists Agency; 1349: AP/Wide World Photos; 1358: Scott, Foresman and Company; 1359: Bettmann/CORBIS; 1360: Alinari/Art Resource, NY; 1364: Bettmann/CORBIS; 1366: John Vickers Theatre Collection; 1435: Martha Swope/TimePix/Getty Images; 1489: John G. Ross; 1500: Andrea Pistolesi/Getty Images; 1501: By courtesy of the National Portrait Gallery, London; 1502: Martha Swope/TimePix/Getty Images; 1524: Photofest; 1566: Photofest; 1603 (top): Martha Swope/TimePix/Getty Images; 1603 (bottom): Photofest; 1723: Hulton | Archive/Getty Images; 1751: Photofest; 1786: By courtesy of the National Portrait Gallery, London; 1809: Bettmann/CORBIS; 1867: Hulton | Archive/Getty Images; 1872: Richard Devin; 1885: Courtesy Milcha Sanchez-Scott; 1969: Bettmann/CORBIS; 1973: Private Collection; 2023: Bettmann/ CORBIS; 2027: Courtesy of the Theatre Arts Department, Drew University; 2043: Susan Johann; 2059: Ted Thai/CORBIS SYGMA; 2063: AP/Wide World Photos; 2114: AP/Wide World Photos.

Index of Authors and Titles

Each page number immediately following a writer's name indicates a quotation from or reference to that writer. A number in **bold** refers you to the page on which you will find the author's biography.

A & P, 15
ABC, 926
ABEYTA, AARON, 1039
   thirteen ways of looking at a tortilla, 1036
ACHEBE, CHINUA, **475**
   Dead Men's Path, 475
Acquainted with the Night, 919
Adam, 1188
ADAMS, RICHARD, 91
ADDONIZIO, KIM
   First Poem for You, 920
Advice to a Friend Who Paints, 758
AESCHYLUS, 1321, 1357, 1364
AESOP, **5**, 212
   Fox and the Grapes, The, 5
After great pain, a formal feeling comes, 1101
Aftermath, 755
ALARCÓN, FRANCISCO X.
   X in My Name, The, 1010
ALBEE, EDWARD, 1869, 1870
ALDRICH, THOMAS BAILEY, 2
ALEXIE, SHERMAN
   Indian Boy Love Song (#1), 1012
ALGER, HORATIO, 21
ALI-SHAH, OMAR
   Our Day's Portion (translation), 1031
ALLENDE, ISABEL
   Judge's Wife, The, 478
Alta Traición, 1058
ALVAREZ, JULIA, 873, 1006, 1007, 1009, 1022
   women on my mother's side were known,
      The, 1006
America, 1007
American Poetry, 1239
American Primitive, 1242
Am I Blue, 2026
AMMONS, A. R.
   Coward, 832
Amorosa Anticipación, 1050
Ancestral Burden, 1058
Ancient Stairway, 933
Anger, 1056
ANDERSON, HANS CHRISTIAN, 9
Andre's Mother, 2060
Anecdote of the Jar, 970
Angel Levine, 631
Annabel Lee, 1088
ANONYMOUS
   Bonny Barbara Allan, 844
   Carnation Milk, 770

Cruel Mother, The, 839
   Epitaph on a Dentist, 925
   Last Words of the Prophet, 1141
   Little Poem Regarding Computer Spell
      Checkers, A, 2128
   Lord Randall, 1138
   O Moon, when I gaze on thy beautiful face,
      1068
   Scottsboro, 771
   Sir Patrick Spence, 708
   Three Ravens, The, 1139
   Twa Corbies, The, 1140
   We four lads from Liverpool are, 1033
   Western Wind, 1141
Anorexic, 1151
ANOUILH, JEAN, 1321
Anthem for Doomed Youth, 1220
Anticipation of Love, 1050
Antigone, 1435
Antigone's Flaw, 1495
anyone lived in a pretty how town, 767
APOLLINAIRE, GUILLAUME, 945
APPACHANA, ANJANA, **485**
   Prophecy, The, 485
APPLE, MAX, 289
Appointment in Samarra, The, 4
AQUINAS, THOMAS, 1077
Araby, 612
ARAGON, LOUIS, 1054
ARISTOPHANES, 1332
ARISTOTLE, 20, 899, 1320, 1321, 1362–63,
      1495, 1868, 1869, 2228
   Defining Tragedy, 1490
ARMSTRONG, LOUIS, 64n, 698
ARNOLD, MATTHEW
   Dover Beach, 1141
Ars Poetica, 1092
Asegura la Confianza de que Ocultará de todo
      un Secreto, 1044
ASHBERY, JOHN, 930, **1269**
   At North Farm, 1142
   Cathedral Is, The, 828
Asian Culture Looks at Shakespeare, An, 1794
As I Walked Out One Evening, 1144
Ask Me, 715
At Home with Dollface, 740
At North Farm, 1142
At the Un-National Monument Along the
      Canadian Border, 740
Atticus, 891

ATWOOD, MARGARET, **497, 1269**
    Happy Endings, 497
    Romantic, 1143
    You fit into me, 828
Aubade, 1019
AUDEN, W. H., 374–75, 377, 714, 841, 849,
    871, 914, 920, 929, 1039, 1094, **1270,** 2119
    As I Walked Out One Evening, 1144
    Funeral Blues, 850
    Iago as a Triumphant Villain, 1792
    James Watt, 925
    Musée des Beaux Arts, 1146
    September 1, 1939, 1081
    Unknown Citizen, The, 733
AUGUSTINE, 788
Aunt Jennifer's Tigers, 707
AUSTEN, JANE, 93, 293
Author to Her Book, The, 719
Autumn Begins in Martins Ferry, Ohio, 1265

BABBITT, IRVING, 1495
BABEL, ISAAC, 122
BAILEY, PHILIP JAMES, 867
BALDWIN, JAMES, **53,** 2204–5
    Race and the African American Writer, 87
    Sonny's Blues, 53
BALÉE, SUSAN
    Psychoanalytic Reading of "The Masque of
        the Red Death," (*translation*) A, 410
Ballad of Birmingham, 847
Ballad of the Landlord, 1121
BALZAC, HONORÉ DE, 14, 124
BAMBER, LINDA
    Female Power in A *Midsummer Night's
        Dream,* 1797
Barn Burning, 178
BARTHES, ROLAND, 2241
    Death of the Author, The, 2241
BASHO, MATSUO, 799, 800, **1270**
    Heat-lightning streak, 799
    In the old stone pool, 799
Batter my heart, three-personed God, for You,
    753
Battle Royal, 555
BAUDELAIRE, CHARLES, 937, 957n, 1807
    On Poe's Genius, 412
BAUERLEIN, MARK
    What Is Cultural Studies?, 2247
Bavarian Gentians, 977
Beaks of Eagles, The, 965
Beat! Beat! Drums!, 903
BEATTIE, ANN, 172
Beauty, 1343
BEAUVOIR, SIMONE DE, 2231
Because I could not stop for Death, 1103
BECK, 840
BECKETT, SAMUEL, 1868–69, 1869
BEERBOHM, MAX, 893
    On the imprint of the first English edition of
        The Works of Max Beerbohm, 893

BEHN, APHRA
    When maidens are young, 866
Being a Bilingual Writer, 1021
BELLOC, HILAIRE
    Fatigue, 925
    Hippopotamus, The, 873
BELLOW, SAUL, 292
BENNETT, BRUCE
    Lady Speaks Again, The, 1035
BENSLEY, CONNIE
    Covetous Cat, The, 737
    Last Haiku, 801
BENTLEY, EDMUND CLERIHEW, 925
    Sir Christopher Wren, 926
BERENDT, JOHN, 291
BERGSON, HENRI, 1332
BETJEMAN, JOHN, 744
    In Westminster Abbey, 735
BETTELHEIM, BRUNO, 2219, 2221, 2222
BIBLE, 760, 778, 914, 935–36, 960, 975, 1067
    Parable of the Good Seed, The, 960
    Parable of the Prodigal Son, The, 241
BIDPAI
    Camel and His Friends, The, 6
BIERCE, AMBROSE, 290, **501**
    Occurrence at Owl Creek Bridge, An, 501
Bilingual / Bilingüe, 1008
Birches, 1175
BISHOP, ELIZABETH, 754, 766n, 809–13, 849,
    1005, 1039, 1094, **1270,** 2210–11
    Filling Station, 1147
    Fish, The, 793
    One Art, 1080
    Sestina, 928
Black and White in *Othello,* 1793
Black Experience in America, 2114
Black Identity in Langston Hughes, 1131
BLAKE, WILLIAM, 705, 725, 779–80, 788, 871,
    878, 888, 895, 981, **1271,** 2212, 2237,
    2249–51
    Chimney Sweeper, The, 739
    Her whole life is an epigram, 923
    London, 778
    Sick Rose, The, 1150
    To see a world in a grain of sand, 820
    Tyger, The, 1149
Blandeur, 763
Blessing, A, 1264
BLOCH, CHANA
    Tired Sex, 802
BLOOM, HAROLD
    Poetic Influence, 2222
BLY, ROBERT, 808, 920, 976, 1094, **1271,**
    2232
    Cricket (*translation*), 799
    Driving to Town Late to Mail a Letter, 803
BODKIN, MAUD
    Lucifer in Shakespeare's *Othello,* 1792
BOGAN, LOUISE, **1272**
    Medusa, 980

BOLAND, EAVAN
  Anorexic, 1151
BONAPARTE, MARIE, 2219
  Psychoanalytic Reading of "The Masque of the Red Death," A, 410
Bonny Barbara Allan, 844
Book of Verses underneath the Bough, A, 1031
BOOTH, WAYNE C., 24n
BORGES, JORGE LUIS, 14, 210, 211, **508**, 937, 1042, **1049**, 1063–64, 1094
  Amorosa Anticipación, 1050
  Enigmas, Los, 1051
  Gospel According to Mark, The, 508
  Riddle of Poetry, The, 1060
Borges and Paz, 1063
Born Again, 800
Boston Evening Transcript, The, 956
BOSWELL, JAMES, 759
BOTTOME, PHYLLIS, 122
BOWLES, PAUL, 27
BOYLE, T. CORAGHESSAN, **143**
  Greasy Lake, 143
BRADLEY, A. C.
  Hamlet's Melancholy, 1787
BRADSTREET, ANNE, 719–20, 723
  Author to Her Book, The, 719
Break, Break, Break, 889
BRECHT, BERTOLT, 1808
BRETON, ANDRÉ, 705n, 1053, 1054
BREUGHEL, PIETER, 939, 1146
BRIDGES, ROBERT
  Triolet, 928
Brief Bio, 914
Bright star! would I were steadfast as thou art, 801
BRINKMEYER, ROBERT, JR.
  Flannery O'Connor and Her Readers, 465
BRITTEN, BENJAMIN, 849
BROCK, VAN K., 824
BRODSKY, JOSEPH, 1007
broken bowl, 800
BRONTË, CHARLOTTE, 284, 2234
BRONTË, EMILY, 2234
BROOKS, CLEANTH
  Formalist Critic, The, 2203
BROOKS, GWENDOLYN, 697, 1094, **1272**
  Hearing "We Real Cool," 905
  independent man, the, 781
  Mother, The, 1152
  preacher ruminates: behind the sermon, the, 1153
  Queen of the Blues, 856
  We Real Cool, 889
BROWN, JOHN RUSSELL
  Recognizing Love in *A Midsummer Night's Dream,* 1795
BROWN, STERLING A., 849
BROWNING, ELIZABETH BARRETT, 1106, **1272**, 2234
  How Do I Love Thee? Let Me Count the Ways, 1154
BROWNING, ROBERT, 704, 711, 731, 744, 887, 888, 897, 1067, 1106, **1273**, 2202, 2205–7
  My Last Duchess, 712
  Soliloquy of the Spanish Cloister, 1154
BRUTSCHY, JENNIFER
  Born Again, 800
Buffalo Bill 's, 938
Bull Calf, The, 1204
BUNYAN, JOHN, 251, 960, 962
BURGESS, ANTHONY
  Asian Culture Looks at Shakespeare, An, 1794
BURGON, JOHN, 825
BURNS, ROBERT, 761–62, 841, 872, **1273**
  Oh, my love is like a red, red rose, 833
BURROUGHS, WILLIAM, 291, 293
BUSON, TANIGUCHI, 791, 798, 799, 958, **1274**
  I go, 799
  On the one-ton temple bell, 799
  piercing chill I feel, The, 790
Bustle in a House, The, 1104
BUTLER, SAMUEL, 878
BYNNER, WITTER, 866
BYRON, GEORGE GORDON, LORD, 847, 872, 894, 901, 952, 1070

California Hills in August, 1179
Camel and His Friends, The, 6
CAMP, JAMES, 1033
CAMPBELL, JOSEPH, 2223
CAMPION, THOMAS, 840, 899, 2215
  Rose-cheeked Laura, 899
CAMPO, RAFAEL
  What the Body Told, 968
CAMUS, ALBERT, 21, 93
CAPOTE, TRUMAN, 291
Care and Feeding, 1159
Cargoes, 777
CARLYLE, THOMAS, 958, 1093
Carnation Milk, 770
Carrie, 968
CARROLL [CHARLES LUTWIDGE DODGSON] LEWIS, 945
  Humpty Dumpty Explicates "Jabberwocky," 773
  Jabberwocky, 771
CARVER, RAYMOND, **109**, 172–73
  Cathedral, 109
  Commonplace but Precise Language, 121
CASSIAN, NINA, 1007
Cathedral, 109
Cathedral Is, The, 828
CATHER, WILLA, 125, 292, **513**
  Paul's Case, 513
CATULLUS, 2215
Cavalry Crossing a Ford, 940
Certainty, 1053
Certeza, 1053

CHAPMAN, TRACY, 849
CHAPPELL, FRED
    Narcissus and Echo, 875
CHARLES, DORTHI
    Concrete Cat, 948
CHAUCER, GEOFFREY, 910
    Merciless Beauty, 1156
CHEEVER, JOHN, **528**, 2208
    Five-Forty-Eight, The, 528
CHEKHOV, ANTON, 14, 171, **539**, 958, 1807,
    1886, 2208–10
    Lady with the Pet Dog, The, 539
Chekhov's Attitude to Romantic Love, 2208
CHERRY, KELLY
    Advice to a Friend Who Paints, 758
CHESTERTON, G. K., 826
    Donkey, The, 1157
CHILD, FRANCIS J., 844
Chimney Sweeper, The, 739
CHOPIN, KATE, 125, **127**, 210, 2211–12
    Storm, The, 127
    Story of an Hour, The, 553
CHRISTIAN, BARBARA T.
    "Everyday Use" and the Black Power
        Movement, 2216
Chrysanthemums, The, 253
CHUANG TZU, **8**
    Independence, 8
CHURCHILL, CARYL, 1870
CIARDI, JOHN, 1007
    Most Like an Arch This Marriage, 961
Cien Sonetos de Amor (V), 1047
Cinderella, 990
CINTHIO, GIRALDI, 1501–2
CISNEROS, SANDRA, **554**
    House on Mango Street, The, 554
Civilian, 737
CLARE, JOHN
    Mouse's Nest, 756
CLARK, MICHAEL
    Light and Darkness in "Sonny's Blues,"
        2204
Clean, Well-Lighted Place, A, 174
CLEGHORN, SARAH N.
    Golf Links, The, 736
CLIFTON, LUCILLE
    Homage to my hips, 950
COCTEAU, JEAN, 976
COFER, JUDITH ORTIZ, 1023
    Quinceañera, 1018
COHEN, LEONARD, 840
COLACURCIO, MICHAEL J.
    End of Young Goodman Brown, The, 2239
COLE, WILLIAM
    On my boat on Lake Cayuga, 870
Cólera que Quiebra al Hombre en Niños, La,
    1055
COLERIDGE, SAMUEL TAYLOR, 701, 705, 760,
    763, 825, 841, 847, 898, 1093
    Kubla Khan, 1158

Collective Unconscious and Archetypes, The,
    2223
COLLINS, BILLY, **1274**
    Care and Feeding, 1159
    Embrace, 805
    Names, The, 768
COLLINS, WILLIAM, 825
Colonel, The, 944
Comic Perversion in "Good Country People,"
    472
Commonplace but Precise Language, 121
Composed upon Westminster Bridge, 1263
Concerning "Love Calls Us to the Things of
    This World," 787
Concrete Cat, 948
CONGREVE, WILLIAM, 1333
Con Los Ojos Cerrados, 1053
CONNELL, EVAN, 122
CONNOLLY, CYRIL, 290
CONRAD, JOSEPH, 171, 252, 292
Contemplation, 924
Content Determines Form, 2228
Convergence of the Twain, The, 1182
COOGLER, J. GORDON, 1069
COOK, ELIZA, 886
COOMBES, H., 754
COPE, WENDY, **1274**
    Lonely Hearts, 766
    Nursery Rhyme (as it might have been
        written by William Wordsworth), A, 1034
    Variation on Belloc's "Fatigue," 925
CORMAN, CID
    only one guy (translation), 799
Cosmos in bloom, 800
Counting-out Rhyme, 901
Counting the Beats, 912
Counting the Mad, 1197
Covetous Cat, The, 737
Coward, 832
CRABBE, GEORGE, 910
CRANE, HART, 749, 826
    My Grandmother's Love Letters, 1160
CRANE, STEPHEN, 3, 125n, **215**, 249, 290, 291
    Heart, The, 940
    Open Boat, The, 215
CRAWFORD, DESSA, 824
Crazy Jane Talks with the Bishop, 1267
Creating "Eleanor Rigby," 858
Creating Trifles, 1349
CREELEY, ROBERT, 732, 936
    Oh No, 732
Cricket, 799
Cruel Mother, The, 839
Cuban Swimmer, The, 1870
CULLEN, COUNTEE, 1008, 1129, 1130
    For a Lady I Know, 719
CUMMINGS, E. E., 760, 763, 828, 867, 920, 937,
    1274, 1973
    anyone lived in a pretty how town, 767
    Buffalo Bill 's, 938

in Just-, 949
politician, a, 923
somewhere i have never travelled,gladly
  beyond, 1161
CUNNINGHAM, J. V., 1094, **1275**
Friend, on this scaffold Thomas More lies
  dead, 757
This *Humanist* whom no beliefs constrained,
  924

Daddy, 1222
Dance, The, 939
DANE, DANA, 987
DANTE (DANTE ALIGHIERI), 21, 251, 911, 959,
  1093
Dark house, by which once more I stand, 1249
Darkling Thrush, The, 1183
DAVIDSON, JOHN, 818
DAVIS, DICK
Fatherhood, 924
I Need a Bare Sufficiency (*translation*), 1031
Day of the Butterfly, 234
Dead Men's Path, 475
Death be not proud, 1137, 1162
Death of a Salesman, 1897
Death of Ivan Ilych, The, 294
Death of the Author, The, 2241
Death of the Ball Turret Gunner, The, 1195
Deconstructing "A Good Man Is Hard to Find,"
  471
DE CRISTORO, VIOLET KAZUE
Cosmos in bloom (*translation*), 800
Even the croaking of frogs (*translation*), 800
Rain shower from mountain (*translation*), 800
war (*translation*), The, 800
War forced us from California (*translation*),
  800
Defining Tragedy, 1490
DEFOE, DANIEL, 3, 289–90, 2250
DEGAS, EDGAR, 749
DE LA MARE, WALTER, 788, 789
Listeners, The, 782
DE MAN, PAUL, 2240
DENHAM, JOHN, 911
DERRIDA, JACQUES, 2242
Description of the Morning, A, 1248
Desert Places, 876
Design, 2149
Desire, 1120
Destiny of Oedipus, The, 1491
DEUTSCH, BABETTE
falling flower, The (*translation*), 798
DICK, PHILIP K., 293
DICKENS, CHARLES, 91, 92
DICKEY, JAMES
Heaven of Animals, The, 984
DICKINSON, EMILY, 729, 823, 846, 864, 873,
  894, 957n, 958, 1093, **1097**, 1108–15,
  2232, 2234–35
After great pain, a formal feeling comes, 1101

Because I could not stop for Death, 1103
Bustle in a House, The, 1104
Dying Tiger – moaned for Drink, A, 1069
I felt a Funeral, in my Brain, 1099
I heard a Fly buzz – when I died, 1102
I like to see it lap the Miles, 721
I'm Nobody! Who are you?, 1100
I started Early – Took my Dog, 1102
It dropped so low – in my Regard, 821
Lightning is a yellow Fork, The, 957
Much Madness is divinest Sense, 1101
My Life had stood – a Loaded Gun, 818
Recognizing Poetry, 1105
Route of Evanescence, A, 796
Self-Description, 1106
Some keep the Sabbath going to Church,
  1101, 1107
Soul selects her own Society, The, 1100
Success is counted sweetest, 1098
Tell all the Truth but tell it slant, 1104
There's a certain Slant of light, 1099
This is my letter to the World, 1102
Wild Nights – Wild Nights!, 1098
Dickinson and Death, 1112
Different Image, A, 1228
Digging, 1186
DI GIOVANNI, NORMAN THOMAS
Gospel According to Mark, The (*translation*),
  508
DINESEN, ISAK, 861–62, 869
DI PASQUALE, EMANUEL, 1007
Rain, 866
Direct Style, The, 209
DISCH, THOMAS, 293, 929
Discovery of Emily Dickinson's Manuscripts,
  The, 1109
Discussing *The Metamorphosis*, 371
Disillusionment of Ten O'Clock, 780
DODDS, E. R.
On Misunderstanding *Oedipus,* 1492
Doll's House, A, 1809
DONALDSON, SCOTT, 2208
Donkey, The, 1157
DONLEAVY, J. P., 292
DONNE, JOHN, 714, 885, 895, 1137, **1275**
Batter my heart, three-personed God, for
  You, 753
Death be not proud, 1137, 1162
Flea, The, 1163
Song, 913
Valediction: Forbidding Mourning, A, 1164
Do not go gentle into that good night, 927
Don't Ask, 1029
DOOLITTLE, HILDA. *See* H. D.
DOSTOYEVSKY, FEODOR, 278, 2219
DOVE, RITA, 976, **1276**
Langston Hughes and Harlem, 1129
Summit Beach, 1921, 1165
Dover Beach, 1141
Down, Wanton, Down!, 752

DRAYTON, MICHAEL
  Since there's no help, come let us kiss and
    part, 918
Dream Boogie, 904
Dream Deferred. *See* Harlem
Dream Variations, 1118
Dream within a Dream, A, 1225
DREISER, THEODORE, 125–26, 285, 290
Drinking Alone Beneath the Moon, 1026
Drinking Alone by Moonlight, 1027
Driving to Town Late to Mail a Letter, 803
DRURY, JOHN, 972
DRYDEN, JOHN, 765, 871, 900, 910, 911, 1070
  To the Memory of Mr. Oldham, 1166
DUCHAMP, MARCEL, 1054
Dulce et Decorum Est, 742
D'URFEY, THOMAS, 841
DYER, JOHN, 713–14, 826, 1071
Dying Tiger – moaned for Drink, A, 1069
DYLAN, BOB, 840, 841
  Times They Are a-Changin', The, 854

Eagle, The, 815
Easter Wings, 945
EASTHOPE, ANTHONY, 2246
EBERHART, RICHARD
  Fury of Aerial Bombardment, The, 765
EHRET, TERRY
  from Papyrus, 947
Eight O'Clock, 868
Eingang, 1025
EISLER, RACHEL, 887
Eleanor Rigby, 853
Elegy, 2237
Elegy for Jane, 1233
Elegy for My Father, Who Is Not Dead, 1017
Elegy, Written with His Own Hand, 827
ELIOT, GEORGE, 170, 289, 2234
ELIOT, T. S., 702, 711, 719, 751, 756, 763, 841,
    937, 956–57, 957n, 962, 976, 981, 987,
    1033, 1094, **1276**
  Boston Evening Transcript, The, 956
  Journey of the Magi, 1167
  Love Song of J. Alfred Prufrock, The, 1169
  Music of Poetry, The, 881
  Virginia, 880
  winter evening settles down, The, 792
ELLINGTON, DUKE [CHARLES KENNEDY], 899, 1127
ELLISON, RALPH, **555**
  Battle Royal, 555
Elms, 1261
ÉLUARD, PAUL, 1054
Embrace, 805
EMERSON, RALPH WALDO, 754, 2222
Emperor of Ice-Cream, The, 1247
End, 1122
Endgames: Sor Juana Inés de la Cruz, 1062
End of Young Goodman Brown, The, 2239
Enigmas, Los, 1051
Enigmas, The, 1051

Entrance, 1025
Epigram Engraved on the Collar of a Dog, 923
Epitaph, 781
Epitaph on a Dentist, 925
ERDRICH, LOUISE
  Indian Boarding School: The Runaways,
    1173
Eskimo "A Rose for Emily," An, 2236
ESPAILLAT, RHINA, 1008
  Being a Bilingual Writer, 1021
  Bilingual / Bilingüe, 1008
ESTESS, SYBIL, 810, 811
Ethics, 1220
Etienne de Silhouette, 926
EURIPIDES, 1321, 1361, 1364, 1489, 1490
EVANS, ABBIE HUSTON, 2158–60
  Wing-Spread, 2157
Evening Walk, An, 969
Even the croaking of frogs, 800
Everyday Use, 102
"Everyday Use" and the Black Power
    Movement, 2216
Ex-Basketball Player, 1253
Excerpt from "On Her Own Work": The
    Element of Suspense in "A Good Man Is
    Hard to Find," 459
Excerpt from "The Grotesque in Southern
    Fiction": The Serious Writer and the Tired
    Reader, 462

Facing It, 1012
Factory Windows Are Always Broken, 900
FAGLES, ROBERT
  Antigone (*translation*), 1435
  Oedipus the King (*translation*), 1365
FAIRCHILD, B. H.
  Starlit Night, A, 1174
Fairy Tale Motifs in "Where Are You Going,
    Where Have You Been?," 2220
falling flower, The, 798
Fall of the House of Usher, The, 391
Family Supper, A, 604
Farmer's Bride, The, 1210
Farm on the Great Plains, The, 1244
FARQUHAR, GEORGE, 1333
FARR, JUDITH
  Reading of "My Life had stood – a Loaded
    Gun," A, 1114
Father-Figure in "The Tell-Tale Heart," The,
    408
Fatherhood, 924
Fatigue, 925
FAULKNER, WILLIAM, 14, 25, 27, **29**, 92, 125,
    126, 173, 210, 213, 252, 285, 958, 976,
    2142–43, 2148, 2225–26, 2236–37
  Barn Burning, 178
  Rose for Emily, A, 29
FEELEY, KATHLEEN
  Comic Perversion in "Good Country People,"
    472

FEHLER, GENE, 1033, 1039
  If Richard Lovelace Became a Free Agent,
    1035
FELSTINER, JOHN
  With Our Eyes Shut (*translation*), 1053
Female Power in *A Midsummer Night's Dream*,
    1797
Fern Hill, 1252
FEYDEAU, GEORGES, 1333
FIELD, EUGENE, 2174
FIELDING, HENRY, 92, 292
FIELDS, W. C., 1333
Filling Station, 1147
Final Love Note, 784
FINCH, ANNIE, 873, 887
Fire and Ice, 784
First Confession, 680
First Poem for You, 920
FISH, STANLEY
  Eskimo "A Rose for Emily," An, 2236
Fish, The, 793
FITZGERALD, EDWARD, 1030, 1032
  Book of Verses underneath the Bough
    (*translation*) A, 1031
  from *The Rubaiyat of Omar Khayyam*
    (*translations*), 1032
FITZGERALD, F. SCOTT, 251, 2208
FITZGERALD, ROBERT
  Anticipation of Love (*translation*), 1050
  Translating Sophocles, 1489
Five-Forty-Eight, The, 528
Flannery O'Connor and Her Readers, 465
FLAUBERT, GUSTAVE, 14, 25–26, 1095
Flea, The, 1163
FLEENOR, JULIANN
  Gender and Pathology in "The Yellow
    Wallpaper," 2233
Flight, The, 966
Flower in the Crannied Wall, 819
Fog, 1086
FOLEY, ADELLE
  Learning to Shave, 801
FOLEY, JACK, 937
For a Lady I Know, 719
FORCHÉ, CAROLYN, 937
  Colonel, The, 944
For I will consider my Cat Jeoffry, 1240
Fork, 796
Formalist Critic, The, 2203
For My Daughter, 723
FORSTER, E. M., 92, 475, 894, 2123
For the Anniversary of My Death, 938
For the White Poets Who Would Be Indian,
    1011
FOUCAULT, MICHEL, 2241
Fox and the Grapes, The, 5
FRAYN, MICHAEL, 1333
FRAZER, SIR JAMES, 975
Freedom of Emily Dickinson, The, 2234
FREUD, SIGMUND, 93, 972, 974, 2218

Destiny of Oedipus, The, 1491
Nature of Dreams, The, 2219
FREYTAG, GUSTAV, 1320n
FRIEDMAN, ALBERT B., 846
Friend, on this scaffold Thomas More lies dead,
    757
FROST, ROBERT, 698, 711, 714, 826, 878, 894,
    897, 907, 908, 919, 920, 934, 988, 996,
    1024, 1093, **1276**, 2148, 2149–52, 2153,
    2154–56, 2158–63, 2184
  Acquainted with the Night, 919
  Birches, 1175
  Desert Places, 876
  Design, 2149
  Fire and Ice, 784
  Importance of Poetic Metaphor, The, 834
  In White (draft of "Design"), 2165
  Mending Wall, 1176
  Nothing Gold Can Stay, 976
  "Out, Out—", 710
  Road Not Taken, The, 962
  Secret Sits, The, 832
  Silken Tent, The, 830
  Stopping by Woods on a Snowy Evening, 1177
FRYE, NORTHROP, 980, 2223
  Mythic Archetypes, 2224
FUENTES, CARLOS, 27
Full fathom five thy father lies, 879
FULTON, ALICE
  What I Like, 951
Funeral Blues, 850
Fury of Aerial Bombardment, The, 765
FUSSELL, PAUL, 899

GARCÍA LORCA, FEDERICO, 2026
GARCÍA MÁRQUEZ, GABRIEL, 14, **566**
  Handsomest Drowned Man in the World,
    The, 566
Garret, The, 941
GASCOIGNE, GEORGE, 754
GASS, WILLIAM, 92
GAY, JOHN, 841, 2250
Gender and Pathology in "The Yellow
    Wallpaper," 2233
GIDE, ANDRÉ, 94
GILBERT, SANDRA M., 2232
  Freedom of Emily Dickinson, The, 2234
GILES, HERBERT
  Independence (*translation*), 8
GILGAMESH, 708
GILMAN, CHARLOTTE PERKINS, 285, **571**,
    2233–34
  Yellow Wallpaper, The, 571
GILMAN, RICHARD, 1870
GINSBERG, ALLEN, 936
  Supermarket in California, A, 1178
GIOIA, DANA
  California Hills in August, 1179
  Entrance (*translation*), 1025
  Godfather Death (*translation*), 9

Girl, 617
GLASPELL, SUSAN, **1305**, 1317–21, 1351–55,
    2169–70, 2172–73, 2175–76
  Creating *Trifles*, 1349
  Trifles, 1305
Glass Menagerie, The, 1972
Glass of Beer, A, 729
GLEN, HEATHER
  Stance of Observation in William Blake's
    "London," The, 2249
GLÜCK, LOUISE
  Mock Orange, 804
Go, Lovely Rose, 1258
Godfather Death, 9
God's Grandeur, 875
GOETHE, JOHANN WOLFGANG VON, 291,
    2219
Golf Links, The, 736
Good Country People, 416
GOODDEN, CHRISTINA, 374
Good Man Is Hard to Find, A, 431
Good Source Is Not So Hard to Find: The Real
    Life Misfit, A, 468
GOODWIN, DORIS KEARNS, 2181
GORKY, MAXIM, 1807
Gospel According to Mark, The, 508
GOSSE, SIR EDMUND, 1068n
Grass, 758
GRAVES, ROBERT, 291, 983, **1277**
  Counting the Beats, 912
  Down, Wanton, Down!, 752
  Poetic Inspiration and Poetic Form, 930
  Our Day's Portion (*translation*), 1031
GRAY, THOMAS, 826, 898, 2156
Greasy Lake, 143
GREENE, GRAHAM, 1794
GREER, GERMAINE
  Shakespeare's "Honest Mirth," 1797
GRENNAN, EAMON, 1007
GRIGSON, GEOFFREY, 1032
GRIMM, JAKOB AND WILHELM, **9**, 12–13, 23, 25,
    994
  Godfather Death, 9
GROSHOLZ, EMILY, 823
  Listening, 1014
GROSS, RONALD, 916, 917
  Yield, 915
GUARE, JOHN, 1333
GUBAR, SUSAN
  Freedom of Emily Dickinson, The, 2234
GUEST, EDGAR A., 1070
GUITERMAN, ARTHUR
  On the Vanity of Earthly Greatness, 1078
GUNN, THOM, 914, 1007
  Man with Night Sweats, The, 1180
GURGA, LEE
  Visitor's Room, 800
GWYNN, R. S., 757, 873
  Scenes from the Playroom, 921
GYLYS, BETH, 824

HACKER, MARILYN, 929
HADAS, RACHEL, 870, 873
HAIGH, A. E.
  Irony of Sophocles, The, 1493
HAINES, JOHN
  Winter News, 805
HALL, DONALD, 914
  Names of Horses, 1181
HAMILTON, EDITH, 975, 1363, 1869
Hamlet, Prince of Denmark, 1604
Hamlet and Ophelia, 1788
Hamlet's Melancholy, 1787
HAMMETT, DASHIELL, 26–27
Hands, 833
Handsomest Drowned Man in the World, The,
    566
Hap, 1184
Happy Endings, 497
HARDY, THOMAS, 193, 285, 732, 841, 1070,
    1093, **1277**
  Convergence of the Twain, The, 1182
  Darkling Thrush, The, 1183
  Hap, 1184
  Neutral Tones, 959
  Oxen, The, 977
  Ruined Maid, The, 764
  Workbox, The, 738
Harlem, 1124
Harlem Renaissance, The, 1126
HARRINGTON, SIR JOHN
  Of Treason, 923
Harrison Bergeron, 242
HARTER, PENNY
  broken bowl, 800
HARTMAN, GEOFFREY
  On Wordsworth's "A Slumber Did My Spirit
    Seal," 2243
HASS, ROBERT
  I go (*translation*), 799
Hawk Roosting, 726
HAWTHORNE, NATHANIEL, 14, 124–25, 126,
    251, 284, 289, 291, **584**, 2180, 2239–40
  Young Goodman Brown, 584
HAYDEN, ROBERT, 1008, 1079, **1278**
  Those Winter Sundays, 1185
  Whipping, The, 1079
H. D. [HILDA DOOLITTLE], 799, 997–1001,
    1278
  Heat, 804
  Helen, 979
  Love That I Bear, 832
HEANEY, SEAMUS, 920, **1278**
  Digging, 1186
  Mother of the Groom, 1187
Hearing "We Real Cool," 905
Heart, The, 940
Heat, 804
HEATH-STUBBS, JOHN, 830
Heat-lightning streak, 799
Heaven of Animals, The, 984

HECHT, ANTHONY
  Adam, 1188
Heel & Toe to the End, 902
HEFFERNAN, MICHAEL, 929
HEILBRUN, CAROLYN, 2233
Helen, 979
HELLER, PETER, 374, 376–77
HEMINGWAY, ERNEST, 1, 21, 24n, 173–74, **174**,
    192, 210, 212–13, 252, 290
  Clean, Well-Lighted Place, A, 174
  Direct Style, The, 209
HENLEY, BETH, 1869, **2026**
  Am I Blue, 2026
  Playwright Is Born, A, 2043
HENRY, O., 193
HERBERT, GEORGE, 945, 955, **1279**
  Easter Wings, 945
  Love, 1190
  Pulley, The, 828
  World, The, 960
Her Kind, 730
HERRICK, ROBERT, 704, 761, 839, 870, **1279**,
    2215
  Moderation, 923
  To the Virgins, to Make Much of Time,
    1191
  Upon Julia's Clothes, 761
  Upon Julia's Voice, 868
HERSEY, JOHN, 291
Her whole life is an epigram, 923
HIGGINSON, THOMAS WENTWORTH
  Meeting Emily Dickinson, 1108
High Treason, 1059
HILBERT, DAVID, 290
HILL, GEOFFREY
  Merlin, 782
Hippopotamus, The, 873
HITCHCOCK, ALFRED, 886, 1300
HIX, H. L.
  I Love the World, As Does Any Dancer, 741
HOFFMAN, DANIEL, 2137
  Father-Figure in "The Tell-Tale Heart," The,
    408
Hokku, A Selection of, 1218
HOLDEN, JONATHAN
  Names of the Rapids, The, 983
HOLLAND, NORMAN, 2236
HOLLANDER, JOHN
  Swan and Shadow, 946
HOLT, VICTORIA, 284
Homage to my hips, 950
Home is so Sad, 1202
HOMER, 13, 93, 699, 708, 998, 1361, 1365, 1491
HOOD, THOMAS, 827, 873, 896
HOPE, A. D.
  Imperial Adam, 989
HOPKINS, CRALE, 812
HOPKINS, GERARD MANLEY, 701–2, 706, 760,
    898, 1075, 1093, **1279**, 2119, 2235
  God's Grandeur, 875

No worst, there is none, 1192
Pied Beauty, 797
Spring and Fall, 1191
Windhover, The, 1193
HORACE, 704, 1028, 1093, 2126, 2215
  Don't Ask, 1029
  Horace to Leuconoe, 1029
  New Year's Toast, A, 1030
  Odes I (11), 1028
House on Mango Street, The, 554
HOUSMAN, A. E., 717, 846, 1035, **1280**
  Eight O'Clock, 868
  Loveliest of trees, the cherry now, 1193
  To an Athlete Dying Young, 1194
  When I was one-and-twenty, 902
How Do I Love Thee? Let Me Count the Ways,
    1154
"How Do We Make a Poem?", 2237
HOWE, TINA, 1333, 1870
How soon hath time, 1212
How to Stage The Glass Menagerie, 2023
How to Write a Play, 2063
HUDGINS, ANDREW
  Elegy for My Father, Who Is Not Dead, 1017
HUGHES, LANGSTON, 849, 1008, **1116**, 1128–36
  Ballad of the Landlord, 1121
  Desire, 1120
  Dream Boogie, 904
  Dream Deferred. See Harlem
  Dream Variations, 1118
  End, 1122
  Harlem, 1124
  Harlem Renaissance, The, 1126
  Island, 1122
  I, Too, 1118
  Mother to Son, 1117
  Negro Artist and the Racial Mountain, The,
    1125
  Negro Speaks of Rivers, The, 1117
  Prayer ("Gather up"), 1120
  Prayer ("O, God of dust"), 924
  Sliver, 1124
  Song for a Dark Girl, 1120
  Subway Rush Hour, 1123
  Theme for English B, 1122
  Weary Blues, The, 1119
HUGHES, TED, 1002
  Hawk Roosting, 726
Hughes as an Experimentalist, 1128
HULME, T. E., 808
  Image, 802
HUME, DAVID, 93
HUMPHRIES, ROLFE, 909
Humpty Dumpty Explicates "Jabberwocky," 773
HUNTER, G. K., 1793
HURSTON, ZORA NEALE, 213, **594**
  Sweat, 594
HWANG, DAVID HENRY, 1870, **2044**
  Multicultural Theater, 2059
  Sound of a Voice, The, 2044

I, Too, 1118
Iago as a Triumphant Villain, 1792
IBSEN, HENRIK, 1304, 1319, 1321, 1806, 1807, **1809**, 1867–68, 1886, 1888–91, 2167
   Doll's House, A, 1809
Ibsen and the Familiar Situation, 1867
I felt a Funeral, in my Brain, 1099
If Richard Lovelace Became a Free Agent, 1035
I go, 799
I Hear America Singing, 1259
I heard a Fly buzz – when I died, 1102
I like to see it lap the Miles, 721
I Love the World, As Does Any Dancer, 741
Image, 802
Image, The, 807
Imagism, 2213
I'm Nobody! Who are you?, 1100
Imperial Adam, 989
Importance of Poetic Metaphor, The, 834
In a Station of the Metro, 790, 2214
Independence, 8
independent man, the, 781
Indian Boarding School: The Runaways, 1173
Indian Boy Love Song (#1), 1012
I Need a Bare Sufficiency, 1031
in Just-, 949
In Memoriam John Coltrane, 879
INNAURATO, ALBERT, 1869
In Search of the Present, 1061
Interpreter of Maladies, 37
In the old stone pool, 799
In this strange labyrinth, 1265
In Westminster Abbey, 735
In White, 2165
IONESCO, EUGÈNE, 1869, 1870, 1892
Irony of Sophocles, The, 1493
ISER, WOLFGANG, 1791
I Shall Paint My Nails Red, 951
ISHIGURO, KAZUO, **604**
   Family Supper, A, 604
Island, 1122
ISOU, ISIDORE, 862
ISSA, KOBAYASHI, 799, **1280**
   Cricket, 799
   only one guy, 799
I Stand Here Ironing, 687
I started Early – Took my Dog, 1102
It dropped so low – in my Regard, 821
IVES, DAVID, **1334**, 1343
   Sure Thing, 1334
I Wandered Lonely as a Cloud, 727

Jabberwocky, 771
JACKSON, SHIRLEY, 213, **262**
   The Lottery, 262
JAGGER, MICK, 849
Jailhouse Blues, 849
JAMES, HENRY, 28, 92–93, 122, 124, 251, 292, 293, 958
JAMES, WILLIAM, 27, 278

James Watt, 925
JARMAN, MARK, 873
   Unholy Sonnet: After the Praying, 920
JARRELL, RANDALL, 711, 729, 2153, 2184
   Death of the Ball Turret Gunner, The, 1195
JEFFERS, ROBINSON, 972, **1281**
   Beaks of Eagles, The, 965
   Hands, 833
   To the Stone-cutters, 1196
JEFFERSON, BLIND LEMON, 849
JEMIE, ONWUCHEKWA
   Reading of "Dream Deferred," A, 1134
JESPERSEN, OTTO, 894
Jilting of Granny Weatherall, The, 94
JIN, HA, **200**
   Missed Time, 1096
   Saboteur, 200
Joe Turner's Come and Gone, 2064
JOHNSON, BARBARA
   Rigorous Unreliability, 2242
JOHNSON, JAMES WELDON, 849, 864, 1008, 1129
JOHNSON, ROBERT, 849
JOHNSON, SAMUEL, 714, 758–59, 765, 827, 1093, 1489, 2238, 2249, 2250
JOHNSON, THOMAS H.
   Discovery of Emily Dickinson's Manuscripts, The, 1109
JONES, V. S. VERNON
   The Fox and the Grapes (*translation*) The, 5
JONG, ERICA, 292
JONSON, BEN, 837–38, **1281**, 1722, 1786, 2215
   On His Friend and Rival William Shakespeare, 1786
   On My First Son, 1196
   Slow, slow, fresh fount, keep time with my salt tears, 890
   To Celia, 838
JORDAN, WINTHROP, 1793
JOSEPH, CHIEF, 1095
Journal Entry, 728
Journey of the Magi, 1167
JOYCE, JAMES, 14, 27–28, 93, 125, 213, 252, 289, 291, 293, **612**, 976
   Araby, 612
Judge's Wife, The, 478
JUNG, CARL, 974, 980, 2219, 2223
   Collective Unconscious and Archetypes, The, 2223
JUSTICE, DONALD, 849, **1281**
   Men at Forty, 1015
   Counting the Mad, 1197

KAFKA, FRANZ, 21, 94, 285, 292, **336**, 373–79
   Discussing The Metamorphosis, 371
   Metamorphosis, The, 336
KAHLO, FRIDA, 1042, 1054
   Two Fridas, The, 1055
KAZIN, ALFRED
   Walt Whitman and Abraham Lincoln, 2230
KEATON, BUSTER, 1332

KEATS, JOHN, 749, 791, 825, 847, 894, 909, 1106, **1282**, 2222
Bright star! would I were steadfast as thou art, 801
Ode on a Grecian Urn, 1197
On First Looking into Chapman's Homer, 1199
This living hand, now warm and capable, 910
To Autumn, 1201
When I have fears that I may cease to be, 1200
KEELER, GREG, 887
KEES, WELDON, 920, 2186–87, 2207, 2213
For My Daughter, 723
KENNEDY, X. J.
Heat-lightning streak (*translation*), 799
In the old stone pool (*translation*), 799
On the one-ton temple bell (*translation*), 799
To the Muse, 698
KENNER, HUGH
Imagism, 2213
KENYON, JANE
Suitor, The, 831
KEROUAC, JACK, 2125
KHANWALKAR, ARUNDHATI
Camel and His Friends (*translation*) The, 6
KHAYYAM, OMAR, 1030, 1032
Book of Verses underneath the Bough, A, 1031
I Need a Bare Sufficiency, 1031
Our Day's Portion, 1031
Rubai, 1031
KILMER, JOYCE, 948
KINCAID, JAMAICA, **617**
Girl, 617
KING, B. B., 849
KINGSMILL [HUGH KINGSMILL LUNN], HUGH
What, still alive at twenty-two?, 1034
KIPLING, RUDYARD, 851, 895
Kite Poem, 1209
KNIGHT, ETHERIDGE, 849
Making jazz swing in, 800
KNIGHT, WILSON, 1788
KOCH, KENNETH, 937
KOMUNYAKAA, YUSEF
Facing It, 1012
KOOSER, TED, **1282**
Carrie, 968
KOSTELANETZ, RICHARD, 948
KOTT, JAN
Producing *Hamlet*, 1789
Kubla Khan, 1158
KUNA, FRANZ, 375
KUNITZ, STANLEY, 907
KUSHNER, TONY, 1870
KYD, THOMAS, 1603

Lady Lazarus, 1003
Lady Speaks Again, The, 1035
Lady with the Pet Dog, The, 539

LAFORGUE, JULES, 957n
LAHIRI, JHUMPA, **37**, 252
Interpreter of Maladies, 37
Lai with Sounds of Skin, 880
LAKE, PAUL, 824, 873
Lake Isle of Innisfree, The, 703
LANGBAUM, ROBERT, 2202
On Robert Browning's "My Last Duchess," 2205
LANGER, SUSANNE, 2244
Langston Hughes and Harlem, 1129
Langston Hughes and Jazz, 1132
LARKIN, PHILIP, 823, **1282**
Aubade, 1019
Home is so Sad, 1202
Poetry of Departures, 1203
LA ROCHEFOUCAULD, 956
Last Haiku, 801
Last Words of the Prophet, 1141
LAWRENCE, D. H., 21, 94, **619**, 744, **1283**, 2229–30
Bavarian Gentians, 977
Piano, 706
Rocking-Horse Winner, The, 619
LAYTON, IRVING
Bull Calf, The, 1204
LAZARUS, EMMA
New Colossus, The, 1087
Lazy Man's Haiku, The, 801
LEAR, EDWARD, 867, 881, 925
Learning to love America, 1016
Learning to Shave, 801
Leaving Forever, 831
Leda and the Swan, 874
LEECH, CLIFFORD, 1363
LE GUIN, URSULA K., **272**
Note on "The Ones Who Walk Away from Omelas," 278
Ones Who Walk Away from Omelas, The, 272
LEHMAN, DAVID, 2241
LEITCH, VINCENT B.
Poststructuralist Cultural Critique, 2246
LEITHAUSER, BRAD
Venus Flytrap, A, 924
LEMAITRE, GEORGE, 817
LENNON, JOHN
Eleanor Rigby, 853
Let me not to the marriage of true minds, 917
LEVERTOV, DENISE, 933–34, 1013, **1283**
Ancient Stairway, 933
Leaving Forever, 831
LEVIN, PHILLIS
Brief Bio, 914
LEVINE, PHILIP
They Feed They Lion, 1205
Life, 1068
Light and Darkness in "Sonny's Blues," 2204
LIGHTMAN, ALAN, 817
Lightning is a yellow Fork, The, 957

LIM, SHIRLEY GEOK-LIN, 1007
    Learning to love America, 1016
LINCOLN, ABRAHAM, 2230–31
LINDSAY, VACHEL
    Factory Windows Are Always Broken, 900
LINES, PATRICIA M.
    Antigone's Flaw, 1495
LI PO, 1026–28, **1284**
    Drinking Alone Beneath the Moon, 1026–28
Listeners, The, 782
Listening, 1014
little Learning is a dang'rous Thing, A, 1226
Little Poem Regarding Computer Spell
    Checkers, A, 2128
Living in Sin, 1230
London, 778
LONDON, JACK, **132**, 192, 290, 2228
    To Build a Fire, 132
Lonely Hearts, 766
LONGFELLOW, HENRY WADSWORTH, 713, 823,
    895, 896
    Aftermath, 755
Long Poem Does Not Exist, A, 1089
Looking for Judas, 1206
LORCA. See GARCÍA LORCA
Lord Randall, 1138
Lottery, The, 262
LOUIS, ADRIAN
    Looking for Judas, 1206
Love, 1190
Love Calls Us to the Things of This World, 786
LOVELACE, RICHARD, 1033, 1035
    To Lucasta, 741
Loveliest of trees, the cherry now, 1193
Love Song of J. Alfred Prufrock, The, 1169
Love That I Bear, 832
LOWELL, ROBERT, 936, 1003, 1024
    Skunk Hour, 1206
LOWES, JOHN LIVINGSTON, 1068
LOY, MINA, 1094
LUCAS, GEORGE, 987
Lucifer In Shakespeare's Othello, 1792
LUCRETIUS, 713
LUKACS, GEORG, 2227
    Content Determines Form, 2228
Luke Havergal, 725

MCCARTNEY, PAUL
    Creating "Eleanor Rigby," 858
    Eleanor Rigby, 853
MACDONALD, DWIGHT, 777, 1032
MCDOWELL, ROBERT
    At Home with Dollface, 740
MCFARLANE, JAMES
    Doll's House, A (translation), 1809
MCINERNEY, JAY, 27
MCKAY, CLAUDE, 1007, 1008, 1128
    America, 1007
MCKUEN, ROD
    Thoughts on Capital Punishment, 1072

MACLEISH, ARCHIBALD, 1093, 1095
    Ars Poetica, 1092
MCNALLY, NANCY, 810
MCNALLY, TERRENCE, **2060**
    Andre's Mother, 2060
    How to Write a Play, 2063
MACNEICE, LOUIS, 714
    Plain Speaking, 829
MCPHERSON, SANDRA, 849
MCRAE, WALLACE, 2156
    Reincarnation, 1073
MAETERLINCK, MAURICE, 1807
Magi, The, 1268
MAILER, NORMAN, 291
MAIO, SAMUEL, 2186–87
Making jazz swing in, 800
MALAMUD, BERNARD, **631**
    Angel Levine, 631
MALLARMÉ, STÉPHANE, 749, 957n, 1807
MAMET, DAVID, 1869
MANN, AIMEE, 840
MANN, THOMAS, 292
MANSFIELD, KATHERINE, **639**
    Miss Brill, 639
Man to Send Rain Clouds, The, 693
Man with Night Sweats, The, 1180
MARLOWE, CHRISTOPHER, 888, 897, 1079
MÁRQUEZ, GABRIEL GARCÍA. See GARCÍA
    MÁRQUEZ, GABRIEL
Martian Sends a Postcard Home, A, 821
MARTIN, CHARLES, 873
    Taken Up, 988
MARTIN, JANE, **1343**
    Beauty, 1343
MARVELL, ANDREW, 719, 754, 825, 847, 894,
    2215–16
    To His Coy Mistress, 1208
MARX, GROUCHO, 1333
MASEFIELD, JOHN, 778
    Cargoes, 777
MASON, BOBBIE ANN, 172, **643**
    Shiloh, 643
MASON, DAVID
    Song of the Powers, 904
Masque of the Red Death, The, 386
Master, The, 1214
MATSUSHITA, SUIKO
    Rain shower from mountain, 800
    Cosmos in bloom, 800
MAUGHAM, W. SOMERSET, 4, 5, 126, 193
    Appointment in Samarra, The, 4
MAUPASSANT, GUY DE, 14, **193**
    Necklace, The, 193
Medusa, 980
Meeting Emily Dickinson, 1108
MELE, JOAN F.
    On Poe's Genius (translation), 412
MELVILLE, HERMAN, 92, 251, 252, 827, 955,
    958, 962, 972, 2148, 2243
Memento Mori in Middle School, 985

MENASHE, SAMUEL, 1009
  Shrine Whose Shape I Am, The, 1010
Men at Forty, 1015
MENCKEN, H. L., 2174
Mending Wall, 1176
Merciless Beauty, 1156
Merlin, 782
MERRILL, JAMES
  Kite Poem, 1209
MERRIM, STEPHANIE
  Endgames: Sor Juana Inés de la Cruz, 1062
MERTON, THOMAS
  Anger (translation), 1056
MERWIN, W. S., 2237–39
  Elegy, 2237
  For the Anniversary of My Death, 938
Metamorphosis, The, 336
Metaphors, 820
Method of Translation, The, 1038
MEW, CHARLOTTE
  Farmer's Bride, The, 1210
MICHENER, JAMES A., 290
MICHIE, JAMES
  Don't ask (translation), 1029
MIDDLEBROOK, DIANE, 2219
Midsummer Night's Dream, A, 1723
MILES, JOSEPHINE, 2207
  Civilian, 737
MILLAY, EDNA ST. VINCENT, 920, 1002,
    1022–23, 1284
  Counting-out Rhyme, 901
  Recuerdo, 1211
  What lips my lips have kissed, and where,
    and why, 919
MILLER, ARTHUR, 1897
  Death of a Salesman, 1897
  Tragedy and the Common Man, 1969
MILLER, JAMES, 2237
MILLETT, KATE, 2231
MILLIER, BRETT C.
  On Elizabeth Bishop's "One Art," 2210
MILTON, JOHN, 13, 714, 732, 762, 763, 826,
    862, 866, 867, 896, 909, 919, 931, 958,
    1066, 1077, 1079, 1284, 2215
  How soon hath time, 1212
  When I consider how my light is spent,
    1212
Miniver Cheevy, 1232
Miss Brill, 639
Missed Time, 1096
MISTRAL, GABRIELA, 1042
MITCHELL, JONI, 840
Mock Orange, 804
Moderation, 923
MOLDENHAUER, JOSEPH
  "To His Coy Mistress" and the Renaissance
    Tradition, 2215
MOLIÈRE (JEAN-BAPTISTE POQUELIN), 711
MOMADAY, N. SCOTT
  Simile, 820

MONEGAL, EMIR RODRÍGUEZ
  Borges and Paz, 1063
Money and Labor in "The Rocking-Horse
  Winner," 2229
MOORE, LORRIE, 27
MOORE, MARIANNE, 814, 914, 1285
  Poetry, 1213
  Silence, 751
MOORE, THOMAS, 877
MORGAN, FREDERICK
  Master, The, 1214
MORGAN, SETH, 292
MORITAKE, ARAKIDA
  falling flower, The, 798
MORRIS, WILLIAM, 881
MOSS, HOWARD
  Shall I Compare Thee to a Summer's Day?,
    816
Most Like an Arch This Marriage, 961
Mother, The, 1152
MOTHER GOOSE, 762, 851, 885, 896, 898
Mother of the Groom, 1187
Mother to Son, 1117
Mouse's Nest, 756
Much Madness is divinest Sense, 1101
Muchos Somos, 1046
Multicultural Theater, 2059
MUNRO, ALICE, 234
  Day of the Butterfly, 234
Musée des Beaux Arts, 1146
Music of Poetry, The, 881
Mutability, 770
My Grandmother's Love Letters, 1160
My heart leaps up when I behold, 770
My Last Duchess, 712
My Life had stood – a Loaded Gun, 818
My mistress' eyes are nothing like the sun,
  1238
My Papa's Waltz, 718
Mythic Archetypes, 2224
Myth in Faulkner's "Barn Burning," 2225

NABAKOV, VLADIMIR, 121, 289, 1007, 2124n
Names, The, 768
Names of Horses, 1181
Names of the Rapids, The, 983
Naming of Parts, 1229
Narcissus and Echo, 875
NASHE, THOMAS, 751
NATHAN, GEORGE JEAN, 1301, 1808
Nature of Dreams, The, 2219
Necklace, The, 193
Negro Artist and the Racial Mountain, The,
  1125
Negro Speaks of Rivers, The, 1117
NELSON, MARILYN, 873, 1285
  Langston Hughes and Harlem, 1129
  Strange Beautiful Woman, A, 1215
NEMEROV, HOWARD
  War in the Air, The, 1216

NERUDA, PABLO, **1045**, 1054, 1063
Cien Sonetos de Amor (V), 1047
Muchos Somos, 1046
Towards the Splendid City, 1060
Neutral Tones, 959
New Colossus, The, 1087
NEWTON, JOHN, 846
New Year's Toast, A, 1030
NIEDECKER, LORINE, **1286**
Popcorn-can cover, 970
Sorrow Moves in Wide Waves, 1217
NIMS, JOHN FREDERICK, 929–30
Contemplation, 924
NOGUCHI, YONE
Hokku, A Selection of, 1218
Noiseless Patient Spider, A, 1258
No One's a Mystery, 269
NORMAN, MARSHA, 1869
Note on "The Ones Who Walk Away from
Omelas," 278
Nothing Gold Can Stay, 976
Not marble nor the gilded monuments, 1237
Not Waving but Drowning, 806
No worst, there is none, 1192
Nursery Rhyme (as it might have been written
by William Wordsworth), A, 1034

OATES, JOYCE CAROL, 14, **654**, 2180, 2220–22
Where Are You Going, Where Have You
Been?, 654
O'BRIEN, EDNA, 93
O'BRIEN, TIM, **667**
Things They Carried, The, 667
O Captain! My Captain!, 1084
Occurrence at Owl Creek Bridge, An, 501
O'CONNOR, FLANNERY, **415**, 465–472, 474,
2142–43, 2180
Good Country People, 416
Good Man Is Hard to Find, A, 431
Excerpt from "On Her Own Work": The
Element of Suspense in "A Good Man Is
Hard to Find," 459
Excerpt from "The Grotesque in Southern
Fiction": The Serious Writer and the Tired
Reader, 462
On Her Catholic Faith, 462
Revelation, 443
Yearbook Cartoons, 464
O'CONNOR, FRANK, **680**
First Confession, 680
Ode on a Grecian Urn, 1197
Odes I (11), 1028
Oedipus the King, 1365
O'FAOLAIN, SEAN, 93
Of Treason, 923
Oh, my love is like a red, red rose, 833
Oh No, 732
OLDS, SHARON, **1286**
One Girl at the Boys' Party, The, 1219
Rites of Passage, 734

OLSEN, TILLIE, **687**
I Stand Here Ironing, 687
OLSON, CHARLES, 935
O Moon, when I gaze on thy beautiful face,
1068
One Art, 1080
One Girl at the Boys' Party, The, 1219
One Hundred Love Sonnets (V), 1048
O'NEILL, EUGENE, 1030
On Elizabeth Bishop's "One Art," 2210
Ones Who Walk Away from Omelas, The, 272
On First Looking into Chapman's Homer, 1199
On Her Catholic Faith, 462
On His Friend and Rival William Shakespeare,
1786
On Imagination, 406
only one guy, 799
On Misunderstanding *Oedipus*, 1492
On my boat on Lake Cayuga, 870
On My First Son, 1196
On Poe's Genius, 412
On Robert Browning's "My Last Duchess,"
2205
On the imprint of the first English edition of
The Works of Max Beerbohm, 893
On the one-ton temple bell, 799
On the Vanity of Earthly Greatness, 1078
On Wordsworth's "A Slumber Did My Spirit
Seal," 2243
Open Boat, The, 215
OROZCO, OLGA, 1042, 1054
Realidad y el Deseo, La, 1056
ORTON, JOE, 1333
ORWELL, GEORGE, 252, 1067
Othello, the Moor of Venice, 1502
Our Day's Portion, 1031
"Out, Out—", 710
OVID, 713, 974, 975
OWEN, WILFRED, 743, 871, **1286**
Anthem for Doomed Youth, 1220
Dulce et Decorum Est, 742
War Poetry, 743
Oxen, The, 977
OZAWA, NEIJI
war, The, 800
War forced us from California, 800
Ozymandias, 1078

PACHECO, JOSÉ EMILIO, 1007, 1042
Alta Traición, 1058
PADILLA, HERBERTO, 1007
PAINE, THOMAS, 2250
Pair of Tickets, A, 152
Papyrus, 947
Parable of the Good Seed, The, 960
Parable of the Prodigal Son, The, 241
Paraphrase of "Ask Me," A, 716
PARKER, CHARLIE, 64n
PARKER, DOROTHY, 863
Résumé, 892

PASTAN, LINDA
  Ethics, 1220
PATTON, CHARLEY, 849
Paul's Case, 513
PAZ, OCTAVIO, 1041, 1042, **1052**, 1054,
    1063–64, 1094
  Certeza, 1053
  Con Los Ojos Cerrados, 1053
  In Search of the Present, 1061
Peso Ancestral, 1058
Peter Piper, 852
Peter Quince at the Clavier, 1245
PETRARCH, 917, 1079
PHILLIPS, ROBERT
  Running on Empty, 1221
Philosophy of Composition, The, 407
Piano, 706
Piazza Piece, 1229
Pied Beauty, 797
piercing chill I feel, The, 790
PINCKNEY, DARRYL
  Black Identity in Langston Hughes, 1131
PINSKY, ROBERT
  ABC, 926
PIRANDELLO, LUIGI, 1808
Piute Creek, 803
Plain Speaking, 829
PLATH, SYLVIA, 711, 1002, 1005, 1013, **1287**,
    2208
  Daddy, 1222
  Lady Lazarus, 1003
  Metaphors, 820
PLAUTUS, 1722, 1868
Playwright Is Born, A, 2043
POE, EDGAR ALLAN, 14, 126, 252, **381**,
    408–414, 473, 756, 886, 894, 895, 955,
    958, 1095, 1112, **1287**, 2123–24, 2132–34,
    2135, 2136–38, 2140–41
  Annabel Lee, 1088
  Dream within a Dream, A, 1225
  Fall of the House of Usher, The, 391
  Long Poem Does Not Exist, A, 1089
  Masque of the Red Death, The, 386
  On Imagination, 406
  Philosophy of Composition, 407
  Tale and Its Effect, The, 405
  Tell-Tale Heart, The, 383
Poe's Quest for Supernal Beauty, 413
Poetic Influence, 2222
Poetic Inspiration and Poetic Form, 930
Poetic Symbols, 971
Poetry, 1213
Poetry of Departures, 1203
Poetry of the Future, The, 952
politician, a, 923
Popcorn-can cover, 970
POPE, ALEXANDER, 702, 759, 862, 867, 870, 878,
    888, 901, 911, 1066, 1077, **1287**
  Atticus, 891
  Epigram Engraved on the Collar of a Dog, 923
  little Learning is a dang'rous Thing, A, 1226

True Ease in Writing comes from Art, not
    Chance, 862
PORTER, KATHERINE ANNE, **94**, 122, 285
  Jilting of Granny Weatherall, The, 94
Poststructuralist Cultural Critique, 2246
POUND, EZRA, 711, 751, 790, 791, 799, 841,
    873, 914, 934–35, 947, 1024, 1077, 1085,
    1288, 2123, 2213–14, 2225
  Garret, The, 941
  Image, The, 807
  In a Station of the Metro, 790, 2214
  River-Merchant's Wife: a Letter, The, 1226
POWELL, JAMES HENRY, 1070
Power, 1231
Prayer ("Gather up"), 1120
Prayer ("O, God of dust"), 924
preacher ruminates: behind the sermon, the,
    1153
Presente en que el Cariño Hace Regalo la
    Llaneza, 1044
Producing *Hamlet*, 1789
Prophecy, The, 485
Psychoanalytic Reading of "The Masque of the
    Red Death," A, 410
Pulley, The, 828

Queen of the Blues, 856
Quinceañera, 1018
QUINTON, ANTHONY, 93

RABASSA, GREGORY
  Handsomest Drowned Man in the World,
    The (*translation*), 566
Race and the African American Writer, 87
RADCLIFFE, ANNE, 284
Rain, 866
RAINE, CRAIG
  Martian Sends a Postcard Home, A, 821
RAINEY, MA, 849
Rain shower from mountain, 800
RALPH, JAMES, 702
RAMPERSAD, ARNOLD
  Hughes as an Experimentalist, 1128
RANDALL, DUDLEY, 847, **1288**
  Ballad of Birmingham, 847
  Different Image, A, 1228
RANSOM, JOHN CROWE, 863
  Piazza Piece, 1229
RATUSHINSKAYA, IRINA, 699
Reader-Response Issues in *Hamlet*, 1791
Reading of "Dream Deferred," A, 1134
Reading of "My Life had stood – a Loaded
    Gun," A, 1114
Realidad y el Deseo, La, 1056
Reality and Desire, 1057
Reapers, 797
Recalling "Aunt Jennifer's Tigers," 714
Recital, 865
Recognizing Love in A *Midsummer Night's
    Dream*, 1795

Recognizing Poetry, 1105
Recuerdo, 1211
Red Wheelbarrow, The, 731
REED, HENRY
  Naming of Parts, 1229
REEVE, CLARA, 288
REEVES, JAMES
  Rough Weather, 872
REID, ALASTAIR, **1289**
  High Treason (*translation*), 1059
  Speaking a Foreign Language, 1019
  Translating Neruda, 1063
  We Are Many (*translation*), 1046
Reincarnation, 1073
Reply to Sor Philothea, 1059
Résumé, 892
Revelation, 443
RICH, ADRIENNE, **1289**, 2234
  Aunt Jennifer's Tigers, 707
  Living in Sin, 1230
  Power, 1231
  Recalling "Aunt Jennifer's Tigers," 714
  Women, 1016
Richard Cory (Robinson), 842
Richard Cory (Simon), 843
RICHARDSON, SAMUEL, 289
Riddle of Poetry, The, 1060
Riders to the Sea, 1322
RIDLAND, JOHN, 823
  Lazy Man's Haiku, The, 801
  Rigorous Unreliability, 2242
RILKE, RAINER MARIA, 937
  Eingang, 1025
Rites of Passage, 734
River-Merchant's Wife: a Letter, The, 1226
Road Not Taken, The, 962
ROBBE-GRILLET, ALAIN, 94
ROBINSON, EDWIN ARLINGTON, 711, 725, 732,
  1289
  Horace to Leuconoe (*translation*), 1029
  Luke Havergal, 725
  Miniver Cheevy, 1232
  Richard Cory, 842
Rocking-Horse Winner, The, 619
ROCKWOOD, R. J. R.
  Fairy Tale Motifs in "Where Are You Going,
    Where Have You Been?," 2220
ROETHKE, THEODORE, 706, 718, 745–47, 1013,
  1289
  Elegy for Jane, 1233
  My Papa's Waltz, 718
  Root Cellar, 792
Romantic, 1143
RONSARD, PIERRE DE, 1067
ROOSEVELT, THEODORE, 725
Root Cellar, 792
ROSE, WENDY
  For the White Poets Who Would Be Indian,
    1011
Rose-cheeked Laura, come, 899

Rose for Emily, A, 29
ROSELIEP, RAYMOND, 800
ROSSETTI, CHRISTINA
  Uphill, 963
ROSSINI, CLARE
  Final Love Note, 784
Rough Weather, 872
Route of Evanescence, A, 796
Rubai, 1031
Ruined Maid, The, 764
RUN D.M.C.
  Peter Piper, 852
Runner, The, 802
Running on Empty, 1221
RYAN, KAY, **1290**
  Blandeur, 763
  Turtle, 832
RYMER, THOMAS, 1805

Saboteur, 200
SÁENZ, BENJAMIN ALIRE
  To the Desert, 722
Sailing to Byzantium, 1075
SAINT-EXUPÉRY, ANTOINE DE, 21
SALTER, MARY JO
  Welcome to Hiroshima, 1234
SALTUS, FRANCIS SALTUS, 1070
SANCHEZ, SONIA, 849
SANCHEZ-SCOTT, MILCHA, **1870**
  Cuban Swimmer, The, 1870
  Writing *The Cuban Swimmer*, 1885
SANDBANK, SHIMON, 374
SANDBURG, CARL, 1129, 1132, **1290**
  Fog, 1086
  Grass, 758
SAROYAN, ARAM, 948
SATYAMURTI, CAROLE
  I Shall Paint My Nails Red, 951
Scenes from the Playroom, 921
SCHENCK, MARY JANE
  Deconstructing "A Good Man Is Hard to
    Find," 471
SCHNACKENBERG, GJERTRUD, 873
  Supernatural Love, 963
SCHOLES, ROBERT
  "How Do We Make a Poem?", 2237
SCHULZ, GRETCHEN
  Fairy Tale Motifs in "Where Are You Going,
    Where Have You Been?," 2220
SCOTT, SIR WALTER, 844, 1140n
SCOTT, WILBUR, 2227
Scottsboro, 771
Second Coming, The, 982
Second Hand Coat, 1248
Secret Sits, The, 832
SEDGLY, BEN, 2249
Self-Description, 1106
September 1, 1939, 1081
SERVICE, ROBERT, 886
Sestina, 928

Setting the Voice, 167
SEXTON, ANNE, 872, 987, 996, 1003, **1290**,
    2219
    Cinderella, 990
    Her Kind, 730
    Transforming Fairy Tales, 994
SHAKESPEARE, WILLIAM, 701, 711, 731, 754,
    757, 759, 777, 791, 814, 823, 824, 828,
    840, 847, 887, 894, 895, 896, 909, 910,
    917, 931, 1002, 1067, 1079, **1291**, 1303–4,
    1305, 1318, 1320, 1333, 1363, **1501**,
    1786–1804, 1807, 1868, 1886, 1893, 1896,
    1970, 2123, 2168, 2169, 2170, 2215, 2219,
    2223, 2227
    Full fathom five thy father lies, 879
    Hamlet, Prince of Denmark, 1604
    Let me not to the marriage of true minds, 917
    Midsummer Night's Dream, A, 1723
    My mistress' eyes are nothing like the sun,
        1238
    Not marble nor the gilded monuments, 1237
    Othello, the Moor of Venice, 1502
    Shall I compare thee to a summer's day?, 815
    Take, O, take those lips away, 841
    That time of year thou mayst in me behold,
        1238
    Weary with toil, I haste me to my bed, 1237
    When, in disgrace with Fortune and men's
        eyes, 1236
Shakespeare's "Honest Mirth," 1797
Shall I Compare Thee to a Summer's Day?
    (Moss), 816
Shall I compare thee to a summer's day?
    (Shakespeare), 815
SHAW, GEORGE BERNARD, 976, 1333
    Ibsen and the Familiar Situation, 1867
SHELLEY, PERCY BYSSHE, 817, 911, 1067, 1303
    Ozymandias, 1078
SHEPARD, SAM, 1870, 2059
She Promises to Hold a Secret in Confidence,
    1044
Shiloh, 643
SHOWALTER, ELAINE
    Toward a Feminist Poetics, 2232
Shrine Whose Shape I Am, The, 1010
Sick Rose, The, 1150
Silence, 751
Silken Tent, The, 830
SILKO, LESLIE MARMON, **693**
    Man to Send Rain Clouds, The, 693
SILVERSTEIN, SHEL, 1870
SIMENON, GEORGES, 2148
SIMIC, CHARLES
    Fork, 796
Simile, 820
SIMON, PAUL, 841, 844
    Richard Cory, 843
Simple Gift Made Rich by Affection, A, 1044
SIMPSON, LOUIS
    American Poetry, 1239

Since there's no help, come let us kiss and part,
    918
Sine Qua Non, 922
SINGER, ISAAC BASHEVIS, 192
Sir Christopher Wren, 926
Sir Patrick Spence, 708
SISCOE, JOHN
    Metamorphosis (translation) The, 336
Skunk Hour, 1206
SLAVITT, DAVID R.
    Titanic, 1239
Sliver, 1124
Slow, slow, fresh fount, keep time with my salt
    tears, 890
Slumber Did My Spirit Seal, A, 865
SMART, CHRISTOPHER
    For I will consider my Cat Jeoffry, 1240
SMILES, SAMUEL, 21
SMITH, BESSIE, 849
    Jailhouse Blues, 849
SMITH, GIBBS, 1073
SMITH, STEVIE, 1002, **1291**
    Not Waving but Drowning, 806
    This Englishwoman, 924
SMITH, VIRGINIA LLEWELLYN
    Chekhov's Attitude to Romantic Love, 2208
SMITH, WILLIAM JAY
    American Primitive, 1242
SNODGRASS, W. D., 825, 914, 1003
SNYDER, GARY, 937
    Piute Creek, 803
Soliloquy of the Spanish Cloister, 1154
SOLZHENITSYN, ALEXANDER, 937
Some keep the Sabbath going to Church, 1101,
    1107
somewhere i have never travelled,gladly
    beyond, 1161
Song, 913
SONG, CATHY
    Stamp Collecting, 1243
Song for a Dark Girl, 1120
Song of the Powers, 904
Sonny's Blues, 53
SOPHOCLES, 732, 1304, 1320, 1321, 1332,
    1357–62, **1364**, 1364–65, 1434, 1489,
    1490–97 1807, 1886, 1893, 1970, 2219
    Antigone, 1435
    Oedipus the King, 1365
SOR JUANA, 1041, 1042, **1043**, 1062
    Asegura la Confianza de que Ocultará de
        todo un Secreto, 1044
    Presente en que el Cariño Hace Regalo la
        Llaneza, 1044
    Reply to Sor Philothea, 1059
Sorrow Moves in Wide Waves, 1217
Soul selects her own Society, The, 1100
Sound of a Voice, The, 2044
Source for Alcée Laballière in "The Storm,"
    The, 2211
Sous-Entendu, 1014

Speaking a Foreign Language, 1019
SPENSER, EDMUND, 760, 867, 960
SPIELBERG, STEVEN, 987
splendor falls on castle walls, The, 869
Spring and All, 1261
Spring and Fall, 1191
SQUIRES, RADCLIFFE, 2151
STAFFORD, WILLIAM, 715, 1094, **1292**
    Ask Me, 715
    At the Un-National Monument Along the
       Canadian Border, 740
    Farm on the Great Plains, The, 1244
    Paraphrase of "Ask Me," A, 716
    Traveling Through the Dark, 1072
STALLINGS, A. E.
    New Year's Toast (*translation*), A, 1030
    Sine Qua Non, 922
STALLWORTHY, JON
    Evening Walk, An, 969
Stamp Collecting, 1243
Stance of Observation in William Blake's
    "London," The, 2249
STANISLAVSKY, CONSTANTIN, 1807
Starlit Night, A, 1174
Star Trek, 13
STEELE, TIMOTHY, 873, **1292**
    Epitaph, 781
    Summer, 922
STEINBECK, JOHN, 14, 126, **253**, 280–82
    Chrysanthemums, The, 253
STEINER, GEORGE, 2201
STEPHENS, JAMES, **1292**
    Glass of Beer, A, 729
    Wind, The, 825
STEVENS, WALLACE, 714, 788, 789, 871, 901,
    953, 1054, 1093, **1293**
    Anecdote of the Jar, 970
    Disillusionment of Ten O'Clock, 780
    Emperor of Ice-Cream, The, 1247
    Peter Quince at the Clavier, 1245
    Thirteen Ways of Looking at a Blackbird,
       941
STEVENSON, ANNE, 972, **1293**
    Sous-Entendu, 1014
    Victory, The, 795
STEWART, GEORGE, 91
STILLMAN, MICHAEL
    In Memoriam John Coltrane, 879
STIMPSON, CATHARINE, 2233
STING, 840
STONE, RUTH
    Second Hand Coat, 1248
STOPPARD, TOM, 1333
Stopping by Woods on a Snowy Evening, 1177
Storm, The, 127
STORNI, ALFONSINA, 1042
    Peso Ancestral, 1058
Story of an Hour, The, 553
Strange Beautiful Woman, A, 1215
STRINDBERG, AUGUST, 1806, 1808

Student Card Reports, 2140, 2172
Student Essays, 280, 374, 745, 809, 997, 1351,
    1800, 1888, 2132, 2136, 2149, 2154, 2158,
    2175
Subway Rush Hour, 1123
Success is counted sweetest, 1098
SUGARHILL GANG, 851
Suitor, The, 831
Summer, 922
Summit Beach, 1921, 1165
Supermarket in California, A, 1178
Supernatural Love, 963
Sure Thing, 1334
SURREY, HENRY HOWARD, EARL OF, 862
Swan and Shadow, 946
Sweat, 594
SWIFT, JONATHAN, 288, 731, 847
    Description of the Morning, A, 1248
SWINBURNE, ALGERNON, 823, 915, 929
SYNGE, JOHN MILLINGTON, 1321, **1322**
    Riders to the Sea, 1322

Taken Up, 988
Take, O, take those lips away, 841
Tale and Its Effect, The, 405
TALLENT, ELIZABETH, **269**
    No One's a Mystery, 269
TAN, AMY, **152**, 210, 289
    Pair of Tickets, A, 152
    Setting the Voice, 167
TANNEN, DEBORAH, 1013
TAPSCOTT, STEPHEN
    One Hundred Love Sonnets (V) (*translation*),
      1048
    Reality and Desire (*translation*), 1057
TATE, ALLEN, 2203, 2232
TATE, J. O.
    Good Source Is Not So Hard to Find: The
      Real Life Misfit, A, 468
Tears, Idle Tears, 785
TEASDALE, SARA, 972
    Flight, The, 966
Tell all the Truth but tell it slant, 1104
Tell-Tale Heart, The, 383
Ten Million Flames of Los Angeles, The, 1255
TENNYSON, ALFRED, LORD, 713, 789, 815, 829,
    862, 863, 906, 909, 912–13, 1067, 1069,
    1293
    Break, Break, Break, 889
    Dark House, by which I once more stand,
      1249
    Eagle, The, 815
    Flower in the Crannied Wall, 819
    Splendor falls on castle walls, The, 869
    Tears, Idle Tears, 785
    Ulysses, 1250
TERENCE, 1722
Term, The, 967
TER MAAT, CORNELIUS J.
    Etienne de Silhouette, 926

THACKERAY, WILLIAM MAKEPEACE, 170, 285
That time of year thou mayst in me behold, 1238
Theme for English B, 1122
Themes of Science Fiction, The, 248
There's a certain Slant of light, 1099
They Feed They Lion, 1205
They flee from me that sometime did me sekë, 1266
THIEL, DIANE
 Ancestral Burden (*translation*), 1058
 Memento Mori in Middle School, 985
 She Promises to Hold a Secret in Confidence (*translation*), 1044
 Simple Gift Made Rich by Affection (*translation*), A, 1044
Things They Carried, The, 667
Thirteen Ways of Looking at a Blackbird, 941
thirteen ways of looking at a tortilla, 1036
This Englishwoman, 924
This *Humanist* whom no beliefs constrained, 924
This Is Just to Say, 750
This is my letter to the World, 1102
This living hand, now warm and capable, 910
THOMAS, DYLAN, 714, 766n, 824, 864, 878, 914, **1294**
 Do not go gentle into that good night, 927
 Fern Hill, 1252
THOMPSON, JOHN, 893
Those Winter Sundays, 1185
Thoughts on Capital Punishment, 1072
Three Privations of Emily Dickinson, The, 1111
Three Ravens, The, 1139
TICHBORNE, CHIDIOCK, 1002
 Elegy, Written with His Own Hand, 827
Times They Are a-Changin', The, 854
Tired Sex, 802
Titanic, 1239
To a Locomotive in Winter, 720
To an Athlete Dying Young, 1194
To Autumn, 1201
To Build a Fire, 132
To Celia, 838
To His Coy Mistress, 1208
"To His Coy Mistress" and the Renaissance Tradition, 2215
TOLKIEN, J. R. R., 289
TOLSTOY, LEO, 24, **294**
 Death of Ivan Ilych, The, 294
To Lucasta, 741
TOMLINSON, CHARLES
 Certainty (*translation*), 1053
TOOMER, JEAN, 1008
 Reapers, 797
To see a world in a grain of sand, 820
TOTH, EMILY
 Source for Alcée Laballière in "The Storm," The, 2211
To the Desert, 722

To the Memory of Mr. Oldham, 1166
To the Stone-cutters, 1196
To the Virgins, to Make Much of Time, 1191
To Waken an Old Lady, 1262
Toward a Feminist Poetics, 2232
Towards the Splendid City, 1060
TOWNSEND, PETER
 Langston Hughes and Jazz, 1132
Tragedy and the Common Man, 1969
Transforming Fairy Tales, 994
Translating Neruda, 1063
Translating Sophocles, 1489
Traveling Through the Dark, 1072
TREASONE, GRACE
 Life, 1068
TRETHEWEY, NATASHA, 724–25
 White Lies, 724
TREVOR, WILLIAM, 1079
Trifles, 1305
Triolet, 928
TROLLOPE, ANTHONY, 170, 2125
True Ease in Writing comes from Art, not Chance, 862
Turtle, 832
TUTTLETON, JAMES
 Poe's Quest for Supernal Beauty, 413
Twa Corbies, The, 1140
TWAIN, MARK, 14, 23, 27, 291, 292, 826
Two Fridas, The, 1055
Tyger, The, 1149

Ulysses, 1250
Unholy Sonnet: After the Praying, 920
Unknown Citizen, The, 733
UPDIKE, JOHN, **15**, 122, 171, 192, 976, **1294**, 2126
 A & P, 15
 Enigmas (*translation*), The 1051
 Ex-Basketball Player, 1253
 Recital, 865
 Why Write?, 20
Uphill, 963
Upon Julia's Clothes, 761
Upon Julia's Voice, 868
UYEMATSU, AMY
 Ten Million Flames of Los Angeles, The, 1255

Valediction: Forbidding Mourning, A, 1164
VALÉRY, PAUL, 1095
VALLEJO, CÉSAR, 1042, 1054
 Cólera que Quiebra al Hombre en Niños, La, 1055
Variation on Belloc's "Fatigue," 925
VAUGHAN, VIRGINIA MASON
 Black and White in *Othello*, 1793
VEGA, SUZANNE, 840
Venus Flytrap, A, 924
Victory, The, 795
VIRGIL, 759, 931

Virginia, 880
Virgins, The, 1257
Visitor's Room, 800
VOLPE, EDMOND
   Myth in Faulkner's "Barn Burning," 2225
VONNEGUT, KURT, JR., **242**, 285
   Harrison Bergeron, 242
   Themes of Science Fiction, The, 248

WADA, HAKURO
   Even the croaking of frogs, 800
WALCOTT, DEREK, 1007
   Virgins, The, 1257
WALDROP, KEITH, 1071
WALEY, ARTHUR
   Drinking Alone by Moonlight (*translation*),
     1027
   Method of Translation, The, 1038
WALKER, ALICE, **102**, 289, 2216–18
   Everyday Use, 102
WALLER, EDMUND, 972
   Go, Lovely Rose, 1258
WALPOLE, HORACE, 284
Walt Whitman and Abraham Lincoln, 2230
war, The, 800
War forced us from California, 800
War in the Air, The, 1216
War Poetry, 743
WARREN, AUSTIN, 2202
WARREN, ROBERT PENN, 2202
WASSERSTEIN, WENDY, 1870
WATKINS, DANIEL P.
   Money and Labor in "The Rocking-Horse
     Winner," 2229
WATTS, ALAN, 791
We Are Many, 1046
Weary Blues, The, 1119
Weary with toil, I haste me to my bed, 1237
We four lads from Liverpool are, 1033
Welcome to Hiroshima, 1234
WELLEK, RENÉ, 2202
WELTY, EUDORA, 77, 955
   Why I Live at the P.O., 77
We Real Cool, 889
WEST, REBECCA
   Hamlet and Ophelia, 1788
Western Wind, 1141
What I Like, 951
What Is Cultural Studies?, 2247
What lips my lips have kissed, and where, and
   why, 919
What, still alive at twenty-two?, 1034
What the Body Told, 968
When I consider how my light is spent, 1212
When I have fears that I may cease to be, 1200
When, in disgrace with Fortune and men's eyes,
   1236
When I was one-and-twenty, 902
When maidens are young, 866
When You Are Old, 1268

Where Are You Going, Where Have You
   Been?, 654
Whipping, The, 1079
White Lies, 724
WHITMAN, WALT, 841, 873, 935, 936, 1033,
   1067, 1084, 1106, 1129, **1294**, 2230–31,
   2235
   Beat! Beat! Drums!, 903
   Cavalry Crossing a Ford, 940
   I Hear America Singing, 1259
   Noiseless Patient Spider, A, 1258
   O Captain! My Captain!, 1084
   Poetry of the Future, The, 952
   Runner, The, 802
   To a Locomotive in Winter, 720
WHITNEY, PHYLLIS A., 284
Who Goes with Fergus?, 864
Why I Live at the P.O., 77
Why Write?, 20
WILBUR, RICHARD, 898, 909, 1066, **1295**
   Concerning "Love Calls Us to the Things of
     This World", 787
   Love Calls Us to the Things of This World,
     786
   Three Privations of Emily Dickinson, The,
     1111
   Writer, The, 1260
WILDE, OSCAR, 923, 1332, 2236
Wild Nights – Wild Nights!, 1098
WILLIAMS, C. K.
   Elms, 1261
WILLIAMS, CLARENCE
   Jailhouse Blues, 849
WILLIAMS, RAYMOND, 2245
WILLIAMS, TENNESSEE, 1299, 1893–94, **1972**,
   2123, 2168n
   Glass Menagerie, The, 1972
   How to Stage *The Glass Menagerie*, 2023
WILLIAMS, WILLIAM CARLOS, 706, 748, 750,
   799, 873, 916, 932, 934, 946–47, **1295**,
   2222
   Dance, The, 939
   Heel & Toe to the End, 902
   Red Wheelbarrow, The, 731
   Spring and All, 1261
   Term, The, 967
   This Is Just to Say, 750
   To Waken an Old Lady, 1262
WILSON, AUGUST, 1870, **2064**
   Black Experience in America, 2114
   Joe Turner's Come and Gone, 2064
WILSON, WOODROW, 925
Wind, The, 825
Windhover, The, 1193
WINGARD, JOEL
   Reader-Response Issues in *Hamlet*, 1791
Wing-Spread, 2157
winter evening settles down, The, 792
Winter News, 805
WINTERS, YVOR, 878–79

With Our Eyes Shut, 1053
With serving still, 892
WOLFF, CYNTHIA GRIFFIN
    Dickinson and Death, 1112
Women, 1016
women on my mother's side were known, The,
    1006
WOODWORTH, SAMUEL, 1071
WOOLF, VIRGINIA, 27, 94, 293
WORDSWORTH, DOROTHY
    Journal Entry, 728
WORDSWORTH, WILLIAM, 727, 728, 729, 760,
    825, 872, 1066, 1067, 1086, 1093, **1296**,
    2222, 2238, 2243–45
    Composed upon Westminster Bridge, 1263
    I Wandered Lonely as a Cloud, 727
    Mutability, 770
    My heart leaps up when I behold, 770
    Slumber Did My Spirit Seal, A, 865
    World Is Too Much with Us, The, 978
Workbox, The, 738
World, The, 960
World Is Too Much with Us, The, 978
WRIGHT, JAMES, **1296**
    Autumn Begins in Martins Ferry, Ohio, 1265
    Blessing, A, 1264
WRIGHT, RICHARD, 291
Writer, The, 1260
Writing *The Cuban Swimmer*, 1885
WROTH, MARY SIDNEY
    In this strange labyrinth, 1265
WYATT, SIR THOMAS, **1297**

They flee from me that sometime did me
    sekë, 1266
With serving still, 892

X in My Name, The, 1010

Yearbook Cartoons, 464
YEATS, WILLIAM BUTLER, 703–4, 706, 714, 750,
    792, 873, 886, 896, 897, 908, 920, 957n,
    981, 982, 1076–77, 1085, 1095, **1297**,
    1808, 2180, 2237
    Crazy Jane Talks with the Bishop, 1267
    Lake Isle of Innisfree, The, 703
    Leda and the Swan, 874
    Magi, The, 1268
    Poetic Symbols, 971
    Sailing to Byzantium, 1075
    Second Coming, The, 982
    When You Are Old, 1268
    Who Goes with Fergus?, 864
Yellow Wallpaper, The, 571
Yield, 915
You fit into me, 828
YOST, CHRYSS
    Lai with Sounds of Skin, 880
YOUNG, DAVID P., 1797
Young Goodman Brown, 584

ZAPPA, FRANK, 840
ZAR, JERROLD H., 2128
ZOLA, ÉMILE, 125n, 1807